# Pocket
# Oxford–Duden
# German Dictionary

## Revised second Edition

German ----> English
English ----> German

**Edited by**
the Dudenredaktion
and the German Section of
the Oxford University Press
Dictionary Department

**Chief Editors**
M. Clark
O. Thyen

D0424461

OXFORD
UNIVERSITY PRESS

# OXFORD
UNIVERSITY PRESS

Great Clarendon Street, Oxford OX2 6DP

Oxford University Press is a department of the University of Oxford.
It furthers the University's objective of excellence in research, scholarship,
and education by publishing worldwide in

Oxford New York

Auckland Bangkok Buenos Aires Cape Town Chennai
Dar es Salaam Delhi Hong Kong Istanbul Karachi Kolkata
Kuala Lumpur Madrid Melbourne Mexico City Mumbai Nairobi
São Paulo Shanghai Taipei Tokyo Toronto

Oxford is a registered trade mark of Oxford University Press
in the UK and in certain other countries

Published in the United States
by Oxford University Press Inc., New York

© Oxford University Press and Bibliographisches Institut & F.A.
Brockhaus AG 1992, 1997, 2000, 2003

First edition published 1992
Revised edition published 1997
Second edition published 2000
Revised second edition published 2003

British Library Cataloguing in Publication Data

Data available

Library of Congress Cataloging in Publication Data

Data available

ISBN 0-19-860705-9

3

Designed by Information Design Unit, Newport Pagnell
Typeset in Nimrod, Arial and Meta by Tradespools
Printed in Great Britain by Clays Ltd, Bungay, Suffolk

# Preface

This major new edition of the *Pocket Oxford-Duden German Dictionary* has been enlarged and extensively updated to take account of new vocabulary and recent developments in German, with the needs of both the general and school user in mind.
New words and phrases reflect scientific and technological innovations as well as changes in politics, culture, and society. Reforms to the spelling of German ratified by the governments of Germany, Austria, and Switzerland in 1996 have been fully incorporated and are clearly signposted.

Combining the authority of the *Oxford-Duden German Dictionary* with the convenience of a smaller format and quick-access layout, this easy-to-use pocket dictionary is the ideal reference tool for all those requiring quick and reliable answers to their translation questions. It provides clear guidance on selecting the most appropriate translation, numerous examples to help with problems of usage and construction, and precise information on grammar, style, and pronunciation.
All grammatical terms used are explained in a glossary at the back of the dictionary.

Included as special features in this new edition are a calendar of traditions, festivals, and holidays in German-speaking countries, an A–Z of German life and culture, giving essential encyclopedic and cultural information about contemporary Germany, and a practical guide to letter-writing in German, including sample letters and practical tips about key differences between German and English letter styles and layout.

Designed to meet the needs of a wide range of users, from the student at intermediate level and above to the enthusiastic traveller and business professional, the *Pocket Oxford-Duden German Dictionary* is an invaluable practical resource for learners of modern, idiomatic German at the start of the twenty-first century.

Michael Clark
*Oxford University Press*

# Editors and contributors

## Oxford University Press
Michael Clark
Bernadette Mohan
Robin Sawers
Gunhild Prowe

## Dudenverlag
Olaf Thyen
Werner Scholze-Stubenrecht
Magdalena Seubel

## Data input
Susan Wilkin
Anne McConnell
Anna Cotgreave

## A–Z of German culture Calendar of traditions, festivals, and holidays
*Ella Associates*
Valerie Grundy
Eva Vennebusch

## Abc der britischen und amerikanischen Kultur Festtags-, Feiertags- und Brauchtumskalender
*Ella Associates*
Valerie Grundy
Eva Vennebusch
Annette Haberstock

## Summary of German Grammar
Nicholas Rollin
Marie-Louise Wasmeier

# Inhalt / Contents

# Als Markenzeichen geschützte Wörter / Note on Proprietary Status

Namen und Kennzeichen, die als Marken bekannt sind und entsprechenden Schutz genießen, sind durch die Zeichen ® oder ⓌⓏ gekennzeichnet. Handelsnamen ohne Markencharakter sind nicht gekennzeichnet. Aus dem Fehlen der Zeichen ® oder ⓌⓏ darf im Einzelfall nicht geschlossen werden, dass ein Name oder Zeichen frei ist. Eine Haftung für ein etwaiges Fehlen der Zeichen ® oder ⓌⓏ wird ausgeschlossen.

This dictionary includes some words which have, or are asserted to have, proprietary status as trade marks or otherwise. Their inclusion does not imply that they have acquired for legal purposes a non-proprietary or general significance, nor any other judgement concerning their legal status. In cases where the editorial staff have some evidence that a word has proprietary status, this is indicated in the entry for that word by the abbreviation ® or ⓌⓏ, but no judgement concerning the legal status of such words is made or implied thereby.

# Erläuterungen zum deutsch-englischen Text / Key to German-English Entries

Stichwort •————— **Bịld·schirm** *der* (Ferns., Informationst.) screen
Headword

**Bịldschirm-:** ~**gerät** *das* VDU; visual •——— **Kompositablock.**
display unit; ~**schoner** *der;* ~~s, ~~ **Eine Tilde ersetzt**
(DV) screen saver **jeweils den**
**gemeinsamen**

Die Aussprache- •——— **Blues** /bluːs/ *der;* ~, ~: blues *pl.* **ersten Bestandteil**
angaben (in IPA- **der Komposita**
Lautschrift) stehen **Compound block**
unmittelbar hinter **with a swung dash**
dem Stichwort **representing the**
(s.S.x) **first element of**
Pronunciation is **each compound**
shown in IPA
immediately after the
headword (see p. xi) **dar|bieten** (geh.) *unr. tr. V.* (aufführen,
vortragen) perform; ... •——— **Ein senkrechter**
**Strich nach dem**
**ersten Bestandteil**
**eines zusammen-**
Ein unter einen •——— **darüber** *Adv.* **(a)** over it/them; ~ **stehen** **gesetzten Verbs**
Vokal gesetzter (fig.) be above such things **zeigt an, dass es**
waagerechter Strich **sich um eine**
zeigt die Länge des **unfeste Zusam-**
Vokals und in **mensetzung handelt**
mehrsilbigen **A vertical bar**
Wörtern zugleich **indicates that a**
die Betonung der **compound verb is**
betreffenden Silbe **separable**
an
An underline indicates **darụm** *Adv.* **(a)** [a]round it/them; ...
a long vowel, stressed •——— **Ein unter einen**
in words of more than **Vokal gesetzter**
one syllable **Punkt zeigt die**
**Kürze des Vokals**
**und in mehrsilbigen**
**Wörtern zugleich**
Ein hochgestellter •——— **dạss**, *****dạß** *Konj.* **(a)** that; ... **die Betonung**
Stern vor einem **der betreffenden**
Stichwort zeigt an, **Silbe an**
dass es sich um **An underdot**
eine alte, künftig **indicates a short**
nicht mehr gültige **vowel, stressed in**
Schreibung handelt **words of more than**
An asterisk indicates **one syllable**
an old spelling

**Erst·aufführung** *die* première •——— **Kompositionsfuge**
**Dot marking the**
Grammatische •——— **erstklassig** **1** *Adj.* first-class **juncture of the**
Gliederungspunkte **2** *adv.* superbly **elements of a**
und Wortartangaben **compound**
Grammatical
categories
and parts of speech

# Key to German-English entries

Die Formen des • **Fạlter** *der;* ~s, ~ (Nacht~) moth; (Tag~)
Genitivs und des    butterfly
Plurals eines
Substantivs       **fliehen** /ˈfliːən/ *unr. itr. V.; mit sein* flee • — Der Hinweis *mit sein*
Genitive and plural   (vor + *Dat.* from); ...      zeigt an, dass das
forms of a noun                betreffende Verb die
                       Perfekttempora mit
                       dem Hilfsverb *sein*
                       bildet
Unregelmäßige • **frọmm**; ~er *od.* frömmer, ~st... *od.*     *mit sein* indicates that
Steigerungsformen   frömmst... [1] *Adj.* pious, devout ⟨*person*⟩;   a verb is conjugated
eines Adjektivs                with the auxiliary verb
Irregular comparative               *sein* in its perfect
and superlative forms               tenses
of an adjective

         **Gehạ̈ssigkeit** *die;* ~, ~en (a) (Wesen)    • — Semantische
         spitefulness;           Gliederungspunkte
         (b) (Äußerung) spiteful remark       und Bedeutungs-
Stilistische •  **hạppig** *Adj.* (ugs.) ~e Preise fancy prices   indikatoren
Kennzeichnungen  (coll.)              Sense categories and
Style labels                indicators

         **Haube** *die;* ~, ~n (a) bonnet; (einer
         Krankenschwester) cap;
         (b) (Kfz-W.) bonnet (Brit.); hood (Amer.)
         **heuer** *Adv.* (südd., österr., schweiz.) this year • — Angaben zur
Bereichsangaben • **Icon** /ˈaiˌkən/ *das;* ~s, ~s (DV) icon    räumlichen
Subject labels **Immụn·schwäche** *die* (Med.)       Zuordnung
         immunodeficiency; immune deficiency      Regional labels

         **knạllen** [1] *itr. V.* (a) ⟨*shot*⟩ ring out;  • — Kollokatoren
         ⟨*firework*⟩ go bang; ⟨*cork*⟩ pop; ⟨*door*⟩ slam;  (Wörter, mit denen
         ⟨*whip, rifle*⟩ crack;        zusammen das
         **knạpp** [1] *Adj.* (a) meagre; narrow ⟨*victory*,  Stichwort häufig
         *lead*⟩; narrow, bare ⟨*majority*⟩;     vorkommt) als Hilfe
                       zur Auswahl der für
Beispiele ( jeweils • **mạchen** [1] *tr. V.* (a) make; aus Plastik/  den jeweiligen
mit einer Tilde an   Holz *usw.* gemacht made of plastic/wood *etc.;*  Kontext passenden
Stelle des    sich (*Dat.*) etw. ~ lassen have sth. made; ...  Übersetzung
Stichworts)                Collocators—words
Examples (with               often used with the
a swung dash                headword, shown to
representing the               help select the correct
headword)                translation for each
                       context

         **Ọmi** *die;* ~, ~s ▶ OMA      • — Ein Pfeil verweist
                       auf ein bedeutungs-
Mit *s. auch* wird • **Sạmstag** *der;* ~[e]s, ~e Saturday; *s. auch*  gleiches anderes
auf ein Stichwort   DIENSTAG           Stichwort
verwiesen, unter               An arrow directs the
dem noch                user to another
zusätzliche                headword with the
Informationen                same meaning
zu finden sind
*s. auch* directs the
user to another
headword where
additional information
can be found

# Key to English-German Entries / Erläuterungen zum englisch-deutschen Text

**Headword** •————— **barber** /'bɑːbə(r)/ *n.* [Herren]friseur, *der;*
Stichwort ~'s shop (Brit.) Friseursalon, *der*
**barbiturate** /bɑːˈbɪtjʊrət/ *n.* (Chem.)
Barbiturat, *das*

**bar: ~chart** *n.* Stabdiagramm, *das;*
~**code** *n.* Strichcode, *der*

•———— **Compound block with a swung dash representing the first element of each compound**
Kompositablock. Eine Tilde ersetzt jeweils den gemeinsamen ersten Bestandteil der Komposita

**bear²** ⬚1 *v.t.*, bore /bɔː(r)/, borne /bɔːn/ ...

**Each phrasal verb** •—— ■ **bear 'out** *v.t.* (fig.) bestätigen ⟨Bericht,
**is entered on a new** *Erklärung*⟩; ~ sb. out jmdm. Recht geben.
**line immediately** ■ '**bear with** *v.t.* Nachsicht haben mit
**following the entry for the first element**
Die *Phrasal Verbs* folgen, jedes auf einer neuen Zeile, direkt auf den Eintrag zu ihrem Grundverb

**bemused** /bɪˈmjuːzd/ *adj.* verwirrt

•——— **Pronunciation shown in IPA (see p. xii).**
Ausspracheangaben (in IPA-Lautschrift) (s. S. xiii)

**Stress mark,** •——— '**bin liner** *n.* Müllbeutel, *der*
**showing stress on the following syllable**
Betonungszeichen vor der betonten Silbe

**cart** /kɑːt/ ⬚1 *n.* Wagen, *der*
⬚2 *v.t.* (coll.) schleppen

•——— **Grammatical categories and parts of speech**
Grammatische Gliederungspunkte und Wortartangaben

**Irregular tenses** •——— **choose** /tʃuːz/ ⬚1 *v.t.*, **chose** /tʃəʊz/,
**of a verb** **chosen** /'tʃəʊzn/ (a) wählen
Unregelmäßige Verbformen

**dub** /dʌb/ *v.t.*, **-bb-** (Cinemat.) synchronisieren

•——— **Doubling of a final consonant of a verb before -ed or -ing**
Verdoppelung des Endkonsonanten eines Verbs vor -ed oder -ing

**Irregular** •———— **good** /ɡʊd/ ⬚1 *adj.*, **better** /'betə(r)/, **best**
**comparative and** /best/ (a) gut; günstig ⟨Gelegenheit,
**superlative forms** *Angebot*⟩; ...
**of an adjective**
Unregelmäßige Steigerungsformen eines Adjektivs

**groom** /ɡruːm/ /ɡrʊm/ ⬚1 *n.* (a) (stable boy)
Stallbursche, *der*
(b) (bride~) Bräutigam, *der*

•——— **Sense categories and sense indicators**
Semantische Gliederungspunkte und Bedeutungsindikatoren

**Subject labels** •——— **HTML** *abbr.* (Comp.) **hypertext markup**
Bereichsangaben **language** HTML
**immobilizer** /ɪˈməʊbɪlaɪzə(r)/ *n.* (Motor Veh.)
Wegfahrsperre, *die*

# Key to English-German entries

• • • • • • • • • • • • • • • • • • • • • • • • • • • • • • • • • • • •

**Style labels** •——
Stilistische
Kennzeichnungen

**jam-packed** *adj.* (coll.) knallvoll (ugs.),
proppenvoll (ugs.) **(with** von)

**loch** /lɒx, lɒk/ *n.* (Scot.) See, *der*
**Medicare** /'medɪkeə(r)/ *n.* (Amer.)
[*bundes*]*staatliches*
*Krankenversicherungssystem für Personen*
*über 65 Jahre*

——• **Regional labels**
Angaben zur
räumlichen
Zuordnung

**Collocators** •——
—words often used
with the headword,
shown to help select
the correct transla-
tion for each context.
Kollokatoren (Wörter,
mit denen zusammen
das Stichwort häufig
vorkommt) als Hilfe
zur Auswahl der für
den jeweiligen Kontext
passenden
Übersetzung

**oppress** /ə'pres/ *v.t.* unterdrücken; (fig.)
⟨*Gefühl:*⟩ bedrücken
**oppressive** /ə'presɪv/ *adj.* repressiv; (fig.)
bedrückend ⟨*Ängste, Atmosphäre*⟩; (hot and
close) drückend ⟨*Wetter, Klima, Tag*⟩

**price** /praɪs/ *n.* (lit. or fig.) Preis, *der; at a*
~ *of* zum Preis von; **what is the** ~ **of this?**
was kostet das?; **at/not at any** ~: um jeden/
keinen Preis

——• **Examples (with a
swung dash
representing the
headword)**
Beispiele (jeweils mit
einer Tilde an Stelle
des Stichworts)

**An arrow directs** •——
the user to another
headword with the
same meaning
Ein Pfeil verweist auf
ein bedeutungsglei-
ches anderes
Stichwort

**sitcom** /'sɪtkɒm/ (coll.) ▶ SITUATION COMEDY

**Sunday** /'sʌndeɪ, 'sʌndɪ/ *n.* Sonntag, *der;*
~ **opening** die sonntägliche Öffnung;
~ **trading** sonntägliche Ladenöffnung; *see
also* FRIDAY

——• *see also* **directs the
user to another
headword where
additional
information can be
found**
Mit *see also* wird auf
ein Stichwort
verwiesen, unter dem
noch zusätzliche
Informationen zu
finden sind

# Phonetic symbols used in transcriptions of German words

## Phonetic information given in the German-English section

The pronunciation of German is largely regular, and phonetic transcriptions have only been given where additional help is needed. In all other cases only the position of the stressed syllable and the length of the vowel in that syllable are shown: a long vowel is indicated by an underline, e.g. **Maß**, a short vowel by a dot placed underneath, e.g. **Masse**.

| a | *hạt* | hat |
|---|---|---|
| aː | *Bạhn* | baːn |
| ɐ | *Ọber* | 'oːbɐ |
| ɐ̯ | *Uhr* | uːɐ̯ |
| ã | *Ensemble* | ã'sãːbl̩ |
| ãː | *Abonnement* | abɔnə'mãː |
| ai̯ | *wei̯t* | vai̯t |
| au̯ | *Hau̯t* | hau̯t |
| b | *Bạll* | bal |
| ç | *ịch* | ɪç |
| d | *dạnn* | dan |
| dʒ | *Gịn* | dʒɪn |
| e | *egạl* | e'gaːl |
| eː | *Beet* | beːt |
| ɛ | *mạ̈sten* | 'mɛstn̩ |
| ɛː | *wählen* | 'vɛːlən |
| ɛ̃ | *Mạnnequin* | 'manəkɛ̃ |
| ɛ̃ː | *Cousin* | ku'zɛ̃ː |
| ə | *Nạse* | 'naːzə |
| f | *Fạß* | fas |
| g | *Gạst* | gast |
| h | *hạt* | hat |
| i | *vitạl* | vi'taːl |
| iː | *viẹl* | fiːl |
| i̯ | *Stu̯die* | 'ʃtuːdi̯ə |
| ɪ | *Bịrke* | 'bɪrkə |
| j | *ja̱* | jaː |
| k | *kạlt* | kalt |
| l | *Lạst* | last |
| l̩ | *Nạbel* | 'naːbl̩ |

| | | |
|---|---|---|
| m | *Mast* | mast |
| n | *Naht* | naːt |
| ṇ | *baden* | ˈbaːdṇ |
| ŋ | *lang* | laŋ |
| o | *Moral* | moˈraːl |
| oː | *Boot* | boːt |
| o̯ | *loyal* | lo̯aˈjaːl |
| õ | *Fondue* | fõˈdyː |
| õː | *Fond* | fõː |
| ɔ | *Post* | pɔst |
| ø | *Ökonom* | økoˈnoːm |
| øː | *Öl* | øːl |
| œ | *göttlich* | ˈɡœtlɪç |
| œ̃ | *Parfum* | parˈfœ̃ː |
| ɔy | *Heu* | hɔy |
| p | *Pakt* | pakt |
| pf | *Pfahl* | pfaːl |
| r | *Rast* | rast |
| s | *Hast* | hast |
| ʃ | *schal* | ʃaːl |
| t | *Tal* | taːl |
| ts | *Zahl* | tsaːl |
| tʃ | *Matsch* | matʃ |
| u | *kulant* | kuˈlant |
| uː | *Hut* | huːt |
| u̯ | *aktuell* | akˈtu̯ɛl |
| ʊ | *Pult* | pʊlt |
| v | *was* | vas |
| x | *Bach* | bax |
| y | *Physik* | fyˈziːk |
| yː | *Rübe* | ˈryːbə |
| y̆ | *Nuance* | ˈny̆ãːsə |
| ʏ | *Fülle* | ˈfʏlə |
| z | *Hase* | ˈhaːzə |
| ʒ | *Genie* | ʒeˈniː |

| | |
|---|---|
| ǀ | Glottal stop, e.g. beachten /bəǀaxtṇ/ |
| ː | Length sign, indicating that the preceding vowel is long, e.g. Chrom /kroːm/ |
| ˜ | Indicates a nasal vowel, e.g. Fond /fõː/ |
| ˈ | Stress mark, immediately preceding a stressed syllable, e.g. Ballon /baˈlɔn/ |

# Die für das Englische verwendeten Zeichen der Lautschrift

| | | | | | | |
|---|---|---|---|---|---|---|
| ɑ | *barb* | bɑːb | | p | *pet* | pet |
| ɑ̃ː | *séance* | ˈseɪɑ̃s | | r | *rat* | ræt |
| æ | *fat* | fæt | | s | *sip* | sɪp |
| æ̃ | *lingerie* | ˈlæ̃ʒərɪ | | ʃ | *ship* | ʃɪp |
| aɪ | *fine* | faɪn | | t | *tip* | tɪp |
| aʊ | *now* | naʊ | | tʃ | *chin* | tʃɪn |
| b | *bat* | bæt | | θ | *thin* | θɪn |
| d | *dog* | dɒg | | ð | *the* | ðə |
| dʒ | *jam* | dʒæm | | uː | *boot* | buːt |
| e | *met* | met | | ʊ | *book* | bʊk |
| eɪ | *fate* | feɪt | | ʊə | *tourist* | ˈtʊərɪst |
| eə | *fairy* | ˈfeərɪ | | ʌ | *dug* | dʌg |
| əʊ | *goat* | gəʊt | | v | *van* | væn |
| ə | *ago* | əˈgəʊ | | w | *win* | wɪn |
| ɜː | *fur* | fɜː(r) | | x | *loch* | lɒx |
| f | *fat* | fæt | | z | *zip* | zɪp |
| g | *good* | gʊd | | ʒ | *vision* | ˈvɪʒn |
| h | *hat* | hæt | | ː | Längezeichen, bezeichnet Länge des unmittelbar davor stehenden Vokals, z. B. boot /buːt/ | |
| ɪ | *bit, lately* | bɪt, ˈleɪtlɪ | | | | |
| ɪə | *nearly* | ˈnɪəlɪ | | | | |
| iː | *meet* | miːt | | | | |
| j | *yet* | jet | | ˈ | Betonung, steht unmittelbar vor einer betonten Silbe, z. B. ago /əˈgəʊ/ | |
| k | *kit* | kɪt | | | | |
| l | *lot* | lɒt | | | | |
| m | *mat* | mæt | | (r) | Ein „r" in runden Klammern wird nur gesprochen, wenn im Textzusammenhang ein Vokal unmittelbar folgt, z. B. pare /peə(r)/; pare away /peər əˈweɪ/ | |
| n | *not* | nɒt | | | | |
| ŋ | *sing* | sɪŋ | | | | |
| ɒ | *got* | gɒt | | | | |
| ɔː | *paw* | pɔː | | | | |
| ɔɪ | *boil* | bɔɪl | | | | |

# German spellings in this dictionary

German spellings in this dictionary are in accordance with the reforms ratified by the governments of Germany, Austria, and Switzerland in July 1996 and in force since August 1998. Key points of the reforms are summarized below. In cases of doubt the editors have followed *Duden—Rechtschreibung der deutschen Sprache*, twenty-first edition, 1996.

To help the user who may not yet be familiar with the reforms, the German-English section of the dictionary gives both the new spellings and the old versions which will become 'invalid' in 2005 after a transition period during which both spellings are 'valid'. The old spellings are marked with an asterisk and are cross-referred where necessary to the new. For example, the translations of the compound verb *wiedererkennen* will no longer be found at this headword, since under the new spelling rules the word will vanish from the language. Instead they are covered by two phrases at the entry for *wieder: jemanden/etwas wieder erkennen* (in the form *jmdn./etw. ~ erkennen*) and *er war kaum wieder zu erkennen* (in the form *er war kaum ~ zu erkennen*). Similarly, the translations of the adjective previously written *belemmert* will be found at the new entry for the headword *belämmert*.

In a number of cases, however, implementing the new spelling rules has meant that just some, but not all, uses of a word have had to be transferred from one entry to another. In these cases the headword is not marked with an asterisk, but the entry is provided with a cross-reference to where the transferred information is now to be found. So, for example, the user who consults the entry for *leid* looking for a translation of the phrase previously written *jemandem leid tun* will find a cross-reference to the entry for the noun *Leid*, since according to the new spelling rules the word is written with a capital *L* in this expression. The headword *leid* itself is not marked with an asterisk, since it continues to exist in its own right as an adjective.

## The following summary lists the most important changes:

**1 The ß character** The ß character, which is generally replaced in Switzerland by a double s, will be retained in Germany and Austria, but will only be written after a long vowel (as in Fuß, Füße) and after a diphthong (as in Strauß, Sträuße). *Fluß, Baß, keß, läßt, Nußknacker* become in future: *Fluss, Bass, kess, lässt, Nussknacker*

## 2 Nominalized adjectives

Nominalized adjectives will be written with a capital even in set phrases.

*sein Schäfchen ins trockene bringen, im trüben fischen, im allgemeinen* become in future: *sein Schäfchen ins Trockene bringen, im Trüben fischen, im Allgemeinen*

## 3 Words from the same word family

In certain cases the spelling of words belonging to the same family will be made uniform.

*numerieren, überschwenglich* become in future: *nummerieren* (like Nummer), *überschwänglich* (being related to Überschwang)

## 4 The same consonant repeated three times

When the same consonant repeated three times occurs in compounds, all three will be written even when a vowel follows.

*Brennessel, Schiffahrt* become in future: *Brennnessel, Schifffahrt* (exceptions are dennoch, Drittel, Mittag)

## 5 Verb, adjective and participle compounds

Verb, adjective and participle compounds will be written more frequently than previously in two words.

*spazierengehen, radfahren, ernstgemeint, erdölexportierend* become in future: *spazieren gehen, Rad fahren, ernst gemeint, Erdöl exportierend*

## 6 Compounds containing numbers in figures

Compounds containing numbers in figures will in future be written with a hyphen.

*24karätig, 8pfünder* become in future: *24-karätig, 8-Pfünder*

## 7 The division of words containing st

st will be treated like a normal combination of consonants and no longer be indivisible.

*Ha-stig, Ki-ste* become in future: *has-tig, Kis-te*

## 8 The division of words containing ck

The combination ck will not be divided and will go on to the next line.

*Bäk-ker, schik-ken* become in future: *Bä-cker, schi-cken*

## 9 The division of foreign words

Compound foreign words which are hardly recognized as such today may be divided by syllables, without regard to their original components.

*He-li-ko-pter* (from the Greek helix and pteron) may also become in future: *He-li-kop-ter*

## 10 The comma before und

Where two complete clauses are connected by *und* a comma will not be obligatory.

*Karl war in Schwierigkeiten, und niemand konnte ihm helfen.* may also in future be written: *Karl war in Schwierigkeiten und niemand konnte ihm helfen.*

## 11 The comma with infinitives and participles

Even longer clauses containing an infinitive or participle will not have to be divided off with a comma.

*Er begann sofort, das neue Buch zu lesen. Ungläubig den Kopf schüttelnd, verließ er das Zimmer.* may also in future be written: *Er begann sofort das neue Buch zu lesen. Ungläubig den Kopf schüttelnd verließ er das Zimmer.*

# Abkürzungen / Abbreviations

| | | |
|---|---|---|
| anderes, andere | a. | other, others |
| ähnliches, ähnliche | ä. | similar |
| Abkürzung | abbr. | abbreviation |
| Abkürzung | Abk. | abbreviation |
| absolut | abs. | absolute |
| adjektivisch | adj. | adjective, adjectival |
| Adjektiv | Adj. | adjective |
| Verwaltungssprache | Admin. | Administration, Administrative |
| adverbial | adv. | adverb, adverbial |
| Adverb | Adv. | adverb |
| Flugwesen | Aeronaut. | Aeronautics |
| Landwirtschaft | Agric. | Agriculture |
| Akkusativ | Akk. | accusative |
| Amerika | Amer. | American, America |
| amerikanisch | amerik. | American |
| Amtssprache | Amtsspr. | official language |
| Anatomie | Anat. | Anatomy |
| Anthropologie | Anthrop. | Anthropology |
| veraltet | arch. | archaic |
| Archäologie | Archaeol. | Archaeology |
| Architektur | Archit. | Architecture |
| Artikel | art. | article |
| Astrologie | Astrol. | Astrology |
| Astronomie | Astron. | Astronomy |
| Raumfahrt | Astronaut. | Astronautics |
| Altes Testament | A. T. | Old Testament |
| attributiv | attr., attrib. | attributive |
| Australien | Austral. | Australian, Australia |
| Bauwesen | Bauw. | Construction |
| Bergmannssprache | Bergmannsspr. | Mining terminology |
| besonders | bes. | especially |
| Bezeichnung | Bez. | name |
| biblisch | bibl. | biblical |
| Biologie | Biol. | Biology |
| Buchführung | Bookk. | Bookkeeping |
| Börsenwesen | Börsenw. | Stock Market |
| Botanik | Bot. | Botany |
| Bundesrepublik Deutschland | BRD | Federal Republic of Germany |
| britisch, Großbritannien | Brit. | British, Britain |
| britisch | brit. | British |
| Bruchzahl | Bruchz. | fraction |
| Buchführung | Buchf. | Bookkeeping |
| Buchwesen | Buchw. | Book Trade |
| Chemie | Chem. | Chemistry |

| | | |
|---|---|---|
| chemisch | chem. | chemical |
| Kindersprache | child lang. | child language |
| christlich | christl. | Christian |
| Kinematographie | Cinemat. | Cinematography |
| umgangssprachlich | coll. | colloquial |
| Kollektivum | collect. | collective |
| Kombination | comb. | combination |
| Handel, Handels- | Commerc. | Commerce, Commercial |
| elektronische Datenverarbeitung | Comp. | Computing |
| Komparativ, komparativ | compar. | comparative |
| Konditional, konditional | condit. | conditional |
| Konjunktion | conj. | conjunction |
| Dativ | Dat. | dative |
| Deutsche Demokratische Republik | DDR | German Democratic Republic |
| bestimmt | def. | definite |
| Deklination | Dekl. | declension |
| Demonstrativpronomen | Demonstrativpron. | demonstrative pronoun |
| Zahnmedizin | Dent. | Dentistry |
| abwertend | derog. | derogatory |
| das heißt | d. h. | that is [to say] |
| Dialekt | dial. | dialect |
| dichterisch | dichter. | poetic |
| Damenschneiderei | Dressm. | Dressmaking |
| Druckwesen | Druckw. | Printing |
| deutsch | dt. | German |
| Datenverarbeitung | DV | Data Processing |
| kirchlich | Eccl. | Ecclesiastical |
| Ökologie | Ecol. | Ecology |
| Ökonomik | Econ. | Economics |
| Bildungswesen | Educ. | Education |
| ehemals, ehemalig | ehem. | former, formerly |
| Eisenbahn | Eisenb. | Railways |
| Elektrizität | Electr. | Electricity |
| Elektrotechnik | Elektrot. | Electrical Engineering |
| elektrisch | elektr. | electrical |
| elliptisch | ellipt. | elliptical |
| emphatisch | emphat. | emphatic |
| besonders | esp. | especially |
| etwas | etw. | something |
| euphemistisch | euphem. | euphemistic |
| evangelisch | ev. | Evangelical |
| ausdrückend | expr. | expressing |

| | | | | | |
|---|---|---|---|---|---|
| fachsprachlich | fachspr. | technical | Kindersprache | Kinderspr. | child language |
| familiär | fam. | familiar | Kochkunst | Kochk. | Cookery |
| feminin | fem. | feminine | Komparativ | Komp. | Comparative |
| Fernsehen | Ferns. | Television | Konjunktion | Konj. | conjunction |
| Fernsprechwesen | Fernspr. | Telephony | landschaftlich | landsch. | regional |
| figurativ | fig. | figurative | Landwirtschaft | Landw. | Agriculture |
| Finanzwesen | Finanzw. | Finance | Linguistik | Ling. | Linguistics |
| Flugwesen | Flugw. | Aeronautics | wortwörtlich | lit. | literal |
| Fußball | Footb. | Football | Literatur | Lit. | Literature |
| Forstwesen | Forstw. | Forestry | Literaturwissen- | Literaturw. | Literary Studies |
| Fotografie | Fot. | Photography | schaft | | |
| Gastronomie | Gastr. | Gastronomy | Luftfahrt | Luftf. | Aeronautics |
| gehoben | geh. | elevated | mittelalterlich | ma. | medieval |
| Genitiv | Gen. | genitive | Mittelalter | MA. | Middle Ages |
| Geographie | Geog. | Geography | marxistisch | marx. | Marxist |
| Geologie | Geol. | Geology | maskulin | masc. | masculine |
| Geometrie | Geom. | Geometry | Mathematik | Math. | Mathematics |
| Handarbeit | Handarb. | Handicraft | Maschinenbau | Mech. | Mechanical |
| Heraldik | Her. | Heraldry | | Engin. | Engineering |
| Hilfsverb | Hilfsv. | auxiliary verb | Medizin | Med. | Medicine |
| historisch | hist. | historical | Meereskunde | Meeresk. | oceanography |
| Geschichte, | Hist. | History, historical | Meteorologie | Met. | Meteorology |
| historisch | | | Metallurgie | Metall. | Metallurgy |
| Hochschulwesen | Hoch- | Higher Education | Metallbearbeitung | Metall- | Metalwork |
| | schulw. | | | bearb. | |
| Gartenbau | Hort. | Horticultural | Metallbearbeitung | Metalw. | Metalwork |
| Imperativ, | imper. | imperative | Meterologie | Meteorol. | Meteorology |
| imperativisch | | | Militär | Mil., Milit. | Military |
| unpersönlich | impers. | impersonal | modifizierend | mod. | modifying |
| unbestimmt | indef. | indefinite | Modalverb | Modalv. | modal verb |
| Indefinitpronomen | Indefinit | indefinite | Kraftfahrzeug- | Motor Veh. | Motor Vehicles |
| | -pron. | pronoun | wesen | | |
| Indeklinabel | Indekl. | indeclinable | Musik | Mus. | Music |
| Indikativ | Indik. | indicative | Mythologie | Mythol. | Mythology |
| Infinitiv | Inf. | infinitive | Substantiv | n. | noun |
| Interjektion | Interj., int. | interjection | Seemannssprache | Naut. | Nautical |
| interrogativ | interrog. | interrogative | negativ | neg. | negative |
| intransitiv | intr. | intransitive | Nominativ | Nom. | nominative |
| irisch, Irland | Ir. | Irish, Ireland | norddeutsch | nordd. | North German |
| ironisch | iron. | ironical | nordostdeutsch | nordostd. | North-East |
| Jägersprache | Jägerspr. | hunting language | | | German |
| jemand | jmd. | somebody | Substantive | ns. | nouns |
| jemandem | jmdm. | somebody | | (English) | |
| jemanden | jmdn. | somebody | nationalsozialis- | ns. | National |
| jemandes | jmds. | somebody | tisch | (Deutsch) | Socialist |
| scherzhaft | joc. | jocular | Neues Testament | N. T. | New Testament |
| Journalismus | Journ. | Journalism | Kernphysik | Nucl. Phys. | Nuclear Physics |
| Jugendsprache | Jugend- | young people's | ohne; oben | o. | without; above |
| | spr. | language | Objekt | obj. | object |
| juristisch | jur. | legal | oder | od. | or |
| Kardinalzahl | Kardinalz. | cardinal number | Ordinalzahl | Ordinalz. | ordinal number |
| katholisch | kath. | Catholic | Ornithologie | Ornith. | Ornithology |
| Kaufmanns- | Kauf- | business | österreichisch | österr. | Austrian |
| sprache | mannsspr. | language | Papierdeutsch | Papierdt. | officialese |
| Kraftfahrzeug- | Kfz-W. | Motor Vehicles | Parlament | Parl. | Parliament |
| wesen | | | Partizip | Part. | participle |

| | | | | | | |
|---|---|---|---|---|---|---|
| Passiv | **pass.** | passive | | Wissenschaft | **Sci.** | Science |
| Perfekt | **Perf.** | perfect | | schottisch | **Scot.** | Scottish, Scotland |
| Person | **Pers.** | person | | Schulwesen | **Schulw.** | School System |
| Philosophie | **Philos.** | Philosophy | | Seemannssprache | **Seemanns-spr.** | Nautical |
| Fotografie | **Photog.** | Photography | | | | |
| Phrase(n) | **phr(s).** | Phrase(s) | | Seewesen | **Seew.** | maritime affairs |
| Physik | **Phys.** | Physics | | Singular | **Sg., sing.** | singular |
| Physiologie | **Physiol.** | Physiology | | salopp | **sl.** | slang |
| Plural | **Pl., pl.** | plural | | siehe oben | **s. o.** | see above |
| Plusquamperfekt | **Plusq.** | pluperfect | | Soziologie | **Sociol.** | Sociology |
| dichterisch | **poet.** | poetical | | Soldatensprache | **Soldaten-spr.** | army slang |
| Politik | **Polit.** | Politics | | | | |
| possessiv, Possessiv- | **poss.** | possessive | | Soziologie | **Soziol.** | Sociology |
| nachgestellt | **postpos.** | postpositive | | spöttisch | **spött.** | derisive |
| Postwesen | **Postw.** | Post Office | | Sprichwort | **Spr.** | proverb |
| zweites Partizip | **p.p.** | past participle | | Sprach-wissenschaft | **Sprachw.** | Linguistics |
| prädikativ | **präd.** | predicative | | | | |
| Präposition | **Präp.** | preposition | | Börsenwesen | **St. Exch.** | Stock Exchange |
| Präsens | **Präs.** | present | | Steuerwesen | **Steuerw.** | Taxation |
| Präteritum | **Prät.** | preterite | | etwas | **sth.** | something |
| prädikativ | **pred.** | predicative | | Studentensprache | **Studen-tenspr.** | student slang |
| Präfix | **pref.** | prefix | | | | |
| Präposition | **prep.** | preposition | | siehe unten | **s. u.** | see below |
| Präsens | **pres.** | present | | Subjekt | **Subj.** | subject |
| erstes Partizip | **pres. p.** | present participle | | substantivisch; substantiviert | **subst.** | nominal; nominalized |
| Eigenname | **pr. n.** | proper noun | | | | |
| Pronomen | **Pron., pron.** | pronoun | | Substantiv | **Subst.** | noun |
| | | | | süddeutsch | **südd.** | South German |
| sprichwörtlich | **prov.** | proverbial | | südwestdeutsch | **südwestd.** | South-West German |
| Psychologie | **Psych.** | Psychology | | | | |
| Präteritum | **p.t.** | past tense | | Suffix | **suf.** | suffix |
| Warenzeichen | **®** | Registered Trade Mark | | Superlativ | **Sup., superl.** | superlative |
| Eisenbahn | **Railw.** | Railways | | Landvermessung | **Surv.** | Surveying |
| Raumfahrt | **Raumf.** | Space Travel | | Symbol | **symb.** | symbol |
| römisch-katho-lische Kirche | **RC Ch.** | Roman Catholic Church | | fachsprachlich | **tech.** | technical |
| | | | | Fernsprechwesen | **Teleph.** | Telephony |
| Rechtssprache | **Rechtsspr.** | legal terminology | | Fernsehen | **Telev.** | Television |
| Rechtswesen | **Rechtsw.** | Law | | Textilwesen | **Textilw.** | Textiles |
| reflexiv | **refl.** | reflexive | | Theologie | **Theol.** | Theology |
| regelmäßig | **regelm.** | regular | | Tiermedizin | **Tiermed.** | Veterinary Medicine |
| relativ | **rel.** | relative | | | | |
| Religion | **Rel.** | Religion | | transitiv | **tr.** | transitive |
| Relativpronomen | **Relativ-pron.** | relative pronoun | | Trennung | **Trenn.** | division |
| | | | | und | **u.** | and |
| römisch | **röm.** | Roman | | und Ähnliches | **u. Ä.** | and similar |
| römisch-katholisch | **röm-kath.** | Roman Catholic | | umgangssprachlich | **ugs.** | colloquial |
| Rundfunk | **Rundf.** | Radio | | unbestimmt | **unbest.** | indefinite |
| siehe | **s.** | see | | Universität | **Univ.** | University |
| Seite | **S.** | page | | unpersönlich | **unpers.** | impersonal |
| jemand | **sb.** | somebody | | unregelmäßig | **unr.** | irregular |
| Schule | **Sch.** | School | | gewöhnlich | **usu.** | usually |
| scherzhaft | **scherzh.** | jocular | | und so weiter | **usw.** | et cetera |
| Schülersprache | **Schüler-spr.** | school slang | | von | **v.** | of |
| | | | | Verb | **V.** | verb |
| schweizerisch | **schweiz.** | Swiss | | Hilfsverb | **v. aux.** | auxiliary verb |

# Abkürzungen / Abbreviations

| | | | | | |
|---|---|---|---|---|---|
| veraltet; veraltend | veralt. | obsolete; obsolescent | transitives und in- transitives Verb | v. t. & i. | transitive and intransitive verb |
| Verhaltensfor- schung | Verhal- tensf. | Behavioural Research | vulgär | vulg. | vulgar |
| verhüllend | verhüll. | euphemistic | Werbesprache | Werbespr. | advertising jargon |
| Verkehrswesen | Verkehrsw. | Transport | westdeutsch | westd. | western German |
| Versicherungs- wesen | Versicher- ungsw. | Insurance | Wirtschaft | Wirtsch. | Commerce and Industry |
| Tiermedizin | Vet. Med. | Veterinary Medicine | Wissenschaft | Wissensch. | Science |
| vergleiche | vgl. | compare | Warenzeichen | Wz. | Registered Trade Mark |
| intransitives Verb | v. i. | intransitive verb | Zahnmedizin | Zahnmed. | Dentistry |
| Verkleinerungs- form | Vkl. | diminutive | zum Beispiel | z. B. | for example |
| Völkerkunde | Völkerk. | Ethnology | Zeitungswesen | Zeitungsw. | Newspaper Industry |
| volkstümlich | volkst. | popular, vernacular | Zoologie | Zool. | Zoology |
| reflexives Verb | v. refl. | reflexive verb | Zusammensetzung | Zus. | compound |
| transitives Verb | v. t. | transitive verb | Zusammen- schreibung | Zusschr. | writing as one word |

**a, A** /aː/ *das;* ~, ~ **(a)** (Buchstabe) a/A; **das A und O** (fig.) the essential thing/things (*Gen.* for); **von A bis Z** (fig. ugs.) from beginning to end

**(b)** (Musik) [key of] A

**a** *Abk.* = **Ar**

**à** /a/ *Präp. mit Nom., Akk.* (Kaufmannsspr.) **zehn Marken à 0,56 Euro** ten stamps at 0·56 euro each

**A** *Abk.* = **Autobahn** ≈ M

**Aal** *der;* ~[e]s, ~e eel; ~ **grün** (Kochk.) green eels; stewed eels

**aalen** *refl. V.* (ugs.) stretch out

**aal·glatt** (abwertend) 1 *Adj.* slippery; ~ **sein** be as slippery as an eel 2 *adv.* smoothly

**Aas** *das;* ~es, ~e *od.* **Äser (a)** *Pl.* ~e carrion *no art.;* (Kadaver) [rotting] carcass **(b)** *Pl.* **Äser** (salopp abwertend) swine; (anerkennend) devil

**ab** 1 *Präp. mit Dat.* **(a)** from; **ab 1980** as from 1980; **ab Werk** (Kaufmannsspr.) ex works; **ab Frankfurt fliegen** fly from Frankfurt **(b)** ([Rang]folge) from … on[wards]; **ab 20 Euro** from 20 euros [upwards] 2 *Adv.* **(a)** (weg) off; away; **[an etw. (***Dat.***)] ab sein** (ugs.: sich [von etw.] gelöst haben) have come off [sth.] **(b)** (ugs.: Aufforderung) off; away; **ab nach Hause** get off home **(c) Gewehr ab!** (milit. Kommando) order arms! **(d) ab und zu** *od.* **an** now and then

**ab|ändern** *tr. V.* alter; amend ⟨text⟩

**Ab·änderung** *die* alteration; (eines Textes) amendment

**ab|arbeiten** *tr. V.* work for ⟨meal⟩; work off ⟨debt, amount⟩

**Ab·art** *die* variety

**ab·artig** *Adj.* deviant; abnormal

**Ab·artigkeit** *die;* ~, ~en abnormality; deviancy

**Abb.** *Abk.* = **Abbildung** Fig.

**Ab·bau** *der* **(a)** dismantling; (von Zelten, Lagern) striking **(b)** ▶ ABBAUEN C: cutback (*Gen.* in); pruning; reduction **(c)** (Bergbau) mining; (von Stein) quarrying

**ab|bauen** *tr. V.* **(a)** dismantle; strike ⟨tent, camp⟩ **(b)** (beseitigen) gradually remove; break down ⟨prejudices, inhibitions⟩ **(c)** (verringern) cut back ⟨staff⟩; prune ⟨jobs⟩; reduce ⟨wages⟩ **(d)** (Bergbau) mine; quarry ⟨stone⟩

**ab|beißen** 1 *unr. tr. V.* bite off 2 *unr. itr. V.* have a bite

**ab|bekommen** *unr. tr. V.* **(a)** get **(b) einen Schlag/ein paar Kratzer** ~: get hit/ get a few scratches; **etwas** ~ (getroffen werden) be hit; (verletzt werden) be hurt **(c)** (los-, herunterbekommen) get ⟨paint, lid, chain⟩ off

**ab|berufen** *unr. tr. V.* recall ⟨ambassador, envoy⟩ (**aus, von** from)

**ab|bestellen** *tr. V.* cancel

**ab|bezahlen** *tr. V.* pay off

**ab|biegen** *unr. itr. V.; mit sein* turn off; **links/rechts** ~: turn [off] left/right

**Abbieger** *der;* ~s, ~, **Abbiegerin** *die;* ~, ~nen (Verkehrsw.) motorist/cyclist/car *etc.* turning off

**Ab·bild** *das* (eines Menschen) likeness; (eines Gegenstandes) copy; (fig.) portrayal

**ab|bilden** *tr. V.* copy; reproduce ⟨object, picture⟩; depict ⟨person, landscape⟩; (fig.) portray

**Abbildung** *die* illustration

**ab|binden** *unr. tr. V.* **(a)** (losbinden) untie; undo **(b)** (abschnüren) put a tourniquet on ⟨artery, arm, leg, etc.⟩; tie ⟨umbilical cord⟩

**ab|blasen** *unr. tr. V.* (ugs.) call off

**ab|blättern** *itr. V.; mit sein* flake off

**ab|blenden** *tr., itr. V.* black out; dip (Brit.), dim (Amer.) ⟨headlights⟩; **bei Gegenverkehr frühzeitig** ~: dip *or* (Amer.) dim one's headlights promptly when there is oncoming traffic

**ab|blitzen** *itr. V.; mit sein* (ugs.) **sie ließ alle Verehrer** ~: she gave all her admirers the brush-off

**ab|brausen** *tr. V.* ▶ ABDUSCHEN

**ab|brechen** 1 *unr. tr. V.* **(a)** break off; break ⟨needle, pencil⟩ **(b)** (zerlegen) strike ⟨tent, camp⟩ **(c)** (abreißen) demolish; pull down ⟨building⟩ **(d)** (beenden) break off ⟨negotiations, [diplomatic] relations, discussion, activity⟩; (vorzeitig) cut short ⟨conversation, holiday, activity⟩ **(e)** (DV) cancel 2 *unr. itr. V.* **(a)** *mit sein* break [off] **(b)** (aufhören) break off

**ab|bremsen** 1 *tr. V.* **(a)** brake **(b)** retard ⟨motion⟩ 2 *itr. V.* brake

**ab|brennen** 1 *unr. itr. V.; mit sein* **(a)** be burned down; **das Haus ist abgebrannt** the house has burned down **(b)** ⟨fuse⟩ burn away; ⟨candle⟩ burn down 2 *unr. tr. V.* **(a)** let off ⟨firework⟩ **(b)** burn down ⟨building⟩

**a**

**ab|bringen** *unr. tr. V.* jmdn. davon ~, etw. zu tun dissuade sb. from doing sth; jmdn. vom Kurs ~: make sb. change course

**ab|bröckeln** *itr. V.; mit sein* (auch fig.) crumble away

**Ab-bruch** *der* (a) (Abriss) demolition; pulling down
(b) (Beendigung) breaking-off; (einer Schwangerschaft) termination
(c) einer Sache (*Dat.*) [keinen] ~ tun do [no] harm to sth.

**ab|buchen** *tr. V.* ⟨*bank*⟩ debit (von to); ⟨*creditor*⟩ claim by direct debit (von to); etw. ~ lassen (durch die Bank) pay sth. by standing order; (durch Gläubiger) pay sth. by direct debit

**ab|bügeln** *tr. V.* (ugs.) reject, brush aside ⟨*warning, question, criticism*⟩; rebuff ⟨*person*⟩

**ab|bürsten** *tr. V.* (a) brush off
(b) (säubern) brush ⟨*garment*⟩

**ab|büßen** *tr. V.* serve [out] ⟨*prison sentence*⟩

**Abc** /a(:)be(:)'ts:e:/ *das;* ~ (auch fig.) ABC

**Abc-Schütze** *der,* **Abc-Schützin** *die* child just starting school

**ab|dampfen** *itr. V.; mit sein* (ugs.: abfahren) set off

**ab|danken** *itr. V.* ⟨*ruler*⟩ abdicate; ⟨*government, minister*⟩ resign

**Abdankung** *die;* ~, ~en ▶ ABDANKEN: abdication; resignation

**ab|decken** *tr. V.* (a) open up; ⟨*gale*⟩ take the roof/roofs off ⟨*house*⟩, take the tiles off ⟨*roof*⟩
(b) (herunternehmen, -reißen) take off
(c) (abräumen) clear ⟨*table*⟩; clear away ⟨*dishes*⟩
(d) (schützen) cover ⟨*person*⟩

**ab|dichten** *tr. V.* seal

**ab|drängen** *tr. V.* push away

**ab|drehen** ① *tr. V.* (a) (ausschalten) turn off; den Hahn ~ (fig.) turn off the supply
(b) (abtrennen) twist off
② *itr. V.; meist mit sein* turn off

**Ab-druck** *der; Pl.* Abdrücke mark; (Fuß~) footprint; (Wachs~) impression; (Gips~) cast

**ab|drücken** ① *itr. V.* pull the trigger; shoot
② *tr. V.* (zudrücken) constrict

**ab|dunkeln** *tr. V.* darken ⟨*room*⟩; dim ⟨*light*⟩

**ab|duschen** *tr. V.* sich/jmdn. [warm] ~: take/give sb. a [hot] shower

**ab|düsen** *itr. V.* (ugs.) zoom off

*****abend** ▶ ABEND A

**Abend** *der;* ~s, ~e evening; guten ~! good evening; am [frühen/späten] ~: early/late] in the evening; heute/morgen/gestern ~: this/tomorrow/yesterday evening; zu ~ essen have dinner; (allgemeiner) have one's evening meal; ein bunter ~: a social [evening]

**abend-, Abend-:** ~**akademie** *die*

---
*old spelling - see note on page xiv

evening school; ~**anzug** *der* evening suit; ~**blatt** *das* evening [news]paper; ~**brot** *das* supper; ~**dämmerung** *die* [evening] twilight; ~**essen** *das* dinner; ~**füllend** *Adj.* occupying a whole evening *postpos., not pred.;* ein ~füllendes Programm a full evening's programme; ~**gymnasium** *das* night school, evening classes *pl.* (*leading to the 'Abitur'*); ~**kasse** *die* box office (*open on the evening of the performance*); ~**kleid** *das* evening dress; ~**kurs[us]** *der* evening class

**Abend-land** *das;* ~[e]s West

**abendlich** *Adj.* evening; ⟨*quiet, coolness*⟩ of the evening

**Abend-:** ~**mahl** *das* (Rel.) Communion; (N.T.) Last Supper; ~**programm** *das* evening programmes *pl.;* ~**rot** *das* red glow of the sunset sky

**abends** *Adv.* in the evenings; um sechs Uhr ~: at six o'clock in the evening

**Abend-:** ~**schule** *die* night school; ~**sonne** *die* evening sun; ~**stern** *der* evening star; ~**stunde** *die* evening hour; in den frühen/späten ~stunden early/late in the evening; ~**vorstellung** *die* evening performance; ~**zeitung** *die* ▶ ~BLATT

**Abenteuer** *das;* ~s, ~ (a) (auch fig.) adventure
(b) (Unternehmen) venture
(c) (Liebesaffäre) affair

**abenteuerlich** *Adj.* (a) (riskant) risky
(b) (bizarr) bizarre

**Abenteuer-:** ~**lust** *die* thirst for adventure; ~**roman** *der* adventure novel

**Abenteurer** *der;* ~s, ~: adventurer

**Abenteurerin** *die;* ~, ~nen adventuress

**aber** ① *Konj.* but
② *Partikel* ~ ja/nein! why, yes/no! ~ natürlich! but of course!; du bist ~ groß! aren't you tall!

**Aber-glaube[n]** *der* superstition

**aber-gläubisch** *Adj.* superstitious

**abermals** *Adv.* once again; once more

**Abf.** *Abk.* = Abfahrt dep.

**ab|fahren** ① *unr. itr. V.; mit sein* (a) (wegfahren) leave; wo fährt der Zug nach Paris ab? where does the Paris train leave from?
(b) (hinunterfahren) drive down; (Skisport) ski down
(c) (salopp: sich begeistern) auf jmdn./etw. [voll] ~: be mad about sb./sth.
(d) (salopp: abgewiesen werden) jmdn. ~ lassen tell sb. where he/she can go (sl.)
② *unr. tr. V.* (a) (abtransportieren) take away
(b) (abnutzen) wear out; abgefahrene Reifen worn tyres

**Ab-fahrt** *die* (a) departure
(b) (Skisport) descent; (Strecke) run

**Abfahrts-:** ~**lauf** *der* (Skisport) downhill [racing]; ~**läufer** *der,* ~**läuferin** *die*

(Skisport) downhill racer; **~rennen** *das* (Skisport) downhill [racing]; **~zeit** *die* time of departure; departure time

**Ab·fall** *der* (Küchen~ o Ä.) rubbish, (Amer.) trash *no indef. art., no pl.*; (Fleisch~) offal *no indef. art., no pl.*; (Industrie~) waste *no indef. art.*; (auf der Straße) litter *no indef. art., no pl.*

**Abfall: ~beseitigung** *die* refuse disposal; (industriell) waste disposal; **~eimer** *der* rubbish bin; trash can (Amer.); (auf der Straße) litter bin; trash can (Amer.)

**ab|fallen** *unr. itr. V.; mit sein* **(a)** fall off **(b)** (abschüssig sein) ⟨*land, road, etc.*⟩ drop away, slope **(c)** (übrigbleiben) be left [over]; **für dich wird** [dabei] **auch etwas ~:** you'll get something out of it too **(d) von jmdm. ~:** leave sb.; **vom Glauben ~:** desert the faith

**ab·fällig** ① *Adj.* disparaging ② *adv.* **sich ~ über jmdn. äußern** make disparaging remarks about sb.

**Abfall-: ~produkt** *das* (auch fig.) by-product; (Sekundärstoff) secondary product; **~vermeidung** *die* waste avoidance

**ab|fangen** *unr. tr. V.* **(a)** catch; intercept ⟨*agent, message, aircraft*⟩ **(b)** repel ⟨*charge, assault*⟩; ward off ⟨*blow, attack*⟩

**ab|färben** *itr. V.* **(a)** ⟨*colour, garment, etc.*⟩ run **(b) auf jmdn./etw. ~** (fig.) rub off on sb./sth.

**ab|fassen** *tr. V.* write ⟨*report, letter, etc.*⟩; draw up ⟨*will*⟩

**ab|fegen** *tr. V.* **(a)** brush off; **etw. von etw. ~:** brush sth. off sth. **(b)** (säubern) **etw. ~:** brush sth. clean

**ab|feiern** *tr. V.* use up ⟨*excess hours worked*⟩ (by taking time off)

**ab|fertigen** *tr. V.* dispatch ⟨*mail*⟩; deal with ⟨*applicant*⟩; handle ⟨*passengers*⟩; serve ⟨*customer*⟩; clear ⟨*ship*⟩ for sailing; clear ⟨*aircraft*⟩ for take-off; clear ⟨*lorry*⟩ for departure

**ab|feuern** *tr. V.* fire

**ab|finden** ① *unr. tr. V.* **jmdn. mit etw. ~:** compensate sb. with sth.; **seine Gläubiger ~:** settle with one's creditors ② *unr. refl. V.* **sich ~:** resign oneself; **sich ~ mit** come to terms with; learn to live with ⟨*noise, heat*⟩

**Abfindung** *die* **~, ~en** settlement; **eine ~ in Höhe von ... zahlen** make a settlement of ...

**Abfindungs·summe** *die* ▶ ABFINDUNG

**ab|flauen** *itr. V.; mit sein* die down; subside; ⟨*interest, conversation*⟩ flag; ⟨*business*⟩ become slack; ⟨*noise*⟩ abate

**ab|fliegen** *unr. itr. V.; mit sein* leave

**ab|fließen** *unr. itr. V.; mit sein* flow off

**Ab·flug** *der* departure

**Abflug·zeit** *die* departure time

**Ab·fluss, \*Ab·fluß** *der* drain; (Rohr) drainpipe; (für Abwasser) waste pipe

**Ab·folge** *die* sequence; **die ~ der Jahreszeiten** the cycle of the seasons

**ab|fotografieren** *tr. V.* take pictures of

**ab|fragen** *tr. V.* test; **jmdn. od. jmdm. die Vokabeln ~:** test sb. on his/her vocabulary

**Abfuhr** *die* **~, ~en (a)** removal **(b) jmdm. eine ~ erteilen** (fig. ugs.) rebuff sb.

**ab|führen** ① *tr. V.* **(a)** (nach Festnahme) take away **(b)** (zahlen) pay out **(c)** (abbringen) take away ② *itr. V.* (für Stuhlgang sorgen) be a laxative

**Abführ·mittel** *das* laxative

**ab|füllen** *tr. V.* (in Flaschen) bottle; (in Dosen) can

**Ab·gabe** *die* **(a)** handing in; (eines Briefes, Pakets, Telegramms) delivery; (eines Gesuchs, Antrags) submission **(b)** (Steuer, Gebühr) tax; (auf Produkte) duty **(c)** (Ausstrahlung) release; emission **(d)** (Sport: Abspiel) pass

**Ab·gang** *der* **(a)** leaving; departure; (Abfahrt) departure; (Theater) exit **(b)** (jmd., der ausscheidet) departure; (Schule) leaver **(c)** (bes. Amtsspr.: Todesfall) death **(d)** (Turnen) dismount

**Ab·gas** *das* exhaust

**Abgas·katalysator** *der* (Kfz-W.) catalytic converter

**abgearbeitet** *Adj.* work-worn ⟨*hands*⟩

**ab|geben** ① *unr. tr. V.* **(a)** (aushändigen) hand over; deliver ⟨*letter, parcel, telegram*⟩; hand in, submit ⟨*application*⟩; hand in ⟨*school work*⟩; **den Mantel in der Garderobe ~:** leave one's coat in the cloakroom **(b)** *auch itr.* **jmdm.** [etwas] **von etw. ~:** let sb. have some of sth. **(c)** (abfeuern) fire ② *unr. refl. V.* **sich mit jmdm./etw. ~:** spend time on sb./sth.; (geringschätzig) waste one's time on sb./sth.

**ab-gebrannt** *Adj.* (ugs.) broke (coll.)

**abgebrüht** *Adj.* (ugs.) hardened

**ab-gedroschen** *Adj.* (ugs.) hackneyed

**ab-gegriffen** *Adj.* battered

**ab|gehen** *unr. itr. V.; mit sein* **(a)** (sich entfernen) leave; (Theater) exit **(b)** (ausscheiden) leave **(c)** (abfahren) ⟨*train, ship, bus*⟩ leave, depart **(d)** (abgeschickt werden) ⟨*message, letter*⟩ be sent [off] **(e)** (abzweigen) branch off **(f)** (sich lösen) come off

**abgehetzt** *Adj.* exhausted

**ab-gelegen** *Adj.* remote; (einsam) isolated; out-of-the-way ⟨*district*⟩

**abgemagert** *Adj.* emaciated; wasted

**ab-geneigt** *Adj.* averse (*Dat.* to); [nicht] **~ sein, etw. zu tun** [not] be averse to doing sth.

**a**

**Abgeordnete** *der/die; adj. Dekl.* member [of parliament]; (z.B. in Frankreich) deputy

**ab·gerissen** *Adj.* ragged

**ab·geschieden** *Adj.* secluded; (abgelegen) isolated

**ab·geschlagen** *Adj.* (Sport) [well] beaten

**ab·geschlossen** *Adj.* secluded

**ab·geschnitten** *Adj.* isolated; **von der Außenwelt** ~: cut off from the outside world

**ab·gesehen** *Adv.* ~ **von** apart from; ~ **davon, dass …** apart from the fact that …

**ab·gespannt** *Adj.* weary; exhausted

**ab·gestanden** *Adj.* flat

**ab·gestorben** *Adj.* dead ‹*branch, tree*›; numb ‹*fingers, legs, etc.*›

**ab·getreten** *Adj.* worn down

**abgewetzt** *Adj.* well-worn; battered ‹*case etc.*›

**ab|gewöhnen** *tr. V.:* **jmdm. etw.** ~: make sb. give up sth.; **sich** (*Dat.*) **etw.** ~: give up sth.

**ab|gießen** *unr. tr. V.* pour away ‹*liquid*›; drain ‹*potatoes*›

**abgöttisch** *Adj.* idolatrous

**ab|grenzen** *tr. V.* (a) bound; **etw. gegen** *od.* **von etw.** ~: separate sth. from sth.
(b) (unterscheiden) distinguish

**Ab·grund** *der* abyss; chasm; (Abhang) precipice

**ab|hacken** *tr. V.* chop off; **jmdm. die Hand** *usw.* ~: chop sb.'s hand *etc.* off

**ab|haken** *tr. V.* tick off; check off (Amer.)

**ab|halten** *unr. tr. V.* (a) **jmdn./etw. [von jmdm./etw.]** ~: keep sb./sth. off [sb./sth.]
(b) **jmdn. davon** ~, **etw. zu tun** stop sb. doing sth.
(c) (durchführen) hold ‹*elections, meeting, referendum*›

**ab|handeln** *tr. V.* (a) **jmdm. etw.** ~: do a deal with sb. for sth.
(b) (darstellen) deal with

**abhanden** *Adv.* ~ **kommen** get lost; go astray; **etw. kommt jmdm.** ~: sb. loses sth.

**Ab·handlung** *die* treatise (über + *Akk.* on)

**Ab·hang** *der* slope; incline

**ab|hängen¹** *unr. itr. V.* **von jmdm./etw.** ~: depend on sb./sth.

**ab|hängen²** [1] *tr. V.* (a) take down
(b) (abkuppeln) uncouple
(c) (ugs.) shake off ‹*pursuer, competitor*›
[2] *itr. V.* (den Hörer auflegen) hang up

**abhängig** *Adj.* dependent (**von** on); (süchtig) addicted (**von** to); **von jmdm./etw.** ~ **sein** depend on sb./sth.

**Abhängige** *der/die; adj. Dekl.* (Rechtspr.) dependant; (Untergebene) subordinate

**Abhängigkeit** *die;* ~, ~**en** dependence; (Sucht) addiction

**Abhängigkeits·verhältnis** *das* relationship of dependence (**zu** on)

---

*alte Schreibung - vgl. Hinweis auf S. xiv

**ab|härten** *tr. V.* harden

**ab|hauen** [1] *unr. tr. V.* (a) *Prät.* **haute ab** knock off
(b) *Prät.* **hieb** (geh.) *od.* **haute ab** (mit Schwert, Axt usw.) chop off
[2] *unr. itr. V.; mit sein; Prät.* **haute ab** (salopp) beat it (coll.)

**ab|heben** [1] *unr. tr. V.* (a) lift off ‹*lid, cover, etc.*›; [**den Hörer**] ~: answer [the telephone]
(b) (von einem Konto) withdraw ‹*money*›
[2] *unr. itr. V.* ‹*balloon*› rise; ‹*aircraft, bird*› take off; ‹*rocket*› lift off
[3] *unr. refl. V.* stand out (**von** against)

**ab|heften** *tr. V.* file

**ab|hetzen** *refl. V.* rush [around]; *s. auch* ABGEHETZT

**Ab·hilfe** *die* action to improve matters; ~ **schaffen** put things right

**ab|holen** *tr. V.* collect, pick up ‹*parcel, book, tickets, etc.*›; pick up ‹*person*›

**ab|hören** *tr. V.* (a) **jmdm.** *od.* **jmdn. Vokabeln** ~: test sb.'s vocabulary [orally]; **das Einmaleins** ~: ask questions on the multiplication tables
(b) tap ‹*telephone conversation, telephone*›; bug (coll.) ‹*conversation, premises*›; **jmdn.** ~: tap sb.'s telephone

**abhör·sicher** *Adj.* bug-proof (coll.); tap-proof ‹*telephone*›

**Abi** *das;* ~**s,** ~**s** (Schülerspr.), **Abitur** *das;* ~**s,** ~**e** Abitur (*school-leaving examination at grammar school needed for entry to higher education*); ≈ A levels (Brit.)

**Abiturient** *der;* ~**en,** ~**en, Abiturientin** *die;* ~, ~**nen** sb. who is taking/has passed the 'Abitur'

**ab|jagen** *tr. V.* **jmdm. etw.** ~: finally get sth. away from sb.

**Abk.** *Abk.* = **Abkürzung** abbr.

**ab|kapseln** *tr. V.* encapsulate; **sich gegen die Umwelt** ~ (fig.) isolate oneself from one's surroundings

**ab|kaufen** *tr. V.* **jmdm. etw.** ~: buy sth. from sb.

**Ab·klatsch** *der* (abwertend) pale imitation; poor copy

**ab|klopfen** *tr. V.* (a) knock off
(b) (säubern) knock the dirt/snow/crumbs *etc.* off
(c) (untersuchen) tap

**ab|knallen** *tr. V.* (salopp) shoot down; gun down

**ab|knicken** [1] *tr. V.* snap off
[2] *itr. V.; mit sein* snap

**ab|kochen** *tr. V.* boil

**ab|kommen** *unr. itr. V.; mit sein* (a) **vom Weg** ~: lose one's way; **vom Kurs** ~: go off course; **von der Fahrbahn** ~: leave the road; **vom Thema** ~: stray from the topic
(b) **von einem Plan** ~: abandon a plan

**Ab·kommen** *das;* ~**s,** ~: agreement

**abkömmlich** *Adj.* free; available

**ạb|können** *unr. tr. V.* (nordd.: mögen) stand; (vertragen) take

**ạb|kratzen** 1 *tr. V.* (a) (mit den Fingern) scratch off; (mit einem Werkzeug) scrape off
(b) (säubern) scrape [clean]
2 *itr. V.; mit sein* (derb) snuff it (sl.)

**ạb|kriegen** *tr. V.* (ugs.) ▶ ABBEKOMMEN

**ạb|kühlen** 1 *tr. V.* cool down
2 *itr., refl. V.; itr. meist mit sein* cool down

**Ạb·kühlung** *die* cooling

**ạb|kupfern** *tr. V.* (ugs.) copy mechanically (**bei** from)

**ạb|kürzen** *tr., itr. V.* (a) (räumlich) shorten; **den Weg ~**: take a shorter route
(b) (zeitlich) cut short
(c) (kürzer schreiben) abbreviate (**mit** to)

**Ạbkürzung** *die* (a) (Weg) short cut
(b) (Wort) abbreviation

**ạb|küssen** *tr. V.* cover with kisses

**ạb|laden** *unr. tr., itr. V.* unload

**Ạb·lage** *die* (a) storage place
(b) (Raum) storage room
(c) (Bürow.) filing

**ạb|lagern** *tr. V.* deposit

**ạb|lassen** 1 *unr. tr. V.* let out (**aus** of); let off ⟨*steam*⟩
2 *unr. itr. V.* (a) **von jmdm./etw. ~**: leave sb./sth. alone
(b) **von etw. ~** ⟨etw. aufgeben⟩ give sth. up

**Ạb·lauf** *der* (a) (Verlauf) course; (einer Veranstaltung) passing off
(b) (Ende) **nach ~ eines Jahres** after a year; **nach ~ einer Frist** at the end of a period of time

**ạb|laufen** *unr. itr. V.; mit sein* (a) flow away; (aus einem Behälter) run out
(b) (verlaufen) pass off
(c) ⟨*alarm clock*⟩ run down; ⟨*parking meter*⟩ expire
(d) ⟨*period, contract, passport*⟩ expire

**ạb|lecken** *tr. V.* (a) lick off
(b) (säubern) lick clean

**ạb|legen** 1 *tr. V.* (a) lay *or* put down
(b) (Bürow.) file
(c) stop wearing ⟨*clothes*⟩
(d) give up ⟨*habit*⟩; lose ⟨*shyness*⟩
(e) swear ⟨*oath*⟩; sit ⟨*examination*⟩; make ⟨*confession*⟩
2 *tr., itr. V.* take off; **möchten Sie ~?** would you like to take your coat off?
3 *itr. V.* [**vom Kai**] **~**: cast off

**Ạbleger** *der;* **~s, ~**: layer; (Steckling) cutting

**ạb|lehnen** *tr. V.* (a) decline; decline, turn down ⟨*money, invitation, position*⟩; reject ⟨*suggestion, applicant*⟩
(b) (missbilligen) disapprove of

**Ạblehnung** *die;* **~, ~en** (a) rejection
(b) (Missbilligung) disapproval

**ạb|leiten** *tr. V.* (a) divert
(b) (herleiten) **etw. aus/von etw. ~**: derive sth. from sth.

**Ạb·leitung** *die* derivation

**ạb|lenken** *tr. V.* (a) deflect
(b) **jmdn. von etw. ~**: distract sb. from sth.
(c) (zerstreuen) divert; **sich ~**: amuse oneself

**Ạb·lenkung** *die* ▶ ABLENKEN: deflection; distraction; diversion

**Ạblenkungs·manöver** *das* diversion[ary tactic]

**ạb|lesen** *unr. tr. V.* (a) read ⟨*speech, lecture*⟩; **werden Sie frei sprechen oder ~?** will you be talking from notes or reading your speech?
(b) read ⟨*gas meter, thermometer, etc.*⟩; check ⟨*time, speed, temperature*⟩
(c) (erkennen) see

**ạb|lichten** *tr. V.* (a) (fotokopieren) photocopy
(b) (fotografieren) take a photograph of

**Ạb·lichtung** *die* (a) (das Fotografieren) photographing; (das Fotokopieren) photocopying
(b) (Fotokopie) photocopy

**ạb|liefern** *tr., itr. V.* hand in; deliver ⟨*goods*⟩

**ạb|lösen** 1 *tr. V.* (a) **etw. [von etw.] ~**: get sth. off [sth.]
(b) **jmdn. ~**: relieve sb.; **sich** *od.* **einander ~**: take turns
2 *refl. V.* **sich [von etw.] ~**: come off [sth.]

**Ạb·lösung** *die* (eines Postens) changing; **ich schicke Ihnen jemanden zur ~**: I'll send someone to relieve you

**ạb|machen** *tr. V.* (a) (ugs.) take off; take down ⟨*sign, rope*⟩
(b) (vereinbaren) agree

**Ạbmachung** *die;* **~, ~en** agreement

**ạb|magern** *itr. V.; mit sein* become thin; (absichtlich) slim

**Ạbmagerungs·kur** *die* reducing diet

**ạb|marschieren** *itr. V.; mit sein* depart; (Milit.) march off

**ạb|melden** *tr. V.* (a) **sich/jmdn. ~**: report that one/sb. is leaving
(b) (Umzug melden) notify the authorities that one is moving from an address;
(c) **ein Auto ~**: cancel a car's registration
(d) (DV) ▶ AUSLOGGEN

**Ạb·meldung** *die* (a) (beim Weggehen) report that one is leaving
(b) (beim Umzug) registration of a move with the authorities at one's old address;
(c) **~ eines Autos** cancellation of a car's registration

**Ạb·messung** *die* (Dimension) dimension; measurement

**ạb|montieren** *tr. V.* take off ⟨*part*⟩; dismantle ⟨*machine, equipment*⟩

**ạb|mühen** *refl. V.* toil; **sie mühte sich mit dem schweren Koffer ab** she struggled with the heavy suitcase

**ạb|murksen** *tr. V.* (salopp) do in (sl.)

**Ạbnahme** *die;* **~, ~n** (a) (das Entfernen) removal
(b) (Verminderung) decrease

**a**

**ạb|nehmen** ⟨1⟩ *unr. tr. V.* **(a)** (entfernen) take off; take down ⟨*picture, curtain, lamp*⟩
**(b) jmdm. den Koffer** ∼: take sb.'s suitcase; **jmdm. eine Arbeit** ∼: save sb. a job
**(c) jmdm. ein Versprechen/einen Eid** ∼: make sb. give a promise/swear an oath
**(d)** (prüfen) inspect and approve; test and pass ⟨*vehicle*⟩
**(e) jmdm. etw.** ∼ (wegnehmen) take sth. off sb.
**(f)** (beim Telefon) answer ⟨*telephone*⟩; pick up ⟨*receiver*⟩
**(g)** (Handarb.) decrease
**(h) das nehme ich dir/ihm** *usw.* **nicht ab** I won't buy that (coll.)
⟨2⟩ *unr. itr. V.* **(a)** (Gewicht verlieren) lose weight
**(b)** (sich verringern) decrease; drop; ⟨*attention, interest*⟩ flag; ⟨*brightness*⟩ diminish; **wir haben** ∼**den Mond** there is a waning moon
**(c)** (beim Telefon) answer the telephone
**Ạb-neigung** *die* dislike (**gegen** for)
**ạb|nutzen,** (landsch.:) **ạb|nützen** *tr., refl. V.* wear out; **abgenutzt** worn
**Abonnement** /abonə'mã:/ *das;* ∼s, ∼s subscription (*Gen.* to)
**Abonnẹnt** *der;* ∼en, ∼en, **Abonnẹntin** *die;* ∼, ∼nen subscriber (+ *Gen.* to); (Theater, Oper) season ticket holder
**abonnieren** *tr. V.* subscribe to
**Ạb-ordnung** *die* delegation
**ạb|packen** *tr. V.* pack; wrap ⟨*bread*⟩; **abgepacktes Obst/abgepackte Fleischportionen** packaged fruit/pieces of meat
**ạb|passen** *tr. V.* **(a)** (abwarten) wait for
**(b)** (aufhalten) catch
**ạb|pausen** *tr. V.* trace
**ạb|pfeifen** (Sport) ⟨1⟩ *itr. V.* blow the whistle
⟨2⟩ *tr. V.* [blow the whistle to] stop
**Ạb-pfiff** *der* (Sport) final whistle; (Halbzeit∼) half-time whistle
**ạb|pflücken** *tr. V.* pick
**ạb|plagen** *refl. V.* slave away
**ạb|prallen** *itr. V.; mit sein* rebound; ⟨*bullet, missile*⟩ ricochet
**Ạb-produkt** *das* waste product
**ạb|putzen** *tr. V.* (ugs.); **(a)** wipe off
**(b)** (säubern) wipe; **jmdm./sich das Gesicht** ∼: clean sb.'s/one's face
**ạb|quälen** *refl. V.* **sich [mit etw.]** ∼: struggle [with sth.]
**ạb|rackern** *refl. V.* (ugs.) flog oneself to death (coll.)
**ạb|rasieren** *tr. V.* shave off
**ạb|raten** *unr. itr. V.* **jmdm. von etw.** ∼: advise sb. against sth.
**ạb|räumen** *tr. V.* **(a)** clear away
**(b)** (leer machen) clear ⟨*table*⟩
**ạb|rechnen** ⟨1⟩ *itr. V.* cash up; **mit jmdm.** ∼ (fig.) call sb. to account

⟨2⟩ *tr. V.* **die Kasse** ∼: reckon up the till; **seine Spesen** ∼: claim one's expenses
**Ạb-rechnung** *die* **(a)** cashing up *no art.;* (Aufstellung) statement
**(b)** (fig.: Vergeltung) reckoning
**Ạb-rede** *die* **(a)** arrangement; agreement
**(b) etw. in** ∼ **stellen** deny sth.
**ạb|regen** *refl. V.* (ugs.) calm down; **reg dich ab!** cool it! (coll.); calm down!
**ạb|reiben** *unr. tr. V.* **(a)** rub off
**(b)** (säubern) rub
**Ạb-reise** *die* departure (**nach** for); **bei meiner** ∼: when I left/leave
**ạb|reisen** *itr. V.; mit sein* leave (**nach** for)
**ạb|reißen** ⟨1⟩ *unr. tr. V.* **(a)** tear off; tear down ⟨*poster, notice*⟩; pull off ⟨*button*⟩
**(b)** (niederreißen) demolish, pull down ⟨*building*⟩
⟨2⟩ *unr. itr. V.; mit sein* **(a)** fly off; ⟨*shoelace*⟩ break off
**(b)** (aufhören) come to an end; ⟨*connection, contact*⟩ be broken off
**ạb|richten** *tr. V.* train
**Ạb-riss, *Ạb-riß** *der* **(a)** ▶ ABREISSEN 1B: demolition; pulling down
**(b)** (knappe Darstellung) outline
**ạb|rollen** ⟨1⟩ *tr. V.* unwind
⟨2⟩ *itr. V.; mit sein* unwind [itself]
**ạb|rücken** ⟨1⟩ *tr. V.* (wegschieben) move away
⟨2⟩ *itr. V.; mit sein* move away
**Ạb-ruf** *der:* **auf** ∼: on call; (DV) in retrievable form
**ạb|rufen** *unr. tr. V.* summon; call
**ạb|runden** *tr. V.* **(a)** (auch fig.) round off
**(b)** round ⟨*figure*⟩ up/down (**auf** + **Akk.** to); **etw. nach oben/unten** ∼: round sth. up/down
**abrụpt** ⟨1⟩ *Adj.* abrupt
⟨2⟩ *adv.* abruptly
**ạb|rüsten** *itr., tr. V.* disarm
**Ạb-rüstung** *die;* ∼: disarmament
**ạb|rutschen** *itr. V.; mit sein* **(a)** slip
**(b)** (nach unten rutschen) slide down
**Abs.** *Abk.* **(a)** = **Absender;**
**(b)** = **Absatz**
**ABS** *Abk.* = **Antiblockiersystem** ABS
**Ạb-sage** *die* (auf eine Einladung) refusal; (auf eine Bewerbung) rejection
**ạb|sagen** ⟨1⟩ *tr. V.* cancel; withdraw ⟨*participation*⟩
⟨2⟩ *itr. V.* **jmdm.** ∼: tell sb. one cannot come
**ạb|sägen** *tr. V.* saw off
**Ạb-satz** *der* **(a)** (am Schuh) heel
**(b)** (Textunterbrechung) break
**(c)** (Textabschnitt) paragraph
**(d)** (Kaufmannsspr.) sales *pl.*
**Ạbsatz-:** ∼**chance** *die* (Kaufmannsspr.) sales prospect; ∼**förderung** *die* (Kaufmannsspr.) sales promotion; ∼**markt** *der* (Kaufmannsspr.) market; ∼**steigerung** *die* (Kaufmannsspr.) increase in sales

---

*old spelling - see note on page xiv

**ab|saufen** *unr. itr. V.; mit sein* (ugs.)
⟨*engine, car*⟩ flood

**ab|saugen** *tr. V.* (a) suck away
(b) (säubern) hoover (Brit.)

**ab|schaben** *tr. V.* (a) scrape off
(b) (säubern) scrape [clean]

**ab|schaffen** *tr. V.* (a) (beseitigen) abolish
⟨*capital punishment, regulation, customs
duty, institution*⟩; repeal ⟨*law*⟩; put an end to
⟨*injustice, abuse*⟩
(b) (weggeben) get rid of

**Ab·schaffung** *die* abolition; (von Gesetzen)
repeal; (von Unrecht, Missstand) ending

**ab|schalten** *tr., itr. V.* switch off; shut
down ⟨*power station*⟩

**abschätzig** ① *Adj.* derogatory
② *adv.* derogatorily

**Ab·scheu** *der;* ∼s detestation; abhorrence

**abscheulich** ① *Adj.* (a) disgusting
⟨*smell, taste*⟩; repulsive ⟨*sight*⟩
(b) (verwerflich) disgraceful ⟨*behaviour*⟩;
abominable ⟨*crime*⟩
② *adv.* disgracefully

**ab|schicken** *tr. V.* send [off]

**ab|schieben** *unr. tr. V.* (a) push away
(b) (abwälzen) shift ⟨*responsibility, blame*⟩
(c) (außer Landes bringen) deport

**Ab·schiebung** *die* (Rechtsw.) deportation

**Abschiebungs·haft** *die* (Rechtsw.)
detention prior to deportation

**Abschied** *der;* ∼[e]s, ∼e parting (von
from); farewell (von to); ∼ nehmen take
one's leave (von of)

**Abschieds-:** ∼brief *der* farewell letter;
∼geschenk *das* parting gift; ∼gruß *der*
goodbye; farewell

**ab|schießen** *unr. tr. V.* (a) shoot down
⟨*aeroplane*⟩
(b) fire ⟨*arrow*⟩; launch ⟨*spacecraft*⟩
(c) (töten) take

**ab|schirmen** *tr. V.* (a) (schützen) shield
(b) (fernhalten) screen off ⟨*light, radiation*⟩

**ab|schlachten** *tr. V.* slaughter

**Ab·schlag** *der* (a) (Kaufmannsspr.) discount
(b) (Teilzahlung) interim payment; (Vorschuss)
advance
(c) (Fußball) goalkeeper's kick out

**ab|schlagen** ① *unr. tr. V.* (a) knock off;
(mit dem Beil, Schwert usw.) chop off
(b) (ablehnen) refuse
(c) (abwehren) beat off
② *unr. itr. V.* (Fußball) kick the ball out

**ab|schleifen** *unr. tr. V.* (von Holz) sand off;
(von Metall, Glas usw.) grind off

**Abschlepp·dienst** *der* breakdown
recovery service; tow[ing] service (Amer.)

**ab|schleppen** tow away; take ⟨*ship*⟩ in
tow; **ein Auto zur Werkstatt** ∼: tow a car to
the garage

**Abschlepp:** ∼**seil** *das* tow rope; (aus
Draht) towing cable; ∼**stange** *die* tow bar;
∼**wagen** *der* breakdown vehicle; tow
truck (Amer.); (der Polizei) tow-away vehicle

**ab|schließen** ① *unr. tr. V.* (a) auch itr.
(zuschließen) lock ⟨*door, gate, cupboard*⟩; lock
[up] ⟨*house, flat, room, park*⟩
(b) (verschließen) seal; **etw. luftdicht** ∼: seal
sth. hermetically
(c) (begrenzen) border
(d) (zum Abschluss bringen) conclude; **sein
Studium** ∼: finish one's studies; **Bewerber
mit abgeschlossenem Universitätsstudium**
applicants with a degree
(e) (vereinbaren) strike ⟨*bargain, deal*⟩; make
⟨*purchase*⟩; enter into ⟨*agreement*⟩
② *unr. itr. V.* (aufhören, enden) end; ∼**d sagte
er** ...: in conclusion he said ...

**Ab·schluss, *Ab·schluß** *der* (a)
(Verschluss) seal
(b) (Beendigung) conclusion; end
(c) (eines Geschäfts, Vertrags) conclusion

**Abschluss-, *Abschluß-:** ∼**ball** *der*
final dance; ∼**prüfung** *die* (a) (Schulw.)
leaving or (Amer.) final examination;
(Hochschulw.) final examination; finals *pl.*; (b)
(Wirtsch.) audit

**ab|schmecken** *tr. V.* (a) (kosten) taste; try
(b) (würzen) season

**ab|schmieren** *tr. V.* (Technik) grease

**ab|schminken** *tr. V.* jmdn./sich ∼:
remove sb.'s/one's make-up

**ab|schmirgeln** *tr. V.* rub off with emery;
(mit Sandpapier) sand off

**ab|schnallen** *tr. V.* unfasten

**ab|schneiden** ① *unr. tr. V.* (a) (auch fig.:
isolieren) cut off; cut down ⟨*sth. hanging*⟩; **etw.
von etw.** ∼: cut sth. off sth.; **sich** (*Dat.*) **eine
Scheibe Brot** ∼: cut oneself a slice of bread
(b) (kürzer schneiden) cut
(c) jmdm. den Weg ∼: take a short cut to
get ahead of sb.
② *unr. itr. V.* **bei etw. gut/schlecht** ∼: do
well/badly in sth.

**Ab·schnitt** *der* (a) (Kapitel) section
(b) (Zeitspanne) phase
(c) (Teil eines Formulars) [detachable] portion

**ab|schrauben** *tr. V.* unscrew [and
remove]

**ab|schrecken** *tr. V.* (a) deter
(b) (fernhalten) scare off
(c) (Kochk.) pour cold water over

**Abschreckung** *die;* ∼, ∼en deterrence;
(Mittel zur Abschreckung) deterrent

**ab|schreiben** ① *unr. tr. V.* (a) copy out;
**etw. bei** od. **von jmdm.** ∼ (in der Schule) copy
sth. off sb.; (als Plagiator) plagiarize sth. from
sb.
(b) (Wirtsch.) amortize
② *unr. itr. V.* **bei** od. **von jmdm.** ∼ (in der
Schule) copy off sb.; (als Plagiator) copy from
sb.

**Ab·schreibung** *die* (Wirtsch.) amortization

**Ab·schrift** *die* copy

**ab|schürfen** *tr. V.* graze

**Ab·schuss, *Ab·schuß** *der* (a) (eines
Flugzeugs) shooting down ····⟩

**(b)** (von Geschossen) firing; (eines Raumschiffs) launching

**abschüssig** *Adj.* downward sloping ‹*land*›

**ab|schütteln** *tr. V.* shake off; (herunterschütteln) shake down

**ab|schwächen** ① *tr. V.* **(a)** (mildern) tone down ‹*statement, criticism*›
**(b)** (verringern) lessen ‹*effect, impression*›; cushion ‹*blow, impact*›
② *refl. V.* ‹*interest, demand*› wane

**Abschwächung** *die;* ~ **(a)** (Milderung) toning down
**(b)** (eines Aufpralls, Stoßes usw.) cushioning

**ab|schweifen** *itr. V.; mit sein* digress

**Abschweifung** *die;* ~, ~en digression

**ab|schwören** *unr. itr. V.* dem Teufel/ seinem Glauben ~: renounce the Devil/one's faith; dem Alkohol/Laster ~: forswear alcohol/vice

**absehbar** *Adj.* foreseeable; in ~er Zeit within the foreseeable future

**ab|sehen** ① *unr. tr. V.* **(a)** (voraussehen) predict; foresee ‹*event*›
**(b)** es auf etw. (*Akk.*) abgesehen haben be after sth.; er hat es darauf abgesehen, uns zu ärgern he's out to annoy us; der Chef hat es auf ihn abgesehen the boss has got it in for him
② *unr. itr. V.* **(a)** von etw. ~ (etw. nicht beachten) leave aside sth.; *s. auch* ABGESEHEN;
**(b)** von etw. ~ (auf etw. verzichten) refrain from sth

**ab|seilen** ① *tr. V.* lower [with a rope]
② *refl. V.* (Bergsteigen) abseil

*****ab|sein** ▶ AB 2A

**abseits** ① *Präp. mit Gen.* away from
② *Adv.* **(a)** far away
**(b)** (Ballspiele) ~ sein *od.* stehen be offside

**Abseits** *das;* ~, ~: das war ein klares ~: that was clearly offside

**ab|senden** *unr. od. regelm. tr. V.* dispatch

**Ab·sender** *der,* **Ab·senderin** *die;* ~, ~nen sender; (Anschrift) sender's address

**ab|setzen** ① *tr. V.* **(a)** take off ‹*hat, glasses, etc.*›
**(b)** (hinstellen) put down ‹*bag, suitcase*›
**(c)** (aussteigen lassen) jmdn. ~ (im öffentlichen Verkehr) put sb. down; let sb. out (Amer.); (im privaten Verkehr) drop sb. [off]
**(d)** remove ‹*chancellor, judge*› from office; depose ‹*king, emperor*›
② *refl. V.* **(a)** (sich ablagern) be deposited
**(b)** (flüchten) get away

**Absetzung** *die;* ~, ~en ▶ ABSETZEN 1D: removal; deposition

**ab|sichern** ① *tr. V.* make safe
② *refl. V.* safeguard oneself

**Ab·sicht** *die* intention; etw. mit ~ tun do sth. intentionally; etw. ohne *od.* nicht mit ~ tun do sth. unintentionally

**ab·sichtlich** ① *Adj.* intentional; deliberate

② *adv.* intentionally; deliberately

**ab|sinken** *unr. itr. V.; mit sein* sink

**absolut** *Adj.* absolute

**Absolutismus** *der;* ~ (hist.) absolutism *no art.*

**Absolvent** /...'vɛnt/ *der;* ~en, ~en, **Absolventin** *die;* ~, ~nen (einer Schule) one who has taken the leaving *or* (Amer.) final examination; (einer Akademie) graduate

**absolvieren** *tr. V.* complete

**Absolvierung** *die;* ~: completion

**ab·sonderlich** *Adj.* strange; odd

**ab|sondern** ① *tr. V.* exude; (Physiol.) secrete
② *refl. V.* isolate oneself

**absorbieren** *tr. V.* absorb

**ab|speisen** *tr. V.* jmdn. mit etw. ~: fob sb. off with sth.

**abspenstig** *Adj.* jmdm. etw. ~ machen get sb. to part with sth.

**ab|sperren** *tr. V.* seal off; close off

**Ab·spiel** *das* (Ballspiele) passing

**ab|spielen** ① *tr. V.* **(a)** play ‹*record, tape*›
**(b)** vom Blatt ~: ‹*piece of music*› play at sight
**(c)** (Ballspiele) pass
② *refl. V.* take place

**Ab·sprache** *die* arrangement; eine ~ treffen make an arrangement

**ab|sprechen** *unr. tr. V.* **(a)** jmdm. etw. ~: deny that sb. has sth.
**(b)** (vereinbaren) arrange

**ab|springen** *unr. itr. V.; mit sein* jump off; (herunterspringen) jump down; vom Fahrrad ~: jump off one's bicycle

**Ab·sprung** *der* take-off; (das Herunterspringen) jump

**ab|spülen** ① *tr. V.* **(a)** wash off
**(b)** (reinigen) rinse off; sich (*Dat.*) die Hände usw. ~: rinse one's hands *etc.;* das Geschirr ~ (bes. südd.) wash the dishes
② *itr. V.* (bes. südd.) wash up

**ab|stammen** *itr. V.* be descended (von from)

**Abstammung** *die;* ~, ~en descent

**Ab·stand** *der* **(a)** distance; in 20 Meter ~: at a distance of 20 metres
**(b)** (Unterschied) gap

**ab|stauben** *tr., itr. V.* dust

**Abstecher** *der;* ~s, ~: side trip

**ab|stehen** *unr. itr. V.* ‹*hair*› stand up; ‹pigtail[s]› stick out; ~de Ohren protruding ears

**Ab·steige** *die;* ~, ~n (ugs. abwertend) cheap and crummy hotel (coll. derog.)

**ab|steigen** *unr. itr. V.; mit sein* **(a)** [vom Pferd/Fahrrad] ~: get off [one's horse/ bicycle]
**(b)** (abwärts gehen) go down

**ab|stellen** *tr. V.* **(a)** put down
**(b)** (unterbringen) put; (parken) park
**(c)** (ausschalten, abdrehen) turn off

---

*****alte Schreibung - vgl. Hinweis auf S. xiv

**(d)** (unterbinden) put a stop to

**Abstell-: ~kammer** *die,* **~raum** *der* lumber room

**ab|stempeln** *tr. V.* **(a)** frank ⟨*letter*⟩; cancel ⟨*stamp*⟩
**(b)** (fig.) label, brand (**zu, als** as)

**ab|sterben** *unr. itr. V.; mit sein* **(a)** [gradually] die
**(b)** (gefühllos werden) go numb

**Abstieg** *der;* **~[e]s,** **~e** **(a)** descent
**(b)** (Niedergang) decline

**ab|stimmen** ① *itr. V.* vote (**über** + *Akk.* **on**)
② *tr. V.* etw. mit jmdm. **~**: discuss and agree on sth. with sb.

**Ab·stimmung** *die* **(a)** vote; **während der ~**: during the voting
**(b)** (Absprache) agreement

**abstinent** /apsti'nɛnt/ *Adj.* teetotal; **~ sein** be a teetotaller

**Abstinenz** *die;* **~**: teetotalism

**Abstinenzler** *der;* **~s,** **~**, **Abstinenzlerin** *die;* **~,** **~nen** teetotaller

**ab|stoppen** ① *tr. V.* halt; stop; check ⟨*advance*⟩
② *itr. V.* come to a halt; ⟨*person*⟩ stop

**Ab·stoß** *der* (Fußball) goal kick

**ab|stoßen** *unr. tr. V.* **(a)** push off
**(b)** (beschädigen) chip ⟨*crockery, paintwork, plaster*⟩
**(c)** (verkaufen) sell off
**(d)** (anwidern) repel; put off

**abstoßend** *Adj.* repulsive

**abstrakt** /ap'strakt/ *Adj.* abstract

**ab|streifen** *tr. V.* pull off; strip off ⟨*berries*⟩; **die Asche [von der Zigarette/ Zigarre] ~**: remove the ash [from one's cigarette/cigar]

**ab|streiten** *unr. tr. V.* deny

**Ab·strich** *der* **(a)** (Med.) swab; **einen ~ machen** take a swab
**(b)** (Streichung, Kürzung) cut; **~e machen** make cuts (**an** + *Dat.* in)

**ab|stumpfen** *itr. V.; mit sein* **jmd. stumpft ab** (wird unsensibel) sb.'s mind becomes deadened

**Ab·sturz** *der* fall; (eines Flugzeugs) crash

**ab|stürzen** *itr. V.; mit sein* fall; ⟨*aircraft, pilot, passenger*⟩ crash

**Absturz·ursache** *die* cause of the crash

**ab|stützen** ① *refl. V.* support oneself (**mit** on, **an** + *Dat.* against)
② *tr. V.* support

**ab|suchen** *tr. V.* search (**nach** for)

**absurd** *Adj.* absurd

**absurderweise** *Adv.* absurdly enough

**Absurdität** *die;* **~,** **~en** absurdity; (Ungereimtheit) inconsistency

**Abszess, \*Abszeß** *der;* **Abszesses, Abszesse** **(a)** (Med.) abscess
**(b)** (Geschwür) ulcer

**Abszisse** *die;* **~,** **~n** (Math.) abscissa

**Abt** *der;* **~[e]s,** **Äbte** abbot

**Abt.** *Abk. =* **Abteilung**

**ab|tasten** *tr. V.* etw. **~**: feel sth. all over

**ab|tauen** ① *itr. V.; mit sein* (eis-/schneefrei werden) become clear of ice/snow; ⟨*refrigerator*⟩ defrost
② *tr. V.* melt; thaw; defrost ⟨*refrigerator*⟩

**Abtei** *die;* **~,** **~en** abbey

**Abteil** *das;* **~[e]s,** **~e** compartment

**Ab·teilung** *die* department

**Abteilungs·leiter** *der,* **Abteilungs·leiterin** *die* head of department

**ab|tippen** *tr. V.* (ugs.) type out

**Äbtissin** *die;* **~,** **~nen** abbess

**ab|tönen** *tr. V.* tint

**ab|töten** *tr. V.* destroy ⟨*parasites, germs*⟩; deaden ⟨*nerve, feeling*⟩

**ab|tragen** *unr. tr. V.* (abnutzen) wear out; **abgetragen** well worn

**abträglich** *Adj.* (geh.) **einer Sache** (*Dat.*) **~ sein** be detrimental to sth.

**Ab·transport** *der* ▶ ABTRANSPORTIEREN: taking away; removal

**ab|transportieren** *tr. V.* take away; remove ⟨*dead, injured*⟩

**ab|treiben** ① *unr. tr. V.* **(a)** carry away; **jmdn./ein Schiff vom Kurs ~**: drive sb./a ship off course
**(b)** abort ⟨*foetus*⟩; **ein Kind ~ lassen** have an abortion
② *unr. itr. V.; mit sein* be carried away; ⟨*ship*⟩ be driven off course

**Abtreibung** *die;* **~,** **~en** abortion

**ab|trennen** *tr. V.* detach

**ab|treten** ① *unr. tr. V.* **(a) sich** (*Dat.*) **die Füße/Schuhe ~**: wipe one's feet
**(b)** jmdm. etw. **~**: let sb. have sth.
② *unr. itr. V.; mit sein* **(a)** (Theater) exit; (fig.) make one's exit
**(b)** (zurücktreten) step down; ⟨*monarch*⟩ abdicate

**Abtreter** *der;* **~s,** **~**: doormat

**ab|trocknen** *tr. V.* dry; **sich** (*Dat.*) **die Hände/die Tränen ~**: dry one's hands/tears

**ab|tropfen** *itr. V.; mit sein* drip off

**abtrünnig** *Adj.* (einer Partei) renegade; (einer Religion, Sekte) apostate; **der Kirche/dem Glauben ~ werden** desert the Church/the faith

**ab|tun** *unr. tr. V.* dismiss

**ab|wägen** *unr. od. regelm. tr., itr. V.* weigh up; **abgewogen** carefully weighted; balanced ⟨*judgement*⟩

**ab|wählen** *tr. V.* vote out; drop ⟨*school subject*⟩

**ab|wandeln** *tr. V.* adapt

**ab|wandern** *itr. V.; mit sein* migrate; (in ein anderes Land) emigrate

**Abwanderung** *die* migration; (in ein anderes Land) emigration

**Ab·wandlung** *die* adaptation

**Ab·wärme** *die* (Technik) waste heat

**ab|warten** ① *itr. V.* wait; **sie warteten ab** they awaited events; **warte ab!** wait and see; (als Drohung) just you wait! ② *tr. V.* wait for

**abwärts** *Adv.* downwards; (bergab) downhill; **den Fluss ~:** downstream

**Abwärts·trend** *der* downward trend

**Abwasch** *der;* ~[e]s washing-up (Brit.); washing dishes (Amer.); **den ~ machen** do the washing-up/wash the dishes

**abwaschbar** *Adj.* washable

**ab|waschen** ① *unr. tr. V.* (a) wash off (b) (reinigen) wash down; wash [up] ⟨*dishes*⟩ ② *unr. itr. V.* wash up (Brit.); wash the dishes (Amer.)

**Ab·wasser** *das; Pl.* Abwässer sewage

**Abwasser: ~aufbereitung** *die;* ~~: sewage treatment; **~kanal** *der* sewer

**ab|watschen** *tr. V.* (ugs.) lambaste (coll.)

**ab|wechseln** *refl., itr. V.* alternate; **wir wechselten uns ab** we took turns

**abwechselnd** *Adv.* alternately

**Abwechslung** *die;* ~, ~en variety; (Wechsel) change; **zur ~:** for a change

**Ab·weg** *der:* **auf ~e kommen** *od.* **geraten** go astray

**abwegig** erroneous; false ⟨*suspicion*⟩

**Ab·wehr** *die;* ~ (a) repulsion; (von Schlägen) fending off; (Sport) clearance; clearing (Amer.) (b) (Sport: Hintermannschaft) defence

**ab|wehren** *tr. V.* (a) repulse; fend off ⟨*blow*⟩; (Sport) clear ⟨*ball, shot*⟩ (b) avert ⟨*danger, consequences*⟩

**Abwehr: ~kraft** *die* power of resistance; **~spieler** *der,* **~spielerin** *die* (Sport) defender

**ab|weichen** *unr. itr. V.; mit sein* (a) deviate (b) (sich unterscheiden) differ

**Abweichung** *die;* ~, ~en (a) deviation (b) (Unterschied) difference

**ab|weisen** *unr. tr. V.* turn away; turn down ⟨*applicant, suitor*⟩

**abweisend** *Adj.* cold ⟨*look, tone of voice*⟩; **in ~em Ton** coldly

**Ab·weisung** *die;* ▶ ABWEISEN: turning away; turning down

**ab|wenden** ① *unr. od. regelm. tr. V.* (a) turn away (b) *nur regelm.* (verhindern) avert ② *unr. od. regelm. refl. V.* turn away

**ab|werben** *unr. tr. V.* lure away

**ab|werfen** ① *unr. tr. V.* (a) drop; throw off ⟨*clothing*⟩; jettison ⟨*ballast*⟩; throw ⟨*rider*⟩ (b) (ins Spielfeld werfen) throw out ⟨*ball*⟩ (c) (einbringen) bring in; **Profit ~:** make a profit ② *unr. itr. V.* (Sport) throw the ball out

**ab|werten** *tr., itr. V.* devalue

**abwertend** *Adj.* derogatory ⟨*term*⟩

**Ab·wertung** *die* devaluation

**abwesend** *Adj.* absent

**Abwesenheit** *die;* ~: absence

**ab|wickeln** *tr. V.* (a) unwind (b) (erledigen) deal with ⟨*case*⟩; do ⟨*business*⟩

**Abwicklung** *die;* ~, ~en ▶ ABWICKELN 1B: dealing (Gen. with); doing

**ab|wiegen** *unr. tr. V.* weigh out; weigh ⟨*single item*⟩

**ab|wimmeln** *tr. V.* (ugs.) get rid of

**ab|winken** *itr. V.* uninteressiert ~: wave it/them aside uninterestedly; **Skat dreschen bis zum Abwinken** (ugs.) play skat till you can't stand any more (coll.); **Champagner bis zum Abwinken** (ugs.) more champagne than you can drink

**ab|wischen** *tr. V.* (a) wipe away (b) (säubern) wipe

**Ab·wurf** *der* (a) dropping; (von Ballast) jettisoning (b) **beim ~ stolperte der Torwart** the goalkeeper stumbled as he threw the ball out

**ab|zahlen** *tr. V.* pay off ⟨*debt, loan*⟩

**ab|zählen** *tr. V.* count

**Ab·zahlung** *die* paying off; **etw. auf ~ kaufen/verkaufen** buy/sell sth. on easy terms

**Ab·zeichen** *das* emblem; (Anstecknadel, Plakette) badge

**ab|zeichnen** ① *tr. V.* (a) (kopieren) copy (b) (signieren) initial ② *refl. V.* stand out; (fig.) begin to emerge

**Abzieh·bild** *das* transfer

**ab|ziehen** ① *unr. tr. V.* (a) pull off; peel off ⟨*skin*⟩; strip ⟨*bed*⟩ (b) (Fot.) make a print/prints of (c) (Milit., auch fig.) withdraw (d) (subtrahieren) subtract; take away; (abrechnen) deduct ② *unr. itr. V.; mit sein* (a) (sich verflüchtigen) escape (b) (Milit.) withdraw

**Ab·zug** *der* (a) (an einer Schusswaffe) trigger (b) (Fot.) print (c) (Verminderung) deduction

**abzüglich** *Präp. mit Gen.* (Kaufmannsspr.) less

**ab|zweigen** ① *itr. V.; mit sein* branch off ② *tr. V.* put aside

**Abzweigung** *die;* ~, ~en turn-off; (Gabelung) fork

**ach** *Interj.* (a) (betroffen, mitleidig) oh [dear] (b) (bedauernd, unwirsch) oh (c) (klagend) ah (d) (erstaunt) oh; **~, wirklich?** no, really?; **~, der!** oh, him! (e) **~ so!** oh, I see; **~ was** *od.* **wo!** of course not

**Achat** *der;* ~[e]s, ~e (Min.) agate

**Achse** *die;* ~, ~n (a) (Rad~) axle (b) (Dreh~, Math., Astron.) axis

─────────────────────
*old spelling - see note on page xiv

**Achsel** *die;* ~, ~n (Schulter) shoulder; (~höhle) armpit

**Achsel-:** ~**haare** *Pl.* armpit hair *sing.;* ~**höhle** *die* armpit

**acht**[1] *Kardinalz.* eight; **um** ~ **[Uhr]** at eight [o'clock]; **um halb** ~: at half past seven; **drei viertel** ~, **Viertel vor** ~: [a] quarter to eight; **es steht** ~ **zu** ~/~ **zu zwei** (Sport) the score is eight all/eight to two

**acht**[2]: **sie waren zu** ~: there were eight of them

**acht…** *Ordinalz.* eighth; **der** ~**e September** the eighth of September; **München, [den] 8. Mai 1984** Munich, 8 May 1984

**Acht**[1] *die;* ~, ~en (a) eight
(b) (Figur) figure eight
(c) (Verbiegung) buckle; **mein Rad hat eine** ~: my wheel is buckled

**Acht**[2]: **etw. außer** ~ **lassen** disregard sth.; **sich in** ~ **nehmen** be careful; **sich vor jmdm./etw. in** ~ **nehmen** be wary of sb./sth.; **auf jmdn./etw.** ~ **geben** take care of sb./sth.; ~ **geben** be careful

**Achte** *der/die; adj. Dekl.* eighth

**acht-, Acht-:** ~**eck** *das* octagon; ~**eckig** *Adj.* octagonal; ~**einhalb** *Bruchz.* eight and a half

**achtel** *Bruchz.* eighth

**Achtel** *das* (schweiz. meist *der*); ~**s,** ~: eighth

**Achtel·note** *die* (Musik) quaver

**achten** [1] *tr. V.* respect
[2] *itr. V.* **auf etw.** (*Akk.*) ~: pay heed to sth.

**achtens** *Adv.* eighthly

**Achterbahn** *die* roller coaster

**acht·fach** *Vervielfältigungsz.* eightfold; **die** ~**fache Menge** eight times the quantity; ~**fach vergrößert/verkleinert** magnified/reduced eight times; **das Achtfache kosten** cost eight times as much

*****acht|geben** ▸ ACHT[2]

**acht-:** ~**hundert** *Kardinalz.* eight hundred; ~**jährig** *Adj.* (8 Jahre alt) eight-year-old *attrib.;* eight years old *pred.;* (8 Jahre dauernd) eight-year *attrib.;* ~**köpfig** *Adj.* ⟨family, committee⟩ of eight

**acht·los** [1] *Adj.* heedless
[2] *adv.* heedlessly

**Achtlosigkeit** *die;* ~: heedlessness

**acht-:** ~**mal** *Adv.* eight times; ~**spurig** *Adj.* eight-lane ⟨road⟩; eight-track ⟨cassette⟩; ~**stellig** *Adj.* eight-figure *attrib.;* ~**stellig sein** have eight figures; ~**stimmig** [1] *Adj.* eight-part *attrib.;* [2] *adv.* in eight parts; ~**stöckig** *Adj.* eight-storey *attrib.;* ~**tägig** *Adj.* (8 Tage alt) eight-day-old *attrib.;* (8 Tage dauernd) eight-day[-long] *attrib.;* ~**tausend** *Kardinalz.* eight thousand; ~**teilig** *Adj.* eight-piece ⟨tea service, tool set, etc.⟩; eight-part ⟨series, serial⟩

**Achtung** *die;* ~ (a) respect (**vor** + *Dat.,* **Gen.** for)

(b) ~**!** watch out!; ~**, fertig, los!** on your marks, get set, go!

**acht·zehn** *Kardinalz.* eighteen; **18 Uhr 33** 6.33p.m.; (auf der 24-Stunden-Uhr) 1833

**achtzehn·jährig** *Adj.* (18 Jahre alt) eighteen-year-old *attrib.;* eighteen years old *pred.;* (18 Jahre dauernd) eighteen-year *attrib.*

**achtzig** *Kardinalz.* eighty; **[mit]** ~ **[km/h] fahren** drive at *or* (coll.) do eighty [k.p.h.]; **über/etwa** ~ **[Jahre alt] sein** be over/about eighty [years old]; **mit** ~ **[Jahren]** at eighty [years of age]

**achtzig·jährig** *Adj.* (80 Jahre alt) eighty-year-old *attrib.;* eighty years old *pred.;* (80 Jahre dauernd) eighty-year *attrib.*

**ächzen** *itr. V.* groan

**Acker** *der;* ~**s,** **Äcker** field

**Acker:** ~**bau** *der* arable farming; ~**land** *das* farmland

**A.D.** *Abk.* = **Anno Domini** AD

**ADAC** *Abk.* = **Allgemeiner Deutscher Automobilclub**

**Adams·apfel** *der* (ugs.) Adam's apple

**adäquat** /atˈɛ'kva:t/ *Adj.* appropriate (*Dat.* to); suitable (*Dat.* for)

**addieren** [1] *tr. V.* add [up]
[2] *itr. V.* add

**Addition** *die;* ~, ~en addition

**ade** *Interj.* (veralt., landsch.) farewell (dated); bye (coll.); **jmdm.** ~ *od.* **Ade sagen** bid farewell to sb.

**Adel** *der;* ~**s** nobility; **der niedere/hohe** ~: the lesser nobility/the aristocracy

**adelig** ▸ ADLIG

**Adelige** ▸ ADLIGE

**adeln** *tr. V.* jmdn. ~: give sb. a title; (in den hohen Adel erheben) raise sb. to the peerage

**Adels-:** ~**geschlecht** *das* noble family; ~**stand** *der* nobility; (hoher Adel) nobility; ~**titel** *der* title of nobility

**Ader** *die;* ~, ~n (a) blood vessel
(b) (Anlage, Begabung) streak
(c) (Bot., Geol.) vein
(d) (Elektrot.) core

**adieu** /a'diø:/ *Interj.* (veralt.) adieu

**Adjektiv** *das;* ~**s,** ~**e** (Sprachw.) adjective

**Adjutant** *der;* ~**en,** ~**en, Adjutantin** *die;* ~, ~**nen** adjutant

**Adler** *der;* ~**s,** ~: eagle

**adlig** *Adj.* noble; ~ **sein** be a noble [man/woman]

**Adlige** *der/die; adj. Dekl.* noble [man/woman]

**Admiral** *der;* ~**s,** ~**e** *od.* **Admiräle** admiral

**adoptieren** *tr. V.* adopt

**Adoption** *die;* ~, ~en adoption

**Adoptiv-:** ~**eltern** *Pl.* adoptive parents; ~**kind** *das* adopted child; ~**mutter** *die; Pl.* ~**mütter** adoptive mother; ~**sohn** *der* adoptive *or* adopted son; ~**tochter** *die* adoptive *or* adopted daughter; ~**vater** *der* adoptive father

**Adressat** *der;* ~en, ~en, **Adressatin** *die;* ~, ~nen addressee

**Adress·buch, \*Adreß·buch** *das* directory

**Adresse** *die;* ~, ~n address; **bei jmdm. an die falsche** ~ **kommen** *od.* **geraten** (fig. ugs.) come to the wrong address (fig.)

**adressieren** *tr. V.* address

**adrett** ① *Adj.* smart ② *adv.* smartly

**Advent** /at'vɛnt/ *der;* ~s (a) Advent (b) (Adventssonntag) Sunday in Advent

**Advents-:** ~**kalender** *der* Advent calendar; ~**kranz** *der: garland of evergreens with four candles for the Sundays in Advent*

**Adverb** /at'vɛrp/ *das;* ~s, ~ien (Sprachw.) adverb

**adverbial** (Sprachw.) ① *Adj.* adverbial ② *adv.* adverbially

**Advokat** /atvo'ka:t/ *der;* ~en, ~en, **Advokatin** *die;* ~, ~nen (österr., schweiz., sonst veralt.) lawyer; advocate (arch.)

**Aero-** /aero- *od.* ɛ:ro-/: ~**gramm** *das* air[mail] letter; ~**sol** *das* ~~s, ~~e aerosol

**Affäre** *die;* ~, ~n affair; **sich aus der** ~ **ziehen** (ugs.) get out of it

**Affe** *der;* ~n, ~n (a) monkey; (Menschen~) ape (b) (salopp) (dummer Kerl) oaf; clot (Brit. coll.); (Geck) dandy

**Affekt** *der;* ~[e]s, ~e emotion; **im** ~: in the heat of the moment

**affektiert** (abwertend) ① *Adj.* affected ② *adv.* affectedly

**Affen·theater** *das* (salopp) farce

**Afghane** /af'ga:nə/ *der;* ~n, ~n (a) Afghan (b) (Hund) Afghan hound

**Afghanin** *die;* ~, ~nen Afghan

**afghanisch** *Adj.* Afghan

**Afghanistan** /af'ga:nɪsta:n/ *(das);* ~s Afghanistan

**Afrika** *(das);* ~s Africa

**Afrikaner** *der;* ~s, ~, **Afrikanerin** *die;* ~, ~nen African

**afrikanisch** *Adj.* African

**After** *der;* ~s, ~: anus

**AG** *Abk.* (a) = **Aktiengesellschaft** PLC (Brit.); Ltd. (*private company*) (Brit.); Inc. (Amer.) (b) = **Arbeitsgemeinschaft**

**Agent** *der;* ~en, ~en, **Agentin** *die;* ~, ~nen agent

**Agentur** *die;* ~, ~en agency

**Agentur·bericht** *der,* **Agentur·meldung** *die* agency report

**Aggregat** *das;* ~[e]s, ~e (Technik) unit; (Elektrot.) set

**Aggregat·zustand** *der* (Chemie) state

**Aggression** *die;* ~, ~en aggression

**aggressiv** ① *Adj.* aggressive ② *adv.* aggressively

**Aggressivität** *die;* ~: aggressiveness

**Aggressor** *der;* ~s, ~en, **Aggressorin** *die;* ~, ~nen aggressor

**Agitation** *die;* ~: agitation

**agitieren** *itr. V.* agitate

**Agrar·land** *das* agrarian country

**Ägypten** *(das);* ~s Egypt

**Ägypter** *der;* ~s, ~, **Ägypterin** *die;* ~, ~nen Egyptian

**ägyptisch** *Adj.* Egyptian

**ah** *Interj.* (verwundert) oh; (freudig, genießerisch) ah; (verstehend) oh; ah

**äh** /ɛ(:)/ *Interj.* (a) (angeekelt) ugh (b) (stotternd) er; hum

**aha** /a'ha(:)/ *Interj.* (verstehend) oh[, I see]; (triumphierend) aha

**Ahn** *der;* ~[e]s, *od.* ~en, ~en (geh.), **Ahne** *der;* ~n, ~n forebear; ancestor

**ähneln** *itr. V.* jmdm. ~: resemble *or* be like sb.; jmdm. sehr/wenig ~: strongly resemble *or* be very like sb./bear little resemblance to sb.; **einer Sache** (*Dat.*) ~: be similar to sth.; be like sth.; **sich** (*Dat.*) ~: resemble one another; be alike

**ahnen** *tr. V.* (a) (im Voraus fühlen) have a premonition of (b) (vermuten) suspect; **das konnte ich doch nicht** ~! I had no way of knowing that

**Ahnin** *die;* ~, ~nen ▶ AHN

**ähnlich** ① *Adj.* similar; jmdm. ~ sein be like sb.; ~ wie like ② *adv.* similarly; ⟨answer, react⟩ in a similar way ③ *Präp. mit Dat.* like

**Ähnlichkeit** *die;* ~, ~en similarity; mit jmdm. ~ haben be like sb.

**Ahnung** *die;* ~, ~en (a) (Vorgefühl) premonition (b) (ugs.: Kenntnisse) knowledge; **von etw.** [viel] ~ haben know [a lot] about sth.; **keine** ~! [I've] no idea

**ahnungs·los** *Adj.* (nichts ahnend) unsuspecting; (naiv, unwissend) naïve

**Ahnungslosigkeit** *die;* ~ (Naivität, Unschuld) naïvety; innocence; (Unwissenheit) naïvety

**ahoi** *Interj.* (Seemannsspr.) ahoy

**Ahorn** /'a:hɔrn/ *der;* ~s, ~e maple

**Ähre** *die;* ~, ~n ear

**Aids** /e:ts/ *das;* ~: Aids

**Aids-:** ~**kranke** *der/die* person suffering from Aids; ~**test** *der* Aids test

**Airbag** /'ɛ:ɐbɛk/ *der;* ~s, ~s (Kfz.-W.) air bag

**Akademie** *die;* ~, ~n academy; (Bergbau, Forstw., Bauw.) school; college

**Akademiker** *der;* ~s, ~, **Akademikerin** *die;* ~, ~nen [university/college] graduate

**akademisch** ① *Adj.* academic

2 *adv.* academically

**Akazie** /a'ka:ts:i̯ə/ *die;* ~, ~n acacia

**akklimatisieren** *refl. V.* become *or* get acclimatized

**Akkord** *der;* ~[e]s, ~e **(a)** (Musik) chord **(b)** (Wirtsch.) piecework; (Lohn) piecework pay *no indef. art., no pl.;* (Satz) piece rate

**Akkordeon** *das;* ~s, ~s accordion

**Akku** *der;* ~s, ~s (ugs.), **Akkumulator** *der;* ~s, ~en accumulator (Brit.); storage battery

**akkurat** 1 *Adj.* meticulous
2 *adv.* meticulously

**Akkusativ** *der;* ~s, ~e (Sprachw.) accusative [case]

**Akkusativ·objekt** *das* (Sprachw.) accusative *or* direct object

**Akne** *die;* ~, ~n (Med.) acne

**Akribie** /akri'bi:/ *die;* ~ (geh.) meticulousness; meticulous precision

**akribisch** /a'kri:bɪʃ/ 1 *Adj.* meticulous; meticulously precise
2 *adv.* meticulously; with meticulous precision

**Akrobat** *der;* ~en, ~en acrobat

**Akrobatik** *die;* ~: acrobatics *pl.*

**Akrobatin** *die;* ~, ~nen acrobat

**akrobatisch** *Adj.* acrobatic

**Akt** *der;* ~[e]s, ~e **(a)** (auch Theater, Zirkus-, Varieteeakt) act
**(b)** (Zeremonie) ceremony
**(c)** (Geschlechtsakt) sexual act
**(d)** (Kunst) nude

**Akt-:** ~**aufnahme** *die* nude photograph; ~**bild** *das* nude [picture]

**Akte** *die;* ~, ~n file

**Akten-:** ~**deckel** *der* folder; ~**koffer** *der* attaché case; ~**mappe** *die* briefcase; ~**notiz** *die* note [for the files]; ~**ordner** *der* file; ~**tasche** *die* briefcase; ~**zeichen** *das* reference

**Akteur** /ak'tø:ɐ̯/ *der;* ~s, ~e, **Akteurin** *die;* ~, ~nen person involved

**Akt·foto** *das* nude photo

**Aktie** /'akts:i̯ə/ *die;* ~, ~n (Wirtsch.) share; ~n shares (Brit.); stock (Amer.); **die** ~**n fallen/steigen** share *or* stock prices are falling/rising

**Aktien-:** ~**gesellschaft** *die* joint stock company; ~**kapital** *das* share capital; ~**mehrheit** *die* majority shareholding (Gen. in); ~**paket** *das* block of shares

**Aktion** *die;* ~, ~en **(a)** action *no indef. art.;* (militärisch) operation
**(b)** (Kampagne) campaign

**Aktionär** *der;* ~s, ~e, **Aktionärin** *die;* ~, ~nen shareholder

**aktiv** 1 *Adj.* **(a)** active
**(b)** (Milit.) serving *attrib.* ⟨officer, soldier⟩
2 *adv.* actively

**Aktiv** *das;* ~s, ~e (Sprachw.) active

**Aktive** *der/die; adj. Dekl.* (Sport) participant

**aktivieren** *tr. V.* **(a)** mobilize ⟨party members, group, class, etc.⟩; **den Kreislauf** ~: stimulate the circulation
**(b)** (DV) activate

**Aktivität** *die;* ~, ~en activity

**Akt·modell** *das* nude model

**aktualisieren** *tr. V.* update

**Aktualität** *die;* ~, ~en **(a)** (Gegenwartsbezug) relevance [to the present]
**(b)** (von Nachrichten usw.) topicality

**aktuell** *Adj.* topical; (gegenwärtig) current; (neu) up-to-the-minute; **eine** ~**e Sendung** (Ferns., Rundf.) a [news and] current affairs programme

**Akupunktur** *die;* ~, ~en (Med.) acupuncture

**Akustik** *die;* ~ **(a)** (Lehre vom Schall) acoustics *sing., no art.;*
**(b)** (Schallverhältnisse) acoustics *pl.*

**akustisch** 1 *Adj.* acoustic
2 *adv.* acoustically

**akut** *Adj.* (auch Med.) acute; pressing, urgent ⟨question, issue⟩

**AKW** *Abk.* = **Atomkraftwerk**

**Akzent** *der;* ~[e]s, ~e **(a)** (Sprachw.) (Betonung) stress; (Betonungszeichen) accent
**(b)** (Sprachmelodie, Aussprache) accent

**akzeptabel** 1 *Adj.* acceptable
2 *adv.* acceptably

**akzeptieren** *tr. V.* accept

**à la** /ala/ (Gastr., ugs.) à la

**Alabaster** *der;* ~s, ~: alabaster

**à la carte** /ala'kart/ (Gastr.) à la carte

**Alarm** *der;* ~[e]s, ~e alarm; (Flieger~) air-raid warning; ~ **geben**/(fig. ugs.) **schlagen** raise the alarm; **blinder** ~: false alarm

**alarm-, Alarm-:** ~**anlage** *die* alarm system; ~**bereit** *Adj.* on alert *postpos.;* ~**bereitschaft** *die* alert

**alarmieren** *tr. V.* **(a)** alarm
**(b)** (zu Hilfe rufen) call [out] ⟨doctor, police, fire brigade, etc.⟩

**Alarm-:** ~**sirene** *die* warning siren; ~**stufe** *die* alert stage

**Albaner** *der;* ~s, ~, **Albanerin** *die;* ~, ~nen Albanian

**Albanien** /al'ba:ni̯ən/ (das) ~s Albania

**albanisch** *Adj.* Albanian

**Albatros** *der;* ~, ~se (Zool.) albatross

**Alben** ▶ ALBUM

**albern** *Adj.* **(a)** silly; **sich** ~ **benehmen** act silly
**(b)** (ugs.: nebensächlich) silly; stupid

**Albernheit** *die;* ~, ~en silliness

**Albino** *der;* ~s, ~s albino

**Alb·traum** *der* nightmare

**Album** *das;* ~s, **Alben** album

**Alge** *die;* ~, ~n alga

**Algebra** /österr.: al'ge:bra/ *die;* ~: algebra

**Algerien** /al'ge:ri̯ən/ (das) ~s Algeria

**a**

**Algerier** *der;* ~s, ~, **Algerierin** *die;* ~,
~nen Algerian
**algerisch** *Adj.* Algerian
**alias** *Adv.* alias
**Alibi** *das;* ~s, ~s alibi
**Alkohol** *der;* ~s, ~e alcohol
**alkohol-, Alkohol-:** ~**abhängig** *Adj.*
dependent on alcohol *postpos.;*
~**abhängigkeit** *die* dependence on
alcohol; alcohol dependence; ~**ein-fluss,**
\*~**ein·fluß** *der,* ~**ein·wirkung** *die*
influence of alcohol *or* drink; **unter**
~**einfluss** *od.* ~**einwirkung** [stehen] [be]
under the influence of alcohol *or* drink;
~**fahne** *die* smell of alcohol [on one's
breath]; **eine** ~**fahne haben** smell of alcohol;
~**frei** *Adj.* non-alcoholic
**Alkoholiker** *der;* ~s, ~, **Alkoholikerin**
*die;* ~, ~nen alcoholic
**alkoholisch** *Adj.* alcoholic
**Alkoholismus** *der;* ~: alcoholism *no art.*
**alkohol-, Alkohol-:** ~**konsum** *der*
consumption of alcohol; ~**missbrauch,**
\*~**mißbrauch** *der* alcohol abuse;
~**sucht** *die* alcohol addiction; alcoholism;
~**süchtig** *Adj.* addicted to alcohol *postpos.;*
alcoholic; ~**süchtige** *der/die; adj. Dekl.*
alcoholic; ~**sünder** *der,* ~**sünderin** *die*
(ugs.) drunk[en] driver; ~**vergiftung** *die*
alcohol[ic] poisoning
**all** *Indefinitpron. u. unbest. Zahlw.* [1] *attr.*
(ganz, gesamt...) all; ~**es andere/Weitere/**
**Übrige** everything else; ~**es Schöne**
everything *or* all that is beautiful; ~**es Gute!**
all the best!; **wir/ihr/sie** ~**e** all of us/you/
them; ~**e Anwesenden** all those present; ~**e**
**Bewohner der Stadt** all the inhabitants of the
town; ~**e Jahre wieder** every year; ~**e fünf**
**Minuten/Meter** every five minutes/metres;
**Bücher** ~**er Art** all kinds of books; **in** ~**er**
**Ruhe** in peace and quiet
[2] *allein stehend* (a) ~**e** all; ~**e, die ...:** all
those who ...
(b) ~**es** (auf Sachen bezogen) everything; (auf
Personen bezogen) everybody; **das** ~**es** all that;
**trotz** ~**em** in spite of everything; ~**es in**
~**em** all in all; **vor** ~**em** above all; **das ist**
~**es** that's all *or* (coll.) it; **ist das** ~**es?** is that
all *or* (coll.) it?; ~**es mal herhören!** (ugs.)
listen everybody!; ~**es aussteigen!** (ugs.)
everyone out!; (vom Schaffner gesagt) all
change!
**All** *das;* ~s ▶ WELTALL
**alle** *Adj.* ~ **sein** be all gone; ~ **werden** run
out
**alle·dem** *Pron.* **trotz** ~: in spite of *or*
despite all that
**Allee** *die;* ~, ~n avenue
**allein** [1] *Adj.* (a) (für sich) alone; on one's/its
own; by oneself/itself; **ganz** ~: all on one's/
its own
(b) (einsam) alone

[2] *adv.* (ohne Hilfe) by oneself/itself; on one's/
its own; **etw.** ~ **tun** do sth. oneself; **von** ~
(ugs.) by oneself/itself
[3] *Adv.* (a) (geh.: ausschließlich) alone
(b) [schon] ~ **der Gedanke,** [schon] **der**
**Gedanke** ~: the mere thought [of it]
**alleine** (ugs.) ▶ ALLEIN 1A, 2, 3B
**allein-, Allein-:** \*~**erziehend** *Adj.*
single *(mother, father, parent)*;
~**erziehende** *der/die; adj. Dekl.* single
parent; ~**gang** *der* (fig.) independent
initiative; **im** ~**gang** off one's own bat
**alleinig** *Adj.* sole
\***allein·stehend** *Adj.* *(person)* living
alone; (ledig) single *(person)*
**Alleinstehende** *der/die; adj. Dekl.* person
living alone; (Ledige[r]) single person
**alle·mal** *Adv.* (ugs.) any time (coll.); **was der**
**kann, das kann ich doch** ~: anything he can
do, I can do too; *s. auch* EIN[1] 1
**allen·falls** *Adv.* (a) (höchstens) at [the] most
(b) (bestenfalls) at best
**aller-:** ~**dings** *Adv.* (a) (einschränkend)
though; **es stimmt** ~**dings, dass ...:** it's true
though that ...; (b) (zustimmend) [yes,]
certainly; **das war** ~**dings Pech** that was bad
luck, to be sure; ~**erst...** *Adj.* (a) very
first; **der/die/das** ~**erste** the very first; (b)
(best...) very best
**Allergie** *die;* ~, ~n (Med.) allergy
**allergisch** [1] *Adj.* (Med.) allergic (gegen to)
[2] *adv.* **auf etw.** *(Akk.)* ~ **reagieren** have an
allergic reaction to sth
**aller-, Aller-:** ~**größt...** *Adj.* utmost
*(trouble, care, etc.)*; biggest *(car, house, town,*
*etc.)* of all; tallest *(person)* of all; **am**
~**größten sein** be [the] biggest/tallest of all;
~**hand** *indekl. Adj.* (ugs.) (a) *attr.* all kinds
*or* sorts of; (b) *allein stehend* all kinds *or*
sorts of things; **das ist** ~**hand** (viel) that's a
lot; **das ist ja** ~**hand!** that's just not on! (Brit.
coll.); ~**heiligen** *das;* ~~s (bes. kath. Kirche)
All Saints' Day; ~**herzlichst** [1] *Adj.*
warmest *(thanks, greetings, congratulations)*;
most cordial *(reception, welcome, invitation)*;
[2] most warmly; ~**höchst...** [1] *Adj.*
highest *(building, tree, etc.)* of all; [2] *adv.* **am**
~**höchsten** *(fly, jump, etc.)* the highest of all;
~**höchstens** *Adv.* at the very most
**allerlei** *indekl. Adj.* all kinds *or* sorts of;
*allein stehend* all kinds *or* sorts of things
**Allerlei** *das;* ~s, ~s (Gemisch) pot-pourri;
(Durcheinander) jumble
**aller-:** ~**letzt...** *Adj.* (a) very last; (b) (ugs.
abwertend) most dreadful (coll.); **das ist das**
**Allerletzte** that is the absolute limit;
~**liebst...** [1] *Adj.* most favourite; **es wäre**
**mir am** ~**liebsten** *od.* **das Allerliebste, wenn**
**...:** I should like it best of all if ...; [2] *adv.*
**etw. am** ~**liebsten tun** like best of all; ~**meist...** [1] *Indefinitpron. u. unbest.*
*Zahlw.* by far the most *attrib.;* **das** ~**meiste/**
**am** ~**meisten** most of all/by far the most;
[2] *Adv.* **am** ~**meisten** most of all;

---

**~mindest...** *Adj.* slightest; least; **das ~mindeste** the very least; **~nächst...** 1 *Adj.* very nearest *attrib.*; (Reihenfolge ausdrückend) very next *attrib.*; 2 *adv.* **am ~nächsten** nearest of all; **~neu[e]st...** *Adj.* very latest *attrib.*; **das Allerneu[e]ste** the very latest; **~schlimmst...** *Adj.* very worst *attrib.*; **~schönst...** 1 *Adj.* most beautiful *attrib.*; loveliest *attrib.*; (angenehmst...) very nicest *attrib.*; 2 *adv.* **er singt am ~schönsten** his singing is the most beautiful of all; **~seits** *Adv.* **guten Morgen ~seits!** good morning everyone

**Allerwelts-:** **~gesicht** *das* nondescript face; **~wort** *das* hackneyed word

**allerwenigst...** 1 *Adj.* lest ... of all; *Pl.* fewest ... of all
2 *adv.* **am ~wenigsten** least of all

**alle·samt** *Indefinitpron. u. unbest. Zahlw.* (ugs.) all [of you/us/them]; **wir ~:** we all

**Alles·kleber** *der* all-purpose adhesive

**all·gemein** 1 *Adj.* general; universal ‹*conscription, suffrage*›; **im ~en Interesse** in the common interest; **im Allgemein**, *****~en** in general
2 *adv.* (a) generally; (ausnahmslos) universally; **es ist ~ bekannt, dass ...:** it is common knowledge that ...
(b) (unverbindlich) ‹*write, talk, discuss*› in general terms

**Allgemein-:** **~befinden** *das* (Med.) general state of health; **~bildung** *die* general education

**Allgemeinheit** *die;* **~** (a) generality
(b) **die ~:** the general public

**Allgemein-:** **~medizin** *die* general medicine; **~wohl** *das* public good

**All·heilmittel** *das* (auch fig.) cure-all; panacea

**Alligator** *der;* **~s, ~en** alligator

**Alliierte** *der; adj. Dekl.* ally; **die ~n** the Allies

**all-:** **~jährlich** 1 *Adj.* annual; yearly; 2 *adv.* annually; every year; **~mächtig** *Adj.* all-powerful

**all·mählich** 1 *Adj.* gradual
2 *adv.* gradually
3 *Adv.* **wir sollten ~ gehen** it's time we got going

**all-, All-:** **~morgendlich** 1 *Adj.* regular morning; 2 *adv.* every morning; **~seitig** 1 *Adj.* general; all-round, (Amer.) all-around *attrib.*; 2 *adv.* generally; **~seits** *Adv.* on all sides; **~tag** *der* (a) (Werktag) weekday; (b) (Einerlei) daily routine; **der graue ~:** the dull routine of everyday life; **~täglich** *Adj.* ordinary ‹*face, person, appearance, etc.*›; everyday ‹*topic, event, sight*›; commonplace ‹*remark*›; **ein nicht ~täglicher Anblick** a sight one doesn't see every day; **~tags** *Adv.* [on] weekdays; **~zu** *Adv.* all too; **~zu bald/früh** all too

soon/early; **~zu lange/oft/sehr** too long/ often/much; **~zu viel** too much; **nicht ~zu viele** not too many

*****allzu·bald** *usw.* ▶ ALLZU

**Alm** *die;* **~, ~en** mountain pasture; Alpine pasture

**Alm·hütte** *die* Alpine hut

**Almosen** *das;* **~s, ~:** alms *pl.*

**Alp** *die;* **~, ~en** (bes. schweiz.) ▶ ALM

**Alpaka** *das;* **~s, ~s** alpaca

**Alpen** *Pl.* **die ~:** the Alps

**Alpen-:** **~rose** *die* rhododendron; **~veilchen** *das* cyclamen

**Alpha** *das;* **~[s], ~[s]** alpha

**Alphabet** *das;* **~[e]s, ~e** alphabet

**alphabetisch** 1 *Adj.* alphabetical
2 *adv.* alphabetically

**Alp·horn** *das* alpenhorn

**alpin** *Adj.* Alpine

**Alpinist** *der;* **~en, ~en, Alpinistin** *die;* **~, ~nen** Alpinist

**Alp·traum** ▶ ALBTRAUM

**als** *Konj.* (a) (zeitlich) when; **damals, ~:** [in the days] when; **gerade ~:** just as
(b) (kausal) **um so mehr, ~:** all the more since *or* in that
(c) *Vergleichspartikel* **größer/älter/mehr/ weniger ~:** bigger/older/more/less than; **anders ~ wir sein/leben** be different/live differently from us; **so viel/so weit ~ möglich** as much/as far as possible; **so bald/ schnell ~ möglich** as soon/as quickly as possible; **~ [wenn od. ob]** (+ *Konjunktiv II*) as if; as though; **~ ob ich das nicht wüsste!** as if I didn't know
(d) **~ Rentner/Arzt** as a pensioner/a doctor; **sich ~ wahr/Lüge erweisen** prove to be true/a lie

**also** 1 *Adv.* so; therefore
2 *Partikel* (a) (das heißt) that is
(b) (nach Unterbrechung) well [then]
(c) (verstärkend) **na ~!** there you are[, you see]; **~ schön** well all right then

**alt, älter, ältest...** *Adj.* (a) old; **Alt und Jung** old and young; **seine ~en Eltern** his aged parents; **wie ~ bist du?** how old are you?; **mein älterer/ältester Bruder** my elder/ eldest brother
(b) (nicht mehr frisch) old; **~es Brot** stale bread
(c) (vom letzten Jahr) old; **~e Äpfel/Kartoffeln** last year's apples/potatoes
(d) (langjährig) long-standing ‹*acquaintance*›
(e) (antik, klassisch) ancient
(f) (vertraut) old familiar ‹*streets, sights, etc.*›; **ganz der/die Alte sein** be just the same

**Alt**[1] *der;* **~s, ~e** (Musik) alto; (Frauenstimme) contralto; (im Chor) contraltos *pl.*

**Alt**[2] *das;* **~[s], ~:** top fermented, dark beer

**Altar** *der;* **~[e]s, Altäre** altar

**alt-, Alt-:** **~bau·wohnung** *die* flat (Brit.) *or* (Amer.) apartment in an old building; **~bekannt** *Adj.* well-known; **~bier** *das* ▶ ALT[2]

**a**

**Alte** der/die; adj. Dekl. **(a)** (alter Mensch) old man/woman; Pl. old people **(b)** (salopp) (Vater, Ehemann) old man (coll.); (Mutter, Ehefrau) old woman (coll.); (Chef) governor (coll.); (Chefin) boss (coll.); **die ~n** (Eltern) my/his etc. old man and old woman (coll.) **(c)** Pl. (Tiereltern) parents

**alt·ehrwürdig** Adj. (geh.) venerable; time-honoured ⟨customs⟩

**Alt·englisch** das Old English

**Alten-:** **~pfleger** der, **~pflegerin** die geriatric nurse; **~tages·stätte** die old people's day centre

**Alter** das; ~s, ~: age; (hohes ~) old age; **im ~:** in one's old age; **im ~ von** at the age of

**älter** [1] ▶ ALT
[2] Adj. (nicht mehr jung) elderly

**altern** itr. V.; mit sein age

**alters-, Alters-:** **~beschwerden** Pl. complaints of old age; **~genosse** der, **~genossin** die contemporary; person/child of the same age; **meine ~genossen** my contemporaries; people of my age; **~gruppe** die age group; **~heim** das old people's home; old-age home (Amer.); **~rente** die old-age pension; **~ruhe·geld** das retirement pension; **~schwach** Adj. old and infirm ⟨person⟩; old and weak ⟨animal⟩; **~schwäche** die (bei Menschen) [old] age and infirmity; (bei Tieren) [old] age and weakness; **~starrsinn** der obstinacy of old age; **~stufe** die age; **~unterschied** der age difference; **~versorgung** die provision for one's old age; (System) pension scheme

**Altertum** das; ~s antiquity no art.

**Älteste** der/die; adj. Dekl. **(a)** (Dorf-, Vereins-, Kirchenälteste usw.) elder **(b)** (Sohn, Tochter) eldest

**alt-, Alt-:** **~glas·behälter** der bottle bank; **~griechisch** das classical or ancient Greek; **~hochdeutsch** das Old High German; **~klug;** ~kluger, ~klugst... [1] Adj. precocious; [2] adv. precociously; **~last** die (Ökologie) old, improperly disposed of harmful waste; (fig.) inherited problem

**ältlich** Adj. rather elderly

**alt-, Alt-:** **~metall** das scrap metal; **~modisch** [1] Adj. old-fashioned; [2] adv. in an old-fashioned way; **~papier** das waste paper; **~rosa** Adj. old rose; **~stadt** die old [part of the] town; **~waren·händler** der, **~waren·händlerin** die second-hand dealer

**Alu** das; ~s (ugs.) aluminium

**Alu·folie** die aluminium foil

**Aluminium** das; ~s aluminium; aluminum (Amer.)

**am** Präp. + Art. **(a)** = an dem; **(b)** **Frankfurt am Main** Frankfurt on [the]

Main; **am Marktplatz** on the market square; **am Meer/Fluss** by the sea/on or by the river; **am Anfang/Ende** at the beginning/end; **am 19. November** on 19 November; **am schnellsten laufen** run [the] fastest; **am Verwelken sein** be wilting

**Amalgam** das; ~s, ~e (Chemie, auch fig.) amalgam

**Amalgam·füllung** die (Zahnmed.) amalgam filling

**Amateur** /ama'tø:ɐ̯/ der; ~s, ~e, **Amateurin** die; ~, ~nen amateur

**Amazonas** der; ~: Amazon

**Amboss, *Amboß** der; Ambosses, Ambosse anvil

**ambulant** (Med.) [1] Adj. outpatient attrib.; [2] adv. jmdn. ~ behandeln give sb. outpatient treatment

**Ambulanz** die; ~, ~en **(a)** (in Kliniken) outpatient[s'] department **(b)** (Krankenwagen) ambulance

**Ameise** die; ~, ~n ant

**Ameisen-:** **~bär** der anteater; **~haufen** der anthill

**amen** Adv. amen

**Amen** das; ~s, ~: Amen

**Amerika** (das); ~s America

**Amerikaner** der; ~s, ~ **(a)** American **(b)** (Gebäck) small, flat iced cake

**Amerikanerin** die; ~, ~nen American

**amerikanisch** Adj. American

**Amino·säure** die (Chemie) amino acid

**Ammann** der; ~[e]s, Ammänner (schweiz.) (Gemeinde-, Bezirksamman) ≈ mayor; (Landamman) cantonal president

**Amme** die; ~, ~n wet nurse

**Amnestie** /amnɛs'ti:/ die; ~, ~n amnesty

**amnestieren** tr. V. grant an amnesty to

**Amöbe** die; ~, ~n (Biol.) amoeba

**Amok** der; ~ laufen run amok

**Amok·läufer** der madman

**Amok·läuferin** die madwoman

**Ampel** die; ~, ~n **(a)** traffic lights pl. **(b)** (für Pflanzen) hanging flowerpot

**Amphibie** /am'fi:biə/ die; ~, ~n (Zool.) amphibian

**Amphibien·fahrzeug** das amphibious vehicle

**Amphi·theater** das amphitheatre

**Ampulle** die; ~, ~n (Med.) ampoule

**Amputation** die; ~, ~en (Med.) amputation

**amputieren** tr. V. amputate

**Amsel** die; ~, ~n blackbird

**Amt** das; ~[e]s, Ämter **(a)** (Stellung) post; position; (hohes politisches od. kirchliches ~) office; **im ~ sein** be in office **(b)** (Aufgabe) task; job **(c)** (Behörde) office **(d)** (Fernsprechvermittlung) exchange

**amtieren** itr. V. **(a)** hold office

---
*alte Schreibung - vgl. Hinweis auf S. xiv

**(b)** (vorübergehend) act (**als** as)

**amtlich** ☐1 *Adj.* official; (ugs.: sicher) definite
☐2 *adv.* officially

**Amt·mann** *der; Pl.* ...männer *od.* ...leute,
**Amt·männin** *die;* ∼, ∼nen *senior civil
servant*

**Amts-:** ∼**anmaßung** *die* (Rechtsw.)
unauthorized assumption of authority;
∼**arzt** *der,* ∼**ärztin** *die* medical officer;
∼**eid** *der* oath of office; ∼**gericht** *das*
local *or* district court; ∼**geschäfte** *Pl.*
official duties; ∼**handlung** *die* official act
*or* duty; ∼**leitung** *die* (Fernspr.) exchange
line

**Amulett** *das;* ∼[e]s, ∼e amulet; charm

**amüsant** ☐1 *Adj.* entertaining; amusing
☐2 *adv.* in an entertaining *or* amusing way

**amüsieren** ☐1 *refl. V.* **(a)** (sich vergnügen)
enjoy oneself; **sich mit jmdm.** ∼: have fun *or*
a good time with sb.
**(b)** (belustigt sein) be amused; **sich über jmdn./
etw.** ∼: find sb./sth. funny
☐2 *tr. V.* amuse

**an** ☐1 *Präp. mit Dat.* **(a)** (räumlich) at; (auf) on;
**Frankfurt an der Oder** Frankfurt on [the]
Oder; **Tür an Tür** next door to one another;
**an ... vorbei** past
**(b)** (zeitlich) on; **an jedem Sonntag** every
Sunday; **an Ostern** (bes. südd.) at Easter
**(c)** arm/**reich an Vitaminen** low/rich in
vitamins; **jmdn. an etw. erkennen** recognize
sb. by sth.; **an etw. leiden** suffer from sth.;
**an einer Krankheit sterben** die of a disease
**(d) an [und für] sich** actually
☐2 *Präp. mit Akk.* **(a)** to; (auf, gegen) on
**(b) an etw./jmdn. glauben** believe in sth./sb.;
**an etw. denken** think of sth.; **sich an etw.
erinnern** remember sth.
☐3 *Adv.* **(a)** (Verkehrsspr.) **Köln an: 9.15** arriving
Cologne 09.15
**(b)** (ugs.: in Betrieb) on; **die Waschmaschine/
der Fernseher/das Licht/das Gas ist an** the
washing machine/television/light/gas is on
**(c)** (ugs.: ungefähr) around; about; **an [die]
2 000 Euro** around *or* about 2,000 euros

**Anabolikum** *das;* ∼s, Anabolika (Med.)
anabolic steroid

**analog** ☐1 *Adj.* **(a)** (gleichartig) analogous; ∼
**[zu] diesem Fall** analogous to this case
**(b)** (Technik, DV) analogue
☐2 *adv.* **(a)** (gleichartig) analogously
**(b)** (Technik, DV) ⟨*display, reproduce*⟩ in
analogue form

**Analog-:** ∼**rechner** *der* (DV) analogue
computer; ∼**uhr** *die* analogue clock;
(Armbanduhr) analogue watch

**Analphabet** *der;* ∼en, ∼en,
**Analphabetin** *die;* ∼, ∼nen illiterate
[person]; ∼ **sein** be illiterate

**Analyse** *die;* ∼, ∼n analysis

**analysieren** *tr. V.* analyse

**Analyst** *der;* ∼en, ∼en, **Analystin**, *die;*
∼, ∼nen (Börsenw.) analyst

**analytisch** ☐1 *Adj.* analytical

☐2 *adv.* analytically

**Ananas** *die;* ∼, ∼ *od.* ∼se pineapple

**Anarchie** *die;* ∼, ∼n anarchy

**Anarchist** *der;* ∼en, ∼en, **Anarchistin**
*die;* ∼, ∼nen anarchist

**Anästhesie** *die;* ∼, ∼n (Med.) anaesthesia

**anästhesieren** *tr. V.* (Med.) anaesthetize

**Anästhesist** *der;* ∼en, ∼en,
**Anästhesistin** *die;* ∼, ∼nen (Med.)
anaesthetist

**Anatomie** *die;* ∼, ∼n anatomy

**anatomisch** *Adj.* anatomical

**an|bahnen** ☐1 *tr. V.* initiate ⟨*negotiations,
talks, process, etc.*⟩; develop ⟨*relationship,
connection*⟩
☐2 *refl. V.* ⟨*development*⟩ be in the offing;
⟨*friendship, relationship*⟩ start to develop

**an|bändeln** *itr. V.* **mit jmdm.** ∼ (ugs.) get
off with sb. (Brit. coll.); pick sb. up

**An-bau** *der; Pl.* ∼ten **(a)** building
**(b)** (Gebäude) extension
**(c)** (das Anpflanzen) growing

**an|bauen** ☐1 *tr. V.* **(a)** build on
**(b)** (anpflanzen) grow
☐2 *itr. V.* (das Haus vergrößern) build an
extension

**an-bei** *Adv.* (Amtsspr.) herewith; **Rückporto**
∼: return postage enclosed

**an|beißen** ☐1 *unr. tr. V.* bite into; take a
bite of
☐2 *unr. itr. V.* (auch fig. ugs.) bite

**an|belangen** *tr. V.* **was mich/dies** *usw.*
**anbelangt** as far as I am/this matter is *etc.*
concerned

**an|beten** *tr. V.* (auch fig.) worship

**An-betracht** *der:* **in** ∼ **einer Sache** (*Gen.*)
in view of sth.

**an|betreffen** *unr. tr. V.* ▶ ANBELANGEN

**an|betteln** *tr. V.* **jmdn.** ∼: beg from sb.;
**jmdn. um etw.** ∼: beg sb. for sth.

**Anbetung** *die;* ∼, ∼en (auch fig.) worship

**an|biedern** *refl. V.* **sich [bei jmdm.]** ∼:
curry favour [with sb.]

**an|bieten** ☐1 *unr. tr. V.* offer; **jmdm. etw.**
∼: offer sb. sth.
☐2 *unr. refl. V.* **(a)** offer one's services; **sich**
∼**, etw. zu tun** offer to do sth.
**(b)** (fig.) ⟨*possibility, solution*⟩ suggest itself

**An-bieter** *der,* **An-bieterin** *die* (Wirtsch.)
supplier

**an|binden** *unr. tr. V.* tie [up] (**an** + *Dat. od.
Akk.* to); tie up, moor ⟨*boat*⟩ (**an** + *Dat. od.
Akk.* to); tether ⟨*animal*⟩ (**an** + *Dat. od. Akk.*
to)

**an|blasen** *unr. tr. V.* **(a)** blow at
**(b)** (anfachen) blow on

**An-blick** *der* sight

**an|blicken** *tr. V.* look at

**an|blinzeln** *tr. V.* **(a)** blink at
**(b)** (zuzwinkern) wink at

**an|brechen** ☐1 *unr. tr. V.* **(a)** crack
**(b)** (öffnen) open      ⋯⋗

**(c)** (zu verbrauchen beginnen) break into ⟨*supplies, reserves*⟩ ② *unr. itr. V.; mit sein* (geh.: beginnen) ⟨*dawn, day*⟩ break; ⟨*age, epoch*⟩ dawn

**an|brennen** ① *unr. tr. V.* (anzünden) light ② *unr. itr. V.; mit sein* burn

**an|bringen** *unr. tr. V.* **(a)** (befestigen) put up ⟨*sign, aerial, curtain, plaque*⟩ (an + *Dat.* on) **(b)** (äußern) make ⟨*request, complaint, comment*⟩ **(c)** (zeigen) demonstrate ⟨*knowledge, experience*⟩ **(d)** (ugs.: herbeibringen) bring

**An·bruch** *der* (geh.: Beginn) dawn[ing]; **der ~ des Tages** daybreak

**an|brüllen** *tr. V.* (ugs.) bellow at

**Andacht** *die;* ~, ~en **(a)** (Sammlung) rapt attention; (im Gebet) silent worship *or* prayer **(b)** (Gottesdienst) prayers *pl.*

**andächtig** ① *Adj.* rapt; (ins Gebet versunken) devout ② *adv.* with rapt attention; (ins Gebet versunken) devoutly

**an|dauern** *itr. V.* ⟨*negotiations*⟩ continue, go on; ⟨*weather, rain*⟩ last

**andauernd** ① *Adj.* continual; constant ② *adv.* continually; constantly

**Anden** *Pl. die* ~: the Andes

**An·denken** *das;* ~s, ~ **(a)** memory; **zum ~ an jmdn./etw.** to remind you/us *etc.* of sb./ sth. **(b)** (Erinnerungsstück) memento; (Reise~) souvenir

**ander...** *Indefinitpron.* ① *attr.* **(a)** other; **ein ~er/eine ~e/ein ~es** another; **das Kleid gefällt mir nicht, haben Sie noch ~e/ein ~es?** I don't like that dress, do you have any others/another?; **jemand ~er** *od.* **~es** someone else; (in Fragen) anyone else; **niemand ~er** *od.* **~es** nobody else; **etwas ~es** something else; (in Fragen) anything else; **nichts ~es** nothing else; not anything else **(b)** (verschieden) different ② *allein stehend* **ein ~r/eine ~e:** another [one]; **nicht drängeln, einer nach dem ~n** don't push, one after the other; **ein ~er/eine ~e/ein ~es** another [one]; **ein[e]s nach dem ~[e]n** first things first; **ich will weder das eine noch das ~e** I don't want either

**anderen·falls** *Adv.* otherwise

**anderer·seits** *Adv.* on the other hand

**ander·mal** *Adv.* **ein ~:** another time

**ändern** ① *tr. V.* change; alter; alter ⟨*garment*⟩; change ⟨*person*⟩ ② *refl. V.* change

**andern·falls** *Adv.* otherwise

**anders** *Adv.* **(a)** (verschieden) ⟨*think, act, feel, do*⟩ differently (**als** from *or* (esp. Brit) to); ⟨*be, look, sound, taste*⟩ different (**als** from *or* (esp. Brit.) to); **es war alles ganz ~:** it was all quite different

**(b)** (sonst) else; **niemand ~:** nobody else; **jemand ~:** someone else; (in Fragen) anyone else

**anders-, Anders-: ~artig** *Adj.* different; **~farbig** *Adj.* different-coloured *attrib.;* of a different colour *postpos.;* **~gläubige** *der/ die* person of a different religion; **~herum** *Adv.* the other way round *or* (Amer.) around; **~herum gehen/fahren** go/drive round *or* (Amer.) around the other way; **~wo** *Adv.* (ugs.) elsewhere; **~woher** *Adv.* (ugs.) from somewhere else; **~wohin** *Adv.* (ugs.) somewhere else

**andert·halb** *Bruchz.* one and a half; **~ Stunden** an hour and a half

**Änderung** *die;* ~, ~en change (*Gen.* in); alteration (*Gen.* to)

**Änderungs·schneiderei** *die* tailor's [that does alterations]

**anderweitig** ① *Adj.* other ② *adv.* in another way

**an|deuten** ① *tr. V.* **(a)** (zu verstehen geben) hint **(b)** (nicht vollständig ausführen) outline; (kurz erwähnen) indicate ② *refl. V.* be indicated

**An·deutung** *die* hint

**An·drang** *der* crowd; (Gedränge) crush

**andre...** ▶ ANDER...

**an|drehen** *tr. V.* **(a)** (einschalten) turn on **(b)** jmdm. etw. ~ (ugs.) palm sb. off with sth.

**andrer·seits** *Adv.* on the other hand

**an|drohen** *tr. V.* jmdm. etw. ~: threaten sb. with sth

**An·drohung** *die* threat

**an|drücken** *tr. V.* press down

**an|ecken** *itr. V.; mit sein* **bei jmdm. ~** (fig. ugs.) rub sb. [up (Brit.)] the wrong way

**an|eignen** *refl. V.* **(a)** appropriate **(b)** (lernen) acquire; learn

**an-einander** *Adv.* (zusammen) together; (nebeneinander) next to each other; next to one another; **~ denken** think of each other *or* one another; **~ vorbeigehen** pass each other *or* one another

***aneinander|binden** *usw.* ▶ ANEINANDER

**Anekdote** *die;* ~, ~n anecdote

**an|ekeln** *tr. V.* disgust

**Anemone** *die;* ~, ~n anemone

**an|erkennen** *unr. tr. V.* **(a)** recognize ⟨*country, record, verdict, qualification, document*⟩; acknowledge ⟨*debt*⟩; accept ⟨*demand, bill, conditions, rules*⟩; allow ⟨*claim, goal*⟩ **(b)** (nicht leugnen) acknowledge **(c)** (würdigen) appreciate; respect ⟨*viewpoint, opinion*⟩; **ein ~der Blick** an appreciative look

**anerkennens·wert** *Adj.* commendable

**Anerkennung** *die;* ~, ~en ▶ ANERKENNEN **(a)** recognition; acknowledgement; acceptance; allowance **(b)** acknowledgement **(c)** appreciation; respect (*Gen.* for)

**an|fachen** *tr. V.* fan; (fig.) arouse ⟨*anger, curiosity, enthusiasm*⟩; inflame ⟨*passion*⟩; stir up ⟨*hatred*⟩; inspire ⟨*hope*⟩; ferment ⟨*discord, war*⟩

**an|fahren** **1** *unr. tr. V.* **(a)** run into; hit **(b)** (herbeifahren) deliver **(c)** (ansteuern) stop at ⟨*village etc.*⟩; ⟨*ship*⟩ put in at ⟨*port*⟩ **(d)** (zurechtweisen) shout at **2** *unr. itr. V.; mit sein* **(a)** (starten) start off **(b) angefahren kommen** come driving/riding up

**An·fahrt** *die* **(a)** (das Anfahren) journey **(b)** (Weg) approach

**Anfahrts·skizze** *die* map showing directions

**An·fall** *der* attack; (epileptischer ∼, fig.) fit; **einen ∼ bekommen** *od.* (ugs.) **kriegen** have an attack/a fit

**an·fallen** **1** *unr. tr. V.* attack **2** *unr. itr V.; mit sein* ⟨*costs*⟩ be incurred; ⟨*interest*⟩ accrue; ⟨*work*⟩ come up

**an·fällig** *Adj.* ⟨*person*⟩ with a delicate constitution; ⟨*machine*⟩ susceptible to faults; **gegen** *od.* **für etw. ∼ sein** be susceptible to sth.

**An·fang** *der* beginning; start; (erster Abschnitt) beginning; **am** *od.* **zu ∼:** at first; **von ∼ an** from the outset; **∼ 1984/der Woche** *usw.* at the beginning of 1984/of the week *etc.*

**an·fangen** **1** *unr. itr. V.* **(a)** begin; start; **mit etw. ∼:** start [on] sth.; **∼, etw. zu tun** start to do sth. **(b)** (zu sprechen anfangen) begin; **von etw. ∼:** start on about sth. **(c)** (eine Stelle antreten) start **2** *unr. tr. V.* **(a)** begin; start; (anbrechen) start **(b)** (machen) do

**An·fänger** *der;* **∼s, ∼, An·fängerin** *die;* **∼, ∼nen** beginner

**anfänglich** *Adj.* initial

**anfangs** *Adv.* at first; initially

**Anfangs-:** **∼buchstabe** *der* initial [letter]; **∼stadium** *das* initial stage

**an|fassen** **1** *tr. V.* **(a)** (fassen, halten) take hold of **(b)** (berühren) touch **(c) jmdn. ∼** (an der Hand nehmen) take sb.'s hand **(d)** (angehen) tackle ⟨*problem, task, etc.*⟩ **(e)** (behandeln) treat ⟨*person*⟩ **2** *itr. V.* [mit] **∼:** lend a hand

**anfechtbar** *Adj.:* ▶ ANFECHTEN A: disputable; contestable; challengeable

**an|fechten** *unr. tr. V.* **(a)** dispute ⟨*statement, contract*⟩; contest ⟨*will*⟩; challenge ⟨*decision, law, opinion*⟩ **(b)** (beunruhigen) trouble

**an|fertigen** *tr. V.* make

**an|feuchten** *tr. V.* moisten ⟨*lips, stamp*⟩; dampen ⟨*ironing, cloth, etc.*⟩

**an|feuern** *tr. V.* spur on

**an|fixen** *tr. V.* (Drogenjargon) **jmdn. ∼:** get sb. shooting up for the first time (sl.); **von etw. angefixt sein** (fig.) be hooked on sth. (coll.)

**an|flehen** *tr. V.* beseech; implore

**an|fliegen** **1** *unr. itr. V.; mit sein* fly in; **angeflogen kommen** come flying in; **gegen den Wind ∼:** fly into the wind **2** *unr. tr. V.* fly to ⟨*city, country, airport*⟩

**An·flug** *der* **(a)** approach **(b)** (Hauch) hint **(c)** (Anwandlung) fit; **in einem ∼ von Großzügigkeit** in a fit of generosity

**an|fordern** *tr. V.* ask for; order ⟨*goods, materials*⟩; send for ⟨*ambulance*⟩

**An·forderung** *die* **(a)** (das Anfordern) request (*Gen.* for) **(b)** (Anspruch) demand

**An·frage** *die* inquiry; (Parl.) question

**an|fragen** *itr. V.* inquire; ask

**an|freunden** *refl. V.* become friends

**an|fügen** *tr. V.* add

**an|fühlen** *refl. V.* feel

**an|führen** *tr. V.* **(a)** lead **(b)** (zitieren) quote **(c)** (nennen) give ⟨*example, reason, details, proof*⟩ **(d)** (ugs.: hereinlegen) have on (Brit. coll.); dupe

**An·führer** *der*, **An·führerin** *die* leader; (Rädelsführer) ringleader

**An·führung** *die* **(a)** (das Zitieren, Zitat) quotation **(b)** (Nennung) giving

**Anführungs-:** **∼strich** *der*, **∼zeichen** *das* quotation mark

**An·gabe** *die* **(a)** (das Mitteilen) giving **(b)** (Information) piece of information; **∼n** information *sing.;* **(c)** (Ballspiele) service; serve

**an|geben** **1** *unr. tr. V.* **(a)** give ⟨*reason*⟩; declare ⟨*income, dutiable goods*⟩; name ⟨*witness*⟩ **(b)** (bestimmen) set ⟨*course, direction*⟩; **den Takt ∼:** keep time **2** *unr. itr. V.* **(a)** (prahlen) boast; brag; (sich angeberisch benehmen) show off **(b)** (Ballspiele) serve

**Angeber** *der;* **∼s, ∼:** braggart

**Angeberei** *die;* **∼:** showing-off

**Angeberin** *die;* **∼, ∼nen** ▶ ANGEBER

**angeblich** **1** *Adj.* alleged **2** *adv.* supposedly; allegedly

**an·geboren** *Adj.* innate ⟨*characteristic*⟩; congenital ⟨*disease*⟩

**An·gebot** *das* **(a)** offer **(b)** (Wirtsch.) supply; (Sortiment) range; **∼ und Nachfrage** supply and demand **(c)** (Kaufmannsspr.: Sonder∼) [special] offer; **im ∼:** on [special] offer; **∼ der Woche** bargain of the week

**an·gebracht** *Adj.* appropriate

**a**

**an·gegriffen** Adj. weakened ⟨health, stomach⟩; strained ⟨nerves, voice⟩

**angeheitert** Adj. tipsy

**an|gehen** 1 unr. itr. V.; mit sein **(a)** ⟨radio, light, heating⟩ come on; ⟨fire⟩ catch **(b)** (anwachsen, wachsen) ⟨plant⟩ take root **(c)** es mag noch ∼: it's [just about] acceptable **(d)** gegen etw./jmdn. ∼: fight sth./sb. 2 unr. tr. V. **(a)** (angreifen) attack **(b)** (in Angriff nehmen) tackle ⟨problem, difficulty⟩; take ⟨fence, bend⟩ **(c)** (bitten) ask ⟨um for⟩ **(d)** (betreffen) concern; das geht dich nichts an it's none of your business

**angehend** Adj. budding; (zukünftig) prospective

**an|gehören** itr. V. jmdm./einer Sache ∼: belong to sb./sth.; der Regierung/einer Familie ∼: be a member of the government/a family

**an·gehörig** Adj. belonging (Dat. to)

**Angehörige** der/die; adj. Dekl. **(a)** (Verwandte) relative; relation **(b)** (Mitglied) member

**Angeklagte** der/die; adj. Dekl. accused; defendant

**Angel** die; ∼, ∼n **(a)** fishing rod **(b)** (Tür∼, Fenster∼ usw.) hinge; etw. aus den ∼n heben (fig.) turn sth. upside down

**An·gelegenheit** die matter; (Aufgabe, Problem) affair

**Angel·haken** der fish hook

**angeln** 1 tr. V. (zu fangen suchen) fish for; (fangen) catch 2 itr. V. angle; fish

**Angel·rute** die fishing rod

**Angel·sachse** der, **Angel·sächsin** die Anglo-Saxon

**Angel·schnur** die fishing line

**an·gemessen** Adj. appropriate; reasonable, fair ⟨price, fee⟩

**an·genehm** 1 Adj. pleasant; ∼e Reise/ Ruhe! [have a] pleasant journey/have a good rest; [sehr] ∼! delighted to meet you 2 adv. pleasantly

**an·gesehen** Adj. respected

**angesichts** Präp. mit Gen. (geh.) **(a)** in the face of **(b)** (fig.: in Anbetracht) in view of

**angespannt** Adj. **(a)** close ⟨attention⟩; taut ⟨nerves⟩ **(b)** tense ⟨situation⟩; tight ⟨market, economic situation⟩

**angestellt** Adj. bei jmdm. ∼ sein be employed by sb.; work for sb.

**Angestellte** der/die; adj. Dekl. [salaried] employee

**Angestellten·gewerkschaft** die white-collar union

---

*alte Schreibung - vgl. Hinweis auf S. xiv

**an·getan** Adj. von jmdm./etw. ∼ sein be taken with sb./sth.

**an·getrunken** Adj. [slightly] drunk

**an·gewiesen** Adj. auf jmdn./etw. ∼ sein have to rely on sb./sth.

**an|gewöhnen** tr. V. jmdm. etw. ∼: get sb. used to sth.; jmdm. ∼, etw. zu tun get sb. used to doing sth.; sich (Dat.) etw. ∼: get into the habit of sth.; [es] sich (Dat.) ∼, etw. zu tun get into the habit of doing sth.

**An·gewohnheit** die habit

**an|gleichen** 1 unr. tr. V. etw. einer Sache (Dat.) od. an etw. (Akk.) ∼: bring sth. into line with sth. 2 unr. refl. V. sich jmdm./einer Sache od. an jmdn./etw. ∼: become like sb./sth.

**An·gleichung** die; die ∼ der Löhne an die Preise bringing wages into line with prices

**Angler** der; ∼s, ∼, **Anglerin** die; ∼, ∼nen angler

**Anglikaner** der; ∼s, ∼, **Anglikanerin** die; ∼, ∼nen Anglican

**anglikanisch** Adj. Anglican

**Anglistik** die; ∼: English studies pl., no art.

**Angola** (das); ∼s Angola

**Angora-:** ∼katze die angora cat; ∼wolle die angora [wool]

**an|greifen** 1 unr. tr. V. **(a)** (auch fig.) attack **(b)** (schwächen) affect ⟨health, heart, stomach, intestine, voice⟩; weaken ⟨person⟩ 2 unr. itr. V. (auch fig.) attack

**Angreifer** der; ∼s, ∼, **Angreiferin** die; ∼, ∼nen (auch fig.) attacker

**An·griff** der **(a)** attack; zum ∼ blasen (auch fig.) sound the attack **(b)** etw. in ∼ nehmen tackle sth.

**angst** Adj. jmdm. ist/wird [es] ∼ [und bange] sb. is/becomes frightened

**Angst** die; ∼, Ängste **(a)** (Furcht) fear; ∼ bekommen od. (ugs.) kriegen become frightened; ∼ haben be frightened (vor + Dat. of) **(b)** (Sorge) anxiety; ∼ haben be anxious (um about); keine ∼, ich vergesse es schon nicht! don't worry, I won't forget [it]!

**ängstigen** 1 tr. V. frighten; (beunruhigen) worry 2 refl. V. be frightened; (sich sorgen) worry

**ängstlich** 1 Adj. anxious 2 adv. anxiously

**Ängstlichkeit** die; ∼: timidity

**an|gucken** tr. V. (ugs.) look at; sich (Dat.) etw./jmdn. ∼: have a look at sth./sb.

**an|gurten** tr. V. strap in; sich ∼: put on one's seat belt

**an|haben** unr. tr. V. **(a)** (ugs.: am Körper tragen) have on **(b)** jmdm./einer Sache etwas ∼ können be able to harm sb./sth.

**an|halten** 1 unr. tr. V. **(a)** stop **(b)** (auffordern) urge

2 *unr. itr. V.* **(a)** stop
**(b)** (andauern) go on; last
**anhaltend** 1 *Adj.* constant; continuous
2 *adv.* constantly; continuously
**An·halter** *der* hitch-hiker; per ~ fahren
hitch[-hike]
**An·halterin** *die* hitch-hiker
**Anhalts·punkt** *der* clue (**für** to); (für eine
Vermutung) grounds *pl.*
**an·hand** 1 *Präp. mit Gen.* with the help of
2 *Adv.* ~ **von** with the help of
**An·hang** *der* **(a)** (Buchw.) appendix
**(b)** (Anhängerschaft) following
**(c)** (Verwandtschaft) family
**an|hängen** 1 *tr. V.* **(a)** hang up (**an** +
*Akk.* on)
**(b)** (ankuppeln) couple on (**an** + *Akk.* to); hitch
up ⟨*trailer*⟩ (**an** + *Akk.* to)
**(c)** (anfügen) add (**an** + *Akk.* to)
**(d)** (ugs.: zuschreiben, anlasten) **jmdm. etw.** ~
blame sb. for sth.; blame sth. on sb.; **er will
mir nur was** ~ he just wants to pin
something on me
2 *refl. V.* **(a)** hang on (**an** + *Akk.* to)
**(b)** (ugs.: sich anschließen) **sich [an jmdn.** *od.*
**bei jmdm.]** ~: tag along [with sb.]
**An·hänger** *der* **(a)** (Mensch) supporter
**(b)** (Wagen) trailer
**(c)** (Schmuckstück) pendant
**(d)** (Schildchen) tag
**Anhängerin** *die;* ~, ~nen ▶ ANHÄNGER A
**Anhängerschaft** *die;* ~, ~en supporters
*pl.*
**anhänglich** *Adj.* devoted ⟨*dog, friend*⟩
**Anhänglichkeit** *die;* ~: devotion
**an|hauchen** *tr. V.* breathe on ⟨*mirror,
glasses*⟩; blow on ⟨*fingers, hands*⟩
**an|häufen** *tr. V.* accumulate
**Anhäufung** *die* accumulation
**an|heben** *unr. tr. V.* **(a)** lift [up]
**(b)** (erhöhen) raise ⟨*prices, wages, etc.*⟩
**an|heften** *tr. V.* attach ⟨*label, list*⟩; put up
⟨*sign, notice*⟩
**anheim** (geh.): **[es] jmdm.** ~ **stellen, etw. zu
tun** leave it to sb. to do sth.
***anheim|stellen** ▶ ANHEIM
**An·hieb** *der:* **auf** ~ (ugs.) straight off
**an|himmeln** *tr. V.* worship
**An·höhe** *die* rise
**an|hören** 1 *tr. V.* listen to; **sich** (*Dat.*)
**jmdn./etw.** ~: listen to sb./sth.
2 *refl. V.* sound
**animieren** *tr. V.* encourage
**Anis** *der;* ~es aniseed
**Ank.** *Abk.* = **Ankunft** arr.
**An·kauf** *der* purchase
**an|kaufen** *tr. V.* purchase; buy
**Anker** *der;* ~s, ~ anchor; **vor** ~ **gehen/
liegen** drop anchor/lie at anchor; ~ **werfen**
drop anchor
**ankern** *itr. V.* **(a)** anchor
**(b)** (vor Anker liegen) be anchored

**Anker·platz** *der* anchorage
**An·klage** *die* **(a)** charge; **unter** ~ **stehen**
have been charged (**wegen** with)
**(b)** (~vertretung) prosecution
**Anklage·bank** *die; Pl.* Anklagebänke
dock; **auf der** ~ **sitzen** (auch fig.) be in the
dock
**an|klagen** *tr. V.* **(a)** (Rechtsw.) charge (*Gen.,*
**wegen** with); accuse
**(b)** (geh.: beschuldigen) accuse
**An·kläger** *der,* **An·klägerin** *die*
prosecutor
**an|klammern** 1 *tr. V.* peg (Brit.), pin
(Amer.) ⟨*clothes, washing*⟩ up; clip ⟨*sheet etc.*⟩;
(mit Heftklammern) staple ⟨*sheet etc.*⟩
2 *refl. V.* **sich an jmdn./etw.** ~: cling to sb./
sth.
**An·klang** *der:* [bei jmdm.] ~ **finden** meet
with [sb.'s] approval
**an|kleben** 1 *tr. V.* stick up ⟨*poster, etc.*⟩
2 *itr. V.; mit sein* stick
**an|kleiden** *tr. V.* (geh.) dress; **sich** ~: dress
**an|klicken** *tr. V.* (DV) click on
**an|klopfen** *itr. V.* knock
**an|knüpfen** 1 *tr. V.* **(a)** tie on (**an** + *Akk.*
to)
**(b)** (beginnen) start up ⟨*conversation*⟩;
establish ⟨*relations, business links*⟩; form
⟨*relationship*⟩
2 *itr. V.* **an etw.** (*Akk.*) ~: take sth. up; **ich
knüpfe dort an, wo …** I'll pick up where …
**an|kommen** *unr. itr. V.; mit sein* **(a)**
(eintreffen) arrive; **seid ihr gut angekommen?**
did you arrive safely?
**(b)** [bei jmdm.] [gut] ~ (fig. ugs.) go down
[very] well [with sb.]
**(c)** **gegen jmdn./etw.** ~: be able to deal with
sb./fight sth.
**(d)** *unpers.* **es kommt auf jmdn./etw. an**
(jmd./etw. ist ausschlaggebend) it depends on
sb./sth.; **es kommt auf etw.** (*Akk.*) **an** (etw. ist
wichtig) sth. matters (*Dat.* to); **es kommt
[ganz] darauf** *od.* **drauf an** (ugs.) it [all]
depends
**(e)** *unpers.* **es darauf** *od.* **drauf** ~ **lassen**
(ugs.) chance it; **es auf etw.** (*Akk.*) ~ **lassen**
[be prepared to] risk sth.
**an|koppeln** 1 *tr. V.* couple ⟨*carriage*⟩ up;
hitch ⟨*trailer*⟩ up; dock ⟨*spacecraft*⟩
2 *itr. V.* ⟨*spacecraft*⟩ dock
**an|kreuzen** *tr. V.* mark with a cross
**an|kündigen** 1 *tr. V.* announce
2 *refl. V.* announce itself
**An·kündigung** *die* announcement
**Ankunft** *die;* ~, Ankünfte arrival; „~"
'arrivals'
**Ankunfts-:** ~**halle** *die* arrival[s] hall;
~**tafel** *die* arrivals board
**an|kuppeln** *tr. V.* ▶ ANKOPPELN 1
**an|kurbeln** *tr. V.* **(a)** crank [up]
**(b)** (fig.) boost ⟨*economy, production, etc.*⟩
**Anl.** *Abk.* = **Anlage** encl.
**an|lächeln** *tr. V.* smile at

**an|lachen** ① *tr. V.* smile at
② *refl. V.* **sich** (*Dat.*) **jmdn.** ~ (ugs.) get off
with sb. (Brit. coll.); pick sb. up

**An·lage** *die* (a) (das Anlegen) (einer Kartei)
establishment; (eines Parks, Gartens usw.) laying
out; (eines Parkplatzes, Stausees) construction
(b) (Grünanlage) park; (um ein Schloss usw.
herum) grounds *pl.;*
(c) (Einrichtung) facilities *pl.;* **militärische** ~n
military installations
(d) (Werk) plant
(e) (Musikanlage usw.) system
(f) (Geldanlage) investment
(g) (Konzeption) conception; (Struktur) structure
(h) (Veranlagung) aptitude; (Neigung) tendency
(i) (Beilage zu einem Brief) enclosure

**Anlage-:** ~**berater** *der,* ~**beraterin**
*die* investment advisor; ~**kapital** *das*
investment capital

**Anlass, *Anlaß** *der;* **Anlasses, Anlässe** (a)
cause (**zu** for); **etw. zum** ~ **nehmen, etw. zu
tun** take sth. as an opportunity to do sth.;
**aus aktuellem** ~: because of current events
(b) (Gelegenheit) occasion

**an|lassen** ① *unr. itr. V.* (a) leave ⟨light,
radio, heating, etc.⟩ on; leave ⟨engine⟩
running; leave ⟨candle⟩ burning
(b) keep ⟨coat, gloves, etc.⟩ on
(c) (in Gang setzen) start [up]
② *unr. refl. V.* **sich gut/schlecht** ~: get off to
a good/bad start

**Anlasser** *der;* ~**s,** ~: starter

**an·lässlich, *an·läßlich** *Präp. mit Gen.*
on the occasion of

**An·lauf** *der* (a) run-up; [mehr] ~ **nehmen**
take [more of] a run-up
(b) (Versuch) attempt; **beim** *od.* **im ersten/
dritten** ~: at the first/third attempt

**an|laufen** ① *unr. itr. V.; mit sein* (a)
**angelaufen kommen** come running along; (auf
einen zu) come running up
(b) **gegen jmdn./etw.** ~: run at sb./sth.
(c) (Anlauf nehmen) take a run-up
(d) (zu laufen beginnen) ⟨engine⟩ start [up]; (fig.)
⟨film⟩ open; ⟨production, campaign, search⟩
start
(e) **rot/dunkel** usw. ~: go *or* turn red/dark
*etc.;*
(f) (beschlagen) mist up
② *unr. tr. V.* put in at ⟨port⟩

**an|legen** ① *tr. V.* (a) put *or* lay ⟨domino,
card⟩ [down] (**an** + *Akk.* next to); place,
position ⟨ruler, protractor⟩ (**an** + *Akk.* on);
put ⟨ladder⟩ up (**an** + *Akk.* against)
(b) **die Flügel/Ohren** ~: close its wings/lay
its ears back; **die Arme** ~: put one's arms to
one's sides
(c) (geh.: anziehen, umlegen) don
(d) (schaffen, erstellen) lay out ⟨town, garden,
plantation, street⟩; start ⟨file, album⟩;
compile ⟨statistics, index⟩
(e) (investieren) invest
(f) (ausgeben) spend (**für** on)

*old spelling - see note on page xiv

(g) **es darauf** ~, **etw. zu tun** be determined to
do sth.
② *itr. V.* (a) (landen) moor
(b) (Kartenspiele) lay a card/cards
(c) (Domino) play [a domino/dominoes]
(d) (zielen) aim (**auf** + *Akk.* at)
③ *refl. V.* **sich mit jmdm.** ~: pick an
argument with sb

**Anlege-:** ~**platz** *der* berth; ~**steg** *der*
jetty

**an|lehnen** ① *tr. V.* (a) lean (**an** + *Akk.* od.
*Dat.* against)
(b) leave ⟨door, window⟩ slightly open
② *refl. V.* **sich** [**an jmdn.** *od.* **jmdm./etw.**] ~:
lean [on sb./against sth.]

**Anlehnung** *die;* **in** ~ **an** (+ *Akk.*) in
imitation of; following

**Anleihe** *die;* ~, ~**n** (Finanzw.) bond

**an|leiten** *tr. V.* instruct

**An·leitung** *die* instructions *pl.*

**an|lernen** *tr. V.* train

**an|liegen** *unr. itr. V.* (a) ⟨pullover etc.⟩ fit
tightly
(b) (ugs.: vorliegen) be on

**An·liegen** *das;* ~**s,** ~ (Bitte) request;
(Angelegenheit) matter

**anliegend** *Adj.* (a) (angrenzend) adjacent
(b) (beiliegend) enclosed

**Anlieger** *der;* ~**s,** ~, **Anliegerin** *die;* ~,
~**nen** resident; „~ **frei**" 'access only'

**an|locken** *tr. V.* attract ⟨customers, tourists,
etc.⟩; lure ⟨bird, animal⟩

**an|lügen** *tr. V.* lie to

**an|machen** *tr. V.* (a) put ⟨light, radio,
heating⟩ on; light ⟨fire⟩
(b) mix ⟨cement, plaster, paint, etc.⟩; dress
⟨salad⟩
(c) (ugs.: ansprechen) ⟨woman, girl⟩ give ⟨man,
boy⟩ the come-on (coll.); ⟨man, boy⟩ chat
⟨woman, girl⟩ up (Brit. coll.)
(d) (ugs.: begeistern, erregen) get ⟨audience etc.⟩
going; **das macht mich ungeheuer/nicht an** it
really turns me on (coll.)/does nothing for me
(coll.)
(e) (provozieren) **mach mich nicht an!** leave me
alone!

**an|malen** *tr. V.* paint

**an|maßen** *refl. V.* **sich** (*Dat.*) **etw.** ~: claim
sth. [for oneself]

**an·maßend** ① *Adj.* presumptuous;
(arrogant) arrogant
② *adv.* presumptuously; (arrogant) arrogantly

**Anmaßung** *die;* ~, ~**en** presumption;
(Arroganz) arrogance

**Anmelde·formular** *das* (a) application
form
(b) (einer Meldebehörde) registration form

**an|melden** ① *tr. V.* (a) (als Teilnehmer)
enrol (**zu** for); **sich** ~: enrol (**zu** for)
(b) (melden, anzeigen) license ⟨radio,
television⟩; apply for ⟨patent⟩; register
⟨domicile, change of address, car, trade
mark⟩; **sich** ~: register one's new address

**(c)** (ankündigen) announce; **sind Sie angemeldet?** do you have an appointment?; **sich beim Arzt ∼:** make an appointment to see the doctor
**(d)** (geltend machen) express 〈*reservation, doubt, wish*〉; put forward 〈*demand*〉
2 *refl V.* (DV) log on

**An·meldung** *die* **(a)** (zur Teilnahme) enrolment
**(b)** ▶ ANMELDEN B: licensing; application (*Gen.* for); registration
**(c)** (Ankündigung) announcement; (beim Arzt, Rechtsanwalt usw.) making an appointment

**an|merken** *tr. V.* **(a)** jmdm. seinen Ärger/ seine Verlegenheit *usw.* ∼: notice that sb. is annoyed/embarrassed *etc.;* **man merkt ihm [nicht] an, dass er krank ist** you can[not] tell that he is ill; **sich nichts ∼ lassen** not let it show
**(b)** (geh.: bemerken) note

**Anmerkung** *die;* ∼, ∼en **(a)** (Fußnote) note
**(b)** (geh.: Bemerkung) comment

**an|motzen** *tr. V.* (ugs.) swear at

**Anmut** *die;* ∼ (geh.) grace

**an·mutig** (geh.) 1 *Adj.* graceful 〈*girl, movement, dance*〉; charming, delightful 〈*girl, smile, picture, landscape*〉
2 *adv.* 〈*move, dance*〉 gracefully; 〈*smile, greet*〉 charmingly

**an|nähen** *tr. V.* sew on

**an|nähern** 1 *refl. V.* get closer (*Dat.* to sth)
2 *tr. V.* bring closer (*Dat.* to)

**annähernd** 1 *Adv.* almost; (ungefähr) approximately
2 *adj.* approximate

**Annahme** *die;* ∼, ∼n **(a)** (das Annehmen) acceptance
**(b)** (Vermutung) assumption; **in der ∼, dass ...:** on the assumption that ...

**annehmbar** 1 *Adj.* **(a)** acceptable
**(b)** (recht gut) reasonable
2 *adv.* reasonably [well]

**an|nehmen** 1 *unr. tr. V.* **(a)** accept; take; accept 〈*alms, invitation, condition, help*〉; take 〈*food, telephone call*〉; accept, take up 〈*offer, challenge*〉
**(b)** (Sport) take 〈*ball, pass, etc.*〉
**(c)** (billigen) approve
**(d)** (aufnehmen) take on 〈*worker, patient, pupil*〉
**(e)** (hinnehmen) accept 〈*fate, verdict, punishment*〉
**(f)** (adoptieren) adopt
**(g)** (haften lassen) take 〈*dye, ink*〉
**(h)** (sich aneignen) adopt 〈*habit, mannerism, name, attitude*〉
**(i)** (bekommen) take on 〈*look, appearance, form, dimension*〉
**(j)** (vermuten, voraussetzen) assume; **angenommen, [dass] ...:** assuming [that] ...
2 *unr. refl. V.* (geh.) **sich jmds./einer Sache ∼:** look after sb./sth.

**Annehmlichkeit** *die;* ∼, ∼en comfort; (Vorteil) advantage

**annektieren** *tr. V.* annex

**Annektierung** *die;* ∼, ∼en, **Annexion** *die;* ∼, ∼en annexation

**Annonce** /a'nõːsə/ *die;* ∼, ∼n advertisement; advert (Brit. coll.)

**annoncieren** *itr. V.* advertise

**annullieren** *tr. V.* annul

**Annullierung** *die;* ∼, ∼en annulment

**anonym** 1 *Adj.* anonymous
2 *adv.* anonymously

**Anonymität** *die;* ∼: anonymity

**Anorak** *der;* ∼s, ∼s anorak

**an|ordnen** *tr. V.* **(a)** (arrangieren) arrange
**(b)** (befehlen) order

**An·ordnung** *die* ▶ ANORDNEN: **(a)** arrangement
**(b)** order

**an·organisch** *Adj.* inorganic

**an|packen** 1 *tr. V.* **(a)** (ugs.: anfassen) grab hold of
**(b)** (angehen) tackle
2 *itr. V.* [mit] ∼ (ugs.: mithelfen) lend a hand

**an|passen** 1 *tr. V.* **(a)** (passend machen) fit
**(b)** (abstimmen) suit (*Dat.* to)
2 *refl. V.* adapt [oneself] (*Dat.* to); 〈*animal*〉 adapt

**Anpassung** *die;* ∼, ∼en adaptation (**an** + *Akk.* to)

**anpassungs·fähig** *Adj.* adaptable

**an|pfeifen** 1 *unr. tr. V.* **das Spiel/die zweite Halbzeit ∼:** blow the whistle to start the game/the second half
2 *unr. itr. V.* blow the whistle

**An·pfiff** *der* **(a)** (Sport) whistle for the start of play
**(b)** (salopp: Zurechtweisung) bawling-out (coll.)

**an|pflanzen** *tr. V.* **(a)** plant
**(b)** (anbauen) grow

**an|pöbeln** *tr. V.* (ugs.) abuse

**an|prangern** *tr. V.* denounce (**als** as)

**an|preisen** *unr. tr. V.* extol

**An·probe** *die* fitting

**an|probieren** *tr. V.* try on

**an|rechnen** *tr. V.* **(a)** count
**(b)** **jmdm. etw. ∼** (in Rechnung stellen) charge sb. for sth.

**An·recht** *das* right; **ein ∼ auf etw.** (*Akk.*) **haben** be entitled to sth.

**An·rede** *die* form of address

**an|reden** *tr. V.* address

**an|regen** *tr. V.* **(a)** stimulate 〈*imagination, digestion*〉; whet 〈*appetite*〉
**(b)** (ermuntern) prompt; (vorschlagen) propose

**anregend** *Adj.* stimulating

**An·regung** *die* **(a)** ▶ ANREGEN A: stimulation; whetting
**(b)** (Denkanstoß) stimulus
**(c)** (Vorschlag) proposal

**an|reichern** 1 *tr. V.* enrich    ⋯⃗

**a**

2 *refl. V.* accumulate

**An·reise** *die* journey [there/here]

**an|reisen** *itr. V.; mit sein* travel there/here; **mit der Bahn** ∼: go/come by train

**An·reiz** *der* incentive

**an|rempeln** *tr. V.* barge into; (absichtlich) jostle

**Anrichte** *die;* ∼, ∼n sideboard

**an|richten** *tr. V.* **(a)** arrange ⟨*food*⟩; (servieren) serve
**(b)** cause ⟨*disaster, confusion, devastation, etc.*⟩

**anrüchig** *Adj.* **(a)** disreputable
**(b)** (unanständig) indecent

**an|rücken** *itr. V.; mit sein* ⟨*troops*⟩ advance; ⟨*firemen, police*⟩ move in

**An·ruf** *der* call

**Anruf·beantworter** *der;* ∼s, ∼: [telephone] answering machine

**an|rufen** *unr. tr. V.* **(a)** call *or* shout to ⟨*friend, passer-by*⟩; call ⟨*sleeping person*⟩
**(b)** (geh.: angehen, bitten) appeal to ⟨*person, court*⟩ (um for); call upon ⟨*God*⟩
**(c)** *auch itr.* (telefonisch ∼) call

**Anrufer** *der;* ∼s, ∼, **Anruferin** *die;* ∼, ∼nen caller

**an|rühren** *tr. V.* **(a)** touch
**(b)** (bereiten) mix

**ans** *Präp. + Art.* **(a)** = an das;
**(b)** sich ∼ Arbeiten machen set to work

**An·sage** *die* announcement

**an|sagen** *tr. V.* **(a)** announce
**(b)** (Kartenspiele) bid

**Ansager** *der;* ∼s, ∼, **Ansagerin** *die;* ∼, ∼nen (Radio, Fernsehen) announcer

**an|sammeln** 1 *tr. V.* accumulate; amass ⟨*riches, treasure*⟩
2 *refl. V.* accumulate; (fig.) ⟨*anger, excitement*⟩ build up

**An·sammlung** *die* **(a)** collection
**(b)** (Auflauf) crowd

**ansässig** *Adj.* resident

**An·satz** *der* (erstes Zeichen, Beginn) beginnings *pl.*

**an|schaffen** *tr. V.* [sich (*Dat.*)] etw. ∼ get [oneself] sth.

**An·schaffung** *die* purchase

**an|schalten** *tr. V.* switch on

**an|schauen** *tr. V.* (bes. südd., österr., schweiz.) ▶ ANSEHEN

**anschaulich** 1 *Adj.* vivid
2 *adv.* vividly

**Anschauung** *die;* ∼, ∼en **(a)** (Wahrnehmung) experience
**(b)** (Auffassung) view

**An·schein** *der* appearance; allem *od.* dem ∼ nach to all appearances

**an·scheinend** *Adv.* apparently

**an|schieben** *unr. tr. V.* push ⟨*vehicle*⟩

**an|schießen** *unr. tr. V.* shoot and wound

**An·schlag** *der* **(a)** (Bekanntmachung) notice; (Plakat) poster
**(b)** (Attentat) assassination attempt; (auf ein Gebäude, einen Zug usw.) attack
**(c)** (Texterfassung) keystroke
**(d) mit dem Gewehr im** ∼: with rifle/rifles levelled

**an|schlagen** *unr. tr. V.* **(a)** put up, ⟨*notice, announcement, message*⟩ (an + *Akk.* on)
**(b)** (beschädigen) chip

**an|schließen** 1 *unr. tr. V.* **(a)** connect (an + *Akk. od. Dat.* to); connect up ⟨*electrical device*⟩
**(b)** (festschließen) lock, secure (an + *Dat. od. Akk.* to)
2 *unr. refl. V.* sich jmdm./einer Sache ∼: join sb./sth.

**An·schluss, *An·schluß** *der* connection; **kein** ∼ **unter dieser Nummer** number unobtainable

**Anschluss-, *Anschluß-:** ∼kabel *das* connecting cable *or* (esp. Brit.) lead; ∼zug *der* connecting train

**an|schnallen** *tr. V.* put on ⟨*skis, skates*⟩; sich ∼ (im Auto) put on one's seat belt; (im Flugzeug) fasten one's seat belt

**an|schrauben** *tr. V.* screw on (an + *Akk.* to)

**An·schreiben** *das* covering letter

**an|schreien** *unr. tr. V.* shout at

**An·schrift** *die* address

**Anschuldigung** *die;* ∼, ∼en accusation

**an|schwärzen** *tr. V.* (ugs.) jmdn. ∼ (in Misskredit bringen) blacken sb.'s name; (schlecht machen) run sb. down (bei to); (denunzieren) inform *or* (Brit. sl.) grass on sb. (bei to)

**an|schwellen** *unr. itr. V.; mit sein* **(a)** swell [up]; (fig.) swell; ⟨*water, river*⟩ rise
**(b)** (lauter werden) grow louder; ⟨*noise*⟩ rise

**an|schwemmen** *tr. V.* wash ashore

**an|sehen** *unr. tr. V.* **(a)** look at; watch ⟨*television programme*⟩; see ⟨*play, film*⟩; jmdn. groß/böse ∼: stare at sb./give sb. an angry look; hübsch *usw.* anzusehen sein be pretty *etc.* to look at; sieh [mal] [einer] an! (ugs.) well, I never! (coll.)
**(b)** (erkennen) man sieht ihm sein Alter nicht an he does not look his age; man sieht ihr die Strapazen an she's showing the strain
**(c)** (zusehen bei) etw. [mit] ∼: watch sth.; das kann man doch nicht [mit] ∼: I/you can't just stand by and watch that

**Ansehen** *das;* ∼s [high] standing

**an·sehnlich** *Adj.* **(a)** (beträchtlich) considerable
**(b)** (gut aussehend, stattlich) handsome

***an|sein** ▶ AN 3B

**an|setzen** *tr. V.* **(a)** (in die richtige Stellung bringen) position ⟨*ladder, jack, drill, saw*⟩
**(b)** (anfügen) attach, put on (an + *Akk. od. Dat.* to)
**(c)** (festlegen) fix ⟨*meeting etc.*⟩ (für, auf + *Akk.* for); fix, set ⟨*deadline, date, price*⟩

---

**(d)** (veranschlagen) estimate
**(e)** (anrühren) mix
**An·sicht** *die* **(a)** (Meinung) opinion; view; meiner ∼ nach in my opinion *or* view
**(b)** (Bild) view
**Ansichts·karte** *die* picture postcard
**an|spannen** *tr. V.* **(a)** harness ⟨*horse etc.*⟩ (an + *Akk.* to); yoke up ⟨*oxen*⟩ (an + *Akk.* to); hitch up ⟨*carriage, cart, etc.*⟩ (an + *Akk.* to)
**(b)** (anstrengen) strain
**An·spannung** *die* strain
**an|spielen** *itr. V.* auf jmdn./etw. ∼: allude to sb./sth.
**Anspielung** *die;* ∼, ∼en allusion (auf + *Akk.* to); (verächtlich, böse) insinuation (auf + *Akk.* about)
**Ansporn** *der;* ∼[e]s, ∼e incentive
**an|spornen** *tr. V.* spur on
**An·sprache** *die* speech; address
**an|sprechen** ⒈ *unr. tr. V.* **(a)** speak to
**(b)** (gefallen) appeal to
⒉ *unr. itr. V.* (reagieren) respond (auf + *Akk.* to)
**ansprechend** ⒈ *Adj.* attractive; attractive, appealing ⟨*personality*⟩
⒉ *adv.* attractively
**Ansprech·partner** *der*, **Ansprech·partnerin** *die* contact
**an|springen** ⒈ *unr. itr. V.; mit sein* ⟨*car, engine*⟩ start
⒉ *unr. tr. V.* jump up at
**An·spruch** *der* **(a)** claim; (Forderung) demand; [keine] Ansprüche stellen make [no] demands; in ∼ nehmen take advantage of ⟨*offer*⟩; exercise ⟨*right*⟩; take up ⟨*time*⟩; [einen] ∼/keinen ∼ auf etw. (*Akk.*) haben be/not be entitled to sth.
**(b)** (Anrecht) right
**an·spruchs-** ∼los ⒈ *Adj.* **(a)** (genügsam) undemanding; **(b)** (schlicht) unpretentious; ⒉ *adv.* **(a)** (genügsam) undemandingly; ⟨*live*⟩ modestly; **(b)** (schlicht) unpretentiously; ∼voll *Adj.* discriminating ⟨*reader, audience, gourmet*⟩; (schwierig) demanding; ambitious ⟨*subject*⟩
**an|spucken** *tr. V.* spit at
**Anstalt** *die;* ∼, ∼en institution
**An·stand** *der* decency
**anständig** ⒈ *Adj.* decent; (ehrbar) respectable
⒉ *adv.* decently; (ordentlich) properly
**an|starren** *tr. V.* stare at
**an·statt** *Konj.* ∼ zu arbeiten/∼, dass er arbeitet instead of working
**an|stecken** ⒈ *tr. V.* **(a)** pin on ⟨*badge, brooch*⟩; put on ⟨*ring*⟩
**(b)** (infizieren, auch fig.) infect
⒉ *itr. V.* be infectious
**ansteckend** *Adj.* infectious; (durch Berührung) contagious
**Ansteckung** *die;* ∼, ∼en infection; (durch Berührung) contagion

**Ansteckungs·gefahr** *die* risk *or* danger of infection
**an|stehen** *unr. itr. V.* (Schlange stehen) queue [up], (Amer.) stand in line (nach for)
**an·stelle** ⒈ *Präp. mit Gen.* instead of
⒉ *Adv.* ∼ von instead of
**an|stellen** ⒈ *refl. V.* queue [up], (Amer.) stand in line (nach for)
⒉ *tr. V.* **(a)** (aufdrehen) turn on
**(b)** (einschalten) switch on
**(c)** (einstellen) employ
**An·stellung** *die* **(a)** employment
**(b)** (Stellung) job
**Anstieg** *der;* ∼[e]s rise, increase (+ *Gen.* in)
**an|stiften** *tr. V.* incite
**An·stifter** *der*, **An·stifterin** *die* instigator
**An·stiftung** *die* incitement
**an|stimmen** *tr. V.* start singing ⟨*song*⟩; start playing ⟨*piece of music*⟩; ein Geschrei ∼: start shouting
**An·stoß** *der* **(a)** stimulus (zu for); den [ersten] ∼ zu etw. geben initiate sth.
**(b)** ∼ erregen cause offence (bei to); [keinen] ∼ an etw. (*Dat.*) nehmen [not] object to sth.
**an|stoßen** ⒈ *unr. itr. V.* **(a)** *mit sein* an etw. (*Akk.*) ∼: bump into sth.
**(b)** [mit den Gläsern] ∼: clink glasses; auf jmdn./etw. ∼: drink to sb./sth.
⒉ *unr. tr. V.* jmdn./etw. ∼: give sb./sth. a push; jmdn. aus Versehen ∼: knock into sb. inadvertently
**anstößig** ⒈ *Adj.* offensive
⒉ *adv.* offensively
**an|strahlen** *tr. V.* **(a)** illuminate; (mit Scheinwerfer) floodlight
**(b)** (anblicken) beam at
**an|streben** *tr. V.* (geh.) aspire to; (mit großer Anstrengung) strive for
**an|streichen** *unr. tr. V.* **(a)** paint
**(b)** (markieren) mark
**an|strengen** ⒈ *refl. V.* make an effort; sich mehr/sehr ∼: make more of an effort/a great effort
⒉ *tr. V.* strain ⟨*eyes, ears, voice*⟩; be a strain on ⟨*person*⟩; seine Fantasie ∼: exercise one's imagination
**anstrengend** *Adj.* (körperlich) strenuous; (geistig) demanding
**Anstrengung** *die;* ∼, ∼en **(a)** effort; große ∼en machen, etw. zu tun make every effort to do sth.
**(b)** (Strapaze) strain
**An·strich** *der* paint
**An·sturm** *der* rush (auf + *Akk.* to); (auf Banken, Waren) run (auf + *Akk.* on)
**Antarktika** (*das*); ∼s Antarctica
**Antarktis** *die;* ∼: Antarctic
**antarktisch** *Adj.* Antarctic
**An·teil** *der* share (an + *Dat.* of); ∼ an etw. (*Dat.*) nehmen take an interest in sth.

**a**

**An·teilnahme** *die;* ~ (a) interest (an +
*Dat.* in)
(b) (Mitgefühl) sympathy (an + *Dat.* with)
**Antenne** *die;* ~, ~n aerial; antenna (Amer.)
**anthrazit** *Adj.* anthracite[-grey]
**anthrazit-grau** *Adj.* anthracite-grey
**anti-, Anti-** anti-
**Anti-alkoholiker** *der,*
**Anti-alkoholikerin** *die* teetotaller
**Antibiotikum** *das;* ~s, **Antibiotika** (Med.)
antibiotic
**anti-, Anti-:** ~**blockier-system** *das*
(Kfz-W.) anti-lock braking system;
~**faschist** *der,* ~**faschistin** *die* anti-fascist;
~**faschistisch** *Adj.* anti-fascist
**antik** *Adj.* (a) classical
(b) (aus vergangenen Zeiten) antique *⟨furniture,
fittings, etc.⟩*
**Antike** *die;* ~: classical antiquity *no art.*
**Antilope** *die;* ~, ~n antelope
**Antipathie** *die;* ~, ~n antipathy
**Antiquariat** antiquarian bookshop/
department; (mit neueren gebrauchten Büchern)
second-hand bookshop/department
**Antiquität** *die;* ~, ~en antique
**Antlitz** *das;* ~es, ~e (dichter., geh.)
countenance (literary); face
**Antrag** *der;* ~[e]s, **Anträge** (a) application
(**auf** + *Akk.* for); **einen** ~ **stellen** make an
application
(b) (Formular) application form
**Antrags·formular** *das* application form
**an|treffen** *unr. tr. V.* find; (zufällig) come
across
**an|treiben** *unr. tr. V.* (a) drive *⟨animals,
column of prisoners⟩* on or along; (fig.) urge
(b) (in Bewegung setzen) drive; power *⟨ship,
aircraft⟩*
**an|treten** ① *unr. itr. V.; mit sein* (a) form
up; (in Linie) line up; (Milit.) fall in
(b) (sich stellen) meet one's opponent; (als
Mannschaft) line up; **gegen jmdn.** ~: meet sb./
line up against sb.
② *unr. tr. V.* start *⟨job, apprenticeship⟩*; take
up *⟨position, appointment⟩*; set out on
*⟨journey⟩*; begin *⟨prison sentence⟩*; come into
*⟨inheritance⟩*
**An·trieb** *der* drive
**An·tritt** *der:* **vor** ~ **Ihres Urlaubs** before you
go on holiday (Brit.) *or* (Amer.) vacation; **vor** ~
**der Reise** before setting out on the journey
**an|tun** *unr. tr. V.* (a) **jmdm. ein Leid** ~: hurt
sb.; **jmdm. etwas Böses/ein Unrecht** ~: do sb.
harm/an injustice
(b) **jmd./etw. hat es jmdm. angetan** sb. was
taken with sb./sth.; *s. auch* ANGETAN
**Antwort** *die;* ~, ~en (a) answer; reply; **er
gab mir keine** ~: he didn't answer [me] *or*
reply
(b) (Reaktion) response

**antworten** *itr. V.* (a) answer; reply; **auf
etw.** (*Akk.*) ~: answer sth.; reply to sth.;
**jmdm.** ~: answer sb.; reply to sb.
(b) (reagieren) respond (**auf** + *Akk.* to)
**an|vertrauen** ① *tr. V.* **jmdm. etw.** ~:
entrust sb. with sth.; (fig.: mitteilen) confide
sth. to sb.
② *refl. V.* **sich jmdm./einer Sache** ~: put
one's trust in sb./sth.; **sich jmdm.** ~ (fig.: sich
jmdm. mitteilen) confide in sb.
**an|wachsen** *unr. itr. V.; mit sein* (a) grow
on
(b) (Wurzeln schlagen) take root
(c) (zunehmen) grow
**Anwalt** *der;* ~[e]s, **Anwälte, Anwältin**
*die;* ~, ~nen (a) (Rechtsanwalt, -anwältin)
lawyer; solicitor (Brit.); attorney (Amer.); (vor
Gericht) barrister (Brit.); attorney[-at-law]
(Amer.); advocate (Scot.)
(b) (Fürsprecher) advocate
**An·wärter** *der,* **An·wärterin** *die*
candidate (**auf** + *Akk.* for); (Sport) contender
(**auf** + *Akk.* for)
**an|weisen** *unr. tr. V.* instruct
**An·weisung** *die* instruction
**an|wenden** *unr.* (auch regelm.) *tr. V.* use,
employ *⟨process, trick, method, violence,
force⟩*; use *⟨medicine, money, time⟩*; apply
*⟨rule, paragraph, proverb, etc.⟩* (**auf** + *Akk.*
to)
**Anwender** *der;* ~s, ~ (DV) user
**anwender·freundlich** *Adj.* (bes. DV)
user-friendly
**Anwenderin** *die;* ~, ~nen (DV) user
**An·wendung** *die* (a) ▶ ANWENDEN: use;
employment; application
(b) (DV) application
**An·wesen** *das* property
**anwesend** *Adj.* present (**bei** at); **die
Anwesenden** those present
**Anwesenheit** *die;* ~: presence
**an|widern** *tr. V.* nauseate
**Anwohner** *der;* ~s, ~, **Anwohnerin**
*die;* ~, ~nen resident; **Parken nur für** ~
residents-only parking
**An·zahl** *die;* ~: number; **eine ganze** ~: a
whole lot
**an|zahlen** *tr. V.* put down *⟨sum⟩* as a
deposit (**auf** + *Akk.* on); (bei Ratenzahlung)
make a down payment of *⟨sum⟩* (**auf** + *Akk.*
on)
**An·zahlung** *die* deposit; (bei Ratenzahlung)
down payment
**An·zeichen** *das* sign; indication
**Anzeige** *die;* ~, ~n (a) (Straf~) report
(b) (Inserat) advertisement
(c) (eines Instruments) display
**an|zeigen** *tr. V.* (a) (Strafanzeige erstatten)
**jmdn./etw.** ~: report sb./sth. to the police/the
authorities
(b) (zeigen) show; indicate; show *⟨time, date⟩*
(c) (DV) display

---

*old spelling - see note on page xiv

**a**

**Anzeigen-:** ~**blatt** *das* advertiser; ~**teil** *der* advertisement section *or* pages *pl.*

**an|ziehen** *unr. tr. V.* **(a)** (auch fig.) attract **(b)** draw up ⟨*knees, feet, etc.*⟩ **(c)** tighten ⟨*rope, wire, screw, knot, belt, etc.*⟩; put on ⟨*handbrake*⟩ **(d)** (ankleiden) dress; **sich** ~: get dressed **(e)** (anlegen) put on ⟨*clothes*⟩

**anziehend** *Adj.* attractive

**An·ziehung** *die* attraction

**Anziehungs·kraft** *die* attractive force; (fig.) attraction

**An·zug** *der* **(a)** suit **(b)** **im** ~ **sein** ⟨*storm*⟩ be approaching; ⟨*fever, illness*⟩ be coming on; ⟨*enemy*⟩ be advancing

**anzüglich** [1] *Adj.* insinuating ⟨*remark, question*⟩ [2] *adv.* in an insinuating way

**Anzüglichkeit** *die;* ~, ~**en (a)** (Art) insinuating nature **(b)** (Bemerkung) insinuating remark

**an|zünden** *tr. V.* light; set fire to ⟨*building etc.*⟩

**an|zweifeln** *tr. V.* doubt; question

**apart** [1] *Adj.* individual *attrib.;* [2] *adv.* in an individual style

**Apartheid** *die;* ~: apartheid *no art.*

**Apartheit** *die;* ~: individuality

**Apartment** *das;* ~s, ~s studio flat (Brit.); studio apartment (Amer.)

**Apartment·haus** *das* block of studio flats (Brit.) *or* (Amer.) studio apartments

**Apathie** *die;* ~, ~n apathy

**apathisch** [1] *Adj.* apathetic [2] *adv.* apathetically

**Aperitif** /aperi'ti:f/ *der;* ~s, ~s aperitif

**Apfel** *der;* ~s, Äpfel apple

**Apfel-:** ~**baum** *der* apple tree; ~**kuchen** *der* apple cake; (mit Äpfeln belegt) apple flan; ~**mus** *das* apple purée; ~**saft** *der* apple juice

**Apfelsine** *die;* ~, ~n orange

**Apfel-:** ~**strudel** *der* apfelstrudel; ~**wein** *der* cider

**Apostel** *der;* ~s, ~: apostle

**Apotheke** *die;* ~, ~n **(a)** chemist's [shop] (Brit.); drugstore (Amer.) **(b)** (Hausapotheke) medicine cabinet; (Reise-, Bordapotheke) first-aid kit

**Apotheker** *der;* ~s, ~, **Apothekerin** *die;* ~, ~**nen** [dispensing] chemist (Brit.); druggist

**App.** *Abk.* = **Apparat** ext.

**Apparat** *der;* ~[e]s, ~e **(a)** apparatus *no pl.;* (Haushaltsgerät) appliance; (kleiner) gadget **(b)** (Radio) radio; (Fernseher) television; (Kamera) camera **(c)** (Telefon) telephone; (Nebenstelle) extension; **am** ~! speaking! **(d)** (Personen und Hilfsmittel) organization; (Verwaltungsapparat) system

**Apparate-medizin** *die* (oft abwertend) high-technology medicine

**Appartement** /aparta'mã:, (schweiz. auch:) -'mɛnt/ *das;* ~s, ~s (schweiz. auch: ~e) **(a)** ▶ APARTMENT. **(b)** (Hotelsuite) suite

**Appell** *der;* ~s, ~e **(a)** appeal (**zu** for, **an** + *Akk.* to) **(b)** (Milit.) muster; (Anwesenheits~) roll-call

**appellieren** *itr. V.* appeal (**an** + *Akk.* to)

**Appetit** *der;* ~[e]s, ~e appetite (**auf** + *Akk.* for); **guten** ~! enjoy your meal!

**appetitlich** *Adj.* **(a)** appetizing **(b)** (sauber, ansprechend) attractive and hygienic

**Appetit·losigkeit** *die;* ~: lack of appetite

**applaudieren** *itr. V.* applaud

**Applaus** *der;* ~es, ~e applause

**Aprikose** *die;* ~, ~n apricot

**April** *der;* ~[s], ~e April; **der** ~: April

**apropos** /apro'po:/ *Adv.* apropos; by the way; incidentally

**Aquädukt** *der od. das;* ~[e]s, ~e aqueduct

**Aquarell** *das;* ~s, ~e watercolour [painting]

**Aquarium** *das;* ~s, **Aquarien** aquarium

**Äquator** *der;* ~s equator

**Ar** *das od. der;* ~s, ~e are

**Ära** *die;* ~, Ären era

**Araber** *der;* ~s, ~, **Araberin** *die;* ~, ~**nen** Arab

**Arabien** /a'ra:bjən/ *(das);* ~s Arabia

**arabisch** *Adj.* Arabian; Arabic ⟨*language, numeral, literature, etc.*⟩

**Arbeit** *die;* ~, ~**en (a)** work *no indef. art.;* **vor/nach der** ~ (ugs.) before/after work **(b)** (Produkt, Werk) work **(c)** (Aufgabe) job **(d)** (Klassenarbeit) test

**arbeiten** [1] *itr. V.* work [2] *tr. V.* (herstellen) make

**Arbeiter** *der;* ~s, ~, **Arbeiterin** *die;* ~, ~**nen** worker; (Bau-, Land~) labourer

**Arbeiter-:** ~**kind** *das* working-class child; ~**klasse** *die* working class[es *pl.*]

**Arbeiterschaft** *die;* ~: workers *pl.*

**Arbeit·geber** *der;* ~s, ~: employer

**Arbeitgeber·anteil** *der* employer's contribution

**Arbeit·geberin** *die;* ~, ~**nen** employer

**Arbeitgeber·verband** *der* employers' association *or* organization

**Arbeitnehmer** *der;* ~s, ~ employee

**Arbeitnehmer·anteil** *der* employee's contribution

**Arbeitnehmerin** *die;* ~, ~**nen** employee

**arbeits-, Arbeits-:** ~**amt** *das* job centre (Brit.); ~**anfang** *der* starting time [at work]; ~**bedingungen** *Pl.* working conditions; ~**beginn** *der* ▶ ~ANFANG; ~**belastung** *die* workload; ····⟩

**a**

~**beschaffungs·maßnahme** die job-creation measure; ~**erlaubnis** die work permit; ~**fähig** Adj. fit for work postpos.; (grundsätzlich) able to work postpos.; ~**gang** der operation; ~**genehmigung** die work permit; ~**gericht** das industrial tribunal; ~**kollege** der, ~**kollegin** die (bei Arbeitern) workmate (Brit.); fellow worker; (bei Angestellten, Beamten) colleague; ~**kraft** die (a) capacity for work; (b) (Mensch) worker; ~**last** die burden of work; ~**leben** das (a) (Berufstätigkeit) working life; (b) (Arbeitswelt) world of work; working life no art.; ~**los** Adj. unemployed; sich ~los melden sign on [for the dole] (coll.;) ~**lose** der/die; adj. Dekl. unemployed person/man/woman etc.; die ~losen the unemployed; ~**losengeld** das (full-rate) earnings-related unemployment benefit; ~**losenhilfe** die (a) (Geld) reduced-rate unemployment benefit; (b) (Institution) reduced-rate unemployment benefit system; ~**losigkeit** die; ~~: unemployment no indef. art.; ~**mangel** der lack of work; ~**markt** der labour market; ~**platz** der (a) (Platz im Betrieb) workplace; am ~platz at one's workplace; (b) (~stätte) place of work; den ~platz wechseln change one's place of work; (c) (~verhältnis) job; ~**scheu** Adj. work-shy; ~**suchende** der/die; adj. Dekl. person/man/woman looking for work; die ~suchenden those looking for work: ~**tag** der working day; ~**teilung** die division of labour; ~**unfähig** Adj. unfit for work postpos.; (grundsätzlich) unable to work postpos.; ~**unfähigkeit** die ▸ ~UNFÄHIG: inability to work; unfitness for work; ~**unfall** der industrial accident; er hatte einen ~unfall he had an accident at work; ~**vermittlung** die (a) (Tätigkeit) arranging employment; (b) (Stelle) employment exchange; job centre (Brit.); (Firma) employment agency; ~**vertrag** der contract of employment; ~**zeit** die working hours pl.; die tägliche ~zeit the working day; ~**zeit·konto** das flexitime work record; ~**zimmer** das study

**Archäologe** der; ~n, ~n archaeologist

**Archäologie** die; ~: archaeology no art.

**Archäologin** die; ~, ~nen archaeologist

**archäologisch** Adj. archaeological

**Arche** die; ~, ~n ark; die ~ Noah Noah's Ark

**Architekt** der; ~en, ~en, **Architektin** die; ~, ~nen architect

**Architektur** die; ~ architecture

**Archiv** das; ~s, ~e archives pl.; archive

**Ären** ▸ ÄRA

**Arena** die; ~, Arenen arena; (Stierkampf~, Manege) ring

**arg, ärger, ärgst...** (geh., landsch.) ① Adj. (a) (schlimm) bad; im Argen liegen be in a sorry state (b) (unangenehm groß, stark) severe ⟨pain, hunger, shock, disappointment⟩; serious ⟨error, dilemma⟩; extreme ⟨embarrassment⟩; gross ⟨exaggeration, injustice⟩ ② adv. (äußerst, sehr) extremely

**Ärger** der; ~s (a) annoyance (b) (Unannehmlichkeiten) trouble; ~ bekommen get into trouble

**ärgerlich** ① Adj. (a) annoyed (b) (Ärger erregend) annoying ② adv. (a) with annoyance (b) (Ärger erregend) annoyingly

**ärgern** ① tr. V. (a) annoy (b) (reizen) tease ② refl. V. sich [über jmdn./etw.] ~: be/get annoyed [at sb./about sth.]

**Ärgernis** das; ~ses, ~se annoyance; (etw. Anstößiges) nuisance

**arg-, Arg-:** ~**list** die deceit; (Heimtücke) malice; ~**listig** Adj. deceitful; (heimtückisch) malicious; ~**los** ① Adj. unsuspecting; ② adv. unsuspectingly; ~**losigkeit** die; ~~: unsuspecting nature

**ärgst...** ▸ ARG

**Argument** das; ~[e]s, ~e argument

**Argumentation** die; ~, ~en argumentation

**argumentieren** itr. V. argue

**Argwohn** der; ~[e]s suspicion

**argwöhnisch** (geh.) ① Adj. suspicious ② adv. suspiciously

**Arie** /'aːriə/ die; ~, ~n aria

**arisch** (Völkerk., Sprachw., ns.) Aryan

**Aristokrat** der; ~en, ~en aristocrat

**Aristokratie** die; ~, ~n aristocracy

**Aristokratin** die; ~, ~nen aristocrat

**aristokratisch** ① Adj. aristocratic ② adv. aristocratically

**arithmetisch** ① Adj. arithmetical ② adv. arithmetically

**Arkade** die; ~, ~n arcade

**Arktis** die; ~: Arctic

**arktisch** Adj. Arctic; (fig.) arctic

**arm, ärmer, ärmst...** Adj. poor; Arm und Reich (veralt.) rich and poor [alike]; ~ an Nährstoffen poor in nutrients; der/die Ärmste od. Arme the poor man/boy/woman/girl

**Arm** der; ~[e]s, ~e arm; jmdm. [mit etw.] unter die ~e greifen help sb. out [with sth.]; ein Hemd mit halbem ~: a short-sleeved shirt

**Armaturen·brett** das instrument panel; (im Kfz) dashboard

**Arm-:** ~**band** das bracelet; (Uhr~) strap; ~**band·uhr** die wristwatch

**Armee** die; ~, ~n (auch fig.) army

**Ärmel** der; ~s, ~: sleeve; [sich (Dat.)] etw. aus dem ~ schütteln (ugs.) produce sth. just like that

**Ärmel·kanal** der; ~s [English] Channel

**ärmer** ▶ ARM

**ärmlich** [1] *Adj.* cheap ⟨*clothing*⟩; shabby ⟨*flat, office*⟩; meagre ⟨*meal*⟩
[2] *adv.* cheaply ⟨*furnished, dressed*⟩

**Arm·reif** *der* armlet

**arm·selig** *Adj.* **(a)** miserable; pathetic ⟨*result, figure*⟩; meagre ⟨*meal, food*⟩; paltry ⟨*return, salary, sum, fee*⟩
**(b)** (abwertend: erbärmlich) miserable

**ärmst...** ▶ ARM

**Armut** *die;* ∼: poverty

**Aroma** *das;* ∼s, Aromen (Duft) aroma; (Geschmack) flavour

**aromatisch** *Adj.* aromatic; distinctive ⟨*taste*⟩; ∼ **duften** give off an aromatic fragrance

**arrangieren** /arãˈziːrən/ [1] *tr. V.* (geh., Musik) arrange
[2] *refl. V.* sich ∼: adapt; sich mit jmdm. ∼: come to an accommodation with sb.

**Arrest** *der;* ∼[e]s, ∼e detention

**arrogant** [1] *Adj.* arrogant
[2] *adv.* arrogantly

**Arroganz** *die;* ∼ arrogance

**Arsch** *der;* ∼[e]s, Ärsche (derb) **(a)** arse (Brit. coarse); ass (Amer. sl.); **leck mich am** ∼**!** (fig.) piss off (sl.); **im** ∼ **sein** (fig.) be buggered (coarse)
**(b)** (widerlicher Mensch) arsehole (Brit. coarse); asshole (Amer. coarse.)

**Arsch·loch** *das* (derb) ▶ ARSCH B

**Art** *die;* ∼, ∼en **(a)** kind; sort; **Bücher aller** ∼: all kinds *or* sorts of books; **[so] eine** ∼ ...: a sort of ...; **aus der** ∼ **schlagen** not be true to type; (in einer Familie) be different from all the rest of the family
**(b)** (Biol.) species
**(c)** (Wesen) nature; (Verhaltensweise) way; (gutes Benehmen) behaviour; **die feine englische** ∼ (ugs.) the proper way to behave
**(d)** (Weise) way; **auf diese** ∼: in this way; ∼ **und Weise** way; (Kochk.) **nach** ∼ **des Hauses** à la maison; **nach Schweizer** ∼: Swiss style

**arten-, Arten-:** ∼**reich** *Adj.* (Biol.) species-rich; ∼**reichtum** *der* (Biol.) species-richness; ∼**schutz** *der* protection of species; species protection

**Arterie** /arˈteːriə/ *die;* ∼, ∼n artery

**artig** *Adj.* well-behaved; **sei** ∼: be a good boy/girl/dog *etc.*

**Artikel** *der;* ∼s, ∼ **(a)** article
**(b)** (Ware) item

**Artillerie** *die;* ∼, ∼n artillery

**Artischocke** *die;* ∼, ∼n artichoke

**Artist** *der;* ∼en, ∼en, **Artistin** *die;* ∼, ∼nen [variety/circus] performer

**Arznei** *die;* ∼, ∼en (veralt.), **Arznei·mittel** *das* medicine

**Arzt** *der;* ∼es, Ärzte, **Ärztin** *die;* ∼, ∼nen doctor

**Arzthelferin** *die* doctor's receptionist

**ärztlich** [1] *Adj.* medical; **auf** ∼**e Verordnung** on doctor's orders
[2] *adv.* **sich** ∼ **behandeln lassen** have medical treatment

**\*As** ▶ ASS

**Asbest** *der;* ∼[e]s, ∼e asbestos

**Asche** *die;* ∼, ∼n ash[es *pl.*]; (sterbliche Reste) ashes *pl.*

**Aschen-:** ∼**becher** *der* ashtray; ∼**brödel** *das;* ∼∼s, ∼∼ (auch fig.) Cinderella

**Ascher·mittwoch** *der* Ash Wednesday

**Äser** ▶ AAS

**Asiat** *der;* ∼en, ∼en, **Asiatin** *die;* ∼, ∼nen Asian

**asiatisch** *Adj.* Asian

**Asien** /ˈaːzjən/ (*das*); ∼s Asia

**Askese** *die;* ∼: asceticism

**Asket** *der;* ∼en, ∼en, **Asketin** *die;* ∼, ∼nen ascetic

**asketisch** [1] *Adj.* ascetic
[2] *adv.* ascetically

**asozial** [1] *Adj.* asocial; (gegen die Gesellschaft gerichtet) antisocial
[2] *adv.* asocially

**Aspekt** *der;* ∼[e]s, ∼e aspect

**Asphalt** *der;* ∼[e]s, ∼e asphalt

**Aspik** *der* (österr. auch das); ∼s, ∼e aspic

**aß** *1. u. 3. Pers. Sg. Prät. v.* ESSEN

**Ass** *das;* ∼es, ∼e ace

**Assistent** *der;* ∼en, ∼en, **Assistentin** *die;* ∼, ∼nen assistant

**Ast** *der;* ∼[e]s, Äste branch; **sich** (*Dat.*) **einen** ∼ **lachen** (ugs.) split one's sides [with laughter]

**Aster** *die;* ∼, ∼n aster; (Herbstaster) Michaelmas daisy

**ästhetisch** [1] *Adj.* aesthetic
[2] *adv.* aesthetically

**Asthma** *das;* ∼s asthma

**ast·rein** [1] *Adj.* (ugs.) (in Ordnung) on the level (coll.); (echt) genuine; (salopp: prima, toll) fantastic (coll.); great (coll.)
[2] *adv.* (salopp: prima) fantastically (coll.)

**Astrologe** *der;* ∼n, ∼n astrologer

**Astrologie** *die;* ∼: astrology *no art.*

**Astrologin** *die;* ∼, ∼nen astrologer

**Astronaut** *der;* ∼en, ∼en, **Astronautin** *die;* ∼, ∼nen astronaut

**Astronom** *der;* ∼en, ∼en astronomer

**Astronomie** *die;* ∼: astronomy *no art.*

**Astronomin** *die;* ∼, ∼nen astronomer

**astronomisch** *Adj.* astronomical

**Asyl** *das;* ∼s, ∼e **(a)** asylum
**(b)** (Obdachlosenheim) hostel

**Asylant** *der;* ∼en, ∼en, **Asylantin** *die;* ∼, ∼nen asylum seeker

**Asylanten·heim** *das* asylum seekers' hostel

**Asyl-:** ∼**antrag** *der* application for asylum; ∼**bewerber** *der,* **bewerberin** ⋯⋯>

**a**

*die* person seeking [political] asylum;
**~bewerber·heim** *das* ▶ ASYLANTENHEIM;
**~gesetz** *das* asylum law[s *pl.*];
**~missbrauch,** *\*~mißbrauch* **der*
misuse of asylum; **~recht** *das* (Rechtsw.) **(a)**
right of [political] asylum; **(b)** (eines Staates)
right to grant [political] asylum; **~werber**
*der;* ~~s, ~~, **~werberin** *die;* ~~,
~~nen (österr.) ▶ ▶BEWERBER

**Atelier** /atə'lie:/ *das;* ~s, ~s studio

**Atem** *der;* ~s breath; außer ~ sein/geraten
be/get out of breath

**atem-, Atem-:** **~beraubend** [1] *Adj.*
breathtaking; [2] *adv.* breathtakingly; **~los**
[1] *Adj.* breathless; [2] *adv.* breathlessly;
**~pause** *die* breathing space; **~zug** *der*
breath

**Atheismus** *der;* ~: atheism *no art.*

**Atheist** *der;* ~en, ~en, **Atheistin** *die;* ~,
~nen atheist

**atheistisch** [1] *Adj.* atheistic
[2] *adv.* atheistically

**Athen** *(das);* ~s Athens

**Äther** *der;* ~s, ~: ether

**Äthiopien** /ɛ'tio:piən/ *(das);* ~s Ethiopia

**Athlet** *der;* ~en, ~en **(a)** (Sportler) athlete
**(b)** (ugs.: kräftiger Mann) muscleman

**Athletin** *die;* ~, ~nen athlete

**athletisch** *Adj.* athletic

**Atlanten** ▶ ATLAS[1]

**Atlantik** *der;* ~s Atlantic

**atlantisch** *Adj.* Atlantic; **der Atlantische
Ozean** the Atlantic Ocean

**Atlas** *der;* ~ *od.* ~ses, Atlanten *od.* ~se
atlas

**atmen** *itr., tr. V.* breathe

**Atmosphäre** /atmo'sfɛ:rə/ *die;* ~, ~n (auch
fig.) atmosphere

**Atmung** *die;* ~: breathing

**Atom** *das;* ~s, ~e atom

**atomar** *Adj.* atomic; (Atomwaffen betreffend)
nuclear

**atom-, Atom-:** **~ausstieg** *der*
abandonment of nuclear power; **~bombe**
*die* atom bomb; **~energie** *die* nuclear
energy *no indef. art.;* **~kern** *der* atomic
nucleus; **~kraft** *die* nuclear power *no indef.
art.;* **~kraftwerk** *das* nuclear power
station; **~krieg** *der* nuclear war; **~müll**
*der* nuclear waste; **~physik** *die* nuclear
physics *sing., no art.;* **~pilz** *der* mushroom
cloud; **~reaktor** *der* nuclear reactor;
**~strom** *der* (ugs.) electricity generated by
nuclear power; **~waffe** *die* nuclear
weapon; **~waffen·frei** *Adj.* nuclear-free;
**~waffen·test** *der* nuclear [weapons] test;
**~zeit·alter** *das* nuclear age

**Attacke** *die;* ~, ~n (auch Med.) attack (auf +
*Akk.* on)

---
*\*old spelling - see note on page xiv*

**Attentat** *das;* ~[e]s, ~e assassination
attempt; (erfolgreich) assassination

**Attentäter** *der;* ~s, ~, **Attentäterin**
*die;* ~, ~nen would-be assassin; (erfolgreich)
assassin

**Attest** *das;* ~[e]s, ~e medical certificate

**Attraktion** *die;* ~, ~en attraction

**attraktiv** [1] *Adj.* attractive
[2] *adv.* attractively

**Attraktivität** *die;* ~: attractiveness

**Attrappe** *die;* ~, ~n dummy

**Attribut** *das;* ~[e]s, ~e attribute

**ätzen** [1] *tr. V.* etch
[2] *itr. V.* corrode

**ätzend** [1] *Adj.* corrosive; (fig.) caustic ⟨wit,
remark, criticism⟩; pungent ⟨smell⟩
[2] *adv.* caustically ⟨ironic, critical⟩

**au** *Interj.* **(a)** (bei Schmerz) ouch
**(b)** (bei Überraschung, Begeisterung) oh

**Aubergine** /obɛr'ʒi:nə/ *die;* ~, ~n
aubergine (Brit.); eggplant

**auch** [1] *Adv.* **(a)** as well; too; also; **Klaus
war ~ dabei** Klaus was there as well *or* too;
Klaus was also there; **Ich gehe jetzt. – Ich ~:**
I'm going now – So am I; **Mir ist warm. – Mir
~:** I feel warm – So do I; **das weiß ich ~**
nicht I don't know either
**(b)** (sogar, selbst) even; **~ wenn, wenn ~:** even
if
[2] *Partikel* **(a)** etwas anderes habe ich ~
nicht erwartet I never expected anything else;
**nun hör aber ~ zu!** now listen!
**(b)** bist du dir ~ im Klaren, was das
bedeutet? are you sure you understand what
that means?; bist du ~ glücklich? are you
truly happy?; lügst du ~ nicht? you're not
lying, are you?
**(c)** wo .../wer .../was ... *usw.* ~: wherever/
whoever/whatever *etc.* ...; wie dem ~ sei
however that may be
**(d)** mag er ~ noch so klug sein no matter
how clever he is

**Audienz** *die;* ~, ~en audience

**Auditorium** *das;* ~s, Auditorien **(a)**
(Hörsaal) auditorium
**(b)** (Zuhörerschaft) audience

**auf** [1] *Präp. mit Dat.* **(a)** on; ~ See at sea;
~ dem Baum in the tree; ~ der Erde on
earth; ~ der Welt in the world; ~ der Straße
in the street
**(b)** at ⟨post office, town, hall, police station⟩;
~ seinem Zimmer (ugs.) in his room; Geld ~
der Bank haben have money in the bank; ~
der Schule/Uni at school/university
**(c)** at ⟨party, wedding⟩; on ⟨course, trip,
walk, holiday, tour⟩
[2] *Präp. mit Akk.* **(a)** on; ~ einen Berg
steigen climb up a mountain; ~ die Straße
gehen go [out] into the street
**(b)** ~ die Schule/Uni gehen go to school/
university; ~ einen Lehrgang gehen go on a
course
**(c)** ~ 10 km [Entfernung] for [a distance of]

10 km; **wir näherten uns der Hütte [bis]** ~
**30 m** we approached to within 30m of the
hut
**(d)** ~ **Jahre [hinaus]** for years [to come];
**etw.** ~ **nächsten Mittwoch verschieben**
postpone sth. until next Wednesday; **die**
**Nacht von Sonntag** ~ **Montag** Sunday night;
**das fällt** ~ **einen Montag** it falls on a
Monday
**(e)** ~ **diese Art und Weise** in this way; ~
**Deutsch** in German; ~ **das Sorgfältigste**
(geh.) most carefully
**(f)** ~ **Wunsch** on request; ~ **meine Bitte** at
my request; ~ **Befehl** on command
**(g) ein Teelöffel** ~ **einen Liter Wasser** one
teaspoon to one litre of water; ~ **die**
**Sekunde/den Millimeter [genau]** [precise] to
the second/millimetre; ~ **deine Gesundheit!**
your health; ~ **bald/morgen!** (bes. südd.) see
you soon/tomorrow
**3** *Adv.* **(a)** (aufgerichtet, aufgestanden) up; ~!
(steh/steht auf!) up you get!
**(b) sie waren längst** ~ **und davon** they had
made off long before
**(c)** ~! (bes. südd.: los) come on; ~ **gehts off**
we go; ~ **ins Schwimmbad!** come on, off to
the swimming pool!
**(d)** ~ **und ab** (hin und her) up and down; to
and fro
**(e) Helm/Hut/Brille** ~! helmet/hat/glasses
on!
**(f)** (ugs.: geöffnet, offen) open; **Fenster/Mund** ~!
open the window/your mouth!

**auf|atmen** *itr. V.* breathe a sigh of relief

**auf|bahren** *tr. V.* lay out; **aufgebahrt sein**
lie in state

**Auf·bau** *der;* ~[e]s, ~ten **(a)** building
**(b)** (Struktur) structure
**(c)** *Pl.* (Schiffbau) superstructure *sing.*

**auf|bauen** *tr. V.* **(a)** erect ⟨hut, kiosk,
podium⟩; set up ⟨equipment, train set⟩; build
⟨house, bridge⟩; set up ⟨tent⟩
**(b)** (hinstellen, arrangieren) lay *or* set out ⟨food,
presents, etc.⟩
**(c)** (fig.: schaffen) build ⟨state, economy, etc.⟩;
build up ⟨business, organization, army, spy
network⟩
**(d)** (fig.: strukturieren) structure

**auf|bäumen** *refl. V.* rear up; **sich gegen**
**jmdn./etw.** ~ (fig.) rise up against sb./sth.

**auf|bessern** *tr. V.* improve; increase
⟨pension, wages, etc.⟩

**auf|bewahren** *tr. V.* keep; **etw. kühl** ~:
store sth. in a cool place

**Auf·bewahrung** *die* keeping

**auf|bieten** *unr. tr. V.* exert ⟨strength,
energy, will power, influence, authority⟩; call
on ⟨skill, wit, powers of persuasion or
eloquence⟩

**auf|blasen** *unr. tr. V.* blow up; inflate

**auf|bleiben** *unr. itr. V.; mit sein* **(a)**
(geöffnet bleiben) stay open
**(b)** (nicht zu Bett gehen) stay up

**auf|blenden** *itr. V.* switch to full beam

**auf|blicken** *itr. V.* **(a)** look up; (kurz)
glance up
**(b) zu jmdm.** ~ (fig.) look up to sb.

**auf|blühen** *itr. V.; mit sein* **(a)** come into
bloom; ⟨bud⟩ open
**(b)** (fig.: aufleben) blossom [out]

**auf|brauchen** *tr. V.* use up

**auf|brechen** **1** *unr. tr. V.* break open
⟨lock, safe, box, crate, etc.⟩; break into ⟨car⟩;
force [open] ⟨door⟩
**2** *unr. itr. V.; mit sein* **(a)** ⟨bud⟩ open; ⟨ice
[sheet], surface, ground⟩ break up; ⟨wound⟩
open
**(b)** (losgehen, -fahren) set off

**auf|bringen** *unr. tr. V.* **(a)** find; raise
⟨money⟩; (fig.) summon [up] ⟨strength, energy,
courage⟩; find ⟨patience⟩
**(b)** (kreieren) start ⟨fashion, custom, rumour⟩;
introduce ⟨slogan, theory⟩
**(c) jmdn.** ~: make sb. angry
**(d) jmdn. gegen jmdn./etw.** ~: set sb.
against sb./sth.

**Auf·bruch** *der* departure

**auf|brühen** *tr. V.* brew [up]

**auf|decken** *tr. V.* **(a)** uncover
**(b)** (Kartenspiele) show
**(c)** (fig.) reveal; uncover; (enthüllen) expose

**auf|drängen** **1** *tr. V.* **jmdm. etw.** ~: force
sth. on sb.
**2** *refl. V.* **sich jmdm.** ~: force oneself on sb.

**auf|drehen** *tr. V.* **(a)** unscrew ⟨bottle cap,
nut⟩; undo ⟨screw⟩; turn on ⟨tap, gas, water⟩;
open ⟨valve, bottle, vice⟩
**(b)** (ugs.) turn up ⟨radio, record player, etc.⟩

**auf·dringlich** **1** *Adj.* pushy (coll.)
⟨person⟩; (fig.) insistent ⟨music,
advertisement⟩; pungent ⟨perfume, smell⟩;
loud ⟨colour, wallpaper⟩
**2** *adv.* ⟨behave⟩ pushily (coll.)

**Aufdringlichkeit** *die;* ~ ▶ AUFDRINGLICH:
pushiness (coll.); insistent manner; pungency

**auf·einander** *Adv.* **(a)** on top of one
another; ~ **prallen** crash into one another;
collide; (fig.) ⟨opinions⟩ clash; ~ **treffen** (fig.)
meet
**(b)** ~ **folgen** follow one another; ~**folgend**
successive

**Aufeinander·folge** *die* sequence; **in**
**rascher** ~ in rapid *or* quick succession

***aufeinander|folgen** *usw.*
▶ AUFEINANDER

**Aufenthalt** *der;* ~[e]s, ~e **(a)** stay
**(b)** (Fahrtunterbrechung) stop

**Aufenthalts-:** ~**erlaubnis** *die*
residence permit; ~**raum** *der* (in einer Schule
o. Ä.) common room (Brit.); (in einer
Jugendherberge) day room; (in einem Betrieb o. Ä.)
recreation room

**auf|essen** *unr. tr. V.* (auch itr.) V. eat up

**auf|fahren** **1** *unr. itr. V.; mit sein* **(a) auf**
**ein anderes Fahrzeug** ~ (aufprallen) drive into
the back of another vehicle ⋯⟶

**a**

**(b) auf den Vordermann zu dicht** ∼: drive too close to the car in front
**(c)** (vorfahren) drive up
**(d)** (in Stellung gehen) move up [into position]
**2** *unr. tr. V.* **(a)** (in Stellung bringen) move up
**(b)** (ugs.: auftischen) serve up

**Auf·fahrt** *die* **(a)** drive up
**(b)** (Weg) drive
**(c)** (Autobahnauffahrt) slip road (Brit.); access road (Amer.)
**(d)** (schweiz.) ▶ HIMMELFAHRT

**Auffahr·unfall** *der* rear-end collision

**auf|fallen** *unr. itr. V.; mit sein* stand out; jmdm. fällt etw. auf sb. notices sth.

**auffallend** **1** *Adj.* conspicuous; (eindrucksvoll, bemerkenswert) striking
**2** *adv.* conspicuously; (eindrucksvoll, bemerkenswert) strikingly

**auf·fällig** **1** *Adj.* conspicuous; garish ⟨colour⟩
**2** *adv.* conspicuously

**auf|fangen** *unr. tr. V.* **(a)** catch
**(b)** (aufnehmen, sammeln) collect

**Auffang·lager** *das* reception camp

**auf|fassen** *tr. V.* grasp; **etw. als etw.** ∼: regard sth. as sth.; **etw. persönlich/falsch** ∼: take sth. personally/misunderstand sth.

**Auf·fassung** *die* (Ansicht) view; (Begriff) conception; **der** ∼ **sein, dass** ...: take the view that ...

**auffindbar** *Adj.* findable

**auf|finden** *unr. tr. V.* find

**auf|fordern** *tr. V.* jmdn. ∼, etw. zu tun call upon sb. to do sth.; (einladen, ermuntern) ask sb. to do sth.; jmdn. [zum Tanz] ∼: ask sb. to dance

**Auf·forderung** *die* request; (nachdrücklicher) demand; (Einladung, Ermunterung) invitation

**auf|forsten** **1** *tr. V.* afforest; (wieder ∼) reforest; **einen Wald** ∼: restock a forest
**2** *itr. V.* establish woods; (wieder ∼) reestablish the woods

**Aufforstung** *die;* ∼, ∼en afforestation; (Wieder∼) reforestation; **die** ∼ **der Wälder** restocking the forests

**auf|fressen** *unr. tr. V.* (auch fig.) eat up

**auf|frischen** **1** *tr. V.* freshen up; brighten up ⟨colour, paintwork⟩; renovate ⟨polish, furniture⟩; (restaurieren) restore ⟨tapestry, fresco, etc.⟩; (fig.) revive ⟨old memories⟩; renew ⟨acquaintance, friendship⟩; **seine Englischkenntnisse** ∼: brush up one's [knowledge of] English
**2** *itr. V.; auch mit sein* ⟨wind⟩ freshen

**auf|führen** **1** *tr. V.* **(a)** put on ⟨film⟩; stage ⟨play, ballet, opera⟩; perform ⟨piece of music⟩
**(b)** (auflisten) list
**2** *refl. V.* behave

**Auf·führung** *die* performance

**Auf·gabe** *die* **(a)** task
**(b)** (fig.: Zweck, Funktion) function

**(c)** (Schulw.) (Übung) exercise; (Prüfungs∼) question; (Haus∼) ▶ HAUSAUFGABE
**(d)** (Rechen∼, Mathematik∼) problem
**(e)** (Kapitulation) retirement; (im Schach) resignation; **jmdn. zur** ∼ **zwingen** force sb. to retire/resign
**(f)** (das Aufgeben a) giving up
**(g)** (einer Postsendung) posting (Brit.); mailing (Amer.); (eines Telegramms) handing in; (einer Bestellung, einer Annonce) placing
**(h)** (von Gepäck) checking in

**Aufgaben-:** ∼**bereich** *der*, ∼**gebiet** *das* area of responsibility

**Auf·gang** *der* **(a)** (eines Gestirns) rising
**(b)** (Treppe) stairs *pl.;* staircase; stairway; (in einem Bahnhof, zu einer Galerie, einer Tribüne) steps *pl.*

**auf|geben** **1** *unr. tr. V.* **(a)** give up; (Sport) retire from ⟨race, competition⟩
**(b)** (übergeben, übermitteln) post (Brit.), mail ⟨letter, parcel⟩; hand in, (telefonisch) phone in ⟨telegram⟩; place ⟨advertisement, order⟩; check ⟨luggage, baggage⟩ in
**(c)** (Schulw.: als Hausaufgabe) set (Brit.); assign (Amer.)
**(d)** jmdm. ein Rätsel ∼: set (Brit.) *or* (Amer.) assign sb. a puzzle
**2** *unr. itr. V.* give up; (im Sport) retire; (im Schach) resign

**Auf·gebot** *das* **(a)** contingent; **ein gewaltiges** ∼ **an Polizisten/Fahrzeugen/ Material** a huge force of police/array of vehicles/materials
**(b)** (zur Heirat) notice of an/the intended marriage; (kirchlich) banns *pl.*

**auf|gehen** *unr. itr. V.; mit sein* **(a)** rise
**(b)** (sich öffnen [lassen]) ⟨door, parachute, wound⟩ open; ⟨stage curtain⟩ go up; ⟨knot, button, zip, bandage, shoelace, stitching⟩ come undone; ⟨boil, pimple, blister⟩ burst; ⟨flower, bud⟩ open [up]
**(c)** (keimen) come up
**(d)** (aufgetrieben werden) ⟨dough, cake⟩ rise
**(e)** (Math.) ⟨calculation⟩ work out; ⟨equation⟩ come out
**(f)** etw. geht jmdm. auf sb. realizes sth.

**auf|geilen** *tr. V.* (salopp) jmdn. [mit/durch etw.] ∼: get sb. randy [with sth.]; sich [an etw. (Dat.)] ∼: get randy [with sth.]; (fig.) get worked up [about sth.]

**aufgeklärt** *Adj.* enlightened; ∼ **sein** (sexualkundlich) know the facts of life

**auf·gelegt** *Adj.* gut/schlecht *usw.* ∼ **sein** be in a good/bad *etc.* mood; **zu etw.** ∼ **sein** be in the mood for sth.

**auf·gelöst** *Adj.* distraught ⟨person⟩

**aufgeregt** **1** *Adj.* excited; (nervös, beunruhigt) agitated
**2** *adv.* excitedly; (nervös, beunruhigt) agitatedly

**auf·geschlossen** *Adj.* open-minded (**gegenüber** as regards, about); (interessiert, empfänglich) receptive (Dat., **für** to); (zugänglich) approachable

---

*alte Schreibung - vgl. Hinweis auf S. xiv

**Auf·geschlossenheit** *die*
▶ AUFGESCHLOSSEN: open-mindedness;
receptiveness; approachableness

**aufgeweckt** *Adj.* bright

**Aufgewecktheit** *die;* ~: brightness

**auf|gießen** *unr. tr. V.* make ⟨*coffee, tea*⟩

**auf|gliedern** *tr. V.* subdivide, break down
(in + *Akk.* into)

**Auf·gliederung** *die* subdivision;
breakdown

**auf|greifen** *unr. tr. V.* pick up

**aufgrund** *Präp. mit Gen.* on the basis *or*
strength of; (wegen) because of

**auf|haben** (ugs.) [1] *unr. tr. V.* **(a)** (aufgesetzt
haben) have on
**(b)** (geöffnet haben) have ⟨*zip*⟩ undone; have
⟨*door, window, jacket, blouse*⟩ open
[2] *unr. itr. V.* ⟨*shop, office*⟩ be open

**auf|halsen** *tr. V.* (ugs.) jmdm./sich etw. ~:
saddle sb./oneself with sth.; sich (*Dat.*) etw.
~ **lassen** get oneself saddled with sth.

**auf|halten** [1] *unr. tr. V.* **(a)** halt
**(b)** (stören) hold up
**(c)** (ugs.: geöffnet halten) hold ⟨*sack, door, etc.*⟩
open; **die Augen [und Ohren]** ~: keep one's
eyes [and ears] open
[2] *unr. refl. V.* **(a)** stay
**(b) sich mit jmdm./etw.** ~: spend [a long]
time on sb./sth

**auf|hängen** [1] *tr. V.* **(a)** hang up; hang
⟨*picture, curtains*⟩
**(b)** (erhängen) hang
[2] *refl. V.* hang oneself

**Aufhänger** *der;* ~s, ~: loop

**auf|heben** *unr. tr. V.* **(a)** pick up
**(b)** (aufbewahren) keep
**(c)** (abschaffen) abolish; repeal ⟨*law*⟩; rescind
⟨*order, instruction*⟩; cancel ⟨*contract*⟩; lift
⟨*ban, prohibition*⟩
**(d)** (ausgleichen) cancel out; neutralize ⟨*effect*⟩

**Aufheben** *das;* ~s: **viel** ~[s]/**kein** ~ **von**
jmdm./etw. machen make a great fuss/not
make any fuss about sb./sth.

**Aufhebungs·vertrag** *der* agreement to
terminate a/the contract

**auf|heitern** [1] *tr. V.* cheer up
[2] *refl. V.* ⟨*weather*⟩ brighten up

**Aufheiterung** *die;* ~, ~en **(a)** (des Wetters)
bright period
**(b)** (Erheiterung) cheering up

**auf|hetzen** *tr. V.* incite

**auf|holen** [1] *tr. V.* make up ⟨*time, delay*⟩;
pull back ⟨*lead*⟩
[2] *itr. V.* catch up; ⟨*athlete, competitor*⟩
make up ground

**auf|horchen** *itr. V.* prick up one's ears

**auf|hören** *itr. V.* stop; [damit] ~, etw. zu
tun stop doing sth.

**auf|kaufen** *tr. V.* buy up

**auf|klappen** *tr. V.* open, fold open ⟨*chair,
table*⟩; open [up] ⟨*suitcase, trunk*⟩; open
⟨*book, knife*⟩

**auf|klären** [1] *tr. V.* **(a)** clear up ⟨*matter,*

mystery, question, misunderstanding, error,
confusion*⟩; solve ⟨*crime, problem*⟩; explain
⟨*event, incident, cause*⟩; resolve
⟨*contradiction, disagreement*⟩
**(b)** (unterrichten) enlighten; **ein Kind** ~
(sexualkundlich) tell a child the facts of life
[2] *refl. V.* **(a)** ⟨*misunderstanding, mystery*⟩
be cleared up
**(b)** ⟨*weather*⟩ brighten [up]; ⟨*sky*⟩ brighten

**Auf·klärung** *die* ▶ AUFKLÄREN 1: **(a)**
clearing up; solution; explanation;
resolution
**(b)** enlightenment; **die** ~ **der Kinder** (über
Sexualität) telling the children the facts of life

**auf|kleben** *tr. V.* stick on; (mit Kleister)
paste on

**Auf·kleber** *der* sticker

**auf|knöpfen** *tr. V.* unbutton; undo

**auf|kochen** [1] *tr. V.* bring to the boil
[2] *itr. V.; mit sein* come to the boil

**auf|kommen** *unr. itr. V.; mit sein* **(a)**
⟨*wind*⟩ spring up; ⟨*storm, gale*⟩ blow up;
⟨*fog*⟩ come down; ⟨*rumour*⟩ start; ⟨*suspicion,
doubt, feeling*⟩ arise; ⟨*fashion, style,
invention*⟩ come in; ⟨*boredom*⟩ set in; ⟨*mood,
atmosphere*⟩ develop
**(b)** ~ **für** (bezahlen) bear ⟨*costs*⟩; pay for
⟨*damage*⟩; pay ⟨*expenses*⟩; be liable for
⟨*debts*⟩; stand ⟨*loss*⟩
**(c)** ~ **für** (Verantwortung tragen für) be
responsible for

**auf|krempeln** *tr. V.* roll up

**auf|laden** [1] *unr. tr. V.* **(a)** load (auf +
*Akk.* on [to])
**(b)** jmdm. etw. ~ (ugs.) load sb. with sth.;
(fig.) saddle sb. with sth.
**(c)** charge [up] ⟨*battery*⟩
[2] *unr. refl. V.* ⟨*battery*⟩ charge

**Auf·lage** *die* **(a)** (Buchw.) edition
**(b)** (Verpflichtung) condition

**auflagen·stark** *Adj.* high-circulation
⟨*newspaper, magazine*⟩

**auf|lassen** *unr. tr. V.* (ugs.) **(a)** leave ⟨*door,
window, jacket, etc.*⟩ open
**(b)** keep on ⟨*hat, glasses, etc.*⟩

**auf|lauern** *itr. V.* jmdm. ~: lie in wait for
sb.

**Auf·lauf** *der* **(a)** (Menschen~) crowd
**(b)** (Speise) soufflé

**auf|leben** *itr. V.; mit sein* revive; (fig.: wieder
munter werden) come to life

**auf|legen** [1] *tr. V.* **(a)** put on; **den Hörer**
~: put down the receiver
**(b)** (Buchw.) publish
[2] *itr. V.* (den Hörer auflegen) hang up

**auf|lehnen** *refl. V.* rebel

**Auflehnung** *die;* ~, ~en rebellion

**auf|leuchten** *itr. V.; auch mit sein* light
up; (für kurze Zeit) flash

**auf|lockern** *tr. V.* **(a)** loosen; break up
⟨*soil*⟩
**(b)** (fig.) introduce some variety into ⋯╬

⟨landscape, lesson, lecture⟩; relieve ⟨pattern, façade⟩; make ⟨mood, atmosphere, evening⟩ more relaxed

**Auf·lockerung** die (a) ▶ AUFLOCKERN A:
loosening; breaking up
(b) zur ~ der Stimmung/des Abends to make the mood/evening more relaxed

**auf|lösen** 1 tr. V. dissolve; resolve ⟨difficulty, contradiction⟩; solve ⟨puzzle, equation⟩; break off ⟨engagement⟩; cancel ⟨arrangement, contract, agreement⟩; dissolve ⟨organization⟩
2 refl. V. dissolve (in + Akk. into); ⟨parliament⟩ dissolve itself; ⟨crowd, demonstration⟩ break up; ⟨fog, mist⟩ lift; (fig.) ⟨empire, social order⟩ disintegrate

**Auf·lösung** die (a) ▶ AUFLÖSEN 1:
dissolving; resolution; solution; breaking off; cancellation; dissolution
(b) ▶ AUFLÖSEN 2: dissolving; breaking up lifting; disintegration

**auf|machen** 1 tr. V. (a) open; undo ⟨button, knot⟩
(b) (ugs.: eröffnen) open [up] ⟨shop, business, etc.⟩
2 itr. V. (a) ⟨shop, office, etc.⟩ open
(b) (ugs.: die Tür öffnen) open the door; jmdm. ~: open the door to sb.
(c) (ugs.: eröffnet werden) ⟨shop, business⟩ open [up]

**Aufmachung** die; ~, ~en presentation; (Kleidung) get-up

**Aufmarsch·gebiet** das (Milit.) deployment area

**auf|marschieren** itr. V.; mit sein
assemble; (heranmarschieren) march up;
Truppen sind an der Grenze aufmarschiert troops were deployed along the border

**aufmerksam** 1 Adj. (a) attentive; sharp ⟨eyes⟩; jmdn. auf jmdn./etw. ~ machen draw sb.'s attention to sb./sth.; auf jmdn./etw. ~ werden become aware of sb./sth.; ~ werden notice
(b) (höflich) attentive
2 adv. attentively

**Aufmerksamkeit** die; ~, ~en (a) attention
(b) (Höflichkeit) attentiveness
(c) (Geschenk) small gift

**auf|motzen** tr. V. (ugs.) tart up (Brit. coll.); doll up (coll.)

**auf|muntern** tr. V. (a) cheer up
(b) (beleben) liven up
(c) (ermutigen) encourage

**Aufmunterung** die; ~ ▶ AUFMUNTERN:
cheering up; livening up; encouragement

**Aufnahme** die; ~, ~n (a) ▶ AUFNEHMEN B:
opening; establishment; taking up
(b) (Empfang) reception
(c) ▶ AUFNEHMEN D: admission (in + Akk. into)
(d) (Einschließung) inclusion

(e) (Finanzw.) raising
(f) (Aufzeichnung) taking down; (von Personalien, eines Diktats) taking [down]
(g) ▶ AUFNEHMEN K: taking: photographing; filming
(h) (Bild) shot
(i) (das Aufnehmen auf Tonträger, das Aufgenommene) recording
(j) (Anklang) reception; response (Gen. to)
(k) (Einverleibung, Absorption) absorption

**aufnahme-, Aufnahme-:** ~antrag der
application for membership; ~fähig Adj.
receptive (für to); ich bin nicht mehr ~fähig I can't take any more in; ~fähigkeit die receptivity (für to); ability to take things in; ~land das host country

**auf|nehmen** unr. tr. V. (a) (aufheben) pick up; (fig.) take up ⟨idea, theme, etc.⟩; es mit jmdm./etw. ~/nicht ~ können (fig.) be a/no match for sb./sth.
(b) (beginnen mit) open ⟨negotiations, talks⟩; establish ⟨relations, contacts⟩; take up ⟨studies, activity, occupation⟩; start ⟨production, investigation⟩
(c) (empfangen) receive; (beherbergen) take in
(d) (beitreten lassen) admit (in + Akk. to)
(e) (einschließen, verzeichnen) include
(f) (erfassen) take in ⟨impressions, information, etc.⟩
(g) (absorbieren) absorb
(h) (Finanzw.) raise ⟨mortgage, money, loan⟩
(i) (reagieren auf) receive
(j) (aufschreiben) take down; take [down] ⟨dictation, particulars⟩
(k) (fotografieren) take ⟨picture⟩; photograph, take a photograph of ⟨scene, subject⟩; (filmen) film
(l) (auf Tonträger) record
(m) (auf Videoband) videotape; video

**auf|opfern** refl. V. devote oneself sacrificingly (für to)

**aufopfernd** 1 Adj. self-sacrificing
2 adv. self-sacrificingly

**auf|passen** itr. V. (a) watch out; (konzentriert sein) pay attention; pass mal auf! (ugs.: hör mal zu!) now listen
(b) auf jmdn./etw. ~: keep an eye on sb./sth.

**auf|platzen** itr. V.; mit sein burst open; ⟨seam, cushion⟩ split open; ⟨wound⟩ open up

**Auf·prall** der; ~[e]s, ~e impact

**auf|prallen** itr. V.; mit sein auf etw. (Akk.) ~: hit sth.

**Auf·preis** der additional charge

**auf|pumpen** tr. V. pump up

**auf|putschen** tr. V. stimulate; arouse ⟨passions, urge⟩

**Aufputsch·mittel** das stimulant

**auf|räumen** tr., itr. V. clear up

**Aufräumungs·arbeiten** Pl. clearance work sing.

**auf·recht** 1 Adj. (auch fig.) upright
2 adv. ⟨walk, sit, hold oneself⟩ straight

**aufrecht|erhalten** unr. tr. V. maintain; keep up ⟨deception, fiction, contact, custom⟩

**auf|regen** ① *tr. V.* excite; (ärgern) annoy; irritate; (beunruhigen) agitate
② *refl. V.* get worked up (**über** + *Akk.* about)

**Auf·regung** *die* excitement *no pl.;* (Beunruhigung) agitation *no pl.;* **jmdn. in** ~ **versetzen** make sb. excited/agitated

**auf|reißen** ① *unr. tr. V.* (a) (öffnen) tear open; wrench open ⟨*drawer*⟩; fling open ⟨*door, window*⟩; **die Augen/den Mund** ~: open one's eyes/mouth wide
(b) (beschädigen) tear open; tear ⟨*clothes*⟩; break up ⟨*road, soil*⟩
② *itr. V.; mit sein* ⟨*clothes*⟩ tear; ⟨*seam*⟩ split; ⟨*wound*⟩ open; ⟨*cloud*⟩ break up

**auf|reizen** *tr. V.* excite

**auf·reizend** ① *Adj.* provocative
② *adv.* provocatively

**auf|richten** ① *tr. V.* erect; put up; **den Oberkörper** ~: raise one's upper body; **jmdn.** [**wieder**] ~ (fig.) give fresh heart to sb.
② *refl. V.* stand up [straight]; **sich an jmdm./ etw.** [**wieder**] ~ (fig.) take heart from sb./sth.

**auf·richtig** ① *Adj.* sincere
② *adv.* sincerely

**Auf·richtigkeit** *die* sincerity

**auf|rücken** *itr. V.; mit sein* move up

**Auf·ruf** *der* (a) call
(b) (Appell) appeal (**an** + *Akk.* to)

**auf|rufen** *unr. tr. V.* (a) call
(b) **jmdn.** ~, **etw. zu tun** call upon sb. to do sth.
(c) (Rechtsw.) appeal for ⟨*witnesses*⟩

**Aufruhr** *der;* ~**s,** ~**e** (a) (Widerstand) rebellion
(b) (Erregung) turmoil

**aufführerisch** *Adj.* inflammatory

**auf|rüsten** *tr., itr. V.* (a) arm; **wieder** ~: rearm
(b) (DV) upgrade

**Auf·rüstung** *die* armament

**aufs** *Präp. + Art.* = **auf das**

**auf|sagen** *tr. V.* recite

**auf|sammeln** *tr. V.* gather up

**aufsässig** ① *Adj.* recalcitrant
② *adv.* recalcitrantly

**Aufsässigkeit** *die;* ~, ~**en** (a) recalcitrance
(b) (Handlung) piece of recalcitrance

**Auf·satz** *der* (Text) essay

**auf|saugen** *unr.* (*auch regelm.*) *tr. V.* soak up; (fig.) absorb

**auf|schieben** *unr. tr. V.* postpone

**Auf·schlag** *der* (a) (Aufprall) impact
(b) (Preis~) surcharge
(c) (Ärmel~) cuff; (Hosen~) turn-up; (Revers) lapel
(d) (Tennis usw.) serve

**auf|schlagen** ① *unr. itr. V.* (a) *mit sein* **auf etw.** (*Dat. od. Akk.*) ~: hit sth.
(b) (teurer werden) ⟨*price, rent, costs*⟩ go up
(c) (Tennis usw.) serve

② *unr. tr. V.* (a) (öffnen) crack ⟨*nut, egg*⟩ [open]; knock a hole in ⟨*ice*⟩; **sich** (*Dat.*) **das Knie/den Kopf** ~: cut one's knee/head
(b) open ⟨*book, newspaper, one's eyes*⟩; **schlagt Seite 15 auf!** turn to page 15
(c) turn up ⟨*collar, sleeve, trouser leg*⟩
(d) (aufbauen) set up ⟨*camp*⟩; pitch ⟨*tent*⟩; put up ⟨*bed, hut, scaffolding*⟩
(e) **5 % auf etw.** (*Akk.*) ~: put 5% on sth.

**auf|schließen** ① *unr. tr. V.* unlock
② *unr. itr. V.* [jmdm.] ~: unlock the door/ gate *etc.* [for sb.]

**Auf·schluss, \*Auf·schluß** *der* information *no pl.*

**auf|schneiden** ① *unr. tr. V.* (a) cut open
(b) (zerteilen) cut
② *unr. itr. V.* (ugs.: prahlen) boast (**mit** about)

**Auf·schneider** *der,* **Auf·schneiderin** *die* (ugs. abwertend) boaster; braggart

**Auf·schnitt** *der* [assorted] cold meats *pl.*/ cheeses *pl.*

**auf|schnüren** *tr. V.* undo

**auf|schrauben** *tr. V.* unscrew; unscrew the top of ⟨*bottle, jar, etc.*⟩

**Auf·schrei** *der* cry; (stärker) yell; (schriller) scream; **ein** ~ **der Empörung** *od.* **Entrüstung** (fig.) an outcry

**auf|schreiben** *unr. tr. V.* write down; [**sich** (*Dat.*)] **etw.** ~: make a note of sth.

**auf|schreien** *unr. itr. V.* cry out; (stärker) yell out; (schrill) scream

**Auf·schrift** *die* inscription

**Auf·schub** *der* postponement; **die Sache duldet keinen** ~: the matter brooks no delay

**Auf·schwung** *der* upturn (*Gen.* in)

**Aufsehen** *das;* ~**s** stir; [**großes**] ~ **erregen** cause a [great] stir

**Auf·seher** *der,* **Auf·seherin** *die;* ~, ~**nen** (im Gefängnis) warder (Brit.); [prison] guard (Amer.); (im Park) park-keeper; (im Museum, auf dem Parkplatz) attendant; (auf einem Gut, Sklavenaufseher) overseer

**\*auf|sein** ▸ AUF 3A, F

**auf|setzen** ① *tr. V.* (a) put on
(b) (verfassen) draw up ⟨*text*⟩
② *refl. V.* sit up

**Auf·sicht** *die* supervision; (bei Prüfungen) invigilation (Brit.); proctoring (Amer.)

**auf|spielen** ① *refl. V.* (ugs. abwertend: angeben) put on airs; **sich vor jmdm.** ~: show off in front of sb.
② *itr. V.* (a) (musizieren) play; **zum Tanz** ~: play dance music
(b) (Sport) **groß/eindrucksvoll** ~: give a fine/ impressive display

**auf|springen** *unr. itr. V.; mit sein* (a) jump up
(b) (hinaufspringen) jump on (**auf** + *Akk.* to)
(c) (rissig werden) crack

**auf|stacheln** *tr. V.* incite

**Auf·stand** *der* rebellion

**auf·ständisch** *Adj.* rebellious

**auf|stehen** *unr. itr. V.; mit sein* stand up; (aus dem Liegen) get up

**auf|steigen** *unr. itr. V.; mit sein* **(a)** (auf ein Fahrzeug) get on; **auf etw.** *(Akk.)* ∼: get on [to] sth.
**(b)** (bergan steigen) climb
**(c)** (hochsteigen) ⟨*sap, smoke, mist*⟩ rise
**(d)** (beruflich, gesellschaftlich) rise **(zu** to); **zum Direktor** ∼: rise to be manager

**auf|stellen** [1] *tr. V.* **(a)** put up **(auf** + *Akk.* on); set up ⟨*skittles*⟩; (postieren) post
**(b)** (aufrecht hinstellen) stand up
**(c)** (Sport) select, pick ⟨*team, player*⟩
**(d)** (bilden) put together ⟨*team of experts*⟩; raise ⟨*army*⟩
**(e)** (nominieren) nominate; put up
[2] *refl. V.* position oneself

**Auf·stellung** *die* **(a)** ▶ AUFSTELLEN 1A: putting up; setting up; posting
**(b)** ▶ AUFSTELLEN B: standing up
**(c)** ▶ AUFSTELLEN C: selection; picking
**(d)** ▶ AUFSTELLEN D: putting together; raising
**(e)** (Nominierung) nomination

**Aufstieg** *der;* ∼[e]s, ∼e **(a)** climb
**(b)** ▶ AUFSTEIGEN D: rise

**auf|stoßen** [1] *unr. tr. V.* push open
[2] *unr. itr. V.* belch; ⟨*baby*⟩ bring up wind

**Auf·strich** *der* spread

**auf|stützen** [1] *tr. V.* rest ⟨*one's arms etc.*⟩
[2] *refl. V.* support oneself; **die Arme auf etw.** *(Akk. od. Dat.)* ∼: rest one's arms on sth.

**auf|suchen** *tr. V.* call on; go to ⟨*doctor*⟩

**Auf·takt** *der* **(a)** (fig.) start
**(b)** (Musik) upbeat

**auf|tauchen** *itr. V.; mit sein* **(a)** surface
**(b)** (sichtbar werden) appear

**auf|tauen** [1] *tr. V.* thaw
[2] *itr. V.; mit sein* (auch fig.) thaw

**auf|teilen** *tr. V.* **(a)** divide [up]
**(b)** (verteilen) share out

**Auftrag** *der;* ∼[e]s, **Aufträge (a)** instructions *pl.;* **in jmds.** ∼ *(Dat.)* on sb.'s instructions; **(für** jmdn.) on behalf of sb
**(b)** (Bestellung) order; (bei Künstlern, Architekten usw.) commission
**(c)** (Mission) task; (Aufgabe) job

**auf|tragen** *unr. tr. V.* **(a)** jmdm. ∼, **etw. zu tun** instruct sb. to do sth.
**(b)** (aufstreichen) put on ⟨*paint, make-up, etc.*⟩

**Auftrag·geber** *der;* ∼s, ∼,
**Auftrag·geberin** *die;* ∼, ∼**nen** client

**Auftrags·buch** *das* (Kaufmannsspr.) order book

**auf|treten** *unr. itr. V.; mit sein* **(a)** tread
**(b)** (sich benehmen) behave
**(c)** (eine Vorstellung geben) appear; **als Zeuge/ Kläger** ∼: appear as a witness/a plaintiff
**(d)** (auftauchen) ⟨*problem, difficulty, difference of opinion*⟩ arise; ⟨*symptom, danger, pest*⟩ appear

**Auftreten** *das;* ∼s (Benehmen) manner

*alte Schreibung - vgl. Hinweis auf S. xiv

**Auf·trieb** *der* **(a)** (Physik) (statischer ∼) buoyancy; (dynamischer ∼) lift
**(b)** (fig.) impetus; **das hat ihm** ∼/**neuen** ∼ **gegeben** that has given him a lift/given him new impetus

**Auf·tritt** *der* **(a)** (Vorstellung) appearance
**(b)** (Theater: das Auftreten) entrance; (Szene) scene

**auf|tun** *unr. refl. V.* (geh.) open; (fig.) open up

**auf|wachen** *itr. V.; mit sein* wake up, awaken **(aus** from); (aus Ohnmacht, Narkose) come round **(aus** from)

**auf|wachsen** *unr. itr. V.; mit sein* grow up

**Auf·wand** *der;* ∼[e]s cost; expense

**aufwändig** ▶ AUFWENDIG

**Aufwands·entschädigung** *die* expense allowance

**auf|wärmen** [1] *tr. V.* heat or warm up ⟨*food*⟩
[2] *refl. V.* warm oneself up

**aufwärts** *Adv.* upwards

**Aufwärts·trend** *der* upward trend

**auf|wecken** *tr. V.* wake [up]; waken

**auf|weichen** [1] *tr. V.* soften
[2] *itr. V.; mit sein* become soft; soften up

**auf|wenden** *unr.* (auch regelm.) *tr. V.* use ⟨*skill, influence*⟩; expend ⟨*energy, resources*⟩; spend ⟨*money, time*⟩; **viel Geld/seine ganze Freizeit für etw.** ∼ spend a great deal of money/all one's spare time on sth.

**auf·wendig** [1] *Adj.* lavish; (kostspielig) costly; expensive
[2] *adv.* lavishly; (kostspielig) expensively

**Auf·wendung** *die* **(a)** ▶ AUFWENDEN: using; expenditure; spending; **unter** ∼ **von etw.** by using/expending/spending sth.
**(b)** *Pl.* (Kosten) expenditure *sing.*

**auf|wiegeln** *tr. V.* incite; stir up

**auf|wirbeln** *tr. V.* swirl up

**auf|wischen** *tr. V.* **(a)** wipe or mop up
**(b)** (säubern) wipe ⟨*floor*⟩; (mit Wasser) wash ⟨*floor*⟩

**auf|zählen** *tr. V.* list

**Auf·zählung** *die* **(a)** listing
**(b)** (Liste) list

**auf|zeichnen** *tr. V.* **(a)** record
**(b)** (zeichnen) draw

**Auf·zeichnung** *die* record; (Film-, Tonaufzeichnung) recording; ∼**en** (Notizen) notes

**auf|ziehen** [1] *unr. tr. V.* **(a)** pull open ⟨*drawer*⟩; open, draw [back] ⟨*curtains*⟩; undo ⟨*zip*⟩
**(b)** wind up ⟨*clock, toy, etc.*⟩
[2] *unr. itr. V.; mit sein* come up; ⟨*clouds, storm*⟩ gather

**Auf·zucht** *die* raising; rearing

**Auf·zug** *der* **(a)** (Lift) lift (Brit.); elevator (Amer.)
**(b)** (abwertend: Aufmachung) get-up
**(c)** (Theater: Akt) act

**Aug·apfel** *der* eyeball

**Auge** *das;* ∼s, ∼n eye; **gute/schlechte** ∼n

haben have good/poor eyesight; **auf einem** ~ **blind** blind in one eye; **da wird er** ~**n machen** (fig. ugs.) his eyes will pop out of his head; **ich traute meinen** ~**n nicht** (ugs.) I couldn't believe my eyes; **ein** ~ od. **beide** ~**n zudrücken** (fig.) turn a blind eye; **etw. nicht aus den** ~**n lassen** not take one's eyes off sb./sth.; **ins** ~ **gehen** (fig. ugs.) end in disaster; **unter vier** ~**n** (fig.) in private

**augen; Augen-:** ~**arzt** *der,* ~**ärztin** *die* eye specialist; ~**blick** */auch: ··'·/ der* ▶ MOMENT[1]; ~**blicklich** */auch: ··'··/* ⒈ *Adj.* (a) (sofortig) immediate; (b) (gegenwärtig) present; ⒉ *adv.* (a) (sofort) at once; (b) (zurzeit) at the moment; ~**braue** *die* eyebrow; ~**farbe** *die* colour of one's eyes; ~**klinik** *die* eye hospital; ~**lid** *das* eyelid; ~**maß** *das:* **ein gutes/schlechtes** ~**maß haben** have a good eye/no eye for distances; ~**merk** *das:* **sein** ~**merk auf jmdn./etw. richten** od. **lenken** give one's attention to sb./sth.; ~**optiker** *der,* ~**optikerin** *die* ophthalmic optician

**Augen·schein** *der* (geh.) (a) (Eindruck) appearance; **dem** ~ **nach** by all appearances (b) (Betrachtung) inspection; **jmdn./etw. in** ~ **nehmen** have a close look at sb./sth.; give sb./sth. a close inspection

**augen·scheinlich** (geh.) ⒈ *Adj.* (scheinbar) apparent; evident; (sichtbar) obvious; evident ⒉ *adv.* (scheinbar) apparently; evidently; (sichtbar) obviously; evidently

**augen-, Augen-:** ~**weide** *die* feast for the eyes; ~**zeuge** *der,* ~**zeugin** *die* eyewitness; ~**zwinkernd** ⒈ *Adj.* tacit ⟨agreement⟩; ⒉ *adv.* with a wink

**August** *der;* ~[e]s *od.* ~, ~e August

**Auktion** *die;* ~, ~en auction

**Aula** *die;* ~, Aulen *od.* ~s hall

**aus** ⒈ *Präp. mit Dat.* (a) (aus dem Inneren von) out of (b) (Herkunft, Quelle, Ausgangspunkt angebend, auch zeitlich) from; ~ **Spanien/Köln** *usw.* from Spain/Cologne *etc.;* (c) ~ **der Mode/Übung sein** be out of fashion/training (d) (Grund, Ursache angebend) out of; **etw.** ~ **Erfahrung wissen** know sth. from experience; ~ **Versehen** by mistake (e) (bestehend ~) of; (hergestellt ~) made of; ~ **etw. bestehen** consist of sth. (f) ~ **ihm ist ein guter Arzt geworden** he made a good doctor ⒉ *Adv.* (a) (ugs.: vorbei) over; **wann ist die Vorstellung** ~? what time does the performance end?; **die Schule ist** ~ school is out; ~ **jetzt!** that's enough (b) (ausgeschaltet) off; (erloschen) out (c) **vom Fenster/obersten Stockwerk** ~: from the window/top storey; **von mir** ~ (ugs.) if you like; **von sich** (*Dat.*) ~: of one's own accord

**aus|atmen** *itr., tr. V.* breathe out

**aus|baden** *tr. V.* (ugs.) carry or take the can for (Brit. coll.); take the rap for (coll.)

**Aus·bau** *der;* ~[e]s (a) (Erweiterung) extension (b) (Ausgestaltung) conversion (zu into)

**aus|bauen** *tr. V.* (a) (demontieren) remove (aus from) (b) (erweitern) extend

**Aus·beute** *die* yield

**aus|beuten** *tr. V.* exploit

**Ausbeutung** *die;* ~, ~en exploitation

**aus|bilden** *tr. V.* (a) train (b) (entwickeln) develop

**Aus·bildung** *die* (a) training (b) (Entwicklung) development

**Aus·blick** *der* view (**auf** + *Akk.* of)

**aus|brechen** *unr. itr. V.; mit sein* (a) break out (**aus** of); (fig.) break free (**aus** from) (b) **jmdm. bricht der Schweiß aus** sb. breaks into a sweat (c) ⟨volcano⟩ erupt (d) (beginnen) break out; ⟨crisis⟩ break (e) **in Gelächter/Weinen** ~: burst out laughing/crying; **in Beifall/Tränen** ~: burst into applause/tears

**aus|breiten** ⒈ *tr. V.* spread; spread [out] ⟨map, cloth, sheet, etc.⟩; open out ⟨fan, newspaper⟩; (nebeneinander legen) spread out ⒉ *refl. V.* spread

**Aus·bruch** *der* (a) (Flucht) escape (**aus** from) (b) (Beginn) outbreak (c) (Gefühlsausbruch) outburst (d) (eines Vulkans) eruption

**aus|brüten** *tr. V.* hatch out; (im Brutkasten) incubate

**aus|bürsten** *tr. V.* brush out ⟨dust, dirt⟩ (**aus** of); brush ⟨clothes, upholstery, etc.⟩

**Aus·dauer** *die* stamina

**aus·dauernd** *Adj.* with stamina *postpos.*

**Ausdauer·training** *das* stamina training

**aus|dehnen** ⒈ *tr. V.* (a) stretch; (fig.) extend (**auf** + *Akk.* to) (b) (zeitlich) prolong ⒉ *refl. V.* expand; (zeitlich) go on

**Aus·dehnung** *die* expansion; (fig.) extension; (zeitlich) prolongation

**aus|denken** *unr. refl. V.* **sich** (*Dat.*) **etw.** ~: think sth. up

**aus|diskutieren** *tr. V.* **etw.** ~: discuss sth. fully *or* thoroughly

**Aus·druck** *der; Pl.* **Ausdrücke** expression; (Terminus) term; **etw. zum** ~ **bringen** express sth.

**aus|drucken** *tr. V.* (Nachrichtenw., DV) print out

**aus|drücken** ⒈ *tr. V.* (a) (auspressen) squeeze ⟨juice⟩ out; squeeze [out] ⟨lemon, grape, orange, etc.⟩; squeeze out ⟨sponge⟩; squeeze ⟨boil, pimple⟩ (b) stub out ⟨cigarette⟩ (c) (mitteilen) express

····⊱

2 *refl. V.* (a) express oneself
(b) (offenbar werden) be expressed

**ausdrücklich** /od. ·'--/ 1 *Adj.* express *attrib.* ⟨*command, wish, etc.*⟩; explicit ⟨*reservation*⟩
2 *adv.* expressly; ⟨*mention*⟩ explicitly

**ausdrucks-:** ∼**los** 1 *Adj.* expressionless; 2 *adv.* expressionlessly; ∼**voll** 1 *Adj.* expressive; 2 *adv.* expressively

**aus·ein·ander** *Adv.* (a) (voneinander getrennt) apart; etw. ∼ schreiben write sth. as separate words; ∼ brechen break up; etw. ∼ brechen break sth. up; ∼ gehen part; ⟨*crowd*⟩ disperse; ⟨*opinions, views*⟩ differ; zwei Dinge ∼ halten (unterscheiden) distinguish between two things; ich kann die beiden Brüder nicht ∼ halten I cannot tell the two brothers apart; etw. ∼ nehmen take sth. apart
(b) jmdm. etw. ∼ setzen explain sth. to sb.; sich mit jmdm. ∼ setzen have it out with sb.; sich mit etw. ∼ setzen concern oneself with sth.

**\*auseinander|brechen** *usw.*
▶ AUSEINANDER

**Auseinandersetzung** *die;* ∼, ∼en (a) (Streit) argument
(b) (Kampfhandlung) clash

**Aus·fahrt** *die* exit

**Aus·fall** *der* (a) (das Nichtstattfinden) cancellation
(b) (Einbuße, Verlust) loss
(c) (eines Motors) failure; (einer Maschine, eines Autos) breakdown

**aus|fallen** *unr. itr. V.; mit sein* (a) fall out
(b) (nicht stattfinden) be cancelled; etw. ∼ lassen cancel sth.
(c) (ausscheiden) drop out
(d) (nicht mehr funktionieren) ⟨*engine, brakes, signal*⟩ fail; ⟨*machine, car*⟩ break down
(e) (ein bestimmtes Ergebnis zeigen) turn out

**ausfallend** *Adj.* [gegen jmdn.] ∼ sein/ werden be/become abusive [towards sb.]

**Ausfall·straße** *die* main road out of the/a town/city

**aus·findig** *Adv.* jmdn./etw. ∼ machen find sb./sth.

**Aus·flug** *der* outing

**Ausflügler** *der;* ∼s, ∼, **Ausflüglerin** *die;* ∼, ∼nen day tripper; excursionist (Amer.)

**Ausflugs-:** ∼**dampfer** *der* pleasure steamer; ∼**lokal** *das* restaurant/café catering for [day] trippers; ∼**verkehr** *der* (am Wochenende) weekend holiday traffic; (an Feiertagen) holiday traffic

**aus|fragen** *tr. V.* jmdn. ∼: question sb., ask sb. questions (nach, über + *Akk.* about)

**aus|fransen** *itr. V.; mit sein* fray

**Aus·fuhr** *die;* ∼, ∼en ▶ EXPORT

**aus|führen** *tr. V.* (a) (ausgehen mit) take ⟨*person*⟩ out
(b) (spazieren führen) take ⟨*person, animal*⟩ for a walk
(c) (exportieren) export
(d) (durchführen) carry out; (Sport) take ⟨*penalty, free kick, corner*⟩

**ausführlich** /auch: ·'--/ 1 *Adj.* detailed; full
2 *adv.* in detail

**Ausfuhr·sperre** *die* ▶ AUSFUHRVERBOT

**Aus·führung** *die* (Durchführung) carrying out; (Sport) taking

**Ausfuhr·verbot** *das* (Wirtsch.) export embargo

**aus|füllen** *tr. V.* (a) fill; fill in ⟨*form, crossword puzzle*⟩
(b) (beanspruchen, einnehmen) take up ⟨*space*⟩

**Aus·gabe** *die* (a) (giving out); (von Essen) serving
(b) (Geldausgabe) item of expenditure; ∼n expenditure *sing.* (für on)
(c) (Edition) edition
(d) (DV) output

**Ausgabe·gerät** *das* (DV) output device

**Aus·gang** *der* (a) (Erlaubnis zum Ausgehen) time off; (von Soldaten) leave
(b) (Tür ins Freie) exit (*Gen.* from)
(c) (Anat.) outlet
(d) (Ende) end; (eines Romans, Films usw.) ending
(e) (Ergebnis) outcome; (eines Wettbewerbs) result; ein Unfall mit tödlichem ∼: an accident with fatal consequences

**Ausgangs-:** ∼**punkt** *der* starting point; ∼**sperre** *die* (bes. Milit.) (für Zivilisten) curfew; (für Soldaten) confinement to barracks; [eine] ∼**sperre verhängen** impose a curfew/confine the soldiers/regiment *etc.* to barracks

**aus|geben** *unr. tr. V.* (a) give out; serve ⟨*food, drinks*⟩
(b) (verbrauchen) spend ⟨*money*⟩ (für on)

**ausgebucht** *Adj.* booked up

**ausgedehnt** *Adj.* extensive

**aus·gefallen** *Adj.* unusual

**Ausgeflippte** *der/die; adj. Dekl.* (salopp) dropout (coll.)

**ausgeglichen** *Adj.* balanced; well-balanced ⟨*person*⟩; equable ⟨*climate*⟩

**aus|gehen** *unr. itr. V.; mit sein* (a) go out
(b) (fast aufgebraucht sein) run out
(c) (enden) end; gut/schlecht ∼: turn out well/badly; ⟨*story, film*⟩ end happily/ unhappily
(d) von jmdm./etw. ∼: come from sb./sth.
(e) von etw. ∼ (etw. zugrunde legen) take sth. as one's starting point; (etw. annehmen) assume sth.

**aus·gelassen** 1 *Adj.* exuberant ⟨*mood, person*⟩; lively ⟨*party, celebration*⟩; (wild) boisterous
2 *adv.* exuberantly; (wild) boisterously

---

\*old spelling - see note on page xiv

**aus·gemacht** *Adj.* (a) (beschlossen) agreed; **es ist [eine]** ∼**e Sache, dass ...** it is an accepted fact that ...
(b) (vollkommen) complete; complete, utter ⟨*nonsense*⟩; **eine** ∼**e Dummheit** downright stupidity

**aus·genommen** *Konj.* except

**ausgeprägt** *Adj.* marked

**ausgerechnet** *Adv.* (*ugs.*) ∼ **heute/ morgen** today/tomorrow of all days; ∼ **hier** here of all places; ∼ **Sie** you of all people

**aus·geschlossen** *Adj.* **das ist** ∼: that is out of the question

**aus·geschnitten** *Adj.* low-cut ⟨*dress, blouse, etc.*⟩

**aus·gesprochen** ⒈ *Adj.* definite, marked ⟨*preference, inclination, resemblance*⟩; pronounced ⟨*dislike*⟩; marked ⟨*contrast*⟩; ∼**es Pech/Glück haben** be decidedly unlucky/lucky; **ein** ∼**es Talent für etw.** a definite talent for sth.; **ein** ∼**er Gegner von etw. sein** be a strong opponent of sth.
⒉ *adv.* (besonders) decidedly; downright ⟨*stupid, ridiculous, ugly*⟩

**aus·gestorben** *Adj.* [**wie**] ∼: deserted

**aus·gewogen** *Adj.* (ausgeglichen) balanced; [well-]balanced ⟨*personality*⟩

**Aus·gewogenheit** *die;* ∼: balance

**ausgezeichnet** /*od.* '--'--/ ⒈ *Adj.* excellent; outstanding ⟨*expert*⟩
⒉ *adv.* excellently

**ausgiebig** ⒈ *Adj.* substantial ⟨*meal*⟩
⒉ *adv.* ⟨*profit*⟩ handsomely; ⟨*read*⟩ extensively; **von etw.** ∼ **Gebrauch machen** make full use of sth.

**aus·gießen** *unr. tr. V.* (a) pour out (aus of)
(b) (leeren) empty

**Aus·gleich** *der;* ∼**[e]s,** ∼**e** (a)
▶ AUSGLEICHEN A: evening out; reconciliation
(b) (Schadensersatz) compensation; **als** *od.* **zum** ∼ **für etw.** to make up for sth.

**aus·gleichen** *unr. tr. V.* (a) even out; reconcile ⟨*differences of opinions, contradictions*⟩
(b) compensate for ⟨*damage*⟩; make up for ⟨*misfortune, lack*⟩; **etw. durch etw.** ∼: make up for sth. with sth.; **sich** ∼: balance out; (sich gegenseitig aufheben) cancel each other out

**aus·graben** *unr. tr. V.* dig up; (Archäol.) excavate

**Aus·grabung** *die* (Archäol.) excavation

**Aus·guss, \*Aus·guß** *der* sink

**aus·halten** *unr. tr. V.* stand; bear; endure; withstand ⟨*attack, load, pressure, test, wear and tear*⟩; **er konnte es zu Hause nicht mehr** ∼: he couldn't stand it at home any more; **es ist nicht zum Aushalten** it is unbearable

**aus·handeln** *tr. V.* negotiate

**aus·händigen** *tr. V.* hand over

**Aus·hang** *der* notice; **einen** ∼ **machen** put up a notice

**aus·heben** *unr. tr. V.* dig out ⟨*earth etc.*⟩; dig ⟨*trench, grave, etc.*⟩

**aus·helfen** *unr. itr. V.* help out; **jmdm.** ∼: help sb. out (mit, bei with)

**Aus·hilfe** *die* (a) (das Aushelfen) help
(b) ▶ AUSHILFSKRAFT

**aushilfs-, Aushilfs-:** ∼**kraft** *die* temporary worker; (in Läden, Gaststätten) temporary assistant; (Sekretärin) temporary secretary; temp (coll.); ∼**lehrer** *der,* ∼**lehrerin,** *die* supply teacher; ∼**weise** *adv.* on a temporary basis

**aus·holen** *itr. V.* [**mit dem Arm**] ∼: draw back one's arm; (zum Schlag) raise one's arm

**aus·kennen** *unr. refl. V.* (an einem Ort usw.) know one's way around; (in einem Fach, einer Angelegenheit usw.) know what's what; **sie kennt sich in dieser Stadt aus** she knows her way around the town; **sich [gut] mit/in etw.** (*Dat.*) ∼: know [a lot] about sth.

**Aus·klang** *der* (geh.) end; **zum** ∼ **des Festes** to end *or* close the festival

**aus·kleiden** *tr. V.* (geh.) undress; **sich** ∼: undress

**aus·klingen** *unr. itr. V.; mit sein* end

**aus·klopfen** *tr. V.* (a) beat out (aus + *Dat.* of)
(b) (säubern) beat ⟨*carpet*⟩; knock ⟨*pipe*⟩ out

**aus·kochen** *tr. V.* boil; (keimfrei machen) sterilize ⟨*instruments etc.*⟩ [in boiling water]

**aus·kommen** *unr. itr. V.; mit sein* (a) manage
(b) **mit jmdm.** [**gut**] ∼: get on [well] with sb.

**Auskommen** *das;* ∼**s** livelihood

**Auskunft** *die;* ∼**, Auskünfte** (a) piece of information; **Auskünfte** information *sing.;* [**jmdm. über etw.** (*Akk.*)] ∼ **geben** give [sb.] information [about sth.]
(b) (Stelle) information desk/counter/office/ centre *etc.;* (Fernspr.) directory enquiries *no art.* (Brit.); directory information *no art.* (Amer.)

**Auskunftei** *die;* ∼**,** ∼**en** private detective agency; (Kredit∼) credit reference agency

**Auskunfts-:** ∼**büro** *das* information office; enquiry office (Brit.); ∼**schalter** *der* information counter; ∼**stelle** *die* information office

**aus·kungeln** *tr. V.* (ugs.) reach by wheeling and dealing

**aus·kurieren** *tr. V.* heal ⟨*wound*⟩ [completely]

**aus·lachen** *tr. V.* laugh at

**aus·laden** *unr. tr. V.* unload ⟨*goods etc.*⟩

**Aus·lage** *die* (a) *Pl.* (Unkosten) expenses
(b) (ausgestellte Ware) item on display; ∼**n** goods on display

**aus·lagern** *tr. V.* (a) remove ⟨*art treasures*⟩ for safe-keeping
(b) relocate ⟨*firm, activity*⟩ (nach to); (an einen externen Dienstleister) outsource ⟨*function, activity*⟩

**Aus·land** *das* foreign countries *pl.;* **im/ins** ∼: abroad; **aus dem** ∼: from abroad

**Ausländer** *der;* ∼s, ∼, **Ausländerin** *die;* ∼, ∼nen foreigner

**ausländer·feindlich** *Adj.* hostile to foreigners *postpos.*

**ausländisch** *Adj.* foreign

**Auslands-:** ∼**aufenthalt** *der* stay abroad; ∼**gespräch** *das* (Fernspr.) international call; ∼**korrespondent** *der,* ∼**korrespondentin** *die* foreign correspondent; ∼**reise** *die* trip abroad

**aus|lassen** *unr. tr. V.* (a) (weglassen) leave out
(b) (versäumen) miss ⟨*opportunity, chance, etc.*⟩

**Auslauf** *der* (a) keinen/zu wenig ∼ haben have no/too little chance to run around outside
(b) (Raum) space to run around in

**aus|laufen** *unr. itr. V.; mit sein* (a) run out (aus of)
(b) (leer laufen) empty; ⟨*egg*⟩ run out
(c) (in See stechen) sail (**nach** for)
(d) (erlöschen) ⟨*contract, agreement, etc.*⟩ run out

**Aus·läufer** *der* (a) (Geogr.) foothill *usu. in pl.;*
(b) (Met.) (eines Hochs) ridge; (eines Tiefs) trough

**aus|legen** *tr. V.* (a) (hinlegen) lay out; display ⟨*goods, exhibits*⟩
(b) etw. mit Fliesen/Teppichboden ∼: tile/carpet sth.
(c) (leihen) lend
(d) (interpretieren) interpret; etw. falsch ∼: misinterpret sth.

**Auslegung** *die;* ∼, ∼en interpretation

**aus|leihen** *unr. tr. V.* ▶ LEIHEN

**aus|liefern** *tr. V.* (a) jmdm. etw. od. etw. an jmdn. ∼: hand sth. over to sb.
(b) *auch itr.* (Kaufmannsspr.: liefern) deliver

**Aus·lieferung** *die* (a) (Übergabe) handing over; (an ein Land) extradition; **jmds.** ∼ **fordern** demand that sb. be handed over/extradited
(b) (Kaufmannsspr.: Lieferung) delivery

**Auslieferungs-:** ∼**antrag** *der* application for extradition; ∼**lager** *das* (Wirtsch.) distribution centre

**aus|loggen** *refl. V.* (DV) log off *or* out

**aus|löschen** *tr. V.* (a) extinguish
(b) (beseitigen) erase ⟨*drawing, writing*⟩

**aus|losen** *tr. V.* etw. ∼: draw lots for sth.

**aus|lösen** *tr. V.* (a) trigger ⟨*mechanism, device, alarm, etc.*⟩; release ⟨*camera shutter*⟩
(b) provoke ⟨*discussion, anger, laughter, reaction, outrage, heart attack*⟩; cause ⟨*sorrow, horror, surprise, disappointment, panic, war*⟩; excite, arouse ⟨*interest, enthusiasm*⟩

**Auslöser** *der;* ∼s, ∼ (Fot.) shutter release

---

*alte Schreibung - vgl. Hinweis auf S. xiv

**aus|machen** *tr. V.* (a) (ugs.) put out ⟨*light, fire, cigarette, candle*⟩; switch off ⟨*television, radio, hi-fi*⟩; turn off ⟨*gas*⟩
(b) (vereinbaren) agree [on]; ∼, **dass** ...: agree that ...
(c) (auszeichnen, kennzeichnen) make up
(d) wenig/nichts/viel ∼: make little/no/a great difference
(e) das macht mir nichts aus I don't mind

**Aus·maß** *das* (a) (Größe) size
(b) (Grad) extent

**aus|messen** *unr. tr. V.* measure up

**Aus·nahme** *die;* ∼, ∼n exception; mit ∼ von with the exception of; bei jmdm. eine ∼ machen make an exception in sb.'s case

**Ausnahme-:** ∼**erscheinung** *die* exceptional phenomenon; ∼**zustand** *der* state of emergency

**ausnahms-:** ∼**los** ① *Adj.* unanimous ⟨*approval, agreement*⟩; ② *adv.* without exception; ∼**weise** *Adv.* by way of an exception; **Dürfen wir mitkommen? – Ausnahmsweise [ja]** May we come too? – Yes, just this once

**aus|nehmen** *unr. tr. V.* (a) gut ⟨*fish, rabbit, chicken*⟩
(b) (ausschließen von) exclude; (gesondert behandeln) make an exception of

**aus|nüchtern** *tr., itr., refl. V.* sober up

**Ausnüchterung** *die;* ∼, ∼en sobering up; jmdn. zur ∼ auf die Wache bringen take sb. to the [police] station to sober up

**Ausnüchterungs·zelle** *die* drying-out cell

**aus|nutzen,** (bes. südd., österr.)
**aus|nützen** *tr. V.* (a) take advantage of
(b) (ausbeuten) exploit

**Aus·nutzung** *die,* (bes. südd., österr.)
**Ausnützung** *die;* ∼: use; (Ausbeutung) exploitation; **unter voller** ∼ **einer Sache** (Gen.) making full use of sth.

**aus|packen** ① *tr., itr. V.* unpack; (auswickeln) unwrap
② *itr. V.* (ugs.) (Geheimnisse verraten) talk (coll.); squeal (sl.)

**aus|pressen** *tr. V.* squeeze out ⟨*juice*⟩; squeeze ⟨*orange, lemon*⟩; (keltern) press ⟨*grapes etc.*⟩

**aus|probieren** *tr. V.* try out

**Aus·puff** *der* exhaust

**Auspuffgase** *Pl.* exhaust fumes *pl.*

**aus|radieren** *tr. V.* rub out; erase

**aus|rangieren** *tr. V.* (ugs.) throw out; discard; scrap ⟨*vehicle, machine*⟩; **ausrangierte Fahrzeuge** scrap vehicles

**aus|rasten** *itr. V.; mit sein* (Technik) disengage; er rastete aus, es rastete bei ihm aus (fig. salopp) something snapped in him

**aus|rauben** *tr. V.* rob

**aus|räuchern** *tr. V.* (auch fig.) smoke out; fumigate ⟨*room*⟩

**aus|räumen** ① *tr. V.* (a) clear out (aus of)

**(b)** (fig.) clear up; dispel ⟨*prejudice, suspicion, misgivings*⟩ ☐2 *itr. V.* clear everything out

**aus|rechnen** *tr. V.* work out; **das kannst du dir leicht ~** (ugs.) you can easily work that out [for yourself]

**Aus·rede** *die* excuse

**aus|reden** ☐1 *itr. V.* finish [speaking] ☐2 *tr. V.* **jmdm. etw. ~:** talk sb. out of sth.

**aus|reichen** *itr. V.* be enough *or* sufficient (**zu** for)

**ausreichend** ☐1 *Adj.* sufficient; enough; (als Note) fair ☐2 *adv.* sufficiently

**Aus·reise** *die:* **jmdm. die ~ verweigern** refuse sb. permission to leave [the/a country]; **vor/bei der ~:** before/when leaving the country

**Ausreise·antrag** *der* application to leave the country; application for an exit visa

**aus|reißen** ☐1 *unr. tr. V.* tear out; pull out ⟨*plants, weeds*⟩ ☐2 *unr. itr. V.; mit sein* **(a)** (sich lösen) come off **(b)** (ugs.: weglaufen) run away (*Dat.* from)

**aus|renken** *tr. V.* dislocate

**aus|richten** *tr. V.* **(a) jmdm. etw. ~:** tell sb. sth. **(b)** (einheitlich anordnen) line up **(c)** (erreichen) achieve

**aus|rollen** *tr. V.* roll out

**aus|rotten** *tr. V.* eradicate

**Aus·ruf** *der* cry

**aus|rufen** *unr. tr. V.* **(a)** call out; **„Schön!", rief er aus** 'Lovely', he exclaimed **(b)** (offiziell verkünden) proclaim; declare ⟨*state of emergency*⟩ **(c)** (zum Kauf anbieten) cry

**Ausrufe·zeichen** *das* exclamation mark

**aus|ruhen** *refl., itr. V.* have a rest; [sich] **ein wenig/richtig ~:** rest a little/have a good rest; **ausgeruht sein** be rested

**aus|rüsten** *tr. V.* equip

**Aus·rüstung** *die* **(a)** equipping **(b)** (Gegenstände) equipment *no pl.*

**Ausrüstungs·gegenstand** *der* item of equipment

**aus|rutschen** *itr. V.; mit sein* slip

**aus|säen** *tr. V.* (*auch itr.*) *V.* (auch fig.) sow

**Aus·sage** *die* statement

**aussage-, Aussage-: ~kraft** *die* meaningfulness; (Ausdruckskraft) expressiveness; **~kräftig** *Adj.* meaningful; (ausdruckskräftig) expressive

**aus|sagen** ☐1 *tr. V.* **(a)** say **(b)** (vor Gericht, vor der Polizei) state; (unter Eid) testify ☐2 *itr. V.* make a statement; (unter Eid) testify

**aus|saugen** *regelm.* (*geh. auch unr.*) *tr. V.* **(a)** suck out (**aus** of); (leer saugen) suck dry

**(b)** (fig.: ausbeuten) jmdn./etw. **~:** bleed sb./sth. [white]; **jmdn. bis aufs Blut** *od.* **Mark ~:** bleed sb. white

**aus|schaben** *tr. V.* **(a)** scrape out **(b)** (Med.) remove; (mit der Kürette) curette

**aus|schalten** *tr. V.* **(a)** switch *or* turn off **(b)** (fig.) eliminate; exclude ⟨*emotion, influence*⟩; dismiss ⟨*doubt, objection*⟩; shut out ⟨*feeling, thought*⟩

**Aus·schank** *der;* **~[e]s** serving

**Aus·schau** *die:* **nach jmdm./etw. ~ halten** keep a lookout for sb./sth.

**aus|schauen** *itr. V.* **nach jmdm./etw. ~:** look out for sb./sth.

**aus|scheiden** ☐1 *unr. itr. V.; mit sein* **(a) aus etw. ~:** leave sth.; **aus dem Amt ~:** leave office **(b)** (Sport) be eliminated **(c) diese Möglichkeit/dieser Kandidat scheidet aus** this possibility/candidate has to be ruled out ☐2 *unr. tr. V.* (Physiol.) excrete ⟨*waste*⟩; eliminate, expel ⟨*poison*⟩; exude ⟨*sweat*⟩

**Aus·scheidung** *die* **(a)** (Physiol.) ▶ AUSSCHEIDEN 2: excretion; elimination; expulsion; exudation; **~en** (Ausgeschiedenes) excreta **(b)** (Sport) qualifier

**aus|schenken** *tr. V.* serve

**aus|scheren** *itr. V.; mit sein* pull out

**aus|schildern** *tr. V.* signpost

**aus|schimpfen** *tr. V.* **jmdn. ~:** tell sb. off

**aus|schlachten** *tr. V.* **(a)** (ugs.: brauchbare Teile ausbauen aus) cannibalize ⟨*machine, vehicle*⟩; break ⟨*vehicle*⟩ for spares **(b)** (ugs. abwertend: ausnutzen) exploit; **etw. politisch ~:** make political capital out of sth.

**aus|schlafen** ☐1 *unr. itr., refl. V.* have a good sleep ☐2 *unr. tr. V.* **seinen Rausch ~** sleep off the effects of alcohol

**Aus·schlag** *der* **(a)** (Hautausschlag) rash **(b)** (eines Zeigers, einer Waage) deflection; (eines Pendels) swing; **den ~ geben** (fig.) tip the scales (fig.)

**aus|schlagen** ☐1 *unr. tr. V.* **(a)** knock out **(b)** (ablehnen) turn down ☐2 *unr. itr. V.* **(a)** ⟨*horse*⟩ kick **(b)** ⟨*needle, pointer*⟩ be deflected, swing **(c)** (sprießen) come out [in bud]

**ausschlag·gebend** *Adj.* decisive

**aus|schließen** *unr. tr. V.* **(a)** (ausstoßen) expel (**aus** from) **(b)** (nicht teilnehmen lassen) exclude (**aus** from) **(c)** (fig.) rule out ⟨*possibility*⟩; **jeden Irrtum ~:** rule out all possibility of error **(d)** (aussperren) lock out

**aus·schließlich** /*od.* ·'·-·, ·'·-/ ☐1 *Adj.* exclusive ☐2 *Adv.* exclusively ☐3 *Präp. mit Gen.* excluding

**Ausschließlichkeit** *die;* ~: exclusiveness

**Aus·schluss, *Aus·schluß** *der* exclusion (von from); (aus einer Gemeinschaft) expulsion (aus from); **unter** ~ **der Öffentlichkeit** with the public excluded; (Rechtsw.) in camera

**aus|schmücken** *tr. V.* deck out

**aus|schneiden** *unr. tr. V.* cut out; (DV) cut

**Aus·schnitt** *der* (a) (Zeitungsausschnitt) cutting; clipping
(b) (Halsausschnitt) neck; **ein tiefer** ~: a plunging neckline
(c) (Teil) part; (eines Textes) excerpt; (eines Films) clip; (Bildausschnitt) detail

**aus|schreiben** *unr. tr. V.* (a) (nicht abgekürzt schreiben) etw. ~: write sth. out in full
(b) (ausstellen) make out ⟨cheque, invoice, receipt⟩
(c) (bekannt geben) call ⟨election, meeting⟩; advertise ⟨flat, job⟩; put ⟨supply order etc.⟩ out to tender

**Aus·schreibung** *die* ▶ AUSSCHREIBEN C: calling; advertisement; invitation to tender

**Ausschreitungen** *Pl.* acts of violence

**Aus·schuss, *Aus·schuß** *der* committee

**aus|schütten** *tr. V.* tip out ⟨water, sand, coal, etc.⟩; (ausleeren) empty ⟨bucket, bowl, container⟩

**ausschweifend** ① *Adj.* wild ⟨imagination, emotion, hope, desire, orgy⟩; extravagant ⟨idea⟩; riotous, wild ⟨enjoyment⟩; dissolute ⟨life, person⟩
② *adv.* ~ **leben** lead a dissolute life

**Ausschweifung** *die;* ~, ~en (im Genießen) dissolution

**aus|sehen** *unr. itr. V.* look (**wie** like); **so siehst du aus!** (ugs.) that's what you think!

**Aussehen** *das;* ~s appearance

***aus|sein** *unr. itr. V.; mit sein; nur im Inf. und Part. zusammengeschrieben* (a) ⟨play, film, war⟩ be over; **wann ist die Vorstellung aus?** what time does the performance end?; **die Schule ist aus** school is out
(b) ⟨fire, candle, etc.⟩ be out
(c) ⟨radio, light, etc.⟩ be off

**außen** *Adv.* outside; **die Vase ist** ~ **bemalt** the vase is painted on the outside; **das Fenster geht nach** ~ **auf** the window opens outwards; **von** ~: from the outside

**außen-, Außen-:** ~**dienst** *der:* **im** ~**dienst sein** *od.* **arbeiten, im** ~**dienst machen** *od.* **haben** be working out of the office; ⟨salesman⟩ be on the road; ~**handel** *der* foreign trade *no art.;* ~**handels-bilanz** *die* balance of trade; ~**minister** *der,* ~**ministerin** *die* Foreign Minister; ~**ministerium** *das* Foreign Ministry; ~**politik** *die* foreign politics *sing.;*

~**politisch** ① *Adj.* ⟨question⟩ relating to foreign policy; ② *adv.* as regards foreign policy; ~**seite** *die* outside

**Außenseiter** *der;* ~s, ~,
**Außenseiterin** *die;* ~, ~nen outsider

**Außen:** ~**spiegel** *der* exterior mirror; ~**stände** *Pl.* outstanding debts *or* accounts; ~**wand** *die* external *or* outside wall; ~**welt** *die* outside world

**außer** ① *Präp. mit Dat.* (a) (abgesehen von) apart from; aside from (Amer.)
(b) (außerhalb von) out of; ~ **sich sein** be beside oneself (**vor** + *Dat.* with)
(c) (zusätzlich zu) in addition to
② *Präp. mit Akk.* ~ **sich geraten** become beside oneself (**vor** + *Dat.* with)
③ *Konj.* except

**äußer...** *Adj.* outer; outside ⟨pocket⟩; outlying ⟨district, area⟩; external ⟨injury, form, circumstances, cause, force⟩; outward ⟨appearance, similarity, effect, etc.⟩; foreign ⟨affairs⟩

**außer·dem** /*auch:* --'-/ *Adv.* as well; (überdies) besides

**Äußere** *das; adj. Dekl.* [outward] appearance

**außer-:** ~**ehelich** ① *Adj.* extra-marital; illegitimate ⟨child, birth⟩; ② *adv.* outside marriage; ~**gewöhnlich** ① *Adj.* (a) unusual; (b) (das Gewohnte übertreffend) exceptional; ② *adv.* (a) unusually; (b) (sehr) exceptionally; ~**halb** *Präp. mit Gen.* outside

**äußerlich** ① *Adj.* external ⟨use, injury⟩; outward ⟨appearance, calm, similarity, etc.⟩
② *adv.: s. Adj.:* externally; outwardly

**Äußerlichkeit** *die;* ~, ~en formality; (Unwesentliches) minor point

**äußern** ① *tr. V.* express, voice ⟨opinion, view, criticism, reservations, disapproval, doubt⟩; express ⟨wish⟩; voice ⟨suspicion⟩
② *refl. V.* (a) **sich über etw.** (*Akk.*) ~: give one's view on sth.
(b) ⟨illness⟩ manifest itself (**in** + *Dat.,* **durch** in)

**außer-:** ~**ordentlich** ① *Adj.* (a) extraordinary; (b) (das Gewohnte übertreffend) exceptional; ② *adv.* (sehr) exceptionally; extremely ⟨pleased, relieved⟩; ~**schulisch** *Adj.* outside the school *postpos.*

**äußerst** *Adv.* extremely

**äußerst...** *Adj.* (a) extreme
(b) (letztmöglich) latest possible ⟨date, deadline⟩; (höchst...) highest ⟨price⟩; (niedrigst...) lowest ⟨price⟩
(c) (schlimmst...) worst

**außerstande** *Adv.* ~ **sein, etw. zu tun** (nicht befähigt) be unable to do sth.; (nicht in der Lage) not be in a position to do sth.

**Äußerung** *die;* ~, ~en comment

**aus|setzen** ① *tr. V.* (a) expose (*Dat.* to); **Belastungen ausgesetzt sein** be subject to strains

---

**(b)** (sich selbst überlassen) abandon ⟨*baby, animal*⟩; (auf einer einsamen Insel) maroon
**(c)** an jmdm./etw. etwas auszusetzen haben find fault with sb./sth.
2 *itr. V.* **(a)** (aufhören) stop; ⟨*engine, machine*⟩ cut out
**(b)** (pausieren) ⟨*player*⟩ miss a turn; mit der Arbeit/dem Training [ein paar Wochen] ~: stop work/training [for a few weeks]

**Aus·sicht** *die* **(a)** view (auf + *Akk.* of)
**(b)** (fig.) prospect; ~ auf etw. (*Akk.*) haben, etw. in ~ haben have the prospect of sth.

**aussichts-, Aussichts-:** ~los 1 *Adj.* hopeless; 2 *adv.* hopelessly; ~losigkeit *die;* ~~: hopelessness; ~punkt *der* vantage point; ~reich *Adj.* promising; ~turm *der* lookout tower

**Aus·siedler** *der* (Auswanderer) emigrant; (Evakuierter) evacuee; (Umsiedler) resettled person

**Aussiedler·heim** *das* resettlement hostel (*for German nationals and ethnic Germans from Eastern europe*)
**Aussiedlerin** *die* ▶ AUSSIEDLER

**aus|sortieren** *tr. V.* sort out

**aus|spannen** *itr. V.* take *or* have a break

**aus|sparen** *tr. V.* leave ⟨*line etc.*⟩ blank; (fig.) leave out; omit

**Ausparung** *die;* ~, ~en **(a)** (das Aussparen) leaving blank
**(b)** (Stelle) gap

**aus|sperren** 1 *tr. V.* lock out; shut ⟨*animal*⟩ out
2 *itr. V.* lock the workforce out

**Aus·sperrung** *die* lockout

**aus|spielen** *tr. V.* **(a)** *auch itr.* (Kartenspiel) lead
**(b)** jmdn./etw. gegen jmdn./etw. ~: play sb./sth. off against sb./sth.

**Aus·sprache** *die* **(a)** pronunciation
**(b)** (Gespräch) discussion

**aus|sprechen** 1 *unr. tr. V.* **(a)** pronounce
**(b)** (ausdrücken) express; voice ⟨*suspicion, request*⟩
2 *unr. refl. V.* **(a)** sich lobend/missbilligend usw. über jmdn./etw. ~: speak highly/disapprovingly of *etc.* sb./sth.
**(b)** (offen sprechen) say what's on one's mind; sich bei jmdm. ~: have a heart-to-heart talk with sb.
**(c)** (Strittiges klären) talk things out (mit with)
3 *unr. itr. V.* (zu Ende sprechen) finish [speaking]

**Aus·spruch** *der* remark

**aus|spucken** 1 *itr. V.* spit
2 *tr. V.* spit out

**aus|spülen** *tr. V.* rinse out

**Aus·stand** *der* strike

**aus|statten** /'au:ʃtatn̩/ *tr. V.* provide (mit with); (mit Gerät) equip; (mit Möbeln, Teppichen, Gardinen usw.) furnish

**Ausstattung** *die;* ~, ~en **(a)**
▶ AUSSTATTEN provision; equipping; furnishing
**(b)** (Ausrüstung) equipment; (Innenausstattung eines Autos) trim
**(c)** (Einrichtung) furnishings *pl.*

**aus|stehen** 1 *unr. itr. V.* noch ~ ⟨*debt*⟩ be outstanding; ⟨*decision*⟩ be still to be taken; ⟨*solution*⟩ be still to be found
2 *unr. tr. V.* ich kann ihn/das nicht ~: I can't stand him/it

**aus|steigen** *unr. itr. V.;* **(a)** mit sein get out; (aus einem Zug, Bus) get off
**(b)** (ugs.: sich nicht mehr beteiligen) ~ aus opt out of; give up ⟨*show business, job*⟩; leave ⟨*project;*⟩
**(c)** (ugs.: der Gesellschaft den Rücken kehren) drop out

**Aussteiger** *der;* ~s, ~, **Aussteigerin** *die;* ~, ~nen (ugs.) dropout (coll.)

**aus|stellen** *tr. V.* **(a)** put on display; display; (im Museum, auf einer Messe) exhibit
**(b)** (ausfertigen) make out ⟨*cheque, prescription, receipt, bill*⟩; issue ⟨*visa, passport, certificate*⟩; einen Scheck auf jmdn. ~: make out a cheque to sb.
**(c)** (ugs.: ausschalten) switch off ⟨*cooker, radio, heating, engine*⟩

**Aus·stellung** *die* **(a)** exhibition
**(b)** ▶ AUSSTELLEN B: making out; issuing

**Ausstellungs-:** ~gelände *das* exhibition site; ~katalog *der* exhibition catalogue

**aus|sterben** *unr. itr. V.; mit sein* die out; ⟨*species*⟩ become extinct; vom Aussterben bedroht sein be threatened with extinction

**Aus·steuer** *die* trousseau (*consisting mainly of household linen*)

**Ausstieg** *der;* ~[e]s, ~e **(a)** exit
**(b)** (ugs.) opting out (aus of); der ~ aus einem Projekt/aus der Atomenergie leaving a project/abandoning nuclear energy

**aus|stopfen** *tr. V.* stuff

**Aus·stoß** *der* (Wirtsch.) output

**aus|stoßen** *unr. tr. V.* **(a)** expel; give off, emit ⟨*gas, fumes, smoke*⟩
**(b)** give ⟨*cry, whistle, laugh, sigh, etc.*⟩; let out ⟨*cry, scream, yell*⟩; utter ⟨*curse, threat, etc.*⟩

**aus|strahlen** 1 *tr. V.* **(a)** (auch fig.) radiate; ⟨*lamp*⟩ give out ⟨*light*⟩
**(b)** (Rundf., Ferns.) broadcast
2 *itr. V.* **(a)** radiate; ⟨*light*⟩ be given out; (fig.) ⟨*pain*⟩ spread
**(b)** auf jmdn./etw. ~ (fig.) communicate itself to sb./influence sth.

**Aus·strahlung** *die* (fig.) charisma

**aus|strecken** 1 *tr. V.* stretch out; put out ⟨*feelers*⟩
2 *refl. V.* stretch out

**aus|streichen** *unr. tr. V.* cross out

**aus|strömen** *itr. V.; mit sein* pour out; ⟨*gas, steam*⟩ escape

**a**

**aus|suchen** tr. V. choose; pick

**Aus·tausch** der (a) exchange; **im ~ für** od. **gegen** in exchange for
(b) (das Ersetzen) replacement (**gegen** with)

**aus|tauschen** tr. V. (a) exchange (**gegen** for)
(b) (ersetzen) replace (**gegen** with)

**Austausch-:** **~motor** der replacement engine; **~schüler** der, **~schülerin** die exchange pupil or student

**aus|teilen** tr. V. distribute (**an** + Akk. to); (aushändigen) hand out ⟨books, post, etc.⟩ (**an** + Akk. to); give ⟨orders⟩; deal [out] ⟨cards⟩; give out ⟨marks, grades⟩; serve ⟨food etc.⟩

**Auster** die; ~, ~n oyster

**aus|tragen** unr. tr. V. (a) deliver ⟨newspapers, post⟩
(b) ⟨pregnant woman⟩ carry ⟨child⟩ to full term; (nicht abtreiben) have ⟨child⟩
(c) (ausfechten) settle ⟨conflict, differences⟩; fight out ⟨battle⟩

**Australien** /au:s'tra:liən/ (das); ~s Australia

**Australier** der; ~s, ~, **Australierin** die; ~, ~nen Australian

**australisch** Adj. Australian

**aus|treiben** unr. tr. V. (a) exorcize, cast out ⟨evil spirit, demon⟩
(b) jmdm. etw. ~: cure sb. of sth.

**aus|treten** ① unr. tr. V. (a) tread out ⟨spark, cigarette end⟩; trample out ⟨fire⟩
(b) (bahnen) tread out ⟨path⟩
(c) wear out ⟨shoes⟩
② unr. itr. V.; mit sein (a) (ugs.: zur Toilette gehen) pay a call (coll.)
(b) aus etw. ~ (ausscheiden) leave sth.

**aus|trinken** tr. V. drink up ⟨drink⟩; finish ⟨glass, cup, etc.⟩

**Aus·tritt** der leaving

**aus|trocknen** ① tr. V. dry out; dry up ⟨river bed, marsh⟩
② itr. V.; mit sein dry out; ⟨river bed, pond, etc.⟩ dry up; ⟨skin, hair⟩ become dry

**aus|üben** tr. V. practise ⟨art, craft⟩; follow ⟨profession⟩; carry on ⟨trade⟩; do ⟨job⟩; hold ⟨office⟩; wield ⟨power, right, control⟩

**Aus·verkauf** der sale

**ausverkauft** Adj. sold out

**Aus·wahl** die (a) choice
(b) (Sortiment) range; **viel/wenig ~ haben** have a wide/limited selection (**an** + Dat., **von** of)

**aus|wählen** tr. V. choose (**aus** from)

**Aus·wanderer** der, **Aus·wanderin** die emigrant

**aus|wandern** itr. V.; mit sein emigrate

**Aus·wanderung** die emigration

**auswärtig** Adj. (a) non-local
(b) (das Ausland betreffend) foreign

**auswärts** Adv. (a) (nach außen) outwards

(b) (nicht zu Hause) ⟨sleep⟩ away from home; **~ essen** eat out
(c) (nicht am Ort) in another town; (Sport) away

**Auswärts·spiel** das (Sport) away match

**aus|waschen** unr. tr. V. wash out

**aus|wechseln** tr. V. (a) change (**gegen** + Akk. for)
(b) (ersetzen) replace (**gegen** with); (Sport) substitute ⟨player⟩

**Aus·weg** der way out (**aus** of)

**ausweg·los** ① Adj. hopeless
② adv. hopelessly

**Ausweglosigkeit** die; ~: hopelessness

**aus|weichen** unr. itr. V.; mit sein get out of the way (Dat. of); (Platz machen) make way (Dat. for); **einem Schlag/Angriff ~:** dodge a blow/evade an attack; **dem Feind ~:** avoid [contact with] the enemy; **einer Frage ~:** evade a question; **eine ~de Antwort** an evasive answer

**Ausweich·manöver** das evasive manœuvre

**aus|weinen** refl. V. have a good cry; **sie hat sich bei mir darüber ausgeweint** (ugs.) she had a good cry on my shoulder about it

**Ausweis** der; ~es, ~e card; (Personalausweis) identity card

**aus|weisen** ① unr. tr. V. (a) expel (**aus** from)
(b) jmdn. als etw. ~: show that sb. is/was sth.
② unr. refl. V. prove or establish one's identity [by showing one's papers]; **können Sie sich ~?** do you have any means of identification?

**Ausweis·papiere** Pl. identity papers

**Aus·weisung** die expulsion (**aus** from)

**aus|weiten** tr. V. stretch

**aus·wendig** Adv. etw. ~ **können/lernen** know/learn sth. [off] by heart

**aus|werfen** unr. tr. V. (a) cast ⟨net, anchor, rope, line, etc.⟩
(b) (herausschleudern) throw out ⟨sparks⟩; ⟨volcano⟩ eject, spew out ⟨lava, ash, etc.⟩; eject ⟨cartridge case⟩

**aus|werten** tr. V. analyse and evaluate

**Aus·wertung** die analysis and evaluation

**aus|wirken** refl. V. have an effect (**auf** + Akk. on); **sich günstig ~:** have a favourable effect

**Aus·wirkung** die effect (**auf** + Akk. on)

**Aus·wuchs** der (a) (Wucherung) growth; excrescence (Med., Bot.)
(b) (fig.) unhealthy product; (Exzess) excess

**aus|wuchten** tr. V. (Technik) **die Räder ~:** balance the wheels

**aus|zahlen** ① tr. V. (a) pay out ⟨money⟩
(b) pay off ⟨employee, worker⟩; buy out ⟨business partner⟩
② refl. V. pay

**aus|zählen** tr. V. (a) count [up] ⟨votes etc.⟩
(b) (Boxen) count out

---

\*alte Schreibung - vgl. Hinweis auf S. xiv

**aus|zeichnen** *tr. V.* **(a)** (mit einem Preisschild) mark **(b)** (ehren) honour

**Aus·zeichnung** *die* **(a)** (von Waren) marking **(b)** (Ehrung) honouring; (Orden) decoration; (Preis) award

**aus|ziehen** ⒈ *unr. tr. V.* **(a)** pull out ‹couch›; extend ‹table, tripod, etc.› **(b)** (ablegen) take off ‹clothes› **(c)** (entkleiden) undress; **sich ~:** get undressed ⒉ *unr. itr. V.; mit sein* move out (**aus** of)

**Auszubildende** *der/die; adj. Dekl.* (bes. Amtsspr.) trainee; (im Handwerk) apprentice

**Aus·zug** *der* **(a)** (das Ausziehen) move **(b)** (Bankw.) statement **(c)** (Textpassage) extract

**auszugs·weise** *Adv.* in extracts *or* excerpts; **etw. ~ lesen** read extracts from sth.

**authentisch** *Adj.* authentic

**Autist** *der; ~en, ~en*, **Autistin** *die; ~, ~nen* autistic

**autistisch** *Adj.* (Med.) autistic

**Auto** *das; ~s, ~s* car; automobile (Amer.); **~ fahren** drive; (mitfahren) go in the car

**auto-, Auto-:** **~bahn** *die* motorway (Brit.); expressway (Amer.); **~biografie** /-----'-/ *die* autobiography; **~biografisch** /----'--/ *Adj.* autobiographical; **~bombe** *die* car bomb; **~bus** *der* ▶ BUS; **~dieb** *der,* **~diebin** *die* car thief; **~fähre** *die* car ferry; **~fahren** *das;* **~~s** driving; motoring; **~fahrer** *der,* **~fahrerin** *die* [car] driver; **~fahrt** *die* drive; **~gramm** /--'-/ *das;* **~~s, ~~e** autograph; **~kino** *das* drive-in cinema

**Automat** *der; ~en, ~en* **(a)** (Verkaufs~) [vending] machine; (Spiel~) slot machine **(b)** (in der Produktion) robot

**Automatik** *die; ~, ~en* automatic control mechanism; (Getriebeautomatik) automatic transmission

**automatisch** (auch fig.) ⒈ *Adj.* automatic ⒉ *adv.* automatically

**automatisieren** *tr. V.* automate

**Automatisierung** *die; ~, ~en* automation

**auto-, Auto-:** **~mobil** /---'-/ *das;* **~~s, ~~e** (geh.) motor car; automobile (Amer.); **~nom** /--'-/ ⒈ *Adj.* autonomous; ⒉ *adv.* autonomously; **~nomie** /---'-/ *die; ~~,* **~~n** autonomy; **~nummer** *die* [car] registration number; **~pilot** *der* (Flugw.) autopilot

**Autopsie** /autoˈpsiː/ *die; ~, ~n* post mortem [examination]

**Autor** *der; ~s, ~en* author

**Auto-:** **~radio** *das* car radio; **~reifen** *der* car tyre; **~reise·zug** *der* Motorail train (Brit.); auto train (Amer.); **~reparatur** *die* car repair; repair to the/a car

**Autorin** *die; ~, ~nen* authoress; author

**autoritär** *Adj.* authoritarian

**Autorität** *die; ~, ~en* authority

**Auto-:** **~schalter** *der* drive-in counter; **~schlange** *die* queue of cars; **~schlüssel** *der* car key; **~skooter** /-skuːtɐ/ *der;* **~~s, ~~:** dodgem; bumper car; **~stopp** *der* hitch-hiking; **per ~stopp fahren,** **~stopp machen** hitch-hike; **~telefon** *das* car telephone; **~tür** *die* car door; **~unfall** *der* car accident; **~vermietung** *die* car rental firm; **~wäsche** *die* car wash; **~werkstatt** *die* garage

**Avocado** /avoˈkaːdo/ *die; ~, ~s* avocado [pear]

**Axt** *die; ~, Äxte* axe

**Azalee** /atsaˈleːə/ *die; ~, ~n* azalea

**Azubi** *der; ~s, ~s/die; ~, ~s* (ugs.)
▶ AUSZUBILDENDE

# Bb

**b, B** /be:/ *das;* ~, ~ **(a)** (Buchstabe) b/B
**(b)** (Musik) [key of] B flat

**B** *Abk.* = **Bundesstraße** ≈ A (Brit.)

**Baby** /'be:bi/ *das;* ~s, ~s baby

**Baby·sitter** /'be:bɪsɪtɐ/ *der;* ~s, ~;
**Baby·sitterin** *die;* ~, ~: babysitter

**Bach** *der;* ~[e]s, Bäche **(a)** stream; brook
**(b)** (Rinnsal) stream [of water]

**Back·blech** *das* baking sheet

**Back·bord** *das* (Seew., Luftf.) port [side]

**Backe** *die;* ~, ~n cheek

**backen** 1 *unr. itr. V.* bake
2 *unr. tr. V.* **(a)** bake
**(b)** (bes. südd.) ▶ BRATEN

**Backen·zahn** *der* molar

**Bäcker** *der;* ~s, ~: baker; **er ist** ~: he is a
baker; **zum/beim** ~: to the/at the baker's

**Bäckerei** *die;* ~, ~en baker's [shop]

**Bäckerin** *die;* ~, ~nen baker

**Back-:** ~**fisch** *der* fried fish (*in
breadcrumbs*); ~**form** *die* baking tin (Brit.);
baking pan (Amer.); ~**hähnchen** *das,*
~**hen** *das* (österr.), ~**huhn** *das* fried
chicken (*in breadcrumbs*); ~**ofen** *der* oven;
~**pulver** *das* baking powder; ~**stein** *der*
brick; ~**waren** *Pl.* bread, cakes, and
pastries

**Bad** *das;* ~[e]s, Bäder **(a)** bath; (das
Schwimmen) swim; (im Meer usw.) bathe; **ein** ~
**nehmen** (geh.) take a bath; (schwimmen) go for
a swim; (im Meer usw.) bathe
**(b)** (Badezimmer) bathroom; **ein Zimmer mit** ~:
a room with [private] bath
**(c)** (Schwimm~) [swimming] pool
**(d)** (Heil~) spa; (See~) [seaside] resort

**Bade-:** ~**anzug** *der* bathing costume;
~**hose** *die* bathing trunks *pl.;* ~**mantel**
*der* dressing gown; bathrobe; ~**meister**
*der,* ~**meisterin** *die* swimming-pool
attendant; ~**mütze** *die* bathing cap

**baden** 1 *itr. V.* **(a)** have a bath
**(b)** (schwimmen) bathe; ~ **gehen** go for a
bathe
2 *tr. V.* bath ⟨*child, patient, etc.*⟩; bathe
⟨*wound, eye, etc.*⟩

**Baden-Württemberg** (*das*); ~s Baden-
Württemberg

**Bäder** ▶ BAD

**Bade-:** ~**strand** *der* bathing beach;
~**tuch** *das; Pl.* ~**tücher** bath towel;
~**wanne** *die* bath[tub]; ~**wasser** *das*
bath water; ~**zimmer** *das* bathroom

**Badminton** *das;* ~s badminton

**Bagatelle** *die;* ~, ~n trifle

**Bagger** *der;* ~s, ~: excavator;
(Schwimmbagger) dredger

**Bagger·see** *der* flooded gravel pit

**Bahn** *die;* ~, ~en **(a)** (Weg) path
**(b)** (Route) path; (eines Geschosses) trajectory
**(c)** (Sport) track; (für Pferderennen) course (Brit.);
track (Amer.); (für einzelne Teilnehmer) lane;
(Kegel~) alley; (Bowling~) lane
**(d)** (Eisen~) railways *pl.;* railroad (Amer.);
(Zug) train; **jmdn. zur** ~ **bringen** take sb. to
the station; [**mit der**] ~ **fahren** go by train
**(e)** (Straßen~) tram; streetcar (Amer.)

**bahn-, Bahn-:** ~**beamte** *der,*
~**beamtin** *die* railway *or* (Amer.) railroad
official; ~**brechend** *Adj.* pioneering;
~**brecher** *der,* ~**brecherin** *die;* ~~,
~~**nen** pioneer; ~**bus** *der* railway bus;
~**damm** *der* railway embankment

**bahnen** *tr. V.* clear ⟨*way, path*⟩; **jmdm./einer
Sache einen Weg** ~ (fig.) pave the way for
sb./sth.

**Bahn-:** ~**fahrt** *die* train journey; ~**hof**
*der* [railway *or* (Amer.) railroad] station;
~**reise** *die* train journey; ~**schranke**
*die* level crossing (Brit.) *or* (Amer.) grade
crossing barrier/gate; ~**steig** *der;* ~~[e]s,
~~**e** [station] platform; ~**übergang** *der*
level crossing (Brit.); grade crossing (Amer.);
~**verbindung** *die* train connection

**Bahre** *die;* ~, ~n **(a)** (Trage) stretcher
**(b)** (Totenbahre) bier

**Baiser** /bɛ'ze:/ *das;* ~s, ~s meringue

**Bajonett** *das;* ~[e]s, ~e bayonet

**Bakterie** /bak'te:rjə/ *die;* ~, ~n bacterium

**Balance** /ba'laŋsə/ *die;* ~, ~n balance

**balancieren** *itr., tr. V.; itr. mit sein*
balance

**bald** *Adv.* **(a)** soon; (leicht, rasch) quickly;
easily; **wirds** ~? get a move on, will you; **bis**
~! see you soon
**(b)** (ugs.: fast) almost

**Baldrian** /'baldria:n/ *der;* ~s, ~e valerian

**Balkan** /'balka:n/ *der;* ~s: **der** ~: the
Balkans *pl.;* (Gebirge) the Balkan Mountains
*pl.* **auf dem** ~: in the Balkans

**Balken** *der;* ~s, ~: beam

**Balkon** /bal'kɔŋ, bal'ko:n/ *der;* ~s, ~s
/bal'kɔŋs/ *od.* ~e /bal'ko:nə/ **(a)** balcony
**(b)** (im Theater, Kino) circle

**Ball** *der;* ~[e]s, Bälle **(a)** ball; ~ **spielen** play
ball
**(b)** (Fest) ball

**Ballade** *die;* ~, ~n ballad

**Ballast** *der;* ~[e]s, ~e ballast

**Ballast·stoffe** *Pl.* (Med.) roughage *sing.*
**ballen** ① *tr. V.* clench ⟨*fist*⟩
② *refl. V.* ⟨*fist*⟩ clench
**Ballen** *der;* ~s, ~ (a) (Packen) bale
(b) (Hand-, Fußballen) ball
**Ballerina** *die;* ~, Ballerinen ballerina
**Ballett** *das;* ~[e]s, ~e ballet
**Ballett-:** ~**schuh** *der* ballet shoe;
~**schule** *die* ballet school; ~**tänzer** *der,*
~**tänzerin** *die* ballet dancer
**Ball-:** ~**junge** *der* ballboy; ~**kleid** *das*
ball gown
**Ballon** /ba'lɔŋ/ *der;* ~s, ~s balloon
**Ball-:** ~**saal** *der* ballroom; ~**spiel** *das*
ball game; ~**spielen** *das;* ~~s playing
ball *no art.*
**Ballungs·gebiet** *das* conurbation
**Balsam** *der;* ~s, ~e balsam; (fig.) balm
**Balte** *der;* ~n, ~n, **Baltin** *die;* ~, ~nen
Balt
**Baltikum** *das;* ~s Baltic States *pl.*
**baltisch** *Adj.* Baltic
**Bambus** *der;* ~ *od.* ~ses, ~se bamboo
**banal** *Adj.* (a) banal
(b) (gewöhnlich) commonplace
**Banane** *die;* ~, ~n banana
**Banause** *der;* ~n, ~n, **Banausin** *die;* ~,
~nen (abwertend) philistine
**band** *1. u. 3. Pers. Sg. Prät. v.* BINDEN
**Band¹** *das;* ~[e]s, Bänder (a) (Haar~,
Hut~) band; (Schürzen~) string
(b) (Klebe~, Isolier~, Ton~ usw.) tape; **etw. auf**
~ ⟨*Akk.*⟩ **aufnehmen** tape[-record] sth.
(c) ▶ FÖRDERBAND;
(d) ▶ FLIESSBAND;
(e) **am laufenden** ~ (ugs.) nonstop
(f) (Anat.) ligament
**Band²** *der;* ~[e]s, Bände /'bɛndə/ volume
**Band³** /bɛnt/ *die;* ~, ~s band; (Beat~,
Rock~ usw.) group
**Bande¹** *die;* ~, ~n (a) gang
(b) (ugs.: Gruppe) mob (coll.)
**Bande²** *die;* ~, ~n (Sport) [perimeter]
barrier; (mit Reklame) billboards *pl.;* (Billard)
cushion
**Banden-:** ~**krieg** *der* gang war;
~**werbung** *die:* advertising on hoardings
around the perimeter of a football pitch etc.
**Bänder** ▶ BAND¹
**Bänder-:** ~**riss,** *\**~**riß** *der* (Med.) torn
ligament; ~**zerrung** *die* (Med.) pulled
ligament
**bändigen** *tr. V.* tame ⟨*animal*⟩; control
⟨*person, anger, urge*⟩
**Bandit** *der;* ~en, ~en bandit
**Band·scheibe** *die* [intervertebral] disc
**bang, bange**; banger, bangst... *od.*
bänger, bängst...: ① *Adj.* afraid; scared;
(besorgt) anxious; **mir ist/wurde** ~ [**zumute**] I
am/became scared
② *adv.* anxiously
**bangen** *itr. V.* be anxious

**Bank¹** *die;* ~, Bänke bench; (mit Lehne)
bench seat; (Kirchen~) pew; **etw. auf die lange**
~ **schieben** (ugs.) put sth. off
**Bank²** *die;* ~, ~en bank
**Bankett¹** *das;* ~[e]s, ~e banquet
**Bankett²** *das;* ~[e]s, ~e (an Straßen)
shoulder; (unbefestigt) verge
**Bank·geheimnis** *das* (Wirtsch.) bankers'
duty to maintain confidentiality
**Bankier** /baŋ'kie:/ *der;* ~s, ~s banker
**Bank-:** ~**kauffrau** *die,* ~**kaufmann**
*der* [qualified] bank/building society/stock
market clerk; ~**konto** *das* bank account;
~**leit·zahl** *die* [bank] sort code; ~**note**
*die* banknote; bill (Amer.); ~**raub** *der* bank
robbery; ~**räuber** *der,* ~**räuberin** *die*
bank robber
**bankrott** *Adj.* bankrupt; **Bankrott** *od.* \*~
**gehen** go bankrupt
**Bankrott** *der;* ~[e]s, ~e bankruptcy; ~
**machen** go bankrupt; *s. auch* BANKROTT
**Bankrott·erklärung** *die* declaration of
bankruptcy; (fig.) declaration of [one's own]
failure
**Bank-:** ~**überfall** *der* bank raid;
~**verbindung** *die* particulars of one's
bank account; ~**wesen** *das* banking
system
**Bann** *der;* ~[e]s (fig. geh.) spell
**bar** ① *Adj.* cash
② *adv.* in cash; **etw.** [**in**] ~ **bezahlen** pay for
sth. in cash; pay cash for sth.
**Bar** *die;* ~, ~s bar
**Bär** *der;* ~en, ~en bear
**Baracke** *die;* ~, ~n hut
**Barbar** *der;* ~en, ~en barbarian
**Barbarei** *die;* ~, ~en (a) (Rohheit)
barbarity
(b) (Kulturlosigkeit) barbarism *no indef. art.*
**Barbarin** *die;* ~, ~nen barbarian
**barbarisch** ① *Adj.* (a) (roh) barbarous
(b) (unzivilisiert) barbaric
② *adv.* (a) (roh) barbarously
(b) (unzivilisiert) barbarically
**Bar·dame** *die* barmaid
**bären-, Bären-:** ~**dienst** *der:* jmdm.
**einen** ~**dienst erweisen** do sb. a disservice;
~**hunger** *der* (ugs.) ~**hunger haben/**
**kriegen** be famished (coll.) *or* starving (coll.)/
get famished (coll.) *or* ravenous (coll.);
~**stark** *Adj.* as strong as an ox *postpos.*
**Barett** *das;* ~[e]s, ~e (eines Geistlichen)
biretta; (eines Richters, Professors) cap;
(Baskenmütze) beret
**bar·fuß** *indekl. Adj.; nicht attr.* barefooted;
~ **herumlaufen/gehen** run about/go barefoot
**barg** *1. u. 3. Pers. Sg. Prät. v.* BERGEN
**bar-, Bar-:** ~**geld** *das* cash; ~**geld·los**
*Adj.* cashless; ~**hocker** *der* bar stool
**Bariton** /'ba(:)ritɔn/ *der;* ~s, ~e baritone
**Barkasse** *die;* ~, ~n launch
**barmherzig** (geh.) ① *Adj.* merciful    ⋯✦

**b**

2 *adv.* mercifully

**Barmherzigkeit** *die;* ~ (geh.) mercy

**Barock** *das od. der;* ~[s] (a) baroque
(b) (Zeit) baroque age

**Baro·meter** *das* barometer

**Baron** *der;* ~s, ~e baron; (als Anrede) [**Herr**]
~: ≈ my lord

**Baronin** *die;* ~, ~nen baroness; (als Anrede)
[**Frau**] ~: ≈ my Lady

**Barren** *der;* ~s, ~ (a) (Gold~, Silber~ usw.)
bar
(b) (Turngerät) parallel bars *pl.*

**Barriere** /ba'rie:rə/ *die;* ~, ~n (auch fig.)
barrier

**Barrikade** *die;* ~, ~n barricade

**barsch** 1 *Adj.* curt
2 *adv.* curtly

**Barsch** *der;* ~[e]s, ~e perch

**barst** *1. u. 3. Pers. Sg. Prät. v.* BERSTEN

**Bart** *der;* ~[e]s, Bärte (a) beard; (Oberlippen~,
Schnurr~) moustache
(b) (von Katzen, Mäusen, Robben) whiskers *pl.;*
(c) (am Schlüssel) bit

**Barten·wal** *der* (Zool.) whalebone whale

**bärtig** *Adj.* bearded

**Bart·wuchs** *der* growth of beard

**Bar-:** ~zahlung *die* cash payment;
~zahlungs·rabatt *der* cash discount

**Basalt** *der;* ~[e]s, ~e basalt

**Basar** *der;* ~s, ~e bazaar

**Basis** *die;* ~, Basen (a) (Grundlage) basis
(b) (Math., Archit., Milit.) base

**Baske** *der;* ~n, ~n Basque

**Basken-:** ~land *das* Basque region;
~mütze *die* beret

**Baskin** *die;* ~, ~nen Basque

**Basket·ball** /'ba(:)skət-/ *der* basketball

**Bass, \*Baß** *der;* Basses, Bässe (Musik) (a)
bass
(b) (Instrument) double bass

**Bassin** /ba'sɛ̃/ *das;* ~s, ~s (Schwimmbecken)
pool; (im Garten) pond

**Bassist** *der;* ~en, ~en (Musik) (a) (Sänger)
bass
(b) (Instrumentalist) double-bass player; bassist;
(in einer Rockband) bass guitarist

**Bassistin** *die;* ~, ~nen ▶ BASSIST B

**Bast** *der;* ~[e]s, ~e bast; (Raffia~) raffia

**basta** *Interj.* (ugs.) that's enough; **und damit**
~**!** and that's that!

**Bastelei** *die;* ~, ~en; (a) (Gegenstand) piece
of handicraft work
(b) (ugs.: das Basteln) handicraft work

**basteln** 1 *tr. V.* make
2 *itr. V.* make things [with one's hands]

**Bastion** *die;* ~, ~en bastion

**bat** *1. u. 3. Pers. Sg. Prät. v.* BITTEN

**Bataillon** /batal'joːn/ *das;* ~s, ~e (Milit.)
battalion

**Batik** *der;* ~s, ~en *od. die;* ~, ~en batik

**Batist** *der;* ~[e]s, ~e batiste

**Batterie** *die;* ~, ~n battery

**batterie-, Batterie-:** ~betrieb *der*
battery operation; ~betrieben *Adj.*
battery-operated; ~huhn *das* battery
chicken; (Henne) battery hen

**Batzen** *der;* ~s, ~ (ugs.) (a) (Klumpen) lump
(b) (Menge) pile (coll.)

**Bau**[1] *der;* ~[e]s, ~ten (a) (Errichtung)
building; **im ~ sein** be under construction
(b) (Gebäude) building
(c) **auf dem ~ arbeiten** (Bauarbeiter sein) be in
the building trade
(d) (Struktur) structure

**Bau**[2] *der;* ~[e]s, ~e (Kaninchenbau) burrow;
hole; (Fuchsbau) earth

**Bau·arbeiten** *Pl.* building work *sing.*

**Bauch** *der;* ~[e]s, Bäuche (auch fig.: von
Schiffen, Flugzeugen) belly

**bauchig** *Adj.* bulbous

**Bauch-:** ~laden *der* vendor's tray;
~landung *die* belly landing; ~nabel *der*
(ugs.) belly button (coll.); ~redner *der,*
~rednerin *die* ventriloquist;
~schmerzen *Pl.* stomach ache *sing.;*
~speichel·drüse *die* pancreas; ~tanz
*der* belly dance; ~tänzerin *die* belly
dancer; ~weh *das* (ugs.) tummy ache (coll.);
stomach ache

**Bau·denkmal** *das* architectural
monument

**bauen** 1 *tr. V.* build
2 *itr. V.* (a) build; **wir wollen ~:** we want to
build a house; (bauen lassen) we want to have
a house built
(b) **auf jmdn./etw. ~** (fig.) rely on sb./sth.

**Bauer**[1] *der;* ~n, ~n (a) farmer; (mit niedrigem
sozialem Status) peasant
(b) (Schachfigur) pawn
(c) (Kartenspiele) ▶ BUBE

**Bauer**[2] *das od. der;* ~s, ~: [bird]cage

**Bäuerin** *die;* ~, ~nen (a) ▶ BAUER[1] A:
[lady] farmer; peasant [woman]
(b) (Frau eines Bauern) farmer's wife

**bäuerlich** *Adj.* farming *attrib.;* (ländlich)
rural

**Bauern-:** ~haus *das* farmhouse; ~hof
*der* farm

**bau-, Bau-:** ~fällig *Adj.* ramshackle;
unsafe ⟨roof, ceiling⟩; ~fälligkeit *die* bad
state of dilapidation; badly dilapidated state;
~herr *der,* ~herrin *die* client (*for whom a
house etc. is being built*); ~jahr *das* year of
construction; (bei Autos) year of manufacture;
~kasten *der* construction set; (mit
Holzklötzen) box of bricks;
~kasten·system *das* unit construction
system; ~klotz *der* building brick; ~kran
*der* construction crane

**baulich** *Adj.* structural

**Baum** *der;* ~[e]s, Bäume tree

**Bau-:** ~markt *der* (Kaufhaus) DIY

hypermarket; **~maschine** *die* piece of construction plant *or* machinery; **~maschinen** construction plant *sing. or* machinery

**Bäumchen** *das;* ~s, ~ small tree

**Bau·meister** *der* (hist.) [architect and] master builder

**baumeln** *itr. V.* (ugs.) dangle (**an** + *Dat.* from)

**Baum-:** **~schule** *die* tree nursery; **~stamm** *der* tree trunk; **~sterben** *das;* **~~s,** **~~:** dying-off of trees; **~stumpf** *der* tree stump; **~wolle** *die* cotton

**Bau·platz** *der* site for building

**bäurisch** (abwertend) [1] *Adj.* boorish [2] *adv.* boorishly

**Bau·satz** *der* kit

**Bausch** *der;* ~[e]s, ~e *od.* Bäusche (a) (Watte~) a wad (b) etw. in ~ und Bogen verwerfen/ verdammen reject/condemn sth. wholesale

**bauschen** [1] *tr. V.* billow 〈*sail, curtains, etc.*〉 [2] *refl. V.* 〈*dress, sleeve*〉 puff out; (ungewollt) bunch up; (im Wind) 〈*curtain, flag, etc.*〉 billow [out]

**bauschig** *Adj.* puffed 〈*dress*〉; baggy 〈*trousers*〉

**bau-, Bau-:** **~sparen** *itr. V.; nur Inf. gebr.* save with a building society; **~sparkasse** *die* building society; **~stein** *der* (a) building stone; (b) (Bestandteil) element; (Elektronik, DV) module; (c) (~klotz) building brick; **~stelle** *die* building site; (beim Straßenbau) roadworks *pl.*; **~stoff** *der* building material; **~teil** *das* component

**Bauten** *Pl.:* ▶ BAU

**Bau-:** **~unternehmer** *der,* **~unternehmerin** *die* building contractor; **~weise** *die* method of construction; **~werk** *das* building; (Brücke, Staudamm) structure; **~wirtschaft** *die* building *or* construction industry

**Bayer** *der;* ~n, ~n **Bayerin** *die;* ~, ~nen Bavarian

**bay[e]risch** *Adj.* Bavarian

**Bayern** (*das*); ~s Bavaria

**Bazille** *die;* ~, ~n (ugs.) ▶ BAZILLUS A

**Bazillus** *der;* ~, Bazillen (a) bacillus (b) (fig.) cancer

**Bd.** *Abk.* = **Band** Vol.

**beabsichtigen** *tr. V.* intend

**beachten** *tr. V.* (a) follow 〈*rule, regulations, instruction*〉; heed, follow 〈*advice*〉; obey 〈*traffic signs*〉; observe 〈*formalities*〉 (b) (berücksichtigen) take account of; (achten auf) pay attention to

**beachtlich** [1] *Adj.* considerable [2] *adv.* considerably

**Beachtung** *die;* ~ (a) ▶ BEACHTEN A: following; heeding; obeying

(b) (Berücksichtigung) consideration (c) (Aufmerksamkeit) attention

**Beamte** *der; adj. Dekl.* official; (Staats~) [permanent] civil servant; (Kommunal~) [established] local government officer; (Polizei~) [police] officer

**Beamtin** *die;* ~, ~nen ▶ BEAMTE

**beängstigend** *Adj.* worrying

**beanspruchen** *tr. V.* (a) claim; etw. ~ können be entitled to expect sth. (b) (ausnutzen) make use of 〈*person, equipment*〉; take advantage of 〈*hospitality, services*〉 (c) (erfordern) demand 〈*energy, attention, stamina*〉; take up 〈*time, space, etc.*〉

**Beanspruchung** *die;* ~, ~en demands *pl.* (Gen. on); die ~ durch den Beruf the demands of his/her job

**beanstanden** *tr. V.* take exception to; (sich beklagen über) complain about

**Beanstandung** *die;* ~, ~en complaint

**beantragen** *tr. V.* apply for

**beantworten** *tr. V.* answer; reply to 〈*letter*〉; return 〈*greeting*〉

**bearbeiten** *tr. V.* (a) deal with; handle 〈*case*〉 (b) edit 〈*text, document*〉 (c) (adaptieren) adapt (**für** for)

**Bearbeitung** *die;* ~, ~en (a) die ~ eines Antrags/eines Falles *usw.* dealing with an application/handling a case *etc.;* (b) (Adaption) adaptation

**beaufsichtigen** *tr. V.* supervise; look after 〈*child*〉

**beauftragen** *tr. V.* entrust

**bebauen** *tr. V.* build on; develop

**bebaut** *Adj.* ein [dicht] ~es Gebiet a densely built-up area; ein ~es Gelände a developed site

**Bebauung** *die;* ~, ~en (a) development (b) (Gebäude) buildings *pl.*

**beben** *itr. V.* shake

**Beben** *das;* ~s, ~ ▶ ERDBEBEN

**bebildern** *tr. V.* illustrate

**Bebilderung** *die;* ~, ~en illustrations *pl.*

**Becher** *der;* ~s, ~ (Glas~, Porzellan~) glass; tumbler; (Plastik~) beaker; cup; (Eis~) (aus Glas, Metall) sundae dish; (aus Pappe) tub; (Joghurt~) carton

**Becken** *das;* ~s, ~ (a) (Wasch~) basin; (Abwasch~) sink; (Toiletten~) pan (b) (Anat.) pelvis (c) *Pl.* (Musik) cymbals

**bedacht** *Adj.* auf etw. (*Akk.*) ~ sein be intent on sth.

**bedächtig** [1] *Adj.* (a) deliberate; measured 〈*steps, stride, speech*〉 (b) (besonnen) thoughtful; well-considered 〈*words*〉 [2] *adv.* (a) deliberately (b) (besonnen) thoughtfully

**bedanken** refl. V. say thank you; **sich bei jmdm. [für etw.]** ~: thank sb. [for sth.]

**Bedarf** der; ~[e]s need (**an** + Dat. of); requirement (**an** + Dat. for); (Bedarfsmenge) needs pl.; requirements pl.; **bei** ~: if required

**bedauerlich** Adj. regrettable

**bedauerlicher·weise** Adv. regrettably

**bedauern** tr., itr. V. (a) feel sorry for; **sie lässt sich gerne** ~: she likes being pitied (b) (schade finden) regret; **ich bedaure sehr, dass** ...: I am very sorry that ...

**Bedauern** das; ~s regret; **zu meinem** ~: to my regret

**bedauerns·wert** Adj. (geh.) unfortunate 〈person〉

**bedecken** tr. V. cover

**bedeckt** Adj. overcast 〈sky〉

**bedenken** unr. tr. V. (a) consider (b) (beachten) take into consideration

**Bedenken** das; ~s, ~ reservation (gegen about); **ohne** ~: without hesitation

**bedenken·los** [1] Adj. unhesitating; (skrupellos) unscrupulous [2] adv. without hesitation; (skrupellos) unscrupulously

**bedenklich** [1] Adj. (a) dubious 〈methods, transactions, etc.〉 (b) (bedrohlich) alarming [2] adv. alarmingly

**Bedenk·zeit** die time for reflection

**bedeuten** tr. V. (a) mean; **was soll das** ~? what does that mean? (b) (sein) represent; **das bedeutet ein Wagnis** that is being really daring

**bedeutend** [1] Adj. (a) significant; important (b) (groß) substantial; considerable 〈success〉 [2] adv. considerably

**Bedeutung** die; ~, ~en (a) meaning (b) (Wichtigkeit) importance

**bedeutungs-:** ~**los** Adj. insignificant; ~**voll** [1] Adj. (a) significant; (b) (viel sagend) meaningful; meaning 〈look〉; [2] adv. meaningfully

**bedienen** [1] tr. V. (a) serve; **werden Sie schon bedient?** are you being served? (b) (handhaben) operate 〈machine〉 [2] itr. V. serve [3] refl. V. help oneself; **sich selbst** ~ (im Geschäft, Restaurant usw.) serve oneself

**Bedienstete** der/die; adj. Dekl. (Amtsspr.) employee

**Bedienung** die; ~, ~en (a) (das Bedienen) service; ~ **inbegriffen** service included (b) (das Handhaben) operation (c) (Servierer[in]) waiter/waitress

**Bedienungs·anleitung** die operating instructions pl.

**bedingen** tr. V. cause

**Bedingung** die; ~, ~en condition; **unter der** ~, **dass** ...: on condition that ...

**bedingungs·los** Adj. unconditional

**bedrängen** tr. V. (a) besiege 〈town, fortress, person〉; put 〈opposing player〉 under pressure (b) (belästigen) pester

**Bedrängnis** die; ~, ~se (geh.) (innere Not) distress; (wirtschaftliche Not) [great] difficulties pl.; **in** ~ **geraten/sein** get into/be in great difficulties pl.

**bedrohen** tr. V. threaten

**bedrohlich** [1] Adj. (Unheil verkündend) ominous; (gefährlich) dangerous [2] adv. (Unheil verkündend) ominously; (gefährlich) dangerously

**Bedrohlichkeit** die; ~: dangerousness; (einer Krankheit usw.) dangerous nature

**Bedrohung** die threat (Gen. to)

**bedrucken** tr. V. print

**bedrücken** tr. V. depress

**Beduine** der; ~n, ~n, **Beduinin** die; ~, ~nen Bed[o]uin

**bedürfen** unr. itr. V. **jmds./einer Sache** ~ (geh.) require or need sb./sth.

**Bedürfnis** das; ~ses, ~se need (**nach** for); **das** ~ **haben, etw. zu tun** feel a need to do sth.

**bedürfnislos** Adj. 〈person〉 with few [material] needs; modest, simple 〈life〉; ~ **sein** have few [material] needs

**Bedürfnislosigkeit** die; ~: lack of [material] needs

**bedürftig** Adj. needy

**Beef·steak** /'bi:f-/ das [beef]steak; **deutsches** ~: ≈ beefburger

**beehren** tr. V. (geh.) honour

**beeiden** tr. V. ~, **dass** ...: swear [on oath] that ...; **eine Aussage** ~: swear to the truth of a statement

**beeilen** refl. V. hurry [up (coll.)]

**beeindrucken** tr. V. impress

**beeindruckend** Adj. impressive

**beeinflussen** tr. V. influence

**Beeinflussung** die; ~, ~en influencing

**beeinträchtigen** tr. V. restrict 〈sights, freedom〉; detract from 〈pleasure, enjoyment, value〉; spoil 〈appetite, good humour〉; impair 〈quality, reactions, efficiency, vision, hearing〉; damage, harm 〈sales, reputation〉

**Beeinträchtigung** die; ~, ~en ▶ BEEINTRÄCHTIGEN: restriction; detracting (+ Gen. from); spoiling; impairment; damage (Gen. to)

**beenden, beendigen** tr. V. (a) end; finish 〈piece of work etc.〉; complete 〈studies〉 (b) (DV) quit 〈program〉

**beengen** tr. V. hinder, restrict 〈movements〉; (fig.) restrict 〈freedom [of action]〉; **beengt wohnen** live in cramped surroundings or conditions; **sich beengt fühlen** feel cramped

**beerben** tr. V. jmdn. ~: inherit sb.'s estate

**beerdigen** tr. V. bury

**Beerdigung** die; ~, ~en burial; (Trauerfeier) funeral

**Beerdigungs-institut** das [firm sing. of] undertakers pl.

**Beere** die; ~, ~n berry

**Beet** das; ~[e]s, ~e (Blumenbeet) bed; (Gemüsebeet) plot

**befahrbar** Adj. passable

**befahren** unr. tr. V. (a) drive on ⟨road⟩; drive across ⟨bridge⟩; use ⟨railway line⟩; **die Straße ist stark/wenig ~:** the road is heavily/little used; **eine stark ~e Straße** a busy road
(b) sail ⟨sea⟩; navigate, sail up/down ⟨river, canal⟩

**befallen** unr. tr. V. (a) overcome; ⟨misfortune⟩ befall; **von Panik/Angst ~ werden** be seized with panic/fear
(b) ⟨pests⟩ attack

**befangen** [1] Adj. (a) self-conscious ⟨person⟩
(b) (voreingenommen) biased
[2] adv. self-consciously

**Befangenheit** die; ~ (a) self-consciousness
(b) (Voreingenommenheit) bias

**befassen** refl. V. sich mit etw. ~: occupy oneself with sth.; ⟨article, book⟩ deal with sth.; (etw. studieren) study sth.

**Befehl** der; ~[e]s, ~e (a) order
(b) den ~ über jmdn./etw. haben be in command of sb./sth.

**befehlen** [1] unr. tr., itr. V. order; (Milit.) order; **man befahl ihm zu warten** he was told to wait
[2] unr. itr. V. über jmdn./etw. ~: have command of or be in command of sb./sth.

**Befehls·haber** der; ~s, ~ (Milit.) commander

**befestigen** tr. V. (a) fix; **etw. an der Wand ~:** fix sth. to the wall
(b) (haltbar machen) stabilize ⟨bank, embankment⟩; make up ⟨road, path, etc.⟩
(c) (sichern) fortify ⟨town etc.⟩; strengthen ⟨border⟩

**Befestigung** die; ~, ~en (a) fixing
(b) (Milit.) fortification

**befeuchten** tr. V. moisten; damp ⟨hair, cloth⟩

**befiehlst, befiehlt** 2., 3. Pers. Sg. Präsens v. BEFEHLEN

**befinden** unr. refl. V. be

**Befinden** das; ~s health; (eines Patienten) condition

**befindlich** Adj.(a) to be found postpos.; **das in der Kasse ~e Geld** the money in the till
(b) (in einem Zustand) **die im Bau ~en Häuser** the houses [which are/were] under construction

**Befindlichkeit** die; ~, ~en (geh.) state

**beflecken** tr. V. stain

**befohlen** 2. Part. v. BEFEHLEN

**befolgen** tr. V. follow, obey ⟨instruction, grammatical rule⟩; obey, comply with ⟨law, regulation⟩; follow ⟨advice, suggestion⟩

**Befolgung** die; ~ ▶ BEFOLGEN: following; obedience (Gen. to); compliance (Gen. with)

**befördern** tr. V. (a) carry; transport
(b) (aufrücken lassen) promote

**Beförderung** die; ~, ~en (a) carriage; transport; (von Personen) transport
(b) (das Aufrückenlassen) promotion

**befragen** tr. V. (a) question (über + Akk. about)
(b) (konsultieren) ask

**Befragung** die; ~, ~en (a) questioning
(b) (Konsultation) consultation
(c) (Umfrage) opinion poll

**befreien** [1] tr. V. (a) free; liberate ⟨country, people⟩ (von from)
(b) (freistellen) exempt (von from)
(c) jmdn. von Schmerzen ~: free sb. of pain
[2] refl. V. free oneself (von from)

**Befreier** der, **Befreierin** die; ~, ~nen liberator

**Befreiung** die; ~ (a) ▶ BEFREIEN 1A: freeing; liberation
(b) (Freistellung) exemption
(c) die ~ von Schmerzen release from pain

**befremden** tr. V. jmdn. ~: put sb. off

**Befremden** das; ~s surprise and displeasure

**befremdlich** (geh.) [1] Adj. strange; odd
[2] adv. strangely

**befreunden** refl. V. ▶ ANFREUNDEN; [gut od. eng] befreundet sein be [good or close] friends (mit with)

**befriedigen** tr. V. (a) satisfy; gratify ⟨lust⟩
(b) (ausfüllen) ⟨job, occupation, etc.⟩ fulfil
(c) (sexuell) satisfy; **sich [selbst] ~:** masturbate

**befriedigend** [1] Adj. satisfactory
[2] adv. satisfactorily

**Befriedigung** die; ~ (a) ▶ BEFRIEDIGEN A: satisfaction; gratification
(b) (Genugtuung) satisfaction

**befristet** Adj. temporary ⟨visa⟩; fixed-term ⟨ban, contract⟩

**befruchten** tr. V. fertilize ⟨egg⟩; pollinate ⟨flower⟩; impregnate ⟨female⟩; **ein Tier künstlich ~:** artificially inseminate an animal

**Befruchtung** die; ~, ~en ▶ BEFRUCHTEN: fertilization; pollination; impregnation; **künstliche ~:** artificial insemination

**Befugnis** die; ~, ~se authority

**befühlen** tr. V. feel

**Befund** der (bes. Med.) result[s pl.]

**befürchten** tr. V. fear; **ich befürchte, dass ...:** I am afraid that ...

**befürworten** tr. V. support

**begabt** *Adj.* talented; gifted; **hoch** ~: highly talented *or* gifted

**Begabung** *die;* ~, ~**en** talent; gift

**begann** *1. u. 3. Pers. Sg. Prät. v.* BEGINNEN

**begatten** *tr. V.* mate with; ‹*man*› copulate with; **sich** ~: mate; ‹*persons*› copulate

**Begattung** *die;* ~, ~**en** mating; (bei Menschen) copulation

**begeben** *unr. refl. V.* (geh.) proceed; make one's way; go; **sich zu Bett** ~: retire to bed; **sich an die Arbeit** ~: commence work

**Begebenheit** *die;* ~, ~**en** (geh.) event; occurrence

**begegnen** *itr. V.; mit sein* jmdm. ~: meet sb.; **sich** (*Dat.*) ~: meet [each other]

**Begegnung** *die;* ~, ~**en** (a) meeting (b) (Sport) match

**begehen** *unr. tr. V.* (a) commit ‹*crime, adultery, indiscretion, sin, suicide, faux-pas, etc.*›; make ‹*mistake*›; **eine [furchtbare] Dummheit** ~: do something [really] stupid (b) (geh.: feiern) celebrate

**begehren** *tr. V.* desire

**begehrens·wert** *Adj.* desirable

**begehrlich** ⓵ *Adj.* greedy
⓶ *adv.* greedily

**begehrt** *Adj.* much sought-after

**begeistern** ⓵ *tr. V.* jmdn. [für etw.] ~: fire sb. with enthusiasm [for sth.]
⓶ *refl. V.* get enthusiastic (**für** about)

**begeisternd** *Adj.* rousing

**begeistert** ⓵ *Adj.* enthusiastic (**von** about)
⓶ *adv.* enthusiastically

**Begeisterung** *die;* ~: enthusiasm

**begeisterungs-, Begeisterungs-:**
~**fähig** *Adj.* ‹*children, people, etc.*› who are able to get enthusiastic *or* are capable of enthusiasm; ~**fähigkeit** *die* capacity for enthusiasm; ~**sturm** *der* storm of enthusiastic applause

**Begierde** *die;* ~, ~**n** desire (**nach** for)

**begierig** ⓵ *Adj.* eager
⓶ *adv.* eagerly

**begießen** *unr. tr. V.* water ‹*plants*›

**Beginn** *der;* ~**[e]s** beginning; [**gleich**] **zu** ~: [right] at the beginning

**beginnen** ⓵ *unr. itr. V.* start; begin; **mit dem Bau** ~: start *or* begin building; **dort beginnt der Wald** the forest starts there
⓶ *unr. tr. V.* start; begin; start ‹*argument*›; ~, **etw. zu tun** start to do sth.

**beglaubigen** *tr. V.* certify

**Beglaubigung** *die;* ~, ~**en** certification

**begleichen** *unr. tr. V.* settle ‹*bill, debt*›; pay ‹*sum*›

**Begleit·brief** *der* covering *or* accompanying letter

**begleiten** *tr. V.* accompany; **jmdn. nach Hause** ~: see sb. home

**Begleiter** *der;* ~**s**, ~, **Begleiterin** *die;* ~, ~**nen** companion; (zum Schutz) escort; (Führer[in]) guide

**Begleitung** *die;* ~, ~**en** (a) **er bot uns seine** ~ **an** he offered to accompany us; **in** ~ **eines Erwachsenen** accompanied by an adult (b) (Musik) accompaniment

**beglückwünschen** *tr. V.* congratulate (**zu** on)

**begnadet** *Adj.* (geh.) divinely gifted

**begnadigen** *tr. V.* pardon; reprieve

**Begnadigung** *die;* ~, ~**en** reprieving; (Straferlass) pardon; reprieve

**begnügen** *refl. V.* content oneself

**Begonie** /be'go:njə/ *die;* ~, ~**n** begonia

**begonnen** *2. Part. v.* BEGINNEN

**begraben** *unr. tr. V.* bury

**Begräbnis** *das;* ~**ses**, ~**se** burial; (~feier) funeral

**begreifen** ⓵ *unr. tr. V.* understand; **er konnte nicht** ~, **was geschehen war** he could not grasp what had happened
⓶ *itr. V.* understand; **schnell** *od.* **leicht/langsam** *od.* **schwer** ~: be quick/slow on the uptake

**begreiflich** *Adj.* understandable

**begrenzen** *tr. V.* limit, restrict (**auf** + *Akk.* to)

**Begriff** *der* (a) concept; (Terminus) term (b) (Auffassung) idea; **sich** (*Dat.*) **keinen** ~ **von etw. machen können** not be able to imagine sth.; **ein/kein** ~ **sein** be/not be well known (c) **im** ~ **sein** *od.* **stehen, etw. zu tun** be about to do sth.

**begriffs·stutzig** *Adj.* (abwertend) obtuse

**Begriffsstutzigkeit** *die;* ~ (abwertend) obtuseness

**begründen** *tr. V.* (a) give reasons for (b) (gründen) found; establish ‹*fame, reputation*›

**Begründer** *der;* ~**s**, ~, **Begründerin** *die;* ~, ~**nen** founder

**begründet** *Adj.* well-founded; reasonable ‹*demand, objection, complaint*›

**Begründung** *die;* ~, ~**en** reason[s]; **mit der** ~, **dass ...**: on the grounds that ...

**begrüßen** *tr. V.* (a) greet; ‹*hostess, host*› welcome (b) (fig.) welcome

**Begrüßung** *die;* ~, ~**en** greeting; (von Gästen) welcoming; (Zeremonie) welcome (*Gen.* for)

**begünstigen** *tr. V.* favour

**Begünstigung** *die;* ~: favouring

**begutachten** *tr. V.* (a) examine and report on (b) (ugs.) have a look at

**Begutachtung** *die;* ~, ~**en** examination

**begütert** *Adj.* wealthy

**begütigen** *tr. V.* placate

**behaart** *Adj.* hairy; **stark** ~ **sein** be covered with hair; **stark** ~**e Beine** very hairy legs

---

**behäbig** [1] *Adj.* slow and ponderous
[2] *adv.* slowly and ponderously
**behagen** *itr. V.* etw. behagt jmdm. sb. likes
sth.
**Behagen** *das;* ~s pleasure
**behaglich** [1] *Adj.* comfortable
[2] *adv.* comfortably
**Behaglichkeit** *die;* ~: comfortableness
**behalten** *unr. tr. V.* **(a)** keep; etw. für sich
~: keep sth. to oneself
**(b)** (zurück~) be left with ⟨scar, defect, etc.⟩
**(c)** (sich merken) remember
**Behälter** *der;* ~s, ~ container; (für Abfälle)
receptacle
**behämmert** *Adj.* (salopp) ▶ BEKLOPPT
**behänd, behände** [1] *Adj.* (geschickt) deft;
(flink) nimble
[2] *adv.* s. *Adj.*: deftly; nimbly
**behandeln** *tr. V.* (auch Med.) treat; handle
⟨matter, machine, device⟩; deal with ⟨subject,
question etc.⟩
**Behandlung** *die;* ~, ~en treatment
**behängen** *tr. V.* hang
**beharren** *itr. V.* auf etw. (Dat.) ~ (etw. nicht
aufgeben) persist in sth.; (auf etw. bestehen)
insist on sth.
**beharrlich** [1] *Adj.* dogged
[2] *adv.* doggedly
**Beharrlichkeit** *die;* ~: doggedness
**behauen** *unr. tr. V.* hew
**behaupten** [1] *tr. V.* **(a)** maintain; assert;
~, jmd. zu sein/etw. zu wissen claim to be
sb./know sth.; **man behauptet** *od.* **es wird
behauptet, dass** ...: it is said *or* claimed that
...
**(b)** (verteidigen) maintain ⟨position⟩; retain
⟨record⟩
[2] *refl. V.* **(a)** assert oneself; (nicht untergehen)
hold one's ground; (dableiben) survive
**(b)** (Sport) win through
**Behauptung** *die;* ~, ~en assertion
**Behausung** *die;* ~, ~en dwelling
**beheben** *unr. tr. V.* remove ⟨danger,
difficulty⟩; repair ⟨damage⟩; remedy ⟨abuse,
defect⟩
**Behebung** *die;* ~, ~en ▶ BEHEBEN:
removal; repair; remedying
**beheimatet** *Adj.* an einem Ort/in einem
Land *usw.* ~ sein be native to a place/to a
country *etc.*
**beheizbar** *Adj.* heatable; eine ~e
Heckscheibe a heated rear window
**beheizen** *tr. V.* heat
**behelfen** *unr. refl. V.* make do
**behelfs·mäßig** [1] *Adj.* makeshift
[2] *adv.* in a makeshift way
**behelligen** *tr. V.* bother; (zudringlich werden
gegen) pester
***behend, *behende** ▶ BEHÄND, BEHÄNDE
**beherbergen** *tr. V.* accommodate
**beherrschen** [1] *tr. V.* **(a)** control; rule
⟨country, people⟩

**(b)** (meistern) control ⟨vehicle, animal⟩; be in
control of ⟨situation⟩
**(c)** (bestimmen, dominieren) dominate
⟨townscape, landscape, discussions⟩
**(d)** (zügeln) control ⟨feelings⟩; control, curb
⟨impatience⟩
**(e)** (gut können) have mastered ⟨instrument,
trade⟩; have a good command of ⟨language⟩
[2] *refl. V.* control oneself
**beherrscht** [1] *Adj.* self-controlled
[2] with self-control
**Beherrschung** *die;* ~ **(a)** control; (eines
Volks, Landes usw.) rule
**(b)** (das Meistern) control
**(c)** (Beherrschtheit) self-control
**(d)** (das Können) mastery
**beherzigen** *tr. V.* take ⟨sth.⟩ to heart
**beherzt** [1] *Adj.* spirited
[2] *adv.* spiritedly
**behilflich** *Adj.* [jmdm.] ~ sein help [sb.]
(bei with)
**behindern** *tr. V.* **(a)** hinder; impede
⟨movement⟩; hold up ⟨traffic⟩
**(b)** (Sport, Verkehrsw.) obstruct
**behindert** *Adj.* handicapped
**Behinderte** *der/die; adj. Dekl.*
handicapped person; die ~n the
handicapped; WC für ~: toilet for disabled
persons
**Behinderung** *die;* ~, ~en **(a)** hindrance
**(b)** (Sport, Verkehrsw.) obstruction
**(c)** (Gebrechen) handicap
**Behörde** *die;* ~, ~n authority; (Amt,
Abteilung) department
**behördlich** [1] *Adj.* official
[2] *adv.* officially
**behüten** *tr. V.* protect (vor + Dat. from);
(bewachen) guard
**behutsam** [1] *Adj.* careful
[2] *adv.* carefully
**bei** *Präp. mit Dat.* **(a)** (nahe) near; (dicht an,
neben) by; wer steht da ~ ihm? who is
standing there with him?; etw. ~ sich haben
have sth. with *or* on one; sich ~ jmdm.
entschuldigen apologize to sb.
**(b)** (unter) among; war heute ein Brief für
mich ~ der Post? was there a letter for me
in the post today?
**(c)** (an) by; jmdn. ~ der Hand nehmen take
sb. by the hand
**(d)** (im Wohn-/Lebens-/Arbeitsbereich von); ~ uns
tut man das nicht we don't do that; ~ mir
[zu Hause] at my house; ~ uns um die Ecke/
gegenüber round the corner from us/
opposite us; ~ seinen Eltern leben live with
one's parents; wir sind ~ ihr eingeladen we
have been invited to her house; wir treffen
uns ~ uns/Peter we'll meet at our/Peter's
place; ~ uns in der Firma in our company;
~ Schmidt (auf Briefen) c/o Schmidt; ~ einer
Firma sein be with a company; ~ jmdm./
einem Verlag arbeiten work for sb./a
publishing house
**(e)** (im Bereich eines Vorgangs) at; ~ einer ····❯

**b**

Hochzeit/einem Empfang *usw.* be at a wedding/reception *etc.;* ~ einem Unfall in an accident

**(f)** (im Werk von) ~ **Goethe** in Goethe

**(g)** (im Falle von) in the case of; **wie** ~ **den Römern** as with the Romans; ~ **der Hauskatze** in the domestic cat

**(h)** (modal) ~ **Tag/Nacht** by day/night; ~ **Tageslicht** by daylight; ~ **Nebel** in fog

**(i)** (im Falle des Auftretens von) „~ **Nässe Schleudergefahr"** 'slippery when wet'

**(j)** (angesichts) with; ~ **dieser Hitze** in this heat; ~ **deinen guten Augen/ihrem Talent** with your good eyesight/her talent

**(k)** (trotz) ~ **all seinem Engagement/seinen Bemühungen** in spite of *or* despite *or* for all his commitment/efforts

**bei|behalten** *unr. tr. V.* keep; retain; keep up ⟨*custom, habit*⟩; keep to ⟨*course, method*⟩; preserve, maintain ⟨*way of life; attitude*⟩

**bei|bringen** *unr. tr. V.* **(a)** jmdm. etw. ~: teach sb. sth.

**(b)** (ugs.: mitteilen) jmdm. ~, **dass** ...: break it to sb. that ...

**(c)** (zufügen) jmdm./sich etw. ~: inflict sth. on sb./oneself

**Beichte** *die;* ~, ~n confession *no def. art.*

**beichten** ① *itr. V.* confess

② *tr. V.* (auch fig.) confess

**Beicht-:** ~**stuhl** *der* confessional; ~**vater** *der* father confessor

**beid...** *Indefinitpron. u. Zahlw.* ① *Pl.* ~e both; (der/die/das eine oder der/die/das andere) either *sing.;* **die** ~**en** the two; **die/seine** ~**en Brüder** the/his two brothers; **die** ~**en ersten Strophen** the first two verses; **kennst du die** ~**en?** do you know those two?; **alle** ~**e** both of us/you/them; **ihr/euch** ~**e** you two; **ihr/euch** ~**e nicht** neither of you; **wir/uns** ~**e** the two of us/both of us; **er hat** ~**e Eltern verloren** he has lost both [his] parents; **mit** ~**en Händen** with both hands; **ich habe** ~**e gekannt** I knew both of them; **einer/eins von** ~**en** one of the two; **keiner/keins von** ~**en** neither [of them]

② *Neutr. Sg.;* ~**es** both *pl.;* (das eine oder das andere) either; ~**es ist möglich** either is possible; **ich glaube** ~**es/**~**es nicht** I believe both things/neither thing; **das ist** ~**es nicht richtig** neither of those is correct

**beiderlei** *indekl. Adj.* ~ **Geschlechts** of both sexes

**beider·seits** ① *Präp. mit Gen.* on both sides of

② *Adv.* on both sides

**bei·einander** *Adv.* together; ~ **Trost suchen** seek comfort from each other

**Bei·fahrer** *der,* **Bei·fahrerin** *die* **(a)** passenger

**(b)** (berufsmäßig) co-driver; (im LKW) driver's mate

*old spelling - see note on page xiv

**Beifahrer·sitz** *der* passenger seat; (eines Motorrads) pillion

**Bei·fall** *der* **(a)** applause

**(b)** (Zustimmung) approval

**bei·fällig** ① *Adj.* approving

② *adv.* approvingly

**beige** /beːʃ/ *Adj.* beige

**Beige** /beːʃ/ *das;* ~, ~ *od.* (ugs.) ~s beige

**Bei·geschmack** *der:* einen bitteren *usw.* ~ haben have a slightly bitter *etc.* taste [to it]

**Bei·hilfe** *die* **(a)** aid; (Zuschuss) allowance

**(b)** (Rechtsw.: Mithilfe) aiding and abetting

**bei|kommen** *unr. itr. V.; mit sein* **(a)** (gewachsen sein) jmdm. ~: get the better of sb.

**(b)** (bewältigen) den Schwierigkeiten/der Unruhe/jmds. Sturheit ~: overcome the difficulties/deal with the unrest/cope with sb.'s obstinacy

**Beil** *das;* ~[e]s, ~e axe; (kleiner) hatchet

**Bei·lage** *die* **(a)** (Zeitungs~) supplement

**(b)** (zu Speisen) side dish; (Gemüse) vegetables *pl.*

**bei·läufig** ① *Adj.* casual

② *adv.* casually

**bei|legen** *tr. V.* **(a)** enclose

**(b)** (schlichten) settle ⟨*dispute etc.*⟩

**Bei·leid** *das* sympathy; [mein] herzliches *od.* aufrichtiges ~! please accept my sincere condolences

**bei|liegen** *unr. itr. V.* einem Brief ~: be enclosed with a letter

**bei·liegend** *Adj.* enclosed; ~ **senden wir** ...: please find enclosed ...

**beim** *Präp. + Art.* **(a)** = bei dem;

**(b)** ~ **Film sein** be in films

**(c)** **er will** ~ **Arbeiten nicht gestört werden** he doesn't want to be disturbed when working; ~ **Duschen sein** be taking a shower

**bei|messen** *unr. tr. V.* attach

**Bein** *das;* ~[e]s, ~e leg; jmdm. ein ~ stellen trip sb.; (fig.) put *or* throw a spanner *or* (Amer.) a monkey wrench in sb.'s works; **wieder auf den** ~**en sein** be back on one's feet again

**bei·nah[e]** *Adv.* almost

**Bei·name** *der* epithet

**Bein·bruch** *der:* das ist [doch] kein ~ (ugs.) it's not the end of the world

**beinhalten** *tr. V.* (Papierdt.) involve

**-beinig** *adj.* -legged

**bei|pflichten** *itr. V.* agree (*Dat.* with)

**bei·rren** *tr. V.* sich durch nichts/von niemandem ~ **lassen** not be deterred by anything/anybody

**beisammen** *Adv.* together

**beisammen|haben** *unr. tr. V.* **(a)** have got together

**(b)** **er hat** [sie] **nicht alle beisammen** (ugs.) he's not all there (coll.)

**Beisammen·sein** *das* get-together

**Bei·schlaf** *der* sexual intercourse

**Bei·sein** *das;* in jmds. ~: in the presence of sb. *or* in sb.'s presence

**bei·seite** *Adv.* aside

**Beis[e]l** *das;* ~s, ~ *od.* ~n (österr.) pub (Brit.); bar (Amer.)

**bei|setzen** *tr. V.* lay to rest; inter ⟨ashes⟩

**Bei·setzung** *die;* ~, ~en funeral; burial

**Bei·spiel** *das* example (für of); zum ~: for example; mit gutem ~ vorangehen set a good example

**beispielhaft** *Adj.* exemplary

**beispiel·los** *Adj.* unparalleled

**beispiels·weise** *Adv.* for example

**beißen** ① *unr. tr., itr. V.* (auch fig.) bite ② *unr. refl. V.* (ugs.) ⟨colours, clothes⟩ clash

**beißend** *Adj.* biting ⟨cold⟩; acrid ⟨smoke, fumes⟩; sharp ⟨frost⟩

**Beiß·zange** *die* ▶ KNEIFZANGE

**Bei·stand** *der* (geh.: Hilfe) aid

**bei|stehen** *unr. itr. V.* jmdm. ~: aid sb.

**bei|steuern** *tr. V.* contribute

**Beitrag** *der;* ~[e]s, Beiträge contribution; (Versicherungsbeitrag) premium; (Mitgliedsbeitrag) subscription

**bei|tragen** *unr. tr., itr. V.* contribute (zu to)

**bei|treten** *unr. itr. V.; mit sein* join ⟨union, club, etc.⟩; einem Abkommen/Pakt accede to ⟨pact, agreement⟩

**Bei·tritt** *der* joining

**Bei·wagen** *der* sidecar

**Bei·werk** *das* accessories *pl.*

**bei|wohnen** *itr. V.* einer Sache (*Dat.*) ~ (geh.) be present at sth.

**Beize** *die;* ~, ~n (Holzbearb.) [wood]stain

**beizeiten** *Adv.* in good time

**beizen** *tr. V.* (Holzbearb.) stain

**bejahen** /bə'ja:ən/ *tr. V.* (a) auch itr. answer ⟨sth.⟩ in the affirmative (b) (gutheißen) approve of; das Leben ~: have a positive *or* an affirmative attitude to life

**Bejahung** *die;* ~, ~en (a) affirmative reply (b) (das Gutheißen) approval

**bejammern** *tr. V.* lament

**bejubeln** *tr. V.* cheer; acclaim

**bekämpfen** *tr. V.* (a) fight against (b) combat ⟨disease, epidemic, pest, unemployment, crime, etc.⟩

**Bekämpfung** *die;* ~ (a) fight (*Gen.* against) (b) ▶ BEKÄMPFEN B: combating

**bekannt** *Adj.* (a) well-known; etw. ~ geben announce sth.; etw. ~ machen announce sth.; (der Öffentlichkeit) make sth. public; ~ werden become known; es ist nichts davon ~: nothing is known concerning it (b) jmd./etw. ist jmdm. ~: sb. knows sb./sth.; Darf ich ~ machen? Meine Eltern may I introduce my parents?

**Bekannte** *der/die; adj. Dekl.* acquaintance

**Bekannt·gabe** *die;* ~: announcement

***bekannt|geben** ▶ BEKANNT A

**bekanntlich** *Adv.* as is well known; etw. ist ~ der Fall sth. is known to be the case

***bekannt|machen** ▶ BEKANNT A

**Bekannt·machung** *die;* ~, ~en announcement

**Bekanntschaft** *die;* ~, ~en acquaintance

***bekannt|werden** ▶ BEKANNT A

**bekehren** ① *tr. V.* convert ② *refl. V.* become converted

**Bekehrung** *die;* ~, ~en (auch fig.) conversion (zu to)

**bekennen** ① *unr. tr. V.* (a) confess; ~, dass ... admit that ... (b) (Rel.) profess ② *refl. V.* sich zum Islam ~: profess Islam; sich zu Buddha ~: profess one's faith in Buddha; sich zu seiner Schuld ~: confess one's guilt; sich schuldig/nicht schuldig ~: confess/not confess one's guilt; (vor Gericht) plead guilty/not guilty

**Bekenntnis** *das;* ~ses, ~se (a) confession (b) (Eintreten) ein ~ zum Frieden a declaration for peace (c) (Konfession) denomination

**bekiffen** *refl. V.* (ugs.) get stoned (sl.)

**bekifft** *Adj.* (ugs.) stoned

**beklagen** ① *tr. V.* (geh.) (a) (betrauern) mourn (b) (bedauern) lament ② *refl. V.* complain

**bekleckern** *tr. V.* (ugs.) etw./sich [mit Soße usw.] ~: drop *or* spill sauce *etc.* down sth./oneself

**bekleiden** *tr. V.* (a) clothe; mit etw. bekleidet sein be wearing sth. (b) (geh.: innehaben) occupy ⟨office, position⟩

**Bekleidung** *die;* ~, ~en clothing; clothes *pl.*

**beklemmend** *Adj.* oppressive

**Beklemmung** *die;* ~, ~en oppressive feeling

**beklommen** *Adj.* uneasy; (stärker) apprehensive

**bekloppt** *Adj.* (salopp) barmy (Brit. coll.); loony (coll.)

**beknackt** *Adj.* (salopp) lousy (coll.); ein ~er Typ a berk (Brit. coll.); a jerk (coll.)

**beknien** *tr. V.* (ugs.) beg

**bekommen** ① *unr. tr. V.* (a) get; get, receive ⟨money, letter, reply, news, orders⟩; (erreichen) catch ⟨train, bus, flight⟩; was ~ Sie? (im Geschäft) can I help you?; (im Lokal, Restaurant) what would you like?; was ~ Sie [dafür]? how much is that?; Hunger/Durst ~: get hungry/thirsty; Angst/Mut ~: become frightened/take heart; er bekommt einen Bart he's growing a beard; sie bekommt eine ···❖

Brust her breasts are developing; **Zähne** ~: ⟨baby⟩ teethe; **sie bekommt ein Kind** she's expecting a baby
**(b) etw. durch die Tür/ins Auto** ~: get sth. through the door/into the car
② *unr. V.; in der Funktion eines Hilfsverbs zur Umschreibung des Passivs* get; **etw. geschenkt** ~: get [given] sth. *or* be given sth. as a present
③ *unr. itr. V.; mit sein* **jmdm. gut** ~: do sb. good; **jmdm. [gut]** ~ ⟨food, medicine⟩ agree with sb.; **wohl bekomms!** your [very good] health!

**bekömmlich** *Adj.* easily digestible

**beköstigen** *tr. V.* cater for

**bekräftigen** *tr. V.* reinforce ⟨statement⟩; reaffirm ⟨promise⟩

**bekreuzigen** *refl. V.* (kath. Kirche) cross oneself

**bekriegen** *tr. V.* wage war on; (fig.) fight; **sich** ~: be at war; (fig.) fight

**bekümmern** *tr. V.* **jmdn.** ~: cause sb. worry

**bekümmert** *Adj.* worried; (stärker) distressed

**bekunden** *tr. V.* express

**belächeln** *tr. V.* smile [pityingly/tolerantly etc.] at

**beladen** *unr. tr. V.* load ⟨ship⟩; load [up] ⟨car, wagon⟩; load up ⟨horse, donkey⟩

**Belag** *der;* ~[e]s, **Beläge (a)** coating
**(b)** (Fußbodenbelag) covering; (Straßenbelag) surface; (Bremsbelag) lining
**(c)** (von Kuchen, Scheibe Brot usw.) topping; (von Sandwiches) filling

**belagern** *tr. V.* (auch fig.) besiege

**Belagerung** *die;* ~, ~en siege; (fig.) besieging

**Belang** *der;* ~[e]s, ~e **(a) von/ohne** ~ **sein** be of importance/of no importance
**(b)** *Pl.* (Interessen) interests

**belangen** *tr. V.* (Rechtsw.) sue; (strafrechtlich) prosecute

**belang·los** *Adj.* (trivial) trivial; (unerheblich) of no importance (**für** for)

**Belanglosigkeit** *die;* ~, ~en unimportance; (Trivialität) triviality

**belassen** *unr. tr. V.* leave

**belastbar** *Adj.* tough, resilient ⟨person⟩; **seelisch/körperlich** ~ **sein** be emotionally/physically tough *or* resilient; be able to stand emotional/physical stress; **ein** ~**er Mitarbeiter** an employee who can work under pressure

**Belastbarkeit** *die;* ~, ~n toughness; resilience; (von Mitarbeitern) ability to work under pressure

**belasten** *tr. V.* **(a) etw.** ~: put sth. under strain; (durch Gewicht) put weight on sth.
**(b)** (beeinträchtigen) pollute ⟨atmosphere⟩; put pressure on ⟨environment⟩

**(c)** (in Anspruch nehmen) burden (**mit** with)
**(d)** **jmdn.** ~ ⟨responsibility, guilt⟩ weigh upon sb.; ⟨thought⟩ weigh upon sb.'s mind
**(e)** (Rechtsw.) incriminate
**(f)** (Geldw.) **jmds. Konto mit 100 Euro** ~: debit sb.'s account with 100 euros

**belästigen** *tr. V.* bother; (sehr aufdringlich) pester; (sexuell) molest

**Belästigung** *die* ▶ BELÄSTIGEN: bothering; pestering; molestation

**Belastung** *die;* ~, ~en **(a)** strain; (das Belasten) straining; (durch Gewicht) loading; (Last) load
**(b) die** ~ **der Atmosphäre/Umwelt durch Schadstoffe** the pollution of the atmosphere by harmful substances/the pressure on the environment caused by harmful substances
**(c)** (Bürde, Sorge) burden

**Belastungs-:** ~**EKG** *das* (Med.) electrocardiogram after effort; ~**zeuge** *der,* ~**zeugin** *die* (Rechtsw.) witness for the prosecution

**belaufen** *unr. refl. V.* **sich auf ...** (Akk.) ~: come to ...

**belauschen** *tr. V.* eavesdrop on

**beleben** ① *tr. V.* enliven; stimulate ⟨economy⟩
② *refl. V.* ⟨market, economic activity⟩ revive, pick up

**belebend** ① *Adj.* invigorating
② *adv.* ~ **wirken** have an invigorating effect

**belebt** *Adj.* busy ⟨street, crossing, town, etc.⟩

**Beleg** *der;* ~[e]s, ~e (Beweisstück) piece of [supporting] documentary evidence; (Quittung) receipt

**belegen** *tr. V.* **(a)** (Milit.: beschießen) bombard; (mit Bomben) attack
**(b)** (mit Belag versehen) cover ⟨floor⟩ (**mit** with); fill ⟨flan base, sandwich⟩; top ⟨open sandwich⟩; **eine Scheibe Brot mit Käse** ~: put some cheese on a slice of bread
**(c)** (in Besitz nehmen) occupy ⟨seat, room, etc.⟩
**(d)** (Hochschulw.) enrol for ⟨seminar, lecture course⟩
**(e) den ersten/letzten Platz** ~ (Sport) take first place/come last
**(f)** (nachweisen) prove; give a reference for ⟨quotation⟩

**Belegschaft** *die;* ~, ~en staff

**belegt** *Adj.* **(a) ein** ~**es Brot** an open *or* (Amer.) openface sandwich; (zugeklappt) a sandwich; **ein** ~**es Brötchen** a roll with topping; an open-face roll (Amer.); (zugeklappt) a filled roll; a sandwich roll (Amer.)
**(b)** (mit Belag bedeckt) furred ⟨tongue, tonsils⟩
**(c)** (heiser) husky ⟨voice⟩
**(d)** (nicht mehr frei) ⟨room, flat⟩ occupied

**belehren** *tr. V.* teach; instruct; (aufklären) enlighten; (informieren) inform; **ich lasse mich gern** ~: I'm quite willing to believe otherwise

**Belehrung** *die;* ~, ~en instruction; (Zurechtweisung) lecture

**beleibt** *Adj.* (geh.) portly

**beleidigen** *tr. V.* insult

**beleidigt** *Adj.* insulted; (gekränkt) offended

**Beleidigung** *die;* ~, ~en (a) insult (b) (Rechtsw.) (schriftlich) libel; (mündlich) slander

**belesen** *Adj.* well-read

**beleuchten** *tr. V.* light up; light ⟨stairs, room, street, etc.⟩

**Beleuchtung** *die;* ~, ~en lighting; (Anstrahlung) illumination

**beleumdet** *Adj.* übel/gut ~ sein have a bad/good reputation

**Belgien** /'bɛlgiən/ *(das);* ~s Belgium

**Belgier** *der;* ~s, ~, **Belgierin** *die;* ~, ~nen Belgian

**belgisch** *Adj.* Belgian

**belichten** *tr. V.* (Fot.) expose; *itr.* richtig/falsch/kurz ~: use the right/wrong exposure/a short exposure time

**Belichtung** *die* (Fot.) exposure

**Belieben** *das;* ~s: nach ~: just as you/they *etc.* like

**beliebig** [1] *Adj.* any [2] *adv.* as you like/he likes *etc.;* ~ lange/viele as long/many as you like/he likes *etc.*

**beliebt** *Adj.* popular; favourite *attrib.*

**Beliebtheit** *die;* ~: popularity

**beliefern** *tr. V.* supply

**bellen** *itr. V.* bark

**Belletristik** /bɛle'trɪstɪk/ *die;* ~: belles-lettres *pl.*

**belohnen** *tr. V.* reward ⟨person, thing⟩

**Belohnung** *die;* ~, ~en reward

**belüften** *tr. V.* ventilate

**Belüftung** *die* ventilation

**belügen** *unr. tr. V.* lie to

**belustigen** *tr. V.* amuse

**Belustigung** *die;* ~, ~en amusement

**bemächtigen** *refl. V.* sich jmds./einer Sache ~ (geh.) seize sb./sth.

**bemalen** *tr. V.* paint; (verzieren) decorate

**bemängeln** *tr. V.* find fault with

**bemerkbar** *Adj.* sich ~ machen attract attention [to oneself]; (erkennbar werden) become apparent; (spürbar werden) make itself felt

**bemerken** *tr. V.* (a) (wahrnehmen) notice; ich wurde nicht bemerkt I was unobserved (b) (äußern) remark

**bemerkenswert** [1] *Adj.* remarkable [2] *adv.* remarkably

**Bemerkung** *die;* ~, ~en (a) (Äußerung) remark; comment (b) (Notiz) note; (Anmerkung) comment

**bemitleiden** *tr. V.* pity; feel sorry for

**bemitleidens·wert** *Adj.* pitiable

**bemogeln** *tr. V.* (ugs.) cheat; diddle (Brit. coll.)

**bemühen** *refl. V.* make an effort; sich ~, etw. zu tun endeavour to do sth.; sich um

etw. ~: try to obtain sth.; sich um eine Stelle ~: try to get a job; sich um jmdn. ~ (kümmern) seek to help sb.

**Bemühung** *die;* ~, ~en effort

**benachbart** *Adj.* neighbouring *attrib.*

**benachrichtigen** *tr. V.* notify (von of)

**Benachrichtigung** *die;* ~, ~en notification

**benachteiligen** *tr. V.* put at a disadvantage; (diskriminieren) discriminate against; die sozial benachteiligten Schichten the underprivileged classes

**Benachteiligte** *der/die; adj. Dekl.* disadvantaged person; die ~n the disadvantaged; those at a disadvantage; die sozial ~n the underprivileged; the socially deprived

**benehmen** *unr. refl. V.* behave

**Benehmen** *das;* ~s behaviour; kein ~ haben have no manners *pl.*

**beneiden** *tr. V.* envy; jmdn. um etw. ~: envy sb. sth.

**beneidens·wert** *Adj.* enviable

**Benelux·länder** *Pl.* Benelux countries

**benennen** *unr. tr. V.* name

**Bengel** *der;* ~s, ~ od. (nordd.) ~s (a) (abwertend: junger Bursche) young rascal (b) (fam.: kleiner Junge) little lad

**benommen** *Adj.* dazed; (durch Fieber, Alkohol) muzzy

**benoten** *tr. V.* mark (Brit.); grade (Amer.); einen Test mit „gut" ~: mark a test 'good' (Brit.); assign a grade of 'good' to a test (Amer.)

**benötigen** *tr. V.* need; require

**benutzen** *tr. V.* use

**Benutzer** *der;* ~s, ~: user

**benutzer·freundlich** *Adj.* user-friendly

**Benutzerin** *die;* ~, ~nen user

**Benutzung** *die;* ~: use

**Benzin** *das;* ~s petrol (Brit.); gasoline (Amer.); gas (Amer. coll.); (Wasch~) benzine

**Benzol** *das;* ~s, ~e (Chemie) benzene

**beobachten** *tr. V.* observe; watch

**Beobachter** *der;* ~s, ~, **Beobachterin** *die;* ~, ~nen observer

**Beobachtung** *die;* ~, ~en observation

**bepacken** *tr. V.* load

**bepflanzen** *tr. V.* plant

**bequem** [1] *Adj.* (a) comfortable (b) (abwertend: träge) idle [2] *adv.* (a) comfortably (b) (leicht) easily

**bequemen** *refl. V.* sich dazu ~, etw. zu tun (geh.) condescend to do sth.

**Bequemlichkeit** *die;* ~ (a) comfort (b) (Trägheit) idleness

**berappen** *tr., itr. V.* (ugs.) ▶ BLECHEN

**beraten** [1] *unr. tr. V.* (a) advise; jmdn. gut/schlecht ~: give sb. good/bad advice (b) (besprechen) discuss ⟨plan, matter⟩ ⋯⟶

**b**

2 *unr. itr. V.* über etw. (*Akk.*) ∼: discuss sth.

3 *unr. refl. V.* sich mit jmdm. ∼, ob ...: discuss with sb. whether ...

**Berater** *der;* ∼s, ∼, **Beraterin** *die;* ∼, ∼nen adviser

**beratschlagen** 1 *tr. V.* discuss
2 *itr. V.* über etw. (*Akk.*) ∼: discuss sth.

**Beratung** *die;* ∼, ∼en (a) advice *no indef. art.;* (durch Arzt, Rechtsanwalt) consultation
(b) (Besprechung) discussion

**berauben** *tr. V.* (auch fig.) rob (*Gen.* of)

**berauschen** (geh.) 1 *tr. V.* (auch fig.) intoxicate
2 *refl. V.* become intoxicated (**an** + *Dat.* with)

**Berber** *der;* ∼s, ∼(a) Berber
(b) (Teppich) Berber carpet/rug
(c) (Nichtsesshafter) tramp

**Berberin** *die;* ∼, ∼nen ▶ BERBER A, C

**berechenbar** *Adj.* calculable; predictable (*behaviour*)

**Berechenbarkeit** *die;* ∼: calculability; (des Verhaltens) predictability

**berechnen** *tr. V.* (a) (auch fig.) calculate; predict (*behaviour, consequences*)
(b) (anrechnen) charge; jmdm. 10 Euro für etw. *od.* jmdm. etw. mit 10 Euro ∼: charge sb. 10 euros for sth.; jmdm. zu viel ∼: overcharge sb.

**Berechnung** *die;* ∼, ∼en (a) calculation
(b) (Eigennutz) [calculating] self-interest

**berechtigen** *tr. V.* entitle; *itr.* die Karte **berechtigt zum Eintritt** the ticket entitles the bearer to admission

**berechtigt** *Adj.* (a) (gerechtfertigt) justified
(b) (befugt) authorized

**Berechtigung** *die;* ∼, ∼en (a) (Befugnis) entitlement; (Recht) right
(b) (Rechtmäßigkeit) legitimacy

**bereden** *tr. V.* (a) (besprechen) discuss
(b) jmdn. ∼, etw. zu tun talk sb. into doing sth.

**beredsam** *Adj.* eloquent

**Beredsamkeit** *die;* ∼: eloquence

**beredt** *Adj.* (auch fig.) eloquent

**Bereich** *der;* ∼[e]s, ∼e area; **im privaten/ staatlichen** ∼: in the private/public sector

**bereichern** *refl. V.* get rich

**Bereicherung** *die;* ∼, ∼en (a) money-making
(b) (Nutzen) valuable acquisition

**bereifen** *tr. V.* put tyres on (*car*); put a tyre on (*wheel*)

**Bereifung** *die;* ∼, ∼en [set *sing.* of] tyres *pl.*

**bereinigen** *tr. V.* clear up (*misunderstanding*); settle, resolve (*dispute*)

**bereisen** *tr. V.* travel around *or* about;

travel through (*towns*); (beruflich) (*representative etc.*) cover (*area*); **fremde Länder** ∼: travel in foreign countries

**bereit** *Adj.* ready; ∼ **sein**, etw. zu tun be ready *or* willing to do sth.

**bereiten** *tr. V.* (a) prepare; make (*tea, coffee*)
(b) (verursachen) cause (*trouble, sorrow, difficulty, etc.*)

**bereit-:** ∼|**halten** *unr. tr. V.* have ready; ∼|**legen** *tr. V.* lay out ready; ∼|**liegen** *unr. itr. V.* be ready

**bereits** *Adv.* already

**Bereitschaft** *die;* ∼: readiness; willingness

**Bereitschafts-dienst** *der:* ∼ haben (*doctor, nurse*) be on call; (*policeman, fireman*) be on standby duty; (*chemist's*) be on rota duty (*for dispensing outside normal hours*)

**bereit-:** ∼|**stehen** *unr. itr. V.* be ready; ∼|**stellen** *tr. V.* place ready; get ready (*food, drinks*); ready, make (*money, funds*) available; ∼**willig** 1 *Adj.* willing. 2 *adv.* readily

**Bereitwilligkeit** *die;* ∼: willingness

**bereuen** 1 *tr. V.* regret
2 *itr. V.* be sorry; (Rel.) repent

**Berg** *der;* ∼[e]s, ∼e (a) hill; (im Hochgebirge) mountain
(b) (Haufen) huge pile; (von Akten, Abfall auch) mountain

**berg-, Berg-:** ∼**ab** /-'-/ *Adv.* downhill; ∼**auf** /-'-/ *Adv.* uphill; ∼**bahn** die mountain railway; (Seilbahn) mountain cableway; ∼**bau** *der* mining

**bergen** *unr. tr. V.* (a) rescue, save (*person*); salvage (*ship, cargo, belongings*)
(b) (geh.: enthalten) hold

**Berg-:** ∼**führer** *der,* ∼**führerin** *die;* ∼∼, ∼∼nen mountain guide; ∼**hütte** *die* mountain hut

**bergig** *Adj.* hilly; (mit hohen Bergen) mountainous

**Berg-:** ∼**kette** die range *or* chain of mountains; mountain range *or* chain; ∼**kristall** *der* rock crystal; ∼**land** *das* hilly country *no indef. art;* (mit hohen Bergen) mountainous country *no indef. art.;* ∼**mann** *der; Pl.* ∼**leute** miner; ∼**station** *die* top station; ∼**steigen** *das;* ∼∼s mountaineering *no art.;* ∼**steiger** *der,* ∼**steigerin** *die;* ∼∼, ∼∼nen mountaineer

**Bergung** *die;* ∼, ∼en (a) rescue
(b) (von Schiffen, Gut) salvaging

**Berg-:** ∼**wacht** *die* mountain rescue service; ∼**werk** *das* mine

**Bericht** *der;* ∼[e]s, ∼e report

**berichten** *tr., itr. V.* report

**Bericht-:** ∼**erstatter** *der;* ∼∼s, ∼∼, ∼**erstatterin** *die;* ∼∼, ∼∼nen reporter; ∼**erstattung** *die* reporting *no indef. art.*

**berichtigen** *tr. V.* correct

**Berichtigung** *die;* ~, ~en correction

**berieseln** *tr. V.* **(a)** (bewässern) irrigate **(b) sich ständig mit Musik ~ lassen** (ugs. abwertend) constantly have music on in the background

**Berlin** *(das);* ~s Berlin

**Berliner** 1 *indekl. Adj.* Berlin 2 *der;* ~s, ~: **(a)** Berliner **(b)** (Gebäck) [jam (Brit.) *or* (Amer.) jelly] doughnut

**Berlinerin** *die;* ~, ~nen Berliner

**berlinisch** *Adj.* Berlin *attrib.*

**Bern** *(das);* ~s Bern[e]

**Bernhardiner** *der;* ~s, ~: St. Bernard [dog]

**Bern·stein** *der* amber

**bersten** *unr. itr. V.; mit sein* (geh.) ⟨ice⟩ break up; ⟨glass⟩ shatter [into pieces]; ⟨wall⟩ crack up

**berüchtigt** *Adj.* notorious (**wegen** for); (verrufen) disreputable

**berücksichtigen** *tr. V.* take into account; consider ⟨applicant, application, suggestion⟩

**Berücksichtigung** *die;* ~: **bei ~ aller Umstände** taking all the circumstances into account

**Beruf** *der;* ~[e]s, ~e occupation; (akademischer) profession; (handwerklicher) trade; **was sind Sie von ~?** what do you do for a living?

**berufen¹** 1 *unr. tr. V.* **(a)** (einsetzen) appoint **(b) berufe es nicht!** (ugs.) don't speak too soon! 2 *unr. refl. V.* **sich auf etw.** (*Akk.*) ~: refer to sth.; **sich auf jmdn. ~:** quote *or* mention sb.'s name

**berufen²** *Adj.* **(a)** competent; **aus ~em Munde** from somebody qualified to speak **(b) sich dazu ~ fühlen, etw. zu tun** feel called to do sth.

**beruflich** 1 *Adj.* vocational ⟨training etc.⟩; (bei akademischen Berufen) professional ⟨training etc.⟩ 2 *adv.* **~ erfolgreich sein** be successful in one's career; **sich ~ weiterbilden** undertake further job training

**berufs-, Berufs-:** **~akademie** *die* university of co-operative education; **~ausbildung** *die* vocational training; **~aussichten** *Pl.* job prospects (*in a particular profession etc.*); **~berater** *der*, **~beraterin** *die* vocational adviser; **~beratung** *die* vocational guidance; **~bild** *das* outline of a/the profession/trade as a career; **~erfahrung** *die* [professional] experience; **~geheimnis** *das* professional secret; (Schweigepflicht) professional secrecy; **~krankheit** *die* occupational disease; **~leben** *das* working life; **~schule** *die* vocational school; **~soldat** *der*, **~soldatin** *die* regular

soldier; **~sportler** *der* professional sportsman; **~sportlerin** *die* professional sportswoman; **~tätig** *Adj.* working *attrib.;* **~tätige** *der/die; adj. Dekl.* working person; **~tätige** *Pl.* working people; **~verkehr** *der* rush hour traffic

**Berufung** *die;* ~, ~en **(a)** (für ein Amt) offer of an appointment (**auf, in, an** + *Akk.* to) **(b)** (innerer Auftrag) vocation **(c)** (das Sichberufen) **unter ~** (*Dat.*) **auf jmdn./etw.** referring *or* with reference to sb./sth. **(d)** (Rechtsw.: Einspruch) appeal; **~ einlegen** lodge an appeal

**beruhen** *itr. V.* **auf etw.** (*Dat.*) ~: be based on sth.; **etw. auf sich ~ lassen** let sth. rest

**beruhigen** /bə'ruːɪgn/ 1 *tr. V.* calm [down]; pacify ⟨child, baby⟩; salve ⟨conscience⟩; (trösten) soothe; (von einer Sorge befreien) reassure 2 *refl. V.* ⟨person⟩ calm down; ⟨sea⟩ become calm

**Beruhigung** *die;* ~ ▸ BERUHIGEN 1: calming [down]; pacifying; salving; soothing; reassurance

**Beruhigungs·mittel** *das* tranquillizer

**berühmt** *Adj.* famous

**berühmt-berüchtigt** *Adj.* notorious

**Berühmtheit** *die;* ~, ~en **(a)** (Ruhm) fame **(b)** (Mensch) celebrity

**berühren** *tr. V.* **(a)** touch; (fig.) touch on ⟨topic, issue. etc.⟩; **sich ~:** touch **(b)** (beeindrucken) affect; **das berührt mich nicht** it's a matter of indifference to me

**Berührung** *die;* ~, ~en touch; **mit jmdm./etw. in ~** (*Akk.*) **kommen** (auch fig.) come into contact with sb./sth.

**besagen** *tr. V.* say; (bedeuten) mean

**besänftigen** *tr. V.* calm [down]; pacify; calm, soothe ⟨temper⟩

**Besatz** *der;* ~es, Besätze (Borte) trimming *no indef. art.*

**Besatzung** *die;* ~, ~en **(a)** (Mannschaft) crew **(b)** (Milit.: Verteidigungstruppe) garrison **(c)** (Milit.: Okkupationstruppen) occupying forces *pl.*

**Besatzungs-:** **~macht** *die* occupying power; **~zone** *die* occupied zone

**besaufen** *unr. refl. V.* (salopp) get canned (Brit. sl.) *or* bombed (Amer. sl.)

**Besäufnis** *das;* ~ses, ~se (salopp) booze-up (Brit. coll.): blast (Amer. coll.)

**beschädigen** *tr. V.* damage

**Beschädigung** *die;* ~, ~en **(a)** damaging **(b)** (Schaden) damage

**beschaffen¹** *tr. V.* obtain, get (*Dat.* for)

**beschaffen²** *Adj.* **so ~ sein, dass ...:** be such that ...

**Beschaffenheit** *die;* ~: properties *pl.*

**Beschaffung** *die;* ~: ▸ BESCHAFFEN: obtaining; getting

**beschäftigen** 1 *refl. V.* occupy oneself; ····⟩

**b**

sich viel mit Musik/den Kindern ∼: devote a great deal of one's time to music/the children; **sehr beschäftigt sein** be very busy ②2 *tr. V.* **(a)** (geistig in Anspruch nehmen) **jmdn.** ∼: preoccupy sb.
**(b)** (angestellt haben) employ ⟨*workers, staff*⟩
**(c)** (zu tun geben) occupy; **jmdn. mit etw.** ∼: give sb. sth. to occupy him/her

**Beschäftigte** *der/die; adj. Dekl.* employee

**Beschäftigung** *die;* ∼, ∼en **(a)** (Tätigkeit) activity
**(b)** (Anstellung, Stelle) job
**(c)** (mit einer Frage, einem Problem) consideration (**mit** of); (Studium) study (**mit** of)
**(d)** (von Arbeitskräften) employment

**beschämen** *tr. V.* shame

**beschämend** ①1 *Adj.* **(a)** (schändlich) shameful
**(b)** (demütigend) humiliating
②2 *adv.* shamefully

**beschämt** *Adj.* ashamed

**Beschämung** *die;* ∼: shame

**beschatten** *tr. V.* **(a)** (geh.) shade
**(b)** (überwachen) shadow

**beschaulich** ①1 *Adj.* peaceful ⟨*life, manner, etc.*⟩
②2 *adv.* peacefully

**Beschaulichkeit** *die;* ∼: peacefulness

**Bescheid** *der;* ∼[e]s, ∼e **(a)** (Auskunft) information; (Antwort) answer; reply; **jmdm.** ∼ **geben** *od.* **sagen[, ob ...]** let sb. know or tell sb. [whether ...]; **sage bitte im Hotel** ∼**, dass ...:** please let the hotel know that ...; **[über etw. (*Akk.*)]** ∼ **wissen** know [about sth.]
**(b)** (Entscheidung) decision

**bescheiden**¹ ①1 *unr. tr. V.* **jmdn./etw. abschlägig** ∼: turn sb./sth. down
②2 *unr. refl. V.* (geh.) be content

**bescheiden**² ①1 *Adj.* modest
②2 *adv.* modestly

**Bescheidenheit** *die;* ∼: modesty

**bescheinigen** *tr. V.* confirm ⟨*sth.*⟩ in writing

**Bescheinigung** *die;* ∼, ∼en written confirmation *no indef. art.;* (Schein, Attest) certificate

**bescheißen** *unr. V.* (derb) **jmdn.** ∼: rip sb. off (coll.); screw sb. (coarse)

**beschenken** *tr. V.* give ⟨*sb.*⟩ a present/ presents

**bescheren** *tr. V.* **jmdn. [mit etw.]** ∼: give sb. [sth. as] a Christmas present/Christmas presents

**Bescherung** *die;* ∼, ∼en **(a)** (zu Weihnachten) giving out of the Christmas presents
**(b) das ist ja eine schöne** ∼ (ugs.) this is a pretty kettle of fish

**bescheuert** *Adj.* (salopp) **(a)** (verrückt) barmy (Brit. coll.); nuts (coll.)
**(b)** (unangenehm) stupid ⟨*task, party, etc.*⟩

**beschichten** *tr. V.* (Technik) coat

**Beschichtung** *die;* ∼, ∼en (Technik) coating

**beschießen** *unr. tr. V.* fire at; (mit Artillerie) bombard

**beschimpfen** *tr. V.* abuse; swear at

**Beschimpfung** *die;* ∼, ∼en insult; ∼en abuse *sing.;* insults

**beschissen** *Adj.* (derb) lousy (coll.); shitty (coarse)

**Beschlag** *der;* ∼[e]s, **Beschläge (a)** fitting
**(b) jmdn./etw. mit** ∼ **belegen** *od.* **in** ∼ **nehmen** monopolize sb./sth.

**beschlagen**¹ ①1 *unr. tr. V.* shoe ⟨*horse*⟩
②2 *unr. itr. V.; mit sein* ⟨*window*⟩ mist up (Brit.), fog up (Amer.); (durch Dampf) steam up

**beschlagen**² *Adj.* knowledgeable

**Beschlagnahme** *die;* ∼, ∼n confiscation

**beschlagnahmen** *tr. V.* confiscate

**Beschlagnahmung** *die;* ∼, ∼en
▶ BESCHLAGNAHME

**beschleunigen** ①1 *tr. V.* accelerate; speed up ⟨*work, delivery*⟩; quicken ⟨*pace, step[s], pulse*⟩
②2 *refl. V.* ⟨*heart rate*⟩ increase; ⟨*pulse*⟩ quicken
③3 *itr. V.* ⟨*driver, car, etc.*⟩ accelerate

**Beschleunigung** *die;* ∼, ∼en
▶ BESCHLEUNIGEN 1: acceleration; speeding up; quickening

**beschließen** *unr. tr. V.* **(a)** decide; pass ⟨*law*⟩; ∼**, etw. zu tun** decide or resolve to do sth.
**(b)** (beenden) end

**Beschluss, \*Beschluß** *der;* **Beschlusses, Beschlüsse** decision; (gemeinsam gefasst) resolution; **einen** ∼ **fassen** come to a decision/pass a resolution

**beschluss·fähig, \*beschluß·fähig** *Adj.* quorate

**Beschluss·fähigkeit, \*Beschluß·fähigkeit** *die* presence of a quorum

**beschmieren** *tr. V.* **etw./sich** ∼: get sth./ oneself in a mess

**beschmutzen** *tr. V.* make ⟨*sth.*⟩ dirty

**beschneiden** *unr. tr. V.* **(a)** cut ⟨*hedge*⟩; prune ⟨*bush*⟩; cut back ⟨*tree*⟩; **einem Vogel die Flügel** ∼: clip a bird's wings
**(b)** (Med., Rel.) circumcise

**Beschneidung** *die;* ∼, ∼en **(a)**
▶ BESCHNEIDEN A: cutting; pruning; cutting back
**(b)** (Med., Rel.) circumcision

**beschnüffeln** *tr. V.* sniff at

**beschönigen** *tr. V.* gloss over

**beschränken** ①1 *tr. V.* restrict (**auf** + *Akk.* to)
②2 *refl. V.* **sich auf etw. (*Akk.*)** ∼: restrict oneself to sth.

**beschränkt** ①1 *Adj.* **(a)** (dumm) dull-witted
**(b)** (engstirnig) narrow-minded

---

**b**

**2** *adv.* narrow-mindedly
**Beschränktheit** *die;* ∼: (a) (Dummheit) lack of intelligence
(b) (Engstimigkeit) narrow-mindedness
**Beschränkung** *die;* ∼, ∼en restriction
**beschreiben** *unr. tr. V.* (a) write on; (voll schreiben) write ⟨page, side, etc.⟩
(b) (darstellen) describe
**Beschreibung** *die;* ∼, ∼en description
**beschriften** *tr. V.* label; inscribe ⟨stone⟩; letter ⟨sign, label, etc.⟩; (mit Adresse) address
**beschuldigen** *tr. V.* accuse (*Gen.* of)
**Beschuldigte** *der/die/ adj. Dekl.* accused
**Beschuldigung** *die;* ∼, ∼en accusation
**beschummeln** *tr. V.* (ugs.) cheat; diddle (Brit. coll.)
**Beschuss, \*Beschuß** *der;* Beschusses fire; [heftig *od.* stark] unter ∼ geraten/stehen *od.* liegen (auch fig.) come/be under [heavy] fire
**beschützen** *tr. V.* protect (vor + *Dat.* from)
**Beschützer** *der;* ∼s, ∼, **Beschützerin** *die;* ∼, ∼nen protector
**Beschwerde** *die;* ∼, ∼n (a) complaint (gegen, über + *Akk.* about)
(b) *Pl.* (Schmerz) pain *sing.;* (Leiden) trouble *sing.*
**beschweren** **1** *refl. V.* complain (über + *Akk.*, wegen about); sich bei jmdm. ∼: complain to sb.
**2** *tr. V.* weight down
**beschwerlich** *Adj.* arduous; (ermüdend) exhausting
**beschwichtigen** *tr. V.* pacify; mollify ⟨anger etc.⟩
**Beschwichtigung** *die;* ∼, ∼en pacification; (des Zorns usw.) mollification
**beschwingt** *Adj.* lively
**beschwipst** *Adj.* (ugs.) tipsy
**beschwören** *unr. tr. V.* (a) swear to; ∼, dass ...: swear that ...; eine Aussage ∼: swear a statement on oath
(b) charm ⟨snake⟩
(c) (erscheinen lassen) invoke ⟨spirit⟩
(d) (bitten) implore
**Beschwörung** *die;* ∼, ∼en (a) (Zauberspruch) spell; incantation
(b) ▶ BESCHWÖREN C: invoking
(c) (Bitte) entreaty
**beseitigen** *tr. V.* remove; eliminate ⟨error, difficulty⟩; dispose of ⟨rubbish⟩
**Beseitigung** *die;* ∼: ▶ BESEITIGEN: removal; elimination; disposal
**Besen** *der;* ∼s, ∼ broom; ich fress einen ∼, wenn das stimmt (salopp) I'll eat my hat if that's right (coll.); neue ∼ kehren gut (Spr.) a new broom sweeps clean ( prov.)
**besessen** *Adj.* (a) possessed
(b) (fig.) obsessive ⟨gambler⟩; von einer Idee ∼ sein be obsessed with an idea
**Besessenheit** *die;* ∼ (a) possession

(b) obsessiveness
**besetzen** *tr. V.* (a) (mit Pelz, Spitzen) edge; trim; mit Perlen besetzt set with pearls
(b) (belegen; auch Milit.: erobern) occupy
(c) (vergeben) fill ⟨post, position, role, etc.⟩
**besetzt** *Adj.* occupied; ⟨table, seat⟩ taken *pred.;* (gefüllt) full; (Fernspr.) engaged; busy (Amer.)
**Besetzung** *die;* ∼, ∼en (a) (einer Stellung) filling
(b) (Film, Theater usw.) cast
(c) (Eroberung) occupation
**besichtigen** *tr. V.* see ⟨sights⟩; see the sights of ⟨town⟩; view ⟨house etc. for sale⟩
**Besichtigung** *die;* ∼, ∼en: zur ∼ der Stadt/des Schlosses/der Wohnung to see the sights of the town/to see the castle/to view the flat
**besiedeln** *tr. V.* settle
**besiedelt** *Adj.* dicht/dünn ∼: densely/ thinly populated
**besiegen** *tr. V.* defeat
**besinnen** *unr. refl. V.* (a) think it over
(b) sich [auf jmdn./etw.] ∼: remember [sb./ sth.]
**Besinnung** *die;* ∼: consciousness; die ∼ verlieren faint; [wieder] zur ∼ kommen regain consciousness
**besinnungs-los** **1** *Adj.* unconscious
**2** *adv.* mindlessly
**Besinnungslosigkeit** *die;* ∼: unconsciousness *no art.*
**Besitz** *der* (a) property
(b) (das Besitzen) possession; im ∼ einer Sache (*Gen.*) sein be in possession of sth.
**Besitz-anspruch** *der* claim to ownership
**besitzen** *unr. tr. V.* own; have ⟨quality, talent, etc.⟩; (nachdrücklicher) possess
**Besitzer** *der;* ∼s, ∼, **Besitzerin** *die;* ∼, ∼nen owner
**besoffen** *Adj.* (salopp) canned (Brit. sl.); bombed (Amer. sl.)
**Besoffene** *der/die; adj. Dekl.* (salopp) drunk
**besohlen** *tr. V.* sole; neu ∼: resole
**besonder...** *Adj.* special; ein ∼es Ereignis an unusual *or* a special event; keine ∼e Leistung no great achievement
**Besonderheit** *die;* ∼, ∼en special feature; (Eigenart) peculiarity
**besonders** **1** *Adv.* particularly
**2** *Adj.; nicht attr.; nur verneint* (ugs.) nicht ∼ sein be nothing special
**besonnen** **1** *Adj.* prudent
**2** *adv.* prudently
**Besonnenheit** *die;* ∼: prudence
**besorgen** *tr. V.* (a) get; (kaufen) buy
(b) (erledigen) take care of
**Besorgnis** *die;* ∼, ∼se concern
**besorgt** **1** *Adj.* concerned (um about)
**2** *adv.* with concern
**Besorgung** *die;* ∼, ∼en purchase

**bespitzeln** *tr. V.* spy on

**besprechen** *unr. tr. V.* discuss; (rezensieren) review

**Besprechung** *die;* ~, ~en discussion; (Konferenz) meeting; (Rezension) review

**bespritzen** *tr. V.* **(a)** splash; (mit einem Wasserstrahl) spray

**(b)** (beschmutzen) bespatter

**besprühen** *tr. V.* spray

**besser** ① *Adj.* **(a)** better; umso ~: so much the better

**(b)** (sozial höher gestellt) superior

② *adv.* [immer] alles ~ wissen always know better; es ~ haben be better off; es geht ihr ~: she feels better; ~ gesagt to be [more] precise

③ *Adv.* (lieber) das lässt du ~ sein *od.* (ugs.) bleiben you'd better not do that

*****besser|gehen ▶ BESSER 2

**bessern** ① *refl. V.* improve; ⟨person⟩ mend one's ways

② *tr. V.* improve; reform ⟨criminal⟩

**Besserung** *die;* ~, ~en recovery; gute ~! get well soon

**best...** ① *Adj.* **(a)** best; bei ~er Gesundheit/ Laune sein be in the best of health/spirits *pl.;* im ~en Falle at best; in den ~en Jahren, im ~en Alter in one's prime; ~e Grüße an ... (*Akk.*) best wishes to ...; mit den ~en Grüßen *od.* Wünschen with best wishes; (als Briefschluss) ≈ yours sincerely

**(b)** es ist *od.* wäre das Beste, wenn ...: it would be best if ...; der/die/das nächste Beste ...: the first ... one comes across; einen Witz zum Besten geben entertain [those present] with a joke; das Beste vom Besten the very best; sein Bestes tun do one's best; zu deinem Besten for your benefit

② *adv.* am ~en best

③ *Adv.* am ~en fährst du mit dem Zug it would be best for you to go by train

**Bestand** *der;* ~, Bestände **(a)** existence, (Fort~) continued existence

**(b)** (Vorrat) stock (an + *Dat.* of)

**bestanden** *Adj.* von *od.* mit etw. ~ sein have sth. growing on it; mit Tannen ~e Hügel fir-covered hills

**beständig** ① *Adj.* **(a)** constant

**(b)** (gleich bleibend) constant; steadfast ⟨person⟩; settled ⟨weather⟩

**(c)** (widerstandsfähig) resistant (gegen to)

② *adv.* constantly

**Beständigkeit** *die;* ~ **(a)** steadfastness

**(b)** (Widerstandsfähigkeit) resistance (gegen to)

**Bestand·teil** *der* component

**bestärken** *tr. V.* confirm

**bestätigen** ① *tr. V.* confirm; endorse ⟨document⟩; acknowledge ⟨receipt⟩

② *refl. V.* be confirmed; ⟨rumour⟩ prove to be true

**Bestätigung** *die;* ~, ~en confirmation; (des Empfangs) acknowledgement; (schriftlich) letter of confirmation

**bestatten** *tr. V.* (geh.) inter (formal); bury

**Bestattung** *die;* ~, ~en interment (formal); burial; (Feierlichkeit) funeral

**Bestattungs-:** ~institut *das,* ~unternehmen *das* [firm of] undertakers *pl.* or funeral directors *pl.;* funeral parlor (Amer.)

**bestäuben** *tr. V.* **(a)** dust

**(b)** (Biol.) pollinate

**bestaunen** *tr. V.* marvel at

**bestechen** *unr. tr. V.* bribe

**bestechlich** *Adj.* corruptible; open to bribery *postpos.*

**Bestechung** *die;* ~, ~en bribery *no indef. art.*

**Bestechungs-:** ~geld *das* bribe; ~versuch *der* attempted bribery

**Besteck** *das;* ~[e]s, ~e cutlery setting; (ugs.: Gesamtheit der Bestecke) cutlery

**bestehen** ① *unr. itr. V.* **(a)** exist; es besteht [die] Aussicht/Gefahr, dass ...: there is a prospect/danger that ...; noch besteht die Hoffnung, dass ...: there is still hope that ...; ~ bleiben remain; ⟨regulation⟩ remain in force

**(b)** (fortdauern) survive; last

**(c)** aus etw. ~: consist of sth.; (hergestellt sein) be made of sth.

**(d)** auf etw. (*Dat.*) ~: insist on sth.

② *unr. tr. V.* pass ⟨test, examination⟩

**Bestehen** *das;* ~s existence; die Firma feiert ihr 10-jähriges ~: the firm is celebrating its tenth anniversary

*****bestehen|bleiben ▶ BESTEHEN 1A

**bestehend** *Adj.* existing; current ⟨conditions⟩

**bestehlen** *unr. tr. V.* rob

**besteigen** *unr. tr. V.* **(a)** climb; mount ⟨horse, bicycle⟩; ascend ⟨throne⟩

**(b)** board ⟨ship, aircraft⟩; get on ⟨bus, train⟩

**Besteigung** *die;* ~, ~en ascent

**bestellen** *tr. V.* **(a)** auch itr. order (bei from); würden Sie mir bitte ein Taxi ~? would you order me a taxi?

**(b)** (reservieren lassen) reserve ⟨tickets, table⟩

**(c)** jmdn. [für 10 Uhr] zu sich ~: ask sb. to go/come to see [at 10 o'clock]

**(d)** (ausrichten) jmdm. etw. ~: tell sb. sth.; bestell deinem Mann schöne Grüße von mir give your husband my regards

**Bestellung** *die;* ~, ~en **(a)** order

**(b)** (Reservierung) reservation

**besten·falls** *Adv.* at best

**bestens** *Adv.* extremely well

**besteuern** *tr. V.* tax

**bestialisch** ① *Adj.* **(a)** bestial

**(b)** (ugs.: schrecklich) ghastly (coll.)

② *adv.* **(a)** in a bestial manner

**(b)** (ugs.: schrecklich) awfully (coll.)

**Bestialität** *die;* ~: bestiality

**bestjcken** *tr. V.* embroider

**Bestie** /'bɛstiə/ *die;* ~, ~n beast

**bestjmmen** ⃞1 *tr. V.* **(a)** (festsetzen) decide on; fix ⟨*price, time, etc.*⟩
**(b)** (vorsehen) intend; **das ist für dich bestimmt** that is meant for you
**(c)** (identifizieren) identify; determine ⟨*age, position*⟩; define ⟨*meaning*⟩
**(d)** (prägen) determine the character of
⃞2 *itr. V.* **(a)** make the decisions
**(b)** **über jmdn.** ~: tell sb. what to do; **[frei] über etw.** (*Akk.*) ~: do as one wishes with sth.

**bestjmmend** ⃞1 *Adj.* decisive
⃞2 *adv.* decisively

**bestjmmt** ⃞1 *Adj.* **(a)** (speziell) particular; (gewiss) certain; (genau) definite
**(b)** (festgelegt) fixed; given ⟨*quantity*⟩
**(c)** (Sprachw.) definite ⟨*article etc.*⟩
**(d)** (entschieden) firm
⃞2 *adv.* **(a)** (deutlich) clearly; (genau) precisely
**(b)** (entschieden) firmly
⃞3 *Adv.* for certain; **du weißt es doch [ganz]** ~ **noch** I'm sure you must remember it; **ich habe das** ~ **liegen gelassen** I must have left it behind

**Bestjmmtheit** *die;* ~: firmness; (im Auftreten) decisiveness

**Bestjmmung** *die;* ~, ~en **(a)** (das Festsetzen) fixing
**(b)** (Vorschrift) regulation
**(c)** (Zweck) purpose
**(d)** ▶ BESTIMMEN 1c: identification; determination; definition
**(e)** (Sprachw.) modifier; **adverbiale** ~: adverbial qualification

**bẹst·möglich** *Adj.* best possible

**bestrafen** *tr. V.* punish (**für, wegen** for); **es wird mit Gefängnis bestraft** it is punishable by imprisonment

**Bestrafung** *die;* ~, ~en punishment

**bestrahlen** *tr. V.* **(a)** illuminate; floodlight ⟨*building*⟩
**(b)** (Med.) treat ⟨*tumour, part of body*⟩ using radiotherapy

**Bestrahlung** *die;* ~, ~en (Med.) radiation [treatment] *no indef. art.*

**Bestreben** *das;* ~s endeavour[s *pl.* ]

**bestrebt** *Adj.:* ~ **sein, etw. zu tun** endeavour to do sth.

**Bestrebung** *die;* ~, ~en effort; (Versuch) attempt

**bestreichen** *unr. tr. V.* **A mit B** ~: spread B on A

**bestreiten** *unr. tr. V.* **(a)** dispute; (leugnen) deny
**(b)** (finanzieren) finance ⟨*studies*⟩; pay for ⟨*studies, sb.'s keep*⟩; meet ⟨*costs, expenses*⟩
**(c)** (gestalten) carry ⟨*programme, conversation, etc.*⟩

**bestreuen** *tr. V.* sprinkle

**Bestseller** /'bɛstzɛlɐ/ *der;* ~s, ~: best seller

**bestürzend** *Adj.* disturbing; (erschreckend) alarming

**bestürzt** ⃞1 *Adj.* dismayed
⃞2 *adv.* with dismay

**Bestürzung** *die;* ~: dismay

**Besuch** *der;* ~[e]s, ~e **(a)** visit (*Gen.,* **bei** to); **ein** ~ **bei jmdm.** a visit to sb.; (kurz) a call on sb.
**(b)** (Teilnahme) attendance (*Gen.* at)
**(c)** (Gast) visitor; (Gäste) visitors *pl.;* ~ **haben** have visitors/a visitor

**besuchen** *tr. V.* visit; (weniger formell) go to see ⟨*person*⟩; go to ⟨*exhibition, theatre, museum, etc.*⟩; (zur Besichtigung) go to see ⟨*church, exhibition, etc.*⟩
**(b)** **die Schule/Universität** ~: go to school/ university

**Besucher** *der;* ~s, ~, **Besucherin** *die;* ~, ~nen visitor

**Besuchs-:** ~**erlaubnis** *die* visiting permit; ~**zeit** *die* visiting time *or* hours *pl.;* **es ist keine** ~**zeit** it is not visiting time

**besucht** *Adj.* **gut/schlecht** ~: well/poorly attended ⟨*lecture, performance, etc.*⟩; much/ little frequented ⟨*restaurant etc.*⟩

**Beta·blocker** /-blɔkɐ/ *der;* ~s, ~ (Med.) betablocker

**betagt** *Adj.* (geh.) elderly

**betasten** *tr. V.* feel [with one's fingers]

**betätigen** ⃞1 *refl. V.* occupy oneself; **sich politisch/körperlich** ~: engage in political/ physical activity
⃞2 *tr. V.* operate ⟨*lever, switch, flush, etc.*⟩; apply ⟨*brake*⟩

**Betätigung** *die;* ~, ~en: **(a)** activity
**(b)** ▶ BETÄTIGEN 2: operation; application

**betäuben** *tr. V.* **(a)** (Med.) anaesthetize; deaden ⟨*nerve*⟩; **jmdn. örtlich** ~: give sb. a local anaesthetic
**(b)** (unterdrücken) deaden ⟨*pain*⟩; still ⟨*unease, fear*⟩
**(c)** (benommen machen) daze; (mit einem Schlag) stun

**Betäubung** *die;* ~, ~en: **(a)** (Med.) anaesthetization; (Narkose) anaesthesia
**(b)** (Benommenheit) daze

**Betäubungs·mittel** *das* narcotic; (Med.) anaesthetic

**beteiligen** ⃞1 *refl. V.* take part (**an** + *Dat.* in)
⃞2 *tr. V.* **jmdn. [mit 10 %] an etw.** (*Dat.*) ~: give sb. a [10%] share of sth.

**beteiligt** *Adj.* **(a)** involved (**an** + *Dat.* in)
**(b)** (finanziell) **an einem Unternehmen/am Gewinn** ~ **sein** have a share in a business/ in the profit

**Beteiligte** *der/die; adj. Dekl.* person involved

**Beteiligung** *die;* ~, ~en **(a)** participation (**an** + *Dat.* in)
**(b)** (Anteil) share (**an** + *Dat.* in)

**beten** ⃞1 *itr. V.* pray (**für, um** for)
⃞2 *tr. V.* say ⟨*prayer*⟩

**beteuern** tr. V. affirm; protest ⟨one's innocence⟩

**Beteuerung** die; ~, ~en ▶ BETEUERN: affirmation; protestation

**Beton** /be'tɔŋ, bes. österr.: be'to:n/ der; ~s, ~s /-ɔŋs/ od. (bes. österr.:) ~e /-o:nə/ concrete

**betonen** tr. V. (a) stress ⟨word, syllable⟩ (b) (hervorheben) emphasize

**betonieren** tr. V. concrete; surface ⟨road etc.⟩ with concrete

**betont** ① Adj. (a) stressed (b) (bewusst) studied ② adv. studiedly

**Betonung** die; ~, ~en (a) stressing (b) (Akzent) stress; (Intonation) intonation (c) (Hervorhebung) emphasis

**betören** tr. V. (geh.) captivate

**betr.** Abk. = **betreffs, betrifft** re

**Betr.** Abk. = **Betreff** re

**Betracht**: jmdn./etw. in ~ ziehen consider sb./sth.; jmdn./etw. außer ~ lassen disregard sb./sth.

**betrachten** tr. V. (a) look at (b) jmdn./etw. als etw. ~: regard sb./sth. as sth. (c) (beurteilen) consider

**Betrachter** der; ~s, ~, **Betrachterin** die; ~, ~nen observer

**beträchtlich** ① Adj. considerable ② adv. considerably

**Betrachtung** die; ~, ~en (a) contemplation; (Untersuchung) examination (b) (Überlegung) reflection

**Betrachtungs·weise** die way of looking at things; (Standpunkt) point of view

**Betrag** der; ~[e]s, Beträge amount; „~ dankend erhalten" 'received with thanks'

**betragen** ① unr. itr. V. be; (bei Geldsummen) come to; amount to ② unr. refl. V. behave

**Betragen** das; ~s behaviour

**Betreff** der; ~[e]s, ~e (im Brief) heading

**betreffen** unr. tr. V. concern; ⟨new rule, change, etc.⟩ affect

**betreffend** Adj. concerning; der ~e Sachbearbeiter the person dealing with this matter; in dem ~en Fall in the case in question

**betreffs** Präp. mit Gen. (Amtsspr., Kaufmannsspr.) concerning

**betreiben** unr. tr. V. (a) proceed with, (energisch) press ahead with ⟨task, case, etc.⟩; pursue ⟨policy, studies⟩; carry on ⟨trade⟩; go in for ⟨sport⟩ (b) run ⟨business, shop⟩ (c) (in Betrieb halten) operate

**betreten**¹ unr. tr. V. (hineintreten in) enter; (treten auf) step on to; (begehen) walk on ⟨carpet, grass, etc.⟩; „Betreten verboten" 'Keep off'; (kein Eintritt) 'Keep out'

**betreten**² ① Adj. embarrassed ② adv. with embarrassment

**betreuen** tr. V. look after; care for ⟨invalid⟩; supervise ⟨youth group⟩; see to the needs of ⟨tourists, sportsmen⟩

**Betreuung** die; ~: care no indef. art.

**Betrieb** der; ~[e]s, ~e (a) business; (Firma) firm (b) (das In-Funktion-Sein) operation; außer ~ sein not operate; (wegen Störung) be out of order; in/außer ~ setzen start up/stop ⟨machine etc.⟩ (c) (ugs.: Treiben) bustle; (Verkehr) traffic; es herrscht großer ~, es ist viel ~: it's very busy

**betrieblich** Adj. firm's; company

**Betriebs-**: ~angehörige der/die employee; ~anleitung die, ~anweisung die operating instructions pl.; ~ausflug der staff outing; ~ferien Pl. firm's annual close-down sing.; „Wegen ~ferien geschlossen" 'closed for annual holidays'; ~klima das working atmosphere; ~rat der (a) works committee; (b) (Person) member of a/the works committee; ~rätin die ▶ BETRIEBSRAT B; ~system das (DV) operating system; ~versammlung die meeting of the workforce; ~wirt der, ~wirtin die graduate in business management; ~wirtschaft die business management

**betrinken** unr. refl. V. get drunk

**betroffen** ① Adj. upset; (bestürzt) dismayed ② adv. in dismay

**Betroffenheit** die; ~: dismay

**betrüblich** Adj. gloomy

**betrübt** ① Adj. sad; gloomy ⟨face etc.⟩ ② sadly; (schwermütig) gloomily

**Betrug** der; ~[e]s deception; (Delikt) fraud

**betrügen** ① unr. tr. V. deceive; be unfaithful to ⟨husband, wife⟩; (Rechtsw.) defraud; (beim Spielen) cheat; jmdn. um 100 Euro ~: cheat or (coll.) do sb. out of 100 euros; (arglistig) swindle sb. out of 100 euros ② unr. itr. V. cheat; (bei Geschäften) swindle people

**Betrüger** der; ~s, ~: swindler; (Hochstapler) conman (coll.); (beim Spielen) cheat

**Betrügerei** die; ~, ~en deception; (beim Spielen usw.) cheating; (bei Geschäften) swindling

**Betrügerin** die; ~, ~nen swindler; (beim Spielen) cheat

**betrunken** Adj. drunken attrib.; drunk pred.

**Betrunkene** der/die; adj. Dekl. drunk

**Bett** das; ~[e]s, ~en (a) bed; ins od. zu ~ gehen go to bed; die Kinder ins ~ bringen put the children to bed (b) (Feder~) duvet

**Bett-**: ~bezug der duvet cover; ~decke die blanket; (gesteppt) quilt

**Bettelei** die; ~, ~en begging no art.

---

**betteln** *itr. V.* beg (**um** for)
**bett·lägerig** *Adj.* bedridden
**Bett·laken** *das* sheet
**Bett·lektüre** *die* bedtime reading *no indef. art.*
**Bettler** *der;* ~s, ~, **Bettlerin** *die;* ~, ~nen beggar
**bett-, Bett-:** ~**reif** *Adj.* (ugs.) ready for bed *pred.;* ~**ruhe** *die* bed rest; ~**schwere** *die:* **die nötige** *od.* **notwendige** ~**schwere haben** (ugs.) be ready for one's bed; ~**tuch** *das; Pl.* ~**tücher** sheet; ~**wäsche** *die* bedlinen; ~**zeug** *das* (ugs.) bedclothes *pl.*
**betucht** *Adj.* (ugs.) well-heeled (coll.); well-off
**betupfen** *tr. V.* dab
**Beuge** *die;* ~, ~n (Turnen) bend
**beugen** [1] *tr. V.* (a) bend; bow ⟨*head*⟩ (b) (Sprachw.: flektieren) inflect ⟨*word*⟩ [2] *refl. V.* (a) bend over; **sich nach vorn/ hinten** ~: bend forwards/bend over backwards; **sich aus dem Fenster** ~: lean out of the window (b) (sich fügen) give way
**Beugung** *die;* ~, ~en (Sprachw.) inflexion
**Beule** *die;* ~, ~n bump; (Vertiefung) dent
**beulen** *itr. V.* bulge
**beunruhigen** *tr., refl. V.* worry
**beurlauben** *tr. V.* (a) jmdn. [**für zwei Tage**] ~: give sb. [two days'] leave of absence (b) (suspendieren) suspend
**beurteilen** *tr. V.* judge; assess ⟨*situation etc.*⟩
**Beurteilung** *die;* ~, ~en (a) judgement; (einer Lage usw.) assessment (b) (Gutachten) assessment
**Beute** *die;* ~, ~n (a) (Gestohlenes) haul; loot *no indef. art.;* (b) (von Raubtieren) prey; (eines Jägers) bag
**Beute·kunst** *die* looted art
**Beutel** *der;* ~s, ~ bag; (kleiner, für Tabak usw.) pouch
**bevölkern** *tr. V.* populate
**Bevölkerung** *die;* ~, ~en population; (Volk) people
**Bevölkerungs-:** ~**dichte** *die* population density; ~**explosion** *die* population explosion; ~**zunahme** *die,* ~**zuwachs** *der* increase in population
**bevollmächtigen** *tr. V.* authorize
**Bevollmächtigte** *der/die; adj. Dekl.* authorized representative
**bevor** *Konj.* before; ~ **du nicht unterschrieben hast** until you have signed
**bevor·munden** *tr. V.* jmdn. ~: impose one's will on sb.; **sie wollen sich nicht länger** ~ **lassen** they do not want to be dictated to any longer
**bevor|stehen** *unr. itr. V.* be near; **unmittelbar** ~: be imminent; **jmdm. steht etw. bevor.** is in store for sb.

**bevorstehend** *Adj.* forthcoming; **unmittelbar** ~: imminent
**bevorzugen** *tr. V.* (a) (vorziehen) prefer (**vor** + *Dat.* to) (b) (begünstigen) favour; give preference *or* preferenzial treatment to (**vor** + *Dat.* over)
**bevorzugt** [1] *Adj.* favoured; (privilegiert) privileged; preferenzial ⟨*treatment*⟩ [2] *adv.* jmdn. ~ **behandeln** give sb. preferential treatment
**Bevorzugung** *die;* ~, ~en (Begünstigung) preferential treatment
**bewachen** *tr. V.* guard; **bewachter Parkplatz** car park with an attendant
**Bewacher** *der;* ~s, ~, **Bewacherin** *die;* ~, ~nen guard
**Bewachung** *die;* ~, ~en guarding
**bewaffnen** [1] *tr. V.* arm [2] *refl. V.* (auch fig.) arm oneself (**mit** with)
**bewaffnet** *Adj.* armed; **bis an die Zähne** ~: armed to the teeth
**Bewaffnung** *die;* ~, ~en (a) arming (b) (Waffen) weapons *pl.*
**bewahren** *tr. V.* (a) protect (**vor** + *Dat.* from) (b) (erhalten) **seine Fassung** ~: retain one's composure; **Stillschweigen** ~: remain silent
**bewähren** *refl. V.* prove oneself/itself
**bewährt** *Adj.* proven ⟨*method, design, etc.*⟩; well-tried ⟨*recipe, cure*⟩; reliable ⟨*worker*⟩
**Bewährung** *die;* ~, ~en (Rechtsw.) probation
**Bewährungs-:** ~**frist** *die* (Rechtsw.) period of probation; ~**helfer** *der,* ~**helferin** *die* probation officer; ~**zeit** *die* (Rechtsw.) probation period
**bewaldet** *Adj.* wooded
**bewältigen** *tr. V.* cope with; overcome ⟨*difficulty, problem*⟩; cover ⟨*distance*⟩
**Bewältigung** *die;* ~, ~en ▶ BEWÄLTIGEN: coping with; overcoming; covering
**bewandert** *Adj.* well-versed
**Bewandtnis** *die;* ~, ~se: **mit etw. hat es [s]eine eigene/besondere** ~: there's a [special] story behind sth.
**bewässern** *tr. V.* irrigate
**Bewässerung** *die;* ~, ~en irrigation
**bewegen**[1] [1] *tr. V.* (a) move (b) (ergreifen) move (c) (innerlich beschäftigen) preoccupy [2] *refl. V.* move
**bewegen**[2] *unr. tr. V.* **jmdn. dazu** ~, **etw. zu tun** ⟨*thing*⟩ induce sb. to do sth.; ⟨*person*⟩ prevail upon sb. to do sth.
**Beweg·grund** *der* motive
**beweglich** *Adj.* (a) movable; moving ⟨*target*⟩ (b) (rege) agile ⟨*mind*⟩
**bewegt** *Adj.* eventful; (unruhig) turbulent
**Bewegung** *die;* ~, ~en (a) movement; (bes. Technik, Physik) motion (b) (körperliche ~) exercise ····⟫

**(c)** (Ergriffenheit) emotion
**(d)** (Bestreben, Gruppe) movement
**Bewegungs·freiheit** *die* freedom of movement
**bewegungslos** *Adj.* motionless
**Bewegungslosigkeit** *die;* ~: motionlessness
**Beweis** *der;* ~**es,** ~**e** proof (*Gen., für* of); **belastende** ~**e** incriminating evidence
**beweisbar** *Adj.* provable
**beweisen** *unr. tr. V.* prove
**Beweis-:** ~**material** *das* evidence; ~**mittel** *das* (Rechtsw.) form of evidence; ~**stück** *das* piece of evidence; ~**stücke** evidence *sing.*
**bewenden** *unr. V.* **es bei** *od.* **mit etw.** ~ **lassen** content oneself with sth.
**bewerben** *unr. refl. V.* apply (**bei** to, **um** for)
**Bewerber** *der;* ~**s,** ~, **Bewerberin** *die;* ~, ~**nen** applicant
**Bewerbung** *die* application
**Bewerbungs-:** ~**bogen** *der* application form; ~**schreiben** *das* letter of application; ~**unterlagen** *Pl.* documents in support of an/the application
**bewerfen** *unr. tr. V.* **jmdn./etw. mit etw.** ~: throw sth. at sb./sth.
**bewerkstelligen** *tr. V.* pull off, manage ⟨*deal, sale, etc.*⟩; **es** ~, **etw. zu tun** contrive *or* manage to do sth.
**bewerten** *tr. V.* assess; rate; (dem Geldwert nach) value (**mit** at)
**Bewertung** *die;* ~, ~**en** assessment; (dem Geldwert nach) valuation
**bewilligen** *tr. V.* grant
**Bewilligung** *die;* ~, ~**en** granting
**bewirken** *tr. V.* bring about; cause
**bewirten** *tr. V.* feed; **jmdn. mit etw.** ~: serve sb. sth.
**bewirtschaften** *tr. V.* **(a)** manage ⟨*estate, farm, restaurant, business, etc.*⟩ **(b)** farm ⟨*fields, land*⟩
**Bewirtung** *die;* ~, ~**en** provision of food and drink
**bewog** *1. u. 3. Pers. Sg. Prät. v.* BEWEGEN[2]
**bewohnbar** *Adj.* habitable
**bewohnen** *tr. V.* inhabit, live in ⟨*house, area*⟩; live in ⟨*room, flat*⟩
**Bewohner** *der;* ~**s,** ~, **Bewohnerin** *die;* ~, ~**nen** (eines Hauses, einer Wohnung) occupant; (einer Stadt, eines Gebietes) inhabitant
**bewohnt** *Adj.* occupied ⟨*house etc.*⟩; inhabited ⟨*area*⟩
**bewölken** *refl. V.* cloud over; become overcast
**bewölkt** *Adj.* cloudy; overcast
**Bewölkung** *die;* ~, ~**en** cloud [cover]
**Bewunderer** *der;* ~**s,** ~, **Bewunderin** *die;* ~, ~**nen** admirer

**bewundern** *tr. V.* admire (**wegen, für** for)
**bewunderns·wert** [1] *Adj.* admirable [2] *adv.* admirably
**Bewunderung** *die;* ~: admiration
**bewusst, \*bewußt** [1] *Adj.* conscious ⟨*reaction, behaviour, etc.*⟩; (absichtlich) deliberate ⟨*lie, deception, attack, etc.*⟩; **etw. ist/wird jmdm.** ~: sb. is/becomes aware of sth.; sb. realizes sth.; **sich** (*Dat.*) **einer Sache** (*Gen.*) ~ **sein/werden** be/become aware of something [2] *adv.* consciously; (absichtlich) deliberately
**bewusst·los, \*bewußt·los** *Adj.* unconscious
**Bewusstlosigkeit, \*Bewußtlosigkeit** *die;* ~: unconsciousness
**Bewusst·sein, \*Bewußt·sein** *das* **(a)** consciousness; **das** ~ **verlieren/wiedererlangen** lose/regain consciousness; **bei vollem** ~ **sein** be fully conscious **(b)** (deutliches Wissen) awareness
**bewusstseins-, \*bewußtseins-, Bewusstseins-, \*Bewußtseins-:** ~**erweiternd** *Adj.* mind-expanding; psychedelic; ~**erweiterung** *die* expansion of consciousness; ~**trübung** *die* clouding *or* dimming of consciousness; ~**veränderung** *die* change of awareness *or* outlook
**bezahlbar** *Adj.* affordable
**bezahlen** [1] *tr. V.* pay ⟨*person, bill, taxes, rent, amount*⟩; pay for ⟨*goods etc.*⟩; **das macht sich bezahlt** it pays off [2] *itr. V.* pay; **Herr Ober, ich möchte** ~ *od.* **bitte** ~: waiter, the bill *or* (Amer.) check please
**Bezahl·fernsehen** *das* pay television; pay TV
**Bezahlung** *die;* ~, ~**en** payment; (Lohn, Gehalt) pay
**bezaubernd** [1] *Adj.* enchanting [2] *adv.* enchantingly
**bezeichnen** *tr. V.* **(a)** **jmdn./sich/etw. als etw.** ~: call sb./oneself/sth. sth. **(b)** (Name, Wort sein für) denote
**bezeichnend** *Adj.* characteristic (**für** of)
**Bezeichnung** *die;* ~, ~**en** **(a)** marking; (Angabe durch Zeichen) indication **(b)** (Name) name
**bezeugen** *tr. V.* testify to
**bezichtigen** *tr. V.* accuse
**beziehen** [1] *unr. tr. V.* **(a)** cover ⟨*seat, cushion, etc.*⟩; **die Betten frisch** ~: put clean sheets on the beds **(b)** (einziehen in) move into ⟨*house, office*⟩ **(c)** (Milit.) take up ⟨*position, post*⟩ **(d)** (erhalten) obtain ⟨*goods*⟩; take ⟨*newspaper*⟩; draw ⟨*pension, salary*⟩ **(e)** (in Beziehung setzen) apply (**auf** + *Akk.* to) [2] *unr. refl. V.* **(a)** **es/der Himmel bezieht sich** it/the sky is clouding over *or* becoming overcast

**(b)** sich auf jmdn./etw. ~ (sich berufen auf) ⟨*person, letter, etc.*⟩ refer to sb./sth.; (betreffen) ⟨*question, statement, etc.*⟩ relate to sb./sth.; wir ~ uns auf Ihr Schreiben vom 28. 8. with reference to your letter of 28 August

**Beziehung** *die;* ~, ~en **(a)** relation; (Zusammenhang) connection (**zu** with); zwischen A und B besteht keine/eine ~: there is no/a connection between A and B **(b)** (Freundschaft, Liebes~) relationship **(c)** (Hinsicht) respect; **in mancher** ~: in many respects

**beziehungs-weise** *Konj.* and ... respectively; (oder) or

**beziffern** *tr. V.* estimate (**auf** + *Akk.* at); **den Schaden auf 3 000 Euro** ~: estimate the damage at 3,000 euros

**Bezirk** *der;* ~[e]s, ~e district

***bezug** ▶ BEZUG D

**Bezug** *der* **(a)** (für Kissen usw.) cover; (für Polstermöbel) loose cover; slip cover (Amer.); (für Betten) duvet cover; (für Kopfkissen) pillowcase **(b)** (Erwerb) obtaining; (Kauf) purchase; ~ **einer Zeitung** taking a newspaper **(c)** *Pl.* salary *sing.;* **(d)** (Papierdt.) **mit** *od.* **unter** ~ **auf etw.** (*Akk.*) with reference to sth.; **in** ~ **auf jmdn./etw.** regarding sb./sth.; ~ **nehmend auf unser Telex** with reference to our telex

**bezüglich** *Präp. mit Gen.* regarding

**bezwecken** *tr. V.* aim to achieve

**bezweifeln** *tr. V.* doubt

**bezwingen** *unr. tr. V.* conquer ⟨*enemy, mountain, pain, etc.*⟩; defeat ⟨*opponent*⟩; capture ⟨*fortress*⟩

**BH** /beːˈhaː/ *der;* ~[s], ~[s] *Abk.* = **Büstenhalter** bra

**Bibel** *die;* ~, ~n (auch fig.) Bible

**Biber** *der;* ~s, ~: beaver

**Bibliographie** *die;* ~, ~n bibliography

**bibliographisch** *Adj.* bibliographical

**Bibliothek** *die;* ~, ~en library

**Bibliothekar** *der;* ~s, ~e, **Bibliothekarin** *die;* ~, ~nen librarian

**biblisch** *Adj.* biblical

**Bidet** /biˈdeː/ *das;* ~s, ~s bidet

**bieder** *Adj.* unsophisticated; (langweilig) stolid; (treuherzig) trusting

**biegen** ① *unr. tr. V.* bend ② *unr. refl. V.* bend; (nachgeben) give ③ *unr. itr. V.; mit sein* turn

**biegsam** *Adj.* flexible; pliable ⟨*material*⟩

**Biegsamkeit** *die;* ~ ▶ BIEGSAM: flexibility; pliability

**Biegung** *die;* ~, ~en bend

**Biene** *die;* ~, ~n bee

**Bienen-:** ~**honig** *der* bees' honey; ~**königin** *die* queen bee; ~**korb** *der* straw hive; ~**stock** *der* beehive

**Bier** *das;* ~[e]s, ~e beer

**Bier-:** ~**bauch** *der* (ugs. spött.) beer belly;

~**brauerei** *die* brewery; ~**deckel** *der* beer mat; ~**dose** *die* beer can; ~**fass,** \*~**faß** *das* beer barrel; ~**flasche** *die* beer bottle; ~**garten** *der* beer garden; ~**glas** *das* beer glass; ~**kasten** *der* beer crate; ~**trinker** *der,* ~**trinkerin** *die* beer drinker; ~**zelt** *das* beer tent

**Biest** *das;* ~[e]s, ~er (ugs. abwertend) **(a)** (Tier, Gegenstand) wretched thing **(b)** (Mensch) wretch

**bieten** ① *unr. tr. V.* **(a)** offer; put on ⟨*programme etc.*⟩; provide ⟨*shelter, guarantee, etc.*⟩ **(b)** **ein schreckliches Bild** ~: present a terrible picture; **einen prächtigen Anblick** ~: be a splendid sight ② *unr. refl. V.* **sich jmdm.** ~: present itself to sb. ③ *unr. itr. V.* bid

**Bigamie** *die;* ~: bigamy no def. art.

**Bigamist** *der;* ~en, ~en, **Bigamistin** *die;* ~, ~nen bigamist

**Bikini** *der;* ~s, ~s bikini

**Bilanz** *die;* ~, ~en **(a)** balance sheet **(b)** (Ergebnis) outcome; ~ **ziehen** take stock

**Bild** *das;* ~[e]s, ~er **(a)** picture **(b)** (Anblick) sight **(c)** (Metapher) image

**bilden** ① *tr. V.* **(a)** form (**aus** from); (modellieren) mould (**aus** from); **eine Gasse** ~: make a path; **sich** (*Dat.*) **ein Urteil** ~: form an opinion **(b)** (ansammeln) build up ⟨*fund, capital*⟩ **(c)** (darstellen) be ⟨*exception etc.*⟩ **(d)** (erziehen) educate ② *refl. V.* **(a)** form **(b)** (lernen) educate oneself

**bildend** *Adj.* **(a)** **die** ~**e Kunst, die** ~**en Künste** the plastic arts *pl.* (including *painting and architecture*) **(b)** (belehrend) educational

**Bilder-:** ~**buch** *das* picture book (*for children*); ~**geschichte** *die* picture story; ~**rahmen** *der* picture frame; ~**rätsel** *das* picture puzzle; (Rebus) rebus

**bild-, Bild-:** ~**hauer** *der* sculptor; ~**hauerin** *die;* ~~, ~~**nen** sculptress; ~**hübsch** *Adj.* really lovely; stunningly beautiful ⟨*girl*⟩

**bildlich** ① *Adj.* pictorial; (übertragen) figurative ② *adv.* pictorially; (übertragen) figuratively

**Bildnis** /ˈbɪltnɪs/ *das;* ~ses, ~se portrait

**Bild-:** ~**qualität** *die* picture quality; ~**röhre** *die* (Ferns.) picture tube

**Bild-schirm** *der* (Ferns., Informationst.) screen

**Bildschirm-:** ~**gerät** *das* VDU; visual display unit; ~**schoner** *der;* ~~s, ~~ (DV) screen saver

**bild-, Bild-:** ~**schön** *Adj.* really lovely; stunningly beautiful ⟨*girl, woman*⟩; ~**telefon** *das* video telephone

**b**

**Bildung** die; ~, ~en (a) (Erziehung) education; (Kultur) culture
(b) (das Formen) formation

**Bildungs-:** ~**lücke** die gap in one's education; ~**wesen** das education system; das ~wesen education

**Bild·unterschrift** die caption

**Billard** /'bɪljart, österr.: bi'ja:ɐ̯/ das; ~s, ~e billiards

**Billard-:** ~**kugel** die billiard ball; ~**stock** der billiard cue; ~**tisch** der billiard table

**Billett** /bɪl'jɛt/ das; ~[e]s, ~e od. ~s (schweiz., veralt.) ticket

**Billiarde** die; ~, ~n thousand million million; quadrillion (Amer.)

**billig** [1] Adj. (a) cheap
(b) (abwertend: primitiv) cheap ⟨trick⟩; feeble ⟨excuse⟩
[2] adv. cheaply

**Billig·angebot** das special or cut-price offer

**billigen** tr. V. approve

**Billig-:** ~**flug** der cheap flight; ~**lohn·land** das low-wage country

**Billigung** die; ~: approval

**Billion** die; ~, ~en trillion; million million

**bimmeln** itr. V. (ugs.) ring

**bin** 1. Pers. Sg. Präsens v. SEIN[1]

**binär** Adj. binary

**Binde** die; ~, ~n (a) (Verband) bandage; (Augenbinde) blindfold
(b) (Armbinde) armband

**Binde-:** ~**gewebe** das (Anat.) connective tissue; ~**haut** die (Anat.) conjunctiva

**binden** [1] unr. tr. V. (a) (auch fig.) tie; knot ⟨tie⟩; make up ⟨wreath, bouquet⟩; jmdn. an sich (Akk.) ~ (fig.) make sb. dependent on one
(b) (fesseln, festhalten, zusammenhalten, fig.: verpflichten, Buchw.) bind
(c) (Kochk.: legieren) thicken ⟨sauce⟩
[2] unr. refl. V. tie oneself down

**Binder** der; ~s, ~ tie

**Binde-strich** der hyphen

**Bind·faden** der string

**Bindung** die; ~, ~en (a) (Beziehung) relationship (an + Akk. to)
(b) (Verbundenheit) attachment (an + Akk. to)
(c) (Skibindung) binding

**binnen** Präp. mit Dat. od. (geh.) Gen. within

**Binnenmarkt** der (Wirtsch.) domestic or home market; europäischer ~: internal European market

**Binsen·weisheit** die truism

**Bio-** (ugs.) organic ⟨farmer, garden, vegetables, etc.⟩

**bio-, Bio-:** ~**abfall** der biowaste; ~**chemie** die biochemistry; ~**graf** der; ~en, ~en biographer; ~**grafie** die;

~, ~n biography; ~**grafin** die; ~, ~nen biographer; ~**grafisch** Adj. biographical; ~**loge** die; ~n, ~n biologist; ~**logie** die; ~: biology no art.; ~**login** der; ~, ~nen biologist; ~**logisch** Adj. (a) biological; (b) (natürlich) natural ⟨medicine, cosmetic, etc.⟩; ~**masse** die biomass; ~**müll** der biowaste; ~**top** der od. das; ~s, ~e (Biol.) biotope

**Birke** die; ~, ~n birch [tree]; (Holz) birch[wood]

**Birma** (das); ~s Burma

**Birn·baum** der pear tree

**Birne** die; ~, ~n (a) pear
(b) (Glühlampe) [light]bulb
(c) (salopp: Kopf) nut (coll.)

**bis** [1] Präp. mit Akk. (a) (zeitlich) until; till; (die ganze Zeit über und bis zu einem bestimmten Zeitpunkt) up until; up till; (nicht später als) by
(b) (räumlich) to; dieser Zug fährt nur ~ Offenburg this train only goes as far as Offenburg; ~ 5000 Euro up to 5,000 euros
(c) ~ auf (einschließlich) down to; (mit Ausnahme von) except for
[2] Adv. ~ zu 6 Personen up to six people
[3] Konj. (a) (nebenordnend) to
(b) (unterordnend) until; till; (österr.: sobald) when

**Bisam·ratte** die muskrat

**Bischof** der; ~s, Bischöfe, **Bischöfin** die; ~, ~nen bishop

**bischöflich** Adj. episcopal

**bi·sexuell** [1] Adj. bisexual
[2] adv. bisexually

**bis·her** Adv. up to now; (aber jetzt nicht mehr) until now; till now

**bisherig** Adj. (vorherig) previous; (momentan) present

**Biskaya** /bɪs'ka:ja/ die; ~: the Bay of Biscay

**Biskuit** /bɪs'kvi:t/ das od. der; ~[e]s, ~s od. ~e (a) sponge biscuit
(b) (~teig) sponge

**bis·lang** Adv.: ▶ BISHER

**Bison** der; ~s, ~s bison

**Biss, *Biß** der; Bisses, Bisse bite

**bisschen, *bißchen** indekl. Indefinitpron. (a) adj. ein ~ Geld/Wasser a bit of or a little money/a drop of or a little water; ein/kein ~ Angst haben be a bit/not a bit frightened
(b) adv. ein/kein ~: a bit or a little/not a or one bit
(c) subst. ein ~: a bit; a little; (bei Flüssigkeiten) a drop; a little; das/kein ~: the little [bit]/not a or one bit

**Bissen** der; ~s, ~: mouthful

**bissig** [1] Adj. (a) ~ sein ⟨dog⟩ bite; ein ~er Hund a dog that bites; „Vorsicht, ~er Hund" 'beware of the dog'
(b) cutting ⟨remark, tone, etc.⟩
[2] adv. ⟨say⟩ cuttingly

**Biss·wunde, *Biß·wunde** die bite

---

*alte Schreibung - vgl. Hinweis auf S. xiv

**bist** 2. Pers. Sg. Präsens v. SEIN[1]

**Bistum** /'bɪstuːm/ das; ~s, **Bistümer** bishopric; diocese

**bis·weilen** Adv. (geh.) from time to time

**Bit** /bɪt/ das; ~s, ~[s] (DV) bit

**bitte** [1] Adv. please

[2] Interj. **(a)** (Bitte, Aufforderung) please; **zwei Tassen Tee, ~:** two cups of tea, please; **~[, nehmen Sie doch Platz]!** do take a seat; **Noch eine Tasse Tee? – [Ja] ~!** Another cup of tea? – Yes, please

**(b)** (Aufforderung, etw. entgegenzunehmen) ~ **[schön** od. **sehr]!** there you are!

**(c)** (Ausdruck des Einverständnisses) ~ **[gern]!** certainly; of course; **Entschuldigung! – Bitte!** [I'm] sorry! – That's all right!

**(d)** ~ **[schön** od. **sehr]!** (im Laden, Lokal) yes, please?

**(e) [wie] ~?** (Nachfrage) sorry

**(f) Vielen Dank! – Bitte [schön** od. **sehr]** Many thanks! – Not at all or you're welcome

**Bitte** die; ~, ~n request; (inständig) plea

**bitten** unr. tr. V. **(a)** auch itr. ask (**um** for); **darf ich Sie um Feuer/ein Glas Wasser ~?** could I ask you for a light/a glass of water, please?

**(b)** (einladen) ask

**bitter** [1] Adj. **(a)** bitter; plain ‹chocolate›

**(b)** (fig.) (verbittert) bitter

**(c)** (schmerzlich) bitter, painful, hard ‹loss›; hard ‹time, fate, etc.›; dire ‹need›; desperate ‹poverty›; grievous ‹injustice, harm›

[2] adv. (sehr stark) desperately; ‹regret› bitterly

**bitter-:** ~**böse** [1] Adj. furious; [2] adv. furiously; ~**kalt** Adj. bitterly cold

**bitterlich** [1] Adj. slightly bitter ‹taste›

[2] adv. (heftig) ‹cry, complain, etc.› bitterly

**bitter-süß** Adj. (auch fig.) bitter-sweet

**Bitt·steller** der; ~s, ~, **Bitt·stellerin** die; ~, ~nen petitioner

**Biwak** das; ~s, ~s (bes. Milit., Bergsteigen) bivouac

**bizarr** [1] Adj. bizarre

[2] adv. bizarrely

**Bizeps** der; ~[es], ~e biceps

**Blähung** die; ~, ~en flatulence no art., no pl.

**Blamage** /bla'maːʒə/ die; ~, ~n disgrace

**blamieren** [1] tr. V. disgrace

[2] refl. V. disgrace oneself; (sich lächerlich machen) make a fool of oneself

**blank** Adj. shiny

**Blanko-:** ~**scheck** der (auch fig.) blank cheque; ~**vollmacht** die (auch fig.) carte blanche

**Bläschen** /'blɛːsçən/ das; ~s, ~ **(a)** [small] bubble

**(b)** (in der Haut) [small] blister

**Blase** die; ~, ~n **(a)** bubble

**(b)** (in der Haut) blister

**(c)** (Harn~) bladder

**Blase·balg** der; ~s, **Blasebälge** bellows pl.

**blasen** [1] unr. itr. V. blow

[2] unr. tr. V. **(a)** blow

**(b)** (spielen) play ‹musical instrument, tune, melody, etc.›

**Bläser** der; ~s, ~, **Bläserin** die; ~, ~nen (Musik) wind player

**blasiert** (abwertend) [1] Adj. blasé

[2] adv. in a blasé way

**Blas-:** ~**instrument** das wind instrument; ~**kapelle** die brass band; ~**musik** die brass-band music

**Blasphemie** /blasfe'miː/ die; ~, ~n blasphemy

**Blas·rohr** das blowpipe

**blass, \*blaß** [1] Adj. pale

[2] adv. palely

**Blässe** die; ~: paleness

**Blatt** das; ~[e]s, **Blätter (a)** (von Pflanzen) leaf

**(b)** (Papier) sheet

**(c)** (Buchseite usw.) page; **etw. vom ~ spielen** sight-read sth.

**(d)** (Zeitung) paper

**(e)** (Spielkarten) hand

**(f)** (am Werkzeug, Ruder) blade

**Blättchen** das; ~s, ~ **(a)** (von Pflanzen) [small] leaf

**(b)** (Papier) [small] sheet

**blättern** itr. V. **in einem Buch ~:** leaf through a book

**Blätter·teig** der puff pastry

**Blatt-:** ~**gold** das gold leaf; ~**grün** das chlorophyll; ~**laus** die aphid

**blau** Adj. blue; **ein ~er Fleck** a bruise; ~ **sein** (fig. ugs.) be tight (coll.); **das Blaue vom Himmel herunterlügen** (ugs.) lie like anything

**Blau** das; ~s, ~ od. (ugs.:) ~s blue

**blau-, Blau-:** ~**äugig** Adj. **(a)** blue-eyed;

**(b)** (naiv) naive; ~**beere** die bilberry; ~**grau** Adj. blue-grey; ~**grün** Adj. blue-green

**bläulich** Adj. bluish

**blau-, Blau-:** ~**licht** das flashing blue light; ~|**machen** itr. V. (ugs.) skip work; ~**mann** der; Pl. ~**männer** (ugs.) boiler suit; ~**säure** die (Chemie) prussic acid; ~**stichig** Adj. (Fot.) with a blue cast postpos., not pred.; ~**stichig sein** have a blue cast

**Blazer** /'bleːzɐ/ der; ~s, ~: blazer

**Blech** das; ~[e]s, ~e **(a)** sheet metal; (Stück Blech) metal sheet

**(b)** (Back~) [baking] tray

**Blech-:** ~**bläser** der, ~**bläserin** die brass player; **die ~bläser** (im Orchester) the brass [section] sing; ~**büchse** die, ~**dose** die tin

**blechen** tr., itr. V. (ugs.) cough up (coll.)

**blechern** [1] Adj. (metallisch klingend) tinny ‹sound, voice›

[2] adv. tinnily

**Blech-:** ~**musik** die (abwertend) brass-band music; ~**napf** der metal bowl

**Blęchner** der; ~s, ~, **Blęchnerin** die;
~, ~nen (südd.) ▶ KLEMPNER

**Blęch-:** ~**schaden** der (Kfz-W.) damage no
indef. art. to the bodywork; ~**trommel** die
tin drum

**blęcken** tr. V. die Zähne ~: bare one's/its
teeth

**Blẹi** das; ~[e]s, ~e lead

**Blẹibe** die; ~, ~n place to stay

**blẹiben** unr. itr. V.; mit sein (a) stay;
remain; ~ Sie bitte am Apparat hold the line
please; wo bleibt er so lange? where has he
got to?; auf dem Weg ~: keep to the path;
sitzen ~: stay or remain sitting down or
seated; bei etw. ~ (fig.: an etw. festhalten) keep
to sth.
(b) (übrig bleiben) be left; remain
(c) etw. ~ lassen give sth. a miss

**blẹibend** Adj. lasting; permanent ⟨damage⟩

*****blẹiben|lassen** ▶ BLEIBEN C

**blẹich** Adj. pale

**blẹichen**[1] tr. V. bleach

**blẹichen**[2] regelm., veralt. auch unr. itr. V.
become bleached

**blẹi-, Blẹi-:** ~**frei** Adj. unleaded ⟨fuel⟩;
~**kristall** das lead crystal; ~**kugel** die
lead ball; (Geschoss) lead bullet; ~**schwer**
Adj. heavy as lead postpos.; ~**stift** der
pencil; mit ~stift in pencil; ~**stift·spitzer**
der pencil sharpener

**Blẹnde** die; ~, ~n (a) (Lichtschutz) shade; (am
Fenster) blind
(b) (Optik, Film, Fot.) diaphragm; (Blendenzahl)
aperture setting

**blẹnden** [1] tr. V. (a) (auch fig.) dazzle
(b) (blind machen) blind
[2] itr. V. ⟨light⟩ be dazzling

**blẹndend** [1] Adj. es geht mir ~: I feel
wonderfully well
[2] adv. wir haben uns ~ amüsiert we had a
marvellous time

**blịch** 1. u. 3. Pers. Sg. Prät. v. BLEICHEN[2]

**Blịck** der; ~[e]s, ~e (a) look; (flüchtig) glance
(b) (Ausdruck) look in one's eyes; mit
misstrauischem ~: with a suspicious look in
one's eye
(c) (Aussicht) view; ein Zimmer mit ~ aufs
Meer a room with a sea view
(d) (Urteil[skraft]) eye

**blịcken** [1] itr. V. look; (flüchtig) glance
[2] tr. V. sich ~ lassen put in an appearance

**Blịck-:** ~**fang** der eye-catcher; als ~fang
dienen serve to catch the eye; ~**feld** das
field of vision; ~**kontakt** der eye contact;
~**punkt** der view; ~**winkel** der (a) angle
of vision; (b) (fig.) point of view; viewpoint

**blịeb** 1. u. 3. Pers. Sg. Prät. v. BLEIBEN

**blịes** 1. u. 3. Pers. Sg. Prät. v. BLASEN

**blịnd** [1] Adj. (a) (auch fig.) blind; ~ werden
go blind
(b) (trübe) clouded ⟨glass⟩

(c) ein ~er Passagier a stowaway
(d) ~er Alarm a false alarm
[2] adv. (a) (ohne hinzusehen) without looking;
(wahllos) blindly
(b) (unkritisch) ⟨trust⟩ implicitly; ⟨obey⟩ blindly

**Blịnd-:** ~**bewerbung** die unsolicited
application; ~**darm** der (a) caecum; (b)
(volkst.: Wurmfortsatz) appendix

**Blịnde** der/die; adj. Dekl. blind person;
blind man/woman; die ~n the blind

**Blịnde·kuh:** ~ spielen play blind man's
buff

**Blịnden-:** ~**hund** der guide dog;
~**schrift** die Braille

**Blịndheit** die; ~ (auch fig.) blindness

**blịndlings** Adv. blindly; ⟨trust⟩ implicitly

**blịnd-, Blịnd-:** ~**schleiche** die; ~, ~n
slowworm; ~**wütig** [1] Adj. raging ⟨anger,
hatred, fury, etc.⟩; wild ⟨rage⟩; [2] adv. in a
blind rage

**blịnken** [1] itr. V. (a) ⟨light, glass, crystal⟩
flash; ⟨star⟩ twinkle; ⟨metal, fish⟩ gleam
(b) (Verkehrsw.) indicate
[2] tr. V. flash

**Blịnker** der; ~s, ~: indicator [light]

**Blịnk-:** ~**licht** das (a) flashing light; (b)
▶ BLINKER; ~**zeichen** das flashlight signal

**blịnzeln** itr. V. blink; (mit einem Auge, um ein
Zeichen zu geben) wink

**Blịtz** der; ~es, ~e (a) lightning no indef.
art.; ein ~: a flash of lightning; [schnell] wie
der ~: like lightning
(b) (Blitzlicht) flash

**blịtz-, Blịtz-:** ~**ab·leiter** der lightning
conductor; ~**artig** [1] Adj. lightning;
[2] adv. like lightning; ⟨disappear⟩ in a flash;
~**blạnk** Adj. (ugs.) ~blank [geputzt]
sparkling clean; brightly polished ⟨shoes⟩

**blịtzeblạnk** ▶ BLITZBLANK

**blịtzen** itr. V. (a) unpers. es blitzte (einmal)
there was a flash of lightning; (mehrmals)
there was lightning
(b) (glänzen) ⟨light, glass, crystal⟩ flash;
⟨metal⟩ gleam

**blịtz-, Blịtz-:** ~**gerät** das flash [unit];
~**licht** das flash[light]; ~**schnell** [1] Adj.
lightning attrib.; ~schnell sein be like
lightning; [2] adv. like lightning; ⟨disappear⟩
in a flash; ~**start** der lightning start

**Blọck** der; ~[e]s, Blöcke od. ~s (a) Pl. nur
Blöcke (Brocken) block
(b) (Wohnblock) block
(c) Pl. nur Blöcke (Gruppierung von politischen
Kräften, Staaten) bloc
(d) (Schreibblock) pad

**Blockạde** die; ~, ~n blockade

**Blọck-:** ~**flöte** die recorder; ~**haus** das,
~**hütte** die log cabin

**blockịeren** tr. V. block; jam ⟨telephone
line⟩; halt ⟨traffic⟩; lock ⟨wheel, machine, etc.⟩

**Blọck·schrift** die block capitals pl.

**blöd[e]** (ugs.) [1] Adj. (a) (dumm) stupid;
idiotic (coll.)

---

*old spelling - see note on page xiv

**(b)** (unangenehm) stupid
2 *adv.* stupidly; idiotically (coll.)
**Blödelei** *die;* ~, ~en silly joke
**blödeln** *itr. V.* make silly jokes
**Blödheit** *die;* ~, ~en stupidity
**blöd-, Blöd-:** ~**mann** *der; Pl.* ~männer
(salopp) stupid idiot (coll.); ~**sinn** *der* (ugs.)
nonsense; **mach doch keinen** ~**sinn!** don't be
stupid; (ugs.) 1 *Adj.* idiotic (coll.);
2 *adv.* idiotically (coll.)
**blöken** *itr. V.* ⟨sheep⟩ bleat; ⟨cattle⟩ low
**blond** *Adj.* fair-haired, blond ⟨man, race⟩;
blonde ⟨woman⟩; blond/blonde, fair ⟨hair⟩
**Blondine** *die;* ~, ~n blonde
**bloß** 1 *Adj.* **(a)** (nackt) naked
**(b)** (nichts als) mere ⟨words, promises,
triviality, suspicion, etc.⟩; **der** ~**e Gedanke
daran** the mere thought of it
2 *Adv.* (ugs.: nur) only
3 *Partikel* **was hast du dir** ~ **dabei
gedacht?** what on earth were you thinking
of?
**Blöße** *die;* ~: **sich** (*Dat.*) **eine/keine** ~
**geben** show a/not show any weakness
**bloß|stellen** *tr. V.* show up; expose
⟨swindler, criminal, etc.⟩
**Blouson** /bluˈzõː/ *das od. der;* ~s, ~s
blouson
**blubbern** *itr. V.* (ugs.) bubble
**Bluejeans** /ˈbluːdʒiːns/ *Pl. od. die;* ~, ~:
[blue] jeans *pl.*
**Blues** /bluːs/ *der;* ~, ~: blues *pl.*
**Bluff** *der;* ~s, ~s bluff
**bluffen** *tr., itr. V.* bluff
**blühen** *itr. V.* **(a)** ⟨plant⟩ flower, be in
flower or bloom; ⟨flower⟩ be in bloom, be
out; ⟨tree⟩ be in blossom; ~**de Gärten**
gardens full of flowers
**(b)** (florieren) thrive
**(c)** (ugs.: bevorstehen) jmdm. ~: be in store for
sb.; **das kann dir auch noch** ~: the same
could happen to you
**blühend** *Adj.* **(a)** (frisch, gesund) glowing
⟨colour, complexion, etc.⟩; radiant ⟨health⟩
**(b)** (übertrieben) vivid ⟨imagination⟩
**Blümchen** *das;* ~s, ~: [little] flower
**Blume** *die;* ~, ~n **(a)** flower
**(b)** (des Weines) bouquet
**(c)** (des Biers) head
**blumen-, Blumen-:** ~**beet** *das* flower
bed; ~**erde** *die* potting compost;
~**geschäft** *das* florist's;
~**geschmückt** *Adj.* flower-bedecked;
adorned with flowers *postpos.;* ~**kasten**
*der* flower box; (vor einem Fenster) window
box; ~**kohl** *der* cauliflower; ~**strauß** *der;*
*Pl.* ~sträuße bunch of flowers; (Bukett)
bouquet of flowers; ~**topf** *der* flowerpot;
~**vase** *die* [flower] vase; ~**zwiebel** *die*
bulb
**Bluse** *die;* ~, ~n blouse
**Blut** *das;* ~[e]s blood
**blut-, Blut-:** ~**arm** *Adj.* (Med.) anaemic;

~**armut** *die* (Med.) anaemia; ~**bad** *das*
bloodbath; ~**bahn** *die* bloodstream;
~**bank** *die; Pl.* ~~en (Med.) blood bank;
~**befleckt** *Adj.* bloodstained;
~**beschmiert** *Adj.* smeared with blood
*postpos.;* ~**buche** *die* copper beech;
~**druck** *der; Pl.* ~drücke blood pressure;
**Blüte** *die;* ~, ~n **(a)** flower; bloom; (eines
Baums) blossom; ~**n treiben** flower; ⟨tree⟩
blossom
**(b)** (das Blühen) flowering; (Baumblüte)
blossoming
**Blut-egel** *der;* ~s, ~: leech
**bluten** *itr. V.* bleed (**aus** from)
**blüten-, Blüten-:** ~**blatt** *das* petal;
~**honig** *der* blossom honey; ~**staub** *der*
pollen; ~**weiß** *Adj.* sparkling white
**Bluter** *der;* ~s, ~, **Bluterin** *die;* ~, ~nen
(Med.) haemophiliac
**Blut-erguss, \*Blut-erguß** *der*
haematoma; (blauer Fleck) bruise
**Bluter-krankheit** *die* haemophilia *no art.*
**Blut-:** ~**fleck[en]** *der* bloodstain;
~**gefäß** *das* (Anat.) blood vessel;
~**gerinnsel** *das;* ~~s, ~~ blood clot;
~**gruppe** *die* blood group;
~**hochdruck** *der* high blood pressure;
~**hund** *der* bloodhound
**blutig (a)** bloody; jmdn. ~ **schlagen** beat
sb. to a pulp
**(b)** (fig. ugs.: völlig) complete ⟨beginner,
layman, etc.⟩
**blut-, Blut-:** ~**jung** *Adj.* very young;
~**konserve** *die* container of stored blood;
~**konserven** stored blood; ~**körperchen**
*das;* ~~s, ~~: blood corpuscle; **rote/weiße**
~**körperchen** red/white corpuscles;
~**krebs** *der* leukaemia; ~**kreislauf** *der*
blood circulation; ~**lache** *die* pool of
blood; ~**leer** *Adj.* bloodless; ~**leere** *die*
restricted blood supply; ~**orange** *die*
blood orange; ~**plasma** *das* (Physiol.) blood
plasma; ~**probe** *die* **(a)** (~entnahme,
~untersuchung) blood test; **(b)** (kleine ~menge)
blood sample; ~**rache** *die* blood revenge;
~**rot** *Adj.* blood-red; ~**rünstig** 1 *Adj.*
bloodthirsty; 2 *adv.* bloodthirstily;
~**schande** *die* incest; ~**spende** *die* (das
Spenden) giving *no indef. art.* of blood;
(~menge) blood donation; ~**spender** *der;*
~**spenderin** *die* blood donor; ~**spur** *die*
trail of blood; ~**stillend** *Adj.* styptic
**bluts-, Bluts-:** ~**tropfen** *der* drop of
blood; ~**verwandt** *Adj.* related by blood
*postpos.;* ~**verwandtschaft** *die* blood
relationship
**Blut-:** ~**tat** *die* (geh.) bloody deed;
~**transfusion** *die* blood transfusion;
~**übertragung** *die* blood transfusion
**Blutung** *die;* ~, ~en **(a)** bleeding *no indef.
art., no pl.;*
**(b)** (Regelblutung) period
**blut-, Blut-:** ~**unterlaufen** *Adj.*
suffused with blood *postpos.;* bloodshot ┈┊

〈eyes〉; ~**vergießen** das; ~~s bloodshed; ~**vergiftung** die blood poisoning no indef. art., no pl.; ~**wurst** die black pudding; ~**zucker·spiegel** der (Physiol.) blood-sugar level

**Bö** die; ~, ~en gust [of wind]

**Bob** der; ~, ~s bob[sleigh]

**Bob-:** ~**bahn** die bob[sleigh] run; ~**fahrer** der, ~**fahrerin** die bobber

**Bock**[1] der; ~[e]s, Böcke (a) (Reh~, Kaninchen~) buck; (Ziegen~) billy goat; he-goat; (Schafs~) ram; **einen/keinen ~ auf etw.** (Akk.) **haben** (ugs.) fancy/not fancy sth.; **einen/keinen ~ haben, etw. zu tun** (ugs.) fancy/not fancy doing sth. (b) (Gestell) trestle (c) (Turngerät) buck

**Bock**[2] das; ~s (Bier) bock [beer]

**Bock·bier** das bock [beer]

**bocken** itr. V. refuse to go on; (vor einer Hürde) refuse; (sich aufbäumen) buck

**bockig** [1] Adj. stubborn and awkward [2] adv. stubbornly [and awkwardly]

**Bocks·horn** das: **sich ins ~ jagen lassen** (ugs.) let oneself be browbeaten

**Bock-:** ~**springen** das; ~~s (Turnen) vaulting [over the buck]; ~**wurst** die bockwurst

**Boden** der; ~s, Böden (a) (Erd~) ground; (Fuß~) floor; **am ~ zerstört [sein]** (ugs.) [be] shattered (coll.); **bleiben wir doch auf dem ~ der Tatsachen** (fig.) let's stick to the facts (b) (unterste Fläche) bottom; (Torten~) base (c) (Dach~, Heu~) loft

**boden-, Boden-:** ~**belag** der floor-covering; ~**ertrag** der crop yield; ~**fläche** die land area; ~**frost** der ground frost; ~**kammer** die attic; ~**los** Adj. (a) bottomless; (b) (ugs.: unerhört) incredible 〈foolishness, meanness, etc.〉; ~**nebel** der ground fog/mist; ~**satz** der sediment; ~**schätze** Pl. mineral resources

**Boden·see** der; ~s Lake Constance

**boden-, Boden-:** ~**ständig** Adj. indigenous 〈culture, population, etc.〉; ~**turnen** das floor exercises pl.; ~**welle** die bump

**Bodybuilding** /ˈbɔdibɪldɪŋ/ das; ~s bodybuilding no art.

**Böe** die; ~, ~n ▶ BÖ

**bog** 1. u. 3. Pers. Sg. Prät. v. BIEGEN

**Bogen** der; ~s, ~, (südd., österr.:) Bögen (a) curve; (Math.) arc (b) (Archit.) arch (c) (Waffe, Musik: Geigen~ usw.) bow (d) (Papier~) sheet

**bogen-, Bogen-:** ~**fenster** das arched window; ~**förmig** Adj. arched; ~**schießen** das; ~~s archery no art.

**Boheme** /boˈeːm/ die; ~: bohemian society

**Bohemien** /boeˈmjɛ̃ː/ der; ~s, ~s bohemian

**Bohle** die; ~, ~n [thick] plank

**Böhnchen** das; ~s, ~: [small] bean

**Bohne** die; ~, ~n bean; **nicht die ~** (ugs.) not one little bit

**Bohnen-:** ~**eintopf** der bean stew; ~**kaffee** der real coffee; ~**kraut** das savory; ~**stange** die (auch ugs.: Mensch) beanpole; ~**stroh** das: **dumm wie ~stroh** (ugs.) as thick as two short planks (coll.); ~**suppe** die bean soup

**bohnern** tr., itr. V. polish

**Bohner·wachs** das floor polish

**bohren** [1] tr. V. (a) bore; (mit Bohrer, Bohrmaschine) drill, bore 〈hole〉; sink 〈well, shaft, pole, post etc.〉 (in + Akk. into) (b) (bearbeiten) drill 〈wood, concrete, etc.〉 (c) (drücken in) poke (in + Akk. in[to]) [2] itr. V. (a) drill; **in der Nase ~:** pick one's nose; **nach Öl/Wasser** usw. ~: drill for oil/water etc.; (b) (ugs.: drängen, fragen) keep on [3] refl. V. bore its way

**bohrend** Adj. (a) gnawing 〈pain, hunger, remorse〉 (b) (hartnäckig) piercing 〈look etc.〉; probing 〈question〉

**Bohrer** der; ~s, ~ drill

**Bohr-:** ~**insel** die drilling rig; ~**maschine** die drill; ~**schrauber** der power drill/screwdriver; ~**turm** der derrick

**Bohrung** die; ~, ~en drill hole

**böig** Adj. gusty

**Boiler** /ˈbɔylɐ/ der; ~s, ~: water heater

**Boje** die; ~, ~n buoy

**Bolivien** /boˈliːvi̯ən/ (das); ~s Bolivia

**Böller·schuss, *Böller·schuß** der gun salute

**Boll·werk** das bulwark; (fig.) bulwark; bastion; stronghold

**Bolschewik** der; ~en, ~i, (abwertend:) ~en, **Bolschewikin** die; ~, ~nen Bolshevik

**Bolschewismus** der; ~: Bolshevism no art.

**Bolschewist** der; ~en, ~en, **Bolschewistin** die; ~, ~nen Bolshevist

**bolschewistisch** Adj. Bolshevik

**bolzen** (ugs.) itr. V. kick the ball about

**Bolzen** der; ~s, ~: bolt

**bombardieren** tr. V. (a) bomb (b) (fig. ugs.) bombard

**Bombardierung** die; ~, ~en (a) (Milit.) bombing (b) (fig. ugs.) bombardment

**bombastisch** [1] Adj. bombastic [2] adv. bombastically

**Bombe** die; ~, ~n bomb

**bomben-, Bomben-:** ~**angriff** der bomb attack; ~**anschlag** der bomb attack; ~**attentat** das bomb attack; ~**drohung**

---

*alte Schreibung - vgl. Hinweis auf S. xiv

*die* bomb threat; **∼erfolg** *der* (ugs.) smash hit (coll.); **∼fest** *Adj.* (ugs.: unveränderbar) dead certain; **∼fest stehen** be dead certain; be a dead cert (Brit. coll.); **∼form** *die* (ugs.) top form; **∼sicher** *Adj.* (ugs.: gewiss) dead certain; **das ist eine ∼sichere Sache** that's dead certain; that's a dead cert (Brit. coll.) *or* a sure thing (Amer.); **∼stjmmung** *die* (ugs.) tremendous *or* fantastic atmosphere (coll.); **∼trichter** *der* bomb crater

**Bomber** *der;* ∼s, ∼: bomber

**Bon** /bõŋ/ *der;* ∼s, ∼s **(a)** voucher; coupon **(b)** (Kassenzettel) receipt

**Bonbon** /bõŋ'bõŋ/ *der od.* (österr. nur) *das;* ∼s, ∼s sweet (Brit.); candy (Amer.); (fig.) treat

**bongen** *tr. V.* (ugs.) ring up; **gebongt sein** (ugs.) be fine; **ist gebongt!** (ugs.) fine!

**Bongo** *das;* ∼[s], ∼s *od. die;* ∼, ∼s bongo [drum]

**Bonmot** /bõ'mo:/ *das;* ∼s, ∼s bon mot

**Bonze** *der;* ∼n, ∼n bigwig (coll.)

**Boom** /bu:m/ *der;* ∼s, ∼s boom

**Boot** *das;* ∼[e]s, ∼e boat

**Boots-:** **∼fahrt** *die* boat trip; **∼haus** *das* boathouse; **∼steg** *der* landing stage; **∼verleih** *der* boat hire

**Bord**¹ *das;* ∼[e]s, ∼e shelf

**Bord**² *der;* ∼[e]s, ∼e (eines Schiffes) side; **an ∼:** on board; **über ∼:** overboard

**Bordell** *das;* ∼s, ∼e brothel

**Bord·stein** *der* kerb

**Bordüre** *die;* ∼, ∼n edging

**borgen** *tr. V.:* ▶ LEIHEN

**Borke** *die;* ∼, ∼n bark

**Borken·käfer** *der* bark beetle

**borniert** ⟨1⟩ *Adj.* bigoted ⟨2⟩ *adv.* in a bigoted way

**Börse** *die;* ∼, ∼n stock market; (Gebäude) stock exchange

**Börsen-:** **∼krach** *der* stock market crash; **∼makler** *der* stockbroker

**Borste** *die;* ∼, ∼n bristle

**borstig** *Adj.* bristly

**Borte** *die;* ∼, ∼n braiding *no indef. art.;* edging *no indef. art.*

**bös** ▶ BÖSE

**bös·artig** ⟨1⟩ *Adj.* **(a)** (heimtückisch) malicious ⟨*person, remark, etc.*⟩; vicious ⟨*animal*⟩ **(b)** (Med.) malignant ⟨2⟩ *adv.* maliciously

**Bös·artigkeit** *die;* ∼ **(a)** maliciousness; (von Tieren) viciousness **(b)** (Med.) malignancy

**Böschung** *die;* ∼, ∼en embankment

**böse** ⟨1⟩ *Adj.* **(a)** wicked; evil **(b)** (übel) bad ⟨*times, illness, dream, etc.*⟩; nasty ⟨*experience, affair, situation, trick, surprise, etc.*⟩ **(c)** (ugs.) (wütend) mad (coll.); (verärgert) cross (coll.) **(d)** (fam.: ungezogen) naughty

**(e)** (ugs.: arg) terrible (coll.) ⟨*pain, fall, shock, disappointment, storm, etc.*⟩ ⟨2⟩ *adv.* **(a)** (übel) ⟨*end*⟩ badly; **es war doch nicht ∼ gemeint** I didn't mean it nastily **(b)** (ugs.) (wütend) angrily; (verärgert) crossly (coll.) **(c)** (ugs.: sehr) terribly (coll.)

**boshaft** ⟨1⟩ *Adj.* malicious ⟨2⟩ *adv.* maliciously

**Boshaftigkeit** *die;* ∼, ∼en **(a)** maliciousness **(b)** (Bemerkung) malicious remark

**Bosheit** *die;* ∼, ∼en **(a)** malice **(b)** (Bemerkung) malicious remark

**Boss, *Boß** *der;* Bosses, Bosse (ugs.) boss (coll.)

**bös·willig** ⟨1⟩ *Adj.* malicious; wilful ⟨*desertion*⟩ ⟨2⟩ *adv.* maliciously; wilfully ⟨*desert*⟩

**Bös·willigkeit** *die;* ∼: malice; maliciousness

**bot** *1. u. 3. Pers. Sg. Prät. v.* BIETEN

**Botanik** *die;* ∼: botany *no art.*

**botanisch** ⟨1⟩ *Adj.* botanical ⟨2⟩ *adv.* botanically

**Bötchen** *das;* ∼s, ∼: little boat

**Bote** *der;* ∼n, ∼n **(a)** messenger **(b)** (Laufbursche) errand boy

**Botin** *die;* ∼, ∼nen ▶ BOTE: **(a)** messenger **(b)** errand girl

**Botschaft** *die;* ∼, ∼en **(a)** message **(b)** (diplomatische Vertretung) embassy

**Botschafter** *der;* ∼s, ∼, **Botschafterin** *die;* ∼, ∼nen ambassador

**Böttcher** *der;* ∼s, ∼, **Böttcherin** *die;* ∼, ∼nen cooper

**Bottich** *der;* ∼s, ∼e tub

**Bouillon** /bul'jõŋ/ *die;* ∼, ∼s bouillon

**Boulevard** /bulə'va:ɐ̯/ *der;* ∼s, ∼s boulevard

**Boulevard-:** **∼blatt** *das* ▶ BOULEVARDZEITUNG; **∼presse** *die* (abwertend) popular press; **∼stück** *das* (Theater) boulevard drama; **∼zeitung** *die* (abwertend) popular rag (derog.); tabloid

**Bourgeoisie** /burʒoa'zi:/ *die;* ∼, ∼n bourgeoisie

**Boutique** /bu'ti:k/ *die;* ∼, ∼s *od.* ∼n boutique

**Bowle** /'bo:lə/ *die;* ∼, ∼n punch (made of wine, champagne, sugar, and fruit or spices)

**bowlen** /'bo:lən/ *itr. V.* bowl

**Bowling** /'boʊlɪŋ/ *das;* ∼s, ∼s [tenpin] bowling

**Bowling-bahn** *die* bowling alley

**Box** *die;* ∼, ∼en **(a)** box **(b)** (Lautsprecher) speaker **(c)** (Pferdebox) [loose] box **(d)** (Motorsport) pit

**boxen** ⟨1⟩ *itr. V.* box; **gegen jmdn. ∼:** fight sb.; box [against] sb. ⟨2⟩ *tr. V.* punch

**Bọxer** *der;* ~s, ~ (Sportler, Hund) boxer

**Bọxerin** *die;* ~, ~nen boxer

**Bọx-:** ~**handschuh** *der* boxing glove; ~**kampf** *der* boxing match; (im Streit) fist fight; ~**ring** *der* boxing ring; ~**sport** *der* boxing *no art.*

**Boy** /bɔy/ *der;* ~s, ~s servant; (im Hotel) pageboy

**Boykott** /bɔy'kɔt/ *der;* ~[e]s, ~s boycott

**boykottieren** *tr. V.* boycott

**brach¹** *1. u. 3. Pers. Sg. Prät. v.* BRECHEN

**brach²** *Adj.* fallow; (auf Dauer) uncultivated

**Brachial·gewalt** *die* brute force

**Brach·land** *das* fallow [land]; (auf Dauer) uncultivated land

**brach|liegen** *unr. itr. V.* (auch fig.) lie fallow; (auf Dauer) lie waste

**brạchte** *1. u. 3. Pers. Sg. Prät. v.* BRINGEN

**Branche** /'brã:ʃə/ *die;* ~, ~n [branch of] industry

**Branchen-verzeichnis** *das* classified directory; (Telefonbuch) Yellow Pages ® *pl.*

**Brand** *der;* ~[e]s, Brände fire; **beim** ~ **der Scheune** when the barn caught fire; **etw. in** ~ **stecken** set fire to sth.

**Brand·anschlag** *der* arson attack (**auf** + *Akk.* on)

**branden** *itr. V.* (geh.) break

**Branden·burg** (*das*); ~s Brandenburg

**brand-, Brand-:** ~**marken** *tr. V.* brand ⟨person⟩; denounce ⟨thing⟩; ~**neu** *Adj.* (ugs.) brand-new; ~**salbe** *die* ointment for burns; ~**schaden** *der* fire damage *no pl., no indef. art.;* ~**stelle** *die* burn; ~**stifter** *der,* ~**stifterin** *die* arsonist; ~**stiftung** *die* arson

**Brandung** *die;* ~, ~en surf

**Brand·wunde** *die* burn

**brannte** *1. u. 3. Pers. Sg. Prät. v.* BRENNEN

**Brannt·wein** *der* spirits *pl.;* (Sorte) spirit

**Brasilianer** *der;* ~s, ~, **Brasilianerin** *die;* ~, ~nen Brazilian

**brasilianisch** *Adj.* Brazilian

**Brasilien** /bra'zi:liən/ (*das*); ~s Brazil

**brät** *3. Pers. Sg. Präsens v.* BRATEN

**Brat·apfel** *der* baked apple

**braten** *unr. tr., itr. V.* fry; (im Backofen) roast

**Braten** *der;* ~s, ~ (a) joint (b) roast [meat] *no indef. art.*

**Braten-:** ~**saft** *der* meat juice[s *pl.*]; ~**soße** *die* gravy

**Brat-:** ~**fett** *das* [cooking] fat; ~**fisch** *der* fried fish; ~**hähnchen** *das,* (südd., österr.) ~**hendl** *das* roast chicken; (gegrillt) broiled chicken; ~**hering** *der* fried herring; ~**kartoffeln** *Pl.* fried potatoes; home fries (Amer.); ~**pfanne** *die* frying pan; ~**spieß** *der* spit; ~**wurst** *die* [fried/grilled] sausage

**Brauch** *der;* ~[e]s, Bräuche custom

**brauchbar** *Adj.* useful; (benutzbar) usable; wearable ⟨clothes⟩

**brauchen** ① *tr. V.* (a) (benötigen) need (b) (aufwenden müssen) **mit dem Auto braucht er zehn Minuten** it takes him ten minutes by car; **wie lange brauchst du dafür?** how long will it take you?; (im Allgemeinen) how long does it take you? (c) (benutzen, gebrauchen) use; **ich könnte es gut** ~: I could do with it ② *mod. V.; 2. Part* **brauchen:** need; **du brauchst nicht zu helfen** there is no need [for you] to help; **du brauchst doch nicht gleich zu weinen** there's no need to start crying

**Brauchtum** /'braʊxtuːm/ *das;* ~s, Brauchtümer custom

**Braue** *die;* ~, ~n [eye]brow

**brauen** *tr. V.* brew

**Brauerei** *die;* ~, ~en brewery

**braun** *Adj.* brown; ~ **werden** (sonnengebräunt) get a tan; ~ **gebrannt** [sun]-tanned

**Braun** *das;* ~s, ~, (ugs.) ~s brown

**Braun·bär** *der* brown bear

**Bräune** *die;* ~: [sun]tan

**bräunen** *tr. V.* (a) tan; **sich** ~: get a tan (b) (Kochk.) brown

**braun-, Braun-:** *\**~**gebrannt** ▶ BRAUN; ~**kohle** *die* brown coal; lignite

**bräunlich** *Adj.* brownish

**Bräunung** *die;* ~, ~en browning

**Braus** ▶ SAUS

**Brause** *die;* ~, ~n (a) fizzy drink; (~pulver) sherbet (b) (veralt.: Dusche) shower

**brausen** ① *itr. V.* (a) ⟨wind, water, etc.⟩ roar (b) (sich schnell bewegen) race (c) *auch refl.:* ▶ DUSCHEN 1; ② *tr. V.* ▶ DUSCHEN 2

**Brause-:** ~**pulver** *das* sherbet; ~**tablette** *die* effervescent tablet

**Braut** *die;* ~, Bräute bride

**Bräutigam** *der;* ~s, ~e [bride]groom

**Braut-:** ~**jungfer** *die* bridesmaid; ~**kleid** *das* wedding dress; ~**paar** *das* bride and groom

**brav** ① *Adj.* (a) (artig) good (b) (redlich) honest ② *adv.* **nun iss schön** ~ **deine Suppe** be a good boy/girl and eat up your soup

**bravo** /'braːvo/ *Interj.* bravo

**Bravo** *das;* ~s, ~s cheer

**Bravo·ruf** *der* cheer

**BRD** *Abk.* = **Bundesrepublik Deutschland** FRG

**Brech-:** ~**bohne** *die* green bean; ~**eisen** *das* crowbar

**brechen** ① *unr. tr. V.* (a) break; **sich** (*Dat.*) **den Arm/das Genick** ~: break one's arm/neck (b) (ablenken) break ⟨waves⟩; refract ⟨light⟩

**(c)** (bezwingen) overcome ⟨*resistance*⟩; break ⟨*will, silence, record, blockade, etc.*⟩

**(d)** (nicht einhalten) break ⟨*agreement, contract, promise, the law, etc.*⟩

**(e)** (ugs.: erbrechen) bring up

**2** *unr. itr. V.* **(a)** *mit sein* break; **brechend voll sein** be full to bursting

**(b)** *mit jmdm.* ~: break with sb.

**(c)** *mit sein durch etw.* ~: break through sth.

**(d)** (ugs.: sich erbrechen) throw up

**3** *unr. refl. V.* ⟨*waves etc.*⟩ break; ⟨*rays etc.*⟩ be refracted

**Brẹcher** *der;* ~s, ~: breaker

**Brẹch-:** ~**mittel** *das* emetic; ~**reiz** *der* nausea; ~**stange** *die* crowbar

**Bredouille** /breˈdʊljə/ *die;* ~, ~n (ugs.) **in der** ~ **sein** *od.* **sitzen** be in real trouble; **in die** ~ **kommen** get into real trouble

**Brei** *der;* ~[e]s, ~e (Hafer~) porridge (Brit.), oatmeal (Amer.) *no indef. art.;* (Reis~) rice pudding; (Grieß~) semolina *no indef. art.*

**breiig** *Adj.* mushy

**breit** **1** *Adj.* **(a)** wide; broad, wide ⟨*hips, face, shoulders, forehead, etc.*⟩; **etw.** ~**er machen** widen sth.; **die Beine** ~ **machen** open one's legs; **ein 5 cm** ~**er Saum** a hem 5 cm wide

**(b)** (groß) **die** ~**e Masse** the general public

**(c) sich** ~ **machen** take up room; (sich ausbreiten) be spreading

**2** *adv.* ~ **gebaut** sturdily built

**breit·beinig** **1** *Adj.* rolling ⟨*gait*⟩

**2** *adv.* with one's legs apart

**Breite** *die;* ~, ~n **(a)** ▶ BREIT 1A: width; breadth

**(b)** (Geogr.) latitude

**breiten** (geh.) *tr., refl. V.* spread

**Breiten-:** ~**grad** *der* degree of latitude; parallel (~kreis); ~**kreis** *der* parallel

**breit-, Breit-:** *\**~**|machen** ▶ BREIT 1C; ~**schult[e]rig** *Adj.* broad-shouldered; ~**seite** *die* long side; (eines Schiffes) side; ~**|treten** *unr. tr. V.* (ugs. abwertend) go on about; ~**wand** *die* (Kino) big screen

**Bremen** (*das*)*;* ~s Bremen

**Brẹms-:** ~**backe** *die* brake shoe; ~**belag** *der* brake lining

**Brẹmse**[1] *die;* ~, ~n brake

**Brẹmse**[2] *die;* ~, ~n (Insekt) horsefly

**brẹmsen** *tr. V.* **(a)** *auch itr.* brake

**(b)** (fig.) slow down ⟨*rate, development, production, etc.*⟩; restrict ⟨*imports etc.*⟩

**Brẹms-:** ~**klotz** *der* brake pad; ~**licht** *das* brake light; ~**pedal** *das* brake pedal; ~**spur** *die* skid mark; ~**weg** *der* braking distance; ~**zug** *der* brake cable

**brẹnn·bar** *Adj.* combustible

**brẹnnen** **1** *unr. itr. V.* **(a)** burn; ⟨*house etc.*⟩ be on fire; ⟨*schnell/leicht* ~: catch fire quickly/easily; **es brennt!** fire!

**(b)** (glühen) be alight

**(c)** (leuchten) be on; **das Licht** ~ **lassen** leave the light on

**(d) die Sonne brannte** the sun was burning down

**(e)** (schmerzen) ⟨*wound etc.*⟩ sting; ⟨*feet etc.*⟩ be sore

**(f) darauf** ~, **etw. zu tun** be dying to do sth.

**2** *unr. tr. V.* **(a)** burn ⟨*hole, pattern, etc.*⟩; **einem Tier ein Zeichen ins Fell** ~: brand an animal

**(b)** (mit Hitze behandeln) fire ⟨*porcelain etc.*⟩; distil ⟨*spirits*⟩

**(c)** (rösten) roast ⟨*coffee beans, almonds, etc.*⟩

**brẹnnend** **1** *Adj.* (auch fig.) burning; lighted ⟨*cigarette*⟩; urgent ⟨*topic*⟩

**2** *adv.* **es interessiert mich** ~, **ob** ...: I'm dying to know whether ...

**Brẹnner** *der;* ~s, ~: burner

**Brennerei** *die;* ~, ~en distillery

***Brẹnnessel** *die;* ~, ~n ▶ BRENNNESSEL

**Brẹnn-:** ~**glas** *das* burning glass; ~**holz** *das* firewood; ~**material** *das* fuel; ~**nessel** *die* stinging nettle; ~**ofen** *der* kiln; ~**punkt** *der* focus; ~**spiritus** *der* methylated spirits *pl.;* ~**stoff** *der* fuel; ~**weite** *die* (Optik) focal length

**brẹnzlig** *Adj.* **(a)** ⟨*smell, taste, etc.*⟩ of burning *not pred.;*

**(b)** (ugs.: gefährlich) dicey (coll.)

**Brẹsche** *die;* ~, ~n gap; breach; [**für jmdn.] in die** ~ **springen** stand in [for sb.]

**Brẹtt** *das;* ~[e]s, ~er **(a)** board; (lang und dick) plank; (Diele) floorboard; **schwarzes** ~: noticeboard; **ein** ~ **vor dem Kopf haben** (fig. ugs.) be thick

**(b)** *Pl.* (Ski) skis

**Brẹtter-:** ~**wand** *die* wooden partition; ~**zaun** *der* wooden fence

**Brẹtt·spiel** *das* board game

**Brẹzel** *die;* ~, ~n pretzel

**Bridge** /brɪtʃ/ *das;* ~: bridge

**Brief** *der;* ~[e]s, ~e letter

**Brief-:** ~**beschwerer** *der;* ~s, ~: paperweight; ~**block** *der; Pl.* ~~s *od.* ~**blöcke** writing pad; ~**bogen** *der* sheet of writing paper; ~**freund** *der,* ~**freundin** *die* penfriend; pen pal (coll.); ~**freundschaft** *die* penfriendship; ~**geheimnis** *das* privacy of the post; ~**karte** *die* correspondence card; ~**kasten** *der* **(a)** postbox; **(b)** ( privat) letter box; ~**kopf** *der* **(a)** letter heading; **(b)** (aufgedruckt) letterhead; ~**kuvert** *das* (veralt.) ▶ ~UMSCHLAG

**brieflich** **1** *Adj.* written

**2** *adv.* by letter

**Brief·marke** *die* [postage] stamp

**Briefmarken-:** ~**album** *das* stamp album; ~**sammler** *der,* ~**sammlerin** *die* stamp collector; ~**sammlung** *die* stamp collection

**Brief-:** ~**öffner** *der* letter-opener; ~**papier** *das* writing paper; ~**partner** ····⟩

*der,* ~**partnerin** *die* penfriend;
~**schreiber** *der,* ~**schreiberin** *die*
[letter-]writer; ~**tasche** *die* wallet;
~**taube** *die* carrier pigeon; ~**träger** *der*
postman; letter-carrier (Amer.); ~**trägerin**
*die* postwoman; [female] letter-carrier (Amer.);
~**umschlag** *der* envelope; ~**waage** *die*
letter scales *pl.;* ~**wahl** *die* postal vote;
~**wechsel** *der* correspondence

**Bries** *das;* ~**es,** ~**e** (Kochk.) sweetbreads *pl.*

**briet** *1. u. 3. Pers. Sg. Prät. v.* BRATEN

**Brigade** *die;* ~, ~**n** (Milit.) brigade

**Brikett** *das;* ~**s,** ~**s** briquette

**brillant** /brɪlˈjant/ **1** *Adj.* brilliant
**2** *adv.* brilliantly

**Brillant** *der;* ~**en,** ~**en** brilliant

**Brillant-:** ~**ring** *der* (brilliant-cut) diamond
ring; ~**schmuck** *der* (brilliant-cut) diamond
jewellery

**Brillanz** /brɪlˈjants:/ *die;* ~: brilliance

**Brille** *die;* ~, ~**n** (a) glasses *pl.;* spectacles
*pl.;* **eine** ~: a pair of glasses *or* spectacles;
**eine** ~ **tragen** wear glasses *or* spectacles
(b) (ugs.: Klosettbrille) [lavatory] seat

**Brillen-:** ~**etui** *das,* ~**futteral** *das*
glasses case; spectacle case; ~**glas** *das*
[spectacle] lens; ~**schlange** *die* spectacled
cobra; ~**träger** *der,* ~**trägerin** *die*
person who wears glasses; ~**träger/-trägerin**
**sein** wear glasses

**Brimborium** *das;* ~**s** (ugs. abwertend) hoo-ha
(coll.)

**bringen** *unr. tr. V.* (a) (her~) bring; (hin~)
take; **jmdm. Glück/Unglück** ~: bring sb.
[good] luck/bad luck; **jmdm. eine Nachricht**
~: bring sb. news
(b) (begleiten) take; **jmdn. nach Hause/zum**
**Bahnhof** ~: take sb. home/to the station
(c) **es zu etwas/nichts** ~: get somewhere/get
nowhere
(d) **jmdn. ins Gefängnis** ~ ⟨crime, misdeed⟩
land sb. in gaol; **jmdn. wieder auf den**
**rechten Weg** ~ (fig.) get sb. back on the
straight and narrow; **jmdn. zum Lachen/zur**
**Verzweiflung** ~: make sb. laugh/drive sb. to
despair; **jmdn. dazu** ~, **etw. zu tun** get sb. to
do sth.; **etw. hinter sich** ~ (ugs.) get sth. over
and done with
(e) **jmdn. um seinen Besitz** ~: do sb. out of
his property
(f) (präsentieren) present; (veröffentlichen)
publish; (senden) broadcast
(g) **ein Opfer** ~: make a sacrifice
(h) **einen großen Gewinn/hohe Zinsen** ~:
make a large profit/earn high interest
(i) **das bringt es mit sich, dass ...:** that
means that ...
(j) (verursachen) cause

**brisant** *Adj.* explosive

**Brisanz** *die;* ~: explosiveness

**Brise** *die;* ~, ~**n** breeze

**Britannien** ⟨*das*⟩*;* ~**s** Britain; (hist.)
Britannia

**Brite** *der;* ~**n,** ~**n** Briton; **die** ~**n** the
British; **er ist [kein]** ~: he is [not] British

**Britin** *die;* ~, ~**nen** Briton; British girl/
woman

**britisch** *Adj.* British; **die Britischen Inseln**
the British Isles

**bröckelig** *Adj.* crumbly

**bröckeln** **1** *itr. V.* (a) crumble
(b) *mit sein* **von der Wand** ~: crumble away
from the wall
**2** *tr. V.* crumble

**Brocken** *der;* ~**s,** ~ (von Brot) hunk; (von
Fleisch) chunk; (von Lehm, Kohle, Erde) lump; **ein**
**paar** ~ **Englisch** (fig.) a smattering of English

**brodeln** *itr. V.* bubble

**Broiler** /ˈbrɔylɐ/ *der;* ~**s,** ~ (regional)
▶ BRATHÄHNCHEN

**Brokat** *der;* ~**[e]s,** ~**e** brocade

**Brokkoli** *der;* ~**s,** ~**[s]** broccoli

**Brom-beere** *die* blackberry

**Bronchie** /ˈbrɔnçiə/ *die;* ~, ~**n** bronchial
tube

**Bronchitis** *die;* ~, bronchitis

**Bronze** /ˈbrõːsə/ *die;* ~: bronze

**Bronze-:** ~**medaille** *die* bronze medal;
~**zeit** *die* Bronze Age

**Brosche** *die;* ~, ~**n** brooch

**Broschüre** *die;* ~, ~**n** booklet

**Brösel** *der;* ~**s,** ~: breadcrumb

**bröselig** *Adj.* crumbly

**bröseln** *itr. V.* crumble

**Brot** *das;* ~**[e]s,** ~**e** bread *no pl., no indef.*
*art.;* (Laib) loaf [of bread]; (Scheibe) slice [of
bread]

**Brot-:** ~**aufstrich** *der* spread; ~**belag**
*der* topping; (im zusammenklappten Brot) filling

**Brötchen** *das;* ~**s,** ~: roll

**Brot-:** ~**erwerb** *der* way to earn a living;
~**korb** *der* bread basket; ~**laib** *der* loaf [of
bread]; ~**messer** *das* bread knife;
~**rinde** *die* [bread] crust; ~**zeit** *die* (südd.)
(a) (Pause) [tea/coffee/lunch] break; (b)
(Vesper) snack; (Vesperbrot) sandwiches *pl.*

**Browser** /ˈbrauzɐ/ *der;* ~**s,** ~ (DV) browser

**Bruch** *der;* ~**[e]s,** **Brüche** (a) break; **in die**
**Brüche gehen** (zerbrechen) get broken; (fig.)
break up
(b) (Med.: Knochen~) fracture; break
(c) (Med.: Eingeweide~) hernia
(d) (fig.) (eines Versprechens) breaking; (eines
Abkommens, Gesetzes) violation
(e) (Math.) fraction

**brüchig** *Adj.* (a) brittle ⟨rock, brickwork⟩
(b) (fig.) crumbling ⟨relationship, marriage,
etc.⟩

**Bruch-:** ~**landung** *die* crash-landing;
~**rechnen** *das* fractions *pl.;* ~**strich** *der*
fraction line; ~**stück** *das* fragment; ~**teil**
*der* fraction; **im** ~**teil einer Sekunde** in a
split second

**Brücke** *die;* ∼, ∼n **(a)** (auch: Kommandobrücke, Zahnmed., Bodenturnen, Ringen) bridge **(b)** (Landungsbrücke) gangway **(c)** (Teppich) rug

**Brücken-:** ∼**bogen** *der* arch [of a/the bridge]; ∼**geländer** *das* parapet; ∼**kopf** *der* (Milit., auch fig.) bridgehead

**Bruder** *der;* ∼s, Brüder brother

**Brüderchen** *das;* ∼s, ∼: little brother

**brüderlich** [1] *Adj.* brotherly [2] *adv.* in a brotherly way

**Brüderlichkeit** *die;* ∼: brotherliness

**Brüderschaft** *die;* ∼: [mit jmdm.] ∼ trinken drink to close friendship [with sb.] (*agreeing to use the familiar 'du' form*)

**Brühe** *die;* ∼, ∼n **(a)** stock; (als Suppe) clear soup **(b)** (ugs. abwertend) (Getränk) muck; (verschmutztes Wasser) filthy water

**brühen** *tr. V.* **(a)** blanch **(b)** (auf∼) brew, make ⟨*tea*⟩; make ⟨*coffee*⟩

**brüh-, Brüh-:** ∼**warm** *Adj.* etw. ∼warm weitererzählen (ugs.) pass sth. on straight away; ∼**würfel** *der* stock cube

**brüllen** [1] *itr. V.* **(a)** ⟨*bull, cow, etc.*⟩ bellow; ⟨*lion, tiger, etc.*⟩ roar **(b)** (ugs.) (schreien) roar; (weinen) howl [2] *tr. V.* yell

**brummen** *tr., itr. V.* **(a)** ⟨*insect*⟩ buzz; ⟨*bear*⟩ growl; ⟨*engine etc.*⟩ drone **(b)** (unmelodisch singen) drone **(c)** (mürrisch sprechen) mumble

**Brummer** *der;* ∼s, ∼ (ugs.) **(a)** (Fliege) bluebottle **(b)** (LKW) heavy lorry (Brit.) or truck

**brummig** *Adj.* (ugs.) grumpy

**Brumm-:** ∼**kreisel** *der* humming top; ∼**schädel** *der* (ugs.) thick head

**brünett** *Adj.* dark-haired ⟨*person*⟩; dark ⟨*hair*⟩

**Brünette** *die;* ∼, ∼n brunette

**Brunnen** *der;* ∼s, ∼ **(a)** well **(b)** (Springbrunnen) fountain

**Brunnen·kresse** *die* watercress

**Brunst** *die;* ∼, Brünste (von männlichen Tieren) rut; (von weiblichen Tieren) heat

**Brunst·zeit** *die* (bei männlichen Tieren) rutting season; (bei weiblichen Tieren) [season of] heat

**brüsk** [1] *Adj.* brusque [2] *adv.* brusquely

**brüskieren** *tr. V.* offend; (stärker) insult; (schneiden) snub

**Brüssel** (*das*); ∼s Brussels

**Brust** *die;* ∼, Brüste **(a)** chest **(b)** (der Frau) breast **(c)** (Hähnchen∼) breast; (Rinder∼) brisket **(d)** (Brustschwimmen) breaststroke

**brüsten** *refl. V.* sich mit etw. ∼: boast about sth.

**brust-, Brust-:** ∼**kasten** (ugs.) chest;

∼**korb** *der* (Anat.) thorax (Anat.); ∼**krebs** *der* breast cancer; ∼**schwimmen** *unr. itr. V.; nur im Inf.* do [the] breaststroke; ∼**schwimmen** *das* breaststroke; ∼**tasche** *die* breast pocket

**Brüstung** *die;* ∼, ∼en parapet; (Balkon∼) balustrade

**Brust·warze** *die* nipple

**Brut** *die;* ∼, ∼en **(a)** brooding **(b)** (Jungtiere, auch fig. scherzh.: Kinder) brood

**brutal** [1] *Adj.* brutal; violent ⟨*attack, programme, etc.*⟩; brute ⟨*force, strength*⟩ [2] *adv.* brutally

**Brutalität** *die;* ∼, ∼en **(a)** brutality **(b)** (Handlung) act of brutality

**brüten** *itr. V.* **(a)** brood **(b)** (grübeln) ponder (über + *Dat.* over); brütend: ∼ heiß (ugs.) boiling hot

**Brüter** *der;* ∼s, ∼ (Kernphysik) breeder

**Brut-:** ∼**kasten** *der* incubator; ∼**reaktor** *der* (Kernphysik) breeder reactor; ∼**stätte** *die* (auch fig.) breeding ground

**brutto** *Adv.* gross

**Brutto-:** ∼**einkommen** *das* gross income; ∼**gehalt** *das* gross salary; ∼**sozialprodukt** *das* (Wirtsch.) gross national product

**brutzeln** [1] *itr. V.* sizzle [2] *tr. V.* (ugs.) fry [up]

**BSE** /beːsˈeː/ *die;* ∼: BSE

**Bub** *der;* ∼en, ∼en (südd., österr., schweiz.) boy; lad

**Bube** *der;* ∼n, ∼n (Kartenspiele) jack; knave

**Bubi** *der;* ∼s, ∼s **(a)** [little] boy or lad **(b)** (salopp: Schnösel) young lad

**Buch** *das;* ∼[e]s, Bücher book; (Dreh∼) script; über etw. (*Akk.*) ∼ führen keep a record of sth.

**Buch-:** ∼**besprechung** *die* book review; ∼**binder** *der,* ∼**binderin** *die;* ∼∼, ∼∼nen bookbinder; ∼**druck** *der* letterpress printing

**Buche** *die;* ∼, ∼n **(a)** beech [tree] **(b)** (Holz) beech[wood]

**Buch·ecker** *die;* ∼, ∼n beech nut

**buchen** *tr. V.* **(a)** enter **(b)** (vorbestellen) book

**Bücher·brett** *das* bookshelf

**Bücherei** *die;* ∼, ∼en library

**Bücher-:** ∼**regal** *das* bookshelves *pl.;* ∼**schrank** *der* bookcase; ∼**wurm** *der* (scherzh.) bookworm; ∼**verbrennung** *die* burning of books

**Buch-:** ∼**fink** *der* chaffinch; ∼**führung** *die* bookkeeping; ∼**halter** *der,* ∼**halterin** *die* bookkeeper; ∼**haltung** *die* **(a)** accountancy; **(b)** (Abteilung) accounts department; ∼**händler** *der,* ∼**händlerin** *die* bookseller; ∼**handlung** *die* bookshop; ∼**klub** *der* book club; ∼**laden** *der; Pl.* ∼**läden** ▶ HANDLUNG; ∼**messe** *die* book fair; ∼**rücken** *der* spine

**Buchs·baum** /'bʊks-/ *der* box [tree]

**Buchse** /'bʊksə/ *die;* ~, ~n (a) (Elektrot.) socket
(b) (Technik) bush

**Büchse** /'bʏksə/ *die;* ~, ~n (a) tin
(b) (ugs.: Sammel~) [collecting] box
(c) (Gewehr) rifle; (Schrot~) shotgun

**Büchsen-** ▶ DOSEN-

**Buchstabe** *der;* ~ns, ~n letter; (Druckw.) character; **ein großer/kleiner** ~: a capital [letter]/small letter

**buchstabieren** *tr. V.* spell

**buchstäblich** *Adv.* literally

**Bucht** *die;* ~, ~en bay

**Buchung** *die;* ~, ~en (a) entry
(b) (Vorbestellung) booking

**Buckel** *der;* ~s, ~ (a) hump; **einen** ~ **machen** ⟨cat⟩ arch its back; ⟨person⟩ hunch one's shoulders
(b) (ugs.: Rücken) back; **rutsch mir den** ~ **runter!** (salopp) get lost! (coll.)

**buckeln** *itr. V.* (ugs.) bow and scrape; **vor jmdm.** ~: kowtow to sb.

**bücken** *refl. V.* bend down

**bucklig** *Adj.* hunchbacked

**Bucklige** *der/die; adj. Dekl.* hunchback

**Bückling¹** *der;* ~s, ~e (ugs. scherzh.: Verbeugung) bow

**Bückling²** *der;* ~s, ~e (Hering) bloater

**buddeln** *itr., tr. V.* (ugs.) dig

**Buddha** /'bʊda/ *der;* ~s, ~s Buddha

**Buddhismus** *der;* ~: Buddhism *no art.*

**Buddhist** *der;* ~en, ~en, **Buddhistin** *die;* ~, ~nen Buddhist

**buddhistisch** *Adj.* Buddhist *attrib.*

**Bude** *die;* ~, ~n (a) kiosk; (Markt~) stall; (Jahrmarkts~) booth
(b) (Bau~) hut
(c) (ugs.) (Haus) dump (coll.); (Zimmer) room; digs *pl.* (Brit. coll.)

**Budget** /by'dʒe:/ *das;* ~s, ~s budget

**Büfett** *das;* ~[e]s, ~s *od.* ~e (a) sideboard
(b) (Schanktisch) bar
(c) (Verkaufstisch) counter
(d) **kaltes** ~: cold buffet

**Büffel** *der;* ~s, ~: buffalo

**büffeln** (ugs.) ⓵ *itr. V.* swot (Brit. coll.); cram
⓶ *tr. V.* swot up (Brit. coll.); cram

**Buffet** /by'fe:/ *das;* ~s, ~s ▶ BÜFETT

**Bug** *der;* ~[e]s, ~e *u.* Büge bow

**Bügel** *der;* ~s, ~ (a) (Kleider~) hanger
(b) (Brillen~) earpiece
(c) (an einer Tasche, Geldbörse) frame

**bügel-, Bügel-:** ~**brett** *das* ironing board; ~**eisen** *das* iron; ~**falte** *die* [trouser] crease; ~**frei** *Adj.* non-iron

**bügeln** *tr., itr. V.* iron

**bugsieren** /bʊ'ksi:rən/ *tr. V.* (ugs.) shift; manœuvre; steer ⟨person⟩

**buh** *Interj.* boo

**Buh** *das;* ~s, ~s (ugs.) boo

**buhen** *itr. V.* (ugs.) boo

**buhlen** *itr. V.* (geh. abwertend) **um jmds. Gunst** ~: court sb.'s favour

**Buh·mann** *der* whipping boy

**Buhne** /'bu:nə/ *die;* ~, ~n groyne

**Bühne** *die;* ~, ~n (a) stage; **ein Stück auf die** ~ **bringen** put on *or* stage a play
(b) (Theater) theatre

**bühnen-, Bühnen-:** ~**arbeiter** *der*, ~**arbeiterin** *die* stagehand; ~**ausstattung** *die* stage set; ~**bild** *das* [stage] set; ~**bildner** *der;* ~~s, ~~, ~**bildnerin** *die;* ~~, ~~nen stage designer; ~**reif** *Adj.* ⟨play etc.⟩ ready for the stage; ⟨imitation etc.⟩ worthy of the stage; dramatic ⟨entrance etc.⟩

**Buh·ruf** *der* boo

**buk** *1. u. 3. Pers. Sg. Prät. v.* BACKEN

**Bukett** *das;* ~s, ~s *od.* ~e (geh.) bouquet

**Bulette** *die;* ~, ~n (bes. berl.) rissole

**Bulgare** *der;* ~n, ~n Bulgarian

**Bulgarien** /bʊl'ga:riən/ (das); ~s Bulgaria

**Bulgarin** *die;* ~, ~nen Bulgarian

**bulgarisch** *Adj.* Bulgarian

**Bull-:** ~**auge** *das* circular porthole; ~**dogge** *die* bulldog; ~**dozer** /-do:zə/ *der;* ~~s, ~~: bulldozer

**Bulle** *der;* ~n, ~n (a) bull
(b) (salopp: Polizist) cop (coll.)

**Bullen·hitze** *die* (ugs.) sweltering *or* boiling heat

**Bulletin** /byl'tɛ̃:/ *das;* ~s, ~s bulletin

**bullig** ⓵ *Adj.* (a) beefy ⟨person, appearance, etc.⟩; chunky ⟨car⟩
(b) (drückend) sweltering ⟨heat⟩
⓶ *adv.* ~ **heiß** boiling hot

**Bull·terrier** *der* bull terrier

**bum** *Interj.* bang

**Bumerang** *der;* ~s, ~e *od.* ~s boomerang

**Bummel** *der;* ~s, ~ (a) stroll (**durch** around)
(b) (durch Lokale) pub crawl (coll.)

**Bummelei** *die;* ~, ~en (ugs.) (a) dawdling
(b) (Faulenzerei) loafing about

**bummelig** (ugs.) ⓵ *Adj.* (a) slow
(b) (nachlässig) slipshod
⓶ *adv.* (a) slowly
(b) (nachlässig) in a slipshod way

**bummeln** *itr. V.* (a) **mit sein** stroll (**durch** around); **durch die Kneipen** ~: go on a pub crawl (Brit. coll.)
(b) (trödeln) dawdle
(c) (faulenzen) laze about

**bums** *Interj.* bang

**Bums** *der;* ~es, ~e (ugs.) bang; (dumpfer) thud

**bumsen** *itr. V.* (ugs.) (a) bang; (dumpfer) thump; *unpers.* **es bumste ganz furchtbar** there was a terrible bang/thud
(b) *mit sein* (stoßen) bang

---

*old spelling - see note on page xiv

**Bund**[1] *der;* ~[e]s, **Bünde (a)** (Vereinigung) association; (Bündnis, Pakt) alliance
**(b)** (föderativer Staat) federation
**(c)** (an Röcken, Hosen) waistband

**Bund**[2] *das;* ~[e]s, ~e bunch

**Bündchen** *das;* ~s, ~ band

**Bündel** *das;* ~s, ~ bundle

**bündeln** *tr. V.* bundle up ⟨*newspapers, old clothes, rags, etc.*⟩; tie ⟨*banknotes etc.*⟩ into bundles/a bundle; tie ⟨*flowers, radishes, carrots, etc.*⟩ into bunches/a bunch; sheave ⟨*straw, hay, etc.*⟩

**Bundes-** federal; (in Namen, Titeln) Federal

**bundes-, Bundes-:** ~**bürger** *der,* ~**bürgerin** *die* (veralt.) West German citizen; ~**deutsch** *Adj.* (veralt.) West German; ~**ebene** *die:* auf ~**ebene** at federal *or* national level; ~**gerichtshof** *der* Federal Supreme Court; ~**kabinett** *das* Federal Cabinet; ~**kanzler** *der* **(a)** Federal Chancellor; **(b)** (schweiz.) Chancellor of the Confederation; ~**land** *das* [federal] state; (österr.) province; ~**liga** *die* national division; ~**minister** *der,* ~**ministerin** *die* Federal Minister; ~**ministerium** *das* Federal Ministry; ~**präsident** *der,* ~**präsidentin** *die* **(a)** [Federal] President; **(b)** (schweiz.) President of the Confederation; ~**rat** *der* Bundesrat; ~**regierung** *die* Federal Government; ~**republik** *die* federal republic; **die** ~**republik Deutschland** The Federal Republic of Germany; ~**straße** *die* federal highway; ≈ A road (Brit.); ~**tag** *der* Bundestag

**Bundestags-:** ~**abgeordnete** *der/die* member of parliament; member of the Bundestag; ~**präsident** *der,* ~**präsidentin** *die* President of the Bundestag; ~**wahl** *die* parliamentary *or* general election

**bundes-, Bundes-:** ~**trainer** *der,* ~**trainerin** *die* national team manager; ~**verfassungs·gericht** *das* Federal Constitutional Court; ~**verwaltungs·gericht** *das* Supreme Administrative Court; ~**wehr** *die* [Federal] Armed Forces *pl.;* ~**weit** *Adj., adv.* nationwide

**Bund-:** ~**falten** *Pl.* pleats; ~**falten·hose** *die* pleat[ed]-front trousers *pl.;* ~**hose** *die* knee breeches

**bündig** [1] *Adj.* **(a)** succinct
**(b)** (schlüssig) conclusive
[2] *adv.* **(a)** succinctly
**(b)** (schlüssig) conclusively

**Bündnis** *das;* ~ses, ~se alliance

**Bungalow** /'bʊŋgalo/ *der;* ~s, ~s bungalow

**Bunker** *der;* ~s, ~ **(a)** bunker
**(b)** (Luftschutzbunker) air-raid shelter

**bunt** [1] *Adj.* **(a)** colourful; (farbig) coloured; ~**e Farben/Kleidung** bright colours/brightly coloured clothes
**(b)** (fig.) varied ⟨*programme etc.*⟩

[2] *adv.* **(a)** colourfully; ~ **bemalt** brightly painted
**(b)** (fig.) **ein** ~ **gemischtes Programm** a varied programme

**bunt-, Bunt-:** *\**~**bemalt** ► BUNT 2A; ~**papier** *das* coloured paper; ~**specht** *der* spotted woodpecker; ~**stift** *der* coloured pencil/crayon

**Bürde** *die;* ~, ~n (geh.) weight; load

**Burg** *die;* ~, ~en castle
**(b)** (Strand~) wall of sand

**Bürge** *der;* ~n, ~n guarantor

**bürgen** *itr. V.* **(a)** für jmdn./etw. ~: vouch for sb./sth.
**(b)** (fig.) guarantee

**Bürger** *der;* ~s, ~, **Bürgerin** *die;* ~, ~nen citizen

**Bürger-:** ~**initiative** *die* citizens' action group; ~**krieg** *der* civil war

**bürgerlich** *Adj.* **(a)** (staats~) civil ⟨*rights, marriage, etc.*⟩; civic ⟨*duties*⟩
**(b)** (dem Bürgertum zugehörig) middle-class; **die** ~**e Küche** good plain cooking
**(c)** (Polit.) non-socialist; (nicht marxistisch) non-Marxist

**bürger-, Bürger-:** ~**meister** *der,* ~**meisterin** *die* mayor; ~**nah** *Adj.* which/who reflects the general public's interests *postpos., not pred.;* ~**pflicht** *die* duty as a citizen; ~**steig** *der;* ~s, ~e pavement (Brit.); sidewalk (Amer.)

**Bürgertum** /'--tuːm/ *das;* ~s **(a)** middle class
**(b)** (Großbürgertum) bourgeoisie

**Bürgin** *die;* ~, ~nen ► BÜRGE

**Bürgschaft** *die;* ~, ~en **(a)** guarantee
**(b)** (Betrag) penalty

**Büro** *das;* ~s, ~s office

**Büro-:** ~**angestellte** *der/die* office worker; ~**artikel** *der* item of office equipment; ~**haus** *das* office block; ~**klammer** *die* paper clip; ~**kraft** *die* clerical worker

**Bürokrat** *der;* ~en, ~en bureaucrat

**Bürokratie** *die;* ~, ~n bureaucracy

**Bürokratin** *die;* ~, ~nen bureaucrat

**bürokratisch** [1] *Adj.* bureaucratic
[2] *adv.* bureaucratically

**Büro·technik** *die* office technology

**Bürschchen** /'bʏrʃçən/ *das;* ~, ~: little fellow

**Bursche** *der;* ~n, ~n **(a)** boy; lad
**(b)** (abwertend: Kerl) guy (coll.)

**burschikos** [1] *Adj.* **(a)** sporty ⟨*look, clothes*⟩; [tom]boyish ⟨*behaviour, girl, haircut*⟩
**(b)** (ungezwungen) casual ⟨*comment, behaviour, etc.*⟩
[2] *adv.* **(a)** [tom]boyishly
**(b)** (ungezwungen) in a colloquial way

**Bürste** *die;* ~, ~n brush

**bürsten** *tr. V.* brush

**Bus** *der;* ~ses, ~se bus

**Bus-bahnhof** *der* bus station

**Busch** *der;* ~[e]s, Büsche bush; **auf den ~ klopfen** (fig. ugs.) sound things out

**Büschel** *das;* ~s, ~: tuft; (von Heu, Stroh) handful

**Busen** *der;* ~s, ~ bust

**Bus-:** ~**fahrer** *der,* ~**fahrerin** *die* bus driver; ~**haltestelle** *die* bus stop; ~**linie** *die* bus route

**Bussard** *der;* ~s, ~e buzzard

**Buße** *die;* ~, ~n (Rel.) penance *no art.*

**büßen** ① *tr. V.* **(a)** atone for **(b)** (fig.) pay for ② *itr. V.* **(a) für etw.** ~: atone for sth. **(b)** (fig.) pay

**Buß-geld** *das* (Rechtsw.) fine

**Buß- und Bettag** *der* (ev. Kirche) Day of Prayer and Repentance (*Wednesday eleven days before the first Sunday in Advent*)

**Büsten-halter** *der* bra; brassière (formal)

**Butan-gas** *das* butane gas

**Butt** *der;* ~[e]s, ~e flounder; butt

**Bütten-papier** *das* handmade paper (*with deckle edge*)

**Butter** *die;* ~: butter; **es ist alles in ~** (ugs.) everything's fine

**butter-, Butter-:** ~**berg** *der* (ugs.) butter mountain; ~**blume** *die* (Sumpfdotterblume) marsh marigold; (Hahnenfuß) buttercup; ~**brot** *das* slice of bread and butter; (zugeklappt) sandwich; ~**creme** *die* buttercream; ~**milch** *die* buttermilk; ~**weich** *Adj.* beautifully soft

**b. w.** *Abk.* = **bitte wenden** p.t.o.

**Bypass** /'baipɑs/ *der;* ~es, Bypässe (Med.) bypass

**Byte** /bait/ *das;* ~s, ~[s] (DV) byte

**bzw.** *Abk.* = **beziehungsweise**

# Cc

**c, C** /tsͤeː/ *das;* ~, ~: **(a)** (Buchstabe) c/C **(b)** (Musik) [key of] C

**C** *Abk.* = **Celsius** C

**ca.** *Abk.* = **cirka** c.

**Café** *das;* ~s, ~s café

**Cafeteria** *die;* ~, ~s cafeteria

**cal** *Abk.* = **[Gramm]kalorie** cal.

**Callboy** /'kɔːlbɔi/ *der;* ~s, ~s call-boy

**Callgirl** /'kɔːlgøːl/ *das;* ~s, ~s call girl

**Camp** /kɛmp/ *das;* ~s, ~s camp

**campen** *itr. V.* camp

**Camping** *das;* ~s camping

**Camping-:** ~**bus** *der* motor caravan; camper; ~**kocher** *der* camping stove; ~**platz** *der* campsite; campground (Amer.)

**Canasta** *das;* ~s canasta

**Cannabis** /'kanabis/ *der;* ~: cannabis

**Cantilever-bremse** /'kæntiliːvɐ-/ *die* cantilever brake

**Caravan** /'ka(ː)ravan/ *der;* ~s, ~s (Wohnwagen) caravan; trailer (Amer.)

**Cashflow** /kæʃ'floʊ/ *der;* ~s (Wirtsch.) [gross] cash flow

**Castor-:** ~**behälter** *der* Castor container; Castor cask; ~**transport** *der* Castor transport

**Catcher** /'kɛtʃɐ/ *der;* ~s, ~, **Catcherin** *die;* ~, ~nen all-in wrestler

**Cayenne-pfeffer** /ka'jɛn-/ *der* cayenne [pepper]

**CD** /tsͤeː'deː/ *die;* ~, ~s CD

**CD-ROM** /tsͤeːdeː'rɔm/ *die;* ~, ~[s] (DV) CD-ROM

**CD-ROM-Laufwerk** *das* (DV) CD-ROM drive

**CD-Spieler** /tsͤeː'deː-/ *der* CD player

**CDU** *Abk.* = **Christlich-Demokratische Union [Deutschlands]** [German] Christian Democratic Party

**C-Dur** /'tsͤeː-/ *das* C major

**Cellist** /tʃɛ'lɪst/ *der;* ~en, ~en, **Cellistin** *die;* ~, ~nen cellist

**Cello** /'tʃɛlo/ *das;* ~s, ~s *od.* Celli cello

**Celsius: 20 Grad ~:** 20 degrees Celsius *or* centigrade

**Cembalo** /'tʃɛmbalo/ *das;* ~s, ~s *od.* Cembali harpsichord

**Cent** *der;* ~[s], ~[s] cent; **50 ~** 50 cents

**Champagner** /ʃam'panjɐ/ *der;* ~s, ~ champagne (from Champagne)

**Champignon** /'ʃampɪnjɔn/ *der;* ~s, ~s mushroom

**Chance** /'ʃãːsə/ *die;* ~, ~n **(a)** chance **(b)** *Pl.* (Aussichten) prospects; **[bei jmdm]** ~n **haben** stand a chance [with sb.]

**Chancen-gleichheit** *die* (Soziol.) equality *no art.* of opportunity

---

*alte Schreibung - vgl. Hinweis auf S. xiv

**Chaos** /'k.../ *das;* ~: chaos *no art.*

**Chaot** /ka'o:t/ *der;* ~en, ~en, **Chaotin** *die;* ~, ~nen(a) (Politik) anarchist (trying to undermine society)
(b) (salopp: unordentlicher Mensch) **ein [furchtbarer]** ~ **sein** be [terribly] disorganized

**chaotisch** [1] *Adj.* chaotic
[2] *adv.* chaotically; **es geht** ~ **zu** there is chaos

**Charakter** /ka.../ *der;* ~s, ~e /...'te:rə/ character

**charakterisieren** *tr. V.* characterize

**charakteristisch** *Adj.* characteristic (**für** of)

**charakterlich** [1] *Adj.* character *attrib.;*
[2] *adv.* in [respect of] character

**charakter·los** *Adj.* unprincipled; (niederträchtig) despicable; (labil) spineless

**Charisma** /'ça:rɪsma/ *das;* ~s, **Charismen** charisma

**charismatisch** /çarɪs'ma:tɪʃ/ *Adj.* charismatic

**charmant** /ʃar'mant/ [1] *Adj.* charming
[2] *adv.* charmingly

**Charme** /ʃarm/ *der;* ~s charm

**Charter-** /'tʃartɐ-/: ~**flug** *der* charter flight; ~**maschine** *die* chartered aircraft

**Charts** /tʃarts/ *Pl.* charts

**Chassis** /ʃa'si:/ *das;* ~ /ʃa'si:(s),/ ~ /ʃa'si:s/ chassis

**chatten** /'tʃɛtn/ *itr. V.* (DV Jargon) chat

**Chauffeur** /ʃo'fø:ɐ̯/ *der;* ~s, ~e, **Chauffeurin** /ʃo'fø:rɪn/ *die;* ~, ~nen driver; ( privat angestellt) chauffeur

**checken** /'tʃɛkn/ *tr. V.* (a) (bes. Technik: kontrollieren) check; examine
(b) (salopp: begreifen) twig (coll.); (bemerken) spot; **ich habe das noch nicht gecheckt** I haven't got it yet

**Check·liste** *die* checklist; (Passagierliste) passenger list

**Chef** /ʃɛf/ *der;* ~s, ~s, **Chefin** /'ʃɛfɪn/ *die;* ~, ~nen (Leiter[in]) head; (der Polizei, des Generalstabs) chief; (einer Partei, Bande) leader; (Vorgesetzte[r]) superior; boss (coll.)

**Chef-:** ~**koch** *der,* ~**köchin** *die* chef; head cook; ~**sekretärin** *die* director's secretary

**Chemie** *die;* ~ (a) chemistry *no art.;*
(b) (ugs.: Chemikalien) chemicals *pl.*

**Chemikalie** /çemi'ka:liə/ *die;* ~, ~n chemical

**Chemiker** *der;* ~s, ~, **Chemikerin** *die;* ~, ~nen (graduate) chemist

**chemisch** [1] *Adj.* chemical
[2] *adv.* chemically

**Chemo·therapie** *die* (Med.) chemotherapy

**Chicorée** /'ʃikore/ *der;* ~s *od. die;* ~: chicory

**Chiffon** /'ʃɪfõ/ *der;* ~s, ~s chiffon

**Chiffre** /'ʃɪfrə/ *die;* ~, ~n (a) (Zeichen) symbol
(b) (Geheimzeichen) cipher
(c) (in Annoncen) box number

**Chile** /'tʃi:le, 'çi:lə/ (*das*); ~s Chile

**Chilene** /tʃi'le:nə, çi'le:nə/ *der;* ~n, ~n, **Chilenin** *die;* ~, ~nen Chilean

**chilenisch** *Adj.* Chilean

**Chili** /'tʃi:li/ *der;* ~s, ~es (a) *Pl.* (Schoten) chillies
(b) (Gewürz) chilli [powder]

**China** (*das*); ~s China

**Chinese** *der;* ~n, ~n, **Chinesin** *die;* ~, ~nen Chinese

**chinesisch** *Adj.* Chinese

**Chip** /tʃɪp/ *der;* ~s, ~s (a) (Spielmarke) chip
(b) (Kartoffel~) [potato] crisp (Brit.) *or* (Amer.) chip
(c) (Elektronik) [micro]chip

**Chip·karte** *die* smart card

**Chirurg** *der;* ~en, ~en surgeon

**Chirurgie** *die;* ~, ~n (a) surgery *no art.;*
(b) (Abteilung) surgical department; (Station) surgical ward

**Chirurgin** *die;* ~, ~nen surgeon

**chirurgisch** [1] *Adj.* surgical
[2] *adv.* surgically; by surgery

**Chlor** /k.../ *das;* ~s chlorine

**Chloroform** /k.../ *das;* ~s chloroform

**Chlorophyll** /k.../ *das;* ~s chlorophyll

**Cholera** *die;* ~: cholera

**cholerisch** *Adj.* irascible; choleric *⟨temperament⟩*

**Cholesterin** *das;* ~s cholesterol

**Chor** *der;* ~[e]s, Chöre /'kø:rə/ (auch Archit.) choir; (in Oper, Sinfonie, Theater; Komposition) chorus; **im** ~ **rufen** shout in chorus

**Choral** *der;* ~s, Choräle (Kirchenlied) chorale

**Choreograph** /koreo'gra:f/ *der;* ~en, ~en choreographer

**Choreographie** *die;* ~, ~n choreography

**Choreographin** *die;* ~, ~nen choreographer

**choreographisch** *Adj.* choreographic

**Chose** /'ʃo:zə/ *die;* ~, ~n (ugs.) stuff; **die ganze** ~: the whole lot (coll.) *or* (coll.) shoot

**Chow-Chow** /tʃau tʃau/ *der;* ~s, ~s chow

**Christ** /k.../ *der;* ~en, ~en Christian

**Christ-:** ~**baum** *der* (bes. südd.) Christmas tree; ~**demokrat** *der,* ~**demokratin** *die* (Politik) Christian Democrat

**Christenheit** *die;* ~: Christendom *no art.*

**Christentum** *das;* ~s Christianity *no art.;* (Glaube) Christian faith

**Christin** *die;* ~, ~nen Christian

**Christ·kind** *das* Christ-child (*as bringer of Christmas gifts*)

**christlich** [1] *Adj.* Christian
[2] *adv.* in a [truly] Christian spirit

**Christ-:** ~**messe** *die* (kath. Rel.) Christmas ⸬

Mass; ~**mette** *die;* ~~, ~~**n** (kath. Rel.) Christmas Mass; (ev. Rel.) midnight service [on Christmas Eve]; ~**rose** *die* Christmas rose; ~**stollen** *der* stollen; [German] Christmas loaf (*with candied fruit, almonds, etc.*)

**Christus** (*der*) ~ *od.* Christi Christ

**Chrom** /k.../ *das;* ~s chromium

**Chromosom** /k.../ *das;* ~s, ~en (Biol.) chromosome

**Chromosomen·satz** *der* (Biol.) chromosome set

**Chronik** /k.../ *die;* ~, ~en chronicle

**chronisch** *Adj.* chronic

**Chrysantheme** /k.../ *die;* ~, ~n chrysanthemum

**City** /'sɪti/ *die;* ~, ~s city centre

**clean** /kliːn/ *Adj.* (ugs.) clean (coll.); ~ **werden** come off drugs

**clever** /'klɛvɐ/ **1** *Adj.* (raffiniert) shrewd; (intelligent, geschickt) clever
**2** *adv.: s. Adj.:* shrewdly; cleverly

**Clique** /'klɪkə/ *die;* ~, ~n (a) (abwertend) clique
(b) (Freundeskreis) set; (größere Gruppe) crowd (coll.)

**Clown** /klaʊn/ *der;* ~s, ~s, **Clownin** /'klaʊnɪn/ *die;* ~, ~nen clown

**Club** ▶ KLUB

**cm** *Abk.* = **Zentimeter** cm.

**Co.** *Abk.* = **Compagnie** Co.

**Coach** /koʊtʃ/ *der;* ~s, ~s (Sport) coach; (bes. Fußball: Trainer) manager

**coachen** /'koʊtʃn/ *tr., itr. V.* (Sport) coach; (Trainer sein) manage

**Cockpit** *das;* ~s, ~s cockpit

**Cocktail** /'kɔkteɪl/ *der;* ~s, ~s cocktail

**Cognac** (Wz) /'kɔnjak/ *der;* ~s, ~s Cognac

**Cola** /'koːla/ *das;* ~s, ~s *od. die;* ~, ~s (ugs.) Coke ®

**Color-** (Fot.) colour (*film, slide, etc.*)

**Colt** (Wz) *der;* ~s, ~s Colt ® [revolver]

**Comeback** /kam'bɛk/ *das;* ~s, ~s comeback; **ein** ~ **feiern** stage a comeback

**Comic·heft** *das* comic

**Computer** /kɔm'pjuːtɐ/ *der;* ~s, ~: computer

**computer·gestützt** *Adj.* computer-aided; computer-assisted

**computerisieren** *tr. V.* computerize (*data, system*); (aufbereiten) make (*data*) computer-compatible

**computer-, Computer-:** ~**raum** *der* computer rooom; ~**spiel** *das* computer game ~**unterstützt** *Adj.* computer-aided; computer-assisted

**Container** /kɔn'teːnɐ/ *der;* ~s, ~: container; (für Müll) [refuse] skip

**cool** /kuːl/ (ugs.) **1** *Adj.* cool; ~ **bleiben** keep one's cool (coll.)
**2** *adv.* coolly (coll.)

**Cord** *der;* ~[e]s, ~e *od.* ~s cord; (~samt) corduroy

**Corned Beef** /'kɔːnd'biːf/ *das;* ~s corned beef

**Couch** /kaʊtʃ/ *die,* (schweiz. auch:) *der;* ~, ~es sofa

**Coup** /kuː/ *der;* ~s, ~s coup

**Coupon** /ku'põː/ *der;* ~s, ~s coupon; voucher

**Courage** /ku'raːʒə/ *die;* ~ (ugs.) courage

**Cousin** /ku'zɛ̃ː/ *der;* ~s, ~s, **Cousine** *die;* ~, ~n cousin

**Cover** /'kavɐ/ *das;* ~s, ~s (a) (von Illustrierten) cover
(b) (von Schallplatten) sleeve

**covern** /'kavɐn/ *tr. V.* cover (*song, record*)

**Cowboy** /'kaʊbɔy:/ *der;* ~s, ~s cowboy

**Credo** ▶ KREDO

**Creme** /kreːm/ *die;* ~, ~s, (schweiz.:) ~n cream

**CSU** *Abk.* = **Christlich-Soziale Union** CSU

**CT** (Med.) *Abk.*
= **Computertomographie** CT

**Curry** /'kœri/ *das;* ~s, ~s curry powder

**Curry·wurst** *die:* sliced fried sausage sprinkled with curry powder and served with ketchup

**Cursor** /'kɔːsɐ/ *der;* ~s, ~s (DV) cursor

**Cyberspace** /'saɪbɐspeɪs/ *der;* ~ (DV) cyberspace

# Dd

**d, D** /de:/ *das;* ~, ~ **(a)** (Buchstabe) d/D
**(b)** (Musik) [key of] D

**D** *Abk.* = **Damen**

**da** ⓵ *Adv.* **(a)** (dort) there; **da draußen/**
**drinnen/drüben/unten** out/in/over/down
there; **da, wo** where
**(b)** (hier) here
**(c)** (zeitlich) then; (in dem Augenblick) at that
moment
**(d)** (deshalb) **der Zug war schon weg, da habe**
**ich den Bus genommen** the train had
already gone, so I took the bus
**(e)** (ugs.: in diesem Fall) **da kann man nichts**
**machen** there's nothing one can do about it
**(f) da sein** (existieren) exist; (übrig sein) be left;
(anwesend sein) be about *or* around; (im Haus,
zu Hause sein) be in; (zu sprechen sein) be
available; (angekommen, eingetroffen sein) have
arrived; (fig.) ⟨*case*⟩ have occurred; ⟨*moment*⟩
have arrived; ⟨*situation*⟩ have arisen; **ich bin**
**gleich wieder da** I'll be right *or* straight
back
⓶ *Konj.* (weil) as; since

**da·bei** *Adv.* **(a)** with it/him/her/them; **nahe**
~: close by; ~ **sein** (anwesend sein) be there;
be present (**bei** at); (teilnehmen) take part (**bei**
in)
**(b)** (währenddessen) at the same time; (bei
diesem Anlass) then; on that occasion; **die** ~
**entstehenden Kosten** the expense involved;
[**gerade**] ~ **sein, etw. zu tun** be just doing
sth.
**(c)** (außerdem) ~ [**auch**] what is more
**(d)** (hinsichtlich dessen) about it/them; **was hast**
**du dir denn** ~ **gedacht?** what 'were you
thinking of?

**dabei-:** ~|**bleiben** *unr. itr. V.; mit sein*
stay there; be there; ~|**haben** *unr. tr. V.*
have with one; *\**~|**sein** ▶ DABEI A, B;
~|**stehen** *unr. itr. V.* stand there

**da|bleiben** *unr. itr. V.; mit sein* stay there;
(hier bleiben) stay here

**Dach** *das;* ~[e]s, Dächer roof

**Dach-:** ~**antenne** *die* roof aerial;
~**boden** *der* loft; **auf dem** ~**boden** in the
loft; ~**decker** /-dɛkɐ/ *der;* ~~s, ~~,
~**deckerin** *die;* ~~, ~~nen roofer;
~**fenster** *das* skylight; (~gaube) dormer
window; ~**garten** *der* roof garden;
~**gaube** *die* dormer window;
~**gepäckträger** *der* (Kfz-W.) roof rack;
~**geschoss,** *\**~**geschoß** *das* attic
[storey]; ~**kammer** *die* attic [room];
~**luke** *die* skylight; ~**pappe** *die* roofing
felt; ~**rinne** *die* gutter

**Dachs** /daks/ *der;* ~es, ~e badger

**Dach·stuhl** *der* roof truss

**dachte** *1. u. 3. Pers. Sg. Prät. v.* DENKEN

**Dach-:** ~**terrasse** *die* roof terrace;
~**wohnung** *die* attic flat (Brit.) *or* (Amer.)
apartment; ~**ziegel** *der* roof tile;
~**zimmer** *das* attic room

**Dackel** *der;* ~s, ~: dachshund

**da·durch** *Adv.* **(a)** through it/them
**(b)** (durch diesen Umstand) as a result; (durch
dieses Mittel) by this [means]

**da·für** *Adv.* **(a)** for it/them; ~, **dass** ... (wenn
man berücksichtigt, dass) considering that ...;
(damit) so that ...; ~ **sorgen [, dass** ...] see to
it [that ...]
**(b)** ~ **sein** be in favour [of it]; **ein Beispiel**
~ **ist** ...: an example of this is ...
**(c)** (als Gegenleistung) in return [for it]; (beim
Tausch) in exchange; (stattdessen) instead
**(d) etwas/nichts** ~ **können** be/not be
responsible

*\****dafür|können** ▶ DAFÜR D

**dagegen** *Adv.* **(a)** against it/them; **etwas**
~ **haben** have sth. against it; **ich habe**
**nichts** ~: I've no objection; ~ **sein** be
against it
**(b)** (im Vergleich dazu) by *or* in comparison

**da·heim** *Adv.* (bes. südd., österr., schweiz.) **(a)**
(zu Hause) at home; (nach Präp.) home
**(b)** (in der Heimat) [back] home

**da·her** *Adv.* **(a)** from there
**(b)** (durch diesen Umstand) hence
**(c)** (deshalb) therefore; so

**daher|kommen** *unr. itr. V.* come along

**da·hin (a)** there
**(b)** (fig.) ~ **musste es kommen** it had to
come to that
**(c) bis** ~: to there; (zeitlich) until then
**(d)** ~ **sein** be *or* have gone
**(e)** (in diesem Sinne) ~ **[gehend], dass** ...: to
the effect that ...

**da·hinten** *Adv.* over there

**da·hinter** *Adv.* behind it/them; (folgend)
after it/them

**Dahlie** /ˈdaːljə/ *die;* ~, ~n dahlia

**da-:** ~|**lassen** *unr. tr. V.* (ugs.) leave
[there]; (hier lassen) leave here; ~|**liegen**
*unr. itr. V.* lie there

**dalli** *Adv.* (ugs.) [~] ~! get a move on!

**damalig** *Adj.* at that *or* the time *postpos.*

**damals** *Adv.* at that time

**Damast** *der;* ~[e]s, ~e damask

**Dame** *die;* ~, ~n **(a)** (Frau) lady
**(b)** (Schach, Kartenspiele) queen
**(c)** (Spiel) draughts (Brit.); checkers (Amer.)

**Damen-:** ~**binde** *die* sanitary towel (Brit.)
*or* (Amer.) napkin; ~**friseur** *der,*

**∼friseurin** *die* ladies' hairdresser; **∼rad** *das* lady's bicycle; **∼toilette** *die* ladies' toilet

**da·mịt** ① *Adv.* (a) with it/them (b) (gleichzeitig) with that (c) (daher) thus ② *Konj.* so that

**dämlich** (ugs. abwertend) ① *Adj.* stupid ② *adv.* stupidly

**Dạmm** *der;* ∼[e]s, Dämme embankment; levee (Amer.); (Deich) dike; (Stau∼) dam

**dämmern** *itr. V.* es dämmert (morgens) it is getting light; (abends) it is getting dark

**Dämmerung** *die;* ∼, ∼en (a) (Abend∼) twilight; dusk (b) (Morgen∼) dawn

**Dämon** *der;* ∼s, ∼en /dɛ'mo:nən/ demon

**dämonisch** *Adj.* demonic

**dämonisieren** *tr. V.* demonize; portray as a demon/demons

**Dạmpf** *der;* ∼[e]s, Dämpfe steam *no pl., no indef. art.*

**Dạmpf·bügel·eisen** *das* steam iron

**dạmpfen** *itr. V.* steam (vor + *Dat.* with)

**dämpfen** *tr. V.* (a) (garen) steam 〈fish, vegetables, potatoes〉 (b) (mildern) muffle 〈sound〉; cushion, absorb 〈blow, impact, shock〉

**Dạmpfer** *der;* ∼s, ∼: steamer

**Dạmpf-:** **∼kochtopf** *der* pressure cooker; **∼maschine** *die* steam engine; **∼nudel** *die* (südd., Kochk.) steamed yeast dumpling; **∼walze** *die* steamroller

**da·nạch** *Adv.* (a) (zeitlich) after it/that; then (b) (räumlich) after it/them (c) (entsprechend) in accordance with it/them

**Däne** *der;* ∼n, ∼n Dane

**da·neben** *Adv.* (a) beside him/her/it/them *etc.;* (b) (im Vergleich dazu) in comparison

**daneben-:** **∼benehmen** *unr. refl. V.* (ugs.) blot one's copybook (coll.); **∼gehen** *unr. itr. V.; mit sein* miss [the target]; **∼schießen** *unr. itr. V.* miss [the target]

**Dänemark** (*das*); ∼s Denmark

**Dänin** *die;* ∼, ∼nen Dane; Danish woman/ girl

**dänisch** *Adj.* Danish

**dạnk** *Präp. mit Dat. u. Gen.* thanks to

**Dạnk** *der;* ∼[e]s thanks *pl.;* mit [vielem od. bestem] ∼ zurück thanks for the loan; (bes. geschrieben) returned with thanks!; vielen/ besten/herzlichen ∼! thank you very much

**dạnkbar** ① *Adj.* grateful; (anerkennend) appreciative 〈child, audience, etc.〉; [jmdm.] für etw. ∼ sein be grateful [to sb.] for sth. ② *adv.* gratefully

**Dạnkbarkeit** *die;* ∼: gratitude

**dạnke** *Höflichkeitsformel* thank you; (ablehnend) no, thank you; ∼ schön/sehr/ vielmals thank you very much

**dạnken** ① *itr. V.* (Dank aussprechen) thank; ich danke Ihnen vielmals thank you very much; na, ich danke! (ugs.) no, 'thank you! ② *tr. V.* [aber bitte,] nichts zu ∼: don't mention it

**Dạnke·schön** *das;* ∼s thank-you

**dạnn** *Adv.* (a) then; was ∼? what happens then?; noch drei Tage, ∼ ist Ostern another three days and it will be Easter; bis ∼: see you then; ∼ und wann now and then (b) (in diesem Falle) then; in that case; ∼ will ich nicht weiter stören in that case I won't disturb you any further; [na,] ∼ eben nicht! in that case, forget it!; nur ∼, wenn ...: only if ...

**daran** /da'ran/ *Adv.* (a) (an dieser/diese Stelle, an diesem/diesen Gegenstand) on it/them; dicht ∼: close to it/them; nahe ∼ sein, etw. zu tun be on the point of doing sth. (b) (hinsichtlich dieser Sache) about it/them; ∼ ist nichts zu machen there's nothing one can do about it; kein Wort ∼ ist wahr not a word of it is true; mir liegt viel ∼: it means a lot to me (c) ich wäre beinahe ∼ erstickt I almost choked on it; er ist ∼ gestorben he died of it

**daran|setzen** *tr. V.* devote 〈energy etc.〉 to it; summon up 〈ambition〉 for it; (aufs Spiel setzen) risk 〈one's life, one's honour〉 for it

**darauf** *Adv.* (a) on it/them; (oben ∼) on top of it/them (b) er hat ∼ geschossen he shot at it/them (c) (danach) after that; ein Jahr ∼/kurz ∼ starb er he died a year later/shortly afterwards; ∼ folgend following

**darauf-:** *∼folgend ▶ DARAUF C; ∼hin /-'-/ *Adv.* (a) thereupon; (b) (unter diesem Gesichtspunkt) with a view to this/that

**daraus** *Adv.* (a) from it/them; out of it/ them (b) mach dir nichts ∼: don't worry about it; was ist ∼ geworden? what has become of it?

**dar|bieten** (geh.) *unr. tr. V.* (aufführen, vortragen) perform; es wurden Gedichte und Lieder dargeboten a recital of poems and songs was presented

**Darbietung** *die;* ∼, ∼en (geh.) (a) presentation (b) (Aufführung) performance; (beim Varieté usw.) act

**dạrf** 1. u. 3. Pers. Sg. Präsens v. DÜRFEN

**dạrfst** 2. Pers. Sg. Präsens v. DÜRFEN

**darịn** *Adv.* (a) in it/them (b) (in dieser Hinsicht) in that respect

**dar|legen** *tr. V.* explain; set forth 〈reasons, facts〉

**Darlehen** *das;* ∼s, ∼: loan; ein ∼ aufnehmen get or raise a loan; jmdm. ein ∼ gewähren give or grant sb. a loan

**Dạrm** *der;* ∼[e]s, Därme intestines *pl.;* bowels *pl.*

---

*alte Schreibung - vgl. Hinweis auf S. xiv

**dar|stellen** tr. V. (a) depict; portray; **etw. grafisch ~:** present sth. graphically
(b) (verkörpern) play; act
(c) (schildern) describe ⟨person, incident, etc.⟩; present ⟨matter, argument⟩
(d) (sein, bedeuten) represent

**Darsteller** der; ~s, ~: actor

**Darstellerin** die; ~, ~nen actress

**Darstellung** die (a) representation; (Schilderung) portrayal; (Bild) picture; **grafische/schematische ~:** diagram; (Graph) graph
(b) (Beschreibung, Bericht) description; account;
(c) (einer Theaterrolle) interpretation; **seine ~ des Mephisto** his portrayal or interpretation of Mephisto

**darüber** Adv. (a) over it/them; **~ stehen** (fig.) be above such things
(b) **~ hinaus** in addition [to that]; (noch obendrein) what is more
(c) (über dieser/diese Angelegenheit) about it/them
(d) (über diese Grenze, dieses Maß hinaus) over [that]

***darüber|stehen** ▶ DARÜBER A

**darum** Adv. (a) [a]round it/them
(b) (diesbezüglich) **ich sorge mich ~:** I worry about it
(c) /'--/ (deswegen) for that reason

**darunter** Adv. (a) (unter dem Genannten/das Genannte) under it/them
(b) (unter dieser Grenze, diesem Maß) less; **Bewerber im Alter von 40 Jahren und ~:** applicants aged 40 and under

**das** ① best. Art. Nom. u. Akk. the
② Demonstrativpron. (a) attr. **das Kind war es** it was 'that child
(b) allein stehend **das** [da] that one; **das** [hier] this one [here]
③ Relativpron. (Mensch) who; that; (Sache, Tier) which; that

***da|sein** ▶ DA 1F

**Da·sein** das existence

**Daseins·berechtigung** die right to exist; **das findet darin** od. **dadurch seine ~:** this justifies its existence

**da|sitzen** unr. itr. V. sit there

**dasjenige** ▶ DERJENIGE

**dass, *daß** Konj. (a) that; **entschuldigen Sie bitte, ~ ich mich verspätet habe** please forgive me for being late; **ich verstehe nicht, ~ sie ihn geheiratet hat** I don't understand why she married him
(b) (nach Pronominaladverbien o. Ä.) [the fact] that; **das liegt daran, ~ du nicht aufgepasst hast** that comes from your not paying attention
(c) (im Konsekutivsatz) that; [**so**]~: so that
(d) (im Finalsatz) so that
(e) (im Ausruf) **~ mir das passieren musste!** why did it have to [go and] happen to me!

**dasselbe** ▶ DERSELBE

**da|stehen** unr. itr. V. (a) stand there

(b) (fig.) **gut ~:** be in a good position; [**ganz**] **allein ~:** be [all] alone in the world

**Datei** /da'tai:/ die; ~, ~en data file

**Daten** ① ▶ DATUM
② Pl. data

**Daten-:** ~**autobahn** die (DV) data highway; ~**bank** die; Pl. ~~en data bank; ~**erfassung** die data collection or capture; ~**schutz** der data protection no def. art.; ~**träger** der data carrier; ~**verarbeitung** die data processing no def. art.

**datieren** tr. V. date

**Dativ** der; ~s, ~e (Sprachw.) dative [case]

**Dativ·objekt** das (Sprachw.) indirect object

**Dattel** die; ~, ~n date

**Dattel·palme** die date palm

**Datum** das; ~s, Daten date

**Dauer** die; ~ (a) length; **für die ~ eines Jahres** od. **von einem Jahr** for a period of one year
(b) (Fortbestehen) **von ~ sein** last [long]; **auf die ~:** in the long run; **auf ~:** permanently

**dauer-, Dauer-:** ~**auftrag** der (Bankw.) standing order; ~**haft** ① Adj. (a) [long-]lasting ⟨peace, friendship, etc.⟩; (b) (haltbar) durable; ② adv. lastingly; ~**karte** die season ticket; ~**lauf** der jogging no art.; **ein ~lauf** a jog

**dauern** itr. V. last; ⟨job etc.⟩ take; **einen Moment, es dauert nicht lange** just a minute, it won't take long

**dauernd** ① Adj. constant ⟨noise, interruptions, etc.⟩; permanent ⟨institution⟩
② adv. constantly; **er kommt ~ zu spät** he keeps on arriving late

**Dauer-:** ~**regen** der continuous rain; ~**stellung** die permanent position; ~**welle** die perm; ~**wurst** die smoked sausage ⟨with good keeping properties, esp. salami⟩; ~**zustand** der permanent state [of affairs]; **zum ~zustand werden** become permanent or a permanent state

**Daumen** der; ~s, ~: thumb

**Daune** die; ~, ~n down [feather]; ~**n down** sing.

**davon** Adv. (a) (von dieser Stelle entfernt, weg) from it/them; (von dort) from there; (mit Entfernungsangabe) away [from it/them]
(b) (hinsichtlich dieser Sache) about it/them
(c) (durch diese Angelegenheit verursacht) by it/them; **das kommt ~!** (ugs.) [there you are,] that's what happens
(d) **ich hätte gern ein halbes Pfund ~:** I would like half a pound of that/those
(e) **~ kann man nicht leben** you can't live on that

**davon-:** ~**|fahren** unr. itr. V.; mit sein leave; (mit dem Auto) drive off; (mit dem Fahrrad, Motorrad) ride off; ~**|kommen** unr. itr. V.; mit sein get away; ~**|laufen** unr. itr. V.; mit sein run away; ~**|tragen** unr. tr. V. (a) ⋯✥

carry away; take away ⟨*rubbish*⟩; **(b)** (geh.: erringen) gain ⟨*a victory, fame*⟩; **(c)** (geh.: sich zuziehen) receive ⟨*injuries*⟩

**da·vor** *Adv.* **(a)** in front of it/them; ∼ **liegen/stehen** *usw.* lie/stand *etc.* in front of it/them
**(b)** (zeitlich) before [it/them]

***davor|liegen** *usw.* ▶ DAVOR A

**Dax** *der;* ∼: Dax [index]

**da·zu** *Adv.* **(a)** (zusätzlich zu dieser Sache) with it/them; (gleichzeitig) at the same time; (außerdem) what is more
**(b)** (diesbezüglich) about it/them
**(c)** (zu diesem Zweck) for it
**(d)** (zu diesem Ergebnis) to it; ∼ **reicht unser Geld nicht** we haven't enough money for that

**dazu-:** ∼|**geben** *unr. tr. V.* add; ∼|**gehören** *tr. V.* belong to it/them; ∼|**kommen** *unr. itr. V.; mit sein* **(a)** (hinkommen) arrive; **(b)** (hinzukommen) **kommt noch etwas dazu?** is there anything else [you would like]?; ∼ **kommt, dass ...** (fig.) what's more, ...; on top of that ...; ∼|**rechnen** *tr. V.* add on; ∼|**tun** *unr. tr. V.* (ugs.) add

**da·zwischen** *Adv.* in between; between them; (darunter) among them

**dazwischen-:** ∼|**kommen** *unr. itr. V.; mit sein* **(a)** **mit dem Finger** ∼**kommen** get one's finger caught [in it]; **(b)** (es verhindern) prevent it; **es ist mir etwas** ∼**gekommen** I had problems; ∼|**reden** *itr. V.* interrupt

**DDR** *Abk.* = **Deutsche Demokratische Republik** GDR; East Germany

**Deal** /di:l/ *der od. das;* ∼**s,** ∼**s** (salopp) deal

**dealen** /ˈdiːlən/ *itr. V.* (ugs.) push drugs; **mit LSD** ∼: push LSD

**Dealer** *der;* ∼**s,** ∼, **Dealerin** *die;* ∼, ∼**nen** (ugs.) pusher

**Debatte** *die;* ∼, ∼**n** debate (**über** + *Akk.* on); **zur** ∼ **stehen** be under discussion

**Debüt** /deˈbyː/ *das;* ∼**s,** ∼**s** debut

**Deck** *das;* ∼[e]**s,** ∼**s** deck

**Deck·bett** *das* ▶ OBERBETT

**Decke** *die;* ∼, ∼**n** **(a)** (Tisch∼) tablecloth
**(b)** (Woll∼, Pferde∼, fig.) blanket; (Reise∼) rug
**(c)** (Zimmer∼) ceiling

**Deckel** *der;* ∼**s,** ∼ **(a)** lid; (auf Flaschen, Gläsern usw.) top; (Schacht∼, Uhr∼, Buch∼ usw.) cover
**(b)** (Bier∼) beer mat

**decken** ⓵ *tr. V.* **(a)** etw. über etw. (*Akk.*) ∼: spread sth. over sth.
**(b)** roof ⟨*house*⟩; cover ⟨*roof*⟩
**(c)** **den Tisch** ∼: lay the table
**(d)** (schützen; Finanzw., Versicherungsw.) cover
**(e)** (befriedigen) meet ⟨*need, demand*⟩
⓶ *itr. V.* (den Tisch decken) lay the table

**Deck·mantel** *der* cover

**Deckung** *die;* ∼, ∼**en (a)** (Schutz; auch fig.) cover (esp. Mil.); (Boxen) guard; (bes. Fußball) defence; **in** ∼ **gehen** take cover
**(b)** (Befriedigung) meeting
**(c)** (Finanzw., Versicherungsw.) cover[ing]

**deckungs·gleich** *Adj.* (Geom.) congruent

**defekt** *Adj.* defective; faulty; ∼ **sein** have a defect; be faulty; (nicht funktionieren) not be working

**Defekt** *der;* ∼[e]**s,** ∼**e** defect, fault (**an** + *Dat.* in)

**defensiv** ⓵ *Adj.* defensive
⓶ *adv.* defensively

**Defensive** *die;* ∼, ∼**n** defensive; **in der** ∼: on the defensive; **die** ∼ (Sport) defensive play

**definieren** *tr. V.* define

**Definition** *die;* ∼, ∼**en** definition

**definitiv** ⓵ *Adj.* definitive
⓶ *adv.* finally

**Defizit** *das;* ∼**s,** ∼**e (a)** deficit
**(b)** (Mangel) deficiency

**deformieren** *tr. V.* **(a)** (verformen) distort
**(b)** (entstellen) deform (also fig.)

**deftig** *Adj.* (ugs.) **(a)** [good] solid *attrib.* ⟨*meal etc.*⟩; [nice] big ⟨*sausage etc.*⟩
**(b)** (derb) crude, coarse ⟨*joke, speech, etc.*⟩

**Degen** *der;* ∼**s,** ∼ **(a)** (Waffe) [light] sword
**(b)** (Fechtsport) épée

**degradieren** *tr. V.* demote

**Degradierung** *die;* ∼, ∼**en (a)** (im Rang) demotion
**(b)** (Herabwürdigung) degradation; reduction (**zu** to the level of)

**dehnbar** *Adj.* **(a)** (elastisch) ⟨*material etc.*⟩ that stretches *not pred.;* elastic ⟨*waistband etc.*⟩
**(b)** (fig.: vage) elastic; **das ist ein** ∼**er Begriff** it's a loose concept

**Dehnbarkeit** *die;* ∼: elasticity

**dehnen** *tr., refl. V.* stretch

**Deich** *der;* ∼[e]**s,** ∼**e** dike

**Deichsel** /ˈdaiksl̩/ *die;* ∼, ∼**n** shaft

**deichseln** *tr. V.* (ugs.) fix

**dein** *Possessivpron.* your; **viele Grüße von** ∼**em Emil** with best wishes, yours Emil; **das Buch dort, ist das** ∼[e]**s?** that book over there, is it yours?; **du und die Deinen** (geh.) you and yours

**deiner** *Gen. des Personalpronomens* **du** (geh.) of you

**deiner·seits** *Adv.* (von deiner Seite) on your part; (auf deiner Seite) for your part

**deinet·wegen** *Adv.* because of you; (für dich) on your behalf; (dir zuliebe) for your sake

**Dekade** /deˈkaːdə/ *die;* ∼, ∼**n** decade

**dekadent** *Adj.* decadent

**Dekadenz** *die;* ∼ (decadence)

**deklamieren** *tr., itr. V.* recite

**Deklination** *die;* ∼, ∼**en** (Sprachw.) declension

**deklinieren** *tr. V.* (Sprachw.) decline

**dekodieren** *tr. V.* (fachspr.) decode

---

*old spelling - see note on page xiv

**Dekolleté** /dekɔl'teː/ das; ~s, ~s low[-cut] neckline; décolletage

**Dekor** das; ~s, ~s od. ~e decoration; (Muster) pattern

**Dekorateur** /dekora'tøːɐ̯/ der; ~s, ~e, **Dekorateurin** die; ~, ~nen (Schaufenster~) window dresser; (von Innenräumen) interior designer

**Dekoration** die; ~, ~en decorations pl.; (Schaufenster~) window display

**dekorativ** [1] Adj. decorative [2] adv. decoratively

**dekorieren** tr. V. decorate ‹room etc.›; dress ‹shop window›

**Deko-stoff** der furnishing fabric

**Dekret** das; ~[e]s, ~e decree

**Delegation** die; ~, ~en delegation

**delegieren** tr. V. (a) send as a delegate/as delegates (b) delegate ‹task etc.› (an + Akk. to)

**Delegierte** der/die; adj. Dekl. delegate

**Delfin** ▶ DELPHIN

**delikat** Adj. (a) delicious; (fein) delicate ‹bouquet, aroma› (b) (heikel) delicate

**Delikatesse** die; ~, ~n delicacy

**Delikt** das; ~[e]s, ~e offence

**Delinquent** der; ~en, ~en, **Delinquentin** die; ~, ~nen offender

**Delirium** das; ~s, Delirien delirium

**Delle** die; ~, ~n (ugs.) dent

**Delphin** der; ~s, ~e dolphin

**dem** [1] best. Art., Dat. Sg. v. DER¹ 1 u. DAS 1: to the; (nach Präp.) the [2] Demonstrativpron., Dat. Sg. v. DER¹ 2 u. DAS 2: (a) attr. that; gib es dem Mann give it to 'that man (b) allein stehend gib es nicht dem, sondern dem da! don't give it to him, give it to that man/child etc.; [3] Relativpron., Dat. Sg. v. DER¹ 3 u. DAS 3 (Person) that/whom; (Sache) that/which; der Mann/das Kind, dem ich das Geld gab the man/the child I gave the money to

**Demagoge** der; ~n, ~n, **Demagogin** die; ~, ~nen demagogue

**demagogisch** Adj. demagogic

**Dementi** das; ~s, ~s denial

**dementieren** [1] tr. V. deny [2] itr. V. deny it

**dem-:** ~entsprechend [1] Adj. appropriate; [2] adv. accordingly; (vor Adjektiven) correspondingly; ~gemäß Adv. (a) (infolgedessen) consequently; (b) (entsprechend) accordingly; ~jenigen ▶ DERJENIGE; ~nach Adv. therefore; ~nächst Adv. shortly

**Demo** die; ~, ~s (ugs.) demo; auf der ~: at the demo

**Demokrat** der; ~en, ~en democrat; (Parteimitglied) Democrat

**Demokratie** die; ~, ~n democracy

**Demokratin** die; ~, ~nen ▶ DEMOKRAT

**demokratisch** [1] Adj. democratic [2] adv. democratically

**demokratisieren** tr. V. democratize

**demolieren** tr. V. wreck; smash up ‹furniture›

**Demonstrant** der; ~en, ~en, **Demonstrantin** die; ~, ~nen demonstrator

**Demonstration** die; ~, ~en demonstration (für in support of, gegen against)

**demonstrativ** [1] Adj. (a) pointed (b) (Sprachw.) demonstrative [2] adv. pointedly

**Demonstrativ·pronomen** das (Sprachw.) demonstrative pronoun

**demonstrieren** [1] itr. V. demonstrate (für in support of, gegen against) [2] tr. V. demonstrate

**dem·selben** ▶ DERSELBE

**Demut** die; ~: humility

**demütig** [1] Adj. humble [2] adv. humbly

**demütigen** [1] tr. V. humiliate [2] refl. V. humble oneself

**Demütigung** die; ~, ~en humiliation

**dem·zufolge** Adv. consequently

**den¹** [1] best. Art., Akk. Sg. v. DER¹ 1: the [2] Demonstrativpron., Akk. Sg. v. DER¹ 2: (a) attr. that; ich meine den Mann I mean 'that man (b) allein stehend ich meine den [da] I mean 'that one [3] Relativpron., Akk. Sg. v. DER¹ 3 (Person) that/whom; (Sache) that/which; der Mann, den ich gesehen habe the man that I saw

**den²** [1] best. Art., Dat. Pl. v. DER¹ 1, DIE¹ 1, DAS 1: the [2] Demonstrativpron. Dat. Pl. v. DER¹ 2A, DIE¹ 2A, DAS 2A: those

**denen** [1] Demonstrativpron., Dat. Pl. v. DER¹ 2B, DIE¹ 2B, DAS 2B them; gib es ~, nicht den anderen give it to 'them, not to the others [2] Relativpron., Dat. Pl. v. DER¹ 3, DIE¹ 3, DAS 3 (Personen) that/whom; (Sachen) that/which; die Menschen, ~ wir Geld gegeben haben the people to whom we gave money; die Tiere, ~ er geholfen hat the animals that he helped

**denjenigen** ▶ DERJENIGE

**denkbar** [1] Adj. conceivable [2] adv. (sehr, äußerst) extremely

**denken** [1] unr. itr. V. think (an + Akk. of, über + Akk. about); wie denkst du darüber? what do you think about it?; what's your opinion of it?; schlecht von jmdm. ~: think badly of sb.; denk daran, dass .../zu ...: don't forget that .../to ...; ich denke nicht daran! ···⫶·

no way!; not on your life!; **ich denke nicht daran, das zu tun** I've no intention of doing that
② *unr. tr. V.* think; **wer hätte das gedacht?** who would have thought it?; **eine gedachte Linie** an imaginary line
③ *unr. refl. V.* (a) (sich vorstellen) imagine (b) *sich (Dat.)* **bei etw. etwas ~:** mean something by sth.; **ich habe mir nichts [Böses] dabei gedacht** I didn't mean any harm [by it]

**Denken** *das;* ~s thinking; (Denkweise) thought

**Denker** *der;* ~s, ~, **Denkerin** *die;* ~, ~nen thinker

**denk·faul** *Adj.* mentally lazy

**Denk-:** ~**fehler** *der* flaw in one's reasoning; ~**mal** *das; Pl.* ~**mäler** *od.* ~**e** monument; memorial; **jmdm. ein ~ errichten** *od.* **setzen** erect *or* put up a memorial to sb.

**Denkmal[s]·schutz** *der* protection of historic monuments; **unter ~ stehen/stellen** be/put under a preservation order

**denk-, Denk-:** ~**pause** *die* pause for thought; ~**sport·aufgabe** *die* brain teaser; ~**vermögen** *das* ability to think [creatively]; ~**würdig** *Adj.* memorable; ~**zettel** *der* lesson

**denn** ① *Konj.* (a) (kausal) for; because (b) (geh.: als) than
② *Adv.* **es sei ~, ...:** unless ...
③ *Partikel* (in Fragesätzen) **wie geht es dir ~?** tell me, how are you?; **wie heißt du ~?** tell me your name; **warum ~ nicht?** why ever not?

**dennoch** *Adv.* nevertheless

**denselben** ▶ DERSELBE

**Denunziant** *der;* ~en, ~en, **Denunziantin** *die;* ~, ~nen informer; grass (sl.)

**denunzieren** *tr. V.* denounce; (bei der Polizei) inform against; grass on (sl.) **(bei** to)

**Deo** *das;* ~s, ~s, **Deodorant** *das;* ~s, ~s (auch:) ~e deodorant

**Deo·spray** *das* deodorant spray

**Deponie** *die;* ~, ~n tip (Brit.); dump

**deponieren** *tr. V.* put; (im Safe o. Ä.) deposit

**Deportation** *die;* ~, ~en transportation; (ins Ausland) deportation

**deportieren** *tr. V.* transport; (ins Ausland) deport

**Deportierte** *der/die; adj. Dekl.* transportee; (ins Ausland) deportee

**Depot** /de'po:/ *das;* ~s, ~s (a) depot; (Lagerhaus) warehouse; (für Möbel usw.) depository; (im Freien, für Munition o. Ä.) dump; (in einer Bank) strongroom; safe deposit (b) (hinterlegte Wertgegenstände) deposits *pl.*

**Depp** *der;* ~en (auch:) ~s, ~en (auch:) ~e (bes. südd., österr., schweiz. abwertend) ▶ DUMMKOPF

**Depression** *die;* ~, ~en depression

**depressiv** ① *Adj.* depressive
② *adv.* **~ veranlagt sein** have a tendency towards depression

**deprimieren** *tr. V.* depress

**deprimierend** *Adj.* depressing

**deprimiert** ① *Adj.* depressed
② *adv.* dejectedly

**der¹** ① *best. Art. Nom.* the; **der Tod** death; **der „Faust"** 'Faust'; **der Bodensee/Mount Everest** Lake Constance/Mount Everest; **der Iran/Sudan** Iran/the Sudan; **der Mensch/Mann ist ...:** man is .../men are ...
② *Demonstrativpron.* (a) *attr.* that; **der Mann war es** it was 'that man
(b) *allein stehend* he; **der war es** it was 'him; **der [da]** (Person) that man/boy; (Sache) that one; **der [hier]** (Person) this man/boy; (Sache) this one
③ *Relativpron.* (Person) who/that; (Sache) which/that; **der Mann, der da drüben entlanggeht** the man walking along over there
④ *Relativ- u. Demonstrativpron.* the one who

**der²** ① *best. Art.* (a) *Gen. Sg. v.* DIE¹ 1: **der Hut der Frau** the woman's hat; **der Henkel der Tasse** the handle of the cup
(b) *Dat. Sg. v.* DIE¹ 1 to the; (nach Präp.) the
(c) *Gen. Pl. v.* DER¹ 1, DIE¹ 1, DAS 1: **das Haus der Freunde** our/their *etc.* friends' house; **das Bellen der Hunde** the barking of the dogs
② *Demonstrativpron.* (a) *Gen. Sg. v.* DIE¹ 2: of the; of that
(b) *Dat. Sg. v.* DIE¹ 2 *attr.* **der Frau [da/hier] gehört es** it belongs to that woman there/this woman here
(c) *Gen. Pl. v.* DER¹ 2A, DIE¹ 2A, DAS 2A: of those
③ *Relativpron.; Dat. Sg. v.* DIE¹ 3: **die Frau, der ich es gegeben habe** the woman I gave it to; **die Katze, der er einen Tritt gab** the cat [that] he kicked

**der·art** *Adv.* so; **es hat lange nicht mehr ~ geregnet** it hasn't rained as hard as that for a long time; **sie hat ~ geschrien, dass ...:** she screamed so much that ...

**der·artig** ① *Adj.* such
② *adv.* ▶ DERART

**derb** ① *Adj.* (a) tough ‹material›; stout, ‹shoes›
(b) (kraftvoll, deftig) earthy ‹scenes, humour›
② *adv.* (a) strongly ‹made, woven, etc.›
(b) (kraftvoll, deftig) earthily

**deren** ① *Relativpron.* (a) *Gen. Sg. v.* DIE¹ 3 (Personen) whose; (Sachen) of which
(b) *Gen. Pl. v.* DER¹ 3, DIE¹ 3, DAS 3 (Personen) whose; (Sachen) **Maßnahmen, ~ Folgen wir noch nicht absehen können** measures, the consequences of which we cannot yet foresee
② *Demonstrativpron.* (a) *Gen. Sg. v.* DIE¹ 2: **meine Tante, ihre Freundin und ~ Hund** my aunt, her friend and her dog

---

\*alte Schreibung - vgl. Hinweis auf S. xiv

**(b)** *Gen. Pl. v.* DER¹ 2, DIE¹ 2, DAS 2: **meine Verwandten und ~ Kinder** my relatives and their children

**derent-:** **~wegen** *Adv.* [1] *relativ* (Personen) because of whom; (Sachen) because of which; [2] *demonstrativ* because of them; **~willen** *Adv.* **um ~willen** (Personen) for whose sake; (Sachen) for the sake of which

**derer** *Demonstrativpron.; Gen. Pl. v.* DER¹ 2, DIE¹ 2, DAS 2 of those

**der·gleichen** *indekl. Demonstrativpron.* **(a)** *attr.* such; like that *postpos., not pred.;* **(b)** *allein stehend* that sort of thing

**Derivat** *das;* ~[e]s, ~e derivative

**der·jenige, die·jenige, das·jenige** *Demonstrativpron.* **(a)** *attr.* that; *Pl.* those **(b)** *allein stehend* that one; *Pl.* those

**derlei** *indekl. Demonstrativpron.:* ▶ DERGLEICHEN

**der·maßen** *Adv.* **~ schön** *usw.,* **dass …:** so beautiful *etc.* that …

**derselbe, dieselbe, dasselbe** *Demonstrativpron.* **(a)** *attr.* the same **(b)** *allein stehend* the same one; *Pl.* the same people; **er sagt immer dasselbe** he always says the same thing; **noch einmal dasselbe, bitte** (ugs.) [the] same again please

**der·zeit** *Adv.* at present

**der·zeitig** *Adj.* present; current

**des** [1] *best. Art.; Gen. Sg. v.* DER¹ 1, DAS 1: **die Mütze des Jungen** the boy's cap; **das Klingeln des Telefons** the ringing of the telephone [2] *Demonstrativpron.; Gen. Sg. v.* DER¹ 2, DAS 2: **er ist der Sohn des Mannes, der …:** he's the son of the man who …

**Deserteur** /dezɛr'tøːɐ̯/ *der;* ~s, ~e, **Deserteurin** /dezɛr'tøːrɪn/ *die;* ~, ~nen deserter

**desertieren** *itr. V.; mit sein* desert

**des·gleichen** *Adv.* likewise; **er ist Arzt, ~ sein Sohn** he is a doctor, as is his son

**des·halb** *Adv.* for that reason; **~ bin ich zu dir gekommen** that is why I came to you

**Design** /di'zaɪn/ *das;* ~s, ~s design

**Designer** /di'zaɪnɐ/ *der;* ~s, ~, **Designerin** *die;* ~, ~nen designer

**Designer·droge** /-'----/ *die;* ~, ~n designer drug

**Desinfektion** *die;* ~, ~nen disinfection

**Desinfektions·mittel** *das* disinfectant

**desinfizieren** *tr. V.* disinfect

**Desinteresse** *das;* ~s lack of interest

**Despot** /dɛs'poːt/ *der;* ~en, ~en, **Despotin** *die;* ~, ~nen despot; (fig. abwertend) tyrant

**despotisch** [1] *Adj.* despotic [2] *adv.* despotically

**des·selben** ▶ DERSELBE

**dessen** [1] *Relativpron.; Gen. Sg. v.* DER¹ 3, DAS 3 *attr.* (Person) whose; (Sache) of which

[2] *Demonstrativpron.; Gen. Sg. v.* DER¹ 2, DAS 2: **mein Onkel, sein Sohn und ~ Hund** my uncle, his son, and 'his dog

**Dessert** /dɛ'seːɐ̯/ *das;* ~s, ~s dessert

**Destille** *die;* ~, ~n distillery

**destillieren** *tr. V.* (Chemie) distil

**desto** *Konj., vor Komp.* **je eher, ~ besser** the sooner the better

**des·wegen** *Adv.* ▶ DESHALB

**Detail** /de'tai/ *das;* ~s, ~s detail

**detailliert** [1] *Adj.* detailed [2] *adv.* in detail; **sehr ~:** in great detail

**Detektiv** *der;* ~s, ~e, **Detektivin** *die;* ~, ~nen [private] detective

**Detonation** *die;* ~, ~en detonation; explosion

**detonieren** *itr. V.; mit sein* detonate; explode

**Deut** **keinen ~:** not one bit

**deuten** [1] *itr. V.* point; **[mit dem Finger] auf jmdn./etw. ~:** point [one's finger] at sb./ sth. [2] *tr. V.* interpret

**deutlich** [1] *Adj.* clear [2] *adv.* clearly

**Deutlichkeit** *die;* **~ (a)** clarity **(b)** (Eindeutigkeit) clearness

**deutsch** [1] *Adj.* German; **Deutsche Mark** Deutschmark; German mark [2] *adv.* **Deutsch sprechen/schreiben** speak/ write German

**Deutsch** *das;* ~[s] German; **gutes/fließend ~ sprechen** speak good/fluent German; **auf od. in ~:** in German; **auf [gut] ~** (ugs.) in plain English

**Deutsche¹** *der/die; adj. Dekl.* German; **er ist ~r** he is German

**Deutsche²** *das; adj. Dekl.* **das ~:** German; **aus dem ~n/ins ~ übersetzen** translate from/into German

**Deutschland** *(das);* ~s Germany

**deutsch-, Deutsch-:** **~lehrer** *der,* **~lehrerin** *die* German teacher; **~sprachig** *Adj.* **(a)** German-speaking; **(b)** German-language *attrib.;* **~unterricht** *der* German teaching; (Unterrichtsstunde) German lesson

**Deutung** *die;* ~, ~en interpretation

**Devise** *die;* ~, ~n motto

**Devisen** *Pl.* foreign currency *sing.*

**Devisen-:** **~börse** *die* foreign exchange market; **~kurs** *der* exchange rate; rate of exchange

**Dezember** *der;* ~s, ~: December

**dezent** [1] *Adj.* quiet ⟨colour, pattern, suit⟩; subdued ⟨lighting, music⟩ [2] *adv.* discreetly; ⟨dress⟩ unostentatiously

**dezimal** *Adj.* decimal

**Dezimal-:** **~system** *das* decimal system; **~zahl** *die* decimal [number]

**dezimieren** *tr. V.* decimate

**dgl.** *Abk.* = **dergleichen, desgleichen**

**d. h.** *Abk.* = **das heißt** i.e.

**Di.** *Abk.* = **Dienstag** Tue[s].

**Dia** *das;* ∼s, ∼s slide

**Diabetes** *der;* ∼: diabetes

**Diabetiker** *der;* ∼s, ∼, **Diabetikerin** *die;* ∼, ∼nen diabetic

**Diagnose** /diaˈgnoːzə/ *die;* ∼, ∼n diagnosis

**diagonal** ① *Adj.* diagonal ② *adv.* diagonally

**Diagonale** *die;* ∼, ∼n diagonal

**Diagramm** *das* graph; (von Gegenständen) diagram

**Dialekt** *der;* ∼[e]s, ∼e dialect

**Dialog** *der;* ∼[e]s, ∼e dialogue

**Dialog-fenster** *das* (DV) dialogue box

**Dialyse** /diaˈlyːzə/ *die;* ∼, ∼n (Physik, Chemie, Med.) dialysis

**Diamant** *der;* ∼en, ∼en diamond

**\*diät** ▶ DIÄT

**Diät** *die;* ∼, ∼en diet; **eine ∼ einhalten** keep to a diet; **∼ essen** be on a diet; **∼ kochen** cook according to a/one's diet

**Diäten** *Pl.* [parliamentary] allowance *sing.*

**dich** ① *Akk. von* DU you ② *Akk. des Reflexivpron. der 2. Pers. Sg.* yourself

**dicht** ① *Adj.* (a) thick; dense ⟨*forest, hedge, crowd*⟩; heavy, dense ⟨*traffic*⟩ (b) (undurchlässig) (für Luft) airtight; (für Wasser) watertight ② *adv.* (a) densely ⟨*populated, wooded*⟩; ∼ **bebaut** heavily built up (b) (undurchlässig) tightly (c) *mit Präp.* (nahe) ∼ **neben** right next to

**\*dicht·bebaut** ▶ DICHT 2A

**Dichte** *die;* ∼ (Physik, fig.) density

**dichten** ① *itr. V.* write poetry ② *tr. V.* (verfassen) write; compose

**Dichter** *der;* ∼s, ∼: poet; (Schriftsteller) writer; author

**Dichterin** *die;* ∼, ∼nen poet[ess]; (Schriftstellerin) writer; author[ess]

**dichterisch** *Adj.* poetic; (schriftstellerisch) literary

**dicht|machen** *tr., itr. V.* (ugs.) shut; (endgültig) shut down

**Dichtung¹** *die;* ∼, ∼en seal; (am Hahn usw.) washer; (am Vergaser, Zylinder usw.) gasket

**Dichtung²** *die;* ∼, ∼en (a) work of literature; (in Versform) poetic work; poem (b) (Dichtkunst) literature; (in Versform) poetry

**dick** ① *Adj.* (a) thick; stout ⟨*tree*⟩; fat ⟨*person, legs, etc.*⟩; swollen ⟨*cheek, ankle, tonsils, etc.*⟩; ∼ **werden** get fat; **5 cm ∼ sein** be 5 cm thick (b) (ugs.) big ⟨*mistake*⟩; hefty ⟨*salary*⟩ ② *adv.* thickly; **etw. ∼ unterstreichen** underline sth. heavily; **sich ∼ anziehen** wrap

up warm[ly]; **etw. 5 cm ∼ schneiden** cut sth. 5 cm. thick; **∼ geschwollen** (ugs.) badly swollen

**Dicke¹** *die;* ∼: thickness; (von Menschen, Körperteilen) fatness

**Dicke²** *der/die; adj. Dekl.* (ugs.) fatty (coll.)

**dick·fellig** (ugs.) *Adj.* thick-skinned

**Dickfelligkeit** *die;* ∼ (ugs.) insensitivity

**Dickicht** /ˈdɪkɪçt/ *das;* ∼[e]s, ∼e thicket

**dick-, Dick-:** ∼**kopf** *der* (ugs.) mule (coll.); **ein ∼kopf sein** be stubborn as a mule; **einen ∼kopf haben** be pigheaded; ∼**köpfig** *Adj.* (ugs.) pigheaded; ∼**macher** *der* (ugs.) fattening food; ∼**milch** *die* sour milk

**die¹** ① *best. Art. Nom.* the; **die Helga** (ugs.) Helga; **die Frau/Menschheit** women *pl.*/ mankind ② *Demonstrativpron.* (a) *attr.* **die Frau war es** it was 'that woman (b) *allein stehend* **die** [da] (Person) that woman/girl; (Sache) that one ③ *Relativpron. Nom.* (Person) who; that; (Sache, Tier) which; that ④ *Relativ- u. Demonstrativpron.* the one who

**die²** ① *best. Art.* (a) *Akk. Sg. v.* DIE¹ 1 the; **ich sah die Frau** I saw the women (b) *Nom. u. Akk. Pl. v.* DER¹ 1, DIE¹ 1, DAS 1: the ② *Demonstrativpron. Nom. u. Akk. Pl. v.* DER¹ 1, DIE¹ 1, DAS 1: *attr.* **ich meine die Männer, die ...** I mean those men who ...; *allein stehend* **ich meine die** [da] I mean 'them ③ *Relativpron.* (a) *Akk. Sg. v.* DIE¹ 3 (Person) who; (Sache) that (b) *Nom. u. Akk. Pl. v.* DER¹ 3, DIE¹ 3, DAS 3 (Personen) whom; (Sachen) which; **die Männer, die ich gesehen habe** the men I saw

**Dieb** *der;* ∼[e]s, ∼e thief

**Diebin** *die;* ∼, ∼nen [woman] thief

**diebisch** ① *Adj.* (a) thieving (b) (verstohlen) mischievous ② *adv.* mischievously

**Diebstahl** *der;* ∼[e]s, **Diebstähle** theft

**die-jenige** ▶ DERJENIGE

**Diele** *die;* ∼, ∼n hall[way]

**dienen** *itr. V.* serve; **womit kann ich ∼?** what can I do for you?

**Diener** *der;* ∼s, ∼: servant; **einen ∼ machen** (ugs.) bow; make a bow

**Dienerin** *die;* ∼, ∼nen maid; servant

**dienlich** *Adj.* helpful

**Dienst** *der;* ∼[e]s, ∼e (a) (Tätigkeit) work; (von Soldaten, Polizeibeamten, Krankenhauspersonal usw.) duty; **seinen ∼ antreten** start work/go on duty; **∼ haben** be at work/on duty; ⟨*doctor*⟩ be on call; ⟨*chemist*⟩ be open (b) (Arbeitsverhältnis) post; **Major außer ∼:** retired major (c) (Tätigkeitsbereich) service; *s. auch* ÖFFENTLICH; (d) (Hilfe) service

---

**Diens·tag** *der* Tuesday; **am** ∼: on Tuesday; ∼, **der 1. Juni** Tuesday, 1 June; **er kommt** ∼: he is coming on Tuesday; **ab nächsten** ∼: from next Tuesday [onwards]; ∼ **in einer Woche** a week on Tuesday; ∼ **vor einer Woche** a week last Tuesday

**diens·tags** *Adv.* on Tuesday[s]

**dienst-, Dienst-:** ∼**bereit** *Adj.* ⟨*chemist*⟩ open *pred.*; ⟨*doctor*⟩ on call; ⟨*dentist*⟩ on duty; ∼**bote** *der,* ∼**botin** *die* servant; ∼**eifrig** *Adj.* zealous; ∼**frei** *Adj.* free ⟨*time*⟩; ∼**geheimnis** *das* (a) professional secret; (im Staatsdienst) official secret; (b) professional secrecy; (im Staatsdienst) official secrecy; ∼**grad** *der* (Milit.) rank; ∼**leister** *der;* ∼∼s, ∼∼, ∼**leisterin** *die;* ∼∼, ∼∼nen (Firma, auch DV) service provider; ∼**leistung** *die* (auch Wirtsch.) service

**Dienstleistungs-:** ∼**branche** *die* (Wirtsch.) (a) service industry; (b) ▶ ∼SEKTOR; ∼**sektor** *der* (Wirtsch.) service sector

**dienstlich** [1] *Adj.* business ⟨*call*⟩; (im Staatsdienst) official ⟨*letter, call, etc.*⟩ [2] *adv.* on business; (im Staatsdienst) on official business

**Dienst-:** ∼**reise** *die* business trip; ∼**stelle** *die* office; ∼**wagen** *der* official car; (Geschäftswagen) company car; ∼**weg** *der* official channels *pl.;* ∼**zeit** *die* (a) period of service; (b) (tägliche Arbeitszeit) working hours *pl.*

**dies** ▶ DIESER

**dies·bezüglich** *adv.* regarding this

**diese** ▶ DIESER

**Diesel** *der;* ∼s, ∼: diesel

**die·selbe** ▶ DERSELBE

**Diesel·motor** *der* diesel engine

**dieser, diese, dieses, dies** *Demonstrativpron.* (a) *attr.* this; *Pl.* these (b) *allein stehend* this one; *Pl.* these; **dies alles** all this; **dies und das,** (geh.) **dieses und jenes** this and that

**diesig** *Adj.* hazy

**dies-:** ∼**mal** *Adv.* this time; ∼**seits** [1] *Präp. mit Gen.* on this side of; [2] *Adv.* ∼**seits von** on this side of

**Dietrich** *der;* ∼s, ∼e picklock

**diffamieren** *tr. V.* defame

**Diffamierung** *die;* ∼, ∼en defamation

**Differential** *usw.* ▶ DIFFERENZIAL *usw.*

**Differenz** *die;* ∼, ∼en difference; (Meinungsverschiedenheit) difference [of opinion]

**Differenzial** /dɪfəren'tsi:a:l/ *das;* ∼s, ∼e (a) (Math.) differential (b) (Technik) differential [gear]

**Differenzial·rechnung** *die* (Math.) differential calculus

**differenziert** *Adj.* complex; subtly differentiated ⟨*methods, colours*⟩; sophisticated ⟨*taste*⟩

**diffus** [1] *Adj.* (a) (Physik, Chemie) diffuse

(b) (geh.) vague; vague and confused ⟨*idea, statement, etc.*⟩ [2] *adv.* in a vague and confused way

**digital** (DV) [1] *Adj.* digital [2] *adv.* digitally

**Digital-** digital ⟨*clock, display, etc.*⟩

**digitalisieren** *tr. V.* (DV) digitalize

**Diktat** *das;* ∼[e]s, ∼e dictation

**Diktator** *der;* ∼s, ∼en, **Diktatorin** *die;* ∼, ∼nen dictator

**diktatorisch** [1] *Adj.* dictatorial [2] *adv.* dictatorially

**Diktatur** *die;* ∼, ∼en dictatorship

**diktieren** *tr. V.* dictate

**Diktier·gerät** *das* dictating machine

**Dilemma** *das;* ∼s, ∼s dilemma

**Dilettant** /dilɛ'tant/ *der;* ∼en, ∼en, **Dilettantin** *die;* ∼, ∼nen dilettante

**dilettantisch** [1] *Adj.* dilettante; amateurish [2] *adv.* amateurishly

**Dill** *der;* ∼[e]s, ∼e dill

**Dimension** *die;* ∼, ∼en (Physik, fig.) dimension

**DIN** /diːn/ *Abk.* = **Deutsche Industrie-Norm[en]** *German Industrial Standard[s];* DIN; **DIN-A4-Format** A4

**Ding**[1] *das;* ∼[e]s, ∼e (a) thing (b) **nach Lage der** ∼e the way things are; **persönliche/private** ∼e personal/private matters; **ein** ∼ **der Unmöglichkeit sein** be quite impossible; **vor allen** ∼en above all (c) **guter** ∼**e sein** (geh.) be in good spirits

**Ding**[2] *das;* ∼[e]s, ∼er (ugs.) thing; **das ist ja ein** ∼! that's really something

**Dinkel** *der;* ∼s, ∼ (Landw.) spelt

**Dino** *der;* ∼s, ∼s (ugs.) dinosaur

**Dino·saurier** *der;* ∼s, ∼: dinosaur

**Diode** *die;* ∼, ∼n (Elektrot.) diode

**Dioden·rücklicht** *das* LED rear light

**Dioxin** *das;* ∼s (Chemie) dioxin

**Diözese** *die;* ∼, ∼n diocese

**Dipl.-Ing.** *Abk.* = **Diplomingenieur** *academically qualified engineer*

**Diplom** *das;* ∼s, ∼e ≈ [first] degree (*in a scientific or technical subject*); (für einen Handwerksberuf) diploma

**Diplom-** qualified

**Diplomat** *der;* ∼en, ∼en, **Diplomatin** *die;* ∼, ∼nen diplomat

**diplomatisch** [1] *Adj.* diplomatic [2] *adv.* diplomatically

**dir** [1] *Dat. von* DU to you; (nach Präp.) you; **Freunde von** ∼: friends of yours [2] *Dat. des Reflexivpron. der 2. Pers. Sg.* yourself

**direkt** [1] *Adj.* direct [2] *adv.* straight; directly; **etw.** ∼ **übertragen** broadcast sth. live

**Direkt·flug** *der* direct flight

**d**

**Direktion** *die;* ~, ~en management; (Büroräume) managers' offices *pl.*

**Direktor** *der;* ~s, ~en, **Direktorin** *die;* ~, ~nen director; (einer Schule) headmaster/ headmistress; (einer Strafanstalt) governor; (einer Abteilung) manager

**Direkt-übertragung** *die* live broadcast

**Dirigent** *der;* ~en, ~en, **Dirigentin** *die;* ~, ~nen conductor

**dirigieren** *tr. V.* (a) *auch itr.* conduct (b) (führen) steer

**Disc-jockey** /'dɪskdʒɔke/ *der* disc jockey

**Disco** /'dɪsko:/ *die;* ~, ~s disco

**Diskette** *die;* ~, ~n (DV) floppy disk

**Disketten-laufwerk** *das* (DV) [floppy-]disk drive

**Diskont-satz** *der* (Finanzw.) discount rate

**Diskothek** *die;* ~, ~en discothèque

**Diskrepanz** *die;* ~, ~en discrepancy

**diskret** ① *Adj.* (vertraulich) confidential; (taktvoll) discreet; tactful
② *adv.* (vertraulich) confidentially; (taktvoll) discreetly; tactfully

**Diskretion** *die;* ~ (a) (Verschwiegenheit, Takt) discretion
(b) (Unaufdringlichkeit) discreetness

**diskriminieren** *tr. V.* discriminate against

**Diskriminierung** *die;* ~, ~en discrimination

**Diskussion** *die;* ~, ~en discussion; **zur** ~ **stehen** be under discussion

**Diskussions-:** ~**beitrag** *der* contribution to a/the discussion; ~**leiter** *der* chair[man] [of the discussion]; ~**leiterin** *die* chair[woman] [of the discussion]

**diskutieren** ① *itr. V.* **über etw.** (*Akk.*) ~: discuss sth.
② *tr. V.* discuss

**Disqualifikation** *die;* ~, ~en (auch Sport) disqualification

**disqualifizieren** *tr. V.* disqualify

**Distanz** *die;* ~, ~en (auch fig.) distance

**distanzieren** *refl. V.* **sich von jmdm./etw.** ~ (fig.) dissociate oneself from sb./sth.

**distanziert** *Adj.* reserved

**Distel** *die;* ~, ~n thistle

**Distel-fink** *der* goldfinch

**Disziplin** *die;* ~, ~en discipline; (Selbstbeherrschung) [self-]discipline

**disziplinieren** ① *tr. V.* discipline
② *refl. V.* discipline oneself

**diszipliniert** ① *Adj.* well-disciplined; (beherrscht) disciplined
② *adv.* in a well-disciplined way; (beherrscht) in a disciplined way

**divers...** /di'vɛrs.../ *Adj.* various; (mehrer...) several

**Dividende** /divi'dɛndə/ *die;* ~, ~n (Wirtsch.) dividend

**dividieren** *tr. V.* divide

**Division** *die;* ~, ~en (auch Milit.) division

**DM** *Abk.* = **Deutsche Mark** DM

**D-Mark** /'de:-/ *die* Deutschmark

**DNS** *Abk.* (Chemie) = **Desoxyribonukleinsäure** DNA

**Do.** *Abk.* = **Donnerstag** Thur[s].

**doch** ① *Konj.* but
② *Adv.* (a) (jedoch) but
(b) (dennoch) all the same; still
(c) (geh.: nämlich) **wusste er** ~, **dass** ...: because he knew that ...
(d) (entgegen allen gegenteiligen Behauptungen, Annahmen) **er war also** ~ **der Mörder!** so he 'was the murderer!
(e) (ohnehin) in any case
③ *Interj.* **Das stimmt nicht. – Doch!** That's not right. – [Oh] yes it is!; **Hast du keinen Hunger? – Doch!** Aren't you hungry? – Yes [I am]!
④ *Partikel* (a) (Ungeduld ausdrückend) **pass** ~ **auf!** [oh] do be careful!; **das ist** ~ **nicht zu glauben** that's just incredible
(b) (Zweifel ausdrückend) **du hast** ~ **meinen Brief erhalten?** you did get my letter, didn't you?
(c) (Überraschung ausdrückend) **das ist** ~ **Karl!** there's Karl!
(d) (verstärkt Bejahung/Verneinung ausdrückend) **gewiss/sicher** ~: [why] certainly; of course; **ja** ~: [yes], all right; **nicht** ~! (abwehrend) [no], don't!
(e) (Wunsch verstärkend) **wäre es** ~ ...: if only it were ...

**Docht** *der;* ~[e]s, ~e wick

**Dock** *das;* ~s, ~s dock

**Dogge** *die;* ~, ~n: [deutsche] ~: Great Dane

**Dogma** *das;* ~s, **Dogmen** (auch fig.) dogma

**dogmatisch** (Theol., auch fig.) *Adj.* dogmatic

**Dohle** *die;* ~, ~n jackdaw

**Doktor** *der;* ~s, ~en (auch ugs.: Arzt) doctor; (Titel) Doctor

**Doktor-arbeit** *die* doctoral thesis

**Doktor-grad** *der* doctorate; doctor's degree

**Doktorin** *die;* ~, ~nen ▶ DOKTOR

**Doktor-titel** *der* title of doctor

**Doktrin** *die;* ~, ~en doctrine

**Dokument** *das;* ~[e]s, ~e document

**Dokumentar-:** ~**bericht** *der* documentary report; ~**film** *der* documentary [film]

**Dokumentation** *die;* ~, ~en (a) documentation
(b) (Bericht) documentary report

**dokumentieren** *tr. V.* (a) document; (fig.) demonstrate
(b) (festhalten) record

**Dolch** *der;* ~[e]s, ~e dagger

**Dolde** *die;* ~, ~n (Bot.) umbel

**doll** (bes. nordd., salopp) ① *Adj.* (a) (ungewöhnlich) incredible

---

*alte Schreibung - vgl. Hinweis auf S. xiv

**(b)** (großartig) great (coll.)
**2** *adv.* **(a)** (großartig) fantastically [well] (coll.)
**(b)** (sehr) ⟨*hurt*⟩ dreadfully (coll.), like mad

**Dollar** *der;* ~s, ~s dollar; **zwei** ~: two
dollars

**dolmetschen** *itr. V.* act as interpreter

**Dolmetscher** *der;* ~s, ~,
**Dolmetscherin** *die;* ~, ~nen
interpreter

**Dom** *der;* ~[e]s, ~e cathedral

**dominieren** *itr. V.* dominate

**dominikanisch** *Adj.* Dominican; **die
Dominikanische Republik** the Dominican
Republic

**Domino** *das;* ~s, ~s (Spiel) dominoes *sing.*

**Domizil** *das;* ~s, ~e (geh.) domicile;
residence

**Dom·pfaff** *der;* ~en *od.* ~s, ~en (Zool.)
bullfinch

**Dompteur** /dɔmp'tøːɐ/ *der;* ~s, ~e,
**Dompteurin** /dɔmp'tøːrɪn/ *die;* ~, ~nen,
**Dompteuse** /dɔmp'tøːzə/ *die;* ~, ~n
tamer

**Donau** *die;* ~: Danube

**Donner** *der;* ~s, ~: thunder

**donnern** *itr. V.* **(a)** (*unpers.*) thunder
**(b)** (fig.) thunder; ⟨*engine*⟩ roar

**Donners·tag** *der* Thursday; *s. auch*
DIENSTAG

**donnerstags** *Adv.* on Thursday[s]; *s.
auch* DIENSTAGS

**Donner·wetter** *das* (ugs.) **(a)** (Krach) row
**(b)** /'--'--/ **zum** ~ **[noch einmal]!** damn it!; ~!
my word

**doof** (ugs.) **1** *Adj.* stupid; dumb (coll.)
**2** *adv.* stupidly

**Doping** /'doːpɪŋ/ *das;* ~s (Sport) taking
drugs

**Doping·kontrolle** *die* (Sport) drug[s] test

**Doppel** *das,* ~s, ~ **(a)** (Kopie) duplicate;
copy
**(b)** (Sport) doubles *sing. or pl.*

**doppel-, Doppel-:** ~**bett** *das* double
bed; ~**bock** *das* extra-strong bock beer;
~**decker** *der;* ~~s, ~~: biplane;
~**deutig** /-dɔy·tɪç/ **1** *Adj.* **(a)** ambiguous;
**(b)** (anzüglich) suggestive; **2** *adv.* **(a)**
ambiguously; **(b)** (anzüglich) suggestively;
~**fenster** *das* double-glazed window;
~**gänger** *der;* ~~s, ~~, ~**gängerin**
*die;* ~~, ~~nen double; ~**haus** *das* pair
of semi-detached houses; ~**haus·hälfte**
*die* semi[-detached house]; ~**kinn** *das*
double chin; ~**klick** *der;* ~~s, ~~s (DV)
double click; ~**moral** *die* double standards
*pl.;* ~**pass,** *** ~paß** *der* (ugs.) der ~pass
dual nationality *no art.;* ~**punkt** *der* colon;
~**stunde** *die* double period

**doppelt** **1** *Adj.* double; **die** ~**e Menge**
twice the quantity; **mit** ~**er Kraft arbeiten**
work with twice as much energy

**2** *adv.* ~ **so groß/alt wie ...:** twice as large/
old as ...; **sich** ~ **anstrengen** try twice as
hard

**Doppelte** *das; adj. Dekl.* **das** ~ **bezahlen**
pay twice as much; pay double

**Doppel-:** ~**tür** *die* double door;
~**zentner** *der* 100 kilograms; ~**zimmer**
*das* double room

**Dorf** *das;* ~[e]s, Dörfer village; **auf dem** ~:
in the country

**Dorf-:** ~**bewohner** *der,*
~**bewohnerin** *die* villager; ~**depp** *der*
(bes. südd., österr.) village idiot; ~**trottel** *der*
village idiot

**Dorn** *der;* ~[e]s, ~en thorn; **jmdm. ein** ~ **im
Auge sein** annoy sb. intensely

**dornig** *Adj.* thorny

**Dorn·röschen** (*das*) the Sleeping Beauty

**dörren** *tr. V.* dry

**Dörr-:** ~**fleisch** *das* (südd.) lean bacon;
~**obst** *das* dried fruit

**Dorsch** *der;* ~[e]s, ~e cod

**dort** *Adv.* there; ~ **bleiben** stay there; *s.
auch* DA 1A

**dort-:** *** ~**|bleiben** ▶ DORT; ~**her** *Adv.*
[von] ~her from there; ~**hin** *Adv.* there

**dortig** *Adj.* there

**Dose** *die;* ~, ~n **(a)** (Blech~) tin; (Pillen~)
box; (Zucker~) bowl
**(b)** (Konserven~) can; tin (Brit.); (Bier~) can

**dösen** *itr. V.* (ugs.) doze

**Dosen-:** ~**bier** *das* canned beer; ~**milch**
*die* canned *or* (Brit.) tinned milk; ~**öffner**
*der* can-opener; tin-opener (Brit.)

**dosieren** *tr. V.* **etw.** ~: measure out the
required dose of sth.

**Dosierung** *die;* ~, ~en **(a)** measuring out;
(das Zuführen) administering; (fig.) dispensing
**(b)** ▶ DOSIS

**Dosis** *die;* ~, Dosen dose

**Dossier** /dɔ'sjeː/ *das,* (veraltet:) *der;* ~s, ~s
dossier

**Dotter** *der od. das;* ~s, ~: yolk

**Dotter·blume** *die* marsh marigold

**doubeln** /'duːbl̩n/ *tr. V.* stand in for
⟨*actor*⟩; use a stand-in for ⟨*scene*⟩; **sich** ~
**lassen** use *or* have a stand-in

**Dozent** *der;* ~en, ~en, **Dozentin** *die;* ~,
~nen lecturer (**für** in)

**dpa** *Abk.* = **Deutsche Presse-
Agentur** German Press Agency

**Dr.** *Abk.* = **Doktor** Dr

**Drache** *der;* ~n, ~n (Myth.) dragon

**Drachen** *der;* ~s, ~ **(a)** kite
**(b)** (Fluggerät) hang-glider

**Dragee, Dragée** /dra'ʒeː/ *das;* ~s, ~s
dragee

**Draht** *der;* ~[e]s, Drähte **(a)** wire
**(b)** (Leitung) wire; (Telefonleitung) line; wire
**(c)** (Telefonverbindung) line

**draht-, Draht-:** ~**los** (Nachrichtenw.)
**1** *Adj.* wireless; **2** *adv.* **etw.** ~**los**    ⋯⋗

d

telegrafieren/übermitteln radio sth.; ∼**seil**
*das* [steel] cable; ∼**seil·bahn** *die* cable
railway; ∼**zieher** *der;* ∼∼s, ∼∼,
∼**zieherin** *die;* ∼∼, ∼∼nen (fig.) wire
puller

**drall** *Adj.* strapping ⟨*girl*⟩; full, rounded
⟨*cheeks, face, bottom*⟩

**Drama** *das;* ∼s, Dramen drama; (fig., ugs.)
disaster

**Dramatiker** *der;* ∼s, ∼, **Dramatikerin**
*die;* ∼, ∼nen dramatist

**dramatisch** ⊡ *Adj.* dramatic
⊡ *adv.* dramatically

**dramatisieren** *tr. V.* dramatize

**dramaturgisch** *adj.* dramaturgical

**dran** *Adv.* (ugs.) (a) häng das Schild ∼! put
the sign up!
(b) arm ∼ sein be in a bad way; gut/schlecht
∼ sein be well off/badly off; früh/spät ∼ sein
be early/late; ich bin ∼: it's my turn

**dran|bleiben** *unr. itr. V.; mit sein* (ugs.) (am
Telefon) hang on (coll.)

**drang** *1. u. 3. Pers. Sg. Prät. v.* DRINGEN

**Drang** *der;* ∼[e]s, Dränge urge

**dränge** *1. u. 3. Pers. Sg. Konjunktiv II v.*
DRINGEN

**drängeln** (ugs.) ⊡ *itr. V.* (a) push [and
shove]
(b) (auf jmdn. einreden) go on (coll.)
⊡ *tr. V.* (a) push; shove
(b) (einreden auf) go on at (coll.)
⊡ *refl. V.* sich nach vorn ∼: push one's way
to the front

**drängen** ⊡ *itr. V.* (a) push
(b) die Zeit drängt time is pressing
⊡ *tr. V.* (a) push
(b) (antreiben) press; urge
⊡ *refl. V.* crowd

**drangsalieren** *tr. V.* (quälen) torment;
(plagen) plague

**dran-:** ∼**|halten** *unr. refl. V.* (ugs.) get a
move on (coll.); ∼**|kommen** *unr. itr. V.; mit
sein* (ugs.) have one's turn; ∼**|nehmen** *unr.
tr. V.* (ugs.) (beim Friseur usw.) see to; (beim Arzt)
see

**drastisch** ⊡ *Adj.* drastic ⟨*measure, means*⟩
⊡ *adv.* drastically; ⟨*punish*⟩ severely

**drauf** *Adv.* (ugs.) on it

**drauf-, Drauf-:** ∼**gänger** *der;* ∼∼s, ∼∼,
∼**gängerin** *die;* ∼∼, ∼∼nen daredevil;
∼**gängerisch** *Adj.* daring; ∼**|gehen**
*unr. itr. V.; mit sein* (ugs.) (a) (umkommen) kick
the bucket (coll.); (b) (verbraucht werden) go (**für**
on); ∼**|zahlen** (ugs.) ⊡ *tr. V.* noch etwas/50
Euro ∼zahlen fork out (coll.) *or* pay a bit
more/an extra 50 euros; ⊡ *itr. V.* (Unkosten
haben) ich zahle dabei noch ∼: it's costing
me money

**draußen** *Adv.* outside; hier/da ∼: out here/
there; von/nach ∼: from outside/outside

**Dreck** *der;* ∼[e]s (a) (ugs.) dirt; (sehr viel)
filth; (Schlamm) mud
(b) (salopp abwertend: Angelegenheit) **mach
deinen ∼ allein** do it yourself; **das geht dich
einen [feuchten] ∼ an** (salopp) none of your
damned business (coll.)
(c) (salopp abwertend: Zeug) junk *no indef. art.*

**Dreck·arbeit** *die* (auch fig.) dirty work *no
indef. art., no pl.*/dirty job

**dreckig** ⊡ *Adj.* (ugs., auch fig.) dirty;
(sehr schmutzig) filthy
(b) (salopp: unverschämt) cheeky
⊡ *adv.* (a) es geht ihm ∼ (ugs.) he's in a bad
way
(b) (salopp: unverschämt) cheekily

**Dreck-:** ∼**sau** *die,* ∼**schwein** *das* (derb)
filthy swine

**Dreh** *der;* ∼s, ∼s (ugs.) (a) den ∼
heraushaben have [got] the knack
(b) [so] um den ∼: about that

**Dreh-:** ∼**arbeiten** *Pl.* (Film) shooting *sing.*
(zu of); ∼**bank** *die; Pl.* ∼bänke lathe;
∼**buch** *das* screenplay; [film] script

**drehen** ⊡ *tr. V.* (a) turn
(b) (formen) twist ⟨*rope, thread*⟩; roll
⟨*cigarette*⟩
(c) (Film) shoot ⟨*scene*⟩; film ⟨*report*⟩; make
⟨*film*⟩
⊡ *itr. V.* (a) ⟨*car*⟩ turn; ⟨*wind*⟩ change
(b) an etw. (*Dat.*) ∼: turn sth.
(c) (Film) shoot; film
⊡ *refl. V.* (a) turn
(b) (ugs.: zum Gegenstand haben) sich um etw.
∼: be about sth.

**Dreh-:** ∼**kreuz** *das* turnstile; ∼**orgel** *die*
barrel organ; ∼**ort** *der* (Film) location;
∼**restaurant** *das* revolving restaurant;
∼**stuhl** *der* swivel chair; ∼**tür** *die*
revolving door

**Drehung** *die;* ∼, ∼en turn; (um einen
Mittelpunkt) revolution

**Dreh-:** ∼**zahl** *die* revolutions *or* (coll.) revs
(*esp. per minute*); ∼**zahl·messer** *der;*
∼∼s, ∼∼: revolution counter; rev counter
(coll.); tachometer

**drei** *Kardinalz.* three;

**Drei** *die;* ∼, ∼en three; eine ∼ schreiben
(Schulw.) get a C

**drei-, Drei-:** ∼**eck** *das* (Geom.) triangle;
∼**eckig** *Adj.* triangular; ∼**ein·halb**
*Bruchz.* three and a half

**Dreier** *der;* ∼s, ∼ (ugs.) three

**dreierlei** *indekl. Adj.* (a) *attr.* three kinds
*or* sorts of; three different
(b) *subst.* three [different] things

**drei-, Drei-:** ∼**fach** *Vervielfältigungsz.*
triple; **die** ∼**fache Menge** three times the
amount; ∼**fache** *das; adj. Dekl.* **das**
∼**fache kosten** cost three times as much; **das**
∼**fache von 3 ist 9** three times three is nine;
∼**faltigkeit** *die;* ∼ (christl. Rel.) Trinity;
∼**hundert** *Kardinalz.* three hundred;
∼**jährig** *Adj.* (3 Jahre alt) three-year-old
*attrib.;* (3 Jahre dauernd) three-year *attrib.;*

~**kampf** der (Sport) triathlon; ~**klang** der triad; ~**köpfig** Adj. ⟨family, crew⟩ of three; ~**mal** Adv. three times; ~**malig** Adj. eine ~malige Wiederholung three repeats

**drein** (ugs.) ▶ DAREIN

**drein-:** ~|**blicken,** ~|**schauen** itr. V. look

**drei-, Drei-:** ~**rad** das tricycle; ~**satz** der rule of three; ~**seitig** Adj. three-sided ⟨figure⟩; three-page ⟨letter, leaflet, etc.⟩

**dreißig** Kardinalz. thirty; s. auch ACHTZIG

**dreißigjährig** Adj. (30 Jahre alt) thirty-year-old attrib.; (30 Jahre dauernd) thirty-year attrib.

**dreißigst...** Ordinalz. thirtieth

**Dreißigstel** das; ~s, ~: thirtieth

**dreist** ① Adj. brazen; barefaced ⟨lie⟩ ② adv. brazenly

**drei-stellig** Adj. three-figure attrib.

**Dreistigkeit** die; ~, ~en (a) brazenness (b) (Handlung) brazen act

**drei-, Drei-:** ~**tausend** Kardinalz. three thousand; ~**teilig** Adj. three-part attrib.; three-piece attrib. ⟨suit⟩; *~**viertel** ▶ VIERTEL; ~**viertel-stunde** /---'--/ die three-quarters of an hour; ~**viertel-takt** /-'---/ der three-four time; ~**zehn** Kardinalz. thirteen; s. auch ACHTZEHN

**Dresche** die; ~ (salopp) walloping (coll.); thrashing

**dreschen** ① unr. tr. V. (a) thresh (b) (salopp: schlagen) wallop (coll.); thrash ② unr. itr. V. thresh

**dressieren** tr. V. train ⟨animal⟩

**Dressur** die; ~, ~en training

**Drill** der; ~[e]s drilling; (Milit.) drill

**drillen** tr. V. (auch Milit.) drill

**Drilling** der; ~s, ~e triplet

**drin** Adv. (ugs.) (a) in it (b) ▶ DRINNEN

**dringen** unr. itr. V. (a) mit sein durch/in etw. ~: penetrate sth. (b) mit sein in jmdn. ~ (geh.) press sb. (c) auf etw. (Akk.) ~: insist upon sth.

**dringend** ① Adj. urgent; strong ⟨suspicion, advice⟩ ② adv. urgently; ⟨advise, suspect⟩ strongly; ~ erforderlich essential

**dringlich** ① Adj. urgent ② adv. urgently

**Dringlichkeit** die; ~: urgency

**drinnen** Adv. inside; (im Haus) indoors; inside

**dritt** in wir waren zu ~: there were three of us

**dritt...** Ordinalz. third

**Drittel** das, (schweiz. meist der); ~s, ~: third

**dritteln** tr. V. split or divide three ways

**drittens** Adv. thirdly

**DRK** Abk. = **Deutsches Rotes Kreuz** German Red Cross

**Dr. med.** Abk. = **doctor medicinae** MD

**droben** Adv. (südd., österr., sonst geh.) up there

**Droge** die; ~, ~n drug

**drogen-, Drogen-:** ~**abhängig** Adj. addicted to drugs postpos.; ~**abhängige** der/die; adj. Dekl. drug addict; ~**abhängigkeit** die drug addiction; ~**beratungs-stelle** die drug advice centre; ~**gefährdet** Adj. at risk from drugs postpos.; ~**handel** der drug trafficking; ~**konsum** der drug-taking; ~**konsument** der, ~**konsumentin** die drug user; ~**missbrauch**, *~**mißbrauch** der drug abuse; ~**rausch** der [state of] drug intoxication; etw. im ~rausch tun do sth. while under the influence of drugs or while [high (coll.)] on drugs; ~**süchtig** Adj. ▶ ~ABHÄNGIG; ~**szene** die drug scene

**Drogerie** die; ~, ~n chemist's [shop] (Brit.); drugstore (Amer.)

**Drogist** der; ~en, ~en, **Drogistin** die; ~, ~nen chemist (Brit.); druggist (Amer.)

**drohen** itr., mod. V. threaten; (bevorstehen) be threatening; jmdm. droht etw. sb. is threatened with sth.

**drohend** Adj. threatening; (bevorstehend) impending

**Drohne** die; ~, ~n drone

**dröhnen** itr. V. boom ⟨machine⟩ roar

**Drohung** die; ~, ~en threat

**drollig** ① Adj. funny; comical; (niedlich) sweet; cute (Amer.) ② adv.: s. Adj.: comically; sweetly; cutely (Amer.)

**Dromedar** das; ~s, ~e dromedary

**Drops** der od. das; ~, ~: fruit or (Brit.) acid drop

**drosch** 1. u. 3. Pers. Sg. Prät. v. DRESCHEN

**Drossel** die; ~, ~n thrush

**drosseln** tr. V. (a) turn down ⟨heating, air conditioning⟩; throttle back ⟨engine⟩ (b) (herabsetzen) reduce

**Dr. phil.** Abk. = **doctor philosophiae** Dr

**drüben** Adv. dort od. da ~: over there; ~ auf der anderen Seite over on the other side

**Druck¹** der; ~[e]s, Drücke (a) (auch fig.) pressure (b) ein ~ auf den Knopf a touch of the button

**Druck²** der; ~[e]s, ~e (a) printing; in ~ gehen go to press (b) (Produkt) print

**Druck-buchstabe** der printed letter

**drucken** tr., itr. V. print

**drücken** ① tr. V. (a) press; press, push ⟨button⟩; squeeze ⟨juice, pus⟩ (aus out of); jmdm. die Hand ~: squeeze sb.'s hand (b) (liebkosen) jmdn. ~: hug [and squeeze] sb. (c) ⟨shoe etc.⟩ pinch ···⊱

**(d)** (herabsetzen) push down ⟨price, rate⟩; depress ⟨sales⟩; bring down ⟨standard⟩ ② *itr. V.* **(a)** press; **auf den Knopf** ~: press or push the button; „**bitte** ~": 'push' **(b)** (Druck verursachen) ⟨shoe etc.⟩ pinch ③ *refl. V.* (ugs.: sich entziehen) shirk; **sich vor etw.** (*Dat.*) ~: get out of sth.

**drückend** *Adj.* **(a)** heavy ⟨debt, taxes⟩; serious ⟨worries⟩; grinding ⟨poverty⟩ **(b)** (schwül) oppressive

**Drucker** *der;* ~s, ~: printer

**Druckerei** *die;* ~, ~en printing works; (Firma) printing house; printer's

**Druckerin** *die;* ~, ~nen printer

**druck-, Druck-:** ~**fehler** *der* misprint; printer's error; ~**knopf** *der* press stud (Brit.); snap fastener; ~**luft** *die* compressed air; ~**mittel** *das* means of bringing pressure to bear (**gegenüber** on); ~**reif** ① *Adj.* ready for publication; (~fertig) ready for press; ② *adv.* ⟨speak⟩ in a polished manner; ~**sache** *die* (Postw.) printed matter; ~**schrift** *die* **(a)** printed writing; **(b)** (Schriftart) type[face]; **(c)** (Schriftwerk) pamphlet

**drum** *Adv.* (ugs.) **(a)** ▶ DARUM; **(b)** [a]round; **alles** *od.* **das [ganze] Drum und Dran** (bei einer Mahlzeit) all the trimmings; (bei einer Feierlichkeit) all the palaver that goes with it (coll.)

**Drum·herum** *das;* ~s everything that goes/went with it

**drunter** *Adv.* (ugs.) underneath; **es** *od.* **alles geht** ~ **und drüber** everything is topsy-turvy

**Drüse** *die;* ~, ~n gland

**Dschungel** /'dʒʊŋl/ *der;* ~s, ~ (auch fig.) jungle

**dt.** *Abk.* = **deutsch** G.

**Dtzd.** *Abk.* = **Dutzend** doz.

**du** *Personalpron.;* 2. *Pers. Sg. Nom.* you; **Du zueinander sagen** use the familiar form in addressing one another; *s. auch* (*Gen.*) DEINER, (*Dat.*) DIR, (*Akk.*) DICH

**Dübel** *der;* ~s, ~: plug

**ducken** ① *refl. V.* duck ② *itr. V.* (fig. abwertend) humble oneself (**vor** + *Dat.* before)

**Duckmäuser** *der;* ~s, ~, **Duckmäuserin** *die;* ~, ~nen (abwertend) moral coward

**Duckmäusertum** *das;* ~s (abwertend) moral cowardice

**Dudel·sack** *der* bagpipes *pl.*

**Duell** *das;* ~s, ~e duel

**duellieren** *refl. V.* fight a duel

**Duett** *das;* ~[e]s, ~e (Musik) duet; **im** ~ **singen** sing a duet

**Duft** *der;* ~[e]s, Düfte scent; (von Parfüm, Blumen) scent; fragrance; (von Kaffee usw.) aroma

**duften** *itr. V.* smell (**nach** of)

**dulden** *tr. V.* tolerate; put up with

**duldsam** ① *Adj.* tolerant (**gegen** towards) ② *adv.* tolerantly

**Duma** *die:* **die** ~: the Duma

**dumm, dümmer, dümmst...** ① *Adj.* **(a)** stupid **(b)** (unvernünftig) foolish **(c)** (ugs.: töricht, albern) idiotic; silly **(d)** (ugs.: unangenehm) nasty ⟨feeling⟩; annoying ⟨habit⟩; **das wird mir jetzt zu** ~ (ugs.) I've had enough of it ② *adv.* (ugs.) idiotically

**Dumme** *der/die; adj. Dekl.* fool; **der/die** ~ **sein** (ugs.) be the loser

**dummer·weise** *Adv.* **(a)** unfortunately; (ärgerlicherweise) annoyingly **(b)** (törichterweise) foolishly

**Dummheit** *die;* ~, ~en **(a)** stupidity **(b)** (unkluge Handlung) stupid thing

**Dumm·kopf** *der* (ugs.) nitwit (coll.)

**dumpf** ① *Adj.* **(a)** dull ⟨thud, rumble of thunder⟩; muffled ⟨sound, thump⟩ **(b)** (muffig) musty **(c)** (stumpfsinnig) dull ② *adv.* **(a)** ⟨echo⟩ hollowly **(b)** (stumpfsinnig) apathetically

**Dumping** /'dampɪŋ/ *das;* ~s (Wirtsch.) dumping

**Dumping·preis** *der* dumping price

**Düne** *die;* ~, ~n dune

**düngen** ① *tr. V.* fertilize ⟨soil, lawn⟩; spread fertilizer on ⟨field⟩; scatter fertilizer around ⟨plants⟩ ② *itr. V.* **gut** ~ ⟨substance⟩ be a good fertilizer

**Dünger** *der;* ~s, ~: fertilizer

**dunkel** ① *Adj.* **(a)** (auch fig.) dark; (tief) deep ⟨voice, note⟩; (undeutlich) vague ② *adv.* **(a)** (tief) ⟨speak⟩ in a deep voice **(b)** (undeutlich) vaguely

**Dünkel** *der;* ~s (geh.) arrogance; (Einbildung) conceit[edness]

**dunkel-:** ~**blond** *Adj.* light brown ⟨hair⟩; ⟨person⟩ with light brown hair; ~**häutig** *Adj.* dark-skinned

**Dunkelheit** *die;* ~: darkness

**Dunkel·kammer** *die* darkroom

**dunkeln** *itr. V.* (unpers.) **es dunkelt** (geh.) it is growing dark

**Dunkel·ziffer** *die* number of unrecorded cases

**dünn** ① *Adj.* thin; slim ⟨book⟩; fine ⟨stocking⟩; watery ⟨coffee, tea, beer⟩ ② *adv.* thinly ⟨sliced, populated⟩; lightly ⟨dressed⟩

**Dunst** *der;* ~[e]s, Dünste **(a)** haze; (Nebel) mist **(b)** (Geruch) smell

**dünsten** *tr. V.* steam ⟨fish, vegetables⟩; braise ⟨meat⟩; stew ⟨fruit⟩

**dunstig** *Adj.* hazy

**Duo** *das;* ~s, ~s (Musik) duet; (fig. scherzh.) duo; pair

**Duplikat** *das;* ~[e]s, ~e duplicate

**duplizieren** *tr. V.* duplicate

**Dur** *das;* ~ (Musik) major [key]

**durch** ① *Präp. mit Akk.* (a) (räumlich) through

(b) (modal) by; ~ **Boten** by courier; **zehn** [geteilt] ~ **zwei** ten divided by two

② *Adv.* (a) (hin~) **das ganze Jahr** ~: throughout the whole year

(b) (ugs.: vorbei) **es war 3 Uhr** ~: it was gone 3 o'clock

(c) ~ **und** ~ **nass/überzeugt** wet through [and through]/completely *or* totally convinced

(d) [durch etw.] ~ **sein** be through [sth.]

(e) ~ **sein** (abgefahren sein) ⟨*train, bus, etc.*⟩ have gone

(f) ~ **sein** (fertig sein) have finished; **durch etw.** ~ **sein** have got through sth.

(g) ~ **sein** ⟨*cheese*⟩ be ripe; ⟨*meat*⟩ be well done

**durch|arbeiten** ① *tr. V.* work through ② *itr. V.* work through; **die Nacht** ~: work through the night

**durch·aus** *Adv.* absolutely; perfectly, quite ⟨*correct, possible, understandable*⟩; **das ist** ~ **richtig** that is entirely right; ~ **nicht** by no means

**durch|beißen** *unr. tr. V.* bite through

**durch|blättern** *tr. V.* leaf through

**Durch·blick** *der* (ugs.) **den** [absoluten] ~ **haben** know [exactly] what's going on

**durch|blicken** *itr. V.* (a) look through; **durch etw.** ~: look through sth.

(b) ~ **lassen, dass** .../**wie** ...: hint that .../at how ...

**Durch·blutung** *die* flow of blood (+ *Gen.* to); [blood] circulation

**Durchblutungs·störung** *die* disturbance of the blood supply

**durch|bohren**[1] *tr. V.* drill through ⟨*wall, plank*⟩; drill ⟨*hole*⟩

**durch·bohren**[2] *tr. V.* pierce

**durch|brechen**[1] ① *unr. tr. V.* **etw.** ~: break sth. in two

② *unr. itr. V.; mit sein* (a) break in two

(b) (hervorkommen) ⟨*sun*⟩ break through

(c) (einbrechen) fall through ⟨*ice, floor, etc.*⟩

**durch·brechen**[2] *unr. tr. V.* break through

**durch|brennen** *unr. itr. V.; mit sein* (a) ⟨*heating coil, lightbulb*⟩ burn out; ⟨*fuse*⟩ blow

(b) (ugs.: weglaufen) (von zu Hause) run away; (mit der Kasse, mit dem Geliebten/der Geliebten) run off

**durch|bringen** *unr. tr. V.* get through; (bei Wahlen) **jmdn.** ~: get sb. elected; **seine Familie/sich** ~: support one's family/oneself

**Durch·bruch** *der* (fig.) breakthrough

**durch·dacht** *Adj.* **ein wenig/gut** ~**er Plan** a badly/well thought-out plan; **nicht** [genügend] ~ **sein** not be sufficiently well thought-out

**durch|drehen** ① *tr. V.* put ⟨*meat*⟩ through the mincer *or* (Amer.) grinder

② *itr. V.* auch mit sein (ugs.) crack up (coll.)

**durch|dringen** *unr. tr. V.; mit sein* ⟨*rain, sun*⟩ come through

**durch·dringen**[2] *unr. tr. V.* penetrate; **jmdn.** ~ ⟨*idea*⟩ take hold of sb. [completely]

**durch·einander** *Adv.* ~ **bringen** (+ *Akk.*) (in Unordnung bringen) get ⟨*room, flat*⟩ into a mess; get ⟨*papers, file*⟩ into a muddle; muddle up ⟨*papers, file*⟩; (verwirren) confuse; (verwechseln) confuse ⟨*names, etc*⟩; get ⟨*names etc.*⟩ mixed up; ~ **sein** ⟨*papers, desk, etc.*⟩ be in a muddle; (verwirrt sein) be confused; (aufgeregt sein) be flustered

**Durcheinander** *das;* ~s (a) muddle; mess

(b) (Wirrwarr) confusion

***durcheinander|bringen**
▶ DURCHEINANDER

**durch|exerzieren** *tr. V.* (ugs.) go through, practise ⟨*rules, multiplication tables*⟩; rehearse ⟨*situation*⟩

**durch|fahren** *unr. itr. V.; mit sein* (a) [durch etw.] ~: drive through [sth.]

(b) (nicht anhalten) go straight through; (mit dem Auto) drive straight through; **der Zug fährt** [in H.] **durch** the train doesn't stop [at H.]

**Durch·fahrt** *die* (a) „~ **verboten**" 'no entry except for access'; **auf der** ~ **sein** be passing through

(b) (Weg) thoroughfare; „**bitte** [die] ~ **freihalten**" 'please do not obstruct'

**Durch·fall** *der* diarrhoea *no art.*

**durch|fallen** *unr. itr. V.; mit sein* (a) fall through

(b) (ugs.: nicht bestehen) fail

**durch|finden** *unr. refl. V.* find one's way through

**durchführbar** *Adj.* practicable

**Durchführbarkeit** *die;* ~: practicability;

**durch|führen** ① *tr. V.* carry out; put into effect ⟨*decision, programme*⟩; perform ⟨*operation*⟩; hold ⟨*meeting, election, examination*⟩

② *itr. V.* **durch etw./unter etw.** (*Dat.*) ~ ⟨*track, road*⟩ go through/under sth.

**Durch·führung** *die* carrying out; (einer Operation) performing; (einer Versammlung, Wahl, Prüfung) holding; (eines Wettbewerbs) staging

**Durch·gang** *der* (a) passage[way]; „**kein** ~", „~ **verboten**" 'no thoroughfare'

(b) (Phase) stage; (einer Versuchsreihe) run; (Sport, Wahlen) round

**Durchgangs-:** ~**straße** *die* through road; ~**verkehr** *der* through traffic

**durch|geben** *unr. tr. V.* announce ⟨*news*⟩; ···:·

give ⟨results, weather report⟩; **eine Meldung im Radio/Fernsehen** ∼: make an announcement on the radio/on television

**durch·gefroren** Adj. frozen stiff; chilled to the bone

**durch|gehen** 1 unr. itr. V.; mit sein (a) [durch etw.] ∼: go or walk through [sth.] (b) (hindurchdringen) [durch etw.] ∼: ⟨rain, water⟩ come through [sth.] (c) (direkt zum Ziel führen) ⟨train etc.⟩ go [right] through (bis to); ⟨flight⟩ go direct (d) (andauern) go on (bis zu until) (e) (hingenommen werden) ⟨discrepancy⟩ be tolerated; ⟨mistake, discourtesy⟩ be allowed to pass; **jmdm. etw.** ∼ **lassen** let sb. get away with sth. (f) ⟨horse⟩ bolt 2 unr. tr. V.; mit sein go through ⟨newspaper, text⟩

**durch·gehend** 1 Adj. (a) continuous ⟨line, pattern, etc.⟩; constantly recurring ⟨motif⟩ (b) (direkt) through ⟨train, carriage⟩; direct ⟨flight, connection⟩ 2 adv. ∼ **geöffnet haben/bleiben** be/stay open all day

**durchgeknallt** Adj. (ugs.) crazy

**durch·geschwitzt** Adj. ⟨person⟩ soaked or bathed in sweat; ⟨clothes⟩ soaked with sweat; sweat-soaked attrib. ⟨clothes⟩

**durch|greifen** unr. itr. V. [hart] ∼: take drastic measures or steps

**durch|halten** 1 unr. itr. V. hold out; (bei einer schwierigen Aufgabe) see it through 2 unr. tr. V. stand

**durch|hängen** unr. itr. V. sag

**durch|kämmen** tr. V. (a) comb ⟨hair⟩ through (b) (durchsuchen) comb ⟨area etc.⟩

**durch|kommen** unr. itr. V.; mit sein (a) come through; (mit Mühe) get through (b) (ugs.: beim Telefonieren) get through (c) (durchgehen, -fahren usw.) **durch etw.** ∼: come through sth. (d) (ugs.: überleben) pull through

**durch|kreuzen**[1] tr. V. cross out

**durch·kreuzen**[2] tr. V. (vereiteln) frustrate

**durch|lassen** unr. tr. V. (a) **jmdn. [durch etw.]** ∼: let sb. through [sth.] (b) (durchlässig sein) let ⟨light, water, etc.⟩ through

**durchlässig** Adj. permeable; (porös) porous; (undicht) leaky; ⟨raincoat, shoe⟩ that lets in water

**Durch·lauf** der (Sport, DV) run

**durch|laufen**[1] 1 unr. itr. V.; mit sein (a) [durch etw.] ∼: run through [sth.]; (durchrinnen) trickle through [sth.] (b) ⟨passieren⟩ ⟨runners⟩ run or pass through (c) (ohne Pause laufen) run without stopping 2 unr. tr. V. go through ⟨soles⟩

*old spelling - see note on page xiv

**durch·laufen**[2] unr. tr. V. go through ⟨phase, stage⟩

**durchlaufend** 1 Adj. continuous 2 adv. ⟨numbered, marked⟩ in sequence

**durch|lesen** unr. tr. V. etw. [ganz] ∼: read sth. [all the way] through

**durch·leuchten** tr. V. x-ray; (fig.) investigate ⟨case, matter, problem, etc.⟩ thoroughly

**durch·löchern** tr. V. make holes in

**durch|machen** (ugs.) 1 tr. V. (a) undergo ⟨change⟩; complete ⟨training course⟩; go through ⟨stage, phase⟩; serve ⟨apprenticeship⟩ (b) (erleiden) go through (c) (durcharbeiten) work through ⟨lunch break etc.⟩ 2 itr. V. (durcharbeiten) work [right] through; (durchfeiern) celebrate all night/day etc.; keep going all night/day etc.

**Durchmesser** der; ∼s, ∼: diameter

**durch|nehmen** unr. tr. V. (Schulw.: behandeln)

**durch|pauken** tr. V. (ugs.) force through ⟨law, regulation, etc.⟩

**durch|peitschen** tr. V. (ugs. abwertend) railroad ⟨law, application, etc.⟩ through

**durch|probieren** tr. V. taste ⟨wines, cakes, etc.⟩ one after another

**durch·queren** tr. V. cross; travel across ⟨country⟩; ⟨train⟩ go through ⟨country⟩

**durch|rechnen** tr. V. calculate ⟨costs etc.⟩ [down to the last penny]; check ⟨bill⟩ thoroughly

**Durch·reise** die journey through

**durch|reisen** itr. V.; mit sein travel through

**Durchreise·visum** das transit visa

**durch|reißen** 1 unr. tr. V. etw. ∼: tear sth. in two or in half 2 unr. itr. V.; mit sein ⟨fabric, garment⟩ rip, tear; ⟨thread, rope⟩ snap [in two]

**durch|rosten** itr. V.; mit sein rust through

**durchs** Präp. + Art. = **durch das**

**Durch·sage** die announcement; (an eine bestimmte Person) message

**durchschaubar** Adj. transparent; **leicht** ∼: easy to see through

**durch·schauen** tr. V. see through ⟨person, plan, etc.⟩; see ⟨situation⟩ clearly

**durch|schlafen** unr. itr. V. sleep [right] through

**Durch·schlag** der (a) (Kopie) carbon [copy] (b) (Küchengerät) strainer

**durch|schlagen** unr. tr. V. etw. ∼: chop sth. in two

**durchschlagend** Adj. resounding ⟨success⟩; decisive ⟨effect, measures⟩; conclusive ⟨evidence⟩

**durch|schneiden** unr. tr. V. cut through

⟨thread, cable⟩; cut ⟨ribbon, sheet of paper⟩ in two; cut ⟨throat, umbilical cord⟩; **etw. in der Mitte** ∼: cut sth. in half

**Durch·schnitt** der average; **im** ∼: on average; **über/unter dem** ∼ **liegen** be above/ below average

**durchschnittlich** [1] Adj. (a) nicht präd. average ⟨growth, performance, output⟩ (b) (ugs.: nicht außergewöhnlich) ordinary ⟨life, person, etc.⟩ (c) (mittelmäßig) modest; ordinary ⟨appearance⟩ [2] adv. ⟨earn etc.⟩ on [an] average; ∼ **groß** of average height

**Durchschnitts-:** ∼**alter** das average age; ∼**geschwindigkeit** die average speed; ∼**mensch** der average person; (Alltagsmensch) ordinary person; ∼**temperatur** die average temperature; ∼**wert** der average or mean value

**Durch·schrift** die carbon [copy]

**durch|sehen** [1] unr. itr. V. [durch etw.] ∼: look through [sth.] [2] unr. tr. V. look through

*durch|sein ▶ DURCH 2 D–G

**durch|setzen** [1] tr. V. carry through; achieve ⟨objective⟩; enforce ⟨demand, claim⟩ [2] refl. V. assert oneself; ⟨idea etc.⟩ find or gain acceptance

**Durch·sicht** die: **nach** ∼ **der Unterlagen** after looking or checking through the documents

**durchsichtig** Adj. (auch fig.) transparent

**durch|sprechen** unr. tr. V. talk ⟨matter etc.⟩ over; discuss ⟨matter etc.⟩ thoroughly

**durch|stehen** unr. tr. V. stand ⟨pace, boring job⟩; come through ⟨difficult situation⟩; get over ⟨illness⟩

**durch|stellen** tr. V. put ⟨call⟩ through (in + Akk., **auf** + Akk. to)

**durch|streichen** unr. tr. V. cross out; (in Formularen) delete

**durch·suchen** tr. V. search (**nach** for); search, scour ⟨area⟩ (**nach** for)

**Durchsuchung** die; ∼, ∼en search

**durch|treten** unr. tr. V. press ⟨clutch pedal, brake pedal⟩ right down

**durchtrieben** (abwertend) [1] Adj. crafty; sly [2] adv. craftily; slyly

**durch·wachsen** Adj. ∼**er Speck** streaky bacon

**Durch·wahl** die (a) direct dialling; **mein Apparat hat keine** ∼: I don't have an outside line (b) ▶ DURCHWAHLNUMMER

**durch|wählen** itr. V. (a) dial direct (b) (bei Nebenstellenanlagen) dial straight through

**Durchwahl·nummer** die number of the/ one's direct line

**durch|zählen** tr. V. count; count up

**durch|ziehen** [1] unr. tr. V. jmdn./etw. [durch etw.] ∼: pull sb./sth. through [sth.]; **ein Gummiband [durch etw.]** ∼: draw an elastic through [sth.] [2] unr. itr. V.; mit sein pass through; ⟨soldiers⟩ march through

**Durch·zug** der draught

**dürfen** [1] unr. Modalverb; 2. Part. **dürfen:** (a) **etw. tun** ∼: be allowed to do sth.; **darf ich rauchen?** may I smoke?; **was darf es sein?** can I help you? (b) Konjunktiv II + Inf. **das dürfte der Grund sein** that is probably the reason [2] unr. tr., itr. V. **er hat nicht gedurft** he was not allowed to

**durfte** 1. u. 3. Pers. Sg. Prät. v. DÜRFEN

**dürfte** 1. u. 3. Pers. Sg. Konjunktiv II v. DÜRFEN

**dürr** Adj. (a) withered; arid, barren ⟨ground, earth⟩ (b) (mager) scrawny

**Dürre** die; ∼, ∼n drought

**Durst** der; ∼[e]s thirst; ∼ **haben** be thirsty; **ich habe** ∼ **auf ein Bier** I could just drink a beer

**durstig** Adj. thirsty

**durst-, Durst-:** ∼**löscher** der thirst-quencher; ∼**stillend** Adj. thirst-quenching; ∼**strecke** die lean period or time

**Dusche** die; ∼, ∼n shower

**duschen** itr., refl. V. have a shower

**Düse** die; ∼, ∼n (Technik) nozzle; (eines Vergasers) jet

**Düsen-:** ∼**flugzeug** das jet aircraft; ∼**motor** der jet engine

**düster** [1] Adj. (a) dark; gloomy; dim ⟨light⟩ (b) (fig.) gloomy; sombre ⟨colour, music⟩ [2] adv. (fig.) gloomily

**Dutzend** das; ∼s, ∼e dozen; **zwei** ∼: two dozen

**dutzend·weise** Adv. in [their] dozens (coll.)

**duzen** tr. V. call ⟨sb.⟩ 'du' (the familiar form of address)

**Duz·freund** der, **Duz·freundin** die good friend (whom one addresses with 'du')

**dynamisch** [1] Adj. (auch fig.) dynamic [2] adv. dynamically

**Dynamit** das; ∼s dynamite

**Dynamo** der; ∼s, ∼s dynamo

**Dynastie** die; ∼, ∼n dynasty

**D-Zug** /ˈdeː-/ der express train

# Ee

**e, E** /eː/ *das;* ~, ~ **(a)** (Buchstabe) e/E
**(b)** (Musik) [key of] E

**Ebbe** *die;* ~, ~n ebb tide; (Zustand) low tide;
**es ist** ~: the tide is out

**eben** [1] *Adj.* **(a)** flat
**(b)** (glatt) level
[2] *adv.* **(a)** (gerade jetzt) just
**(b)** (kurz) [for] a moment

**Ebene** *die;* ~, ~n **(a)** plain; **in der** ~: on
the plain
**(b)** (Geom., Physik) plane
**(c)** (fig.) level

**eben·falls** *Adv.* likewise; as well; **danke,** ~:
thank you, [and] [the] same to you

**Eben·holz** *das* ebony

**eben·so** *Adv.* **(a)** *mit Adjektiven, Adverbien*
just as; **ich mag Erdbeeren** ~ **gern** [**wie...**] I
like strawberries just as much [as ...]; ~
**gern würde ich an den Strand gehen** I would
just as soon go to the beach; ~ **gut** just as
well
**(b)** *mit Verben* in exactly the same way

**\*ebenso·gern** *usw.* ▶ EBENSO A

**Eber** *der;* ~s, ~: boar

**Eber·esche** *die* rowan; mountain ash

**ebnen** *tr. V.* level ⟨*ground*⟩

**Echo** *das;* ~s, ~s echo

**echt** [1] *Adj.* **(a)** genuine; real ⟨*love,
friendship*⟩
**(b)** (typisch) real, typical
[2] *adv.* **(a)** (ugs. verstärkend) really
**(b)** (typisch) typically

**Eck** *das;* ~s, ~e (südd., österr.:) ~e corner

**Eck-:** ~**ball** *der* (Sport) corner [kick/hit/
throw]; **einen** ~**ball treten** take a corner;
~**bank** *die; Pl.* ~**bänke** corner seat

**Ecke** *die;* ~, ~n corner; **an der** ~: on *or* at
the corner; **um die** ~: round the corner

**eckig** *Adj.* square; angular

**Eck·zahn** *der* canine tooth

**edel** *Adj.* **(a)** thoroughbred ⟨*horse*⟩; species
⟨*rose*⟩
**(b)** (großmütig) noble[-minded], high-minded
⟨*person*⟩; noble ⟨*thought, gesture, feelings,
deed*⟩; honourable ⟨*motive*⟩

**Edel-:** ~**metall** *das* precious metal;
~**nutte** *die* (salopp) high-class tart (sl.);
~**pilz·käse** *der* blue[-veined] cheese;
~**stahl** *der* stainless steel; ~**stein** *der*
precious stone; gem[stone]

**Edition** *die;* ~, ~en edition

**Edutainment** /ɛdjuˈtɛmmənt/ *das;* ~s
edutainment

---

**EDV** *Abk.* = **elektronische
Datenverarbeitung** EDP

**EEG** *Abk.*
= **Elektroenzephalogramm** EEG; **ein
EEG machen lassen** have an EEG

**Efeu** *der;* ~s ivy

**Effekt** *der;* ~[e]s, ~e effect

**effekt·voll** *Adj.* effective; dramatic ⟨*pause,
gesture, entrance*⟩

**EG** *Abk.* **(a)** = **Europäische
Gemeinschaft** EC
**(b)** = **Erdgeschoss**

**egal** *Adj.* (ugs.: einerlei) **es ist jmdm.** ~: it's all
the same to sb.; **[ganz]** ~, **wie/wer** *usw.* ...:
no matter how/who *etc.* ...

**Egge** *die;* ~, ~n harrow

**E-Gitarre** *die* electric guitar

**Egoist** *der;* ~en, ~en, **Egoistin** *die;* ~,
~nen egoist

**egoistisch** [1] *Adj.* egoistic[al]
[2] *adv.* egoistically

**ehe** *Konj.* before

**Ehe** *die;* ~, ~n marriage

**Ehe-:** ~**bett** *das* marriage bed; (Doppelbett)
double bed; ~**bruch** *der* adultery; ~**frau**
*die* wife; (verheiratete Frau) married woman;
~**krach** *der* (ugs.) row; ~**leute** *Pl.*
married couple

**ehelich** *Adj.* marital; matrimonial; conjugal
⟨*rights, duties*⟩; legitimate ⟨*child*⟩

**ehemalig** *Adj.* former

**ehe-, Ehe-:** ~**mann** *der; Pl.* ~**männer**
husband; (verheirateter Mann) married man;
~**mündig** *Adj.* (Rechtsspr.) of marriageable
age *postpos.;* ~**mündig sein** be of
marriageable age *or* of an age to marry;
~**mündigkeit** *die* (Rechtsspr.) being of
marriageable age; ~**paar** *das* married
couple

**eher** *Adv.* **(a)** (früher) earlier; sooner
**(b)** (lieber) rather; sooner

**Ehe-:** ~**ring** *der* wedding ring;
~**scheidung** *die* divorce; ~**vertrag** *der*
(Rechtsw.) marriage contract

**Ehre** *die;* ~, ~n honour; **jmdm.** ~ **antun** pay
tribute to sb.

**ehren** *tr. V.* **(a)** honour; **Sehr geehrter Herr
Müller!/Sehr geehrte Frau Müller!** Dear Herr
Müller/Dear Frau Müller
**(b)** (Ehre machen) **deine Hilfsbereitschaft ehrt
dich** your willingness to help does you credit

**ehren-, Ehren-:** ~**amt** *das* honorary
position *or* post; ~**amtlich** [1] *Adj.*

honorary ⟨*position, membership*⟩; voluntary
⟨*help, worker*⟩; **2** *adv.* in an honorary
capacity; (freiwillig) on a voluntary basis
**ehrenhaft** *Adj.* honourable
**ehren-, Ehren-:** ~**rührig** *Adj.*
defamatory ⟨*allegations*⟩; ~**sache** *die:* das
ist ~sache that is a point of honour;
~sache! you can count on me!; ~**voll** *Adj.*
honourable; ~**wert** *Adj.* (geh.) worthy;
~**wort** *das; Pl.* ~~e: ~wort [!/?] word of
honour [!/?]
**ehrerbietig** *Adj.* (geh.) respectful
**Ehr·furcht** *die* reverence (**vor** + *Dat.* for)
**ehrfürchtig** *Adj.* reverent
**ehr-, Ehr-:** ~**gefühl** *das* sense of honour;
~**geiz** *der* ambition; ~**geizig** *Adj.*
ambitious
**ehrlich** *Adj.* honest; genuine ⟨*concern,
desire, admiration*⟩; upright ⟨*character*⟩
**Ehrlichkeit** *die;* ~ ▶ EHRLICH: honesty;
genuineness; uprightness
**ehr·los** *Adj.* dishonourable
**Ehrung** *die;* ~, ~en: **die** ~ **der Preisträger**
the prize-giving (Brit.) *or* (Amer.) awards
ceremony; **bei der** ~ **der Sieger** when the
winners were awarded their medals/
trophies
**ehr·würdig** *Adj.* venerable
**Ei** *das;* ~[e]s, ~er egg
**Eiche** *die;* ~, ~n oak [tree]; (Holz) oak
[wood]
**Eichel** *die;* ~, ~n acorn
**eichen** *tr. V.* calibrate ⟨*measuring
instrument, thermometer*⟩; standardize
⟨*weights, measures, containers, products*⟩;
adjust ⟨*weighing scales*⟩
**Eich·hörnchen** *das* squirrel
**Eid** *der;* ~[e]s, ~e oath
**Eidechse** /'ai:dɛksə/ *die;* ~, ~n lizard
**eides·stattlich** *Adj.* (Rechtsw.) **eine** ~**e**
**Erklärung** a statutory declaration
**Ei·dotter** *der od. das* egg yolk
**Eier-:** ~**becher** *der* eggcup; ~**kuchen**
*der* pancake; (Omelett) omelette; ~**likör** *der*
egg flip; ~**stock** *der* (Physiol., Zool.) ovary;
~**uhr** *die* egg timer
**Eifer** *der;* ~s eagerness
**Eifer·sucht** *die* jealousy (**auf** + *Akk.* of)
**eifer·süchtig** *Adj.* jealous (**auf** + *Akk.* of)
**eifrig** *Adj.* eager
**Ei·gelb** *das;* ~[e]s, ~e egg yolk
**eigen** *Adj.* own; (selbstständig) separate
**eigen-, Eigen-:** ~**art** *die* (Wesensart)
particular nature; (Zug) peculiarity; **eine**
~**art dieser Stadt** one of the characteristic
features of this city; ~**artig** *Adj.* peculiar;
strange; odd; ~**artigerweise** *Adv.*
strangely [enough]; oddly [enough];
~**artigkeit** *die* peculiarity; strangeness;
oddness; ~**brötelei** *die;* ~~, ~~en
taking an [unduly] independent line;
~**brötler** *der;* ~~s, ~~, ~**brötlerin**

*die;* ~~, ~~**nen** loner; lone wolf;
~**dynamik** *die* inherent dynamism;
~**händig** **1** *Adj.* personal ⟨*signature*⟩;
holographic ⟨*will, document*⟩; **2** *adv.*
⟨*present, sign*⟩ personally; ~**heim** *das*
house of one's own
**Eigenheit** *die;* ~, ~en peculiarity
**eigen-, Eigen-:** ~**initiative** *die*
initiative of one's own; ~**lob** *das* self-
praise; ~**mächtig** *Adj.* unauthorized;
~**name** *der* proper name; ~**nützig** *Adj.*
self-seeking; selfish ⟨*motive*⟩
**eigens** *Adv.* specially
**Eigenschaft** *die;* ~, ~en quality;
characteristic; (von Sachen, Stoffen) property
**Eigenschafts·wort** *das; Pl.*
**Eigenschaftswörter** adjective
**eigen-, Eigen-:** ~**sinn** *der* obstinacy;
~**sinnig** *Adj.* obstinate; ~**ständig** *Adj.*
independent; ~**ständigkeit** *die;* ~~:
independence
**eigentlich** **1** *Adj.* (wirklich) actual; real;
(wahr) true; (ursprünglich) original
**2** *Adv.* actually
**3** *Partikel* **wie spät ist es** ~? tell me, what
time is it?; **was willst du** ~? what exactly do
you want?
**Eigen·tor** *das* (Ballspiele, fig.) own goal
**Eigentum** *das;* ~s property; (einschließlich
Geld usw.) assets *pl.*
**Eigentümer** *der;* ~s, ~: owner; (Hotel~,
Geschäfts~) proprietor
**Eigentümerin** *die;* ~, ~nen owner;
(Hotel~, Geschäfts~) proprietress; proprietor
**Eigentums·wohnung** *die* owner-
occupied flat (Brit.); condominium apartment
(Amer.)
**eigen-, Eigen-:** ~**vorsorge** private
[pension] provision; ~**willig** *Adj.* self-
willed
**eignen** *refl. V.* be suitable
**Eigner** *der;* ~s, ~, **Eignerin** *die;* ~,
~nen owner
**Eignung** *die;* ~: suitability; **seine** ~ **zum**
**Fliegen** his aptitude for flying
**Eignungs-:** ~**prüfung** *die,* ~**test** *der*
aptitude test
**Eil-:** ~**bote** *der,* ~**botin** *die* special
messenger; „**durch** *od.* **per** ~**boten**" (veralt.)
'express'; ~**brief** *der* express letter
**Eile** *die;* ~: hurry; **in** ~ **sein** be in a hurry
**eilen** *itr. V.* **(a)** *mit sein* hurry; (besonders
schnell) rush
**(b)** (dringend sein) be urgent; „**eilt!**" 'urgent'
**eilig** **1** *Adj.* **(a)** hurried; **es** ~ **haben** be in
a hurry
**(b)** (dringend) urgent
**2** *adv.* hurriedly
**Eil·zug** *der* semi-fast train
**Eimer** *der;* ~s, ~: bucket; (Milch~) pail;
(Abfall~) bin; **ein** ~ **[voll] Wasser** a bucket of
water; **im** ~ **sein** (salopp) be up the spout
(coll.)

**ein**¹ ① *Kardinalz.* one; ~ für alle Mal, *~ für allemal once and for all
② *unbest. Art.* a/an
③ *Indefinitpron.* ▶ IRGENDEIN A; *s. auch* EINER

**ein**² (elliptisch) ~ – aus (an Schaltern) on – off

**Einakter** *der;* ~s, ~: one-act play

**einander** *reziprokes Pron.; Dat. u. Akk.* (geh.) each other; one another

**ein|arbeiten** *tr. V.* train ⟨employee⟩

**ein·armig** *Adj.* one-armed

**ein|äschern** *tr. V.* cremate

**ein|atmen** *tr., itr. V.* breathe in

**ein·äugig** *Adj.* one-eyed

**Ein·bahn·straße** *die* one-way street

**Ein·band** *der; Pl.* Einbände binding

**Ein·bau** *der; Pl.* ~ten fitting; (eines Motors) installation

**ein|bauen** *tr. V.* build in, fit; install ⟨engine, motor⟩

**Einbau·küche** *die* fitted kitchen

**ein·beinig** *Adj.* one-legged

**ein|berufen** *unr. tr. V.* summon; call

**Ein·berufung** *die* (a) (das Einberufen) calling (b) (zur Wehrpflicht) call-up; conscription; draft (Amer.)

**Einbett·zimmer** *das* single room

**ein|beziehen** *unr. tr. V.* include

**ein|biegen** *unr. itr. V.; mit sein* turn

**ein|bilden** *refl. V.* (a) sich *(Dat.)* etw. ~: imagine sth.
(b) (ugs.) sich *(Dat.)* etwas ~: be conceited (auf + *Akk.* about)

**Ein·bildung** *die* (a) imagination
(b) (falsche Vorstellung) fantasy
(c) (Hochmut) conceitedness

**ein|binden** *unr. tr. V.* bind ⟨book⟩; etw. neu ~: rebind sth.

**ein|blenden** *tr. V.* (Rundf., Fems., Film) insert

**Ein·blick** *der* (a) view; ~ in etw. *(Akk.)* haben be able to see into sth.
(b) (Durchsicht) jmdm. ~ in etw. *(Akk.)* gewähren allow sb. to look at *or* examine sth.
(c) (Kenntnis) insight

**ein|brechen** *unr. itr. V.* (a) *mit haben od. sein* break in; **in eine Bank** ~: break into a bank; **bei jmdm.** ~: burgle sb.
(b) *mit sein* (einstürzen) ⟨roof, ceiling⟩ cave in
(c) *mit sein* (durchbrechen) fall through

**Einbrecher** *der;* ~s, ~, **Einbrecherin** *die;* ~, ~nen burglar

**ein|bringen** *unr. tr. V.* (a) bring in ⟨harvest⟩
(b) (verschaffen) Gewinn/Zinsen ~: yield a profit/bring in interest; **jmdm. Ruhm** ~: bring sb. fame
(c) (Parl.: vorlegen) introduce ⟨bill⟩
(d) invest ⟨capital, money⟩

**Ein·bruch** *der* (a) burglary; **ein** ~ **in eine Bank** a break-in at a bank
(b) (das Einstürzen) collapse

**einbürgern** ① *tr. V.* naturalize
② *refl. V.* ⟨custom, practice⟩ become established; ⟨person, plant, animal⟩ become naturalized

**Einbürgerung** *die;* ~, ~en naturalization

**Ein·buße** *die* loss

**ein|büßen** *tr. V.* lose; (durch eigene Schuld) forfeit

**ein|checken** *tr., itr. V.* (Flugw.) check in

**ein|cremen** *tr. V.* put cream on ⟨hands etc.⟩; **sich** ~: put cream on

**ein|dämmen** *tr. V.* (fig.) check; stem

**ein|decken** ① *refl. V.* stock up
② *tr. V.* (ugs.: überhäufen) jmdn. mit Arbeit ~: swamp sb. with work

**Eindecker** *der;* ~s, ~ (Flugw.) monoplane

**eindeutig** *Adj.* clear

**Eindeutigkeit** *die;* ~, ~en clarity

**ein|dringen** *unr. itr. V.; mit sein* in etw. *(Akk.)* ~: penetrate into sth.; ⟨bullet⟩ pierce sth.; (allmählich) ⟨water, sand, etc.⟩ seep into sth.

**ein·dringlich** *Adj.* urgent; impressive ⟨voice⟩; forceful, powerful ⟨words⟩

**Eindringling** *der;* ~s, ~e intruder

**Ein·druck** *der; Pl.* Eindrücke impression

**ein|drücken** *tr. V.* smash in ⟨mudguard, bumper⟩; stave in ⟨side of ship⟩; smash ⟨pier, column, support⟩; break ⟨window⟩; crush ⟨ribs⟩; flatten ⟨nose⟩

**eindrucks·voll** ① *Adj.* impressive
② *adv.* impressively

**eine** ▶ EIN¹

**ein|ebnen** *tr. V.* level

**eineiig** /'ai:n|ai:ɪç/ *Adj.* identical ⟨twins⟩

**ein-ein-halb** *Bruchz.* one and a half; ~ Stunden an hour and a half

**ein|engen** *tr. V.* (a) jmdn. ~: restrict sb.'s movement[s]
(b) (fig.) restrict

**einer, eine, eines, eins** *Indefinitpron.* (man) one; (jemand) someone; somebody; (fragend, verneint) anyone; anybody; **kaum einer** hardly anybody; **ein[e]s ist sicher** one thing is for sure

**Einer** *der;* ~s, ~ (a) (Math.) unit
(b) (Sport) single sculler; **im** ~: in the single sculls

**einerlei** *Adj.* ~, ob/wo/wer *usw.* no matter whether/where/who *etc.;* **es ist** ~: it makes no difference

**Einerlei** *das;* ~s monotony

**einerseits** *Adv.* on the one hand

**ein·fach** ① *Adj.* (a) simple
(b) (nicht mehrfach) single ⟨knot, ticket, journey⟩
② *Partikel* simply; just

**Einfachheit** *die;* ~ simplicity

**ein|fädeln** ① *tr. V.* thread (in + *Akk.* into)

**2** *refl. V.* (Verkehrsw.) filter in

**ein|fahren** **1** *unr. itr. V.; mit sein* come in; ⟨*train*⟩ pull in; **in den Bahnhof ∼:** pull into the station

**2** *unr. tr. V.* **(a)** bring in ⟨*harvest*⟩ **(b)** (beschädigen) knock down ⟨*wall*⟩; smash in ⟨*mudguard*⟩

**Ein·fahrt** *die* **(a)** (das Hineinfahren) entry; **Vorsicht bei der ∼ des Zuges!** stand clear [of the edge of the platform], the train is approaching **(b)** (Zufahrt) entrance; (Autobahn∼) slip road; „**keine ∼**" 'no entry'

**Ein·fall** *der* **(a)** (Idee) idea **(b)** (Licht∼) incidence (Optics)

**ein|fallen** *unr. itr. V.; mit sein* **(a)** jmdm. **∼:** occur to sb.; **was fällt dir denn ein!** what do you think you're doing? **(b)** (in Erinnerung kommen) **ihr Name fällt mir nicht ein** I cannot think of her name; **plötzlich fiel ihr ein, dass ...:** suddenly she remembered that ... **(c)** (von Licht) come in

**einfalls-, Einfalls-:** **∼los** *Adj.* unimaginative; lacking in ideas; **∼losigkeit** *die;* ∼∼: unimaginativeness; lack of ideas; **∼reich** *Adj.* imaginative; full of ideas; **∼reichtum** *der* imaginativeness; wealth of ideas; **∼tor** *das* gateway

**Ein·falt** *die;* ∼: simpleness; simple-mindedness

**ein·fältig** *Adj.* simple; naïve; naïve ⟨*remarks*⟩

**Ein·familien·haus** *das* house (as opposed to block of flats etc.)

**ein|fangen** *unr. tr. V.* catch

**ein|fassen** *tr. V.* border; edge; frame ⟨*picture*⟩; set ⟨*gem*⟩; edge ⟨*grave, lawn, etc.*⟩

**Ein·fassung** *die* ▶ EINFASSEN: border; edging; frame; setting

**ein|fetten** *tr. V.* grease; dubbin ⟨*leather*⟩; **sich** (*Dat.*) **die Haut/Hände ∼:** rub cream into one's skin/hands

**ein|finden** *unr. refl. V.* arrive; (sich treffen) meet; ⟨*crowd*⟩ gather

**ein|fliegen** *unr. tr. V.* fly in

**ein|flößen** *tr. V.* **(a)** jmdm. Tee **∼:** pour tea into sb.'s mouth **(b)** (fig.) jmdm. Angst **∼:** put fear into sb.

**Ein·fluss, *Ein·fluß** *der* influence

**einfluss-, *einfluß-, Einfluss-, *Einfluß-:** **∼bereich** *der* sphere of influence; **∼nahme,** *die;* ∼∼: exertion of influence (**auf** + *Akk.* on); **∼reich** *Adj.* influential

**ein·förmig** *Adj.* monotonous

**ein|frieren** **1** *unr. itr. V.; mit sein* freeze; ⟨*pipes*⟩ freeze up **2** *unr. tr. V.* **(a)** deep-freeze ⟨*food*⟩ **(b)** (fig.) freeze

**ein|fügen** *tr. V.* **(a)** fit in; **etw. in etw.** (*Akk.*) **∼:** fit sth. into sth. **(b)** (DV) insert; paste

**ein|fühlen** *refl. V.* **sich in jmdn. ∼:** empathize with sb.

**einfühlsam** *Adj.* understanding

**Ein·fühlung** *die;* ∼: empathy (**in** + *Akk.* with)

**Ein·fuhr** *die;* ∼, ∼en ▶ IMPORT

**ein|führen** *tr. V.* **(a)** (als Neuerung) introduce ⟨*fashion, method, technology*⟩ **(b)** (importieren) import

**Einfuhr-:** **∼sperre** *die,* **∼stopp** *der* embargo *or* ban on imports

**Ein·führung** *die* introduction

**Einfuhr·verbot** *das* ▶ ∼SPERRE

**Ein·gabe** *die* **(a)** (Gesuch) petition; (Beschwerde) complaint **(b)** (DV) input

**Eingabe·gerät** *das* (DV) input device

**Ein·gang** *der* entrance; „**kein ∼**" 'no entry'

**ein·gängig** *Adj.* catchy

**eingangs** *Adv.* at the beginning *or* start

**Eingangs-:** **∼halle** *die* entrance hall; (eines Hotels, Theaters) foyer; **∼tür** *die* (von Kaufhaus, Hotel usw.) [entrance] door; (von Wohnung, Haus usw.) front door

**ein|geben** *unr. tr. V.* (DV) feed in; **etw. in den Computer ∼:** feed sth. into the computer

**ein·gebildet** *Adj.* **(a)** imaginary ⟨*illness*⟩ **(b)** (arrogant) conceited

**Eingeborene** *der/die; adj. Dekl.* (veralt.) native

**ein·gefahren** *Adj.* long-established; deep-rooted ⟨*prejudice*⟩; **sich** *od.* **in ∼en Bahnen** *od.* **Gleisen bewegen** go on in the same old way

**ein|gehen** **1** *unr. itr. V.; mit sein* **(a)** arrive **(b)** (fig.) **in die Geschichte ∼:** go down in history **(c)** (schrumpfen) shrink **(d)** **auf eine Frage ∼/nicht ∼:** go into *or* deal with/ignore a question; **auf jmdn. ∼:** be responsive to sb.; **auf jmdn. nicht ∼:** ignore sb.'s wishes **2** *unr. tr. V.* enter into ⟨*contract, matrimony*⟩; take ⟨*risk*⟩; accept ⟨*obligation*⟩

**ein·gehend** *Adj.* detailed

**Ein·gemachte** *das; adj. Dekl.* preserved fruit/vegetables

**ein|gemeinden** *tr. V.* incorporate ⟨*village*⟩ (**in** + *Akk.,* nach into)

**ein·geschnappt** *Adj.* (ugs.) huffy

**Ein·geständnis** *das* confession; admission

**ein|gestehen** *unr. tr. V.* admit

**Eingeweide** *das;* ∼s, ∼: entrails *pl.;* innards *pl.*

**ein|gewöhnen** *refl. V.* get used to one's new surroundings

**ein|gießen** *unr. tr., itr. V.* pour in

**ein|gliedern** *tr. V.* integrate (**in** + *Akk.* into); incorporate ⟨*village, company*⟩ (**in** + *Akk.* into); (einordnen) include (**in** + *Akk.* in)

**Ein·gliederung** *die* ▶ EINGLIEDERN: integration; incorporation; inclusion

**ein|graben** *unr. tr. V.* bury (**in** + *Akk.* in); sink ⟨*pile, pipe*⟩ (**in** + *Akk.* into)

**ein|gravieren** *tr. V.* engrave (**in** + *Akk.* on)

**ein|greifen** *unr. itr. V.* intervene (**in** + *Akk.* in)

**Ein·griff** *der* (a) intervention (**in** + *Akk.* in) (b) (Med.) operation

**ein|haken** ⊡ *tr. V.* (a) (mit Haken befestigen) fasten (b) **sich** ∼: link arms ⊡ *refl. V.* **sich bei jmdm.** ∼: link arms with sb.

**Ein·halt** *der:* **jmdm./einer Sache** ∼ **gebieten** *od.* **tun** (geh.) halt sb./sth.

**ein|halten** ⊡ *unr. tr. V.* keep ⟨*appointment*⟩; meet ⟨*deadline, commitments*⟩; keep to ⟨*diet, speed limit, agreement*⟩; observe ⟨*regulation*⟩ ⊡ *unr. itr. V.* (geh.) stop

**ein·heimisch** *Adj.* native; home *attrib.* ⟨*team*⟩

**Einheimische** *der/die; adj. Dekl.* local

**Einheit** *die;* ∼, ∼**en** unity

**einheitlich** ⊡ *Adj.* unified; (unterschiedslos) uniform ⟨*dress*⟩; standard ⟨*procedure, practice*⟩ ⊡ *adv.* ∼ **gekleidet sein** be dressed the same

**einhellig** ⊡ *Adj.* unanimous ⊡ *adv.* unanimously

**ein|holen** ⊡ *tr. V.* (a) catch up with ⟨*person, vehicle*⟩ (b) make up ⟨*arrears, time*⟩ ⊡ *itr. V.* (ugs.) ▶ EINKAUFEN 1

**ein·hundert** *Kardinalz.* ▶ HUNDERT

**einig** *Adj.* **sich** (*Dat.*) ∼ **sein** be agreed; **sich** (*Dat.*) ∼ **werden** reach agreement

**einig...** *Indefinitpron. u. unbest. Zahlwort* some; ∼**e wenige** a few; ∼**e Hundert** several hundred

**einigen** ⊡ *tr. V.* unite ⊡ *refl. V.* reach an agreement

**einigermaßen** *Adv.* somewhat

**Einigkeit** *die;* ∼ (a) unity (b) (Übereinstimmung) agreement

**ein·jährig** *Adj.* (ein Jahr alt) one-year-old *attrib.;* one year old *pred.;* (ein Jahr dauernd) one-year *attrib.*

**Ein·kauf** *der* (a) **Einkäufe machen** do some shopping (b) (eingekaufte Ware) purchase (c) (Abteilung) purchasing department

**ein|kaufen** ⊡ *itr. V.* shop; ∼ **gehen** go shopping ⊡ *tr. V.* buy; purchase

**Ein-käufer** *der,* **Ein-käuferin** *die* buyer; purchaser

**Einkaufs-:** ∼**bummel** *der* [leisurely] shopping expedition; ∼**liste** *die* shopping list; ∼**preis** *der* (Kaufmannsspr.) wholesale price; ∼**tasche** *die* shopping bag; ∼**zentrum** *das* shopping centre; ∼**zettel** *der* shopping list

**ein|kehren** *itr. V.; mit sein* stop; **in einem Wirtshaus** ∼: stop at an inn

**ein|klammern** *tr. V.* **etw.** ∼: put sth. in brackets; bracket sth.

**Ein·klang** *der* harmony; **in** *od.* **im** ∼ **stehen** accord

**ein|kleben** *tr. V.* stick in

**ein|kleiden** *tr. V.* clothe

**ein|klemmen** *tr. V.* (a) (quetschen) catch (b) (fest einfügen) clamp

**ein|kochen** *tr. V.* preserve ⟨*fruit etc.*⟩

**Einkommen** *das;* ∼**s,** ∼: income

**Einkommen·steuer** *die* income tax

**ein|kreisen** *tr. V.* (a) **etw.** ∼: put a circle round sth. (b) (umzingeln) surround

**Einkünfte** *Pl.* income *sing.;* **feste** ∼: a regular income

**ein|laden**[1] *unr. tr. V.* load ⟨*goods*⟩

**ein|laden**[2] *unr. tr. V.* invite ⟨*person*⟩ (**zu** for)

**einladend** *Adj.* inviting

**Ein·ladung** *die* invitation

**Ein·lage** *die* (a) (in Brief) enclosure (b) (Kochk.) *vegetables, dumplings, etc. added to a clear soup;* (c) (Schuh∼) arch support (d) (Programm∼) interlude

**ein|lagern** *tr. V.* store; lay in ⟨*stores*⟩

**Einlass,** *\**Einlaß** *der;* **Einlasses, Einlässe** admission

**ein|lassen** *unr. tr. V.* (a) (hereinlassen) admit; let in (b) (einfüllen) run ⟨*water*⟩

**Ein·lauf** *der* (Med.) enema

**ein|laufen** ⊡ *unr. itr. V.; mit sein* (a) ⟨*ship*⟩ come in (b) (kleiner werden) shrink ⊡ *unr. tr. V.* wear in ⟨*shoes*⟩

**ein|leben** *refl. V.* settle down

**ein|legen** *tr. V.* (a) load ⟨*film*⟩; engage ⟨*gear*⟩ (b) (Kochk.) pickle

**ein|leiten** *tr. V.* (a) introduce (b) induce ⟨*birth*⟩ (c) lead in; **etw. in etw.** (*Akk.*) ∼: lead sth. into sth.

**Ein·leitung** *die* (a) introduction (b) (einer Geburt) induction

**ein|leuchten** *itr. V.* **jmdm.** ∼: be clear to sb.

**einleuchtend** *Adj.* plausible

**ein|liefern** *tr. V.* take ⟨*letter, person*⟩ (**bei, in** + *Akk.* to)

---

\*alte Schreibung - vgl. Hinweis auf S. xiv

**Einlieger·wohnung** *die* ≈ granny flat

**ein|lösen** *tr. V.* cash ⟨cheque⟩

**ein|machen** *tr. V.* preserve ⟨fruit etc.⟩; (in Gläser) bottle

**einmal** ⓵ *Adv.* (a) once; **noch ~ so groß [wie]** twice as big [as]; **etw. noch ~ tun** do sth. again
(b) /'--/ (später) one day; (früher) once; **es war ~ ...:** once upon a time there was ...
⓶ *Partikel* **nicht ~:** not even; **wieder ~:** yet again

**Einmal·eins** *das;* **~:** [multiplication] tables *pl.*

**einmalig** ⓵ *Adj.* (a) unique; one-off ⟨payment, purchase⟩
(b) (ugs.) fantastic (coll.)
⓶ *adv.* (ugs.) really fantastically (coll.)

**Ein·marsch** *der* (a) entry
(b) (Besetzung) invasion (**in** + *Akk.* of)

**ein|marschieren** *itr. V.; mit sein* march in

**ein|massieren** *tr. V.* massage *or* rub in

**ein|mauern** *tr. V.* (a) immure ⟨prisoner, traitor⟩; wall in ⟨relic, treasure⟩
(b) (ins Mauerwerk einfügen) **etw. in die Wand usw. ~:** set sth. into the wall *etc.*

**ein|mischen** *refl. V.* interfere (**in** + *Akk.* in)

**ein|motten** *tr. V.* **etw. ~:** put sth. into mothballs; (fig.) mothball

**Ein·mündung** *die* (von Straßen) junction

**einmütig** ⓵ *Adj.* unanimous
⓶ *adv.* unanimously

**ein|nähen** *tr. V.* sew in

**Einnahme** *die;* **~, ~n** (a) income; (Staats~) revenue; (Kassen~) takings *pl.;*
(b) (von Arzneimitteln) taking
(c) (einer Stadt, Burg) taking

**Einnahme·quelle** *die* source of income; (des Staates) source of revenue

**ein|nehmen** *unr. tr. V.* (a) take; (verdienen) earn
(b) (ausfüllen) take up ⟨amount of room⟩
(c) (beeinflussen) **jmdn. für sich ~:** win sb. over

**einnehmend** *Adj.* winning ⟨manner⟩; **ein ~es Wesen haben** (scherzh.) take everything one can get

**Ein·öde** *die* barren waste

**ein|ölen** *tr. V.* (a) (mit Öl einreiben) **sich/jmdn. ~:** put *or* rub oil on oneself/sb.
(b) (ölen) oil

**ein|ordnen** ⓵ *tr. V.* arrange; put in order
⓶ *refl. V.* (a) (Verkehrsw.) get into the correct lane; **„~" 'get in lane'**
(b) (sich einfügen) fit in

**ein|packen** ⓵ *tr. V.* pack (**in** + *Akk.* in); (einwickeln) wrap [up]
⓶ *itr. V.* (ugs.) **er kann ~:** he's had it (coll.)

**ein|parken** *tr., itr. V.* park

**ein|pflanzen** *tr. V.* (a) plant
(b) (Med., fig.) implant

**ein|prägen** *tr. V.* (a) stamp (**in** + *Akk.* into, on)
(b) (fig.) **sich** (*Dat.*) **etw. ~:** memorize sth.; **jmdm. etw. ~:** impress sth. on sb.

**einprägsam** *Adj.* easily remembered

**ein|pudern** *tr. V.* powder; **sich** (*Dat.*) **das Gesicht ~:** powder one's face

**ein|rahmen** *tr. V.* frame

**ein|räumen** *tr. V.* (a) put away
(b) (füllen) **seinen Schrank ~:** put one's things away in one's cupboard; **ein Zimmer ~:** put the furniture into a room
(c) (zugestehen) admit

**ein|reden** ⓵ *tr. V.* **jmdm. etw. ~:** talk sb. into believing sth.; **sich** (*Dat.*) **~, dass ...:** persuade oneself that ...
⓶ *itr. V.* **auf jmdn. ~:** talk insistently to sb.

**ein|regnen** *refl. V.; unpers.* **es hat sich eingeregnet** it's begun to rain steadily

**ein|reiben** *unr. tr. V.* rub ⟨substance⟩ in; **etw. mit Öl ~:** rub oil into sth.

**ein|reichen** *tr. V.* submit; lodge ⟨complaint⟩; tender ⟨resignation⟩

**ein|reihen** ⓵ *refl. V.* **sich in etw.** (*Akk.*) **~:** join sth.
⓶ *tr. V.* **jmdn. in eine Kategorie ~:** place sb. in a category

**Einreiher** *der;* **~s, ~:** single-breasted suit/jacket

**Ein·reise** *die* entry

**Einreise·erlaubnis** *die* entry permit

**ein|reisen** *itr. V.; mit sein* enter; **nach Schweden ~:** enter Sweden

**ein|reißen** ⓵ *unr. tr. V.* (a) pull down ⟨building⟩
(b) (einen Riss machen in) tear; rip
⓶ *unr. itr. V.; mit sein* tear; rip

**ein|renken** *tr. V.* (a) (Med.) set
(b) (ugs.: bereinigen) sort out

**ein|richten** ⓵ *refl. V.* **sich schön ~:** furnish one's home beautifully; **sich häuslich ~:** make oneself at home
⓶ *tr. V.* furnish ⟨flat, house⟩; fit out ⟨shop⟩; equip ⟨laboratory⟩

**Ein·richtung** *die* (a) furnishing
(b) (Mobiliar) furnishings *pl.*

**ein|rollen** ⓵ *tr. V.* roll up ⟨carpet etc.⟩; put ⟨hair⟩ in curlers
⓶ *itr. V.; mit sein* roll in

**ein|rosten** *itr. V.; mit sein* go rusty

**ein|rücken** ⓵ *itr. V.; mit sein* (einmarschieren) move in
⓶ *tr. V.* indent ⟨line, heading, etc.⟩

**eins** ⓵ *Kardinalz.* one; **es ist ~:** it is one o'clock; **~ zu null** one-nil; **~ zu ~:** one all; **„~, zwei, drei"** 'ready, steady, go'
⓶ *Adj.* **mir ist alles ~:** it's all the same to me
⓷ *Indefinitpron.* ▶ IRGENDEIN A

**Eins** *die;* **~, ~en** (a) one
(b) (Schulnote) one; A

**einsam** *Adj.* (a) lonely ⟨person, decision⟩
(b) (einzeln) solitary ⟨tree, wanderer⟩ ⋯∤

**(c)** (abgelegen) isolated
**(d)** (menschenleer) deserted
**Einsamkeit** *die;* ~ **(a)** loneliness
**(b)** (Alleinsein) solitude
**(c)** (Abgeschiedenheit) isolation
**ein|sammeln** *tr. V.* **(a)** (auflesen) pick up; gather up
**(b)** (sich aushändigen lassen) collect in; collect ⟨*tickets*⟩
**Ein·satz** *der* **(a)** (aus Stoff) inset; (in Kochtopf, Nähkasten usw.) compartment
**(b)** (Betrag) stake
**(c)** (Gebrauch) use; (von Truppen) deployment
**Einsatz-:** ~**befehl** *der* order to go into action; den ~befehl haben have operational command; ~**leiter** *der,* ~**leiterin** *die* head of operations; ~**wagen** *der* (der Polizei) police car; (der Feuerwehr) fire engine; (Notarztwagen) ambulance
**ein|saugen** *unr.* (*auch regelm.*) *tr. V.* suck in; breathe [in] ⟨*fresh air*⟩
**ein|schalten** ① *tr. V.* **(a)** switch on ⟨*radio, TV, electricity, etc.*⟩
**(b)** (fig.) call in ⟨*press, police, expert, etc.*⟩
② *refl. V.* **(a)** switch [itself] on
**(b)** (eingreifen) intervene (**in** + *Akk.* in)
**Einschalt·quote** *die* (Rundf.) listening figures *pl.;* (Ferns.) viewing figures *pl.*
**ein|schärfen** *tr. V.* jmdm. etw. ~: impress sth. [up]on sb.
**ein|schätzen** *tr. V.* judge ⟨*person*⟩; assess ⟨*situation, income, damages*⟩; (schätzen) estimate
**Ein·schätzung** *die* ▶ EINSCHÄTZEN: judging; assessment; estimation
**ein|schenken** *tr., itr. V.* **(a)** (eingießen) pour [out]; jmdm. etw. ~: pour out sth. for sb.
**(b)** (füllen) fill [up] ⟨*glass, cup*⟩
**ein|scheren** *itr. V.; mit sein* **auf eine Fahrspur** ~: get *or* move into a lane
**ein|schicken** *tr. V.* send in
**ein|schieben** *unr. tr. V.* **(a)** push in
**(b)** (einfügen) insert; put on ⟨*trains, buses*⟩
**ein|schiffen** *tr., refl. V.* embark
**einschl.** *Abk.* = **einschließlich** incl.
**ein|schlafen** *unr. itr. V.; mit sein* **(a)** fall asleep
**(b)** (verhüll.: sterben) pass away
**(c)** (gefühllos werden) go to sleep
**ein|schläfern** *tr. V.* **(a)** jmdn. ~: send sb. to sleep, (betäuben) put sb. to sleep
**(b)** (schmerzlos töten) ein Tier ~: put an animal to sleep
**einschläfernd** ① *Adj.* soporific
② *adv.* ~ wirken have a soporific effect
**ein|schlagen** ① *unr. tr. V.* **(a)** knock in
**(b)** (zertrümmern) smash [in]
**(c)** (einwickeln) wrap up ⟨*present*⟩; cover ⟨*book*⟩

② *unr. itr. V.* **(a)** ⟨*bomb*⟩ land; ⟨*lightning*⟩ strike
**(b)** **auf jmdn./etw.** ~: rain blows on sb./sth.
**einschlägig** ① *Adj.* specialist ⟨*journal, shop*⟩; relevant ⟨*literature, passage*⟩
② *adv.* er ist ~ vorbestraft he has previous convictions for a similar offence/similar offences
**ein|schleichen** *unr. refl. V.* steal in
**ein|schließen** *unr. tr. V.* **(a)** etw. in etw. (*Dat.*) ~: lock sth. up [in sth.]; jmdn./sich ~: lock sb./oneself in
**(b)** (umgeben) surround
**einschließlich** ① *Präp. mit Gen.* including; ~ der Unkosten including expenses
② *adv.* bis ~ 30. Juni up to and including 30 June
**ein|schmeicheln** *refl. V.* sich bei jmdm. ~: ingratiate oneself with sb.
**ein|schmuggeln** *tr. V.* smuggle in
**ein|schneiden** *unr. tr. V.* **(a)** make a cut in
**(b)** (einritzen) carve
**einschneidend** *Adj.* drastic
**ein|schneien** *itr. V.; mit sein* get snowed in
**Ein·schnitt** *der* cut
**ein|schränken** ① *tr. V.* **(a)** reduce, curb ⟨*expenditure, consumption*⟩
**(b)** (einengen) limit; restrict; jmdn. in seinen Rechten ~: limit *or* restrict sb.'s rights
② *refl. V.* economize
**Einschränkung** *die;* ~, ~en **(a)** restriction; limitation
**(b)** (Vorbehalt) reservation
**ein|schrauben** *tr. V.* screw in
**ein|schreiben** *unr. tr. V.* **(a)** (Postw.) register ⟨*letter*⟩
**(b)** (eintragen) sich/jmdn. ~: enter one's/sb.'s name
**Ein·schreiben** *das* (Postw.) registered letter; per ~: by registered mail
**ein|schreiten** *unr. itr. V.* intervene
**ein|schrumpfen** *itr. V.; mit sein* shrivel up; (fig.) dwindle
**ein|schüchtern** *tr. V.* intimidate
**ein|schulen** *tr. V.* eingeschult werden start school
**ein|sehen** *unr. tr. V.* **(a)** (überblicken) see into
**(b)** (prüfend lesen) look at
**(c)** (erkennen) realize
**(d)** (begreifen) see
**ein|seifen** *tr. V.* lather
**ein·seitig** ① *Adj.* **(a)** on one side *postpos.;*
**(b)** (tendenziös) one-sided
② *adv.* **(a)** on one side
**(b)** (tendenziös) one-sidedly
**ein|senden** *unr.* (*auch regelm.*) *tr. V.* send [in]

**Ein·sender** der, **Ein·senderin** die; ~, ~nen sender; (bei einem Preisausschreiben) entrant

**Einsende·schluss,** *****Einsende·schluß** der closing date

**ein|setzen** 1 tr. V. (a) (hineinsetzen) put in
(b) put on ⟨special train etc.⟩
(c) (ernennen) appoint
(d) (in Aktion treten lassen) use
(e) (aufs Spiel setzen) stake ⟨money⟩
(f) (riskieren) risk
2 itr. V. begin; ⟨storm⟩ break
3 refl. V. (sich engagieren) **ich werde mich dafür ~, dass ...:** I shall do what I can to see that ...; **sich nicht genug ~:** ⟨pupil⟩ be lacking application; ⟨minister⟩ be lacking in commitment

**Ein·sicht** die (a) view (**in** + Akk. into)
(b) (Einblick) ~ **in die Akten nehmen** take or have a look at the files
(c) (Erkenntnis) insight

**einsichtig** Adj. (a) (verständnisvoll) understanding
(b) (verständlich) comprehensible

**Ein·siedler** der, **Ein·siedlerin** die hermit

**ein·silbig** Adj. (a) monosyllabic ⟨word⟩
(b) (fig.) taciturn ⟨person⟩

**Einsilbigkeit** die; ~ (fig.) taciturnity

**ein|sinken** unr. itr. V. sink in

**ein|sitzen** unr. itr. V. (Rechtsw.) serve a prison sentence; **er sitzt für drei Jahre ein** he is serving three years or a three-year sentence

**Einsitzer** der; ~s, ~: single-seater

**einsitzig** Adj. single-seater attrib.

**ein|spannen** tr. V. harness ⟨horse⟩; put in ⟨paper⟩: fix ⟨fabric⟩; clamp ⟨work⟩

**ein|sparen** tr. V. save

**Einsparung** die; ~, ~en saving (**an** + Dat. in); ~**en an Kosten/Energie/Material** savings or economies in costs/energy/materials

**ein|speichern** tr. V. (DV) feed in; input

**ein|speisen** tr. V. (Technik, DV) feed in

**ein|sperren** tr. V. lock up

**einsprachig** Adj. monolingual

**ein|springen** unr. itr. V.; mit sein stand in; (aushelfen) step in and help out

**ein|spritzen** tr. V. inject; **jmdm. etw. ~:** inject sb. with sth.

**Einspritz·motor** der fuel-injection engine

**Ein·spruch** der objection (**gegen** to)

**einspurig** 1 Adj. single-track ⟨road⟩
2 adv. **die Autobahn ist nur ~ befahrbar** only one lane of the motorway is open

**einst** Adv. (geh.) once

**ein|stampfen** tr. V. pulp ⟨books⟩

**Ein·stand** der; **seinen ~ geben** celebrate starting a new job

**ein|stecken** tr. V. (a) put in
(b) (mitnehmen) put ⟨sth.⟩ in one's pocket/bag etc.

**ein|stehen** unr. itr. V. **für jmdn. ~:** vouch for sb.; **für etw. ~:** take responsibility for sth.

**ein|steigen** unr. itr. V.; mit sein (a) (in ein Fahrzeug) get in; **in ein Auto ~:** get into a car; **in den Bus ~:** get on the bus
(b) (eindringen) climb in

**einstellbar** Adj. adjustable

**ein|stellen** 1 tr. V. (a) (einordnen) put away ⟨books etc.⟩
(b) (unterstellen) put in ⟨car, bicycle⟩
(c) (beschäftigen) take on ⟨workers⟩
(d) (regulieren) adjust
(e) (beenden) stop; call off ⟨search, strike⟩
(f) (Sport) equal ⟨record⟩
2 refl. V. (a) arrive
(b) ⟨pain, worry⟩ begin; ⟨success⟩ come; ⟨symptoms, consequences⟩ appear
(c) **sich auf etw.** (Akk.) **~:** prepare oneself for sth.; **sich schnell auf neue Situationen ~:** adjust quickly to new situations

**ein·stellig** Adj. single-figure attrib.

**Ein·stellung** die (a) (von Arbeitskräften) employment
(b) (Regulierung) adjustment
(c) (Beendigung) stopping
(d) (Sport) **die ~ eines Rekordes** the equalling of a record
(e) (Ansicht) attitude; **ihre politische/religiöse ~:** her political/religious views pl.;
(f) (Film) take

**Ein·stich** der (a) insertion
(b) (~stelle) puncture; prick

**Ein·stieg** der; ~[e]s, ~e (Eingang) entrance; (Tür) door/doors; „**kein ~**" 'exit only'

**Einstiegs·droge** die come-on drug

**ein|stimmen** 1 itr. V. join in
2 tr. V. **jmdn. auf etw.** (Akk.) **~:** get sb. in the [right] mood for sth.

**einstimmig** 1 Adj. (a) (Musik) for one voice
(b) (einmütig) unanimous ⟨decision, vote⟩
2 adv. (a) (Musik) in unison
(b) (einmütig) unanimously

**ein·stöckig** Adj. single-storey attrib.

**ein|stöpseln** tr. V. plug in ⟨telephone, electrical device⟩

**Ein·strahlung** die irradiation; (Sonnen~) insolation

**ein|streichen** unr. tr. V. (ugs.: für sich behalten) pocket ⟨money, winnings, etc.⟩; (ugs. abwertend) rake in (coll.) ⟨money, profits, etc.⟩

**ein|studieren** tr. V. rehearse

**ein|stufen** tr. V. classify; categorize

**ein·stündig** Adj. one-hour attrib.

**ein|stürmen** itr. V. **mit Fragen auf jmdn. ~:** besiege sb. with questions

**Ein·sturz** der collapse

**ein|stürzen** itr. V.; mit sein collapse

**einst·weilen** Adv. for the time being

**eintägig** Adj. one-day attrib.

**Eintags·fliege** die (Zool.) mayfly; (fig. ugs.) seven-day wonder

e

**ein|tauchen** ① *tr. V.* dip; (untertauchen) immerse
  ② *itr. V.; mit sein* dive in; ⟨*submarine*⟩ dive

**ein|tauschen** *tr. V.* exchange (**gegen** for)

**ein-tausend** *Kardinalz.:* ▸ TAUSEND

**ein|teilen** *tr. V.* (a) divide up; classify ⟨*plants, species*⟩
  (b) (disponieren, verplanen) organize

**einteilig** *Adj.* one-piece

**ein|tippen** *tr. V.* (in die Kasse) register; (in einen Rechner) key in

**eintönig** ① *Adj.* monotonous
  ② *adv.* monotonously

**Eintönigkeit** *die; ∼:* monotony

**Ein-topf** *der* stew

**Ein-tracht** *die* harmony

**ein-trächtig** *Adj.* harmonious

**Eintrag** *der; ∼[e]s, Einträge* entry

**ein|tragen** *unr. tr. V.* (a) enter
  (b) (Amtsspr.) register

**einträglich** *Adj.* lucrative

**ein|treffen** *unr. itr. V.; mit sein* (a) arrive
  (b) (verwirklicht werden) come true

**ein|treiben** *unr. tr. V.* collect ⟨*taxes, debts*⟩; (durch Gerichtsverfahren) recover ⟨*debts, money*⟩

**Eintreibung** *die; ∼, ∼en* (von Steuern, Schulden) collection; (durch Gerichtsverfahren) recovery

**ein|treten** ① *unr. itr. V.; mit sein* (a) enter; **bitte, treten Sie ein!** please come in
  (b) (Mitglied werden) **in einen Verein/einen Orden ∼:** join a club/enter a religious order
  (c) (Raumfahrt) enter
  ② *unr. tr. V.* kick in ⟨*door, window, etc.*⟩

**ein|trichtern** *tr. V.* (salopp) **jmdm. etw. ∼:** drum sth. into sb.

**Ein-tritt** *der* (a) entry; entrance; **vor dem ∼ in die Verhandlungen** (fig.) before entering into negotiations
  (b) (Beitritt) **der ∼ in einen Verein/einen Orden** joining a club/entering a religious order
  (c) (von Raketen) entry
  (d) (Zugang, Eintrittsgeld) admission
  (e) (Beginn) onset; **∼ der Dunkelheit** nightfall

**Eintritts-: ∼geld** *das* admission fee; **∼karte** *die* admission ticket; **∼preis** *der* admission charge

**ein|trocknen** *itr. V.; mit sein* dry; ⟨*water, toothpaste*⟩ dry up; ⟨*leather*⟩ dry out; ⟨*berry, fruit*⟩ shrivel

**ein|üben** *tr. V.* practise

**Ein-vernehmen** *das; ∼s* harmony; (Übereinstimmung) agreement

**ein-vernehmlich** (Amtsspr.) ① *Adv.* conjointly
  ② *adj.* conjoint

**einverstanden** *Adj.* **∼ sein** agree; **mit jmdm./etw. ∼ sein** approve of sb./sth.

**Ein-verständnis** *das* consent (**zu** to)

**Ein-waage** *die* (Kaufmannsspr.) contents *pl.*

**ein|wachsen** *unr. itr. V.; mit sein* grow into the flesh; **eingewachsen** ingrown ⟨*toenail*⟩

**Einwand** *der; ∼[e]s, Einwände* objection (**gegen** to)

**Ein-wanderer** *der,* **Ein-wanderin** *die* immigrant

**ein|wandern** *itr. V.; mit sein* immigrate (**in + Akk.** into)

**Ein-wanderung** *die* immigration

**Einwanderungs-: ∼behörde** *die* immigration authorities *pl.;* **∼land** *das* country of immigration

**einwand-frei** ① *Adj.* flawless; impeccable ⟨*behaviour*⟩; indisputable ⟨*proof*⟩
  ② *adv.* flawlessly; ⟨*behave*⟩ impeccably; ⟨*prove*⟩ beyond question

**ein|wechseln** *tr. V.* (a) change ⟨*money*⟩
  (b) (Sport) substitute ⟨*player*⟩

**ein|wecken** *tr. V.* preserve; bottle

**Ein-weg-: ∼flasche** *die* non-returnable bottle; **∼spritze** *die* disposable [hypodermic] syringe

**ein|weichen** *tr. V.* soak

**ein|weihen** *tr. V.* open [officially] ⟨*bridge, road*⟩; dedicate ⟨*monument*⟩

**Einweihung** *die; ∼, ∼en* ▸ EINWEIHEN: [official] opening; dedication

**ein|weisen** *unr. tr. V.* (a) (in eine Tätigkeit) introduce
  (b) (in ein Amt) install

**ein|wenden** *unr. (auch regelm.) tr. V.* **dagegen lässt sich vieles ∼:** there is a lot to be said against that

**ein|werfen** *unr. tr. V.* (a) mail ⟨*letter*⟩; insert ⟨*coin*⟩
  (b) smash ⟨*window*⟩
  (c) throw in ⟨*ball*⟩
  (d) (bemerken, sagen) throw in ⟨*remark*⟩

**ein|wickeln** *tr. V.* wrap [up]

**ein|willigen** *itr. V.* agree (**in + Akk.** to)

**Einwilligung** *die; ∼, ∼en* agreement

**ein|winken** *tr. V.* (Verkehrsw.) guide in ⟨*aircraft, car*⟩

**ein|wirken** (a) (beeinflussen) **auf jmdn. ∼:** influence sb.
  (b) (eine Wirkung ausüben) have an effect (**auf + Akk.** on)

**Ein-wirkung** *die* (Einfluss) influence; (Wirkung) effect

**Einwohner** *der; ∼s, ∼,* **Einwohnerin** *die; ∼, ∼nen* inhabitant

**Einwohner-zahl** *die* population

**Ein-wurf** *der* (a) insertion; (von Briefen) mailing
  (b) (Ballspiele) throw-in
  (c) (Bemerkung) interjection

**Ein-zahl** *die* singular

**ein|zahlen** *tr. V.* pay in; **Geld auf ein Konto ∼:** pay money into an account

**Ein-zahlung** *die* payment

**ein|zäunen** *tr. V.* fence in; enclose

**Einzäunung** *die;* ~, ~en fencing-in
**ein|zeichnen** *tr. V.* draw or mark in
**einzeilig** *Adj.* one-line *attrib.*
**Einzel** *das;* ~s, ~ (Sport) singles *pl.*
**Einzel-:** ~**bett** *das* single bed; ~**fall** *der*
(a) particular case; (b) (Ausnahme) isolated
case; ~**gänger** *der;* ~~s, ~~,
~**gängerin** *die;* ~~, ~~**nen** loner;
~**haft** *die* solitary confinement;
**Einzel·handel** *der* retail trade
**Einzelhandels·preis** *der* retail price
**Einzel·händler** *der,* ~**händlerin** *die*
retailer
**Einzelheit** *die;* ~, ~en (a) detail
(b) (einzelner Umstand) particular
**Einzel·kind** *das* only child
**Einzeller** *der;* ~s, ~ (Biol.) unicellular
organism
**einzeln** *Adj.* (a) (für sich allein) individual
(b) (allein stehend) solitary ‹building, tree›;
single ‹lady, gentleman›
(c) ~e (wenige) a few; (einige) some
(d) *substantivisch* der/jeder Einzelne the/
each individual; Einzelnes (manches) some
things *pl.;* das Einzelne the particular
**Einzel-:** ~**preis** *der* individual price;
~**teil** *das* individual part; ~**zelle** *die*
single cell; ~**zimmer** *das* single room
**ein|ziehen** ① *unr. tr. V.* (a) put in; thread
in ‹tape, elastic›
(b) (einholen) haul in ‹net›
(c) (einatmen) breathe in ‹scent, fresh air›;
inhale ‹smoke›
(d) (einberufen) call up ‹recruits›
(e) (beitreiben) collect
② *unr. itr. V.; mit sein* (a) ‹liquid› soak in
(b) (einkehren) enter
(c) (in eine Wohnung) move in
**einzig** ① *Adj.* only; kein ~es Wort not a
single word
② *adv.* (a) *intensivierend bei Adj.*
extraordinarily
(b) (ausschließlich) only; das ~ Wahre the only
thing
**einzig·artig** ① *Adj.* unique
② *adv.* uniquely
**Einzigartigkeit** *die,* **Einzigkeit** *die*
uniqueness
**Ein·zug** *der* (a) entry (in + *Akk.* into)
(b) (in eine Wohnung) move
**Einzugs·bereich** *der* catchment area
**Eis** *das;* ~es (a) ice; ~ laufen ice-skate
(b) (Speise~) ice cream; ein ~ am Stiel an
ice lolly (Brit.) or (Amer.) ice pop
**Eis-:** ~**bahn** *die* ice rink; ~**bär** *der* polar
bear; ~**becher** *der* ice cream sundae;
~**bein** *das* (Kochk.) knuckle of pork;
~**berg** *der* iceberg; ~**beutel** *der* ice bag;
~**blume** *die* frost flower; ~**bombe** *die*
(Gastr.) bombe glacée; ~**brecher** *der* ice-
breaker; ~**café** *das* ice cream parlour
**Eis·schnee** *der* stiffly beaten egg white
**Eis·diele** *die* ice cream parlour

**Eisen** *das;* ~s, ~: iron
**Eisen·bahn** *die* (a) railway; railroad
(Amer.); mit der ~ fahren go by train
(b) (Bahnstrecke) railway line; railroad track
(Amer.)
**Eisenbahn·abteil** *das* railway or (Amer.)
railroad compartment
**Eisenbahner** *der;* ~s, ~: railwayman;
railway worker; railroader (Amer.)
**Eisenbahnerin** *die;* ~, ~nen railway
worker
**Eisenbahn·unglück** *das* train crash
**Eisen-:** ~**erz** *das* iron ore; ~**kette** *die*
iron chain; ~**ring** *der* iron ring;
~**stange** *die* iron bar; ~**waren** *Pl.*
ironmongery *sing.;* ~**zeit** *die* Iron Age
**eisern** ① *Adj.* (auch fig.) iron
② *adv.* resolutely; ‹save, train› with iron
determination; ~ durchgreifen take drastic
measures
**eis-, Eis-:** ~**fach** *das* freezing
compartment; ~**frei** *Adj.* ice-free;
~**gekühlt** *Adj.* iced; ~**glatt** *Adj.* (a) icy
‹road›; (b) /'--/ (ugs.) ‹floor, steps› as
slippery as ice; ~**glätte** *die* black ice;
~**hockey** *das* ice hockey
**eisig** ① *Adj.* (a) icy ‹wind, cold›; icy [cold]
‹water›
(b) (fig.) frosty
② *adv.* (a) ~ kalt sein be icy cold
(b) (fig.) ‹smile› frostily
*eisig·kalt** *Adj.* ▶ EISKALT 1A
**eis-, Eis-:** ~**kaffee** *der* iced coffee;
~**kalt** ① *Adj.* (a) ice-cold ‹drink›; freezing
cold ‹weather›; (b) (gefühllos) icy; ice-cold
‹look›; ② *adv.* es lief mir ~kalt über den
Rücken a cold shiver went down my spine;
~**kunst·lauf** *der* figure skating;
~**kunst·läufer** *der,* ~**kunst·läuferin**
*die* figure skater; ~**lauf** *der* ice skating;
*~**laufen** ▶ EIS A; ~**laufen** *das;* ~~s
ice skating; ~**läufer** *der,* ~**läuferin** *die*
ice skater
**Ei·sprung** *der* (Physiol.) ovulation
**Eis-:** ~**regen** *der* sleet; ~**schrank** *der*
refrigerator; ~**sport** *der* ice sports *pl.;*
~**tanz** *der* (Sport) ice dancing; ~**waffel**
*die* [ice cream] wafer; ~**wein** *der: wine
made from grapes frozen on the vine;*
~**würfel** *der* ice cube; ~**zapfen** *der*
icicle; ~**zeit** *die* ice age
**eitel** *Adj.* vain
**Eitelkeit** *die;* ~, ~en vanity
**Eiter** *der;* ~s pus
**eitern** *itr. V.* suppurate
**eitrig** *Adj.* suppurating
**Ei·weiß** *das;* ~es, ~e (a) egg white
(b) (Protein) protein
**eiweiß-:** ~**arm** *Adj.* low-protein *attrib.;*
low in protein *postpos.;* ~**reich** *Adj.* high-
protein *attrib.;* rich in protein *postpos.*
**Ejakulation** *die;* ~, ~en (Physiol.)
ejaculation

**Ekel**[1] *der;* ~s revulsion; [einen] ~ vor etw. (*Dat.*) **haben** have a revulsion for sth.

**Ekel**[2] *das;* ~s, ~ (ugs. abwertend) horror; **er ist ein [altes]** ~: he is quite obnoxious

**ekelhaft** *Adj.* revolting ⟨sight⟩; horrible ⟨weather, person⟩

**ekeln** [1] *refl. V.* be disgusted; **sich vor etw.** (*Dat.*) ~: find sth. repulsive
[2] *tr., itr. V.* (*unpers.*) **es ekelt mich** *od.* **mir ekelt davor** I find it revolting

**eklig** *Adj.* (a) ▶ EKELHAFT;
(b) (ugs.: gemein) nasty

**Ekstase** /ɛkˈstaːzə/ *die;* ~, ~n ecstasy

**Ekzem** *das;* ~s, ~e (Med.) eczema

**Elan** *der;* ~s zest; vigour

**elastisch** *Adj.* elasticated ⟨material⟩; springy ⟨surface⟩; supple ⟨person, body⟩

**Elastizität** *die;* ~: elasticity; (Federkraft) springiness; (Geschmeidigkeit) suppleness

**Elch** *der;* ~[e]s, ~e elk; (in Nordamerika) moose

**Elefant** *der;* ~en, ~en elephant

**elegant** [1] *Adj.* elegant
[2] *adv.* elegantly

**Eleganz** *die;* ~: elegance

**elektrifizieren** *tr. V.* electrify

**Elektrifizierung** *die;* ~, ~en electrification

**Elektriker** *der;* ~s, ~, **Elektrikerin** *die;* ~, ~nen electrician

**elektrisch** [1] *Adj.* electric; electrical ⟨resistance, wiring, system⟩
[2] *adv.* ~ **kochen** cook with electricity; ~ **geladen sein** be electrically charged

**elektrisieren** [1] *tr. V.* (Med.) treat using electricity
[2] *refl. V.* get an electric shock

**Elektrizität** *die;* ~ electricity

**Elektrizitäts·werk** *das* power station

**elektro-, Elektro-:** ~**artikel** *der* electrical appliance; ~**auto** *das* electric car; ~**gerät** *das* electrical appliance; ~**geschäft** *das* electrical shop *or* (Amer.) store; ~**herd** *der* electric cooker; ~**magnet** *der* electromagnet; ~**magnetisch** [1] *Adj.* electromagnetic; [2] *adv.* electromagnetically; ~**mobil** *das;* ~~s, ~~e electric car; ~**motor** *der* electric motor

**Elektron** *das;* ~s, ~en /-ˈtroːnən/ electron

**Elektronen-:** ~[ge]**hirn** *das* (ugs.) electronic brain (coll.); ~**hülle** *die* electron shell; ~**rechner** *der* electronic computer

**Elektronik** *die;* ~ (a) electronics *sing., no art.;*
(b) (Teile) electronics *pl.*

**Elektronik·schrott** *der* scrapped electrical appliances *pl.*

**elektronisch** [1] *Adj.* electronic
[2] *adv.* electronically

**elektro-, Elektro-:** ~**rasierer** *der* electric shaver; ~**smog** *der* (Jargon) electronic smog; ~**statisch** [1] *Adj.* electrostatic; [2] *adv.* electrostatically; ~**technik** *die* electrical engineering *no art.;* ~**techniker** *der,* ~**technikerin** *die* (a) electronics engineer; (b) (Elektriker) electrician

**Element** *das;* ~[e]s, ~e element

**elementar** *Adj.* (a) (grundlegend) fundamental
(b) (einfach) elementary ⟨knowledge⟩
(c) (naturhaft) elemental ⟨force⟩

**Elementar·teilchen** *das* (Physik) elementary particle

**elend** *Adj.* wretched; miserable

**Elend** *das;* ~s misery

**Elends-:** ~**quartier** *das* slum [dwelling]; ~**viertel** *das* slum area

**elf** *Kardinalz.* eleven

**Elf** *die;* ~, ~en (a) eleven
(b) (Sport) team; side

**Elfe** *die;* ~, ~n fairy

**Elfen·bein** *das* ivory

**Elfenbein-:** ~**schnitzerei** *die* ivory carving; ~**turm** *der* (fig.) ivory tower

**Elf·meter** *der* (Fußball) penalty; **einen** ~ **schießen** take a penalty

**Elfmeter·schießen** *das;* ~s (Fußball) **durch** ~: by *or* on penalties

**eliminieren** *tr. V.* eliminate

**elitär** *adj.* élitist; **ein** ~**es Bewusstsein** an élite-awareness

**Elite** *die;* ~, ~n élite

**Elite·truppe** *die* (Milit.) élite *or* crack force

**Ell·bogen** *der; Pl.* ~: elbow

**Elle** *die;* ~, ~n (a) (Anat.) ulna
(b) (frühere Längeneinheit) cubit
(c) (veralt.: Maßstock) ≈ yardstick

**Ellen·bogen** *der; Pl.* ~: ▶ ELLBOGEN

**Ellipse** *die;* ~, ~n ellipse

**Elsass, *Elsaß** *das;* ~ *od.* **Elsasses** Alsace

**Elster** *die;* ~, ~n magpie

**elterlich** *Adj.* parental

**Eltern** *Pl.* parents *pl.*

**eltern-, Eltern-:** ~**abend** *der* (Schulw.) parents' evening; ~**bei·rat** *der* (Schulw.) parents' association; ~**haus** *das* home; ~**los** *Adj.* orphaned; ~**teil** *der* parent

**Email** /eˈmaɪ/ *das;* ~s, ~s, **Emaille** /eˈmaljə/ *die;* ~, ~n enamel

**E-Mail** /ˈiːmeɪl/ *die;* ~, ~s (DV) e-mail

**Emanzipation** *die;* ~, ~en emancipation

**emanzipieren** *refl. V.* emancipate

**emanzipiert** *Adj.* emancipated; emancipated, liberated ⟨woman⟩

**Embargo** *das;* ~s, ~s embargo

**Emblem** *das;* ~s, ~e emblem

**Embryo** *der;* ~s, ~nen /-ˈyˈoːnən/ *od.* ~s embryo

---

**Emigrant** der; ~en, ~en, **Emigrantin**
die; ~, ~nen emigrant; (Flüchtling) emigré
**Emigration** die; ~, ~en (das Emigrieren)
emigration
**emigrieren** itr. V.; mit sein emigrate
**Emission** (a) (Physik, Ökologie) emission
(b) (Ausgabe [von Briefmarken, Wertpapieren])
issue
**Emotion** die; ~, ~en emotion
**emotional** ① Adj. emotional; emotive
‹topic, question›
② adv. emotionally
**Empfang** der; ~[e]s, Empfänge reception;
(Entgegennahme) receipt
**empfangen** unr. tr. V. receive
**Empfänger** der; ~s, ~ (a) recipient; (eines
Briefs) addressee
(b) (Empfangsgerät) receiver
**Empfängerin** die; ~, ~nen ▶ EMPFÄNGER
A
**empfänglich** Adj. (a) receptive (für to)
(b) (beeinflussbar) susceptible
**Empfänglichkeit** die; ~ (a)
(Zugänglichkeit) receptivity, receptiveness (für
to)
(b) (Beeinflussbarkeit) susceptibility (für to)
**Empfängnis** die; ~: conception
**Empfängnis-verhütung** die
contraception
**empfangs-, Empfangs-:**
~berechtigt Adj. authorized to receive
payment/goods postpos.; ~chef der head
receptionist; ~dame die receptionist;
~halle die reception lobby
**empfehlen** ① unr. tr. V. recommend
② unr. refl. V. (a) take one's leave
(b) unpers. es empfiehlt sich, ... zu ...: it's
advisable to ...
**empfehlens-wert** Adj. (a) to be
recommended postpos.; recommendable
(b) (ratsam) advisable
**Empfehlung** die; ~, ~en (a)
recommendation
(b) (Empfehlungsschreiben) letter of
recommendation
**empfiehl** Imperativ Sg. v. EMPFEHLEN
**empfiehlst** 2. Pers. Sg. Präsens v.
EMPFEHLEN
**empfiehlt** 3. Pers. Sg. Präsens v.
EMPFEHLEN
**empfinden** unr. tr. V. (a) (wahrnehmen) feel
(b) (auffassen) etw. als Beleidigung ~: feel
sth. to be an insult
**Empfinden** das; ~s feeling; für mein od.
nach meinem ~: to my mind
**empfindlich** ① Adj. (a) sensitive; fast
‹film›
(b) (leicht beleidigt) sensitive
(c) (anfällig) zart und ~: delicate
(d) (spürbar) severe ‹punishment, shortage›
② adv. ~ auf etw. (Akk.) reagieren (sensibel)
be susceptible to sth.; (beleidigt) react
oversensitively to sth.

**Empfindlichkeit** die; ~, ~en
▶ EMPFINDLICH: sensitivity; severity; (eines
Films) speed
**empfindsam** Adj. sensitive ‹nature›
**Empfindung** die; ~, ~en (Gefühl) feeling
**empfing** 1. u. 3. Pers. Sg. Prät. v.
EMPFANGEN
**empfohlen** ① 2. Part. v. EMPFEHLEN;
② Adj. recommended
**empirisch** ① Adj. empirical
② adv. empirically
**empor** Adv. (geh.) upwards
**Empore** die; ~, ~n gallery
**empören** ① tr. V. fill with indignation;
outrage
② refl. V. become indignant or outraged
**empörend** Adj. outrageous
**empört** Adj. outraged
**Empörung** die; ~, ~en outrage
**emsig** ① Adj. industrious ‹person›;
bustling ‹activity›
② adv. industriously
**Emu** der; ~s, ~s (Zool.) emu
**Ende** das; ~s, ~n end; am ~ der Straße/
Stadt at the end of the road/town; am/bis/
gegen ~ des Monats at/by/towards the end
of the month; ~ April at the end of April; zu
~ sein ‹patience, war› be at an end; ‹school›
be over; ‹film, game› have finished; ~ gut,
alles gut all's well that ends well (prov.)
**End-effekt** der im ~: in the end; in the
final analysis
**enden** itr. V. (a) end; ‹programme› finish
(b) in der Gosse ~: end up in the gutter;
(dort sterben) die in the gutter
**end-, End-:** ~ergebnis das final result;
~gültig ① Adj. final ‹consent, decision›;
conclusive ‹evidence›; ② adv. das ist
~gültig vorbei that's all over and done with;
sich ~gültig trennen separate for good;
~haltestelle die terminus; ~kampf
der (Sport) final; (Milit.) final battle; ~lauf
der (Sport) final
**endlich** ① Adv. (a) (nach langer Zeit) at last
(b) (schließlich) in the end
② Adj. finite
**end-, End-:** ~los ① Adj. (a) (ohne Ende)
infinite; (ringförmig) continuous; (b) (nicht
enden wollend) endless; interminable ‹speech›;
② adv. ~los lange dauern be interminably
long; ~lösung die (ns. verhüll.) Final
Solution (to the Jewish question);
~resultat das final result; ~runde die
(Sport) final; ~spiel das (Sport) final;
~spurt der (bes. Leichtathletik) final spurt;
~stadium das final stage; (Med.) terminal
stage; ~station die terminus; ~summe
die [sum] total
**Endung** die; ~, ~en (Sprachw.) ending
**End-:** ~verbraucher der,
~verbraucherin die (Wirtsch.) consumer; ⋯⫶

~**ziffer** *die* final number; **das Los mit der** ~**ziffer 4** the coupon with a number ending in 4

**Energie** *die;* ~, ~**n** energy

**energie-, Energie-:** ~**bewusst,** *\*~**bewußt** *Adj.* energy-conscious; ~**mix** *der* mix of energy sources; ~**politik** *die* energy policy; ~**quelle** *die* energy source; ~**spar·lampe** *die* energy-saving lamp; ~**verbrauch** *der* energy consumption; ~**versorgung** *die* energy supply; ~**wirtschaft** *die* energy sector

**energisch** ☐1 *Adj.* (a) energetic ‹*person*›; firm ‹*action*›
(b) forceful ‹*voice, words*›
☐2 *adv.* (a) energetically; ~ **durchgreifen** take drastic action
(b) ‹*reject, say*› forcefully; ‹*stress*› emphatically; ‹*deny*› strenuously

**eng** /ɛŋ/ ☐1 *Adj.* (a) (schmal) narrow
(b) (dicht) close ‹*writing*›
(c) (fest anliegend) close-fitting
(d) (beschränkt) narrow
(e) (nahe) close ‹*friend*›
☐2 *adv.* (a) (dicht) ~ [zusammen]sitzen/stehen sit/stand close together
(b) (fest anliegend) ~ **anliegen/sitzen** fit closely
(c) (beschränkt) **etw. zu** ~ **auslegen** interpret sth. too narrowly
(d) (nahe) closely

**Engagement** /ãgaʒə'mãː/ *das;* ~s, ~s
(a) (Einsatz) involvement; **sein** ~ **für etw.** his commitment to sth.; **sein** ~ **gegen etw.** his committed stand against sth.
(b) (eines Künstlers) engagement

**engagiert** *Adj.* committed ‹*literature, film, director*›; **politisch/sozial** ~ **sein** be politically/socially committed *or* involved

**Engagiertheit** *die;* ~: commitment; involvement

**Enge** *die;* ~, ~**n** confinement

**Engel** *der;* ~**s,** ~: angel

**eng·herzig** *Adj.* petty

**England** *(das);* ~**s** England

**Engländer** *der;* ~**s,** ~: Englishman/ English boy; **er ist** ~: he is English; **die** ~: the English

**Engländerin** *die;* ~, ~**nen** Englishwoman/ English girl; **sie ist** ~: she is English

**englisch** ☐1 *Adj.* English; **die** ~**e Sprache/ Literatur** the English language/English literature
☐2 *adv.* ~ **sprechen** speak English

**Englisch** *das;* ~**[s]** English

**englisch-, Englisch-:** ~**lehrer** *der,* ~**lehrerin** *die* English teacher; ~**sprachig** *Adj.* (a) English-language ‹*book, magazine*›; (b) (Englisch sprechend) English-speaking ‹*population, country*›; ~**unterricht** *der* English teaching; (Unterrichtsstunde) English lesson

---

**Eng·pass, \*Eng·paß** *der* (a) defile
(b) (fig.) bottleneck

**eng·stirnig** *Adj.* narrow-minded

**Enkel** *der;* ~**s,** ~: grandson

**Enkelin** *die;* ~, ~**nen** granddaughter

**Enkel·kind** *das* grandchild

**enorm** ☐1 *Adj.* enormous ‹*sum, costs*›; tremendous (coll.) ‹*effort*›; immense ‹*strain*›
☐2 *adv.* tremendously (coll.)

**Ensemble** /ã'sãːbl̩/ *das;* ~, ~**s** ensemble; (Theater~) company

**entarten** *itr. V.; mit sein* degenerate

**entbehren** *tr. V.* (verzichten auf) do without

**entbehrlich** *Adj.* dispensable

**Entbehrung** *die;* ~, ~**en** privation

**entbinden** ☐1 *unr. tr. V.* (a) **jmdn. von einem Versprechen** ~: release sb. from a promise; **seines Amtes** *od.* **von seinem Amt entbunden werden** be relieved of [one's] office
(b) **jmdn.** ~ (Med.) deliver sb.'s baby
☐2 *unr. itr. V.* give birth

**Entbindung** *die* (Med.) delivery

**Entbindungs·station** *die* maternity ward

**entblößen** ☐1 *refl. V.* take one's clothes off; ‹*exhibitionist*› expose oneself
☐2 *tr. V.* uncover ‹*one's arm etc.*›

**entdecken** *tr. V.* (a) discover
(b) (ausfindig machen) **jmdn.** ~: find sb.; **etw.** ~: find *or* discover sth.

**Entdecker** *der;* ~**s,** ~, **Entdeckerin** *die;* ~, ~**nen** discoverer

**Entdeckung** *die;* ~, ~**en** discovery

**Ente** *die;* ~, ~**n** duck

**entehren** *tr. V.* dishonour; ~**d** degrading

**enteignen** *tr. V.* expropriate

**Enteignung** *die;* ~, ~**en** expropriation

**enterben** *tr. V.* disinherit

**entern** *tr., itr. V.* board ‹*ship*›

**entfachen** *tr. V.* (geh.) (a) kindle, light ‹*fire*›
(b) (fig.) provoke ‹*quarrel, argument*›; arouse ‹*passion, enthusiasm*›

**entfallen** *unr. itr. V.; mit sein* (a) (aus dem Gedächtnis) **es ist mir** ~: it escapes me
(b) (zugeteilt werden) **auf jmdn./etw.** ~: be allotted to sb./sth.
(c) (wegfallen) lapse

**entfalten** ☐1 *tr. V.* (a) open [up]; unfold ‹*map etc.*›
(b) (fig.) display ‹*ability, talent*›
☐2 *refl. V.* (a) open [up]
(b) (fig.) ‹*personality, talent, etc.*› develop

**Entfaltung** *die;* ~, ~**en** (fig.) (a) (Entwicklung) development
(b) ▶ ENTFALTEN 1B: display

**entfernen** ☐1 *tr. V.* remove; take out ‹*tonsils etc.*›
☐2 *refl. V.* go away

**entfernt** ☐1 *Adj.* (a) (fern) remote; **das ist**

od. **liegt weit ~ von der Stadt** it is a long way from the town; **10 km/zwei Stunden ~:** 10 km/two hours away
**(b)** slight ⟨*acquaintance*⟩; distant ⟨*relation*⟩; slight ⟨*resemblance*⟩
**2** *adv.* **(a)** (fern) remotely
**(b)** slightly ⟨*acquainted*⟩; distantly ⟨*related*⟩
**Entfernung** *die; ~, ~en* **(a)** (Abstand) distance
**(b)** (das Beseitigen) removal
**entfesseln** *tr. V.* unleash
**entflammen** **1** *tr. V.* arouse ⟨*enthusiasm etc*⟩
**2** *itr. V.; mit sein* flare up
**entfliehen** *unr. itr. V.; mit sein* escape; **jmdm. ~:** escape from sb.
**entfremden** **1** *tr. V.* **(a)** **etw. seinem Zweck ~:** use sth. for a different purpose
**(b)** (Philos., Soziol.) **entfremdet** alienated
**2** *refl. V.* **sich jmdm./einer Sache ~:** become estranged from sb./unfamiliar with sth.
**Entfremdung** *die; ~, ~en* alienation; estrangement
**entführen** *tr. V.* kidnap ⟨*child etc.*⟩; hijack ⟨*plane, lorry, etc.*⟩
**Entführer** *der,* **Entführerin** *die* ▶ ENTFÜHREN: kidnapper; hijacker
**Entführung** *die* ▶ ENTFÜHREN: kidnapping; hijacking
**entgegen** **1** *Adv.* towards
**2** *Präp. mit Dat.* **~ meinem Wunsch** against my wishes; **~ dem Befehl** contrary to orders
**entgegen-, Entgegen-:** **~|bringen** *unr. tr. V.* (fig.) show ⟨*love, understanding*⟩; **~|fahren** *unr. itr. V.; mit sein* jmdm. **~fahren** come/go to meet sb.; **~|gehen** *unr. itr. V.; mit sein* **(a)** jmdm. **~gehen** go to meet sb.; **(b)** (fig.) be heading for ⟨*catastrophe, hard times*⟩; **~gesetzt** **1** *Adj.* **(a)** (umgekehrt) opposite ⟨*end, direction*⟩; **(b)** (gegensätzlich) opposing; **2** *adv.* **genau ~gesetzt handeln/denken** do/think exactly the opposite; **~|kommen** *unr. itr. V.; mit sein* jmdm. **~kommen** come to meet sb.; (Zugeständnisse machen) be accommodating towards sb.; **~kommen** *das;* **~~s** cooperation; (Zugeständnis) concession; **~kommend** *Adj.* obliging; **~|nehmen** *unr. itr. V.* receive; **~|treten** *unr. itr. V.; mit sein* go/come up to; (fig.) stand up to ⟨*difficulties*⟩
**entgegnen** *tr. V.* retort; reply
**entgehen** *unr. itr. V.; mit sein* **(a)** (entkommen) escape
**(b)** jmdm. **entgeht etw.** sb. misses sth.
**entgeistert** *Adj.* dumbfounded
**Entgelt** *das;* **~[e]s,** **~e** payment; fee
**entgiften** *tr. V.* decontaminate ⟨*substance etc.*⟩; detoxicate ⟨*body etc.*⟩
**entgleisen** *itr. V.; mit sein* **(a)** be derailed
**(b)** (fig.) make a/some faux pas
**entgräten** *tr. V.* fillet

**enthaaren** *tr. V.* remove hair from
**Enthaarungs·mittel** *das* hair remover
**enthalten¹** **1** *unr. tr. V.* contain
**2** *unr. refl. V.* **sich einer Sache** (Gen.) **~:** abstain from sth.; **sich der Stimme ~:** abstain
**enthalten²** *Adj.* **in etw.** (Dat.) **~ sein** be contained in sth.; **das ist im Preis ~:** that is included in the price
**enthaltsam** **1** *Adj.* abstemious; (sexuell) abstinent
**2** *adv.* **~ leben** live in abstinence
**Enthaltsamkeit** *die; ~:* abstinence
**Enthaltung** *die; ~, ~en* abstention
**enthaupten** *tr. V.* (geh.) behead
**enthäuten** *tr. V.* skin
**entheben** *unr. tr. V.* (geh.) relieve
**enthemmt** *Adj.* uninhibited
**enthüllen** *tr. V.* unveil ⟨*monument etc.*⟩; reveal ⟨*face, truth, secret*⟩
**Enthüllung** *die; ~, ~en* ▶ ENTHÜLLEN: unveiling; revelation
**Enthusiasmus** /ɛntuˈzĭasmʊs/ *der; ~:* enthusiasm
**Enthusiast** *der; ~en, ~en,* **Enthusiastin** *die; ~, ~nen* enthusiast
**enthusiastisch** **1** *Adj.* enthusiastic
**2** *adv.* enthusiastically
**entkalken** *tr. V.* decalcify
**entkleiden** *tr. V.* (geh.) **(a)** undress
**(b)** (berauben) strip
**entkommen** *unr. itr. V.; mit sein* escape
**entkorken** *tr. V.* uncork ⟨*bottle*⟩
**entkräften** *tr. V.* **(a)** weaken; **völlig ~:** exhaust
**(b)** (fig.) refute ⟨*argument etc.*⟩
**Entkräftung** *die; ~, ~en* **(a)** debility; **völlige ~:** exhaustion
**(b)** (fig.) refutation
**entladen** **1** *unr. tr. V.* unload
**2** *unr. refl. V.* **(a)** ⟨*storm*⟩ break
**(b)** (fig.) ⟨*anger etc.*⟩ erupt; ⟨*aggression etc.*⟩ be released
**entlang** **1** *Präp. mit Akk. u. Dat.* along
**2** *Adv.* along; **hier/dort ~, bitte!** this/that way please!
**entlang-:** **~|fahren** *unr. itr. V.; mit sein* **(a)** drive along; **(b)** (streichen) go along; **~|gehen** *unr. itr. V.; mit sein* ⟨*person*⟩ go or walk along; **~|laufen** *unr. itr. V.; mit sein* **(a)** walk/run along; **(b)** (verlaufen) go or run along
**entlarven** *tr. V.* expose
**entlassen** *unr. tr. V.* **(a)** (aus dem Gefängnis) release; (aus dem Krankenhaus, der Armee) discharge
**(b)** (aus einem Arbeitsverhältnis) dismiss; (wegen Arbeitsmangels) make redundant (Brit.); lay off
**Entlassung** *die; ~, ~en* ▶ ENTLASSEN: release; discharge; dismissal; redundancy (Brit.); laying off
**entlasten** *tr. V.* **(a)** relieve ⋯⟩

**(b)** (Rechtsw.) exonerate ⟨*defendant*⟩

**Entlastung** *die;* ~, ~en **(a)** relief
**(b)** (Rechtsw.) exoneration; defence

**entlaufen** *unr. itr. V.; mit sein* run away;
ein ~er Sträfling/Sklave an escaped convict/a
runaway slave

**entlausen** *tr. V.* delouse

**entledigen** *refl. V.* sich jmds./einer Sache
(*Gen.*) ~ (geh.) rid oneself of sb./sth.

**entleeren** *tr. V.* empty; evacuate ⟨*bowels,
bladder*⟩

**entlegen** *Adj.* remote

**entleihen** *unr. tr. V.* borrow

**entlocken** *tr. V.* (geh.) jmdm. etw. ~: elicit
sth. from sb.

**entlohnen** *tr. V.* pay

**Entlohnung** *die;* ~, ~en payment; (Lohn)
pay

**entlüften** *tr. V.* ventilate

**Entlüfter** *der;* ~s, ~: ventilator

**entmachten** *tr. V.* deprive of power

**entmilitarisieren** *tr. V.* demilitarize

**entmündigen** *tr. V.* incapacitate

**Entmündigung** *die;* ~, ~en
incapacitation

**entmutigen** *tr. V.* discourage

**Entnahme** *die;* ~, ~n (von Wasser) drawing;
(von Blut) extraction

**Entnazifizierung** *die;* ~, ~en
denazification

**entnehmen** *unr. tr. V.* **(a)** etw. [einer
Sache (*Dat.*)] ~: take sth. [from sth.]
**(b)** (ersehen aus) gather (*Dat.* from)

**entnervend** *Adj.* nerve-racking

**entnervt** *Adj.* ~ sein be worn down; have
reached *or* be at the end of one's tether; er
gab ~ auf he had reached the end of his
tether and gave up

**entpuppen** *refl. V.* sich als etw./jmd. ~:
turn out to be sth./sb.

**entrahmen** *tr. V.* skim ⟨*milk*⟩

**entreißen** *unr. tr. V.* jmdm. etw. ~: snatch
sth. from sb.

**entrichten** *tr. V.* (Amtsspr.) pay ⟨*fee*⟩

**entrümpeln** *tr. V.* clear out

**Entrümpelung** *die;* ~, ~en clear-out

**entrüsten** ① *refl. V.* sich [über etw. (*Akk.*)]
~: be indignant [at *or* about sth.]
② *tr. V.* (empören) jmdn. ~: make sb.
indignant

**Entrüstung** *die;* ~, ~en indignation (über
+ *Akk.* at, about)

**Entsafter** *der;* ~s, ~: juice extractor

**entsagen** *itr. V.* einer Sache (*Dat.*) ~ (geh.)
renounce sth.

**Entsagung** *die;* ~, ~en (geh.) renunciation

**entschädigen** *tr. V.* compensate **(für** for);
jmdn. für etw. ~ (fig.) make up for sth.

**Entschädigung** *die;* ~, ~en
compensation

**entschärfen** *tr. V.* defuse; tone down
⟨*discussion, criticism*⟩

**entscheiden** ① *unr. refl. V.* **(a)** decide
**(b)** (*unpers.*) morgen entscheidet es sich,
ob ...: I/we/you will know tomorrow
whether ...
② *unr. itr. V.* über etw. (*Akk.*) ~: settle sth.
③ *unr. tr. V.* decide on ⟨*dispute*⟩; decide
⟨*outcome, result*⟩

**entscheidend** ① *Adj.* crucial; decisive
⟨*action*⟩
② *adv.* jmdn./etw. ~ beeinflussen have a
decisive influence on sb./sth.

**Entscheidung** *die;* ~, ~en decision

**entschieden** ① *Adj.* **(a)** (entschlossen)
determined; resolute
**(b)** (eindeutig) definite
② *adv.* resolutely; das geht ~ zu weit that is
going much too far

**Entschiedenheit** *die;* ~: decisiveness;
etw. mit ~ behaupten/verneinen state/deny
sth. categorically; etw. mit ~ fordern demand
sth. emphatically

**entschlafen** *unr. itr. V.; mit sein* pass
away

**entschließen** *unr. refl. V.* decide

**Entschließung** *die;* ~, ~en resolution

**entschlossen** *Adj.* determined

**Entschlossenheit** *die;* ~: determination

**Entschluss, *Entschluß** *der;*
Entschlusses, Entschlüsse decision

**entschlüsseln** *tr. V.* decipher

**entschuldigen** ① *refl. V.* apologize
② *tr.* (*auch itr.*) *V.* excuse ⟨*person*⟩; sich ~
lassen ask to be excused; ~ Sie [bitte]! (bei
Fragen, Bitten) excuse me; (bedauernd) I'm sorry

**Entschuldigung** *die;* ~, ~en **(a)** apology
**(b)** (Grund) excuse
**(c)** (Höflichkeitsformel) ~! (bei Fragen, Bitten)
excuse me; (bedauernd) [I'm] sorry

**entschwinden** *unr. itr. V.; mit sein* (geh.)
disappear; vanish

**entsetzen** ① *refl. V.* be horrified
② *tr. V.* horrify; über etw. (*Akk.*) entsetzt
sein be horrified by sth.

**Entsetzen** *das;* ~s horror

**entsetzlich** ① *Adj.* **(a)** horrible ⟨*accident,
crime, etc.*⟩
**(b)** (ugs.: stark) terrible ⟨*thirst, hunger*⟩
② *adv.* terribly (coll.)

**entsinnen** *unr. refl. V.* sich jmds./einer
Sache ~: remember sb./sth.

**entsorgen** *tr. V.* (Amtsspr., Wirtsch.) dispose
of ⟨*waste etc.*⟩

**Entsorgung** *die;* ~, ~en (Amtsspr., Wirtsch.)
waste disposal

**entspannen** ① *tr. V.* relax
② *refl. V.* **(a)** ⟨*person*⟩ relax
**(b)** (fig.) ⟨*situation, tension*⟩ ease

**Entspannung** *die;* ~ **(a)** relaxation
**(b)** ( politisch) easing of tension; détente

---

*old spelling - see note on page xiv

**Entspannungs·politik** *die* policy of détente

**entsprechen** *unr. itr. V.* **(a)** (übereinstimmen mit) **einer Sache** (*Dat.*) ~: correspond to sth.; **der Wahrheit/den Tatsachen** ~: be in accordance with the truth/the facts **(b)** (nachkommen) **einem Wunsch** ~: comply with a request; **den Anforderungen** ~: meet the requirements

**entsprechend** ① *Adj.* **(a)** corresponding; (angemessen) appropriate **(b)** (dem~) in accordance *postpos.;* ② *adv.* **(a)** (angemessen) appropriately **(b)** (dem~) accordingly ③ *Präp. mit Dat.* in accordance with

**entspringen** *unr. itr. V.; mit sein* **(a)** ⟨*river*⟩ rise **(b)** (entstehen aus) **einer Sache** (*Dat.*) ~: spring from sth.

**entstehen** *unr. itr. V.; mit sein* **(a)** originate⟨*quarrel, friendship, etc.*⟩ arise **(b)** (gebildet werden) be formed (**aus** from, **durch** by) **(c)** (sich ergeben) occur; (als Folge) result

**Entstehung** *die;* ~: origin

**entsteinen** *tr. V.* stone

**entstellen** *tr. V.* **(a)** disfigure **(b)** (verfälschen) distort ⟨*text, facts*⟩

**Entstellung** *die;* ~, ~en **(a)** disfigurement **(b)** (Verfälschung) distortion

**entstören** *tr. V.* (Elektrot.) suppress ⟨*engine, electrical appliance*⟩

**Entstörungs·stelle** *die* fault repair service

**enttarnen** *tr. V.* uncover

**enttäuschen** *tr. V.* disappoint

**enttäuschend** *Adj.* disappointing

**enttäuscht** *Adj.* disappointed; dashed ⟨*hopes*⟩

**Enttäuschung** *die;* ~, ~en disappointment

**entwachsen** *unr. itr. V.; mit sein* **einer Sache** (*Dat.*) ~: grow out of sth.

**entwaffnen** *tr. V.* (auch fig.) disarm

**entwaffnend** *Adj.* disarming

**entwarnen** *itr. V.* sound the all-clear

**Entwarnung** *die;* ~, ~en all-clear

**entwässern** *tr. V.* drain

**Entwässerung** *die;* ~, ~en drainage

**entweder** *Konj.:* ~ ... **oder** either ... or

**entweichen** *unr. itr. V.; mit sein* escape

**entwenden** *tr. V.* (geh.) purloin

**entwerfen** *unr. tr. V.* design ⟨*furniture, dress*⟩; draft ⟨*novel etc.*⟩; draw up ⟨*plans etc.*⟩

**entwerten** *tr. V.* **(a)** cancel ⟨*ticket, postage stamp*⟩ **(b)** devalue ⟨*currency*⟩

**Entwerter** *der;* ~s, ~: ticket-cancelling machine

**entwickeln** ① *refl. V.* develop

② *tr. V.* produce ⟨*vapour, smell*⟩; display ⟨*ability, characteristic*⟩; develop ⟨*equipment, photograph, film*⟩; elaborate ⟨*theory, ideas*⟩

**Entwicklung** *die;* ~, ~en **(a)** development; (von Dämpfen usw.) production; **in der** ~ **sein** ⟨*young person*⟩ be adolescent **(b)** (Darlegung) elaboration **(c)** (Fot.) developing

**Entwicklungs-:** ~**helfer** *der,* ~**helferin** *die* development aid worker; ~**hilfe** *die* [development] aid; ~**land** *das* developing country; ~**politik** *die* development aid policy

**entwirren** *tr. V.* disentangle

**entwischen** *itr. V.; mit sein* (ugs.) get away

**entwöhnen** *tr. V.* wean

**entwürdigend** *Adj.* degrading

**Entwurf** *der;* ~, Entwürfe **(a)** design **(b)** (Konzept) draft

**entwurzeln** *tr. V.* uproot

**entziehen** ① *unr. tr. V.* **(a)** take away **(b)** (nicht zugestehen) withdraw ② *unr. refl. V.* **sich seinen Pflichten** (*Dat.*) ~: evade one's duty; **das entzieht sich meiner Kontrolle** that is beyond my control

**Entziehung** *die;* ~, ~en **(a)** withdrawal **(b)** (Entziehungskur) withdrawal treatment *no indef. art.*

**entziffern** *tr. V.* decipher

**entzückend** *Adj.* delightful

**entzückt** *Adj.* delighted

**Entzug** *der;* ~[e]s withdrawal

**Entzugs·erscheinung** *die* withdrawal symptom

**entzündbar** *Adj.* [in]flammable

**entzünden** ① *tr. V.* light ⟨*fire*⟩; strike ⟨*match*⟩ ② *refl. V.* **(a)** ignite **(b)** (anschwellen) become inflamed

**entzündlich** *Adj.* **(a)** [in]flammable ⟨*substance*⟩ **(b)** (Med.) inflammatory

**Entzündung** *die;* ~, ~en inflammation

**entzwei** *Adj.* (geh.) in pieces

**entzweien** *refl. V.* fall out

**entzwei|gehen** *unr. itr. V.; mit sein* (geh.) break

**Enzian** *der;* ~s, ~e gentian

**Enzyklika** *die;* ~, Enzykliken encyclical

**Enzyklopädie** *die;* ~, ~n encyclopaedia

**enzyklopädisch** *Adj.* encyclopaedic

**Epen** ▶ EPOS

**Epidemie** *die;* ~, ~n epidemic

**epidemisch** *Adj.* (geh.) ▶ EPIDEMISCH

**epigonal** *Adj.* (geh.) ▶ EPIGONENHAFT

**Epigone** *der;* ~n, ~n (geh.) imitator

**epigonenhaft** *Adj.* (geh.) imitative; unoriginal

**Epigonin** *die;* ~, ~nen ▶ EPIGONE

**Epik** /'e:pɪk/ *die;* ~ (Literaturw.) epic poetry

**Epilepsie** *die;* ~, ~n (Med.) epilepsy *no art.*
**Epileptiker** *der;* ~s, ~, **Epileptikerin** *die;* ~, ~nen epileptic
**epileptisch** *Adj.* epileptic
**episch** *Adj.* epic
**Episode** *die;* ~, ~n episode
**Epoche** *die;* ~, ~n epoch
**Epos** /'e:pɔs/ *das;* ~, Epen epic [poem]; epos
**er** *Personalpron. 3. Pers. Sg. Nom. Mask.* he; (betont) him; (bei Dingen/Tieren) it; *s. auch* IHM; IHN; SEINER
**erachten** *tr. V.* (geh.) consider; **etw. als** *od.* **für seine Pflicht** ~: consider sth. [to be] one's duty
**erarbeiten** *tr. V.* work for
**Erb·anlage** *die* hereditary disposition
**erbarmen** *refl. V.* (geh.) take pity (Gen. on)
**Erbarmen** *das;* ~s pity
**erbärmlich** [1] *Adj.* **(a)** (elend) wretched **(b)** (unzulänglich) pathetic **(c)** (abwertend: gemein) mean; wretched **(d)** (sehr groß) terrible ⟨hunger, fear, etc.⟩ [2] *adv.* terribly
**erbauen** [1] *tr. V.* **(a)** build **(b)** (geh.: erheben) uplift [2] *refl. V.* **sich an etw.** (Dat.) ~: be uplifted by sth.
**Erbauer** *der;* ~s, ~, **Erbauerin** *die;* ~, ~nen architect
**Erbe**[1] *das;* ~s **(a)** inheritance **(b)** (Vermächtnis) legacy
**Erbe**[2] *der;* ~n ~n heir
**erben** *tr.* (auch itr.) *V.* inherit
**erbetteln** *tr. V.* get by begging
**erbeuten** *tr. V.* carry off, get away with ⟨valuables, prey, etc.⟩; capture ⟨enemy plane, tank, etc.⟩
**Erb-:** ~**faktor** *der* hereditary factor; ~**folge** *die* succession; ~**gut** *das* (Biol.) genetic make-up
**Erbin** *die;* ~, ~nen heiress
**erbitten** *unr. tr. V.* (geh.) request
**erbittern** *tr. V.* enrage
**erbittert** [1] *Adj.* bitter [2] *adv.* ~ **kämpfen** wage a bitter struggle
**Erb·krankheit** *die* hereditary disease
**erblassen** *itr. V.; mit sein* (geh.) turn pale; blanch (literary)
**erbleichen** *itr. V.; mit sein* (geh.) ► ERBLASSEN
**erblich** *Adj.* hereditary ⟨title, disease⟩
**erblicken** *tr. V.* (geh.) catch sight of; (fig.) see
**erblinden** *itr. V.; mit sein* lose one's sight
**erblühen** *itr. V.; mit sein* (geh.) bloom; blossom
**Erb·masse** *die* (Biol.) genetic make-up
**erbost** *Adj.* furious
**erbrechen** [1] *unr. tr. V.* bring up ⟨food⟩

[2] *unr. itr., refl. V.* vomit
**Erbrechen** *das;* ~s vomiting
**erbringen** *unr. tr. V.* produce
**Erbschaft** *die;* ~, ~en inheritance
**Erbschaft[s]·steuer** *die* estate *or* death duties *pl.*
**Erb-:** ~**schleicher** *der;* ~~s, ~~ (abwertend) legacy hunter; ~**schleicherei** *die;* ~~, ~~en (abwertend) legacy hunting; ~**schleicherin** *die;* ~~, ~~nen ► ~SCHLEICHER
**Erbse** *die;* ~, ~n pea
**Erb-:** ~**stück** *das* heirloom; ~**sünde** *die* original sin; ~**teil** *das* share of an/the inheritance
**Erd-:** ~**achse** *die* earth's axis; ~**anziehung** *die* earth's gravitational pull; ~**apfel** *der* (bes. österr.) ► KARTOFFEL; ~**atmosphäre** *die* earth's atmosphere; ~**beben** *das* earthquake; ~**beere** *die* strawberry; ~**boden** *der* ground; earth; **etw. dem** ~**boden gleichmachen** raze sth. to the ground
**Erde** *die;* ~, ~n **(a)** (Erdreich) soil; earth **(b)** (fester Boden) ground **(c)** (Welt) earth; world **(d)** (Planet) Earth
**erdenklich** *Adj.* conceivable
**Erd-:** ~**gas** *das* natural gas; ~**geschoss**, *\**~**geschoß** *das* ground floor; first floor (Amer.); ~**kugel** *die* terrestrial globe; earth; ~**kunde** *die* geography; ~**magnetismus** *der* terrestrial magnetism; ~**nuss**, *\**~**nuß** *die* peanut; ~**oberfläche** *die* earth's surface; ~**öl** *das* oil; ~**öl exportierende Länder** oil-exporting countries
**erdöl-, Erdöl-:** *\**~**exportierend** ► ERDÖL; ~**gewinnung** *die* oil production; ~**leitung** *die* oil pipeline
**erdrosseln** *tr. V.* strangle
**erdrücken** *tr. V.* **(a)** crush **(b)** (fig.: belasten) overwhelm
**erdrückend** *Adj.* overwhelming; oppressive ⟨heat, silence⟩
**Erd-:** ~**rutsch** *der* landslide; ~**rutsch·sieg** *der* (Politik) landslide victory; ~**teil** *der* continent
**erdulden** *tr. V.* endure ⟨sorrow, misfortune⟩; tolerate ⟨insults⟩; (über sich ergehen lassen) undergo
**Erd-:** ~**umdrehung** *die* rotation of the earth; ~**umlauf·bahn** *die* orbit [of the earth]
**ereifern** *refl. V.* get excited
**ereignen** *refl. V.* happen; ⟨accident, mishap⟩ occur
**Ereignis** *das;* ~ses, ~se event; occurrence
**ereignis·reich** *Adj.* eventful
**Eremit** *der;* ~en, ~en, **Eremitin** *die;* ~, ~nen hermit
**ererbt** *Adj.* inherited

---

**erfahren¹** *unr. tr. V.* **(a)** find out; learn; (hören) hear
**(b)** (geh.: erleben) experience; (erleiden) suffer

**erfahren²** *Adj.* experienced

**Erfahrung** *die;* ∼, ∼en experience; ∼en sammeln gain experience *sing.;* **etw. in** ∼ **bringen** discover sth.

**erfahrungs·gemäß** *Adv.* in our/my experience

**erfassen** *tr. V.* **(a)** (mitreißen) catch
**(b)** (begreifen) grasp ⟨situation, etc.⟩
**(c)** (registrieren) record

**Erfassung** *die;* ∼, ∼en registration

**erfinden** *unr. tr. V.* invent; **das ist alles erfunden** it is pure fabrication

**Erfinder** *der;* ∼s, ∼, **Erfinderin** *die;* ∼, ∼nen **(a)** inventor
**(b)** (Urheber) creator

**erfinderisch** *Adj.* inventive; (schlau) resourceful

**Erfindung** *die;* ∼, ∼en invention

**erflehen** *tr. V.* (geh.) beg

**Erfolg** *der;* ∼[e]s, ∼e success; **keinen** ∼ **haben** be unsuccessful

**erfolgen** *itr. V.; mit sein* take place; occur; **es erfolgte keine Reaktion** there was no reaction

**erfolg-, Erfolg-:** ∼los ①*Adj.* unsuccessful; ②*adv.* unsuccessfully; ∼losigkeit *die;* ∼∼: lack of success; ∼reich ①*Adj.* successful; ②*adv.* successfully

**Erfolgs·erlebnis** *das* feeling of achievement

**erfolg·versprechend** *Adj.* promising

**erforderlich** *Adj.* required; necessary

**erfordern** *tr. V.* require; demand

**erforschen** *tr. V.* discover ⟨facts, causes, etc.⟩; explore ⟨country⟩

**Erforschung** *die;* ∼ research (+ *Gen.* into); (eines Landes usw.) exploration

**erfreuen** ①*tr. V.* please
②*refl. V.* **sich an etw.** (*Dat.*) ∼: take pleasure in sth.

**erfreulich** *Adj.* pleasant

**erfreulicherweise** *Adv.* happily

**erfrieren** ①*unr. itr. V.; mit sein* freeze to death; ⟨plant, harvest, etc.⟩ be damaged by frost
②*unr. refl. V.* **sich** (*Dat.*) **die Finger** ∼: get frostbite in one's fingers

**Erfrierung** *die;* ∼, ∼en frostbite *no pl.;* ∼en an den Händen/Füßen frostbitten hands/feet

**erfrischen** ①*tr.* (*auch itr.*) *V.* refresh
②*refl. V.* freshen oneself up

**erfrischend** (auch fig.) *Adj.* refreshing

**Erfrischung** *die;* ∼, ∼en (auch fig.) refreshment

**Erfrischungs-:** ∼getränk *das* soft

drink; ∼raum *der* refreshment room; ∼tuch *das; Pl.* ∼tücher tissue wipe; towelette

**erfüllen** ①*tr. V.* grant ⟨wish, request⟩; fulfil ⟨contract⟩; carry out ⟨duty⟩; meet ⟨condition⟩
②*refl. V.* ⟨wish⟩ come true

**Erfüllung** *die;* **in** ∼ **gehen** come true

**erfunden** *Adj.* fictional ⟨story⟩

**ergänzen** *tr. V.* **(a)** (vervollständigen) complete; (erweitern) add to
**(b)** (hinzufügen) add ⟨remark⟩

**Ergänzung** *die;* ∼, ∼en **(a)** (Vervollständigung) completion; (Erweiterung) enlargement
**(b)** (Zusatz) addition; (zu einem Gesetz) amendment

**ergattern** *tr. V.* (ugs.) manage to grab

**ergaunern** *tr. V.* get by underhand means

**ergeben¹** ①*unr. refl. V.* **(a) sich in etw.** (*Akk.*) ∼: submit to sth.
**(b)** (kapitulieren) surrender (*Dat.* to)
**(c)** (folgen, entstehen) arise (**aus** from)
②*unr. tr. V.* result in

**ergeben²** *Adj.* **(a)** (zugeneigt) devoted
**(b)** (resignierend) **mit** ∼er **Miene** with an expression of resignation

**Ergebnis** *das;* ∼ses, ∼se result

**ergebnis·los** *Adj.* fruitless

**ergehen** *unr. refl. V.* **sich in etw.** (*Dat.*) ∼: indulge in sth.

**ergiebig** *Adj.* rich ⟨deposits, resources⟩; fertile ⟨topic⟩

**Ergiebigkeit** *die;* ∼ ▶ ERGIEBIG: richness; fertility

**ergonomisch** ①*Adj.* ergonomic
②*adv.* ergonomically

**ergötzen** (geh.) ①*tr. V.* enthrall
②*refl. V.* **sich an etw.** (*Dat.*) ∼: be delighted by sth.

**ergrauen** *itr. V.; mit sein* go grey

**ergreifen** *unr. tr. V.* **(a)** (greifen) grab
**(b)** (festnehmen) catch ⟨thief etc.⟩
**(c)** (fig.: erfassen) seize
**(d)** (fig.: aufnehmen) take up ⟨career⟩; take ⟨initiative, opportunity⟩
**(e)** (fig.: bewegen) move

**ergreifend** *Adj.* moving

**ergriffen** *Adj.* moved

**Ergriffenheit** *die;* ∼: **voller** ∼: deeply moved

**ergründen** *tr. V.* ascertain; discover ⟨cause⟩

**Erguss, \*Erguß** *der* (geh. abwertend) outburst; **ein poetischer** ∼: a poetic outpouring

**erhaben** *Adj.* solemn ⟨moment⟩; awe-inspiring ⟨sight⟩; sublime ⟨beauty⟩; **über etw.** (*Akk.*) ∼ **sein** be above sth.

**Erhalt** *der;* ∼ (Amtsdt.) receipt

**erhalten** *unr. tr. V.* (a) receive ⟨letter, news, gift⟩; be given ⟨order⟩; get ⟨good mark, impression⟩
(b) (bewahren) preserve ⟨town, building⟩
**erhältlich** *Adj.* obtainable
**Erhaltung** *die;* ~: preservation; (des Friedens) maintenance
**erhängen** *tr. V.* hang
**erhärten** *tr. V.* strengthen ⟨suspicion, assumption⟩; substantiate ⟨claim⟩
**erheben** [1] *unr. tr. V.* (a) raise
(b) (verlangen) levy ⟨tax⟩; charge ⟨fee⟩
[2] *unr. refl. V.* (a) rise
(b) (rebellieren) rise up (gegen against)
**erhebend** *Adj.* uplifting
**erheblich** [1] *Adj.* considerable
[2] *adv.* considerably
**Erhebung** *die;* ~, ~en (a) (Anhöhe) elevation
(b) (Aufstand) uprising
(c) (Umfrage) survey
(d) (Einziehen) (von Steuern) levying; (von Gebühren) charging
**erheitern** *tr. V.* jmdn. ~: cheer sb. up
**Erheiterung** *die;* ~, ~en amusement
**erhellen** *tr. V.* light up
**erhitzen** [1] *tr. V.* heat ⟨liquid⟩; jmdn. ~: make sb. hot
[2] *refl. V.* heat up; ⟨person⟩ become hot
**erhoffen** *tr. V.* sich ⟨Dat.⟩ viel/wenig von etw. ~: expect a lot/little from sth.
**erhöhen** [1] *tr. V.* increase ⟨prices, productivity, etc.⟩
[2] *refl. V.* ⟨rent, prices⟩ rise
**Erhöhung** *die;* ~, ~en increase (Gen. in)
**erholen** *refl. V.* (auch fig.) recover (von from); (sich ausruhen) have a rest
**erholsam** *Adj.* restful
**Erholung** *die;* ~: ▶ ERHOLEN: recovery; rest; ~ brauchen need a rest
**erholungs-bedürftig** *Adj.* in need of a rest *postpos.*
**Erholungs-urlaub** *der* holiday for convalescence
**erhören** *tr. V.* (geh.) hear
**Erika** *die;* ~, ~s *od.* Eriken (Bot.) erica
**erinnern** [1] *refl. V.* sich an jmdn./etw. ~: remember sb./sth.; sich [daran] ~, dass ...: remember *or* recall that ...
[2] *tr. V.* jmdn. an etw./jmdn. ~: remind sb. of sth./sb.
**Erinnerung** *die;* ~, ~en memory (an + Akk. of); etw. [noch gut] in ~ haben [still] remember sth. [well]; zur ~ an jmdn./etw. in memory of sb./sth.
**Erinnerungs-lücke** *die* gap in one's memory
**erjagen** *tr. V.* (a) catch
(b) (gewinnen) win ⟨fame⟩; make ⟨money, fortune⟩

**erkalten** *tr. V.; mit sein* cool
**erkälten** *refl. V.* catch cold
**Erkältung** *die;* ~, ~en cold
**Erkältungs-krankheit** *die* cold
**erkämpfen** *tr. V.* win; den Sieg ~: gain a victory
**erkaufen** *tr. V.* (a) (durch Opfer) win
(b) (durch Geld) buy
**erkennbar** *Adj.* recognizable; (sichtbar) visible
**erkennen** *unr. tr. V.* (a) recognize
(b) (deutlich sehen) make out
**erkenntlich** *Adj.* (a) sich [für etw.] ~ zeigen show one's appreciation for sth.
(b) ▶ ERKENNBAR
**Erkenntnis** *die;* ~, ~se discovery; zu der ~ kommen, dass ...: come to the realization that ...
**Erkennungs-:** ~melodie *die* (einer Sendung) theme music; (eines Senders) signature tune; ~zeichen *das* sign [to recognize sb. by]
**Erker** *der;* ~s, ~: bay window
**Erker-fenster** *das* bay window
**erklärbar** *Adj.* explicable
**erklären** [1] *tr. V.* (a) explain
(b) (mitteilen) state; declare
(c) jmdn. für tot ~: pronounce someone dead; jmdn. zu etw. ~: name sb. as sth
[2] *refl. V.* sich einverstanden/bereit ~: declare oneself [to be] in agreement/willing
**erklärlich** *Adj.* understandable
**erklärt** *Adj.* declared
**Erklärung** *die;* ~, ~en (a) (Darlegung) explanation
(b) (Mitteilung) statement
**erklimmen** *unr. tr. V.* (geh.) climb
**erklingen** *unr. itr. V.; mit sein* ring out
**erkranken** *itr. V.; mit sein* become ill (an + Dat. with); schwer erkrankt sein be seriously ill
**Erkrankung** *die;* ~, ~en illness; (eines Körperteils) disease
**erkunden** *tr. V.* reconnoitre ⟨terrain⟩
**erkundigen** *refl. V.* sich nach jmdn./etw. ~: ask after sb./enquire about sth.
**Erkundigung** *die;* ~, ~en enquiry
**Erkundung** *die;* ~, ~en (meist Milit.) reconnaissance
**Erkundungs-:** ~fahrt *die* exploratory trip; ~flug *der* reconnaissance flight
**erlahmen** *itr. V.; mit sein* tire; ⟨strength⟩ flag
**erlangen** *tr. V.* gain; obtain ⟨credit, visa⟩; reach ⟨age⟩
**Erlass, *Erlaß** *der;* Erlasses, Erlasse decree
**erlassen** *unr. tr. V.* (a) enact ⟨law⟩; declare ⟨amnesty⟩; issue ⟨warrant⟩
(b) (verzichten auf) remit ⟨sentence⟩
**erlauben** [1] *tr. V.* (a) allow
(b) (ermöglichen) permit

② *refl. V.* sich (*Dat.*) etw. ~: permit oneself sth

**Erlaubnis** *die;* ~, ~se permission; (Schriftstück) permit

**erläutern** *tr. V.* explain; comment on ⟨*picture etc.*⟩; annotate ⟨*text*⟩

**Erläuterung** *die* explanation

**Erle** *die;* ~, ~n alder

**erleben** *tr. V.* experience; **etwas Schreckliches ~**: have a terrible experience; **er wird das nächste Jahr nicht mehr ~**: he won't see next year; **du kannst was ~!** (ugs.) you won't know what's hit you!

**Erlebnis** *das;* ~ses, ~se experience

**erledigen** ① *tr. V.* deal with ⟨*task*⟩; settle ⟨*matter*⟩; **ich muss noch einige Dinge erledigen** I must see to a few things; **sie hat alles pünktlich erledigt** she got everything done on time
② *refl. V.* ⟨*matter, problem*⟩ resolve itself; **vieles erledigt sich von selbst** a lot of things sort them'selves out

**erledigt** *Adj.* closed ⟨*case*⟩; (ugs.) worn out ⟨*person*⟩

**erlegen** *tr. V.* shoot ⟨*animal*⟩

**erleichtern** *tr. V.* **(a)** make easier
**(b)** (befreien) relieve

**Erleichterung** *die;* ~, ~en **(a) zur ~ der Arbeit** to make the work easier
**(b)** (Befreiung) relief
**(c)** (Verbesserung, Milderung) alleviation

**erleiden** *unr. tr. V.* suffer

**erlernbar** *Adj.* learnable

**erlernen** *tr. V.* learn

**erlesen** *Adj.* superior ⟨*wine*⟩; choice ⟨*dish*⟩

**erleuchten** *tr. V.* **(a)** light
**(b)** (geh.: mit Klarheit erfüllen) inspire

**Erleuchtung** *die;* ~, ~en inspiration

**erliegen** *unr. itr. V.; mit sein* succumb (*Dat.* to); **einem Irrtum ~**: be misled; **einer Krankheit** (*Dat.*) ~: die from an illness

**erlogen** *Adj.* made up

**Erlös** *der;* ~es, ~e proceeds *pl.*

**erlöschen** *unr. itr. V.; mit sein* ⟨*fire*⟩ go out; **ein erloschener Vulkan** an extinct volcano

**erlösen** *tr. V.* save, rescue **(von** from)

**Erlöser** *der;* ~s, ~ **(a)** saviour
**(b)** (christl. Rel.) redeemer

**Erlöserin** *die;* ~, ~nen ▶ ERLÖSER A

**Erlösung** *die;* ~, ~en release **(von** from)

**ermächtigen** *tr. V.* authorize

**Ermächtigung** *die;* ~, ~en authorization

**ermahnen** *tr. V.* admonish; tell (coll.); (warnen) warn

**Ermahnung** *die;* ~, ~en admonition; (Warnung) warning

**Ermang[e]lung** *die;* ~: **in ~** (+ *Gen.*) (geh.) in the absence of

**ermäßigen** *tr. V.* reduce

**Ermäßigung** *die;* ~, ~en reduction

**ermatten** (geh.) ① *itr. V.; mit sein* become exhausted
② *tr. V.* exhaust, tire

**ermessen** *unr. tr. V.* estimate, gauge

**Ermessen** *das;* ~s estimation

**ermitteln** ① *tr. V.* ascertain ⟨*facts*⟩; discover ⟨*culprit, address*⟩; establish ⟨*identity, origin*⟩; decide ⟨*winner*⟩; calculate ⟨*quota, rates, data*⟩
② *itr. V.* (Rechtsw.) investigate

**Ermittlung** *die;* ~, ~en **(a)** (das Ermitteln)
▶ ERMITTELN A: ascertainment; discovery; establishment
**(b)** (Untersuchung) investigation

**ermöglichen** *tr. V.* enable

**ermorden** *tr. V.* murder

**Ermordung** *die;* ~, ~en murder

**ermüden** ① *itr. V.; mit sein* tire
② *tr. V.* tire; make tired

**ermüdend** *Adj.* tiring

**Ermüdung** *die;* ~, ~en tiredness

**ermuntern** *tr. V.* encourage

**ermunternd** *Adj.* encouraging

**ermutigen** *tr. V.* encourage

**Ermutigung** *die;* ~, ~en encouragement

**ernähren** ① *tr. V.* **(a)** feed ⟨*young, child*⟩
**(b)** (unterhalten) keep ⟨*family, wife*⟩
② *refl. V.* feed oneself

**Ernährer** *der;* ~s, ~, **Ernährerin** *die;* ~, ~nen breadwinner

**Ernährung** *die;* ~: feeding; (Nahrung) diet

**Ernährungs·wissenschaft** *die* dietetics *sing.*, no art.

**ernennen** *unr. tr. V.* appoint

**Ernennung** *die* appointment **(zu** as)

**erneuerbar** *Adj.* renewable; ~e **Energien** renewable sources of energy

**erneuern** *tr. V.* **(a)** replace
**(b)** (wiederherstellen) renovate ⟨*roof, building*⟩; (fig.) thoroughly reform ⟨*system*⟩

**Erneuerung** *die;* ~, ~en **(a)** replacement
**(b)** (Wiederherstellung) renovation

**erneut** ① *Adj.* renewed
② *adv.* once again

**erniedrigen** *tr. V.* humiliate

**Erniedrigung** *die;* ~, ~en humiliation

**ernst** ① *Adj.* **(a)** serious
**(b)** (aufrichtig) genuine ⟨*intention, offer*⟩
**(c)** (gefahrvoll) serious ⟨*injury*⟩; grave ⟨*situation*⟩
② *adv.* seriously; **jmdn./etw. ~ nehmen** take sb./sth. seriously; **~ gemeint** serious; sincere ⟨*wish*⟩

**Ernst** *der;* ~[e]s **(a)** seriousness; **das ist mein [voller] ~**: I mean that [quite] seriously; **etw. im ~ meinen** mean sth. seriously
**(b)** (Wirklichkeit) **daraus wurde [blutiger/ bitterer] ~**: it became [deadly] serious; **der ~ des Lebens** the serious side of life

**ernst-, Ernst-:** ~**fall** *der:* **im ~fall** when the real thing happens; *\*~***gemeint** ⋯⟶

e

▶ ERNST 2; **~haft** [1] *Adj.* serious; [2] *adv.* seriously; **~haftigkeit** *die;* ~~: seriousness

**ernstlich** [1] *Adj.* (a) serious
(b) (aufrichtig) genuine ⟨*wish*⟩
[2] *adv.* (a) seriously
(b) (aufrichtig) genuinely ⟨*sorry, repentant*⟩

**Ernte** *die;* ~, ~n (a) harvest
(b) (Ertrag) crop; **die ~ einbringen** bring in the harvest

**Ernte·dank·fest** *das* harvest festival

**ernten** *tr. V.* harvest

**ernüchtern** *tr. V.* sober up; (fig.) bring down to earth; **~d** sobering

**Ernüchterung** *die;* ~, ~en (fig.) disillusionment

**Eroberer** *der;* ~s, ~, **Eroberin** *die;* ~, ~nen conqueror

**erobern** *tr. V.* (a) conquer; take ⟨*town, fortress*⟩
(b) seize ⟨*power*⟩

**Eroberung** *die;* ~, ~en conquest; (einer Stadt, Festung) taking

**eröffnen** *tr. V.* (a) open; start ⟨*business, practice*⟩
(b) (mitteilen) jmdm. etw. ~: reveal sth. to sb.
(c) **ein Testament ~:** read a will

**Eröffnung** *die;* ~, ~en (a) opening; (einer Sitzung) start
(b) (Mitteilung) revelation
(c) (Testaments~) reading

**erogen** *Adj.* erogenous ⟨*zone*⟩

**erörtern** *tr. V.* discuss

**Erörterung** *die;* ~, ~en discussion

**Eros·Center** *das* [licensed] brothel; eros centre

**Erosion** *die;* ~, ~en erosion

**Erotik** *die;* ~: eroticism

**erotisch** *Adj.* erotic

**Erpel** *der;* ~s, ~: drake

**erpicht** *Adj.* **in auf etw.** (*Akk.*) ~ **sein** be keen on sth.

**erpressbar, \*erpreßbar** *Adj.* blackmailable; susceptible to blackmail *postpos.*

**Erpressbarkeit, \*Erpreßbarkeit** *die;* ~: susceptibility to blackmail

**erpressen** *tr. V.* (a) (nötigen) blackmail
(b) (erlangen) extort ⟨*money etc.*⟩

**Erpresser** *der;* ~s, ~, **Erpresserin** *die;* ~, ~nen blackmailer

**Erpressung** *die;* ~, ~en blackmail *no indef. art.;* (von Geld, Geständnis) extortion

**Erpressungs·versuch** *der* blackmail attempt

**erproben** *tr. V.* test ⟨*medicine*⟩ (**an** + *Akk.* on)

**Erprobung** *die;* ~, ~en testing

**erquickend** *Adj.* (geh.) refreshing

**erraten** *unr. tr. V.* guess

**errechnen** *tr. V.* calculate

**erregen** [1] *tr. V.* (a) annoy
(b) (sexuell) arouse
(c) (verursachen) arouse
[2] *refl. V.* get excited

**erregend** *Adj.* exciting; (sexuell) arousing

**Erreger** *der;* ~s, ~ (Med.) pathogen

**erregt** *Adj.* excited; (sexuell) aroused

**Erregung** *die;* ~, ~en excitement

**erreichbar** *Adj.* (a) within reach *postpos.;*
(b) **der Ort ist mit dem Zug ~:** the place can be reached by train

**erreichen** *tr. V.* (a) reach; **den Zug ~:** catch the train; **er ist telefonisch zu ~:** he can be contacted by telephone
(b) (durchsetzen) achieve ⟨*goal, aim*⟩

**errichten** *tr. V.* (a) build ⟨*house, bridge, etc.*⟩
(b) (aufstellen) erect

**erringen** *unr. tr. V.* gain ⟨*victory*⟩; reach ⟨*first etc. place*⟩

**erröten** *itr. V.; mit sein* blush

**Errungenschaft** *die;* ~, ~en achievement

**Ersatz** *der;* ~es (a) replacement
(b) (Entschädigung) compensation

**Ersatz-:** **~frau** *die* replacement; (Sport) substitute; **~kasse** *die* private health insurance company; **~mann** *der; Pl.* **~männer** *od.* **~leute** *die* replacement; (Sport) substitute; **~rad** *das* spare wheel; **~reifen** *der* spare tyre; **~spieler** *der*, **~spielerin** *die* (Sport) substitute [player]; **~teil** *das* (bes. Technik) spare part; spare (Brit.)

**ersaufen** *unr. itr. V.; mit sein* (salopp) drown

**ersäufen** *tr. V.* drown

**erschaffen** *unr. tr. V.* create

**Erschaffung** *die* creation

**erschaudern** *itr. V.; mit sein* (geh.) shudder (**bei** at)

**erscheinen** *unr. itr. V.; mit sein* ⟨*book*⟩ be published

**Erscheinung** *die;* ~, ~en (a) (Vorgang) phenomenon
(b) (äußere Gestalt) appearance
(c) (Vision) apparition; **eine ~ haben** see a vision

**Erscheinungs-:** **~bild** *das* appearance; **~form** *die* manifestation; **~weise** *die* **~weise einer Zeitung** the frequency of publication of a newspaper; **wöchentliche/ monatliche ~weise** weekly/monthly publication

**erschießen** *unr. tr. V.* shoot dead

**Erschießung** *die;* ~, ~en shooting

**erschlaffen** *itr. V.; mit sein* ⟨*muscle, limb*⟩ become limp; ⟨*skin*⟩ grow slack

**erschlagen¹** *unr. tr. V.* strike dead; kill

**erschlagen²** *Adj.* (ugs.) (a) (erschöpft) worn out

---

\*alte Schreibung - vgl. Hinweis auf S. xiv

**(b)** (verblüfft) **wie ~ sein** be flabbergasted (coll.) *or* thunderstruck

**erschließen** *unr. tr. V.* develop ⟨area, building land⟩; tap ⟨resources⟩

**erschöpfen** *tr. V.* exhaust

**erschöpfend** *Adj.* exhaustive

**erschöpft** *Adj.* exhausted

**Erschöpfung** *die; ~, ~en* exhaustion

**Erschöpfungs·zustand** *der* state of exhaustion

**erschrecken**[1] *unr. itr. V.; mit sein* be startled; **vor etw. (Dat.) od. über etw. (Akk.) ~:** be startled by sth.

**erschrecken**[2] *tr. V.* frighten; scare

**erschrecken**[3] *unr. od. regelm. refl. V.* get a fright

**erschreckend** *Adj.* alarming

**erschrocken** [1] 2. *Part. v.* ERSCHRECKEN[1]; [2] *Adj.* frightened

**erschüttern** *tr. V.* (auch fig.) shake

**erschütternd** *Adj.* deeply distressing; deeply shocking ⟨conditions⟩

**Erschütterung** *die; ~, ~en* **(a)** vibration; (der Erde) tremor **(b)** (Ergriffenheit) shock; (Trauer) distress

**erschweren** *tr. V. etw. ~:* make sth. more difficult

**erschwerend** [1] *Adj.* complicating ⟨factor⟩ [2] *adv.* **es kommt ~ hinzu, dass er ...:** to make matters worse he ...

**Erschwernis** *die; ~, ~se* difficulty

**erschwinglich** *Adj.* reasonable

**ersehen** *unr. tr. V.* see; **aus etw. zu ~ sein** be evident from sth.

**ersetzen** *tr. V.* **(a)** replace **(durch** by) **(b)** (erstatten) reimburse ⟨expenses⟩; **jmdm. einen Schaden ~:** compensate sb. for damages

**Ersetzung** *die; ~, ~en* (von Kosten usw.) reimbursement; **die ~ von Schäden** compensation for damage

**ersichtlich** *Adj.* apparent

**ersinnen** *unr. tr. V.* (geh.) devise

**erspähen** *tr. V.* (geh.) espy (literary); catch sight of

**ersparen** *tr. V.* save

**Ersparnis** *die; ~, ~se* saving

**ersprießlich** *Adj.* (geh.) fruitful ⟨contacts, collaboration⟩

**erst** [1] *Adv.* **(a)** (zu~) first; **~ einmal** first [of all] **(b)** (nicht eher als) **eben ~:** only just; **~ nächste Woche** not until next week; **er war ~ zufrieden, als ...:** he was not satisfied until ... **(c)** (nicht mehr als) only [2] *Partikel* **so was lese ich gar nicht ~:** I don't even start reading that sort of stuff

**erst...** *Ordinalz.* **(a)** first; **etw. das ~e Mal**

tun do sth. for the first time; **am Ersten [des Monats]** on the first [of the month]; **als Erster/Erste etw. tun** be the first to do sth. **(b)** (best...) **das ~e Hotel** the best hotel; **der/die Erste [der Klasse]** the top boy/girl [of the class]

**erstarren** *itr. V.; mit sein* ⟨jelly, plaster⟩ set; ⟨limbs, fingers⟩ grow stiff

**erstatten** *tr. V.* **(a)** reimburse ⟨expenses⟩ **(b)** **Anzeige gegen jmdn. ~:** report sb. [to the police]

**Erstattung** *die; ~, ~en* (von Kosten) reimbursement

**Erst·aufführung** *die* première

**erstaunen** *tr. V.* astonish

**Erstaunen** *das; ~s* astonishment

**erstaunlich** [1] *Adj.* astonishing [2] *adv.* astonishingly

**erstaunlicher·weise** *Adv.* astonishingly *or* amazingly [enough]

**erstaunt** *Adj.* astonished; amazed

**Erst·ausgabe** *die* first edition

**erstechen** *unr. tr. V.* stab [to death]

**erstehen** (geh.) [1] *unr. tr. V.* (kaufen) purchase [2] *unr. itr. V.; mit sein* ⟨difficulties, problems⟩ arise

**ersteigen** *unr. tr. V.* climb

**ersteigern** *tr. V.* buy [at an auction]

**erstellen** *tr. V.* (Papierdt.) **(a)** (bauen) build **(b)** (anfertigen) make ⟨assessment⟩; draw up ⟨plan, report, list⟩

*****erste·mal** ▶ MAL[1]
*****ersten·mal** ▶ MAL[1]

**erstens** *Adv.* firstly; in the first place

**erster...** *Adj.* the former

**erst·geboren** *Adj.* first-born

**ersticken** [1] *itr. V.; mit sein* suffocate; (sich verschlucken) choke [2] *tr. V.* **(a)** (töten) suffocate **(b)** smother ⟨flames⟩

**erstklassig** [1] *Adj.* first-class [2] *adv.* superbly

**erstmals** *Adv.* for the first time

**erstrangig** *Adj.* **(a)** first-class **(b)** (vordringlich) of top priority *postpos.*

**erstreben** *tr. V.* strive for

**erstrebens·wert** *Adj.* ⟨ideals etc.⟩ worth striving for; desirable ⟨situation⟩

**erstrecken** *refl. V.* **(a)** (sich ausdehnen) stretch **(b)** (dauern) **sich über 10 Jahre ~:** carry on for 10 years

**Erst·stimme** *die* first vote

**erstürmen** *tr. V.* take by storm

**ersuchen** *tr. V.* (geh.) ask; **jmdn. ~, etw. zu tun** request sb. to do sth.

**ertappen** *tr. V.* catch ⟨thief, burglar⟩

**erteilen** *tr. V.* give ⟨advice, information⟩; give, grant ⟨permission⟩

**Erteilung** die; ~, ~en giving; (einer Genehmigung) granting

**ertönen** itr. V.; mit sein sound

**Ertrag** der; ~[e]s, Erträge (a) yield
(b) (Gewinn) return

**ertragen** unr. tr. V. bear

**erträglich** Adj. tolerable; bearable ⟨pain⟩

**ertrag·reich** Adj. lucrative ⟨business⟩; productive ⟨land, soil⟩

**ertränken** tr. V. drown

**ertrinken** unr. itr. V.; mit sein be drowned; drown

**erübrigen** ① tr. V. spare ⟨money, time⟩
② refl. V. be unnecessary

**erwachen** itr. V.; mit sein (geh.) awake

**Erwachen** das; ~s (auch fig.) awakening

**erwachsen¹** unr. itr. V.; mit sein (a) grow (aus out of); ⟨rumour⟩ spread
(b) (sich ergeben) ⟨difficulties, tasks⟩ arise

**erwachsen²** Adj. grown-up attrib.; ~ sein be grown up

**Erwachsene** der/die; adj. Dekl. adult; grown-up

**erwägen** unr. tr. V. consider

**Erwägung** die; ~, ~en consideration; etw. in ~ ziehen take sth. into consideration

**erwählen** tr. V. (geh.) choose

**erwähnen** tr. V. mention

**erwähnens·wert** Adj. worth mentioning postpos.

**Erwähnung** die; ~, ~en mention

**erwärmen** ① tr. V. heat
② refl. V. (warm werden) ⟨air, water⟩ warm up

**Erwärmung** die; ~: eine ~ der Luft/des Wassers an increase in air/water temperature; bei ~ der Flüssigkeit when the liquid is heated

**erwarten** tr. V. expect; jmdn. am Bahnhof ~: wait for sb. at the station

**Erwartung** die; ~, ~en expectation

**erwartungs-:** ~gemäß Adv. as expected; ~voll Adj. expectant

**erwecken** tr. V. (a) (auf~) wake
(b) (erregen) arouse ⟨longing, pity⟩

**erweichen** tr. V. soften

**erweisen** ① unr. tr. V. (a) prove
(b) (bezeigen) jmdm. Achtung ~: show respect to sb.
② unr. refl. V. sich als etw. ~: prove to be sth.

**erweitern** ① tr. V. widen ⟨river, road⟩; expand ⟨library, business⟩; enlarge ⟨collection⟩; dilate ⟨pupil, blood vessel⟩
② refl. V. ⟨road, river⟩ widen; ⟨pupil, blood vessel⟩ dilate

**Erweiterung** die; ~, ~en ▶ ERWEITERN: widening; expansion; enlargement; dilation

**Erwerb** der; ~[e]s (a) (Aneignung) acquisition
(b) (Kauf) purchase

**erwerben** unr. tr. V. (a) (verdienen) earn
(b) (sich aneignen) gain
(c) (kaufen) acquire

**erwerbs-, Erwerbs-:** ~fähig Adj. capable of gainful employment postpos.; able to work postpos.; ~fähigkeit die ability to work; ~los Adj.: ▶ ARBEITSLOS; ~lose der/die; adj. Dekl.: ▶ ARBEITSLOSE; ~tätig Adj. gainfully employed; ~unfähig Adj. incapable of gainful employment postpos.; unable to work postpos.

**Erwerbung** die acquisition; (Gekauftes) purchase

**erwidern** tr. V. (a) reply
(b) (reagieren auf) return ⟨greeting, visit⟩; reciprocate ⟨sb.'s feelings⟩

**Erwiderung** die; ~, ~en (a) reply (auf + Akk. to)
(b) ▶ ERWIDERN B: return; reciprocation

**erwiesen** Adj. proved; proven ⟨fact⟩

**erwiesener·maßen** Adv. as has been proved

**erwirken** tr. V. obtain

**erwirtschaften** tr. V. etw. ~: obtain sth. by careful management

**erwischen** tr. V. (ugs.) (a) catch ⟨culprit, train, bus⟩
(b) (greifen) grab
(c) (bekommen) manage to get
(d) (unpers.) es hat ihn erwischt (ugs.) (er ist tot) he's bought it (sl.); (er ist krank) he's got it; (er ist verletzt) he's been hurt; (scherzh.: er ist verliebt) he's got it bad (coll.)

**erwünscht** Adj. wanted

**erwürgen** tr. V. strangle

**Erz** /ɛrts: od. e:rts:/ das; ~es, ~e ore

**erzählen** tr. (auch itr.) V. tell ⟨joke, story⟩; jmdm. etw. ~: tell sb. sth.

**Erzähler** der, **Erzählerin** die storyteller; (Autor[in]) writer [of stories]; narrative writer

**Erzählung** die; ~, ~en narration; (Bericht) account; (Literaturw.) story

**Erz-:** ~bischof der archbishop; ~bistum das, ~diözese die archbishopric; archdiocese; ~engel der archangel

**erzeugen** tr. V. produce; generate ⟨electricity⟩

**Erzeuger** der; ~s, ~ (Vater) father

**Erzeugnis** das; ~ses, ~se product

**Erzeugung** die; ~, ~en (von Lebensmitteln usw.) production; (von Industriewaren) manufacture; (Strom~) generation

**Erz·feind** der, **Erz·feindin** die arch enemy

**erziehen** unr. tr. V. bring up; (in der Schule) educate; ein Kind zu Sauberkeit und Ordnung ~: bring a child up to be clean and tidy

**Erzieher** der; ~s, ~, **Erzieherin** die; ~, ~nen educator; (Pädagoge) educationalist; (Lehrer) teacher

**Erziehung** die; ~, ~en upbringing; (Schul~) education

---

**Erziehungs-:** ~**berechtig⸱e** *der/die;*
*adj. Dekl.* parent or [legal] guardian;
~**urlaub** *der* child-rearing leave

**erzielen** *tr. V.* reach ⟨*agreement,
compromise, speed*⟩; achieve ⟨*result, effect*⟩;
make ⟨*profit*⟩; obtain ⟨*price*⟩

**erzürnen** (geh.) *tr. V.* anger; (stärker) incense

**erzwingen** *unr. tr. V.* force

**es** *Personalpron.; 3. Pers. Sg. Nom. u. Akk.
Neutr.* **(a)** (*s. auch Gen.* **seiner;** *Dat.* **ihm**)
(Sache) it; (weibliche Person) she/her; (männliche
Person) he/him
**(b)** *ohne Bezug auf ein bestimmtes Subst.,
mit unpers. konstruierten Verben, als
formales Satzglied* it; **ich bin es** it's me; **wir
sind traurig, ihr seid es auch** we are sad, and
so are you; **es sei denn, [dass]** ...: unless ...;
**es ist genug!** that's enough; **es hat geklopft**
there was a knock; **es klingelt** someone is
ringing; **es wird schöner** the weather is
improving; **es geht ihm gut/schlecht** he is
well/unwell; **es wird gelacht** there is
laughter; **es lässt sich aushalten** it is
bearable; **er hat es gut** he has it good; **er
meinte es gut** he meant well

**Esche** *die;* ~, ~**n** (Bot.) ash

**Esel** *der;* ~**s,** ~ **(a)** donkey; ass
**(b)** (ugs.: Dummkopf) ass (coll.)

**Esels-:** ~**brücke** *die* (ugs.) mnemonic;
~**ohr** *das* (ugs.: umgeknickte Stelle) dog-ear

**Eskalation** *die;* ~, ~**en** escalation

**eskalieren** *tr., itr. V.* escalate

**Eskapade** /ɛska'paːdə/ *die;* ~, ~**n**
escapade; (Seitensprung) amorous adventure

**Eskimo** *der;* ~[s], ~[s] Eskimo

**Eskimo·frau** *die* Eskimo woman

**Eskorte** *die;* ~, ~**n** escort

**eskortieren** *tr. V.* escort

**Espe** *die;* ~, ~**n** aspen

**Essay** /'ɛse/ *der od. das;* ~**s,** ~**s** essay

**essbar, \*eßbar** *Adj.* edible; **nicht** ~:
inedible

**essen** *unr. tr., itr. V.* eat; **etw. gern** ~: like
sth.; **sich satt** ~: eat one's fill; **gut** ~: have a
good meal; (immer) eat well; ~ **gehen** go out
for a meal

**Essen** *das;* ~**s,** ~ (Mahlzeit) meal; (Speise)
food; [**das**] ~ **machen/kochen** get/cook the
meal

**Essen[s]-:** ~**marke** *die* meal ticket;
~**zeit** *die* mealtime

**Essenz** *die;* ~, ~**en** essence

**Esser** *der;* ~**s,** ~, **Esserin** *die;* ~, ~**nen:**
**er ist ein schlechter Esser** he has a poor
appetite

**Essig** *der;* ~**s,** ~**e** vinegar

**Essig·gurke** *die* pickled gherkin

**Ess-, \*Eß-:** ~**kastanie** *die* sweet
chestnut; ~**löffel** *der* (Suppenlöffel) soup
spoon; (für Nach-, Vorspeise) dessert spoon;
~**stäbchen** *das* chopstick; ~**teller** *der*

dinner plate; ~**tisch** *der* dining table;
~**waren** *Pl.* food *sing.;* ~**zimmer** *das*
dining room

**Establishment** /ɪs'tɛblɪʃmənt/ *das;* ~**s,**
~**s** Establishment

**Este** *der;* ~**n,** ~**n, Estin** *die;* ~, ~**nen**
Estonian

**Est·land** (*das*)*;* ~**s** Estonia

**Estragon** /'ɛstragɔn/ *der;* ~**s** tarragon

**Estrich** /'ɛstrɪç/ *der;* ~**s,** ~**e** composition
floor

**Eszett** /ɛs'tsɛt/ *das;* ~, ~ [the letter] ß

**etablieren** *tr. V.* establish; set up

**etabliert** *Adj.* established

**Etablissement** /etablɪs(ə)'mãː/ *das;* ~**s,**
~**s** establishment

**Etage** /e'taːʒə/ *die;* ~, ~**n** floor; storey

**Etappe** *die;* ~, ~**n** stage

**Etat** /e'taː/ *der;* ~**s,** ~**s** budget

**etepetete** /eːtəpeˈteːtə/ *Adj.* (ugs.) fussy;
finicky

**Ethik** *die;* ~, ~**en (a)** ethics *sing.;*
**(b)** (sittliche Normen) ethics *pl.*

**ethisch** *Adj.* ethical

**ethnisch** [1] *Adj.* ethnic; ~**e Säuberung**
ethnic cleansing
[2] *adv.* ethnically

**Etikett** *das;* ~[**e**]**s,** ~**en** *od.* ~**e** *od.* ~**s**
label

**Etikette** *die;* ~, ~**n** etiquette

**Etiketten·schwindel** *der* (abwertend)
playing with names

**etikettieren** *tr. V.* label

**etlich...** *Indefinitpron. u. unbest. Zahlwort:
Sg.* quite a lot of; *Pl.* quite a few

**Etüde** *die;* ~, ~**n** (Musik) étude

**Etui** /ɛt'viː/ *das;* ~**s,** ~**s** case

**etwa** [1] *Adv.* **(a)** (ungefähr) about; ~ **so groß
wie** ...: about as large as ...; ~ **so** roughly
like this
**(b)** (beispielsweise) for example
[2] *Partikel* **störe ich** ~? am I disturbing
you at all?

**etwaig...** /'ɛtva(ː)ɪg.../ *Adj.* possible

**etwas** *Indefinitpron.* **(a)** something; (fragend,
verneinend) anything; **irgend**~: something
**(b)** (Bedeutsames) **aus ihm wird** ~: he'll make
something of himself
**(c)** (ein Teil) some; (fragend, verneinend) any; ~
**von dem Geld** some of the money
**(d)** (ein wenig) a little; ~ **lauter/besser** a little
louder/better

**Etymologie** *die;* ~, ~**n** etymology

**EU** *Abk.* = **Europäische Union** EU

**euch** [1] *Dat. u. Akk. Pl. des Personalpron.*
**ihr** you
[2] *Dat. u. Akk. Pl. des Reflexivpron. der 2.
Pers. Pl.* yourselves

**euer¹** *Possessivpron.* your; **Grüße von
eu[e]rer Helga/eu[e]rem Hans** Best wishes,
Yours, Helga/Hans

**euer²** *Gen. des Personalpron.* **ihr** (geh.) **wir werden** ~ **gedenken** we will remember you

**Eule** *die;* ~, ~n owl; ~n **nach Athen tragen** carry coals to Newcastle

**Eunuch** *der;* ~en, ~en eunuch

**Euphorie** *die;* ~, ~n (bes. Med., Psych.) euphoria

**euphorisch** (bes. Med., Psych.) ☐1 *Adj.* euphoric
☐2 *adv.* euphorically

**eure** ▸ EUER¹

**eurer·seits** ▸ DEINERSEITS

**euret·wegen** *Adv.* ▸ DEINETWEGEN

**Euro** *der;* ~[s], ~[s] euro; **50** ~ 50 euros

**Eurocheque** /'ɔyːroʃɛk/ *der;* ~s, ~s Eurocheque

**Europa** (*das*); ~s Europe

**Europäer** *der;* ~s, ~, **Europäerin** *die;* ~, ~nen European

**europäisch** *Adj.* European; **die Europäische Union** the European Union

**Europa-:** ~**meister** *der,* ~**meisterin** *die* (Sport) European champion; ~**meisterschaft** *die* (Sport) **(a)** (Wettbewerb) European Championship; **(b)** (Sieg) European title; ~**parlament** *das* European Parliament; ~**pokal** *der* (Sport) European cup; ~**rat** *der* Council of Europe; ~**straße** *die* European long-distance road

**Euro·scheck** *der* ▸ EUROCHEQUE

**Euter** *das od. der;* ~s, ~: udder

**ev.** *Abk.* = **evangelisch** ev.

**e.V., E.V.** *Abk.* = **eingetragener Verein**

**evakuieren** /evaku'iːrən/ *tr. V.* evacuate

**Evakuierung** *die;* ~, ~en evacuation

**evangelisch** /evaŋ'geːlɪʃ/ *Adj.* Protestant

**Evangelium** *das;* ~s, **Evangelien (a)** (auch fig.) gospel
**(b)** (christl. Rel.) Gospel

**Event** /i'vɛnt/ *der od. das;* ~s, ~s event

**Eventualität** /evɛntʊali'tɛːt/ *die;* ~, ~en eventuality; contingency

**eventuell** ☐1 *Adj.* possible
☐2 *adv.* possibly; perhaps

**Evolution** /evolu'tsjoːn/ *die;* ~, ~en evolution

**evtl.** *Abk.* = **eventuell**

**EWG** *Abk.* = **Europäische Wirtschaftsgemeinschaft** EEC

**ewig** ☐1 *Adj.* eternal; (abwertend) never-ending
☐2 *adv.* eternally; for ever

**Ewig·gestrige** *der/die; adj. Dekl.* (abwertend) **ein** ~**r sein** be an old reactionary

**Ewigkeit** *die;* ~, ~en **(a)** eternity
**(b)** (ugs.) **es dauert eine** ~: it takes ages (coll.)

**ex** *Adv.* (ugs.) **etw. ex trinken** drink sth. down in one (coll.)

**Ex-** (vor Personenbez.: vormalig) ex-

**exakt** *Adj.* exact; precise

**Exaktheit** *die;* ~: precision; exactness

**Examen** *das;* ~s, ~ *od.* **Examina** examination

**exekutieren** *tr. V.* **(a)** execute
**(b)** (österr.) ▸ PFÄNDEN

**Exekution** *die;* ~, ~en **(a)** execution
**(b)** (österr.) ▸ PFÄNDUNG

**Exekutive** *die;* ~, ~n (Rechtsw., Politik) executive

**Exempel** *das;* ~s, ~: example

**Exemplar** *das;* ~s, ~e specimen; (Buch, Zeitung usw.) copy

**exemplarisch** *Adj.* exemplary

**exerzieren** *tr., itr. V.* drill

**Exhibitionist** *der;* ~en, ~en, **Exhibitionistin** *die;* ~, ~nen (Psych., fig.) exhibitionist

**exhibitionistisch** (Psych.) ☐1 *Adj.* exhibitionist
☐2 *adv.* **er ist** ~ **veranlagt** he has exhibitionist tendencies

**Exil** *das;* ~s, ~e exile

**exiliert** *Adj.* exiled

**Exil·regierung** *die* government in exile

**existentiell** ▸ EXISTENZIELL

**Existenz** *die;* ~, ~en **(a)** existence
**(b)** (Lebensgrundlage) livelihood
**(c)** (Mensch) character

**Existenz·grundlage** *die* basis of one's livelihood

**existenziell** *Adj.* existential; **in etw.** (*Dat.*) **eine** ~**e Bedrohung sehen** see in sth. a threat to one's existence

**Existenz-:** ~**kampf** *der* struggle for existence; ~**minimum** *das* subsistence level

**existieren** *itr. V.* exist

**Exitus** *der;* ~ (Med.) death

**exkl.** *Abk.* = **exklusiv[e]** excl.

**exklusiv** ☐1 *Adj.* exclusive
☐2 *adv.* exclusively

**exklusive** *Präp.* + *Gen.* exclusive of

**Exklusiv·vertrag** *der* exclusive contract

**Exkommunikation** *die;* ~, ~en excommunication

**Exkursion** *die;* ~, ~en study trip

**exotisch** ☐1 *Adj.* exotic
☐2 *adv.* exotically

**expandieren** *tr., itr. V.* expand

**Expansion** *die;* ~, ~en expansion

**Expedition** *die;* ~, ~en expedition

**Experiment** *das;* ~[e]s, ~e experiment

**experimentell** ☐1 *Adj.* experimental
☐2 *adv.* experimentally

**experimentieren** *itr. V.* experiment

**Experte** *der;* ~n, ~n, **Expertin** *die;* ~, ~nen expert (**für** in)

**Experten·system** *das* (DV) expert system

**explizit** ☐1 *Adj.* explicit

---

*alte Schreibung - vgl. Hinweis auf S. xiv

2 *adv.* ‹*describe, define*› explicitly

**explodieren** *itr. V.; mit sein* (auch fig.) explode; ‹*costs*› rocket

**Explosion** *die;* ~, ~en explosion

**explosiv** 1 *Adj.* (auch fig.) explosive
2 *adv.* explosively

**Exponent** *der;* ~en, ~en (Math.) exponent

**exponiert** *Adj.* exposed

**Export¹** *der;* ~[e]s, ~e export

**Export²** *das;* ~s, ~e (Bier) export; zwei ~: two export

**Export-:** ~artikel *der* export; ~bier *das* export beer

**Exporteur** /ɛkspɔr'tøːɐ̯/ *der;* ~s, ~e, **Exporteurin** *die;* ~, ~nen (Wirtsch.) exporter

**Export-:** ~firma *die* exporter; ~handel *der* export trade

**exportieren** *tr., itr. V.* export

**Express-gut, *Expreß-gut** *das* express freight

**Expressionismus** *der;* ~: expressionism *no art.*

**expressionistisch** *Adj.* expressionist

**exquisit** 1 *Adj.* exquisite
2 *adv.* exquisitely

**extern** *Adj.* external

**extra** *Adv.* (a) (gesondert) ‹*pay*› separately
(b) (zusätzlich, besonders) extra
(c) (eigens) especially

**Extra** *das;* ~s, ~s extra

**Extra-blatt** *das* special edition

**Extrakt** *der;* ~[e]s, ~e extract

**extra-terrestrisch** *Adj.* (Astron.) extraterrestrial

**extravagant** /-va'gant/ *Adj.* flamboyant; flamboyantly furnished ‹*flat*›

**Extravaganz** /-va'gants:/ *die;* ~, ~en
(a) flamboyance
(b) *Pl.* seine ~en his flamboyance *sing.*

**extravertiert** /-vɛr'tiːɐ̯t/ *Adj.* (Psych.) extrovert[ed]

**Extravertiertheit** *die;* ~ (Psych.) extroversion

**Extra-wurst** *die* (fig. ugs.) eine ~ bekommen get special treatment *or* special favours

**extrem** *Adj.* extreme

**Extrem** *das;* ~s, ~e extreme

**Extrem-fall** *der* extreme case

**Extremismus** *der;* ~: extremism

**Extremist** *der;* ~en, ~en, **Extremistin** *die;* ~, ~nen extremist

**extremistisch** *Adj.* extremist

**Extremität** /ɛkstremi'tɛːt/ *die;* ~, ~en
(a) extremity
(b) (das Extremsein) extremeness

**Extrem-wert** *der* (Math.) extremum

**Exzellenz** *die;* ~, ~en Excellency

**Exzentriker** *der;* ~s, ~, **Exzentrikerin** *die;* ~, ~nen eccentric

**exzentrisch** 1 *Adj.* eccentric
2 *adv.* eccentrically

**Exzess, *Exzeß** *der;* Exzesses, Exzesse excess

**exzessiv** /ɛksts:ɛ'siːf/ 1 *Adj.* excessive
2 *adv.* excessively

# Ff

**f, F** /ɛf/ *das;* ~, ~ (a) (Buchstabe) f/F
(b) (Musik) [key of] F

**f.** *Abk.* = **folgend** f.

**Fa.** *Abk.* = **Firma**

**Fabel** *die;* ~, ~n fable; (Kern einer Handlung) plot

**fabelhaft** 1 *Adj.* (ugs.: großartig) fantastic (coll.)
2 *adv.* (ugs.) fantastically (coll.)

**Fabrik** *die;* ~, ~en factory

**Fabrikant** *der;* ~en, ~en manufacturer

**Fabrikat** *das;* ~[e]s, ~e product; (Marke) make

**Fabrikation** *die;* ~: production

**Fabrikations-fehler** *der* manufacturing fault; factory fault

**Fabrik-:** ~besitzer *der,* ~besitzerin *die* factory owner; ~direktor *der,* ~direktorin *die* works manager

**fabrizieren** *tr. V.* (ugs. abwertend) knock together (coll.)

**fabulieren** *itr. V.* invent stories; spin yarns

**Fach** *das;* ~[e]s, Fächer (a) compartment; (für Post) pigeonhole
(b) (Studien~, Unterrichts~) subject; (Wissensgebiet) field; (Berufszweig) trade; ein Mann vom ~: an expert

**Fach-:** ~arbeiter *der,* ~arbeiterin *die* skilled worker; ~arzt *der,* ~ärztin *die* specialist (für in); ~bereich *der* (Hochschulw.) faculty; school; (in der Schule) department

**fächer-übergreifend** *Adj.:*
▶ FACHÜBERGREIFEND

**Fạch-:** ~**frau** die expert; ~**geschäft** das specialist shop; ~**hochschule** die college (offering courses in a special subject)

**fạchlich** Adj. specialist ⟨knowledge, work⟩; technical ⟨problem, explanation, experience⟩

**fạch-, Fạch-:** ~**mann** der; Pl. ~**männer** od. ~**leute** expert; ~**terminus** der specialist/technical term; ~**übergreifend** ① Adj. interdisciplinary ⟨teaching⟩; ② adv. ⟨think, argue⟩ along interdisciplinary lines; ⟨teach⟩ using interdisciplinary methods; ~**werk** das (Bauweise) half-timbered construction; ~**werk·haus** das half-timbered house; ~**zeitschrift** die specialist/technical journal

**Fạckel** die; ~, ~n torch

**fade** Adj. insipid; **ein** ~**r Beigeschmack** (fig.) a flat aftertaste

**Faden** der; ~s, **Fäden** thread; **ein** ~: a piece of thread

**faden·scheinig** Adj. threadbare; flimsy ⟨excuse⟩

**Fagọtt** das; ~[e]s, ~e bassoon

**fähig** Adj. (a) (begabt) able; capable (b) **zu etw.** ~ **sein** be capable of sth.

**Fähigkeit** die; ~, ~en (a) ability; capability; **geistige** ~en intellectual faculties (b) (Imstandesein) ability (**zu** to)

**fahl** Adj. pale; pallid; wan ⟨light⟩

**fahnden** itr. V. search (**nach** for)

**Fahndung** die; ~, ~en search

**Fahne** die; ~, ~n flag

**Fahr·bahn** die carriageway

**Fähr·betrieb** der ferry service; (von mehreren Fähren) ferry services pl.

**Fähre** die; ~, ~n ferry

**fahren** ① unr. itr. V.; mit sein (a) (als Fahrzeuglenker) drive; (mit dem Fahrrad, Motorrad usw.) ride (b) (als Mitfahrer; mit öffentlichem Verkehrsmittel) go (**mit** by); (mit dem Aufzug/der Rolltreppe/der Seilbahn) take the lift (Brit.) or (Amer.) elevator/ escalator/cable car; (per Anhalter) hitch-hike (c) (reisen) go; **in Urlaub** ~: go on holiday (d) (los~) go; leave (e) ⟨motor vehicle, train, lift, cable car⟩ go; ⟨ship⟩ sail; **mein Auto fährt nicht** my car won't go (f) (verkehren) ⟨train etc.⟩ run (g) **etw.** ~ **lassen** (loslassen) let sth. go; (fig.: aufgeben) abandon sth. ② unr. tr. V. (a) (fortbewegen) drive ⟨car, lorry, train, etc.⟩; ride ⟨bicycle, motor cycle⟩ (b) **50/80 km/h** ~: do 50/80 k.p.h.; **hier muss man 50 km/h** ~: you've got to keep to 50 k.p.h. here; sail ⟨boat⟩; **Auto** ~: drive [a car]; **Kahn** od. **Boot/Kanu** ~: go boating/canoeing; **Ski** ~: ski; **U-Bahn** ~: ride on the underground (Brit.) or (Amer.) subway (c) (befördern) take

**Fahrenheit: 70 Grad** ~: 70 degrees Fahrenheit

*****fahren|lassen** ▶ FAHREN 1G

**Fahrer** der; ~s, ~: driver

**Fahrerflucht** die: **wegen** ~: for failing to stop after [being involved in] an accident; ~ **begehen** fail to stop after [being involved in] an accident

**Fahrerin** die; ~, ~nen driver

**Fahr-:** ~**gast** der passenger; ~**geld** das fare

**fahrig** Adj. nervous

**fahr-, Fahr-:** ~**karte** die ticket; ~**karten·automat** der ticket machine; ~**karten·schalter** der ticket window; ~**lässig** ① Adj. negligent ⟨behaviour⟩; ~**lässige Tötung/Körperverletzung** (Rechtsw.) causing death/injury through [culpable] negligence; ② adv. negligently; ~**lehrer** der, ~**lehrerin** die driving instructor

**Fähr·mann** der; Pl. **Fährmänner** od. **Fährleute** ferryman

**fahr-, Fahr-:** ~**plan** der timetable; schedule (Amer.); ~**plan·mäßig** ① Adj. scheduled ⟨departure, arrival⟩; ② adv. ⟨depart, arrive⟩ according to schedule, on time; ~**preis** der fare; ~**prüfung** die driving test; ~**rad** das bicycle; cycle; **mit dem** ~**rad fahren** cycle; ride a bicycle; ~**rad·kurier** der, ~**rad·kurierin** die bicycle or bike messenger; bicycle or bike courier; ~**rad·ständer** der bicycle rack; ~**schein** der ticket; ~**schein·automat** der ticket machine; ~**schein·entwerter** der ticket cancelling machine; ~**schule** die driving school; ~**spur** die traffic lane

**fährst** 2. Pers. Sg. Präsens v. FAHREN

**Fahr-:** ~**stuhl** der lift (Brit.); elevator (Amer.); (für Lasten) hoist; ~**stunde** die driving lesson

**Fahrt** die; ~, ~en (a) journey; **freie** ~ **haben** have a clear run; (Schiffsreise) voyage; (kurze Reise, Ausflug) trip (b) (Geschwindigkeit) **in voller** ~: at full speed

**fährt** 3. Pers. Sg. Präsens v. FAHREN

**Fährte** die trail; **jmds.** ~ **verfolgen** track sb.

**Fahrt·kosten** Pl. (für öffentliche Verkehrsmittel) fare/fares; (für Autoreisen) travel costs

**Fahr·treppe** die escalator

**Fahrt·richtung** die direction; **in** ~ **parken** park in the direction of the traffic; **die** ~ **ändern** change direction

**fahr·tüchtig** Adj. ⟨driver⟩ fit to drive; ⟨vehicle⟩ roadworthy

**Fahrt-:** ~**wind** der airflow; ~**ziel** das destination

**Fahr-:** ~**wasser** das shipping channel; fairway; **in ein gefährliches** ~**wasser geraten** (fig.) get on to dangerous ground; ~**werk** das (Flugw.) undercarriage; ~**zeit** die travelling time; ~**zeug** das vehicle; (Luft~) aircraft; (Wasser~) vessel; ~**zeug·papiere** Pl. vehicle documents pl.

**fair** /fɛːɐ̯/ [1] *Adj.* fair (**gegen** to)
[2] *adv.* fairly
**Fäkalien** /fɛːˈkaːli̯ən/ *Pl.* faeces *pl.*
**Fakten** ▶ FAKTUM
**faktisch** [1] *Adj.* real; actual
[2] *adv.* **das bedeutet** ~ ...: it means in
effect ...
**Faktor** *der;* ~s, ~en (auch Math.) factor
**Faktum** *das;* ~s, **Fakten** fact
**Fakultät** *die;* ~, ~en (Hochschulw.) faculty
**Falke** *der;* ~n, ~n (auch Politik fig.) hawk
**Fall** *der;* ~[e]s, **Fälle** (a) (Sturz) fall; **zu** ~
**kommen** have a fall; **jmdn. zu** ~ **bringen** (fig.)
bring about sb.'s downfall
(b) (das Fallen) descent; **der freie** ~: free fall
(c) (Ereignis; Rechtsw., Med., Grammatik) case; (zu
erwartender Umstand) eventuality; **es ist [nicht]
der** ~: it is [not] the case; **gesetzt den** ~:
assuming; **auf jeden** ~, **in jedem** ~, **auf alle
Fälle** in any case; **auf keinen** ~: on no
account
**Falle** *die;* ~, ~n (auch fig.) trap
**fallen** *unr. itr. V.; mit sein* (a) fall; **jmdn./
etw.** ~ **lassen** drop sb./sth.
(b) (hin~, stürzen) fall [over]; **über einen Stein**
~: trip over a stone
(c) ⟨*prices, light, glance, choice*⟩ fall;
⟨*temperature, water level*⟩ fall, drop; ⟨*fever*⟩
subside; ⟨*shot*⟩ be fired
(d) (im Kampf sterben) die; fall (literary)
**fällen** *tr. V.* (a) fell ⟨*tree, timber*⟩
(b) **ein Urteil** ~ ⟨*judge*⟩ pass sentence; ⟨*jury*⟩
return a verdict
***fallen|lassen** ▶ FALLEN A
**fällig** *Adj.* due
**Fall-obst** *das* windfalls *pl.*
**Fallout** /fɔːlˈʔaʊt/ *der;* ~s, ~s (Kernphysik)
fallout
**falls** *Konj.* (a) (wenn) if
(b) (für den Fall, dass) in case
**Fall-schirm** *der* parachute; **mit dem** ~
**abspringen** (im Notfall) parachute out; (als
Sport) make a [parachute] jump
**falsch** [1] *Adj.* (a) (unecht, imitiert) false ⟨*teeth,
plait*⟩; imitation ⟨*jewellery*⟩
(b) (gefälscht) forged; assumed ⟨*name*⟩
(c) (irrig, fehlerhaft) wrong
[2] *adv.* wrongly; **die Uhr geht** ~: the clock
is wrong
**fälschen** *tr. V.* forge
**Fälscher** *der;* ~s, ~, **Fälscherin** *die;* ~,
~nen forger
**Falschgeld** *das* counterfeit money
**fälschlich** [1] *Adj.* false
[2] *adv.* falsely
**Falsch-meldung** *die* false report
**Fälschung** *die;* ~, ~en fake
**Falt-blatt** *das* leaflet; (in Zeitungen,
Zeitschriften, Büchern) insert
**Falte** *die;* ~, ~n (a) crease
(b) (im Stoff) fold; (mit scharfer Kante) pleat
(c) (Haut~) wrinkle

**falten** [1] *tr. V.* fold; **die Hände** ~: fold one's
hands
[2] *refl. V.* (auch Geol.) fold; ⟨*skin*⟩ become
wrinkled
**Falten-rock** *der* pleated skirt
**Falter** *der;* ~s, ~ (Nacht~) moth; (Tag~)
butterfly
**faltig** (a) *Adj.* ⟨*clothes*⟩ gathered [in folds];
wrinkled ⟨*skin, hands*⟩
(b) (zerknittert) creased
**-fältig** *Adj., adv.* -fold
**Falz** *der;* ~es, ~e fold
**falzen** *tr. V.* fold; seam
**familiär** *Adj.* (a) family ⟨*problems, worries*⟩
(b) (zwanglos) familiar; informal
**Familie** /faˈmiːli̯ə/ *die;* ~, ~n family; ~
**Meyer** the Meyer family
**Familien-:** ~**angehörige** *der/die*
member of the family; ~**feier** *die* family
party; ~**grab** *das* family grave; ~**leben**
*das* family life; ~**name** *der* surname;
~**planung** *die* family planning *no art.;*
~**stand** *der* marital status; ~**vater** *der:*
~**vater sein** be the father of a family; **ein
guter** ~**vater** a good husband and father
**Fan** /fɛn/ *der;* ~s, ~s fan
**Fanatiker** *der;* ~s, ~, **Fanatikerin** *die;*
~, ~nen fanatic; (religiös) fanatic; zealot
**fanatisch** [1] *Adj.* fanatical
[2] *adv.* fanatically
**fanatisieren** *tr. V.* rouse to fanaticism;
**der fanatisierte Mob** the fanatically excited
mob
**fand** *1. u. 3. Pers. Sg. Prät. v.* FINDEN
**Fanfare** *die;* ~, ~n (Signal) fanfare
**Fang** *der;* ~[e]s, **Fänge** (a) (Tier~) trapping;
(von Fischen) catching
(b) (Beute) bag; (von Fischen) catch
**fangen** [1] *unr. tr. V.* catch; capture
⟨*fugitive etc.*⟩; **jmdn./ein Tier gefangen halten**
hold sb. prisoner/keep an animal in
captivity; **jmdn. gefangen nehmen** take sb.
prisoner
[2] *unr. refl. V.* (a) (in eine Falle geraten) be
caught
(b) (wieder in die normale Lage kommen) **sich
[gerade] noch** ~: [just] manage to steady
oneself
**Fang-frage** *die* catch question
**Fantasie** *die;* ~, ~n (a) imagination
(b) (Produkt der ~) fantasy
**fantasie-los** [1] *Adj.* unimaginative
[2] *adv.* unimaginatively
**Fantasielosigkeit** *die;* ~: lack of
imagination; (Eintönigkeit) dullness
**fantasieren** *itr. V.* (a) indulge in
fantasies, fantasize (**von** about)
(b) (Med.: irrereden) talk deliriously.
**fantasievoll** [1] *Adj.* imaginative
[2] *adv.* imaginatively
**fantastisch** [1] *Adj.* (a) fantastic; ⟨*idea*⟩
divorced from reality
(b) (ugs.: großartig) fantastically (coll.)

**f**

**Farb-:** ~**bild** das (Foto) colour photo; ~**dia** das colour slide; ~**drucker** der (DV) colour printer

**Farbe** die; ~, ~n (a) colour (b) (für Textilien) dye; (zum Malen, Anstreichen) paint; ~**n mischen/auftragen** mix/apply paint

**farb·echt** Adj. colour-fast

**färben** 1 tr. V. dye
2 refl. V. change colour; **sich schwarz/rot usw.** ~: turn black/red etc.
3 itr. V. (ugs.: ab~) ⟨material, blouse etc.⟩ run

**-farben** Adj. coloured

**farben-, Farben-:** ~**blind** Adj. colour-blind; ~**froh** Adj. colourful; ~**pracht** die colourful splendour; ~**prächtig** Adj. vibrant with colour postpos.

**Farb-:** ~**fernsehen** das colour television; ~**fernseher** der (ugs.) colour telly (coll.) or television; ~**film** der colour film; ~**foto** das colour photo

**farbig** 1 Adj. (a) coloured (b) (bunt, auch fig.) colourful
2 adv. colourfully

**-farbig** Adj. -coloured

**Farbige** der/die; adj. Dekl. coloured man/woman; Pl. coloured people

**farblich** 1 Adj. in colour postpos.; as regards colour postpos.
2 adv. etw. ~ **abstimmen** match sth. in colour

**farb-, Farb-:** ~**los** Adj. (auch fig.) colourless; clear ⟨varnish⟩; neutral ⟨shoe polish⟩; ~**losigkeit** die; ~~ (auch fig.) colourlessness; ~**stift** der coloured pencil; ~**stoff** der (a) (Med., Biol.) pigment; (b) (für Textilien) dye; (c) (für Lebensmittel) colouring; ~**ton** der; Pl. ~**töne** shade; ~**tupfen,** ~**tupfer** der spot of colour

**Färbung** die; ~, ~en colouring

**Farn** der; ~[e]s, ~e, **Farn·kraut** das fern

**Fasan** der; ~[e]s, ~e[n] pheasant

**Fasching** der; ~s, ~e od. ~s [pre-Lent] carnival

**Faschismus** der; ~: fascism no art.

**Faschist** der; ~en, ~en, **Faschistin** die; ~, ~nen fascist

**faschistisch** Adj. fascist

**faseln** itr. V. (ugs. abwertend) drivel

**Faser** die; ~, ~n fibre

**fasern** itr. V. fray

**Fass, *Faß** das; **Fasses, Fässer** barrel; (Öl~) drum; (kleines Bier~) keg; (kleines Sherry~ usw.) cask; **Bier vom** ~: draught beer; **ein** ~ **ohne Boden** an endless drain on sb.'s resources

**Fassade** die; ~, ~n façade

**fassbar, *faßbar** Adj. (a) tangible ⟨results⟩

(b) (verständlich) comprehensible

**Fass·bier, *Faß·bier** das draught beer; beer on draught

**fassen** 1 tr. V. (a) (greifen) grasp; take hold of
(b) (festnehmen) catch ⟨thief, culprit⟩
(c) (aufnehmen können) ⟨hall, tank⟩ hold
(d) (begreifen) **ich kann es nicht** ~: I cannot take it in
(e) **einen Entschluss** ~: make or take a decision
2 itr. V. (greifen) **nach etw.** ~: reach for sth.; **in etw.** (Akk.) ~: put one's hand in sth.

**fasslich, *faßlich** Adj. comprehensible

**Fasson** /fa'sõ:/ die; ~, ~s style; shape

**Fassung** die; ~, ~en (a) (Form) version (b) (Selbstbeherrschung) composure; **die** ~ **bewahren** keep one's composure; **die** ~ **verlieren** lose one's self-control; **jmdn. aus der** ~ **bringen** upset sb. (c) (für Glühlampen) holder

**fassungs·los** Adj. stunned

**fast** Adv. almost; nearly; ~ **nie** hardly ever

**fasten** itr. V. fast

**Fast·nacht** die carnival; ~ **feiern** celebrate Shrovetide or the carnival

**Fastnachts-:** ~**brauch** der Shrovetide custom; ~**dienstag** der Shrove Tuesday; ~**zug** der carnival procession

**faszinieren** tr. V. fascinate

**faszinierend** 1 Adj. fascinating
2 adv. fascinatingly

**fatal** Adj. (a) (peinlich, misslich) awkward (b) (verhängnisvoll) fatal

**fauchen** itr. V. ⟨cat⟩ hiss; ⟨tiger, person⟩ snarl

**faul** Adj. (a) (verdorben) rotten; bad ⟨food, tooth⟩; foul ⟨water, air⟩ (b) (träge) lazy

**Fäule** die; ~: foulness

**faulen** itr. V.; meist mit sein rot; ⟨water⟩ go foul; ⟨meat, fish⟩ go off

**faulenzen** itr. V. laze about; loaf about (derog.)

**Faulenzer** der; ~s, ~, **Faulenzerin** die; ~, ~nen idler; lazybones sing. (coll.)

**Faulheit** die; ~: laziness

**faulig** Adj. stagnating ⟨water⟩; ~ **schmecken/riechen** taste/smell off

**Fäulnis** die; ~: rottenness

**Faul-:** ~**pelz** der (fam.) lazybones sing. (coll.); ~**tier** das (a) (Zool.) sloth; (b) (ugs.: Faulenzer[in]) ▶ ~**PELZ**

**Fauna** die; ~, **Faunen** (Zool.) fauna

**Faust** die; ~, **Fäuste** fist; **eine** ~ **machen** clench one's fist; **das passt wie die** ~ **aufs Auge** (ugs.) (passt nicht) that clashes horribly; (passt) that matches perfectly; **auf eigene** ~: on one's own initiative

**Fäustchen** das; ~s, ~: **sich** (Dat.) **ins** ~ **lachen** laugh up one's sleeve

---

**faust·dick** *Adj.* as thick as a man's fist *postpos.*; (fig.) barefaced ⟨*lie*⟩

**Fäustling** *der;* ~s, ~e mitten

**Faust·regel** *die* rule of thumb

**Favorit** /favo'riːt/ *der;* ~en, ~en, **Favoritin** *die;* ~, ~nen favourite

**Fax** *das;* ~, ~[e] fax

**Fax·anschluss, \*Fax·anschluß** *der* fax line

**faxen** *tr. V.* fax

**Faxen** *Pl.* (ugs.) fooling around

**Fax-:** ~**gerät** *das* fax machine; ~**nachricht** *der* fax message; ~**nummer** *die* fax number

**Fazit** *das;* ~s, ~s *od.* ~e result

**FCKW** *Abk.* = **Fluorchlorkohlenwasserstoff** CFC

**FCKW-frei** *Adj* CFC-free

**FDP, F.D.P.** *Abk.* = **Freie Demokratische Partei**

**Feature** /'fiːtʃɐ/ *das;* ~s, ~s (Rundf., Ferns., Zeitungsw.) feature

**Februar** *der;* ~[s], ~e February

**fechten** *unr. itr., tr. V.* fence

**Fechter** *der;* ~s, ~, **Fechterin** *die;* ~, ~nen fencer

**Feder** *die;* ~, ~n **(a)** (Vogel~) feather **(b)** (zum Schreiben) nib **(c)** (Technik) spring

**feder-, Feder-:** ~**ball** *der* **(a)** (Spiel) badminton; **(b)** (Ball) shuttlecock; ~**bett** *das* duvet (Brit.); stuffed quilt (Amer.); ~**führend** *Adj.* in charge *postpos.*; ~**halter** *der* fountain pen; ~**leicht** *Adj.* ⟨*person*⟩ as light as a feather; featherweight ⟨*object*⟩; ~**lesen** *das:* nicht viel ~lesen[s] mit jmdm./etw. machen give sb./sth. short shrift

**federn** ① *itr. V.* ⟨*springboard, floor, etc.*⟩ be springy
② *tr. V.* (mit einer Federung versehen) spring; **das Bett ist gut gefedert** the bed is well-sprung

**Federung** *die;* ~, ~en (Kfz-W.) suspension

**Fee** *die;* ~, ~n fairy

**Feedback** /'fiːdbæk/ *das;* ~s, ~s feedback

**Fege·feuer** *das* purgatory

**fegen** ① *tr. V.* **(a)** (bes. nordd.: säubern) sweep **(b)** (schnell entfernen) brush
② *itr. V.* sweep up

**Fehde** *die;* ~, ~n feud

**Fehde·hand·schuh** *der* jmdm. den ~ hinwerfen throw down the gauntlet to sb.

**fehl** *Adv.* ~ am Platz[e] sein be out of place

**Fehl·anzeige** *die:* ~! (ugs.) no chance! (coll.)

**fehlen** *itr. V.* **(a)** (nicht vorhanden sein) **ihm fehlt das Geld** he has no money **(b)** (ausbleiben) be absent

**(d)** (verschwunden sein) be missing; **in der Kasse fehlt Geld** money is missing from the till

**(d)** (vermisst werden) **er/das wird mir ~:** I shall miss him/that

**(e)** (erforderlich sein) be needed; **ihm ~ noch zwei Punkte zum Sieg** he needs only two points to win; **es fehlte nicht viel, und ich wäre eingeschlafen** I all but fell asleep

**(f)** *unpers.* (mangeln) **es fehlt an Lehrern** there is a lack of teachers

**(g)** (krank sein) **was fehlt Ihnen?** what seems to be the matter?; **fehlt dir etwas?** is there something wrong?

**Fehl-:** ~**entscheidung** *die* wrong decision; ~**entwicklung** *die* abortive development

**Fehler** *der;* ~s, ~ **(a)** (Irrtum) mistake; error; (Sport) fault **(b)** (schlechte Eigenschaft) fault

**fehler·frei** *Adj.* faultless

**fehlerhaft** *Adj.* faulty; defective; imperfect ⟨*pronunciation*⟩

**Fehler·quelle** *die* source of error

**fehl-, Fehl-:** ~**geburt** *die* miscarriage; ~**investition** *die* (bes. Wirtsch.) bad investment; ~**planung** *die* [piece of] bad planning *no art.;* ~**schlag** *der* failure; ~|**schlagen** *unr. itr. V.; mit sein* fail; ~**start** *der* (Leichtathletik) false start; ~**tritt** *der* (fig. geh.) slip; ~**urteil** *das* **(a)** (Rechtsw.) **ein ~urteil fällen** ⟨*jury*⟩ return a wrong verdict; ⟨*judge*⟩ pass a wrong judgement **(b)** (falsche Beurteilung) error of judgement; ~**verhalten** *das* (fehlerhaftes Verhalten) incorrect conduct; ~**zündung** *die* (Technik) misfire

**Feier** *die;* ~, ~n **(a)** (Veranstaltung) party; (aus festlichem Anlass) celebration **(b)** (Zeremonie) ceremony

**Feier·abend** *der* (Arbeitsschluss) finishing time; **nach ~:** after work; ~ **machen** finish work

**feierlich** ① *Adj.* ceremonial ⟨*act etc.*⟩; solemn ⟨*silence*⟩
② *adv.* solemnly; ceremoniously

**Feierlichkeit** *die;* ~, ~en **(a)** solemnity **(b)** (Veranstaltung) celebration

**feiern** ① *tr. V.* **(a)** celebrate ⟨*birthday, wedding, etc.*⟩ **(b)** acclaim ⟨*artist, sportsman, etc.*⟩
② *itr. V.* celebrate

**Feier·tag** *der* holiday; **ein gesetzlicher/ kirchlicher ~:** a public holiday/religious festival

**feig[e]** ① *Adj.* cowardly
② *adv.* in a cowardly way

**Feige** *die;* ~, ~n fig

**Feigheit** *die;* ~: cowardice

**Feigling** *der;* ~s, ~e coward

**Feile** *die;* ~, ~n file

**feilen** *tr., itr. V.* file

**feilschen** *itr. V.* haggle (**um** over)

**fein** [1] *Adj.* **(a)** fine; finely-ground ⟨*flour*⟩; finely-granulated ⟨*sugar*⟩ **(b)** (hochwertig) high-quality ⟨*fruit, soap, etc.*⟩; fine ⟨*silver, gold, etc.*⟩; fancy ⟨*cakes, pastries, etc.*⟩ **(c)** (ugs.: erfreulich) great (coll.) **(d) sich ~ machen** (ugs.) dress up [2] *adv.* **~ [he]raus sein** (ugs.) be sitting pretty (coll.)

**Feind** *der;* ~[e]s, ~e, **Feindin** *die;* ~, ~nen enemy

**feindlich** [1] *Adj.* **(a)** hostile **(b)** (Milit.) enemy ⟨*attack, activity*⟩ [2] *adv.* in a hostile manner

**Feindschaft** *die;* ~, ~en enmity

**feind·selig** *Adj.* hostile

**Feind·seligkeit** *die;* ~, ~en hostility; ~en (Milit.) hostilities

**Feinheit** *die;* ~, ~en **(a)** fineness; delicacy **(b)** (Nuance) subtlety

**fein-, Fein-:** ~**kost·geschäft** *das* delicatessen; *\*~|machen* ▶ FEIN 1D; ~**schmecker** *der;* ~~s, ~~, ~**schmeckerin** *die;* ~~, ~~nen gourmet; ~**sinnig** *Adj.* sensitive and subtle; ~**waschmittel** *das* mild detergent

**feist** *Adj.* (meist abwertend) fat

**Feld** *das;* ~[e]s, ~er **(a)** field **(b)** (Sport: Spiel~) pitch; field **(c)** (auf Formularen) box; space; (auf Brettspielen) space; (auf dem Schachbrett) square **(d)** (Tätigkeitsbereich) field; sphere

**Feld-:** ~**herr** *der* (veralt.) commander; ~**marschall** *der* Field Marshal; ~**salat** *der* corn salad; ~**stecher** *der;* ~~s, ~~ binoculars *pl.;* ~**versuch** *der* (Wissensch.) field experiment; ~**webel** *der;* ~~s, ~~ (Milit.) sergeant; ~**weg** *der* path; track; ~**zug** *der* (Milit., fig.) campaign

**Felge** *die;* ~, ~n [wheel] rim

**Fell** *das;* ~[e]s, ~e **(a)** (Haarkleid) fur; (Pferde~, Hunde~, Katzen~) coat; (Schaf~) fleece **(b)** (Material) fur **(c)** (abgezogen) hide; **ein dickes ~ haben** (ugs.) be thick-skinned

**Fels** *der;* ~en, ~en rock

**Felsen** *der;* ~s, ~: rock; (an der Steilküste) cliff

**felsen-, Felsen-:** ~**fest** *Adj.* firm; unshakeable ⟨*opinion, belief*⟩; ~**küste** *die* rocky coast *or* coastline

**felsig** *Adj.* rocky

**Fels-:** ~**spalte** *die* crevice [in the rock]; ~**wand** *die* rock face

**feminin** *Adj.* feminine

**Feminismus** *der;* ~: feminism *no art.*

**Feminist** *der;* ~en, ~en, **Feministin** *die;* ~, ~nen feminist

**Fenchel** *der;* ~s fennel

**Fenster** *das;* ~s, ~: window

**Fenster-:** ~**bank** *die Pl.* ~bänke window sill; ~**laden** *der* [window] shutter; ~**leder** *das* wash leather; ~**platz** *der* window seat; ~**putzer** *der;* ~~s, ~~, ~**putzerin** *die;* ~~, ~~nen window cleaner; ~**rahmen** *der* window frame; ~**scheibe** *die* window pane

**Ferien** /'fe:riən/ *Pl.* holiday[s *pl.*] (Brit.); vacation (Amer.); **in die ~ fahren** go on holiday/vacation; **~ haben** have a *or* be on holiday/vacation

**Ferien-:** ~**arbeit** *die* vacation work; **eine ~arbeit** a vacation job; ~**haus** *das* holiday house (Brit.); vacation house (Amer.); ~**job** *der* vacation job; ~**ort** *der* holiday resort (Brit.); vacation resort (Amer.); ~**paradies** *das* holiday[maker's] paradise (Brit.); vacationer['s] paradise (Amer.); ~**wohnung** *die* holiday flat *or* apartment (Brit.); vacation apartment (Amer.)

**Ferkel** *das;* ~s, ~: piglet

**fern** [1] *Adj.* distant; **jmdn./etw. ~ halten** keep sb./sth. away [2] *adv.* **~ von der Heimat** far from home [3] *Präp. mit Dat.* (geh.) far [away] from

**fern-, Fern-:** ~**bedienung** *die* remote control; ~**|bleiben** *unr. itr. V.; mit sein* (geh.) stay away

**Ferne** *die;* ~, ~n distance

**ferner** *Adv.* furthermore

**fern-, Fern-:** ~**fahrer** *der,* ~**fahrerin** *die* long-distance lorry driver (Brit.) *or* (Amer.) trucker; ~**flug** *der* long-distance *or* long-haul flight; ~**gelenkt** *Adj.* remote-controlled; ~**gespräch** *das* long-distance call; ~**gesteuert** *Adj.* ▶ ~GELENKT; ~**glas** *das* binoculars *pl.;* *\*~|halten* ▶ FERN 1; ~**heizung** *die* district heating system; ~**lenkung** *die* remote control; ~**licht** *das* (Kfz-W.) full beam; ~**melde·amt** *das* telephone exchange; ~**ost: in/aus/nach ~ost** in/from/to the Far East; ~**rohr** *das* telescope; ~**ruf** *der* telephone number; ~**schreiben** *das* telex [message]; ~**schreiber** *der* telex [machine]

**Fernseh-:** ~**antenne** *die* television aerial (Brit.) *or* (Amer.) antenna; ~**apparat** *der* television [set]

**fern|sehen** *unr. itr. V.* watch television

**Fern·sehen** *das;* ~s television; **im ~:** on television

**Fern·seher** *der;* ~s, ~ (ugs.) telly (Brit. coll.); TV

**Fernseh-:** ~**gebühren** *Pl.* television licence fee; ~**gerät** *das* television [set]; ~**journalist** *der,* ~**journalistin** *die* television reporter; ~**kanal** *der* television channel; ~**programm** *das* **(a)** (Sendungen) television programmes *pl.;* **(b)** (Kanal) television channel; **(c)** (Blatt, Programmheft) television [programme] guide; ~**publikum** *das* viewing public; ~**sender** *der*

---

\*old spelling - see note on page xiv

television transmitter; **∼sendung** *die* television programme; **∼serie** *die* television series; **∼spiel** *das* television play; **∼zuschauer** *der*, **∼zuschauerin** *die* television viewer

**Fern·sicht** *die* (Aussicht) view; (gute Sicht) visibility

**Fern·sprecher** *der* telephone

**Fernsprech-:** **∼gebühren** *Pl.* telephone charges; **∼teilnehmer** *der*, **∼teilnehmerin** *die* telephone subscriber; telephone customer (Amer.)

**Fern-:** **∼steuerung** *die* (Technik) remote control; **∼straße** *die* major road; **∼studium** *das* correspondence course; ≈ Open University course (Brit.); **∼unterricht** *der* correspondence courses *pl.*; **∼verkehr** *der* long-distance traffic; **∼zug** *der* long-distance train

**Ferse** *die;* ∼, ∼n heel

**fertig** *Adj.* (a) finished ⟨*manuscript, picture, etc.*⟩; **das Essen ist ∼:** lunch/dinner *etc.* is ready; [mit etw.] ∼ sein/werden have finished/finish [sth.]; etw. ∼ machen finish sth.

(b) (bereit, verfügbar) ready (**zu, für** for) (c) (ugs.: erschöpft) shattered (coll.); jmdn. ∼ machen (erschöpfen) wear sb. out; (schikanieren) wear sb. down; (deprimieren) get sb. down (d) etw. ∼ bekommen *od.* bringen *od.* (ugs.) kriegen manage sth; etw. ∼ stellen complete sth.

**fertig-, Fertig-:** **∼bau** *der; Pl.* ∼∼ten prefabricated building; **∼bauweise** *die* prefabricated construction; prefabrication; ***∼bringen** ▶ FERTIG D

**fertigen** *tr. V.* make

**Fertig-:** **∼gericht** *das* ready-to-serve meal; **∼haus** *das* prefabricated house; prefab (coll.)

**Fertigkeit** *die;* ∼, ∼en skill

**fertig-, Fertig-:** ***∼machen** ▶ FERTIG A, C; ***∼stellen** ▶ FERTIG D; **∼stellung** *die* completion

**Fertigung** *die;* ∼: production; manufacture

**Fessel** *die;* ∼, ∼n fetter; shackle; (Kette) chain

**fesseln** *tr. V.* (a) tie up; **ans Bett/ans Haus/ an den Rollstuhl gefesselt sein** (fig.) be confined to [one's] bed/tied to the house/ confined to a wheelchair (b) (faszinieren) ⟨*book*⟩ grip; ⟨*work, person*⟩ fascinate

**fesselnd** ① *Adj.* compelling ② *adv.* compellingly

**fest** ① *Adj.* (a) (nicht flüssig od. gasförmig) solid (b) (fest) firm ⟨*bandage*⟩; sound ⟨*sleep*⟩; sturdy ⟨*shoes*⟩; strong ⟨*fabric*⟩; solid ⟨*house, shell*⟩; steady ⟨*voice*⟩; **der ∼en Überzeugung sein, dass ...:** be of the firm opinion that ... (c) (dauernd) permanent ⟨*address*⟩; fixed ⟨*income*⟩

② *adv.* (a) ⟨*tie, grip*⟩ tight[ly]

(b) (ugs. auch ∼e) ⟨*work*⟩ with a will; ⟨*eat*⟩ heartily; ⟨*sleep*⟩ soundly (c) ⟨*believe, be convinced*⟩ firmly; **sich auf jmdn./etw.** ∼ **verlassen** rely one hundred per cent on sb./sth. (d) (endgültig) firmly; **etw.** ∼ **vereinbaren** come to a firm arrangement about sth. (e) (auf Dauer) permanently; ∼ **befreundet sein** be close friends; (als Paar) be going steady

**Fest** *das;* ∼[e]s, ∼e (a) celebration; (Party) party (b) (Feiertag) festival; **frohes** ∼! happy Christmas/Easter!

**fest-, Fest-:** **∼akt** *der* ceremony; **∼|binden** *unr. tr. V.* tie [up]; **∼|bleiben** *unr. itr. V.;* mit sein stand firm; **∼essen** *das* banquet; **∼|fahren** *unr. itr., refl. V.* (itr. V. mit sein) get stuck; (fig.) get bogged down; **∼|halten** ① *unr. tr. V.* (a) (halten, packen) hold on to; (b) (nicht weiterleiten) withhold ⟨*letter, parcel, etc.*⟩; (c) (verhaftet haben) hold, detain ⟨*suspect*⟩; ② *unr. refl. V.* **sich an** jmdm./etw. **∼halten** hold on to sb./sth.

**festigen** ① *tr. V.* strengthen; consolidate ⟨*position*⟩ ② *refl. V.* ⟨*friendship, ties*⟩ become stronger

**Festival** /ˈfɛstivəl/ *das;* ∼s, ∼s festival

**fest-, Fest-:** **∼|kleben** *tr., itr. V.; mit sein* stick (**an** + *Dat.* to); **∼land** *das* (Kontinent) continent; (im Gegensatz zu den Inseln) mainland; **∼|legen** *tr. V.* (a) fix ⟨*time, deadline, price*⟩; arrange ⟨*programme*⟩; (b) (verpflichten) **sich [auf etw. (*Akk.*)]** ∼legen [lassen] commit oneself [to sth.]; jmdn. [auf etw. (*Akk.*)] ∼legen tie sb. down [to sth.]

**festlich** ① *Adj.* festive ⟨*atmosphere*⟩; formal ⟨*dress*⟩ ② *adv.* festively; formally

**fest-, Fest-:** **∼|machen** *tr. V.* (a) (befestigen) fix; (b) (fest vereinbaren) arrange ⟨*meeting etc.*⟩; **∼|nageln** *tr. V.* (a) (befestigen) nail (**an** + *Dat.* to); (b) (ugs.: festlegen) jmdn. [auf etw. (*Akk.*)] ∼nageln tie sb. down [to sth.]; **∼nahme** *die;* ∼∼, ∼∼n arrest; **bei seiner ∼nahme** when he was/is arrested; **∼|nehmen** *unr. tr. V.* arrest; **∼platte** *die* (DV) fixed disk; **∼rede** *die* speech; **∼|schnallen** *tr. V.* tie (**an** + *Dat.* to); **∼|sitzen** *unr. itr. V.* be stuck; **∼|stehen** *unr. itr. V.* ⟨*order, appointment, etc.*⟩ have been fixed; ⟨*decision*⟩ be definite; ⟨*fact*⟩ be certain; **∼|stellen** *tr. V.* (a) establish ⟨*identity, age, facts*⟩; (b) (wahrnehmen) detect; diagnose ⟨*illness*⟩; **∼stellung** *die* (a) establishment; (b) (Wahrnehmung) realization; **die ∼stellung machen, dass ...:** realize that ...

**Fest·tag** *der* holiday; (Ehrentag) special day

**Festung** *die;* ∼, ∼en fortress

**fest-, Fest-:** **∼zeit** *die* holiday (Brit.) *or* (Amer.) vacation [period]; **∼zelt** *das* marquee; **∼|ziehen** *unr. tr. V.* pull tight

**Fete** *die;* ∼, ∼n (ugs.) party

**fett** 1 *Adj.* **(a)** fatty ⟨*food*⟩; ~**er Speck** fat bacon
**(b)** (sehr dick) fat
**(c)** (Druckw.) bold
2 *adv.* **(a)** ~ **essen** eat fatty foods
**(b)** ~ **gedruckt** bold
**Fett** *das;* ~[e]s, ~e fat; ~ **ansetzen** ⟨*animal*⟩ fatten up; ⟨*person*⟩ put on weight
**fett-, Fett-:** ~**arm** *Adj.* low-fat ⟨*food*⟩; low in fat *pred.;* ~**auge** *das* speck of fat; ~**creme** *die* enriched [skim] cream; ~**druck** *der* bold type; ~**fleck[en]** *der* grease mark; *\*~**gedruckt** ▶ FETT 2B; ~**gehalt** *der* fat content
**fettig** *Adj.* greasy
**fett-, Fett-:** ~**leibig** *Adj.* obese; ~**leibigkeit** *die;* ~~: obesity; ~**näpfchen** *das:* ins ~**näpfchen treten** (scherzh.) put one's foot in it; ~**polster** *das* subcutaneous fat *no indef. art.;* fat pad; ~**reich** *Adj.* high-fat; ~**säure** *die* (Chemie) fatty acid; ~**wanst** *der* (salopp abwertend) fatso (coll.)
**Fetus** *der;* ~ *od.* ~ses, ~se *od.* Feten (Med.) foetus
**Fetzen** *der;* ~s, ~: scrap
**feucht** *Adj.* damp; humid ⟨*climate*⟩
**feucht·fröhlich** *Adj.* (ugs. scherzh.) merry ⟨*company*⟩; boozy (coll.) ⟨*evening*⟩
**Feuchtigkeit** *die* moisture
**Feuchtigkeits·creme** *die* (Kosmetik) moisturizing cream; moisturizer
**feucht-:** ~**kalt** *Adj.* cold and damp; ~**warm** *Adj.* muggy
**feudal** *Adj.* **(a)** feudal ⟨*system*⟩
**(b)** aristocratic ⟨*regiment etc.*⟩
**(c)** (ugs.: vornehm) plush ⟨*hotel etc.*⟩
**Feuer** *das;* ~s, ~ **(a)** fire; jmdm. ~ **geben** give sb. a light
**(b)** (Brand) fire; blaze; ~**!** fire!
**(c)** (Milit.) das ~ **einstellen** cease fire
**feuer-, Feuer-:** ~**alarm** *der* fire alarm; ~**eifer** *der* enthusiasm; zest; ~**fest** *Adj.* heat-resistant ⟨*dish, plate*⟩; fireproof ⟨*material*⟩; ~**gefährlich** *Adj.* [in]flammable; ~**holz** *das* firewood; ~**leiter** *die* (bei Häusern) fire escape; (beim ~wehrauto) [fireman's] ladder; ~**löscher** *der;* ~~s, ~~: fire extinguisher; ~**melder** *der;* ~~s, ~~: fire alarm
**feuern** 1 *tr. V.* **(a)** (ugs.: entlassen) fire (coll.); sack (coll.)
**(b)** (ugs.: schleudern, werfen) fling
2 *itr. V.* (Milit.) fire (**auf** + *Akk.* at)
**feuer-, Feuer-:** ~**rot** *Adj.* fiery red; ~**schlucker** *der,* ~**schluckerin** *die;* ~~, ~~**nen** fire-eater; ~**sirene** *die* fire siren; ~**stein** *der* flint; ~**versicherung** *die* fire insurance; ~**waffe** *die* firearm; ~**wehr** *die;* ~~, ~~**en** fire service; ~**wehr·auto** *das* fire engine; ~**wehr·mann** *der;* *Pl.* ~**männer** *od.*

~**leute** fireman; ~**wehr·wagen** *der* fire engine; ~**werk** *das* firework display; (~werkskörper) fireworks *pl.;* ~**werks·körper** *der* firework; ~**zeug** *das* lighter
**Feuilleton** /fœjə'tõ:/ *das;* ~s, ~s arts section
**feurig** *Adj.* fiery
**ff.** *Abk.* = **folgende [Seiten]** ff.
**Ffm.** *Abk.* = **Frankfurt am Main**
**Fiaker** /'fjakɐ/ *der;* ~s, ~ (österr.) cab
**Fiasko** *das;* ~s, ~s fiasco
**Fibel** *die;* ~, ~n reader; primer
**ficht** /fɪçt/ *Imperativ Sg. u. 3. Pers. Sg. Präsens v.* FECHTEN
**Fichte** *die;* ~, ~n spruce
**ficken** *tr., itr. V.* (vulg.) fuck (coarse)
**fick[e]rig** *Adj.* (landsch.: nervös) nervous
**fidel** *Adj.* (ugs.) jolly
**Fieber** *das;* ~s [high] temperature; (über 38°C) fever; ~ **haben** have a [high] temperature/a fever; **bei jmdm.** ~ **messen** take sb.'s temperature
**fieber·frei** *Adj.* ⟨*person*⟩ free from fever
**fieberhaft** *Adj.* feverish
**fieberig** *Adj.* feverish
**fiebern** *itr. V.* have a temperature
**Fieber·thermometer** *das* [clinical] thermometer
**fiebrig** *Adj.* feverish
**Fiedel** *die;* ~, ~n (veralt., scherzh.) fiddle
**fiel** 1 *u. 3. Pers. Sg. Prät. v.* FALLEN
**fiepen** *itr. V.* ⟨*dog*⟩ whimper; ⟨*bird*⟩ cheep
**fies** 1 *Adj.* (ugs.) nasty ⟨*person, character*⟩
2 *adv.* in a nasty way
**Figur** *die;* ~, ~en **(a)** (einer Frau) figure; (eines Mannes) physique
**(b)** (Bildwerk) figure
**(c)** (geometrisches Gebilde) shape
**(d)** (Spielstein) piece
**(e)** (Persönlichkeit) figure
**(f)** (literarische Gestalt) character
**fiktiv** *Adj.* fictitious
**Filet** /fi'le:/ *das;* ~s, ~s fillet
**Filiale** *die;* ~, ~n branch
**Filigran** *das;* ~s, ~e filigree
**Film** *der;* ~[e]s, ~e **(a)** (Fot.) film
**(b)** (Kino~) film; movie (Amer. coll.)
**Filme·macher** *der,* **Filme·macherin** *die* film-maker
**filmen** *tr., itr. V.* film
**Film-:** ~**festival** *das* film festival; ~**festspiele** *Pl.* film festival *sing.;* ~**industrie** *die* film industry; ~**kamera** *die* film camera; (Schmalfilmkamera) cine camera; ~**kunst** *die* cinematic art; ~**musik** *die* film music; (eines einzelnen ~s) theme music; ~**plakat** *das* film poster; ~**produzent** *der,* ~**produzentin** *die* film producer; ~**regisseur** *der,* ~**regisseurin** *die* film director;

~**schauspieler** *der,*
~**schauspielerin** *die* film actor; ~**star**
*der* film star

**Filter** *der,* ~s, ~: filter

**filtern** *tr. V.* filter

**Filter-:** ~**papier** *das* filter paper;
~**zigarette** *die* [filter-]tipped cigarette

**Filz** *der;* ~es, ~e felt

**filzen** *tr. V.* (ugs.: durchsuchen) search ⟨*room,
car, etc.*⟩; frisk ⟨*person*⟩

**Filz·stift** *der* felt-tip pen

**Fimmel** *der;* ~s, ~: einen ~ für etw. haben
(ugs. abwertend) have a thing about sth. (coll.)

**Finale** *das;* ~s, ~[s] (a) (Sport) final
(b) finale

**Finalist** *der;* ~en, ~en, **Finalistin** *die;*
~, ~nen (Sport) finalist

**Finanz** *die;* ~: finance *no art.*

**Finanz-:** ~**amt** *das* (a) (Behörde) ≈ Inland
Revenue; (b) (Gebäude) tax office;
~**beamte** *der,* ~**beamtin** *die* tax officer

**Finanzen** *Pl.* finances

**finanziell** /finan'tsi̯ɛl/ *Adj.* financial

**finanzieren** *tr. V.* finance

**Finanzierung** *die;* ~, ~en financing

**finanz-, Finanz-:** ~**kraft** *die* financial
strength; ~**kräftig** *Adj.* financially
powerful; ~**lage** *die* financial situation;
~**minister** *der,* ~**ministerin** *die*
minister of finance; ~**politik** *die* (des
Staates, eines Unternehmens) financial policy;
(allgemeine) politics of finance

**Findel·kind** *das* foundling

**finden** *unr. tr. V.* (a) find
(b) Freunde ~: make friends
(c) (einschätzen, beurteilen) etw. gut/richtig ~:
think sth. is good/right; wie ~ Sie dieses
Bild? what do you think of this painting?

**Finder** *der;* ~s, ~: finder

**Finder·lohn** *der* reward [for finding sth.]

**findig** *Adj.* resourceful

**Findling** *der;* ~s, ~e (a) (Findelkind)
foundling
(b) (Geol.) erratic block

**fing** *1. u. 3. Pers. Sg. Prät. v.* FANGEN

**Finger** *der;* ~s, ~: finger; lange ~ machen
(ugs.) get itchy fingers

**Finger-:** ~**abdruck** *der* fingerprint;
~**fertigkeit** *die* dexterity;
~**handschuh** *der* glove [with fingers];
~**hut** *der* thimble; ~**kuppe** *die* fingertip

**fingern** *itr. V.* fiddle; an etw. (*Dat.*) ~:
fiddle with sth.; nach etw. ~: fumble
[around] for sth.

**Finger-:** ~**nagel** *der* fingernail; ~**spitze**
*die* fingertip; ~**spitzen·gefühl** *das*
feeling

**fingieren** *tr. V.* fake; ein fingierter Name a
false name

**Fink** *der;* ~en, ~en finch

**Finne** *der;* ~n, ~n, **Finnin** *die;* ~, ~nen
Finn

**finnisch** *Adj.* Finnish

**Finnland** (*das*); ~s Finland

**finster** 1 *Adj.* dark; dimly-lit ⟨*pub,
district*⟩
2 *adv.* jmdn. ~ ansehen give sb. a black
look

**Finsternis** *die;* ~, ~se darkness; (auch bibl.,
fig.) dark

**Finte** *die;* ~, ~n trick; jmdn. durch eine ~
täuschen deceive sb. by trickery

**Firlefanz** *der;* ~es (ugs. abwertend) frippery;
trumpery

**firm** *Adj.* in etw. (*Dat.*) ~ sein be well up in
sth.

**Firma** *die;* ~, Firmen firm; company

**Firmen-:** ~**inhaber** *der,* ~**inhaberin**
*die* owner of the/a company; ~**schild** *das*
company's name plate; ~**zeichen** *das*
trademark

**Firmung** *die;* ~, ~en confirmation

**First** *der;* ~[e]s, ~e ridge

**Fisch** *der;* ~[e]s, ~e (a) fish; [fünf] ~e
fangen catch [five] fish; kleine ~e (fig.) small
fry
(b) (Astrol.) die ~e Pisces; er ist [ein] ~: he is
a Piscean

**fischen** 1 *tr. V.* (a) fish for
(b) (ugs.) etw. aus etw. ~: fish sth. out of sth.
2 *itr. V.* fish; nach etw. ~: fish for sth.

**Fischer** *der;* ~s, ~: fisherman

**Fischer-:** ~**boot** *das* fishing boat; ~**dorf**
*das* fishing village

**Fischerei** *die;* ~: fishing

**Fischerin** *die;* ~, ~nen fisherwoman

**Fisch-:** ~**fang** *der:* vom ~fang leben
make a/one's living by fishing; auf ~fang
gehen go fishing; ~**geschäft** *das*
fishmonger's [shop] (Brit.); fish store (Amer.);
~**grät[en]·muster** *das* (Textilw.)
herringbone pattern; ~**industrie** *die*
fishing industry; ~**konserve** *die* canned
fish; ~**kutter** *der* fishing trawler;
~**stäbchen** *das* (Kochk.) fish finger;
~**sterben** *das* death of the fish

**Fiskus** *der;* ~, Fisken *od.* ~se Government
(*as managing the State finances*)

**Fitness·zentrum** *das* fitness centre

**Fittich** *der;* ~[e]s, ~e (dichter.) wing

**fix** 1 *Adj.* (ugs.) quick; ein ~er Bursche a
bright lad; ~ und fertig quite finished; (völlig
erschöpft) completely shattered (coll.)
2 *adv.* (ugs.) quickly; mach ~! hurry up!

**fixen** *itr. V.* (Drogenjargon) fix (sl.)

**Fixer** *der;* ~s, ~, **Fixerin** *die;* ~, ~nen
(Drogenjargon) fixer

**fixieren** *tr. V.* (a) fix one's gaze on; jmdn.
scharf ~: gaze sharply at sb.
(b) (geh.: schriftlich niederlegen) take down

**Fix·stern** *der* (Astron.) fixed star

**Fjord** /fjɔrt/ *der;* ~[e]s, ~e fiord

**FKK** /ɛf ka: 'ka:/ Abk.
= **Freikörperkultur** nudism no art.;
naturism no art.

**FKK-Strand** der nudist beach

**flach** Adj. (a) flat
(b) (niedrig) low
(c) (nicht tief) shallow ‹water, dish›

**Fläche** die; ~, ~n (a) area
(b) (Ober~) surface
(c) (Geom.) area; (einer dreidimensionalen Figur) side

**Flächen-:** ~**inhalt** der area; ~**maß** das unit of square measure; ~**staat** der territorial state

**flach, Flach-:** ~|**fallen** itr. V.; mit sein (ugs.) ‹trip› fall through; ‹event› be cancelled; ~**land** das lowland

**Flachs** der; ~es flax

**flachsen** itr. V. mit jmdm. ~ (ugs.) joke with sb.

**Flach·zange** die flat tongs pl.

**flackern** itr. V. flicker

**Fladen** der; ~s, ~: flat, round unleavened cake made with oat or barley flour

**Flagge** die; ~, ~n flag

**flaggen** itr. V. put out the flags

**flambieren** tr. V. (Kochk.) flambé

**Flamme** die; ~, ~n (a) flame
(b) (Brennstelle) burner

**Flanell** der; ~s, ~e flannel

**flanieren** itr. V.; mit Richtungsangabe mit sein stroll

**Flanke** die; ~, ~n (a) (Weiche) flank
(b) (Ballspiele: Vorlage) centre
(c) (Teil des Spielfeldes) wing

**Flasche** die; ~, ~n bottle; eine ~ Wein a bottle of wine; dem Kind die ~ geben feed the baby

**Flaschen-:** ~**bier** das bottled beer; ~**öffner** der bottle-opener; ~**post** die message in a/the bottle; ~**zug** der block and tackle

**flatterhaft** Adj. fickle

**flattern** itr. V.; mit Richtungsangabe mit sein flutter

**flau** Adj. (a) slack ‹breeze›
(b) (leicht übel) queasy ‹feeling›

**Flaum** der; ~[e]s fuzz

**Flausch** der; ~[e]s, ~e brushed wool

**flauschig** Adj. fluffy

**Flause** die; ~, ~n; meist Pl. (ugs.) er hat nur ~n im Kopf he can never think of anything sensible

**Flaute** die; ~, ~n (a) (Seemannsspr.) calm
(b) (Kaufmannsspr.) fall[-off] in trade

**Flechte** die; ~, ~n (a) (Bot.) lichen
(b) (Med.) eczema

**flechten** unr. tr. V. plait ‹hair›; weave ‹basket, mat›

**Fleck** der; ~[e]s, ~e (a) stain

(b) (andersfarbige Stelle) patch

**flecken** itr. V. stain

**flecken·los** ①Adj. spotless
②adv. spotlessly

**Fleck·entferner** der stain or spot remover

**fleckig** Adj. stained; blotchy ‹face, skin›

**Fleder·maus** die bat

**Flegel** der; ~s, ~ (abwertend) lout

**Flegelei** die; ~, ~en (abwertend) loutish behaviour

**flegelhaft** Adj. (abwertend) loutish

**flegeln** refl. V. (abwertend) sich auf ein Sofa/in einen Sessel ~: flop on to a sofa/into an armchair

**flehen** /'fle:ən/ itr. V. plead (um for)

**Fleisch** das; ~[e]s (a) flesh; ~ fressend (Biol.) carnivorous
(b) (Nahrungsmittel) meat

**Fleisch·brühe** die bouillon; consommé

**Fleischer** der; ~s, ~: butcher

**Fleischerei** die; ~, ~en butcher's shop

**fleisch·fressend** Adj. carnivorous

**Fleisch·fresser** der (Biol.) carnivore

**fleischig** Adj. plump ‹hands, face›; fleshy ‹leaf, fruit›

**Fleisch-:** ~**käse** der; ~~s, ~~: meat loaf; ~**klößchen** das; ~~s, ~~: small meat ball; ~**pastete** die (Kochk.) pâté; ~**salat** der (Kochk.) meat salad; ~**vergiftung** die food poisoning [from meat]; ~**waren** Pl. meat products; ~**wolf** der mincer; ~**wunde** die flesh wound; ~**wurst** die pork sausage

**Fleiß** der; ~es hard work; (Eigenschaft) diligence

**fleißig** ①Adj. hard-working
②adv. hard; ~ lernen learn as much as one can

**flennen** itr. V. (ugs.) blubber

**fletschen** tr., itr. V. die Zähne od. mit den Zähnen ~: bare one's teeth

**Fleurop** Ⓦ /'flɔy:rɔp/ die Interflora ®

**flexibel** ①Adj. flexible
②adv. flexibly

**flicht** Imperativ Sg. u. 3. Pers. Sg. Präsens v. FLECHTEN

**flicken** tr. V. mend; repair ‹engine, cable›

**Flicken** der; ~s, ~: patch

**Flick-:** ~**werk** das (abwertend) botched-up job; ~**zeug** das repair kit

**Flieder** der; ~s, ~: lilac

**Fliege** die; ~, ~n (a) fly
(b) (Schleife) bow tie

**fliegen** ①unr. itr. V.; mit sein (a) fly
(b) (ugs.: fallen) vom Pferd/Fahrrad ~: fall off a/the horse/bicycle
(c) (ugs.: entlassen werden) get the sack (coll.); von der Schule ~: be chucked out [of the school] (coll.)
②unr. tr. V. fly

---

**Fliegen-:** ~**draht** *der* fly screen;
~**fenster** *das* wire-mesh window;
~**gewicht** *das* (Schwerathletik) flyweight;
~**pilz** *der* fly agaric
**Flieger** *der;* ~**s,** ~: pilot
**Flieger·alarm** *der* air-raid warning
**Fliegerin** *die;* ~, ~**nen** pilot
**fliegerisch** *Adj.* aeronautical
**fliehen** /ˈfliːən/ *unr. itr. V.; mit sein* flee
(**vor** + *Dat.* from); (aus dem Gefängnis usw.)
escape (**aus** from); **ins Ausland/über die
Grenze** ~: flee the country/escape over the
border
**Flieh·kraft** *die* (Physik) centrifugal force
**Fliese** *die;* ~, ~**n** tile
**Fließ·band** *das* conveyor belt; **am** ~
**arbeiten** *od.* (ugs.) **stehen** work on the
assembly line
**fließen** *unr. itr. V.; mit sein* flow; ~**des
Wasser** running water; **eine Sprache** ~**d
sprechen** speak a language fluently
**Flimmer·kasten** *der,* **Flimmer·kiste**
*die* (ugs.) telly (coll.); box (coll.)
**flimmern** *itr. V.* shimmer
**flink** ① *Adj.* nimble ⟨*fingers*⟩; sharp ⟨*eyes*⟩;
quick ⟨*hands*⟩
② *adv.* quickly
**Flinkheit** *die;* ~ ▶ FLINK 1: nimbleness;
sharpness; quickness
**Flinte** *die;* ~, ~**n** shotgun; **die** ~ **ins Korn
werfen** (fig.) throw in the towel
**Flirt** *der;* ~**s,** ~**s** flirtation
**flirten** *itr. V.* flirt
**Flittchen** *das;* ~**s,** ~ (ugs. abwertend)
floozie
**Flitter** *der;* ~**s** frippery; trumpery
**Flitter·wochen** *Pl.* honeymoon *sing.*
**flitzen** *itr. V.; mit sein* (ugs.) shoot; dart
**Flitzer** *der;* ~**s,** ~ (ugs.) sporty job (coll.)
**floaten** /ˈfloʊtn̩/ *tr., itr. V.* (Wirtsch.) float
**flocht** *1. u. 3. Pers. Sg. Prät. v.* FLECHTEN
**Flocke** *die;* ~, ~**n** (a) flake
(b) (Staub~) piece of fluff
**flockig** *Adj.* fluffy
**flog** *1. u. 3. Pers. Sg. Prät. v.* FLIEGEN
**floh** *1. u. 3. Pers. Sg. Prät. v.* FLIEHEN
**Floh** *der;* ~**[e]s,** Flöhe flea
**Floh-:** ~**markt** *der* flea market; ~**zirkus**
*der* flea circus
**Flora** *die;* ~, Floren flora
**Florett** *das;* ~**[e]s,** ~**e** foil
**florieren** *itr. V.* flourish
**Florist** *der;* ~**en,** ~**en,** **Floristin** *die;* ~,
~**nen** [qualified] flower arranger
**Floskel** *die;* ~, ~**n** cliché
**floss** *1. u. 3. Pers. Sg. Prät. v.* FLIESSEN
**Floß** *das;* ~**es,** Flöße raft
**Flosse** *die;* ~, ~**n** (a) (Zool., Flugw.) fin
(b) (zum Tauchen) flipper
**flößen** *tr., itr. V.* float

**Flößer** *der;* ~**s,** ~: raftsman
**Flößerin** *die;* ~, ~**nen** raftswoman
**Flöte** *die;* ~, ~**n** flute; (Block~) recorder
**flöten** ① *itr. V.* ⟨*bird*⟩ flute; ~ **gehen** (ugs.)
⟨*money*⟩ go down the drain; ⟨*time*⟩ be wasted
② *tr. V.* whistle
*****flöten|gehen** ▶ FLÖTEN 1
**flott** ① *Adj.* (a) (schwungvoll) lively
(b) (schick) smart
② *adv.* ⟨*work*⟩ quickly; ⟨*dance, write*⟩ in a
lively manner; ⟨*be dressed*⟩ smartly
**Flotte** *die;* ~, ~**n** fleet
**flott|machen** *tr. V.* refloat ⟨*ship*⟩; get
⟨*car*⟩ back on the road
**Flöz** *das;* ~**es,** ~**e** (Bergbau) seam
**Fluch** *der;* ~**[e]s,** Flüche curse; oath
**fluchen** *itr. V.* curse; swear
**Flucht** *die;* ~: flight
**flucht·artig** ① *Adj.* hurried; hasty
② *adv.* hurriedly; hastily
**flüchten** ① *itr. V.; mit sein* **vor jmdm./etw.**
~: flee from sb./sth.; **vor der Polizei** ~: run
away from the police
② *refl. V.* take refuge
**Flucht-:** ~**fahrzeug** *das* getaway vehicle;
~**helfer** *der,* ~**helferin** *die* person who
aids/aided an/the escape; ~**hilfe** *die* aiding
an escape
**flüchtig** ① *Adj.* (a) fugitive
(b) cursory; superficial ⟨*insight*⟩
② *adv.* (a) (oberflächlich) cursorily
(b) (eilig) hurriedly
**Flüchtigkeit** *die;* ~, ~**en** cursoriness
**Flüchtigkeits·fehler** *der* slip
**Flüchtling** *der;* ~**s,** ~**e** refugee
**Flüchtlings-:** ~**elend** *das* hardship
among refugees; ~**hilfe** *die* refugee relief;
(Organisation) refugee relief agency; ~**lager**
*das* refugee camp; ~**treck** *der* long stream
of refugees
**Flucht·weg** *der* escape route
**Flug** *der;* ~**[e]s,** Flüge flight
**Flug-:** ~**bahn** *die* trajectory; ~**blatt** *das*
pamphlet; leaflet
**Flügel** *der;* ~**s,** ~ (a) wing
(b) (Klavier) grand piano
**Flügel·mutter** *die; Pl.* ~**n** wing nut
**Flug·gast** *der* [air] passenger
**flügge** *Adj.* fully-fledged
**Flug-:** ~**gesellschaft** *die* airline;
~**hafen** *der* airport; ~**hafen·steuer** *die*
airport tax; ~**linie** *die* (a) (Strecke) air
route; (b) (Gesellschaft) airline; ~**lotse** *der,*
~**lotsin** *die* air traffic controller; ~**platz**
*der* airfield; ~**schein** *der* air ticket;
~**schreiber** *der* flight recorder;
~**verbindung** *die* air connection;
~**verkehr** *der* air traffic
**Flug·zeug** *das* aeroplane (Brit.); airplane
(Amer.); aircraft
**Flugzeug-:** ~**absturz** *der* plane crash;
~**entführer** *der,* ~**entführerin** *die* ···⟩

[aircraft] hijacker; ~**entführung** *die* [aircraft] hijack[ing]; ~**katastrophe** *die* air disaster; ~**träger** *der* aircraft carrier

**Flunder** *die;* ~, ~n flounder

**flunkern** *itr. V.* tell stories

**Fluor** *das;* ~s (Chemie) fluorine

**Fluor·chlor·kohlen·wasserstoff** *der* (Chemie) chlorofluorocarbon

**Flur¹** *der;* ~[e]s, ~e (Korridor) corridor; (Diele) [entrance] hall; **im/auf dem** ~: in the corridor/hall

**Flur²** *die;* ~, ~en farmland *no indef. art.*

**Fluss, *Fluß** *der;* Flusses, Flüsse river; (fließende Bewegung) flow

**fluss-, *fluß-, Fluss-, *Fluß-:** ~**ab[wärts]** *Adv.* downstream; ~**auf[wärts]** *Adv.* upstream; ~**bett** *das* river bed

**Flüsschen, *Flüßchen** *das;* ~s, ~: small river

**Fluss·diagramm** *das* (DV, Arbeitswiss.) flow chart

**flüssig** ① *Adj.* (a) liquid (b) (fließend, geläufig) fluent (c) **einen Betrag** ~ **machen** make a sum of money available ② *adv.* ⟨write, speak⟩ fluently

**Flüssig·gas** *das* liquid gas

**Flüssigkeit** *die;* ~, ~en (a) liquid; (auch Gas) fluid (b) (Geläufigkeit) fluency

**Flüssig·kristall·anzeige** *die* (Technik) liquid crystal display

***flüssig|machen** ▸ FLÜSSIG 1c

**Fluss·pferd, *Fluß·pferd** *das* hippopotamus

**flüstern** *itr., tr. V.* whisper

**Flut** *die;* ~, ~en (a) tide (b) (geh.: Wassermasse) flood

**fluten** *itr. V.; mit sein* (geh.) flood

**Flut·licht** *das* floodlight

**focht** *1. u. 3. Pers. Sg. Prät. v.* FECHTEN

**Föderalismus** *der;* ~: federalism *no art.*

**föderalistisch** *Adj.* federalist

**Fohlen** *das;* ~s, ~: foal

**Föhn** *der;* ~[e]s, ~e (a) föhn (b) (Haartrockner) hair-drier

**föhnen** *tr. V.* blow-dry

**Folge** *die;* ~, ~n (a) (Auswirkung) consequence; (Ergebnis) consequence; result (b) (Aufeinander~) succession; (zusammengehörend) sequence (c) (Fortsetzung) (einer Sendung) episode; (eines Romans) instalment

**Folge·erscheinung** *die* consequence

**folgen** *itr. V.; mit sein* follow; **jmdm. im Amt/ in der Regierung** ~: succeed sb. in office/in government; **auf etw.** (*Akk.*) ~: follow sth.; **aus etw.** ~: follow from sth.

**folgend** *Adj.* following; **der/die/das**

Folgende the next in order; **im Folgenden** *od.* **in Folgendem** [in the course of] the following discussion/passage *etc.*

**folgendermaßen** *Adv.* as follows; (so) in the following way

**folge·richtig** ① *Adj.* logical; consistent ⟨behaviour, action⟩ ② *adv.* logically; ⟨act, behave⟩ consistently

**Folge·richtigkeit** *die* (einer Entscheidung, Schlussfolgerung) logicality; (eines Verhaltens, einer Handlung) consistency

**folgern** ① *tr. V.* etw. aus etw. ~: infer sth. from sth. ② *itr. V.* **richtig** ~: draw a/the correct conclusion

**Folgerung** *die;* ~, ~en conclusion

**Folge·schaden** *der* (a) damaging after-effects (b) (Versicherungsw.) consequential damage

**folglich** *Adv.* consequently

**folgsam** ① *Adj.* obedient ② *adv.* obediently

**Folgsamkeit** *die;* ~: obedience

**Folie** /ˈfoːli̯ə/ *die;* ~, ~n (Metall~) foil; (Plastik~) film

**Folklore** *die;* ~ (a) folklore (b) (Musik) folk music

**folkloristisch** ① *Adj.* folkloric ② *adv.* in a folkloric way

**Folter** *die;* ~, ~n torture; **jmdn. auf die** ~ **spannen** (fig.) keep sb. in an agony of suspense

**Folterer** *der;* ~s, ~, **Folterin** *die;* ~, ~nen torturer

**foltern** *tr. V.* torture; (fig.) torment

**Folterung** *die;* ~, ~en torture

**Fön** Ⓦ *der;* ~[e]s, ~e hairdrier

**Fond** /foː/ *der;* ~s, ~s (geh.) back

**Fonds** /foː/ *der;* ~ /foː(s),/ ~ /foːs/ fund

**Fondue** /fõˈdyː/ *die;* ~, ~s *od. das;* ~s, ~s (Kochk.) fondue

***fönen** ▸ FÖHNEN

**Fontäne** *die;* ~, ~n jet; (Springbrunnen) fountain

**forcieren** /fɔrˈsiːrən/ *tr. V.* step up ⟨production⟩; intensify ⟨efforts⟩; push forward ⟨developments⟩

**Förderer** *der;* ~s, ~: patron

**Förderin** *die;* ~, ~nen patroness

**fordern** *tr. V.* (a) demand (b) (in Anspruch nehmen) make demands on

**fördern** *tr. V.* (a) promote; patronize, support ⟨artist, art⟩; further ⟨investigation⟩; foster ⟨talent, tendency⟩; improve ⟨appetite⟩; aid ⟨digestion, sleep⟩ (b) (Bergbau, Technik) mine ⟨coal, ore⟩; extract ⟨oil⟩

**Forderung** *die;* ~, ~en (a) demand (b) (Kaufmannsspr.) claim (an + *Akk.* against)

**Förderung** *die;* ~, ~en (a) ▸ FÖRDERN A: promotion; patronage; support; furthering; fostering; improvement; aiding

---

*alte Schreibung - vgl. Hinweis auf S. xiv

**(b)** (Bergbau, Technik) output; (das Fördern) mining; (von Erdöl) extraction

**Forelle** *die;* ~, ~n trout

**Form** *die;* ~, ~en **(a)** shape; **in** ~ **von Tabletten** in the form of tablets
**(b)** (bes. Sport: Verfassung) form; **in** ~ **sein** be on form
**(c)** (vorgeformtes Modell) mould; (Back~) baking tin
**(d)** (Darstellungs~, Umgangs~) form

**formal** [1] *Adj.* formal
[2] *adv.* formally

**formalisieren** *tr. V.* formalize

**Formalität** *die;* ~, ~en formality

**Format** *das;* ~[e]s, ~e **(a)** size; (Buch~, Papier~, Bild~) format
**(b)** (Persönlichkeit) format

**formatieren** *tr. V.* (DV) format

**formbar** *Adj.* malleable

**Form-:** ~**blatt** *das* form; ~**brief** *der* form letter

**Formel** *die;* ~, ~n formula

**formell** *Adj.* formal

**formen** *tr. V.* **(a)** (gestalten) form; shape
**(b)** (bilden, prägen) mould, form ‹*character, personality*›

**Form·fehler** *der* irregularity

**formieren** *tr., refl. V.* form

**förmlich** [1] *Adj.* **(a)** formal
**(b)** (regelrecht) positive
[2] *adv.* **(a)** formally
**(b)** (geradezu) **sich** ~ **fürchten** be really afraid

**form·los** *Adj.* **(a)** informal
**(b)** (gestaltlos) shapeless

**Form·sache** *die* formality

**Formular** *das;* ~s, ~e form

**formulieren** *tr. V.* formulate

**Formulierung** *die;* ~, ~en **(a)** (das Formulieren) formulation; (eines Entwurfes, Gesetzes) drafting
**(b)** (formulierter Text) formulation

**form·vollendet** [1] *Adj.* perfectly executed ‹*pirouette, bow, etc.*›; ‹*poem*› perfect in form
[2] *adv.* faultlessly

**forsch** *Adj.* forceful

**forschen** *itr. V.* **(a)** **nach jmdm./etw.** ~: search *or* look for sb./sth.
**(b)** (als Wissenschaftler) research

**Forscher** *der;* ~s, **Forscherin** *die;* ~, ~nen researcher

**Forschung** *die;* ~, ~en research

**Forschungs-:** ~**reaktor** *der* research reactor; ~**reisende** *der/die* explorer

**Forst** *der;* ~[e]s, ~e[n] forest

**Förster** *der;* ~s, ~, **Försterin** *die;* ~, ~nen forest warden

**Forst·wirtschaft** *die* forestry

**Forsythie** /fɔr'zyːtsi̯ə/ *die;* ~, ~n forsythia

**fort** *Adv.* **(a)** ▶ WEG;

**(b)** (weiter) **und so** ~: and so on

**fort-, Fort-:** ~**an** /-'-/ *Adv.* from now/then on; ~**bestand** *der* continuation; (eines Staates) continued existence; ~|**bewegen** [1] *tr. V.* move; shift; [2] *refl. V.* move [along]; ~|**bilden** *tr. V.* sich/jmdn. ~bilden continue one's/sb.'s education; ~**bildung** *die* further education; (beruflich) further training; ~**bildungs·kurs** *der* further education course; (beruflich) training course; ~|**bleiben** *unr. itr. V.; mit sein* fail to come; ~|**bringen** *unr. tr. V.:*
▶ WEGBRINGEN; ~**dauer** *die* continuation; ~|**dauern** *itr. V.* continue; ~|**fahren** [1] *unr. itr. V.* **(a)** *mit sein* leave; **(b)** *auch mit sein* (weitermachen) continue; go on; [2] *unr. tr. V.* drive away; ~|**führen** *tr. V.* **(a)** lead away; **(b)** (fortsetzen) continue; ~**gang** *der* **(a)** departure **(aus** from); **(b)** (Weiterentwicklung) progress; ~|**gehen** *unr. itr. V.; mit sein* leave; geh ~! go away!; ~**geschritten** *Adj.* advanced; ~**geschrittene** *der/die; adj. Dekl.* advanced student/player; ~|**kommen** *unr. itr. V.; mit sein* ▶ WEGKOMMEN A, B; ~|**laufen** *unr. itr. V.; mit sein* **(a)**
▶ WEGLAUFEN; **(b)** (sich ~setzen) continue; ~**laufend** [1] *Adj.* continuous; [2] *adv.* continuously; ~|**pflanzen** *refl. V.* **(a)** reproduce [oneself/itself]; **(b)** (sich verbreiten) ‹*idea, mood*› spread; ‹*sound, light*› travel; ~**pflanzung** *die;* ~~: reproduction; ~|**schaffen** *tr. V.* take away; ~|**schreiben** *unr. tr. V.* update; (in die Zukunft) project forward; ~**schreibung** *die* updating; (in die Zukunft) forward projection; ~|**schreiten** *unr. itr. V.; mit sein* ‹*process*› continue; ‹*time*› move on; ~**schritt** *der* progress; ~**schritte** progress *sing.;* **ein** ~**schritt** a step forward; ~**schrittlich** [1] *Adj.* progressive; [2] *adv.* progressively; ~**schrittlichkeit** *die* ~~: progressiveness; ~|**setzen** [1] *tr. V.* continue; [2] *refl. V.* continue; ~**setzung** *die;* ~~, ~~en **(a)** (das ~setzen) continuation; **(b)** (anschließender Teil) instalment; ~**setzungs·roman** *der* serial; serialized novel; ~|**während** [1] *Adj.* continual; [2] *adv.* continually; ~|**werfen** *unr. tr. V.:* ▶ WEGWERFEN

**fossil** *Adj.* fossilized; fossil *attrib.*

**Foto** *das;* ~s, ~s photo; ~**s machen** take photos

**Foto-:** ~**album** *das* photo album; ~**apparat** *der* camera

**fotogen** *Adj.* photogenic

**Foto·graf** *der;* ~en, ~en photographer

**Fotografie** *die;* ~, ~n **(a)** photography *no art.*
**(b)** (Lichtbild) photograph

**fotografieren** *tr. V.* photograph; take a photograph/photographs of

**Fotografin** *die;* ~, ~nen photographer

**foto-, Foto-:** ~**kopie** die photocopy;
~**kopieren** tr., itr. V. photocopy;
~**kopierer** der photocopier

**Foto-:** ~**labor** das photographic
laboratory; ~**modell** das photographic
model

**Foul** /faʊl/ das; ~s, ~s (Sport) foul (an +
Dat. on)

**Foul·spiel** /'faʊl-/ das foul

**Foyer** /foa'je:/ das; ~s, ~s foyer

**FPÖ** Abk. = **Freiheitliche Partei
Österreichs**

**Fr.** Abk. (a) = **Franken** SFr.
(b) = **Frau;**
(c) = **Freitag** Fri.

**Fracht** die; ~, ~en (Schiffs~, Luft~) cargo;
freight; (Bahn~, LKW-~) goods pl.; freight

**Fracht·brief** der consignment note;
waybill

**Frachter** der; ~s, ~: freighter

**Fracht-:** ~**gut** das slow freight; slow goods
pl.; ~**schiff** das cargo ship

**Frack** der; ~[e]s, Fräcke tails pl.; evening
dress

**Frage** die; ~, ~n question; (Angelegenheit)
issue; in ~: ▶ INFRAGE

**Fragebogen** der questionnaire; (Formular)
form

**fragen** ① tr., itr. V. (a) ask
(b) (sich erkundigen) **nach etw.** ~: ask or
inquire about sth.
(c) (nachfragen) ask for
② refl. V. **sich** ~, **ob** ...: wonder whether ...

**Frage·zeichen** das question mark

**fraglich** Adj. (a) doubtful
(b) (betreffend) in question postpos.; relevant

**Fragment** das; ~[e]s, ~e fragment

**frag·würdig** Adj. (a) questionable
(b) (zwielichtig) dubious

**Fragwürdigkeit** die; ~, ~en
(a) questionableness
(b) (Zwielichtigkeit) dubiousness

**Fraktion** die; ~, ~en parliamentary party;
(mit zwei Parteien) parliamentary coalition

**Fraktions-** (Parl.)**:** ~**führer** der,
~**führerin** die leader of the parliamentary
party/coalition; ~**zwang** der obligation to
vote in accordance with party policy

**frank** Adv. ~ **und frei** frankly and openly;
openly and honestly

**Franken** der; ~s ~: [Swiss] franc

**Frankfurter** die; ~, ~ (Wurst) frankfurter

**frankieren** tr. V. frank

**Frank·reich** (das); ~s France

**Franse** die; ~, ~n strand [of a/the fringe]

**Franzose** der; ~n, ~n Frenchman; **er ist**
~: he is French; **die** ~**n** the French

**Französin** die; ~, ~nen Frenchwoman

**französisch** Adj. French

**Französisch** das; ~[s] French

**Fräse** die; ~, ~n (für Holz) moulding
machine; (für Metall) milling machine

**fraß** 1. u. 3. Pers. Sg. Prät. v. FRESSEN

**Fraß** der; ~es (derb) muck

**Fratze** die; ~, ~n (a) hideous face
(b) (ugs.: Grimasse) grimace

**Frau** die; ~, ~en (a) woman
(b) (Ehe~) wife
(c) (Titel, Anrede) ~ **Schulze** Mrs Schulze; (in
Briefen) **Sehr geehrte** ~ **Schulze** Dear Madam;
(bei persönlicher Bekanntschaft) Dear Mrs/Miss/
Ms Schulze

**Frauen-:** ~**arzt** der, ~**ärztin** die
gynaecologist; ~**bewegung** die women's
movement; ~**emanzipation** die female
emancipation; women's emancipation;
~**gefängnis** das women's prison;
~**gruppe** die women's group; ~**haus** das
battered wives' refuge; ~**klinik** die
gynaecological hospital or clinic;
~**misshandlung, \*~mißhandlung**
die abuse of women; ~**recht** das women's
right; ~**rechtlerin** die; ~~, ~~**nen**
feminist; Women's Libber (coll.);
~**zeitschrift** die women's magazine;
~**zimmer** das (abwertend) female

**Fräulein** das; ~s, ~ (ugs. ~s) (a) (junges
~) young lady; (ältliches ~) spinster
(b) (Titel, Anrede) ~ **Mayer/Schulte** Miss
Mayer/Schulte

**fraulich** ① Adj. feminine
② adv. in a feminine way

**frech** ① Adj. (a) impertinent; cheeky;
barefaced ⟨lie⟩
(b) (keck, kess) saucy
② adv. impertinently; cheekily

**Frech·dachs** der (ugs., meist scherzh.)
cheeky little thing

**Frechheit** die; ~, ~en (a) impertinence;
cheek
(b) (Äußerung) impertinent or cheeky remark

**frei** ① Adj. (a) (unabhängig) free
(b) (nicht angestellt) freelance
(c) (ungezwungen) free and easy
(d) (nicht mehr in Haft) free
(e) (offen) open; **im Freien sitzen/übernachten**
sit out of doors/spend the night in the open;
**ständig im Freien übernachten** sleep rough
(f) (unbesetzt) vacant; free
(g) (kostenlos) free ⟨food, admission⟩
(h) (verfügbar) spare; free ⟨time⟩
② adv. freely

**frei-, Frei-:** ~**bad** das open-air swimming
pool; ~**|bekommen** ① unr. itr. V. (ugs.)
get time off; ② unr. tr. V. jmdn./etw.
~**bekommen** get sb./sth. released;
~**beruflich** ① Adj. self-employed;
freelance; ⟨doctor, lawyer⟩ in private
practice; ② adv. ~**beruflich tätig sein/**
**arbeiten** work freelance/practise privately;
~**betrag** der (Steuerw.) [tax] allowance;
~**bier** das free beer

**Freier** der; ~s, ~ (veralt.) suitor

**frei-, Frei-:** ~**exemplar** das (Buch) free

copy; (Zeitung) free issue; **∼frau** *die* baroness; **∼gabe** *die* release; **∼|geben** *unr. tr. V.* release; **∼gebig** *Adj.* generous; open-handed; **∼gebigkeit** *die;* **∼∼:** generosity; open-handedness; **∼gehege** *das* outdoor enclosure; **∼gepäck** *das* baggage allowance; **∼hafen** *der* free port; **∼|halten** *unr. tr. V.* (a) treat; (b) (offen halten) keep ⟨*entrance, roadway*⟩ clear; Einfahrt **∼halten!** no parking in front of entrance; **∼handels·zone** *die* free-trade zone; **∼händig** *adv.* ⟨*cycle*⟩ without holding on

**Freiheit** *die;* **∼, ∼en** (a) freedom; **∼,** Gleichheit, Brüderlichkeit Liberty, Equality, Fraternity
(b) (Vorrecht) freedom; privilege

**freiheitlich** [1] *Adj.* liberal ⟨*philosophy, conscience*⟩; **∼** und demokratisch free and democratic
[2] *adv.* liberally

**Freiheits-:** **∼beraubung** *die* ( jur.) wrongful detention; **∼strafe** *die* (Rechtsw.) term of imprisonment; prison sentence

**frei-, Frei-:** **∼herr** *der* baron; **∼karte** *die* complimentary ticket; **∼|kaufen** *tr. V.* ransom ⟨*hostage*⟩; buy the freedom of ⟨*slave*⟩; **∼|kommen** *unr. itr. V.* aus dem Gefängnis **∼kommen** be released from prison; **∼körper·kultur** *die* nudism no art.; naturism no art.; **∼land** *das* open ground; **∼|lassen** *unr. tr. V.* set free; release; **∼|legen** *tr. V.* uncover

**freilich** *Adv.* of course

**Frei·licht-:** **∼bühne** *die,* **∼theater** *das* open-air theatre

**frei-, Frei-:** **∼|machen** [1] *refl. V.* (ugs.: frei nehmen) take time off; [2] *tr. V.* (Postw.) frank; etw. mit 0,56 Euro **∼machen** put a 0.56 euro stamp on sth.; **∼marke** *die* postage stamp; **∼mütig** [1] *Adj.* candid; frank; [2] *adv.* candidly; frankly; **∼mütigkeit** *die;* **∼∼:** candidness; frankness; **∼schaffend** *Adj.* freelance; **∼schärler** *der;* **∼∼s, ∼∼,** **∼schärlerin** *die;* **∼∼, ∼∼nen** irregular [soldier]; **∼|schwimmen** *unr. refl. V.* sich **∼schwimmen** pass the 15-minute swimming test; **∼|sprechen** *unr. tr. V.* (a) (Rechtsw.) acquit; (b) (für unschuldig erklären) exonerate (von from); **∼spruch** *der* (Rechtsw.) acquittal; **∼|stellen** *tr. V.* (a) jmdm. etw. **∼stellen** leave sth. up to sb.; (b) (befreien) release ⟨*person*⟩; jmdn. vom Wehrdienst **∼stellen** exempt sb. from military service; **∼stoß** *der* (Fußball) free kick

**Frei·tag** *der* Friday; s. auch DIENSTAG usw.

**freitags** *Adv.* on Friday[s]; s. auch DIENSTAGS

**frei-, Frei-:** **∼tod** *der* (verhüll.) suicide no art.; **∼treppe** *die* [flight of] steps; **∼übung** *die; meist Pl.* (Sport) keep-fit exercise; **∼wild** *das* fair game; **∼willig**

[1] *Adj.* voluntary ⟨*decision*⟩; optional ⟨*subject*⟩; [2] *adv.* voluntarily; sich **∼willig** melden volunteer; **∼willige** *der/die; adj. Dekl.* volunteer; **∼zeichen** *das* ringing tone;

**Frei·zeit** *die* spare time

**Freizeit-:** **∼beschäftigung** *die* hobby; leisure pursuit; **∼gestaltung** *die* (Soziol., Päd.) leisure activity; **∼park** *der* amusement park

**frei-, Frei-:** **∼zügig** *Adj.* (a) generous; (b) (gewagt, unmoralisch) risqué ⟨*remark, film, dress*⟩; **∼zügigkeit** *die;* **∼∼** (a) generosity; (b) (freie Wahl des Wohnsitzes) freedom of domicile

**fremd** *Adj.* (a) foreign
(b) (nicht eigen) other people's; of others *postpos.;*
(c) (unbekannt) strange

**fremd-, Fremd-:** **∼arbeiter** *der,* **∼arbeiterin** *die* (veralt., schweiz.) foreign worker; **∼artig** *Adj.* strange

**Fremde¹** *der/die; adj. Dekl.* (a) stranger
(b) (Ausländer) foreigner

**Fremde²** *die;* **∼** (geh.) die **∼:** foreign parts *pl.*

**fremden-, Fremden-:** **∼feindlich** *Adj.* xenophobic; hostile to strangers/ foreigners *postpos.;* **∼feindlichkeit** *die* xenophobia; hostility towards foreigners; **∼führer** *der,* **∼führerin** *die* tourist guide; **∼hass, \*∼haß** *der* xenophobia; hatred of foreigners; **∼verkehr** *der* tourism no art.; **∼zimmer** *das* room

**fremd-, Fremd-:** **∼|gehen** *unr. itr. V.; mit sein* (ugs.) be unfaithful; **∼herrschaft** *die* foreign domination; **∼ländisch** *Adj.* foreign; (exotisch) exotic

**Fremdling** *der;* **∼s, ∼e** (veralt.) stranger

**fremd-, Fremd-:** **∼sprache** *die* foreign language; **∼sprachen·assistent** *der,* **∼sprachen·assistentin** *die* foreign-language assistant; **∼sprachig** *Adj.* bilingual/multilingual ⟨*staff, secretary*⟩; foreign ⟨*literature*⟩; foreign-language ⟨*edition, teaching*⟩; **∼sprachlich** *Adj.* foreign-language ⟨*teaching*⟩; foreign ⟨*word*⟩; **∼wort** *das; Pl.* **∼wörter** foreign word

**frenetisch** [1] *Adj.* frenetic
[2] *adv.* frenetically

**Frequenz** *die;* **∼, ∼en** (Physik) frequency; (Med.: Puls∼) rate

**Fressalien** /frɛ'saljən/ *Pl.* (ugs. scherzh.) grub (coll.)

**Fresse** *die;* **∼, ∼n** (derb) (a) (Mund) gob (sl.)
(b) (Gesicht) mug (coll.)

**fressen** [1] *unr. tr. V.* (a) ⟨*animal*⟩ eat; (sich ernähren von) feed on
(b) (ugs.: verschlingen) swallow up ⟨*money, time, distance*⟩; drink ⟨*petrol*⟩
(c) (zerstören) eat away
(d) (derb: von Menschen) guzzle
[2] *unr. itr. V.* (von Tieren) feed; (derb: von Menschen) stuff one's face (sl.)

**Fressen** *das;* ~s (a) (für Hunde, Katzen usw.)
food; (für Vieh) feed
  (b) (derb: Essen) grub (coll.)
**Fresserei** *die;* ~, ~en (derb) guzzling
**Freude** *die;* ~, ~n joy; (Vergnügen) pleasure;
  ~ an etw. (*Dat.*) haben take pleasure in sth.
**Freuden-:** ~**fest** *das* celebration; ein
  ~**fest feiern** hold a celebration; ~**haus** *das*
  house of pleasure; ~**tag** *der* happy day
**freudestrahlend** *Adj.* beaming with joy;
**freudig** *Adj.* joyful; joyous ⟨*heart*⟩;
  delightful ⟨*surprise*⟩;
**freud-los** *Adj.* joyless;
**freuen** 1 *refl. V.* be glad (**über** + *Akk.*
  about); (froh sein) be happy; **sich auf etw.**
  (*Akk.*) ~: look forward to sth.
  2 *tr. V.* please; **es freut mich, dass ...** I am
  pleased *or* glad that ...; **das hat ihn sehr**
  **gefreut** he was very pleased about it
**Freund** *der;* ~es, ~e (a) friend
  (b) (Verehrer, Geliebter) boyfriend
**Freundes-kreis** *der* circle of friends; **im**
  **engen** ~: among close friends
**Freundin** *die;* ~, ~nen (a) friend
  (b) (Geliebte) girlfriend; (älter) lady friend
**freundlich** 1 *Adj.* (a) kind ⟨*face*⟩; friendly
  ⟨*reception*⟩
  (b) (angenehm) pleasant
  (c) (freundschaftlich) friendly
  2 *adv.* jmdm. ~ **danken** thank sb. kindly
**Freundlichkeit** *die;* ~: kindness
**Freundschaft** *die;* ~, ~en friendship; **mit**
  jmdm. ~ **schließen** make friends with sb.
**freundschaftlich** 1 *Adj.* friendly
  2 *adv.* in a friendly way
**Frevel** /'freːfl̩/ *der;* ~s, ~ (geh., veralt.)
  crime; outrage
**frevelhaft** (geh.) 1 *Adj.* wicked ⟨*deed,*
  *rebellion, person*⟩; criminal ⟨*stupidity*⟩
  2 *adv.* wickedly
**Friede** *der;* ~ns, ~n (älter, geh.) ▶ FRIEDEN
**Frieden** *der;* ~s, ~: peace
**Friedens-:** ~**abkommen** *das* peace
  agreement; (Friedensvertrag) peace treaty;
  ~**bewegung** *die* peace movement;
  ~**bruch** *der* violation of the peace;
  ~**forschung** *die* peace studies *pl., no art.;*
  ~**konferenz** *die* peace conference;
  ~**nobelpreis** *der* Nobel Peace Prize;
  ~**pfeife** *die* pipe of peace; ~**richter** *der,*
  ~**richterin** *die:* lay magistrate dealing
  *with minor offences;* ≈ Justice of the Peace;
  ~**taube** *die* dove of peace;
  ~**verhandlungen** *Pl.* peace negotiations;
  ~**vertrag** *der* peace treaty; ~**zeiten** *Pl.*
  peacetime *sing.*
**fried-fertig** *Adj.* peaceable ⟨*person,*
  *character*⟩
**Fried-fertigkeit** *die;* ~: peaceableness
**Fried-hof** *der* cemetery; (Kirchhof) graveyard
**friedlich** 1 *Adj.* peaceful

2 *adv.* peacefully
**Friedlichkeit** *die;* ~: peacefulness
**fried-liebend** *Adj.* peace-loving
**frieren** *unr. itr. V.* (a) be *or* feel cold
  (b) *mit sein* (gefrieren) freeze
**Frikadelle** *die;* ~, ~n rissole
**frisch** 1 *Adj.* fresh; new-laid ⟨*egg*⟩; clean
  ⟨*linen, underwear*⟩; wet ⟨*paint*⟩
  2 *adv.* freshly
**Frische** *die;* ~ freshness; **geistige** ~:
  mental alertness; **körperliche** ~: physical
  fitness
**Frisch-:** ~**fleisch** *das* fresh meat;
  ~**halte-beutel** *der* airtight bag; ~**luft**
  *die* fresh air; ~**milch** *die* fresh milk
**Friseur** /friˈzøːɐ̯/ *der;* ~s, ~e, **Friseuse**
  /friˈzøːzə/ *die;* ~, ~n hairdresser
**frisieren** *tr. V.* jmdn./sich ~: do sb.'s/one's
  hair; **sich** ~ **lassen** have one's hair done
**friss, \*friß** *Imperativ Sg. v.* FRESSEN
**frisst, \*frißt** 2. u. 3. Pers. Sg. Präsens v.
  FRESSEN
**Frist** *die;* ~, ~en (a) time; period; **die** ~
  **verlängern** extend the deadline
  (b) (begrenzter Aufschub) extension
**frist-:** ~**gemäß,** ~**gerecht** *Adj., adv.*
  within the specified time *postpos.;* (bei
  Anmeldung usw.) before the closing date
  *postpos.;* ~**los** 1 *Adj.* instant; 2 *adv.*
  without notice
**Frisur** *die;* ~, ~en hairstyle
**fritieren** *tr. V.* deep-fry
**frivol** /friˈvoːl/ *Adj.* (a) (schamlos) suggestive
  ⟨*remark, picture, etc.*⟩; risqué ⟨*joke*⟩; earthy
  ⟨*man*⟩; flighty ⟨*woman*⟩
  (b) (leichtfertig) frivolous
**froh** *Adj.* (a) happy; cheerful ⟨*person, mood*⟩;
  good ⟨*news*⟩
  (b) (ugs.: erleichtert) pleased, glad (**über** + *Akk.*
  about)
**fröhlich** *Adj.* cheerful; happy
**Fröhlichkeit** *die;* ~: cheerfulness; (eines
  Festes, einer Feier) gaiety
**Froh-:** ~**natur** *die* cheerful person; ~**sinn**
  *der* cheerfulness; gaiety
**fromm;** ~**er** *od.* **frömmer,** ~**st...** *od.*
  **frömmst...** 1 *Adj.* pious, devout ⟨*person*⟩;
  devout ⟨*Christian*⟩
  2 *adv.* piously
**Frömmigkeit** *die;* ~: piety; devoutness
**Fron-leichnam** /froːn-/ (*das*) ~s [the
  feast of] Corpus Christi
**Front** *die;* ~, ~en (a) (Gebäude~) front;
  façade
  (b) (Kampfgebiet) front [line]
**frontal** 1 *Adj.* head-on ⟨*collision*⟩; frontal
  ⟨*attack*⟩
  2 *adv.* ⟨*collide*⟩ head-on; ⟨*attack*⟩ from the
  front
**Front-antrieb** *der* (Kfz-W.) front-wheel
  drive
**fror** *1. u. 3. Pers. Sg. Prät. v.* FRIEREN

---

\*alte Schreibung - vgl. Hinweis auf S. xiv

**Frosch** *der;* ~[e]s, Frösche frog
**Frosch-:** ~**mann** *der; Pl.* ~**männer**
frogman; ~**perspektive** *die* worm's-eye
view; ~**schenkel** *der* frog's leg
**Frost** *der;* ~[e]s, Fröste frost
**Frostbeule** *die* chilblain
**frösteln** *itr. V.* feel chilly
**Frost·grenze** *die* (Met.) 0° C isotherm;
(Geol.) frost line
**frostig** ① *Adj.* (auch fig.) frosty
② *adv.* frostily
**Frostigkeit** *die;* ~: frostiness
**Frost-:** ~**schaden** *der* frost damage;
~**schutz·mittel** *das* (a) frost protection
agent; (b) (Kfz-W.) antifreeze
**Frottee** *das* u. *der;* ~s, ~s terry towelling
**Frottee·handtuch** *das* terry towel
**frottieren** *tr. V.* rub; towel
**frotzeln** ① *tr. V.* tease
② *itr. V.* **über jmdn./etw.** ~: make fun of
sb./sth.
**Frucht** *die;* ~, Früchte fruit
**frucht·bar** *Adj.* fertile; fruitful ‹work, idea,
etc.›
**Fruchtbarkeit** *die;* ~: fertility;
fruitfulness
**Frucht·becher** *der* fruit sundae
**fruchten** *tr. V.* **nichts** ~: be no use
**fruchtig** *Adj.* fruity
**frucht·los** *Adj.* fruitless, vain ‹efforts›
**Frucht·losigkeit** *die;* ~~: fruitlessness
**Frucht-:** ~**saft** *der* fruit juice;
~**wasser** *das; Pl.* ~wässer (Anat.)
amniotic fluid; waters *pl.* (coll.)
**früh** ① *Adj.* (a) early
(b) (vorzeitig) premature
② *adv.* early; **heute** ~: this morning
**früh·auf:** **von** ~ from early childhood
on[wards]
**Frühaufsteher** *der;* ~s, ~,
**Frühaufsteherin** *die;* ~, ~nen early
riser
**Frühe** *die;* ~: **in aller** ~: at the crack of
dawn
**früher** ① *Adj., nicht präd.* (a) (vergangen)
earlier; former
(b) (ehemalig) former ‹owner, occupant,
friend›
② *adv.* formerly; ~ **war er ganz anders** he
used to be quite different
**Früh·erkennung** *die* (Med.) early
recognition
**frühestens** *Adv.* at the earliest
**Früh·geburt** *die* (a) premature birth
(b) (Kind) premature baby
**Früh·jahr** *das* spring
**Frühjahrsmüdigkeit** *die* springtime
tiredness
**Frühling** *der;* ~s, ~e spring
**Frühlings·anfang** *der* first day of
spring

**früh-, Früh-:** ~**reif** *Adj.* precocious
‹child›; ~**schoppen** *der* morning drink;
(um Mittag) lunchtime drink; ~**sport** *der*
early-morning exercise
**Früh·stück** *das;* ~s, ~e breakfast
**frühstücken** *itr. V.* have breakfast
**Frühstücks-:** ~**fernsehen** *das*
breakfast television; ~**pause** *die* morning
break; coffee break
**früh-, Früh-:** ~**warn·system** *das* early
warning system; ~**zeitig** ① *Adj.* early;
(vorzeitig) premature; ② *adv.* early; (vorzeitig)
prematurely
**Frustration** *die;* ~, ~en (Psych.)
frustration
**frustrieren** *tr. V.* frustrate
**Fuchs** *der;* ~es, Füchse fox
**fuchsen** *tr. V.* annoy; vex
**fuchs·teufels·wild** *Adj.* (ugs.) livid (coll.)
**Fuchtel** *die;* ~: **unter jmds.** ~ (ugs.) under
sb.'s thumb
**fuchteln** *itr. V.* (ugs.) **mit etw.** ~: wave sth.
about
**Fuder** *das;* ~s, ~: cartload
**Fuge**[1] *die;* ~, ~n joint; (Zwischenraum) gap
**Fuge**[2] *die;* ~, ~n (Musik) fugue
**fügen** ① *tr. V.* place; set; **etw zu etw.** ~ (fig.)
add sth. to sth.
② *refl. V.* (a) (sich ein~) **sich in etw.** (Akk.)
~: fit into sth.
(b) (gehorchen) **sich** ~: fall into line
**fügsam** *Adj.* obedient
**fühlbar** *Adj.* noticeable
**fühlen** ① *tr.*, *itr. V.* feel
② *refl. V.* **sich krank** ~: feel sick
**Fühler** *der;* ~s, ~: feeler; antenna
**Fühlungnahme** *die;* ~: initial contact
**fuhr** 1. u. 3. Pers. Sg. Prät. v. FAHREN
**Fuhre** *die;* ~, ~n load
**führen** ① *tr. V.* (a) lead; **jmdn. durch ein**
**Haus/eine Stadt** ~: show sb. around a
house/town; **durch das Programm führt [Sie]**
**Klaus Frank** Klaus Frank will present the
programme
(b) (verkaufen) stock, sell ‹goods›
(c) (durch~) **Gespräche/Verhandlungen** ~:
hold conversations/negotiations; **eine**
**glückliche Ehe** ~: be happily married
(d) (leiten) manage, run ‹company, business,
pub, etc.›; lead ‹party, country›; command
‹regiment›
(e) (Amtsspr.) drive ‹train, motor, vehicle›
(f) (als Kennzeichnung, Bezeichnung haben) bear;
**einen Titel/Künstlernamen** ~: have a title/
use a stage name
(g) (angelegt haben) keep ‹diary, list, file›
(h) (registrieren) **jmdn. in einer Liste/Kartei** ~:
have sb. on a list/on file
(i) (tragen) **etw. bei od. mit sich** ~: have sth.
on one; **eine Waffe/einen Ausweis bei sich**
~: carry a weapon/a pass
② *itr. V.* (a) lead
(b) (an der Spitze liegen) lead; be ahead

**f**

**führend** *Adj.* leading; high-ranking ⟨*official*⟩; prominent ⟨*position*⟩

**Führer** *der;* ~s, ~ (a) (Leiter) leader (b) (Fremdenführer, Buch) guide

**Führerin** *die;* ~, ~nen ▶ FÜHRER

**führer-, Führer-:** ~**los** [1] *Adj.* leaderless; (ohne Lenker) driverless ⟨*car*⟩ [2] *adv.* ▶ 1: without a leader; without a driver; ~**schein** *der* driving licence (Brit.); driver's license (Amer.); ~**schein-entzug** *der* disqualification from driving; driving ban

**Führung** *die;* ~, ~en (a) ▶ FÜHREN 1D: management; running; leadership; command (b) (Fremdenführung) guided tour (c) (führende Position) lead

**Führungs-:** ~**kraft** *die* manager; ~**spitze** *die* (Politik) top leadership; (im Betrieb) top management; ~**zeugnis** *das:* document issued by police certifying that holder has no criminal record

**Fuhr-:** ~**unternehmer** *der,* ~**unternehmerin** *die* haulage contractor; ~**werk** *das* cart

**Fülle** *die;* ~ (a) wealth; abundance (b) (Körper~) corpulence

**füllen** [1] *tr. V.* (a) fill; (Kochk.) stuff (b) (fig.) fill in ⟨*gap, time*⟩ [2] *refl. V.* (voll werden) fill [up]

**Füller** *der;* ~s, ~ (ugs.) [fountain] pen

**Füll·federhalter** *der* fountain pen

**füllig** *Adj.* corpulent, portly ⟨*person*⟩; ample ⟨*figure, bosom*⟩

**Füllung** *die;* ~, ~en stuffing; (Kochk.; Zahnmed.) filling; (in Schokolade) centre

**fummeln** *itr. V.* (ugs.) (a) (fingern) fiddle (b) (erotisch) pet

**Fund** *der;* ~[e]s, ~e (auch Archäol.) find

**Fundament** *das;* ~[e]s, ~e (a) (Bauw.) foundations *pl.;* (b) (Basis) base; basis

**fundamental** *Adj.* fundamental

**Fundamentalismus** *der;* ~: fundamentalism

**Fundamentalist** *der;* ~en, ~en, **Fundamentalistin** *die;* ~, ~nen fundamentalist

**Fund-:** ~**büro** *das* lost property office (Brit.); lost and found office (Amer.); ~**grube** *die* treasure house

**fundieren** *tr. V.* underpin

**fündig** *Adj.* ~ sein yield something; ~ werden make a find; (bei Bohrungen) make a strike

**Fund·ort** *der* place or site where sth. is/was found

**fünf** *Kardinalz.* five

**Fünf** *die;* ~, ~en five; (Schulnote) E

**fünf-, Fünf-:** ~**eck** *das;* pentagon; ~**fach** *Vervielfältigungsz.* fivefold; ~**fache** *das;*

*adj. Dekl.* five times as much; ~**hundert** *Kardinalz.* five hundred; ~**kampf** *der* (Sport) pentathlon

**Fünfling** *der;* ~s, ~e quintuplet; quin (coll.)

**fünf-:** ~**mal** *Adv.* five times; ~**stellig** *Adj.* five-figure

**fünft...** *Ordinalz.* fifth

**Fünf·tagewoche** *die* five-day [working] week

**fünf·tausend** *Kardinalz.* five thousand

**fünftel** *Bruchz.* fifth

**Fünftel** *das* (schweiz. meist *der*); ~s, ~: fifth

**fünftens** *Adv.* fifthly

**fünf·zehn** *Kardinalz.* fifteen

**fünfzig** *Kardinalz.* fifty

**Fünfzig** *die;* ~: fifty

**fünfziger** *indekl. Adj.* **die Fünfzigerjahre** the fifties

**Fünfziger** *der;* ~s, ~ (a) (ugs.) fifty-pfennig piece/fifty-euro note *etc.* (b) (50-Jähriger) fifty-year-old

**Fünfzig-:** ~**mark·schein** *der* fifty-mark note; ~**pfennig·stück** *das* fifty-pfennig piece

**fünfzigst...** *Ordinalz.* fiftieth

**fungieren** *itr. V.* als etw. ~ ⟨*person*⟩ act as sth.; ⟨*word etc.*⟩ function as sth.

**Funk** *der;* ~s radio

**Funk·ausstellung** *die* radio and television exhibition

**Funke** *der;* ~ns, ~n (auch fig.) spark

**funkeln** *itr. V.* ⟨*light, star*⟩ twinkle; ⟨*gold, diamonds*⟩ glitter; ⟨*eyes*⟩ blaze

**funken** *tr. V.* radio; ⟨*transmitter*⟩ broadcast

**Funker** *der;* ~s, ~, **Funkerin** *die;* ~, ~nen radio operator

**Funk-:** ~**gerät** *das* radio set; (tragbar) walkie-talkie; ~**haus** *das* broadcasting centre; ~**kolleg** *das* radio-based [adult education] course; ~**sprech-gerät** *das* radiophone; (tragbar) walkie-talkie; ~**spruch** *der* radio signal; (Nachricht) radio message; ~**station** *die,* ~**stelle** *die* radio station; ~**stille** *die* radio silence; ~**streife** *die* [police] radio patrol; ~**taxi** *das* radio taxi; ~**telefon** *das* radio-telephone

**Funktion** *die;* ~, ~en function

**Funktionär** *der;* ~s, ~e official; functionary

**funktionieren** *itr. V.* work; function

**funktions·tüchtig** *Adj.* working; sound ⟨*organ*⟩

**Funk-:** ~**turm** *der* radio tower; ~**verbindung** *die* radio contact

**Funzel** *die;* ~, ~n (ugs.) useless light

**für** *Präp. mit Akk.* for; etw. ~ ungültig erklären declare sth. invalid; *s. auch* WAS 1

**Furche** *die;* ~, ~n (a) furrow (b) (Wagenspur) rut

---
*old spelling - see note on page xiv

**Furcht** *die;* ~: fear; ~ vor jmdm./etw. haben fear sb./sth.

**furchtbar** 1 *Adj.* **(a)** dreadful **(b)** (ugs.: unangenehm) terrible (coll.) 2 *adv.* (ugs.) terribly (coll.)

**fürchten** 1 *refl. V.* **sich [vor jmdm./etw.]** ~: be afraid *or* frightened [of sb./sth.] 2 *tr. V.* be afraid of; **ich fürchte, [dass]** ...: I'm afraid [that] ...

**fürchterlich** *Adj., adv.* ▶ FURCHTBAR

**furcht·los** 1 *Adj.* fearless 2 *adv.* fearlessly

**furchtsam** 1 *Adj.* timid 2 *adv.* timidly

**für·einander** *Adv.* for one another; for each other

**Furie** /'fu:riə/ *die;* ~, ~n Fury

**Furnier** *das;* ~s, ~e veneer

**Für·sorge** *die;* ~ **(a)** care **(b)** (veralt.: Sozialhilfe) welfare **(c)** (veralt.: Sozialamt) social services *pl.*

**für·sorglich** 1 *Adj.* considerate 2 *adv.* considerately

**Für·sprache** *die* support

**Für·sprecher** *der,* **Für·sprecherin** *die* advocate

**Fürst** *der;* ~en, ~en prince

**Fürstentum** *das;* ~s, Fürstentümer principality

**Fürstin** *die;* ~, ~nen princess

**fürstlich** 1 *Adj.* **(a)** royal **(b)** (fig.: üppig) lavish 2 *adv.* lavishly

**Furt** *die;* ~, ~en ford

**Furunkel** *der od. das;* ~s, ~: boil; furuncle

**Für·wort** *das; Pl.* -wörter pronoun

**Furz** *der;* ~es, Fürze (derb) fart (coarse); **einen** ~ **lassen** let off a fart; **jeder** ~ (fig.) the slightest thing

**furzen** *itr. V.* (derb) fart (coarse)

**Fusion** *die;* ~, ~en amalgamation; (von Konzernen) merger

**fusionieren** *itr. V.* merge

**Fuß** *der;* ~es, Füße foot; (einer Lampe, Säule) base; (von Möbeln) leg; **zu** ~ **gehen** go on foot;

walk; **bei** ~! heel!; (fig.) **auf freiem** ~ **sein** be at large; **auf großem** ~ **leben** live in great style

**Fuß·ball** *der* **(a)** (Ballspiel) [Association] football **(b)** (Ball) football

**Fußballer** *der;* ~s, ~, **Fußballerin** *die;* ~, ~nen footballer

**Fußball-:** ~**platz** *der* football ground; (Spielfeld) football pitch; ~**spiel** *das* **(a)** football match; **(b)** (Sportart) football *no art.;* ~**spieler** *der,* ~**spielerin** *die* football player

**Fuß·boden** *der* floor

**Fußboden·heizung** *die* underfloor heating

**fußen** *itr. V.* **auf etw.** (*Dat.*) ~: be based on sth.

**Fuß·ende** *das* foot

**Fußgänger** *der;* ~s, ~, **Fußgängerin** *die;* ~, ~nen pedestrian

**Fußgänger-:** ~**brücke** *die* footbridge; ~**übergang** *der,* ~**überweg** *der* pedestrian crossing; ~**unterführung** *die* pedestrian subway; ~**zone** *die* pedestrian precinct

**Fuß-:** ~**nagel** *der* toenail; ~**note** *die* footnote; ~**stapfen** *der;* ~~s, ~~: footprint; ~**tritt** *der* kick; ~**volk** *das* **(a)** (hist.) footmen *pl.;* **(b)** (abwertend: Untergeordnete) lower ranks *pl.;* ~**weg** *der* footpath

**futsch** *Adj.* (salopp) ~ **sein** have gone for a burton (Brit. coll.)

**Futter**[1] *das;* ~s (Tiernahrung) feed; (für Pferde, Kühe) fodder

**Futter**[2] *das;* ~s, ~ (von Kleidungsstücken usw.) lining

**Futteral** *das;* ~s, ~e case

**Futter·mittel** *das* animal food

**füttern**[1] *tr. V.* feed

**füttern**[2] *tr. V.* (mit Futter[2] ausstatten) line

**Futter·pflanze** *die* fodder plant; forage plant

**Fütterung** *die;* ~, ~en feeding

**Futur** *das;* ~s, ~e (Sprachw.) future [tense]

**Fuzzi** *der;* ~s, ~s (salopp) bozo (sl.)

# Gg

**g, G** /geː/ *das;* ~, ~ (a) (Buchstabe) g/G
(b) (Musik) [key of] G
**g** *Abk.* (a) = **Gramm** g
(b) = **Groschen**
**gab** *1. u. 3. Pers. Sg. Prät. v.* GEBEN
**Gabe** *die;* ~, ~n (a) (geh.: Geschenk, Talent)
gift
(b) (Almosen, Spende) alms *pl.*
**Gabel** *die;* ~, ~n fork; (Telefon~) cradle
**gabeln** *refl. V.* fork
**Gabel-:** ~**schlüssel** *der* flat spanner;
~**stapler** *der;* ~~s, ~~: forklift truck
**Gabelung** *die;* ~, ~en fork
**Gaben-tisch** *der* gift table
**gackern** *itr. V.* (a) cluck
(b) (ugs.: lachen) cackle
**gaffen** *itr. V.* (abwertend) gape; gawp (coll.)
**Gaffer** *der;* ~s, ~, **Gafferin** *die;* ~, ~nen
gaper; starer
**Gag** /gɛk/ *der;* ~s, ~s (a) (Theater, Film) gag
(b) (Besonderheit) gimmick
**Gage** /'gaːʒə/ *die;* ~, ~n salary; (für einzelnen
Auftritt) fee
**gähnen** *itr. V.* (auch fig.) yawn
**Gala** /'gaːla, *auch* 'gala/ *die;* ~: formal dress
**galant** ① *Adj.* gallant; (amourös) amorous
② *adv.* gallantly
**Gala-vorstellung** *die* gala performance
**Galeere** *die;* ~, ~n galley
**Galerie** *die;* ~, ~n gallery
**Galgen** *der* gallows *sing.*
**Galgen-:** ~**frist** *die* reprieve; ~**humor**
*der* gallows humour
**Galle** *die;* ~, ~n (a) (Gallenblase) gall
[bladder]
(b) (Sekret) (bei Tieren) gall; (bei Menschen) bile
**Galopp** *der;* ~s, ~s *od.* ~e gallop
**galoppieren** *itr. V.; meist mit sein* gallop
**galt** *1. u. 3. Pers. Sg. Prät. v.* GELTEN
**galvanisch** /gal'vaːnɪʃ/ *Adj.* galvanic
**Gamasche** *die;* ~, ~n gaiter; (bis zum
Knöchel reichend) spat
**Gambe** *die;* ~, ~n (Musik) viola da gamba
**Gamma-strahlen** *Pl.* (Physik, Med.) gamma
rays
**gammelig** *Adj.* (ugs.) (a) bad; rotten
(b) (unordentlich) scruffy
**gammeln** *itr. V.* (a) (ugs.) go off
(b) (nichts tun) loaf around; bum around (Amer.
coll.)
**Gammler** *der;* ~s, ~, **Gammlerin** *die;*
~, ~nen (ugs.) dropout (coll.)

**Gämse** *die;* ~, ~n chamois
**gang:** ~ und gäbe sein be quite usual
**Gang** *der;* ~[e]s, Gänge (a) walk; gait
(b) (Besorgung) errand
(c) (Verlauf) course
(d) (Technik) gear
(e) (Flur) (in Zügen, Gebäuden usw.) corridor;
(Verbindungs~) passage[way]; (im Theater, Kino,
Flugzeug) aisle
(f) (Kochk.) course
**gangbar** *Adj.* passable; (fig.) practicable
**Gängel-band** *das:* jmdn. am ~ führen keep
sb. in leading reins
**gängeln** *tr. V.* (ugs.) jmdn. ~: boss sb.
around
**gang-genau** *Adj.* accurate
**Gang-genauigkeit** *die* accuracy
**gängig** *Adj.* (a) (üblich) common; (aktuell)
current
(b) (leicht verkäuflich) popular
**Gang-schaltung** *die* (Technik) gear system;
(Art) gear change
**Gangway** /'gæŋweɪ/ *die;* ~, ~s gangway
**Ganove** /ga'noːvə/ *der;* ~n, ~n (ugs.
abwertend) crook (coll.)
**Gans** *die;* ~, Gänse goose
**Gänse-:** ~**blümchen** *das* daisy;
~**braten** *der* roast goose; ~**füßchen** *das;*
~~s, ~~ (ugs.) ▶ ANFÜHRUNGSZEICHEN;
~**haut** *die* (fig.) gooseflesh; goose pimples
*pl.;* ~**marsch** im ~marsch in single *or*
Indian file
**Gänserich** *der;* ~s, ~e gander
**ganz** ① *Adj.* (a) (gesamt) whole; entire; **den**
~**en Tag/das** ~**e Jahr** all day/year
(b) (ugs.: alle) **die** ~**en Kinder/Leute/Gläser**
*usw.* all the children/people/glasses *etc.;*
(c) (vollständig) whole
(d) (ugs.: ziemlich [groß]) **eine** ~**e Menge/ein**
~**er Haufen** quite a lot/quite a pile
(e) (ugs.: unversehrt) intact; **etw. wieder** ~
**machen** mend sth.
② *adv.* quite
**Ganze** *das; adj. Dekl.* (a) whole
(b) (alles) **das** ~: the whole thing
**gänzlich** *Adv.* entirely
**ganz-:** ~**tägig** ① *Adj.* all-day; **eine**
~**tägige Arbeit** a full-time job; ② *adv.* all
day; ~**tags** *Adv.* arbeiten work full-time
**Ganztags-:** ~**schule** *die* all-day school;
(System) all-day schooling *no art.;* ~**stelle**
*die* full-time job
**gar**[1] *Adj.* cooked; done *pred.*
**gar**[2] *Partikel* (a) (überhaupt) ~ **nicht** [**wahr**]
not [true] at all; ~ **nichts** nothing at all; ~

---

**niemand** od. **keiner** nobody at all; ~ **keines** not a single one; ~ **kein Geld** no money at all

**(b)** (südd., österr., schweiz.: verstärkend) ~ **zu** only too

**(c)** (geh.: sogar) even

**Garage** /ga'ra:ʒə/ die; ~, ~n garage

**Garagen-:** ~**firma** die garage startup; ~**wagen** der garaged car

**Garant** der; ~en, ~en guarantor

**Garantie** die; ~, ~n guarantee

**Garantie-frist** die guarantee period

**garantieren** ⏻ tr. V. guarantee ⏼ itr. V. für etw. ~: guarantee sth.

**garantiert** Adv. (ugs.) wir kommen ~ zu spät we're dead certain to arrive late (coll.)

**Garantie-schein** der guarantee [certificate]

**Garantin** die; ~, ~nen guarantor

**Garaus** /'ga:ɐ̯|au:s/: jmdm. den ~ machen do sb. in (coll.)

**Garbe** die; ~, ~n (a) sheaf (b) (Geschoss~) burst of fire

**Garde** die; ~, ~n guard

**Garderobe** die; ~, ~n (a) wardrobe; clothes pl.; (b) (Flur~) coat rack (c) (im Theater usw.) cloakroom; checkroom (Amer.)

**Garderoben-frau** die cloakroom or (Amer.) checkroom attendant

**Gardine** die; ~, ~n (a) net curtain (b) (landsch., veralt.) curtain

**Gardinen-:** ~**predigt** die (ugs.) telling-off (coll.); (einer Ehefrau zu ihrem Mann) curtain lecture; ~**stange** die curtain rail

**garen** tr., itr. V. cook

**gären** regelm. (auch unr.) itr. V. ferment; (fig.) seethe

**Garn** das; ~[e]s, ~e (a) thread; (Näh~) cotton (b) (Seew.) yarn

**Garnele** die; ~, ~n shrimp

**garnieren** tr. V. (a) decorate (b) (Gastr.) garnish

**Garnison** die; ~, ~en garrison

**Garnitur** die; ~, ~en (a) set; (Wäsche) set of [matching] underwear; (Möbel) suite (b) (ugs.) die erste/zweite ~: the first/second-rate people pl.

**garstig** Adj. nasty; bad ‹behaviour›

**Garstigkeit** die; ~, ~en (a) nastiness (b) (Handlung) piece of nastiness

**Gärtchen** das; ~s, ~: little garden

**Garten** der; ~s, Gärten garden

**Garten-:** ~**abfall** der garden waste; ~**abfälle** garden waste; ~**arbeit** die gardening; ~**bau** der horticulture; ~**fest** das garden party; ~**haus** das summer house; ~**laube** die summerhouse; garden house; ~**lokal** das beer garden; (Restaurant) open-air café; ~**schau** die horticultural

show; ~**wirtschaft** die ▶ ~LOKAL; ~**zwerg** der (a) garden gnome; (b) (salopp abwertend) little runt

**Gärtner** der; ~s, ~: gardener

**Gärtnerei** die; ~, ~en nursery

**Gärtnerin** die; ~, ~nen gardener

**Gärung** die; ~, ~en fermentation

**Gas** das; ~es, ~e (a) gas (b) (Treibstoff) petrol (Brit.); gasoline (Amer.); gas (Amer. coll.); ~ **wegnehmen** take one's foot off the accelerator; ~ **geben** accelerate; put one's foot down (coll.)

**gas-, Gas-:** ~**flasche** die gas cylinder; (für einen Herd, Ofen) gas bottle; ~**förmig** Adj. gaseous; ~**hahn** der gas tap; ~**herd** der gas cooker; ~**kammer** die gas chamber; ~**leitung** die gas pipe; (Hauptrohr) gas main; ~**maske** die gas mask; ~**pedal** das accelerator [pedal]; gas pedal (Amer.); ~**pistole** die pistol that fires gas cartridges

**Gasse** die; ~, ~n lane; (österr.) street

**Gassen-junge** der (abwertend) street urchin

**Gast** der; ~[e]s, Gäste (a) guest (b) (Besucher eines Lokals) patron (c) (Besucher) visitor

**Gast-:** ~**arbeiter**, der, ~**arbeiterin** die immigrant or guest worker; ~**dozent** der, ~**dozentin** die (Hochschulw.) visiting lecturer

**Gäste-:** ~**buch** das guest book; ~**haus** das guest house; ~**zimmer** das (privat) guest room; spare room; (im Hotel) room

**gast-, Gast-:** ~**freundlich** Adj. hospitable; ~**freundlichkeit** die, ~**freundschaft** die hospitality; ~**geber** der host; ~**geberin** die hostess; ~**haus** das, ~**hof** der inn

**gastieren** itr. V. give a guest performance

**gastlich** Adj. hospitable

**Gastlichkeit** die; ~: hospitality

**Gast-professor** der, **Gast-professorin** die visiting professor

**Gastronom** der; ~en, ~en restaurateur

**Gastronomie** die; ~: catering no art.; (Gaststättengewerbe) restaurant trade

**Gastronomin** die; ~, ~nen restaurateur

**Gast-:** ~**spiel** das guest performance; ~**stätte** die public house; (Speiselokal) restaurant; ~**wirt** der publican; landlord; (eines Restaurants) [restaurant] proprietor; (Pächter) restaurant manager; ~**wirtin** die ▶ ~WIRT: publican; landlady; [restaurant] proprietress or owner; restaurant manageress; ~**wirtschaft** die ▶ ~STÄTTE

**Gas-:** ~**vergiftung** die gas poisoning no indef. art.; ~**versorgung** die gas supply; ~**werk** das gasworks sing.; ~**zähler** der gas meter

**Gatte** der; ~n, ~n husband

**Gatter** das; ~s, ~ (a) (Zaun) fence; (Lattenzaun) fence; paling

**(b)** (Tor) gate

**Gattin** *die;* ∼, ∼**nen** (geh.) wife

**Gattung** *die;* ∼, ∼**en (a)** kind; sort;
(Kunst∼) genre; form
**(b)** (Biol.) genus

**GAU** *der;* ∼**s,** ∼**s** *Abk.* = **größter**
**anzunehmender Unfall** MCA;
maximum credible accident

**Gaudi** *das;* ∼**s** (bayr., österr.) *die;* ∼ (ugs.) bit
of fun

**Gaukler** *der;* ∼**s,** ∼, **Gauklerin** *die;* ∼,
∼**nen (a)** (veralt.: Taschenspieler[in]) itinerant
entertainer
**(b)** (geh.: Betrüger[in]) charlatan

**Gaul** *der;* ∼[e]**s,** Gäule nag (derog.)

**Gaumen** *der;* ∼**s,** ∼: palate

**Gauner** *der;* ∼**s,** ∼ (abwertend) crook (coll.);
rogue

**Gaunerei** *die;* ∼, ∼**en** swindle

**Gaunerin** *die;* ∼, ∼**nen** ▶ GAUNER

**Gauner·sprache** *die* thieves' cant *or*
Latin

**Gaze** /'gaːzə/ *die;* ∼, ∼**n** gauze

**geächtet** *Adj.* respected

**Geäst** *das;* ∼[e]**s** branches *pl.*

**geb.** *Abk.* **(a)** = **geboren;**
**(b)** = **geborene**

**Gebäck** *das;* ∼[e]**s,** ∼**e** cakes and pastries
*pl.;* (Kekse) biscuits *pl.;* (Törtchen) tarts *pl.*

**gebacken** 2. *Part. v.* BACKEN

**Gebälk** *das;* ∼[e]**s,** ∼**e** beams *pl.;* (Dach∼)
rafters *pl.*

**gebar** 1. u. 3. *Pers. Sg. Prät. v.* GEBÄREN

**Gebärde** *die;* ∼, ∼**n** gesture

**gebärden** *refl. V.* behave

**gebären** *unr. tr. V.* bear; give birth to; *s.*
*auch* GEBOREN

**gebär·fähig** *Adj.* **Frauen im** ∼**en Alter**
women of child-bearing age.

**Gebär·mutter** *die; Pl.* Gebärmütter womb

**Gebäude** *das;* ∼**s,** ∼ **(a)** building
**(b)** (Gefüge) structure

**gebaut** *Adj.* **gut** ∼ **sein** have a good figure

**Gebein** *das;* ∼[e]**s,** ∼**e** *Pl.* (geh.) bones *pl.;*
(sterbliche Reste) [mortal] remains

**Gebell** *das;* ∼[e]**s** barking; (der Jagdhunde)
baying

**geben** ⊡ *unr. tr. V.* give; jmdm. **die Hand**
∼: shake sb.'s hand; ∼ **Sie mir bitte Herrn N.**
please put me through to Mr N.; **Unterricht**
∼: teach; **eins plus eins gibt zwei** one and
one is *or* makes two; **etw. von sich** ∼: utter
sth.
⊡ *unr. tr. V.* (unpers.) **es gibt** there is/are;
**heute gibts Fisch** we're having fish today;
**morgen gibt es Schnee** it'll snow tomorrow
⊡ *intr. V.* **(a)** (Karten austeilen) deal
**(b)** (Sport: aufschlagen) serve
⊡ *unr. refl. V.* **(a)** sich [natürlich/steif] ∼:
act *or* behave [naturally/stiffly]

**(b) das gibt sich noch** it will get better

**Gebet** *das;* ∼[e]**s,** ∼**e** prayer

**gebeten** 2. *Part. v.* BITTEN

**Gebets-:** ∼**mühle** *die* prayer wheel;
∼**teppich** *der* (islam. Rel.) prayer mat

**gebiert** 3. *Pers. Sg. Präsens v.* GEBÄREN

**Gebiet** *das;* ∼[e]**s,** ∼**e** region; area;
(Staats∼) territory; (Bereich, Fach) field

**gebieten** (geh.) **(a)** command; order
**(b)** (erfordern) demand

**Gebieter** *der;* ∼**s,** ∼ (veralt.) master

**Gebieterin** *die;* ∼, ∼**nen** (veralt.) mistress

**gebieterisch** (geh.) *Adj.* imperious;
(herrisch) domineering; peremptory ⟨tone⟩

**Gebiets·anspruch** *der* territorial claim

**Gebilde** *das;* ∼**s,** ∼: object; (Bauwerk)
structure

**gebildet** *Adj.* educated

**Gebimmel** *das;* ∼**s** (ugs.) ringing; (von
kleinen Glocken) tinkling

**Gebirge** *das;* ∼**s,** ∼: mountain range; **im**
∼: in the mountains

**gebirgig** *Adj.* mountainous

**Gebiss, \*Gebiß** *das;* Gebisses, Gebisse
**(a)** set of teeth; teeth *pl.;*
**(b)** (Zahnersatz) denture; plate (coll.); (für beide
Kiefer) dentures *pl.*

**gebissen** 2. *Part. v.* BEISSEN

**geblasen** 2. *Part. v.* BLASEN

**geblichen** 2. *Part. v.* BLEICHEN

**geblümt** *Adj.* flowered

**Geblüt** *das;* ∼[e]**s** (geh.) blood

**gebogen** 2. *Part. v.* BIEGEN

**geboren** ① 2. *Part. v.* GEBÄREN;
② *Adj.* blind/taub ∼ sein be born blind/deaf;
**Frau Anna Schmitz** ∼**e Meyer** Mrs Anna
Schmitz née Meyer

**geborgen** ① 2. *Part. v.* BERGEN;
② *Adj.* safe; secure

**Geborgenheit** *die;* ∼: security

**geborsten** 2. *Part. v.* BERSTEN

**gebot** 1. u. 3. *Pers. Sg. Prät. v.* GEBIETEN

**Gebot** *das;* ∼[e]**s,** ∼**e (a)** (Grundsatz) precept;
**die Zehn** ∼**e** (Rel.) the Ten Commandments
**(b)** (Vorschrift) regulation

**geboten** ① 2. *Part. v.* BIETEN, GEBIETEN;
② *Adj.* (ratsam) advisable; (notwendig)
necessary

**Gebr.** *Abk.* = **Gebrüder** Bros.

**gebracht** 2. *Part. v.* BRINGEN

**gebrannt** 2. *Part. v.* BRENNEN

**gebraten** 2. *Part. v.* BRATEN

**Gebrauch** *der* **(a)** use
**(b)** (Brauch) custom

**gebrauchen** *tr. V.* use

**gebräuchlich** *Adj.* **(a)** normal;
customary
**(b)** (häufig) common

**gebrauchs-, Gebrauchs-:**
∼**anweisung** *die* instructions *pl.* [for

---

\*old spelling - see note on page xiv

use]; ~**fertig** *Adj.* ready for use *pred.;*
~**gegenstand** *der* item of practical use;
~**wert** *der* utility value

**gebraucht** *Adj.* second-hand; used ⟨car⟩

**Gebraucht·wagen** *der* used car

**Gebrechen** *das;* ~s, ~ (geh.) affliction

**gebrechlich** *Adj.* infirm

**Gebrechlichkeit** *die;* ~: infirmity

**gebrochen** ① *2. Part. v.* BRECHEN;
② *Adj.* ~es Englisch/Deutsch broken
English/German
③ *adv.* ~ Deutsch sprechen speak broken
German

**Gebrüder** *Pl.:* die ~ Meyer Meyer Brothers

**Gebrüll** *das;* ~[e]s roaring

**Gebrumm** *das;* ~[e]s (von Bären) growling;
(von Flugzeugen, Bienen) droning; (von Insekten)
buzz[ing]

**gebückt** *Adj.* in ~er Haltung bending
forward

**Gebühr** *die;* ~, ~en charge; (Maut) toll;
(Anwalts~) fee

**gebühren** (geh.) *itr. V.* jmdm. gebührt
Achtung *usw.* sb. deserves respect *etc.*

**Gebühren·anzeiger** *der* (Fernspr.)
telephone meter

**gebührend** ① *Adj.* fitting
② *adv.* fittingly

**gebühren-, Gebühren-:**
~**ermäßigung** *die* reduction of charges/
fees; ~**frei** ① *Adj.* free of charge *pred.;*
② *adv.* free of charge; ~**pflichtig** *Adj.*
eine ~pflichtige Verwarnung a fine and a
caution; ~**vignette** *die* [Swiss] motorway
fee sticker

**gebunden** ① *2. Part. v.* BINDEN;
② *Adj.* (verpflichtet) bound

**Geburt** *die;* ~, ~en birth

**Geburten-:** ~**kontrolle** *die* birth
control; ~**rate** *die* birth rate; ~**ziffer** *die*
birth rate

**gebürtig** *Adj.* ein ~er Schwabe a Swabian
by birth

**Geburts-:** ~**anzeige** *die* birth
announcement; ~**datum** *das* date of birth;
~**haus** *das:* das ~haus Beethovens the
house where Beethoven was born;
Beethoven's birthplace; ~**helfer** *der,*
~**helferin** *die* (Arzt, Ärztin) obstetrician;
~**hilfe** *die* (Med.) obstetrics *sing.;* (von einer
Hebamme) midwifery; ~**stadt** *die* native
town/city; ~**ort** *der* place of birth; ~**tag**
*der* birthday; jmdm. zum ~tag gratulieren
wish sb. many happy returns of the day;
~**ur·kunde** *die* birth certificate

**Gebüsch** *das;* ~[e]s, ~e bushes *pl.*

**gedacht** *2. Part. v.* DENKEN, GEDENKEN

**Gedächtnis** *das;* ~ses, ~se (a) memory
(b) (Andenken) memory

**Gedächtnis-:** ~**lücke** *die* gap in one's
memory; ~**schwund** *der* loss of memory

**gedämpft** *Adj.* subdued ⟨mood⟩; subdued,
soft ⟨light⟩; muffled ⟨sound⟩

**Gedanke** *der;* ~ns, ~n (a) thought; der ~
an etw. (*Akk.*) the thought of sth.
(b) *Pl.* (Meinung) ideas
(c) (Einfall) idea

**gedanken-, Gedanken-:** ~**gang** *der*
train of thought; ~**gut** *das* thought;
christliches ~gut Christian thought;
staatszersetzendes ~gut subversive ideas
*pl.;* ~**los** ① *Adj.* unconsidered; (zerstreut)
absent-minded; ② *adv.* without thinking;
(zerstreut) absent-mindedly; ~**losigkeit** *die;*
~~ (Zerstreutheit) absent-mindedness;
(Unüberlegtheit) lack of thought; ~**strich** *der*
dash; ~**verloren** *Adv.* lost in thought;
~**voll** ① *Adj.* pensive; ② *adv.* pensively

**gedanklich** ① *Adj.* intellectual
② *adv.* intellectually

**Gedärm** *das;* ~[e]s, ~e intestines *pl.;*
bowels *pl.,* (eines Tieres) entrails *pl.*

**Gedeck** *das;* ~[e]s, ~e (a) place setting;
cover
(b) (Menü) set meal
(c) (Getränk) drink [with a cover charge]

**gedeihen** *unr. itr. V.; mit sein* (a) thrive;
(wirtschaftlich) flourish; prosper
(b) (fortschreiten) progress

**gedenken** *unr. itr. V.* (a) jmds./einer
Sache ~ (geh.) remember sb./sth.; (in einer
Feier) commemorate sb./sth.
(b) etw. zu tun ~: intend to do *or* doing sth.

**Gedenk·stätte** *die* memorial

**Gedicht** *das;* ~[e]s, ~e poem

**gediegen** ① *Adj.* solid ⟨furniture⟩; sound
⟨piece of work⟩
② *adv.* ~ gebaut/verarbeitet solidly built/
made

**gedieh** *1. u. 3. Pers. Sg. Prät. v.* GEDEIHEN

**gediehen** *2. Part. v.* GEDEIHEN

**Gedränge** *das;* ~s (a) pushing and
shoving; (Menge) crush; crowd
(b) ins ~ kommen *od.* geraten get into
difficulties

**gedroschen** *2. Part. v.* DRESCHEN

**gedrungen** ① *2. Part. v.* DRINGEN;
② *Adj.* stocky; thickset

**Geduld** *die;* ~: patience

**gedulden** *refl. V.* be patient; ~ Sie sich
bitte ein paar Minuten please be so good as
to wait a few minutes

**geduldig** ① *Adj.* patient
② *adv.* patiently

**Gedulds-:** ~**probe** *die* trial of one's
patience; ~**spiel** *das* puzzle

**gedurft** *2. Part. v.* DÜRFEN

**geeignet** *Adj.* suitable; (richtig) right

**Gefahr** *die;* ~, ~en (a) danger; (Bedrohung)
danger; threat (für to); bei ~: in case of
emergency
(b) (Risiko) risk; auf eigene ~: at one's own
risk

**gefährden** tr. V. endanger; jeopardize ⟨enterprise, success, position, etc.⟩

**gefährdet** Adj. ⟨people, adolescents, etc.⟩ at risk postpos.

**Gefährdung** die; ~, ~en (a) endangering; (eines Unternehmens, einer Position usw.) jeopardizing
(b) (Gefahr) threat (+ Gen. to)

**gefahren** 2. Part. v. FAHREN

**gefährlich** ① Adj. dangerous; (gewagt) risky
② adv. dangerously

**gefahr·los** ① Adj. safe
② adv. safely

**Gefährt** das; ~[e]s, ~e (geh.) vehicle

**Gefährte** der; ~n, ~n, **Gefährtin** die; ~, ~nen (geh.) companion; (Ehemann/Ehefrau) partner in life

**Gefälle** das; ~s, ~: slope; incline; (einer Straße) gradient

**gefallen**¹ unr. itr. V. (a) das gefällt mir [gut] I like it [a lot]
(b) sich (Dat.) etw. ~ lassen put up with sth.

**gefallen**² 2. Part. v. FALLEN, GEFALLEN

**Gefallen**¹ der; ~s, ~: favour

**Gefallen**² das; ~s pleasure

**Gefallene** der; adj. Dekl. soldier killed in action; die ~n the fallen

**Gefälle·strecke** die incline

**gefällig** ① Adj. (a) obliging; helpful
(b) (anziehend) pleasing; agreeable ⟨programme, behaviour⟩
② adv. pleasingly; agreeably

**Gefälligkeit** die; ~, ~en favour

**gefälligst** Adv. (ugs.) kindly

**gefangen** 2. Part. v. FANGEN

**Gefangene** der/die; adj. Dekl. prisoner

**gefangen-:** *~|halten, *~|nehmen
▶ FANGEN 1

**Gefangenschaft** die; ~, ~en captivity

**Gefängnis** das; ~ses, ~se (a) prison; gaol
(b) (Strafe) imprisonment

**Gefängnis-:** ~strafe die prison sentence; ~wärter der, ~wärterin die [prison] warder

**Gefasel** das; ~s (ugs. abwertend) twaddle (coll.); drivel (derog.)

**Gefäß** das; ~es, ~e (a) vessel; container
(b) (Anat.) vessel

**gefasst,** *gefaßt Adj. (a) calm; composed
(b) in auf etw. (Akk.) [nicht] ~ sein [not] be prepared for sth.

**Gefecht** das; ~[e]s, ~e battle

**Gefieder** das; ~s, ~: plumage; feathers pl.

**gefiedert** Adj. feathered

**geflissentlich** ① Adj. deliberate
② adv. deliberately

**geflochten** 2. Part. v. FLECHTEN

**geflogen** 2. Part. v. FLIEGEN

**geflohen** 2. Part. v. FLIEHEN

**geflossen** 2. Part. v. FLIESSEN

**Geflügel** das; ~s poultry

**Geflügel·schere** die poultry shears pl.

**geflügelt** Adj. winged ⟨insect, seed⟩; ein ~es Wort (fig.) a standard or familiar quotation

**gefochten** 2. Part. v. FECHTEN

**Gefolge** das; ~s, ~: entourage

**Gefolgschaft** die; ~, ~en: jmdm. ~ leisten obey or follow sb.; give one's allegiance to sb.; jmdm. die ~ verweigern refuse to obey or follow sb.; refuse to give sb. one's allegiance

**gefragt** Adj. in great demand postpos.; sought-after

**gefräßig** Adj. (abwertend) greedy

**Gefreite** der; adj. Dekl. (Milit.) lance corporal (Brit.); private first class (Amer.); (Marine) able seaman; (Luftw.) aircraftman first class (Brit.); airman third class (Amer.)

**gefressen** 2. Part. v. FRESSEN

**gefrieren** unr. itr. V.; mit sein freeze

**gefrier-, Gefrier-:** ~fach das freezing compartment; ~punkt der freezing point; ~schrank der freezer; ~|trocknen tr. V.; meist im Inf. u. 2. Part. freeze-dry; ~truhe die [chest] freezer

**gefroren** 2. Part. v. FRIEREN, GEFRIEREN

**gefrustet** Adj. (ugs.) frustrated

**Gefüge** das; ~s, ~: structure

**gefügig** Adj. compliant; docile ⟨animal⟩

**Gefühl** das; ~s, ~e (a) sensation; feeling
(b) (Gemütsverfassung) feeling

**gefühl·los** Adj. (a) numb
(b) (herzlos, kalt) unfeeling

**gefühls-, Gefühls-:** ~betont Adj. emotional; ~duselei die; ~~ (ugs. abwertend) mawkishness; ~mäßig Adj. emotional ⟨reaction⟩; ⟨action⟩ based on emotion; ~regung die emotion

**gefühl·voll** ① Adj. sensitive; (ausdrucksvoll) expressive
② adv. sensitively; expressively

**gefüllt** 2. Part. v. FÜLLEN

**gefunden** 2. Part. v. FINDEN; s. auch FRESSEN B

**Gegacker** das; ~s (a) (dauerndes Gackern) cackling
(b) (ugs.: Kichern) giggling

**gegangen** 2. Part. v. GEHEN

**gegeben** 2. Part. v. GEBEN

**gegebenen·falls** Adv. should the occasion arise

**gegen** Präp. mit Akk. (a) against; ~ etw. stoßen knock into sth.; ein Mittel ~ Krebs a cure for cancer; ~ die Abmachung contrary to the agreement
(b) ~ Abend/Morgen towards evening/dawn; ~ vier Uhr around 4 o'clock
(c) (im Vergleich zu) compared with

---

**(d)** (im Ausgleich für) for; ~ **Quittung** against a receipt

**Gegen-:** ~**angriff** der counter-attack; ~**argument** das counter-argument; ~**besuch** der return visit

**Gegend** die; ~, ~**en (a)** area **(b)** (Körperregion) region

**Gegen-:** ~**darstellung** die: eine ~darstellung [der Sache] an account [of the matter] from an opposing point of view; ~**druck** der counter pressure

**gegen·einander** Adv. against each other or one another

**gegen-, Gegen-:** ~**gewicht** das counterweight; ein ~gewicht zu od. gegen etw. bilden (fig.) counterbalance sth.; ~**gift** das antidote; ~**kandidat** der, ~**kandidatin** die opposing candidate; rival candidate; ~**leistung** die service in return; ~**mittel** das (gegen Gift) antidote; (gegen Krankheit) remedy; ~**partei** die opposing side; other side; (Sport) opposing side or team; ~**probe** die cross-check; ~**satz** der **(a)** (Gegenteil) opposite; im ~satz zu in contrast to or with; unlike **(b)** (Widerspruch) conflict; ~**sätzlich** Adj. conflicting; ~**schlag** der counterstroke; zum ~schlag ausholen prepare to counterattack or strike back; ~**seite** die **(a)** (einer Straße, eines Flusses usw.) other side; far side; **(b)** ▶ ~PARTEI; ~**seitig** ⒈ Adj. (wechselseitig) mutual; ⒉ adv. sich ~seitig helfen/überbieten help/outdo each other or one another; ~**seitigkeit** die; ~~: reciprocity; auf ~seitigkeit (Dat.) beruhen be mutual; ~**spieler** der, ~**spielerin** die opponent; (Sport) opposite number

**Gegen·stand** der object; (Thema) subject; topic

**gegenständlich** Adj. (Kunst) representational; (Philos.) objective

**gegenstands·los** Adj. **(a)** (hinfällig) invalid **(b)** (grundlos, unbegründet) unfounded ‹accusation, complaint, jealousy›; baseless ‹fear›

**gegen-, Gegen-:** ~**stimme** die vote against; ohne ~stimme unanimously; ~**stück** das companion piece; (fig.) counterpart; ~**teil** das opposite; im ~teil on the contrary; ~**teilig** Adj. opposite; contrary; ~**tor** das (Sport) goal for the other side

**gegen·über** Präp. mit Dat. **(a)** opposite **(b)** (in Bezug auf) ~ jmdm. od. jmdm. ~ freundlich sein be kind to sb. **(c)** (im Vergleich zu) compared with

**gegenüber-, Gegenüber-:** ~|**stehen** unr. itr. V. **(a)** jmdm./einer Sache ~stehen stand facing sb./sth.; (fig.) face sb./sth.; **(b)** jmdm./einer Sache feindlich/wohlwollend ~stehen be ill/well disposed towards sb./sth.; ~|**stellen** tr. V. confront; ~**stellung** die **(a)** confrontation; **(b)**

(Vergleich) comparison; **(c)** (zur Identifizierung) identification parade; ~|**treten** unr. itr. V.; mit sein jmdm./einer Sache ~treten (auch fig.) face sb./sth.

**Gegen·verkehr** der oncoming traffic

**Gegenwart** die; ~ **(a)** present **(b)** (Anwesenheit) presence **(c)** (Grammatik) present [tense]

**gegenwärtig** ⒈ Adj. present ⒉ adv. at present; at the moment

**Gegen-:** ~**wehr** die resistance; ~**wert** der equivalent; ~**wind** der head wind; ~**zug** der (Brettspiele, fig.) countermove

**gegessen** 2. Part. v. ESSEN

**geglichen** 2. Part. v. GLEICHEN

**geglitten** 2. Part. v. GLEITEN

**Gegner** der; ~s, ~, **Gegnerin** die; ~, ~**nen (a)** adversary; opponent **(b)** (Sport) opponent

**gegnerisch** Adj. opposing; opponents' ‹goal›

**Gegnerschaft** die; ~ (Einstellung) hostility; antagonism

**gegolten** 2. Part. v. GELTEN

**gegoren** 2. Part. v. GÄREN

**gegossen** 2. Part. v. GIESSEN

**gegriffen** 2. Part. v. GREIFEN

**Gehabe** das; ~s (abwertend) affected behaviour; ihr wichtigtuerisches ~: her pompous behaviour

**gehabt** Adj. (ugs.: schon da gewesen) same old (coll.); usual; wie ~: as before

**Gehalt¹** der; ~[e]s, ~e **(a)** meaning **(b)** (Anteil) content

**Gehalt²** das (österr. auch: der); ~[e]s, **Gehälter** salary

**gehalten** 2. Part. v. HALTEN

**Gehalts-:** ~**abrechnung** die salary statement; payslip; ~**empfänger** der, ~**empfängerin** die salary earner; ~**erhöhung** die salary increase; ~**zettel** der salary slip

**gehalt·voll** Adj. nutritious ‹food›; ‹novel, speech› rich in substance

**gehässig** Adj. (abwertend) spiteful

**Gehässigkeit** die; ~, ~**en (a)** (Wesen) spitefulness **(b)** (Äußerung) spiteful remark

**gehauen** 2. Part. v. HAUEN

**gehäuft** Adj. ein ~er Teelöffel/Esslöffel a heaped teaspoon/tablespoon

**Gehäuse** das; ~s, ~ (einer Maschine) casing; housing; (einer Kamera, Uhr) case

**geh·behindert** Adj. able to walk only with difficulty postpos.; disabled

**Gehege** das; ~s, ~ **(a)** (Jägerspr.) preserve; jmdm. ins ~ kommen (fig.) poach on sb.'s preserve; sich (Dat.) [gegenseitig] ins ~ kommen (fig.) encroach on each other's territory **(b)** (im Zoo) enclosure

**geheim** 1 *Adj.* **(a)** secret; **etw.** ~ **halten** keep sth. secret
**(b)** (mysteriös) mysterious
2 *adv.* ~ **abstimmen** vote by secret ballot

**geheim-, Geheim-:** ~**agent** *der,* ~**agentin** *die* secret agent; ~**dienst** *der* secret service; *\*~|**halten** ▶ GEHEIM 1A

**Geheimnis** *das;* ~ses, ~se secret

**Geheimnis·tuerei** *die;* ~ (ugs.) secretiveness

**geheimnis·voll** *Adj.* mysterious

**Geheim·nummer** *die* **(a)** (Bankw.) personal identification number; PIN
**(b)** (Telefonnummer) ex-directory number; unlisted number (Amer.)

**Geheim·zahl** *die* ▶ GEHEIMNUMMER A

**Geheiß** *das:* **auf jmds.** ~ (geh.) at sb.'s behest

**gehen** 1 *unr. itr. V.; mit sein* **(a)** walk; go; **über die Straße** ~: cross the street
**(b)** (sich irgendwohin begeben) go
**(c)** (regelmäßig besuchen) attend
**(d)** (weg~) go; leave
**(e)** (in Funktion sein) work; **meine Uhr geht falsch** my watch is wrong
**(f)** (möglich sein) **ja, das geht** yes, I/we can manage that; **das geht nicht** that can't be done
**(g)** (ugs.: gerade noch angehen) **Hast du gut geschlafen? – Es geht** Did you sleep well? – Not too bad
**(h)** (sich entwickeln) **der Laden/das Geschäft geht gut/gar nicht** the shop/business is doing well/not doing well at all; **es ist gut gegangen** it turned out well
**(i)** (*unpers.*) **wie geht es dir?** How are you?; **jmdm. geht es gut/schlecht** (gesundheitlich) sb. is well/not well; (geschäftlich) sb. is doing well/badly
**(j)** (*unpers.*) (sich um etw. handeln); **worum geht es hier?** what is this all about?
**(k) sich** ~ **lassen** (sich nicht beherrschen) lose control of oneself; (sich vernachlässigen) let oneself go
**(l)** (ein Liebespaar sein) **mit jmdm.** ~: go out with sb.
2 *unr. tr. V.* (zurücklegen) **10 km** ~: walk 10 km

*\***gehen|lassen** ▶ GEHEN 1K

**geheuer** *Adj.* **(a)** **in diesem Gebäude ist es nicht** ~: this building is eerie
**(b)** **ihr war doch nicht [ganz]** ~: she felt [a little] uneasy
**(c)** **die Sache ist [mir] nicht ganz** ~: [I feel] there's something odd about this business

**Gehilfe** *der;* ~n, ~n, **Gehilfin** *die;* ~, ~nen assistant

**Gehirn** *das;* ~[e]s, ~e brain

**Gehirn-:** ~**erschütterung** *die* concussion; ~**schlag** *der* stroke; ~**wäsche** *die* brainwashing *no indef. art.*

**gehoben** 1 2. *Part. v.* HEBEN;

2 *Adj.* **(a)** higher; senior ⟨*position*⟩
**(b)** (gewählt) elevated, refined

**geholfen** 2. *Part. v.* HELFEN

**Gehör** *das;* ~[e]s [sense of] hearing; **[etw.] nach dem** ~ **singen/spielen** sing/play [sth.] by ear; **das absolute** ~ (Musik) absolute pitch

**gehorchen** *itr. V.* **jmdm.** ~: obey sb.

**gehören** 1 *itr. V.* **(a)** **jmdm.** ~: belong to sb.
**(b)** (Teil eines Ganzen sein) **zu jmds. Freunden/Aufgaben** ~: be one of sb.'s friends/part of sb.'s duties
**(c)** (passend sein) **dein Roller gehört nicht in die Küche!** your scooter does not belong in the kitchen!
**(d)** (nötig sein) **es hat viel Fleiß dazu gehört** it took a lot of hard work; **dazu gehört sehr viel** that takes a lot
2 *refl. V.* (sich schicken) be fitting; **es gehört sich [nicht], ... zu ...:** it is [not] good manners to ...

**gehörig** 1 *Adj.* **(a)** proper
**(b)** (ugs.: beträchtlich) **ein** ~**er Schrecken/eine** ~**e Portion Mut** a good fright/a good deal of courage
2 *adv.* (ugs.: beträchtlich) ~ **essen/trinken** eat/drink heartily

**gehorsam** *Adj.* obedient

**Gehorsam** *der;* ~s obedience

**Geh·steig** *der;* ~[e]s, ~e pavement (Brit.); sidewalk (Amer.)

**Geht·nicht·mehr** *das:* **bis zum** ~ (salopp) ad nauseam

**Gehupe** *das;* ~s honking; hooting

**Geier** *der;* ~s, ~: vulture

**Geige** *die;* ~, ~n violin

**Geiger** *der;* ~s, ~, **Geigerin** *die;* ~, ~nen violin player; violinist

**Geiger·zähler** *der* (Physik) Geiger counter

**geil** *Adj.* **(a)** (oft abwertend: sexuell erregt) randy; horny (sl.); (lüstern) lecherous
**(b)** (Jugendspr.) great (coll.); fabulous (coll.)

**Geilheit** *die;* ~ ▶ GEIL A randiness; horniness (sl.); lecherousness

**Geisel** *die;* ~, ~n hostage

**Geisel-:** ~**nahme** *die;* ~~, ~~n taking of hostages; ~**nehmer** *der;* ~~s, ~~, ~**nehmerin** *die;* ~~, ~~nen terrorist/guerrilla *etc.* holding the hostages

**Geißel** *die;* ~, ~n (hist., auch fig.) scourge

**Geist** *der;* ~[e]s, ~er **(a)** (Verstand) mind
**(b)** (Scharfsinn) wit
**(c)** (innere Einstellung) spirit
**(d)** (denkender Mensch) mind; intellect; **ein großer/kleiner** ~: a great mind/a person of limited intellect
**(e)** (überirdisches Wesen) spirit; **der Heilige** ~ (christl. Rel.) the Holy Ghost *or* Spirit
**(f)** (Gespenst) ghost

**Geister-:** ~**bahn** *die* ghost train; ~**fahrer** *der;* ~**fahrerin** *die: person driving on the wrong side of the road or the wrong carriageway*

---

*\*old spelling - see note on page xiv

**geisterhaft** *Adj.* ghostly; eerie ⟨*atmosphere*⟩

**Geister·hand** *die;* wie von *od.* durch ∼: as if by an invisible hand

**geistes-, Geistes-:** ∼**abwesend** ① *Adj.* absent-minded; ② *adv.* absent-mindedly; ∼**blitz** *der* (ugs.) brainwave; ∼**gegenwart** *die* presence of mind; ∼**gegenwärtig** ① *Adj.* quick-witted; ② *adv.* with great presence of mind; ∼**krank** *Adj.* mentally ill; ∼**krankheit** *die* mental illness; ∼**wissenschaften** *Pl.* arts; humanities; ∼**wissenschaftler** *der,* ∼**wissenschaftlerin** *die* arts scholar; scholar in the humanities; ∼**zustand** *der* mental state

**geistig** ① *Adj.* (a) intellectual; (Psych.) mental
(b) alcoholic ⟨*drinks*⟩
② *adv.* intellectually; (Psych.) mentally

**geistlich** *Adj.* sacred ⟨*song, music*⟩; religious ⟨*order, book, writings*⟩

**Geistliche** *der; adj. Dekl.* clergyman

**geist-, Geist-:** ∼**los** *Adj.* dim-witted; (trivial) trivial; ∼**losigkeit** *die;* ∼∼: dim-wittedness; (Trivialität) triviality; ∼**reich** ① *Adj.* witty; (klug) clever; ② *adv.:* wittily; cleverly; ∼**tötend** *Adj.* soul-destroying ⟨*work, job*⟩; stupefyingly boring ⟨*chatter, drivel*⟩

**Geiz** *der;* ∼**es** meanness; (Knauserigkeit) miserliness

**geizen** *itr. V.* be mean

**Geiz·hals** *der* (abwertend) skinflint

**geizig** *Adj.* mean; (knauserig) miserly

**gekannt** *2. Part. v.* KENNEN

**Gekicher** *das;* ∼**s** giggling

**geklungen** *2. Part. v.* KLINGEN

**geknickt** *Adj.* (ugs.) dejected

**gekniffen** *2. Part. v.* KNEIFEN

**gekommen** *2. Part. v.* KOMMEN

**gekonnt** ① *2. Part. v.* KÖNNEN; ② *Adj.* accomplished; (hervorragend ausgeführt) masterly

**gekrochen** *2. Part. v.* KRIECHEN

**gekünstelt** ① *Adj.* artificial ② *adv.* er lächelte ∼: he gave a forced smile

**Gelächter** *das;* ∼**s,** ∼: laughter

**geladen** *2. Part. v.* LADEN

**Gelände** *das;* ∼**s,** ∼ (a) (Landschaft) ground; terrain
(b) (Grundstück) site; (von Schule, Krankenhaus usw.) grounds *pl.*

**Geländer** *das;* ∼**s,** ∼: banisters *pl.;* handrail; (am Balkon, an einer Brücke) railing[s *pl.*]; (aus Stein) parapet

**gelang** *3. Pers. Sg. Prät. v.* GELINGEN

**gelangen** *itr. V.; mit sein* an etw. (*Akk.*)/zu etw. ∼: reach sth.; (fig.) zu Ansehen ∼: gain esteem

**gelassen** ① *2. Part. v.* LASSEN; ② *Adj.* calm; (gefasst) composed

**Gelassenheit** *die;* ∼: calmness; (Gefasstheit) composure

**Gelatine** /ʒelaˈtiːnə/ *die;* ∼: gelatine

**gelaufen** *2. Part. v.* LAUFEN

**geläufig** *Adj.* (vertraut) common ⟨*expression, concept*⟩

**gelaunt** *Adj.* gut ∼: cheerful; schlecht ∼: bad-tempered; gut/schlecht ∼ sein be in a good/bad mood

**gelb** *Adj.* yellow

**Gelb** *das;* ∼**s,** ∼ *od.* (ugs.) ∼**s** yellow

**gelblich** *Adj.* yellowish; yellowed ⟨*paper*⟩; sallow ⟨*skin*⟩

**Gelb·sucht** *die* (Med.) jaundice

**Geld** *das;* ∼**es,** ∼**er** money; großes ∼: large denominations *pl.;* kleines/bares ∼: change/cash

**geld-, Geld-:** ∼**automat** *der* cash dispenser; ∼**beutel** *der* (bes. südd.) purse; ∼**börse** *die* purse; ∼**buße** *die* fine; ∼**gier** *die* avarice; ∼**gierig** *Adj.* avaricious; ∼**institut** *das* financial institution; ∼**mangel** *der* lack of money; ∼**mittel** *Pl.* financial resources; ∼**preis** *der* cash prize; ∼**rück·gabe** *die* (a) ∼rückgabe verlangen ask for one's money back; Anspruch auf ∼rückgabe haben be entitled to one's money back; (b) (eines Automaten) coin return; ∼**schein** *der* banknote; bill (Amer.); ∼**schrank** *der* safe; ∼**schwierigkeiten** *Pl.* financial difficulties *or* straits; ∼**spende** *die* donation; contribution; ∼**strafe** *die* fine; ∼**stück** *das* coin; ∼**wechsel** *der* exchanging of money; „∼wechsel" 'bureau de change'

**Gelee** /ʒeˈleː/ *der od. das;* ∼**s,** ∼**s** jelly

**gelegen** ① *2. Part. v.* LIEGEN; ② *Adj.* (passend) convenient

**Gelegenheit** *die;* ∼, ∼**en** opportunity; (Anlass) occasion

**Gelegenheits-:** ∼**arbeit** *die* casual work; ∼**kauf** *der* bargain

**gelegentlich** ① *Adj.* occasional ② *adv.* occasionally

**gelehrig** *Adj.* ⟨*child*⟩ who is quick to learn; ⟨*animal*⟩ that is quick to learn

**gelehrt** *Adj.* learned

**Gelehrte** *der/die; adj. Dekl.* scholar

**Geleit** *das;* ∼[e]s, ∼e (geh.) sie bot uns ihr ∼ an she offered to accompany us

**geleiten** *tr. V.* (geh.) escort

**Geleit·schutz** *der* (Milit.) escort

**Gelenk** *das;* ∼[e]s, ∼e joint

**gelenkig** ① *Adj.* agile ⟨*person*⟩; supple ⟨*limb*⟩ ② *adv.* agilely

**Gelenkigkeit** *die;* ∼: agility; (von Gliedmaßen) suppleness

**gelernt** *Adj.* qualified

**gelesen** *2. Part. v.* LESEN

**Geliebte** *der/die; adj. Dekl.* lover/mistress

**geliefert** *Adj.:* ~ **sein** (salopp) have had it (coll.)

**geliehen** 2. *Part. v.* LEIHEN

**gelind[e]** ⟦1⟧ *Adj.* mild
⟦2⟧ *adv.* mildly; ~e **gesagt** to put it mildly

**gelingen** *unr. itr. V.; mit sein* succeed

**Gelingen** *das;* ~s success

**gelitten** 2. *Part. v.* LEIDEN

**gellen** *itr. V.* **(a)** (hell schallen) ring out
**(b)** (nachhallen) ring

**geloben** *tr. V.* (geh.) vow; **das Gelobte Land** the Promised Land

**gelogen** 2. *Part. v.* LÜGEN

**gelöst** *Adj.* relaxed

**gelten** ⟦1⟧ *unr. itr. V.* **(a)** (gültig sein) be valid; ⟨banknote, coin⟩ be legal tender; ⟨law etc.⟩ be in force
**(b)** (angesehen werden) **als etw.** ~: be regarded as sth.
**(c)** (+ *Dat.*) (bestimmt sein für) be directed at
⟦2⟧ *unr. tr. V.* **(a)** (wert sein) **sein Wort gilt viel/ wenig** his word carries a lot of/little weight
**(b)** *unpers.* **es gilt, etw. zu tun** it is essential to do sth.

**geltend: etw.** ~ **machen** assert sth.

**Geltung** *die;* ~ **(a)** (validity; **für jmdn.** ~ **haben** apply to sb.
**(b)** (Wirkung) recognition; **zur** ~ **kommen** show to [its best] advantage

**Geltungs·bedürfnis** *das* need for recognition

**gelungen** ⟦1⟧ 2. *Part. v.* GELINGEN;
⟦2⟧ *Adj.* **(a)** (ugs.: spaßig) priceless
**(b)** (ansprechend) inspired

**gemächlich** /gə'mɛ(ː)çlɪç/ ⟦1⟧ *Adj.* leisurely
⟦2⟧ *adv.* in a leisurely manner

**Gemächlichkeit** *die;* ~: leisureliness

**gemacht: ein** ~er **Mann sein** (ugs.) be a made man

**Gemahl** *der;* ~s, ~e (geh.) consort; husband

**Gemahlin** *die;* ~, ~nen (geh.) consort; wife

**Gemälde** *das;* ~s, ~: painting

**gemäß** *Präp. + Dat.* in accordance with

**gemäßigt** *Adj.* moderate; qualified ⟨optimism⟩; temperate ⟨climate⟩

**Gemecker[e]** *das;* ~s **(a)** (von Schafen, Ziegen) bleating
**(b)** (ugs. abwertend: Nörgelei) griping (coll.); grousing (coll.); moaning

**gemein** ⟦1⟧ *Adj.* **(a)** vulgar ⟨joke, expression⟩; nasty ⟨person⟩
**(b)** (niederträchtig) mean; dirty ⟨lie⟩; mean ⟨trick⟩
⟦2⟧ *adv.* in a mean *or* nasty way

**Gemeinde** *die;* ~, ~n **(a)** municipality; (Bewohner) community
**(b)** (Pfarr~) parish
**(c)** (versammelte Gottesdienstteilnehmer) congregation

---

**Gemeinde-:** ~**rat** *der* (a) (Gremium) local council; (b) (Mitglied) local councillor;
~**rätin** *die* local councillor;
~**schwester** *die* district nurse;
~**verwaltung** *die* local administration

**gemein·gefährlich** *Adj.* dangerous to the public

**Gemein·gut** *das* (geh.) common property

**Gemeinheit** *die;* ~, ~en **(a)** meanness
**(b)** (Handlung) mean trick

**gemein·nützig** *Adj.* serving the public good *postpos., not pred.;* (wohltätig) charitable

**gemeinsam** ⟦1⟧ *Adj.* **(a)** common ⟨interests, characteristics⟩; mutual ⟨acquaintance, friend⟩; joint ⟨property, account⟩; shared ⟨experience⟩; ~e **Interessen/Merkmale haben** have interests/characteristics in common
**(b)** (miteinander unternommen) joint; **viel Gemeinsames haben** have a lot in common
⟦2⟧ *adv.* together

**Gemeinsamkeit** *die;* ~, ~en common feature

**Gemeinschaft** *die;* ~, ~en **(a)** community
**(b)** (Verbundenheit) coexistence

**gemeinschaftlich** ▸ GEMEINSAM

**gemein·verständlich** *Adj.* generally comprehensible

**Gemein·wohl** *das* public good

**gemessen** ⟦1⟧ 2. *Part. v.* MESSEN;
⟦2⟧ *Adj.* (würdevoll) measured ⟨steps, tones, language⟩; deliberate ⟨words, manner of speaking⟩

**Gemetzel** *das;* ~s, ~: massacre

**gemieden** 2. *Part. v.* MEIDEN

**Gemisch** *das;* ~[e]s, ~e mixture (**aus, von** of)

**gemocht** 2. *Part. v.* MÖGEN

**gemolken** 2. *Part. v.* MELKEN

***Gemse** ▸ GÄMSE

**Gemurmel** *das;* ~s murmuring

**Gemüse** *das;* ~s, ~: vegetables *pl.*

**gemusst, * gemußt** 2. *Part. v.* MÜSSEN

**Gemüt** *das;* ~[e]s, ~er **(a)** nature
**(b)** (Empfindungsvermögen) heart
**(c)** (Mensch) soul

**gemütlich** ⟦1⟧ *Adj.* snug; cosy; (bequem) comfortable; (ungezwungen) informal
⟦2⟧ *adv.* cosily; (bequem) comfortably; ~ **beisammensitzen** sit pleasantly together

**Gemütlichkeit** *die;* ~: snugness; (Zwanglosigkeit) informality

**gemüts-, Gemüts-:** ~**krank** *Adj.* (Med., Psych.) emotionally disturbed; ~**mensch** *der* (ugs.) even-tempered person

**gemüt·voll** *Adj.* warm-hearted; (empfindsam) sentimental

**Gen** *das;* ~s, ~e (Biol.) gene

**genannt** 2. *Part. v.* NENNEN

**genas** 1. u. 3. *Pers. Sg. Prät. v.* GENESEN

**genau** ⟦1⟧ *Adj.* **(a)** (exakt) exact; precise

**(b)** (sorgfältig, gründlich) meticulous; ⟨person⟩; careful ⟨study⟩

[2] adv. **(a)** exactly; precisely; ~ **um 8⁰⁰** at 8 o'clock precisely

**(b)** (gerade, eben) just

**(c)** (als Verstärkung) just

**(d)** (als Zustimmung) exactly; precisely

**(e)** (sorgfältig) ~ **arbeiten/etw.** ~ **durchdenken** work/think sth. out meticulously; ~ **genommen** strictly speaking

\***genau·genommen** ▶ GENAU 2E

**Genauigkeit** die; ~ **(a)** (Exaktheit) exactness; precision; (einer Waage) accuracy

**(b)** (Sorgfalt) meticulousness

**genau·so** Adv. **(a)** mit Adjektiven just as

**(b)** mit Verben in exactly the same way; (in demselben Maße) just as much

**genaustens** Adv. **etw.** ~ **durchdenken/ beachten** think sth. out/observe sth. most meticulously

**Gendarm** /ʒan'darm/ der; ~**en,** ~**en** (österr., sonst veralt.) village or local policeman or constable

**Gendarmerie** /ʒandarmə'ri:/ die; ~, ~**n** (österr., sonst veralt.) village or local constabulary

**genehm** Adj. **jmdm.** ~ **sein** (geh.) (jmdm. passen) be convenient to sb.; (jmdm. angenehm sein) be acceptable to sb.

**genehmigen** tr. V. approve ⟨plan, alterations, application⟩; authorize ⟨stay⟩; grant ⟨request⟩; give permission for ⟨demonstration⟩; **sich** (Dat.) **etw.** ~ (ugs.) treat oneself to sth.

**Genehmigung** die; ~, ~**en (a)** ▶ GENEHMIGEN; approval; authorization; granting; permission (Gen. for)

**(b)** (Schriftstück) permit; (Lizenz) licence

**geneigt** Adj. **in** ~ **sein, etw. zu tun** be inclined to do sth.

**General** der; ~**s,** ~**e** od. **Generäle** general

**General-:** ~**direktor** der chairman; president (Amer.); ~**direktorin** die chairwoman; president (Amer.)

**generalisieren** tr., itr. V. generalize

**Generalisierung** die; ~, ~**en** generalization

**general-, General-:** ~**probe** die (auch fig.) dress rehearsal; ~**streik** der general strike; ~**überholen** tr. V.; nur im Inf. und 2. Part. gebr. (bes. Technik) **etw.** ~**überholen** give sth. a general overhaul; ~**vertreter** der, ~**vertreterin** die general representative; ~**vollmacht** die (Rechtsw.) full or unlimited power of attorney

**Generation** die; ~, ~**en** generation

**Generations·konflikt** der generation gap

**Generator** der; ~**s,** ~**en** generator

**generell** [1] Adj. general

[2] adv. generally

**genervt** Adj. annoyed

**genesen** unr. itr. V.; mit sein (geh.) recover

**Genesung** die; ~, ~**en** (geh.) recovery

**genetisch** (Biol.) Adj. genetic

**Genf** (das); ~**s** Geneva

**Genfer** [1] der; ~**s,** ~: Genevese

[2] Adj. Genevese; **der** ~ See Lake Geneva

**Genferin** die; ~, ~**nen** Genevese

**Gen·forschung** die (Biol.) genetic research

**genial** Adj. brilliant

**Genialität** die; ~: genius

**Genick** das; ~[e]s, ~**e** back or nape of the neck

**Genie** /ʒe'ni:/ das; ~**s,** ~**s** genius

**genieren** /ʒe'ni:rən/ refl. V. be embarrassed

**genießbar** Adj. (essbar) edible; (trinkbar) drinkable; **er ist heute nicht** ~ (fig. ugs.) he is unbearable today

**genießen** unr. tr. V. enjoy

**Genießer** der; ~**s,** ~, **Genießerin** die; ~, ~**nen: er ist ein richtiger Genießer** he is a regular 'bon viveur'; **sie ist eine stille Genießerin** she enjoys life [to the full] in her own quiet way

**genießerisch** [1] Adj. appreciative

[2] adv. appreciatively; ⟨drink, eat⟩ with relish

**Genitale** das; ~**s,** **Genitalien** /geni'ta:liən/, **Genital·organ** das genital organ

**Genitiv** der; ~**s,** ~**e** (Sprachw.) genitive [case]

**Gen·manipulation** die genetic manipulation

**gen·manipuliert** Adj. genetically engineered; genetically manipulated

**Genom** /ge'no:m/ das; ~**s,** ~**e** (Biol.) genome

**genommen** 2. Part. v. NEHMEN

**genoss, \*genoß** 1. u. 3. Pers. Sg. Prät. v. GENIESSEN

**Genosse** der; ~**n,** ~**n** comrade

**genossen** 2. Part. v. GENIESSEN

**Genossenschaft** die; ~, ~**en** cooperative

**Genossin** die; ~, ~**nen** comrade

**gen-, Gen-:** ~**technik** die genetic engineering no art.; ~**technisch** [1] Adj. genetic engineering ⟨techniques, research etc.⟩; ⟨research, developments etc.⟩ in genetic engineering [2] adv. by genetic engineering; ~**technisch verändert** genetically altered or modified; altered or modified by genetic engineering; ~**technologie** die genetic engineering no art.

**genug** Adv. enough

**genügen** itr. V. **(a)** be enough

**(b)** einer Sache (Dat.) ~: satisfy sth.

**genügend** [1] Adj. **(a)** enough

**(b)** (befriedigend) satisfactory

[2] adv. enough

**genügsam** Adj. modest

**Genugtuung** /-tu:ʊŋ/ die; ~, ~**en** satisfaction

g

**Genus** *das;* ~, **Genera** (Sprachw.) gender

**Genuss, \*Genuß** *der;* **Genusses, Genüsse**
(a) consumption
(b) (Wohlbehagen) etw. mit ~ essen/lesen eat
sth. with relish/enjoy reading sth.

**genüsslich, \*genüßlich** *Adv.* ⟨*eat,
drink*⟩ with relish

**Geograph** *der;* ~en, ~en geographer

**Geographie** *die;* ~: geography *no art.*

**Geographin** *die;* ~, ~nen geographer

**geographisch** *Adj.* geographic[al]

**Geologe** *der;* ~n, ~n geologist

**Geologie** *die;* ~: geology *no art.*

**Geologin** *die;* ~, ~nen geologist

**geologisch** *Adj.* geological

**Geometrie** *die;* ~: geometry *no art.*

**geometrisch** *Adj.* geometric[al]

**Gepäck** *das;* ~[e]s luggage (Brit.); baggage
(Amer.); (am Flughafen) baggage

**Gepäck-:** ~**annahme** *die* (a) checking
in the luggage/baggage; (b) (Schalter) [in-
counter of the] luggage office (Brit.) *or*
baggage office (Amer.); (zur Aufbewahrung) [in-
counter of the] left-luggage office (Brit.) *or*
checkroom (Amer.); (am Flughafen) baggage
check-in; ~**aufbewahrung** *die* left-
luggage office (Brit.); checkroom (Amer.);
(Schließfächer) luggage lockers (Brit.); baggage
lockers (Amer.); ~**ausgabe** *die* [out-counter
of the] luggage office (Brit.) *or* (Amer.) baggage
office; (zur Aufbewahrung) [out-counter of the]
left-luggage office (Brit.) *or* (Amer.) checkroom;
(am Flughafen) baggage reclaim; ~**kontrolle**
*die* baggage check; ~**netz** *das* luggage rack
(Brit.); baggage rack (Amer.); ~**schalter** *der*
▶ ~ANNAHME B; ~**schein** *der* luggage
ticket (Brit.); baggage check (Amer.); ~**träger**
*der* (a) porter; (b) (am Fahrrad) carrier; rack

**Gepard** *der;* ~s, ~e cheetah; hunting
leopard

**gepfeffert** *Adj.* (ugs.) steep (coll.) ⟨*price,
rent, etc.*⟩

**Gepfeife** *das;* ~s (ugs. abwertend)
[continuous, tuneless] whistling

**gepfiffen** 2. *Part. v.* PFEIFEN

**gepflegt** *Adj.* (a) well-groomed; spruce
⟨*appearance*⟩; neat ⟨*clothing*⟩
(b) (hochwertig) choice ⟨*food, drink*⟩

**Gepflogenheit** *die;* ~, ~en (geh.) custom;
(Gewohnheit) habit

**Geplapper** *das;* ~s (ugs., oft abwertend)
prattling

**geplättet** *Adj.* (salopp) flabbergasted

**Gepolter** *das;* ~s clatter

**gepriesen** 2. *Part. v.* PREISEN

**Gequake** *das;* ~s (ugs.) croaking; (von
Enten) quacking

**Gequäke** *das;* ~s (ugs.) bawling

**gequält** *Adj.* forced ⟨*smile, gaiety*⟩; pained
⟨*expression*⟩

**gequollen** 2. *Part. v.* QUELLEN

**gerade** ① *Adj.* (a) straight; etw. ~ biegen
bend sth. straight; straighten sth. [out]; ~
stehen stand up straight
(b) (nicht schief) upright
(c) (aufrichtig) forthright; direct
(d) (Math.) even ⟨*number*⟩
② *Adv.* just; (direkt) right

**Gerade** *die;* ~, ~n; *auch adj. Dekl.* (Geom.)
straight line

**gerade-:** ~**aus** *Adv.* straight ahead;
~**|biegen** *unr. tr. V.* (ugs.: bereinigen)
straighten out; ~**heraus** /----'-/ (ugs.) *Adv.*
etw. ~heraus sagen say sth. straight out;
~**so** *Adv.* ~so groß/lang wie ...: just as big/
long as ...; ~**|stehen** *unr. itr. V.* (fig.:
einstehen) für etw. ~stehen accept
responsibility for sth.; ~**zu** *Adv.* really;
(beinahe) almost

**gerad-, Gerad-:** ~**linig** ① *Adj.* (a)
straight; direct, lineal ⟨*descent, descendant*⟩
(b) (aufrichtig) straightforward; ② *adv.*
(a) ~linig verlaufen run in a straight line
(b) (aufrichtig) ~linig handeln/denken be
straightforward; ~**linigkeit** *die;* ~~
(a) straightness; (b) (Aufrichtigkeit)
straightforwardness

**gerammelt** *Adv.* ~ **voll** (ugs.) [jam-]packed
(coll.); packed out (coll.)

**Geranie** /ge'ra:niə/ *die;* ~, ~n geranium

**gerann** 3. *Pers. Sg. Prät. v.* GERINNEN

**gerannt** 2. *Part. v.* RENNEN

**gerät** 3. *Pers. Sg. Präsens v.* GERATEN¹

**Gerät** *das;* ~[e]s, ~e (a) piece of
equipment; (Fernseher, Radio) set; (Garten~)
tool
(b) (Turnen) piece of apparatus

**geraten¹** *unr. itr. V.; mit sein* (a) (gelangen)
get
(b) (werden) turn out; (gut ~) turn out well

**geraten²** ① 2. *Part. v.* RATEN, GERATEN¹
② *Adj.* advisable

**Geratewohl:** aufs ~ (ugs.) ⟨*select*⟩ at
random; wir fuhren aufs ~ los (ugs.) we went
for a drive just to see where we ended up

**geraum** *Adj.* (geh.) considerable

**geräumig** *Adj.* spacious ⟨*room*⟩; roomy
⟨*cupboard etc.*⟩

**Geräusch** *das;* ~[e]s, ~e sound;
(unerwünscht) noise

**geräusch-, Geräusch-:** ~**arm** ① *Adj.*
quiet; ② *adv.* quietly; ~**los** ① *Adj.* silent
② *adv.* (a) silently; (b) (fig. ugs.) without
[any] fuss; ~**pegel** *der* noise level; ~**voll**
*Adj.* noisy

**gerben** *tr. V.* tan ⟨*hides, skins*⟩

**gerecht** ① *Adj.* just; (unparteiisch) fair
② *adv.* justly

**gerechtfertigt** *Adj.* justified

**Gerechtigkeit** *die;* ~: justice

**Gerechtigkeits·sinn** *der* sense of justice

**Gerede** *das;* ~s (abwertend) (a) (ugs.) talk
(b) (Klatsch) gossip

**geregelt** *Adj.* regular, steady ⟨*job*⟩

**gereizt** *Adj.* irritable

**Gericht¹** *das;* ∼[e]s, ∼e court; (Richter) bench; (Gebäude) court [house]; **das Jüngste** ∼ (Rel.) the Last Judgement

**Gericht²** *das;* ∼[e]s, ∼e dish

**gerichtlich** ⟨1⟩ *Adj.* judicial; legal ⟨*proceedings*⟩
⟨2⟩ *adv.* jmdn. ∼ verfolgen take sb. to court

**Gerichts-:** ∼**hof** *der* Court of Justice; ∼**kosten** *Pl.* legal costs; ∼**saal** *der* courtroom; ∼**verfahren** *das* legal proceedings *pl.;* **ein** ∼**verfahren einleiten** institute legal *or* court proceedings; **ohne** ∼**verfahren** without trial; ∼**vollzieher** *der;* ∼∼s, ∼∼, ∼**vollzieherin** *die;* ∼∼, ∼∼**nen** bailiff

**gerieben** 2. *Part. v.* REIBEN

**geriffelt** *Adj.* corrugated ⟨*surface, sheet metal*⟩; fluted ⟨*column*⟩; ribbed ⟨*glass*⟩

**gering** *Adj.* (a) low; little ⟨*value*⟩; small ⟨*quantity, amount*⟩; short ⟨*distance, time*⟩ (b) (unbedeutend) slight; minor ⟨*role*⟩; **nicht im Geringsten** not in the slightest *or* least; **jmdn./etw.** ∼ **achten** *od.* **schätzen** have a low opinion of *or* think very little of sb./sth.; **den Erfolg/Reichtümer** ∼ **achten** *od.* **schätzen** set little store by success/riches

**geringfügig** ⟨1⟩ *Adj.* slight; minor ⟨*alteration, injury*⟩; trivial ⟨*amount, detail*⟩
⟨2⟩ *adv.* slightly

**Geringfügigkeit** *die;* ∼, ∼en triviality

**\*gering|schätzen** ▸ GERING B

**geringschätzig** *Adj.* disdainful; disparaging ⟨*remark*⟩

**gerinnen** *unr. itr. V.; mit sein* ⟨*blood*⟩ clot; ⟨*milk*⟩ curdle

**Gerippe** *das;* ∼s, ∼: skeleton

**gerippt** *Adj.* ribbed; fluted ⟨*glass, column*⟩

**gerissen** ⟨1⟩ 2. *Part. v.* REISSEN
⟨2⟩ *Adj.* (ugs.) crafty

**geritten** 2. *Part. v.* REITEN

**geritzt** *Adj.* (salopp) etw. ist ∼: sth. is [all] settled; **ist** ∼**!** will do! (coll.)

**Germane** *der;* ∼n, ∼n, **Germanin** *die;* ∼, ∼**nen** (hist.) ancient German; Teuton

**germanisch** *Adj.* (auch fig.) Germanic; Teutonic

**Germanistik** *die;* ∼: German studies *pl.,* no art.

**gern[e]; lieber, am liebsten** *Adv.* (a) etw. ∼ **tun** like *or* enjoy doing sth.; **er spielt lieber Tennis als Golf** he prefers playing tennis to golf; **etw.** ∼**/am liebsten essen** like sth./like sth. best; **ja,** ∼**/aber** ∼: yes, of course; certainly!
(b) (durchaus) **das glaube ich** ∼: I can well believe that

**gerochen** 2. *Part. v.* RIECHEN

**Geröll** *das;* ∼s, ∼e debris; (größer) boulders *pl.*

**geronnen** 2. *Part. v.* RINNEN, GERINNEN

**Gerste** *die;* ∼: barley

**Gersten·korn** *das* (Med.) sty

**Gerte** *die;* ∼, ∼n switch

**Geruch** *der;* ∼[e]s, Gerüche smell; (von Blumen) scent

**Gerücht** *das;* ∼[e]s, ∼e rumour

**gerufen** 2. *Part. v.* RUFEN

**geruhsam** ⟨1⟩ *Adj.* peaceful; leisurely ⟨*stroll*⟩
⟨2⟩ *adv.* leisurely; quietly

**Geruhsamkeit** *die;* ∼: peacefulness; (eines Spaziergangs) leisureliness

**Gerümpel** *das;* ∼s junk

**gerungen** 2. *Part. v.* RINGEN

**Gerüst** *das;* ∼[e]s, ∼e scaffolding *no pl., no indef. art.*

**gesamt** *Adj.* whole; entire

**gesamt-, Gesamt-:** ∼**deutsch** *Adj.* all-German; ∼**eindruck** *der* general impression

**Gesamtheit** *die;* **die** ∼ **der Bevölkerung** the entire population

**Gesamt-:** ∼**schule** *die* comprehensive [school]; ∼**werk** *das* œuvre; (Bücher) complete works *pl.*

**gesandt** 2. *Part. v.* SENDEN

**Gesandte** *der/die; adj. Dekl.* envoy

**Gesandtschaft** *die;* ∼, ∼en legation

**Gesang** *der;* ∼[e]s, Gesänge (a) singing (b) (Lied) song

**Gesang-:** ∼**buch** *das* hymn book; ∼**verein** *der* choral society

**Gesäß** *das;* ∼es, ∼e backside; buttocks *pl.*

**geschaffen** 2. *Part. v.* SCHAFFEN 1

**Geschäft** *das;* ∼[e]s, ∼e (a) business; (Transaktion) [business] deal; **mit jmdm.** ∼**e/ein** ∼ **machen** do business with sb./strike a bargain *or* do a deal with sb.; **ein gutes** ∼ **machen** make a good profit (b) (Laden) shop; store (Amer.)

**Geschäfte-macher** *der,* **Geschäfte-macherin** *die* (abwertend) profit-seeker

**geschäftig** *Adj.* bustling

**geschäftlich** ⟨1⟩ *Adj.* business *attrib.*
⟨2⟩ *adv.* on business

**geschäfts-, Geschäfts-:** ∼**bedingungen** *Pl.* terms [and conditions] of trade; ∼**brief** *der* business letter; ∼**frau** *die* businesswoman; ∼**freund** *der,* ∼**freundin** *die* business associate; ∼**führer** *der* manager; (Vereinswesen) secretary; ∼**führerin** *die* ▸ ∼FÜHRER: manageress; secretary; ∼**führung** *die* management; ∼**gebaren** *das* business *no art.;* business practices *pl.;* ∼**inhaber** *der,* ∼**inhaberin** *die* owner of the/a business; ∼**jahr** *das* financial year; ∼**kosten** *Pl.* auf ∼**kosten** on expenses; ∼**lage** *die* [business] position; ∼**leitung** *die* ▸ ∼FÜHRUNG; ∼**leute** ▸ ∼MANN; ∼**mann** *der; Pl.* ∼**leute** businessman; ····⟩

**g**

~**ordnung** die standing orders pl.; (im Parlament) [rules pl. of] procedure;

~**partner** der, ~**partnerin** die business partner; ~**reise** die business trip; ~**schluss** der closing time; ~**stelle** die branch; (einer Partei, eines Vereins) office;

~**straße** die shopping street; ~**tüchtig** Adj. able, ⟨businessman, landlord, etc.⟩; ~**viertel** das business quarter; (Einkaufszentrum) shopping district; ~**wagen** der company car; ~**zeit** die business hours pl.; (im Büro) office hours pl.

**geschah** 3. Pers. Sg. Prät. v. GESCHEHEN

**geschehen** unr. itr. V.; mit sein happen; occur; (ausgeführt werden) be done; **jmdm. geschieht etw.** sth. happens to sb.

**gescheit** Adj. **(a)** (intelligent) clever **(b)** (ugs.: vernünftig) sensible

**Gescheitheit** die; ~: cleverness

**Geschenk** das; ~[e]s, ~e present; gift

**Geschenk-:** ~**artikel** der gift; ~**packung** die gift pack

**Geschichte** die; ~, ~n **(a)** history **(b)** (Erzählung) story

**geschichtlich** Adj. **(a)** historical **(b)** (bedeutungsvoll) historic

**Geschichts-:** ~**atlas** der historical atlas; ~**buch** das history book

**Geschick**[1] das; ~[e]s, ~e (geh.) fate

**Geschick**[2] das; ~[e]s skill

**Geschicklichkeit** die; ~: skilfulness; skill

**geschickt** [1] Adj. **(a)** skilful **(b)** (klug) clever; adroit [2] adv. **(a)** (gewandt) skilfully **(b)** (klug) cleverly; adroitly

**geschieden** 2. Part. v. SCHEIDEN

**geschienen** 2. Part. v. SCHEINEN

**Geschirr** das; ~[e]s, ~e **(a)** crockery; (benutzt) dishes pl.; **(b)** (für Zugtier) harness

**Geschirr-:** ~**spül·maschine** die dishwasher; ~**tuch** das; Pl. ~**tücher** tea towel; dish towel (Amer.)

**geschissen** 2. Part. v. SCHEISSEN

**geschlafen** 2. Part. v. SCHLAFEN

**geschlagen** 2. Part. v. SCHLAGEN

**Geschlecht** das; ~[e]s, ~er **(a)** sex **(b)** (Generation) generation **(c)** (Sippe) family **(d)** (Sprachw.) gender

**geschlechtlich** Adj. sexual

**geschlechts-, Geschlechts-:** ~**akt** der sex[ual] act; ~**chromosom** das (Biol.) sex chromosome; ~**krank** Adj. ⟨person⟩ suffering from VD; ~**krankheit** die venereal disease; ~**organ** das sex[ual] organ; genital organ; ~**teil** das genitals pl.; ~**verkehr** der sexual intercourse; ~**wort** das ▶ ARTIKEL A

**geschlichen** 2. Part. v. SCHLEICHEN

**geschliffen** [1] 2. Part. v. SCHLEIFEN; [2] Adj. polished

**geschlossen** [1] 2. Part. v. SCHLIESSEN; [2] Adj. united ⟨action, front⟩; unified ⟨procedure⟩; **eine ~e Ortschaft** a built-up area

**Geschlossenheit** die; ~: unity

**geschlungen** 2. Part. v. SCHLINGEN

**Geschmack** der; ~[e]s, Geschmäcke taste

**geschmacklos** [1] Adj. tasteless [2] adv. tastelessly

**Geschmacklosigkeit** die; ~, ~en lack of [good] taste; bad taste; (Äußerung) tasteless remark

**Geschmack[s]·sache** die **das ist ~:** that is a question or matter of taste

**geschmack·voll** [1] Adj. tasteful [2] adv. tastefully

**Geschmatze** das; ~s (ugs. abwertend) smacking one's lips no art.; (beim Essen) noisy eating no art.

**Geschmeide** das; ~s, ~ (geh.) jewellery no pl.

**geschmeidig** [1] Adj. **(a)** sleek ⟨hair, fur⟩; soft ⟨leather, boots, skin⟩ **(b)** (gelenkig) supple ⟨fingers⟩; lithe ⟨body, movement, person⟩ [2] adv. (gelenkig) agilely

**Geschmeidigkeit** die; ~: ▶ GESCHMEIDIG 1: sleekness; suppleness; softness; litheness

**geschmissen** 2. Part. v. SCHMEISSEN

**geschmolzen** 2. Part. v. SCHMELZEN

**Geschmuse** das; ~s (ugs.) cuddling; (eines Pärchens) kissing and cuddling

**Geschnetzelte** das; adj. Dekl.: small, thin slices of meat [cooked in sauce]

**geschnitten** 2. Part. v. SCHNEIDEN

**geschoben** 2. Part. v. SCHIEBEN

**geschollen** 2. Part. v. SCHALLEN

**gescholten** 2. Part. v. SCHELTEN

**Geschöpf** das; ~[e]s, ~e creature

**geschoren** 2. Part. v. SCHEREN

**Geschoss**[1], *****Geschoß** das; Geschosses, Geschosse projectile; (Kugel) bullet; (Rakete) missile

**Geschoss**[2], *****Geschoß** das; Geschosses, Geschosse floor; storey

**geschossen** 2. Part. v. SCHIESSEN

**geschraubt** Adj. (ugs.) stilted

**Geschrei** das; ~s **(a)** shouting; (von Verletzten, Tieren) screaming; screams pl.; **(b)** (ugs. fig) fuss

**geschrieben** 2. Part. v. SCHREIBEN

**geschrie[e]n** 2. Part. v. SCHREIEN

**geschritten** 2. Part. v. SCHREITEN

**geschunden** 2. Part. v. SCHINDEN

**Geschütz** das; ~es, ~e [big] gun

**Geschütz·feuer** das artillery fire; shell fire

**geschützt** Adj. **(a)** sheltered

---

*alte Schreibung - vgl. Hinweis auf S. xiv

**(b)** (unter Naturschutz) protected
**(c)** ~er Geschlechtsverkehr sex with a
condom
**Geschwader** *das;* ~s, ~ (Marine)
squadron; (Luftwaffe) wing (Brit.); group (Amer.)
**Geschwätz** *das;* ~es (ugs. abwertend)
prattling; (Klatsch) gossip
**geschwätzig** *Adj.* (abwertend) talkative
**geschweige** *Konj.* ~ [denn] let alone;
never mind
**geschwiegen** 2. *Part. v.* SCHWEIGEN
**geschwind** (bes. südd.) **1** *Adj.* swift; quick
**2** *adv.* swiftly; quickly
**Geschwindigkeit** *die;* ~, ~en speed
**Geschwindigkeits-:** ~begrenzung
*die,* ~beschränkung *die* speed limit
**Geschwister** *Pl.* brothers and sisters
**geschwollen** **1** 2. *Part. v.* SCHWELLEN;
**2** *Adj.* **(a)** swollen
**(b)** (fig. abwertend) pompous
**3** *adv.* pompously
**geschwommen** 2. *Part. v.* SCHWIMMEN
**geschworen** 2. *Part. v.* SCHWÖREN
**Geschworene** *der/die; adj. Dekl.* juror
**Geschwulst** *die;* ~, Geschwülste tumour
**geschwunden** 2. *Part. v.* SCHWINDEN
**geschwungen** **1** 2. *Part. v.* SCHWINGEN;
**2** *Adj.* curved
**Geschwür** *das;* ~s, ~e ulcer; (Furunkel)
boil
**gesehen** 2. *Part v.* SEHEN
**Geseire** *das;* ~s (ugs.) drivel
**Geselle** *der;* ~n, ~n journeyman; (Kerl)
fellow
**gesellen** *refl. V.* sich zu jmdm. ~: join sb.
**gesellig** *Adj.* sociable; ein ~er Abend/~es
Beisammensein a convivial evening/a
friendly get-together
**Geselligkeit** *die;* ~: die ~ lieben enjoy
[good] company
**Gesellin** *die;* ~, ~nen journeyman;
journeywoman (rare)
**Gesellschaft** *die;* ~, ~en **(a)** society
**(b)** (Veranstaltung) party
**(c)** (Kreis von Menschen) group of people
**(d)** (Wirtschaft) company
**Gesellschafter** *der;* ~s, ~ **(a)** ein guter
~ sein be good company
**(b)** (Wirtsch.) partner; (Teilhaber) shareholder
**Gesellschafterin** *die;* ~, ~nen **(a)**
[lady] companion
**(b)** (Wirtsch.) partner; (Teilhaberin) shareholder
**gesellschaftlich** *Adj.* social
**gesellschafts-, Gesellschafts-:**
~fähig *Adj.* (auch fig.) socially acceptable;
~ordnung *die* social order; ~reise *die*
group tour; ~schicht *die* stratum of
society; ~spiel *das* party game
**gesessen** 2. *Part. v.* SITZEN
**Gesetz** *das;* ~es, ~e **(a)** law; (geschrieben)
statute
**(b)** (Regel) rule

**gesetz-, Gesetz-:** ~buch *das* statute
book; ~gebend *Adj.* legislative; ~geber
*der* legislator; (Organ) legislature;
~gebung *die;* ~: legislation
**gesetzlich** **1** *Adj.* legal; statutory
⟨holiday⟩; lawful ⟨heir, claim⟩
**2** *adv.* legally
**gesetz-, Gesetz-:** ~los *Adj.* lawless;
~losigkeit *die;* ~~: lawlessness;
~mäßig **1** *Adj.* **(a)** law-governed;
~mäßig sein be governed by *or* obey a
[natural] law/[natural] laws; **(b)** (gesetzlich)
legal; (rechtmäßig) lawful; **2** *adv.* in
accordance with a [natural] law/[natural]
laws; ~mäßigkeit *die* **(a)** conformity to a
[natural] law/[natural] laws; **(b)**
(Gesetzlichkeit) legality; (Rechtmäßigkeit)
lawfulness
**gesetzt** *Adj.* staid
**Gesetztheit** *die;* ~: staidness
**gesetz·widrig** *Adj.* illegal; unlawful
**Gesetz·widrigkeit** *die* illegality;
unlawfulness
**Gesicht** *das;* ~[e]s, ~er face; (fig.) das ~
einer Stadt the appearance of a town
**Gesichts-:** ~ausdruck *der* expression;
look; ~creme *die* face cream; ~punkt
*der* point of view; ~wasser *das* face
lotion; ~züge *Pl.* features
**Gesindel** *das;* ~s (abwertend) rabble
**gesinnt** *Adj.* christlich/sozial ~ [sein] [be]
Christian-minded/public-spirited; jmdm.
freundlich ~ sein be well-disposed towards
sb.
**Gesinnung** *die;* ~, ~en [basic]
convictions *pl.;* [fundamental] beliefs *pl.*
**gesinnungs-, Gesinnungs-:** ~los
(abwertend) *Adj.* unprincipled; ~wandel
*der* change of attitude
**gesittet** *Adj.* well-behaved; well-mannered
**gesogen** 2. *Part. v.* SAUGEN
**gesondert** **1** *Adj.* separate
**2** *adv.* separately
**gesonnen** *Adj.* ~ sein, etw. zu tun feel
disposed to do sth.
**gesotten** 2. *Part. v.* SIEDEN
**Gespann** *das;* ~[e]s, ~e **(a)** (Zugtiere) team
**(b)** (Wagen) horse and carriage
**(c)** (Menschen) couple; pair
**gespannt** *Adj.* **(a)** eager; rapt ⟨attention⟩;
~ zuhören listen with rapt attention
**(b)** tense ⟨situation, atmosphere⟩; strained
⟨relationships⟩
**Gespenst** *das;* ~[e]s, ~er **(a)** ghost
**(b)** (geh.: Gefahr) spectre
**gespenstig, gespenstisch** *Adj.*
ghostly; eerie ⟨building, atmosphere⟩
**gespie[e]n** 2. *Part. v.* SPEIEN
**gesponnen** 2. *Part. v.* SPINNEN
**Gespött** *das;* ~[e]s mockery; ridicule
**Gespräch** *das;* ~[e]s, ~e conversation;
(Diskussion) discussion; (Telefon~) call (**mit** to)

**g**

**gesprächig** *Adj.* talkative

**Gesprächs-:** ~**partner** *der,*
~**partnerin** *die:* wer war dein ~partner/
deine ~partnerin? who were you talking to?;
~**stoff** *der* topics *pl.* of conversation;
~**thema** *das* topic of conversation

**gesprochen** *2. Part. v.* SPRECHEN

**gesprossen** *2. Part. v.* SPRIESSEN

**gesprungen** *2. Part. v.* SPRINGEN

**Gespür** *das;* ~s feel

**gest.** *Abk.* = **gestorben** d.

**Gestalt** *die;* ~, ~en (a) build
(b) (Mensch, Persönlichkeit) figure
(c) (in der Dichtung) character
(d) (Form) form

**gestalten** *tr. V.* fashion; lay out ⟨*public gardens*⟩; shape ⟨*character, personality*⟩; arrange ⟨*party, conference, etc.*⟩

**Gestaltung** *die;* ~, ~en ▸ GESTALTEN:
fashioning; laying out; arranging

**gestand** *1. u. 3. Pers. Sg. Prät. v.* GESTEHEN

**gestanden** ⟨1⟩ *2. Part. v.* STEHEN, GESTEHEN;
⟨2⟩ *Adj.* ein ~er Mann a grown man; ein ~er
Parlamentarier an experienced *or* seasoned
parliamentarian

**geständig** *Adj.:* ~ sein have confessed

**Geständnis** *das;* ~ses, ~se confession

**Gestank** *der;* ~[e]s (abwertend) stench; stink

**Gestapo** *die;* ~ (ns.) Gestapo

**gestatten** ⟨1⟩ *tr., itr. V.* permit; allow; ~
Sie, dass ich ...? may I ...?
⟨2⟩ *refl. V.* sich (*Dat.*) etw. ~: allow oneself
sth.

**Geste** /ˈɡɛstə, ˈɡeːstə/ *die;* ~, ~n (auch fig.)
gesture

**Gesteck** *das;* ~[e]s, ~e flower
arrangement

**gestehen** *tr., itr. V.* confess

**Gestein** *das;* ~[e]s, ~e rock

**Gestell** *das;* ~[e]s, ~e (a) (für Weinflaschen)
rack; (zum Wäschetrocknen) horse
(b) (Unterbau) frame

**gestern** *Adv.* yesterday

**gestiegen** *2. Part. v.* STEIGEN

**gestikulieren** *itr. V.* gesticulate

**Gestirn** *das;* ~[e]s, ~e star

**gestochen** ⟨1⟩ *2. Part. v.* STECHEN;
⟨2⟩ *Adj.* extremely neat ⟨*handwriting*⟩

**gestohlen** *2. Part. v.* STEHLEN

**Gestöhne** *das;* ~s groaning

**gestorben** *2. Part. v.* STERBEN

**gestoßen** *2. Part. v.* STOSSEN

**Gestrampel** *das;* ~s (ugs.) kicking about;
(beim Radfahren) pedalling

**Gesträuch** *das;* ~[e]s, ~e shrubbery;
bushes *pl.*

**gestreift** *Adj.* striped

**gestrichen** ⟨1⟩ *2. Part. v.* STREICHEN;
⟨2⟩ *Adj.* level ⟨*measure*⟩

**gestrig** *Adj.* yesterday's

**gestritten** *2. Part. v.* STREITEN

**Gestrüpp** *das;* ~[e]s, ~e undergrowth

**gestunken** *2. Part. v.* STINKEN

**Gestüt** *das;* ~[e]s, ~e stud [farm]

**Gesuch** *das;* ~[e]s, ~e request (um for);
(Antrag) application (um for)

**gesucht** *Adj.* (a) [much] sought-after
(b) (gekünstelt) laboured

**gesund;** gesünder, *seltener:* ~er,
gesündest..., *seltener:* ~est... *Adj.* healthy;
wieder ~ werden get better; bleib ~! look
after yourself!

**gesunden** *itr. V.; mit sein* ⟨person⟩ recover,
get well, regain one's health

**Gesundheit** *die;* ~: health; ~! (ugs.) bless
you!

**gesundheitlich** ⟨1⟩ *Adj.; nicht präd.* ~e
Betreuung health care; sein ~er Zustand [the
state of] his health
⟨2⟩ *adv.* wie geht es Ihnen ~? how are you?

**gesundheits-, Gesundheits-:** ~**amt**
*das* [local] public health department;
~**gefährdend** *Adj.* ~gefährdend sein be
a danger to health; ~gefährdende Bakterien/
Produkte bacteria that are a danger to
health/products that are a health risk;
~**gefährdung** *die* risk to health;
~**schädlich** *Adj.* detrimental to [one's]
health *postpos.;* ~**zeugnis** *das* certificate
of health; ~**zustand** *der* state of health

**gesungen** *2. Part. v.* SINGEN

**gesunken** *2. Part. v.* SINKEN

**getan** *2. Part. v.* TUN

**Getier** *das;* ~[e]s (geh.) animals *pl.*

**Getöse** *das;* ~s [thunderous] roar; (von
vielen Menschen) din

**getragen** *2. Part. v.* TRAGEN

**Getränk** *das;* ~[e]s, ~e drink; beverage
(formal)

**getrauen** *refl. V.* dare

**Getreide** *das;* ~s grain

**Getreide-:** ~**anbau** *der* growing of
cereals; ~**handel** *der* corn trade

**getrennt** ⟨1⟩ *Adj.* separate
⟨2⟩ *adv.* ⟨pay⟩ separately; ⟨sleep⟩ in separate
rooms

**getreten** *2. Part. v.* TRETEN

**getreu** ⟨1⟩ *Adj.* (geh.) exact; faithful ⟨image⟩
⟨2⟩ *adv.* (geh.) ⟨report, describe⟩ faithfully

**Getriebe** *das;* ~s, ~: gears *pl.;* (in einer
Maschine) gear system

**getrieben** *2. Part. v.* TREIBEN

**getroffen** *2. Part. v.* TREFFEN, TRIEFEN

**getrogen** *2. Part. v.* TRÜGEN

**getrost** ⟨1⟩ *Adj.* confident
⟨2⟩ *adv.* confidently; du kannst es mir ~
glauben you can take my word for it

**getrunken** *2. Part. v.* TRINKEN

**Getto** *das;* ~s, ~s ghetto

**Getue** *das;* ~s (ugs. abwertend) fuss (**um** about)

**Getümmel** *das;* ~s tumult

**geübt** *Adj.* accomplished; practised ⟨*eye, ear*⟩

**Gewächs** *das;* ~es, ~e plant

**gewachsen** ⁜1⁜ 2. *Part. v.* WACHSEN; ⁜2⁜ jmdm./einer Sache ~ **sein** be a match for sb./be equal to sth.

**gewagt** *Adj.* daring; (gefährlich) risky; (fast anstößig) risqué ⟨*joke etc.*⟩

**gewählt** ⁜1⁜ *Adj.* refined ⁜2⁜ *adv.* in a refined manner

**Gewähr** *die;* ~: guarantee; **keine** ~ übernehmen be unable to guarantee sth.

**gewähren** *tr. V.* grant; give ⟨*pleasure, joy*⟩

**gewähr·leisten** *tr. V.* guarantee

**Gewahrsam** *der;* ~s (a) (Obhut) safe-keeping (b) (Haft) custody

**Gewährs·mann** *der; Pl.* ~männer *od.* ~leute, **Gewährs·person** *die* informant; source

**Gewalt** *die;* ~, ~en (a) power (b) (Willkür) force (c) (körperliche Kraft) force; violence

**gewalt-, Gewalt-:** ~**akt** *der* act of violence; ~**anwendung** *die* use of force *or* violence ~**bereit** *Adj.* ⟨*person*⟩ prone to violence; ⟨*group, organization*⟩ prepared to resort *or* use violence; ~**bereitschaft** *die: s.* ~BEREIT: propensity to violence; willingness to resort to *or* use violence

**Gewalten·teilung** *die* separation of powers

**gewaltig** ⁜1⁜ *Adj.* (a) (immens) huge (b) (imponierend) mighty, huge, massive ⟨*building etc*⟩; monumental ⟨*literary work etc.*⟩ ⁜2⁜ *adv.* (ugs.) very much

**gewalt·los** ⁜1⁜ *Adj.* non-violent ⁜2⁜ *adv.* without violence

**Gewalt·losigkeit** *die;* ~: non-violence

**gewaltsam** ⁜1⁜ *Adj.* forcible ⟨*expulsion*⟩; enforced ⟨*separation*⟩; violent ⟨*death*⟩ ⁜2⁜ *adv.* forcibly

**gewalt·tätig** *Adj.* violent

**Gewalt·tätigkeit** *die* (a) (gewalttätige Art) violence (b) ▶ GEWALTAKT

**Gewand** *das;* ~[e]s, Gewänder (geh.) robe; gown

**gewandt** ⁜1⁜ 2. *Part. v.* WENDEN; ⁜2⁜ *Adj.* skilful; (körperlich) agile ⁜3⁜ *adv.* skilfully; (körperlich) agilely

**Gewandtheit** *die;* ~: ▶ GEWANDT 2: skill; skilfulness; agility

**gewann** 1. *u.* 3. *Pers. Sg. Prät. v.* GEWINNEN

**gewaschen** 2. *Part. v.* WASCHEN

**Gewässer** *das;* ~s, ~: stretch of water

**Gewebe** *das;* ~s, ~ (a) (Stoff) fabric (b) (Med., Biol.) tissue

**Gewehr** *das;* ~[e]s, ~e rifle; (Schrot~) shotgun

**Geweih** *das;* ~[e]s, ~e antlers *pl.*

**Gewerbe** *das;* ~s, ~: business; (Handel, Handwerk) trade

**Gewerbe-:** ~**freiheit** *die* right to carry on a business *or* trade; ~**ordnung** *die* laws *pl.* governing trade and industry; ~**schein** *der* licence to carry on a business *or* trade; ~**treibende** *der/die; adj. Dekl.* tradesman/tradeswoman; ~**zweig** *der* branch of trade

**gewerblich** ⁜1⁜ *Adj.* commercial; business *attrib.*; (industriell) industrial ⁜2⁜ *adv.* ~ tätig sein work

**gewerbs·mäßig** *Adj.* professional

**Gewerkschaft** *die;* ~, ~en trade union

**Gewerkschaft[l]er** *der;* ~s, ~, **Gewerkschaft[l]erin** *die;* ~, ~nen trade unionist

**gewerkschaftlich** ⁜1⁜ *Adj.* [trade] union *attrib.;* ⁜2⁜ *adv.* ~ organisiert sein belong to a [trade] union

**Gewerkschafts·funktionär** *der,* **Gewerkschafts·funktionärin** *die* [trade] union official

**gewesen** 2. *Part. v.* SEIN¹

**gewichen** 2. *Part. v.* WEICHEN

**Gewicht** *das;* ~[e]s, ~e (auch fig.) weight; [nicht] ins ~ **fallen** be of [no] consequence

**Gewicht·heben** *das;* ~s weightlifting

**gewichtig** *Adj.* weighty

**Gewichts·klasse** *die* (Sport) weight [division *or* class]

**gewieft** *Adj.* (ugs.) cunning

**gewiesen** 2. *Part. v.* WEISEN

**gewillt** *Adj.* in [nicht] ~ sein, etw. zu tun be [un]willing to do sth.

**Gewimmel** *das;* ~s throng; (von Insekten) teeming mass

**Gewinde** *das;* ~s, ~ (Technik) thread

**Gewinn** *der;* ~[e]s, ~e (a) profit (b) (Preis einer Lotterie) prize; (beim Spiel) winnings *pl.;* (c) (Sieg) win

**Gewinn·beteiligung** *die* (Wirtsch.) profit sharing; (Betrag) profit-sharing bonus

**gewinn·bringend** *Adj.* lucrative

**gewinnen** ⁜1⁜ *unr. tr. V.* win; gain ⟨*time, influence, validity, etc.*⟩ ⁜2⁜ *unr. itr. V.* win (**bei** at)

**gewinnend** *Adj.* winning

**Gewinner** *der;* ~s, ~, **Gewinnerin** *die;* ~, ~nen winner

**Gewinn-:** ~**quote** *die* share of prize money; ~**spanne** *die* profit margin; ~**sucht** *die* greed for profit

**Gewinnung** *die;* ~ (a) (von Kohle, Erz usw.) mining; extraction; (von Öl) recovery; (von Metall aus Erz) extraction (b) (Erzeugung) production

**Gewinn·zahl** *die* winning number

**Gewirr** *das;* ∼[e]s **(a)** tangle
**(b)** (Durcheinander) **ein** ∼ **von Ästen** a maze of branches

**gewiss, \*gewiß** [1] *Adj.* certain
[2] *adv.* certainly

**Gewissen** *das;* ∼s, ∼: conscience

**gewissenhaft** [1] *Adj.* conscientious
[2] *adv.* conscientiously

**gewissen·los** *Adj.* unscrupulous

**Gewissens·bisse** *Pl.* pangs of conscience

**gewissermaßen** *Adv.* (sozusagen) as it were; (in gewissem Sinne) to a certain extent

**Gewissheit, \*Gewißheit** *die;* ∼, ∼en certainty

**Gewitter** *das;* ∼s, ∼: thunderstorm

**Gewitter·wolke** *die* thundercloud

**gewittrig** *Adj.* thundery

**gewitzt** *Adj.* shrewd

**gewoben** 2. *Part. v.* WEBEN

**gewogen** [1] 2. *Part. v.* WIEGEN
[2] *Adj.* (geh.) well disposed (+ *Dat.* towards)

**gewöhnen** [1] *tr. V.* **jmdn. an jmdn./etw.** ∼: get sb. used to sb./sth.; accustom sb. to sb./sth.
[2] *refl. V.* **sich an jmdn./etw.** ∼: get used *or* get *or* become accustomed to sb./sth.; accustom oneself to sb./sth.

**Gewohnheit** *die;* ∼, ∼en habit

**gewohnheits-, Gewohnheits-:**
∼**mäßig** [1] *Adj.* habitual ⟨*drinker etc.*⟩; automatic ⟨*reaction etc.*⟩; [2] *adv.* (regelmäßig) habitually; ∼**mensch** *der* creature of habit; ∼**tier** *das* (scherzh.) creature of habit; ∼**trinker** *der,* ∼**trinkerin** *die* habitual drinker; ∼**verbrecher** *der,* ∼**verbrecherin** *die* (Rechtsw.) habitual criminal

**gewöhnlich** [1] *Adj.* **(a)** normal; ordinary
**(b)** (gewohnt, üblich) usual
**(c)** (abwertend: ordinär) common
[2] *adv.* **(a)** [für] ∼: usually; **wie** ∼: as usual
**(b)** (abwertend: ordinär) in a common way

**gewohnt** *Adj.* **(a)** usual
**(b)** etw. (*Akk.*) ∼ **sein** be used to sth.

**Gewölbe** *das;* ∼s, ∼: vault

**gewonnen** 2. *Part. v.* GEWINNEN

**geworben** 2. *Part. v.* WERBEN

**geworfen** 2. *Part. v.* WERFEN

**gewrungen** 2. *Part. v.* WRINGEN

**Gewühl** *das;* ∼[e]s milling crowd

**gewunden** 2. *Part. v.* WINDEN

**Gewürz** *das;* ∼es, ∼e spice; (würzende Zutat) seasoning

**Gewürz-:** ∼**gurke** *die* pickled gherkin; ∼**nelke** *die* clove

**gewusst, \*gewußt** 2. *Part. v.* WISSEN

**gez.** *Abk.* = **gezeichnet** sgd.

**Gezeit** *die;* ∼, ∼en tide

**Gezerre** *das;* ∼s wrangling

**gezielt** [1] *Adj.* specific ⟨*questions, measures, etc.*⟩; deliberate ⟨*insult, indiscretion*⟩; well-directed ⟨*advertising campaign*⟩
[2] *adv.* ⟨*proceed, act*⟩ purposefully

**geziemen** (geh. veralt.) [1] *itr. V.* **jmdm.** [nicht] ∼: [ill] befit sb
[2] *refl. V.* be proper; **sich für jmdn.** ∼: befit sb.

**geziert** [1] *Adj.* (abwertend) affected
[2] *adv.* (abwertend) affectedly

**gezogen** 2. *Part. v.* ZIEHEN

**Gezwitscher** *das;* ∼s twittering

**gezwungen** [1] 2. *Part. v.* ZWINGEN
[2] *Adj.* forced

**gezwungenermaßen** *Adv.* of necessity

**gib** *Imperativ Sg. Präsens v.* GEBEN

**gibst** 2. *Pers. Sg. Präsens v.* GEBEN

**gibt** 3. *Pers. Sg. Präsens v.* GEBEN

**Gicht** *die;* ∼: gout

**Giebel** *der;* ∼s, ∼: gable

**Gier** *die;* ∼: greed (nach for)

**gierig** [1] *Adj.* greedy
[2] *adv.* greedily

**gießen** [1] *unr. tr. V.* **(a)** pour (in + *Akk.* into, über + *Akk.* over)
**(b)** (verschütten) spill (über + *Akk.* over)
**(c)** (begießen) water
[2] *unpers.* (ugs.) pour [with rain]

**Gießer** *der;* ∼s, ∼: caster

**Gießerei** *die;* ∼, ∼en foundry

**Gießerin** *die;* ∼, ∼nen caster

**Gift** *das;* ∼[e]s, ∼e poison; (Schlangen∼) venom

**gift·grün** *Adj.* garish green

**giftig** *Adj.* poisonous; venomous ⟨*snake*⟩; toxic, poisonous ⟨*substance, gas, chemical*⟩; (fig.) venomous

**Gift-:** ∼**mord** *der* [murder by] poisoning; ∼**mörder** *der,* ∼**mörderin** *die* poisoner; ∼**müll** *der* toxic waste; ∼**pilz** *der* poisonous mushroom; [poisonous] toadstool; ∼**schlange** *die* venomous snake; ∼**schrank** *der* poison cabinet *or* cupboard; ∼**stachel** *der* poisonous sting; ∼**zahn** *der* poison fang

**Gigant** *der;* ∼en, ∼en giant

**gigantisch** *Adj.* gigantic

**Gilde** *die;* ∼, ∼n (hist.) guild

**gilt** 3. *Pers. Sg. Präsens v.* GELTEN

**Gimpel** *der;* ∼s, ∼: bullfinch

**Gin** /dʒɪn/ *der;* ∼s, ∼s gin

**ging** 1. u. 3. *Pers. Sg. Prät. v.* GEHEN

**Ginster** *der;* ∼s, ∼: broom

**Gipfel** *der;* ∼s, ∼: peak; (höchster Punkt des Berges) summit; (fig.) height

**Gipfel·konferenz** *die* summit conference

**gipfeln** *itr. V.* in etw. (*Dat.*) ∼: culminate in sth.

**Gipfel·treffen** *das* summit meeting

---

\*alte Schreibung - vgl. Hinweis auf S. xiv

**Gips** *der;* ~es, ~e plaster; gypsum (Chem.)

**Gips·abdruck** *der* plaster cast

**gipsen** *tr. V.* plaster; put ‹*leg, arm, etc.*› in plaster

**Gips·verband** *der* plaster cast

**Giraffe** *die;* ~, ~n giraffe

**Girlande** *die;* ~, ~n festoon

**Giro** /'ʒiːro/ *das;* ~s, ~s, *österr. auch* **Giri** (Finanzw.) giro

**Giro·konto** *das* (Finanzw.) current account

**gis, Gis** *das;* ~, ~ (Musik) G sharp

**Gischt** *der;* ~[e]s, ~e *od.* die; ~, ~en spray

**Gitarre** *die;* ~, ~n guitar

**Gitarrist** *der;* ~en, ~en, **Gitarristin** *die;* ~, ~nen guitarist

**Gitter** *das;* ~s, ~: bars *pl.;* (vor Fenster-, Türöffnungen) grille; (in der Straßendecke, im Fußboden) grating; (Geländer) railing[s *pl.*]

**Gitter·fenster** *das* barred window

**Glacé·hand·schuh** /glaˈseː:.../ *der* kid glove

**Gladiole** *die;* ~, ~n gladiolus

**Glanz** *der;* ~es (a) (von Licht, Sternen, Augen) brightness; (von Haar, Metall, Perlen, Leder usw.) lustre; sheen **(b)** (der Jugend, Schönheit) radiance; (des Adels usw.) splendour

**glänzen** *itr. V.* **(a)** (Glanz ausstrahlen) shine; ‹*hair, metal, etc.*› gleam; ‹*elbows, trousers, etc.*› be shiny **(b)** (Bewunderung erregen) shine (**bei** at)

**glänzend** (ugs.) ⓵ *Adj.* **(a)** shining; gleaming ‹*hair, metal, etc.*›; shiny ‹*elbows, trousers, etc.*› **(b)** (bewundernswert) brilliant; splendid ‹*references, marks, results, etc.*› ⓶ *adv.* ~ **mit** jmdm. auskommen get on very well with sb.; **es geht mir/uns** ~: I am/ we are very well

**glanz-, Glanz-:** ~**leistung** *die* (auch iron.) brilliant performance; ~**los** *Adj.* dull; lacklustre; ~**nummer** *die* star turn; ~**voll** ⓵ *Adj.* brilliant; sparkling ‹*variety number*›; ⓶ *adv.* brilliantly

**Glas** *das;* ~es, Gläser **(a)** glass **(b)** (Trinkgefäß) glass; **zwei** ~ *od.* **Gläser Wein** two glasses of wine **(c)** (Behälter) jar

**Glas:** ~**bläser** *der,* **Glas·bläserin** *die* glass-blower; ~**container** *der* bottle bank

**Gläschen** *das;* ~s, ~ **(a)** [little] glass **(b)** (kleines Gefäß) [little] [glass] jar

**Glaser** *der;* ~s, ~, **Glaserin** *die;* ~, ~nen glazier

**gläsern** *Adj.* glass

**Glas·faser** *die* glass fibre

**glasieren** *tr. V.* **(a)** glaze **(b)** (Kochk.) ice; glaze ‹*meat*›

**glasig** *Adj.* **(a)** glassy **(b)** (Kochk.) transparent

**Glas·malerei** *die* stained glass

**Glasur** *die;* ~, ~en **(a)** glaze **(b)** (Kochk.) icing; (auf Fleisch) glaze

**glatt** ⓵ *Adj.* **(a)** smooth; (rutschig) slippery **(b)** (ugs.: offensichtlich) downright ‹*lie*›; outright ‹*deception, fraud*›; flat ‹*refusal*› ⓶ *adv.* **(a)** smoothly; ~ **gehen** (ugs.) go smoothly **(b)** (ugs.: rückhaltlos) jmdm. etw. ~ **ins Gesicht sagen** tell sb. sth. straight to his/her face; ‹*reject, deny*› flatly

**Glätte** *die;* ~: smoothness; (Rutschigkeit) slipperiness

**Glatt·eis** *das* glaze; ice; (auf der Straße) black ice

**glätten** *tr. V.* smooth out ‹*piece of paper, etc.*›; smooth [down] ‹*feathers, fur, etc.*›; plane ‹*wood etc.*›

**glatt-:** \*~\|**gehen** ▶ GLATT 2A; ~**weg** *Adv.* (ugs.) etw. ~weg ablehnen/ignorieren turn sth. down flat/simply ignore sth.; **das ist** ~weg erlogen/erfunden that's a downright lie/that's pure invention

**Glatze** *die;* ~, ~n bald head; **eine** ~ **haben/bekommen** be/go bald

**Glaube** *der;* ~ns faith (**an** + *Akk.* in); (Überzeugung, Meinung) belief (**an** + *Akk.* in)

**glauben** ⓵ *tr. V.* **(a)** (meinen) think **(b)** (für wahr halten) believe; **das glaube ich dir nicht** I don't believe you; **das glaubst du doch selbst nicht!** [surely] you can't be serious; **sie glaubt ihm jedes Wort** she believes every word he says; **ob du es glaubst oder nicht ...** believe it or not ...; **das ist doch kaum zu** ~ (ugs.) it's incredible ⓶ *itr. V.* believe (**an** + *Akk.* in)

**Glaubens-:** ~**bekenntnis** *das* creed; ~**freiheit** *die* religious freedom; ~**krieg** *der* religious war; ~**sache** *die* (ugs.) matter of faith *or* belief

**glaubhaft** ⓵ *Adj.* credible ⓶ *adv.* convincingly

**gläubig** ⓵ *Adj.* devout; (vertrauensvoll) trusting ⓶ *adv.* devoutly; (vertrauensvoll) trustingly

**Gläubige** *der/die; adj. Dekl.* believer

**Gläubiger** *der;* ~s, ~: creditor

**glaub·würdig** ⓵ *Adj.* credible ⓶ *adv.* convincingly

**Glaubwürdigkeit** *die;* ~: credibility

**gleich** ⓵ *Adj.* **(a)** (identisch, von derselben Art) same; ~ **bleiben** remain the same; ‹*speed, temperature, etc.*› remain constant; ~ **bleibend** constant, steady ‹*temperature, speed, etc.*›; (~berechtigt, ~wertig, Math.) equal **(b)** (ugs.: gleichgültig) **es ist mir völlig** *od.* **ganz** ~: I couldn't care less (coll.); **ganz** ~, **wer anruft, ...**: no matter who calls, ... ⓶ *adv.* **(a)** (übereinstimmend) ~ **groß/alt** *usw.* **sein** be the same height/age *etc.;* ~ **gut/ schlecht** *usw.* equally good/bad *etc.;* **(b)** (in derselben Weise) ~ **aufgebaut/gekleidet** having the same structure/wearing identical clothes ⸱⸱⸱⸱▸

**(c)** (sofort) at once; straight away; (bald) in a moment

**(d)** (räumlich) right; just; ~ rechts/links immediately on the right/left

**gleich-, Gleich-:** ~**alt[e]rig** /-alt(ə)rɪç/ Adj. of the same age (mit as); ~**artig** ① Adj. of the same kind postpos. (+ Dat. as); (sehr ähnlich) very similar (+ Dat. to); ② adv. in the same way; ~**berechtigt** Adj. having equal rights postpos.; ~berechtigte Partner equal partners; ~**berechtigung** die equal rights pl.; *~|**bleiben**, ~**bleibend** ▶ GLEICH 1A

**gleichen** unr. itr. V. jmdm./einer Sache ~: be like or resemble sb./sth.;

**gleichermaßen** Adv. equally

**gleich-, Gleich-:** ~**falls** Adv. (auch) also; (ebenfalls) likewise; danke ~falls! thank you, [and] the same to you; ~**förmig** ① Adj. (a) (einheitlich) uniform; (b) (monoton) monotonous; ② adv. (a) (einheitlich) uniformly; (b) (monoton) monotonously; ~**geschlechtlich** Adj. homosexual; ~**gewicht** das balance; ~**gewichts-störung** die disturbance of one's sense of balance; ~**gültig** ① Adj. indifferent (gegenüber towards); (belanglos) trivial; das ist mir ~gültig it's a matter of indifference to me; ② adv. indifferently; ~**gültigkeit** die indifference (gegenüber towards)

**Gleichheit** die; ~, ~en (a) identity; (Ähnlichkeit) similarity

**(b)** (gleiche Rechte) equality

**Gleichheits-zeichen** das equals sign

**gleich-, Gleich-:** ~|**kommen** unr. itr. V.; mit sein (a) (entsprechen) be tantamount to; (b) (die gleiche Leistung erreichen) jmdm./einer Sache [an etw. (Dat.)] ~kommen equal sb./sth. [in sth.]; ~|**machen** tr. V. make equal; ~**macherei** die; ~~, ~~en (abwertend) levelling down (derog.); egalitarianism; ~**mäßig** ① Adj. regular (interval, rhythm); uniform (acceleration, distribution); even (heat); ② adv. (breathe) regularly; etw. ~mäßig verteilen/auftragen distribute sth. equally/apply sth. evenly; ~**mut** der equanimity; ~**mütig** ① Adj. calm; composed; ② adv. with equanimity; calmly; ~**namig** Adj.(a) of the same name postpos.; (b) (Math.) ~namige Brüche fractions with a common denominator; Brüche ~namig machen reduce fractions to a common denominator

**Gleichnis** das; ~ses, ~se (Allegorie) allegory; (Parabel) parable

**gleichsam** Adv. (geh.) as it were

**gleich-, Gleich-:** ~|**schalten** tr. V. force into line; ~**schenk[e]lig** Adj. (Math.) isosceles; ~**schritt** der marching in step; ~**seitig** Adj. (Math.) equilateral; ~|**setzen** tr. V. equate; ~|**stellen** tr. V. equate; ~**strom** der (Elektrot.) direct current

**Gleichung** die; ~, ~en equation

**gleich-:** ~**wertig** Adj. of the same value postpos.; ~**wohl** /-'-- od. '--/ Adv. nevertheless; ~**zeitig** ① Adj. simultaneous; ② adv. at the same time

**Gleis** das; ~es, ~e track; (Bahnsteig) platform; (einzelne Schiene) rail

**gleiten** unr. itr. V.; mit sein glide; (hand) slide

**Gleit-:** ~**flug** der glide; ~**zeit** die flexitime; flexible working hours Pl.

**Gletscher** der; ~s, ~: glacier

**Gletscher-spalte** die crevasse

**glich** 1. u. 3. Pers. Sg. Prät. v. GLEICHEN

**Glied** das; ~[e]s, ~er (a) limb; (Finger~, Zehen~) joint

**(b)** (Ketten~, auch fig.) link

**(c)** (Teil eines Ganzen) section; (Mitglied) member

**gliedern** ① tr. V. structure; organize (thoughts)

② refl. V. sich in Gruppen/Abschnitte usw. ~: be divided into groups/sections etc.

**Gliederung** die; ~, ~en structure

**Glied-:** ~**maße** /-ma:sə/ die; ~, ~n limb; ~**satz** der (Sprachw.) subordinate clause

**glimmen** unr. od. regelm. itr. V. glow

**Glimm-stängel, *Glimm-stengel** der (ugs. scherzh.) fag (coll.); ciggy (coll.)

**glimpflich** ① Adj. (a) der Unfall nahm ein ~es Ende the accident turned out not to be too serious

**(b)** (mild) lenient (sentence, punishment)
② adv. (a) (ohne Schaden) ~ davonkommen get off lightly

**(b)** (mild) leniently

**glitschig** Adj. (ugs.) slippery

**glitt** 1. u. 3. Pers. Sg. Prät. v. GLEITEN

**glitzern** itr. V. (star) twinkle; (diamond, decorations) sparkle; (snow, eyes, tears) glisten

**global** ① Adj. (a) global; worldwide

**(b)** (umfassend) all-round (education); overall (control, planning, etc.)

**(c)** (allgemein) general
② adv. (a) worldwide

**(b)** (umfassend) in overall terms

**(c)** (allgemein) in general terms

**globalisieren** tr. V. globalize

**Globalisierung** die; ~, ~en globalization

**Globen** ▶ GLOBUS

**Globetrotter** der; ~s, ~: globetrotter

**Globus** der; ~ od. ~ses, Globen globe

**Glöckchen** das; ~s, ~: [little] bell

**Glocke** die; ~, ~n bell

**Glocken-:** ~**blume** die (Bot.) campanula; ~**rock** der widely flared skirt; ~**spiel** das (a) carillon; (mit einer Uhr gekoppelt auch) chimes pl.; (b) (Instrument) glockenspiel

**glomm** 1. u. 3. Pers. Sg. Prät. v. GLIMMEN

**Glorien-schein** /'glo:riən-/ der glory; (um den Kopf, fig.) halo

**glorifizieren** tr. V. glorify

**Glorifizierung** *die;* ~, ~en glorification

**glor·reich** [1] *Adj.* glorious
[2] *adv.* gloriously

**Glossar** *das;* ~s, ~e glossary

**Glosse** *die;* ~, ~n commentary; (spöttische Bemerkung) sneering comment

**Glotze** *die;* ~, ~n (salopp) box (coll.); goggle-box (Brit. coll.)

**glotzen** *itr. V.* (abwertend) goggle; gawp (coll.)

**Glotz·kiste** *die* (salopp) box (coll.); goggle-box (Brit. coll.)

**Glück** *das;* ~[e]s **(a)** luck; [es ist] ein ~, dass ...: it's lucky that ...; [kein] ~ haben be [un]lucky; **viel ~!** [the] best of luck!; **zum ~** *od.* **zu meinem/seinem** *usw.* ~: luckily *or* fortunately [for me/him *etc.*]
**(b)** happiness

**Glucke** *die;* ~, ~n brood hen

**glücken** *tr. V.; mit sein* succeed; **etw. glückt jmdm.** sb. is successful with sth.

**gluckern** *itr. V.* gurgle; glug

**glücklich** [1] *Adj.* **(a)** happy (**über** + *Akk.* about)
**(b)** (erfolgreich) lucky ⟨*winner*⟩; successful ⟨*outcome*⟩; safe ⟨*journey*⟩
**(c)** (vorteilhaft) fortunate
[2] *adv.* **(a)** (erfolgreich) successfully
**(b)** (vorteilhaft, zufrieden) happily ⟨*chosen, married*⟩

**glücklicher·weise** *Adv.* fortunately; luckily

**glück·selig** [1] *Adj.* blissfully happy
[2] *adv.* blissfully

**Glück·seligkeit** *die;* ~: bliss

**glucksen** *itr. V.* **(a)** ▶ GLUCKERN;
**(b)** (lachen) chuckle

**Glücks-:** ~**klee** *der* four-leaf clover; ~**pfennig** *der* lucky penny; ~**pilz** *der* (ugs.) lucky devil (coll.)

**Glück[s]·sache** *die:* **das ist** ~: it's a matter of luck

**Glücks·spiel** *das* game of chance

**glück·strahlend** *Adj.* radiantly happy

**Glücks·zahl** *die* lucky number

**Glück·wunsch** *der* congratulations *pl.;* **herzlichen** ~ **zum Geburtstag!** happy birthday!

**Glüh·birne** *die* lightbulb

**glühen** *itr. V.* glow

**glühend** [1] *Adj.* red-hot ⟨*metal etc.*⟩; blazing ⟨*heat*⟩; ardent ⟨*admirer etc.*⟩; passionate ⟨*words, letter, etc.*⟩
[2] *adv.* ⟨*love*⟩ passionately; ⟨*admire*⟩ ardently; ~ **heiß** blazing hot

**Glüh-:** ~**wein** *der* mulled wine; ~**würmchen** *das;* ~~s, ~ (ugs.) (weiblich) glow-worm; (männlich) firefly

**Glut** *die;* ~, ~en **(a)** embers *pl.;*
**(b)** (geh.: Leidenschaft) passion

**glut·rot** *Adj.* fiery red

**Glyzerin** *das;* ~s glycerine

**GmbH** *Abk.* = **Gesellschaft mit beschränkter Haftung** ≈ plc, PLC

**Gnade** *die;* ~, ~n (Gunst) favour; (Rel.) grace; (Milde) mercy

**gnaden-, Gnaden-:** ~**brot** *das:* jmdm./einem Tier das ~**brot geben** keep sb./an animal in his/her/its old age; ~**frist** *die* reprieve; ~**gesuch** *das* plea for clemency; ~**los** (auch fig.) [1] *Adj.* merciless; [2] *adv.* mercilessly; ~**losigkeit** *die;* ~~: mercilessness; ~**schuss,** *\****~schuß** *der* coup de grâce (*by shooting*)

**gnädig** *Adj.* gracious; (glimpflich) lenient ⟨*sentence etc.*⟩

**Gnom** *der;* ~en, ~en gnome

**Gockel** *der;* ~s, ~ (bes. südd., sonst ugs. scherzh.) cock

**Gold** *das;* ~[e]s gold

**Gold·barren** *der* gold bar

**golden** [1] *Adj.* (aus Gold) gold; (herrlich) golden ⟨*days, memories, etc.*⟩
[2] *adv.* like gold

**Gold-:** ~**fisch** *der* goldfish; ~**füllung** *die* gold filling; ~**grube** *die* (auch fig.) gold mine; ~**hamster** *der* golden hamster

**goldig** *Adj.* sweet

**gold-, Gold-:** ~**richtig** (ugs.) *Adj.* absolutely right; ~**schmied** *der,* ~**schmiedin** *die* goldsmith; ~**schnitt** *der* gilt; ~**währung** *die* (Wirtsch.) currency tied to the gold standard

**Golf**[1] *der;* ~[e]s, ~e gulf

**Golf**[2] *das;* ~s (Sport) golf

**Golf-:** ~**platz** *der* golf course; ~**schläger** *der* golf club; ~**spieler** *der,* ~**spielerin** *die* golfer; ~**strom** *der* Gulf Stream

**Gondel** *die;* ~, ~n gondola

**gondeln** *itr. V.; mit sein* (ugs.) **(a)** (mit einem Boot) cruise
**(b)** (reisen) travel around
**(c)** (herumfahren) cruise around

**Gong** *der;* ~s, ~s gong

**gongen** *itr. V.* **es hat gegongt** the gong has sounded

**gönnen** *tr. V.* **jmdm. etw.** ~: not begrudge sb. sth.; **sich/jmdm. etw.** ~: allow oneself/sb. sth.

**Gönner** *der;* ~s, ~: patron

**gönnerhaft** (abwertend) *Adj.* patronizing

**Gönnerin** *die;* ~, ~nen patroness

**gor** *3. Pers. Sg. Prät. v.* GÄREN

**Göre** *die;* ~, ~n (nordd., oft abwertend) kid (coll.)

**Gorilla** *der;* ~s, ~s gorilla

**goss,** *\****goß** *1. u. 3. Pers. Sg. Prät. v.* GIESSEN

**Gosse** *die;* ~, ~n gutter

**Gotik** *die;* ~ (Stil) Gothic [style]; (Epoche) Gothic period

**gotisch** *Adj.* Gothic

**Gott** *der;* ~es, Götter **(a)** God; **grüß [dich]** ····⟫

~! (landsch.) hello!; **um** ~**es Willen** (bei Erschrecken) for God's sake; (bei einer Bitte) for heaven's sake
**(b)** (übermenschliches Wesen) god

**Gottes-:** ~**dienst** der service; ~**haus** das (geh.) house of God; ~**lästerung** die blasphemy

**Gottheit** die; ~, ~en deity

**Göttin** die; ~, ~nen goddess

**göttlich** ① Adj. (auch fig.) divine
② adv. divinely

**gott-, Gott-:** ~**lob** adv. thank goodness; ~**los** ① Adj. **(a)** ungodly ‹life etc.›; impious ‹words, speech, etc.›; **(b)** (Gott leugnend) godless ‹theory etc.›; ② adv. (verwerflich) irreverently; ~**vater** der God the Father; ~**verlassen** Adj. (ugs.: abseits) godforsaken; ~**vertrauen** das trust in God

**Götze** der; ~n, ~n (auch fig.) idol

**Götzen-:** ~**bild** das idol; ~**diener** der idolater; ~**dienerin** die idolatress

**Gouverneur** /guvɛrˈnøːɐ̯/ der; ~s, ~e governor

**Grab** das; ~[e]s, Gräber grave; **das Heilige** ~: the Holy Sepulchre; **das** ~ **des Unbekannten Soldaten** the tomb of the Unknown Warrior

**graben** unr. tr., itr. V. dig

**Graben** der; ~s, Gräben ditch; (Schützen~) trench; (Festungs~) moat

**Grab-:** ~**hügel** der grave mound; ~**kammer** die burial chamber; ~**mal** das; Pl. ~mäler, geh. ~male monument; ~**schändung** die desecration of a/the grave/of [the] graves

**grabschen** ① tr. V. grab; snatch
② itr. V. **nach etw.** ~: grab at sth.

**gräbst** 2. Pers. Sg. Präsens v. GRABEN

**gräbt** 3. Pers. Sg. Präsens v. GRABEN

**Grab·stein** der gravestone

**Grabung** die; ~, ~en (bes. Archäol.) excavation

**Gracht** die; ~, ~en canal

**Grad** der; ~[e]s, ~e degree; (Milit.) rank

**grade** (ugs.) ▶ GERADE

**Grad·messer** der gauge, yardstick (**für** of)

**graduell** ① Adj. gradual; slight ‹difference etc.›
② adv. gradually; ‹different› in degree

**graduiert** Adj. graduate; **ein** ~**er Ingenieur** an engineering graduate

**Graf** der; ~en, ~en count; (britischer ~) earl

**Graffito** der od. das; ~[s], Graffiti **(a)** (Kunst) graffito
**(b)** Pl. (Kritzelei) graffiti

**Grafik** die; ~, ~en graphic art[s pl.]; (Kunstwerk) graphic; (Druck) print

**Grafiker** der; ~s, ~, **Grafikerin** die; ~, ~nen [graphic] designer; (Künstler[in]) graphic artist

**grafisch** ① Adj. graphic
② adv. graphically

**Gräfin** die; ~, ~nen countess

**Grafschaft** die; ~, ~en **(a)** count's land; (in Großbritannien) earldom
**(b)** (Verwaltungsbezirk) county

**Gram** der; ~[e]s (geh.) grief; sorrow

**grämen** ① tr. V. grieve
② refl. V. grieve (**über** + Akk., **um** over)

**Gramm** das; ~s, ~e gram

**Grammatik** die; ~, ~en grammar

**grammatisch** ① Adj. grammatical
② adv. grammatically

**Grammophon** Ⓦ das; ~s, ~e gramophone; phonograph (Amer.)

**Granat** der; ~[e]s, ~e (Schmuckstein) garnet

**Granat·apfel** der pomegranate

**Granate** die; ~, ~n shell; (Hand~) grenade

**Granat·feuer** das shellfire no pl., no indef. art.

**grandios** ① Adj. magnificent
② adv. magnificently

**Granit** der; ~s, ~e granite

**grantig** (südd., österr. ugs.) ① Adj. bad-tempered
② adv. bad-temperedly

**Grapefruit** /ˈgreːpfruːt/ die; ~, ~s grapefruit

**Graph** der; ~en, ~en (Math., Naturw.) graph

**Graphik** usw.: ▶ GRAFIK usw.

**Graphit** der; ~s, ~e graphite

**Gras** das; ~es, Gräser **(a)** grass; **über etw.** (Akk.) ~ **wachsen lassen** (ugs.) let the dust settle on sth.
**(b)** (Drogenjargon) grass (sl.)

**grasen** itr. V. graze

**Gras-:** ~**halm** der blade of grass; ~**land** das grassland; ~**narbe** die turf

**grässlich, \*gräßlich** ① Adj. **(a)** (abscheulich) horrible; terrible ‹accident›
**(b)** (ugs.: unangenehm) dreadful (coll.)
**(c)** (ugs.: sehr stark) terrible (coll.)
② adv. **(a)** (abscheulich) horribly; terribly
**(b)** (ugs.: unangenehm) terribly (coll.)
**(c)** (ugs.: sehr) terribly (coll.)

**Grässlichkeit, \*Gräßlichkeit** die; ~, ~enz **(a)** (Abscheulichkeit) horribleness; (eines Unfalls) terribleness
**(b)** (unangenehme Art) dreadfulness (coll.)

**Grat** der; ~[e]s, ~e ridge

**Gräte** die; ~, ~n [fish] bone

**Gratifikation** die; ~, ~en bonus

**gratinieren** tr. V. (Gastr.) brown [the top of]; **gratinierter Blumenkohl** cauliflower au gratin

**gratis** Adv. free [of charge]; gratis

**Gratis-:** ~**aktie** die (Börsenw.) bonus share; ~**muster** das, ~**probe** die free sample

**Grätsche** die; ~, ~n (Turnen) straddle; (Sprung) straddle vault

---

**Gratulant** der; ~en, ~en, **Gratulantin** die; ~, ~nen well-wisher

**Gratulation** die; ~, ~en congratulations pl.

**gratulieren** itr. V. jmdm. ~: congratulate sb.; jmdm. zum Geburtstag ~: wish sb. many happy returns [of the day]

**Grat·wanderung** die ridge walk; (fig.) balancing act

**grau** Adj. grey; (trostlos) dreary; drab; ~ meliert greying ⟨hair⟩

**Gräuel** der; ~s, ~ (a) etw./jmd. ist jmdm. ein ~: sb. loathes or detests sth./sb.
(b) (geh.) (~tat) atrocity

**Gräuel·tat** die atrocity

**grauen**[1] itr. V. (geh.) der Morgen/der Tag graut morning/day is breaking

**grauen**[2] itr. V. (unpers.) ihm graut [es] davor/vor ihr he dreads [the thought of] it/he's terrified of her

**Grauen** das; ~s, ~: horror (vor + Dat. of)

**grauen·haft**[1] Adj. horrifying; (ugs.: sehr unangenehm) terrible (coll.)
[2] adv. horrifyingly; (ugs.: sehr unangenehm) terribly (coll.)

**grauhaarig** Adj. grey-haired

**gräulich**[1] Adj. (a) horrifying
(b) (unangenehm) awful
[2] adv. (a) horrifyingly
(b) (unangenehm) terribly

\***grau·meliert** ▶ GRAU

**Graupe** die; ~, ~n (a) grain of pearl barley
(b) Pl. (Gericht) pearl barley sing.

**Graupel** die; ~, ~n soft hail pellet; ~n soft hail; graupel

**graupeln** itr. V. (unpers.) es graupelt there's soft hail falling

**grausam**[1] Adj. (a) cruel
(b) (furchtbar) terrible; dreadful
[2] adv. (a) cruelly
(b) (furchtbar) terribly, dreadfully

**Grausamkeit** die; ~, ~en (a) cruelty
(b) (Handlung) act of cruelty

**grausen**[1] tr., itr. V. (unpers.) es grauste ihm od. ihn davor/vor ihr he dreaded it/he was terrified of her
[2] refl. V. sich vor etw./jmdm. ~: dread sth./be terrified of sb.

**Grausen** das; ~s horror

**grausig** Adj., adv. ▶ GRAUENHAFT

**gravieren** tr. V. engrave

**gravierend** Adj. serious, grave

**Gravierung** die; ~, ~en engraving

**Gravitation** die; ~ (Physik, Astron.) gravitation

**Gravur** /graˈvuːɐ̯/ die; ~, ~en engraving

**Grazie** /ˈɡraːtsi̯ə/ die; ~, ~n (a) (Anmut) gracefulness
(b) (Myth.) Grace

**greif·bar**[1] Adj. (a) in ~er Nähe (fig.)

within reach; der Urlaub ist in ~e Nähe gerückt (fig.) the holiday is just coming up [now]
(b) (deutlich) tangible; concrete
(c) (ugs.: verfügbar) available
[2] adv. ~ nahe (fig.) within reach

**greifen**[1] unr. tr. V. (a) (ergreifen) take hold of; grasp; (rasch ~) seize
(b) (fangen) catch
[2] unr. itr. V. (a) in/unter/hinter etw./sich (Akk.) ~: reach into/under/behind sth./one; nach etw. ~: reach for sth.; (hastig) make a grab for sth.
(b) (Technik) grip

**Greis** der; ~es, ~e old man

**Greisin** die; ~, ~nen old woman

**grell**[1] Adj. (a) (hell) glaring, ⟨light, sun, etc.⟩
(b) (auffallend) garish ⟨colour etc.⟩; loud ⟨dress, pattern, etc.⟩
(c) (schrill) shrill, ⟨cry, voice, etc.⟩
[2] adv. (a) (hell) with glaring brightness
(b) (auffallend) gegen od. von etw. ~ abstechen contrast sharply with sth.
(c) (schrill) shrilly

**Gremium** das; ~s, Gremien committee

**Grenze** die; ~, ~n (a) boundary; (Staats~) border; (gedachte Trennungslinie) borderline
(b) (fig.) limit

**grenzen** itr. V. an etw. (Akk.) ~: border [on] sth.

**grenzen·los**[1] Adj. boundless; (fig.) boundless, unbounded ⟨joy, wonder, jealousy, grief, etc.⟩; unlimited ⟨wealth, power⟩; limitless ⟨patience, ambition⟩; extreme ⟨tiredness, anger, foolishness⟩
[2] adv. endlessly; (fig.) beyond all measure

**Grenzen·losigkeit** die; ~: boundlessness

**Grenz-:** ~gänger der; ~~s, ~~, ~gängerin die; ~~, ~~nen [regular] commuter across the border or frontier; ~konflikt der border or frontier conflict; ~land das border or frontier area; ~posten der border or frontier guard; ~stein der boundary stone; ~übergang der border crossing-point; ~übertritt der crossing of the border; der ungesetzliche ~übertritt crossing the border illegally; ~verkehr der [cross-]border traffic

**Gretchen·frage** die crucial question; sixty-four-thousand-dollar question (coll.)

\***Greuel** ▶ GRÄUEL

\***Greueltat** ▶ GRÄUELTAT

\***greulich** ▶ GRÄULICH

**Grieche** der; ~n, ~n Greek

**Griechen·land** (das); ~s Greece

**griechisch**[1] Adj. Greek
[2] adv. ⟨speak, write⟩ in Greek

**Griechisch** das; ~[s] Greek no art.

**Griechin** die; ~, ~nen Greek

**griesgrämig**[1] Adj. grumpy
[2] adv. in a grumpy manner

**Grieß** der; ~es, ~e semolina

**Grieß·brei** der semolina

**griff** 1. u. 3. Pers. Sg. Prät. v. GREIFEN

**Griff** der; ~[e]s, ~e **(a)** grip; grasp
  **(b)** (Knauf, Henkel) handle

**griff·bereit** Adj. ready to hand postpos.

**Griffel** der; ~s, ~: slate pencil

**griffig** Adj. **(a)** (handlich) handy
  **(b)** (gut greifend) that grips well postpos., not
  pred.; non-slip (surface, floor)

**Grill** der; ~s, ~s grill; (Rost) barbecue

**Grille** die; ~, ~n **(a)** cricket
  **(b)** (sonderbarer Einfall) whim

**grillen** 1 tr. V. grill
  2 itr. V. im Garten ~: have a barbecue in
  the garden

**Grill·platz** der barbecue area

**Grimasse** die; ~, ~n grimace

**grimmig** 1 Adj. furious (person); grim
  ⟨expression⟩
  2 adv. grimly

**grinsen** itr. V. grin; (höhnisch) smirk

**Grippe** die; ~, ~n **(a)** influenza; flu (coll.)
  **(b)** (volkst.: Erkältung) cold

**Grips** der; ~es brains pl.

**grob** 1 Adj. **(a)** coarse; thick ⟨wire⟩; rough
  ⟨work⟩
  **(b)** (ungefähr) rough
  **(c)** (schwerwiegend) gross; flagrant ⟨lie⟩
  **(d)** (barsch) rude
  2 adv. **(a)** coarsely
  **(b)** (ungefähr) roughly
  **(c)** (schwerwiegend) grossly
  **(d)** (barsch) rudely

**Grobheit** die; ~, ~en **(a)** rudeness
  **(b)** (Äußerung) rude remark

**Grobian** der; ~[e]s, ~e lout

**Grog** der; ~s, ~s grog

**groggy** Adj. **(a)** (Boxen) groggy
  **(b)** (ugs.: erschöpft) whacked [out] (coll.); all in
  (coll.)

**grölen** 1 tr. V. (ugs. abwertend) bawl [out];
  roar, howl ⟨approval⟩
  2 itr. V. bawl

**Groll** der; ~[e]s (geh.) rancour

**grollen** itr. V. (geh.) **(a)** [mit] jmdm. ~: bear
  a grudge against sb.
  **(b)** ⟨thunder⟩ rumble

**Grönland** (das); ~s Greenland

**Gros** /groː/ das; ~ /groːs/, ~ /groːs/ bulk

**Groschen** der; ~s, ~ **(a)** (österreichische
  Münze) groschen
  **(b)** (ugs.: Zehnpfennigstück) ten-pfennig piece;
  (fig.) penny; cent (Amer.)

**groß**; größer, größt... 1 Adj. **(a)** big, large;
  great ⟨length, width, height⟩; tall ⟨person⟩;
  wide ⟨selection⟩; ~: 1m² in area; im
  **Großen und Ganzen** by and large
  **(b)** (älter) big ⟨brother, sister⟩; (erwachsen)
  grown-up
  **(c)** (lange dauernd) long, lengthy

---

*old spelling - see note on page xiv

**(d)** intense ⟨heat, cold⟩; high ⟨speed⟩; great,
  major ⟨event, artist, work⟩
  2 adv. (ugs.: besonders) greatly; ~
  **geschrieben werden** (ugs.) be stressed; s. auch
  GROSSSCHREIBEN

**groß-, Groß-:** ~**abnehmer** der,
  ~**abnehmerin** die bulk buyer or
  purchaser; ~**aktionär** der,
  ~**aktionärin** die (Wirtsch.) principal or
  major shareholder; ~**artig** 1 Adj.
  magnificent; splendid; 2 adv. magnificently;
  splendidly; ~**auftrag** der (Wirtsch.) large
  order

**Großbritannien** (das); ~s the United
  Kingdom; [Great] Britain

**Groß·buchstabe** der capital [letter]

**Größe** die; ~, ~n size; (Höhe, Körper~)
  height; (fig.) greatness; **die ~ der Katastrophe**
  the [full] extent of the catastrophe

**Groß·eltern** Pl. grandparents

**Größen·ordnung** die order [of
  magnitude]; **in einer ~ von einer Milliarde
  Euro** in the order of a thousand million or a
  billion euros

**großen·teils** Adv. largely; for the most
  part

**Größen·wahn** der delusions pl. of
  grandeur

**größer** ▶ GROSS

**Groß-:** ~**fahndung** die large-scale search;
  ~**familie** die (Soziol.) extended family;
  (mehrere Kleinfamilien) composite family;
  ~**handel** der wholesale trade; ~**händler**
  der, ~**händlerin** die wholesaler;
  ~**industrielle** der/die; adj. Dekl. big
  industrialist

**Grossist** der; ~en, ~en, **Grossistin** die;
  ~, ~nen (Kaufmannsspr.) wholesaler

**groß-, Groß-:** ~**macht** die great power;
  ~**maul** das (ugs. abwertend) bigmouth (coll.);
  ~**mut** die; ~~: generosity; ~**mütig** Adj.
  generous; ~**mutter** die; Pl. ~**mütter**
  grandmother; ~**rechner** der (DV)
  mainframe [computer]; ~**reinemachen**
  das; ~~s (ugs.) thorough cleaning;
  ~**|schreiben** unr. tr. V. write ⟨word⟩ with
  a capital; s. auch GROSS 2; ~**spurig**
  (abwertend) 1 Adj. boastful; (hochtrabend)
  pretentious; 2 adv. boastfully; (hochtrabend)
  pretentiously; ~**stadt** die city; large town;
  ~**städter** der, ~**städterin** die city-
  dweller

**größt...** ▶ GROSS

**Groß·teil** der **(a)** (Hauptteil) major part
  **(b)** (nicht unerheblicher Teil) large part

**größten·teils** Adv. for the most part

**größt·möglich** Adj. greatest possible

**groß-, Groß-:** ~**|tun** unr. itr. V. boast;
  ~**unternehmen** das (Wirtsch.) large-scale
  enterprise; big concern; ~**vater** der
  grandfather; ~**verbraucher** der,
  ~**verbraucherin** die bulk or large
  consumer; ~**|ziehen** unr. tr. V. bring up;

raise; rear ⟨animal⟩; ~**zügig** [1] Adj.
generous; grand and spacious ⟨building,
garden, etc.⟩; [2] adv. generously;
~**zügigkeit** die; ~~: generosity

**grotęsk** [1] Adj. grotesque
[2] adv. grotesquely

**Grǫtte** die; ~, ~n grotto

**grub** 1. u. 3. Pers. Sg. Prät. v. GRABEN

**Grübchen** das; ~s, ~: dimple

**Grube** die; ~, ~n pit; (Bergbau) mine

**grübeln** itr. V. ponder (**über** + Dat. on,
over)

**Gruben·arbeiter** der,
**Gruben·arbeiterin** die miner;
mineworker

**grüęzi** Interj. (schweiz.) hallo

**Gruft** die; ~, Grüfte vault; (in einer Kirche)
crypt

**grün** Adj. green

**Grün** das; ~s, ~ od. (ugs.) ~s (a) green
(b) (Pflanzen) greenery

**Grün·anlage** die green space; (Park) park

**Grund** der; ~[e]s, Gründe (a) ground; (eines
Gewässers) bottom; **im** ~**e** [**genommen**]
basically
(b) (Ursache, Veranlassung) reason; **auf** ~:
▶ AUFGRUND

**Grund-:** ~**besitz** der (a) (Eigentum an Land)
ownership of land; (b) (Land) land; ~**buch**
das land register

**gründen** [1] tr. V. (a) found; set up,
establish ⟨business⟩; start [up] ⟨club⟩
(b) (aufbauen) base ⟨plan, theory, etc.⟩ (**auf** +
Akk. on)
[2] itr. V. **auf** od. **in etw.** (Dat.) ~: be based
on sth.
[3] refl. V. **sich auf etw.** (Akk.) ~: be based
on sth.

**Gründer** der; ~s, ~, **Gründerin** die; ~,
~nen founder

**Grund·erwerb[s]·steuer** die (Steuerw.)
land transfer tax

**Grund·gesetz** das Basic Law

**grundieren** tr. V. prime

**Grundierung** die; ~, ~en (a) (das
Grundieren) priming
(b) (erster Anstrich) priming coat

**grund-, Grund-:** ~**kenntnis** die basic
knowledge no pl. (**in** + Dat. of); ~**lage** die
basis; foundation

**Grundlagen·forschung** die basic
research

**grund·legend** [1] Adj. fundamental, basic
(**für** to); seminal ⟨idea, work⟩
[2] adv. fundamentally

**gründlich** [1] Adj. thorough
[2] adv. thoroughly

**Gründlichkeit** die; ~: thoroughness

**grund·los** [1] Adj. groundless
[2] adv. **sich** ~ **aufregen/ängstigen** be
needlessly agitated/alarmed

**Grund·nahrungsmittel** das basic
food[stuff]

**Grün·dǫnnerstag** der Maundy Thursday

**Grund-:** ~**ordnung** die basic
fundamental [constitutional] order;
~**prinzip** das fundamental principle;
~**recht** das basic or constitutional right;
~**riss**, *~**riß** der (a) (Bauw.) [ground] plan;
(b) (Leitfaden) outline; ~**satz** der principle

**grund·sätzlich** [1] Adj. (a) fundamental
⟨difference, question, etc.⟩
(b) (aus Prinzip) ⟨opponent etc.⟩ on principle
(c) (allgemein) ⟨agreement etc.⟩ in principle
[2] adv. (a) fundamentally
(b) (aus Prinzip) on principle
(c) (allgemein) in principle

**Grund-:** ~**schule** die primary school;
~**stein** der foundation stone;
~**stein·legung** die; ~~, ~~en laying of
the foundation stone; ~**stück** das plot [of
land]

**Gründung** die; ~, ~en ▶ GRÜNDEN 1A:
foundation; setting up; establishing; starting
[up]

**Grund-:** ~**wasser** das (Geol.) ground
water; ~**wortschatz** der (Sprachw.) basic
vocabulary; ~**zug** der essential feature

**Grüne**[1] das; adj. Dekl. green; **im** ~**n/ins** ~:
[out] in/into the country

**Grüne**[2] der/die; adj. Dekl. (Politik) member of
the Green Party; **die** ~**n** the Greens

**Grün-:** ~**fläche** die green space; (im Park)
lawn; ~**gürtel** der green belt; ~**land** das
(Landw.) (Wiese) meadow land; (Weide)
pastureland; ~**pflanze** die foliage plant;
~**schnabel** der (abwertend) [young]
whippersnapper; (Neuling) greenhorn;
~**span** der verdigris; ~**streifen** der
central reservation ⟨grassed and often with
trees and bushes⟩

**grunzen** tr., itr. V. grunt

**Gruppe** die; ~, ~n (a) group
(b) (Klassifizierung) class; category

**Gruppen-:** ~**druck** der group pressure;
~**dynamik** die (Sozialpsych.) group
dynamics sing., no art.; ~**leiter** der,
~**leiterin** die group leader; ~**reise** die
(Touristik) group travel no pl., no art.; **eine**
~**reise nach London machen** travel to
London with a group; ~**sieg** der (Sport) top
place in the group

**gruppieren** [1] tr. V. arrange
[2] refl. V. form a group/groups

**Gruppierung** die; ~, ~en grouping

**gruselig** Adj. eerie; creepy

**gruseln** [1] tr., itr. V. ⟨unpers.⟩ **es gruselt**
**jmdn.** od. **jmdm.** sb.'s flesh creeps
[2] refl. V. be frightened

**Gruß** der; ~es, Grüße (a) greeting; (Milit.)
salute
(b) (im Brief) **mit herzlichen Grüßen** [with]
best wishes; **mit bestem** ~/**freundlichen**
**Grüßen** yours sincerely

**grüßen** ① *tr. V.* **(a)** greet; (Milit.) salute **(b)** (Grüße senden) **grüße deine Eltern [ganz herzlich] von mir** please give your parents my [kindest] regards; **grüß dich!** (ugs.) hello *or* (coll.) hi [there]!
② *itr. V.* say hello; (Milit.) salute

**Grütze** *die;* ~, ~n groats *pl.;* **rote** ~: red fruit pudding *(made with fruit juice, fruit and cornflour, etc.)*

**gucken** *itr. V.* (ugs.) **(a)** look; (heimlich) peep **(b)** (hervorsehen) stick out **(c)** (dreinschauen) look

**Guck·loch** *das* spyhole

**Guerilla** /geˈrɪlja/ *die;* ~, ~s guerrilla war; (Einheit) guerrilla unit

**Gulasch** /ˈɡʊlaʃ, ˈɡuːlaʃ/ *das od. der;* ~[e]s, ~e *od.* ~s goulash

**Gulden** *der;* ~s, ~: guilder

**gültig** *Adj.* valid; current ⟨note, coin⟩

**Gültigkeit** *die;* ~: validity; ~ **haben/ erlangen** be/become valid

**Gummi** *der od. das;* ~s, ~[s] rubber

**Gummi-:** ~**band** *das* rubber *or* elastic band; (in Kleidung) elastic *no indef. art.;* ~**bärchen** *das;* ~~s, ~~: jelly baby; ~**baum** *der* rubber plant

**gummieren** *tr. V.* gum

**Gummi-:** ~**handschuh** *der* rubber glove; ~**knüppel** *der* [rubber] truncheon; ~**sohle** *die* rubber sole; ~**stiefel** *der* rubber boot; (für Regenwetter) wellington [boot] (Brit.).

**Gunst** *die;* ~ **(a)** favour; goodwill **(b) zu** ~**en** ▶ ZUGUNSTEN

**günstig** ① *Adj.* favourable; propitious ⟨sign⟩; auspicious ⟨moment⟩; beneficial ⟨influence⟩; good
② *adv.* favourably; **etw.** ~ **beeinflussen** have *or* exert a beneficial influence on sth.

**günstig[st]en·falls** *Adv.* at best

**Gurgel** *die;* ~, ~n throat; **jmdm. die** ~ **zudrücken** throttle sb.

**gurgeln** *itr. V.* gargle

**Gurke** *die;* ~, ~n cucumber; (eingelegt) gherkin

**gurren** *itr. V.* (auch fig.) coo

**Gurt** *der;* ~[e]s, ~e strap; (im Auto, Flugzeug) [seat] belt

**Gürtel** *der;* ~s, ~: belt

**Gürtel-:** ~**linie** *die* waist[line]; **das war ein Schlag unter die** ~**linie** (fig. ugs.) that was hitting below the belt (fig. coll.); ~**reifen** *der* radial[-ply] tyre

**Gurt·straffer** *der;* ~s, ~ (Kfz.-W.) [seat-]belt tensioner

**Guru** *der;* ~s, ~s guru

**GUS** *Abk.* = **Gemeinschaft Unabhängiger Staaten** CIS

**Guss, \*Guß** *der;* Gusses, Güsse **(a)** (das Gießen) casting

**(b)** (ugs.: Regenschauer) downpour

**Guss-eisen, \*Guß·eisen,** *das* cast iron **guss·eisern, \*guß·eisern** *Adj.* cast-iron

**gut; besser, best...** ① *Adj.* good; fine ⟨wine⟩; **ein** ~**es neues Jahr** a happy new year; ~ **tun** do good; **mir ist nicht** ~: I'm not feeling well; ~ **aussehend** good-looking; ~**en Appetit!** enjoy your lunch/dinner *etc.!;* **eine** ~**e Stunde [von hier]** a good hour [from here]
② *adv.* **(a)** well; ~ **gemeint** well-meant; **so** ~ **wie nichts** next to nothing
**(b)** (mühelos) easily; *s. auch* BESSER, BEST...

**Gut** *das;* ~[e]s, Güter **(a)** property; (Besitztum, auch fig.) possession **(b)** (landwirtschaftlicher Grundbesitz) estate **(c)** (Fracht~, Ware) item; Güter goods; (Fracht~) freight *sing.;* goods (Brit.).

**gut-, Gut-:** ~**achten** *das;* ~~s, ~~: [expert's] report; ~**artig** *Adj.* **(a)** good-natured; **(b)** (nicht gefährlich) benign; ~**artigkeit** *die* **(a)** good nature; goodnaturedness; **(b)** (Ungefährlichkeit) benignity; \*~**aussehend** ▶ GUT 1; ~**bürgerlich** *Adj.* good middle-class; ~**bürgerliche Küche** good plain cooking; ~**dünken** *das;* ~~s discretion

**Güte** *die;* ~: goodness; kindness; (Qualität) quality

**Gute·nacht·kuss, \*Gute·nacht·kuß** *der* goodnight kiss

**Güter-:** ~**abfertigung** *die* **(a)** (Abfertigung von Waren) dispatch of freight *or* (Brit.) goods; **(b)** (Annahmestelle) freight *or* (Brit.) goods office; ~**bahnhof** *der* freight depot; goods station (Brit.); ~**wagen** *der* goods wagon (Brit.); freight car (Amer.); ~**zug** *der* goods train (Brit.); freight train (Amer.)

**gut-, Gut-:** \*~**|gehen** ▶ GEHEN H, I; \*~**gelaunt** ▶ GELAUNT; \*~**gemeint** ▶ GUT 2a; ~**gläubig** *Adj.* innocently trusting; ~**haben** *das;* ~~s, ~~: credit balance; ~**|heißen** *unr. tr. V.* approve of; ~**herzig** *Adj.* kind-hearted

**gütig** ① *Adj.* kindly ② *adv.* ~ **lächeln** give a kindly smile

**gütlich** *Adj.* amicable

**gut-, Gut-:** ~**|machen** *tr. V.* make good ⟨damage⟩; put right ⟨omission, mistake, etc.⟩; ~**mütig** *Adj.* good-natured; ~**mütigkeit** *die;* ~~: good nature

**Guts·besitzer** *der,* **Guts·besitzerin** *die* owner of a/the estate; landowner

**gut-, Gut-:** ~**schein** *der* voucher, coupon (**für, auf** + *Akk.* for); ~**|schreiben** *unr. tr. V.* credit; ~**schrift** *die* credit

**Guts·hof** *der* estate; manor

**gut-:** \*~**|tun** ▶ GUT 1; ~**willig** ① *Adj.* willing; (entgegenkommend) obliging; ② *adv.* **etw.** ~**willig herausgeben/versprechen** hand sth. over voluntarily/promise sth. willingly

**Gymnasium** *das;* ~s, Gymnasien ≈ grammar school

---

**Gymnastik** *die;* ∼: physical exercises *pl.;* (Turnen) gymnastics *sing.*

**Gynäkologe** *der;* ∼n, ∼n,
**Gynäkologin** *die;* ∼, ∼nen gynaecologist

# H h

**h, H** /ha:/ *das;* ∼, ∼(a) (Buchstabe) h/H
(b) (Musik) [key of] B

**h** *Abk.* (a) = **Uhr** hrs
(b) = **Stunde** hr[s]

**H** *Abk.* (a) = **Herren;**
(b) = **Haltestelle**

**ha¹** /ha(:)/ *Interj.* (a) (Überraschung) ah
(b) (Triumph) aha

**ha²** *Abk.* = **Hektar** ha

**Haar** *das;* ∼[e]s, ∼e hair; **blonde** ∼**e** *od.*
**blondes** ∼ **haben** have fair hair; (fig.) ∼**e auf**
**den Zähnen haben** (ugs. scherzh.) be a tough
customer; **um ein** ∼ (ugs.) very nearly

**Haar-:** ∼**ausfall** *der* hair loss; ∼**bürste**
*die* hairbrush; ∼**büschel** *das* tuft of hair

**haaren** *itr. V.* moult

**Haares·breite** *die;* **um** ∼: by a hair's
breadth

**haar-, Haar-:** ∼**festiger** *der;* ∼s, ∼:
setting lotion; ∼**genau** (ugs.) ① *Adj.* exact;
② *adv.* exactly

**haarig** *Adj.* hairy

**haar-, Haar-:** ∼**klemme** *die* hairgrip;
∼**nadel** *die* hairpin; ∼**nadel·kurve** *die*
hairpin bend; ∼**schnitt** *der* haircut;
(modisch) hairstyle; ∼**spalterei** *die;* ∼∼,
∼∼en (abwertend) hair-splitting; **das ist doch**
∼**spalterei** that's splitting hairs; ∼**spange**
*die* hairslide; ∼**sträubend** *Adj.* (a)
(grauenhaft) hair-raising; (b) (empörend)
outrageous; shocking; ∼**teil** *das* hairpiece;
∼**waschmittel** *das* shampoo;
∼**wasser** *das* hair lotion

**Habe** *die;* ∼ (geh.) possessions *pl.*

**haben** ① *unr. tr. V.* have; have got; **heute**
∼ **wir schönes Wetter** the weather is fine
today; **es gut/schlecht/schwer** ∼: have it
good (coll.)/have a bad time [of it]/have a
difficult time; **du hast zu gehorchen** you
must obey; **das Jahr hat 12 Monate** there are
12 months in a year
② *refl. V.* (ugs.: sich aufregen) make a fuss
③ *Hilfsverb* have; **ich habe/hatte ihn eben**
**gesehen** I've/I'd just seen him; **er hat es**
**gewusst** he knew it
④ *mod. V.* **du hast zu gehorchen** you must
obey; **er hat sich nicht einzumischen** he's not
to interfere

**Haben** *das;* ∼s, ∼ (Kaufmannsspr.) credit

**Habe·nichts** *der;* ∼, ∼e pauper

**Haben-:** ∼**seite** *die* (Kaufmannsspr.) credit
side; ∼**zinsen** *Pl.* interest *sing.* on
deposits

**Hab·gier** *die* (abwertend) greed

**hab·gierig** ① *Adj.* (abwertend) greedy
② *adv.* greedily

**Habicht** *der;* ∼s, ∼e hawk

**Hab-:** ∼**seligkeiten** *Pl.* [meagre]
belongings; ∼**sucht** *die;* (abwertend) greed;
avarice

**Hachse** *die;* ∼, ∼n (südd.) knuckle

**Hack** *das;* ∼s (ugs., bes. nordd.) mince

**Hack·braten** *der* meat loaf

**Hacke¹** *die;* ∼, ∼n hoe; (Pickel) pick[axe]

**Hacke²** *die;* ∼, ∼n (bes. nordd. u. md.) heel

**hacken** ① *itr. V.* (a) hoe
(b) (picken) peck
② *tr. V.* (a) hoe ⟨garden, flower bed, etc.⟩
(b) (zerkleinern) chop; chop [up] ⟨meat,
vegetables, etc.⟩

**Hacker** *der;* ∼s, ∼, **Hackerin** *die;* ∼,
∼nen (DV-Jargon) hacker

**hacke·zu** *Adj.* (salopp) paralytic [drunk]
(coll.)

**Hack·fleisch** *das* minced meat; mince

**Häcksel** *der od. das;* ∼s (Landw.) chaff

**hadern** *itr. V.* (geh.) **mit etw.** ∼: be at odds
with sth.

**Hafen** *der;* ∼s, Häfen harbour; port

**Hafen-:** ∼**arbeiter** *der,* ∼**arbeiterin**
*die* dock worker; docker; ∼**kneipe** *die*
dockland pub (Brit.) *or* (Amer.) bar;
∼**rundfahrt** *die* trip round the harbour;
∼**stadt** *die* port; ∼**viertel** *das* dock area

**Hafer** *der;* ∼s oats *pl.*

**Hafer-:** ∼**brei** *der* porridge; ∼**flocken**
*Pl.* porridge oats

**Haff** *das;* ∼[e]s, ∼s *od.* ∼e lagoon

**-haft** *Adj., adv.* -like

**Haft** *die;* ∼ (a) (Gewahrsam) custody; (aus
politischen Gründen) detention
(b) (Freiheitsstrafe) imprisonment

**haftbar** *Adj.* (bes. Rechtsspr.) **für etw.** ∼ **sein**
be liable for sth.

**Haft·befehl** *der* (Rechtsw.) warrant [of
arrest]

**haften¹** *itr. V.* stick (sich festsetzen) ⟨smell,
dirt, etc.⟩; cling (**an** + *Dat.* to); ∼ **bleiben** ····⁘

stick; (**an/auf** + *Dat.* to); ⟨*smell, smoke*⟩ cling
(**an/auf** + *Dat.* to); (ugs.: im Gedächtnis bleiben)
stick

**haften²** *itr. V.* **für jmdn./etw. ~:** be
responsible for sb./liable for sth.; (Rechtsw.,
Wirtsch.) be liable

*****haften|bleiben** ▶ HAFTEN¹

**Häftling** *der;* ~s, ~e prisoner

**Haft·pflicht** *die* liability (**für** for)

**Haftpflicht·versicherung** *die* personal
liability insurance; (für Autofahrer) third party
insurance

**Haft-:** ~**prüfung** *die* (Rechtsw.) review of a/
the remand in custody; ~**schale** *die*
contact lens; ~**strafe** *die* (Rechtsspr. veralt.)
prison sentence

**Haftung** *die;* ~, ~en liability; **Gesellschaft
mit [un]beschränkter ~:** [un]limited
[liability] company

**Hagebutte** *die;* ~, ~n (a) (Frucht) rose hip
(b) (ugs.: Heckenrose) dog rose

**Hagel** *der;* ~s, ~ (auch fig.) hail

**hageln** *itr., tr. V.* (*unpers.*) hail

**Hagel-:** ~**schaden** *der* damage *no pl.*
caused by hail; ~**schauer** *der* [short]
hailstorm; ~**schlag** *der* hail

**hager** *Adj.* gaunt

**haha** /ha'ha(:)/ *Interj.* ha ha

**Häher** *der;* ~s, ~: jay

**Hahn¹** *der;* ~[e]s, **Hähne** cock; (Wetter~)
weathercock

**Hahn²** *der;* ~[e]s, **Hähne,** *fachspr.:* ~**en** (a)
tap; faucet (Amer.)
(b) (bei Waffen) hammer

**Hähnchen** *das;* ~s, ~: chicken

**Hahnen·fuß** *der* buttercup

**Hai** *der;* ~s, ~e shark

**Häkchen** *das;* ~s, ~ (a) [small] hook
(b) (Zeichen) mark; (beim Abhaken) tick

**häkeln** *tr., itr. V.* crochet

**Häkel·nadel** *die* crochet hook

**haken** ⟦1⟧ *tr. V.* hook (**an** + *Akk.* on to)
⟦2⟧ *itr. V.* (klemmen) be stuck

**Haken** *der;* ~s, ~ (a) hook
(b) (Zeichen) tick
(c) (ugs.: Schwierigkeit) catch
(d) (Boxen) hook

**haken-, Haken-:** ~**förmig** ⟦1⟧ *Adj.*
hooked; hook-shaped; ⟦2⟧ *adv.* ~**förmig
gebogen** hooked; hook-shaped; ~**kreuz** *das*
swastika; ~**nase** *die* hooked nose; hook
nose

**halb** ⟦1⟧ *Adj. u. Bruchz.* half; **eine ~e
Stunde/ein ~er Meter** half an hour/a metre;
**zum ~en Preis** [at] half price; ~ **Europa/die
~e Welt** half of Europe/half the world; **es ist
~ eins** it's half past twelve; **die ~e Wahrheit**
half [of] the truth; **[noch] ein ~es Kind sein**
be hardly more than a child
⟦2⟧ *adv.* ~ **voll/leer** half-full/-empty; ~ **offen**

*****old spelling - see note on page xiv

half-open; ~ **angezogen** half dressed; ~
**links/rechts** (Fußball) ⟨*play*⟩ [at] inside left/
right

**Halb·dunkel** *das* semi-darkness

**Halbe** *der* od. die od. das; *adj. Dekl.* (ugs.)
half litre (*of beer etc.*)

**Halb·edelstein** *der* (veralt.) semi-precious
stone

**halber** *Präp. mit Gen.; nachgestellt* (wegen)
on account of; (um ... willen) for the sake of

**halb-, Halb-:** ~**finale** *das* (Sport) semi-
final; ~**gar** *Adj.* half-cooked;
~**gefror[e]ne** *das; adj. Dekl.* soft ice
cream

**Halbheit** *die;* ~, ~en (abwertend) half
measure

**halbieren** *tr. V.* cut/tear ⟨*object*⟩ in half;
halve ⟨*amount, number*⟩

**halb-, Halb-:** ~**insel** *die* peninsula;
~**jahr** *das* six months *pl.;* half year;
~**jährlich** ⟦1⟧ *Adj.* six-monthly; ⟦2⟧ *adv.*
every six months; ~**kreis** *der* semicircle;
~**kugel** *die* hemisphere; ~**lang** *Adj.* mid-
length ⟨*hair*⟩; mid-calf length ⟨*coat, dress,
etc.*⟩; ~**links** /-'-/ *Adv.* (Fußball) ⟨*play*⟩ [at]
inside left; ~**mast** *Adv.* at half-mast;
~**mond** *der* (a) (Mond) half-moon; (b) (Figur)
crescent; *****offen** *Adj.:* ▶ HALB 2;
~**pension** *die* half-board; ~**rechts** /-'-/
*Adv.* (Fußball) ⟨*play*⟩ [at] inside right;
~**schlaf** *der* light sleep; **im ~schlaf liegen**
be half asleep; doze; ~**schuh** *der* shoe;
~**starke** *der; adj. Dekl.* (ugs. abwertend)
[young] hooligan

**halb·tags** *Adv.* ⟨*work*⟩ part-time; (morgens/
nachmittags) ⟨*work*⟩ [in the] mornings/
afternoons

**Halbtags-:** ~**arbeit** *die,*
~**beschäftigung** *die* part-time job;
(morgens/nachmittags) morning/afternoon job;
~**schule** *die* half-day school; ~**stelle** *die*
part-time job; (morgens/nachmittags) morning/
afternoon job

**halb-, Halb-:** *****voll** *Adj.:* ▶ HALB 2;
~**wegs** *Adv.* to some extent; ~**wüchsig**
/-vy:ksɪç/ *Adj.* adolescent; ~**wüchsige**
*der/die; adj. Dekl.* adolescent; ~**zeit** *die* (bes.
Fußball) (a) half; (b) (Pause) half-time;
~**zeit·pause** *die* (Sport) half-time

**Halde** *die;* ~, ~n (Bergbau) slag heap

**half** *1. u. 3. Pers. Sg. Prät. v.* HELFEN

**Hälfte** *die;* ~, ~n (a) half
(b) (ugs.: Teil) part

**Halfter¹** *der* od. *das;* ~s, ~: halter

**Halfter²** *die;* ~, ~n; *auch das;* ~s, ~:
holster

**Hall** *der;* ~[e]s, ~e (a) (geh.) reverberation
(b) (Echo) echo

**Halle** *die;* ~, ~n hall; (Fabrik~) shed; (Hotel~,
Theater~) foyer

**hallen** *itr. V.* (a) reverberate; ⟨*shot, bell,
cry*⟩ ring out
(b) (widerhallen) echo

**Hạllen-** indoor ⟨*swimming pool, handball*⟩

**Hạllig** *die;* ~, ~**en** small low island (*particularly one of those off Schleswig-Holstein*)

**hạllo** *Interj.* hello

**Hạllo** *das;* ~**s,** ~**s** cheering

**Halluzinatiọn** *die;* ~, ~**en** hallucination

**Hạlm** *der;* ~[e]s, ~**e** stalk; stem

**Hạls** *der;* ~**es,** Hälse neck; (Kehle) throat; ~ **über Kopf** (ugs.) in a rush

**hạls-, Hạls-:** ~**ab·schneider** *der,* ~**ab·schneiderin** *die* (ugs. abwertend) shark; ~**band** *das* (für Tiere) collar; ~**bruch** *der:* ▶ ~ **- UND BEINBRUCH;** ~**entzündung** *die* inflammation of the throat; ~**kette** *die* necklace; ~-**Nasen-Ohren-Arzt** *der,* ~-**Nasen-Ohren-Ärztin** *die* ear, nose, and throat specialist; ~**schlagader** *die* carotid [artery]; ~**schmerzen** *Pl.* sore throat *sing.;* ~**starrig** *Adj.* (abwertend) stubborn; obstinate; ~**tuch** *das; Pl.* ~**tücher** cravat; (des Cowboys) neckerchief; ~**- und Beinbruch** *Interj.* (scherzh.) good luck; ~**weh** *das* (ugs.) ▶ ~SCHMERZEN

**hạlt** *Interj.* stop

**Hạlt** *der;* ~[e]s, ~**e (a)** hold **(b)** (Stopp) stop; ~ **machen** stop

**hạltbar** *Adj.* **(a)** ~ **sein** ⟨*food*⟩ keep [well]; ~ **bis 5. 3.** use by 5 March **(b)** (nicht verschleißend) hard-wearing ⟨*material, clothes*⟩ **(c)** (aufrechtzuerhalten) tenable ⟨*hypothesis etc.*⟩

**Hạltbarkeit** *die;* ~ (Strapazierfähigkeit) durability

**Hạlte·bucht** *die* (Verkehrsw.) lay-by (Brit.); turnout (Amer.)

**hạlten** 1 *unr. tr. V.* **(a)** (auch Milit.) hold; **die Hand vor den Mund** ~: put one's hand in front of one's mouth **(b)** (Ballspiele) save ⟨*shot, penalty, etc.*⟩ **(c)** (bewahren) keep; (beibehalten, aufrechterhalten) keep up ⟨*speed etc.*⟩; maintain ⟨*temperature, equilibrium*⟩ **(d)** (erfüllen) keep; **sein Wort/ein Versprechen** ~: keep one's word/a promise **(e)** (besitzen, beschäftigen, beziehen) keep ⟨*chickens etc.*⟩; take ⟨*newspaper, magazine, etc.*⟩ **(f)** (einschätzen) **jmdn. für reich/ehrlich** ~: think sb. is rich/honest; **viel von jmdm.** ~: think a lot of sb. **(g)** (ab~, veranstalten) give, ⟨*speech, lecture*⟩ 2 *unr. itr. V.* **(a)** (stehen bleiben) stop **(b)** (unverändert, an seinem Platz bleiben) last **(c)** (Sport) save **(d)** (beistehen) **zu jmdm.** ~: stand by sb. 3 *unr. refl. V.* **(a)** (sich durchsetzen, behaupten) **wir werden uns/die Stadt wird sich nicht länger** ~ **können** we/the town won't be able to hold out much longer **(b)** (sich bewähren) **sich gut** ~: do well **(c)** (unverändert bleiben) ⟨*weather, flowers, etc.*⟩ last; ⟨*milk, meat, etc.*⟩ keep

**(d)** (Körperhaltung haben) **sich schlecht/gerade** ~: hold oneself badly/straight **(e)** (bleiben) **sich auf den Beinen/im Sattel** ~: stay on one's feet/in the saddle; **sich links/ rechts** ~: keep [to the] left/right; **sich an etw.** (*Akk.*) ~: keep to sth.

**Hạlte·punkt** *der* stop

**Hạlter** *der;* ~**s,** ~ **(a)** (Fahrzeug~) keeper **(b)** (Tier~) owner **(c)** (Vorrichtung) holder

**Hạlterin** *die;* ~, ~**nen (a)** ▶ HALTER A: keeper **(b)** ▶ HALTER B: owner

**Hạlterung** *die;* ~, ~**en** support

**Hạlte-:** ~**stelle** *die* stop; ~**verbot** *das* **(a)** „~**verbot**" 'no stopping'; **hier ist** ~**verbot** this is a no-stopping zone; **(b)** (Stelle) no-stopping zone; ~**verbots·schild** *das* no-stopping sign

**-haltig,** (österr.) **-hältig: vitamin**~**/silber**~ *usw.* containing vitamins/silver etc. *postpos., not pred.;* **vitamin**~ **sein** contain vitamins

**hạlt-, Hạlt-:** ~**los** *Adj.* **(a)** (labil) ~**los sein** be a weak character; **ein** ~**loser Mensch** a weak character; **(b)** (unbegründet) unfounded; ~**losigkeit** *die;* ~~ **(a)** (Labilität) weakness of character; **(b)** (mangelnde Begründung) unfoundedness; \*~**|machen** ▶ HALT B

**Hạltung** *die;* ~, ~**en (a)** (Körper~) posture **(b)** (Pose) manner **(c)** (Einstellung) attitude **(d)** (Fassung) composure

**Halụnke** *der;* ~**n,** ~**n** scoundrel; villain

**Hạmburger** *der;* ~**s,** ~ (Frikadelle) hamburger

**hämisch** 1 *Adj.* malicious 2 *adv.* maliciously

**Hạmmel** *der;* ~**s,** ~ **(a)** wether **(b)** (Fleisch) mutton

**Hạmmel·fleisch** *das* mutton

**Hạmmer** *der;* ~**s,** Hämmer **(a)** hammer; (Holz~) mallet; ~ **und Sichel** hammer and sickle **(b)** (Technik) ram

**hämmern** *itr., tr. V.* hammer

**Hämorrhoiden** /hɛmɔroˈiːdn̩/ *Pl.* (Med.) haemorrhoids; piles

**Hạmpel·mann** *der* **(a)** jumping jack **(b)** (ugs. abwertend) puppet

**hạmpeln** *itr. V.* (ugs.) jump about

**Hạmster** *der;* ~**s,** ~ hamster

**hạmstern** *tr., itr. V.* **(a)** (horten) hoard **(b)** (Lebensmittel tauschen) barter goods for [food]

**Hạnd** *die;* ~, Hände hand; **eine** ~ **voll** a handful; **jmdm. die** ~ **geben** shake sb.'s hand; ~ **und Fuß/weder** ~ **noch Fuß haben** (ugs.) make sense/no sense; **alle** *od.* **beide Hände damit voll haben, etw. zu tun** (ugs.) have one's hands full doing sth.; **die Hände in den Schoß legen** sit back and do nothing; **etw. aus der** ~ **geben** let sth. out of one's hands; ~ **in** ~ **arbeiten** work hand in hand; ⋯⬦

etw. zur ~ haben have sth. handy; zu
Händen [von] Herrn Müller attention Herr
Müller; unter der ~ (fig.) on the quiet

**Hand-:** ~**arbeit** die (a) handicraft; etw. in
~arbeit herstellen make sth. by hand; (b)
(Gegenstand) handmade article; (c) (Nadelarbeit)
[piece of] needlework; ~**ball** der handball;
~**besen** der brush; ~**betrieb** der
manual operation; ~**bewegung** die (a)
movement of the hand; (b) (Geste) gesture;
~**bremse** die handbrake; ~**buch** das
handbook; (technisches ~buch) manual

**Händchen** das; ~s, ~: [little] hand

**Hände** ▶ HAND

**Hände-:** ~**druck** der; Pl. ~drücke
handshake; ~**klatschen** das; ~~s
clapping

**Handel** der; ~s trade; ~ treiben trade; ~
treibend trading ⟨nation⟩

**handeln** [1] itr. V. (a) trade; deal
(b) (feilschen) haggle
(c) (agieren) act
(d) (sich verhalten) behave
(e) von etw. od. über etw. (Akk.) ~ ⟨book,
film, etc.⟩ be about or deal with sth.
[2] refl. V. (unpers.) es handelt sich um …:
it is a matter of …; (es dreht sich um) it's
about …

**handels-, Handels-:** ~**abkommen**
das trade agreement; ~**bank** die; Pl. ~~en
merchant bank; ~**bilanz** die (a) (eines
Betriebes) balance sheet; (b) (eines Staates)
balance of trade; ~**einig, ~eins:** mit
jmdm. ~einig od. ~eins werden/sein agree/
have agreed terms with sb.; ~**flotte** die
merchant fleet; ~**gesellschaft** die
company; ~**kammer** die: ▶ INDUSTRIE- UND
HANDELSKAMMER; ~**klasse** die grade;
~**marine** die merchant navy; ~**partner**
der, ~**partnerin** die trading partner;
~**register** das register of companies;
~**schiff** das merchant ship; ~**schule** die
commercial college; ~**straße** die (hist.)
trade route; ~**üblich** Adj. ~übliche
Praktiken/Größen standard business
practices/standard [commercial] sizes;
~**unternehmen** das trading concern;
~**vertreter** der, ~**vertreterin** die
[sales] representative; travelling salesman/
saleswoman; ~**vertretung** die trade
mission; ~**zentrum** das trading centre

**hände·ringend** Adv. (ugs.: dringend) ⟨need⟩
urgently; ⟨search for sb./sth.⟩ desperately

**hand-, Hand-:** ~**feger** der brush; ~**fest**
Adj. (a) robust; sturdy; (b) substantial ⟨meal
etc.⟩; (c) solid ⟨proof⟩; concrete ⟨suggestion⟩;
complete ⟨lie⟩; well-founded ⟨argument⟩;
~**fläche** die palm [of one's/the hand]; flat
of one's/the hand; ~**gas** das (Kfz-W.) hand
throttle; ~**gearbeitet** Adj. handmade;
~**gelenk** das wrist; ~**gemenge** das
fight; ~**gepäck** das hand baggage;
~**geschrieben** Adj. handwritten;

~**granate** die hand grenade; ~**greiflich**
Adj. (a) (tätlich) ~greiflich werden start using
one's fists; (b) tangible ⟨success, advantage,
proof, etc.⟩; palpable ⟨contradiction, error⟩;
obvious ⟨fact⟩; ~**griff** der (a) mit einem
~griff/wenigen ~griffen in one movement/
without much trouble; (schnell) in no time at
all/next to no time; (b) (am Koffer, an einem
Werkzeug) handle; ~**habe** die; ~~, ~~n:
eine [rechtliche] ~habe [gegen jmdn.] a legal
handle [against sb.]; ~**haben** tr. V. (a)
handle; operate ⟨device, machine⟩; (b)
(praktizieren) implement ⟨law etc.⟩; ~**habung**
die; ~~, ~~en (a) handling; (eines Gerätes,
einer Maschine) operation; (b) (Durchführung)
implementation

**Handikap** /ˈhɛndikɛp/ das; ~s, ~s (auch
Sport) handicap

**handikapen** /ˈhɛndikɛpn/ tr. V. handicap

**Hand-:** ~**käse** der (landsch.) small, hand-
formed curd cheese; ~**koffer** der [small]
suitcase; ~**kuss, \*~~s, ~~,
~langer** der; ~~s, ~~,
~**langerin** die; ~~, ~~nen (ungelernter
Arbeiter) labourer; (abwertend) lackey; ~**lauf**
der handrail

**Händler** der; ~s, ~, **Händlerin** die; ~,
~nen trader

**handlich** Adj. handy; easily carried ⟨parcel,
suitcase⟩; easily portable ⟨television, camera⟩

**Handlung** die; ~, ~en (a) (Vorgehen) action;
(Tat) act
(b) (Fabel) plot

**handlungs-, Handlungs-:** ~**arm** Adj.
short on action pred.; ~**fähig** Adj. able to
act pred.; working attrib. ⟨majority⟩;
~**freiheit** die freedom of action;
~**reisende** der/die ▶ HANDELSVERTRETER;
~**weise** die conduct

**hand-, Hand-:** ~**puppe** die glove or
hand puppet; ~**schelle** die handcuff;
~**schlag** der handshake; ~**schrift** die
handwriting; ~**schriftlich** [1] Adj.
handwritten; [2] adv. by hand; ~**schuh** der
glove; ~**schuh·fach** das glove
compartment; ~**signiert** Adj. signed;
~**spiegel** der hand mirror; ~**stand** der
(Turnen) handstand; ~**tasche** die handbag;
~**tuch** das; Pl. -tücher towel;
~**umdrehen:** im ~umdrehen in no time at
all; ~**verlesen** Adj. hand-picked; \*~**voll**
▶ HAND; ~**wäsche** die washing by hand

**Hand·werk** das craft; (als Beruf) trade; sein
~ kennen/beherrschen know one's job

**Handwerker** der; ~s, ~: tradesman

**Handwerkerin** die; ~, ~nen
tradeswoman;

**handwerklich** Adj. ein ~er Beruf a
[skilled] trade

**Handwerks·zeug** das tools pl.

**Handy** /ˈhɛndi/ das; ~s, ~s mobile [phone]

**Hand·zeichen** das sign [with one's hand];
(eines Autofahrers) hand signal; (Abstimmung)
show of hands

---
\*alte Schreibung - vgl. Hinweis auf S. xiv

**Hanf** *der;* ~[e]s hemp

**Hang** *der;* ~[e]s, **Hänge** slope; (Neigung) tendency

**Hänge-:** ~**brücke** *die* suspension bridge; ~**lampe** *die* pendant light; ~**matte** *die* hammock

**hängen¹** *unr. itr. V.; südd., österr., schweiz. mit sein* hang (**an** + *Dat.* from); (an einem Fahrzeug) be hitched (**an** + *Dat.* to); [mit der Ärmel *usw.* an/in etw. (*Dat.*) ~ bleiben] one's sleeve *etc.* caught on/in sth.; ~ bleiben (ugs.: haften) stick (**an/auf** + *Dat.*) to; (ugs.: verweilen) get stuck (coll.)

**hängen²** ① *tr. V.* (a) hang (**in/über** + (*Akk.*) in/over; **an/auf** + *Akk.* on) (b) (befestigen) hitch up (**an** + *Akk.* to); couple on ⟨*railway carriage, etc.*⟩ (**an** + *Akk.* to) ② *refl. V.* (a) **sich an etw.** (*Akk.*) ~: hang on to sth. (b) (sich festsetzen) cling (**an** + *Akk.* to)

**\*hängen|bleiben** ▸ HÄNGEN¹

**hängend** *Adj.* hanging

**Hänge-schrank** *der* wall cupboard

**Hang-lage** *die* hillside location

**Hansaplast** Ⓦ *das;* ~[e]s sticking plaster; Elastoplast ®

**hänseln** *tr. V.* tease

**Hanse-stadt** *die* Hanseatic city

**Hantel** *die;* ~, ~n (Sport) (kurz) dumb-bell; (lang) barbell

**hantieren** *itr. V.* be busy

**Häppchen** *das;* ~s, ~ (a) [small] morsel (b) (Appetithappen) canapé

**Happen** *der;* ~s, ~: morsel

**happig** *Adj.* (ugs.) ~e Preise fancy prices (coll.)

**Happyend, Happy-End** /ˈhɛpiˈ|ɛnt/ *das;* ~[s], ~s happy ending

**Hardware** /ˈhɑːdwɛə/ *die;* ~, ~s (DV) hardware

**Harfe** *die;* ~, ~n harp

**Harke** *die;* ~, ~n rake

**harken** *tr. V.* rake

**harm-los** ① *Adj.* (a) (ungefährlich) harmless; slight ⟨*injury, cold, etc.*⟩; mild ⟨*illness*⟩; safe ⟨*medicine, bend, road, etc.*⟩ (b) (arglos) innocent; harmless ⟨*fun, pastime, etc.*⟩ ② *adv.* (a) (ungefährlich) harmlessly (b) (arglos) innocently

**Harmlosigkeit** *die;* ~ (a) (Ungefährlichkeit) harmlessness; (einer Krankheit) mildness; (eines Medikamentes) safety (b) (Arglosigkeit, harmloses Verhalten) innocence

**Harmonie** *die;* ~, ~n (auch fig.) harmony

**harmonieren** *itr. V.* (a) harmonize (b) (miteinander auskommen) get on well

**Harmonika** *die;* ~, ~s *od.* **Harmoniken** harmonica

**harmonisch** ① *Adj.* harmonious; (Musik) harmonic ② *adv.* harmoniously; (Musik) harmonically

**harmonisieren** *tr. V.* coordinate; etw. mit etw. ~ (Wirtsch.) bring sth. into line with sth.

**Harmonisierung** *die;* ~, ~en (Wirtsch.) harmonization

**Harmonium** *das;* ~s, **Harmonien** harmonium

**Harn** *der;* ~[e]s, ~e (Med.) urine

**Harn-blase** *die* bladder

**Harnisch** *der;* ~s, ~e armour

**Harpune** *die;* ~, ~n harpoon

**harpunieren** *tr. V.* harpoon

**harren** *itr. V.* (geh.) jmds./einer Sache *od.* auf jmdn./etw. ~: await sb./sth.

**harsch** ① *Adj.* (a) (vereist) crusted (b) (barsch) harsh ② *adv.* harshly

**Harsch** *der;* ~[e]s crusted snow

**hart;** härter, härtest… ① *Adj.* (a) hard; ~ gekocht hard-boiled ⟨*egg*⟩ (b) tough ⟨*situation, job*⟩; harsh ⟨*reality, truth*⟩ (c) (streng) harsh ⟨*penalty, punishment, judgement*⟩; tough ⟨*measure, law, course*⟩ (d) (rau) rough ⟨*game, opponent*⟩ ② *adv.* hard chair; (a) (mühevoll) ⟨*work*⟩ hard (b) (streng) harshly (c) (nahe) close (**an** + *Dat.* to)

**Härte** *die;* ~, ~n (a) (auch Physik) hardness (b) (Widerstandsfähigkeit) toughness (c) (schwere Belastung) hardship (d) (Strenge) harshness (e) (Heftigkeit) (eines Aufpralls usw.) force; (eines Streits) violence (f) (Rauheit) roughness

**Härte-fall** *der* (a) case of hardship (b) (ugs.: Person) hardship case

**härten** *tr., itr. V.* harden

**härter** ▸ HART

**härtest…** ▸ HART

**hart-, Hart-:** \*~gekocht ▸ HART 1A; ~**geld** *das* coins *pl.*; ~**gummi** *das* hard rubber; ~**herzig** ① *Adj.* hard-hearted ② *adv.* hard-heartedly; ~**herzigkeit** *die;* ~~: hard-heartedness; ~**käse** *der* hard cheese; ~**näckig** ① *Adj.* (a) (eigensinnig) obstinate; stubborn; (b) (ausdauernd) dogged ② *adv.* (a) (eigensinnig) obstinately; stubbornly; (b) (ausdauernd) doggedly; ~**näckigkeit** *die;* ~~ (a) (Eigensinn) obstinacy; stubbornness; (b) (Ausdauer) doggedness

**Härtung** *die;* ~, ~en hardening; (von Stahl auch) tempering

**Hart-wurst** *die* dry sausage

**Harz** *das;* ~es, ~e resin

**Harzer Käse** *der;* ~ ~s, ~ ~: Harz [Mountain] cheese

**Haschee** (Kochk.) *das;* ~s, ~s hash

**Haschen¹** *tr. V.* (veralt.) catch

**haschen²** *itr. V.* (ugs.) smoke [hash] (coll.)

**Häschen** /ˈhɛːsçən/ *das;* ~, ~s bunny

**Haschisch** *das od. der;* ~[s] hashish

**Haschisch·rausch** der [state of] hashish intoxication; **etw. im** od. **bei einem ~rausch tun** do sth. while under the effects of hashish or while [high (coll.)] on hashish

**Hase** der; ~n, ~n (a) hare
(b) (landsch.) ▸ KANINCHEN

**Hasel·nuss, \*Hasel·nuß** die hazelnut

**Hasen-: ~fuß** der (spöttisch abwertend) coward; chicken (coll.); **~scharte** die (Med.) harelip

**Haspel** die; ~, ~n (Technik) (für Garn) reel; (für ein Seil, Kabel) drum

**Hass, \*Haß** der; **Hasses** hatred (**auf +** Akk., **gegen** of, for)

**hassen** tr., itr. V. hate

**hass·erfüllt, \*haß·erfüllt** Adj. filled with hatred postpos.

**hässlich, \*häßlich** ⒈ Adj. (a) ugly
(b) (gemein) nasty
(c) (unangenehm) awful ⟨weather, cold, situation, etc.⟩
⒉ adv. (a) ⟨dress⟩ unattractively
(b) (gemein) nastily

**Hässlichkeit, \*Häßlichkeit** die; ~, ~en (a) (Aussehen) ugliness
(b) (Gesinnung) nastiness

**hast** 2. Pers. Sg. Präsens v. HABEN

**Hast** die; ~: haste

**hasten** itr. V.; mit sein hurry

**hastig** ⒈ Adj. hasty; hurried
⒉ adv. hastily; hurriedly

**hat** 3. Pers. Sg. Präsens v. HABEN

**hätscheln** tr. V. caress

**hatschi** Interj. atishoo

**hatte** 1. u. 3. Pers. Sg. Prät. v. HABEN

**hätte** 1. u. 3. Pers. Sg. Konjunktiv II v. HABEN

**Haube** die; ~, ~n (a) bonnet; (einer Krankenschwester) cap
(b) (Kfz-W.) bonnet (Brit.); hood (Amer.)

**Hauch** der; ~[e]s, ~e (geh.) (a) (Atem, auch fig.) breath
(b) (Luftzug) breath of wind
(c) (leichter Duft) delicate smell
(d) (dünne Schicht) [gossamer-]thin layer

**hauch·dünn** Adj. gossamer-thin ⟨material, dress⟩; wafer-thin ⟨layer, slice, majority⟩

**hauchen** itr. V. breathe (**gegen, auf +** Akk. on)

**Haue** die; ~, ~n (a) (südd., österr.: Hacke) hoe
(b) (ugs.: Prügel) a hiding (coll.)

**hauen** ⒈ unr. tr. V. (a) (ugs.: schlagen) belt; clobber (coll.)
(b) (ugs.: auf einen Körperteil) belt (coll.); hit
(c) (herstellen) carve ⟨figure, statue, etc.⟩ (**in +** Akk. in)
⒉ unr. itr. V. (a) (ugs.: prügeln) **er haut immer gleich** he's quick to hit out
(b) (auf einen Körperteil) belt (coll.); hit
(c) (ugs.: auf/gegen etw. schlagen) thump

\*old spelling - see note on page xiv

⒊ unr. refl. V. (ugs.: sich prügeln) have a punch-up (coll.)

**Hauer** der; ~s, ~ (Jägerspr.) tusk; (fig.) fang

**Haufen** der; ~s, ~: heap; pile; (Gruppe) bunch (coll.)

**häufen** ⒈ tr. V. heap, pile (**auf +** Akk. on to); (aufheben) hoard ⟨money, supplies⟩
⒉ refl. V. (sich mehren) pile up

**häufig** ⒈ Adj. frequent
⒉ adv. frequently; often

**Häufigkeit** die; ~, ~en frequency

**Häufung** die; ~, ~en increasing frequency

**Haupt** das; ~[e]s, **Häupter** (geh., auch fig.) head

**haupt-, Haupt-: ~bahnhof** der main station; **~beruflich** ⒈ Adj. seine ~berufliche Tätigkeit his main occupation; ⒉ adv. **er ist ~beruflich als Elektriker tätig** his main occupation is that of electrician; **~darsteller** der (Theater, Film) male lead; **~darstellerin** die (Theater, Film) female lead; **~eingang** der main entrance; **~einschalt·zeit** die peak or prime viewing time; **~fach** das major; **~figur** die main character; **~film** der main feature; **~gang** der (a) main corridor;
(b) ▸ ~GERICHT; **~gebäude** das main building; **~gericht** das main course; **~gewinn** der first prize

**Häuptling** der; ~s, ~e chief[tain]

**haupt-, Haupt-: ~mahlzeit** die main meal; **~mann** der; Pl. **~leute** (Milit.) captain; **~person** die central figure; **~postamt** das main post office; **~quartier** das (Milit., auch fig.) headquarters sing. or pl.; **~reise·zeit** die high season; peak [holiday] season; **~rolle** die main role; lead; **die ~rolle spielen** (fig.) play the leading role; **~sache** die main thing; **~sächlich** ⒈ Adv. mainly; principally; ⒉ Adj.; nicht präd. main; principal; **~saison** die high season; **~satz** der main clause; (allein stehend) sentence; **~schalter** der (Elektrot.) mains switch; **~schlagader** die aorta; **~schul·abschluss, \*~schul·abschluß** der ≈ secondary school leaving certificate; **~schule** die ≈ secondary modern school; **~schüler** der, **~schülerin** die ≈ secondary modern school pupil; **~sitz** der head office; headquarters pl.; **~stadt** die capital [city]; **~städtisch** Adj. metropolitan; **~straße** die main street; **~thema** das main topic or theme; (Musik) main theme; **~verkehr** der bulk of the traffic

**Hauptverkehrs-: ~straße** die main road ~**zeit** die rush hour

**Haupt·: ~versammlung** die (Wirtsch.) shareholders' meeting; **~wache** die main police station; **~wort** das (Sprachw.) noun

**hau ruck** Interj. heave[-ho]

**Haus** das; ~es, **Häuser (a)** house; (Amts-,

Firmengebäude usw.) building; (Heim) home;
**nach** ~**e** home; **zu** ~**e** at home; **das erste** ~
**am Platze** the best hotel in the town
**(b)** ~ **halten** be economical

**haus-, Haus-:** ~**angestellte** der/die
domestic servant; ~**apotheke** die
medicine cabinet; ~**arbeit** die housework;
(Schulw.) homework; ~**arrest** der house
arrest; ~**arzt** der, ~**ärztin** die family
doctor; ~**aufgabe** die homework;
~**backen** ① Adj. plain; unadventurous
⟨clothes⟩; ② adv. ⟨dress⟩ unadventurously;
~**besetzer** der; ~~s, ~~,
~**besetzerin** die; ~~, ~~**nen** squatter;
~**besitzer** der houseowner; (Vermieter)
landlord; ~**besitzerin** die houseowner;
(Vermieterin) landlady; ~**besuch** der house
call; ~**boot** das houseboat

**Häuschen** /'hɔy:sçən/ das; ~s, ~: small
house; **aus dem** ~ **sein** (ugs.) be over the
moon (coll.)

**hausen** itr. V. **(a)** (ugs. abwertend) live
**(b)** (Verwüstungen anrichten) **[furchtbar]** ~:
wreak havoc

**Häuser·block** der block [of houses]

**haus-, Haus-:** ~**flur** der hall[way]; (im
Obergeschoss) landing; ~**frau** die housewife;
~**freund** der **(a)** friend of the family; **(b)**
(verhüll.: Liebhaber) man friend (euphem.);
~**freundin** die friend of the family;
~**friedens·bruch** der (Rechtsw.) trespass;
~**gebrauch** der domestic use; **das reicht
für den** ~**gebrauch** (ugs.) it's good enough to
get by (coll.); ~**gehilfin** die [home] help;
~**gemacht** Adj. home-made

**Haus·halt** der **(a)** household
**(b)** (Arbeit im ~) housekeeping; **jmdm. den** ~
**führen** keep house for sb.
**(c)** (Politik) budget

\***haus|halten** ▶ HAUS B

**Haushälterin** die; ~, ~**nen** housekeeper

**Haushalts-:** ~**artikel** der household
article; ~**debatte** die (Politik) budget
debate; ~**geld** das housekeeping money;
~**jahr** das financial year; ~**kasse** die
housekeeping money; ~**plan** der budget;
~**waren** Pl. household goods

**haus-, Haus-:** ~**herr** der **(a)**
(Familienoberhaupt) head of the household; **(b)**
(als Gastgeber) host; **(c)** (Rechtsspr.) (Eigentümer)
owner; (Mieter) occupier ~**herrin** die **(a)**
▶ ~HERR A; **(b)** ▶ ~HERR B; ~**hoch** ① Adj.
as high as a house; (fig.) overwhelming;
② adv. (fig.) ~**hoch gewinnen** win hands
down

**hausieren** itr. V. **[mit etw.]** ~: hawk [sth.];
peddle [sth.]; „**Hausieren verboten**" 'no
hawkers'

**Hausierer** der; ~s, ~, **Hausiererin** die;
~, ~**nen** pedlar; hawker

**häuslich** Adj. **(a)** domestic
**(b)** (das Zuhause liebend) home-loving

**Hausmacher·art** die: **nach** ~: home-
made-style attrib.

**Haus·mann** der: man who stays at home
and does the housework; (Ehemann)
househusband

**Hausmanns·kost** die plain cooking

**Haus-:** ~**marke** die **(a)** house wine; **(b)**
(ugs.: bevorzugtes Getränk) favourite tipple
(coll.); ~**meister** der, ~**meisterin** die
caretaker; ~**mittel** das household remedy;
~**musik** die music at home; ~**nummer**
die house number; ~**ordnung** die house
rules pl.; ~**putz** der spring-clean;
(regelmäßig) clean-out

**Haus·rat** der household goods pl.

**Hausrat·versicherung** die [household
or home] contents insurance

**Haus-:** ~**schlüssel** der front-door key;
house key; ~**schuh** der slipper; ~**segen**
der: **bei ihnen hängt der** ~**segen schief** (ugs.
scherzh.) they've been having a row

**Haussuchung** die; ~, ~**en** house search

**Haussuchungs·befehl** der search
warrant

**Haus-:** ~**telefon** das internal telephone;
~**tier** das **(a)** pet; **(b)** (Nutztier) domestic
animal; ~**tür** die front door; ~**verbot** das
ban on entering the house/pub/restaurant
etc.; ~**verwalter** der, ~**verwalterin**
die manager [of the block]; ~**wirt** der
landlord; ~**wirtin** die landlady;
~**wirtschaft** die domestic science and
home economics; ~**zelt** das ridge tent

**Haut** die; ~, **Häute** skin; **aus der** ~ **fahren**
(ugs.) go up the wall (coll.)

**Haut-:** ~**arzt** der, ~**ärztin** die skin
specialist; ~**ausschlag** der [skin] rash

**häuten** ① tr. V. skin; flay
② refl. V. shed its skin/their skins

**haut-, Haut-:** ~**eng** Adj. skintight;
~**farbe** die [skin] colour; ~**krankheit**
die skin disease; ~**krebs** der skin cancer

**Häutung** die; ~, ~**en (a)** ▶ HÄUTEN 1:
skinning; flaying
**(b)** (das Sichhäuten) **eine Eidechse bei der** ~:
a lizard shedding its skin

**Haxe** die; ~, ~**n** ▶ HACHSE

**he** Interj. (ugs.) hey

**Heb·amme** die midwife

**Hebel** der; ~s, ~: lever

**heben** unr. tr. V. **(a)** lift; raise ⟨baton,
camera, glass⟩
**(b)** (verbessern) raise ⟨standard, level⟩;
increase ⟨turnover, self-confidence⟩; improve
⟨mood⟩; enhance ⟨standing⟩; boost ⟨morale⟩

**hecheln**[1] itr. V. (ugs. abwertend) gossip

**hecheln**[2] itr. V. pant [for breath]

**Hecht** der; ~[e]s, ~e pike

**Hecht·sprung** der **(a)** (Turnen) Hecht vault
**(b)** (Schwimmen) racing dive; (vom Sprungturm)
pike-dive

**Heck** das; ~[e]s, ~e od. ~s stern;
(Flugzeug~) tail; (Auto~) rear

**Heck·antrieb** der (Kfz-W.) rear-wheel drive

**Hecke** *die;* ~, ~n (a) hedge
(b) (wild wachsend) thicket

**Hecken-:** ~**rose** *die* dogrose; ~**schütze**
*der,* ~**schützin** *die* sniper

**Heck·scheibe** *die* rear window

**Heer** *das;* ~[e]s, ~e armed forces *pl.;* (für
den Landkrieg, fig.) army

**Hefe** *die;* ~, ~n yeast

**Hefe·teig** *der* yeast dough

**Heft**[1] *das;* ~[e]s, ~e (geh.) haft; handle

**Heft**[2] *das;* ~[e]s, ~e (a) (bes. Schule)
exercise book
(b) (Nummer einer Zeitschrift) issue

**Heftchen** *das;* ~s, ~: book [of tickets/
stamps *etc.*]

**heften** [1] *tr. V.* (a) (mit einer Nadel) pin; (mit
einer Klammer) clip; (mit Klebstoff) stick
(b) (Schneiderei) tack
(c) (Buchbinderei) stitch; (mit Klammern) staple
[2] *refl. V.* **sich an jmds. Fersen** (*Akk.*) ~:
stick hard on sb.'s heels

**Hefter** *der;* ~s, ~: [loose-leaf] file

**heftig** [1] *Adj.* violent; heavy ⟨*rain, shower,*
*blow*⟩; severe ⟨*pain*⟩; ⟨*person*⟩ with a violent
temper
[2] *adv.* ⟨*rain, snow, breathe*⟩ heavily; ⟨*hit*⟩
hard; ⟨*quarrel*⟩ violently

**Heftigkeit** *die;* ~: ▶ HEFTIG 1: violence;
heaviness; severity

**Heft-:** ~**klammer** staple; ~**pflaster** *das*
sticking plaster; ~**zwecke** *die*
▶ REISSZWECKE

**hegen** *tr. V.* (a) (bes. Forstw., Jagdw.) look
after, tend
(b) (geh.: umsorgen) look after
(c) (fig.) feel ⟨*contempt, hatred, mistrust*⟩;
cherish ⟨*hope, wish, desire*⟩; harbour
⟨*grudge, suspicion*⟩

**Hehl** *der od. das:* **kein[en]** ~ **aus etw.**
**machen** make no secret of sth.

**Hehler** *der;* ~s, ~: receiver [of stolen
goods]

**Hehlerei** *die;* ~, ~en (Rechtsw.) receiving
[stolen goods] *no art.*

**Hehlerin** *die;* ~, ~nen ▶ HEHLER

**Heide**[1] *der;* ~n, ~n heathen

**Heide**[2] *die;* ~, ~n heath; (Landschaft)
heathland

**Heide-:** ~**kraut** *das* heather; ~**land** *das*
moorland; heathland

**Heidel·beere** *die* bilberry

**Heidin** *die;* ~, ~nen heathen

**heidnisch** *Adj.* heathen

**heikel** *Adj.* (a) (schwierig) delicate, ticklish
⟨*matter, subject*⟩; ticklish tricky ⟨*problem,*
*question, situation*⟩
(b) (wählerisch) fussy (**in Bezug auf** + *Akk.*
about)

**heil** *Adj.* (nicht entzwei) in one piece; **wieder** ~
**sein** ⟨*injured part*⟩ have healed [up]

---

*alte Schreibung - vgl. Hinweis auf S. xiv

**Heil** *das;* ~s (a) (Wohlergehen) benefit
(b) (Rel.) salvation

**Heiland** *der;* ~[e]s, ~e Saviour

**Heil·anstalt** *die* (Anstalt für Kranke od.
Süchtige) sanatorium; (psychiatrische Klinik)
mental hospital

**heilbar** *Adj.* curable

**Heil·butt** *der* halibut

**heilen** [1] *tr. V.* cure; heal ⟨*wound*⟩
[2] *itr. V.;* mit sein ⟨*wound*⟩ heal [up];
⟨*fracture*⟩ mend

**heil·froh** *Adj.* very glad

**heilig** *Adj.* (a) holy; **die Heiligen Drei Könige**
the Three Kings *or* Wise Men; the Magi; **die**
**Heilige Schrift** the Holy Scriptures *pl.;* **der**
**Heilige Abend** Christmas Eve
(b) (geh.: unantastbar) sacred ⟨*right, tradition,*
*cause, etc.*⟩

**Heilig·abend** *der* Christmas Eve

**Heilige** *der/die; adj. Dekl.* saint

**heiligen** *tr. V.* keep ⟨*tradition, Sabbath,*
*etc.*⟩; **der Zweck heiligt die Mittel** the end
justifies the means

**Heiligen·schein** *der* gloriole; (um den
Kopf) halo

**Heiligkeit** *die;* ~: holiness

**Heiligtum** *das;* ~s, Heiligtümer shrine

**Heil-:** ~**kraut** *das* medicinal herb;
~**mittel** *das* (auch fig.) remedy (**gegen** for);
(Medikament) medicament; ~**praktiker** *der,*
~**praktikerin** *die* non-medical
practitioner

**heilsam** *Adj.* salutary

**Heils·armee** *die* Salvation Army

**Heilung** *die;* ~, ~en (einer Wunde) healing;
(von Krankheit, Kranken) curing

**Heim** *das;* ~[e]s, ~e (a) (Zuhause) home
(b) (Anstalt, Alters~) home; (für Obdachlose)
hostel

**Heim·arbeit** *die* outwork

**Heimat** *die;* ~, ~en (a) (Ort) home; home
town/village; (Land) home; homeland
(b) (Ursprungsland) natural habitat

**Heimat-:** ~**kunde** *die* local history,
geography, and natural history; ~**land** *das*
native land; (fig.) home

**heimatlich** *Adj.* native ⟨*dialect*⟩; nostalgic
⟨*emotions*⟩

**heimat-, Heimat-:** ~**los** *Adj.* homeless;
~**museum** *das* museum of local history;
~**ort** *der* home town/village; ~**stadt** *die*
home town; ~**vertriebene** *der/die; adj.*
*Dekl.* expellee [from his/her homeland]

**heim-, Heim-:** ~|**bringen** *unr. tr. V.* (a)
jmdn. ~: take *or.* see sb. home; (b) bring
home; ~**computer** *der* home computer;
~|**fahren** [1] *unr. itr. V.;* mit sein drive
home; [2] *unr. tr. V.* drive home; ~**fahrt** *die*
journey home; (mit dem Auto) drive home;
~|**gehen** *unr. itr. V.;* mit sein go home

**heimisch** *Adj.* (einheimisch) indigenous,

native ⟨*plants, animals, etc.*⟩ (**in** + *Dat.* to);
domestic ⟨*industry*⟩; **sich ∼ fühlen** feel at
home; **∼ werden** [**in** (+ *Dat.*)] settle in[to]
**heim-, Heim-:** ∼**kehr** *die;* ∼∼: return
home; homecoming; ∼|**kehren** *itr. V.; mit
sein* return home (**aus** from); ∼|**kommen**
*unr. itr. V.; mit sein* come home

**heimlich** ①*Adj.* secret
② *adv.* secretly

**Heimlichkeit** *die;* ∼, ∼**en** secret

**heim-, Heim-:** ∼**reise** *die* journey home;
∼**spiel** *das* (Sport) home match *or* game;
∼|**suchen** *tr. V.* ⟨*storm, earthquake,
epidemic*⟩ strike; ⟨*disease*⟩ afflict;
⟨*nightmares, doubts*⟩ plague; ∼**suchung**
*die;* ∼, ∼**en** affliction; visitation;
∼**tückisch** ①*Adj.* (bösartig) malicious;
(fig.) insidious ⟨*disease*⟩; ② *adv.* maliciously;
∼**wärts** *Adv.* (nach Hause zu) home; (in
Richtung Heimat) homeward[s]; ∼**weg** *der*
way home; ∼**weh** *das* homesickness;
∼**weh haben** be homesick (**nach** for);
∼|**zahlen** *tr. V.* jmdm. etw. ∼**zahlen** pay
sb. back for sth.

**Heinzel·männchen** *das* brownie

**Heirat** *die;* ∼, ∼**en** marriage

**heiraten** ①*itr. V.* get married
② *tr. V.* marry

**Heirats-:** ∼**antrag** *der:* jmdm. einen
∼**antrag machen** propose to sb.; ∼**anzeige**
*die* announcement of a/the forthcoming
marriage; ∼**schwindler** *der,*
∼**schwindlerin** *die:* person who makes a
spurious offer of marriage for purposes of
fraud

**heiser** ①*Adj.* hoarse
② *adv.* in a hoarse voice

**Heiserkeit** *die;* ∼: hoarseness

**heiß** ①*Adj.* hot; jmdm. **ist** ∼: sb. feels hot;
**etw.** ∼ **machen** heat sth. up; heated ⟨*debate,
argument*⟩; fierce ⟨*fight, battle*⟩; ardent
⟨*wish, love*⟩; **ein** ∼**es Thema** a controversial
subject
② *adv.* ⟨*fight*⟩ fiercely; ⟨*love*⟩ dearly; ⟨*long*⟩
fervently

**heißen** *unr. itr. V.* (den Namen tragen) be
called; (bedeuten) mean; (lauten) ⟨*saying*⟩ go;
(*unpers.*) **es heißt, dass ...:** they say that ...;
**in dem Artikel heißt es ...:** in the article it
says that ...

**Heiß·luft** *die* hot air

**Heißluft·backofen** *der* fan oven

**heiter** *Adj.* cheerful, happy ⟨*person,
nature*⟩; happy, merry ⟨*laughter*⟩; fine
⟨*weather, day*⟩

**Heiterkeit** *die;* ∼ (a) (Frohsinn)
cheerfulness
**(b)** (Belustigung) merriment

**heizbar** *Adj.* heated

**Heiz·decke** *die* electric blanket

**heizen** ①*itr. V.* have the heating on
② *tr. V.* heat ⟨*room etc.*⟩

**Heizer** *der;* ∼**s**, ∼, **Heizerin** *die;* ∼,
∼**nen** stoker
**Heiz-:** ∼**kissen** *das* heating pad;
∼**körper** *der* radiator; ∼**ofen** *der* stove;
heater; ∼**platte** *die* hotplate
**Heizung** *die;* ∼, ∼**en** (a) [central] heating
*no pl., no indef. art.;*
**(b)** (ugs.: Heizkörper) radiator

**Hektar** *das od. der;* ∼**s**, ∼**e** hectare

**Hektik** *die;* ∼: hectic rush; (des Lebens)
hectic pace

**hektisch** *Adj.* hectic

**Held** *der;* ∼**en**, ∼**en** hero

**heldenhaft** ①*Adj.* heroic
② *adv.* heroically

**Heldentum** *das;* ∼**s** heroism

**Heldin** *die;* ∼, ∼**nen** heroine

**helfen** *unr. itr. V.* help; jmdm. [**bei etw.**] ∼:
help sb. [with sth.]; (*unpers.*) **es hilft nichts**
it's no use *or* good

**Helfer** *der;* ∼**s**, ∼, **Helferin** *die;* ∼, ∼**nen**
helper; (Mitarbeiter[in]) assistant; (eines
Verbrechens) accomplice

**Helikopter** *der;* ∼**s**, ∼: helicopter

**hell** ①*Adj.* **(a)** (von Licht erfüllt) light; well-lit
⟨*stairs*⟩
**(b)** (klar) bright ⟨*day, sky, etc.*⟩
**(c)** (viel Licht spendend) bright ⟨*light, lamp,
star, etc.*⟩
**(d)** (blass) light ⟨*colour*⟩; fair ⟨*skin, hair*⟩;
light-coloured ⟨*clothes*⟩
**(e)** (akustisch) high, clear ⟨*sound, voice*⟩;
ringing ⟨*laugh*⟩
**(f)** (klug) bright
**(g)** (ugs.: absolut) sheer, utter ⟨*madness,
foolishness, despair*⟩
② *adv.* brightly

**hell-:** ∼**blau** *Adj.* light blue; ∼**blond** *Adj.*
very fair; light blonde

**Helle** *das; adj. Dekl.* ≈ lager

**Heller** *der;* ∼**s**, ∼: heller; **bis auf den
letzten** ∼/**bis auf** ∼ **und Pfennig** (ugs.) down
to the last penny *or* (Amer.) cent

**hell-:** ∼**grün** *Adj.* light green; ∼**häutig**
*Adj.* fair-skinned

**Helligkeit** *die;* ∼, ∼**en** (auch Physik)
brightness

**hell-, Hell-:** ∼**rot** *Adj.* light red;
∼**sehen** *unr. itr. V.; nur im Inf.* ∼**sehen
können** have second sight; ∼**seher** *der,*
∼**seherin** *die* clairvoyant; ∼**wach** *Adj.*
wide awake

**Helm** *der;* ∼**[e]s**, ∼**e** helmet

**Hemd** *das;* ∼**[e]s**, ∼**en** shirt; (Unterhemd)
[under]vest; undershirt

**Hemds·ärmel** *der* shirtsleeve

**hemmen** *tr. V.* **(a)** (verlangsamen) slow
[down]
**(b)** (aufhalten) check; stem ⟨*flow*⟩
**(c)** (beeinträchtigen) hinder

**Hemmung** *die;* ∼, ∼**en** (a) (Gehemmtheit)
inhibition
**(b)** (Bedenken) scruple

**hemmungs·los** ①Adj. unrestrained ②adv. unrestrainedly

**Hendl** das; ~s, ~[n] (bayr., österr.) chicken; (Brathähnchen) [roast] chicken

**Hengst** der; ~[e]s, ~e (Pferd) stallion

**Henkel** der; ~s, ~: handle

**Henker** der; ~s, ~: hangman; (Scharfrichter, auch fig.) executioner

**Henne** die; ~, ~n hen

**her** /heːɐ̯/ Adv. ~ damit give it to me; give it here (coll.); **vom Fenster** ~: from the window; **wo ist er** ~? where is he from?; **von ihrer Kindheit** ~: since childhood; **von der Konzeption** ~: as far as the basic design is concerned; **hinter jmdm.** (ugs.)/**etw.** ~ **sein** be after sb./sth.; **einen Monat/lange** ~ **sein** be a month/a long time ago; **es ist lange** ~, **dass wir...**: it is a long time since we...

**herab** Adv. down; **von oben** ~ (fig.) condescendingly

**herab-:** ~|**hängen** unr. itr. V. hang [down] (**von** from); ~**hängende Schultern** drooping shoulders; ~|**lassen** ① unr. tr. V. let down; lower; ② unr. refl. V. (iron.: bereit sein) **sich** ~**lassen, etw. zu tun** condescend to do sth.; ~**lassend** ① Adj. condescending; patronizing (**zu** towards); ② adv. condescendingly; patronizingly; ~|**sehen** unr. itr. V. **auf jmdn.** ~**sehen** look down on sb.; ~|**setzen** tr. V. (a) reduce; (b) (abwerten) belittle

**heran** Adv. **an etw.** (Akk.) ~: right up to sth.

**heran-, Heran-:** ~|**bilden** tr. V. train [up]; (auf der Schule, Universität) educate; ~|**bringen** unr. tr. V. (a) bring [up] (**an** + Akk., **zu** to); (b) (vertraut machen) **jmdn. an etw.** (Akk.) ~**bringen** introduce sb. to sth.; ~|**fahren** unr. itr. V.; mit sein drive up (**an** + Akk. to); ~|**kommen** unr. itr. V.; mit sein **an etw.** (Akk.) ~**kommen** come near to sth.; (erreichen) reach sth.; (erwerben) obtain sth.; ~|**reifen** itr. V.; mit sein ⟨fruit, crops⟩ ripen; **zur Frau** ~**reifen** mature into a woman; ~|**treten** unr. itr. V.; mit sein (sich wenden) **an jmdn.** ~**treten** approach sb.; ~|**wachsen** unr. itr. V.; mit sein grow up; ~**wachsende** der/die; adj. Dekl. young person; ~|**ziehen** unr. tr. V. pull over; pull up ⟨chair⟩; **etw. zu sich** ~**ziehen** pull sth. towards one

**herauf** Adv. up

**herauf-:** ~|**beschwören** tr. V. (a) (verursachen) cause ⟨disaster, war, crisis⟩; (b) (erinnern) evoke ⟨memories etc.⟩; ~|**kommen** unr. itr. V.; mit sein (nach oben kommen) come up; ~|**setzen** tr. V. increase, put up ⟨prices, rents, interest rates, etc.⟩

**heraus** Adv. ~ **aus den Federn!/dem Bett!** rise and shine!/out of bed!

**heraus-, Heraus-:** ~|**bekommen** unr. tr. V. (a) (entfernen) get out (**aus** of); (b) (ugs.:

lösen) work out ⟨problem, answer, etc.⟩; solve ⟨puzzle⟩; (c) (ermitteln) find out; (d) (als Wechselgeld bekommen) **5 Euro** ~**bekommen** get back 5 euros change; **ich bekomme noch 5 Euro** ~: I still have 5 euros [change] to come; ~|**bringen** unr. tr. V. (a) (nach außen bringen) bring out (**aus** of); (b) (nach draußen begleiten) show out; (c) (veröffentlichen) bring out; (aufführen) put on, stage ⟨play⟩; screen ⟨film⟩; (d) (auf den Markt bringen) bring out; (e) (populär machen) make widely known; ~|**fahren** ① unr. itr. V.; mit sein (a) (nach außen fahren) **aus etw.** ~**fahren** drive/ride out of sth.; (b) (fahrend herauskommen) come out; ② unr. tr. V. **den Wagen [aus dem Hof]** ~**fahren** drive the car out [of the yard]; **jmdn.** ~**fahren** drive sb. out (**zu** to); ~|**finden** ① unr. tr. V. find out; trace ⟨fault⟩; ② unr. itr. V. find one's way out (**aus** of); ~|**fordern** ① tr. V. (a) (auch Sport) challenge; (b) (heraufbeschwören) provoke ⟨person, resistance, etc.⟩; invite ⟨criticism⟩; court ⟨danger⟩; ② itr. V. **zu etw.** ~**fordern** provoke sth.; ~**forderung** die (auch Sport) challenge; (Provokation) provocation; ~|**geben** ① unr. tr. V. (a) (aushändigen) hand over ⟨property, person, hostage, etc.⟩; (zurückgeben) give back; (b) (als Wechselgeld zurückgeben) **5 Euro/zu viel** ~**geben** give 5 euros/too much change; (c) (veröffentlichen) publish; (d) issue ⟨stamp, coin, etc.⟩; ② unr. itr. V. give change; ~**geber** der; ~s, ~, ~**geberin** die; ~~, ~~nen publisher; (Redakteur[in]) editor; ~|**gehen** unr. itr. V.; mit sein (a) go out (**aus** of); (b) (sich entfernen lassen) ⟨stain etc.⟩ come out; ~|**halten** unr. refl. V. keep out; ~|**hängen** tr. V. hang out (**aus** of); ~|**helfen** unr. itr. V. **jmdm.** ~**helfen** (auch fig.) help sb. out (**aus** of); ~|**holen** tr. V. (a) (nach außen holen) bring out; (b) (ugs.: erwirken) win ⟨wage increase, advantage, etc.⟩; ~|**kommen** unr. itr. V.; mit sein (a) come out (**aus** of); (b) (erscheinen; ugs.: auf den Markt kommen, bekannt werden) come out; ~|**nehmen** unr. tr. V. (a) take out (**aus** of); (b) (ugs.: entfernen) take out ⟨appendix, tonsils, tooth, etc.⟩; ~|**reden** refl. V. (ugs.) talk one's way out (**aus** of); ~|**reißen** unr. tr. V. (a) tear out (**aus** of); pull up ⟨plant⟩; (b) (aus der Umgebung, der Arbeit) tear away (**aus** from); **die Krankheit hat ihn aus der Arbeit** ~**gerissen** the illness has interrupted his work; (c) (Mängel ausgleichen) **den zunächst etwas langweiligen Abend** ~**reißen** rescue what had been rather a boring evening; **die Eins im Aufsatz reißt die Drei im Diktat heraus** the A for the essay makes up for the C in the dictation; ~|**rutschen** itr. V.; mit sein (ugs.) ⟨remark etc.⟩ slip out; ~|**stellen** refl. V. **es stellte sich** ~, **dass ...**: it turned out that ...; ~|**suchen** tr. V. pick out; look out ⟨file⟩

**herb** Adj. [slightly] sharp ⟨taste⟩; dry ⟨wine⟩; [slightly] sharp ⟨smell, perfume⟩; bitter ⟨disappointment⟩; severe ⟨face, features⟩; austere ⟨beauty⟩; harsh ⟨words, criticism⟩

**herbei-:** ~|**eilen** itr. V.; mit sein hurry over; ~|**laufen** unr. itr. V.; mit sein come running up

**Herberge** die; ~, ~n (veralt.: Gasthaus) inn

**Herbergs-:** ~**mutter** die; Pl. ~mütter, ~**vater** der warden [of the/a youth hostel]

**her|bringen** unr. tr. V. etw. ~: bring sth. [here]

**Herbst** der; ~[e]s, ~e autumn; fall (Amer.); s. auch FRÜHLING

**Herbst-anfang** der beginning of autumn

**herbstlich** Adj. autumn attrib.; autumnal

**Herd** der; ~[e]s, ~e cooker; (fig.) centre (of disturbance/rebellion)

**Herde** die; ~, ~n herd

**Herd-platte** die hot-plate

**herein-:** ~|**bitten** unr. tr. V. jmdn. ~ bitten ask or invite sb. in; ~|**brechen** unr. itr. V.; mit sein (geh.) ⟨night, evening, dusk⟩ fall; ⟨winter⟩ set in; ⟨storm⟩ strike, break; ~|**bringen** unr. tr. V. bring in; ~|**fallen** unr. itr. V.; mit sein (ugs.) be taken for a ride (coll.); be done (coll.); ~|**kommen** unr. itr. V.; mit sein come in; ~|**lassen** unr. tr. V. let in; ~|**legen** tr. V. (ugs.) jmdn. ~legen take sb. for a ride (coll.) (**mit, bei** with); ~|**platzen** itr. V.; mit sein (ugs.) burst in; ~|**schneien** unr. itr. V.; mit sein (ugs.) turn up out of the blue (coll.)

**her-, Her-:** ~**fahrt** die journey here; ~**fallen** unr. itr. V.; mit sein **über** jmdn. ~fallen attack sb.; (gierig zu essen beginnen) **über etw.** (Akk.) ~fallen fall upon sth.; ~**gang** der: der ~gang der Ereignisse the sequence of events; ~|**geben** unr. tr. V. hand over; (weggeben) give away; ~|**gehen** unr. itr. V.; mit sein **neben/vor/hinter** jmdm. ~gehen walk along beside/in front of/ behind sb.; ~|**haben** unr. tr. V. (ugs.) **wo hat er/sie das** ~? where did he/she get that from?; ~|**halten** unr. itr. V. ~halten **müssen [für** jmdn./etw.] be the one to suffer [for sb./sth.]; ~|**hören** itr. V. listen

**Hering** der; ~s, ~e (a) herring (b) (Zeltpflock) peg

**her-:** ~|**kommen** unr. itr. V.; mit sein come here; ~**kömmlich** Adj. conventional; traditional ⟨custom⟩

**Herkunft** die; ~, Herkünfte origin

**Herkunfts-land** das country of origin

**her-:** ~|**laufen** unr. itr. V.; mit sein **vor/ hinter/neben** jmdm. ~laufen run [along] in front of/behind/alongside sb.; (nachlaufen) **hinter** jmdm. ~laufen run after sb. (fig.) chase sb. up; ~|**leiten** tr., refl. V. derive (**aus, von** from); ~|**machen** (ugs.) refl. V. **sich über etw.** (Akk.) ~machen get stuck into sth. (coll.)

**Hermelin** der; ~s, ~e (Pelz) ermine

**hermetisch** [1] Adj. hermetic [2] adv. hermetically

**Heroin** das; ~s heroin

**Heroin-sucht** die heroin addiction

**heroin-süchtig** Adj. addicted to heroin postpos.

**Herr** der; ~n, ~en (a) (Mann) gentleman (b) (Titel, Anrede) ~ **Schulze** Mr Schulze; **Sehr geehrter** ~ **Schulze!** Dear Sir; (bei persönlicher Bekanntschaft) Dear Mr Schulze; **meine** ~**en** gentlemen (c) (Gebieter) master

**herren-, Herren-:** ~**ausstatter** der [gentle]men's outfitter; ~**los** Adj. abandoned ⟨car, luggage⟩; stray ⟨dog, cat⟩; ~**salon** der men's hairdressing salon; ~**schuh** der man's shoe; ~**schuhe** men's shoes; ~**toilette** die [gentle]men's toilet

**Herr-gott** der; ~s: **der [liebe]/unser** ~: the Lord [God]; God

**Herrgotts-frühe** die **in aller** ~: at the crack of dawn

**her|richten** tr. V. (bereitmachen) get ⟨room, refreshments, etc.⟩ ready; arrange ⟨table⟩; (in Ordnung bringen) renovate

**Herrin** die; ~, ~en mistress

**herrisch** [1] Adj. overbearing; imperious [2] adv. imperiously

**herrlich** [1] Adj. marvellous; magnificent ⟨view, clothes⟩ [2] adv. marvellously

**Herrlichkeit** die; ~, ~en (a) (Schönheit) magnificence; splendour (b) (herrliche Sache) marvellous thing

**Herrschaft** die; ~, ~en (a) rule; (Macht) power (b) Pl. (Damen u. Herren) ladies and gentlemen

**herrschen** itr. V. rule; ⟨monarch⟩ reign, rule; **draußen** ~ 30° **Kälte** it's 30° below outside

**Herrscher** der; ~s, ~, **Herrscherin** die; ~, ~nen ruler

**herrsch-, Herrsch-:** ~**sucht** die thirst for power; (herrisches Wesen) domineering nature; ~**süchtig** Adj. domineering

**her-:** ~|**rühren** itr. V. **von** jmdm./etw. ~rühren come from sb./stem from sth.; *~|**sein** ▸ HER; ~|**stellen** tr. V. produce; manufacture; make

**Hersteller** der; ~s, ~, **Herstellerin** die; ~, ~nen producer

**Her-stellung** die production; manufacture

**herüber** Adv. over

**herum** Adv. **um ...** ~ (Richtung) round; (Anordnung) around; **um Weihnachten** ~: around Christmas; ~ **sein** (ugs.: vergangen sein, vorüber sein) have passed

**herum-:** ~|**ärgern** refl. V. (ugs.) **sich mit** jmdm./etw. ~ärgern keep getting annoyed with sb./sth.; ~|**drehen** [1] tr. V. (ugs.) turn ⟨key⟩; turn over ⟨coin, mattress, hand, etc.⟩ [2] refl. V. turn [a]round; ~|**fahren** (ugs.) [1] unr. itr. V.; mit sein (sich plötzlich herumdrehen) spin round; [2] unr. tr. V. jmdn. **[in der Stadt]** ~fahren drive sb. around the town; ~|**führen** [1] tr. V. jmdn. **[in der Stadt]** ~führen show sb. around the town;    ···✦

**h**

② *itr. V.* **um etw. ~führen** ⟨*road etc.*⟩ go round sth.; **~gehen** *unr. itr. V.; mit sein* (vergehen) pass; **um etw. ~gehen** go round sth.; **etw. ~gehen lassen** circulate sth.; pass; **~|kommandieren** (ugs.) ① *tr. V.* jmdn. ~kommandieren boss (coll.) *or* order sb. around *or* about; ② *itr. V.* boss (coll.) *or* order people around *or* about; **~|kommen** *unr. itr. V.; mit sein* (ugs.) **(a)** (vermeiden können) **um etw. [nicht] ~kommen** [not] be able to get out of sth.; **(b)** (viel reisen) get around *or* about; **in der Welt ~kommen** see a lot of the world; **~|laufen** *unr. itr. V.; mit sein* **(a)** walk/(schneller) run around *or* about; **um etw. ~laufen** go round sth.; **(b)** (gekleidet sein) **wie ein Hippie ~laufen** go about looking like a hippie; **~|lungern** *itr. V.* (salopp) loaf around; **~|schlagen** *unr. refl. V.* (ugs.) **sich mit Problemen/Einwänden ~schlagen** grapple with problems/battle against objections; *\*~|sein ▶* HERUM; **~|sitzen** *unr. itr. V.* (ugs.) sit around *or* about; **~|sprechen** *unr. refl. V.* get around *or* about; **~|stöbern** *itr. V.* (ugs.) keep rummaging around *or* about (**in** + *Dat.* in); **~|treiben** *unr. refl. V.* (ugs. abwertend) **sich auf den Straßen/in Discos ~treiben** hang around the streets/in discos; **sich in der Welt ~treiben** roam about the world

**herụnter** *Adv.* **(a)** (nach unten) down; [körperlich] **~ sein** be in poor health **(b)** (fort) off; **~ vom Sofa!** [get] off the sofa!

**herụnter-:** **~|bringen** *unr. tr. V.* bring down; **~|fallen** *unr. itr. V.; mit sein* fall down; **vom Tisch/Stuhl ~fallen** fall off the table/chair; **~|gehen** *unr. itr. V.; mit sein* **(a)** come down; **(b)** (niedriger werden) ⟨*temperature*⟩ drop; ⟨*prices*⟩ come down, fall; **~gekommen** ① *2. Part. v.* ~KOMMEN; ② *Adj.* poor ⟨*health*⟩; dilapidated ⟨*building*⟩; run-down ⟨*area*⟩; down and out ⟨*person*⟩; **~|handeln** *tr. V.* (ugs.) **einen Preis ~handeln** beat down a price; **~|hängen** *unr. itr. V.* hang down; **~|hauen** *unr. tr. V.* (ugs.) **jmdm. eine ~hauen** give sb. a clout round the ear (coll.); **~|kommen** *unr. itr. V.; mit sein* **(a)** come down; **(b)** (ugs.: verfallen) go to the dogs (coll.); **~|lassen** *unr. tr. V.* lower; **~|schlucken** *tr. V.* swallow; *\*~|sein ▶* HERUNTER A; **~|spielen** *tr. V.* (ugs.) play down

**hervọr** *Adv.* **aus ... ~:** out of

**hervọr-:** **~|heben** *unr. tr. V.* stress; **~ragend** ① *Adj.* outstanding[ly good]; ② *adv.* **~ragend geschult** outstandingly well trained; **~ragend spielen/arbeiten** play/work outstandingly well; **~|tun** *unr. refl. V.* distinguish oneself; (wichtig tun) show off

**Hẹrz** *das;* **~ens,** **~en** heart; (Kartenspiel) hearts *pl.;* **von ~en kommen** come from the heart; **ein ~ für die Armen haben** feel for the poor; **ein ~ für Kinder haben** have a love of children; **schweren ~ens** with a heavy

heart; **etw. auf dem ~en haben** have sth. on one's mind; **es nicht übers ~ bringen, etw. zu tun** not have the heart to do sth.; **sich** (*Dat.*) **etw. zu ~en nehmen** take sth. to heart

**Hẹrz-:** **~an·fall** *der* heart attack; **~beschwerden** *Pl.* heart trouble *sing.*

**hẹrzens-, Hẹrzens-:** **~gut** /'--'-/ *Adj.* kind-hearted; **~lust** *die:* **nach ~lust** to one's heart's content

**hẹrzhaft** ① *Adj.* hearty; (nahrhaft) hearty ⟨*meal*⟩; (von kräftigem Geschmack) tasty ② *adv.* heartily; (nahrhaft) **er isst gern ~:** he likes to have a hearty meal

**her|ziehen** *unr. itr. V.; mit sein od. haben* (ugs.) **über jmdn./etw. ~** run sb./sth. down

**hẹrzig** ① *Adj.* sweet; delightful ② *adv.* sweetly; delightfully

**hẹrz-, Hẹrz-:** **~infarkt** *der* heart attack; **~klappen·fehler** *der* (Med.) valvular defect *or* insufficiency; **~klopfen** *das;* **~~s:** **jmd. hat ~klopfen** sb.'s heart is pounding; **~krank** *Adj.* ⟨*person*⟩ with a heart condition; **~kranz·gefäß** *das* coronary vessel

**hẹrzlich** ① *Adj.* warm ⟨*smile, reception*⟩; kind ⟨*words, regards*⟩; (ehrlich gemeint) sincere; **~en Dank** many thanks ② *adv.* warmly; (ehrlich gemeint) sincerely; ⟨*congratulate*⟩ heartily; **~ wenig** very *or* (coll.) precious little

**Hẹrzlichkeit** *die;* **~:** warmth; kindness; (Aufrichtigkeit) sincerity

**hẹrz·los** ① *Adj.* heartless ② *adv.* heartlessly

**Hẹrzog** *der;* **~s, Herzöge** duke

**Hẹrzogin** *die;* **~, ~nen** duchess

**Hẹrz·rhythmus·störung** *die* (Med.) disturbance of the heart *or* cardiac rhythm

**hẹrz-, Hẹrz-:** **~schlag** *der* heartbeat; (Herzversagen) heart failure; **~schmerz** *der* pain in the region of the heart; **~schrittmacher** *der* (Anat., Med.) [cardiac] pacemaker; **~transplantation** *die* (Med.) heart transplantation; **~zerreißend** ① *Adj.* heart-rending; ② *adv.* heart-rendingly

**Hẹssen** (*das*); **~s** Hesse

**hetero·sexuẹll** *Adj.* heterosexual

**Hẹtze** *die;* **~ (a)** [mad] rush **(b)** (abwertend) smear campaign

**hẹtzen** ① *tr. V.* **(a)** hunt **(b)** (antreiben) rush ② *itr. V.* **(a)** (in großer Eile sein) rush **(b)** *mit sein* (hasten) rush; (rennen) dash; race

**Hẹtz-:** **~kampagne** *die* (abwertend) smear campaign; (gegen eine Minderheit) hate campaign; **~rede** *die* (abwertend) inflammatory speech

**Heu** *das;* **~[e]s** hay

**Heuchelei** *die;* **~:** hypocrisy

**heucheln** ① *itr. V.* be a hypocrite ② *tr. V.* feign

---

\*alte Schreibung - vgl. Hinweis auf S. xiv

**Heuchler** der; ~s, ~, **Heuchlerin** die; ~, ~nen hypocrite

**heuchlerisch** [1] Adj. hypocritical [2] adv. hypocritically

**heuer** Adv. (südd., österr., schweiz.) this year

**Heuer** die; ~, ~n (Seemannsspr.) pay; wages pl.

**Heu-ernte** die (a) hay harvest (b) (Ertrag) hay crop

**heulen** itr. V. (a) howl; ‹siren etc.› wail (b) (ugs.: weinen) howl; bawl

**Heurige** der; adj. Dekl. (bes. österr.) (a) (Wein) new wine (b) (Weinlokal) inn with new wine on tap

**Heu-:** ~**schnupfen** der hay fever; ~**schrecke** die grasshopper

**heute** Adv. today; ~ früh early this morning; ~ Morgen/Abend this morning/evening; ~ Mittag [at] midday today; ~ Nacht tonight; (letzte Nacht) last night; ~ in einer Woche a week [from] today; today week; ~ vor einer Woche a week ago today

**heutig** Adj. (a) (von diesem Tag) today's; der ~e Tag today (b) (gegenwärtig) today's; of today postpos.; in der ~en Zeit nowadays

**heut-zu-tage** Adv. nowadays

**Hexe** die; ~, ~n witch

**hexen** itr. V. work magic

**Hexen-schuss, *Hexen-schuß** der lumbago no indef. art.

**Hexerei** die; ~, ~en witchcraft; (von Kunststücken usw.) magic

**Hickhack** das od. der; ~s, ~s (ugs.) squabbling; bickering

**hieb** 1. u. 3. Pers. Sg. Prät. v. HAUEN

**Hieb** der; ~[e]s, ~e (a) (Schlag) blow; (mit der Peitsche) lash (b) Pl. (ugs.: Prügel) hiding sing.

**hieb-fest** Adj.: hieb- und stichfest watertight; cast-iron

**hielt** 1. u. 3. Pers. Sg. Prät. v. HALTEN

**hier** Adv. (a) here; [von] ~ oben/unten [from] up/down here (b) (jetzt) now; von ~ an from now on

**hieran** Adv. here; sich ~ festhalten hold on to this; (fig.) im Anschluss ~: immediately after this

**Hierarchie** /hierar'çi:/ die; ~, ~n hierarchy

**hierauf** Adv. (a) on here; (darauf) on this; wir werden ~ zurückkommen we'll come back to this (b) (danach) after that; then (c) (infolgedessen) whereupon

**hieraus** Adv. out of here; (aus dieser Tatsache, Quelle) from this

**hier-:** ~|**behalten** unr. tr. V. jmdn./etw. ~behalten keep sb./sth. here; ~**bei** Adv. (a) (bei dieser Gelegenheit) Diese Übung ist sehr schwierig. Man kann sich ~bei leicht verletzen. This exercise is very difficult. You can easily injure yourself doing it; (b) (bei der erwähnten Sache) here; ~|**bleiben** unr. itr. V.; mit sein stay here; ~**durch** Adv. through here; (aufgrund dieser Sache) because of this; ~**für** Adv. for this

**hier-her** Adv. here; ich gehe bis ~ und nicht weiter I'm going this far and no further; ~**gehören** belong here; (hierfür wichtig sein) be relevant [here]; ~**kommen** mit sein come here

**hier-hin** Adv. here; bis ~: up to here

**hier-:** ~**in** Adv. (a) (räumlich) in here; (b) in this; ~**mit** Adv. with this/these; ~mit ist der Fall erledigt that puts an end to the matter; ~**nach** Adv. (anschließend) after that

**Hieroglyphe** /hiero.../ die; ~, ~n hieroglyph

**hier-:** *~**sein** ▸ HIER A; ~**über** Adv. (a) (über dem Erwähnten) above here; (über das Erwähnte) over here; (b) (das Erwähnte betreffend) about this/these; ~**von** Adv. of this/these; ~**zu** Adv. with this; (hinsichtlich dieser Sache) about this; ~zu gehört/gehören ...: this includes/these include; ~zu reicht mein Geld nicht I haven't got enough money for that; ~**zu-lande** Adv. [here] in this country

**hiesig** Adj. local

**hieß** 1. u. 3. Pers. Sg. Prät. v. HEISSEN

**Hi-Fi-Anlage** /'hai:fi-/ die hi-fi system

**high** /hai/ Adj. (ugs.) high (coll.)

**Hightech-, High-Tech-** /'hai'tɛk-/ high-tech

**Hilfe** die; ~, ~n (a) help; (für Notleidende) aid; relief; zu ~! help! (b) (Hilfskraft) help; (im Geschäft) assistant

**Hilfe-:** ~**leistung** die help; ~**ruf** der cry for help; ~**stellung** die (Turnen) jmdm. ~stellung geben act as spotter for sb.

**hilflos** [1] Adj. helpless [2] adv. helplessly

**Hilflosigkeit** die; ~ helplessness

**hilfs-, Hilfs-:** ~**bedürftig** Adj. (a) (schwach) in need of help postpos.; (b) (notleidend) in need; needy; ~**bereit** Adj. helpful; ~**bereitschaft** die helpfulness; ~**gelder** Pl. aid money sing.; ~**kraft** die assistant; ~**mittel** das aid; ~**organisation** die aid or relief organization; ~**programm** das aid or relief programme; ~**verb** das, ~**zeitwort** das (Sprachw.) auxiliary [verb]

**Himalaja** der; ~[s]: der/im ~: the/in the Himalayas pl.

**Him-beere** die raspberry

**Himmel** der; ~s, ~ sky; (Rel.) heaven; ~ noch [ein]mal! for Heaven's sake!

**himmel-, Himmel-:** ~**bett** das four-poster bed; ~**blau** Adj. sky-blue; clear blue ‹eyes›; ~**fahrt** die (Rel.) (a) Christi/Mariä ~fahrt the Ascension of Christ/the Assumption of the Virgin Mary; (b) (Festtag) [Christi] ~: Ascension Day no art.

**Himmels-:** ~**richtung** *die* point of the
compass; ~**schlüsselchen** *das;* ~~s,
~~: cowslip

**himmel·weit** *Adj.* enormous, vast
⟨*difference*⟩

**himmlisch** *Adj.* (auch fig.) heavenly

**hin** *Adv.* **(a)** (räumlich) **zur Straße** ~ **liegen**
face the road
**(b)** (zeitlich) **gegen Mittag** ~: towards midday
**(c)** (in Verbindungen) **nach außen** ~: outwardly;
**auf meinen Rat** ~: on my advice; **auf seine
Bitte** ~: at his request
**(d)** (in Wortpaaren) ~ **und zurück** there and
back; **einmal Köln** ~ **und zurück** a return
[ticket] to Cologne; ~ **und her** to and fro;
back and forth; ~ **und wieder** [every] now
and then
**(e)** ~ **sein** (ugs.: verloren sein); be gone; (ugs.:
nicht mehr brauchbar sein); have had it (coll.);
⟨*car*⟩ be a write-off; (salopp: tot sein) have
snuffed it (sl.); **von jmdm./etw. ganz** ~ **sein**
(ugs.: hingerissen sein) be mad about sb./bowled
over by sth.

**hinab** *Adv.* ▶ HINUNTER

**hinab|-** ▶ HINUNTER-

**hinauf** *Adv.* up; **bis** ~ **zu** up to

**hinauf-:** ~|**fahren** *unr. itr. V.; mit sein* go
up; (im Auto) drive up; (mit einem Motorrad) ride
up; ~|**gehen** *unr. itr. V.; mit sein* **(a)** (nach
oben gehen) go up; **(b)** (nach oben führen) lead
up; **(c)** (ugs.: steigen) ⟨*prices, taxes, etc.*⟩ go up;
rise; ~|**klettern** *itr. V.; mit sein* climb up;
~|**steigen** *unr. itr. V.; mit sein* climb up;
~|**ziehen** ① *unr. tr. V.* pull up; ② *unr. itr.
V.; mit sein* move up; ③ *unr. refl. V.* (sich
erstrecken) stretch up

**hinaus** *Adv.* **(a)** (räumlich) out
**(b)** (zeitlich) **auf Jahre** ~: for years to come
**(c)** (etw. überschreitend) **über etw.** (*Akk.*) ~: in
addition to sth.
**(d)** **über etw.** (*Akk.*) ~ **sein** be past sth.

**hinaus-:** ~|**bringen** *unr. tr. V.* jmdn./etw.
~**bringen** see sb. out/take sth. out (**aus** of);
~|**fahren** ① *unr. itr. V.; mit sein* **aus etw.**
~**fahren** (mit dem Auto) drive out of sth.; (mit
dem Zweirad) ride out of sth.; ⟨*car, bus*⟩ go out
of sth.; ⟨*train*⟩ pull out of sth.; **zum Flugplatz**
~**fahren** drive out to the airport; ② *unr. itr.
V.* jmdn./etw. ~**fahren** drive sb./take sth. out;
~|**fallen** *unr. itr. V.; mit sein* fall out (**aus**
of); ~|**finden** *unr. itr. V.* find one's way out
(**aus** of); ~|**gehen** *unr. itr. V.; mit sein* **(a)**
go out (**aus** of); **(b)** (gerichtet sein) **das Zimmer
geht zum Garten/nach Westen** ~: the room
looks out on to the garden/faces west;
~|**kommen** *unr. itr. V.; mit sein* come out
(**aus** of); ~|**laufen** *unr. itr. V.; mit sein* **(a)**
run out (**aus** of); **(b)** (als Ergebnis haben) **auf
etw.** (*Akk.*) ~**laufen** lead to sth.; ~|**sehen**
*unr. itr. V.* look out; **zum Fenster** ~**sehen**
look out of the window; *\*~|**sein** ▶ HINAUS
D; ~|**tragen** *unr. tr. V.* jmdn./etw. ~**tragen**
carry sb./sth. out; ~|**werfen** *unr. tr. V.*

(auch ugs. fig.) throw out (**aus** of); ~|**ziehen**
① *unr. itr. V.* **(a)** (nach draußen ziehen) jmdn./
etw. ~**ziehen** pull sb./sth. out (**aus** of); tow
⟨*ship*⟩ out; **(b)** (verzögern) put off; delay;
② *unr. refl. V.* be delayed; ~|**zögern** ① *tr.
V.* delay; ② *refl. V.* be delayed

**hin-, Hin-:** ~|**blick** *der:* **im** *od.* **in** ~**blick
auf etw.** (*Akk.*) (wegen) in view of; (hinsichtlich)
with regard to; ~|**bringen** *unr. tr. V.*
jmdn./etw. ~**bringen** take sb./sth. [there];
~|**denken** *unr. itr. V.* **wo denkst du hin?**
(ugs.) whatever are you thinking of?

**hinderlich** *Adj.* ~ **sein** get in the way

**hindern** *tr. V.* **(a)** (abhalten) jmdn. ~: stop sb.
(**an** + *Dat.* from)
**(b)** (behindern) hinder

**Hindernis** *das;* ~ses, ~se obstacle

**hin|deuten** *itr. V.* **(a)** auf jmdn./etw. *od.* zu
jmdm./etw. ~: point to sb./sth.
**(b)** auf etw. (*Akk.*) ~ (fig.) point to sth.

**Hindu** *der;* ~[s], ~[s] Hindu

**Hinduismus** *der;* ~ Hinduism *no art.*

**hin-durch** *Adv.* **(a)** (räumlich) **durch den Wald**
~: through the wood
**(b)** (zeitlich) **das ganze Jahr** ~: throughout
the year

**hinein** *Adv.* **(a)** (räumlich) in; **in etw.** (*Akk.*)
~: into sth.
**(b)** (zeitlich) **bis in den Morgen/tief in die
Nacht** ~: till morning/far into the night

**hinein-:** ~|**bringen** *unr. tr. V.* take in;
~|**fahren** (mit dem Auto) drive in; (mit dem
Zweirad) ride in; **in etw.** (*Akk.*) ~**fahren** drive/
ride into sth.; ~|**fallen** *unr. itr. V.; mit sein*
fall in; **in etw.** (*Akk.*) ~**fallen** fall into sth.;
~|**gehen** *unr. itr. V.; mit sein* go in; **in etw.**
(*Akk.*) ~**gehen** go into sth.; ~|**gucken** *itr.
V.* (ugs.) look in; **in etw.** (*Akk.*) ~**gucken** look
in[to] sth.; ~|**kommen** *unr. itr. V.; mit sein*
**(a)** come in; **in etw.** (*Akk.*) ~**kommen** come
into sth.; **(b)** (gelangen, auch fig.) get in; **in etw.**
(*Akk.*) ~**kommen** get into sth.; ~|**reden** *itr.
V.* jmdm. **in seine Angelegenheiten/
Entscheidungen** *usw.* ~**reden** interfere in
sb.'s affairs/decisions *etc.*; ~|**sehen** *unr.
itr. V.* look in; **in etw.** (*Akk.*) ~**sehen** look
into sth.; ~|**versetzen** *refl. V.* **sich in**
jmdn. *od.* jmds. **Lage** ~**versetzen** put oneself
in sb.'s position; ~|**ziehen** *unr. tr. V.* **(a)**
pull or draw in; **etw./jmdn. in etw.** (*Akk.*)
~**ziehen** pull or draw sth./sb. into sth.;
**(b)** (verwickeln) jmdn. **in eine Angelegenheit/
einen Streit/Skandal** ~**ziehen** drag sb. into
an affair/a dispute/scandal

**hin-, Hin-:** ~|**fahren** ① *unr. itr. V.; mit
sein* go there; ② *unr. tr. V.* jmdn. ~**fahren**
drive sb. there; ~|**fahrt** *die* journey there;
(Seereise) voyage out; ~|**fallen** *unr. itr. V.;
mit sein* **(a)** fall over; **(b)** jmdm. **fällt etw.** ~:
sb. drops sth.; **etw.** ~**fallen lassen** drop sth.;
~**fällig** *Adj.* **(a)** infirm; frail; **(b)** (ungültig)
invalid; ~|**fliegen** *unr. itr. V.; mit sein* fly
there; ~**flug** *der* outward flight

**hing** *1. u. 3. Pers. Sg. Prät. v.* HÄNGEN

**Hin·gabe** *die;* ~: devotion; (Eifer) dedication

**Hingebung** *die;* ~: devotion

**hingebungs·voll** ① *Adj.* devoted ② *adv.* devotedly; with devotion; ⟨listen⟩ with rapt attention; ⟨dance, play⟩ with abandon

**hin·gegen** *Konj., Adv.* (jedoch) however; (andererseits) on the other hand

**hin-, Hin-:** ~|**gehen** *unr. itr. V.; mit sein* (a) go [there]; **zu jmdm./etw.** ~**gehen** go to sb./sth.; (b) (verstreichen) ⟨time⟩ go by; ~|**halten** *unr. tr. V.* (a) hold out; (b) (warten lassen) **jmdn.** ~**halten** keep sb. waiting; ~**halte·taktik** *die* delaying tactics *pl.;* ~|**hören** *itr. V.* listen

**hinken** /'hɪŋkn̩/ *itr. V.* (a) walk with a limp (b) *mit sein* (hinkend gehen) limp

**hin-, Hin-:** ~|**kommen** *unr. itr. V.; mit sein* (a) get there; (b) (an einen Ort gehören) go; belong; (c) (ugs.: stimmen) be right; ~**länglich** ① *Adj.* sufficient; (angemessen) adequate; ② *adv.* sufficiently; (angemessen) adequately; ~|**legen** ① *tr. V.* put; (weglegen) put down; ② *refl. V.* lie down; ~**reichend** ① *Adj.* sufficient; (angemessen) adequate; ② *adv.* sufficiently; (angemessen) adequately; ~**reise** *die* journey there; (mit dem Schiff) voyage out; ~**reißend** *Adj.* enchanting ⟨person, picture, view⟩; captivating ⟨speaker, play⟩; ~|**richten** *tr. V.* execute; ~**richtung** *die* execution

**Hinrichtungs·kommando** *das* firing squad

**hin-, Hin-:** ~|**sehen** *unr. itr. V.* look; *\*~|sein ▶ HIN E;* ~|**setzen** ① *tr. V.* put; ② *refl. V.* sit down; ~**sicht** *die* in gewisser ~**sicht** in a way/in some respects *or* ways; in jeder ~**sicht** in every respect; in finanzieller ~**sicht** financially; ~**sichtlich** *Präp. mit Gen.* (Amtsspr.) with regard to; (in Anbetracht) in view of; ~|**stellen** ① *tr. V.* put; put up ⟨building⟩; (absetzen) put down; ② *refl. V.* stand

**hinten** *Adv.* at the back; **sich** ~ **anstellen** join the back of the queue (Brit.) *or* (Amer.) line; **weiter** ~: further back; (in einem Buch) further on; **die Adresse steht** ~ **auf dem Brief** the address is on the back of the envelope; **nach** ~ **hinaus liegen/gehen** be at the back; **die anderen sind ganz weit** ~: the others are a long way back

**hinter** ① *Präp. mit Dat.* behind; (nach) after; **3 km** ~ **der Grenze** 3 km beyond the frontier; **eine Prüfung** ~ **sich haben** (fig.) have got an examination over [and done] with; **viele Enttäuschungen/eine Krankheit** ~ **sich haben** have experienced many disappointments/have got over an illness ② *Präp. mit Akk.* behind

**hinter…** *Adj.; nicht präd.* back

**hinter-, Hinter-:** ~**einander** *Adv.* (a) (räumlich) one behind the other; (b) (zeitlich) one after another *or* the other; ~**gedanke** *der* ulterior motive; ~**gehen** /-'--/ *unr. tr. V.* deceive; ~**grund** *der* background; ~**grund·bericht** *der* background report; ~**gründig** ① *Adj.* enigmatic; ② *adv.* enigmatically; ~**grund·information** *die* item *or* piece of background information; ~**grundinformationen** [items *or* pieces of] background information *sing.;* ~**halt** *der* ambush; ~**hältig** ① *Adj.* underhand; ② *adv.* in an underhand manner; ~**her** *Adv.* (räumlich) behind; (nachher) afterwards; ~**hof** *der* courtyard; ~**land** *das* hinterland; (Milit.) back area; ~**lassen** /-'--/ *unr. tr. V.* leave; ~**legen** /-'--/ *tr. V.* deposit (bei with); ~**list** *die* guile; deceit; ~**listig** *Adj.* deceitful; ~**mann** *der* (a) person behind; (b) (Gewährsmann) [secret] informant

**Hintern** *der;* ~s, ~ (ugs.) backside; bottom

**hinter-, Hinter-:** ~**rad** *das* rear wheel; ~**sinn** *der* deeper meaning; ~**sinnig** *Adj.* ⟨remark, story, etc.⟩ with a deeper meaning; ~**teil** *das* backside; behind; ~**treffen** *das* (ugs.): **ins** ~**treffen geraten** *od.* **kommen** fall behind; ~**treiben** /-'--/ *unr. tr. V.* foil ⟨plan⟩; prevent ⟨marriage, promotion⟩; block ⟨law, investigation, reform⟩; ~**treppe** *die* back stairs *pl.;* ~**tür** *die* back door; ~**wäldler** *der;* ~~s, ~~ (spött.) backwoodsman; ~**wäldlerin** *die;* ~~, ~~nen backwoodswoman; ~**wäldlerisch** *Adj.* (spött.) backwoods *attrib.* ⟨views, attitudes, manners, etc.⟩

**hinüber** *Adv.* over; across

**Hin- und Rück·fahrt** *die* journey there and back; round trip (Amer.)

**hinunter** *Adv.* down

**hinunter-:** ~|**fahren** ① *unr. itr. V.; mit sein* go down; (mit dem Auto) drive down; (mit dem Fahrrad) ride down; ② *unr. tr. V.* **jmdn./ein Auto/eine Ladung** ~**fahren** drive sb. down/drive a car down/take a load down; ~|**gehen** *unr. itr. V.; mit sein* go down; ⟨aircraft⟩ descend; ~|**klettern** *itr. V.; mit sein* climb down; ~|**reichen** ① *tr. V.* hand down; ② *itr. V.* (sich bis hinunter erstrecken) reach down (bis auf + Akk. to)

**hin·weg** *Adv.* (a) (geh.) ~ **mit dir!** away with you! (b) **über etw.** ~: over sth.

**Hin·weg** *der* way there

**hinweg-:** ~|**gehen** *unr. itr. V.; mit sein* **über etw.** (Akk.) ~**gehen** pass over sth.; ~|**kommen** *unr. itr. V.; mit sein* **über etw.** (Akk.) ~**kommen** get over sth.; ~|**setzen** *refl. V.* **sich über etw.** (Akk.) ~**setzen** ignore sth.

**Hinweis** /'hɪnvaɪ̯s/ *der;* ~es, ~e hint; **unter** ~ **auf** (+ Akk.) with reference to

**hin-:** ~|**weisen** ① *unr. itr. V.* **auf jmdn./etw.** ~**weisen** point to sb./sth.; ② *unr. tr. V.* **jmdn. auf etw.** (Akk.) ~**weisen** point sth. out to sb.; ~**weisend** *Adj.* (Grammatik) demonstrative; ~|**werfen** *unr. tr. V.* throw ···❖

down; ∼|**ziehen** [1] *unr. tr. V.* pull, draw (**zu** to, towards); [2] *unr. itr. V.; mit sein* (umziehen) move there; **wo ist sie** ∼**gezogen?** where did she move to?; [3] *unr. refl. V.* (a) (sich erstrecken) drag on (**über** + *Akk.* for); (b) (sich verzögern) be delayed

**hinzu-:** ∼|**fügen** *tr. V.* add; ∼|**kommen** *unr. itr. V.; mit sein* (a) come along; (b) (hinzugefügt werden) **zu etw.** ∼**kommen** be added to sth.; **es kommt noch** ∼**, dass ...** (fig.) there is also the fact that ...; ∼|**tun** *unr. tr. V.* (ugs.) add

**Hiobs·botschaft** *die* bad news

**Hirn** *das;* ∼[e]s, ∼e (a) brain (b) (Speise; ugs.: Verstand) brains *pl.*

**Hirsch** *der;* ∼[e]s, ∼e deer; (Rothirsch) red deer; (männlicher Rothirsch) stag; (Speise) venison

**Hirse** *die;* ∼, ∼n millet

**Hirt** *der;* ∼en, ∼en, **Hirte** *der;* ∼n, ∼n herdsman; (Schaf∼) shepherd

**Hirtin** *die;* ∼, ∼nen shepherdess

**hissen** *tr. V.* hoist

**historisch** *Adj.* (a) historical (b) (geschichtlich bedeutungsvoll) historic

**Hit** *der;* ∼[s], ∼s (ugs.) hit

**Hitler·jugend** *die* Hitler Youth

**Hit·parade** *die* hit parade

**Hitze** *die;* ∼: heat

**hitze-, Hitze-:** ∼**beständig** *Adj.* heat-resistant; ∼**frei** *Adj.* ∼**frei haben** have the rest of the day off [school/work] because of excessively hot weather; ∼**periode** *die* hot spell; spell *or* period of hot weather; ∼**welle** *die* heat wave

**hitzig** *Adj.* (a) hot-tempered (b) (erregt) heated ⟨*discussion etc.*⟩

**hitz-, Hitz-:** ∼**kopf** *der* hothead; ∼**köpfig** *Adj.* hot-headed; ∼**schlag** *der* heatstroke

**HIV-:** ∼**-Anti·körper** *der* HIV antibody; ∼**-Infektion** *die* HIV infection; ∼**-infiziert** *Adj.* HIV-infected; ∼**-kontaminiert** *Adj.* HIV-contaminated; ∼**-positiv** *Adj.* HIV-positive; ∼**-Test** *der* HIV test; ∼**-verseucht** *Adj.* HIV-contaminated

**hl** *Abk.* = **Hektoliter** hl

**H-Milch** *die;* ∼ long-life *or* UHT milk

**HNO-Arzt** *der,* **HNO-Ärztin** *die* ENT specialist

**hob** *1. u. 3. Pers. Sg. Prät. v.* HEBEN

**Hobby** *das;* ∼s, ∼s hobby

**Hobel** *der;* ∼s, ∼ (a) plane (b) (Küchengerät) [vegetable] slicer

**Hobel·bank** *die; Pl.* **Hobel·bänke** woodworker's bench

**hobeln** *tr., itr. V.* (a) plane (b) (schneiden) slice

**hoch; höher, höchst...** [1] *Adj.* high; tall

⟨*tree, mast*⟩; long ⟨*grass*⟩; deep ⟨*snow, water*⟩; heavy ⟨*fine*⟩; large ⟨*sum, amount*⟩; severe, extensive ⟨*damage*⟩; senior ⟨*official, officer, post*⟩; high-level ⟨*diplomacy, politics*⟩; **höchste Gefahr** extreme danger; **es ist höchste Zeit, dass ...:** it is high time that ...; **das hohe C** top C; **vier** ∼ **zwei** (Math.) four to the power [of] two; four squared [2] *adv.* (in großer Höhe) high; (nach oben) up; (zahlenmäßig viel, sehr) highly; ∼ **begabt** highly gifted; ∼ **empfindlich** highly sensitive ⟨*instrument, device, material, etc.*⟩; fast ⟨*film*⟩; extremely delicate ⟨*fabric*⟩; ∼ **gestellt** ⟨*person*⟩ in a high position; important ⟨*person*⟩; ∼ **verschuldet/versichert** heavily in debt/insured for a large sum [of money]; **etw.** ∼ **und heilig versprechen** promise sth. faithfully

**Hoch** *das;* ∼s, ∼s (a) (Hochruf) **ein [dreifaches]** ∼ **auf jmdn. ausbringen** give three cheers for sb. (b) (Met.) high

**Hoch·achtung** *die* great respect

**hochachtungs·voll** *Adv.* (Briefschluss) yours faithfully

**hoch-, Hoch-:** ∼**aktuell** *Adj.* highly topical; ∼**amt** *das* (kath. Rel.) high mass; ∼|**arbeiten** *refl. V.* work one's way up; ∼**begabt** *Adj.* highly gifted; ∼**betagt** *Adj.* aged; ∼**betrieb** *der* (ugs.) **es herrschte** ∼**betrieb im Geschäft** the shop was at its busiest; ∼**blüte** *die* golden age; ∼**burg** *die* stronghold; ∼**deutsch** *Adj.* High German; ∼**deutsch** *das,* ∼**deutsche** *das* High German; ∼**druck** *der; Pl.* ∼**drücke** (Physik, Met.) high pressure; *\**∼**empfindlich** ▶ HOCH 2; ∼|**fahren** *unr. itr. V.; mit sein* (a) (ugs.) go up; (mit dem Auto) drive up; (mit dem Fahrrad, Motorrad) ride up; (b) (auffahren) start up; **aus dem Sessel** ∼**fahren** start [up] from one's chair; (c) (aufbrausen) flare up; ∼**finanz** *die* high finance; ∼**fliegend** *Adj.* ambitious; ∼**form** *die* top form; ∼**gebirge** *das* [high] mountains *pl.;* ∼**gefühl** *das* [feeling of] elation; ∼|**gehen** *unr. itr. V.; mit sein* (ugs.) go up; (zornig werden) blow one's top (coll.); explode; (explodieren) ⟨*bomb, mine*⟩ go off; ∼**genuss,** *\**∼**genuß** *der:* **ein** ∼**genuss sein** be a real delight; ∼**geschlossen** *Adj.* high-necked ⟨*dress*⟩; *\**∼**gestellt** ▶ HOCH 2; ∼**glanz** *der:* **etw. auf** ∼**glanz bringen** give sth. a high polish; (fig.) make sth. spick and span; ∼**gradig** [1] *Adj.* extreme; [2] *adv.* extremely; ∼|**halten** *unr. tr. V.* hold up; ∼**haus** *das* high-rise building; ∼|**heben** *unr. tr. V.* lift up; raise ⟨*arm, leg, hand*⟩; ∼**interessant** *Adj.* extremely interesting; ∼**kant** *Adv.* (ugs.): **jmdn.** ∼**kant hinauswerfen** chuck sb. out (coll.); throw sb. out on his/her ear (coll.); ∼|**kommen** *unr. itr. V.; mit sein* (ugs.) come up; (vorwärts kommen) get on; ∼|**konjunktur** *die* (Wirtsch.) boom; **auf dem Automarkt herrscht** ∼**konjunktur** the car market is booming;

---

*\*alte Schreibung - vgl. Hinweis auf S. xiv

**∼|krempeln** *tr. V.* roll up; **∼land** *das* highlands *Pl.;* **∼|leben** *itr. V.* jmdn./etw. **∼leben lassen** cheer sb./sth.; **er lebe ∼!** three cheers for him; **∼leistungs·sport** *der* top-level sport; **∼modern** *Adj.* ultramodern; **∼mut** *der* arrogance; **∼mütig** *Adj.* arrogant; **∼näsig** *Adj.* (abwertend) stuck-up; **∼|nehmen** *unr. tr. V.* (ugs.: verspotten) jmdn. **∼nehmen** pull sb.'s leg; **∼ofen** *der* blast furnace; **∼prozentig** *Adj.* high-proof ⟨spirits⟩; **∼|rechnen** project; **∼rechnung** *die* (Statistik) projection; **∼ruf** *der* cheer; **∼saison** *die* high season; **∼|schlagen** ⒈ *unr. tr. V.* turn up ⟨collar, brim⟩; ⒉ *unr. itr. V.; mit sein* ⟨water, waves⟩ surge up; ⟨flames⟩ leap up; **∼schule** *die* college; (Universität) university

**Hochsee·fischerei** *die* deep-sea fishing *no art.*

**hoch-, Hoch-: ∼sitz** *der* (Jägerspr.) raised hide; **∼sommer** *der* high summer; **∼spannung** *die* (Elektrot.) high voltage; **∼|spielen** *tr. V.* blow up

**höchst** *Adv.* extremely; most

**höchst...** ▸ HOCH

**Hoch·stapler** /-ʃtaːplɐ/ *der;* **∼s, ∼:** confidence trickster; conman (coll.); (Aufschneider) fraud

**höchsten·falls** *Adv.* at [the] most *or* the outside; at the very most

**höchstens** *Adv.* at most; (bestenfalls) at best

**Höchst-: ∼fall** *der:* **im ∼fall** at [the] most; **∼form** *die* (bes. Sport) peak form; **∼geschwindigkeit** *die* top speed; (Geschwindigkeitsbegrenzung) speed limit

**Hoch·stimmung** *die* high spirits *pl.*

**höchst-, Höchst-: ∼leistung** *die* supreme performance; (Ergebnis) supreme achievement; **∼maß** *das:* **ein ∼maß an etw.** (*Dat.*) a very high degree of sth.; **∼persönlich** ⒈ *Adj.* personal; ⒉ *adv.* in person; **∼temperatur** *die* maximum *or* highest temperature; **∼wahrscheinlich** *Adv.* very probably; **∼wert** *der* maximum value

**hoch-, Hoch-: ∼tour** *die:* **auf ∼touren laufen** run at full speed; (intensiv betrieben werden) be in full swing; **∼trabend** (abwertend) ⒈ *Adj.* high-flown; ⒉ *adv.* in a high-flown manner; **∼|treiben** *unr. tr. V.* force up ⟨prices etc.⟩; **∼verrat** *der* high treason; (Überschwemmung) flood; **∼wasser** *das* (Flut) high tide; **∼wertig** *Adj.* high-quality ⟨goods⟩; highly nutritious ⟨food⟩; **∼würden** *der;* **∼∼[s]** (veralt.) Reverend Father

**Hoch·zeit** *die;* **∼, ∼en** wedding

**Hochzeits-: ∼feier** *die* wedding; **∼nacht** *die* wedding night; **∼reise** *die* honeymoon [trip]

**Hocke** *die;* **∼, ∼n (a)** (Körperhaltung) squat; crouch

**(b)** (Turnen) squat vault

**hocken** ⒈ *itr. V.* **(a)** *mit haben od.* (südd.) *sein* squat; crouch

**(b)** *mit haben od.* (südd.) *sein* (ugs.: sich aufhalten) sit around

⒉ *refl. V.* crouch down

**Hocker** *der;* **∼s, ∼:** stool

**Höcker** *der;* **∼s, ∼:** hump; (auf der Nase) bump; (auf dem Schnabel) knob

**Hockey** /ˈhɔki/ *das;* **∼s** hockey

**Hoden** *der;* **∼s, ∼:** testicle

**Hoden·bruch** *der* (Med.) scrotal hernia

**Hof** *der;* **∼[e]s, Höfe (a)** courtyard; (Schul∼) playground; (Gefängnis∼) [prison] yard **(b)** (Bauern∼) farm **(c)** (Herrscher, Hofstaat) court

**Hof·dame** *die* lady of the court; (Begleiterin der Königin) lady-in-waiting

**hof·fähig** *Adj.* presentable at court *pred.*

**hoffen** ⒈ *tr. V.* hope ⒉ *itr. V.* hope; **auf etw.** (*Akk.*) **∼:** hope for sth.; (Vertrauen setzen auf) **auf jmdn./etw. ∼:** put one's faith in sb./sth.

**hoffentlich** *Adv.* hopefully; **∼!** let's hope so

**Hoffnung** *die;* **∼, ∼en** hope

**hoffnungs-, Hoffnungs-: ∼los** ⒈ *Adj.* hopeless; despairing ⟨person⟩; ⒉ *adv.* hopelessly; **∼losigkeit** *die;* **∼∼:** despair; (der Lage) hopelessness; **∼voll** ⒈ *Adj.* **(a)** hopeful; full of hope *pred.;* **(b)** (erfolgversprechend) promising; ⒉ *adv.* **(a)** full of hope; **(b)** (erfolgversprechend) promisingly

**höflich** ⒈ *Adj.* polite ⒉ *adv.* politely

**Höflichkeit** *die;* **∼:** politeness

**hoh...** ▸ HOCH

**Höhe** /ˈhøːə/ *die;* **∼, ∼n** height; **etw. in die ∼ heben** lift sth. up; **das ist ja die ∼!** (fig. ugs.) that's the limit!

**Hoheit** *die;* **∼, ∼en** sovereignty (**über** + *Akk.* over); **Seine/Ihre ∼:** His/Your Highness

**Hoheits-: ∼gebiet** *das* [sovereign] territory; **∼gewässer** *das* territorial waters

**Höhen-: ∼angst** *die* fear of heights; **∼flug** *der* (fig.) flight; **∼lage** *die* altitude; **∼luft** *die* mountain air; **∼messer** *der* altimeter; **∼sonne** *die* (Med.) sun lamp; **∼unterschied** *der* difference in altitude; **∼zug** *der* (Geogr.) range of hills; (Bergkette) range of mountains; mountain range

**Höhe·punkt** *der* high point; (einer Veranstaltung) high spot; highlight; (einer Laufbahn, des Ruhms) peak; pinnacle; (Orgasmus; eines Stückes) climax

**höher** /ˈhøːɐ/ ▸ HOCH

**hohl** *Adj.* hollow

**Höhle** *die;* **∼, ∼n (a)** cave; (größer) cavern **(b)** (Tierbau) lair

**Hohl-:** ~**maß** das measure of capacity;
~**raum** der cavity; [hollow] space;
~**spiegel** der concave mirror
**Hohn** der; ~[e]s scorn; derision
**höhnen** (geh.) itr. V. jeer
**höhnisch** [1] Adj. scornful
[2] adv. scornfully
**Hokuspokus** der; ~: hocus-pocus;
(abwertend: Drum und Dran) fuss
**hold** Adj. (dichter. veralt.) fair; lovely; lovely
⟨sight, smile⟩
**holen** [1] tr. V. (a) fetch; get
(b) (ab~) fetch
(c) (ugs.: erlangen) get ⟨prize etc.⟩; carry off
⟨medal, trophy, etc.⟩
[2] refl. V. (ugs.: sich zuziehen) catch; **sich** (Dat.)
**[beim Baden] einen Schnupfen** ~: catch a
cold [swimming]
**Holland** (das); ~s Holland
**Holländer** der; ~s, ~: Dutchman
**Holländerin** die; ~, ~nen Dutchwoman
**holländisch** Adj. Dutch
**Hölle** die; ~, ~n hell no art.
**Höllen-lärm** der (ugs.) diabolical noise or
row (coll.)
**höllisch** [1] Adj. (a) infernal; ⟨spirits,
torments⟩ of hell
(b) (ugs.: sehr groß) tremendous (coll.)
[2] adv. (ugs.: sehr) hellishly (coll.)
**Holm** der; ~[e]s, ~e (Turnen) bar
**Holocaust** der; ~[s] Holocaust
**holpern** itr. V. mit sein (fahren) jolt; bump
**holprig** Adj. (a) bumpy; rough
(b) (stockend) halting ⟨speech⟩; clumsy ⟨verses,
style, language, etc.⟩
**Holunder** der; ~s, ~: elder
**Holz** das; ~es, Hölzer wood; (Bau~, Tischler~)
timber; wood
**Holz-:** ~**bein** das wooden leg; ~**bläser**
der, **Holz·bläserin** die woodwind player
**hölzern** Adj. (auch fig.) wooden
**holz-, Holz-:** ~**fäller** der; ~~s, ~~:
woodcutter; lumberjack (Amer.); ~**frei** Adj.
wood-free ⟨paper⟩
**holzig** Adj. woody
**Holz-:** ~**klotz** der block of wood; (als
Spielzeug) wooden block; ~**kohle** die
charcoal; ~**kopf** der (salopp abwertend)
blockhead; ~**pantoffel** der clog;
~**scheit** das piece of wood; (Brenn~) piece
of firewood; ~**schnitt** der (a) (Technik)
woodcutting no art.; (b) (Blatt) woodcut;
~**schuh** der clog; ~**stoß** der pile of wood;
~**weg** der: auf dem ~weg sein be on the
wrong track (fig.); ~**wolle** die wood wool;
~**wurm** der woodworm
**homogen** Adj. homogeneous
**homöopathisch** Adj. homoeopathic
**Homo·sexualität** die; ~: homosexuality
**homo·sexuell** [1] Adj. homosexual

[2] adv. ~ **veranlagt sein** have homosexual
tendencies
**Honig** der; ~s, ~e honey
**Honig·kuchen** der honey cake
**Honig·wabe** die honeycomb
**Honorar** das; ~s, ~e fee; (Autoren~) royalty
**Honoratioren** /honora'ts:jo:rən/ Pl.
notabilities
**honorieren** tr. V. (a) jmdn. ~: pay sb. [a/
his/her fee]
(b) (würdigen) appreciate; (belohnen) reward
**Hopfen** der; ~s, ~: hop; **bei ihm ist** ~ **und**
**Malz verloren** (ugs.) he's a hopeless case
**hopp** Interj. quick; look sharp
**hoppeln** itr. V.; mit sein hop; (über + Akk.
across, over)
**hoppla** Interj. oops; whoops
**hopsen** itr. V.; mit sein (ugs.) (springen) jump;
(hüpfen) ⟨animal⟩ hop; ⟨child⟩ skip; ⟨ball⟩
bounce
**Hopser** der; ~s, ~ (ugs.) [little] jump
**Hör·apparat** der hearing aid
**hörbar** [1] Adj. audible
[2] adv. audibly; (geräuschvoll) noisily
**Hör·buch** das audiobook
**horchen** itr. V. listen (auf + Akk. to);
(heimlich zuhören) eavesdrop
**Horde** die; ~, ~n horde; (von Halbstarken)
mob
**hören** [1] tr. V. hear; (anhören) listen to
[2] itr. V. hear; (zuhören) listen; **auf jmdn./**
**jmds. Rat** ~: listen to sb./sb.'s advice
**Hören·sagen** das: vom ~: from hearsay
**Hörer** der; ~s, ~ (a) listener
(b) (Telefon~) receiver
**Hörerin** die; ~, ~nen listener
**Hörerschaft** die; ~, ~en audience
**Hör-:** ~**fehler** der (a) **das war ein** ~**fehler**
he/she etc. misheard; (b) (Schwerhörigkeit)
hearing defect; ~**funk** der radio; **im** ~**funk**
on the radio; ~**funk·sendung** die radio
programme; ~**gerät** das hearing aid
**hörig** Adj.: jmdm. ~ **sein** be submissively
dependent on sb.; (sexuell) be sexually
enslaved to sb.
**Horizont** der; ~[e]s, ~e (auch Geol., fig.)
horizon
**horizontal** [1] Adj. horizontal
[2] adv. horizontally
**Horizontale** die; ~, ~n (a) (Linie)
horizontal line
(b) (Lage) **die** ~: the horizontal
**Hormon** das; ~s, ~e hormone
**Horn** das; ~[e]s, Hörner horn
**Hörnchen** das; ~s, ~ (Gebäck) croissant
**Horn·haut** die (a) callus; hard skin no
indef. art.;
(b) (am Auge) cornea
**Hornisse** die; ~, ~n hornet
**Horoskop** das; ~s, ~e horoscope

---

*old spelling - see note on page xiv

**horrend** *Adj.* shocking (coll.), horrendous (coll.) ‹price›; colossal (coll.) ‹sum, amount, rent›

**Hör·rohr** *das* stethoscope

**Horror** *der;* ~s horror

**Horror-:** ~**film** *der* horror film; ~**roman** *der* horror novel

**Hör-:** ~**saal** *der* lecture theatre *or* hall; ~**spiel** *das* radio play

**Horst** *der;* ~[e]s, ~e eyrie

**Hort** *der;* ~[e]s, ~e ▸ KINDERHORT

**horten** *tr. V.* hoard; stockpile ‹raw materials›

**Hortensie** /hɔr'tɛnzi̯ə/ *die;* ~, ~n hydrangea

**Hör·weite** *die:* in/außer ~weite in/out of earshot

**Höschen** /'høːsçən/ *das;* ~s, ~: trousers *pl.;* pair of trousers; (kurzes ~) shorts *pl.;* pair of shorts

**Hose** *die;* ~, ~n (a) trousers *pl.;* pants *pl.* (Amer.); (Unter~) pants *pl.;* (Freizeit~) slacks *pl.;* (Bund~) breeches *pl.;* (Reit~) riding breeches *pl.;* **eine** ~: a pair of trousers/ pants/slacks *etc.;* (b) (fig.) **die** ~**n anhaben** (ugs.) wear the trousers; **die** ~**n runterlassen** (salopp) come clean (coll.); **in die** ~[**n**] **gehen** (salopp) be a [complete] flop (coll.); **es ist tote** ~ (Jugendspr.) there's nothing doing (coll.)

**Hosen-:** ~**anzug** *der* trouser suit (Brit.); pant suit; ~**matz** *der;* ~~es, ~~e *od.* ~**mätze** (ugs. scherzh.) toddler; ~**rock** *der* culottes *pl.;* ~**tasche** *die* trouser pocket; pants pocket (Amer.); ~**träger** *Pl.* braces; suspenders (Amer.); pair of braces/ suspenders

**Hospital** *das;* ~s, ~e *od.* **Hospitäler** hospital

**Hospiz** *das;* ~es, ~e hospice

**Hostie** /'hɔsti̯ə/ *die;* ~, ~n (christl. Rel.) host

**Hotel** *das;* ~s, ~s hotel

**Hotel·bar** *die* hotel bar

**Hotel garni** /- gar'ni:/ *das;* ~ ~, ~s ~s /- gar'ni:/ bed-and-breakfast hotel

**Hotelier** /hotɛ'li̯e:/ *der;* ~s, ~s hotelier

**Hotline** /'hɔtlam/ *die;* ~, ~s hotline

**hüben** *Adv.* over here

**hübsch** ① *Adj.* pretty; nice ‹area, flat, voice, tune, etc.›; nice-looking ‹boy, person›; **ein** ~es **Sümmchen** (ugs.) a tidy sum (coll.); a nice little sum; **das ist eine** ~e **Geschichte** (ugs. iron.) this is a fine *or* pretty kettle of fish (coll.) ② *adv.* prettily; (ugs.: sehr) ~ **kalt** perishing cold

**Hub·schrauber** *der;* ~s, ~: helicopter

**Hubschrauber·lande·platz** *der* heliport; (kleiner) helicopter pad; landing pad

**huckepack** *Adv.* jmdn. ~ **tragen** (ugs.) give sb. a piggyback

**hudeln** *itr. V.* (bes. südd., österr.) be sloppy (**bei** in)

**Huf** *der;* ~[e]s, ~e hoof

**huf-, Huf-:** ~**eisen** *das* horseshoe; ~**eisen·förmig** ① *Adj.* horseshoe-shaped; ② *adv.* in [the shape of] a horseshoe; ~**schmied** *der* farrier

**Hüfte** *die;* ~, ~n hip

**Hüft-:** ~**gelenk** *das* (Anat.) hip joint; ~**gürtel** *der* girdle

**Hügel** *der;* ~s, ~ hill

**hügelig** *Adj.* hilly

**Huhn** *das;* ~[e]s, **Hühner** chicken; (Henne) chicken; hen

**Hühnchen** *das;* ~s, ~: small chicken; **mit jmdm. [noch] ein** ~ **zu rupfen haben** (ugs.) [still] have a bone to pick with sb.

**Hühner-:** ~**auge** *das* (am Fuß) corn; ~**brühe** *die* chicken broth

**hui** /hui/ *Interj.* whoosh

**huldigen** *itr. V.* jmdm. ~: pay tribute to sb.

**Huldigung** *die;* ~, ~en tribute

**Hülle** *die;* ~, ~n cover

**hüllen** *tr. V.* (geh.) wrap

**Hülse** *die;* ~, ~n (a) case (b) (Bot.) pod

**Hülsen·frucht** *die* (a) (Frucht) fruit of a leguminous plant; **Hülsenfrüchte** pulse *sing.;* (b) (Pflanze) legume; leguminous plant

**human** *Adj.* humane

**Humanismus** *der;* ~: humanism; (Epoche) Humanism *no art.*

**humanitär** *Adj.* humanitarian

**Humbug** *der;* ~s (ugs.) humbug

**Hummel** *die;* ~, ~n bumble-bee

**Hummer** *der;* ~s, ~: lobster

**Humor** *der;* ~s humour; (Sinn für ~) sense of humour; **den** ~ **nicht verlieren** remain good-humoured

**Humorist** *der;* ~en, ~en, **Humoristin** *die;* ~, ~nen (a) (Autor[in]) humorist (b) (Vortragskünstler[in]) comedian

**humoristisch** *Adj.* humorous

**humor-:** ~**los** *Adj.* humourless; ~**losigkeit** *die;* ~~: humourlessness; lack of humour; ~**voll** *Adj.* humorous

**humpeln** *itr. V.* (a) *auch mit sein* walk with a limp (b) *mit sein* (sich ~d fortbewegen) limp

**Hund** *der;* ~es, ~e (a) dog; **auf den** ~ **kommen** (ugs.) go to the dogs (coll.); **vor die** ~e **gehen** (ugs.) go to the dogs (coll.); (sterben) kick the bucket (coll.) (b) (abwertend) bastard (sl.)

**hunde-, Hunde-:** ~**elend** *Adj.* (ugs.) [really] wretched *or* awful; ~**hütte** *die* [dog] kennel; ~**kuchen** *der* dog biscuit; ~**müde** *Adj.* (ugs.) dog-tired; ~**rasse** *die* breed of dog

**hundert** *Kardinalz.* (a) *or* one hundred (b) (ugs.: viele) hundreds of

**Hundert¹** *das;* ~s, ~e hundred

**Hundert²** *die;* ~, ~en hundred

**Hunderter** *der;* ~s, ~ (ugs.) hundred-euro/ -mark/-dollar *etc.* note

**hundert·mal** *Adv.* a hundred times; **auch wenn du dich** ~ **beschwerst** (ugs.) however much you complain

**Hundert-:** ~**mark·schein** *der* hundred-mark note; ~**meter·lauf** *der* (Leichtathletik) hundred metres *sing.*

**hundert·prozentig** ① *Adj.* (a) [one-]hundred per cent *attrib.;* **(b)** (ugs.: völlig) a hundred per cent **(c)** (ugs.: ganz sicher) absolutely reliable ② *adv.* (ugs.) **ich bin nicht** ~ **sicher** I'm not a hundred per cent sure

**hundertst...** /'hʊndɐts:t.../ *Ordinalz.* hundredth

**hundertstel** /'hʊndɐts:tl̩/ *Bruchz.* hundredth

**Hundertstel** *das* (schweiz. meist *der*); ~s, ~: hundredth

**hundert·tausend** *Kardinalz.* a or one hundred thousand

**Hunde-:** ~**scheiße** *die* (derb) dog shit (coarse); ~**steuer** *die* dog licence fee; ~**zwinger** *der* dog run

**Hündin** *die;* ~, ~nen bitch

**Hüne** *der;* ~n, ~n giant

**Hünen·grab** *das* megalithic tomb; (Hügelgrab) barrow

**Hunger** *der;* ~s (a) ~ **bekommen/haben** get/be hungry **(b)** (geh.: Verlangen) hunger; (nach Ruhm, Macht) craving

**Hunger·kur** *die* starvation diet

**hungern** *itr. V.* go hungry; starve; **nach etw.** ~: (fig.) hunger for sth.

**Hungers·not** *die* famine

**Hunger-:** ~**streik** *der* hunger strike; ~**tuch** *das:* **am** ~**tuch nagen** (ugs. scherzh.) be on the breadline

**hungrig** *Adj.* (auch geh. fig.) hungry (**nach** for)

**Hupe** *die;* ~, ~n horn

**hupen** *itr. V.* sound one's horn; **dreimal** ~: hoot three times

**hüpfen** *itr. V.; mit sein* hop; ⟨ball⟩ bounce

**Hürde** *die;* ~, ~n hurdle

**Hürden·lauf** *der* (Leichtathletik) hurdling; (Wettbewerb) hurdles *pl.*

**Hure** *die;* ~, ~n (abwertend) whore

**huren** *itr. V.* (abwertend) whore

**hurra** *Interj.* hurray; hurrah; ~/**Hurra schreien** cheer

**Hurra** *das;* ~s, ~s cheer

**hurtig** ① *Adj.* rapid ② *adv.* quickly

**huschen** *itr. V.; mit sein* (lautlos u. leichtfüßig)

⟨person⟩ steal; (lautlos u. schnell) dart; ⟨mouse, lizard, etc.⟩ dart; ⟨smile⟩ flit; ⟨light⟩ flash; ⟨shadow⟩ slide quickly

**hüsteln** *itr. V.* give a slight cough

**husten** ① *itr. V.* cough; (Husten haben) have a cough ② *tr. V.* cough up ⟨blood, phlegm⟩

**Husten** *der;* ~s, ~: cough

**Husten-:** ~**anfall** *der* coughing fit; fit of coughing; ~**bonbon** *das* cough drop; ~**reiz** *der* tickling in the throat; ~**saft** *der* cough mixture; ~**tropfen** *Pl.* cough drops

**Hut¹** *der;* ~es, Hüte hat; (fig.) **da geht einem/ mir der** ~ **hoch** (ugs.) it makes you/me mad (coll.); **das kann er sich** (*Dat.*) **an den** ~ **stecken** (ugs. abwertend) he can keep it (coll.)

**Hut²** *die;* ~ (geh.) keeping; care; **auf der** ~ **sein** be on one's guard

**hüten** ① *tr. V.* look after; tend ⟨sheep, cattle⟩ ② *refl. V.* be on one's guard

**Hut·schnur** *die:* **das geht mir über die** ~ (ugs.) that's going too far

**Hütte** *die;* ~, ~n (a) hut; (ärmliches Haus) shack; hut **(b)** (Eisen~) iron [and steel] works *sing.* or *pl.* **(c)** (Jagd~) [hunting] lodge

**Hütten-:** ~**käse** *der* cottage cheese; ~**schuh** *der* slipper sock

**Hyäne** *die;* ~, ~n hyena

**Hyazinthe** *die;* ~, ~n hyacinth

**Hydrant** *der;* ~en, ~en hydrant

**Hydrat** *das;* ~[e]s, ~e (Chemie) hydrate

**Hydraulik** *die;* ~ (Technik) (a) (Theorie) hydraulics *sing., no art.;* **(b)** (Vorrichtungen) hydraulics *pl.*

**hydraulisch** (Technik) ① *Adj.* hydraulic ② *adv.* hydraulically

**Hydro·kultur** *die* (Gartenbau) hydroponics *sing.*

**Hygiene** *die;* ~ (a) (Gesundheitspflege) health care **(b)** (Sauberkeit) hygiene

**hygienisch** ① *Adj.* hygienic ② *adv.* hygienically

**Hymne** /'hʏmnə/ *die;* ~, ~n hymn; (National~) national anthem

**Hypnose** *die;* ~, ~n hypnosis

**hypnotisieren** *tr. V.* hypnotize

**Hypochonder** /hypoˈxɔndɐ/ *der;* ~s, ~, **Hypochondrin** *die;* ~, ~nen hypochondriac

**hypochondrisch** *Adj.* hypochondriac

**Hypotenuse** *die;* ~, ~n (Math.) hypotenuse

**Hypothek** *die;* ~, ~en (Bankw.) mortgage; (fig.) burden

**Hypothese** *die;* ~, ~n hypothesis

**hypothetisch** ① *Adj.* hypothetical ② *adv.* hypothetically

**Hysterie** *die;* ~, ~n hysteria

**hysterisch** ① *Adj.* hysterical ② *adv.* hysterically

---

# I i

**i, I** /i:/ *das;* ~, ~ i/I; **das Tüpfelchen** *od.* **der Punkt auf dem** ~ (fig.) the final touch
**i** *Interj.* ugh; **i bewahre, i wo** (ugs.) [good] heavens, no!
**i.A.** *Abk.* = **im Auftrag[e]** p.p.
**IC** *Abk.* = **Intercity** IC
**ICE** *Abk.* = **Intercityexpress[zug]** ICE
**ich** *Personalpron.; 1. Pers. Sg. Nom.* I; **immer** ~ (ugs.) [it's] always me; ~ **nicht** not me; **Menschen wie du und** ~: people like you and me; *s. auch (Gen.)* MEINER, *(Dat.)* MIR, *(Akk.)* MICH
**Ich** *das;* ~[s], ~[s] **(a)** self
**(b)** (Psych.) ego
**Ichform** *die* first person
**Icon** /'ai:kən/ *das;* ~s, ~s (DV) icon
**ideal** [1] *Adj.* ideal
[2] *adv.* ideally
**Ideal** *das;* ~s, ~e ideal
**Ideal-:** ~**bild** *das* ideal; ~**fall** *der* ideal case; ~**gewicht** *das* ideal weight
**idealisieren** *tr. V.* idealize
**Idealismus** *der;* ~ (auch Philos.) idealism
**Idealist** *der;* ~en, ~en, **Idealistin** *die;* ~, ~nen idealist
**idealistisch** (auch Philos.) [1] *Adj.* idealistic
[2] *adv.* idealistically
**Idee** *die;* ~, ~n **(a)** idea
**(b)** (ein bisschen) **eine** ~: a shade; **eine** ~ [Salz/Pfeffer] a touch [of salt/pepper]
**ideell** *Adj.* non-material; (geistig-seelisch) spiritual
**ideen·los** *Adj.* [completely] lacking in ideas *postpos.*
**Identifikation** /idɛntifika'ts:jo:n/ *die;* ~, ~en (auch Psych.) identification
**identifizieren** [1] *tr. V.* identify
[2] *refl. V.* (auch Psych.) **sich mit jmdm./etw.** ~: identify with sb./sth.
**identisch** *Adj.* identical
**Identität** *die;* ~: identity
**Ideologe** *der;* ~n, ~n ideologue
**Ideologie** *die;* ~, ~n /-i:ən/ ideology
**Ideologin** *die;* ~, ~nen ideologue
**ideologisch** [1] *Adj.* ideological
[2] *adv.* ideologically
**Idiot** *der;* ~en, ~en (auch ugs. abwertend) idiot
**idioten-, Idioten-:** ~**hügel** *der* (ugs. scherzh.) nursery slope; ~**sicher** *Adj.* (ugs. scherzh.) foolproof
**Idiotie** *die;* ~, ~n /-i:ən/ **(a)** idiocy
**(b)** (ugs. abwertend: Dummheit) madness
**Idiotin** *die;* ~, ~nen (auch ugs. abwertend) idiot

**idiotisch** [1] *Adj.* **(a)** (Psych.) severely subnormal
**(b)** (ugs. abwertend) idiotic
[2] *adv.* (auch ugs. abwertend) idiotically
**Idol** *das;* ~s, ~e (auch bild. Kunst) idol
**Idyll** *das;* ~s, ~e idyll
**Idylle** *die;* ~, ~n idyll
**idyllisch** *Adj.* idyllic
**Igel** *der;* ~s, ~: hedgehog
**Iglu** *der od. das;* ~s, ~s igloo
**Ignoranz** /ɪgno'rants:/ *die;* ~: ignorance
**ignorieren** *tr. V.* ignore
**ihm** *Dat. von* ER, ES: (bei männlichen Personen) him; (bei weiblichen Personen) her; (bei Dingen, Tieren) it; **gib es** ~: give it to him; give him it; **Freunde von** ~: friends of his
**ihn** *Akk. von* ER (bei männlichen Personen) him; (bei Dingen, Tieren) it
**ihnen** *Dat. von* SIE, *Pl.* them; **gib es** ~: give it to them; give them it; **Freunde von** ~: friends of theirs
**Ihnen** *Dat. von* SIE you; **ich habe es** ~ **gegeben** I gave it to you; **Freunde von** ~: friends of yours
**ihr¹** /i:ɐ̯/ *Dat. von* SIE, *Sg.* (bei Personen) her; (bei Dingen, Tieren) it
**ihr²**, *Personalpron.; 2. Pers. Pl. Nom.* you
**ihr³** *Possessivpron.* **(a)** *Sg.* (einer Person) her; (eines Tieres, einer Sache) its
**(b)** *Pl.* their
**Ihr** *Possessivpron.* (Anrede) your; ~ **Hans Meier** (Briefschluss) yours, Hans Meier; **welcher Mantel ist** ~**er?** which coat is yours?
**ihrer (a)** *Gen. von* SIE, *Sg.* (geh.) **wir gedachten** ~: we remembered her
**(b)** *Gen. von* SIE, *Pl.* (geh.) **wir werden** ~ **gedenken** we will remember them; **es waren** ~ **zwölf** there were twelve of them
**Ihrer** *Gen. von* SIE (geh.) **wir werden** ~ **gedenken** we will remember you
**ihrerseits** *Adv.* for her/their part; (von ihr/ ihnen) on her/their part
**Ihrerseits** *Adv.:* ▶ DEINERSEITS
**ihres·gleichen** *indekl. Pron.* people *pl.* like her/them; (abwertend) the likes of her/ them
**Ihres·gleichen** *indekl. Pron.* people *pl.* like you; (abwertend) the likes of you
**ihret·wegen** *Adv.:* ▶ MEINETWEGEN: because of her/them; for her/their sake; about her/them; as far as she is/they are concerned
**Ihret·wegen** *Adv.:* ▶ DEINETWEGEN
**Ikone** *die;* ~, ~n icon

**illegal** ① *Adj.* illegal
② *adv.* illegally
**Illegalität** *die;* ∼, ∼en illegality
**illegitim** *Adj.* (geh.) illegitimate
**illuminieren** *tr. V.* illuminate
**Illusion** *die;* ∼, ∼en illusion
**illusorisch** *Adj.* illusory; (zwecklos) pointless
**Illustration** *die;* ∼, ∼en illustration
**illustrieren** *tr. V.* illustrate
**Illustrierte** *die; adj. Dekl.* magazine
**Iltis** *der;* ∼ses, ∼se polecat; (Pelz) fitch
**im** *Präp. + Art.* (a) = in dem;
(b) (räumlich) in the; **im Theater** at the theatre; **im Fernsehen** on television; **im Bett** in bed
(c) (zeitlich) **im Mai** in May; **im letzten Jahr** last year; **im Alter von** ... at the age of ...
(d) (Verlauf) etw. **im Sitzen tun** do sth. [while] sitting down; **im Gehen sein** be going
**Image** /'ɪmɪtʃ:/ *das;* ∼[s], ∼s image
**imaginär** *Adj.* (geh., Math.) imaginary
**Imbiss, *Imbiß** *der;* Imbisses, Imbisse (a) (kleine Mahlzeit) snack
(b) ▶ IMBISSSTUBE
**Imbiss-stube, *Imbiß-stube** *die* café
**Imitation** *die;* ∼, ∼en imitation
**imitieren** *tr. V.* imitate
**Imker** *der;* ∼s, ∼, **Imkerin** *die;* ∼, ∼nen bee-keeper
**Immatrikulation** *die;* ∼, ∼en (Hochschulw.) registration
**immatrikulieren** *tr., refl. V.* (Hochschulw.) register
**immer** *Adv.* (a) always; **schon** ∼: always; ∼ **wieder** time and time again; ∼, **wenn** every time that
(b) immer + *Komp.:* ∼ **dunkler** darker and darker; ∼ **mehr** more and more
(c) (ugs.: jeweils) ∼ **drei Stufen auf einmal** three steps at a time
(d) (auch) **wo/wer/wann/wie [auch]** ∼: wherever/whoever/whenever/however
(e) (verstärkend) ∼ **noch, noch** ∼: still
(f) (ugs.: bei Aufforderung) ∼ **geradeaus!** keep [going] straight on
**immer-, Immer-:** ∼**fort** *Adv.* all the time; ∼**grün** *Adj.* evergreen; ∼**grün** *das* periwinkle; ∼**hin** *Adv.* (a) (wenigstens) at any rate; (b) (trotz allem) all the same; (c) (schließlich) after all; ∼**zu** *Adv.* (ugs.) the whole time
**Immigrant** *der;* ∼en, ∼en, **Immigrantin** *die;* ∼, ∼nen immigrant
**Immigration** *die;* ∼, ∼en immigration
**immigrieren** *itr. V.; mit sein* immigrate
**Immobilien** *Pl.* property *sing.;* real estate *sing.*
**immun** (a) (Med., fig.) immune (**gegen** to)
(b) (Rechtsspr.) ∼ **sein** have immunity

**Immunität** *die;* ∼, ∼en (a) (Med.) immunity (**gegen** to)
(b) (Rechtsspr.) immunity (**gegen** from)
**Immun-schwäche** *die* (Med.) immunodeficiency; immune deficiency
**Imperativ** *der;* ∼s, ∼e (a) (Sprachw.) imperative
(b) (Philos.) [kategorischer] ∼: [categorical] imperative
**Imperfekt** *das;* ∼s, ∼e (Sprachw.) imperfect [tense]
**Imperialismus** *der;* ∼: imperialism *no art.*
**imperialistisch** *Adj.* imperialistic
**Imperium** *das;* ∼s, Imperien (hist., fig.) empire
**impfen** *tr. V.* vaccinate; inoculate
**Impf-:** ∼**pass, *∼paß** *der* vaccination certificate; ∼**stoff** *der* vaccine
**Impfung** *die;* ∼, ∼en vaccination
**implantieren** *tr. V.* (Med.) implant
**imponieren** *itr. V.* impress
**imponierend** ① *Adj.* impressive
② *adv.* impressively
**Imponier-gehabe** *das* (Verhaltensf.) display; (fig.) showing off
**Import** *der;* ∼[e]s, ∼e import
**Importeur** /ɪmpɔr'tøːɐ̯/ *der;* ∼s, ∼e, **Importeurin** *die;* ∼, ∼nen importer
**importieren** *tr., itr. V.* import
**imposant** ① *Adj.* imposing; impressive ⟨achievement⟩
② *adv.* imposingly
**impotent** *Adj.* impotent
**Impotenz** *die;* ∼: impotence
**imprägnieren** *tr. V.* impregnate; (wasserdicht machen) waterproof
**Improvisation** *die;* ∼, ∼en improvisation
**improvisieren** *tr., itr. V.* improvise
**Impuls** *der;* ∼es, ∼e stimulus; (innere Regung) impulse
**impulsiv** ① *Adj.* impulsive
② *adv.* impulsively
**imstande** *Adv.* ∼ **sein, etw. zu tun** be able to do sth.
**in¹** ① *Präp. mit Dat.* (auf die Frage: wo?/wann?/ wie?) in; **er hat** ∼ **Tübingen studiert** he studied at Tübingen; *s. auch* IM;
② *Präp. mit Akk.* (auf die Frage: wohin?) into; *s. auch* INS
**in²** *Adj.:* ∼ **sein** (ugs.) be in
**In-anspruchnahme** *die;* ∼, ∼n (starke Belastung) demands *pl.*
**In-begriff** *der* quintessence
**inbegriffen** *Adj.* included
**In-betrieb-nahme** *die;* ∼, ∼n, **In-betrieb-setzung** *die;* ∼, ∼n bringing into service
**In-brunst** *die;* ∼ (geh.) fervour; (der Liebe) ardour

**in·brünstig** (geh.) [1] *Adj.* fervent; ardent
⟨*love*⟩
[2] *adv.* fervently; ⟨*love*⟩ ardently

**in·dem** *Konj.* (a) (während) while; (gerade als)
as
(b) (dadurch, dass) ~ **man etw. tut** by doing
sth.

**Inder** *der;* ~s, ~, **Inderin** *die;* ~, ~nen
Indian

**in·dessen** [1] *Konj.* (geh.) (a) (während)
while
(b) (wohingegen) whereas
[2] *Adv.* (a) (inzwischen) meanwhile; in the
mean time
(b) ( jedoch) however

**Index** *der;* ~ *od.* ~es, ~e *od.* **Indizes (a)** *Pl.*
~e *od.* **Indizes** (Register) index
(b) *Pl.* ~e (kath. Kirche) Index

**Indianer** *der;* ~s, ~: [American] Indian

**Indianer·häuptling** *der* Indian chief

**Indianerin** *die;* ~, ~nen [American]
Indian

**indianisch** *Adj.* Indian

**Indien** /'ɪndiən/ *(das);* ~s India

**in·different** *Adj.* indifferent

**Indikativ** *der;* ~s, ~e /-i:və/ (Sprachw.)
indicative [mood]

**Indikator** *der;* ~s, ~en (auch Chemie,
Technik) indicator

**in·direkt** [1] *Adj.* indirect
[2] *adv.* indirectly

**indisch** *Adj.* Indian

**in·diskret** *Adj.* indiscreet

**In·diskretion** *die;* ~, ~en indiscretion

**Individualist** *der;* ~en, ~en,
**Individualistin** *die;* ~, ~nen (geh.)
individualist

**Individualität** *die;* ~, ~en (geh.) (a)
individuality
(b) (Persönlichkeit) personality

**individuell** [1] *Adj.* individual; private
⟨*property, vehicle, etc.*⟩
[2] *adv.* individually

**Individuum** *das;* ~s, **Individuen** (auch
Chemie, Biol.) individual

**Indiz** *das;* ~es, ~ien (a) (Rechtsw.) piece of
circumstantial evidence; ~ien
circumstantial evidence *sing.;*
(b) (Anzeichen) sign (**für** of)

**Indizes** ▶ INDEX

**Indizien·beweis** *der* (Rechtsw.) piece of
circumstantial evidence; ~e circumstantial
evidence *sing.*

**indoktrinieren** *tr. V.* indoctrinate

**Indonesien** /ɪndo'ne:ziən/ *(das);* ~s
Indonesia

**Indonesier** *der;* ~s, ~, **Indonesierin**
*die;* ~, ~nen Indonesian

**indonesisch** *Adj.* Indonesian

**industrialisieren** *tr. V.* industrialize

**Industrialisierung** *die;* ~:
industrialization

**Industrie** *die;* ~, ~n industry

**Industrie-:** ~**betrieb** *der* industrial
firm; ~**gebiet** *das* industrial area;
~**kauffrau** *die,* ~**kaufmann** *der: person
with three years' business training employed
on the business side of an industrial
company*

**industriell** [1] *Adj.* industrial
[2] *adv.* industrially

**Industrielle** *der/die; adj. Dekl.*
industrialist

**Industrie-:** ~**staat** *der* industrial nation;
~**stadt** *die* industrial town

**Industrie- und Handels·kammer** *die*
Chamber of Industry and Commerce

**Industriezweig** *der* branch of industry

**in·einander** *Adv.* ~ greifen mesh together
(lit. or fig); ~ **verliebt sein** be in love with
each other *or* one another; ~ **verschlungene**
Ornamente intertwined decorations

**\*ineinander|greifen** ▶ INEINANDER

**infam** [1] *Adj.* disgraceful
[2] *adv.* disgracefully

**Infanterie** *die;* ~, ~n (Milit.) infantry

**infantil** (Psych., Med., sonst abwertend) [1] *Adj.*
infantile
[2] *adv.* in an infantile way

**Infarkt** *der;* ~[e]s, ~e (Med.) infarction

**Infekt** *der;* ~[e]s, ~e (Med.) infection

**Infektion** *die;* ~, ~en (Med.) (a) (Ansteckung)
infection
(b) (ugs.: Entzündung) inflammation

**Infektions-:** ~**gefahr** *die* (Med.) risk of
infection; ~**herd** *der* (Med.) seat of the/an
infection; ~**krankheit** *die* (Med.)
infectious disease

**Inferno** *das;* ~s (geh.) inferno

**Infinitiv** *der;* ~s, ~e (Sprachw.) infinitive

**infizieren** [1] *tr. V.* infect
[2] *refl. V.* become infected; **sich bei jmdm.**
~: be infected by sb.

**in flagranti** *Adv.* (geh.) in flagrante
[delicto]

**Inflation** *die;* ~, ~en (Wirtsch.) inflation;
(Zeit der ~) period of inflation

**inflationär** *Adj.* inflationary

**Inflations·rate** *die* inflation rate; rate of
inflation

**in·folge** [1] *Präp. + Gen.* as a result of
[2] *Adv.* ~ **von etw.** (Dat.) as a result of sth.

**infolge·dessen** *Adv.* consequently

**Informatik** *die;* ~: computer science *no
art.*

**Informatiker** *der;* ~s, ~,
**Informatikerin** *die;* ~, ~nen computer
scientist

**Information** *die;* ~, ~en (a) information
*no pl., no indef. art.* (**über** + *Akk.* about, on);
**eine** ~: [a piece of] information
(b) (Büro) information bureau; (Stand)
information desk

**Informations-:** ~**büro** *das* information ⋯⫶

bureau *or* office; **~freiheit** *die* freedom of information; **~material** *das* informational literature; **~quelle** *die* source of information; **~vielfalt** *die* variety of information

**informativ** *Adj.* informative

**informieren** 1 *tr. V.* inform (über + *Akk.* about)
2 *refl. V.* inform oneself, find out (über + *Akk.* about)

**in·frage:** ~ kommen be possible; das kommt nicht ~ (ugs.) that is out of the question

**Infra·rot** *das* (Physik) infra-red radiation

**Infra·struktur** *die* infrastructure

**Infusion** *die;* ~, ~en (Med.) infusion

**Ing.** *Abk.* = **Ingenieur**

**In·gebrauch·nahme** *die;* ~, ~n: vor ~ des Geräts before operating the appliance

**Ingenieur** /ɪnʒe'niø:ɐ̯/ *der;* ~s, ~e, **Ingenieurin** *die;* ~, ~nen [qualified] engineer

**Ingwer** *der;* ~s, ~: ginger

**Inhaber** *der;* ~s, ~, **Inhaberin** *die;* ~, ~nen (a) holder
(b) (Besitzer) owner

**inhaftieren** *tr. V.* take into custody; detain

**Inhaftierung** *die;* ~, ~en detention

**inhalieren** *tr. V.* inhale

**Inhalt** *der;* ~[e]s, ~e (a) contents *pl.;*
(b) (einer Geschichte usw.) content
(c) (bes. Math.) (Flächen~) area; (Raum~) volume

**inhaltlich** 1 *Adj.* an ~en Gesichtspunkten gemessen from the point of view of content
2 *adv.* ~ ist der Aufsatz gut the essay is good as regards content; ~ übereinstimmen be the same in content

**Inhalts-:** **~angabe** *die* summary [of contents]; synopsis; (eines Films, Dramas) synopsis; **~verzeichnis** *das* table of contents; (auf einem Paket) list of contents

**in·human** *Adj.* (a) (unmenschlich) inhuman
(b) (rücksichtslos) inhumane

**Initiale** *die;* ~, ~n initial [letter]

**Initiative** *die;* ~, ~n initiative

**Initiator** *der;* ~s, ~en, **Initiatorin** *die;* ~, ~nen initiator; (einer Organisation) founder

**Injektion** *die;* ~, ~en (Med.) injection

**injizieren** *tr. V.* (Med.) inject

**Inkarnation** *die;* ~, ~en incarnation

**inkl.** *Abk.* = **inklusive** incl.

**inklusive** /ɪnklu'zi:və/ 1 *Präp.* + *Gen.* (bes. Kaufmannsspr.) including
2 *Adv.* inclusive

**inkognito** *Adv.* (geh.) incognito

**in·kompetent** *Adj.* incompetent

**In·kompetenz** *die* incompetence

**in·konsequent** 1 *Adj.* inconsistent
2 *adv.* inconsistently

**In·konsequenz** *die* inconsistency

**in·korrekt** 1 *Adj.* incorrect
2 *adv.* incorrectly

**In·korrektheit** *die;* ~, ~en
(a) (Fehlerhaftigkeit) incorrectness
(b) (Fehler) mistake

**In·kraft·treten** *das;* ~s: mit [dem] ~ des Gesetzes when the law comes/came into force

**Inkubations·zeit** *die;* ~, ~en (Med.) incubation period

**In·land** *das* (a) im ~: at home
(b) (Binnenland) interior; inland; im/ins ~: inland

**inländisch** *Adj.* domestic; home-produced ⟨goods⟩

**Inlands-:** **~markt** *der* domestic market; **~porto** *das* inland postage

**in·mitten** 1 *Präp.* + *Gen.* (geh.) in the midst of
2 *Adv.* ~ von in the midst of

**inne|haben** *unr. tr. V.* hold, occupy ⟨position⟩; hold ⟨office⟩

**innen** *Adv.* inside; (auf/an der Innenseite) on the inside

**innen-, Innen-:** **~architekt** *der,* **~architektin** *die* interior designer; **~aufnahme** *die* (Fot.) indoor photo[graph]; (Film) interior shot; **~einrichtung** *die* furnishings *pl.;* **~hof** *der* inner courtyard; **~leben** *das* (a) [inner] thoughts and feelings *pl.;* (b) (oft scherzh.: Ausstattung) inside; **~minister** *der,* **~ministerin** *die* Minister of the Interior; ≈ Home Secretary (Brit.); ≈ Secretary of the Interior (Amer.); **~ministerium** *das* Ministry of the Interior; ≈ Home Office (Brit.); ≈ Department of the Interior (Amer.); **~politik** *die* (eines Staates) home affairs *pl.;* (einer Regierung) domestic policy/policies *pl.;* **~politisch** ▶ ~POLITIK: 1 *Adj.* ~politische Fragen matters of domestic policy; 2 *adv.* as regards home affairs/domestic policy; **~stadt** *die* town centre; downtown (Amer.); (einer Großstadt) city centre

**inner...** *Adj.* inner; (inländisch; Med.) internal; inside ⟨pocket, lane⟩

**Innere** *das; adj. Dekl.* inside; (eines Gebäudes, Wagens, Schiffes) interior; inside; (eines Landes) interior

**Innereien** *Pl.* entrails; (Kochk.) offal *sing.*

**inner·halb** 1 *Präp.* + *Gen.* (a) within; ~ der Familie/Partei (fig.) within the family/party
(b) (binnen) within; ~ einer Woche within a week
2 *Adv.* (a) ~ von within
(b) (im Verlauf) ~ von zwei Jahren within two years

**innerlich** 1 *Adj.* inner
2 *adv.* inwardly

**innerst...** *Adj.* innermost

**Innerste** *das; adj. Dekl.* innermost being

**inne|wohnen** itr. V. (geh.) **etw. wohnt jmdm./einer Sache** ~: sb./sth. possesses sth.

**innig** [1] Adj. deep ⟨affection, sympathy⟩; fervent ⟨wish⟩; intimate ⟨friendship⟩; **mein** ~**ster Dank** my sincerest thanks [2] adv. ⟨love⟩ with all one's heart

**Innigkeit** die; ~: depth; (einer Beziehung) intimacy

**innovativ** Adj. innovative

**Innung** /'ɪnʊŋ/ die; ~, ~en [trade] guild

**in-offiziell** [1] Adj. unofficial [2] adv. unofficially

**in puncto** as regards

**ins** Präp. + Art. (a) = **in das** (b) (räumlich) to the; ~ **Bett gehen** go to bed (c) ~ **Schlendern geraten** go into a skid

**Insasse** der; ~n, ~n, **Insassin** die; ~, ~nen (a) (Fahrgast) passenger (b) (Bewohner[in]) inmate

**ins·besond[e]re** Adv. particularly; in particular

**In·schrift** die inscription

**Insekt** /ɪn'zɛkt/ das; ~s, ~en insect

**Insel** die; ~, ~n island

**Insel-:** ~**bewohner** der, ~**bewohnerin** die islander; ~**gruppe** die group of islands; ~**staat** die island state; ~**welt** die islands pl.

**Inserat** das; ~[e]s, ~e advertisement (in a newspaper)

**Inserent** der; ~en, ~en, **Inserentin** die; ~, ~nen advertiser

**inserieren** itr. V. advertise

**ins·geheim** Adv. secretly

**ins·gesamt** Adv. in all; altogether; (alles in allem) all in all

**insofern** [1] Adv. /ɪn'zo:fɛrn/ (in dieser Hinsicht) to this extent; ~ **als** in so far as [2] Konj. /ɪnzo'fɛrn/ (falls) provided [that]

**Insolvenz·verfahren** das insolvency proceedings pl.

**insoweit** [1] adv. /ɪn'zo:vaɪt/ ▶ INSOFERN 1; [2] Konj. /ɪnzo'vaɪt/ ▶ INSOFERN 2

**in spe** /ɪn 'spe:/ future attrib.; **mein Schwiegersohn** ~ ~: my future son-in-law

**Inspektion** die; ~, ~en inspection; (Kfz-W.) service

**Inspiration** die; ~, ~en inspiration

**inspirieren** tr. V. inspire

**inspizieren** tr. V. inspect

**Installateur** /ɪnstala'tø:ɐ̯/ der; ~s, ~e, **Installateurin** die; ~, ~nen plumber; (Gas~) [gas] fitter; (Heizungs~) heating engineer; (Elektro~) electrician

**Installation** die; ~, ~en installation; (Rohre) plumbing no pl.

**installieren** tr. V. install

**in·stand** Adv. **etw. ist gut/schlecht** ~: sth. is in good/poor condition; **etw.** ~ **halten** keep sth. in good condition; **etw.** ~ **setzen/ bringen** repair sth.

**Instand·haltung** die maintenance

**in·ständig** [1] Adj. urgent [2] adv. urgently

**Instand·setzung** die; ~, ~en repair; (Renovierung) renovation

**Instanz** /ɪn'stants:/ die; ~, ~en (a) authority (b) (Rechtsw.) **[die] erste/zweite/dritte** ~: the court of original jurisdiction/the appeal court/the court of final appeal; **durch alle** ~**en gehen** go through all the courts

**Instinkt** /ɪn'stɪŋkt/ der; ~[e]s, ~e instinct

**instinktiv** [1] Adj. instinctive [2] adv. instinctively

**Institut** /ɪnstɪ'tu:t/ das; ~[e]s, ~e institute

**Institution** die; ~, ~en (auch fig.) institution

**Instruktion** /ɪnstrʊk'ts:i̯o:n/ die; ~, ~en instruction

**Instrument** /ɪnstru'mɛnt/ das; ~[e]s, ~e instrument

**instrumental** (Musik) [1] Adj. instrumental [2] adv. instrumentally

**Insulin** das; ~s insulin

**inszenieren** tr. V. stage; put on; (Regie führen bei) direct; (fig.) (einfädeln) engineer; (organisieren) stage

**Inszenierung** die; ~, ~en staging; (Regie) direction; (Aufführung) production

**intakt** Adj. (a) (unbeschädigt) intact (b) (funktionsfähig) in [proper] working order postpos.; healthy ⟨economy⟩

**integer** Adj. **eine integre Persönlichkeit** a person of integrity; ~ **sein** be a person of integrity

**Integral** das; ~s, ~e (Math.) integral

**Integration** die; ~, ~en (auch Math.) integration

**integrieren** tr. V. integrate

**Intellekt** der; ~[e]s intellect

**intellektuell** Adj. intellectual

**Intellektuelle** der/die; adj. Dekl. intellectual

**intelligent** [1] Adj. intelligent [2] adv. intelligently

**Intelligenz** die; ~, ~en (a) intelligence (b) (Gesamtheit der Intellektuellen) intelligentsia

**Intelligenz·quotient** der intelligence quotient

**Intendant** der; ~en, ~en, **Intendantin** die; ~, ~nen (Theater) manager and artistic director; (Fernseh~, Rundfunk~) director general

**Intensität** die; ~: intensity

**intensiv** [1] Adj. (gründlich) intensive (kräftig) intense [2] adv. intensively

**intensivieren** tr. V. intensify; increase ⟨exports⟩; strengthen ⟨connections⟩

**Intensiv·station** die intensive-care unit

**interaktiv** Adj. interactive

**Intercityzug** der inter-city train

**interessant** [1] Adj. interesting ····>

2 *adv.* ~ **schreiben** write in an interesting way

**interessanterweise** *Adv.* interestingly enough

**Interesse** *das;* ~s, ~n interest; ~ **an** jmdm./etw. **haben** be interested in sb./sth.

**interesse-halber** *Adv.* out of interest

**Interessen-gebiet** *das* field of interest

**Interessent** *der;* ~en, ~en, **Interessentin** *die;* ~, ~nen interested person; (möglicher Käufer/mögliche Käuferin) potential buyer

**Interessen-verband** *der* [organized] interest group

**Interessen-vertretung** *die* (a) representation

(b) (Vertreter von Interessen) representative body

**interessieren** 1 *refl. V.* **sich für** jmdn./ etw. ~: be interested in sb./sth.

2 *tr. V.* interest; **das interessiert mich nicht** I'm not interested [in it]

**interessiert** *Adj.* interested (**an** + *Dat.* in)

**Interjektion** *die;* ~, ~en interjection

**Inter-:** ~**kontinental-rakete** *die* (Milit.) intercontinental ballistic missile; ~**mezzo** *das;* ~~s, ~~s *od.* ~**mezzi** (Theat., Musik) intermezzo; (fig.) interlude; intermezzo

**intern** 1 *Adj.* internal

2 *adv.* internally

**Internat** *das;* ~[e]s, ~e boarding school

**inter-, Inter-:** ~**national** 1 *Adj.* international; 2 *adv.* internationally; ~**nationale** *die;* ~, ~n (a) International; Internationale; (b) (Lied) Internationale

**Internats-:** ~**schule** *die* boarding school; ~**schüler** *der,* ~**schülerin** *die* boarding school pupil; boarder

**Internet** /ˈɪntɛnɛt/ *das;* ~s Internet; **im** ~: on the Internet

**Internet-anschluss** *der,* *Internet-anschluß** *der* Internet connection; connection to the Internet; **einen** ~ **haben** be connected to the Internet

**internieren** *tr. V.* (Milit.) intern

**Internierung** *die;* ~, ~en internment

**Internist** *der;* ~en, ~en, **Internistin** *die;* ~, ~nen (Med.) internist

**Interpol** *die;* ~: Interpol *no art.*

**Interpret** *der;* ~en, ~en interpreter (*of music, text, events, etc.*)

**Interpretation** *die;* ~, ~en interpretation (*of music, text, events, etc.*)

**interpretieren** *tr. V.* interpret ‹*music, texts, events, etc.*›

**Interpretin** *die;* ~, ~nen ▶ INTERPRET

**Interpunktion** *die;* ~ (Sprachw.) punctuation

**Intervall** /ɪntɛˈval/ *das;* ~s, ~e (Musik, Math.) interval

**intervenieren** *itr. V.* (geh., Politik) intervene

**Intervention** *die;* ~, ~en (geh., Politik) intervention; (Protest) representations *pl.*

**Interview** /ˈɪntɐˈvjuː/ *das;* ~s, ~s interview

**interviewen** /ɪntɐˈvjuːən/ *tr. V.* interview

**Interviewer** *der;* ~s, ~, **Interviewerin** *die;* ~, ~nen interviewer

**intialisieren** *tr. V.* (DV) initialize

**intim** 1 *Adj.* intimate

2 *adv.* ~ **befreundet sein** be intimate friends

**Intimität** *die;* ~, ~en intimacy

**Intim-:** ~**partner** *der,* ~**partnerin** *die* intimate partner; sexual partner; ~**sphäre** *die* private life

**in-tolerant** *Adj.* intolerant

**In-toleranz** *die* intolerance (**gegenüber** of)

**Intonation** *die;* ~, ~en intonation

**Intranet** *das;* ~s, ~s (DV) Intranet

**in-transitiv** 1 *Adj.* (Sprachw.) intransitive

2 *adv.* intransitively

**intravenös** (Med.) 1 *Adj.* intravenous

2 *adv.* intravenously

**Intrige** *die;* ~, ~n intrigue

**Intuition** *die;* ~, ~en intuition

**intuitiv** 1 *Adj.* intuitive

2 *adv.* intuitively

**intus:** etw. ~ **haben** (ugs.) (begriffen haben) have got sth. into one's head; (gegessen od. getrunken haben) have put sth. away (coll.)

**Invalide** *der; adj. Dekl.* invalid

**Invasion** *die;* ~, ~en invasion

**Inventar** *das;* ~s, ~e (einer Firma) fittings and equipment *pl.;* (eines Hauses, Büros) furnishings and fittings *pl.*

**inventarisieren** *tr. V.* inventory; draw up *or* make an inventory of

**Inventur** *die;* ~, ~en stock-taking

**investieren** *tr., itr. V.* (auch fig.) invest (**in** + *Akk.* in)

**Investition** *die;* ~, ~en investment

**Investitions-güter** *Pl.* (Wirtsch.) capital goods

**Investor** *der;* ~s, ~en /-ˈtoːrən/, **Investorin** *die;* ~, ~nen (Wirtsch.) investor

**in-wie-fern** *Adv.* in what way; (bis zu welchem Grade) to what extent

**in-wie-weit** *Adv.* to what extent

**In-zahlung-nahme** *die;* ~, ~n part exchange; trade in (Amer.)

**Inzest** *der;* ~[e]s, ~e incest

**In-zucht** *die;* ~: inbreeding

**in-zwischen** *Adv.* (a) (seither) in the meantime; since [then]

(b) (bis zu einem Zeitpunkt) (in der Gegenwart) by now; (in der Vergangenheit/Zukunft) by then

(c) (währenddessen) meanwhile

**IOK** *Abk.* Internationales Olympisches Komitee IOC

**Ion** /iːn/ *das;* ~s, ~en (Physik, Chemie) ion

**ionisieren** *tr. V.* (Physik, Chemie) ionize

**Iono·sphäre** *die* ionosphere
**Irak** *(das);* ~s *od. der;* ~[s] Iraq
**Iraker** *der;* ~s, ~, **Irakerin** *die;* ~, ~nen Iraqi
**irakisch** Iraqi
**Iran** *(das);* ~s *od. der;* ~[s] Iran
**Iraner** *der;* ~s, ~, **Iranerin** *die;* ~, ~nen Iranian
**iranisch** *Adj.* Iranian
**irden** *Adj.* earthen[ware]
**irdisch** *Adj.* (a) earthly; worldly ⟨*goods, pleasures, possessions*⟩ (b) (zur Erde gehörig) terrestrial; **das** ~**e Leben** life on earth
**Ire** *der;* ~n, ~n Irishman
**irgend** *Adv.* (a) ~ **so ein Politiker** (ugs.) some politician [or other]; ~ **so etwas** something like that (b) (irgendwie) **wenn** ~ **möglich** if at all possible
**irgend-:** ~**ein** *Indefinitpron.* (a) *attr.* some; (fragend, verneinend) any; (b) *subst.* ~**einer**/~**eine** someone; somebody; (fragend, verneinend) anyone; anybody; ~**eines** *od.* (ugs.) ~**eins** any one; ~**einmal** *Adv.* sometime; ~**etwas** something; (fragend, verneinend) anything; ~**jemand** *Indefinitpron.* someone; somebody; (fragend, vereinend) anyone; somebody; (fragend, verneinend) anyone; anybody; ~**wann** *Adv.* [at] some time [or other]; (zu jeder beliebigen Zeit) [at] any time; ~**was** *Indefinitpron.* (ugs.) something [or other]; (fragend, verneinend) anything; ~**welch** *Indefinitpron.* some; (fragend, verneinend) any; ~**wer** *Indefinitpron.* (ugs.) somebody or other (coll.); (fragend, verneinend) anyone; anybody; ~**wie** *Adv.* somehow; ~**wo** *Adv.* somewhere; (fragend, verneinend) anywhere; ~**woher** *Adv.* from somewhere; (fragend, verneinend) from anywhere; ~**wohin** *Adv.* somewhere; (fragend, verneinend) anywhere
**Irin** *die;* ~, ~nen Irishwoman
**Iris** *die;* ~, ~ (Bot., Anat.) iris
**irisch** *Adj.* Irish
**Irland** *(das);* ~s Ireland
**Ironie** *die;* ~, ~n irony
**ironisch** ① *Adj.* ironic; ironical ② *adv.* ironically
**ir·rational** ① *Adj.* irrational ② *adv.* irrationally
**irre** ① *Adj.* (a) insane (b) (salopp: faszinierend) amazing (coll.) ② *adv.* (salopp) terribly (coll.)
**Irre** *der/die; adj. Dekl.* madman/madwoman; lunatic; (fig.) lunatic
**irre-, Irre-:** ~|**führen** *tr. V.* mislead; (täuschen) deceive; ~**führung** *die:* **eine bewusste** ~**führung** a deliberate attempt to mislead; ~**führung der Öffentlichkeit** misleading the public
**ir·relevant** *Adj.* irrelevant (**für** to)
**irre|machen** *tr. V.* disconcert; put off

**irren** ① *refl. V.* be mistaken; **Sie haben sich in der Nummer geirrt** you've got the wrong number ② *itr. V.* (a) **da** ~ **Sie** you are wrong there (b) *mit sein* (ziellos umherstreifen) wander
**Irren-:** ~**anstalt** *die* (veralt. abwertend) mental home; ~**haus** *das* (abwertend) [lunatic] asylum
**ir·reparabel** *Adj.* irreparable
**Irr·fahrt** *die* wandering
**irriger·weise** *Adv.* mistakenly
**Irritation** *die;* ~, ~en irritation
**irritieren** *tr., itr. V.* (a) (verwirren) put off (b) (stören) disturb
**irr-, Irr-:** ~**licht** *das* will o' the wisp; ~**sinn** *der* (a) insanity; madness; (b) (ugs. abwertend) lunacy; ~**sinnig** ① *Adj.* (a) (geistig gestört) insane; mad; (absurd) idiotic; (b) (ugs.: extrem) terrible (coll.); terrific (coll.) ⟨*speed, heat, cold*⟩; ② *adv.* (ugs.) terribly (coll.)
**Irrtum** *der;* ~s, Irrtümer mistake; ~! wrong!; **im** ~ **sein** be wrong *or* mistaken
**irrtümlich** ① *Adj.* incorrect ② *adv.* by mistake
**Irr·weg** *der* error; **diese Methode hat sich als** ~ **erwiesen** this method has proved to be wrong
**Ischias** *der od. das od.* (Med.) *die;* ~: sciatica
**Islam** /ɪsˈlaːm *od.* ˈɪslam/ *der;* ~[s] Islam
**islamisch** *Adj.* Islamic
**Islamismus** *der;* ~: Islamic fundamentalism; Islamism
**Islamist** *der;* ~en, ~en, **Islamistin** *die;* ~, ~nen Islamic fundamentalist; Islamist
**islamistisch** *Adj.* Islamic fundamentalist; Islamist
**Island** *(das);* ~s Iceland
**Isländer** *der;* ~s, ~, **Isländerin** *die;* ~, ~nen Icelander
**isländisch** *Adj.* Icelandic
**Isolation** *die;* ~, ~en ▶ ISOLIERUNG
**Isolator** *der;* ~s, ~en insulator
**Isolier·band** *das* insulating tape
**isolieren** *tr. V.* (a) isolate (b) (Technik) insulate ⟨*wiring, wall, etc.*⟩; lag ⟨*boilers, pipes, etc.*⟩
**Isolier·station** *die* (Med.) isolation ward
**Isolierung** *die;* ~, ~en (a) isolation (b) (Technik) ▶ ISOLIEREN B: insulation; lagging
**Isotop** *das;* ~s, ~e isotope
**Israel** /ˈɪsraeːl/ *(das);* ~s Israel
**Israeli** *der;* ~[s], ~[s]/*die;* ~, ~[s] Israeli
**israelisch** *Adj.* Israeli
**Israelit** *der;* ~en, ~en, **Israelitin** *die;* ~, ~nen Israelite
**israelitisch** *Adj.* Israelite
**iss, *iß** *Imperativ Sg. v.* ESSEN
**isst, *ißt** *2. u. 3. Pers. Sg. Präsens v.* ESSEN

**ist** *3. Pers. Sg. Präsens v.* SEIN
**Italien** /i'ta:lien/ *(das);* ~s Italy
**Italiener** *der;* ~s, ~, **Italienerin** *die;* ~,
~nen Italian

**italienisch** *Adj.* Italian
**I-Tüpfel[chen]** *das;* ~s, ~: final touch;
**bis aufs [letzte]** ~: down to the last detail
**i.V.** *Abk.* = **in Vertretung**

# Jj

**j, J** /jɔt, *österr.:* je:/ *das;* ~, ~: j/J
**ja** ⓵ *Interj.* yes; (nachgestellt: nicht wahr?) won't
you/doesn't it *etc.?*
⓶ *Partikel* **Sie wissen ja, dass ...:** you know,
of course, that ...; **da seid ihr ja!** there you
are!
**Ja** *das;* ~[s], ~[s] yes; **mit** ~ **stimmen** vote
yes
**Jacht** *die;* ~, ~en yacht
**Jacke** *die;* ~, ~n jacket; (gestrickt) cardigan
**Jacken·kleid** *das* dress and jacket
combination
**Jacket·krone** /'dʒɛkɪt-/ *die* (Zahnmed.)
jacket crown
**Jackett** /ʒa'kɛt/ *das;* ~s, ~s jacket
**Jade** *die;* ~: jade
**Jagd** *die;* ~, ~en (a) die ~: shooting;
hunting; **auf die** ~ **gehen** go hunting/
shooting
(b) (Veranstaltung) shoot; (Hetzjagd) hunt
(c) (Verfolgung) hunt; (Verfolgungsjagd) chase; **auf**
jmdn./etw. ~ **machen** hunt for sb./sth.
**Jagd-:** ~**beute** *die* bag; kill; ~**bomber**
*der* (Luftwaffe) fighter-bomber; ~**flieger** *der,*
~**fliegerin** *die* (Luftwaffe) fighter pilot;
~**flugzeug** *das* (Luftwaffe) fighter aircraft;
~**gewehr** *das* sporting gun; ~**horn** *das*
hunting horn; ~**hund** *der* gun dog;
~**hütte** *die* shooting box; ~**revier** *das*
preserve; shoot; ~**schein** *der* game
licence; ~**wurst** *die* chasseur sausage;
~**zeit** *die* open season
**jagen** ⓵ *tr. V.* (a) hunt *⟨game, fugitive,
criminal, etc.⟩*; shoot *⟨game, game birds⟩*;
(hetzen) chase *⟨fugitive, criminal, etc.⟩*
(b) (treiben) drive; **jmdn. aus dem Haus** ~:
throw sb. out of the house
⓶ *itr. V.* (die Jagd ausüben) go shooting *or*
hunting
**Jäger** *der;* ~s, ~: (a) hunter
(b) (Milit.) rifleman
(c) (Soldatenspr.: Jagdflugzeug) fighter
**Jäger·hut** *der* huntsman's hat
**Jägerin** *die;* ~, ~nen huntress
**Jäger-:** ~**latein** *das* (scherzh.) [hunter's]
tall story/stories; **das ist das reinste** ~**latein**

that's all wild exaggeration; ~**rock** *der*
hunting jacket; ~**schnitzel** *das* (Kochk.)
escalope chasseur
**Jaguar** *der;* ~s, ~e jaguar
**jäh** ⓵ *Adj.* (geh.) (a) sudden; abrupt *⟨change,
movement, stop⟩*; sudden, sharp *⟨pain⟩*
(b) (steil) steep; precipitous
⓶ *adv.* (a) *⟨change⟩* abruptly
(b) (steil) *⟨fall, drop⟩* steeply
**jählings** *Adv.* (geh.) (a) (plötzlich) *⟨change,
end, stop⟩* suddenly, abruptly; *⟨die⟩* suddenly
(b) (steil) steeply
**Jahr** *das;* ~[e]s, ~e year; **ein halbes** ~: six
months; **im** ~[e] **1908** in [the year] 1908; **er
ist zwanzig** ~e [alt] he is twenty years old;
**Kinder bis zu zwölf** ~en children up to the
age of twelve; **zwischen den** ~en between
Christmas and the New Year
**jahr·aus** *Adv.* ~, **jahrein** year in, year out
**jahre·lang** ⓵ *Adj.* [many] years of; long-
standing *⟨feud, friendship⟩*
⓶ *adv.* for [many] years
**jähren** *refl. V.* **heute jährt sich zum zehnten
Mal, dass ...:** it is ten years ago today that ...
**Jahres-:** ~**bilanz** *die* (Wirtsch.,
Kaufmannsspr.) annual balance [of accounts];
(Dokument) annual balance sheet;
~**einkommen** *das* annual income;
~**ende** *das* end of the year; ~**frist:** **in** *od.*
**innerhalb** *od.* **binnen** ~**frist** within [a period
of] a *or* one year; ~**hälfte** *die:* **die erste/
zweite** ~**hälfte** the first/second half *or* six
months of the year; ~**karte** *die* yearly
season ticket; ~**tag** *der* anniversary;
~**umsatz** *der* annual turnover; ~**urlaub**
*der* annual holiday *or* (formal) leave *or* (Amer.)
vacation; ~**wechsel** *der* turn of the year;
**zum** ~**wechsel die besten Wünsche** best
wishes for the New Year; ~**zahl** *die* date;
~**zeit** *die* season
**Jahr·gang** *der* (a) (Altersklasse) year; **der** ~
**1900** those born in 1900
(b) (eines Weines) vintage
(c) (einer Zeitschrift) set [of issues] for a/the
year
**Jahr·hundert** *das* century
**Jahrhundert·wende** *die* turn of the
century
**-jährig** (a) (... Jahre alt) **ein elfjähriges Kind**
an eleven-year-old child

---

*alte Schreibung - vgl. Hinweis auf S. xiv

**(b)** (... Jahre dauernd) ... year's/years'; **nach vierjähriger Vorbereitung** after four years' preparation; **mit dreijähriger Verspätung** three years late

**jährlich** [1] *Adj.;* annual; yearly [2] *adv.* annually; yearly; **zweimal** ~: twice a year

**Jahr-:** ~**markt** *der* fair; funfair; ~**tausend** *das* thousand years; millennium; ~**tausend·wende** *die* turn of the millennium; ~**zehnt** *das* decade

**jahrzehnte·lang** [1] *Adj.; nicht präd.* decades of ⟨*practice, experience, etc.*⟩ [2] *adv.* for decades

**Jäh·zorn** *der* violent anger

**jäh·zornig** [1] *Adj.* violent-tempered [2] *adv.* in a blind rage

**ja·ja** *Part.* (ugs.) **(a)** (seufzend) ~[, **so ist das Leben**] oh well[, that's life] **(b)** (ungeduldig) ~[, **ich komme schon**]! all right, all right[, I'm coming]!

**Jalousie** /ʒalu'zi:/ *die;* ~, ~**n** Venetian blind

**Jamaika** (*das*)*;* -**s** Jamaica

**Jamaikaner** *der;* ~**s**, ~, **Jamaikanerin** *die;* ~, ~**nen** Jamaican

**Jammer** *der;* ~**s** [mournful] wailing; (Elend) misery

**jämmerlich** [1] *Adj.* **(a)** pitiful **(b)** wretched ⟨*appearance, existence, etc.*⟩; paltry, meagre ⟨*quantity*⟩ [2] *adv.* pitifully

**jammern** *itr. V.* wail; (sich beklagen) moan

**jammer·schade** *Adj.* (ugs.) **es ist** ~, **dass** ...: it's a crying shame that ...; **es ist** ~ **um ihn** it's a great pity about him

**Janker** *der;* ~**s**, ~ (südd., österr.) Alpine jacket

**Januar** *der;* ~[**s**], ~**e** January

**Japan** (*das*) ~**s** Japan

**Japaner** *der;* ~**s**, ~, **Japanerin** *die;* ~, ~**nen** Japanese

**japanisch** *Adj.* Japanese

**japsen** *itr. V.* (ugs.) pant

**Jargon** /jar'gõ:/ *der;* ~**s**, ~**s** jargon

**Jasmin** *der;* ~**s**, ~**e** jasmine

**Ja·stimme** *die* yes-vote

**jäten** *tr., itr. V.* weed; **Unkraut** ~: weed

**Jauche** *die;* ~, ~**n** liquid manure

**Jauche·grube** *die* liquid-manure reservoir

**jauchzen** *itr. V.* cheer; **vor Freude** ~: shout for joy

**Jauchzer** *der;* ~**s**, ~: cry of delight

**jaulen** *itr. V.* howl

**Jause** *die;* ~, ~**n** (österr.) **(a)** snack; **eine** ~ **machen** have a snack **(b)** (Nachmittagskaffee) [afternoon] tea

**ja·wohl** *Part.* certainly

**Ja·wort** *das* consent; **jmdm. das** ~ **geben** consent to marry sb.

**Jazz** /dʒæz od. dʒɛs od. jats:/ *der;* ~: jazz

**jazzen** /'dʒɛsn̩/ *od.* 'jatsn̩/ *itr. V.* play jazz

**Jazzer** /'dʒɛsɐ od. 'jats:ɐ/ *der;* ~**s**, ~, **Jazzerin** *die;* ~, ~**nen** jazz musician

**Jazz-:** ~**keller** *der* jazz cellar; ~**tanz** *der* jazz dance

**je**[1] [1] *Adv.* **(a)** (jemals) ever; **mehr/besser denn je** more/better than ever **(b)** (jeweils) **je zehn Personen** ten people at a time; **sie kosten je 30 Euro** they cost 30 euros each **(c)** (entsprechend) **je nach Gewicht** according to weight [2] *Präp. mit Akk.* per; for each [3] *Konj.* **je länger, je lieber** the longer the better; **je nachdem** it all depends

**je**[2] *Interj.* **ach je, wie schade!** oh dear, what a shame!

**Jeans** /dʒi:nz/ *Pl. od. die;* ~, ~: jeans *pl.;* denims *pl.*

**jede** ▸ JEDER

**jeden·falls** *Adv.* **(a)** in any case **(b)** (zumindest) at any rate

**jeder, jede, jedes** *Indefinitpron. u. unbest. Zahlwort* [1] *attr.* **(a)** (alle) every **(b)** (alle einzeln) each **(c)** (jeglicher) all [2] *allein stehend* **(a)** (alle) everyone; everybody **(b)** (alle einzeln) **jedes der Kinder** each of the children

**jeder-:** ~**mann** *Indefinitpron.* everyone; everybody; ~**zeit** *Adv.* [at] any time

**jedes** ▸ JEDER

*****jedes·mal** ▸ MAL[1]

**je·doch** *Konj., Adv.* however

**je·her** /od. '-'-/ *Adv.* **seit** *od.* **von** ~: always; since time immemorial

**jemals** *Adv.* ever

**jemand** *Indefinitpron.* someone; somebody; (fragend, verneinend) anyone; anybody

**Jemen** (*das*)*;* ~**s** *od.* **der;** ~[**s**] Yemen

**jener, jene, jenes** *Demonstrativpron.* (geh.) [1] *attr.* that; (im Pl.) those [2] *allein stehend* that one; (im Pl.) those

**jenseits** [1] *Präp. mit Gen.* on the other side of; (in größerer Entfernung) beyond [2] *Adv.* on the other side; ~ **von** on the other side of

**Jenseits** *das;* ~: hereafter; beyond

**Jersey**[1] /'dʒø:ɐzi/ *der;* ~[**s**], ~**s** (Textilind.) jersey

**Jersey**[2] *das;* ~**s**, ~**s** (Sport: Trikot) jersey

**Jesus** (*der*)*;* **Jesu** Jesus

**Jet** /dʒɛt/ *der;* ~[**s**], ~**s** jet; **mit einem** ~ **fliegen/reisen** fly/travel by jet

**jetzig** *Adj.* current

**jetzt** *Adv.* **(a)** just now; **bis** ~: up to now; **bis** ~ **noch nicht** not yet; **von** ~ **an** *od.* **ab** from now on[wards]; **erst** ~ *od.* ~ **erst** only just; **schon** ~: already **(b)** (heutzutage) now; nowadays

**jeweilig** Adj. (a) (in einem bestimmten Fall) particular
(b) (zu einer bestimmten Zeit) current; of the time postpos., not pred.;
(c) (zugehörig, zugewiesen) respective

**jeweils** Adv. (a) (jedesmal) ~ am ersten/ letzten Mittwoch des Monats on the first/last Wednesday of each month
(b) (zur Zeit) at the time

**Jg.** Abk. = **Jahrgang**

**Jh.** Abk. = **Jahrhundert** c.

**JH** Abk. = **Jugendherberge**

**jiddisch** /'jɪdɪʃ/ Adj. Yiddish

**Job** /dʒɔp/ der; ~s (ugs.; auch DV) job

**jobben** /dʒɔbn̩/ itr. V. (ugs.) do a job/jobs

**Job-:** ~**killer** der destroyer of jobs;
~**sharing** /'-ʃɛərɪŋ/ das; ~~s jobsharing

**Joch** das; ~[e]s, ~e yoke

**Jockei, Jockey** /'dʒɔke od. 'dʒɔki/ der; ~s, ~s jockey

**Jod** das; ~[e]s iodine

**jodeln** itr., tr. V. yodel

**jod·haltig** Adj. iodiferous

**Joga** der od. das; ~[s] yoga

**joggen** /'dʒɔgn̩/ itr. V.; mit Richtungsangabe mit sein jog

**Jogging·anzug** der jogging suit

**Joghurt** /'joːgʊrt/ der od. das; ~[s], ~[s] yoghurt

**Joghurt·becher** der yoghurt pot (Brit.) or (Amer.) container

**Johannis·beere** die currant; rote/weiße/ schwarze ~n redcurrants/white currants/ blackcurrants

**johlen** itr. V. yell; (vor Wut) howl

**Joint** /dʒɔɪnt/ der; ~s, ~s (ugs.) joint (sl.)

**Jolle** die; ~, ~n keel-centreboard yawl

**Jongleur** /ʒɔŋ'løːɐ̯/ der; ~s, ~e, **Jongleurin** die; ~, ~nen juggler

**jonglieren** tr., itr. V. juggle

**Joppe** die; ~, ~n heavy jacket

**Jordanien** (das); ~s Jordan

**Jordanier** der; ~s, ~, **Jordanierin** die; ~, ~nen Jordanian

**jordanisch** Adj. Jordanian

**Jot** das; ~, ~: j, J

**Journalismus** /ʒʊr.../ der; ~: journalism no art.

**Journalist** der; ~en, ~en, **Journalistin** die; ~, ~nen journalist

**journalistisch** 1 Adj. journalistic; eine ~e Ausbildung a training in journalism
2 adv. journalistically; ~ tätig sein be a journalist

**Joystick** /'dʒɔystik/ der; ~s, ~s (DV) joystick

**jr.** Abk. = **junior** Jr.

**Jubel** der; ~s rejoicing; jubilation; (laut) cheering

**Jubel·jahr** das jubilee; **alle** ~**e [einmal]** once in a blue moon

**jubeln** itr. V. cheer; **über etw.** (Akk.) ~: rejoice over sth.

**Jubilar** der; ~s, ~e man celebrating his anniversary/birthday

**Jubilarin** die; ~, ~nen woman celebrating her anniversary/birthday

**Jubiläum** das; ~s, Jubiläen anniversary; (eines Monarchen) jubilee

**jubilieren** itr. V. (geh.) jubilate (literary); rejoice

**juchzen** itr. V. (ugs.) shout with glee

**jucken** 1 tr., itr. V. (a) **mir juckt die Haut** I itch; **es juckt mich hier** I've got an itch here
(b) (Juckreiz verursachen) irritate
2 tr. V. (reizen, verlocken) **es juckt mich, das zu tun** I am itching to do it
3 refl. V. (ugs.: sich kratzen) scratch

**Juck·reiz** der itch

**Jude** der; ~n, ~n Jew

**Juden:** ~**hass,** *~**haß** der anti-Semitism; hatred of [the] Jews; ~**stern** der (ns.) Star of David

**Judentum** das; ~s (a) (Volk) Jewry; Jews pl.;
(b) (Kultur u. Religion) Judaism

**Juden·verfolgung** die persecution of [the] Jews

**Jüdin** die; ~, ~nen Jewess

**jüdisch** Adj. Jewish

**Judo** das; ~[s] judo no art.

**Jugend** die; ~ (a) youth
(b) (Jugendliche) young people

**jugend-, Jugend-:** ~**amt** das youth office (agency responsible for education and welfare of young people);
~**arbeitslosigkeit** die youth unemployment; ~**arrest** der detention in a community home; ~**bewegung** die (hist.) [German] youth Movement; ~**buch** das book for young people; ~**frei** Adj. ⟨film, book, etc.⟩ suitable for persons under 18; **nicht** ~**frei** ⟨film⟩ not U-certificate pred.;
~**gefährdend** Adj. liable to have an undesirable influence on the moral development of young people postpos.;
~**heim** das youth centre; ~**herberge** die youth hostel; ~**klub** der youth club; ~**kriminalität** die juvenile delinquency

**jugendlich** Adj. (a) young ⟨offender, customer, etc.⟩
(b) (für Jugendliche charakteristisch) youthful

**Jugendliche** der/die; adj. Dekl. young person; **die** ~**n** the young people

**Jugend-:** ~**liebe** die sweetheart of one's youth; ~**schutz** der protection of young people; ~**schutz·gesetz** das laws pl. protecting young people; ~**sprache** die young people's language no art.; ~**stil** der art nouveau; (in Deutschland) Jugendstil; ~**strafanstalt** die detention centre;

---

*old spelling - see note on page xiv

~**strafe** *die* youth custody sentence; ~**sünde** *die* youthful folly; ~**zeit** *die* youth; ~**zentrum** *das* youth centre

**Jugo·sla̲we** *der* Yugoslav

**Jugo·sla̲wien** (*das*); ~s Yugoslavia

**Jugo·sla̲win** *die* Yugoslav

**jugo·sla̲wisch** *Adj.* Yugoslav[ian]

**Jule̲i** *der;* ~[s], ~s ▶ JULI

**Ju̲li** *der;* ~[s], ~s July; *s. auch* APRIL

**ju̲ng** *Adj.;* jünger, jüngst... (a) young; new ‹*project, undertaking, sport, marriage, etc.*› (b) (*letzt...*) recent; **in jüngster Zeit** recently

**Ju̲nge¹** *der;* ~n, ~n *od.* (ugs.) Jung[en]s boy

**Ju̲nge²** *das; adj. Dekl.* **ein** ~s one of the young; ~ **kriegen** give birth to young

**ju̲ngen** *itr. V.* give birth to young; ‹*cat*› have kittens; ‹*dog*› have pups

**ju̲ngenhaft** *Adj.* boyish

**jünger** *Adj.* youngish; **sie ist noch** ~: she is still quite young; *s. auch* JUNG

**Jünger** *der;* ~s, ~, **Jüngerin** *die;* ~, ~nen follower

**Ju̲ngfer** *die;* ~, ~n (abwertend: ältere ledige Frau) spinster

**Ju̲ngfern·fahrt** *die* maiden voyage

**Ju̲ngfern·häutchen** *das;* ~s, ~: hymen

**Ju̲ng·frau** *die* (a) virgin (b) (Astrol.) Virgo

**ju̲ng·fräulich** *Adj.* (geh., auch fig.) virgin

**Ju̲ng·geselle** *der* bachelor

**Ju̲ng·gesellin** *die* bachelor girl

**Jüngling** *der;* ~s, ~e (geh., spött.) youth; boy

**jüngst** *Adv.* (geh.) recently

**jüngst...** ▶ JUNG

**Jüngste** *der/die; adj. Dekl.* youngest [one]

**Ju̲ng-:** ~**verheiratete** *der/die; adj.*

*Dekl.,* young married man/woman; **die** ~**verheirateten** the newly-weds; ~**wähler** *der,* ~**wählerin** *die* first-time voter

**Ju̲ni** *der;* ~[s], ~s June; *s. auch* APRIL

**ju̲nior** *indekl. Adj.; nach Personennamen* junior

**Ju̲nior** *der;* ~s, ~en (a) (oft scherzh.) junior (joc.) (b) (Kaufmannsspr.) junior partner

**Ju̲nior-:** ~**chef** *der* owner's *or* (coll.) boss's son; ~**chefin** *die* owner's *or* (coll.) boss's daughter

**Ju̲no** *der;* ~[s], ~s ▶ JUNI

**Ju̲nta** /'xʊnta/ *die;* ~, Ju̲nten junta

**Ju̲ra** law *sing.;* ~ **studieren** read Law

**Juri̲st** *der;* ~en, ~en, **Juri̲stin** *die;* ~, ~nen lawyer; jurist

**juri̲stisch** *Adj.* legal

**Jury** /ʒy'riː/ *die;* ~, ~s (a) (Preisrichter) panel [of judges]; jury (b) (Sachverständige) panel [of experts]

**ju̲st** *Adv.* (veralt., noch scherzh.) just; ~ **in diesem Augenblick** just at that moment; at that very moment

**justi̲eren** *tr. V.* adjust

**Justi̲erung** *die;* ~, ~en adjustment

**Justi̲z** *die;* ~: justice; (Behörden) judiciary

**Justi̲z-:** ~**irrtum** *der* miscarriage of justice; ~**minister** *der,* ~**ministerin** *die* Minister of Justice; ~**ministerium** *das* Ministry of Justice; ~**mord** *der* judicial murder; ~**vollzugs·anstalt** *die* (Amtsspr.) penal institution (formal); prison

**Ju̲te** *die;* ~: jute

**Jütland** (*das*); ~s Jutland

**Juwe̲l** *das od. der;* ~s, ~en piece of jewellery; (Edelstein) jewel

**Juwelier** /juvə'liːɐ̯/ *der;* ~s jeweller

**Juwelier·geschäft** *das* jeweller's shop

**Ju̲x** *der;* ~es, ~e (ugs.) joke

# Kk

**k, K** /ka:/ *das;* ~, ~: k/K

**Kabarett** *das;* ~s, ~s *od.* ~e (a) satirical revue
**(b)** (Ensemble) cabaret act

**Kabarettist** *der;* ~en, ~en,
**Kabarettistin** *die;* ~, ~nen revue performer

**kabarettistisch** *Adj.* [satirical] revue *attrib.;* ~e **Szenen** scenes in the style of a [satirical] revue

**kabbeln** *refl. V.* (ugs.) bicker (**mit** with)

**Kabel** *das;* ~s, ~: cable; (für kleineres Gerät) flex

**Kabel·fernsehen** *das* cable television

**Kabeljau** *der;* ~s, ~s *od.* ~s cod

**kabeln** *tr., itr. V.* (veralt.) cable

**Kabine** *die;* ~, ~n (a) cabin
**(b)** (Umkleideraum, abgeteilter Raum) cubicle
**(c)** (einer Seilbahn) [cable] car

**Kabinett** *das;* ~s, ~e Cabinet

**Kabrio** *das;* ~s, ~s, **Kabriolett** *das;* ~s, ~s convertible

**Kachel** *die;* ~, ~n [glazed] tile

**kacheln** *tr. V.* tile

**Kachel·ofen** *der* tiled stove

**Kacke** *die;* ~ (derb; auch fig.) shit (coarse); crap (coarse)

**kacken** *itr. V.* (derb) shit (coarse); crap (coarse)

**Kadaver** *der;* ~s, ~: carcass

**Kader** *der od.* (schweiz.) *das;* ~s, ~ (a) cadre
**(b)** (Sport) squad

**Käfer** *der;* ~s, ~: beetle

**Kaff** *das;* ~s, ~s *od.* **Käffer** (ugs. abwertend) dump (coll.)

**Kaffee** /'kafe *od.* (österr.) ka'fe:/ *der;* ~s, ~s
**(a)** coffee
**(b)** (Nachmittags~) afternoon coffee; ~ **trinken** have afternoon coffee

**Kaffee-:** ~**kanne** *die* coffee pot; ~**kränzchen** *das* (veralt.) **(a)** (Zusammentreffen) coffee afternoon; **(b)** (Gruppe) coffee circle; ~**maschine** *die* coffee maker; ~**mühle** *die* coffee grinder; ~**satz** *der* coffee grounds *pl.;* ~**tante** *die* (ugs. scherzh.) coffee addict

**Käfig** *der;* ~s, ~e cage

**kahl** *Adj.* **(a)** (ohne Haare) bald; jmdn. ~ **scheren** shave sb.'s head
**(b)** (ohne Grün, schmucklos) bare; etw. ~ **fressen** strip sth. bare

**kahl-, Kahl-:** *\*~|**fressen** ▶ KAHL B;

~**köpfig** *Adj.* bald[-headed]; *\*~|**scheren** ▶ KAHL A; ~**schlag** *der* **(a)** clear-felling *no indef. art.;* **(b)** (Waldfläche) clear-felled area

**Kahn** *der;* ~[e]s, **Kähne** (a) (Ruder~) rowing boat; (Stech~) punt
**(b)** (Lastschiff) barge

**Kai** *der;* ~s, ~s quay

**Kaiser** *der;* ~s, ~: emperor

**Kaiserin** *die;* ~, ~nen empress

**Kaiser-:** ~**krone** *die* imperial crown; ~**reich** *das* empire; ~**schnitt** *der* Caesarean section; ~**wetter** *das* (scherzh.) glorious, sunny weather (*for an event*)

**Kajüte** *die;* ~, ~n (Seemannsspr.) cabin

**Kakao** /ka'kau:/ *der;* ~s, ~s cocoa; jmdn./ etw. durch den ~ **ziehen** (ugs.) make fun of sb./sth.

**Kakerlak** *der;* ~s *od.* ~en, ~en cockroach

**Kaktus** *der;* ~, **Kakteen** cactus

**Kalauer** *der;* ~s, ~: corny joke (coll.); (Wortspiel) atrocious *or* (coll.) corny pun

**Kalb** *das;* ~[e]s, **Kälber** (a) calf
**(b)** (ugs.: ~fleisch) veal

**kalben** *itr. V.* calve

**Kalb·fleisch** *das* veal

**Kalbs-:** ~**braten** *der* (Kochk.) roast veal *no indef. art.;* (Gericht) roast of veal; ~**leder** *das* calfskin; ~**schnitzel** *das* veal cutlet

**Kalender** *der;* ~s, ~: calendar; (Taschen~) diary

**Kalender-:** ~**jahr** *das* calendar year; ~**monat** *der* calendar month

**Kalesche** *die;* ~, ~n (hist.) barouche

**Kali** *das;* ~s, ~s potash

**Kaliber** *das;* ~s, ~: **(a)** (Technik, Waffenkunde) calibre
**(b)** (ugs., oft abwertend) sort; kind

**Kalifornien** /kali'fɔrniən/ *(das);* ~s California

**Kalium** (Chemie) *das;* ~s potassium

**Kalk** *der;* ~[e]s, ~e calcium carbonate; (Baustoff) lime; quicklime

**kalken** *tr. V.* whitewash

**Kalk-:** ~**mangel** *der* calcium deficiency; ~**stein** *der* limestone

**Kalkül** *das od. der;* ~s, ~e (geh.) calculation

**Kalkulation** *die;* ~, ~en (auch Wirtsch.) calculation

**kalkulieren** *tr. V.* calculate ⟨cost, price⟩; cost ⟨product, article⟩

**Kalorie** *die;* ~, ~n calorie

**kalorien-, Kalorien-:** ~**arm** ⓵ *Adj.*

low-calorie *attrib.;* ~**arm sein** be low in calories; ☒ *adv.* ~**arm kochen** cook low-calorie meals; ~**gehalt** *der* calorie content

**kalt; kälter, kältest...** ① *Adj.* cold; frosty ⟨*atmosphere, smile*⟩; ~ **bleiben** (fig.) remain unmoved; **jmdn.** ~ **lassen** (ugs.) leave sb. unmoved; (nicht interessieren) leave sb. cold (coll.)

☒ *adv.* **(a)** ~ **duschen** have a cold shower **Getränke/Sekt** ~ **stellen** cool drinks/chill champagne **(b)** (nüchtern) coldly **(c)** (abweisend, unfreundlich) frostily

**kalt-, Kalt-:** *~|bleiben ▶ KALT 1; ~blütig ① *Adj.* **(a)** cool-headed; **(b)** (abwertend: skrupellos) cold-blooded; ☒ *adv.* **(a)** coolly; **(b)** (abwertend: skrupellos) cold-bloodedly; ~**blütigkeit** *die;* ~~: ▶ ~BLÜTIG A, B: cool-headedness; cold-bloodedness

**Kälte** *die;* ~ cold; (fig.) coldness **Kälte-:** ~**einbruch** *der* (Met.) sudden onset of cold weather; ~**grad** *der* degree of frost

**kälter ▶ KALT**

**kältest... ▶ KALT**

**Kälte·welle** *die* cold spell

**kalt-, Kalt-:** ~**gepresst,** *~**gepreßt** *Adj.* cold-pressed; ~**herzig** *Adj.* cold-hearted; *~**lächelnd** *Adv.* (ugs. abwertend) **etw.** ~**lächelnd tun** take callous pleasure in doing sth.; *~|**lassen ▶ KALT 1;** ~|**machen** *tr. V.* (salopp) **jmdn.** ~**machen** do sb. in (sl.); ~**miete** *die* rent exclusive of heating; ~**schale** *die: cold sweet soup made with fruit, beer, wine, or milk;* ~**schnäuzig** (ugs.) ① *Adj.* cold and insensitive; (frech) insolent; ☒ *adv.* coldly and insensitively; (frech) insolently; ~|**stellen** *tr. V.* (coll.) ~|**stellen** put sb. out of the way (coll. joc.)

**kam** *1. u. 3. Pers. Prät. v. KOMMEN*

**Kambodscha** (*das*)*; ~s* Cambodia

**käme** *1. u. 3. Pers. Konjunktiv II v. KOMMEN*

**Kamel** *das;* ~s, ~e camel

**Kamera** *die;* ~, ~s camera

**Kamerad** *der;* ~en, ~en, **Kameradin** *die;* ~, ~nen companion; (Freund[in]) friend; (Mitschüler[in]) mate; (Soldat[in]) comrade; (Sport) teammate

**Kameradschaft** *die;* ~: comradeship

**kameradschaftlich** ① *Adj.* comradely ☒ *adv.* in a comradely way

**Kamera-:** ~**frau** *die* camerawoman; ~**mann** *der Pl.;* ~**männer** *od.* ~**leute** cameraman; ~**team** *das* camera crew

**Kamerun** /'kaməru:n/ (*das*); ~s Cameroon; the Cameroons *pl.*

**Kamille** *die;* ~, ~n camomile

**Kamin** *der, schweiz.: das;* ~s, ~e fireplace

**Kamin·feger** *der,* **Kamin·fegerin** *die* (bes. südd.) ▶ SCHORNSTEINFEGER

**Kamm** *der;* ~[e]s, **Kämme (a)** comb

**(b)** (bei Hühnern usw.) comb **(c)** (Gebirgs~) ridge

**kämmen** *tr. V.* comb

**Kammer** *die;* ~, ~n **(a)** storeroom **(b)** (Biol., Med., Technik, Waffenkunde) chamber **(c)** (Parl.) chamber

**Kammer-:** ~**diener** *der* (veralt.) valet; ~**jäger** *der,* ~**jägerin** *die* pest controller; ~**musik** *die* chamber music; ~**sänger** *der,* ~**sängerin** *die: title awarded to singer of outstanding merit;* ~**zofe** *die* (veralt.) lady's maid

**Kamm·garn** *das* worsted

**Kampagne** /kam'panjə/ *die;* ~, ~n campaign

**Kampf** *der;* ~[e]s, **Kämpfe (a)** (militärisch) battle (**um** for) **(b)** (zwischen persönlichen Gegnern) fight; (fig.) struggle **(c)** (Wett~) contest; (Boxen) contest; bout **(d)** (Einsatz aller Mittel) fight (**um, für** for; **gegen** against)

**kampf-, Kampf-:** ~**abstimmung** *die* (Politik) crucial vote; ~**bereit** *Adj.* ready to fight *postpos.;* ⟨*army, troops*⟩ ready for battle

**kämpfen** *itr. V.* **(a)** fight **(b)** (Sport: sich messen) ⟨*team*⟩ play; ⟨*wrestler, boxer*⟩ fight

**Kampfer** *der;* ~s camphor

**Kämpfer** *der;* ~s, ~, **Kämpferin** *die;* ~, ~nen fighter

**kampf-, Kampf-:** ~**fähig** *Adj.* ⟨*troops*⟩ fit for action; ⟨*boxer etc.*⟩ fit to fight; ~**handlungen** *Pl.* fighting *sing.;* ~**preis** *der* (Wirtsch.) cut price; ~**richter** *der,* ~**richterin** *die* (Sport) judge; ~**unfähig** *Adj.* ⟨*troops*⟩ unfit for action; ⟨*boxer etc.*⟩ unfit to fight

**kampieren** *itr. V.* camp

**Kanada** (*das*)*; ~s* Canada

**Kanadier** /ka'na:diɐ/ *der;* ~s, ~, **Kanadierin** *die;* ~, ~nen Canadian

**kanadisch** *Adj.* Canadian

**Kanal** *der;* ~s, **Kanäle (a)** canal **(b)** (Geogr.) **der ~:** the [English] Channel **(c)** (für Abwässer) sewer **(d)** (zur Entwässerung, Bewässerung) channel; (Graben) ditch **(e)** (Rundf., Ferns., Weg der Information) channel

**Kanalisation** *die;* ~, ~en sewerage system; sewers *pl.*

**kanalisieren** *tr. V.* **(a)** (lenken) channel ⟨*energies, goods, etc.*⟩ **(b)** (schiffbar machen) canalize

**Kanal·tunnel** *der* Channel Tunnel

**Kanaren** *Pl.* Canaries

**Kanarien·vogel** /ka'na:riən-/ *der* canary

**Kanarische Inseln** *Pl.* Canary Islands

**Kandare** *die;* ~, ~n curb bit; **jmdn. an die ~ nehmen** (fig.) take sb. in hand

**Kandidat** *der;* ~en, ~en, **Kandidatin** *die;* ~, ~nen **(a)** candidate **(b)** (beim Quiz usw.) contestant

**k**

**Kandidatur** die; ~, ~en candidature (auf + Akk. for)

**kandidieren** itr. V. stand [as a candidate] (für for)

**kandieren** tr. V. candy; kandiert crystallized ⟨orange, petal⟩; glacé ⟨cherry, pear⟩; candied ⟨peel⟩

**Kandis** der; ~, **Kandis·zucker** der rock candy

**Känguru**, *\*Känguruh** das; ~s, ~s kangaroo

**Kaninchen** das; ~s, ~: rabbit

**Kanister** der; ~s, ~: can; [metal/plastic] container

**kann** 1. u. 3. Pers. Sg. Präsens v. KÖNNEN

**Kännchen** das; ~s, ~: [small] pot; (für Milch) [small] jug

**Kanne** die; ~, ~n (a) pot; (für Milch, Wein, Wasser) jug
(b) (Henkel~) can; (für Milch) pail; (beim Melken) churn

**kannst** 2. Pers. Sg. Präsens v. KÖNNEN

**kannte** 1. u. 3. Pers. Sg. Prät. v. KENNEN

**Kanon** der; ~s, ~s canon

**Kanone** die; ~, ~n cannon; (fig. ugs.: Könner) ace

**Kantate** die; ~, ~n (Musik) cantata

**Kante** die; ~, ~n edge

**kantig** Adj. square-cut ⟨timber, stone⟩; rough-edged ⟨rock⟩; angular ⟨face⟩; square ⟨chin⟩

**Kantine** die; ~, ~n canteen

**Kanton** der; ~s, ~e canton

**kantonal** 1 Adj. cantonal
2 adv. on a cantonal basis

**Kantor** der; ~s, ~en choirmaster and organist

**Kantorin** die; ~, ~nen choirmistress and organist

**Kanu** das; ~s, ~s canoe

**Kanüle** die; ~, ~n (Med.) cannula

**Kanzel** die; ~, ~n (a) pulpit
(b) (Flugw.) cockpit

**Kanzlei** die; ~, ~en (a) (veralt.: Büro) office
(b) (Anwalts~) chambers pl. ⟨of barrister⟩; office ⟨of lawyer⟩

**Kanzler** der; ~s, ~ chancellor

**Kap** das; ~s, ~s cape

**Kapazität** die; ~, ~en (a) capacity
(b) (Experte) expert

**Kapelle** die; ~, ~n (a) (Archit.) chapel
(b) (Musik~) band; [light] orchestra

**Kapell·meister** der,
**Kapell·meisterin** die bandmaster/ -mistress; (im Orchester) conductor; (im Theater usw.) musical director

**Kaper** die; ~, ~n caper usu. in pl.

**kapern** tr. V. (a) (hist.) capture

(b) (ugs.) jmdn. [für etw.] ~: rope sb. in[to sth.]

**kapieren** (ugs.) 1 tr. V. (ugs.) get (coll.)
2 itr. V. kapiert? got it? (coll.)

**Kapital** das; ~s, ~e od. ~ien (a) capital
(b) (fig.) asset

**Kapital·anlage** die (Wirtsch.) capital investment

**Kapitalismus** der; ~: capitalism no art.

**Kapitalist** der; ~en, ~en, **Kapitalistin** die; ~, ~nen capitalist

**kapitalistisch** Adj. capitalistic

**Kapital·verbrechen** das serious offence; (mit Todesstrafe bedroht) capital offence

**Kapitän** der; ~s, ~e, **Kapitänin** die; ~, ~nen captain

**Kapitel** das; ~s, ~: chapter

**Kapitulation** die; ~, ~en surrender; capitulation; seine ~ erklären admit defeat

**kapitulieren** itr. V. (a) surrender; capitulate
(b) (fig.: aufgeben) give up; vor etw. (Dat.) ~: give up in the face of sth.

**Kaplan** der; ~s, Kapläne (kath. Kirche) chaplain; (Hilfsgeistlicher) curate

**Kappe** die; ~, ~n cap

**kappen** tr. V. (a) (Seemannsspr.) cut
(b) (beschneiden) cut back ⟨hedge etc.⟩; (abschneiden) cut off ⟨branches etc.⟩

**Käppi** das; ~s, ~s garrison cap

**Kapsel** die; ~, ~n capsule

**Kapstadt** (das); ~s Cape Town

**kaputt** Adj. (a) broken; das Telefon ist ~: the phone is not working
(b) (ugs.: erschöpft) shattered (coll.)

**kaputt-:** ~|gehen unr. itr. V.; mit sein (ugs.) (entzweigehen) break; ⟨machine⟩ break down, (coll.) pack up; ⟨lightbulb⟩ go; (zerbrechen) be smashed; ~|lachen refl. V. (ugs.) kill oneself [laughing] (coll.); ~|machen (ugs.) 1 tr. V. break; spoil ⟨sth. made with effort⟩; ruin ⟨clothes, furniture, etc.⟩; finish ⟨person⟩ off; 2 refl. V. wear oneself out

**Kapuze** die; ~, ~n hood; (bei Mönchen) cowl; hood

**Kapuziner** der; ~s, ~: Capuchin [friar]

**Karabiner** der; ~s, ~: carbine

**Karaffe** die; ~, ~n carafe; (mit Glasstöpsel) decanter

**Karambolage** /karambo'la:ʒə/ die; ~, ~n (ugs.) crash; collision

**\*Karamel** usw. ▶ KARAMELL usw.

**Karamell** der (schweiz.: das); ~s caramel

**Karamell·bonbon** der od. das caramel [toffee]

**Karat** das; ~[e]s, ~e carat

**Karate** das; ~[s] karate

**Karawane** die; ~, ~n caravan

**Kardinal** der; ~s, Kardinäle (kath. Kirche) cardinal

**Kardinal-:** ~**fehler** der cardinal error; ~**tugend** die cardinal virtue; ~**zahl** die cardinal [number]

**Karenz** die; ~, ~en, **Karenz·zeit** die waiting period

**Kar·freitag** der Good Friday

**karg** ⬚1 Adj. meagre ⟨wages etc.⟩; frugal ⟨meal etc.⟩; poor ⟨light, accommodation⟩; (wenig fruchtbar) barren ⬚2 adv. ~ **bemessen sein** ⟨helping⟩ be mingy (Brit. coll.); ⟨supply⟩ be scanty; ~ **leben** live frugally

**kärglich** ⬚1 Adj. meagre, poor ⟨wages etc.⟩; poor ⟨light⟩; frugal ⟨meal⟩; scanty ⟨supply⟩ ⬚2 adv. poorly ⟨lit, paid, rewarded⟩

**karibisch** Adj. Caribbean

**kariert** Adj. check, checked ⟨material, pattern⟩; check ⟨jacket etc.⟩; squared ⟨paper⟩

**Karies** /'kaːri̯ɛs/ die; ~: caries

**Karikatur** die; ~, ~en cartoon; (Porträt) caricature

**Karikaturist** der; ~en, ~en, **Karikaturistin** die; ~, ~nen cartoonist; (Porträtist) caricaturist

**karikieren** tr. V. caricature

**kariös** Adj. (Zahnmed.) carious

**karitativ** Adj. charitable

**Karl** /karl/ (der) Charles; ~ **der Große** Charlemagne

**Karneval** /'karnəval/ der; ~s, ~e od. ~s carnival; ~ **feiern** join in the carnival festivities

**karnevalistisch** Adj. carnival attrib.

**Karnevals-:** ~**kostüm** das carnival costume; ~**verein** der carnival society; ~**zug** der carnival procession

**Karnickel** das; ~s, ~ (landsch.) rabbit

**Kärnten** (das); ~s Carinthia

**Karo** das; ~s, ~s (a) square; (auf der Spitze stehend) diamond (b) (Karomuster) check (c) (Kartenspiel: Farbe) diamonds pl.; (d) (Kartenspiel: Karte) diamond

**Karosse** die; ~, ~n [state] coach

**Karosserie** die; ~, ~n bodywork

**Karotte** die; ~, ~n small carrot

**Karpaten** Pl. Carpathians; Carpathian Mountains

**Karpfen** der; ~s, ~: carp

**Karre** die; ~, ~n (bes. nordd.) (a) ▶ KARREN; (b) (abwertend: Fahrzeug) [old] heap (coll.)

**Karree** das; ~s, ~s: ums ~ **gehen/fahren** walk/drive round the block

**karren** tr. V. (a) cart (b) (salopp: mit einem Auto) run (coll.)

**Karren** der; ~s, ~ (bes. südd., österr.) cart; (zweirädrig) barrow

**Karriere** /ka'ri̯eːrə/ die; ~, ~n career; ~ **machen** make a [successful] career for oneself

**Kärrner·arbeit** die donkey work

**Kar·samstag** der Easter Saturday

**Karte** die; ~, ~n card; (Speise~) menu; (Fahr~, Flug~, Eintritts~) ticket; (Land~) map; **alles auf eine** ~ **setzen** stake everything on one chance

**Kartei** die; ~, ~en card file

**Kartei-:** ~**karte** die file card; ~**kasten** der file-card box

**Kartell** das; ~s, ~e (Wirtsch., Politik) cartel

**Kartell-:** ~**amt** das: government body concerned with the control and supervision of cartels; ≈ Monopolies and Mergers Commission (Brit.); ~**gesetz** das law relating to cartels; ≈ monopolies law (Brit.)

**Karten-:** ~**haus** das house of cards; ~**spiel** das (a) (Spiel mit Karten) card game; (b) (Satz Spielkarten) pack or (Amer.) deck [of cards]; ~**telefon** das cardphone; ~**vorverkauf** der advance booking

**Kartoffel** die; ~, ~n potato

**Kartoffel-:** ~**brei** der mashed potatoes pl.; mash (coll.); ~**chips** Pl. [potato] crisps (Brit.) or (Amer.) chips; ~**käfer** der Colorado beetle; ~**kloß** der potato dumpling; ~**puffer** der potato pancake (made from grated raw potatoes); ~**püree** das; ▶ ~BREI

**Karton** /kar'tɔŋ/ der; ~s, ~s (a) (Pappe) card[board] (b) (Schachtel) cardboard box

**Karussell** das; ~s, ~s od. ~e merry-go-round; carousel (Amer.); (kleineres) roundabout

**Kar·woche** die Holy Week

**karzinogen** Adj. (Med.) carcinogenic

**Karzinom** das; ~s, ~e (Med.) carcinoma

**kaschieren** tr. V. conceal; hide; disguise ⟨fault⟩

**Kaschmir¹** (das); ~s Kashmir

**Kaschmir²** der; ~s, ~e (Textilw.) cashmere

**Käse** der; ~s, ~: cheese; (ugs. abwertend: Unsinn) rubbish

**Käse-:** ~**blatt** das (salopp abwertend) rag; ~**glocke** die cheese dome

**Kaserne** die; ~, ~n barracks sing. or pl.

**käse·weiß** Adj. (ugs.) [as] white as a sheet

**käsig** Adj. (ugs.) pasty; pale

**Kasino** das; ~s, ~s (a) (Spiel~) casino (b) (Offiziers~) [officers'] mess (c) (Speiseraum) canteen

**Kasko·versicherung** die (Voll~) comprehensive insurance; (Teil~) insurance against theft, fire, or act of God

**Kasper** der; ~s, ~: ≈ Punch; (fig. ugs.) clown

**Kasperl** das; ~s, ~[n] (österr.), **Kasperle** das od. der; ~s, ~: ▶ KASPER

**Kasper-:** ~**puppe** die ≈ Punch and Judy puppet; ~**theater** das ≈ Punch and Judy show; (Puppenbühne) ≈ Punch and Judy theatre

**Kasse** die; ~, ~n (a) cash box; (Registrier~) till ⋯⟶

**(b)** (Ort zum Bezahlen) cash desk; (im Supermarkt) checkout; (in einer Bank) counter
**(c)** (Kassenraum) cashier's office
**(d)** (Theater~, Kino~) box office

**Kasseler** *das;* ~s smoked loin of pork

**Kassen-:** ~**arzt** *der,* ~**ärztin** *die:* doctor *who treats members of health insurance schemes;* ~**bon** *der* sales slip; receipt; ~**lage** *die* financial situation; **die** ~**lage der Firma** the state of the company's finances; **nach** ~**lage** as finances allow/allowed; **eine Rentenpolitik nach** ~**lage** a pensions policy dependent on what finances will allow; ~**patient** *der,* ~**patientin** *die:* patient *who is a member of a health insurance scheme;* ~**wart** *der;* ~~s, ~~e, ~**wartin** *die;* ~~, ~~nen treasurer; ~**zettel** *der:* ▶ ~BON

**Kassette** *die;* ~, ~n **(a)** box; case
**(b)** (mit Büchern, Schallplatten) boxed set; (Tonband~, Film~) cassette

**Kassetten-:** ~**deck** *das* cassette deck; ~**recorder,** ~**rekorder** *der;* ~~s, ~~: cassette recorder

**kassieren** [1] *tr. V.* **(a)** collect
**(b)** (ugs.: wegnehmen) confiscate; take away ‹driving licence›
[2] *itr. V.* **bei jmdm.** ~: give sb. his/her bill or (Amer.) check; (ohne Rechnung) settle up with sb.; **darf ich bei Ihnen** ~? would you like your bill?/can I settle up with you?

**Kassierer** *der;* ~s, ~, **Kassiererin** *die;* ~, ~nen cashier; (bei einem Verein) treasurer

**Kastanie** /kas'ta:niə/ *die;* ~, ~n chestnut

**kastanien-braun** *Adj.* chestnut

**Kästchen** *das;* ~s, ~ **(a)** small box
**(b)** (vorgedrucktes Quadrat) square; (auf Fragebögen) box

**Kaste** *die;* ~, ~n caste

**kasteien** *refl. V.* **(a)** (als Bußübung) chastise oneself
**(b)** (sich Entbehrungen auferlegen) deny oneself

**Kasteiung** *die;* ~, ~en **(a)** (als Bußübung) self-chastisement
**(b)** (Auferlegung von Entbehrungen) self-denial

**Kastell** *das;* ~s, ~e **(a)** (hist.: röm. Lager) fort
**(b)** (Burg) castle

**Kasten** *der;* ~s, Kästen **(a)** box; (für Flaschen) crate
**(b)** (ugs.: Briefkasten) postbox
**(c)** (ugs. abwertend) (Gebäude) barracks *sing.* or *pl.;* (Auto) heap (coll.); (fig. ugs.) heap; **etw. auf dem** ~ **haben** have got it up top (coll.)

**Kasten-brot** *das* tin [loaf]

**Kastration** /kastra'ts:jo:n/ *die;* ~, ~en castration

**kastrieren** *tr. V.* castrate

**Kat** *der;* ~s, ~s (ugs.) ▶ KATALYSATOR B

**Katalog** *der;* ~[e]s, ~e (auch fig.) catalogue

**katalogisieren** *tr. V.* catalogue

**Katalysator** *der;* ~s, ~en **(a)** (Chemie, fig.) catalyst
**(b)** (Kfz-W.) catalytic converter

**Katamaran** *der od. das;* ~s, ~e catamaran

**katapultieren** *tr. V.* (auch fig.) catapult; eject ‹pilot›

**Katarrh** /ka'tar/ *der;* ~s, ~e (Med.) catarrh

**katastrophal** /katastro'fa:l/ [1] *Adj.* disastrous; (stärker) catastrophic
[2] *adv.* disastrously; (stärker) catastrophically

**Katastrophe** /katas'tro:fə/ *die;* ~, ~n (Unglück) disaster; (stärker, auch Literaturw.) catastrophe

**Katastrophen-:** ~**alarm** *der* disaster alert; ~**gebiet** *das* disaster area; ~**schutz** *der* (Organisation) emergency services *pl.;* (Maßnahmen) disaster procedures *pl.*

**Kategorie** *die;* ~, ~n category

**kategorisch** [1] *Adj.* categorical
[2] *adv.* categorically

**Kater** *der;* ~s, ~ **(a)** tomcat
**(b)** (ugs.) hangover

**Kathedrale** *die;* ~, ~n cathedral

**Katholik** *der;* ~en, ~en, **Katholikin** *die;* ~, ~nen [Roman] Catholic

**katholisch** *Adj.* [Roman] Catholic

**Katholizismus** *der;* ~: [Roman] Catholicism *no art.*

**Katz** *die* ~ **und Maus [mit jmdm.] spielen** (ugs.) play cat and mouse [with sb.]; **für die** ~ **sein** (salopp) be a waste of time

**Kätzchen** *das;* ~s, ~ **(a)** little cat; pussy; ‹junge Katze› kitten
**(b)** *meist Pl.* catkin

**Katze** *die;* ~, ~n cat

**katzen-, Katzen-:** ~**auge** *das* reflector; Cat's-eye ®; ~**jammer** *der* **(a)** (Kater) hangover; **(b)** (fig.) mood of depression; ~**musik** *die* (ugs. abwertend) terrible row (coll.); ~**sprung** *der* stone's throw; ~**wäsche** *die* (ugs.) ~**wäsche machen** have a lick and a promise (coll.)

**Kauderwelsch** *das;* ~[s] gibberish *no indef. art.*

**kauen** *tr., itr. V.* chew; **[die] Nägel** ~: bite one's nails

**kauern** *itr., refl. V.* crouch [down]; (ängstlich) cower

**Kauf** *der;* ~[e]s, Käufe **(a)** (das Kaufen) buying; purchasing (formal)
**(b)** (das Gekaufte) purchase

**kaufen** [1] *tr. V.* buy; purchase
[2] *itr. V.* (einkaufen) shop

**Käufer** *der;* ~s, ~, **Käuferin** *die;* ~, ~nen buyer; purchaser (formal)

**Kauf-:** ~**frau** *die* (Geschäftsfrau) businesswoman; (Händlerin) trader; ~**haus** *das* department store; ~**kraft** *die* (Wirtsch.)
**(a)** (Wert des Geldes) purchasing power; **(b)** (Zahlungsfähigkeit) spending power

---

**käuflich** ① *Adj.* (a) for sale *postpos.;*
(b) (bestechlich) venal; ~ **sein** be easily
bought
② *adv.* etw. ~ **erwerben/erstehen** purchase
sth.

**Kauf·mann** *der; Pl.* **Kaufleute (a)**
(Geschäftsmann) businessman; (Händler) trader
(b) (Besitzer) shopkeeper; (eines
Lebensmittelladens) grocer

**kaufmännisch** *Adj.* commercial;
business *attrib.*

**Kauf-:** ~**preis** *der* purchase price;
~**vertrag** *der* contract of sale; (beim
Hauskauf) title deed

**Kau·gummi** *der od. das;* ~**s,** ~**s** chewing
gum

**Kaukasus** *der;* ~: the Caucasus

**Kaulquappe** *die;* ~**,** ~**n** tadpole

**kaum** *Adv.* hardly; scarcely; ~ **hatte er**
**Platz genommen, als ...:** no sooner had he
sat down than ...

**kausal** *Adj.* (geh., Sprachw.) causal

**Kau·tabak** *der* chewing tobacco

**Kaution** *die;* ~**,** ~**en (a)** (bei Freilassung eines
Gefangenen) bail
(b) (beim Mieten einer Wohnung) deposit

**Kautschuk** *der;* ~**s,** ~**e** rubber

**Kauz** *der;* ~**es,** **Käuze (a)** (Wald~) tawny
owl; (Stein~) little owl
(b) (Sonderling) strange fellow; oddball (coll.)

**Kavalier** /kava'liːɐ̯/ *der;* ~**s,** ~**e** gentleman

**Kavaliers·delikt** *das* trifling offence

**Kavallerie** /kavalə'riː/ *die;* ~**,** ~**n** (Milit.
hist.) cavalry

**Kavallerist** *der;* ~**en,** ~**en** cavalryman

**Kaviar** /'kaːviɐ̯/ *der;* ~**s,** ~**e** caviare

**kcal** *Abk.* = **Kilo[gramm]kalorie** kcal

**keck** ① *Adj.* **(a)** cheeky; saucy (Brit.)
(b) (veralt.: verwegen) bold
(c) (flott) jaunty, pert ⟨*hat etc.*⟩
② *adv.* **(a)** cheekily; saucily (Brit.)
(b) (veralt.: verwegen) boldly
(c) (flott) jauntily

**Keckheit** *die;* ~**,** ~**en (a)** cheek; sauce
(Brit.)
(b) (veralt.: Kühnheit) boldness

**Kegel** *der;* ~**s,** ~ **(a)** cone
(b) (Spielfigur) skittle; (beim Bowling) pin

**Kegel-:** ~**bahn** *die* skittle alley;
~**förmig** *Adj.* conical

**kegeln** ① *itr. V.* play skittles *or* ninepins
② *tr. V.* **eine Partie** ~: play a game of
skittles *or* ninepins; **eine Neun** ~: score a
nine

**Kehle** *die;* ~**,** ~**n** throat

**Kehl·kopf** *der* (Anat.) larynx

**Kehlkopf·krebs** *der* (Med.) cancer of the
larynx

**Kehre** *die;* ~**,** ~**n** sharp bend

**kehren**¹ ① *tr. V.* turn
② *refl. V.* turn

**kehren²** ① *itr. V.* (bes. südd.) sweep; do the
sweeping
② *tr. V.* sweep; (mit einem Handfeger) brush

**Kehricht** *der od. das;* ~**s** (schweiz.: Müll)
refuse; garbage (Amer.)

**Kehr·seite** *die* **(a)** back; (einer Münze,
Medaille) reverse; (scherzh.) (Gesäß) backside
(b) (nachteiliger Aspekt) drawback;
disadvantage

**kehrt|machen** *itr. V.* (ugs.) turn [round
and go] back

**keifen** *itr. V.* (abwertend) nag

**Keil** *der;* ~**[e]s,** ~**e (a)** (zum Spalten) wedge
(b) (zum Festklemmen) chock; (unter einer Tür)
wedge

**keilen** *refl. V.* (ugs.: sich prügeln) fight; scrap

**Keiler** *der;* ~**s,** ~ (Jägerspr.) wild boar

**Keilerei** *die;* ~**,** ~**en** (ugs.) punch-up (coll.);
fight

**Keil-:** ~**riemen** *der* (Technik) V-belt;
~**schrift** *die* cuneiform script

**Keim** *der;* ~**[e]s,** ~**e** (Bot.) shoot; (Biol.)
embryo

**Keim-:** ~**bahn** *die* (Biol.) germ line;
~**drüse** *die* (Zool., Med.) gonad

**keimen** *itr. V.* germinate; (fig.) ⟨*hope*⟩ stir

**keim-, Keim-:** ~**frei** *Adj.* germ-free;
sterile; ~**zelle** *die* nucleus

**kein** *Indefinitpron.* **(a)** no
(b) (ugs.: nicht ganz, nicht einmal) less than

**kein...** *Indefinitpron.* ~**er/**~**e** nobody; no
one; ~**s von beiden** neither [of them]

**keinerlei** *indekl. Adj.* no ... what[so]ever

**keines-:** ~**falls** *Adv.* on no account;
~**wegs** *Adv.* by no means

**kein·mal** *Adv.* not [even] once

**Keks** *der;* ~ *od.* ~**es,** ~ *od.* ~**e** biscuit
(Brit.); cookie (Amer.)

**Kelch** *der;* ~**[e]s,** ~**e** goblet; (Rel.) chalice

**Kelle** *die;* ~**,** ~**n (a)** ladle
(b) (Signalstab) signalling disc
(c) (Maurer~) trowel

**Keller** *der;* ~**s,** ~: cellar; (~geschoss)
basement

**Keller·assel** *die;* ~**,** ~**n** woodlouse

**Kellerei** *die;* ~**,** ~**en** winery; (Kellerräume)
[wine] cellars *pl.*

**Keller-:** ~**geschoss,** *\**~**geschoß** *das*
basement; ~**wohnung** *die* basement flat
(Brit.) *or* (Amer.) apartment

**Kellner** *der;* ~**s,** ~: waiter

**Kellnerin** *die;* ~**,** ~**nen** waitress

**kellnern** *itr. V.* (ugs.) work as a waiter/
waitress

**Kelte** *der;* ~**n,** ~**n** Celt

**Kelter** *die;* ~**,** ~**n** winepress

**keltern** *tr. V.* press ⟨*grapes etc.*⟩

**Keltin** *die;* ~**,** ~**nen** Celt

**keltisch** *Adj.* Celtic

**Kenia** (*das*); ~**s** Kenya

**Keni̱aner** *der; ~s, ~*, **Keni̱anerin** *die;*
*~, ~nen* Kenyan

**ke̱nnen** *unr. tr. V.* know; jmdn./etw. *~*
lernen get to know sb./sth.; jmdn. *~* lernen
( jmdm. erstmals begegnen) meet sb.; jmdn. als
etw. *~* lernen come to know sb. as sth.

**Ke̱nner** *der; ~s, ~*: expert (+ *Gen.* on); (von
Wein, Speisen) connoisseur

**Ke̱nner·blick** *der* expert eye; mit *~*: with
an expert eye

**Ke̱nnerin** *die; ~, ~nen* ▶ KENNER

**Ke̱nn·marke** *die* [police] identification
badge; ≈ [police] warrant card *or* (Amer.) ID
card

**ke̱nntlich** *Adj.:* *~* sein be recognizable (an
by); etw./jmdn. *~* machen mark sth./make
sb. [easily] identifiable

**Ke̱nntnis** *die; ~, ~se* knowledge

***ke̱nnen|lernen* ▶ KENNEN**

**Ke̱nntnisnahme** *die; ~* (Papierdt.) nach *~*
der Akten after giving the documents my/his
*etc.* attention

**ke̱nntnis·reich** *Adj.* well-informed;
knowledgeable

**ke̱nn-, Ke̱nn-:** *~wort das; Pl.* *~wörter*
code word; (Parole) password; code word;
*~zahl die* index; *~zeichen das* (a) sign;
(b) (Erkennungszeichen) badge; (auf einem
Behälter, einer Ware usw.) label; (am Fahrzeug)
registration number; *~zeichnen tr. V.* (a)
mark; label; mark *⟨way⟩*; (b) (charakterisieren)
characterize; *~zeichnend Adj.* typical,
characteristic (für of)

**ke̱ntern** *itr. V. mit sein* capsize

**Kera̱mik** *die; ~, ~en* ceramics *pl.;* pottery;
(Gegenstand) piece of pottery

**Ke̱rbe** *die; ~, ~n* notch

**Ke̱rbel** *der; ~s* chervil

**Ke̱rb·holz** *das:* etwas auf dem *~* haben
(ugs.) have done a job (sl.)

**Ke̱rker** *der; ~s, ~* (hist.) dungeons *pl.;*
(einzelne Zelle) dungeon

**Ke̱rl** *der; ~s, ~e* (nordd., md. auch: *~s*)
(ugs.) fellow (coll.); bloke (Brit. coll.)

**Ke̱rn** *der; ~[e]s, ~e* pip; (von Steinobst) stone;
(von Nüssen usw.) kernel; (Atom*~*) nucleus; (fig.)
der *~* einer Sache the heart of a matter; der
harte *~*: the hard core

**ke̱rn-, Ke̱rn-:** *~energie die* nuclear
energy *no art.;* *~gehäuse das* core;
*~geschäft das* core business; *~gesund*
*Adj.* fit as a fiddle *pred.*

**ke̱rnig** *Adj.* earthy *⟨language⟩;* forceful
*⟨speech⟩;* pithy *⟨saying⟩*

**ke̱rn-, Ke̱rn-:** *~kraft die* nuclear power;
*~kraftwerk das* nuclear power station *or*
plant; *~los Adj.* seedless; *~obst das*
pomaceous fruit; *~physik die* nuclear
physics *sing., no art.;* *~reaktor der*
nuclear reactor; *~seife die* washing soap;
*~spaltung die* (Physik) nuclear fission *no*

*art.;* *~spin·tomographie*
/ˈkɛrnspɪntomografiː/ *die;* *~~* (Med.)
[nuclear] magnetic resonance imaging;
*~waffe die* nuclear weapon; *~zeit die*
core time

**Ke̱rze** *die; ~, ~n* candle

**ke̱rzen-, Ke̱rzen-:** *~gerade,* (ugs.)
*~grade* ① *Adj.* dead straight; ② *adv.* bolt
upright; *~halter der* candle holder;
*~leuchter der* candlestick; *~licht das*
the light of a candle/of candles; bei *~licht* by
candlelight

**ke̱ss, *ke̱ß** ① *Adj.* (a) pert; jaunty *⟨hat,*
*dress, etc.⟩*
(b) (frech) cheeky
② *adv.* (a) (flott) jauntily
(b) (frech) cheekily

**Ke̱ssel** *der; ~s, ~* (a) kettle; (zum Kochen)
pot; (Wasch*~*) copper
(b) (Berg*~*) basin-shaped valley
(c) (Milit.) encircled area

**Ke̱ssel-:** *~stein der* scale; *~treiben*
*das* (Hetzkampagne) witch-hunt

**Ke̱tte** *die; ~, ~n* chain; (Hals*~*) necklace;
(von Ereignissen) string

**ke̱tten** *tr. V.* chain (an + *Akk.* to)

**Ke̱tten-:** *~hund der* guard dog (*kept on a*
*chain*); *~rauchen das;* *~~s* chain-
smoking *no art.;* *~raucher der,*
*~raucherin die* chain-smoker; *~säge*
*die* chain saw; *~schaltung die* derailleur
gears *pl.*

**Ke̱tzer** *der; ~s, ~* (auch fig.) heretic

**Ketzere̱i** *die; ~, ~en* (auch fig.) heresy

**Ke̱tzerin** *die; ~, ~nen* ▶ KETZER

**ke̱uchen** *itr. V.* gasp for breath

**Ke̱uch·husten** *der* whooping cough *no*
*art.*

**Ke̱ule** *die; ~, ~n* (a) club
(b) (Kochk.) leg

**ke̱usch** ① *Adj.* chaste
② *adv.* *~* leben lead a chaste life

**Ke̱uschheit** *die; ~*: chastity

**Kfz** *Abk.* = **Kraftfahrzeug**

**kg** *Abk.* = **Kilogramm** kg

**KG** *Abk.* = **Kommanditgesellschaft**

**ki̱chern** *itr. V.* giggle

**ki̱cken** (ugs.) ① *itr. V.* play football
② *tr. V.* kick

**ki̱dnappen** /ˈkɪtnɛpn̩/ *tr. V.* kidnap

**Ki̱dnapper** *der; ~s, ~*, **Ki̱dnapperin**
*die; ~, ~nen* kidnapper

**Ki̱ebitz** *der; ~es, ~e* lapwing; peewit

**Ki̱efer¹** *der; ~s, ~*: jaw; (~knochen) jawbone

**Ki̱efer²** *die; ~, ~n* pine[tree]

**Ki̱efer·höhle** *die* (Anat.) maxillary sinus

**Ki̱efern·holz** *das* pine [wood]

**Ki̱el** *der; ~[e]s, ~e* keel

**ki̱el·holen** *tr. V.* (Seemannsspr.) keelhaul
*⟨person⟩*

**Ki̱el·wasser** *das* wake

---

*old spelling - see note on page xiv

**Kieme** *die;* ~, ~n gill

**Kien** *der;* ~[e]s resinous wood

**Kies** *der;* ~es, ~e gravel; (auf dem Strand) shingle

**Kiesel** *der;* ~s, ~: pebble

**Kiesel·stein** *der* pebble

**Kies-:** ~**grube** *die* gravel pit; ~**weg** *der* gravel path

**kiffen** *itr. V.* (ugs.) smoke pot (sl.) *or* grass (sl.)

**Kiffer** *der;* ~s, ~, **Kifferin** *die;* ~, ~nen (ugs.) pothead (sl.)

**kikeriki** /kikəri'ki:/ *Interj.* (Kinderspr.) cock-a-doodle-doo

**Killer** *der;* ~s, ~, **Killerin** *die;* ~, ~nen (salopp) killer; (gegen Bezahlung) hit man

**Kilo** *das;* ~s, ~[s] kilo

**Kilo·gramm** *das* kilogram

**Kilometer** *der;* ~s, ~: kilometre

**kilometer-, Kilometer-:** ~**lang** [1] *Adj.* miles long *pred.;* [2] *adv.* for miles [and miles]; ~**stand** *der* mileage reading

**Kilowatt·stunde** *die* (Physik; bes. Elektrot.) kilowatt-hour

**Kimme** *die;* ~, ~n sighting notch

**Kimono** *der;* ~s, ~s kimono

**Kind** *das;* ~[e]s, ~er (a) child; **ein** ~ **erwarten** be expecting (b) [~er,] ~er! my goodness!

**Kinder-:** ~**arzt** *der,* ~**ärztin** *die* paediatrician; ~**betreuung** *die* child care; ~**bett** *das* cot; (für größeres Kind) child's bed; ~**dorf** *das* children's village

**Kinderei** *die;* ~, ~en childishness *no indef. art., no pl.*

**kinder-, Kinder-:** ~**erziehung** *die* bringing up of children; ~**feindlich** *Adj.* hostile to children *pred.;* ~**freundlich** *Adj.* fond of children *pred.;* ⟨town, resort⟩ which caters for children; ⟨planning, policy⟩ which caters for the needs of children; ~**garten** *der* nursery school; ~**gärtnerin** *die* nusery-school teacher; ~**geld** *das* child benefit; ~**heilkunde** *die* paediatrics *sing., no art.;* ~**hort** *der* day home for schoolchildren; ~**krankheit** *die* (a) (Infektionskrankheit) children's disease *or* illness; (b) *Pl.* (fig.: Anfangsschwierigkeiten) teething troubles; ~**krippe** *die* crèche; day nursery; ~**lähmung** *die* poliomyelitis; ~**leicht** (ugs.) *Adj.* childishly simple; dead easy; **das ist** ~**leicht** it's kid's stuff (coll.); it's child's play; ~**lieb** *Adj.* fond of children *pred.;* ~**los** *Adj.* childless; ~**reich** *Adj.* with many children *postpos., not pred.;* ~**sterblichkeit** *die* child mortality; ~**stube** *die* **eine gute/schlechte** ~**stube gehabt haben** have been well/badly brought up; ~**tages·heim** *das,* ~**tages·stätte** *die* day nursery; crèche ~**teller** *der* (auf der Speisekarte) children's menu; ~**wagen** *der* pram (Brit.); baby carriage (Amer.); (Sportwagen) pushchair (Brit.); stroller (Amer.)

**Kindes-:** ~**alter** *das* childhood; ~**misshandlung, *****~mißhandlung** *die* (Rechtsw.) child abuse

**Kindheit** *die;* ~: childhood

**kindisch** [1] *Adj.* childish, infantile; naïve ⟨ideas⟩ [2] *adv.* childishly

**kindlich** [1] *Adj.* childlike [2] *adv.* ⟨behave⟩ in a childlike way

**Kinkerlitzchen** *Pl.* (ugs.) trifles

**Kinn** *das;* ~[e]s, ~e chin

**Kinn-:** ~**haken** *der* hook to the chin; ~**lade** *die* jaw

**Kino** *das;* ~s, ~s cinema (Brit.); movie theater (Amer.)

**Kino-:** ~**gänger** *der;* ~~s, ~~, ~**gängerin** *die;* ~~, ~~nen cinema-goer (Brit.); movie-goer (Amer.); ~**karte** *die* cinema ticket (Brit.); movie ticket (Amer.)

**Kiosk** *der;* ~[e]s, ~e kiosk

**Kippe¹** *die;* ~, ~n (ugs.) cigarette end; dog-end (coll.)

**Kippe²** *die;* ~, ~n (a) (Bergmannsspr.) slag heap (b) **etw. steht auf der** ~ (fig.) it's touch and go with sth.; (etw. ist noch nicht entschieden) sth. hangs in the balance

**kippen** [1] *tr. V.* (a) tip [up] (b) (ausschütten) tip [out] (c) (ugs.: trinken) knock back (coll.); **einen** ~: have a quick one (coll.) *or* a drink [2] *itr. V.; mit sein* tip over; ⟨top-heavy object⟩ topple over; ⟨person⟩ topple; ⟨boat⟩ overturn; ⟨car⟩ roll over

**Kipp-:** ~**fenster** *das* horizontally pivoted window; ~**schalter** *der* tumbler switch

**Kirche** *die;* ~, ~n church; **in die** ~ **gehen** go to church

**Kirchen-:** ~**fest** *das* church festival; ~**lied** *das* hymn; ~**musik** *die* church music; ~**steuer** *die* church tax

**Kirch-:** ~**gänger** *der;* ~~s, ~~, ~**gängerin** *die;* ~~, ~~nen churchgoer; ~**hof** *der* (veralt.) churchyard

**kirchlich** [1] *Adj.* ecclesiastical; church *attrib.* ⟨wedding, funeral⟩ [2] *adv.* ~ **getraut/begraben werden** have a church wedding/funeral

**Kirch-:** ~**turm** *der* [church] steeple; (ohne Turmspitze) church tower; ~**weih** *die;* ~~, ~~en fair (held on the anniversary of the consecration of a church)

**Kirmes** *die;* ~, **Kirmessen** (bes. md., niederd.) ▶ KIRCHWEIH

**Kirsch·baum** *der* cherry [tree]

**Kirsche** *die;* ~, ~n cherry

**Kirsch-:** ~**torte** *die* cherry gateau; (mit Tortenboden) cherry flan; ~**wasser** *das; Pl.* ~**wässer** kirsch

**Kissen** *das;* ~s, ~: cushion; (Kopf~) pillow

**k**

**Kiste** *die;* ∼, ∼n box; (Truhe) chest; (Latten∼) crate

**Kita** *die;* ∼, ∼s day nursery; crèche

**Kitsch** *der;* ∼[e]s kitsch

**kitschig** *Adj.* kitschy

**Kitt** *der;* ∼[e]s, ∼e putty; (für Porzellan, Kacheln usw.) cement

**Kittchen** *das;* ∼s, ∼ (ugs.) clink (sl.)

**Kittel** *der;* ∼s, ∼ (a) overall; (eines Arztes usw.) white coat
(b) (hemdartige Bluse) smock

**kitten** *tr. V.* cement [together]

**Kitz** *das;* ∼es, ∼e (Reh∼) fawn; (Ziegen∼, Gämsen∼) kid

**kitzeln** *tr., itr. V.* tickle

**kitzlig** *Adj.* (auch fig.) ticklish

**KKW** *Abk.* = **Kernkraftwerk**

**Klacks** *der;* ∼es, ∼e (ugs.) dollop (coll.); (∼ Senf) dab; **etw. ist nur ein ∼ [für jmdn.]** (fig.) sth. is no trouble at all [for sb.]

**Kladde** *die;* ∼, ∼n rough book

**Kladderadatsch** *der;* ∼[e]s, ∼e (ugs.) unholy mess (coll.)

**klaffen** *itr. V.* yawn; ⟨hole, wound⟩ gape

**kläffen** *itr. V.* (abwertend) yap

**Kläffer** *der;* ∼s, ∼ (ugs. abwertend) yapping dog; yapper

**Klafter** *der od. das;* ∼s, ∼ (Raummaß für Holz) cord

**Klage** *die;* ∼, ∼n (a) (Äußerung der Trauer) lament
(b) (Beschwerde) complaint
(c) (Rechtsw.) action; (im Strafrecht) charge

**klagen** ① *itr. V.* (a) (geh.: jammern) wail; (stöhnend) moan
(b) (sich beschweren) complain (**über** + *Akk.* about)
(c) (bei Gericht) take legal action
② *tr. V.* **jmdm. sein Leid/seine Not ∼:** pour out one's sorrows *pl.*/troubles *pl.*

**Kläger** *der;* ∼s, ∼, **Klägerin** *die;* ∼, ∼nen (im Zivilrecht) plaintiff; (im Strafrecht) prosecuting party; (bei einer Scheidung) petitioner

**kläglich** *Adj.* (a) (Mitleid erregend) pitiful
(b) (minderwertig) pathetic
(c) (erbärmlich) despicable ⟨behaviour, role, compromise⟩; pathetic ⟨result, defeat⟩

**Klamauk** *der;* ∼s (ugs. abwertend) fuss; (Lärm, Krach) row (coll.)

**klamm** *Adj.* (a) (feucht) cold and damp
(b) (steif) numb

**Klammer** *die;* ∼, ∼n (Wäsche∼) peg; (Haar∼) [hair]grip; (Zahn∼) brace; (Büro∼) paper clip; (Heft∼) staple; (Schriftzeichen) bracket

**klammern** ① *refl. V.* **sich an jmdn./etw. ∼** (auch fig.) cling to sb./sth.
② *tr. V.* (a) **eine Wunde ∼:** close a wound with a clip/clips
(b) (mit einer Büroklammer) clip; (mit einer Heftmaschine) staple; (mit Wäscheklammern) peg

**Klamotten** *Pl.* (salopp) (Kleidung) gear *sing.* (coll.); (Kram) stuff *sing.*

**Klampfe** *die;* ∼, ∼n (volkst.: Gitarre) guitar

**klang** *1. u. 3. Pers. Sg. Prät. v.* KLINGEN

**Klang** *der;* ∼[e]s, **Klänge** (a) (Ton) sound
(b) (∼farbe) tone

**Klapp·bett** *das* folding bed

**Klappe** *die;* ∼, ∼n (a) [hinged] lid; (am LKW) tailgate; (seitlich) side gate; (am Kombiwagen) back; (am Ofen) [drop-]door
(b) (an Musikinstrumenten) key; (an einer Trompete) valve
(c) (Filmjargon) clapperboard
(d) (salopp: Mund) trap (sl.)

**klappen** ① *tr. V.* **nach oben/unten ∼:** turn up/down ⟨collar, hat brim⟩; lift up/put down ⟨lid⟩; **nach vorne/hinten ∼:** tilt forward/back ⟨seat⟩
② *itr. V.* (a) ⟨door, shutter⟩ bang
(b) (stoßen) bang
(c) (ugs.: gelingen) work out all right

**klapperig** *Adj.* rickety

**klappern** *itr. V.* (a) rattle
(b) (ein Klappern erzeugen) make a clatter

**Klapper·schlange** *die* rattlesnake

**Klapp·fahrrad** *das* folding bicycle

**klapprig** *Adj.* rickety

**Klapp-:** ∼**sitz** *der* tip-up seat; ∼**stuhl** *der* folding chair

**Klaps** *der;* ∼es, ∼e (ugs.) smack; slap

**Klaps·mühle** *die* (salopp) loony bin (sl.)

**klar** ① *Adj.* (a) clear; straight ⟨question, answer⟩; **sich** (*Dat.*) **über etw.** (*Akk.*) ∼ **werden** realize sth.; **jmdm. ∼ werden** become clear to sb.; **sich** (*Dat.*) **über etw.** (*Akk.*) **im Klaren sein** realize sth.; **etw. ∼ machen** (ugs.) make sth. clear
(b) (fertig) ready
② *adv.* clearly; ∼ **sehen** understand the matter

**Klär·anlage** *die* sewage treatment plant

**Klare** *der;* ∼n, ∼n schnapps

**klären** ① *tr. V.* settle ⟨question, issue, matter⟩; clarify ⟨situation⟩; clear up ⟨case, affair, misunderstanding⟩
(b) (reinigen) purify; treat ⟨effluent, sewage⟩
② *refl. V.* (a) ⟨situation⟩ become clear; ⟨question, issue, matter⟩ be settled
(b) (rein werden) ⟨liquid, sky⟩ clear; ⟨weather⟩ clear [up]

**klar|gehen** *unr. itr. V.; mit sein* (ugs.) go OK (coll.)

**Klarheit** *die;* ∼: clarity; **sich** (*Dat.*) **über etw.** (*Akk.*) ∼ **verschaffen** clarify sth.

**Klarinette** *die;* ∼, ∼n clarinet

**klar-:** ∼**machen** *tr. V.* (Seemannsspr.) get ready; *∼*∼**|sehen** ▸ KLAR 2

**klaro** *Adj., Interj.* (ugs.) of course; it goes without saying; ∼, **dass** ...: it goes without saying that ...

---

**Klarsicht·folie** die transparent film
**klar|stellen** tr. V. clear up; clarify
**Klar·text** der (auch DV) clear text; **im ~text** (fig.) in plain language
**Klärung** die; ~, ~en (a) clarification
(b) (Reinigung) purification; (von Abwässern) treatment
***klar|werden** ▶ KLAR 1A
**Klär·werk** das sewage works sing. or pl.
**klasse** (ugs.) ⓵ indekl. Adj. great (coll.)
⓶ adv. marvellously
**Klasse** die; ~, ~n (a) (Schul~) class; (Raum) classroom; (Stufe) year; grade (Amer.)
(b) (Sport) league; (Boxen) division
(c) (Fahrzeug~, Boots~, Qualitätsstufe) class; **das ist einsame** od. **ganz große ~!** (ugs.) that's [just] great (coll.) or marvellous!
**klassen-, Klassen-:** ~**arbeit** die (Schulw.) [written] class test; ~**buch** das (Schulw.) book recording details of pupils' attendance, behaviour, and of topics covered in each lesson; ≈ [class] register; ~**fahrt** die (Schulw.) class outing; ~**gesellschaft** die (Soziol.) class society; ~**kampf** der (marx.) class struggle; ~**lehrer** der, ~**lehrerin** die (Schulw.) class teacher; ~**los** Adj. (Soziol.) classless; ~**sprecher** der, ~**sprecherin** die (Schulw.) class spokesman; ~**treffen** das (Schulw.) class reunion; ~**ziel** das (Schulw.) required standard (for pupils in a particular class); ~**zimmer** das (Schulw.) classroom
**klassifizieren** tr. V. classify (als as)
**Klassifizierung** die; ~, ~en classification
**Klassik** die; ~ (a) (Antike) classical antiquity no art.;
(b) (Zeit kultureller Höchstleistung) classical period
**Klassiker** der; ~s, ~, **Klassikerin** die; ~, ~nen classical writer/composer
**klassisch** Adj. classical; (vollendet, zeitlos; auch iron.) classic
**Klassizismus** der; ~: classicism
**Klatsch** der; ~[e]s, ~e (a) (ugs. abwertend) gossip
(b) (Geräusch) smack
**Klatsch·base** die (ugs. abwertend) gossip
**klatschen** itr. V. (a) auch mit sein ⟨waves, wet sails⟩ slap
(b) (mit den Händen; applaudieren) clap
(c) (schlagen) slap
(d) (ugs. abwertend: reden) gossip (über + Akk. about)
**klatschhaft** Adj. gossipy; fond of gossip pred.
**klatsch-, Klatsch-:** ~**mohn** der corn poppy; ~**nass**, *~**naß** Adj. (ugs.) sopping wet; dripping wet ⟨hair⟩; ~**spalte** die (ugs. abwertend) gossip column
**Klaue** die; ~, ~n (a) claw; (von Raubvögeln) talon; (salopp: Hand) mitt (coll.)
(b) (salopp abwertend: Schrift) scrawl

**klauen** (ugs.) ⓵ tr. V. pinch (coll.); **jmdm. etw. ~:** pinch sth. from sb.
⓶ itr. V. pinch (coll.) things
**Klause** die; ~, ~n hermitage; (Klosterzelle) cell
**Klausel** die; ~, ~n clause; (Bedingung) condition; (Vorbehalt) proviso
**Klausur** die; ~, ~en [examination] paper; (Examen) examination; **eine ~ schreiben** take a[n examination] paper/an examination
**Klausur-:** ~**arbeit** die [examination] paper; ~**tagung** die private meeting
**Klavier** /kla'viːɐ̯/ das; ~s, ~e piano
**Klebe·folie** die adhesive film
**kleben** ⓵ itr. V. (a) stick (an + Dat. to)
(b) (ugs.: klebrig sein) be sticky (von, vor + Dat. with)
⓶ tr. V. (a) (befestigen) stick; (mit Klebstoff) glue; **jmdm. eine ~** (salopp) belt sb. one (coll.)
(b) (reparieren) stick or glue ⟨vase etc.⟩ back together
**Kleber** der; ~s, ~: adhesive; glue
**klebrig** Adj. sticky
**Kleb-:** ~**stoff** der adhesive; glue; ~**streifen** der adhesive or sticky tape
**kleckern** (ugs.) itr. V. make a mess
**Klecks** der; ~es, ~e (a) stain; (nicht aufgesogen) blob; (Tintenfleck) [ink] blot
(b) (ugs.: kleine Menge) spot; (von Senf, Mayonnaise) dab
**klecksen** itr. V. (a) make a stain/stains; (mit Tinte) make a blot/blots; ⟨pen⟩ blot
(b) (ugs. abwertend: schlecht malen) daub
**Klee** der; ~s clover
**Klee·blatt** das cloverleaf
**Kleid** das; ~es, ~er (a) dress
(b) Pl. (Kleidung) clothes
**kleiden** ⓵ refl. V. dress
⓶ tr. V. (a) dress
(b) ⟨jmdm. stehen⟩ suit
**Kleider-:** ~**bügel** der clothes hanger; coat hanger; ~**bürste** die clothes brush; ~**haken** der coat hook; ~**schrank** der wardrobe; ~**spende** die donation of [second-hand] clothes or clothing; ~**ständer** der coat stand
**kleidsam** Adj. becoming
**Kleidung** die; ~: clothes pl.
**Kleidungs·stück** das garment
**klein** ⓵ Adj. (a) little; small; **er ist ~er als ich** he is shorter than me; **etw. ~ schneiden** cut sth. into small pieces; **Zwiebeln ~ schneiden/hacken** chop up onions [small]
(b) (jung) little; **von ~ auf** from an early age
(c) (von kurzer Dauer) little, short ⟨while⟩; short ⟨walk, break, holiday⟩; brief ⟨moment⟩
(d) (von geringer Menge) small; low ⟨price⟩; ~**es Geld haben** have some [small] change
(e) (von geringem Ausmaß) small ⟨party, gift⟩; scant ⟨attention⟩; slight ⟨cold, indisposition, mistake, irregularity⟩; minor ⟨event, error⟩ ⋯⋗

**k**

**(f)** (unbedeutend) lowly ⟨*employee*⟩; minor ⟨*official*⟩; ~ **anfangen** (ugs.) start off in a small way

**2** *adv.* **die Heizung ~/~er einstellen** turn the heating down low/lower; **ein Wort ~ schreiben** write a word with a small initial letter

**klein-, Klein-: ~aktionär** *der,* **~aktionärin** *die* (Wirtsch.) small shareholder; **~anzeige** *die* (Zeitungsw.) small *or* classified advertisement; **~asien** (*das*) Asia Minor; **~buchstabe** *der* small letter; **~bürger** *der,* **~bürgerin** *die* lower middle-class person; (abwertend: Spießbürger) petit bourgeois; **~bürgerlich** *Adj.* **(a)** (das Kleinbürgertum betreffend) lower middle-class; **(b)** (abwertend: spießbürgerlich) petit bourgeois

**Kleine**[1] *der; adj. Dekl.* **(a)** (kleiner Junge) little boy

**(b)** (ugs. Anrede) little man

**Kleine**[2] *die; adj. Dekl.* **(a)** (kleines Mädchen) little girl

**(b)** (ugs. Anrede) love; (abwertend) little madam

**klein-, Klein-: ~familie** *die* (Soziol.) nuclear family; **~geld** *das* [small] change; **~gläubig** *Adj.* sceptical

**Kleinigkeit** *die; ~, ~en* small thing; (Einzelheit) [small] detail; **ich habe noch eine ~ zu erledigen** I still have a small matter to attend to; **eine ~ essen** have a [small] bite to eat; **eine ~ für jmdn. sein** be no trouble for sb.

**klein-, Klein-: ~kind** *das* small child; **~kram** *der* (ugs.) odds and ends *pl.*; (unbedeutende Dinge) trivial matters *pl.*; **~kredit** *der* (Bankw.) personal loan (*repayable within two years*); **~|kriegen** *tr. V.* (ugs.) **(a)** (zerkleinern) crush [to pieces]; **(b)** (zerstören) smash; break; **(c)** (aufbrauchen) get through; **(d)** jmdn. **~kriegen** get sb. down (coll.); (durch Drohungen) intimidate sb.; (gefügig machen) bring sb. into line; **~kunst** *die* cabaret; **~laut** **1** *Adj.* subdued; (verlegen) sheepish; **2** *adv.* in a subdued fashion; (verlegen) sheepishly

**kleinlich** (abwertend) **1** *Adj.* pernickety; (ohne Großzügigkeit) mean; (engstirnig) small-minded; petty

**2** *adv.* meticulously

**Kleinod** *das; ~[e]s, ~e od. ~ien* (geh.) **(a)** (Schmuckstück) piece of jewellery; (Edelstein) jewel

**(b)** (Kostbarkeit) gem

**klein-, Klein-: ~|rechnen** *tr. V.* undercalculate; **\*~|schneiden** ▶ KLEIN 1A; **~stadt** *die* small town; **~städter** *der,* **~städterin** *die* small-town dweller

**Kleinste** *der/die/das; adj. Dekl.* youngest boy/girl/child

**klein|stellen** *tr. V.* turn down [low]

**Klein·wagen** *der* small car

**Kleister** *der; ~s, ~:* paste

**Klementine** *die; ~, ~n* clementine

**Klemme** *die; ~, ~n* clip; **in der ~ sein** *od.* **sitzen** (ugs.) be in a fix (coll.)

**klemmen** **1** *tr. V.* **(a)** (befestigen) tuck; stick (coll.)

**(b)** (quetschen) **sich** (*Dat.*) **den Fuß/die Hand ~:** get one's foot/hand caught *or* trapped

**2** *refl. V.* **sich hinter etw.** (*Akk.*) **~** (fig. ugs.) put some hard work into sth.

**3** *itr. V.* ⟨*door, drawer, etc.*⟩ stick

**Klempner** *der; ~s, ~,* **Klempnerin** *die; ~, ~nen* tinsmith; (Installateur[in]) plumber

**Kleptomanie** *die; ~* (Psych.) kleptomania *no art.*

**klerikal** *Adj.* (auch abwertend) clerical; church ⟨*property*⟩

**Klerus** *der; ~:* clergy

**Klette** *die; ~, ~n* bur; (Pflanze) burdock

**klettern** *itr. V.; mit sein* (auch fig.) climb; **auf einen Baum ~:** climb a tree

**Kletter·pflanze** *die* creeper; (Bot.) climbing plant; climber

**Klett·verschluss, \*Klett·verschluß** *der* Velcro ® fastening

**klicken** *itr. V.* click

**Klient** *der; ~en, ~en,* **Klientin** *die; ~, ~nen* client

**Klima** *das; ~s, ~s od.* **Klimate** climate

**Klima·anlage** *die* air conditioning *no indef. art.*

**klimatisch** *Adj.* climatic

**klimatisieren** *tr. V.* air-condition

**Klima·wechsel** *der* change of climate

**Klimm·zug** *der* (Turnen) pull-up

**klimpern** **1** *itr. V.* jingle

**2** *tr. V.* (ugs. abwertend) plunk out ⟨*tune etc.*⟩

**Klinge** *die; ~, ~n* blade

**Klingel** *die; ~, ~n* bell

**Klingel-: ~beutel** *der* offertory bag; collection bag; **~knopf** *der* bell push

**klingeln** *itr. V.* ring; ⟨*alarm clock*⟩ go off; **es klingelt** (an der Tür) there is a ring at the door; (Telefon) the telephone is ringing

**klingen** *unr. V.* sound; **die Glocken klangen** the bells were ringing

**Klinik** *die; ~, ~en* hospital; (spezialisiert) clinic

**Klinke** *die; ~, ~n* door handle

**Klinker** *der; ~s, ~:* [Dutch] clinker

**klipp** *Adv.* **~ und klar** (ugs.) quite plainly

**Klippe** *die; ~, ~n* rock

**klirren** *itr. V.* clink; ⟨*weapons in fight*⟩ clash; ⟨*window pane*⟩ rattle; ⟨*chains, spurs*⟩ rattle; ⟨*harness*⟩ jingle

**Klischee** *das; ~s, ~s* cliché

**klitsch·nass, \*klitsch·naß** *Adj.* (ugs.) sopping wet; (tropfnass) dripping wet

**klitze·klein** *Adj.* (ugs.) teeny[-weeny] (coll.)

**Klo** *das;* ~s, ~s (ugs.) loo (Brit. coll.); john (Amer. coll.)

**Kloake** *die;* ~, ~n cesspit; (Kanal) sewer

**klobig** *Adj.* heavy and clumsy[-looking] ⟨*shoes, furniture*⟩; bulky ⟨*figure*⟩; (plump) clumsy

**Klon** *der;* ~s, ~e (Biol.) clone

**klonen** *tr. V.* clone

**Klo·papier** *das* (ugs.) loo paper (Brit. coll.); toilet paper

**klopfen** 1 *itr. V.* (a) (schlagen) knock
(b) (pulsieren) ⟨*heart*⟩ beat; ⟨*pulse*⟩ throb
2 *tr. V.* beat ⟨*carpet*⟩

**Klöppel** *der;* ~s, ~ (Glocken~) clapper

**klöppeln** *tr., itr. V.* [etw.] ~: make [sth. in] pillow lace

**Klops** *der;* ~es, ~e (nordostd.) meat ball

**Klosett** *das;* ~s, ~s *od.* ~e lavatory

**Kloß** *der;* ~es, Klöße dumpling; (Fleisch~) meat ball

**Kloster** *das;* ~s, Klöster (Mönchs~) monastery; (Nonnen~) convent

**Klotz** *der;* ~es, Klötze block [of wood]; (Stück eines Baumstamms) log

**Klub** *der;* ~s, ~s club

**Klub·sessel** *der* club chair

**Kluft**[1] *die;* ~, ~en (ugs.) gear (coll.); (Uniform) garb

**Kluft**[2] *die;* ~, Klüfte (veralt.) (Spalte) cleft; (im Gletscher) crevasse; (Abgrund) chasm; (fig.) gulf

**klug**; klüger, klügst... *Adj.* clever; bright ⟨*child, pupil*⟩; intelligent ⟨*eyes*⟩; (vernünftig) wise; sound ⟨*advice*⟩; (geschickt) shrewd ⟨*politician, negotiator, question*⟩; astute ⟨*businessman*⟩

**Klugheit** *die;* ~ ▶ KLUG: cleverness; brightness; intelligence; wisdom; soundness; shrewdness; astuteness

**klumpen** *itr. V.* go lumpy

**Klumpen** *der;* ~s, ~: lump; ein ~ Gold a gold nugget

**km** *Abk.* = **Kilometer** km.

**knabbern** 1 *tr. V.* nibble
2 *itr. V.* an etw. (*Dat.*) ~: nibble [at] sth.

**Knabe** *der;* ~n, ~n (geh. veralt./südd., österr., schweiz.) boy; (ugs.: Bursche) chap (coll.)

**knabenhaft** 1 *Adj.* boyish
2 *adv.* boyishly

**Knäcke·brot** *das* crispbread; (Scheibe) slice of crispbread

**knacken** 1 *itr. V.* (a) ⟨*bed, floor, etc.*⟩ creak
(b) mit sein (ugs.: zerbrechen) snap; ⟨*window*⟩ crack
2 *tr. V.* (a) crack ⟨*nut, shell*⟩
(b) (salopp: aufbrechen) crack ⟨*safe*⟩ [open]; break into ⟨*car, bank, etc.*⟩

**knackig** *Adj.* (a) crisp
(b) (ugs.: attraktiv) delectable

**Knacks** *der;* ~es, ~e (ugs.) crack; (fig.: Defekt) einen ~ bekommen ⟨*person*⟩ have a breakdown; ⟨*health*⟩ suffer

**Knall** *der;* ~[e]s, ~e bang

**knallen** 1 *itr. V.* (a) ⟨*shot*⟩ ring out; ⟨*firework*⟩ go bang; ⟨*cork*⟩ pop; ⟨*door*⟩ slam; ⟨*whip, rifle*⟩ crack; mit der Tür ~: slam the door
(b) (ugs.: schießen) shoot, fire (auf + *Akk.* at)
(c) (Ballspiele ugs.) aufs Tor ~: belt the ball/puck at the goal (coll.)
2 *tr. V.* (a) (ugs.) slam down; (werfen) sling (coll.)
(b) (ugs.: schlagen) jmdm. eine ~ (salopp) belt sb. one (coll.)

**knall-:** ~hart (ugs.) 1 *Adj.* very tough ⟨*demands, measures, etc.*⟩; ⟨*person*⟩ as hard as nails; 2 *adv.* brutally; gegen etw. ~hart vorgehen take very tough action against sth.; ~rot *Adj.* bright *or* vivid red; sie wurde ~rot she turned as red as a beetroot

**knapp** 1 *Adj.* (a) meagre; narrow ⟨*victory, lead*⟩; narrow, bare ⟨*majority*⟩; die Vorräte wurden ~: supplies ran short; vor einer ~en Stunde just under an hour ago
(b) (eng) tight-fitting ⟨*garment*⟩; (zu eng) tight ⟨*garment*⟩
(c) (kurz) terse ⟨*reply, greeting*⟩; succinct ⟨*description, account, report*⟩
2 *adv.* (a) ~ bemessen sein be meagre, ⟨*time*⟩ be limited; ~ gewinnen/verlieren win/lose narrowly; er ist ~ fünfzig he is just this side of fifty
(b) (eng) ~ sitzen fit tightly; (zu eng) be a tight fit
(c) (kurz) ⟨*reply*⟩ tersely; ⟨*describe, summarize*⟩ succinctly

**Knappheit** *die;* ~ (a) (Mangel) shortage (an + *Dat.* of)
(b) (Kürze) (einer Antwort, eines Grußes) terseness; (einer Beschreibung, eines Berichts) succinctness

**Knarre** *die;* ~, ~n (salopp: Gewehr) shooting iron (coll.)

**knarren** *itr. V.* creak

**Knast** *der;* ~[e]s, Knäste *od.* ~e (ugs.) (a) (Strafe) bird (sl.); time
(b) (Gefängnis) clink (sl.); prison

**Knatsch** *der;* ~[e]s (ugs.: Ärger) trouble

**knattern** *itr. V.* clatter; ⟨*sail*⟩ flap; ⟨*radio*⟩ crackle

**Knäuel** *der od. das;* ~s, ~ ball; (wirres ~) tangle

**Knauf** *der;* ~[e]s, Knäufe knob; (eines Schwertes, Dolches) pommel

**knauserig** *Adj.* (ugs. abwertend) stingy; tight-fisted

**knausern** *itr. V.* (ugs. abwertend) be stingy; skimp

**knautschen** (ugs.) 1 *tr. V.* crumple; crease ⟨*dress*⟩
2 *itr. V.* ⟨*dress, material*⟩ crease

**Knebel** *der;* ~s, ~ (a) gag
(b) (Griff) toggle

**knebeln** *tr. V.* gag

**Knecht** *der;* ~[e]s, ~e farm labourer

**knẹchten** *tr. V.* (geh.) reduce to slavery; enslave; (unterdrücken) oppress

**Knẹchtschaft** *die;* ∼, ∼en (geh.) bondage; slavery

**kneifen** ① *unr. tr., itr. V.* pinch
② *unr. itr. V.* (a) ⟨clothes⟩ be too tight
(b) (ugs.: sich drücken) chicken (coll.) out (**vor** + *Dat.* of)

**Kneif·zange** *die* pincers *pl.*

**Kneipe** *die;* ∼, ∼n (ugs.) pub (Brit. coll.); bar (Amer.)

**Kneipen·tour** *die* (ugs.) pub crawl

**kneippen** *itr. V.* (ugs.) take a Kneipp cure

**Kneipp·kur** *die* Kneipp cure

**kneten** *tr. V.* (a) (bearbeiten) knead ⟨dough, muscles⟩; work ⟨clay⟩
(b) (formen) model ⟨figure⟩

**Knẹt·masse** *die* Plasticine ®

**Knịck** *der;* ∼[e]s, ∼e sharp bend; (Falz) crease

**knịcken** ① *tr. V.* (a) (brechen) snap
(b) (falten) crease ⟨page, paper, etc.⟩
② *itr. V.; mit sein* snap

**knịck[e]rig** *Adj.* (ugs. abwertend) stingy

**Knịck[e]rigkeit** *die;* ∼ (ugs. abwertend) stinginess

**Knịcks** *der;* ∼es, ∼e curtsy

**knịcksen** *itr. V.* curtsy (**vor** + *Dat.* to)

**Knie** *das;* ∼s, ∼ /'kni:(ə)/ (a) knee
(b) (Biegung) sharp bend

**knie-, Knie-:** ∼**beuge** *die* knee bend; ∼**bund·hose** *die* knee breeches *pl.;* ∼**fall** *der:* einen ∼fall tun *od.* machen (auch fig.) go down on one's knees (**vor** + *Dat.* before); ∼**kehle** *die* hollow of the knee

**knien** /'kni:(ə)n/ ① *itr. V.* kneel
② *refl. V.* kneel [down]

**Knie-:** ∼**scheibe** *die* kneecap; ∼**strumpf** *der* knee-length sock

**Kniff** *der;* ∼[e]s, ∼e (a) pinch
(b) (Falte) crease
(c) (Kunstgriff) trick

**knịpsen** *tr. V.* (a) (entwerten) clip; punch
(b) (fotografieren) take a snap[shot] of

**Knịrps** *der;* ∼es, ∼e (a) ⟨Ⓦ Taschenschirm⟩ telescopic umbrella
(b) (ugs.: Junge) nipper (coll.)

**knịrschen** *itr. V.* crunch; **mit den Zähnen** ∼: grind one's teeth

**knịstern** *itr. V.* rustle; ⟨wood, fire⟩ crackle

**knịttern** *tr., itr. V.* crease; crumple

**knobeln** *itr. V.* (mit Würfeln) play dice

**Knob·lauch** *der* garlic

**Knoblauch·zehe** *die* clove of garlic

**Knọ̈chel** *der;* ∼s, ∼: ankle; (am Finger) knuckle

**Knọchen** *der;* ∼s, ∼: bone

**knọchen-, Knọchen-:** ∼**bau** *der* bone structure; ∼**bruch** *der* fracture; ∼**hart** *Adj.* (ugs.) rock-hard; ∼**mark** *das* bone marrow

**knọchig** *Adj.* bony

**Knọ̈del** *der;* ∼s, ∼ (bes. südd., österr.) dumpling

**Knọ̈llchen** *das;* ∼s, ∼ (ugs.: Strafzettel) [parking] ticket

**Knọlle** *die;* ∼, ∼n tuber

**Knọpf** *der;* ∼[e]s, Knöpfe button; (Knauf) knob

**knọ̈pfen** *tr. V.* button [up]

**Knọpf·loch** *das* buttonhole

**Knọrpel** *der;* ∼s, ∼ (Anat.) cartilage; (im Steak o. Ä.) gristle

**knọrrig** *Adj.* gnarled

**Knọspe** *die;* ∼, ∼n bud

**knọspen** *itr. V.* bud

**knọten** *tr. V.* knot

**Knọten** *der;* ∼s, ∼: knot; (Haartracht) bun; knot; (Med.) lump

**Knọten·punkt** *der* junction; intersection

**Know-how** /noʊˈhaʊ:/ *das;* ∼[s] know-how

**knuffen** *tr. V.* poke

**Knụ̈ller** *der;* ∼s, ∼ (ugs.) sensation; (Angebot, Verkaufsartikel) sensational offer

**knụ̈pfen** *tr. V.* (a) tie (**an** + *Akk.* to); **Bedingungen an etw.** (*Akk.*) ∼: attach conditions to sth.
(b) (durch Knoten herstellen) knot; make ⟨net⟩

**Knụ̈ppel** *der;* ∼s, ∼ cudgel; (Polizei∼) truncheon

**knụ̈ppel-, Knụ̈ppel-:** ∼**dịck** *Adv.* (ugs.) **es kam** ∼dick it was one disaster after the other; ∼**schaltung** *die* (Kfz-W.) floor[-type] gear change

**knụrren** *itr. V.* (a) ⟨animal⟩ growl; (wütend) snarl; (fig.) ⟨stomach⟩ rumble
(b) (murren) grumble (**über** + *Akk.* about)

**knụsprig** *Adj.* crisp; crusty ⟨bread, roll⟩

**knụtschen** (ugs.) ① *tr. V.* smooch with (coll.); (sexuell berühren) pet; **sich** ∼: smooch (coll.)/pet
② *itr. V.* smooch (coll.); (sich sexuell berühren) pet

**k. o.** /ka:ˈ|o:/ *Adj.* (a) (Boxen) **jmdn. k. o. schlagen** knock sb. out
(b) (ugs.: übermüdet) all in (coll.)

**koalieren** *itr. V.* (Politik) form a coalition (**mit** with)

**Koalition** *die;* ∼, ∼en coalition

**Koax·kabel** *das* (Technik Jargon) coax [cable]; coaxial cable

**Kobalt** *das;* ∼s (Chemie) cobalt

**Kobold** *der;* ∼[e]s, ∼e goblin

**Kobra** *die;* ∼, ∼s cobra

**Koch** *der;* ∼[e]s, Köche cook; (Küchenchef) chef

**Koch·buch** *das* cookery book (Brit.); cookbook (Amer.)

---

*alte Schreibung - vgl. Hinweis auf S. xiv

**kọchen** ☐1 *tr. V.* **(a)** boil; (zubereiten) cook ⟨*meal*⟩; make ⟨*purée, jam*⟩; **Tee** ∼: make some tea
**(b)** (waschen) boil
☐2 *itr. V.* **(a)** (Speisen zubereiten) cook
**(b)** (sieden) ⟨*water, milk, etc.*⟩ boil
**Kọcher** *der;* ∼s, ∼ [small] stove; (Kochplatte) hotplate
**Kọcher** *der;* ∼s, ∼ (für Pfeile) quiver
**Kọch·feld** *das* ceramic hob
**Kọchin** *die;* ∼, ∼nen cook
**Kọch-:** ∼**löffel** *der* wooden spoon; ∼**nische** *die* kitchenette; ∼**salz** *das* common salt; ∼**topf** *der* [cooking] pot; ∼**wäsche** *die* washing that is to be boiled
**Kọder** *der;* ∼s, ∼: bait
**kọdern** *tr. V.* lure
**Koffein** *das;* ∼s caffeine
**koffein·frei** *Adj.* decaffeinated
**Kọffer** *der;* ∼s, ∼: [suit]case
**Kọffer-:** ∼**kuli** *der* luggage trolley; ∼**radio** *das* portable radio; ∼**raum** *der* boot (Brit.); trunk (Amer.)
**Kognak** /'kɔnjak/ *der;* ∼s, ∼s brandy; *s. auch* COGNAC
**Kohl** *der;* ∼[e]s **(a)** cabbage
**(b)** (ugs. abwertend: Unsinn) rubbish; rot (coll.)
**Kohl·dampf** *der* (salopp) ∼ **haben** be ravenously hungry
**Kohle** *die;* ∼, ∼n **(a)** coal
**(b)** (salopp: Geld) dough (coll.)
**Kohle·hydrat** ▶ KOHLENHYDRAT
**kohlen**[1] *itr. V.* smoulder; ⟨*wick*⟩ smoke
**kohlen**[2] *itr. V.* (fam.) (lügen) tell fibs; (übertreiben) exaggerate
**Kohlen-:** ∼**dioxid**, ∼**dioxyd** /-'---/ *das* (Chemie) carbon dioxide; ∼**grube** *die* coal mine; ∼**händler** *der*, ∼**händlerin** *die* coal merchant; ∼**hydrat** *das* (Chemie) carbohydrate; ∼**monoxid**, ∼**monoxyd** /-'---/ *das* (Chemie) carbon monoxide; ∼**säure** *die* carbonic acid; ∼**stoff** *der* carbon
**Kohle·papier** *das* carbon paper
**Köhler** *der;* ∼s, ∼: charcoal burner
**Kohle·zeichnung** *die* charcoal drawing
**Kohl-:** ∼**kopf** *der* [head of] cabbage; ∼**rübe** *die* swede
**Koitus** *der;* ∼, Koitus (geh.) sexual intercourse; coitus (formal)
**Koje** *die;* ∼, ∼n **(a)** (Seemannsspr.) bunk; berth
**(b)** (Ausstellungsstand) stand
**(c)** (ugs. scherzh.: Bett) bed
**Kokain** *das;* ∼s cocaine
**kokẹtt** ☐1 *Adj.* coquettish
☐2 *adv.* coquettishly
**kokettieren** *itr. V.* mit etw. ∼: make much play with sth.
**Kokos·nuss, \*Kokos·nuß** *die* coconut
**Koks** *der;* ∼es coke
**Kọlben** *der;* ∼s, ∼ **(a)** (Technik) piston

**(b)** (Chemie: Glas∼) flask
**(c)** (Teil des Gewehrs) butt
**Kolchose** /kɔl'çoːzə/ *die;* ∼, ∼n kolkhoz; Soviet collective farm
**Kolibri** *der;* ∼s, ∼s hummingbird
**Kolik** *die;* ∼, ∼en colic
**Kollaborateur** /kɔlabora'tøːɐ̯/ *der;* ∼s, ∼e, **Kollaborateurin** *die;* ∼, ∼nen collaborator
**Kollaps** *der;* ∼es, ∼e collapse
**Kolleg** *das;* ∼s, ∼s lecture
**Kollege** *der;* ∼n, ∼n colleague
**kollegial** ☐1 *Adj.* helpful and considerate
☐2 *adv.* ⟨*act etc.*⟩ like a good colleague/good colleagues
**Kollegin** *die;* ∼, ∼nen colleague
**Kollegium** *das;* ∼s, Kollegien **(a)** (Gruppe) group; (unmittelbar zusammenarbeitend) team
**(b)** (Lehrkörper) [teaching] staff
**Kollekte** *die;* ∼, ∼n collection
**Kollektion** *die;* ∼, ∼en collection; (Sortiment) range
**kollektiv** ☐1 *Adj.* collective
☐2 *adv.* collectively
**kollidieren** *itr. V.* **(a)** *mit sein* collide
**(b)** (fig.) conflict
**Kollier** /kɔ'liːe/ *das;* ∼s, ∼s necklace
**Kollision** *die;* ∼, ∼en collision
**Köln** *(das)* ∼s Cologne
**Kölner** ☐1 *indekl. Adj.* Cologne *attrib.*; (in Köln) in Cologne *postpos., not pred*; ⟨*suburb, archbishop, mayor, speciality*⟩ of Cologne
☐2 *der;* ∼s, ∼: inhabitant of Cologne; (von Geburt) native of Cologne
**Kölnerin** *die;* ∼, ∼nen ▶ KÖLNER 2
**Kolonialisierung** *die;* ∼, ∼en colonialization
**Kolonialismus** *der;* ∼: colonialism *no art.*
**Kolonie** *die;* ∼, ∼n colony
**kolonisieren** *tr. V.* colonize
**Kolonisierung** *die;* ∼, ∼en colonization
**Kolonne** *die;* ∼, ∼n column
**Koloss, \*Koloß** *der;* Kolọsses, Kolọsse (auch fig. ugs.) giant
**kolossal** ☐1 *Adj.* **(a)** colossal; gigantic
**(b)** (ugs.: sehr groß) tremendous (coll.); incredible (coll.) ⟨*rubbish, nonsense*⟩
☐2 *adv.* (ugs.) tremendously (coll.)
**Kolumbianer** *der;* ∼s, ∼, **Kolumbianerin** *die;* ∼, ∼nen Colombian
**Kolumbien** /ko'lʊmbiən/ *(das)* ∼s Colombia
**Kombination** *die;* ∼, ∼en **(a)** combination
**(b)** (gedankliche Verknüpfung) deduction; piece of reasoning
**(c)** (Kleidungsstücke) ensemble; suit; (Herren∼) suit
**kombinieren** ☐1 *tr. V.* combine
☐2 *itr. V.* deduce; reason

**Kombi-:** ~**wagen** der estate [car]; station wagon (Amer.); ~**zange** die combination pliers pl.

**Komet** der; ~en, ~en comet

**Komfort** /kɔmˈfoːɐ̯/ der; ~s comfort

**komfortabel** ① Adj. comfortable ② adv. comfortably

**Komik** die; ~: comic effect; (komisches Element) comic element

**Komiker** der; ~s, ~, **Komikerin** die; ~, ~en (a) (Vortragskünstler[in]) comedian (b) (Darsteller[in]) comic actor

**komisch** Adj. (a) comical; funny (b) (seltsam) funny

**Komitee** das; ~s, ~s committee

**Komma** das; ~s, ~s od. ~ta comma; (Math.) decimal point; **zwei** ~ **acht** two point eight

**Kommandant** der; ~en, ~en (Milit.) commanding officer

**Kommandeur** /kɔmanˈdøːɐ̯/ der; ~s, ~e (Milit.) ▶ KOMMANDANT

**kommandieren** ① tr. V. (a) command; be in command of; order ⟨retreat, advance⟩ (b) (ugs.) jmdn. ~: boss sb. about (coll.) ② itr. V. (ugs.) boss people about (coll.)

**Kommandit-gesellschaft** die (Wirtsch.) limited partnership

**Kommando** das; ~s, ~s command

**kommen** unr. itr. V.; mit sein (a) come; **angelaufen** ~: come running along; (auf jmdn. zu) come running up (b) (gelangen, geraten) get; **unter ein Auto** ~: be knocked down by a car; **wie kommst du darauf?** what gives you that idea? (c) ~ **lassen** (bestellen) order ⟨taxi⟩; **den Arzt/ die Polizei** ~ **lassen** send for a doctor/the police (d) (aufgenommen werden) **zur Schule/aufs Gymnasium** ~: start school/grammar school (e) (auftauchen) ⟨seeds, plants⟩ come up; ⟨buds, flowers⟩ come out; ⟨teeth⟩ come through (f) (seinen festen Platz haben) go; belong; **in die Schublade** ~: go or belong in the drawer; (seinen Platz erhalten) **in die Mannschaft** ~: get into the team; **auf den ersten Platz** ~: go into first place (g) (Gelegenheit haben) **dazu** ~, **etw. zu tun** get round to doing sth. (h) (sich ereignen) come about; **wie kommt es, dass ...:** how is it that ...; how come that ... (coll.) (i) (etw. erlangen) **zu Geld** ~: become wealthy; **zu Erfolg/Ruhm** usw. ~: gain success/fame etc.

**kommend** Adj. (a) (folgend) next; **in den** ~**en Jahren** in years to come (b) (mit großer Zukunft) **der** ~**e Mann/Meister** the coming man/future champion

**Kommentar** der; ~s, ~e commentary; (Stellungnahme) comment; **kein** ~! no comment!

**Kommentator** der; ~s, ~en, **Kommentatorin** die; ~, ~nen commentator

**kommentieren** tr. V. (a) (erläutern) furnish with a commentary ⟨text, work⟩ (b) (Stellung nehmen zu) comment on

**kommerziell** ① Adj. commercial ② adv. commercially

**Kommiss, \*Kommiß** der; Kommisses (Soldatenspr.) army

**Kommissar** der; ~s, ~e, **Kommissarin** die; ~, ~nen (a) (Beamter/ Beamtin der Polizei) detective superintendent (b) (staatlicher Beauftragter/staatliche Beauftragte) commissioner

**Kommission** die; ~, ~en (a) (Gremium) committee; (Prüfungs~) commission (b) etw. in ~ nehmen/haben/geben (Wirtsch.) take/have sth. on commission/give sth. to a dealer for sale on commission

**Kommode** die; ~, ~n chest of drawers

**kommunal** Adj. local; (bei einer städtischen Gemeinde) municipal; local

**Kommunal-wahl** die local [government] elections pl.

**Kommunikation** die; ~, ~en (Sprachw., Soziol.) communication

**Kommunion** die; ~, ~en (kath. Kirche) [Holy] Communion

**Kommuniqué** /kɔmyniˈkeː/ das; ~s, ~s communiqué

**Kommunismus** der; ~: communism

**Kommunist** der; ~en, ~en, **Kommunistin** die; ~, ~nen communist

**kommunistisch** ① Adj. communist ② adv. Communist-⟨influenced, led, ruled, etc.⟩

**kommunizieren** itr. V. (a) (geh.) communicate (b) (kath. Kirche) receive [Holy] Communion

**Komödiant** der; ~en, ~en, **Komödiantin** die; ~, ~nen (veralt.) actor/ actress; player; (abwertend: Heuchler[in]) play-actor

**Komödie** /koˈmøːdi̯ə/ die; ~, ~n comedy; (Theater) comedy theatre

**Kompagnon** /kɔmpanˈjõː/ der; ~s, ~s (Wirtsch.) partner; associate

**kompakt** Adj. solid

**Kompanie** die; ~, ~n company

**Komparativ** der; ~s, ~e (Sprachw.) comparative

**Kompass, \*Kompaß** der; Kompasses, Kompasse compass

**kompatibel** Adj. (Nachrichtenw., Sprachw.) compatible

**Kompatibilität** die; ~, ~en compatibility

**Kompensation** die; ~, ~en (Wirtsch., Physik, geh.) compensation

**kompensieren** tr. V. etw. mit etw. od. durch etw. ~: compensate for sth. by sth.

**kompetent** Adj. competent

**Kompetenz** die; ~, ~en competence; (bes. Rechtsw.) authority

**komplett** [1] Adj. complete
[2] adv. fully ⟨furnished, equipped⟩; (ugs.: ganz und gar) completely

**komplettieren** tr. V. complete

**Komplett·preis** der all-inclusive price

**komplex** Adj. complex

**Komplex** der; ~es, ~e (auch Psych.) complex

**Komplexität** die; ~: complexity

**Komplikation** die; ~, ~en (auch Med.) complication

**Kompliment** das; ~[e]s, ~e compliment

**Komplize** der; ~n, ~n (abwertend) accomplice

**komplizieren** tr. V. complicate

**kompliziert** [1] Adj. complicated
[2] adv. ~ aufgebaut sein have a complicated or complex structure

**Kompliziertheit** die; ~: complexity; complicatedness

**Komplizin** die; ~, ~nen ▶ KOMPLIZE

**Komplott** das; ~[e]s, ~e plot; conspiracy

**komponieren** tr., itr. V. compose

**Komponist** der; ~en, ~en,
**Komponistin** die; ~, ~nen composer

**Komposition** die; ~, ~en composition

**Kompost** der; ~[e]s, ~e compost

**Kompost·haufen** der compost heap

**kompostierbar** Adj. compostable

**kompostieren** tr. V. compost

**Kompott** das; ~[e]s, ~e stewed fruit; compote

**Kompresse** die; ~, ~n (Med.) **(a)** (Umschlag) [wet] compress
**(b)** (Mull) [gauze] pad

**Kompression** die; ~, ~en (Physik, Technik, Med., DV) compression

**Kompressor** der; ~s, ~en (Technik) compressor

**komprimieren** tr. V. (auch Physik, Technik, DV) compress

**Kompromiss, \*Kompromiß** der; Kompromisses, Kompromisse compromise

**kompromiss-, \*kompromiß-, Kompromiss-, \*Kompromiß-:**
~**bereit** Adj. willing to compromise pred.;
~**los** [1] Adj. uncompromising; [2] adv. uncompromisingly; ~**vorschlag** der compromise proposal

**kompromittieren** tr. V. compromise

**Kondensation** die; ~, ~en (Physik, Chemie) condensation

**Kondensator** der; ~s, ~en (Elektrot.) capacitor

**kondensieren** tr., itr. V. (itr. auch mit sein) (Physik, Chemie) condense

**Kondens-:** ~**milch** die condensed milk;
~**streifen** der condensation trail;
~**wasser** das condensation

**Kondition** die; ~, ~en condition; **eine gute/schlechte** ~ **haben** be/not be in good condition or shape; **keine** ~ **haben** be out of condition; (fig.) have no stamina

**Konditional·satz** der (Sprachw.) conditional clause

**Konditions·training** das fitness training

**Konditor** der; ~s, ~en pastry cook

**Konditorei** die; ~, ~en cake shop; (Lokal) café

**kondolieren** itr. V. offer one's condolences; **jmdm. [zu jmds. Tod]** ~: offer one's condolences to sb. [on sb.'s death]

**Kondom** das od. der; ~s, ~e condom

**Konfekt** das; ~[e]s **(a)** confectionery; sweets pl. (Brit.); candies pl. (Amer.)
**(b)** (bes. südd., österr., schweiz.: Teegebäck) [small] fancy biscuits pl. (Brit.) or (Amer.) cookies pl.

**Konfektion** die; ~, ~en ready-made garments pl.

**Konferenz** die; ~, ~en conference; (Besprechung) meeting

**konferieren** itr. V. confer (**über** + Akk. on, about)

**Konfession** die; ~, ~en denomination

**konfessionell** [1] Adj. denominational
[2] adv. as regards denomination; ~ **[un]gebunden sein** have [no] denominational ties

**Konfetti** das; ~[s] confetti

**Konfirmand** der; ~en, ~en,
**Konfirmandin** die; ~, ~nen (ev. Rel.) confirmand

**Konfirmation** die; ~, ~en (ev. Rel.) confirmation

**konfirmieren** tr. V. (ev. Rel.) confirm

**konfiszieren** tr. V. (bes. Rechtsw.) confiscate

**Konfitüre** die; ~, ~n jam

**Konflikt** der; ~[e]s, ~e conflict

**Konföderation** die; ~, ~en confederation

**konform** Adj. concurring attrib.; ~ **gehen** be in agreement

**Konformismus** der; ~: conformism

**Konformist** der; ~en, ~en,
**Konformistin** die; ~, ~: conformist

**konformistisch** [1] Adj. conformist
[2] adv. in a conformist way

**Konfrontation** die; ~, ~en confrontation

**konfrontieren** tr. V. confront

**konfus** [1] Adj. confused
[2] adv. in a confused fashion

**Kongo¹** der; ~[s] (Fluss) Congo

**Kongo²** (das); ~s od. der; ~[s] (Staat) the Congo

**Kongress, \*Kongreß** der; Kongresses, Kongresse congress; conference; **der** ~ (USA): Congress

**Kongress·halle, \*Kongreß·halle** die conference hall

**König** *der;* ~s, ~e king
**Königin** *die;* ~, ~nen queen
**königlich** ① *Adj.* (a) royal
(b) (vornehm) regal
(c) (reichlich) princely ‹*gift, salary, wage*›
② *adv.* ‹*pay*› handsomely; (ugs.: außerordentlich) ‹*enjoy oneself*› immensely (coll.)
**König·reich** *das* kingdom
**Königs·haus** *das* royal house
**Königtum** *das;* ~s, Königtümer (a) (Monarchie) monarchy
(b) (veralt.: Reich) kingdom
**Konjugation** *die;* ~, ~en (Sprachw.) conjugation
**konjugieren** *tr. V.* (Sprachw.) conjugate
**Konjunktion** *die;* ~, ~en (Sprachw.) conjunction
**Konjunktiv** *der;* ~s, ~e (Sprachw.) subjunctive
**Konjunktur** *die;* ~, ~en (Wirtsch.) (a) (wirtschaftliche Lage) [level of] economic activity; economy; (Tendenz) economic trend
(b) (Hoch~) boom; (Aufschwung) upturn [in the economy]
**konjunkturell** *Adj.* economic
**Konjunktur·politik** *die* (Wirtsch.) measures *pl.* aimed at avoiding violent fluctuations in the economy
**konkav** (Optik) ① *Adj.* concave
② *adv.* concavely
**konkret** ① *Adj.* concrete
② *adv.* in concrete terms
**konkretisieren** *tr. V.* etw. ~: put sth. in concrete terms
**Konkurrent** *der;* ~en, ~en, **Konkurrentin** *die;* ~, ~nen (Sport, Wirtsch.) competitor
**Konkurrenz** *die;* ~, ~en (Sport, Wirtsch.) competition
**konkurrenz-, Konkurrenz-:** ~**fähig** *Adj.* competitive; ~**kampf** *der* competition; (zwischen zwei Menschen) rivalry
**konkurrieren** *itr. V.* compete
**Konkurs** *der;* ~es, ~e (a) (Bankrott) bankruptcy; ~ machen od. in ~ gehen go bankrupt
(b) (gerichtliches Verfahren) bankruptcy proceedings *pl.*
**können** ① *unr. Modalverb; 2. Part.* können: (a) be able to; er kann gut reden/tanzen he is a good talker/dancer; ich kann nicht schlafen I cannot *or* (coll.) can't sleep; kann das explodieren? could it explode?; man kann nie wissen you never know; es kann sein, dass ...: it could be that ...; kann ich Ihnen helfen? can I help you?
(b) (Grund haben) du kannst ganz ruhig sein you don't have to worry; das kann man wohl sagen! you could well say that
(c) (dürfen) kann ich gehen? can I go?; ~ wir mit[kommen]? can we come too?

② *unr. tr. V.* (beherrschen) know ‹*language*›; be able to play ‹*game*›; sie kann das [gut] she can do that [well]; etw./nichts für etw. ~: be/not be responsible for sth.
③ *unr. itr. V.* (a) (fähig sein) er kann nicht anders there's nothing else he can do; (es ist seine Art) he can't help it (coll.)
(b) (Zeit haben) ich kann heute nicht I can't today (coll.)
(c) (ugs.: Kraft haben) kannst du noch [weiter]? can you go on?
(d) (ugs.: umgehen ~) [gut] mit jmdm. ~: get on [well] with sb.
**Können** *das;* ~s ability
**Könner** *der;* ~s, ~, **Könnerin** *die;* ~, ~nen expert
**konnte** *1. u. 3. Pers. Sg. Prät. v.* KÖNNEN
**könnte** *1. u. 3. Pers. Sg. Konjunktiv II v.* KÖNNEN
**Konsens·gespräch** *das* (Politik) discussion aimed at reaching a consensus
**konsequent** ① *Adj.* consistent; (folgerichtig) logical
② *adv.* consistently; (folgerichtig) logically
**Konsequenz** *die;* ~, ~en (a) (Folge) consequence
(b) (Unbeirrbarkeit) determination
**konservativ** ① *Adj.* conservative
② *adv.* conservatively
**Konservative** *der/die; adj. Dekl.* conservative
**Konservatorium** *das;* ~s, Konservatorien conservatoire; conservatory (Amer.)
**Konserve** *die;* ~, ~n (a) (Büchse) can; tin (Brit.)
(b) (konservierte Lebensmittel) preserved food; (in Dosen) canned *or* (Brit.) tinned food
**Konserven-:** ~**büchse** *die*, ~**dose** *die* can; tin (Brit.)
**konservieren** *tr. V.* preserve; conserve ‹*work of art*›
**Konservierung** *die;* ~, ~en preservation
**Konservierungs·mittel** *das* preservative
**konsolidieren** *tr. V.* consolidate
**Konsolidierung** *die;* ~, ~en (Festigung) consolidation
**Konsonant** *der;* ~en, ~en consonant
**Konsortium** *das;* ~s, Konsortien (Wirtsch.) consortium
**konspirativ** /kɔnspira'tiːf/ *Adj.* conspiratorial
**konstant** /kɔn'stant/ ① *Adj.* (a) constant
(b) (beharrlich) persistent
② *adv.* (a) constantly
(b) (beharrlich) persistently
**Konstellation** /kɔnstɛla'tsi̯oːn/ *die;* ~, ~en (von Parteien usw.) grouping; (von Umständen) combination
(b) (Astron., Astrol.) constellation
**konstituieren** /kɔnstitu'iːrən/ ① *tr. V.* (gründen) constitute; set up
② *refl. V.* be constituted

**Konstitution** /kɔnstitu'tsːi̯oːn/ die; ~,
~en constitution
**konstruieren** /kɔnstru'iːrən/ tr. V. (a)
(entwerfen) design
(b) (aufbauen, Geom. Sprachw.) construct
(c) (abwertend) fabricate
**Konstrukteur** /kɔnstrʊk'tøːɐ̯/ der; ~s,
~e, **Konstrukteurin** die; ~, ~nen
designer; design engineer
**Konstruktion** /kɔnstrʊk'tsi̯oːn/ die; ~,
~en (a) (Aufbau, Geom., Sprachw.)
construction; (das Entwerfen) designing
(b) (Entwurf) design; (Bau) construction
**konstruktiv** ⁅1⁆ Adj. constructive
⁅2⁆ adv. constructively
**Konsul** der; ~s, ~n (Dipl., hist.) consul
**Konsulat** das; ~[e]s, ~e (Dipl., hist.)
consulate
**Konsulin** die; ~, ~nen ▶ KONSUL
**konsultieren** tr. V. (auch fig.) consult
**Konsum** der; ~s consumption
**Konsument** der; ~en, ~en,
**Konsumentin** die; ~, ~nen consumer
**Konsum-gesellschaft** die consumer
society
**konsumieren** tr. V. consume
**Kontakt** der; ~[e]s, ~e contact; mit od. zu
jmdm. ~ haben/halten be/remain in contact
with sb.
**kontakt-, Kontakt-:** ~**freudig** Adj.
sociable; ~**linse** die contact lens; ~**mann**
der; Pl.: ~männer od. ~leute (Agent) contact;
~**person** die (Med.) contact
**Kontamination** die; ~, ~en
contamination
**kontaminieren** tr. V. contaminate
**Konten** ▶ KONTO
**kontern** tr., itr. V. (Boxen, auch fig.) counter;
(Ballspiele) counter-attack
**Konter·revolution** die counter-
revolution
**Kontinent** der; ~[e]s, ~e continent
**kontinental** Adj. continental
**Kontingent** das; ~[e]s, ~e quota
**kontinuierlich** ⁅1⁆ Adj. steady
⁅2⁆ adv. steadily
**Kontinuität** die; ~: continuity
**Konto** das; ~s, Konten od. Konti account;
ein laufendes ~: a current account
**Konto-:** ~**auszug** der (Bankw.) [bank]
statement; ~**bewegung** die transaction;
~**nummer** die account number
**Kontor** das; ~s, ~e branch; (einer Reederei)
office
**Konto·stand** der (Bankw.) balance; state of
an/one's account
**kontra** ⁅1⁆ Präp. mit Akk. (Rechtsspr., auch
fig.) versus
⁅2⁆ Adv. against
**Kontra** das; ~s, ~s (Kartenspiele) double;
jmdm. ~ geben (fig. ugs.) flatly contradict sb.

**Kontrahent** der; ~en, ~en,
**Kontrahentin** die; ~, ~nen adversary;
opponent
**konträr** Adj. contrary; opposite
**Kontrast** der; ~[e]s, ~e contrast
**Kontroll·abschnitt** der stub
**Kontrolle** die; ~, ~n (a) (Überwachung)
surveillance
(b) (Überprüfung) check; (bei Waren, bei
Lebensmitteln) inspection
(c) (Herrschaft) control; die ~ über etw. (Akk.)
verlieren lose control of sth.
**Kontrolleur** /kɔntrɔ'løːɐ̯/ der; ~s, ~e,
**Kontrolleurin** die; ~, ~nen inspector
**Kontroll·gang** der tour of inspection;
(eines Nachtwächters) round; (eines Polizisten)
patrol
**kontrollieren** tr. V. (a) (überwachen) check;
monitor
(b) (überprüfen) check; inspect ‹goods, food›
(c) (beherrschen) control
**Kontrollturm** der control tower
**kontrovers** ⁅1⁆ Adj. conflicting; (strittig)
controversial
⁅2⁆ adv. sich ~ zu etw. äußern express
conflicting opinions on sth.
**Kontroverse** /kɔntro'vɛrzə/ die; ~, ~n
controversy (um, über + Akk. about)
**Kontur** die; ~, ~en contour; outline
**Konvention** /kɔnvɛn'tsi̯oːn/ die; ~, ~en
convention
**konventionell** ⁅1⁆ Adj. (a) conventional
(b) (förmlich) formal
⁅2⁆ adv. (a) conventionally
(b) (förmlich) formally
**Konversation** /kɔnvɛrza'tsi̯oːn/ die; ~,
~en conversation
**Konversations-lexikon** das
encyclopaedia
**konvertieren** ⁅1⁆ itr. V.; auch mit sein
(Rel.) be converted
⁅2⁆ tr. V. (Wirtsch., DV) convert
**konvex** /kɔn'vɛks/ (Optik) ⁅1⁆ Adj. convex
⁅2⁆ adv. convexly
**Konvoi** /kɔn'vɔy̯/ der; ~s, ~s (bes. Milit.)
convoy
**Konzentration** die; ~, ~en
concentration
**Konzentrations-:** ~**fähigkeit** die
ability to concentrate; ~**lager** das (bes. ns.)
concentration camp
**konzentrieren** refl., tr. V. concentrate;
sich auf etw. (Akk.) ~: concentrate on sth.
**konzentriert** ⁅1⁆ Adj. concentrated
⁅2⁆ adv. with concentration
**Konzept** das; ~[e]s, ~e (a) [rough] draft
(b) (Programm) programme; (Plan) plan
**Konzern** der; ~[e]s, ~e (Wirtsch.) group [of
companies]
**Konzert** das; ~[e]s, ~e (a) (Komposition)
concerto
(b) (Veranstaltung) concert

k

**Konzẹrt·saal** *der* concert hall

**Konzessiọn** *die;* ~, ~en (a) (Amtsspr.) licence
(b) (Zugeständnis) concession

**Konzịl** *das;* ~s, ~e *od.* ~ien (kath. Kirche) council

**konzipịeren** *tr. V.* draft; design ‹*device, car, etc.*›

**Kooperatiọn** *die;* ~, ~en cooperation *no indef. art.*

**kooperatịv** 1 *Adj.* cooperative
2 *adv.* cooperatively

**kooperịeren** *tr. V.* cooperate

**Koordinạte** *die;* ~, ~n coordinate

**Koordinạten·system** *das* (Math.) system of coordinates

**koordinịeren** *tr. V.* coordinate

**Kopenhạgen** *(das);* ~s Copenhagen

**Kopf** *der;* ~[e]s, Köpfe (a) head; **ein ~ Salat** a lettuce; **~ an ~:** shoulder to shoulder; (im Wettlauf) neck and neck; (fig.) **~ stehen** (ugs.: überrascht sein) be bowled over; **nicht wissen, wo einem der ~ steht** not know whether one is coming or going; **~ hoch!** chin up!; **den ~ hängen lassen** become disheartened
(b) (Person) person; **ein kluger/fähiger ~ sein** be a clever/able man/woman; **pro ~:** per head; **die führenden Köpfe der Wirtschaft** the leading minds in the field of economics
(c) (Wille) **seinen ~ durchsetzen** make sb. do what one wants
(d) (Verstand) mind; head; **sich** (*Dat.*) **den ~ zerbrechen** (ugs.) rack one's brains (**über +** *Akk.* over)

**Kopf-:** ~**bahnhof** *der* terminal station; ~**bedeckung** *die* headgear; **ohne** ~**bedeckung** without anything on one's head

**Köpfchen** *das;* ~s, ~: **brains** *pl.;* **~ muss man haben** you've got to have it up here (coll.)

**köpfen** *tr. V.* (a) decapitate; (hinrichten) behead
(b) (Fußball) head

**kopf-, Kopf-:** ~**ende** *das* head end; ~**haut** *die* [skin of the] scalp; ~**hörer** *der* headphones *pl.;* ~**kissen** *das* pillow; ~**lastig** *Adj.* down by the head *pred.;* ~**los** 1 *Adj.* rash; (in Panik) panic-stricken; 2 *adv.* rashly; ~**los davonrennen** flee in panic; ~**rechnen** *itr. V.; nur im Inf. gebr.* do mental arithmetic; ~**rechnen** *das* mental arithmetic; ~**salat** *der* head lettuce; ~**schmerz** *der* headache; ~**schmerzen haben** have a headache *sing.;* ~**sprung** *der* header; ~**stand** *der* headstand; *\*~|***stehen** ▶ KOPF A; ~**stein·pflaster** *das* cobblestones *pl.;* ~**tuch** *das; Pl.* ~**tücher** headscarf; ~**weh** *das* (ugs.) headache; ~**weh haben** have a headache; ~**zerbrechen** *das;* ~s: **etw. bereitet** *od.*

---
*\*old spelling - see note on page xiv*

**macht jmdm. ~zerbrechen** sb. has to rack his/her brains about sth.; (etw. macht jmdm. Sorgen) sth. is a worry to sb.

**Kopịe** *die;* ~, ~n copy; (Durchschrift) carbon copy; (Fotokopie) photocopy; (Fot., Film) print

**kopịeren** *tr. V.* copy; (fotokopieren) photocopy; (Fot., Film) print

**Kopịerer** *der;* ~s, ~: [photo]copier

**Kopịer·gerät** *das* photocopier

**Kopilọt** *der;* ~en, ~en, **Kopilọtin** *die;* ~, ~nen (Flugw.) co-pilot

**Kọppel**[1] *das;* ~s, ~, österr.: *die;* ~, ~n (Gürtel) [leather] belt (*as part of a uniform*)

**Kọppel**[2] *die;* ~, ~n paddock

**kọppeln** *tr. V.* couple (**an +** *Akk.* to); dock ‹*spacecraft*›

**Kọppelung** ▶ KOPPLUNG

**Kọpplung** *die;* ~, ~en coupling; (Raumf.) docking

**kopulịeren** *itr. V.* copulate

**Korạlle** *die;* ~, ~n coral

**Korạn** *der;* ~s, ~e Koran

**Korb** *der;* ~es, Körbe (a) basket
(b) **jmdm. einen ~ geben** turn sb. down

**Kọrb·ball** *der* netball

**Kọrd** *der;* ~[e]s (a) corduroy; cord
(b) ▶ KORDSAMT

**Kọrdel** *die;* ~, ~n cord

**Kọrd·samt** *der* cord velvet

**Korẹa** *(das)* ~s Korea

**Koreạner** *der;* ~s, ~, **Koreạnerin** *die;* ~, ~nen Korean

**koreạnisch** *Adj.* Korean

**Korịnthe** *die;* ~, ~n currant

**Kọrk** *der;* ~s, ~e cork

**Kọrken** *der;* ~s, ~: cork

**Kọrken·zieher** *der;* ~s, ~: corkscrew

**Kọrn**[1] *das;* ~[e]s, Körner (a) (Frucht) grain; (Getreide~) grain [of corn]; (Pfeffer~) corn
(b) *o. Pl.* (Getreide) corn; grain
(c) (Salz~, Sand~) grain; (Hagel~) stone

**Kọrn**[2] *der;* ~[e]s, ~ (ugs.) corn schnapps; corn liquor (Amer.)

**Kọrn·blume** *die* cornflower

**Kọrnchen** *das;* ~s, ~: tiny grain; (von Sand usw.) [tiny] grain; granule

**Kọrner** ▶ KORN

**Kọrn·feld** *das* cornfield

**kọrnig** *Adj.* granular

**Korọna** *die;* ~, Koronen crowd (coll.)

**Kọrper** *der;* ~s, ~: body

**körper-, Körper-:** ~**bau** *der* physique; ~**behindert** *Adj.* physically handicapped; ~**behinderte** *der/die* physically handicapped person; ~**behinderte** *Pl.* physically handicapped people; ~**geruch** *der* body odour; BO (coll.); ~**größe** *die* height

**körperlich** 1 *Adj.* physical
2 *adv.* physically

**Kọrper·pflege** *die* body care *no art.*

**Körperschaft[s]·steuer** *die* (Steuerw.) corporation tax

**Körper-:** ~**spray** *der od. das* deodorant spray; ~**teil** *der* part of the/one's body; ~**verletzung** *die* (Rechtsw.) bodily harm *no indef. art.*

**Korps** /koːɐ̯/ *das;* ~ /koːɐ̯(s),/ ~ /koːɐ̯s/ **(a)** (Milit.) corps
**(b)** (Studentenverbindung) student duelling society

**korpulent** *Adj.* corpulent

**korrekt** [1] *Adj.* correct
[2] *adv.* correctly

**korrekter·weise** *Adv.* to be [strictly] correct

**Korrektheit** *die;* ~: correctness

**Korrektor** *der;* ~s, ~en /-'toːrən/, **Korrektorin** *die;* ~, ~nen proof-reader

**Korrektur** *die;* ~, ~en correction

**Korrespondent** *der;* ~en, ~en, **Korrespondentin** *die;* ~, ~nen correspondent

**Korrespondenz** *die;* ~, ~en correspondence

**korrespondieren** *itr. V.* correspond **(mit** with**)**

**Korridor** *der;* ~s, ~e corridor

**korrigieren** *tr. V.* correct; revise ‹*opinion, view*›

**korrodieren** *tr., itr. V.* (*itr. mit sein*) (bes. Chemie, Geol.) corrode

**Korrosion** *die;* ~, ~en (auch Geol., Med.) corrosion

**korrosions-, Korrosions-:** ~**beständig** *Adj.,* ~**fest** *Adj.* corrosion-resistant; ~**schutz** *der* protection against corrosion

**korrupt** *Adj.* corrupt

**Korruption** *die;* ~, ~en corruption

**Korsett** *das;* ~s, ~s *od.* ~e corset

**Korsika** (*das*); ~s Corsica

**Kortison** *das;* ~s (Med.) cortisone

**koscher** *Adj.* kosher

**Kose-:** ~**form** *die* familiar form; ~**name** *der* pet name

**Kosinus** *der;* ~, ~ *od.* ~se (Math.) cosine

**Kosmetik** *die;* ~ **(a)** beauty culture *no art.;*
**(b)** (fig.) cosmetic procedures *pl.*

**Kosmetikerin** *die;* ~, ~nen cosmetician; beautician

**Kosmetikum** *das;* ~s, **Kosmetika** cosmetic

**kosmetisch** [1] *Adj.* (auch fig.) cosmetic
[2] *adv.* jmdn. ~ beraten give sb. advice on beauty care; sich ~ behandeln lassen have beauty treatment

**kosmisch** *Adj.* cosmic ‹*ray, dust, etc.*›; space ‹*age, station, research, etc.*›; meteoric ‹*iron*›

**Kosmos** *der;* ~: cosmos

**Kost** *die;* ~: food; ~ und **Logis** board and lodging

**kostbar** [1] *Adj.* valuable; precious ‹*time*›
[2] *adv.* expensively ‹*dressed*›; luxuriously ‹*decorated*›

**Kostbarkeit** *die;* ~, ~en **(a)** (Sache) treasure
**(b)** (Eigenschaft) value

**kosten**[1] [1] *tr. V.* taste; try
[2] *itr. V.* (probieren) have a taste

**kosten**[2] *tr. V.* **(a)** cost
**(b)** (erfordern) take; cost ‹*lives*›

**Kosten** *Pl.* cost *sing.;* costs; (Auslagen) expenses; (Rechtsw.) costs; **auf jmds.** ~: at sb.'s expense

**kosten-, Kosten-:** ~**deckend** *Adj.* that covers/cover [one's] costs *postpos., not pred.;* ~**erstattung** *die* reimbursement of costs; ~**los** [1] *Adj.* free; [2] *adv.* free of charge; ~**pflichtig** (Rechtsw.) [1] *Adj.* eine ~pflichtige Verwarnung a fine and a caution; [2] *adv.* eine Klage ~pflichtig abweisen dismiss a case with costs; ein Auto ~pflichtig abschleppen tow a car away at the owner's expense; ~**punkt** *der* (ugs.) ~punkt? how much is it/are they?; ~punkt 25 Euro it costs/they cost 25 euros; ~**stelle** *die* (Wirtsch.) cost centre; ~**vor·anschlag** *der* estimate

**Kost·gänger** *der;* ~s, ~, **Kost·gängerin** *die;* ~, ~nen (veralt.) boarder

**köstlich** [1] *Adj.* delicious; (unterhaltsam) delightful
[2] *adv.* ‹*taste*› delicious; sich ~ amüsieren/ unterhalten enjoy oneself enormously (coll.)

**Köstlichkeit** *die;* ~, ~en (Sache) delicacy

**Kost·probe** *die;* ~, ~n taste

**kost·spielig** *Adj.* costly

**Kostüm** *das;* ~s, ~e **(a)** suit
**(b)** (Theater~, Verkleidung) costume

**kostümieren** *tr. V.* dress up

**Kot** *der;* ~[e]s, ~e excrement

**Kotangens** *der;* ~, ~ (Math.) cotangent

**Kotelett** /kɔt'lɛt/ *das;* ~s, ~s chop; (vom Nacken) cutlet

**Koteletten** *Pl.* side whiskers

**Köter** *der;* ~s, ~ (abwertend) cur

**Kot·flügel** *der* (Kfz-W.) wing

**kotzen** *itr. V.* (derb) puke (coarse)

**KP** *Abk.* = **Kommunistische Partei** CP

**Krabbe** *die;* ~, ~n (a) (Zool.) crab
**(b)** (ugs.: Garnele) shrimp; (größer) prawn

**krabbeln** [1] *itr. V.; mit sein* crawl
[2] *tr. V.* (ugs.: kraulen) tickle

**Krach** *der;* ~[e]s, **Kräche** (a) (Lärm) noise; row
**(b)** (lautes Geräusch) crash
**(c)** (ugs.: Streit) row

**krachen** [1] *itr. V.* **(a)** (Krach auslösen) ‹*thunder*› crash; ‹*shot*› ring out     ⸳⸳⸳⸻⸻▸

**(b)** *mit sein* (ugs.: bersten) ⟨ice⟩ crack; ⟨bed⟩ collapse
**(c)** *mit sein* (ugs.: mit Krach auftreffen) crash
② *refl. V.* (ugs.) row (coll.)

**krächzen** *itr. V.* ⟨raven, crow⟩ caw; ⟨parrot⟩ squawk; ⟨person⟩ croak

**kraft** *Präp. + Gen.* (Amtsspr.) ~ [meines] Amtes by virtue of my office; ~ **Gesetzes** by law

**Kraft** *die;* ~, **Kräfte** strength; (Wirksamkeit) power; (Physik) force; (Arbeits~) employee; **mit letzter** ~: with one's last ounce of strength; **aus eigener** ~: by one's own efforts; **mit vereinten Kräften werden wir ...:** if we join forces *or* combine our efforts we will ...; **außer** ~ **setzen** repeal ⟨law⟩; countermand ⟨order⟩; **außer** ~ **sein/treten** no longer be/ cease to be in force; **in** ~ **treten/sein/bleiben** come into/be in/remain in force

**Kraft-:** ~**aufwand** *der* effort; ~**brühe** *die* strong meat broth; ~**fahrer** *der,* ~**fahrerin** *die* driver; motorist;

**Kraft·fahrzeug** *das* motor vehicle

**Kraftfahrzeug-:** ~**brief** *der* vehicle registration document; logbook (Brit.); ~**schein** *der* vehicle registration document; ~**steuer** *die* vehicle tax

**kräftig** ① *Adj.* strong; vigorous ⟨plant, shoot⟩; powerful, hefty ⟨blow, kick, etc.⟩; nourishing ⟨soup, bread, meal, etc.⟩
② *adv.* powerfully ⟨built⟩; ⟨rain, snow⟩ heavily; ⟨eat⟩ heartily

**kräftigen** *tr. V.* ⟨holiday, air, etc.⟩ invigorate; ⟨food etc.⟩ fortify

**kraft-, Kraft-:** ~**meier** *der;* ~~s, ~~ (ugs.: abwertend) muscleman; ~**probe** *die* trial of strength; ~**rad** *das* (Amtsspr.) motorcycle; ~**stoff** *der* (Kfz-W.) fuel; ~**stoff·verbrauch** *der* fuel consumption; ~**voll** ① *Adj.* powerful; ② *adv.* powerfully; ~**wagen** *der* motor vehicle; ~**werk** *das* power station

**Kragen** *der;* ~s, ~, (südd., österr. u. schweiz. auch:) **Krägen** collar

**Kragen·weite** *die* collar size

**Krähe** /'krɛːə/ *die;* ~, ~n crow

**krähen** *itr. V.* (auch fig.) crow

**Krähen·füße** *Pl.* (ugs.) crow's feet

**krakeelen** *itr. V.* (ugs.) kick up a row (coll.)

**krakeln** *tr., itr. V.* (ugs.) scrawl

**kraklig** *Adj.* (ugs. abwertend) scrawly

**Kralle** *die;* ~, ~n claw

**krallen** ① *refl. V.* sich an etw. (Akk.) ~ ⟨cat⟩ dig its claws into sth.; ⟨person⟩ clutch sth. [tightly]
② *tr. V.* (fest greifen) **die Finger in/um etw.** (Akk.) ~: dig one's fingers into sth./clutch sth. [tightly] with one's fingers

**Kram** *der;* ~[e]s (ugs.) **(a)** stuff; (Gerümpel) junk
**(b)** (Angelegenheit) affair

**kramen** ① *itr. V.* in etw. (Dat.) ~: rummage about in sth.
② *tr. V.* (ugs.) **etw. aus etw.** ~: fish (coll.) sth. out of sth.

**Krämer** *der;* ~s, ~, **Krämerin** *die;* ~, ~nen grocer

**Kram·laden** *der* (ugs. abwertend) junk shop

**Krampf** *der;* ~[e]s, **Krämpfe (a)** cramp; (Zuckung) spasm
**(b)** (painful strain; (sinnloses Tun) senseless waste of effort

**Krampf·ader** *die* varicose vein

**krampfhaft** ① *Adj.* convulsive; (verbissen) desperate
② *adv.* convulsively; (verbissen) desperately

**Kran** *der;* ~[e]s, **Kräne (a)** crane
**(b)** (südwestd.: Wasserhahn) tap; faucet (Amer.)

**Kranich** *der;* ~s, ~e crane

**krank**; kränker, kränkst... *Adj.* ill *usu. pred.;* sick; bad ⟨leg, tooth⟩; diseased ⟨plant, organ⟩; (fig.) ailing ⟨economy, business⟩; ~ **werden** be taken ill

**Kranke** *der/die; adj. Dekl.* sick man/woman; (Patient) patient

**kränkeln** *itr. V.* be in poor health

**kränken** *tr. V.* jmdn. ~: hurt sb. *or* sb.'s feelings

**Kranken-:** ~**geld** *das* sickness benefit; ~**gymnastik** *die* remedial *or* medical gymnastics *sing.;* physiotherapy; ~**gymnastin** *die;* ~~, ~~nen remedial gymnast; medical gymnast; physiotherapist; ~**haus** *das* hospital; ~**kasse** *die* health insurance scheme; (Körperschaft) health insurance institution; (privat) health insurance company; ~**pfleger** *der* male nurse; ~**schein** *der* health insurance certificate; ~**schwester** *die* nurse; ~**versicherung** *die* **(a)** (Versicherung) health insurance; **(b)** (Unternehmen) health insurance company; ~**wagen** *der* ambulance

**kränker** ▶ KRANK

**krank|feiern** *itr. V.* (ugs.) skive off work (coll.) [pretending to be ill]

**krankhaft** ① *Adj.* pathological; morbid ⟨growth, state, swelling, etc.⟩
② *adv.* pathologically; morbidly ⟨swollen, sensitive⟩

**Krankheit** *die;* ~, ~en **(a)** illness; (bestimmte Art, von Pflanzen, Organen) disease
**(b)** (Zeit des Krankseins) illness

**Krankheits·erreger** *der* pathogen

**kränklich** *Adj.* ailing

**krank|schreiben** *tr. V.* give ⟨person⟩ a medical certificate

**kränkst...** ▶ KRANK

**Kränkung** *die;* ~, ~en: **eine** ~: an injury to one's/sb.'s feelings

**Kranz** *der;* ~es, **Kränze** wreath; garland; (auf einem Grab usw.) wreath

**Kränzchen** *das;* ~s, ~: coffee circle; coffee klatch (Amer.)

---

**k**

**Krapfen** der; ~s, ~: doughnut

**krass, \*kraß** [1] Adj. blatant ⟨case⟩; flagrant ⟨injustice⟩; stark ⟨contrast⟩; complete ⟨contradiction⟩; sharp ⟨difference⟩; out-and-out ⟨egoist⟩

[2] adv. sich ~ ausdrücken put sth. bluntly; sich von etw. ~ unterscheiden be in stark contrast to sth

**Krater** der; ~s, ~: crater

**Kratz·bürste** die (ugs. scherzh.) prickly so-and-so

**kratzen** [1] tr. V. scratch; (entfernen) scrape

[2] itr. V. (a) scratch

(b) (jucken) itch

**Kratzer** der; ~s, ~ (ugs.) scratch

**kratzig** Adj. itchy ⟨material⟩

**Kraul** das; ~s (Sport) crawl

**kraulen**[1] [1] itr. V. do the crawl

[2] tr. V.; auch mit sein eine Strecke ~: cover a distance using the crawl

**kraulen**[2] tr. V. jmdm. das Kinn ~: tickle sb. under the chin; jmdn. in den Haaren ~: run one's fingers through sb.'s hair

**kraus** Adj. creased ⟨skirt etc.⟩; frizzy ⟨hair⟩

**Krause** die; ~, ~n (Kragen) ruff; (am Ärmel) ruffle

**kräuseln** [1] tr. V. ruffle ⟨water, surface⟩; gather ⟨material etc.⟩; frizz ⟨hair⟩

[2] refl. V. ⟨hair⟩ go frizzy; ⟨water⟩ ripple; ⟨smoke⟩ curl up

**Kraut** das; ~[e]s, Kräuter (a) herb

(b) (bes. südd., österr.: Kohl) cabbage

**Kraut·salat** der coleslaw

**Krawall** der; ~s, ~e (a) riot

(b) (ugs.: Lärm) row (coll.)

**Krawatte** die; ~, ~n tie

**kraxeln** itr. V.; mit sein (bes. südd., österr. ugs.) climb; (mit Mühe) clamber

**kreativ** [1] Adj. creative

[2] adv. ~ veranlagt sein have a creative bent

**Kreativität** die; ~: creativity

**Kreatur** die; ~, ~en creature

**Krebs** der; ~es, ~e (a) crustacean; (Fluss~) crayfish; (Krabbe) crab

(b) (Krankheit) cancer

(c) (Astrol.) Cancer; the Crab

**krebs-, Krebs-:** ~ erregend, ~erzeugend Adj. carcinogenic; ~forschung die cancer research; ~geschwulst die cancerous growth or tumour; ~geschwür das (volkst.) cancerous ulcer; (fig. geh.) cancer; ~krank Adj. ~krank sein have cancer; ~rot Adj. as red as a lobster postpos.

**Kredit** der; ~[e]s, ~e credit; (Darlehen) loan

**kredit-, Kredit-:** ~institut das credit institution; ~karte die credit card; mit ~karte bezahlen pay by credit card; ~nehmer der; ~s, ~, ~nehmerin die; ~~, ~~nen borrower; ~würdig Adj. (Finanzw.) creditworthy

**Kreide** die; ~, ~n chalk

**kreide·bleich** Adj. as white as a sheet postpos.

**Kreide·felsen** der chalk cliff

**kreieren** /kre'i:rən/ tr. V. create

**Kreis** der; ~es, ~e circle; (Verwaltungsbezirk) district; (Wahl~) ward

**Kreis·bahn** die orbit

**kreischen** itr. V. screech; ⟨door⟩ creak

**Kreisel** der; ~s, ~ (Kinderspielzeug) top; (ugs.: Kreisverkehr) roundabout

**kreisen** itr. V.; auch mit sein ⟨planet⟩ revolve (um around); ⟨satellite etc.⟩ orbit; ⟨aircraft, bird⟩ circle

**kreis-, Kreis-:** ~förmig Adj. circular; ~lauf der (Physiol.) circulation; (der Natur, des Lebens usw.) cycle; ~lauf·störungen Pl. (Med.) circulatory trouble sing.; ~rund Adj. [perfectly] round; ~säge die circular saw

**Kreiß·saal** der (Med.) delivery room

**Kreis-:** ~stadt die chief town of a/the district; ~verkehr der roundabout

**Krem** die; ~, ~s ▶ CREME

**Krematorium** das; ~s, Krematorien crematorium

**Krempe** die; ~, ~n brim

**Krempel** der; ~s (ugs. abwertend) stuff; (Gerümpel) junk

**krepieren** itr. V.; mit sein (salopp) ⟨person⟩ snuff it (sl.)

**Krepp** der; ~s, ~s od. ~e crêpe

**\*Kreppapier** das, **Krepp·papier** das crêpe paper

**Kresse** die; ~, ~n (Bot.) cress

**Kreta** (das); ~s Crete

**Kreuz** das; ~es, ~e (a) cross; (Kreuzzeichen) sign of the cross

(b) (Teil des Rückens) small of the back; jmdn. aufs ~ legen (salopp) take sb. for a ride (coll.)

(c) (Kartenspiel) (Farbe) clubs pl.; (Karte) club

(d) (Autobahn) interchange

(e) (Musik) sharp

**kreuzen** [1] tr. V. (auch Biol.) cross

[2] refl. V. (a) ⟨überschneiden⟩ cross

(b) (zuwiderlaufen) clash (mit with)

[3] itr. V.; mit haben od. sein (fahren) cruise

**Kreuz-:** ~fahrer der (hist.) crusader; ~fahrt die cruise; ~feuer das (Milit., auch fig.) crossfire; ~gang der cloister

**kreuzigen** tr. V. crucify

**Kreuzigung** die; ~, ~en crucifixion

**Kreuz-:** ~otter die adder; [common] viper; ~ritter der (hist.) crusader; ~schlitz·schraube die Phillips screw ®; ~schmerzen Pl. pain sing. in the small of the back; ~spinne die cross spider; garden spider

**Kreuzung** die; ~, ~en (a) crossroads sing.

(b) (Biol.) crossing; cross-breeding; (Ergebnis) cross

**kreuz-, Kreuz-:** ~verhör das cross-  ⋯⁑

examination; ~**weise** *Adv.* crosswise;
~**wort·rätsel** *das* crossword [puzzle];
~**zug** *der* (hist., fig.) crusade

**kribbelig** *Adj.* (ugs.) (vor Ungeduld) fidgety;
(nervös) edgy

**kribbeln** *itr. V.* (jucken) tickle; (prickeln)
tingle

**kriechen** *unr. itr. V.* (a) *mit sein* ‹insect,
baby› crawl; ‹plant› creep; ‹person, animal›
creep, crawl
(b) *auch mit sein* (fig. abwertend) crawl (vor +
*Dat.* to)

**Kriecher** *der;* ~s, ~, **Kriecherin** *die;* ~,
~nen (abwertend) crawler

**Kriech·spur** *die* (Verkehrsw.) crawler lane

**Krieg** *der;* ~[e]s, ~e war; ~ führend
warring; belligerent

**kriegen** *tr. V.* (ugs.) get; (erreichen) catch
‹train, bus, etc.›

**Krieger** *der;* ~s, ~, **Kriegerin** *die;* ~,
~nen warrior

**kriegerisch** *Adj.* (a) (kampflustig) warlike
(b) (militärisch) military; eine ~e
Auseinandersetzung an armed conflict

*****krieg·führend** ▶ KRIEG

**kriegs-, Kriegs-:** ~**beil** *das* tomahawk;
das ~beil begraben (scherzh.) bury the
hatchet; ~**bemalung** *die* (Völkerk.)
warpaint; ~**beschädigt** *Adj.* war-
disabled; ~**beschädigte** *der/die; adj.
Dekl.* war invalid; ~**dienst** *der* (a) (im
Krieg) active service; (b) (Wehrdienst) military
service; den ~dienst verweigern be a
conscientious objector;
~**dienst·verweigerer** *der* conscientious
objector; ~**ende** *das* end of the war; bei/
vor ~ende at/before the end of the war;
~**erklärung** *die* declaration of war;
~**gefangene** *der* prisoner of war; POW;
~**gefangenschaft** *die* captivity;
~**opfer** *das* war victim; ~**schiff** *das*
warship; ~**verbrechen** *das* (Rechtsw.) war
crime; ~**verbrecher** *der*,
~**verbrecherin** *die* war criminal;
~**waise** *die* war orphan

**Krimi** *der;* ~[s], ~[s] (ugs.) crime thriller

**Kriminal·beamte** *der*,
**Kriminal·beamtin** *die* [plain-clothes]
detective

**kriminalisieren** *tr. V.* jmdn. ~: make sb.
turn to crime

**kriminalistisch** ① *Adj.* ‹methods,
practice› of criminalistics; ‹abilities› in the
field of criminalistics
② *adv.* ‹proceed etc.› using the methods of
criminalistics

**Kriminalität** *die;* ~: crime *no art.*

**Kriminal-:** ~**polizei** *die* criminal
investigation department; ~**roman** *der*
crime novel; (mit Detektiv als Held) detective
novel

*****old spelling - see note on page xiv

**kriminell** ① *Adj.* criminal
② *adv.* ~ veranlagt sein have criminal
tendencies; ~ handeln act illegally

**Kriminelle** *der/die; adj. Dekl.* criminal

**Krimskrams** *der;* ~[es] (ugs.) stuff

**Kringel** *der;* ~s, ~ (Kreis) [small] ring;
(Kritzelei) round squiggle; (Gebäck) [ring-
shaped] biscuit

**kringeln** *refl. V.* curl [up]; ‹hair› go curly;
sich ~ [vor Lachen] (ugs.) kill oneself
[laughing] (coll.)

**Kripo** *die;* ~ (ugs.) die ~: ≈ the CID

**Krippe** *die;* ~, ~n (a) (Futtertrog) manger;
crib
(b) (Weihnachts~) model of a nativity scene
(c) (Kinder~) crèche

**Krise** *die;* ~, ~n (auch Med.) crisis

**kriseln** *itr. V.* (unpers.) es kriselt in ihrer
Ehe/in der Partei their marriage is in
trouble/the party is in a state of crisis

**Krisen-:** ~**gebiet** *das* crisis area; ~**herd**
*der* trouble spot

**Kristall**[1] /krɪsˈtal/ *der;* ~s, ~e crystal

**Kristall**[2] *das;* ~s crystal *no indef. art.*

**Kristallisation** *die;* ~, ~en (bes. Chemie)
crystallization

**kristallisieren** *itr. V.* (bes. Chemie)
crystallize

**Kriterium** *das;* ~s, Kriterien criterion

**Kritik** *die;* ~, ~en (a) criticism *no indef.
art.* (an + *Dat.* of); an jmdm./etw. ~ üben
criticize sb./sth.
(b) (Besprechung) review

**Kritiker** *der;* ~s, ~, **Kritikerin** *die;* ~,
~nen critic

**kritik·los** ① *Adj.* uncritical
② *adv.* uncritically

**kritisch** ① *Adj.* critical
② *adv.* critically

**kritisieren** *tr. V.* criticize; review ‹book,
play, etc.›

**kritzeln** ① *itr. V.* (schreiben) scribble;
(zeichnen) doodle
② *tr. V.* scribble

**Kroatien** /kroˈaːtsjən/ (*das*) ~s Croatia

**kroatisch** *Adj.* Croatian

**kroch** *1. u. 3. Pers. Sg. Prät. v.* KRIECHEN

**Krokant** *der;* ~s praline

**Krokette** *die;* ~, ~n (Kochk.) croquette

**Krokodil** *das;* ~s, ~e crocodile

**Krokodils·tränen** *Pl.* (ugs.) crocodile
tears

**Krokus** *der;* ~, ~ *od.* ~se crocus

**Krone** *die;* ~, ~n crown; (eines Baumes) top;
crown; (einer Welle) crest; die ~ der
Schöpfung the pride of creation

**krönen** *tr. V.* (auch fig.) crown

**Kronen·korken** *der* crown cork

**Kron-:** ~**juwelen** *Pl.* Crown jewels;

~**leuchter** *der* chandelier; ~**prinz** *der* crown prince; ~**prinzessin** *die* crown princess

**Krönung** *die;* ~, ~en coronation; (fig.) culmination

**Kron·zeuge** *der,* **Kron·zeugin** *die* (Rechtsw.) person who turns Queen's/King's evidence; **als ~ auftreten** turn Queen's/King's evidence

**Kropf** *der;* ~[e]s, Kröpfe (Med.) goitre

**Kröte** *die;* ~, ~n (a) toad
(b) *Pl.* (salopp: Geld) **ein paar/eine ganze Menge** ~n **verdienen** earn a few bob (Brit. coll.)/a fair old whack (coll.)

**Krücke** *die;* ~, ~n crutch

**Krück·stock** *der* walking stick

**Krug** *der;* ~[e]s, Krüge jug; (größer) pitcher; (Bier~) mug

**Krume** *die;* ~, ~n crumb

**Krümel** *der;* ~s, ~: crumb

**krümeln** *itr. V.* (a) crumble
(b) (Krümel machen) make crumbs

**krumm** ① *Adj.* (a) bent ⟨nail, back⟩; crooked ⟨stick, branch, etc.⟩; bandy ⟨legs⟩; **sich über etw.** (Akk.) ~ **lachen** (ugs.) fall about laughing over sth.
(b) (ugs.: unrechtmäßig) crooked
(c) etw. ~ **nehmen** (ugs.) take sth. the wrong way
② *adv.* crookedly

**krümmen** ① *tr. V.* bend
② *refl. V.* (a) (sich winden) writhe
(b) (krumm verlaufen) ⟨road, path, river⟩ bend

**krumm-:** *~|lachen ▶ KRUMM 1A;
*~|nehmen ▶ KRUMM 1c

**Krümmung** *die;* ~, ~en bend

**Krüppel** *der;* ~s, ~: cripple

**Kruste** *die;* ~, ~n crust; (vom Braten) crisp

**Kruzifix** *das;* ~es, ~e crucifix

**Krypta** *die;* ~, Krypten (Archit.) crypt

**Kuba** (*das*) ~s Cuba

**Kubaner** *der;* ~s, ~, **Kubanerin** *die;* ~, ~nen Cuban

**Kübel** *der;* ~s, ~: pail

**Kubik-** cubic ⟨metre, foot, etc.⟩

**Küche** *die;* ~, ~n kitchen; (Einrichtung) kitchen furniture *no indef. art.;* (Kochk.) cooking; cuisine; **kalte/warme** ~: cold/hot food

**Kuchen** *der;* ~s, ~: cake; (Obst~) flan; (Torte) gateau

**Küchen-:** ~**abfälle** *Pl.* kitchen scraps; ~**chef** *der,* ~**chefin** *die* chef

**Kuchen-:** ~**form** *die* cake tin; ~**gabel** *die* pastry fork

**Küchen-:** ~**gerät** *das* kitchen utensil; (als Kollektivum) kitchen utensils *pl.;*
~**maschine** *die* food processor; ~**meister** *der,* ~**meisterin** *die* chef; ~**messer** *das* kitchen knife; ~**schabe** *die* cockroach; ~**schrank** *der* kitchen cupboard; ~**tisch** *der* kitchen table

**Kuckuck** *der;* ~s, ~e (a) cuckoo; **zum ~ [noch mal]!** (salopp) for crying out loud! (coll.)
(b) (scherzh.: Pfandsiegel) bailiff's seal (*placed on distrained goods*)

**Kuckucks·uhr** *die* cuckoo clock

**Kufe** *die;* ~, ~n runner; (von Flugzeugen, Hubschraubern) skid

**Kugel** *die;* ~, ~n (a) ball; (Geom.) sphere; (Kegeln) bowl; (beim Kugelstoßen) shot
(b) (ugs.: Geschoss) bullet

**Kugel·lager** *das* (Technik) ball bearing

**kugeln** ① *tr. V.* roll
② *refl. V.* **sich [vor Lachen]** ~ (ugs.) double or roll up [laughing]

**kugel-, Kugel-:** ~**rund** /-'-'-/ *Adj.* round as a ball *postpos.;* (scherzh.: dick) rotund; tubby; ~**schreiber** *der* ball pen; Biro ®; ~**sicher** *Adj.* bulletproof; ~**stoßen** *das;* ~~s shot[-put]; (Disziplin) putting the shot *no art.*

**Kuh** *die;* ~, Kühe cow

**Kuh-:** ~**fladen** *der* cowpat; ~**handel** *der* (ugs. abwertend) shady horse-trading *no indef. art.;* **ein** ~**handel** a bit of shady horse-trading; ~**haut** *die:* **das geht auf keine** ~**haut** (fig. salopp) it's absolutely staggering

**kühl** ① *Adj.* cool; **etw.** ~ **lagern** keep sth. in a cool place
② *adv.* coolly

**Kuhle** *die;* ~, ~n (ugs.) hollow

**Kühle** *die;* ~: coolness

**kühlen** ① *tr. V.* cool; chill ⟨wine⟩; refrigerate ⟨food⟩
② *itr. V.* ⟨cold compress, ointment, breeze, etc.⟩ have a cooling effect

**Kühler** *der;* ~s, ~ (a) (am Auto) radiator; (Kühlerhaube) bonnet (Brit.); hood (Amer.)
(b) (Sekt~) ice bucket

**Kühler·haube** *die* bonnet (Brit.); hood (Amer.)

**Kühl-:** ~**fach** *das* frozen food compartment; ~**haus** *das* cold store; ~**raum** *der* cold store; cold-storage room; ~**schrank** *der* refrigerator; fridge (Brit. coll.); icebox (Amer.); ~**truhe** *die* [chest] freezer; (im Lebensmittelgeschäft) freezer [cabinet]

**Kühlung** *die;* ~, ~en cooling; (Vorrichtung) cooling system; (für Lebensmittel) refrigeration system

**Kühl·wasser** *das* cooling water

**kühn** ① *Adj.* bold; (dreist) audacious
② *adv.* boldly; (gewagt) daringly; (dreist) audaciously

**Kühnheit** *die;* ~: boldness; (Gewagtheit) daringness; (Dreistigkeit) audacity

**Kuh·stall** *der* cowshed

**Küken** *das;* ~s, ~: chick

**kulant** *Adj.* obliging; fair ⟨terms⟩

**Kulanz** *die;* ~: willingness to oblige

**Kuli** *der;* ~s, ~s (a) coolie
(b) (ugs.) ballpoint; Biro ®

**kulinarisch** *Adj.* culinary

**Kulisse** *die;* ~, ~n piece of scenery; flat; (Hintergrund) backdrop; **die** ~n the scenery *sing.;* **hinter den** ~n (fig.) behind the scenes

**kullern** (ugs.) *itr. V. mit sein* roll

**Kult** *der;* ~[e]s, ~e (auch fig.) cult

**Kult·film** *der* cult film

**kultivieren** *tr. V.* (auch fig.) cultivate

**kultiviert** 1 *Adj.* cultured; (vornehm) refined
2 *adv.* in a cultured manner; (vornehm) in a refined manner

**Kultur** *die;* ~, ~en (a) culture; (kultivierte Lebensart) refinement; **ein Mensch von** ~: a cultured person
(b) (Zivilisation, Lebensform) civilization

**Kultur·:** ~**abkommen** *das* cultural agreement; ~**austausch** *der* cultural exchange; ~**beutel** *der* sponge bag (Brit.); toilet bag

**kulturell** 1 *Adj.* cultural
2 *adv.* culturally

**Kultur·:** ~**film** *der* documentary film; ~**geschichte** *die* history of civilization; (einer bestimmten Kultur) cultural history; ~**politik** *die* cultural and educational policy

**Kultus·minister** *der,* **Kultus·ministerin** *die* minister for education and cultural affairs

**Kümmel** *der;* ~s, ~: caraway [seed]; (Branntwein) kümmel

**Kummer** *der;* ~s sorrow; grief; (Ärger, Sorgen) trouble; ~ **um** *od.* **über jmdn.** grief for sb.; **jmdm.** ~ **machen** give sb. trouble

**kümmerlich** *Adj.* (a) (schwächlich) puny; stunted ⟨*vegetation, plants*⟩
(b) (ärmlich) wretched; miserable
(c) (abwertend: gering) miserable; meagre ⟨*knowledge, leftovers*⟩

**kümmern** 1 *refl. V.* (a) sich um jmdn./etw. ~: take care of sb./sth.
(b) (sich befassen mit) **sich nicht um Politik** ~: not be interested in politics
2 *tr. V.* concern

**Kumpan** *der;* ~s, ~e, **Kumpanin** *die;* ~, ~nen (ugs.) (a) pal (coll.); buddy (coll.)
(b) (abwertend: Mittäter[in]) accomplice

**Kumpel** *der;* ~s, ~ (a) (Bergmannsspr.) miner
(b) (salopp: Kamerad) pal (coll.); buddy (coll.)

**Kumulus·wolke** *die* (Met.) cumulus cloud

**kündbar** *Adj.* terminable ⟨*contract*⟩; redeemable ⟨*loan, mortgage*⟩

**Kunde¹** *der;* ~n, ~n customer; (eines Architekten-, Anwaltbüros, einer Versicherung usw.) client

**Kunde²** *die;* ~ (geh.) tidings *pl.* (literary)

**Kunden·dienst** *der* service to customers; (Wartung) after-sales service

**Kundgebung** *die;* ~, ~en rally

**kundig** *Adj.* (kenntnisreich) knowledgeable; (sachverständig) expert

**kündigen** 1 *tr. V.* cancel ⟨subscription, membership⟩; terminate ⟨contract, agreement⟩; **seine Stellung** ~: hand in one's notice (bei to)
2 *unr. itr. V.* (a) (ein Mietverhältnis beenden) ⟨tenant⟩ give notice; **jmdm.** ~ ⟨landlord⟩ give sb. notice to quit; **zum 1. Juli** ~: give notice for 1 July
(b) (ein Arbeitsverhältnis beenden) ⟨employee⟩ hand in one's notice (bei to); **jmdm.** ~ ⟨employer⟩ give sb. his/her notice

**Kündigung** *die;* ~, ~en (a) (der Mitgliedschaft, eines Abonnements) cancellation; (eines Vertrags) termination
(b) (eines Arbeitsverhältnisses) **jmdm. die** ~ **aussprechen** give sb. his/her notice

**Kündigungs·:** ~**frist** *die* period of notice; ~**schutz** *der* protection against wrongful dismissal

**Kundin** *die;* ~, ~nen customer/client

**Kundschaft** *die;* ~, ~en ▸ KUNDE¹: customers *pl.;* clientele

**Kundschafter** *der;* ~s, ~, **Kundschafterin** *die;* ~, ~nen scout

**kund|tun** (geh.) *unr. tr. V.* announce

**künftig** 1 *Adj.* future
2 *adv.* in future

**Kunst** *die;* ~, Künste (a) art; **die bildende** ~, **die bildenden Künste** the plastic arts *pl.;* **die schönen Künste** [the] fine arts
(b) (das Können) skill; **die ärztliche** ~: medical skill; **das ist keine** ~! (ugs.) there's nothing 'to it

**kunst-, Kunst-:** ~**ausstellung** *die* art exhibition; ~**buch** *das* art book; ~**druck** *der; Pl.* ~~**e** (a) [fine] art print; (b) (Druckw.) fine-art printing; ~**erzieher** *der,* ~**erzieherin** *die* art teacher; ~**faser** *die* synthetic fibre; ~**führer** *der* guide to cultural and artistic monuments [of an/the area]; ~**genuss**, *\**~**genuß** *der* enjoyment of art; (Ereignis) artistic treat; ~**gerecht** 1 *Adj.* expert; 2 *adv.* expertly; ~**geschichte** *die* art history; ~**geschichtlich** 1 *Adj.* art historical ⟨studies, evidence, expertise⟩; ⟨work⟩ on art history; 2 *adv.* ~ **geschichtlich interessiert/ versiert** interested/well versed in art history; ~**gewerbe** *das* arts and crafts *pl.;* ~**griff** *der* trick; dodge; ~**halle** *die* art gallery; ~**händler** *der,* ~**händlerin** *die* [fine-]art dealer; ~**handwerk** *das* craftwork; ~**kritiker** *der,* ~**kritikerin** *die* art critic; ~**leder** imitation leather

**Künstler** *der;* ~s, ~, **Künstlerin** *die;* ~, ~nen (a) artist; (Zirkus~, Varietee~) artiste
(b) (Könner) genius (**in** + *Dat.* at)

**künstlerisch** 1 *Adj.* artistic
2 *adv.* artistically

**Künstler·name** *der* stage name

**künstlich** 1 *Adj.* (a) artificial

**(b)** (gezwungen) forced ⟨*laugh, cheerfulness, etc.*⟩
2 *adv.* artificially

**kunst-, Kunst-:** ~**licht** *das* artificial light; ~**los** *Adj.* plain; ~**postkarte** *die* art postcard; ~**saal** *der* art room; ~**sammler** *der*, ~**sammlerin** *die* art collector; ~**sammlung** *die* art collection; ~**schatz** *der* art treasure; ~**stoff** *der* synthetic material; plastic; ~**stück** *das* trick; **das ist kein** ~**stück** (ugs.) it's no great feat; ~**turnen** *das* gymnastics *sing.*; ~**voll** 1 *Adj.* ornate and artistic; (kompliziert) elaborate; 2 *adv.* **(a)** ornately *or* elaborately and artistically; **(b)** (geschickt) skilfully; ~**werk** *das* work of art

**kunter·bunt** 1 *Adj.* multi-coloured; (abwechslungsreich) varied; (ungeordnet) jumbled ⟨*confusion, muddle, etc.*⟩
2 *adv.* ⟨*painted, printed*⟩ in many colours; ~ **durcheinander sein** be higgledy-piggledy

**Kupfer** *das;* ~s **(a)** copper
**(b)** (~geschirr) copperware; (~geld) coppers *pl.*

**Kupfer-:** ~**geld** *das* coppers *pl.;* ~**stich** *der* **(a)** copperplate engraving *no art.;* **(b)** (Blatt) copperplate print *or* engraving

**Kuppe** *die;* ~, ~n **(a)** [rounded] hilltop
**(b)** (Finger~) tip; end

**Kuppel** *die;* ~, ~n dome; (kleiner) cupola

**Kuppelei** *die;* ~: procuring

**kuppeln** *itr. V.* operate the clutch

**Kuppelung** ▶ KUPPLUNG

**Kuppler** *der;* ~s, ~: procurer

**Kupplerin** *die;* ~, ~nen procuress

**Kupplung** *die;* ~, ~en **(a)** (Kfz-W.) clutch
**(b)** (Technik: Vorrichtung zum Verbinden) coupling

**Kur** *die;* ~, ~en [health] cure; (ohne Aufenthalt im Badeort) course of treatment

**Kür** *die;* ~, ~en (Eiskunstlauf) free programme; (Turnen) optional exercises *pl.*

**Kurbel** *die;* ~, ~n crank [handle]; (an Spieldosen, Grammophonen) winder; (an einem Brunnen) [winding] handle

**kurbeln** *tr. V.* etw. nach oben/unten ~: wind sth. up/down

**Kurbel·welle** *die* (Technik) crankshaft

**Kürbis** *der;* ~ses, ~se pumpkin

**Kurde** *der;* ~n, ~n, **Kurdin** *die;* ~, ~nen Kurd

**kurdisch** *Adj.* Kurdish

**Kur-:** ~**fürst** *der* (hist.) Elector; ~**gast** *der* visitor to a/the spa; (Patient) patient at a/the spa

**Kurier** *der;* ~s, ~e courier

**kurieren** *tr. V.* (auch fig.) cure (**von** of)

**Kurierin** *die;* ~, ~nen ▶ KURIER

**kurios** 1 *Adj.* curious
2 *adv.* curiously; strangely; oddly

**Kuriosität** *die;* ~, ~en **(a)** strangeness
**(b)** (Gegenstand) curiosity; curio

**Kur-:** ~**konzert** *das* concert [at a spa]; ~**ort** *der* spa; ~**pfuscher** *der*, ~**pfuscherin** *die* (ugs. abwertend) quack

**Kurs** *der;* ~es, ~e **(a)** (Richtung) course; **ein harter/weicher** ~ (fig.) a hard/soft line
**(b)** (von Wertpapieren) price; (von Devisen) exchange rate; **der** ~ **des Dollars** the dollar rate
**(c)** (Lehrgang) course; (Teilnehmer) class

**Kürschner** *der;* ~s, ~, **Kürschnerin** *die;* ~, ~nen furrier

**kursieren** *itr. V.; auch mit sein* circulate

**Kurs·teilnehmer** *der*, **Kurs·teilnehmerin** *die* course participant

**Kursus** *der;* ~, Kurse ▶ KURS

**Kurs·wagen** *der* (Eisenb.) through carriage

**Kur·taxe** *die;* visitors' tax (*at a spa*)

**Kurve** *die;* ~, ~n **(a)** (einer Straße) bend
**(b)** (Geom.) curve
**(c)** (in der Statistik, Temperatur~ usw.) graph

**kurven** *itr. V.; mit sein* **(a)** ⟨*aircraft*⟩ circle; ⟨*tanks etc.*⟩ circle [round]
**(b)** (ugs.: fahren) drive around

**kurven·reich** *Adj.* winding; twisting

**kurz; kürzer, kürzest...** 1 *Adj.* short; (zeitlich; knapp) short, brief; quick ⟨*look*⟩
2 *adv.* **(a)** (zeitlich) briefly; (knapp) ~ **gesagt** in a word
**(b)** (wenig) just; ~ **vor/hinter der Kreuzung** just before/past the crossroads; ~ **vor/nach Pfingsten** just before/after Whitsun

**kurz-, Kurz-:** ~**arbeit** *die* short-time working; ~**ärm[e]lig** *Adj.* short-sleeved

**Kürze** *die;* ~ **(a)** shortness
**(b)** (geringe Dauer) shortness; brevity; **in** ~: shortly
**(c)** (Knappheit) brevity

**Kürzel** *das;* ~s, ~: shorthand symbol

**kürzen** *tr. V.* shorten; abridge ⟨*article, book*⟩; cut ⟨*pension, budget*⟩

**kürzer** ▶ KURZ

**kurzer·hand** *Adv.* without more ado

**kürzest...** ▶ KURZ

**kurz-, Kurz-:** ~**fristig** 1 *Adj.* **(a)** ⟨*refusal, resignation, etc.*⟩ at short notice; **(b)** (für kurze Zeit) short-term; 2 *adv.* **(a)** at short notice; **(b)** (für kurze Zeit) for a short time; (auf kurze Sicht) in the short term; (in kurzer Zeit) without delay; ~**geschichte** *die* short story; ~**haar·frisur** *die* bob; bobbed hairstyle; ~**lebig** *Adj.* (auch fig.) short-lived; ~**lebigkeit** *die;* ~~: short-livedness

**kürzlich** *Adv.* recently; not long ago

**kurz-, Kurz-:** ~**meldung** *die* brief report; (während einer anderen Sendung) news flash; ~**parker** *der;* ~~s, ~~, ~**parkerin** *die;* ~~, ~~nen short-stay (Brit.) *or* short-term parker; ~**schluss**, *~*~**schluß** *der* (Elektrot.) short circuit; ~**sichtig** (auch fig.) 1 *Adj.* short-sighted; 2 *adv.* short-sightedly; ~**sichtigkeit** *die;* ~~ (auch fig.) short-sightedness

**k**

**Kurzstrecken·rakete** *die* short-range missile

**Kürzung** *die;* ∼, ∼en cut

**kurz-, Kurz-:** ∼**waren** *Pl.* haberdashery *sing.* (Brit.); notions (Amer.); ∼**welle** *die* (Physik, Rundf.) short wave; ∼**weilig** *Adj.* entertaining; ∼**zeitig** [1] *Adj.* brief; [2] *adv.* briefly

**kuschelig** *Adj.* cosy

**kuscheln** *refl. V.* sich an jmdn. ∼: snuggle up to sb.

**Kuschel·tier** *das* cuddly toy

**kuschen** *itr. V.* knuckle under (**vor** + *Dat.* to)

**Kusine** *die;* ∼, ∼n ▶ COUSINE

**Kuss, *Kuß** *der;* Kusses, Küsse kiss

**kuss·echt, *kuß·echt** *Adj.* kissproof

**küssen** *tr., itr. V.* kiss

**Kuss·hand, *Kuß·hand** *die:* jmdm. eine ∼ zuwerfen blow sb. a kiss; **mit** ∼ (ugs.) gladly

**Küste** *die;* ∼, ∼n coast

**Küsten-:** ∼**linie** *die* coastline; ∼**wache** *die* coastguard [service]

**Küster** *der;* ∼s, ∼, **Küsterin** *die;* ∼, ∼nen sexton

**Kutsche** *die;* ∼, ∼n coach

**Kutscher** *der;* ∼s, ∼, **Kutscherin** *die;* ∼, ∼nen coach driver

**kutschieren** [1] *itr. V.; mit sein* drive, ride [in a coach]
[2] *tr. V.* jmdn. ∼: drive sb. [in a coach]

**Kutte** *die;* ∼, ∼n [monk's/nun's] habit

**Kutter** *der;* ∼s, ∼: cutter

**Kuvert** /ku'veːɐ̯/ *das;* ∼s, ∼s envelope; (geh.: Gedeck) cover

**Kuwait** /ku'vaiːt/ (*das*); ∼s Kuwait

**Kybernetik** *die;* ∼: cybernetics *sing.*

**Kybernetiker** *der;* ∼s, ∼, **Kybernetikerin** *die;* ∼, ∼nen cybernetician; cyberneticist

**kybernetisch** *Adj.* cybernetic

**KZ** *Abk.* = **Konzentrationslager**

**KZ-Häftling** *der,* **KZler** *der;* ∼s, ∼, **KZlerin** *die;* ∼, ∼nen concentration-camp prisoner

# L l

**l, L** /ɛl/ *das;* ∼, ∼: l/L

**l** *Abk.* = **Liter** l.

**Lab** *das;* ∼[e]s, ∼e rennet

**labberig** *Adj.* (ugs. abwertend) **(a)** (fade) wishy-washy; ∼ **schmecken** taste of nothing **(b)** (weich) floppy, limp ⟨*material*⟩; floppy ⟨*trousers, dress, etc.*⟩

**laben** (geh.) [1] *tr. V.* jmdn. ∼: give sb. refreshment
[2] *refl. V.* refresh oneself (**an** + *Dat.,* **mit** with)

**labern** *itr. V.* (ugs. abwertend) rabbit (Brit. coll.) or babble on

**labil** *Adj.* **(a)** (Med.) delicate ⟨*constitution, health*⟩; poor ⟨*circulation*⟩ **(b)** (auch Psych.) unstable ⟨*person, character, situation, etc.*⟩

**Labor** *das;* ∼s, ∼s, *auch:* ∼e laboratory

**Laboratorium** *das;* ∼s, **Laboratorien** laboratory

**Labyrinth** *das;* ∼[e]s, ∼e maze; labyrinth

**Lache¹** *die;* ∼, ∼n (ugs.) laugh

**Lache²** /'la(ː)xə/ *die;* ∼, ∼n puddle; (von Blut, Öl) pool

**lächeln** *itr. V.* smile (**über** + *Akk.* at)

**Lächeln** *das;* ∼s smile

**lachen** [1] *itr. V.* laugh (**über** + *Akk.* at)
[2] *tr. V.* was gibt es denn zu ∼? what's so funny?

**Lachen** *das;* ∼s laughter; **ein lautes** ∼: a loud laugh

**lächerlich** [1] *Adj.* ridiculous; ludicrous ⟨*argument, statement*⟩
[2] *adv.* ridiculously

**Lächerlichkeit** *die;* ∼: ridiculousness; (von Argumenten, Behauptungen usw.) ludicrousness

**lachhaft** *Adj.* ridiculous

**Lachs** *der;* ∼es, ∼e salmon

**Lack** *der;* ∼[e]s, ∼e varnish; (für Metall, Lackarbeiten) lacquer

**lackieren** *tr. V.* varnish; spray ⟨*car*⟩

**Lack·leder** *das* patent leather

**Lade** *die;* ∼, ∼n (landsch.) drawer

**Lade·hemmung** *die* jam

**laden¹** [1] *unr. tr. V.* load; (Physik) charge
[2] *unr. itr. V.* load [up]

**laden²** *unr. tr. V.* **(a)** (Rechtsspr.) summon **(b)** (geh.: einladen) invite

**Laden** *der;* ∼s, Läden **(a)** shop; store (Amer.); **der** ∼ **läuft** (ugs.) business is good **(b)** (Fensterladen) shutter

**Laden-:** ∼**dieb** *der,* ∼**diebin** *die* shoplifter; ∼**diebstahl** *der* shoplifting;

---

*old spelling - see note on page xiv

~**schluss,** *~**schluß** *der* shop *or* (Amer.) store closing time; ~**tisch** *der* [shop] counter

**Lade-:** ~**rampe** *die* loading ramp; ~**raum** *der* (beim Auto) luggage space; (beim Flugzeug, Schiff) hold; (bei LKWs) payload space

**lädieren** *tr. V.* damage

**lädst** *2. Pers. Sg. Präsens v.* LADEN

**lädt** *3. Pers. Sg. Präsens v.* LADEN

**Ladung** *die;* ~, ~**en** (a) (Schiffs~, Flugzeug~) cargo; (eines LKW) load (b) (beim Sprengen, Schießen; Physik) charge (c) (Rechtsspr.: Vor~) summons *sing.*

**lag** *1. u. 3. Pers. Sg. Prät. v.* LIEGEN

**Lage** *die;* ~, ~**n** (a) situation; **eine gute** ~ **haben** be well situated (b) (Art des Liegens) position (c) (Situation) situation

**Lage-plan** *der* map of the area

**Lager** *das;* ~**s,** ~ (a) camp (b) storeroom; (in Geschäften, Betrieben) stockroom (c) (Warenbestand) stock

**Lager-:** ~**bestand** *der* (Wirtsch.) stock; **den** ~**bestand aufnehmen** do a stocktake; ~**feuer** *das* campfire; ~**halle** *die* warehouse

**lagern** ① *tr. V.* (a) store (b) (hinlegen) lay down ② *itr. V.* (a) camp (b) (liegen) lie; ⟨foodstuffs, medicines, etc.⟩ be kept

**Lager-:** ~**platz** *der* campsite; ~**raum** storeroom; (im Geschäft, Betrieb) stockroom

**Lagerung** *die;* ~, ~**en** storage

**Lagune** *die;* ~, ~**n** lagoon

**lahm** *Adj.* (a) (gelähmt) lame; (ugs.: unbeweglich) stiff (b) (ugs.: unzureichend) lame ⟨excuse, explanation, etc.⟩ (c) (ugs. abwertend: matt) dreary

**lahmen** *itr. V.* be lame

**lähmen** *tr. V.* paralyse; (fig.) paralyse ⟨economy, industry⟩; bring ⟨traffic⟩ to a standstill

**Lähmung** *die;* ~, ~**en** paralysis; (fig.) (der Wirtschaft, Industrie) paralysis; **zu einer** ~ **des Verkehrs führen** bring traffic to a standstill

**Laib** *der;* ~**[e]s,** ~**e** loaf; **ein [halber]** ~ **Brot** [half] a loaf of bread

**Laich** *der;* ~**[e]s,** ~**e** spawn

**laichen** *itr. V.* spawn

**Laie** *die;* ~**n,** ~**n** (Mann) layman; (Frau) laywoman

**Lakai** *der;* ~**en,** ~**en** lackey; liveried footman

**Lake** *die;* ~, ~**n** brine

**Laken** *das;* ~**s,** ~ (bes. nordd.) sheet

**Lakritze** *die;* ~, ~**n** liquorice

**lallen** *tr., itr. V.* ⟨baby⟩ babble; ⟨drunk/drowsy person⟩ mumble

**Lamelle** *die;* ~, ~**n** (einer Jalousie) slat; (eines Heizkörpers) rib

**lamentieren** *itr. V.* (ugs.) moan (**über** + *Akk.* about)

**Lametta** *das;* ~**s** lametta

**Lamm** *das;* ~**[e]s,** **Lämmer** lamb

**lamm-, Lamm-:** ~**fell** *das* lambskin; ~**fleisch** *das* lamb; ~**fromm** ① *Adj.* ⟨person⟩ as meek as a [little] lamb; ② *adv.* ⟨answer⟩ like a lamb

**Lämpchen** *das;* ~**s,** ~: small *or* little light; **ein rotes** ~: a little red light

**Lampe** *die;* ~, ~**n** light; (Tisch~, Öl~, Signal~) lamp

**Lampen-:** ~**fieber** *das* stage fright; ~**schirm** *der* [lamp]shade

**Lampion** /lamˈpiɔŋ/ *der;* ~**s,** ~**s** Chinese lantern

**Land** *das;* ~**es,** **Länder** *od.* (veralt.) ~**e** (a) land *no indef. art.;* (dörfliche Gegend) country *no indef. art.;* **an** ~: ashore; **auf dem** ~ **wohnen** live in the country (b) (Staat) country; **hier zu** ~**e** [here] in this country (c) (Bundesland) Land; state; (österr.) province

**Land-:** ~**arbeiter** *der,* ~**arbeiterin** *die* agricultural worker; farm worker; ~**bevölkerung** *die* rural population

**Lande-:** ~**anflug** *der* (Flugw.) [landing] approach; ~**bahn** *die* (Flugw.) [landing] runway; ~**erlaubnis** *die* (Flugw.) permission to land *no art.*

**landen** ① *itr. V.; mit sein* (a) land; (ankommen) arrive (b) (ugs.: gelangen) land up ② *tr. V.* (a) land ⟨aircraft, troops, passengers, fish, etc.⟩ (b) (ugs.: zustande bringen) pull off ⟨victory, coup⟩; have ⟨smash hit⟩

**Ländereien** *Pl.* estates

**Länder-:** ~**kampf** *der* (Sport) international match; ~**spiel** *das* (Sport) international [match]

**Landes-:** ~**innere** *das* interior [of the country]; ~**kunde** *die* regional studies *pl., no art.;* ~**regierung** *die* government of a/ the Land/province; ~**sprache** *die* language of the country

**Lande-steg** *der* landing stage; jetty

**Landes-:** ~**tracht** *die* national costume *or* dress; ~**verrat** *der* (Rechtsw.) treason; ~**währung** *die* currency of a/the country

**land-, Land-:** ~**flucht** *die* migration from the land *or* countryside [to the towns]; ~**friedens-bruch** *der* (Rechtsw.) breach of the peace; ~**gewinnung** *die* reclamation of land; ~**haus** *das* country house; ~**karte** *die* map; ~**kreis** *der* district; ~**läufig** *Adj.* widely accepted

**ländlich** *Adj.* rural; country *attrib.* ⟨life⟩

**Land-:** ~**luft** *die* country air; ~**plage** *die* (fig.) pest; nuisance; ~**ratte** *die* (ugs.) landlubber

**Landschaft** *die;* ~, ~en landscape;
(ländliche Gegend) countryside
**landschaftlich** ⓵ *Adj.* regional
⓶ *adv.* ~ herrlich gelegen sein be in a
glorious natural setting; **die Umgebung der
Stadt ist** ~ **sehr schön** the town is in *or* has
a beautiful natural setting
**Land·schul·heim** *das* ▶ SCHULLANDHEIM
**Lands-:** ~**mann** *der; Pl.* ~**leute** fellow
countryman; compatriot; ~**männin** *die;*
~~, ~~**nen** fellow countrywoman;
compatriot
**Land-:** ~**straße** *die* country road; (im
Gegensatz zur Autobahn) ordinary road;
~**streicher** *der;* ~~**s**, ~~,
~**streicherin** *die;* ~~, ~~**nen** tramp;
~**strich** *der* area; ~**tag** *der* Landtag; state
parliament; (österr.) provincial parliament
**Landung** *die;* ~, ~en landing
**Landungs·brücke** *die* [floating] landing
stage
**land-, Land-:** ~**weg** *der* overland route;
**auf dem** ~**weg** overland; ~**wirt** *der,*
~**wirtin** *die* farmer; ~**wirtschaft** *die*
agriculture *no art.;* farming *no art.;*
~**wirtschaftlich** ⓵ *Adj.* agricultural;
⓶ *adv.* ~**wirtschaftlich genutzt werden** be
used for agricultural purposes; ~**zunge** *die*
(Geogr.) tongue of land
**lang; länger, längst...** ⓵ *Adj.* long; (ugs.:
groß) tall
⓶ *adv.* [for] a long time; **eine Sekunde/
mehrere Stunden** ~: for a second/several
hours
**lang-:** ~**ärm[e]lig** *Adj.* long-sleeved;
~**atmig** ⓵ *Adj.* long-winded; ⓶ *adv.* long-
windedly; ⟨relate⟩ at great length
**lange; länger, am längsten** *Adv.* **(a)** a long
time; **bist du schon** ~ **hier?** have you been
here long?
**(b)** (bei weitem) **ich bin noch** ~ **nicht fertig** I'm
nowhere near finished; **hier is es** ~ **nicht so
schön** it isn't nearly as nice here
**Länge** *die;* ~, ~n length; (Geogr.) longitude
**langen** (ugs.) ⓵ *itr. V.* **(a)** be enough
**(b)** (greifen) reach (**in** + *Akk.* into; **auf** + *Akk.*
on to; **nach** for)
⓶ *tr. V.* **jmdm. eine** ~ (ugs.) give sb. a clout
[around the ear] (coll.)
**Längen·grad** *der* (Geogr.) degree of
longitude
**länger** ⓵ ▶ LANG, LANGE;
⓶ *Adj.* **seit** ~**er Zeit** for quite some time
**Lange·weile** *die;* ~ *od.* **Langenweile**
boredom; ~ **haben** be bored
**lang-, Lang-:** ~**fristig** ⓵ *Adj.* long-term;
long-dated ⟨loan⟩; ⓶ *adv.* on a long-term
basis; ~**jährig** *Adj.* ⟨customer, friend⟩ of
many years' standing; long-standing
⟨friendship⟩; ~**jährige Erfahrung** many years

of experience; ~**lauf** *der* (Skisport) cross-
country; ~**lebig** *Adj.* long-lived ⟨animals,
organisms⟩; durable ⟨goods, materials⟩
**länglich** *Adj.* oblong
**lang-, Lang-:** ~**mut** *die;* ~~:
forbearance; ~**mütig** *Adj.* forbearing;
~**mütigkeit** *die;* ~~: forbearance
**längs** ⓵ *Präp.* + *Gen. od.* (selten) *Dat.* along
⓶ *Adv.* lengthways
**Längs·achse** *die* longitudinal axis
**langsam** ⓵ *Adj.* slow
⓶ *adv.* **(a)** slowly; ~, **aber sicher** (ugs.)
slowly but surely
**(b)** (allmählich) gradually
**Lang-:** ~**schläfer** *der,* ~**schläferin** *die*
late riser; ~**spiel·platte** *die* long-playing
record; LP
**Längs·schnitt** *der* longitudinal section
**längst** *Adv.* **(a)** (schon lange) a long time ago
**(b)** (bei weitem) **hier ist es** ~ **nicht so schön** it
isn't nearly as nice here
**längst...** ▶ LANG
**längstens** *Adv.* (ugs.) (höchstens) at [the]
most; (spätestens) at the latest
**Languste** *die;* ~, ~n spiny lobster
**lang-, Lang-:** ~**weilen** ⓵ *tr. V.* bore;
⓶ *refl. V.* be bored; ~**weilig** ⓵ *Adj.*
boring; dull ⟨place⟩; ⓶ *adv.* boringly;
~**welle** *die* (Physik, Rundf.) long wave;
~**wierig** *Adj.* lengthy; prolonged ⟨search⟩
**Lanze** *die;* ~, ~n lance; (zum Werfen) spear
**Laos** (das); Laos' Laos
**Laote** *der;* ~n, ~n, **Laotin** *die;* ~, ~nen
Laotian
**lapidar** ⓵ *Adj.* (kurz, aber wirkungsvoll)
succinct; (knapp) terse
⓶ *adv.* succinctly/tersely
**Lappalie** /la'pa:li̯ə/ *die;* ~, ~n trifle
**Lappe** *der;* ~n, ~n Lapp
**Lappen** *der;* ~s, ~: cloth; (Fetzen) rag;
(Wasch~) flannel
**Lappin** *die;* ~, ~nen Lapp
**läppisch** *Adj.* silly
**Lapp·land** (das); ~s Lapland
**Laptop** *der;* ~s, ~s (DV) laptop
**Lärche** *die;* ~, ~n larch
**Lärm** *der;* ~[e]s noise; (Krach) din; row (coll.)
**Lärm·belästigung** *die* disturbance
caused by noise
**lärmen** *itr. V.* make a noise *or* (coll.) row
**Lärm-:** ~**pegel** *der* noise level; ~**schutz**
*der* **(a)** protection against noise;
**(b)** (Vorrichtung) noise barrier; noise *or* sound
insulation *no indef. art.;* ~**schutz·wand**
*die* sound-insulating wall
**Larve** *die;* ~, ~n grub; larva
**las** *1. u. 3. Pers. Sg. Prät. v.* LESEN
**lasch** ⓵ *Adj.* limp ⟨handshake⟩; feeble
⟨action, measure⟩; lax ⟨upbringing⟩
⓶ *adv.* s. *Adj.*: limply; feebly; laxly

**Lasche** *die;* ~, ~n (Gürtel~) loop; (eines Briefumschlags) flap; (Schuh~) tongue
**Laser** /'leɪzɐ/ *der;* ~s, ~ (Physik) laser
**Laser-:** ~**drucker** *der* (DV) laser printer; ~**pointer** *der* (DV) laser pointer
**lass, \*laß** *Imperativ Sg. v.* LASSEN
**lassen** ① *unr. tr. V.* (a) *mit Inf. + Akk.* (2. *Part.* lassen) (veranlassen) etw. tun/machen/ bauen/waschen ~: have *or* get sth. done/ made/built/washed; jmdn. warten ~: keep sb. waiting; jmdn. grüßen ~: send one's regards to sb.; jmdn. kommen/rufen ~: send for sb.
(b) *mit Inf. + Akk.* (2.*Part.* lassen) (erlauben) jmdn. etw. tun ~: let sb. do sth.; allow sb. to do sth.
(c) (belassen) jmdn. in Frieden ~: leave sb. in peace
(d) (hinein~/heraus~) let *or* allow (in + *Akk.* into, aus out of)
(e) (unterlassen) stop
(f) (zurück~; bleiben ~) leave
(g) (überlassen) jmdm. etw. ~: let sb. have sth.
(h) (als Aufforderung) lass/lasst uns gehen/ fahren! let's go!
(i) (verlieren) lose; (ausgeben) spend
② *unr. refl. V.* die Tür lässt sich leicht öffnen the door opens easily; das lässt sich nicht beweisen it can't be proved
③ *unr. itr. V.* (a) (ugs.) Lass mal. Ich mache das schon Leave it. I'll do it
(b) (veranlassen) ich lasse bitten would you ask him/her/them to come in
**lässig** ① *Adj.* casual
② *adv.* casually
**lässt, \*läßt** *3. Pers. Sg. Präsens v.* LASSEN
**Last** *die;* ~, ~en load; (Gewicht) weight; (Bürde) burden
**lasten** *itr. V.* be a burden; auf jmdm./etw. ~: weigh heavily [up]on sb./sth.
**Laster¹** *der;* ~s, ~ (ugs.: Lkw) truck; lorry (Brit.)
**Laster²** *das;* ~s, ~: vice
**lasterhaft** *Adj.* (abwertend) depraved
**lästern** ① *itr. V.* (abwertend) über jmdn./etw. ~: make malicious remarks about sb./sth.
② *tr. V.* (veralt.) blaspheme against
**lästig** *Adj.* tiresome; troublesome ⟨*illness, cough, etc.*⟩
**Last-:** ~**schrift** *die* debit; ~**wagen** *der* truck; lorry (Brit.)
**Lasur** *die;* ~, ~en varnish; (farbig) glaze
**Latein** *das;* ~s Latin
**Latein·amerika** ⟨*das*⟩ Latin America
**lateinisch** *Adj.* Latin
**latent** *Adj.* latent
**Laterne** *die;* ~, ~n (a) (Leuchte) lamp; lantern (Naut.)
(b) (Straßen~) street light
**Laternen·pfahl** *der* lamp post
**Latrine** *die;* ~, ~n latrine

**latschen** *itr. V.; mit sein* (salopp) trudge; (schlurfend) slouch
**Latschen** *der;* ~s, ~ (ugs.) old worn-out shoe/slipper
**Latte** *die;* ~, ~n (a) lath; (Zaun~) pale
(b) (Sport: Quer~ des Tores) [cross]bar
(c) (Leichtathletik) bar
**Latten-:** ~**rost** *der* (auf dem Boden) duckboards *pl.;* (eines Bettes) slatted frame ~**zaun** *der* paling fence
**Latz** *der;* ~es, Lätze bib
**Lätzchen** *das;* ~s, ~: bib
**lau** *Adj.* tepid, lukewarm ⟨*water etc.*⟩; mild ⟨*wind, air, evening, etc.*⟩
**Laub** *das;* ~[e]s leaves *pl.;* dichtes ~: thick foliage
**Laub·baum** *der* broad-leaved tree
**Laube** *die;* ~, ~n summer house; (überdeckter Sitzplatz) bower; arbour
**Laub-:** ~**frosch** *der* tree frog; ~**säge** *die* fretsaw; ~**wald** *der* deciduous wood/forest
**Lauch** *der;* ~[e]s (Porree) leek
**Lauer** *die;* ~: auf der ~ liegen *od.* sein (ugs.) (jmdm. auflauern) lie in wait
**lauern** *itr. V.* (auch fig.) lurk
**Lauf** *der;* ~[e]s, Läufe (a) running
(b) (Sport: Wettrennen) heat
(c) (Ver~) course; im ~[e] der Zeit in the course of time; im ~[e] der Jahre/des Tages over the years/during the day
(d) (von Schusswaffen) barrel
**Lauf·bahn** *die* (a) (Werdegang) career
(b) (Leichtathletik) running track
**laufen** ① *unr. itr. V.; mit sein* (a) run; (beim Eislauf) skate; (beim Ski~) ski; (gehen) go; (zu Fuß gehen) walk; in ⟨*Akk.*⟩/gegen etw. ~: walk into sth.; dauernd zum Arzt ~ (ugs.) keep running to the doctor
(b) (im Gang sein) ⟨*machine*⟩ be running; ⟨*radio, television, etc.*⟩ be on; (funktionieren) ⟨*machine*⟩ run; ⟨*radio, television, etc.*⟩ work
(c) (gelten) ⟨*contract, agreement, engagement, etc.*⟩ run
(d) (gespielt werden) ⟨*programme, play, etc.*⟩ be on
② *unr. tr. u. itr. V.* (a) *mit sein* (zurücklegen) (zu Fuß) walk; (rennen) run
(b) *mit sein* (erzielen) einen Rekord ~: set up a record
(c) *mit haben od. sein* Ski/Schlittschuh/ Rollschuh ~: ski/skate/roller-skate
**laufend** ① *Adj.* (a) (ständig) regular ⟨*interest, income*⟩; recurring ⟨*costs*⟩
(b) (gegenwärtig) current ⟨*issue, year, month, etc.*⟩
② *adv.* constantly; ⟨*increase*⟩ steadily
**Läufer** *der;* ~s, ~ (a) (Sport) runner; (Handball; Fußball veralt.) halfback
(b) (Teppich) ⟨*long narrow*⟩ carpet
**Läuferin** *die;* ~, ~nen ▶ LÄUFER A
**Lauf·feuer** *das* brush fire; wie ein ~: like wildfire
**Lauf-:** ~**masche** *die* ladder; ~**pass,** ···⁖

**\*~paß** *der:* er hat seiner Freundin den ~pass gegeben (ugs.) he finished with his girlfriend (coll.); **~schritt** *der:* im ~schritt, marsch, marsch! at the double, quick march!

**läufst** 2. *Pers. Sg. Präsens v.* LAUFEN

**Lauf·stall** *der* playpen

**läuft** 3. *Pers. Sg. Präsens v.* LAUFEN

**Laufwerk** *das* (Technik) mechanism; (DV) drive

**Lauge** *die;* ~, ~n (a) soapy water (b) (Chemie) alkaline solution

**Laugen·brezel** *die* (südd.) pretzel

**Laune** *die;* ~, ~n mood

**launenhaft** *Adj.* temperamental; (unberechenbar) capricious

**launig** witty

**launisch** *Adj.:* ▶ LAUNENHAFT

**Laus** *die;* ~, Läuse louse

**Laus·bub** *der* little rascal

**Lausch·aktion** *die,* **Lausch·angriff** *der* bugging operation (coll.)

**lauschen** *itr. V.* (a) (horchen) listen (b) (zuhören) listen [attentively]

**Lauscher** *der;* ~s, **Lauscherin** *die;* ~, ~nen eavesdropper

**lauschig** *Adj.* cosy, snug ⟨corner⟩

**lausig** [1] *Adj.* (ugs.) (a) (abwertend: unangenehm, schäbig) lousy (coll.); rotten (coll.) (b) (sehr groß) perishing (Brit. coll.), freezing ⟨cold⟩; terrible (coll.) ⟨heat⟩ [2] *adv.* terribly (coll.)

**laut¹** [1] *Adj.* loud; (geräuschvoll) noisy [2] *adv.* loudly; (geräuschvoll) noisily

**laut²** *Präp. + Gen. od. Dat.* (Amtsspr.) according to

**Laut** *der;* ~[e]s, ~e sound

**Laute** *die;* ~, ~n lute

**lauten** *itr. V.* ⟨answer, instruction, slogan⟩ be, run; ⟨letter, passage, etc.⟩ read, go; ⟨law⟩ state

**läuten** [1] *tr., itr. V.* ring; ⟨alarm clock⟩ go off
[2] *itr. V.* (bes. südd.: klingeln) ring; es läutete the bell rang *or* went (**zu** for)

**lauter¹** *Adj.* (geh.) honourable ⟨person, intentions, etc.⟩; honest ⟨truth⟩

**lauter²** *indekl. Adj.* nothing but; sheer ⟨nonsense, joy, etc.⟩

**läutern** *tr. V.* (geh.) reform ⟨character⟩; purify ⟨soul⟩

**Läuterung** *die;* ~, ~en (geh.) reformation; (der Seele) purification

**laut·hals** *Adv.* at the top of one's voice; ~ lachen roar with laughter

**lautlich** [1] *Adj.* phonetic [2] *adv.* phonetically

**laut-, Laut-:** ~**los** [1] *Adj.* silent; soundless; (wortlos) silent; [2] *adv.* silently; soundlessly; ~**schrift** *die* (Phon.) phonetic alphabet; (Umschrift) phonetic transcription;

---

**~sprecher** *der* loudspeaker; (einer Stereoanlage usw.) speaker; ~**stark** [1] *Adj.* loud; vociferous, loud ⟨protest⟩; [2] *adv.* loudly; ⟨protest⟩ vociferously; ~**stärke** *die* volume

**lau·warm** *Adj.* lukewarm

**Lava** *die;* ~, Laven (Geol.) lava

**Lavendel** *der;* ~s, ~: lavender

**Lawine** *die;* ~, ~n (auch fig.) avalanche; **eine** ~ **von Protesten** (fig.) a storm of protest

**Lawinen·gefahr** *die* danger of avalanches

**lax** [1] *Adj.* lax [2] *adv.* laxly

**Laxheit** *die;* ~: laxness; laxity

**Layout** /ˈleːˈaʊt/ *das;* ~s, ~s (Druckw., Elektronik) layout

**Lazarett** *das;* ~[e]s, ~e military hospital

**Lead·sänger** /ˈliːt-/ *der,*
**Lead·sängerin** *die* lead singer

**leasen** /ˈliːzn̩/ *tr. V.* rent; (für längere Zeit mieten) lease ⟨car etc.⟩

**leben** *itr. V.* live; (lebendig sein) be alive; leb[e] wohl! farewell!; **von seiner Rente/seinem Gehalt** ~: live on one's pension/salary

**Leben** *das;* ~s, ~ (a) life; **das** ~: life; **sich** (*Dat.*) **das** ~ **nehmen** take one's [own] life; **am** ~ **sein/bleiben** be/stay alive; **ums** ~ **kommen** lose one's life (b) (Betriebsamkeit) **auf dem Markt herrschte ein reges** ~: the market was bustling with activity; **das** ~ **auf der Straße** the comings and goings in the street

**lebend** *Adj.* living; live ⟨animal⟩

**lebendig** [1] *Adj.* living; (lebhaft) lively [2] *adv.* (lebhaft) in a lively way

**Lebendigkeit** *die;* ~: liveliness

**lebens-, Lebens-:** ~**abend** *der* (geh.) evening of one's life (literary); ~**art** *die* (a) way of life; (b) (Umgangsformen) manners *pl.*; ~**aufgabe** *die* life's work; ~**bejahend** *Adj.* ⟨person⟩ with a positive attitude to life; ~**bereich** *der* area of life; ~**dauer** *die* lifespan; ~**ende** *das* end [of one's life]; ~**erinnerungen** *Pl.* memories of one's life; (aufgezeichnet) memoirs; ~**erwartung** *die* life expectancy; ~**fähig** *Adj.* (auch fig.) viable; ~**freude** *die* zest for life; ~**froh** *Adj.* full of zest for life *postpos.*; ~**gefahr** *die* mortal danger; „Achtung, ~**gefahr!**" 'danger'; ~**gefährlich** [1] *Adj.* highly dangerous; critical ⟨injury⟩; [2] *adv.* critically ⟨injured, ill⟩; ~**gefährte** *der,* ~**gefährtin** *die* (geh.) companion through life (literary); ~**geister** *Pl.* jmds. ~**geister [wieder] wecken** put new life into sb.; ~**groß** *Adj.* life-size; ~**größe** *die:* **eine Statue in** ~**größe** a life-size statue

**Lebens·haltung** *die* cost of living

**Lebenshaltungs-:** ~**index** *der* (Wirtsch.) cost-of-living index; ~**kosten** *Pl.* cost of living *sing.*

**lebens-, Lebens-:** ~**jahr** *das* year of [one's] life; ~**kraft** *die* vitality;

---

~**künstler** der, ~**künstlerin** die: ein [echter/wahrer] ~**künstler** a person who always knows how to make the best of things; ~**lage** die situation [in life]; ~**lang** ① Adj. lifelong; ② adv. all one's life; ~**länglich** ① Adj. ~länglicher Freiheitsentzug life imprisonment; ② adv. jmdn. ~länglich gefangen halten keep sb. imprisoned for life; ~**lauf** der curriculum vitae; c.v.; ~**licht** das (geh.) flame of life (literary); jmdm. das ~licht ausblasen od. auspusten (ugs.) send sb. to kingdom come (coll.); ~**lustig** Adj. ⟨person⟩ full of the joys of life

**Lebens·mittel** das food[stuff]; ~ Pl. food sing.

**Lebensmittel-:** ~**abteilung** die food department; ~**geschäft** das food shop; ~**vergiftung** die food poisoning

**lebens-, Lebens-:** ~**müde** Adj. weary of life pred.; ~**notwendig** Adj. essential; ~**raum** der (a) (Umkreis) lebensraum; (b) (Biol.) ▸ BIOTOP; ~**retter** der, ~**retterin** die rescuer; ~**standard** der standard of living; ~**unterhalt** der: seinen ~unterhalt verdienen/bestreiten earn one's living/ support oneself; ~**versicherung** die life insurance; ~**wandel** der way of life; ~**weg** der ⟨journey through⟩ life; ~**weise** die way of life; ~**zeichen** das sign of life; ~**zeit** die life[span]; auf ~zeit for life

**Leber** die; ~, ~n liver

**Leber-:** ~**fleck** der liver spot; ~**käse** der: meat loaf made with mincemeat, [minced liver,] eggs, and spices; ~**tran** der fish-liver oil; (des Kabeljaus) cod-liver oil; ~**wurst** die liver sausage; ~**zirrhose** die (Med.) cirrhosis of the liver

**Lebe-:** ~**wesen** das living being; ~**wohl** /-'--/ das; ~~[e]s, ~~ od. ~~e (geh.) farewell

**lebhaft** ① Adj. (a) lively; busy ⟨traffic⟩; brisk ⟨business⟩ (b) (deutlich) vivid ⟨idea, picture, etc.⟩ (c) (kräftig) bright ⟨colour⟩; vigorous ⟨applause, opposition⟩ ② adv. (a) in a lively way (b) (deutlich) vividly (c) (kräftig) brightly ⟨coloured⟩

**leb-, Leb-:** ~**kuchen** der ≈ gingerbread; ~**los** Adj. lifeless; ~**zeiten** Pl. bei od. zu jmds. ~zeiten during sb.'s lifetime

**lechzen** itr. V. (geh.) nach einem Trunk ~: long for a drink; nach Rache usw. ~: thirst for revenge etc.

**leck** Adj. leaky; ~ sein leak

**Leck** das; ~[e]s, ~s leak

**lecken¹** ① tr. V. lick ② itr. V. an etw. (Dat.) ~: lick sth.

**lecken²** itr. V. (leck sein) leak

**lecker** Adj. tasty ⟨meal⟩; delicious ⟨cake etc.⟩; good ⟨smell, taste⟩

**Lecker·bissen** der delicacy; ein musikalischer ~ (fig.) a musical treat

**Leckerei** die; ~, ~en (ugs.) dainty; (Süßigkeit) sweet [meat]

**led.** Abk. = **ledig**

**Leder** das; ~s, ~: leather

**Leder-:** ~**handschuh** der leather glove; ~**hose** die leather shorts pl.; lederhosen pl.; (lang) leather trousers; ~**jacke** die leather jacket; ~**riemen** der [leather] strap; ~**waren** Pl. leather goods

**ledig** Adj. single; eine ~e Mutter an unmarried mother

**Ledige** der/die; adj. Dekl. single person

**lediglich** Adj. merely

**leer** Adj. empty; clean ⟨sheet of paper⟩; ~ stehend empty, unoccupied

**Leere** die; ~ (auch fig.) emptiness

**leeren** tr., refl. V. empty

**leer-, Leer-:** ~**gefegt** Adj. deserted ⟨street, town⟩; wie ~gefegt deserted; ~**lauf** der im ~lauf den Berg hinunterfahren ⟨driver⟩ coast down the hill in neutral; ⟨cyclist⟩ freewheel down the hill; *~**stehend** ▸ LEER; ~**taste** die space bar

**Leerung** die; ~, ~en emptying; (von Briefkästen) collection

**Lefze** die; ~, ~n lip

**legal** ① Adj. legal ② adv. legally

**legalisieren** tr. V. legalize

**Legalisierung** die; ~, ~en legalization

**Legalität** die; ~: legality

**legen** ① tr. V. (a) lay [down] (b) (verlegen) lay ⟨pipe, cable, carpet, tiles, etc.⟩ ② tr., itr. V. ⟨hen⟩ lay ③ refl. V. (a) lie down (b) (nachlassen) die down; abate; ⟨enthusiasm⟩ wear off, subside

**legendär** Adj. legendary

**Legende** die; ~, ~n legend

**leger** /le'ʒeːɐ̯/ ① Adj. casual ② adv. casually

**legieren** tr. V. alloy

**Legierung** die; ~, ~en alloy

**Legislative** die; ~, ~n (Politik) legislature

**Legislatur·periode** die legislative period

**legitim** Adj. legitimate

**Legitimation** die; ~, ~en (a) legitimation (b) (Ausweis) proof of identity

**legitimieren** ① tr. V. (a) (rechtfertigen) justify (b) (bevollmächtigen) authorize (c) (für legitim erklären) legitimize ⟨child, relationship⟩ ② refl. V. show proof of one's identity

**Legitimität** die; ~: legitimacy

**Lehm** der; ~s (Ton) clay

**Lehne** die; ∼, ∼n (Rücken∼) back; (Arm∼) arm

**lehnen** [1] tr., refl. V. lean (an + Akk., **gegen** against)

[2] itr. V. be leaning (an + Dat. against)

**Lehn-:** ∼**stuhl** der armchair; ∼**wort** das; Pl. ∼wörter loanword

**Lehr-:** ∼**auftrag** der lectureship; ∼**buch** das textbook

**Lehre** die; ∼, ∼n (a) apprenticeship (b) (Weltanschauung) doctrine (c) (Theorie, Wissenschaft) theory (d) (Erfahrung) lesson

**lehren** tr., itr. V. teach

**Lehrer** der; ∼s, ∼ (auch fig.) teacher; (Ausbilder) instructor

**Lehrer-:** ∼**ausbildung** die teacher training no art.; ∼**ausflug** die staff outing

**Lehrerin** die; ∼, ∼nen teacher

**Lehrer-:** ∼**kollegium** das teaching staff; faculty (Amer.); ∼**konferenz** das staff meeting; ∼**zimmer** das staffroom

**Lehr-:** ∼**gang** der course (für, in + Dat. in); ∼**jahr** das year as an apprentice; ∼**körper** der (Amtsspr.) teaching staff; faculty (Amer.)

**Lehrling** der; ∼s, ∼e apprentice; (in kaufmännischen Berufen) trainee

**lehr-, Lehr-:** ∼**plan** der (Schulw.) syllabus; (Gesamtlehrgang) curriculum; ∼**reich** Adj. informative; ∼**stelle** die apprenticeship; (in kaufmännischen Berufen) trainee post; ∼**stoff** der (Schulw.) syllabus

**Leib** der; ∼[e]s, ∼er (geh.) body; mit ∼ und Seele Arzt/Krankenschwester usw. sein be a dedicated doctor/nurse etc.; mit ∼ und Seele dabei sein put one's whole heart into it

**Leibes-:** ∼**übungen** Pl. (Schulw.) physical education sing.; PE; ∼**visitation** die; ∼∼, ∼∼en body search

**Leib·gericht** das favourite dish

**leibhaftig** Adj. in person postpos.; (echt) real

**leiblich** Adj. physical ⟨well-being⟩; (blutsverwandt) real

**Leib-:** ∼**schmerzen** Pl. abdominal pain sing.; ∼**wächter** der, ∼**wächterin** die bodyguard

**Leiche** die; ∼, ∼n [dead] body; corpse

**Leichen** der hearse

**leichen-, Leichen-:** ∼**blass**, \*∼**blaß** Adj. deathly pale; ∼**schau·haus** das morgue; ∼**wagen** der hearse

**Leichnam** der; ∼s, ∼e (geh.) body

**leicht** [1] Adj. light; lightweight ⟨suit, material⟩; easy ⟨task, question, job, etc.⟩; slight ⟨accent, illness, wound, doubt, etc.⟩; mild ⟨cigar, cigarette⟩; ∼ fallen be easy; das fällt mir ∼: it's easy for me; jmdm./sich etw. ∼ machen make sth. easy for sb./oneself; etw. ∼ nehmen make light of sth.

\*alte Schreibung - vgl. Hinweis auf S. xiv

[2] adv. lightly ⟨built⟩; (einfach, schnell, spielend) easily; (geringfügig) slightly; ∼ **verletzt** slightly injured

**leicht-, Leicht-:** ∼**athletik** die [track and field] athletics sing.; \*∼**fallen** ▶ LEICHT 1; ∼**fertig** [1] Adj. careless ⟨behaviour, person⟩; rash ⟨promise⟩; ill-considered, slapdash ⟨plan⟩; [2] adv. carelessly; ∼**gläubig** Adj. gullible

**Leichtigkeit** die; ∼ (geringes Gewicht) lightness; (Mühelosigkeit) ease

**leicht-, Leicht-:** \*∼**machen** ▶ LEICHT 1; \*∼**nehmen** ▶ LEICHT 1; ∼**sinn** der carelessness no indef. art.; (mit Gefahr verbunden) recklessness no indef. art.; ∼**sinnig** [1] Adj. careless; (sich, andere gefährdend) reckless; (fahrlässig) negligent; [2] adv. carelessly; (gefährlich) recklessly; ⟨promise⟩ rashly; ∼**sinniger·weise** Adv. carelessly; (gefährlicherweise) recklessly; ⟨promise⟩ rashly; \*∼**verletzt** ▶ LEICHT 2

**leid** Adj. etw./jmdn. ∼ sein/werden (ugs.) be/ get fed up with sth./sb. (coll.); s. auch LEID[2]

**Leid**[1] das; ∼[e]s (a) (Schmerz) suffering; (Kummer) grief; sorrow (b) (Unrecht) wrong; (Böses) harm

**Leid**[2]: es tut mir ∼, [dass]...: I'm sorry [that]...; er tut mir ∼: I feel sorry for him

**leiden** [1] unr. itr. V. suffer (an, unter + Dat. from)

[2] unr. tr. V. (a) jmdn. [gut] ∼ können od. mögen like sb. (b) (geh.: ertragen müssen) suffer ⟨hunger, thirst, etc.⟩

**Leiden** das; ∼s, ∼ (a) (Krankheit) illness; (Gebrechen) complaint (b) (Qual) suffering

**leidend** Adj. (a) (krank) ailing (b) (schmerzvoll) strained ⟨voice⟩; martyred ⟨expression⟩

**Leidenschaft** die; ∼, ∼en passion (zu, für for)

**leidenschaftlich** [1] Adj. passionate; vehement ⟨protest⟩

[2] adv. passionately; (eifrig) dedicatedly; etw. ∼ gern tun adore doing sth.

**Leidens·genosse** der, **Leidens·genossin** die fellow sufferer

**leider** Adv. unfortunately

**leidig** Adj. tiresome

**leidlich** Adj. reasonable

**Leid·tragende** der/die; adj. Dekl. victim

**Leier** die; ∼, ∼n lyre

**leihen** unr. tr. V. (a) jmdm. etw. ∼: lend sb. sth. (b) (entleihen) borrow

**Leih-:** ∼**gabe** die loan (Gen. from); ∼**gebühr** die hire or (Amer.) rental charge; (bei Büchern) borrowing fee; ∼**haus** das pawnbroker's; pawnshop; ∼**mutter** die; Pl. ∼mütter surrogate mother; ∼**wagen** der hire or (Amer.) rental car

**Leim** der; ∼[e]s glue

**leimen** *tr. V.* glue (an + *Akk.* to)

**Leine** *die;* ~, ~n rope; (Wäsche~, Angel~) line; (Hunde~) lead (esp. Brit.); leash; ~ **ziehen** (ugs.) clear off

**leinen** *Adj.* linen ⟨*tablecloth, sheet, etc.*⟩

**Leinen** *das;* ~s **(a)** (Gewebe) linen **(b)** (Buchw.) cloth

**Leinen·band** *der* cloth-bound volume

**Lein·wand** *die* **(a)** linen; (grob) canvas **(b)** (des Malers) canvas **(c)** (für Filme und Dias) screen

**leise** ① *Adj.* **(a)** quiet; soft ⟨*steps, music, etc.*⟩ **(b)** (leicht) faint; slight; slight, gentle ⟨*touch*⟩ ② *adv.* **(a)** quietly **(b)** (leicht; kaum merklich) slightly; ⟨*touch, rain*⟩ gently

**Leiste** *die;* ~, ~n strip; (Holz~) batten; (profiliert) moulding

**leisten** ① *tr. V.* do ⟨*work*⟩; (schaffen) achieve ⟨*a lot, nothing*⟩; **jmdm. Hilfe** ~: help sb. ② *refl. V.* (ugs.) **sich** (*Dat.*) **etw.** ~: treat oneself to sth.; **sich** (*Dat.*) **etw. [nicht]** ~ **können** [not] be able to afford sth.

**Leisten·bruch** *der* rupture

**Leistung** *die;* ~, ~en **(a)** (Qualität bzw. Quantität der Arbeit) performance **(b)** (Errungenschaft) achievement; (im Sport) performance **(c)** (Leistungsvermögen, Physik: Arbeits~) power **(d)** (Zahlung, Zuwendung) payment; (Versicherungsw.) benefit **(e)** (Dienst~) service

**leistungs-, Leistungs-:** ~**druck** *der* (bei Arbeitnehmern) pressure to work harder; (bei Sportlern, Schülern) pressure to achieve *or* to do well; ~**fähig** *Adj.* capable ⟨*person*⟩; (körperlich) able-bodied; ~**gesellschaft** *die* competitive society; ~**prinzip** *das* competitive principle; ~**sport** *der* competitive sport *no art.*

**Leit·artikel** *der* (Zeitungsw.) leading article; leader

**leiten** *tr. V.* **(a)** (anführen) lead; head; be head of ⟨*school*⟩; (verantwortlich sein für) be in charge of ⟨*project, expedition, etc.*⟩; manage ⟨*factory, enterprise*⟩; (den Vorsitz führen bei) chair; conduct ⟨*orchestra, choir*⟩; ~**der Angestellter** manager **(b)** (begleiten, führen) lead **(c)** (lenken) direct; route ⟨*traffic*⟩; (um~) divert

**Leiter**[1] *der;* ~s, ~: leader; (einer Abteilung) head; (eines Instituts) director; (einer Schule) head teacher; headmaster (Brit.); principal (esp. Amer.); (Vorsitzender) chair[man]

**Leiter**[2] *die;* ~, ~n ladder

**Leiterin** *die;* ~, ~nen ▶ LEITER[1]; (einer Schule) head teacher; headmistress (Brit.); principal (esp. Amer.)

**Leit-:** ~**motiv** *das* (Musik, Literaturw., fig.) **(a)** leitmotiv; **(b)** (Leitgedanke) dominant *or* central theme; ~**planke** *die* crash barrier; guardrail (Amer.)

**Leitung** *die;* ~, ~en **(a)** ▶ LEITEN A: leading; heading; being in charge; management; chairing **(b)** (einer Expedition usw.) leadership; (Verantwortung) responsibility (*Gen.* for); (eines Betriebes, Unternehmens) management; (einer Sitzung, Diskussion) chairmanship **(c)** (leitende Personen) management; (einer Schule) head and senior staff **(d)** (Rohr~) pipe; (Haupt~) main **(e)** (Draht, Kabel) cable; (für ein Gerät) lead **(f)** (Telefon~) line

**Leitungs·wasser** *das* tap water

**Leit·zins[satz]** *der* (Finanzw.) discount rate; ≈ base rate

**Lektion** /lɛkˈtsi̯oːn/ *die;* ~, ~en lesson

**Lektor** *der;* ~s, ~en **(a)** (Hochschulw.) *junior university teacher in charge of practical or supplementary classes etc.;* **(b)** (im Verlag) [publisher's] editor

**Lektüre** *die;* ~, ~n **(a)** reading **(b)** (Lesestoff) reading [matter]

**Lende** *die;* ~, ~n loin

**Lenden-:** ~**gegend** *die* loins *pl.;* lumbar region (Anat.); ~**schurz** *der* loincloth; ~**wirbel** *der* (Anat.) lumbar vertebra

**lenken** *tr. V.* **(a)** *auch itr.* steer; be at the controls of ⟨*aircraft*⟩; guide ⟨*missile*⟩; (fahren) drive ⟨*car etc.*⟩ **(b)** direct ⟨*thoughts etc.*⟩ (auf + *Akk.* to); turn ⟨*attention*⟩ (auf + *Akk.* to) **(c)** (kontrollieren) control ⟨*person, press, economy*⟩; govern ⟨*state*⟩

**Lenker** *der;* ~s, ~ **(a)** handlebars *pl.;* **(b)** (Fahrer) driver

**Lenkerin** *die;* ~, ~nen ▶ LENKER B

**Lenk-:** ~**rad** *das* steering wheel; ~**rad·schloss**, *\**~**rad·schloß** *das* (Kfz-W.) steering [wheel] lock; ~**stange** *die* handlebars *pl.*

**Lenz** *der;* ~es, ~e (dichter. veralt.) spring

**Leopard** *der;* ~en, ~en leopard

**Lepra** *die;* ~: leprosy *no art.*

**Lerche** *die;* ~, ~n lark

**lernen** ① *itr. V.* study; (als Lehrling) train ② *tr. V.* learn (aus from)

**lesbar** *Adj.* legible; (klar) lucid ⟨*style*⟩; (verständlich) comprehensible

**Lesbe** *die;* ~, ~n (ugs.) lesbian

**Lesbierin** /ˈlɛsbi̯ərɪn/ *die;* ~, ~nen lesbian

**lesbisch** *Adj.* Lesbian

**Lese-:** ~**brille** *die* reading glasses *pl.;* ~**buch** *das* reader

**lesen**[1] *unr. tr., tr., itr. V.* read

**lesen**[2] *unr. tr. V.* **(a)** pick ⟨*grapes, berries, fruit*⟩; gather ⟨*firewood*⟩; **Ähren** ~: glean [ears of corn] **(b)** (aussondern) pick over

**Leser** *der;* ~s, ~: reader

**Leserbrief** der reader's letter; ~e readers' letters; „~e" (Zeitungsrubrik) 'Letters to the editor'
**Leserin** die; ~, ~nen reader
**Leserkreis** der readership
**leserlich** ① Adj. legible ② adv. legibly
**Lese·zeichen** das bookmark
**Lesung** die; ~, ~en reading
**Lette** die; ~n, ~n, **Lettin** die; ~, ~nen Latvian
**lettisch** Adj. Latvian; Lettish ⟨language⟩
**Lett·land** (das); ~s Latvia
**Letzt:** zu guter ~: in the end
**letzt...** Adj. last; ~en Endes in the end; (äußerst...) ultimate; (neuest...) latest ⟨news⟩
***letzte·mal:** ▸ MAL¹
***letzen·mal:** ▸ MAL¹
**letzter...** Adj. latter
**letztlich** Adv. ultimately; in the end
**Leucht·diode** die light-emitting diode; LED
**Leuchte** die; ~, ~n light
**leuchten** itr. V. (a) ⟨moon, sun, star, etc.⟩ be shining; ⟨fire, face⟩ glow (b) shine a/the light; jmdm. ~: light the way for sb.
**leuchtend** Adj. (a) shining ⟨eyes⟩; brilliant ⟨colours⟩; bright ⟨blue, red, etc.⟩ (b) (großartig) shining ⟨example⟩
**Leuchter** der; ~s, ~: candelabrum; (für eine Kerze) candlestick
**Leucht-:** ~farbe die luminous paint; ~kugel die flare; ~reklame die neon sign; ~stoff·lampe die fluorescent light or lamp; ~turm der lighthouse; ~ziffer·blatt das luminous dial
**leugnen** ① tr. V. deny ② itr. V. deny it
**Leukämie** die; ~, ~n (Med.) leukaemia
**Leumund** der; ~[e]s (geh.) reputation
**Leute** Pl. people; die reichen/alten ~: the rich/the old
**Leutnant** der; ~s, ~s second lieutenant
**leut·selig** ① Adj. affable ② adv. affably
**Lexikon** das; ~s, Lexika od. Lexiken encyclopaedia (Gen., für of)
**Libanese** der; ~n, ~n, **Libanesin** die; ~, ~nen Lebanese
**Libanon** (das) od. der; ~s Lebanon
**Libelle** die; ~, ~n dragonfly
**liberal** ① Adj. liberal ② adv. liberally
**Liberale** der/die; adj. Dekl. liberal
**liberalisieren** tr. V. liberalize; relax ⟨import controls⟩
**Libero** der; ~s, ~s (Fußball) sweeper

**Libyen** (das); ~s Libya
**libysch** Adj. Libyan
**licht** Adj. (a) light (b) (dünn bewachsen) sparse; thin
**Licht** das; ~[e]s, ~er (a) light (b) (elektrisches) light (c) Pl. auch ~e (Kerze) candle
**licht-, Licht-:** ~bild das [small] photograph (for passport etc.); ~empfindlich Adj. sensitive to light
**lichten¹** ① tr. V. thin out ⟨trees etc.⟩ ② refl. V. ⟨trees⟩ thin out; ⟨hair⟩ grow thin; ⟨fog, mist⟩ lift
**lichten²** tr. V. (Seemannsspr.) den/die Anker ~: weigh anchor
**lichterloh** ① Adj. blazing ⟨fire⟩; leaping ⟨flames⟩ ② adv. ~ brennen be blazing fiercely
**Lichter·meer** das sea of lights
**Licht-:** ~hupe die headlight flasher; ~jahr das (Astron.) light year; ~kegel der beam; ~maschine die (Kfz-W.) (mit Gleichstrom) dynamo; (mit Wechselstrom) alternator; generator (esp. Amer.); ~reklame die neon sign; ~schalter der light switch; ~schranke die photoelectric beam; ~schutz·faktor der protection factor (against sunburn)
**Lichtung** die; ~, ~en clearing
**Lid** das; ~[e]s, ~er eyelid
**lieb** ① Adj. (a) (liebevoll) kind ⟨words, gesture⟩ (b) (liebenswert) likeable; nice; (stärker) lovable ⟨child, girl, pet⟩; ~ aussehen look sweet or (Amer.) cute (c) (artig) good ⟨child, dog⟩ (d) (geschätzt) dear; sein liebstes Spielzeug his favourite toy; ~er Hans/~e Else! (am Briefanfang) dear Hans/Else (e) (angenehm) welcome; es wäre mir ~/~er, wenn ...: I should be glad/should prefer it if ... (f) jmdn. ~ haben love sb.; (gern haben) be fond of sb. ② adv. (a) (liebenswert) kindly (b) (artig) nicely
**Liebe** die; ~, ~n (a) love; ~ zu jmdm./zu etw. love for sb./of sth.; aus ~ [zu jmdm.] for love [of sb.]; tu mir die ~ und ...: do me a favour and ...; mit ~: lovingly; with loving care (b) (ugs.: geliebter Mensch) love
**Liebelei** die; ~, ~en flirtation
**lieben** ① tr. V. (a) love sb.; (sexuell) make love to sb.; sich ~: be in love; (sexuell) make love (b) etw. ~: be fond of sth.; (stärker) love sth. ② itr. V. be in love
**liebend** Adv. etw. ~ gern tun [simply] love doing sth.
**liebens·würdig** Adj. kind; charming ⟨smile⟩
**lieber** Adv. (a) ▸ GERN;

**(b)** better; **lass das ~:** better not do that

**Liebes-: ~brief** der love letter; **~paar** das courting couple; **~roman** der romantic novel

**liebe·voll** [1] Adj. loving attrib. ⟨care⟩; affectionate ⟨embrace, gesture, person⟩ [2] adv. lovingly; affectionately; (mit Sorgfalt) lovingly

***lieb|haben** ▶ LIEB 1F

**Liebhaber** der; **~s, ~ (a)** lover **(b)** (Interessierter, Anhänger) enthusiast (Gen. for); (Sammler) collector

**Liebhaberei** die; **~, ~:** hobby

**Liebhaberin** die; **~, ~nen** ▶ LIEBHABER

**lieblich** [1] Adj. charming; (angenehm) sweet ⟨scent, sound⟩ [2] adv. sweetly; (angenehm) pleasingly

**Liebling** der; **~s, ~e** (bes. als Anrede) darling; (bevorzugte Person) favourite

**Lieblings-** favourite

**lieb·los** [1] Adj. loveless [2] adv. **(a)** without affection **(b)** (ohne Sorgfalt) without proper care

**liebsten: am ~:** ▶ GERN

**Liechtenstein** (das); **~s** Liechtenstein

**Lied** das; **~[e]s, ~er** song

**liederlich** Adj. slovenly; messy ⟨hairstyle, person⟩

**Lieder-: ~macher** der; **~~s, ~~, ~macherin** die; **~~, ~~nen** singer-songwriter

**lief** 1. u. 3. Pers. Sg. Prät. v. LAUFEN

**Lieferant** der; **~en, ~en, Lieferantin** die; **~, ~nen** supplier

**lieferbar** Adj. available; (vorrätig) in stock

**Liefer·bedingungen** Pl. terms of delivery

**liefern** tr. V. **(a)** (bringen) deliver (an + Akk. to); (zur Verfügung stellen) supply **(b)** (hervorbringen) produce; provide ⟨eggs, honey, examples, raw material, etc.⟩

**Liefer-: ~schein** der delivery note; **~termin** der delivery date

**Lieferung** die; **~, ~en** delivery

**Liefer-: ~wagen** der [delivery] van; **~zeit** die delivery time

**Liege** die; **~, ~n** daybed; (zum Ausklappen) bed settee; (als Gartenmöbel) sunlounger

**liegen** unr. itr. V. lie; ⟨person⟩ be lying down; (sich befinden) be; ⟨object⟩ be [lying]; ⟨town, house, etc.⟩ be [situated]; **im Bett ~:** lie in bed; **~ bleiben** (liegen gelassen werden) stay; be left; (vergessen werden) be left behind; (unerledigt bleiben) be left undone; (nicht aufstehen) stay [lying]; [im Bett] **~ bleiben** stay in bed; **etw. ~ lassen** leave sth.; (vergessen) leave sth. [behind]; (unerledigt lassen) leave sth. undone; **einen Brief ~ lassen** (nicht abschicken) leave a letter unposted; (nicht öffnen) leave a letter unopened; **das liegt an ihm** od. **bei ihm** it is up to him; (ist seine Schuld) it is his fault; **es**

**liegt mir nicht** it doesn't suit me; (es spricht mich nicht an) it doesn't appeal to me; (ich mag es nicht) I don't like it; **daran liegt ihm viel/wenig/nichts** he sets great/little/no store by that

**liegen-: *~|bleiben** ▶ LIEGEN; ***~|lassen** ▶ LIEGEN

**Liege-: ~stuhl** der deckchair; **~stütz** der; **~~es, ~~e** press-up; **~wagen** der couchette car; **~wiese** die sunbathing lawn

**lieh** 1. u. 3. Pers. Sg. Prät. v. LEIHEN

**lies** Imperativ Sg. v. LESEN

**ließ** 1. u. 3. Pers. Sg. Prät. v. LASSEN

**liest** 3. Pers. Sg. Präsens v. LESEN

**Lift** der; **~[e]s, ~e** od. **~s (a)** lift (Brit.); elevator (Amer.) **(b)** Pl.: **~e** (Ski~, Sessel~) lift

**Liga** die; **~, Ligen** league; (Sport) division

**Likör** der; **~s, ~e** liqueur

**lila** indekl. Adj. mauve; (dunkel~) purple

**Lila** das; **~s, ~** od. (ugs.) **~s** mauve; (Dunkel~) purple

**Lilie** /ˈliːliə/ die; **~, ~n** lily

**Liliputaner** der; **~s, ~, Liliputanerin** die; **~, ~nen** dwarf

**Limit** das; **~s, ~s** limit

**Limo** die, auch: das; **~, ~[s]** (ugs.) fizzy drink

**Limonade** die; **~, ~n** fizzy drink; (Zitronen~) lemonade

**Limousine** die; **~, ~n** [large] saloon (Brit.) or (Amer.) sedan

**Linde** die; **~, ~n** lime [tree]

**lindern** tr. V. relieve ⟨suffering, pain⟩; slake ⟨thirst⟩

**Lineal** das; **~s, ~e** ruler

**Linie** /ˈliːniə/ die; **~, ~n** line; (Verkehrsstrecke) route; **die ~ 12** (Verkehrsw.) the number 12; **auf die [schlanke] ~ achten** (ugs. scherzh.) watch one's figure; **auf der ganzen ~** (fig.) all along the line

**linien-, Linien-: ~bus** der regular bus; **~flug** der scheduled flight; **~richter** der, **~richterin** die (Fußball usw.) linesman; (Tennis) line judge; (Rugby) touch judge; **~treu** [1] Adj. loyal to the party line postpos.; [2] adv. ⟨act⟩ in accordance with the party line

**linieren, liniieren** tr. V. rule

**link...** Adj. **(a)** left **(b)** (innen, nicht sichtbar) wrong, reverse ⟨side⟩ **(c)** (in der Politik) left-wing

**linkisch** [1] Adj. awkward [2] adv. awkwardly

**links** Adv. on the left; (Politik) on the left wing

**links-, Links-: ~abbieger** der, **~abbiegerin** die (Verkehrsw.) motorist/cyclist/car etc. turning left; **~außen** der; **~~, ~~** (Ballspiele) left wing; outside left; **~extremist** der, **~extremistin** die ⋯⟩

(Politik) left-wing extremist; ∼**händer** der;
∼∼s, ∼∼, ∼**händerin** die; ∼∼, ∼∼nen
left-hander; ∼**kurve** die left-hand bend;
∼**radikal** (Politik) [1] Adj. radical left-
wing; [2] adv. eine ∼radikal orientierte Gruppe
a group with a radical left-wing orientation;
∼**radikale** der/die left-wing radical;
∼**radikalismus** der left-wing radicalism;
∼**verkehr** der driving no art. on the left
**Linoleum** das; ∼s linoleum; lino
**Linse** die; ∼, ∼n (a) (Bot., Kochk.) lentil
(b) (Med., Optik) lens
**Lippe** die; ∼, ∼n lip
**Lippen·stift** der lipstick
**liquid** Adj. (Wirtsch.) liquid ⟨funds, resources⟩;
solvent ⟨business⟩
**liquidieren** (verhüll.: töten; Wirtsch.) liquidate
**lispeln** itr. V. lisp
**Lissabon** (das); ∼s Lisbon
**List** die; ∼, ∼en (a) [cunning] trick
(b) (listige Art) cunning
**Liste** die; ∼, ∼n list; schwarze ∼: blacklist
**listig** [1] Adj. cunning; crafty
[2] adv. cunningly; craftily
**Litauen** (das); ∼s Lithuania
**Litauer** der; ∼s, ∼, **Litauerin** die; ∼,
∼nen Lithuanian
**litauisch** Adj. Lithuanian
**Liter** der, auch: das; ∼s, ∼: litre
**literarisch** Adj. literary
**Literatur** die; ∼, ∼en literature
**Literatur-:** ∼**geschichte** die literary
history; history of literature;
∼**verzeichnis** das list of references
**liter·weise** Adv. by the litre; in litres
**Litfaß·säule** die advertising column
**Lithografie, Lithographie** die; ∼, ∼n
(Druck) lithograph
**litt** 1. u. 3. Pers. Sg. Prät. v. LEIDEN
**Litze** die; ∼, ∼n braid
**live** /laiːf/ (Rundf., Ferns.); [1] Adj. live
[2] adv. live; in dieser Sendung wird nur ∼
gesungen in this programme all the singing
is live
**Live-:** ∼**sendung,** *∼**-Sendung** die
(Rundf., Ferns.) live programme;
∼**übertragung** die (Rundf., Ferns.) live
broadcast
**Lizenz** die; ∼, ∼en licence
**Lizenz·gebühr** die licence fee; (Verlagsw.)
royalty
**Lkw, LKW** /ɛlkaːˈveː/ der; ∼[s], ∼[s] Abk.
= **Lastkraftwagen** truck; lorry (Brit.)
**Lob** das; ∼[e]s, ∼e praise no indef. art.
**Lobby** /ˈlɔbi/ die; ∼, ∼s od. **Lobbies** lobby
**loben** tr. V. praise
**lobens·wert** [1] Adj. praiseworthy;
laudable; commendable
[2] adv. laudably; commendably

**löblich** Adj. commendable
**Lob·lied** das song of praise
**Loch** das; ∼[e]s, **Löcher** hole
**lochen** tr. V. punch holes/a hole in; punch
⟨ticket⟩
**Locher** der; ∼s, ∼: punch
**löcherig** Adj. full of holes pred.
**Locke** die; ∼, ∼n curl
**locken** tr. V. (a) lure
(b) (reizen) tempt
**Locken·wickler** der [hair] curler
**locker** [1] Adj. loose; (entspannt) relaxed
⟨position, muscles⟩; slack ⟨rope, rein⟩; (fig.)
relax ⟨regulation, law, etc.⟩
[2] adv. ∼ sitzen ⟨tooth, screw, nail⟩ be loose;
(entspannt, ungezwungen) loosely
**locker|lassen** unr. itr. V. (ugs.) nicht ∼:
not give up
**lockern** [1] tr. V. loosen; slacken [off] ⟨rope
etc.⟩; relax ⟨muscles, limbs⟩
[2] refl. V. ⟨brick, tooth, etc.⟩ work itself loose;
⟨person⟩ loosen up
**Lockerung** die; ∼, ∼en (a) loosening; (fig.:
von Bestimmung, Gesetz usw.) relaxation
(b) (Entspannung) loosening up; relaxation
**lockig** Adj. curly
**Lock·vogel** der decoy
**Loden·mantel** der loden coat
**Löffel** der; ∼s, ∼: spoon; (als Maßangabe)
spoonful; (Jägerspr.) ear
**löffeln** tr. V. spoon [up]
**log** 1. u. 3. Pers. Sg. Prät. v. LÜGEN
**Logarithmus** der; ∼, **Logarithmen** (Math.)
logarithm; log
**Loge** /ˈloːʒə/ die; ∼, ∼n box
**logieren** itr. V. (veralt.) stay
**Logik** die; ∼: logic
**logisch** [1] Adj. logical
[2] adv. logically
**logischer·weise** Adv. logically;
(selbstverständlich) naturally
**logo** Adj. (salopp) [ist doch] ∼! you bet! (coll.);
of course!
**Lohn** der; ∼[e]s, **Löhne (a)** wage[s pl.]; pay
no indef. art., no pl.
(b) (Belohnung) reward
**Lohn·büro** das payroll office
**lohnen** [1] refl., itr. V. be worth it
[2] tr. V. be worth
**lohnend** Adj. rewarding
**Lohn·steuer** die income tax
**Lohn-:** ∼**steuer·karte** die income-tax
card; ∼**streifen** der payslip; ∼**tüte** die
pay packet (Brit.); wage packet
**lokal** Adj. local
**Lokal** das; ∼s, ∼e pub (Brit. coll.); bar (Amer.);
(Speise∼) restaurant
**Lokalität** die; ∼, ∼en locality
**Lokal-:** ∼**blatt** das local paper;
∼**patriotismus** der local patriotism;

---

*alte Schreibung - vgl. Hinweis auf S. xiv

~**teil** der (Zeitungsw.) local section;
~**termin** der (Rechtsspr.) visit to the scene
[of the crime]

**Lok·führer** der, **Lok·führerin** die:
▶ LOKOMOTIVFÜHRER

**Lokomotive** /lokomoˈtiːvə/ die; ~, ~n
locomotive

**Lokomotiv·führer** der,
**Lokomotiv·führerin** die engine driver
(Brit.); engineer (Amer.)

**Lokus** der; ~ od. ~ses, ~ od. ~se (salopp)
loo (Brit. coll.); john (Amer. coll.)

**London** (das) ~s London

**Londoner** ① indekl. Adj. London
② der; ~s, ~: Londoner

**Londonerin** die; ~, ~nen Londoner

**Lorbeer** der; ~s, ~en (a) laurel
(b) (Gewürz) bayleaf

**Lore** die; ~, ~n car; (kleiner) tub

**los** ① Adj. (a) (gelöst, ab) off
(b) es ist etwas ~: there is something going
on
(c) jmdn./etw. ~ sein be rid of sb./sth.
② Adv. (als Aufforderung) come on!

**Los** das; ~es, ~e (a) lot
(b) (Lotterie~) ticket

**Lösch·blatt** das piece of blotting paper

**löschen** tr. V. (a) put out; extinguish;
**seinen Durst** ~ (fig.) quench one's thirst
(b) (tilgen) delete ⟨entry⟩; erase ⟨recording,
memory, etc.⟩

**Lösch-:** ~**fahrzeug** das fire engine;
~**papier** das blotting paper

**lose** ① Adj. loose
② adv. loosely

**Löse·geld** das ransom

**losen** itr. V. draw lots (um for)

**lösen** ① tr. V. (a) remove ⟨stamp,
wallpaper⟩; **etw. von etw.** ~: remove sth.
from sth.
(b) (lockern) undo ⟨screw, belt, tie⟩
(c) (klären) solve; resolve ⟨contradiction,
conflict⟩
(d) (annullieren) break off ⟨engagement⟩;
cancel ⟨contract⟩; sever ⟨relationship⟩
(e) (kaufen) buy, obtain ⟨ticket⟩
② refl. V. (a) (lose werden) come off; (sich
lockern) ⟨wallpaper, plaster⟩ come off;
⟨packing, screw⟩ come loose
(b) (sich klären) ⟨puzzle, problem⟩ be solved
(c) (sich auflösen) dissolve

**los-:** ~**fahren** unr. itr. V.; mit sein set off;
(wegfahren) move off; ~**gehen** unr. itr. V.;
mit sein (a) (aufbrechen) set off; (b) (ugs.:
beginnen) start; (c) (ugs.: abgehen) ⟨button,
handle, etc.⟩ come off; ~**kommen** unr.
itr. V.; mit sein (ugs.) (a) get away; (b)
(freikommen) get free; ~**lassen** unr. tr. V.
(a) (nicht festhalten) let go of; (b) (freilassen) let
⟨person, animal⟩ go; ~**legen** itr. V. (ugs.)
get going

**löslich** Adj. soluble

**Löslichkeit** die; ~: solubility

**los|machen** tr. V. (ugs.) let ⟨animal⟩ loose;
untie ⟨string, line, rope⟩; unhitch ⟨trailer⟩

**Los·nummer** die [lottery-]ticket number

**los-:** ~**reißen** unr. refl. V. break free or
loose; ~**sagen** refl. V. sich von jmdm./etw.
~**sagen** break with sb./sth.; ~**schlagen**
unr. itr. V. (bes. Milit.) attack; launch one's
attack

**Löss, *Löß** der; Lösses, Lösse (Geol.) loess

**Losung** die; ~, ~en slogan; (Milit.: Kennwort)
password

**Lösung** die; ~, ~en (a) solution (Gen., für
to)
(b) ▶ LÖSEN 1D: breaking off; cancellation;
severing

**los|werden** unr. tr. V.; mit sein get rid of

**Lot** das; ~[e]s, ~e plumb [bob]; [nicht] im ~
sein be [out of] plumb

**löten** tr. V. solder

**Lotion** die; ~, ~en lotion

**Löt·kolben** der soldering iron

**lot·recht** ① Adj. perpendicular; vertical
② adv. perpendicularly; vertically

**Lotse** der; ~n, ~n (Seew.) pilot

**lotsen** tr. V. guide

**Lotsin** die ▶ LOTSE

**Lotterie** die; ~, ~n lottery

**Lotto** das; ~s, ~s national lottery

**Lotto-:** ~**schein** der national-lottery
coupon; ~**zahlen** Pl. winning national-
lottery numbers

**Löt·zinn** das [tin-lead] solder

**Löwe** der; ~n, ~n (a) lion
(b) (Astrol.) Leo; the Lion

**Löwen-:** ~**anteil** der lion's share;
~**mäulchen** das; ~~s, ~~: snapdragon;
~**zahn** der dandelion

**Löwin** die; ~, ~nen lioness

**loyal** /loaˈjaːl/ ① Adj. loyal
② adv. loyally

**Loyalität** die; ~: loyalty

**LP** /ɛlˈpeː/ die; ~, ~[s] Abk.
= Langspielplatte LP

**LSD** /ɛl|ɛsˈdeː/ das; ~[s] LSD

**Luchs** der; ~es, ~e lynx

**Lücke** die; ~, ~n gap

**lücken-, Lücken-:** ~**büßer** der, ~~s,
~~, ~**büßerin** die; ~~, ~~nen (ugs.)
stopgap; ~**haft** Adj. sketchy; ~**los** Adj.
complete

**lud** 1. u. 3. Pers. Sg. Prät. v. LADEN

**Luder** das; ~s, ~ (salopp) so-and-so (coll.)

**Luft** die; ~, Lüfte air; **an die frische** ~
**gehen** get out in[to] the fresh air; **die** ~
**anhalten** hold one's breath; **tief** ~ **holen** take
a deep breath; **in die** ~ **gehen** (fig. ugs.) blow
one's top (coll.)

**luft-, Luft-:** ~**angriff** der (Milit.) air raid;
~**ballon** der balloon; ~**brücke** die
airlift; ~**dicht** Adj. airtight; ~**druck** der
(a) (Physik) air pressure; (b) (Druckwelle) blast

**lüften** ☐1 *tr. V.* **(a)** air ⟨*room, clothes, etc.*⟩
**(b)** raise ⟨*hat*⟩
**(c)** disclose ⟨*secret*⟩
☐2 *itr. V.* air the room/house *etc*

**luft-, Luft-:** ~**fahrt** *die* aviation *no art.;*
~**feuchtigkeit** *die* [atmospheric]
humidity; ~**gekühlt** *Adj.* air-cooled;
~**getrocknet** *Adj.* air-dried; ~**gewehr**
*das* air rifle; airgun

**luftig** *Adj.* airy ⟨*room, building, etc.*⟩; light
⟨*clothes*⟩

**Luft·kissen·boot** *das* hovercraft

**luft-, Luft-:** ~**leer** *Adj.* ein ~leerer Raum
a vacuum; ~**linie** *die* 1000 km ~linie 1,000
km. as the crow flies; ~**loch** *das* air hole;
~**matratze** *die* airbed; air mattress; Lilo
®; ~**pirat** *der,* ~**piratin** *die* [aircraft]
hijacker; ~**post** *die* airmail; **etw. per** *od.*
**mit** ~**post schicken** send sth. [by] airmail;
~**pumpe** *die* air pump; (für Fahrrad) [bicycle]
pump; ~**röhre** *die* (Anat.) windpipe;
~**schiff** *das* airship; ~**schloss,**
*~**schloß** *das* castle in the air; ~**schutz**
*der* air-raid protection *no art.;*
~**schutz·bunker,** ~**schutz·keller,**
~**schutz·raum** *der* air-raid shelter;
~**verschmutzung** *die* air pollution;
~**waffe** *die* air force; ~**zug** *der* [gentle]
breeze; (in Zimmern, Gebäuden) draught

**Lüge** *die;* ~, ~n lie

**lügen** *itr., tr. V.* lie; **das ist gelogen!** that's a
lie!

**Lügner** *der;* ~s, ~, **Lügnerin** *die;* ~,
~nen liar

**Luke** *die;* ~, ~n (Dach~) skylight; (bei
Schiffen) hatch; (Keller~) trapdoor

**lukrativ** ☐1 *Adj.* lucrative
☐2 *adv.* lucratively

**Lümmel** *der;* ~s, ~: lout; (ugs., fam.: Bengel)
rascal

**Lump** *der;* ~en, ~en scoundrel

**lumpen** (ugs.) *tr. V.* **sich nicht** ~ **lassen**
splash out (coll.)

**Lumpen** *der;* ~s, ~ rag

**Lumpen-:** ~**sammler** *die* rag-and-bone
man; ~**sammlerin** *die* rag-and-bone
woman

**Lunge** *die;* ~, ~n lungs *pl.*

**Lungen-:** ~**entzündung** *die* pneumonia
*no indef. art.;* ~**krebs** *der* lung cancer;
~**zug** *der* inhalation

**Lunte** *die;* ~, ~n fuse; match

**Lupe** *die;* ~, ~n magnifying glass

**Lurch** *der;* ~[e]s, ~e amphibian

**Lust** *die;* ~ **(a)** ~ **haben, etw. zu tun** feel
like doing sth.
**(b)** (Vergnügen) pleasure; joy

**lustig** ☐1 *Adj.* **(a)** merry; jolly; enjoyable
⟨*time*⟩
**(b)** (komisch) funny
☐2 *adv.* **(a)** merrily
**(b)** (komisch) funnily

**lust-, Lust-:** ~**los** ☐1 *Adj.* listless; ☐2 *adv.*
listlessly; ~**spiel** *das* comedy

**lutherisch** *Adj.* Lutheran

**lutschen** ☐1 *tr. V.* suck
☐2 *itr. V.* suck; **an etw.** (*Dat.*) ~: suck sth.

**Luxemburg** (*das*) ~s Luxembourg

**luxuriös** ☐1 *Adj.* luxurious
☐2 *adv.* luxuriously

**Luxus** *der;* ~: luxury

**Lymphe** *die;* ~, ~n lymph

**Lymph·knoten** *der* lymph node

**lynchen** *tr. V.* lynch

**Lyrik** *die;* ~: lyric poetry

**Lyriker** *der;* ~s, ~, **Lyrikerin** *die;* ~,
~nen lyric poet; lyricist

**lyrisch** *Adj.* lyrical; lyric ⟨*poetry*⟩

**Lyzeum** *das;* ~s, Lyzeen girls' high school

# M m

**m, M** /ɛm/ *das;* ~, ~ m/M

**m** *Abk.* = **Meter** m

**Mach·art** *die* style; (Schnitt) cut

**machbar** *Adj.* feasible

**machen** ☐1 *tr. V.* **(a)** make; **aus Plastik/Holz**
*usw.* **gemacht** made of plastic/wood *etc.;* **sich**
(*Dat.*) **etw.** ~ **lassen** have sth. made; **etw. aus**
**jmdm.** ~: make sb. into sth.; **jmdn. zum**
**Präsidenten** *usw.* ~: make sb. president *etc.;*

**jmdm./sich [einen] Kaffee** ~: make [some]
coffee for sb./oneself
**(b)** (verursachen) **jmdm. Arbeit** ~: make [extra]
work for sb.; **das macht das Wetter** that's
[because of] the weather
**(c)** (ausführen) do ⟨*job, repair, etc.*⟩; **einen**
**Spaziergang** ~: go for a walk; **eine Reise** ~:
go on a journey; **einen Besuch [bei jmdm.]**
~: pay [sb.] a visit
**(d)** (tun) do; **was machst du da?** what are you
doing?; **so etwas macht man nicht** that [just]
isn't done
**(e)** **was macht ...?** (wie ist es um ... bestellt?)

---

*old spelling - see note on page xiv

how is ...?; **was macht die Gesundheit/ Arbeit?** how are you keeping/how is the job [getting on]?

**(f)** (ergeben) (beim Rechnen) be; (bei Geldbeträgen) come to; **zwei mal zwei macht vier** two times two is four; **das macht 12 Euro** that is 12 euros; (Endsumme) that comes to 12 euros

**(g)** (schaden) **was macht das schon?** what does it matter?; **macht nichts!** (ugs.) it doesn't matter

**(h)** (teilnehmen an) **einen Kursus** od. **Lehrgang ~:** take a course

**(i) mach's gut!** (ugs.) look after yourself!; (auf Wiedersehen) so long!

②refl. V. **(a) sich an etw.** (Akk.) **~:** get down to sth.

**(b)** (ugs.: sich entwickeln) do well

**(c) mach dir nichts daraus!** (ugs.) don't let it bother you

③itr. V. **(a) mach schon!** (ugs.) get a move on! (coll.)

**(b) das macht hungrig/durstig** it makes you hungry/thirsty; **das macht dick** it's fattening

**Machenschaften** Pl. (abwertend) wheeling and dealing sing.

**Macher** der; ~s, ~, **Macherin** die; ~, ~nen (ugs.) doer; **der Typ des Machers** the dynamic type who just gets on with things

**Macho** /'matʃ:o/ der; ~s, ~s (abwertend) macho

**Macht** die; ~, **Mächte** power; **an die ~ kommen** come to power

**Macht-:** ~**bereich** der sphere of influence; ~**haber** der; ~~s, ~~, ~**haberin** die; ~~, ~~nen ruler

**mächtig** ①Adj. **(a)** powerful
**(b)** (beeindruckend groß) mighty
②adv. (ugs.) terribly (coll.)

**macht-, Macht-:** ~**kampf** der power struggle; ~**los** Adj. powerless; **gegen etw. ~los sein** be powerless in the face of sth.; ~**probe** die trial of strength

**Mach·werk** das (abwertend) shoddy effort

**Macke** die; ~, ~n **(a)** (salopp: Tick) fad
**(b)** (ugs.: Defekt) defect

**Mädchen** das; ~s, ~ **(a)** girl
**(b)** (Haus~) maid

**mädchenhaft** Adj. girlish

**Mädchen·name** der **(a)** girl's name
**(b)** (Name vor der Ehe) maiden name

**Made** die; ~, ~n maggot

**madig** Adj. maggoty; **jmdn./etw. ~ machen** (ugs.) run sb./sth. down

**Madonna** die; ~, **Madonnen** madonna

**mag** 1. u. 3. Pers. Sg. Präsens v. MÖGEN

**Magazin** das; ~s, ~e **(a)** (Lager) store; (für Waren) stockroom
**(b)** (für Patronen, Dias, Film usw.; Zeitschrift) magazine

**Magazin·sendung** die magazine programme

**Magen** der; ~s, **Mägen** od. ~: stomach

**magen-, Magen-:** ~**bitter** der; ~~s, ~~: bitters pl.; ~**geschwür** das stomach ulcer; ~**krebs** der cancer of the stomach; ~**schmerzen** Pl. stomach ache sing.

**mager** Adj. **(a)** thin
**(b)** (fettarm) low-fat; low in fat pred.; lean ⟨meat⟩
**(c)** (fig.) poor ⟨soil, harvest⟩; meagre ⟨profit, increase, success, report, etc.⟩; thin ⟨programme⟩

**Mager-:** ~**milch** die skim[med] milk; ~**quark** der low-fat curd cheese; ~**sucht** die (Med.) wasting disease; (Anorexie) anorexia

**Magie** die; ~: magic

**Magier** /'ma:giɐ/ der; ~s, ~, **Magierin** die; ~, ~nen (auch fig.) magician

**magisch** Adj. magic ⟨powers⟩; (geheimnisvoll) magical

**Magistrat** der; ~[e]s, ~e City Council

**Magnat** der; ~en, ~en magnate

**Magnet** der; ~en od. ~[e]s, ~e magnet

**Magnet·band** das; Pl. **Magnet·bänder** magnetic tape

**magnetisch** ①Adj. magnetic
②adv. magnetically

**magnetisieren** tr. V. magnetize

**Magnetismus** der; ~: magnetism

**Magnet·nadel** die [compass] needle

**Mahagoni** das; ~s mahogany

**Mäh·drescher** der combine harvester

**mähen** ①tr. V. mow; cut ⟨corn⟩
②itr. V. mow; (Getreide ~) reap

**Mahl** das; ~[e]s, **Mähler** (geh.) meal; repast (formal)

**mahlen** unr. tr., itr. V. grind

**Mahl·zeit** meal

**Mähne** die; ~, ~n mane

**mahnen** tr. V. urge; remind ⟨debtor⟩

**Mahn-:** ~**mal** das; Pl. ~~e od. ~**mäler** memorial (erected as a warning to future generations); ~**schreiben** das reminder

**Mahnung** die; ~, ~en **(a)** (exhortation; (Warnung) admonition
**(b)** ▶ MAHNSCHREIBEN

**Mai** der; ~[e]s od. ~: May

**Mai-:** ~**baum** der maypole; ~**feiertag** der May Day no def. art.; ~**glöckchen** das lily of the valley; ~**käfer** der May bug

**Mais** der; ~es maize; corn (esp. Amer.); (als Gericht) sweet corn

**Mais·kolben** der corn cob; (als Gericht) corn on the cob

**Majestät** die; ~, ~en **(a)** (Titel) Majesty; **Eure ~:** Your Majesty
**(b)** (geh.) majesty

**majestätisch** ①Adj. majestic
②adv. majestically

**Majonäse** die; ~, ~n mayonnaise

**Major** der; ~s, ~e (Milit.) major

**Majoran** der; ~s, ~e marjoram

**makaber** Adj. macabre

**Makedonien** /makeˈdoːni̯ən/ *(das); ~*s Macedonia

**Makel** *der; ~s, ~* (geh.) **(a)** (Schmach) stigma
**(b)** (Fehler) blemish

**makel·los** [1] *Adj.* flawless; spotless ⟨*white, cleanness*⟩
[2] *adv.* immaculately; spotlessly ⟨*clean*⟩

**Make-up** /meːkˈʔap/ *das; ~s, ~s* make-up

**Makkaroni** *Pl.* macaroni *sing.*

**Makler** *der; ~s, ~*, **Maklerin** *die; ~*, *~nen* **(a)** (Häusermakler) estate agent (Brit.); realtor (Amer.)
**(b)** (Börsenmakler) broker

**Makrele** *die; ~, ~n* mackerel

**Makro** *der od. das; ~s, ~s* (DV) macro

**Makrone** *die; ~, ~n* macaroon

**mal** [1] *Adv.* times; (bei Flächen) by
[2] *Partikel* **komm ~ her!** come here!

**Mal**[1] *das; ~[e]s, ~e* time; **das erste/zweite ~, zum ersten/zweiten ~:** for the first/second time; **beim ersten/zweiten ~:** the first/second time; **das letzte, zum letzten ~:** for the last time; **letztes, beim letzten ~:** last time; **jedes ~:** every time; **mit einem ~[e]** all at once

**Mal**[2] *das; ~[e]s, ~e od.* **Mäler** mark; (Muttermal) birthmark; (braun) mole

**Malaie** *der; ~n, ~n*, **Malaiin** *die; ~, ~nen* Malay

**Malaria** *die; ~:* malaria

**Malaysia** *(das); ~s* Malaysia

**Mal·buch** *das* colouring book

**malen** *tr., itr. V.* paint; decorate ⟨*flat, room, walls*⟩

**Maler** *der; ~s, ~:* painter

**Malerei** *die; ~, ~en* painting

**Malerin** *der; ~, ~nen* painter

**malerisch** [1] *Adj.* picturesque
[2] *adv.* picturesquely

**mal‖nehmen** *unr. tr., itr. V.* multiply (**mit** by)

**malträtieren** *tr. V.* maltreat; ill-treat

**Malz·bier** *das* malt beer

**Mama** *die; ~, ~s* (fam.) mamma

**Mami** *die; ~, ~s* (fam.) mummy (Brit. coll.); mommy (Amer. coll.)

**Mammut** *das; ~s, ~e od. ~s* mammoth

**mampfen** *tr., itr. V.* (salopp) munch; nosh (coll.)

**man** *Indefinitpron. im Nom.* one; you *2nd person;* (irgendjemand) somebody; (die Behörden; die Leute dort) they *pl.;* (die Menschen im Allgemeinen) people *pl;* **~ hat mir gesagt ...:** I was told ...

**Management** /ˈmɛnɪdʒmənt/ *das; ~s, ~s* management

**managen** /ˈmɛnɪdʒn̩/ *tr. V.* **(a)** (ugs.) fix; organize
**(b)** (betreuen) manage ⟨*singer, artist, player*⟩

**Manager** /ˈmɛnɪdʒɐ/ *der; ~s, ~*, **Managerin** *die; ~, ~nen* manager; (eines Fußballvereins) club secretary

**manch** *Indefinitpron.* **(a)** *attr.* many a; **in [so] ~er Beziehung** in many respects
**(b)** *allein stehend* ~er many a person/man; ~e *Pl.* some; (viele) many; **[so] ~es** a number of things; (allerhand Verschiedenes) all kinds of things

**mancherlei** *indekl. Adj.* **(a)** *attr.* various; a number of
**(b)** *allein stehend* various things

**manch·mal** *Adv.* sometimes

**Mandant** *der; ~en, ~en*, **Mandantin** *die; ~, ~nen* client

**Mandarine** *die; ~, ~n* mandarin [orange]

**Mandel** *die; ~, ~n* **(a)** almond
**(b)** (Anat.) tonsil

**Mandel·entzündung** *die* tonsillitis *no indef. art.*

**Manege** /maˈneːʒə/ *die; ~, ~n* (im Zirkus) ring; (in der Reitschule) arena

**Mangel**[1] *der; ~s,* **Mängel** **(a)** (Fehlen) lack (**an** + *Dat.* of); (Knappheit) shortage, lack (**an** + *Dat.* of)
**(b)** (Fehler) defect

**Mangel**[2] *die; ~, ~n* [large] mangle

**mangelhaft** [1] *Adj.* faulty ⟨*goods, German, English, etc.*⟩; (unzulänglich) inadequate ⟨*knowledge, lighting*⟩; (Schulw.) **die Note „~"** the mark 'unsatisfactory'; (bei Prüfungen) the fail mark
[2] *adv.* faultily; (unzulänglich) inadequately

**mangeln**[1] *itr. V.; unpers.* **es mangelt an etw.** (*Dat.*) (etw. fehlt) there is a lack of sth.; (etw. ist unzureichend vorhanden) there is a shortage of sth.; **jmdm./einer Sache mangelt es an etw.** (*Dat.*) sb./sth. lacks sth.

**mangeln**[2] *tr. V.* mangle

**mangels** *Präp. mit Gen.* in the absence of

**Mango** *die; ~, ~s* mango

**Mangold** *der; ~[e]s* [Swiss] chard

**Manie** *die; ~, ~n* mania

**Manier** *die; ~, ~en* **(a)** manner
**(b)** *Pl.* (Umgangsformen) manners

**manierlich** [1] *Adj.* **(a)** (fam.) well-mannered; well-behaved ⟨*child*⟩
**(b)** (ugs.: einigermaßen gut) decent
[2] *adv.* **(a)** (fam.) nicely
**(b)** (ugs.: einigermaßen gut) **ganz/recht ~:** quite/really nicely

**Manifest** *das; ~[e]s, ~e* manifesto

**Maniküre** *die; ~:* manicure

**maniküren** *tr. V.* manicure

**Manipulation** *die; ~, ~en* (geh.) manipulation

**manipulieren** *tr. V.* manipulate; rig ⟨*election result etc.*⟩

**Manko** *das; ~s, ~s* shortcoming; deficiency

**Mann** *der; ~[e]s,* **Männer** **(a)** man
**(b)** (Ehemann) husband

**Männchen** *das; ~s, ~* **(a)** little man

**(b)** (Tier∼) male; ∼ **machen** ‹*animal*› sit up and beg

**Mannequin** /'manǝkē/ *das;* ∼s, ∼s mannequin; [fashion] model

**männer-, Männer-:** ∼**beruf** *der* all-male profession; (überwiegend von Männern ausgeübt) male-dominated profession; ∼**mordend** *Adj.* (ugs. scherzh.) man-eating (fig.); ∼**sache** *die:* **das ist** ∼**sache** that's men's business; ∼**überschuss**, *∗*∼**überschuß** *der* surplus of men

**mannig·fach** *Adj.* multifarious

**männlich** ⟨1⟩ *Adj.* **(a)** male
**(b)** ▶ MASKULIN 1;
⟨2⟩ *adv.* in a masculine way

**Mannschaft** *die;* ∼, ∼en (Sport, auch fig.) team; (Schiffs-, Flugzeugbesatzung) crew; (Milit.) unit

**Mannschafts-:** ∼**führer** *der,* ∼**führerin** *die* (Sport) team captain; ∼**kapitän** *der,* ∼**kapitänin** *die* (Sport) team captain; ∼**spiel** *das* (Sport) team game

**Manöver** *das;* ∼s, ∼ **(a)** (Milit.) exercise; ∼ *Pl.* manœuvres
**(b)** (Bewegung; fig. abwertend: Trick) manœuvre

**manövrieren** *itr., tr. V.* manœuvre

**Mansarde** *die;* ∼, ∼n attic; (Zimmer) attic room

**Manschette** *die;* ∼, ∼n cuff

**Manschetten·knopf** *der* cuff link

**Mantel** *der;* ∼s, Mäntel coat

**Manteltarif·vertrag** *der* (Wirtsch.) framework collective agreement [on working conditions]

**Manuskript** *das;* ∼[e]s, ∼e **(a)** manuscript; (Typoskript) typescript
**(b)** (Notizen) notes *pl.*

**Mappe** *die;* ∼, ∼n **(a)** folder
**(b)** (Aktentasche) briefcase; (Schul∼) schoolbag

**Marathon·lauf** /...tɔn.../ *der* marathon

**Märchen** *das;* ∼s, ∼: fairy story; fairy tale; (ugs.: Lüge) [tall] story (coll.)

**Märchen·buch** *das* book of fairy stories

**märchenhaft** ⟨1⟩ *Adj.* magical
⟨2⟩ *adv.* magically; (ugs.) fantastically (coll.)

**Margarine** *die;* ∼: margarine

**Margerite** *die;* ∼, ∼n ox-eye daisy

**Maria** (*die*); ∼s *od.* (Rel.) Mariä Mary

**Marien·käfer** *der* ladybird

**Marihuana** *das;* ∼s marijuana

**Marinade** *die;* ∼, ∼n (Kochk.) marinade; (Salatsoße) [marinade] dressing

**Marine** *die;* ∼, ∼n fleet; (Kriegs∼) navy

**marinieren** *tr. V.* marinade; **marinierte Heringe** soused herrings

**Marionette** *die;* ∼, ∼n puppet; marionette

**Marionetten·theater** *das* puppet theatre

**Mark¹** *die;* ∼, ∼: mark; **Deutsche** ∼: Deutschmark

**Mark²** *das;* ∼[e]s **(a)** (Knochen∼) marrow
**(b)** (Frucht∼) pulp

**markant** *Adj.* striking; prominent ‹*figure, nose, chin*›; clear-cut ‹*features, profile*›

**Marke** *die;* ∼, ∼n **(a)** (Waren∼) brand; (Fabrikat) make
**(b)** (Brief∼, Rabatt∼, Beitrags∼) stamp
**(c)** (Essen∼) meal ticket
**(d)** (Erkennungs∼) [identification] disc; (Dienst∼) [police] identification badge; ≈ warrant card (Brit.) *or* (Amer.) ID card

**Marken-:** ∼**artikel** *der* proprietary *or* (Brit.) branded article; ∼**zeichen** *das* trade mark

**Marketing** *das;* ∼s (Wirtsch.) marketing

**markieren** ⟨1⟩ *tr. V.* **(a)** mark
**(b)** (ugs.: vortäuschen) sham ‹*illness, breakdown, etc.*›
⟨2⟩ *itr. V.* (ugs.: simulieren) put it on (coll.)

**Markierung** *die;* ∼, ∼en marking

**Markt** *der;* ∼[e]s, Märkte market; (∼platz) market place *or* square; **freitags ist** ∼: Friday is market day

**markt-, Markt-:** ∼**anteil** *der* share of the market; ∼**beherrschend** *Adj.* market-dominating *attrib.;* ∼**einführung** *die* launch; ∼**forschung** *die* market research *no def. art.;* ∼**frau** *die* market woman; ∼**führer** *der,* ∼**führerin** *die* market leader; ∼**halle** *die* covered market; ∼**lücke** *die* gap in the market; ∼**platz** *der* market place; ∼**stand** *der* market stall; ∼**wirtschaft** *die* market economy

**Marmelade** *die;* ∼, ∼n jam; (Orangen∼) marmalade

**Marmor** *der;* ∼s marble

**Marokkaner** *der;* ∼s, ∼, **Marokkanerin** *die;* ∼, ∼nen Moroccan

**marokkanisch** *Adj.* Moroccan

**Marokko** (*das*); ∼s Morocco

**Marone** *die;* ∼, ∼n [sweet] chestnut

**Mars** *der;* ∼: Mars *no def. art.*

**Marsch¹** *der;* ∼[e]s, Märsche march; (Wanderung) [long] walk

**Marsch²** *die;* ∼, ∼en fertile marshland

**Marsch·flug·körper** *der* cruise missile

**marschieren** *itr. V.; mit sein* march; (wandern) walk

**Marsch-:** ∼**musik** *die* march music; ∼**verpflegung** *die* (Milit.) marching rations *pl.;*

**Mars-:** ∼**mensch** *der* Martian; ∼**sonde** *die* (Raumfahrt) Mars probe

**Marter** *die;* ∼, ∼n (geh.) torture; (seelisch) torment

**martern** *tr. V.* (geh.) torture

**Märtyrer** *der;* ∼s, ∼, **Märtyrerin** *die;* ∼, ∼nen martyr

**Martyrium** *das;* ∼s, Martyrien martyrdom

**Marxismus** *der;* ∼: Marxism *no art.*

**Marxist** *der;* ∼en, ∼en, **Marxistin** *die;* ∼, ∼nen Marxist

**marxistisch** *Adj.* Marxist

**März** *der;* ∼[es] March

m

**Marzipan** *das;* ~s marzipan

**Masche** *die;* ~, ~n stitch; (Lauf~) run; ladder (Brit.); (beim Netz) mesh

**Maschen-draht** *der* wire netting

**Maschine** *die;* ~, ~n (a) (auch ugs.: Motorrad) machine
(b) (ugs.: Automotor) engine
(c) (Flugzeug) [aero]plane
(d) (Schreib~) typewriter; ~ **schreiben** type

**maschine-geschrieben** *Adj.* typewritten

**maschinell** 1 *Adj.* machine *attrib.;* by machine *postpos.;*
2 *adv.* by machine; ~ **hergestellt** machine-made

**Maschinen-:** ~**gewehr** *das* machine gun; ~**pistole** *die* sub-machine gun; ~**schlosser** *der,* ~**schlosserin** *die* fitter

\***maschine|schreiben** ▶ MASCHINE D

**Masern** *Pl.* measles *sing. or pl.*

**Maserung** *die;* ~, ~en [wavy] grain

**Maske** *die;* ~, ~n mask

**Masken-:** ~**ball** *der* masked ball; ~**bildner** *der;* ~~s, ~~, ~**bildnerin** *die;* ~~, ~~nen make-up artist

**Maskerade** *die;* ~, ~n [fancy-dress] costume

**maskieren** 1 *tr. V.* mask
2 *refl. V.* put on a mask/masks

**Maskottchen** *das;* ~s, ~: [lucky] mascot

**maskulin** /*auch:* '---/ 1 *Adj.* (auch Sprachw.) masculine
2 *adv.* in a masculine way

**Masochismus** *der;* ~ (Psych.) masochism *no art.*

**Masochist** *der;* ~en, ~en, **Masochistin** *die;* ~, ~nen (Psych.) masochist

**masochistisch** (Psych.) 1 *Adj.* masochistic
2 *adv.* masochistically; ~ **veranlagt sein** have masochistic tendencies

**maß** *1. u. 3. Pers. Sg. Prät. v.* MESSEN

**Maß¹** *das;* ~es, ~e (a) measure (für of); (fig.) **das** ~ **ist voll** enough is enough
(b) (Größe) measurement
(c) (Grad) degree (an + *Dat.* of); **in großem/gewissem** ~**e** to a great/certain extent
(d) ~ **halten** exercise moderation

**Maß²** *die;* ~, ~[e] (bayr., österr.) litre [of beer]

**Massage** /ma'sa:ʒə/ *die;* ~, ~n massage

**Massaker** *das;* ~s, ~: massacre

**Maß-:** ~**anzug** *der* made-to-measure suit; ~**arbeit** *die* (a) custom-made item; (Kleidungsstück) made-to-measure item; (b) (genaue Arbeit) neat work

**Masse** *die;* ~, ~n (a) mass
(b) (Gemisch) mixture

**Maß-einheit** *die* unit of measurement

**Massen-:** ~**arbeitslosigkeit** *die* mass unemployment; ~**entlassungen** *Pl.* mass redundancies *pl.;* ~**grab** *das* mass grave

**massenhaft** 1 *Adj.* in huge numbers *postpos.;*
2 *adv.* on a huge scale

**massen-, Massen-:** ~**karambolage** *die* multiple crash; ~**kommunikations-mittel** *das* medium of mass communication; mass medium; ~**medium** *das* mass medium; ~**mörder** *der,* ~**mörderin** *die* mass murderer; ~**produktion** *die* mass production; ~**vernichtung** *die* mass extermination; ~**vernichtungs-waffen** *Pl.* weapons of mass destruction; ~**weise** *Adv.* in huge numbers

**Masseur** /ma'søːɐ̯/ *der;* ~s, ~e masseur

**Masseurin** *die;* ~, ~nen, **Masseuse** /ma'søːzə/ *die;* ~, ~n masseuse

**maß-gebend, maß-geblich** 1 *Adj.* authoritative 〈book, expert, opinion〉; definitive 〈text〉; influential 〈person, circles, etc.〉; decisive 〈factor, influence, etc.〉
2 *adv.* 〈influence〉 to a considerable extent; (entscheidend) decisively

\***maß|halten** ▶ MAß¹ D

**massieren** *tr. V.* massage

**mäßig** 1 *Adj.* moderate; (mittel~) mediocre
2 *adv.* in moderation; moderately 〈gifted, talented〉; (mittel~) indifferently

**mäßigen** *refl. V.* (geh.) (a) practise *or* exercise moderation
(b) (sich beherrschen) control *or* restrain oneself

**Mäßigkeit** *die;* ~: moderation

**Mäßigung** *die;* ~: moderation

**massiv** 1 *Adj.* (a) solid
(b) (heftig) massive 〈demand〉; crude 〈accusation, threat〉; strong 〈attack, criticism, pressure〉
2 *adv.* 〈attack〉 strongly; 〈accuse, threaten〉 crudely

**maß-, Maß-:** ~**krug** *der* (südd., österr.) litre beer mug; (aus Steingut) stein; ~**los** 1 *Adj.* extreme; gross 〈exaggeration, insult〉; excessive 〈demand, claim〉; boundless 〈ambition, greed, sorrow, joy〉; 2 *adv.* extremely; 〈exaggerate〉 grossly; ~**nahme** *die;* ~~, ~~n measure; ~**regel** *die* regulation; (Maßnahme) measure; ~**regeln** *tr. V.* (zurechtweisen) reprimand; (bestrafen) discipline; ~**stab** *der* (a) standard; (b) (einer Karte, eines Modells usw.) scale; ~**voll** 1 *Adj.* moderate; 2 *adv.* in moderation

**Mast** *der;* ~[e]s, ~en, *auch:* ~e (Schiffs~, Antennen~) mast; (Stange, Fahnen~) pole; (Hochspannungs~) pylon

**mästen** *tr. V.* fatten

**Masturbation** *die;* ~, ~en masturbation

**masturbieren** *itr., tr. V.* masturbate

---

\*old spelling - see note on page xiv

**Match** /mɛtʃ/ *das od.* **der;** ∼[e]s, ∼s *od.* ∼e match

**Material** *das;* ∼s, ∼ien material; (Bau∼; Hilfsmittel) materials *pl.*

**Materialismus** *der;* ∼: materialism

**Materialist** *der;* ∼en, ∼en, **Materialistin** *die;* ∼, ∼nen materialist

**materialistisch** [1] *Adj.* materialistic [2] *adv.* materialistically

**Materie** *die;* ∼, ∼n **(a)** matter **(b)** (geh.: Thema, Gegenstand) subject matter

**materiell** [1] *Adj.* (finanziell) financial [2] *adv.* materially; (finanziell) financially

**Mathe** *die;* ∼ (ugs.) maths *sing.* (Brit. coll.); math (Amer. coll.)

**Mathematik** *die;* ∼: mathematics *sing., no art.*

**mathematisch** [1] *Adj.* mathematical [2] *adv.* mathematically

**Matjes** *der;* ∼, ∼: matie [herring]

**Matratze** *die;* ∼, ∼n mattress

**Matrose** *der;* ∼n, ∼n sailor; seaman

**Matsch** *der;* ∼[e]s (ugs.) mud; (breiiger Schmutz) sludge; (Schnee∼) slush

**matschig** *Adj.* (ugs.) **(a)** muddy; slushy ⟨*snow*⟩ **(b)** (weich) mushy; squashy ⟨*fruit*⟩

**matt** [1] *Adj.* **(a)** weak; feeble ⟨*applause, reaction*⟩ **(b)** (glanzlos) matt; dull ⟨*metal, mirror, etc.*⟩ **(c)** (undurchsichtig) frosted ⟨*glass*⟩; pearl ⟨*lightbulb*⟩ **(d)** subdued; (Schach) checkmated; ∼! checkmate! [2] *adv.* **(a)** (kraftlos) weakly **(b)** (mäßig) ⟨*protest, contradict*⟩ feebly

**Matte** *die;* ∼, ∼n mat

**Matt·scheibe** *die* (ugs.) telly (Brit. coll.); box (coll.)

**Matur** *die;* ∼ (schweiz.), **Matura** *die;* ∼a (österr., schweiz.) ▶ ABITUR

**Mätzchen** *das;* ∼s, ∼: ∼ machen (ugs.) fool about *or* around

**Mauer** *die;* ∼, ∼n wall

**mauern** [1] *tr. V.* build [2] *itr. V.* lay bricks

**Mauer-:** ∼**segler** *der* swift; ∼**werk** *das* **(a)** masonry; (aus Ziegeln) brickwork; **(b)** (Mauern) walls *pl.*

**Maul** *das;* ∼[e]s, Mäuler (von Tieren) mouth; (derb: Mund) gob (sl.)

**Maul-:** ∼**esel** *der* mule; ∼**korb** *der* (auch fig.) muzzle; ∼**tier** *das* mule

**Maul·wurf** *der* mole

**Maulwurfs-:** ∼**haufen** *der*, ∼**hügel** *der* molehill

**Maurer** *der;* ∼s, ∼, **Maurerin** *die;* ∼, ∼nen bricklayer

**Maus** *die;* ∼, Mäuse mouse

**Mauschelei** *die;* ∼, ∼en (ugs. abwertend) shady wheeling and dealing *no indef. art.*

**mauscheln** *itr. V.* (ugs. abwertend) engage in shady wheeling and dealing

**Mäuschen** *das;* ∼s, ∼: little mouse

**mäuschen·still** *Adj.* ∼ sein be as quiet as a mouse

**Mause-falle** *die* mousetrap

**mausern** *refl. V.* moult

**Maus:** ∼**klick** *der;* ∼∼s, ∼∼s (DV) mouse click; ∼**taste** *die* (DV) mouse button; ∼**zeiger** *der* (DV) mouse pointer

**Maut** *die;* ∼, ∼en toll

**maximal** [1] *Adj.* maximum [2] *adv.* ∼ zulässige Geschwindigkeit maximum permitted speed

**Maxime** *die;* ∼, ∼n maxim

**maximieren** *tr. V.* maximize

**Maximum** *das;* ∼s, Maxima maximum (an + *Dat.* of)

**Maxi·single** *die* maxi-single

**Mayonnaise** /majɔ'nɛːzə/ *die;* ∼, ∼n mayonnaise

**Mäzen** *der;* ∼s, ∼e (geh.) patron

**Mäzenin** *die;* ∼, ∼nen patroness

**MdB, M.d.B.** *Abk.* = **Mitglied des Bundestages** Member of the Bundestag

**m. E.** *Abk.* = **meines Erachtens** in my opinion *or* view

**Mechanik** *die;* ∼: mechanics *sing., no art.*

**Mechaniker** *der;* ∼s, ∼, **Mechanikerin** *die;* ∼, ∼nen mechanic

**mechanisch** [1] *Adj.* mechanical; power attrib. ⟨*loom, press*⟩ [2] *adv.* mechanically

**Mechanismus** *der;* ∼, Mechanismen mechanism

**meckern** *itr. V.* **(a)** (auch fig.) bleat **(b)** (ugs.: nörgeln) grumble; moan

**Mecklenburg-Vorpommern** *(das);* ∼s Mecklenburg-Western Pomerania

**Medaille** /me'daljə/ *die;* ∼, ∼n medal

**Medaillen·gewinner** *der*, **Medaillen·gewinnerin** *die* medallist; medal winner

**Medaillon** /medal'jõ:/ *das;* ∼s, ∼s **(a)** locket **(b)** (Kochk., bild. Kunst) medallion

**medial** *Adj.* (in den Medien) in the media *postpos.*; (von den Medien) by the media *postpos.*; eine ∼e Präsenz a media presence; ein ∼es Spektakel a media spectacle

**Medien-:** ∼**angebot** *das* range of media; ∼**konzern** *der* media concern; ∼**landschaft** *die* media scene; ∼**politik** *die* media policy; ∼**präsenz** *die* media presence

**Medikament** *das;* ∼[e]s, ∼e medicine; (Droge) drug

**Meditation** *die;* ∼, ∼en meditation

**meditieren** *itr. V.* meditate (über + *Akk.* [up]on)

**Medium** *das;* ∼s, Medien medium

**Medizin** die; ~, ~en medicine

**Mediziner** der; ~s, ~, **Medizinerin** die; ~, ~nen doctor; (Student[in]) medical student

**medizinisch** [1] Adj. medical; medicinal ⟨bath etc.⟩; medicated ⟨toothpaste, soap, etc.⟩ [2] adv. medically

**Meer** das; ~[e]s, ~e (auch fig.) sea; am ~: by the sea

**Meer·enge** die straits pl.; strait

**Meeres-:** ~**boden** der sea bed or bottom or floor; ~**bucht** die bay; ~**früchte** Pl. (Kochk.) seafood sing.; ~**kunde** die oceanography no art.; ~**spiegel** der sea level

**Meer-:** ~**jungfrau** die mermaid; ~**katze** die guenon; ~**rettich** der horseradish; ~**schweinchen** das; ~~s, ~~: guinea pig; ~**wasser** das sea water

**Meeting** /'mi:tɪŋ/ das; ~s, ~s meeting

**mega-, Mega-** mega-

**Mega·byte** das (DV) megabyte

**Megaphon** das; ~s, ~e megaphone; loud hailer

**Mehl** das; ~[e]s flour

**mehlig** Adj. (a) floury
(b) mealy ⟨potato, apple, etc.⟩

**Mehl-:** ~**sack** der flour sack; (Sack voll Mehl) sack of flour; ~**tau** der mildew; ~**wurm** der mealworm

**mehr** [1] Indefinitpron. more
[2] Adv. (a) more
(b) nicht ~: not … any more; no longer; es war niemand ~ da there was no one left; das wird nie ~ vorkommen it will never happen again; da ist nichts ~ zu machen there is nothing more to be done

**mehr-, Mehr-:** ~**bändig** Adj. in several volumes postpos.; ~**bereichs·öl** das (Technik) multi-purpose oil; ~**deutig** [1] Adj. ambiguous; [2] adv. ambiguously

**mehren** (geh.) refl. V. increase

**mehrer…** Indefinitpron. u. unbest. Zahlwort
(a) attr. several
(b) allein stehend ~e several people; ~es several things pl.

**mehr·fach** [1] Adj. multiple; (wiederholt) repeated
[2] adv. several times; (wiederholt) repeatedly

**Mehrheit** die; ~, ~en majority

**Mehrheits-:** ~**beschluss**, *~**beschluß** der, ~**entscheidung** die majority decision

**mehr-, Mehr-:** ~**jährig** Adj. lasting several years postpos.; ~**malig** Adj.; nicht präd. repeated; ~**mals** Adv. several times; (wiederholt) repeatedly; ~**parteien·system** das multi-party system; ~**sprachig** Adj. multilingual; ~**stimmig** (Musik) [1] Adj. for several voices postpos.; ein ~stimmiges Lied a part-song; [2] adv. ~stimmig singen sing in harmony; ~**teilig** Adj. in several parts postpos.

**Mehrweg-:** ~**flasche** die returnable or reusable bottle; ~**verpackung** die reusable packaging

**Mehr-:** ~**wert** der (Wirtsch.) surplus value; ~**wert·steuer** die (Wirtsch.) value added tax (Brit.); VAT (Brit.); sales tax (Amer.); ~**zahl** die (a) (Sprachw.) plural; (b) (Mehrheit) majority

**meiden** unr. tr. V. (geh.) avoid

**Meile** die; ~, ~n mile

**mein** Possessivpron. my; ~e Damen und Herren ladies and gentlemen; das Buch dort, ist das ~[e]s? that book over there, is it mine?

**Mein·eid** der perjury no indef. art.; einen ~ schwören commit perjury

**meinen** [1] itr. V. think
[2] tr. V. (a) think
(b) (sagen wollen, im Sinn haben) mean
(c) (beabsichtigen) mean; intend; es gut mit jmdm. ~: mean well by sb.
(d) (sagen) say

**meiner** Gen. von ICH (geh.) gedenkt ~: remember me; erbarme dich ~: have mercy upon me

**meinerseits** Adv. for my part; ganz ~: the pleasure is [all] mine

**meinetwegen** Adv. (a) because of me; (mir zuliebe) for my sake; (um mich) about me
(b) /auch: --'--/ (von mir aus) as far as I'm concerned; ~! if you like

**Meinung** die; ~, ~en opinion (zu on, über + Akk. about); er ist der ~, dass … he is of the opinion or takes the view that …; meiner ~ nach in my opinion; ganz meine ~! I agree entirely; einer ~ sein be of the same opinion

**Meinungs-:** ~**forschung** die opinion research; ~**freiheit** die freedom to form and express one's own opinions; (Redefreiheit) freedom of speech; ~**umfrage** die [public] opinion poll; ~**verschiedenheit** die difference of opinion

**Meise** die; ~, ~n tit[mouse]

**Meißel** der; ~s, ~: chisel

**meißeln** tr. V. chisel; carve ⟨statue, sculpture⟩ with a chisel

**meist** Adv. mostly

**meist…** Indefinitpron. u. unbest. Zahlw. most; die ~en Leute …: most people …; am ~en most

**meistens** Adv. ▶ MEIST

**Meister** der; ~s, ~ (a) master
(b) (Werk~, Polier) foreman
(c) (Sport) champion

**Meister·brief** der master craftsman's diploma or certificate

**meisterhaft** [1] Adj. masterly
[2] adv. in a masterly manner

**Meisterin** die; ~, ~nen ▶ MEISTER A,C

**meistern** *tr. V.* master

**Meister·prüfung** *die* examination for the/one's master craftsman's diploma *or* certificate

**Meisterschaft** *die;* ∼, ∼en (a) mastery **(b)** (Sport) championship

**Meister-:** ∼**stück** *das* masterpiece (an + *Dat.* of); ∼**titel** *der* (Sport) championship [title]; ∼**werk** *das* masterpiece (an + *Dat.* of)

**Melancholie** /melaŋkoːˈliː/ *die;* ∼ (Gemütszustand) melancholy; (Psych.) melancholia

**melancholisch** ① *Adj.* melancholy; melancholy, melancholic ⟨*person, temperament*⟩ ② *adv.* melancholically

**melden** ① *tr. V.* report; (registrieren lassen) register ⟨*birth, death, etc.*⟩ (*Dat.* with) ② *refl. V.* **(a)** report **(b)** (am Telefon) answer **(c)** (ums Wort bitten) put one's hand up **(d)** (von sich hören lassen) get in touch (**bei** with)

**Meldung** *die;* ∼, ∼en (a) report; (Nachricht) piece of news **(b)** (Wort∼) request to speak

**meliert** *Adj.* mottled; [grau] ∼es Haar hair streaked with grey

**melken** *regelm.* (*auch unr.*) *tr. V.* milk

**Melodie** *die;* ∼, ∼n melody; (Weise) tune

**melodisch** ① *Adj.* melodic ② *adv.* melodically

**Melone** *die;* ∼, ∼n (a) melon **(b)** (ugs.: Hut) bowler [hat]

**Membran** *die;* ∼, ∼en (a) (Technik) diaphragm **(b)** (Biol., Chemie) membrane

**Memoiren** /meˈmoaːrən/ *Pl.* memoirs

**Menge** *die;* ∼, ∼n (a) quantity; amount **(b)** (große) lot (coll.); eine ∼ (ugs.) lots [of it/them] (coll.) **(c)** (Menschen∼) crowd **(d)** (Math.) set

**Mengen-:** ∼**lehre** *die* set theory *no art.;* ∼**rabatt** *der* bulk discount

**Meniskus** *der;* ∼, Menisken (Anat., Optik) meniscus

**Menopause** *die;* ∼, ∼n (Physiol.) menopause

**Mensa** *die;* ∼, ∼s *od.* Mensen refectory, canteen (*of university, college*)

**Mensch** *der;* ∼en, ∼en (a) (Gattung) der ∼: man; die ∼en man *sing.;* human beings; mankind *sing.;* **(b)** (Person) person; man/woman; ∼en people

**menschen-, Menschen-:** ∼**affe** *der* anthropoid [ape]; ∼**auflauf** *der* crowd [of people]; ∼**feind** *der,* ∼**feindin** *die* misanthropist; ∼**fresser** *der* (ugs.) cannibal; ∼**freund** *der,* ∼**freundin** *die* philanthropist; ∼**handel** *der* trade *or* traffic in human beings; ∼**kenner** *der,*

∼**kennerin** *die* judge of human nature; ∼**kenntnis** *die;* ability to judge human nature; ∼**leben** *das* life; ∼**leer** *Adj.* deserted; ∼**menge** *die* crowd [of people]; ∼**recht** *das* human right; ∼**schlag** *der* breed [of people]; ∼**seele** *die:* keine ∼seele not a [living] soul

**Menschens·kind:** ∼! (salopp) (erstaunt) good heavens; good grief; (vorwurfsvoll) for heaven's sake

**menschen-, Menschen-:** ∼**unwürdig** ① *Adj.* ⟨*accommodation*⟩ unfit for human habitation; ⟨*conditions*⟩ unfit for human beings; ⟨*behaviour*⟩ unworthy of a human being; ② *adv.* ⟨*treat*⟩ in a degrading and inhumane way; ⟨*live, be housed*⟩ in conditions unfit for human beings; ∼**verstand** *der* human intellect; ∼**würde** *die* human dignity *no art.*

**Menschheit** *die;* ∼: mankind *no art.;* humanity *no art.;* human race

**menschlich** ① *Adj.* **(a)** human **(b)** (annehmbar) civilized **(c)** (human) humane ⟨*person, treatment, etc.*⟩ ② *adv.* **(a)** er ist mir ∼ sympathisch I like him as a person **(b)** (human) humanely

**Menschlichkeit** *die;* ∼: humanity *no art.*

**Mensen** ▶ MENSA

**Menstruation** *die;* ∼, ∼en (Physiol.) menstruation; (Periode) [menstrual] period

**Mentalität** *die;* ∼, ∼en mentality

**Menü** *das;* ∼s, ∼s (auch DV) menu

**Menü·leiste** *die* (DV) menu bar

**merkbar** ① *Adj.* noticeable ② *adv.* noticeably

**Merk·blatt** leaflet

**merken** ① *tr. V.* notice ② *refl. V.* sich (*Dat.*) etw. ∼: remember sth.

**merklich** ▶ MERKBAR

**Merkmal** *das;* ∼s, ∼e feature

**Merkur** *der;* ∼s Mercury

**merkwürdig** ① *Adj.* strange; odd ② *adv.* strangely; oddly

**messbar, \*meßbar** *Adj.* measurable

**Messe**[1] *die;* ∼, ∼n (Gottesdienst, Musik) mass

**Messe**[2] *die;* ∼, ∼n (Ausstellung) [trade] fair

**messen** ① *unr. tr. V.* **(a)** *auch itr.* measure **(b)** (beurteilen) judge (**nach** by) ② *unr. refl. V.* (geh.) compete (**mit** with)

**Messer** *das;* ∼s, ∼: knife

**messer-, Messer-:** ∼**scharf** ① *Adj.* razor-sharp; (fig.) incisive ⟨*logic*⟩; razor-sharp ⟨*wit, intellect*⟩; ② *adv.* (fig. ugs.) ⟨*argue*⟩ incisively; ∼**stecherei** *die;* ∼∼, ∼∼en knife fight; fight with knives; ∼**stich** *der* knife thrust; (Wunde) knife wound

**Mess·gerät, \*Meß·gerät** *das* measuring device; (Zähler) meter

**Messias** *der;* ∼, ∼se Messiah

**m**

**Messing** *das;* ~s brass
**Mess·instrument, \*Meß·instrument**
*das* measuring instrument
**Messung** *die;* ~, ~en measurement
**Metall** *das;* ~s, ~e metal
**metallic** *indekl. Adj.* metallic [grey/blue/
etc.]
**Metall·industrie** *die* metal-processing and
metal-working industries *pl.*
**metallisch** *Adj.* metallic; metal *attrib.*,
metallic ⟨*conductor*⟩
**Metapher** *die;* ~, ~n metaphor
**metaphorisch** (Stilk.) [1] *Adj.* metaphorical
[2] *adv.* metaphorically
**Meta·physik** *die;* ~: metaphysics *sing., no
art.*
**Metastase** *die;* ~, ~n (Med.) metastasis
**Meteor** *der;* ~s, ~e meteor
**Meteorit** *der;* ~en *od.* ~s, ~e[n] meteorite
**Meteorologe** *der;* ~n, ~n meteorologist
**Meteorologie** *die;* ~: meteorology *no art.*
**Meteorologin** *die;* ~, ~nen meteorologist
**meteorologisch** [1] *Adj.* meteorological
[2] *adv.* meteorologically
**Meter** *der od. das;* ~s, ~: metre
**meter-, Meter-:** ~**dick** *Adj.* (sehr dick)
metres thick *postpos.;* ~**hoch** *Adj.* metres
high *postpos.;* ⟨*snow*⟩ metres deep; ~**maß**
*das* tape measure; (Stab) [metre] rule
**Methan** *das;* ~s methane
**Methode** *die;* ~, ~n method
**methodisch** [1] *Adj.* methodological; (nach
einer Methode vorgehend) methodical
[2] *adv.* methodologically; (nach einer Methode)
methodically
**Metier** /me'tje:/ *das;* ~s, ~s profession
**Metrik** *die;* ~, ~en metrics
**metrisch** [1] *Adj.*(a) (Verslehre, Musik)
metrical
(b) (auf den Meter bezogen) metric
[2] *adv.* metrically
**Metropole** *die;* ~, ~n metropolis
**Mett·wurst** *die;* soft smoked sausage made
of minced pork and beef
**Metzger** *der;* ~s, ~ (bes. westmd., südd.,
schweiz.) butcher
**Metzgerei** *die;* ~, ~en (bes. westmd., südd.,
schweiz.) butcher's [shop]
**Meute** *die;* ~, ~n (a) (Jägerspr.) pack
(b) (ugs. abwertend) mob
**Meuterei** *die;* ~, ~en mutiny
**meutern** *itr. V.* (a) mutiny; ⟨*prisoners*⟩ riot
(b) (ugs.: Unwillen äußern) moan
**Mexikaner** *der;* ~s, ~, **Mexikanerin**
*die;* ~, ~ Mexican
**mexikanisch** *Adj.* Mexican
**Mexiko** *(das);* ~s Mexico
**MEZ** *Abk.* = **mitteleuropäische Zeit**
CET

**mg** *Abk.* = **Milligramm** mg
**MG** /ɛm'ge:/ *das;* ~s, ~s *Abk.*
= **Maschinengewehr**
**Mi.** *Abk.* = **Mittwoch** Wed.
**miau** *Interj.* miaow
**miauen** *itr. V.* miaow
**mich** [1] *Akk. von* ICH me
[2] *Akk. des Reflexivpron. der 1.Pers. Sg.*
myself
**mick[e]rig** *Adj.* (ugs.) miserable; measly
(coll.); puny ⟨*person*⟩
**mied** *1. u. 3. Pers. Sg. Prät. v.* MEIDEN
**Mieder·waren** *Pl.* corsetry *sing.*
**Miene** *die;* ~, ~n expression
**mies** (ugs.) [1] *Adj.* lousy (coll.)
[2] *adv.* lousily (coll.)
**Mies-:** ~**macher** *der,* ~**macherin** *die*
(ugs. abwertend) carping critic; (Spielverderber)
killjoy; ~**muschel** *die* [common] mussel
**Miete** *die;* ~, ~n rent; (für ein Auto, Boot) hire
charge; **zur** ~ **wohnen** live in rented
accommodation
**mieten** *tr. V.* rent; (für kürzere Zeit) hire
**Mieter** *der;* ~s, ~, **Mieterin** *die;* ~, ~nen
tenant
**Miets·haus** *das* block of rented flats (Brit.)
*or* (Amer.) apartments
**Miet-:** ~**erhöhung** *die* rent increase;
~**vertrag** *der* tenancy agreement;
~**wagen** *der* hire car
**Migräne** *die;* ~, ~n migraine
**Migrant** *der;* ~en, ~en, **Migrantin** *die;*
~, ~nen migrant
**mikro-, Mikro-** micro-
**Mikrobe** *die;* ~, ~n microbe
**mikro-, Mikro-:** ~**film** *der* microfilm;
~**phon** /-'-/ *das;* ~s, ~e microphone;
~**skop** /-'-/ *das;* ~s, ~e microscope;
~**skopisch** /-'-'-/ [1] *Adj.* microscopic;
[2] *adv.* microscopically; ~**welle** *die* (ugs.)
microwave [oven]
**Milbe** *die;* ~, ~n mite
**Milch** *die;* ~: milk
**Milch·flasche** *die* milk bottle
**milchig** [1] *Adj.* milky
[2] *adv.* ~ **weiß** milky-white
**Milch-:** ~**kaffee** *der* coffee with plenty of
milk; ~**kännchen** *das;* ~s, ~~: milk
jug; ~**reis** *der* rice pudding; ~**straße** *die*
Milky Way; Galaxy; ~**zahn** *der* milk tooth
**mild, milde** [1] *Adj.* mild; lenient ⟨*judge,
judgement*⟩; soft ⟨*light*⟩; smooth ⟨*brandy*⟩
[2] *adv.* (gütig) leniently; (gelinde) mildly
**Milde** *die;* ~: mildness; (Güte) leniency
**mildern** *tr. V.* moderate; mitigate
⟨*punishment*⟩
**Milderung** *die;* ~: ▶ MILDERN: moderation;
mitigation
**Milieu** /mi'ljø:/ *das;* ~s, ~s environment
**militant** *Adj.* militant

**Militär¹** *das;* ~s armed forces *pl.;* military; (Soldaten) soldiers *pl.*

**Militär²** *der;* ~s, ~s [high-ranking military] officer

**Militär-:** ~**dienst** *der* military service; ~**diktatur** *die* military dictatorship

**militärisch** *Adj.* military

**militarisieren** *tr. V.* militarize

**Militarismus** *der;* ~ (abwertend) militarism

**Militarist** *der;* ~en, ~en (abwertend) militarist

**Militär-:** ~**macht** *die* military power; ~**putsch** *der* military putsch

**Military** /ˈmɪlɪtərɪ/ *die;* ~, ~s (Reiten) three-day event

**Miliz** *die;* ~, ~en militia; (Polizei) police

**Mill.** *Abk.* = **Million** m.

**milli-, Milli-** milli-

**Milliarde** *die;* ~, ~n billion

**Milli-:** ~**gramm** *das* milligram; ~**meter** *der od. das* millimetre; ~**meter-papier** *das* [graph] paper ruled in millimetre squares

**Million** *die;* ~, ~en million

**Millionär** *der;* ~s, ~e millionaire

**Millionen-:** ~**schaden** *der* damage no *pl.,* no *indef. art.* running into millions; ~**stadt** *die* town with over a million inhabitants

**millionst...** *Ordinalz.* millionth

**Milz** *die;* ~: spleen

**Mimik** *die;* ~: gestures and facial expressions *pl.*

**Mimose** *die;* ~, ~n **(a)** mimosa **(b)** (fig.) oversensitive person

**mimosenhaft** ⓵ *Adj.* oversensitive ⓶ *adv.* oversensitively

**minder** *Adv.* (geh.) less

**minder...** *Adj.* inferior ⟨*goods, brand*⟩

**minder-bemittelt** *Adj.* without much money *postpos., not pred.;* ~ **sein** not have much money; **geistig** ~ (fig. salopp abwertend) not all that bright (coll.)

**Minderheit** *die;* ~, ~en minority

**minder-jährig** *Adj.* ⟨*child etc.*⟩ who is/was a minor

**Minder-jährige** *der/die; adj. Dekl.* minor

**mindern** *tr. V.* (geh.) reduce

**Minderung** *die;* ~, ~en reduction (*Gen.* in)

**minder-wertig** *Adj.* inferior

**mindest...** *Adj.* least; (geringst...) slightest; **das ist das Mindeste** *od.* ~**e, was du tun kannst** it is the least you can do

**mindestens** *Adv.* at least

**Mindest-haltbarkeits-datum** *das* best-before date

**Mine** *die;* ~, ~n **(a)** (Bergwerk, Sprengkörper) mine **(b)** (Bleistift~) lead; (Kugelschreiber~, Filzschreiber~) refill

**Mineral** *das;* ~s, ~e *od.* **Mineralien** mineral

**Mineralogie** *die;* ~: mineralogy no *art.*

**Mineral-:** ~**öl** *das* mineral oil; ~**wasser** *das* mineral water

**Mini** *das;* ~s, ~s (Mode) mini

**Mini-** mini-

**Miniatur** *die;* ~, ~en miniature

**minimal** ⓵ *Adj.* minimal; marginal ⟨*advantage, lead*⟩; very slight ⟨*benefit, profit*⟩ ⓶ *adv.* minimally

**Minimum** *das;* ~s, **Minima** minimum (**an** + *Dat.* of)

**minimieren** *tr. V.* (bes. Math.) minimize

**Minister** *der;* ~s, ~, **Ministerin** *die;* ~, ~nen minister (**für** for); (eines britischen Hauptministeriums) Secretary of State (**für** for); (eines amerikanischen Hauptministeriums) Secretary (**für** of)

**Ministerium** *das;* ~s, **Ministerien** Ministry; Department (Amer.)

**Minister-präsident** *der,* **Minister-präsidentin** *die* **(a)** (eines deutschen Bundeslandes) minister-president **(b)** (Premierminister[in]) Prime Minister

**Minister-rat** *der* Council of Ministers

**Ministrant** *der;* ~en, ~en, **Ministrantin** *die;* ~, ~nen (kath. Kirche) server

**Minorität** *die;* ~, ~en ▶ MINDERHEIT

**minus** *Konj., Adv.* (bes. Math.) minus

**Minus** *das;* ~: deficit

**Minus-zeichen** *das* minus sign

**Minute** *die;* ~, ~n minute

**minuten-lang** ⓵ *Adj.* lasting [for] several minutes *postpos.;* ⓶ *adv.* for several minutes

**Minuten-zeiger** *der* minute hand

**Mio.** *Abk.* = **Million[en]** m.

**mir** ⓵ *Dat. von* ICH to me; (nach Präpositionen) me; **Freunde von** ~: friends of mine; **gehen wir zu** ~: let's go to my place; **von** ~ **aus** as far as I'm concerned ⓶ *Dat. des Reflexivpron. der 1. Pers. Sg.* myself

**Mirabelle** *die;* ~, ~n mirabelle

**Misch-:** ~**brot** *das* bread made from wheat and rye flour; ~**ehe** *die* mixed marriage

**mischen** ⓵ *tr. V.* mix ⓶ *refl. V.* **(a)** (sich ver~) mix (**mit** with); ⟨*smell, scent*⟩ blend (**mit** with) **(b)** (sich ein~) **sich in etw.** (*Akk.*) ~: interfere in sth.

**Misch-farbe** *die* non-primary colour

**Mischling** *der;* ~s, ~e half-caste

**Mischmasch** *der;* ~[e]s, ~e (ugs., meist abwertend) hotchpotch; mishmash

**Misch-pult** *das* (Film, Rundf., Ferns.) mixing desk *or* console

**Mischung** *die;* ~, ~en mixture; (Tee~, Kaffee~, Tabak~) blend; (Pralinen~) assortment

m

**Misch·wald** der mixed [deciduous and coniferous] forest

**miserabel** (ugs.) ⟨1⟩ Adj. dreadful (coll.) ⟨2⟩ adv. dreadfully (coll.); **ihm geht es gesundheitlich ~:** he's in a bad way

**Misere** die; ~, ~n (geh.) wretched or dreadful state; (Elend) misery; (Not) distress

**miss, *miß** Imperativ Sg. v. MESSEN

**miss·achten, *miß·achten** tr. V. (a) (ignorieren) disregard; ignore (b) (geringschätzen) be contemptuous of

**miss·billigen, *miß·billigen** tr. V. disapprove of

**Miss·billigung, *Miß·billigung** die disapproval

**Miss·brauch, *Miß·brauch** der: ▶ MISSBRAUCHEN: abuse; misuse

**miss·brauchen, *miß·brauchen** tr. V. abuse; misuse; abuse ⟨trust⟩

**missen** tr. V. (geh.) jmdn./etw. nicht ~ mögen not want to be without sb./sth.

**Miss·erfolg, *Miß·erfolg** der failure

**Misse·tat** die (geh. veralt.) misdeed

**miss·fallen, *miß·fallen** unr. itr. V. etw. missfällt jmdm. sb. dislikes sth.

**Missfallen, *Mißfallen** das; ~s displeasure; (Missbilligung) disapproval

**Miss·geschick, *Miß·geschick** das mishap

**miss·glücken, *miß·glücken** itr. V.; mit sein fail

**miss·gönnen, *miß·gönnen** tr. V. jmdm. etw. ~: begrudge sb. sth.

**Miss·griff, *Miß·griff** der error of judgement

**miss·handeln, *miß·handeln** tr. V. maltreat

**Miss·handlung, *Miß·handlung** die maltreatment

**Mission** die; ~, ~en mission

**Missionar** der; ~s, ~e, **Missionarin** die; ~, ~nen missionary

**Miss·kredit, *Miß·kredit** der: jmdn./etw. in ~ bringen bring sb./sth. into discredit

**misslang, *mißlang** 1. u. 3. Pers. Sg. Prät. v. MISSLINGEN

**missliebig, *mißliebig** Adj. unpopular

**misslingen, *mißlingen** unr. itr. V.; mit sein fail

**Misslingen, *Mißlingen** das; ~s failure

**misslungen, *mißlungen** 2. Part. v. MISSLINGEN

**Miss·mut, *Miß·mut** der ill humour no indef. art.

**miß·mutig, *miss·mutig** ⟨1⟩ Adj. bad-tempered; sullen ⟨face⟩ ⟨2⟩ adv. bad-temperedly

**Miss·stand, *Miß·stand** der deplorable state of affairs no pl.

**misst, *mißt** 2. u. 3. Pers. Sg. Präsens v. MESSEN

**miss·trauen, *miß·trauen** itr. V. jmdm./einer Sache ~: mistrust or distrust sb./sth.

**Misstrauen, *Miß·trauen** das; ~s mistrust, distrust (gegen of)

**misstrauisch, *miß·trauisch** ⟨1⟩ Adj. mistrustful; distrustful ⟨2⟩ adv. mistrustfully; distrustfully

**miss·verständlich, *miß·verständlich** ⟨1⟩ Adj. unclear; ⟨formulation, concept, etc.⟩ that could be misunderstood ⟨2⟩ adv. ⟨express oneself, describe⟩ in a way that could be misunderstood

**Miss·verständnis, *Miß·verständnis** das misunderstanding

**miss·verstehen, *miß·verstehen** unr. tr. V. ich missverstehe, missverstanden, misszuverstehen misunderstand

**Miss·wirtschaft, *Miß·wirtschaft** die mismanagement

**Mist** der; ~[e]s (a) dung; (Dünger) manure; (mit Stroh usw. gemischt) muck (b) (Misthaufen) dung/manure/muck heap (c) (ugs. abwertend) (Unsinn) rubbish no indef. art.; (Minderwertiges) junk no indef. art.

**Mistel** die; ~, ~n mistletoe

**Mist·haufen** der dung/manure/muck heap

**mit** ⟨1⟩ Präp. mit Dat. with; **ein Zimmer ~ Frühstück** a room with breakfast included; ~ **50 [km/h] fahren** drive at 50 [k.p.h]; ~ **der Bahn/dem Auto fahren** go by train/car; ~ **20 [Jahren]** at [the age of] twenty ⟨2⟩ adv. (a) too; as well (b) **seine Arbeit war ~ am besten** (ugs.) his work was among the best

**Mit·arbeit** die collaboration (**bei/an** + Dat. on); (Mithilfe) assistance (**bei, in** + Dat. in); (Beteiligung) participation (**in** + Dat. in)

**mit|arbeiten** itr. V. collaborate (**bei/an** + Dat. on) (sich beteiligen) participate (**in** + Dat. in)

**Mit·arbeiter** der, **Mit·arbeiterin** die (a) collaborator; **freier ~:** freelance worker (b) (Angestellter) employee

**mit|bekommen** unr. tr. V. (a) **etw. ~:** be given sth. to take with one (b) (wahrnehmen) be aware of; (durch Hören, Sehen) hear/see

**mit|bestimmen** ⟨1⟩ itr. V. have a say ⟨2⟩ tr. V. have an influence on

**Mit·bestimmung** die participation (**bei** in); (der Arbeitnehmer) co-determination

**mit|bringen** unr. tr. V. (a) **etw. ~:** bring sth. with one; **jmdm./sich etw. ~:** bring sth. with one for sb./bring sth. back for oneself (b) (haben) have ⟨ability, gift, etc.⟩

**Mitbringsel** das; ~s, ~: [small] present; (Andenken) [small] souvenir

**Mịt·bürger** *der,* **Mịt·bürgerin** *die* fellow citizen; **ältere Mitbürger** (Amtsspr.) senior citizens

**mit·einạnder** *Adv.* **(a)** with each other *or* one another; ~ **sprechen** talk to each other *or* one another
**(b)** (gemeinsam) together

**mịt|erleben** *tr. V.* **(a)** witness ‹events etc.›
**(b)** (mitmachen) be alive during

**mịt|fahren** *unr. itr. V.; mit sein* **bei jmdm.** [im Auto] ~: go/travel with sb. [in his/her car]; (mitgenommen werden) get a lift with sb. [in his/her car]

**mịt·fühlend** 1 *Adj.* sympathetic
2 *adv.* sympathetically

**mịt|führen** *tr. V.* **(a)** (Amtsspr.: bei sich tragen) **etw.** ~: carry sth. [with one]
**(b)** (transportieren) ‹river, stream› carry along

**mịt|geben** *unr. tr. V.* **jmdm. etw.** ~: give sb. sth. to take with him/her; (fig.) provide sb. with sth.

**Mịt·gefühl** *das* sympathy

**mịt|gehen** *unr. itr. V.; mit sein* **(a)** go too; **mit jmdm.** ~: go with sb.
**(b)** (sich mitreißen lassen) **begeistert** ~: respond enthusiastically

**Mịt·gift** *die;* ~, ~en (veralt.) dowry

**Mịt·glied** *das* member (*Gen.,* **in** + *Dat.* of)

**Mịtglieder·versammlung** *die* general meeting

**Mịtglieds-:** ~**ausweis** *der* membership card; ~**beitrag** *der* membership subscription

**Mịtgliedschaft** *die;* ~: membership (+ *Gen.,* **in** + *Dat.*) of

**Mịtglied[s]·staat** *der* member state *or* country

**mịt|halten** *unr. itr. V.* keep up (**bei** in, **mit** with)

**mịt|helfen** *unr. itr. V.* help (**bei, in** + *Dat.* with)

**mit·hilfe** 1 *Präp. mit Gen.* with the help *or* aid of
2 *Adv.* ~ **von** with the help *or* aid of

**Mịt·hilfe** *die* help; assistance

**mịt|hören** 1 *tr. V.* listen to; (zufällig) overhear ‹conversation, argument, etc.›; (abhören) listen in on
2 *itr. V.* listen; (zufällig) overhear

**mịt|kommen** *unr. itr. V.; mit sein* **(a)** come too; **kommst du mit?** are you coming [with me/us]?
**(b)** (Schritt halten) keep up

**Mịt·läufer** *der,* **Mịt·läuferin** *die* (abwertend) [mere] supporter

**Mịt·laut** *der* consonant

**Mịt·leid** *das* pity, compassion (**mit** for); (Mitgefühl) sympathy (**mit** for)

**Mịt·leidenschaft** *die:* **jmdn./etw. in** ~ **ziehen** affect sb./sth.

**mịt·leidig** 1 *Adj.* compassionate; (mitfühlend) sympathetic

2 *adv.* compassionately; (mitfühlend) sympathetically

**mịt|machen** 1 *tr. V.* **(a)** (teilnehmen an) go on ‹trip›; join in ‹joke›; follow ‹fashion›; fight in ‹war›; do ‹course, seminar›; **das mache ich nicht mit** (ugs.) I can't go along with it
**(b)** (ugs.: erleiden) **zwei Weltkriege/viele Bombenangriffe mitgemacht haben** have been through two world wars/many bomb attacks
2 *itr. V.* **(a)** (sich beteiligen) join in
**(b)** (ugs.: funktionieren) **mein Herz/Kreislauf macht nicht mit** my heart/circulation can't take it

**Mịt·mensch** *der* fellow human being

**mịt|nehmen** *unr. tr. V.* **(a)** **jmdn.** ~: take sb. with one; **etw.** ~: take sth. with one; (verhüll.: stehlen) walk off with sth. (coll.); (kaufen) take sth.; **Essen/Getränke zum Mitnehmen** food/drinks to take away *or* (Amer.) to go
**(b)** (in Mitleidenschaft ziehen) **jmdn.** ~: take it out of sb.

**mịt|reden** *itr. V.* **(a)** join in the conversation
**(b)** (mitbestimmen) have a say

**Mịt·reisende** *der/die* fellow passenger

**mịt|reißen** *unr. tr. V.* **die Begeisterung/ seine Rede hat alle Zuhörer mitgerissen** the audience was carried away with enthusiasm/by his speech

**mit·sạmt** *Präp. mit Dat.* together with

**mịt|schneiden** *unr. tr. V.* (Rundf., Fers.) record [live]

**Mịt·schuld** *die* share of the blame *or* responsibility (**an** + *Dat.* for)

**Mịt·schüler** *der,* **Mịt·schülerin** *die* schoolfellow

**mịt|spielen** *itr. V.* **(a)** join in the game
**(b)** (in einem Film ~: be in a film; **in einem Orchester/in** *od.* **bei einem Fußballverein** ~: play in an orchestra/for a football club

**Mịt·spieler** *der,* **Mịt·spielerin** *die* player; (in derselben Mannschaft) teammate

*\****mịttag** ▶ MITTAG

**Mịttag** *der;* ~**s,** ~**e (a)** midday *no art.;* **gegen** ~: around midday; **zu** ~ **essen** have lunch; **heute/Montag** ~: at midday today/on Monday
**(b)** (ugs.: Mittagspause) lunch hour

**Mịttag·essen** *das* lunch

**mịttags** *Adv.* at midday; **12 Uhr** ~: 12 noon

**Mịttags-:** ~**pause** *die* lunch hour; ~**ruhe** *die* period of quiet after lunch; ~**zeit** *die* **(a)** (Zeit gegen 12 Uhr) lunchtime *no art.;* **(b)** (Mittagspause) lunch hour

**Mịtte** *die;* ~, ~**n** middle; (eines Kreises, einer Kugel, Stadt) centre; ~ **des Monats/Jahres** in the middle of the month/year

**mịt|teilen** *tr. V.* **jmdm. etw.** ~: tell sb. sth.; (informieren) inform sb. of sth.

m

**mitteilsam** *Adj.* communicative; (gesprächig) talkative

**Mit·teilung** *die* communication; (Bekanntgabe) announcement

**Mittel** *das;* ~s, ~ (a) means; (Methode) way; method; (Werbe~, Propaganda~ usw.) device (*Gen.* for); **mit allen ~n versuchen, etw. zu tun** try by every means to do sth.
(b) (Arznei) **ein ~ gegen Husten** *usw.* a cure for coughs *etc.;*
(c) *Pl.* (Geldmittel) funds; [financial] resources; (Privatmittel) means

**Mittel·alter** *das* Middle Ages *pl.*

**mittel·alterlich** *Adj.* medieval

**mittelbar** ① *Adj.* indirect
② *adv.* indirectly

**mittel-, Mittel-:** ~**ding** *das* **ein ~ding sein** be something in between; ~**europa** (*das*) Central Europe; ~**finger** *der* middle finger; ~**gebirge** *das* low mountains *pl.;* ~**groß** *Adj.* medium-sized; ⟨*person*⟩ of medium height; ~**klasse·wagen** *der* medium-sized car; ~**linie** *die* centre line; (Fußball) half-way line; ~**los** *Adj.* without means *postpos.;* ~**mäßig** *Adj.* mediocre; ~**meer** *das* Mediterranean [Sea]; ~**punkt** *der* (a) (Geom.) centre; (einer Strecke) midpoint; (b) (Mensch/Sache im Zentrum) centre of attention; ~**scheitel** *der* centre parting; ~**schule** *die* ▶ REALSCHULE; ~**stand** *der* middle class; ~**strecken·rakete** *die* medium-range missile; ~**streifen** *der* central reservation; median strip (Amer.); ~**weg** *der* middle course; ~**welle** *die* (Physik, Rundf.) medium wave

**mitten** *Adv.* ~ **an/auf etw.** (*Akk./Dat.*) in the middle of sth.; ~ **durch die Stadt** right through the town

**mitten-:** ~**drin** *Adv.* [right] in the middle; ~**durch** *Adv.* [right] through the middle

**Mitter·nacht** *die* midnight *no art.*

**Mitternachts·sonne** *die* midnight sun

**Mittler** *der;* ~s, ~ mediator

**mittler...** *Adj.* middle; moderate ⟨*speed*⟩; medium-sized ⟨*company, town*⟩; medium ⟨*quality, size*⟩; (durchschnittlich) average; **die ~e Reife** (Schulw.) *standard of achievement for school-leaving certificate at a Realschule or for entry to the sixth form in a Gymnasium*

**Mittlerin** *die;* ~, ~nen mediator

**Mittler·rolle** *die* mediating role

**mittler·weile** *Adv.* since then; (bis jetzt) by now; (unterdessen) in the meantime

**Mittwoch** *der;* ~[e]s, ~e Wednesday; *s. auch* DIENSTAG

**mittwochs** *Adv.* on Wednesday[s]

**mit·unter** *Adv.* from time to time

**mit·wirken** *itr. V.* **an etw.** (*Dat.*)/**bei etw.** ~: collaborate on/be involved in sth.; **in einem Orchester/Theaterstück** ~: play in an orchestra/act *or* appear in a play

**Mitwirkende** *der/die adj. Dekl.* (an einer Sendung) participant; (in einer Show) performer; (in einem Theaterstück) actor

**Mit·wisser** *der;* ~s ~, **Mit·wisserin** *die;* ~, ~nen: ~ **einer Sache** (*Gen.*) **sein** be an accessory to sth.

**mixen** *tr. V.* mix; **sich** (*Dat.*) **einen Drink** ~: fix oneself a drink

**Mixer** *der;* ~s, ~, (a) (Bar~) barman; bartender (Amer.)
(b) (Gerät) blender and liquidizer

**Mixerin** *die;* ~, ~nen barmaid

**mm** *Abk.* = **Millimeter** mm.

**Mo.** *Abk.* = **Montag** Mon.

**Mob** *der;* ~s (abwertend) mob

**Möbel** *das;* ~s, ~ (a) *Pl.* furniture *sing., no indef. art.;*
(b) piece of furniture

**Möbel·wagen** *der* furniture van; removal van

**mobil** *Adj.* (a) mobile; *s. auch* MOBILMACHEN;
(b) (ugs.) (lebendig) lively

**Mobiliar** *das;* ~s furnishings *pl.*

**mobilisieren** *tr. V.* (a) (Milit., fig.) mobilize
(b) (aktivieren) activate

**mobil|machen** *itr. V.* mobilize

**Mobilmachung** *die;* ~, ~en mobilization

**Mobil·telefon** *das* cellular phone

**möblieren** *tr. V.* furnish

**mochte** *1. u. 3. Pers. Sg. Prät. v.* MÖGEN

**möchte** *1. u. 3. Pers. Sg. Konjunktiv II v.* MÖGEN

**Mode** *die;* ~, ~n fashion

**Mode·farbe** *die* fashionable colour

**Modell** *das;* ~s, ~e (auch fig.) model; **jmdm.** ~ **sitzen** *od.* **stehen** sit for sb.

**modellieren** *tr. V.* model, mould ⟨*figures, objects*⟩; mould ⟨*clay, wax*⟩

**Modell·kleid** *das* model dress

**Modem** *der od. das;* ~s, ~s (DV) modem

**Moden·schau** *die* fashion show

**Moder** *der;* ~s mould; (~geruch) mustiness

**Moderation** *die;* ~, ~en (Rundf., Ferns.) presentation

**Moderator** *der;* ~s, ~en, **Moderatorin** *die;* ~, ~nen (Rundf., Ferns.) presenter

**moderieren** *tr. V.* (Rundf., Ferns.) present ⟨*programme*⟩

**modern¹** *itr. V.; auch mit sein* go mouldy

**modern²** ① *Adj.* modern; (modisch) fashionable
② *adv.* in a modern manner; (modisch) fashionably

**modernisieren** *tr. V.* modernize

**Mode-:** ~**schöpfer** *der* couturier; ~**schöpferin** *die* couturière; ~**wort** *das; Pl.* ~**wörter** vogue word; ~**zeitschrift** *die* fashion magazine

**modifizieren** *tr. V.* (geh.) modify

**modisch** ① *Adj.* fashionable
② *adv.* fashionably

---

*old spelling - see note on page xiv

**Mofa** das; ~s, ~s [low-powered] moped
**Mogelei** die; ~, ~en (ugs.) cheating no pl.
**mogeln** itr. V. cheat
**Mogel-packung** die (abwertend) deceptive packaging
**mögen** ① unr. Modalverb; 2.Part. mögen:
(a) (wollen) want to; **das hätte ich sehen ~**: I would have liked to see that
(b) (geh.: sollen) **das mag genügen** that should be enough
(c) (Vermutung, Möglichkeit) **sie mag/mochte vierzig sein** she must be/must have been [about] forty; [das] **mag sein** maybe
(d) Konjunktiv II (den Wunsch haben) **ich/sie möchte gern wissen** ...: I would/she would like to know ...
② unr. tr. V. like; **sie mag keine Rosen** she does not like roses; **sie ~ sich** they're fond of one another; **möchten Sie ein Glas Wein?** would you like a glass of wine?; **ich möchte lieber Tee** I would prefer tea
③ unr. itr. V. (a) (es wollen) like to
(b) **ich möchte nach Hause** I want to go home; **er möchte zu Herrn A** he would like to see Mr A
**möglich** Adj. possible; **es war ihm nicht ~** [zu kommen] he was unable [to come]; **alles Mögliche** (ugs.) all sorts of things; [**das ist doch] nicht ~!** impossible!; **sein Möglichstes tun** do one's utmost
**möglicher-weise** Adv. possibly
**Möglichkeit** die; ~, ~en (a) possibility; (Methode) way; **es besteht die ~, dass** ...: there is a possibility that ...
(b) (Gelegenheit) opportunity; chance
**möglichst** Adv. (a) if [at all] possible
(b) **~ schnell** as fast as possible
**Mohammed** (der) Muhammad
**Mohammedaner** der; ~s, ~,
**Mohammedanerin** die; ~, ~nen Muslim; Muhammadan
**mohammedanisch** Adj. Muslim; Muhammadan
**Mohn** der; ~s poppy; (Samen) poppy seed; (auf Brot, Kuchen) poppy seeds pl.
**Mohn-:** ~**blume** die poppy; ~**brötchen** das poppy-seed roll; ~**kuchen** der poppy-seed cake
**Möhre** die; ~, ~n carrot
**Mohren-kopf** der chocolate marshmallow
**Mohr-rübe** die carrot
**mokieren** refl. V. (geh.) sich über etw. (Akk.) ~: scoff at sth.; **sich über jmdn. ~**: mock sb.
**Mokka** der; ~s strong black coffee
**Molch** der; ~[e]s, ~e newt
**Mole** die; ~, ~n [harbour] mole
**Molekül** das; ~s, ~e molecule
**molekular** Adj. molecular
**molk** 1. u. 3. Pers. Sg. Prät. v. MELKEN
**Molkerei** die; ~, ~en dairy
**Moll** das; ~ (Musik) minor [key]

**mollig** ① Adj. (a) (rundlich) plump
(b) (warm) snug
② adv. snugly; ~ **warm** warm and snug
**Moment**[1] der; ~[e]s, ~e moment; **jeden ~** (ugs.) [at] any moment; **im ~**: at the moment
**Moment**[2] das; ~[e]s, ~e factor, element (für in)
**momentan** ① Adj. (a) present
(b) (vorübergehend) temporary; (flüchtig) momentary
② adv. (a) at present
(b) (vorübergehend) temporarily
**Monaco** (das); ~s Monaco
**Monarch** der; ~en, ~en monarch
**Monarchie** die; ~, ~n monarchy
**Monarchin** die; ~, ~nen monarch
**Monat** der; ~s, ~e month; **im ~ April** in the month of April
**monatelang** ① Adj. lasting for months postpos., not pred.;
② adv. for months [on end]
**monatlich** ① Adj. monthly
② adv. every month; (pro Monat) per month
**Monats-:** ~**ende** das end of the month; ~**erste** der; adj. Dekl. first [day] of the month; ~**hälfte** die half of the month; ~**karte** die monthly season ticket; ~**letzte** der; adj. Dekl. last day of the month
**Mönch** der; ~[e]s, ~e monk
**Mond** der; ~[e]s, ~e moon; **auf** od. **hinter dem ~ leben** (fig. ugs.) be a bit behind the times; **nach dem ~ gehen** (ugs.) ⟨clock, watch⟩ be hopelessly wrong
**Mond-:** ~**fähre** die (Raumf.) lunar module; ~**finsternis** die eclipse of the moon; ~**landung** die moon landing; ~**licht** das moonlight; ~**phase** die moon's phase
**Mongole** der; ~n, ~n (a) Mongol
(b) (Bewohner der Mongolei) Mongolian
**Mongolei** die; ~: Mongolia
**Mongolin** die; ~, ~nen ▶ MONGOLE
**Monitor** der; ~s, ~en monitor
**mono-, Mono-:** mono-
**Mono-gramm** das; ~s, ~e monogram
**Monographie** die; ~, ~n monograph
**Monolog** der; ~s, ~e monologue
**Monopol** das; ~s, ~e monopoly (auf + Akk., für in, of)
**monoton** ① Adj. monotonous
② adv. monotonously
**Monotonie** die; ~, ~n monotony
**Monster** das; ~s, ~: monster; (hässlich) [hideous] brute
**Monstren** ▶ MONSTRUM
**monströs** Adj. monstrous
**Monstrum** das; ~s, Monstren (a) monster
(b) (Sache) hulking great thing (coll.)
**Monsun** der; ~s, ~e (Geogr.) monsoon
**Mon-tag** der Monday; s. auch DIENSTAG
**Montage** /mɔn'taːʒə/ die; ~, ~n (a) ⋯⟫

(Zusammenbau) assembly; (Einbau) installation; (Aufstellen) erection; (Anbringen) fitting (an + *Akk. od. Dat.* to); mounting (auf + *Akk. od. Dat.* on)
**(b)** (Film, bild. Kunst, Literaturw.) montage

**montags** *Adv.* on Monday[s]

**montieren** *tr. V.* **(a)** (zusammenbauen) assemble (aus from); erect ⟨*building*⟩ **(b)** (anbringen) fit (an + *Akk. od. Dat.* to; auf + *Akk. od. Dat.* on); (einbauen) install (in + *Akk.* in); (befestigen) fix (an + *Akk. od. Dat.* to)

**Monument** *das;* ~[e]s, ~e monument

**monumental** *Adj.* monumental

**Moor** *das;* ~[e]s, ~e bog; (Bruch) marsh

**Moos** *das;* ~es, ~e moss

**Moped** /'mo:pɛt/ *das;* ~s, ~s moped

**Mops** *der;* ~es, Möpse pug [dog]; (salopp: dicke Person) podge (coll.)

**Moral** *die;* ~ **(a)** (Norm) morality **(b)** (Sittlichkeit) morals *pl.;* **(c)** (Selbstvertrauen) morale **(d)** (Lehre) moral

**moralisch** ⓵ *Adj.* **(a)** moral **(b)** (tugendhaft) virtuous ⓶ *adv.* **(a)** morally **(b)** (tugendhaft) virtuously

**moralisieren** *itr. V.* (geh.) moralize

**Moralist** *der;* ~en, ~en, **Moralistin** *die;* ~, ~nen moralist

**Moral·predigt** *die* (abwertend) [moralizing] lecture; homily

**Morast** *der;* ~[e]s, ~e od. Moräste **(a)** bog; swamp **(b)** (Schlamm) mud

**Mord** *der;* ~[e]s, ~e murder (an + *Dat.* of); (durch ein Attentat) assassination; **einen** ~ **begehen** commit murder

**Mord-:** ~**anschlag** *der* attempted murder (auf + *Akk.* of); (Attentat) assassination attempt (auf + *Akk.* on); ~**drohung** *die* murder threat

**morden** *tr., itr. V.* murder

**Mörder** *der;* ~s, ~: murderer (esp. Law); killer; (politischer) assassin

**Mörderin** *die;* ~, ~nen murderer; murderess; (politische) assassin

**mörderisch** ⓵ *Adj.* murderous ⓶ *adv.* (ugs.) dreadfully (coll.)

**Mord·fall** *der* murder case

**mords-, Mords-** (ugs.) terrific (coll.)

**mords·mäßig** *Adj.* terrific (coll.); tremendous (coll.); (entsetzlich) terrible (coll.)

**Mord-:** ~**verdacht** *der* suspicion of murder; ~**versuch** *der* attempted murder; (Attentat) assassination attempt; ~**waffe** *die* murder weapon

**morgen** *Adv.* tomorrow; ~ **in einer Woche** tomorrow week; a week tomorrow; ~ **um diese Zeit** this time tomorrow; **bis** ~! until tomorrow!; see you tomorrow!

---

*alte Schreibung - vgl. Hinweis auf S. xiv

**Morgen** *der;* ~s, ~: morning; **am** ~: in the morning; **am folgenden** od. **nächsten** ~: next morning; **früh am** ~, **am frühen** ~: early in the morning; **heute** ~: this morning; **guten** ~! good morning!

**morgendlich** *Adj.* morning

**Morgen-:** ~**grauen** *das* daybreak; ~**mantel** *der* dressing gown; ~**rot** *das* (geh.) rosy dawn

**morgens** *Adv.* in the morning; (jeden Morgen) every morning; **Dienstag** od. **dienstags** ~: on Tuesday morning[s]; **von** ~ **bis abends** from morning to evening

**morgig** *Adj.* tomorrow's

**Morphium** *das;* ~s morphine

**morphium·süchtig** *Adj.* addicted to morphine *pred.*

**morsch** *Adj.* (auch fig.) rotten

**Mörser** *der;* ~s, ~ (Gefäß, Geschütz) mortar

**Mörtel** *der;* ~s mortar

**Mosaik** *das;* ~s, ~en od. ~e mosaic

**Mosambik** (*das*) ~s Mozambique

**Moschee** *die;* ~, ~n mosque

**Moschus** *der;* ~: musk

**Mosel** *die;* ~: Moselle

**Mosel·wein** *der* Moselle [wine]

**mosern** *itr. V.* (ugs.) gripe (coll.) (über + *Akk.*)

**Moskau** (*das*) ~s Moscow

**Moskauer** ⓵ *indekl. Adj.* Moscow *attrib.;* ⓶ *der;* ~s, ~: Muscovite

**Moskauerin** *die;* ~, ~nen Muscovite

**Moskito** *der;* ~s, ~s mosquito

**Moslem** *der;* ~s, ~s ▶ MUSLIM

**Moslemin** *die;* ~, ~nen ▶ MUSLIMIN

**moslemisch** ▶ MUSLIMISCH

**Most** *der;* ~[e]s, ~e **(a)** [cloudy fermented] fruit juice **(b)** (landsch.: neuer Wein) new wine

**Mostrich** *der;* ~s (nordostd.) mustard

**Motel** *das;* ~s, ~s motel

**Motiv** *das;* ~s, ~e **(a)** motive **(b)** (fachspr.: Thema) motif; theme; (Kunst) subject

**Motor** *der;* ~s, ~en engine; (Elektro~) motor

**Motor·haube** *die* (Kfz-W.) bonnet (Brit.); hood (Amer.)

**motorisieren** *tr. V.* motorize

**Motor-:** ~**rad** *das* motor cycle; ~**rad·fahrer** *der,* ~**rad·fahrerin** *die* motorcyclist; ~**roller** *der* motor scooter; ~**schaden** *der* engine trouble *no indef. art.*

**Motte** *die;* ~, ~n moth

**Motten·kugel** *die* mothball

**Motto** *das;* ~s, ~s motto; (Schlagwort) slogan

**Möwe** *die;* ~, ~n gull

**Mrd.** *Abk.* = **Milliarde** bn.

**Mücke** *die;* ~, ~n midge; (größer) mosquito

**Mücken·stich** *der* midge/mosquito bite

**Mucks** *der;* ~es, ~e (ugs.) murmur [of protest]; **keinen ~ sagen** not utter a [single] word

**müde** 1 *Adj.* tired; (ermattet) weary; (schläfrig) sleepy; **jmdn./etw.** *od.* **jmds./einer Sache ~ sein** (geh.) be tired of sb./sth.
2 *adv.* wearily; (schläfrig) sleepily

**Müdigkeit** *die;* ~: tiredness

**muffelig** (ugs.) 1 *Adj.* grumpy
2 *adv.* grumpily

**muffig** *Adj.* musty

**Mühe** *die;* ~, ~n trouble; **sich** (*Dat.*) **mit jmdm./etw. ~ geben** take [great] pains over sb./sth.; **mit Müh und Not** with great difficulty

**mühelos** 1 *Adj.* effortless
2 *adv.* effortlessly

**mühe·voll** *Adj.* laborious; painstaking ⟨*work*⟩

**Mühle** *die;* ~, ~n (a) mill; (Kaffee~) [coffee] grinder
(b) (Spiel) nine men's morris

**Mühsal** *die;* ~, ~e (geh.) tribulation; (Strapaze) hardship

**mühsam** 1 *Adj.* laborious
2 *adv.* laboriously

**müh·selig** (geh.) 1 *Adj.* laborious; arduous ⟨*journey, life*⟩
2 *adv.* with [great] difficulty

**Mulde** *die;* ~, ~n hollow

**Mull** *der;* ~[e]s (Stoff) mull; (Verband~) gauze

**Müll** *der;* ~s refuse; rubbish; garbage (Amer.); trash (Amer.); (Industrie~) [industrial] waste

**Müll-:** ~**abfuhr** *die* refuse *or* (Amer.) garbage collection; ~**ablade·platz** *der* [refuse] dump *or* (Brit.) tip

**Mull·binde** *die* gauze bandage

**Müll·deponie** *die* (Amtsspr.) refuse disposal site

**Müller** *der;* ~s, ~: miller

**Müll-:** ~**halde** *die* refuse dump; ~**kippe** *die* ▸ MÜLLABLADEPLATZ; ~**mann** *der;* (ugs.) dustman (Brit.); garbage man (Amer.); ~**sack** *der* refuse bag; ~**schlucker** *der* rubbish *or* (Amer.) garbage chute; ~**tonne** *die* dustbin (Brit.); garbage *or* trash can (Amer.); ~**tüte** *die* bin bag; ~**wagen** *der* dustcart (Brit.); garbage truck (Amer.)

**mulmig** *Adj.* (ugs.) uneasy

**Multimedia·technik** *die* (DV) multimedia technology

**Multiplex** *das;* ~es, ~e multiplex

**Multiplikation** *die;* ~, ~en (Math.) multiplication

**multiplizieren** *tr. V.* multiply (mit by)

**Mumie** /'mu:mjə/ *die;* ~, ~n mummy

**Mumm** *der;* ~s (ugs.) (Mut) guts *pl.* (coll.); (Tatkraft) drive; zap (coll.); (Kraft) muscle power

**Mumps** *der od. die;* ~: mumps *sing.*

**München** (*das*)*;* ~s Munich

**Münch[e]ner** 1 *indekl. Adj.* Munich *attrib*
2 *der;* ~s, ~: inhabitant/native of Munich

**Münch[e]nerin** *die;* ~, ~nen
▸ MÜNCH[E]NER 2

**Mund** *der;* ~[e]s, Münder mouth; **er küsste sie auf den ~:** he kissed her on the lips; **mit vollem ~ sprechen** speak with one's mouth full; **den ~ nicht aufmachen** (fig. ugs.) not say anything; **den** *od.* **seinen ~ halten** (ugs.) (zu sprechen aufhören) shut up (coll.); (nichts sagen) not say anything; (nichts verraten) keep quiet (**über** + *Akk.* about); **sie ist nicht auf den ~ gefallen** (fig. ugs.) she's never at a loss for words

**Mund·art** *die* dialect

**münden** *itr. V.; mit sein in etw.* (*Akk.*) ~: ⟨*river*⟩ flow into sth.; ⟨*corridor, street*⟩ lead into sth.

**mund-, Mund-:** ~**faul** *Adj.* (ugs.) uncommunicative; ~**gerecht** *Adj.* bite-sized; ~**geruch** *der* bad breath *no indef. art.;* ~**harmonika** *die* mouth organ

**mündig** *Adj.* of age *pred.;* ~ **werden** come of age

**mündlich** 1 *Adj.* oral
2 *adv.* orally

**Mund·stück** *das* mouthpiece; (bei Zigaretten) tip

**mund·tot** *Adj.* **jmdn. ~ machen** silence sb.

**Mündung** *die;* ~, ~en (a) mouth; (größere Trichter~) estuary
(b) (bei Feuerwaffen) muzzle

**Mund·wasser** *das; Pl.* ~wässer mouthwash

**Mund-zu-Mund-Beatmung** *die* mouth-to-mouth resuscitation

**Munition** *die;* ~: ammunition

**munkeln** *tr., itr. V.* (ugs.) **man munkelt, dass ...:** there is a rumour that ...

**Münster** *das;* ~s, ~: minster; (Dom) cathedral

**munter** 1 *Adj.* (a) cheerful; (lebhaft) lively ⟨*eyes, game*⟩
(b) (wach) awake
2 *adv.* cheerfully

**Munterkeit** *die;* ~: cheerfulness

**Münz·automat** *der* slot machine

**Münze** *die;* ~, ~n coin

**Münz-:** ~**fernsprecher** *der* payphone; pay station (Amer.); ~**tankstelle** *die* coin-in-the-slot petrol (Brit.) *or* (Amer.) gas station; ~**wechsler** *der* change machine

**mürbe** *Adj.* crumbly ⟨*biscuit, cake, etc.*⟩; tender ⟨*meat*⟩; soft ⟨*fruit*⟩; **jmdn. ~ machen** (fig.) wear sb. down

**Murmel** *die;* ~, ~n marble

**murmeln** *tr., itr. V.* mumble; mutter; (sehr leise) murmur

**Murmel·tier** *das* marmot

**murren** *itr. V.* grumble

**mürrisch** 1 *Adj.* grumpy ⋯▸

② *adv.* grumpily

**Mus** *das od. der;* ∼es, ∼e purée

**Muschel** *die;* ∼, ∼n **(a)** mussel; (Schale) [mussel] shell
**(b)** (am Telefon) (Hör∼) earpiece; (Sprech∼) mouthpiece

**Muse** *die;* ∼, ∼n muse

**Museum** *das;* ∼s, Museen museum

**Musik** *die;* ∼, ∼en music

**musikalisch** ① *Adj.* musical
② *adv.* musically

**Musikant** *der;* ∼en, ∼en, **Musikantin** *die;* ∼, ∼nen musician

**Musik-box** *die* jukebox

**Musiker** *der;* ∼s, ∼, **Musikerin** *die;* ∼, ∼nen musician

**Musik-:** ∼**hochschule** *die* college of music; ∼**instrument** *das* musical instrument; ∼**saal** *der* (in der Schule) music room; ∼**sender** *der* music station; ∼**stück** *das* piece of music; **ein** ∼**stück** **Chopins/von Chopin** a piece by Chopin; ∼**stunde** *die* music lesson; ∼**szene** *die* music scene

**musisch** ① *Adj.* artistic; ⟨*education*⟩ in the arts
② *adv.* artistically

**musizieren** *itr. V.* play music; (bes. unter Laien) make music

**Muskat** *der;* ∼[e]s, ∼e nutmeg

**Muskat-nuss,** *****Muskat-nuß** *die* nutmeg

**Muskel** *der;* ∼s, ∼n muscle

**Muskel-:** ∼**kater** *der* stiff muscles *pl.;* ∼**kraft** *die* muscle power; ∼**krampf** *der* cramp; ∼**pille** *die* (scherzh.) muscle-building pill; muscle builder ∼**protz** *der* (ugs.) muscleman; ∼**zerrung** *die* (Med.) pulled muscle; **sich** (*Dat.*) **eine** ∼**zerrung zuziehen** pull a muscle

**Muskulatur** *die;* ∼, ∼en musculature; muscular system

**muskulös** *Adj.* muscular

**Müsli** *das;* ∼s, ∼s muesli

**Muslim** *der;* ∼s, ∼e *od.* ∼s Muslim

**Muslimin** *die;* ∼, ∼nen Muslim [woman]

**muslimisch** ① *Adj.* Muslim
② *adv.* on Muslim principles; ∼ **erzogen werden** be brought up in the Muslim faith

**muss,** *****muß** *1. u. 3.Pers. Sg. Präsens v.* MÜSSEN

**Muss,** *****Muß** *das;* ∼: necessity; must (coll.)

**Muße** *die;* ∼: leisure

**müssen** ① *unr. Modalverb; 2.Part.* müssen: **(a)** have to; **er muss es tun** he must do it; he has to *or* (coll.) has got to do it; **das muss 1968 gewesen sein** it must have been in 1968; **er muss gleich hier sein** he will be here at any moment

**(b)** *Konjunktiv II* **es müsste doch möglich sein** it ought to be possible; **reich müsste man sein!** how nice it would be to be rich!
② *unr. itr. V.* **ich muss nach Hause** I have to *or* must go home; **ich muss mal** (fam.) I need to spend a penny (Brit. coll.) *or* (Amer. coll.) go to the john

**müßig** ① *Adj.* idle ⟨*person*⟩; ⟨*hours, weeks, life*⟩ of leisure
② *adv.* idly

**Müßig-:** ∼**gang** *der* leisure; (Untätigkeit) idleness ∼**gänger** *der;* ∼∼s, ∼∼, ∼**gängerin** *die;* ∼, ∼∼nen idler; ∼**gänger** *Pl.* people with time on their hands

**musste,** *****mußte** *1. u. 3. Pers. Sg. Prät. v.* MÜSSEN

**Muster** *das;* ∼s, ∼ **(a)** (Vorlage) pattern
**(b)** (Vorbild) model **(an** + *Dat.* of)
**(c)** (Verzierung) pattern
**(d)** (Warenprobe) sample

**muster-, Muster-:** ∼**beispiel** *das* perfect example; ∼**gültig** ① *Adj.* exemplary; impeccable ⟨*order*⟩; ② *adv.* in an exemplary fashion; ∼**prozess,** *****prozeß** *der* test case

**mustern** *tr. V.* **(a)** eye
**(b)** (Milit.: ärztlich untersuchen) **jmdn.** ∼: give sb. his medical

**Musterung** *die;* ∼, ∼en **(a)** scrutiny
**(b)** (Milit.: von Wehrpflichtigen) medical examination; medical

**Mut** *der;* ∼[e]s courage

**mutig** ① *Adj.* brave
② *adv.* bravely

**mut-los** *Adj.* dejected; (entmutigt) disheartened

**Mut-losigkeit** *die;* ∼: dejection

**mutmaßen** *tr., itr. V.* conjecture

**mutmaßlich** *Adj.* supposed; suspected ⟨*murderer etc.*⟩

**Mutmaßung** *die;* ∼, ∼en conjecture

**Mut-probe** *die* test of courage

**Mutter¹** *die;* ∼, Mütter mother

**Mutter²** *die;* ∼, ∼n nut

**mütterlich** ① *Adj.* **(a)** maternal ⟨*line, love, instincts, etc.*⟩
**(b)** (fürsorglich) motherly ⟨*woman, care*⟩
② *adv.* in a motherly way

**mütterlicher-seits** *Adv.* on the/his/her *etc.* mother's side

**Mütterlichkeit** *die;* ∼: motherliness; (mütterliche Gefühle) motherly feeling

**Mutter-:** ∼**liebe** *die* motherly love *no art.;* ∼**mal** *das;* ∼∼e birthmark

**Mutterschaft** *die;* ∼: motherhood

**Mutterschafts-urlaub** *der* maternity leave

**mutter-, Mutter-:** ∼**seelen-allein** *Adj.* all alone; ∼**söhnchen** *das* mummy's *or* (Amer.) mama's boy; ∼**sprache** *die* mother tongue; ∼**tag** *der* Mother's Day *no def. art.*

---

*old spelling - see note on page xiv

**Mụtti** *die;* ~, ~s mummy (Brit. coll.); mum (Brit. coll.); mommy (Amer. coll.); mom (Amer. coll.)

**mut·willig** ① *Adj.* wilful; wanton ⟨*destruction*⟩ ② *adv.* wilfully

**Mütze** *die;* ~, ~n cap

**MW** *Abk.* (Rundf.) = **Mittelwelle** MW

**Mw.-St., MwSt.** *Abk.* Mehrwertsteuer VAT

**mysteriös** ① *Adj.* mysterious ② *adv.* mysteriously

**Mystik** *die;* ~: mysticism

**Mystery-** /ˈmɪstəri/ mystery *attrib.*

**Mythologie** *die;* ~, ~n mythology

**mythologisch** *Adj.* mythology

**Mythos** *der;* ~, Mythen myth

# Nn

**n, N** /ɛn/ *das;* ~, ~: n/N

**N** *Abk.* = **Nord[en]** N

**na** *Interj.* (ugs.) well; **na so [et]was!** well I never!; **na und?** (wennschon) so what?; (beschwichtigend) **na, na, na!** now, now, come along; (triumphierend) **na also!** there you are!; (unsicher) **na, ich weiß nicht** hmm, I'm not sure; (ärgerlich) **na, was soll das denn?** now what's all this about?; (drohend) **na warte!** just [you] wait!

**Nabe** *die;* ~, ~n hub

**Nabel** *der;* ~s, ~: navel

**Nabel-:** ~**bruch** *der* (Med.) umbilical hernia; ~**schnur** *die* umbilical cord

**Naben·schaltung** *die* hub gear

**nach** ① *Präp. mit Dat.* (a) (räumlich) to; **der Zug ~ München** the train for Munich *or* the Munich train; ~ **Hause gehen** go home; ~ **Osten [zu]** eastwards; [towards the] east (b) (zeitlich) after; **zehn [Minuten] ~ zwei** ten [minutes] past two (c) (mit bestimmten Verben, bezeichnet das Ziel der Handlung) for (d) (bezeichnet [räumliche und zeitliche] Reihenfolge) after; ~ **Ihnen/dir!** after you (e) (gemäß) according to; ~ **meiner Ansicht** *od.* **Meinung, meiner Ansicht** *od.* **Meinung ~:** in my view *or* opinion; ~ **der neusten Mode gekleidet** dressed in [accordance with] the latest fashion; **dem Gesetz ~:** in accordance with the law; by law; ~ **etw. schmecken/riechen** taste/smell of sth. ② *Adv.* (a) (räumlich) [alle] **mir ~!** [everybody] follow me! (b) (zeitlich) ~ **und ~:** little by little; gradually; ~ **wie vor** still

**nach|ahmen** *tr. V.* imitate

**Nachahmung** *die;* ~, ~en imitation

**Nachbar** *der;* ~n, ~n neighbour

**Nachbar·haus** *das* house next door

**Nachbarin** *die;* ~, ~nen neighbour

**Nachbar·land** *das* neighbouring country

**Nachbarschaft** *die;* ~, ~en (a) the whole neighbourhood (b) (Beziehungen) **gute ~:** good neighbourliness (c) (Gegend) neighbourhood; (Nähe) vicinity

**Nach·beben** *das* aftershock

**nach|bestellen** *tr. V.* [noch] etw. ~: order more of sth.; ⟨*shop*⟩ reorder sth.

**Nach·bildung** *die* (a) copying (b) (Gegenstand) copy

**nach|blicken** *tr. V.* (geh.) jmdm./einer Sache ~: gaze after sb./sth.

**nach|datieren** *tr. V.* backdate

**nach·dem** *Konj.* (a) after (b) ▶ JE¹ 3

**nach|denken** *unr. itr. V.* think; **denk mal [gut** *od.* **scharf] nach** have a [good] think

**Nach·denken** *das* thought

**nachdenklich** ① *Adj.* thoughtful ② *adv.* thoughtfully

**Nach·druck** *der; Pl.* ~e (a) **mit ~:** emphatically (b) (Druckw.) reprint

**nachdrücklich** ① *Adj.* emphatic ② *adv.* emphatically

**Nachdrücklichkeit** *die;* ~: emphatic nature

**nach|dunkeln** *itr. V.; mit sein* get darker

**Nach·durst** *der* morning-after thirst

**nach|eifern** *itr. V.* jmdm. ~: emulate sb.

**nach-einander** *Adv.* one after the other

**nach|empfinden** *unr. tr. V.* empathize with ⟨*feeling*⟩; share ⟨*delight, sorrow*⟩

**Nach-erzählung** *die* retelling [of a story]; (Schulw.) reproduction

**Nachfahr** *der;* ~en, ~en, **Nachfahrin** *die;* ~, ~nen (geh.) descendant

**nach|fahren** *unr. itr. V.; mit sein* follow [on]; jmdm. ~: follow sb.

**Nach·folge** *die* succession

**Nachfolger** *der;* ~s, ~, **Nachfolgerin** *die;* ~, ~nen successor

**Nach·forschung** *die* investigation

**Nach·frage** *die* demand (**nach** for)

**nach|fragen** *itr. V.* ask; inquire; **bei jmdm.** ∼: ask sb.; **ob ich mal** ∼ **soll?** should I ask about it *or* make inquiries?

**nach|fühlen** *tr. V.* empathize with; **das kann ich dir** ∼! I know how you feel!

**nach|füllen** *tr. V.* top up; **Salz/Wein** ∼: put [some] more salt/wine in

**nach|geben** *unr. itr. V.* give way

**Nach·gebühr** *die* excess postage

**nach|gehen** *unr. itr. V.; mit sein* **(a)** jmdm./einer Sache ∼: follow sb./sth.; **einer Sache** ∼ (fig.) look into a matter; **einem Beruf** ∼: practise a profession **(b)** (nicht aus dem Kopf gehen) **jmdm.** ∼: remain on sb.'s mind **(c)** ⟨*clock, watch*⟩ be slow; **[um] eine Stunde** ∼: be an hour slow

**Nach·geschmack** *der* aftertaste

**nach·giebig** *Adj.* indulgent

**Nachgiebigkeit** *die;* ∼: indulgence

**nach·haltig** ⟨1⟩ *Adj.* **(a)** lasting **(b)** (Ökologie) sustainable ⟨2⟩ *adv.* **(a)** (auf längere Zeit) for a long time **(b)** (Ökologie) sustainably

**Nach·hause·weg** *der* way home

**nach|helfen** *unr. itr. V.* help

**nach·her** /*auch:* '--/ *Adv.* afterwards; (später) later [on]; **bis** ∼! see you later!

**Nach·hilfe** *die* coaching

**Nachhilfe·unterricht** *der* coaching

***nach·hinein, Nachhinein: im** ∼ (nachträglich) afterwards; later; (zurückblickend) with hindsight

**nach|holen** *tr. V.* (nachträglich erledigen) catch up on ⟨*work, sleep*⟩; make up for ⟨*working hours missed*⟩

**nach|jagen** *itr. V.; mit sein* **jmdm./einer Sache** ∼: chase after sb./sth.

**Nachkomme** *der;* ∼n, ∼n descendant

**nach|kommen** *unr. itr. V.; mit sein* follow [later]; come [on] later

**Nachkommenschaft** *die;* ∼: descendants *pl.*

**Nachkömmling** *der;* ∼s, ∼e much younger child (*than the rest*)

**Nach·kriegs-** post-war ⟨*generation, period, etc.*⟩

**Nach·lass, *Nach·laß** *der;* Nachlasses, Nachlasse *od.* Nachlässe **(a)** estate **(b)** (Kaufmannsspr.: Rabatt) discount

**nach|lassen** ⟨1⟩ *unr. itr. V.* let up; ⟨*pain, stress, pressure*⟩ ease; ⟨*effect*⟩ wear off; ⟨*interest, enthusiasm, strength, courage*⟩ wane; ⟨*health, hearing, memory*⟩ deteriorate; ⟨*business*⟩ drop off ⟨2⟩ *unr. tr. V.* (Kaufmannsspr.) give a discount of

**nach·lässig** ⟨1⟩ *Adj.* careless

⟨2⟩ *adv.* carelessly

**Nach·lässigkeit** *die;* ∼, ∼en carelessness

**Nachlass·verwalter** *der,* **Nachlass·verwalterin,** *die* (Rechtsw.) executor

**nach|laufen** *unr. itr. V.; mit sein* **jmdm./ einer Sache** ∼: run after sb./sth.

**nach|lesen** *unr. itr. V.* look up

**nach|lösen** ⟨1⟩ *tr. V.* **eine Fahrkarte** ∼: buy a ticket [on the train, bus, etc.] ⟨2⟩ *itr. V.* pay the excess [fare]

**nach|machen** *tr. V.* (auch tun) copy; (imitieren) imitate; (genauso herstellen) reproduce ⟨*period furniture etc.*⟩; forge ⟨*signature*⟩

***nach·mittag** ▶ NACHMITTAG

**Nach·mittag** *der* afternoon; **am** ∼: in the afternoon; **am späten** ∼: late in the afternoon; **heute** ∼: this afternoon

**nach·mittags** *Adv.* in the afternoon; **dienstags** *od.* **Dienstag** ∼: on Tuesday afternoons; **um vier Uhr** ∼: at four in the afternoon; at 4 p.m.

**Nachnahme** *die;* ∼, ∼n: per ∼: cash on delivery; COD

**Nach·name** *der* surname

**Nach·porto** *das* excess postage

**nachprüfbar** *Adj.* verifiable

**nach|prüfen** *tr., itr. V.* check

**nach|rechnen** *tr. V.* check ⟨*figures*⟩

**Nach·rede** *die:* **üble** ∼: malicious gossip; (Rechtsw.) defamation [of character]

**nach|rennen** *unr. itr. V.:* ▶ NACHLAUFEN

**Nachricht** *die;* ∼, ∼en **(a)** news *no pl.;* **das ist eine gute** ∼: that is [a piece of] good news; **eine** ∼ **hinterlassen** leave a message **(b)** *Pl.* (Ferns., Rundf.) news *sing.;* ∼en **hören** listen to the news

**Nachrichten-:** ∼**sprecher** *der,* ∼**sprecherin** *die* newsreader

**nach|rücken** *itr. V.; mit sein* move up

**Nach·ruf** *der* obituary (**auf** + *Akk.* of)

**nach|rufen** *unr. tr., itr. V.* **jmdm. [etw.]** ∼: call [sth.] after sb.

**nach|rüsten** ⟨1⟩ *itr. V.* counter-arm ⟨2⟩ *tr. V.* (Technik: zusätzlich ausstatten) **mit etw.** ∼ (+ *Akk.*) equip additionally with sth.; upgrade ⟨*television, hi-fi, etc.*⟩ with sth.

**nach|sagen** *tr. V.* **(a)** (wiederholen) repeat **(b)** **man sagt ihm nach, er sei ...:** he is said to be ...; **jmdm. Schlechtes** ∼: speak ill of sb.

**Nach·saison** *die* late season

**nach|schicken** *tr. V.* **(a)** (durch die Post o. Ä.) forward **(b)** **jmdm. jmdn.** ∼: send sb. after sb.

**Nach·schlag** *der* (ugs.: zusätzliche Portion) second helping; seconds *pl.*

**nach|schlagen** ⟨1⟩ *unr. tr. V.* look up ⟨2⟩ *unr. itr. V.* **im Lexikon/Wörterbuch** ∼: consult the encyclopaedia/dictionary

**Nachschlage·werk** *das* work of reference

**Nach·schlüssel** *der* duplicate key

**n**

**nach|schmeißen** *unr. tr. V.* (ugs.) **man kriegt sie nachgeschmissen** you get them for next to nothing

**Nach·schub** *der* (Milit.) (a) supply (an + Dat. of)
(b) (~material) supplies *pl.* (an + Dat. of)

**nach|sehen** ⊞ *unr. itr. V.* (a) jmdm./einer Sache ~: gaze after sb./sth.
(b) (kontrollieren) check
(c) (nachschlagen) have a look
⊡ *unr. tr. V.* (a) (nachlesen) look up
(b) (überprüfen) check [over]

**Nach·sehen** *das:* das ~ haben not get a look-in; (nichts abbekommen) be left with nothing

**nach|senden** *unr. od. regelm. tr. V.* forward

**Nach·sicht** *die* leniency

**nachsichtig** ⊞ *Adj.* lenient (gegen, mit towards)
⊡ *adv.* leniently

**Nachsichtigkeit** *die;* ~: leniency

**Nach·silbe** *die* (Sprachw.) suffix

**nach|sitzen** *unr. itr. V.* be in detention; [eine Stunde] ~ müssen have [an hour's] detention

**Nach·spann** *der;* ~[e]s, ~e (Film, Ferns.) [final] credits *pl.*

**Nach·speise** *die* dessert; sweet

**Nach·spiel** *das:* die Sache wird noch ein ~ haben this affair will have repercussions; ein gerichtliches ~ haben result in court proceedings

**nach|spionieren** *itr. V.* jmdm. ~: spy on sb.

**nach|sprechen** *unr. tr. V.* [jmdm.] etw. ~: repeat sth. [after sb.]

**nächst...** *Sup. zu* NAH: *Adj.* next; (kürzest) shortest ⟨way⟩; am ~en Tag the next day; beim ~en Mal, das ~e Mal the next time; der ~e bitte! next [one], please; wer kommt als ~er dran? whose turn is it next?

**Nächste** *der; adj. Dekl.* (geh.) neighbour

**nach|stehen** *unr. itr. V.* jmdm. an etw. (Dat.) nicht ~: be sb.'s match in sth.; jmdm./ einer Sache in nichts ~: be in no way inferior to sb./sth.

**nach·stehend** ⊞ *Adj.* following
⊡ *adv.* below

**Nächsten·liebe** *die* charity [to one's neighbour]

**nächstens** *Adv.* (a) shortly
(b) (ugs.: wenn es so weitergeht) if it goes on like this

**nächst-:** ~liegend *Adj.* first, immediate ⟨problem⟩; [most] obvious ⟨explanation etc.⟩; ~möglich *Adj.* earliest possible

**nach|suchen** *itr. V.* (geh.) um etw. ~: request sth.; (bes. schriftlich) apply for sth.

**\*nacht** ▸ NACHT

**Nacht** *die;* ~, Nächte night; gestern/ morgen/Dienstag ~: last night/tomorrow

night/on Tuesday night; heute ~: tonight; bei ~, in der ~: at night[-time]; über ~ bleiben stay overnight; gute ~! good night!

**nacht-, Nacht-:** ~arbeit *die* night work *no art.;* ~blind *Adj.* night-blind; ~blindheit *die* night blindness; ~creme *die* night cream; ~dienst *der* night duty; ~dienst haben be on night duty; ⟨chemist's shop⟩ be open late

**Nacht·teil** *der* disadvantage

**nachteilig** ⊞ *Adj.* detrimental; harmful
⊡ *adv.* detrimentally; harmfully

**Nacht-:** ~essen *das* (bes. südd., schweiz.) ▸ ABENDESSEN; ~hemd *das* nightshirt

**Nachtigall** *die;* ~, ~en nightingale

**nächtigen** *itr. V.* (österr., sonst geh.) spend the night

**Nacht·tisch** *der* dessert; sweet

**nächtlich** *Adj.* nocturnal; night ⟨sky⟩; ⟨darkness, stillness⟩ of the night

**Nacht·lokal** *das* night spot (coll.)

**nach|tragen** *unr. tr. V.* (schriftlich ergänzen) insert; add

**nach·tragend** *Adj.* unforgiving; (rachsüchtig) vindictive

**nachträglich** ⊞ *Adj.* later; subsequent ⟨apology⟩; (verspätet) belated ⟨greetings, apology⟩
⊡ *adv.* afterwards; subsequently; (verspätet) belatedly

**nach|trauern** *itr. V.* jmdm./einer Sache ~: bemoan the passing of sb./sth.

**Nacht·ruhe** *die* night's sleep

**nachts** *Adv.* at night; Montag *od.* montags ~: on Monday nights; um 3 Uhr ~: at 3 o'clock in the morning

**Nacht-:** ~schicht *die* night shift; ~schwester *die* night nurse; ~tisch *der* bedside table; ~tisch·lampe *die* bedside light; ~topf *der* chamber pot; ~wächter *der*, ~wächterin *die* nightwatchman

**Nach·untersuchung** *die* follow-up examination; check-up

**nach|vollziehen** *unr. tr. V.* reconstruct; (begreifen) comprehend

**nach|wachsen** *unr. itr. V.; mit sein* [wieder] ~: grow again

**Nach·wehen** *Pl.* (Med.) afterpains; (fig. geh.) unpleasant after-effects

**Nachweis** *der;* ~es, ~e proof *no indef. art.* (Gen., über + Akk. of); (Zeugnis) certificate (über + Akk. of)

**nachweisbar** ⊞ *Adj.* demonstrable ⟨fact, truth, error, defect, guilt⟩; detectable ⟨substance, chemical⟩
⊡ *adv.* demonstrably

**nach|weisen** *unr. tr. V.* prove

**nachweislich** *Adv.* as can be proved

**Nach·welt** *die* posterity *no art.;* future generations *pl., no art.*

n

**nach|winken** *itr. V.* jmdm./einer Sache ∼:
wave after sb./sth.

**Nach·wirkung** *die* after-effect

**Nach·wort** *das; Pl.* ∼e afterword

**Nach·wuchs** *der* (a) (fam.: Kind[er])
offspring

(b) (junge Kräfte) new blood; (für eine Branche
usw.) new recruits *pl.;* (in der Ausbildung)
trainees *pl.*

**nach|zahlen** *tr., itr. V.* (a) pay later

(b) (zusätzlich zahlen) **25 Euro** ∼: pay another
25 euros

**nach|zählen** *tr., itr. V.* [re]count

**Nach·zahlung** *die* additional payment

**nach|ziehen** *unr. itr. V.* (a) (ugs.: ebenso
handeln) do likewise; follow suit

(b) *mit sein* (nachträglich übersiedeln) **jmdm.** ∼:
[go to] join sb.

**Nachzügler** *der;* ∼s, ∼, **Nachzüglerin**
*die;* ∼, ∼nen straggler; (spät Ankommende[r])
latecomer

**Nackedei** *der;* ∼s, ∼s (fam. scherzh.)
[kleiner] ∼: naked little thing

**Nacken** *der;* ∼s, ∼: back *or* nape of the
neck; (Hals) neck

**nackt** *Adj.* naked; bare ⟨*feet, legs, arms,
skin, fists*⟩; (fig.) plain ⟨*truth, fact*⟩; bare
⟨*existence*⟩

**Nackt·bade·strand** *der* nudist beach

**Nackte** *der/die; adj. Dekl.* naked man/
woman

**Nackt·foto** *das* nude photo

**Nadel** *die;* ∼, ∼n needle; (Steck∼, Hut∼,
Haar∼) pin; **an der** ∼ **hängen** (fig. ugs.) be on
the needle (sl.)

**Nadel·baum** *der* conifer

**Nadeldrucker** *der* (DV) dot-matrix printer

**nadeln** *itr. V.* ⟨*tree*⟩ shed its needles

**Nadel·wald** *der* coniferous forest

**Nagel** *der;* ∼s, Nägel nail; **den** ∼ **auf den
Kopf treffen** (fig. ugs.) hit the nail on the head

**Nagel-:** ∼**bürste** *die* nailbrush; ∼**feile**
*die* nail file; ∼**lack** *der* nail varnish (Brit.);
nail polish

**nageln** *tr. V.* nail (**an** + *Akk.* to, **auf** + *Akk.*
on); (Med.) pin

**nagel·neu** *Adj.* (ugs.) brand-new

**Nagel·schere** *die* nail scissors *pl.*

**nagen** ⓵ *itr. V.* gnaw; **an etw.** (*Dat.*) ∼:
gnaw [at] sth.

⓶ *tr. V.* gnaw off; **ein Loch ins Holz** ∼: gnaw
a hole in the wood

**Nage·tier** *das* rodent

**nah** ▶ NAHE

**Nah·aufnahme** *die* (Fot.) close-up
[photograph]

**nahe** /'na:ə,/ näher /'nɛːɐ,/ nächst... ⓵ *Adj.*
(a) (räumlich) near *pred.;* close *pred.;* nearby
*attrib.;*

(b) (zeitlich) imminent; near *pred.*

(c) (eng) close ⟨*relationship etc.*⟩

⓶ *adv.* (a) (räumlich) ∼ **an** (+ *Dat./Akk.*), ∼
**bei** close to; ∼ **gelegen** nearby; **von** ∼m from
close up; **jmdm.** ∼ **gehen** affect sb. deeply;
**eine Sache** (*Dat.*) ∼ **kommen** come close to
sth.; ⟨*amount*⟩ approximate to sth.; **jmdm/
sich** [menschlich] ∼ **kommen** get to know
sb./one another well; **jmdm/sich** [menschlich]
**näher kommen** get on closer terms with sb.;
**jmdm.** ∼ **stehen** be on intimate terms with
sb.; **jmdm. etw.** ∼ **legen** (fig.) suggest sth. to
sb.; **einen Verdacht/einen Gedanken** *usw.* ∼
**legen** give rise to a suspicion/thought *etc.;*
∼ **liegen** (fig.) ⟨*thought*⟩ suggest itself;
⟨*suspicion, question*⟩ arise

(b) (zeitlich) ∼ **an die achtzig** (ugs.) pushing
eighty (coll.)

(c) (eng) closely

⓷ *Präp. mit Dat.* (geh.) near; close to

**Nähe** *die;* ∼: closeness

**nahe-:** ∼**bei** *Adv.* nearby; close by;
∼|**gehen** *usw.* ▶ NAHE 2A; ∼**liegend** *Adj.*
obvious ⟨*reason, solution*⟩

**nahen** *itr. V.; mit sein* (geh.) draw near; **sein/
ihr** *usw.* **Ende nahte** the end was near

**nähen** ⓵ *itr. V.* sew; (Kleider machen) make
clothes

⓶ *tr. V.* (a) sew ⟨*seam, hem*⟩; make ⟨*dress
etc.*⟩

(b) (Med.) stitch

**näher** ⓵ *Komp. zu* nahe;

⓶ *Adj.* (a) (kürzer) shorter ⟨*way, road*⟩

(b) (genauer) more precise ⟨*information*⟩;
closer ⟨*investigation, inspection*⟩

⓷ *adv.* (a) **bitte treten Sie** ∼! please come
in/nearer/this way

(b) (genauer) more closely; (im Einzelnen) in
[more] detail

**\*näher|kommen** ▶ NAHE 2A

**nähern** *refl. V.* approach; **sich jmdm./einer
Sache** ∼: approach sb./sth.

**nahe-:** **\***∼|**stehen** ▶ NAHE 2A; ∼**zu** *Adv.*
almost; nearly; (mit Zahlenangabe) close on

**Näh-:** ∼**garn** *das* [sewing] cotton;
∼**kasten** *der* sewing box

**nahm** *1. u. 3. Pers. Sg. Prät. v.* NEHMEN

**Näh-:** ∼**maschine** *die* sewing machine;
∼**nadel** *die* sewing needle

**nah·östlich** *Adj.* Middle Eastern

**Nähr·boden** *der* culture medium; (fig.)
breeding ground

**nähren** ⓵ *tr. V.* feed (**mit** on)

⓶ *refl. V.* (geh.) **sich von etw.** ∼: live on sth.;
⟨*animal*⟩ feed on sth.

**nahrhaft** *Adj.* nourishing

**Nahrung** *die;* ∼: food

**Nahrungs·mittel** *das* food [item]; ∼ *Pl.*
foodstuffs

**Nähr·wert** *der* nutritional value

**Näh·seide** *die* sewing silk

**Naht** *die;* ∼, Nähte seam

**naht·los** ⓵ *Adj.* seamless; (fig.) perfectly
smooth ⟨*transition*⟩

**2** *adv.* Studium und Beruf gehen nicht ∼ ineinander über there is not a perfectly smooth transition from study to work

**Nah-:** ∼**verkehr** *der* local traffic; ∼**verkehrs·zug** *der* local train

**Näh·zeug** *das* sewing things *pl.*

**naiv** **1** *Adj.* naïve
**2** *adv.* naïvely

**Naivität** *die;* ∼: naïvety

**Name** *der;* ∼ns, ∼n name

**namens** *Adv.* by the name of

**Namens-:** ∼**schild** *das* (a) (an Türen usw.) nameplate; (b) (zum Anstecken) name badge; ∼**tag** *der* name day

**namentlich** **1** *Adj.* by name *postpos.;*
**2** *adv.* by name
**3** *Adv.* (besonders) particularly

**namhaft** *Adj.* (a) (berühmt) noted
(b) (ansehnlich) noteworthy ⟨*sum, difference*⟩; notable ⟨*contribution, opportunity*⟩

**nämlich** *Adv.* (a) er kann nicht kommen, er ist ∼ krank he cannot come, as he is ill
(b) (und zwar) namely

**nannte** *1. u. 3. Pers. Sg. Prät. v.* NENNEN

**nanu** *Interj.* ∼, was machst du denn hier? hello, what are you doing here?; ∼, Sie gehen schon? what, you're going already?

**Napf** *der;* ∼[e]s, Näpfe bowl (esp. for animal's food)

**Narbe** *die;* ∼, ∼n scar

**narbig** *Adj.* scarred

**Narkose** *die;* ∼, ∼n (Med.) narcosis

**narkotisieren** *tr. V.* (Med.) anaesthetize ⟨*patient*⟩; put ⟨*patient*⟩ under a general anaesthetic

**Narr** *der;* ∼en, ∼en fool

**Narren·freiheit** *die* freedom to do as one pleases

**Närrin** *die;* ∼, ∼nen fool

**närrisch** **1** *Adj.* crazy; carnival-crazy ⟨*season*⟩
**2** *adv.* crazily

**Narzisse** *die;* ∼, ∼n narcissus

**naschen** **1** *itr. V.* (Süßes essen) eat sweet things; (heimlich essen) have a nibble
**2** *tr. V.* eat ⟨*sweets, chocolate, etc.*⟩; er hat Milch genascht he has been at the milk

**Nascherei** *die;* ∼, ∼en (a) [continually] eating sweet things; hör auf mit der ∼! don't keep eating sweet things all the time!
(b) (Süßigkeit) ∼en sweets

**naschhaft** *Adj.* sweet-toothed; ∼ sein have a sweet tooth

**Nase** *die;* ∼, ∼n nose; die ∼ voll haben (ugs.) have had enough

**Nasen-:** ∼**bluten** *das;* ∼∼s bleeding from the nose; ∼**loch** *das* nostril; ∼**spitze** *die* tip of the/one's nose; jmdm. etw. an der ∼spitze ansehen (fig. ugs.) tell sth. by sb.'s face; ∼**tropfen** *Pl.* nose drops; ∼**wurzel** *die* root of the nose

**nase-:** ∼**rümpfend** **1** *Adj.* disapproving

**2** *adv.* disdainfully; ∼**weis** **1** *Adj.* precocious; pert ⟨*remark, reply*⟩; **2** *adv.* precociously

**Nas·horn** *das* rhinoceros

**nass,** *\***naß;** nasser *od.* nässer, nassest... *od.* nässest...: *Adj.* wet; sich/das Bett ∼ machen wet oneself/one's bed

**Nässe** *die;* ∼: wetness

**nass·kalt,** *\***naß·kalt** *Adj.* cold and wet

**Nass·rasur,** *\***Naß·rasur** *die* wet shaving *no art.*

**Nation** *die;* ∼, ∼en nation

**national** **1** *Adj.* national
**2** *adv.* nationally

**National-:** ∼**elf** *die* (Fußball) national side; ∼**hymne** *die* national anthem

**Nationalisierung** *die;* ∼, ∼en nationalization

**Nationalismus** *der;* ∼: nationalism *usu. no art.*

**nationalistisch** **1** *Adj.* nationalist; nationalistic
**2** *adv.* nationalistically

**Nationalität** *die;* ∼, ∼en nationality

**national,- National-:** ∼**mannschaft** *die* national team; ∼**sozialismus** *der* National Socialism; ∼**sozialist** *der,* ∼**sozialistin** *die* National Socialist; ∼**sozialistisch** *Adj.* National Socialist; ∼**spieler** *der,* ∼**spielerin** *die* (Sport) national player; international; ∼**staat** *der* nation state; ∼**stolz** *der* national pride; ∼**versammlung** *die* National Assembly

**NATO, Nato** *die;* ∼: NATO, Nato *no art.*

**Natron** *das;* ∼s [doppeltkohlensaures] ∼: sodium bicarbonate; [kohlensaures] ∼: sodium carbonate

**Natter** *die;* ∼, ∼n colubrid

**Natur** *die;* ∼, ∼en nature; die freie ∼: [the] open countryside

**Naturalien** /natuˈraːli̯ən/ *Pl.* natural produce *sing.* (used as payment); in ∼ (*Dat.*) bezahlen pay in kind

**Naturalismus** *der;* ∼: naturalism

**naturalistisch** **1** *Adj.* naturalistic
**2** *adv.* naturalistically

**Naturell** *das;* ∼s, ∼e temperament

**natur-, Natur-:** ∼**erscheinung** *die* natural phenomenon; ∼**farben** *Adj.* natural-coloured; ∼**freund** *der,* ∼**freundin** *die* nature lover; ∼**gemäß** *Adv.* naturally; ∼**geschichte** *die* natural history; ∼**gesetz** *das* law of nature; ∼**getreu** **1** *Adj.* lifelike ⟨*portrait, imitation*⟩; faithful ⟨*reproduction*⟩; **2** *adv.* ⟨*draw*⟩ true to life; ⟨*reproduce*⟩ faithfully; ∼**heilkunde** *die* naturopathy *no art.;* ∼**katastrophe** *die* natural disaster

**natürlich** **1** *Adj.* natural
**2** *adv.* ⟨*laugh, behave*⟩ naturally
**3** *Adv.* (a) (selbstverständlich, wie erwartet) naturally; of course
(b) (zwar) of course

**n**

**Natürlichkeit** *die;* ~: naturalness
**natur-, Natur-:** ~**park** *der* ≈ national
park; ~**produkt** *das* natural product;
~**schutz** *der* [nature] conservation; **unter**
~**schutz** *(Dat.)* **stehen** be protected by law;
be a protected species/variety/area *etc.*;
~**schutz·gebiet** *das* nature reserve;
~**talent** *das* [great] natural talent *or* gift;
(begabter Mensch) naturally talented *or* gifted
person; ~**verbunden** *Adj.* ⟨*person*⟩ in
tune with nature; ~**volk** *das* primitive
people; ~**wissenschaft** *die* natural
science *no art.*; ~**wissenschaftler** *der,*
~**wissenschaftlerin** *die* [natural]
scientist; ~**wissenschaftlich** [1] *Adj.*
scientific; [2] *adv.* scientifically; ~**wunder**
*das* miracle *or* wonder of nature
**Navigation** *die;* ~: navigation *no art.*
**navigieren** *tr., itr. V.* navigate
**n. Chr.** *Abk.* = **nach Christus** AD
**Neandertaler** *der;* ~s, ~: Neanderthal
man
**Nebel** *der;* ~s, ~: fog; (weniger dicht) mist
**nebelig** ▶ NEBLIG
**Nebel-:** ~**scheinwerfer** *der* fog lamp;
~**schluss·leuchte**,
\*~**schluß·leuchte** *die* rear fog lamp;
~**schwaden** *Pl.* swathes of mist;
~**wand** *die* wall of fog
**neben** [1] *Präp. mit Dat.* **(a)** (Lage) next to;
beside
**(b)** (außer) apart from; aside from (Amer.)
**(c)** (verglichen mit) beside
[2] *Präp. mit Akk.* (Richtung) next to; beside
**neben-, Neben-:** ~**an** *Adv.* next door;
~**bei** *Adv.* **(a)** ⟨*work*⟩ on the side; (zusätzlich)
as well; **(b)** (beiläufig) ⟨*remark, ask*⟩ by the
way; ⟨*mention*⟩ in passing; ~**beruf** *der*
second job; sideline; ~**beruflich** [1] *Adj.*
eine ~berufliche Tätigkeit a second job;
[2] *adv.* on the side; **er arbeitet** ~**beruflich als**
**Übersetzer** he translates as a sideline;
~**beschäftigung** *die* second job;
sideline; ~**buhler** *der,* ~**buhlerin** *die*
rival
**neben·einander** *Adv.* **(a)** next to each
other; ⟨*be sitting, standing*⟩ next to one
another, side by side; (fig.: zusammen) ⟨*live,*
*exist*⟩ side by side; ~ **wohnen** live next door
to each other; ~ **legen** (+ *Akk.*) lay *or* place
⟨*objects*⟩ next to each other *or* side by side
**(b)** (gleichzeitig) together
\***nebeneinander|legen** *usw.*
▶ NEBENEINANDER A
**Neben-:** ~**erwerb** *der* secondary
occupation; ~**fach** *das* subsidiary subject;
minor (Amer.); ~**fluss,** \*~**fluß** *der*
tributary; ~**gebäude** *das* **(a)** annexe;
outbuilding **(b)** (Nachbargebäude) neighbouring
building; ~**geräusch** *das* background
noise; ~**haus** *das* house next door
**neben·her** *Adv.* ▶ NEBENBEI

**nebenher-:** ~|**fahren** *unr. itr. V.; mit*
*sein* drive/ride alongside; ~|**gehen** *unr. itr.*
*V.; mit sein* walk alongside
**neben-, Neben-:** ~**höhle** *die* (Anat.)
paranasal sinus; ~**kläger** *der,*
~**klägerin** *die* (Rechtsw.) accessory
prosecutor; ~**kosten** *Pl.* **(a)** additional
costs; **(b)** (bei Mieten) heating, lighting, and
services; ~**produkt** *das* by-product;
~**rolle** *die* supporting role; ~**sache** *die*
minor matter; ~**sachen** inessentials;
~**sächlich** *Adj.* of minor importance
*postpos.;* unimportant; minor ⟨*detail*⟩;
~**sächlichkeit** *die;* ~~, ~~en
(Unwichtiges) matter of minor importance;
unimportant matter; ~**satz** *der* (Sprachw.)
subordinate clause; ~**stelle** *die* extension;
~**straße** *die* side street; ~**tätigkeit** *die*
second job; sideline; ~**tisch** *der* next table;
~**verdienst** *der* additional income;
~**wirkung** *die* side effect; ~**zimmer** *das*
next room
**neblig** *Adj.* foggy; (weniger dicht) misty
**Necessaire** /nɛsɛˈsɛːɐ̯/ *das;* ~s, ~s
sponge bag (Brit.); toilet bag (Amer.)
**necken** *tr. V.* tease
**Neckerei** *die;* ~: teasing
**nee** (ugs.) no; nope (Amer. coll.)
**Neffe** *der;* ~n, ~n nephew
**negativ** [1] *Adj.* negative
[2] *adv.* ⟨*answer*⟩ in the negative
**Negativ** *das;* ~s, ~e (Fot.) negative
**Neger** *der;* ~s, ~: Negro
**Negerin** *die;* ~, ~nen Negress
**nehmen** *unr. tr. V.* take; **sich** *(Dat.)* **etw.** ~:
take sth.; (sich bedienen) help oneself to sth.;
**auf sich** *(Akk.)* ~: take on ⟨*responsibility,*
*burden*⟩; **jmdm./einer Sache etw.** ~: deprive
sb./sth. of sth.; **was nehmen Sie dafür?** how
much do you charge for it?
**Neid** *der;* ~[e]s envy; jealousy
**neiden** *tr. V.* (geh.) **jmdm. etw.** ~: envy sb.
[for] sth.
**Neid·hammel** *der* (salopp abwertend) envious
sod (sl.)
**neidisch** [1] *Adj.* envious
[2] *adv.* enviously
**neigen** [1] *tr. V.* tip; tilt; incline ⟨*head,*
*upper part of body*⟩
[2] *refl. V.:* ⟨*person*⟩ lean; ⟨*ship*⟩ heel over,
list; ⟨*scales*⟩ tip
[3] *itr. V.* **(a)** **zu Erkältungen/Krankheiten** ~:
be prone to colds/illnesses
**(b)** (tendieren) tend
**Neigung** *die;* ~, ~en **(a)** (Vorliebe)
inclination
**(b)** (Tendenz) tendency
**nein** *Interj.* no
**Nein** *das;* ~[s], ~[s] no
**Nein·stimme** *die* no-vote
**Nektar** *der;* ~s, ~e (Bot.) nectar
**Nektarine** *die;* ~, ~n nectarine

---

\*alte Schreibung - vgl. Hinweis auf S. xiv

**Nelke** *die;* ~, ~n (a) pink; (Dianthus caryophyllus) carnation
(b) (Gewürz) clove

**nennen** ① *unr. tr. V.* (a) call
(b) (angeben) give ⟨*name, date of birth, address, reason, price, etc.*⟩
(c) (anführen) give ⟨*example*⟩; (erwähnen) mention ⟨*person, name*⟩
② *unr. refl. V.* ⟨*person, thing*⟩ be called

**nennens·wert** *Adj.* considerable ⟨*influence, changes, delays, damage*⟩; kaum ~e **Veränderungen** changes scarcely worth mentioning

**Nenner** *der;* ~s, ~ (Math.) denominator

**neo-, Neo-** neo-

**Neon** *das;* ~s neon

**Neon-:** ~**licht** *das* neon light; ~**röhre** *die* neon tube

**Nepal** (*das*); ~s Nepal

**Nepp** *der;* ~s (ugs. abwertend) daylight robbery *no art.;* rip-off (coll.)

**neppen** *tr. V.* (ugs. abwertend) rook; rip ⟨*tourist, customer, etc.*⟩ off (sl.)

**Nepper** *der;* ~s, ~, **Nepperin** *die;* ~, ~nen (ugs. abwertend) shark; rip-off merchant (coll.)

**Nepp·lokal** *das* (ugs. abwertend) clip joint (coll.)

**Nerv** *der;* ~s, ~en nerve; die ~en verlieren lose control [of oneself]; jmdm. auf die ~en gehen *od.* fallen get on sb.'s nerves

**nerven** (salopp) ① *tr. V.* jmdn. ~: get on sb.'s nerves
② *itr. V.* be wearing on the nerves

**nerven-, Nerven-:** ~**aufreibend** *Adj.* nerve-racking; ~**bündel** *das* (ugs.) bundle of nerves (coll.); ~**gift** *das* neurotoxin; ~**heil·anstalt** *die* (veralt.) psychiatric hospital; ~**krank** *Adj.* ⟨*person*⟩ suffering from a nervous disease; ~**probe** *die* mental trial; ~**säge** *die* (salopp) pain in the neck (coll.); ~**zusammen·bruch** *der* nervous breakdown

**nervig** *Adj.* (auch fig.) sinewy

**nervlich** *Adj.* nervous ⟨*strain*⟩

**nervös** ① *Adj.* (auch Med.) nervous; jittery ⟨*person*⟩
② *adv.* nervously

**Nervosität** *die;* ~ nervousness

**nerv·tötend** *Adj.* nerve-racking ⟨*wait*⟩; soul-destroying ⟨*activity, work*⟩

**Nerz** *der;* ~es, ~e mink

**Nerz·mantel** *der* mink coat

**Nessel** *die;* ~, ~n nettle

**Nest** *das;* ~[e]s, ~er (a) nest
(b) (fam.: Bett) bed
(c) (ugs. abwertend: kleiner Ort) little place

**nett** ① *Adj.* nice; (freundlich) kind
② *adv.* nicely; (freundlich) nicely; kindly

**netter·weise** *Adv.* kindly

**netto** *Adv.* ⟨*weigh, earn, etc.*⟩ net

**Netto-:** ~**einkommen** *das* net income; ~**gehalt** *das* net salary; ~**preis** *der* net price

**Netz** *das;* ~es, ~e (a) net; (Einkaufs~) string bag; (Gepäck~) [luggage] rack
(b) (Spinnen~) web
(c) (Netzwerk) network; (für Strom, Wasser, Gas) mains *pl.*

**Netz-:** ~**haut** *die* (Anat.) retina; ~**werk** *das* (auch Elektrot.) network

**neu** ① *Adj.* new; die ~este Mode the latest fashion; das ist mir ~: that is news to me; der/die Neue the new man/woman/boy/girl
② *adv.* (a) ~ tapeziert/gestrichen repapered/repainted; sich ~ einrichten refurnish one's home
(b) (gerade erst) diese Ware ist ~ eingetroffen this item has just come in; ~ eröffnet newly-opened; (wieder eröffnet) reopened

**neu·artig** *Adj.* new; ~e Lebensmittel novel foods

**Neu·artigkeit** *die;* ~~: novelty

**neu-, Neu-:** ~**bau** *der; Pl.* ~~ten new house/building; ~**bau·wohnung** *die* flat (Brit.) *or* (Amer.) apartment in a new block/ house; ~**beginn** *der* new beginning

**neuerdings** *Adv.* er trägt ~ eine Brille he has recently started wearing glasses

**\*neu·eröffnet** ▶ NEU 2B

**Neu·eröffnung** *die* (a) opening
(b) (Wiedereröffnung) reopening

**Neuerung** *die;* ~, ~en innovation

**neu·geboren** *Adj.* newborn

**Neu·gier, Neugierde** *die;* ~: curiosity; (Wissbegierde) inquisitiveness

**neu·gierig** ① *Adj.* curious; inquisitive; inquisitive ⟨*person*⟩; ich bin ~, was er dazu sagt I'm curious to know what he'll say about it
② *adv.* ⟨*ask*⟩ inquisitively; ⟨*peer*⟩ nosily (coll. derog.)

**Neuheit** *die;* ~, ~en (a) novelty
(b) (Neues) new product/gadget/article *etc.*

**Neuigkeit** *die;* ~, ~en piece of news; ~en news *sing.*

**Neu:** ~**jahr** *das* New Year's Day; ~**land** *das* (fig.) new ground

**neulich** *Adv.* recently; ~ morgens the other morning

**Neuling** *der;* ~s, ~e newcomer; (auf einem Gebiet) novice

**Neu·mond** *der* new moon

**neun** *Kardinalz.* nine

**Neun** *die;* ~, ~en nine

**neun-:** ~**hundert** *Kardinalz.* nine hundred; ~**jährig** *Adj.* (9 Jahre alt) nine-year-old *attrib.;* (9 Jahre dauernd) nine-year *attrib.;* ~**mal** *Adv.* nine times

**neunt...** *Ordinalz.* ninth

**neun·tausend** *Kardinalz.* nine thousand

**Neuntel** *das* (schweiz. meist *der*); ~s, ~: ninth

**neuntens** *Adv.* ninthly
**neun·zehn** *Kardinalz.* nineteen
**neunzig** *Kardinalz.* ninety
**neunziger** *indekl. Adj.* die ~ Jahre the nineties
**neunzigst...** *Ordinalz.* ninetieth
**neuralgisch** *Adj.* (a) (Med.) neuralgic (b) (empfindlich) das ist mein ~er Punkt it's a sore *or* touchy point with me.
**neu·reich** *Adj.* nouveau riche
**Neurodermitis** *die;* ~, Neurodermitiden (Med.) neurodermatitis
**Neurologe** *der;* ~n, ~n neurologist
**Neurologie** *die;* ~: neurology
**Neurologin** *die;* ~, ~nen neurologist
**neurologisch** *Adj.* neurological
**Neurose** *die;* ~, ~n (Med., Psych.) neurosis
**Neurotiker** *der;* ~s, ~, **Neurotikerin** *die;* ~, ~nen (Med., Psych., auch ugs.) neurotic
**neurotisch** *Adj.* (Med., Psych., auch ugs.) neurotic
**Neu·see·land** *(das);* ~s New Zealand
**Neuseeländer** *der;* ~s, ~, **Neuseeländerin** *die;* ~, ~nen New Zealander
**neutral** ① *Adj.* neutral ② *adv.* sich ~ verhalten remain neutral
**Neutralität** *die;* ~, ~en neutrality
**Neutron** *das;* ~s, ~en neutron
**Neutrum** *das;* ~s, **Neutra** (österr. nur so) *od.* **Neutren** (Sprachw.) neuter
**neu-, Neu-:** ~wert *der* value when new; ~wertig *Adj.* as new; ~zeit *die* modern age; ~zeitlich *Adj.* modern
**nicht** *Adv.* not; ~! [no,] don't!; ~ rostend non-rusting ⟨blade⟩; stainless ⟨steel⟩; ~ [wahr]? isn't it/he/she *etc.;* don't you/we/they *etc.;* du magst das, ~ [wahr]? you like that, don't you?; was du ~ sagst! you don't say!
**nicht-, Nicht-** non-
**Nicht·angriffs·pakt** *der* nonaggression pact
**Nichte** *die;* ~, ~n niece
**nichtig** *Adj.* (a) (geh.) vain ⟨things, pleasures, etc.⟩; trivial ⟨reason⟩ (b) (Rechtsspr.) void
**Nicht·raucher** *der* non-smoker; „~raucher" 'no smoking'
***nicht·rostend** ▶ NICHT
**nichts** *Indefinitpron.* nothing; ich möchte ~: I don't want anything; ~ sagend (fig.) empty; (ausdruckslos) expressionless ⟨face⟩
**nichts·desto·weniger** *Adv.* nevertheless; none the less
**nichts-, Nichts-:** ~nutz *der;* ~es, ~e (veralt.) good-for-nothing; ~nutzig *Adj.* (veralt.) good-for-nothing *attrib.;* worthless ⟨existence⟩; *~sagend ▶ NICHTS; ~tun das idleness no art.

*old spelling - see note on page xiv

**Nickel** *das;* ~s nickel
**nicken** *itr. V.* nod
**nie** *Adv.* never
**nieder** ① *Adj.; nicht präd.* lower ⟨class, intelligence⟩; minor ⟨official⟩; lowly ⟨family, origins, birth⟩; menial ⟨task⟩ ② *Adv.* down
**nieder-, Nieder-:** ~gang *der* fall; decline; ~|gehen *unr. itr. V.; mit sein* ⟨plane etc., rain, avalanche⟩ come down; ~geschlagen *Adj.* dejected; ~geschlagenheit *die;* ~: dejection; ~lage *die* defeat
**Nieder·lande** *Pl.:* die ~: the Netherlands
**Niederländer** *der;* ~s, ~: Dutchman
**Niederländerin** *die;* ~, ~nen Dutchwoman
**niederländisch** *Adj.* Dutch; Netherlands *attrib.* ⟨government, embassy, etc.⟩
**nieder-, Nieder-:** ~|lassen *unr. refl. V.* (a) set up in business; ⟨doctor, lawyer⟩ set up in practice; (b) (seinen Wohnsitz nehmen) settle; ~lassung *die;* ~, ~en (Wirtsch.) branch; ~|legen *tr. V.* (a) (geh.: hinlegen) lay *or* put down; lay ⟨wreath⟩; (b) (fig.) resign [from] ⟨office⟩; relinquish ⟨command⟩
**Nieder·sachsen** *(das)* Lower Saxony
**nieder-, Nieder-:** ~schlag *der* precipitation; ~|schlagen *unr. tr. V.* (a) jmdn. ~schlagen knock sb. down; (b) (beenden) suppress, put down ⟨revolt, uprising, etc.⟩; (c) (senken) lower ⟨eyes, eyelids⟩; ~schmetternd *Adj.* shattering ⟨experience, news⟩; devastating ⟨result, review⟩; ~trächtig ① *Adj.* malicious ⟨person, slander, lie, etc.⟩; (verachtenswert) despicable ⟨person⟩; base ⟨misrepresentation, slander, lie⟩; ② *adv.* ⟨betray, lie, treat⟩ in a despicable way; ~trächtigkeit *die;* ~, ~~en (a) ▶ ~TRÄCHTIG 1: maliciousness; despicableness; baseness; (b) (gemeine Handlung) despicable act
**Niederung** *die;* ~, ~en low-lying area; (an Flussläufen, Küsten) flats *pl.;* (Tal) valley
**niedlich** ① *Adj.* sweet; cute (Amer. coll.) ② *adv.* sweetly
**niedrig** ① *Adj.* low; lowly ⟨origins, birth⟩; base ⟨instinct, desire, emotion⟩; vile ⟨motive⟩ ② *adv.* ⟨hang, fly⟩ low
**Niedrig-:** ~lohn·land *das* country with a low-wage country; ~wasser *das* (a) (von Seen/Flüssen) bei ~wasser when the [level of the] lake/river is low; (b) (bei Ebbe) low tide; low water; bei ~wasser at low tide *or* low water
**niemals** *Adv.* never
**niemand** *Indefinitpron.* nobody; no one
**Niemands·land** *das* (auch fig.) no man's land
**Niere** *die;* ~, ~n kidney
**Nieren-:** ~entzündung *die* nephritis; ~stein *der* kidney stone
**nieseln** *unpers. itr. V.* drizzle

**Niesel·regen** der drizzle
**niesen** itr. V. sneeze
**Niete**[1] die; ~, ~n (a) (Los) blank
(b) (ugs.: Mensch) dead loss (coll.) (in + Dat. at)
**Niete**[2] die; ~, ~n rivet
**nieten** tr. V. rivet
**niet- und nagelfest**: [alles] was nicht ~
ist (ugs.) [everything] that's not nailed or
screwed down
**Nikolaus** /'nɪkolaʊs/ der; ~, ~e (ugs.)
Nikoläuse (a) St Nicholas
(b) (Tag) St Nicholas' Day
**Nikotin** das; ~s nicotine
**nikotin·arm** Adj. low-nicotine attrib.; low
in nicotine pred.
**Nikotin·sucht** die nicotine addiction
**Nil** der; ~[s] Nile
**Nil·pferd** das hippopotamus
**nimm** Imperativ Sg. v. NEHMEN
**nippen** itr. V. sip
**nirgends, nirgend·wo** Adv. nowhere
**Nische** die; ~, ~n niche; (Erweiterung eines
Raumes) recess
**nisten** itr. V. nest
**Nitrat** das; ~[e]s, ~e nitrate
**Niveau** /ni'vo:/ das; ~s, ~s level;
(Qualitäts~) standard
**Nixe** die; ~, ~n nixie; (mit Fischschwanz)
mermaid
**nobel** Adj. (a) (geh.) noble; noble[-minded]
⟨person⟩
(b) (oft spött.: luxuriös) elegant; posh (coll.)
**Nobel·preis** der Nobel prize
**noch** [1] Adv. (a) ([wie] bisher) still; ~ nicht
not yet; sie sind immer ~ nicht da they're
still not here; ich habe Großvater ~ gekannt
I'm old enough to have known grandfather;
er hat ~ Glück gehabt he was lucky; das
geht ~: that's [still] all right
(b) (als Rest einer Menge) ich habe [nur] ~
zehn Euro I've [only] ten euros left; es sind
~ 10 km bis zur Grenze it's another 10 km.
to the border
(c) (bevor etw. anderes geschieht) just; ich will ~
[schnell] duschen I just want to have a
[quick] shower
(d) (irgendwann einmal) some time; one day; er
wird ~ anrufen/kommen he will still call/
come
(e) (womöglich) if you're/he's etc. not careful;
du kommst ~ zu spät! you'll be late if
you're not careful
(f) (drückt eine geringe zeitliche Distanz aus) only;
gestern habe ich ihn ~ gesehen I saw him
only yesterday
(g) (nicht später als) ~ am selben Abend the
[very] same evening
(h) (außerdem, zusätzlich) wer war ~ da? who
else was there?; ~ etwas Kaffee? [would you
like] some more coffee?; Geld/Kleider usw. ~
und ~ heaps and heaps of money/clothes
etc. (coll.)
(i) er ist ~ größer [als Karl] he is even taller

[than Karl]; er will ~ mehr haben he wants
even more; jeder ~ so dumme Mensch
versteht das anyone, however stupid, can
understand that
(j) wie heißt sie [doch] ~? [now] what's her
name again?
[2] Partikel das ist ~ Qualität! that's what I
call quality; der wird sich ~ wundern (ugs.)
he's in for a surprise; er kann ~ nicht
einmal lesen he can't even read
[3] Konj. (und auch nicht) nor; weder ... noch
neither ... nor
**noch·mals** Adv. again
**Nominativ** der; ~s, ~e (Sprachw.)
nominative [case]
**nominieren** tr. V. nominate
**Nominierung** die; ~, ~en nomination
**Nonne** die; ~, ~n nun
**Nord** (bes. Seemannsspr., Met.) ▶ NORDEN
**nord-, Nord-:** ~afrika (das) North
Africa; ~amerika (das) North America;
~deutsch Adj. North German
**Norden** der; ~s north; der ~: the North;
nach ~: northwards
**Nord·irland** (das) Northern Ireland
**nordisch** Adj. Nordic
**Nord·kap** das North Cape
**nördlich** [1] Adj. (a) (im Norden gelegen)
northern
(b) (nach, aus dem Norden) northerly
(c) (aus dem Norden kommend, für den Norden
typisch) Northern
[2] adv. northwards; ~ von ...: [to the] north
of ...
[3] Präp. mit Gen. [to the] north of
**Nord-:** ~licht das northern lights pl.;
aurora borealis; ein ~licht/~lichter the
northern lights; ~pol der North Pole
**Nordrhein-Westfalen** (das); ~s North
Rhine-Westphalia
**Nord·see** die; ~: North Sea
**nord·wärts** Adv. northwards
**Nord·wind** der northerly wind
**Nörgelei** die; ~ (abwertend) grumbling
**nörgeln** itr. V. (abwertend) moan, grumble
(an + Dat. about)
**Norm** die; ~, ~en (a) norm
(b) (geforderte Arbeitsleistung) quota
(c) (Sport) qualifying standard
(d) (technische, industrielle ~) standard
**normal** [1] Adj. normal
[2] adv. normally
**Normal·benzin** das ≈ two-star petrol
(Brit.); regular (Amer.)
**normalerweise** Adv. normally
**normalisieren** [1] tr. V. normalize
[2] refl. V. return to normal
**Normalität** die; ~: normality no def. art.
**Normal·zustand** der normal state
**Normandie** die; ~: Normandy
**normen** tr. V., **normieren** tr. V.
standardize

**Norwegen** (das); ~s Norway
**Norweger** der; ~s, ~, **Norwegerin** die;
~, ~nen Norwegian
**norwegisch** Adj. Norwegian
**Nostalgie** die; ~: nostalgia
**Not** die; ~, **Nöte** (a) (Gefahr) **in** ~ **sein** be in
desperate straits
**(b)** (Mangel, Armut) need; poverty [and
hardship]; ~ **leiden** suffer poverty [and
hardship]; **in** ~ **geraten/sein** encounter hard
times/be suffering want [and deprivation]
**(c)** (Verzweiflung) distress
**(d)** (Sorge, Mühe) trouble; **mit knapper** ~: by
the skin of one's teeth
**(e)** (veralt.: Notwendigkeit) necessity; **zur** ~: if
need be
**Notar** der; ~s, ~e notary
**Notariat** das; ~[e]s, ~e (a) (Amt)
notaryship
**(b)** (Kanzlei) notary's office
**not-, Not-:** ~**arzt** der doctor on
[emergency] call; ~**aufnahme** die
casualty department; casualty no art.;
~**ausgang** der emergency exit;
~**bremse** die emergency brake; ~**dienst**
der ▶ BEREITSCHAFTSDIENST; ~**durft** die; ~
(geh.) **seine [große/kleine]** ~**durft verrichten**
relieve oneself; ~**dürftig** [1] Adj. makeshift
⟨shelter, repair⟩; scanty ⟨cover, clothing⟩;
[2] adv. scantily ⟨clothed⟩
**Note** die; ~, ~n (a) (Zeichen) note
**(b)** Pl. (Text) music sing.;
**(c)** (Schul~) mark
**(d)** (Eislauf, Turnen) score
**Notebook** /'noutbʊk/ das; ~s, ~s (DV)
notebook [computer]
**not-, Not-:** ~**fall** der (a) emergency; **(b) im**
~**fall** (nötigenfalls) if need be; ~**falls** Adv. if
need be; ~**gedrungen** Adv. of necessity
**notieren** [1] tr. V. [**sich** (Dat.)] **etw.** ~:
make a note of sth.
[2] itr. V. (Börsenw., Wirtsch.) be quoted (**mit** at)
**Notierung** die; ~, ~en (Börsenw., Wirtsch.)
quotation; (Preis) quoted [price] (**für** for); (von
Devisen) rate (**für** for)
**nötig** [1] Adj. necessary; **etw./jmdn.** ~ **haben**
need sth./sb.
[2] adv. **er braucht** ~ **Hilfe** he is in urgent
need of help
**nötigen** tr. V. compel; force; (Rechtsspr.)
coerce
**Nötigung** die; ~, ~en (bes. Rechtsspr.)
intimidation; coercion
**Notiz** die; ~, ~en note; (Zeitungs~) brief
report; **von jmdm./etw. [keine]** ~ **nehmen**
take [no] notice of sb./sth.
**Notiz-:** ~**block** der; Pl. ~blocks, schweiz.:
~blöcke notepad; ~**buch** das notebook
**not-, Not-:** ~**lage** die serious difficulties
pl.; ~**landen** itr. V.; mit sein; **ich notlande**,
**notgelandet, notzulanden** do an emergency

landing; ~**landung** die emergency landing;
~**leidend** Adj. needy; (als Gegensatz zum
stopgap; ~**lüge** die evasive lie; (aus
Rücksichtnahme) white lie
**notorisch** [1] Adj. notorious
[2] adv. notoriously
**Not-:** ~**ruf** der (a) (Hilferuf) emergency call;
(eines Schiffes) Mayday call; **(b)** (Nummer)
emergency number; ~**ruf-nummer** die
emergency number; ~**ruf-säule** die
emergency telephone (mounted in a pillar);
~**stand** der crisis; (Staatsrecht) state of
emergency; ~**unterkunft** die emergency
accommodation no pl., no indef. art.;
~**wehr** die self-defence
**not·wendig** Adj. necessary
**Notwendigkeit** die; ~, ~en necessity
**Not·zucht** die (Rechtsw. veralt.) rape; ~ [**an**
**jmdm.**] **begehen** od. **verüben** commit rape [on
sb.]
**Novelle** die; ~, ~n (Literaturw.) novella
**November** der; ~[s], ~: November
**Novität** die; ~, ~en novelty; (neue Erfindung)
innovation; (neue Schallplatte) new release;
(neues Buch) new publication
**Nr.** Abk. = **Nummer** No
**Nu** der: **im Nu** in no time
**Nuance** /'nÿãːsə/ die; ~, ~n nuance; (Grad)
shade
**nüchtern** [1] Adj. (nicht betrunken; realistisch)
sober; (ungeschminkt) bare, plain ⟨fact⟩; **der**
**Patient muss** ~ **sein** the patient's stomach
must be empty
[2] adv. soberly
**Nüchternheit** die; ~: sobriety
**nuckeln** (ugs.) itr. V. suck (**an** + Dat. at)
**Nudel** die; ~, ~n piece of spaghetti/
vermicelli/tortellini etc.; (als Suppeneinlage)
noodle; ~**n** (Teigwaren) pasta sing.; (als
Suppeneinlage) noodles
**Nugat** /'nuːgat/ der; auch das; ~s nougat
**nuklear** [1] Adj. nuclear
[2] adv. ~ **angetrieben** nuclear-powered
**Nuklear-:** ~**medizin** die nuclear
medicine no art.; ~**waffe** die nuclear
weapon
**null** Kardinalz. nought; ~ **Komma sechs**
[nought] point six; **gegen** ~ **Uhr** around
twelve midnight
**Null** die; ~, ~en (a) nought; zero; **in** ~
**Komma nichts** (ugs.) in less than no time;
**gleich** ~ **sein** (fig.) be practically zero; **auf** ~
**stehen** ⟨indicator, needle, etc.⟩ be at zero
**(b)** (ugs.: Versager) failure; dead loss (coll.)
**Null-:** ~**punkt** der zero;
~**summen·spiel** das zero-sum game
*****numerieren** tr. V. number
*****Numerierung** die; ~, ~en numbering
**Numerus clausus** der; ~: fixed number
of students admissible to a university to study
a particular subject; numerus clausus
**Nummer** die; ~, ~n (a) number; **ein Wagen**

**n**

mit [einer] Münchner ~: a car with a Munich registration; **ich bin unter der ~ 242679 zu erreichen** I can be reached on 242679
**(b)** (Ausgabe) issue
**(c)** (Größe) size
**Nummern·schild** *das* number plate; license plate (Amer.)
**nummerieren** *tr. V.* number
**Nummerierung** *die;* ~, ~en numbering
**nun** [1] *adv.* now
[2] *Partikel* now; **das hast du ~ davon!** it serves you right!; **kommst du ~ mit oder nicht?** now are you coming or not?; **~ gut** [well,] all right; **~, ~!** now, come on; **~ ja** ...: well, yes ...
**nur** [1] *adv.* **(a)** (nicht mehr als) only; just
**(b)** (ausschließlich) only; **nicht ~ ..., sondern auch ...:** not only ..., but also ...; **~ so zum Spaß** just for fun
[2] *Konj.* but; **ich kann dir das Buch leihen, ~ nicht heute** I can lend you the book, only not today
[3] *Partikel* **wenn er ~ hier wäre** if only he were here; **~ zu!** go ahead; **lass dich ~ nicht erwischen** just don't let me/them *etc.* catch you; **was sollen wir ~ tun?** what on earth are we going to do?; **so schnell er ~ konnte** just as fast as he could
**Nürnberg** *(das);* ~s Nuremberg
**nuscheln** *tr., itr. V.* (ugs.) mumble
**Nuss, \*Nuß** *die;* ~, Nüsse nut
**Nuss-, \*Nuß-:** ~**baum,** *der* walnut tree; ~**knacker** *der* nutcrackers *pl.;* ~**schale** *die* nutshell
**Nüster** *die;* ~, ~n nostril
**Nut** *die;* ~, ~en (Technik) groove

**Nutte** *die;* ~, ~n (derb) tart (sl.); hooker (Amer. sl.)
**nutz-:** ~**bar** *Adj.* usable; exploitable, utilizable ⟨*mineral resources, invention*⟩; cultivatable ⟨*land, soil*⟩; ~**bringend**
[1] *Adj.* useful; (gewinnbringend) profitable
[2] *adv.* profitably
**nutzen** [1] *tr. V.* **(a)** use; exploit, utilize ⟨*natural resources*⟩; cultivate ⟨*land, soil*⟩; harness ⟨*energy source*⟩; exploit ⟨*advantage*⟩
**(b)** (be-, ausnutzen) use; make use of
[2] *itr. V.* ▶ NÜTZEN 1
**Nutzen** *der;* ~s **(a)** benefit; **[jmdm.] von ~ sein** be of use [to sb.]
**(b)** (Profit) profit
**nützen** [1] *itr. V.* be of use (*Dat.* to); **nichts ~:** be no use
[2] *tr. V.* ▶ NUTZEN 1
**nützlich** *Adj.* useful
**Nützlichkeit** *die;* ~: usefulness
**nutzlos** [1] *Adj.* useless; (vergeblich) vain *attrib.;* in vain *pred.;*
[2] *adv.* uselessly; (vergeblich) in vain
**Nutz·losigkeit** *die;* ~: uselessness; (Vergeblichkeit) futility
**Nutznießer** *der;* ~s, ~, **Nutznießerin** *die;* ~, ~nen beneficiary
**Nutzung** *die;* ~, ~en use; (des Landes, des Bodens) cultivation; (von Bodenschätzen) exploitation; utilization; (einer Energiequelle) harnessing
**Nylon** Ⓦ /'nailɔn/ *das;* ~s nylon
**Nymphe** *die;* ~, ~n (Myth., Zool.) nymph
**Nymphomanin** *die;* ~, ~nen (Psych.) nymphomaniac

# Oo

**o, O** *das;* ~, ~: o/O
**ö, Ö** *das;* ~, ~: o/O umlaut
**O** *Abk.* = **Ost[en]** E
**Oase** *die;* ~, ~n (auch fig.) oasis
**ob** *Konj.* **(a)** whether
**(b) und ob!** of course!
**OB** *Abk.* = **Oberbürgermeister[in]**
**Obacht** *die;* ~ (bes. südd.) caution; **~ auf jmdn./etw. geben** take care of sb./sth.; (aufmerksam sein) pay attention to sb./sth.
**Obdach** *das;* ~[e]s (geh.) shelter
**obdach·los** *Adj.* homeless
**Obdachlose** *der/die; adj. Dekl.* homeless person/man/woman; **die ~n** the homeless
**Obdachlosen-:** ~**heim** *das* hostel for the homeless; ~**siedlung** *die* estate of houses for the homeless

**Obdachlosigkeit** *die;* ~: homelessness
**Obduktion** *die;* ~, ~en (Med., Rechtsw.) post mortem [examination]; autopsy
**obduzieren** *tr. V.* carry out *or* perform a/ the postmortem [examination] *or* autopsy on
**O-Beine** *Pl.* bandy legs; bow legs
**oben** *Adv.* **(a)** hier/dort ~: up here/there; **weiter ~:** further up; **nach ~:** upwards; **von ~:** from above; **von ~ herab** (fig.) condescendingly
**(b)** (im Gebäude) upstairs; **nach ~:** upstairs
**(c)** (am oberen Ende, zum oberen Ende hin) at the top; **nach ~ [hin]** towards the top; **von ~:** from the top; **~ ohne** topless
**(d)** (an der Oberseite) on top
**(e)** (in einer Hierarchie, Rangfolge) at the top
**(f)** ([weiter] vorn im Text) above; **~ genannt** above-mentioned

**\*oben·genannt** ▶ OBEN F

**Ober** *der;* ~s, ~: waiter; **Herr** ~! waiter!

**ober...** *Adj.* upper *attrib.;* top *attrib.*

**Ober-:** ~**arm** *der* upper arm;
~**bekleidung** *die* outer clothing;
~**bürgermeister** *der* mayor; ~**fläche**
*die* surface; (Flächeninhalt) surface area

**oberflächlich** ① *Adj.* superficial
② *adv.* superficially

**Ober·geschoss, \*Ober·geschoß** *das*
upper storey; **im fünften** ~: on the fifth floor
(Brit.) *or* (Amer.) the sixth floor

**ober·halb** ① *Adv.* above; ~ **von** above
② *Präp. mit Gen.* above

**Ober-:** ~**hand** *die* die ~hand [über jmdn./
etw.] haben have the upper hand [over sb./
sth.]; die ~hand [über jmdn./etw.] gewinnen/
bekommen gain *or* get the upper hand [over
sb./sth.]; ~**haupt** *das* head; (einer
Verschwörung) leader; ~**hemd** *das* shirt;
~**kiefer** *der* upper jaw; ~**körper** *der*
upper part of the body; ~**lippen·bart** *der*
moustache; ~**schenkel** *der* thigh;
~**schicht** *die* (Soziol.) upper class;
~**schule** *die* secondary school; ~**seite**
*die* top

**oberst...** ▶ OBER...

**Ober-:** ~**stufe** *die* (Schulw.) upper school;
~**teil** *das od. der* top [part]; (eines Bikinis,
Anzugs, Kleids usw.) top [half]; ~**wasser** *das*
headwater; (fig.) ~wasser haben feel in a
strong position; ~wasser bekommen/kriegen
have one's hand strengthened

**ob·gleich** *Konj.* ▶ OBWOHL

**obig** *Adj.* above

**Objekt** *das;* ~s, ~e object; (Kaufmannsspr.:
Immobilie) property

**objektiv** ① *Adj.* objective
② *adv.* objectively

**Objektiv** *das;* ~s, ~e lens

**Objektivität** *die;* ~: objectivity

**Obrigkeit** *die;* ~, ~en authorities *pl.*

**ob·schon** *Konj.* (geh.) although

**Obst** *das;* ~[e]s fruit

**Obst-:** ~**baum** *der* fruit tree; ~**garten**
*der* orchard; ~**kuchen** *der* fruit flan

**Obstler** *der;* ~s, ~ (bes. südd.) fruit brandy

**Obst-:** ~**saft** *der* fruit juice; ~**salat** *der*
fruit salad; ~**wein** *der* fruit wine

**obszön** ① *Adj.* obscene
② *adv.* obscenely

**Obszönität** *die;* ~, ~en obscenity

**ob·wohl** *Konj.* although; though

**Ochse** /'ɔksə/ *der;* ~n, ~n (a) ox; bullock
(b) (salopp) numskull (coll.)

**Ochsen·schwanz·suppe** *die* oxtail
soup

**od.** *Abk.* = **oder**

**öde** *Adj.* (a) deserted; desolate ⟨*area,
landscape*⟩

(b) (unfruchtbar) barren

(c) (langweilig) tedious; dreary ⟨*life, time,
existence*⟩

**Öde** *die;* ~ ▶ ÖDE A–C: desertedness;
desolateness; barrenness; tediousness;
dreariness

**oder** *Konj.* or; (in Fragen) **er ist doch hier,** ~?
he is here, isn't he? (zweifelnd) he is here – or
isn't he?

**Öd·land** *das* uncultivated land

**Oeuvre** /'øːvrə/ *das;* ~, ~s (geh.) œuvre

**OEZ** *Abk.* = **osteuropäische Zeit** EET

**Ofen** *der;* ~s, **Öfen** heater; (Kohle~) stove;
(Back~) oven; (Brenn~, Trocken~) kiln

**Ofen·rohr** *das* [stove] flue

**offen** ① *Adj.* (a) open; ~ **bleiben** stay open;
**etw.** ~ **lassen** leave sth. open; ~ **stehen** be
open; **ein** ~**es Hemd** a shirt with the collar
unfastened; ~ **haben** *od.* **sein** be open; ~**es
Licht** a naked light

(b) (frei) vacant ⟨*job, post*⟩

(c) (ungewiss, ungeklärt) open ⟨*question*⟩;
uncertain ⟨*result*⟩; ~ **bleiben** remain open;
⟨*decision*⟩ be left open

(d) (noch nicht bezahlt) outstanding ⟨*bill*⟩

(e) (freimütig, aufrichtig) frank [and open]
⟨*person*⟩; frank, candid ⟨*look, opinion, reply*⟩
② *adv.* openly; ~ **gesagt** frankly; to be
frank

**offen·bar** ① *Adj.* obvious
② *adv.* obviously

**Offenbarung** *die;* ~, ~en revelation

**\*offen|bleiben** ▶ OFFEN 1A, C

**Offen·heit** *die;* ~ ▶ OFFEN E: frankness
[and openness]; candour

**offen-:** ~**kundig** ① *Adj.* obvious; ② *adv.*
obviously; **\*~|lassen** ▶ OFFEN 1A;
~**sichtlich** ① *Adj.* obvious; ② *adv.*
obviously

**offensiv** ① *Adj.* (a) offensive
(b) (Sport) attacking
② *adv.* (a) offensively
(b) (Sport) ~ **spielen** play an attacking game

**Offensive** *die;* ~, ~n (auch Sport) offensive

**\*offen|stehen** ▶ OFFEN 1A

**öffentlich** ① *Adj.* public; state *attrib.*;
[state-]maintained ⟨*school*⟩; **der** ~**e Dienst**
the civil service
② *adv.* publicly; ⟨*perform, appear*⟩ in public

**Öffentlichkeit** *die;* ~: public

**offiziell** ① *Adj.* official
② *adv.* officially

**Offizier** *der;* ~s, ~e, **Offizierin** *die;* ~,
~nen officer

**öffnen** ① *tr. V.* open; turn on ⟨*tap*⟩; undo
⟨*coat, blouse, button, zip*⟩
② *itr. V.* (a) [jmdm.] ~: open the door [to
sb.]
(b) (geöffnet werden) ⟨*shop, bank, etc.*⟩ open
③ *refl. V.* open

**Öffner** *der;* ~s, ~: opener

**Öffnung** *die;* ~, ~en opening

**Öffnungs·zeiten** *Pl.* opening times

---
\*old spelling - see note on page xiv

**Offroader** /ɔfˈrəʊdɐ/ *der;* ~s, ~: offroader

**oft** *Adv.* öfter, am öftesten often; **wie oft soll ich dir noch sagen, dass ...?** how many [more] times do I have to tell you that ...?

**öfter** *Adv.* now and then

**oftmals** *Adv.* often; frequently

**OG** *Abk.* = **Obergeschoss**

**ohne** [1] *Präp. mit Akk.* without; ~ **mich!** [you can] count me out!; ~ **weiteres** (leicht, einfach) easily; (ohne Einwand) readily [2] *Konj.* ~ **zu zögern** without hesitation

**ohne·hin** *Adv.* anyway

**Ohnmacht** *die;* ~, ~en (a) faint; **in** ~ **fallen** faint (b) (Machtlosigkeit) powerlessness; impotence

**ohnmächtig** [1] *Adj.* (a) unconscious; ~ **werden** faint; ~ **sein** have fainted (b) (machtlos) powerless; impotent [2] *adv.* impotently; ~ **zusehen** watch helplessly

**Ohr** *das;* ~[e]s, ~en ear; **gute/schlechte** ~**en haben** have good/poor hearing *sing.;* **jmdn. übers** ~ **hauen** (fig. ugs.) put one over on sb. (coll.)

**Öhr** *das;* ~[e]s, ~e eye

**ohren-, Ohren-:** ~**arzt,** *der,* ~**ärztin,** *die* otologist; ear specialist; ~**betäubend** [1] *Adj.* ear-splitting; deafening; deafening ⟨applause⟩; [2] *adv.* deafeningly; ~**sausen** *das;* ~~s ringing in the *or* one's ears; tinnitus (Med.); ~**schmerz** *der* earache; ~**schmerzen haben** have [an] earache *sing.*

**ohr-, Ohr-:** ~**feige** *die* box on the ears; ~**feigen** *tr. V.* jmdn. ~**feigen** box sb.'s ears; **ich könnte mich** ~**feigen!** (ugs.) I could kick myself!; ~**läppchen** *das* ear lobe; ~**ring** *der* earring; ~**wurm** *der* (a) earwig; (b) (ugs.: Melodie) catchy tune; **ein** ~**wurm sein** be really catchy

**okay** /oˈke/ (ugs.) *Interj., Adj., adv.* OK (coll.); okay (coll.)

**öko-, Öko-** eco-

**Ökologie** *die;* ~: ecology

**ökologisch** [1] *Adj.* ecological [2] *adv.* ecologically

**ökonomisch** [1] *Adj.* (a) economic (b) (sparsam) economical [2] *adv.* economically

**Öko-:** ~**produkt** *das* ecoproduct; environmentally friendly *or* safe product; ~**steuer** *die* eco-tax; ~**system** *das* ecosystem

**Oktober** *der;* ~[s], ~: October

**ökumenisch** *Adj.* (christl. Rel.) ecumenical

**Öl** *das;* ~[e]s, ~e oil; **in Öl malen** paint in oils

**ölen** *tr. V.* oil

**Öl-:** ~**embargo** *das* oil embargo; ~**farbe** *die* (a) oil-based paint; (b) (zum Malen) oil paint; ~**gemälde** *das* oil painting

**ölig** *Adj.* oily

**Olive** *die;* ~, ~n olive

**Oliven-:** ~**baum** *der* olive tree; ~**öl** *das* olive oil

**Öl-:** ~**ofen** *der* oil heater; ~**pest** *die* oil pollution *no indef. art.;* ~**quelle** *die* oil well; ~**sardine** *die* sardine in oil; **eine Dose** ~**sardinen** a tin of sardines; ~**teppich** *der* oil slick; ~**wechsel** *der* (bes. Kfz-W.) oil change

**Olympiade** *die;* ~, ~n Olympic Games *pl.;* Olympics *pl.*

**Olympia-:** ~**sieger** *der,* ~**siegerin** *die* Olympic champion; ~**stadion** *das* Olympic stadium

**olympisch** *Adj.* Olympic; **die Olympischen Spiele** the Olympic Games; the Olympics

**Oma** *die;* ~, ~s (fam.) granny (coll./child lang.)

**Omelett** /ɔm(ə)ˈlɛt/ *das;* ~[e]s, ~e *od.* ~s omelette

**Omi** *die;* ~, ~s ▶ OMA

**Omnibus** *der;* ~ses, ~se omnibus (formal); (Privat- und Reisebus auch) coach

**Onanie** *die;* ~: onanism *no art.;* masturbation *no art.*

**onanieren** *itr. V.* masturbate

**Onkel** *der;* ~s, ~ *od.* (ugs.) ~s uncle

**online** /ˈɔnlam/ [1] *Adj.* online; ~ **gehen** go online [2] *Adv.* online

**Online·shopping** *das* online shopping

**OP** /oːˈpeː/ *der;* ~[s], ~[s] *Abk.* = **Operationssaal**

**Opa** *der;* ~s, ~s (fam.) grandad (coll./child lang.)

**Opal** *der;* ~s, ~e opal

**OPEC** /ˈoːpɛk/ *die;* ~: *Abk.* OPEC

**Oper** *die;* ~, ~n opera; (Opernhaus) Opera; opera house

**Operation** *die;* ~, ~en operation

**Operations·saal** *der* operating theatre (Brit.) *or* room

**operativ** [1] *Adj.*(Med.) operative [2] *adv.* (Med.) by operative surgery; **etw.** ~ **entfernen** operate to remove sth.

**Operette** *die;* ~, ~n operetta

**operieren** [1] *tr. V.* operate on ⟨patient⟩ [2] *itr. V.* operate

**Opern·glas** *das* opera glass[es *pl.*]

**Opfer** *das;* ~s, ~ (a) sacrifice (b) (Geschädigter) victim

**opfern** *tr. V.* (auch fig.) sacrifice; offer up ⟨fruit, produce, etc.⟩

**Opi** *der;* ~s, ~s ▶ OPA

**Opium** *das;* ~s opium

**opponieren** *itr. V.* gegen jmdn./etw. ~: oppose sb./sth.

**Opposition** *die;* ~, ~en opposition

**oppositionell** *Adj.* opposition *attrib.* ⟨group, movement, etc.⟩; ⟨newspaper, writer, artist, etc.⟩ opposed to the government

**Optik** *die;* ~: optics *sing., no art.*

**Optiker** *der;* ~s, ~, **Optikerin** *die;* ~,
~nen optician

**optimal** [1] *Adj.* optimal; optimum *attrib.;*
[2] *adv.* jmdn. ~ **beraten** give sb. the best
possible advice

**optimieren** *tr. V.* optimize

**Optimierung** *die;* ~, ~en optimization

**Optimismus** *der;* ~: optimism

**Optimist** *der;* ~en, ~en, **Optimistin** *die;*
~, ~nen optimist

**optimistisch** [1] *Adj.* optimistic
[2] *adv.* optimistically

**optisch** [1] *Adj.* optical; visual ⟨*impression*⟩;
eine ~e Täuschung an optical illusion
[2] *adv.* optically; visually ⟨*impressive,*
*effective*⟩

**orange** /o'rã:ʒ(ə)/ *indekl. Adj.* orange

**Orange** *die;* ~, ~n orange

**Orangen-:** ~**marmelade** *die* orange
marmalade; ~**saft** *der* orange juice

**Orchester** /ɔr'kɛstɐ/ *das;* ~s, ~: orchestra

**Orden** *der;* ~s, ~ (a) order
(b) (Ehrenzeichen) decoration

**ordentlich** [1] *Adj.* (a) [neat and] tidy; neat
⟨*handwriting, clothes*⟩
(b) (anständig) respectable; proper ⟨*manners*⟩
(c) (planmäßig) ordinary ⟨*meeting*⟩; ~es
Mitglied full member
(d) (ugs.: richtig) proper; real; ein ~es Stück
Kuchen a nice big piece of cake
(e) (ugs.: recht gut) decent ⟨*wine, flat, marks,*
*etc.*⟩; ganz ~: pretty good
[2] *adv.* (a) tidily; neatly; ⟨*write*⟩ neatly
(b) (anständig) properly
(c) (ugs.: gehörig) ~ feiern have a real good
celebration (coll.)
(d) (ugs.: recht gut) ⟨*ski, speak, etc.*⟩ really well

**ordern** *tr., itr. V.* (Kaufmannsspr.) order

**Ordinal·zahl** *die* ordinal [number]

**ordinär** [1] *Adj.* vulgar
[2] *adv.* vulgarly

**Ordinate** *die;* ~, ~n (Math.) ordinate

**ordnen** *tr. V.* arrange; sein Leben/seine
Finanzen ~: straighten out one's life/put
one's finances in order

**Ordner** *der;* ~s, ~ (Hefter) file

**Ordnung** *die;* ~, ~en order; (geregelter
Ablauf) routine; ~ halten keep things tidy; in
~ sein (ugs.) be OK (coll.) *or* all right; hier ist
etw. nicht in ~: there's something wrong
here; sie ist in ~ (ugs.) she's OK (coll.); in ~!
(ugs.) OK! (coll.); all right!

**ordnungs-, Ordnungs-:** ~**gemäß**
[1] *Adj.* ⟨*conduct etc.*⟩ in accordance with the
regulations; [2] *adv.* in accordance with the
regulations; ~**halber** *Adv.* as a matter of
form; ~**widrig** (Rechtsw.) [1] *Adj.* ⟨*actions,*
*behaviour, etc.*⟩ contravening the regulations;
illegal ⟨*parking*⟩; [2] *adv.* ~widrig parken

park illegally; ~**widrigkeit** *die* (Rechtsw.)
infringement of the regulations; ~**zahl** *die*
ordinal [number]

**Organ** *das;* ~s, ~e organ; (ugs.: Stimme)
voice

**Organisation** *die;* ~, ~en organization

**Organisator** *der;* ~s, ~en,
**Organisatorin** *die;* ~, ~nen organizer

**organisatorisch** *Adj.* organizational

**organisch** [1] *Adj.* organic
[2] *adv.* organically

**organisieren** [1] *tr. V.* organize
[2] *itr. V.* gut ~ können be a good organizer
[3] *refl. V.* organize

**Organismus** *der;* ~, Organismen organism

**Organist** *der;* ~en, ~en, **Organistin** *die;*
~, ~nen organist

**Organ·spender** *der,*
**Organ·spenderin** *die* organ donor

**Orgasmus** *der;* ~, Orgasmen orgasm

**Orgel** *die;* ~, ~n organ

**Orgie** /'ɔrgiə/ *die;* ~, ~n (auch fig.) orgy

**Orient** /'o:riɛnt/ *der;* ~s Middle East and
south-western Asia (*including Afghanistan
and Nepal*); der Vordere ~: the Middle East

**orientalisch** *Adj.* oriental

**orientieren** [1] *refl. V.* (a) get one's
bearings
(b) sich über etw. (*Akk.*) ~ (fig.) inform
oneself about sth.
(c) sich an etw. (*Dat.*) ~ (fig.) be oriented
towards sth.; ⟨*policy, advertising*⟩ be geared
towards sth.
[2] *tr. V.* (unterrichten) inform (über + *Akk.*
about)

**Orientierung** *die;* ~ (a) die ~ verlieren
lose one's bearings
(b) (Unterrichtung) zu Ihrer ~: for your
information

**Orientierungs·sinn** *der* sense of
direction

**original** [1] *Adj.* original
[2] *adv.* ~ italienischer Espresso genuine
Italian espresso coffee; etw. ~ übertragen
broadcast sth. live

**Original** *das;* ~s, ~e original

**Original-:** ~**fassung** *die* original version;
~**gemälde** *das* original painting

**Originalität** *die;* ~: originality

**Original·ton** *der; Pl.* Original-töne (Film,
Ferns.) direct sound; original sound

**originell** [1] *Adj.* original
[2] *adv.* with originality

**Orkan** *der;* ~[e]s, ~e hurricane

**Ornament** *das;* ~[e]s, ~e ornament

**Ort**[1] /ɔrt/ *der;* ~[e]s, ~e place; (Dorf) village;
(Stadt) town; an ~ und Stelle there and then

**Ort**[2]**:** vor ~ (fig.) on the spot

**orthodox** *Adj.* orthodox

**Orthographie** *die;* ~, ~n orthography

**orthographisch** [1] *Adj.* orthographic; ~e
Fehler spelling mistakes

---

*alte Schreibung - vgl. Hinweis auf S. xiv

269 **Orthopäde ⋯⟶ Packen** ⋯⋯

**2** *adv.* orthographically
**Orthopäde** *der;* ~n, ~n orthopaedic
specialist
**orthopädisch** **1** *Adj.* orthopaedic
**2** *adv.* orthopaedically
**örtlich** **1** *Adj.* (auch Med.) local
**2** *adv.* (auch Med.) locally; ~ **betäubt werden**
be given a local anaesthetic
**Ortschaft** *die;* ~, ~en (Dorf) village; (Stadt)
town
**Orts-:** ~**gespräch** *das* (Fernspr.) local call;
~**name** *der* place name;
~**netz·kennzahl** *die* (Fernspr.) dialling
code; area code (Amer.)
**Öse** *die;* ~, ~n eye
**Ossi** *der;* ~s, ~s (salopp) East German
**Ost** (bes. Seemannsspr., Met.) ▶ OSTEN
**ost-, Ost-:** ~**block** *der* Eastern bloc;
~**deutsch** *Adj.* Eastern German; (hist.: auf
die DDR bezogen) East German;
~**deutschland** (*das*) Eastern Germany;
(hist.: DDR) East Germany
**Osten** *der;* ~s east; **der** ~: the East; **der**
**Ferne** ~: the Far East; **der Nahe** ~: the
Middle East
**Oster-:** ~**ei** *das* Easter egg; ~**glocke** *die*
daffodil; ~**hase** *der* Easter hare (*said to*
*bring children their Easter Eggs*);
~**montag** *der* Easter Monday *no def. art.*
**Ostern** *das;* ~, ~: Easter; **Frohe** *od.*
**Fröhliche** ~: Happy Easter! **zu** ~: at Easter
**Österreich** (*das*); ~s Austria
**Österreicher** *der;* ~s,
**Österreicherin** *die* ~, ~nen Austrian
**österreichisch** *Adj.* Austrian

**Oster·sonntag** *der* Easter Sunday *no def.*
*art.*
**Ost·europa** (*das*) Eastern Europe
**Ostler** *der;* ~s, ~, **Ostlerin** *die;* ~, ~nen
(ugs.) East German
**östlich** **1** *Adj.* **(a)** (im Osten gelegen) eastern
**(b)** (nach, aus dem Osten) easterly
**(c)** (aus dem Osten kommend, für den Osten
typisch; Politik) Eastern; ⟨*influence, policies*⟩ of
the East
**2** *adv.* eastwards; ~ **von** ...: [to the] east
of ...
**3** *Präp. mit Gen.* [to the] east of
**Ost·see** *die;* ~: Baltic [Sea]
**ost·wärts** *Adv.* eastwards
**Ost·wind** *der* easterly wind
**Otter¹** *der;* ~s, ~ (Fisch~) otter
**Otter²** *die;* ~, ~n (Viper) adder; viper
**Otto·motor** *der* Otto engine
**out** /au̯t/ *Adj.* ~ **sein** (ugs.) be out
**Outfit** /'au̯tfɪt/ *das;* ~[s], ~s outfit
**Ouvertüre** /uvɐ'tyːrə/ *die;* ~, ~n (auch
fig.) overture (*Gen.* to)
**oval** *Adj.* oval
**Ovation** *die;* ~, ~en ovation; jmdm. ~**en**
darbringen give sb. an ovation
**Ozean** *der;* ~s, ~e ocean
**Ozean·dampfer** *der* ocean liner
**Ozon** *der od. das;* ~s ozone
**Ozon-:** ~**alarm** *der* ozone alert; ~**loch**
*das* hole in the ozone layer; ~**schicht** *die*
ozone layer; ~**zerstörung** *die* ozone
destruction

**p**

# Pp

**p, P** /peː/ *das;* ~, ~: p/P
**paar** *indekl. Indefinitpron.* **ein** ~ ...: a few
...; (zwei od. drei) a couple of ...
**Paar** *das;* ~[e]s, ~e pair; (Mann und Frau)
couple; **ein** ~ **Würstchen** two sausages
**paaren** *refl. V.* ⟨*animals*⟩ mate; ⟨*people*⟩
copulate
**Paar·lauf** *der* pairs *pl.*
**paar·mal** *Adv.* **ein** ~ a few times; (zwei- oder
dreimal) a couple of times
**Paarung** *die;* ~, ~en (Zool.) mating
**paar·weise** *Adv.* in pairs
**Pacht** *die;* ~, ~en lease; **etw. in** ~ **nehmen**
lease sth.; **etw. in** ~ **haben** have sth. on
lease; **etw. in** ~ **geben** lease sth.
**pachten** *tr. V.* lease

**Pächter** *der;* ~s, ~, **Pächterin** *die;* ~,
~nen leaseholder; (eines Hofes) tenant
**Pacht-:** ~**vertrag** *der* lease; ~**zins** *der;*
*Pl.* ~~e rent
**Pack¹** *der;* ~[e]s, ~e *od.* **Päcke (a)** pack
**(b)** ▶ PACKEN
**Pack²** *das;* ~[e]s (ugs. abwertend) rabble
**Päckchen** *das;* ~s, ~ **(a)** package; (auch
Postw.) small parcel; (Bündel) packet
**(b)** ▶ PACKUNG A
**packen** **1** *tr. V.* **(a)** pack
**(b)** (fassen) grab [hold of]; (fig.) **Furcht packte**
**ihn/er wurde von Furcht gepackt** he was
seized with fear
**2** *itr. V.* (Koffer usw. ~) pack
**Packen** *der;* ~s, ~: pile; (zusammengeschnürt)
bundle; (von Geldscheinen) wad

**packend** [1] *Adj.* gripping
[2] *adv.* grippingly
**Pack·papier** *das* [stout] wrapping paper
**Packung** *die;* ∼, ∼en (a) packet; pack (esp. Amer.)
(b) (Med., Kosmetik) pack
**Pädagoge** *der;* ∼n, ∼n (Erzieher, Lehrer) teacher; (Wissenschaftler) educationalist
**Pädagogik** *die;* ∼: [theory and methodology of] education
**Pädagogin** *die;* ∼, ∼nen ▶ PÄDAGOGE
**pädagogisch** [1] *Adj.* educational; **seine** ∼en Fähigkeiten his teaching ability *sing.;* [2] *adv.* educationally ⟨*sound, wrong*⟩
**Paddel** *das;* ∼s, ∼: paddle
**Paddel·boot** *das* canoe
**paddeln** *itr. V.; mit sein* paddle; (als Sport) canoe
**Päderast** *der;* ∼en, ∼en pederast
**pädophil** *Adj.* paedophile
**Pädophile** *der; adj. Dekl.* paedophile
**paffen** [1] *tr. V.* puff at ⟨*pipe etc.*⟩
[2] *itr. V.* puff away
**Page** /ˈpaːʒə/ *der;* ∼n, ∼n bellboy
**Paket** *das;* ∼[e]s, ∼e pile; (zusammengeschnürt) bundle; (Eingepacktes, Post∼) parcel; (Packung) packet; pack (esp. Amer.)
**Paket-:** ∼**karte** *die* parcel dispatch form; ∼**schalter** *der* parcels counter
**Pakistan** (*das*); ∼s Pakistan
**Pakistaner** *der;* ∼s, ∼, **Pakistanerin** *die;* ∼, ∼nen, **Pakistani** *der;* ∼[s], ∼[s] Pakistani
**pakistanisch** *Adj.* Pakistani
**Pakt** *der;* ∼[e]s, ∼e pact
**paktieren** *itr. V.* make *or* do a deal/deals
**Palast** *der;* ∼[e]s, **Paläste** palace
**Palästina** (*das*); ∼s Palestine
**Palästinenser** *der;* ∼s, ∼, **Palästinenserin** *die;* ∼, ∼nen Palestinian
**palästinensisch** *Adj.* Palestinian
**Palaver** /paˈlaːvɐ/ *das;* ∼s, ∼ (ugs. abwertend) palaver
**palavern** *itr. V.* (ugs. abwertend) palaver
**Palette** *die;* ∼, ∼n (a) palette
(b) (bes. Werbespr.: Vielfalt) diverse range; **die ganze** ∼: the whole range
(c) (Technik, Wirtsch.: Untersatz) pallet
**paletti** *Adj.* **alles** ∼ (ugs.) everything's OK (coll.) *or* all right
**Palme** *die;* ∼, ∼n palm [tree]
**Pampelmuse** *die;* ∼, ∼n grapefruit
**Panade** *die;* ∼, ∼n (Kochk.) breadcrumb coating
**Panama** (*das*); ∼s Panama
**Panama·kanal** *der;* ∼s Panama Canal
**Panel** /ˈpɛnl/ *das;* ∼s, ∼s panel

**Pan·flöte** *die* pan pipes *pl.*
**panieren** *tr. V.* bread; coat ⟨*sth.*⟩ with breadcrumbs
**Panier·mehl** *das* breadcrumbs *pl.*
**Panik** *die;* ∼, ∼en panic
**Panik-:** ∼**mache** *die;* ∼∼ (abwertend) panicmongering; ∼**macher** *der,* ∼**macherin** *die* (abwertend) panicmonger
**Panne** *die;* ∼, ∼n (a) breakdown; (Reifen∼) puncture; flat [tyre]
(b) (Missgeschick) mishap
**Pannen·dienst** *der* breakdown service
**Panorama** *das;* ∼s, **Panoramen** panorama
**Panter**, *****Panther** *der;* ∼s, ∼: panther
**Pantoffel** *der;* ∼s, ∼n backless slipper
**Pantomime** *die;* ∼, ∼n mime
**Panzer** *der;* ∼s, ∼ (a) (Milit.) tank
(b) (Zool.) armour *no indef. art.;* (von Schildkröten, Krebsen) shell
**Panzer·glas** *das* bulletproof glass
**panzern** *tr. V.* armour[-plate]
**Panzer·schrank** *der* safe
**Papa** *der;* ∼s, ∼s (ugs.) daddy (coll.)
**Papagei** *der;* ∼en *od.* ∼s, ∼e[n] parrot
**Paparazzo** *der;* ∼s, **Paparazzi** paparazzo
**Paperback** /ˈpeɪpəbæk/ *das;* ∼s, ∼s paperback
**Papi** *der;* ∼s, ∼s (ugs.) daddy (coll.)
**Papier** *das;* ∼s, ∼e (a) paper
(b) *Pl.* (Ausweis[e]) [identity] papers
(c) (Finanzw.: Wert∼) security
**Papier-:** ∼**geld** *das* paper money; ∼**korb** *der* waste-paper basket
**Pappe** *die;* ∼, ∼n cardboard
**Pappel** *die;* ∼, ∼n poplar
**päppeln** *tr. V.* feed up
**Papp·karton** *der* cardboard box
**Paprika** *der;* ∼s, ∼[s] (a) pepper
(b) (Gewürz) paprika
**Papst** *der;* ∼[e]s, **Päpste**, **Päpstin** *die;* ∼, ∼nen pope
**päpstlich** *Adj.* papal
**Para** *der;* ∼s, ∼s para (coll.)
**Parabel** *die;* ∼, ∼n (a) (bes. Literaturw.) parable
(b) (Math.) parabola
**Parade** *die;* ∼, ∼n parade
**Parade·beispiel** *das* perfect example
**Paradeiser** *der;* ∼s, ∼ (österr.) tomato
**Paradies** *das;* ∼es, ∼e paradise
**paradiesisch** *Adj.* paradisical; (herrlich) heavenly
**Paradigma** *das;* ∼s, **Paradigmen** paradigm
**paradox** *Adj.* paradoxical
**Para·gleiten** *das;* ∼s, **Para·gliding** /ˈparaglaːdɪŋ/ *das;* ∼s paragliding
**Paragraph** *der;* ∼en, ∼en section; (in Vertrag) clause
**parallel** [1] *Adj.* parallel
[2] *adv.* ∼ **verlaufen** run parallel (**mit, zu** to)

---

**Parallele** *die;* ~, ~n parallel
**Parallelogramm** *das;* ~s, ~e
parallelogram
**Parallel-straße** *die* street running
parallel (*Gen.* to)
**Para·nuss, \*Para·nuß** *die* Brazil nut
**Parasit** *der;* ~en, ~en (auch fig.) parasite
**parat** *Adj.* ready
**Pardon** /par'dõ/ *der od. das;* ~s pardon; ~!
I beg your pardon
**Parfum** /par'fœː/, **Parfüm** *das;* ~s, ~s
perfume
**Parfümerie** *die;* ~, ~en perfumery
**parfümieren** *tr. V.* perfume
**Pariser** 1 *indekl. Adj.* Parisian; Paris
*attrib.;*
2 *der;* ~s, ~ (a) (Einwohner) Parisian
(b) (ugs.: Kondom) French letter (coll.)
**Pariserin** *die;* ~, ~nen Parisian
**Parität** *die;* ~, ~en parity
**Park** /park/ *der;* ~s, ~s park; (Schloss~
usw.) grounds *pl.*
**Parka** *der;* ~s, ~s parka
**parken** *tr., itr. V.* park; „Parken verboten!"
'No Parking'
**Parkett** *das;* ~[e]s, ~e (a) parquet floor
(b) (Theater) [front] stalls *pl.;* parquet (Amer.)
**Parkett-:** ~[fuß]boden *der* parquet
floor; ~handel *der* (Börsenw.) floor trading
**Park-:** ~gebühr *die* parking fee; ~haus
*das* multi-storey car park
**parkieren** *tr., itr. V.* (schweiz.) ▶ PARKEN
**Park-:** ~lücke *die* parking space; ~platz
*der* car park; parking lot (Amer.); (für ein
einzelnes Fahrzeug) parking space;
~scheibe *die* parking disc; ~schein
*der* car park ticket; ~uhr *die* parking
meter; ~verbot *das* ban on parking; im
~verbot stehen be parked illegally;
~verbots·schild *das* no-parking sign
**Parlament** *das;* ~[e]s, ~e parliament
**Parlamentarier** *der;* ~s, ~,
**Parlamentarierin** *die;* ~, ~nen
member of parliament
**parlamentarisch** *Adj.* parliamentary
**Parodie** *die;* ~, ~n parody (auf + *Akk.* of)
**Parole** *die;* ~, ~n (a) (Wahlspruch) motto;
(Schlagwort) slogan
(b) (bes. Milit.: Kennwort) password
**Partei** *die;* ~, ~en (a) (Politik, Rechtsw.) party
(b) (Gruppe, Mannschaft) side; **für jmdn.** ~
**ergreifen** *od.* nehmen side with sb.
**Partei·gänger** *der;* ~~s, ~~,
**Partei·gängerin** *die;* ~~~, ~~~nen (oft
abwertend) [loyal] party supporter
**parteiisch** 1 *Adj.* biased
2 *adv.* in a biased manner
**parteilich** 1 *Adj.* (parteiisch) biased
2 *adv.* in a biased manner
**Parteilichkeit** *die;* ~ (einseitige Parteinahme)
bias; partiality
**partei-, Partei-:** ~los *Adj.* (Politik)

independent ⟨*MP*⟩; ~lose *der/die; adj.*
*Dekl.* (Politik) independent; person not
attached to a party; ~nahme *die;* ~~,
~~n partisanship; taking sides *no art.;*
~politik *die* party politics *sing.;*
~politisch 1 *Adj.* party political;
2 *adv.* from a party political point of view;
~tag *der* party conference *or* (Amer.)
convention
**Parterre** *das;* ~s, ~s ground floor; first
floor (Amer.)
**Partie** *die;* ~, ~n (a) part
(b) (Spiel, Sport: Runde) game; (Golf) round
(c) **eine gute** ~ [für jmdn.] sein be a good
match [for sb.]
**Partisan** *der;* ~s *od.* ~en, ~en,
**Partisanin** *die,* ~, ~nen guerrilla; (gegen
Besatzungstruppen im Krieg) partisan
**Partitur** *die;* ~, ~en (Musik) score
**Partizip** *das;* ~s, ~ien /-'tsiːpiən/ (Sprachw.)
participle
**Partner** *der;* ~s, ~, **Partnerin** *die;* ~,
~nen partner
**Partnerschaft** *die;* ~, ~en partnership
**partnerschaftlich** 1 *Adj.* ⟨cooperation
*etc.*⟩ on a partnership basis
2 *adv.* in a spirit of partnership
**Partner-:** ~schule *die* partner school;
~stadt *die* twin town (Brit.); sister city *or*
town (Amer.); ~vermittlung *die* (a)
matchmaking; (b) (Agentur) [introduction
and] matchmaking agency;
~vermittlungs·büro *das:* ▶
PARTNERVERMITTLUNG B
**Party** /'paːɐti/ *die;* ~, ~s party
**Parzelle** *die;* ~, ~n [small] plot [of land]
**Pass, \*Paß** *der;* Passes, Pässe (a)
(Reisepass) passport
(b) (Gebirgspass; Ballspiele) pass
**passabel** 1 *Adj.* reasonable; presentable
⟨appearance⟩
2 *adv.* reasonably well
**Passage** /pa'saːʒə/ *die;* ~, ~n (a)
[shopping] arcade
(b) (Abschnitt) passage
**Passagier** /pasa'ʒiːɐ/ *der;* ~s, ~e
passenger; **blinder** ~: stowaway
**Passagier-:** ~dampfer *der* passenger
steamer; ~flugzeug *das* passenger
aircraft
**Passagierin** *die;* ~, ~nen passenger
**Passagier·liste** *die* passenger list
**Pass·amt, \*Paß·amt** *das* passport office
**Passant** *der;* ~en, ~en, **Passantin** *die;*
~, ~nen passer-by
**Pass·bild, \*Paß·bild** *das* passport
photograph
**Pässe** ▶ PASS
**passen** *itr. V.* (a) (die richtige Größe/Form
haben) fit
(b) (geeignet sein) be suitable (**auf** + *Akk.,* **zu**
for); (harmonieren) ⟨colour *etc.*⟩ match; **zu etw.**/ ···⫶

jmdm. ~: go well with sth./be well suited to
sb.; **zueinander** ~ ⟨things⟩ go well together;
⟨two people⟩ be suited to each other
(c) (genehm sein) jmdm. ~ ⟨time⟩ suit sb.
(d) (Kartenspiel) pass

**passend** Adj. (a) (geeignet) suitable ⟨dress,
present, etc.⟩; right ⟨words, expression,
moment⟩
(b) (harmonierend) matching ⟨shoes etc.⟩

**Pass·foto, *Paß·foto** das ▶ PASSBILD

**passierbar** Adj. passable ⟨road⟩; navigable
⟨river⟩; negotiable ⟨path⟩

**passieren** 1 tr. V. pass; die Grenze ~:
cross the border
2 itr. V.; mit sein happen

**Passion** die; ~, ~en (a) passion
(b) (christl. Rel.) Passion

**passioniert** Adj. passionate ⟨collector, card
player, huntsman⟩

**passiv** 1 Adj. passive
2 adv. passively

**Passiv** das; ~s, ~e (Sprachw.) passive

**Passivität** die; ~: passivity

**Pass-, *Paß-:** ~kontrolle die passport
check; ~straße die [mountain] pass road;
~wort das; Pl. ~wörter (DV) password;
~zwang der obligation to carry a passport

**Paste** die; ~, ~n paste

**Pastell** das; ~[e]s, ~e (a) (Farbton) pastel
shade
(b) (Maltechnik) pastel no art.

**Pastell-:** ~farbe die pastel colour; ~ton
der pastel shade

**Pastete** die; ~, ~n (a) (gefüllte) vol-au-vent
(b) (in einer Schüssel o. Ä. gegart) pâté; (in einer
Hülle aus Teig gebacken) pie

**pasteurisieren** tr. V. pasteurize

**Pastille** die; ~, ~n pastille

**Pastor** der; ~s, ~en, **Pastorin** die; ~,
~nen pastor

**Pate** der; ~n, ~n godfather; (männlich od.
weiblich) godparent

**Paten-:** ~kind das godchild; ~onkel der
godfather; ~stadt die ▶ PARTNERSTADT

**patent** (ugs.) 1 Adj. (a) (tüchtig) capable
(b) (zweckmäßig) ingenious
2 adv. ingeniously; neatly ⟨solved⟩

**Patent** das; ~[e]s, ~e (a) (Schutz) patent;
etw. zum od. als ~ anmelden apply for a
patent for sth.
(b) (Erfindung) [patented] invention

**Patent·amt** das Patent Office

**Paten·tante** die godmother

**patentieren** tr. V. patent

**Patent-:** ~lösung die patent remedy (für,
zu for); ~rezept das patent remedy
(gegen, für for)

**Pater** der; ~s, ~ od. **Patres** (kath. Kirche)
Father

**Paternoster** der; ~s, ~ (Aufzug)
paternoster [lift]

**pathetisch** 1 Adj. emotional ⟨speech,
manner⟩; melodramatic ⟨gesture⟩; pompous
⟨voice⟩
2 adv. emotionally; (dramatisch)
[melo]dramatically

**Pathos** das; ~: emotionalism

**Patience** /pa'sjã:s/ die; ~, ~n [game of]
patience; ~n/eine ~ legen play patience/a
game of patience

**Patient** /pa'ts:i̯ent/ der; ~en, ~en,
**Patientin** die; ~, ~nen patient

**Patin** die; ~, ~nen godmother

**Patres** ▶ PATER

**Patriot** der; ~en, ~en, **Patriotin** die; ~,
~nen patriot

**patriotisch** 1 Adj. patriotic
2 adv. patriotically

**Patriotismus** der; ~: patriotism

**Patrone** die; ~, ~n cartridge

**Patrouille** /pa'truljə/ die; ~, ~n patrol

**patrouillieren** /patrul'ji:rən/ itr. V.; auch
mit sein be on patrol

**Patsche** die; ~, ~n (ugs.) ▶ KLEMME

**patschen** itr. V., mit sein (ugs.) splash

**patsch·nass, *patsch·naß** Adj. (ugs.)
sopping wet

**patt** Adj. (Schach) stalemated

**Patt** das; ~s, ~s (Schach; auch fig.) stalemate

**Patt·situation** die [position of] stalemate

**Patzer** der; ~s, ~ (ugs.) slip (coll.); boob
(coll.)

**patzig** (ugs.) 1 Adj. snotty (coll.); (frech)
cheeky
2 adv. snottily (coll.); (frech) cheekily

**Pauke** die; ~, ~n kettledrum; auf die ~
hauen (ugs.) (feiern) paint the town red (coll.);
(sich lautstark äußern) come right out with it

**pauken** (ugs.) 1 tr. V. swot up (Brit. sl.),
bone up on (Amer. coll.) ⟨facts, figures, etc.⟩;
Latein/Mathe ~: swot up one's Latin/maths
2 itr. V. swot (Brit. sl.); (fürs Examen) cram
(coll.)

**pausbäckig** Adj. chubby-faced; chubby
⟨face⟩

**pauschal** 1 Adj. (a) all-inclusive ⟨price,
settlement⟩
(b) (verallgemeinernd) sweeping ⟨judgement,
criticism, statement⟩; indiscriminate
⟨prejudice⟩; wholesale ⟨discrimination⟩
2 adv. (a) ⟨cost⟩ all in all; ⟨pay⟩ in a lump
sum
(b) (ohne zu differenzieren) wholesale

**Pauschale** die; ~, ~n flat-rate payment

**Pauschal-:** ~preis der flat rate;
(Inklusivpreis) all-in price; ~reise die package
holiday; (mit mehreren Reisezielen) package tour

**Pause** die; ~, ~n break; (Ruhe~) rest;
(Theater) interval (Brit.); intermission (Amer.)

**pausen** tr. V. trace; (eine Lichtpause machen)
Photostat (Brit. ®)

**p**

**pausen-, Pausen-:** ∼**brot** das sandwich (eaten during break); ∼**hof** der school yard; ∼**los** [1] Adj. incessant (noise, moaning, questioning); continous (work, operation)
[2] adv. incessantly; (work) non-stop

**Pavian** /ˈpaːvi̯aːn/ der; ∼s, ∼e baboon

**Pavillon** /ˈpaviljon/ der; ∼s, ∼s pavilion

**Pazifik** der; ∼s Pacific

**pazifisch** Adj. Pacific (area); **der Pazifische Ozean** the Pacific Ocean

**Pazifismus** der; ∼: pacifism no art.

**Pazifist** der; ∼en, ∼en, **Pazifistin** die; ∼, ∼nen pacifist

**pazifistisch** [1] Adj. pacifist
[2] adv. in a pacifist way

**PC** der; ∼[s], ∼[s] (DV) PC

**PDS** Abk. = **Partei des Demokratischen Sozialismus** Party of Democratic Socialism

**Peanuts** /ˈpiːnʌts/ Pl. peanuts (coll.)

**Pech** das; ∼[e]s, ∼e **(a)** pitch
**(b)** (Missgeschick) bad luck

**pech·schwarz** Adj. (ugs.) jet-black

**Pedal** das; ∼s, ∼e pedal

**Pedant** der; ∼en, ∼en, **Pedantin** die; ∼, ∼nen pedant

**pedantisch** [1] Adj. pedantic
[2] adv. pedantically

**Pediküre** die; ∼, ∼n pedicure

**pediküren** tr. V. pedicure

**Pegel** der; ∼s, ∼ **(a)** water level indicator; (Tide∼) tide gauge
**(b)** (Wasserstand) water level

**peilen** tr. V. take a bearing on (transmitter, fixed point)

**Pein** die; ∼ (geh.) torment

**peinigen** tr. V. (geh.) torment; (foltern) torture

**peinlich** [1] Adj. **(a)** embarrassing; awkward (question, position, pause); **es ist mir sehr ∼:** I feel very bad (coll.) or embarrassed about it
**(b)** (äußerst genau) meticulous
[2] adv. **(a)** unpleasantly (surprised)
**(b)** (überaus [genau]) meticulously

**Peinlichkeit** die; ∼, ∼en **(a)** embarrassment; **die ∼ der Situation** the awkwardness of the situation
**(b)** (Genauigkeit) meticulousness
**(c)** (peinliche Situation) embarrassing situation

**Peitsche** die; ∼, ∼n whip

**peitschen** tr. V. whip; (fig.) (storm, waves, rain) lash

**Pelikan** der; ∼s, ∼e pelican

**Pelle** die; ∼, ∼n (bes. nordd.) skin; (abgeschält) peel

**pellen** (bes. nordd.) tr., refl. V. peel

**Pell·kartoffel** die potato boiled in its skin

**Pelz** der; ∼es, ∼e **(a)** fur; coat; (des toten Tieres) skin; pelt
**(b)** (Material) fur; (∼mantel) fur coat

**Pelz·mantel** der fur coat

**Pendel** das; ∼s, ∼: pendulum

**pendeln** itr. V. **(a)** swing [to and fro]; (mit weniger Bewegung) dangle
**(b)** mit sein (bus, ferry, etc.) operate a shuttle service; (person) commute

**Pendler** der; ∼s, ∼, **Pendlerin** die; ∼, ∼nen commuter

**penetrant** [1] Adj. **(a)** penetrating (smell, taste); overpowering (stink, perfume)
**(b)** (aufdringlich) pushing, (coll.) pushy (person); overbearing (tone, manner); aggressive (question)
[2] adv. **(a)** overpoweringly
**(b)** (aufdringlich) overbearingly

**penibel** [1] Adj. over-meticulous (person); (pedantisch) pedantic
[2] adv. painstakingly; over-meticulously (dressed)

**Penis** der; ∼, ∼se penis

**pennen** itr. V. (salopp) **(a)** (schlafen) kip (coll.)
**(b)** (fig.: nicht aufpassen) be half asleep
**(c)** (koitieren) **mit jmdm. ∼:** sleep with sb.

**Penner** der; ∼s, ∼, **Pennerin** die; ∼, ∼nen (salopp) tramp (Brit.); hobo (Amer.)

**Pensen** ▸ PENSUM

**Pension** /pãˈzi̯oːn/ die; ∼, ∼en **(a)** (Ruhestand) **in ∼ gehen** retire; **in ∼ sein** be retired
**(b)** (Ruhegehalt) [retirement] pension
**(c)** (Haus für [Ferien]gäste) guest house
**(d)** (Unterkunft u. Verpflegung) board

**Pensionär** /pãzi̯oˈnɛːɐ̯/ der; ∼s, ∼e, **Pensionärin** die; ∼, ∼nen retired civil servant

**pensionieren** tr. V. pension off; retire; **sich [vorzeitig] ∼ lassen** take [early] retirement; **ein pensionierter Schulmeister/Politiker** a retired schoolmaster/politician

**Pensionierung** die; ∼, ∼en retirement

**Pensions-:** ∼**alter** das retirement age; ∼**anspruch** der pension entitlement

**Pensum** das; ∼s, **Pensen** work quota

**per** Präp. mit Akk. **(a)** (mittels) by; **∼ Adresse X** care of X; c/o X
**(b)** (Kaufmannsspr.: [bis] zum) by; (am) on
**(c)** (Kaufmannsspr.: pro) per

**perfekt** [1] Adj. **(a)** perfect (crime, host); faultless (English, French, etc.)
**(b)** ∼ **sein** (ugs.: abgeschlossen, fertig sein) be finalized
[2] adv. perfectly

**Perfekt** das; ∼s (Sprachw.) perfect

**Perfektion** die; ∼: perfection

**perfektionieren** tr. V. perfect

**Perfektionismus** der; ∼: perfectionism

**Perfektionist** der; ∼en, ∼en, **Perfektionistin** die; ∼, ∼nen perfectionist

**perfektionistisch** [1] Adj. perfectionist (standards etc.)
[2] adv. in a perfectionist manner

**Pergament·papier** *das* greaseproof paper

**Periode** *die;* ~, ~n period

**Perle** *die;* ~, ~n **(a)** (auch fig.) pearl
**(b)** (aus Holz, Glas o. Ä.) bead

**Perlmutt** *das;* ~s mother-of-pearl

**Perlon** ⓦ *das;* ~s ≈ nylon

**Perser** *der;* ~s, ~ **(a)** Persian
**(b)** ▶ PERSERTEPPICH

**Perserin** *die;* ~, ~nen Persian

**Perser·teppich** *der* Persian carpet

**Persianer** *der;* ~s, ~ (Mantel) Persian lamb
coat

**Persien** (*das*) ~s Persia

**persisch** *Adj.* Persian

**Person** *die;* ~, ~en person; (in der Dichtung,
im Film) character

**Personal** *das;* ~s (in einem Betrieb o. Ä.) staff;
(im Haushalt) domestic staff *pl.*

**Personal-:** ~**abbau** *der* reduction in
staff; (in mehreren Abteilungen/Betrieben) staff cuts
*pl.;* ~**abteilung** *die* personnel department;
~**ausweis** *der* identity card; ~**büro** *das*
personnel office; ~**chef** *der,* ~**chefin** *die*
personnel manager

**Personalien** *Pl.* personal particulars

**Personal-:** ~**kosten** *Pl.* (Wirtsch.,
Verwaltung) staff costs; ~**mangel** *der* staff
shortage; ~**pronomen** *das* (Sprachw.)
personal pronoun; ~**rat** *der* **(a)** (Ausschuss)
staff council (*for civil servants*); **(b)** (Mitglied)
staff council representative; ~**rätin** *die;*
▶ ~RAT B

**Personen-:** ~**kraftwagen** *der* (bes.
Amtsspr.) private car *or* (Amer.) automobile;
~**name** *der* personal name; ~**wagen** *der*
(Auto) [private] car; automobile (Amer.); (im
Unterschied zum Lastwagen) passenger car *or*
(Amer.) automobile; ~**zug** *der* stopping train

**Personifikation** *die;* ~, ~en
personification

**personifizieren** *tr. V.* personify

**Personifizierung** *die;* ~, ~en
personification

**persönlich** ① *Adj.* personal; ~ werden get
personal
② *adv.* personally; (auf Briefen) 'private [and
confidential]'

**Persönlichkeit** *die;* ~, ~en **(a)**
personality
**(b)** (Mensch) person of character; eine ~ sein
have a strong personality; ~en des
öffentlichen Lebens public figures

**Perspektive** *die;* ~, ~n perspective;
(Blickwinkel) angle; (Zukunftsaussicht) prospect

**Peru** (*das*) ~s Peru

**Peruaner** *der;* ~s, ~, **Peruanerin** *die;*
~, ~nen Peruvian

**peruanisch** *Adj.* Peruvian

**Perücke** *die;* ~, ~n wig

**pervers** *Adj.* perverted

**Perversion** *die;* ~, ~en perversion

**Pessimismus** *der;* ~: pessimism

**Pessimist** *der;* ~en, ~en, **Pessimistin**
*die;* ~, ~nen pessimist

**pessimistisch** ① *Adj.* pessimistic
② *adv.* pessimistically

**Pest** *die;* ~: plague

**Pestizid** *das;* ~s, ~e pesticide

**Petersilie** /petɐˈziːliə/ *die;* ~: parsley

**Petition** *die;* ~, ~en (Amtsspr.) petition

**Petroleum** /peˈtroːleʊm/ *das;* ~s paraffin
(Brit.); kerosene (Amer.)

**Petrus** (*der*)*;* **Petri** (christl. Rel.: Apostel) St
Peter

**petzen** (Schülerspr.) ① *itr. V.* tell tales; sneak
(Brit. school coll.)
② *tr. V.* ~, dass …: tell teacher/sb.'s parents
that …

**Pf** *Abk.* = **Pfennig**

**Pfad** *der;* ~[e]s, ~e path

**Pfad-:** ~**finder** *der* Scout; ~**finderin** *die;*
~, ~nen Guide (Brit.); girl scout (Amer.)

**Pfaffe** *der;* ~n, ~n (abwertend) cleric; Holy
Joe (derog.)

**Pfahl** *der;* ~[e]s, Pfähle post; stake

**Pfand** *das;* ~[e]s, Pfänder **(a)** security;
pledge (esp. fig.)
**(b)** (für Flaschen usw.) deposit (auf + *Dat.* on)

**pfänden** *tr. V.* seize [under distress] (Law)
⟨*goods, chattels*⟩; attach ⟨*wages etc.*⟩ (Law)

**Pfand·flasche** *die* returnable bottle (*on
which a deposit is payable*)

**Pfändung** *die;* ~, ~en seizure; distraint
(Law); (von Geldsummen, Vermögensrechten)
attachment (Law)

**Pfanne** *die;* ~, ~n [frying] pan

**Pfann·kuchen** *der* **(a)** pancake
**(b)** (Berliner) doughnut

**Pfarrei** *die;* ~, ~en **(a)** (Bezirk) parish
**(b)** (Dienststelle) parish office
**(c)** ▶ PFARRHAUS

**Pfarrer** *der;* ~s, ~ pastor; (anglikanisch)
vicar; (von Freikirchen) minister

**Pfarrerin** *die;* ~, ~nen [woman] pastor; (in
Freikirchen) [woman] minister

**Pfarr·haus** *das* vicarage; (katholisch)
presbytery; (in Schottland) manse

**Pfau** *der;* ~[e]s, ~en peacock

**Pfauen·auge** *das* peacock butterfly

**Pfd.** *Abk.* = **Pfund** lb.

**Pfeffer** *der;* ~s, ~: pepper

**Pfeffer-:** ~**kuchen** *der* ≈ gingerbread;
~**minze** *die* peppermint [plant];
~**minz·tee** *der* peppermint tea; ~**mühle**
*die* pepper mill

**pfeffern** *tr. V.* season with pepper

**Pfeffer·streuer** *der;* ~s, ~: pepper pot

**Pfeife** *die;* ~, ~n pipe; (Triller~) whistle

**pfeifen** ① *unr. itr. V.* whistle; ⟨*bird*⟩ sing;

(auf einer Trillerpfeife o. Ä.) ⟨*policeman, referee, etc.*⟩ blow one's whistle; **auf jmdn./etw.** ∼ (ugs.) not give a damn about sb./sth. ② *unr. tr. V.* whistle ⟨*tune etc.*⟩; ⟨*bird*⟩ sing ⟨*song*⟩; (auf einer Pfeife) pipe, play ⟨*tune etc.*⟩

**Pfeil** *der;* ∼[e]s, ∼e arrow

**Pfeiler** *der;* ∼s, ∼: pillar; (Brücken∼) pier

**Pfennig** *der;* ∼s, ∼e pfennig; **es kostete damals 20** ∼: it cost 20 pfennig[s] at that time

**pferchen** *tr. V.* cram; pack

**Pferd** *das;* ∼[e]s, ∼e horse; (Schachfigur) knight; **mit ihr kann man** ∼**e stehlen** (ugs.) she's game for anything

**Pferde-:** ∼**rennen** *das* horse race; (Sportart) horseracing; ∼**schwanz** *der* (Frisur) ponytail; ∼**stall** *der* stable

**pfiff** *1. u. 3. Pers. Sg. Prät. v.* PFEIFEN

**Pfiff** *der;* ∼[e]s, ∼e **(a)** whistle **(b)** (ugs.: besonderer Reiz) style

**Pfifferling** *der;* ∼s, ∼e chanterelle; **keinen** *od.* **nicht einen** ∼ **wert sein** (ugs.) be not worth a bean (coll.)

**pfiffig** ① *Adj.* smart; bright ⟨*idea*⟩; artful ⟨*smile, expression*⟩ ② *adv.* artfully

**Pfingsten** *das;* ∼, ∼: Whitsun

**Pfingst-:** ∼**montag** *der* Whit Monday *no def. art.;* ∼**sonntag** *der* Whit Sunday *no def. art.*

**Pfirsich** *der;* ∼s, ∼e peach

**Pflanze** *die;* ∼, ∼n plant

**pflanzen** *tr. V.* plant

**Pflanzen-öl** *das* vegetable oil

**pflanzlich** *Adj.* plant *attrib.* ⟨*life, motif*⟩; vegetable ⟨*dye, fat*⟩

**Pflaster** *das;* ∼s, ∼ **(a)** (Straßen∼) road surface; (auf dem Gehsteig) pavement; **ein teures/gefährliches** ∼ (ugs.) an expensive/ dangerous place *or* spot to be **(b)** (Wund∼) sticking plaster

**pflastern** *tr.* (*auch itr.*) *V.* surface; (mit Kopfsteinpflaster, Steinplatten) pave

**Pflaster-stein** *der* paving stone; (Kopfstein) cobblestone

**Pflaume** *die;* ∼, ∼n plum; **getrocknete** ∼**n** [dried] prunes

**Pflege** *die;* ∼: care; (Maschinen∼, Fahrzeug∼) maintenance; (fig.: von Beziehungen, Kunst, Sprache) cultivation; **jmdn./etw. in** ∼ (*Akk.*) **nehmen** look after sb./sth.

**pflege-, Pflege-:** ∼**bedürftig** *Adj.* needing care *or* attention *postpos.;* ⟨*person*⟩ in need of care; ∼**bedürftig sein** need looking after; need attention; ∼**eltern** *Pl.* foster-parents; ∼**fall** *der:* **ein** ∼**fall sein** be in [permanent] need of nursing; ∼**heim** *das* nursing home (esp. Brit.); ∼**kind** *das* foster-child; ∼**leicht** *Adj.* easy-care *attrib.* ⟨*textiles, flooring*⟩

**pflegen** ① *tr. V.* look after; care for; take care of ⟨*skin, teeth, floor*⟩; look after ⟨*bicycle,*

*car, machine*⟩; look after, tend ⟨*garden, plants*⟩; cultivate ⟨*relations, arts, interests*⟩; foster ⟨*contacts, cooperation*⟩; pursue ⟨*hobby*⟩ ② *mod. V.* **etw. zu tun** ∼: usually do sth.

**Pflege-personal** *das* nursing staff

**Pfleger** *der;* ∼s, ∼ **(a)** (Krankenpfleger) [male] nurse **(b)** (Tierpfleger) keeper

**Pflegerin** *die;* ∼, ∼nen **(a)** (Krankenpflegerin) nurse **(b)** (Tierpflegerin) keeper

**Pflege-versicherung** *die* (*long-term*) [nursing-]care insurance

**Pflicht** *die;* ∼, ∼en duty

**pflicht-, Pflicht-:** ∼**bewusst,** *\**∼**bewußt** ① *Adj.* conscientious; ② *adv.* with a sense of duty; ∼**bewusstsein,** *\**∼**bewußtsein** *das,* sense of duty; ∼**fach** *das* compulsory subject; ∼**gefühl** *das* sense of duty; ∼**übung** *die* (fig.) ritual exercise; ∼**verteidiger** *der,* ∼**verteidigerin** *die* (Rechtsw.) *defense counsel appointed by the court;* assigned counsel

**Pflock** *der;* ∼[e]s, Pflöcke peg

**pflücken** *tr. V.* pick

**Pflug** *der;* ∼[e]s, Pflüge plough

**pflügen** *tr.,* *itr. V.* plough

**Pforte** *die;* ∼, ∼n (Tor) gate; (Tür) door; (Eingang) entrance

**Pförtner** *der;* ∼s, ∼, **Pförtnerin** *die;* ∼, ∼nen porter; (eines Wohnblocks, Büros) doorkeeper; (am Tor) gatekeeper

**Pförtner-loge** *die* porter's lodge

**Pfosten** *der;* ∼s, ∼: post

**Pfote** *die;* ∼, ∼n paw

**Pfropf** *der;* ∼[e]s, ∼e blockage

**pfropfen** *tr. V.* (ugs.) cram; stuff; **gepfropft voll** crammed [full]; packed

**Pfropfen** *der;* ∼s, ∼: stopper; (Korken) cork; (für Fässer) bung

**pfui** *Interj.* ugh; ∼ **rufen** boo

**Pfund** *das;* ∼[e]s, ∼e pound

**Pfusch** *der;* ∼[e]s **(a)** (ugs. abwertend) **das ist** ∼: it's a botch-up **(b)** (österr.: Schwarzarbeit) work done on the side (*and not declared for tax*); (nach Feierabend) moonlighting (coll.)

**pfuschen** *itr. V.* **(a)** (ugs. abwertend) botch it; do a botched-up job **(b)** (österr.: schwarzarbeiten) do work on the side (*not declared for tax*); (nach Feierabend) moonlight (coll.)

**Pfütze** *die;* ∼, ∼n puddle

**Phänomen** *das;* ∼s, ∼e phenomenon

**Phantasie** *usw.:* ▶ FANTASIE *usw.*

**Pharma-:** ∼**berater** *der,* ∼**beraterin** *die:* ▶ ∼REFERENT; ∼**industrie** *die* pharmaceutical industry

**Pharmakologie** *die;* ∼: pharmacology *no art.*

**Pharma·referent** *der*,
**Pharma·referentin** *die* pharmaceutical
representative
**pharmazeutisch** *Adj.* pharmaceutical
**Phase** *die;* ~, ~n phase
**Philosoph** *der;* ~en, ~en philosopher
**Philosophie** *die;* ~, ~n philosophy
**philosophieren** *itr.* (*auch tr.*) *V.*
philosophize
**Philosophin** *die;* ~, ~nen philosopher
**philosophisch** ①*Adj.* philosophical;
⟨*dictionary, principles*⟩ of philosophy
②*adv.* philosophically
**Phosphat** *das;* ~[e]s, ~e (Chemie)
phosphate
**Photo** *das;* ~s, ~s ▶ FOTO
**Phrase** *die;* ~, ~n (abwertend) [empty]
phrase; cliché
**Physik** *die;* ~: physics *sing., no art.*
**physikalisch** *Adj.* physics *attrib.*
⟨*experiment, formula, research, institute*⟩;
physical ⟨*map, process*⟩
**Physiker** *der;* ~s, ~, **Physikerin** *die;* ~,
~nen physicist
**physisch** ①*Adj.* physical
②*adv.* physically
**Pianist** *der;* ~en, ~en, **Pianistin** *die;* ~,
~nen pianist
**Pickel** *der;* ~s, ~: pimple
**picken** ①*itr.* *V.* peck (**nach** at; **an** + *Akk.*,
**gegen** on, against)
②*tr.* *V.* ⟨*bird*⟩ peck; (ugs.) ⟨*person*⟩ pick
**Picknick** *das;* ~s, ~e *od.* ~s picnic
**piek·fein** (ugs.) ①*Adj.* posh (coll.)
②*adv.* poshly (coll.)
**piepe, piep·egal** *Adj.* [jmdm.] ~ **sein**
(ugs.) not matter at all [to sb.]; **es ist mir** ~
(ugs.) I don't give a damn
**Piepen** *Pl.* (salopp: Geld) dough *sing.* (coll.)
**piep[s]en** *itr.* *V.* (ugs.) squeak; ⟨*small bird*⟩
cheep; **bei dir piept's wohl!** (salopp) you must
be off your rocker (coll.); **zum Piepen sein**
(ugs.) be a hoot *or* a scream (coll.)
**Pietät** /piɛˈtɛːt/ *die;* ~: respect; (Ehrfurcht)
reverence
**Pik** *das;* ~[s], ~[s] (Kartenspiel) **(a)** (Farbe)
spades *pl.;*
**(b)** (Karte) spade
**pikant** ①*Adj.* **(a)** piquant
**(b)** (fig.: witzig) ironical
**(c)** (verhüll.: schlüpfrig) racy ⟨*joke, story*⟩
②*adv.* piquantly ⟨*seasoned*⟩
**pikiert** ①*Adj.* piqued
②*adv.* ⟨*reply, say*⟩ in an aggrieved tone
**Pilger** *der;* ~s, ~, **Pilgerin** *die;* ~, ~nen
pilgrim
**pilgern** *itr.* *V.* go on a pilgrimage
**Pille** *die;* ~, ~n pill
**Pilot** *der;* ~en, ~en, **Pilotin** *die;* ~, ~nen
pilot

**Pils** *das;* ~, ~: Pils
**Pilz** *der;* ~es, ~e fungus; (Speise~, auch fig.)
mushroom
**Pinguin** *der;* ~s, ~e penguin
**Pinie** /ˈpiːnjə/ *die;* ~, ~n [stone *or*
umbrella] pine
**pinkeln** *itr.* *V.* (salopp) pee (coll.)
**Pinsel** *der;* ~s, ~: brush; (Mal~) paintbrush
**Pinzette** *die;* ~, ~n tweezers *pl.*
**Pionier** *der;* ~s, ~e (Milit.) sapper; (fig.:
Wegbereiter) pioneer
**Pionierin** *die;* ~, ~nen pioneer
**Pionier·arbeit** *die* pioneering work
**Pipi** *das;* ~s (Kinderspr.) ~ **machen** do wee-
wees (sl.); ~ **müssen** have to do wee-wees *or*
have a wee (sl.)
**Pirat** *der;* ~en, ~en, **Piratin** *die;* ~, ~nen
pirate
**pissen** *itr.* *V.* (derb) piss (coarse)
**Pistazie** /pɪsˈtaːtsiə/ *die;* ~, ~n pistachio
**Piste** *die;* ~, ~n (Ski~) piste; (Renn~)
course; (Flugw.) runway
**Pistole** *die;* ~, ~n pistol
**Pizza** *die;* ~, ~s *od.* Pizzen pizza
**Pkw, PKW** /ˈpeːkaːveː/ *der;* ~[s], ~[s]
[private] car; automobile (Amer.)
**plädieren** *itr.* *V.* (Rechtsw.) plead (**auf** + *Akk.*
for); (fig.) argue
**Plädoyer** /plɛdoaˈjeː/ *das;* ~s, ~s (Rechtsw.)
summing up (*for the defence/prosecution*);
(fig.) plea
**Plage** *die;* ~, ~n **(a)** nuisance
**(b)** (ugs.: Mühe) bother; trouble
**plagen** ①*tr.* *V.* **(a)** torment
**(b)** (ugs.: bedrängen) harass; (mit Bitten, Fragen)
pester
②*refl.* *V.* **(a)** (sich abmühen) slave away
**(b)** (leiden) **sich mit etw.** ~: be bothered by
sth.
**Plagiat** *das;* ~[e]s, ~e plagiarism *no art.*
**Plakat** *das;* ~[e]s, ~e poster
**Plakette** *die;* ~, ~n badge
**Plan** *der;* ~[e]s, Pläne **(a)** plan
**(b)** (Karte) map; plan
**Plane** *die;* ~, ~n tarpaulin
**planen** *tr., itr.* *V.* plan
**Planet** *der;* ~en, ~en planet
**planieren** *tr.* *V.* level; grade
**Planier·raupe** *die* bulldozer
**Planke** *die;* ~, ~n plank
**plan·:** ~**los** ①*Adj.* aimless; (ohne System)
unsystematic; ②*adv.* ▶1: aimlessly;
unsystematically; ~**mäßig** ①*Adj.* **(a)**
scheduled ⟨*service, steamer*⟩; ~**mäßige**
**Ankunft/Abfahrt** scheduled time of arrival/
departure; **(b)** (systematisch) systematic
②*adv.* **(a)** (wie geplant) according to plan;
(pünktlich) on schedule; **(b)** (systematisch)
systematically
**Plansch·becken** *das* paddling pool
**planschen** *itr.* *V.* splash [about]

**Plantage** /plan'ta:ʒə/ die; ~, ~n plantation

**Planung** die; ~, ~en planning

**Plan·wirtschaft** die planned economy

**Plastik¹** die; ~, ~en sculpture

**Plastik²** das; ~s (ugs.) plastic

**Plastik·beutel** der, **Plastik·tüte** die plastic bag

**Platane** die; ~, ~n plane tree

**Platin** das; ~s platinum

**platschen** itr. V. (a) splash
(b) mit sein (~d auftreffen) splash (an + Akk., gegen against)

**plätschern** itr. V. (a) splash; ⟨rain⟩ patter; ⟨stream⟩ burble
(b) mit sein ⟨stream⟩ burble along

**platt** Adj. flat; **ein Platter** (ugs.) a flat (coll.); etw. ~ **machen** (salopp abwertend) close sth. down

**Platt** das; ~[s] [local] Low German dialect

**Plättchen** das; ~s, ~: small plate or disc

**platt·deutsch** Adj. Low German

**Platte** die; ~, ~n (a) (Stein~) slab; (Metall~) plate; sheet; (Span~, Hartfaser~ usw.) board; (Tisch~) [table] top; (Grab~) [memorial] slab
(b) (Koch~) hotplate
(c) (Schall~) [gramophone] record
(d) (Teller) plate; (zum Servieren, aus Metall) dish; **kalte** ~: selection of cold meats [and cheese]

**Platten·spieler** der record player

**Platt·fuß** der (a) flat foot
(b) (ugs.: Reifenpanne) flat (coll.)

**Platz** der; ~es, Plätze (a) square
(b) (Sport~) ground; (Spielfeld) field; (Tennis~, Volleyball~ usw.) court; (Golf~) course
(c) (Stelle, wo jmd., etw. hingehört) place; **nicht** od. **fehl am** ~[e] **sein** (fig.) be out of place
(d) (Sitz~) seat; (am Tisch, Steh~ usw.) place; ~ **nehmen** sit down
(e) (bes. Sport: Platzierung) place
(f) (Ort) place; **am** ~: in the town/village
(g) (Raum) space; room; ~ **machen** make room (Dat. for)

**Platz·angst** die (volkst.: Klaustrophobie) claustrophobia

**Plätzchen** das; ~s, ~ (a) little place
(b) (Keks) biscuit (Brit.); cookie (Amer.)

**platzen** itr. V.; mit sein (a) burst; (explodieren) explode
(b) (ugs.: scheitern) fall through; **der Wechsel/ das Treffen ist geplatzt** the bill has bounced (coll.)/the meeting is off
(c) **in eine Versammlung** ~ (ugs.) burst into a meeting

**Platz-: ~karte** die reserved-seat ticket; ~**konzert** das open-air concert (by a military or brass band); ~**mangel** der lack of space; ~**not** die [acute] lack of space; ~**regen** der cloudburst; ~**wunde** die lacerated wound

**Plauderei** die; ~, ~en chat

**plaudern** itr. V. chat

**plausibel** Adj. plausible

**Play·boy** /'pleɪbɔɪ/ der playboy

**Player** /'pleɪɐ/ der: ~, ~: player

**pleite** (ugs.) ~ **sein** ⟨person⟩ be broke (coll.); ⟨company⟩ have gone bust (coll.); s. auch PLEITE A

**Pleite** die; ~, ~n (ugs.) (a) (Bankrott) bankruptcy no def. art.; ~ **gehen/machen** go bust (coll.)
(b) (Misserfolg) washout (coll.)

**Pleite-: ~geier** der (ugs.) spectre of bankruptcy; ~**wirtschaft** die (ugs.) bankrupt economy

**Plissee** das; ~s, ~s accordion pleats pl.

**Plombe** die; ~, ~n (a) (Siegel) [lead] seal
(b) (veralt.: Zahnfüllung) filling

**plombieren** tr. V. (a) (versiegeln) seal
(b) (veralt.) fill ⟨tooth⟩

**plötzlich** ① Adj. sudden
② adv. suddenly

**Plötzlichkeit** die; ~: suddenness

**plump** ① Adj. (a) (dick) plump; (unförmig) ungainly ⟨shape⟩; (rundlich) bulbous
(b) (schwerfällig) clumsy ⟨movements, style⟩
(c) (fig.) (dreist) crude ⟨lie, deception, trick⟩; (leicht durchschaubar) blatantly obvious; (unbeholfen) clumsy ⟨excuse, advances⟩; crude ⟨joke, forgery⟩
② adv. (a) (schwerfällig) clumsily
(b) (fig.) in a blatantly obvious manner

**Plumpheit** die; ~ (a) (Dicke) plumpness; (Unförmigkeit) ungainliness; (Rundlichkeit) bulbousness
(b) (Schwerfälligkeit) clumsiness
(c) (abwertend: Dreistigkeit) blatant nature

**plumps** Interj. bump; thud; (ins Wasser) splash; ~ **machen** go bump

**Plumps** der; ~es, ~e (ugs.) bump; thud; (ins Wasser) splash

**plumpsen** itr. V. fall with a bump; thud; (ins Wasser) splash

**Plünderer** der; ~s, ~, **Plünderin** die; ~, ~nen looter

**plündern** itr., tr. V. (a) loot; plunder ⟨town⟩
(b) (scherzh.) raid ⟨larder, fridge, account⟩

**Plünderung** die; ~, ~en looting; (einer Stadt) plundering; ~en cases of looting/ plundering

**Plural** der; ~s, ~e plural

**Pluralismus** der; ~: pluralism

**pluralistisch** ① Adj. pluralistic
② adv. pluralistically; along pluralistic lines

**plus** Konj., Adv. plus

**Plus** das; ~: surplus; (Vorteil) advantage

**Plüsch** der; ~[e]s, ~e plush

**Plusquam·perfekt** das pluperfect [tense]

**PLZ** Abk. = Postleitzahl

**Po** der; ~s, ~s (ugs.) bottom

**Pöbel** der; ~s rabble

**pöbeln** itr. V. make rude or coarse remarks

**pochen** *itr. V.* (klopfen) knock (**gegen**/**an** +
*Akk.* at, on); (geh.: pulsieren) ⟨*heart*⟩ pound
**Pocken** *Pl.* smallpox *sing.*
**Podest** *das od. der;* ∼[e]s, ∼e rostrum
**Podium** *das;* ∼s, Podien (Plattform) platform;
(Bühne) stage; (trittartige Erhöhung) rostrum
**Poesie** *die;* ∼: poetry
**Poet** *der;* ∼en, ∼en (veralt.) poet; bard
(literary)
**poetisch** ⒈ *Adj.* poetic[al]
⒉ *adv.* poetically
**Pogrom** *das od. der;* ∼s, ∼e pogrom
**Pointe** /'po̯ɛ̃:tə/ *die;* ∼, ∼n (eines Witzes)
punch line; (einer Geschichte) point; (eines
Sketches) curtain line
**pointiert** /po̯ɛ̃'ti:ɐ̯t/⒈ *Adj.* pointed
⟨*remark*⟩
⒉ *adv.* pointedly
**Pokal** *der;* ∼s, ∼e (a) (Trinkgefäß) goblet
(b) (Siegestrophäe, ∼wettbewerb) cup
**Pökel·fleisch** *das* salt meat
**pökeln** *tr. V.* salt
**Poker** *das od. der;* ∼s poker
**Poker·gesicht** *das* poker face
**pokern** *itr. V.* play poker
**Pol** *der;* ∼s, ∼e pole
**Polar·licht** *das* aurora; polar lights *pl.*
**Polaroid·kamera** Ⓦ *die* Polaroid
camera ®
**Pole** *der;* ∼n, ∼n Pole
**polemisch** ⒈ *Adj.* polemic[al]
⒉ *adv.* polemically
**Polen** *das;* ∼s Poland
**Polente** *die;* ∼ (salopp) cops *pl.* (coll.)
**Police** /po'li:sə/ *die;* ∼, ∼n (Versicherungsw.)
policy
**polieren** *tr. V.* polish
**Poli·klinik** *die* outpatients' clinic
**Polin** *die;* ∼n, ∼nen Pole
**Polit·büro** *das* politburo
**Politik** *die;* ∼, ∼en (a) politics *sing.*, no art.
(b) (eine spezielle ∼) policy
**Politiker** *der;* ∼s, ∼, **Politikerin** *die;* ∼,
∼nen politician
**politisch** ⒈ *Adj.* political
⒉ *adv.* politically
**politisieren** ⒈ *itr. V.* talk politics
⒉ *tr. V.* make politically active
**Politur** *die;* ∼, ∼en polish
**Polizei** *die;* ∼, ∼en police *pl.*
**Polizei-:** ∼**auto** *das* police car;
∼**beamte** *der* police officer; ∼**kontrolle**
*die* police check
**polizeilich** ⒈ *Adj.* police; ∼e Meldepflicht
obligation to register with the police
⒉ *adv.* by the police
**Polizei-:** ∼**präsidium** *das* police
headquarters *sing. or pl.*; ∼**revier** *das*

police station; ∼**streife** *die* police patrol;
∼**stunde** *die* closing time; ∼**wache** *die*
police station
**Polizist** *der;* ∼en, ∼en policeman
**Polizistin** *die;* ∼, ∼nen policewoman
**Pollen** *der;* ∼s, ∼ (Bot.) pollen
**Poller** *der;* ∼s, ∼: bollard
**polnisch** *Adj.* Polish
**Polster** *das;* ∼s, ∼: upholstery no pl., no
indef. art.
**Polster·möbel** *Pl.* upholstered furniture
*sing.*
**polstern** *tr. V.* upholster ⟨*furniture*⟩
**poltern** *itr. V.* (a) crash about
(b) mit sein der Karren polterte über das
Pflaster the cart clattered over the
cobblestones
**Polyp** *der;* ∼en, ∼en (Zool., Med.) polyp
**Pommern** (*das*); ∼s Pomerania
**Pommes frites** /pɔm'frit/ *Pl.* chips (Brit.);
French fries (Amer.)
**pompös** ⒈ *Adj.* grandiose
⒉ *adv.* grandiosely
**Pony**[1] /'pɔni/ *das;* ∼s, ∼s pony
**Pony**[2] *der;* ∼s, ∼s (Frisur) fringe
**Popel** *der;* ∼s, ∼ (ugs.) bogy (sl.)
**popelig** (ugs. abwertend) ⒈ *Adj.* crummy
(coll.); lousy (coll.); (durchschnittlich) second-rate
⒉ *adv.* crummily (sl.)
**Popeline·mantel** *der* poplin coat
**popeln** *itr. V.* (ugs.) [in der Nase] ∼: pick
one's nose
**Pop-:** ∼**musik** *die* pop music; ∼**star** *der*
pop star
**populär** ⒈ *Adj.* popular (**bei** with)
⒉ *adv.* popularly
**popularisieren** *tr. V.* popularize
**Popularität** *die;* ∼: popularity
**Pore** *die;* ∼, ∼n pore
**Porno** *der;* ∼s, ∼s (ugs.) porn[o] film/
magazine *etc.*
**Pornographie** *die;* ∼: pornography
**pornographisch** ⒈ *Adj.* pornographic
⒉ *adv.* pornographically
**Porree** *der;* ∼s leek
**Portal** *das;* ∼s, ∼e portal
**Portemonnaie** /pɔrtmɔ'ne:/ *das;* ∼s, ∼s
purse
**Porti** *Pl.* ▶ PORTO
**Portier** /pɔr'tje:/ *der;* ∼s, ∼s, österr.:
/pɔr'ti:ɐ̯/ *der;* ∼s, ∼e porter
**Portion** /pɔr'ts:i̯o:n/ *die;* ∼, ∼en (a) (beim
Essen) portion; helping
(b) (ugs.: Anteil) amount
**Porto** *das;* ∼s, ∼s od. Porti postage (**für** on,
for)
**Portugal** (*das*); ∼s Portugal
**Portugiese** *der;* ∼n, ∼n, **Portugiesin**
*die;* ∼, ∼nen Portuguese
**portugiesisch** *Adj.* Portuguese
**Portwein** *der* port

**Porzellan** *das;* ~s porcelain; china
**Posaune** *die;* ~, ~n trombone
**Position** /pozi'tsɪoːn/ *die;* ~, ~en position
**positiv** [1] *Adj.* positive
  [2] *adv.* positively
**Positiv** *das;* ~s, ~e (Fot.) positive
**Possessiv·pronomen** *das* (Sprachw.)
possessive pronoun
**Post** *die;* ~, ~en (a) post (Brit.); mail; **etw.
mit der** *od.* **per** ~ **schicken** send sth. by post
*or* mail; **die** ~ **geht ab** (fig. ugs.) it's all
happening; **ab 20 Uhr geht die** ~ **ab** (fig. ugs.)
it'll all be happening from 8 o'clock; **auch
beim Publikum geht die** ~ **ab** (fig. ugs.) the
audience is having a ball too (coll.)
  (b) (Postamt) post office
**Post-:** ~**amt** *das* post office;
~**anweisung** *die* postal remittance form;
~**auto** *das* mail van; ~**bote** *der* (ugs.)
postman (Brit.); mailman (Amer.); ~**botin** *die*
(ugs.) postwoman (Brit.); mailwoman (Amer.)
**Posten** *der;* ~s, ~ (a) post
  (b) (bes. Milit.: Wachmann) sentry
**post-, Post-:** ~**fach** *das* post office *or* PO
box; (im Büro, Hotel usw.) pigeonhole; ~**karte**
*die* postcard; ~**lagernd** *Adj., adv.* poste
restante; general delivery (Amer.);
~**leit·zahl** *die* postcode; Zip code (Amer.);
~**stempel** *der* (Abdruck) postmark;
~**wendend** *Adv.* by return [of post]
**potent** *Adj.* potent
**Potenz** *die;* ~, ~en (a) potency
  (b) (Math.) power
**potenzieren** *tr. V.* (Math.) **mit 5** ~**:** raise to
the power [of] 5
**Pracht** *die;* ~: splendour
**prächtig, pracht·voll** [1] *Adj.* splendid
  [2] *adv.* splendidly
**prädestiniert** *Adj.* predestined
**Prädikat** *das;* ~[e]s, ~e (a) (Auszeichnung)
rating
  (b) (Sprachw.) predicate
**Prag** *(das)* ~s Prague
**prägen** *tr. V.* (a) emboss
  (b) mint ‹coin›
  (c) (fig.: beeinflussen) shape
**prägnant** [1] *Adj.* concise; succinct
  [2] *adv.* concisely; succinctly
**Prägung** *die;* ~, ~en embossing; (von
Münzen) minting
**prahlen** *itr. V.* boast, brag (mit about)
**Prahler** *der;* ~s, ~: boaster; braggart
**Prahlerei** *die;* ~, ~en (abwertend) boasting;
bragging; ~en boasts
**Prahlerin** *die;* ~, ~nen boaster; braggart
**Praktik** *die;* ~, ~en practice
**Praktika** ▶ PRAKTIKUM
**praktikabel** *Adj.* practicable; practical
**Praktikant** *der;* ~en, ~en,
  **Praktikantin** *die;* ~, ~nen (a) (in einem
Betrieb) student trainee

  (b) (an der Hochschule) physics/chemistry
student (doing a period of practical training)
**Praktikum** *das;* ~s, **Praktika** period of
practical training
**praktisch** [1] *Adj.* practical; ~**er Arzt**
general practitioner
  [2] *adv.* practically; (auf die Praxis bezogen;
wirklich) in practice
**praktizieren** *tr. V.* practise
**Praline** *die;* ~, ~n [filled] chocolate
**prall** *Adj.* (a) hard ‹ball›; bulging ‹sack,
wallet, bag›; big strong attrib. ‹thighs,
muscles, calves›; well-rounded ‹breasts›
  (b) (intensiv) blazing ‹sun›
**prallen** *itr. V.; mit sein* crash (**gegen/auf/an**
+ *Akk.* into); collide (**gegen/auf/an** + *Akk.*
with)
**Prämie** /'prɛːmiə/ *die;* ~, ~n (a)
(Leistungs~; Wirtschaft) bonus; (Belohnung)
reward; (Spar~, Versicherungs~) premium
  (b) (einer Lotterie) [extra] prize
**prämieren** *tr. V.* award a prize to ‹person,
film›; give an award for ‹best essay etc.›
**Pranger** *der;* ~s, ~ (hist.) pillory
**Pranke** *die;* ~, ~n paw
**Präparat** *das;* ~[e]s, ~e preparation
**präparieren** [1] *tr. V.* prepare
  [2] *refl. V.* (geh.: sich vorbereiten) prepare
oneself
**Präposition** *die;* ~, ~en (Sprachw.)
preposition
**Prärie** *die;* ~, ~n prairie
**Präsens** /'prɛːzɛns/ *das;* ~ (Sprachw.)
present [tense]
**präsentieren** *tr. V.* present
**Präservativ** *das;* ~s, ~e condom
**Präsident** *der;* ~en, ~en, **Präsidentin**
*die;* ~, ~nen president
**Präsidium** *das;* ~s, **Präsidien** (a)
committee
  (b) (Vorsitz) chairmanship
  (c) (Polizei~) police headquarters *sing. or pl.*
**prasseln** *itr. V.* pelt down; ‹shots› clatter;
‹fire› crackle
**prassen** *itr. V.* live extravagantly;
(schlemmen) feast
**Präteritum** *das;* ~s (Sprachw.) preterite
[tense]
**Prävention** *die;* ~, ~en prevention
**Praxis** *die;* ~, **Praxen** (a) (im Unterschied zur
Theorie) practice *no art.;* (Erfahrung) [practical]
experience
  (b) (eines Arztes, Anwalts usw.) practice; (Räume)
(eines Arztes) surgery (Brit.); office (Amer.);
(eines Anwalts usw.) office
**präzise** [1] *Adj.* precise
  [2] *adv.* precisely
**Präzision** *die;* ~: precision
**predigen** [1] *itr. V.* deliver a/the sermon
  [2] *tr. V.* preach
**Prediger** *der;* ~s, ~, **Predigerin** *die;* ~,
~nen preacher

**p**

**Predigt** die; ~, ~en sermon

**Preis** der; ~es, ~e: (a) (Kaufpreis) price (**für** of)
(b) (Belohnung) prize

**Preis-:** ~**anstieg** der rise or increase in prices; ~**aus·schreiben** das [prize] competition; ~**bindung** die (Wirtsch.) price-fixing

**Preisel·beere** die cranberry

**preisen** unr. tr. V. (geh.) praise

**preis-, Preis-:** ~**erhöhung** die price increase or rise; ~**geld** das prize money; ~**günstig** ①Adj. ⟨goods⟩ available at unusually low prices; ⟨purchases⟩ at favourable prices; inexpensive ⟨holiday⟩; **das** ~**günstigste Angebot** the best bargain or value; **das ist [sehr]** ~**günstig** that is [very] good value; ②adv. at a low price; **etw.** ~**günstig herstellen/verkaufen/bekommen** produce/sell/get sth. at a low price; ~**kampf** der price war; ~**liste** die price list; ~**nachlass**, *~**nachlaß** der price reduction; ~**richter** der, ~**richterin** die judge; ~**schild** das price tag; ~**senkung** die price reduction or cut; ~**steigerung** die rise or increase in prices; ~**tafel** die price list; ~**träger** der, ~**trägerin** die prizewinner; ~**verleihung** die presentation [of prizes/awards]; ~**wert** ①Adj. good value pred.; ②adv. ⟨eat⟩ at a reasonable price; **dort kann man** ~**wert einkaufen** you get good value for money there

**prellen** tr. V. (a) (betrügen) cheat (**um** out of); **die Zeche** ~: avoid paying the bill
(b) (verletzen) bash; bruise

**Prellung** die; ~, ~en bruise

**Premiere** /prə'mie̯:rə/ die; ~, ~n opening night

**Presse** die; ~, ~n (a) press; (Zitronen~) squeezer
(b) (Zeitungen) press

**Presse-:** ~**erklärung** die press statement; ~**freiheit** die freedom of the press; ~**information** die press release; ~**konferenz** die press conference; ~**meldung** die press report

**pressen** tr. V. press

**Presse·sprecher** der, ~**sprecherin** die spokesman; press officer

**Press·luft-**, *Preß·luft-: ~**bohrer** der pneumatic drill; ~**hammer** der pneumatic hammer

**Prestige** /prɛs'ti:ʒə/ das; ~s prestige

**prickeln** itr. V. tingle

**pries** 1. u. 3. Pers. Sg. Prät. v. PREISEN

**Priester** der; ~s, ~: priest

**Priesterin** die; ~, ~nen priestess

**prima** (ugs.) ①indekl. Adj. great (coll.)
②adv. ⟨taste⟩ great (coll.); ⟨sleep⟩ fantastically well (coll.)

**primär** ①Adj. primary
②adv. primarily

**Primel** die; ~, ~n primula; (Schlüsselblume) cowslip

**primitiv** ①Adj. primitive; (einfach, schlicht) simple
②adv. primitively; (einfach, schlicht) in a simple manner

**Prim·zahl** die (Math.) prime [number]

**Prinz** der; ~en, ~en prince

**Prinzessin** die; ~, ~nen princess

**Prinzip** das; ~s, ~ien /-'tsi:pi̯ən/ principle; **aus** ~: on principle; **im** ~: in principle

**prinzipiell** ①Adj. in principle postpos., not pred.; ⟨rejection⟩ on principle
②adv. (im Prinzip) in principle; (aus Prinzip) on principle

**Prion** das; ~s, ~en (Biol.) prion

**Prise** die; ~, ~n pinch

**privat** ①Adj. private; (persönlich) personal
②adv. privately

**Privat-:** ~**adresse** die private or home address; ~**angelegenheit** die private matter; ~**besitz** der private property; ~**eigentum** das private property

**privatisieren** tr. V. (Wirtsch.) privatize; transfer into private ownership

**Privatisierung** die; ~, ~en (Wirtsch.) privatization; transfer into private ownership

**Privat-:** ~**leben** das private life; ~**lehrer** der, ~**lehrerin** die private tutor; ~**patient** der, ~**patientin** die private patient; ~**schule** die private school; (Eliteschule in Großbritannien) public school; ~**unterricht** der private tuition; ~**vermögen** das private fortune; ~**versicherung** die private insurance; ~**weg** der private way; ~**wirtschaftlich** Adj. private-sector attrib.

**privilegiert** Adj. privileged

**pro** Präp. mit Akk. per; ~ **Stück** each; a piece

**pro-** pro-; ~**westlich**/~**kommunistisch** pro-western/pro-communist

**Probe** die; ~, ~n (a) test
(b) (Muster, Teststück) sample
(c) (Theater~, Orchester~) rehearsal

**Probe-:** ~**fahrt** die trial run; (vor dem Kauf, nach einer Reparatur) test drive; ~**jahr** das probationary year

**proben** tr., itr. V. rehearse

**probe·weise** Adv. ⟨employ⟩ on a trial basis

**Probe·zeit** die probationary period

**probieren** ①tr. V. (a) try; have a go at
(b) (kosten) taste; try
(c) (aus~) try out; (an~) try on ⟨clothes, shoes⟩
②itr. V. (a) (versuchen) try
(b) (kosten) have a taste

**Problem** das; ~s, ~e problem

**problematisch** *Adj.* problematic[al]

**problematisieren** *tr. V.* etw. ~: expound the problems of sth.

**problem·los** [1] *Adj.* problem-free
[2] *adv.* without any problems

**Product-placement**
/'prɔdaktpleɪsmənt/ *das;* ~s, ~ product placement

**Produkt** *das;* ~[e]s, ~e (auch Math., fig.) product

**Produktion** *die;* ~, ~en production

**produktiv** [1] productive; prolific ⟨writer, artist, etc.⟩
[2] *adv.* ⟨work, cooperate⟩ productively

**Produktivität** *die;* ~: productivity

**Produzent** *der;* ~en, ~en,
**Produzentin** *die;* ~, ~nen producer

**produzieren** *tr. V.* produce

**Prof.** *Abk.* = **Professor** Prof.

**professionell** [1] *Adj.* professional
[2] *adv.* professionally

**Professor** *der;* ~s, ~en, **Professorin**
*die;* ~, ~nen professor

**Professur** *die;* ~, ~en professorship, chair (**für** in)

**Profi** *der;* ~s, ~s (ugs.) pro (coll.)

**Profil** *das;* ~s, ~e (a) (Seitenansicht) profile; **im** ~: in profile
(b) (von Reifen, Schuhsohlen) tread

**Profit** *der;* ~[e]s, ~e profit

**profitieren** *itr. V.* profit (**von, bei** by)

**profund** *Adj.* (geh.) profound; deep

**Prognose** *die;* ~, ~n prognosis; (Wetter~, Wirtschafts~) forecast

**prognostizieren** *tr. V.* (geh.) forecast; predict

**Programm** *das;* ~s, ~e programme; program (Amer., Computing); (Ferns.: Sender) channel

**Programm-:** ~**fehler** *der* (DV) program error; error in the/a program; ~**heft** *das* programme; ~**hinweis** *der* programme announcement

**programmieren** *tr. V.* (a) (DV) program
(b) (auf etw. festlegen) programme

**Programmierer** *der;* ~s, ~,
**Programmiererin** *die;* ~, ~nen (DV) programmer

**Programm-:** ~**vorschau** *die* (im Fernsehen) preview [of the week's/evening's *etc.* viewing]; (im Kino) trailers *pl.;*
~**zeitschrift** *die* radio and television magazine

**progressiv** [1] *Adj.* progressive
[2] *adv.* progressively

**Projekt** *das;* ~[e]s, ~e project

**Projekt·management** *das* project management

**Projektor** /proˈjɛktɔr/ *der;* ~s, ~en
/-ˈtoːrən/ projector

**Projekt·tage** *Pl.* (Schulw.) project[-work] days

**projizieren** /proˈjitsiːrən/ *tr. V.* (Optik) project

**proklamieren** *tr. V.* proclaim

**Prolet** *der;* ~en, ~en (abwertend) peasant

**Proletariat** *das;* ~[e]s proletariat

**Proletarier** /proleˈtaːri̯ɐ/ *der;* ~s, ~: proletarian

**proletarisch** *Adj.* proletarian

**prollig** *Adj.* (salopp) boorish

**Promenade** *die;* ~, ~n promenade

**Promille** *das;* ~s, ~: [part] per thousand; **er fährt nur ohne** ~ (ugs.) he never drinks and drives; **er hatte 1,8** ~: he had a blood alcohol level of 1.8 per thousand

**Promille·grenze** *die* (ugs.) legal [alcohol] limit

**prominent** *Adj.* prominent

**Prominente** *der/die; adj. Dekl.* prominent figure

**Prominenz** *die;* ~: prominent figures *pl.*

**Promotion** /promoˈtsi̯oːn/ *die;* ~ (Wirtsch.) promotion; **für etw.** ~ **machen** promote sth.

**promovieren** [1] *itr. V.* (a) (die Doktorwürde erlangen) gain *or* obtain a/one's doctorate
(b) (eine Dissertation schreiben) do a doctorate (**über** + *Akk.* on)
[2] *tr. V.* confer a doctorate *or* the degree of doctor on

**prompt** [1] *Adj.* prompt
[2] *adv.* (a) promptly
(b) (ugs., meist iron.: wie erwartet) [and] sure enough

**Promptheit** *die;* ~: promptness

**Pronomen** *das;* ~s, ~ *od.* **Pronomina** (Sprachw.) pronoun

**Propaganda** *die;* ~: propaganda

**propagieren** *tr. V.* propagate

**Propan·gas** *das* propane

**Propeller** *der;* ~s, ~ propeller

**Prophet** *der;* ~en, ~en, **Prophetin** *die;* ~, ~nen prophet

**prophezeien** *tr. V.* prophesy (*Dat.* for); predict ⟨result, weather⟩

**Proportion** *die;* ~, ~en proportion

**Prosa** *die;* ~: prose

**Prosa·literatur** *die* prose writing

**prosit** *Interj.* your [very good] health; ~ **Neujahr!** happy New Year!

**Prospekt** *der od.* (bes. österr.) *das;* ~[e]s, ~e (Werbeschrift) brochure; (Werbezettel) leaflet

**prost** *Interj.* (ugs.) cheers (Brit. coll.)

**Prostituierte** *die/der; adj. Dekl.* prostitute

**Prostitution** *die;* ~: prostitution *no art.*

**Protagonist** *der;* ~en, ~en,
**Protagonistin** *die;* ~, ~nen (geh.) protagonist

**Protest** *der;* ~[e]s, ~e protest

**Protestant** *der;* ~en, ~en,
**Protestantin** *die;* ~, ~nen Protestant

**protestantisch** *Adj.* Protestant

P

**Protestantịsmus** *der;* ∼: Protestantism
*no art.*

**protestieren** *itr. V.* protest, make a
protest (**gegen** against, about)

**Protẹst·kundgebung** *die* protest rally

**Prothese** *die;* ∼, ∼n artificial limb;
prosthesis (Med.); (Zahn∼) set of dentures;
dentures *pl.*

**Protokọll** *das;* ∼s, ∼e **(a)** (wörtlich
mitgeschrieben) transcript; (Ergebnis∼) minutes
*pl.;* (bei Gericht) record; **etw. zu** ∼ **geben** make
a statement about sth.
**(b)** (diplomatisches Zeremoniell) protocol

**protokollieren** ①️ *tr. V.* take down; take
the minutes of ⟨*meeting*⟩; minute ⟨*remark*⟩
②️ *itr. V.* take the minutes; (bei Gericht) keep
the record

**protzen** *itr. V.* (ugs.) swank (coll.); show off;
**mit etw.** ∼: show sth. off

**protzig** (ugs. abwertend) ①️ *Adj.* swanky (coll.);
showy
②️ *adv.* swankily (coll.)

**Proviạnt** *der;* ∼s, ∼e provisions *pl.*

**Provịnz** *die;* ∼, ∼en province

**provinziẹll** ①️ *Adj.* provincial
②️ *adv.* provincially

**Provision** *die;* ∼, ∼en (Kaufmannsspr.)
commission

**provisorisch** ①️ *Adj.* provisional;
temporary
②️ *adv.* temporarily

**Pro·vitamin** *das* provitamin

**Provokation** *die;* ∼, ∼en provocation

**provozieren** *tr. V.* provoke

**Prozedur** *die;* ∼, ∼en procedure

**Prozẹnt** *das;* ∼[e]s, ∼e **(a)** *nach
Zahlenangaben Pl. ungebeugt* per cent *sing.;*
**fünf** ∼: five per cent
**(b)** *Pl.* (ugs.) (Gewinnanteil) share *sing.* of the
profits; (Rabatt) discount *sing.;* **auf etw.** (*Akk.*)
∼**e bekommen** get a discount on sth.

**-prozẹntig** *adj.* -per-cent

**Prozẹnt-:** ∼**punkt** *der* percentage point;
∼**rechnung** *die* percentage calculation;
∼**satz** *der* percentage

**prozentual** ①️ *Adj.* percentage
②️ *adv.* ∼ **am Gewinn beteiligt sein** have a
percentage share in the profits

**Prozẹß, \*Prozẹß** *der;* Prozẹsses,
Prozẹsse **(a)** trial; (Fall) [court] case; **einen** ∼
**gewinnen/verlieren** win/lose a case
**(b)** (Vorgang) process

**prozessieren** *itr. V.* go to court; **gegen
jmdn.** ∼: bring an action against sb.

**Prozẹß·kosten, \*Prozẹß·kosten** *Pl.*
legal costs

**Prozẹssor** *der;* ∼s, ∼en (DV) [central]
processor

**prüde** (abwertend) ①️ *Adj.* prudish
②️ prudishly

**Prüderie** *die* ∼ (abwertend) prudery;
prudishness

**prüfen** *tr. V.* **(a)** *auch itr.* examine ⟨*pupil,
student, etc.*⟩; **mündlich/schriftlich geprüft
werden** have an oral/a written examination
**(b)** (untersuchen) examine (**auf** + *Akk.* for);
check ⟨*device, machine, calculation*⟩ (**auf** +
*Akk.* for); investigate ⟨*complaint*⟩; (testen) test
(**auf** + *Akk.* for)
**(c)** (kontrollieren) check; examine ⟨*accounts,
books*⟩
**(d)** (vor einer Entscheidung) check ⟨*price*⟩;
examine ⟨*offer*⟩; consider ⟨*application*⟩

**Prüfer** *der;* ∼s, ∼, **Prüferin** *die;* ∼, ∼nen
**(a)** inspector; (Buch∼) auditor
**(b)** (im Examen) examiner

**Prüfling** *der;* ∼s, ∼e examinee;
[examination] candidate

**Prüfung** *die;* ∼, ∼en **(a)** examination; exam
(coll.); **eine** ∼ **machen** *od.* **ablegen** take an
examination
**(b)** ▶ PRÜFEN B–D: examination; check;
investigation; test; consideration

**Prügel** *Pl.* (Schläge) beating *sing.;* (als Strafe
für Kinder) hiding (coll.)

**Prügelei** *die;* ∼, ∼en (ugs.) punch-up (coll.);
fight

**Prügel·knabe** *der* whipping boy

**prügeln** ①️ *tr. (auch itr.) V.* beat
②️ *refl. V.* **sich** ∼: fight; **sich mit jmdm.** [**um
etw.**] ∼: fight sb. [over *or* for sth.]

**Prunk** *der;* ∼[e]s splendour; magnificence

**Prunk-:** ∼**bau** *der; Pl.* ∼∼ten magnificent
building; ∼**stück** *das* showpiece

**PS** /pe:'|ɛs/ *das;* ∼, ∼; *Abk.*
= **Pferdestärke** h.p.

**Psalm** *der;* ∼s, ∼en psalm

**Psychiater** *der;* ∼s, ∼, **Psychiaterin**
*die;* ∼, ∼nen psychiatrist

**Psychiatrie** *die;* ∼; psychiatry *no art.*

**psychisch** ①️ *Adj.* psychological; mental
⟨*process, illness*⟩
②️ *adv.* psychologically; ∼ **gesund/krank
sein** be mentally fit/ill

**psycho-: Psycho-** /psyço-/: ∼**loge** *der;*
∼∼n, ∼∼n psychologist; ∼**logie** *die;* ∼∼:
psychology; ∼**login** *die;* ∼∼, ∼∼nen
psychologist; ∼**logisch** ①️ *Adj.*
psychological; ②️ *adv.* psychologically;
∼**path** *der;* ∼∼en, ∼∼en, ∼**pathin** *die;*
∼∼, ∼∼nen psychopath

**Psychose** *die;* ∼, ∼n psychosis

**psychotisch** *Adj.* psychotic

**pubertär** *Adj.* pubertal

**Pubertät** *die;* ∼: puberty

**pubertieren** *itr. V.* reach puberty; ∼**d**
pubescent

**publịk** *Adj.* ∼ **sein/werden** be/become
public knowledge

**Publikum** *das;* ∼s **(a)** (Zuschauer, Zuhörer)
audience; (bei Sportveranstaltungen) crowd
**(b)** (Kreis von Interessierten) public; (eines
Schriftstellers) readership

p

**(c)** (Besucher) clientele

**Publikums-: ~erfolg** der success with the public; **~liebling** der idol of the public; **~sport** der spectator sport

**publizieren** tr. (auch itr.) V. publish

**Publizität** die; ~: publicity

**Pudding** der; ~s, ~e od. ~s thick, usually flavoured, milk-based dessert; ≈ blancmange

**Pudel** der; ~s, ~: poodle

**Puder** der; ~s, ~: powder

**Puder-dose** die powder compact

**pudern** tr. V. powder

**Puder-zucker** der icing sugar (Brit.); confectioners' sugar (Amer.)

**Puff¹** der; ~[e]s, Püffe (ugs.) **(a)** (Stoß) thump; (leichter/kräftiger Stoß mit dem Ellenbogen) nudge/dig
**(b)** (Knall) bang

**Puff²** der od. das; ~s, ~s (salopp: Bordell) knocking shop (Brit. sl.); brothel

**puffen** (ugs.) tr. V.: ▶ PUFF¹ A: thump; nudge; dig

**Puff-reis** der puffed rice

**Pulli** der; ~s, ~s (ugs.), **Pullover** der; ~s, ~: pullover; sweater

**Pullunder** der; ~s, ~: slipover

**Puls** der; ~es, ~e pulse

**Puls-ader** die artery

**Pult** das; ~[e]s, ~e desk; (Lese~) lectern

**Pulver** das; ~s, ~: powder

**pulverisieren** tr. V. pulverize; powder

**Pulver-kaffee** der instant coffee

**pumm[e]lig** Adj. (ugs.) chubby

**Pumpe** die; ~, ~n pump

**pumpen** tr., itr. V. **(a)** (auch fig.) pump
**(b)** (salopp) ▶ LEIHEN A, B

**Pump-: ~spray** das pump spray; **~zerstäuber** der pump-action atomizer

**Punkt** der; ~[e]s, ~e **(a)** (Tupfen) dot; (größer) spot
**(b)** (Satzzeichen) full stop
**(c)** (I-Punkt) dot
**(d)** (Stelle) point; **ein schwacher/wunder ~** (fig.) a weak/sore point
**(e)** (Gegenstand, Thema, Abschnitt) point; (einer Tagesordnung) item
**(f)** (Bewertungs~) point; (bei einer Prüfung) mark
**(g)** ~ **12 Uhr** at 12 o'clock on the dot

**pünktlich** ⏽ Adj. punctual
⏽ adv. punctually; on time

**Pünktlichkeit** die; ~: punctuality

**Punsch** der; ~[e]s, ~e od. Pünsche punch

**Pupille** die; ~, ~n pupil

**Puppe** die; ~, ~n **(a)** doll[y]
**(b)** (Marionette) puppet; marionette

**Puppen-: ~stube** die doll's house; dollhouse (Amer.); **~wagen** der doll's pram

**pur** Adj. **(a)** (rein) pure
**(b)** (unvermischt) neat ⟨whisky etc.⟩; straight

**Püree** das; ~s, ~s **(a)** purée
**(b)** ▶ KARTOFFELBREI

**pürieren** tr. V. (Kochk.) purée ⟨potatoes, apples, etc.⟩; (zerstampfen) mash

**Purpur** der; ~s crimson

**purzeln** itr. V.; mit sein (fam.) tumble

**pushen** tr. V. **(a)** (Drogenjargon) push
**(b)** (Journalistenjargon) push

**Puste** die; ~ (salopp) puff; breath

**Pustel** die; ~, ~n pimple; pustule (Med.)

**pusten** (ugs.) tr., itr. V. blow

**Pute** die; ~, ~n turkey hen; (als Braten) turkey

**Puter** der; ~s, ~: turkeycock; (als Braten) turkey

**Putsch** der; ~[e]s, ~e putsch; coup [d'état]

**putschen** itr. V. organize a putsch or coup

**Putsch-versuch** der attempted putsch or coup

**Putz** der; ~es plaster; (für Außenmauern) rendering

**putzen** tr. V. **(a)** (blank reiben) polish
**(b)** (säubern) clean; groom ⟨horse⟩; [sich (Dat.)] **die Zähne/die Nase ~:** clean or brush one's teeth/blow one's nose
**(c)** auch itr. (sauber machen) clean ⟨room, shop, etc.⟩; **~ gehen** work as a cleaner
**(d)** (vorbereiten) wash and prepare ⟨vegetables⟩

**Putz-: ~fimmel** der (ugs. abwertend) mania for cleaning; **~frau** die cleaner

**putzig** Adj. (ugs.) (entzückend) sweet; cute (Amer.); (possierlich) funny; comical

**Putz-: ~lappen** der [cleaning] rag; cloth; **~leute** Pl. cleaners; **~mann** der cleaner; **~mittel** das cleaning agent; **~tuch** das; Pl. ~tücher cloth; (Lappen) [cleaning] rag

**puzzeln** /'pʊzln/ itr. V. do jigsaw puzzles/a jigsaw [puzzle]

**Puzzle** /'pʊzl/ das; ~s, ~s, **Puzzlespiel** das jigsaw [puzzle]

**Pyjama** /pʏ'dʒaːma/ der (österr., schweiz. auch: das); ~s, ~s pyjamas pl.

**Pyramide** die; ~, ~n pyramid

**pyramiden-förmig** Adj. pyramidal; pyramid-shaped

**Python** der; ~s, ~s od. ~en, **Python-schlange** die python

p

# Qq

**q, Q** /ku:/ *das;* ~, ~: q/Q
**Quacksalber** *der;* ~s, ~,
  **Quacksalberin** *die;* ~, ~nen (abwertend)
quack [doctor]
**Quader** *der;* ~s, ~ *od.* (österr.:) ~n **(a)**
(Steinblock) ashlar block; [rectangular] block
of stone
  **(b)** (Geom.) rectangular parallelepiped;
cuboid
**Quadrat** *das;* ~[e]s, ~e square
**quadratisch** *Adj.* square
**Quadrat-:** ~**meter** *der od. das* square
metre; ~**wurzel** *die* (Math.) square root (**aus**
of); ~**zahl** *die* square number
**quaken** *itr. V.* ⟨duck⟩ quack; ⟨frog⟩ croak
**Qual** *die;* ~, ~en **(a)** torment
  **(b)** (Schmerzen) agony; ~en pain *sing.;* agony
*sing.;* (seelisch) torment *sing.*
**quälen** *tr. V.* **(a)** torment ⟨person, animal⟩;
be cruel to ⟨animal⟩; (foltern) torture
  **(b)** (plagen) ⟨cough etc.⟩ plague; (belästigen)
pester
**Quälerei** *die;* ~, ~en **(a)** torment; (Folter)
torture; (Grausamkeit) cruelty
  **(b)** (das Belästigen) pestering
**Qualifikation** *die;* ~, ~en **(a)** (Ausbildung)
qualifications *pl.*
  **(b)** (Sport) qualification
**qualifizieren** *refl. V.* **(a)** gain
qualifications
  **(b)** (Sport) qualify
**qualifiziert** *Adj.* **(a)** ⟨work, post⟩ requiring
particular qualifications
  **(b)** (sachkundig) competent; skilled ⟨work⟩
**Qualität** *die;* ~, ~en quality
**qualitativ** ①*Adj.* qualitative; ⟨difference,
change⟩ in quality
  ②*adv.* with regard to quality
**Qualitäts-erzeugnis** *das* quality product
**Qualle** *die;* ~, ~n jellyfish
**Qualm** *der;* ~[e]s [thick] smoke
**qualmen** *itr. V.* **(a)** give off clouds of [thick]
smoke
  **(b)** (ugs.: rauchen) puff away
**qualmig** *Adj.* (ugs.) thick with smoke
*postpos.;* smoke-filled
**qual-voll** ①*Adj.* agonizing
  ②*adv.* agonizingly
**Quantität** *die;* ~, ~en quantity
**quantitativ** ①*Adj.* quantitative
  ②*adv.* quantitatively
**Quantum** *das;* ~s, **Quanten** quota (**an** +
*Dat.* of); (Dosis) dose

**Quarantäne** /karan'tɛ:nə/ *die;* ~, ~n
quarantine
**Quark** *der;* ~s quark
**Quark·speise** *die* quark dish
**Quartal** *das;* ~s, ~e quarter [of the year]
**Quartett** *das;* ~[e]s, ~e **(a)** quartet
  **(b)** (Spiel) ≈ Happy Families; (Satz von vier
Karten) set [of four]
**Quartier** *das;* ~s, ~e accommodation *no
indef. art.;* accommodations *pl.* (Amer.); place
to stay; (Mil.) quarters *pl.*
**Quarz** *der;* ~es, ~e quartz
**Quarz·uhr** *die* quartz clock; (Armbanduhr)
quartz watch
**quasi** *Adv.* [so] ~: more or less; (so gut wie)
as good as
**quasseln** (ugs.)①*itr. V.* chatter; rabbit on
(Brit. sl.) (**von** about)
  ②*tr. V.* spout, babble ⟨nonsense⟩
**Quaste** *die;* ~, ~n tassel
**Quatsch** *der;* ~[e]s (ugs.) **(a)** (Äußerung)
rubbish
  **(b)** (Handlung) nonsense; (Unfug) messing
about; **lass den** ~ stop that nonsense
**quatschen** (ugs.)①*itr. V.* **(a)** (dumm reden)
rabbit on (Brit. coll.)
  **(b)** (klatschen) gossip; **es wird so viel
gequatscht** there is so much gossip
  **(c)** (sich unterhalten) [have a] chat *or* (coll.)
natter
  ②*tr. V.* (äußern) spout ⟨nonsense, rubbish⟩
**Quatsch·kopf** *der* (salopp) stupid
chatterbox; (Schwätzer, Schwafler) windbag
**Queck·silber** *das* mercury
**Quell·bewölkung** *die* (Met.) cumulus
clouds *pl.*
**Quelle** *die;* ~, ~n spring; (eines Flusses; fig.)
source
**quellen** *unr. itr. V.; mit sein* **(a)** ⟨liquid⟩
gush, stream; (aus der Erde) well up; ⟨smoke⟩
billow
  **(b)** (sich ausdehnen) swell [up]
**Quell·wasser** *das; Pl.* ~ *od.* **Quell·wässer**
spring water
**quengeln** *itr.* (auch *tr.*) *V.* (ugs.) **(a)** (weinen)
⟨baby⟩ whimper, (coll.) grizzle
  **(b)** (drängen) nag
  **(c)** (nörgeln) carp
**quer** *Adv.* sideways; (schräg) diagonally;
(rechtwinklig) at right angles; ~ **durch/über**
(+ *Akk.*) straight through/across
**Quer-:** ~**achse** *die* transverse axis;
~**denker** *der,* ~**denkerin** *die* lateral
thinker

**q**

**Quere** *die* jmdm. in die ∼ kommen bump into sb. (coll.); (fig.: jmdn. behindern) get in sb.'s way (coll.)

**quer-, Quer-:** ∼**flöte** *die* transverse flute; ∼**format** *das* landscape format; ∼**kopf** *der* (ugs.) awkward cuss (coll.); (komischer Kauz) oddball (coll.); ∼**köpfig** *Adj.* awkward; perverse; ∼**schläger** *der* deflected shot; ricochet; ∼**schnitt** *der* (*auch fig.*) cross section; ∼**schnitt[s]·gelähmt** *Adj.* (Med.) paraplegic; ∼**straße** *die* intersecting road; ∼**treiber** *der;* ∼∼**s**, ∼∼, ∼**treiberin** *die;* ∼∼, ∼∼**nen** (ugs. abwertend) troublemaker

**Querulant** *der;* ∼**en**, ∼**en**, **Querulantin** *die;* ∼, ∼**nen** (abwertend) malcontent

**quetschen** *tr. V.* crush; sich (*Dat.*) die Hand ∼: get one's hand caught

**Quetschung** *die;* ∼, ∼**en** bruise; contusion (Med.)

**quietschen** *itr. V.* squeak; ⟨brakes, tyres⟩ squeal, screech; (ugs.) ⟨person⟩ squeal, shriek

**Quirl** *der;* ∼**[e]s**, ∼**e** *long-handled blender with a star-shaped head*

**quirlig** *Adj.* lively; (flink) nimble

**quitt** *Adj.* (ugs.) quits

**Quitte** *die;* ∼, ∼**n** quince

**quittieren** *tr. V.* **(a)** *auch itr.* acknowledge, confirm ⟨receipt, condition⟩; give a receipt for ⟨sum, invoice⟩
**(b)** etw. mit etw. ∼: react *or* respond to sth. with sth.

**Quittung** *die;* ∼, ∼**en** **(a)** receipt
**(b)** (fig.) come-uppance (coll.)

**Quiz** /kvɪs/ *das;* ∼, ∼: quiz

**quoll** *1. u. 3. Pers. Sg. Prät. v.* QUELLEN

**Quote** *die;* ∼, ∼**n** proportion

**Quoten·regelung** *die: requirement that women should be adequately represented*

**Quotient** *der;* ∼**en**, ∼**en** (Math.) quotient (**aus** of)

# Rr

**r, R** /ɛr/ *das;* ∼, ∼: r/R

**Rabatt** *der;* ∼**[e]s**, ∼**e** discount

**Rabatte** *die;* ∼, ∼**n** border

**Rabbi** *der;* ∼**[s]**, ∼**nen** *od.* ∼**s** **(a)** (Titel) Rabbi
**(b)** (Person) rabbi

**Rabbiner** *der;* ∼**s**, ∼: rabbi

**Rabe** *der;* ∼**n**, ∼**n** raven

**Rabenmutter** *die; Pl.* Rabenmütter (abwertend) uncaring [brute of a] mother

**rabiat** ⟨1⟩ *Adj.* violent; brutal; ruthless ⟨methods⟩
⟨2⟩ *adv.* (gewalttätig) violently; brutally

**Rache** *die;* ∼: revenge; [an jmdm.] ∼ nehmen take revenge [on sb.]

**Rache·akt** *der* (geh.) act of revenge, reprisal (*Gen.* by, on the part of)

**Rachen** *der;* ∼**s**, ∼ **(a)** (Schlund) pharynx (Anat.)
**(b)** (Maul) mouth; maw (literary); (fig.) jaws *pl.*

**rächen** ⟨1⟩ *tr. V.* avenge ⟨person, crime⟩; take revenge for ⟨insult, crime⟩
⟨2⟩ *refl. V.* **(a)** take one's revenge
**(b)** ⟨mistake etc.⟩ take its/their toll

**Rachitis** *die;* ∼ (Med.) rickets *sing.*

**Rach·sucht** *die* (geh.) lust for revenge

**rach·süchtig** (geh.) ⟨1⟩ *Adj.* vengeful
⟨2⟩ *adv.* vengefully

**Rad** *das;* ∼**es**, Räder **(a)** wheel; das fünfte ∼ am Wagen sein (fig. ugs.) be superfluous; ein ∼ abhaben (fig. ugs.) have a screw loose (coll.)

**(b)** (Fahrrad) bicycle; bike (coll.); ∼ fahren cycle; ride a bicycle *or* (coll.) bike

**Radar** *der od. das;* ∼**s** radar

**Radar-:** ∼**falle** *die* (ugs.) [radar] speed trap; ∼**kontrolle** *die* [radar] speed check; ∼**schirm** *der* radar screen

**Rad·dampfer** *der* paddle steamer

**radeln** *itr. V.; mit sein* (ugs., bes. südd.) cycle

**Rädels·führer** *der*, **Rädels·führerin** *die* (abwertend) ringleader

**rad-, Rad-:** *∗*∼|**fahren** ▶ RAD B; ∼**fahrer** *der*, ∼**fahrerin** *die* cyclist

**Radien** ▶ RADIUS

**radieren** *tr. V.* (*auch itr.*) *V.* erase

**Radier·gummi** *der* rubber [eraser]

**Radierung** *die;* ∼, ∼**en** (Grafik) etching

**Radieschen** *das;* ∼**s**, ∼: radish

**radikal** ⟨1⟩ *Adj.* radical; drastic ⟨measure, method, cure⟩
⟨2⟩ *adv.* radically; (vollständig) totally

**Radikalismus** *der;* ∼: radicalism

**Radikalität** *die;* ∼: radicalness; radical nature

**Radio** *das* (südd., schweiz. auch: *der*); ∼**s**, ∼**s** radio; ∼ hören listen to the radio

**radio-, Radio-:** ∼**aktiv** /----'-/ ⟨1⟩ *Adj.* radioactive; ⟨2⟩ *adv.* radioactively; ∼**aktivität** /-----'-/ *die* radioactivity; ∼**sender** *der* radio station; ∼**wecker** *der* radio alarm clock

**Radius** *der;* ∼, **Radien** radius

**Rad-:** ~**kappe** *die* hubcap; ~**lager** *das* wheel bearing
**Radler** *der;* ~s, ~: (a) cyclist
(b) (bes. südd.: Getränk) shandy
**Radlerin** *die;* ~, ~nen cyclist
**Rad-:** ~**rennbahn** *die* cycle racing track; ~**rennen** *das* cycle race; (Sport) cycle racing; ~**sport** *der* cycling *no def. art.;* ~**tour** *die* cycling tour; ~**weg** *der* cycle path *or* track
**raffen** *tr. V.* (a) snatch; rake in (coll.) ⟨*money*⟩; etw. [an sich] ~: seize sth.; (eilig) snatch sth.
(b) gather ⟨*material, curtain*⟩
**Raffinerie** *die;* ~, ~n refinery
**Raffinesse** *die;* ~, ~n (a) (Schlauheit) guile; ingenuity
(b) (Finesse) refinement
**raffiniert** ⌐1⌐ *Adj.* (a) ingenious ⟨*plan, design*⟩; (verfeinert) refined, subtle ⟨*colour, scheme, effect*⟩; sophisticated ⟨*dish, cut (of clothes)*⟩
(b) (gerissen) cunning ⟨*person, trick*⟩
⌐2⌐ *adv.* (a) ingeniously; (verfeinert) with great refinement/sophistication
(b) (gerissen) cunningly
**Raffiniertheit** *die;* ~ (a) (Klugheit) ingenuity; (Verfeinerung) refinement; sophistication
(b) (Gerissenheit) cunning
**Raft** *das;* ~s, ~s raft
**raften** *itr. V.* raft
**Rafting** *das;* ~s rafting
**Rage** /'ra:ʒə/ *die;* ~ (ugs.) fury
**ragen** *itr. V.* (a) (vertikal) rise [up]; ⟨*mountains*⟩ tower up
(b) (horizontal) project, stick out (**in** + *Akk.* into; **über** + *Akk.* over)
**Ragout** /ra'gu:/ *das;* ~s, ~s ragout
**Rahm** *der;* ~[e]s cream
**rahmen** *tr. V.* frame
**Rahmen** *der;* ~s, ~ (a) frame; (Fahrgestell) chassis
(b) (fig.) framework
**Rakete** *die;* ~, ~n rocket; (Lenkflugkörper) missile
**rammen** *tr. V.* ram
**Rampe** *die;* ~, ~n (a) (Lade~) [loading] platform
(b) (schiefe Fläche) ramp
**Rampen·licht** *das:* im ~ [der Öffentlichkeit] stehen be in the limelight
**Ramsch** *der;* ~[e]s, ~e (ugs.) (a) (Ware) trashy goods *pl.;*
(b) (Kram) junk
**ran** *Adv.* (ugs.) (a) ▶ HERAN;
(b) (fang[t] an) off you go; (fangen wir an) let's go
(c) (greif[t] an) go at him/them!
**Rand** *der;* ~[e]s, Ränder (a) edge; (Einfassung)

border; (Hut~) brim; (Brillen~, Gefäß~, Krater~) rim; (eines Abgrunds) brink; (auf einem Schriftstück) margin; (Weg~) verge; (Stadt~) outskirts *pl.;*
(b) (Schmutz~) mark; (rund) ring
**randalieren** *itr. V.* riot
**Randalierer** *der;* ~s, ~,
**Randaliererin** *die;* ~, ~nen hooligan
**rand-, Rand-:** ~**bemerkung** *die* marginal note *or* comment; ~**gruppe** *die* (Soziol.) fringe *or* marginal group; ~**stein** *der* kerb; ~**voll** *Adj.* ⟨*glass etc.*⟩ full to the brim
**rang** *1. u. 3. Pers. Sg. Prät. v.* RINGEN
**Rang** *der;* ~[e]s, Ränge (a) rank; (in der Gesellschaft) status
(b) (im Theater) circle; **erster** ~: dress circle; **zweiter** ~: upper circle; **dritter** ~: gallery
**rangieren** /raŋ'ʒi:rən/ *tr. V.* shunt ⟨*trucks etc.*⟩; switch ⟨*cars*⟩ (Amer.)
**Rang-:** ~**liste** *die* ranking list; **Nummer eins der internationalen** ~**liste** number one in the world rankings; ~**ordnung** *die* order of precedence; (Verhaltensf.) pecking order
**Ranke** *die;* ~, ~n (Bot.) tendril
**ranken** *refl. V.* climb, grow (**an** + *Dat.* up, **über** + *Akk.* over)
**Ranking** /'ræŋkɪŋ/ *das;* ~s ranking
**rann** *1. u. 3. Pers. Sg. Prät. v.* RINNEN
**rannte** *1. u. 3. Pers. Sg. Prät. v.* RENNEN
**Ranzen** *der;* ~s, ~: satchel
**ranzig** *Adj.* rancid
**Rap** /ræp/ *der;* ~[s], ~s rap
**Rappe** *der;* ~n, ~n black horse
**rappen** /'ræpn̩/ *itr. V.* rap
**Rappen** *der;* ~s, ~: [Swiss] centime
**Rapper**/'ræpɐ/ *der;* ~s, ~, **Rapperin** *die;* ~, ~nen rapper
**Raps** *der;* ~es (Bot.) rape
**rar** *Adj.* scarce; (selten) rare
**Rarität** *die;* ~, ~en rarity
**rasant** (ugs.) ⌐1⌐ *Adj.* tremendously fast (coll.) ⟨*car, horse, etc.*⟩
⌐2⌐ *adv.* at terrific speed (coll.)
**rasch** ⌐1⌐ *Adj.* quick; speedy, swift ⟨*end, action, decision, progress*⟩
⌐2⌐ *adv.* quickly; ⟨*decide, end, proceed*⟩ swiftly, rapidly
**rascheln** *itr. V.* rustle; ⟨*mouse etc.*⟩ make a rustling noise
**rasen** *itr. V.* (a) *mit sein* (ugs.: eilen) dash *or* rush [along]; (fahren) tear *or* race along; (fig.) ⟨*pulse*⟩ race
(b) (toben) ⟨*person*⟩ rage
**Rasen** *der;* ~s, ~: grass *no indef. art.;* (gepflegte Rasenfläche) lawn
**rasend** ⌐1⌐ *Adj.* (a) (sehr schnell) breakneck *attrib.* ⟨*speed*⟩
(b) (tobend) raging
(c) (heftig) violent
⌐2⌐ *adv.* (ugs.) incredibly (coll.)

**Rasen·mäher** *der;* ∼s, ∼: lawn-mower
**Raser** *der;* ∼s, ∼ (ugs. abwertend) speed merchant (coll.); (rücksichtslos) road hog
**Raserei** *die;* ∼, ∼en (ugs.) tearing along *no art.*
**Raserin** *die;* ∼, ∼nen ▶ RASER
**Rasier·apparat** *der* [safety] razor; (elektrisch) electric shaver
**rasieren** *tr. V.* shave; **sich** ∼: shave; **sich nass/trocken/elektrisch** ∼: have a wet shave/have a dry shave/use an electric shaver
**Rasierer** *der;* ∼s, ∼ (ugs.) [electric] shaver
**Rasier-:** ∼**klinge** *die* razor blade; ∼**messer** *das* cutthroat razor; ∼**pinsel** *der* shaving brush; ∼**schaum** *der* shaving foam; ∼**seife** *die* shaving soap; ∼**wasser** *das* aftershave; (vor der Rasur) pre-shave lotion
**Räson** /rɛˈzɔŋ/ *die* zur ∼ kommen come to one's senses; jmdn. zur ∼ bringen make sb. see reason
**Rasse** *die;* ∼, ∼n (a) breed
(b) (Menschen∼) race
**Rassel** *die;* ∼, ∼n rattle
**rasseln** *itr. V.* rattle
**Rassen-:** ∼**hass**, *∼**haß** *der* racial hatred *no art.;* ∼**krawall** *der* race riot; ∼**trennung** *die* racial segregation *no art.*
**Rassismus** *der;* ∼: racism; racialism
**Rassist** *der;* ∼en, ∼en, **Rassistin** *die;* ∼, ∼nen racist; racialist
**rassistisch** *Adj.* racist; racialist
**Rast** *die;* ∼, ∼en rest; ∼ machen stop for a break
**rasten** *itr. V.* rest; take a rest *or* break
**Raster** *der;* ∼s, ∼ (a) (Druckw.) screen
(b) (fig.) [conceptual] framework; set pattern
**Rast-:** ∼**haus** *das* roadside café; (an der Autobahn) motorway restaurant; ∼**hof** *der* [motorway] motel [and service area]; ∼**platz** *der* (a) place to rest; (b) (an Autobahnen) parking place (*with benches and WCs*); picnic area; ∼**stätte** *die* service area
**Rasur** *die;* ∼, ∼en shave
**Rat** *der;* ∼[e]s, Räte (a) advice; ein ∼: a word of advice
(b) (Gremium) council
**rät** *3. Pers. Sg. Präsens v.* RATEN
**Rate** *die,* ∼, ∼n (a) (Teilbetrag) instalment; etw. auf ∼n kaufen buy sth. by instalments *or* (Brit.) on hire purchase *or* (Amer.) on the installment plan
(b) (Statistik) rate
**raten** ①️ *unr. itr. V.* (a) jmdm. ∼: advise sb.
(b) (schätzen) guess
②️ *tr. V.* (a) jmdm. ∼, etw. zu tun advise sb. to do sth.
(b) (erraten) guess
**Raten·zahlung** *die* payment by instalments

**Rat·haus** *das* town hall
**Ratifizierung** *die;* ∼, ∼en ratification
**Rätin** *die;* ∼, ∼nen councillor
**Ration** *die;* ∼, ∼en ration
**rational** *Adj.* rational
**rationalisieren** *tr., itr. V.* rationalize
**rationell** ①️ *Adj.* efficient; (wirtschaftlich) economic
②️ *adv.* efficiently; (wirtschaftlich) economically
**rationieren** *tr. V.* ration
**rat·los** ①️ *Adj.* baffled; helpless ⟨*look*⟩
②️ *adv.* helplessly
**Rat·losigkeit** *die;* ∼: helplessness
**ratsam** *Adj.* advisable
**Ratschlag** *der* [piece of] advice
**Rätsel** *das;* ∼s, ∼ (a) riddle; (Bilder∼, Kreuzwort∼ usw.) puzzle
(b) (Geheimnis) mystery
**rätselhaft** ①️ *Adj.* mysterious; (unergründlich) enigmatic
②️ *adv.* mysteriously; (unergründlich) enigmatically
**rätseln** *itr. V.* puzzle, rack one's brains (über + *Akk.* over); ∼, wer …/ob …: try to work out who …/whether …
**Ratte** *die;* ∼, ∼n (auch fig.) rat⁻
**rau** ①️ *Adj.* (a) (nicht glatt) rough
(b) (nicht mild) harsh, raw ⟨*climate, winter*⟩; raw ⟨*wind*⟩
(c) (kratzig) husky, hoarse ⟨*voice*⟩
(d) (entzündet) sore ⟨*throat*⟩
(e) (grob, nicht feinfühlig) rough; harsh ⟨*words, tone*⟩
②️ *adv.* (a) (kratzig) ⟨*speak etc.*⟩ huskily, hoarsely
(b) (grob, nicht feinfühlig) roughly
**Raub** *der;* ∼[e]s (a) robbery
(b) (Beute) stolen goods *pl.*
**Raub·bau** *der* overexploitation (an + *Dat.* of); ∼ an etw. (*Dat.*) treiben over-exploit sth.
**rauben** *tr. V.* steal; kidnap ⟨*person*⟩; jmdm. etw. ∼: rob sb. of sth.; (geh.: wegnehmen) deprive sb. of sth.
**Räuber** *der;* ∼s, ∼, **Räuberin** *die;* ∼, ∼nen robber
**Raub-:** ∼**fisch** *der* predatory fish; ∼**kopie** *die* pirated copy; ∼**mord** *der* (Rechtsw.) murder (an + *Dat.* of) in the course of a robbery *or* with robbery as motive; ∼**tier** *das* predator; ∼**überfall** *der* robbery (auf + *Akk.* of); ∼**vogel** *der* bird of prey
**Rauch** *der;* ∼[e]s smoke
**rauchen** ①️ *itr. V.* smoke
②️ *tr.* (*auch itr.*) *V.* smoke ⟨*cigarette, pipe, etc.*⟩; „Rauchen verboten" 'No smoking'
**Raucher** *der;* ∼s, ∼: smoker
**Raucher-:** ∼**abteil** *das* smoking compartment; smoker; ∼**husten** *der* smoker's cough
**Raucherin** *die;* ∼, ∼nen smoker
**räuchern** *tr. V.* smoke ⟨*meat, fish*⟩

**r**

**rauchig** *Adj.* smoky; husky ⟨*voice*⟩

**Rauch-:** ∼**melder** *der* smoke detector;
∼**schwaden** *der* cloud of smoke;
∼**verbot** *das* ban on smoking; ∼**wolke**
*die* cloud of smoke

**räudig** *Adj.* mangy

**rauf** *Adv.* (ugs.) up; ∼ mit euch! up you go!;
*s. auch* HERAUF; HINAUF

**Rau·faser·tapete** *die* woodchip wallpaper

**raufen** ⓵ *itr., refl. V.* fight
⓶ *tr. V.* sich (*Dat.*) die Haare/den Bart ∼:
tear one's hair/at one's beard

**Rauferei** *die;* ∼, ∼en fight

***rauh** *usw.* ▶ RAU *usw.*

**Raum** *der;* ∼[e]s, Räume (a) (Wohn∼, Nutz∼)
room
(b) (Gebiet) area; region
(c) (Platz) room; space

**räumen** *tr. V.* (a) clear [away]; clear ⟨*snow*⟩
(b) (an einen Ort) clear; move
(c) (freimachen) clear ⟨*street, building,
warehouse, stocks, etc.*⟩
(d) (verlassen) vacate

**Raum·fahrt** *die;* ∼: space travel

**räumlich** ⓵ *Adj.* (a) spatial; aus ∼en
Gründen for reasons of space
(b) (dreidimensional) three-dimensional;
stereoscopic ⟨*vision*⟩
⓶ *adv.* (a) spatially
(b) (dreidimensional) three-dimensionally

**Räumlichkeit** *die;* ∼, ∼en (a) Pl. rooms
(b) (räumliche Wirkung) three-dimensionality

**Raum-:** ∼**schiff** *das* spaceship; ∼**sonde**
*die* space probe

**Räumung** *die;* ∼, ∼en (a) clearing
(b) (das Verlassen) vacation; vacating
(c) (wegen Gefahr) evacuation
(d) (eines Lagers) clearance

**Räumungs·verkauf** *der* (Kaufmannsspr.)
clearance sale

**raunen** *tr., itr. V.* (geh.) whisper

**Raupe** *die;* ∼, ∼n caterpillar

**Rau·reif** *der* hoar frost

**raus** *Adv.* (ugs.) out; ∼ mit euch! out you go!;
*s. auch* HERAUS; HINAUS

**Rausch** *der;* ∼[e]s, Räusche (a) state of
drunkenness
(b) (starkes Gefühl) transport; der ∼ der
Geschwindigkeit the exhilaration *or* thrill of
speed

**rauschen** *itr. V.* ⟨*water, wind, torrent*⟩
rush; ⟨*trees, leaves*⟩ rustle; ⟨*skirt, curtains,
silk*⟩ swish; ⟨*waterfall, strong wind*⟩ roar;
⟨*rain*⟩ pour down

**Rausch·gift** *das* drug; narcotic; ∼ nehmen
take drugs; be on drugs

**Rauschgift-:** ∼**händler** *der,*
∼**händlerin** *die* drug trafficker; ∼**sucht**
*die* drug addiction

**raus|fliegen** *unr. itr. V.; mit sein* (ugs.) be
fired (coll.)

**räuspern** *refl. V.* clear one's throat

**raus|schmeißen** *unr. tr. V.* (ugs.) chuck
(coll.) ⟨*objects*⟩ out *or* away; give ⟨*employee*⟩
the push (coll.) *or* sack (coll.); chuck (coll.) *or*
throw ⟨*customer, drunk, tenant*⟩ out (aus of)

**Raute** *die;* ∼, ∼n (Geom.) rhombus

**Rave** /reɪv/ *der;* ∼s, ∼s rave

**Raver** /ˈreɪvɐ/ *der;* ∼s, ∼, **Raverin** *die;* ∼,
∼nen raver

**Razzia** *die;* ∼, Razzien raid

**reagieren** *itr. V.* react (auf + *Akk.* to)

**Reaktion** *die;* ∼, ∼en reaction (auf + *Akk.*
to)

**reaktionär** *Adj.* reactionary

**Reaktionär** *der;* ∼s, ∼e reactionary

**Reaktor** *der;* ∼s, ∼en /-ˈtoːrən/ reactor

**real** ⓵ *Adj.* real
⓶ *adv.* actually

**realisieren** *tr. V.* (geh.) realize

**Realismus** *der;* ∼: realism

**Realist** *der;* ∼en, ∼en, **Realistin** *die;* ∼,
∼nen realist

**realistisch** ⓵ *Adj.* realistic
⓶ *adv.* realistically

**Realität** *die;* ∼, ∼en reality

**Real·schule** *die* ≈ secondary modern
school (Brit. Hist.)

**Rebe** *die;* ∼, ∼n (a) vine shoot
(b) (Weinstock) [grape] vine

**Rebell** *der;* ∼en, ∼en, **Rebellin** *die;* ∼,
∼nen rebel

**rebellieren** *itr. V.* rebel (gegen against)

**Rebellion** *die;* ∼, ∼en rebellion

**rebellisch** *Adj.* rebellious

**Reb-:** ∼**huhn** *das* partridge; ∼**stock** *der*
vine

**rechen** *tr. V.* (bes. südd.) rake

**Rechen** *der;* ∼s, ∼ (bes. südd.) rake

**Rechen-:** ∼**fehler** *der* arithmetical error;
∼**maschine** *die* calculator

**Rechenschaft** *die;* ∼: account; jmdn. für
etw. zur ∼ ziehen call *or* bring sb. to account
for sth.

**Rechenschafts·bericht** *der* report

**Recherche** /reˈʃɛrʃə/ *die;* ∼, ∼n (a) (geh.)
investigation; enquiry
(b) (DV) search

**recherchieren** *itr., tr. V.* (geh.) investigate

**rechnen** ⓵ *tr. V.* (a) eine Aufgabe ∼: work
out a problem
(b) (veranschlagen) reckon; estimate; gut/rund
gerechnet at a generous/rough estimate
(c) (berücksichtigen) take into account
(d) (einbeziehen) count
⓶ *itr. V.* (a) do *or* make a calculation/
calculations; gut/schlecht ∼ können be good/
bad at figures
(b) (zählen) reckon
(c) (ugs.: berechnen) calculate; estimate

**(d)** (wirtschaften) budget carefully
**(e)** auf jmdn./etw. *od.* mit jmdm./etw. ∼:
count on sb./sth.
**(f)** mit etw. ∼ (etw. einkalkulieren) reckon with
sth.; (etw. erwarten) expect sth.
**Rechnen** *das;* ∼s arithmetic
**Rechner** *der;* ∼s, ∼: calculator; (Computer)
computer
**rechnerisch** *Adj.* arithmetical
**Rechnung** *die;* ∼, ∼en **(a)** calculation
**(b)** (schriftliche Kosten∼) bill; invoice
(Commerc.); [jmdm.] etw. in ∼ **stellen** charge
[sb.] for sth.
**recht** 1 *Adj.* **(a)** (geeignet, richtig) right
**(b)** (gesetzmäßig, anständig) right; proper; ∼
**und billig** right and proper
**(c)** (wunschgemäß) jmdm. ∼ **sein** be all right
with sb.
**(d)** (wirklich, echt) real
2 *adv.* **(a)** (geeignet) **du kommst gerade** ∼:
you are just in time
**(b)** (richtig) correctly
**(c)** (gesetzmäßig, anständig) properly
**(d)** (wunschgemäß) **es jmdm.** ∼ **machen** please
sb.
**(e)** (wirklich, echt) really
**(f)** (ziemlich) quite; rather; *s. auch* RECHT D
**Recht** *das;* ∼[e]s, ∼e **(a)** (Rechtsordnung) law
**(b)** (Rechtsanspruch) right; **sein** ∼ **fordern** *od.*
**verlangen** demand one's rights
**(c)** (Berechtigung) right (auf + *Akk.* to);
**gleiches** ∼ **für alle!** equal rights for all!; **im**
∼ **sein** be in the right; **zu** ∼: rightly
**(d)** ∼ **haben** be right; **jmdm.** ∼ **geben** admit
that sb. is right
**recht...** *Adj.* **(a)** right; right[-hand] ⟨edge⟩
**(b)** (außen, sichtbar) right ⟨side⟩
**(c)** (in der Politik) right-wing
**recht·fertigen** *tr. V.* justify (**vor** + *Dat.* to)
**Recht·fertigung** *die* justification
**rechtlich** 1 *Adj.* legal
2 *adv.* legally
**Rechtlichkeit** *die;* ∼ *s.:* RECHTMÄSSIGKEIT
**recht·los** *Adj.* without rights *postpos.*
**Rechtlosigkeit** *die;* ∼: lack of rights
**rechtmäßig** 1 *Adj.* lawful; rightful;
legitimate ⟨claim⟩
2 *adv.* lawfully; rightfully
**Rechtmäßigkeit** *die;* ∼: legality; (eines
Anspruchs) legitimacy
**rechts** *Adv.* **(a)** on the right; **von** ∼: from
the right
**(b)** (Politik) on the right wing
**Rechts-:** ∼**abbieger** *der,*
∼**abbiegerin** *die* (Verkehrsw.) motorist/
cyclist/car *etc.* turning right; ∼**anwalt**
*der,* ∼**anwältin** *die* lawyer; solicitor (Brit.);
attorney (Amer.); (vor Gericht) barrister (Brit.);
attorney[-at-law] (Amer.); advocate (Scot.);
∼**außen** /-'--/ *der;* ∼, ∼ (Ballspiele) right
wing; outside right
**recht-, Recht-:** ∼**schaffen** 1 *Adj.*

honest; 2 *adv.* honestly;
∼**schreib·fehler** *der* spelling mistake;
∼**schreibung** *die* orthography
**rechts-, Rechts-:** ∼**empfinden** *das*
sense of [what is] right and wrong;
∼**extremist** *der,* ∼**extremistin** *die*
(Politik) right-wing extremist; ∼**händer** *der;*
∼**s,** ∼**,** ∼**händerin** *die;* ∼**,** ∼**nen**
right-hander; ∼**kräftig** (Rechtsw.) 1 *Adj.*
final [and absolute] ⟨decision, verdict, etc.⟩;
2 *adv.* jmdn. ∼**kräftig verurteilen** pass a
final sentence on sb.; ∼**kurve** *die* right-
hand bend
**Recht·sprechung** *die;* ∼, ∼en
administration of justice; (eines Gerichts)
jurisdiction
**rechts-, Rechts-:** ∼**radikal** (Politik)
1 *Adj.* radical right-wing; 2 *adv.* **eine**
∼**radikal orientierte Gruppe** a group with a
radical right-wing orientation; ∼**radikale**
*der/die* right-wing radical;
∼**radikalismus** *der* right-wing
radicalism; ∼**staat** *der* [constitutional]
state founded on the rule of law;
∼**staatlich** *Adj.* founded on the rule of
law *postpos.;* ∼**verkehr** *der* driving *no art.*
on the right; ∼**verletzung** *die* (Rechtsw.)
infringement *or* violation of the law;
∼**widrig** 1 *Adj.* unlawful; 2 *adv.*
unlawfully; ∼**widrigkeit** *die* **(a)**
unlawfulness; **(b)** (Handlung) unlawful act
**recht-:** ∼**wink[e]lig** *Adj.* right-angled;
∼**zeitig** 1 *Adj.* timely; (pünktlich) punctual;
2 *adv.* in time; (pünktlich) on time
**Reck** *das;* ∼[e]s, ∼e *od.* ∼s horizontal bar
**recken** 1 *tr. V.* stretch
2 *refl. V.* stretch oneself
**recyceln** /ri'sai:kln̩/ *tr. V.;* 2. *Part.* **recycelt**
recycle
**Recycling** /ri'sai:klɪŋ/ *das;* ∼s recycling
**Recycling·papier** /ri'sai:klɪŋ-/ *das*
recycled paper
**Redakteur** /redak'tø:ɐ̯/ *der;* ∼s, ∼e,
**Redakteurin** *die;* ∼, ∼nen editor
**Redaktion** *die;* ∼, ∼en **(a)** (Redakteure)
editorial staff
**(b)** (Büro) editorial department *or* office/
offices *pl.*
**redaktionell** 1 *Adj.* editorial
2 *adv.* editorially
**Rede** *die;* ∼, ∼n **(a)** (Ansprache) address;
speech; **eine** ∼ **halten** give *or* make a speech
**(b)** (Vortrag) rhetoric
**(c)** (Äußerung, Ansicht) **nicht der** ∼ **wert sein**
be not worth mentioning; **jmdn. zur** ∼
**stellen** make someone explain himself/
herself; **von jmdm./etw. ist die** ∼: there is
some talk about sb./sth.; **es ist die** ∼ **davon,**
**dass ...:** it is being said *or* people are saying
that ...; **davon kann keine** ∼ **sein** it's out of
the question
**reden** 1 *tr. V.* talk; **Unsinn** ∼: talk
nonsense; **kein Wort** ∼: not say *or* speak a
word ⸱⸱⸱⟶

② *itr. V.* **(a)** (sprechen) talk; speak; **viel/wenig** ~: talk a lot (coll.)/not talk much
**(b)** (sich äußern, eine Rede halten) speak; **gut ~ können** be a good speaker
**(c)** (sich unterhalten) talk; **mit jmdm./über jmdn. ~**: talk to/about sb.

**Redens·art** *die* **(a)** expression; (Sprichwort) saying
**(b)** *Pl.* (Phrase) empty *or* meaningless words

**Rede·wendung** *die* (Sprachw.) idiom

**redlich** ① *Adj.* honest
② *adv.* honestly

**Redlichkeit** *die;* ~: honesty

**Redner** *der;* ~s, ~, **Rednerin** *die* ~, ~nen **(a)** speaker
**(b)** (Rhetoriker) orator

**red·selig** *Adj.* talkative

**reduzieren** ① *tr. V.* reduce (**auf** + *Akk.* to)
② *refl. V.* decrease; diminish

**Reeder** *der;* ~s, ~: shipowner

**Reederei** *die;* ~, ~en shipping firm

**Reederin** *die;* ~, ~nen shipowner

**reell** ① *Adj.* honest, straight ‹person, deal, etc.›; sound, solid ‹business, firm, etc.›; straight ‹offer›
② *adv.* honestly

**Reet** *das;* ~s (nordd.) reeds *pl.*

**Referat** *das;* ~[e]s, ~e **(a)** paper
**(b)** (kurzer schriftlicher Bericht) report

**Referendar** *der;* ~s, ~e, **Referendarin** *die;* ~, ~nen *candidate for a higher civil-service post who has passed the first state examination and is undergoing in-service training*

**Referenz** *die;* ~, ~en (Person, Stelle) referee; **jmdn. als ~ angeben** give sb.'s name *or* give sb. as a reference

**referieren** *itr. V.* **über etw.** (*Akk.*) ~: present a paper on sth.; (zusammenfassend) give a report on sth.

**reflektieren** *itr. V.* reflect

**Reflex** *der;* ~es, ~e reflex

**Reflexion** *die;* ~, ~en reflection

**Reflexiv·pronomen** *das* (Sprachw.) reflexive pronoun

**Reform** *die;* ~, ~en reform

**Reformation** *die;* ~ (hist.) Reformation

**Reformations·fest** *das* Reformation Day

**Reform·haus** *das* health food shop

**reformieren** *tr. V.* reform

**Refrain** /rə'frɛ̃ː/ *der;* ~s, ~s chorus

**Regal** *das;* ~s, ~e [set *sing.* of] shelves *pl.*

**rege** ① *Adj.* **(a)** (betriebsam) busy ‹traffic›; brisk ‹demand, trade, business, etc.›
**(b)** (lebhaft) lively; keen ‹interest›
② *adv.* **(a)** (betriebsam) actively
**(b)** (lebhaft) actively

**Regel** *die;* ~, ~n **(a)** rule; **nach allen ~n der Kunst** (fig.) well and truly

**(b)** rule; custom; **die ~ sein** be the rule; **in der** *od.* **aller ~:** as a rule
**(c)** (Menstruation) period

**regel·mäßig** ① *Adj.* regular
② *adv.* regularly

**Regel·mäßigkeit** *die* regularity

**regeln** ① *tr. V.* **(a)** settle ‹matter, question, etc.›; put ‹finances, affairs, etc.› in order
**(b)** (einstellen, regulieren) regulate; (steuern) control
② *refl. V.* take care of itself

**regelrecht** ① *Adj.* (ugs.: richtiggehend) proper (coll.); real; real ‹shock›; real, absolute ‹scandal›; complete, utter ‹flop, disaster›; **ich hatte ~e Angst** I was really afraid
② *adv.* (ugs.: richtiggehend) really

**Regelung** *die;* ~, ~en **(a)** ▶ REGELN 1A, B: settlement; putting in order; regulation; control
**(b)** (Vorschrift) regulation

**regen** ① *tr. V.* (geh.) move
② *refl. V.* **(a)** (sich bewegen) move
**(b)** (geh.) ‹hope, doubt, desire, conscience› stir

**Regen** *der;* ~s, ~ **(a)** rain; **vom** *od.* **aus dem ~ in die Traufe kommen** (fig.) jump out of the frying pan into the fire
**(b)** (fig.) shower

**Regen-:** ~**bogen** *der* rainbow; ~**mantel** *der* raincoat; mackintosh; ~**schirm** *der* umbrella; ~**tag** *der* rainy day; ~**wald** *der* (Geogr.) rainforest; ~**wasser** *das* rainwater; ~**wetter** *das* wet weather; ~**wolke** *die* rain cloud; ~**wurm** *der* earthworm; ~**zeit** *die* rainy season

**Regie** /re'ʒiː/ *die;* ~ **(a)** (Theater, Film, Ferns., Rundf.) direction; **die ~ bei etw. haben** *od.* **führen** direct sth.
**(b)** (Leitung, Verwaltung) management

**regieren** ① *itr. V.* rule (**über** + *Akk.* over); ‹party, administration› govern
② *tr. V.* rule; govern; ‹monarch› reign over

**Regierung** *die;* ~, ~en **(a)** (Herrschaft) rule; (eines Monarchen) reign
**(b)** (Kabinett) government

**Regierungs·sitz** *der* seat of government

**Regiment** *das;* ~[e]s, ~e *od.* ~er **(a)** *Pl.* ~e (Herrschaft) rule
**(b)** *Pl.* ~er (Milit.) regiment

**Region** *die;* ~, ~en region

**regional** ① *Adj.* regional
② *adv.* regionally

**Regisseur** /reʒɪ'søːɐ̯/ *der;* ~s, ~e, **Regisseurin** *die;* ~, ~nen director

**Register** *das;* ~s, ~ **(a)** index
**(b)** (amtliche Liste) register
**(c)** (Musik) (bei Instrumenten) register; (Orgel~) stop

**registrieren** *tr. V.* **(a)** register
**(b)** (bewusst wahrnehmen) note; register

**Regler** *der;* ~s, ~ (Technik) regulator; (Kybernetik) control

**reg·los** *Adj.* motionless

r

*old spelling - see note on page xiv

**regnen** [1] *itr., tr. V.* (*unpers.*) rain; **es regnet** it is raining
[2] *itr. V.; mit sein* (fig.) rain down
**regnerisch** *Adj.* rainy
**regulär** *Adj.* (a) proper; normal ⟨*working hours*⟩
(b) (normal, üblich) normal
**regulieren** *tr. V.* regulate
**Regulierung** *die;* ~, ~en regulation
**Regung** *die;* ~, ~en (geh.: Gefühl) stirring
**regungs·los** *Adj.* motionless
**Reh** *das;* ~[e]s, ~e roe deer
**Rehabilitation** *die;* ~, ~en rehabilitation
**rehabilitieren** *tr. V.* rehabilitate
**Reh-:** ~**bock** *der* roebuck; ~**kitz** *das* fawn [of a/the roe deer]
**Reibach** *der;* ~s (ugs.) profits *pl.;* **einen** [kräftigen] ~ **machen** make a killing (coll.)
**Reibe** *die;* ~, ~n, **Reib·eisen** *das* grater
**reiben** [1] *unr. tr. V.* (a) rub
(b) (zerkleinern) grate
[2] *unr. itr. V.* rub (**an** + *Dat.* on)
**Reib·fläche** *die* striking surface (*of matchbox*)
**Reibung** *die;* ~, ~en (Physik, fig.) friction
**reibungs·los** [1] *Adj.* smooth
[2] *adv.* smoothly
**reich** [1] *Adj.* (a) (vermögend) rich
(b) ( prächtig) costly ⟨*goods, gifts*⟩; rich ⟨*décor, finery*⟩
(c) (üppig) rich; abundant ⟨*harvest*⟩; abundant ⟨*mineral resources*⟩; ~ **an etw.** (*Dat.*) **sein** be rich in sth.
(d) (vielfältig) rich ⟨*collection, possibilities*⟩; wide, large ⟨*selection, choice*⟩; wide ⟨*knowledge, experience*⟩
[2] *adv.* richly
**Reich** *das;* ~[e]s, ~e (a) empire; (König~) kingdom; realm; **das [Deutsche]** ~ (hist.) the German Reich *or* Empire; **das Dritte** ~ (hist.) the Third Reich
(b) (fig.) realm
**reichen** [1] *itr. V.* (a) (ausreichen) be enough; **das Geld reicht nicht** I/we *etc.* haven't got enough money; **jetzt reichts mir aber!** now I've had enough!; **danke, es reicht** that's enough, thank you
(b) (sich erstrecken) reach; ⟨*forest, fields, etc.*⟩ extend
[2] *tr. V.* (a) pass; hand; **jmdm. die Hand** ~: hold out one's hand to sb.; **sich** (*Dat.*) **die Hand** ~: shake hands
(b) (servieren) serve ⟨*food, drink*⟩
**reich·haltig** *Adj.* extensive; varied ⟨*programme*⟩; substantial ⟨*meal*⟩
**Reich·haltigkeit** *die;* ~~: extensiveness; (eines Programms) varied content; (einer Mahlzeit) substantialness
**reichlich** [1] *Adj.* large; ample ⟨*space, time*⟩; good ⟨*hour, year*⟩
[2] *adv.* (a) amply
(b) (mehr als) over; more than

(c) (ugs.: ziemlich, sehr) a bit too ⟨*cheeky, dear, late*⟩
**Reichtum** *der;* ~s, **Reichtümer** (a) wealth (**an** + *Dat.* of)
(b) *Pl.* (Vermögenswerte) riches
**Reich·weite** *die* reach; (eines Geschützes, Senders, Flugzeugs) range
**reif** *Adj.* (a) ripe ⟨*fruit, grain, cheese*⟩; mature ⟨*brandy, cheese*⟩; ~ **für etw. sein** (ugs.) be ready for sth.
(b) (erwachsen, ausgewogen) mature
**Reif**[1] *der;* ~[e]s hoar frost
**Reif**[2] *der;* ~[e]s, ~e (geh.) ring; (Arm~) bracelet; (Diadem) circlet
**Reife** *die;* ~ (a) ripeness; (von Menschen, Gedanken, Produkten) maturity
(b) (Reifung) ripening
(c) **mittlere** ~ (Schulw.) *school-leaving certificate usually taken after the fifth year of secondary school*
**reifen** [1] *itr. V.; mit sein* (a) ⟨*fruit, cereal, cheese*⟩ ripen
(b) (geh.: älter, reifer werden) mature (**zu** into)
(c) ⟨*idea, plan, decision*⟩ mature
[2] *tr. V.* ripen ⟨*fruit, cereal*⟩
**Reifen** *der;* ~s, ~ (a) hoop
(b) (Gummi~) tyre
(c) ▶ REIF[2]
**Reifen-:** ~**druck** *der; Pl.* ~drücke tyre pressure; ~**panne** *die* puncture; ~**wechsel** *der* tyre change
**Reif·glätte** *die* ice on the roads
**reiflich** [1] *Adj.* [very] careful
[2] *adv.* [very] carefully
**Reifung** *die;* ~: ▶ REIFEN 1: ripening; maturing; maturation
**Reigen** *der;* ~s, ~ (a) round dance
(b) (fig.) **den** ~ **eröffnen** start off
**Reihe** *die;* ~, ~n (a) row; **in Reih und Glied** (Milit.) in rank and file; **aus der** ~ **tanzen** (fig. ugs.) be different
(b) (Reihenfolge) series; **er/sie** *usw.* **ist an der** ~: it's his/her *etc.* turn; **der** ~ **nach, nach der** ~: in turn
(c) (größere Anzahl) number
**reihen** (geh.) *tr. V.* string; thread
**Reihen-:** ~**folge** *die* order; ~**haus** *das* terraced house
**Reiher** *der;* ~s, ~: heron
**Reim** *der;* ~[e]s, ~e rhyme
**reimen** [1] *itr. V.* make up rhymes
[2] *tr., refl. V.* rhyme (**auf** + *Akk.* with)
**rein**[1] *Adv.* (ugs.) ~ **mit dir!** in you go/come!
**rein**[2] [1] *Adj.* (a) (unvermischt) pure
(b) (nichts anderes als) pure; sheer; plain, unvarnished ⟨*truth*⟩
(c) (frisch, sauber) clean; fresh ⟨*clothes, sheet of paper, etc.*⟩; pure, clean ⟨*water, air*⟩; clear ⟨*complexion*⟩; **etw. ins Reine schreiben** make a fair copy of sth.; **etw. ins Reine bringen** clear sth. up
[2] *Adv.* purely; ~ **gar nichts** (ugs.) absolutely nothing

**Rein·fall** der (ugs.) let-down
**rein|fallen** unr. itr. V.; mit sein (ugs.)
▶ HEREINFALLEN
**Rein·gewinn** der net profit
**Reinheit** die; ~ (a) purity
(b) (Sauberkeit) cleanness; (des Wassers, der Luft)
purity; (der Haut) clearness
**reinigen** tr. V. clean; purify ⟨effluents, air,
water, etc.⟩; Kleider [chemisch] ~ lassen
have clothes [dry-]cleaned
**Reinigung** die; ~, ~en (a) ▶ REINIGEN:
cleaning; purification; dry-cleaning
(b) (Betrieb) [dry-]cleaner's
**reinlich** Adj. cleanly
**Reinlichkeit** die; ~: cleanliness
**rein, Rein-:** ~rassig Adj. thoroughbred
⟨animal⟩; ~|reiten tr. V. (ugs.) jmdn.
~reiten drag sb. in (fig.); ~schrift die fair
copy
**rein|ziehen** unr. tr. V. (a) ▶ HINEINZIEHEN;
(b) sich (Dat.) etw. ~ziehen (salopp) take
⟨drug⟩; watch ⟨film, show, video⟩
**Reis** der; ~es rice
**Reis·brei** der rice pudding
**Reise** die; ~, ~n journey; (kürzere Fahrt,
Geschäfts~) trip; (Ausflug) outing; trip;
(Schiffs~) voyage; eine ~ machen go on a
trip/an outing; auf ~n sein travel; (nicht zu
Hause sein) be away; glückliche od. gute ~!
have a good journey
**reise-, Reise-:** ~andenken das
souvenir; ~boom das tourist boom;
~büro das travel agent's; travel agency;
~bus der coach; ~freiheit die freedom of
travel; ~führer der (a) (Reiseleiter) courier;
(b) (Buch) guidebook; ~führerin die
courier; ~gepäck das luggage (Brit.);
baggage (Amer.); (am Flughafen) baggage;
~gesellschaft die (a) (Reisegruppe) party
of tourists; (b) (ugs.: Reiseveranstalter) tour
operator; ~kosten Pl. travel expenses;
~krank Adj. travel-sick; ~krankheit die
travel sickness no pl.; ~leiter der,
~leiterin die courier
**reisen** itr. V.; mit sein (a) travel
(b) (abreisen) leave; set off
**Reisende** der/die; adj. Dekl. traveller;
(Fahrgast) passenger
**Reise-:** ~pass, *~paß der passport;
~planung die travel planning; die
~planung umstellen change one's travel
plans; ~prospekt der travel brochure;
~route die route; ~scheck der
traveller's cheque; ~tasche die holdall;
~verkehr der holiday traffic;
~wetterbericht der holiday weather
forecast; ~ziel das destination
**Reisig** das; ~s brushwood
**Reiß·brett** das drawing board
**reißen** ① unr. itr. V. (a) tear; (in Stücke) tear
up

(b) (ziehen an) pull; (heftig) yank (coll.)
(c) (werfen, ziehen) jmdn. zu Boden/in die Tiefe
~: knock sb. to the ground/drag sb. down
into the depths
(d) (töten) ⟨wolf, lion, etc.⟩ kill ⟨prey⟩
(e) etw. an sich ~ (fig.) seize sth.
② unr. itr. V. (a) mit sein ⟨paper, fabric⟩
tear, rip; ⟨rope, thread⟩ break, snap; ⟨film⟩
break; ⟨muscle⟩ tear
(b) (ziehen) an etw. (Dat.) ~: pull at sth.
③ unr. refl. V. (ugs.: sich bemühen um) sie ~
sich um die Eintrittskarten they are fighting
each other to get tickets
**reißend** Adj. rapacious ⟨animal⟩; raging
⟨torrent⟩; ~en Absatz finden sell like hot
cakes
**reißerisch** (abwertend) ① Adj. sensational;
lurid ⟨headline⟩; garish, lurid ⟨colour⟩
② adv. sensationally
**Reiß-:** ~leine die (Flugw.) ripcord;
~nagel der; ▶ ~ZWECKE; ~verschluss,
*~verschluß der zip [fastener];
~zwecke die drawing pin (Brit.);
thumbtack (Amer.)
**reiten** ① unr. itr. V.; meist mit sein ride
② unr. tr. V.; auch mit sein ride; Schritt/
Trab/Galopp ~: ride at a walk/trot/gallop
**Reiten** das; ~s riding no art.
**Reiter** der; ~s, ~, **Reiterin** die; ~, ~nen
rider
**Reit-:** ~hose die riding breeches pl.;
~pferd das saddle horse; ~stiefel der
riding boot
**Reiz** der; ~es, ~e (a) (Physiol.) stimulus
(b) (Anziehungskraft) attraction; appeal no pl.;
(des Verbotenen, der Ferne usw.) lure
(c) (Zauber) charm
**reizbar** Adj. irritable
**Reizbarkeit** die; ~: irritability
**reizen** ① tr. V. (a) annoy; tease ⟨animal⟩;
(herausfordern, provozieren) provoke; s. auch
GEREIZT
(b) (Physiol.) irritate
(c) (Interesse erregen bei) jmdn. ~: attract sb.;
appeal to sb.
(d) (Kartenspiele) bid
② itr. V. (Kartenspiele) bid
**reizend** ① Adj. charming; delightful, lovely
⟨child⟩
② adv. charmingly
**reizlos** Adj. unattractive; ⟨landscape,
scenery⟩ lacking in charm
**reizvoll** Adj. (a) (hübsch) charming
(b) (interessant) attractive
**rekeln** refl. V. (ugs.) stretch
**Reklamation** /reklama'ts:jo:n/ die; ~,
~en complaint (wegen about)
**Reklame** die; ~, ~n (a) advertising no
indef. art.; ~ für jmdn./etw. machen promote
sb./advertise or promote sth.
(b) (ugs.: Werbemittel) advert (Brit. coll.); ad (coll.);
(im Fernsehen, Radio auch) commercial

---

**Reklame-:** ～**schild** *das* advertising sign; ～**tafel** *die* advertising hoarding; (klein) advertising board

**reklamieren** ① *itr. V.* complain
② *tr. V.* (a) complain about (**bei** to, **wegen** on account of)
(b) (beanspruchen) claim

**rekonstruieren** *tr. V.* reconstruct

**Rekord** *der;* ～[e]s, ～e record

**Rekord-halter** *der*, **Rekord-halterin** *die*, **Rekord-inhaber** *der*, **Rekord-inhaberin** *die* record holder

**Rekrut** *der;* ～en, ～en (Milit.) recruit

**Rektor** *der;* ～s, ～en (a) (einer Schule) head[master]
(b) (Universitäts～) Rector; ≈ Vice-Chancellor (Brit.); (einer Fachhochschule) principal

**Rektorin** *die;* ～, ～nen (a) (einer Schule) head[mistress]
(b) ▶ REKTOR B

**Relation** *die;* ～, ～en relation

**relativ** ① *Adj.* relative
② *adv.* relatively

**relativieren** *tr. V.* relativize

**Relativierung** *die;* ～, ～en relativization

**Relativ-:** ～**pronomen** *das* (Sprachw.) relative pronoun; ～**satz** *der* (Sprachw.) relative clause

**relaxed** /riˈlɛkst/ *Adj.* (salopp) laid-back (coll.)

**relevant** /releˈvant/ *Adj.* relevant (**für** to)

**Relevanz** *die;* ～: relevance (**für** to)

**Relief** *das;* ～s, ～en *od.* ～e relief

**Religion** *die;* ～, ～en religion

**religiös** ① *Adj.* religious
② *adv.* in a religious manner

**Religiosität** *die;* ～: religiousness

**Relikt** *das;* ～[e], ～e relic

**Reling** *die;* ～, ～s *od.* ～e [deck] rail

**Reliquie** /reˈliːkvi̯ə/ *die;* ～, ～n relic

**Remis** *das;* ～ /rəˈmiː(s)/, ～ /rəˈmiːs/ (bes. Schach) draw

**Ren** *das;* ～s, ～s *od.* ～e reindeer

**Renaissance** /rənɛˈsãːs/ *die;* ～, ～n (a) Renaissance
(b) (Wiederaufleben) revival

**Rendezvous** /rãdeˈvuː/ *das;* ～ /...ˈvuː(s)/, ～ /ˈrãdeˈvuːs/ rendezvous

**Renn-bahn** *die* (Sport) racetrack; (für Pferde) racecourse

**rennen** *unr. itr. V.; mit sein* run; **an/gegen** *jmdn./etw.* ～: run *or* bang into sb./sth.

**Rennen** *das;* ～s, ～: running; (Pferde～, Auto～) racing; (Wettbewerb) race

**Renner** *der;* ～s, ～ (ugs.: Verkaufserfolg) big seller

**Renn-:** ～**fahrer** *der*, ～**fahrerin** *die* racing driver; ～**pferd** *das* racehorse; ～**rad** *das* racing cycle; ～**wagen** *der* racing car

**renommiert** *Adj.* renowned

**renovieren** *tr. V.* renovate; redecorate ‹room, flat›

**Renovierung** *die;* ～, ～en renovation; (eines Zimmers, einer Wohnung) redecoration

**rentabel** ① *Adj.* profitable
② *adv.* profitably

**Rentabilität** *die;* ～ (bes. Wirtsch.) profitability

**Rente** *die;* ～, ～n (a) pension
(b) (Kapitalertrag) annuity

**Renten-:** ～**alter** *das* pensionable age *no art.;* ～**empfänger** *der*, ～**empfängerin** *die* pensioner; ～**versicherung** *die* pension scheme

**Ren-tier** *das* reindeer

**rentieren** *refl. V.* be profitable; ‹equipment, machinery› pay its way

**Rentner** *der;* ～s, ～, **Rentnerin** *die;* ～, ～nen pensioner

**Reparatur** *die;* ～, ～en repair (**an** + *Dat.* to)

**Reparatur-werkstatt** *die* repair [work]shop; (für Autos) garage

**reparieren** *tr. V.* repair; mend

**Repertoire** /repɛˈto̯aːɐ̯/ *das;* ～s, ～s repertoire

**Report** *der;* ～[e]s, ～e, **Reportage** /reporˈtaːʒə/ *die;* ～, ～n report

**Reporter** *der;* ～s, ～, **Reporterin** *die;* ～, ～nen reporter

**Repräsentant** *der;* ～en, ～en, **Repräsentantin** *die;* ～, ～nen representative

**repräsentativ** *Adj.* representative

**repräsentieren** *tr. V.* represent

**Repressalie** /reprɛˈsaːli̯ə/ *die;* ～, ～n repressive measure

**Reproduktion** *die* reproduction

**reproduzieren** *tr. V.* reproduce

**Reptil** *das;* ～s, ～ien reptile

**Republik** *die;* ～, ～en republic

**republikanisch** *Adj.* republican

**Reservat** *das;* ～[e]s, ～e (a) reservation
(b) (Naturschutzgebiet) reserve

**Reserve** *die;* ～, ～n reserve

**Reserve-:** ～**rad** *das* spare wheel; ～**reifen** *der* spare tyre

**reservieren** *tr. V.* reserve

**reserviert** ① *Adj.* reserved
② *adv.* in a reserved way

**Reserviertheit** *die;* ～: reserve

**Reservierung** *die;* ～, ～en reservation

**Reservoir** /rezɛrˈvo̯aːɐ̯/ *das;* ～s, ～e (auch fig.) reservoir (**an** + *Dat.* of)

**Residenz** *die;* ～, ～en (a) residence
(b) (Hauptstadt) [royal] capital

**Resignation** *die;* ～, ～en resignation

**resignieren** *itr. V.* give up

**resigniert** ① *Adj.* resigned
② *adv.* resignedly

**resolut** ① *Adj.* resolute ····⊱

2 *adv.* resolutely

**Resolution** *die;* ~, ~en resolution

**Resonanz** *die;* ~, ~en resonance

**resozialisieren** *tr. V.* (bes. Rechtsspr.) reintegrate into society

**Resozialisierung** *die;* ~, ~en (bes. Rechtsspr.) reintegration into society

**Respekt** *der;* ~[e]s (a) (Achtung) respect (**vor** + *Dat.* for)
(b) (Furcht) **jmdm.** ~ **einflößen** intimidate sb.

**respektabel** 1 *Adj.* respectable
2 *adv.* respectably

**respektieren** *tr. V.* respect

**respekt·los** 1 *Adj.* disrespectful
2 *adv.* disrespectfully

**Respekt·losigkeit** *die;* ~: disrespectfulness

**respekt·voll** 1 *Adj.* respectful
2 *adv.* respectfully

**Ressort** /rɛˈsoːɐ̯/ *das;* ~s, ~s area of responsibility; (Abteilung) department

**Ressource** /rɛˈsʊrsə/ *die;* ~, ~n resource

**Rest** *der;* ~[e]s, ~e (a) rest; **ein** ~ **von a** little bit of
(b) (Endstück) remnant
(c) (Math.) remainder

**Rest·alkohol** *der* residual alcohol

**Restaurant** /rɛstoˈrãː/ *das;* ~s, ~s restaurant

**restaurieren** *tr. V.* restore

**restlich** *Adj.* remaining

**rest·los** 1 *Adj.* complete
2 *adv.* completely

**Rest·müll** *der* general waste; non-recyclable waste

**Resultat** *das;* ~[e]s, ~e result

**resultieren** *itr. V.* result

**Retorte** *die;* ~, ~n retort

**Retorten·baby** *das* (ugs.) test tube baby

**Retrospektive** *die;* ~, ~n (a) (Rückblick) retrospective view; **in der** ~: in retrospect
(b) (Ausstellung) retrospective

**retten** 1 *tr. V.* save; (vor Gefahr) save; rescue; (befreien) rescue; **jmdm. das Leben** ~: save sb.'s life
2 *refl. V.* (fliehen) escape (**aus** from)

**Retter** *der;* ~s, ~, **Retterin** *die;* ~, ~nen rescuer

**Rettich** *der;* ~s, ~e radish

**Rettung** *die* rescue; (vor Zerstörung) saving

**rettungs-, Rettungs-:** ~**aktion** *die* rescue operation; ~**boot** *das* lifeboat; ~**hubschrauber** *der* rescue helicopter; ~**los** 1 *Adj.* hopeless; inevitable ⟨*disaster*⟩; 2 *adv.* hopelessly; ~**ring** *der* lifebelt

**Reue** *die;* ~: remorse (**über** + *Akk.* for); (Rel.) repentance

**reuen** *tr. V.* **etw. reut jmdn.** sb. regrets sth.

**reu·mütig** *Adj.* remorseful; repentant ⟨*sinner*⟩

**Reuse** *die;* ~, ~n fish trap

**Revanche** /reˈvãːʃ(ə)/ *die;* ~, ~n revenge; (Sport) return match/fight/game

**revanchieren** *refl. V.* (a) get one's revenge, (coll.) get one's own back (**bei** on)
(b) **sich bei jmdm. für eine Einladung** ~ (ugs.) return sb.'s invitation

**Revers** /rəˈveːɐ̯/ *das od.* (österr.) *der;* ~ /rəˈveːɐ̯(s)/, ~ /rəˈveːɐ̯s/ lapel

**reversibel** /revɛrˈziːbl̩/ *Adj.* (Technik, Med.) reversible

**revidieren** /reviˈdiːrən/ *tr. V.* (abändern) revise; amend ⟨*law, contract*⟩

**Revier** /reˈviːɐ̯/ *das;* ~s, ~e (a) (Aufgabenbereich) province
(b) (Zool.) territory
(c) (Polizei~) (Dienststelle) [police] station; (Bereich) district; (des einzelnen Polizisten) beat

**Revision** /reviˈzi̯oːn/ *die;* ~, ~en (a) revision; (Änderung) amendment
(b) (Rechtsw.) appeal [on a point/points of law]; ~ **einlegen, in die** ~ **gehen** lodge an appeal [on a point/points of law]

**Revolte** /reˈvɔltə/ *die;* ~, ~n revolt

**revoltieren** /revɔlˈtiːrən/ *itr. V.* revolt, rebel (**gegen** against); (fig.) ⟨*stomach*⟩ rebel

**Revolution** /revoluˈts̯i̯oːn/ *die;* ~, ~en (auch fig.) revolution

**revolutionär** 1 *Adj.* revolutionary
2 *adv.* in a revolutionary way

**Revolutionär** *der;* ~s, ~e, **Revolutionärin** *die;* ~, ~nen revolutionary

**Revolver** /reˈvɔlvɐ/ *der;* ~s, ~: revolver

**Rezept** *das;* ~[e]s, ~e (a) (Med.) prescription
(b) (Anleitung) recipe

**rezept·frei** 1 *Adj.* ~e Mittel medicines obtainable without a prescription
2 *adv.* etw. ~ verkaufen/erhalten sell/obtain sth. without a prescription *or* over the counter

**Rezeption** *die;* ~, ~en reception *no art.*

**rezept·pflichtig** *Adj.* ⟨*drug etc.*⟩ obtainable only on prescription

**Rezession** *die;* ~, ~en (Wirtsch.) recession

**R-Gespräch** /ˈɛr-/ *das* (Fernspr.) reverse-charge call (Brit.); collect call (Amer.)

**Rhabarber** *der;* ~s rhubarb

**Rhein** *der;* ~[e]s Rhine

**rheinisch** *Adj.* Rhenish; ⟨*speciality etc.*⟩ of the Rhine region

**Rhein·land** *das;* ~[e]s Rhineland

**Rheinland-Pfalz** (*das*); ~: the Rhineland-Palatinate

**Rhetorik** *die;* ~, ~en rhetoric

**Rheuma** *das;* ~s (ugs.) rheumatism

**rheumatisch** (Med.) 1 *Adj.* rheumatic
2 *adv.* rheumatically

**Rheumatismus** *der;* ~, **Rheumatismen**
(Med.) rheumatism

**Rhinozeros** *das;* ~[ses], ~se rhinoceros;
rhino (coll.)

**Rhododendron** *der od. das;* ~s,
**Rhododendren** rhododendron

**rhythmisch** ⊡ *Adj.* rhythmical; rhythmic
⊡ *adv.* rhythmically

**Rhythmus** *der;* ~, **Rhythmen** (auch fig.)
rhythm

**richten** ⊡ *tr. V.* (a) direct ⟨*gaze*⟩ (auf +
*Akk.* at, towards); turn ⟨*eyes, gaze*⟩ (auf +
*Akk.* towards); point ⟨*torch, telescope, gun*⟩
(auf + *Akk.* at); aim ⟨*gun, missile, telescope,
searchlight*⟩ (auf + *Akk.* on); (fig.) direct
⟨*activity, attention*⟩ (auf + *Akk.* towards);
address ⟨*letter, remarks, words*⟩ (an + *Akk.*
to); level ⟨*criticism*⟩ (an + *Akk.* at)
(b) (geraderichten) straighten
(c) (aburteilen) judge; (verurteilen) condemn; *s.
auch* ZUGRUNDE A;
⊡ *refl. V.* (a) (sich hinwenden) **sich auf jmdn./
etw.** ~ (auch fig.) be directed towards sb./sth.
(b) **sich an jmdn./etw.** ~ ⟨*person*⟩ turn on
sb./sth.; ⟨*appeal, explanation*⟩ be directed at
sb./sth.; **sich gegen jmdn./etw.** ~ ⟨*person*⟩
criticize sb./sth.; ⟨*criticism, accusations, etc.*⟩
be aimed *or* levelled at sb./sth.
(c) (sich orientieren) **sich nach jmdm./jmds.
Wünschen** ~: fit in with sb./sb.'s wishes
(d) (abhängen) **sich nach jmdm./etw.** ~:
depend on sb./sth.
⊡ *itr. V.* (urteilen) judge

**Richter** *der;* ~s, ~, **Richterin** *die;* ~,
~nen judge

**Richt·geschwindigkeit** *die*
recommended maximum speed

**richtig** ⊡ *Adj.* (a) right; (zutreffend) right;
correct; accurate ⟨*prophecy, premonition*⟩;
**etw.** ~ **stellen** correct sth.
(b) (ordentlich) proper
(c) (wirklich, echt) real
⊡ *adv.* (a) right; correctly
(b) (ordentlich) properly
(c) (richtiggehend) really

**richtig·gehend** ⊡ *Adj.* real; proper (coll.)
⊡ *adv.* really

**Richtigkeit** *die;* ~: correctness; **etw. hat
seine** ~, **mit etw. hat es seine** ~: sth. is
right; **das wird schon seine** ~ **haben** I'm
sure it's all right *or* (coll.) OK

***richtig|stellen** ▶ RICHTIG 1A

**Richt-:** ~**linie** *die* guideline; ~**schnur**
*die; Pl.* ~~en (fig.) guiding principle

**Richtung** *die;* ~, ~en (a) direction; **in** ~
**Ulm** in the direction of Ulm
(b) (fig.: Tendenz) movement; trend

**richtung·weisend** *Adj.* ⟨*idea, resolution,
paper, speech*⟩ that points the way ahead

**rieb** *1. u. 3. Pers. Sg. Prät. v.* REIBEN

**riechen** ⊡ *unr. tr. V.* (a) smell
(b) (wittern) ⟨*dog etc.*⟩ pick up the scent of
⊡ *unr. itr. V.* (a) smell; **an jmdm./etw.** ~:
smell sb./sth.

(b) (einen Geruch haben) smell (**nach** of)

**rief** *1. u. 3. Pers. Sg. Prät. v.* RUFEN

**Riegel** *der;* ~s, ~ (a) bolt
(b) **ein** ~ **Schokolade** a bar of chocolate

**Riemen** *der;* ~s, ~ (a) strap; (Treib~, Gürtel)
belt; **sich am** ~ **reißen** (ugs.) pull oneself
together; get a grip on oneself
(b) (Ruder) [long] oar

**Riese** *der;* ~n, ~n giant

**rieseln** *itr. V.; mit Richtungsangabe mit
sein* trickle [down]; ⟨*snow*⟩ fall gently

**Riesen-** giant; enormous ⟨*selection, profit,
portion*⟩; tremendous (coll.) ⟨*effort, rejoicing,
success*⟩; terrific (coll.), terrible (coll.)
⟨*stupidity, scandal, fuss*⟩

**riesen-, Riesen-:** ~**groß** *Adj.*
enormous; huge; terrific (coll.) ⟨*surprise*⟩;
~**schritt** *der* giant stride

**riesig** ⊡ *Adj.* enormous; huge; vast
⟨*country*⟩; tremendous ⟨*effort, progress*⟩
⊡ *adv.* (ugs.) tremendously (coll.); terribly
(coll.)

**Riesin** *die;* ~, ~nen giantess

**Riesling** *der;* ~s, ~e Riesling

**riet** *1. u. 3. Pers. Sg. Prät. v.* RATEN

**Riff** *das;* ~[e]s, ~e reef

**rigoros** ⊡ *Adj.* rigorous
⊡ *adv.* rigorously

**Rille** *die;* ~, ~n groove

**Rind** *das;* ~[e]s, ~er (a) cow; (Stier) bull;
~**er** cattle *pl.;*
(b) (~fleisch) beef

**Rinde** *die;* ~, ~n (a) (Baum~) bark
(b) (Brot~) crust; (Käse~) rind

**Rinder·braten** *der* roast beef *no indef.
art.;* (roh) roasting beef *no indef. art.*

**Rinder·wahnsinn** *der* mad cow disease

**Rind-:** ~**fleisch** *das* beef; ~**vieh** *das* (a)
cattle *pl.;* (b) (ugs. abwertend) ass; [stupid] fool

**Ring** *der;* ~[e]s, ~e ring

**Ringel·natter** *die* ring snake

**ringen** ⊡ *unr. tr. V.* (Sport, fig.) wrestle; (fig.:
kämpfen) struggle, fight (**um** for; **gegen, mit**
with); **nach Luft** ~: struggle for breath
⊡ *unr. tr. V.* **die Hände** ~: wring one's
hands

**Ringen** *das;* ~s (Sport) wrestling *no art.*

**Ring-:** ~**finger** *der* ring finger; ~**kampf**
*der* (a) [stand-up] fight; (b) (Sport) wrestling
bout

**rings** *Adv.* all around

**rings·herum** *Adv.* all around [it/them *etc.*]

**Ring·straße** *die* ring road

**rings-:** ~**um**, ~**umher** *Adv.* all around

**Rinne** *die;* ~, ~n channel; (Dach~, Rinnstein)
gutter; (Abfluss) drainpipe

**rinnen** *unr. itr. V.; mit sein* run

**Rinn·stein** *der* gutter

**Rippchen** *das;* ~s, ~ (Kochk. südd.) rib [of
pork]

**Rippe** *die;* ~, ~n rib

**Rippen·bruch** *der* (Med.) rib fracture

**Risiko** *das;* ~s, **Risiken** risk

**Risiko-:** ~**faktor** *der* risk factor;
~**gruppe** *die* risk group

**riskant** ① *Adj.* risky
② *adv.* riskily

**riskieren** *tr. V.* risk

**riss, *riß** *1. u. 3. Pers. Sg. Prät. v.* REISSEN

**Riss, *Riß** *der;* **Risses, Risse** tear; (Spalt, Sprung) crack

**rissig** *Adj.* cracked; chapped ⟨lips⟩

**ritt** *1. u. 3. Pers. Sg. Prät. v.* REITEN

**Ritt** *der;* ~[e]s, ~e ride

**Ritter** *der;* ~s, ~: knight

**Ritter·sporn** *der* delphinium

**rittlings** *Adv.* astride

**Ritze** *die;* ~, ~n crack; [narrow] gap

**ritzen** *tr. V.* scratch

**Rivale** *der;* ~n, ~n, **Rivalin** *die;* ~, ~nen rival

**Rivalität** *die;* ~, ~en rivalry *no indef. art.*

**Roastbeef** /'ro:stbi:f/ *das;* ~s, ~s roast [sirloin (Brit.) of] beef

**Robbe** *die;* ~, ~n seal

**Robe** *die;* ~, ~n robe; (schwarz) gown

**Roboter** *der;* ~s, ~: robot

**robust** *Adj.* robust

**roch** *1. u. 3. Pers. Sg. Prät. v.* RIECHEN

**Rochade** *die;* ~, ~n (Schach) castling

**röcheln** *itr. V.* give the death rattle

**Rock¹** *der;* ~[e]s, **Röcke** skirt

**Rock²** *der;* ~[s] (Musik) rock [music]

**Rock and Roll** /'rɔk ɛnt 'rɔl/ *der;* ~[s], ~[s] rock and roll *no pl.*

**Rock·band** *die* rock band

**rocken** *itr. V.* rock

**Rocker** *der;* ~s, ~: rocker

**rockig** *Adj.* rock ⟨music⟩; rock-like ⟨jazz etc.⟩

**Rock·musik** *die* rock music

**Rodel·bahn** *die* toboggan run; (Sport) luge run

**rodeln** *itr. V.; mit sein* sledge; toboggan

**roden** *tr. V.* clear ⟨wood, land⟩; (ausgraben) grub up ⟨tree⟩

**Rogen** *der;* ~s, ~: roe

**Roggen** *der;* ~s rye

**Roggen-:** ~**brot** *das* rye bread; **ein** ~**brot** a loaf of rye bread; ~**brötchen** *das* rye-bread roll

**roh** ① *Adj.* (a) raw ⟨food⟩; unboiled ⟨milk⟩; unfinished ⟨wood⟩
(b) (ungenau) rough
(c) (brutal) brutish; brute *attrib.* ⟨force⟩
② *adv.* (a) (ungenau) roughly
(b) (brutal) brutishly; (grausam) callously; (grob) coarsely

**Roh-:** ~**bau** *der* shell [of a/the building];

~**kost** *die* raw fruit and vegetables *pl.;*
~**material** *das* raw material; ~**öl** *das* crude oil

**Rohr** *das;* ~[e]s, ~e (a) (Leitungs~) pipe; (als Bauteil) tube
(b) *o. Pl.* (Röhricht) reeds *pl.;*
(c) *o. Pl.* (Werkstoff) reed

**Röhre** *die;* ~, ~n tube; (Elektronen~) valve (Brit.); tube (Amer.)

**Roh·stoff** *der* raw material

**Rokoko** *das;* ~[s] rococo

***Rolladen** ▶ ROLLLADEN

**Roll·bahn** *die* (Flugw.) taxiway

**Rolle** *die;* ~, ~n (a) (Spule) reel
(b) (zylindrischer [Hohl]körper; Zusammengerolltes) roll
(c) (Walze) roller
(d) (Rad) [small] wheel; (an Möbeln usw.) castor; (für Gardine, Schiebetür usw.) runner
(e) (Turnen, Kunstflug) roll
(f) (Theater, Film usw., fig.) role; part; (Soziol.) role; **es spielt keine** ~: it is of no importance; (es macht nichts aus) it doesn't matter

**rollen** ① *tr. V.* roll
② *itr. V. mit sein* ⟨ball, wheel, etc.⟩ roll; ⟨vehicle⟩ move; ⟨aircraft⟩ taxi

**Roller** *der;* ~s, ~: scooter

**Roll-:** ~**feld** *das* runway[s] and taxiway[s]; ~**kragen** *der* polo neck; ~**laden** *der* [roller] shutter; ~**mops** *der* rollmops; ~**schuh** *der* roller skate; ~**schuh laufen** roller-skate; ~**splitt** *der* loose chippings *pl.;* ~**stuhl** *der* wheelchair; ~**treppe** *die* escalator

**Rom** (*das*) ~s Rome

**Roman** *der;* ~s, ~e novel

**Romantik** *die;* ~: romanticism; **die** ~: Romanticism

**romantisch** ① *Adj.* romantic
② *adv.* romantically

**Romanze** *die;* ~, ~n romance

**Römer** *der;* ~s, ~, **Römerin** *die;* ~, ~nen Roman

**römisch-katholisch** *Adj.* Roman Catholic

**röntgen** *tr. V.* X-ray

**Röntgen-:** ~**aufnahme** *die,* ~**bild** *das* X-ray [image/photograph *or* picture]; ~**strahlen** *Pl.* X-rays

**rosa** ① *indekl. Adj.* pink
② *adv.* pink

**Rosa** *das;* ~s, ~ *od.* ~s pink

**Rose** *die;* ~, ~n rose

**rosé** *indekl. Adj.* pale pink

**Rosé** *der;* ~s, ~s rosé [wine]

**Rosen-:** ~**kohl** *der* [Brussels] sprouts *pl.;* ~**kranz** *der* (kath. Kirche) rosary; **einen** ~**kranz beten** say a rosary; ~**montag** *der* the day before Shrove Tuesday

**rosig** *Adj.* (a) rosy; pink ⟨piglet etc.⟩
(b) (fig.) rosy; optimistic ⟨mood⟩

**Rosine** *die;* ~, ~n raisin
**Rosmarin** *der;* ~s rosemary
**Ross, *Roß** *das;* **Rosses, Rosse** *od.* **Rösser**
horse; steed (poet./joc.); **hoch zu** ~: on
horseback; **auf dem** *od.* **seinem hohen** ~
**sitzen** (fig.) be on one's high horse
**Ross-, *Roß-:** ~**haar** *das* horsehair;
~**kastanie** *die* horse chestnut
**Rost¹** *der;* ~[e]s, ~e **(a)** (Gitter) grating;
(eines Ofens, einer Feuerstelle) grate; (Brat~) grill
**(b)** (Bett~) base
**Rost²** *der;* ~[e]s rust
**Rost-:** ~**braten** *der* grilled steak;
~**bratwurst** *die* grilled sausage
**rosten** *itr. V.; auch mit sein* rust
**rösten** /'rœstn̩, 'røːstn̩/ *tr. V.* roast; toast
⟨bread⟩
**rost·frei** *Adj.* stainless ⟨steel⟩
**Rösti** *die;* ~ (schweiz. Kochk.) thinly sliced
fried potatoes *pl.*
**rostig** *Adj.* rusty
**rot** [1] *Adj.* red; ~ **werden** turn red; ⟨person⟩
blush; ⟨traffic light⟩ change to red
[2] *adv.* red
**Rot** *das;* ~s, ~ *od.* ~s red
**Rot·barsch** *der* rosefish
**Röte** *die;* ~: red[ness]
**röten** [1] *tr. V.* redden
[2] *refl. V.* go *or* turn red
**rot·haarig** *Adj.* red-haired
**Rot·hirsch** *der* red deer
**rotieren** *itr. V.* **(a)** rotate
**(b)** (ugs.: hektisch sein) get into a flap (coll.)
**Rot-:** ~**käppchen** *das;* ~~s Little Red
Riding Hood; ~**kehlchen** *das;* ~~s, ~~:
robin [redbreast]; ~**kohl** *der,* (bes. südd.,
österr.) ~**kraut** *das* red cabbage
**rötlich** *Adj.* reddish
**Rot-:** ~**licht** *das* red light; **bei** ~**licht**
under a red light; ~**stift** *der* red pencil
**Rötung** *die;* ~, ~en reddening
**Rot·wein** *der* red wine
**Rotz** *der;* ~es (salopp) snot (sl.)
**rotzen** (derb) [1] *itr. V.* **(a)** blow one's nose
loudly
**(b)** (Schleim in den Mund ziehen) sniff back
one's snot (sl.)
**(c)** (ausspucken) gob (sl.)
[2] *tr. V.* spit
**rotz·frech** (salopp) [1] *Adj.* insolent; snotty
(sl.)
[2] *adv.* insolently; snottily (sl.)
**Rouge** /ruːʒ/ *das;* ~s, ~s rouge
**Roulade** /ruːlaːdə/ *die;* ~, ~n (Kochk.)
[beef/veal/pork] olive
**Route** /'ruːtə/ *die;* ~, ~n route
**Routine** /ruˈtiːnə/ *die;* ~ **(a)** (Erfahrung)
experience; (Übung) practice
**(b)** (Gewohnheit) routine *no def. art.*
**routiniert** /rutiˈniːɐ̯t/ [1] *Adj.* (gewandt)
expert; skilled; (erfahren) experienced

[2] *adv.* expertly; skilfully
**Rowdy** /'rauːdi/ *der;* ~s, ~s (abwertend)
hooligan
**Rübe** *die;* ~, ~n turnip; **Rote** ~: beetroot;
**Gelbe** ~ (südd.) carrot
**rüber** *Adv.* (ugs.) over
**Rubin** *der;* ~s, ~e ruby
**Rubrik** *die;* ~, ~en column; (fig.: Kategorie)
category
**Ruck** *der;* ~[e]s, ~e jerk
**Rück·blick** *der* look back (**auf** + *Akk.* at);
retrospective view (**auf** + *Akk.* of)
**rücken** *itr., tr. V.* move
**Rücken** *der;* ~s, ~: back; (Buch~) spine
**Rücken-:** ~**deckung** *die* **(a)** (bes. Milit.)
rear cover; **(b)** (fig.) backing; ~**lehne** *die*
[chair/seat] back; ~**mark** *das* (Anat.) spinal
cord; ~**schmerzen** *Pl.* backache *sing.;*
~**schwimmen** *das* backstroke; ~**wind**
*der* tail wind
**rück-, Rück-:** ~|**erstatten** *tr. V.; nur*
*im Inf. u. 2. Part.* repay; ~**erstattung** *die*
repayment; ~**fahr·karte** *die,*
~**fahr·schein** *der* return [ticket];
~**fahrt** *die* return journey; ~**fall** *der* (Med.,
auch fig.) relapse; ~**fällig** *Adj.* (Med., auch fig.)
relapsed ⟨patient, alcoholic, etc.⟩; ~**fällig**
**werden** have a relapse; ⟨alcoholic etc.⟩ go
back to one's old ways; ⟨criminal⟩ commit a
second offence; ~**flug** *der* return flight;
~**frage** *die* query; ~**gabe** *die* return;
~**gang** *der* drop, fall (Gen. in); ~**gängig**
*Adj.* ~**gängig machen** cancel ⟨agreement,
decision, etc.⟩; ~**grat** *das;* ~~[e]s, ~~e
spine; (bes. fig.) backbone; ~**halt** *der*
support; backing; ~**halt·los** [1] *Adj.*
unreserved, unqualified ⟨support⟩; [2] *adv.*
unreservedly; ~**kehr** *die;* ~~: return;
~**kopp[e]lung** *die* (Elektrot.) feedback;
~**lage** *die* savings *pl.;* ~**läufig** *Adj.*
decreasing ⟨number⟩; declining ⟨economic
growth etc.⟩; falling ⟨rate, production, etc.⟩;
~**licht** *das* rear *or* tail light
**rücklings** *Adv.* on one's back
**Rück-:** ~**nahme** *die;* ~~: taking back;
~**reise** *die* return journey; ~**ruf** *der*
(Fernspr.) return call
**Ruck·sack** *der* rucksack; (Touren~)
backpack
**Rucksack·urlaub** *der* backpacking
holiday
**rück-, Rück-:** ~**schlag** *der* setback;
~**schritt** *der* retrograde step; ~**seite** *die*
back; (einer Münze usw.) reverse; far side;
~**sicht** *die* consideration; ~**sicht auf jmdn.**
**nehmen** show consideration for *or* towards
sb.; ~**sicht·nahme** *die;* ~~:
consideration; ~**sichts·los** [1] *Adj.*
inconsiderate; thoughtless; (verantwortungslos)
reckless ⟨driver⟩; (schonungslos) ruthless;
[2] *adv. s. Adj:* inconsiderately; recklessly;
ruthlessly; ~**sichtslosigkeit** *die;* ~~,
~~en ▶ RÜCKSICHTSLOS: lack of
consideration; recklessness; ruthlessness; ⸱⸱⸱⸱▸

~**sichts·voll** [1] *Adj.* considerate; [2] *adv.*
considerately; ~**sitz** *der* back seat;
~**spiegel** *der* rear-view mirror;
~**sprache** *die* consultation; ~**stand** *der*
(a) (Rest) residue; (b) (ausstehende Zahlung)
arrears *pl.*; (c) (Zurückbleiben hinter dem gesetzten
Ziel) backlog; (bes. Sport: hinter dem Gegner)
deficit; [mit etw.] im ~**stand** sein/in ~**stand**
(*Akk.*) geraten be/get behind [with sth.];
~**ständig** *Adj.* (a) backward; (b) (schon
länger fällig) outstanding ‹*payment, amount*›;
‹*wages*› still owing; ~**strahler** *der*
reflector; ~**tritt** *der* resignation (**von** from);
(von einer Kandidatur, einem Vertrag usw.)
withdrawal (**von** from)

**rückwärts** *Adv.* backwards

**Rückwärts·gang** *der* reverse [gear]

**rück-, Rück-:** ~**weg** *der* return journey;
~**wirkend** [1] *Adj.* retrospective;
backdated ‹*pay increase*›; [2] retrospectively;
~**zahlung** *die* repayment; ~**zug** *der*
retreat

**Rüde** *der;* ~**n,** ~**n** [male] dog

**Rudel** *das;* ~**s,** ~: herd; (von Wölfen, Hunden)
pack

**Ruder** *das;* ~**s,** ~ (a) (Riemen) oar
(b) (Steuer~) rudder

**Ruder·boot** *das* rowboat; rowing boat (Brit.)

**Rudergänger** *der;* ~~**s,** ~~, ~**gast** *der*
(Seemannsspr.) helmsman

**rudern** [1] *itr. V.; mit sein* row
[2] *tr. V.* row

**Ruder·regatta** *die* rowing regatta

**Ruf** *der;* ~**[e]s,** ~**e** (a) call; (Schrei) shout;
cry; (Tierlaut) call
(b) (fig.: Forderung) call (**nach** for)
(c) (Telefonnummer) telephone [number]
(d) (Leumund) reputation

**rufen** [1] *unr. itr. V.* call (**nach** for); (schreien)
shout (**nach** for); ‹*animal*› call
[2] *unr. tr. V.* (a) (ausrufen) call; (schreien)
shout
(b) (herbeirufen, anrufen) jmdn. ~: call sb.;
jmdn. zu Hilfe ~: call to sb. to help

**Ruf-:** ~**mord** *der* character assassination;
~**mord·kampagne** *die* smear campaign;
~**name** *der* first name (*by which one is
generally known*); ~**nummer** *die* telephone
number

**Rüge** *die;* ~, ~**n** reprimand

**rügen** *tr. V.* reprimand ‹*person*› (**wegen** for);
censure ‹*carelessness etc.*›

**Ruhe** *die;* ~ (a) (Stille) silence; ~ [bitte]!
quiet *or* silence [please]!
(b) (Ungestörtheit) peace; jmdn. mit etw. in ~
lassen stop bothering sb. with sth.
(c) (Unbewegtheit) rest
(d) (Erholung) rest *no def. art.;*
(e) (Gelassenheit) calm[ness]; composure; [die]
~ bewahren/die ~ verlieren keep calm/lose
one's composure; in [aller] ~: [really] calmly

**ruhe·los** [1] *Adj.* restless
[2] *adv.* restlessly

**ruhen** *itr. V.* (a) (ausruhen) rest
(b) (geh.: schlafen) sleep
(c) (stillstehen) ‹*work, business*› have stopped;
‹*production, firm*› be at a standstill

**Ruhe-:** ~**pause** *die* break; ~**stand** *der*
retirement; in den ~**stand** gehen/versetzt
werden go into retirement/be retired;
~**störung** *die* disturbance; (Rechtsw.)
disturbance of the peace; ~**tag** *der* closing
day; „Dienstag ~**tag**" 'closed on Tuesdays'

**ruhig** [1] *Adj.* (a) (still, leise) quiet
(b) (friedlich, ungestört) peaceful ‹*times, life,
valley, etc.*›; quiet ‹*talk, reflection, life*›
(c) (unbewegt) calm ‹*sea, weather*›; still ‹*air*›;
(fig.) peaceful ‹*melody*›; (gleichmäßig) steady
‹*breathing, hand, steps*›; smooth ‹*flight,
crossing*›
(d) (gelassen) calm ‹*voice etc.*›; quiet, calm
‹*person*›
[2] *adv.* (a) (still, leise) quietly; sich ~
verhalten keep quiet
(b) (friedlich, ohne Störungen) peacefully; (ohne
Zwischenfälle) uneventfully; ‹*work, think*› in
peace
(c) (unbewegt) ‹*sit, lie, stand*› still; (gleichmäßig)
‹*burn, breathe*› steadily; ‹*run, fly*› smoothly
(d) (gelassen) ‹*speak, watch, sit*› calmly
[3] *Adv.* by all means

**Ruhm** *der;* ~**[e]s** fame

**rühmen** [1] *tr. V.* praise
[2] *refl. V.* boast (+ *Gen.* about)

**ruhm·reich** *Adj.* glorious ‹*victory, history*›;
celebrated ‹*general, army, victory*›

**Ruhr** *die;* ~, ~**en** dysentery *no art.*

**Rühr·ei** *das* scrambled egg[s *pl.*]

**rühren** [1] *tr. V.* (a) (umrühren) stir; (einrühren)
stir ‹*egg, powder, etc.*› (**an, in** + *Akk.* into)
(b) (bewegen) move ‹*limb, fingers, etc.*›
(c) (fig.) move; touch
[2] *itr. V.* (a) (umrühren) stir
(b) (geh.: herrühren) das rührt daher, dass ...:
that stems from the fact that ...
[3] *refl. V.* (a) (sich bewegen) move
(b) (Milit.) rührt euch! at ease!

**rührend** [1] *Adj.* touching
[2] *adv.* touchingly

**rühr·selig** [1] *Adj.* (a) emotional ‹*person*›
(b) (allzu gefühlvoll) over-sentimental; ‹*manner,
mood, etc.*›; maudlin, (coll.) tear-jerking ‹*play,
song, etc.*›
[2] *adv.* (allzu gefühlvoll) in an over-sentimental
manner

**Rühr·seligkeit** *die* sentimentality

**Rührung** *die;* ~: emotion

**Ruine** *die;* ~, ~**n** ruin

**ruinieren** *tr. V.* ruin

**rülpsen** *itr. V.* (ugs.) burp

**rum** *Adv.* (ugs.) ▶ HERUM

**Rum** *der;* ~**s,** ~**s** rum

**Rumäne** *der;* ~**n,** ~**n** Romanian

**Rumänien** (*das*); ~**s** Romania

---

**Rumänin** *die;* ~, ~nen Romanian
**rumänisch** *Adj.* Romanian
**Rummel** *der;* ~s (ugs.) **(a)** commotion; (Aufhebens) fuss (**um** about)
**(b)** (Jahrmarkt) fair
**Rummel·platz** *der* (bes. nordd.) fairground
**Rumpel·kammer** *die* (ugs.) boxroom (Brit.); junk room
**rumpeln** *itr. V.* (ugs.) bump and bang about
**Rumpf** *der;* ~[e]s, Rümpfe **(a)** trunk [of the body]
**(b)** (beim Schiff) hull
**(c)** (beim Flugzeug) fuselage
**rümpfen** *tr. V.* **die Nase [bei etw.]** ~: wrinkle one's nose [at sth.]; **über jmdn./etw. die Nase rümpfen** (fig.) look down one's nose at sb./turn up one's nose at sth.
**Rumpsteak** /'rʊmpsteːk/ *das;* ~s, ~s rump steak
**rum|treiben** *unr. refl. V.* (ugs.)
▶ HERUMTREIBEN
**rund** ⎡1⎤ *Adj.* **(a)** round
**(b)** (dicklich) plump ⟨*arms etc.*⟩; chubby ⟨*cheeks*⟩; fat ⟨*stomach*⟩
**(c)** (ugs.: ganz) round ⟨*dozen, number, etc.*⟩
⎡2⎤ *Adv.* **(a)** (ugs.: etwa) about
**(b)** ~ **um jmdn./etw.** [all] around sb./sth.
**Rund-:** ~**blick** *der* panorama; view in all directions; ~**brief** *der* circular [letter]
**Runde** *die;* ~, ~n **(a)** (Sport: Strecke) lap
**(b)** (Sport: Durchgang usw.) round; **über die** ~**n kommen** (fig. ugs.) get by; manage
**(c)** (Personenkreis) circle; (Gesellschaft) company
**(d)** (Rundgang) round
**(e)** (Lage) round
**rund-, Rund-:** ~**erneuern** *tr. V.;* **ich runderneuere, runderneuert, rundzuerneuern** (Kfz-W.) remould; ~**fahrt** *die* tour (**durch** of); ~**funk** *der* **(a)** radio; **(b)** (Einrichtung, Gebäude) radio station
**Rundfunk-:** ~**anstalt** *die* broadcasting corporation; ~**gebühren** *Pl.* radio licence fees; ~**gerät** *das* radio set; ~**sendung** *die* radio programme; ~**sprecher** *der,* ~**sprecherin** *die* radio announcer
**rund-, Rund-:** ~**gang** *der* round (**durch** of); ~**herum** *Adv.* **(a)** (ringsum) all around; **(b)** (völlig) completely
**rundlich** *Adj.* **(a)** roundish
**(b)** (mollig) plump

**Rund-:** ~**reise** *die* [circular] tour (**durch** of); ~**schreiben** *das:* ▶ ~BRIEF; ~**weg** *der* circular path *or* walk
**runter** *Adv.* (ugs.) ~ [**da**]! get off [there]; *s. auch* HERUNTER; HINUNTER
**Runzel** *die;* ~, ~n wrinkle
**runz[e]lig** *Adj.* wrinkled
**runzeln** *tr. V.* **die Stirn/die Brauen** ~: wrinkle one's brow/knit one's brows; (ärgerlich) frown
**rupfen** *tr. V.* **(a)** pluck ⟨*goose, hen, etc.*⟩
**(b)** (abreißen) pull up ⟨*weeds, grass*⟩; pull off ⟨*leaves etc.*⟩
**ruppig** *Adj.* (abwertend) gruff ⟨*person, behaviour*⟩; sharp ⟨*tone*⟩; **er war** ~ **zu ihr** he was short with her; he snapped at her
**Rüsche** *die;* ~, ~n ruche; frill
**Ruß** *der;* ~es soot
**Russe** *der;* ~n, ~n Russian
**Rüssel** *der;* ~s, ~ (des Elefanten) trunk; (des Schweins) snout; (bei Insekten u. Ä.) proboscis
**rußen** *itr. V.* give off sooty smoke
**Russin** *die;* ~, ~nen Russian
**russisch** ⎡1⎤ *Adj.* Russian
⎡2⎤ *adv.* (auf ~) in Russian
**Russisch** *das;* ~[s] Russian
**Russ·land, \*Ruß·land** (*das*); ~s Russia
**rüsten** *itr. V.* arm
**rüstig** *Adj.* sprightly; active
**rustikal** ⎡1⎤ *Adj.* country-style ⟨*food, inn, clothes, etc.*⟩; rustic ⟨*furniture*⟩
⎡2⎤ *adv.* in [a] country style
**Rüstung** *die;* ~, ~en **(a)** armament *no art.;* (Waffen) arms *pl.;* weapons *pl.*
**(b)** (hist.) suit of armour
**Rüstungs-:** ~**industrie** *die* armaments *or* arms industry; ~**kontrolle** *die* arms control; ~**stopp** *der* arms freeze; ~**wettlauf** *der* arms race
**Rute** *die;* ~, ~n switch; (Birken~, Angel~, Wünschel~) rod
**Rutsch** *der* **guten** ~ [**ins neue Jahr**]! (ugs.) happy New Year!
**Rutsch·bahn** *die* slide
**Rutsche** *die;* ~, ~n chute
**rutschen** *itr. V.; mit sein* slide; ⟨*clutch, carpet*⟩ slip
**rutschig** *Adj.* slippery
**rütteln** *tr., itr. V.* shake

# Ss

**s, S** /ɛs/ *das;* ~, ~ s/S

**s** *Abk.* = **Sekunde** sec.; s.

**s.** *Abk.* = **siehe**

**S** *Abk.* **(a)** = **Süden** S.
**(b)** (österr.) = **Schilling** Sch.

**S.** *Abk.* = **Seite** p.

**Sa.** *Abk.* = **Samstag** Sat.

**Saal** *der;* ~[e]s, **Säle (a)** hall; (Ballsaal)
ballroom
**(b)** (Publikum) audience

**Saar·land** *das;* ~[e]s Saarland; Saar (esp.
Hist.)

**Saat** *die;* ~, ~en **(a)** (das Gesäte) [young]
crops *pl.*
**(b)** (das Säen) sowing
**(c)** (Samenkörner) seed[s *pl.*]

**Säbel** *der;* ~s, ~: sabre

**Sabotage** /zabo'ta:ʒə/ *die;* ~, ~n sabotage
*no art.*

**Sabotage·akt** *der* act of sabotage

**sabotieren** *tr. V.* sabotage

**Sach-:** ~**bearbeiter** *der,*
~**bearbeiterin** *die* person responsible
(für for); (Experte) specialist, expert (für on);
~**beschädigung** *die* (Rechtsw.) wilful
damage to property; ~**buch** *das* [popular]
non-fiction book; ~**bücher lesen** read non-
fiction *sing.*

**sach·dienlich** *Adj.* useful

**Sache** *die;* ~, ~n **(a)** things
**(b)** (Angelegenheit) matter; business (esp.
derog.); **zur** ~ **kommen** come to the point
**(c)** (Rechtssache) case
**(d)** (Anliegen) cause

**sach-, Sach-:** ~**gebiet** *das* subject
[area]; field; ~**gemäß, ~gerecht**
[1] *Adj.* proper; correct; [2] *adv.* properly;
correctly; ~**kenntnis** *die* expertise;
knowledge of the subject; ~**kundig** [1] *Adj.*
with a knowledge of the subject *postpos., not
pred.;* [2] *adv.* expertly

**sachlich** [1] *Adj.* **(a)** (objektiv) objective;
(nüchtern) functional ‹building, style, etc.›;
matter-of-fact ‹letter etc.›
**(b)** (sachbezogen) factual ‹error›
[2] *adv.* **(a)** objectively; ‹state› as a
matter of fact; (nüchtern) ‹furnished› in a
functional style; ‹written› in a matter-of-fact
way
**(b)** (sachbezogen) factually ‹wrong›

**sächlich** *Adj.* (Sprachw.) neuter

**Sachlichkeit** *die;* ~: objectivity;
(Nüchternheit) functionalism

**Sach-:** ~**register** *das* [subject] index;
~**schaden** *der* damage [to property] *no
indef. art.*

**Sachse** *der;* ~n, ~n Saxon

**Sachsen** (*das*); ~s Saxony

**Sachsen-Anhalt** (*das*); ~s Saxony-
Anhalt

**Sächsin** *die;* ~, ~nen Saxon

**sacht, sachte** [1] *Adj.* **(a)** (behutsam)
gentle
**(b)** (leise) quiet
[2] *adv.* **(a)** gently
**(b)** (leise) quietly

**Sach-:** ~**verhalt** *der;* ~~[e]s, ~~e facts
*pl.* [of the matter]; ~**verstand** *der*
expertise; grasp of the subject;
~**verständige** *der/die; adj. Dekl.* expert

**Sack** *der;* ~[e]s, **Säcke** sack; (aus Papier,
Kunststoff) bag

**Sack-:** ~**gasse** *die* cul-de-sac; ~**hüpfen**
*das;* ~~s sack race

**Sadismus** *der;* ~: sadism *no art.*

**Sadist** *der;* ~en, ~en, **Sadistin** *die;* ~,
~nen sadist

**sadistisch** [1] *Adj.* sadistic
[2] *adv.* sadistically

**säen** *tr.* (*auch itr.*) *V.* sow

**Saft** *der;* ~[e]s, **Säfte (a)** juice
**(b)** (in Pflanzen) sap

**saftig** *Adj.* **(a)** juicy; sappy ‹stem›; lush
‹meadow, green›
**(b)** (ugs.) hefty ‹slap, blow›; steep (coll.)
‹prices, bill›; crude ‹joke, song, etc.›;
strongly-worded ‹letter etc.›

**saft-, Saft-:** ~**laden** *der* (salopp abwertend)
lousy outfit (coll.); ~**los** *Adj.* **(a)** juiceless
**(b)** (fig.) feeble, anodyne ‹language›; ~ **und
kraftlos** feeble, wishy-washy; (adv.) without
any zest; ~**sack** *der* (derb abwertend) bastard
(coll.)

**Sage** *die;* ~, ~n legend; (bes. nordische) saga

**Säge** *die;* ~, ~n saw

**Säge-:** ~**blatt** *das* saw blade; ~**mehl**
sawdust

**sagen** [1] *tr. V.* **(a)** say; **was ich noch** ~
**wollte** [oh] by the way; **unter uns gesagt**
between you and me
**(b)** (mitteilen) **jmdm. etw.** ~: say sth. to sb.;
(zur Information) tell sb. sth.
**(c)** (nennen) **zu jmdm./etw. X** ~: call sb./sth. X
**(d)** (anordnen, befehlen) tell
[2] *refl. V.* **sich** (*Dat.*) **etw.** ~: say sth. to
oneself

**sägen** *tr., itr. V.* saw

---

**Säge-:** ∼**späne** *Pl.* wood shavings;
∼**werk** *das* sawmill

**sah** *1. u. 3. Pers. Sg. Prät. v.* SEHEN

**Sahne** *die;* ∼: cream

**Saison** /zɛ'zõː/ *die;* ∼, ∼s season

**saisonal** /zɛzo'naːl/ [1] *Adj.* seasonal
[2] *adv. ⟨fluctuate⟩* according to the season

**Saite** *die;* ∼, ∼n string

**Saiten·instrument** *das* stringed
instrument

**Sakko** *der od. das;* ∼s, ∼s jacket

**Sakrament** *das;* ∼[e]s, ∼e sacrament

**Sakristei** *die;* ∼, ∼en sacristy

**säkularisieren** *tr. V.* secularize *⟨property,
art, etc.⟩*; deconsecrate *⟨church⟩*

**Salami** *die;* ∼, ∼[s] salami

**Salami·taktik** *die* step-by-step policy

**Salat** *der;* ∼[e]s, ∼e **(a)** salad
**(b)** [grüner] ∼: lettuce; **ein Kopf** ∼: a [head
of] lettuce

**Salat-:** ∼**besteck** *das* salad servers *pl.;*
∼**soße** *die* salad dressing

**Salbe** *die;* ∼, ∼n ointment

**Salbei** *der od. die. die;* ∼: sage

**Saldo** *der;* ∼s, ∼s *od.* **Saldi** (Buchf., Finanzw.)
balance

**Säle** ▶ SAAL

**Salmiak** *der od. das;* ∼: sal ammoniac

**Salmonelle** *die;* ∼, ∼n salmonella

**Salon** /za'lõː/ *der;* ∼s, ∼s **(a)** (Raum)
drawing room
**(b)** (Geschäft) [hair *etc.*] salon

**salopp** [1] *Adj.* casual *⟨clothes⟩*; informal
*⟨behaviour⟩*
[2] *adv. ⟨dress⟩* casually

**Salto** *der;* ∼s, ∼s *od.* **Salti** somersault; (beim
Turnen auch) salto

**Salut** *der;* ∼[e]s, ∼e (Milit.) salute; ∼
**schießen** fire a salute

**salutieren** *itr. V.* (bes. Milit.) salute

**Salut·schuss, \*Salut·schuß** *der* (Milit.)
gun salute

**Salve** *die;* ∼, ∼n (Milit.) salvo; (aus Gewehren)
volley

**Salz** *das;* ∼es, ∼e salt

**salzen** *tr. V.* salt

**salzig** *Adj.* salty

**Salz-:** ∼**kartoffel** *die* boiled potato;
∼**säure** *die* (Chemie) hydrochloric acid;
∼**stange** *die* salt stick; ∼**streuer** *der;*
∼∼**s,** ∼∼: salt sprinkler; salt shaker
(Amer.); ∼**wasser** *das* **(a)** (zum Kochen)
salted water; **(b)** (Meerwasser) salt water

**Sambia** *(das);* ∼s Zambia

**Samen** *der;* ∼s, ∼ **(a)** (Samenkorn) seed
**(b)** (Samenkörner) seed[s *pl.*]
**(c)** (Sperma) sperm; semen

**Samen-:** ∼**bank** *die; Pl.* ∼∼en (Med.,
Tiermed.) sperm bank; ∼**erguss,**
\*∼**erguß** *der* ejaculation; ∼**korn** *das* seed

**Sammel-:** ∼**büchse** *die* collecting box;
∼**mappe** *die* folder; file

**sammeln** [1] *tr. (auch itr.) V.* **(a)** collect;
gather *⟨honey, firewood, fig.: experiences,
impressions, etc.⟩*; gather, pick *⟨berries etc.⟩*
**(b)** (zusammenkommen lassen) gather *⟨people⟩*
[together]; assemble *⟨people⟩*; cause *⟨light
rays⟩* to converge
[2] *refl. V.* gather [together]

**Sammler** *der;* ∼s, ∼: collector

**Sammlung** *die;* ∼, ∼en **(a)** collection
**(b)** [innere] ∼: composure

**Samstag** *der;* ∼[e]s, ∼e Saturday; *s. auch*
DIENSTAG

**samstags** *Adv.* on Saturdays

**samt** [1] *Präp. mit Dat.* together with
[2] *Adv.* ∼ **und sonders** one and all

**Samt** *der;* ∼[e]s, ∼e velvet

**samten** *Adj.* velvet

**Samt·handschuh** *der* velvet glove; **jmdn.
mit** ∼**en anfassen** (fig.) handle sb. with kid
gloves

**samtig** *Adj.* velvety

**sämtlich** *Indefinitpron. u. unbest. Zahlwort*
all the

**Sand** *der;* ∼[e]s sand

**Sandale** *die;* ∼, ∼n sandal

**Sand-:** ∼**bank** *die; Pl.* ∼**bänke** sandbank;
∼**dorn** *der; Pl.* ∼∼e (Bot.) hippopha;
[Echter] ∼**dorn** sea buckthorn ∼**düne** *die*
sand dune

**sandig** *Adj.* sandy

**sand-, Sand-:** ∼**kasten** *der* [child's]
sandpit; sandbox (Amer.); ∼**kuchen** *der*
Madeira cake; ∼**mann** *der,*
∼**männchen** *das* sandman; ∼**stein** *der*
sandstone; ∼**strahlen** *tr. V.* (Technik)
sandblast; ∼**strand** *der* sandy beach

**sandte** *1. u. 3. Pers. Sg. Prät. v.* SENDEN

**sanft** [1] *Adj.* gentle; (leise) soft; (friedlich)
peaceful
[2] *adv.* gently; (leise) softly; (friedlich)
peacefully

**Sänfte** *die;* ∼, ∼n litter; (geschlossen) sedan
chair

**Sanftheit** *die;* ∼: gentleness; (von Klängen,
Licht, Farben) softness

**Sanftmut** *die;* ∼: gentleness; **mit** ∼:
gently; (nachsichtig) leniently

**sanftmütig** [1] *Adj.* gentle; docile *⟨horse⟩*
[2] *adv.* gently

**Sanftmütigkeit** *die;* ∼: gentleness;
(Fügsamkeit) docility

**sang** *1. u. 3. Pers. Sg. Prät. v.* SINGEN

**Sänger** *der;* ∼s, ∼, **Sängerin** *die;* ∼,
∼**nen** singer

**sanieren** [1] *tr. V.* **(a)** redevelop *⟨area⟩*;
rehabilitate *⟨building⟩*; (renovieren) renovate
[and improve] *⟨flat etc.⟩*
**(b)** (Wirtsch.) restore *⟨firm⟩* to profitability  ····⊹

[2] *refl. V.* ⟨*company etc.*⟩ restore itself to profitability; ⟨*person*⟩ get oneself out of the red

**Sanierung** *die;* ~, ~en (a) ▶ SANIEREN A: redevelopment; rehabilitation; renovation
(b) ▶ SANIEREN B: restoration to profitability

**sanitär** *Adj.* sanitary

**Sanitäter** *der;* ~s, ~, **Sanitäterin** *die;* ~, ~nen first-aid worker; (im Krankenwagen) ambulance worker

**sank** *1. u. 3. Pers. Sg. Prät. v.* SINKEN

**Sanktion** *die;* ~, ~en sanction

**sanktionieren** *tr. V.* sanction

**Sanktionierung** *die;* ~, ~en sanctioning *no indef. art.*

**sann** *1. u. 3. Pers. Sg. Prät. v.* SINNEN

**Saphir** *der;* ~s, ~e sapphire

**Sardelle** *die;* ~, ~n anchovy

**Sardine** *die;* ~, ~n sardine

**Sarg** *der;* ~[e]s, **Särge** coffin

**Sarkasmus** *der;* ~: sarcasm

**sarkastisch** [1] *Adj.* sarcastic
[2] *adv.* sarcastically

**saß** *1. u. 3. Pers. Sg. Prät. v.* SITZEN

**Satan** *der* (bibl.) Satan *no def. art.*

**Satellit** *der;* ~en, ~en satellite

**Satelliten-:** ~**fernsehen** *das* satellite television; ~**schüssel** *die* (ugs.) satellite dish; ~**technologie** *die* satellite technology

**Satire** *die;* ~, ~n satire

**satirisch** [1] *Adj.* satirical
[2] *adv.* satirically; with a satirical touch

**satt** *Adj.* (a) full [up] *pred.;* well-fed; **sich** ~ **essen/trinken** eat/drink as much as one wants; eat/drink one's fill
(b) jmdn./etw. ~ **haben** (ugs.) be fed up with sb./sth. (coll.)

**Sattel** *der;* ~s, **Sättel** saddle

**satteln** [1] *tr. V.* saddle
[2] *itr. V.* saddle the/one's horse

**sättigen** *itr. V.* be filling

**Sattler** *der;* ~s, ~, **Sattlerin** *die;* ~, ~nen saddler; (allgemein) leather worker

**Satz** *der;* ~es, **Sätze** (a) (sprachliche Einheit) sentence
(b) (Musik) movement
(c) (Tennis, Volleyball) set; (Tischtennis, Badminton) game
(d) (Sprung) leap; jump
(e) (Amtsspr.: Tarif) rate
(f) (Set) set
(g) (Bodensatz) sediment; (von Kaffee) grounds *pl.*

**Satz·glied** *das,* **Satz·teil** *der* (Sprachw.) component part [of a/the sentence]

**Satzung** *die;* ~, ~en articles of association *pl.;* statutes *pl.*

**Satz·zeichen** *das* punctuation mark

**Sau** *die;* ~, **Säue** (a) (weibliches Schwein) sow

(b) (bes. südd.: Schwein) pig
(c) **die** ~ **rauslassen** (fig. ugs.) let one's hair down

**sau-, Sau-** (salopp) bloody ... (Brit. sl.); damn ... (coll.)

**sauber** [1] *Adj.* (a) clean; etw. ~ **machen** clean sth.; ~ **machen** ( putzen) clean; do the cleaning
(b) (sorgfältig) neat
[2] *adv.* (a) (sorgfältig) neatly
(b) (fehlerlos) [sehr] ~: [quite] perfectly

**Sauberkeit** *die;* ~: cleanness

**säuberlich** [1] *Adj.* neat
[2] *adv.* neatly; **fein** ~ **geordnet/verpackt** *usw.* neatly arranged/packed *etc.*

*\***sauber|machen** ▶ SAUBER 1A

**säubern** *tr. V.* (a) clean
(b) (befreien) clear, rid (von of); purge ⟨*party, government, etc.*⟩ (von of)

**Säuberung** *die;* ~, ~en (a) cleaning
(b) (Entfernung) purging
(c) (Politik) purge; **ethnische** ~ (verhüll.) ethnic cleansing

**Säuberungs·aktion** *die* (Politik) purge; clean-up operation

**Sauce** ▶ SOSSE

**Saudi** *der;* ~s, ~s Saudi

**Saudi-Arabien** (*das*) Saudi Arabia

**sauer** [1] *Adj.* (a) sour; pickled ⟨*herring, gherkin, etc.*⟩; acid[ic] ⟨*wine, vinegar*⟩; **saurer Regen** acid rain
(b) (ugs.: verärgert) cross, annoyed (**auf** + *Akk.* with)
[2] *adv.* in vinegar

**Sauer·braten** *der:* braised beef marinated in vinegar and herbs; sauerbraten (Amer.)

**Sauerei** *die;* ~, ~en (salopp abwertend) (a) (Unflätigkeit) obscenity
(b) (Gemeinheit) bloody scandal (coll.)

**Sauer-:** ~**kirsche** *die* sour cherry; ~**kraut** *das* sauerkraut

**säuerlich** *Adj.* [leicht] ~: slightly sour; slightly sharp ⟨*sauce*⟩

**Sauer-:** ~**stoff** *der* oxygen; ~**stoff-gerät** *das* oxygen apparatus; ~**stoff-mangel** *der* lack of oxygen; ~**teig** *der* leaven

**saufen** [1] *unr. itr. V.* (salopp: trinken) drink; swig (coll.); (Alkohol trinken) drink; booze (coll.)
[2] *unr. tr. V.* (salopp: trinken) drink

**Säufer** *der;* ~s, ~ (salopp) boozer (coll.)

**säuft** *3. Pers. Sg. Präsens v.* SAUFEN

**saugen** [1] *tr. V.* (a) *auch unr.* suck
(b) *auch itr.* (staubsaugen) vacuum; hoover (coll.)
[2] *regelm.* (*auch unr.*) *itr. V.* **an etw.** (*Dat.*) ~: suck [at] sth.
[3] *unr.* (*auch regelm.*) *refl. V.* **sich voll etw.** ~: become soaked with sth.

**säugen** *tr. V.* suckle

**Säuge·tier** *das* (Zool.) mammal

**Säugling** *der;* ~s, ~e baby

**Säuglings-:** ~**alter** das infancy; babyhood; ~**pflege** die baby care

**Säule** die; ~, ~n column; (nur als Stütze, auch fig.) pillar

**Saum** der; ~[e]s, Säume hem

**säumen** tr. V. hem; (fig. geh.) line

**säumig** (geh.) Adj. tardy

**Sauna** die; ~, ~s od. Saunen sauna

**Säure** die; ~, ~n (a) (von Früchten) sourness; (von Wein, Essig) acidity; (von Soßen) sharpness **(b)** (Chemie) acid

**säure-:** ~**beständig** Adj. acid-resistant; ~**frei** Adj. acid-free

**Saure-gurken-zeit, Saure-Gurken-Zeit** die (ugs.) silly season (Brit.)

**Saurier** /'zauːriɐ/ der; ~s, ~: large prehistoric reptile

**Saus:** in ~ und Braus leben live the high life

**säuseln** [1] itr. V. ⟨leaves, branches, etc.⟩ rustle; ⟨wind⟩ murmur
[2] tr. V. (iron.: sagen) whisper

**sausen** itr. V. (a) ⟨wind⟩ whistle; ⟨storm⟩ roar; ⟨head, ears⟩ buzz
**(b)** mit sein ⟨person⟩ rush; ⟨vehicle⟩ roar
**(c)** mit sein ⟨whip, bullet, etc.⟩ whistle

**sau-, Sau-:** ~**stall** der (fig. salopp abwertend) hole (coll.); dump (coll.); ~**stark** Adj. (salopp) bloody brilliant (sl.); ~**wetter** das (salopp abwertend) lousy weather (coll.); ~**wohl** Adj. sich ~wohl fühlen (salopp) feel bloody (Brit. sl.) or (coll.) damn good or great

**Savanne** /zaˈvanə/ die; ~, ~n savannah

**Saxophon** das; ~s, ~e saxophone

**SB-** /ɛsˈbeː-/ self-service attrib.

**S-Bahn** /ˈɛs-/ die city and suburban railway

**Scanner** /ˈskænɐ/ der; ~s, ~ (DV, Med., graf. Technik) scanner

**Schabe** die; ~, ~n cockroach

**schaben** tr., itr. V. scrape

**Schaber** der; ~s, ~: scraper

**schäbig** [1] Adj. (a) (abgenutzt) shabby
**(b)** (jämmerlich, gering) pathetic
**(c)** (gemein) shabby
[2] adv. (a) (abgenutzt) shabbily
**(b)** (jämmerlich) miserably
**(c)** (gemein) meanly

**Schablone** die; ~, ~n pattern

**Schach** das; ~s, ~s (a) (Spiel) chess
**(b)** (Stellung) check; jmdn./etw. in ~ halten (ugs. fig.) keep sb./sth. in check

**Schach-:** ~**brett** das chessboard; ~**figur** die chess piece; ~**spiel** das (a) (Spiel) chess; (das Spielen) chess-playing; **(b)** (Brett und Figuren) chess set

**Schacht** der; ~[e]s, Schächte shaft

**Schachtel** die; ~, ~n (a) box; eine ~ Zigaretten a packet or (Amer.) pack of cigarettes
**(b)** alte ~ (salopp abwertend) old bag (sl.)

**schade** Adj. [ach, wie] ~! [what a] pity or

shame; [es ist] ~ um jmdn./etw. it's a pity or shame about sb./sth.; für jmdn./für od. zu etw. zu ~ sein be too good for sb./sth.

**Schädel** der; ~s, ~: skull; (Kopf) head

**Schädel-basis-bruch** der (Med.) basal skull fracture

**Schädel-bruch** der (Med.) skull fracture

**schaden** itr. V. jmdm./einer Sache ~: damage or harm sb./sth.

**Schaden** der; ~s, Schäden (a) damage no pl., no indef. art.; ein kleiner/großer ~: little/ major damage
**(b)** (Nachteil) disadvantage

**schaden-, Schaden-:** ~**ersatz** der (Rechtsw.) damages pl.; ~**freude** die malicious pleasure; ~**froh** [1] Adj. gloating; ~froh sein gloat; [2] adv. with malicious pleasure

**schadhaft** Adj. defective

**Schadhaftigkeit** die; ~: defectiveness

**schädigen** tr. V. damage ⟨health, reputation, interests⟩; harm, hurt ⟨person⟩; cause losses to ⟨firm, industry, etc.⟩

**Schädigung** die; ~, ~en damage no pl., no indef. art. (Gen. to)

**schädlich** Adj. harmful

**Schädling** der; ~s, ~e pest

**Schad-stoff** der harmful chemical

**schadstoff-arm** Adj. (bes. Kfz-W.) low in harmful substances postpos.; clean-exhaust attrib. ⟨vehicle⟩

**Schaf** das; ~[e]s, ~e (a) sheep
**(b)** (ugs.: Dummkopf) twit (Brit. coll.)

**Schaf-bock** der ram

**Schäfchen** das; ~s, ~: [little] sheep; (Lamm) lamb

**Schäfchen-wolke** die fleecy cloud

**Schäfer** der; ~s, ~: shepherd

**Schäfer-hund** der sheepdog; [deutscher] ~: Alsatian

**Schäferin** die; ~, ~nen shepherdess

**Schaf-fell** das sheepskin

**schaffen** [1] unr. tr. V. (a) create
**(b)** auch regelm. (herstellen) create ⟨conditions, jobs, situation, etc.⟩; make ⟨room, space, fortune⟩
[2] tr. V. (a) (bewältigen) manage; es ~, etw. zu tun manage to do sth.
**(b)** (ugs.: erschöpfen) wear out
**(c)** etw. aus etw./in etw. (Akk.) ~: get sth. out of/into sth.
[3] itr. V. (a) (südd.: arbeiten) work
**(b)** sich (Dat.) zu ~ machen busy oneself; jmdm. zu ~ machen cause sb. trouble

**Schaffner** der; ~s ~ (im Bus) conductor; (im Zug) guard (Brit.); conductor (Amer.)

**Schaffnerin** die; ~, ~nen (im Bus) conductress (Brit.); (im Zug) guard (Brit.); conductress (Amer.)

**Schaffung** die; ~: creation

**Schafott** das; ~[e]s, ~e scaffold

**Schafs-käse** der sheep's milk cheese

**Schaf·wolle** *die* sheep's wool
**Schakal** *der;* ~s, ~e jackal
**schal** *Adj.* stale ⟨*drink, taste, smell, joke*⟩; empty ⟨*words, feeling*⟩
**Schal** *der;* ~s, ~s *od.* ~e scarf
**Schale** *die;* ~, ~n (a) (Obstschale) skin; (abgeschälte ~) peel *no pl.;* (b) (Nussschale, Eierschale) shell (c) (Schüssel) bowl; (flacher) dish (d) **sich in ~ werfen** *od.* **schmeißen** (ugs.) get dressed [up] to the nines
**schälen** [1] *tr. V.* peel ⟨*fruit, vegetable*⟩; shell ⟨*egg, nut, pea*⟩ [2] *refl. V.* peel
**Schall** *der;* ~[e]s, ~e *od.* **Schälle** sound
**Schall·dämpfer** *der* (a) silencer (b) (Musik) mute
**schall·dicht** *Adj.* soundproof
**schallen** *regelm.* (*auch unr.*) *itr. V.* ring out; ~**des Gelächter** ringing laughter
**Schall-:** ~**geschwindigkeit** *die* speed *or* velocity of sound; ~**mauer** *die* sound *or* sonic barrier; ~**platte** *die* record
**Schalotte** *die;* ~, ~n shallot
**schalt** *1. u. 3. Pers. Sg. Prät. v.* SCHELTEN
**schalten** [1] *tr. V.* switch [2] *itr. V.* (a) (Schalter betätigen) switch, turn (**auf** + *Akk.* to) (b) ⟨*machine*⟩ switch (**auf** + *Akk.* to) (c) (im Auto) change [gear] (d) ~ **und walten** manage one's affairs (e) (ugs.: begreifen) twig (coll.); catch on (coll.)
**Schalter** *der;* ~s, ~ (a) switch (b) (Post-, Bankschalter usw.) counter
**Schalter-:** ~**beamte** *der,* ~**beamtin** *die* counter clerk; (im Bahnhof) ticket clerk; ~**halle** *die* hall; (im Bahnhof) booking hall (Brit.); ticket office
**Schalt·jahr** *das* leap year
**Schaltung** *die;* ~, ~en (Elektrot.) circuit; wiring system
**Scham** *die;* ~: shame
**schämen** *refl. V.* be ashamed (*Gen.,* **für, wegen** of)
**Scham·gefühl** *das* sense of shame
**schamhaft** [1] *Adj.* bashful [2] *adv.* bashfully
**scham·los** [1] *Adj.* (a) (skrupellos, dreist) shameless (b) (unanständig) indecent; shameless ⟨*person*⟩ [2] *adv.* (a) (skrupellos, dreist) shamelessly (b) (unanständig) indecently
**Schampon** *das;* ~s, ~s ▶ SHAMPOO
**schamponieren** *tr. V.* shampoo
**Schande** *die;* ~: disgrace
**schändlich** [1] *Adj.* disgraceful [2] *adv.* disgracefully
**Schändlichkeit** *die;* ~: disgracefulness
**Schar** *die;* ~, ~en crowd; horde
**scharen·weise** *Adv.* in swarms *or* hordes

**scharf;** **schärfer, schärfst...** [1] *Adj.* (a) sharp (b) (stark gewürzt, brennend, stechend) hot; strong ⟨*drink, vinegar, etc.*⟩; caustic ⟨*chemical*⟩; pungent ⟨*smell*⟩ (c) (durchdringend) shrill; (hell) harsh; (kalt) biting ⟨*cold, wind, etc.*⟩; sharp ⟨*frost*⟩ (d) (deutlich wahrnehmend) keen (e) (schnell) fast; hard ⟨*ride, gallop, etc.*⟩ (f) (explosiv) live; (Ballspiele) powerful ⟨*shot*⟩ (g) **das** ~**e S** (bes. österr.) the letter 'ß' (h) ~ **auf jmdn./etw. sein** (ugs.) really fancy sb. (coll.)/be really keen on sth. [2] *adv.* (a) ~ **würzen/abschmecken** season/flavour highly; ~ **riechen** smell pungent (b) (durchdringend) shrilly; (hell) harshly; (kalt) bitingly (c) (deutlich wahrnehmend) ⟨*listen, watch, etc.*⟩ closely, intently; ⟨*think, consider, etc.*⟩ hard (d) (deutlich hervortretend) sharply (e) (schonungslos) ⟨*attack, criticize, etc.*⟩ sharply, strongly; ⟨*watch, observe, etc.*⟩ closely (f) (schnell) fast; ~ **bremsen** brake hard *or* sharply
**Schärfe** *die;* ~ (a) sharpness (b) (von Geschmack) hotness; (von Chemikalien) causticity; (von Geruch) pungency (c) (Intensität) shrillness; (des Frostes) sharpness
**schärfen** [1] *tr. V.* (auch fig.) sharpen [2] *refl. V.* become sharper *or* keener
**scharf-, Scharf-:** ~**kantig** *Adj.* sharp-edged; ~**macher** *der* (ugs.) rabble-rouser; ~**macherei** *die;* ~~, ~~**en** (ugs.) rabble-rousing; ~**macherin** *die:* ▶ ~MACHER; ~**sichtig** *Adj.* sharp-sighted; perspicacious; ~**sinn** *der* astuteness; ~**sinnig** [1] *Adj.* astute; [2] *adv.* astutely
**Scharlach** *der;* ~s (Med.) scarlet fever
**Scharlatan** *der;* ~s, ~e (abwertend) charlatan
**Scharnier** *das;* ~s, ~e hinge
**scharren** [1] *itr. V.* (a) scrape (b) (wühlen) scratch [2] *tr. V.* scrape, scratch out ⟨*hole, hollow, etc.*⟩
**Schaschlik** *der od. das;* ~s, ~s (Kochk.) shashlik
**Schatten** *der;* ~s, ~ (a) shadow (b) (schattiger Bereich) shade
**Schatten-:** ~**kabinett** *das* (Politik) shadow cabinet; ~**riss, \***~**riß** *der* silhouette; ~**seite** *die* shady side; **die** ~**seiten des Lebens kennen lernen** (fig.) get to know the dark side of life
**schattig** *Adj.* shady
**Schatz** *der;* ~es, **Schätze** treasure *no indef. art.*
**schätzen** [1] *tr. V.* (a) estimate; **sich glücklich** ~: deem oneself lucky (b) (ugs.: annehmen) reckon (c) (würdigen, hoch achten) **jmdn.** ~: hold sb. in high esteem

─────────────

**\*** alte Schreibung - vgl. Hinweis auf S. xiv

**2** *itr. V.* guess

**Schätzung** *die;* ~, ~en estimate

**Schätz·wert** *der* estimated value

**Schau** *die;* ~, ~en (a) (Ausstellung) exhibition
**(b)** (Vorführung) show
**(c)** zur ~ stellen (ausstellen) exhibit; display; (offen zeigen) display

**Schauder** *der;* ~s, ~: shiver

**schauderhaft 1** *Adj.* terrible
**2** *adv.* terribly

**schaudern** *itr. V.* (a) (vor Kälte) shiver
**(b)** (vor Angst) shudder

**schauen** (bes. südd., österr., schweiz.)
**1** *itr. V.* (a) look
**(b)** (sich kümmern um) nach jmdm./etw. ~: take *or* have a look at sb./sth.
**(c)** (achten) auf etw. (*Akk.*) ~: set store by sth.
**(d)** (ugs.: sich bemühen) schau, dass du ...: see *or* mind that you ...
**(e)** (nachsehen) have a look
**2** *tr. V.* Fernsehen ~: watch television

**Schauer** *der;* ~s, ~: shower

**Schauer·geschichte** *die* horror story

**schauerlich 1** *Adj.* (a) horrifying
**(b)** (ugs.: fürchterlich) terrible (coll.)
**2** (ugs.: fürchterlich) terribly (coll.)

**Schaufel** *die;* ~, ~n shovel; (Kehr~) dustpan

**schaufeln** *tr. V.* shovel; (graben) dig

**Schau·fenster** *das* shop window

**Schaufenster-:** ~**bummel** *der:* einen ~bummel machen go window shopping; ~**einbruch** *der* raid on a shop window

**Schaukel** *die;* ~, ~n (a) swing
**(b)** (Wippe) see-saw

**schaukeln 1** *itr. V.* (a) swing; (im Schaukelstuhl) rock
**(b)** (sich hin und her bewegen) sway [to and fro]; (sich auf und ab bewegen) ⟨*ship, boat*⟩ pitch and toss; ⟨*vehicle*⟩ bump [up and down]
**2** *tr. V.* rock

**Schaukel-:** ~**pferd** *das* rocking horse; ~**stuhl** *der* rocking chair

**Schau·lustige** *der/die; adj. Dekl.* curious onlooker

**Schaum** *der;* ~s, Schäume (a) foam; (von Seife usw.) lather; (von Getränken, Suppen usw.) froth
**(b)** (Geifer) foam; froth

**schäumen** *itr. V.* foam; froth; ⟨*soap etc.*⟩ lather; ⟨*beer, fizzy drink, etc.*⟩ froth [up]

**Schaum·gummi** *der* foam rubber

**schaumig** *Adj.* frothy; Butter und Zucker ~ rühren beat butter and sugar until fluffy

**Schaum-:** ~**schläger** *der* (abwertend) boaster; ~**schlägerei** *die* (abwertend) boasting; ~**schlägerin** *die:* ▶ ~SCHLÄGER; ~**stoff** *der* [plastic] foam; ~**wein** *der* sparkling wine

**Schau·platz** *der* scene

**schaurig** *Adj.* (furchtbar) dreadful; frightful; (unheimlich) eerie

**Schau-:** ~**spiel** *das* (a) (Drama) drama *no art.;* (b) (ernstes Stück) play; (c) (geh.: Anblick) spectacle; ~**spieler** *der* actor; ~**spielerin** *die* actress; ~**steller** *der;* ~~s, ~~: showman; ~**stellerin** *die;* ~~, ~~nen showwoman

**Scheck** *der;* ~s, ~s cheque

**Scheck-:** ~**heft** *das* chequebook; ~**karte** *die* cheque card

**scheel** (ugs.) **1** *Adj.* disapproving; (neidisch) envious; jealous
**2** *adv.* disapprovingly; (neidisch) enviously; jealously

**scheffeln** *tr. V.* (ugs.) rake in (coll.)

**Scheibe** *die;* ~, ~n (a) disc
**(b)** (abgeschnittene) slice
**(c)** (Glasscheibe) pane [of glass]; (Fensterscheibe) [window] pane

**Scheiben-:** ~**bremse** *die* disc brake; ~**wasch·anlage** *die* (Kfz-W.) windscreen washer system *or* unit; ~**wischer** *der* windscreen wiper

**Scheide** *die;* ~, ~n (a) sheath
**(b)** (Anat.) vagina

**scheiden** *unr. tr. V.* dissolve ⟨*marriage*⟩; divorce ⟨*married couple*⟩; sich ~ lassen get divorced *or* get a divorce

**Scheidung** *die;* ~, ~en divorce

**Schein** *der;* ~[e]s, ~e (a) (Lichtschein) light
**(b)** (Anschein) appearances *pl., no art.;* (Täuschung) pretence; etw. nur zum ~ tun [only] pretend to do sth.; make a show of doing sth.
**(c)** (Geldschein) note

**scheinbar 1** *Adj.* apparent; seeming
**2** *adv.* seemingly

**scheinen** *unr. itr. V.* (a) shine
**(b)** (den Eindruck erwecken) seem; appear; mir scheint, [dass] ...: it seems *or* appears to me that ...

**schein-, Schein-:** ~**heilig 1** *Adj.* hypocritical; **2** *adv.* hypocritically; ~**heiligkeit** *die* hypocrisy; ~**tot** *Adj.* (a) (Med.) apparently *or* seemingly dead; (b) (salopp: sehr alt) with one foot in the grave *postpos.;* ~**werfer** *der* floodlight; (am Auto) headlight; ~**werfer·licht** *das* floodlight; (des Autos) headlights *pl.;* (im Theater, Museum usw.) spotlight [beam]

**Scheiße** *die;* ~ (derb) shit (coarse); crap (coarse)

**scheiß·egal** *Adj.* (derb) ~ sein not matter a damn (sl.); das ist mir ~: I don't give a damn (sl.) *or* (coarse) shit

**scheißen** *unr. itr. V.* (derb) [have *or* (Amer.) take a] shit (coarse); crap (coarse); have a crap (coarse)

**Scheiß·kerl** *der* (derb) bastard (coll.)

**Scheitel** *der;* ~s, ~: parting

**scheiteln** *tr. V.* part ⟨*hair*⟩

**S**

**scheitern** itr. V.; mit sein fail; ⟨talks, marriage⟩ break down; ⟨plan, project⟩ fail, fall through

**Schelle** die; ~, ~n bell

**schellen** itr. V. (westd.) ▶ KLINGELN

**Schell·fisch** der haddock

**Schelm** der; ~[e]s, ~e rascal; rogue

**schelmisch** ①Adj. roguish
②adv. roguishly

**Schelte** die; ~, ~n (geh.) scolding

**schelten** (südd., geh.) ①unr. itr. V. auf od. über jmdn./etw. ~: moan about sb./sth.
②unr. tr. V. scold

**Schema** das; ~s, ~s od. ~ta od. **Schemen** pattern

**schematisch** ①Adj. (a) diagrammatic
(b) (mechanisch) mechanical
②adv. (a) in diagram form
(b) (mechanisch) mechanically

**Schemel** der; ~s, ~ (a) stool
(b) (südd.: Fußbank) footstool

**Schenkel** der; ~s, ~: thigh

**schenken** tr. V. (a) give; jmdm. etw. [zum Geburtstag] ~: give sb. sth. or sth. to sb. [as a birthday present or for his/her birthday]
(b) (ugs.: erlassen) jmdm./sich etw. ~: spare sb./oneself sth.

**scheppern** itr. V. (ugs.) clank

**Scherbe** die; ~, ~n fragment

**Schere** die; ~, ~n (a) scissors pl.; eine ~: a pair of scissors
(b) (Zool.) claw

**scheren**¹ unr. tr. V. crop; (von Haar befreien) shear, clip ⟨sheep⟩

**scheren**² tr., refl. V. sich um jmdn./etw. nicht ~: not care about sb./sth.

**Scherereien** Pl. (ugs.) trouble no pl.

**Scherz** der; ~es, ~e joke

**scherzen** itr. V. joke

**scherzhaft** ①Adj. jocular
②adv. jocularly

**scheu** ①Adj. shy; timid ⟨animal⟩; (ehrfürchtig) awed
②adv. shyly; (von Tieren) timidly

**Scheu** die; ~ (a) shyness; (Ehrfurcht) awe
(b) (von Tieren) timidity

**scheuchen** tr. V. shoo; drive

**scheuen** ①tr. V. shrink from; shun ⟨people, light, company, etc.⟩
②refl. V. sich vor etw. (Dat.) ~: be afraid of or shrink from sth.
③itr. V. ⟨horse⟩ shy (vor + Dat. at)

**scheuern** ①tr., itr. V. (a) (reinigen) scour; scrub
(b) (reiben) rub; chafe
②tr. V. (reiben an) rub

**Scheuer-:** ~pulver das scouring powder; ~tuch das; Pl. ~tücher scouring cloth

**Scheune** die; ~, ~n barn

**Scheusal** das; ~s, ~e monster

**scheußlich** ①Adj. (a) dreadful
(b) (ugs.: äußerst unangenehm) dreadful (coll.); ghastly (coll.) ⟨weather, taste, smell⟩
②adv. (a) dreadfully
(b) (ugs.: sehr) dreadfully (coll.)

**Scheußlichkeit** die; ~, ~en (a) dreadfulness
(b) (etw. Scheußliches) dreadful thing

**Schi** usw. ▶ SKI usw.

**Schicht** die; ~, ~en (a) (Lage) layer; (Geol.) stratum; (von Farbe) coat; (sehr dünn) film
(b) (Gesellschaftsschicht) stratum
(c) (Arbeitsschicht) shift; ~ arbeiten work shifts; be on shift work

**Schicht·arbeit** die shift work

**schichten** tr. V. stack

**schick** ①Adj. (a) stylish; chic ⟨clothes, fashions⟩; smart ⟨woman, girl, man⟩
(b) (ugs.: großartig, toll) great (coll.); fantastic (coll.)
②adv. stylishly; smartly ⟨furnished, decorated⟩

**schicken** ①tr. V. send; jmdm. etw. ~, etw. an jmdn. ~: send sth. to sb.; send sb. sth.
②itr. V. nach jmdm. ~: send for sb.
③refl. V. (veralt.: sich ziemen) be proper or fitting

**Schickeria** die; ~ (ugs.) smart set

**Schicksal** das; ~s, ~e: [das] ~: fate; destiny; (schweres Los) fate

**Schicksals·schlag** der stroke of fate

**Schiebe·dach** das sunroof

**schieben** ①unr. tr. V. (a) push
(b) (stecken) put
(c) etw. auf jmdn./etw. ~: blame sb./sth. for sth.
②unr. refl. V. sich durch die Menge ~: push one's way through the crowd
③unr. itr. V. push; (heftig) shove

**Schiebe·tür** die sliding door

**Schiebung** die; ~, ~en (ugs.) (a) shady deal
(b) (Begünstigung) pulling strings

**schied** 1. u. 3. Pers. Sg. Prät. v. SCHEIDEN

**Schieds·richter** der, **Schieds·richterin** die referee; (Tennis, Hockey, Kricket) umpire

**schief** ①Adj. (a) (schräg) leaning ⟨wall, fence, post⟩; (nicht parallel) crooked; sloping ⟨surface⟩; worn[-down] ⟨heels⟩
(b) (fig.: verzerrt) distorted ⟨picture, presentation, view, impression⟩; false ⟨comparison⟩
②adv. (a) (schräg) das Bild hängt/der Teppich liegt ~: the picture/carpet is crooked; der Tisch steht ~: the table isn't level
(b) (fig.: verzerrt) etw. ~ darstellen give a distorted account of sth.
(c) ~ gehen od. laufen (ugs.) go wrong

**Schiefer** der; ~s (Gestein) slate

**\*schief-:** ~|gehen, ~|laufen ▶ SCHIEF

**s**

**schielen** itr. V. (a) squint; **auf dem rechten Auge** ∼: have a squint in one's right eye (b) (ugs.: blicken) look out of the corner of one's eye

**schien** 1. u. 3. Pers. Sg. Prät. v. SCHEINEN

**Schien·bein** das shinbone

**Schiene** die; ∼, ∼n (a) rail (b) (Gleitschiene) runner (c) (Med.: Stütze) splint

**schienen** tr. V. jmds. Arm/Bein ∼: put sb.'s arm/leg in a splint/splints

**schießen** ① unr. itr. V. (a) shoot; **auf jmdn./etw.** ∼: shoot/fire at sb./sth. (b) mit sein (strömen) gush; (spritzen) spurt (c) mit sein (schnell wachsen) shoot up ② unr. tr. V. (a) shoot; fire ⟨bullet, missile, rocket⟩ (b) (Fußball) score ⟨goal⟩ (c) (ugs.: fotografieren) **einige Aufnahmen** ∼: take a few snaps

**Schießerei** die; ∼, ∼en (a) shooting no indef. art., no pl.; (b) (Schusswechsel) gun battle

**Schiff** das; ∼[e]s, ∼e (a) ship; **mit dem** ∼: by ship or sea (b) (Archit.) (Mittelschiff) nave; (Querschiff) transept; (Seitenschiff) aisle

**\*Schiffahrt** ▶ SCHIFFFAHRT

**schiffbar** Adj. navigable

**Schiff-:** ∼**bau** der shipbuilding no art.; ∼**bruch** der (veralt.) shipwreck; [**mit etw.**] ∼**bruch erleiden** (fig.) fail [in sth.]; ∼**brüchige** der/die; adj. Dekl. shipwrecked man/woman

**Schiffer** der; ∼s, ∼, **Schifferin** die; ∼, ∼nen boatman/boatwoman; (eines Lastkahns) bargee; (Kapitän[in]) skipper

**Schiff·fahrt** die shipping no indef. art.; (Schifffahrtskunde) navigation

**Schiffs-:** ∼**arzt** der ship's doctor; ∼**brücke** die pontoon bridge; ∼**junge** der ship's boy; ∼**reise** die voyage; (Vergnügungsreise) cruise; ∼**verkehr** der shipping traffic

**Schikane** die; ∼, ∼n (a) harassment no indef. art. (b) **mit allen** ∼n (ugs.) ⟨kitchen, house⟩ with all mod cons (Brit. coll.); ⟨car, bicycle, stereo⟩ with all the extras

**schikanieren** tr. V. harass

**Schild¹** der; ∼[e]s, ∼e shield

**Schild²** das; ∼[e]s, ∼er sign; (Nummernschild) number plate; (Namensschild) nameplate; (auf Denkmälern, Gebäuden usw.) plaque; (Etikett) label

**Schild·drüse** die (Med.) thyroid [gland]

**schildern** tr. V. describe

**Schild·kröte** die tortoise; (Meeresschildkröte) turtle

**Schilf** das; ∼[e]s (a) reed (b) (Röhricht) reeds pl.

**schillern** itr. V. shimmer

**Schilling** der; ∼s, ∼e schilling

**schilt** 3. Pers. Sg. Präsens v. SCHELTEN

**Schimmel** der; ∼s, ∼ (a) mould; (auf Leder, Papier) mildew (b) (Pferd) white horse

**schimmelig** Adj. mouldy; mildewy ⟨paper, leather⟩

**schimmeln** itr. V.; auch mit sein go mouldy; ⟨leather, paper⟩ get covered with mildew

**Schimmel·pilz** der mould

**Schimmer** der; ∼s (Schein) gleam; (von Seide) shimmer; sheen; **keinen** ∼ [**von etw.**] **haben** (ugs.) not have the faintest idea [about sth.] (coll.)

**schimmern** itr. V. gleam; ⟨water, sea⟩ glisten, shimmer; ⟨metal⟩ glint, gleam; ⟨silk etc.⟩ shimmer

**schimmlig** ▶ SCHIMMELIG

**Schimpanse** der; ∼n, ∼n chimpanzee

**schimpfen** ① itr. V. (a) carry on (coll.) (auf, über + Akk. about); (meckern) grumble, moan (auf, über + Akk. at) (b) mit jmdm. ∼: tell sb. off; scold sb. ② tr. V. jmdn. ∼: tell sb. off

**Schimpf·wort** das; Pl. Schimpf·wörter (Beleidigung) insult; (derbes Wort) swear word

**schinden** unr. tr. V. maltreat; ill-treat; **Zeit** ∼ (ugs.) play for time

**Schinderei** die; ∼, ∼en (Strapaze, Qual) struggle; (Arbeit) toil

**Schinken** der; ∼s, ∼: ham

**Schinken·speck** der bacon

**Schippe** die; ∼, ∼n (Schaufel) shovel

**Schirm** der; ∼[e]s, ∼e umbrella; brolly (Brit. coll.); (Sonnenschirm) sunshade

**Schirm-:** ∼**herr** der patron; ∼**herrin** die patroness; ∼**herrschaft** die patronage; ∼**ständer** der umbrella stand

**schiss, \*schiß** 1. u. 3. Pers. Sg. Prät. v. SCHEISSEN

**Schlacht** die; ∼, ∼en battle

**schlachten** tr. (auch itr.) V. slaughter; kill ⟨rabbit, chicken, etc.⟩

**Schlachter** der; ∼s, ∼ (nordd.) butcher

**Schlachterei** die; ∼, ∼en (nordd.) butcher's [shop]

**Schlacht-:** ∼**feld** das battlefield; ∼**hof** der abattoir; ∼**tier** das animal kept for meat; (kurz vor der Schlachtung) animal for slaughter

**Schlachtung** die; ∼, ∼en slaughter[ing]

**Schlacht·vieh** das animals pl. kept for meat; (kurz vor der Schlachtung) animals pl. for slaughter

**Schlacke** die; ∼, ∼n cinders pl.; (Hochofen∼) slag

**Schlaf** der; ∼[e]s sleep; **einen leichten/ festen/gesunden** ∼ **haben** be a light/heavy/ good sleeper

**Schlaf·anzug** der pyjamas pl.

**Schläfchen** das; ∼s, ∼: nap; snooze (coll.)

**Schläfe** die; ∼, ∼n temple

**schlafen** *unr. itr. V.* **(a)** (auch fig.) sleep; **tief od. fest ~:** be sound asleep; **lange ~:** sleep for a long time; (am Morgen) sleep in; **~ gehen** go to bed
**(b)** (ugs.: nicht aufpassen) be asleep

**Schläfer** *der; ~s, ~,* **Schläferin** *die; ~, ~nen* sleeper

**schlaff** [1] *Adj.* **(a)** slack; flabby ⟨*stomach, muscles*⟩
**(b)** (schlapp, matt) limp ⟨*body, hand, handshake*⟩; shaky ⟨*knees*⟩
[2] *adv.* **(a)** slackly
**(b)** (schlapp, matt) limply

**Schlaf-: ~gelegenheit** *die* place to sleep; **~mittel** *das* sleep-inducing drug

**schläfrig** [1] *Adj.* sleepy
[2] *adv.* sleepily

**Schläfrigkeit** *die; ~:* sleepiness

**Schlaf-: ~saal** *der* dormitory; **~sack** sleeping bag

**schläft** *3. Pers. Sg. Präsens v.* SCHLAFEN

**Schlaf-: ~tablette** *die* sleeping pill; **~wagen** *der* sleeping car; sleeper; **~zimmer** *das* bedroom

**Schlag** *der; ~[e]s,* **Schläge (a)** blow; (Faust~) punch; (Klaps) slap; (Tennis, Golf) stroke; shot; **~ auf ~** (fig.) in quick succession
**(b)** (Aufprall) bang; (dumpf) thud; (Klopfen) knock
**(c)** (des Herzens, Pulses) beating; (eines Pendels) swinging
**(d)** (einzelne rhythmische Bewegung) beat; (eines Pendels) swing
**(e)** (Töne) (einer Uhr) striking; (einer Glocke) ringing
**(f)** (einzelner Ton) (Stundenschlag) stroke; (Glockenschlag) ring; **~ acht Uhr** on the stroke of eight

**schlag-, Schlag-: ~ader** *die* artery; **~anfall** *der* stroke; **~artig** [1] *Adj.* very sudden; [2] *adv.* quite suddenly; **~baum** *der* barrier; **~bohrer** *der,* **~bohr·maschine** *die* percussion drill; hammer drill

**schlagen** [1] *unr. tr. V.* **(a)** hit; beat; strike; (mit der Faust) punch; hit; (mit der flachen Hand) slap
**(b)** (mit Richtungsangabe) hit ⟨*ball*⟩; **einen Nagel in etw. (Akk.) ~:** knock a nail into sth.
**(c)** (rühren) beat ⟨*mixture*⟩; whip ⟨*cream*⟩; (mit einem Schneebesen) whisk
**(d)** (läuten) ⟨*clock*⟩ strike; ⟨*bell*⟩ ring
**(e)** (legen) throw
**(f)** (einwickeln) wrap (**in** + *Akk.* in)
**(g)** (besiegen, übertreffen) beat
[2] *unr. itr. V.* **(a)** **er schlug mit der Faust auf den Tisch** he beat the table with his fist
**(b)** **mit den Flügeln ~** ⟨*bird*⟩ beat or flap its wings

**(c)** *mit sein* (prallen) bang; **mit dem Kopf auf etw. (Akk.)/gegen etw. ~:** bang one's head on/against sth.
**(d)** *mit sein* **jmdm. auf den Magen ~:** affect sb.'s stomach
**(e)** (pulsieren) ⟨*heart, pulse*⟩ beat; (heftig) ⟨*heart*⟩ pound; ⟨*pulse*⟩ throb
**(f)** (läuten) ⟨*clock*⟩ strike; ⟨*bell*⟩ ring
[3] *unr. refl. V.* fight; **sich mit jmdm. ~:** fight with sb.

**Schlager** *der; ~s, ~* **(a)** pop song
**(b)** (Erfolg) (Buch) best seller; (Ware) best-selling line; (Film, Stück, Lied) hit

**Schläger** *der; ~s, ~* **(a)** (Raufbold) tough; thug
**(b)** (Tennis, Federball, Squash) racket; (Tischtennis, Kricket) bat; ([Eis]hockey, Polo) stick; (Golf) club

**Schlägerei** *die; ~, ~en* brawl; fight

**Schlägerin** *die; ~, ~nen* ▶ SCHLÄGER A

**Schlager·sänger** *der,* **Schlager·sängerin** *die* pop singer

**schlag-, Schlag-: ~fertig** *Adj.* quick-witted ⟨*reply*⟩; ⟨*person*⟩ who is quick at repartee; **~fertigkeit** *die* quickness at repartee; **~licht** *das* (Kunst, Fot.) shaft of light; **ein ~licht auf etw. werfen** highlight sth.; **~loch** *das* pothole; **~obers** *das; ~~* (österr.), **~rahm** *der* (bes. südd., österr., schweiz.), **~sahne** *die* whipping cream; (geschlagen) whipped cream; **~seite** *die* list; **[starke od. schwere] ~seite haben/bekommen** be listing [heavily] *or* have a [heavy] list/develop a [heavy] list; **~stock** *der* cudgel; (für Polizei) truncheon; **~wort** *das* **(a)** *Pl. meist ~~e* (Parole) slogan; catchphrase; **(b)** *Pl. ~wörter* (Buchw.: Stichwort) headword; **~zeile** *die* headline; **~zeug** *das* drums *pl.*

**schlaksig** (ugs.) *Adj.* gangling; lanky

**Schlamassel** *der od. das; ~s* (ugs.) mess

**Schlamm** *der; ~[e]s, ~e od.* **Schlämme (a)** mud
**(b)** (Schlick) sludge

**schlammig** *Adj.* **(a)** muddy
**(b)** (schlickig) sludgy; muddy

**Schlamperei** *die; ~, ~en* (ugs. abwertend) sloppiness

**schlampig** (ugs. abwertend) [1] *Adj.* **(a)** (liederlich) slovenly
**(b)** (nachlässig) sloppy, slipshod ⟨*work*⟩
[2] *adv.* **(a)** (liederlich) in a slovenly way
**(b)** (nachlässig) sloppily

**schlang** *1. u. 3. Pers. Sg. Prät. v.* SCHLINGEN

**Schlange** *die; ~, ~n* **(a)** snake
**(b)** (Warteschlange) queue; line (Amer.); **~ stehen** queue; stand in line (Amer.)
**(c)** (Autoschlange) tailback (Brit.); backup (Amer.)

**schlängeln** *refl. V.* ⟨*snake*⟩ wind [its way]; ⟨*road*⟩ wind, snake [its way]

**Schlangen·linie** *die* wavy line

**schlank** *Adj.* slim ⟨*person*⟩; slim, slender ⟨*build, figure*⟩

**Schlankheit** *die;* ~ ▶ SCHLANK: slimness; slenderness

**Schlankheits·kur** *die* slimming diet

**schlapp** *Adj.* **(a)** worn out; tired out; (wegen Schwüle) listless; (wegen Krankheit) run-down

**(b)** (ugs.: ohne Schwung) wet (coll.); feeble

**(c)** slack ⟨*rope, cable*⟩; loose ⟨*skin*⟩; flabby ⟨*stomach, muscles*⟩

**Schlappe** *die;* ~, ~n setback

**schlapp|machen** *itr. V.* (ugs.) flag; (zusammenbrechen) flake out (coll.); (aufgeben) give up

**Schlaraffen·land** *das;* ~[e]s Cockaigne

**schlau** [1] *Adj.* **(a)** shrewd; astute; (gerissen) wily; crafty; cunning

**(b)** (ugs.: gescheit) clever; bright; smart; **aus jmdm. nicht ~ werden** (ugs.) not be able to make sb. out

[2] *adv.* shrewdly; astutely; (gerissen) craftily; cunningly

**Schlauch** *der;* ~[e]s, **Schläuche (a)** hose

**(b)** (im Reifen) tube

**Schlauch·boot** *das* rubber dinghy; inflatable [dinghy]

**schlauchen** (ugs.) *tr., auch itr. V.* **jmdn. ~:** take it out of sb.

**schlauch·los** *Adj.* tubeless ⟨*tyre*⟩

**Schläue** *die;* ~: shrewdness; astuteness; (Gerissenheit) wiliness; craftiness; cunning

**Schlaufe** *die;* ~, ~n loop

**schlecht** [1] *Adj.* **(a)** bad; poor, bad ⟨*food, quality, style, harvest, health, circulation*⟩; poor ⟨*salary, eater, appetite*⟩; poor-quality ⟨*goods*⟩; bad, weak ⟨*eyes*⟩; **um jmdn./mit etw. steht es ~:** sb./sth. is in a bad way; **jmdn. ~ machen** run sb. down; disparage sb.

**(b)** (böse) bad; wicked

**(c)** (ungenießbar) off; **das Fleisch ist ~ geworden** the meat has gone off

[2] *adv.* **(a)** badly; **er sieht/hört ~:** his sight is poor/he has poor hearing; **über jmdn. od. von jmdm. ~ sprechen** speak ill of sb.; **~ bezahlt** badly *or* poorly paid

**(b)** (schwer) **heute geht es ~:** today is difficult

**(c)** **~ und recht, mehr ~ als recht** after a fashion

**schlecht-:** \*~**bezahlt** ▶ SCHLECHT 2A; \*~**|gehen** ▶ GEHEN I; \*~**gelaunt** ▶ GELAUNT

**Schlechtigkeit** *die;* ~: badness; wickedness

\***schlecht|machen** ▶ SCHLECHT 1A

**schlecken** (bes. südd., österr.) *tr. V.* lap up

**schleichen** [1] *unr. itr. V.; mit sein* creep; (heimlich) creep; sneak; ⟨*cat*⟩ slink, creep; (langsam fahren) crawl along

[2] *unr. refl. V.* creep; sneak; ⟨*cat*⟩ slink, creep

**schleichend** *Adj.* insidious ⟨*disease*⟩; slow[-acting] ⟨*poison*⟩; creeping ⟨*inflation*⟩; gradual ⟨*crisis*⟩

**Schleich·werbung** *die* surreptitious advertising

**Schleier** *der;* ~s, ~: veil

**schleier·haft** *Adj.* **jmdm. ~ sein/bleiben** be/remain a mystery to sb.

**Schleife** *die;* ~, ~n **(a)** bow; (Fliege) bow tie

**(b)** (starke Biegung) loop

**schleifen**[1] *unr. tr. V.* grind; cut ⟨*diamond, glass*⟩; (mit Schleifpapier usw.) sand; (schärfen) sharpen

**schleifen**[2] [1] *tr. V.* **(a)** (auch fig.) drag

**(b)** (niederreißen) raze ⟨*sth.*⟩ [to the ground]

[2] *itr. V.; auch mit sein* drag; **die Kupplung ~ lassen** (Kfz-W.) slip the clutch

**Schleim** *der;* ~[e]s, ~e mucus; (im Hals) phlegm; (von Schnecken) slime

**schleimig** *Adj.* (auch fig.) slimy; (Physiol., Zool.) mucous

**schlemmen** *itr. V.* have a feast

**Schlemmer** *der;* ~s, ~: gourmet

**schlendern** *itr. V.; mit sein* stroll

**Schlenker** *der;* ~s, ~ (ugs.) swerve; **einen ~ machen** swerve

**schlenkern** *tr., itr. V.* swing; **mit den Armen ~:** swing one's arms

**Schleppe** *die;* ~, ~n train

**schleppen** [1] *tr. V.* **(a)** (ziehen) tow ⟨*vehicle, ship*⟩

**(b)** (tragen) carry; lug

**(c)** (ugs.: mitnehmen) drag

[2] *refl. V.* drag *or* haul oneself

**schleppend** *Adj.* (nicht zügig) slow

**Schlepper** *der;* ~s, ~ **(a)** (Schiff) tug

**(b)** (Traktor) tractor

**Schlepper·organisation** *die;* organization smuggling illegal immigrants and emigrants

**Schlepp-:** ~**lift** *der* T-bar [lift]; ~**tau** *das* towline; **in jmds. ~tau** (fig.) in sb.'s wake

**Schleswig-Holstein** *(das);* ~s Schleswig-Holstein

**Schleuder** *die;* ~, ~n sling; (mit Gummiband) catapult (Brit.); slingshot (Amer.)

**schleudern** [1] *tr. V.* hurl

[2] *itr. V.; mit sein* ⟨*vehicle*⟩ skid

**schleunigst** *Adv.* **(a)** (auf der Stelle) at once; immediately; straight away

**(b)** (eilends) hastily; with all haste

**Schleuse** *die;* ~, ~n lock

**schlich** *1. u. 3. Pers. Sg. Prät. v.* SCHLEICHEN

**schlicht** [1] *Adj.* **(a)** simple; plain ⟨*pattern, furniture*⟩

**(b)** (unkompliziert) simple, unsophisticated ⟨*person, view, etc.*⟩

[2] *adv.* simply; simply, plainly ⟨*dressed, furnished*⟩

**schlichten** [1] *tr. V.* settle ⟨*argument etc.*⟩; settle ⟨*industrial dispute etc.*⟩ by mediation

[2] *itr. V.* mediate

**Schlichtheit** *die;* ~ ▶ SCHLICHT A, B:
simplicity; plainness; unsophisticatedness
**Schlick** *der;* ~[e]s, ~e silt
**schlief** *1. u. 3. Pers. Sg. Prät. v.* SCHLAFEN
**Schließe** *die;* ~, ~n clasp; (Schnalle) buckle
**schließen** ① *unr. tr. V.* (a) close; shut;
turn off ‹*tap*›; fasten ‹*belt, bracelet*›; do up
‹*button, zip*›; close ‹*street, route, border,
electrical circuit*›; fill, close ‹*gap*›
(b) (außer Betrieb setzen) close [down] ‹*shop,
school*›
(c) etw./jmdn./sich in etw. (*Akk.*) ~: lock
sth./sb./oneself in sth.
(d) (beenden) close ‹*meeting, proceedings,
debate*›; end, conclude ‹*letter, speech, lecture*›
(e) (eingehen, vereinbaren) conclude ‹*treaty,
pact, ceasefire, agreement*›; reach ‹*settlement,
compromise*›; enter into ‹*contract*›
(f) (folgern) infer (**aus** from)
② *unr. itr. V.* (a) close, shut
(b) (enden) end; conclude
(c) [aus etw.] auf etw. (*Akk.*) ~: infer sth.
[from sth.]
③ *unr. refl. V.* ‹*door, window*› close, shut;
‹*wound, circle*› close
**Schließ·fach** *das* locker; (bei der Post) PO
box; (bei der Bank) safe-deposit box
**schließlich** *Adv.* (a) finally; in the end
(b) (immerhin, doch) after all
**schliff** *1. u. 3. Pers. Sg. Prät. v.* SCHLEIFEN
**Schliff** *der;* ~[e]s, ~e (a) cutting; (von
Messern, Sensen usw.) sharpening
(b) (Art, wie etw. geschliffen wird) cut; (von
Messern, Scheren usw.) edge
(c) einem Brief/Text *usw.* den letzten ~
geben put the finishing touches *pl.* to a
letter/text *etc.*
**schlimm** ① *Adj.* (a) grave, serious ‹*error,
mistake, accusation, offence*›; bad, serious
‹*error, mistake*›
(b) (übel) bad; nasty, bad ‹*experience*›; [das ist
alles] halb so ~: it's not as bad as all that;
ist nicht ~! [it] doesn't matter
② *adv.* ~ dran sein be in a bad way; (in einer
Notlage) be in dire straits
**schlimmsten·falls** *Adv.* if the worst
comes to the worst
**Schlinge** *die;* ~, ~n (a) loop; (für den Arm)
sling; (zum Erhängen) noose
(b) (Fanggerät) snare
**Schlingel** *der;* ~s, ~: rascal; rogue
**schlingen** ① *unr. tr. V.* etw. um etw. ~:
loop sth. round sth.
② *unr. refl. V.* sich um etw. ~: wind itself
round sth.
③ *unr. itr. V.* bolt one's food
**schlingern** *itr. V.; mit sein* ‹*ship, boat*› roll;
‹*train, vehicle*› lurch from side to side
**Schlips** *der;* ~es, ~e tie
**Schlitten** *der;* ~s, ~: sledge; sled;
(Pferdeschlitten) sleigh; (Rodelschlitten) toboggan;
~ fahren go tobogganing

---

*old spelling - see note on page xiv

**schlittern** *itr. V.* slide
**Schlitt-:** ~**schuh** *der* [ice] skate; ~**schuh**
laufen *od.* fahren [ice-]skate;
~**schuh·laufen** *das* [ice] skating *no art.;*
~**schuh·läufer** *der,* ~**schuh·läuferin**
*die* [ice] skater
**Schlitz** *der;* ~es, ~e (a) slit; (am Briefkasten,
Automaten) slot
(b) (Hosenschlitz) flies *pl.;* fly
**schlitz-, Schlitz-:** ~**auge** *das* slit eye;
~**äugig** *Adj.* slit-eyed; ~**ohr** *das* (ugs.)
wily *or* crafty devil; ~**ohrig** (ugs.) ① *Adj.*
wily; crafty; ② *adv.* craftily
**schloss, *schloß** *1. u. 3. Pers. Sg. Prät. v.*
SCHLIESSEN
**Schloss, *Schloß** *das;* Schlosses,
Schlösser (a) lock; (Vorhänge~) padlock;
hinter ~ und Riegel (ugs.) behind bars
(b) (Verschluss) clasp
(c) (Wohngebäude) castle; (Palast) palace;
(Herrschaftshaus) mansion
**Schlosser** *der;* ~s, ~, **Schlosserin** *die;*
~, ~nen metalworker; (Maschinenschlosser)
fitter; (für Schlösser) locksmith
**Schlot** *der;* ~[e]s, ~e *od.* Schlöte chimney
[stack]; (eines Schiffes) funnel
**schlottern** *itr. V.* (a) shake
(b) ‹*clothes*› hang loose
**Schlucht** *die;* ~, ~en ravine
**schluchzen** *itr. V.* sob
**Schluck** *der;* ~[e]s, ~e *od.* Schlücke
swallow; mouthful; (großer ~) gulp; (kleiner ~)
sip
**Schluck·auf** *der;* ~s hiccups *pl.*
**Schlückchen** *das;* ~s, ~: sip
**schlucken** ① *tr. V.* swallow; etw. hastig
~: gulp sth. down
② *itr. V.* swallow
**Schlucker** *der;* ~s, ~: armer ~ (ugs.) poor
devil *or* (Brit. coll.) blighter
**schluderig** ▶ SCHLUDRIG
**schludern** *itr. V.* (ugs.) work sloppily
**schludrig** (ugs.) ① *Adj.* (a) slipshod ‹*work,
examination*›; botched ‹*job*›; slapdash
‹*person, work*›
(b) (schlampig [aussehend]) scruffy
② *adv.* (a) in a slipshod *or* slapdash way
(b) (schlampig) scruffily
**schlug** *1. u. 3. Pers. Sg. Prät. v.* SCHLAGEN
**Schlummer** *der;* ~s (geh.) slumber ( poet./
rhet.)
**schlummern** *itr. V.* (geh.) slumber ( poet./
rhet.)
**Schlund** *der;* ~[e]s, Schlünde [back of the]
throat; pharynx (Anat.)
**schlüpfen** *itr. V.; mit sein* slip; [aus dem
Ei] ~ ‹*chick*› hatch out
**Schlüpfer** *der;* ~s, ~ (für Damen) knickers
*pl.* (Brit.); panties *pl.;* (für Herren) [under]pants
*pl. or* trunks *pl.*
**schlüpfrig** *Adj.* (a) slippery
(b) (anstößig) lewd

**Schlüpfrigkeit** *die;* ~, ~en (a) (feuchte Glätte) slipperiness
**(b)** (Anstößigkeit) lewdness
**schlurfen** *itr. V.; mit sein* shuffle
**schlürfen** ⟦1⟧ *tr. V.* slurp [up] (coll.)
⟦2⟧ *itr. V.* slurp (coll.)
**Schluss, *Schluß** *der;* Schlusses, Schlüsse **(a)** end; (eines Vortrags o. Ä.) conclusion; (eines Buchs, Schauspiels usw.) ending; **am** *od.* **zum** ~: at the end; (schließlich) in the end
**(b)** (Folgerung) conclusion
**Schlüssel** *der;* ~s, ~: key
**Schlüssel-:** ~**bein** *das* collarbone; clavicle (Anat.); ~**blume** *die* cowslip; (Primel) primula; ~**bund** *der od. das* bunch of keys; ~**figur** *die* key figure; ~**loch** *das* keyhole; ~**stellung** *die* key position
**schluss·folgern, *schluß·folgern** *tr. V.* conclude (aus from)
**Schluss·folgerung, *Schluß·folgerung** *die* conclusion, inference (aus from); ~**en ziehen** draw conclusions
**schlüssig** ⟦1⟧ *Adj.* **(a)** conclusive ⟨proof, evidence⟩; convincing, logical ⟨argument, conclusion⟩
**(b) sich** (*Dat.*) ~ **werden** make up one's mind
⟦2⟧ *adv.* conclusively
**Schlüssigkeit** *die;* ~: conclusiveness
**Schluss-, *Schluß-:** ~**licht** *das* tail *or* rear light; ~**strich** *der* [bottom] line; ~**verkauf** *der* [end-of-season] sale[s *pl.*]
**schmächtig** *Adj.* slight
**schmackhaft** *Adj.* tasty
**Schmähung** *die;* ~, ~en diatribe; ~en abuse *sing.;* invective *sing.*
**schmal;** ~er *od.* schmäler, ~st... *od.* schmälst... *Adj.* narrow; slim, slender ⟨hips, hands, figure, etc.⟩; thin ⟨lips, face, nose, etc.⟩
**schmälern** *tr. V.* diminish; restrict ⟨rights⟩
**Schmalz¹** *das;* ~es dripping; (Schweineschmalz) lard
**Schmalz²** *der;* ~es (abwertend) schmaltz (coll.)
**Schmalz·brot** *das* slice of bread and dripping
**schmalzig** (abwertend) ⟦1⟧ *Adj.* schmaltzy (coll.)
⟦2⟧ *adv.* with slushy sentimentality
**schmarotzen** *itr. V.* (fig.) sponge; freeload (coll.)
**Schmarren** *der;* ~s, ~ (österr., auch südd.) *pancake broken up with a fork after frying*
**schmatzen** *itr. V.* smack one's lips; (geräuschvoll essen) eat noisily
**Schmaus** *der;* ~es, Schmäuse (veralt., scherzh.) [good] spread (coll.)
**schmecken** ⟦1⟧ *itr. V.* taste (nach of); [gut] ~: taste good; **schmeckt es [dir]?** are you enjoying it *or* your meal?

⟦2⟧ *tr. V.* taste; (kosten) sample
**schmeicheln** *itr. V.* jmdm. ~: flatter sb.
**Schmeichler** *der;* ~s, ~,
**Schmeichlerin** *die;* ~, ~nen flatterer
**schmeißen** (ugs.) ⟦1⟧ *unr. tr. V.* chuck (coll.); sling (coll.); (schleudern) fling; hurl
⟦2⟧ *unr. refl. V.* throw oneself; (mit Wucht) hurl oneself
⟦3⟧ *unr. itr. V.* **mit etw. [nach jmdm.]** ~: chuck sth. [at sb.] (coll.)
**Schmeiß·fliege** *die* blowfly; (blaue) bluebottle
**schmelzen** ⟦1⟧ *unr. itr. V.; mit sein* melt; (fig.) ⟨doubts, apprehension, etc.⟩ dissolve, fade away
⟦2⟧ *unr. tr. V.* melt; smelt ⟨ore⟩; render ⟨fat⟩
**Schmelz-:** ~**käse** *der* processed cheese; ~**wasser** *das* melted snow and ice; meltwater (Geol.)
**Schmerz** *der;* ~es, ~en **(a)** (physisch) pain; (dumpf u. anhaltend) ache; **wo haben Sie** ~**en?** where does it hurt?; ~**en haben** be in pain
**(b)** (psychisch) pain; (Kummer) grief
**schmerz·empfindlich** *Adj.* sensitive to pain *pred.*
**Schmerz·empfindlichkeit** *die;* ~: sensitivity to pain
**schmerzen** ⟦1⟧ *tr. V.* jmdn. ~: hurt sb.; (jmdm. Kummer bereiten) grieve sb.; cause sb. sorrow
⟦2⟧ *itr. V.* hurt
**schmerz·frei** *Adj.* free of pain *pred.;* painless ⟨operation⟩
**Schmerz·grenze** *die* (fig.) jetzt/dann ist die ~ erreicht this/that is the absolute limit
**schmerzhaft** *Adj.* painful
**schmerzlich** ⟦1⟧ *Adj.* painful; distressing
⟦2⟧ *adv.* painfully
**schmerz-, *Schmerz-:** ~**lindernd** *Adj.* pain-relieving; ~**los** ⟦1⟧ *Adj.* painless; ⟦2⟧ *adv.* painlessly; ~**stillend** *Adj.* pain-killing; ~**tablette** *die* pain-killing tablet
**Schmetterling** *der;* ~s, ~e butterfly
**schmettern** ⟦1⟧ *tr. V.* **(a)** hurl (an + *Akk.* at, **gegen** against)
**(b)** (laut spielen, singen usw.) blare out ⟨march, music⟩; ⟨person⟩ sing lustily ⟨song⟩
**(c)** (Tennis usw.) smash ⟨ball⟩
⟦2⟧ *itr. V.* ⟨trumpet, music, etc.⟩ blare out
**Schmied** *der;* ~[e]s, ~e blacksmith
**Schmiede** *die;* ~, ~n smithy; forge
**schmieden** *tr. V.* (auch fig.) forge
**Schmiedin** *die;* ~, ~nen ▶ SCHMIED
**schmiegen** ⟦1⟧ *refl. V.* snuggle, nestle (in + *Akk.* in); **sich an jmdn.** ~: snuggle [close] up to sb.
⟦2⟧ *tr. V.* press (an + *Akk.* against)
**schmieren** ⟦1⟧ *tr. V.* **(a)** lubricate
**(b)** (streichen) spread ⟨butter, jam, etc.⟩ (auf + *Akk.* on); **Brote** ~: spread slices of bread
⟦2⟧ *itr. V.* **(a)** ⟨oil, grease⟩ lubricate
**(b)** (ugs: unsauber schreiben) ⟨person⟩ scrawl, scribble; ⟨pen, ink⟩ smudge, make smudges

**S**

**schmierig** *Adj.* greasy

**Schmier-:** ~**mittel** *das* lubricant;
~**seife** *die* soft soap

**schmilzt** *2. u. 3. Pers. Sg. Präsens v.*
SCHMELZEN

**Schminke** *die;* ~, ~**n** make-up

**schminken** 1 *tr. V.* make up ⟨face, eyes⟩
2 *refl. V.* make oneself up

**schmirgeln** *tr. V.* rub down; (bes. mit
Sandpapier) sand

**Schmirgel·papier** *das* emery paper;
(Sandpapier) sandpaper

**schmiss, \*schmiß** *1. u. 3. Pers. Sg. Prät.*
*v.* SCHMEISSEN

**Schmöker** *der;* ~**s**, ~ (ugs.) lightweight
adventure story/romance

**schmökern** (ugs.) 1 *itr. V.* bury oneself in
a book
2 *tr. V.* bury oneself in ⟨book⟩

**schmollen** *itr. V.* sulk

**Schmoll·mund** *der* pouting mouth

**schmolz** *1. u. 3. Pers. Sg. Prät. v.*
SCHMELZEN

**Schmor·braten** *der* braised beef

**schmoren** 1 *tr. V.* braise
2 *itr. V.* **(a)** braise
**(b)** (ugs.: schwitzen) swelter

**schmuck** *Adj.* attractive

**Schmuck** *der;* ~**[e]s (a)** jewelry; jewellery
(esp. Brit.)
**(b)** ▶ SCHMUCKSTÜCK
**(c)** (Zierde) decoration

**schmücken** *tr. V.* decorate; embellish
⟨writings, speech⟩

**schmuck-, Schmuck-:** ~**kästchen**
*das,* ~**kasten** *der* jewelry or (esp. Brit.)
jewellery box; ~**los** *Adj.* plain; bare ⟨room⟩;
~**losigkeit** *die;* ~~: plainness; (eines
Zimmers) bareness; ~**stück** *das* piece of
jewelry or (esp. Brit.) jewellery

**schmuddelig** *Adj.* (ugs.) grubby; mucky
(coll.); (schmutzig u. unordentlich) messy; grotty
(Brit. coll.)

**Schmuggel** *der;* ~**s** smuggling *no art.*

**schmuggeln** *tr., itr. V.* smuggle (**in** + *Akk.*
into; **aus** out of)

**Schmuggler** *der;* ~**s**, ~,
**Schmugglerin** *die;* ~, ~**nen** smuggler

**schmunzeln** *itr. V.* smile to oneself

**schmusen** *itr. V.* (ugs.) cuddle; ⟨couple⟩
kiss and cuddle

**Schmutz** *der;* ~**es** dirt; (Schlamm) mud

**schmutzen** *itr. V.* get dirty

**schmutzig** *Adj.* dirty

**Schmutz·wasser** *das* dirty water;
(Abwasser) sewage

**Schnabel** *der;* ~**s**, **Schnäbel (a)** beak
**(b)** (ugs.: Mund) gob (sl.)

**Schnake** *die;* ~, ~**n (a)** daddy-long-legs
**(b)** (bes. südd.: Stechmücke) mosquito

**Schnalle** *die;* ~, ~**n** buckle

**schnallen** *tr. V.* **(a)** (mit einer Schnalle
festziehen) buckle ⟨shoe, belt⟩; fasten ⟨strap⟩
**(b)** (mit Riemen/Gurten befestigen) strap (**auf** +
*Akk.* on to)

**schnalzen** *itr. V.* [mit der Zunge/den
Fingern] ~: click one's tongue/snap one's
fingers

**Schnäppchen** *das;* ~**s**, ~ (ugs.) snip (Brit.
coll.); [real] bargain; **ein** ~ **machen** get a
[real] bargain

**schnappen** 1 *itr. V.* **nach** jmdm./etw. ~
⟨animal⟩ snap at sb./sth.; **nach Luft** ~: gasp
for breath
2 *tr. V.* ⟨dog, bird, etc.⟩ snatch; [sich (*Dat.*)]
jmdn./etw. ~ (ugs.) ⟨person⟩ grab sb./sth.; (mit
raschem Zugriff) snatch sb./sth

**Schnapp·schuss, \*Schnapp·schuß**
*der* snapshot

**Schnaps** *der;* ~**es**, **Schnäpse (a)** spirit;
(Klarer) schnapps
**(b)** (Spirituosen) spirits *pl.*

**schnarchen** *itr. V.* snore

**schnattern** *itr. V.* **(a)** ⟨goose etc.⟩ cackle,
gaggle
**(b)** (ugs.: eifrig schwatzen) jabber [away];
chatter

**schnauben** *itr. V.* snort (**vor** with)

**schnaufen** *itr. V.* puff (**vor** with)

**Schnauze** *die;* ~, ~**n (a)** (von Tieren)
muzzle; (der Maus usw.) snout; (Maul) mouth
**(b)** (derb: Mund) gob (sl.); [**halt die**] ~! shut
your trap! (sl.)

**schnauzen** *tr., itr. V.* (ugs.) bark; (ärgerlich)
snap; snarl

**Schnecke** *die* snail; (Nacktschnecke) slug

**Schnecken·haus** *das* snail shell

**Schnee** *der;* ~**s** snow

**schnee-, Schnee-:** ~**ball** *der* snowball;
~**besen** *der* whisk; ~**flocke** *die*
snowflake; ~**gestöber** *das* snow flurry;
~**glöckchen** *das* snowdrop; ~**kette** *die*
snow chain; ~**matsch** *der* slush; ~**pflug**
*der* snowplough; ~**schmelze** *die;* ~~,
~~**n** melting of the snow; thaw; ~**sturm**
*der* snowstorm; ~**treiben** *das* driving
snow; ~**wehe** *die* snowdrift; ~**weiß** *Adj.*
snow-white; as white as snow *postpos.*

**Schneewittchen** *das;* ~**s** Snow White

**Schneid·brenner** *der* (Technik) cutting
torch; oxyacetylene cutter

**Schneide** *die;* ~, ~**n** [cutting] edge

**schneiden** 1 *unr. itr. V.* cut (**in** + *Akk.*
into)
2 *unr. tr. V.* **(a)** cut; (in Scheiben) slice
⟨bread, sausage, etc.⟩; (klein ~) cut up, chop
⟨wood, vegetables⟩; (stutzen) prune ⟨tree,
bush⟩; trim ⟨beard⟩; cut, mow ⟨grass⟩; **sich**
(*Dat.*) **die Haare** ~ **lassen** have one's hair cut
**(b)** **eine Kurve** ~: cut a corner

**Schneider** *der;* ~**s**, ~: tailor;
(Damenschneider) dressmaker

---

**Schneiderei** *die;* ~, ~en tailor's shop;
(Damenschneider) dressmaker's shop
**Schneiderin** *die;* ~, ~nen ▶ SCHNEIDER
**schneidern** *tr. V.* make; make, tailor
⟨*suit*⟩
**Schneide-zahn** *der* incisor
**schneien** ①*itr., tr. V.* (*unpers.*) snow; **es
schneit** it is snowing
②*itr. V.; mit sein* (fig.) rain down; fall like
snow
**Schneise** *die;* ~, ~n (Wald~) aisle; (als
Feuerschutz) firebreak
**schnell** ①*Adj.* quick ⟨*journey, decision,
service, etc.*⟩; fast ⟨*car, skis, road, track, etc.*⟩;
quick, swift ⟨*progress, movement, blow,
action*⟩
②*adv.* quickly; ⟨*drive, move, etc.*⟩ fast,
quickly; ⟨*spread*⟩ quickly, rapidly; (bald) soon
⟨*sold, past, etc.*⟩; **mach** ~! (ugs.) move it!
(coll.)
**schnellen** *itr. V.; mit sein* shoot (**aus** +
*Dat.* out of; **in** + *Akk.* into)
**Schnelligkeit** *die;* ~, ~en speed
**Schnell-: ~imbiss, *~imbiß** der*
snackbar; **~koch·topf** *der* pressure
cooker
**schnellstens** *Adv.* as quickly as possible
**Schnell-: ~straße** *die* expressway;
**~zug** *der* express [train]
**Schnepfe** *die;* ~, ~n snipe
**schneuzen** ①*tr. V.* **sich/einem Kind die
Nase** ~: blow one's/a child's nose
②*refl. V.* blow one's nose
**schnippeln** (ugs.) ①*itr. V.* snip [away] (**an**
+ *Dat.* at)
②*tr. V.* shred ⟨*vegetables*⟩; chop ⟨*beans etc.*⟩
[finely]
**schnippen** ①*itr. V.* snap one's fingers
(**nach** at)
②*tr. V.* flick (**von** off, from)
**schnippisch** ①*Adj.* pert ⟨*reply, tone, etc.*⟩
②*adv.* pertly
**Schnipsel** *der od. das;* ~s, ~: scrap; (aus
Papier, Stoff) snippet; shred
**schnipseln** ▶ SCHNIPPELN
**schnitt** *1. u. 3. Pers. Sg. Prät. v.* SCHNEIDEN
**Schnitt** *der;* ~[e]s, ~e (a) cut
(b) (das Mähen) (von Gras) mowing; (von
Getreide) harvest
**Schnitt-: ~blume** *die* cut flower;
**~bohne** *die* French bean
**Schnittchen** *das;* ~s, ~: canapé; [small]
open sandwich
**Schnitte** *die;* ~, ~n slice; **eine** ~ [Brot] a
slice of bread
**Schnitt·fläche** *die* cut surface
**schnittig** ①*Adj.* stylish, smart ⟨*suit,
appearance, etc.*⟩; (sportlich) racy ⟨*car, yacht,
etc.*⟩
②*adv.* stylishly; (sportlich) racily
**Schnitt-: ~lauch** *der* chives *pl.;*
**~menge** *die* (Math.) intersection; **~punkt**

*der* intersection; (Geom.) point of
intersection; **~stelle** *die* (DV) interface;
**~wunde** *die* cut; (lang u. tief) gash
**Schnitzel** *das;* ~s, ~ (a) (Fleisch) [veal/
pork] escalope
(b) (von Papier) scrap; (von Holz) shaving
**schnitzeln** *tr. V.* chop up ⟨*vegetables*⟩ [into
small pieces]; shred ⟨*cabbage*⟩
**schnitzen** *tr., itr. V.* carve
**schnodderig** (ugs.) ①*Adj.* brash
②*adv.* brashly
**schnöde** (geh.) ①*Adj.* (a) (verachtenswert)
contemptible
(b) (gemein) contemptuous, scornful ⟨*glance,
reply, etc.*⟩
②*adv.* (gemein) contemptuously; ⟨*exploit,
misuse*⟩ flagrantly
**Schnorchel** *der;* ~s, ~: snorkel
**Schnörkel** *der;* ~s, ~: scroll; (der
Handschrift, in der Rede) flourish
**schnorren** *tr., itr. V.* (ugs.) scrounge (coll.)
(**bei, von** + *Dat.* off)
**Schnorrer** *der;* ~s, ~, **Schnorrerin**
*die;* ~, ~nen (ugs.) scrounger (coll.)
**Schnösel** *der;* ~s, ~ (ugs. abwertend) young
whippersnapper
**schnüffeln** *itr. V.* (a) sniff
(b) (ugs.: spionieren) snoop [about] (coll.)
(c) (Drogenjargon: Dämpfe ~) sniff [glue/paint
etc.]
**Schnüffler** *der;* ~s, ~, **Schnüfflerin**
*die;* ~, ~nen (a) (ugs.) Nosey Parker; (Spion)
snooper (coll.)
(b) (Drogenjargon) [glue-, paint-, *etc.*]sniffer
**Schnulze** *die;* ~, ~n (ugs. abwertend) (Lied/
Melodie) slushy song/tune; (Theaterstück, Film,
Fernsehspiel) tear jerker (coll.); slushy play
**schnupfen** ①*tr. V.* sniff; **Tabak** ~: take
snuff
②*itr. V.* take snuff
**Schnupfen** *der;* ~s, ~: [head] cold; [den
*od.* einen] ~ **haben** have a [head] cold
**Schnupf·tabak** *der* snuff
**schnuppe: das/er ist mir** ~/**mir völlig** ~
(ugs.) I don't care/I couldn't care less about
it/him (coll.)
**schnuppern** *itr. V.* sniff; **an etw.** (*Dat.*) ~:
sniff sth.
**Schnur** *die;* ~, **Schnüre** (a) (Bindfaden) piece
of string; (Kordel) piece of cord
(b) (ugs.: Kabel) flex (Brit.); lead; cord (Amer.)
**schnüren** *tr. V.* tie ⟨*bundle, string, etc.*⟩;
tie, lace up ⟨*shoe, corset, etc.*⟩
**schnur·los** *Adj.* cordless
**Schnurr·bart** *der* moustache
**schnurren** *itr. V.* ⟨*cat*⟩ purr; ⟨*machine*⟩
hum
**Schnür-: ~schuh** *der* lace-up shoe;
**~senkel** *der;* ~s, ~ (bes. nordd.)
[shoe]lace; (für Stiefel) bootlace
**schnur·stracks** *Adv.* (ugs.) straight
**schob** *1. u. 3. Pers. Prät. v.* SCHIESSEN

**Schock** *der;* ∼[e]s, ∼s shock

**schockieren** *tr. V.* shock; **über etw.** (*Akk.*) **schockiert sein** be shocked at sth.

**Schöffe** *der;* ∼n, ∼n lay judge (*acting together with another lay judge and a professional judge*)

**Schöffen·gericht** *das:* court presided over by a professional judge and two lay judges

**Schöffin** *die;* ∼, ∼nen ▶ SCHÖFFE

**Schokolade** *die;* ∼, ∼n (a) chocolate (b) (Getränk) [drinking] chocolate

**Schokolade[n]-:** ∼**eis** *das* chocolate ice cream; ∼**guss,** *\**∼**guß** *der* chocolate icing; ∼**pudding** *der* chocolate blancmange; ∼**torte** *die* chocolate cake *or* gateau

**scholl** *1. u. 3. Pers. Sg. Prät. v.* SCHALLEN

**Scholle** *die;* ∼, ∼n (a) (Erdscholle) clod [of earth]
(b) (Eisscholle) [ice] floe
(c) (Fisch) plaice

**schon** 1 *Adv.* (a) (bereits) (oft nicht übersetzt) already; (in Fragen) yet; **wie lange bist du** ∼ **hier?** how long have you been here?
(b) (fast gleichzeitig) there and then
(c) (jetzt) ∼ **[mal]** now; (inzwischen) meanwhile
(d) (selbst, sogar) even; (nur) only
(e) (ohne Ergänzung, ohne weiteren Zusatz) on its own; **[allein]** ∼ **der Gedanke daran** the mere thought of it; ∼ **deshalb** for this reason alone
(f) (wohl) really; **Lust hätte ich** ∼**, aber** ...: I'd certainly like to, but ...
2 *Partikel* (a) (ugs. ungeduldig: endlich) **nun komm** ∼**!** come on!; hurry up!
(b) (beruhigend: bestimmt) all right
(c) (durchaus) **das ist** ∼ **möglich** that is quite possible

**schön** 1 *Adj.* (a) beautiful; handsome ⟨youth, man⟩
(b) (angenehm) pleasant, nice ⟨day, holiday, dream, relaxation, etc.⟩; fine ⟨weather⟩; (nett) nice; **das war eine** ∼**e Zeit** those were wonderful days
(c) (gut) good
(d) (in Höflichkeitsformeln) ∼**e Grüße** best wishes; **recht** ∼**en Dank für** ...: thank you very much for ...
(e) ∼**!** (ugs.: einverstanden) OK (coll.); all right
(f) (iron.: leer) ∼**e Worte** fine[-sounding] words; (schmeichlerisch) honeyed words
(g) (ugs.: beträchtlich) handsome, (coll.) tidy ⟨sum, fortune, profit⟩; considerable ⟨quantity, distance⟩; pretty good ⟨pension⟩
(h) (iron.: unerfreulich) nice (coll. iron.); **das sind ja** ∼**e Aussichten!** this is a fine lookout *sing.* (iron.)
(i) **sich** ∼ **machen** smarten oneself up
2 *adv.* (a) beautifully
(b) (angenehm, erfreulich) nicely; ∼ **warm/ weich/langsam** nice and warm/soft/slow
(c) (gut) well

(d) (in Höflichkeitsformeln) **bitte** ∼**, können Sie mir sagen,** ...: excuse me, could you tell me ...
(e) (iron.) **wie es so** ∼ **heißt, wie man so** ∼ **sagt** as they say
(f) (ugs.: beträchtlich) really; (vor einem Adjektiv) pretty; **ganz** ∼ **arbeiten müssen** have to work jolly hard (Brit. coll.)
3 *Partikel* (ugs.) **bleib** ∼ **liegen!** lie there and be good

**schonen** 1 *tr. V.* treat ⟨clothes, books, furniture, etc.⟩ with care; (schützen) protect ⟨hands, furniture⟩; (nicht strapazieren) spare ⟨voice, eyes, etc.⟩; conserve ⟨strength⟩
2 *refl. V.* take things easy

**Schönheit** *die;* ∼, ∼en beauty

**Schönheits-:** ∼**chirurgie** *die* cosmetic surgery *no art.;* ∼**pflege** *die* beauty care *no art.*

**Schon·kost** *die* light food

*\****schön|machen** (ugs.) ▶ SCHÖN 1I

**Schonung** *die;* ∼, ∼en (a) (Nachsicht) consideration; (nachsichtige Behandlung) considerate treatment; (nach Krankheit/ Operation) [period of] rest; (von Gegenständen) careful treatment
(b) (Jungwald) [young] plantation

**schonungs·los** 1 *Adj.* unsparing, ruthless ⟨criticism etc.⟩; blunt ⟨frankness⟩
2 *adv.* unsparingly; ⟨say⟩ without mincing one's words

**Schonungslosigkeit** *die;* ∼: ruthlessness; (Strenge) rigour

**Schopf** *der;* ∼[e]s, Schöpfe shock of hair

**schöpfen** *tr. V.* (a) scoop [up] ⟨water, liquid⟩; (mit einer Kelle) ladle ⟨soup⟩
(b) (geh.: einatmen) draw, take ⟨breath⟩

**Schöpfer** *der;* ∼s, ∼: creator; (Gott) Creator

**Schöpferin** *die;* ∼, ∼nen creator

**schöpferisch** 1 *Adj.* creative
2 *adv.* creatively

**Schöpf-:** ∼**kelle** *die,* ∼**löffel** *der* ladle

**Schöpfung** *die;* ∼, ∼en (geh.) creation; **die** ∼ (die Welt) Creation

**Schoppen** *der;* ∼s, ∼: [quarter-litre/half-litre] glass of wine/beer

**schor** *1. u. 3. Pers. Sg. Prät. v.* SCHEREN

**Schorf** *der;* ∼[e]s, ∼e scab

**Schorle** *die;* ∼, ∼n wine with mineral water; ≈ spritzer

**Schorn·stein** *der* chimney; (Lokomotive, Schiff usw.) funnel

**Schornstein·feger** *der;* ∼s, ∼, **Schornstein·fegerin** *die;* ∼, ∼nen chimney sweep

**schoss,** *\****schoß** *1. u. 3. Pers. Sg. Prät. v.* SCHIESSEN

**Schoß** *der;* ∼es, Schöße lap

**Schote** *die;* ∼, ∼n pod

**Schotte** *der;* ∼n, ∼n Scot; Scotsman; **die** ∼n the Scots; the Scottish

---

*\*old spelling - see note on page xiv

**Schotten·rock** *der* tartan skirt; (Kilt) kilt

**Schottin** *die;* ~, ~nen Scot; Scotswoman

**schottisch** *Adj.* Scottish; ~er Whisky Scotch whisky

**Schottland** *(das);* ~s Scotland

**schräg** ①*Adj.* diagonal ⟨line, beam, cut, etc.⟩; sloping ⟨surface, roof, wall, side, etc.⟩; slanting, slanted ⟨writing, eyes, etc.⟩; tilted ⟨position of the head etc., axis⟩
② *adv.* at an angle; (diagonal) diagonally

**Schräge** *die;* ~, ~n (a) (schräge Fläche) sloping surface
**(b)** (Neigung) slope

**Schräg·strich** *der* oblique stroke

**schrak** *1. u. 3. Pers. Sg. Prät. v.* SCHRECKEN

**Schramme** *die;* ~, ~n scratch

**schrammen** *tr. V.* scratch

**Schrank** *der;* ~[e]s, Schränke cupboard; closet (Amer.); (Glas~; kleiner Wand~) cabinet; (Kleiderschrank) wardrobe; (Bücher~) bookcase

**Schränkchen** *das;* ~s, ~: cabinet

**Schranke** *die;* ~, ~n (a) (auch fig.) barrier
**(b)** (fig.: Grenze) limit

**Schraube** *die;* ~, ~n bolt; (Holz-, Blechschraube) screw

**schrauben** *tr. V.* (a) ▶ SCHRAUBE: bolt/ screw (an, auf + Akk. on to)
**(b)** (drehen) screw ⟨nut, hook, lightbulb, etc.⟩ (auf + Akk. on to; in + Akk. into)

**Schrauben-:** ~schlüssel *der* spanner; ~zieher *der;* ~s, ~: screwdriver

**Schraub·verschluss, *Schraub·verschluß** *der* screw top

**Schreber·garten** *der* ≈ allotment (cultivated primarily as a garden)

**Schreck** *der;* ~[e]s, ~e fright; scare; (Schock) shock; jmdm. einen ~ einjagen give sb. a fright

**schrecken** *regelm. (auch unr.) itr. V.* start [up]; aus dem Schlaf ~: awake with a start; start from one's sleep

**Schrecken** *der;* ~s, ~: fright; scare; (Entsetzen) horror; (große Angst) terror; jmdm. einen ~ einjagen give sb. a fright

**schreckhaft** *Adj.* easily scared

**Schreckhaftigkeit** *die;* ~: easily scared nature; tendency to take fright

**schrecklich** ① *Adj.* terrible
② *adv.* terribly

**Schredder** *der;* ~s, ~: shredder

**schreddern** *tr. V.* shred

**Schrei** *der;* ~[e]s, ~e cry; (lauter Ruf) shout; (durchdringend) yell; (gellend) scream; (kreischend) shriek

**Schreib·block** *der; Pl.* ~s *od.* Schreib·blöcke writing pad

**schreiben** ① *unr. itr. V.* write; (mit der Schreibmaschine) type; an einem Roman *usw.* ~: be writing a novel *etc.;* jmdm. *od.* an jmdn. ~: write to sb.

② *unr. tr. V.* write; (mit der Schreibmaschine) type; wie schreibt man dieses Wort? how is this word spelt?
③ *unr. refl. V.* be spelt

**Schreiben** *das;* ~s, ~ (a) writing *no def. art.;*
**(b)** (Brief) letter

**Schreiber** *der;* ~s, ~: writer; (Verfasser) author

**Schreiberin** *die;* ~, ~en writer; (Verfasserin) authoress

**Schreib-:** ~marke *die* (DV) cursor; ~maschine *die* typewriter; ~maschinen·papier *das* typing paper; ~papier *das* writing paper; ~schutz *der* (DV) write protection; ~tisch *der* desk

**Schreibung** *die;* ~, ~en spelling

**Schreib-:** ~waren *Pl.* stationery *sing.;* ~waren·geschäft *das* stationer's

**schreien** *unr. itr. V.* ⟨person⟩ cry [out]; (laut rufen/sprechen) shout; (durchdringend) yell; (gellend) scream; ⟨baby⟩ yell, bawl; zum Schreien sein (ugs.) be a scream (coll.)

**Schrei·hals** *der* (ugs.) (a) (Kind) bawler
**(b)** (abwertend: Randalierer) rowdy

**Schreiner** *der;* ~s, ~, (bes. südd.)
▶ TISCHLER

**Schreinerei** *die;* ~, ~en (bes. südd.)
▶ TISCHLEREI

**Schreinerin** *die;* ~, ~nen (bes. südd.)
▶ TISCHLERIN

**schreiten** *unr. itr. V.; mit sein* (geh.) walk; (mit großen Schritten) stride

**schrickst** *2. Pers. Sg. Präsens v.*
SCHRECKEN

**schrickt** *3. Pers. Sg. Präsens v.* SCHRECKEN

**schrie** *1. u. 3. Pers. Sg. Prät. v.* SCHREIEN

**schrieb** *1. u. 3. Pers. Sg. Prät. v.* SCHREIBEN

**Schrieb** *der;* ~[e]s, ~e (ugs.) missive (coll.)

**Schrift** *die;* ~, ~en (a) (System) script; (Alphabet) alphabet
**(b)** (Handschrift) [hand]writing
**(c)** (Werk) work

**Schrift·art** *die* (Druckw.) [type]face

**schriftlich** ① *Adj.* written
② *adv.* in writing

**Schrift-:** ~steller *der;* ~s, ~, ~stellerin *die;* ~, ~nen writer; ~stück *das* [official] document; ~wechsel *der* correspondence; ~zeichen *das* character; ~zug *der* (Namenszug) lettering; (als Firmenzeichen) logo

**schrill** ① *Adj.* shrill
② *adv.* shrilly

**schrillen** *itr. V.* shrill; sound shrilly

**schritt** *1. u. 3. Pers. Sg. Prät. v.* SCHREITEN

**Schritt** *der;* ~[e]s, ~e (a) step; einen ~ machen *od.* tun take a step
**(b)** *Pl.* (Geräusch) footsteps
**(c)** (Entfernung) pace
**(d)** (Gleich~) aus dem ~ kommen get out of step ··⫶

S

**(e)** (Gangart) walk; **seinen ~ verlangsamen/ beschleunigen** slow/quicken one's pace; [**mit jmdm./etw.**] **~ halten** (auch fig.) keep up *or* keep pace [with sb./sth.]
**(f)** (Schrittgeschwindigkeit) walking pace; „**~ fahren**" 'dead slow'
**(g)** (fig.: Maßnahme) step; measure

**Schritt-: ~geschwindigkeit** *die* walking pace; **~macher** *der,* **~macherin** *die* pacemaker

**schroff** 1 *Adj.* **(a)** precipitous ⟨*rock etc.*⟩
**(b)** (plötzlich) sudden ⟨*transition, change*⟩; (krass) stark ⟨*contrast*⟩
**(c)** (barsch) curt ⟨*refusal, manner*⟩; brusque ⟨*manner, behaviour, tone*⟩
2 *adv.* **(a)** ⟨*rise, drop*⟩ sheer; ⟨*fall away*⟩ precipitously
**(b)** (plötzlich, unvermittelt) suddenly
**(c)** (barsch) curtly; ⟨*interrupt*⟩ abruptly; ⟨*treat*⟩ brusquely

**schröpfen** *tr. V.* (ugs.) fleece

**Schrot** *der od. das;* ~[e]s, ~e **(a)** coarse meal; (aus Getreide) whole meal (Brit.); whole grain
**(b)** (Munition) shot

**schroten** *tr. V.* grind ⟨*grain etc.*⟩ [coarsely]; crush ⟨*malt*⟩ [coarsely]

**Schrot-: ~flinte** *die* shotgun; **~kugel** *die* pellet

**Schrott** *der;* ~[e]s, ~e **(a)** scrap [metal]; **ein Auto zu ~ fahren** (ugs.) write a car off
**(b)** (salopp fig.) rubbish

**schrott·reif** *Adj.* ready for the scrap heap *postpos.*

**schrubben** *tr.* (*auch itr.*) *V.* scrub

**Schrubber** *der;* ~s, ~: [long-handled] scrubbing brush

**Schrulle** *die;* ~, ~n cranky idea; (Marotte) quirk

**schrumpelig** *Adj.* (ugs.) wrinkly

**schrumpeln** *itr. V.; mit sein* (ugs.) ⟨*skin*⟩ go wrinkled; ⟨*apple etc.*⟩ shrivel

**schrumpfen** *itr. V.; mit sein* shrink; ⟨*metal, rock*⟩ contract; ⟨*apple etc.*⟩ shrivel; ⟨*skin*⟩ go wrinkled; (abnehmen) decrease; ⟨*supplies, capital, hopes*⟩ dwindle

**Schrumpf-: ~leber** *die* cirrhotic liver; **~niere** *die* cirrhotic kidney

**Schub** *der;* ~[e]s, Schübe **(a)** (Physik) thrust
**(b)** (Med.: Phase) phase; stage
**(c)** (Gruppe, Anzahl) batch

**Schuber** *der;* ~s, ~: slip case

**Schub-: ~fach** *das* drawer; **~karre** *die,* **~karren** *der* wheelbarrow; **~lade** *die* drawer

**Schubs** *der;* ~es, ~e (ugs.) shove

**schubsen** *tr.* (*auch itr.*) *V.* (ugs.) push; shove

**schub·weise** *Adv.* (Med.) in phases *or* stages

**schüchtern** 1 *Adj.* **(a)** shy ⟨*person, smile, etc.*⟩; shy, timid ⟨*voice, knock, etc.*⟩
**(b)** (fig.: zaghaft) tentative, cautious ⟨*attempt, beginnings, etc.*⟩
2 *adv.* shyly; ⟨*knock, ask, etc.*⟩ timidly

**Schüchternheit** *die;* ~: shyness

**Schuft** *der;* ~[e]s, ~e scoundrel

**schuften** (ugs.) *itr. V.* slave away

**Schufterei** *die;* ~ (ugs.) slaving away *no indef. art.;* slog

**Schuh** *der;* ~[e]s, ~e shoe; (hoher ~, Stiefel) boot; **jmdm. etw. in die ~e schieben** (fig. ugs.) pin the blame for sth. on sb.

**Schuh-: ~anzieher** *der;* ~~s, ~~: shoehorn; **~band** *das; Pl.* **~bänder** (bes. südd.) shoelace; **~creme** *die* shoe polish; **~größe** *die* shoe size; **welche ~größe hast du?** what size shoe[s] do you take?; **~löffel** *der* shoehorn; **~macher** *der,* **~macherin** *die* shoemaker; **~sohle** *die* sole [of a/one's shoe]

**Schul-: ~abschluss, *\~abschluß** *der* school-leaving qualification; **~arbeit** *die* **(a)** ▶ ~AUFGABE; **(b)** (österr.: Klassenarbeit) [written] class test; **~aufgabe** *die* item of homework; **~aufgaben** homework *sing.;* **~beirat** *der* school advisory board; **~buch** *das* school book; **~bus** *der* school bus

**schuld** ▶ SCHULD B

**Schuld** *die;* ~, ~en **(a)** guilt; **er ist sich** (*Dat.*) **keiner ~ bewusst** he is not conscious of having done any wrong
**(b)** (Verantwortlichkeit) blame; **es ist [nicht] seine ~:** it is [not] his fault; [**an etw.** (*Dat.*)] **~ haben** *od.* **schuld sein** be to blame [for sth.]
**(c)** (Verpflichtung zur Rückzahlung) debt; **5 000 Euro ~en haben** have debts of 5,000 euros; **owe 5,000 euros**

**schuld·bewusst, *schuld·bewußt**
1 *Adj.* guilty ⟨*look, face, etc.*⟩
2 *adv.* guiltily

**schulden** *tr. V.* owe; **was schulde ich Ihnen?** how much do I owe you?

**Schuld·gefühl** *das* feeling of guilt

**schuldig** *Adj.* **(a)** guilty; **der [an dem Unfall] ~e Autofahrer** the driver to blame [for the accident]
**(b)** **jmdm. etw. ~ sein/bleiben** owe sb. sth.
**(c)** (gebührend) due; proper

**Schuldige** *der/die; adj. Dekl.* guilty person; (im Strafprozess) guilty party

**Schuldigkeit** *die;* ~, ~en duty; **meine [verdammte] Pflicht und ~:** my bounden duty; **seine ~ getan haben** (fig.) have served its/his purpose

**Schul·direktor** *der,* **Schul·direktorin** *die* head teacher; headmaster/headmistress

**schuld-, Schuld-: ~los** *Adj.* innocent (**an** + *Dat.* of); **~spruch** *der* verdict of guilty

---
*\*alte Schreibung - vgl. Hinweis auf S. xiv

**Schule** *die;* ~, ~n school; **zur** *od.* **in die** ~ **gehen, die** ~ **besuchen** go to school; **auf** *od.* **in der** ~: at school

**schulen** *tr. V.* train

**Schüler** *der;* ~s, ~: pupil; (Schuljunge) schoolboy

**Schüler·austausch** *der* school exchange

**Schülerin** *die;* ~, ~nen pupil; (Schulmädchen) schoolgirl

**Schüler·mit·verwaltung** *die* pupil participation *no art.* in school administration

**schul-, Schul-:** ~**ferien** *Pl.* school holidays *or* (Amer.) vacation *sing.;* ~**fernsehen** *das* educational television; television for schools; ~**fest** *das* school open day; ~**frei** *Adj.* ⟨day⟩ off school; **morgen ist/haben wir** ~**frei** there is/we have no school tomorrow; ~**frei bekommen** be let off school; ~**hof** *der* school yard; ~**jahr** *das* (a) school year; (b) (Klasse) year; ~**junge** *der* schoolboy; ~**kind** *das* schoolchild; ~**klasse** *die* [school] class; ~**land·heim** *das* [school's] country hostel (*visited by school classes*); ~**mädchen** *das* schoolgirl; ~**ordnung** *die* school rules *pl.;* ~**pflicht** *die* obligation to attend school; **die Einführung der [allgemeinen]** ~**pflicht** the introduction of compulsory school attendance [for all children]; ~**pflichtig** *Adj.* required to attend school *postpos.;* ~**pflichtig sein** have to attend school; **im** ~**pflichtigen Alter** of school age; ~**ranzen** *der* [school] satchel; ~**sportfest** *das* inter-school sports day; ~**sprecher** *der* pupils' representative; ≈ head boy; ~**sprecherin** *die* pupils' representative; ≈ head girl; ~**tag** *der* school day; ~**tasche** *die* schoolbag; (Ranzen) [school] satchel; ~**uniform** *die* school uniform

**Schulter** *die;* ~, ~n shoulder; **jmdm. auf die** ~ **klopfen** pat sb. on the shoulder *or* (fig.) back

**Schulter·blatt** *das* (Anat.) shoulder blade

**schultern** *tr. V.* shoulder; **das Gewehr** ~: shoulder arms

**Schul-:** ~**weg** *der* way to school; ~**zeit** *die* schooldays *pl.*

**Schummelei** *die;* ~, ~en (ugs.) ▶ MOGELEI

**schummeln** *itr., tr., refl. V.* (ugs.) ▶ MOGELN

**schummerig** *Adj.* dim ⟨light etc.⟩; dimly lit ⟨room etc.⟩

**Schummler** *der;* ~s, ~, **Schummlerin** *die;* ~, ~nen (ugs.) cheat

**Schund** *der;* ~[e]s trash

**Schuppe** *die;* ~, ~n (a) scale (b) *Pl.* (auf dem Kopf) dandruff *sing.;* (auf der Haut) flaking skin *sing.*

**schuppen** [1] *tr. V.* scale ⟨fish⟩ [2] *refl. V.* ⟨skin⟩ flake; ⟨person⟩ have flaking skin

**Schuppen** *der;* ~s, ~ (a) shed

(b) (ugs.: Lokal) joint (coll.)

**schüren** *tr. V.* (a) poke ⟨fire⟩ (b) (fig.) stir up ⟨hatred, envy, etc.⟩

**schürfen** [1] *itr. V.* scrape [2] *tr. V.* (a) **sich** ⟨Dat.⟩ **das Knie** *usw.* ~: graze one's knee *etc.;* (b) (Bergbau) mine ⟨ore etc.⟩ open-cast *or* (Amer.) opencut

**Schürf·wunde** *die* graze; abrasion

**Schurke** *der;* ~n, ~n, **Schurkin** *die;* ~, ~nen rogue

**Schur·wolle** *die* new wool

**Schürze** *die;* ~, ~n apron; (Latzschürze) pinafore

**Schuss, \*Schuß** *der;* Schusses, Schüsse (a) shot (**auf** + *Akk.* at); **weit** *od.* **weitab vom** ~ (fig. ugs.) well away from the action (b) (Menge Munition/Schießpulver) round; **drei** ~ **Munition** three rounds of ammunition (c) (Schusswunde) gunshot wound (d) (kleine Menge) dash (e) (Drogenjargon) shot; fix (sl.) (f) (Skisport) schuss; ~ **fahren** schuss (g) (ugs.) **etw. in** ~ **bringen/halten** get sth. into/keep sth. in [good] shape

**Schüssel** *die;* ~, ~n bowl; (flacher) dish

**schusselig** (ugs.) [1] *Adj.* scatterbrained [2] *adv.* in a scatterbrained way

**Schusseligkeit** *die;* ~ (ugs.) scatterbrained way

**Schuss-, \*Schuß-:** ~**linie** *die* line of fire; **in die/jmds.** ~**linie geraten** *od.* **kommen** (auch fig.) come under fire/come under fire from sb.; ~**verletzung** *die* gunshot wound; ~**waffe** *die* weapon (firing a projectile); (Gewehr usw.) firearm; ~**wechsel** *der* exchange of shots

**Schuster** *der;* ~s, ~, **Schusterin** *die;* ~, ~nen (ugs.) shoemaker; (jmd., der Schuhe repariert) shoe repairer

**Schutt** *der;* ~[e]s rubble; „~ **abladen verboten**" 'no tipping'; 'no dumping'

**Schüttel·frost** *der* [violent] shivering fit

**schütteln** [1] *tr. V.* (a) shake; **den Kopf [über etw.** ⟨Akk.⟩**]** ~: shake one's head [over sth.]; **jmdm. die Hand** ~: shake sb.'s hand; **jmdn. by the hand** (b) (*unpers.*) **es schüttelte ihn [vor Kälte]** he was shaking [with *or* from cold] [2] *refl. V.* shake oneself/itself [3] *itr. V.* **mit dem Kopf** ~: shake one's head

**schütten** [1] *tr. V.* pour ⟨liquid, flour, etc.⟩; (unabsichtlich) spill ⟨liquid, flour, etc.⟩; tip ⟨rubbish, coal, etc.⟩ [2] *itr. V.* (*unpers.*) (ugs.: regnen) pour [down]

**schütter** *Adj.* sparse; thin

**Schutt-:** ~**halde** *die* pile *or* heap of rubble; ~**haufen** *der* pile of rubble; (Abfallhaufen) rubbish heap

**Schutz** *der;* ~es protection (**vor** + *Dat.,* **gegen** against); (Zuflucht) refuge; ~ **suchend** seeking protection *postpos.*

**schutz-, Schutz-:** ~**bedürftig** *Adj.* in ⋯⋮

**S**

need of protection *postpos.;*
**∼behauptung** *die* (bes. Rechtsw.) attempt
to justify one's behaviour; **∼blech** *das*
mudguard; **∼brief** *der* (Kfz-W.) travel
insurance; (Dokument) travel insurance
certificate

**Schütze** *der;* ∼n, ∼n **(a)** marksman
**(b)** (Fußball usw.) scorer
**(c)** (Milit.: einfacher Soldat) private
**(d)** (Astrol.) Sagittarius

**schützen** 1 *tr. V.* protect (vor + *Dat.* from,
gegen against); safeguard ⟨interest, property,
etc.⟩ (vor + *Dat.* from, gegen against); **gesetzlich geschützt**
registered [as a trade mark]
2 *itr. V.* provide or give protection (vor +
*Dat.* from, gegen against); (vor Wind, Regen)
give shelter (vor + *Dat.* from)

**Schützen·fest** *das: shooting competition
with fair*

**Schutz·engel** *der* guardian angel

**Schützen-:** **∼graben** *der* trench;
**∼panzer** *der* armoured personnel carrier;
**∼verein** *der* rifle club

**Schutz-:** **∼helm** *der* helmet; (bei
Motorradfahrern usw.) crash helmet; (bei
Bauarbeitern usw.) safety helmet; **∼hütte** *die*
**(a)** (Unterstand) shelter; **(b)** (Berghütte)
mountain hut; **∼impfung** *die* vaccination

**Schützin** *die;* ∼, ∼nen **(a)** markswoman
**(b)** (Fußball usw.) scorer

**Schützling** *der;* ∼s, ∼e protégé;
(Anvertrauter) charge

**schutz-, Schutz-:** **∼los** *Adj.* defenceless;
**∼mann** *der; Pl.* ∼männer *od.* ∼leute (ugs.
veralt.) [police] constable; copper (Brit. coll.);
**∼patron** *der,* **∼patronin** *die* patron
saint; **∼schicht** *die* protective layer (aus
of); (flüssig aufgetragen) protective coating;
*****∼suchend** ▶ SCHUTZ; **∼umschlag** *der*
dust jacket

**schwabbelig** *Adj.* flabby ⟨stomach,
person, etc.⟩; wobbly ⟨jelly etc.⟩

**schwabbeln** *itr. V.* (ugs.) wobble

**Schwabe** *der;* ∼n, ∼n Swabian

**Schwaben** *(das);* ∼s Swabia

**Schwäbin** *die;* ∼, ∼nen Swabian

**schwäbisch** *Adj.* Swabian

**schwach; schwächer, schwächst...** 1 *Adj.*
**(a)** weak; weak, delicate ⟨child, woman⟩;
frail ⟨invalid, old person⟩; low-powered
⟨engine, bulb, amplifier, etc.⟩; weak, poor
⟨eyesight, memory, etc.⟩; poor ⟨hearing⟩;
delicate ⟨health, constitution⟩; **∼ werden**
grow weak; (fig.: schwanken) weaken; (fig.:
nachgeben) give in
**(b)** (nicht gut) poor ⟨pupil, player,
performance, result, etc.⟩; weak ⟨argument,
opponent, play, film, etc.⟩
**(c)** (gering, niedrig) poor, low ⟨attendance etc.⟩;
slight ⟨effect, resistance, gradient, etc.⟩; light

⟨wind, rain, current⟩; faint ⟨voice, pressure,
hope, smile, smell⟩; weak, faint ⟨pulse⟩; faint,
dim ⟨light⟩; pale ⟨colour⟩
**(d)** (wenig konzentriert) weak ⟨solution, coffee,
poison, etc.⟩
**(e)** (Sprachw.) weak
2 *adv.* **(a)** weakly
**(b)** (nicht gut) poorly
**(c)** (in geringem Maße) poorly ⟨attended,
developed⟩; slightly ⟨poisonous, sweetened,
inclined⟩; ⟨rain⟩ slightly; ⟨remember, glow,
smile⟩ faintly
**(d)** (Sprachw.) ∼ **gebeugt** weak

**Schwäche** *die;* ∼, ∼n weakness; **eine ∼
für jmdn./etw. haben** have a soft spot for sb./
a weakness for sth.

**Schwäche·anfall** *der* sudden feeling of
faintness

**schwächen** *tr. V.* weaken

**schwächlich** *Adj.* weakly ⟨person⟩; frail
⟨old person, constitution⟩

**Schwächling** *der;* ∼s, ∼e weakling

**schwach-, Schwach-:** **∼punkt** *der*
weak point; **∼sinn** *der* **(a)** (Med.) mental
deficiency; **(b)** (ugs.) [idiotic (coll.)] rubbish;
**∼sinnig** 1 *Adj.* **(a)** (Med.) mentally
deficient; **(b)** (ugs.) idiotic (coll.), nonsensical
⟨measure, policy, etc.⟩; rubbishy ⟨film etc.⟩;
2 *adv.* (ugs.) idiotically (coll.); stupidly

**Schwächung** *die;* ∼, ∼en weakening

**Schwaden** *der;* ∼s, ∼: [thick] cloud

**schwafeln** 1 *itr. V.* rabbit on (Brit.
coll.), waffle (von about)
2 *tr. V.* blether ⟨nonsense⟩

**Schwager** *der;* ∼s, Schwäger brother-in-
law

**Schwägerin** *die;* ∼, ∼nen sister-in-law

**Schwalbe** *die;* ∼, ∼n swallow

**Schwall** *der;* ∼[e]s, ∼e torrent

**schwamm** 1. u. 3. Pers. Sg. Prät. v.
SCHWIMMEN

**Schwamm** *der;* ∼[e]s, Schwämme **(a)**
sponge; ∼ **drüber!** (ugs.) [let's] forget it
**(b)** (südd., österr.: Pilz) mushroom

**Schwammerl** *das;* ∼s, ∼[n] (bayr., österr.)
mushroom

**schwammig** 1 *Adj.* **(a)** spongy
**(b)** (aufgedunsen) flabby, bloated ⟨face, body,
etc.⟩
2 *adv.* (unpräzise) vaguely

**Schwammigkeit** *die;* ∼ **(a)** sponginess
**(b)** (abwertend: Aufgedunsenheit) flabbiness;
bloated appearence
**(c)** (abwertend: Vagheit) woolliness

**Schwan** *der;* ∼[e]s, Schwäne swan

**schwand** 1. u. 3. Pers. Sg. Prät. v.
SCHWINDEN

**schwang** 1. u. 3. Pers. Sg. Prät. v.
SCHWINGEN

**schwanger** *Adj.* pregnant (von by)

---

*old spelling - see note on page xiv

**Schwangere** *die; adj. Dekl.* expectant mother; pregnant woman

**schwängern** *tr. V.* make ⟨*woman*⟩ pregnant

**Schwangerschaft** *die;* ∼, ∼en pregnancy

**Schwangerschafts-:** ∼**abbruch** *der* termination of pregnancy; abortion; ∼**verhütung** *die* contraception; ∼**vertretung** *die* (a) maternity[-leave] cover; **die** ∼**vertretung für jmdn. machen** cover for sb. while she is on maternity leave; **(b)** (Person) person covering [a period of] maternity leave

**Schwank** *der;* ∼[e]s, Schwänke comic tale; (auf der Bühne) farce

**schwanken** *itr. V.; mit Richtungsangabe mit sein* (a) sway; ⟨*boat*⟩ rock; (heftiger) roll; ⟨*ground, floor*⟩ shake
**(b)** (fig.: unbeständig sein) ⟨*prices, temperature, etc.*⟩ fluctuate; ⟨*number, usage, etc.*⟩ vary
**(c)** (fig.: unentschieden sein) waver; (zögern) hesitate

**Schwankung** *die;* ∼, ∼en variation; (der Kurse usw.) fluctuation

**Schwanz** *der;* ∼es, Schwänze (a) tail
**(b)** (salopp: Penis) prick (coarse); cock (coarse)

**Schwänzchen** *das;* ∼s, ∼(a) [little] tail
**(b)** (fam.: Penis) willy (coll.)

**schwänzeln** *itr. V.* wag its tail/their tails

**schwänzen** *tr., itr. V.* (ugs.) skip, cut ⟨*lesson etc.*⟩; [die Schule] ∼: play truant *or* (Amer.) hookey

**schwappen** *itr. V.* slosh

**Schwarm** *der;* ∼[e]s, Schwärme (a) swarm
**(b)** (fam.: Angebetete[r]) idol; heart-throb

**schwärmen** *itr. V.* (a) *mit Richtungsangabe mit sein* swarm
**(b)** (begeistert sein) **für jmdn./etw.** ∼: be mad about *or* really keen on sb./sth.; **von etw.** ∼: go into raptures about sth.

**schwärmerisch** [1] *Adj.* rapturous
[2] *adv.* rapturously

**Schwarte** *die;* ∼, ∼n (a) rind
**(b)** (ugs.: dickes Buch) tome

**schwarz;** schwärzer, schwärzest... [1] *Adj.*
**(a)** black; Black ⟨*person*⟩; filthy[-black] ⟨*hands, fingernails, etc.*⟩; **mir wurde Schwarz vor den Augen** everything went black **der** ∼**e Erdteil** *od.* Kontinent the Dark Continent; **das Schwarze Meer** the Black Sea; **ins Schwarze treffen** (fig.) hit the nail on the head
**(b)** (illegal) illicit ⟨*deal, exchange, etc.*⟩; **der** ∼**e Markt** the black market
**(c)** ∼ **sehen** look on the black side; be pessimistic (**für** about)
[2] *adv.* (illegal) illegally

**Schwarz** *das;* ∼[es], ∼: black

**Schwarz·brot** *das* black bread

**Schwarze** *der/die; adj. Dekl.* Black

**schwärzen** *tr. V.* blacken

**schwarz-, Schwarz-:** ∼|**fahren** *unr.*

*itr. V.; mit sein* dodge paying the fare; ∼**fahrer** *der,* ∼**fahrerin** *die* fare dodger; ∼**haarig** *Adj.* black-haired; ∼**handel** *der* black market (**mit** in); (Tätigkeit) black marketeering (**mit** in); ∼**markt** *der* black market; ∼|**sehen** *unr. itr. V.* watch television without a licence; *s. auch* SCHWARZ 1c; ∼**seher** *der,* ∼**seherin** *die* (a) (ugs.) pessimist; **(b)** (jmd, der schwarz fernsieht) [television] licence dodger

**Schwärzung** *die;* ∼, ∼en blackening

**schwarz-, Schwarz-:** ∼**wald** *der;* ∼[e]s Black Forest; ∼**weiß** *Adj.* black and white; ∼**weiß-film** *der* black and white film; ∼**weiß-foto** *das* black and white photo; ∼**wurzel** *die* black salsify

**schwatzen,** (bes. südd.) **schwätzen**
[1] *itr. V.* chat; (über belanglose Dinge) chatter; natter (coll.)
[2] *tr. V.* say; talk ⟨*nonsense, rubbish*⟩

**Schwätzer** *der;* ∼s, ∼, **Schwätzerin** *die;* ∼, ∼nen chatterbox; (klatschhafter Mensch) gossip

**schwatzhaft** *Adj.* talkative; (klatschhaft) gossipy

**Schwatzhaftigkeit** *die;* ∼: talkativeness; (Klatschsucht) gossipiness

**Schwebe** *die;* **in der** ∼ **sein/bleiben** (fig.) be/remain in the balance

**Schwebe-:** ∼**bahn** *die* cableway; ∼**balken** *der* (Turnen) [balance] beam

**schweben** *itr. V.* (a) ⟨*bird, balloon, etc.*⟩ hover; ⟨*cloud, balloon, mist*⟩ hang; **in Gefahr** ∼ (fig.) be in danger
**(b)** *mit sein* (durch die Luft) float

**Schwede** *der;* ∼n, ∼n Swede

**Schweden** *(das);* ∼s Sweden

**Schwedin** *die;* ∼, ∼nen Swede

**schwedisch** *Adj.* Swedish

**Schwefel** *der;* ∼s sulphur

**Schwefel-:** ∼**dioxid,** ∼**dioxyd** *das* (Chemie) sulphur dioxide; ∼**säure** *die* (Chemie) sulphuric acid; ∼**wasserstoff** *der* (Chemie) hydrogen sulphide

**Schweif** *der;* ∼[e]s, ∼e tail

**schweifen** *itr. V.; mit sein* (geh.; auch fig.) wander

**Schweige·geld** *das* hush money

**schweigen** *unr. itr. V.* remain *or* stay silent; say nothing; **ganz zu** ∼ **von** ...: not to mention ...

**Schweigen** *das;* ∼s silence

**schweigsam** *Adj.* silent; quiet

**Schweigsamkeit** *die;* ∼: silence; quietness

**Schwein** *das;* ∼[e]s, ∼e (a) pig
**(b)** (Fleisch) pork
**(c)** (salopp: gemeiner Mensch) swine; (Schmutzfink) mucky devil (coll.); mucky pig (coll.)
**(d)** (salopp: Mensch) **ein armes** ∼: a poor devil; **kein** ∼ **war da** there wasn't a bloody (Brit. sl.) *or* (coll.) damn soul there ···ᐳ

**(e)** (ugs.: Glück) [großes] ∼ haben have a [big] stroke of luck; (davonkommen) get away with it (coll.)

**Schweine-:** ∼**braten** der roast pork *no indef. art.;* ∼**fleisch** das pork; ∼**kotelett** das (Kochk.) pork chop

**Schweinerei** die; ∼, ∼en (ugs.) **(a)** (Schmutz) mess
**(b)** (Gemeinheit) mean *or* dirty trick

**Schweine-:** ∼**schnitzel** das escalope of pork; ∼**stall** der (auch fig.) pigsty; pigpen (Amer.); ∼**steak** das pork steak;

**schweinisch** (ugs.) *Adj.* **(a)** (schmutzig) filthy
**(b)** (unanständig) dirty; smutty

**Schweins-leder** das pigskin

**Schweiß** der; ∼es sweat; **mir brach der** ∼ **aus** I broke out in a sweat

**Schweiß-:** ∼**ausbruch** der sweat; ∼**brenner** der welding torch; ∼**drüse** die (Anat.) sweat gland

**schweißen** tr., itr. V. weld

**Schweißer** der; ∼s, ∼, **Schweißerin** die; ∼, ∼nen welder

**schweiß-, Schweiß-:** ∼**fuß** sweaty foot; ∼**gebadet** Adj. bathed in sweat *postpos.;* ∼**nass**, *∗*∼**naß** Adj. sweaty; damp with sweat *pred.;* ∼**perle** die bead of sweat

**Schweiz** die; ∼: Switzerland *no art.*

**Schweizer** der; ∼s, ∼: Swiss

**schweizer-deutsch** Adj. Swiss German

**Schweizerin** die; ∼, ∼nen Swiss

**schweizerisch** Adj. Swiss

**schwelen** (auch fig.) smoulder

**schwelgen** itr. V. feast

**Schwelle** die; ∼, ∼n **(a)** threshold
**(b)** (Eisenbahnschwelle) sleeper (Brit.); [cross] tie (Amer.)

**schwellen** unr. itr. V.; mit sein swell; ⟨limb, face, cheek, etc.⟩ swell [up]

**Schwellen-land** das: country at the stage of economic take-off

**Schwellung** die; ∼, ∼en (Med.) swelling

**Schwemme** die; ∼, ∼n glut (an + Dat. of)

**Schwemm-land** das alluvial land

**Schwengel** der; ∼s, ∼ **(a)** (der Glocke) clapper
**(b)** (der Pumpe) handle

**Schwenk** der; ∼s, ∼s **(a)** (Drehung) swing
**(b)** (Film, Ferns.) pan

**schwenken** [1] tr. V. **(a)** swing; wave ⟨flag, handkerchief⟩
**(b)** (spülen) rinse
[2] itr. V.; mit sein ⟨marching column⟩ swing, wheel; ⟨camera⟩ pan; ⟨path, road, car⟩ swing

**schwer** [1] Adj. **(a)** heavy; **2 Kilo** ∼ **sein** weigh two kilos
**(b)** (mühevoll) heavy ⟨work⟩; hard, tough ⟨job⟩; hard ⟨day⟩; difficult ⟨birth⟩; **es** ∼/**nicht** ∼

**S**

haben have it hard/easy; **sich mit** *od.* **bei etw.** ∼ **tun** (ugs.) have trouble with sth.; **jmdm. fällt etw.** ∼: sb. finds sth. difficult; **jmdm./ sich etw.** ∼ **machen** make sth. difficult for sb./oneself
**(c)** (schlimm) severe ⟨shock, disappointment, strain, storm⟩; serious, grave ⟨wrong, injustice, error, illness, blow, reservation⟩; serious ⟨accident, injury⟩; heavy ⟨punishment, strain, loss, blow⟩; **etw.** ∼ **nehmen** take sth. seriously
[2] adv. **(a)** heavily ⟨built, laden, armed⟩; ∼ **tragen** be carrying sth. heavy [with difficulty]
**(b)** ⟨work⟩ hard; ⟨breathe⟩ heavily; ∼ **hören** be hard of hearing
**(c)** (schwierig) with difficulty; ∼ **verdaulich** (auch fig.) hard to digest *pred.*
**(d)** (sehr) seriously ⟨injured, ill⟩; greatly, deeply ⟨disappointed⟩; ⟨punish⟩ severely, heavily; ∼ **verunglücken** have a serious accident

**Schwer-:** ∼**arbeiter** der worker engaged in heavy physical work; ∼**behinderte** der/die severely handicapped person; (körperlich auch) severely disabled person; **die** ∼**behinderten** the severely handicapped/ disabled; ∼**beschädigte** der/die/ adj. Dekl. severely disabled person

**Schwere** die; ∼ **(a)** weight
**(b)** (Schwerkraft) gravity
**(c)** ▶ SCHWER 1C: severity; seriousness; gravity; heaviness

**schwere-los** Adj. weightless

**Schwerelosigkeit** die; ∼: weightlessness

**schwer-, Schwer-:** *∗*∼|**fallen** ▶ SCHWER 1B; ∼**fällig** [1] Adj. (auch fig.) ponderous; cumbersome ⟨bureaucracy, procedure⟩; [2] adv. ponderously; ∼**fälligkeit** die: ▶ ∼FÄLLIG: ponderousness; cumbersomeness; ∼**gewicht** das **(a)** (Sport) heavyweight; **(b)** (Schwerpunkt) main focus; ∼**hörig** Adj. hard of hearing *pred.;* ∼**hörigkeit** die; ∼∼: hardness of hearing; ∼**industrie** die heavy industry; ∼**kraft** die gravity; *∗*∼**krank** ▶ SCHWER 2D

**schwerlich** Adv. hardly

**schwer-, Schwer-:** *∗*∼|**machen** ▶ SCHWER 1B; ∼**metall** das heavy metal; ∼**mütig** [1] Adj. melancholic; [2] adv. melancholically; *∗*∼|**nehmen** ▶ SCHWER 1C; ∼**punkt** der centre of gravity; (fig.) main focus; (Hauptgewicht) main stress

**Schwert** das; ∼[e]s, ∼er sword

**Schwert-:** ∼**fisch** der swordfish; ∼**lilie** die iris

**schwert|tun** ▶ SCHWER 1B

**Schwert-wal** der (Orka) killer whale

**schwer-, Schwer-:** ∼**verbrecher** der, ∼**verbrecherin** die serious offender; *∗*∼**verdaulich** ▶ SCHWER 2C; *∗*∼**verletzt** ▶ SCHWER 2D; ∼**wiegend** Adj. serious; momentous ⟨decision⟩

**Schwester** die; ∼, ∼n **(a)** sister

**(b)** (Krankenschwester) nurse

**schwesterlich** ⓵ *Adj.* sisterly
⓶ *adv.* ~ handeln act in a sisterly way

**schwieg** *1. u. 3. Pers. Prät. v.* SCHWEIGEN

**Schwieger-:** ~**eltern** *Pl.* parents-in-law;
~**mutter** *die; Pl.* ~**mütter** mother-in-law;
~**sohn** *der* son-in-law; ~**tochter** *die*
daughter-in-law; ~**vater** *der* father-in-law

**Schwiele** *die;* ~, ~n callus; ~n an den
Händen horny hands

**schwielig** *Adj.* callused; ~e Hände horny
hands

**schwierig** *Adj.* difficult

**Schwierigkeit** *die;* ~, ~en difficulty

**Schwierigkeits·grad** *der* degree of
difficulty; (von Lehrmaterial usw.) level of
difficulty

**Schwimm-:** ~**bad** *das* swimming baths
*pl.* (Brit.); swimming pool; ~**becken** *das*
swimming pool

**schwimmen** ⓵ *unr. itr. V.* **(a)** *meist mit
sein* swim
**(b)** *meist mit sein* (treiben, nicht untergehen)
float
**(c)** (ugs.: unsicher sein) be all at sea; **ins
Schwimmen geraten** start to flounder
⓶ *unr. tr. V.; auch mit sein* swim

**Schwimmen** *das;* ~s: swimming *no art.*

**Schwimmer** *der;* ~s, ~ **(a)** swimmer
**(b)** (Technik) float

**Schwimmerin** *die;* ~, ~nen swimmer

**Schwimm-:** ~**flosse** *die* flipper;
~**lehrer** *der,* ~**lehrerin** *die* swimming
instructor; ~**weste** *die* life jacket

**Schwindel** *der;* ~s **(a)** dizziness;
giddiness
**(b)** (Betrug) swindle; (Lüge) lie

**schwindel·frei** *Adj.* ~ sein have a head
for heights

**schwindelig** ▶ SCHWINDLIG

**schwindeln** *itr. V.* **(a)** (unpers.) mich od.
mir schwindelt I feel dizzy *or* giddy
**(b)** (lügen) tell fibs

**schwinden** *unr. itr. V.; mit sein* fade;
⟨supplies, money⟩ run out; ⟨effect⟩ wear off;
⟨fear, mistrust⟩ lessen; ⟨powers, influence⟩
wane

**Schwindler** *der;* ~s, ~, **Schwindlerin**
*die;* ~, ~nen (Lügner[in]) liar; (Betrüger[in])
swindler; (Hochstapler[in]) confidence trickster

**schwindlig** *Adj.* dizzy; giddy; **jmdm. wird
es** ~: sb. gets dizzy *or* giddy

**schwingen** ⓵ *unr. itr. V.* **(a)** *mit sein*
swing
**(b)** (vibrieren) vibrate
⓶ *unr. tr. V.* swing; wave ⟨flag, wand⟩;
brandish ⟨sword, axe, etc.⟩
⓷ *unr. refl. V.* sich aufs Pferd/Fahrrad ~:
leap on to one's horse/bicycle

**Schwingung** *die;* ~, ~en **(a)** swinging;
(Vibration) vibration
**(b)** (Physik) oscillation

**Schwips** *der;* ~es, ~e (ugs.) einen ~
haben be tipsy

**schwirren** *itr. V. mit sein* ⟨arrow, bullet,
etc.⟩ whiz; ⟨bird⟩ whirr; ⟨insect⟩ buzz

**schwitzen** *itr. V.* (auch fig.) sweat

**schwor** *1. u. 3. Pers. Sg. Prät. v.* SCHWÖREN

**schwören** ⓵ *unr. tr., itr. V.* swear
⟨fidelity, friendship⟩; swear, take ⟨oath⟩
⓶ *unr. itr. V.* swear an/the oath

**Schwuchtel** *die;* ~, ~n (salopp) queen (sl.)

**schwul** *Adj.* (ugs.) gay (coll.)

**schwül** *Adj.* sultry; close

**Schwule** *der; adj. Dekl.* (ugs.) gay (coll.);
(abwertend) queer (sl.)

**Schwüle** *die;* ~: sultriness

**schwülstig** ⓵ *Adj.* bombastic; pompous;
over-ornate ⟨art, architecture⟩
⓶ *adv.* bombastically; pompously

**Schwund** *der;* ~[e]s decrease, drop (Gen.
in); (an Interesse) waning; falling off

**Schwung** *der;* ~[e]s, Schwünge **(a)**
(Bewegung) swing
**(b)** (Linie) sweep
**(c)** (Geschwindigkeit) momentum; ~ holen
build *or* get up momentum
**(d)** (Antrieb) drive; energy
**(e)** (mitreißende Wirkung) sparkle

**schwung·haft** *Adj.* thriving; brisk,
flourishing ⟨trade, business⟩

**schwung·voll** ⓵ *Adj.* **(a)** lively
**(b)** (kraftvoll) vigorous; sweeping ⟨movement,
gesture⟩; bold ⟨handwriting, line, stroke⟩
⓶ *adv.* spiritedly; (kraftvoll) with great vigour

**Schwur** *der;* ~[e]s, Schwüre **(a)** (Gelöbnis)
vow
**(b)** (Eid) oath

**Schwur·gericht** *das:* court with a jury

**sechs** *Kardinalz.* six

**Sechs** *die;* ~, ~en six

**sechs-, Sechs-:** ~**eck** *das* hexagon;
~**eckig** *Adj.* hexagonal; ~**fach**
*Vervielfältigungsz.* sixfold; ~**hundert**
*Kardinalz.* six hundred; ~**mal** *Adv.* six
times

**sechst...** *Ordinalz.* sixth

**sechs·tausend** *Kardinalz.* six thousand

**sechstel** *Bruchz.* sixth

**Sechstel** *das,* (schweiz. meist *der*); ~s, ~:
sixth

**sechstens** *Adv.* sixthly

**sechzehn** *Kardinalz.* sixteen

**sechzig** *Kardinalz.* sixty

**sechzigst...** *Ordinalz.* sixtieth

**SED** *Abk.* (DDR) = **Sozialistische
Einheitspartei Deutschlands**
Socialist Unity Party of Germany (state
party of the former DDR)

**See**[1] *der;* ~s, ~n lake

**See**[2] *die;* ~: die ~: the sea; **an die ~ fahren**
go to the seaside; **auf hoher ~:** on the high
seas

**see-, See-:** ~**bad** *das* seaside health   ···⟩

**S**

resort; ∼**fahrt** *die* seafaring *no art.;* sea travel *no art.;* ∼**gang** *der* leichter/starker *od.* hoher *od.* schwerer ∼**gang** light/heavy *or* rough sea; ∼**hund** *der* [common] seal; (Pelz)seal[skin]; ∼**igel** *der* sea urchin; ∼**krank** *Adj.* seasick; ∼**krankheit** *die* seasickness; ∼**lachs** *der* pollack

**Seele** *die;* ∼, ∼n soul; (Psyche) mind

**Seelen·leben** *das* (geh.) inner life

**seelen·ruhig** ① *Adj.* calm; unruffled ② *adv.* calmly

**seelisch** ① *Adj.* psychological ⟨cause, damage, tension⟩; mental ⟨equilibrium, breakdown, illness, health⟩
② *adv.* ∼ bedingt sein have psychological causes; ∼ krank mentally ill

**Seel·sorge** *die* pastoral care

**Seelsorger** *der;* ∼s, ∼, **Seelsorgerin** *die;* ∼, ∼nen pastoral worker; (Geistliche[r]) pastor

**see-, See-:** ∼**macht** *die* sea power; ∼**mann** *der; Pl.* ∼leute seaman; sailor; ∼**meile** *die* nautical mile; ∼**not** *die* distress [at sea]; **in** ∼**not geraten** get into difficulties *pl.;* ∼**pferd[chen]** *das* sea horse; ∼**räuber** *der,* ∼**räuberin** *die* pirate; ∼**reise** *die* voyage; (Kreuzfahrt) cruise; ∼**rose** *die* waterlily; ∼**stern** *der* starfish; ∼**tüchtig** *Adj.* seaworthy; ∼**zunge** *die* sole

**Segel** *das;* ∼s, ∼: sail

**Segel-:** ∼**boot** *das* sailing boat; ∼**flieger** *der,* ∼**fliegerin** *die* glider pilot; ∼**flugzeug** *das* glider

**segeln** *itr. V.; mit sein* sail

**Segel-:** ∼**schiff** *das* sailing ship; ∼**tuch** *das; Pl.* ∼e sailcloth

**Segen** *der;* ∼s, ∼: blessing; (Gebet in der Messe) benediction

**Segler** *der;* ∼s, ∼: yachtsman

**Seglerin** *die;* ∼, ∼nen yachtswoman

**segnen** *tr. V.* bless

**seh·behindert** *Adj.* partially sighted; visually handicapped

**sehen** ① *unr. itr. V.* (a) see; schlecht/gut ∼: have bad/good eyesight; mal ∼, wir wollen *od.* werden ∼ (ugs.) we'll see; siehste! (ugs.) there, you see!
(b) (hinsehen) look (auf + *Akk.* at); sieh mal *od.* doch! look!; siehe da! lo and behold!
② *unr. tr. V.* (a) (auch fig.) see; jmdn./etw. [nicht] zu ∼ bekommen [not] get to see sb./sth.; ich habe ihn kommen [ge]∼: I saw him coming
(b) (ansehen) watch ⟨television programme⟩

**sehens·wert** *Adj.* worth seeing *postpos.*

**Sehens·würdigkeit** *die;* ∼, ∼en sight

**Seher** *der;* ∼s, ∼, **Seherin** *die;* ∼, ∼nen seer; prophet/prophetess

**Seh-:** ∼**fehler** *der* sight defect; defect of vision; ∼**kraft** *die* sight

**Sehne** *die;* ∼, ∼n (a) tendon
(b) (Bogen∼) string

**sehnen** *refl. V.* sich nach jmdm./etw. ∼: long *or* yearn for sb./sth.

**sehnig** *Adj.* (a) stringy ⟨meat⟩
(b) (kräftig) sinewy ⟨figure, legs, etc.⟩

**sehnlichst** ① *Adj.* das ist mein ∼es Verlangen/mein ∼er Wunsch that's what I long for most/that's my dearest wish
② *adv.* etw. ∼ herbeiwünschen look forward longingly to sth.

**Sehn·sucht** *die* longing; ∼ nach jmdm. haben long to see sb.

**sehn·süchtig** *Adj.* longing *attrib.,* yearning *attrib.* ⟨desire, look, gaze, etc.⟩

**sehr** *Adv.* (a) *mit Adj. u. Adv.* very; ∼ viel a great deal; jmdn. ∼ gern haben like sb. a lot (coll.) *or* a great deal
(b) *mit Verben* very much; greatly; danke ∼! thank you *or* thanks [very much]; bitte ∼, Ihr Steak! here's your steak, sir/madam

**Seh-:** ∼**schärfe** *die* visual acuity; ∼**test** *der* eye test; ∼**vermögen** *das* sight

**sei** *1. u. 3. Pers. Sg. Präsens Konjunktiv u. Imperativ Sg. v.* SEIN

**seicht** ① *Adj.* (auch fig.) shallow
② *adv.* (fig.) shallowly

**Seichtheit** *die;* ∼ (auch fig.) shallowness

**seid** *2. Pers. Pl. Präsens u. Imperativ Pl. v.* SEIN

**Seide** *die;* ∼, ∼n silk

**Seidel** *das;* ∼s, ∼: beer mug

**seiden** *Adj.* silk

**Seiden·papier** *das* tissue paper

**seidig** ① *Adj.* silky
② *adv.* silkily

**Seife** *die;* ∼, ∼n soap

**Seifen-:** ∼**blase** *die* soap bubble; ∼**oper** *die* (ugs.) soap opera; ∼**schale** *die* soap dish; ∼**schaum** *der* lather

**Seil** *das;* ∼s, ∼e rope; (Drahtseil) cable

**Seil·bahn** *die* cableway

**seil|hüpfen** *itr. V.; nur im Inf. u. 2. Part.; mit sein* ▶ SEILSPRINGEN

**Seilschaft** *die;* ∼, ∼en (Bergsteigen) rope; (fig.) followers *pl.*

**seil-, Seil-:** ∼|**springen** *unr. itr. V.; nur im Inf. u. 2. Part.; mit sein* skip; ∼**tänzer** *der,* ∼**tänzerin** *die* tightrope walker; ∼**winde** *die* cable winch

**sein¹** ① *unr. itr. V.* be; (existieren) be; exist; (sich ereignen) be; happen; **wie dem auch sei** be that as it may; **er ist Schwede/Lehrer** he is Swedish *or* a Swede/a teacher; **bist du es?** is that you?; **mir ist kalt/besser** I am *or* feel cold/better; **mir ist schlecht** I feel sick; **drei und vier ist** *od.* (ugs.) **sind sieben** three and four is *or* makes seven; **es ist drei Uhr/Mai/Winter** it is three o'clock/May/winter; **er ist aus Berlin** he is *or* comes from Berlin; **was darf es** ∼? (im Geschäft) what can I get you?; **es war einmal ein Prinz** once upon a time there was a prince

---
*old spelling - see note on page xiv

**2** *mod. V.* (in der Funktion von können/müssen + *Passiv*) **es ist niemand zu sehen** there's no one to be seen; **das war zu erwarten** that was to be expected; **die Schmerzen sind kaum zu ertragen** the pain is hardly bearable; **die Richtlinien sind strengstens zu beachten** the guidelines are to be strictly followed
**3** *Hilfsverb* **(a)** (zur Perfektumschreibung) have; **er ist gestorben** he has died
**(b)** (zur Bildung des Zustandspassivs) be; **wir sind gerettet worden/wir waren gerettet** we were saved

**sein²** *Possessivpron.* (einer männlichen Person) his; (einer weiblichen Person) her; (einer Sache, eines Tiers) its; (nach man) one's; his (Amer.)

**Sein** *das;* ~s (Philos.) being; (Dasein) existence; ~ **und Schein** appearance and reality

**seiner** (geh.) *Gen. von* ER: **sich** ~ **erbarmen** have pity on him; ~ **gedenken** remember him

**seiner-:** ~**seits** *Adv.* for his part; (von ihm) on his part; ~**zeit** *Adv.* at that time

**seines·gleichen** *indekl. Pron.* his own kind

**seinet·wegen** *Adv.* ▶ MEINETWEGEN: because of him; for his sake; about him; as far as he is concerned

**seismo-, Seismo-:** ~**graph** *der;* ~~ en, ~~en seismograph; ~**loge** *der;* ~~n, ~~n seismologist; ~**logie** *die;* ~~: seismology *no art.;* ~**login** *die;* ~~, ~~nen seismologist; ~**logisch** **1** *Adj.* seismological; **2** *adv.* seismologically

**seit** **1** *Präp. mit Dat.* (Zeitpunkt) since; (Zeitspanne) for; **ich bin** ~ **zwei Wochen hier** I've been here [for] two weeks
**2** *Konj.* since; ~ **du hier wohnst** since you have been living here

**seit·dem** **1** *Adv.* since then
**2** *Konj.* ▶ SEIT 2

**Seite** *die;* ~, ~n **(a)** side; **zur od. auf die** ~ **gehen** move aside *or* to one side; ~ **an** ~: side by side; **jmdm. zur** ~ **stehen** stand by sb.; **von allen** ~n (auch fig.) from all sides; **nach allen** ~n in all directions; (fig.) on all sides
**(b)** (Buch-, Zeitungsseite) page

**Seiten-:** ~**ansicht** *die* side view; ~**aufprall·schutz** *der* side impact protection; ~**hieb** *der* (fig.) sideswipe (**auf** + *Akk.* at); ~**ruder** *das* (Flugw.) rudder

**seitens** *Präp. mit Gen.* (Papierdt.) on the part of

**Seiten-:** ~**sprung** *der* infidelity; ~**straße** *die* side street; ~**wind** *der* side wind; crosswind; ~**zahl** *die* **(a)** page number; **(b)** (Anzahl der Seiten) number of pages

**seit·her** *Adv.* since then

**seitlich** **1** *Adj.* at the side (postpos.)
**2** *adv.* (an der Seite) at the side; (von der Seite) from the side; (nach der Seite) to the side

**seit·wärts** *Adv.* sideways

**Sekretär** *der;* ~s, ~e **(a)** secretary **(b)** (Schreibschrank) bureau (Brit.)

**Sekretariat** *das;* ~[e]s, ~e [secretary's/ secretaries'] office

**Sekretärin** *die;* ~, ~nen secretary

**Sekt** *der;* ~[e]s, ~e high-quality sparkling wine; ≈ champagne

**Sekte** *die;* ~, ~n sect

**Sektor** *der;* ~s, ~en **(a)** (Fachgebiet) field; sphere; **industrieller/wirtschaftlicher** ~: industrial/economic sector
**(b)** (Geom.; Besatzungszone) sector

**sekundär** **1** *Adj.* secondary
**2** *adv.* secondarily

**Sekundar-:** ~**schule** *die* (schweiz.) secondary school; ~**stufe** *die* secondary stage (*of education*)

**Sekunde** *die;* ~, ~n **(a)** (auch Math., Musik) second
**(b)** (ugs.: Augenblick) second; moment

**Sekunden·zeiger** *der* second hand

**selb...** *Demonstrativpron.* same;

**selber** *indekl. Demonstrativpron.* ▶ SELBST 1

**selbst** **1** *indekl. Demonstrativpron.* myself/ yourself/himself/herself/itself/ourselves/ yourselves/themselves; **von** ~: automatically; ~ **gemacht** home-made
**2** *Adv.* even

**Selbst·achtung** *die* self-respect; self-esteem

**selb·ständig** **1** *Adj.* independent; self-employed ⟨*business man, tradesman, etc.*⟩; **sich** ~ **machen** set up on one's own
**2** *adv.* independently; ~ **denken** think for oneself

**Selbständigkeit** *die;* ~: independence

**selbst-, Selbst-:** ~**auslöser** *der* (Fot.) delayed-action shutter release;
~**bedienung** *die* self-service *no art.;*
~**befriedigung** *die* masturbation *no art.;*
~**beherrschung** *die* self-control *no art.;*
~**bestätigung** *die* (Psych.) self-affirmation *no art.;* ~**bewusst,**
*\**~**bewußt** **1** *Adj.* self-confident; **2** *adv.* self-confidently; ~**bewusstsein,**
*\**~**bewußtsein** *das* self-confidence *no art.;* ~**erkenntnis** *die* self-knowledge *no art.;* ~**gefällig** **1** *Adj.* self-satisfied; smug; **2** *adv.* smugly; ~**gefälligkeit** *die* self-satisfaction; smugness; *\**~**gemacht** ▶ SELBST 1; ~**gespräch** *das* conversation with oneself; ~**hilfe** *die* self-help *no art.;* **Hilfe zur** ~**hilfe leisten** help people to help themselves; ~**hilfe·gruppe** *die* self-help group; ~**los** **1** *Adj.* selfless; **2** *adv.* selflessly; unselfishly; ~**mord** *der* suicide *no art.;* ~**mörder** *der,* ~**mörderin** *die* suicide; ~**sicher** **1** *Adj.* self-confident; **2** *adv.* in a self-confident manner;
~**ständig** *usw.;* ▶ SELBSTÄNDIG *usw.;*
~**süchtig** **1** *Adj.* selfish; **2** *adv.* selfishly; ~**tätig** **1** *Adj.* automatic;                ⸱⸱⸱⸳

2 *adv.* automatically; ~**verständlich**
1 *Adj.* natural; **etw. für** ~**verständlich halten** regard sth. as a matter of course; (für gegeben hinnehmen) take sth. for granted; 2 *adv.* naturally; of course; ~**verständlichkeit** *die* matter of course; **etw. mit der größten** ~**verständlichkeit tun** do sth. as if it were the most natural thing in the world; ~**vertrauen** *das* self-confidence; ~**verwaltung** *die* self-government *no art.*; ~**zweck** *der* end in itself

**selektieren** *tr. V.* select; pick out

**Selektion** *die;* ~, ~**en** selection

**selektiv** 1 *Adj.* selective
2 *adv.* selectively

**selig** 1 *Adj.* (a) (Rel.) blessed
(b) (tot) late [lamented]
(c) (glücklich) blissful ⟨*idleness, slumber, etc.*⟩; blissfully happy ⟨*person*⟩
2 *adv.* blissfully

**Seligkeit** *die;* ~, ~**en** bliss *no pl.;* [blissful] happiness *no pl.*

**Sellerie** *der;* ~s, ~[s] *od.* die; ~, ~: celeriac; (Stangen~) celery

**selten** 1 *Adj.* rare; infrequent ⟨*visit, visitor*⟩
2 *adv.* (a) rarely
(b) (sehr) exceptionally; uncommonly

**Seltenheit** *die;* ~, ~**en** rarity

**Seltenheits·wert** *der;* ~[es] rarity value

**Selters·wasser** *das* seltzer [water]

**seltsam** 1 *Adj.* strange; odd
2 *adv.* strangely

**Semester** *das;* ~s, ~: semester

**Semester·ferien** *Pl.* [university] vacation *sing.*

**Semi·finale** *das* (Sport) semi-final

**Semi·kolon** *das;* ~s, ~s semicolon

**Seminar** *das;* ~s, ~e (a) seminar (über + *Akk.* on)
(b) (Institut) department

**Semit** *der;* ~**en**, ~**en**, **Semitin** *die;* ~, ~**nen** Semite

**semitisch** *Adj.* Semitic

**Semmel** *die;* ~, ~**n** (bes. österr., bayr., ostmd.) [bread] roll

**Semmel·knödel** *der* (bayr., österr.) bread dumpling

**Senat** *der;* ~[e]s, ~e senate

**Senator** *der;* ~s, ~**en**, **Senatorin** *die;* ~, ~**nen** senator

**senden**[1] *unr.* (auch regelm.) *tr. V.* (geh.) send

**senden**[2] *regelm.* (schweiz. unr.) *tr., itr. V.* broadcast ⟨*programme, play, etc.*⟩; transmit ⟨*signals, Morse, etc.*⟩

**Sender** *der;* ~s, ~: [broadcasting] station; (Anlage) transmitter

**Sende·reihe** *die* series [of programmes]

**Sender·such·lauf** *der* (Rundf., Ferns.) [automatic] station search

**Sende·schluss, \*Sende·schluß** *der* close down

**Sende·zeit** *die* (Rundf., Ferns.) broadcasting time; **die** ~ **um zehn Minuten überschreiten** overrun by ten minutes

**Sendung** *die;* ~, ~**en** (a) consignment
(b) (Rundf., Ferns.) programme

**Senf** *der;* ~[e]s, ~e mustard

**senil** 1 *Adj.* (Med., auch abwertend) senile
2 *adv.* in a senile manner

**senior** *nach Personennamen* senior

**Senior** *der;* ~s, ~**en** (a) (Kaufmannsspr.) senior partner
(b) (Sport) senior [player]
(c) (Rentner) senior citizen

**Senioren·heim** *das* home for the elderly

**Seniorin** *die;* ~, ~**nen** ▶ SENIOR

**Senke** *die;* ~, ~**n** hollow

**senken** 1 *tr. V.* lower
2 *refl. V.* ⟨*curtain, barrier, etc.*⟩ fall, come down; ⟨*ground, building, road*⟩ subside, sink; ⟨*water level*⟩ fall, sink

**senk-, Senk-:** ~**fuß** *der* flat foot;
~**recht** 1 *Adj.* vertical; ~**recht zu etw.** perpendicular to sth.; 2 *adv.* vertically;
~**rechte** *die;* ~~, ~~**n**; *auch adj. Dekl.* vertical; (Geom.: Gerade) perpendicular

**Sensation** *die;* ~, ~**en** sensation

**sensationell** 1 *Adj.* sensational
2 *adv.* sensationally

**Sense** *die;* ~, ~**n** scythe

**sensibel** 1 *Adj.* sensitive
2 *adv.* sensitively

**sensibilisieren** *tr. V.* (geh.) make ⟨*person*⟩ more sensitive (**für** to)

**Sensibilität** *die;* ~: sensitivity

**sentimental** 1 *Adj.* sentimental
2 *adv.* sentimentally

**Sentimentalität** *die;* ~, ~**en** sentimentality

**separat** 1 *Adj.* separate; self-contained ⟨*flat etc.*⟩
2 *adv.* separately

**September** *der;* ~[s], ~: September

**Serbe** *der;* ~**n**, ~**n** Serb; Serbian

**Serbien** (*das*); ~s Serbia

**Serbin** *die;* ~, ~**nen** ▶ SERBE

**serbisch** *Adj.* Serbian

**Serenade** *die;* ~, ~**n** serenade

**Serie** /ˈzeːri̯ə/ *die;* ~, ~**n** series

**serien·mäßig** 1 *Adj.* standard ⟨*product, model, etc.*⟩
2 *adv.* (a) ~ **gefertigt** *od.* **gebaut** produced in series
(b) (nicht als Sonderausstattung) ⟨*fitted, supplied, etc.*⟩ as standard

**seriös** *Adj.* respectable ⟨*person, hotel, etc.*⟩; trustworthy ⟨*firm, partner, etc.*⟩; serious ⟨*offer, applicant, artist, etc.*⟩

**Seriosität** *die;* ~ (geh.) **(a)** (Solidität) respectability; (Vertrauenswürdigkeit) trustworthiness
**(b)** (Ernsthaftigkeit) seriousness

**Serpentine** *die;* ~, ~n hairpin bend

**Serum** *das;* ~s, Seren serum

**Service¹** /zɛr'viːs/ *das;* ~, ~: [dinner *etc.*] service

**Service²** /'zøːɐ̯vɪs/ *der;* ~, ~s /'zøːɐ̯vɪsɪs/ (Bedienung, Kundendienst) service

**servieren** *tr. V.* serve

**Serviererin** *die;* ~, ~nen waitress

**Serviette** /zɛr'vjɛtə/ *die;* ~, ~n napkin; serviette (Brit.)

**Servo-:** ~**bremse** *die* servo[-assisted] brake; ~**lenkung** *die* power[-assisted] steering *no indef. art.*

**Servus** /'zɛrvʊs/ *Interj.* (bes. südd., österr.) (beim Abschied) goodbye; so long (coll.); (zur Begrüßung) hello

**Sesam** *der;* ~s sesame seeds *pl.*

**Sessel** *der;* ~s, ~ **(a)** armchair
**(b)** (österr.: Stuhl) chair

**Sessel·lift** *der* chairlift

**sesshaft, \*seßhaft** *Adj.* settled; ~ werden settle down

**Sesshaftigkeit, \*Seßhaftigkeit** *die;* ~: settled way of life

**Set** *das od. der;* ~[s], ~s **(a)** set, combination (aus of)
**(b)** (Deckchen) table- *or* place mat

**setzen** [1] *refl. V.* **(a)** sit [down]; **setzen Sie sich** sit down; take a seat; **sich aufs Sofa** *usw.* ~: sit on the sofa *etc.;*
**(b)** ⟨*coffee, froth, etc.*⟩ settle; ⟨*sediment*⟩ sink to the bottom
[2] *tr. V.* **(a)** put
**(b)** (einpflanzen) plant ⟨*tomatoes, potatoes, etc.*⟩
**(c)** (aufziehen) hoist ⟨*flag etc.*⟩; set ⟨*sails, navigation lights*⟩
**(d)** (Druckw.) set ⟨*manuscript etc.*⟩
[3] *itr. V.* **(a)** *meist mit sein* (springen) leap; jump
**(b) über einen Fluss** ~ (mit einer Fähre o. Ä.) cross a river
**(c)** (beim Wetten) bet; **auf ein Pferd/auf Rot** ~: back a horse/put one's money on red

**Setzer** *der;* ~s, ~, **Setzerin** *die;* ~, ~nen (Druckw.) [type]setter

**Setzling** *der;* ~s, ~e seedling

**Seuche** *die;* ~, ~n epidemic

**Seuchen·gefahr** *die* danger of an epidemic

**seufzen** *itr., tr. V.* sigh

**Seufzer** *der;* ~s, ~: sigh

**Sex** *der;* ~[es] sex *no art.*

**Sexismus** *der;* ~: sexism *no art.*

**sexistisch** [1] *Adj.* sexist
[2] *adv.* ⟨*behave, think, etc.*⟩ in a sexist manner

**Sexualität** *die;* ~: sexuality *no art.*

**Sexual-:** ~**kunde** *die* (Schulw.) sex education *no art.;* ~**leben** *das* sex life; ~**partner** *der,* ~**partnerin** *die* sexual partner; ~**trieb** *der* sex[ual] drive *or* urge; ~**verbrechen** *das* sex crime; ~**verbrecher** *der* sex offender

**sexuell** [1] *Adj.* sexual
[2] *adv.* sexually

**sezieren** *tr. V.* dissect ⟨*corpse*⟩

**sfr., sFr.** *Abk.* **Schweizer Franken**

**Shampoo** /ʃam'puː/, **Shampoon** /ʃam'poːn/ *das;* ~s, ~s shampoo

**Shareholdervalue** /'ʃeəhoʊldəvælju:/ *der;* ~s, ~s shareholder value

**Sherry** /'ʃɛrɪ/ *der;* ~s, ~s sherry

**Show** /ʃoʊ/ *die;* ~, ~s show

**siamesisch** *Adj.* Siamese

**Siam·katze** *die* Siamese cat

**Sibirien** (*das*); ~s Siberia

**sich** *Reflexivpron. der 3. Pers. Sg. und Pl. Akk. und Dat.* **(a)** himself/herself/itself/ themselves; (auf man bezogen) oneself; (auf das Anredepronomen Sie bezogen) yourself/ yourselves; ~ **freuen/wundern/schämen/ täuschen** be pleased/surprised/ashamed/ mistaken; ~ **sorgen** worry
**(b)** (reziprok) one another, each other

**Sichel** *die;* ~, ~n sickle

**sicher** [1] *Adj.* **(a)** safe ⟨*road, procedure, etc.*⟩; secure ⟨*job, investment, etc.*⟩
**(b)** reliable ⟨*evidence, source*⟩; certain ⟨*proof*⟩; reliable, sure ⟨*judgment, taste, etc.*⟩
**(c)** (selbstbewusst) [self-]assured ⟨*person, manner*⟩
**(d)** (gewiss) certain; sure
[2] *adv.* **(a)** safely
**(b)** (zuverlässig) reliably; ~ **[Auto] fahren** be a safe driver
**(c)** (selbstbewusst) [self-]confidently
[3] *Adv.* certainly

**sicher|gehen** *unr. itr. V.; mit sein* play safe

**Sicherheit** *die;* ~, ~en **(a)** safety; (der Öffentlichkeit) security; **jmdn./etw. in** ~ **[vor etw. (***Dat.***)] bringen** save *or* rescue sb./sth. [from sth.]
**(b)** (Gewissheit) certainty
**(c)** (Wirtsch.: Bürgschaft) security

**sicherheits-, Sicherheits-:** ~**abstand** *der* (Verkehrsw.) safe distance between vehicles; ~**gurt** *der* seat belt; ~**halber** *Adv.* to be on the safe side; ~**nadel** *die* safety pin; ~**schloss, \*~schloß** *das* safety lock

**sicherlich** *Adv.* certainly

**sichern** *tr. V.* **(a)** make ⟨*door etc.*⟩ secure; (garantieren) safeguard ⟨*rights, peace*⟩; (schützen) protect ⟨*rights etc.*⟩; **sich (***Dat.***) etw.** ~: secure sth.
**(b)** (DV) back up

**sicher|stellen** *tr. V.* **(a)** impound ⟨*goods, vehicle*⟩
**(b)** guarantee ⟨*supply, freedom, etc.*⟩

**S**

**Sicher·stellung** *die* (a) ▶ SICHERSTELLEN
A: impounding
(b) (Gewährleistung) guarantee

**Sicherung** *die;* ~, ~en (a) safeguarding;
(das Schützen) protection
(b) (Elektrot.) fuse
(c) (techn. Vorrichtung) safety catch

**Sicherungs·kopie** *die* (DV) back-up
[copy]

**Sicht** *die;* ~: view (auf + *Akk.,* in + *Akk.* of);
**gute** *od.* **klare/schlechte** ~: good/poor
visibility; **in** ~ **kommen** come into sight;
**außer** ~ **sein** be out of sight

**sichtbar** [1] *Adj.* visible; (fig.) apparent
⟨*reason*⟩
[2] *adv.* visibly

**sichten** *tr. V.* sight

**sichtlich** [1] *Adj.* obvious; evident
[2] *adv.* obviously; evidently; visibly
⟨*impressed*⟩

**Sichtung** *die;* ~, ~en sighting

**Sicht-:** ~**verhältnisse** *Pl.* visibility
*sing.;* ~**vermerk** *der* visa; ~**weite** *die*
visibility *no art.;* **außer/in** ~**weite sein** be out
of/in sight

**sickern** *itr. V.; mit sein* seep; (spärlich fließen)
trickle

**sie** [1] *Personalpron.;* 3. *Pers. Sg. Nom. Fem.*
she; (betont) her; (bei Dingen, Tieren) it; *s. auch*
IHR[1], IHRER A
[2] *Personalpron.;* 3. *Pers. Pl. Nom.* they;
(betont) them; *s. auch* IHNEN; IHRER B;
[3] *Akk. von* SIE 1: her; (bei Dingen, Tieren) it
[4] *Akk. von* SIE 2A: them

**Sie** *Personalpron.;* 3. *Pers. Pl. Nom. u. Akk;*
*Anrede an eine od. mehrere Personen* you; *s.*
*auch* IHNEN; IHRER

**Sieb** *das;* ~[e]s, ~e sieve; (für Tee) strainer

**sieben**[1] *tr. V.* (a) sieve ⟨*flour etc.*⟩; riddle
⟨*sand, gravel, etc.*⟩
(b) (auswählen) screen ⟨*candidates*⟩

**sieben**[2] *Kardinalz.* seven

**Sieben** *die;* ~, ~en seven

**sieben-, Sieben-:** ~**fach**
*Vervielfältigungsz.* sevenfold; ~**mal** *Adj.*
seven times; ~**sachen** *Pl.* (ugs.) **meine/**
**deine** *usw.* ~**sachen** my/your *etc.* belongings
*or* (coll.) bits and pieces

**siebt...** *Ordinalz.* seventh

**siebtel** *Bruchz.* seventh

**Siebtel** *das,* (schweiz. meist *der*); ~s, ~:
seventh

**siebtens** *Adv.* seventhly

**sieb·zehn** *Kardinalz.* seventeen

**siebzig** *Kardinalz.* seventy

**siebzigst...** *Ordinalz.* seventieth

**siedeln** *itr. V.* settle

**sieden** *unr. od. regelm. itr. V.* boil

**Siede·punkt** *der* (auch fig.) boiling point

**Siedler** *der;* ~s, ~: settler

**Siedlung** *die;* ~, ~en (a) (Wohngebiet)
[housing] estate
(b) (Niederlassung) settlement

**Sieg** *der;* ~[e]s, ~e victory, (bes. Sport) win
(**über** + *Akk.* over)

**Siegel** *das;* ~s, ~: seal; (von Behörden) stamp

**siegen** *itr. V.* win; **über jmdn.** ~: gain *or*
win a victory over sb.; (bes. Sport) win
against sb.; beat sb.

**Sieger** *der;* ~s, ~: winner; (Mannschaft)
winners *pl.;* (einer Schlacht) victor

**Sieger·ehrung** *die* presentation ceremony;
awards ceremony

**Siegerin** *die;* ~, ~nen winner

**sieges·sicher** [1] *Adj.* confident of victory
*pred.;*
[2] *adv.* confident of victory

**sieg·gewohnt** *Adj.* ⟨*army*⟩ accustomed to
victory; ⟨*team*⟩ used to winning

**sieh, siehe** *Imperativ Sg. v.* SEHEN

**siehst** 2. *Pers. Sg. Präsens v.* SEHEN

**sieht** 3. *Pers. Sg. Präsens v.* SEHEN

**siezen** *tr. V.* call ⟨*sb.*⟩ 'Sie' (*the polite form*
*of address*)

**Signal** *das;* ~s, ~e signal

**signalisieren** *tr. V.* indicate ⟨*danger,*
*change, etc.*⟩

**Signatur** *die;* ~, ~en (a) initials *pl.;* (Kürzel)
abbreviated signature; (des Künstlers)
autograph
(b) (Unterschrift) signature
(c) (in einer Bibliothek) shelf mark

**signieren** *tr. V.* sign; autograph ⟨*one's own*
*work*⟩

**Silbe** *die;* ~, ~n syllable

**Silber** *das;* ~s (a) silver
(b) (silbernes Gerät) silver[ware]

**Silber·medaille** *die* silver medal

**silbern** [1] *Adj.* silver; silvery ⟨*moonlight,*
*shade, gleam, etc.*⟩
[2] *adv.* ⟨*shine, shimmer, etc.*⟩ with a silvery
lustre

**Silber·papier** *das* silver paper

**Silhouette** /ziˈlʊɛtə/ *die;* ~, ~n silhouette

**Silicium** *das;* ~s silicon

**Silikon** *das;* ~s, ~e (Chemie) silicone

**Silo** *der od. das;* ~s, ~s silo

**Silvester** *der od. das;* ~s, ~: New Year's
Eve

**Silvester·nacht** *die* night of New Year's
Eve

**Simbabwe** (*das*); ~s Zimbabwe

**simpel** [1] *Adj.* (a) simple ⟨*question, task*⟩
(b) (beschränkt) simple-minded ⟨*person*⟩;
simple ⟨*mind*⟩
[2] *adv.* (a) simply
(b) (beschränkt) in a simple-minded manner

**Simpel** *der;* ~s, ~ (bes. südd. ugs.)
simpleton; fool

**Sims** *der od. das;* ~es, ~e ledge; sill;
(Kamin~) mantelpiece

---

*old spelling - see note on page xiv

**Simulant** *der;* ~en, ~en **Simulantin**
*die;* ~, ~nen malingerer
**Simulation** *die;* ~, ~en simulation
**simulieren** [1] *tr. V.* feign, sham ‹*illness,
emotion, etc.*›; simulate ‹*situation, condition,
etc.*›
[2] *itr. V.* feign illness
**simultan** [1] *Adj.* simultaneous
[2] *adv.* simultaneously
**sind** *1. u. 3. Pers. Pl. Präsens v.* SEIN[1]
**Sinfonie** *die;* ~, ~n symphony
**Sinfonie-orchester** *das* symphony
orchestra
**singen** *unr. tr., itr. V.* sing
**Single**[1] /'zɪŋl/ *die;* ~, ~s (Schallplatte) single
**Single**[2] *der;* ~s, ~s single person; ~s
single people *no art.*
**Single**[3] *das;* ~s, ~s (Badminton, Tennis)
singles *sing. or pl.*
**Singular** *der;* ~s singular
**Sing-vogel** *der* songbird
**sinken** *unr. itr. V.; mit sein* (a) ‹*ship, sun*›
sink, go down; ‹*plane, balloon*› descend, go
down
(b) (niedersinken) fall
(c) (niedriger werden) ‹*temperature, level*› fall,
drop
(d) (an Wert verlieren; nachlassen; abnehmen) fall,
go down
**Sinn** *der;* ~[e]s, ~e (a) sense
(b) *Pl.* (geh.: Bewusstsein) senses; mind *sing.;*
**nicht bei** ~**en sein** be out of one's senses *or*
mind
(c) (Gefühl, Verständnis) feeling
(d) (Bedeutung) meaning
(e) (Ziel u. Zweck) point
**Sinn-bild** *das* symbol
**Sinnes-:** ~**organ** *das* sense organ;
sensory organ; ~**täuschung** *die* trick of
the senses
**sinn-gemäß** [1] *Adj.* eine ~e Übersetzung
a translation which conveys the general
sense
[2] *adv.* etw. ~ übersetzen/wiedergeben
translate the general sense of sth./give the
gist of sth.
**sinnlich** *Adj.* sensory ‹*impression,
perception, stimulus*›; sensual ‹*love, mouth*›;
sensuous ‹*pleasure, passion*›
**Sinnlichkeit** *die;* ~: sensuality
**sinn-los** [1] *Adj.* (a) senseless
(b) (zwecklos) pointless
[2] *adv.* (a) senselessly
(b) (zwecklos) pointlessly
**Sinnlosigkeit** *die;* ~ (a) senselessness
(b) (Zwecklosigkeit) pointlessness
**sinn-voll** [1] *Adj.* (a) (vernünftig) sensible
(b) (einen Sinn ergebend) meaningful
[2] *adv.* (a) (vernünftig) sensibly
(b) (einen Sinn ergebend) meaningfully
**Sint-flut** *die* Flood; Deluge
**sintflut-artig** [1] *Adj.* torrential
[2] *adv.* in torrents

**Sinto** *der;* ~, **Sinti** Sinte
**Sippe** *die;* ~, ~n (a) (Völkerk.) sib
(b) (ugs.: Verwandtschaft) clan
**Sippschaft** *die;* ~, ~en (ugs.) ▶ SIPPE B
**Sirene** *die;* ~, ~n siren
**Sirup** *der;* ~s, ~e syrup
**Sitte** *die;* ~, ~n (a) (Brauch) custom;
tradition
(b) (moralische Norm) common decency
(c) *Pl.* (Benehmen) manners
**sitten-widrig** *Adj.* (a) (Rechtsw.) illegal
‹*methods, advertising, etc.*›
(b) (unmoralisch) immoral ‹*behaviour*›
**sittlich** [1] *Adj.* moral
[2] *adv.* morally
**Sittlichkeit** *die;* ~: morality
**Sittlichkeits-:** ~**verbrechen** *das*
sexual crime; ~**verbrecher** *der,*
~**verbrecherin** *die* sex offender
**Situation** *die;* ~, ~en situation
**situiert** *Adj.* gut/schlechter (usw.) ~ well
off/worse off *etc.*
**Sitz** *der;* ~es, ~e (a) seat
(b) (Verwaltungssitz) headquarters *sing. or pl.;*
(c) (von Kleidungsstücken) fit
**Sitz-bank** *die; Pl.* Sitzbänke bench
**sitzen** *unr. itr. V.; südd., österr., schweiz.
mit sein* (a) sit
(b) (sein) be
(c) ([gut] passen) fit
(d) ~ **bleiben** (nicht versetzt werden) stay down
[a year]; (unverheiratet bleiben) be left on the
shelf; **auf etw.** (*Dat.*) ~ **bleiben** (für etw. keinen
Käufer finden) be left *or* (coll.) stuck with sth.;
**jmdn.** ~ **lassen** (ugs.) (nicht heiraten) jilt sb.; (im
Stich lassen) leave sb. in the lurch; **etw. nicht
auf sich** (*Dat.*) ~**lassen** not take sth.
**sitzen-:** *\**~**|bleiben** ▶ SITZEN D;
*\**~**|lassen** ▶ SITZEN D
**Sitz-platz** *der* seat
**Sitzplatz-stadion** *das* all-seater stadium
**Sitzung** *die;* ~, ~en meeting; (eines
Parlaments) sitting; session
**Sitzungs-saal** *der* conference hall
**Skala** *die;* ~, Skalen scale
**Skalp** *der;* ~s, ~e scalp
**Skalpell** *das;* ~s, ~e scalpel
**skalpieren** *tr. V.* scalp
**Skandal** *der;* ~s, ~e scandal
**skandalös** *Adj.* scandalous
**Skandinavien** (*das*); ~s Scandinavia
**Skandinavier** *der;* ~s, ~: Scandinavian
**skandinavisch** *Adj.* Scandinavian
**Skat** *der;* ~[e]s, ~e *od.* ~s skat
**Skateboard** /'skeɪtbɔːd/ *das;* ~s, ~s
skateboard
**Skateboarder** /'skeɪtbɔːdɐ/ *der;* ~s, ~,
**Skateboarderin** *die;* ~, ~nen
skateboarder
**Skelett** *das;* ~[e]s, ~e skeleton
**Skepsis** *die;* ~: scepticism

**S**

**skeptisch** ☐1 *Adj.* sceptical
☐2 *adv.* sceptically
**Ski** /ʃiː/ *der;* ~s, ~er *od.* ~: ski; ~ **laufen**
*od.* **fahren** ski
**Ski-:** ~**läufer** *der,* ~**läuferin** *die* skier;
~**lehrer** *der,* ~**lehrerin** *die* ski
instructor; ~**lift** *der* ski lift; ~**springen**
*das;* ~~s ski jumping *no art.*
**Skinhead** /'skɪnhɛd/ *der;* ~s, ~s skinhead
**Skizze** *die;* ~, ~n sketch
**Skizzen·block** *der* sketch pad
**skizzieren** *tr. V.* sketch
**Sklave** *der;* ~n, ~n slave
**Sklaven·händler** *der,*
  **Sklaven·händlerin** *die* slave trader
**Sklaverei** *die;* ~: slavery *no art.*
**Sklavin** *die;* ~, ~nen slave
**sklavisch** ☐1 *Adj.* slavish
☐2 *adv.* slavishly
**Skonto** *der od. das;* ~s, ~s (Kaufmannsspr.)
[cash] discount
**Skorbut** *der;* ~[e]s scurvy *no art.*
**Skorpion** *der;* ~s, ~e scorpion; (Astrol.)
Scorpio
**Skrupel** *der;* ~s, ~: scruple
**skrupel·los** ☐1 *Adj.* unscrupulous
☐2 *adv.* unscrupulously
**Skrupellosigkeit** *die;* ~:
unscrupulousness
**Skulptur** *die;* ~, ~en sculpture
**skurril** ☐1 *Adj.* absurd; droll ⟨person⟩
☐2 *adv.* absurdly
**Skurrilität** *die;* ~, ~en absurdity
**Slalom** *der;* ~s, ~s slalom
**Slawe** *der;* ~n, ~n, **Slawin** *die;* ~, ~nen
Slav
**slawisch** *Adj.* Slav[ic]; Slavonic
**Slip** *der;* ~s, ~s briefs *pl.*
**Slogan** /'sloːɡn̩/ *der;* ~s, ~s slogan
**Slowake** *der;* ~n, ~n Slovak
**Slowakei** *die;* ~: Slovakia *no art.*
**Slowakin** *die;* ~, ~nen Slovak
**Slowene** *der;* ~n, ~n Slovene; Slovenian
**Slowenien** /sloˈveːnjən/ *(das);* ~s Slovenia
**Slowenin** *die;* ~, ~nen Slovene; Slovenian
**Slum** /slam/ *der;* ~s, ~s slum
**Smaragd** *der;* ~[e]s, ~e emerald
**Smog** *der;* ~[s], ~s smog
**Smoking** *der;* ~s, ~s dinner jacket *or*
(Amer.) tuxedo and dark trousers
**Snowboard** /'snoʊbɔːd/ *das;* ~s, ~s
snowboard
**Snowboarder** /'snoʊbɔːdɐ/ *der;* ~s, ~,
  **Snowboarderin** *die;* ~, ~nen
snowboarder
**so** ☐1 *Adv.* (a) (auf diese Weise; in, von dieser Art)
like this/that; this/that way; **weiter so!** carry
on in the same way!; **so gennant** so-called
(b) (dermaßen, überaus) so

(c) (genauso) as; **so wenig/viel wie** *od.* **als** as
little/much as; **halb/doppelt so viel** half/
twice as much; **so weit wie möglich** as far as
possible; **so weit** (im großen Ganzen) by and
large; (bis jetzt) up to now; **so weit sein** (ugs.)
be ready; **so gut ich konnte** as best I could
(d) (ugs.: solch) such; **so ein Idiot!** what an
idiot!; **so einer/eine/eins** one like that
(e) *betont* (eine Zäsur ausdrückend) right; OK
(coll.)
(f) (ugs.: schätzungsweise) about
☐2 *Partikel* (a) just; **ach, das hab' ich nur so
gesagt** oh, I didn't mean anything by that
(b) (in Aufforderungssätzen verstärkend) **so komm
doch** come on now
**s. o.** *Abk.* = **siehe oben**
**So.** *Abk.* = **Sonntag** Sun.
**Soap** /soʊp/ *die;* ~, ~s soap [opera]
**sobald** *Konj.* as soon as
**Socke** *die;* ~, ~n sock
**Sockel** *der;* ~s, ~ (a) (einer Säule, Statue)
plinth
(b) (unterer Teil eines Hauses, Schrankes) base
**so·dass**, *****sodaß** *Konj.* (a) (damit) so that
(b) (und deshalb) and so
**Soda·wasser** *das* soda; soda water
**Sod·brennen** *das;* ~s heartburn
**so·eben** *Adv.* just
**Sofa** *das;* ~s, ~s sofa; settee
**so·fern** *Konj.* provided [that]
**soff** *1. u. 3. Pers. Sg. Prät. v.* SAUFEN
**so·fort** *Adv.* immediately; at once
**sofortig** *Adj.* (unmittelbar) immediate
**Sofort·maßnahme** *die* immediate
measure
**Software** /'sɔftvɛːɐ̯/ *die;* ~, ~s (DV)
software
**sog** *1. u. 3. Pers. Sg. Prät. v.* SAUGEN
**Sog** *der;* ~[e]s, ~e suction; (bei Schiffen)
wake; (bei Fahr-, Flugzeugen) slipstream; (von
Wasser, auch fig.) current
**so·gar** *Adv.* even
*****so·genannt** ▶ SO 1A
**so·gleich** *Adv.* immediately; at once
**Sohle** *die;* ~, ~n (a) (Schuh~) sole;
(Einlege~) insole
(b) (Fuß~) sole [of the foot]
**Sohn** *der;* ~es, Söhne son
**Soja-:** ~**bohne** *die* soy[a] bean; ~**soße**
*die* soy[a] sauce
**so·lang[e]** *Konj.* so *or* as long as
**solar** *Adj.* solar
**Solar·energie** *die* (Physik.) solar energy
**Solarium** *das;* ~s, Solarien solarium
**Solar-:** ~**kraftwerk** *das:*
▶ SONNENKRAFTWERK; ~**technik** *die*
(Energietechnik) solar technology *no art.;*
~**zelle** *die* (Physik, Elektrot.) solar cell
**solch** *Demonstrativpron.* (a) *attr.* such; **das
macht** ~**en Spaß!** it's so much fun!
(b) *allein stehend* ~**e wie die** people like that

**Sold** *der;* ~[e]s, ~e [military] pay

**Soldat** *der;* ~en, ~en soldier

**Soldaten-friedhof** *der* military *or* war cemetery

**Soldatin** *die;* ~, ~nen [female *or* woman] soldier

**soldatisch** ① *Adj.* military ⟨*discipline, expression, etc.*⟩; soldierly ⟨*figure, virtue*⟩ ② *adv.* in a military manner

**Söldner** *der;* ~s, ~, **Söldnerin** *die;* ~, ~nen mercenary

**solidarisch** ① *Adj.* ~es Verhalten zeigen show one's solidarity ② *adv.* ~ handeln/sich ~ verhalten act in/ show solidarity

**solidarisieren** *refl. V.* show [one's] solidarity

**Solidarität** *die;* ~: solidarity

**solide** ① *Adj.* (a) solid; sturdy ⟨*shoes, material*⟩; [good-]quality ⟨*goods*⟩ (b) (gut fundiert) sound ⟨*work, education, knowledge*⟩; solid ⟨*firm*⟩ (c) (anständig) respectable ⟨*person, life, profession*⟩ ② *adv.* (a) solidly ⟨*built*⟩; sturdily ⟨*made*⟩ (b) (gut fundiert) soundly ⟨*educated, constructed*⟩ (c) (anständig) ⟨*live*⟩ respectably, steadily

**Solidität** *die;* ~: ▶ SOLIDE 1 A-C: solidness; sturdiness; soundness; respectability

**Solist** *der;* ~en, ~en, **Solistin** *die;* ~, ~nen soloist

**Soll** *das;* ~[s], ~[s] (a) (Bankw.) debit (b) (Arbeits~) quota; sein ~ erfüllen *od.* erreichen achieve one's target

**sollen** ① *unr. Modalverb; 2. Part.* sollen: (a) (bei Aufforderung, Anweisung, Auftrag) **was soll ich als Nächstes tun?** what should I do next?; [sagen Sie ihm,] **er soll hereinkommen** tell him to come in (b) (bei Wunsch, Absicht, Vorhaben) **das sollte ein Witz sein** that was meant to be a joke; **was soll denn das heißen?** what is that supposed to mean? (c) (bei Ratlosigkeit) **was soll ich nur machen?** what am I to do? (d) (Notwendigkeit ausdrückend) **man soll so etwas nicht unterschätzen** it shouldn't be taken so lightly (e) *häufig im Konjunktiv II* (Erwartung, Wünschenswertes ausdrückend) **du solltest dich schämen** you ought to be ashamed of yourself; **das hättest du besser nicht tun** ~: it would have been better if you hadn't done that (f) (jmdm. beschieden sein) **er sollte seine Heimat nicht wieder sehen** he was never to see his homeland again (g) *im Konjunktiv II* (eine Möglichkeit ausdrückend) **wenn du ihn sehen solltest, sage ihm bitte ...:** if you should see him, please tell him ... (h) *im Präsens* (sich für die Wahrheit nicht

verbürgend) **das Restaurant soll sehr teuer sein** the restaurant is supposed *or* said to be very expensive (i) *im Konjunktiv II* (Zweifel ausdrückend) **sollte das sein Ernst sein?** is he really being serious? (j) (können) **mir soll es gleich sein** it's all the same to me ② *tr., itr. V.* **was soll das?** what's the idea?; **was soll ich dort?** what would I do there?

**Solo** *das;* ~s, ~s *od.* **Soli** solo

**so-mit** /*auch:* '--/ *Adv.* consequently; therefore

**Sommer** *der;* ~s, ~: summer

**Sommer-ferien** *Pl.* summer holidays

**sommerlich** ① *Adj.* summer; summery ⟨*warmth, weather*⟩; summer's *attrib.* ⟨*day, evening*⟩ ② *adv.* **es war ~ warm** it was as warm as summer

**sommer-, Sommer-:** ~**reifen** *der* standard tyre; ~**schluss-verkauf,** *\**~**schluß-verkauf** *der* summer sale/ sales; ~**sprosse** *die* freckle; ~**sprossig** *Adj.* freckled; ~**zeit** *die* (Uhrzeit) summer time

**Sonate** *die;* ~, ~n (Musik) sonata

**Sonde** *die;* ~, ~n probe; (zur Ernährung) tube

**Sonder-:** ~**angebot** *das* special offer; ~**ausgabe** *die* (a) special edition; (b) (Steuerw.: private Aufwendungen) tax-deductible expenditure; (c) (Extraausgabe) extra expense

**sonderbar** ① *Adj.* strange; odd ② *adv.* strangely; oddly

**sonderbarer-weise** *Adv.* strangely *or* oddly enough

**Sonder-:** ~**fall** *der* special case; ~**genehmigung** *die* special permit

**sonder-gleichen** *Adv., nachgestellt* **eine Frechheit/Unverschämtheit ~:** the height of cheek/impudence

**sonderlich** *Adv.* particularly

**Sonderling** *der;* ~s, ~e strange *or* odd person

**Sonder-:** ~**marke** *die* special issue [stamp]; ~**müll** *der* hazardous waste

**sondern**[1] *tr. V.* (geh.) separate (von from)

**sondern**[2] *Konj.* but; **nicht nur ..., ~ [auch] ...:** not only ... but also ...

**Sonder-:** ~**nummer** *die* special edition *or* issue; ~**preis** *der* special *or* reduced price; ~**schule** *die* special school; ~**schul-lehrer** *der,* ~**schul-lehrerin** *die* teacher at a special school; ~**wunsch** *der* special request *or* wish; ~**zug** *der* special train

**sondieren** *tr. V.* sound out

**Sonett** *das;* ~[e]s, ~e sonnet

**Sonn-abend** *der* (bes. nordd.) Saturday; *s. auch* DIENSTAG

**sonn-abends** *Adv.* on Saturday[s]

**Sonne** *die;* ~, ~n sun; (Licht der ~) sun[light]

**S**

**sonnen** *refl. V.* sun oneself
**sonnen-, Sonnen-:** ∼**aufgang** *der*
sunrise; ∼**baden** *itr. V.* sunbathe;
∼**blume** *die* sunflower; ∼**brand** *der*
sunburn *no indef. art.;* ∼**brille** *die*
sunglasses *pl.;* ∼**energie** *die* solar energy;
∼**finsternis** *die* solar eclipse; ∼**hut** *der*
sun hat; ∼**kollektor** *der* (Energietechnik)
solar collector; ∼**kraftwerk** *das* solar
power station; ∼**licht** *das* sunlight;
∼**milch** *die* suntan lotion; ∼**öl** *das* sun oil;
∼**schein** *der* sunshine; ∼**schirm** *der*
sunshade; ∼**schutz·creme** *die* suntan
lotion; ∼**stich** *der* sunstroke *no indef. art.;*
∼**strahl** *der* ray of sun[shine]; ∼**uhr** *die*
sundial; ∼**untergang** *der* sunset
**sonnig** *Adj.* sunny
**Sonn·tag** *der* Sunday; *s. auch* DIENSTAG
**sonn·täglich** ① *Adj.* Sunday *attrib.;*
② *adv.* ∼ **gekleidet** dressed in one's Sunday
best
**sonntags** *Adv.* on Sunday[s]
**sonst** *Adv.* (a) **der** ∼ **so freundliche Mann**
...: the man, who is/was usually so friendly,
...; **alles war wie** ∼: everything was [the
same] as usual; ∼ **was** (ugs.) something else;
(fragend, verneint) anything else; ∼ **wer** (ugs.)
somebody else; (fragend, verneint) anybody else;
∼ **wo** (ugs.) somewhere else; (fragend, verneint)
anywhere else; ∼ **noch was?** (ugs., auch iron.)
anything else?; **wer/was/wie/wo [denn]** ∼?
who/what/how/where else?
(b) (andernfalls) otherwise; or
**sonstig...** *Adj.* other; further
*\***sonst·was** *usw.* ▶ SONST A
**so·oft** *Konj.* whenever
**sophistisch** ① *Adj.* sophistic[al]
② *adv.* sophistically
**Sopran** *der;* ∼**s,** ∼**e** (Musik) soprano; (im
Chor) sopranos *pl.*
**Sopranistin** *die;* ∼**,** ∼**nen** soprano
**Sorge** *die;* ∼**,** ∼**n** worry; **keine** ∼**!** don't
[you] worry!
**sorgen** ① *refl. V.* worry (**um** about)
② *itr. V.* **für jmdn./etw.** ∼: take care of sb./
sth.
**sorgen-, Sorgen-:** ∼**frei** ① *Adj.*
carefree; ② *adv.* ∼**frei leben** live in a
carefree manner; ∼**kind** *das* (auch fig.)
problem child; ∼**voll** ① *Adj.* worried;
② *adv.* worriedly
**Sorg·falt** *die;* ∼: care
**sorg·fältig** ① *Adj.* careful
② *adv.* carefully
**sorg·los** ① *Adj.* (a) (ohne Sorgfalt) careless
(b) (unbekümmert) carefree
② *adv.* ∼ **mit etw. umgehen** treat sth.
carelessly
**Sorglosigkeit** *die;* ∼ (a) (Mangel an Sorgfalt)
carelessness
(b) (Unbekümmertheit) carefreeness

**sorgsam** ① *Adj.* careful
② *adv.* carefully
**Sorte** *die;* ∼**,** ∼**n** (a) sort; type; kind
(b) *Pl.* (Devisen) foreign currency *sing.*
**Sorten·kurs** *der* (Bankw.) exchange rate
**sortieren** *tr. V.* sort [out] ⟨pictures, letters,
washing, etc.⟩; grade ⟨goods etc.⟩
**Sortiment** *das;* ∼**[e]s,** ∼**e** range (**an** + *Dat.*
of)
**so·sehr** *Konj.* however much
**Soße** *die;* ∼**,** ∼**n** sauce; (Bratensoße) gravy;
sauce; (Salatsoße) dressing
**sott** *1. u. 3. Pers. Sg. Prät. v.* SIEDEN
**Souffleur** /zu'flø:ɐ̯/ *der;* ∼**s,** ∼**e,**
**Souffleuse** /zu'flø:zə/ *die;* ∼**,** ∼**n**
prompter
**soufflieren** /zu'fli:rən/ *tr. V.* prompt
**Sound-:** ∼**check** /'saʊndʃɛk/ *der;* ∼**s,**
∼∼**s** sound check; ∼**karte** *die* (DV) sound
card
**Souvenir** /suvə'ni:ɐ̯/ *das;* ∼**s,** ∼**s** souvenir
**souverän** /zuvə'rɛːn/ *Adj.* sovereign
**Souveränität** *die;* ∼: sovereignty
**so·viel** *Konj.* as *or* so far as; *s. auch* SO 1B
**so·weit** *Konj.* (a) as *or* so far as; *s. auch*
SO 1B;
(b) (in dem Maße, wie) [in] so far as; *s. auch*
SO 1B
*\***so·wenig** ▶ SO 1B
**so·wie** *Konj.* (a) (und) as well as
(b) (sobald) as soon as
**so·wie·so** *Adv.* anyway
**sowjetisch** *Adj.* Soviet
**Sowjet·union** *die* (1922–1991) Soviet Union
**so·wohl** *Konj.* ∼ ... **als** *od.* **wie [auch]** ...:
both ... and ...; ... as well as ...
**sozial** ① *Adj.* social
② *adv.* socially
**sozial-, Sozial-:** ∼**abgaben** *Pl.* social
welfare contributions; ∼**arbeiter** *der,*
∼**arbeiterin** *die* social worker;
∼**demokrat** *der,* ∼**demokratin** *die*
Social Democrat; ∼**demokratisch** *Adj.*
social democratic; ∼**dienst** *der* community
services department; ∼**hilfe** *die* social
welfare; ∼**hilfe·empfänger** *der,*
∼**hilfe·empfängerin** *die* welfare
recipient
**Sozialismus** *der;* ∼: socialism *no art.;*
**Sozialist** *der;* ∼**en,** ∼**en,** **Sozialistin** *die;*
∼**,** ∼**nen** socialist
**sozialistisch** ① *Adj.* socialist
② ∼ **regierte Länder** countries with socialist
governments
**Sozial-:** ∼**kunde** *die* social studies *sing.,*
*no art.;* ∼**politik** *die* social policy;
∼**produkt** *das* (Wirtsch.) national product;
∼**staat** *der* welfare state
**Soziologe** *der;* ∼**n,** ∼**n** sociologist
**Soziologie** *die;* ∼: sociology
**Soziologin** *die;* ∼**,** ∼**nen** sociologist
**soziologisch** ① *Adj.* sociological

**s**

**2** *adv.* sociologically

**Sozius** *der;* ~, ~se **(a)** *Pl. auch:* **Sozii** (Wirtsch.: Teilhaber) partner
**(b)** (beim Motorrad) pillion

**so·zu·sagen** *Adv.* as it were

**Spachtel** *der;* ~s, ~ *od. die;* ~, ~n putty knife; (zum Malen) palette knife

**Spachtel·masse** *die* filler

**spachteln** *tr. V.* **(a)** stop, fill ⟨*hole, crack, etc.*⟩; smooth over ⟨*wall, panel, surface, etc.*⟩
**(b)** (ugs.: essen) put away (coll.) ⟨*food, meal*⟩

**Spagat** *der od. das;* ~[e]s, ~e splits *pl.;* [einen] ~ **machen** do the splits

**Spaghetti** *Pl.* spaghetti *sing.*

**spähen** *itr. V.* peer; (durch ein Loch, eine Ritze usw.) peep

**Späher** *der;* ~s, ~, **Späherin** *die;* ~, ~nen (Milit.) scout; (Posten) lookout; (Spitzel) informer

**Spalier** *das;* ~s, ~e **(a)** trellis
**(b)** (Ehren~) guard of honour; ~ **stehen** line the route; ⟨*soldiers*⟩ form a guard of honour

**Spalt** *der;* ~[e]s, ~e opening; (im Fels) fissure; crevice; (zwischen Vorhängen) chink; gap; (langer Riss) crack

**Spalte** *die;* ~, ~n **(a)** crack; (Felsspalte) crevice
**(b)** (Druckw.) column

**spalten** *unr. (auch regelm.) tr., refl. V.* split

**Spaltung** *die;* ~, ~en (auch fig.) splitting; (fig.: das Gespaltensein) split

**Span** *der;* ~[e]s, **Späne** (Hobelspan) shaving

**Span·ferkel** *das* suckling pig

**Spange** *die;* ~, ~n clasp; (Haarspange) hairslide (Brit.); barrette (Amer.); (Armspange) bracelet; bangle

**Spaniel** /'ʃpa:niəl/ *der;* ~s, ~s spaniel

**Spanien** /'ʃpa:niən/ *(das);* ~s Spain

**Spanier** /'ʃpa:niɐ/ *der;* ~s, ~, **Spanierin** *die;* ~, ~nen Spaniard

**spanisch** *Adj.* Spanish

**Span·korb** *der* chip basket; chip

**spann** *1. u. 3. P. Sing. Prät. v.* SPINNEN

**spannen** **1** *tr. V.* **(a)** tighten ⟨*violin string, violin bow, etc.*⟩; draw ⟨*bow*⟩; tension ⟨*spring, tennis net, drumhead, saw blade*⟩; stretch ⟨*fabric, shoe, etc.*⟩; draw or pull ⟨*line*⟩ tight or taut; flex ⟨*muscle*⟩; cock ⟨*gun, camera shutter*⟩
**(b)** (befestigen) put up ⟨*washing line*⟩; stretch ⟨*net, wire, tarpaulin, etc.*⟩ (**über** + *Akk.* over)
**(c)** (schirren) harness (**vor, an** + *Akk.* to)
**2** *refl. V.* **(a)** become or go taut; ⟨*muscles*⟩ tense
**(b)** (geh.: sich wölben) **sich über etw.** (*Akk.*) ~: span sth.
**3** *itr. V.* ⟨*clothing*⟩ be [too] tight; ⟨*skin*⟩ be taut

**spannend** **1** *Adj.* exciting; (stärker) thrilling
**2** *adv.* excitingly; (stärker) thrillingly

**Spannung** *die;* ~, ~en **(a)** excitement; (Neugier) suspense
**(b)** (eines Romans, Films usw.) suspense
**(c)** (Zwistigkeit, Nervosität) tension
**(d)** (Elektrot.) voltage

**Spannungs·gebiet** *das* (Politik.) area of tension

**Spann·weite** *die* [wing]span

**Span·platte** *die* chipboard

**Spar-:** ~**buch** *das* savings book; ~**büchse** *die* money box

**sparen** **1** *tr. V.* save
**2** *itr. V.* **(a)** save; **für** *od.* **auf etw.** (*Akk.*) ~: save up for sth.
**(b)** (sparsam wirtschaften) economize (**mit** on); **an etw.** (*Dat.*) ~: be sparing with sth.; (beim Einkauf) economize on sth.

**Sparer** *der;* ~s, ~, **Sparerin** *die;* ~, ~nen saver

**Spargel** *der;* ~s, ~, (schweiz. auch) *die;* ~, ~n asparagus *no pl., no indef. art.*

**Spar-:** ~**groschen** *der* (ugs.) nest egg; savings *pl.;* ~**kasse** *die* savings bank; ~**konto** *das* savings *or* deposit account

**spärlich** **1** *Adj.* sparse ⟨*vegetation, beard, growth*⟩; thin ⟨*hair, applause*⟩; scanty ⟨*leftovers, knowledge, news, evidence, clothing*⟩; poor ⟨*lighting*⟩
**2** *adv.* sparsely, thinly ⟨*populated, covered*⟩; poorly ⟨*lit, attended*⟩; scantily ⟨*dressed*⟩

**sparsam** **1** *Adj.* thrifty ⟨*person*⟩; (wirtschaftlich) economical; **mit etw.** ~ **sein** be economical with sth.
**2** *adv.* ~ **mit der Butter/dem Papier umgehen** use butter/paper sparingly; economize on butter/paper

**Sparsamkeit** *die;* ~: thrift[iness]; (Wirtschaftlichkeit) economicalness

**Sparte** *die;* ~, ~n **(a)** (Teilbereich) area; (eines Geschäfts) line [of business]
**(b)** (Rubrik) section

**Sparten·kanal** *der* special-interest channel

**Spar-:** ~**vertrag** *der* savings agreement; ~**zins** *der; Pl.* ~~**en** interest *no pl.* on a savings account

**Spaß** *der;* ~es, **Späße (a)** (Vergnügen) fun; ~ **an etw.** (*Dat.*) **haben** enjoy sth.; **[jmdm.]** ~ **machen** be fun [for sb.]; **viel** ~! have a good time!
**(b)** (Scherz) joke; (Streich) prank; **er macht nur** ~: he's only joking; ~ **beiseite!** joking aside; ~ **muss sein!** there's no harm in a joke; ~ **verstehen** be able to take a joke; **im** *od.* **zum** *od.* **aus** ~: as a joke; for fun

**spaßen** *itr. V.* **(a)** (Spaß machen) joke
**(b) er lässt nicht mit sich** ~: he won't stand for any nonsense; **mit ihm/damit ist nicht zu** ~: he/it is not to be trifled with

**spaßes·halber** *Adv.* for the fun of it; for fun

**spaßig** *Adj.* funny; comical; amusing

**Spaß·macher** *der,* **Spaß·macherin** *die* joker

**S**

**spät** ⓵ *Adj.* late; **wie ~ ist es?** what time is it?

⓶ *adv.* late; **~ am Abend** late in the evening

**Spaten** *der;* ~s, ~: spade

**später** ⓵ *Adj.* (a) later ⟨*years, generations, etc.*⟩

(b) (zukünftig) future ⟨*owner, wife, etc.*⟩

⓶ *Adv.* later; **bis ~!** see you later!

**spätestens** *Adv.* at the latest

**Spatz** *der;* ~en, ~en (a) sparrow

(b) (fam.: Liebling) pet

**Spätzle** *Pl.* spaetzle; *kind of noodles*

**spazieren** *itr. V.; mit sein* stroll; **~ gehen** go for a walk; **~ fahren** go for a ride; **ein Kind [im Kinderwagen] ~ fahren** take a baby for a walk [in a pram]

**\*spazieren|fahren** *usw.* ▶ SPAZIEREN

**Spazier-:** **~gang** *der* walk; **~gänger** *der;* ~~s, ~~, **~gängerin** *die;* ~~, ~~nen person out for a walk

**SPD** ~ *Abk.* = **Sozialdemokratische Partei Deutschlands** SPD

**Specht** *der;* ~[e]s, ~e woodpecker

**Speck** *der;* ~[e]s, ~e (a) bacon fat; (Schinkenspeck) bacon

(b) (ugs. scherzh.: Fettpolster) fat; flab (coll.)

**speckig** *Adj.* greasy

**Spediteur** /ʃpediˈtøːɐ̯/ *der;* ~s, ~e, **Spediteurin** *die;* ~, ~nen carrier; haulage contractor; (Möbelspediteur) furniture remover

**Spedition** *die;* ~, ~en ▶ SPEDITIONSFIRMA

**Speditions-firma** *die* forwarding agency; ( per Schiff) shipping agency; (Transportunternehmen) haulage firm; firm of hauliers; ( per Schiff) firm of carriers; (Möbelspedition) removal firm

**Speer** *der;* ~[e]s, ~e (a) spear

(b) (Sportgerät) javelin

**Speichel** *der;* ~s saliva

**Speicher** *der;* ~s, ~ (a) storehouse; (Lagerhaus) warehouse

(b) (südd.: Dachboden) loft

(c) (Elektronik) memory

**Speicher-kapazität** *die* storage capacity; (DV) memory *or* storage capacity

**speichern** *tr. V.* store

**speien** (geh.) *unr. tr., itr. V.* spit

**Speise** *die;* ~, ~n (a) (Gericht) dish

(b) (geh.: Nahrung) food

**Speise-:** **~eis** *das* ice cream; **~fisch** *der* food fish; **~gaststätte** *die* restaurant; **~kammer** *die* larder; **~karte** *die* menu; **~lokal** *das* restaurant

**speisen** (geh.) ⓵ *itr. V.* eat; (dinieren) dine

⓶ *tr. V.* eat; (dinieren) dine on

**Speise-:** **~saal** *der* dining hall; (im Hotel, in einer Villa usw.) dining room; **~wagen** *der* restaurant car (Brit.); **~zettel** *der* menu

---

**Spektakel** *der;* ~s, ~ (ugs.) (Lärm) row (coll.); rumpus (coll.)

**spektakulär** ⓵ *Adj.* spectacular

⓶ *adv.* spectacularly

**Spekulation** *die;* ~, ~en speculation

**spekulieren** *itr. V.* (a) (ugs.) **darauf ~, etw. tun zu können** count on being able to do sth.

(b) (Wirtsch.) speculate (**mit** in)

**Spelunke** *die;* ~, ~n (ugs. abwertend) dive (coll.)

**Spelze** *die;* ~, ~n husk

**Spende** *die;* ~, ~n donation; contribution

**spenden** *tr., itr. V.* (a) donate; give

(b) (fig. geh.) give ⟨*light*⟩; afford, give ⟨*shade*⟩; give off ⟨*heat*⟩

**Spenden-aktion** *die* campaign for donations

**Spender** *der;* ~s, ~, **Spenderin** *die;* ~, ~nen donor; donator; (Organspender, Blutspender) donor

**Spender-organ** *das* donar organ

**spendieren** *tr. V.* (ugs.) get, buy ⟨*drink, meal, etc.*⟩; stand ⟨*round*⟩

**Spengler** *der;* ~s, ~, **Spenglerin** *die;* ~, ~nen (südd., österr., schweiz.) ▶ KLEMPNER

**Sperling** *der;* ~s, ~e sparrow

**Sperma** *das;* ~s, Spermen sperm; semen

**Sperma-bank** *die; Pl.* ~en sperm bank

**sperr-, Sperr-:** **~angel-weit** *Adv.* (ugs.) **~angel-weit offen** *od.* **geöffnet** wide open; **~bezirk** *der* (a) restricted *or* prohibited area; (b) (für Prostituierte) *area in which prostitution is prohibited;* (c) (Gesundheitswesen) infected area

**Sperre** *die;* ~, ~n (a) barrier; (Straßensperre) roadblock; (Milit.) obstacle

(b) (fig.) ban; (Handelssperre) embargo; (Import-, Exportsperre) blockade; (Nachrichten~) [news] blackout

**sperren** ⓵ *tr. V.* (a) close; close off ⟨*area*⟩; block ⟨*entrance, access, etc.*⟩; lock ⟨*mechanism etc.*⟩

(b) cut off ⟨*water, gas, electricity, etc.*⟩

(c) (Bankw.) stop ⟨*cheque, overdraft facility*⟩; freeze ⟨*bank account*⟩

(d) (einsperren) **ein Tier/jmdn. in etw.** (*Akk.*) **~:** shut an animal/sb. in sth.

(e) (Sport: von der Teilnahme ausschließen) ban

(f) (Druckw.: spationieren) print ⟨*word, text*⟩ with the letters spaced

⓶ *refl. V.* **sich [gegen etw.] ~:** balk [at sth.]

**Sperr-holz** *das* plywood

**sperrig** *Adj.* unwieldy

**Sperr-:** **~müll** *der* bulky refuse (*for which there is a separate collection service*); **~sitz** *der* (im Kino) seat in the back stalls; (im Zirkus) front seat; (im Theater) seat in the front stalls; **~stunde** *die* closing time

**Sperrung** *die;* ~, ~en ▶ SPERREN A-C, E: closing; closing off; cutting off; stopping; freezing; banning

**Spesen** *Pl.* expenses; **auf ~:** on expenses

**Spezi** *der;* ∼s, ∼[s] (südd., österr., schweiz. ugs.) [bosom] pal (coll.); chum (coll.)

**spezialisieren** *refl. V.* specialize (**auf** + *Akk.* in)

**Spezialist** *der;* ∼en, ∼en, **Spezialistin** *die;* ∼, ∼nen specialist

**Spezialität** *die;* ∼, ∼en speciality

**speziell** ⟦1⟧ *Adj.* special; specific ⟨*question, problem, etc.*⟩
⟦2⟧ *Adv.* especially; (eigens) specially

**spezifisch** ⟦1⟧ *Adj.* specific; characteristic ⟨*smell, style*⟩
⟦2⟧ *adv.* specifically

**Sphäre** *die;* ∼, ∼n (auch fig.) sphere

**spicken** *tr. V.* lard

**spie** *1. u. 3. Pers. Sg. Prät. v.* SPEIEN

**Spiegel** *der;* ∼s, ∼ (a) mirror
(b) (Wasserspiegel, fig.: Konzentration) level

**spiegel-, Spiegel-:** ∼**bild** *das* reflection; ∼**blank** *Adj.* shining; ∼**ei** *das* fried egg; ∼**glatt** *Adj.* like glass *postpos.;* as smooth as glass *postpos.*

**spiegeln** ⟦1⟧ *itr. V.* (a) (glänzen) shine; gleam
(b) (als Spiegel wirken) reflect the light
⟦2⟧ *tr. V.* reflect; mirror
⟦3⟧ *refl. V.* be mirrored *or* reflected

**Spiegel·reflex·kamera** *die* reflex camera

**Spiegelung** *die;* ∼, ∼en (a) (auch fig., Math.) reflection
(b) (Med.) speculum examination

**spiegel·verkehrt** ⟦1⟧ *Adj.* back-to-front ⟨*lettering*⟩; **eine** ∼**e Abbildung** a mirror image
⟦2⟧ *adv.* **etw.** ∼ **abbilden** reproduce sth. as a *or* in mirror image

**Spiel** *das;* ∼[e]s, ∼e (a) play
(b) (Glücks, Gesellschaftsspiel) game; (Wettspiel) game; match; **auf dem** ∼ **stehen** be at stake; **etw. aufs** ∼ **setzen** put sth. at stake; risk sth.

**Spiel·bank** *die; Pl.* ∼en casino

**spielen** ⟦1⟧ *itr. V.* (a) play; **auf der Gitarre** ∼: play the guitar; **um Geld** ∼: play for money
(b) (als Schauspieler) act; perform
(c) **der Roman/Film spielt im 17. Jahrhundert/in Berlin** the novel/film is set in the 17th century/in Berlin
(d) (fig.) **das Blau spielt ins Violette** the blue is tinged with purple
⟦2⟧ *tr. V.* (a) play; **Cowboy** ∼: play at being a cowboy; **Geige** *usw.* ∼: play the violin *etc.;*
(b) (aufführen, vorführen) put on ⟨*play*⟩; show ⟨*film*⟩; perform ⟨*piece of music*⟩; play ⟨*record*⟩; **den Beleidigten/Unschuldigen** ∼ (fig.) act offended/play the innocent

**spielend** *Adv.* easily

**Spieler** *der;* ∼s, ∼: player; (Glücksspieler) gambler

**Spielerei** *die;* ∼, ∼en (a) playing *no art.;* (im Glücksspiel) gambling *no art.;*

(b) **eine** ∼ **mit Worten/Zahlen** playing [around] with words/numbers

**Spiel·ergebnis** *das* match result

**Spielerin** *die;* ∼, ∼nen ▶ SPIELER

**spielerisch** *Adj.* playful

**Spiel-:** ∼**feld** *das* field; pitch (Brit.); (Tennis, Squash, Volleyball usw.) court; ∼**film** *der* feature film; ∼**kamerad** *der* playmate; ∼**karte** *die* playing card; ∼**leitung** *die* (a) (Sport) control of the match; (b) ▶ REGIE; ∼**plan** *der* programme; ∼**platz** *der* playground; ∼**raum** *der* room to move (fig.); scope; latitude; ∼**regel** *die* (auch fig.) rule of the game; **gegen die** ∼**regeln verstoßen** (auch fig.) break the rules; ∼**sachen** *Pl.* toys; ∼**verderber** *der;* ∼∼s, ∼∼, ∼**verderberin** *die;* ∼∼, ∼∼nen spoilsport; ∼**waren** *Pl.* toys; ∼**zeit** *die* (a) (Theater: Saison) season; (b) (Sport) playing time; **die normale** ∼**zeit** normal time; ∼**zeug** *das* (a) toy; (fig.) toy; plaything; (b) (Gesamtheit) toys *pl.*

**Spieß** *der;* ∼es, ∼e (a) (Waffe) spear; **den** ∼ **umdrehen** *od.* **umkehren** (ugs.) turn the tables
(b) (Bratspieß) spit
(c) (Fleischspieß) kebab
(d) (Soldatenspr.) [company] sergeant major

**Spieß·bürger** *der,* **Spießbürgerin** *die* (abwertend) [petit] bourgeois

**Spießer** *der;* ∼s, ∼, **Spießerin** *die;* ∼, ∼nen (abwertend) [petit] bourgeois

**spießig** (abwertend) ⟦1⟧ *Adj.* [petit] bourgeois
⟦2⟧ *adv.* ⟨*think, behave, etc.*⟩ in a [petit] bourgeois way

**Spinat** *der;* ∼[e]s, ∼e spinach

**Spind** *der od. das;* ∼[e]s, ∼e locker

**Spindel** *die;* ∼, ∼n spindle

**Spinne** *die;* ∼, ∼n spider

**spinnen** ⟦1⟧ *unr. tr. V.* spin (fig.); plot ⟨*intrigue*⟩; think up ⟨*idea*⟩; hatch ⟨*plot*⟩
⟦2⟧ *unr. itr. V.* (a) spin
(b) (ugs.: verrückt sein) be crazy *or* (coll.) nuts

**Spinnen·netz** *das* spider's web

**Spinner** *der;* ∼s, ∼ (a) (Beruf) spinner
(b) (ugs. abwertend) nutcase (coll.); idiot

**Spinnerei** *die;* ∼, ∼en spinning mill

**Spinnerin** *die;* ∼, ∼nen ▶ SPINNER

**Spinn-:** ∼**rad** *das* spinning wheel; ∼**webe** *die;* ∼∼, ∼∼n cobweb

**Spion** *der;* ∼s, ∼e (a) spy
(b) (Guckloch) spyhole

**Spionage** /ʃpio'na:ʒə/ *die;* ∼: spying; espionage

**spionieren** *itr. V.* spy

**Spionin** *die;* ∼, ∼nen spy

**Spirale** *die;* ∼, ∼n spiral

**Spiral·feder** *die* coil spring

**Spirituose** *die;* ∼, ∼n spirit *usu. in pl.*

**Spiritus** *der;* ∼, ∼se spirit; ethyl alcohol

**Spiritus·kocher** *der* spirit stove

**S**

**Spital** *das;* ∿s, **Spitäler** (bes. österr., schweiz.) hospital

**spitz** [1] *Adj.* (a) pointed; sharp ⟨*pencil, needle, stone, etc.*⟩; fine ⟨*pen nib*⟩; (Geom.) acute ⟨*angle*⟩
(b) (schrill) shrill ⟨*cry etc.*⟩
(c) (boshaft) cutting ⟨*remark etc.*⟩
[2] *adv.* (a) ∿ **zulaufen** taper to a point; ∿ **zulaufend** pointed
(b) (boshaft) cuttingly

**Spitz** *der;* ∿es, ∿e spitz

**spitz-, Spitz-:** ∿**bart** *der* goatee; ∿**bube** *der* (scherzh.: Schlingel) rascal; ∿**bübisch** [1] *Adj.* mischievous; [2] *adv.* mischievously

**spitze** *indekl. Adj.* (ugs.) ▶ KLASSE

**Spitze** *die;* ∿, ∿n (a) point; (Pfeil∿, Horn∿ usw.) tip
(b) (oberes Ende) top; (eines Berges) summit
(c) (Zigarren-, Haar-, Zweigspitze) end; (Schuhspitze) toe; (Finger-, Nasenspitze) tip
(d) (vorderes Ende) front; **an der** ∿ **liegen** (Sport) be in the lead *or* in front
(e) (führende Position) top
(f) (einer Firma, Organisation usw.) head; (einer Hierarchie) top; (leitende Gruppe) management
(g) (Höchstwert) maximum; peak
(h) [absolute/einsame] ∿ **sein** (ugs.) be [absolutely] great (coll.)
(i) (fig.: Angriff) dig (**gegen** at)
(j) (Textilwesen) lace

**Spitzel** *der;* ∿s, ∿: informer

**spitzen** *tr. V.* sharpen ⟨*pencil*⟩; purse ⟨*lips, mouth*⟩; prick up ⟨*ears*⟩

**Spitzen-:** ∿**erzeugnis** *das* top-quality product; ∿**kandidat** *der,* ∿**kandidatin** *die* leading *or* top candidate; ∿**klasse** *die* top class; ∿**qualität** *die* top quality; ∿**reiter** *der* (a) top rider; (fig.) leader; (b) (Mannschaft) top team; (c) (Ware) top *or* best seller; ∿**reiterin** *die:* ▶ ∿REITER A; ∿**sportler** *der* top sportsman; ∿**sportlerin** *die* top sportswoman

**Spitzer** *der;* ∿s, ∿: [pencil] sharpener

**spitz-, Spitz-:** ∿**findig** *Adj.* hairsplitting; ∿**findigkeit** *die;* ∿, ∿∿en (a) hair-splitting; (b) (etwas Spitzfindiges) nicety; ∿**hacke** *die* pick; ∿|**kriegen** *tr. V.* (ugs.) tumble to (coll.); ∿**maus** *die* shrew; ∿**name** *der* nickname

**Spleen** /ʃpliːn/ *der;* ∿s, ∿e *od.* ∿s strange habit; eccentricity

**Splitt** *der;* ∿[e]s, ∿e (stone) chippings *pl.;* (zum Streuen) grit

**Splitter** *der;* ∿s, ∿: splinter; (Granat-, Bombensplitter) splinter

**splitter·faser·nackt** *Adj.* (ugs.) absolutely stark naked; completely **starkers** *pred.* (Brit. coll.)

**splittern** *itr. V.* (a) (Splitter bilden) splinter
(b) *mit sein* (in Splitter zerbrechen) ⟨*glass, windscreen, etc.*⟩ shatter

---

*old spelling - see note on page xiv

**splitter·nackt** *Adj.* (ugs.) stark naked; **starkers** *pred.* (Brit. coll.)

**Splitter·partei** *die* splinter party

**SPÖ** *Abk.* = **Sozialistische Partei Österreichs** Austrian Socialist Party

**sponsern** *tr. V.* sponsor

**Sponsor** *der;* ∿s, ∿en sponsor

**spontan** [1] *Adj.* spontaneous
[2] *adv.* spontaneously

**Spontaneität** /ʃpɔntaneiˈtɛːt/ *die;* ∿: spontaneity

**sporadisch** [1] *Adj.* sporadic
[2] *adv.* sporadically

**Spore** *die;* ∿, ∿n spore

**Sporn** *der;* ∿[e]s, **Sporen** (des Reiters) spur; **einem Pferd die Sporen geben** spur a horse

**Sport** *der;* ∿[e]s (a) sport; (als Unterrichtsfach) sport; PE; ∿ **treiben** do sport
(b) (Hobby, Zeitvertreib) hobby; pastime

**Sport-:** ∿**art** *die* [form of] sport; ∿**fest** *das* sports festival; (einer Schule) sports day; ∿**flugzeug** *das* sports plane; ∿**geist** *der* sportsmanship; ∿**halle** *die* sports hall; ∿**journalist** *der,* ∿**journalistin** *die* sports journalist; ∿**kleidung** *die* sportswear

**Sportler** *der;* ∿s, ∿: sportsman

**Sportlerin** *die;* ∿, ∿nen sportswoman

**sportlich** [1] *Adj.* (a) sporting *attrib.;*
(b) (fair) sportsmanlike; sporting
(c) (fig.: flott, rasant) sporty ⟨*car, driving, etc.*⟩
(d) (zu sportlicher Leistung fähig) sporty, athletic ⟨*person*⟩
(e) (jugendlich wirkend) sporty, smart but casual ⟨*clothes*⟩; smart but practical ⟨*hairstyle*⟩
[2] *adv.* (a) as far as sport is concerned
(b) (fair) sportingly
(c) (fig.: flott, rasant) in a sporty manner

**Sport-:** ∿**platz** *der* sports field; (einer Schule) playing field/fields *pl.;* ∿**schuh** *der* sports shoe; ∿**stadion** *das* [sports] stadium; ∿**teil** *der* sport[s] section; ∿**verein** *der* sports club; ∿**wagen** *der* (a) (Auto) sports car; (b) (Kinderwagen) pushchair (Brit.); stroller (Amer.); ∿**zentrum** *das* sports centre

**Spot** /spɔt/ *der;* ∿s, ∿s (a) (Werbespot) commercial; advertisement; ad (coll.)
(b) (Leuchte) spotlight; spotlamp

**Spott** *der;* ∿[e]s mockery; (höhnischer) ridicule; derision

**spott·billig** *Adj., adv.* (ugs.) dirt cheap

**spötteln** *itr. V.* mock [gently]; poke *or* make [gentle] fun

**spotten** *itr. V.* (a) mock; poke *or* make fun; (höhnischer) ridicule; be derisive
(b) *einer Sache* (Gen.) ∿: be contemptuous of *or* scorn sth.

**Spötter** *der;* ∿s, ∿, **Spötterin** *die;* ∿, ∿nen mocker

**spöttisch** [1] *Adj.* mocking; (höhnischer) derisive
[2] *adv.* mockingly

**Spott·preis** *der* (ugs.) ridiculously low price

**sprach** *1. u. 3. Pers. Sg. Prät. v.* SPRECHEN

**Sprache** *die;* ~, ~n **(a)** language; **in englischer** ~: in English **(b)** (Sprechweise) way of speaking; speech; (Stil) style **(c)** etw. zur ~ **bringen** bring sth. up; raise sth.; **heraus mit der** ~! come on, out with it!

**Sprachen·schule** *die* language school

**Sprach-:** ~**fehler** *der* speech impediment *or* defect; ~**führer** *der* phrase book; ~**grenze** *die* language boundary; ~**kenntnisse** *Pl.* knowledge *sing.* of a language/languages; ~**kurs** *der* language course; ~**labor** *das* language laboratory *or* (coll.) lab

**sprachlich** [1] *Adj.* linguistic [2] *adv.* linguistically

**sprach-, Sprach-:** ~**los** *Adj.* (überrascht) speechless; ~**problem** *das* language problem; ~**rohr** *das* (Repräsentant) spokesman; (Propagandist) mouthpiece; ~**schule** *die* language school; ~**unterricht** *der* language teaching

**sprang** *1. u. 3. Pers. Sg. Prät. v.* SPRINGEN

**Spray** /ʃpreː/ *das od. der;* ~s, ~s spray

**Spray·dose** *die* aerosol [can]

**sprayen** *tr., itr. V.* spray

**Sprech-:** ~**anlage** *die* intercom (coll.); ~**chor** *der* chorus

**sprechen** [1] *unr. itr. V.* speak (**über** + *Akk.* about; **von** about, of); (sich besprechen, sich besprechen) talk (**über** + *Akk.*, **von** about); ⟨parrot etc.⟩ talk; **deutsch/flüsternd** ~: speak German/in a whisper; **für/gegen** etw. ~: speak in favour of/against sth.; **mit** jmdm. ~: speak *or* talk with *or* to sb.; **mit wem spreche ich?** who is speaking please? [2] *unr. tr. V.* **(a)** speak ⟨language, dialect⟩; say ⟨word, sentence⟩; „**Hier spricht man Deutsch**" 'German spoken' **(b)** (rezitieren) say, recite ⟨poem, text⟩; say ⟨prayer⟩ **(c)** jmdn. ~: speak to sb. **(d)** (aussprechen) pronounce ⟨name, word, etc.⟩

**Sprecher** *der;* ~s, ~, **Sprecherin** *die;* ~, ~**nen (a)** spokesman/spokeswoman **(b)** (Ansager[in]) announcer; (Nachrichtensprecher[in]) newscaster; newsreader **(c)** (Kommentator[in], Erzähler[in]) narrator

**Sprech-:** ~**funk·gerät** *das* radio-telephone; (Walkie-talkie) walkie-talkie; ~**stunde** *die* consultation hours *pl.;* (eines Arztes) surgery; ~**stunden·hilfe** *die* (eines Arztes) receptionist; (eines Zahnarztes) assistant; ~**zimmer** *das* consulting room

**spreizen** *tr. V.* spread ⟨fingers, toes, etc.⟩; **die Beine** ~: spread one's legs apart; open one's legs

**Spreiz·fuß** *der* (Med.) spread foot

**sprengen** *tr. V.* **(a)** blow up; blast ⟨rock⟩; **etw. in die Luft** ~: blow sth. up **(b)** (gewaltsam öffnen, aufbrechen) force [open] ⟨door⟩; force ⟨lock⟩; burst, break ⟨bonds, chains⟩; (fig.) break up ⟨meeting, demonstration⟩ **(c)** (besprengen) water ⟨flower bed, lawn⟩; sprinkle ⟨street, washing⟩ with water; (verspritzen) sprinkle; (mit dem Schlauch) spray

**Spreng-:** ~**stoff** *der* explosive; ~**stoff·anschlag** *der* bomb attack

**Sprenkel** *der;* ~s, ~: spot; dot; speckle

**sprenkeln** *tr. V.* sprinkle spots of ⟨colour⟩; sprinkle ⟨water⟩

**Spreu** *die;* ~: chaff

**sprich** *Imperativ Sg. v.* SPRECHEN

**sprichst** *2. Pers. Sg. Präsens v.* SPRECHEN

**spricht** *3. Pers. Sg. Präsens v.* SPRECHEN

**Sprich·wort** *das; Pl.* Sprichwörter proverb

**sprießen** *unr. itr. V.; mit sein* ⟨leaf, bud⟩ shoot, sprout; ⟨seedlings⟩ come *or* spring up; ⟨beard⟩ sprout

**Spring·brunnen** *der* fountain

**springen** [1] *unr. itr. V.* **(a)** *mit sein* (auch Sport) jump; (mit Schwung) leap; spring; jump; ⟨frog, flea⟩ hop, jump; (sich in Sprüngen fortbewegen) bound **(b)** *mit sein* (fig.) ⟨pointer, milometer, etc.⟩ jump (**auf** + *Akk.* to); ⟨traffic lights⟩ change (**auf** + *Akk.* to); ⟨spark⟩ leap; ⟨ball⟩ bounce **(c)** *mit sein* ⟨string, glass, porcelain, etc.⟩ break; (Risse, Sprünge bekommen) crack [2] *unr. tr. V.; auch mit sein* (Sport) perform ⟨somersault, twist dive, etc.⟩

**Springer** *der;* ~s, ~ **(a)** (Sport) jumper **(b)** (Schachfigur) knight

**Springerin** *die;* ~, ~nen (Sport) jumper

**spring·lebendig** *Adj.* extremely lively; full of beans *pred.* (coll.)

**Spring·reiten** *das* showjumping *no art.*

**Sprinkler** *der;* ~s, ~: sprinkler

**sprinten** *itr. V.* (auch tr.) *V.; mit sein* sprint

**Sprinter** *der;* ~s, ~, **Sprinterin** *die;* ~, ~nen (Sport) sprinter

**Sprit** *der;* ~[e]s, ~e **(a)** (ugs.: Treibstoff) gas (Amer. coll.); juice (sl.); petrol (Brit.) **(b)** (ugs.: Schnaps) shorts *pl.*

**Spritze** *die;* ~, ~n **(a)** syringe **(b)** (Injektion) injection **(c)** (der Feuerwehr) hose; (Löschfahrzeug) fire engine

**spritzen** [1] *tr. V.* **(a)** (versprühen) spray; (verspritzen) splash; (in Form eines Strahls) spray, squirt ⟨water, foam, etc.⟩; pipe ⟨cream etc.⟩ **(b)** (bespritzen, besprühen) water ⟨lawn, tennis court⟩; water, spray ⟨street, yard⟩; spray ⟨plants, crops, etc.⟩; (mit Lack) spray ⟨car etc.⟩; **jmdn. nass** ~: splash sb.; (mit Wasserpistole, Schlauch) spray sb. **(c)** (injizieren) inject ⟨drug etc.⟩; (ugs.: einer Injektion unterziehen) **jmdn./sich** ~: give sb. an injection/inject oneself   ⋯⟩

2 *itr. V.; mit Richtungsangabe mit sein* ⟨*hot fat*⟩ spit; ⟨*mud etc.*⟩ spatter, splash; ⟨*blood, water*⟩ spurt

**Spritzer** *der;* ~s, ~ (kleiner Tropfen) splash; (von Farbe) splash; spot

**spritzig** 1 *Adj.* (a) sparkling ⟨*wine*⟩; tangy ⟨*fragrance, perfume*⟩
(b) lively ⟨*show, music, article*⟩; sparkling ⟨*performance*⟩; racy ⟨*style*⟩; nippy (coll.); zippy ⟨*car, engine*⟩; agile ⟨*person*⟩
2 *adv.* sparklingly ⟨*produced, performed, etc.*⟩; racily ⟨*written*⟩

**Spritz·tour** *die* (ugs.) spin

**spröd, spröde** *Adj.* (a) brittle ⟨*glass, plastic, etc.*⟩; dry ⟨*hair, lips, etc.*⟩; (rissig) chapped ⟨*lips, skin*⟩; (rauh) rough ⟨*skin*⟩
(b) (fig.: abweisend) aloof ⟨*person, manner, nature*⟩

**Sprödheit, Sprödigkeit** *die;* ~ (a)
▶ SPRÖDE A: brittleness; dryness; roughness
(b) (fig.: abweisendes Wesen) aloofness

**spross, *sproß** *1. u. 3. Pers. Sg. Prät. v.*
SPRIESSEN

**Spross, *Sproß** *der;* Sprosses, Sprosse (Bot.) shoot

**Sprosse** *die;* ~, ~n (a) (auch fig.) rung
(b) (eines Fensters) glazing bar

**Sprössling, *SpRößling** *der;* ~s, ~e (ugs. scherzh.) offspring; **seine** ~e his offspring *pl.*

**Sprotte** *die;* ~, ~n sprat

**Spruch** *der;* ~[e]s, Sprüche (Wahlspruch) motto; (Sinnspruch) maxim; (Ausspruch) saying; aphorism; (Zitat) quotation

**spruch·reif** *Adj.* **das ist noch nicht** ~: that's not definite, so people mustn't start talking about it yet

**Sprudel** *der;* ~s, ~ (a) sparkling mineral water
(b) (österr.) fizzy drink

**sprudeln** *itr. V.; mit sein* bubble; ⟨*lemonade, champagne, etc.*⟩ fizz, effervesce

**Sprudel·wasser** *das* sparkling mineral water

**Sprüh·dose** *die* aerosol [can]

**sprühen** 1 *tr. V.* spray
2 *itr. V.; mit Richtungsangabe mit sein* ⟨*sparks, spray*⟩ fly; (fig.) ⟨*eyes*⟩ sparkle (**vor** + *Dat.* with); ⟨*intellect, wit*⟩ sparkle

**Sprüh·regen** *der* drizzle; fine rain

**Sprung** *der;* ~[e]s, Sprünge (a) (auch Sport) jump; (schwungvoll) leap; (Satz) bound; (fig.) leap; **keine großen Sprünge machen können** (fig. ugs.) not be able to afford many luxuries; **auf dem** ~[e] **sein** (fig. ugs.) be in a rush
(b) (ugs.: kurze Entfernung) stone's throw
(c) (Riss) crack

**Sprung·brett** *das* (auch fig.) springboard

**sprunghaft** 1 *Adj.* (a) erratic ⟨*person, character, manner*⟩; disjointed ⟨*conversation, thoughts*⟩

(b) (unvermittelt) sudden
(c) (ruckartig) rapid ⟨*change*⟩; sharp ⟨*increase*⟩
2 *adv.* ▶ 1B–c: disjointedly; suddenly; rapidly; sharply

**Sprunghaftigkeit** *die;* ~: ▶ SPRUNGHAFT 1A: erraticness; disjointedness

**Sprung·tuch** *das; Pl.* **Sprungtücher** safety blanket

**Spucke** *die;* ~: spit

**spucken** 1 *itr. V.* spit; **in die Hände** ~ (fig.: an die Arbeit gehen) go to work with a will
2 *tr. V.* spit; cough up ⟨*blood, phlegm*⟩

**Spuk** *der;* ~[e]s, ~e [ghostly *or* supernatural] manifestation

**spuken** *itr. V.; unpers.* **hier/in dem Haus spukt es** this place/the house is haunted

**Spül·bürste** *die* washing-up brush

**Spule** *die;* ~, ~n spool; (für Tonband, Film) spool; reel

**Spüle** *die;* ~, ~n sink unit; (Becken) sink

**spulen** *tr., itr. V.* spool; (am Tonbandgerät) wind

**spülen** 1 *tr. V.* (a) rinse; bathe ⟨*wound*⟩
(b) (landsch.: abwaschen) wash up ⟨*dishes, glasses, etc.*⟩; **Geschirr** ~: wash up
2 *itr. V.* (a) (beim WC) flush [the toilet]
(b) (den Mund ausspülen) rinse out [one's mouth]
(c) (landsch.) ▶ ABWASCHEN 2

**Spül-:** ~**maschine** *die* dishwasher; ~**mittel** *das* washing-up liquid; ~**tuch** *das; Pl.* ~**tücher** dish cloth; ~**wasser** *das* (a) rinse water; (b) (Abwaschwasser) dishwater

**Spund** *der;* ~[e]s, ~e/Spünde (a) *Pl.* Spünde (Zapfen) bung
(b) *Pl.* ~e (ugs.) [**junger** *od.* **grüner**] ~ young greenhorn *or* tiro

**Spur** *die;* ~, ~en (a) (Abdruck im Boden) track; (Folge von Abdrücken) tracks *pl.;* **eine heiße** ~ (fig.) a hot trail; **jmdm./einer Sache auf der** ~ **sein** be on to the track *or* trail of sb./sth.
(b) (Anzeichen) trace; (eines Verbrechens) clue (*Gen.* to)
(c) (sehr kleine Menge; auch fig.) trace
(d) (Verkehrsw.: Fahrspur) lane; **die** ~ **wechseln** change lanes

**spürbar** 1 *Adj.* noticeable; distinct, perceptible ⟨*improvement*⟩; evident ⟨*relief, embarrassment*⟩
2 *adv.* noticeably; perceptibly; (sichtlich) clearly ⟨*relieved, on edge*⟩

**spüren** *tr. V.* feel; (instinktiv) sense

**spur·los** 1 *Adj.* total, complete ⟨*disappearance*⟩
2 *adv.* ⟨*disappear*⟩ completely *or* without trace

**Spür·sinn** *der* (feiner Instinkt) intuition

**Spurt** *der;* ~[e]s, ~s *od.* ~e spurt

**spurten** *itr. V.* (a) mit Richtungsangabe mit sein spurt
(b) mit sein (ugs.: schnell laufen) sprint

**sputen** *refl. V.* (veralt.) make haste

**St.** *Abk.* **(a)** = **Sankt** St.
**(b)** = **Stück**

**Staat** *der;* ~[e]s, ~en state

**staatlich** ① *Adj.* state *attrib.; ⟨power, unity, etc.⟩* of the state; state-owned *⟨factory etc.⟩*
② *adv.* by the state; ~ **anerkannt/geprüft** state-approved/-certified

**staats-, Staats-:** ~**angehörige** *der/ die* national; ~**angehörigkeit** *die* nationality; ~**anwalt** *der,* ~**anwältin** *die* public prosecutor; ~**bürger** *der,* ~**bürgerin** *die* citizen; **er ist deutscher** ~**bürger** he is a German citizen *or* national; ~**bürgerlich** *Adj.* civil *⟨rights⟩;* civic *⟨duties, loyalty⟩; ⟨education, attitude⟩* as a citizen; ~**bürgerschaft** *die*
▶ ~ANGEHÖRIGKEIT; ~**gewalt** *die* authority of the state; (Exekutive) executive power; ~**grenze** *die* state frontier *or* border; ~**mann** *der; Pl.* -**männer** statesman; ~**oberhaupt** *das* head of state; ~**präsident** *der,* ~**präsidentin** *die* [state] president; ~**sicherheit** *die* **(a)** state security; **(b)** (DDR ugs.)
▶ ~SICHERHEITSDIENST;
~**sicherheits-dienst** *der* (DDR) State Security Service

**Stab** *der;* ~[e]s, Stäbe **(a)** rod; (länger) pole; (eines Käfigs, Gitters, Geländers) bar
**(b)** (Milit.) staff
**(c)** (Team) team

**Stäbchen** *das;* ~s, ~ **(a)** (kleiner Stab) little rod; [small] stick
**(b)** (Essstäbchen) chopstick

**stabil** ① *Adj.* sturdy *⟨chair, cupboard⟩;* robust, sound *⟨health⟩;* stable *⟨prices, government, economy, etc.⟩*
② *adv.* ~ **gebaut** solidly built

**stabilisieren** ① *tr. V.* stabilize
② *refl. V.* **(a)** stabilize
**(b)** *⟨health, circulation, etc.⟩* become stronger

**Stabilität** *die;* ~ **(a)** (einer Konstruktion) sturdiness; (von Gesundheit, Konstitution usw.) robustness; soundness
**(b)** (das Beständigsein) stability

**Stab-lampe** *die* torch (Brit.); flashlight (Amer.)

**Stabs-arzt** *der,* **Stabs-ärztin** *die* (Milit.) medical officer, MO *(with the rank of captain)*

**stach** *1. u. 3. Pers. Sg. Prät. v.* STECHEN

**Stachel** *der;* ~s, ~n **(a)** spine; (Dorn) thorn
**(b)** (Giftstachel) sting
**(c)** (Spitze) spike; (an Stacheldraht) barb

**Stachel-:** ~**beere** *die* gooseberry;
~**draht** *der* barbed wire

**stachelig** *Adj.* prickly

**Stadion** *das;* ~s, Stadien stadium

**Stadium** *das;* ~s, Stadien stage

**Stadt** *die;* ~, Städte **(a)** town; (Großstadt) city; **die** ~ **Basel** the city of Basel; **in die** ~ **gehen** go into town; go downtown (Amer.)
**(b)** (Verwaltung) town council; (in der Großstadt) city council; city hall *no art.* (Amer.)

**Stadt-:** ~**bahn** *die* urban railway;
~**bummel** *der* (ugs.) **einen** ~**bummel machen** take a stroll through the town/city centre

**Städter** *der;* ~s, ~, **Städterin** *die;* ~, ~nen **(a)** town-dweller; (Großstädter, -städterin) city-dweller
**(b)** (Stadtmensch) townie (coll.)

**Städte-tour** *die* city tour

**Stadt-:** ~**führer** *der* town/city guidebook;
~**führung** *die* guided tour of the town/ city; ~**gespräch** *das;* ~**gespräch sein** be the talk of the town

**städtisch** ① *Adj.* **(a)** (kommunal) municipal
**(b)** (urban) urban *⟨life, way of life, etc.⟩*
② *adv.* (kommunal) municipally

**Stadt-:** ~**mauer** *die* town/city wall;
~**mitte** *die* town centre; (einer Großstadt) city centre; downtown area (Amer.); ~**park** *der* municipal park; ~**plan** *der* [town/city] street plan *or* map; ~**rand** *der* outskirts *pl.* of the town/city; **am** ~**rand** on the outskirts of the town/city; ~**rundfahrt** *die* sightseeing tour round a/the town/city;
~**teil** *der* district; part [of a/the town];
~**tor** *das* town/city gate; ~**viertel** *das* district

**Staffel** *die;* ~, ~n **(a)** (Sport: Mannschaft) relay team
**(b)** (Sport: Staffellauf) relay race
**(c)** (Luftwaffe: Einheit) flight
**(d)** (Eskorte) escort formation

**Staffelei** *die;* ~, ~en easel

**staffeln** *tr. V.* **(a)** (aufstellen, formieren) arrange in a stagger *or* in an echelon
**(b)** (einteilen, abstufen) grade *⟨salaries, fees, prices⟩;* stagger *⟨times, arrivals, starting places⟩*

**stahl** *1. u. 3. Pers. Sg. Prät. v.* STEHLEN

**Stahl** *der;* ~[e]s, Stähle *od.* ~e steel

**Stahl-:** ~**beton** *der* reinforced concrete;
~**blech** *das* sheet steel

**stählern** *Adj.* steel

**stak** *1. u. 3. Pers. Sg. Prät. v.* STECKEN

**Stall** *der;* ~[e]s, Ställe (Pferde-, Rennstall) stable; (Kuhstall) cowshed; (Hühnerstall) [chicken] coop; (Schweinestall) [pig]sty; (für Kaninchen, Kleintiere) hutch; (für Schafe) pen

**Stallung** *die;* ~, ~en (Pferdestall) stable; (Kuhstall) cowshed; (Schweinestall) [pig]sty

**Stamm** *der;* ~[e]s, Stämme **(a)** (Baumstamm) trunk
**(b)** (Volksstamm) tribe

**Stamm-:** ~**aktie** *die* (Wirtsch.) ordinary share; ~**baum** *der* family tree; (eines Tieres) pedigree

**stammeln** *tr., itr. V.* stammer

**S**

**stạmmen** *itr. V.* come (**aus, von** from);
(datieren) date (**aus, von** from)

**Stạmm-:** ~**gast** *der* (im Lokal/Hotel) regular
customer/visitor; regular (coll.); ~**tisch** *der*
(a) (Tisch) regulars' table (coll.); (b) (Runde)
group of regulars (coll.); (c) (Treffen) get-
together with the regulars (coll.)

**stạmpfen** [1] *itr. V.* (a) (laut auftreten) stamp
(b) *mit sein* (sich fortbewegen) tramp; (mit
schweren Schritten) trudge
[2] *tr. V.* (a) mit den Füßen den Rhythmus ~:
tap the rhythm with one's feet
(b) (feststampfen) compress
(c) (zerkleinern) mash ⟨*potatoes*⟩

**stạnd** *1. u. 3. Pers. Sg. Prät. v.* STEHEN

**Stạnd** *der;* ~[e]s, Stände (a) (das Stehen)
standing position; [bei jmdm. od. gegen
jmdn.] einen schweren ~ haben (fig.) have a
tough time [of it] [with sb.]
(b) (Standort) position
(c) (Verkaufsstand; Box für ein Pferd) stall;
(Messestand, Informationsstand) stand;
(Zeitungsstand) [newspaper] kiosk
(d) (erreichte Stufe; Zustand) state; **etw. auf den
neu[e]sten ~ bringen** bring sth. up to date;
**außer** ~[e] ▶ AUSSERSTANDE; **im** ~[e]
▶ IMSTANDE;
(e) (des Wassers, Flusses) level; (des
Thermometers, Zählers, Barometers) reading; (der
Kasse, Finanzen) state; (eines Himmelskörpers)
position
(f) (Familienstand) status
(g) (Gesellschaftsschicht) class; (Berufsstand)
trade; (Ärzte, Rechtsanwälte) [professional]
group

**Stạndard** *der;* ~s, ~s standard

**standardisieren** *tr. V.* standardize

**Standardisierung** *die;* ~, ~en
standardization

**Ständchen** *das;* ~s, ~: serenade; **jmdm.
ein ~ bringen** serenade sb.

**Ständer** *der;* ~s, ~: stand; (Kleider~) coat
stand; (Wäsche~) clothes horse

**stạndes-, Stạndes-:** ~**amt** *das* registry
office; ~**amtlich** [1] *Adj.* registry office
⟨*wedding, document*⟩; [2] *adv.* ~**amtlich
heiraten** get married in a registry office;
~**beamte** *der*, ~**beamtin** *die* registrar

**stạnd-, Stạnd-:** ~**fest** *Adj.* steady;
stable; strong ⟨*stalk, stem*⟩; ~**haft** [1] *Adj.*
steadfast; [2] *adv.* steadfastly; ~**haftigkeit**
*die;* ~~: steadfastness; ~|**halten** *unr. itr.
V.* stand firm; **einer Sache** (*Dat.*) ~**halten**
withstand sth.

**stạndig** [1] *Adj.* constant ⟨*noise, worry,
pressure, etc.*⟩; permanent ⟨*residence,
correspondent, staff, member, etc.*⟩; standing
⟨*committee*⟩; regular ⟨*income*⟩
[2] *adv.* constantly

**Stạnd-:** ~**licht** *das* (Kfz-W.) sidelights *pl.;*
~**ort** *der* (a) position; (eines Betriebes usw.)
location; site; (b) (Milit.: Garnison) garrison;

base; ~**punkt** *der* (fig.) point of view;
viewpoint; **auf dem** ~**punkt stehen, dass ...:**
take the view that ...; ~**spur** *die* (Verkehrsw.)
hard shoulder; ~**uhr** *die* grandfather clock

**Stạnge** *die;* ~, ~**n** pole; (aus Metall) bar;
(dünner) rod; (Kleiderstange) rail; (Vogelstange)
perch; **ein Anzug von der** ~ (ugs.) an off-the-
peg-suit

**Stạngel** *der;* ~s, ~: stem; stalk

**Stạngen-:** ~**brot** *das* French bread;
~**spargel** *der* asparagus spears *pl.*

**stạnk** *1. u. 3. Pers. Sg. Prät. v.* STINKEN

**Stạpel** *der;* ~s, ~: pile; **ein** ~ **Holz** a pile *or*
stack of wood

**stạpeln** [1] *tr. V.* pile up; stack
[2] *refl. V.* pile up

**stạpfen** *itr. V.; mit sein* tramp

**Star**[1] *der;* ~[e]s, ~e *od.* (schweiz.) ~en (Vogel)
starling

**Star**[2] *der;* ~s, ~s (berühmte Persönlichkeit) star

**Star**[3] *der;* ~[e]s (Med.) **grauer** ~: cataract;
**grüner** ~: glaucoma

**stạrb** *1. u. 3. Pers. Sg. Prät. v.* STERBEN

**stạrk; stärker, stärkst...** [1] *Adj.* (a) strong;
potent ⟨*drink, medicine, etc.*⟩; powerful
⟨*engine, lens, voice, etc.*⟩; (ausgezeichnet)
excellent; *s. auch* STÜCK C;
(b) (dick) thick; stout ⟨*rope, string*⟩; (verhüll.:
korpulent) well-built (euphem.)
(c) (zahlenmäßig groß, umfangreich) sizeable,
large; big ⟨*demand*⟩; **eine 100 Mann** ~**e
Truppe** a 100-strong unit
(d) (heftig, intensiv) heavy; severe ⟨*frost, pain*⟩;
strong ⟨*impression, current, resistance,
dislike*⟩; grave ⟨*doubt, reservations*⟩; great
⟨*exaggeration, interest*⟩; loud ⟨*applause*⟩
(e) (Jugendspr.: großartig) great (coll.); fantastic
(coll.)
[2] *adv.* (a) (sehr, überaus, intensiv) (mit Adj.)
very; heavily ⟨*indebted, stressed*⟩; greatly
⟨*increased, reduced, enlarged*⟩; strongly
⟨*emphasized, characterized*⟩; badly ⟨*damaged,
worn, affected*⟩; (mit Verb) heavily ⟨*exaggerate,
impress*⟩ greatly; ⟨*enlarge, reduce, increase*⟩
considerably; ⟨*support, oppose, suspect*⟩
strongly; ⟨*remind*⟩ very much; ~ **erkältet
sein** have a heavy *or* bad cold
(b) (Jugendspr.: großartig) fantastically (coll.)

**Stạrk-bier** *das* strong beer

**Stärke** *die;* ~, ~**n** (a) strength; (eines Motors)
power; (einer Glühbirne) wattage
(b) (Dicke) thickness; (Technik) gauge
(c) (zahlenmäßige Größe) strength
(d) (besondere Fähigkeit, Vorteil) strength; **jmds.**
~/**nicht jmds.** ~ **sein** be sb.'s forte/not be
sb.'s strong point
(e) (Intensität) strength; (von Sturm, Schmerzen,
Abneigung) intensity; (von Frost) severity; (von
Lärm, Verkehr) volume
(f) (organischer Stoff) starch

**stärken** [1] *tr. V.* (a) strengthen; boost
⟨*power, prestige*⟩; ⟨*drink, food, etc.*⟩ fortify
⟨*person*⟩
(b) (steif machen) starch ⟨*washing etc.*⟩

---

*old spelling - see note on page xiv

**2** *refl. V.* refresh oneself

**Stärkung** *die;* ~, ~en (a) strengthening
(b) (Erfrischung) refreshment

**starr** **1** *Adj.* (a) rigid; (steif) stiff (vor +
*Dat.* with); fixed *(expression, smile, stare)*
(b) (nicht abwandelbar) inflexible, rigid *(law,
rule, principle)*
(c) (unnachgiebig) inflexible *(person, attitude,
etc.)*
**2** *adv.* rigidly; (steif) stiffly

**starren** *itr. V.* (a) stare (**in** + *Akk.* into, **auf,
an, gegen** + *Akk.* at); **jmdm. ins Gesicht** ~:
stare sb. in the face
(b) **vor/von Schmutz** ~: be filthy

**starr-, Starr-:** ~**sinn** *der* pigheadedness;
~**sinnig** *Adj.* pigheaded; ~**sinnigkeit**
*die* pigheadedness

**Start** *der;* ~[e]s, ~s start; (eines Flugzeugs)
take-off; (einer Rakete) launch

**Start·bahn** *die* [take-off] runway

**start·bereit** *Adj.* ready to start *postpos.;*
*(aircraft)* ready for take-off

**starten** **1** *itr. V.; mit sein* (a) start;
*(aircraft)* take off; *(rocket)* blast off, be
launched
(b) (den Motor anlassen) start the engine
**2** *tr. V.* start; launch *(rocket, satellite,
attack)*; start [up] *(engine, machine, car)*

**Stasi** *die;* ~: *Abk.* (DDR ugs.)
**Staatssicherheit**

**Stasi·akte** *die* Stasi file

**Station** *die;* ~, ~en (a) station
(b) (Haltestelle) stop
(c) (Zwischenhalt, Aufenthalt) stopover; ~
**machen** stop over *or* off
(d) (im Krankenhaus) ward

**stationär** **1** *Adj.* (Med.) *(treatment)* in
hospital, as an inpatient
**2** *adv.* (Med.) in hospital; **jmdn.** ~
**behandeln** treat sb. as an inpatient

**stationieren** *tr. V.* station *(troops)*; deploy
*(weapons, bombers, etc.)*

**Stationierung** *die;* ~, ~en stationing;
(von Waffen, Raketen usw.) deployment

**Stations-:** ~**arzt** *der,* ~**ärztin** *die* ward
doctor; ~**schwester** *die* ward sister;
~**taste** *die* (Rundf.) preset [tuning] button;
preset

**statisch** *Adj.* static

**Statistik** *die;* ~: statistics *sing., no art.*

**statistisch** **1** *Adj.* statistical
**2** *adv.* statistically

**statt** **1** *Präp. mit Gen.* instead of; *s. auch*
STATTDESSEN;
**2** *Konj.* ▶ ANSTATT

**statt·dessen** *Adv.* instead [of this]

**statt|finden** *unr. itr. V.* take place;
*(process, development)* occur

**statthaft** *Adj.* permissible

**stattlich** **1** *Adj.* (a) well-built; imposing
*(figure, stature, building, etc.)*; fine *(farm,
estate)*; impressive *(trousseau, collection)*
(b) (beträchtlich) considerable

**2** *adv.* impressively

**Statue** *die;* ~, ~n statue

**Statur** *die;* ~, ~en build

**Status** *der;* ~, ~ /'ʃtaːtuːs/ status

**Status quo** *der;* ~ (geh.) status quo

**Statut** *das;* ~[e]s, ~en statute

**Stau** *der;* ~[e]s, ~s *od.* ~e (a) build-up
(b) (von Fahrzeugen) tailback (Brit.); backup
(Amer.)

**Staub** *der;* ~[e]s dust; ~ **wischen** dust; ~
**saugen** vacuum; *or* (Brit. coll.) hoover; **sich
aus dem** ~[e] **machen** (fig. ugs.) make oneself
scarce (coll.)

**stauben** *itr. V.* cause dust

**staubig** *Adj.* dusty

**staub-, Staub-:** ~**saugen** *itr., tr. V.* **ich
staubsauge, staubgesaugt, staubzusaugen**
vacuum; (Brit. coll.) hoover; ~**sauger** *der*
vacuum cleaner; Hoover (*Brit.* ®); ~**tuch**
*das; Pl.* ~**tücher** duster

**Stau·damm** *der* dam

**Staude** *die;* ~, ~n (Bot.) herbaceous
perennial

**stauen** **1** *tr. V.* dam [up] *(stream, river)*;
staunch *(blood)*
**2** *refl. V.* *(water, blood, etc.)* accumulate,
build up; *(people)* form a crowd; *(traffic)*
form a tailback/tailbacks (Brit.) *or* (Amer.)
backup/backups

**staunen** *itr. V.* be amazed *or* astonished
(**über** + *Akk.* at); (beeindruckt sein) marvel
(**über** + *Akk.* at); ~**d** with *or* in amazement

**Staunen** *das;* ~s amazement (**über** + *Akk.*
at); (Bewunderung) wonderment

**Stau-:** ~**see** *der* reservoir; ~**stufe** *die*
barrage

**Stauung** *die;* ~, ~en (a) (eines Bachs,
Flusses) damming; (des Blutes, Wassers)
stemming the flow; (das Sichstauen) build-up
(b) (Verkehrsstau) tailback (Brit.); backup
(Amer.); jam

**Std.** *Abk.* = **Stunde** hr.

**Steak** /steːk/ *das;* ~s, ~s steak

**stechen** **1** *unr. itr. V.* (a) prick; *(wasp,
bee)* sting; *(mosquito)* bite
(b) (hineinstechen) **mit etw. in etw.** (*Akk.*) ~:
stick *or* jab sth. into sth.
**2** *unr. tr. V.* (mit dem Messer, Schwert) stab;
(mit der Nadel, mit einem Dorn usw.) prick; *(bee,
wasp)* sting; *(mosquito)* bite; **sich in den
Finger** ~: prick one's finger

**stechend** *Adj.* penetrating, pungent
*(smell)*; penetrating *(glance, eyes)*

**Stech-:** ~**mücke** *die* mosquito; gnat;
~**uhr** *die* time clock

**Steck-:** ~**brief** *der* description [of a/the
wanted person]; (Plakat) 'wanted' poster;
~**dose** *die* socket; power point

**stecken** **1** *tr. V.* (a) put
(b) (mit Nadeln) pin *(hem, lining, etc.)*; pin
[on] *(badge)*; pin up *(hair)*
**2** *itr. V.* be; ~ **bleiben** get stuck; **den
Schlüssel [im Schloss]** ~ **lassen** leave the ⋯⋗

**S**

key in the lock; **wo steckt meine Brille?** (ugs.) where have my glasses got to *or* gone?; **hinter etw.** (*Dat.*) ~ (fig. ugs.) be behind sth.

**stecken-, Stecken-:** \*~|**bleiben**
▶ STECKEN 2; \*~|**lassen** ▶ STECKEN 2;
~**pferd** *das* (a) (Spielzeug) hobby horse; (b) (Liebhaberei) hobby

**Stecker** *der;* ~s, ~: plug

**Steck·nadel** *die* pin

**Steg** *der;* ~[e]s, ~e (Brücke) [narrow] bridge; (Laufbrett) gangplank; (Boots~) landing stage

**Steg·reif** *der:* aus dem ~: impromptu

**Steh·auf·männchen** *das* tumbling figure; tumbler

**stehen** *unr. itr. V.; südd., österr., schweiz. mit sein* (a) stand
(b) (sich befinden) be; ⟨upright object, building⟩ stand
(c) (einen bestimmten Stand haben) **auf etw.** (*Dat.*) ~ ⟨needle, hand⟩ point to sth.; **das Barometer steht tief/auf Regen** the barometer is reading low/indicating rain; **das Spiel/es steht 1:1** (Sport) the score is one all; **die Sache steht gut/schlecht** things are going well/badly
(d) (einen bestimmten Kurs, Wert haben) ⟨currency⟩ stand (bei at); **wie steht das Pfund?** what is the rate for the pound?
(e) (nicht in Bewegung sein) be stationary; ⟨machine etc.⟩ be at a standstill; **meine Uhr steht** my watch has stopped; ~ **bleiben** (anhalten) stop; ⟨traffic⟩ come to a standstill; (stehen gelassen werden) stay; be left; (zurückgelassen werden) be left behind; (der Zerstörung entgehen) ⟨building⟩ be left standing; **etw.** ~ **lassen** (nicht entfernen) leave sth.; (vergessen) leave sth. [behind]
(f) (geschrieben, gedruckt sein) be; **in der Zeitung steht, dass ...:** it says in the paper that ...
(g) (Sprachw.: gebraucht werden) ⟨subjunctive etc.⟩ occur; be found
(h) jmdm. [gut] ~ ⟨dress etc.⟩ suit sb. [well]
(i) **auf etw.** (*Akk.*) ~ (ugs., bes. Jugendspr.: mögen) be into sth. (coll.); **sie steht total auf ihn** she's nuts about him

\*stehen|**bleiben,** \*ste͟hen|**lassen**
▶ STEHEN E

**Steh·lampe** *die* standard lamp (Brit.); floor lamp (Amer.)

**stehlen** *unr. tr., itr. V.* steal; *s. auch* GESTOHLEN 2

**Steh·platz** *der* (im Theater usw.) standing place; (im Bus) space to stand

**Steiermark** *die;* ~: Styria *no art.*

**steif** ① *Adj.* (a) stiff; (ugs.: erigiert) erect ⟨penis⟩
(b) (Seemannsspr.: stark) stiff ⟨wind, breeze⟩
(c) (förmlich) stiff; formal
② *adv.* stiffly

**Steifheit** *die;* (a) ~ stiffness
(b) (Förmlichkeit) formality; stiffness

**steigen** ① *unr. itr. V.; mit sein* (a) climb; ⟨mist, smoke, sun⟩ rise; ⟨balloon⟩ climb, rise;

**auf die Leiter** ~: get on to the ladder; **in den/aus dem Bus/Zug** ~: board *or* get on/get off *or* out of the bus/train
(b) (ansteigen, zunehmen) rise ⟨price, cost, salary, output⟩ increase, rise; ⟨debts, tension⟩ increase, mount; ⟨chances⟩ improve
② *unr. tr. V.; mit sein* climb ⟨stairs, steps⟩

**Steiger** *der;* ~s, ~ (Bergbau) overman

**steigern** ① *tr. V.* (a) increase ⟨speed, value, sales, consumption, etc.⟩ (auf + *Akk.* to); step up ⟨demands, production, etc.⟩; raise ⟨standards, requirements⟩; (verstärken) intensify ⟨fear, tension⟩; heighten ⟨effect⟩
(b) (Sprachw.) compare ⟨adjective⟩
② *refl. V.* ⟨confusion, speed, profit, etc.⟩ increase; ⟨pain, excitement, tension, etc.⟩ become more intense; ⟨costs⟩ escalate; ⟨effect⟩ be heightened

**Steigerung** *die;* ~, ~en (a) increase (*Gen.* in); (Verstärkung) intensification; (einer Wirkung) heightening; (Verbesserung) improvement (*Gen.* in); (bes. Sport: Leistungssteigerung) improvement [in performance]
(b) (Sprachw.) comparison

**Steigung** *die;* ~, ~en gradient

**steil** ① *Adj.* steep; meteoric ⟨career⟩; rapid ⟨rise⟩
② *adv.* steeply

**Steil-:** ~**hang** *der* steep escarpment; ~**küste** *die* (Geogr.) cliffs *pl.*

**Stein** *der;* ~[e]s, ~e stone; (Fels) rock; (Baustein) [stone]block; ⟨stone⟩block; **mir fällt ein ~ vom Herzen** that's a weight off my mind

**Stein-:** ~**bock** *der* (a) ibex; (b) (Astrol.) Capricorn; the Goat; ~**bruch** *der* quarry

**steinern** *Adj.* stone

**Stein·gut** *das* earthenware

**stein·hart** *Adj.* rock-hard

**steinig** *Adj.* stony

**steinigen** *tr. V.* stone ⟨person⟩

**Stein-:** ~**kohle** *die* [hard] coal; ~**metz** *der;* ~~en, ~~en, ~**metzin** *die;* ~~, ~~nen stonemason; ~**obst** *das* stone fruit; ~**pilz** *der* cep; ~**schlag** *der* rock fall; „Achtung ~**schlag**" 'beware falling rocks'; ~**zeit** *die* (fig.) stone age

**Steiß·bein** *das* (Anat.) coccyx

**Stelle** *die;* ~, ~n (a) place; **an jmds.** ~ **treten** take sb.'s place; **ich an deiner** ~ ...: ... if I were you; **an achter** ~ **liegen** be in eighth place; **die erste** ~ **hinter** *od.* **nach dem Komma** (Math.) the first decimal place; **an** ~ (+ *Gen.*) instead of; **auf der** ~ (z2): immediately
(b) (begrenzter Bereich) patch; (am Körper) spot
(c) (Passage) passage; (Punkt im Ablauf einer Rede usw.) point
(d) (Arbeitsstelle) job; post; **eine freie** ~: a vacancy
(e) (Dienststelle) office; (Behörde) authority

**stellen** ① *tr. V.* (a) put; (mit Sorgfalt) place; (aufrecht hin~) stand
(b) (ein~) set ⟨points, clock, scales⟩; **den**

**Wecker auf 6 Uhr** ∿: set the alarm for 6 o'clock; **die Heizung höher/niedriger** ∿: turn the heating up/down
**(c)** (bereitstellen) provide
**(d) jmdn. besser** ∿: ⟨*firm*⟩ improve sb.'s pay; **gut/schlecht/besser gestellt** comfortably/badly/better off
**(e)** *verblasst* put ⟨*question*⟩; set ⟨*task, topic, condition*⟩; make ⟨*application, demand, request*⟩; **jmdm. eine Frage** ∿: ask sb. a question
2 *refl. V.* **(a)** place oneself; **sich auf die Zehenspitzen** ∿: stand on tiptoe
**(b) sich schlafend/taub/tot** *usw.* ∿: feign sleep/deafness/death *etc.;* pretend to be asleep/deaf/dead *etc.*

**stellen-, Stellen-:** ∿**angebot** *das* offer of a job; (Inserat) job advertisement; „∿**angebote**" 'situations vacant'; ∿**anzeige** *die* job advertisement; ∿**gesuch** *das* 'situation wanted' advertisement; ∿**markt** *der* job market; ∿**profil** *das* job profile; ∿**suche** *die* job-hunting *no art.;* search for a job; ∿**weise** *Adv.* in places; ∿**wert** *der* **(a)** (Math.) place value; **(b)** (fig.: Bedeutung) standing; status

**Stellung** *die;* ∿, ∿**en** position; **zu etw.** ∿ **nehmen** express one's opinion on sth.

**Stellungnahme** *die;* ∿, ∿**n** opinion; (kurze Äußerung) statement

**stell-, Stell-:** ∿**vertretend** 1 *Adj.* acting; (von Amts wegen) deputy ⟨*minister, director, etc.*⟩; 2 *adv.* as a deputy; ∿**vertreter** *der,* ∿**vertreterin** *die* deputy

**Stelze** *die;* ∿, ∿**n** stilt

**stelzen** *itr. V.; mit sein* strut; stalk

**stemmen** 1 *tr. V.* **(a)** (hochstemmen) lift [above one's head]
**(b)** (drücken) brace ⟨*feet, knees*⟩ **(gegen** against)
2 *refl. V.* **sich gegen etw.** ∿: brace oneself against sth.

**Stempel** *der;* ∿**s,** ∿: stamp; (Poststempel) postmark

**stempeln** *tr. V.* stamp ⟨*passport, form*⟩; postmark ⟨*letter*⟩; cancel ⟨*postage stamp*⟩

***Stengel** ▶ STÄNGEL

**steno-, Steno-:** ∿**gramm** *das* shorthand text; ∿**graph** *der;* ∿∿**en,** ∿∿**en** stenographer; ∿**graphie** *die;* ∿∿, ∿∿**n** stenography *no art.;* shorthand *no art.;* ∿**graphieren** *itr. V.* do shorthand; ∿**graphin** *die;* ∿∿, ∿∿**nen** stenographer; ∿**typistin** *die;* ∿∿, ∿∿**nen** shorthand typist

**Stepp-decke** *die* quilt

**Steppe** *die;* ∿, ∿**n** steppe

**steppen¹** *tr.* (*auch itr.*) *V.* backstitch

**steppen²** *itr. V.* (tanzen) tap dance

**Steppke** *der;* ∿**s,** ∿**s** (ugs., bes. berlin.) lad; nipper (coll.)

**sterben** *unr. itr. V.; mit sein* die; **im Sterben liegen** lie dying

**sterbens-krank** *Adj.* mortally ill

**sterblich** *Adj.* mortal

**Sterbliche** *der/die; adj. Dekl.* mortal; **ein gewöhnlicher** ∿**r** an ordinary mortal *or* person

**Sterblichkeit** *die;* ∿: mortality

**stereo** *Adv.* in stereo

**Stereo** *das;* ∿**s** stereo

**Stereo-:** ∿**anlage** *die* stereo [system]; ∿**aufnahme** *die* stereo recording

**steril** *Adj.* sterile

**Sterling** /'stɛːlɪŋ/: **Pfund** ∿: pound/pounds sterling

**Stern** *der;* ∿**[e]s,** ∿**e** star

**Sternchen** *das;* ∿**s,** ∿ (Druckw.) asterisk

**Stern·schnuppe** *die;* ∿, ∿**n** shooting star

**Stethoskop** *das;* ∿**s,** ∿**e** (Med.) stethoscope

**Steuer¹** *das;* ∿**s,** ∿: [steering] wheel; (von Schiffen) helm

**Steuer²** *die;* ∿, ∿**n** tax

**steuer-, Steuer-:** ∿**belastung** *die* tax burden; ∿**berater** *der,* ∿**beraterin** *die* tax consultant *or* adviser; ∿**bord** *das od.* (österr.) *der* (Seew., Flugw.) starboard; ∿**erhöhung** *die* tax increase; ∿**erklärung** *die* tax return; ∿**ermäßigung** *die* tax relief; ∿**frau** *die* (Rudersport) cox; ∿**frei** *Adj.* tax-free

**steuerlich** 1 *Adj.* tax ⟨*advantages, benefits, etc.*⟩
2 *adv.* ∿ **absetzbar** tax-deductible

**Steuer·mann** *der; Pl.* ∿**leute** *od.* ∿**männer** (Rudersport) cox

**steuern** 1 *tr. V.* (fahren) steer; (fliegen) pilot, fly ⟨*aircraft*⟩; fly ⟨*course*⟩
2 *itr. V.* **(a)** be at the wheel; (auf dem Schiff) be at the helm
**(b)** *mit sein* (Kurs nehmen, ugs.: sich hinbewegen; auch fig.) head

**Steuer-:** ∿**oase** *die* (ugs.) tax haven; ∿**senkung** *die* (Steuerw.) tax cut; reduction in taxation

**Steuerung** *die;* ∿, ∿**en (a)** (System) controls *pl.;*
**(b)** ▶ STEUERN 1: steering; piloting; flying

**Steward** /'stjuːɐt/ *der;* ∿**s,** ∿**s** steward

**Stewardess** *, *Stewardeß** /'stjuːɐdɛs/ *die;* ∿, **Stewardessen** stewardess

**stich** *Imper. Sg. v.* STECHEN

**Stich** *der;* ∿**[e]s,** ∿**e (a)** (mit einer Waffe) stab
**(b)** (mit einem Dorn, einer Nadel) prick; (von Wespe, Biene usw.) sting; (Mückenstich usw.) bite
**(c)** (Stichwunde) stab wound
**(d)** (beim Nähen) stitch
**(e)** (Schmerz) stabbing *or* shooting pain
**(f)** (Kartenspiel) trick ⋯⋗

**(g)** jmdn./etw. im ∼ **lassen** leave sb. in the lurch/abandon sth.

**Stichelei** die; ∼, ∼en (ugs. abwertend) **(a)** (Bemerkung) dig; gibe

**(b)** hör auf mit deiner ∼: stop getting at me/him etc. (coll.)

**sticheln** itr. V. make snide remarks (coll.) (**gegen** about)

**stich-, Stich-:** ∼**flamme** die tongue of flame; ∼**haltig** Adj. sound ⟨argument, reason⟩; valid ⟨assertion, reply⟩; conclusive ⟨evidence⟩; ∼**haltigkeit** die; ∼∼:
▶ ∼HALTIG: soundness; validity; conclusiveness

**Stichling** der; ∼s, ∼e stickleback

**Stich-probe** die [random] sample; (bei Kontrollen) spot check

**stichst** 2. Pers. Sg. Präsens v. STECHEN

**sticht** 3. Pers. Sg. Präsens v. STECHEN

**Stich-:** ∼**tag** der set date; deadline; ∼**wunde** die stab wound

**sticken** ① itr. V. do embroidery ② tr. V. embroider

**Stickerei** die; ∼, ∼en embroidery no pl.; (gestickte Arbeit) piece of embroidery

**Stick-garn** das embroidery thread

**stickig** Adj. stuffy; stale ⟨air⟩

**Stick-:** ∼**oxid,** ∼**oxyd** das nitrogen oxide; ∼**oxid-emission,** ∼**oxyd-emission** die nitrogen oxide emission; ∼**stoff** der nitrogen; ∼**stoff-oxid,** ∼**stoff-oxyd** das nitrogen oxide

**Stief-** step ⟨brother, child, mother, etc.⟩

**Stiefel** der; ∼s, ∼ boot

**stief-, Stief-:** ∼**mutter** die; Pl. ∼mütter stepmother; ∼**mütterchen** das; ∼∼s, ∼∼ (Bot.) pansy; ∼**mütterlich** ① Adj. poor, shabby ⟨treatment⟩; ② adv. ∼mütterlich behandeln treat ⟨person⟩ poorly or shabbily; neglect ⟨pet, flowers, doll, problem⟩; ∼**vater** der stepfather

**stieg** 1. u. 3. Pers. Sg. Prät. v. STEIGEN

**Stieglitz** der; ∼s, ∼e goldfinch

**stiehl** Imp. Sg. v. STEHLEN

**stiehlst** 2. Pers. Sg. Präsens v. STEHLEN

**stiehlt** 3. Pers. Sg. Präsens v. STEHLEN

**Stiel** der; ∼[e]s, ∼e (Griff) handle; (Besenstiel) [broom]stick; (für Süßigkeiten) stick; (bei Gläsern) stem; (bei Blumen) stem; (an Obst usw.) stalk

**Stier** der; ∼[e]s, ∼e bull; (Astrol.) Taurus; the Bull

**stieren** itr. V. stare [vacantly] (**auf** + Akk. at)

**Stier-kampf** der bullfight

**stieß** 1. u. 3. Pers. Sg. Prät. v. STOSSEN

**Stift** der; ∼[e]s, ∼e **(a)** (aus Metall) pin; (aus Holz) peg

**(b)** (Bleistift) pencil; (Malstift) crayon; (Schreibstift) pen

**stiften** tr. V. **(a)** found, establish ⟨monastery, hospital, etc.⟩; endow ⟨prize, scholarship⟩; (als Spende) donate, give (**für** to)

**(b)** (herbeiführen) cause, create ⟨unrest, confusion, strife, etc.⟩; bring about ⟨peace, order, etc.⟩; arrange ⟨marriage⟩

**Stifter** der; ∼s, ∼, **Stifterin** die; ∼, ∼nen founder; (Spender) donor

**Stiftung** die; ∼, ∼en (Rechtsspr.) foundation; endowment

**Stift-zahn** der (Zahnmed.) post crown

**stigmatisieren** tr. V. stigmatize

**Stil** der; ∼[e]s, ∼e style

**Stil-bruch** der inconsistency of style

**stilistisch** ① Adj. stylistic ② adv. stylistically

**still** ① Adj. quiet; (ohne Geräusche) silent; still; (reglos) still; (wortlos) silent; (heimlich) secret; **der Stille Ozean** the Pacific [Ocean] ② adv. quietly; (geräuschlos) silently; (wortlos) in silence

**Stille** die; ∼: quiet; (Geräuschlosigkeit) silence; stillness

**\*stillegen** ▶ STILLLEGEN

**stillen** ① tr. V. **(a)** ein Kind ∼: breastfeed a baby

**(b)** (befriedigen) satisfy; quench ⟨thirst⟩

**(c)** (eindämmen) stop ⟨bleeding, tears, pain⟩ ② itr. V. breastfeed

**still-, Still-:** ∼**halten** unr. itr. V. keep or stay still; ∼**legen** tr. V. close or shut down; close ⟨railway line⟩; ∼**schweigen** das silence; ∼**schweigen bewahren** maintain silence; keep silent; ∼**schweigend** ① Adj. silent; (ohne Abmachung) tacit ⟨assumption, agreement⟩; ② adv. in silence; (ohne Abmachung) tacitly; ∼**sitzen** unr. itr. V. sit still; ∼**stand** der standstill; ∼**stehen** unr. itr. V. **(a)** ⟨factory, machine⟩ stand idle; ⟨traffic⟩ be at a standstill; ⟨heart etc.⟩ stop); **(b)** (Milit.) stand to attention

**Stimm-bruch** der: er ist im ∼: his voice is breaking

**Stimme** die; ∼, ∼n **(a)** voice

**(b)** (bei Wahlen) vote

**stimmen** ① itr. V. **(a)** be right or correct; **stimmt es, dass ...?** is it true that ...?

**(b)** (seine Stimme geben) vote; **mit Ja** ∼: vote yes or in favour ② tr. V. **(a)** (in eine Stimmung versetzen) make

**(b)** (Musik) tune ⟨instrument⟩

**Stimm-:** ∼**enthaltung** die abstention; ∼**gabel** die (Musik) tuning fork

**stimmig** Adj. harmonious; **die Argumentation ist [in sich (Dat.)]** ∼: the argument is consistent

**Stimm-:** ∼**lage** die **(a)** voice; **(b)** (Musik) voice; register; ∼**recht** das right to vote

**Stimmung** die; ∼, ∼en **(a)** mood

**(b)** (Atmosphäre) atmosphere

**stimmungs-voll** ① Adj. atmospheric ② adv. ⟨describe, light⟩ atmospherically; ⟨sing, recite⟩ with great feeling

**Stimm·zettel** *der* ballot paper
**stimulieren** *tr. V.* stimulate
**Stink·bombe** *die* stink bomb
**stinken** *unr. itr. V.* stink (**nach** of)
**stink·faul** *Adj.* (salopp abwertend) bone idle (coll.)
**stinkig** *Adj.* (salopp abwertend) stinking; smelly
**stink-:** ~**normal** (salopp) [1] *Adj.* dead (coll.) *or* boringly ordinary; [2] *adv.* in a dead ordinary way (coll.); ~**reich** *Adj.* (salopp) stinking rich (coll.)
**Stipendium** *das;* ~s, Stipendien (als Auszeichnung) scholarship; (als finanzielle Unterstützung) grant
**stirb** *Imp. Sg. v.* STERBEN
**stirbst** *2. Pers. Sg. Präsens v.* STERBEN
**stirbt** *3. Pers. Sg. Präsens v.* STERBEN
**Stirn** *die;* ~, ~en forehead; brow
**Stirn-:** ~**höhle** *die* (Anat.) frontal sinus; ~**runzeln** *das;* ~s frown; ~**seite** *die* front [side]
**stöbern** *itr. V.* (ugs.) rummage
**stochern** *itr. V.* poke
**Stock**[1] *der;* ~[e]s, Stöcke (a) stick; (Zeigestock) pointer; stick; (Taktstock) baton; (Skistock) pole; stick
(b) (Pflanze) (Rosenstock) [rose] bush; (Rebstock) vine
**Stock**[2] *der;* ~[e]s, ~ (Etage) floor; storey; **in welchem** ~? on which floor?
**stock·dunkel** *Adj.* (ugs.) pitch-dark
**stocken** *itr. V.* (a) ⟨traffic⟩ be held up; ⟨conversation, production⟩ stop; ⟨business⟩ slacken; ⟨journey⟩ be interrupted
(b) (innehalten) falter
**stock·finster** *Adj.* (ugs.) pitch-dark
**Stöckel·schuhe** *Pl.* high heels
**-stöckig** -storey *attr.;* -storeyed
**stock·nüchtern** *Adj.* (ugs.) stone-cold sober
**Stockung** *die;* ~, ~en hold-up (Gen. in)
**Stockwerk** *das* floor; storey
**Stoff** *der;* ~[e]s, ~e (a) material; fabric
(b) (Materie) substance
(c) (Philos.) matter
(d) (Thema) subject [matter]; (Gesprächsthema) topic
(e) (salopp: Rauschgift) stuff (sl.); dope (sl.)
**stofflich** *Adj.* material
**Stofflichkeit** *die;* ~: materiality
**Stoff·wechsel** *der* metabolism
**stöhnen** *itr. V.* moan; (vor Schmerz) groan
**Stola** *die;* ~, Stolen shawl; (Pelzstola) stole
**Stollen** *der;* ~s, ~ (a) (Kuchen) Stollen
(b) (Bergbau) gallery
(c) (bei Sportschuhen) stud
**stolpern** *itr. V.; mit sein* stumble; trip
**stolz** [1] *Adj.* proud (**auf** + Akk. of); **eine** ~**e Summe** (ugs.) a tidy sum
[2] *adv.* proudly
**Stolz** *der;* ~es pride (**auf** + Akk. in)

**stolzieren** *itr. V.; mit sein* strut
**stop** /stɔp/ *Interj.* stop; (Verkehrsw.) halt
**stopfen** *tr. V.* (a) darn
(b) (hineintun) stuff
(c) (füllen) stuff ⟨cushion, quilt, etc.⟩; fill ⟨pipe⟩; plug, stop [up] ⟨hole, leak⟩
**Stopf-:** ~**garn** *das* darning cotton; ~**nadel** *die* darning needle
**Stopp** *der;* ~s, ~s stop; (Einstellung) freeze (Gen. on)
**Stoppel** *die;* ~, ~n stubble *no pl.*
**stoppelig** *Adj.* stubbly
**stoppen** *tr., itr. V.* stop
**Stopp-:** ~**licht** *das* stop light; ~**schild** *das* stop sign; ~**uhr** *die* stopwatch
**Stöpsel** *der;* ~s, ~: plug
**Stör** *der;* ~s, ~e sturgeon
**Storch** *der;* ~[e]s, Störche stork
**stören** [1] *tr. V.* (a) disturb; disrupt ⟨court proceedings, lecture, church service, etc.⟩; interfere with ⟨transmitter, reception⟩
(b) (missfallen) bother
[2] *itr. V.* (a) disturb
(b) (Unruhe stiften) make *or* cause trouble
[3] *refl. V.* sich an jmdm./etw. ~: take exception to sb./sth.
**Störenfried** *der;* ~[e]s, ~e troublemaker
**Stör·fall** *der* (Technik) fault
**störrisch** [1] *Adj.* stubborn
[2] *adv.* stubbornly
**Störung** *die;* ~, ~en (a) disturbance; (einer Gerichtsverhandlung, Vorlesung, eines Gottesdienstes usw.) disruption; **bitte entschuldigen Sie die** ~, **aber** ...: I'm sorry to bother you, but ...
(b) **eine technische** ~: a technical fault
**Stoß** *der;* ~es, Stöße (a) (mit der Faust) punch; (mit dem Fuß) kick; (mit dem Kopf, den Hörnern) butt; (mit dem Ellbogen) dig
(b) (mit einer Waffe) (Stich) thrust; (Schlag) blow
(c) (beim Schwimmen, Rudern) stroke
(d) (Stapel) pile; stack
**stoßen** [1] *unr. tr. V.* (a) *auch itr.* (mit der Faust) punch; (mit dem Fuß) kick; (mit dem Kopf, den Hörnern) butt; (mit dem Ellbogen) dig
(b) (hineintreiben) plunge, thrust ⟨dagger, knife⟩; push ⟨stick, pole⟩
(c) (schleudern) push; **die Kugel** ~: put the shot
[2] *unr. itr. V.* (a) *mit sein* (auftreffen) bump (**gegen** into); **mit dem Kopf gegen etw.** ~: bump one's head on sth.
(b) *mit sein* (fig.) **auf etw.** (Akk.) ~ (etw. entdecken) come upon sth.; **auf Ablehnung** ~ (abgelehnt werden) meet with disapproval
(c) (grenzen) **an etw.** (Akk.) ~ ⟨room, property, etc.⟩ be [right] next to sth.
[3] *unr. refl. V.* bump *or* knock oneself; **sich an etw.** (Dat.) ~ (fig.) object to sth.
**Stoß-:** ~**seufzer** *der* heartfelt groan; ~**stange** *die* bumper
**stößt** *3. Pers. Sg. Präsens v.* STOSSEN
**stoß-, Stoß-:** ~**weise** *Adv.* (a) ⋯⦂

spasmodically; **(b)** (in Stapeln) by the pile; in piles; ~**zahn** der tusk; ~**zeit** die peak time; (Hauptverkehrszeit) rush hour

**Stotterer** der; ~s, ~, **Stotterin** die; ~, ~nen stutterer

**stottern** ① itr. V. stutter
② tr. V. stutter [out]

**Str.** Abk. **Straße** St./Rd.

**stracks** Adv. **(a)** (direkt) straight
**(b)** (sofort) straight away

**straf·bar** Adj. punishable

**Strafe** die; ~, ~n punishment; (Rechtsspr.) penalty; (Freiheitsstrafe) sentence; (Geldstrafe) fine

**strafen** tr. V. punish

**straff** ① Adj. **(a)** tight, taut ⟨rope, lines, etc.⟩; firm ⟨breasts, skin⟩
**(b)** (energisch) tight ⟨organization, planning, etc.⟩; strict ⟨discipline, leadership, etc.⟩
② adv. **(a)** [zu] ~ sitzen ⟨clothes⟩ be [too] tight
**(b)** (energisch) tightly, strictly

**straf·fällig** Adj. ~ werden commit a criminal offence

**straffen** tr. V. **(a)** tighten; firm ⟨skin⟩
**(b)** (fig.) tighten up ⟨text, procedure, organization, etc.⟩

**straf-, Straf-:** ~**frei** Adj. ~frei ausgehen go unpunished; ~**freiheit** die exemption from punishment; ~**gefangene** der/die prisoner; ~**gericht** das (fig.) judgement; ein ~gericht des Himmels divine judgement; ~**gesetz·buch** das penal code

**sträflich** ① Adj. criminal
② adv. criminally

**Sträfling** der; ~s, ~e prisoner

**straf-, Straf-:** ~**los** Adj. unpunished; ~**rechtlich** ① Adj. criminal attrib. ⟨case, investigation, responsibility⟩; ② adv. under criminal law; etw. ~rechtlich verfolgen prosecute sth.; ~**tat** die criminal offence; ~**täter** der, ~**täterin** die offender; ~**verfahren** das criminal proceedings pl.; ~**vollzug** der (System) penal system; ~**zettel** der (ugs.) [parking, speeding, etc.] ticket

**Strahl** der; ~[e]s, ~en (auch Phys., Math., fig.) ray; (von Scheinwerfern, Taschenlampen) beam; (von Flüssigkeit) jet

**Strahle·mann** der (ugs.) man/boy with the smiling face

**strahlen** itr. V. **(a)** shine; bei ~dem Wetter/ Sonnenschein in glorious sunny weather/in glorious sunshine; ~d weiß sparkling white
**(b)** (glänzen) sparkle
**(c)** (lächeln) beam (vor + Dat. with)

**Strahler** der; ~s, ~ **(a)** radiator
**(b)** (Heizstrahler) radiant heater

**Strahlung** die; ~, ~en radiation

**Strähne** die; ~, ~n strand; eine graue ~: a grey streak

**strähnig** ① Adj. straggly ⟨hair⟩
② adv. in strands

**stramm** ① Adj. **(a)** (straff) tight, taut ⟨rope, line, etc.⟩; tight ⟨clothes⟩
**(b)** (kräftig) strapping ⟨girl, boy⟩; sturdy ⟨legs, body⟩
**(c)** (gerade) upright, erect ⟨posture, etc.⟩
② adv. **(a)** (straff) tightly
**(b)** (kräftig) sturdily ⟨built⟩

**strampeln** itr. V. ⟨baby⟩ kick [his/her feet]

**Strand** der; ~[e]s, Strände beach; am ~: on the beach

**Strand-:** ~**bad** das bathing beach (on river, lake); ~**burg** die sand den (built as a windbreak)

**stranden** itr. V.; mit sein ⟨ship⟩ run aground

**Strand-:** ~**korb** der basket chair; ~**urlaub** der beach holiday; beach vacation (Amer.)

**Strang** der; ~[e]s, Stränge rope

**Strapaze** die; ~, ~n strain no pl.

**strapazieren** tr. V. be a strain on ⟨person, nerves⟩

**strapazier·fähig** Adj. hard-wearing ⟨clothes, shoes⟩; durable ⟨material⟩

**Straße** die; ~, ~n (in Ortschaften) street; road; (außerhalb) road

**Straßen-:** ~**bahn** die tram (Brit.); streetcar (Amer.); ~**bahn·haltestelle** die tram stop (Brit.); ~**bau·arbeiten** Pl. roadworks; ~**café** das pavement café; street café; ~**ecke** die street corner; ~**feger** der, ~**fegerin** die; ~~, ~~nen (bes. nordd.) road sweeper; ~**graben** der ditch [at the side of the road]; ~**karte** die road map; ~**kehrer** der; ~~s, ~~, ~**kehrerin** die; ~~, ~~nen (bes. südd.) road sweeper; ~**kriminalität** die street crime; ~**musikant** der, ~**musikantin** die street musician; busker; ~**raub** der street robbery; (gewalttätig) mugging; ~**räuber** der, ~**räuberin** die street robber; (gewalttätig) mugger; ~**schild** das street name sign; ~**sperre** die roadblock; ~**verkehr** der traffic

**Strategie** die; ~, ~n strategy

**strategisch** ① Adj. strategic
② adv. strategically

**Strato·sphäre** die stratosphere

**sträuben** ① tr. V. ruffle [up] ⟨feathers⟩; bristle ⟨fur, hair⟩
② refl. V. **(a)** ⟨hair, fur⟩ bristle, stand on end; ⟨feathers⟩ become ruffled
**(b)** (sich widersetzen) resist

**Strauch** der; ~[e]s, Sträucher shrub

**straucheln** itr. V.; mit sein (geh.) stumble

**Strauß**[1] der; ~es, Sträuße bunch of flowers; bouquet [of flowers]

**Strauß**[2] der; ~es, ~e (Vogel) ostrich

**Sträußchen** das; ~s, ~: posy

**streben** itr. V. **(a)** mit sein make one's way briskly

---

**(b)** (trachten) strive (**nach** for)

**Streber** *der;* ~**s**; ~ (abwertend) pushy person (coll.); (in der Schule) swot (Brit. coll.); grind (Amer. coll.)

**strebsam** *Adj.* ambitious and industrious

**Strecke** *die;* ~, ~**n** distance; (Abschnitt, Route) route; (Eisenbahn~) line

**strecken** ⓵ *tr. V.* (gerade machen) stretch ⟨*arms, legs*⟩; (dehnen) stretch [out] ⟨*arms, legs, etc.*⟩; **den Kopf aus dem Fenster** ~: stick one's head out of the window (coll.) ⓶ *refl. V.* stretch out

**strecken·weise** *Adv.* in places; (fig.: zeitweise) at times

**Streich** *der;* ~**[e]s**, ~**e** trick; prank; **jmdm. einen** ~ **spielen** play a trick on sb.

**streicheln** *tr. V.* stroke

**streichen** ⓵ *unr. tr. V.* **(a)** stroke **(b)** (anstreichen) paint; „**frisch gestrichen**" 'wet paint' **(c)** (auftragen) spread ⟨*butter, jam, ointment, etc.*⟩; (bestreichen) **ein Brötchen mit Butter/mit Honig** ~: butter a roll/spread honey on a roll **(d)** (tilgen) delete; cancel ⟨*train, flight*⟩ ⓶ *unr. itr. V.* **(a)** stroke; **jmdm. über den Kopf** ~: stroke sb.'s head **(b)** (anstreichen) paint

**Streicher** *der;* ~**s**, ~, **Streicherin** *die;* ~, ~**nen** (Musik) string player; **die Streicher:** the strings

**Streich-:** ~**holz** *das* match; ~**instrument** *das* string[ed] instrument; ~**käse** *der* cheese spread; ~**wurst** *die* [soft] sausage for spreading; ≈ meat spread

**Streife** *die;* ~, ~**n (a)** (Personen) patrol **(b)** (Streifengang) patrol

**streifen** ⓵ *tr. V.* **(a)** (leicht berühren) touch; ⟨*shot*⟩ graze **(b)** (kurz behandeln) touch [up]on ⟨*problem, subject, etc.*⟩ **(c)** **den Ring vom Finger** ~: slip the ring off one's finger; **die Ärmel nach oben** ~: pull/push up one's sleeves ⓶ *itr. V. mit sein* roam

**Streifen** *der;* ~**s**, ~ **(a)** stripe **(b)** (Stück, Abschnitt) strip

**Streifen·wagen** *der* patrol car

**streifig** *Adj.* streaky

**Streif·licht** *das* streak of light; **ein** ~**licht auf etw.** (*Akk.*) **werfen** (fig.) highlight sth.

**Streik** *der;* ~**[e]s**, ~**s** strike; **in den** ~ **treten** come out *or* go on strike

**Streik·brecher** *der*, **Streik·brecherin** *die;* ~, ~**nen** strike-breaker; blackleg (derog.)

**streiken** *itr. V.* **(a)** strike; be on strike; (in den Streik treten) come out *or* go on strike; strike **(b)** (ugs.: nicht mitmachen) go on strike **(c)** (ugs.: nicht funktionieren) pack up (coll.)

**Streikende** *der/die; adj. Dekl.* striker

**Streik·posten** *der* picket

**Streit** *der;* ~**[e]s**, ~**e** (Zank) quarrel; (Auseinandersetzung) dispute; argument

**streiten** *unr. itr., refl. V.* quarrel; argue; (sich zanken) quarrel

**Streiterei** *die;* ~, ~**en** arguing *no pl., no indef. art.;* (Gezänk) quarrelling *no pl.*

**Streitigkeit** *die;* ~, ~**en** *meist Pl.* **(a)** quarrel; argument **(b)** (Streitfall) dispute

**Streit·kräfte** *Pl.* armed forces

**streng** ⓵ *Adj.* **(a)** strict; severe ⟨*punishment*⟩; stringent, strict ⟨*rule, regulation, etc.*⟩; stringent ⟨*measure*⟩; rigorous ⟨*examination, check, test, etc.*⟩; stern ⟨*reprimand, look*⟩; absolute ⟨*discretion*⟩; complete ⟨*rest*⟩ **(b)** (schmucklos, herb) austere, severe ⟨*cut, collar, style, etc.*⟩; severe ⟨*face, features, hairstyle, etc.*⟩ **(c)** (durchdringend) pungent, sharp ⟨*taste, smell*⟩ **(d)** (rau) severe ⟨*winter*⟩; sharp, severe ⟨*frost*⟩ ⓶ *adv.* ⟨*mark, judge, etc.*⟩ strictly, severely; ⟨*punish*⟩ severely; ⟨*look, reprimand*⟩ sternly; ⟨*smell*⟩ strongly

**Strenge** *die;* ~ **(a)** ▶ STRENG A: strictness; severity; stringency; rigour; sternness **(b)** (von [Gesichts]zügen) severity **(c)** (von Geruch, Geschmack) pungency; sharpness **(d)** ▶ STRENG D: severity; sharpness

**strengstens** *Adv.* [most] strictly

**Stress, \*Streß** *der;* **Stresses** stress

**stressen** (ugs.) ⓵ *tr. V.* **jmdn.** ~: put sb. under stress; **vollkommen gestresst sein** be under an enormous amount of stress; **die gestressten Großstädter** the stressed city-dwellers ⓶ *itr. V.* be stressful

**Streu** *die;* ~, ~**en** straw

**streuen** *tr. V.* **(a)** spread ⟨*manure, sand, grit*⟩; sprinkle ⟨*salt, herbs, etc.*⟩; strew, scatter ⟨*flowers*⟩ **(b)** *auch itr.* **die Straßen [mit Sand/Salz]** ~: grit/salt the roads

**streunen** *itr. V.; meist mit sein* wander *or* roam about *or* around; ~**de Katzen/Hunde** stray cats/dogs

**Streusel·kuchen** *der* streusel cake

**strich** *1. u. 3. Pers. Sg. Prät. v.* STREICHEN

**Strich** *der;* ~**[e]s**, ~**e** (Linie) line; (Gedankenstrich) dash; (Schrägstrich) diagonal; (Binde-, Trennungsstrich) hyphen; **auf den** ~ **gehen** (salopp) walk the streets

**stricheln** *tr. V.* **(a)** sketch in [with short lines] **(b)** (schraffieren) hatch

**Strich-:** ~**junge** *der* (salopp) [young] male prostitute; ~**mädchen** *das* (salopp) streetwalker; hooker (Amer. sl.); ~**punkt** *der* semicolon

**Strick** *der;* ~**[e]s**, ~**e** cord; (Seil) rope; **jmdm. aus etw. einen** ~ **drehen** (fig.) use sth. against sb.

**S**

**stricken** tr., itr. V. knit

**Strick-:** ~**jacke** die cardigan; ~**nadel** die knitting needle; ~**zeug** das knitting

**striegeln** tr. V. groom ⟨horse⟩

**strikt** ⓵ Adj. strict
⓶ adv. strictly

**Strip** der; ~s, ~s strip[tease]

**Strippe** die; ~, ~n (ugs.) string; **an der** ~ **hängen** (fig.) be on the phone (coll.); (dauernd) hog the phone (coll.)

**Stripper** der; ~s, ~, **Stripperin** die; ~, ~**nen** (ugs.) stripper

**Striptease** /'ʃtrɪptiːs/ der od. das; ~: striptease

**stritt** 1. u. 3. Pers. Sg. Prät. v. STREITEN

**strittig** Adj. contentious ⟨point, problem⟩; disputed ⟨territory⟩; ⟨question⟩ in dispute, at issue

**Stroh** das; ~[e]s straw

**Stroh-:** ~**blume** die (a) (Immortelle) immortelle; (b) (Korbblütler) strawflower; ~**halm** der straw; ~**witwe** die (ugs. scherzh.) grass widow; ~**witwer** der (ugs. scherzh.) grass widower

**Strolch** der; ~[e]s, ~e (fam. scherzh.: Junge) rascal

**Strom** der; ~[e]s, Ströme river; (fig.) stream; (Strömung; Elektrizität) current; (~versorgung) electricity; **unter** ~ **stehen** be live

**strom-:** ~**abwärts** Adv. downstream; ~**auf**[**wärts**] Adv. upstream

**strömen** itr. V.; mit sein stream

**Strömung** die; ~, ~en current; (Met.) airstream; (fig.) trend

**Strophe** die; ~, ~n verse; (einer Ode) strophe

**strotzen** itr. V. von od. vor etw. (Dat.) ~: be full of sth.; **von** od. **vor Gesundheit** ~: be bursting with health

**strubbelig** Adj. tousled

**Strudel** der; ~s, ~ (a) whirlpool (b) (bes. südd., österr.: Gebäck) strudel

**Struktur** die; ~, ~en structure

**strukturieren** tr. V. structure; **neu** ~: restructure

**Strumpf** der; ~[e]s, Strümpfe stocking; (Socke, Knie~) sock

**Strumpf-:** ~**band** das garter; (Straps) suspender (Brit.); garter (Amer.); ~**hose** die tights pl. (Brit.); pantyhose (esp. Amer.)

**Strunk** der; ~[e]s, Strünke stem; stalk; (Baumstrunk) stump

**struppig** Adj. shaggy; tangled, tousled ⟨hair⟩

**Stube** die; ~, ~n (a) (veralt.: Wohnraum) [living] room; parlour (dated) (b) (Milit.) [barrack] room

**Stuben·fliege** die [common] housefly

**Stück** das; ~[e]s, ~e (a) piece; (kleines) bit; (Teil, Abschnitt) part; **ein** ~ **Kuchen** a piece or

slice of cake; **ein** ~ **Zucker/Seife** a lump of sugar/a piece or bar of soap; **im** od. **am** ~: unsliced ⟨sausage, cheese, etc.⟩
(b) (Einzelstück) item; (Exemplar) specimen; **ich nehme 5** ~: I'll take five [of them]; **30 Cent das** ~: thirty cents each; ~ **für** ~: piece by piece; (eins nach dem andern) one by one; **das ist** [ja] **ein starkes** ~ (ugs.) that's a bit much; **ein faules/freches** ~ (salopp) a lazy/cheeky thing or devil
(c) (Bühnenstück) play; (Musikstück) piece

**Stückchen** das; ~s, ~: [little] piece; bit

**stückeln** tr. V. put together ⟨sleeve, curtain⟩ with patches

**Student** der; ~en, ~en (a) student (b) (österr.: Schüler) [secondary-school] pupil

**Studenten·wohnheim** das student hostel; hall of residence

**Studentin** die; ~, ~nen ▶ STUDENT

**Studie** /'ʃtuːdjə/ die; ~, ~n study

**Studien-:** ~**aufenthalt** der study visit (in + Dat. to); ~**dauer** die length of study; **eine neunsemestrige** ~**dauer** nine semesters of study; ~**freund** der, ~**freundin** die university/college friend; ~**gebühr** die tuition fee; ~**platz** der university/college place; ~**reise** die study trip

**studieren** tr., itr. V. study

**Studierende** der/die; adj. Dekl. student

**Studio** das; ~s, ~s studio

**Studium** das; ~s, Studien study; (Studiengang) course of study

**Stufe** die; ~, ~n (a) step; (einer Treppe) stair; „**Vorsicht,** ~!" 'mind the step'
(b) (Raketenstufe, Geol., fig.: Stadium) stage; (Niveau) level; (Grad) degree; (Rang) grade

**Stuhl** der; ~[e]s, Stühle chair

**Stuhl-:** ~**gang** der bowel movement[s]; (Kot) stool; ~**lehne** die (Rückenlehne) chair back; (Armlehne) chair arm

**stülpen** tr. V. etw. auf od. über etw. (Akk.) ~: pull/put sth. on to or over sth.

**stumm** Adj. dumb ⟨person⟩; (schweigsam) silent; (wortlos) wordless; mute ⟨glance, gesture⟩

**Stumme** der/die; adj. Dekl. mute; **die** ~**n** the dumb

**Stummel** der; ~s, ~: stump; (Bleistiftstummel) stub; (Zigaretten-/Zigarrenstummel) [cigarette/cigar] butt

**Stumm·film** der silent film

**Stümper** der; ~s, ~: botcher; bungler

**stümperhaft** ⓵ Adj. incompetent; botched ⟨job⟩; (laienhaft) amateurish ⟨attempt, drawing⟩
⓶ adv. incompetently; (laienhaft) amateurishly

**Stümperin** die; ~, ~nen botcher; bungler

**stümpern** itr. V. work incompetently; (pfuschen) bungle

**stumpf** Adj. (a) blunt ⟨pin, needle, knife, etc.⟩

---
*old spelling - see note on page xiv

**(b)** (glanzlos, matt) dull ⟨*paint, hair, metal, colour, etc.*⟩

**Stumpf** der; ~[e]s, Stümpfe stump

**Stumpf·sinn** der **(a)** apathy
**(b)** (Monotonie) monotony; tedium

**stumpf·sinnig** ⚀ Adj. **(a)** apathetic; vacant ⟨*look*⟩
**(b)** (monoton) tedious; soul-destroying ⟨*job, work*⟩
⚁ adv. **(a)** apathetically; ⟨*stare*⟩ vacantly
**(b)** (monoton) tediously

**Stunde** die; ~, ~n hour; (Unterrichts~) lesson; eine ~ Aufenthalt/Pause an hour's stop/break; a stop/break of an hour

**stünde** 1. u. 3. Pers. Sg. Konjunktiv II v. STEHEN

**stunden** tr. V. jmdm. einen Betrag usw. ~: allow sb. to defer payment of a sum etc.

**stunden-, Stunden-:** ~**kilometer** der kilometre per hour; k.p.h.; ~**lang** ⚀ Adj. lasting hours postpos.; ⚁ adv. for hours; ~**lohn** der hourly wage; ~**plan** der timetable; ~**zeiger** der hour hand

**-stündig** adj. -hour

**stündlich** Adj., adv. hourly

**-stündlich** adj. -hourly; zwei~/halb~: two-hourly/half-hourly; adv. every two hours/half an hour

**Stundung** die; ~, ~en deferment of payment

**Stups** der; ~es, ~e (ugs.) push; shove; (leicht) nudge

**stupsen** tr. V. (ugs.) push; shove; (leicht) nudge

**Stups·nase** die snub nose

**stur** (ugs.) ⚀ Adj. **(a)** obstinate; dogged ⟨*insistence*⟩; (phlegmatisch) dour
**(b)** (unbeirrbar) dogged; persistent
**(c)** (stumpfsinnig) tedious
⚁ adv. **(a)** obstinately
**(b)** (unbeirrbar) doggedly
**(c)** (stumpfsinnig) tediously; ⟨*learn, copy*⟩ mechanically

**stürbe** 1. u. 3. Pers. Sg. Konjunktiv II v. STERBEN

**Sturheit** die; ~ (ugs.) **(a)** obstinacy; pigheadedness; (phlegmatisches Wesen) dourness
**(b)** (Stumpfsinnigkeit) deadly monotony

**Sturm** der; ~[e]s, Stürme **(a)** storm; (heftiger Wind) gale
**(b)** (Milit.) assault (auf + Akk. on); ~ klingeln ring the [door]bell like mad

**stürmen** ⚀ itr. V. **(a)** unpers. es stürmt [heftig] it's blowing a gale
**(b)** mit sein (rennen) rush; (verärgert) storm
⚁ tr. V. (Milit.) storm ⟨*town, position, etc.*⟩; (fig.) besiege ⟨*booking office, shop, etc.*⟩

**Stürmer** der; ~s, ~ (Sport) striker; forward

**stürmisch** ⚀ Adj. **(a)** stormy; (fig.) tempestuous, turbulent
**(b)** (ungestüm) tumultuous ⟨*applause,*

welcome, reception⟩; wild ⟨*enthusiasm*⟩; passionate ⟨*lover, embrace, temperament*⟩; vehement ⟨*protest*⟩
⚁ adv. ⟨*protest*⟩ vehemently; ⟨*embrace*⟩ impetuously, passionately; ⟨*demand*⟩ clamorously; ⟨*applaud*⟩ wildly

**Sturz** der; -es, Stürze **(a)** fall; (Unfall) accident
**(b)** (fig.: von Preis, Temperatur usw.) [sharp] fall, drop (Gen. in)
**(c)** (Verlust des Amtes, der Macht) fall; (Absetzung) overthrow; (Amtsenthebung) removal from office

**Sturz·bach** der [mountain] torrent; (fig.: von Fragen usw.) torrent

**sturz·besoffen** Adj (ugs.) paralytic [drunk] (coll.)

**stürzen** ⚀ itr. V.; mit sein **(a)** fall; (fig.) ⟨*temperature, exchange rate, etc.*⟩ drop [sharply]; ⟨*prices*⟩ tumble; ⟨*government*⟩ fall, collapse
**(b)** (laufen) rush; dash
**(c)** (fließen) stream; pour
⚁ refl. V. sich auf jmdn./etw. ~ (auch fig.) pounce on sb./sth.; sich in etw. (Akk.) ~: throw oneself into sth.
⚂ tr. V. **(a)** throw; (mit Wucht) hurl
**(b)** (umdrehen) upturn ⟨*mould*⟩; turn out ⟨*pudding, cake, etc.*⟩
**(c)** (des Amtes entheben) oust ⟨*person*⟩ [from office]; (gewaltsam) overthrow ⟨*leader, government*⟩

**Sturz-:** ~**flug** der (Flugw.) [nose]dive; im ~**flug** in a [nose]dive; ~**helm** der crash helmet

**Stuss, *Stuß** der; Stusses (ugs. abwertend) rubbish; twaddle (coll.)

**Stute** die; ~, ~n mare

**Stütze** die; ~, ~n (auch fig.) support

**stutzen¹** itr. V. stop short

**stutzen²** tr. V. trim; dock ⟨*tail*⟩; clip ⟨*ear, hedge, wing*⟩; prune ⟨*tree, bush*⟩

**stützen** ⚀ tr. V. support; (mit Pfosten o. Ä.) prop up; (aufstützen) rest ⟨*head, hands, arms, etc.*⟩
⚁ refl. V. sich auf jmdn./etw. ~: lean or support oneself on sb./sth.

**stutzig** Adj. ~ werden begin to wonder; jmdn. ~ machen make sb. wonder

**Styropor** Ⓦ das; ~s polystyrene [foam]

**s. u.** Abk. = siehe unten see below

**Subjekt** das; ~[e]s, ~e **(a)** subject
**(b)** (abwertend: Mensch) creature

**subjektiv** ⚀ Adj. subjective
⚁ adv. subjectively

**Subjektivität** die; ~: subjectivity

***substantiell** ▶ SUBSTANZIELL

**Substantiv** das; ~s, ~e (Sprachw.) noun

**Substanz** die; ~, ~en **(a)** (auch fig.) substance
**(b)** (Grundbestand) die ~: the reserves pl.

**substanziell** ⚀ Adj. substantial
⚁ adv. substantially

**S**

**subtil** ⓵ *Adj.* subtle
⓶ *adv.* subtly
**Subtilität** *die;* ~, ~en subtlety
**sub·tropisch** *Adj.* subtropical
**Subvention** *die;* ~, ~en (Wirtsch.) subsidy
**Suche** *die;* ~, ~n search (nach for); **auf der**
~ [nach jmdm./etw.] **sein** be looking/
(intensiver) searching [for sb./sth.]
**suchen** ⓵ *tr. V.* (a) look for; (intensiver)
search for; „**Leerzimmer gesucht**"
'unfurnished room wanted'
(b) (bedacht sein auf, sich wünschen) seek
⟨protection, advice, company, warmth, etc.⟩;
look for ⟨adventure⟩
⓶ *itr. V.* search; **nach jmdm./etw.** ~: look/
search for sb./sth.
**Sucherei** *die;* ~, ~en (ugs., oft abwertend)
[endless] searching *no pl.*
**Sucht** *die;* ~, Süchte *od.* ~en (a) addiction
(nach to); [bei jmdm.] **zur** ~ **werden** (auch fig.)
become addictive [in sb.'s case]
(b) *Pl.* Süchte (übermäßiges Verlangen) craving
(nach for)
**süchtig** *Adj.* (a) addicted
(b) (fig.) **nach etw.** ~ **sein** be obsessed with
sth.
**Sucht·kranke** *die/der* addict
**Süd** (bes. Seemannsspr., Met.) ▶ SÜDEN
**Süd-:** ~**afrika** (das) South Africa;
~**amerika** (das) South America
**Sudan** (das); ~s *od. der;* ~s Sudan
**Süden** *der;* ~s south; **der** ~: the South;
**Süd·frucht** *die* tropical [or sub-tropical]
fruit
**Südländer** *der;* ~s, ~, **Südländerin**
*die;* ~, ~nen Southern European
**südländisch** *Adj.* Southern [European];
Latin ⟨temperament⟩; ~ **aussehen** have Latin
looks
**südlich** ⓵ *Adj.* (a) southern
(b) (nach, von Süden) southerly
(c) (aus dem Süden) Southern
⓶ *adv.* southwards
⓷ *Präp. mit Gen.* [to the] south of
**süd-, Süd-:** ~**licht** *das* southern lights *pl.;*
(einzelne Erscheinung) display of the southern
lights; ~**pol** *der* South Pole; ~**see** *die;*
~~: **die** ~**see:** the South Seas *pl.;*
~**see·insel** *die* South Sea island; ~**tirol**
(das) South Tyrol; ~**wärts** *Adv.*
southwards; ~**wind** *der* south *or* southerly
wind
**Sues·kanal** *der;* ~s Suez Canal
**Sühne** *die;* ~, ~n (geh.) atonement;
expiation
**sühnen** *tr., itr. V.* [für] **etw.** ~: atone for *or*
pay the penalty for sth.
**Sultanine** *die;* ~, ~n sultana
**Sülze** *die;* ~, ~n (a) diced meat/fish in
aspic; (vom Schweinskopf) brawn
(b) (Aspik) aspic

**sülzen** *tr., itr. V.* (salopp) ▶ QUATSCHEN 1A, 2
**Summe** *die;* ~, ~n sum
**summen** ⓵ *itr. V.* hum; (lauter, heller) buzz
⓶ *tr. V.* hum ⟨tune, song, etc.⟩
**summieren** *refl. V.* add up (**auf** + *Akk.* to)
**Sumpf** *der;* ~[e]s, Sümpfe marsh; (bes. in den
Tropen) swamp
**sumpfig** *Adj.* marshy
**Sund** *der;* ~[e]s, ~e (Geogr.) sound
**Sünde** *die;* ~, ~n sin; (fig.) misdeed;
transgression
**Sünden·bock** *der* (ugs.) scapegoat
**Sünder** *der;* ~s, ~, **Sünderin** *die;* ~,
~nen sinner
**sündigen** *itr. V.* sin
**Super** *das;* ~s, ~: four star (Brit.); premium
(Amer.)
**super-** ultra- ⟨long, high, fast, modern,
masculine, etc.⟩
**Super-** super⟨hero, car, group, etc.⟩; terrific
(coll.), tremendous (coll.) ⟨success, offer,
chance, idea, etc.⟩
**Super·benzin** *das* four-star petrol (Brit.);
premium (Amer.)
**Superlativ** *der;* ~s, ~e (Sprachw.)
superlative
**Super-:** ~**macht** *die* super power;
~**markt** *der* supermarket
**Suppe** *die;* ~; ~n soup
**Suppen·löffel** *der* soup spoon
**Surf·brett** /'sə:f-/ *das* surfboard
**surfen** /'sə:fn/ *itr. V.* surf
**Surfer** /'sə:fɐ/ *der;* ~s, ~, **Surferin** *die;*
~, ~nen surfer
**surren** *itr. V.* (a) (summen) hum; ⟨camera,
fan⟩ whirr
(b) *mit sein* (schwirren) whirr
**suspekt** ⓵ *Adj.* suspicious; **jmdm.** ~ **sein**
arouse sb.'s suspicions
⓶ *adv.* suspiciously
**süß** ⓵ *Adj.* sweet
⓶ *adv.* sweetly
**süßen** *tr. V.* sweeten
**Süßigkeit** *die;* ~, ~en sweet (Brit.); candy
(Amer.); ~**en** sweets (Brit.); candy *sing.* (Amer.);
(als Ware) confectionery *sing.*
**süßlich** ⓵ *Adj.* (a) [slightly] sweet; on the
sweet side *pred.;*
(b) (sentimental) mawkish
⓶ *adv.* ⟨write, paint⟩ mawkishly
**süß-, Süß-:** ~**most** *der* unfermented fruit
juice; ~**sauer** ⓵ *Adj.* sweet-and-sour; (fig.)
wry ⟨smile, face⟩; ⓶ *adv.* (a) etw. ~**sauer**
zubereiten give sth. a sweet-and-sour flavour;
(b) (fig.) ⟨smile⟩ wryly; ~**speise** *die* sweet;
dessert; ~**stoff** *der* sweetener; ~**wasser**
*das* fresh water
**Symbol** *das;* ~s, ~e symbol
**symbolisch** ⓵ *Adj.* symbolic
⓶ *adv.* symbolically
**Sympathie** *die;* ~, ~n sympathy (**für** with)

## sympathisch ···⫶ Tagebuch ····

**sympathisch** ① *Adj.* congenial, likeable ‹*person, manner*›; appealing ‹*voice, appearance, material*› ② *adv.* in an appealing way; (angenehm) agreeably

**Symphonie** *usw.* ▶ SINFONIE *usw.*

**Symptom** *das;* ~s, ~e (Med., geh.) symptom (*Gen.*, **für, von** of)

**symptomatisch** (Med., geh.) *Adj.* symptomatic (**für** of)

**Synagoge** *die;* ~, ~n synagogue

**synchron** ① *Adj.* **(a)** synchronous **(b)** (Sprachw.) synchronic ② *adv.* **(a)** synchronously **(b)** (Sprachw.) synchronically

**Synchronisation** *die;* ~, ~en ▶ SYNCHRONISIERUNG

**synchronisieren** *tr. V.* **(a)** (Film) dub ‹*film*› **(b)** (Technik, fig.) synchronize ‹*watches, operations, etc.*›; **synchronisiertes Getriebe** synchromesh [gearbox]

**Synchronisierung** *die;* ~, ~en **(a)** (Film) dubbing **(b)** (Technik, fig.) synchronization

**Synthese** *die;* ~, ~n synthesis (*Gen.*, **von, aus** of)

**Synthesizer** /'sɪntəsaiːzɐ/ *der;* ~s, ~ (Musik) synthesizer

**synthetisch** ① *Adj.* synthetic ② *adv.* synthetically

**Syrer** *der;* ~s, ~, **Syrerin** *die;* ~, ~nen Syrian

**Syrien** /'zyːriən/ *(das);* ~s Syria

**syrisch** *Adj.* Syrian

**System** *das;* ~, ~e system

**systematisch** ① *Adj.* systematic ② *adv.* systematically

**System·fehler** *der* fault in the system

**Szenario** *das;* ~s, ~s scenario

**Szene** /'stsːeːnə/ *die;* ~, ~n (auch fig.) scene

**Szenen·wechsel** *der* (Theater) scene change

# Tt

**t, T** /teː/ *das;* ~, ~: t/T

**t** *Abk.* = **Tonne** t

**Tab.** *Abk.* = **Tabelle**

**Tabak** *der;* ~s, ~e tobacco

**Tabaks·pfeife** *die* [tobacco] pipe

**tabellarisch** *Adj.* tabular; **ein** ~**er Lebenslauf** a curriculum vitae in tabular form

**Tabelle** *die;* ~, ~n table

**Tabellen·kalkulation** *die* (DV) performing calculations using a spreadsheet; (Program) spreadsheet program

**Tabernakel** *das od. der;* ~s, ~: tabernacle

**Tablett** *das;* ~[e]s, ~s *od.* ~e tray

**Tablette** *die;* ~, ~n tablet

**tabletten·süchtig** *Adj.* addicted to pills *postpos.*

**tabu** *Adj.* taboo

**Tabu** *das;* ~s, ~s taboo

**tabuisieren** *tr. V.* **etw.** ~: taboo sth.; make sth. taboo

**Ta·cheles** [**mit jmdm.**] ~ **reden** (ugs.) do some straight talking [to sb.]

**Tacho** *der;* ~s, ~s (ugs.) speedo (coll.)

**Tacho-:** ~**meter** *der od. das* speedometer; ~**stand** *der* (ugs.: Kilometerstand) mileometer *or* odometer reading

**Tadel** *der;* ~s, ~ **(a)** censure **(b)** (im Klassenbuch) black mark

**tadel·los** ① *Adj.* impeccable; immaculate ‹*hair, clothing, suit, etc.*›; perfect ‹*condition, teeth, pronunciation, German, etc.*› ② *adv.* ‹*dress*› impeccably; ‹*fit, speak, etc.*› perfectly; ‹*live, behave, etc.*› irreproachably

**tadeln** *tr. V.* **jmdn.** [**für** *od.* **wegen etw.**] ~: rebuke sb. [for sth.]

**Tafel** *die;* ~, ~n **(a)** (Schiefertafel) slate; (Wandtafel) blackboard **(b)** (plattenförmiges Stück) slab; **eine** ~ **Schokolade** a bar of chocolate **(c)** (Gedenktafel) plaque **(d)** (geh.: festlicher Tisch) table

**Täfelchen** *das;* ~s, ~: ▶ TAFEL B: [small] slab; [small] bar

**tafeln** *itr. V.* (geh.) feast

**täfeln** *tr. V.* panel

**Tafel-:** ~**spitz** *der* (österr.) boiled fillet of beef; ~**wasser** *das* [bottled] mineral water; ~**wein** *der* table wine

**taff** *Adj.* (ugs.) tough

**Taft** *der;* ~[e]s, ~e taffeta

**Tag** *der;* ~[e]s, ~e day; **am** ~[e] during the day[time]; **guten** ~! hello; (bei Vorstellung) how do you do?; **an diesem** ~: on this day; **dreimal am** ~: three times a day; **am folgenden** ~: the next day; **eines** ~**es** one day; some day

**tag·aus** *Adv.* ~, **tagein** day in, day out; day after day

**Tage·buch** *das* diary

**tag-ein** Adv. ▶ TAGAUS

**tage-lang** ① Adj. lasting for days postpos.; nach ~em Regen after days of rain ② adv. for days [on end]

**tagen** itr. V. meet; das Gericht/Parlament tagt the court/parliament is in session

**tages-, Tages-:** ~aktuell Adj. die ~aktuellen Nachrichten the [current] news of the day; die ~aktuellen Kurse the rates of exchange current on the day; ~anbruch der daybreak; dawn; ~ausflug der day's outing; ~karte die (a) (Gastron.) menu of the day; (b) (Fahr-, Eintrittskarte) day ticket; ~kasse die (a) box office (open during the day); (b) (Tageseinnahme) day's takings pl.; ~licht das daylight; ~licht-projektor der overhead projector; ~zeit die time of day; ~zeitung die daily newspaper; daily

**-tägig** (a) (... Tage alt) ein sechstägiges Küken a six-day-old chick (b) (... Tage dauernd) nach dreitägiger Vorbereitung after three days' preparation

**täglich** ① Adj. daily ② adv. every day; zweimal ~: twice a day; ~ drei Tabletten einnehmen take three tablets daily

**tags** Adv. (a) by day; in the daytime (b) ~ zuvor/davor the day before; ~ darauf the next or following day; the day after

**tags-über** Adv. during the day

**tag-täglich** (intensivierend) ① Adj. day-to-day; daily ② adv. every single day

**Tagung** die; ~, ~en conference

**Taifun** der; ~s, ~e typhoon

**Taille** /'taljə/ die; ~, ~n waist

**Taiwan** (das); ~s Taiwan

**Takt** der; ~[e]s, ~e (a) (Musik) time; (Einheit) bar; measure (Amer.); aus dem ~ kommen lose the beat (b) (rhythmischer Bewegungsablauf) rhythm (c) (Feingefühl) tact

**Takt-gefühl** das sense of tact

**taktieren** itr. V. proceed tactically; vorsichtig/klug ~: use caution/clever tactics

**Taktik** die; ~, ~en: [eine] ~: tactics pl.

**taktisch** ① Adj. tactical ② adv. tactically

**taktlos** ① Adj. tactless ② adv. tactlessly

**Taktlosigkeit** die; ~, ~en (a) (taktlose Art) tactlessness (b) (taktlose Handlung) piece of tactlessness

**taktvoll** ① Adj. tactful ② adv. tactfully

**Tal** das; ~[e]s, Täler valley

**Talent** das; ~[e]s, ~e talent (zu, für for); (Mensch) talented person

**talentiert** Adj. talented

**Talg** der; ~[e]s, ~e suet; (zur Herstellung von Seife, Kerzen usw.) tallow

**Talisman** der; ~s, ~e talisman

**Tampon** der; ~s, ~s tampon

**Tamtam** das; ~s (ugs. abwertend) [großes] ~: [a big] fuss

**Tang** der; ~[e]s, ~e seaweed

**Tangente** die; ~, ~n (Math.) tangent

**Tank** der; ~s, ~s tank

**tanken** tr., itr. V. fill up; Öl ~: fill up with oil

**Tanker** der; ~s, ~: tanker

**Tank-:** ~säule die petrol pump (Brit.); gasoline pump (Amer.); ~stelle die petrol station (Brit.); gas station (Amer.); ~wagen der tanker; ~wart der; ~s, ~e, ~wartin die; ~, ~nen petrol pump attendant (Brit.); gas station attendant (Amer.)

**Tanne** die; ~, ~n fir [tree]

**Tannen-:** ~baum der (ugs.) fir tree; (Weihnachtsbaum) Christmas tree; ~grün das fir sprigs pl.; ~zapfen der fir cone; ~zweig der fir branch

**Tansania** (das); ~s Tanzania

**Tante** die; ~, ~n (a) aunt (b) (Kinderspr.: Frau) lady (c) (ugs.: Frau) woman

**Tanz** der; ~es, Tänze dance

**Tanz-:** ~abend der evening dance; ~bar die night spot (coll.) with dancing; ~café das coffee house with dancing

**tanzen** itr., tr. V. dance

**Tänzer** der; ~s, ~, **Tänzerin** die; ~, ~nen dancer; (Balletttänzer[in]) ballet dancer

**Tanz-:** ~fläche die dance floor; ~lokal das café/restaurant with dancing; ~orchester das dance band; ~stunde die (a) (~kurs) dancing class; (b) (einzelne Stunde) dancing lesson

**Tapete** die; ~, ~n wallpaper

**Tapeten-wechsel** der (ugs.) change of scene

**tapezieren** tr. V. [wall]paper

**tapfer** ① Adj. brave ② adv. bravely

**Tapferkeit** die; ~: courage; bravery

**tappen** itr. V. (a) mit sein patter (b) (tastend greifen) grope (nach for)

**Taps** der; ~es, ~e (ugs. abwertend) clumsy oaf

**Tarif** der; ~s, ~e charge; (Post-, Wassertarif) rate; (Verkehrstarif) fares pl.; (Zolltarif) tariff; (Lohntarif) [wage] rate; (Gehaltstarif) [salary] scale

**tarnen** ① tr., itr. V. camouflage ② refl. V. camouflage oneself

**Tasche** die; ~, ~n bag; (in Kleidung, Rucksack usw.) pocket; jmdm. auf der ~ liegen (fig. ugs.) live off sb.

**Taschen-:** ~buch das paperback; ~dieb der, ~diebin die pickpocket; ~geld das pocket money; ~lampe die [pocket] torch (Brit.) or (Amer.) flashlight;

---

**∼messer** das penknife; **∼rechner** der pocket calculator; **∼tuch** das; Pl. **∼tücher** handkerchief; **∼uhr** die pocket watch

**Tasse** die; ∼, ∼n cup

**Tastatur** die; ∼, ∼en keyboard

**Taste** die; ∼, ∼n (a) (eines Musikinstruments, einer Schreibmaschine) key
(b) (Pedal) pedal [key]
(c) (am Telefon, Radio, Fernsehgerät, Taschenrechner usw.) button

**tasten** 1 itr. V. (fühlend suchen) grope, feel (nach for)
2 refl. V. (sich tastend bewegen) grope or feel one's way

**Tasten·telefon** das push-button telephone

**tat** 1. u. 3. Pers. Sg. Prät. v. TUN

**Tat** die; ∼, ∼en act; (das Tun) action; **eine gute ∼**: a good deed; **in der ∼** (verstärkend) actually; (zustimmend) indeed

**Tatar** das; ∼[s] steak tartare

**Tat·bestand** der (a) facts pl. [of the matter or case]
(b) (Rechtsw.) elements pl. of an offence

**Täter** der; ∼s, ∼, **Täterin** die; ∼, ∼nen culprit

**tätig** Adj. (a) ∼ sein work
(b) (rührig, aktiv) active

**tätigen** tr. V. (Kaufmannsspr., Papierdt.) transact ⟨business, deal, etc.⟩

**Tätigkeit** die; ∼, ∼en activity; (Arbeit) job

**tat-, Tat-:** **∼kraft** die energy; drive; **∼kräftig** 1 Adj. energetic ⟨person⟩; 2 adv. energetically

**tätlich** 1 Adj. physical ⟨clash, attack, resistance, etc.⟩; **gegen jmdn. ∼ werden** become violent towards sb.
2 adv. physically; **jmdn. ∼ angreifen** attack sb. physically; assault sb.

**Tat·ort** der scene of a/the crime

**tätowieren** tr. V. tattoo

**Tätowierung** die; ∼, ∼en tattoo

**Tat·sache** die fact

**tatsächlich** 1 Adj. actual; real
2 adv. actually; really

**tätscheln** tr. V. pat

**Tattoo** /tɛ'tu:/ das; ∼s, ∼s tattoo

**tat·verdächtig** Adj. suspected

**Tat·waffe** die weapon [used in the crime]

**Tatze** die; ∼, ∼n paw

**Tat·zeit** die time of the crime

**Tau¹** der; ∼[e]s dew

**Tau²** das; ∼[e]s, ∼e (Seil) rope

**taub** Adj. (a) deaf
(b) (wie abgestorben) numb
(c) empty ⟨nut⟩

**Taube¹** die; ∼, ∼n pigeon; (Turteltaube; auch Politik fig.) dove

**Taube²** der/die; adj. Dekl. deaf person; deaf man/woman; **die ∼n** the deaf

**Taubheit** die; ∼: deafness

**taub·stumm** Adj. deaf and dumb

**Taub·stumme** der/die; adj. Dekl. deaf mute

**tauchen** 1 itr. V. (a) auch mit sein dive (nach for)
(b) mit sein (eintauchen) dive; (auftauchen) rise; emerge
2 tr. V. (a) (eintauchen) dip
(b) (untertauchen) duck

**Taucher** der; ∼s, ∼: diver; (mit Flossen und Atemgerät) skin diver

**Taucher-:** **∼anzug** der diving suit; **∼brille** die diving goggles pl.

**Taucherin** die; ∼, ∼nen ▶ TAUCHER

**Tauch·sieder** der; ∼s, ∼: portable immersion heater

**tauen** 1 itr. V. (a) unpers. **es taut** it's thawing
(b) mit sein (schmelzen) melt
2 tr. V. melt; thaw

**Taufe** die; ∼, ∼n (christl. Rel.) (a) (Sakrament) baptism
(b) (Zeremonie) christening; baptism

**taufen** tr. V. (a) baptize
(b) (einen Namen geben) christen

**taugen** itr. V. **nichts/nicht viel/etwas ∼**: be no/not much/some good or use

**tauglich** Adj. [nicht] ∼: [un]suitable; (für Militärdienst) fit [for service]

**Taumel** der; ∼s (a) [feeling of] dizziness
(b) (Rausch) frenzy; fever

**taumelig** Adj. dizzy; giddy

**taumeln** itr. V. (a) auch mit sein (wanken) reel, sway (vor + Dat. with)
(b) mit sein (taumelnd gehen) stagger

**Tausch** der; ∼[e]s, ∼e exchange; **ein guter/schlechter ∼**: a good/bad deal

**tauschen** 1 tr. V. exchange (gegen for); **sie tauschten die Plätze** they changed places
2 itr. V. **mit jmdm. ∼** (fig.) change places with sb.

**täuschen** 1 tr. V. deceive; **wenn mich nicht alles täuscht** unless I'm completely mistaken
2 itr. V. be deceptive
3 refl. V. be wrong or mistaken (in + Dat. about)

**täuschend** 1 Adj. remarkable, striking ⟨similarity, imitation⟩
2 adv. remarkably

**Täuschung** die; ∼, ∼en deception; (Selbst∼) delusion

**tausend** Kardinalz. (a) a or one thousand
(b) (ugs.: sehr viele) thousands of; **∼ Dank/Küsse** a thousand thanks/kisses

**Tausend** das; ∼s, ∼e thousand

**tausend·ein[s]** Kardinalz. a or one thousand and one

**Tausender** der; ∼s, ∼ (ugs.) (Tausendmarkschein usw.) thousand-mark/-dollar etc. note; (Betrag) thousand marks/dollars etc.

**tausenderlei** *indekl. Adj.* (ugs.) a thousand and one different ⟨*answers, kinds, etc.*⟩

**tausend·mal** *Adv.* a thousand times

**Tausend·mark·schein** *der* thousand-mark note

**tausendst...** *Ordinalz.* thousandth; *s. auch* ACHT...

**tausendstel** *Bruchz.* thousandth

**Tausendstel** *das* (schweiz. meist *der*); ~s, ~: thousandth

**Tau-:** ~**wasser** *das* meltwater; ~**wetter** *das* thaw; ~**ziehen** *das;* ~~s (auch fig.) tug-of-war

**Taxe** *die;* ~, ~n (a) (Taxi) taxi (b) (Gebühr) charge

**Taxi** *das;* ~s, ~s taxi

**taxieren** *tr. V.* estimate

**Taxi-:** ~**fahrer** *der,* ~**fahrerin** *die* taxi driver; ~**stand** *der* taxi rank (Brit.); taxi stand

**Tb** /te:'be:/, **Tbc** /te:be:'ts:e:/ *die;* ~: *Abk.* = **Tuberkulose** TB

**Team** /ti:m/ *das;* ~s, ~s team

**Team·arbeit** *die* teamwork

**Technik** *die;* ~, ~en (a) technology; (Studienfach) engineering *no art.;* (b) (technische Ausrüstung) equipment (c) (Arbeitsweise, Verfahren) technique

**Techniker** *der;* ~s, ~, **Technikerin** *die;* ~, ~nen technical expert

**technisch** ①*Adj.* technical; technological ⟨*progress, age*⟩ ② *adv.* technically; technologically ⟨*advanced*⟩

**Techno** /'tɛkno/ *das od. der;* ~s techno

**Technologie** *die;* ~, ~n technology

**technologisch** ①*Adj.* technological ② *adv.* technologically

**Techno·party** *die* techno party

**Tee** *der;* ~s, ~s tea

**TEE** /te:|e:'|e:/ *der;* ~[s], ~[s] *Abk.* = **Trans-Europ-Express** TEE

**Tee-:** ~**beutel** *der* tea bag; ~**kanne** *die* teapot; ~**löffel** *der* teaspoon

**Teenie** /'ti:ni/ *der;* ~s, ~s (ugs.) young teenager

**Tee-:** ~**sieb** *das* tea strainer; ~**tasse** *die* teacup

**Teich** *der;* ~[e]s, ~e pond

**Teig** *der;* ~[e]s, ~e dough; (Kuchen-, Biskuitteig) pastry; (Pfannkuchen-, Waffelteig) batter

**Teig·waren** *Pl.* pasta *sing.*

**Teil** (a) *der;* ~[e]s, ~e part; **fünfter** ~: fifth (b) *der od. das;* ~[e]s, ~e (Anteil; Beitrag) share (c) *der;* ~[e]s, ~e (beteiligte Person[en]; Rechtsw.: Partei) party (d) *das;* ~[e]s, ~e (Einzelteil) part

**teil·bar** *Adj.* divisible (**durch** by)

**Teilbarkeit** *die;* ~: divisibility

**Teilchen** *das;* ~s, ~ (a) (kleines Stück) [small] part (b) (Partikel) particle

**teilen** ①*tr. V.* (a) divide (**durch** by) (b) (aufteilen) share (**unter** + *Dat.* among) ② *refl. V.* **sich** (*Dat.*) etw. [**mit** jmdm.] ~: share sth. [with sb.]

**Teiler** *der;* ~s, ~ (Math.) factor

**teil|haben** *unr. itr. V.* share (**an** + *Dat.* in)

**Teilhaber** *der;* ~s, ~, **Teilhaberin** *die;* ~, ~nen partner

**Teil·kasko·versicherung** *die: insurance giving limited cover*

**Teilnahme** *die;* ~, ~n (a) participation (**an** + *Dat.* in); ~ **an einem Kurs** attendance at a course (b) (Interesse) interest (**an** + *Dat.* in) (c) (geh.: Mitgefühl) sympathy

**teilnahms·los** *Adj.* indifferent

**Teilnahmslosigkeit** *die;* ~: indifference

**teilnahms·voll** ①*Adj.* compassionate ② *adv.* compassionately

**teil|nehmen** *unr. itr. V.* [**an** etw. (*Dat.*)] ~: take part [in sth.]; [**an einem Lehrgang**] ~: attend [a course]

**Teilnehmer** *der;* ~s, ~, **Teilnehmerin** *die;* ~, ~nen (a) participant (*Gen.,* **an** + *Dat.* in); (bei Wettbewerb auch) competitor, contestant (**an** + *Dat.* in) (b) (Fernspr.) subscriber

**teils** *Adv.* partly

**Teilung** *die;* ~, ~en division

**teil·weise** ①*Adv.* partly ② *adj.* partial

**Teilzeit-:** ~**arbeit** *die* part-time work *no indef. art.;* ~**job** *der* part-time job

**Teint** /tɛ̃:/ *der;* ~s, ~s complexion

**Telefon** /'te:lefo:n, *auch* tele'fo:n/ *das;* ~s, ~e telephone; phone; **ans** ~ **gehen** answer the [tele]phone

**Telefon-:** ~**anruf** *der* [tele]phone call; ~**anschluss,** *\**~**anschluß** *der* telephone; line; ~**apparat** *der* telephone

**Telefonat** *das;* ~[e]s, ~e telephone call

**Telefon-:** ~**buch** *das* [tele]phone book *or* directory; ~**gespräch** *das* telephone conversation

**telefonieren** *itr. V.* make a [tele]phone call; **mit** jmdm. ~: talk to sb. [on the telephone]

**telefonisch** ①*Adj.* telephone *attrib.* ② *adv.* by telephone

**Telefonist** *der;* ~en, ~en, **Telefonistin** *die;* ~, ~nen telephonist; (in einer Firma) switchboard operator

**Telefon-:** ~**karte** *die* phonecard; ~**nummer** *die* [tele]phone number; ~**rechnung** *die* [tele]phone bill; ~**verzeichnis** *das* [tele]phone list; ~**zelle** *die* [tele]phone booth *or* (Brit.) box; call box (Brit.); ~**zentrale** *die* telephone exchange

---

*\*alte Schreibung - vgl. Hinweis auf S. xiv

**Telegraf** *der;* ~en, ~en telegraph
**Telegrafie** *die;* ~: telegraphy *no art.*
**telegrafieren** *itr., tr. V.* telegraph
**telegrafisch** ⓵ *Adj.* telegraphic
  ⓶ *adv.* by telegraph *or* telegram
**Telegramm** *das* telegram
**Tele-objektiv** *das* (Fot.) telephoto lens
**Tele-text** *der* teletext *no art.*
**Teller** *der;* ~s, ~: plate
**Tempel** *der;* ~s, ~: temple
**Temperament** *das;* ~[e]s, ~e (a)
  (Wesensart) temperament
  **(b)** (Schwung) **eine Frau mit** ~: a woman with
  spirit; **das** ~ **geht oft mit mir durch** I often
  lose my temper
**temperament·voll** *Adj.* spirited ⟨*person,
  speech, dance, etc.*⟩
**Temperatur** *die;* ~, ~en temperature
**Temperatur-:** ~**anstieg** *der* rise in
  temperature; ~**rückgang** *der* drop *or* fall
  in temperature
**Tempo** *das;* ~s, ~s *od.* **Tempi** (a) *Pl.* ~s
  speed
  **(b)** (Musik) tempo; time
**Tempo·limit** *das* (Verkehrsw.) speed limit
**Tempus** *das;* ~, **Tempora** (Sprachw.) tense
**Tendenz** *die;* ~, ~en trend
**tendieren** *itr. V.* tend (**zu** towards)
**Teneriffa** (*das*)*;* ~s Tenerife
**Tennis** *das;* ~: tennis *no art.*
**Tennis-:** ~**ball** *der* tennis ball; ~**platz**
  *der* tennis court; ~**schläger** *der* tennis
  racket; ~**schuh** *der* tennis shoe;
  ~**schule** *die* tennis school; ~**spieler**
  *der,* ~**spielerin** *die* tennis player
**Tenor** *der;* ~s, **Tenöre**, (österr. auch:) ~e
  (Musik) tenor; (im Chor) tenors *pl.;* tenor
  voices *pl.*
**Teppich** *der;* ~s, ~e carpet; (kleiner) rug
**Teppich·boden** *der* fitted carpet
**Termin** *der;* ~s, ~e date; (Anmeldung)
  appointment; (Verabredung) engagement;
  (Rechtsw.) hearing
**Terminal** /'tø:ɐminəl/ *das;* ~s, ~s
  terminal
**Termin-:** ~**geschäft** *das* (Börsenw.)
  forward transaction *or* operation;
  ~**kalender** *der* appointments book
**Terminus** *der;* ~, **Termini** term
**Terpentin** *das,* (österr. meist:) *der;* ~s (a)
  (Harz) turpentine
  **(b)** (ugs.: Terpentinöl) turps *sing.* (coll.)
**Terpentin·öl** *das* oil of turpentine
**Terrain** /tɛ'rɛ̃:/ *das;* ~s, ~s terrain
**Terrasse** *die;* ~, ~n terrace
**Terrier** /'tɛriɐ/ *der;* ~s, ~: terrier
**Terrine** *die;* ~, ~n tureen
**Territorium** *das;* ~s, **Territorien** territory
**Terror** *der;* ~s terrorism *no art.*
**Terror·anschlag** *der* terrorist attack
**terrorisieren** *tr. V.* (a) terrorize

**(b)** (ugs.: belästigen) pester
**Terrorismus** *der;* ~: terrorism *no art.*
**Terrorist** *der;* ~en, ~en, **Terroristin**
  *die;* ~, ~nen terrorist
**Terz** *die;* ~, ~en (Musik) third
**Test** *der;* ~[e]s, ~s *od.* ~e test
**Testament** *das;* ~[e]s, ~e (a) will
  **(b)** (christl. Rel.) Testament
**Test·bogen** *der* test paper
**testen** *tr. V.* test (**auf** + *Akk.* for)
**teuer** ⓵ *Adj.* expensive; dear *usu. pred.;*
  **wie** ~ **war das?** how much did that cost?
  ⓶ *adv.* expensively; dearly; **etw.** ~ **kaufen/
  verkaufen** pay a great deal for sth./sell sth.
  at a high price
**Teuerung** *die;* ~, ~en rise in prices
**Teuerungs·rate** *die* rate of price
  increases
**Teufel** *der;* ~s, ~: devil
**Teufels·zeug** *das* (ugs.) terrible stuff (coll.)
**teuflisch** ⓵ *Adj.* (a) devilish, fiendish
  ⟨*plan, trick, etc.*⟩; diabolical ⟨*laughter,
  pleasure, etc.*⟩
  **(b)** (ugs.: groß, intensiv) terrible (coll.); dreadful
  (coll.)
  ⓶ *adv.* (a) diabolically
  **(b)** (ugs.) terribly (coll.)
**Text** *der;* ~[e]s, ~e text; (Wortlaut) wording;
  (eines Theaterstücks) script; (einer Oper) libretto;
  (eines Liedes, Chansons usw.) words *pl.;* (eines
  Schlagers) words *pl.;* lyrics *pl.;* (zu einer
  Abbildung) caption
**texten** *tr. V.* write ⟨*song, advertisement,
  etc.*⟩
**Textilien** *Pl.* (a) textiles
  **(b)** (Fertigwaren) textile goods
**Textil·industrie** *die* textile industry
**Text·verarbeitung** *die* text processing;
  word processing
**Thailand** (*das*)*;* ~s Thailand
**Theater** *das;* ~s, ~ (a) theatre; **ins** ~
  **gehen** go to the theatre; **im** ~: at the
  theatre; ~ **spielen** act; (fig.) play-act; pretend
  **(b)** (fig. ugs.) fuss
**Theater-:** ~**abonnement** *das* theatre
  subscription [ticket]; ~**stück** *das* [stage]
  play
**Theke** *die;* ~, ~n (a) (Schanktisch) bar
  **(b)** (Ladentisch) counter
**Thema** *das;* ~s, **Themen** subject; topic;
  (einer Abhandlung) subject; theme; (Leitgedanke)
  theme
**Themse** *die;* ~: Thames
**Theologe** *der;* ~n, ~n theologian
**Theologie** *die;* ~, ~n theology *no art.*
**Theologin** *die;* ~, ~: theologian
**theologisch** ⓵ *Adj.* theological
  ⓶ *adv.* theologically
**theoretisch** ⓵ *Adj.* theoretical
  ⓶ *adv.* theoretically
**Theorie** *die;* ~, ~n theory

**Therap<u>eu</u>t** *der;* ~en, ~en,
  **Therap<u>eu</u>tin** *die;* ~, ~nen therapist;
therapeutist
**therap<u>eu</u>tisch** ⨐ *Adj.* therapeutic
  ⨑ *adv.* therapeutically
**Therap<u>ie</u>** *die;* ~, ~n therapy (**gegen** for)
**therap<u>ie</u>ren** *tr. V.* treat
**Thermo-m<u>e</u>ter** *das (österr. u. schweiz. der*
*od. das)* thermometer
**Th<u>e</u>rmos-flasche** Ⓦⓩ *die* Thermos flask
®; vacuum flask
**Thermost<u>a</u>t** *der;* ~[e]s *od.* ~en, ~e *od.*
~en thermostat
**Th<u>e</u>se** *die;* ~, ~n thesis
**Thr<u>o</u>n** *der;* ~[e]s, ~e throne
**Th<u>u</u>n-fisch** *der* tuna
**Th<u>ü</u>ringen** *(das);* ~s Thuringia
**Th<u>ü</u>ringer Wald** *der;* ~ ~[e]s Thuringian
Forest
**Th<u>y</u>mian** *der;* ~s, ~e thyme
**T<u>i</u>ck** *der;* ~[e]s, ~s (a) (ugs.: Schrulle) quirk;
thing (coll.)
  **(b)** (ugs.: Nuance) tiny bit; shade
**t<u>i</u>cken** *itr. V.* tick; **du tickst wohl nicht**
**richtig** (salopp) you must be off your rocker
(coll.)
**Ticket** *das;* ~s, ~s ticket
**t<u>ie</u>f** ⨐ *Adj.* (auch fig.) deep; (niedrig) low; low
⟨neckline, bow⟩; deep; intense ⟨pain,
suffering⟩
  ⨑ *adv.* deep; (niedrig) low; (intensiv) deeply;
⟨stoop, bow⟩ low; ⟨breathe, inhale⟩ deeply
**T<u>ie</u>f** *das;* ~s, ~s (Met.) low
**t<u>ie</u>f-blau** *Adj.* deep blue
**T<u>ie</u>f-druck** *der* (Met.) low pressure
**T<u>ie</u>fe** *die;* ~, ~n depth; **in die** ~ **stürzen**
plunge into the depths
**t<u>ie</u>f-, T<u>ie</u>f-:** ~**garage** *die* underground
car park; ~**greifend** ⨐ *Adj.* profound;
profound, deep ⟨crisis⟩; far-reaching
⟨improvement⟩; ⨑ *adv.* profoundly;
~**gründig** *Adj.* profound; ~|**kühlen** *tr. V.*
[deep-]freeze
**T<u>ie</u>f-kühl-:** ~**fach** *das* freezer
[compartment]; ~**kost** *die* frozen food
**t<u>ie</u>f-, T<u>ie</u>f-:** ~**punkt** *der* low [point];
~**schlag** *der* (Boxen) low punch; punch
below the belt (lit. or fig.); ~**see** *die* (Geogr.)
deep sea; ~**sinnig** ⨐ *Adj.* profound;
⨑ *adv.* profoundly
**T<u>ie</u>fst-temperatur** *die* minimum *or*
lowest temperature
**T<u>ie</u>gel** *der;* ~s, ~ (zum Kochen) pan;
(Schmelztiegel) crucible; (Behälter) pot
**T<u>ie</u>r** *das;* ~[e]s, ~e animal
**T<u>ie</u>r-:** ~**arzt** *der,* ~**ärztin** *die* veterinary
surgeon; vet; ~**garten** *der* zoo; zoological
garden; ~**heim** *das* animal home
**t<u>ie</u>risch** ⨐ *Adj.* (a) animal *attrib.;* savage
⟨cruelty, crime⟩

  **(b)** (ugs.: unerträglich groß) terrible (coll.); ~**er**
**Ernst** deadly seriousness
  ⨑ *adv.* **(a)** ⟨roar⟩ like an animal; savagely
⟨cruel⟩
  **(b)** (ugs.: unerträglich) terribly (coll.)
**t<u>ie</u>r-, T<u>ie</u>r-:** ~**kreis** *der* (Astron., Astrol.)
zodiac; ~**kreis-zeichen** *das* (Astron.,
Astrol.) sign of the zodiac; ~**lieb** *Adj.* animal-
loving *attrib.;* fond of animals *postpos.;*
~**park** *der* zoo; ~**pfleger** *der,*
~**pflegerin** *die* animal keeper;
~**quälerei** /---'-/ *die* cruelty to animals;
~**reich** *das* animal kingdom
**T<u>i</u>ger** *der;* ~s, ~: tiger
**t<u>i</u>lgen** *tr. V.* **(a)** (geh.) delete ⟨word, letter,
error⟩; erase ⟨record, endorsement⟩; (fig.) wipe
out ⟨shame, guilt, traces⟩
  **(b)** (Wirtsch., Bankw.) repay; pay off
**T<u>i</u>lgung** *die;* ~, ~en **(a)** (geh.) ▶ TILGEN A:
deletion; erasure; wiping out
  **(b)** (Wirtsch., Bankw.) repayment
**T<u>i</u>lsiter** *der;* ~s, ~: Tilsit [cheese]
**T<u>i</u>nte** *die;* ~, ~n ink; **in der** ~ **sitzen** (ugs.)
be in the soup (coll.)
**T<u>i</u>nten-:** ~**fisch** *der* cuttlefish; (Krake)
octopus; ~**strahl-drucker** *der* (DV) ink-jet
printer
**\*T<u>i</u>p, T<u>i</u>pp** *der;* ~s, ~s **(a)** (ugs.) tip
  **(b)** (bei Toto, Lotto usw.) [row of] numbers
**t<u>i</u>ppen** ⨐ *itr. V.* **(a)** an/**gegen etw.** *(Akk.)* ~:
tap sth.
  **(b)** (ugs.: Maschine schreiben) type
  **(c)** (wetten) do the pools/lottery *etc.;* **im Lotto**
~: do the lottery
  ⨑ *tr. V.* **(a)** tap
  **(b)** (ugs.: mit der Maschine schreiben) type
  **(c)** (setzen auf) choose; **sechs Richtige** ~:
make six correct selections
**T<u>i</u>pp-:** ~**fehler** *der* typing error *or*
mistake; ~**gemeinschaft** *die* pools/
lottery *etc.* syndicate
**t<u>i</u>pp-t<u>o</u>pp** (ugs.) ⨐ *Adj.* (tadellos)
immaculate; (erstklassig) tip-top
  ⨑ *adv.* immaculately
**Tir<u>o</u>l** *(das);* ~s [the] Tyrol
**Tir<u>o</u>ler** *der;* ~s, ~, **Tir<u>o</u>lerin** *die;* ~,
~nen Tyrolese; Tyrolean
**T<u>i</u>sch** *der;* ~[e]s, ~e table; **reinen** ~
**machen** (ugs.) sort things out
**T<u>i</u>sch-:** ~**dame** *die* dinner partner;
~**decke** *die* tablecloth; ~**gebet** *das* grace
*no pl.;* ~**herr** *der* dinner partner; ~**lampe**
*die* table lamp
**T<u>i</u>schler** *der;* ~s, ~: joiner; (bes. Kunst~)
cabinetmaker
**T<u>i</u>schlerei** *die;* ~, ~en ▶ TISCHLER: **(a)**
(Werkstatt) joiner's/cabinetmaker's [workshop]
  **(b)** (Handwerk) joinery/cabinetmaking
**T<u>i</u>schlerin** *die;* ~, ~nen ▶ TISCHLER
**T<u>i</u>sch-:** ~**nachbar** *der* person next to one
[at table]; ~**platte** *die* table top; ~**tennis**
*das* table tennis; ~**tuch** *das; Pl.* ~**tücher**

tablecloth; ~**wäsche** *die* table linen;
~**wein** *der* table wine; ~**zeit** *die*
lunchtime
**Titel** *der;* ~s, ~ (a) title
(b) (ugs.: Musikstück, Song usw.) number
**Titel-:** ~**bild** *das* cover picture; ~**blatt**
*das* title page; ~**rolle** *die* title role;
~**seite** *die* (a) (einer Zeitung, Zeitschrift) [front]
cover; (b) (eines Buchs) title page
**Titte** *die;* ~, ~n (derb) tit (coarse)
**titulieren** *tr. V.* call
**tja** /tja(:)/ *Interj.* [yes] well; (Resignation
ausdrückend) oh, well
**Toast** /to:st/ *der;* ~[e]s, ~e *od.* ~s toast
**Toast-brot** *das* [sliced white] bread for
toasting
**toasten** *tr. V.* toast
**Toaster** *der;* ~s, ~: toaster
**toben** *itr. V.* (a) go wild (**vor** + *Dat.* with);
(fig.) ⟨*storm, sea, battle*⟩ rage
(b) (tollen) romp *or* charge about
(c) *mit sein* (laufen) charge
**Tochter** *die;* ~, Töchter (a) daughter
(b) (Wirtsch.) subsidiary
**Tochter·gesellschaft** *die* (Wirtsch.)
subsidiary [company]
**Tod** *der;* ~[e]s, ~e death; **eines natürlichen/
gewaltsamen** ~**es sterben** die a natural/
violent death; **jmdn. zum** ~**e verurteilen**
sentence sb. to death
**tod·ernst** ①*Adj.* deadly serious
②*adv.* deadly seriously
**Todes-:** ~**anzeige** *die* (a) (in einer Zeitung)
death notice; (b) (Karte) card announcing a
*person's death;* ~**fall** *der* death; (in der
Familie) bereavement; ~**nachricht** *die*
news of his/her/their *etc.* death; ~**opfer**
*das* death; fatality; ~**strafe** *die* death
penalty; ~**ursache** *die* cause of death;
~**urteil** *das* death sentence;
~**verachtung** *die* [utter] fearlessness in
the face of death; **etw. mit** ~**verachtung
essen/trinken** (ugs.) force sth. down [without
showing one's distaste]
**Tod·feind** *der,* Tod·feindin *die* deadly
enemy
**tod·krank** *Adj.* critically ill
**tödlich** ①*Adj.* (a) fatal ⟨*accident, illness,
outcome, etc.*⟩; lethal, deadly ⟨*poison, bite,
shot, trap, etc.*⟩; lethal ⟨*dose*⟩
(b) (sehr groß, ausgeprägt) deadly ⟨*hatred,
seriousness, certainty, boredom*⟩
②*adv.* (a) fatally
(b) (sehr) terribly (coll.)
**tod-, Tod-:** ~**müde** *Adj.* dead tired;
~**schick** (ugs.) ①*Adj.* dead smart (coll.);
②*adv.* dead smartly (coll.); ~**sicher** (ugs.)
①*Adj.* sure-fire (coll.); ②*adv.* for certain *or*
sure; ~**sünde** *die* (auch fig.) deadly *or*
mortal sin; ~**unglücklich** *Adj.* (ugs.)
extremely *or* desperately unhappy
**Toilette** /tǫa'lɛtǝ/ *die;* ~, ~n toilet
**Toiletten·papier** *das* toilet paper

**toi, toi, toi** /'tɔy: 'tɔy: 'tɔy:/ *Interj.* good
luck!; (unberufen!) touch wood!
**Tokio** (*das*); ~s Tokyo
**tolerant** ①*Adj.* tolerant (**gegen** of)
②*adv.* tolerantly
**Toleranz** *die;* ~: tolerance
**tolerierbar** *Adj.* tolerable
**tolerieren** *tr. V.* tolerate
**toll** ①*Adj.* (a) (ugs.) (großartig) great (coll.);
fantastic (coll.); (erstaunlich) amazing; (heftig,
groß) enormous ⟨*respect*⟩; terrific (coll.) ⟨*noise,
storm*⟩
(b) (wild) wild
②*adv.* (a) (ugs.: großartig) terrifically well
(coll.)
(b) (ugs.: heftig) ⟨*rain, snow*⟩ like billy-o (coll.)
(c) (wild) **bei dem Fest ging es** ~ **zu** it was a
wild party
**Tolle** *die;* ~, ~n quiff
**tollen** *itr. V.* (a) romp about
(b) *mit sein* romp
**toll-, Toll-:** ~**kühn** ①*Adj.* daredevil
*attrib.;* daring; ②*adv.* daringly; ~**wut** *die*
rabies *sing.;* ~**wütig** *Adj.* rabid
**Tollpatsch** *der;* ~[e]s, ~e (ugs.) clumsy *or*
awkward creature
**tollpatschig** (ugs.) ①*Adj.* clumsy;
awkward
②*adv.* clumsily; awkwardly
***Tolpatsch** *usw.* ▶ TOLLPATSCH *usw.*
**Tölpel** *der;* ~s, ~: fool
**tölpelhaft** ①*Adj.* foolish
②*adv.* foolishly
**Tomate** *die;* ~, ~n tomato
**Tomaten·mark** *das* tomato purée
**Tombola** *die;* ~, ~s raffle
**Ton¹** *der;* ~[e]s, ~e clay
**Ton²** *der;* ~[e]s, Töne (a) (auch Physik, Musik;
beim Telefon) tone; (Klang) note
(b) (Film, Ferns. usw., Tonwiedergabe) sound
(c) (ugs.: Äußerung) word
(d) (Farb~) shade
(e) (Akzent) stress
**ton-, Ton-:** ~**angebend** *Adj.*
predominant; ~**art** *die* (a) (Musik) key; (b)
(fig.) tone; ~**band** *das; Pl.* ~bänder tape;
~**band-gerät** *das* tape recorder;
~**effekt** *der* sound effect
**tönen** ①*itr. V.* (geh.) sound; ⟨*bell*⟩ sound,
ring; (schallen, widerhallen) resound
②*tr. V.* (färben) tint
**Ton-:** ~**fall** *der* tone; (Intonation) intonation;
~**höhe** *die* pitch; ~**leiter** *die* (Musik) scale
**Tonne** *die;* ~, ~n (a) (Behälter) drum;
(Mülltonne) bin; (Regentonne) water butt
(b) (Gewicht) tonne
**tonnen·weise** *Adv., adj.* by the ton
**Ton·qualität** *die* sound quality
**Tönung** *die;* ~, ~en tint; shade
**Tool** /tu:l/ *das;* ~s, ~s (DV) tool
**Topf** *der;* ~es, Töpfe (a) pot; (Braten~,
Schmor~) casserole; (Stielkasserolle) saucepan ⋯▸

**(b)** (zur Aufbewahrung) pot
**(c)** (Krug) jug
**(d)** (Nachttopf) chamber pot; (für Kinder) potty (Brit. coll.)
**(e)** (Blumentopf) [flower]pot
**Topf·blume** die [flowering] pot plant
**Töpfchen** das; ~s, ~: potty (Brit. coll.)
**Töpfer** der; ~s, ~ potter
**Töpferei** die; ~, ~en **(a)** (Handwerk) pottery no art.;
**(b)** (Werkstatt) pottery; potter's workshop
**(c)** (Erzeugnis) piece of pottery; ~en pottery sing.
**Töpferin** die; ~, ~nen ▶ TÖPFER
**Topf-:** ~**lappen** der oven cloth; ~**pflanze** die pot plant
**Tor¹** das; ~[e]s, ~e **(a)** gate; (einer Garage, Scheune) door; (fig.) gateway
**(b)** (Ballspiele) goal
**(c)** (Ski) gate
**Tor²** der; ~en, ~en (geh.: Narr) fool
**Torf** der; ~[e]s, ~e peat
**Torheit** die; ~, ~en (geh.) **(a)** foolishness
**(b)** (Handlung) foolish act
**Tor·hüter** der, **Tor·hüterin** die (Ballspiele) goalkeeper
**töricht** (geh.) ☐1 Adj. foolish
☐2 adv. foolishly
**torkeln** itr. V.; mit sein stagger
**Tor·mann** der; Pl. **Tormänner** od. **Torleute** (Ballspiele) goalkeeper
**Tornister** /tɔrˈnɪstɐ/ der; ~s, ~: knapsack; (Schulranzen) satchel
**torpedieren** tr. V. (Milit., fig.) torpedo
**Torpedo** der; ~s, ~s torpedo
**Törtchen** das; ~s, ~: tartlet
**Torte** die; ~, ~n (Creme-, Sahnetorte) gateau; (Obsttorte) [fruit] flan
**Torten-:** ~**boden** der flan case; (ohne Rand) flan base; ~**guss**, *~**guß** der glaze; ~**heber** der; ~s, ~: cake slice
**Tortur** die; ~, ~en **(a)** ordeal
**(b)** (veralt.: Folter) torture
**Tor-:** ~**wart** der; ~~[e]s, ~~e, ~**wartin** die; ~~, ~~**nen** (Ballspiele) goalkeeper; ~**weg** der gateway
**tosen** itr. V. roar; ⟨storm⟩ rage
**tot** Adj. dead; ~ umfallen drop dead; sich ~ stellen pretend to be dead; play dead; ~ geboren stillborn
**total** ☐1 Adj. total
☐2 adv. totally
**Total·ausverkauf** der clearance sale
**totalitär** (Politik) ☐1 Adj. totalitarian
☐2 adv. in a totalitarian way; ⟨organized, run⟩ along totalitarian lines
**Total·schaden** der (Versicherungsw.) an beiden Fahrzeugen entstand ~: both vehicles were a write-off
**tot|ärgern** refl. V. (ugs.) get livid (coll.)

---

**Tote** der/die; adj. Dekl. dead person; **die** ~**n** the dead
**töten** tr., itr. V. kill; deaden ⟨nerve etc.⟩
**toten-, Toten-:** ~**blass**, *~**blaß**, ~**bleich** Adj. deathly pale; ~**gräber** der; ~~s, ~~, ~~**gräberin** die; ~~, ~~**nen** gravedigger; ~**kopf** der **(a)** skull; **(b)** (als Symbol) death's head; (mit gekreuzten Knochen) skull and crossbones; ~**schädel** der skull; ~**sonntag** der (ev. Kirche) Sunday before Advent on which the dead are commemorated; ~**still** Adj. deathly quiet; ~**stille** die deathly silence; ~**wache** die vigil by the body
**tot-, Tot-:** ~|**fahren** unr. tr. V. [run over and] kill; *~**geboren** ▶ TOT; ~**geburt** die still birth; ~|**lachen** refl. V. (ugs.) kill oneself laughing; zum Totlachen sein be killing (coll.)
**Toto** das od. der; ~s, ~s **(a)** (Pferdetoto) tote (coll.); im ~: on the tote
**(b)** (Fußballtoto) [football] pools pl.; [im] ~ spielen do the pools
**Toto·schein** der; ▶ TOTO: pools coupon/ (coll.) tote ticket
**tot-, Tot-:** ~|**schießen** unr. tr. V. (ugs.) jmdn. ~**schießen** shoot sb. dead; ~**schlag** der (Rechtsw.) manslaughter no indef. art.; ~|**schlagen** unr. tr. V. beat to death; *~|**stellen** ▶ TOT; ~|**treten** unr. tr. V. trample ⟨person⟩ to death; step on and kill ⟨insect⟩
**Tötung** die; ~, ~en killing; **fahrlässige** ~ (Rechtsspr.) manslaughter by culpable negligence
**Touch** /tatʃ/ der; ~s, ~s (ugs.) touch
**tough** /taf/ Adj. (ugs.) tough
**Toupet** /tuˈpe:/ das; ~s, ~s toupee
**toupieren** /tuˈpiːrən/ tr. V. backcomb
**Tour** /tuːɐ̯/ die; ~, ~en tour (**durch** of); (kürzere Fahrt, Ausflug) trip; (mit dem Auto) drive; (mit dem Fahrrad) ride; (feste Strecke) route; **in einer** ~ (ugs.) the whole time
**touren** /ˈtuːrən/ itr. V.; mit sein tour
**Tourismus** /tuˈrɪsmʊs/ der; ~: tourism no art.
**Tourismus·branche** die tourism industry; tourist industry;
**Tourist** der; ~en, ~en tourist
**Touristen-:** ~**klasse** die tourist class; ~**zentrum** das tourist centre
**Touristin** die; ~, ~nen tourist
**Tournee** /tʊrˈne:/ die; ~, ~s od. ~n tour; **auf** ~ **sein/gehen** be/go on tour
**Trab** der; ~[e]s trot; **im** ~: at a trot; **im** ~ **reiten** trot
**traben** itr. V.; mit sein (auch ugs.: laufen) trot
**Tracht** die; ~, ~en **(a)** (Volkstracht) national costume; (Berufstracht) uniform
**(b)** **eine** ~ **Prügel** a thrashing; (als Strafe) a hiding
**trachten** itr. V. (geh.) strive (**nach** for, after)
**Tradition** die; ~, ~en tradition

**traditionell** [1] *Adj.* traditional
[2] *adv.* traditionally

**traf** *1. u. 3. Pers. Sg. Prät. v.* TREFFEN

**träfe** *1. u. 3. Pers. Sg. Konjunktiv II v.*
TREFFEN

**Trafik** *die;* ~, ~en (österr.) tobacconist's
[shop]

**Trag·bahre** *die* stretcher

**tragbar** *Adj.* (a) portable
(b) wearable ⟨*clothes*⟩
(c) (finanziell) supportable ⟨*cost, debt, etc.*⟩
(d) (erträglich) bearable; tolerable

**träge** [1] *Adj.* sluggish
[2] *adv.* sluggishly

**Trage** *die;* ~, ~n (a) (Bahre) stretcher
(b) (Traggestell) pannier

**tragen** [1] *unr. tr. V.* (a) carry
(b) (bringen) take
(c) (ertragen) bear ⟨*fate, destiny*⟩; bear, endure
⟨*suffering*⟩
(d) (halten) hold; **einen/den linken Arm in der
Schlinge** ~: have one's arm/one's left arm
in a sling
(e) (von unten stützen) support
(f) (belastbar sein durch) be able to carry *or*
take ⟨*weight*⟩
(g) (übernehmen, aufkommen für) bear, carry
⟨*costs etc.*⟩; take ⟨*blame, responsibility,
consequences*⟩
(h) (am Körper) wear ⟨*clothes, wig, glasses,
jewellery, etc.*⟩
(i) have ⟨*false teeth, beard, etc.*⟩
(j) (hervorbringen) ⟨*tree*⟩ bear ⟨*fruit*⟩; ⟨*field*⟩
produce ⟨*crops*⟩
[2] *unr. itr. V.* (a) carry
(b) (am Körper) **man trägt [wieder] kurz/lang**
short/long skirts are in fashion [again]
(c) **der Baum trägt gut** the tree produces a
good crop

**tragend** *Adj.* (Stabilität gebend) load-bearing;
supporting ⟨*wall, column, function, etc.*⟩

**Träger** *der;* ~s, ~ (a) porter
(b) (Austräger) paper boy/girl; delivery boy/
girl
(c) (Bauw.) girder; [supporting] beam
(d) (an Kleidung) strap; (Hosenträger) braces *pl.;*
(e) (Inhaber) (eines Amts) holder; (eines Namens,
Titels) bearer; (eines Preises) winner

**Trägerin** *die;* ~, ~nen ▶ TRÄGER A, B, E

**Trage·tasche** *die* carrier bag

**Trag-:** ~**fähigkeit** *die* load-bearing
capacity; ~**fläche** *die* wing;
~**flügel·boot** *das* hydrofoil

**Trägheit** *die;* ~, ~en sluggishness

**Tragik** *die;* ~: tragedy

**tragi·komisch** [1] *Adj.* tragicomic
[2] *adv.* tragicomically

**tragisch** [1] *Adj.* tragic; **das ist nicht [so]**
~ (ugs.) it's not the end of the world (coll.)
[2] *adv.* tragically

**Tragödie** /tra'gøːdiə/ *die;* ~, ~n tragedy

**Trag·weite** *die* consequences *pl.*

**Trainer** /'trɛːnɐ/ *der;* ~s, ~, **Trainerin**
*die;* ~, ~nen coach; trainer; (einer
Fußballmannschaft) manager

**trainieren** [1] *tr. V.* (a) train; coach
⟨*swimmer, tennis player*⟩; manage ⟨*football
team*⟩; exercise ⟨*muscles etc.*⟩
(b) (üben, einüben) practise ⟨*exercise, jump,
etc.*⟩; **Fußball** ~: do football training
[2] *itr. V.* train

**Training** /'trɛːnɪŋ/ *das;* ~s, ~s training *no
indef. art.*

**Trainings-:** ~**anzug** *der* track suit;
~**hose** *die* track-suit bottoms *pl.* ~**lager**
*das* training camp

**Trakt** *der;* ~[e]s, ~e section; (Flügel) wing

**Traktor** *der;* ~s, ~en tractor

**trällern** *itr., tr. V.* warble

**trampeln** [1] *itr. V.* (a) [mit den Füßen] ~:
stamp one's feet
(b) *mit sein* (treten) trample (**auf** + *Akk.* on)
[2] *tr. V.* trample

**Trampel·pfad** *der* [beaten] path

**trampen** /'trɛmpn̩/ *itr. V. mit sein* hitch-
hike

**Tramper** *der;* ~s, ~, **Tramperin** *die;* ~,
~nen hitch-hiker

**Trampolin** *das;* ~s, ~e trampoline

**Tramway** /'tramve/ *die;* ~, ~s (österr.)
tram (Brit.); streetcar (Amer.)

**Tran** *der;* ~[e]s train-oil

**Trance** /'trãːs(ə)/ *die;* ~, ~n trance; **in** ~:
in a trance

**tranchieren** /trã'ʃiːrən/ *tr. V.* carve

**Träne** *die;* ~, ~n tear; ~**n lachen** laugh till
one cries

**tränen** *itr. V.* ⟨*eyes*⟩ water

**tranig** *Adj.* (ugs. abwertend: langsam) sluggish;
slow

**trank** *1. u. 3. Pers. Sg. Prät. v.* TRINKEN

**Tränke** *die;* ~, ~n watering place

**tränken** *tr. V.* (a) water
(b) (sich voll saugen lassen) soak

**Transfer** *der;* ~s, ~s (bes. Wirtsch., Sport)
transfer

**Transfer·summe** *die* transfer fee

**Trans·formator** *der;* ~s, ~en
transformer

**Transistor** *der;* ~s, ~en transistor

**Transit** /tran'ziːt, *auch:* 'tranzɪt/ *das;* ~s,
~s transit visa

**transitiv** (Sprachw.) [1] *Adj.* transitive
[2] *adv.* transitively

**Transit·verkehr** *der* transit traffic

**transparent** *Adj.* transparent; (Licht
durchlassend) translucent

**Transparent** *das;* ~[e]s, ~e (Spruchband)
banner; (Bild) transparency

**Transparenz** *die;* ~ transparency

**Transport** *der;* ~[e]s, ~e (a)
transportation        ···⟩

**(b)** (beförderte Lebewesen od. Sachen) (mit dem Zug) trainload; (mit mehreren Fahrzeugen) convoy; (Fracht) consignment

**transportabel** *Adj.* transportable; (tragbar) portable

**Transporteur** /...'tøːɐ̯/ *der;* ~s, ~e, **Transporteurin** *die;* ~, ~nen carrier

**transport·fähig** *Adj.* moveable

**transportieren** *tr. V.* transport ⟨goods, people⟩; move ⟨patient⟩

**Transport·kosten** *Pl.* carriage *sing.;* transport costs

**Transvestit** *der;* ~en, ~en transvestite

**Trapez** *das;* ~es, ~e **(a)** (Geom.) trapezium (Brit.); trapezoid (Amer.)
**(b)** (im Zirkus) trapeze

**trappeln** *itr. V.; mit sein* patter [along]; ⟨feet⟩ patter; ⟨hoofs⟩ go clip-clop

**Trara** *das;* ~s (ugs.) razzmatazz (coll.)

**Trasse** *die;* ~, ~n (Verkehrsweg) [marked-out] route *or* line

**trat** *1. u. 3. Pers. Sg. Prät. v.* TRETEN

**Tratsch** *der;* ~[e]s (ugs.) gossip; tittle-tattle

**tratschen** *itr. V.* (ugs.) gossip; (schwatzen) chatter

**Traube** *die;* ~, ~n **(a)** bunch; (von Johannisbeeren usw.) cluster
**(b)** (Weinbeere~) grape
**(c)** (Menschenmenge) bunch; cluster

**trauen** ① *itr. V.* jmdm./einer Sache ~: trust sb./sth.
② *refl. V.* dare
③ *tr. V.* (verheiraten) ⟨vicar, registrar, etc.⟩ marry

**Trauer** *die;* ~ **(a)** grief (über + Akk. over); (um einen Toten) mourning (um + Akk. for);
**(b)** (Trauerzeit) [period of] mourning
**(c)** ~ tragen be in mourning

**Trauer-:** ~fall *der* bereavement; ~feier *die* memorial ceremony; (beim Begräbnis) funeral ceremony; ~karte *die* [pre-printed] card of condolence; ~kleidung *die* mourning clothes *pl.*

**trauern** *itr. V.* mourn; um jmdn. ~: mourn for sb.

**Trauer-:** ~spiel *das* tragedy; (fig. ugs.) deplorable business; ~weide *die* weeping willow

**träufeln** *tr. V.* [let] trickle (in + Akk. into); drip ⟨ear drops etc.⟩

**Traum** *der;* ~[e]s, Träume /'trɔy:mə/ dream

**Trauma** *das;* ~s, Traumen *od.* ~ta (Psych., Med.) trauma

**traumatisch** (Psych., Med.) ① *Adj.* traumatic
② *adv.* traumatically

**träumen** ① *itr. V.* dream (von of, about); (unaufmerksam sein) [day]dream
② *tr. V.* dream

**Träumer** *der;* ~s, ~, **Träumerin** *die;* ~, ~nen dreamer

**träumerisch** ① *Adj.* dreamy
② *adv.* dreamily

**traumhaft** (ugs.) ① *Adj.* marvellous; fabulous (coll.)
② *adv.* fabulously (coll.)

**Traum·urlaub** *der* dream holiday

**traurig** ① *Adj.* **(a)** sad; unhappy ⟨childhood, youth⟩; painful ⟨duty⟩
**(b)** (kümmerlich) sorry ⟨state etc.⟩; miserable ⟨result⟩
② *adv.* sadly

**Traurigkeit** *die;* ~: sadness; sorrow

**Trau-:** ~ring *der* wedding ring; ~schein *der* marriage certificate

**Trauung** *die;* ~, ~en wedding [ceremony]

**Trau·zeuge** *der,* **Trau·zeugin** *die* witness ⟨at wedding ceremony⟩

**Trecker** *der;* ~s, ~: tractor

**Treff** *der;* ~s, ~s (ugs.) rendezvous; (Ort) meeting place

**treffen** ① *unr. tr. V.* **(a)** hit; ⟨punch, blow, object⟩ strike; ihn trifft keine Schuld he is in no way to blame
**(b)** (erschüttern) affect [deeply]; (verletzen) hurt
**(c)** (begegnen) meet
**(d)** (vorfinden) come upon, find ⟨anomalies etc.⟩; es gut/schlecht ~: be *or* strike lucky/be unlucky
**(e)** (als Funktionsverb) make ⟨arrangements, choice, preparations, decision, etc.⟩
② *unr. itr. V.* **(a)** ⟨person, shot, etc.⟩ hit the target; nicht ~: miss [the target]
**(b)** *mit sein* auf etw. (Akk.) ~: come upon sth.; auf Widerstand/Ablehnung/Schwierigkeiten ~: meet with resistance/rejection/difficulties
③ *unr. refl. V.* **(a)** sich mit jmdm. ~: meet sb.
**(b)** *unpers.* es trifft sich gut/schlecht it is convenient/inconvenient

**Treffen** *das;* ~s, ~: meeting

**treffend** ① *Adj.* apt
② *adv.* aptly

**Treffer** *der;* ~s, ~ **(a)** (Milit., Boxen, Fechten usw.) hit; (Schlag) blow; (Ballspiele) goal
**(b)** (Gewinn) win; (Los) winner

**trefflich** (geh.) ① *Adj.* excellent; splendid ⟨person⟩
② *adv.* excellently; splendidly

**treff-, Treff-:** ~punkt *der* meeting place; ~sicher ① *Adj.* accurate ⟨language, mode of expression⟩; unerring ⟨judgement⟩; ② *adv.* accurately; ~sicherheit *die* accuracy

**Treib·eis** *das* drift-ice

**treiben** ① *unr. tr. V.* **(a)** drive
**(b)** (sich beschäftigen mit) go in for ⟨farming, cattle breeding, etc.⟩; study ⟨French etc.⟩; carry on, pursue ⟨studies, trade, craft⟩; viel Sport ~: do a lot of sport; es wüst/übel/toll ~ (ugs.) lead a dissolute/bad life/live it up

2 *unr. itr. V. meist, mit Richtungsangabe*
*nur, mit sein* drift
**Treiben** *das;* ~s **(a)** (Durcheinander) bustle
**(b)** (Tun) activities *pl.;* doings *pl.*

**Treib-:** ~**gas** *das* propellant; ~**haus** *das*
hothouse; ~**haus-effekt** *der* greenhouse
effect; ~**haus-gas** *das* greenhouse gas;
~**stoff** *der* fuel

**Trekking** *das;* ~s trekking

**Trenchcoat** /'trɛntʃkoʊt/ *der;* ~s, ~s
trench coat

**Trend** *der;* ~s, ~s trend (**zu** + *Dat.*
towards); (Mode) vogue

**trendig** *Adj.* (ugs.) modern and fashionable

**trennen** 1 *tr. V.* **(a)** separate (**von** from);
sever ⟨*head, arm*⟩
**(b)** (auftrennen) unpick ⟨*dress, seam*⟩
**(c)** (teilen) divide ⟨*word, parts of a room etc.,*
*fig.: people*⟩
2 *refl. V.* **(a)** (voneinander weggehen) part
[company]
**(b)** (eine Partnerschaft auflösen) ⟨*couple,*
*partners*⟩ split up
**(c)** sich von etw. ~: part with sth.

**Trennung** *die;* ~, ~**en** (von Menschen)
separation (**von** from); (von Gegenständen)
parting; (von Wörtern) division

**trepp-:** ~**ab** *Adv.* down the stairs; ~**auf**
*Adv.* up the stairs

**Treppe** *die;* ~, ~**n** staircase; [flight *sing.*
of] stairs *pl.;* (im Freien, auf der Bühne) [flight
*sing.* of] steps *pl.*

**Treppen-:** ~**absatz** *der* half-landing;
~**geländer** *das* banisters *pl.;* ~**haus** *das*
stairwell; ~**stufe** *die* stair; (im Freien) step

**Tresen** *der;* ~s, ~ (bes. nordd.) bar;
(Ladentisch) counter

**Tresor** *der;* ~s, ~e safe

**Tret-boot** *das* pedalo

**treten** 1 *unr. itr. V.* **(a)** *mit sein* step (**in** +
*Akk.* into, **auf** + *Akk.* on to)
**(b)** (seinen Fuß setzen) **auf etw.** (*Akk.*) ~ tread
on sth.
**(c)** (ausschlagen) kick
2 *unr. tr. V.* **(a)** (Tritt versetzen) kick ⟨*person,*
*ball, etc.*⟩
**(b)** (trampeln) trample ⟨*path*⟩
**(c)** (mit dem Fuß niederdrücken) step on ⟨*brake,*
*pedal*⟩; operate ⟨*bellows, clutch*⟩

**treu** 1 *Adj.* faithful; loyal; faithful
⟨*husband, wife*⟩; loyal ⟨*ally, subject*⟩; **jmdm.**
~ **sein** be true to sb.; **sich selbst** (*Dat.*)/
**seinem Glauben** ~ **bleiben** be true to
oneself/one's faith
2 *adv.* faithfully; loyally

**Treue** *die;* ~ **(a)** loyalty; (von [Ehe]partnern)
fidelity
**(b)** (Genauigkeit) accuracy

**treu-, Treu-:** ~**hand[anstalt]** *die*
(Wirtschaft) German privatization agency;
~**herzig** 1 *Adj.* ingenuous; (naiv) naïve;
(unschuldig) innocent; 2 *adv.* ingenuously;
(naiv) naïvely; (unschuldig) innocently;

~**herzigkeit** *die;* ~~: ingenuousness;
(Naivität) naivety; (Unschuld) innocence; ~**los**
1 *Adj.* disloyal; faithless ⟨*friend, person*⟩;
unfaithful ⟨*husband, wife, lover*⟩; 2 *adv.*
faithlessly

**Tribunal** *das;* ~s, ~e tribunal

**Tribüne** *die;* ~, ~**n** [grand]stand

**Tribut** *der;* ~[e]s, ~e (fig.) due; **einer Sache**
(*Dat.*) ~ **zollen** pay the price for sth.

**Trichter** *der;* ~s, ~ funnel

**Trick** *der;* ~s, ~s trick; (fig.: List) ploy

**Trick-film** *der* animated cartoon [film]

**trieb** *1. u. 3. Pers. Sg. Prät. v.* TREIBEN

**Trieb** *der;* ~[e]s, ~e **(a)** (innerer Antrieb)
impulse; (Drang) urge; (Verlangen) [compulsive]
desire
**(b)** (Spross) shoot

**trieb-, Trieb-:** ~**feder** *die* mainspring;
(fig.) driving *or* motivating force; ~**haft**
1 *Adj.* compulsive; carnal ⟨*sensuality*⟩;
2 *adv.* compulsively; ~**täter** *der,*
~**täterin** *die,* ~**verbrecher** *der,*
~**verbrecherin** *die: offender committing*
*a crime in gratifying a compulsive desire;*
(Sexualtäter) sexual offender; ~**wagen** *der*
(Eisenb.) railcar; ~**werk** *das* engine

**triefen** *unr. od. regelm. itr. V.* **(a)** *mit sein*
(fließen) (in Tropfen) drip; (in kleinen Rinnsalen)
trickle
**(b)** (nass sein) be dripping wet; ⟨*nose*⟩ run

**triff** *Imperativ Sg. v.* TREFFEN

**trifft** *3. Pers. Sg. Präsens v.* TREFFEN

**triftig** *Adj.* good ⟨*reason, excuse*⟩; valid,
convincing ⟨*motive, argument*⟩

**Trikot¹** /tri'ko:/ *der od. das;* ~s, ~s (Stoff)
cotton jersey

**Trikot²** /tri'ko:/ *das;* ~s, ~ (ärmellos)
singlet; (eines Tänzers) leotard; (eines
Fußballspielers) shirt

**Triller** *der;* ~s, ~: trill

**trillern** 1 *itr. V.* trill
2 *tr. V.* warble ⟨*song*⟩

**Triller-pfeife** *die* police/referee's whistle

**Trillion** *die;* ~, ~**en** quintillion

**Trimm-dich-Pfad** *der* keep-fit trail

**trimmen** *tr. V.* (durch Sport) get ⟨*person*⟩ into
shape

**trinken** 1 *unr. itr. V.* drink; **auf jmdn./etw.**
~: drink to sb./sth.
2 *unr. tr. V.* drink; **einen Kaffee/ein Bier** ~:
have a coffee/beer

**Trinker** *der;* ~s, ~: alcoholic

**Trinkerei** *die;* ~, ~**en** drinking *no art.*

**Trinkerin** *die;* ~, ~**nen** alcoholic

**Trink-:** ~**geld** *das* tip; ~**halle** *die* **(a)** (in
einem Heilbad) pump room; **(b)** (Kiosk)
refreshment kiosk; (größer) refreshment stall;
~**wasser** *das* drinking water; „**kein**
~**wasser**" 'not for drinking'

**Trio** *das;* ~s, ~s (Musik, fig.) trio

**Trip** *der;* ~s, ~s **(a)** (ugs.: Ausflug) trip; jaunt
**(b)** (Drogenjargon: Rausch) trip (coll.) ⋯▸

**(c)** (Drogenjargon: Dosis) fix (sl.)

**trippeln** *itr. V.; mit sein* trip; ⟨*child*⟩ patter

**trist** *Adj.* dreary; dismal

**tritt** *Imperativ Sg. u. 3. Pers. Sg. Präsens v.* TRETEN

**Tritt** *der;* ∼[e]s, ∼e (Schritt; Trittbrett) step; (Fußtritt) kick

**Tritt-:** ∼**brett** *das* step; ∼**brett·fahrer** *der,* ∼**brett·fahrerin** *die* (fig. abwertend) ≈ free rider (Amer.); *person who profits from another's work*

**Triumph** *der;* ∼[e]s, ∼e triumph

**triumphieren** *itr. V.* **(a)** exult
**(b)** (siegen) be triumphant; triumph (lit. or fig.) (über + *Akk.* over)

**trivial** ①*Adj.* **(a)** (platt) banal; trite; (unbedeutend) trivial
**(b)** (alltäglich) humdrum ⟨*life, career*⟩
② *adv.* ( platt) banally; ⟨*say etc.*⟩ tritely

**trocken** ①*Adj.* (auch fig.) dry
② *adv.* drily

**Trocken·haube** *die* (hood-type) hairdrier

**Trockenheit** *die;* ∼, ∼en **(a)** dryness
**(b)** (Dürreperiode) drought

**trocken-, Trocken-:** ∼|**legen** *tr. V.* **(a)** ein Baby ∼legen change a baby's nappies (Brit.) *or* (Amer.) diapers; **(b)** (entwässern) drain ⟨*marsh, pond, etc.*⟩; ∼**milch** *die* dried milk; ∼|**reiben** *unr. V.* rub ⟨*hair, child, etc.*⟩ dry; wipe ⟨*crockery, window, etc.*⟩ dry

**trocknen** ①*itr. V.; meist mit sein* dry
② *tr. V.* dry

**Troddel** *die;* ∼, ∼n tassel

**Trödel** *der;* ∼s (ugs.) junk; (für den Flohmarkt) jumble

**trödeln** *itr. V.* **(a)** (ugs.) dawdle (**mit** over)
**(b)** *mit sein* (ugs.: schlendern) saunter

**Trödler** *der;* ∼s, ∼, **Trödlerin** *die;* ∼, ∼nen (ugs.) junk dealer

**troff** *1. u. 3. Pers. Sg. Prät. v.* TRIEFEN

**trog** *1. u. 3. Pers. Sg. Prät. v.* TRÜGEN

**Trog** *der;* ∼[e]s, Tröge trough

**trollen** (ugs.) *refl. V.* push off (coll.)

**Trommel** *die;* ∼, ∼n drum

**Trommel·bremse** *die* drum brake

**trommeln** *itr. V.* **(a)** beat the drum; (als Beruf, Hobby usw.) play the drums
**(b)** ([auf etw.] schlagen, auftreffen) drum (**auf** + *Akk.* on, **an** + *Akk.* against)

**Trommel·wirbel** *der* drum roll

**Trommler** *der;* ∼s, ∼ drummer

**Trompete** *die;* ∼, ∼n trumpet

**trompeten** ①*itr. V.* play the trumpet; (fig.) ⟨*elephant*⟩ trumpet
② *tr. V.* play ⟨*piece*⟩ on the trumpet

**Trompeter** *der;* ∼s, ∼, **Trompeterin** *die;* ∼, ∼nen trumpeter

**Tropen** *Pl.* tropics

**Tropen-** tropical

**Tropen·helm** *der* sun helmet

**Tropf** *der;* ∼[e]s, ∼e (Med.) drip

**Tröpfchen** *das;* ∼s, ∼: droplet; (kleine Menge) drop

**tröpfeln** ①*itr. V.* **(a)** *mit sein* drip (**auf** + *Akk.* on to, **aus, von** from)
**(b)** *unpers.* (ugs.: leicht regnen) es tröpfelt it's spitting [with rain]
② *tr. V.* let ⟨*sth.*⟩ drip (**in** + *Akk.* into, **auf** + *Akk.* on to)

**tropfen** ①*itr. V.; mit Richtungsangabe mit sein* drip; ⟨*tears*⟩ fall; *unpers.* es tropft [vom Dach *usw.*] water is dripping from the roof etc.;
② *tr. V.* let ⟨*sth.*⟩ drip (**in** + *Akk.* into, **auf** + *Akk.* on to)

**Tropfen** *der;* ∼s, ∼ drop; ein guter/edler ∼: a good/fine vintage

**Tropf·stein·höhle** *die* limestone cave with stalactites and/or stalagmites

**Trophäe** *die;* ∼, ∼n (hist., Jagd, Sport) trophy

**tropisch** *Adj.* tropical

**Tross, *Troß** *der;* Trosses, Trosse
**(a)** (Milit.) baggage train
**(b)** (Gefolge) retinue; (fig.: Zug) procession [of hangers-on]

**Trost** *der;* ∼[e]s consolation; (bes. geistlich) comfort; nicht [ganz *od.* recht] bei ∼ sein (ugs.) be out of one's mind

**trösten** ①*tr. V.* comfort, console (**mit** with)
② *refl. V.* console oneself

**tröstlich** *Adj.* comforting

**trost·los** *Adj.* **(a)** hopeless; (verzweifelt) in despair *postpos.;*
**(b)** (deprimierend, öde) miserable; dreary; hopeless ⟨*situation*⟩

**Trostlosigkeit** *die;* ∼ **(a)** (einer Person, der Lage usw.) hopelessness; (Verzweiflung) despair
**(b)** (Öde) dreariness

**Trost·preis** *der* consolation prize

**Tröstung** *die;* ∼, ∼en comfort *no indef. art.*

**Trott** *der;* ∼[e]s, ∼e trot; (fig.) routine

**Trottel** *der;* ∼s, ∼ (ugs.) fool

**trottelig** (ugs.) ①*Adj.* doddery
② *adv.* in a feeble-minded way

**trotten** *itr. V.; mit sein* trot [along]

**trotz** *Präp. mit Gen., seltener mit Dat.* in spite of; despite

**Trotz** *der;* ∼es defiance

**trotz·dem** /*auch:* '-'-/ *Adv.* nevertheless

**trotzen** *itr. V.* **(a)** (geh.: widerstehen) jmdm./ einer Sache ∼ (auch fig.) defy sb./sth.
**(b)** (trotzig sein) be contrary

**trotzig** ①*Adj.* defiant; (widerspenstig) contrary; difficult ⟨*child*⟩
② *adv.* defiantly

**trüb[e]** ①*Adj.* **(a)** (nicht klar) murky ⟨*stream, water*⟩; cloudy ⟨*liquid, wine, juice*⟩; (schlammig) muddy ⟨*puddle*⟩; (schmutzig) dirty ⟨*glass, window pane*⟩; dull ⟨*eyes*⟩

**t**

**(b)** (nicht hell) dim ⟨*light*⟩; dull, dismal ⟨*day, weather*⟩; grey, overcast ⟨*sky*⟩
2 *adv.* ⟨*shine, light*⟩ dimly

**Trubel** *der;* ~s [hustle and] bustle; **sie stürzten sich in den dicksten** ~: they plunged into the thick of the hurly-burly

**trüben** 1 *tr. V.* **(a)** make ⟨*liquid*⟩ cloudy; cloud ⟨*liquid*⟩
**(b)** (beeinträchtigen) dampen ⟨*mood*⟩; mar ⟨*relationship*⟩; cloud ⟨*judgement*⟩
2 *refl. V.* ⟨*liquid*⟩ become cloudy; ⟨*eyes*⟩ become dull; ⟨*sky*⟩ darken

**Trübsal** *die;* ~, ~e (geh.) **(a)** (Leiden) affliction
**(b)** (Kummer) grief; ~ **blasen** (ugs.) mope (**wegen** over, about)

**trüb-, Trüb-:** ~**selig** 1 *Adj.* **(a)** (öde) dreary, depressing ⟨*place, area, colour*⟩; **(b)** (traurig) gloomy; 2 *adv.* (traurig) gloomily; ~**seligkeit** *die:* **(a)** (Ödheit) dreariness; **(b)** (Traurigkeit) gloom; ~**sinn** *der* melancholy; ~**sinnig** 1 *Adj.* melancholy; 2 *adv.* gloomily

**Trübung** *die;* ~, ~en **(a)** clouding; (des Auges) dimming
**(b)** (Beeinträchtigung) deterioration; (der Stimmung) dampening

**trudeln** *itr. V. mit sein* roll

**Trüffel** *die;* ~, ~n truffle

**trug** *1. u. 3. Pers. Prät. v.* TRAGEN

**trüge** *1. u. 3. Pers. Sg. Konjunktiv II v.* TRAGEN

**trügen** 1 *unr. tr. V.* deceive
2 *unr. itr. V.* be deceptive; ⟨*feeling, deception*⟩ be a delusion

**trügerisch** 1 *Adj.* deceptive; false ⟨*hope, sign, etc.*⟩; treacherous ⟨*ice*⟩
2 *adv.* deceptively

**Truhe** *die;* ~, ~n chest

**Trümmer** *Pl.* (eines Gebäudes) rubble *sing.;* (Ruinen) ruins; (eines Flugzeugs usw.) wreckage *sing.;* (kleinere Teile) debris *sing.*

**Trümmer·haufen** *der* pile *or* heap of rubble

**Trumpf** *der;* ~[e]s, Trümpfe (auch fig.) trump [card]; (Farbe) trumps *pl.;* ~ **sein** (fig.: Mode sein) be the in thing

**trumpfen** *itr. V.* play a trump

**Trunk** *der;* ~[e]s, Trünke (geh.) (Getränk) drink; beverage (formal)

**Trunkenheit** *die;* ~: drunkenness; ~ **am Steuer** drink-driving

**Trunk·sucht** *die* alcoholism *no art.*

**trunk·süchtig** *Adj.* alcoholic; ~ **sein** be an alcoholic

**Trupp** *der;* ~s, ~s troop; (von Arbeitern, Gefangenen) gang; (von Soldaten, Polizisten) squad

**Truppe** *die;* ~, ~n **(a)** (Einheit der Streitkräfte) unit
**(b)** *Pl.* (Soldaten) troops
**(c)** (Streitkräfte) [armed] forces *pl.;* (Heer) army
**(d)** (Gruppe von Schauspielern, Artisten) troupe; (von Sportlern) squad

**Trut·hahn** *der* turkey [cock]

**tschau** *Interj.* (ugs.) ciao (coll.)

**Tscheche** *der;* ~n, ~n Czech

**Tschechien** (*das*); ~s Czech Republic

**Tschechin** *die;* ~, ~nen Czech

**tschechisch** *Adj.* Czech

**Tschechoslowakei** *die;* ~ (hist.) Czechoslovakia *no art.*

**tschechoslowakisch** *Adj.* (hist.) Czechoslovak[ian]

**tschüs** *Interj.* (ugs.) bye (coll.)

**Tsd.** *Abk.* = **Tausend**

**T-Shirt** /'tiːʃəːt/ *das;* ~s, ~s T-shirt

**Tube** *die;* ~, ~n tube

**Tuberkulose** *die;* ~, ~n (Med.) tuberculosis *no art.*

**Tuch** *das;* ~[e]s, Tücher *od.* ~e **(a)** *Pl.* Tücher cloth; (Kopf-, Halstuch) scarf
**(b)** *Pl.* ~e (Gewebe) cloth

**Tuch·fühlung** *die* (scherzh.) physical contact

**tüchtig** 1 *Adj.* **(a)** efficient; (fähig) capable, competent (**in** + *Dat.* at)
**(b)** (ugs.: beträchtlich) sizeable ⟨*piece, portion*⟩; big ⟨*gulp*⟩; hearty ⟨*eater, appetite*⟩
2 *adv.* **(a)** efficiently; (fähig) competently
**(b)** (ugs.: sehr) really ⟨*cold, warm*⟩; ⟨*snow, rain*⟩ good and proper (coll.); ⟨*eat*⟩ heartily

**Tüchtigkeit** *die;* ~: efficiency; (Fähigkeit) ability; competence; (Fleiß) industry

**Tücke** *die;* ~, ~n **(a)** (Hinterhältigkeit) deceit[fulness]; (List) guile
**(b)** ([verborgene] Gefahr/Schwierigkeit) [hidden] danger/difficulty

**tuckern** *itr. V.; mit Richtungsangabe mit sein* chug

**tückisch** 1 *Adj.* **(a)** (hinterhältig) wily; (betrügerisch) deceitful
**(b)** (gefährlich) treacherous ⟨*bend, slope, spot, etc.*⟩
2 *adv.* craftily

**tüfteln** *itr. V.* (ugs.) fiddle (**an** + *Dat.* with); do finicky work (**an** + *Dat.* on); (geistig) rack one's brains (**an** + *Dat.* over)

**Tugend** *die;* ~, ~en virtue

**tugendhaft** 1 *Adj.* virtuous
2 *adv.* virtuously

**Tüll** *der;* ~s, ~e tulle

**Tülle** *die;* ~, ~n (bes. nordd.) spout

**Tulpe** *die;* ~, ~n tulip

**tummeln** *refl. V.* romp [about]

**Tummel·platz** *der* (auch fig.) playground

**Tumor** *der;* ~s, ~en (Med.) tumour

**Tümpel** *der;* ~s, ~: pond

**Tumult** *der;* ~[e]s, ~e tumult; commotion; (Protest) uproar

**tun** 1 *unr. tr. V.* **(a)** do; **so etwas tun man nicht** that is just not done; **[etwas] mit etw./jmdm. zu** ~ **haben** be concerned with sth./ have dealings with sb.
**(b)** *als Funktionsverb* make ⟨*remark, catch, etc.*⟩; take ⟨*step, jump*⟩; do ⟨*deed*⟩ ⋯⟶

**(c)** (bewirken) work, perform ‹*miracle*›
**(d)** (antun) jmdm. etw. ~: do sth. to sb.
**(e)** es ~ (ugs.: genügen) be good enough
**(f)** (ugs.: irgendwohin bringen) put
[2] *unr. itr. V.* **(a)** (ugs.: funktionieren) work
**(b)** freundlich/geheimnisvoll ~: pretend to be
*or* (coll.) act friendly/act mysteriously
[3] *unr. refl. V.; unpers.* **es hat sich einiges
getan** quite a bit has happened
**Tünche** *die;* ~, ~n distemper; wash;
[weiße] ~: whitewash
**tünchen** *tr.* (*auch itr.*) *V.* distemper; **weiß**
~: whitewash
**Tunell** *das;* ~s, ~s (südd., österr., schweiz.)
▶ TUNNEL
**tunen** /'tjuːnən/ *tr. V.* (Kfz-W.) tune
**Tuner** /'tjuːnɐ/ *der;* ~s, ~(a) (Elektronik)
tuner
**(b)** (Kfz-W.) tuner; tuning expert
**Tunesien** /tuˈneːzi̯ən/ (*das*) ~s Tunisia
**tunesisch** *Adj.* Tunisian
**Tunke** *die;* ~, ~n (bes. ostmd.) sauce;
(Bratensoße) gravy
**tunken** *tr. V.* (bes. ostmd.) dip
**tunlichst** *Adv.* (geh.) **(a)** (möglichst) as far as
possible
**(b)** (unbedingt) at all costs
**Tunnel** *der;* ~s, ~ *od.* ~s tunnel
**tupfen** *tr. V.* **(a)** dab
**(b)** (mit Tupfen versehen) dot
**Tupfen** *der;* ~s, ~: dot; (größer) spot
**Tupfer** *der;* ~s, ~ (Med.) swab
**Tür** *die;* ~, ~n door; (Garten~) gate; **an die
~ gehen** (öffnen) [go and] answer the door;
**vor die ~ gehen** go outside
**Turban** *der;* ~s, ~e turban
**Turbine** *die;* ~, ~n turbine
**turbulent** [1] *Adj.* (auch fachspr.) turbulent
[2] *adv.* (auch fachspr.) turbulently
**Turbulenz** *die;* ~, ~en (auch Physik, Astron.,
Met.) turbulence *no pl.*
**Tür·griff** *der* door handle
**Türke** *der;* ~n, ~n Turk
**Türkei** *die;* ~: Turkey *no art.*
**türken** *tr. V.* (ugs.) fake ‹*scene, letter,
document, etc.*›; make up ‹*story, report*›
**Türkin** *die;* ~, ~nen Turk
**türkis** *indekl. Adj.* turquoise
**Türkis** *der;* ~es, ~e turquoise
**türkisch** *Adj.* Turkish
**Tür·klinke** *die* door handle
**Turm** *der;* ~[e]s, Türme **(a)** tower; (spitzer
Kirchturm) spire; steeple
**(b)** (Schach) rook
**(c)** (Sprungturm) diving platform
**Türmchen** *das;* ~s, ~: turret

**türmen¹** [1] *tr. V.* (stapeln) stack up; (häufen)
pile up
[2] *refl. V.* be piled up; ‹*clouds*› gather
**türmen²** *itr. V.; mit sein* (salopp) scarper (Brit.
coll.)
**Turm·falke** *der* kestrel
**turnen** [1] *itr. V.* do gymnastics; (Schulw.) do
gym
[2] *tr. V.* do, perform ‹*exercise, routine*›
**Turnen** *das;* ~s gymnastics *sing., no art.;*
(Schulw.) gym *no art.;* PE *no art.*
**Turner** *der;* ~s, ~, **Turnerin** *die;* ~,
~nen gymnast
**Turn-:** ~halle *die* gymnasium; ~hemd
*das* [gym] singlet; ~hose *die* gym shorts
*pl.*
**Turnier** *das;* ~s, ~e (auch hist.) tournament;
(Reitturnier) show; (Tanzturnier) competition
**Turn·schuh** *der* gym shoe
**Turnus** *der;* ~, ~se regular cycle
**Turn·verein** *der* gymnastics club
**Tür-:** ~öffner *der* door-opener;
~rahmen *der* doorframe
**turteln** *itr. V.* (scherzh.: zärtlich sein) bill and
coo
**Tusch** *der;* ~[e]s, ~e fanfare
**Tusche** *die;* ~, ~n Indian (Brit.) *or* (Amer.)
India ink
**Tuschelei** *die;* ~, ~en **(a)** (das Tuscheln)
whispering
**(b)** (Äußerung) whisper
**tuscheln** *itr., tr. V.* whisper
**Tussi** *die;* ~, ~s (salopp) female (derog.)
**Tüte** *die;* ~, ~n bag
**tuten** *itr. V.* hoot; ‹*siren, [fog]horn*› sound
**Tutor** *der;* ~s, ~en, **Tutorin** *die;* ~, ~nen
(Päd.) tutor
**Tycoon** /taiˈkuːn/ *der;* ~s, ~s tycoon
**Typ** *der;* ~s, ~en **(a)** type
**(b)** *Gen. auch* ~en (ugs.: Mann) bloke (Brit. coll.)
**Type** *die;* ~, ~n (Druck-, Schreibmaschinentype)
type
**Typhus** *der;* ~: typhoid [fever]
**typisch** [1] *Adj.* typical (für of)
[2] *adv.* typically
**Typographie** *die;* ~, ~n (Druckw.)
typography
**typographisch** (Druckw.) [1] *Adj.*
typographical
[2] *adv.* typographically
**Tyrann** *der;* ~en, ~en (auch fig.) tyrant
**Tyrannei** *die;* ~, ~en (auch fig.) tyranny
**Tyrannin** *die;* ~, ~nen ▶ TYRANN
**tyrannisch** [1] *Adj.* tyrannical
[2] *adv.* tyrannically
**tyrannisieren** *tr. V.* tyrannize

# U u

**u, U** /u:/ *das;* ~, ~: u/U

**u.** *Abk.* = **und**

**ü, Ü** /y:/ *das;* ~, ~: u umlaut

**U-Bahn** *die* underground (Brit.); subway (Amer.); (bes. in London) tube

**U-Bahnhof** *der;* U̲-Bahn-Station *die* underground station (Brit.); subway station (Amer.); (bes. in London) tube station

**übel** *Adj.* **(a)** foul, nasty ‹*smell, weather*›; bad, nasty ‹*headache, cold, taste*›; nasty ‹*consequences, situation*›; sorry ‹*state, affair*›; foul, (coll.) filthy ‹*mood*›; **nicht** ~ (ugs.) not bad at all

**(b)** (unwohl) jmdm. ist/wird ~: sb. feels sick

**(c)** (verwerflich) bad; wicked; nasty, dirty ‹*trick*›

**(d)** jmdm. etw. ~ nehmen hold sth. against sb.; etw. ~ nehmen take offence at sth.

**Übel** *das;* ~s, ~: evil

**Übelkeit** *die;* ~, ~en nausea

***übel|nehmen** ▶ ÜBEL D

**Übel·täter** *der,* **Übel·täterin** *die* wrongdoer

**üben** *tr. V.* **(a)** (*auch itr.*) practise; rehearse ‹*scene, play*›; practise on ‹*musical instrument*›

**(b)** (trainieren, schulen) exercise ‹*fingers*›; train ‹*memory*›

**über** [1] *Präp. mit Dat.* **(a)** (Lage, Standort) over; above; (in einer Rangfolge) above; ~ jmdm. wohnen live above sb.; **zehn Grad ~ Null** ten degrees above zero; **sie trug eine Jacke ~ dem Kleid** she wore a jacket over her dress

**(b)** (während) during; ~ **dem Lesen/der Arbeit einschlafen** fall asleep over one's book/ magazine *etc.*/over one's work

[2] *Präp. mit Akk.* **(a)** (Richtung) over; (quer hinüber) across; ~ **Ulm nach Stuttgart** via Ulm to Stuttgart

**(b)** (während) over; (für die Dauer von) for

**(c)** (betreffend) about; ~ **etw. reden/schreiben** talk/write about sth.; **ein Scheck/eine Rechnung ~ 100 Euro** a cheque/bill for 100 euros

**(d)** Kinder ~ 10 Jahre children over ten [years of age]

[3] *Adv.* **(a)** (mehr als) over

**(b)** ~ **und** ~: all over

**über·all** /*od.* -'-/ *Adv.* **(a)** everywhere

**(b)** (bei jeder Gelegenheit) always

**überall-:** ~**her** *Adv.* from all over the place; ~**hin** *Adv.* everywhere

**Über·angebot** *das* surplus (**an** + *Dat.* of); (Schwemme) glut (**an** + *Dat.* of)

**über·anstrengen** *tr. V.;* **ich**

überanstrenge, überanstrengt, zu überanstrengen overtax ‹*person, energy*›; strain ‹*eyes, nerves, heart*›; **sich** ~: overexert oneself

**über·arbeiten** [1] *tr. V.* rework; revise ‹*text, edition*›

[2] *refl. V.* overwork

**über·aus** *Adv.* (geh.) extremely

**über·backen** *unr. tr. V.* etw. mit Käse *usw.* ~: top sth. with cheese *etc.* and brown it lightly [under the grill/in a hot oven]

**Über·bein** *das* (Med.) ganglion

**überbelichten** *tr. V.;* ich überbelichte, überbelichtet, überzubelichten (Fot.) overexpose

**über·bieten** *unr. tr. V.* **(a)** outbid (**um** by)

**(b)** (übertreffen) surpass; outdo ‹*rival*›; break ‹*record*› (**um** by); exceed ‹*target*› (**um** by)

**Über·blick** *der* **(a)** view; **einen guten ~ über etw. (*Akk.*) haben** have a good view over sth.

**(b)** (Abriss) survey

**(c)** (Einblick) overall view

**über·blicken** *tr. V.* ▶ ÜBERSEHEN A, B

**über·bringen** *unr. tr. V.* deliver; convey ‹*greetings, congratulations*›

**über·brücken** *tr. V.* bridge ‹*gap, gulf*›; reconcile ‹*difference*›

**Über·brückung** *die;* ~, ~en (fig.) bridging; (von Gegensätzen) reconciliation

**über·buchen** *tr. V.* overbook

**überdacht** *Adj.* covered ‹*terrace, station platform, etc.*›

**über·dauern** *tr. V.* survive ‹*war, separation, hardship*›

**über·dehnen** *tr. V.* overstretch; strain ‹*muscle*›

**über·dies** *Adv.* moreover

**Über·dosis** *die* overdose

**Über·druck** *der; Pl.* Überdrücke excess pressure

**Über·druss, *Überdruß** *der;* Überdrusses surfeit (**an** + *Dat.* of)

**überdrüssig** *Adj.* jmds./einer Sache ~ sein/werden be/grow tired of sb./sth.

**über·eignen** *tr. V.* jmdm. etw. ~: transfer sth. *or* make sth. over to sb.

**Über·eignung** *die* transfer (**an** + *Akk.* to)

**über·eilen** *tr. V.* rush; **übereilt** overhasty

**über·einander** *Adv.* **(a)** one on top of the other; Holzscheite *usw.:* ~ **legen** lay pieces of wood *etc.* one on top of the other; **Arme/ Beine ~ schlagen** fold one's arms/cross one's legs

**(b)** ‹*talk etc.*› about each other

**\*übereinander|legen** *usw.*
▶ ÜBEREINANDER A

**überein|kommen** *unr. itr. V.; mit sein*
agree; come to an agreement

**Überein·kommen** *das;* ~s, ~,
**Übereinkunft** *die;* ~, Übereinkünfte
agreement

**überein|stimmen** *itr. V.* (a) (einer Meinung
sein) agree (**in** + *Dat.* on)
(b) (sich gleichen) *‹colours, styles›* match;
*‹figures, statements, reports, results›* tally,
agree; *‹views, opinions›* coincide

**Überein·stimmung** *die* agreement (**in** +
*Dat.* on; *Gen.* between)

**über·empfindlich** ⓵ *Adj.* oversensitive
(**gegen** to); (Med.) hypersensitive (**gegen** to)
⓶ *adv.* oversensitively; (Med.)
hypersensitively

**Über·empfindlichkeit** *die*
oversensitivity (**gegen** to); (Med.)
hypersensitivity (**gegen** to)

**über|fahren¹** ⓵ *unr. tr. V.* jmdn. ~: ferry
*or* take sb. over
⓶ *unr. itr. V.; mit sein* cross over

**über·fahren²** *unr. tr. V.* (a) run over
(b) (hinwegfahren über) cross; go over
*‹crossroads›*

**Über·fahrt** *die* crossing (**über** + *Akk.* of)

**Über·fall** *der* attack (**auf** + *Akk.* on); (aus
dem Hinterhalt) ambush (**auf** + *Akk.* on); (mit
vorgehaltener Waffe) hold-up; (auf eine Bank o. Ä.)
raid (**auf** + *Akk.* on)

**über·fallen** *unr. tr. V.* (a) attack; raid
*‹bank, enemy position, village, etc.›;*
(hinterrücks) ambush; (mit vorgehaltener Waffe)
hold up
(b) (überkommen) *‹tiredness, homesickness,
fear›* come over

**über·fällig** *Adj.* overdue

**über·fliegen** *unr. tr. V.* (a) fly over; overfly
(formal)
(b) (flüchtig lesen) skim [through]

**über·flügeln** *tr. V.* outshine; outstrip

**Über·fluss, \*Über·fluß** *der* abundance
(**an** + *Dat.* of); (Wohlstand) affluence

**über·flüssig** *Adj.* superfluous; unnecessary
*‹purchase, words, work›*

**über·fluten** *tr. V.* (auch fig.) flood

**Über|flutung** *die;* ~, ~en (auch fig.)
flooding

**über·fordern** *tr. V.* jmdn. [mit etw.] ~:
overtax sb. [with sth.]; ask *or* demand too
much of sb. [with sth.]

**über·fragen** *tr. V.* da bin ich überfragt
I don't know the answer to that

**über·fremden** *tr. V.* überfremdet werden/
sein *‹country›* be dominated [by foreign
influences]

**Über·fremdung** *die;* ~, ~en domination
[by foreign influences]

---

**über·frieren** *unr. itr. V.; mit sein* freeze
over; ~de Nässe black ice

**über|führen¹** *tr. V.* transfer

**über·führen²** *tr. V.* (a) ▶ ÜBERFÜHREN¹;
(b) jmdn. [eines Verbrechens] ~: find sb.
guilty [of a crime]; convict sb. [of a
crime]

**Über·führung** *die* (a) transfer
(b) (eines Verdächtigen) conviction
(c) (Brücke) bridge; (Hochstraße) overpass; (für
Fußgänger) [foot]bridge

**über·füllt** *Adj.* crammed full (**von** with); (mit
Menschen) overcrowded (**von** with);
oversubscribed *‹course›*

**Über·gabe** *die* (a) handing over (**an** + *Akk.*
to); (von Macht) handing over
(b) (Auslieferung an den Gegner) surrender (**an** +
*Akk.* to)

**Über·gang** *der* (a) crossing
(b) (Stelle zum Überqueren) crossing;
(Bahnübergang) level crossing (Brit.); grade
crossing (Amer.); (Grenzübergang) crossing point
(c) (Wechsel, Überleitung) transition (**zu, auf** +
*Akk.* to)

**über·geben** ⓵ *unr. tr. V.* (a) hand over;
pass *‹baton›*
(b) (übereignen) transfer, make over (*Dat.* to)
(c) (ausliefern) surrender (*Dat.,* **an** + *Akk.* to)
(d) eine Straße dem Verkehr ~: open a road
to traffic
⓶ *unr. refl. V.* (sich erbrechen) vomit

**über|gehen¹** *unr. itr. V.; mit sein* (a) pass
(b) zu etw. ~: go over to sth.
(c) in etw. (*Akk.*) ~ (zu etw. werden) turn into
sth.

**über·gehen²** *unr. tr. V.* (a) (nicht beachten)
ignore
(b) (auslassen, überspringen) skip [over]
(c) (nicht berücksichtigen) pass over

**über·geordnet** *Adj.* higher *‹court,
authority, position›;* greater *‹significance›;*
superordinate *‹concept›*

**Über·gewicht** *das* (a) excess weight
(b) (fig.) predominance

**über·gewichtig** *Adj.* overweight

**über·glücklich** *Adj.* blissfully happy;
(hocherfreut) overjoyed

**über|greifen** *unr. itr. V.* auf etw. (*Akk.*) ~:
spread to sth.

**Über·griff** *der* (unrechtmäßiger Eingriff)
encroachment (**auf** + *Akk.* on); infringement
(**auf** + *Akk.* of); (Angriff) attack (**auf** + *Akk.*
on)

**Über·größe** *die* outsize

**überhand**: ~ nehmen get out of hand;
*‹attacks, muggings, etc.›* increase alarmingly;
*‹weeds›* run riot

**über|hängen** *tr. V.* sich (*Dat.*) eine Jacke
~: put a jacket round one's shoulders; sich
(*Dat.*) das Gewehr/die Tasche ~: hang the
rifle/bag over one's shoulder

**über·häufen** *tr. V.* jmdn. mit etw. ~: heap
*or* shower sth. on sb.

---

\*alte Schreibung - vgl. Hinweis auf S. xiv

**überhaupt** *Adv.* (a) in general
(b) ~ **nicht** not at all; ~ **keine Zeit haben**
have no time at all; ~ **nichts** nothing at all
**überheblich** ①*Adj.* arrogant;
supercilious ‹*grin*›
②*adv.* arrogantly; ‹*grin*› superciliously
**Überheblichkeit** *die;* ~: arrogance
**über·holen** ①*tr. V.* (a) overtake (esp. Brit.);
pass (esp. Amer.)
(b) (übertreffen) outstrip
(c) (wieder instand setzen) overhaul
②*itr. V.* overtake (esp. Brit.); pass (esp. Amer.)
**Überholspur** *die* overtaking lane (esp.
Brit.); pass lane (esp. Amer.)
**überholt** *Adj.* (veraltet) outdated
**Überholung** *die;* ~, ~en overhaul
**Überhol·verbot** *das* ban on overtaking
**über·hören** *tr. V.* not hear
**über·irdisch** ①*Adj.* celestial; heavenly;
(übernatürlich) supernatural
②*adv.* celestially; (übernatürlich)
supernaturally
**über|kochen** *itr. V.; mit sein* (auch fig. ugs.)
boil over
**über·kommen** *unr. tr. V.* **Mitleid/Ekel/
Furcht überkam mich** I was overcome by
pity/revulsion/fear
**über·laden** *unr. tr. V.* (auch fig.) overload
**über·lassen** *unr. tr. V.* (a) **jmdm. etw.** ~:
let sb. have sth.
(b) **sich** (*Dat.*) **selbst** ~ **sein** be left to one's
own devices
(c) **etw. jmdm.** ~ (etw. jmdn. entscheiden/tun
lassen) leave sth. to sb.
**über·lasten** *tr. V.* overload; overtax
‹*person*›; (mit Arbeit) overwork ‹*person*›
**Über·lauf** *der* overflow
**über|laufen**[1] *unr. itr. V.; mit sein* (a)
overflow
(b) (auf die gegnerische Seite überwechseln)
defect; ‹*partisan*› go over to the other side
**über·laufen**[2] *unr. tr. V.* seize; **ein
Frösteln/Schauer überlief mich, es überlief
mich** [eis]kalt a cold shiver ran down my
spine
**überlaufen**[3] *Adj.* overcrowded
**Über·läufer** *der,* **Über·läuferin** *die*
(auch fig.) defector
**über·leben** *tr. V.* survive
**Über·lebende** *der/die; adj. Dekl.* survivor
**über|legen**[1] *tr. V.* **jmdm. etw.** ~: put sth.
over sb.
**über·legen**[2] ①*tr. V.* consider; think
about; **es sich anders** ~: change one's mind
②*itr. V.* think
**überlegen**[3] ①*Adj.* (a) superior; clear,
convincing ‹*win, victory*›; **jmdm.** ~ **sein** be
superior to sb. (**an** + *Dat.* in)
(b) (herablassend) supercilious
②*adv.* (a) in a superior manner; ‹*play*›
much the better: ‹*win, argue*› convincingly
(b) (herablassend) superciliously

**Überlegenheit** *die;* ~: superiority
**überlegt** ①*Adj.* carefully considered
②*adv.* in a carefully considered way
**Überlegung** *die;* ~, ~en (a) thought
(b) (Gedanke) idea; ~en (Gedankengang)
thoughts
**über·liefern** *tr. V.* hand down
**Über·lieferung** *die* tradition
**überlisten** *tr. V.* outwit
**überm** *Präp. + Art.* = **über dem**
**Über·macht** *die* superior strength;
(zahlenmäßig) superior numbers *pl.*
**über·mannen** *tr. V.* overcome
**Über·maß** *das* excessive amount, excess
(**an** + *Dat.* of)
**über·mäßig** ①*Adj.* excessive
②*adv.* excessively
**über·menschlich** *Adj.* superhuman
**über·mitteln** *tr. V.* send; (als Mittler
weitergeben) pass on, convey ‹*greetings,
regards, etc.*›
**über·morgen** *Adv.* the day after
tomorrow
**über·müden** *tr. V.* overtire; **übermüdet**
overtired; exhausted
**Übermüdung** *die;* ~: overtiredness;
exhaustion
**Über·mut** *der* high spirits *pl.*
**übermütig** ①*Adj.* high-spirited
②*adv.* high-spiritedly
**über·nächst...** *Adj.* **im** ~**en Jahr,** ~**es
Jahr** the year after next; **am** ~**en Tag** two
days later
**über·nachten** *itr. V.* stay overnight
**übernächtigt** *Adj.* ‹*person*› tired *or* worn
out [through lack of sleep]; tired ‹*face, look,
etc.*›
**Übernachtung** *die;* ~, ~en overnight
stay; ~ **und Frühstück** bed and breakfast
**Übernahme** *die;* ~ (von Waren, einer
Sendung) taking delivery *no art.;* (einer Idee
usw.) adoption, taking over *no indef. art.;* (der
Macht, einer Praxis usw.) take over
**über·natürlich** *Adj.* supernatural
**über·nehmen** ①*unr. tr. V.* (a) take
delivery of ‹*goods, consignment*›; take over
‹*power, practice, business, etc.*›; take on ‹*job,
position, etc.*›; undertake to pay ‹*costs*›
(b) (sich zu Eigen machen) adopt ‹*ideas,
methods, subject, etc.*› (**von** from); borrow
‹*word, phrase*› (**von** from)
②*unr. refl. V.* overdo things or it; **sich mit
etw.** ~: take on too much with sth.
**Über·produktion** *die* (Wirtsch., Med.)
overproduction
**über·prüfen** *tr. V.* check (**auf** + *Akk.* for);
review ‹*issue, situation, results*›
**Über·prüfung** *die* (a) checking *no indef.
art.* (**auf** + *Akk.* for)
(b) (Kontrolle) check; (einer Lage, Frage usw.)
review
**über·queren** *tr. V.* cross

**u**

**über·ragen** tr. V. (a) jmdn./etw. ~: tower above sb./sth.
(b) (übertreffen) jmdn. an etw. (Dat.) ~: be head and shoulders above sb. in sth.

**überragend** [1] Adj. outstanding
[2] adv. outstandingly

**über·raschen** tr. V. surprise

**Überraschung** die; ~, ~en surprise

**über·reden** tr. V. persuade

**Überredung** die; ~: persuasion

**über·regional** [1] Adj. national ⟨newspaper, radio station⟩
[2] adv. nationally

**über·reichen** tr. V. [jmdm.] etw. ~: present sth. [to sb.]

**Überreichung** die; ~: presentation

**über·reif** Adj. over-ripe

**über·rumpeln** tr. V. jmdn. ~: take sb. by surprise

**über·runden** tr. V. (a) (Sport) lap
(b) (übertreffen) outstrip

**übers** Präp. + Art. = über das

**über·sättigen** tr. V. supersaturate ⟨solution⟩; glut ⟨market⟩; satiate ⟨public⟩

**Überschall-:** ~flugzeug das supersonic aircraft; ~geschwindigkeit die supersonic speed

**über·schatten** tr. V. overshadow; cast its/their shadow over; (fig.) cast a shadow over

**über·schätzen** tr. V. overestimate; overrate ⟨artist, talent, etc.⟩

**Überschätzung** die ▶ ÜBERSCHÄTZEN: overestimation; overrating

**überschaubar** Adj. eine ~e Menge/Zahl a manageable quantity/number

**über·schauen** tr. V. ▶ ÜBERSEHEN A, B

**Über·schlag** der (a) rough calculation or estimate
(b) (Turnen) handspring
(c) ▶ LOOPING

**über|schlagen**[1] [1] unr. tr. V. die Beine ~: cross one's legs
[2] unr. itr. V.; mit sein ⟨wave⟩ break

**über·schlagen**[2] [1] unr. tr. V. (a) skip ⟨chapter, page, etc.⟩
(b) (ungefähr berechnen) calculate or estimate roughly
[2] unr. refl. V. go head over heels; ⟨car⟩ turn over

**über|schnappen** itr. V.; mit sein (ugs.) go crazy

**über·schneiden** unr. refl. V. cross, intersect; (fig.) overlap

**über·schreiben** unr. tr. V. (a) entitle; head ⟨chapter, section⟩
(b) etw. jmdm. od. auf jmdn. ~: transfer sth. to sb.

**über·schreiten** unr. itr. V. cross; (fig.) exceed

**Über·schrift** die heading; (in einer Zeitung) headline; (Titel) title

**Über·schuss, \*Über·schuß** der surplus (an + Dat. of)

**überschüssig** Adj. surplus

**über·schütten** tr. V. cover

**Überschwang** der; ~[e]s exuberance

**über·schwänglich** [1] Adj. effusive ⟨words etc.⟩; wild ⟨joy, enthusiasm⟩
[2] adv. effusively

**über·schwemmen** tr. V. (auch fig.) flood

**Überschwemmung** die; ~, ~en flood; (das Überschwemmen) flooding no pl.

**\*über·schwenglich** ▶ ÜBERSCHWÄNGLICH

**Über·see:** aus od. von ~: from overseas; in/nach ~: overseas

**über·sehen** unr. tr. V. (a) look out over
(b) (abschätzen) assess ⟨damage, situation, consequences, etc.⟩
(c) (nicht sehen) overlook; miss; miss ⟨turning, signpost⟩
(d) (ignorieren) ignore

**über·senden** unr. (auch regelm.) tr. V. send

**über|setzen**[1] [1] tr. V. ferry over
[2] itr. V.; auch mit sein cross [over]

**über·setzen**[2] tr., itr. V. (auch fig.) translate

**Über·setzer** der, **Übersetzerin** die; ~, ~nen translator

**Übersetzung** die; ~, ~en translation

**Über·sicht** die (a) overall view, overview (über + Akk. of)
(b) (Darstellung) survey; (Tabelle) summary

**über·sichtlich** [1] Adj. clear; ⟨crossroads⟩ which allows a clear view
[2] adv. clearly

**Übersichtlichkeit** die; ~: clarity; (einer Kreuzung) clear layout

**über|siedeln**[1], **über·siedeln**[2] itr. V.; mit sein move (nach to)

**Über·siedler** der, **Über·siedlerin** die migrant

**überspannt** Adj. exaggerated ⟨ideas, behaviour, gestures⟩; extreme ⟨views⟩; inflated ⟨demands, expectations⟩

**über·spielen** tr. V. (a) (hinweggehen über) cover up; smooth over ⟨difficult situation⟩
(b) (aufnehmen) [auf ein Tonband] ~: transfer ⟨record⟩ to tape; put ⟨record⟩ on tape

**über·spitzen** tr. V. etw. ~: push or carry sth. too far

**über·springen** unr. tr. V. (a) jump ⟨obstacle⟩
(b) (auslassen) miss out

**über|stehen**[1] unr. itr. V.; südd., österr., schweiz. mit sein jut out

**über·stehen**[2] unr. tr. V. come through ⟨danger, war, operation⟩; get over ⟨illness⟩

**über·steigen** unr. tr. V. (a) climb over
(b) (fig.) exceed

**über·stimmen** tr. V. outvote

**über|streifen** *tr. V.* [sich (*Dat.*)] etw. ∼:
slip sth. on
**über|stülpen** *tr. V.* pull on ⟨*hat etc.*⟩
**Über·stunde** *die:* ∼n machen do overtime
**über·stürzen** ① *tr. V.* rush
② *refl. V.* rush; (rasch aufeinander folgen)
⟨*events, news, etc.*⟩ come thick and fast
**überstürzt** ① *Adj.* hurried ⟨*escape,
departure*⟩; overhasty ⟨*decision*⟩
② *adv.* ⟨*decide, act*⟩ overhastily; ⟨*depart*⟩
hurriedly
**über·tölpeln** *tr. V.* dupe; con (coll.)
**über·tönen** *tr. V.* drown out
**Übertrag** *der;* ∼[e]s, **Überträge** (bes. Buchf.)
carry-over
**über·tragbar** *Adj.* transferable (**auf** + *Akk.*
to); (auf etw. anderes anwendbar) applicable (**auf**
+ *Akk.* to); (übersetzbar) translatable;
(ansteckend) infectious ⟨*disease*⟩
**über·tragen** *unr. tr. V.* (a) transfer (**auf** +
*Akk.* to); transmit ⟨*power, torque, etc.*⟩ (**auf** +
*Akk.* to); communicate ⟨*disease, illness*⟩ (**auf**
+ *Akk.* to); carry over ⟨*subtotal*⟩; (auf etw.
anderes anwenden) apply (**auf** + *Akk.* to);
(übersetzen) translate
(b) (senden) broadcast ⟨*concert, event, match,
etc.*⟩; (im Fernsehen) televise
(c) (geben) jmdm. **Aufgaben/Pflichten** *usw.* ∼:
hand over tasks/duties *etc.* to sb.;
(anvertrauen) entrust sb. with tasks/duties *etc.*
**Übertragung** *die;* ∼, ∼en (a)
▶ ÜBERTRAGEN A: transference; transmission;
communication; carrying over; application;
translation
(b) (das Senden) broadcasting; (Sendung)
broadcast; (im Fernsehen) televising/television
broadcast
**über·treffen** *unr. tr. V.* (a) surpass, outdo
(**an** + *Dat.* in); break ⟨*record*⟩
(b) (übersteigen) exceed
**über·treiben** *unr. tr. V.* (a) auch itr.
exaggerate
(b) (zu weit treiben) overdo
**Übertreibung** *die;* ∼, ∼en exaggeration
**über|treten¹** *unr. itr. V.; mit sein* change
sides; **zum Katholizismus/Islam** ∼: convert
to Catholicism/Islam
**über·treten²** *unr. tr. V.* contravene ⟨*law*⟩;
violate ⟨*regulation, prohibition*⟩
**Übertretung** *die;* ∼, ∼en (a)
▶ ÜBERTRETEN²: contravention; violation
(b) (Vergehen) misdemeanour
**übertrieben** *Adj.* ① exaggerated;
(übermäßig) excessive ⟨*care, thrift, etc.*⟩
② *adv.* excessively
**Über·tritt** *der* change of allegiance, switch
(**zu** to); (Rel.) conversion (**zu** to)
**über·trumpfen** *tr. V.* outdo
**über·tünchen** *tr. V.* cover with
whitewash; (fig.) cover up
**über·vorteilen** *tr. V.* cheat
**über·wachen** *tr. V.* keep under
surveillance ⟨*suspect, agent, area, etc.*⟩;

supervise ⟨*factory, workers, process*⟩; control
⟨*traffic*⟩; monitor ⟨*progress, production
process, experiment, patient*⟩
**Überwachung** *die;* ∼, ∼en
▶ ÜBERWACHEN: surveillance; supervision;
controlling; monitoring
**über·wältigen** *tr. V.* (a) overpower
(b) (fig.) ⟨*sleep, emotion, fear, etc.*⟩ overcome;
⟨*sight, impressions, beauty, etc.*⟩ overwhelm
**überwältigend** ① *Adj.* overwhelming
⟨*sight, impression, victory, majority, etc.*⟩;
overpowering ⟨*smell*⟩; stunning ⟨*beauty*⟩
② *adv.* stunningly ⟨*beautiful*⟩
**über·weisen** *unr. tr. V.* (a) transfer
⟨*money*⟩ (**an, auf** + *Akk.* to)
(b) refer ⟨*patient*⟩ (**an** + *Akk.* to)
**Über·weisung** *die* (a) transfer (**an, auf** +
*Akk.* to)
(b) (Summe) remittance
(c) (eines Patienten) referral (**an** + *Akk.* to)
**überwiegend** ① /*auch* --'--/ *Adj.*
overwhelming
② *adv.* mainly
**über·winden** ① *unr. tr. V.* overcome; get
past ⟨*stage*⟩
② *unr. refl. V.* overcome one's reluctance;
**sich [dazu]** ∼, etw. zu tun bring oneself to
do sth.
**Über·windung** *die* (a) ▶ ÜBERWINDEN 1:
overcoming; getting past
(b) (das Sichüberwinden) **es war eine große** ∼
**für ihn** it cost him a great effort
**über·wuchern** *tr. V.* overgrow
**Über·zahl** *die* majority
**überzählig** *Adj.* surplus
**über·zeugen** ① *tr. V.* convince
② *itr. V.* be convincing
**überzeugend** ① *Adj.* convincing
② *adv.* convincingly
**überzeugt** *Adj.* convinced
**Über·zeugung** *die* (feste Meinung)
conviction
**über|ziehen¹** *unr. tr. V.* pull on
**über·ziehen²** *unr. tr. V.* (a) etw. mit etw.
∼: cover sth. with sth.
(b) overdraw ⟨*account*⟩ (**um by**)
**Überziehungs·kredit** *der* (Finanzw.)
overdraft facility
**überzüchtet** *Adj.* overbred; over-
sophisticated ⟨*engines, systems*⟩
**Überzug** *der* (a) (Beschichtung) coating
(b) (Bezug) cover
**üblich** *Adj.* usual; (normal) normal;
(gebräuchlich) customary
**üblicher·weise** *Adv.* usually
**U-Boot** *das* submarine; sub (coll.)
**übrig** *Adj.* remaining *attrib.;* (ander...) other;
**alle** ∼en Gäste ...: all the other guests ...; **im
Übrigen** besides; **es ist etwas** ∼: there is
some left; ∼ **bleiben** be left; ⟨*food, drink*⟩ be
left over; ∼ **lassen** (+ *Akk.*) leave; leave
⟨*food, drink*⟩ over

**u**

**\*übrig|bleiben** ▶ ÜBRIG

**übrigens** *Adv.* by the way

**\*übrig|lassen** ▶ ÜBRIG

**Übung** *die;* ~, ~en (a) exercise
(b) (das Üben, Geübtsein) practice

**UdSSR** *Abk. die;* ~ (1922–1991) = **Union der Sozialistischen Sowjetrepubliken** USSR

**Ufer** *das;* ~s, ~: bank; (des Meers) shore

**UG** *Abk.* = **Untergeschoss**

**Uganda** *(das);* ~s Uganda

**Uhr** *die;* ~, ~en (a) clock; (Armband-, Taschenuhr) watch; (Wasser-, Gasuhr) meter; (an Messinstrumenten) dial; gauge; **auf die od.** nach der ~ sehen look at the time; **rund um die** ~ (ugs.) round the clock
(b) acht ~: eight o'clock; **wie viel** ~ **ist es?** what's the time?; what time is it?

**Uhr-:** ~armband *das* watch strap; ~kette *die* watch chain; ~macher *der,* ~macherin *die* watchmaker/clockmaker; ~werk *das* clock/watch mechanism; ~zeiger *der* clock/watch hand; ~zeiger·sinn *der:* im/entgegen dem ~zeigersinn clockwise/anticlockwise; ~zeit *die* time; jmdn. nach der ~zeit fragen ask sb. the time

**Uhu** *der;* ~s, ~s eagle owl

**Ukraine** *die;* ~: Ukraine

**Ukrainer** *der;* ~s, ~, **Ukrainerin** *die;* ~, ~nen Ukrainian

**UKW** *Abk.* = **Ultrakurzwelle** VHF

**UKW-Sender** *der* VHF station; ≈ FM station

**Ulk** *der;* ~s, ~e lark (coll.); (Streich) trick; [practical] joke

**ulkig** (ugs.) ① *Adj.* funny
② *adv.* in a funny way

**Ulme** *die;* ~, ~n elm

**Ultimatum** *das;* ~s, Ultimaten ultimatum

**Ultra·kurz·welle** *die* ultra-short wave; (Rundf.: Wellenbereich) very high frequency; VHF

**Ultra·schall** *der* (Physik, Med.) ultrasound

**Ultraschall-untersuchung** *die* (Med.) ultrasound examination

**ultra·violett** *Adj.* ultraviolet

**um** ① *Präp. mit Akk.* (a) (räumlich) [a]round; um die Ecke round the corner
(b) (zeitlich) (genau) at; (etwa) around [about]
(c) Tag um Tag/Stunde um Stunde day after day/hour after hour
(d) (bei Maß- u. Mengenangaben) by
② *Adv.* around; about; **um [die] 10 Euro/50 Personen [herum]** around *or* about 10 euros/50 people
③ *Konj.* (a) (final) um ... zu [in order] to
(b) (konsekutiv) er ist groß genug/ist noch zu klein, um ... zu ...: he is big enough/is still too young to ...

---

**um|ändern** *tr. V.* change; revise ⟨*text, novel*⟩; alter ⟨*garment*⟩

**um-armen** *tr. V.* embrace; (an sich drücken) hug

**Umarmung** *die;* ~, ~en embrace; hug

**Um·bau** *der;* ~[e]s, ~ten ▶ UMBAUEN: rebuilding; alteration; conversion; (fig.) reorganization

**um|bauen** *tr., auch itr. V.* rebuild; (leicht ändern) alter; (zu etw. anderem) convert (**zu** into); (fig.) reorganize ⟨*system, administration, etc.*⟩

**um|benennen** *unr. tr. V.* change the name of; rename

**um|biegen** *unr. tr. V.* ① bend
② *unr. itr. V.; mit sein* turn

**um|binden** *unr. tr. V.* put on

**um|blättern** ① *tr. V.* turn [over]
② *itr. V.* turn the page/pages

**um|blicken** *refl. V.* (a) look around
(b) (zurückblicken) [turn to] look back (**nach** at)

**um|bringen** *unr. tr. V.* kill

**Um·bruch** *der* (a) radical change; (Umwälzung) upheaval
(b) (Druckw.) make-up; (Ergebnis) page proofs *pl.*

**um|buchen** ① *tr. V.* change (**auf** + *Akk.* to)
② *itr. V.* change one's booking (**auf** + *Akk.* to)

**Um·buchung** *die* change of booking

**um|datieren** *tr. V.* change the date of; redate ⟨*contract, letter, etc.*⟩

**um|denken** *unr. itr. V.* revise one's thinking; rethink; **ein Prozess des Umdenkens** a process of rethinking

**um|drehen** ① *tr. V.* turn round; turn over ⟨*coin, hand, etc.*⟩; turn ⟨*key*⟩
② *refl. V.* turn round; (den Kopf wenden) turn one's head
③ *itr. V.; auch mit sein* (ugs.: umkehren) turn back; (ugs.: wenden) turn round

**Um·drehung** *die* turn; (eines Motors usw.) revolution; rev (coll.)

**um-einander** *Adv.* sich ~ kümmern/sorgen take care of/worry about each other *or* one another

**um|fahren¹** *unr. tr. V.* knock down

**um·fahren²** *unr. tr. V.* go round; make a detour round ⟨*obstruction etc.*⟩; (im Auto) drive round; (im Schiff) sail round; (auf einer Umgehungsstraße) bypass ⟨*town, village, etc.*⟩

**um|fallen** *unr. itr. V.; mit sein* (a) fall over
(b) (zusammenbrechen) collapse; **tot** ~: fall down dead

**Um·fang** *der* (a) circumference; (eines Quadrats usw.) perimeter; (eines Baums, Menschen usw.) girth
(b) (Größe) size
(c) (Ausmaß) extent

**umfang·reich** *Adj.* extensive; substantial ⟨*book*⟩

**um·fassen** *tr. V.* (a) grasp; (umarmen) embrace

**(b)** (enthalten) contain; (einschließen) include; span, cover ⟨*period*⟩

**umfassend** ⟦1⟧ *Adj.* full ⟨*reply, information, survey, confession*⟩; extensive, wide ⟨*knowledge, powers*⟩ ⟦2⟧ *adv.* ⟨*inform*⟩ fully

**Um·feld** *das* (Psych., Soziol.) milieu

**um|formen** *tr. V.* reshape; revise ⟨*poem, novel*⟩; transform ⟨*person*⟩

**Um·frage** *die* survey; (Politik) opinion poll

**um|füllen** *tr. V.* etw. in etw. (*Akk.*) ∼: transfer sth. into sth.

**um|funktionieren** *tr. V.* change the function of; etw. zu etw. ∼: turn sth. into sth.

**Um·gang** *der* **(a)** (gesellschaftlicher Verkehr) contact **(b)** (das Umgehen) den ∼ mit Pferden lernen learn how to handle horses

**umgänglich** *Adj.* affable; (gesellig) sociable

**Umgangs-:** ∼**form** *die* gute/schlechte/ keine ∼formen haben have good/bad/no manners; ∼**sprache** *die* colloquial language

**um·garnen** *tr. V.* beguile

**um·geben** *unr. tr. V.* **(a)** surround; ⟨*hedge, fence, wall, etc.*⟩ enclose **(b)** etw. mit etw. ∼: surround sth. with sth.; (einfrieden) enclose sth. with sth.

**Umgebung** *die;* ∼, ∼en surroundings *pl.;* (Nachbarschaft) neighbourhood; (eines Ortes) surrounding area

**um|gehen¹** *unr. itr. V.; mit sein* **(a)** (im Umlauf sein) ⟨*list, rumour, etc.*⟩ go round, circulate; ⟨*illness, infection*⟩ go round **(b)** (spuken) hier geht ein Gespenst um this place is haunted **(c)** (behandeln) mit jmdm. freundlich/liebevoll *usw.* ∼: treat sb. kindly/lovingly *etc.;* er kann mit Geld nicht ∼: he can't handle money

**um·gehen²** *unr. tr. V.* **(a)** go round; make a detour round; (auf einer Umgehungsstraße) bypass ⟨*town etc.*⟩ **(b)** (vermeiden) avoid; evade ⟨*question, issue*⟩ **(c)** (nicht befolgen) circumvent ⟨*law, restriction, etc.*⟩; evade ⟨*obligation, duty*⟩

**umgehend** ⟦1⟧ *Adj.* immediate ⟦2⟧ *adv.* immediately

**Umgehung** *die;* ∼, ∼en **(a)** durch ∼ der Innenstadt by bypassing *or* avoiding the town centre **(b)** ▶ UMGEHEN² c: circumvention; evasion

**Umgehungs·straße** *die* bypass

**umgekehrt** ⟦1⟧ *Adj.* inverse ⟨*ratio, proportion*⟩; reverse ⟨*order*⟩; opposite ⟨*sign*⟩ ⟦2⟧ *adv.* inversely ⟨*proportional*⟩; vom Englischen ins Deutsche und ∼ übersetzen translate from English into German and vice versa

**um|gestalten** *tr. V.* reshape; remodel; redesign ⟨*square, park, room, etc.*⟩

**um|graben** *unr. tr. V.* dig over

**Um·hang** *der* cape

**um|hängen** *tr. V.* **(a)** etw. ∼: hang sth. somewhere else **(b)** jmdm./sich einen Mantel/eine Decke ∼: drape a coat/blanket round sb.'s/one's shoulders

**um|hauen** *unr. tr. V.* fell; (fig.) knock down

**um·her-** *Adv.* around

**umher-** ▶ HERUM-

**um|hören** *refl. V.* keep one's ears open; (direkt fragen) ask around

**um|jubeln** *tr. V.* cheer

**um|kehren** ⟦1⟧ *itr. V.; mit sein* turn back ⟦2⟧ *tr. V.* turn upside down; turn over ⟨*sheet of paper*⟩; (nach links drehen) turn ⟨*garment etc.*⟩ inside out; (nach rechts drehen) turn ⟨*garment etc.*⟩ right side out

**um|kippen** ⟦1⟧ *itr. V.; mit sein* **(a)** fall over; ⟨*boat*⟩ capsize, turn over; ⟨*vehicle*⟩ overturn **(b)** (ugs.: ohnmächtig werden) keel over **(c)** (Ökologie) ⟨*river, lake*⟩ reach the stage of biological collapse ⟦2⟧ *tr. V.* tip over; knock over ⟨*lamp, vase, glass, cup*⟩; capsize ⟨*boat*⟩; turn ⟨*boat*⟩ over; overturn ⟨*vehicle*⟩

**um|klappen** *tr. V.* fold down

**Um·kleide·kabine** *die* changing cubicle

**um|knicken** *itr. V.; mit sein* **[mit dem Fuß]** ∼: go over on one's ankle **(b)** bend; ⟨*branch*⟩ bend and snap

**um|kommen** *unr. itr. V.; mit sein* die; (bei einem Unglück, durch Gewalt) get killed; die; ⟨*food*⟩ go off

**Um·kreis** *der* surrounding area; im ∼ von 5 km within a radius of 5 km.

**um·kreisen** *tr. V.* circle; ⟨*spacecraft, satellite*⟩ orbit; ⟨*planet*⟩ revolve [a]round

**Um·lauf** *der* **(a)** (von Planeten) revolution **(b)** (Zirkulation) circulation; in *od.* im ∼ sein be circulating; ⟨*coin, banknote*⟩ be in circulation; in ∼ bringen circulate; bring ⟨*coin, banknote*⟩ into circulation

**Umlauf·bahn** *die* (Astron., Raumf.) orbit

**Um·laut** *der* (Sprachw.) umlaut

**um|legen** *tr. V.* **(a)** (um einen Körperteil) put on **(b)** (verlegen) transfer ⟨*patient, telephone call*⟩ **(c)** (salopp: ermorden) jmdn. ∼: bump sb. off (coll.)

**um|leiten** *tr. V.* divert

**Um·leitung** *die* diversion

**umliegend** *Adj.* surrounding ⟨*area*⟩; (nahe) nearby ⟨*building*⟩

**um|modeln** *tr. V.* (ugs.) change ⟨*house, flat*⟩ round; refashion, alter ⟨*jacket etc.*⟩

**um·nachtet** *Adj.* (geh.) deranged

**Umnachtung** *die;* ∼, ∼en (geh.) derangement

**um|pflanzen** *tr. V.* transplant

**um|pflügen** *tr. V.* plough up

**um|räumen** ⟦1⟧ *tr. V.* rearrange ⟦2⟧ *itr. V.* rearrange things

u

**um|rechnen** *tr. V.* convert (in + *Akk.* into)

**Um-rechnung** *die* conversion (in + *Akk.* into)

**Umrechnungs-kurs** *der* exchange rate

**um|reißen¹** *unr. tr. V.* pull ⟨*mast, tree*⟩ down; knock ⟨*person*⟩ down; ⟨*wind*⟩ tear ⟨*tent etc.*⟩ down

**um·reißen²** *unr. tr. V.* outline; summarize ⟨*subject, problem, situation*⟩

**um|rennen** *unr. tr. V.* [run into and] knock down

**um·ringen** *tr. V.* surround

**Um·riss, \*Um·riß** *der* (auch fig.) outline

**um|rühren** *tr. (auch itr.) V.* stir

**um|rüsten** *tr. V.* (Technik) convert (auf + *Akk.* to, zu into)

**ums** /ʊms/ *Präp. + Art.* (a) = um das; (b) ~ Leben kommen lose one's life

**um|satteln** *itr. V.* (ugs.) change jobs; ⟨*student*⟩ change courses

**Um·satz** *der* turnover; (Verkauf) sales *pl.* (an + *Dat.* of); ~ machen (ugs.) make money

**um|säumen** *tr. V.* hem

**um|schalten** **1** *tr. V.* (auch fig.) switch [over] (auf + *Akk.* to); move ⟨*lever*⟩ **2** *itr. V.* switch *or* change over (auf + *Akk.* to)

**Um·schlag** *der* (a) cover (b) (Briefumschlag) envelope (c) (Schutzumschlag) jacket; (einer Broschüre, eines Heftes) cover (d) (Med.: Wickel) compress; (warm) poultice

**um|schlagen** **1** *unr. tr. V.* (a) turn up ⟨*sleeve, collar, trousers*⟩; turn over ⟨*page*⟩ (b) (umladen, verladen) turn round, trans-ship ⟨*goods*⟩ **2** *unr. itr. V.; mit sein* change (in + *Akk.* into); ⟨*wind*⟩ veer [round]

**um|schreiben¹** *unr. tr. V.* rewrite

**um·schreiben²** *unr. tr. V.* (a) (in Worte fassen) describe; (definieren) define ⟨*meaning, sb.'s task, etc.*⟩; (paraphrasieren) paraphrase ⟨*word, expression*⟩ (b) (Sprachw.) construct (mit with)

**Um·schreibung** *die* description; (Definition) definition; (Verhüllung) circumlocution (*Gen.* for)

**Um·schrift** *die* (Sprachw.) transcription

**um|schulen** **1** *tr. V.* (beruflich) retrain **2** *itr. V.* retrain (auf + *Akk.* as)

**Umschulung** *die;* ~: retraining (auf + *Akk.* as)

**um|schütten** *tr. V.* (a) pour [into another container]; decant ⟨*liquid*⟩ (b) (verschütten) spill

**Um·schweif** *der* circumlocution; ohne ~e without beating about the bush

**Um·schwung** *der* complete change; (in der Politik usw.) U-turn

*\*old spelling - see note on page xiv*

**um|sehen** *unr. refl. V.* (a) look; sich im Zimmer ~: look [a]round the room (b) (zurücksehen) look round *or* back

**umseitig** *Adj., adv.* overleaf

**um|setzen** *tr. V.* (a) move; (auf anderen Posten usw.) move, transfer (in + *Akk.* to); (umpflanzen) transplant; (in anderen Topf) repot (b) (verwirklichen) implement ⟨*plan*⟩; translate ⟨*plan, intention, etc.*⟩ into action *or* reality; realize ⟨*ideas*⟩ (c) (Wirtsch.) turn over, have a turnover of ⟨*x euros etc.*⟩; sell ⟨*shares, goods*⟩

**Um·sicht** *die* circumspection

**um·sichtig** **1** *Adj.* circumspect **2** *adv.* circumspectly

**um|siedeln** **1** *tr. V.* resettle **2** *itr. V.; mit sein* move (in + *Akk.*, nach to)

**um·so** *Konj.* je ... ~: the ..., the; ~ besser/ schlimmer! all the better/worse!

**um·sonst** *Adv.* (a) (unentgeltlich) free; for nothing (b) (vergebens) in vain

**Um·stand** *der* (a) (Gegebenheit) circumstance; (Tatsache) fact; unter Umständen possibly (b) (Aufwand) business; macht keine [großen] Umstände please don't go to any bother

**umstände·halber** *Adv.* owing to circumstances; „~ zu verkaufen" 'forced to sell'

**umständlich** **1** *Adj.* involved, elaborate ⟨*procedure, method, description, explanation, etc.*⟩; elaborate, laborious ⟨*preparation, check, etc.*⟩; awkward, difficult ⟨*journey, job*⟩; (weitschweifig) long-winded; (Umstände machend) awkward ⟨*person*⟩ **2** *adv.* in an involved *or* roundabout way; (weitschweifig) at great length

**Umstands·kleid** *das* maternity dress

**umstehend** *Adj.* standing round *postpos.*

**um|steigen** *unr. itr. V.* change (in + *Akk.* [on] to)

**um|stellen¹** **1** *tr. V.* (a) rearrange, change round ⟨*furniture, books, etc.*⟩; reorder ⟨*words etc.*⟩; transpose ⟨*two words*⟩ (b) (anders einstellen) reset ⟨*lever, switch, points, clock*⟩ (c) (ändern) change *or* switch over (auf + *Akk.* to) **2** *refl. V.* adjust (auf + *Akk.* to)

**um·stellen²** *tr. V.* surround

**um|stimmen** *tr. V.* win ⟨*person*⟩ round

**um|stoßen** *unr. tr. V.* (a) knock over (b) (rückgängig machen) change ⟨*plan, decision*⟩; (zunichte machen) upset, wreck ⟨*plan, theory*⟩

**umstritten** *Adj.* disputed; controversial ⟨*book, author, policy, etc.*⟩

**Um·sturz** *der* coup

**um|stürzen** **1** *tr. V.* overturn; (fig.) topple, overthrow ⟨*political system, government*⟩ **2** *itr. V.* overturn; ⟨*wall, building, chimney*⟩ fall down

**umstürzlerisch** *Adj.* subversive

**u**

**Ụmsturz·versuch** *der* attempted coup

**Ụm·tausch** *der* exchange

**ụm|tauschen** *tr. V.* exchange ⟨*goods, article*⟩ (**gegen** for); change ⟨*dollars, pounds, etc.*⟩ (**in** + *Akk.* into)

**ụm|topfen** *tr. V.* repot ⟨*plant*⟩

**Ụm·trunk** *der* communal drink

**ụm|tun** *unr. refl. V.* (ugs.) look [a]round; **sich nach etw.** ∼: be on the lookout for sth.

**Ụmwälzung** *die;* ∼, ∼**en** (fig.) revolution

**ụm|wandeln** *tr. V.* convert ⟨*substance, building, etc.*⟩ (**in** + *Akk.* into); (ändern) change; alter

**Ụm·weg** *der* detour

**Ụm·welt** *die* (a) environment

(b) (Menschen) people *pl.* around sb.

**ụmwelt-, Ụmwelt-:** ∼**bedingt** *Adj.* caused by the *or* one's environment *postpos.;* ∼**belastung** *die* environmental pollution *no indef. art.;* ∼**bewusst, *** ∼**bewußt** *Adj.* environmentally conscious *or* aware; ∼**feindlich** [1] *Adj.* inimical to the environment *postpos.;* ecologically undesirable; [2] *adv.* in an ecologically undesirable way; ⟨*drive, behave*⟩ without regard for the environment; ∼**freundlich** [1] *Adj.* environmentally friendly; [2] *adv.* in an environmentally friendly way; ∼**katastrophe** *die* environmental disaster; ∼**schädlich** [1] *Adj.* harmful to the environment *postpos.;* ecologically harmful; [2] *adv.* in an ecologically harmful way; ∼**schutz** *der* environmental protection *no art.;* ∼**schützer** *der;* ∼**s,** ∼∼, ∼**schützerin** *die;* ∼∼, ∼, ∼**nen** environmentalist; conservationist; ∼**verschmutzung** *die* pollution [of the environment]

**ụm|wenden** *regelm.* (*auch unr.*) *tr. V.* (a) turn over ⟨*page, joint, etc.*⟩

(b) turn round ⟨*vehicle, horse*⟩

**um·wẹrben** *unr. tr. V.* court; woo; **viel umworben** much-courted

**ụm|werfen** *unr. tr. V.* (a) knock over; knock ⟨*person*⟩ down *or* over; (fig. ugs.: aus der Fassung bringen) bowl ⟨*person*⟩ over; stun ⟨*person*⟩

(b) (fig. ugs.: umstoßen) knock ⟨*plan*⟩ on the head (coll.)

**ụmwerfend** (ugs.) [1] *Adj.* fantastic (coll.); stunning (coll.)

[2] *adv.* fantastically [well] (coll.); brilliantly

**um·wịckeln** *tr. V.* wrap; bind; (mit einem Verband) bandage

**Umzäunung** *die;* ∼, ∼**en** fence, fencing (*Gen.* round)

**ụm|ziehen** [1] *unr. itr. V.; mit sein* move (**an** + *Akk.,* **in** + *Akk.,* **nach** to)

[2] *unr. tr. V.* jmdn. ∼: change sb. *or* get sb. changed; **sich** ∼: change *or* get changed

**um·zịngeln** *tr. V.* surround; encircle

**Umzịngelung** *die;* ∼: encirclement

**Ụm·zug** *der* (a) move; (von Möbeln) removal

(b) (Festzug) procession

**UN** *Pl.* UN *sing.*

**unabạ̈nderlich** [1] *Adj.* unalterable; irrevocable ⟨*decision*⟩

[2] *adv.* irrevocably

**ụnabhängig** [1] *Adj.* independent (**von** of); (unbeeinflusst) unaffected (**von** by)

[2] *adv.* independently (**von** of); ∼ **davon, ob** …/**was** …/**wo** … *usw.* irrespective *or* regardless of whether …/what …/where … etc

**Ụnabhängigkeit** *die;* ∼: independence

**unabkọ̈mmlich** *Adj.* indispensable; **sie ist im Moment** ∼: she is otherwise engaged

**ụnablässig** [1] *Adj.* incessant

[2] *adv.* incessantly

**ụnabsichtlich** [1] *Adj.* unintentional

[2] *adv.* unintentionally

**unabwẹndbar** *Adj.* inevitable

**ụnachtsam** [1] *Adj.* (a) inattentive

(b) (nicht sorgfältig) careless

[2] *adv.* (ohne Sorgfalt) carelessly

**Ụnachtsamkeit** *die;* ∼ (a) inattentiveness

(b) (mangelnde Sorgfalt) carelessness

**ụnangebracht** *Adj.* inappropriate

**ụnangefochten** *Adj.* unchallenged; (Rechtsw.) uncontested ⟨*verdict, will, etc.*⟩

**ụnangenehm** [1] *Adj.* unpleasant (*Dat.* for); (peinlich) embarrassing ⟨*question, situation*⟩

[2] *adv.* unpleasantly

**unannẹhmbar** *Adj.* unacceptable

**Ụnannehmlichkeit** *die;* ∼, ∼**en** trouble

**ụnansehnlich** *Adj.* unprepossessing; plain ⟨*girl*⟩

**ụnanständig** [1] *Adj.* improper; (anstößig) indecent; dirty ⟨*joke*⟩; rude ⟨*word, song*⟩

[2] *adv.* improperly

**Ụnanständigkeit** *die;* ∼, ∼**en** impropriety; indecency; (Obszönität) obscenity

**ụnappetitlich** [1] *Adj.* unappetizing; (fig.) unsavoury ⟨*joke*⟩; disgusting ⟨*washbasin, nails, etc.*⟩

[2] *adv.* unappetizingly

**Ụnart** *die;* ∼, ∼**en** bad habit

**ụnartig** *Adj.* naughty

**ụnästhetisch** *Adj.* unpleasant ⟨*sight etc.*⟩; ugly ⟨*building etc.*⟩

**ụnauffällig** [1] *Adj.* inconspicuous; unobtrusive ⟨*scar, defect, skill, behaviour, surveillance, etc.*⟩; discreet ⟨*signal, elegance*⟩

[2] *adv.* inconspicuously; unobtrusively

**unauffịndbar** *Adj.* untraceable; ∼ **sein** *od.* **bleiben** be nowhere to be found

**ụnaufgefordert** *Adv.* without being asked

**unaufhạltsam** [1] *Adj.* inexorable

[2] *adv.* inexorably

**ụnaufmerksam** *Adj.* inattentive (**gegenüber** to); careless ⟨*driver*⟩

**ụnaufrichtig** *Adj.* insincere

**Unaufrichtigkeit** *die;* ~, ~en insincerity
**unausbleiblich** *Adj.* inevitable
**unausgegoren** *Adj.* (abwertend) immature
**unausstehlich** *Adj.* unbearable ⟨*person, noise, smell, etc.*⟩; insufferable ⟨*person*⟩; intolerable ⟨*noise, smell*⟩.
**unausweichlich** *Adj.* unavoidable; inevitable
**unbändig** [1] *Adj.* **(a)** boisterous **(b)** (überaus groß/stark) unbridled [2] *adv.* **(a)** wildly **(b)** (sehr, äußerst) unrestrainedly; tremendously (coll.)
**unbarmherzig** *Adj.* merciless
**unbeabsichtigt** [1] *Adj.* unintentional [2] *adv.* unintentionally
**unbeachtet** *Adj.* unnoticed
**unbedacht** [1] *Adj.* rash; thoughtless [2] *adv.* rashly; thoughtlessly
**unbedenklich** *adv.* without second thoughts
**unbedeutend** [1] *Adj.* insignificant; minor ⟨*artist, poet*⟩; slight, minor ⟨*improvement, change, error*⟩ [2] *adv.* slightly
**unbedingt** [1] *Adj.* absolute [2] *adv.* absolutely [3] *Adv.* (auf jeden Fall) whatever happens
**unbefangen** *Adj.* **(a)** (ungehemmt) uninhibited **(b)** (unvoreingenommen) impartial
**Unbefangenheit** *die;* ▶ UNBEFANGEN A, B: uninhibitedness; impartiality
**unbefriedigend** *Adj.* unsatisfactory
**unbefristet** [1] *Adj.* for an indefinite period *postpos.;* indefinite ⟨*strike*⟩; unlimited ⟨*visa*⟩ [2] *adv.* for an indefinite period
**unbefugt** [1] *Adj.* unauthorized [2] *adv.* without authorization
**unbegreiflich** *Adj.* incomprehensible (*Dat.,* für to); incredible ⟨*love, goodness, stupidity, carelessness, etc.*⟩
**unbegrenzt** [1] *Adj.* unlimited [2] *adv.* ⟨*stay, keep, etc.*⟩ indefinitely
**Unbehagen** *das;* ~s uneasiness, disquiet; (Sorge) concern (an + *Dat.* about)
**unbehaglich** [1] *Adj.* uneasy ⟨*feeling, atmosphere*⟩; uncomfortable ⟨*thought, room*⟩ [2] *adv.* uneasily
**unbeherrscht** *Adj.* uncontrolled; er ist ~: he has no self-control
**Unbeherrschtheit** *die;* ~: lack of self-control
**unbeholfen** [1] *Adj.* clumsy [2] *adv.* clumsily
**unbekannt** *Adj.* **(a)** unknown; (nicht vertraut) unfamiliar; unidentified ⟨*caller, donor*⟩; „Empfänger ~" 'not known at this address'

**(b)** (nicht vielen bekannt) little known; obscure ⟨*poet, painter, etc.*⟩
**Unbekannte**[1] *der/die; adj. Dekl.* unknown *or* unidentified man/woman; (Fremde[r]) stranger
**Unbekannte**[2] *die; adj. Dekl.* (Math.; auch fig.) unknown
**unbekleidet** *Adj.* without any clothes on *postpos.;* bare ⟨*torso etc.*⟩; naked ⟨*corpse*⟩
**unbekümmert** [1] *Adj.* carefree; (ohne Bedenken, lässig) casual [2] *adv.* **(a)** in a carefree way **(b)** (ohne Bedenken) without caring *or* worrying
**unbeleuchtet** *Adj.* unlit ⟨*street, corridor, etc.*⟩; ⟨*vehicle*⟩ without [any] lights
**unbeliebt** *Adj.* unpopular (bei with)
**unbemannt** *Adj.* unmanned
**unbemerkt** *Adj., adv.* unnoticed
**unbenutzt** *Adj.* unused
**unbequem** [1] *Adj.* **(a)** uncomfortable **(b)** (lästig) awkward, embarrassing ⟨*question, opinion*⟩; troublesome ⟨*politician etc.*⟩; unpleasant ⟨*criticism, truth, etc.*⟩ [2] *adv.* uncomfortably
**unberechenbar** [1] *Adj.* unpredictable [2] *adv.* unpredictably
**unberechtigt** *Adj.* **(a)** (ungerechtfertigt) unjustified **(b)** (unbefugt) unauthorized
**unberührt** *Adj.* untouched; sie ist noch ~: she is still a virgin
**unbescheiden** *Adj.* presumptuous
**unbeschrankt** *Adj.* ⟨*crossing*⟩ without gates, with no gates
**unbeschreiblich** [1] *Adj.* indescribable; unimaginable ⟨*fear, beauty*⟩; ⟨*fear, beauty*⟩ beyond description [2] *adv.* indescribably ⟨*beautiful*⟩; unbelievably ⟨*busy*⟩
**unbesorgt** *Adj.* unconcerned; seien Sie ~: don't [you] worry
**unbeständig** *Adj.* changeable ⟨*weather*⟩; fickle ⟨*lover etc.*⟩
**unbestimmt** [1] *Adj.* **(a)** indefinite; indeterminate ⟨*age, number*⟩; (ungewiss) uncertain **(b)** (ungenau) vague **(c)** (Sprachw.) indefinite ⟨*article, pronoun*⟩ [2] *adv.* (ungenau) vaguely
**unbestreitbar** *Adj.* indisputable; unquestionable
**unbestritten** [1] *Adj.* undisputed; ~ ist, dass ... it is undisputed that ...; there is no disputing that ... [2] *adv.* indisputably
**unbewacht** *Adj.* unsupervised; unattended ⟨*car park*⟩
**unbewaffnet** *Adj.* unarmed
**unbeweglich** *Adj.* motionless; still ⟨*air, water*⟩; fixed ⟨*gaze, expression*⟩

**u**

---
*alte Schreibung - vgl. Hinweis auf S. xiv

**unbewegt** *Adj.* motionless; fixed ⟨*expression*⟩

**unbewohnbar** *Adj.* uninhabitable

**unbewohnt** *Adj.* uninhabited ⟨*area*⟩; unoccupied ⟨*house, flat*⟩

**unbewusst, \*unbewußt** *Adj.* unconscious

**unbrauchbar** *Adj.* unusable; (untauglich) useless ⟨*method, person*⟩

**und** *Konj.* and; (folglich) [and] so; **ich** ~ **tanzen?** what, me dance?; **sei so gut** ~ **mach das Fenster zu** be so good as to shut the window

**Undank** *der;* ~[e]s: ingratitude

**undankbar** *Adj.* ungrateful ⟨*person, behaviour*⟩

**undenkbar** *Adj.* unthinkable; inconceivable

**undeutlich** 1 *Adj.* unclear; indistinct; (ungenau) vague ⟨*idea, memory, etc.*⟩
2 *adv.* indistinctly; (ungenau) vaguely

**undicht** *Adj.* leaky; leaking; ~**e Fenster** windows which do not fit tightly

**Unding** *das* **ein** ~ **sein** be preposterous *or* ridiculous

**undurchführbar** *Adj.* impracticable

**undurchlässig** *Adj.* impermeable; (wasserdicht) watertight; waterproof; (luftdicht) airtight

**uneben** *Adj.* uneven

**Unebenheit** *die;* ~, ~**en (a)** unevenness **(b)** (unebene Stelle) lumpy *or* uneven patch

**unehelich** *Adj.* illegitimate ⟨*child*⟩; unmarried ⟨*mother*⟩

**unehrlich** 1 *Adj.* dishonest
2 *adv.* dishonestly; by dishonest means

**uneigennützig** *Adj.* unselfish

**Uneigennützigkeit** *die;* ~: unselfishness

**uneinig** *Adj.* ⟨*party*⟩ divided by disagreement; [**sich** (*Dat.*)] ~ **sein** disagree

**Uneinigkeit** *die;* ~: disagreement (**in** + *Dat.* on)

**uneins** *Adj.* ~ **sein** be divided (**in** + *Dat.* on); ⟨*persons*⟩ be at variance *or* at cross purposes (**in** + *Dat.* over)

**unempfindlich** *Adj.* **(a)** insensitive (**gegen** to)
**(b)** (immun) immune (**gegen** to, against)
**(c)** (strapazierfähig) hard-wearing

**unendlich** 1 *Adj.* infinite; boundless; (zeitlich) endless; (Math.) infinite
2 *adv.* infinitely ⟨*lovable, sad*⟩; immeasurably ⟨*happy*⟩; ⟨*happy*⟩ beyond measure

**unentbehrlich** *Adj.* indispensable (*Dat.*, **für** to)

**unentgeltlich** */od.* '⎯⎯/ 1 *Adj.* free
2 *adv.* free of charge; ⟨*work*⟩ for nothing, without pay

**unentschieden** 1 *Adj.* unsettled; undecided ⟨*question*⟩; (Sport, Schach) drawn

2 *adv.* ~ **spielen** draw

**Unentschieden** *das;* ~**s,** ~ (Sport, Schach) draw

**unentwegt** */od.* -⎻'-/ 1 *Adj.* **(a)** (beharrlich) persistent ⟨*fighter, champion, efforts*⟩
**(b)** (unaufhörlich) constant; incessant
2 *adv.* **(a)** (beharrlich) persistently
**(b)** (unaufhörlich) constantly; incessantly

**unerbittlich** 1 *Adj.* (auch fig.) inexorable; unsparing ⟨*critic*⟩; relentless ⟨*battle, struggle*⟩; implacable ⟨*hate, enemy*⟩
2 *adv.* (auch fig.) inexorably

**unerfahren** *Adj.* inexperienced

**unerfreulich** 1 *Adj.* unpleasant; bad ⟨*news*⟩
2 *adv.* unpleasantly

**unerheblich** *Adj.* insignificant

**unerhört** 1 *Adj.* (empörend) outrageous
2 *adv.* outrageously

**unerlaubt** 1 *Adj.* unauthorized
2 *adv.* without authorization

**unerledigt** *Adj.* not dealt with *postpos.*

**unermüdlich** 1 *Adj.* tireless, untiring (**bei, in** + *Dat.* in)
2 *adv.* tirelessly

**unerreichbar** *Adj.* inaccessible; (fig.) unattainable

**unerreicht** *Adj.* unequalled

**unersättlich** *Adj.* insatiable

**unerschöpflich** *Adj.* inexhaustible

**unersetzlich** *Adj.* irreplaceable

**unerträglich** */od.* '⎯⎯/ *Adj.* unbearable; intolerable ⟨*situation, conditions, etc.*⟩

**unerwartet** 1 *Adj.* unexpected; **es kam für alle** ~: it came as a surprise to everybody
2 *adv.* unexpectedly

**unerwünscht** *Adj.* unwanted; unwelcome ⟨*interruption, visit, visitor*⟩; undesirable ⟨*side effects*⟩

**unfähig** *Adj.* **(a)** ~ **sein, etw. zu tun** (ständig) be incapable of doing sth.; (momentan) be unable to do sth.
**(b)** (inkompetent) incompetent

**Unfähigkeit** *die* **(a)** inability
**(b)** (Inkompetenz) incompetence

**unfair** 1 *Adj.* unfair (**gegen** to)
2 *adv.* unfairly

**Un·fall** *der;* ~[e]s, **Unfälle** accident

**Unfall-:** ~**arzt** *der,* ~**ärztin** *die* casualty doctor; ~**flucht** *die* (Rechtsspr.) ~**flucht begehen** fail to stop after [being involved in] an accident; ~**opfer** *das* accident victim; ~**stelle** *die* scene of an/the accident; ~**versicherung** *die* accident insurance

**unfehlbar** *Adj.* infallible

**Unfehlbarkeit** *die;* ~: infallibility

**unförmig** *Adj.* shapeless; huge ⟨*legs, hands, body*⟩; bulky, ungainly ⟨*shape, shoes, etc.*⟩

**unfrei** *Adj.* not free *pred.;* subject, dependent ⟨*people*⟩; ⟨*life*⟩ of bondage

**u**

**unfreiwillig** 1 *Adj.* involuntary;
(erzwungen) enforced ⟨*stay*⟩; (nicht beabsichtigt)
unintended ⟨*publicity, joke, humour*⟩
2 *adv.* involuntarily; without wanting to;
(unbeabsichtigt) unintentionally

**unfreundlich** 1 *Adj.* unfriendly (**zu**,
**gegen** to); unkind ⟨*words, remark*⟩
2 *adv.* in an unfriendly way

**Unfreundlichkeit** *die;* ∼: unfriendliness

**unfrisiert** *Adj.* ungroomed ⟨*hair*⟩

**unfruchtbar** *Adj.* infertile; (fig.)
unproductive

**Unfruchtbarkeit** *die;* ∼: infertility; (fig.)
unproductiveness

**Unfug** *der;* ∼[e]s (a) [piece of] mischief;
grober ∼: public nuisance
(b) (Unsinn) nonsense

**Ungar** *der;* ∼n, ∼n, **Ungarin** *die;* ∼,
∼nen Hungarian

**ungarisch** *Adj.* Hungarian

**Ungarn** *(das);* ∼s Hungary

**ungeachtet** *Präp. mit Gen.* (geh.)
notwithstanding; despite

**ungebildet** *Adj.* uneducated

**ungeboren** *Adj.* unborn

**ungebräuchlich** *Adj.* uncommon; rare;
rarely used ⟨*method, process*⟩

**ungebrochen** *Adj.* (fig.) unbroken ⟨*will,
person*⟩; undiminished ⟨*strength, courage*⟩

**ungedeckt** *Adj.* uncovered ⟨*cheque*⟩

**Ungeduld** *die;* ∼: impatience

**ungeduldig** 1 *Adj.* impatient
2 *adv.* impatiently

**ungeeignet** *Adj.* unsuitable; (für eine
Aufgabe) unsuited (**für, zu** to, for)

**ungefähr** 1 *Adj.* approximate; rough
⟨*idea, outline*⟩
2 *adv.* approximately; roughly

**ungefährlich** *Adj.* safe; harmless ⟨*animal,
person, illness, etc.*⟩

**ungeheizt** *Adj.* unheated

**ungeheuer** 1 *Adj.* enormous; tremendous
⟨*strength, energy, effort, enthusiasm, fear,
success, pressure, etc.*⟩; vast, immense
⟨*fortune, knowledge*⟩; (schrecklich) terrible
(coll.), terrific (coll.) ⟨*pain, rage*⟩
2 *adv.* tremendously; terribly (coll.)
⟨*difficult, clever*⟩

**Ungeheuer** *das;* ∼s, ∼ (auch fig.) monster

**ungeheuerlich** *Adj.* monstrous;
outrageous

**Ungeheuerlichkeit** *die;* ∼, ∼en (a)
monstrous nature; outrageousness
(b) (Vorgang) monstrous *or* outrageous thing

**ungehindert** *Adj.* unimpeded

**ungehörig** 1 *Adj.* improper; (frech)
impertinent
2 *adv.* improperly; (frech) impertinently

**ungehorsam** *Adj.* disobedient (**gegenüber**
to)

**Ungehorsam** *der;* ∼s disobedience
(**gegenüber** to)

**ungekürzt** *Adj.* unabridged ⟨*edition, book*⟩;
uncut ⟨*film, speech*⟩

**ungelegen** 1 *Adj.* **das kommt mir sehr** ∼/
**nicht** ∼: that is very inconvenient *or*
awkward/quite convenient for me
2 *adv.* inconveniently

**ungelernt** *Adj.* unskilled

**ungemütlich** 1 *Adj.* uninviting, cheerless
⟨*room, flat*⟩; uncomfortable, unfriendly
⟨*atmosphere*⟩
2 *adv.* uncomfortably ⟨*furnished*⟩

**ungenau** 1 *Adj.* inaccurate; imprecise,
inexact ⟨*definition, formulation, etc.*⟩;
(undeutlich) vague ⟨*memory, idea, impression*⟩
2 *adv.* inaccurately; ⟨*define*⟩ imprecisely,
inexactly; ⟨*remember*⟩ vaguely

**ungeniert** /'ʊnʒeniːɐ̯t/ 1 *Adj.* free and
easy; uninhibited
2 *adv.* openly; ⟨*yawn*⟩ unconcernedly;
⟨*undress etc.*⟩ without any embarrassment

**ungenießbar** *Adj.* (nicht essbar) inedible;
(nicht trinkbar) undrinkable; (fig. ugs.)
unbearable

**ungenügend** 1 *Adj.* inadequate; **die Note**
„∼"**/ein Ungenügend** (Schulw.) the/an
'unsatisfactory' [mark]
2 *adv.* inadequately

**ungepflegt** *Adj.* neglected ⟨*garden, park,
car, etc.*⟩; unkempt ⟨*person, appearance,
hair*⟩; uncared-for ⟨*hands*⟩

**ungerade** *Adj.* odd ⟨*number*⟩

**ungerecht** 1 *Adj.* unjust, unfair (**gegen,
zu, gegenüber** to)
2 *adv.* unjustly; unfairly

**Ungerechtigkeit** *die;* ∼, ∼en injustice

**ungern** *Adv.* reluctantly; **etw.** ∼ **tun** not like
*or* dislike doing sth.

**ungerührt** *Adj.* unmoved

**ungeschält** *Adj.* unpeeled ⟨*fruit*⟩

**ungeschehen** *Adj.* **etw.** ∼ **machen** undo
sth.

**Ungeschicklichkeit** *die;* ∼, ∼en
(a) clumsiness
(b) (etwas Ungeschicktes) piece of clumsiness

**ungeschickt** 1 *Adj.* clumsy; awkward
2 *adv.* clumsily; awkwardly

**ungesetzlich** 1 *Adj.* unlawful; illegal
2 *adv.* unlawfully; illegally

**ungestempelt** *Adj.* uncancelled ⟨*stamp*⟩

**ungestört** *Adj.* undisturbed; uninterrupted
⟨*development*⟩

**ungesund** *Adj.* (auch fig.) unhealthy

**Ungetüm** *das;* ∼s, ∼e monster

**ungewiss, \*ungewiß** *Adj.* uncertain;
**über etw.** (*Akk.*) **im Ungewissen sein** be
uncertain *or* unsure about sth.

**Ungewissheit, \*Ungewißheit** *die;* ∼,
∼en uncertainty

**ungewöhnlich** 1 *Adj.* (a) unusual

**(b)** (sehr groß) exceptional ⟨*strength, beauty, ability, etc.*⟩; outstanding ⟨*achievement, success*⟩
2 *adv.* **(a)** ⟨*behave*⟩ abnormally, strangely
**(b)** (enorm) exceptionally

**ungewohnt** 1 *Adj.* unaccustomed; (nicht vertraut) unfamiliar ⟨*method, work, surroundings, etc.*⟩
2 *adv.* unusually

**ungewollt** 1 *Adj.* unwanted; (unbeabsichtigt) unintentional; inadvertent
2 *adv.* unintentionally; inadvertently

**Ungeziefer** *das;* ∼s vermin *pl.*

**ungezogen** 1 *Adj.* naughty; badly behaved; bad ⟨*behaviour*⟩; (frech) cheeky
2 *adv.* naughtily; ⟨*behave*⟩ badly

**ungezwungen** *Adj.* natural, unaffected ⟨*person, behaviour, cheerfulness*⟩; (nicht förmlich) informal, free and easy ⟨*tone, conversation, etc.*⟩

**ungläubig** 1 *Adj.* **(a)** disbelieving
**(b)** (Rel.) unbelieving
2 *adv.* in disbelief

**unglaublich** 1 *Adj.* incredible
2 *adv.* (ugs.: äußerst) incredibly (coll.)

**unglaubwürdig** *Adj.* implausible; untrustworthy, unreliable ⟨*witness etc.*⟩

**ungleich** 1 *Adj.* unequal; odd, unmatching ⟨*socks, gloves, etc.*⟩; (unähnlich) dissimilar
2 *adv.* **(a)** unequally
**(b)** (ungleichmäßig) unevenly

**ungleichmäßig** 1 *Adj.* uneven
2 *adv.* unevenly

**Unglück** *das;* ∼[e]s, ∼e **(a)** (Unfall) accident; (Flugzeugunglück, Zugunglück) crash; accident
**(b)** (Not) misfortune; (Leid) suffering
**(c)** (Pech) bad luck; ∼ haben be unlucky; das bringt ∼: that's unlucky
**(d)** (Schicksalsschlag) misfortune

**unglücklich** 1 *Adj.* **(a)** unhappy
**(b)** (nicht vom Glück begünstigt) unfortunate ⟨*person*⟩; (bedauernswert, arm) hapless ⟨*person, animal*⟩
**(c)** (ungünstig, ungeschickt) unfortunate ⟨*moment, combination, meeting, etc.*⟩; unhappy ⟨*end, choice, solution*⟩
2 *adv.* **(a)** unhappily
**(b)** (ungünstig) unfortunately; (ungeschickt) unhappily, clumsily ⟨*translated, expressed*⟩

**unglücklicher·we̲i̲se** *Adv.* unfortunately

**Unglücks·fall** *der* accident

**Ungnade** *die* [bei jmdm.] in ∼ (*Akk.*) fallen/in ∼ (*Dat.*) sein fall/be out of favour [with sb.]

**ungnädig** *Adj.* bad-tempered; grumpy

**ungültig** *Adj.* invalid; void (esp. Law); spoilt ⟨*vote, ballot paper*⟩; disallowed ⟨*goal*⟩

**Ungunst** *die* zu jmds. ∼en to sb.'s disadvantage

**ungünstig** 1 *Adj.* **(a)** unfavourable; unfortunate, bad ⟨*shape, layout*⟩
**(b)** (unpassend) inconvenient ⟨*time*⟩; (ungeeignet) inappropriate, inconvenient ⟨*time, place*⟩
2 *adv.* **(a)** unfavourably; badly ⟨*designed, laid out*⟩
**(b)** (unpassend) inconveniently

**ungut** *Adj.* nichts für ∼! no offence [meant]! (coll.)

**unhandlich** *Adj.* unwieldy

**Unheil** *das;* ∼s disaster

**unheilbar** 1 *Adj.* incurable
2 *adv.* incurably

**unheil·voll** *Adj.* disastrous; (verhängnisvoll) fateful

**unheimlich** 1 *Adj.* **(a)** eerie
**(b)** (ugs.) (schrecklich) terrible (coll.) ⟨*hunger, headache, etc.*⟩ terrific (coll.) ⟨*fun etc.*⟩
2 *adv.* **(a)** eerily
**(b)** (ugs.: äußerst) terribly (coll.); incredibly (coll.) ⟨*quick, long*⟩

**unhöflich** 1 *Adj.* impolite
2 *adv.* impolitely

**Unhöflichkeit** *die;* ∼, ∼en impoliteness

**unhygienisch** 1 *Adj.* unhygienic
2 *adv.* unhygienically

**Uni** *die;* ∼, ∼s (ugs.) university

**Uniform** *die;* ∼, ∼en uniform

**uninteressant** *Adj.* uninteresting; (nicht von Belang) of no interest *postpos.;* unimportant

**Union** *die;* ∼, ∼en union

**Universität** *die;* ∼, ∼en university

**Universum** *das;* ∼s universe

**unkenntlich** *Adj.* unrecognizable ⟨*person, face*⟩; indecipherable ⟨*writing, stamp*⟩

**Unkenntnis** *die;* ∼: ignorance

**unklar** *Adj.* unclear; sich (*Dat.*) über etw. (*Akk.*) im Unklaren sein be unclear *or* unsure about sth.

**unkonventionell** 1 *Adj.* unconventional
2 *adv.* unconventionally

**Unkosten** *Pl.* **(a)** [extra] expense *sing.;* expenses
**(b)** (ugs.: Ausgaben) costs; expenditure *sing.*

**Unkosten·beitrag** *der* contribution towards expenses

**Unkraut** *das;* ∼[e]s, Unkräuter weeds *pl.*

**unkultiviert** *Adj.* uncultivated

**unlauter** *Adj.* (geh.) dishonest; ∼er Wettbewerb (Rechtsspr.) unfair competition

**unleserlich** 1 *Adj.* illegible
2 *adv.* illegibly

**unmäßig** 1 *Adj.* immoderate; excessive
2 *adv.* excessively; ⟨*eat, drink*⟩ to excess

**Unmenge** *die* mass; enormous number/ amount

**Unmensch** *der;* ∼en, ∼en brute

**unmenschlich** 1 *Adj.* **(a)** inhuman; brutal; appalling ⟨*conditions*⟩
**(b)** (entsetzlich) appalling ┄┅➤

2 *adv.* (a) in an inhuman way
(b) (entsetzlich) appallingly (coll.)

**unmissverständlich,**
\***unmißverständlich** 1 *Adj.* (a)
(eindeutig) unambiguous
(b) (offen, direkt) blunt ⟨*answer, refusal*⟩;
unequivocal ⟨*language*⟩
2 *adv.* (a) (eindeutig) unambiguously
(b) (offen, direkt) bluntly; unequivocally

**unmittelbar** 1 *Adj.* immediate; direct
⟨*contact, connection, influence, etc.*⟩
2 *adv.* immediately; directly

**unmöbliert** *Adj.* unfurnished

**unmodern** 1 *Adj.* old-fashioned; (nicht
modisch) unfashionable
2 *adv.* in an old-fashioned way; (nicht
modisch) unfashionably

**unmöglich** 1 *Adj.* impossible; (ugs.:
seltsam) incredible
2 *adv.* (ugs.) ⟨*behave*⟩ impossibly; ⟨*dress*⟩
ridiculously
3 *Adv.* (ugs.) ich/es *usw.* kann ∼ ...: I/it *etc.*
can't possibly ...

**unmoralisch** 1 *Adj.* immoral
2 *adv.* immorally

**unmündig** *Adj.* under-age

**Unmut** *der;* ∼[e]s (geh.) displeasure;
annoyance

**unnachsichtig** 1 *Adj.* merciless;
unmerciful
2 *adv.* mercilessly; ⟨*punish*⟩ unmercifully

**unnahbar** *Adj.* unapproachable

**unnatürlich** 1 *Adj.* unnatural; forced
⟨*laugh*⟩
2 *adv.* unnaturally; ⟨*laugh*⟩ in a forced way;
⟨*speak*⟩ affectedly

**unnötig** 1 *Adj.* unnecessary
2 *adv.* unnecessarily

**unnütz** *Adj.* useless

**UNO** *die;* ∼: UN

**unordentlich** 1 *Adj.* (a) untidy
(b) (ungeregelt) disorderly ⟨*life*⟩
2 *adv.* untidily; ⟨*tie, treat, etc.*⟩ carelessly

**Unordnung** *die;* ∼: disorder; mess

**unparteiisch** 1 *Adj.* impartial
2 *adv.* impartially

**unpassend** 1 *Adj.* inappropriate;
unsuitable ⟨*dress etc.*⟩
2 *adv.* inappropriately; unsuitably ⟨*dressed
etc.*⟩

**unpersönlich** 1 *Adj.* impersonal; distant,
aloof ⟨*person*⟩
2 *adv.* impersonally; ⟨*answer, write*⟩ in
impersonal terms

**unpraktisch** 1 *Adj.* unpractical
2 *adv.* in an unpractical way

**unproblematisch** *Adj.* unproblematic

**unproduktiv** *Adj.* unproductive

**unpünktlich** 1 *Adj.* unpunctual ⟨*person*⟩;
late, unpunctual ⟨*payment*⟩
2 *adv.* late

**Unpünktlichkeit** *die;* ∼: lack of
punctuality

**Unrecht** *das;* ∼[e]s wrong; zu ∼: wrongly;
∼ haben be wrong; jmdm. ∼ tun do sb. an
injustice

**unrechtmäßig** 1 *Adj.* unlawful
2 *adv.* unlawfully

**unredlich** (geh.) 1 *Adj.* dishonest
2 *adv.* dishonestly

**Unredlichkeit** *die;* ∼, ∼en (a) dishonesty
(b) (Handlung) dishonest act

**unregelmäßig** 1 *Adj.* irregular
2 *adv.* irregularly

**Unregelmäßigkeit** *die;* ∼, ∼en
irregularity

**unreif** *Adj.* (a) unripe
(b) (nicht erwachsen) immature

**unrentabel** *Adj.* unprofitable

**Unruhe** *die;* ∼, ∼n (auch fig.) unrest; (Lärm)
noise; (Unrast) restlessness; (Besorgnis) anxiety

**unruhig** 1 *Adj.* (a) restless; (besorgt)
anxious; unsettled, troubled ⟨*time*⟩
(b) (laut) noisy
(c) (ungleichmäßig) uneven ⟨*breathing, pulse,
etc.*⟩; fitful ⟨*sleep*⟩; disturbed ⟨*night*⟩
2 *adv.* (a) restlessly; (besorgt) anxiously
(b) (ungleichmäßig) unevenly; ⟨*sleep*⟩ fitfully

**uns** 1 (a) *Akk. von* WIR us
(b) *Dat. von* WIR; gib es ∼: give it to us; bei
∼: at our home *or* (coll.) place
2 *Reflexivpron. der 1. Pers. Pl.* (a) *refl.*
ourselves
(b) *reziprok* one another

**unsachlich** 1 *Adj.* unobjective
2 *adv.* without objectivity

**unsauber** 1 *Adj.* (a) dirty
(b) (nachlässig) untidy; sloppy
2 *adv.* (nachlässig) untidily

**unschädlich** *Adj.* harmless

**unscharf** *Adj.* blurred ⟨*photo, picture*⟩

**unscheinbar** *Adj.* inconspicuous

**unschlagbar** *Adj.* unbeatable

**Unschuld** *die;* ∼: innocence; (Jungfräulichkeit)
virginity

**unschuldig** 1 *Adj.* innocent
2 *adv.* innocently

**unselbständig, unselbstständig**
*Adj.* dependent [on other people]

**unser**[1] *Possessivpron. der 1. Pers. Pl.* our;
das ist ∼s that is ours

**unser**[2] *Gen. von* WIR (geh.) of us; in ∼ aller/
beider Interesse in the interest of all/both of
us

**unser·einer, unsereins** *Indefinitpron.*
(ugs.) the likes of us *pl.;* our sort (coll.)

**unserer·seits** *Adv.* for our part; (von uns)
on our part

**unser[e]s-gleichen** *indekl. Indefinitpron.*
people *pl.* like us

**unsert·wegen** *Adv.:* ▶ MEINETWEGEN:
because of us; for our sake; about us; as far
as we are concerned

**ụnsicher** [1] *Adj.* uncertain; (nicht selbstsicher) insecure
[2] *adv.* ⟨*walk, stand, etc.*⟩ unsteadily; (nicht selbstsicher) ⟨*smile, look*⟩ diffidently

**Ụnsicherheit** *die;* ~: uncertainty; (fehlende Selbstsicherheit) insecurity

**ụnsichtbar** *Adj.* invisible (**für** to)

**Ụnsinn** *der;* ~[e]s nonsense; ~ **machen** mess *or* fool about

**ụnsinnig** *Adj.* nonsensical ⟨*statement, talk, etc.*⟩; absurd, ridiculous ⟨*demand etc.*⟩

**Ụnsitte** *die;* ~, ~n bad habit

**ụnsittlich** [1] *Adj.* indecent
[2] *adv.* indecently

**unsr...** ▶ UNSER[1]

**unstẹrblich** *Adj.* immortal

**Unstẹrblichkeit** *die;* ~: immortality

**ụnstreitig** [1] *Adj.* indisputable
[2] *adv.* indisputably

**ụnsympathisch** *Adj.* uncongenial, disagreeable ⟨*person*⟩; unpleasant ⟨*characteristic, nature, voice*⟩

**Ụntat** *die;* ~, ~en misdeed; evil deed

**ụntätig** *Adj.* idle; ~ **herumsitzen/zusehen** sit around doing nothing/stand idly by

**ụntauglich** *Adj.* unsuitable; (für Militärdienst) unfit [for service] *postpos.*

**ụnten** *Adv.* (a) down; **hier/da** ~: down here/there; **von** ~: from below
(b) (in Gebäuden) downstairs; **nach** ~: downstairs
(c) (am unteren Ende, zum unteren Ende hin) at the bottom; ~ **[links] auf der Seite/im Schrank** at the bottom [left] of the page/cupboard
(d) (an der Unterseite) underneath
(e) (im Text) below; ~ **genannt** undermentioned (Brit.); mentioned below *postpos.*

**\*ụnten·genannt** ▶ UNTEN E

**ụnter** [1] *Präp. mit Dat.* (Lage, Standort) under; (zwischen) among[st]; **Mengen** ~ **100 Stück** quantities of less than 100; ~ **Angst/ Tränen** in *or* out of fear/in tears
[2] *Präp. mit Akk.* under; (zwischen) among[st]; ~ **Null sinken** drop below zero
[3] *Adv.* less than; ~ **30** [**Jahre alt**] **sein** be under 30 [years of age]

**ụnter...** *Adj.* lower; bottom; (ganz unten) bottom; (in der Rangfolge o. Ä.) lower

**Ụnter·arm** *der* forearm

**ụnterbelichten** *tr. V.;* **ich unterbelichte, unterbelichtet, unterzubelichten** (Fot.) underexpose

**Ụnter·bewusstsein, \*Ụnter·bewußtsein** *das* subconscious

**unter·bleiben** *unr. itr. V.; mit sein* etw. unterbleibt sth. does not occur *or* happen

**unter·brẹchen** *unr. tr. V.* interrupt; break ⟨*journey, silence*⟩

**Ụnter·brẹchung** *die* ▶ UNTERBRECHEN: interruption; break (*Gen.* in)

**ụnter|bringen** *unr. tr. V.* (a) put
(b) (beherbergen) put up

**Ụnterbringung** *die;* ~, ~en accommodation *no indef. art.*

**ụnter|buttern** *tr. V.* (ugs.) push aside (fig.)

**\*unter·der·hạnd** ▶ HAND

**unter·dẹssen** ▶ INZWISCHEN

**unter·drụcken** *tr. V.* suppress; hold back ⟨*comment, question, answer, criticism, etc.*⟩; oppress ⟨*minority etc.*⟩

**Unterdrụckung** *die;* ~, ~en (a) (das Unterdrücken) suppression
(b) (das Unterdrücktwerden, -sein) oppression

**unter·einạnder** *Adv.* (a) (räumlich) one below the other
(b) (miteinander) among[st] ourselves/ themselves *etc.*

**ụnter·ernährt** *Adj.* undernourished

**Ụnter·ernährung** *die* malnutrition

**Ụnter·führung** *die* underpass; (für Fußgänger) subway (Brit.); [pedestrian] underpass (Amer.)

**unter-, Ụnter-:** ~**gang** *der* (a) (Sonnenuntergang, Monduntergang usw.) setting;
(b) (von Schiffen) sinking; (c) (das Zugrundegehen) decline; ~|**gehen** *unr. itr. V.; mit sein* (a) ⟨*sun, star, etc.*⟩ set; ⟨*ship*⟩ sink, go down; ⟨*person*⟩ drown, go under; (b) (zugrunde gehen) come to an end;
~**geordnet** *Adj.* secondary ⟨*role, importance, etc.*⟩; subordinate ⟨*position, post, etc.*⟩; ~**geschoss, \*~geschoß** *das* basement; ~**gewicht** *das* underweight;
~**grund** *der* (bes. Politik) underground;
~**grund·bahn** *die* underground [railway] (Brit.); subway (Amer.); ~|**haken** *tr. V.* (ugs.) jmdn. ~haken take sb.'s arm; ~**halb** [1] *Adv.* below; ~halb **von** below; [2] *Präp. mit Gen.* below; ~**halt** *der* (a) living; (b) (Zahlung) maintenance; (c) (Instandhaltung[skosten]) upkeep

**unter-, Ụnter-:** ~**halten** [1] *unr. tr. V.* (a) support; (b) (instand halten) maintain ⟨*building*⟩; (c) (betreiben) run, keep ⟨*car, hotel*⟩; (d) (pflegen) maintain, keep up ⟨*contact, correspondence*⟩; (e) entertain ⟨*guest, audience*⟩; [2] *unr. refl. V.* (a) talk; converse; (b) (sich vergnügen) enjoy oneself;
~**haltsam** *Adj.* entertaining; ~**haltung** *die* (a) (Versorgung) support; (b) (Instandhaltung) maintenance; (c) (Gespräch) conversation; (d) (Zeitvertreib) entertainment

**unter-, Ụnter-:** ~**händler** *der,* ~**händlerin** *die* (bes. Politik) negotiator;
~**hemd** *das* vest (Brit.); undershirt (Amer.);
~**holz** *das* underwood; undergrowth;
~**hose** *die* (für Männer) briefs *pl.;* [under]pants *pl.;* (für Frauen) panties *pl.;* knickers *pl.* (Brit.); ~**irdisch** [1] *Adj.* underground; [2] *adv.* underground;
~|**jubeln** *tr. V.* (ugs.) jmdm. etw. ~jubeln palm sth. off on sb.; ~**kiefer** *der* lower

**u**

jaw; ~|**kommen** *unr. itr. V.; mit sein* find accommodation; ~**kühlt** *Adj.* ~**kühlt sein** be suffering from hypothermia *or* exposure

**Unterkunft** *die;* ~, Unterkünfte accommodation *no indef. art.;* lodging *no indef. art.;* ~ **und Frühstück** bed and breakfast; ~ **und Verpflegung** board and lodging

**Unter·lage** *die* (a) (Schreibunterlage) pad; (für eine Schreibmaschine usw.) mat (b) *Pl.* documents; papers

**unter-, Unter-:** ~**lassen** *unr. tr. V.* refrain from [doing]; ~**lassung** *die;* ~~, ~~**en** omission; failure; ~**lassungs·sünde** *die* (ugs.) sin of omission; ~**laufen** *unr. itr. V.; mit sein* occur; **jmdm. ist ein Fehler/Irrtum** ~**laufen** sb. made a mistake; ~**legen** *Adj.* inferior; **jmdm.** ~**legen sein** be inferior to sb. (**an** + *Dat.* in); ~**leib** *der* lower abdomen

**unter·liegen** *unr. itr. V.* (a) *mit sein* (besiegt werden) lose; be beaten *or* defeated (b) (unterworfen sein) be subject to

**Unter·lippe** *die* lower lip

**unterm** *Präp.* + *Art.* = **unter dem**

**unter·malen** *tr. V.* accompany

**Unter·malung** *die;* ~, ~**en** accompaniment (*Gen.* to)

**unter·mauern** *tr. V.* (mit Argumenten, Fakten absichern) back up

**Unter-:** ~**miete** *die* subtenancy; sublease; ~**mieter** *der,* ~**mieterin** *die* subtenant; lodger

**untern** (ugs.) *Präp.* + *Art.* = **unter den**

**unter-, Unter-:** ~**nehmen** *unr. tr. V.* (a) (durchführen) undertake; make; take ⟨*steps*⟩; (b) **etwas** ~**nehmen** do something; ~**nehmen** *das;* ~~s, ~~ (a) (Vorhaben) enterprise; (b) (Firma) concern; ~**nehmer** *der;* ~~s, ~~, ~**nehmerin** *die;* ~~, ~~**nen** employer

**unternehmerisch** [1] *Adj.* entrepreneurial [2] *adv.* ⟨think⟩ in an entrepreneurial *or* businesslike way

**unter·nehmungs·lustig** *Adj.* active; **sie ist sehr** ~ she is always out doing things

**Unter·offizier** *der* (a) non-commissioned officer (b) (Dienstgrad) corporal

**unter|ordnen** [1] *tr. V.* subordinate [2] *refl. V.* accept a subordinate role

**Unterredung** *die;* ~, ~**en** discussion

**Unterricht** *der;* ~[e]s, ~**e** instruction; (Schulunterricht) teaching; (Schulstunden) classes *pl.*

**unterrichten** [1] *tr. V.* (a) teach (b) (informieren) inform (**über** + *Akk.* of, about) [2] *itr. V.* (Unterricht geben) teach [3] *refl. V.* (sich informieren) inform oneself (**über** + *Akk.* about)

**Unterrichts·stunde** *die* lesson; period

---

**Unter·rock** *der* [half] slip

**unter|rühren** *tr. V.* stir in

**unters** *Präp.* + *Art.* = **unter das**

**unter·sagen** *tr. V.* forbid; prohibit

**Unter·satz** *der* ▸ UNTERSETZER

**unter-, Unter-:** ~**schätzen** *tr. V.* underestimate ⟨amount, effect, etc.⟩; underrate ⟨talent, ability, etc.⟩; ~**scheiden** [1] *unr. tr. V.* distinguish; [2] *unr. refl. V.* differ (**durch** in, **von** from); ~**scheidung** *die* (Vorgang) differentiation; (Resultat) distinction

**Unter-:** ~**schenkel** *der* shank; lower leg; ~**schicht** *die* (Soziol.) lower class

**Unter·schied** *der;* ~[e]s, ~**e** difference

**unterschiedlich** [1] *Adj.* different; (uneinheitlich) variable; varying [2] *adv.* [sehr/ganz] ~: in [very/quite] different ways

**unterschieds·los** [1] *Adj.* uniform; equal ⟨treatment⟩ [2] *adv.* ⟨treat⟩ equally; (ohne Benachteiligung) without discrimination

**unter·schlagen** *unr. tr. V.* embezzle ⟨money, funds, etc.⟩; (unterdrücken) intercept ⟨letter⟩; withhold ⟨fact, news, information, etc.⟩

**Unter·schlupf** *der;* ~[e]s, ~**e** shelter; (Versteck) hiding place; hideout

**unter|schlüpfen** *itr. V.; mit sein* (ugs.) hide out

**unter·schreiben** *unr. itr., tr. V.* sign

**Unter-:** ~**schrift** *die* signature; (Bild~) caption; ~**see·boot** *das* submarine; ~**setzer** *der* mat; (für Gläser) coaster

**untersetzt** *Adj.* stocky

**Unter·stand** *der* (Schutzbunker) dugout; (Unterschlupf) shelter

**unter|stehen** [1] *unr. itr. V.* **jmdm.** ~: be subordinate *or* answerable to sb. [2] *unr. refl. V.* dare

**unter|stellen¹** [1] *tr. V.* (zur Aufbewahrung) keep; store ⟨furniture⟩ [2] *refl. V.* take shelter

**unter·stellen²** *tr. V.* (a) **jmdm. eine Abteilung** ~: put sb. in charge of a department; **die Behörde ist dem Ministerium unterstellt** the office is under the ministry (b) (unterschieben) **jmdm. böse Absichten** *usw.* ~: insinuate that sb.'s intentions *etc.* are bad

**Unter·stellung** *die* (falsche Behauptung) insinuation

**unter·streichen** *unr. tr. V.* (a) underline (b) (hervorheben) emphasize

**Unter·streichung** *die;* ~, ~**en** (a) underlining (b) (das Betonen) emphasizing

**unter·stützen** *tr. V.* support

**Unter·stützung** *die;* ~, ~**en** (a) support (b) (finanzielle Hilfe) allowance; (für Arbeitslose) [unemployment] benefit *no art.*

**unter·suchen** *tr. V.* examine; (überprüfen)

test (**auf** + *Akk.* for); (aufzuklären suchen)
investigate; (durchsuchen) search (**auf** + *Akk.*,
**nach** for)

**Untersuchung** *die;* ~, ~en **(a)**
▶ UNTERSUCHEN: examination; test;
investigation; search
**(b)** (wissenschaftliche Arbeit) study

**Untersuchungs·haft** *die* imprisonment
*or* detention while awaiting trial

**Unter·tasse** *die* saucer

**unter|tauchen** ① *itr. V.; mit sein* **(a)** (im
Wasser) dive [under]
**(b)** (verschwinden) disappear
② *tr. V.* duck

**Unter·teil** *das od. der* bottom part

**unter·teilen** *tr. V.* divide; (gliedern)
subdivide

**Unter·titel** *der* subtitle

**unter·treiben** *unr. itr. V.* play things
down

**Untertreibung** *die;* ~, ~en
understatement

**unter·vermieten** *tr., itr. V.* sublet

**unter·wandern** *tr. V.* infiltrate

**Unter·wanderung** *die* infiltration *no
indef. art.*

**Unter·wäsche** *die* underwear

**unterwegs** *Adv.* on the way; (nicht zu
Hause) out [and about]

**unter·weisen** *unr. tr. V.* (geh.) instruct

**Unter·welt** *die;* ~: underworld

**unter·werfen** ① *unr. tr. V.* **(a)** subjugate
⟨*people, country*⟩
**(b)** (unterziehen) subject (*Dat.* to)
② *unr. refl. V.* **sich [jmdm./einer Sache]** ~:
submit [to sb./sth.]

**Unterwerfung** *die;* ~, ~en **(a)** (das
Unterwerfen) subjugation (**unter** + *Akk.* to)
**(b)** (das Sichunterwerfen) submission (**unter** +
*Akk.* to)

**unterwürfig** ① *Adj.* obsequious
② *adv.* obsequiously

**unter·zeichnen** *tr. V.* sign

**unter·ziehen** ① *unr. tr. V.* **etw. einer
Untersuchung/Überprüfung** (*Dat.*) ~:
examine/check sth.
② *unr. refl. V.* **sich einer Operation** (*Dat.*) ~:
undergo *or* have an operation

**untragbar** *Adj.* unbearable

**untreu** *Adj.* disloyal; (in der Ehe, Liebe)
unfaithful

**Untreue** *die;* ~: disloyalty; (in der Ehe, Liebe)
unfaithfulness

**untröstlich** *Adj.* inconsolable

**Untugend** *die;* ~, ~en bad habit

**unüberlegt** ① *Adj.* rash
② *adv.* rashly

**unübersehbar** ① *Adj.* **(a)** (offenkundig)
conspicuous
**(b)** (sehr groß) enormous
② *adv.* (sehr) extremely

**unübersichtlich** ① *Adj.* unclear;
confusing ⟨*arrangement*⟩; blind ⟨*bend*⟩;
broken ⟨*country etc.*⟩
② *adv.* unclearly; confusingly ⟨*arranged*⟩

**unübertrefflich** ① *Adj.* superb
② *adv.* superbly

**unübertroffen** *Adj.* unsurpassed

**unumgänglich** *Adj.* [absolutely]
necessary

**Unumgänglichkeit** *die;* ~: absolute
necessity

**unumwunden** ① *Adj.* frank
② *adv.* frankly; openly

**ununterbrochen** ① *Adj.* incessant
② *adv.* incessantly

**unveränderlich** *Adj.* unchangeable

**unverantwortlich** ① *Adj.* irresponsible
② *adv.* irresponsibly

**unverbesserlich** *Adj.* incorrigible

**unverbindlich** ① *Adj.* **(a)** not binding
*pred.;* without obligation *postpos;*
**(b)** (reserviert) non-committal ⟨*answer,
words*⟩; impersonal ⟨*attitude*⟩
② *adv.* ⟨*send, reserve*⟩ without obligation

**unverbleit** *Adj.* unleaded

**unverblümt** ① *Adj.* blunt
② *adv.* bluntly

**unverbraucht** *Adj.* untouched; unspent
⟨*energy*⟩; fresh ⟨*air*⟩

**unverdaut** *Adj.* undigested

**unverdorben** *Adj.* unspoilt

**unverdrossen** *Adj.* undeterred; (unverzagt)
undaunted

**unvereinbar** *Adj.* incompatible (**mit** with)

**Unvereinbarkeit** *die;* ~: incompatibility
(**mit** with)

**unverfänglich** *Adj.* harmless

**unverfroren** *Adj.* insolent; impudent

**unvergänglich** *Adj.* immortal ⟨*fame*⟩;
unchanging ⟨*beauty*⟩; abiding ⟨*recollection*⟩

**unvergesslich, \*unvergeßlich** *Adj.*
unforgettable

**unvergleichlich** ① *Adj.* incomparable
② *adv.* incomparably

**unverheiratet** *Adj.* unmarried

**unverhofft** ① *Adj.* unexpected
② *adv.* unexpectedly

**unverhohlen** ① *Adj.* unconcealed
② *adv.* openly

**unverkäuflich** *Adj.* **diese Vase ist** ~: this
vase is not for sale/(nicht absetzbar)
unsaleable

**unvermeidlich** *Adj.* unavoidable; (sich als
Folge ergebend) inevitable

**Unvermögen** *das;* ~s lack of ability

**unvermutet** ① *Adj.* unexpected
② *adv.* unexpectedly

**unvernünftig** *Adj.* stupid; foolish

**unverrichtet** *Adj.* ~**er Dinge** without
having achieved anything

**u**

**unverschämt** ① *Adj.* (a) impertinent
⟨*person, manner, words, etc.*⟩; barefaced ⟨*lie*⟩
(b) (ugs.: sehr groß) outrageous ⟨*price, luck, etc.*⟩
② *adv.* impertinently; ⟨*lie*⟩ barefacedly; blatantly
**Unverschämtheit** *die;* ∼, ∼en impertinence
**unversehens** *Adv.* suddenly
**unversehrt** *Adj.* unscathed; (unbeschädigt) undamaged
**unverständlich** *Adj.* incomprehensible
**Unverständnis** *das;* ∼ses lack of understanding
**unverträglich** *Adj.* (a) quarrelsome
(b) incompatible ⟨*blood groups, medicines, transplant tissue*⟩
**unverwechselbar** *Adj.* unmistakable; distinctive
**unverwüstlich** *Adj.* indestructible
**unverzeihlich** *Adj.* unforgivable
**unverzüglich** ① *Adj.* prompt
② *adv.* promptly
**unvollkommen** ① *Adj.* (a) imperfect
(b) (unvollständig) incomplete
② *adv.* (a) imperfectly
(b) (unvollständig) incompletely
**Unvollkommenheit** *die;* ∼: (a) imperfectness
(b) (Unvollständigkeit) incompleteness
**unvollständig** *Adj.* incomplete
**Unvollständigkeit** *die;* ∼: incompleteness
**unvorhergesehen** *Adj.* unforeseen; unexpected ⟨*visit*⟩
**unvorhersehbar** *Adj.* unforeseeable
**unvorsichtig** ① *Adj.* careless; (unüberlegt) rash
② *adv.* carelessly; (unüberlegt) rashly
**Unvorsichtigkeit** *die;* ∼ ▶ UNVORSICHTIG 1: carelessness; rashness
**unvorstellbar** ① *Adj.* inconceivable
② *adv.* unimaginably
**unvorteilhaft** *Adj.* (a) unattractive ⟨*figure, appearance*⟩
(b) (ohne Vorteil) unfavourable, poor ⟨*purchase, exchange*⟩; unprofitable ⟨*business*⟩
**unwahr** *Adj.* untrue
**Unwahrheit** *die;* ∼, ∼en (a) untruthfulness
(b) (Äußerung) untruth
**unwahrscheinlich** ① *Adj.* (a) improbable; unlikely
(b) (ugs.: sehr viel) incredible (coll.)
② *adv.* (ugs.: sehr) incredibly (coll.)
**Unwahrscheinlichkeit** *die;* ∼: improbability
**unwegsam** *Adj.* [almost] impassable
**unweiblich** *Adj.* unfeminine
**unweigerlich** ① *Adj.* inevitable

---

*alte Schreibung - vgl. Hinweis auf S. xiv

② *adv.* inevitably
**Unwesen** *das:* sein ∼ treiben (abwertend) be up to one's mischief *or* one's tricks
**Unwetter** *das;* ∼s, ∼: [thunder]storm
**unwichtig** *Adj.* unimportant
**Unwichtigkeit** *die;* ∼, ∼en (a) unimportance
(b) (etw. Unwichtiges) unimportant thing
**unwiderruflich** ① *Adj.* irrevocable
② *adv.* irrevocably
**unwiderstehlich** *Adj.* irresistible
**unwiederbringlich** (geh.) ① *Adj.* irretrievable
② *adv.* irretrievably
**Unwille[n]** *der;* Unwillens displeasure
**unwillig** ① *Adj.* indignant; (widerwillig) unwilling
② *adv.* indignantly; (widerwillig) unwillingly
**unwillkürlich** ① *Adj.* (a) spontaneous ⟨*cry, sigh*⟩; instinctive ⟨*reaction, movement, etc.*⟩
(b) (Physiol.) involuntary ⟨*movement etc.*⟩
② *adv.* (a) ⟨*shout etc.*⟩ spontaneously; ⟨*react, move, etc.*⟩ instinctively
(b) (Physiol.) ⟨*move etc.*⟩ involuntarily
**unwirklich** (geh.) *Adj.* unreal
**Unwirklichkeit** *die;* ∼, ∼en unreality
**unwirksam** *Adj.* ineffective
**Unwirksamkeit** *die;* ∼: ineffectiveness
**unwirsch** ① *Adj.* surly; ill-natured
② *adv.* ill-naturedly
**unwirtschaftlich** ① *Adj.* uneconomic ⟨*procedure etc.*⟩; (nicht sparsam) uneconomical ⟨*driving etc.*⟩
② *adv.* ⟨*work, drive, etc.*⟩ uneconomically
**Unwissenheit** *die;* ∼: ignorance
**unwissentlich** ① *Adj.* unconscious
② *adv.* unknowingly; unwittingly
**unwohl** *Adv.* unwell; mir ist ∼: I don't feel well
**Unwohlsein** *das;* ∼s indisposition
**unwürdig** *Adj.* (a) undignified ⟨*person, behaviour*⟩; degrading ⟨*treatment*⟩
(b) (unangemessen) unworthy
**unzählig** *Adj.* innumerable; countless
**Unze** *die;* ∼, ∼n ounce
**unzeitgemäß** *Adj.* anachronistic
**unzerbrechlich** *Adj.* unbreakable
**unzertrennlich** *Adj.* inseparable
**Unzucht** *die;* ∼ treiben fornicate; gewerbsmäßige ∼: prostitution
**unzüchtig** ① *Adj.* obscene ⟨*letter, gesture*⟩
② *adv.* ⟨*touch, approach, etc.*⟩ indecently; ⟨*speak*⟩ obscenely
**unzufrieden** *Adj.* dissatisfied; (stärker) unhappy
**Unzufriedenheit** *die;* ∼: dissatisfaction; (stärker) unhappiness
**unzugänglich** *Adj.* inaccessible ⟨*area, building, etc.*⟩; unapproachable ⟨*character, person, etc.*⟩

**unzulänglich** (geh.) ⓵ *Adj.* insufficient
⓶ *adv.* insufficiently

**unzumutbar** *Adj.* unreasonable

**unzurechnungsfähig** *Adj.* not
responsible for one's actions *pred.;*
(geistesgestört) of unsound mind *postpos.*

**unzustellbar** *Adj.* (Postw.) „∼": 'not
known [at this address]'

**unzutreffend** *Adj.* inappropriate; (falsch)
incorrect

**unzuverlässig** *Adj.* unreliable

**Unzuverlässigkeit** *die;* ∼: unreliability

**unzweckmäßig** ⓵ *Adj.* unsuitable;
(unpraktisch) impractical
⓶ *adv.* unsuitably; (unpraktisch) impractically

**Update** /'apdeit/ *das;* ∼s, ∼s (DV) update

**üppig** ⓵ *Adj.* lush ⟨*vegetation*⟩; thick ⟨*hair,
beard*⟩; full ⟨*bosom, lips*⟩; voluptuous ⟨*figure,
woman*⟩; (fig.) sumptuous, opulent ⟨*meal*⟩
⓶ *adv.* luxuriantly; (fig.) sumptuously

**Ur·abstimmung** *die* [*esp.* strike] ballot

**Ural** *der;* ∼[s] Urals *pl.;* Ural Mountains *pl.*

**ur·alt** *Adj.* very old; ancient

**Uran** *das;* ∼s uranium

**Ur·aufführung** *die* première; first night *or*
performance; (eines Films) première; first
showing

**urbar** *Adj.* ein Stück Land ∼ machen
cultivate a piece of land

**Ur·einwohner** *der,* **Ur·einwohnerin**
*die* native inhabitant

**Ur·enkel** *der* great-grandson

**Urgroß-:** ∼**eltern** *Pl.* great-grandparents;
∼**mutter** *die; Pl.* ∼mütter great-
grandmother; ∼**vater** *der* great-
grandfather

**Ur·heber** *der;* ∼s, ∼: originator; initiator;
(bes. Rechtsspr.: Verfasser, Autor) author

**Urheber·recht** *das* copyright

**urig** *Adj.* natural ⟨*person*⟩; real ⟨*beer*⟩; cosy
⟨*pub*⟩

**Urin** *der;* ∼s, ∼e (Med.) urine

**urinieren** *itr. V.* urinate

**Ur·knall** *der* big bang

**Ur·kunde** *die;* ∼, ∼n document;
(Bescheinigung, Siegerurkunde, Diplom usw.)
certificate

**Urlaub** *der;* ∼[e]s, ∼e holiday[s] (Brit.);
vacation (esp. Amer.); (bes. Milit.) leave

**urlaubs-, Urlaubs-:** ∼**geld** *das* holiday
pay *or* money; (gespartes Geld) holiday
money; ∼**ort** *der* holiday resort; ∼**reif**
*Adj.* ∼reif sein (ugs.) be ready for a holiday;
∼**reise** *die* holiday [trip]; ∼**zeit** *die*
holiday period *or* season

**Urne** *die;* ∼, ∼n urn; (Wahlurne) [ballot] box

**Ur·oma** *die* (fam.) great-granny (coll./child
lang.)

**Ur·opa** *der* (fam.) great-grandpa (coll./child
lang.)

**Ur·sache** *die* cause

**Ur·sprung** *der* origin

**ur·sprünglich** ⓵ *Adj.* (a) original ⟨*plan,
price, form, material, etc.*⟩
(b) (natürlich) natural
⓶ *adv.* (a) originally
(b) (natürlich) naturally

**Urteil** *das;* ∼s, ∼e judgement; (Strafe)
sentence; (Gerichtsurteil) verdict

**urteilen** *itr. V.* form an opinion; judge;
über etw./jmdn. ∼: judge sth./sb.

**urteils-, Urteils-:** ∼**fähig** *Adj.*
competent *or* able to judge *postpos.;*
∼**fähigkeit** *die* competence *or* ability to
judge; ∼**vermögen** *das* competence to
judge

**Ur·wald** *der* primeval forest; (tropisch)
jungle

**ur·wüchsig** *Adj.* natural ⟨*landscape,
power*⟩; earthy ⟨*language, humour*⟩

**Urwüchsigkeit** *die;* ∼ ▶ URWÜCHSIG:
naturalness; earthiness

**USA** *Pl.* USA

**User** /'ju:zɐ/ *der;* ∼s, ∼, **Userin** *die;* ∼,
∼nen (bes. DV, Drogenjargon) user

**usw.** *Abk.* = **und so weiter** etc.

**Utensil** *das;* ∼s, ∼ien /...jən/ piece of
equipment; ∼ien equipment *sing.*

**Utopie** *die;* ∼, ∼n utopian dream

**utopisch** *Adj.* utopian

**UV** *Abk.* = **Ultraviolett** UV

**u**

# Vv

**v, V** /vau:/ *das;* ~, ~: v/V

**v.** *Abk.* = **von**

**vage** /'va:gə/ ☐ *Adj.* vague
☐ *adv.* vaguely

**Vagina** /va'gi:na/ *die;* ~, Vaginen (Anat.)
vagina

**vaginal** *Adj.* (Anat.) vaginal

**vakant** /va'kant/ *Adj.* vacant

**Vakuum** *das;* ~s, Vakuen vacuum

**vakuum·verpackt** *Adj.* vacuum-packed

**Valentins·tag** /'va:lɛnti:ns-/ *der* [St]
Valentine's Day

**Van** /væn/ *der;* ~s, ~s (Kfz.-W.) multi-
purpose vehicle; MPV

**Vandale** /van'da:la/ *usw.* ▶ WANDALE

**Vanille** /va'nɪljə/ *die;* ~: vanilla

**Vanille-:** ~**eis** *das* vanilla ice cream;
~**pudding** *der* vanilla pudding; ~**zucker**
*der* vanilla sugar

**variabel** /va'ria:bl̩/ ☐ *Adj.* variable
☐ *adv.* variably

**Variante** /va'riantə/ *die;* ~, ~n (geh.)
variant; variation

**variieren** *tr., itr. V.* vary

**Vase** /'va:zə/ *die;* ~, ~n vase

**Vaseline** /vaze'li:nə/ *die;* ~: Vaseline ®

**Vater** *der;* ~s, Väter father; Gott ~: God the
Father

**Vater·land** *das* fatherland

**väterlich** ☐ *Adj.* (a) paternal ‹line, love,
instincts, etc.›
(b) (fürsorglich) fatherly
☐ *adv.* in a fatherly way

**väterlicherseits** *Adv.* on the/his/her *etc.*
father's side

**Vaterschaft** *die;* ~, ~en fatherhood

**Vater-:** ~**tag** *der* Father's Day *no def. art.;*
~**unser** *das;* ~~s, ~~: Lord's Prayer

**Vati** *der;* ~s, ~s (fam.) dad[dy] (coll.)

**Vatikan** /vati'ka:n/ *der;* ~s Vatican

**v. Chr.** *Abk.* = **vor Christus** BC

**Vegetarier** /vege'ta:riɐ/ *der;* ~s, ~,
**Vegetarierin** *die;* ~, ~nen vegetarian

**vegetarisch** ☐ *Adj.* vegetarian
☐ *adv.* er isst *od.* lebt ~: he is a vegetarian

**Vegetation** *die;* ~, ~en vegetation *no
indef. art.*

**vegetieren** *itr. V.* vegetate

**Veilchen** *das;* ~s, ~: violet

**Vene** /'ve:nə/ *die;* ~, ~n vein

**Venedig** /ve'ne:dɪç/ *(das);* ~s Venice

**Venezolaner** /venets:o'la:nɐ/ *der;* ~s, ~,
**Venezolanerin** *die;* ~, ~nen Venezuelan

**venezolanisch** *Adj.* Venezuelan

**Venezuela** *(das);* ~s Venezuela

**Ventil** /vɛn'ti:l/ *das;* ~s, ~e valve

**Ventilator** /vɛnti'la:tɔr/ *der;* ~s, ~en
ventilator

**Venus** /'ve:nʊs/ *die;* ~: Venus *no def. art.*

**verabreden** ☐ *tr. V.* arrange
☐ *refl. V.* sich im Park/zum Tennis/für den
folgenden Abend ~: arrange to meet in the
park/for tennis/next evening

**Verabredung** *die;* ~, ~en (a)
arrangement
(b) (verabredete Zusammenkunft) appointment;
eine ~ absagen call off a meeting

**verabscheuen** *tr. V.* detest; loathe

**verabschieden** ☐ *tr. V.* (a) say goodbye
to
(b) (aus dem Dienst) retire ‹general, civil
servant, etc.›
☐ *refl. V.* sich [von jmdm.] ~: say goodbye
[to sb.]

**Verabschiedung** *die;* ~, ~en (a) leave-
taking
(b) (aus dem Dienst) retirement

**verachten** *tr. V.* despise

**verächtlich** ☐ *Adj.* (a) contemptuous
(b) (verachtenswürdig) contemptible
☐ *adv.* contemptuously

**Verächtlichkeit** *die;* ~: contempt;
contemptuousness

**Verachtung** *die;* ~: contempt

**verallgemeinern** *tr., itr. V.* generalize

**Verallgemeinerung** *die;* ~, ~en
generalization

**veralten** *itr. V.; mit sein* become obsolete

**Veranda** /ve'randa/ *die;* ~, Veranden
veranda; porch

**veränderlich** *Adj.* changeable

**verändern** *tr., refl. V.* change

**Veränderung** *die;* ~, ~en change (Gen.
in)

**verängstigen** *tr. V.* frighten; scare

**verankern** *tr. V.* fix ‹tent, mast, pole, etc.›;
(mit einem Anker) anchor

**veranlagen** *tr. V.* (Steuerw.) assess (mit at)

**veranlagt** *Adj.* künstlerisch/praktisch ~
sein have an artistic bent/be practically
minded

**Veranlagung** *die;* ~, ~en [pre]disposition

**veranlassen** *tr. V.* cause; induce; ~, **dass**
... see to it that ...

---

**Veranlassung** *die;* ~, ~en reason
**veranschaulichen** *tr. V.* illustrate
**veranschlagen** *tr. V.* estimate (**mit** at)
**veranstalten** *tr. V.* organize; hold, give ⟨*party*⟩; hold ⟨*auction*⟩; do ⟨*survey*⟩
**Veranstalter** *der;* ~s, ~,
**Veranstalterin** *die;* ~, ~nen organizer
**Veranstaltung** *die;* ~, ~en (a) (das Veranstalten) organizing; organization
(b) (etw., was veranstaltet wird) event
**verantworten** [1] *tr. V.* etw. ~: take responsibility for sth.
[2] *refl. V.* sich für etw. ~: answer for sth.; sich vor jmdm. ~: answer to sb
**verantwortlich** *Adj.* responsible
**Verantwortung** *die;* ~, ~en responsibility (**für** for)
**verantwortungs-:** ~**bewusst,**
\*~**bewußt** *Adj.* responsible; ~**los** *Adj.* irresponsible; ~**voll** *Adj.* responsible
**verarbeiten** *tr. V.* use; etw. zu etw. ~: make sth. into sth.; (geistig bewältigen) assimilate ⟨*film, experience, impressions*⟩
**Verarbeitung** *die;* ~, ~en (a) (das Verarbeiten) use
(b) (Art der Fertigung) finish; Schuhe in erstklassiger ~: shoes with a first-class finish
**verärgern** *tr. V.* annoy
**verarzten** *tr. V.* (ugs.) patch up (coll.) ⟨*person*⟩; fix (coll.) ⟨*wound etc.*⟩
**verausgaben** *refl. V.* wear oneself out; sie hat sich total verausgabt (finanziell) she has completely spent out
**veräußern** *tr. V.* dispose of ⟨*property*⟩
**Verb** /vɛrp/ *das;* ~s, ~en verb
**verbal** /vɛrˈbaːl/ *Adj.* [1] (auch Sprachw.) verbal
[2] *adv.* verbally
**Verband** *der* (a) (Binde) bandage; dressing
(b) (Vereinigung) association
**verbandeln** *tr. V.* link closely
**Verband[s]-:** ~**kasten** *der* first-aid box; ~**material** *das* dressing materials *pl.*
**Verband-zeug** *das* first-aid things *pl.*
**Verbannung** *die;* ~, ~en banishment
**verbeamten** *tr. V.* make ⟨*person*⟩ a civil servant
**verbergen** *unr. tr. V.* hide; conceal
**verbessern** [1] *tr. V.* (a) improve
(b) (korrigieren) correct
[2] *refl. V.* (a) improve
(b) ([beruflich] aufsteigen) better oneself
**Verbesserung** *die* (a) improvement
(b) (Korrektur) correction
**Verbesserungs-vorschlag** *der* suggestion for improvement
**verbeugen** *refl. V.* bow (**vor** + *Dat.* to)
**Verbeugung** *die;* ~, ~en bow
**verbeulen** *tr. V.* dent
**verbieten** *unr. tr. V.* (a) forbid; jmdm. etw.

~: forbid sb. sth.; „**Betreten des Rasens/ Rauchen verboten**" 'keep off the grass'/'no smoking'
(b) (für unzulässig erklären) ban
**verbinden** [1] *unr. tr. V.* (a) (bandagieren) bandage; dress
(b) (zubinden) bind; jmdm. die Augen ~: blindfold sb.
(c) (zusammenfügen) join
(d) (in Beziehung bringen) connect (**durch** by); link ⟨*towns, lakes, etc.*⟩ (**durch** by)
(e) (verknüpfen) combine ⟨*abilities, qualities, etc.*⟩
(f) *auch itr.* (telefonisch) jmdn. [mit jmdm.] ~: put sb. through [to sb.]
[2] *unr. refl. V.* (a) (auch Chemie) combine (**mit** with)
(b) (sich zusammentun) join [together]; join forces
**verbindlich** [1] *Adj.* (a) friendly
(b) (bindend) obligatory; compulsory; binding ⟨*agreement, decision, etc.*⟩
[2] *adv.* (a) (freundlich) in a friendly manner
(b) ~ zusagen definitely agree; jmdm. etw. ~ zusagen make sb. a firm offer of sth
**Verbindung** *die;* ~, ~en (a) (das Verknüpfen) linking
(b) (Zusammenhalt) join; connection
(c) (verknüpfende Strecke) link
(d) (durch Telefon, Funk, Verkehrsmittel) connection (**nach** to)
(e) (Kombination) combination; in ~ mit etw. in conjunction with sth.
(f) (Kontakt) contact; sich mit jmdm. in ~ setzen get in touch *or* contact with sb.
(g) (Zusammenhang) connection
**verbissen** [1] *Adj.* dogged; doggedly determined
[2] *adv.* doggedly
**verbitten** *unr. refl. V.* sich (*Dat.*) etw. ~: refuse to tolerate sth.
**verbittern** *tr. V.* embitter
**Verbitterung** *die;* ~, ~en bitterness; embitterment
**verblassen** *itr. V.; mit sein* (auch fig. geh.) fade
**Verbleib** *der;* ~[e]s (geh.) whereabouts *pl.*
**verbleiben** *unr. itr. V.; mit sein* remain; wie seid ihr verblieben? what did you arrange?
**verbleien** *tr. V.* (Technik) lead ⟨*petrol*⟩
**Verblendung** *die;* ~, ~en blindness
**verblüffen** *tr.* (auch itr.) *V.* amaze
**verblüffend** [1] *Adj.* amazing
[2] *adv.* amazingly
**Verblüffung** *die;* ~, ~en amazement
**verblühen** *itr. V.; mit sein* (auch fig.) fade
**verbluten** *itr.* (auch refl.) *V.; mit sein* bleed to death
**verbohrt** *Adj.* pigheaded
**verborgen** *Adj.* (abgelegen) secluded; (nicht sichtbar) hidden
**Verbot** *das;* ~[e]s, ~e ban (*Gen.,* **von** on)

**Verbots·schild** *das; Pl.* ~er sign
( prohibiting sth.); (Verkehrsw.) prohibitive sign

**Verbrauch** *der;* ~[e]s consumption (**von**,
**an** + *Dat.* of)

**verbrauchen** *tr. V.* use; consume *(food,
drink)*; use up *(provisions)*; spend *(money)*;
consume, use *(fuel)*; (fig.) use up *(strength,
energy)*

**Verbraucher** *der;* ~s, ~,
**Verbraucherin** *die;* ~, ~nen consumer

**Verbraucher·schutz** *der* consumer
protection

**Verbrechen** *das;* ~s, ~: crime (**an** + *Dat.*,
**gegen** against)

**Verbrechens-:** ~**rate** *die* crime rate;
~**verhütung** *die* crime prevention

**Verbrecher** *der;* ~s, ~, **Verbrecherin**
*die;* ~, ~nen criminal

**verbrecherisch** *Adj.* criminal

**verbreiten** [1] *tr. V.* spread; radiate
*(optimism, calm, etc.)*
[2] *refl. V.* spread

**Verbreitung** *die;* ~, ~en (a) ▶ VERBREITEN
1: spreading; radiation
(b) (Ausbreitung) spread

**verbrennen** [1] *unr. itr. V.; mit sein* burn
[2] *tr. V.* burn; cremate *(dead person)*; **sich**
(*Dat.*) **den Mund** ~ (fig.) say too much

**Verbrennung** *die;* ~, ~en (a)
▶ VERBRENNEN 2: burning; cremation
(b) (Wunde) burn

**verbringen** *unr. tr. V.* spend

**verbummeln** *tr. V.* (ugs.) (a) waste *(time)*
(b) (vergessen) forget [all] about; clean forget;
(verlieren) lose

**verbünden** *refl. V.* form an alliance

**Verbündete** *der/die; adj. Dekl.* ally

**verbüßen** *tr. V.* serve *(sentence)*

**Verdacht** *der;* ~[e]s, ~e *od.* **Verdächte**
suspicion; **wen hast du in** ~? who do you
suspect?

**verdächtig** [1] *Adj.* suspicious
[2] *adv.* suspiciously

**Verdächtige** *der/die; adj. Dekl.* suspect

**verdächtigen** *tr. V.* suspect

**Verdächtigung** *die;* ~, ~en suspicion

**verdammen** *tr. V.* condemn; (Rel.) damn
*(sinner)*

**verdampfen** [1] *itr. V.; mit sein* evaporate
[2] *tr. V.* evaporate

**verdanken** *tr. V.* jmdm./einer Sache etw.
~: owe sth. to sb./sth.

**verdarb** *1. u. 3. Pers. Sg. Prät. v.* VERDERBEN

**verdattert** (ugs.) *Adj.* flabbergasted;
(verwirrt) dazed; stunned

**verdauen** [1] *tr. V.* (auch fig.) digest
[2] *itr. V.* digest [one's food]

**verdaulich** *Adj.* digestible

**Verdauung** *die;* ~: digestion

---

**Verdeck** *das;* ~[e]s, ~e top; hood (Brit.); (bei
Kinderwagen) hood

**verdecken** *tr. V.* hide; cover

**verderben** [1] *unr. itr. V.; mit sein* go bad
*or* off; spoil
[2] *unr. tr. V.* spoil; (stärker) ruin; spoil
*(appetite, enjoyment, fun, etc.)*
[3] *unr. refl. V.* **sich** (*Dat.*) **den Magen/die
Augen** ~: give oneself an upset stomach/
ruin one's eyesight

**Verderben** *das;* ~s ruin

**verderblich** *Adj.* perishable *(food)*;
pernicious *(influence, effect, etc.)*

**verdeutlichen** *tr. V.* **etw.** ~: make sth.
clear; (erklären) explain sth.

**verdichten** *refl. V.* *(fog, smoke)* thicken,
become thicker; (fig.) *(suspicion, rumour)*
grow; *(feeling)* intensify

**verdienen** [1] *tr. V.* (a) earn
(b) (wert sein) deserve
[2] *itr. V.* **beide Eheleute** ~: husband and
wife are both earning

**Verdiener** *der;* ~s, ~, **Verdienerin** *die;*
~, ~nen wage earner

**Verdienst¹** *der;* ~[e]s, ~e income;
earnings *pl.*

**Verdienst²** *das;* ~[e]s, ~e merit

**verdienst·voll** [1] *Adj.* commendable;
*(person)* of outstanding merit
[2] *adv.* commendably

**verdient** [1] *Adj.* (a) *(person)* of
outstanding merit; **sich um etw.** ~ **machen**
render outstanding services to sth.
(b) (gerecht, zustehend) well-deserved
[2] *adv.* deservedly

**verdientermaßen** *Adv.* deservedly

**verdoppeln** [1] *tr. V.* double; (fig.) double,
redouble *(efforts etc.)*
[2] *refl. V.* double

**verdorben** 2. *Part. v.* VERDERBEN

**verdorren** *itr. V.; mit sein* wither [and die];
*(meadow)* scorch

**verdrängen** *tr. V.* (a) drive out
*(inhabitants)*; (fig.: ersetzen) displace
(b) (Psych.) repress; (bewusst) suppress

**verdrehen** *tr. V.* (a) twist *(joint)*; roll *(eyes)*
(b) (ugs. abwertend: entstellen) twist *(words,
facts, etc.)*

**verdrießen** *unr. tr. V.* (geh.) irritate; annoy

**verdrießlich** [1] *Adj.* morose
[2] *adv.* morosely

**verdross, *verdroß** *1. u. 3. Pers. Sg.
Prät. v.* VERDRIESSEN

**verdrossen** [1] *Adj.* (missmutig) morose;
(missmutig und lustlos) sullen
[2] *adv.* (missmutig) morosely; (missmutig und
lustlos) sullenly

**Verdruss, *Verdruß** *der;* Verdrusses,
Verdrusse annoyance

**verdunkeln** *tr. V.* darken; (vollständig) black
out *(room, house, etc.)*

**Verdunk[e]lung** *die;* ~, ~en darkening; (vollständig) blackout

**verdünnen** *tr. V.* dilute

**verdunsten** *itr. V.; mit sein* evaporate

**verdünnen** *tr. V.* dilute

**verdunsten** *itr. V.; mit sein* evaporate

**Verdunstung** *die;* ~: evaporation

**verdursten** *itr. V.; mit sein* die of thirst

**verdutzt** *Adj.* taken aback *pred.;* nonplussed; (verwirrt) baffled

**Verdutztheit** *die;* ~: bafflement

**verehren** *tr. V.* (a) venerate
(b) (geh.: bewundern) admire; (ehrerbietig lieben) worship

**Verehrer** *der;* ~s, ~, **Verehrerin** *die;* ~, ~en admirer

**Verehrung** *die;* ~ (a) veneration
(b) (Bewunderung) admiration

**vereidigen** *tr. V.* swear in

**Vereidigung** *die;* ~, ~en swearing in

**Verein** *der;* ~s, ~e organization; (der Kunstfreunde usw.) association; society; (Sportverein) club

**vereinbar** *Adj.* compatible

**vereinbaren** *tr. V.* agree; arrange ⟨*meeting etc.*⟩

**Vereinbarung** *die;* ~, ~en (a) agreeing; (eines Termins usw.) arranging
(b) (Abmachung) agreement

**vereinfachen** *tr. V.* simplify

**Vereinfachung** *die;* ~, ~en simplification

**vereinheitlichen** *tr. V.* standardize

**Vereinheitlichung** *die;* ~, ~en standardization

**vereinigen** *tr., refl. V.* unite; (in der Wirtschaft) merge

**vereinigt** *Adj.* united

**Vereinigung** *die;* ~, ~en (a) organization
(b) (das Vereinigen) uniting; (von Unternehmen) merging

**vereinsamen** *itr. V.; mit sein* become [increasingly] lonely *or* isolated

**Vereinsamung** *die;* ~: loneliness; isolation

**vereinzelt** [1] *Adj.* occasional
[2] *adv.* (zeitlich) occasionally; (örtlich) here and there

**Vereinzelung** *die;* ~, ~en isolation

**vereisen** *itr. V.; mit sein* freeze *or* ice over; ⟨*wing*⟩ ice up; ⟨*lock*⟩ freeze up

**vereiteln** *tr. V.* thwart

**Vereitelung** *die;* ~: thwarting

**vereitern** *itr. V.; mit sein* go septic

**verenden** *itr. V.; mit sein* perish; die

**verengen** *refl. V.* narrow; ⟨*pupils*⟩ contract

**vererben** *tr. V.* leave, bequeath ⟨*property*⟩ (*Dat.,* an + *Akk.* to)

**Vererbung** *die;* ~, ~en heredity *no art.*

**verewigen** [1] *tr. V.* immortalize

[2] *refl. V.* (ugs.: Spuren hinterlassen) leave one's mark

**verfahren** [1] *unr. refl. V.* lose one's way
[2] *unr. itr. V.; mit sein* proceed

**Verfahren** *das;* ~s, ~ (a) procedure; (Technik) process; (Methode) method
(b) (Rechtsw.) proceedings *pl.*

**Verfall** *der;* ~[e]s (a) decay; (fig.: der Preise, einer Währung) collapse
(b) (Auflösung) decline

**verfallen** *unr. itr. V.; mit sein* (a) (baufällig werden) fall into disrepair
(b) (körperlich) ⟨*strength*⟩ decline
(c) (untergehen) ⟨*empire*⟩ decline; ⟨*morals, morale*⟩ deteriorate
(d) (ungültig werden) expire

**Verfalls-datum** *das* use-by date; (ugs.: Mindesthaltbarkeitsdatum) best-before date

**verfälschen** *tr. V.* distort, misrepresent ⟨*statement, message*⟩; falsify, misrepresent ⟨*facts, history, truth*⟩; falsify ⟨*painting, banknote*⟩; adulterate ⟨*wine, milk, etc.*⟩

**Verfälschung** *die* ▶ VERFÄLSCHEN: distortion; misrepresentation; falsification; adulteration

**verfassen** *tr. V.* write; draw up ⟨*resolution*⟩

**Verfasser** *der;* ~s, ~, **Verfasserin** *die;* ~, ~nen writer; (eines Buchs, Artikels usw.) author; writer

**Verfassung** *die;* ~, ~en (a) (Politik) constitution
(b) (Zustand) state [of health/mind]; **in guter/ schlechter** ~ **sein** be in good/poor shape

**verfassungs-gemäß** [1] *Adj.* constitutional; in accordance with the constitution *postpos.;*
[2] *adv.* constitutionally; in accordance with the constitution

**verfaulen** *itr. V.; mit sein* rot

**verfehlen** *tr. V.* miss

**Verfehlung** *die;* ~, ~en misdemeanour; (Rel.: Sünde) transgression

**verfeinden** *refl. V.* **sich** ~ **mit** make an enemy of

**verfeinern** *tr. V.* improve; refine ⟨*method, procedure*⟩

**Verfeinerung** *die;* ~, ~en ▶ VERFEINERN: improvement; refinement

**verfertigen** *tr. V.* produce

**verfilmen** *tr. V.* film; make a film of

**Verfilmung** *die;* ~, ~en (a) (das Verfilmen) filming
(b) (Film) film [version]

**verfinstern** [1] *tr. V.* obscure ⟨*sun etc.*⟩
[2] *refl. V.* (auch fig.) darken

**Verfinsterung** *die;* ~, ~en darkening

**verflixt** (ugs.) [1] *Adj.* (a) (ärgerlich) awkward, unpleasant ⟨*situation, business, etc.*⟩
(b) (verdammt) blasted (Brit.); blessed; confounded; ~ **[noch mal]!** [damn and] blast! (Brit. coll.)

⋯⊹

**(c)** (sehr groß) **er hat ~es Glück gehabt** he was damned lucky (coll.)

**2** *adv.* (sehr) damned (coll.)

**verflossen** *Adj.* (ugs.) former

**verfluchen** *tr. V.* curse

**verflucht** **1** *Adj.* (salopp) damned (coll.); bloody (Brit. sl.); **~ [noch mal]!** damn [it]! (coll.)

**2** *adv.* (sehr) damned (coll.)

**verfolgen** *tr. V.* pursue; hunt, track ⟨*animal*⟩; **etw. [strafrechtlich] ~:** prosecute sth.

**Verfolgte** *der/die; adj. Dekl.* victim of persecution

**Verfolgung** *die; ~, ~en* **(a)** pursuit; (eines Ziels, Plans usw.) pursuance

**(b)** [strafrechtliche] **~:** prosecution

**Verfolgungs-: ~jagd** *die* pursuit; chase; **~wahn** *der* (Psych.) persecution mania

**verfressen** *Adj.* (salopp) greedy

**verfügen** **1** *tr. V.* (anordnen) order; (dekretieren) decree

**2** *itr. V.* **über etw.** (*Akk.*) **[frei] ~ können** be free to decide what to do with sth.; **über etw.** (*Akk.*) **~** (etw. haben) have sth. at one's disposal

**Verfügung** *die; ~, ~en* **(a)** (Anordnung) order; (Dekret) decree

**(b)** (Disposition) **etw. zur ~ haben** have sth. at one's disposal; **jmdm. etw. zur ~ stellen** put sth. at sb.'s disposal

**verführen** *tr. V.* **(a)** (verleiten) tempt

**(b)** (sexuell) seduce

**Verführer** *der; ~s, ~:* seducer

**Verführerin** *der; ~, ~nen* seductress

**verführerisch** **1** *Adj.* **(a)** (verlockend) tempting

**(b)** (aufreizend) seductive

**2** *adv.* **(a)** (verlockend) temptingly

**(b)** (aufreizend) seductively

**Verführung** *die; ~, ~en* **(a)** temptation

**(b)** (sexuell) seduction

**vergangen** *Adj.* **(a)** (vorüber, vorbei) bygone, former ⟨*times, years, etc.*⟩

**(b)** (letzt...) last ⟨*year, week, etc.*⟩

**Vergangenheit** *die; ~* **(a)** past

**(b)** (Grammatik: Präteritum) past tense

**vergänglich** *Adj.* transient; transitory; ephemeral

**Vergänglichkeit** *die; ~:* transience

**Vergaser** *der; ~s, ~:* carburettor

**vergaß** *1. u. 3. Pers. Sg. Prät. v.* VERGESSEN

**Vergasung** *die; ~, ~en* **(a)** (von Kohle) gasification

**(b)** (Tötung) gassing

**(c)** **bis zur ~** (ugs.) ad nauseam

**vergeben** *unr. tr. V.* **(a)** *auch itr.* (geh.: verzeihen) forgive; **jmdm. etw. ~:** forgive sb. [for] sth.

**(b)** throw away ⟨*chance, goal, etc.*⟩

**(c)** (geben) place ⟨*order*⟩ (**an** + *Akk.* with); award ⟨*grant, prize*⟩ (**an** + *Akk.* to)

**vergebens** **1** *Adv.* in vain; vainly

**2** *adj.* **es war ~:** it was of *or* to no avail

**vergeblich** **1** *Adj.* futile; vain, futile ⟨*attempt, efforts*⟩

**2** *adv.* in vain

**Vergebung** *die; ~:* (geh.) forgiveness

**vergegenwärtigen** /od. ---'---/ *refl. V.* **sich** (*Dat.*) **etw. ~:** imagine sth.; (erinnern) recall sth.

**vergehen** *unr. itr. V.; mit sein* ⟨*time*⟩ pass [by], go by; ⟨*pain*⟩ wear off, pass; ⟨*pleasure*⟩ fade

**Vergehen** *das; ~s, ~:* crime; (Rechtsspr.) offence

**vergeigen** *tr. V.* (ugs.) botch up ⟨*test, performance, etc.*⟩; lose ⟨*game, match*⟩

**vergelten** *unr. tr. V.* repay

**vergessen** *unr. tr. V.* (*auch itr.*) *V.* forget

**Vergessenheit** *die; ~:* oblivion

**vergesslich, \*vergeßlich** *Adj.* forgetful

**vergeuden** *tr. V.* waste

**Vergeudung** *die; ~, ~en* waste

**vergewaltigen** *tr. V.* rape

**Vergewaltigung** *die; ~, ~en* rape

**vergewissern** *refl. V.* make sure (*Gen.* of)

**vergießen** *unr. tr. V.* spill; **Tränen ~:** shed tears

**vergiften** *tr. V.* (auch fig.) poison

**Vergiftung** *die; ~, ~en* poisoning

**vergiss, \*vergiß** *Imper. Sg. v.* VERGESSEN

**Vergiss-mein-nicht, \*Vergiß-mein-nicht** *das; ~[e]s, ~[e]* forget-me-not

**vergisst, \*vergißt** *2. u. 3. Pers. Sg. Präs. v.* VERGESSEN

**Vergleich** *der; ~[e]s, ~e* **(a)** comparison; **im ~ zu** *od.* **mit etw.** in comparison with sth.; compared with *or* to sth.

**(b)** (Rechtsw.) settlement

**vergleichbar** *Adj.* comparable

**vergleichen** *unr. tr. V.* compare

**Vergleichs·form** *die* (Sprachw.) comparative/superlative form

**verglühen** *itr. V.; mit sein* ⟨*log, wick, fire, etc.*⟩ smoulder and go out; ⟨*satellite, rocket, wire, etc.*⟩ burn out

**vergnügen** *refl. V.* enjoy oneself; have a good time

**Vergnügen** *das; ~s, ~:* pleasure; (Spaß) fun; **viel ~!** (auch iron.) have fun!

**vergnüglich** *Adj.* amusing; entertaining

**vergnügt** **1** *Adj.* cheerful

**2** *adv.* cheerfully

**Vergnügungs·viertel** *das* pleasure district

**vergolden** *tr. V.* gold-plate ⟨*jewellery etc.*⟩; (mit Blattgold) gild

**vergraben** *unr. tr. V.* bury

**vergrämt** *Adj.* careworn

---

\*old spelling - see note on page xiv

**vergraulen** tr. V. (ugs.) put off
**vergreifen** unr. refl. V. sich an jmdm. ~: assault sb.
**vergriffen** Adj. out of print pred.
**vergrößern** ① tr. V. (a) (erweitern) extend ⟨room, area, building, etc.⟩
(b) (vermehren) increase
(c) (größer reproduzieren) enlarge ⟨photograph etc.⟩
② refl. V. (a) (größer werden) ⟨firm, business, etc.⟩ expand
(b) (zunehmen) increase
③ itr. V. ⟨lens etc.⟩ magnify
**Vergrößerung** die; ~, ~en (a) ▶ VERGRÖSSERN 1, 2: extension; increase; enlargement; expansion
(b) (Foto) enlargement
**Vergrößerungs·glas** das magnifying glass
**Vergünstigung** die; ~, ~en privilege
**vergüten** tr. V. (a) (erstatten) jmdm. etw. ~: reimburse sb. for sth.
(b) (bes. Papierdt.: bezahlen) remunerate, pay for ⟨work, services⟩
**Vergütung** die; ~, ~en (a) (Rückerstattung) reimbursement
(b) (Geldsumme) remuneration
**verhaften** tr. V. arrest; Sie sind verhaftet you are under arrest
**Verhaftung** die; ~, ~en arrest
**verhalten** unr. refl. V. (a) behave; (reagieren) react
(b) (beschaffen sein) be
**Verhalten** das; ~s behaviour
**Verhaltens·weise** die behaviour
**Verhältnis** das; ~ses, ~se (a) ein ~ von drei zu eins a ratio of three to one
(b) (persönliche Beziehung) relationship (zu with); mit jmdm. ein ~ haben (ugs.) have an affair with sb.
(c) Pl. (Umstände) conditions
**verhältnis·mäßig** Adv. relatively; comparatively
**Verhältnis·wort** das; Pl. ~wörter (Sprachw.) preposition
**verhandeln** ① itr. V. (a) negotiate (über + Akk. about)
(b) (strafrechtlich) try a case; (zivilrechtlich) hear a case
② tr. V. (a) etw. ~: negotiate over sth.
(b) (strafrechtlich) try ⟨case⟩; (zivilrechtlich) hear ⟨case⟩
**Verhandlung** die; ~, ~en (a) ~en negotiations
(b) (strafrechtlich) trial; (zivilrechtlich) hearing; die ~ gegen X the trial of X
**verhängen** tr. V. impose ⟨fine, punishment⟩ (über + Akk. on); declare ⟨state of emergency, state of siege⟩; (Sport) award, give ⟨penalty etc.⟩
**Verhängnis** das; ~ses, ~se undoing
**verhängnis·voll** Adj. disastrous
**verharmlosen** tr. V. play down

**Verharmlosung** die; ~, ~en playing down
**verhärmt** Adj. careworn
**verharren** itr. V. (geh.) remain
**verhärten** ① tr. V. harden; make ⟨person⟩ hard
② refl. V. ⟨tissue⟩ become hardened
**verhasst, *verhaßt** Adj. hated; detested
**verhätscheln** tr. V. (ugs.) pamper
**verhauen** (ugs.) unr. tr. V. beat up; (als Strafe) beat
**verheben** unr. refl. V. do oneself an injury [while lifting sth.]
**verheeren** tr. V. devastate; lay waste [to]
**verheerend** Adj. (a) devastating
(b) (ugs.: scheußlich) ghastly (coll.)
**verhehlen** tr. V. (geh.) conceal (Dat. from)
**verheilen** itr. V.; mit sein ⟨wound⟩ heal [up]
**verheimlichen** tr. V. [jmdm.] etw. ~: keep sth. secret [from sb.]
**Verheimlichung** die; ~, ~en concealment
**verheiraten** refl. V. get married; sich mit jmdm. ~: marry sb.; get married to sb.
**Verheiratete** der/die; adj. Dekl. married person; married man/woman
**Verheiratung** die; ~, ~en marriage
**verheizen** tr. V. (a) burn; use as fuel
(b) (abwertend: rücksichtslos einsetzen) burn out ⟨athlete, skier, etc.⟩; use ⟨troops⟩ as cannon fodder
**verhelfen** unr. itr. V. jmdm./einer Sache zu etw. ~: help sb./sth. to get/achieve sth.
**verherrlichen** tr. V. glorify
**Verherrlichung** die; ~, ~en glorification
**verheult** Adj. (ugs.) ⟨eyes⟩ red from crying; ⟨face⟩ puffy or swollen from crying
**verhexen** tr. V. (auch fig.) bewitch
**verhindern** tr. V. prevent
**Verhinderung** die; ~, ~en prevention
**verhöhnen** tr. V. mock
**Verhöhnung** die; ~, ~en mockery
**Verhör** das; ~[e]s, ~e interrogation; questioning; (bei Gericht) examination
**verhören** ① tr. V. interrogate; question; (bei Gericht) examine
② refl. V. mishear
**verhüllen** tr. V. cover; (fig.) disguise
**verhüllend** Adj. (Literaturw.) euphemistic
**Verhüllung** die; ~, ~en covering; (fig.) disguising
**verhungern** itr. V.; mit sein die of starvation; starve [to death]
**verhunzen** tr. V. (ugs. abwertend) ruin; mess up; ruin ⟨landscape, townscape, etc.⟩
**verhüten** tr. V. prevent
**Verhütung** die; ~, ~en prevention; (Empfängnisverhütung) contraception
**Verhütungs·mittel** das contraceptive

**verirren** *refl. V.* (a) get lost; lose one's way; ⟨*animal*⟩ stray
(b) (irgendwohin gelangen) stray (**in, an** + *Akk.* into)
**verjagen** *tr. V.* chase away
**verjüngen** 1 *tr. V.* rejuvenate
2 *refl. V.* (schmaler werden) taper; become narrower; narrow
**verkalken** *itr. V.; mit sein* (a) ⟨*tissue*⟩ calcify; ⟨*arteries*⟩ become hardened
(b) (ugs.: senil werden) become senile
**Verkauf** *der;* ~[e]s, Verkäufe sale
**verkaufen** *tr. V.* (auch fig.) sell (*Dat.,* an + *Akk.* to); „zu ~" 'for sale'
**Verkäufer** *der;* ~s, ~ **Verkäuferin** *die;* ~, ~nen (a) seller; vendor (formal)
(b) (Berufsbez.) sales *or* shop assistant; (im Außendienst) salesman/saleswoman
**verkäuflich** *Adj.* (zum Verkauf geeignet) saleable; (zum Verkauf bestimmt) for sale *postpos.*
**verkaufs·offen** *Adj.* der ~e Samstag Saturday on which the shops are open all day
**Verkaufs·preis** *der* retail price
**Verkehr** *der;* ~s (a) traffic
(b) (Kontakt) contact; communication
(c) (Geschlechtsverkehr) intercourse
**verkehren** *itr. V.* (a) auch mit sein (fahren) run; ⟨*aircraft*⟩ fly
(b) (in Kontakt stehen) mit jmdm. ~: associate with sb.
(c) (zu Gast sein) bei jmdm. ~: visit sb. regularly
**verkehrs-, Verkehrs-:** ~ampel *die* traffic lights *pl.;* ~amt *das* tourist information office; ~aufkommen *das* volume of traffic; ~hindernis *das* obstruction to traffic; ~knotenpunkt *der* [traffic] junction; ~kontrolle *die* traffic check; ~meldung *die* traffic announcement *or* flash; ~mittel *das* means of transport; die öffentlichen ~mittel public transport *sing.;* ~polizist *der* traffic policeman; ~polizistin *die* traffic policewoman; ~schild *das; Pl.* ~~er traffic sign; road sign; ~sicher *Adj.* roadworthy; ~teilnehmer *der,* ~teilnehmerin *die* road user; ~unfall *der* road accident; ~weg *der* traffic route; ~zeichen *das* traffic sign; road sign
**verkehrt** 1 *Adj.* wrong
2 *adv.* wrongly; alles ~ machen do everything wrong
**verkennen** *unr. tr. V.* fail to recognize; misjudge ⟨*situation*⟩
**verklagen** *tr. V.* sue; take to court; eine Firma auf Schadenersatz ~: sue a company for damages
**verkleben** 1 *itr. V.; mit sein* stick together
2 *tr. V.* (zukleben) seal up ⟨*hole*⟩; (festkleben) stick [down] ⟨*floor covering etc.*⟩

**verkleiden** *tr. V.* disguise; (kostümieren) dress up; sich ~: disguise oneself/dress [oneself] up
**Verkleidung** *die;* ~, ~en (a) disguising; (das Kostümieren) dressing up
(b) (Kleidung) disguise; (bei einer Party) fancy dress
**verkleinern** 1 *tr. V.* (a) make smaller
(b) (verringern) reduce ⟨*size, number, etc.*⟩
(c) (kleiner reproduzieren) reduce ⟨*photograph etc.*⟩
2 *refl. V.* become smaller; ⟨*number*⟩ decrease
**Verkleinerungs·form** *die* (Sprachw.) diminutive form
**verknallen** *refl. V.* (ugs.: sich verlieben) fall head over heels in love (**in** + *Akk.* with); in jmdn. verknallt sein be crazy about sb. (coll.)
**verknittern** *tr. V.* crumple
**verknoten** *tr. V.* tie; knot
**verknüpfen** *tr. V.* (a) (knoten) tie; knot
(b) (in Beziehung setzen) link
**verkochen** *itr. V.; mit sein* (a) boil away
(b) (breiig werden, zerfallen) boil down to a pulp
**verkohlen** *itr. V.* char
**verkommen**[1] *unr. itr. V.; mit sein* go to the dogs; (moralisch, sittlich) go to the bad
**verkommen**[2] *Adj.* depraved
**verköstigen** *tr. V.* feed; provide with meals
**verkraften** *tr. V.* cope with
**verkrampfen** *refl. V.* ⟨*muscle*⟩ become cramped; ⟨*person*⟩ tense up
**Verkrampfung** *die;* ~, ~en tenseness; tension
**verkriechen** *unr. refl. V.* ⟨*animal*⟩ creep [away]; ⟨*person*⟩ hide [oneself away]
**verkrümeln** *refl. V.* (ugs.: sich entfernen) slip off *or* away
**verkrümmt** *Adj.* bent ⟨*person*⟩; crooked ⟨*finger*⟩; curved ⟨*spine*⟩
**Verkrümmung** *die;* ~, ~en crookedness
**verkrüppeln** *tr. V.* cripple
**verkümmern** *itr. V.; mit sein* ⟨*person, animal*⟩ go into a decline; ⟨*plant etc.*⟩ become stunted; ⟨*talent, emotional life, etc.*⟩ wither away
**verkünden** *tr. V.* announce; pronounce ⟨*judgement*⟩; promulgate ⟨*law, decree*⟩
**verkündigen** *tr. V.* (geh.) announce; proclaim
**Verkündigung** *die;* ~, ~en announcement; proclamation
**Verkündung** *die;* ~, ~en announcement; (von Urteilen) pronouncement; (von Gesetzen, Verordnungen) promulgation
**verkürzen** *tr. V.* (a) (verringern) reduce; (abkürzen) shorten
(b) (abbrechen) cut short ⟨*stay, life*⟩; put an end to, end ⟨*suffering*⟩
**verladen** *unr. tr. V.* load

**Verlag** *der;* ∼[e]s, ∼e publishing house *or* firm; publisher's

**verlagern** *tr. V.* shift; (an einen anderen Ort) move; (fig.) transfer; shift ⟨*emphasis*⟩

**Verlagerung** *die* moving; **eine** ∼ **des Schwergewichts** (fig.) a shift in emphasis

**verlanden** *itr. V.; mit sein* silt up

**Verlandung** *die;* ∼, ∼en silting up

**verlangen** *tr. V.* demand; (nötig haben) ⟨*task etc.*⟩ require, call for ⟨*patience, knowledge, experience, skill, etc.*⟩; (berechnen) charge; (sehen/sprechen wollen) ask for; **du wirst am Telefon verlangt** you're wanted on the phone (coll.)

**Verlangen** *das;* ∼s, ∼ (a) desire (**nach** for)
(b) **auf** ∼: on request

**verlängern** *tr. V.* extend; lengthen, make longer ⟨*skirt, sleeve, etc.*⟩; renew ⟨*passport, driving licence, etc.*⟩

**Verlängerung** *die;* ∼, ∼en ▶ VERLÄNGERN: extension; lengthening; renewal

**Verlängerungs·schnur** *die* extension lead *or* (Amer.) cord

**verlangsamen** *tr. V.* **das Tempo/seine Schritte** ∼: reduce speed/slacken one's pace; slow down

**verlassen¹** [1] *unr. refl. V.* rely, depend (**auf +** *Akk.* on)
[2] *unr. tr. V.* (a) leave
(b) (sich trennen von) desert; abandon; forsake; leave, desert ⟨*wife, family, etc.*⟩

**verlassen²** *Adj.* deserted ⟨*street etc.*⟩; empty ⟨*house*⟩; (öd) desolate ⟨*region etc.*⟩

**verlässlich, \*verläßlich** [1] *Adj.* reliable
[2] *adv.* reliably

**Verlauf** *der;* ∼[e]s, Verläufe course

**verlaufen** [1] *unr. itr. V.; mit sein* (a) (sich erstrecken) run
(b) (ablaufen) ⟨*test, rehearsal, etc.*⟩ go; ⟨*party etc.*⟩ go off
[2] *unr. refl. V.* get lost; lose one's way

**Verlaufs·form** *die* (Sprachw.) progressive *or* continuous form

**verlautbaren** *tr. V.* announce [officially]

**Verlautbarung** *die;* ∼, ∼en announcement

**verlauten** *itr. V.; mit sein* be reported; **wie verlautet** according to reports

**verleben** *tr. V.* spend

**verlebt** *Adj.* dissipated

**verlegen¹** *tr. V.* (a) mislay
(b) (verschieben) postpone (**auf +** *Akk.* until); (vor∼) bring forward (**auf +** *Akk.* to); **einen Termin** ∼: alter an appointment
(c) (verlagern) move; transfer ⟨*patient*⟩
(d) (legen) lay ⟨*cable, pipe, carpet, etc.*⟩

**verlegen²** [1] *Adj.* embarrassed
[2] *adv.* in embarrassment

**Verlegenheit** *die;* ∼, ∼en (a) (Befangenheit) embarrassment; **jmdn. in** ∼ **bringen** embarrass sb.
(b) (Unannehmlichkeit) embarrassing situation

**Verleger** *der;* ∼s, ∼, **Verlegerin** *die;* ∼, ∼nen publisher

**Verleih** *der;* ∼[e]s, ∼e (a) hiring out; (von Autos) renting *or* hiring out
(b) (Unternehmen) hire firm; (Filmverleih) distribution company; (Videoverleih) video library; (Autoverleih) rental *or* hire firm

**verleihen** *unr. tr. V.* (a) hire out; rent *or* hire out ⟨*car*⟩; (umsonst) lend [out]
(b) (überreichen) award; confer ⟨*award, honour*⟩

**Verleihung** *die;* ∼, ∼en (a) ▶ VERLEIHEN A: hiring out; renting out; lending [out]
(b) ▶ VERLEIHEN B: awarding; conferring; (Zeremonie) award; conferment

**verleiten** *tr. V.* jmdn. dazu ∼, etw. zu tun lead *or* induce sb. to do sth.

**verlernen** *tr. V.* forget

**verlesen** [1] *unr. tr. V.* read out
[2] *unr. refl. V.* (falsch lesen) make a mistake/ mistakes in reading

**verletzen** *tr. V.* (a) injure; (durch Schuss, Stich) wound
(b) (kränken) hurt ⟨*person, feelings*⟩
(c) (verstoßen gegen) violate; infringe ⟨*regulation*⟩; break ⟨*agreement, law*⟩

**verletzlich** *Adj.* vulnerable

**Verletzlichkeit** *die;* ∼: vulnerability

**Verletzte** *der/die; adj. Dekl.* casualty; (durch Schuss, Stich) wounded person

**Verletzung** *die;* ∼, ∼en (a) (Wunde) injury
(b) (Kränkung) hurting
(c) ▶ VERLETZEN C: violation; infringement; breaking

**verleugnen** *tr. V.* deny; disown ⟨*friend, relation*⟩

**Verleugnung** *die;* ∼, ∼en denial; (eines Freundes, Verwandten) disownment

**verleumden** *tr. V.* slander; (schriftlich) libel

**verleumderisch** *Adj.* slanderous; (in Schriftform) libellous

**Verleumdung** *die;* ∼, ∼en slander; (in Schriftform) libel

**verlieben** *refl. V.* fall in love (**in +** *Akk.* with)

**Verliebte** *der/die; adj. Dekl.* lover

**verlieren** *unr. tr., itr. V.* lose

**Verlierer** *der;* ∼s, ∼, **Verliererin** *die;* ∼, ∼nen loser

**verloben** *refl. V.* get engaged; **verlobt sein** be engaged

**Verlobte** *der/die; adj. Dekl.* fiancé/fiancée

**verlockend** *Adj.* tempting

**Verlockung** *die;* ∼, ∼en temptation

**verlogen** *Adj.* lying, mendacious ⟨*person*⟩; false ⟨*morality etc.*⟩

**verlor** *1. u. 3. Pers. Sg. Prät. v.* VERLIEREN

**verloren** [1] *2. Part. v.* VERLIEREN  ⋯⟶

**2** *Adj.* lost; wasted ⟨*effort*⟩; ~ **gehen** get lost
**\*verloren|gehen** ▶ VERLOREN 2
**verlosen** *tr. V.* raffle
**Verlosung** *die;* ~, ~**en** raffle; draw
**verlottern** *itr. V.; mit sein* ⟨*person*⟩ go to seed
**Verlust** *der;* ~[e]s, ~**e** loss (an + *Dat.* of)
**vermachen** *tr. V.* jmdm. etw. ~: leave *or* bequeath sth. to sb.; (fig.: schenken, überlassen) give sth. to sb.
**vermählen** *refl. V.* (geh.) sich [jmdm. *od.* mit jmdm.] ~: marry *or* wed [sb.]
**Vermählung** *die;* ~, ~**en** (geh.) **(a)** marriage
**(b)** (Fest) wedding ceremony
**vermarkten** *tr. V.* market ⟨*goods etc.*⟩
**Vermarktung** *die;* ~, ~**en** marketing
**vermehren** **1** *tr. V.* increase (um by)
**2** *refl. V.* **(a)** increase
**(b)** (sich fortpflanzen) reproduce
**Vermehrung** *die;* ~, ~**en** **(a)** increase (*Gen.* in)
**(b)** (Fortpflanzung) reproduction
**vermeiden** *unr. tr. V.* avoid
**Vermeidung** *die;* ~, ~**en** avoidance
**vermeintlich** *Adj.* supposed
**vermengen** *tr. V.* mix (miteinander together)
**Vermerk** *der;* ~[e]s, ~**e** note; (amtlich) remark
**vermerken** *tr. V.* make a note of; note [down]; (in Akten, Wachbuch usw.) record
**vermessen**¹ *unr. tr. V.* measure; survey ⟨*land, site*⟩
**vermessen²** *Adj.* (geh.) presumptuous
**vermieten** *tr.* (*auch itr.*) *V.* rent [out], let [out] (an + *Akk.* to); hire [out] ⟨*boat, car, etc.*⟩; „Zimmer zu ~" "room to let"
**Vermieter** *der;* ~**s**, ~: landlord
**Vermieterin** *die;* ~, ~**nen** landlady
**Vermietung** *die;* ~, ~**en** ▶ VERMIETEN: renting [out]; letting [out]; hiring [out]
**vermindern** **1** *tr. V.* reduce; decrease; reduce, lessen ⟨*danger, stress*⟩; lower ⟨*resistance*⟩; reduce ⟨*debt*⟩
**2** *refl. V.* decrease; ⟨*resistance*⟩ diminish
**Verminderung** *die* ▶ VERMINDERN 1: reduction; decreasing; lessening; lowering; eine ~ der Einnahmen a decrease in revenues
**verminen** *tr. V.* mine
**vermischen** **1** *tr. V.* mix (miteinander together); blend ⟨*teas, tobaccos, etc.*⟩
**2** *refl. V.* mix; (fig.) mingle ⟨*races, animals*⟩ interbreed
**Vermischung** *die;* ~ ▶ VERMISCHEN: mixing; blending; (fig.) mingling
**vermissen** *tr. V.* **(a)** miss
**(b)** (nicht haben) ich vermisse meinen Ausweis my identity card is missing

**Vermisste, \*Vermißte** *der/die; adj. Dekl.* missing person
**vermitteln** **1** *itr. V.* mediate, act as [a] mediator (in + *Dat.* in)
**2** *tr. V.* **(a)** (herbeiführen) arrange; negotiate ⟨*transaction, ceasefire, compromise*⟩
**(b)** (besorgen) jmdm. eine Stelle ~: find sb. a job
**(c)** (weitergeben) impart ⟨*knowledge, insight, values, etc.*⟩; communicate ⟨*message, information, etc.*⟩; convey ⟨*feeling*⟩; pass on ⟨*experience*⟩
**Vermittler** *der;* ~**s**, ~, **Vermittlerin** *die;* ~, ~**nen** **(a)** (Mittler) mediator
**(b)** ▶ VERMITTELN 2c: imparter; communicator; conveyer
**(c)** (von Berufs wegen) agent
**Vermittlung** *die;* ~, ~**en** **(a)** (Schlichtung) mediation
**(b)** ▶ VERMITTELN 2A: arrangement; negotiation
**(c)** ▶ VERMITTELN 2c: imparting; communicating; conveying
**(d)** (Telefonzentrale) exchange; (in einer Firma) switchboard
**vermöbeln** *tr. V.* (ugs.) beat up; (als Strafe) thrash
**vermögen** (geh.) *unr. tr. V.* etw. zu tun ~: be able to do sth.; be capable of doing sth.
**Vermögen** *das;* ~**s**, ~ **(a)** (geh.: Fähigkeit) ability
**(b)** (Besitz) fortune; er hat ~: he has money
**vermögend** *Adj.* wealthy; well-off
**Vermögen[s]·steuer** *die* wealth tax
**vermummen** *tr. V.* wrap up [warmly]; (verbergen) disguise
**vermurksen** *tr. V.* (ugs.) mess up; muck up (Brit. sl.)
**vermuten** *tr. V.* suspect; das ist zu ~: that is what one would suppose *or* expect; we may assume that;
**vermutlich** **1** *Adj.* probable
**2** *Adv.* presumably; (wahrscheinlich) probably
**Vermutung** *die;* ~, ~**en** supposition
**vernachlässigen** *tr. V.* neglect; (unberücksichtigt lassen) ignore; disregard
**Vernachlässigung** *die;* ~, ~**en** neglect
**vernarben** *itr. V.; mit sein* [form a] scar; heal (lit. or fig.)
**vernehmbar** *Adj.* (geh.) audible
**vernehmen** *unr. tr. V.* **(a)** (geh.: hören, erfahren) hear
**(b)** (verhören) question
**vernehmlich** **1** *Adj.* [clearly] audible
**2** *adv.* audibly
**Vernehmung** *die;* ~, ~**en** questioning
**verneigen** *refl. V.* (geh.) bow (vor + *Dat.* to, (literary) before)
**verneinen** *tr.* (*auch itr.*) *V.* **(a)** say 'no' to ⟨*question*⟩; answer ⟨*question*⟩ in the negative
**(b)** (Sprachw.) negate
**Verneinung** *die;* ~, ~**en** (Sprachw.) negation

**vernetzen** tr. V. (Chemie, Technik) interlink

**vernichten** tr. V. destroy; exterminate ⟨pests, vermin⟩

**vernichtend** ① Adj. crushing ⟨defeat⟩; shattering ⟨blow⟩; (fig.) devastating ⟨criticism⟩; devastating, withering ⟨glance⟩ ② adv. **den Feind** ∼ **schlagen** inflict a crushing defeat on the enemy

**Vernichtung** die; ∼, ∼en destruction; (von Schädlingen) extermination

**Vernichtungs-:** ∼**lager** das extermination camp; ∼**waffe** die weapon of annihilation

**Vernunft** die; ∼: reason

**vernünftig** ① Adj. (a) sensible (b) (ugs.: ordentlich, richtig) decent ② adv. (a) sensibly (b) (ugs.: ordentlich, richtig) ⟨talk, eat⟩ properly; ⟨dress⟩ sensibly

**veröffentlichen** tr. V. publish

**Veröffentlichung** die; ∼, ∼en publication

**verordnen** tr. V. [jmdm. etw.] ∼: prescribe [sth. for sb.]

**Verordnung** die; ∼, ∼en prescribing

**verpachten** tr. V. lease

**verpacken** tr. V. pack; wrap up ⟨present, parcel⟩

**Verpackung** die (a) packing (b) (Umhüllung) packaging no pl.; wrapping

**verpassen** tr. V. miss

**verpennen** (salopp) ① itr. V. oversleep ② tr. V. (a) (vergessen) forget (b) (verschlafen) sleep through ⟨morning etc.⟩

**verpesten** tr. V. (abwertend) pollute

**Verpestung** (abwertend) die; ∼, ∼en pollution

**verpflanzen** tr. V. (auch Med.) transplant; graft ⟨skin⟩

**Verpflanzung** die; ∼, ∼en (Med.) transplant[ing]; (von Haut) graft

**verpflegen** tr. V. cater for; feed

**Verpflegung** die; ∼, ∼en (a) catering no indef. art. (Gen. for) (b) (Nahrung) food; **Unterkunft und** ∼: board and lodging

**verpflichten** ① tr. V. (a) oblige; commit; (festlegen, binden) bind (b) (einstellen, engagieren) engage ⟨manager, actor, etc.⟩ ② refl. V. undertake; promise; **sich vertraglich** ∼: sign a contract

**Verpflichtung** die; ∼, ∼en (a) obligation; commitment (b) (Engagement) engaging; engagement

**verpfuschen** tr. V. (ugs.) make a mess of; muck up (Brit. sl.)

**verpissen** refl. V. (salopp) piss off (Brit. sl.); beat it (coll.)

**verpönt** Adj. scorned; (tabu) taboo

**verprügeln** tr. V. beat up; (zur Strafe) thrash

**Verputz** der; ∼es plaster; (auf Außenwänden) rendering

**verputzen** tr. V. plaster; render ⟨outside wall⟩

**verquer** Adj. (absonderlich) weird, outlandish ⟨idea⟩

**verquirlen** tr. V. mix [with a whisk]; whisk

**verquollen** Adj. swollen

**verrammeln** tr. V. barricade

**Verrat** der; ∼[e]s betrayal (an + Dat. of)

**verraten** unr. tr. V. (a) betray (an + Akk. to) (b) (ugs.: mitteilen) **jmdm. den Grund usw.** ∼: tell sb. the reason etc.; (c) (erkennen lassen) show, betray ⟨feelings, surprise, fear, etc.⟩; show ⟨influence, talent⟩

**Verräter** der; ∼s, ∼: traitor

**Verräterin** die; ∼, ∼nen traitress

**verräterisch** Adj. treacherous ⟨plan, purpose, act, etc.⟩

**verraucht** Adj. smoke-filled; smoky

**verrechnen** ① tr. V. include ⟨amount etc.⟩; (gutschreiben) credit ⟨cheque etc.⟩ to another account ② refl. V. miscalculate

**Verrechnungs-scheck** der crossed cheque

**verregnen** itr. V.; mit sein be spoilt or ruined by rain

**verreiben** unr. tr. V. rub in

**verreisen** itr. V.; mit sein go away

**verrenken** tr. V. dislocate

**Verrenkung** die; ∼, ∼en dislocation

**verrichten** tr. V. perform

**verriegeln** tr. V. bolt

**verringern** ① tr. V. reduce ② refl. V. decrease

**Verringerung** die; ∼: reduction; decrease (Gen., von in)

**Verriss, \*Verriß** der (ugs.) damning review or criticism (**über** + Akk. of)

**verrosten** itr. V.; mit sein rust; **verrostet** rusty

**verrückt** (ugs.) ① Adj. (a) mad; ∼ **werden** go mad or insane (b) (überspannt, ausgefallen) crazy ⟨idea, fashion, prank, day, etc.⟩ ② adv. crazily; ⟨behave⟩ crazily or like a madman; ⟨dress etc.⟩ in a mad or crazy way

**Verrückte** der/die; adj. Dekl. (ugs.) madman/madwoman; lunatic

**verrufen** Adj. disreputable

**verrühren** tr. V. stir together; mix

**verrutschen** itr. V. slip

**Vers** der; ∼es, ∼e verse

**versagen** itr. V. fail; ⟨machine, engine⟩ stop [working]; **menschliches Versagen** human error

**Versager** der; ∼s, ∼, **Versagerin** die; ∼, ∼nen failure

**versalzen** *unr. tr. V.* put too much salt in/ on; (fig. ugs.) spoil

**versammeln** *tr., refl. V.* assemble

**Versammlung** *die;* ~, ~en (a) meeting (b) (Gremium) assembly

**Versand** *der;* ~[e]s (a) dispatch (b) (ugs.: Versandhaus) mail order firm

**Versand-:** ~**handel** *der* mail order business; ~**haus** *das* mail order firm

**versauen** *tr. V.* (salopp) (a) (verschmutzen) mess up; make mucky (coll.) (b) (verderben) foul up (coll.)

**versäumen** *tr. V.* (a) (verpassen) miss; lose ⟨time, sleep⟩ (b) (vernachlässigen, unterlassen) neglect ⟨duty, task⟩

**verschaffen** *tr. V.* jmdm. etw. ~: provide sb. with sth.; get sb. sth.; **sich** (*Dat.*) **etw.** ~: get hold of sth.; obtain sth.

**verschämt** ⊡ *Adj.* bashful ⊡ *adv.* bashfully

**verschandeln** *tr. V.* (ugs.) spoil; ruin

**verschenken** *tr. V.* give away

**verscheuchen** *tr. V.* chase away

**verscheuern** *tr. V.* (ugs.) flog (Brit. sl.) (*Dat.,* **an** + *Akk.* to)

**verschicken** *tr. V.* ▶VERSENDEN

**verschieben** ⊡ *unr. tr. V.* (a) shift; move (b) (aufschieben) put off, postpone (**auf** + *Akk.* till) ⊡ *unr. refl. V.* be postponed (**um** for); ⟨start⟩ be put back *or* delayed (**um** by)

**Verschiebung** *die;* ~, ~en postponement

**verschieden** ⊡ *Adj.* (a) different (**von** from) (b) (vielfältig) various; **die** ~**sten** ...: all sorts of ...; **die** ~**en** ...: the various ... (c) **Verschiedenes** various things *pl.;* ⊡ *adv.* differently

**verschieden·artig** ⊡ *Adj.* different in kind *pred.;* (mehr als zwei) diverse ⊡ *adv.* diversely

**Verschiedenheit** *die;* ~, ~en difference; (unter mehreren) diversity

**verschiedentlich** *Adv.* on various occasions

**verschimmeln** *itr. V.; mit sein* go mouldy; **verschimmelt** mouldy

**verschlafen**¹ ⊡ *unr. itr. (auch refl.) V.* oversleep ⊡ *unr. tr. V.* (a) (schlafend verbringen) sleep through ⟨morning, journey, etc.⟩ (b) (versäumen) not wake up in time for ⟨appointment⟩; not wake up in time to catch ⟨train, bus⟩ (c) (ugs.: vergessen) forget about ⟨appointment etc.⟩

**verschlafen**² *Adj.* half asleep; (fig.) sleepy ⟨town⟩

**Verschlag** *der;* ~[e]s, **Verschläge** shed

**verschlagen**¹ *unr. tr. V.* die Seite ~: lose one's place *or* page; jmdm. die Sprache ~: leave sb. speechless

**verschlagen**² ⊡ *Adj.* sly; shifty ⊡ *adv.* slyly; shiftily

**verschlechtern** ⊡ *tr. V.* make worse ⊡ *refl. V.* get worse; deteriorate

**Verschlechterung** *die;* ~, ~en worsening, deterioration (Gen. in)

**Verschleiß** *der;* ~es, ~e (a) wear *no indef. art.;* (b) (Verbrauch) consumption (**an** + *Dat.* of)

**verschleißen** ⊡ *unr. itr. V.; mit sein* wear out ⊡ *unr. tr. V.* wear out; (fig.) run down, ruin ⟨one's nerves, one's health⟩; use up ⟨energy, ability, etc.⟩

**verschleppen** *tr. V.* (a) carry off; take away ⟨person⟩ (b) (weiterverbreiten) carry, spread ⟨disease, bacteria, mud, etc.⟩ (c) (verzögern) delay; (in die Länge ziehen) draw out; let ⟨illness⟩ drag on [and get worse]

**verschleudern** *tr. V.* (a) sell dirt cheap (coll.); (mit Verlust) sell at a loss (b) (verschwenden) squander

**verschließbar** *Adj.* closable; lockable ⟨suitcase, drawer, etc.⟩; [luftdicht] ~: sealable ⟨container etc.⟩

**verschließen** *unr. tr. V.* (a) close; stop, (mit einem Korken) cork ⟨bottle⟩ (b) (abschließen) lock; lock up ⟨house etc.⟩ (c) (wegschließen) lock away (**in** + *Dat. od. Akk.* in)

**verschlimmern** ⊡ *tr. V.* make worse ⊡ *refl. V.* get worse; ⟨position, conditions⟩ deteriorate, worsen

**Verschlimmerung** *die;* ~, ~en worsening

**verschlingen** *unr. tr. V.* (a) [inter]twine ⟨threads etc.⟩ (**zu** into) (b) (essen, fressen) devour ⟨food⟩; (fig.) devour ⟨novel, money, etc.⟩

**verschlissen** *2. Part. v.* VERSCHLEISSEN 2

**verschlossen** *Adj.* (wortkarg) taciturn; (zurückhaltend) reserved

**Verschlossenheit** *die;* ~: taciturnity; (Zurückhaltung) reserve

**verschlucken** ⊡ *tr. V.* swallow ⊡ *refl. V.* choke

**Verschluss, *Verschluß** *der* (am BH, an Schmuck usw.) fastener; fastening; (an Taschen, Schmuck) clasp; (an Schuhen, Gürteln) buckle; (am Schrank, Fenster, Koffer usw.) catch; (an Flaschen) top; (Stöpsel) stopper

**verschmähen** *tr. V.* (geh.) spurn

**verschmerzen** *tr. V.* get over

**verschmieren** *tr. V.* smear ⟨window etc.⟩; (beim Schreiben) mess up ⟨paper⟩; scrawl all over ⟨page⟩; smudge ⟨ink⟩

**verschmitzt** ⊡ *Adj.* mischievous ⊡ *adv.* mischievously

---

V

**verschmutzen** ☐1 *itr. V.; mit sein* get dirty; ⟨*river etc.*⟩ become polluted
☐2 *tr. V.* dirty; soil; pollute ⟨*air, water, etc.*⟩
**Verschmutzung** *die;* ~, ~en (der Umwelt) pollution; (von Stoffen, Teppichen usw.) soiling

**verschnaufen** *itr. V. (auch refl.)* V. have *or* take a breather

**verschneit** *Adj.* snow-covered *attrib.;* covered with snow *postpos.*

**verschnörkelt** *Adj.* ornate

**verschnüren** *tr. V.* tie up

**verschollen** *Adj.* missing

**verschonen** *tr. V.* spare; **jmdn. mit etw.** ~: spare sb. sth.

**verschönern** *tr. V.* brighten up

**verschränken** *tr. V.* fold ⟨*arms*⟩; cross ⟨*legs*⟩; clasp ⟨*hands*⟩

**verschrecken** *tr. V.* frighten *or* scare [off *or* away]

**verschreiben** ☐1 *unr. tr. V.* (Med.: verordnen) prescribe
☐2 *unr. refl. V.* **(a)** make a slip of the pen **(b) sich einer Sache** (*Dat.*) ~: devote oneself to sth.

**verschreibungs-pflichtig** *Adj.* available only on prescription *postpos.*

**verschrie[e]n** *Adj.* notorious (**wegen** for)

**verschroben** *Adj.* eccentric, cranky ⟨*person*⟩; cranky, weird ⟨*ideas*⟩

**verschrotten** *tr. V.* scrap

**Verschrottung** *die;* ~, ~en scrapping

**verschulden** ☐1 *tr. V.* be to blame for ⟨*accident, death, etc.*⟩
☐2 *refl. V.* get into debt

**Verschulden** *das;* ~s guilt; **durch eigenes** ~: through one's own fault

**verschuldet** *Adj.* in debt *postpos.* (**bei** to); **hoch** ~: deeply in debt

**verschütt:** ~ **gehen** (ugs.) do a vanishing trick *or* disappearing act (coll.)

**verschütten** *tr. V.* **(a)** spill **(b)** (begraben) bury ⟨*person*⟩ [alive]

***verschütt|gehen** ▶ VERSCHÜTT

**verschwägert** *Adj.* related by marriage *postpos.*

**verschweigen** *unr. tr. V.* conceal (*Dat.* from)

**verschwenden** *tr. V.* waste (**an** + *Akk.* on)

**Verschwender** *der;* ~s, ~, **Verschwenderin** *die;* ~, ~nen (von Geld) spendthrift; (von Dingen) wasteful person

**verschwenderisch** ☐1 *Adj.* wasteful ⟨*person*⟩; ⟨*life*⟩ of extravagance
☐2 *adv.* wastefully

**Verschwendung** *die;* ~, ~en wastefulness; extravagance

**verschwiegen** *Adj.* discreet; (still, einsam) secluded

**Verschwiegenheit** *die;* ~: secrecy; (Diskretion) discretion

**verschwimmen** *unr. itr. V.; mit sein* blur

**verschwinden** *unr. itr. V.; mit sein* disappear; vanish; **verschwinde [hier]!** off with you!; go away!; hop it! (coll.); **ich muss mal** ~ (ugs. verhüll.) I have to pay a visit (coll.) *or* (Brit. coll.) spend a penny

**verschwindend** ☐1 *Adj.* tiny
☐2 *adv.* ~ **klein** tiny; minute; ~ **wenig** a tiny amount

**verschwommen** ☐1 *Adj.* blurred ⟨*photograph, vision*⟩; blurred, hazy ⟨*outline*⟩; vague, woolly ⟨*idea, concept, formulation, etc.*⟩
☐2 *adv.* vaguely; ⟨*remember*⟩ hazily

**versehen** ☐1 *unr. tr. V.* **(a)** (ausstatten) provide; equip ⟨*car, factory, machine, etc.*⟩ **(b)** (ausüben, besorgen) perform ⟨*duty etc.*⟩
☐2 *unr. refl. V.* make a slip; slip up

**Versehen** *das;* ~s, ~: oversight; slip; **aus** ~: by mistake; inadvertently

**versehentlich** ☐1 *Adv.* by mistake; inadvertently
☐2 *adj.* inadvertent

**Versehrte** *der/die; adj. Dekl.* disabled person; **die** ~**n** the disabled

**versenden** *unr. (auch regelm.) tr. V.* send ⟨*letter, parcel*⟩; send out ⟨*invitations*⟩; dispatch ⟨*goods*⟩

**versetzen** ☐1 *tr. V.* **(a)** move; transfer, move ⟨*employee*⟩; (in die nächsthöhere Klasse) move ⟨*pupil*⟩ up, (Amer.) promote ⟨*pupil*⟩ (**in** + *Akk.* to); (umpflanzen) transplant, move ⟨*plant*⟩; (fig.) transport (**in** + *Akk.* to) **(b)** (nicht geradlinig anordnen) stagger **(c)** (verpfänden) pawn **(d)** (verkaufen) sell **(e)** (ugs.: vergeblich warten lassen) stand ⟨*person*⟩ up (coll.) **(f)** (vermischen) mix **(g)** (erwidern) retort **(h) etw. in Bewegung/Tätigkeit** ~: set sth. in motion/operation; **jmdn. in die Lage** ~, **etw. zu tun** put sb. in a position to do sth.; **jmdm. einen Stoß/Fußtritt/Schlag** *usw.* ~: give sb. a push/kick/deal sb. a blow *etc.;*
☐2 *refl. V.* **sich in jmds. Lage** (*Akk.*) ~: put oneself in sb.'s position *or* place

**Versetzung** *die;* ~, ~en (eines Schülers) moving up, (Amer.) promotion (**in** + *Akk.* to); (eines Angestellten) transfer

**verseuchen** *tr. V.* (auch fig.) contaminate; **radioaktiv** ~: contaminate with radioactivity

**Verseuchung** (auch fig.) *die;* ~, ~en contamination

**Versicherer** *der;* ~s, ~, **Versicherin** *die;* ~, ~nen insurer

**versichern** *tr. V.* **(a)** assert ⟨*sth.*⟩ **(b)** (vertraglich schützen) insure (**bei** with)

**Versicherte** *der/die; adj. Dekl.* insured [person]

**Versicherung** *die* **(a)** (Beteuerung) assurance
**(b)** (Schutz durch Vertrag) insurance; (Vertrag) insurance [policy] (**über** + *Akk.* for); (Gesellschaft) insurance [company]

**Versicherungs-:** ~**beitrag** der insurance premium; ~**betrug** der insurance fraud; ~**gesellschaft** die insurance company; ~**nehmer** der; ~~s, ~~, ~**nehmerin** die; ~~, ~~**nen** policy holder; ~**police** die insurance policy

**versickern** itr. V.; mit sein ⟨river etc.⟩ drain or seep away

**versiegeln** tr. V. seal

**versiegen** itr. V.; mit sein (geh.) dry up; run dry

**versinken** unr. itr. V.; mit sein sink; **im Schlamm** ~: sink into the mud

**verslumen** /...'slamən/ itr. V.; mit sein turn into a slum; **ein verslumter Stadtteil** a slum district

**versoffen** Adj. (salopp abwertend) boozy (coll.)

**versöhnen** ① refl. V. sich [miteinander] ~: become reconciled; **sich mit jmdm.** ~: make it up with sb.
② tr. V. reconcile

**Versöhnung** die; ~, ~en reconciliation

**versonnen** ① Adj. dreamy
② adv. dreamily

**versorgen** tr. V. (a) supply
(b) (unterhalten, ernähren) provide for ⟨children, family⟩
(c) (sorgen für) look after; **jmdn. ärztlich** ~: give sb. medical care; (kurzzeitig) give sb. medical attention

**Versorger** der; ~s, ~, **Versorgerin** die; ~, ~nen breadwinner

**Versorgung** die; ~, ~en (a) supply[ing]
(b) (Unterhaltung, Ernährung) support[ing]
(c) (Bedienung, Pflege) care; **ärztliche** ~: medical care or treatment; (kurzzeitig) medical attention

**Verspannung** die (Med.: der Muskulatur) tension

**verspäten** refl. V. be late

**verspätet** Adj. late ⟨arrival etc.⟩; belated ⟨greetings, thanks⟩; ~ **eintreffen** arrive late

**Verspätung** die; ~, ~en lateness; (verspätetes Eintreffen) late arrival; [**fünf Minuten**] ~ **haben** be [five minutes] late

**versperren** tr. V. block; obstruct ⟨view⟩

**verspielen** tr. V. gamble away; (fig.) squander, throw away ⟨opportunity, chance⟩; forfeit ⟨right, credibility, etc⟩

**verspielt** ① Adj. (auch fig.) playful; fanciful, fantastic ⟨form, design, etc.⟩
② adv. playfully (lit. or fig.); ⟨dress, designed⟩ fancifully, fantastically

**verspotten** tr. V. mock; ridicule

**Verspottung** die; ~, ~en mocking; ridiculing

**versprechen** ① unr. tr. V. promise; **sich** (Dat.) **etw. von etw./jmdm.** ~: hope for sth. or to get sth. from sth./sb.
② unr. refl. V. make a slip/slips of the tongue

**Versprechen** das; ~s, ~, **Versprechung** die; ~, ~en promise

**versprühen** tr. V. spray

**verspüren** tr. V. feel

**verstaatlichen** tr. V. nationalize

**Verstaatlichung** die; ~, ~en nationalization

**Verstand** der; ~[e]s (Fähigkeit zu denken) reason no art.; (Fähigkeit, Begriffe zu bilden) mind; (Vernunft) [common] sense no art.; **hast du denn den** ~ **verloren?** (ugs.) have you taken leave of your senses?

**verständig** ① Adj. sensible
② adv. sensibly

**verständigen** ① tr. V. notify, inform (von, über + Akk. of)
② refl. V. (a) make oneself understood; **sich mit jmdm.** ~: communicate with sb.
(b) (sich einigen) **sich [mit jmdm.] über/auf etw.** (Akk.) ~: come to an understanding [with sb.] about or. on sth

**Verständigkeit** die; ~: understanding; intelligence

**Verständigung** die; ~, ~en (a) notification
(b) (das Sichverständlichmachen) communication no art.;
(c) (Einigung) understanding

**Verständigungs-schwierigkeit** die difficulty of communication

**verständlich** ① Adj. (a) comprehensible; (deutlich) clear ⟨pronunciation, presentation, etc.⟩; **sich** ~ **machen** make oneself understood; **jmdm. etw.** ~ **machen** make sth. clear to sb.
(b) (begreiflich, verzeihlich) understandable
② adv. comprehensibly; (deutlich) ⟨speak, express oneself, present⟩ clearly

**verständlicher-weise** Adv. understandably

**Verständlichkeit** die; ~: comprehensibility; clarity

**Verständnis** das; ~ses, ~se understanding; **ich habe volles** ~ **dafür, dass** ...: I fully understand that ...; **für die Unannehmlichkeiten bitten wir um [Ihr]** ~: we apologize for the inconvenience caused

**verständnis-:** ~**los** ① Adj. uncomprehending; ② adv. uncomprehendingly; ~**voll** ① Adj. understanding; ② adv. understandingly

**verstärken** ① tr. V. (a) strengthen
(b) (zahlenmäßig) reinforce ⟨troops etc.⟩ (um by); enlarge ⟨orchestra, choir⟩ (um by)
(c) (intensiver machen) intensify, increase ⟨effort, contrast⟩; strengthen, increase ⟨impression, suspicion⟩; (größer machen) increase ⟨pressure, voltage, effect, etc.⟩; (lauter machen) amplify ⟨signal, sound, guitar, etc.⟩
② refl. V. increase

**Verstärker** der; ~s, ~: amplifier

**Verstärkung** die; ~, ~en (a) strengthening

**(b)** (zahlenmäßig) reinforcement (esp. Mil.)
**(c)** (Zunahme) increase (*Gen.* in); (der Lautstärke) amplification
**(d)** (zusätzliche Person[en]) reinforcements *pl.*
**verstauben** *itr. V.; mit sein* get dusty; gather dust (lit. or fig.)
**verstaubt** *Adj.* (fig. abwertend) old-fashioned; outmoded
**verstauchen** *tr. V.* sprain; **sich** (*Dat.*) **den Fuß/die Hand** ~: sprain one's ankle/wrist
**Verstauchung** *die;* ~, ~en sprain
**verstauen** *tr. V.* pack (**in** + *Dat. od. Akk.* in[to]); (bes. im Boot/Auto) stow (**in** + *Dat. od. Akk.* in)
**Versteck** *das;* ~[e]s, ~e hiding place: ~ **spielen** play hide-and-seek
**verstecken** [1] *tr. V.* hide (**vor** + *Dat.* from)
[2] *refl. V.* **sich** [vor jmdm./etw.] ~: hide [from sb./sth.]
**versteckt** *Adj.* hidden; (heimlich) secret ⟨*malice, activity, etc.*⟩; disguised ⟨*foul*⟩
**verstehen** [1] *unr. tr. V.* understand; **wie soll ich das** ~? how am I to interpret that?; **jmdn./etw. falsch** ~: misunderstand sb./sth.
[2] *unr. refl. V.* **sich mit jmdm.** ~: get on with sb.; **das versteht sich** [von selbst] that goes without saying
**versteigern** *tr. V.* auction; **etw.** ~ **lassen** put sth. up for auction
**Versteigerung** *die;* ~, ~en auction
**versteinern** *itr. V.; mit sein* ⟨*plant, animal*⟩ fossilize, become fossilized; ⟨*wood etc.*⟩ petrify, become petrified
**Versteinerung** *die;* ~, ~en **(a)** (das Versteinern) fossilization; (von Holz) petrification
**(b)** (Fossil) fossil
**verstellbar** *Adj.* adjustable
**verstellen** [1] *tr. V.* **(a)** (falsch platzieren) misplace
**(b)** (anders einstellen) adjust ⟨*seat etc.*⟩; alter [the adjustment of] ⟨*mirror etc.*⟩; reset ⟨*alarm clock, points, etc.*⟩
**(c)** (versperren) block, obstruct
**(d)** (zur Täuschung verändern) disguise ⟨*voice, handwriting*⟩
[2] *refl. V.* pretend
**Verstellung** *die;* ~, ~en pretence; (der Stimme, Schrift) disguising
**versteuern** *tr. V.* pay tax on
**verstimmen** *tr. V.* put ⟨*person*⟩ in a bad mood; (verärgern) annoy
**verstimmt** *Adj.* **(a)** (Musik) out of tune *pred.;*
**(b)** (verärgert) put out, peeved, disgruntled (**über** + *Akk.* by, about); **ein** ~**er Magen** an upset stomach
**Verstimmung** *die;* ~, ~en bad mood
**verstockt** *Adj.* obdurate; stubborn
**Verstocktheit** *die;* ~: obduracy; stubbornness
**verstohlen** [1] *Adj.* furtive

[2] *adv.* furtively
**verstopfen** [1] *tr. V.* block; **verstopft sein** ⟨*pipe, drain, jet, nose, etc.*⟩ be blocked [up] (**durch, von** with)
[2] *itr. V.; mit sein* become blocked
**Verstopfung** *die;* ~, ~en (Med.) constipation
**verstorben** *Adj.* late (*deceased*)
**Verstorbene** *der/die; adj. Dekl.* (geh.) deceased
**verstören** *tr. V.* distress
**verstört** *Adj.* distraught
**Verstoß** *der;* ~es, **Verstöße** violation (**gegen** of)
**verstoßen** [1] *unr. tr. V.* disown
[2] *unr. itr. V.* **gegen etw.** ~: infringe sth
**verstreichen** [1] *unr. tr. V.* apply, put on ⟨*paint*⟩; spread ⟨*butter etc.*⟩
[2] *unr. itr. V.; mit sein* (geh.) ⟨*time*⟩ pass [by]
**verstreuen** *tr. V.* scatter; put down ⟨*bird food, salt*⟩; (versehentlich) spill
**verstricken** [1] *tr. V.* **jmdn. in etw.** (*Akk.*) ~: involve sb. in sth.; draw sb. into sth.
[2] *refl. V.* **sich in etw.** (*Akk.*) ~: become entangled *or* caught up in sth
**verstümmeln** *tr. V.* mutilate; (fig.) garble ⟨*report*⟩; chop, mutilate ⟨*text*⟩
**verstummen** *itr. V.; mit sein* (geh.) fall silent; ⟨*music, noise, conversation*⟩ cease
**Versuch** *der;* ~[e]s, ~e attempt; (Experiment) experiment (**an** + *Dat.* on); (Probe) test
**versuchen** *tr. V.* **(a)** try; attempt
**(b)** ( probieren) try ⟨*cake etc.*⟩
**versündigen** *refl. V.* **sich an jmdm./etw.** ~: sin against sb./sth.
**versüßen** *tr. V.* **jmdm./sich etw.** ~ (fig.) make sth. more pleasant for sb./oneself
**vertauschen** *tr. V.* exchange; switch; reverse ⟨*roles, poles*⟩; **etw. mit** *od.* **gegen etw.** ~: exchange sth. for sth.
**verteidigen** *tr. V.* defend
**Verteidiger** *der;* ~s, ~, **Verteidigerin** *die;* ~, ~nen (auch Sport) defender; (Rechtsw.) defence counsel
**Verteidigung** *die;* ~, ~en defence
**Verteidigungs-minister** *der,* **Verteidigungs-ministerin** *die* minister of defence
**verteilen** *tr. V.* distribute, hand out ⟨*leaflets, prizes, etc.*⟩ (**an** + *Akk.* to, **unter** + *Akk.* among); share [out], distribute ⟨*money, food*⟩ (**an** + *Akk.* to, **unter** + *Akk.* among); allocate ⟨*work*⟩; distribute ⟨*weight etc.*⟩ (**auf** + *Akk.* over); spread ⟨*cost*⟩ (**auf** + *Akk.* among); distribute, spread ⟨*butter, seed, dirt, etc.*⟩
**Verteilung** *die;* ~, ~en distribution; (der Rollen, der Arbeit) allocation
**verteuern** [1] *tr. V.* make ⟨*goods*⟩ more expensive
[2] *refl. V.* become more expensive

V

**verteufeln** *tr. V.* condemn; denigrate

**Verteufelung** *die; ~, ~en* condemnation; denigration

**vertiefen** [1] *tr. V.* (auch fig.) deepen (**um** by) [2] *refl. V.* **sich ~ in** (+ *Akk.*) bury oneself in ⟨*book, work, etc.*⟩; **in etw.** (*Akk.*) **vertieft sein** be engrossed in sth

**Vertiefung** *die; ~, ~en* (Mulde) depression; hollow

**vertikal** [1] *Adj.* vertical [2] *adv.* vertically

**Vertikale** *die; ~, ~n* ▶ SENKRECHTE

**vertilgen** *tr. V.* (a) (vernichten) exterminate ⟨*vermin*⟩; kill off ⟨*weeds*⟩ (b) (ugs.: verzehren) devour, (joc.) demolish ⟨*food*⟩

**vertonen** *tr. V.* set ⟨*text, poem*⟩ to music

**Vertonung** *die; ~, ~en* setting

**Vertrag** *der; ~[e]s, Verträge* contract; (zwischen Staaten) treaty

**vertragen** [1] *unr. tr. V.* endure; tolerate (esp. Med.); (aushalten, leiden können) stand; bear; **ich vertrage keinen Kaffee** coffee disagrees with me [2] *unr. refl. V.* **sich mit jmdm. ~:** get on *or* along with sb.; (passen) **sich mit etw. ~:** go with sth

**vertraglich** [1] *Adj.* contractual [2] *adv.* contractually; by contract

**verträglich** *Adj.* (a) digestible ⟨*food*⟩ (b) (umgänglich) goodnatured; easy to get on with *pred.*

**vertrauen** *itr. V.* jmdm./einer Sache ~: trust sb./sth.; **auf etw.** (*Akk.*) ~: [put one's] trust in sth.

**Vertrauen** *das; ~s* trust; confidence; **jmdn. ins ~ ziehen** take sb. into one's confidence

**vertrauen-erweckend** *Adj.* inspiring

**vertrauens-, Vertrauens-:** ~**bruch** *der* breach of trust; ~**lehrer** *der,* ~**lehrerin** *die* (Schulw.) liaison teacher (liaising between staff and pupils); ~**person** *die* person in a position of trust; ~**sache** *die* matter *or* question of trust; ~**selig** *Adj.* all too trusting; ~**voll** [1] *Adj.* trusting ⟨*relationship*⟩; ⟨*collaboration, cooperation*⟩ based on trust; (zuversichtlich) confident; [2] *adv.* trustingly; (zuversichtlich) confidently; ~**würdig** *Adj.* trustworthy

**vertraulich** [1] *Adj.* (a) confidential (b) (freundschaftlich, intim) familiar ⟨*manner, tone, etc.*⟩; intimate ⟨*conversation*⟩ [2] *adv.* (a) confidentially (b) (freundschaftlich, intim) in a familiar way

**Vertraulichkeit** *die; ~, ~en* (a) confidentiality (b) (vertrauliche Information) confidence (c) (distanzloses Verhalten) familiarity; (Intimität) intimacy

**vertraut** *Adj.* (a) close ⟨*friend etc.*⟩; intimate ⟨*circle, conversation, etc.*⟩

---

(b) (bekannt) familiar; **jmdn./sich mit etw. ~ machen** familiarize sb./oneself with sth.

**Vertraute** *der/die; adj. Dekl.* close friend

**vertreiben** *unr. tr. V.* (a) drive out (**aus** of); drive away ⟨*animal, smoke, clouds*⟩ (**aus** from); fight off ⟨*tiredness, troubles*⟩ (b) (verkaufen) sell

**vertreten** [1] *unr. tr. V.* (a) stand in *or* deputize for ⟨*colleague etc.*⟩; ⟨*teacher*⟩ cover for ⟨*colleague*⟩ (b) (eintreten für, repräsentieren) represent ⟨*person, firm, interests, constituency, country, etc.*⟩; (Rechtsw.) act for ⟨*person, prosecution, etc.*⟩; ~ **sein** be represented (c) (einstehen für, verfechten) support ⟨*point of view, principle*⟩; hold ⟨*opinion*⟩; advocate ⟨*thesis etc.*⟩ [2] *unr. refl. V.* **sich** (*Dat.*) **die Füße** *od.* **Beine ~** (ugs.) stretch one's legs

**Vertreter** *der; ~s, ~,* **Vertreterin** *die; ~, ~nen* (a) (Stellvertreter[in]) deputy; stand-in (b) (Repräsentant[in]) representative; (Handelsvertreter[in]) sales representative; commercial traveller (c) (Verfechter[in], Anhänger[in]) supporter; advocate

**Vertretung** *die; ~, ~en* deputy; (Delegierte[r]) representative; (Delegation) delegation (Handelsvertretung) [sales] agency; **eine diplomatische ~:** a diplomatic mission

**Vertriebene** *der/die; adj. Dekl.* expellee [from his/her homeland]

**vertrocknen** *itr. V.; mit sein* dry up

**vertrödeln** *tr. V.* (ugs. abwertend) dawdle away, waste ⟨*time*⟩

**vertrösten** *tr. V.* put ⟨*person*⟩ off (**auf** + *Akk.* until)

**vertun** [1] *unr. tr. V.* waste [2] *unr. refl. V.* (ugs.) make a slip

**vertuschen** *tr. V.* hush up ⟨*scandal etc.*⟩; keep ⟨*truth etc.*⟩ secret

**Vertuschung** *die; ~, ~en* hushing up; **eine ~:** a hush-up *or* cover-up

**verübeln** *tr. V.* **jmdm. eine Äußerung usw. ~:** take sb.'s remark *etc.* amiss

**verüben** *tr. V.* commit ⟨*crime etc.*⟩

**verunglücken** *itr. V.; mit sein* have an accident; ⟨*car etc.*⟩ be involved in an accident; **mit dem Auto/Flugzeug ~:** be in a car/an air accident *or* crash

**Verunglückte** *der/die; adj. Dekl.* accident victim; casualty

**verunreinigen** *tr. V.* pollute; contaminate ⟨*water, milk, flour, oil*⟩

**verunsichern** *tr. V.* **jmdn. ~:** make sb. feel unsure *or* uncertain

**verunstalten** *tr. V.* disfigure

**Verunstaltung** *die; ~, ~en* disfigurement

**veruntreuen** *tr. V.* embezzle

**Veruntreuung** *die; ~, ~en* embezzlement

**verunzieren** *tr. V.* spoil the look of

**verursachen** *tr. V.* cause

**verurteilen** *tr. V.* pass sentence on; sentence; (fig.) condemn ⟨*behaviour, action*⟩; **jmdn. zum Tode ~:** sentence *or* condemn sb. to death

**Verurteilte** *der/die; adj. Dekl.* convicted man/woman

**Verurteilung** *die; ~, ~en* sentencing; (fig.) condemnation

**vervollkommnen** *tr. V.* perfect

**vervollständigen** *tr. V.* complete

**verwachsen** *Adj.* deformed

**verwählen** *refl. V.* misdial

**verwahren** ① *tr. V.* keep [safe]
② *refl. V.* protest

**verwahrlosen** *itr. V.; mit sein* get in a bad state; ⟨*house, building*⟩ fall into disrepair; ⟨*garden, hedge*⟩ become overgrown; ⟨*person*⟩ let oneself go; **verwahrlost** neglected; overgrown ⟨*hedge, garden*⟩; dilapidated ⟨*house, building*⟩; unkempt ⟨*person, appearance, etc.*⟩; (in der Kleidung) ragged ⟨*person*⟩

**Verwahrlosung** *die; ~:* (eines Gebäudes) dilapidation; (einer Person) advancing decrepitude

**verwaisen** *itr. V.* be orphaned

**verwalten** *tr. V.* (a) administer ⟨*estate, property*⟩; run ⟨*house*⟩; hold ⟨*money*⟩ in trust
(b) (leiten) run, manage ⟨*hostel, kindergarten, etc.*⟩; (regieren) administer ⟨*area, colony, etc.*⟩; govern ⟨*country*⟩

**Verwalter** *der; ~s, ~,* **Verwalterin** *die; ~, ~nen* administrator; (eines Amts usw.) manager; (eines Nachlasses) trustee

**Verwaltung** *die; ~, ~en* (a) administration; (eines Landes) government; (eines Amtes) tenure; (einer Aufgabe) performance
(b) (Organ) administration

**verwandeln** ① *tr. V.* convert (**in** + *Akk.,* **zu** into); (völlig verändern) transform (**in** + *Akk.,* **zu** into)
② *refl. V.* **sich in etw.** (*Akk.*) *od.* **zu etw. ~:** turn *or* change into sth.; (bei chemischen Vorgängen usw.) be converted into sth

**Verwandlung** *die; ~, ~en* conversion (**in** + *Akk.,* **zu** into); (völlige Veränderung, das Sichverwandeln) transformation (**in** + *Akk.,* **zu** into)

**verwandt¹** 2. *Part. v.* VERWENDEN

**verwandt²** *Adj.* related (**mit** to); (fig.) similar ⟨*views, ideas, forms*⟩

**Verwandte** *der/die; adj. Dekl.* relative; relation

**Verwandtschaft** *die; ~, ~en* (a) relationship (**mit** to); (fig.) affinity
(b) (Verwandte) relatives *pl.;* relations *pl.;* **die ganze ~:** all one's relatives

**verwandtschaftlich** *Adj.* family ⟨*ties, relationships, etc.*⟩

**verwarnen** *tr. V.* warn, caution (**wegen** for)

**Verwarnung** *die; ~, ~en* warning; caution

**verwechseln** *tr. V.* (a) [miteinander] **~:** confuse ⟨*two things/people*⟩; **etw. mit etw./ jmdn. mit jmdm. ~:** mistake sth. for sth./sb. for sb.; confuse sth. with sth./sb. with sb.
(b) (vertauschen) mix up

**Verwechslung** *die; ~, ~en* (a) [case of] confusion
(b) (Vertauschung) mixing up; **eine ~:** a mix-up

**verwegen** ① *Adj.* daring; (auch fig.) audacious
② *adv.* (auch fig.) audaciously

**Verwegenheit** *die; ~:* daring; (auch fig.) audacity

**verwehren** *tr. V.* **jmdm. etw. ~:** refuse *or* deny sb. sth.

**Verwehung** *die; ~, ~en* [snow]drift

**verweigern** *tr. V.* refuse

**Verweigerung** *die; ~, ~en* refusal

**Verweis** *der; ~es, ~e* (a) reference (**auf** + *Akk.* to); (Querverweis) cross reference
(b) (Tadel) reprimand

**verweisen** *unr. tr. V.* (a) **jmdn./einen Fall usw. an jmdn./etw. ~** (auch Rechtsspr.) refer sb./a case *etc.* to sb./sth.
(b) (wegschicken) **jmdn. von der Schule/aus dem Saal ~:** expel sb. from the school/send sb. out of the room; **einen Spieler vom Platz ~:** send a player off [the field]
(c) *auch itr.* (hinweisen) **[jmdn.] auf etw.** (*Akk.*) **~:** refer [sb.] to sth.

**verwelken** *itr. V.; mit sein* wilt

**verwendbar** *Adj.* usable

**Verwendbarkeit** *die; ~:* usability

**verwenden** *unr. od. regelm. tr. V.* (a) use (**zu, für** for)
(b) (aufwenden) spend ⟨*time*⟩ (**auf** + *Akk.* on)

**Verwendung** *die; ~, ~en* use

**verwerfen** *unr. tr. V.* reject; dismiss ⟨*thought*⟩

**verwerflich** (geh.) ① *Adj.* reprehensible
② *adv.* reprehensibly

**verwertbar** *Adj.* utilizable; usable

**verwerten** *tr. V.* utilize, use (**zu** for); make use of ⟨*suggestion, experience, knowledge, etc.*⟩

**verwesen** *itr. V.; mit sein* decompose

**Verwesung** *die; ~:* decomposition

**verwickeln** ① *refl. V.* get tangled up *or* entangled; **sich in etw.** (*Akk. od. Dat.*) **~:** get caught [up] in sth.
② *tr. V.* involve

**Verwicklung** *die; ~, ~en* complication

**verwildern** *itr. V.* ⟨*garden*⟩ become overgrown; ⟨*domestic animal*⟩ return to the wild

**verwirklichen** ① *tr. V.* realize ⟨*dream*⟩; realize, put into practice ⟨*plan, proposal, idea, etc.*⟩; carry out ⟨*project, intention*⟩
② (a) *refl. V.* ⟨*hope, dream*⟩ be realized ⋯⟩

**(b)** (sich voll entfalten) **sich [selbst]** ∼: realize one's [full] potential; fulfil oneself

**Verwirklichung** *die;* ∼, ∼en realization; (eines Wunsches, einer Hoffnung) fulfilment

**verwirren** *tr.* (*auch itr.*) *V.* confuse; **verwirrt** confused; ∼d bewildering

**Verwirrung** *die;* ∼, ∼en confusion

**verwischen** *tr. V.* smudge ⟨*signature, writing, etc.*⟩; smear ⟨*paint*⟩; (fig.) cover up ⟨*tracks*⟩

**verwittern** *itr. V.; mit sein* weather

**Verwitterung** *die;* ∼, ∼en weathering

**verwitwet** *Adj.* widowed

**verwöhnen** *tr. V.* spoil

**verwöhnt** *Adj.* spoilt; (anspruchsvoll) discriminating; ⟨*taste, palate*⟩ of a gourmet

**verworren** *Adj.* confused, muddled ⟨*ideas, situation, etc.*⟩

**verwunden** *tr. V.* wound; injure

**Verwundete** *der/die; adj. Dekl.* casualty; **die** ∼n the wounded

**Verwundung** *die;* ∼, ∼en wound

**verwünschen** *tr. V.* curse

**verwüsten** *tr. V.* devastate

**Verwüstung** *die;* ∼, ∼en devastation

**verzagen** *itr. V.; mit sein od. haben* despair; lose heart; **verzagt sein** be despondent

**Verzagtheit** *die;* ∼: despondency; despair

**verzählen** *refl. V.* miscount

**verzanken** *refl. V.* (ugs.) **sich [mit jmdm. wegen etw.]** ∼: fall out [with sb. over sth.]

**verzaubern** *tr. V.* cast a spell on; bewitch; (fig.) enchant; **jmdn. in etw.** (*Akk.*) ∼: transform sb. into sth.

**Verzehr** *der;* ∼[e]s consumption

**verzehren** *tr. V.* consume

**Verzeichnis** *das;* ∼ses, ∼se list; (Register) index

**verzeihen** *unr. tr., itr. V.* forgive; (entschuldigen) excuse ⟨*behaviour, remark, etc.*⟩; ∼ **Sie [bitte], können Sie mir sagen ...?** excuse me, could you tell me ...?

**Verzeihung** *die;* ∼: forgiveness; ∼**!** sorry!; **jmdn. um** ∼ **bitten** apologize to sb.

**verzerren** *tr. V.* **(a)** contort ⟨*face etc.*⟩ (**zu** into)
**(b)** (akustisch, optisch) distort ⟨*sound, image*⟩; **etw. verzerrt darstellen** (fig.) present a distorted account *or* picture of sth.

**Verzicht** *der;* ∼[e]s, ∼e **(a)** renunciation (**auf** + *Akk.* of)
**(b)** (auf Reichtum, ein Amt usw.) relinquishment (**auf** + *Akk.* of)

**verzichten** *itr. V.* do without; ∼ **auf** (+ *Akk.*) do without; (sich enthalten) refrain from; (aufgeben) give up ⟨*share, smoking, job, etc.*⟩; renounce ⟨*inheritance*⟩; relinquish ⟨*right, privilege*⟩; (opfern) sacrifice ⟨*holiday, salary*⟩

**verziehen¹** 2. *Part. v.* VERZEIHEN

**verziehen²** ① *unr. tr. V.* **(a)** screw up ⟨*face, mouth, etc.*⟩
**(b)** (schlecht erziehen) spoil
② *unr. refl. V.* **(a)** (aus der Form geraten) go out of shape; ⟨*wood*⟩ warp
**(b)** (wegziehen) ⟨*clouds, storm*⟩ move away, pass over; ⟨*fog, mist*⟩ disperse
**(c)** (ugs.: weggehen) take oneself off
③ *unr. itr. V.; mit sein* move [away]; „**Empfänger [unbekannt] verzogen**" 'no longer at this address'

**verzieren** *tr. V.* decorate

**Verzierung** *die;* ∼, ∼en decoration

**verzögern** ① *tr. V.* **(a)** delay (**um** by)
**(b)** (verlangsamen) slow down
② *refl. V.* be delayed (**um** by)

**Verzögerung** *die;* ∼, ∼en delay (*Gen.* in); (Verlangsamung) slowing down

**verzollen** *tr. V.* pay duty on

**Verzug** *der;* ∼[e]s delay; **im** ∼ **sein/in** ∼ **kommen** be/fall behind

**verzweifeln** *itr. V.; mit sein* despair; **über etw./jmdn.** ∼: despair at sth./of sb.

**verzweifelt** ① *Adj.* despairing ⟨*person*⟩; desperate ⟨*situation, attempt, effort, struggle, etc.*⟩; ∼ **sein** be in despair
② *adv.* desperately

**Verzweiflung** *die;* ∼: despair

**verzweigen** *refl. V.* branch [out]

**Veteran** /vete'raːn/ *der;* ∼en, ∼en,
**Veteranin** *die;* ∼, ∼nen (auch fig.) veteran

**Vetter** *der;* ∼s, ∼n cousin

**vgl.** *Abk.* = **vergleiche** cf.

**v. H.** *Abk.* = **vom Hundert** per cent

**via** /'viːa/ *Präp.* via

**Viadukt** /via'dʊkt/ *das od. der;* ∼[e]s, ∼e viaduct

**Viagra** ⓦ /'viagra/ *das;* ∼s Viagra ®

**vibrieren** /vi'briːrən/ *itr. V.* vibrate

**Video** *das;* ∼s, ∼s (ugs.) video

**video-, Video-** /'viːdeo-/: video

**Video-:** ∼**clip** *der;* ∼s, ∼s video; ∼**gerät** *das* video machine; ∼**kassette** *die* video cassette; ∼**recorder, ∼rekorder** *der* video recorder; ∼**text** *der* videotex[t]

**Videothek** *die;* ∼, ∼en video library

**Vieh** *das;* ∼[e]s **(a)** (Nutztiere) livestock *sing. or pl.;*
**(b)** (Rinder) cattle *pl.*

**Vieh-zucht** *die* [live]stock/cattle breeding *no art.*

**viel** ① *Indefinitpron. u. unbest. Zahlw.* **(a)** *Sg.* a great deal of; a lot of (coll.); **wie/nicht/zu** ∼: how/not/too much; ∼**[es]** (vielerlei) much; **der** ∼**e Regen** all the rain; **um** ∼**es jünger** a great deal younger
**(b)** *Pl.* many; **gleich** ∼**[e]** the same number of; **die** ∼**en Menschen** all the people
② *Adv.* **(a)** (oft, lange) a great deal; a lot (coll.)
**(b)** (wesentlich) much; a great deal; a lot (coll.); ∼ **zu klein** much too small

---

*old spelling - see note on page xiv

**V**

**vielerlei** *indekl. Adj.* **(a)** *attr.* many different; all kinds *or* sorts of **(b)** *allein stehend* all kinds of things

**viel-, Viel-:** ~**fach** [1] *Adj.* **(a)** multiple; **die** ~**fache Menge** many times the amount; **(b)** (vielfältig) many kinds of; [2] *adv.* many times; ~**falt** *die;* ~~: diversity; ~**fältig** [1] *Adj.* many and diverse; [2] *adv.* in many different ways

**vielleicht** *Adv.* perhaps; maybe

**viel-:** ~**mals** *Adv.* **ich bitte** ~**mals um Entschuldigung** I'm very sorry; **danke** ~**mals** thank you very much; ~**mehr** /od. ·'·/ *Konj. u. Adv.* rather; ~**sagend** [1] *Adj.* meaningful; [2] *adv.* meaningfully; ~**seitig** *Adj.* versatile 〈*person*〉; ~**versprechend** [1] *Adj.* [very] promising; [2] *adv.* [very] promisingly

**vier** *Kardinalz.* four

**Vier** *die;* ~, ~**en** four; **eine** ~ **schreiben/ bekommen** (Schulw.) ≈ get a D

**vier-, Vier-:** (s. auch ACHT-, ACHT-); ~**beiner** *der;* ~~s, ~~ (ugs.) four-legged friend; ~**beinig** *Adj.* four-legged; ~**eck** *das* quadrilateral; (Rechteck) rectangle; (Quadrat) square; ~**eckig** *Adj.* quadrilateral; (rechteckig) rectangular; ~**fach** *Vervielfältigungsz.* fourfold; quadruple; ~**fache** *das; adj. Dekl.* **um das** ~**fache:** fourfold; by four times the amount; ~**hundert** *Kardinalz.* four hundred

**Vierling** *der;* ~s, ~e quadruplet

**vier-, Vier-:** ~**mal** *Adv.* four times; ~**spurig** *Adj.* four-lane 〈*road, motorway*〉; ~**spurig sein** have four lanes; ~**stellig** *Adj.* four-figure *attrib.;* ~**sterne·hotel** /·'·---/ *das* four-star hotel

**viert...** *Ordinalz.* fourth

**vier·tausend** *Kardinalz.* four thousand;

**viertel** /'fɪrtl̩ / *Bruchz.* quarter; **ein** ~ **Pfund** a quarter of a pound; **drei** ~ **Liter** three quarters of a litre

**Viertel** /'fɪrtl̩ / *das* (schweiz. meist *der*); ~s, ~ **(a)** quarter; ~ **vor/nach eins** [a] quarter to/past one; **drei** ~: three-quarters **(b)** (Stadtteil) quarter; district

**viertel-, Viertel-:** ~**finale** *das* (Sport) quarter-final; ~**jahr** *das* three months *pl.;* ~**jährlich** [1] *Adj.* quarterly; [2] *adv.* quarterly; ~**liter** *der* quarter of a litre; ~**note** *die* (Musik) crotchet (Brit.); quarter note (Amer.); ~**pfund** *das* quarter [of a] pound; ~**stunde** *die* quarter of an hour; ~**stündig** *Adj.* quarter-of-an-hour; ~**stündlich** [1] *Adj.* every quarter of an hour *postpos.;* [2] *adv.* every quarter of an hour

**viertens** *Adv.* fourthly

**viertürig** *Adj.* four-door *attrib.;* ~ **sein** have four doors

**Vierwaldstätter See,** (schweiz.:) **Vierwaldstättersee** *der* Lake Lucerne

**vier-** /'fɪr·:/ ~**zehn** *Kardinalz.* fourteen; **für**

**vierzehn Tage** for a fortnight; ~**zehn·tägig** *Adj.* two-week; ~**zehn·täglich** [1] *Adj.* fortnightly; [2] *adv.* fortnightly

**vierzig** /'fɪrtsɪç/ *Kardinalz.* forty; *s. auch* ACHTZIG

**vierzigst...** *Ordinalz.* fortieth; *s. auch* ACHT...

**Vikar** /vi'kaːɐ̯/ *der;* ~s, ~e, **Vikarin** *die;* ~, ~**nen (a)** (kath. Kirche) locum tenens **(b)** (ev. Kirche) ≈ [trainee] curate

**Villa** /'vɪla/ *die;* ~, **Villen** villa

**Villen·viertel** *das* exclusive residential district

**violett** /vio'lɛt/ purple; violet

**Violett** *das;* ~s, ~e od. ugs. ~s purple; violet; (im Spektrum) violet

**Violine** /vio'liːnə/ *die;* ~, ~n (Musik) violin

**Viper** /'viːpɐ/ *die;* ~, ~n viper; adder

**Viren** ▶ VIRUS

**virtuell** /vɪr'tu̯ɛl/ [1] *Adj.* **(a)** potential **(b)** (DV, Optik) virtual 〈*memory, image;*〉 ~**e Wirklichkeit** virtual reality [2] *adv.* virtually

**virtuos** /vɪr'tu̯oːs/ [1] *Adj.* virtuoso 〈*performance etc.*〉 [2] *adv.* in a virtuoso manner

**Virtuose** *der;* ~n, ~n, **Virtuosin** *die;* ~, ~**nen** virtuoso

**Virtuosität** *die;* ~: virtuosity

**Virus** /'viːrʊs/ *das;* ~, **Viren** virus

**Visa** ▶ VISUM

**Visage** /vi'zaːʒə/ *die;* ~, ~n (salopp abwertend) mug (coll.); (Miene) expression

**Visen** ▶ VISUM

**Visier** /vi'ziːɐ̯/ *das;* ~s, ~e (am Helm) visor; (an der Waffe) backsight

**Vision** /vi'zi̯oːn/ *die;* ~, ~en vision

**Visite** /vi'ziːtə/ *die;* ~, ~n round; ~ **machen** do one's round

**Visiten·karte** *die* visiting card

**Visum** /'viːzʊm/ *das;* ~s, **Visa** od. **Visen** visa

**vital** *Adj.* vital

**Vitalität** *die;* ~: vitality

**Vitamin** /vita'miːn/ *das;* ~s, ~e vitamin

**vitamin-, Vitamin-:** ~**arm** *Adj.* low in vitamins *postpos.;* ~**mangel** *der* vitamin deficiency; ~**reich** *Adj.* rich in vitamins *postpos.*

**Vitrine** /vi'triːnə/ *die;* ~, ~n display case; (Möbel) display cabinet

**Vize-** vice-

**Vogel** *der;* ~s, **Vögel** bird; **einen** ~ **haben** (salopp) be off one's rocker (coll.)

**Vogel-:** ~**käfig** *der* birdcage; ~**nest** *das* bird's nest; ~**perspektive** *die* bird's-eye view; ~**scheuche** *die;* ~~, ~~n scarecrow

**Vokabel** /vo'kaːbl̩ / *die;* ~, ~n word; ~n vocabulary *sing.*

**V**

**Vokal** /vo'ka:l/ *der;* ~s, ~e (Sprachw.) vowel

**Volk** *das;* ~[e]s, Völker people

**volks-, Volks-:** ~**abstimmung** *die* plebiscite; ~**eigen** *Adj.* (DDR) publicly *or* nationally owned; ~**entscheid** *der* (Politik) referendum; ~**fest** *das* public festival; (Jahrmarkt) fair; ~**hochschule** *die* adult education centre; ~**kammer** *die* (DDR) Volkskammer; People's Chamber; ~**kunde** *die* folklore; ~**lied** *das* folk song; ~**musik** *die* folk music; ~**polizei** *die* (DDR) People's Police; ~**republik** *die* People's Republic; ~**stamm** *der* tribe; ~**tanz** *der* folk dance; ~**tracht** *die* traditional costume; (eines Landes) national costume; ~**trauer·tag** *der* (Bundesrepublik Deutschland) national remembrance day

**volkstümlich** ① *Adj.* popular ② *adv.* ~ schreiben write in terms readily comprehensible to the layman

**volks-, Volks-:** ~**verhetzung** *die;* ~~: incitement of the people; ~**vertreter** *der,* ~**vertreterin** *die* representative of the people; ~**wirt** *der,* ~**wirtin** *die* economist; ~**wirtschaft** *die* national economy; (Fach) economics *sing., no art.;* ~**wirtschaftlich** ① *Adj.* economic; ② *adv.* economically; ~**zählung** *die* [national] census; ~**zorn** *der* public anger

**voll** ① *Adj.* full; ample ⟨bosom⟩; (salopp: betrunken) plastered (sl.); ~ von *od.* mit etw. sein be full of sth.; ~ laufen fill up; etw. ~ laufen lassen fill sth. [up]; etw. ~ füllen fill sth. up; etw. ~ gießen fill sth. [up]; etw. ~ tanken fill sth. up; bitte ~ tanken fill it up, please; etw. ~ machen fill sth. up; [sich] (*Dat.*)] die Hosen/Windeln ~ machen (ugs.) mess one's pants/nappy; jmdn. nicht für ~ nehmen not take sb. seriously ② *adv.* fully; ~ und ganz completely

*\***vollabern▶** VOLLLABERN

**voll·auf** /*od.* '--/ *Adv.* completely

*\***vollaufen ▶** VOLL 1

**voll-, Voll-:** ~**automatisch** ① *Adj.* fully automatic; ② *adv.* fully automatically; ~**bad** *das* bath; ~**bart** *der* full beard; ~**bringen** /-'--/ *unr. tr. V.* (geh.) accomplish; achieve

**Völle·gefühl** *das* feeling of fullness

**voll·enden** *tr. V.* complete

**vollendet** ① *Adj.* accomplished ⟨performance⟩; perfect ⟨gentleman, host, manners, reproduction⟩ ② *adv.* ⟨play⟩ in an accomplished manner

**vollends** *Adv.* completely

**Voll·endung** *die* completion

**voller** *indekl. Adj.* full of; ~ Flecken covered with stains

**Volley·ball** /'vɔlibal/ *der* volleyball

**voll-, Voll-:** ~**führen** /-'--/ *tr. V.* perform;

*\*alte Schreibung - vgl. Hinweis auf S. xiv*

~|**füllen ▶** VOLL 1; ~**gas** *das* ~gas geben put one's foot down; mit ~gas at full throttle; *\**~|**gießen ▶** VOLL 1

**völlig** ① *Adj.* complete; total ② *adv.* completely; totally; du hast ~ Recht you are absolutely right

**voll-, Voll-:** ~**jährig** *Adj.* of age *pred.;* ~jährig werden come of age; ~**jährigkeit** *die;* ~: majority *no art.;* ~**kasko·versicherung** *die* fully comprehensive insurance

**voll·kommen** ① *Adj.* (a) /-'-- *od.* '---/ (vollendet) perfect (b) /'---/ (vollständig) complete; total ② /'---/ *adv.* completely; totally

**voll-, Voll-:** ~**korn·brot** *das* wholemeal (Brit.) *or* (Amer.) wholewheat bread; ~|**labern** *tr. V.* (ugs.) jmdn. ~labern rabbit on at sb. (coll.); *\**~|**laufen ▶** VOLL 1; *\**~|**machen ▶** VOLL 1; ~**macht** *die;* ~~, ~~en (a) authority; (b) (Urkunde) power of attorney; ~**milch** *die* full-cream milk; ~**milch·schokolade** *die* full-cream milk chocolate; ~**mond** *der* full moon; ~**pension** *die* full board *no art.;* ~**ständig** ① *Adj.* complete; full ⟨text, address, etc.⟩; ② *adv.* completely; ⟨list⟩ in full; ~**ständigkeit** *die;* ~: completeness; ~**strecken** /-'--/ *tr. V.* enforce ⟨penalty, fine, law⟩; carry out ⟨sentence⟩ (an + *Dat.* on); *\**~|**tanken ▶** VOLL 1; ~**treffer** *der* direct hit; ein ~treffer sein (fig.) hit the bull's eye; ~**versammlung** *die* general meeting; (der UNO) General Assembly; ~**zählig** *Adj.* complete

**voll·ziehen** *unr. tr. V.* carry out (an + *Dat.* on); execute, carry out ⟨order⟩; perform ⟨sacrifice, ceremony, sexual intercourse⟩

**Voll·zug** *der:* ▶ VOLLZIEHEN: carrying out; execution; performance

**Volt** /vɔlt/ *das;* ~ *od.* ~[e]s, ~: (Physik; Elektrot.) volt

**Volumen** /vo'lu:mən/ *das;* ~s, ~: volume

**vom** *Präp.* + *Art.* (a) = von dem; (b) (räumlich) from the; links/rechts ~ Eingang to the left/right of the entrance; ~ Stuhl aufspringen jump up out of one's chair (c) (zeitlich) ~ Morgen bis zum Abend from morning till night; ~ ersten Januar an [as] from the first of January (d) (zur Angabe der Ursache) das kommt ~ Rauchen/Alkohol that comes from smoking/drinking alcohol; jmdn. ~ Sehen kennen know sb. by sight

**von** *Präp. mit Dat.* (a) (räumlich) from; nördlich/südlich ~ Mannheim to the north/south of Mannheim; rechts/links ~ mir on my right/left; ~ hier an *od.* (ugs.) ab from here on[ward]; ~ Mannheim aus from Mannheim (b) (zeitlich) from; ~ jetzt an *od.* (ugs.) ab from now on; ~ heute/morgen an [as] from today/tomorrow; starting today/tomorrow; in der

Nacht ∼ **Freitag auf** *od.* **zu Samstag** during
Friday night; **das Brot ist** ∼ **gestern** it's
yesterday's bread
**(c)** (anstelle eines Genitivs) of; **acht** ∼ **hundert/
zehn** eight out of a hundred/ten
**(d)** (zur Angabe des Urhebers, der Ursache, beim
Passiv) by; **der Roman ist** ∼ **Fontane** the
novel is by Fontane; **müde** ∼ **der Arbeit sein**
be tired from work[ing]; **sie hat ein Kind** ∼
**ihm** she has a child by him
**(e)** (zur Angabe von Eigenschaften) of; **eine Fahrt**
∼ **drei Stunden** a three-hour drive
**von·ein·ander** *Adv.* from each other *or*
one another

**vonstatten** *Adv.* ∼ **gehen** proceed

**vor** ⑴ *Präp. mit Dat.* **(a)** (räumlich) in front
of; (weiter vorn) ahead of; in front of; (nicht ganz
so weit wie) before; (außerhalb) outside; **kurz** ∼
**der Abzweigung** just before the turn-off; ∼
**der Stadt** outside the town; **etw.** ∼ **sich
haben** (fig.) have sth. before one; **das liegt
noch** ∼ **mir** (fig.) I still have that to come *or*
have that ahead of me
**(b)** (zeitlich) before; **es ist fünf [Minuten]** ∼
**sieben** it is five [minutes] to seven
**(c)** (bei Reihenfolge, Rangordnung) before; **knapp**
∼ **jmdm. siegen** win just ahead *or* in front
of sb.
**(d)** (aufgrund von) with; ∼ **Freude strahlen**
beam with joy; ∼ **Hunger/Durst umkommen**
(ugs.) die of hunger/thirst
**(e)** ∼ **fünf Minuten/10 Jahren/Wochen** *usw.*
five minutes/ten years/weeks ago; **heute** ∼
**einer Woche** a week ago today
⑵ *Präp. mit Akk.* in front of; ∼ **sich hin** to
oneself

**Vor·abend** *der* evening before; (fig.) eve

**Vor·ahnung** *die* premonition;
presentiment; **dunkle/schlimme** ∼**en** dark
forebodings

**vor·an** *Adv.* forward[s] ahead; first

**voran-:** ∼**|gehen** *unr. itr. V.; mit sein* **(a)**
go first; **(b)** (Fortschritte machen) make
progress; ∼**|kommen** *unr. itr. V.; mit sein*
**(a)** make headway; **(b)** (Fortschritte machen)
make progress; ∼**|treiben** *unr. tr. V.* push
ahead

**Vor·arbeiter** *der* foreman

**Vor·arbeiterin** *die* forewoman

**vor·aus** ⑴ /'-/ *Präp. mit Dat., nachgestellt*
in front; **jmdm./seiner Zeit** ∼ **sein** (fig.) be
ahead of sb./one's time
⑵ *Adv.* **im Voraus** /'--/ in advance

**voraus-, Voraus-:** ∼**|gehen** *unr. itr. V.;
mit sein* **(a)** go [on] ahead; **(b)** (zeitlich) **einem
Ereignis** ∼**gehen** precede an event; ∼**sage**
*die* ▶ VORHERSAGE; ∼**|sagen** *tr. V.* predict;
∼**|sehen** *unr. tr. V.* foresee; ∼**|setzen**
*tr. V.* **(a)** (als gegeben ansehen) assume;
∼**gesetzt, [dass]** ...: provided [that] ...; **(b)**
(erfordern) require ⟨*skill, experience, etc.*⟩;
presuppose ⟨*good organization, planning,
etc.*⟩; ∼**setzung** *die;* ∼∼, ∼∼**en** **(a)**
(Annahme) assumption; (Prämisse) premiss;

**(b)** (Vorbedingung) prerequisite; **unter der**
∼**setzung, dass** ...: on condition *or* on the
precondition that ...; ∼**sichtlich** ⑴ *Adj.*
anticipated; ⑵ *adv.* probably

**Vor·bau** *der; Pl.* ∼**ten** porch

**Vorbehalt** *der;* ∼**[e]s,** ∼**e** reservation;
**unter dem** ∼**, dass** ...: with the reservation
that ...

**vor|behalten** *unr. tr. V.* **sich** (*Dat.*) **etw.**
∼: reserve oneself sth.; „**Änderungen** ∼“
'subject to alterations'

**vorbehalt·los** ⑴ *Adj.* unreserved;
unconditional
⑵ *adv.* unreservedly; without reservation[s]

**vor·bei** *Adv.* **(a)** (räumlich) past; by; **an etw.**
(*Dat.*) ∼: past sth.
**(b)** (zeitlich) past; over; (beendet) finished;
over; **es ist acht Uhr** ∼ (ugs.) it is past *or*
gone eight o'clock

**vorbei-:** ∼**|fahren** *unr. itr. V.; mit sein* **(a)**
drive/ride past; pass; **an jmdm.** ∼**fahren**
drive/ride past *or* pass sb.; **(b)** (ugs.: einen
kurzen Besuch machen) **[bei jmdm./der Post]**
∼**fahren** drop in (coll.) [at sb.'s/at the post
office]; ∼**|gehen** *unr. itr. V.; mit sein* **(a)**
pass; go past; **an jmdm./etw.** ∼**gehen** pass *or*
go past sb./sth.; **der Schuss ist** ∼**gegangen**
the shot missed; **(b)** (ugs.: einen kurzen Besuch
machen) **[bei jmdm./der Post]** ∼**gehen** drop in
(coll.) [at sb.'s/at the post office]; **(c)** (vergehen)
pass; ∼**|kommen** *unr. itr. V.; mit sein*
pass; **an etw.** (*Dat.*) ∼**kommen** pass sth.;
∼**|reden** *itr. V.* **an etw.** (*Dat.*) ∼**reden** talk
round sth. without getting to the point;
**aneinander** ∼**reden** talk at cross purposes;
∼**|schießen** *unr. itr. V.* miss

**vor·belastet** *Adj.* handicapped (**durch** by);
**erblich** ∼ **sein** have an inherited defect

**vor|bereiten** *tr. V.* prepare; **jmdn./sich auf**
*od.* **für etw.** ∼: prepare sb./oneself for sth.

**Vor·bereitung** *die;* ∼, ∼**en** preparation;
∼**en [für etw.] treffen** make preparations for
sth.

**vor|bestellen** *tr. V.* order in advance

**Vor·bestellung** *die* advance order

**vor·bestraft** *Adj.* with a previous
conviction/previous convictions *postpos., not
pred.*

**vor|beugen** ⑴ *tr. V.* bend ⟨*head, upper
body*⟩ forward; **sich** ∼: lean forward
⑵ *itr. V.* **einer Sache** (*Dat.*) *od.* **gegen etw.**
∼: prevent sth.

**Vor·beugung** *die* prevention (**gegen** of);
**zur** ∼: as a preventive

**Vor·bild** *das* model; **jmdm. ein gutes** ∼ **sein**
be a good example to sb.

**vor·bildlich** ⑴ *Adj.* exemplary
⑵ *adv.* in an exemplary way

**vor|bringen** *unr. tr. V.* say; **eine
Forderung/ein Anliegen** ∼: make a demand/
express a desire; **Argumente** ∼: present
arguments

**vor·christlich** *Adj.* pre-Christian

**v**

**vor|datieren** *tr. V.* postdate

**vorder...** *Adj.* front; **der Vordere Orient** the Middle East

**Vorder-:** ~**grund** *der* foreground; **im** ~**grund stehen** (fig.) be prominent *or* to the fore; ~**mann** *der; Pl.* ~**männer** person in front; **jmdn. auf** ~**mann bringen** (ugs.) lick sb. into shape

**vor|drängen** *refl. V.* push [one's way] forward *or* to the front; (fig.) push oneself forward

**vor|dringen** *unr. itr. V.; mit sein* push forward; advance

**vor·dringlich** ① *Adj.* (a) priority *attrib.* ⟨*treatment*⟩
(b) (dringlich) urgent
② *adv.* (a) as a matter of priority
(b) (dringlich) as a matter of urgency

**Vor·druck** *der; Pl.* ~**e** form

**vor·eilig** ① *Adj.* rash
② *adv.* rashly

**vor·einander** *Adv.* (a) one in front of the other
(b) (einer dem anderen gegenüber) opposite each other; face to face
(c) **Angst** ~ **haben** be afraid of each other

**vor·eingenommen** *Adj.* prejudiced; biased; **für/gegen jmdn.** ~ **sein** be prejudiced in sb.'s favour/against sb.

**Vor·eingenommenheit** *die;* ~, ~**en** prejudice; bias

**vorenthalten** *unr. tr. V.; ich enthalte vor (od. seltener:* **vorenthalte**), **vorenthalten**, **vorzuenthalten: jmdm. etw.** ~: withhold sth. from sb.

**vor·erst** /*od.* ‑'‑/ *Adv.* for the present

**Vor·fahr** *der;* ~**en**, ~**en** forefather

**vor|fahren** *unr. itr. V.; mit sein* (a) (ankommen) drive/ride up
(b) (weiter nach vorn fahren) ⟨*person*⟩ drive *or* move forward; ⟨*car*⟩ move forward
(c) (vorausfahren) drive *or* go on ahead

**Vor·fahrt** *die* right of way; „~ **beachten/gewähren"** 'give way'

**Vorfahrt[s]-:** ~**schild** *das; Pl.* ~~**er** right-of-way sign; ~**straße** *die* main road

**Vor·fall** *der* incident; occurrence

**vor|fallen** *unr. itr. V.; mit sein* (a) (sich ereignen) happen; occur
(b) (nach vorn fallen) fall forward

**Vor·film** *der* supporting film

**vor|finden** *unr. tr. V.* find

**Vor·freude** *die* anticipation

**vor|führen** *tr. V.* show ⟨*film, slides, etc.*⟩; present ⟨*circus act, programme*⟩; perform ⟨*play, trick, routine*⟩; (demonstrieren) demonstrate; **jmdn. dem Richter** ~: bring sb. before the judge

**Vor·führung** *die* show; (eines Theaterstücks) performance

**Vor·gang** *der* occurrence; (Amtsspr.) file

**Vor·gänger** *der;* ~**s**, ~, **Vorgängerin** *die;* ~, ~**nen** predecessor

**Vor·garten** *der* front garden

**vor|geben** *unr. tr. V.* pretend

**Vor·gebirge** *das* promontory

**vor·gefasst, \*vor·gefaßt** *Adj.* preconceived

**vor|gehen** *unr. itr. V.; mit sein* (a) (ugs.: nach vorn gehen) go forward
(b) (vorausgehen) go on ahead; **jmdn.** ~ **lassen** let sb. go first
(c) ⟨*clock*⟩ be fast
(d) (einschreiten) **gegen jmdn./etw.** ~: take action against sb./sth.
(e) (verfahren) proceed
(f) (sich abspielen) happen; go on
(g) (Vorrang haben) have priority; come first

**Vor·geschmack** *der* foretaste

**Vor·gesetzte** *der/die; adj. Dekl.* superior

**vor·gestern** *Adv.* the day before yesterday

**vor|greifen** *unr. itr. V.* **jmdm.** ~: anticipate sb.; jump in ahead of sb.

**vor|haben** *unr. tr. V.* intend; (geplant haben) plan

**Vor·haben** *das;* ~**s**, ~: plan; (Projekt) project

**Vor·halle** *die* entrance hall; (eines Theaters, Hotels) foyer

**vor|halten** *unr. tr. V.* (a) hold up; **mit vorgehaltener Schusswaffe** at gunpoint
(b) (zum Vorwurf machen) **jmdm. etw.** ~: reproach sb. for sth.

**Vor·haltungen** *Pl.* **jmdm. [wegen etw.]** ~ **machen** reproach sb. [for sth.]

**vorhanden** *Adj.* existing; (verfügbar) available; ~ **sein** exist *or* be in existence/be available

**Vor·hang** *der* (auch Theater) curtain

**Vorhänge·schloss, \*Vorhänge·schloß** *das* padlock

**Vor·haut** *die* foreskin

**vor·her** /*od.* ‑'‑/ *Adv.* beforehand; (davor) before

**vorher|gehen** *unr. itr. V.; mit sein* **in den** ~**den Wochen** in the preceding weeks

**Vor·herrschaft** *die* supremacy

**vor|herrschen** *itr. V.* predominate

**vorher-, Vorher-:** ~**sage** *die* prediction; (des Wetters) forecast; ~|**sagen** *tr. V.* predict; forecast ⟨*weather*⟩; ~|**sehen** *unr. tr. V.* ▶ VORAUSSEHEN

**vor·hin** /*od.* ‑'‑/ *Adv.* a short time *or* while ago

**vorig...** *Adj.* last

**Vor·jahr** *das* previous year

**vor·jährig** *Adj.* of the previous year

**Vor·kämpfer** *der*, **Vor·kämpferin** *die* pioneer

**Vorkehrungen** *Pl.* precautions

**Vor·kenntnis** *die* background knowledge

**vor|kommen** *unr. itr. V.; mit sein* **(a)** (sich ereignen) happen
**(b)** (vorhanden sein) occur
**(c)** (erscheinen) seem; **das Lied kommt mir bekannt vor** I seem to know the song

**Vorkommnis** *das;* ~**ses**, ~**se** incident; occurrence

**vor|laden** *unr. tr. V.* summon

**Vor·ladung** *die* summons

**Vor·lage** *die* **(a)** ▸ VORLEGEN: presentation; showing; production; submission; tabling
**(b)** (Entwurf) draft
**(c)** (Muster) pattern; (Modell) model

**Vor·lauf** *der* (eines Bandgeräts) fast forward

**Vor·läufer** *der,* **Vor·läuferin** *die* precursor; forerunner

**vor·läufig** **1** *Adj.* temporary; provisional; interim ⟨*order, agreement*⟩
**2** *adv.* for the time being

**vor·laut** **1** *Adj.* forward
**2** *adv.* forwardly

**vor|legen** *tr. V.* present; show, produce ⟨*certificate, identity card, etc.*⟩; show ⟨*sample*⟩; submit ⟨*evidence*⟩; table ⟨*parliamentary bill*⟩

**vor|lesen** *unr. tr., itr. V.* read aloud *or* out; read ⟨*story, poem, etc.*⟩ aloud; **jmdm. [etw.]** ~: read [sth.] to sb.

**Vor·lesung** *die* lecture; (Vorlesungsreihe) series *or* course of lectures

**vor·letzt...** *Adj.* last but one; penultimate ⟨*page, episode, etc.*⟩

**vorlieb**: **mit jmdm./etw.** ~ **nehmen** put up with sb./sth.; (sich begnügen) make do with sb./sth.

**Vor·liebe** *die* preference

*****vorlieb|nehmen** ▸ VORLIEB

**vor|liegen** *unr. itr. V.* **jmdm.** ~: be with sb.; **die Ergebnisse liegen uns noch nicht vor** we do not have the results yet; **im** ~**den Fall** in the present case

**vor|lügen** *unr. tr. V.* (ugs.) **jmdm. etwas** ~: lie to sb.

**vorm** *Präp. + Art.* **(a)** = vor dem;
**(b)** (räumlich) in front of the
**(c)** (zeitlich, bei Reihenfolge) before the

**vor|machen** *tr. V.* (ugs.) **jmdm. etw.** ~: show sb. sth.; (vortäuschen) kid (coll.) *or* fool sb.

**vormalig** *Adj.* former

**vormals** *Adv.* formerly

**Vor·marsch** *der* (auch fig.) advance

**vor|merken** *tr. V.* make a note of; **ich habe Sie für den Kurs vorgemerkt** I've put you down for the course

*****vor·mittag** ▸ VORMITTAG

**Vor·mittag** *der* morning; **heute/morgen/gestern** ~: this/tomorrow/yesterday morning

**vor·mittags** *Adv.* in the morning

**Vor·mund** *der; Pl.* ~**e** *od.* **Vormünder** guardian

**Vor·name** *der* first *or* Christian name

**vorn[e]** *Adv.* at the front; **nach** ~: to the front; **von** ~: from the front; **noch einmal von** ~ **anfangen** start afresh; **von** ~ **bis hinten** (ugs.) from beginning to end

**vornehm** **1** *Adj.* (nobel; adelig) noble; (kultiviert) distinguished; (elegant) exclusive ⟨*district, hotel, restaurant, resort*⟩; elegant ⟨*villa, clothes*⟩
**2** *adv.* nobly; (elegant) elegantly

**vor|nehmen** *unr. refl. V.* **sich** (*Dat.*) **etw.** ~: plan sth.; **sich** (*Dat.*) ~, **mit dem Rauchen aufzuhören** resolve to give up smoking

**vorn-**: ~**herein**: **von** ~**herein** from the outset; ~**über** *Adv.* forwards

**Vor·ort** *der* suburb

**vor|programmieren** *tr. V.* (auch fig.) pre-programme

**Vor·rang** *der* **(a)** priority (vor + *Dat.* over)
**(b)** (bes. österr.: Vorfahrt) right of way

**Vor·rat** *der* supply, stock (an + *Dat.* of)

**vorrätig** *Adj.* in stock *postpos.*

**Vor·raum** *der* anteroom

**vor|rechnen** *tr. V.* **jmdm. etw.** ~: work sth. out *or* calculate sth. for sb.; **jmdm. seine Fehler** ~ (fig.) enumerate sb.'s mistakes

**Vor·recht** *das* privilege

**Vor·redner** *der,* **Vor·rednerin** *die* previous speaker; **mein Vorredner**: the previous speaker

**Vor·richtung** *die* device

**vor|rücken** **1** *tr. V.* move forward; advance ⟨*chess piece*⟩
**2** *itr. V.; mit sein* move forward; **auf den 5. Platz** ~: move up to fifth place

**Vor·ruhestand** *der* early retirement

**vors** *Präp. + Art.* = vor das

**vor|sagen** *tr. V.* **(a)** *auch itr.* **jmdm. [die Antwort]** ~: tell sb. the answer; (flüsternd) whisper the answer to sb.
**(b)** (aufsagen) recite

**Vor·saison** *die* start of the season; early [part of the] season

**Vor·satz** *der* intention

**vorsätzlich** **1** *Adj.* intentional; wilful ⟨*murder, arson, etc.*⟩
**2** *adv.* intentionally

**Vor·schau** *die* preview

**Vor·schein** *der*: **zum** ~ **kommen** appear; (entdeckt werden) come to light

**vor|schieben** *unr. tr. V.* **(a)** push ⟨*bolt*⟩ across
**(b)** (nach vorn schieben) push forward

**vor|schießen** *unr. tr. V.* **jmdm. Geld** ~: advance sb. money

**Vorschlag** *der* suggestion; proposal

**vor|schlagen** *unr. tr. V.* **[jmdm.] etw.** ~: suggest *or* propose sth. [to sb.]

**vor|schreiben** *unr. tr. V.* stipulate, set ⟨*conditions*⟩; lay down ⟨*rules*⟩; prescribe ⟨*dose*⟩

V

**Vor·schrift** *die* instruction; order; (gesetzliche od. amtliche Bestimmung) regulation

**vorschrifts·mäßig** ⬜1 *Adj.* correct; proper
⬜2 *adv.* correctly; properly

**Vor·schub** *der* jmdm./einer Sache ~ leisten encourage sb./encourage *or* promote *or* foster sth.

**Vorschul·alter** *das* preschool age

**Vor·schuss, \*Vor·schuß** *der* advance

**vor|schwärmen** *itr. V.* jmdm. von jmdm./etw. ~: rave about sb./sth. to sb. (coll.)

**vor|schweben** *itr. V.* jmdm. schwebt etw. vor sb. has sth. in mind

**vor|sehen** ⬜1 *unr. tr. V.* (a) plan; etw. für/als etw. ~: intend sth. for/as sth.
(b) ⟨law, plan, contract, etc.⟩ provide for
⬜2 *unr. refl. V.* sich [vor jmdm./etw.] ~: be careful [of sb./sth.]

**vor|setzen** *tr. V.* jmdm. etw. ~: serve sb. sth.; (fig.) serve *or* dish sb. up sth.

**Vor·sicht** *die* care; (bei Risiko, Gefahr) caution; care; zur ~: as a precaution; ~! be careful!; „~, Stufe!" 'mind the step!'

**vorsichtig** ⬜1 *Adj.* careful; (bei Risiko, Gefahr) cautious; sei ~! be careful!; take care!
⬜2 *adv.* carefully; with care

**vorsichts·halber** *Adv.* as a precaution; to be on the safe side

**Vorsichts·maßnahme** *die* precautionary measure; precaution

**Vor·silbe** *die* [monosyllabic] prefix

**vor|singen** *unr. tr. V.* [jmdm.] etw. ~: sing sth. [to sb.]

**Vor·sitz** *der* chairmanship

**Vorsitzende** *der/die; adj. Dekl.* chair[person]; (bes. Mann) chairman; (Frau auch) chairwoman

**Vor·sorge** *die* precautions *pl.;* (für den Todesfall, Krankheit, Alter) provisions *pl.*

**vor|sorgen** *itr. V.* für etw. ~: make provisions for sth.; provide for sth.

**Vorsorge·untersuchung** *die* (Med.) medical check-up

**vorsorglich** *adv.* as a precaution

**Vor·spann** *der* (Film, Ferns.) opening credits *pl.*

**Vor·speise** *die* starter; hors d'œuvre

**Vor·spiel** *das* (Theater) prologue; (Musik) prelude

**vor|spielen** *tr. V.* (a) play ⟨piece of music⟩ (Dat. to, for); act out, perform ⟨scene⟩ (Dat. for, in front of)
(b) (vorspiegeln) jmdm. etw. ~: feign sth. to sb.

**vor|sprechen** ⬜1 *unr. tr. V.* (a) (zum Nachsprechen) jmdm. etw. ~: pronounce *or* say sth. first for sb.
(b) (zur Prüfung) recite
⬜2 *unr. itr. V.* audition

**Vor·sprung** *der* lead (vor + Dat. over)

**Vor·stadt** *die* suburb

**Vor·stand** *der* (einer Firma) board [of directors]; (eines Vereins, einer Gesellschaft) executive committee; (einer Partei) executive

**vor|stehen** *unr. itr. V.* (a) project; jut out; ⟨teeth, chin⟩ stick out; ~de Zähne buck teeth; projecting teeth
(b) (geh.: leiten) einer Institution ~: be the head of an institution

**vorstell·bar** *Adj.* conceivable; imaginable; es ist durchaus/[nur] schwer ~, dass ...: it is quite/scarcely conceivable that ...

**vor|stellen** ⬜1 *tr. V.* jmdn./sich jmdm. ~: introduce sb./oneself to sb.; (bei Bewerbung) sich ~: come/go for [an] interview; die Uhr [um eine Stunde] ~: put the clock forward [one hour]
⬜2 *refl. V.* sich (Dat.) etw. ~: imagine sth.

**Vor·stellung** *die* (a) (Begriff) idea
(b) (Fantasie) imagination
(c) (Aufführung) performance; (im Kino) showing

**Vorstellungs·gespräch** *das* interview

**Vor·stoß** *der* advance

**vor|stoßen** *unr. itr. V.; mit sein* advance; push forward

**Vor·strafe** *die* previous conviction

**vor|strecken** *tr. V.* stretch ⟨arm, hand⟩ out; advance ⟨money, sum⟩

**Vor·tag** *der* day before

**vor|täuschen** *tr. V.* feign; simulate ⟨reality etc.⟩; fake ⟨crime⟩

**Vor·teil** /od. 'fortail/ *der* advantage

**vorteilhaft** ⬜1 *Adj.* advantageous
⬜2 *adv.* advantageously

**Vortrag** *der;* ~[e]s, Vorträge talk; (wissenschaftlich) lecture; einen ~ halten give a talk/lecture

**vor|tragen** *unr. tr. V.* (a) sing ⟨song⟩; perform, play ⟨piece of music⟩; recite ⟨poem⟩
(b) (darlegen) present ⟨case, matter, request, demands⟩; lodge, make ⟨complaint⟩; express ⟨wish, desire⟩

**vor·trefflich** ⬜1 *Adj.* excellent
⬜2 *adv.* excellently

**Vor·trefflichkeit** *die;* ~: excellence

**vorüber** *Adv.* over; (räumlich) past

**vorüber|gehen** *unr. itr. V.; mit sein* (a) go *or* walk past; pass by; an jmdm./etw. ~: go past sb./sth.; pass sb./sth.; (achtlos) pass sb./sth. by
(b) (vergehen) pass; ⟨pain⟩ go

**vorübergehend** ⬜1 *Adj.* temporary; passing ⟨interest, infatuation⟩; brief ⟨illness, stay⟩
⬜2 *adv.* temporarily; (für kurze Zeit) for a short time; briefly

**Vor·urteil** *das* bias; (voreilige Schlussfolgerung) prejudice

**Vor·vergangenheit** *die* (Sprachw.) pluperfect

**Vor·verkauf** *der* advance sale of tickets

---

\*alte Schreibung - vgl. Hinweis auf S. xiv

**vor|verlegen** *tr. V.* (zeitlich) bring forward (auf + *Akk.* to; **um** by)

**Vor·wahl** *die,* **Vorwähl·nummer** *die* (Fernspr.) dialling code

**Vorwand** *der;* ∼[e]s, Vorwände pretext; (Ausrede) excuse

**vor|warnen** *tr. V.* jmdn. ∼: give sb. advance warning; warn sb. [in advance]; **vorgewarnt sein** be forewarned

**Vor·warnung** *die* [advance] warning

**vor·wärts** *Adv.* forwards; (weiter) onwards; ∼ **kommen** make progress; (im Beruf, Leben) get on; get ahead

**\*vorwärts|kommen** ▶ VORWÄRTS

**vor·weg** *Adv.* beforehand

**vorweg|nehmen** *unr. tr. V.* anticipate

**vor|weisen** *unr. tr. V.* produce

**vor|werfen** *unr. tr. V.* jmdm. etw. ∼: reproach sb. with sth.; (beschuldigen) accuse sb. of sth.

**vor·wiegend** *Adv.* mainly

**vor·witzig** *Adj.* bumptious; pert ⟨*child*⟩

**Vor·wort** *das; Pl.* ∼e foreword

**Vor·wurf** *der* reproach; (Beschuldigung) accusation

**vorwurfs·voll** ⒈ *Adj.* reproachful ⒉ *adv.* reproachfully

**Vor·zeichen** *das* (a) (Omen) omen (b) (Math.) [algebraic] sign

**vor|zeigen** *tr. V.* produce; show

**Vor·zeit** *die* prehistory

**vorzeitig** ⒈ *Adj.* premature; early ⟨*retirement*⟩ ⒉ *adv.* prematurely

**vor|ziehen** *unr. tr. V.* prefer

**Vor·zimmer** *das* outer office

**Vor·zug** *der* (a) preference (**gegenüber** over) (b) (gute Eigenschaft) good quality; merit

**vorzüglich** ⒈ *Adj.* excellent; first-rate ⒉ *adv.* excellently

**vulgär** /vʊlˈgɛːɐ̯/ ⒈ *Adj.* vulgar ⒉ *adv.* in a vulgar way

**Vulgarität** /vʊlgariˈtɛːt/ *die;* ∼, ∼en vulgarity

**Vulkan** /vʊlˈkaːn/ *der;* ∼s, ∼e volcano

**vulkanisch** *Adj.* volcanic

**vulkanisieren** *tr. V.* vulcanize

**v. u. Z.** *Abk.* = **vor unserer Zeit[rechnung]** BC

# Ww

**w, W** /veː/ *das;* ∼s, ∼: w/W

**W** *Abk.* (a) = **West, Westen** W. (b) = **Watt** W.

**Waage** *die;* ∼, ∼n (a) [pair *sing.* of] scales *pl.* (b) (Astrol.) [die] ∼: Libra; **er ist [eine]** ∼: he is a Libra *or* Libran

**waage·recht** ⒈ *Adj.* horizontal ⒉ *adv.* horizontally

**Waage·rechte** *die;* ∼, ∼n; *also adj. Dekl.* horizontal

**Waag·schale** *die* scale pan

**Wabe** *die;* ∼, ∼n honeycomb

**wach** ⒈ *Adj.* awake ⒉ *adv.* alertly; attentively

**Wache** *die;* ∼, ∼n (a) (Milit.) guard *or* sentry duty; (Seew.) watch [duty] (b) (Wächter, Milit.) guard; (Seew.) watch (c) (Polizei∼) police station

**wachen** *itr. V.* (geh.) be awake; **bei jmdm.** ∼: stay up at sb.'s bedside; sit up with sb.

**Wachheit** *die;* ∼: alertness

**Wach·hund** *der* guard dog

**Wacholder** *der;* ∼s, ∼: juniper

**Wach·posten** *der* (Milit.) guard

**Wachs** *das;* ∼es, ∼e wax

**wachsam** *Adj.* watchful; vigilant

**Wachsamkeit** *die;* ∼: vigilance

**wachsen¹** *unr. itr. V.; mit sein* grow

**wachsen²** *tr. V.* wax

**Wachs-:** ∼**figur** *die* waxwork; ∼**figuren·kabinett** *das* waxworks *sing. or pl.;* waxworks museum

**wächst** *2. u. 3. Pers. Sg. Präsens v.* WACHSEN

**Wachs·tuch** *das Pl.* Wachstücher (Tischtuch) oilcloth tablecloth

**Wachstum** *das;* ∼s growth

**Wachtel** *die;* ∼, ∼n quail

**Wächter** *der;* ∼s, ∼: guard; (Nacht-, Turmwächter) watchman; (Parkwächter) [park-]keeper

**Wächterin** *die;* ∼, ∼nen ▶ WÄCHTER

**Wach[t]·turm** *der* watchtower

**wackelig** *Adj.* (a) wobbly ⟨*chair, table, etc.*⟩; loose ⟨*tooth*⟩ (b) (ugs.: kraftlos, schwach) frail

**Wackel·kontakt** *der* (Elektrot.) loose connection

**wackeln** *itr. V.* wobble; ⟨*tooth etc.*⟩ be loose; ⟨*house, window, etc.*⟩ shake; **mit dem Kopf/den Ohren** ∼: waggle one's head/ears

**wacker** (veralt.) ⒈ *Adj.* upright   ⋯⋗

2 *adv.* valiantly; **sich ~ halten** put up a good show

**Wade** *die;* ~, ~n (Anat.) calf

**Waden·krampf** *der* cramp in one's calf

**Waffe** *die;* ~, ~n weapon

**Waffel** *die;* ~, ~n waffle; (dünne Waffel, Eiswaffel) wafer; (Eistüte) cone

**Waffen-:** ~**gewalt** *die* mit ~gewalt by force of arms; ~**handel** *der* arms trade; ~**händler** *der*, ~**händlerin** *die* arms dealer; ~**schein** *der* firearms licence; ~**stillstand** *der* armistice

**Wage·mut** *der* daring

**wage·mutig** *Adj.* daring

**wagen** 1 *tr. V.* risk; [es] ~, etw. zu tun dare to do sth.
2 *refl. V.* **sich irgendwohin/nicht irgendwohin ~:** venture somewhere/not dare to go somewhere

**Wagen** *der;* ~s, ~: (PKW) car; (Pferdewagen) cart; (Eisenb.: Personenwagen) coach; (Eisenb.: Güterwagen) truck; (Straßenbahnwagen) car; (Kinder-, Puppenwagen) pram (Brit.); baby carriage (Amer.); (Sportwagen) pushchair (Brit.); stroller (Amer.)

**Wagen·heber** *der* jack

**Waggon** /va'gɔŋ, *südd., österr.:* va'goːn/ *der;* ~s, ~s, *südd., österr.:* ~s, ~e wagon; truck (Brit.); car (Amer.)

**waghalsig** 1 *Adj.* daring; (leichtsinnig) reckless
2 *adv.* daringly; ⟨speculate⟩ riskily; (leichtsinnig) recklessly

**Wagnis** *das;* ~ses, ~se daring exploit *or* feat; (Risiko) risk

**Wahl** *die;* ~, ~en (a) choice; **eine/seine ~ treffen** make a/one's choice
(b) (in ein Gremium, Amt usw.) election; **geheime ~:** secret ballot

**wahl·berechtigt** *Adj.* eligible *or* entitled to vote *postpos.*

**Wahl·beteiligung** *die* turn-out

**wählen** 1 *tr. V.* (a) choose; (aus~) select
(b) (Fernspr.) dial ⟨number⟩
(c) (durch Stimmabgabe) elect
(d) (stimmen für) vote for ⟨party, candidate⟩
2 *itr. V.* (a) choose
(b) (Fernspr.) dial
(c) (stimmen) vote

**Wähler** *der;* ~s, ~: voter

**Wahl·ergebnis** *das* election result

**Wählerin** *die;* ~, ~nen voter

**wählerisch** *Adj.* choosy; particular (**in +** *Dat.* about)

**Wählerschaft** *die;* ~, ~en electorate; **die ~ der SPD** the SPD's voters *pl.;* those who vote for the SPD

**wahl-, Wahl-:** ~**fach** *das* (Schulw.) optional subject; ~**gang** *der* ballot; ~**geheimnis** *das* secrecy of the ballot; ~**geschenk** *das* pre-election bonus;

~**kabine** *die* polling booth; ~**kampf** *der* election campaign; ~**kreis** *der* constituency; ~**lokal** *das* polling station; ~**los** 1 *Adj.* indiscriminate; 2 *adv.* indiscriminately; ~**niederlage** *die* election defeat; ~**recht** *das* right to vote

**Wähl·scheibe** *die* (Fernspr.) dial

**Wahl-:** ~**sieg** *der* election victory; ~**spruch** *der* motto; ~**system** *das* electoral system; ~**urne** *die* ballot box

**Wahn** *der;* ~[e]s mania; delusion

**Wahn·sinn** *der* (a) insanity; madness
(b) (ugs.: Unvernunft) madness; lunacy

**wahnsinnig** 1 *Adj.* (a) (geistesgestört) insane; mad
(b) (ugs.: ganz unvernünftig) mad; crazy
(c) (ugs.: groß, heftig, intensiv) terrific (coll.) ⟨effort, speed, etc.⟩; terrible (coll.) ⟨fright, job, pain⟩
2 *adv.* (ugs.) incredibly (coll.); terribly (coll.)

**wahr** *Adj.* (a) true; **nicht ~?** *translation depends on preceding verb form:* **du hast Hunger, nicht ~?** you're hungry, aren't you?; **nicht ~, er weiß es doch?** he does know, doesn't he?
(b) (wirklich) real ⟨reason, motive, feelings, joy, etc.⟩; actual ⟨culprit⟩; (echt) true, real ⟨friend, friendship, love, art⟩

**wahren** *tr. V.* (geh.) preserve ⟨balance, equality, neutrality, etc.⟩; maintain ⟨authority, right⟩; (verteidigen) defend

**währen** *itr. V.* (geh.) last

**während** 1 *Konj.* (a) (zeitlich) while
(b) (adversativ) whereas
2 *Präp. mit Gen.* during; (über einen Zeitraum von) for

**wahr|haben** *unr. tr. V.* **etw. nicht ~ wollen** not want to admit sth.

**wahrhaft** (geh.) 1 *Adj.* true
2 *adv.* truly

**wahrhaftig** 1 *Adj.* (geh.) truthful ⟨person⟩
2 *adv.* really; genuinely

**Wahrheit** *die;* ~, ~en truth

**wahrheits·getreu** 1 *Adj.* truthful; faithful ⟨account⟩
2 *adv.* truthfully; ⟨portray⟩ faithfully

**wahr|nehmen** *unr. tr. V.* (a) (mit den Sinnen erfassen) perceive; (spüren) feel; detect ⟨sound, smell⟩; (bemerken) notice; (erkennen, ausmachen) make out
(b) (nutzen) take advantage of ⟨opportunity⟩; exploit ⟨advantage⟩; exercise ⟨right⟩
(c) (vertreten) look after ⟨sb.'s interests, affairs⟩
(d) (erfüllen, ausführen) carry out, perform ⟨function, task, duty⟩; fulfil ⟨responsibility⟩

**Wahrnehmung** *die;* ~, ~en (a) perception; (eines Sachverhalts) awareness; (eines Geruchs, eines Tons) detection
(b) (Nutzung) (eines Rechts) exercise; (einer Gelegenheit, eines Vorteils) exploitation
(c) (Vertretung) representation
(d) (einer Funktion, Aufgabe, Pflicht) performance; execution; (einer Verantwortung) fulfilment

---

*old spelling - see note on page xiv

**wahr·sagen** 2. *Part.* gewahrsagt ⊡ *itr. V.* tell fortunes
⊡ *tr. V.* predict, foretell ⟨*future*⟩

**Wahrsager** *der;* ∼s, ∼, **Wahrsagerin** *die;* ∼, ∼nen fortune-teller

**wahrscheinlich** ⊡ *Adj.* probable; likely
⊡ *adv.* probably

**Wahrscheinlichkeit** *die;* ∼, ∼en probability; likelihood

**Währung** *die;* ∼, ∼en currency

**Währungs-:** ∼**reform** *die* currency reform; ∼**union** *die* currency union; ∼-, Wirtschafts- und Sozialunion social, economic, and currency union

**Wahr·zeichen** *das* symbol; (einer Stadt, einer Landschaft) [most famous] landmark

**Waise** *die;* ∼, ∼n orphan

**Waisen·haus** *das* orphanage

**Wal** *der;* ∼[e]s, ∼e whale

**Wald** *der;* ∼[e]s, Wälder wood; (größer) forest

**Wald·brand** *der* forest fire

**Wäldchen** *das;* ∼s, ∼: copse

**Wald-:** ∼**meister** *der* (Bot.) woodruff; ∼**sterben** *das;* ∼∼s death of the forest [as a result of pollution]

**Wal·fang** *der* whaling *no def. art.;* auf ∼ gehen/sein go/be whaling

**Waliser** *der;* ∼s, ∼: Welshman

**Waliserin** *die;* ∼, ∼nen Welshwoman

**walisisch** *Adj.* Welsh

**Walkman** ⓦ /'wɔkmən/ *der;* ∼s, Walkmen /'wɔkmən/ Walkman ®; personal stereo

**Wall** *der;* ∼[e]s, Wälle earthwork; embankment; rampart (esp. Mil.)

**Wall-:** ∼**fahrer** *der* pilgrim; ∼**fahrt** *die* pilgrimage; ∼**fahrts·ort** *der* place of pilgrimage

**Wal·nuss, *Wal·nuß** *die* walnut

**Wal·ross, *Wal·roß** *das; Pl.* -rosse walrus

**walten** *itr. V.* (geh.) ⟨*good sense, good spirit*⟩ prevail; ⟨*peace, silence, harmony, etc.*⟩ reign

**Walze** *die;* ∼, ∼n roller; (Straßen∼) [road] roller; (Schreib∼) platen

**walzen** *tr. V.* roll ⟨*field, road, steel, etc.*⟩

**wälzen** ⊡ *tr. V.* roll; heave ⟨*heavy object*⟩; (fig.) shove ⟨*blame, responsibility*⟩ (auf + *Akk.* on); etw. in Mehl *usw.* ∼ (Kochk.) toss sth. in flour *etc.;* Probleme ∼ (fig. ugs.) mull over problems
⊡ *refl. V.* roll; (auf der Stelle) roll about *or* around; (im Krampf, vor Schmerzen) writhe around

**Walzer** *der;* ∼s, ∼: waltz

**wand** *1. u. 3. Pers. Sg. Prät. v.* WINDEN

**Wand** *die;* ∼, Wände wall; (Trennwand) partition; (bewegliche Trennwand) screen; (eines Behälters, Schiffs) side

**Wandale** *die;* ∼n, ∼n, **Wandalin** *die;* ∼, ∼nen vandal

**Wandalismus** *der;* ∼: vandalism

**Wandel** *der;* ∼s change

**wandeln** *refl., tr. V.* change (in + *Akk.* into)

**Wanderer** *der;* ∼s, ∼, **Wanderin** *die;* ∼, ∼nen rambler; hiker

**Wander·karte** *die* rambler's [path] map

**wandern** *itr. V.; mit sein* (a) hike; ramble (b) (ugs.: gehen; fig.) wander (lit. or fig.) (c) (ziehen, reisen) travel; (ziellos) roam; ⟨*exhibition, circus, theatre*⟩ tour, travel; ⟨*animal, people, tribe*⟩ migrate

**Wander·tag** *der* day's hike (*for a class or school*)

**Wanderung** *die;* ∼, ∼en (a) hike; walking tour; eine ∼ machen go on a hike *or* a walking tour (b) (Zool., Soziol.) migration

**Wander-:** ∼**urlaub** *der* walking holiday; ∼**weg** *der* footpath (*constructed for ramblers*)

**Wand-:** ∼**gemälde** *das* mural; ∼**lampe** *die* wall light

**Wandlung** *die;* ∼, ∼en change; (grundlegend) transformation

**Wand-:** ∼**malerei** *die* (Bild) mural; ∼**schrank** *der* wall cupboard *or* (Amer.) closet

**wandte** *1. u. 3. Pers. Prät. v.* WENDEN

**Wange** *die;* ∼, ∼n (geh.) cheek

**Wankelmut** *der* (geh.) vacillation

**wankel·mütig** *Adj.* (geh.) vacillating

**wanken** *itr. V.* (a) sway; ⟨*person*⟩ totter; (unter einer Last) stagger (b) *mit sein* (unsicher gehen) stagger; totter

**wann** *Adv.* when; seit ∼ wohnst du dort? how long have you been living there?

**Wanne** *die;* ∼, ∼n bath[tub]

**Wanze** *die;* ∼, ∼n bug (coll.)

**Wappen** *das;* ∼s, ∼: coat of arms

**wappnen** *refl. V.* (geh.) forearm oneself

**war** *1. u. 3. Pers. Sg. Prät. v.* SEIN

**warb** *1. u. 3. Pers. Sg. Prät. v.* WERBEN

**ward** (geh.) *1. u. 3. Pers. Sg. Prät. v.* WERDEN

**Ware** *die;* ∼, ∼n (a) ∼n [n] goods *pl.;* (b) (Artikel) article; commodity (Econ., fig.); (Erzeugnis) product

**Waren-:** ∼**angebot** *das* supply [of goods]; (Sortiment) range of goods; ∼**haus** *das* department store; ∼**korb** *der* (Statistik) basket of goods; ∼**lager** *das* (einer Fabrik o. Ä.) stores *pl.;* (eines Geschäftes) stockroom; (größer) warehouse; ∼**muster** *das,* ∼**probe** *die* sample; ∼**zeichen** *das* trade mark

**warf** *1. u. 3. Pers. Sg. Prät. v.* WERFEN

**warm; wärmer, wärmst ...** ⊡ *Adj.* (auch fig.) warm; hot ⟨*meal, food, bath, spring*⟩; keen, lively ⟨*interest*⟩ das Essen ∼ machen heat up the food; „∼" (auf Wasserhahn) 'hot'
⊡ *adv.* warmly; ∼ essen/duschen have a hot meal/shower

**Wärme** *die;* ∼: warmth; (Hitze; auch Physik) heat

**wärmen** ①  *tr. V.* warm; (aufwärmen) warm
up ⟨*food, drink*⟩
② *itr. V.* be warm; (warm halten) keep one
warm

**Wärme-pumpe** *die* (Technik) heat pump

**Warm-front** *die* (Met.) warm front

**warm|halten** *unr. tr. V.* (ugs.) sich (*Dat.*)
jmdn. ~: keep on the right side of sb.

**Warm-wasser-:** **~bereiter** *der;* ~s, ~:
water heater; **~heizung** *die* hot-water
heating

**Warn-:** **~blinkanlage** *die* (Kfz-W.) hazard
warning lights *pl.;* **~dreieck** *das* (Kfz-W.)
hazard warning triangle

**warnen** *tr.* (*auch itr.*) *V.* warn (**vor** + *Dat.*
of, about); jmdn. [**davor**] ~, etw. zu tun warn
sb. against doing sth.

**Warn-:** **~schild** *das; Pl.* ~~er warning
sign; **~schuss,** *\*~schuß der* warning
shot; **~signal** *das* warning signal;
**~streik** *der* token strike

**Warnung** *die;* ~, ~en warning (**vor** + *Dat.*
of, about)

**Warschau** (*das*)*;* ~s Warsaw

**Warte-:** **~halle** *die* waiting room; (Flugw.)
departure lounge; **~liste** *die* waiting list

**warten** ① *itr. V.* wait (**auf** + *Akk.* for)
② *tr. V.* service ⟨*car etc.*⟩

**Wärter** *der;* ~s, ~, **Wärterin** *die;* ~,
~nen attendant; (Tier-, Zoo-, Leuchtturmwärter[in])
keeper; (Krankenwärter[in]) orderly;
(Gefängniswärter[in]) warder

**Warte-:** **~saal** *der* waiting room;
**~zimmer** *das* waiting room

**Wartung** *die;* ~, ~en service; (das Warten)
servicing; (Instandhaltung) maintenance

**warum** *Adv.* why

**Warze** *die;* ~, ~n wart; (Brust~) nipple

**was** ① *Interrogativpron. Nom. u. Akk. u.*
(*nach Präp.*) *Dat. Neutr.;* ~ **kostet das?** what
or how much does that cost?; **ach** ~! (ugs.)
oh, come on!; ~ **für ein** .../~ **für** ...: what
sort or kind of ...
② *Relativpron. Nom. u. Akk. u.* (*nach Präp.*)
*Dat. Neutr.;* [**das,**] ~: what; **alles,** ~ ...:
everything or all that ...; **vieles/nichts/etwas,**
~ ...: much/nothing/something that ...; ~
**mich betrifft,** [**so**] ...: as far as I'm concerned,
...
③ *Indefinitpron. Nom. u. Akk. u.* (*nach*
*Präp.*) *Dat. Neutr.* (ugs.) ▶ ETWAS;
④ *Adv.* (ugs.) (warum, wozu) why; what ... for

**Wasch-:** **~anlage** *die* car wash;
**~automat** *der* washing machine;
**~becken** *das* washbasin

**Wäsche** *die;* ~, ~n (a) (zu waschende Textilien)
washing; (für die Wäscherei) laundry
(b) (Unterwäsche) underwear
(c) (das Waschen) washing *no pl.;* (einmalig)
wash; **in der** ~ **sein** be in the wash

**wasch-echt** *Adj.* (a) colour-fast ⟨*textile,*
*clothes*⟩; fast ⟨*colour*⟩
(b) (fig.) genuine

**Wäsche-:** **~klammer** *die* clothes peg
(Brit.); clothespin (Amer.); **~korb** *der* laundry
basket; **~leine** *die* clothes line

**waschen** ① *unr. tr. V.* wash; sich ~: wash
[oneself]; have a wash; **Wäsche** ~: do the/
some washing
② *unr. itr. V.* do the washing

**Wäscherei** *die;* ~, ~en laundry

**Wäsche-:** **~schleuder** *die* spin drier;
**~trockner** *der* (a) (Maschine) tumble drier;
(b) (Gestell) clothes airer

**wasch-, Wasch-:** **~gelegenheit** *die*
washing facilities *pl.;* **~küche** *die* laundry
room; **~lappen** *der* [face] flannel;
washcloth (Amer.); **~maschine** *die*
washing machine; **~maschinen-fest**
*Adj.* machine washable; **~mittel** *das*
detergent; **~pulver** *das* washing powder;
**~raum** *der* washing room; **~schüssel**
*die* washing bowl; **~straße** *die* [automatic]
car wash

**wäscht** *3. Pers. Sg. Präsens v.* WASCHEN

**Wasch-wasser** *das* washing water

**Wasser** *das;* ~s, ~/Wässer (a) water
(b) *Pl.* Wässer (Mineral-, Tafelwasser) mineral
water; (Heilwasser) water
(c) (Gewässer) **ein fließendes/stehendes** ~: a
moving/stagnant stretch of water
(d) ~ **lassen** pass water

**wasser-, Wasser-:** **~bad** *das* (Kochk.)
bain-marie; **~ball** *der* (a) beachball; (b)
(Spiel) water polo; **~dampf** *der* steam;
**~dicht** *Adj.* waterproof ⟨*clothing, watch,*
*etc.*⟩; watertight ⟨*container, seal, etc.*⟩; **~fall**
*der* waterfall; **~farbe** *die* watercolour;
**~hahn** *der* water tap; faucet (Amer.)

**wässerig** ▶ WÄSSRIG

**Wasser-:** **~kessel** *der* kettle; **~leitung**
*die* water pipe; (Hauptleitung) water main;
**~mann** *der* (Astrol.) [der] ~mann Aquarius;
er/sie ist [ein] ~~: he/she is an
Aquarian

**wassern** *itr. V.; mit sein* land [on the
water]

**wässern** *tr. V.* soak; (Fot.) wash ⟨*negative,*
*print*⟩

**wasser-, Wasser-:** **~pflanze** *die*
aquatic plant; **~qualität** *die* water quality;
**~rohr** *das* water pipe; **~scheu** *Adj.*
scared of water; **~schlauch** *der* [water]
hose; **~schutz-polizei** *die* river/lake
police; **~ski¹** *der* waterski; **~ski fahren**
waterski; **~ski²** *das;* ~~s waterskiing *no*
*art.;* **~spiegel** *der* (a) (Oberfläche) surface
[of the water]; (b) (Niveau) water level;
**~sport** *der* water sport *no art.;*
**~spülung** *die* flush

**Wasser-stoff** *der* hydrogen

**Wasser-stoff-:** **~bombe** *die* hydrogen

bomb; **~per·oxid, ~per·oxyd, ~super·oxid, ~super·oxyd** *das* (Chemie) hydrogen peroxide

**Wasser-: ~strahl** *der* jet of water; **~straße** *die* waterway; **~temperatur** *die* water temperature; **~tiefe** *die* depth of the water; **~tropfen** *der* drop of water; **~turm** *der* water tower; **~werfer** *der* water cannon; **~werk** *das* waterworks *sing.;* **~zeichen** *das* watermark

**wässrig, \*wäßrig** *Adj.* watery

**waten** *itr. V.; mit sein* wade

**Waterloo** *das;* ~s, ~s Waterloo *no art.;* **sein** ~ **erleben** meet one's Waterloo

**watscheln** *itr. V.; mit sein* waddle

**Watt¹** *das;* ~[e]s, ~en mudflats *pl.*

**Watt²** *das;* ~s, ~ (Technik, Physik) watt

**Watte** *die;* ~, ~n cotton wool

**Watte·bausch** *der* wad of cotton wool

**Watten·meer** *das* tidal shallows *pl.*

**wattiert** *Adj.* quilted; padded ‹*shoulder etc., envelope*›

**WC** *das;* ~[s], ~[s] toilet; WC

**weben** *tr., itr. V.* weave

**Weber** *der;* ~s, ~, **Weberin** *die;* ~, ~nen weaver

**Website** /web'sait/ *die;* ~, ~s (DV) Web site

**Web·stuhl** *der* loom

**Wechsel** *der;* ~s, ~ (a) (das Auswechseln) change; (Geldwechsel) exchange **(b)** (Aufeinanderfolge) alternation; **im** ~: alternately; (bei mehr als zwei) in rotation **(c)** (das Überwechseln) move; (Sport) transfer **(d)** (Bankw.) bill of exchange (**über** + *Akk.* for)

**wechsel-, Wechsel-: ~geld** *das* change; **~haft** *Adj.* changeable; **~jahre** *Pl.* change of life *sing.;* menopause *sing.;* **~kurs** *der* exchange rate

**wechseln** ① *tr. V.* (a) change; **das Hemd** ~: change one's shirt; **die Wohnung** ~: move home **(b)** ([aus]tauschen) exchange ‹*letters, glances, etc.*› **(c)** (umwechseln) change ‹*money, note, etc.*› (**in** + *Akk.* into) ② *itr. V.* change

**wechsel-, Wechsel-: ~seitig** ① *Adj.* mutual; ② *adv.* mutually; **~strom** *der* (Elektrot.) alternating current; **~stube** *die* bureau de change; **~wähler** *der,* **~wählerin** *die* (Politik) floating voter; **~wirkung** *die* interaction

**wecken** *tr. V.* jmdn. [aus dem Schlaf] ~: wake sb. [up]; (fig.: hervorrufen) arouse ‹*interest, curiosity, anger*›

**Wecker** *der;* ~s, ~: alarm clock

**wedeln** *itr. V.* ‹*tail*› wag; [mit dem Schwanz] ~ ‹*dog*› wag its tail

**weder** *Konj.* ~ **A noch B** neither A nor B

**weg** *Adv.* away; (verschwunden, weggegangen)

gone; **er ist schon seit einer Stunde** ~: he left an hour ago; **weit** ~: far away; a long way away

**Weg** *der;* ~[e]s, ~e (a) (Fußweg) path; (Feldweg) track **(b)** (Zugang) way; (Passage, Durchgang) passage; **sich** (*Dat.*) **einen** ~ **durch etw. bahnen** clear a path *or* way through sth. **(c)** (Route, Verbindung) way; route **(d)** (Strecke, Entfernung) distance; (Gang) walk; (Reise) journey; **auf dem kürzesten** ~: by the shortest route; **auf halbem** ~[e] (auch fig.) half-way; **sich auf den** ~ **machen** set off; **etw. in die** ~e **leiten** get sth. under way **(e)** (ugs.: Besorgung) errand **(f)** (Methode) way; (Mittel) means

**weg-: ~|bleiben** *unr. itr. V.; mit sein* (nicht kommen) stay away; (nicht nach Hause kommen) stay out; **~|bringen** *unr. itr. V.* take away; (zur Reparatur, Wartung usw.) take in

**Wegelagerei** *die;* ~: highway robbery

**Wegelagerer** *der;* ~s, ~: highwayman

**Wegelagerin** *die;* ~, ~nen highwaywoman

**wegen** *Präp. mit Gen.* (a) because of; ~ **Umbau[s] geschlossen** closed for alterations **(b)** (um … willen) for the sake of; ~ **der Kinder**/(ugs.) **dir** for the children's/your sake **(c)** (bezüglich) about; regarding

**weg-: ~|fahren** ① *unr. itr. V.; mit sein* (a) leave; (im Auto) drive off; (losfahren) set off; **(b)** (irgendwohin fahren) go away; ② *unr. tr. V.* drive away; (mit dem Handwagen usw.) take away; **~|fallen** *unr. itr. V.; mit sein* be discontinued; (nicht mehr zutreffen) no longer apply; **~|fliegen** *unr. itr. V.; mit sein* fly away; (weggeblasen werden) fly off; **~|gehen** *unr. itr. V.* (a) leave; (ugs.: ausgehen) go out; (ugs.: wegziehen) move away; **(b)** (verschwinden) ‹*spot, fog, etc.*› go away; **(c)** (sich entfernen lassen) ‹*stain*› come out; **~|jagen** *tr. V.* chase away; **~|kommen** *unr. itr. V.; mit sein* (a) get away; **(b)** (abhanden kommen) go missing; **(c)** gut/schlecht *usw.* [bei etw.] ~kommen (ugs.) come off well/badly *etc.* [in sth.]; **~|kriegen** *tr. V.* get rid of ‹*cold, pain, etc.*›; get out, get rid of ‹*stain*›; **~|lassen** *unr. tr. V.* (a) jmdn. ~lassen let sb. go; (ausgehen lassen) let sb. go out; **(b)** (auslassen) leave out; omit; **~|laufen** *unr. itr. V.; mit sein* run away (**von, vor** + *Dat.* from); **~|legen** *tr. V.* put aside; (an seinen Platz legen) put away; **~|nehmen** *unr. tr. V.* (a) take away; move ‹*head, arm*›; **(b)** jmdm. etw. ~nehmen take sth. away from sb.; **~|schicken** *tr. V.* (a) send off ‹*letter, parcel*›; **(b)** send ‹*person*› away; **~|schmeißen** *tr. V.* (ugs.) chuck away (coll.); **~|schnappen** *tr. V.* (ugs.) jmdm. etw. ~schnappen/vor der Nase ~schnappen snatch sth. away from sb./from under sb.'s nose; **~|schütten** *tr. V.* pour away; **~|sehen** *unr. itr. V.* look away; **~|stellen** *tr. V.* put away; (beiseite stellen) ⋯❖

**w**

put aside; ~|**stoßen** *unr. tr. V.* push *or* shove away; ~|**tragen** *unr. tr. V.* carry away

**Weg·weiser** *der;* ~s, ~: signpost

**weg-:** ~|**werfen** *unr. tr. V.* (auch fig.) throw away; ~**werfend** *Adj.* dismissive ‹gesture, remark›; ~|**wischen** *tr. V.* wipe away; ~**zappen** (ugs.) [1] *tr. V.* etw. ~**zappen** switch sth. off [by changing channels]; [2] *itr. V.* switch to another channel; ~**ziehen** [1] *unr. tr. V.* pull away; draw back curtain; pull off blanket; [2] *unr. itr. V.; mit sein* (a) (umziehen) move away; (b) (wandern) ‹animals, nomads, etc.› leave [on their migration]

**weh** (ugs.) *Adj.* sore; *s. auch* WEHTUN

**Wehe** *die;* ~, ~n: ~n haben have contractions; **in den** ~n **liegen** be in labour

**wehen** *itr. V.* (a) (blasen) blow (b) (flattern) flutter

**weh-, Weh-:** ~**leidig** (abwertend) [1] *Adj.* (überempfindlich) soft; (weinerlich) whining *attrib.;* [2] *adv.* self-pityingly; (weinerlich) whiningly; ~**mut** *die;* ~ (geh.) wistful nostalgia; ~**mütig** *Adj.* wistfully nostalgic

**Wehr¹** *die;* ~, ~en: **sich [gegen jmdn./etw.] zur** ~ **setzen** make a stand [against sb./sth.]; resist [sb./sth.]

**Wehr²** *das;* ~[e]s, ~e weir

**Wehrdienst** *der* military service *no art.;* **seinen** ~ **ableisten** do one's military service

**Wehr·dienst-:** ~**verweigerer** *der;* ~s, ~: conscientious objector; ~**verweigerung** *die* conscientious objection

**wehren** *refl. V.* defend oneself

**wehr-, Wehr-:** ~**los** *Adj.* defenceless; ~**losigkeit** *die;* ~~: defencelessness; ~**pflicht** *die* military service; **die allgemeine** ~**pflicht** compulsory military service; ~**pflichtig** *Adj.* liable for military service *postpos.;* ~**sold** *der* military pay; ~**übung** *die* reserve duty [re]training exercise

**weh|tun** *unr. itr. V.* (ugs.) hurt; **mir tut der Magen/Kopf/Rücken weh** my stomach/head/back is aching *or* hurts; **jmdm./sich** ~: hurt sb./oneself

**Weib** *das;* ~[e]s, ~er (veralt., ugs.) woman; female (derog.)

**Weibchen** *das;* ~s, ~: female

**Weiber·held** *der* (ugs.) ladykiller

**weiblich** [1] *Adj.* (a) female (b) (für die Frau typisch; Sprachw.) feminine [2] *adv.* femininely

**Weiblichkeit** *die;* ~: femininity

**Weibs·bild** *das* (a) (ugs.) woman (b) (salopp abwertend) female

**weich** [1] *Adj.* (auch fig.) soft; **ein** ~**es** *od.* ~ **gekochtes Ei** a soft-boiled egg [2] *adv.* softly

**Weiche¹** *die;* ~, ~n (Flanke) flank

**Weiche²** *die;* ~, ~n points *pl.* (Brit.); switch (Amer.)

**weichen** *unr. itr. V.; mit sein* move; **vor jmdm./einer Sache** ~: give way to sb./sth.

***weich-gekocht** ▶ WEICH 1

**weichlich** [1] *Adj.* soft; (ohne innere Festigkeit) weak [2] *adv.* softly

**Weich·macher** *der* (Chemie, Technik) plasticizer

**Weide¹** *die;* ~, ~n willow

**Weide²** *die;* ~, ~n pasture

**weiden** *itr., tr. V.* graze

**Weiden·kätzchen** *das* willow catkin

**weigern** *refl. V.* refuse

**Weigerung** *die;* ~, ~en refusal

**Weih·bischof** *der* (kath. Kirche) suffragan bishop

**Weihe** *die;* ~, ~n (Rel.) consecration; (kath. Kirche: Priester-, Bischofsweihe) ordination

**weihen** *tr. V.* (a) (Rel.) consecrate; (zueignen) dedicate (*Dat.* to) (b) (kath. Kirche: ordinieren) ordain

**Weiher** *der;* ~s, ~: [small] pond

**Weihnachten** *das;* ~, ~: Christmas; **frohe** *od.* **fröhliche** *od.* **gesegnete** ~! Merry *or* Happy Christmas!

**weihnachtlich** *Adj.* Christmassy

**Weihnachts-:** ~**baum** *der* Christmas tree; ~**feiertag** *der:* der erste/zweite ~**feiertag** Christmas Day/Boxing Day; ~**fest** *das* Christmas; ~**geld** *das* Christmas bonus; ~**geschenk** *das* Christmas present *or* gift; ~**lied** *das* Christmas carol; ~**mann** *der; Pl.* ~**männer** Father Christmas; Santa Claus; ~**markt** *der* Christmas fair; ~**tag** *der:* ▶ ~FEIERTAG; ~**zeit** *die* Christmas time

**Weih-:** ~**rauch** *der* incense; ~**wasser** *das* (kath. Kirche) holy water

**weil** *Konj.* because

**Weile** *die;* ~: while

**weilen** *itr. V.* (geh.) stay; (sein) be

**Wein** *der;* ~[e]s, ~e wine

**Wein-:** ~**berg** *der* vineyard; ~**berg·schnecke** *die* [edible] snail; ~**brand** *der* brandy

**weinen** *itr. V.* cry (über + *Akk.* over, about); (aus Trauer, Kummer) cry, weep (um for)

**weinerlich** [1] *Adj.* tearful; weepy [2] *adv.* tearfully

**wein-, Wein-:** ~**essig** *der* wine vinegar; ~**flasche** *die* wine bottle; ~**glas** *das* wineglass; ~**handlung** *die* wine merchant's; ~**karte** *die* wine list; ~**krampf** *der* crying fit; fit of crying; ~**lokal** *das* wine bar; ~**probe** *die* wine-tasting [session]; ~**rebe** *die* grapevine; ~**rot** *Adj.* wine-red; ~**schaum·creme**

W

*die* (Kochk.) zabaglione; ⁓**stock** *der; Pl.*
⁓stöcke [grape]vine; ⁓**st⋅ube** *die* wine
bar; ⁓**traube** *die* grape
**weise** ① *Adj.* wise
② *adv.* wisely
**Weise** *die;* ⁓, ⁓**n (a)** (Art, Verfahren) way
**(b)** (Melodie) tune; melody
**weisen** ① *unr. tr. V.* (geh.: zeigen) show;
**jmdn. aus dem Zimmer** ⁓: send sb. out of
the room
② *unr. itr. V.* (irgendwohin zeigen) point
**Weisheit** *die;* ⁓, ⁓**en (a)** wisdom
**(b)** (Erkenntnis) wise insight; (Spruch) wise
saying
**Weisheits·zahn** *der* wisdom tooth
**weis|machen** *tr. V.* (ugs.) **das kannst du
mir nicht** ⁓! you can't expect me to swallow
that!
**weiß¹** *1. u. 3. Pers. Sg. Präsens v.* WISSEN
**weiß²** *Adj.* white
**Weiß** *das;* ⁓[e]s, ⁓: white
**weis·sagen** *tr. V.* prophesy
**Weissagung** *die;* ⁓, ⁓**en** prophecy
**Weiß-:** ⁓**bier** *das* wheat beer; white beer;
⁓**brot** *das* white bread; ⁓**dorn** *der;* ⁓⁓**s,**
⁓⁓**e** hawthorn
**Weiße** *der/die; adj. Dekl.* white; white man/
woman
**weißen** *tr. V.* paint white; (tünchen)
whitewash
**weiß-, Weiß-:** ⁓**gold** *das* white gold;
⁓**haarig** *Adj.* white-haired; ⁓**haarig sein**
have white hair; ⁓**herbst** *der* ≈ rosé
wine; ⁓**kohl** *der,* (bes. südd., österr.)
⁓**kraut** *das* white cabbage
**weißlich** *Adj.* whitish
**Weiß·macher** *der* whitener
**weißt** *2. Pers. Sg. Präsens v.* WISSEN
**Weiß-:** ⁓**wein** *der* white wine; ⁓**wurst**
*die* veal sausage
**Weisung** *die;* ⁓, ⁓**en** (geh., sonst Amtsspr.)
instruction; (Direktive) directive
**Weisungs·befugnis** *die* authority to
issue instructions/directives
**weit** ① *Adj.* wide; long ‹way›; **jmdm. zu** ⁓
**sein** ‹clothes› be too loose on sb.
② *adv.* **(a)** (räumlich ausgedehnt) ⁓ **geöffnet**
wide open; ⁓ **und breit war niemand zu
sehen** there was no one to be seen
anywhere; ⁓ **verbreitet** widespread;
common; common ‹plant, animal›; ⁓ **gereist**
widely travelled
**(b)** (lang) far; ⁓**er** further; farther; **am**
⁓**esten** [the] furthest *or* farthest; ⁓ **[entfernt
od. weg] wohnen** live a long way away *or*
off; live far away; ⁓ **reichend** long-range;
(fig.) far-reaching ‹importance, consequences›;
sweeping ‹changes, powers›; extensive
‹relations, influence›; **von** ⁓**em** from a
distance; **das geht zu** ⁓ (fig.) that is going
too far
**(c)** (zeitlich entfernt) ⁓ **nach Mitternacht** well
past midnight

**(d)** (in der Entwicklung) far
**Weit·blick** *der* far-sightedness
**Weite** *die;* ⁓, ⁓**n (a)** (räumliche Ausdehnung)
expanse
**(b)** (bes. Sport: Entfernung) distance
**(c)** (eines Kleidungsstückes) width
**weiten** ① *tr. V.* widen
② *refl. V.* widen; ‹pupil› dilate
**weiter** *Adv.* **(a)** ▶ WEIT 2;
**(b) und so** ⁓: and so on
**(c)** (weithin, anschließend) then
**(d)** (außerdem, sonst) ⁓ **nichts** nothing more
*or* else
**weiter...** *Adj.* further; **bis auf** ⁓**es** for the
time being; *s. auch* OHNE
**weiter-, Weiter-:** ⁓**|bilden** *tr. V.:*
▶ FORTBILDEN; ⁓**bildung** *die:*
▶ FORTBILDUNG; ⁓**|bringen** *unr. tr. V.* **die
Diskussion brachte uns nicht** ⁓: the
discussion did not get us any further
[forward]; ⁓**|erzählen** *tr. V.* **(a)** continue
telling; *itr.* **erzähl weiter!** do carry *or* go on;
**(b)** (⁓sagen) pass on; ⁓**|fahren** *unr. itr. V.;*
*mit sein* continue [on one's way]; (weiterreisen)
travel on; ⁓**|führen** *tr., itr. V.* continue;
⁓**|geben** *unr. tr. V.* pass on; ⁓**|gehen**
*unr. itr. V.; mit sein* go on; **bitte** ⁓**gehen!**
please move along *or* keep moving!; ⁓**hin**
*Adv.* **(a)** (immer noch) still; **(b)** (künftig) in
future; **(c)** (außerdem) in addition;
⁓**|kommen** *unr. itr. V.; mit sein* **(a)** get
further; **(b)** (Fortschritte machen) make
progress; **im Beruf** ⁓**kommen** get on in one's
career; ⁓**|machen** (ugs.) *itr. V.* carry on;
go on; ⁓**|reichen** *tr. V.* pass on;
⁓**|sagen** *tr. V.* pass on; ⁓**|sehen** *unr.*
*itr. V.* see
**Weiterungen** *Pl.* complications;
difficulties
**weiter-, Weiter-:**
⁓**verarbeiten** *tr. V.* process;
⁓**verarbeitung** *die* processing
**weit-, Weit-:** ⁓**gehend** ① *Adj.*
extensive, wide, sweeping ‹powers›; far-
reaching ‹support, concessions, etc.›; wide
‹support, agreement, etc.›; general
‹renunciation›; ② *adv.* to a large *or* great
extent; *\**⁓**gereist** ▶ WEIT 2A; ⁓**hin** *Adv.*
for miles around; ⁓**läufig** ① *Adj.* **(a)**
(ausgedehnt) extensive; (geräumig) spacious; **(b)**
(entfernt) distant; ② *adv.* **(a)** (ausgedehnt)
spaciously; **(b)** (entfernt) distantly;
⁓**räumig** ① *Adj.* spacious ‹room, area,
etc.›; wide ‹gap, space›; ② *adv.* spaciously;
*\**⁓**reichend** ▶ WEIT 2B; ⁓**sichtig** *Adj.*
long-sighted; ⁓**sichtigkeit** *die;* ⁓⁓: long-
sightedness; ⁓**sprung** *der* (Sport) long
jump (Brit.); broad jump (Amer.);
*\**⁓**verbreitet** ▶ WEIT 2A;
⁓**winkel·objektiv** *das* wide-angle lens
**Weizen** *der;* ⁓**s** wheat
**Weizen·bier** *das:* ▶ WEISSBIER
**welch** ① *Interrogativpron.* (bei Wahl aus einer ⋯⊹

unbegrenzten Menge) what; (bei Wahl aus einer begrenzten Menge) *(adj.)* which; *(subst.)* which one

[2] *Relativpron.* (bei Menschen) who; (bei Sachen) which

[3] *Indefinitpron.* some; (in Fragen) any

**welk** *Adj.* withered ‹*skin, hands, etc.*›; wilted ‹*leaves, flower*›; limp ‹*lettuce*›

**welken** *itr. V.; mit sein* ‹*plant, flower*› wilt

**Well·blech** *das* corrugated iron

**Welle** *die;* ~*,* ~**n (a)** (auch fig.) wave; (Rundf.: Wellenlänge) wavelength
**(b)** (Technik) shaft

**wellen-, Wellen-:** ~**bad** *das* artificial wave pool; ~**bereich** *der* (Rundf.) waveband; ~**brecher** *der* breakwater; ~**gang** *der* swell; **bei starkem** ~**gang** in heavy seas; ~**länge** *die* wavelength; ~**sittich** *der* budgerigar

**Well·fleisch** *das* boiled belly pork

**wellig** *Adj.* wavy ‹*hair*›; undulating ‹*scenery, hills, etc.*›; uneven ‹*surface, track, etc.*›

**Well·pappe** *die* corrugated cardboard

**Wels** *der;* ~**es,** ~**e** catfish

**Welt** *die;* ~*,* ~**en (a)** world; **auf der** ~: in the world; **die Alte/Neue** ~: the Old/New World; **die Dritte/Vierte** ~ the Third/Fourth World; **auf die** *od.* **zur** ~ **kommen** be born; **alle** ~ (fig. ugs.) the whole world; everybody
**(b)** (Weltall) universe

**welt-, Welt-:** ~**all** *das* universe; ~**anschauung** *die* world view; ~**ausstellung** *die* world fair; ~**berühmt** *Adj.* world-famous; ~**bevölkerung** *die* world population; population of the world

**Welten·bummler** *der;* ~**s,** ~*,* **Welten·bummlerin** *die;* ~*,* ~**nen** globetrotter

**welt-, Welt-:** ~**erfolg** *der* worldwide success; ~**fremd** [1] *Adj.* unworldly; [2] *adv.* unrealistically; ~**frieden** *der* world peace; ~**karte** *die* map of the world; ~**klima** *das* world climate; ~**krieg** *der* world war; **der Erste/Zweite** ~**krieg** the First/Second World War

**weltlich** *Adj.* **(a)** worldly
**(b)** (nicht geistlich) secular

**welt-, Welt-:** ~**literatur** *die* world literature *no art.;* ~**macht** *die* world power; ~**markt** *der* (Wirtsch.) world market; ~**meister** *der,* ~**meisterin** *die* world champion; ~**meisterschaft** *die* world championship; ~**politik** *die* world politics *pl.;* ~**rangliste** *die* world ranking list; world rankings *pl.;* ~**raum** *der* space *no art.;* ~**reise** *die* world tour; ~**rekord** *der* world record; ~**religion** *die* world religion; ~**sicherheits·rat** *der* (Pol.) [United Nations] Security Council; ~**sprache** *die* world language; ~**stadt**

*die* cosmopolitan city; ~**weit** [1] *Adj.* worldwide; [2] *adv.* throughout the world; ~**wirtschaft** *die* world economy; ~**wunder** *das:* **die sieben** ~**wunder** the Seven Wonders of the World

**wem** *Dat. von* WER [1] *Interrogativpron.* to whom; who ... to; **mit/von/zu** ~: with/from/ to whom; who ... with/from/to
[2] *Relativpron.* the person to whom ...; the person who ... to
[3] *Indefinitpron.* (ugs.: jemandem) to somebody *or* someone; (fragend *od.* verneint) to anybody *or* anyone

**wen** *Akk. von* WER [1] *Interrogativpron.* whom; who (coll.); **an/für** ~: to/for whom ...; who ... to/for
[2] *Relativpron.* the person whom
[3] *Indefinitpron.* (ugs.: jemanden) somebody; someone; (fragend *od.* verneint) anybody; anyone

**Wende** *die;* ~*,* ~**n** change (**zu** for)

**Wende·kreis** *der* **(a)** (Geogr.) tropic
**(b)** (Kfz-W.) turning circle

**Wendel·treppe** *die* spiral staircase

**wenden¹** [1] *tr., auch itr. V.* (auf die andere Seite) turn [over]; (in die entgegengesetzte Richtung) turn [round]; **bitte** ~**!** please turn over
[2] *itr. V.* turn [round]
[3] *refl. V.* **sich zum Besseren/Schlechteren** ~: take a turn for the better/worse

**wenden²** [1] *unr.* (auch regelm.) *tr. V.* turn
[2] *unr.* (auch regelm.) *refl. V.* **(a)** ‹*person*› turn
**(b)** (sich richten) **sich an jmdn.** [**um Rat**] ~: turn to sb. [for advice]

**Wende-:** ~**platz** *der* turning area; ~**punkt** *der* turning point

**wendig** [1] *Adj.* **(a)** agile; manœuvrable ‹*vehicle, boat, etc.*›
**(b)** (gewandt) astute
[2] *adv.* **(a)** (beweglich) agilely
**(b)** (gewandt) astutely

**Wendigkeit** *die;* ~ **(a)** agility; (eines Flugzeugs) manœuvrability
**(b)** (Gewandtheit) astuteness

**Wendung** *die;* ~*,* ~**en (a)** (Änderung der Richtung) turn
**(b)** (Veränderung) change

**wenig** [1] *Indefinitpron. u. unbest. Zahlw.*
**(a)** *Sing.* little; **das ist** ~: that isn't much; **zu** ~ **Zeit/Geld haben** not have enough time/ money; **ein Exemplar/50 Euro zu** ~: one copy too few/50 euros too little
**(b)** *Pl.* a few; **mit** ~**en Worten** in a few words
[2] *Adv.* little; ~ **mehr** not much more

**weniger** [1] *Komp. von* WENIG; *Indefinitpron. u. unbest. Zahlw.* (+ *Sg.*) less; (+ *Pl.*) fewer; **immer** ~: less and less
[2] *Komp. von* WENIG; *Adv.* less; **das ist** ~ **angenehm/erfreulich/schön** that is not very pleasant/pleasing/nice; *s. auch* MEHR 1;
[3] *Konj.* less; **fünf** ~ **drei** five, take away three

**wenigst...** ⒈ *Sup. von* WENIG 1; least; **am ∼en** least
⒉ *Sup. von* WENIG 2: **am ∼en** the least

**wenigstens** *Adv.* at least

**wenn** *Konj.* (a) (konditional) if; **außer ∼:** unless; **∼ es nicht anders geht** if there's no other way
(b) (temporal) when; **jedes Mal** *od.* **immer, ∼:** whenever
(c) (konzessiv) **wenn ... auch** even though
(d) (in Wunschsätzen) if only

**wenn·gleich** *Konj.* (geh.) even though; although

**wer** *Nom. Mask. u. Fem.; s. auch* (*Gen.*) WESSEN; (*Dat.*) WEM; (*Akk.*) WEN
⒈ *Interrogativpron.* who; **∼ von ...:** which of ...
⒉ *Relativpron.* the person who; ( jeder, der) anyone *or* anybody who
⒊ *Indefinitpron.* (ugs.: jemand) someone; (in Fragen, Konditionalsätzen) anyone; anybody

**Werbe-:** **∼abteilung** *die* advertising *or* publicity department; **∼agentur** *die* advertising agency; **∼aktion** *die* advertising campaign; **∼block** *der; pl.* **∼blöcke** commercial break; **∼fernsehen** *das* television commercials *pl.;* **∼funk** *der* radio commercials *pl.;* **∼geschenk** *das* [promotional] free gift

**werben** ⒈ *unr. itr. V.* advertise; **für etw. ∼:** advertise sth.
⒉ *unr. tr. V.* attract ⟨*readers, customers, etc.*⟩; recruit ⟨*soldiers, members, etc.*⟩

**Werbe-:** **∼pause** *die* commercial break; **∼spot** *der* commercial; advertisement; ad (coll.); **∼spruch** *der* advertising slogan

**Werbung** *die; ∼:* advertising; **für etw. ∼ machen** advertise sth.

**Werde·gang** *der* career

**werden** ⒈ *unr. itr. V.; mit sein* become; get; **älter ∼:** get *or* grow old[er]; **wahnsinnig** *od.* **verrückt ∼:** go mad; **das muss anders ∼:** things have to change; **wach ∼:** wake up; **rot ∼:** go *or* turn red; **Arzt/Professor ∼:** become a doctor/professor; **zu etw. ∼:** become sth.; **es wird [höchste] Zeit** it is [high] time; **es wird 10 Uhr** it is nearly 10 o'clock; **weil Herbst wird** autumn is coming; **sind die Fotos [etwas] geworden?** (ugs.) have the photos turned out [well]?
⒉ *Hilfsverb; 2. Part.* **worden (a)** (zur Bildung des Futurs) **wir ∼ uns um ihn kümmern** we will take care of him; **es wird gleich regnen** it is going to rain any minute; **es wird um die 80 Euro kosten** (ich vermute, es kostet um die 80 Euro) it will cost around 80 euros
(b) (zur Bildung des Passivs) **du wirst gerufen** you are being called; **er wurde gebeten** he was asked

**werfen** ⒈ *unr. tr. V.* throw; drop ⟨*bombs*⟩
⒉ *unr. itr. V.* (a) throw; **mit etw. ∼:** throw sth.
(b) (Junge kriegen) give birth; ⟨*dog, cat*⟩ litter

⒊ *unr. refl. V.* throw oneself; **sich vor einen Zug ∼:** throw oneself under a train

**Werft** *die; ∼, ∼en* shipyard

**Werk** *das; ∼[e]s, ∼e* (a) work
(b) (Betrieb, Fabrik) factory; works *sing. or pl.;* **ab ∼:** ex works

**Werk·bank** *die; Pl.* **Werkbänke** workbench

**werken** *itr. V.* work

**Werken** *das; ∼s* (Schulw.) handicraft

**Werk[s]-:** **∼angehörige** *der/die* factory *or* works employee; **∼arzt** *der,* **∼ärztin** *die* factory *or* works doctor

**werk-, Werk-:** **∼statt** *die;* **∼statt, ∼stätten** workshop; (Kfz-W.) garage; **∼stoff** *der* material; **∼tag** *der* working day; workday; **∼tags** *Adv.* on weekdays; **∼tätig** *Adj.* working; **∼tätige** *der/die; adj. Dekl.* worker; **∼zeug** *das* (auch fig.) tool; (Gesamtheit von Werkzeugen) tools *pl.*

**Werkzeug-:** **∼kasten** *der* toolbox; **∼macher** *der,* **∼macherin** *die* tool maker

**Wermut** *der; ∼[e]s, ∼s* (a) (Pflanze) wormwood
(b) (Wein) vermouth

**wert** *Adj.* (geh.) esteemed; (als Anrede) my dear ...; **etw./nichts ∼ sein** be worth sth./be worthless

**Wert** *der; ∼[e]s, ∼e* value; **im ∼[e] von ...:** worth ...; **∼ auf etw.** (*Akk.*) **legen** set great store by *or* on sth.

**wert·beständig** *Adj.* of lasting value *postpos.*

**werten** *tr., itr. V.* judge; assess

**wert-, Wert-:** **∼gegenstand** *der* valuable object; **∼gegenstände** valuables; **∼los** *Adj.* worthless; valueless; **∼papier** *das* (Wirtsch.) security; **∼sache** *die* valuable item; **∼sachen** valuables; **∼sendung** *die* (Postw.) registered item; **∼stoff** *der* recyclable material

**Wertung** *die; ∼, ∼en* judgement

**Wert·urteil** *das* value judgement

**wert·voll** *Adj.* valuable; (moralisch) estimable

**Wesen** *das; ∼s* nature

**wesentlich** ⒈ *Adj.* fundamental (für to); **im W∼en** essentially
⒉ *adv.* (erheblich) considerably; much

**wes·halb** *Adv.* ▶ WARUM

**Wespe** *die; ∼, ∼n* wasp

**Wespen·nest** *das* wasp's nest; **in ein ∼stechen** (fig. ugs.) stir up a hornets' nest

**wessen** *Interrogativpron.* (a) *Gen. von* WER whose
(b) *Gen. von* WAS: **∼ wird er beschuldigt?** what is he accused of?

**Wessi** *der; ∼s, ∼s* (salopp) West German

**West** (bes. Seemannsspr., Met.) ▶ WESTEN

**west·deutsch** *Adj.* Western German; (hist.: auf die alte BRD bezogen) West German

**W**

**West·deutschland** (das) Western Germany; (hist.: alte BRD) West Germany

**Weste** die; ~, ~n waistcoat (Brit.); vest (Amer.)

**Westen** der; ~s west; der ~: the West

**Western** der; ~[s], ~: western

**West·europa** (das) Western Europe

**Westfalen** (das); ~s Westphalia

**westfälisch** Adj. Westphalian

**West·indien** (das) the West Indies pl.

**westlich** 1 Adj. (a) western
(b) (nach Westen) westerly
(c) (aus dem Westen) Western
2 adv. westwards
3 Präp. mit Gen. [to the] west of

**west·wärts** Adv. [to the] west

**West·wind** der west[erly] wind

**wes·wegen** Adv. ▶ WARUM

**Wett·bewerb** der; ~[e]s, ~e (a) competition
(b) (Wirtsch.) competition no indef. art.

**Wette** die; ~, ~n bet; eine ~ [mit jmdm.] abschließen make a bet [with sb.]; mit jmdm. um die ~ laufen race sb.

**wett·eifern** itr. V.; 2. Part. gewetteifert: mit jmdm. [um etw.] ~: compete with sb. [for sth.]

**wetten** itr. V. bet; mit jmdm. ~: have a bet with sb.; mit jmdm. um etw. ~: bet sb. sth.

**Wetter** das; ~s weather

**wetter-, Wetter-:** ~aussichten Pl. weather outlook sing.; ~bericht der weather report; (Vorhersage) weather forecast; ~dienst der weather or meteorological service; ~fühlig Adj. sensitive to [changes in] the weather postpos.; ~fühligkeit die; ~~: sensitivity to [changes in] the weather; ~karte die weather chart; weather map; ~lage die weather situation; ~satellit der weather satellite; ~vorhersage die weather forecast; ~warte die weather station

**wett-, Wett-:** ~kampf der competition; ~lauf der race; ~|machen tr. V. make up for (durch with); ~rennen das race; ~rüsten das; ~~s arms race; ~streit der contest

**wetzen** tr. V. sharpen; whet

**WEZ** Abk. = **Westeuropäische Zeit** GMT

**Whirlpool** /'wə:lpu:l/ der; ~s, ~s whirlpool [bath]

**Whiskey** /'vɪski/ der; ~s ~s whiskey

**Whisky** /'vɪski/ der; ~s, ~s whisky

**wich** 1. u. 3. Pers. Sg. Prät. v. WEICHEN

**wichtig** Adj. important

**Wichtigkeit** die; ~: importance

**Wicke** die; ~, ~n vetch; (im Garten) sweet pea

**Wickel** der; ~s, ~: compress

**wickeln** tr. V. wind; (einwickeln) wrap (in + Akk. in); (auswickeln) unwrap (aus + Dat. from); (abwickeln) unwind (von from); ein Kind ~: change a baby's nappy

**Widder** der; ~s, ~: (a) ram
(b) (Astrol.) Aries

**wider** Präp. mit Akk. (geh.) against

**wider-:** ~fahren unr. itr. V.; mit sein (geh.) etw. ~fährt jmdm. sth. happens to sb.; ~legen tr. V. etw. ~legen refute sth.; jmdn. ~legen prove sb. wrong

**widerlich** 1 Adj. revolting; repulsive ⟨person, behaviour, etc.⟩; awful ⟨headache etc.⟩
2 adv. revoltingly; ⟨behave⟩ in a repugnant or repulsive manner; awfully ⟨cold, sweet, etc.⟩

**Widerlichkeit** die; ~, ~en (abwertend)
(a) repulsiveness
(b) (Äußerung/Handlung) revolting remark/action

**wider-, Wider-:** ~rede die: keine ~rede! don't argue!; ~ruf der retraction; [bis] auf ~ruf until revoked; ~rufen /-'-'-/ unr. tr., auch itr. V. retract ⟨statement, claim, confession, etc.⟩; ~setzen /-'-'-/ refl. V. sich jmdm./einer Sache ~setzen oppose sb./sth.; ~spenstig 1 Adj. unruly; stubborn ⟨horse, mule, etc.⟩; 2 adv. wilfully; ~|spiegeln, ~spiegeln /-'-'-/ 1 tr. V. mirror; (fig.) reflect; 2 refl. V. be mirrored; (fig.) be reflected; ~sprechen /-'-'-/ unr. itr. V. contradict; ~spruch der (a) (Widerrede, Protest) opposition; protest; (b) (etw. Unvereinbares) contradiction; in ~spruch zu od. mit etw. stehen contradict sth.; be contradictory to sth.; ~sprüchlich Adj. contradictory ⟨news, statements, etc.⟩; inconsistent ⟨behaviour, attitude, etc.⟩

**Wider·stand** der (a) resistance (gegen to)
(b) (Hindernis) opposition

**widerstands-, Widerstands-:** ~fähig Adj. robust; resistant ⟨material etc.⟩; hardy ⟨animal, plant⟩; ~fähigkeit die robustness; (von Material usw.) resistance; (von Tier, Pflanze) hardiness; ~los Adj., adv. without resistance postpos.

**wider-, Wider-:** ~stehen /-'-'-/ unr. itr. V. (a) (nicht nachgeben) [jmdm./einer Sache] ~stehen resist [sb./sth.]; (b) (standhalten) jmdm./einer Sache ~stehen withstand sb./sth.; ~streben /-'-'-/ itr. V. etw. ~strebt jmdm. sb. dislikes or detests sth.; ~wärtig 1 Adj. revolting, repugnant ⟨smell, taste, etc.⟩; offensive ⟨person, behaviour, etc.⟩; 2 adv. ⟨behave etc.⟩ in an offensive manner; ~wille der aversion (gegen to); ~willig 1 Adj. reluctant; unwilling; 2 adv. reluctantly; unwillingly

**widmen** 1 tr. V. (a) dedicate
(b) (verwenden für/auf) devote
2 refl. V. sich jmdm./einer Sache ~: attend to sb./sth.; (ausschließlich) devote oneself to sb./sth.

---

*old spelling - see note on page xiv

**Wịdmung** *die;* ~, ~en dedication (an + *Akk.* to)

**wịdrig** *Adj.* unfavourable; adverse

**Wịdrigkeit** *die;* ~, ~en adversity

**wie** ① *Interrogativadv.* how; ~ viel/viele how much/many; ~ [bitte]? [I beg your] pardon?; ~ spät ist es? what time is it? ② *Relativadv.* ~ er es tut the way *or* manner in which he does it ③ *Konj.* (a) *Vergleichspartikel* as; [so] ... ~ ...: as ... as ...; ich fühlte mich ~ ...: I felt as if I were ...; „N" ~ „Nordpol" N for November (b) (zum Beispiel) like; such as (c) (und, sowie) as well as; both

**wieder** *Adv.* again; alles ist ~ beim Alten everything is back as it was before; ich bin gleich ~ da I'll be right back (coll.); etw. ~ finden find sth. again; etw. ~ gutmachen make sth. good; put sth. right; den Schaden ~ gutmachen pay for the damage; jmdn. ~ wählen re-elect sb.; jmdn. ~ beleben revive *or* resuscitate sb.; jmdn./etw. ~ erkennen recognize sb./sth.

**wieder-, Wieder-:** ~aufbau /--'--/ *der* reconstruction; rebuilding; der wirtschaftliche ~aufbau economic recovery; ~|bekommen *unr. tr. V.* get back; *\**~|beleben ▶ WIEDER; ~belebungs·versuch *der* attempt at resuscitation; ~eingliederung *die* reintegration (in + *Akk.* in); *\**~|erkennen ▶ WIEDER; *\**~|finden ▶ WIEDER; ~gabe *die* (Bericht) report; (Übersetzung) rendering; (Reproduktion) reproduction; ~|geben *unr. tr. V.* (a) (zurückgeben) give back; (b) (berichten) report; (wiederholen) repeat; ~geburt *die* (christl. Rel., fig. geh.) rebirth

**\*wieder·gut|machen** ▶ WIEDER

**wieder|haben** *unr. tr. V.* (auch fig.) have back

**wieder-:** ~her|stellen *tr. V.* (a) re-establish ⟨contact, peace⟩; (b) (reparieren) restore ⟨building⟩; ~|holen ① *tr. V.* repeat; (repetieren) revise ⟨lesson, vocabulary, etc.⟩; ② *refl. V.* (a) (wieder dasselbe sagen) repeat oneself; (b) (erneut geschehen) happen again; (c) (wiederkehren) be repeated; recur

**wieder|holen** *tr. V.* fetch *or* get back

**wiederholt** ① *Adj.* repeated ② *adv.* repeatedly

**Wiederholung** *die;* ~, ~en repetition; (eines Fußballspiels usw.) replay; (einer Sendung) repeat; (einer Aufführung) repeat performance; (von Lernstoff) revision

**Wiederholungs·täter** *der,* **Wiederholungs·täterin** *die* habitual offender

**Wieder·hören** *das:* [auf *od.* Auf] ~! goodbye! (*at end of telephone call*)

**wieder-, Wieder-:** ~kehr *die;* ~~ (geh.) return; ~|kehren *itr. V.; mit sein* (geh.) return; ~|kommen *unr. itr. V.; mit sein* (a) (zurückkommen) return; come back; (b)

(noch einmal kommen) come back *or* again; (c) (sich noch einmal ereignen) ⟨opportunity, past⟩ come again; ~|kriegen *tr. V.* (ugs.) get back; ~schauen *das:* [auf] ~schauen! (südd., österr.) goodbye!; ~|sehen *unr. tr. V.* see again; ~sehen *das;* ~s, ~: reunion; [auf] ~sehen! goodbye!; ~um *Adv.* (a) (erneut) again; (b) (andererseits) on the other hand; ~verwendung *die* reuse; ~verwertung *die* recycling; ~wahl *die* re-election; *\**~|wählen *tr. V.* WIEDER

**Wiege** *die;* ~, ~n (auch fig.) cradle

**wiegen¹** *unr. itr., tr. V.* weigh

**wiegen²** *tr. V.* rock; shake ⟨head⟩

**Wiegen·lied** *das* lullaby; cradle song

**wiehern** *itr. V.* whinny; (lauter) neigh

**Wien** (*das*) ~s Vienna

**Wiener¹** *der;* ~s, ~: Viennese

**Wiener²** *Adj.* Viennese; *s. auch* WÜRSTCHEN

**Wienerin** *die;* ~, ~nen Viennese

**wienerisch** *Adj.* Viennese

**wies** *1. u. 3. Pers. Sg. Prät. v.* WEISEN

**Wiese** *die;* ~, ~n meadow; (Rasen) lawn

**wie·so** *Interrogativadv.* why

**\*wie·viel** /*od.* '--/ ▶ VIEL, WIE, UHR B

**wie·viel·mal** /*od.* -'--/ *Interrogativadv.* how many times

**wievielt...** /*od.* '--/ *Interrogativadj.* der ~e Band? which number volume?; der Wievielte ist heute? what is the date today?

**wie·weit** *Interrogativadv.* to what extent; how far

**wild** ① *Adj.* (auch fig.) wild; (wütend) furious ⟨cursing, shouting, etc.⟩; ~es Parken illegal parking; ~er Streik wildcat strike; ~ auf etw./jmdn. sein (ugs.) be mad *or* crazy about sth./sb. (coll.); ~ werden get furious; jmdn. ~ machen infuriate sb. ② *adv.* (a) wildly; wie ~ (ugs.) like mad (coll.) (b) (ordnungswidrig) illegally

**Wild** *das;* ~[e]s (a) (Tiere, Fleisch) game (b) (einzelnes Tier) [wild] animal

**Wild·bret** /-brɛt/ *das;* ~s (geh.) game

**Wilde** *der/die; adj. Dekl.* savage

**Wilderei** *die;* ~, ~en poaching *no pl., no art.*

**Wilderer** *der;* ~s, ~, **Wilderin** *die;* ~, ~nen poacher

**wild·fremd** *Adj.* completely strange

**Wild·gans** *die* wild goose

**Wildheit** *die;* ~: wildness

**Wild-:** ~katze *die* wild cat; ~leder *das* suede

**Wildnis** *die;* ~, ~se wilderness

**Wild-:** ~pferd *das* wild horse; ~schwein *das* wild boar; ~wasser *das Pl.* ~~: mountain torrent; ~wechsel *der* game crossing; ~west·film *der* western

**will** *1. u. 3. Pers. Sg. Präsens v.* WOLLEN

**Wille** *der;* ~ns will; (Wunsch) wish

W

**willen** *Präp. mit Gen.* **um jmds./einer Sache**
∼: for sb.'s/sth.'s sake
**Willen** *der;* ∼s ▶ WILLE
**willen·los** ☐1 *Adj.* will-less
☐2 *adv.* will-lessly
**willens** *Adj.* ∼ **sein, etw. zu tun** (geh.) be
willing to do sth.
**willens-, Willens-:** ∼**schwach** *Adj.*
weak-willed; ∼**schwäche** *die* weakness of
will; ∼**stark** *Adj.* strong-willed; ∼**stärke**
*die* strength of will
**willentlich** ☐1 *Adj.* deliberate
☐2 *adv.* deliberately; on purpose
**willig** ☐1 *Adj.* willing
☐2 *adv.* willingly
**will·kommen** *Adj.* welcome; **jmdn.** ∼
**heißen** welcome sb.
**Will·kür** *die;* ∼: arbitrary use of power;
(Handlung o. Ä.) arbitrariness
**willkürlich** ☐1 *Adj.* arbitrary; (vom Willen
gesteuert) voluntary ⟨*muscle, movement, etc.*⟩
☐2 *adv.* arbitrarily; (vom Willen gesteuert)
voluntarily
**wimmeln** *itr. V.* **von Fischen/Fehlern** ∼: be
teeming with fish/mistakes
**wimmern** *itr. V.* whimper
**Wimpel** *der;* ∼s, ∼: pennant
**Wimper** *die;* ∼, ∼n [eye]lash
**Wimpern·tusche** *die* mascara
**Wind** *der;* ∼[e]s, ∼e wind
**Wind·beutel** *der* cream puff
**Winde** *die;* ∼, ∼n winch
**Windel** *die;* ∼, ∼n nappy (Brit.); diaper
(Amer.)
**Windel·höschen** *das* nappy pants *pl.*
**winden** ☐1 *unr. tr. V.* (geh.) make ⟨*wreath,
garland*⟩; **etw. um etw.** ∼: wind sth. around
sth.
☐2 *unr. refl. V.* ⟨*plant, tendrils*⟩ wind (**um**
around); ⟨*snake*⟩ coil [itself], wind itself (**um**
around); **sich vor Schmerzen** ∼: writhe in
pain
**Windes·eile** *die:* **in** ∼: in next to no time
**Wind-:** ∼**hose** *die* (Met.) whirlwind;
∼**hund** *der* greyhound
**windig** *Adj.* windy
**Wind-:** ∼**kanal** *der* (Technik) wind tunnel;
∼**mühle** *die* windmill; ∼**pocken** *Pl.*
chickenpox *sing.;* ∼**schatten** *der* lee;
∼**schutz·scheibe** *die* windscreen (Brit.);
windshield (Amer.); ∼**stärke** *die:* ∼stärke
**7/9** *usw.* wind force 7/9 *etc.;* ∼**still** *Adj.*
windless; still; ∼**stoß** *der* gust of wind;
∼**surfer** *der,* ∼**surferin** *die* windsurfer;
∼**surfing** *das;* ∼∼∼s windsurfing *no art.*
**Windung** *die;* ∼, ∼en (a) bend
(b) (spiralförmiger Verlauf) spiral; (einer Spule
usw.) winding
**Wink** *der;* ∼[e]s, ∼e sign; (Hinweis) hint;
(Ratschlag) tip; hint

**Winkel** *der;* ∼s, ∼ (a) (Math.) angle; **toter** ∼:
blind spot
(b) (Ecke; auch fig.) corner
**winkelig** *Adj.* twisty ⟨streets⟩
**winken** ☐1 *itr. V.* (a) wave; **mit etw.** ∼:
wave sth.
(b) (auffordern heranzukommen) **jmdm.** ∼: beckon
sb. over; **einem Taxi** ∼: hail a taxi
☐2 *tr. V.* beckon; **jmdn. zu sich** ∼: beckon sb.
over [to one]
**winklig** *Adj.* ▶ WINKELIG
**winseln** *itr. V.* ⟨dog⟩ whimper
**Winter** *der;* ∼s, ∼: winter
**Winter-:** ∼**anfang** *der* beginning of
winter; ∼**garten** *der* conservatory
**winterlich** ☐1 *Adj.* wintry; winter *attrib.*
⟨clothing, break⟩
☐2 *adv.* ∼ **kalt** cold and wintry
**Winter-:** ∼**reifen** *der* winter tyre;
∼**schlussverkauf,**
*∼**schlußverkauf** *der* winter sale[s *pl.*];
∼**sport** *der* winter sports *pl.;* ∼**urlaub**
*der* winter holiday; ∼**zeit** *die* wintertime
**Winzer** *der;* ∼s, ∼, **Winzerin** *die;* ∼,
∼**nen** winegrower
**winzig** ☐1 *Adj.* tiny
☐2 *adv.* ∼ **klein** tiny; minute
**Winzigkeit** *die;* ∼, ∼en (a) tininess;
minuteness
(b) (Kleinigkeit) tiny thing; triviality
**Wipfel** *der;* ∼s, ∼: treetop
**Wippe** *die;* ∼, ∼n see-saw
**wippen** *itr. V.* bob up and down; (hin und her)
bob about; (auf einer Wippe) see-saw
**wir** *Personalpron.; 1. Pers. Pl. Nom.* we; *s.
auch* (Gen.) UNSER; (Dat.) UNS; (Akk.) UNS
**wirb** *Imperativ Sg. v.* WERBEN
**Wirbel** *der;* ∼s, ∼ (a) (kreisende Bewegung) (im
Wasser) whirlpool; (in der Luft) whirlwind;
(kleiner) eddy; (von Rauch, beim Tanz) whirl
(b) (Trubel) hurly-burly
(c) (Aufsehen) fuss
(d) (Anat.) vertebra
**wirbeln** ☐1 *itr. V.* **mit sein** whirl; ⟨water,
snowflakes⟩ swirl
☐2 *tr. V.* swirl ⟨leaves, dust⟩; whirl ⟨dancer⟩
**Wirbel-:** ∼**säule** *die* spinal column;
∼**sturm** *der* cyclone
**wirbt** *3. Pers. Sg. Präsens v.* WERBEN
**wird** *3. Pers. Sg. Präsens v.* WERDEN
**wirf** *Imperativ Sg. v.* WERFEN
**wirft** *3. Pers. Sg. Präsens v.* WERFEN
**wirken** *itr. V.* (a) (eine Wirkung haben) have an
effect; **gegen etw.** ∼: be effective against sth.
(b) (erscheinen) seem; appear
**wirklich** ☐1 *Adj.* real
☐2 *Adv.* really
**Wirklichkeit** *die;* ∼, ∼en reality; **in** ∼: in
reality
**wirksam** ☐1 *Adj.* effective
☐2 *adv.* effectively
**Wirksamkeit** *die;* ∼: effectiveness

---

*alte Schreibung - vgl. Hinweis auf S. xiv

**Wirk·stoff** *der* active agent

**Wirkung** *die;* ~, ~en effect (**auf** + *Akk.* on); **mit** ~ **vom 1. Juli** (Amtsspr.) with effect from 1 July

**wirkungs-, Wirkungs-:** ~**grad** *der* (Technik) efficiency; ~**los** ① *Adj.* ineffective; ② *adv.* ineffectively; ~**losigkeit** *die;* ~~: ineffectiveness; ~**voll** ① *Adj.* effective; ② *adv.* effectively

**wirr** *Adj.* (unordentlich) tousled ‹*hair, beard*›; tangled ‹*ropes, roots*›; (unklar, verwirrt) confused

**Wirren** *Pl.* turmoil *sing.*

**Wirrwarr** *der;* ~s chaos; (von Stimmen) clamour

**Wirsing** *der;* ~s, **Wirsing·kohl** *der* savoy [cabbage]

**Wirt** *der;* ~[e]s, ~e landlord

**Wirtin** *die;* ~, ~nen landlady

**Wirtschaft** *die;* ~, ~en (a) economy; (Geschäftsleben) commerce and industry (**b**) (Gaststätte) public house; pub (Brit. coll.); bar (Amer.) (**c**) (Haushalt) household (**d**) (ugs. abwertend: Unordnung) mess; shambles *sing.*

**wirtschaften** *itr. V.* **mit dem Geld gut** ~: manage one's money well; **mit Verlust/ Gewinn** ~: run at a loss/profit

**wirtschaftlich** ① *Adj.* (a) economic (**b**) (finanziell) financial (**c**) (sparsam, rentabel) economical ② *adv.; s. Adj.:* economically; financially

**Wirtschaftlichkeit** *die;* ~: economic viability

**Wirtschafts-:** ~**hilfe** *die* economic aid *no indef. art.;* ~**krieg** *der* economic war; (Kriegsführung) economic warfare; ~**kriminalität** *die* economic crime *no art.;* ~**krise** *die* economic crisis; ~**lehre** *die* economics *sing.;* ~**minister** *der,* ~**ministerin** *die* minister for economic affairs; ~**politik** *die* economic policy; ~**union** *die* economic union; *s. auch* WÄHRUNGSUNION; ~**wunder** *das* (ugs.) economic miracle

**Wirts-:** ~**haus** *das* pub (Brit. coll.); ~**leute** *Pl.* landlord and landlady

**Wisch** *der;* ~[e]s, ~e (salopp) piece *or* bit of paper

**wischen** *itr., tr. V.* wipe; **Staub** ~: do the dusting; dust

**wispern** *itr., tr. V.* whisper

**wiss-, \*wiß-, Wiss, \*Wiß-:** ~**begier,** ~**begierde** *die* thirst for knowledge; ~**begierig** *Adj.* eager for knowledge; ‹*child*› eager to learn

**wissen** ① *unr. tr. V.* know; **von jmdm./etw. nichts [mehr]** ~ **wollen** want to have nothing [more] to do with sb./sth. ② *unr. itr. V.* **von etw./um etw.** ~: know about sth.

**Wissen** *das;* ~s knowledge; **meines/ unseres** ~s to my/our knowledge

**Wissenschaft** *die;* ~, ~en science

**Wissenschaftler** *der;* ~s ~, **Wissenschaftlerin** *die;* ~, ~nen academic; (Naturwissenschaft) scientist

**wissenschaftlich** ① *Adj.* scholarly; (naturwissenschaftlich) scientific ② *adv.* in a scholarly manner; (naturwissenschaftlich) scientifically

**wissens·wert** *Adj.* ~ **sein** be worth knowing

**wissentlich** ① *Adj.* deliberate ② *adv.* knowingly; deliberately

**wittern** ① *itr. V.* sniff the air ② *tr. V.* get wind of; (fig.: ahnen) sense

**Witterung** *die;* ~, ~en (a) (Wetter) weather *no indef. art;* (**b**) (Jägerspr.) (Geruchssinn) sense of smell; (Geruch) scent

**Witwe** *die;* ~, ~n widow; ~ **werden** be widowed

**Witwen·rente** *die* widow's pension

**Witwer** *der;* ~s, ~: widower; ~ **werden** be widowed

**Witz** *der;* ~es, ~e joke

**Witz-:** ~**blatt** *das* humorous magazine; ~**bold** *der;* ~~es, ~~e joker

**Witzelei** *die;* ~, ~en (a) teasing (**b**) (witzelnde Bemerkung) joke

**witzeln** *itr. V.* joke (**über** + *Akk.* about)

**Witz·figur** *die* (a) (in Witzen) joke character (**b**) (ugs. abwertend) figure of fun

**witzig** ① *Adj.* funny ② *adv.* amusingly

**witz·los** *Adj.* (a) dull (**b**) (ugs.: sinnlos) pointless

**wo** ① *Adv.* where ② *Konj.* (a) (da, weil) seeing that (**b**) (obwohl) although; when

**wo·anders** *Adv.* somewhere else

**wo·bei** *Adv.* (a) (interrogativ) ~ **hast du sie ertappt?** what did you catch her doing? (**b**) (relativisch) **er gab sechs Schüsse ab,** ~ **einer der Täter getötet wurde** he fired six shots – one of the criminals was killed

**Woche** *die;* ~, ~n week; **in dieser/der nächsten/der letzten** ~: this/next/last week; **heute in/vor einer** ~: a week today/a week ago today

**wochen-, Wochen-:** ~**bett** *das;* im ~**bett liegen** be lying in; ~**ende** *das* weekend; ~**lang** ① *Adj.* lasting weeks *postpos;* ② *adv.* for weeks [on end]; ~**stunde** *die* (Schulw.) period per week; ~**tag** *der* weekday (*including Saturday*); ~**tags** *Adv.* on weekdays [and Saturdays]

**wöchentlich** *Adj., adv.* weekly

**Wochen·zeitung** *die* weekly newspaper

**-wöchig** (a) (... Wochen alt) ... -week-old (**b**) (... Wochen dauernd) ... week's/weeks'; ...-week

**Wöchnerin** *die;* ~, ~nen woman who has just given birth

**Wodka** *der;* ~s, ~s vodka

**wo·durch** *Adv.* (a) (interrogativ) how (b) (relativisch) as a result of which

**wo·für** *Adv.* (a) (interrogativ) for what (b) (relativisch) for which

**wog** *1. u. 3. Pers. Sg. Prät. v.* WIEGEN

**Woge** *die;* ~, ~n wave

**wo·gegen** ⓵ *Adv.* (a) (interrogativ) against what; what … against (b) (relativisch) against which; which … against ⓶ *Konj.* whereas

**wogen** *itr. V.* (geh.) ‹*sea*› surge; (fig.) ‹*corn*› wave

**wo·her** *Adv.* (a) (interrogativ) where … from; ~ weißt du das? how do you know that? (b) (relativisch) where … from

**wo·hin** *Adv.* (a) (interrogativ) where [… to] (b) (relativisch) where

**wo·hingegen** *Konj.* whereas

**wohl** ⓵ *Adv.* (a) well; jmdm. ist nicht ~, jmd. fühlt sich nicht ~: sb. does not feel well (b) (behaglich) at ease; happy; leb ~!/leben Sie ~! farewell! (c) (durchaus) well (d) (ungefähr) about (e) etw. tut jmdm. ~: sth. does sb. good ⓶ *Partikel* probably; ~ kaum hardly

**Wohl** *das;* ~[e]s welfare; auf jmds. ~ trinken drink sb.'s health; zum ~! cheers!

**wohl-, Wohl-:** ~auf /-ˈ-/ *Adj.* (geh.) ~auf sein be well; ~befinden *das* well-being; ~behagen *das* sense of well-being; ~behalten *Adj.* safe and well ‹*person*›; undamaged ‹*thing*›; ~fahrts·staat *der* welfare state; ~gefallen *das;* ~s pleasure; ~gemerkt *Adv.* please note; ~habend *Adj.* prosperous; ~habenheit *die;* ~~: prosperity

**wohlig** ⓵ *Adj.* pleasant; agreeable ⓶ *adv.* ‹*sigh, purr, etc.*› with pleasure

**wohl-, Wohl-:** ~klang *der* (geh.) melodious sound; ~schmeckend *Adj.* (geh.) delicious; ~stand *der* prosperity; ~stands·gesellschaft *die* affluent society; ~tat *die* (a) (gute Tat) good deed; (Gefallen) favour; (b) (*Genuss*) blissful relief; ~tätig *Adj.* charitable; ~tuend *Adj.* agreeable; *~tun ▶* WOHL 1 E; ~verdient *Adj.* well-earned; ~weislich *Adv.* deliberately; ~wollen *das;* ~~s goodwill; ~wollend ⓵ *Adj.* benevolent; favourable ‹*judgement, opinion*›; ⓶ *adv.* benevolently; ‹*judge, consider*› favourably

**Wohn-:** ~anhänger *der* caravan; trailer (Amer.); ~block *der; Pl.* ~~s, *od.* ~blöcke residential block

**wohnen** *itr. V.* live; (kurzfristig) stay

**wohn-, Wohn-:** ~gemeinschaft *die*

group sharing a flat (Brit.) *or* (Amer.) apartment/house; ~haft *Adj.* resident (**in** + *Dat.* in); ~heim *das* (für Alte, Behinderte) home; (für Obdachlose, Lehrlinge) hostel; (für Studenten) hall of residence

**wohnlich** *Adj.* homely

**Wohn-:** ~mobil *das;* ~~s, ~~e motor home; ~ort *der* place of residence; ~siedlung *die* residential estate; (mit gleichartigen Häusern) housing estate; ~sitz *der* place of residence; **ohne festen** ~sitz of no fixed abode

**Wohnung** *die;* ~, ~en (a) flat (Brit.); apartment (Amer.) (b) (Unterkunft) lodging

**Wohnungs-:** ~not *die* housing crisis; serious housing shortage; ~schlüssel *der* key to the flat (Brit.) *or* (Amer.) apartment; ~suche *die* search for a flat (Brit.) *or* (Amer.) apartment; **auf** ~suche **sein** be flat-hunting; ~tür *die* door of the flat (Brit.) *or* (Amer.) apartment; ~verlust *der* loss of one's home

**Wohn-:** ~verhältnisse *Pl.* living conditions; ~wagen *der* caravan; trailer (Amer.); ~zimmer *das* living room

**wölben** ⓵ *tr. V.* curve; vault, arch ‹*roof, ceiling*› ⓶ *refl. V.* curve; ‹*bridge, ceiling*› arch

**Wölbung** *die;* ~, ~en curve; (einer Decke) arch; vault

**Wolf** *der;* ~[e]s, Wölfe wolf

**Wolke** *die;* ~, ~n cloud

**wolken-, Wolken-:** ~bruch *der* cloudburst; ~bruch·artig *Adj.* torrential; ~decke *die* [unbroken] cloud *no indef. art.;* **die** ~decke **riss auf** the clouds broke; ~kratzer *der* skyscraper; ~los *Adj.* cloudless

**wolkig** *Adj.* cloudy

**Wolle** *die;* ~, ~n wool

**wollen¹** *Adj.* woollen

**wollen²** ⓵ *unr. Modalverb; 2. Part.* wollen: etw. tun ~ (den Wunsch haben, etw. zu tun) want to do sth.; (die Absicht haben, etw. zu tun) be going to do sth.; **die Wunde will nicht heilen** the wound [just] won't heal ⓶ *unr. itr. V.* **du musst nur** ~, **dann …** you only have to want to enough, then … **ganz wie du willst** just as you like; **ich will nach Hause** (ugs.) I want to go home; **zu wem** ~ **Sie?** whom do you want to see? ⓷ *unr. tr. V.* want; **das habe ich nicht gewollt** I never meant that to happen

**wo·mit** *Adv.* (a) (interrogativ) ~ **schreibst du?** what do you write with? (b) (relativisch) ~ **du schreibst** which *or* that you write with; (more formal) with which you write

**wo·möglich** *Adv.* possibly

**wo·nach** *Adv.* (a) (interrogativ) after what; what … after; ~ **suchst du?** what are you looking for?

**(b)** (relativisch) after which; which ... after

**Wonne** *die;* ~, ~n (geh.) bliss *no pl.;*
ecstasy; (etw., was Freude macht) joy

**wonnig** *Adj.* sweet

**woran** *Adv.* **(a)** (interrogativ) ~ **denkst du?**
what are you thinking of?
**(b)** (relativisch) **nichts,** ~ **man sich anlehnen
könnte** nothing one could lean against

**worauf (a)** (interrogativ) ~ **wartest du?** what
are you waiting for?
**(b)** (relativisch) **etwas,** ~ **man sich verlassen
kann** something one can rely on
**(c)** (relativisch: woraufhin) whereupon

**woraus** *Adv.* **(a)** (interrogativ) ~ **schließt du
das?** what do you infer from that?
**(b)** (relativisch) **es gab nichts,** ~ **wir den Wein
hätten trinken können** there was nothing for
us to drink the wine out of

**worden** *2. Part. v.* WERDEN 2

**worin** *Adv.* **(a)** (interrogativ) in what; what ...
in
**(b)** (relativisch) in which; which ... in

**Workaholic** /wə:kə'hɔlık/ *der;* ~s, ~s:
workaholic

**Wort** *das;* ~[e]s, Wörter/~e **(a)** *Pl.* **Wörter,**
(auch:) ~e word; ~ **für** ~: word for word;
**1 000 €** (in ~en: tausend) 1,000 € (in words:
one thousand)
**(b)** *Pl.* ~e (Äußerung) word; **mir fehlen die** ~e
I'm lost for words; **Dr. Meyer hat das** ~: it's
Dr Meyer's turn to speak
**(c)** *Pl.* ~e (Spruch) saying; (Zitat) quotation
**(d)** *Pl.* ~e (geh.: Text) words *pl.;* **in** ~ **und
Bild** in words and pictures
**(e)** *Pl.* ~e (Versprechen) word; [sein] ~ **halten**
keep one's word

**Wort·bruch** *der* breaking one's word *no
art.*

**wort·brüchig** *Adj.* ~ **werden** break one's
word

**Wörter·buch** *das* dictionary

**wort-, Wort-:** ~**getreu** *Adj.* word-for-
word; ~**karg** ⎯1⎯ *Adj.* taciturn ⟨*person*⟩;
⎯2⎯ *adv.* taciturnly; ~**kargheit** *die*
taciturnity; ~**laut** *der* wording; **im [vollen]**
~**laut** verbatim

**wörtlich** ⎯1⎯ *Adj.* **(a)** word-for-word
**(b)** (der eigentlichen Bedeutung entsprechend)
literal
⎯2⎯ *adv.: s. Adj.:* word for word; literally

**wort-, Wort-:** ~**los** ⎯1⎯ *Adj.* silent;
wordless; ⎯2⎯ *adv.* without saying a word;
~**meldung** *die:* gibt es noch
~**meldungen?** does anyone else wish to
speak?; ~**spiel** *das* play on words; pun;
~**wechsel** *der* exchange of words;
~**wörtlich** *Adj.* word-for-word

**worüber** *Adv.* **(a)** (interrogativ) over what ...;
what ... over
**(b)** (relativisch) over which; which ... over

**worum** *Adv.* **(a)** (interrogativ) around what;
what ... around

**(b)** (relativisch) around which; which ...
around

**worunter** *Adv.* **(a)** (interrogativ) under what;
what ... under
**(b)** (relativisch) under which; which ... under

**wo·von** *Adv.* **(a)** (interrogativ) from where;
where ... from
**(b)** (relativisch) from which; which ... from

**wo·vor** *Adv.* **(a)** (interrogativ) in front of what;
what ... in front of
**(b)** (relativisch) in front of which; which ... in
front of

**wo·zu** *Adv.* **(a)** (interrogativ) to what; what ...
to; (wofür) what ... for
**(b)** (relativisch) ~ **du dich auch entschließt**
whatever you decide on

**Wrack** *das;* ~[e]s, ~s *od.* ~e wreck

**wrang** *1. und 3. Pers. Sg. Prät. v.* WRINGEN

**wringen** *unr. tr. V.* (bes. nordd.) wring

**Wucher** *der;* ~s profiteering; (beim Verleihen
von Geld) usury

**wuchern** *itr. V.* **(a)** *auch mit sein* ⟨plants,
weeds, etc.⟩ proliferate, run wild
**(b)** (Wucher treiben) [mit etw.] ~: profiteer [on
sth.]; (beim Verleihen von Geld) lend [sth.] at
extortionate interest rates

**Wucherung** *die;* ~, ~en growth

**wuchs** *1. u. 3. Pers. Sg. Prät. v.* WACHSEN

**Wuchs** *der;* ~es (Gestalt) stature

**Wucht** *die;* ~: force; (von Schlägen) power;
weight

**wuchtig** ⎯1⎯ *Adj.* **(a)** (voller Wucht) powerful;
mighty
**(b)** (schwer, massig) massive
⎯2⎯ *adv.* powerfully

**wühlen** ⎯1⎯ *itr. V.* **(a)** dig; (mit der Schnauze,
dem Schnabel) root **(nach** for); ⟨mole⟩ tunnel,
burrow
**(b)** (ugs.: suchen) rummage [around] **(nach**
for)
⎯2⎯ *tr. V.* burrow; tunnel out ⟨burrow⟩

**wulstig** *Adj.* bulging

**wund** *Adj.* sore; **sich** ~ **liegen** get bed sores

**Wunde** *die;* ~, ~n wound

**wunder, Wunder**[1] (ugs.): **er denkt, er sei**
~ **wer** he thinks he's really something; **sie
bildet sich** ~ **was darauf ein** she's terribly
pleased with herself about it (coll.)

**Wunder**[2] *das;* ~s, ~ **(a)** miracle; ~ **wirken**
(fig. ugs.) work wonders; **ein/kein** ~ **sein**
(ugs.) be a/no wonder
**(b)** (etw. Erstaunliches) wonder

**wunderbar** ⎯1⎯ *Adj.* **(a)** miraculous
**(b)** (sehr schön, herrlich) wonderful; marvellous
⎯2⎯ *adv.* **(a)** (sehr schön, herrlich) wonderfully;
marvellously
**(b)** (ugs.: sehr) wonderfully

**Wunder-:** ~**kerze** *die* sparkler; ~**kind**
*das* child prodigy

**wunderlich** ⎯1⎯ *Adj.* strange; odd
⎯2⎯ *adv.* strangely; oddly

**W**

**wundern** 1 *tr. V.* surprise; **mich wundert**
*od.* **es wundert mich, dass …:** I'm surprised
that …
2 *refl. V.* **sich über jmdn./etw. ~:** be
surprised at sb./sth

**wunder-: ~schön** 1 *Adj.* simply
beautiful; (herrlich) simply wonderful; 2 *adv.*
quite beautifully; **~voll** 1 *Adj.* wonderful;
2 *adv.* wonderfully

*****wund|liegen** ▶ WUND

**Wund·starr·krampf** *der* (Med.) tetanus

**Wunsch** *der;* **~[e]s, Wünsche** wish (**nach** to
have); (Sehnen) desire (**nach** for); **haben Sie**
[sonst] **noch einen ~?** will there be
anything else?; **auf jmds. ~:** at sb.'s wish;
**mit den besten/herzlichsten Wünschen** with
best/warmest wishes

**wünschbar** *Adj.* (bes. schweiz.) desirable

**Wünschel-: ~rute** *die* divining rod;
**~ruten·gänger** *der;* **~~s, ~~,**
**~ruten·gängerin** *die;* **~~, ~~nen**
diviner

**wünschen** *tr. V.* **(a) sich** (*Dat.*) **etw. ~:**
want sth.; (im Stillen) wish for sth.
**(b)** (in formelhaften Wünschen) wish; **jmdm. alles**
**Gute/frohe Ostern ~:** wish sb. all the best/a
happy Easter
**(c)** *auch itr. V.* (begehren) want; **was ~ Sie?,**
**Sie ~?** (im Lokal) what would you like?; (in
einem Geschäft) can I help you?

**Wunsch-: ~kind** *das* wanted child;
**~konzert** *das* request concert; (im
Rundfunk) request programme; **~zettel** *der*
(zum Geburtstag *usw.*) list of presents one
would like

**wurde** *1. u. 3. Pers. Sg. Prät. v.* WERDEN

**würde** *1. u. 3. Pers. Sg. Konjunktiv II v.*
WERDEN

**Würde** *die;* **~:** dignity

**würde·los** 1 *Adj.* undignified; (schimpflich)
disgraceful
2 *adv.* in an undignified way; (schimpflich)
disgracefully

**Würdelosigkeit** *die;* **~** ▶ WÜRDELOS: lack
of dignity; disgracefulness

**Würden·träger** *der,* **Würden·trägerin**
*die* dignitary

**würde·voll** 1 *Adj.* dignified
2 *adv.* with dignity

**würdig** 1 *Adj.* **(a)** dignified
**(b)** (wert) worthy
2 *adv.* **(a)** with dignity
**(b)** (angemessen) worthily

**würdigen** *tr. V.* **(a)** (anerkennen, beachten)
recognize; (schätzen) appreciate; (lobend
hervorheben) acknowledge
**(b)** (für wert halten) **jmdn. keines Blickes/keiner**
**Antwort ~:** not deign to look at/answer sb.

**Wurf** *der;* **~[e]s, Würfe (a)** throw; (beim
Kegeln) bowl

**(b)** *o. Pl.* (das Werfen) throwing/pitching/
bowling
**(c)** (Zool.) litter

**Würfel** *der;* **~s, ~:** cube; (Spielwürfel) dice;
die (formal)

**Würfel·becher** *der* dice cup

**würfeln** 1 *itr. V.* throw the dice; **um etw.**
**~:** play dice for sth.
2 *tr. V.* **(a)** throw
**(b)** (in Würfel schneiden) dice

**Würfel-: ~spiel** *das* dice; (Brettspiel) dice
game; **~zucker** *der* cube sugar

**Wurf·geschoss,** *****Wurf·geschoß** *das*
missile

**würgen** 1 *tr. V.* strangle; throttle
2 *itr. V.* (Brechreiz haben) retch

**Wurm** *der;* **~[e]s, Würmer** worm; (Made)
maggot

**wurmig** *Adj.,* **wurm·stichig** *Adj.* worm-
eaten; (madig) maggoty

**Wurst** *die;* **~, Würste** sausage; **es geht um**
**die ~** (fig. ugs.) the crunch has come; **jmdm.**
**ist jmd./etw. ~** (ugs.) sb. doesn't care about
sb./sth.

**Wurst·bude** *die* ▶ WÜRSTCHENBUDE

**Würstchen** *das;* **~s, ~ (a)** [small] sausage;
**Frankfurter/Wiener ~:** frankfurter/
wienerwurst
**(b)** (fig. ugs.) nobody; (hilfloser Mensch) poor
soul

**Würstchen·bude** *die* sausage stand

**Wurstelei** *die;* **~, ~en** (ugs. abwertend)
pottering about *no pl.*

**wursteln** *itr. V.* (ugs.) potter

**Wurst·salat** *der: piquant salad with pieces*
*of sausage, onion rings, boiled eggs and/or*
*cheese*

**Würze** *die;* **~, ~n** spice; seasoning

**Wurzel** *die;* **~, ~n** (auch fig.) root

**wurzeln** *itr. V.* take root

**würzen** *tr. V.* season

**würzig** *Adj.* tasty; full-flavoured ⟨beer,
wine⟩; aromatic ⟨fragrance⟩; tangy ⟨air⟩

**Würzigkeit** *die;* **~** ▶ WÜRZIG 1: tastiness;
full flavour; aromatic fragrance; tanginess

**wusch** *1. u. 3. Pers. Sg. Prät. v.* WASCHEN

**wusste,** *****wußte** *1. und 3. Pers. Sg. Prät.*
*v.* WISSEN

**wüsste,** *****wüßte** *1. und 3. Pers. Sg.*
*Konjunktiv II v.* WISSEN

**wüst** 1 *Adj.* **(a)** (öde) desolate
**(b)** (unordentlich) chaotic
**(c)** (ungezügelt) wild; (unanständig) rude
2 *adv.* **(a)** (unordentlich) chaotically
**(b)** (ungezügelt) wildly

**Wust** *der;* **~[e]s** (abwertend) jumble; (fig.)
welter; **ein ~ von Daten/Vorschriften** a mass
of data/regulations

**Wüste** *die;* **~, ~n** desert

**Wut** *die;* **~:** rage; fury

---

**wüten** *itr. V.* (auch fig.) rage; (zerstören) wreak havoc

**wütend** [1] *Adj.* furious; angry ⟨*voice, mob*⟩
[2] *adv.* furiously; in a fury

# Xx

**x¹, X** /ɪks/ *das;* ∼, ∼: x/X
**x²** *unbest. Zahlwort* (ugs.) umpteen (coll.)
**x-Achse** *die* (Math.) x-axis
**X-Beine** *Pl.* knock knees
**x-beinig** *Adj.* knock-kneed
**x-beliebig** *Adj.* (ugs.) [irgend]ein ∼er/ [irgend]eine ∼e/[irgend]ein ∼es any old (coll. attrib.); jeder ∼e Ort any old place (coll.)

**X-Chromosom** *das* (Biol.) X-chromosome
**x-fach** [1] *Vervielfältigungsz.* die ∼e Menge (Math.) x times the amount; (ugs.) umpteen times the amount (coll.)
[2] *adv.* (ugs.) ∼ erprobt sein ⟨*tested etc.*⟩ umpteen times (coll.)
**x-mal** *Adv.* (ugs.) umpteen times (coll.)
**x-t...** *Ordinalz.* (ugs.) umpteenth (coll.)
**Xylophon** *das;* ∼s, ∼e xylophone

# Yy

**y, Y** /ˈʏpsilɔn/ *das;* ∼, ∼: y/Y
**y-Achse** *die* (Math.) y-axis
**Yacht** ▶ JACHT
**Y-Chromosom** *das* (Biol.) Y-chromosome

**Yoga** ▶ JOGA
**Ypsilon** *das;* ∼[s], ∼s y, Y; (im griechischen Alphabet) upsilon

# Zz

**z, Z** /tsɛt/ *das;* ∼, ∼: z/Z
**Zack**: auf ∼ sein (ugs.: tüchtig sein) be on the ball (coll.) *or* one's toes; jmdn. auf ∼ bringen (ugs.) knock sb. into shape (coll.)
**Zacke** *die;* ∼, ∼n point; peak; (einer Säge, eines Kamms) tooth; (einer Gabel, Harke) prong
**Zacken** *der;* ∼s: ▶ ZACKE
**zackig** [1] *Adj.* (a) (gezackt) jagged; (mit kleinen, regelmäßigen Zacken) serrated
(b) (schneidig) dashing; smart; rousing ⟨*music*⟩; brisk ⟨*orders, tempo*⟩; lively ⟨*organization*⟩
[2] *adv.* (a) (gezackt) jaggedly
(b) (schneidig) smartly; ⟨*play music*⟩ rousingly
**zaghaft** [1] *Adj.* timid; (zögernd) hesitant
[2] *adv.* timidly; (zögernd) hesitantly
**Zaghaftigkeit** *die;* ∼: timidity; (Zögern) hesitancy
**zäh** [1] *Adj.* (a) tough; heavy ⟨*dough, soil*⟩; (dickflüssig) glutinous; viscous ⟨*oil*⟩

(b) (widerstandsfähig) tough ⟨*person*⟩
(c) (beharrlich) tenacious; tough ⟨*negotiations*⟩; dogged ⟨*resistance*⟩
[2] *adv.* (beharrlich) tenaciously; ⟨*resist*⟩ doggedly
**Zähheit** *die;* ∼: (a) (Festigkeit) toughness; (des Teigs, Bodens) heaviness; (Dickflüssigkeit) glutinousness; (von Öl) viscosity
(b) (Widerstandsfähigkeit) toughness
(c) (Beharrlichkeit) tenacity; (des Widerstands) doggedness
**Zähigkeit** *die;* ∼ (a) (Widerstandsfähigkeit) toughness
(b) (Beharrlichkeit) tenacity; mit ∼: tenaciously
**Zahl** *die;* ∼, ∼en number; (Ziffer) numeral; (Zahlenangabe, Geldmenge) figure; in den roten/ schwarzen ∼en in the red/black
**zahlbar** *Adj.* (Kaufmannsspr.) payable
**zahlen** [1] *tr. V.* pay (an + *Akk.* to) ⋯⋗

2 *itr. V.* pay; [ich möchte] bitte ~ (im Lokal) [can I have] the bill, please!

**zählen** 1 *itr. V.* (a) count; **zu einer Gruppe** *usw.* ~: be one of *or* belong to a group *etc.;* (b) **auf jmdn./etw.** ~: count on sb./sth 2 *tr. V.* count; **jmdn. zu seinen Freunden** ~: count sb. among one's friends

**zahl-, Zahl-:** ~**karte** *die* (Postw.) paying-in slip; ~**los** *Adj.* countless; ~**reich** *Adj.* numerous

**Zahlung** *die;* ~, ~**en** payment

**Zählung** *die;* ~, ~**en** counting; **eine** ~: a count

**zahlungs-, Zahlungs-:** ~**bilanz** *die* (Wirtsch.) balance of payments; ~**fähig** *Adj.* solvent; ~**fähigkeit** *die* solvency; ~**mittel** *das* means of payment; ~**unfähig** *Adj.* insolvent; ~**unfähigkeit** *die* insolvency

**Zahl·wort** *das; Pl.* **Zahl·wörter** (Sprachw.) numeral

**zahm** 1 *Adj.* tame 2 *adv.* tamely

**zähmen** *tr. V.* (auch fig.) tame

**Zahn** *der;* ~[e]s, **Zähne** tooth; (Reißzahn) fang; (an einer Briefmarke usw.) serration

**Zahn-:** ~**arzt** *der,* ~**ärztin** *die* dentist; (mit chirurgischer Ausbildung) dental surgeon; ~**bürste** *die* toothbrush

**zahnen** *itr. V.* ⟨baby⟩ be teething

**zahn-, Zahn-:** ~**ersatz** *der* denture; ~**fleisch** *das* gum; (als Ganzes) gums *pl.;* ~**fleisch·bluten** *das;* ~~**s** bleeding gums *pl.;* ~**los** *Adj.* toothless; ~**lücke** *die* gap in one's teeth; ~**pasta** *die;* ~~, ~**pasten** toothpaste; ~**pflege** *die* dental care; ~**prothese** *die* dentures *pl.;* [set *sing.* of] false teeth *pl.;* ~**rad** *das* gearwheel; (für Ketten) sprocket; ~**schmerzen** *Pl.* toothache *sing.;* ~**seide** *die* dental floss; ~**spange** *die* [tooth] brace; ~**stein** *der* tartar; ~**stocher** *der;* ~~**s**, ~~: toothpick; ~**weh** *das* (ugs.) toothache

**Zange** *die;* ~, ~**n** (a) (Werkzeug) pliers *pl.;* (Eiswürfel-, Zuckerzange) tongs *pl.;* (Geburtszange) forceps *pl.;* (Kneifzange) pincers *pl.;* **eine** ~: a pair of pliers/tongs/forceps/pincers (b) (bei Tieren) pincer

**Zank** *der;* ~[e]s squabble; row

**zanken** *refl.* (auch itr.) V. squabble, bicker (**um** od. **über** + Akk. over)

**zänkisch** *Adj.* quarrelsome

**Zäpfchen** *das;* ~**s**, ~: suppository

**zapfen** *tr. V.* tap, draw ⟨beer, wine⟩

**Zapfen** *der;* ~**s**, ~ (a) (Bot.) cone (b) (Stöpsel) plug

**Zapf·säule** *die* petrol pump (Brit.); gasoline pump (Amer.)

**zappeln** *itr. V.* wriggle; ⟨child⟩ fidget

**zappen** /'zɛpn/ *itr. V.* (ugs.) zap (coll.)

**Zar** *der;* ~**en**, ~**en** (hist.) Tsar

**Zarin** *die;* ~, ~**nen** (hist.) Tsarina

**zart** 1 *Adj.* (auch fig.) delicate; soft ⟨skin⟩; tender ⟨bud, shoot; meat, vegetables⟩; fine ⟨biscuits⟩; gentle ⟨kiss, touch⟩; soft ⟨pastel colours⟩ 2 *adv.* (empfindlich) delicately; ⟨kiss, touch⟩ gently

**Zartheit** *die;* ~: delicacy; (der Haut) softness; (von Fleisch, Gemüse) tenderness; (eines Kusses, einer Berührung) gentleness

**zärtlich** 1 *Adj.* tender 2 *adv.* tenderly

**Zärtlichkeit** *die;* ~, ~**en** (a) (Zuneigung) tenderness; affection (b) (Liebkosung) caress

**Zauber** *der;* ~**s**, ~ (a) (auch fig.) magic; (Bann) [magic] spell (b) (ugs. abwertend: Aufheben) fuss

**Zauberei** *die;* ~, ~**en** (a) (das Zaubern) magic (b) (Zaubertrick) magic trick

**Zauberer** *der;* ~**s**, ~: magician

**zauber·haft** 1 *Adj.* enchanting 2 *adv.* enchantingly

**Zauberin** *die;* ~, ~**nen** (a) sorceress (b) (Zauberkünstlerin) conjurer

**Zauber·künstler** *der,* **Zauberkünstlerin** *die* conjurer; magician

**zaubern** 1 *itr. V.* (a) do magic (b) (Zaubertricks ausführen) do conjuring tricks 2 *tr. V.* (auch fig.) conjure

**zaudern** *itr. V.* (geh.) delay

**Zaum** *der;* ~[e]s, **Zäume** bridle

**zäumen** *tr. V.* bridle

**Zaum·zeug** *das* bridle

**Zaun** *der;* ~[e]s, **Zäune** fence

**Zaun·könig** *der* wren

**z. B.** *Abk.* = **zum Beispiel** e.g.

**ZDF** *das;* ~: *Abk.* = **Zweites Deutsches Fernsehen** Second German Television Channel

**Zebra** *das;* ~**s**, ~**s** zebra

**Zebra·streifen** *der* zebra crossing (Brit.); pedestrian crossing

**Zeche** *die;* ~, ~**n** (a) (Rechnung) bill (Brit.); check (Amer.) (b) (Bergwerk) pit; mine

**zechen** *itr. V.* (veralt., scherzh.) tipple

**Zecke** *die;* ~, ~**n** (Zool.) tick

**Zeder** *die;* ~, ~**n** cedar

**Zedern·holz** *das* cedarwood

**Zeh** *der;* ~**s**, ~**en**, **Zehe** *die;* ~, ~**n** (a) toe (b) (Knoblauchzehe) clove

**Zehen·spitze** *die:* **auf** ~**n** on tiptoe

**zehn** *Kardinalz.* ten

**Zehn** *die;* ~, ~**en** ten

**Zehner** *der;* ~**s**, ~ (a) (ugs.: Geldschein, Münze) ten (b) (ugs.: Autobus) number ten (c) (Math.) ten

z (circled letter in left margin)

**zehn·fach** *Vervielfältigungsz.* tenfold

**Zehnfache** *das; adj. Dekl.* **das** ∼: ten times as much

**zehn-, Zehn-:** ∼**kampf** *der* (Sport) decathlon; ∼**mal** *Adv.* ten times; ∼**mark·schein** *der* ten-mark note; ∼**pfennig-[brief]marke** *die* ten-pfennig stamp; ∼**pfennig·stück** *das* ten-pfennig piece

**zehnt...** *Ordinalz.* tenth;

**zehn·tausend** *Kardinalz.* ten thousand

**zehntel** *Bruchz.* tenth

**Zehntel** *das* (schweiz. meist *der*); ∼**s**, ∼: tenth

**zehntens** *Adv.* tenthly

**zehren** *itr. V.* **von etw.** ∼: live on or off sth.

**Zeichen** *das;* ∼**s**, ∼: sign; (Markierung) mark; (Chemie, Math., auf Landkarten usw.) symbol; (Schrift∼) character; **jmdm. ein** ∼ **geben** signal to sb.

**Zeichen-:** ∼**setzung** *die;* ∼∼: punctuation; ∼**sprache** *die* sign language

**zeichnen** [1] *tr. V.* draw; (fig.) portray ⟨character⟩ [2] *itr. V.* draw

**Zeichner** *der;* ∼**s**, ∼, **Zeichnerin** *die;* ∼, ∼**nen** graphic artist; (Technik) draughtsman/-woman

**Zeichnung** *die;* ∼, ∼**en** drawing

**zeichnungs·berechtigt** *Adj.* with signatory powers *postpos.;* ∼ **sein** have signatory powers

**Zeige·finger** *der* index finger; forefinger

**zeigen** [1] *itr. V.* point [2] *tr. V.* show [3] *refl. V.* **(a)** (sich sehen lassen) appear **(b)** (sich erweisen) prove to be; **es wird sich** ∼, ...: time will tell ...

**Zeiger** *der;* ∼**s**, ∼: pointer; (Uhrzeiger) hand

**Zeile** *die;* ∼, ∼**n** line; (Reihe) row

**zeit** *Präp. mit Gen.* ∼ **meines** *usw./*unseres *usw.* **Lebens** all my *etc.* life/our *etc.* lives

**Zeit** *die;* ∼, ∼**en (a)** time *no art.;* **mit der** ∼: with *or* in time; (allmählich) gradually; **eine** ∼ **lang** for a while **(b)** (Zeitpunkt) time; **alles zu seiner** ∼: all in good time; *\*zur* ∼: at the moment **(c)** (Zeit-, Lebensabschnitt) time; period; (Geschichtsabschnitt) age; period **(d)** (Sprachw.) tense

**zeit-, Zeit-:** ∼**alter** *das* age; era; ∼**arbeit** *die* (Wirtsch.) temporary work; work as a temp (coll.); ∼**druck** *der* pressure of time; **unter** ∼**druck** under pressure; **unter** ∼**druck stehen** be pressed for time; ∼**geist** *der* spirit of the age; ∼**gemäß** *Adj.* (modern) up-to-date; (aktuell) topical ⟨theme⟩; contemporary ⟨views⟩; ∼**genosse** *der,* ∼**genossin** *die* contemporary; ∼**genössisch** *Adj.* contemporary; ∼**geschehen** *das:* **das** [aktuelle] ∼**geschehen** current events *pl.;* ∼**geschichte** *die* contemporary history *no art.*

**zeitig** *Adj., adv.* early

**zeit-, Zeit-:** ∼**karte** *die* (Verkehrsw.) season ticket; *\**∼**lang** ▶ ZEIT A; ∼**lebens** *Adv.* all my/his/her *etc.* life

**zeitlich** [1] *Adj.* ⟨length, interval⟩ in time; chronological ⟨order, sequence⟩ [2] *adv.* with regard to time

**zeit-, Zeit-:** ∼**los** [1] *Adj.* timeless; classic ⟨fashion, shape⟩; [2] *adv.* timelessly; ∼**lupe** *die* slow motion; ∼**mangel** *der* lack of time; ∼**punkt** *der* moment; ∼**raubend** *Adj.* time-consuming; ∼**raum** *der* period; ∼**schrift** *die* magazine; (bes. wissenschaftlich) journal; periodical; ∼**spanne** *die* period

**Zeitung** *die;* ∼, ∼**en** [news]paper

**Zeitungs-:** ∼**ausschnitt** *der* newspaper cutting; ∼**notiz** *die* newspaper item

**zeit-, Zeit-:** ∼**unterschied** *der* time difference; ∼**verschwendung** *die* waste of time; ∼**vertreib** *der;* ∼∼[e]s, ∼∼e pastime; **zum** ∼**vertreib** to pass the time; ∼**weilig** [1] *Adj.* temporary; [2] *adv.* temporarily; ∼**weise** *Adv.* (gelegentlich) occasionally; (von Zeit zu Zeit) from time to time; ∼**wort** *das; Pl.* ∼**wörter** (Sprachw.) verb; ∼**zünder** *der* time fuse

**Zelle** *die;* ∼, ∼**n** cell

**Zelluloid** /tsɛlu'lɔyt/ *das;* ∼[e]s celluloid

**Zelt** *das;* ∼[e]s, ∼e tent; (Festzelt) marquee; (Zirkuszelt) big top

**zelten** *itr. V.* camp

**Zelt-:** ∼**lager** *das* camp; ∼**plane** *die* tarpaulin

**Zement** *der;* ∼[e]s, ∼e cement

**Zensur** *die;* ∼, ∼**en (a)** (Schulw.: Note) mark; grade (Amer.) **(b)** (Kontrolle) censorship **(c)** (Behörde) censors *pl.*

**Zenti-:** ∼**meter** *der, auch: das* centimetre; ∼**meter·maß** *das* [centimetre] measuring tape

**Zentner** *der;* ∼**s**, ∼ **(a)** metric hundredweight **(b)** (österr., schweiz.) ▶ DOPPELZENTNER

**zentral** [1] *Adj.* central [2] *adv.* centrally

**Zentral·bank** *die; Pl.* ∼**en** (Finanzw.) central bank

**Zentrale** *die;* ∼, ∼**n (a)** (zentrale Stelle) head *or* central office; (der Polizei, einer Partei) headquarters *sing. or pl.;* (Funkzentrale) control centre **(b)** (Telefonzentrale) [telephone] exchange; (eines Hotels, einer Firma o. Ä.) switchboard

**Zentral-:** ∼**figur** *die* central figure; ∼**heizung** *die* central heating; ∼**speicher** *der* (DV) main memory

**Zentren** ▶ ZENTRUM

**Zentrifugal·kraft** *die* (Physik) centrifugal force

**Z**

**Zentrifuge** *die;* ∼, ∼n centrifuge

**Zentrum** *das;* ∼s, Zentren centre; **im** ∼: at the centre; (im Stadtzentrum) in the town/city centre

**Zeppelin** *der;* ∼s, ∼e Zeppelin

**Zepter** *das, auch: der;* ∼s, ∼: sceptre

**zerbeißen** *unr. tr. V.* bite in two

**zerbersten** *unr. itr. V.; mit sein* burst apart

**zerbrechen** [1] *unr. itr. V.; mit sein* break [into pieces]; smash [to pieces]; ⟨glass⟩ shatter; (fig.) ⟨marriage, relationship⟩ break up
[2] *unr. tr. V.* break; smash, shatter ⟨dishes, glass⟩

**zerbrechlich** *Adj.* fragile; (fig.) frail

**Zerbrechlichkeit** *die;* ∼: fragility; (fig.) frailty

**zerbröckeln** [1] *itr. V.; mit sein* crumble away
[2] *tr. V.* break into small pieces

**zerdrücken** *tr. V.* mash

**Zeremonie** *die;* ∼, ∼n ceremony; (fig.) ritual

**Zeremoniell** *das;* ∼s, ∼e ceremonial

**zerfallen** *unr. itr. V.; mit sein* (auch fig.) disintegrate (**in** + *Akk.,* **zu** into); ⟨building⟩ fall into ruin, decay; ⟨corpse⟩ decompose, decay

**zerfetzen** *tr. V.* rip *or* tear to pieces; (fig.) tear apart ⟨body, limb⟩

**zerfleischen** *tr. V.* tear ⟨person, animal⟩ limb from limb

**zerfressen** *unr. tr. V.* **(a)** eat away; ⟨moth etc.⟩ eat holes in
**(b)** (zersetzen) corrode ⟨metal⟩; eat away ⟨bone⟩

**zergehen** *unr. itr. V.; mit sein* melt; (in Wasser, im Mund) ⟨tablet etc.⟩ dissolve

**zerhacken** *tr. V.* chop up (**zu** into)

**zerhauen** *unr. tr. V.* chop up

**zerkleinern** *tr. V.* chop up; (zermahlen) crush ⟨rock etc.⟩

**zerknautschen** *tr. V.* (ugs.) crumple

**zerknirscht** [1] *Adj.* remorseful
[2] *adv.* remorsefully

**zerknittern** *tr. V.* crease; crumple

**zerknüllen** *tr. V.* crumple up [into a ball]

**zerkratzen** *tr. V.* scratch

**zerkrümeln** *tr. V.* crumble up

**zerlegen** *tr. V.* **(a)** dismantle; take to pieces
**(b)** (zerschneiden) cut up ⟨animal, meat⟩; carve ⟨joint⟩

**zerlumpt** *Adj.* ragged ⟨clothes, person⟩

**zerplatzen** *itr. V.; mit sein* burst

**Zerr·bild** *das* distorted image

**zerreiben** *unr. tr. V.* crush

**zerreißen** [1] *unr. tr. V.* **(a)** tear up; (in kleine Stücke) tear to pieces; break ⟨thread⟩

**(b)** (beschädigen) tear ⟨stocking, trousers, etc.⟩ (**an** + *Dat.* on)
[2] *unr. itr. V.; mit sein* ⟨thread, string, rope⟩ break; ⟨paper, cloth, etc.⟩ tear

**Zerreiß·probe** *die* acid test

**zerren** [1] *tr. V.* **(a)** drag
**(b) sich** (*Dat.*) **einen Muskel/eine Sehne** ∼: pull a muscle/tendon
[2] *tr. V.* **an etw.** (*Dat.*) ∼: tug *or* pull at sth

**Zerrung** *die;* ∼, ∼en pulled muscle/tendon

**zerrütten** *tr. V.* ruin; shatter ⟨nerves⟩

**zerschellen** *itr. V.; mit sein* be dashed *or* smashed to pieces

**zerschlagen** [1] *unr. tr. V.* smash ⟨plate, windscreen, etc.⟩; smash up ⟨furniture⟩; (fig.) smash ⟨spy ring etc.⟩
[2] *unr. refl. V.* ⟨plan, deal⟩ fall through

**zerschmettern** *tr. V.* smash; shatter ⟨glass, leg, bone⟩

**zerschneiden** *unr. tr. V.* cut; (in Stücke) cut up; (in zwei Teile) cut in two

**zersetzen** *tr. V.* corrode ⟨metal⟩; decompose ⟨organism⟩

**zersplittern** *itr. V.; mit sein* ⟨wood, bone⟩ splinter; ⟨glass⟩ shatter

**zerspringen** *unr. itr. V.; mit sein* shatter; (Sprünge bekommen) crack

**zerstäuben** *tr. V.* spray

**zerstören** *tr. V.* destroy; ⟨hooligan⟩ smash up, vandalize; (fig.) ruin ⟨health, life⟩

**Zerstörung** *die;* ∼, ∼en ▶ ZERSTÖREN: destruction; smashing up; vandalization; (fig.) ruin[ation]

**Zerstörungs·wut** *die* destructive frenzy

**zerstreuen** [1] *tr. V.* scatter; disperse ⟨crowd⟩; **jmdn./sich** ∼ (ablenken) take sb.'s/ one's mind off things
[2] *refl. V.* disperse; (schneller) scatter

**zerstreut** [1] *Adj.* distracted; (vergesslich) absent-minded
[2] *adv.* absentmindedly

**Zerstreuung** *die;* ∼, ∼en (Ablenkung) diversion

**zerstückeln** *tr. V.* break ⟨sth.⟩ up into small pieces; (zerschneiden) cut *or* chop ⟨sth.⟩ up into small pieces; dismember ⟨corpse⟩

**zerteilen** *tr. V.* divide into pieces; (zerschneiden) cut into pieces; cut up

**Zertifikat** *das;* ∼[e]s, ∼e certificate

**zertrampeln** *tr. V.* trample all over ⟨flower bed etc.⟩; trample ⟨child etc.⟩ underfoot

**zertreten** *unr. tr. V.* stamp on; stamp out ⟨cigarette, match⟩

**zertrümmern** *tr. V.* smash; smash, shatter ⟨glass⟩; smash up ⟨furniture⟩; wreck ⟨car, boat⟩; reduce ⟨building⟩ to ruins

**Zerwürfnis** *das;* ∼ses, ∼se (geh.) quarrel; dispute; (Bruch) rift

**zerzausen** *tr. V.* ruffle; **zerzaust aussehen** look dishevelled

**zetern** *itr. V.* scold [shrilly]; (sich beklagen) moan (**über** + *Akk.* about)

---

*\*alte Schreibung · vgl. Hinweis auf S. xiv

**Zettel** *der;* ~s, ~: slip *or* piece of paper; (mit einigen Zeilen) note; (Bekanntmachung) notice; (Formular) form; (Kassenzettel) receipt; (Handzettel) leaflet

**Zeug** *das;* ~[e]s, ~e (a) (ugs.) stuff; **dummes** ~: nonsense; rubbish (b) (Kleidung) things *pl.*

**Zeuge** *der;* ~n, ~n witness

**zeugen** *tr. V.* procreate; ⟨man⟩ father ⟨child⟩

**Zeugen·aussage** *die* testimony

**Zeugin** *die;* ~, ~nen witness

**Zeugnis** *das;* ~ses, ~se (a) (Schulw.) report (b) (Arbeitszeugnis) reference; testimonial (c) (Gutachten) certificate

**Zeugung** *die;* ~, ~en procreation; (eines Kindes) fathering

**zeugungs·fähig** *Adj.* fertile

**z. Hd.** *Abk.* = **zu Händen** attn.

**Zicke** *die;* ~, ~n (a) ▶ ZIEGE; (b) *Pl.* (ugs.: Dummheiten) stupid tricks; monkey business *sing.* (coll.); ~n **machen** mess about; (Schwierigkeiten machen) make trouble

**Zickzack** *der;* ~[e]s, ~e zigzag

**Ziege** *die;* ~, ~n goat; (Schimpfwort: Frau) cow (sl. derog.)

**Ziegel** *der;* ~s, ~ brick; (Dachziegel) tile

**Ziegelei** *die;* ~, ~en brickworks *sing.*

**Ziegel·stein** *der* brick

**Ziegen-:** ~**bock** *der* he- *or* billy goat; ~**käse** *der* goat's cheese

**ziehen** ① *unr. tr. V.* (a) pull; (sanfter) draw; (zerren) tug; (schleppen) drag; **etw. nach sich** ~ (fig.) result in sth.; entail sth.
(b) (herausziehen) extract ⟨tooth⟩; take out, remove ⟨stitches⟩; draw ⟨cord, sword, pistol⟩; **den Hut** ~: raise one's hat; **die [Quadrat]wurzel** ~ (Math.) extract the square root
(c) (dehnen) stretch ⟨elastic etc.⟩; stretch out ⟨sheets etc.⟩
(d) (Gesichtspartien bewegen) make ⟨face, grimace⟩
(e) (bei Brettspielen) move ⟨chessman etc.⟩
(f) (zeichnen) draw ⟨line etc.⟩
(g) (anlegen) dig ⟨trench⟩; build ⟨wall⟩; erect ⟨fence⟩; put up ⟨washing line⟩; run, lay ⟨cable, wires⟩; draw ⟨frontier⟩
(h) (aufziehen) grow ⟨plants, flowers⟩; breed ⟨animals⟩
② *unr. itr. V.* (a) (reißen) pull; **an etw.** (Dat.) ~: pull on sth.
(b) (funktionieren) ⟨stove, pipe, chimney⟩ draw
(c) *mit sein* (umziehen) move (**nach, in** + *Akk.* to)
(d) *mit sein* (gehen) go; (marschieren) march; (umherstreifen) roam; (weggehen) go away; leave; ⟨fog, clouds⟩ drift
(e) (saugen) draw; **an einer Zigarette/Pfeife** ~: draw on a cigarette/pipe
(f) ⟨tea, coffee⟩ draw
(g) (Kochk.) simmer
(h) *unpers.* **es zieht** there's a draught

③ *unr. refl. V.* ⟨road⟩ run, stretch; ⟨frontier⟩ run

**Zieh·harmonika** *die* piano accordion

**Ziehung** *die;* ~, ~en draw

**Ziel** *das;* ~[e]s, ~e (a) destination (b) (Sport) finish; (Ziellinie) finishing line; (Pferderennen) finishing post (c) (Zielscheibe; auch Milit.) target (d) (Zweck) aim; goal; **sein** ~ **erreichen** achieve one's objective *or* aim

**ziel·bewusst, *ziel·bewußt** ① *Adj.* determined ② *adv.* determinedly

**zielen** *itr. V.* aim (**auf** + *Akk.*, at); (fig.) **auf jmdn./etw.** ~ ⟨reproach, efforts, etc.⟩ be aimed at sb./sth.

**ziel-, Ziel-:** ~**gruppe** *die* target group; ~**los** ① *Adj.* aimless; ② *adv.* aimlessly; ~**losigkeit** *die;* ~~: aimlessness; ~**scheibe** *die* (auch fig.) target (*Gen.* for); ~**strebig** ① *Adj.* (a) purposeful; (b) (energisch) single-minded ⟨person⟩; ② *adv.* (a) purposefully; (b) (energisch) single-mindedly; ~**strebigkeit** *die;* ~~ ▶ ~STREBIG: (a) purposefulness; (b) single-mindedness; ~**wahl** *die* (Fernspr.) one-touch dialling

**ziemlich** ① *Adj.* (ugs.) fair, sizeable ⟨quantity, number⟩ ② *adv.* (a) quite; fairly (b) (ugs.: fast) pretty well

**Zierde** *die;* ~, ~n (auch fig.) ornament

**zieren** *refl. V.* be coy

**zierlich** ① *Adj.* dainty; petite, dainty ⟨woman, figure⟩ ② *adv.* daintily

**Zierlichkeit** *die;* ~: daintiness; (einer Frau, Gestalt) petiteness; daintiness

**Zier·pflanze** *die* ornamental plant

**Ziffer** *die;* ~, ~n numeral; (in einer mehrstelligen Zahl) digit; figure

**Ziffer·blatt** *das* dial; face

**zig** *unbest. Zahlwort* (ugs.) umpteen (coll.)

**Zigarette** *die;* ~, ~n cigarette

**Zigaretten·werbung** *die* cigarette advertising

**Zigarillo** *der od. das;* ~s, ~s cigarillo; small cigar

**Zigarre** *die;* ~, ~n cigar

**Zigeuner** *der;* ~s, ~, **Zigeunerin** *die;* ~, ~nen gypsy

**zig·mal** *Adv.* (ugs.) umpteen times (coll.)

**zig·tausend** *unbest. Zahlwort* (ugs.) umpteen thousand (coll.)

**Zimmer** *das;* ~s, ~: room

**Zimmer·mädchen** *das* chambermaid

**zimmern** *tr. V.* make ⟨shelves etc.⟩

**Zimmer-:** ~**suche** *die* room-hunt; ~**vermittlung** *die* accommodation office

**zimperlich** ① *Adj.* timid; (leicht angeekelt) squeamish; (prüde) prissy ② *adv.: s. Adj.:* timidly; squeamishly; prissily

**Zimperlichkeit** *die;* ~, ~en (abwertend) timidity; (Neigung zum Ekel) squeamishness; (Prüderie) prissiness

**Zimt** *der;* ~[e]s, ~e cinnamon

**Zink** *das;* ~[e]s zinc

**Zinke** *die;* ~, ~n prong; (eines Kamms) tooth

**Zinn** *das;* ~[e]s tin; (Gegenstände) pewter[ware]

**Zins** *der;* ~es, ~en interest

**Zinses-zins** *der* compound interest

**zins-los** ⓵ *Adj.* interest-free ⓶ *adv.* free of interest

**Zins-satz** *der* interest rate

**Zipfel** *der;* ~s, ~ (einer Decke, eines Tisch-, Handtuchs usw.) corner; (Wurstzipfel, eines Halstuchs) [tail] end

**Zipfel-mütze** *die* [long-]pointed cap

**zirka** *Adv.* about; approximately

**Zirkulation** *die,* ~, ~en circulation

**zirkulieren** *itr. V.; auch mit sein* circulate

**Zirkus** *der;* ~, ~se (a) circus (b) (ugs.) (Trubel) hustle and bustle; (Krach) to-do

**zirpen** *itr. V.* chirp

**zischeln** *tr. V.* whisper angrily

**zischen** *itr. V.* (a) hiss; ‹hot fat› sizzle (b) *mit sein* hiss

**Zitat** *das;* ~[e]s, ~e quotation (aus from)

**zitieren** *tr., itr. V.* (a) quote; (Rechtsspr.) cite (b) (rufen) summon

**Zitronat** *das;* ~[e]s candied lemon peel

**Zitrone** *die;* ~, ~n lemon

**Zitronen-:** ~**limonade** *die* lemonade; ~**presse** *die* lemon squeezer; ~**saft** *der* lemon juice

**Zitrus-frucht** *die* citrus fruit

**zittern** *itr. V.* tremble (vor + *Dat.* with); (vor Kälte) shiver; (beben) ‹walls, windows› shake; **vor jmdm./etw.** ~: be terrified of sb./sth.

**Zitter-partie** *die* nail-biting affair

**zittrig** *Adj.* shaky; doddery ‹old man›

**Zitze** *die;* ~, ~n teat

**zivil** ⓵ *Adj.* (a) civilian; non-military ‹purposes›; civil ‹aviation, marriage, law, defence› (b) (annehmbar) decent ⓶ *adv.* (annehmbar) decently

**Zivil** *das;* ~s civilian clothes *pl.*

**Zivil-bevölkerung** *die* civilian population

**Zivilisation** /tsivili̯za'tsi̯o:n/ *die;* ~, ~en civilization

**zivilisieren** *tr. V.* civilize

**zivilisiert** ⓵ *Adj.* civilized ⓶ *adv.* in a civilized way

**Zivilist** *der;* ~en, ~en, **Zivilistin** *die;* ~, ~nen civilian

**Zivil-kleidung** *die* civilian clothes *pl.*

**Zofe** *die;* ~, ~n (hist.) lady's maid

**zoffen** *refl. V.* (ugs.) quarrel (**mit** with)

---

*old spelling - see note on page xiv

**zog** *1. u. 3. Pers. Sg. Prät. v.* ZIEHEN

**zögerlich** ⓵ *Adj.* hesitant; tentative ⓶ *adv.* hesitantly; tentatively

**zögern** *itr. V.* hesitate; **ohne zu** ~: without hesitation

**Zoll** *der;* ~[e]s, Zölle (a) [customs] duty (b) (Behörde) customs *pl.*

**zoll-, Zoll-:** ~**amt** *das* customs house *or* office; ~**beamte** *der,* ~**beamtin** *die* customs officer; ~**erklärung** *die* customs declaration; ~**frei** ⓵ *Adj.* duty-free; free of duty *pred.;* ⓶ *adv.* free of duty; ~**kontrolle** *die* customs examination *or* check; ~**stock** *der* folding rule

**Zone** *die;* ~, ~n zone

**Zoo** *der;* ~s, ~s zoo

**Zoologe** *der;* ~n, ~n zoologist

**Zoologie** *die;* ~: zoology *no art.*

**Zoologin** *die;* ~, ~nen zoologist

**zoologisch** *Adj.* zoological; ~**er Garten** zoological gardens *pl.*

**Zoom** *das;* ~s, ~s (Film, Fot.) zoom

**Zoom-objektiv** *das* (Film, Fot.) zoom lens

**Zopf** *der;* ~[e]s, Zöpfe plait; (am Hinterkopf) pigtail

**Zorn** *der;* ~[e]s anger; (stärker) wrath; fury

**zornig** ⓵ *Adj.* furious ⓶ *adv.* furiously

**Zote** *die;* ~, ~n dirty joke

**zotig** ⓵ *Adj.* smutty; dirty ‹joke› ⓶ *adv.* smuttily

**zottig** *Adj.* shaggy

**zu** ⓵ *Präp. mit Dat.* (a) (Richtung) to; **zu ... hin** towards ... (b) (zusammen mit) with; **zu dem Käse gab es Wein** there was wine with the cheese (c) (Lage) at; **zu beiden Seiten** on both sides (d) (zeitlich) at; **zu Weihnachten** at Christmas (e) (Art u. Weise) **zu meiner Zufriedenheit/ Überraschung** to my satisfaction/surprise; (bei Mengenangaben) **zu Dutzenden/zweien** by the dozen/in twos (f) (ein Zahlenverhältnis ausdrückend) **ein Verhältnis von 3 zu 1** a ratio of 3 to 1 (g) (einen Preis zuordnend) at; for (h) (Zweck) for (i) (Ziel, Ergebnis) into; **zu etw. werden** turn into sth. (j) (über) about; on; **sich zu etw. äußern** comment on sth. (k) (gegenüber) freundlich/hässlich **zu jmdm. sein** be friendly/nasty to sb.; *s. auch* ZUM; ZUR; ⓶ *Adv.* (a) (allzu) too; **zu sehr/viel** too much; **zu wenig** too little (b) *nachgestellt* (Richtung) towards ⓷ *Konj.* (a) *mit Infinitiv* too; **was gibts da zu lachen?** what is there to laugh about? (b) *mit 1. Part.* **die zu erledigende Post** the letters *pl.* to be dealt with

**Zubehör** *das;* ~[e]s, ~e *od. schweiz.* ~**den** accessories *pl.;* (eines Staubsaugers, Mixers usw.) attachments *pl.;* (Ausstattung) equipment

**z**

**zu|bereiten** *tr. V.* prepare ‹*meal etc.*›; make up ‹*medicine, ointment*›; (kochen) cook ‹*fish, meat, etc.*›

**zu|billigen** *tr. V.* jmdm. etw. ~: grant *or* allow sb. sth.

**zu|binden** *unr. tr. V.* tie [up]

**zu|blinzeln** *itr. V.* jmdm. ~: wink at sb.

**zu|bringen** *unr. tr. V.* spend

**Zu·bringer** *der;* ~s, ~ (a) (Straße) access road
(b) (Verkehrsmittel) shuttle

**Zucht** *die;* ~, ~en (a) breeding; (von Pflanzen) cultivation; **ein Pferd aus deutscher** ~: a German-bred horse
(b) (geh.: Disziplin) discipline

**züchten** *tr. V.* (auch fig.) breed; cultivate ‹*plants*›; culture ‹*bacteria, pearls*›

**Züchter** *der;* ~s, ~, **Züchterin** *die;* ~, ~nen breeder; (von Pflanzen) grower [of new varieties]

**züchtigen** *tr. V.* (geh.) beat; thrash; (fig.: bestrafen) castigate

**Züchtigung** *die;* ~, ~en (geh.) beating; thrashing; (fig.: Bestrafung) castigation

**Züchtung** *die;* ~, ~en (a) breeding; (von Pflanzen) cultivation
(b) (Zuchtergebnis) strain

**zucken** *itr. V.; mit Richtungsangabe mit sein* twitch; ‹*body, arm, leg, etc.*› jerk; (vor Schreck) start; ‹*flames*› flicker; **mit den Achseln/Schultern** ~: shrug one's shoulders

**zücken** *tr. V.* draw ‹*sword, dagger, knife*›

**Zucker** *der;* ~s, ~ (a) sugar
(b) (ugs.: Diabetes) diabetes; ~ **haben** be a diabetic

**zucker-, Zucker-:** ~**dose** *die* sugar bowl; ~**hut** *der* sugar loaf; ~**krank** *Adj.* diabetic

**zuckern** *tr. V.* sugar

**Zucker·wasser** *das* sugar water

**Zuckung** *die;* ~, ~en twitch

**zu|decken** *tr. V.* cover up; cover [over] ‹*well, ditch*›; jmdn./sich ~: tuck sb./oneself up

**zu|drehen** *tr. V.* (a) (abdrehen) turn off
(b) (zuwenden) jmdm. den Rücken ~: turn one's back on sb.

**zu·dringlich** 1 *Adj.* pushy (coll.), pushing ‹*person, manner*›; (sexuell) importunate ‹*person, manner*›; prying ‹*glance*›
2 *adv.* importunately

**Zu·dringlichkeit** *die;* ~, ~en (a) pushiness (coll.); (in sexueller Hinsicht) importunate manner
(b) (Handlung) ~en insistent advances *or* attentions

**zu|drücken** *tr. V.* press shut; push ‹*door*› shut; jmdm. die Kehle ~: choke *or* throttle sb.

**zu·einander** *Adv.* to one another

**zu·erst** *Adv.* (a) first
(b) (anfangs) at first; to start with

(c) (erstmals) first

**Zu·fahrt** *die* (a) access [for vehicles]
(b) (Straße, Weg) access road; (zum Haus) driveway

**Zufahrts·straße** *die* access road

**Zu·fall** *der* chance; (zufälliges Zusammentreffen von Ereignissen) coincidence; **durch** ~: by chance

**zu|fallen** *unr. itr. V.; mit sein* (a) ‹*door etc.*› slam shut; ‹*eyes*› close
(b) (zukommen) jmdm. ~ ‹*task*› fall to sb.; ‹*prize, inheritance*› go to sb.

**zu·fällig** 1 *Adj.* accidental; chance attrib. ‹*meeting, acquaintance*›; random ‹*selection*›
2 *adv.* by chance; **wissen Sie** ~, **wie spät es ist?** (ugs.) do you by any chance know the time?

**Zufalls·treffer** *der* fluke

**zu|fassen** *itr. V.* make a snatch *or* grab

**zu|faxen** *tr. V.* jmdm. etw. ~: fax sth. to sb.; fax sb. sth.

**zu|fliegen** *unr. itr. V.; mit sein* (ugs.) ‹*door, window, etc.*› slam shut

**Zu·flucht** *die* refuge (vor + *Dat.* from); (vor Unwetter o. Ä.) shelter (vor + *Dat.* from)

**Zufluchts·ort** *der* place of refuge; sanctuary

**Zu·fluss,** *****Zu·fluß** *der* (a) (das Zufließen) inflow; supply; (fig.) influx
(b) (Gewässer) feeder stream/river

**zu|flüstern** *tr. V.* jmdm. etw. ~: whisper sth. to sb.

**zu·folge** *Präp. mit Dat.; nachgestellt* according to

**zu·frieden** 1 *Adj.* contented; (befriedigt) satisfied; **mit etw.** ~ **sein** be satisfied with sth.; **sich** ~ **geben** be satisfied with sth.; **jmdn.** ~ **stellen** satisfy sb.
2 *adv.* contentedly

*****zufrieden|geben** ▶ ZUFRIEDEN 1

**Zufriedenheit** *die;* ~: contentment; (Befriedigung) satisfaction

*****zufrieden|stellen** ▶ ZUFRIEDEN 1

**zufriedenstellend** 1 *Adj.* satisfactory
2 *adv.* satisfactorily

**zu|frieren** *unr. itr. V.; mit sein* freeze over

**zu|fügen** *tr. V.* jmdm. etw. ~: inflict sth. on sb.; **jmdm. Schaden/[ein] Unrecht** ~: do sb. harm/an injustice

**Zufuhr** *die;* ~: supply; (Material) supplies *pl.*

**zu|führen** 1 *itr. V.* auf etw. (*Akk.*) ~: lead towards sth.
2 *tr. V.* (a) (zuleiten) **einer Sache** (*Dat.*) etw. ~: supply sth. to sth.
(b) (bringen) **einer Partei Mitglieder** ~: bring new members to a party

**Zug** *der;* ~[e]s, Züge (a) (Bahn) train
(b) (Kolonne) column; (Umzug) procession; (Demonstrationszug) march
(c) (das Ziehen) pull; traction (Phys.)
(d) (Vorrichtung) pull
(e) (Wanderung) migration
(f) (beim Brettspiel) move

···⊹

**(g)** (Schluck) swig (coll.); mouthful; (großer Schluck) gulp; **das Glas auf einen** *od.* **in einem ∼ leeren** empty the glass at one go
**(h)** (beim Rauchen) pull; drag (coll.)
**(i)** (Atemzug) breath
**(j)** (Zugluft; beim Ofen) draught
**(k)** (Gesichtszug) feature; (Wesenszug) characteristic; trait

**Zu·gabe** *die* **(a)** (Geschenk) [free] gift
**(b)** (im Konzert, Theater) encore

**Zu·gang** *der* **(a)** (Weg, auch fig.) access; (Eingang) entrance
**(b)** (das Hinzukommen) (von Personen) intake; (von Patienten) admission
**(c)** (Zuwachs) increase (**von** in)

**zu·gange:** ∼ **sein** (ugs.) be busy *or* occupied

**zugänglich** *Adj.* **(a)** accessible; (geöffnet) open
**(b)** (zur Verfügung stehend) available (*Dat.,* **für** to); (verständlich) accessible (*Dat.,* **für** to)
**(c)** (aufgeschlossen) approachable ⟨person⟩

**zu|geben** *unr. tr. V.* admit; admit to ⟨deed, crime⟩

**zu·gegen** *Adj.* ∼ **sein** be present

**zu|gehen** *unr. itr. V.; mit sein* **(a)** **auf jmdn./etw.** ∼: approach sb./sth.
**(b)** **jmdm.** ∼ (zugeschickt werden) be sent to sb.
**(c)** (ugs.: sich schließen) close; shut; **die Tür geht nicht zu** the door will not shut

**zu·gehörig** *Adj.* belonging to it/them *postpos., not pred.*

**Zugehörigkeit** *die;* ∼: belonging (**zu** to)

**Zügel** *der;* ∼**s,** ∼: rein

**zügel·los** (fig.) **[1]** *Adj.* unrestrained; unbridled ⟨rage, passion⟩
**[2]** *adv.* without restraint

**Zügellosigkeit** *die;* ∼, ∼**en** lack of restraint; (Unzüchtigkeit) licentiousness

**zügeln** *tr. V.* rein [in] ⟨horse⟩; (fig.) curb, restrain ⟨desire etc.⟩

**zu|gesellen** *refl. V.* **sich jmdm./einer Sache** ∼: join sb./sth.

**Zu·geständnis** *das* concession

**zu|gestehen** *unr. tr. V.* admit; concede

**zu·getan** *Adj.* **jmdm.** [herzlich] ∼ **sein** (geh.) be [very] attached to sb.

**zugig** *Adj.* draughty, (im Freien) windy ⟨corner etc.⟩

**zügig** **[1]** *Adj.* speedy; rapid
**[2]** *adv.* speedily; rapidly

**Zügigkeit** *die;* ∼: speediness; rapidity

**zu·gleich** *Adv.* at the same time

**Zug-:** ∼**luft** *die* draught; ∼**maschine** *die* tractor; (von Sattelzug) tractor [unit]

**zu|greifen** *unr. itr. V.* **(a)** take hold
**(b)** (sich bedienen) help oneself
**(c)** (fleißig arbeiten) [hart *od.* kräftig] ∼: [really] knuckle down to it

**Zu·griff** *der* (Zugang) access (**auf** + *Akk.* to)

**zu·grunde** *Adv.* **(a)** ∼ **gehen** (sterben) die

**(an** + *Dat.* of); (zerstört werden) be destroyed
**(an** + *Dat.* by); ∼ **richten** destroy; (finanziell) ruin ⟨company, person⟩
**(b)** etw. **einer Sache** (*Dat.*) ∼ **legen** base sth. on sth.; etw. **liegt einer Sache** ∼: sth. is based on sth.

**zu|gucken** *itr. V.* (ugs.) ▶ ZUSEHEN

**zu·gunsten** **[1]** *Präp. mit Gen.* in favour of
**[2]** *Adv.* ∼ **von** in favour of

**zu·gute** *Adv.* **jmdm. seine Unerfahrenheit** *usw.* ∼ **halten** (geh.) make allowances for sb.'s inexperience *etc.;* **sich** (*Dat.*) **etwas/viel auf etw.** (*Akk.*) ∼ **tun** *od.* **halten** (geh.) be proud/very proud of sth.; **jmdm./einer Sache** ∼ **kommen** stand sb./sth. in good stead

**zu|haben** *unr. itr. V.* (ugs.) ⟨shop, office⟩ be shut *or* closed

**zu|halten** *unr. tr. V.* hold closed; (nicht öffnen) keep closed

**zu|hängen** *tr. V.* cover ⟨window, cage⟩

**zu|hauen** (ugs.) **[1]** *unr. itr. V.* bang *or* slam ⟨door, window⟩ shut
**[2]** *unr. itr. V.* hit *or* strike out

**Zu·hause** *das;* ∼**s** home

**Zuhilfenahme** *die;* ∼: utilization; **ohne/ unter** ∼ **einer Sache** (*Gen.*)/**von etw.** without/ with the aid of sth.

**zu|hören** *itr. V.* **jmdm./einer Sache** ∼: listen to sb./sth.

**Zu·hörer** *der,* **Zu·hörerin** *die* listener

**zu|kleben** *tr. V.* seal ⟨letter, envelope⟩

**zu|knallen** (ugs.) **[1]** *tr. V.* slam
**[2]** *itr. V.; mit sein* slam

**zu|knöpfen** *tr. V.* button up

**zu|kommen** *itr. V.; mit sein* **auf jmdn.** ∼: approach sb.

**Zukunft** *die;* ∼: future

**Zu·lage** *die* extra pay *no indef. art.;* additional allowance *no indef. art.*

**zu|lassen** *unr. tr. V.* **(a)** allow; permit
**(b)** (teilnehmen lassen) admit
**(c)** (mit einer Lizenz usw. versehen) **jmdn. als Arzt** ∼: register sb. as a doctor
**(d)** (Kfz-W.) register ⟨vehicle⟩
**(e)** (geschlossen lassen) leave closed *or* shut ⟨door, window, etc.⟩

**zu·lässig** *Adj.* permissible; admissible ⟨appeal⟩

**Zulassung** *die;* ∼, ∼**en** registration

**Zu·lauf** *der* [viel] ∼ **haben** ⟨shop, restaurant, etc.⟩ enjoy a large clientele; ⟨doctor, lawyer⟩ have a large practice

**zu|laufen** *unr. itr. V.; mit sein* **(a)** **auf jmdn./etw.** ∼ (auch fig.) run towards sb./sth.
**(b)** **jmdm.** ∼ ⟨cat, dog, etc.⟩ adopt sb. as a new owner

**zu|legen** *refl. V.* **sich** (*Dat.*) **etw.** ∼: get oneself sth.

**zu·letzt** *Adv.* **(a)** last [of all]
**(b)** (als Letzter/Letzte/Letztes) last
**(c)** (fig.: am wenigsten) least of all
**(d)** (schließlich, am Ende) in the end; **bis** ∼: [right up] to *or* until the end

---

*alte Schreibung - vgl. Hinweis auf S. xiv

**z**

**zu·lie̱be** *Adv.* jmdm./einer Sache ∼: for sb.'s sake/for the sake of sth.

**zu̱m** *Präp.* + *Art.* **(a)** = zu dem; **(b)** (räumlich: Richtung) to the **(c)** (räumlich: Lage) **etw.** ∼ **Fenster hinauswerfen** throw sth. out of the window **(d)** (Hinzufügung) **Milch** ∼ **Tee nehmen** take milk with [one's] tea **(e)** (zeitlich) at the; **spätestens** ∼ **15. April** by 15 April at the latest **(f)** (Zweck) ∼ **Spaß/Vergnügen** for fun/ pleasure **(g)** (Folge) ∼ **Ärger seines Vaters** to the annoyance of his father

**zu̱|machen** *tr. V.* close; fasten, do up ⟨*dress*⟩; seal ⟨*envelope, letter*⟩; turn off ⟨*tap*⟩; put the top on ⟨*bottle*⟩; (stilllegen) close *or* shut down ⟨*factory, mine, etc.*⟩

**zu·ma̱l** [1] *Adv.* especially; particularly [2] *Konj.* especially *or* particularly since

**zumi̱ndest** *Adv.* at least

**zu̱|müllen** *tr. V.* (ugs.) **etw.** ∼: bury sth. under rubbish; **mit etw. zugemüllt werden** be buried under sth.; **von etw. zugemüllt werden** (fig.) be buried under sth.

**zu·mu̱te** *Adj.* **jmdm. ist unbehaglich** *usw.* ∼: sb. feels uncomfortable *etc.;* **mir war nicht danach** ∼: I didn't feel like it *or* in the mood

**zu̱|muten** *tr. V.* **jmdm. etw.** ∼ (abverlangen) expect *or* ask sth. of sb.; (antun) expect sb. to put up with sth.

**Zu̱mutung** *die;* ∼, ∼**en** unreasonable demand; **eine** ∼ **sein** be unreasonable

**zu·nä̱chst** *Adv.* **(a)** (als erstes) first; (anfangs) at first **(b)** (im Moment, vorläufig) for the moment

**Zu̱nahme** *die;* ∼, ∼**n** increase (*Gen.,* **an** + *Dat.* in)

**Zu·name** *der* surname; last name

**zünden** [1] *tr. V.* ignite ⟨*gas, fuel, etc.*⟩; detonate ⟨*bomb, explosive device, etc.*⟩; let off ⟨*fireworks*⟩; fire ⟨*rocket*⟩ [2] *itr. V.* ⟨*rocket, engine*⟩ fire; ⟨*lighter, match*⟩ light; ⟨*gas, fuel, explosive*⟩ ignite

**Zünd-:** ∼**holz** *das* (bes. südd., österr.) match; ∼**schlüssel** *der* (Kfz-W.) ignition key

**Zündung** *die;* ∼, ∼**en (a)** ▶ ZÜNDEN 1: ignition; detonation; letting off; firing **(b)** (Kfz-W.: Anlage) ignition

**zu̱|nehmen** *unr. itr. V.* **(a)** increase (**an** + *Dat.* in); ⟨*moon*⟩ wax **(b)** (schwerer werden) put on *or* gain weight

**Zu·neigung** *die* affection

**Zu̱nge** *die;* ∼, ∼**n** tongue; **[jmdm.] die** ∼ **herausstrecken** put one's tongue out [at sb.]

**zu·ni̱chte** *Adj.* **etw.** ∼ **machen** ruin sth.

**zu·o̱berst** *Adv.* [right] on [the] top

**zu·pa̱ss,** *\****zu·pa̱ß:** **jmdm.** ∼ **kommen** come [to sb.] at just the right time *or* moment

**zupfen** [1] *itr. V.* **an etw.** (*Dat.*) ∼: pluck *or* pull at sth.

[2] *tr. V.* **(a)** etw. aus/von *usw.* etw. ∼: pull sth. out of/from *etc.* sth. **(b)** (auszupfen) pull out; pluck ⟨*eyebrows*⟩ **(c)** pluck ⟨*string, guitar, tune*⟩ **(d)** jmdn. am Ärmel ∼: pull *or* tug [at] sb.'s sleeve

**zur** *Präp.* + *Art.* **(a)** = zu der; **(b)** (räumlich, fig.: Richtung) to the; ∼ **Schule/ Arbeit gehen** go to school/work **(c)** (räumlich: Lage) ∼ **Tür hereinkommen** come [in] through the door **(d)** (Zusammengehörigkeit, Hinzufügung) with the **(e)** (zeitlich) at the; ∼ **Stunde** at the moment; at present ∼ **Zeit** ▶ ZURZEIT **(f)** (Zweck) ∼ **Entschuldigung** by way of [an] excuse **(g)** (Folge) ∼ **vollen Zufriedenheit ihres Chefs** to the complete satisfaction of her boss

**zurechnungs·fähig** *Adj.* sound of mind *pred.*

**zurecht-:** ∼|**finden** *unr. refl. V.* find one's way [around]; ∼|**kommen** *unr. itr. V.; mit sein* get on (mit with); ∼|**legen** *tr. V.* lay out [ready]; **jmdm. etw.** ∼**legen** lay sth. out ready for sb.; ∼|**machen** *tr. V.* (ugs.) **(a)** (vorbereiten) get ready; **(b)** (herrichten) do up; **(c)** jmdn./sich ∼**machen** get sb. ready [oneself] ready; (schminken) make sb. up/put on one's make-up; ∼|**weisen** *unr. tr. V.* rebuke; reprimand ⟨*pupil, subordinate, etc.*⟩

**zu̱|reden** *itr. V.* **jmdm.** ∼: persuade sb.; (ermutigen) encourage sb.

**Zürich** *(das);* ∼**s** Zurich

**zu·rü̱ck** *Adv.* back; (weiter hinten) behind; **einen Schritt** ∼: a step backwards; ∼**!** get *or* go back!

**zurück-, Zurück-:** ∼|**behalten** *unr. tr. V.* **(a)** keep [back]; retain; **(b)** be left with ⟨*scar, heart defect, etc.*⟩; ∼|**bekommen** *unr. tr. V.* get back; **Sie bekommen 10 Euro** ∼: you get 10 euros change; ∼|**bleiben** *unr. itr. V.; mit sein* **(a)** remain; **(b)** (nicht mithalten) lag behind; (fig.) fall behind; **(c)** (bleiben) remain; ∼|**blicken** *itr. V.* look back; ∼|**erstatten** *tr. V.* refund; **jmdm. etw.** ∼**erstatten** refund sth. to sb.; ∼|**fahren** *unr. itr. V.; mit sein* **(a)** go back; return; **(b)** (nach hinten fahren) go back[wards]; ∼|**fallen** *unr. itr. V.; mit sein* **(a)** (in Rückstand geraten) fall behind; **(b)** (auf einen niedrigeren Rang) drop (**auf** + *Akk.* to); **(c)** an jmdn. ∼**fallen** ⟨*property*⟩ revert to sb.; **(d)** auf jmdn. ∼**fallen** ⟨*actions, behaviour*⟩ reflect [up]on sb.; ∼|**fliegen** *unr. itr. V.; mit sein* fly back; ∼|**führen** *tr. V.* etw. auf etw. (*Akk.*) ∼**führen** attribute sth. to sth.; ∼|**geben** *unr. tr. V.* give back; return; take back ⟨*defective goods*⟩; ∼|**gehen** *unr. itr. V.; mit sein* **(a)** go back; return; **(b)** (nach hinten) go back; **(c)** (verschwinden) disappear; ⟨*swelling, inflammation*⟩ go down; ⟨*pain*⟩ subside; **(d)** (sich verringern) decrease; ⟨*fever*⟩ abate; ⟨*flood*⟩ subside; ⟨*business*⟩ fall off; **(e)** (zurückgeschickt werden) be returned *or* sent back; ∼|**greifen** *unr. itr. V.* auf jmdn./etw. ···⟩

∼zurückgreifen fall back on sb./sth.;
∼|**halten** 1 *unr. tr. V.* (a) jmdn. ∼halten
hold sb. back; (von etw. abhalten) stop sb.; (b)
(am Vordringen hindern) keep back ⟨*crowd, mob,
etc.*⟩; (c) (behalten) withhold ⟨*news, letter, etc.*⟩;
(d) (nicht austreten lassen) hold back ⟨*tears etc.*⟩;
2 *unr. refl. V.* restrain *or* control oneself;
**sich in einer Diskussion** ∼halten keep in the
background in a discussion; ∼**haltend**
1 *Adj.* (a) reserved; (b) (kühl, reserviert) cool,
restrained ⟨*reception, response*⟩; (c) (Wirtsch.:
schwach) slack ⟨*demand*⟩; 2 *adv.* ⟨*behave*⟩
with reserve *or* restraint; (kühl, reserviert)
coolly; ∼**haltung** *die* reserve; (Kühle,
Reserviertheit) coolness; (Wirtsch.) caution;
∼|**kehren** *itr. V.; mit sein* return; come
back; ∼|**kommen** *unr. itr. V.; mit sein*
come back; return; (zurückgelangen) get back;
∼kommen **auf** (+ *Akk.*) come back to
⟨*subject, question, point, etc.*⟩; ∼|**kriegen**
*tr. V.* (ugs.) ▶ ∼BEKOMMEN; ∼|**lassen** *unr.*
*tr. V.* leave; ∼|**legen** *tr. V.* (a) put back; (b)
(reservieren) put aside, keep (*Dat.*, **für** for); (c)
(sparen) put away; (d) (hinter sich bringen) cover
⟨*distance*⟩; ∼|**lehnen** *refl. V.* lean back;
∼|**nehmen** *unr. tr. V.* (auch fig. widerrufen)
take back; ∼|**rufen** *unr. tr. V.* (a) call back;
recall ⟨*ambassador*⟩; (b) *auch itr.* (telefonisch)
call *or* (Brit.) ring back; ∼|**schauen** *itr. V.*
(bes. südd., österr., schweiz.) ▶ ∼BLICKEN;
∼|**schicken** *tr. V.* send back;
∼|**schlagen** 1 *unr. tr. V.* (a) (nach hinten
schlagen) fold back ⟨*cover, hood, etc.*⟩; turn
down ⟨*collar*⟩; (b) (durch einen Schlag
zurückbefördern) hit back; (mit dem Fuß) kick
back; (c) (zum Rückzug zwingen, abwehren) beat
off, repulse ⟨*enemy, attack*⟩; 2 *unr. itr. V.* (a)
hit back; ⟨*enemy*⟩ strike back, retaliate; (b)
*mit sein* ⟨*pendulum*⟩ swing back;
∼|**schrecken** *regelm.*, (veralt.) *unr., itr. V.,
mit sein* **vor etw.** (*Dat.*) ∼schrecken (fig.)
shrink from sth.; **er schreckt vor nichts** ∼:
he will stop at nothing; ∼|**senden** *unr. od.
regelm. tr. V.* (geh.) ▶ ∼SCHICKEN; ∼|**treten**
*unr. itr. V.; mit sein* step back; (von einem Amt)
resign; step down; ⟨*government*⟩ resign; (von
einem Vertrag usw.) withdraw (**von** from); back
out (**von** of); (fig.: in den Hintergrund treten)
become less important; ∼|**weisen** *unr.
tr. V.* reject ⟨*proposal, question, demand,
application, etc.*⟩; turn down, refuse ⟨*offer,
request, help, etc.*⟩; turn away ⟨*petitioner,
unwelcome guest*⟩; repudiate ⟨*accusation,
claim, etc.*⟩; ∼|**werfen** *unr. tr. V.* throw
back; reflect ⟨*light, sound*⟩; repulse ⟨*enemy*⟩;
(fig.: in einer Entwicklung) set back; ∼|**zahlen**
*tr. V.* pay back; ∼|**ziehen** 1 *unr. tr. V.* (a)
pull back; draw back ⟨*bolt, curtains, one's
hand, etc.*⟩; (b) (abziehen, zurückbeordern)
withdraw ⟨*troops*⟩; recall ⟨*ambassador*⟩; (c)
(rückgängig machen) withdraw; cancel ⟨*order,
instruction*⟩; 2 *unr. refl. V.* withdraw
**Zu·ruf** *der* shout

**zu**|**rufen** *unr. tr. V.* jmdm. etw. ∼: shout sth.
to sb.

**zur·zeit** *Adv.* at the moment

**Zu·sage** *die* (a) (auf eine Einladung hin)
acceptance; (auf eine Stellenbewerbung hin) offer
(b) (Versprechen) promise; undertaking

**zu**|**sagen** 1 *itr. V.* (a) accept
(b) jmdm. ∼ (gefallen) appeal to sb.
2 *tr. V.* promise

**zusammen** *Adv.* together; ∼ **sein**
(zusammenleben) be *or* live together

**zusammen-, Zusammen-:** ∼**arbeit**
*die* cooperation *no indef. art.;* ∼|**arbeiten**
*itr. V.* cooperate; ∼|**binden** *unr. tr. V.* tie
together; ∼|**brechen** *unr. itr. V.; mit sein*
collapse; (fig.) ⟨*order, communications, system,
telephone network*⟩ break down; ⟨*traffic*⟩
come to a standstill; ∼**bruch** *der* collapse;
(fig., auch psychisch, nervlich) breakdown;
∼|**drücken** *tr. V.* press together;
∼|**fahren** *unr. itr. V.; mit sein*
(zusammenzucken) start; jump; ∼|**fallen** *unr.
itr. V.; mit sein* (a) collapse; (b) [zeitlich]
∼fallen coincide; ∼|**fassen** *tr. V.*
summarize; ∼**fassung** *die* summary;
∼|**fegen** *tr. V.* (bes. nordd.) sweep together;
∼|**fließen** *unr. itr. V.; mit sein* ⟨*rivers,
streams*⟩ flow into each other; ∼**fluss**,
*∼**fluß** *der* confluence; ∼|**fügen** *tr. V.* fit
together; ∼|**führen** *tr. V.* bring together;
∼|**gehören** *itr. V.* belong together;
∼|**gehörig** *Adj.* [closely] related *or*
connected ⟨*subjects, problems, etc.*⟩; matching
*attrib.* ⟨*pieces of tea service, cutlery, etc.*⟩;
∼**gehörigkeit** *die;* ∼∼: **ein starkes**
**Gefühl der** ∼**gehörigkeit** a strong sense of
belonging together;
∼**gehörigkeits·gefühl** *das* sense *or*
feeling of belonging together; ∼**hang** *der*
connection; (einer Geschichte, Rede) coherence;
(Kontext) context; ∼|**hängen** *unr. itr. V.* (a)
be joined [together]; (b) mit etw. ∼hängen
(fig.) be related to sth.; (durch etw. [mit]
verursacht sein) be a result of sth.;
∼|**kehren** *tr. V.* (bes. südd.) sweep together;
∼**klappbar** *Adj.* folding; ∼|**klappen** *tr.
V.* fold up; ∼|**kommen** *unr. itr. V.; mit sein*
(a) meet; mit jmdm. ∼kommen meet sb.; (b)
(zueinanderkommen; auch fig.) get together;
(gleichzeitig auftreten) occur *or* happen together;
∼**kunft** *die;* ∼, ∼künfte meeting;
∼|**laufen** *unr. itr. V.; mit sein* (a) ⟨*people,
crowd*⟩ gather, congregate; (b) ⟨*rivers,
streams*⟩ flow into each other, join up;
∼|**leben** *itr. V.* live together; ∼**leben** *das*
living together *no art.;* ∼|**legen** 1 *tr. V.*
(a) put *or* gather together; (b) (zusammenfalten)
fold [up]; (c) (miteinander verbinden)
amalgamate, merge ⟨*classes, departments,
etc.*⟩; combine ⟨*events*⟩; (d) put ⟨*patients,
guests, etc.*⟩ together [in the same room];
2 *itr. V.* club together; ∼|**nehmen** 1 *unr.
tr. V.* summon up ⟨*courage, strength,
understanding*⟩; 2 *unr. refl. V.* get *or* take a
grip on oneself; **nimm dich** ∼! pull yourself

together!; ~|**passen** *itr. V.* go together; ⟨*persons*⟩ be suited to each other; ~**prall** *der;* ~~[e]s, ~~e collision; ~|**prallen** *itr. V.; mit sein* collide (mit with); ~|**schlagen** *unr. tr. V.* (verprügeln) beat up; *~|**sein** ▶ zusammen; ~|**setzen** ① *tr. V.* put together; ② *refl. V.* (a) sich aus etw. ~setzen be made up *or* composed of sth.; (b) (sich zueinander setzen) sit together; (zu einem Gespräch) get together; ~**setzung** *die;* ~~, ~~en (a) putting together; (b) (Aufbau) composition; „~setzung: ...“ (als Aufschrift auf Medikamentenpackung) 'ingredients: ...'; (c) (Sprachw.) compound; ~**spiel** *das* (a) (von Musikern) ensemble playing; (von Darstellern) ensemble acting; (einer Mannschaft) teamwork; (b) (fig.) interplay; ~|**stehen** *unr. itr. V.* stand together; ~|**stellen** *tr. V.* put together; draw up ⟨*list*⟩; ~**stoß** *der* collision; (fig.) clash (mit with); ~|**stoßen** *unr. itr. V.; mit sein* collide (mit with); ~|**treffen** *unr. itr. V.; mit sein* (a) meet; mit jmdm. ~treffen meet sb.; (b) (zeitlich) coincide; ~|**wachsen** *unr. itr. V.; mit sein* grow together; join [up]; ⟨*bones*⟩ knit together; (fig.) ⟨*towns*⟩ merge into one; ~|**zählen** *tr. V.* add up; ~|**ziehen** *unr. itr. V.; mit sein* move in together; mit jmdm. ~ziehen move in with sb.; ~|**zucken** *itr. V.; mit sein* start; jump

**Zu·satz** *der* addition; (Zugesetztes, Additiv) additive

**zusätzlich** ① *Adj.* additional ② *adv.* in addition

**zu|schauen** *itr. V.* (südd., österr., schweiz.) ▶ zusehen

**Zu·schauer** *der,* **Zu·schauerin** *die;* ~, ~nen spectator; (im Theater, Kino) member of the audience; (an einer Unfallstelle) onlooker; (Fernsehzuschauer) viewer; die Zuschauer (im Theater, Kino) the audience *sing.*

**zu|schicken** *tr. V.* send; jmdm. etw. ~: send sth. to sb.

**zu|schieben** *unr. tr. V.* (a) push ⟨*drawer, door*⟩ shut (b) (fig.) jmdm. die Schuld ~: lay the blame on sb.

**Zu·schlag** *der* (a) additional *or* extra charge; (für Nacht-, Feiertagsarbeit usw.) additional *or* extra payment (b) (Eisenb.) supplement

**zu|schlagen** ① *unr. tr. V.* bang *or* slam ⟨*door, window, etc.*⟩ shut; close ⟨*book*⟩; (heftig) slam ⟨*book*⟩ shut ② *unr. itr. V.* (a) *mit sein* ⟨*door, trap*⟩ slam *or* bang shut (b) (einen Schlag/Schläge führen) throw a blow/ blows; (losschlagen) hit *or* strike out; (fig.) ⟨*army, police, murderer*⟩ strike

**zu|schließen** ① *unr. tr. V.* lock ② *unr. itr. V.* lock up

**zu|schnüren** *tr. V.* tie up

**zu|schrauben** *tr. V.* screw the lid *or* top on ⟨*jar, flask*⟩; screw ⟨*lid, top*⟩ on

**Zu·schrift** *die* letter; (auf eine Anzeige) reply

**Zu·schuss,** *Zu·schuß* *der* contribution (zu towards)

**zu|sehen** *unr. itr. V.* (a) watch; jmdm. [beim Arbeiten *usw.*] ~: watch sb. [working *etc.*] (b) (dafür sorgen) make sure; see to it

**zu|senden** *unr. od. regelm. tr. V.* ▶ zuschicken

**Zu·sendung** *die* sending

**zu|spitzen** *refl. V.* become aggravated

**zu|sprechen** ① *unr. tr. V.* (a) er sprach ihr Trost/Mut zu his words gave her comfort/ courage (b) jmdm. ein Erbe *usw.* ~: award sb. an inheritance *etc.*; ② *unr. itr. V.* jmdm. ermutigend/tröstend *usw.* ~: speak encouragingly/comfortingly to sb.

**Zu·stand** *der* (a) condition; (bes. abwertend) state (b) (Stand der Dinge) state of affairs

**zu·stande** *Adv.* etw. ~ bringen [manage to] bring about sth.; ~ kommen come into being; (geschehen) take place

**zu·ständig** *Adj.* appropriate relevant ⟨*authority, office, etc.*⟩; [für etw.] ~ sein (verantwortlich) be responsible [for sth.]

**Zuständigkeit** *die;* ~, ~en (Verantwortlichkeit) responsibility; (Kompetenz) competence

**zu|stehen** *unr. itr. V.* etw. steht jmdm. zu sb. is entitled to sth.

**zu|steigen** *unr. itr. V.; mit sein* get on; ist noch jemand zugestiegen? (im Bus) ≈ any more fares, please?; (im Zug) ≈ tickets, please!

**zu|stellen** *tr. V.* deliver ⟨*letter, parcel, etc.*⟩

**zu|stimmen** *itr. V.* agree; jmdm. [in einem Punkt] ~: agree with sb. [on a point]; einer Sache (*Dat.*) ~: agree to sth.

**Zu·stimmung** *die* (Billigung) approval (zu of); (Einverständnis) agreement (zu to, with)

**zu|stoßen** *unr. itr. V.; mit sein* jmdm. ~: happen to sb.

**Zu·tat** *die* ingredient

**zu·teil** *Adv.* jmdm./einer Sache ~ werden (geh.) be granted to sb./sth.

**zu|teilen** *tr. V.* jmdm. jmdn./etw. ~: allot *or* assign sb./sth. to sb.; jmdm. seine Portion ~: mete out his/her share to sb.

**zu|tragen** *unr. refl. V.* (geh.) occur

**zuträglich** *Adj.* healthy ⟨*climate*⟩; jmdm./ einer Sache ~ sein be good for sb./sth.; be beneficial to sb./sth.

**zu|trauen** *tr. V.* jmdm. etw. ~: believe sb. [is] capable of [doing] sth.; sich (*Dat.*) etw. ~: think one can do *or* is capable of doing sth.

**Zutrauen** *das;* ~s confidence, trust (zu in)

**zutraulich** ① *Adj.* trusting ② *adv.* trustingly

Z

**Zutraulichkeit** *die;* ~: trust[fulness]
**zu|treffen** *unr. itr. V.* **(a)** be correct
**(b)** auf *od.* für jmdn./etw. ~: apply to sb./sth.
**zutreffend** 1 *Adj.* **(a)** correct; (treffend)
accurate
**(b)** (geltend) applicable; relevant
2 *adv.* correctly
**zu|trinken** *unr. itr. V.* jmdm. ~: raise one's
glass and drink to sb.
**Zu·tritt** *der* entry; admittance; „kein ~", „~
verboten" 'no entry'; 'no admittance'; ~ [zu
etw.] haben have access [to sth.]
**Zu·tun** *das;* ~s: ohne jmds. ~: without sb.'s
being involved
**zu·unterst** *Adv.* right at the bottom
**zuverlässig** 1 *Adj.* reliable; (verlässlich)
dependable ⟨person⟩
2 *adv.* reliably
**Zuverlässigkeit** *die;* ~: reliability;
(Verlässlichkeit) dependability
**Zuversicht** *die;* ~: confidence
**zuversichtlich** 1 *Adj.* confident
2 *adv.* confidently
*****zuviel** ▶ ZU 2A
**zu·vor** *Adv.* before
**zuvor|kommen** *unr. itr. V.; mit sein* **(a)**
jmdm. ~: beat sb. to it
**(b)** einer Sache (*Dat.*) ~: anticipate sth.
**zuvorkommend** 1 *Adj.* obliging; (höflich)
courteous
2 *adv.* obligingly; (höflich) courteously
**Zuvorkommenheit** *die;* ~:
courteousness; courtesy
**Zuwachs** *der;* ~es, Zuwächse increase
(*Gen.*, an + *Dat.* in)
**Zuwachs·rate** *die* (bes. Wirtsch.) growth
rate
**Zu·wanderer** *der*, **Zu·wanderin** *die*
immigrant
**Zu·wanderung** *die* immigration
**zu·weilen** *Adv.* (geh.) now and again
**zu|weisen** *unr. tr. V.* jmdm. etw. ~:
allocate *or* allot sb. sth.
**zu|wenden** *unr. od. regelm. refl. V.* sich
jmdm./einer Sache ~ (auch fig.) turn to sb./
sth.
*****zu·wenig** ▶ ZU 2A
**zuwider** *Adj.* jmdm. ~ **sein** be repugnant to
sb.
**zu|winken** *itr. V.* jmdm./einander ~: wave
to sb./one another
**zu|zahlen** *tr. V.* pay ⟨*five euros etc.*⟩ extra
**zu|ziehen** 1 *unr. tr. V.* pull ⟨*door*⟩ shut;
draw ⟨*curtain*⟩; do up ⟨*zip*⟩
2 *unr. refl. V.* sich (*Dat.*) eine Krankheit ~:
catch an illness
3 *unr. itr. V.; mit sein* move into the area
**Zu·zug** *der* influx
**zuzüglich** *Präp. mit Gen.* plus
**zwang** *1. u. 3. Pers. Sg. Prät. v.* ZWINGEN

**Zwang** *der;* ~[e]s, Zwänge **(a)** compulsion
**(b)** (unwiderstehlicher Drang) irresistible urge
**zwängen** 1 *tr. V.* squeeze
2 *refl. V.* squeeze [oneself]
**zwanghaft** *Adj.* obsessive
**zwanglos** 1 *Adj.* **(a)** informal; casual
⟨*behaviour*⟩
**(b)** (unregelmäßig) haphazard ⟨*arrangement*⟩
2 *adv.* **(a)** informally
**(b)** (unregelmäßig) haphazardly ⟨*arranged*⟩
**Zwanglosigkeit** *die;* ~: **(a)** informality
**(b)** (Unregelmäßigkeit) haphazard *or* casual
manner
**Zwangs·lage** *die* predicament
**zwangs·läufig** 1 *Adj.* inevitable
2 *adv.* inevitably
**zwanzig** *Kardinalz.* twenty; *s. auch* ACHTZIG
**zwanziger** *indekl. Adj.* die ~ Jahre the
twenties
**Zwanzig·mark·schein** *der* twenty-mark
note
**zwanzigst...** *Ordinalz.* twentieth
**zwar** *Adv.* **(a)** admittedly
**(b)** und ~: to be precise
**Zweck** *der;* ~[e]s, ~e purpose; (Sinn) point;
es hat keinen ~: it's pointless; es hat keinen
~, das zu tun there is no point in doing that
**zweck-, Zweck-:** ~**entfremden** *tr. V.*
use for another purpose; ~**los** *Adj.*
pointless; ~**losigkeit** *die;* ~~:
pointlessness; ~**mäßig** 1 *Adj.*
appropriate; expedient ⟨*behaviour, action*⟩;
functional ⟨*building, fittings, furniture*⟩;
2 *adv.* appropriately ⟨*arranged, clothed*⟩;
⟨*act*⟩ expediently; ⟨*equip, furnish*⟩
functionally; ~**mäßigkeit** *die*
appropriateness; (einer Handlung) expediency;
(eines Gebäudes) functionalism
**zwecks** *Präp. mit Gen.* (Papierdt.) for the
purpose of
**zwei** *Kardinalz.* two; *s. auch* ACHT[1]
**Zwei** *die;* ~, ~en **(a)** (Zahl) two
**(b)** (Schulnote) B
**zwei-, Zwei-:** ~**bettzimmer** *das* twin-
bedded room; ~**deutig** 1 *Adj.* ambiguous;
(fig.: schlüpfrig) suggestive ⟨*remark, joke*⟩;
2 *adv.* ambiguously; (fig.) suggestively;
~**deutigkeit** *die;* ~~, ~~en ambiguity;
(fig.) suggestiveness; ~**dimensional**
1 *Adj.* two-dimensional; 2 *adv.* two-
dimensionally; ~**ein·halb** *Bruchz.* two and
a half
**zweierlei** *indekl. Adj.* **(a)** *attr.* two sorts *or*
kinds of; two different ⟨*sizes, kinds, etc.*⟩; odd
⟨*socks, gloves*⟩
**(b)** *allein stehend* two [different] things
**zwei·fach** *Vervielfältigungsz.* double;
(zweimal) twice
**Zwei·fache** *das; adj. Dekl.* das ~: twice as
much
**Zweifel** *der;* ~s, ~: doubt (an + *Dat.*
about); etw. in ~ ziehen question sth.
**zweifelhaft** *Adj.* **(a)** doubtful

433

**(b)** (fragwürdig) dubious; (suspekt) suspicious

**zwei·fel·los** *Adv.* undoubtedly

**zweifeln** *itr. V.* doubt; **an jmdm./etw.** ∼: doubt sb./sth.; have doubts about sb./sth.

**zweifels-, Zweifels-:** ∼**fall** *der* case of doubt; doubtful *or* problematic case; **im** ∼**fall[e]** in case of doubt; if in doubt; ∼**ohne** *Adv.* undoubtedly; without doubt

**Zweig** *der;* ∼[e]s, ∼e [small] branch; (meist ohne Blätter) twig

**zwei-, Zwei-:** ∼**hundert** *Kardinalz.* two hundred; ∼**mal** *Adv.* twice; ∼**mark·stück** *das* two-mark piece; ∼**pfennig·stück** *das* two-pfennig piece; ∼**reiher** *der* double-breasted suit/coat/jacket; ∼**schneidig** *Adj.* double-edged; ∼**sprachig** ⒈ *Adj.* bilingual; ⟨sign⟩ in two languages; ⒉ *adv.* bilingually; ⟨written⟩ in two languages; ⟨published⟩ in a bilingual edition; ∼**spurig** *Adj.* **(a)** two-lane ⟨road⟩; **(b)** two-track ⟨vehicle⟩; **(c)** two- *or* twin-track ⟨recording⟩; ∼**stellig** *Adj.* two-figure *attrib.* ⟨number, sum⟩; ∼**stöckig** *Adj.* two-storey *attrib.;* ∼**stöckig sein** have two storeys

**zweit...** *Ordinalz.* second; **jeder Zweite** every other one; *s. auch* ERST...

**zwei·tägig** *Adj.* (2 Tage alt) two-day-old *attrib.;* (2 Tage dauernd) two-day *attrib.*

**zweit·ältest...** *Adj.* second oldest

**zwei·tausend** *Kardinalz.* two thousand

**zweit·best...** *Adj.* second best

*****zweite·mal** ▶ MAL[1]

*****zweiten·mal** ▶ MAL[1]

**zweitens** *Adv.* secondly; in the second place

**Zweite[r]-Klasse-Abteil** *das* second-class compartment

**zweit·rangig** *Adj.* of secondary importance *postpos.;* (zweitklassig) second-rate

**Zweit·stimme** *die* second vote

**zwei·türig** *Adj.* two-door ⟨car⟩

**Zweit-:** ∼**wagen** *der* second car; ∼**wohnung** *die* second home

**Zwei·zimmer·wohnung** *die* two-room flat (Brit.) *or* (Amer.) apartment

**Zwerch·fell** *das* (Anat.) diaphragm

**Zwerg** *der;* ∼[e]s, ∼e dwarf; (Gartenzwerg) gnome

**Zwetsche** *die;* ∼, ∼n damson plum

**Zwieback** *der;* ∼[e]s, ∼e *od.* Zwiebäcke rusk; (unzählbar) rusks *pl.*

**Zwiebel** *die;* ∼, ∼n onion; (Blumenzwiebel) bulb

**zwie-, Zwie-:** ∼**gespräch** *das* (geh.) dialogue; ∼**spalt** *der;* ∼∼[e]s, ∼∼e *od.* ∼**spälte** [inner] conflict; ∼**spältig** *Adj.* conflicting ⟨mood, feelings⟩; discordant ⟨impression⟩; (widersprüchlich) contradictory ⟨nature, attitude, person, etc.⟩

**Zwilling** *der;* ∼s, ∼e **(a)** twin **(b)** *Pl.* (Astrol.) Gemini; the Twins; **er/sie ist [ein]** ∼: he/she is a Gemini

**Zwillings-:** ∼**bruder** *der* twin brother; ∼**paar** *das* pair of twins; ∼**schwester** *die* twin sister

**zwingen** *unr. tr. V.* force; **jmdn. [dazu]** ∼, **etw. zu tun** force or compel sb. to do sth.

**zwingend** *Adj.* compelling ⟨reason, logic⟩; conclusive ⟨proof, argument⟩; imperative ⟨necessity⟩

**zwinkern** *itr. V.* [mit den Augen] ∼: blink; (als Zeichen) wink

**Zwirn** *der;* ∼[e]s, ∼e [strong] thread *or* yarn

**zwischen** *Präp. mit Dat./Akk.* between; (mitten unter) among[st]

**zwischen-, Zwischen-:** ∼**durch** /-'-'-/ *Adv.* (zeitlich) between times; (zwischen zwei Zeitpunkten) in between; (von Zeit zu Zeit) from time to time; ∼**fall** *der* incident; ∼**landen** *itr. V.; mit sein* in **X** ∼**landen** land in X on the way; ∼**mahlzeit** *die* snack [between meals]; ∼**menschlich** ⒈ *Adj.* interpersonal ⟨relations⟩; ⟨contacts⟩ between people; ⒉ *adv.* on a personal level; ∼**raum** *der* space; gap; (Lücke) gap; ∼**ruf** *der* interruption; **viele** ∼**rufe** a great deal of heckling *sing.;* ∼**wand** *die* dividing wall; partition; ∼**zeit** *die* interim

**Zwist** *der;* ∼[e]s, ∼e (geh.) strife *no indef. art.;* (Fehde) feud; dispute

**Zwistigkeit** *die;* ∼, ∼en (geh.) dispute

**zwitschern** *itr. V.* (auch tr.) *V.* chirp

**Zwitter** *der;* ∼s, ∼ (Biol.) hermaphrodite

**zwo** *Kardinalz.* (ugs.; bes. zur Verdeutlichung) two

**zwölf** *Kardinalz.* twelve; ∼ **Uhr mittags/nachts** [twelve o'clock] midday/midnight; *s. auch* ACHT[1]

**zwölft...** *Ordinalz.* twelfth; *s. auch* ACHT...

**zwölftel** *Bruchz.* twelfth; *s. auch* ACHTEL

**Zwölftel** *das* (schweiz. meist *der*); ∼s, ∼: twelfth

**zwot...** *Ordinalz.* (ugs.; bes. zur Verdeutlichung) second

**zwotens** *Adv.* (ugs.; bes. zur Verdeutlichung) secondly

**Zylinder** /ts:i'lɪndɐ/ *der;* ∼s, ∼ **(a)** cylinder; **(b)** (Hut) top hat

**zylindrisch** ⒈ *Adj.* cylindrical ⒉ *adv.* cylindrically

**Zyniker** *der;* ∼s, ∼, **Zynikerin** *die;* ∼, ∼nen cynic

**zynisch** ⒈ *Adj.* cynical ⒉ *adv.* cynically

**Zynismus** *der;* ∼: cynicism

**Zypern** (*das*); ∼s Cyprus

**Zyprer** *der;* ∼s, ∼, **Zyprerin** *die;* ∼, ∼nen Cypriot

**Zypresse** *die;* ∼, ∼n cypress

**Zypriot** *der;* ∼en, ∼en, **Zypriotin** *die;* ∼, ∼nen Cypriot

**zypriotisch, zyprisch** *Adj.* Cypriot

**Zyste** *die;* ∼, ∼n (Med.) cyst

• • • • • • • • • • • • • • • • • • • • • • • • • • • • • • • • • • • • • • • • • •

**Kalender / Calendar
Kultur
Culture
Letters / Briefe**

# Festtags-, Feiertags- und Brauchtumskalender / Calendar of traditions, festivals, and holidays

## January

| | | | | |
|---|---|---|---|---|
| 1 | 8 | 15 | 22 | 29 |
| 2 | 9 | 16 | 23 | 30 |
| 3 | 10 | 17 | 24 | 31 |
| 4 | 11 | 18 | 25 | |
| 5 | 12 | 19 | 26 | |
| 6 | 13 | 20 | 27 | |
| 7 | 14 | 21 | 28 | |

## February

| | | | |
|---|---|---|---|
| 1 | 8 | 15 | 22 |
| 2 | 9 | 16 | 23 |
| 3 | 10 | 17 | 24 |
| 4 | 11 | 18 | 25 |
| 5 | 12 | 19 | 26 |
| 6 | 13 | 20 | 27 |
| 7 | 14 | 21 | 28 |

## March

| | | | | |
|---|---|---|---|---|
| 1 | 8 | 15 | 22 | 29 |
| 2 | 9 | 16 | 23 | 30 |
| 3 | 10 | 17 | 24 | 31 |
| 4 | 11 | 18 | 25 | |
| 5 | 12 | 19 | 26 | |
| 6 | 13 | 20 | 27 | |
| 7 | 14 | 21 | 28 | |

## Festtags-, Feiertags- und Brauchtumskalender

**1 Januar** New Year's Day Neujahr ist Feiertag und normalerweise ein ruhiger Tag, an dem man sich von den Silvesterfeierlichkeiten erholt.

**2 Januar** Feiertag in Schottland.

**6 Januar** Epiphany/Twelfth Night (Heilige Drei Könige) Mit diesem Tag sind keine bestimmten Bräuche verbunden, aber traditionellerweise werden Weihnachtsbaum und Weihnachtsschmuck dann weggeräumt.

**25 Januar** Burns Night Der Geburtstag des schottischen Dichters Robert Burns, der im 18. Jh. lebte. Schotten in aller Welt treffen sich an diesem Tag zu *Burns Suppers* (Burns-Essen). Dabei wird das Hauptgericht, der *haggis* (eine dem Saumagen ähnliche schottische Spezialität, die mit Innereien, Haferflocken, Zwiebeln und Gewürzen gefüllt ist), unter Dudelsackbegleitung zu Tisch getragen.

**2 Februar** Groundhog Day An diesem Tag soll einer Wetterregel in den USA zufolge das Murmeltier aus seinem Winterschlaf erwachen. Wenn es dann seinen Schatten sieht (d.h. wenn die Sonne scheint), bedeutet das noch weitere sechs Wochen Winterwetter.

**14 Februar** St Valentine's day (Valentinstag) Der Tag, an dem sich Liebespaare mit Blumen und Geschenken überraschen. Es ist auch üblich, eine anonyme Valentinskarte an jemanden zu schicken, den man mag.

**1 März** St David's Day (Davidstag) Der heilige David ist der Schutzheilige von Wales. Viele Waliser tragen an diesem Tag zu seinen Ehren eine Narzisse am Aufschlag.

**17 März** St. Patrick's Day (Patrickstag) Der heilige Patrick ist der Schutzheilige Irlands. Dieser Tag ist ein Feiertag in Irland und Nordirland und wird auch in den USA begangen. In New York finden Umzüge statt, und Iren in aller Welt treffen sich zu feuchtfröhlichen Feiern mit Musik und Tanz.

**1 April** April Fool's Day (Erster April) An diesem Tag schickt man sich gegenseitig in den April. Wer einem Aprilscherz zum Opfer fällt, gilt als *April Fool.*

**23 April** St George's Day (Georgstag) Der heilige Georg ist der Schutzheilige Englands.

**4 Juli** Independence Day (Unabhängigkeitstag) Ein Feiertag in den USA zum Gedenken an die Unabhängigkeit der Nation. Der Tag wird mit Umzügen, Feuerwerk und Flaggen gefeiert, und man trifft sich zum Essen im Freien oder zu Grillfesten.

**12 Oktober** Columbus Day (Kolumbustag) Feiertag in den USA zum Gedenken an die Entdeckung der Neuen Welt im Jahre 1492 durch Christoph Kolumbus.

**31 Oktober** Halloween Am Abend vor Allerheiligen vermischen sich Bräuche christlichen und heidnischen Ursprungs. Kinder verkleiden sich als Gespenster oder Hexen und spielen *Trick or Treat*, d.h. sie klingeln an den Haustüren in der Nachbarschaft und erwarten Süßigkeiten oder Geld. Wer ihnen nichts gibt, dem spielen sie einen Streich. In den USA feiern viele Familien Kostümfeste.

**5 November** Bonfire Night/Guy Fawkes. Dies ist der Jahrestag des *Gunpowder Plot*, ein von Guy Fawkes und anderen Verschwörern geplanter, aber fehlgeschlagener Sprengstoffanschlag auf die *Houses of Parliament* im Jahre 1605. Es werden Feuerwerke abgebrannt und Freudenfeuer entzündet, in denen eine Puppe, *the Guy*, verbrannt wird.

## April

| | | | | |
|---|---|---|---|---|
| ☐1 | 8 | 15 | 22 | 29 |
| 2 | 9 | 16 | ⦿23 | 30 |
| 3 | 10 | 17 | 24 | |
| 4 | 11 | 18 | 25 | |
| 5 | 12 | 19 | 26 | |
| 6 | 13 | 20 | 27 | |
| 7 | 14 | 21 | 28 | |

## May

| | | | | |
|---|---|---|---|---|
| ◇1 | 8 | 15 | 22 | 29 |
| 2 | 9 | 16 | 23 | 30 |
| 3 | 10 | 17 | 24 | 31 |
| 4 | 11 | 18 | 25 | |
| 5 | 12 | 19 | 26 | |
| 6 | 13 | 20 | 27 | |
| 7 | 14 | 21 | 28 | |

## June

| | | | | |
|---|---|---|---|---|
| 1 | 8 | 15 | 22 | 29 |
| 2 | 9 | 16 | 23 | 30 |
| 3 | 10 | 17 | 24 | |
| 4 | 11 | 18 | 25 | |
| 5 | 12 | 19 | 26 | |
| 6 | 13 | 20 | 27 | |
| 7 | 14 | 21 | 28 | |

**11 November** Veterans' Day
Feiertag in den USA, der am Jahrestag des Endes des Ersten Weltkriegs zu Ehren der amerikanischen Veteranen und der Opfer aller Kriege begangen wird.

**11 November** Remembrance Sunday fällt in Großbritannien auf den Sonntag, der dem 11. November am nächsten liegt. Es ist ein Gedenktag für die Toten beider Weltkriege und späterer Konflikte. Traditionellerweise trägt man eine rote Mohnblume am Aufschlag, und Kränze aus Mohnblumen werden an den Kriegerdenkmälern niedergelegt.

**30 November** St Andrew's Day (Andreastag) Der heilige Andreas ist der Schutzheilige Schottlands.

**24 Dezember** Christmas Eve (Heiligabend, Heiliger Abend) Mit Heiligabend sind keine bestimmten Bräuche verbunden, allerdings gehen manche Leute zur Mitternachtsmesse.

**25 Dezember** Christmas Day (Weihnachten, erster Weihnachtstag) Der erste Weihnachtstag ist Feiertag. Die Bescherung findet morgens unter dem Weihnachtsbaum statt. In vielen Familien in Großbritannien finden die Kinder morgens einen Strumpf mit Süßigkeiten und kleinen Geschenken an ihrem Bett, den der Tradition zufolge *Father Christmas*, auch *Santa Claus* genannt, gebracht hat.

**26 Dezember** Boxing Day (Zweiter Weihnachtstag) Feiertag in Großbritannien.

**26 Dezember** St Stephen's Day (Stephanstag) Feiertag in der Republik Irland.

**31 Dezember** New Year's Eve (Silvester) In Schottland heißt Silvester **Hogmanay**. Dort ist es üblich, Freunde und Nachbarn um Mitternacht zu besuchen, um bis in die Morgenstunden zu essen und zu trinken. Es gibt den Brauch, ein Stück Kohle als Glücksbringer mitzunehmen.

### Bewegliche Feste

**Presidents' Day** Der dritte Montag im Februar, Feiertag in den USA zu Ehren der Präsidenten George Washington und Abraham Lincoln.

**Shrove Tuesday/Pancake Day** (Faschingsdienstag) Traditionelles Fest vor dem Beginn der Fastenzeit, an dem man Pfannkuchen mit Zitronensaft und Zucker isst.

**Mothers' Day/Mothering Sunday** (Muttertag) In Großbritannien und Irland der vierte Sonntag in der Fastenzeit. Mütter bekommen an diesem Tag von ihren Kindern Karten und kleine Geschenke. In den USA (**Mothers' Day**) der zweite Sonntag in Mai.

**Good Friday** (Karfreitag) Feiertag in Großbritannien und Irland.

**Easter Sunday** (Ostern, Ostersonntag) Ostern wird von der Kirche gefeiert, und die Kinder bekommen Ostereier aus Schokolade.

**Easter Monday** (Ostermontag) Feiertag in Großbritannien und Irland.

**Early May Bank Holiday** Der dem 1 Mai am nächsten gelegene Montag ist in Großbritannien und Irland Feiertag.

**Whitsun/Pentecost** (Pfingsten) Pfingsten wird von der Kirche gefeiert, aber sonst nicht. Pfingstmontag war früher ein Feiertag in Großbritannien, wurde aber durch den **Spring Bank Holiday / Late May Bank Holiday** (Frühlingsfeiertag) am letzten Montag im Mai ersetzt.

**Fathers' Day** (Vatertag) Der dritte Sonntag im Juni. Väter bekommen an diesem Tag von ihren Kindern Karten und kleine Geschenke.

**Late Summer Bank Holiday/August Bank Holiday** Feiertag im Vereinigten Königreich am letzten Montag im August.

**Labor Day** (Tag der Arbeit) Wird in den USA am ersten Montag im September volksfestartig (u.a. mit Umzügen und Picknicks) begangen.

**Thanksgiving** In den USA der vierte Donnerstag im November. Ein Tag für Familien- und kirchliche Feiern, dessen Höhepunkt ein großes Essen bildet, bei dem es Truthahn mit Süßkartoffeln und Preiselbeersoße und danach Kürbiskuchen gibt.

**Advent** (Advent) In Großbritannien haben viele Kinder *Advent Calendars* (Adventskalender) mit einem Fenster für jeden Tag vom 1. bis zum 25. Dezember. Jedes Fenster, das geöffnet wird, zeigt ein weihnachtliches Bild.

**Kalender / Calendar**

• • • • • • • • • • • • • • • • • • • • • • • • • • • • • • • • • • • • • • • • • • • • • • • •

## July

| | | | | |
|---|---|---|---|---|
| 1 | 8 | 15 | 22 | 29 |
| 2 | 9 | 16 | 23 | 30 |
| 3 | 10 | 17 | 24 | 31 |
| (4) | 11 | 18 | 25 | |
| 5 | 12 | 19 | 26 | |
| 6 | 13 | 20 | 27 | |
| 7 | 14 | 21 | 28 | |

## August

| | | | | |
|---|---|---|---|---|
| 1 | 8 | 15 | 22 | 29 |
| 2 | 9 | 16 | 23 | 30 |
| 3 | 10 | 17 | 24 | 31 |
| 4 | 11 | 18 | 25 | |
| 5 | 12 | 19 | 26 | |
| 6 | 13 | 20 | 27 | |
| 7 | 14 | 21 | 28 | |

## September

| | | | | |
|---|---|---|---|---|
| 1 | 8 | 15 | 22 | 29 |
| 2 | 9 | 16 | 23 | 30 |
| 3 | 10 | 17 | 24 | |
| 4 | 11 | 18 | 25 | |
| 5 | 12 | 19 | 26 | |
| 6 | 13 | 20 | 27 | |
| 7 | 14 | 21 | 28 | |

**Kalender / Calendar**

## Feast days and festivals in German-speaking countries

**1 January Neujahr** New Year's Day is always a public holiday and tends to be a quiet day when people are recovering from the *Silvester* celebrations.

**6 January Heilige Drei Könige** Epiphany or Twelfth Night is a public holiday in Austria and some parts of southern Germany. In some areas, children dressed up as the Three Kings go from house to house to bless the homes for the coming year and collect money for charity. This is also traditionally the day when the Christmas tree is taken down.

**2 February Mariä Lichtmess** Candlemas is celebrated in the Catholic church but is not a public holiday.

**1 April Erster April** April Fool's Day is the time to make an April fool of your family and friends (*jdn. in den April schicken*) or to play an April fool trick (*Aprilscherz*).

**1 May Erster Mai** May Day is a public holiday in Germany, Austria and Switzerland. It is celebrated by trade unions as *Labour Day*, often with rallies and demonstrations. Many people simply use the day for a family outing or picnic, and in rural areas maypoles are put up in the villages.

**3 October Tag der deutschen Einheit** Germany's national holiday, the *Day of German Unity* commemorates German reunification on 3 October 1990.

**26 October Nationalfeiertag** Austria's national holiday.

**31 October Reformationstag** Reformation Day is a public holiday in some mainly Protestant parts of Germany and commemorates the Reformation.

**1 November Allerheiligen** All Saints' Day is a public holiday in Catholic parts of Germany and Austria.

**2 November Allerseelen** All Souls' Day is the day when Catholics remember their dead by visiting the cemeteries to pray and place wreaths, flowers and lighted candles on the graves. This is often done on 1 November as *Allerseelen* is not a public holiday.

**11 November Martinstag** St Martin's day is not a public holiday, but in Catholic areas the charitable Saint is commemorated with processions where children carry lanterns and sing songs. Traditional food includes the *Martinsgans* (roast goose) and *Martinsbrezel* (a kind of soft pretzel).

**6 December Nikolaustag** On the eve of St. Nicholas' Day, children put out their boots in the hope of finding presents and fruit, nuts and sweets in the morning. The Saint may also turn up in person, looking much like Santa Claus or Father Christmas.

**24 December Heiligabend** Christmas Eve is not a public holiday but many firms and shops close early for the Christmas period. This is the day when traditionally the Christmas tree is put up and decorated. Christmas presents are given in the evening, and many people attend midnight mass.

**25 December Erster Weihnachtstag** Christmas Day is a public holiday in Germany, Austria and Switzerland. It tends to be a quiet day for family get-togethers, often with a traditional lunch of goose or carp.

**26 December Zweiter Weihnachtstag** Boxing Day is a public holiday in Germany, Austria and Switzerland. In Austria and Switzerland it is called *Stephanstag* (St Stephen's day).

**31 December Silvester** New Year's Eve is not a bank holiday, but firms and shops tend to close early. A party, or at least a meal with friends, is a must for *Silvester* evening. At midnight, the new year is toasted in Sekt (German sparkling wine), and everybody goes outside to admire the fireworks.

# Calendar of traditions, festivals, and holidays

. . . . . . . . . . . . . . . . . . . . . . . . . . . . . . . . . . . . . . .

## October

| | | | | |
|---|---|---|---|---|
| 1 | 8 | 15 | 22 | 29 |
| 2 | 9 | 16 | 23 | 30 |
| ◁3▷ | 10 | 17 | 24 | [31] |
| 4 | 11 | 18 | 25 | |
| 5 | (12) | 19 | ◁26▷ | |
| 6 | 13 | 20 | 27 | |
| 7 | 14 | 21 | 28 | |

## November

| | | | | |
|---|---|---|---|---|
| ◁1▷ | 8 | 15 | 22 | 29 |
| ◁2▷ | 9 | 16 | 23 | (30) |
| 3 | 10 | 17 | 24 | |
| 4 | [11] | 18 | 25 | |
| (5) | 12 | 19 | 26 | |
| 6 | 13 | 20 | 27 | |
| 7 | 14 | 21 | 28 | |

## December

| | | | | |
|---|---|---|---|---|
| 1 | 8 | 15 | 22 | 29 |
| 2 | 9 | 16 | 23 | 30 |
| 3 | 10 | 17 | [24] | [31] |
| 4 | 11 | 18 | [25] | |
| 5 | 12 | 19 | [26] | |
| ◁6▷ | 13 | 20 | 27 | |
| 7 | 14 | 21 | 28 | |

### Movable Feasts and festivals

**Rosenmontag** The day before Shrove Tuesday is not an official public holiday but many people, especially in the Rhineland, get the day off work or school to take part in the *Karneval* celebrations, which involve masked balls, fancy-dress parties and parades. The street parades in Düsseldorf, Cologne, Mainz and other cities are attended by thousands of revellers and shown live on television.

**Faschingsdienstag** Shrove Tuesday is the final day of *Fasching* (Carnival) in Southern Germany, with processions and fancy dress parties similar to Rosenmontag in the Northwest. In the far south, ancient customs to drive out the winter with bells and drums survive. The pre-Lent carnival in and around the Rhineland is called Karneval. Almost every town has its own carnival prince and princess, and organizes a street parade with decorated floats, which is watched by thousands of revellers in fancy dress.

**Aschermittwoch** Ash Wednesday marks the end of the carnival season and the beginning of Lent. This day is celebrated in the Catholic church but is not a public holiday.

**Karfreitag** Good Friday is a public holiday and generally a very quiet day. Catholics traditionally eat fish on this day.

**Ostern** Easter traditions include hiding Easter eggs (often dyed hardboiled eggs, or the chocolate variety) in the garden for the children. The *Osterhase* (Easter bunny) is supposed to have brought them. Ostermontag (Easter Monday) is also a public holiday.

**Weißer Sonntag** (Sunday after Easter) In the Catholic Church, first communion is traditionally taken on this Sunday.

**Muttertag** (second Sunday in May) On Mothers' day, children of all ages give their mothers small gifts, cards or flowers.

**Christi Himmelfahrt** (40 days after Easter) Ascension day is a public holiday in Germany, Austria and Switzerland. This day is also Fathers' day when fathers traditionally go out on daytrips or pub crawls.

**Pfingsten** (seventh Sunday after Easter) As *Pfingstmontag* (Whit Monday) is also a public holiday in Germany, Austria and Switzerland, Whitsun is a popular time to have a long weekend away.

**Fronleichnam** (second Thursday after Whitsun) Corpus Christi is a public holiday in Austria and in parts of Germany and Switzerland. In Catholic areas, processions and open-air masses are held.

**Buß- und Bettag** (third Wednesday in November, 11 days before the first Advent Sunday) This 'day of repentance and prayer' is a public holiday only in some parts of Germany.

**Volkstrauertag** (second Sunday before the beginning of Advent) In Germany, this is a national day of mourning to commemorate the dead of both world wars, and the victims of the Nazis.

**Totensonntag** (last Sunday before the beginning of Advent) Protestants remember their dead on this day.

**Advent** The four weeks leading up to Christmas, beginning with the **1. Adventssonntag** (first Sunday in Advent) in late November or early December, still have a special significance in Germany, even for non-religious people. An Advent wreath with four candles is present in almost every German household during this time, and on each Sunday of Advent one more candle is lit.

☐ Celebrated in German and English-speaking countries / In deutsch- und englischsprachigen Ländern begangene Tage

◇ Celebrated in German-speaking countries / In deutschsprachigen Ländern begangene Tage

◯ Celebrated in English-speaking countries / In englischsprachigen Ländern begangene Tage

# Abc der britischen und amerikanischen Kultur

### ABC - American Broadcasting Company
Eine der größten amerikanischen Fernsehanstalten, gehört jetzt zur
Walt Disney Company.

### ACT - American College Test
Ein Test, den Studierende in fast allen Staaten der USA bestehen müssen, um an
einem **College** zugelassen zu werden. Der Test wird normalerweise am Ende der
**HIGH SCHOOL** abgelegt und deckt eine Reihe von Kernfächern einschließlich
Englisch und Mathematik ab.

### African American
Dies ist in den USA z.Z. der gebräuchlichste Begriff für Amerikaner afrikanischer
Abstammung.

### Afro-Caribbean
Dies ist in Großbritannien und den USA zur Zeit der gebräuchlichste Begriff
für Menschen afrikanischer Herkunft, die in der Karibik leben oder aus der
Karibik kommen.

### A level - Advanced level
Ein Examen, das von vielen Schülern in England und Wales, üblicherweise
im letzten Jahr der weiterführenden Schule, abgelegt wird. Die Abschlussnoten
(**grades**) werden in jedem Fach einzeln vergeben. Schüler, die ein Hochschulstudium
(**higher education**) anstreben, absolvieren in der Regel 3 bis 4 *A levels* und werden
von den Universitäten und anderen Institutionen entsprechend ihren
Abschlussnoten, besonders in den für ihr Studienfach relevanten Fächern,
ausgewählt.

### Alliance Party (Northern Ireland)
Eine politische Partei in Nordirland, deren Ziel es ist, ein Ende des Konflikts
zwischen extremen religiösen Gruppen zu bewirken, indem sie Menschen mit
gemäßigten Ansichten beider Seiten zusammenführt.

### American Indian ▶ NATIVE AMERICAN.

### AS level - Advanced Supplementary level
Ein Abschlussexamen in einem bestimmten Fach, das in der Regel im letzten Jahr
der **Secondary School** von vielen Schülern in England und Wales abgelegt wird.
Ein *AS level* liegt zwischen einem **GCSE** und einem **A LEVEL** und zählt für den
Zugang zur Universität halb so viele Punkte wie ein *A level*. Viele Studierende legen
eine Mischung aus *A levels* und *AS levels* ab.

### Asian American
Dies ist z.Z. der gebräuchlichste Begriff für einen Amerikaner asiatischer, besonders
fernöstlicher Abstammung.

### BBC - British Broadcasting Corporation
Eine der wichtigsten britischen Fernseh- und Rundfunkanstalten. Sie erhielt 1927 die
*Royal Charter*, das königliche Privileg, finanziert sich über Fernsehgebühren, nicht
über Werbeeinnahmen, und ist zur unparteilichen Berichterstattung verpflichtet.

## bed and breakfast

Überall in Großbritannien sieht man Schilder mit der Aufschrift *Bed & Breakfast* oder **B&B**. Sie weisen auf Privathäuser hin, die Unterkunft zu meist recht niedrigen Preisen anbieten, wobei im Zimmerpreis das Frühstück mit eingeschlossen ist. Die Gäste erhalten normalerweise ein üppiges traditionelles Frühstück mit Fruchtsaft, Müsli, warmem Essen - dazu gehört vor allem Spiegelei mit Speck - und Toast und Marmelade.

## Big Issue

Eine Zeitung, die von Obdachlosen in vielen größeren und kleineren Städten in Großbritannien verkauft wird. Die Artikel haben oft ein sehr gutes Niveau, sie behandeln hauptsächlich soziale Themen oder Aspekte der Stadtkultur. Die Verkäufer kaufen die Zeitungen von einer zentralen Stelle und verkaufen sie zu einem festgelegten Preis. Den Gewinn dürfen sie behalten in der Hoffnung, dass sie dann leben können, ohne betteln zu müssen.

## broadsheet

Ein Zeitung in Großbritannien, die auf großen Zeitungsbögen gedruckt wird, im Gegensatz zu den **TABLOIDS** , der Boulevardpresse, die auf halb so großen Bögen hergestellt wird. Das *broadsheet*-Format wird normalerweise mit der *quality press* (seriösen Presse) assoziiert, mit Zeitungen wie z.b. **THE GUARDIAN** und **THE TIMES**, während die meisten Zeitungen der *popular press* (Boulevardpresse), wie z.B. **The Mirror** und **The Sun** das *tabloid*-Format benutzen.

## busking

Dies ist der informelle britische Ausdruck für das Musizieren an öffentlichen Plätzen, mit dem Zweck Geld einzunehmen. In den großen britischen Städten gibt es viele *buskers* (Straßenmusikanten), oft auf hohem Niveau. An einigen Plätzen ist es verboten, Straßenmusik zu machen, z.B. in der Londoner U-Bahn.

## Cabinet

Das britische Kabinett ist ein Komitee von etwa 20 *Ministers* (Ministern), die vom Prime Minister (**Premierminister**) berufen werden. Jedes Mitglied ist für ein bestimmtes politisches Ressort verantwortlich und das Kabinett als Ganzes entscheidet über die Regierungspolitik. Das **shadow cabinet** (Schattenkabinett) wird vom Oppositionsführer berufen, so dass es im Fall eines Regierungswechsels, wie z.B. nach einer **general election** (Wahl), die Regierungsgeschäfte übernehmen kann.

## Cambridge Certificate

Ein Sprachzertifikat über das Leistungsniveau von Lernenden, die Englisch als Fremdsprache studieren. Die Examen werden von der Universität Cambridge auf drei verschiedenen Niveaus abgenommen. Auf dem niedrigeren Niveau führt das Examen zum *First Certificate in English*, auf dem mittleren Niveau zum *Advanced Certificate in English*, und auf dem fortgeschrittenen Niveau führt es zum *Certificate of Proficiency in English*. Viele Sprachschulen innerhalb und außerhalb Großbritanniens bereiten Studierende auf diese Examen vor.

## Capitol

Der Sitz des amerikanischen **CONGRESS** auf dem Capitol Hill in Washington.

## CBS - Columbia Broadcasting System

Neben **ABC** und **NBC** eine der drei ersten amerikanischen nationalen Rundfunkgesellschaften.

**Kultur**

## Ceefax

Ein Informationsservice, der in Großbritannien von der **BBC** angeboten wird und eine große Bandbreite abdeckt, von Wetterberichten bis zu Aktienkursen. Die Informationen können über den Fernseher abgerufen werden und erscheinen auf dem Bildschirm.

## Channel Five

Ein britischer privater Fernsehsender, der populäre leichte Unterhaltung ausstrahlt.

## Channel Four

Ein britischer privater Fernsehsender mit einem umfangreichen sozialen und kulturellen Programm. Er hat ein Renommee für exzellente Dokumentationen und für die Berichterstattung über kulturelle und künstlerische Ereignisse.

## City

The City of London ist das Gebiet innerhalb der alten Stadtgrenzen von London. Heute ist es das Geschäfts- und Finanzzentrum Londons und viele Banken und andere Geldinstitute haben dort ihre Hauptstellen. Wenn Leute über die *City* sprechen, beziehen sie sich oft auf diese Institutionen und nicht auf den Ort.

## City Technology College (CTC)

Eine Form der *secondary school* in Großbritannien, die gemeinsam von der Regierung und privaten Unternehmen eingerichtet wurde. Diese Colleges liegen in den Stadtzentren und legen besonderen Wert auf die Vermittlung von Mathematik, Naturwissenschaften und Technologie.

## CNN - Cable News Network

Eine amerikanische Fernsehgesellschaft, die Nachrichten und Informationsprogramme 24 Stunden am Tag über Satellit überträgt.

## college of further education (CFE)

Ein Collegetyp in Großbritannien, der Personen über 16 Jahren Voll- und Teilzeitkurse anbietet. Dazu gehören Vorbereitungskurse für **GCSE** und **A LEVELS** sowie Tages- und Abendkurse in diversen Fächern wie Fremdsprachen, Informatik, bis hin zu Töpferei und Autowartung.

## community college

Ein Collegetyp in den Vereinigten Staaten, der eine Vielzahl von praktischen Kursen für die Allgemeinheit anbietet.

## community service

In Großbritannien gibt es auf kommunaler Ebene ehrenamtliche Helfer, die z.B. Alte oder Behinderte pflegen oder Reparaturen an Gemeindezentren und anderen Einrichtungen ausführen. Diese Art von Sozialdienst wird manchmal auch Straftätern auferlegt, als Alternative zu einer Haftstrafe.

## comprehensive school

Einer Gesamtschule entsprechende große staatliche weiterführende Schule in Großbritannien für Kinder aller Leistungsstufen im Alter von 11 bis 18 Jahren, die in einer bestimmten Gegend leben.

● ● ● ● ● ● ● ● ● ● ● ● ● ● ● ● ● ● ● ● ● ● ● ● ● ● ● ● ● ● ● ● ● ● ● ● ● ● ● ● ● ● ● ● ● ● ●

## Congress
Die nationale gesetzgebende Versammlung in den Vereinigten Staaten. Der Kongress tritt im **CAPITOL** zusammen und besteht aus zwei Kammern, **SENATE** (Senat) und **HOUSE OF REPRESENTATIVES** (Repräsentantenhaus). Die Funktion des Kongresses ist es, Gesetze zu erlassen. Jedes Gesetz muss von beiden Kammern angenommen und anschließend vom **PRESIDENT** (Präsident) verabschiedet werden.

## Conservative Party
Eine der Volksparteien Großbritanniens. Es ist eine Partei der politischen Rechten, die für Kapitalismus, freie Marktwirtschaft und private Industrie und Dienstleistung steht. Sie entwickelte sich etwa 1830 aus der alten *Tory Party* und wird auch heute noch häufig so genannt. Die Farbe der Partei ist Blau.

## council
Gewählte Versammlung, die für die Verwaltung eines bestimmten Gebietes in Großbritannien zuständig ist. Dieses Gebiet kann eine **COUNTY** (Grafschaft) sein, Teil eines Landkreises, eine Stadt oder Teil einer größeren Stadt. Der *council* ist dafür verantwortlich, die Straßen und Gemeinschaftseinrichtungen instand zu halten, und stellt eine breite Palette öffentlicher Dienstleistungen bereit.

## council house
Ein Haus in Großbritannien, das vom lokalen **COUNCIL** zu einem vergleichsweise niedrigen Preis vermietet wird. Diese Häuser und **council flats** (Sozialwohnungen) sind oft im Besitz des *councils*. Allerdings wurden ab 1980 viele dieser Wohnungen an ihre Bewohner verkauft.

## council tax
Eine Steuer, die jeder Haushalt in Großbritannien an die lokale oder kommunale Verwaltung entrichten muss. Die Höhe der *council tax* berechnet sich aus dem Schätzwert des Hauses bzw. der Wohnung sowie aus der Anzahl der Personen im Haushalt.

## county
Ein Verwaltungsbezirk in vielen Teilen Großbritanniens. Die *counties* bilden die Hauptverwaltungseinheiten und viele haben noch die alten Grenzen. Allerdings wurden in den letzten Jahrzehnten viele Grenzen und Namen geändert und die Bezeichnung *county* wird nicht mehr immer verwendet. In Schottland werden die Hauptverwaltungsbezirke jetzt **REGIONS** genannt.

## Daily Telegraph - The Daily Telegraph
Eine britische überregionale Tageszeitung. Der *Sunday Telegraph* wird von demselben Verlagshaus publiziert. Die Zeitung zählt zu den **BROADSHEET**-Zeitungen und damit zur seriösen Presse. Sie vertritt Ansichten der politischen Rechten und wurde in der Vergangenheit durch die Äußerung von sehr rechten Positionen bekannt. Traditionell vertritt sie die Interessen der **CONSERVATIVE PARTY**, äußert jedoch auch oft Kritik an der konservativen Politik.

## Democratic Party
Neben der **REPUBLICAN PARTY** eine der zwei großen politischen Parteien in den USA. Die demokratische Partei gilt als die liberalere, besonders in Fragen der Gesellschaftspolitik. Aus diesem Grund erhält sie viel Unterstützung aus den Reihen der Minderheitengruppierungen und Gewerkschaften.

**Kultur**

## Downing Street

Der Name einer Straße in Westminster im Zentrum von London. Das Haus mit der Nummer 10 in der Downing Street ist der offizielle Sitz des Premierministers und Nummer 11 der des Finanzministers. Unter Journalisten ist der Ausdruck *Downing Street* oder *Number 10* gebräuchlich, wenn vom Amtssitz des Premierministers die Rede ist.

## elementary school

Die Grundschule in den Vereinigten Staaten. Sie unterrichtet Kinder im Alter von sechs bis zwölf oder dreizehn Jahren. Diese Schulstufe wird auch als *grade school* oder *primary school* bezeichnet.

## first school ▶ PRIMARY SCHOOL.

## football pools

Eine dem Fußballtoto ähnliche beliebte Wettform in Großbritannien. Wer mitspielen will, lässt sich einmal wöchentlich *pools coupons* von einer der Toto-Gesellschaften zusenden. Man füllt die Wettscheine aus, indem man die Fußballergebnisse der nächsten Woche in Großbritannien vorhersagt. Für jedes Ergebnis wird gezahlt. Der Gewinn, der sich aus diesen Einzahlungen zusammensetzt, wird an diejenigen ausgezahlt, die dem Resultat am nächsten lagen. Dies kann bedeuten, dass unter Umständen eine sehr hohe Summe an eine einzelne Person ausgezahlt wird.

## further education

In Großbritannien bedeutet *further education* in der Regel jede Form der Fortbildung für Personen über 16 Jahren, mit Ausnahme der Hochschulausbildung, die als **higher education** bezeichnet wird. In den Vereinigten Staaten schließt jedoch der Ausdruck *further education* auch ein Hochschulstudium mit ein.

## Gaelic

Die alte Sprache der Kelten, wie sie noch von einigen Schotten und Iren gesprochen wird. Obgleich es beträchtliche Unterschiede zwischen dem schottischen und dem irischen Gälisch gibt, können die Sprecher einander verstehen. Das schottische Gälisch wird nur von etwa 40.000 Menschen im schottischen Hochland und auf den westschottischen Inseln gesprochen. Irisches Gälisch, das auch **Erse** oder einfach **Irish** genannt wird, erlebte in den letzten 50 Jahren eine bemerkenswerte Wiederbelebung. Es wird nun von vielen gesprochen und an Schulen als offizielle Sprache neben Englisch unterrichtet.

## GCSE

Ein Examen in einem bestimmten Fach, das gewöhnlich im 5. Schuljahr von den meisten Schülern in England und Wales abgelegt wird. Die Abschlussnoten (**grades**) werden in jedem Fach einzeln vergeben. Das *GCSE* können Schüler aller Befähigungen ablegen, die meisten tun dies in einer Reihe von Fächern. Schüler, die danach **A LEVELS** machen wollen, brauchen eine bestimmte Anzahl von *GCSEs*, um dafür zugelassen zu werden. Es ist möglich, *GCSEs* mit den eher beruflich orientierten **GNVQ**s zu kombinieren.

## GNVQ - General National Vocational Qualification

Ein Examen in einem bestimmten Fach, das gewöhnlich im 5. Schuljahr von den meisten Schülern in England und Wales abgelegt wird. *GNVQs* wurden 1992 als Alternative zu den **GCSEs** in einer Reihe von berufs- oder praxisorientierten Fächern eingeführt. Ihr Ziel ist es, Schüler auf das Berufsleben vorzubereiten. Viele Schüler legen ihre Examen mit einer Mischung aus *GNVQs* und **GCSEs** ab.

· · · · · · · · · · · · · · · · · · · · · · · · · · · · · · · · · · · · · · · · · · · · ·

## GP - general practitioner

Ein *GP*, oft auch **family doctor** (Hausarzt) genannt, ist ein Arzt für
Allgemeinmedizin in Großbritannien. In einer Gemeinschaftspraxis arbeiten meist
mehrere *GPs*. Die Patienten der Praxis können den behandelnden Arzt frei wählen.
Durch den **NATIONAL HEALTH SERVICE** müssen Patienten ihren Arzt nicht
bezahlen, die Praxis wird direkt oder indirekt aus staatlichen Geldern finanziert.
Wenn nötig, kann ein *GP* einen Patienten zu einem Spezialisten überweisen oder ins
Krankenhaus einweisen. Die Praxis wird **surgery** genannt.

## graduate school

Das Seminar einer Universität in den USA, das Kurse und Betreuung für graduierte
Studierende organisiert, die ihr Studium und/oder ihre Forschung nach dem 1.
Examen (nach ungefähr 3-4 Jahren Universitätsstudium) fortsetzen wollen.

## grammar school

Eine dem Gymnasium vergleichbare Form der weiterführenden Schule in einigen
Gebieten Englands und Wales' für Schüler zwischen 11 und 18 Jahren. Schüler im
Alter von 11 oder 12 Jahren werden nach bestandener Aufnahmeprüfung zugelassen.
*Grammar schools* wurden seit 1965 größtenteils von **COMPREHENSIVE SCHOOLS**
ersetzt. In den USA ist *grammar school* ein anderer Name für **ELEMENTARY
SCHOOL**.

## grant-maintained school

Eine Form der weiterführenden Schule in England und Wales, die von der Regierung
in London und nicht von der lokalen Regierung finanziert wird.

## green card

Ein offizielles Dokument, das nichtamerikanische Bürger zur Erwerbstätigkeit in
den USA berechtigt. Die *green card* braucht jeder, der beabsichtigt, eine feste Stelle
in den USA anzutreten.

## Green Party

Eine politische Partei in Großbritannien, die sich dem Umweltschutz verpflichtet
und Kritik an Industrien, Transportmitteln und Energiequellen übt, die sie für
umweltschädlich hält. Die Grünen sprechen sich gegen die Nutzung von
Atomenergie aus.

## Greyhound bus

Ein Bus der *Greyhound Lines Company*, der größten Busgesellschaft in den
Vereinigten Staaten. *Greyhound*-Busse verkehren zwischen größeren und kleineren
Städten in den gesamten Vereinigten Staaten und sind vor allem bei jungen Leuten
und Touristen beliebt, die oft lange Strecken mit ihnen zurücklegen.

## Guardian - The Guardian

Eine britische überregionale Tageszeitung. Der *Guardian* ist eine **BROADSHEET**-
Zeitung und zählt zur seriösen Presse. Politisch steht der Guardian links von der
Mitte, er berichtet ausführlich über soziale und kulturelle Themen.

## Guardian Angels

Eine Jugendorganisation in den USA, die gegründet wurde, um Menschen vor
Verbrechen zu schützen. Ihre Mitglieder tragen rote Kappen und T-Shirts mit dem
Motto '*Dare to Care*' ('Trau dich zu helfen'). Sie arbeiten mit der Polizei zusammen
und sind unbewaffnet.

## heritage centre
Ein Museumstyp in Großbritannien, der einem bestimmten Thema wie z.B. der Geschichte der lokalen Architektur oder einer bestimmten traditionellen Industrie oder Aktivität gewidmet ist. *Heritage centres* werden manchmal um alte Gebäude herum entwickelt.

## high school
Eine weiterführende Schule in den USA, normalerweise für Schüler von vierzehn bis achtzehn Jahren. Auch in Großbritannien werden einige weiterführende Schulen als *high schools* bezeichnet.

## House of Commons
Eines der zwei Häuser der britischen **HOUSES OF PARLIAMENT**, das Unterhaus des britischen Parlaments. Die gewählten **MEMBERS OF PARLIAMENT** treten hier zusammen, um innen- und außenpolitische Themen zu debattieren und über Gesetzesvorschläge abzustimmen.

## House of Lords
Eines der zwei Häuser der britischen **HOUSES OF PARLIAMENT**, das Oberhaus des britischen Parlaments. Seine Mitglieder werden nicht gewählt und seine Aufgabe ist es, Gesetze, die vom **HOUSE OF COMMONS** verabschiedet wurden, zu diskutieren und sie entweder anzunehmen oder Änderungen vorzuschlagen. Das **HOUSE OF LORDS** fungiert auch als oberstes Gericht in Großbritannien.

## House of Representatives
Das Unterhaus des amerikanischen **CONGRESS**. Es gibt 435 **REPRESENTATIVES** (Abgeordnete), die alle zwei Jahre gewählt werden. Proportional zu seiner Bevölkerung hat jeder Staat eine bestimmte Anzahl von Repräsentanten. Das *House of Representatives* bringt Gesetzesvorlagen ein und verabschiedet alle neuen Gesetze.

## Houses of Parliament
Die zwei Häuser des britischen Parlaments: **HOUSE OF COMMONS** und **HOUSE OF LORDS**. Der Westminsterpalast, der Gebäudekomplex im Zentrum von London, wo beide Häuser untergebracht sind, ist auch als *Houses of Parliament* bekannt.

## Independent - The Independent
Eine britische überregionale Tageszeitung. Ihr Pendant am Sonntag heißt *The Independent on Sunday*. Obgleich der *Independent* politisch eher links als rechts steht, strebt er, wie der Name schon andeutet, eine unabhängige überparteiliche Berichterstattung an. Der *Independent* ist eine BROADSHEET-Zeitung und zählt zur seriösen Presse.

## independent school
Eine Privatschule in Großbritannien, die sich selbst finanziert, und zwar durch Elternbeiträge. Sie erhält keine staatliche Unterstützung. **PUBLIC SCHOOLS** und **PREPARATORY SCHOOLS** fallen in diese Kategorie.

## infant school
Eine Grundschule in Großbritannien, die für die ersten drei Jahre Schulausbildung sorgt. Schulpflichtiges Alter in Großbritannien ist fünf. Oft ist die *infant school* Teil einer **PRIMARY SCHOOL**, zusammen mit einer **JUNIOR SCHOOL**, die Kinder bis zu ihrem 11. Lebensjahr betreut.

. . . . . . . . . . . . . . . . . . . . . . . . . . . . . . . . . . . . . . . . .

### International Herald Tribune - The International Herald Tribune

Eine internationale amerikanische Zeitung. Sie hat ihren Sitz in Paris, wird täglich in 180 Ländern veröffentlicht und hat eine exzellente Reputation für seriöse und gründliche Berichterstattung. Es ist eine **BROADSHEET**-Zeitung.

### Internet

Das Internet bietet eine Fülle von nützlichen Informationen über britische und amerikanische Kultur, Gesellschaft und Tagespolitik. Alle wichtigen Zeitungen und Zeitschriften haben Webseiten (z.B. http://www.the-times.co.uk und http://www.nytimes.com), ebenso die BBC (http://www.bbc.co.uk) und CNN (http://www.cnn.com).

### interstate (highway)

Durch mehr als einen Bundesstaat führende Autobahn in den USA, *Interstates* haben ein rotblaues Zeichen, auf dem 'I' steht. Nord-Süd-*interstates* haben ungerade Nummern und Ost-West-*interstates* haben gerade. Sie sind in jeder Richtung vierspurig.

### ITV - Independent Television

Die Gruppe von Fernsehgesellschaften, die in Großbritannien auf Channel 3 senden. Es gibt fünfzehn Regionen, von denen jede ihre eigenen Programme und Nachrichten empfangen kann. Daneben werden auf Channel 3 aber auch viele Gemeinschaftssendungen ausgestrahlt.

### Jobcentre

In den meisten britischen Städten gibt es Beratungszentren, die verschiedene Dienste für Arbeitssuchende anbieten, z.B. werden freie Stellen ausgehängt und Bewerbungsgespräche mit Arbeitgebern vermittelt. Jobcentres werden vom *Employment Service* betrieben.

### jobseeker's allowance

Eine staatliche Beihilfe, die Arbeitssuchenden in Großbritannien gewährt wird, wenn sie nachweisen können, dass sie sich um eine Anstellung bemühen.

### junior high school

Eine Schule in den USA, die für die Ausbildung zwischen der **ELEMENTARY SCHOOL** und der **HIGH SCHOOL** sorgt und normalerweise an eine *high school* angeschlossen ist.

### junior school

Eine staatliche Schule in Großbritannien für Kinder von sieben bis elf Jahren.

### Labour Party

Eine der drei großen politischen Parteien in Großbritannien. 1924 übernahm die *Labour Party* zum ersten Mal die Regierung. Ihr Ziel war, die Interessen der Arbeiter und Gewerkschaften zu vertreten. In den letzten 20 Jahren ist die Partei generell von ihren linken Positionen abgerückt. Sie wird daher heute oft als **New Labour** bezeichnet. 1997 wurde die Partei unter der Führung von Tony Blair in die Regierungsverantwortung gewählt.

**Kultur**

### L-driver - learner driver

Eine Person in Großbritannien, die Auto- oder Motorradfahren lernt, indem sie schon vor dem Erwerb eines entsprechenden Führerscheins als Lenker oder Lenkerin eines Kraftfahrzeugs am öffentlichen Straßenverkehr teilnimmt. *L-drivers* müssen von einer Person begleitet werden, die eine gültige *driving licence* (Führerschein) besitzt und müssen so lange *L-plates* vorne und hinten am Auto haben, bis sie ihren driving test (Führerscheinprüfung) erfolgreich abgeschlossen haben. *L-plates* sind viereckige weiße Schilder mit einem roten 'L' darauf.

### Liberal Democratic Party

Inoffiziell oft auch als *Lib Dems* bezeichnet. Die drittgrößte politische Partei Großbritanniens. Sie ging 1988 aus einem Zusammenschluss der *Liberal Party* und Mitgliedern der *Social Democratic Party* hervor.

### Los Angeles Times - The Los Angeles Times

Eine in Los Angeles verlegte Tageszeitung, die zu den besten Zeitungen in den USA gezählt wird. Sie verkauft Artikel an Zeitungen in aller Welt .

### Medicaid

Staatliche Krankenversicherung in den USA für Versicherungsnehmer unter 65 Jahren mit kleinem Einkommen.

### Medicare

Staatliche Gesundheitsversorgung und Krankenversicherung in den USA für Versicherungsnehmer über 65 Jahren.

### Member of Parliament (MP)

Ein Abgeordneter des **HOUSE OF COMMONS**, der eine der 659 *constituencies* (Wahlkreise) in England, Schottland, Wales und Nordirland repräsentiert.

### middle school

Eine staatliche Schule in einigen Teilen von England and Wales, die Kinder im Alter von 8 bis 14 Jahren unterrichtet.

### Mirror - The Mirror

Eine überregionale Tageszeitung. Am Sonntag erscheint ihr Pendant *The Sunday Mirror*. Der Mirror ist gemäßigt links und eine **TABLOID**-Zeitung, also ein Blatt, das zur Boulevardpresse gezählt wird.

### motorway

Eine britische Autobahn. In Großbritannien gibt es ein gut ausgebautes Autobahnnetz, die meisten Autobahnen sind dreispurig. Sie sind mit dem Buchstaben 'M' und einer nachfolgenden Nummer gekennzeichnet und haben eine Geschwindigkeitsbegrenzung von 70 mph (112 kmh). Die britischen Autobahnen sind gebührenfrei.

### National Health Service (NHS)

Das staatliche Gesundheitssystem in Großbritannien, das die ärztliche Versorgung gewährleistet. Es wird größtenteils aus öffentlichen Geldern finanziert. Ein Großteil der medizinischen Versorgung ist kostenlos. Kostenpflichtig sind jedoch Zahnarztbehandlungen und verschriebene Medikamente. Von der Zahlung ausgenommen sind Kinder, Jugendliche unter 18 Jahren und Rentner.

## National Insurance (NI)

Obligatorische Sozialabgaben von Arbeitgebern und Arbeitnehmern in Großbritannien werden **National Insurance Contributions** genannt. Jeder Erwachsene muss eine **National Insurance Number** haben. Mithilfe dieses Systems werden verschiedene staatliche Zuwendungen finanziert wie z.B. die **JOBSEEKERS' ALLOWANCE**, die Altersrenten sowie der **NATIONAL HEALTH SERVICE**.

## National Lottery

Eine Lotterie in Großbritannien, die ihre Einnahmen einer Vielzahl von Projekten in der Kunst, dem Sport, nationalen historischen Stätten und wohltätigen Zwecken zuführt.

## National Trust

Eine Stiftung zur Erhaltung und Pflege von Stätten von historischem Interesse oder besonderer Naturschönheiten. Der *National Trust* finanziert sich aus Stiftungsgeldern und privaten Spenden und ist der größte Privateigner von Land in Großbritannien. Er hat riesige Landflächen, Dörfer und Häuser gekauft oder erhalten, von denen viele zu bestimmten Zeiten öffentlich zugänglich sind.

## Native American

Dies ist die heute akzeptierte Bezeichnung für die Ureinwohner Nord- und Südamerikas sowie der Karibik. Sie wird besonders im offiziellen Kontext dem Ausdruck *American Indian* vorgezogen, da sie akkurater und positiver ist, denn *Indian* rührt daher, dass Kolumbus bei seiner Ankunft in Amerika annahm, in Indien zu sein. *American Indian* hat weiterhin weite Verbreitung und wird von den betreffenden Völkern nicht als diskriminierend empfunden.

## NBC - National Broadcasting Company

Die erste Rundfunkgesellschaft in den USA. Sie wurde 1926 gegründet. Das erste NBC-Nachrichtenprogramm wurde 1940 ausgestrahlt.

## News of the World - The News of the World

Eine britische Sonntagszeitung. Schwerpunkte der Berichterstattung sind die Themen Verbrechen und Sport. Das Blatt ist besonders für seine Sensationsberichterstattung über Prominente und die königliche Familie bekannt. Es ist eine **TABLOID**-Zeitung, Teil der Boulevardpresse und ist in Großbritannien die auflagenstärkste Zeitung.

## NVQ - National Vocational Qualification

Eine Qualifikation in Großbritannien, die man durch Ausbildung und Trainee-Umläufe am Arbeitsplatz oder in bestimmten Colleges und Schulen erhält. Die Fächer sind konkret berufsbezogen und auf verschiedenen Niveaus angesiedelt.

## Observer - The Observer

Eine britische Sonntagszeitung, die für die Qualität ihres investigativen Journalismus bekannt ist. Ihre politische Position ist links von der Mitte, besonders in sozialen Fragen. Der *Observer* ist eine **BROADSHEET**-Zeitung, zählt zur seriösen Presse und gehört nun der **GUARDIAN**-Gruppe an.

**Kultur**

- - - - - - - - - - - - - - - - - - - - - - - - - - - - - - - - - - - - - - - -

## pantomime
Eine Form der Theateraufführung, die traditionell in den Wochen vor und nach Weihnachten auf Bühnen in ganz Großbritannien hauptsächlich für Kinder gezeigt wird. Die Handlung ist oft die komische Adaption eines Märchens oder einer Volkssage und sie bezieht die Zuschauer stark ein. Gemäß der Tradition wird die Rolle des *principal boy* oder Helden von einer Frau gespielt und die Rolle der *dame*, einer grotesken Frauenfigur, von einem Mann.

## Parliament
Das britische Parlament ist die höchste gesetzgebende Gewalt in Großbritannien und besteht aus dem Souverän (dem König oder der Königin), dem **HOUSE OF LORDS** und dem **HOUSE OF COMMONS**.

## PBS - Public Broadcasting Service
Ein staatlich geförderter Rundfunkdienst in den USA, bekannt für seine hohe Programmqualität. Er übermittelt sein Programm an eine Gruppe von lokalen Sendern, die keinen Gewinn anstreben und keine Werbung ausstrahlen.

## Pentagon – The Pentagon
Das Gebäude in Arlington, Virginia, in dem die Verwaltungen des Verteidigungsministeriums untergebracht sind. Mit "das Pentagon" bezeichnen Journalisten oft die militärische Führung in den USA.

## Plaid Cymru
Die nationalistische politische Partei in Wales. Ihr wesentliches Ziel ist die völlige Unabhängigkeit vom Vereinigten Königreich. Im Rahmen dieses Ziels sind Anstrengungen unternommen worden, **WELSH** (das Walisische) wieder zu beleben und die walisische Kultur zu pflegen.

## preparatory school
Eine Privatschule in Großbritannien, auch **prep school** genannt, für Schüler im Alter von sieben bis dreizehn Jahren. Einige sind Tagesschulen, einige Internate und viele eine Mischung aus beidem. Eine *preparatory school* ist normalerweise entweder für Jungen oder für Mädchen, hat also keine gemischten Klassen. Die Eltern zahlen für die Ausbildung ihrer Kinder und andere Angebote innerhalb der Schule Schulgeld. Die meisten Schüler gehen anschließend auf eine **PUBLIC SCHOOL** (Privatschule). *Preparatory schools* und *public schools* nennen sich heute oft **INDEPENDENT SCHOOLS**.

## President
Der Präsident der Vereinigten Staaten ist das Staatsoberhaupt, trägt außenpolitische Verantwortung und hat den Oberbefehl über die Streitkräfte. Er kann Bundesrichter und leitende Minister ernennen und wird vom **CONGRESS** gebeten, neue Gesetze zu bewilligen. Ein Präsident kann maximal für zwei *terms* (Legislaturperioden), also für 8 Jahre regieren.

## primary school
Eine Grundschule in Großbritannien, die Kinder von fünf bis elf betreut.

## public school
Eine Privatschule in England und Wales für Schüler im Alter von dreizehn bis achtzehn Jahren, die vorher meist eine **PREPARATORY SCHOOL** besucht haben. Die meisten *public schools* sind Internate, normalerweise entweder für Jungen oder Mädchen. Die Eltern zahlen für die Ausbildung ihrer Kinder und andere Angebote innerhalb der Schule Schulgeld. In Schottland und den USA ist eine *public school* eine staatliche Schule.

Kultur

. . . . . . . . . . . . . . . . . . . . . . . . . . . . . . . . . . . . . . . . . . . . .

### Queen's Speech
Eine von den Mitgliedern des britischen Parlaments vorbereitete Rede, die von der Königin jährlich zur Parlamentseröffnung im Herbst im **HOUSE OF LORDS** verlesen wird. Dies ist ein wichtiger Anlass, denn in der Rede werden die Pläne der Regierung für das kommende Jahr vorgestellt.

### region
Die größte Verwaltungseinheit in Schottland. Es gibt davon neun, jede mit einem eigenen **COUNCIL**.

### Representative
Ein Mitglied des amerikanischen **HOUSE OF REPRESENTATIVES**.

### Republican Party
Neben der **DEMOCRATIC PARTY** eine der zwei großen politischen Parteien in den USA. Sie wird als die konservativere der beiden Parteien eingestuft.

### SAT
1 - **Scholastic Aptitude Test** Eine standardisierte Eignungsprüfung in den USA, die normalerweise im letzten Schuljahr der **HIGH SCHOOL** abgelegt wird und die für die meisten Colleges und Universitäten als Zulassungsvoraussetzung gilt.
2 - **Standard Assessment Test** Ein Test für Schüler im Alter von 7, 11 und 14 Jahren in allen Schulen in England und Wales zur Kontrolle ihres Wissensstandes.

### Scottish Certificate of Education
Das am weitesten verbreitete Schulabschlusszeugnis in Schottland, das sein eigenes Ausbildungssystem hat. Die erste Prüfung wird mit 16 abgelegt und ist das Äquivalent zu den GCSE-Prüfungen in England, während die zweite Prüfung mit 17 abgelegt wird und das Äquivalent zu den **A-LEVELs** darstellt.

### Scottish National Party (SNP)
Eine schottische Partei, deren Ziel es ist, eine vollkommen unabhängige schottische Regierung zu erwirken.

### Scottish Parliament
Das schottische Parlament, dessen Mitglieder im *Palace of Holyroodhouse* in der Hauptstadt Edinburgh zusammentreten. Es wurde 1999 nach den schottischen Wahlen eröffnet und verleiht Schottland eine größere Autonomie gegenüber dem britischen Parlament in London.

### SDLP - Social Democrat and Labour Party
Eine politische Partei in Nordirland, deren Ziel die rechtliche Gleichstellung von Katholiken und die Vereinigung Nordirlands mit der Republik Irland ist. Sie lehnt Gewalt als Mittel der Politik ab.

### Senate - the United States Senate
Das Oberhaus des amerikanischen **CONGRESS**. Es gibt 100 gewählte **SENATORS** (Senatoren). Neue Gesetze müssen sowohl vom **HOUSE OF REPRESENTATIVES** als auch vom Senat verabschiedet werden.

### Senator
Ein Mitglied des amerikanischen **SENATE**.

Kultur

**Kultur**

## Shadow Cabinet ▶ CABINET

## Silicon Valley
Ein scherzhafter Name für ein Gebiet im kalifornischen Santa Clara Valley, wo es eine besonders hohe Dichte an Computerfirmen und Elektronikunternehmen gibt. Der Name rührt daher, dass in der Elektronik mit Silicium gearbeitet wird.

## Sinn Fein
Name einer 1905 in Irland gegründeten politischen Bewegung und Partei, deren ursprüngliche Ziele die Unabhängigkeit Irlands und eine Wiederbelebung der irischen Kultur waren und die heute, im Verein mit der IRA, ein vereinigtes republikanisches Irland anstrebt.

## Stars and Stripes
Die amerikanische Nationalflagge.

## Star-Spangled Banner
Die amerikanische Nationalhymne.

## state school
Eine direkt oder indirekt vom Staat finanzierte Schule in Großbritannien, die keine Schulgebühren verlangt. Die meisten Kinder in Großbritannien besuchen solche staatlichen Schulen.

## Sun - The Sun
Eine britische Tageszeitung, die für ihre Sensationsschlagzeilen und -berichterstattung sowie für ihre rechten Meinungen bekannt ist. Sie ist eine **TABLOID**-Zeitung, gehört zur Boulevardpresse und ist die auflagenstärkste Tageszeitung in Großbritannien.

## tabloid
Eine Zeitung in Großbritannien, die auf kleinen Zeitungsbögen gedruckt wird, im Gegensatz zu den **BROADSHEETS**, die auf doppelt so großen Zeitungsbögen gedruckt werden. Das *tabloid*-Format wird normalerweise mit der popular press (Boulevardpresse) assoziiert, wie sie z.B. von **THE SUN** und **THE MIRROR** repräsentiert wird, während das *broadsheet-Format* von den meisten Zeitungen der *quality press* (seriösen Presse), wie z.B. **THE GUARDIAN** und **THE TIMES**, benutzt wird.

## The Times, The White House *etc.* ▶ TIMES, WHITE HOUSE *etc.*

## Times - The Times
Eine britische überregionale Tageszeitung, deren Pendant am Sonntag *The Sunday Times* ist. Sie ist eine **BROADSHEET**-Zeitung und zählt zur seriösen Presse. Sie ist politisch unabhängig, wird jedoch gemeinhin als konservativ angesehen. Sie ist die älteste Zeitung in England und wurde erstmals 1785 veröffentlicht.

## TOEFL - Test of English as a Foreign Language
Ein Test zur Feststellung der englischen Sprachkenntnisse für Studierende, die an einer amerikanischen Universität studieren wollen und deren Muttersprache nicht Englisch ist.

## Tory ▶ CONSERVATIVE PARTY.

## Turner Prize

Ein jährlich ausgeschriebener Preis, der von der *Tate Gallery* in London für ein Werk eines britischen Künstlers unter 50 Jahren vergeben wird. Die Preisverleihung erhält ein breites Echo in der Presse und der öffentlichen Diskussion, da viele der Werke avantgardistisch und umstritten sind.

## Ulster Democratic Unionist Party

Eine politische Partei in Nordirland, die stark von den Protestanten unterstützt wird und den Standpunkt vertritt, dass Nordirland Teil des Vereinigten Königreichs bleiben sollte.

## Ulster Unionist Party

Von den politischen Parteien in Nordirland, die die Ansicht vertreten, dass Nordirland Teil des Vereinigten Königreichs bleiben sollte, ist dies die bedeutendste.

## Union Jack

Die Nationalflagge des Vereinigten Königreichs. Sie setzt sich aus dem englischen *St George's Cross*, dem schottischen *St Andrew's Cross* und dem nordirischen *St Patrick's Cross* zusammen.

## Washington Post - The Washington Post

Eine amerikanische überregionale Tageszeitung, die in Washington erscheint. Sie ist bekannt für ihre politische Berichterstattung, ihren investigativen Journalismus auf hohem Niveau und ihre Liberalität.

## Welsh

Die alte keltische Sprache, wie sie in Wales gesprochen wird. Für mehr als 20% der Bevölkerung ist Walisisch noch die erste Sprache und hat, wie viele Minderheitensprachen, in den letzten 40 Jahren eine Wiederbelebung erfahren. Es ist zur Zeit die erste Sprache in vielen walisischen Schulen und offizielle Schilder sind normalerweise sowohl in *Welsh* als auch in Englisch beschriftet.

## Welsh Assembly

Das walisische Parlament, dessen Mitglieder in der Hauptstadt Cardiff zusammentreten. Es wurde 1999 nach den walisischen Wahlen eröffnet und verleiht Wales eine größere Autonomie gegenüber dem britischen Parlament in London.

## Westminster

Ein Stadtteil im Zentrum von London, in dem ein Großteil der Regierungsgebäude liegt. Das wichtigste unter ihnen ist der *Palace of Westminster*, auch **HOUSES OF PARLIAMENT** genannt, in dem beide Häuser des britischen Parlaments tagen. Ebenfalls im Stadtteil liegt die *Westminster Abbey*, wo alle englischen Könige und Königinnen seit William dem Eroberer gekrönt wurden.

## Whitehall

Eine Straße im Zentrum von London, in der sich ein Großteil der Ministerien befindet. Journalisten bezeichnen mit *Whitehall* oft die Regierung und die Verwaltung Großbritanniens.

## White House – The White House

Der offizielle (Arbeits-)Sitz des amerikanischen Präsidenten in Washington. Journalisten bezeichnen mit *the White House* häufig den Präsidenten und seine Berater.

**Kultur**

# A–Z of German life and culture

### Abendbrot, Abendessen
For most Germans, **MITTAGESSEN** is still the main meal of the day.
*Abendbrot* or *Abendessen* normally consists of bread, cheese, meats, perhaps a salad, and a hot drink. It is eaten by the whole family at about 6 or 7 p.m. *Abendessen* can also refer to a cooked meal, especially for people who are out at work all day.

### Abitur
This is the final exam taken by pupils at a **GYMNASIUM**, usually when they are about 19. The result is based on continuous assessment during the last two years before the *Abitur*, plus examinations in four subjects. The *Abitur* is the obligatory qualification for university entrance.

### ADAC - Allgemeiner Deutscher Automobil-Club
Europe's largest motoring organization, based in Munich, the *ADAC* acts as a powerful lobby for the German motorist. The *ADAC-Straßenwacht* provides free breakdown assistance for *ADAC* members.

### Ampel-Koalition
A term describing any coalition between the **SPD** (the party colour is red), the **FDP** (yellow) and the Green Party. This type of coalition has become increasingly common in local government over the last ten years, with some **LÄNDER** ruled in this way.

### AOK - Allgemeine Ortskrankenkasse
The largest health insurance organization in Germany. Foreign visitors to Germany who need medical assistance can get the necessary forms at the local *AOK* office.

### Arbeitsamt
The local employment office to be found in every German town. It provides career guidance, helps the unemployed find new jobs, and processes all claims for **ARBEITSLOSENGELD** and related benefits. Unemployed people have to report to the *Arbeitsamt* once every three months to prove they are still looking for work.

### Arbeitslosengeld
This is the benefit paid to all unemployed people who are looking for a new job and have already made a minimum contribution to the **ARBEITSLOSENVERSICHERUNG**. The benefit is a proportion of the person's previous pay, and is higher for people supporting children. After one year, it is reduced and called *Arbeitslosenhilfe*.

### Arbeitslosenversicherung
This is the compulsory state-run insurance against unemployment. All *Arbeiter* and *Angestellte* have to pay into this scheme and in return are entitled to **ARBEITSLOSENGELD** and related benefits. This area has been subject to wide-ranging reforms in recent years.

### ARD
An umbrella organization for the regional broadcasting stations of the various German **LÄNDER**, financed by licence fees plus a certain amount of advertising. The *ARD* broadcasts **DAS ERSTE**.

. . . . . . . . . . . . . . . . . . . . . . . . . . . . . . . . . . . . . . . . . . .

## Autobahn

Germany's motorway network is very extensive and not subject to a general speed limit, other than a recommended limit of about 80 mph. Many motorways have only two lanes. To ease congestion, lorries are not allowed to use the *Autobahn* on Sundays. German motorways are free, but on Austrian and Swiss motorways all vehicles must display a **VIGNETTE**.

## BAföG - Bundesausbildungsförderungsgesetz

The grant which about a quarter of German students receive from the state. Whether they are entitled to *BAföG*, and how much they get, depends on the students' and their parents' financial circumstances. Half of the money is given in the form of a loan which has to be repaid later.

## Bayern

*Bayern* (Bavaria), Germany's largest and southernmost **LAND**, is known for its beautiful scenery (the Alps and their foothills, as well as forests, rivers, and lakes, picturesque towns and villages), its excellent beer and food, and its lively cosmopolitan capital München (Munich). The Bavarians are said to be warm and hospitable, but also fiercely independent and very conservative.

## Bausparen

German building societies expect people to have saved up a sizeable sum towards the purchase of a house before they will give them a mortgage. For this reason, many Germans have a *Bausparvertrag* (a tax-efficient savings contract for an agreed sum) with a building society, even if they are not planning to buy their **EIGENHEIM** for some time.

## Beamte

This term covers civil servants and other officials, but also occupations like teachers and lecturers. *Beamte* are legally obliged to support the democratic system in Germany and are not allowed to go on strike. In return, they enjoy many privileges, such as total job security, private health insurance, and exemption from social security contributions.

## Berlin

After **WIEDERVEREINIGUNG**, Berlin took over from Bonn as the capital of Germany, but the German government did not start moving there until 1998. This vibrant city in the heart of Europe lies on the river Spree. It has about 3.5 million inhabitants and is a major cultural and industrial centre.

## Berufsausbildung ▶ LEHRE.

## Berufsschule

A college for young people who are doing a **LEHRE**. They attend *Berufsschule* 2 days a week (or sometimes in blocks of several weeks) to continue their general education and receive formal training in their chosen type of job.

## Betriebsrat

The staff in any German company with at least five employees are entitled to have a *Betriebsrat*. This is a committee elected by the workers to represent their interests as opposed to those of management. It allows workers to participate in decisions on pay and other benefits, redundancies, and even some business matters.

## Biergarten

A rustic open-air pub which is traditional in Bavaria but can now be found throughout Germany. It is usually set up for the summer in the yard of a pub or restaurant. A *Biergarten* is the best place to enjoy a beer and a simple meal on a summer's day.

## Bild Zeitung

Germany's largest-selling daily newspaper, *Bild* is a typical tabloid with huge headlines, lots of photos, scandal stories, gossip and nude models. It is known for its right-wing views. *Bild* sells about 4.5 million copies every day, almost eight times more than any other newspaper in Germany. Its Sunday edition is called *Bild am Sonntag*.

## Bodensee

This is the German name for Lake Constance, Germany's biggest lake, bordered by Germany, Switzerland, and Austria. The river Rhine flows through it. This popular recreation area enjoys a particularly mild climate, especially on the three islands Lindau, Mainau, and Reichenau.

## Bonn

Bonn was the capital of the Federal Republic of Germany from 1949 until **BERLIN** was made the capital of a reunified Germany and remains home to a number of government institutions. This relatively small, quiet city of about 300,000 inhabitants enjoys a picturesque location on the river Rhine.

## Bund

This term refers to the federal state as the top level of government, as opposed to the individual **LÄNDER** which make up the Federal Republic. *Bund* and *Länder* have different responsibilities, with the *Bund* in charge of foreign policy, defence, transport, health, employment, etc.

## Bundesbank

Properly called the *Deutsche Bundesbank*, Germany's central bank is located in Frankfurt/Main. With the introduction of the Euro in 1999, some of its functions have passed to the European Central Bank (also in Frankfurt).

## Bundeskanzler

The Chancellor is the head of government in Germany and Austria. The German chancellor is normally elected for 4 years by the MPs in the **BUNDESTAG** after being proposed by the **BUNDESPRÄSIDENT**. He chooses the ministers and decides on government policies.

## Bundesland ▶ LAND.

## Bundespräsident

The President is the head of state in Germany and Austria. The German president is elected for 5 years by the MPs and delegates from the **LÄNDER**. He (so far there have not been any women) acts mainly as a figurehead, representing Germany abroad, and does not get involved in party politics, although he often takes a moral lead in major issues like the reform of the education system.

• • • • • • • • • • • • • • • • • • • • • • • • • • • • • • • • • • • • • • • • • • • • •

## Bundesrat

This is the upper house of the German parliamentary system, where the **LÄNDER** are represented. The *Bundesrat* members are appointed by the Länder governments. It has to approve laws affecting the *Länder*, and also any changes to the **GRUNDGESETZ**. Sometimes the opposition parties actually hold a majority in the *Bundesrat*, which allows them to influence German legislation.

## Bundestag

The lower house of the German parliament, which is elected every four years by the German people. The *Bundestag* is responsible for federal legislation, the federal budget, and electing the **BUNDESKANZLER**. Half of the MPs are elected directly and half by proportional representation, in a complicated voting system where each voter has two votes.

## Bundeswehr

This is the name for the German armed forces, which come under the control of the defence minister. The *Bundeswehr* consists of professional soldiers and conscripts serving their **WEHRDIENST**. Until 1994, the **GRUNDGESETZ** did not allow German forces to be deployed abroad, but they now take part in certain operations, notably UN peacekeeping missions.

## Bündnis 90/Die Grünen

This party came into being in 1993 as the result of a merger of the West German Green party and civil rights movements of the former GDR. It is the third largest force in the German parliament, committed to environmental and social issues.

## CDU - Christlich-Demokratische Union

One of the main German political parties. It was founded in 1945 and is committed to Christian and conservative values. The *CDU* is not active in Bavaria. ▶ **CSU**.

## Christkind

Traditionally, it is *Das Christkind* (the Christ Child) who brings Christmas presents to children on Christmas Eve. The concept of *der Weihnachtsmann* (Father Christmas) is relatively new in Germany.

## CSU - Christlich-Soziale Union

The Bavarian sister party of the **CDU**. It was founded in 1946 and has enjoyed an absolute majority in Bavaria for over 30 years. Politically, it stands to the right of the *CDU*.

## Das Erste

Also called **Erstes Programm**, this is the first German public TV channel, broadcast by **ARD**. Programming includes news, information, films, and entertainment. There is a limited amount of advertising, which is concentrated in 'blocks' at certain times of day and not after 8 p.m.

## Der Spiegel

One of Germany's best-selling weekly news and current affairs magazines, *Der Spiegel* was founded in 1947 and is published in Hamburg. It has a liberal to left-wing outlook and has become synonymous with investigative journalism in Germany, as it has brought to light a number of major scandals in German business and politics over the years.

Culture

### Deutsche Post

The previously state-run German postal system has undergone wide-ranging reforms in recent years which will effectively remove the *Deutsche Post* monopoly by 2002. The number of post offices has been reduced, but small post office agencies can now be found in shops, newsagents, and petrol stations. German letter boxes are yellow. Postal charges are relatively high, but the service is very reliable.

### Deutsche Telekom

The previously state-run German telecommunications service has undergone extensive reforms and gradual privatization and is now a public limited company. Since 1998 when the market was opened up to competition, *Deutsche Telekom* has ceased to have a monopoly.

### Deutsche Welle

The German equivalent of the BBC World Service, this radio station is financed and controlled by the German government and broadcasts programmes on German politics, business, arts, and culture, aimed at listeners abroad.

### DGB - Deutscher Gewerkschaftsbund

The biggest trade-union umbrella organization in Germany, with about 8 million members in 13 individual unions. In recent years, the *DGB* has pursued a policy of moderation in its pay demands.

### Die Republikaner

This ultra right-wing party was founded in 1983 and quickly became notorious for its xenophobic and nationalistic aims. After some success in the early 90s it now has very little support and is not represented in the **BUNDESTAG**.

### Die Welt

A national daily newspaper which was founded in 1946 and is published in Hamburg. It has a large business section and is considered to be right-wing in its views.

### Die Zeit

Germany's 'heaviest' weekly newspaper is published in Hamburg and is considered essential reading for academics and intellectuals. Former **BUNDESKANZLER** Helmut Schmidt is a joint editor. The paper offers in-depth analysis of current issues in politics, society, culture, and the arts.

### documenta

This international contemporary art exhibition takes place in Kassel every 4 to 5 years. The 1997 *documenta* covered drama, music, film, talks and the Internet as well as art. It cost over 20 million DM and was subsidized heavily by the taxpayer and private sponsors.

### Drittes Programm

One of the eight regional television channels run by the **ARD** and focussing on regional affairs and educational programmes.

### Duales System

This is a waste disposal and recycling system which was introduced in Germany in 1993 and is operated by the private company *DSD*. All packaging materials marked with the **GRÜNER PUNKT** symbol are collected separately, and sorted into plastics, glass, paper and metal for recycling. Non-recyclable and compostable waste is still collected by the local refuse collection service.

• • • • • • • • • • • • • • • • • • • • • • • • • • • • • • • • • • • • • • • • • • •

### Eigenheim

The level of home ownership in Germany is rising but still far lower than in Britain. Many people happily live in rented flats or houses, but most dream of buying or building their *Eigenheim* (own home) one day and save up towards it through the system of **BAUSPAREN**. German houses tend to be large and solidly built, usually with cellars, and are therefore relatively expensive. First-time buyers are usually middle-aged and expect to stay in their home for the rest of their lives.

### Einwohnermeldeamt

Anybody who moves to Germany or relocates within Germany is legally obliged to register their address with the *Einwohnermeldeamt* within a week.

### Entwerter

When travelling on buses and trams in Germany it is important to remember that you have to cancel (*entwerten*) your ticket in one of the *Entwerter* machines located inside the bus or tram. Your ticket, even if you have just bought it from the driver, is not valid without the stamp from the *Entwerter*.

### Erste, Das ▶ DAS ERSTE.

### Erziehungsgeld

A state benefit paid for up to two years to any mother or father who stays at home after the birth of a child to look after it. In 98% of cases, it is still the mother who claims *Erziehungsgeld*. Although this benefit is means-tested, almost all families receive some money for the first 6 months of the baby's life. In addition to this, parents receive **Kindergeld** (child benefit) for each child.

### Erziehungsurlaub

A German mother or father who looks after a child at home is entitled to up to three years' extended maternity or paternity leave. At the end of this *Erziehungsurlaub* they are entitled to return to their old job. 95% of German mothers take time out of work for at least one year after the birth.

### Eurocheque

The Eurocheque is the standard cheque issued by banks in Germany. It is backed up by the *Eurochequekarte* which can also be used at cash machines and for payments in shops. Although plastic cards have become more popular in Germany, many people (and shops and restaurants) still prefer cash.

### Fachhochschule

This type of university provides shorter, more vocational and practically-based courses than those available at a **HOCHSCHULE**.

### Fahrschule

Learner drivers in Germany have to take lessons from a qualified driving instructor at a *Fahrschule* (driving school) in a specially adapted car with dual controls. It is quite common to have 20 or 30 driving lessons before sitting the driving test, as there is no other way of getting driving practice on the road.

### FDP - Freie Demokratische Partei

The German Liberal party, which was founded in 1948. This relatively small party tends to gain only 5 to 10% of the vote at general elections, but it has held the balance of power in various coalition governments both with the SPD and the CDU/CSU. It supports a free-market economy and the freedom of the individual.

Culture

## Focus
A relatively new weekly news and current affairs magazine published in Munich. It was set up in 1993 and is aimed at a centre-right readership, especially businesspeople and professionals. *Focus* has become a serious competitor of **DER SPIEGEL**, with shorter, easier-to-read articles and a more modern presentation.

## Frankfurter Allgemeine Zeitung (FAZ)
One of Germany's most serious and widely respected daily newspapers. It was founded in 1945 and is published in Frankfurt/Main. It tends to have a centre-left to liberal outlook.

## Frühstück
Breakfast in Germany typically consists of strong coffee, slices of bread or fresh rolls with butter, jam, honey, sliced cheese and meat, and maybe a boiled egg. For working people and schoolchildren, who have little time for breakfast first thing in the morning, a *zweites Frühstück* is common at around 10 a.m.

## Gastarbeiter
The term used for foreign workers from southern European countries, mainly Turkey, former Yugoslavia, and Italy, many of whom came to Germany in the 60s and 70s. Despite the time that they have lived in Germany and the fact that their children have grown up there, integration is still a widely discussed issue.

## Gemeinde
The lowest level of local government, run by a local council chaired by the *Bürgermeister* (mayor). *Gemeinden* have their own budget, with income from local taxes. They pass local legislation and administer local affairs.

## Gesamthochschule
A type of university established in some **LÄNDER** following reforms in the 60s and combining **HOCHSCHULE** and **FACHHOCHSCHULE** under one roof, thereby offering greater flexibility and a wider choice of subjects to the student.

## Gesamtschule
A comprehensive secondary school introduced in the 70s and designed to replace the traditional division into **GYMNASIUM**, **REALSCHULE,** and **HAUPTSCHULE**. Pupils are taught different subjects at their own level and may take any of the school-leaving exams, including the **ABITUR**.

## Goethe-Institut
An organization for promoting German language and culture abroad. It is based in Munich and runs about 140 institutes in over 70 countries, offering German language classes, cultural events such as exhibitions, films and seminars, and a library of German books and magazines and other documentation, which is open to the public.

## Grundgesetz
The written German constitution which came into force in May 1949. It lays down the basic rights of German citizens, the relationship between **BUND** and **LÄNDER**, and the legal framework of the German state.

## Grundschule
The primary school which all German children attend for four years from the age of 6 (some children do not start until they are 7). Lessons are intense but pupils only attend school for about 4 hours a day. At the end of the *Grundschule*, teachers and parents decide together which type of secondary school the child should attend.

### Grüner Punkt

A symbol used to mark packaging materials which can be recycled. Any packaging carrying this logo is collected separately under the **DUALES SYSTEM** recycling scheme. Manufacturers have to buy a licence from the recycling company *DSD* to entitle them to use this symbol.

### Gymnasium

The secondary school which prepares pupils for the **ABITUR**. The *Gymnasium* is attended after the **GRUNDSCHULE** by the most academically-inclined pupils. They spend nine years at this school, and during the last three years, they have some choice as to which subjects they study. ▶ **SCHULE**.

### Hauptschule

The secondary school which prepares pupils for the **Hauptschulabschluss** (school-leaving certificate). The *Hauptschule* aims to give the least academically-inclined children a sound educational grounding. Pupils stay at the *Hauptschule* for 5 or 6 years after the **GRUNDSCHULE**. ▶ **SCHULE, LEHRE.**

### Hochschule

German *Hochschulen* (universities) do not charge fees, and anybody who has passed the **ABITUR** is entitled to go to university (except for some subjects which have a **NUMERUS CLAUSUS**). They tend to be very large and impersonal institutions. Students may receive a **BAföG** grant and often take more than the minimum 8 semesters (4 years) to complete their course.

### ICE - Intercityexpresszug

This high-speed train runs at two-hour intervals on a number of main routes in Germany, offering shorter journey times and better facilities than ordinary trains. A futuristic new *ICE* station has been built at Frankfurt airport.

### IM - inoffizieller Mitarbeiter

This term refers to 'unofficial collaborators' of the **STASI**. These informers were often ordinary people in the former GDR who had been recruited or pressurized by the Stasi to spy on neighbours, family, and friends. However, some were prominent figures in the West.

### Internet

A wealth of useful information on German politics, culture and so on can be obtained on the Internet, which is very popular in Germany. All the main German newspapers have web sites (e.g. http://www.focus.de), as do the television channels (e.g. http://www.ard.de) and organizations like the *Goethe-Institut* (http://goethe.de). In addition, many German towns and cities have web sites (e.g. http://www.berlin.de).

### Kaffee

This refers not only to coffee as a drink but also to the small meal taken at about 4 in the afternoon, consisting of coffee and cakes or biscuits. It is often a social occasion as it is common to invite family or friends for *Kaffee und Kuchen* (rather than for lunch or dinner), especially on birthdays and other family occasions.

### Kanton

The name for the individual autonomous states that make up Switzerland. There are 26 *Kantone*, with the largest having just over 1 million inhabitants. Each *Kanton* has its own government and its own constitution.

Culture

## Kindergarten

Every German pre-school child has the right to attend *Kindergarten* (nursery or play school) between the ages of 3 and 6. Kindergarten concentrates on play, crafts, singing etc., and aims to foster the child's social and emotional development. There is no formal teaching at all, this being reserved for the **GRUNDSCHULE**.

## Kindertagesstätte

Often called *Kita* for short, this is a day nursery intended for the children of working parents. The age range is usually from babies to 6, although some *Kitas* also offer after-school care for older children.

## Kirchensteuer

Any taxpayer who is a member of one of the established churches in Germany (mainly Catholic and Protestant) has to pay *Kirchensteuer* (church tax). It is calculated as a proportion of income tax and is collected at source by the tax office, which then passes on the money to the relevant church.

## Krankenkasse

There are many different health insurance organizations in Germany with the **AOK** being the largest. Contributions are high, due to the high standard (and cost) of health care in Germany. The *Krankenkassen* issue their members with plastic cards which entitle them to treatment by the doctor of their choice.

## Kur

A health cure in a spa town lasting about 3 to 6 weeks and usually involving a special diet, exercise programmes, physiotherapy, massage etc. These are intended for people with minor complaints or recovering from illness and play an important role in preventative medicine in Germany. *Kuren* are paid for by the **KRANKENKASSEN**, with the patient making a contribution. A number of cutbacks have been made in this area in recent years.

## Ladenschlusszeit

The strict regulations governing shop closing times in Germany were relaxed in 1996. Shops are allowed to stay open until 8 p.m. on weekdays and 4 p.m. on Saturdays, and bakeries may open for 3 hours on Sundays. However, the actual opening times vary, depending on the location and size of the shop.

## Land

Germany is a federal republic consisting of 16 member states called *Länder* or *Bundesländer*. Five so-called neue *Bundesländer* were added after reunification in 1990. The Land has a degree of autonomy and is responsible for all educational and cultural affairs, the police, the environment, and local government. Austria is a federal state consisting of 9 *Länder*, and the Swiss equivalent is a **KANTON**.

## Landtag

The parliament of a **LAND**, which is elected every 4 to 5 years using a similar mixed system of voting as for the **BUNDESTAG** elections.

## Lehre

This type of apprenticeship is still the normal way to learn a trade or train for a practical career in Germany. A *Hauptschulabschluss* is the minimum requirement, although many young people with a *Realschulabschluss* or even *Abitur* opt to train in this way. A *Lehre* takes about 2 to 3 years and involves practial training by a **MEISTER(IN)** backed up by lessons at a **BERUFSSCHULE**, with an exam at the end.

## Love Parade

A Techno music and dance festival which takes place in Berlin every summer, with about 1 million mainly young people attending. Originally a celebration of youth culture, it has become a major tourist attraction.

## Markt

Weekly markets are still held in most German cities and towns, usually laid out very attractively in the picturesque market squares. Fresh fruit and vegetables, flowers, eggs, cheese and other dairy products, bread, meat and fish are available directly from the producer. Many Germans still buy most of their provisions *auf dem Markt*.

## Meister(in)

A master craftsman or craftswoman who has completed rigorous training in his/her trade or vocation and has passed a final exam after several years' experience in a job. A *Meister(in)* is allowed to set up in business and train young people who are doing their **LEHRE**.

## Mittagessen

This is a cooked meal eaten in the middle of the day and is the main meal of the day for most Germans. Schoolchildren come home from school in time for *Mittagessen* and most large companies have canteens where hot meals are served at lunchtime. On a Sunday, *Mittagessen* might consist of a starter like a clear broth, followed by a roast with gravy, boiled potatoes and vegetables, and a dessert.

## Namenstag

This day is celebrated by many Germans, especially Catholics, in the same way as a birthday. It is the day dedicated to the saint whose name the person carries so, for example, someone called Martin would celebrate their *Namenstag* on *Martinstag* (November 11).

## Numerus clausus

The *Numerus clausus* system is used to limit the number of students studying certain oversubscribed subjects such as medicine at German universities.
It means that only those students who have achieved a minimum average mark in their **ABITUR** are admitted.

## Orientierungsstufe

The name given to the first two years at a **HAUPTSCHULE**, a **REALSCHULE**, or a **GYMNASIUM**. During this time pupils can find out if they are suited to the type of school they are attending, and at the end of the two years they may transfer to a different school.

## Ossi

A colloquial and sometimes derogatory term for someone from East Germany, as opposed to a **WESSI** (someone from West Germany).

## Parkscheibe

When parking your car in Germany in an area where the parking time is limited, you have to display a *Parkscheibe* (parking disc) in the windscreen, with the hands of the clock set to your arrival time. These blue cardboard or plastic discs are available at newsagents and department stores.

Culture

∙ ∙ ∙ ∙ ∙ ∙ ∙ ∙ ∙ ∙ ∙ ∙ ∙ ∙ ∙ ∙ ∙ ∙ ∙ ∙ ∙ ∙ ∙ ∙ ∙ ∙ ∙ ∙ ∙ ∙ ∙ ∙ ∙ ∙ ∙ ∙ ∙ ∙ ∙ ∙ ∙ ∙ ∙ ∙ ∙ ∙ ∙ ∙ ∙ ∙ ∙ ∙ ∙ ∙ ∙ ∙ ∙ ∙ ∙ ∙

### PDS - Partei des Demokratischen Sozialismus

A party formed in 1990 from the old East German SED. The ultra left-wing *PDS* is against a free-market economy and demands the redistribution of wealth. It has virtually no support in the former West Germany.

### Pflegeversicherung

Compulsory nursing-care insurance which all employees have to pay into as part of their **SOZIALABGABEN**. It was introduced in Germany in 1995 and pays for the long-term nursing care of the elderly and the severely disabled. Employers and employees make equal contributions to the scheme.

### Polterabend

This is Germany's answer to stag and hen nights. The *Polterabend* usually takes place a few days before the wedding and takes the form of a large party for the family and friends of both bride and groom. Traditionally, the guests smash some crockery, as this is supposed to bring luck to the couple.

### Post ▶ DEUTSCHE POST.

### Premiere

Germany's main Pay-TV channel was introduced in 1991 and can be received via satellite or cable. *Premiere* subscribers can watch the latest feature films, sports events, cutural programmes and documentaries uninterrupted by advertising.

### Pro 7

Germany's third largest private television channel, *Pro 7* is financed entirely by advertising and offers films, documentaries, and news programmes.

### Realschule

The secondary school which prepares pupils for the *Realschulabschluss* (school-leaving certificate).This type of school is in between **HAUPTSCHULE** and **GYMNASIUM**, catering for less academic children who will probably train for a practical career. Pupils stay at the *Realschule* for 6 years after the **GRUNDSCHULE**. ▶ **SCHULE, LEHRE**.

### Rechtschreibreform

After much controversy, a reform aiming to simplify the strict rules governing German spelling and punctuation was finally implemented in 1998. The old spelling is still acceptable for a transitional period until 2005, but most newspapers and some new books already use the new spelling.

### Reichstag

This historic building in the centre of Berlin became the seat of the **BUNDESTAG** in 1999. The refurbishment of the *Reichstag* included the addition of a glass cupola, with a walkway open to visitors, which provides a spectacular viewing platform and addition to the Berlin skyline.

### Rentenversicherung

This is the compulsory state pension insurance in Germany. All employees have to pay into it as part of their **SOZIALABGABEN**, with employers and the state also making a contribution. The amount of the German state pension depends on the contributions made by the individual, with allowances for years spent as a student or carer.

### Republikaner ▶ DIE REPUBLIKANER.

Culture

## RTL

Germany's largest privately-owned television channel is the market leader in commercial television. It broadcasts films, sport, news, and entertainment and regularly achieves the highest viewing figures.

## SAT 1

Germany's second largest privately-owned television channel broadcasts films, news, sport, and entertainment. It was the first commercial channel in the country.

## 3SAT

This satellite TV channel is run jointly by **ARD, ZDF**, and Swiss and Austrian TV.

## Schule

German children do not start school until they are 6, and they are not allowed to leave school until they are at least 15. All children attend the **GRUNDSCHULE** for four years (six in Berlin) and either a **HAUPTSCHULE**, **REALSCHULE**, **GYMNASIUM**, or **GESAMTSCHULE**, depending on their ability. Some students stay at school until they are over 20 due to the system of **"SITZEN BLEIBEN"**.

## Schultag - 1. Schultag

The first day at school is a big event for a German child, involving a ceremony at school and sometimes at church. The child is given a *Schultüte*, a large cardboard cone containing pens, small gifts, and sweets, to mark this special occasion.

## Schützenfest

An annual festival celebrated in most towns, involving a shooting competition, parade and fair. The winners of the shooting competition are crowned *Schützenkönig* and *Schützenkönigin* for the year.

## Schwarzwald

This is the German name for the Black Forest, a mountainous area in south-western Germany and a popular holiday destination for Germans and foreign tourists alike. The name refers to the large coniferous forests in the area.

## sitzen bleiben

If German pupils fail more than one subject in their end-of-year school report, they have to repeat the year. This is colloquially referred to as *sitzen bleiben*, and it means that some pupils do not manage to sit their **ABITUR** until they are 20.

## Skat

A popular card game for three players playing with 32 German cards. Keen players meet regularly for a game or even join a *Skat* club.

## Solidaritätszuschlag

A tax surcharge introduced to help pay for the enormous cost of German reunification and rebuilding the economy in the East. It is payable by every German taxpayer or firm (in 1999 it was 5.5% of income tax and corporation tax).

## Sozialabgaben

This term refers to the contributions every German taxpayer has to make towards the four main state insurance schemes: pension, health, nursing care, and unemployment. Altogether this amounts to over 40% of gross income, with employee and employer paying half each.

Culture

• • • • • • • • • • • • • • • • • • • • • • • • • • • • • • • • • • • • • • • • • • •

**SPD - Sozialdemokratische Partei Deutschlands**

One of the main German political parties and the party with the biggest membership. Re-formed after the war in 1945, it is a workers' party supporting social democratic values.

**Spiegel ▶ DER SPIEGEL.**

**Stammtisch**

A large table reserved for regulars in most German pubs. The word is also used to refer to the group of people who meet around this table for a drink and lively discussion.

**Stasi - Staatssicherheitsdienst**

The secret service in the former GDR. With the help of an extensive network of informers, the *Stasi* built up personal files on over 6 million people, that is one third of the population. It was disbanded a year before re-unification. ▶ IM.

**Süddeutsche Zeitung**

This respected daily national newspaper was founded in 1945 and is published in Munich. It has a liberal outlook and is read mainly in southern Germany.

**Trabant**

A make of car produced in the former GDR. A *Trabant* or *Trabi* with its two-stroke engine and plastic body was a prized possession, and people had to wait for years to get one. After reunification, the *Trabant* came to symbolize the GDR era and has achieved cult status in Germany.

**TÜV - Technischer Überwachungs-Verein**

An independent organization responsible for testing the technical safety of vehicles and all types of machinery. Cars over three years old have to pass a *TÜV* safety and exhaust emission test every two years.

**Vignette**

In order to be able to use Austrian and Swiss motorways, all vehicles must display a sticker on the windscreen called a *Vignette*. These stickers are usually valid for one year, but foreign tourists in Austria can buy stickers for a period of 10 days or two months.

**Volkshochschule (VHS)**

A local adult education centre that can be found in every German town. The *VHS* offers low-cost daytime and evening classes in a wide range of subjects, including crafts, languages, music, and exercise.

**Waldorfschule**

An increasingly popular type of private school originally founded by the Austrian anthroposophist Rudolf Steiner in the 1920s. The main aim of these schools is to develop pupils' creative and cognitive abilities through music, art, and crafts.

**Wehrdienst**

Compulsory military service for young men in Germany (10 months), Switzerland (3 months) and Austria (6 months). Young Germans are generally called up when they are 19, although there are certain exemptions. Conscientious objectors may apply to do **ZIVILDIENST** instead.

Culture

## Weihnachtsmarkt

During the weeks of Advent, these Christmas markets take place in most German towns, selling Christmas decorations, handmade toys and crib figures, traditional Christmas biscuits, and mulled wine to sustain the shoppers.

## Weinstube

A cosy wine bar which offers a wide choice of wines and usually also serves a few dishes which are considered to go well with wine. A *Weinstube* tends be more upmarket than an ordinary pub, or else fairly rustic, especially in wine-growing areas.

## Welt ▶ DIE WELT.

## Wende

This word can refer to any major political or social change or turning point, but it is used especially to refer to the collapse of Communism in 1989, which was symbolized by the fall of the Berlin wall and eventually led to the **WIEDERVEREINIGUNG** in 1990.

## Wessi

A colloquial and sometimes derogatory term for someone from West Germany, as opposed to an **OSSI**. The expression *Besserwessi*, a pun on *Besserwisser* ('know-all') is used by East Germans to describe a *Wessi* who thinks he knows it all.

## Westdeutsche Allgemeine Zeitung (WAZ)

Germany's highest-circulation serious national paper. It was founded in 1948 and is published in Essen, catering mainly for the densely populated Ruhr area.

## Wiedervereinigung

This is the German word for the reunification of Germany which officially took place on 3 October 1990, when the former GDR was incorporated into the Federal Republic. The huge financial and social costs of reunification are still being felt throughout Germany.

## ZDF - Zweites Deutsches Fernsehen

The second German public TV channel which was founded in 1961 and broadcasts the *Zweites Programm* with entertainment, news, information and a limited amount of advertising.

## Zeit ▶ DIE ZEIT.

## Zivildienst

Community service which recognized conscientious objectors in Germany and Austria can choose to carry out instead of **WEHRDIENST**. It lasts 3 months longer than *Wehrdienst* (2 months longer in Austria) and usually involves caring for children, the elderly, the disabled, or the sick.

**Culture**

# Letter-writing / Briefeschreiben

## Holiday postcard

- *Beginnings (informal):* 'Lieber' here because it's a man; if it's a woman, use e.g. Liebe Elke.

  *To two people, repeat* 'Liebe(r)': Lieber Hans, liebe Elke.

  *To a family:* Liebe Schmidts, Liebe Familie Schmidt, *or just* Liebe Leute.

- *Address: Note that the title (Herrn, Frau, Fräulein) stands on the line above the name. Herr always has an n on the end in addresses.*

  *The house number comes after the street name.*

  *The postcode comes before the place, and if you're writing from outside the country put a D- for Germany, A- for Austria or CH- for Switzerland in front of it.*

---

Heidelberg. den 6.8. 2003

Lieber Hans!

Einen schönen Gruß aus Alt-Heidelberg! Wir sind
erst zwei Tage hier. aber schon sehr angetan von
der Stadt und Umgebung. trotz der vielen Touristen.
Allerdings ist es ziemlich schwül. Wir waren
gestern abend in einem Konzert im Schlosshof. eine
wunderbare Stimmung! Und dann die herrliche
Aussicht auf Altstadt und Neckar von der Terrasse.
Morgen machen wir eine Bootsfahrt. dann geht's
am Donnerstag wieder nach Hause. Hoffentlich ist
deine Mutter inzwischen wieder gesund.

Bis bald

Max und Sophie

Herrn

Hans Matthäus

Brucknerstr. 26

91052 Erlangen

---

- *Endings (informal):*
  Herzlich *or* Herzlichst,
  Herzliche Grüße; *more
  affectionately:* Alles
  Liebe; Bis bald = *See
  you soon* .

## Postkarte aus dem Urlaub

■ *Anrede: sehr einfach auf Postkarten, immer 'Dear' und der Vorname, der im englischen Sprachraum viel häufiger verwendet wird. Die Anrede kann auch entfallen.*

■ *Meist keine Ortsangabe, wenn der Ort aus dem Inhalt oder dem Bild auf der Postkarte klar hervorgeht.*
*Datum – in den USA verwendet man die Reihenfolge Monat, Tag, Jahr, wenn ein Datum mit Ziffern angegeben ist – 8.6.2000*

■ *Adresse: Der Titel (Mr, Mrs, Miss, Ms) steht direkt vor dem Namen auf der gleichen Zeile.*

*Das Haus hat oft einen Namen anstelle einer (oder zusätzlich zur) Hausnummer, die übrigens vor dem Straßennamen steht.*

*Es folgen (in GB) Ortschaft, meist auch Grafschaft, dann Postleitzahl (postcode), alles jeweils auf einer eigenen Zeile; in den USA Ortschaft und Postleitzahl (zipcode), mit dem auf zwei Buchstaben abgekürzten Namen des Staates davor:*

*John Splaine Jr.*
*1067 Blackwall Avenue*
*Studio City*
*CA 91604*
*USA*

---

6.8.2000

Dear John,

Greetings from old Heidelberg! Got here ① a couple of days ago, but already in love with the place (in spite of all the tourists). It's pretty sultry though. Last night we went to a concert in the castle courtyard, very atmospheric. And a terrific view of the river and the old town from the terrace. Tomorrow we're taking a boat trip, and then on Thursday we head for home. Hope ① your mother's fully recovered by now.

See you soon,

Mark and Juliet

Mr J. Roberts
The Willows
49 North Terrace
Kings Barton
Nottinghamshire
NG8 4LQ
England

---

■ *Schlussformel:*
*All the best, Best wishes, oder einfach Yours; auch Love (from), wenn man den Addressaten näher steht.*

① *Telegrammstil: die Angabe der Person entfällt auf Postkarten oft.*

## Christmas and New Year wishes

On a card:

Frohe Weihnachten und viel Glück im neuen Jahr

*A bit more formal:* Ein gesegnetes Weihnachtsfest und die besten Wünsche zum neuen Jahr

*A bit less formal:* Fröhliche Weihnachten und einen guten Rutsch ins neue Jahr

In a letter:

- *On most personal letters German speakers don't put their address at the top, but just the name of the place and the date*

Würzburg, den 20.12.2003

Liebe Karin, lieber Ferdinand,

euch und euren Kindern wünschen wir von Herzen frohe Weihnachten und ein glückliches neues Jahr. Wir hoffen, es geht euch allen gut, und dass wir uns bald mal wieder sehen werden. Es kommt uns so vor, als hätten wir uns eine Ewigkeit nicht gesehen.

Das vergangene Jahr war für uns sehr ereignisreich. Thomas hatte im Sommer einen Unfall mit dem Fahrrad, und brach sich den Arm und das Schlüsselbein. Sabine hat das Abitur gerade noch bestanden und ist jetzt an der Uni in Erlangen, studiert Sport. Der arme Michael ist im Oktober arbeitslos geworden und sucht immer noch nach einer Stelle.

Ihr müsst unbedingt vorbeikommen, wenn ihr das nächste Mal in der Gegend seid. Ruft doch einfach ein paar Tage vorher an, damit wir etwas ausmachen können.

Mit herzlichen Grüßen

Eure Gabi und Michael

## Weihnachts- und Neujahrsgrüße

Auf einer Karte:

> [Best wishes for a] Happy ① Christmas and a Prosperous New Year
>
> All best wishes for Christmas and the New Year
>
> Wishing you every happiness this Christmas[tide] and in the New Year

① *Oder etwas altmodisch:* Merry

In einem Brief:

> 44 Louis Gardens
> London NW6 4GM
>
> December 20th 2003
>
> Dear Peter and Claire,
>
> First of all, a very happy Christmas and all the best for the New Year to you and the children.① We hope you're all well② and that we'll see you again soon. It seems ages since we last met up.
>
> We've had a very eventful year. Last summer Gavin came off his bike and broke his arm and collarbone. Kathy scraped through her A levels and is now at Sussex doing European Studies. Poor Tony was made redundant in October and is still looking for a job.
>
> Do come and see us next time you are over this way. Just give us a ring a couple of days before so we can fix something.
>
> All best wishes
>
> Tony and Ann

① *Oder (vor allem, wenn die Kinder älter sind):* to you and the family.
② *Informeller:* flourishing.

. . . . . . . . . . . . . . . . . . . . . . . . . . . . . . . . . . . . . . . . . . . . . . . . . . . . . . . .

## Invitation (informal)

Hamm, den 22.4.2003

Liebe Jennie,

wäre es möglich, dass du ① in den Sommerferien zu uns kommst? Katrin und
Gottfried würden sich riesig freuen (ich und mein Mann natürlich auch). Wir
planen eine Reise zum Bodensee Ende Juli/Anfang August, du ① könntest gerne
mitfahren. Es ist wirklich sehr schön dort unten. Wir werden wahrscheinlich
zelten – hoffentlich hast du ① nichts dagegen!

Schreib bald, ob das für dich ① in Frage kommt.

Herzliche Grüße

Monika Pfortner

- *Beginning: if you put a comma after the name on the first line (which is usual), the letter proper should start with a small letter.*

① du, dich, dein etc.: although many people still write these with a capital in letters, this is not necessary. But the formal Sie, Ihnen, Ihr must always have a capital.

## Invitation (formal)

*Invitations to parties are usually by word of mouth, while for weddings, announcements rather than invitations are usually sent out:*

Irene Brinkmann                    Stefan Hopf

Wir heiraten am Samstag, den 19. April 2003,
um 14 Uhr in der Pfarrkirche Landsberg.

Goethestraße 12                    Ulrichsweg 4

Landsberg                          Altötting

• • • • • • • • • • • • • • • • • • • • • • • • • • • • • • • • • • • • • • • • •

## Einladung (informell)

- Die Absenderadresse befindet sich oben auf dem Brief selbst, entweder rechts oder in der Mitte, darunter das Datum.

- Das Datum im Englischen hat viele Formen: May 10, 10 May, May 10th, 10th May sind alle möglich und gleichermaßen richtig. In den USA verwendet man die Reihenfolge Monat, Tag, Jahr, wenn das Datum in Ziffern angegeben wird: 05/10/2003

.............. 35 Winchester Drive
Stoke Gifford
Bristol
BS34 8PD

April 22nd 2003

Dear Klaus,

Is there any chance of your coming to stay with us in the summer holidays? Roy and Debbie would be delighted if you could (as well as David and me, of course). We hope to go to North Wales at the end of July/beginning of August, and you'd be very welcome to come too. It's really beautiful up there. We'll probably take tents – I hope that's OK by you.

Let me know as soon as possible if you can manage it.

All best wishes

Rachel Hemmings

## Einladung (förmlich)
Zu einer Hochzeit mit anschließendem Empfang

*Mr and Mrs Peter Thompson*

request the pleasure of your company
at the marriage of their daughter

Hannah Louise
to
Steven David Warner

at St. Mary's Church, Little Bourton
on Saturday 26th July 2003 at 2 p.m.
and afterwards at the
Golden Cross Hotel, Billing

R.S.V.P.          23 Santers Lane
Little Bourton
Northampton
NN6 1AZ

**Accepting an invitation**

Edinburgh, den 2.5.2003

Liebe Frau Pfortner,

recht herzlichen Dank für Ihre liebe Einladung. Da ich noch keine festen Pläne für die Sommerferien habe, möchte ich sie sehr gerne annehmen. Allerdings darf ich nicht mehr als vier bis fünf Tage weg sein, da es meiner Mutter nicht sehr gut geht. Sie ① müssen mir sagen, was ich mitbringen soll (außer Edinburgh Rock!). Ist es sehr warm am Bodensee? Kann man im See schwimmen?

Natürlich habe ich nichts gegen Zelten. Auch hier in Schottland bei Wind und Regen macht es mir Spaß!

Ich freue mich auf ein baldiges Wiedersehen.

Herzliche Grüße

Jennie Stewart

① Since this is a letter from a younger person writing to the mother of a friend, she uses the formal Sie form and possessive Ihr (always with capitals), and writes to her as "Frau Pfortner". On the other hand it was quite natural for Frau Pfortner to use the du form to her.

## Antwort auf eine Einladung (informell)

Mozartstraße 5
32756 Detmold
Germany

2 May 2003

Dear Mrs Hemmings,

Many thanks for your letter and kind invitation. Since I don't have anything fixed yet for the summer holidays, I'd be delighted to come. However I mustn't be away for more than four or five days since my mother hasn't been very well.

You must let me know what I should bring. How warm is it in North Wales? Can one swim in the sea? Camping is fine as far as I'm concerned, we take our tent everywhere.

Looking forward to seeing you again soon,

Yours

Klaus

**Letters / Briefe**

## Antwort auf eine Einladung (förmlich)

Greenacres
Westway
Balsall Common
West Midlands
CV7 8RR

■ Man wiederholt die Details von der Einladung, etwas vereinfacht.

**Annahme:**
Richard Willis has great pleasure in accepting Mr and Mrs Peter Thompson's kind invitation to the marriage of their daughter Hannah Louise to Steven Warner at St. Mary's Church, Little Bourton, on Saturday 26th July.

■ Im Falle einer Absage ist es oft höflicher, einen Brief zu schreiben, vor allem wenn man die Brauteltern gut kennt.

**Absage:**
Richard Willis regrets that he is unable to accept Mr and Mrs Peter Thompson's kind invitation ... , due to a prior engagement.

## Replying to a job advertisement

David Baker
67 Whiteley Avenue
St George
Bristol
BS5 6TW

Softwarehaus WSO GmbH
Personalabteilung
Kanalstr. 75
D-75757 Pforzheim                    Bristol, den 26.2.2004

Ihre Stellenanzeige im Tagblatt vom 23.2.2004

Sehr geehrte Damen und Herren, ①

ich interessiere mich für die von Ihnen im Tagblatt vom 23. September ausgeschriebene Stelle eines Computergrafikers und würde mich freuen, wenn Sie mir nähere Informationen zuschicken könnten. ②

Derzeit bin ich bei der Firma Wondersoft Ltd in Bristol tätig, aber mein Vertrag läuft schon Ende des Monats aus, ③ und ich möchte gerne in Deutschland arbeiten. Wie Sie meinem Lebenslauf entnehmen können, verfüge ich über ausgezeichnete Sprachkenntnisse sowie die geforderten Qualifikationen und einschlägige Berufserfahrung.

Zu einem Vorstellungsgespräch stehe ich jederzeit ab dem 6. Oktober zur Verfügung. Sie können mich ab diesem Datum unter der folgenden Adresse in Deutschland erreichen:

bei Gerber
Rudolfstr. 22
81925 München
Tel. (089) 460 99 507

Ich freue mich darauf, von Ihnen zu hören. ④

Mit freundlichen Grüßen

David Baker

Anlage: Lebenslauf

① *Correct if the letter is addressed to the personnel department, but if it is addressed to the personnel manager (An den Personalleiter, …) the letter begins:* Sehr geehrter Herr XY *or* Sehr geehrte Frau XY.

② *Or if you have enough details and want to apply for the job right away:* und möchte mich um diese Stellung bewerben.

③ *Or if you are unemployed:* Derzeit bin ich arbeitslos, …

④ *Or.* Ihre Antwort erwarte ich mit Interesse.

## Bewerbung auf eine Stellenanzeige hin

Humboldtweg 16
60247 Frankfurt a. M.
Germany
Tel. (069) 724 689

13th February 2004

The Personnel Manager ①
Patterson Software plc
Milton Estate
Bath BA6 8YZ

Dear Sir or Madam, ②

I am interested in the post of programmer advertised in the Guardian of 12th February and would be grateful if you could send me further particulars. ③

I am currently working for the Sempo Corporation in Frankfurt, but my contract finishes at the end of the month, and I would like ④ to come and work in the UK. As you can see from my CV (enclosed), I have an excellent command of English and also the required qualifications and experience.

I will be available for interview any time after 6th October, from which date I can be contacted at the following address in the UK:

c/o Lewis
51 Dexter Road
London N7 6BW
Tel. 0207 607 5512

I look forward to hearing from you. ⑤

Yours sincerely

Rita Steinmüller

Encl.

① *Den Brief so addressieren, wenn in der Anzeige kein Name vorkommt; aber wenn es z.B. heißt* "Reply to Angela Summers", *dann* "Ms Angela Summers, ..."

② *Wenn der Name bekannt ist, dann* "Dear Ms Summers", "Dear Mr Wright" *etc.*

③ *Oder falls Sie schon genügend Informationen haben und sich bewerben wollen:* "and would like to apply for this position".

④ *Oder falls Sie arbeitslos sind:* "I am currently unemployed and would like ..."

⑤ *Oder:* "Thanking you in anticipation".

. . . . . . . . . . . . . . . . . . . . . . . . . . . . . . . . . . . . . . . . . . . . .

## Curriculum Vitae (CV) or (*Amer.*) Résumé

---

Lebenslauf

David Baker
67 Whiteley Avenue
St George
Bristol
BS5 6TW
Großbritannien

Tel. +43 (0)117 945 3421

geboren am 30.06.1970 in London, ledig ①

Ausbildung

1986 O Levels in 7 Fächern (ungefähr = mittlere Reife), John Radcliffe School,
Croydon

1988 A Levels in Mathematik, Höherer Mathematik, Informatik, Deutsch
(ungefähr = Abitur), Croydon Sixth Form College

1989 Teilzeitarbeit in München, Abendkurse an der VHS

1990-94 University of Aston, Birmingham, B.Sc in Informatik

Berufstätigkeit

08/94 - 08/97 Traineeausbildung, anschließend Sotwareentwickler bei IBM

seit 09/97 Programmierer bei Wondersoft plc, Bristol

Entwicklung von Programmen für die Industrie; Schwerpunkt: Grafiksoftware

Besondere Kenntnisse

Fremdsprachen: Deutsch (fließend), Französisch (gut)

---

① *Or:* Verheiratet (mit einem Kind/zwei Kindern etc.); Geschieden (mit einem Kind/zwei
Kindern etc.)

## Lebenslauf

---

### CURRICULUM VITAE ①

| | |
|---|---|
| Name: | Rita Steinmüller |
| Address: | Humboldtweg 16 |
| | 60247 Frankfurt a. M. |
| | Germany |
| Telephone: | +44 (0)69 724 689 |
| Nationality: | German |
| Date of Birth: | 11/3/1976 |
| Marital status: | Single ② |

**Education:**

| | |
|---|---|
| 1994-1998 | Degree Course in Information Technology |
| | at Stuttgart University |
| 1987-1994 | Theodor-Heuss-Gymnasium, Eichborn |
| | Abitur examination (approx. A Level) in Mathematics, |
| | Physics, Economics and English |

**Employment:**

| | |
|---|---|
| 1999-present | Program development engineer with Sempo-Informatik, |
| | Frankfurt, specializing in computer graphics |
| 1998-1999 | Trainee programmer with Oregon Germany, Rüsselsheim |

**Further skills:**

| | |
|---|---|
| Languages: | German (mother tongue), English (fluent spoken and written), |
| | French (good) |
| Interests: | Travel (many trips to the UK), chess, tennis |

---

① *Oder (Amer.):* RÉSUMÉ
② *Oder:* Married (with one/two/three etc. children), Divorced (with one/two/three etc. children)

## Enquiry to a tourist office

■ *A simple business-style letter. The recipient's address is on the left and the sender's on the right, with the date below.*

Letters / Briefe

Verkehrsverein Heidelberg e.V.
Friedrich-Ebert-Anlage 2
69117 Heidelberg

Silvia Sommer
Tannenweg 23
48149 Münster

24. April 2003

■ *The subject of the letter is centred.*

**Hotels und Pensionen in Heidelberg**

Sehr geehrte Damen und Herren,

■ *This is the standard formula for starting a business letter addressed to a firm or organization, and not to a particular person.*

würden Sie mir bitte freundlicherweise eine Liste der Hotels und Pensionen (der mittleren Kategorie) am Ort zusenden?

Ich möchte bitte auch Informationen über Busfahrten zu den Sehenswürdigkeiten der Umgebung in der zweiten Augusthälfte haben.

Mit freundlichen Grüßen

*Silvia Sommer*

■ "Mit freundlichen Grüßen" *is the standard ending for a formal or business letter; another possibility is* "Mit besten Grüßen".

## Anfrage an ein Fremdenverkehrsbüro

■ *Diese Anrede verwendet man, wenn der Name des Adressaten nicht bekannt ist. Es wäre hier auch möglich, "The Manager" wegzulassen und das Tourist Office anzuschreiben; in diesem Fall könnte der Brief auch mit "Dear Sirs" anfangen.*

---

Am Grün 28
A-9026 Klagenfurt
Austria

4th May 2003

The Manager
Regional Tourist Office
3 Virgin Road
Canterbury
CT1 3AA

Dear Sir or Madam,

Please send me a list of hotels and guest houses in Canterbury in the medium price range.

I would also like details of coach trips to local sights in the second half of August.

Yours sincerely

*Bruno Angermeyer*

---

■ *"Yours sincerely" ist der übliche Briefschluss für Geschäftsbriefe sowie für persönliche Briefe an Leute, die man nicht sehr gut kennt. "Yours faithfully" ist etwas altmodisch und wird nur noch für sehr formelle Geschäftsbriefe verwendet, vor allem in Rechtssachen.*

# Letter-writing / Briefeschreiben

## Booking a hotel room

| | |
|---|---|
| Hotel Goldener Pflug | Tobias Schwarz |
| Ortsstraße 7 | Gartenstr. 19 |
| 69235 Steinbach | 76530 Baden-Baden |

16. Juli 2003

Sehr geehrte Damen und Herren,

Ich wurde durch die Broschüre "Hotels und Pensionen im Naturpark Odenwald (Ausgabe 2003)" auf ihr Hotel aufmerksam.

Ich möchte für mich und meine Frau für die Zeit vom 2. bis 11. August (neun Nächte) ein ruhiges Doppelzimmer mit Dusche reservieren, sowie ein Einzelzimmer für unseren Sohn.

Falls Sie für diese Zeit etwas Passendes haben, informieren Sie mich doch bitte über den Preis und darüber, ob Sie eine Anzahlung wünschen.

Mit freundlichen Grüßen

Tobias Schwarz

## Booking a campsite

**Camilla Stumpf**
**Saalgasse 10**
**60311 Frankfurt**

Camping am See
Frau Bettina Sattler
Auweg 6-10
87654 Waldenkirchen

■ *For a business letter to a particular person, use "Sehr geehrte(r)" and the name. (If this letter were to a man, it would start "Sehr geehrter Herr Sattler").*

Frankfurt, den 16.04.2003

Sehr geehrte Frau Sattler,

Ihr Campingplatz wurde mir von Herrn Stephan Seidel empfohlen, der schon mehrmals bei Ihnen war. ① Ich würde nun gerne vom 18. bis 25. Juli mit zwei Freunden eine Woche bei Ihnen verbringen. Könnten Sie uns bitte einen Zeltplatz ② möglichst in unmittelbarer Nähe des Sees ③ reservieren?

Würden Sie mir freundlicherweise mitteilen, ob Sie meine Reservierung annehemen können und ob Sie eine Anzahlung wünschen?

Außerdem wäre ich Ihnen dankbar für eine kurze Wegbeschreibung von der Autobahn.

Mit vielem Dank im Voraus und freundlichen Grüßen

Camilla Stumpf

---

① *Or if you have found the campsite in a guide, say e.g.:* "Ich habe Ihre Anschrift dem ACDA-Campingführer 2003 entnommen".
② *Or if you have a caravan:* "einen Stellplatz für einen Wohnwagen".
③ *Alternatives:* "in schattiger/geschützter Lage".

# Letter-writing / Briefeschreiben

## Hotelzimmerreservierung

The Manager
Torbay Hotel
Dawlish
Devon
EX37 2LR

35 Prince Edward Road
Oxford OX7 3AA

Tel. 01865 322435
23rd April 2003

Dear Sir or Madam,

I saw your hotel listed in the Inns of Devon guide for last year, and wish to reserve a double (or twin-bedded) room with shower ① in a quiet position from August 2nd - 11th (nine nights), also a single room for our son.

If you have anything suitable for this period please let me know the price and whether you require a deposit.

Yours sincerely

Charles Fairhurst

① *Alternativen:* "with bath", "with ensuite".

## Campingplatzreservierung

22 Daniel Avenue
Caldwood
Leeds LS8 7RR
Tel. 01132 998767

25th April 2003

Mr Joseph Vale
Lakeside Park
Rydal
Cumbria
LA22 9RZ

Dear Mr Vale

Your campsite was recommended to me by James Dallas, who knows it from several visits.① I and two friends would like to come for a week from July 18th to 25th Could you please reserve us a site for one tent, ② preferably close to the shore.③

Please confirm the booking and let me know if you require a deposit. Would you also be good enough to send me instructions on how to reach you from the motorway.

Yours sincerely

Frances Good

① *Oder falls Sie den Campingplatz einem Führer entnommen haben, etwa:* "I found your site in the Tourist Board's list/ the Good Camper's Guide" *etc.*

② *Oder falls Sie einen Wohnwagen haben:* "a caravan site".

③ *Andere Möglichkeiten:* "in a shady/sheltered spot".

## Cancelling a reservation

Herrn
Hans Knauer
Gasthaus Sonnenblick
Hauptstr. 6
D-94066 Bad Füssing
Germany                                    Aberdeen, den 2.6.2003

Sehr geehrter Herr Knauer,

leider muss ich meine/unsere Reservierung für die Woche vom 7. bis 13. August
① rückgängig machen. Wegen unvorhergesehener Umstände ② muss
ich/müssen wir auf meinen/unseren Urlaub verzichten.

Es tut mir aufrichtig Leid, dass ich so spät abbestellen muss, und hoffe, dass Sie
deswegen keine Unannehmlichkeiten haben.

Mit freundlichen Grüßen

Robert McDonald

① Or: "für die Zeit vom 7. bis 20. August" etc.
② Or more precisely: "Durch den überraschenden Tod meines Vaters/die Krankheit meines
   Mannes" etc.

## Stornierung einer Reservierung

Mrs J. Warrington              Wernerstr. 17
Downlands                      49835 Wietmarschen
Steyning                       Germany
West Sussex
BN44 6LZ

                               July 20th 2003

Dear Mrs Warrington,

Unfortunately I have to cancel my/our reservation for the week
of August 7th. ① Due to unforeseen circumstances ② I/we have
had to abandon my/our holiday plans.

I very much regret having to cancel [at such a late stage] and
hope it does not cause you undue inconvenience.

Yours sincerely

Elke Nordrup

① Oder: "for the period from August 7th to 14th".
② Oder genauer: "Owing to my father's sudden death/my husband's illness" etc

· · · · · · · · · · · · · · · · · · · · · · · · · · · · · · · · · · · · ·

## Sending an e-mail

The illustration shows a typical interface for sending e-mail.

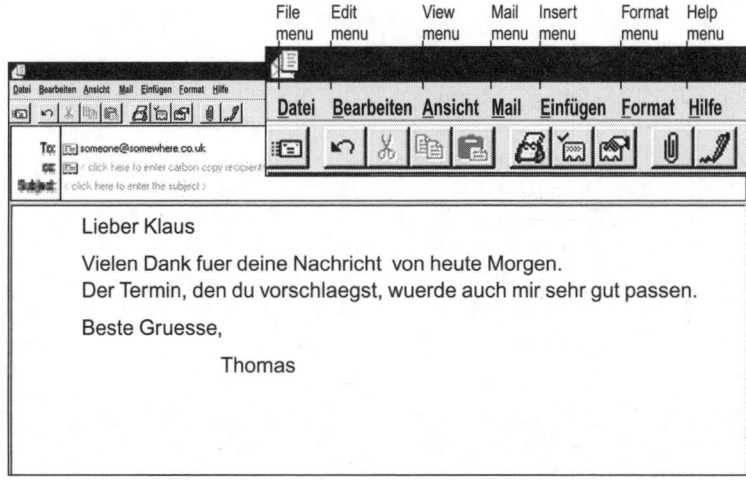

## Das Verschicken von E-Mails

Die Abbildung zeigt eine typische Oberfläche zum Verschicken
von E-Mails.

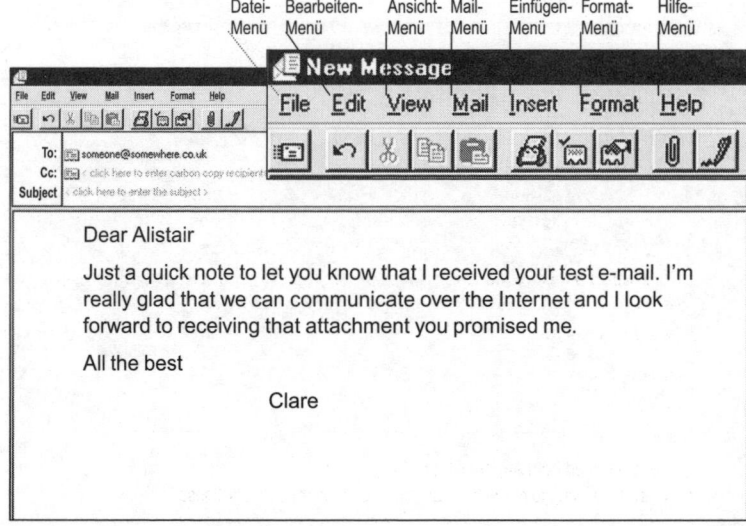

**A, a¹** /eɪ/ n. A, a, das; **A road** Straße 1. Ordnung; ≈ Bundesstraße, die

**a²** /ə, stressed eɪ/ indef. art. ein/eine/ein; **he is a gardener/a Frenchman** er ist Gärtner/ Franzose; **she did not say a word** sie sagte kein Wort

**AA** abbr. (Brit.) = **Automobile Association** britischer Automobilklub

**aback** /ə'bæk/ adv. **be taken ~:** erstaunt sein

**abacus** /'æbəkəs/ n., pl. **~es** or **abaci** /'æbəsaɪ/ Abakus, der

**abandon** /ə'bændən/ v.t. verlassen ⟨Ort, Person⟩; aufgeben ⟨Prinzip⟩; **~ed** verlassen, ausgesetzt ⟨Kind, Tier⟩

**abase** /ə'beɪs/ v.t. erniedrigen

**abashed** /ə'bæʃt/ adj. beschämt

**abate** /ə'beɪt/ v.i. nachlassen

**abattoir** /'æbətwɑː(r)/ n. Schlachthof, der

**abbey** /'æbɪ/ n. Abtei, die

**abbot** /'æbət/ n. Abt, der

**abbreviate** /ə'briːvɪeɪt/ v.t. abkürzen

**ab'breviated dialling** n. (Teleph.) Kurzwahl, die

**abbreviation** /əbriːvɪ'eɪʃn/ n. Abkürzung, die

**abdicate** /'æbdɪkeɪt/ v.t. abdanken

**abdication** /æbdɪ'keɪʃn/ n. Abdankung, die

**abdomen** /'æbdəmən/ n. Bauch, der

**abdominal** /æb'dɒmɪnl/ adj. Bauch-

**abduct** /əb'dʌkt/ v.t. entführen

**abduction** /əb'dʌkʃn/ n. Entführung, die

**aberration** /æbə'reɪʃn/ n. Abweichung, die

**abet** /ə'bet/ v.t., **-tt-** helfen (+ Dat.); **aid and ~:** Beihilfe leisten (+ Dat.)

**abhor** /əb'hɔː(r)/ v.t., **-rr-** verabscheuen

**abhorrent** /əb'hɒrənt/ adj. abscheulich

**abide** /ə'baɪd/ **1** v.i. **~ by** befolgen ⟨Gesetz, Vorschrift⟩; [ein]halten ⟨Versprechen⟩ **2** v.t. ertragen; **I can't ~ dogs** ich kann Hunde nicht ausstehen

**ability** /ə'bɪlɪtɪ/ n. (a) (capacity) Fähigkeit, die; **have the ~ to do sth.** etw. können (b) (cleverness) Intelligenz, die (c) (talent) Begabung, die

**abject** /'æbdʒekt/ adj. elend; bitter ⟨Armut⟩; demütig ⟨Entschuldigung⟩

**ablaze** /ə'bleɪz/ adj. **be ~:** in Flammen stehen

**able** /'eɪbl/ adj. (a) **be ~ to do sth.** etw. tun können (b) (competent) fähig

**able-bodied** /'eɪblbɒdɪd/ adj. kräftig; tauglich ⟨Soldat, Matrose⟩

**ably** /'eɪblɪ/ adv. geschickt; gekonnt

**abnormal** /æb'nɔːml/ adj. abnorm; a[b]normal ⟨Interesse, Verhalten⟩

**abnormality** /æbnɔː'mælɪtɪ/ n. Abnormität, die

**aboard** /ə'bɔːd/ **1** adv. an Bord **2** prep. an Bord (+ Gen.); **~ the bus** imC **~ ship** an Bord

**abode** /ə'bəʊd/ n. **of no fixed ~:** ohne festen Wohnsitz

**abolish** /ə'bɒlɪʃ/ v.t. abschaffen

**abolition** /æbə'lɪʃn/ n. Abschaffung, die

**abominable** /ə'bɒmɪnəbl/ adj. abscheulich; scheußlich

**aborigine** /æbə'rɪdʒɪnɪ/ n. Ureinwohner, der

**abort** /ə'bɔːt/ v.t. abtreiben ⟨Baby⟩

**abortion** /ə'bɔːʃn/ n. Abtreibung, die; 1776991/ann>**back-street ~:** illegale Abtreibung (durch Engelmacherin)

**a'bortion pill** n. Abtreibungspille, die

**abortive** /ə'bɔːtɪv/ adj. misslungen ⟨Plan⟩; fehlgeschlagen ⟨Versuch⟩

**abound** /ə'baʊnd/ v.i. **~ in sth.** an etw. (Dat.) reich sein

**about** /ə'baʊt/ **1** adv. (a) (all around) rings[her]um; (here and there) überall; **all ~:** ringsumher (b) (near) **be ~:** da sein; hier sein (c) **be ~ to do sth.** gerade etw. tun wollen (d) **be out and ~:** aktiv sein (e) (approximately) ungefähr **2** prep. (a) (all round) um [... herum] (b) (concerning) über (+ Akk.); **know ~ sth.** von etw. wissen; **a question ~ sth.** eine Frage zu etw.; **what was it ~?** worum ging es?

**above** /ə'bʌv/ **1** adv. (a) (position) oben; (higher up) darüber (b) (direction) nach oben **2** prep. (position) über (+ Dat.); (direction, more than) über (+ Akk.); **~ all** vor allem

**above 'board** pred. adj. einwandfrei; korrekt

**a'bove-mentioned** adj. oben erwähnt od. genannt

**abrasion** /ə'breɪʒn/ n. (graze) Hautabschürfung, die

**abrasive** /ə'breɪsɪv/ **1** adj. (a) scheuernd; Scheuer- (b) (fig.: harsh) aggressiv **2** n. Scheuermittel, das

**abreast** /ə'brest/ adv. (a) nebeneinander ⋯▶

(b) (fig.) **keep** ~ **of** sth. sich über etw. (*Akk.*) auf dem Laufenden halten

**abroad** /ə'brɔːd/ *adv.* im Ausland; (direction) ins Ausland

**abrupt** /ə'brʌpt/ *adj.*, **a'bruptly** *adv.* (a) (sudden[ly]) abrupt; plötzlich
(b) (brusque[ly]) schroff

**ABS** *abbr.* = **anti-lock brake** *or* **braking system** ABS

**abscess** /'æbsɪs/ *n.* Abszess, *der*

**abscond** /əb'skɒnd/ *v.t.* sich entfernen

**absence** /'æbsəns/ *n.* Abwesenheit, *die;* **the** ~ **of** sth. der Mangel an etw. (*Dat.*)

**absent** /'æbsənt/ *adj.* abwesend; **be** ~ **from school/work** in der Schule/am Arbeitsplatz fehlen

**absentee** /æbsən'tiː/ *n.* Fehlende, *der/die;* Abwesende, *der/die;* ~ **landlord** nicht auf seinem Gut lebender Gutsherr

**absenteeism** /æbsən'tiːɪzm/ *n.* [häufiges] Fernbleiben; (without good reason) Krankfeiern, *das* (ugs.)

**absent-minded** /æbsənt'maɪndɪd/ *adj.* geistesabwesend; (habitually) zerstreut

**absolute** /'æbsəluːt/ *adj.* absolut; ausgemacht ⟨*Lüge, Skandal*⟩; ~ **majority** absolute Mehrheit

**abso'lutely** *adv.* absolut; völlig ⟨*verrückt*⟩; **you're** ~ **right!** du hast völlig Recht; ~ **not!** auf keinen Fall!

**absolve** /əb'zɒlv/ *v.t.* ~ **from** entbinden von ⟨*Pflichten*⟩; lossprechen von ⟨*Schuld*⟩

**absorb** /əb'sɔːb/ *v.t.* (a) aufsaugen ⟨*Flüssigkeit*⟩
(b) abfangen ⟨*Schlag, Stoß*⟩
(c) (fig.: engross) ausfüllen

**absorbency** /əb'sɔːbənsɪ/ *n.* Saugfähigkeit, *die*

**absorbent** /əb'sɔːbənt/ *adj.* saugfähig

**ab'sorbing** *adj.* faszinierend

**abstain** /əb'steɪn/ *v.i.* ~ **from** sth. sich einer Sache (*Gen.*) enthalten; ~ [**from voting**] sich der Stimme enthalten

**abstemious** /əb'stiːmɪəs/ *adj.* enthaltsam

**abstention** /əb'stenʃn/ *n.* (from voting) Stimmenthaltung, *die*

**abstinence** /'æbstɪnəns/ *n.* Abstinenz, *die*

**abstinent** /'æbstɪnənt/ *adj.* abstinent

**abstract** /'æbstrækt/ ① *adj.* abstrakt
② *n.* Zusammenfassung, *die*

**absurd** /əb'sɜːd/ *adj.* absurd; (ridiculous) lächerlich

**absurdity** /əb'sɜːdɪtɪ/ *n.* Absurdität, *die*

**ab'surdly** *adv.* lächerlich

**abundance** /ə'bʌndəns/ *n.* [an] ~ **of** sth. eine Fülle von etw.

**abundant** /ə'bʌndənt/ *adj.* reich (**in an** + *Dat.*)

**abuse** ① /ə'bjuːz/ *v.t.* beschimpfen
② /ə'bjuːs/ *n.* Beschimpfungen *Pl.*

**abusive** /ə'bjuːsɪv/ *adj.* beleidigend; **become** ~: ausfallend werden

**abysmal** /ə'bɪzml/ *adj.* (coll.: bad) katastrophal (ugs.)

**abyss** /ə'bɪs/ *n.* Abgrund, *der*

**AC** *abbr.* = **alternating current** Ws

**academic** /ækə'demɪk/ *adj.* akademisch

**academy** /ə'kædəmɪ/ *n.* Akademie, *die*

**accede** /æk'siːd/ *v.i.* (a) zustimmen (**to** *Dat.*)
(b) ~ [**to the throne**] den Thron besteigen

**accelerate** /ək'seləreɪt/ ① *v.t.* beschleunigen
② *v.i.* sich beschleunigen; ⟨*Auto, Fahrer:*⟩ beschleunigen

**acceleration** /əkselə'reɪʃn/ *n.* Beschleunigung, *die*

**accelerator** /ək'seləreɪtə(r)/ *n.* ~ [**pedal**] Gas[pedal], *das*

**accent** /'æksənt/ *n.* Akzent, *der*

**accentuate** /æk'sentjʊeɪt/ *v.t.* betonen

**accept** /ək'sept/ *v.t.* (a) annehmen; entgegennehmen ⟨*Dank, Spende*⟩; übernehmen ⟨*Verantwortung*⟩
(b) (acknowledge) akzeptieren

**acceptable** /ək'septəbl/ *adj.* akzeptabel; annehmbar ⟨*Preis, Gehalt*⟩

**acceptance** /ək'septəns/ *n.* (a) Annahme, *die*
(b) (acknowledgement) Anerkennung, *die*

**access** /'ækses/ *n.* (a) (admission) **gain** ~: Einlass finden
(b) (opportunity to use or approach) Zugang, *der* (**to** zu)

**accessible** /ək'sesɪbl/ *adj.* (a) (reachable) erreichbar
(b) (available, understandable) zugänglich (**to** für)

**accession** /æk'seʃn/ *n.* Amtsantritt, *der;* ~ [**to the throne**] Thronbesteigung, *die*

**accessory** /ək'sesərɪ/ *n.* (a) **accessories** *pl.* Zubehör, *das*
(b) (dress article) Accessoire, *das*

**'access road** *n.* Zufahrtsstraße, *die*

**accident** /'æksɪdənt/ *n.* (a) Unfall, *der*
(b) (chance) Zufall, *der;* **by** ~: zufällig
(c) (mistake) Versehen, *das;* **by** ~: versehentlich

**accidental** /æksɪ'dentl/ *adj.* (chance) zufällig; (unintended) unbeabsichtigt

**acci'dentally** *adv.* (by chance) zufällig; (by mistake) versehentlich

**'accident-prone** *adj.* ~ **person** Unfäller, *der* (Psych.); **he's such an** ~ **boy** mit dem Jungen ist aber auch immer irgendwas (ugs.)

**acclaim** /ə'kleɪm/ *v.t.* feiern

**acclimatise, acclimatise**
▶ ACCLIMATIZ-

**acclimatization** /əklaɪmətaɪ'zeɪʃn/ *n.* (lit. or fig.) Akklimatisation, *die*

**acclimatize** /ə'klaɪmətaɪz/ *v.t.* **get** *or* **become** ~**d** sich akklimatisieren

**accolade** /'ækəleɪd/ *n.* ~[**s**] (praise) Lob, *das*

**accommodate** /əˈkɒmədeɪt/ *v.t.* **(a)** unterbringen; (hold) Platz bieten (+ *Dat.*) **(b)** (oblige) gefällig sein (+ *Dat.*)

**accommodating** /əˈkɒmədeɪtɪŋ/ *adj.* zuvorkommend

**accommodation** /əkɒməˈdeɪʃn/ *n.* Unterkunft, *die*

**accommo'dation address** *n.* Gefälligkeitsadresse, *die*

**accompaniment** /əˈkʌmpənɪmənt/ *n.* Begleitung, *die*

**accompanist** /əˈkʌmpənɪst/ *n.* Begleiter, *der*/Begleiterin, *die*

**accompany** /əˈkʌmpənɪ/ *v.t.* begleiten

**accomplice** /əˈkʌmplɪs/ *n.* Komplize, *der*/ Komplizin, *die*

**accomplish** /əˈkʌmplɪʃ/ *v.t.* vollbringen ⟨*Tat*⟩; erfüllen ⟨*Aufgabe*⟩

**accomplished** /əˈkʌmplɪʃt/ *adj.* fähig; **he is an ∼ speaker/dancer** er ist ein erfahrener Redner/vollendeter Tänzer

**ac'complishment** *n.* **(a)** (completion) Vollendung, *die* **(b)** (achievement) Leistung, *die;* (skill) Fähigkeit, *die*

**accord** /əˈkɔːd/ ①① *n.* Übereinstimmung, *die;* **of one's own ∼:** aus eigenem Antrieb; **with one ∼:** geschlossen ② *v.t.* **∼ sb. sth.** jmdm. etw. gewähren

**accordance** /əˈkɔːdəns/ *n.* **in ∼ with** in Übereinstimmung mit

**ac'cording** *adv.* **∼ to** nach; **∼ to him** nach seiner Aussage

**ac'cordingly** *adv.* (as appropriate) entsprechend; (therefore) folglich

**accordion** /əˈkɔːdɪən/ *n.* Akkordeon, *das*

**accost** /əˈkɒst/ *v.t.* ansprechen

**account** /əˈkaʊnt/ *n.* **(a)** (Finance) Rechnung, *die;* (at bank, shop) Konto, *das* **(b)** (consideration) **take ∼ of sth., take sth. into ∼:** etw. berücksichtigen; **take no ∼ of sth./ sb.** etw./jmdn. unberücksichtigt lassen; **don't change your plans on my ∼:** ändert nicht meinetwegen eure Pläne; **on ∼ of** wegen; **on no ∼:** auf [gar] keinen Fall **(c)** (report) Bericht, *der* **(d) call sb. to ∼:** jmdn. zur Rechenschaft ziehen

■ **ac'count for** *v.t.* Rechenschaft ablegen über; (explain) erklären

**accountable** /əˈkaʊntəbl/ *adj.* verantwortlich

**accountancy** /əˈkaʊntənsɪ/ *n.* Buchhaltung, *die*

**accountant** /əˈkaʊntənt/ *n.* [Bilanz]buchhalter, *der*/-halterin, *die*

**account:** **∼ holder** *n.* Kontoinhaber, *der*/-inhaberin, *die;* **∼ number** *n.* Kontonummer, *die*

**accredited** /əˈkredɪtɪd/ *adj.* anerkannt ⟨*Schule, Anstalt, Buch, Regierung*⟩; akkreditiert ⟨*Botschafter, Diplomat*⟩; zugelassen ⟨*Journalist*⟩

**accrue** /əˈkruː/ *v.i.* ⟨*Zinsen:*⟩ auflaufen; **∼ to sb.** ⟨*Reichtümer, Einnahmen:*⟩ jmdm. zufließen

**accumulate** /əˈkjuːmjʊleɪt/ ①① *v.t.* sammeln ② *v.i.* ⟨*Menge, Staub:*⟩ sich ansammeln; ⟨*Geld:*⟩ sich anhäufen

**accumulation** /əkjuːmjʊˈleɪʃn/ *n.* [An]sammeln, *das;* (being accumulated) Anhäufung, *die*

**accuracy** /ˈækjʊrəsɪ/ *n.* Genauigkeit, *die*

**accurate** /ˈækjʊrət/ *adj.*, **'accurately** *adv.* genau; (correct[ly]) richtig

**accusation** /ækjuːˈzeɪʃn/ *n.* Anschuldigung, *die;* (Law) Anklage, *die*

**accusative** /əˈkjuːzətɪv/ *adj. & n.* **∼ [case]** Akkusativ, *der*

**accuse** /əˈkjuːz/ *v.t.* beschuldigen; (Law) anklagen (of wegen + *Gen.*)

**accustom** /əˈkʌstəm/ *v.t.* gewöhnen (**to** an + *Akk.*); **grow/be ∼ed to sth.** sich an etw. (*Akk.*) gewöhnen/an etw. (*Akk.*) gewöhnt sein

**accustomed** /əˈkʌstəmd/ *attrib. adj.* gewohnt; üblich

**ace** /eɪs/ ① *n.* As, *das* ② *adj.* (coll.) klasse (ugs.); spitze (ugs.)

**ache** /eɪk/ ① *v.i.* schmerzen; wehtun ② *n.* Schmerz, *der*

**achieve** /əˈtʃiːv/ *v.t.* zustande bringen; erreichen ⟨*Ziel, Standard*⟩

**a'chievement** *n.* **(a)** ▶ ACHIEVE: Zustandebringen, *das;* Erreichen, *das* **(b)** (thing accomplished) Leistung, *die*

**acid** /ˈæsɪd/ ① *adj.* sauer ② *n.* Säure, *die*

**'acid house** *n.* Acidhouse, *das;* **∼ music/ party** Acidhousemusik, *die*/Acidhouseparty, *die*

**'acid: ∼'rain** *n.* saurer Regen; **∼ test** *n.* (fig.) Feuerprobe, *die*

**acidic** /əˈsɪdɪk/ *adj.* säuerlich

**acidity** /əˈsɪdɪtɪ/ *n.* Säure, *die*

**acknowledge** /əkˈnɒlɪdʒ/ *v.t.* **(a)** zugeben ⟨*Tatsache, Fehler, Schuld*⟩ **(b)** sich erkenntlich zeigen für ⟨*Dienste, Bemühungen*⟩; erwidern ⟨*Gruß*⟩ **(c)** bestätigen ⟨*Empfang, Bewerbung*⟩; **∼ a letter** den Empfang eines Briefes bestätigen

**acknowledg[e]ment** /əkˈnɒlɪdʒmənt/ *n.* **(a)** (admission) Eingeständnis, *das* **(b)** (thanks) Dank, *der* (of für) **(c)** (of letter) Bestätigung [des Empfangs]

**acne** /ˈæknɪ/ *n.* Akne, *die*

**acorn** /ˈeɪkɔːn/ *n.* Eichel, *die*

**acoustic** /əˈkuːstɪk/ *adj.* akustisch

**a'coustics** *n. pl.* Akustik, *die*

**acquaint** /əˈkweɪnt/ *v.t.* **be ∼ed with sb.** mit jmdm. bekannt sein

**acquaintance** /əˈkweɪntəns/ *n.* **(a)** **∼ with sb.** Bekanntschaft mit jmdm.; **make sb.'s ∼:** jmds. Bekanntschaft machen ····⊱

**(b)** (person) Bekannte, *der/die*

**acquiesce** /ækwɪ'es/ *v.i.* einwilligen (**in** in + *Akk.*)

**acquire** /ə'kwaɪə(r)/ *v.t.* sich (*Dat.*) anschaffen ⟨*Gegenstände*⟩; erwerben ⟨*Besitz, Kenntnisse*⟩

**acquisition** /ækwɪ'zɪʃn/ *n.* Erwerb, *der;* (thing) Anschaffung, *die*

**acquisitive** /ə'kwɪzɪtɪv/ *adj.* raffsüchtig

**acquit** /ə'kwɪt/ *v.t.,* **-tt-** freisprechen

**acquittal** /ə'kwɪtl/ *n.* Freispruch, *der*

**acre** /'eɪkə(r)/ *n.* Acre, *der*

**acrid** /'ækrɪd/ *adj.* beißend ⟨*Geruch, Rauch*⟩; bitter ⟨*Geschmack*⟩

**acrimonious** /ækrɪ'məʊnɪəs/ *adj.* bitter; erbittert ⟨*Streit*⟩

**acrobat** /'ækrəbæt/ *n.* Akrobat, *der/* Akrobatin, *die*

**acrobatic** /ækrə'bætɪk/ *adj.* akrobatisch

**acrobatics** /ækrə'bætɪks/ *n.* Akrobatik, *die*

**acronym** /'ækrənɪm/ *n.* Akronym, *das*

**across** /ə'krɒs/ ⸤1⸥ *adv.* (from one side to the other) darüber; (from here to there) hinüber; **be 9 miles ~:** 9 Meilen breit sein
⸤2⸥ *prep.* über (+ *Akk.*); (on the other side of) auf der anderen Seite (+ *Gen.*)

**a'cross-the-board** *adj.* pauschal; **an ~ pay rise** eine pauschale *od.* generelle Lohnerhöhung

**acrylic** /ə'krɪlɪk/ ⸤1⸥ *adj.* aus Acryl *nachgestellt;* Acryl-; **~ paint/fibre** Acrylfarbe, *die/*-faser, *die*
⸤2⸥ *n.* Acryl, *das*

**act** /ækt/ ⸤1⸥ *n.* **(a)** (deed) Tat, *die*
**(b)** (Theatre) Akt, *der*
**(c)** (pretence) Theater, *das;* **put on an ~:** Theater spielen
**(d)** (Law) Gesetz, *das*
⸤2⸥ *v.t.* spielen ⟨*Stück*⟩
⸤3⸥ *v.i.* **(a)** (perform actions) handeln
**(b)** (behave) sich verhalten; **~ as** fungieren als
**(c)** (perform play) spielen
**(d)** (have effect) **~ on sth.** auf etw. (*Akk.*) wirken

**'acting** ⸤1⸥ *n.* (Theatre etc.) die Schauspielerei
⸤2⸥ *adj.* (temporary) stellvertretend

**action** /'ækʃn/ *n.* **(a)** (doing sth.) Handeln, *das;* **take ~:** Schritte *od.* etwas unternehmen; **put a plan into ~:** einen Plan in die Tat umsetzen; **put sth. out of ~:** etw. außer Betrieb setzen
**(b)** (act) Tat, *die*
**(c)** (legal process) [Gerichts]verfahren, *das*
**(d)** **the in ~:** im Kampf fallen

**action: ~ committee, ~ group** *ns.* [Eltern-/Bürger- *usw.*]initiative, *die;*
**~-packed** *adj.* spannend ⟨*Buch, Roman*⟩; **an ~-packed film** ein Film mit viel Aktion;
**~'replay** *n.* Wiederholung [in Zeitlupe]

**activate** /'æktɪveɪt/ *v.t.* **(a)** in Gang setzen
**(b)** (Chem., Phys.) aktivieren

**active** /'æktɪv/ *adj.,* **'actively** *adv.* aktiv

**activist** /'æktɪvɪst/ *n.* Aktivist, *der/* Aktivistin, *die*

**activity** /æk'tɪvɪtɪ/ *n.* Aktivität, *die;* **outdoor activities** Betätigung an der frischen Luft; **~ holiday** Aktivurlaub, *der*

**actor** /'æktə(r)/ *n.* Schauspieler, *der*

**actress** /'æktrɪs/ *n.* Schauspielerin, *die*

**actual** /'æktʃʊəl/ *adj.* eigentlich; wirklich ⟨*Name*⟩

**'actually** *adv.* (in fact) eigentlich; (by the way) übrigens; (believe it or not) sogar

**acumen** /'ækjʊmen/ Scharfsinn, *der;* **business ~:** Geschäftssinn, *der*

**acupressure** /'ækjuːpreʃə(r)/ *n.* (Med.) Akupressur, *die*

**acupuncture** /'ækjʊpʌŋktʃə(r)/ *n.* Akupunktur, *die*

**acute** /ə'kjuːt/ *adj.* **(a)** spitz ⟨*Winkel*⟩
**(b)** (critical; Med.) akut

**ad** /æd/ *n.* (coll.) Annonce, *die*

**AD** *abbr.* = **Anno Domini** n.Chr.

**adamant** /'ædəmənt/ *adj.* unnachgiebig; **be ~ that ...:** darauf bestehen, dass ...

**adapt** /ə'dæpt/ *v.t.* **(a)** anpassen (**to** *Dat.*); **~ oneself to sth.** sich an etw. (*Akk.*) gewöhnen
**(b)** bearbeiten ⟨*Text, Theaterstück*⟩

**adaptable** /ə'dæptəbl/ *adj.* anpassungsfähig

**adaptation** /ædəp'teɪʃn/ *n.* **(a)** Anpassung, *die*
**(b)** (version) Adap[ta]tion, *die;* (of story, text) Bearbeitung, *die*

**adapter, adaptor** /ə'dæptə(r)/ *n.* Adapter, *der*

**add** /æd/ ⸤1⸥ *v.t.* hinzufügen (**to** *Dat.*); **~ two and two** zwei und zwei zusammenzählen
⸤2⸥ *v.i.* **~ to** vergrößern ⟨*Schwierigkeiten, Einkommen*⟩

■ **add 'up** ⸤1⸥ *v.i.* **~ up to sth.** (fig.) auf etw. (*Akk.*) hinauslaufen
⸤2⸥ *v.t.* zusammenzählen

**adder** /'ædə(r)/ *n.* Viper, *die*

**addict** ⸤1⸥ /ə'dɪkt/ *v.t.* **be ~ed** süchtig sein (**to** nach); **be ~ed to alcohol/smoking/drugs** alkohol-/nikotin-/drogensüchtig sein
⸤2⸥ /'ædɪkt/ *n.* Süchtige, *der/die*

**addiction** /ə'dɪkʃn/ *n.* Sucht, *die* (**to** nach)

**addictive** /ə'dɪktɪv/ *adj.* **be ~:** süchtig machen

**addition** /ə'dɪʃn/ *n.* **(a)** Hinzufügen, *das;* (adding up) Addieren, *das;* (process) Addition, *die;* **in ~:** außerdem; **in ~ to** zusätzlich zu
**(b)** (thing added) Ergänzung, *die* (**to** zu)

**additional** /ə'dɪʃənl/ *adj.* zusätzlich

**additionally** /ə'dɪʃənəlɪ/ *adv.* außerdem

**additive** /'ædɪtɪv/ *n.* Zusatz, *der*

**'add-on** ⸤1⸥ *n.* (accessory) Zubehörteil, *das;* (for electrical appliance) Zusatzgerät, *das;* (addition) Zusatz, *der*

2 *adj.* ~ **accessory** Zubehörteil, *das*; (for electrical appliance) Zusatzgerät, *das*

**address** /ə'dres/ 1 *v.t.* (a) (mark with ~) adressieren (**to** an + *Akk.*)
(b) (speak to) anreden; sprechen zu ⟨*Zuhörern*⟩
2 *n.* (a) (on letter) Adresse, *die*
(b) (speech) Ansprache, *die*

**ad'dress book** *n.* Adressenbüchlein, *das*

**addressee** /ædre'si:/ *n.* Adressat, *der*/ Adressatin, *die*

**ad'dress label** *n.* Adressenaufkleber, *der*

**adept** /'ædept, ə'dept/ *adj.* geschickt (**in, at** in + *Dat.*)

**adequate** /'ædɪkwət/ *adj.* (a) angemessen (**to** *Dat.*); (suitable) passend
(b) (sufficient) ausreichend

**'adequately** *adv.* (a) (sufficiently) ausreichend
(b) (suitably) angemessen ⟨*gekleidet, qualifiziert usw.*⟩

**adhere** /əd'hɪə(r)/ *v.i.* haften, (by glue) kleben (**to** an + *Dat.*)

**adhesion** /əd'hi:ʒn/ *n.* Haften, *das*

**adhesive** /əd'hi:sɪv/ 1 *adj.* gummiert ⟨*Briefmarke*⟩; Klebe⟨*band*⟩; ~ **plaster** Heftpflaster, *das*
2 *n.* Klebstoff, *der*

**adjacent** /ə'dʒeɪsənt/ *adj.* angrenzend; ~ **to** neben (*position:* + *Dat.; direction:* + *Akk.*)

**adjective** /'ædʒɪktɪv/ *n.* Adjektiv, *das*

**adjoin** /ə'dʒɔɪn/ *v.t.* grenzen an (+ *Akk.*)

**adjourn** /ə'dʒɜ:n/ 1 *v.t.* (break off) unterbrechen; (put off) aufschieben
2 *v.i.* sich vertagen; ~ **for lunch/half an hour** eine Mittagspause/halbstündige Pause einlegen

**a'djournment** *n.* (of court) Vertagung, *die;* (of meeting) Unterbrechung, *die*

**adjudicate** /ə'dʒu:dɪkeɪt/ *v.i.* (in court, tribunal) das Urteil fällen; (in contest) entscheiden

**adjust** /ə'dʒʌst/ 1 *v.t.* einstellen; ~ **sth. [to sth.]** etw. [an etw. (*Akk.*)] anpassen
2 *v.i.* ⟨*Person:*⟩ sich anpassen (**to** an + *Akk.*)

**adjustable** /ə'dʒʌstəbl/ *adj.* einstellbar; verstellbar ⟨*Gerät*⟩

**a'djustment** *n.* Einstellung, *die;* (to situation etc.) Anpassung, *die*

**ad-lib** /æd'lɪb/ 1 *adj.* improvisiert
2 *v.i.,* -**bb**- improvisieren

**adman** /'ædmæn/*n.* Werbe-, Reklamefachmann, *der*

**admin** /'ædmɪn/ *n.* (coll.) Verwaltung, *die;* **an** ~ **problem** ein Verwaltungsproblem

**'aedmzen administer** /æd'mɪnɪstə(r)/ (a) (manage) verwalten
(b) leisten ⟨*Hilfe*⟩; verabreichen ⟨*Medikamente*⟩

**administration** /ədmɪnɪ'streɪʃn/ *n.* Verwaltung, *die*

**administrative** /əd'mɪnɪstrətɪv/ *adj.* Verwaltungs-; **an** ~ **job** ein Verwaltungsposten

**administrator** /əd'mɪnɪstreɪtə(r)/ *n.* Administrator, *der;* Verwalter, *der*

**admirable** /'ædmərəbl/ *adj.* bewundernswert

**admiral** /'ædmərəl/ *n.* Admiral, *der*

**admiration** /ædmə'reɪʃn/ *n.* Bewunderung, *die* (**of, for** für)

**admire** /əd'maɪə(r)/ *v.t.* bewundern

**admirer** /əd'maɪərə(r)/ *n.* Bewunderer, *der*/ Bewunderin, *die*

**admiring** /əd'maɪərɪŋ/ *adj.* bewundernd

**admission** /əd'mɪʃn/ *n.* (a) (entry) Zutritt, *der*
(b) (charge) Eintritt, *der*
(c) (confession) Eingeständnis, *das*

**admission:** ~ **charge,** ~ **fee** *ns.* Eintrittspreis, *der;* ~ **money** *n.* Eintrittsgeld, *das;* ~**price** *n.* Eintrittspreis, *der;* ~ **ticket** *n.* Eintrittskarte, *die*

**admit** /əd'mɪt/ *v.t.,* -**tt**-: (a) (let in) hinein-/ hereinlassen
(b) (acknowledge) zugeben

**admittance** /əd'mɪtəns/ *n.* Zutritt, *der*

**admittedly** /əd'mɪtɪdlɪ/ *adv.* zugegeben[ermaßen]

**admonish** /əd'mɒnɪʃ/ *v.t.* ermahnen

**ado** /ə'du:/ *n.* **without more** ~: ohne weiteres Aufheben

**adolescence** /ædə'lesns/ *n.* die Zeit des Erwachsenwerdens

**adolescent** /ædə'lesnt/ 1 *n.* Heranwachsende, *der/die*
2 *adj.* heranwachsend

**adopt** /ə'dɒpt/ *v.t.* (a) adoptieren
(b) (take over) annehmen ⟨*Glaube, Kultur*⟩
(c) (take up) übernehmen ⟨*Methode*⟩; einnehmen ⟨*Standpunkt, Haltung*⟩

**adoption** /ə'dɒpʃn/ *n.* (a) Adoption, *die*
(b) (taking over) Annahme, *die*
(c) (taking up) Übernahme, *die;* (of point of view) Einnahme, *die*

**adorable** /ə'dɔ:rəbl/ *adj.* bezaubernd

**adoration** /ædə'reɪʃn/ *n.* Verehrung, *die*

**adore** /ə'dɔ:(r)/ *v.t.* verehren

**adorn** /ə'dɔ:n/ *v.t.* schmücken

**a'dornment** *n.* Verzierung, *die;* ~**s** Schmuck, *der*

**adrenalin** /ə'drenəlɪn/ *n.* Adrenalin, *das*

**Adriatic** /eɪdrɪ'ætɪk/ *pr. n.* ~ [**Sea**] Adriatisches Meer

**adrift** /ə'drɪft/ *adj.* **be** ~: treiben

**adroit** /ə'drɔɪt/ *adj.* geschickt

**adulation** /ædjʊ'leɪʃn/ *n.* Vergötterung, *die*

**adult** /'ædʌlt, ə'dʌlt/ 1 *adj.* erwachsen; ein ~ **film/book** *etc.* ein Film/Buch *usw.* [nur] für Erwachsene
2 *n.* Erwachsene, *der/die;* ~ **education** Erwachsenenbildung, *die*

**adulterate** /əˈdʌltəreɪt/ *v.t.* verunreinigen

**adultery** /əˈdʌltərɪ/ *n.* Ehebruch, *der*

**advance** /ədˈvɑːns/ ① *v.t.* (a) (also Mil.) vorrücken lassen
(b) (put forward) vorbringen ⟨*Plan, Meinung*⟩
(c) (further) fördern
(d) (pay before due date) vorschießen; ⟨*Bank:*⟩ leihen
② *v.i.* (a) (also Mil.) vorrücken; ⟨*Prozession:*⟩ sich vorwärts bewegen
(b) (fig.: make progress) vorankommen
③ *n.* (a) Vorrücken, *das;* (fig.: progress) Fortschritt, *der*
(b) *usu.* in pl. (personal approach) Annäherungsversuch, *der*
(c) (on salary) Vorschuss, *der*
(d) in ~: im Voraus

**ad'vance booking** *n.* (for a film, play) [vorherige] Kartenreservierung; (of a table in a restaurant) [vorherige] Tischreservierung

**advanced** /ədˈvɑːnst/ *adj.* fortgeschritten

**advance:** ~ 'notice *n.* a week's ~ notice Benachrichtigung eine Woche [im] Voraus; give sb. ~ notice of sth. jmdn. im Voraus von etw. in Kenntnis setzen; ~ 'payment *n.* Vorauszahlung, *die*

**advantage** /ədˈvɑːntɪdʒ/ *n.* Vorteil, *der;* take ~ of sb. jmdn. ausnutzen; be to one's ~: für jmdn. von Vorteil sein; turn sth. to [one's] ~: etw. ausnutzen

**advantageous** /ædvənˈteɪdʒəs/ *adj.* vorteilhaft

**advent** /ˈædvent/ *n.* Beginn, *der;* A~: Advent, *der*

**adventure** /ədˈventʃə(r)/ *n.* Abenteuer, *das*

**adventure:** ~ holiday *n* Abenteuerurlaub, *der;* ~ playground *n.* (Brit.) Abenteuerspielplatz, *der*

**adventurous** /ədˈventʃərəs/ *adj.* abenteuerlustig

**adverb** /ˈædvɜːb/ *n.* Adverb, *das*

**adversary** /ˈædvəsərɪ/ *n.* (enemy) Widersacher, *der*/Widersacherin, *die;* (opponent) Kontrahent, *der*/Kontrahentin, *die*

**adverse** /ˈædvɜːs/ *adj.* (a) (unfavourable) ungünstig
(b) (contrary) widrig ⟨*Wind, Umstände*⟩

**adversity** /ədˈvɜːsɪtɪ/ *n.* (a) *no pl.* Not, *die*
(b) *usu.* in pl. Widrigkeit, *die*

**advert** /ˈædvɜːt/ (Brit. coll.) ► ADVERTISEMENT

**advertise** /ˈædvətaɪz/ ① *v.t.* werben für; (by small ad) inserieren; ausschreiben ⟨*Stelle*⟩
② *v.i.* werben; (in newspaper) inserieren; annoncieren

**advertisement** /ədˈvɜːtɪsmənt/ *n.* Anzeige, *die;* TV ~: Fernsehspot, *der;* classified ~: Kleinanzeige, *die*

**advertiser** /ˈædvətaɪzə(r)/ *n.* (in newspaper) Inserent, *der*/Inserentin, *die;* (on radio, TV) Auftraggeber/Auftraggeberin [der Werbesendung]

**advertising** /ˈædvətaɪzɪŋ/ *n.* Werbung, *die;*

*attrib.* Werbe-; ~ agency/campaign/industry Werbeagentur, *die*/-kampagne, *die*/-branche, *die*

**advice** /ədˈvaɪs/ *n.* Rat, *der;* take sb.'s ~: jmds. Rat (*Dat.*) folgen

**advisable** /ədˈvaɪzəbl/ *adj.* ratsam

**advise** /ədˈvaɪz/ *v.t.* beraten; ~ sth. zu etw. raten; (inform) unterrichten (of über + *Akk.*); ~ sb. to do sth. jmdm. raten, etw. zu tun

**adviser, advisor** /ədˈvaɪzə(r)/ *n.* Berater, *der*/Beraterin, *die*

**advisory** /ədˈvaɪzərɪ/ *adj.* beratend

**advocate** ① /ˈædvəkət/ *n.* (of a cause) Befürworter, *der*/Befürworterin, *die;* (Law) [Rechts]anwalt, *der*/-anwältin, *die*
② /ˈædvəkeɪt/ *v.t.* befürworten

**advt.** *abbr.* = **advertisement**

**aerial** /ˈeərɪəl/ ① *adj.* Luft-; ~ bombardment Bombardierung [aus der Luft]; ~ photograph/photography Luftaufnahme, *die*/Luftaufnahmen Pl.
② *n.* Antenne, *die*

**aero-** /eərəʊ/ *in comb.* Aero-

**aerobic** /eəˈrəʊbɪk/ *adj.* (Biol.) aerob

**ae'robics** *n.* Aerobic, *das*

**aerody'namic** *adj.* aerodynamisch

**aeronautics** /eərəˈnɔːtɪks/ *n.* Aeronautik, *die*

**aeroplane** /ˈeərəpleɪn/ *n.* (Brit.) Flugzeug, *das*

**aerosol** /ˈeərəsɒl/ *n.* (spray) Spray, *der* od. *das;* (container) ~ [spray] Spraydose, *die*

**'aerospace** *n., no art.* Erdatmosphäre und Weltraum; (technology) Luft- und Raumfahrt, *die*

**aesthetic** /iːsˈθetɪk/ *adj.* ästhetisch

**afar** /əˈfɑː/ *adv.* from ~: aus der Ferne

**affable** /ˈæfəbl/ *adj.* freundlich

**affair** /əˈfeə(r)/ *n.* (a) (concern) Angelegenheit, *die*
(b) *in pl.* (business) Geschäfte Pl.
(c) (love ~) Affäre, *die;* have an ~ with sb. eine Affäre od. ein Verhältnis mit jmdm. haben

**affect** /əˈfekt/ *v.t.* (a) sich auswirken auf (+ *Akk.*)
(b) (emotionally) betroffen machen

**affectation** /æfekˈteɪʃn/ *n.* (studied display) Verstellung, *die;* (artificiality) Affektiertheit, *die*

**affected** /əˈfektɪd/ *adj.* affektiert; gekünstelt ⟨*Sprache, Stil*⟩

**affection** /əˈfekʃn/ *n.* Zuneigung, *die*

**affectionate** /əˈfekʃənət/ *adj.* anhänglich; liebevoll ⟨*Umarmung*⟩

**af'fectionately** *adv.* liebevoll

**affiliate** /əˈfɪlɪeɪt/ *v.t.* be ~d to sth. an etw. (*Akk.*) angegliedert sein

**affinity** /əˈfɪnɪtɪ/ *n.* (a) (relationship) Verwandtschaft, *die* (to mit)
(b) (liking) Neigung, *die* (for zu); feel an ~ to or for sb./sth. sich zu jmdm./etw. hingezogen fühlen

**affirm** /əˈfɜːm/ v.t. (assert) bekräftigen ⟨Absicht⟩; beteuern ⟨Unschuld⟩; (state as a fact) bestätigen

**affirmation** /æfəˈmeɪʃn/ n. (of intention) Bekräftigung, die; (of fact) Bestätigung, die

**affirmative** /əˈfɜːmətɪv/ ① adj. affirmativ; bejahend ⟨Antwort⟩
② n. answer in the ∼: bejahend antworten

**affirmative 'action** n. (Amer.) positive Diskriminierung (fachspr.); Bevorzugung, die

**afflict** /əˈflɪkt/ v.t. (physically) plagen; (mentally) quälen; peinigen; **be ∼ed with sth.** von etw. befallen sein

**affliction** /əˈflɪkʃn/ n. Leiden, das

**affluence** /ˈæfluəns/ n. Reichtum, der

**affluent** /ˈæfluənt/ adj. reich; **the ∼ society** die Überflussgesellschaft

**afford** /əˈfɔːd/ v.t. (a) sich (Dat.) leisten
(b) (provide) bieten; gewähren ⟨Schutz⟩

**affordable** /əˈfɔːdəbl/ adj. erschwinglich

**affray** /əˈfreɪ/ n. Schlägerei, die

**affront** /əˈfrʌnt/ ① v.t. beleidigen
② n. Beleidigung, die

**afield** /əˈfiːld/ adv. **far ∼** (direction) weit hinaus; (place) weit draußen

**afloat** /əˈfləʊt/ pred. adj. (a) (floating) über Wasser; flott ⟨Schiff⟩
(b) (at sea) auf See; **be ∼:** auf dem Meer treiben

**afoot** /əˈfʊt/ pred. adj. im Gange

**aforementioned** /əˈfɔːmenʃnd/,
**aforesaid** /əˈfɔːsed/ adjs. oben erwähnt od. genannt

**afraid** /əˈfreɪd/ adj. **be ∼ [of sb./sth.]** [vor jmdm./etw.] Angst haben; **be ∼ to do sth.** Angst davor haben, etw. zu tun; **I'm ∼ so/ not** ich fürchte ja/nein

**afresh** /əˈfreʃ/ adv. von neuem

**Africa** /ˈæfrɪkə/ pr. n. Afrika (das)

**African** /ˈæfrɪkən/ ① adj. afrikanisch; **sb. is ∼:** jmd. ist Afrikaner/Afrikanerin
② n. Afrikaner, der/Afrikanerin, die

**Afro-Carib'bean** ① adj. afrokaribisch
② n. Mensch afrokaribischer Herkunft od. Abstammung

**after** /ˈɑːftə(r)/ ① adv. (a) (later) danach
(b) (behind) hinterher
② prep. (a) (in time) nach; **two days ∼:** zwei Tage danach
(b) (behind) hinter (+ Dat.)
(c) **ask ∼ sb./sth.** nach jmdm./etw. fragen
(d) **∼ all** schließlich
③ conj. nachdem

**after: ∼care** n. (Med.) Nachbehandlung, die **∼-effect** n. Nachwirkung, die

**aftermath** /ˈɑːftəmæθ, ˈɑːftəmɑːθ/ n. Nachwirkungen Pl.

**after: ∼'noon** n. Nachmittag, der; **this/ tomorrow ∼noon** heute/morgen Nachmittag; **in the ∼noon** am Nachmittag; (regularly) nachmittags; **∼-sales service** n.

Kundendienst, der; **∼shave** n. Aftershave, das; **∼taste** n. Nachgeschmack, der; **∼thought** n. nachträglicher Einfall

**afterwards** /ˈɑːftəwədz/ adv. danach

**again** /əˈgen, əˈgeɪn/ adv. wieder; (one more time) noch einmal; **∼ and ∼, time and [time] ∼:** immer wieder; **back ∼:** wieder zurück

**against** /əˈgenst, əˈgeɪnst/ prep. gegen

**age** /eɪdʒ/ ① n. (a) Alter, das; **what ∼ are you?** wie alt bist du?; **at the ∼ of** im Alter von; **come of ∼:** volljährig werden; **be under ∼:** zu jung sein
(b) (great period) Zeitalter, das; **∼s** (coll.: a long time) eine Ewigkeit
② v.t. altern lassen
③ v.i. altern

**'age bracket** n. Altersstufe, die

**aged** adj. (a) /eɪdʒd/ **be ∼ five** fünf Jahre alt sein; **a boy ∼ five** ein fünfjähriger Junge
(b) /ˈeɪdʒɪd/ (elderly) bejahrt

**'age group** n. Altersgruppe, die

**ageism** /ˈeɪdʒɪzm/ n. Diskriminierung aufgrund des Alters

**ageist** /ˈeɪdʒɪst/ adj. das Alter diskriminierend

**ageless** /ˈeɪdʒlɪs/ adj. nicht alternd ⟨Person⟩; (eternal) zeitlos

**'age limit** n. Altersgrenze, die

**agency** /ˈeɪdʒənsɪ/ n. (business establishment) Geschäftsstelle, die; (news/advertising ∼) Agentur, die

**agenda** /əˈdʒendə/ n. Tagesordnung, die

**agent** /ˈeɪdʒənt/ n. Vertreter, der/ Vertreterin, die; (spy) Agent, der/Agentin, die

**age: ∼-old** adj. uralt; **∼ range** n. Altersstufe, die

**aggravate** /ˈægrəveɪt/ v.t. (a) (make worse) verschlimmern
(b) (annoy) aufregen; ärgern

**aggravating** /ˈægrəveɪtɪŋ/ adj. ärgerlich

**aggravation** /ægrəˈveɪʃn/ n. (a) Verschlimmerung, die
(b) (annoyance) Ärger, der

**aggregate** /ˈægrɪgət/ ① n. Gesamtmenge, die
② adj. gesamt

**aggression** /əˈgreʃn/ n. Aggression, die

**aggressive** /əˈgresɪv/ adj.,
**ag'gressively** adv. aggressiv

**ag'gressiveness** n. Aggressivität, die

**aggressor** /əˈgresə(r)/ n. Aggressor, der

**aggrieved** /əˈgriːvd/ v.t. (resentful) verärgert; (offended) gekränkt

**aggro** /ˈægrəʊ/ n. (Brit. sl.) Zoff, der (ugs.); Krawall, der; **they are looking for ∼:** sie suchen Streit

**aghast** /əˈgɑːst/ pred. adj. bestürzt (**über** + Akk.)

**agile** /ˈædʒaɪl/ adj. beweglich; flink ⟨Bewegung⟩

**agility** /əˈdʒɪlɪtɪ/ n. Beweglichkeit, die; (of movement) Flinkheit, die

**a**

**agitate** /'ædʒɪteɪt/ ① *v.t.* **(a)** (shake) schütteln
**(b)** (disturb) erregen
② *v.i.* agitieren

**agitation** /ædʒɪ'teɪʃn/ *n.* **(a)** (shaking) Schütteln, *das*
**(b)** (emotional) Erregung, *die*

**agitator** /'ædʒɪteɪtə(r)/ *n.* Agitator, *der*

**AGM** *abbr.* = **Annual General Meeting** JHV

**agnostic** /æg'nɒstɪk/ *n.* Agnostiker, *der/* Agnostikerin, *die*

**ago** /ə'gəʊ/ *adv.* ten years ∼: vor zehn Jahren; [not] long ∼: vor [nicht] langer Zeit

**agog** /ə'gɒg/ *pred. adj.* gespannt

**agonize** /'ægənaɪz/ *v.i.* ∼ over sth. sich (*Dat.*) den Kopf über etw. (*Akk.*) zermartern

**agony** /'ægənɪ/ *n.* Todesqualen *Pl.*

**'agony aunt** *n.* (coll.) Briefkastentante, *die* (ugs. scherzh.)

**agoraphobia** /ægərə'fəʊbɪə/ *n.* (Psych.) Agoraphobie, *die;* Platzangst, *die*

**agoraphobic** /ægərə'fəʊbɪk/ *adj.* (Psych.) an Agoraphobie *od.* Platzangst leidend; **be ∼**: an Agoraphobie *od.* Platzangst leiden

**agree** /ə'griː/ ① *v.i.* **(a)** (consent) einverstanden sein (**to, with** mit)
**(b)** (hold similar opinion) einer Meinung sein; they ∼d [with me] sie waren derselben Meinung [wie ich]
**(c)** (reach similar opinion) ∼ on sth. sich über etw. (*Akk.*) einigen
**(d)** (harmonize) übereinstimmen
**(e)** ∼ with sb. (suit) jmdm. bekommen
② *v.t.* vereinbaren

**agreeable** /ə'griːəbl/ *adj.* **(a)** (pleasing) angenehm
**(b)** be ∼ [to sth.] [mit etw.] einverstanden sein

**agreeably** /ə'griːəblɪ/ *adv.* angenehm

**agreed** /ə'griːd/ *adj.* einig; vereinbart ⟨*Summe, Zeit*⟩

**a'greement** *n.* Übereinstimmung, *die;* be in ∼ [about sth.] sich (*Dat.*) [über etw. (*Akk.*)] einig sein

**agricultural** /ægrɪ'kʌltʃərl/ *adj.* landwirtschaftlich

**agriculture** /'ægrɪkʌltʃə(r)/ *n.* Landwirtschaft, *die*

**aground** /ə'graʊnd/ *adj.* go *or* run ∼: auf Grund laufen

**aha** /ɑː'hɑː/ *int.* aha

**ahead** /ə'hed/ *adv.* voraus; ∼ of vor (+ *Dat.*); be ∼ of the others (fig.) den anderen voraus sein

**AI** *abbr.* = **artificial intelligence** KI

**aid** /eɪd/ ① *v.t.* **(a)** ∼ sb. [to do sth.] jmdm. helfen[, etw. zu tun]; ∼ed by unterstützt von
**(b)** (promote) fördern
② *n.* **(a)** (help) Hilfe, *die;* with the ∼ of sth./ sb. mit Hilfe einer Sache (*Gen.*)/mit jmds. Hilfe; in ∼ of sb./sth. zugunsten von jmdm./ etw.

**(b)** (source of help) Hilfsmittel, *das* (to für)

**'aid agency** *n.* Hilfsorganisation, *die;* Hilfswerk, *das*

**aide** /eɪd/ *n.* Berater, *der/*Beraterin, *die*

**Aids** /eɪdz/ *n.* Aids (*das*); ∼ test Aidstest, *der*

**'Aids-related** *adj.* ∼ disease/illness durch Aids hervorgerufene Krankheit

**'aid worker** *n.* Helfer, *der/*Helferin, *die;* ∼s Hilfskräfte *Pl.;* Hilfspersonal, *das*

**ailment** /'eɪlmənt/ *n.* Gebrechen, *das*

**aim** /eɪm/ ① *v.t.* ausrichten ⟨*Schusswaffe, Rakete*⟩; ∼ sth. at sb./sth. etw. auf jmdn./etw. richten
② *v.i.* **(a)** zielen (at auf + *Akk.*)
**(b)** ∼ to do sth. beabsichtigen, etw. zu tun; ∼ at *or* for sth. (fig.) etwas anstreben
③ *n.* Ziel, *das;* take ∼ [at sth./sb.] [auf etw./ jmdn.] zielen

**'aimless** *adj.,* **'aimlessly** *adv.* ziellos

**air** /eə(r)/ ① *n.* **(a)** (Luft, *die;* be/go on the ∼: senden; ⟨*Programm:*⟩ gesendet werden; by ∼: mit dem Flugzeug; (by ∼ mail) mit Luftpost
**(b)** (facial expression) Miene, *die*
**(c)** put on ∼s sich aufspielen
② *v.t.* (ventilate) lüften; (make public) [öffentlich] darlegen

**air:** ∼ bag *n.* (Motor Veh.) Airbag *der;* side ∼ bag Seitenairbag, *der;* ∼base *n.* Luftwaffenstützpunkt, *der;* ∼bed *n.* Luftmatratze, *die;* ∼borne *adj.* be ∼borne sich in der Luft befinden; ∼ brake *n.* Druckluftbremse, *die;* (flap) Luftbremse, *die;* ∼brush *n.* Spritzpistole, *die;* ∼bubble *n.* Luftblase, *die;* ∼ bus *n.* Airbus, *der;* ∼-conditioned *adj.* klimatisiert; ∼ conditioner *n.* Klimaanlage, *die;* ∼ conditioning *n.* Klimaanlage, *die;* ∼-cooled *adj.* luftgekühlt; ∼craft *n., pl.* same Flugzeug, *das;* ∼craft carrier *n.* Flugzeugträger, *der;* ∼ crew *n.* Besatzung, *die;* Flugpersonal, *das;* ∼ cushion *n.* Luftkissen, *das;* ∼ fare *n.* Flugpreis, *der;* ∼field *n.* Flugplatz, *der;* ∼ force *n.* Luftwaffe, *die;* ∼ freshener *n.* Lufterfrischer, *der;* Luftverbesserer, *der;* ∼gun *n.* Luftgewehr, *das;* ∼ hostess *n.* Stewardess, *die*

**airing** /'eərɪŋ/ *n.* Auslüften, *das;* these clothes need a good ∼: diese Kleider müssen gründlich gelüftet werden

**airless** /'eəlɪs/ *adj.* stickig ⟨*Zimmer, Büro*⟩; windstill ⟨*Nacht*⟩

**air:** ∼ letter *n.* Aerogramm, *das;* ∼lift *n.* Luftbrücke, *die;* (of für); ∼line *n.* Fluggesellschaft, *die;* Fluglinie, *die;* ∼line pilot [für eine Fluggesellschaft fliegender] Pilot; ∼ liner *n.* Verkehrsflugzeug, *das;* ∼ mail *n.* Luftpost, *die;* by ∼ mail mit Luftpost; ∼man /'eəmən/ *n., pl.* ∼men / -mən/ Flieger, *der;* ∼ mile *n.* Flugmeile, *die;* ∼plane *n.* (Amer.) Flugzeug, *das;* ∼ play *n.* (Radio) das Spielen einer Platte im Radio;

the record receives *or* gets no/a great deal of
~play die Platte wird [überhaupt] nicht/
wird sehr häufig im Radio gespielt;
~ **pocket** *n.* (Aeronaut.) Luftloch, *das;*
~ **pollution** *n.* Luftverschmutzung, *die;*
~**port** *n.* Flughafen, *der;* ~**port tax**
Flughafengebühr, *die;* ~ **pressure** *n.*
Luftdruck, *der;* ~ **raid** *n.* Luftangriff, *der;*
~**-raid shelter** *n.* Luftschutzraum, *der;*
~ **rifle** *n.* Luftgewehr, *das;* ~**sea**
'**rescue** *n.* Seenotrettungseinsatz aus der
Luft; ~**ship** *n.* Luftschiff, *das;* ~ **show** *n.*
Flugschau, *die;* ~**sick** *adj.* luftkrank;
~**stream** *n.* (Meteorol.) Luftströmung, *die;*
~**strike** *n.* Luftanschlag, *der;*
~ **terminal** *n.* [Air-]Terminal, *der od. das;*
~**tight** *adj.* luftdicht; ~**time** *n.* Sendezeit,
*die;* ~ **traffic** *n.* Flugverkehr, *der;*
~**-traffic control** *n.* Flugsicherung, *die;*
~**-traffic controller** *n.* Fluglotse, *der;*
~ **travel** *n.* Fliegen, *das;* ~**waves** *n. pl.*
Äther, *der*

'**airy** *adj.* luftig ⟨Büro, Zimmer⟩

**aisle** /aɪl/ *n.* Gang, *der;* (of church)
Seitenschiff, *das*

**ajar** /ə'dʒɑː(r)/ *adj.* **be** ~: einen Spaltbreit
offen stehen

**a.k.a.** *abbr.* = **also known as** al.

**akin** /ə'kɪn/ *adj.* **be** ~ **to sth.** einer Sache
(*Dat.*) ähnlich sein

**alarm** /ə'lɑːm/ |1| *n.* (a) Alarm, *der;* **give** *or*
**raise the** ~: Alarm schlagen
**(b)** (fear) Angst, *die*
|2| *v.t.* aufschrecken

**alarm:** ~ **call** *n.* Weck[an]ruf, *der;*
~ '**clock** *n.* Wecker, *der*

**alas** /ə'læs/ *int.* ach

**Albania** /æl'beɪnɪə/ *pr. n.* Albanien (*das*)

**Albanian** /æl'beɪnɪən/ |1| *adj.* albanisch;
**sb. is** ~: jmd. ist Albaner/Albanerin
|2| *n.* (a) (person) Albaner, *der*/Albanerin, *die*
**(b)** (language) Albanisch, *das; see also*
ENGLISH 2 A

**albatross** /'ælbətrɒs/ *n.* Albatros, *der*

**album** /'ælbəm/ *n.* Album, *das*

**alcohol** /'ælkəhɒl/ *n.* Alkohol, *der*

'**alcohol-free** *adj.* alkoholfrei

**alcoholic** /ælkə'hɒlɪk/ |1| *adj.* alkoholisch
|2| *n.* Alkoholiker, *der*/Alkoholikerin, *die*

**Alcoholics A'nonymous** *n.* die
Anonymen Alkoholiker

**alcoholism** /'ælkəhɒlɪzm/ *n.*
Alkoholismus, *der*

**alcopop** /'ælkəʊpɒp/ *n.: alkoholhaltiges
Erfrischungsgetränk*

**alcove** /'ælkəʊv/ *n.* Alkoven, *der*

**ale** /eɪl/ *n.* Ale, *das*

**alert** /ə'lɜːt/ |1| *adj.* wachsam
|2| *n.* Alarmbereitschaft, *die;* **on the** ~: auf
der Hut
|3| *v.t.* alarmieren; ~ **sb. [to sth.]** jmdn. [vor
etw. (*Dat.*)] warnen

'**A level** *n.* (Brit. Sch.) ≈ Abitur, *das*

**algebra** /'ældʒɪbrə/ *n.* Algebra, *die*

**Algeria** /æl'dʒɪərɪə/ *pr. n.* Algerien (*das*)

**Algerian** /æl'dʒɪərɪən/ |1| *adj.* algerisch;
**sb. is** ~: jmd. ist Algerier/Algerierin
|2| *n.* Algerier, *der*/Algerierin, *die*

**alias** /'eɪlɪəs/ |1| *adv.* alias
|2| *n.* angenommener Name

**alibi** /'ælɪbaɪ/ *n.* Alibi, *das*

**alien** /'eɪlɪən/ |1| *adj.* (a) (strange) fremd
**(b)** (foreign) ausländisch
|2| *n.* (a) (from another world) Außerirdische,
*der/die*
**(b)** (Admin.: foreigner) Ausländer, *der*/
Ausländerin, *die*

**alienate** /'eɪlɪəneɪt/ *v.t.* befremden

**alienation** /eɪlɪə'neɪʃn/ *n.* Entfremdung,
*die*

**alight**[1] /ə'laɪt/ *v.i.* (a) aussteigen (**from** aus)
**(b)** ⟨Vogel:⟩ sich niedersetzen

**alight**[2] *adj.* **be/catch** ~: brennen; **set sth.**
~: etw. in Brand setzen

**align** /ə'laɪn/ *v.t.* (a) (place in a line)
ausrichten
**(b)** (bring into line) in eine Linie bringen

**a'lignment** *n.* Ausrichtung, *die;* **out of** ~:
nicht richtig ausgerichtet

**alike** /ə'laɪk/ *pred. adj.* ähnlich;
(indistinguishable) gleich

**alimony** /'ælɪmənɪ/ *n.* Unterhaltszahlung,
*die*

**alive** /ə'laɪv/ *pred. adj.* (a) lebendig
**(b)** (aware) **be** ~ **to sth.** sich (*Dat.*) einer
Sache (*Gen.*) bewusst sein
**(c)** (swarming) **be** ~ **with** wimmeln von

**alkali** /'ælkəlaɪ/ *n., pl.* ~**s** *or* ~**es** Alkali,
*das*

**alkaline** /'ælkəlaɪn/ *adj.* alkalisch

**all** /ɔːl/ |1| *attrib. adj.* (a) (entire extent or
quantity of) ganz; ~ **day** den ganzen Tag;
~ **my money** all mein Geld; mein ganzes
Geld
**(b)** (entire number of) alle; ~ **the books** alle
Bücher; ~ **my books** all[e] meine Bücher;
~ **the others** alle anderen
**(c)** (any whatever) jeglicher/jegliche/jegliches
**(d)** (greatest possible) **in** ~ **innocence** in aller
Unschuld
|2| *n.* (a) (~ persons) alle; ~ **of us** wir alle;
**the happiest of** ~: der/die Glücklichste
unter *od.* von allen
**(b)** (every bit) ~ **of it** alles; ~ **of the money**
das ganze Geld
**(c)** ~ **of** (coll.: as much as) **be** ~ **of seven feet
tall** gut sieben Fuß groß sein
**(d)** (~ things) alles; ~ **I need is the money**
ich brauche nur das Geld; **that is** ~: das ist
alles; **the most beautiful of** ~: der/die/das
Schönste von allen; **most of** ~: am meisten;
**it was** ~ **but impossible** es war fast
unmöglich; **it's** ~ **the same to me** es ist mir
ganz egal; **can I help you at** ~? kann ich
Ihnen irgendwie behilflich sein?; **she has no
talent at** ~: sie hat überhaupt kein Talent; ⋯⊹

nothing at ∼: gar nichts; not at ∼ happy/well überhaupt nicht glücklich/gesund; not at ∼! überhaupt nicht!; (acknowledging thanks) gern geschehen!; if at ∼: wenn überhaupt; in ∼: insgesamt; ∼ in ∼: alles in allem (e) (Sport) two [goals] ∼: zwei zu zwei; (Tennis) thirty ∼: dreißig beide
**3** *adv.* ganz; ∼ but fast; ∼ the better/worse [for that] um so besser/schlimmer; ∼ at once (suddenly) plötzlich; be ∼ 'in (exhausted) total erledigt sein (ugs.); sth. is ∼ right etw. ist in Ordnung; (tolerable) etw. ist ganz gut; I'm ∼ right mir geht es ganz gut; yes, ∼ right ja, gut; it's ∼ right by me das ist mir recht

**allay** /ə'leɪ/ *v.t.* zerstreuen ‹*Besorgnis, Befürchtungen*›

**all:** ∼-'clear *n.* Entwarnung, *die;* ∼-**day** *adj.* ganztägig ‹*Ausflug, Versammlung*›

**allegation** /ælɪ'ɡeɪʃn/ *n.* Behauptung, *die;* make ∼s against sb. Beschuldigungen gegen jmdn. erheben

**allege** /ə'ledʒ/ *v.t.* behaupten

**alleged** /ə'ledʒd/ *adj.,* **allegedly** /ə'ledʒɪdlɪ/ *adv.* angeblich

**allegiance** /ə'liːdʒəns/ *n.* Loyalität, *die* (to gegenüber)

**allegorical** /ælɪ'ɡɒrɪkl/ *adj.* allegorisch

**allegory** /'ælɪɡərɪ/ *n.* Allegorie, *die*

**allergic** /ə'lɜːdʒɪk/ *adj.* allergisch (to gegen)

**allergy** /'ælədʒɪ/ *n.* Allergie, *die*

**alleviate** /ə'liːvɪeɪt/ *v.t.* abschwächen

**alley** /'ælɪ/ *n.* [schmale] Gasse

**alliance** /ə'laɪəns/ *n.* Bündnis, *das;* (league) Allianz, *die*

**allied** /'ælaɪd/ *adj.* be ∼ to *or* with sb./sth. mit jmdm./etw. verbündet sein

**alligator** /'ælɪɡeɪtə(r)/ *n.* Alligator, *der*

**all:** ∼-in *adj.* Pauschal-; ∼-**night** *adj.* die ganze Nacht dauernd ‹*Sitzung*›; nachts durchgehend geöffnet ‹*Gaststätte*›

**allocate** /'æləkeɪt/ *v.t.* zuweisen, zuteilen (to *Dat.*)

**allocation** /ælə'keɪʃn/ *n.* Zuweisung, *die;* (ration) Zuteilung, *die*

**allot** /ə'lɒt/ *v.t.,* -tt-: ∼ sth. to sb. jmdm. etw. zuteilen

**al'lotment** *n.* (Brit.: plot of land) ≈ Schrebergarten, *der*

**all:** ∼-**out** *attrib. adj.* mit allen [verfügbaren] Mitteln *nachgestellt;* ∼-**over** *attrib. adj.* ∼-**over** tan nahtlose Bräune

**allow** /ə'laʊ/ **1** *v.t.* erlauben; zulassen; ∼ sb. to do sth. jmdm. erlauben, etw. zu tun; be ∼ed to do sth. etw. tun dürfen
**2** *v.i.* ∼ for etw. etw. berücksichtigen

**allowance** /ə'laʊəns/ *n.* (a) Zuteilung, *die;* (for special expenses) Zuschuss, *der* (b) make ∼s for sth./sb. etw./jmdn. berücksichtigen

**alloy** /'ælɔɪ/ *n.* Legierung, *die*

**all:** ∼-**purpose** *adj.* Universal-; Allzweck-; ∼-**risks** *attrib. adj.* an ∼-risks insurance

eine alle gängigen Risiken abdeckende Versicherung; ∼-**round** *adj.* Allround-; ∼-'**rounder** *n.* Allroundtalent, *das;* ∼-**seater** *adj.* voll bestuhlt ‹*Stadion*›; ∼-**time** *adj.* ∼-time record absoluter Rekord

**allude** /ə'luːd/ *v.i.* ∼ to sich beziehen auf (+ *Akk.*); (indirectly) anspielen auf (+ *Akk.*)

**allusion** /ə'luːʒn/ *n.* Hinweis, *der;* (indirect) Anspielung, *die*

**ally** /'ælaɪ/ *n.* Verbündete, *der/die;* the Allies die Alliierten

**almighty** /ɔːl'maɪtɪ/ *adj.* allmächtig; the A∼: der Allmächtige

**almond** /'ɑːmənd/ *n.* Mandel, *die*

**almost** /'ɔːlməʊst/ *adv.* fast; beinahe

**alms** /ɑːmz/ *n.* Almosen, *das*

**alone** /ə'ləʊn/ **1** *pred. adj.* allein; alleine (ugs.)
**2** *adv.* allein

**along** /ə'lɒŋ/ **1** *prep.* entlang (*position:* + *Dat.; direction:* + *Akk.*)
**2** *adv.* weiter; I'll be ∼ shortly ich komme gleich; all ∼: die ganze Zeit [über]

**along'side** **1** *adv.* daneben
**2** *prep.* neben (*position:* + *Dat.; direction:* + *Akk.*)

**aloof** /ə'luːf/ **1** *adv.* abseits; hold ∼ from sb. sich von jmdm. fern halten
**2** *adj.* distanziert

**aloud** /ə'laʊd/ *adv.* laut; read [sth.] ∼: [etw.] vorlesen

**alphabet** /'ælfəbet/ *n.* Alphabet, *das*

**alphabetical** /ælfə'betɪkl/ *adj.,* **alpha'betically** *adv.* alphabetisch

**alpine** /'ælpaɪn/ *adj.* alpin

**Alps** /ælps/ *pr. n. pl.* the ∼: die Alpen

**already** /ɔːl'redɪ/ *adv.* schon

**Alsation** /æl'seɪʃn/ *n.* [deutscher] Schäferhund

**also** /'ɔːlsəʊ/ *adv.* auch; (moreover) außerdem

**altar** /'ɔːltə(r), 'ɒltə(r)/ *n.* Altar, *der*

**alter** /'ɔːltə(r), 'ɒltə(r)/ **1** *v.t.* ändern
**2** *v.i.* sich verändern

**alteration** /ɔːltə'reɪʃn, ɒltə'reɪʃn/ *n.* Änderung, *die*

**alternate** **1** /ɔːl'tɜːnət/ *adj.* sich abwechselnd
**2** /'ɔːltəneɪt/ *v.t.* abwechseln lassen
**3** /'ɔːltəneɪt/ *v.i.* sich abwechseln

**al'ternately** *adv.* abwechselnd

**'alternating current** *n.* (Electr.) Wechselstrom, *der*

**alternative** /ɔːl'tɜːnətɪv/ **1** *adj.* alternativ; Alternativ-
**2** *n.* (a) (choice) Alternative, *die;* ∼ fuel Alternativkraftstoff, *der* (*für Verbrennungsmotoren*); ∼ medicine Alternativmedizin, *die* (b) (possibility) Möglichkeit, *die*

**al'ternatively** *adv.* oder aber; or ∼: oder aber auch

**although** /ɔːlˈðəʊ/ *conj.* obwohl

**altimeter** /ˈæltɪmiːtə(r)/ *n.* Höhenmesser, *der*

**altitude** /ˈæltɪtjuːd/ *n.* Höhe, *die*

**altogether** /ɔːltəˈgeðə(r)/ *adv.* völlig; (on the whole) im Großen und Ganzen; (in total) insgesamt; **not** ∼ **[true/convincing]** nicht ganz [wahr/überzeugend]

**altruist** /ˈæltruɪst/ *n.* Altruist, *der*/ Altruistin, *die* (geh.)

**altruistic** /æltruˈɪstɪk/ *adj.* altruistisch

**aluminium** /æljʊˈmɪnɪəm/ (Brit.), **aluminum** /əˈluːmɪnəm/ (Amer.) *ns.* Aluminium, *das*

**always** /ˈɔːlweɪz/ *adv.* immer; (repeatedly) ständig

**Alzheimer's disease** /ˈæltshaɪmez dɪziːz/ *n.* Alzheimerkrankheit, *die*

**am** ▶ BE

**AM** *abbr.* = **amplitude modulation** AM

**a.m.** /eɪˈem/ *adv.* vormittags; [at] one/four ∼: [um] ein/vier Uhr früh

**amalgamate** /əˈmælgəmeɪt/ ① *v.t.* vereinigen
② *v.i.* sich vereinigen; ⟨Firmen:⟩ fusionieren

**amalgamation** /əmælgəˈmeɪʃn/ *n.* Vereinigung, *die;* (of firms) Fusion, *die*

**amass** /əˈmæs/ *v.t.* anhäufen

**amateur** /ˈæmətə(r)/ *n.* Amateur, *der; attrib.* Amateur-; Laien-

**ˈamateurish** *adj.* laienhaft; amateurhaft

**amaze** /əˈmeɪz/ *v.t.* verblüffen; verwundern

**aˈmazement** *n.* Verblüffung, *die;* Verwunderung, *die*

**amazing** /əˈmeɪzɪŋ/ *adj.* (remarkable) erstaunlich; (astonishing) verblüffend

**Amazon** /ˈæməzən/ *pr. n.* **the** ∼: der Amazonas

**ambassador** /æmˈbæsədə(r)/ *n.* Botschafter, *der*/Botschafterin, *die*

**amber** /ˈæmbə(r)/ ① *n.* **(a)** Bernstein, *der* **(b)** (traffic light) Gelb, *das*
② *adj.* Bernstein-; (colour) bernsteinfarben; gelb ⟨Verkehrslicht⟩

**ambiguity** /æmbɪˈgjuːɪtɪ/ *n.* Zweideutigkeit, *die*

**ambiguous** /æmˈbɪgjʊəs/ *adj.* zweideutig

**ambition** /æmˈbɪʃn/ *n.* Ehrgeiz, *der;* (aspiration) Ambition, *die*

**ambitious** /æmˈbɪʃəs/ *adj.* ehrgeizig

**ambivalent** /æmˈbɪvələnt/ *adj.* ambivalent

**amble** /ˈæmbl/ *v.i.* schlendern

**ambulance** /ˈæmbjʊləns/ *n.* Krankenwagen, *der;* Ambulanz, *die*

**ambulance:** ∼ **chaser** *n.* (Amer.) *Anwalt oder sein Agent, der Unfallopfer dazu überredet, auf Schadenersatz zu klagen;*

∼ **driver** *n.* Fahrer/Fahrerin eines/des Krankenwagens; ∼ **man** *n.* Sanitäter, *der;* ∼ **service** *n.* Rettungsdienst, *der*

**ambush** /ˈæmbʊʃ/ ① *n.* Hinterhalt, *der;* **lie in** ∼: im Hinterhalt liegen
② *v.t.* [aus dem Hinterhalt] überfallen

**amen** /ɑːˈmen, eɪˈmen/ ① *int.* amen
② *n.* Amen, *das*

**amenable** /əˈmiːnəbl/ *adj.* zugänglich, aufgeschlossen **(to** Dat.**)**

**amend** /əˈmend/ *v.t.* berichtigen; abändern ⟨Gesetzentwurf, Antrag⟩

**aˈmendment** *n.* (to motion) Abänderungsantrag, *der;* (to bill) Änderungsantrag, *der*

**amends** /əˈmendz/ *n. pl.* **make** ∼ **[to sb.]** es [bei jmdm.] wieder gutmachen; **make** ∼ **for sth.** etw. wieder gutmachen

**amenity** /əˈmiːnɪtɪ/ *n.,* usu. in pl. **amenities** (of town) kulturelle und Freizeiteinrichtungen

**America** /əˈmerɪkə/ *pr. n.* Amerika (*das*)

**American** /əˈmerɪkən/ ① *adj.* amerikanisch; **sb. is** ∼: jmd. ist Amerikaner/Amerikanerin; ∼ **English** amerikanisches Englisch
② *n.* (person) Amerikaner, *der*/ Amerikanerin, *die*

**American:** ∼ **ˈfootball** *n.* Football, *der;* ∼ **ˈIndian** *n.* Indianer, *der*/Indianerin, *die*

**Americanism** /əˈmerɪkənɪzm/ *n.* (Ling.) Amerikanismus, *der*

**Americanization** /əmerɪkənaɪˈzeɪʃn/ *n.* Amerikanisierung, *die*

**Americanize** /əˈmerɪkənaɪz/ *v.t.* amerikanisieren

**amiable** /ˈeɪmɪəbl/ *adj.* umgänglich

**amicable** /ˈæmɪkəbl/ *adj.* freundschaftlich; gütlich ⟨Einigung⟩

**amicably** /ˈæmɪkəblɪ/ *adv.* in [aller] Freundschaft

**amid[st]** /əˈmɪd(st)/ *prep.* inmitten; (fig.: during) bei

**amiss** /əˈmɪs/ ① *pred. adj.* verkehrt; **is anything** ∼? stimmt irgendetwas nicht?
② *adv.* **take sth.** ∼: etw. übel nehmen

**ammonia** /əˈməʊnɪə/ *n.* Ammoniak, *das*

**ammunition** /æmjʊˈnɪʃn/ *n.* Munition, *die*

**amnesia** /æmˈniːzɪə/ *n.* Amnesie, *die*

**amnesty** /ˈæmnɪstɪ/ *n.* Amnestie, *die*

**amniocentesis** /æmnɪəʊsenˈtiːsɪs/ *n.* (Med.) Fruchtwasserentnahme, *die*

**amok** /əˈmɒk/ *adv.* **run** ∼: Amok laufen

**among[st]** /əˈmʌŋ(st)/ *prep.* unter (+ Dat.); ∼ **other things** unter anderem; **they often quarrel** ∼ **themselves** sie streiten oft miteinander

**amoral** /eɪˈmɒrl/ *adj.* amoralisch

**amorous** /ˈæmərəs/ *adj.* verliebt; amourös ⟨Abenteuer, Beziehung⟩

**amorphous** /əˈmɔːfəs/ *adj.* formlos; amorph ⟨Masse⟩

**a**

**amount** /ə'maʊnt/ [1] *v.i.* ~ **to sth.** sich auf etw. (*Akk.*) belaufen; (fig.) etw. bedeuten [2] *n.* (a) (total) Betrag, *der;* Summe, *die* (b) (quantity) Menge, *die*

**amp** /æmp/ *n.* Ampere, *das*

**amphetamine** /æm'fetəmɪn/ *n.* (Med.) Amphetamin, *das*

**amphibian** /æm'fɪbɪən/ [1] *adj.* amphibisch [2] *n.* Amphibie, *die*

**amphibious** /æm'fɪbɪəs/ *adj.* amphibisch

**amphitheatre** /'æmfɪθɪətə(r)/ *n.* Amphitheater, *das*

**ample** /'æmpl/ *adj.* (a) (spacious) weitläufig ⟨*Garten, Räume*⟩; reichhaltig ⟨*Mahl*⟩ (b) (enough) ~ **room/food** reichlich Platz/zu essen

**amplifier** /'æmplɪfaɪə(r)/ *n.* Verstärker, *der*

**amplify** /'æmplɪfaɪ/ *v.t.* verstärken; (enlarge on) weiter ausführen

**amputate** /'æmpjʊteɪt/ *v.t.* amputieren

**amputation** /æmpjʊ'teɪʃn/ *n.* Amputation, *die*

**amuse** /ə'mjuːz/ *v.t.* (a) (interest) unterhalten; ~ **oneself by doing sth.** sich (*Dat.*) die Zeit damit vertreiben, etw. zu tun (b) (make laugh or smile) amüsieren

**a'musement** *n.* Belustigung, *die;* ~ **arcade** Spielhalle, *die*

**amusing** /ə'mjuːzɪŋ/ *adj.* amüsant

**an** /ən, *stressed* æn/ *indef. art. see also* A²: ein/eine/ein

**anaemia** /ə'niːmɪə/ *n.* Blutarmut, *die;* Anämie, *die*

**anaemic** /ə'niːmɪk/ *adj.* blutarm; anämisch

**anaesthetic** /ænɪs'θetɪk/ *n.* Anästhetikum, *das;* **general** ~: Narkosemittel, *das;* **local** ~: Lokalanästhetikum, *das*

**anaesthetist** /ə'niːsθətɪst/ *n.* Anästhesist, *der*/Anästhesistin, *die;* Narkose[fach]arzt, *der*/-ärztin, *die*

**anagram** /'ænəgræm/ *n.* Anagramm, *das*

**analgesia** /ænæl'dʒiːzɪə/ *n.* (Med.) Analgesie, *die*

**analgesic** /ænæl'dʒiːsɪk/ (Med.) [1] *adj.* analgetisch [2] *n.* Analgetikum, *das*

**analog** (Amer.) ▶ ANALOGUE

**analogue** /'ænəlɒg/ *n.* Entsprechung, *die;* Analogon, *das* (geh.); ~ **computer** Analogrechner, *der;* ~ **watch** Analoguhr, *die*

**analogy** /ə'nælədʒɪ/ *n.* Analogie, *die*

**analyse** /'ænəlaɪz/ *v.t.* analysieren

**analysis** /ə'næləsɪs/ *n., pl.* **analyses** /ə'næləsiːz/ Analyse, *die*

**analyst** /'ænəlɪst/ *n.* (a) (Psych.) Analytiker, *der*/Analytikerin, *die* (b) (Econ., Polit., etc.) Experte, *der*/Expertin, *die*

**analytic** /ænə'lɪtɪk/, **analytical** /ænə'lɪtɪkl/ *adj.* analytisch

**analyze** (Amer.) ▶ ANALYSE

**anarchic** /ə'nɑːkɪk/, **anarchical** /ə'nɑːkɪkl/ *adj.* anarchisch; (anarchistic) anarchistisch

**anarchist** /'ænəkɪst/ *n.* Anarchist, *der*/Anarchistin, *die*

**anarchy** /'ænəkɪ/ *n.* Anarchie, *die*

**anatomical** /ænə'tɒmɪkl/ *adj.* anatomisch

**anatomy** /ə'nætəmɪ/ *n.* Anatomie, *die*

**ANC** *abbr.* = **African National Congress** ANK

**ancestor** /'ænsestə(r)/ *n.* Vorfahr, *der*

**ancestry** /'ænsestrɪ/ *n.* Abstammung, *die*

**anchor** /'æŋkə(r)/ [1] *n.* Anker, *der* [2] *v.t.* verankern [3] *v.i.* ankern

**anchorage** /'æŋkərɪdʒ/ *n.* Ankerplatz, *der*

**anchorman** /'æŋkəmæn/ *n.* (Telev., Radio) Moderator, *der*

**anchovy** /'æntʃəvɪ/ *n.* Sardelle, *die*

**ancient** /'eɪnʃənt/ *adj.* alt; historisch ⟨*Gebäude usw.*⟩; (of antiquity) antik

**and** /ənd, *stressed* ænd/ *conj.* und; **for weeks** ~ **weeks** wochenlang; **better** ~ **better** immer besser

**androgynous** /æn'drɒdʒɪnəs/ *adj.* (Biol.) zwittrig

**anecdote** /'ænɪkdəʊt/ *n.* Anekdote, *die*

**anemia, anemic** (Amer.) ▶ ANAEM-

**anesthetic** *etc.* (Amer.) ▶ ANAESTHETIC *etc.*

**angel** /'eɪndʒl/ *n.* Engel, *der*

**angelic** /æn'dʒelɪk/ *adj.* engelhaft

**anger** /'æŋgə(r)/ [1] *n.* Zorn, *der* (at über + Akk.); (fury) Wut, *die* (at über + Akk.) [2] *v.t.* verärgern; (infuriate) wütend machen

**angina [pectoris]** /æn'dʒaɪnə ('pektərɪs)/ *n.* (Med.) Angina pectoris, *die*

**angle¹** /'æŋgl/ *n.* (a) (Geom.) Winkel, *der;* **at an** ~ **of 60°** im Winkel von 60°; **at an** ~: schief (b) (fig.) Gesichtspunkt, *der*

**angle²** *v.i.* angeln; (fig.) ~ **for sth.** sich um etw. bemühen

**angle:** ~ **brackets** *n. pl.* spitze Klammern; ~ **grinder** *n.* Winkelschleifer, *der;* (with cutting disc) Flex, *die;* ~**-parking** *n.* Schrägparken, *das*

**angler** /'æŋglə(r)/ *n.* Angler, *der*/Anglerin, *die*

**Anglican** /'æŋglɪkən/ [1] *adj.* anglikanisch [2] *n.* Anglikaner, *der*/Anglikanerin, *die*

**Anglo-** /æŋgləʊ/ *in comb.* anglo-/Anglo-

**Anglo-Saxon** /-'sæksn/ [1] *n.* Angelsachse, *der*/Angelsächsin, *die;* (language) Angelsächsisch, *das* [2] *adj.* angelsächsisch

**angora [wool]** /æŋ'gɔːrə/ *n.* Angorawolle, *die;* Mohair, *der*

**angrily** /'æŋgrɪlɪ/ *adv.* verärgert; (stronger) zornig

**angry** /'æŋgrɪ/ *adj.* böse; verärgert ⟨*Person, Stimme, Geste*⟩; (stronger) zornig; wütend; **be**

~ **at** or **about sth.** wegen etw. böse sein; **be** ~ **with** or **at sb.** mit jmdm. od. auf jmdn. böse sein; **get** ~: böse werden

**anguish** /'æŋgwɪʃ/ n. Qualen Pl.

**angular** /'æŋgjʊlə(r)/ adj. eckig ‹Gebäude, Struktur›; kantig ‹Gesicht›

**animal** /'ænɪməl/ ① n. Tier, das ② adj. tierisch

**animal: A**~ **Libe'ration Front** n. Tierbefreiungsfront, die; ~ **lover** n. Tierfreund, der/-freundin, die; ~ **pro'tectionist** n. Tierschützer, der/ -schützerin, die; ~ **'rights** n. pl. Tierrechte Pl.; ~ **rights supporter** Tierrechtler, der/ Tierrechtlerin, die

**animate** ① /'ænɪmeɪt/ v.t. beleben ② /'ænɪmət/ adj. beseelt ‹Leben, Körper›; belebt ‹Objekt, Welt›

**animated** /'ænɪmeɪtɪd/ adj. lebhaft ‹Diskussion, Gebärde›; ~ **cartoon** Zeichentrickfilm, der

**animation** /ænɪ'meɪʃn/ n. (a) Lebhaftigkeit, die (b) (Cinemat.) Animation, die

**animosity** /ænɪ'mɒsɪtɪ/ n. Feindseligkeit, die

**aniseed** /'ænɪsiːd/ n. Anis[samen], der

**ankle** /'æŋkl/ n. Fußgelenk, das

**ankle:** ~**-deep** adj. knöcheltief; ~ **sock** n. Socke, die; (esp. for children) Söckchen, das

**annex** ① /ə'neks/ v.t. annektieren ‹Land, Territorium› ② /'æneks/ n. Anbau, der

**annexation** /ænɪk'seɪʃn/ n. Annexion, die; Annektierung, die

**annexe** ▶ ANNEX 2

**annihilate** /ə'naɪleɪt/ v.t. vernichten

**annihilation** /ənaɪ'leɪʃn/ n. Vernichtung, die

**anniversary** /ænɪ'vɜːsərɪ/ n. Jahrestag, der; **wedding** ~: Hochzeitstag, der

**annotate** /'ænəteɪt/ v.t. kommentieren

**announce** /ə'naʊns/ v.t. bekannt geben; ansagen ‹Programm›; (over Tannoy etc.) durchsagen; (in newspaper) anzeigen ‹Heirat usw.›

**an'nouncement** n. Bekanntgabe, die; (over Tannoy etc.) Durchsage, die; (in newspaper) Anzeige, die

**an'nouncer** n. Ansager, der/Ansagerin, die

**annoy** /ə'nɔɪ/ v.t. (a) ärgern (b) (harass) schikanieren

**annoyance** /ə'nɔɪəns/ n. Verärgerung, die; (nuisance) Plage, die

**annoyed** /ə'nɔɪd/ adj. **be** ~ [at or with sb./ sth.] ärgerlich [auf od. über jmdn./über etw.] sein; **he got very** ~: er hat sich darüber sehr geärgert

**an'noying** adj. ärgerlich; lästig ‹Gewohnheit, Person›

**annual** /'ænjʊəl/ ① adj. (a) (reckoned by the year) Jahres-; ~ **income/subscription/rent/ turnover/production/leave/salary** Jahreseinkommen, das/-abonnement, das/ -miete, die/-umsatz, der/-produktion, die/ -urlaub, der/-gehalt, das; ~ **rainfall** jährliche Regenmenge (b) (recurring yearly) [all]jährlich ‹Ereignis, Feier›; Jahres‹bericht, -hauptversammlung› ② n. (a) Jahrbuch, das; (of comic etc.) Jahresalbum, das (b) (plant) einjährige Pflanze

**'annually** adv. jährlich

**annul** /ə'nʌl/ v.t., **-ll-** annullieren; auflösen ‹Vertrag›

**anodyne** /'ænədaɪn/ adj. (fig.) wohltuend; (soothing) einlullend

**anon.** /ə'nɒn/ abbr. = **anonymous [author]** anon.

**anonymity** /ænə'nɪmɪtɪ/ n. Anonymität, die

**anonymous** /ə'nɒnɪməs/ adj. anonym

**anorak** /'ænəræk/ n. Anorak, der

**anorexia** /ænə'reksɪə/ n. Anorexie, die (Med.); Magersucht, die

**anorexic** /ænə'reksɪk/ adj. anorektisch (fachspr.); magersüchtig; **be** ~: an Anorexie (Med.) od. Magersucht leiden

**another** /ə'nʌðə(r)/ ① pron. (a) (an additional one) noch einer/eine/eins; ein weiterer/eine weitere/ein weiteres (b) (counterpart) wieder einer/eine/eins (c) (a different one) ein anderer/eine andere/ ein anderes ② adj. (a) (additional) noch ein/eine; ein weiterer/eine weitere/ein weiteres; **after** ~ **six weeks** nach weiteren sechs Wochen (b) (different) ein anderer/eine andere/ein anderes

**answer** /'ɑːnsə(r)/ ① n. (a) (reply) Antwort, die (to auf + Akk.) (b) (to problem) Lösung, die (to Gen.); (to calculation) Ergebnis, das ② v.t. (a) beantworten ‹Brief, Frage›; antworten auf (+ Akk.) ‹Frage, Hilferuf, Einladung, Inserat›; eingehen auf (+ Akk.) ‹Angebot, Vorschlag›; sich stellen zu ‹Beschuldigung›; erhören ‹Gebet›; erfüllen ‹Bitte, Wunsch›; ~ **sb.** jmdm. antworten (b) ~ **the door/bell** an die Tür gehen ③ v.i. (a) (reply) antworten; ~ **to sth.** sich zu etw. äußern (b) (be responsible) ~ **for sth.** für etw. die Verantwortung übernehmen (c) ~ **to a description** einer Beschreibung (Dat.) entsprechen

**answerable** /'ɑːnsərəbl/ adj. verantwortlich (for für; to Dat.)

**answering:** ~**machine** n. Anrufbeantworter, der; ~ **service** n. Fernsprechauftragsdienst, der

**'answerphone** (Brit.) ▶ ANSWERING MACHINE

**ant** /ænt/ n. Ameise, die

**a**

**antagonism** /æn'tægənɪzm/ n.
Feindseligkeit, die (towards, against
gegenüber)

**antagonist** /æn'tægənɪst/ n. Gegner, der/
Gegnerin, die

**antagonistic** /æntægə'nɪstɪk/ adj.
feindlich

**antagonize** /æn'tægənaɪz/ v.t. ~ sb. sich
(Dat.) jmdn. zum Feind machen

**antarctic** /ænt'ɑːktɪk/ [1] adj. antarktisch
[2] n. the A~: die Antarktis

**antelope** /'æntɪləʊp/ n. Antilope, die

**antenatal** /æntɪ'neɪtl/ adj. (concerning
pregnancy) Schwangerschafts-; Schwangeren-;
~ care Schwangerenfürsorge, die; ~ clinic
Klinik für werdende Mütter

**antenna** /æn'tenə/ n. (a) pl. ~e /æn'teniː/
(Zool.) Fühler, der
(b) pl. ~s (tech., Amer.: aerial) Antenne, die

**anthem** /'ænθəm/ n. Chorgesang, der

**anthology** /æn'θɒlədʒɪ/ n. Anthologie, die

**anthropologist** /ænθrə'pɒlədʒɪst/ n.
Anthropologe, der/Anthropologin, die

**anthropology** /ænθrə'pɒlədʒɪ/ n.
Anthropologie, die

**anti** /'æntɪ/ [1] prep. gegen
[2] adj. ablehnend

**anti-** /æntɪ/ pref. anti-/Anti-

**anti: ~a'bortion** attrib. adj. ~-abortion
protester Abtreibungsgegner, der/-gegnerin,
die; ~-abortion protest/law Protest/Gesetz
gegen Abtreibung; ~-abortion
demonstration/movement
Antiabtreibungsdemonstration, die/
-bewegung, die; ~-**abortionist**
/æntɪə'bɔːʃənɪst/ n. Abtreibungsgegner, der/
-gegnerin, die; ~-'**aircraft** adj. (Mil.)
Flugabwehr-; ~-aircraft gun Flak, die

**antibiotic** /æntɪbaɪ'ɒtɪk/ n. Antibiotikum,
das

**'antibody** n. Antikörper, der

**antic** /'æntɪk/ n. (trick) Mätzchen, das (ugs.);
(of clown) Possen, der

**anticipate** /æn'tɪsɪpeɪt/ v.t. (a) (expect)
erwarten; (foresee) voraussehen; ~ trouble
mit Ärger rechnen
(b) (consider before due time) vorwegnehmen

**anticipation** /æntɪsɪ'peɪʃn/ n. Erwartung,
die

**anti'climax** n. Abstieg, der

**anti'clockwise** adv., adj. gegen den
Uhrzeigersinn

**anti'cyclone** n. Hochdruckgebiet, das

**antidepressant** /æntɪdɪ'presənt/ n.
Antidepressivum, das

**antidote** /'æntɪdəʊt/ n. Gegenmittel, das
(for, against, to gegen)

**'antifreeze** n. Frostschutzmittel, das

**'anti-hero** n. Antiheld, der

**antihistamine** /æntɪ'hɪstəmɪn/ n. (Med.)
Antihistamin[ikum], das

**'anti-lock** adj. Antiblockier-; ~ brake or
braking system Antiblockiersystem, das

**anti'nuclear** adj. Anti-Atom[kraft]-

**antipathy** /æn'tɪpəθɪ/ n. Antipathie, die;
Abneigung, die

**anti-person'nel** adj. gegen Menschen
gerichtet; ~ mine Schützenmine, die

**antiperspirant** /æntɪ'pɜːspɪrənt/ [1] adj.
schweißhemmend; ~ spray Deodorantspray,
der od. das
[2] n. Antitranspirant, das

**antiquated** /'æntɪkweɪtɪd/ adj. antiquiert;
veraltet

**antique** /æn'tiːk/ [1] adj. antik ⟨Möbel,
Schmuck usw.⟩
[2] n. Antiquität, die; ~ shop
Antiquitätenladen, der

**antiquity** /æn'tɪkwɪtɪ/ n. Altertum, das;
Antike, die

**anti-Semitic** /æntɪsɪ'mɪtɪk/ adj.
antisemitisch; judenfeindlich

**anti-Semitism** /æntɪ'semɪtɪzm/ n.
Antisemitismus, der; Judenhass, der

**anti'septic** [1] adj. antiseptisch
[2] n. Antiseptikum, das

**anti'social** adj. asozial

**anti-'theft** attrib. adj. Antidiebstahl-

**antithesis** /æn'tɪθəsɪs/ n., pl. **antitheses**
/æn'tɪθəsiːz/ Gegensatz, das (of, to zu)

**anti-** ~'**toxin** n. (Med.) Antitoxin, das;
~'**virus** attrib. adj. (Comp.) Antivirus-;
~virus software Antivirensoftware, die

**antivivisectionist** /æntɪvɪvɪ'sekʃənɪst/
n. Vivisektionsgegner, der/-gegnerin, die

**antler** /'æntlə(r)/ n. Geweihsprosse, die;
[pair of] ~s Geweih, das

**anvil** /'ænvɪl/ n. Amboss, der

**anxiety** /æŋ'zaɪətɪ/ n. Angst, die; (concern
about future) Sorge, die (about wegen)

**anxious** /'æŋkʃəs/ adj. (a) (troubled) besorgt
(about um)
(b) (eager) sehnlich; be ~ for sth. sich nach
etw. sehnen

**'anxiously** adv. (a) besorgt
(b) (eagerly) sehnsüchtig

**any** /'enɪ/ [1] adj. (a) (some) [irgend]ein/
[irgend]eine; not ~: kein/keine; have you
~ wool/wine? haben Sie Wolle/Wein?
(b) (one) ein/eine
(c) (all, every) jeder/jede/jedes; [at] ~ time
jederzeit
(d) (whichever) jeder/jede/jedes [beliebige];
choose ~ [one] book/~ books you like
suchen Sie sich (Dat.) irgendein Buch/
irgendwelche Bücher aus
[2] pron. (a) (some) in condit., interrog., or
neg. sentence (replacing sing. n.) einer/eine/
ein[e]s; (replacing collect. n.) welcher/welche/
welches; (replacing pl. n.) welche; not ~:
keiner/keine/kein[e]s/Pl. keine; without ~:
ohne
(b) (no matter which) irgendeiner/irgendeine/
irgendein[e]s/irgendwelche Pl.

**3** *adv.* **do you feel ~ better today?** fühlen Sie sich heute [etwas] besser?; **if it gets ~ colder** wenn es noch kälter wird; **I can't wait ~ longer** ich kann nicht [mehr] länger warten

**'anybody** *n. & pron.* **(a)** (whoever) jeder **(b)** (somebody) [irgend]jemand; *after neg.* niemand

**'anyhow** *adv.* **(a)** ▶ ANYWAY **(b)** (haphazardly) irgendwie

**'anyone** ▶ ANYBODY

**'anything** **1** *n. & pron.* **(a)** (whatever thing) was [immer]; alles, was **(b)** (something) irgendetwas; *after neg.* nichts **(c)** (a thing of any kind) alles **2** *adv.* **not ~ like as ... as** keineswegs so ... wie

**'anyway** *adv.* **(a)** (in any case, besides) sowieso **(b)** (at any rate) jedenfalls

**'anywhere** *adv.* **(a)** (in any place) (wherever) überall, wo; wo [immer]; (somewhere) irgendwo; **not ~ near as ... as** (coll.) nicht annähernd so ... wie **(b)** (to any place) (wherever) wohin [auch immer]; (somewhere) irgendwohin

**aorta** /eɪˈɔːtə/ *n.* (Anat.) Aorta, *die*

**apart** /əˈpɑːt/ *adv.* **(a)** (separately) getrennt; **~ from ...:** außer ... **(b)** (into pieces) auseinander

**apartheid** /əˈpɑːteɪt/ *n.* Apartheid, *die*

**apartment** /əˈpɑːtmənt/ *n.* **(a)** (room) Apartment, *das* **(b)** (Amer.: flat) Wohnung, *die*

**apathetic** /æpəˈθetɪk/ *adj.* apathisch (**about** gegenüber)

**apathy** /ˈæpəθɪ/ *n.* Apathie, *die* (**about** gegenüber)

**ape** /eɪp/ **1** *n.* [Menschen]affe, *der* **2** *v.t.* nachahmen

**aperitif** /əperɪˈtiːf/ *n.* Aperitif, *der*

**aperture** /ˈæpətʃə(r)/ *n.* Öffnung, *die*

**apex** /ˈeɪpeks/ *n.* Spitze, *die*

**aphid** /ˈeɪfɪd/ *n.* Blattlaus, *die*

**aphrodisiac** /æfrəˈdɪzɪæk/ *n.* Aphrodisiakum, *das*

**apiece** /əˈpiːs/ *adv.* je; **they cost a penny ~:** sie kosten einen Penny das Stück

**apolitical** /eɪpəˈlɪtɪkl/ *adj.* apolitisch; unpolitisch

**apologetic** /əpɒləˈdʒetɪk/ *adj.* entschuldigend; **be ~:** sich entschuldigen

**apologize** /əˈpɒlədʒaɪz/ *v.i.* sich entschuldigen (**to** bei)

**apology** /əˈpɒlədʒɪ/ *n.* Entschuldigung, *die;* **make an ~:** sich entschuldigen (**to** bei)

**apoplectic** /æpəˈplektɪk/ *adj.* apoplektisch; **~ fit** Schlaganfall, *der*

**apoplexy** /ˈæpəpleksɪ/ *n.* Apoplexie, *die* (fachspr.); Schlaganfall, *der*

**apostle** /əˈpɒsl/ *n.* Apostel, *der*

**apostrophe** /əˈpɒstrəfɪ/ *n.* Apostroph, *der;* Auslassungszeichen, *das*

**appal** (*Amer.:* **appall**) /əˈpɔːl/ *v.t.,* **-ll-** entsetzen

**ap'palling** *adj.* entsetzlich

**apparatus** /æpəˈreɪtəs/ *n.* (equipment) Gerät, *das;* (gymnastic ~) Geräte *Pl.;* (machinery, lit. or fig.) Apparat, *der;* **a piece of ~:** ein Gerät

**apparel** /əˈpærəl/ *n.* Kleidung, *die;* Gewänder *Pl.* (geh.)

**apparent** /əˈpærənt/ *adj.* **(a)** (clear) offensichtlich; offenbar ⟨*Bedeutung, Wahrheit*⟩ **(b)** (seeming) scheinbar

**ap'parently** *adv.* **(a)** (clearly) offensichtlich **(b)** (seemingly) scheinbar

**apparition** /æpəˈrɪʃn/ *n.* [Geister]erscheinung, *die*

**appeal** /əˈpiːl/ **1** *v.i.* **(a)** (Law etc.) Einspruch einlegen **(b)** (make earnest request) **~ to sb. for sth./to do sth.** jmdn. um etw. ersuchen/jmdn. ersuchen, etw. zu tun **(c)** (address oneself) **~ to sb./sth.** an jmdn./ etw. appellieren **(d)** (be attractive) **~ to sb.** jmdm. zusagen **2** *n.* **(a)** (Law etc.) Einspruch, *der* (**to** bei); (to higher court) Berufung, *die* (**to** bei) **(b)** (request) Appell, *der;* **an ~ to sb. for sth.** eine Bitte an jmdn. um etw. **(c)** (attraction) Reiz, *der*

**ap'pealing** *adj.* **(a)** (imploring) flehend **(b)** (attractive) ansprechend; verlockend ⟨*Idee*⟩

**appear** /əˈpɪə(r)/ *v.i.* **(a)** (become visible, arrive) erscheinen; ⟨*Licht, Mond:*⟩ auftauchen; (present oneself) auftreten **(b)** (occur) vorkommen **(c)** (seem) **~ [to be] ...:** scheinen ... [zu sein]

**appearance** /əˈpɪərəns/ *n.* **(a)** (becoming visible) Auftauchen, *das;* (arrival) Erscheinen, *das;* (of performer etc.) Auftritt, *der* **(b)** (look) Äußere, *das;* **to all ~s** allem Anschein nach **(c)** (semblance) Anschein, *der* **(d)** (occurrence) Vorkommen, *das*

**appease** /əˈpiːz/ *v.t.* besänftigen; (Polit.) beschwichtigen

**append** /əˈpend/ *v.t.* anhängen (**to** an + *Akk.*); (add) anfügen (+ *Dat.*)

**appendage** /əˈpendɪdʒ/ *n.* Anhängsel, *das;* (addition) Anhang, *der*

**appendicitis** /əpendɪˈsaɪtɪs/ *n.* Blinddarmentzündung, *die*

**appendix** /əˈpendɪks/ *n., pl.* **appendices** /əˈpendɪsiːz/ *or* **~es (a)** Anhang, *der* (**to** zu) **(b)** (Anat.) Blinddarm, *der*

**appetite** /ˈæpɪtaɪt/ *n.* **(a)** Appetit, *der* (**for** auf + *Akk.*) **(b)** (fig.) Verlangen, *das* (**for** nach)

**appetizer** /ˈæpɪtaɪzə(r)/ *n.* Appetitanreger, *der*

**appetizing** /ˈæpɪtaɪzɪŋ/ *adj.* appetitlich

**applaud** /ə'plɔːd/ 1 v.i. applaudieren; [Beifall] klatschen
2 v.t. applaudieren (+ Dat.)

**applause** /ə'plɔːz/ n. Beifall, der; Applaus, der

**apple** /'æpl/ n. Apfel, der

**apple:** ~ 'pie gedeckte Apfeltorte; ~ 'sauce n. Apfelmus, das

**applet** /'æplɪt/ n. (Comp.) Applet, das

**'apple tree** n. Apfelbaum, der

**appliance** /ə'plaɪəns/ n. Gerät, das

**applicable** /ə'plɪkəbl/ adj. (a) anwendbar (to auf + Akk.)
(b) (appropriate) geeignet; zutreffend ⟨Fragebogenteil⟩

**applicant** /'æplɪkənt/ n. Bewerber, der/ Bewerberin, die (for um); (claimant) Antragsteller, der/-stellerin, die

**application** /æplɪ'keɪʃn/ n. (a) (request) Bewerbung, die (for um); (for passport, licence, etc.) Antrag, der (for auf + Akk.); ~ form Antragsformular, das
(b) (putting) Auftragen, das (to auf + Akk.)
(c) (use) Anwendung, die
(d) (Comp.) Applikation, die

**applicator** /'æplɪkeɪtə(r)/ n. Applikator, der

**apply** /ə'plaɪ/ 1 v.t. (a) auftragen ⟨Creme, Farbe⟩ (to auf + Akk.)
(b) (make use of) anwenden
2 v.i. (a) (have relevance) zutreffen (to auf + Akk.)
(b) ~ [to sb.] for sth. [jmdn.] um etw. bitten; (for passport etc.) [bei jmdm.] etw. beantragen; (for job) sich [bei jmdm.] um etw. bewerben

**appoint** /ə'pɔɪnt/ v.t. (a) (fix) bestimmen; festlegen ⟨Zeitpunkt, Ort⟩
(b) (to job) einstellen; (to office) ernennen

**appointee** /əpɔɪn'tiː/ n. Ernannte, der/die; Berufene, der/die

**ap'pointment** n. (a) (to job) Einstellung, die; (to office) Ernennung, die (as zum/zur)
(b) (job) Stelle, die
(c) (arrangement) Termin, der; make an ~ with sb. sich (Dat.) von jmdm. einen Termin geben lassen; by ~: nach Anmeldung

**appraisal** /ə'preɪzl/ n. (evaluation) Bewertung, die

**appraise** /ə'preɪz/ v.t. (evaluate) bewerten

**appreciable** /ə'priːʃəbl/ adj. (a) (perceptible) nennenswert ⟨Unterschied, Einfluss⟩; spürbar ⟨Veränderung, Wirkung⟩; merklich ⟨Verringerung, Anstieg⟩
(b) (considerable) beträchtlich

**appreciably** /ə'priːʃəblɪ/ adv. (a) (perceptibly) spürbar ⟨verändern⟩; merklich ⟨sich unterscheiden⟩
(b) (considerably) beträchtlich

**appreciate** /ə'priːʃɪeɪt/ 1 v.t. (a) ([correctly] estimate) [richtig] einschätzen; (understand) verstehen; (be aware of) sich (Dat.) bewusst sein (+ Gen.)
(b) (be grateful for) schätzen; (enjoy) genießen

2 v.i. im Wert steigen

**appreciation** /əpriːʃɪ'eɪʃn/ n. (a) ([correct] estimation) [richtige] Einschätzung; (understanding) Verständnis, das (of für); (awareness) Bewusstsein, das
(b) (gratefulness) Dankbarkeit, die; (enjoyment) Gefallen, das (of an + Dat.)

**appreciative** /ə'priːʃətɪv/ adj. (grateful) dankbar (of für); (approving) anerkennend

**apprehend** /æprɪ'hend/ v.t. (a) (arrest) festnehmen
(b) (understand) erfassen

**apprehension** /æprɪ'henʃn/ n. Besorgnis, die

**apprehensive** /æprɪ'hensɪv/ adj. besorgt

**apprentice** /ə'prentɪs/ n. Lehrling, der (to bei)

**ap'prenticeship** n. (training) Lehre, die; (learning period) Lehrzeit, die

**approach** /ə'prəʊtʃ/ 1 v.i. sich nähern; (in time) nahen
2 v.t. (a) (come near to) sich nähern (+ Dat.)
(b) (approximate to) nahe kommen (+ Dat.)
(c) (appeal to) sich wenden an (+ Akk.)
3 n. (a) [Heran]nahen, das
(b) (approximation) Annäherung, die (to an + Akk.)
(c) (appeal) Herantreten, das (to an + Akk.)
(d) (access) Zugang, der; (road) Zufahrtsstraße, die

**approachable** /ə'prəʊtʃəbl/ adj. (a) (friendly) umgänglich
(b) (accessible) zugänglich

**ap'proach road** n. Zufahrtsstraße, die

**appropriate** 1 /ə'prəʊprɪət/ adj. geeignet (to, for für)
2 /ə'prəʊprɪeɪt/ v.t. sich (Dat.) aneignen

**appropriately** /ə'prəʊprɪətlɪ/ adv. gebührend; passend ⟨gekleidet, genannt⟩

**approval** /ə'pruːvl/ n. (a) (sanctioning) Genehmigung, die; (of proposal) Billigung, die; (agreement) Zustimmung, die
(b) on ~ (Commerc.) zur Probe

**approve** /ə'pruːv/ 1 v.t. (a) (sanction) genehmigen ⟨Plan, Projekt⟩; billigen ⟨Vorschlag⟩
(b) (find good) gutheißen
2 v.i. ~ of billigen; zustimmen (+ Dat.) ⟨Plan⟩

**approving** /ə'pruːvɪŋ/ adj. zustimmend ⟨Worte⟩; anerkennend ⟨Blicke⟩

**approx.** /ə'prɒks/ abbr. = **approximately** ca.

**approximate** /ə'prɒksɪmət/ adj. ungefähr attr.

**ap'proximately** adv. ungefähr

**approximation** /əprɒksɪ'meɪʃn/ n. (a) Annäherung, die (to an + Dat.)
(b) (estimate) Annäherungswert, der

**APR** abbr. = **annualized percentage rate** Jahreszinssatz, der

**Apr.** abbr. = **April** Apr.

**après-ski** /ˈæpreɪˈskiː/ n. Après-Ski, der; attrib. Après-Ski-

**apricot** /ˈeɪprɪkɒt/ n. Aprikose, die

**April** /ˈeɪprəl/ n. April, der; ∼ **fool** April[s]narr, der; see also AUGUST

**apron** /ˈeɪprən/ n. Schürze, die

**apt** /æpt/ adj. **(a)** (suitable) passend; treffend ⟨Bemerkung⟩
**(b)** be ∼ **to do** sth. dazu neigen, etw. zu tun

**aptitude** /ˈæptɪtjuːd/ n. Begabung, die

'**aptly** adv. passend

**aqualung** /ˈækwəlʌŋ/ n. Tauchgerät, das

**aquaplane** /ˈækwəpleɪn/ v.i. ⟨Reifen:⟩ aufschwimmen; ⟨Fahrzeug:⟩ [durch Aquaplaning] ins Rutschen geraten

**aquarium** /əˈkweərɪəm/ n., pl. ∼s or aquaria /əˈkweərɪə/ Aquarium, das

**Aquarius** /əˈkweərɪəs/ n. (Astrol., Astron.) der Wassermann

**aquatic** /əˈkwætɪk/ adj. aquatisch; Wasser-; ∼ **plant** Wasserpflanze, die

**aqueduct** /ˈækwɪdʌkt/ n. Aquädukt, der od. das

**aqueous** /ˈeɪkwɪəs, ˈækwɪəs/ adj. wässerig; wässrig

**Arab** /ˈærəb/ **1** adj. arabisch
**2** n. Araber, der/Araberin, die

**Arabian** /əˈreɪbɪən/ **1** adj. arabisch
**2** n. Araber, der/Araberin, die

**Arabic** /ˈærəbɪk/ **1** adj. arabisch
**2** n. Arabisch, das; see also ENGLISH 2A

**arable** /ˈærəbl/ adj. bebaubar, landwirtschaftlich nutzbar ⟨Land⟩; ∼ **land** (cultivated) Ackerland, das

**arbitrary** /ˈɑːbɪtrərɪ/ adj. willkürlich

**arbitrate** /ˈɑːbɪtreɪt/ **1** v.t. schlichten ⟨Streit⟩
**2** v.i. ∼ [upon sth.] [in einer Sache] vermitteln

**arbitration** /ɑːbɪˈtreɪʃn/ n. Vermittlung, die; (in industry) Schlichtung, die

**arbitrator** /ˈɑːbɪtreɪtə(r)/ n. Vermittler, der; (in industry) Schlichter, der

**arboretum** /ɑːbəˈriːtəm/ n., pl. arboreta /ɑːbəˈriːtə/ or (Amer.) ∼s Arboretum, das; Baumgarten, der

**arbour** /ˈɑːbə(r)/ n. (Brit.) Laube, die

**arc** /ɑːk/ n. [Kreis]bogen, der; ∼ **lamp**, ∼ **light** Lichtbogenlampe, die; ∼ **welding** Lichtbogen-, Elektroschweißung, die

**arcade** /ɑːˈkeɪd/ n. Arkade, die

**arch** /ɑːtʃ/ **1** n. Bogen, der; (of foot) Wölbung, die
**2** v.t. beugen ⟨Rücken⟩; ∼ **its back** ⟨Katze:⟩ einen Buckel machen

**arch-** pref. Erz-

**archaeological** /ɑːkɪəˈlɒdʒɪkl/ adj. archäologisch

**archaeologist** /ɑːkɪˈɒlədʒɪst/ n. Archäologe, der/Archäologin, die

**archaeology** /ɑːkɪˈɒlədʒɪ/ n. Archäologie, die

**archaic** /ɑːˈkeɪɪk/ adj. veraltet

**arch'bishop** n. Erzbischof, der

**arch-'enemy** n. Erzfeind, der/Erzfeindin, die

**archeology** etc. (Amer.) ▶ ARCHAEOLOGY etc.

**archer** /ˈɑːtʃə(r)/ n. Bogenschütze, der

**archery** /ˈɑːtʃərɪ/ n. Bogenschießen, das

**archetype** /ˈɑːkɪtaɪp/ n. (original) Urfassung, die; (typical specimen) Prototyp, der

**architect** /ˈɑːkɪtekt/ n. Architekt, der/Architektin, die

**architectural** /ɑːkɪˈtektʃərl/ adj. architektonisch

**architecture** /ˈɑːkɪtektʃə(r)/ n. Architektur, die

**archive** /ˈɑːkaɪv/ **1** n. Archiv, das; ∼s Archiv, die
**2** v.t. archivieren

**arctic** /ˈɑːktɪk/ **1** adj. arktisch; **A**∼ **Circle** nördlicher Polarkreis; **A**∼ **Ocean** Nordpolarmeer, das
**2** n. the **A**∼: die Arktis

**ardent** /ˈɑːdənt/ adj. leidenschaftlich; brennend ⟨Wunsch⟩; (eager) begeistert

**ardor** (Amer.), **ardour** (Brit.) /ˈɑːdə(r)/ n. Leidenschaft, die

**arduous** /ˈɑːdjʊəs/ adj. anstrengend

**are** ▶ BE

**area** /ˈeərɪə/ n. **(a)** (surface measure) Fläche, die; Flächeninhalt, der
**(b)** (region) Gelände, das; (of wood, marsh, desert) Gebiet, das; (of city, country) Gegend, die; **parking/picnic** ∼: Park-/Picknickplatz, der
**(c)** (subject field) Gebiet, das

'**area code** n. (Amer. Teleph.) Gebietsvorwahl[nummer], die

**arena** /əˈriːnə/ n. Arena, die; **the political** ∼: die politische Arena

**aren't** /ɑːnt/ (coll.) = **are not;** ▶ BE

**Argentina** /ɑːdʒənˈtiːnə/ pr. n. Argentinien (das)

**Argentinian** /ɑːdʒənˈtɪnɪən/ **1** adj. argentinisch; **sb. is** ∼: jmd. ist Argentinier/Argentinierin
**2** n. Argentinier, der/Argentinierin, die

**arguable** /ˈɑːgjʊəbl/ adj. (questionable) fragwürdig

**arguably** /ˈɑːgjʊəblɪ/ adv. möglicherweise

**argue** /ˈɑːgjuː/ **1** v.t. **(a)** (maintain) ∼ **that** ...: die Ansicht vertreten, dass ...
**(b)** (with reasoning) darlegen ⟨Grund, Standpunkt⟩
**2** v.i. ∼ **with** sb. sich mit jmdm. streiten; ∼ **for/against** sth. für/gegen etw. eintreten; ∼ **about** sth. sich über/um etw. (Akk.) streiten

**argument** /ˈɑːgjʊmənt/ n. **(a)** (reason) Begründung, die; ∼s **for/against** sth. Argumente für/gegen etw.
**(b)** (reasoning process) Argumentieren, das ⋯⁖

**(c)** (disagreement, quarrel) Auseinandersetzung, *die*

**argumentative** /ɑːgjʊ'mentətɪv/ *adj.* widerspruchsfreudig

**arid** /'ærɪd/ *adj.* trocken

**Aries** /'eəriːz/ *n.* (Astrol; Astron.) der Widder

**arise** /ə'raɪz/ *v.i.*, **arose** /ə'rəʊz/, **arisen** /ə'rɪzn/ **(a)** (originate) entstehen
**(b)** (present itself) auftreten; ⟨*Gelegenheit:*⟩ sich bieten
**(c)** (result) ∼ **from** *or* **out of sth.** von etw. herrühren

**aristocracy** /ærɪ'stɒkrəsɪ/ *n.* Aristokratie, *die*

**aristocrat** /'ærɪstəkræt/ *n.* Aristokrat, *der*/ Aristokratin, *die*

**aristocratic** /ærɪstə'krætɪk/ *adj.* aristokratisch

**arithmetic** /ə'rɪθmətɪk/ *n.* Arithmetik, *die*

**arm¹** /ɑːm/ *n.* Arm, *der*

**arm²** ① *n.* **(a)** *usu. in pl.* (weapon) Waffe, *die;* **up in** ∼**s** (fig.) in Harnisch (**about** wegen)
**(b)** *in pl.* (heraldic device) Wappen, *das*
② *v.t.* bewaffnen

**armada** /ɑː'mɑːdə/ *n.* Armada, *die*

**arm:** ∼**band** *n.* Armbinde, *die;* ∼**chair** *n.* Sessel, *der;* ∼**chair politician/strategist** politischer Amateur/Amateurstratege, *der;* ∼**chair critic** Hobby- *od.* Amateurkritiker, *der;* ∼**chair travel** Reisen *Pl.* in der Fantasie

**armed** /ɑːmd/ *adj.* bewaffnet; ∼ **forces** Streitkräfte *Pl.*

**armistice** /'ɑːmɪstɪs/ *n.* Waffenstillstand, *der*

**armor** (Amer.), **armour** (Brit.) /'ɑːmə(r)/ *n.* **(a)** (Hist.) Rüstung, *die*
**(b)** (steel plates) Panzerung, *die*

**arm:** ∼**pit** *n.* Achselhöhle, *die;* ∼**rest** *n.* Armlehne, *die*

**arms:** ∼ **control** *n.* Rüstungskontrolle, *die; attrib.* Rüstungskontroll-; ∼ **race** *n.* Rüstungswettlauf, *der;* ∼ **trade** *n.* Waffenhandel, *der*

**army** /'ɑːmɪ/ *n.* Heer, *das;* **join the** ∼: zum Militär gehen

**aroma** /ə'rəʊmə/ *n.* Duft, *der*

**aromatherapy** /ərəʊmə'θerəpɪ/ *n.* Aromatherapie, *die*

**aromatic** /ærə'mætɪk/ *adj.* aromatisch

**arose** ▶ ARISE

**around** /ə'raʊnd/ ① *adv.* **(a)** (on every side) [all] ∼: überall
**(b)** (round) herum
**(c)** (in various places) **ask/look** ∼: herumfragen/sich umsehen
② *prep.* **(a)** um [… herum]
**(b)** (approximately) ∼ **3 o'clock** gegen 3 Uhr; **sth.** [**costing**] ∼ **£2** etw. für ungefähr 2 Pfund

**arouse** /ə'raʊz/ *v.t.* **(a)** (awake) [auf]wecken
**(b)** (excite) erregen; erwecken ⟨*Interesse, Begeisterung*⟩; ∼ **suspicion** Verdacht erregen

**arrange** /ə'reɪndʒ/ ① *v.t.* **(a)** (order) anordnen
**(b)** (settle, agree) ausmachen, vereinbaren ⟨*Termin*⟩; planen ⟨*Urlaub*⟩; **they** ∼**d to meet the following day** sie verabredeten sich für den nächsten Tag
② *v.i.* (plan) sorgen (**for** für)

**ar'rangement** *n.* **(a)** (ordering, order) Anordnung, *die*
**(b)** (settling, agreement) Vereinbarung, *die*
**(c)** *in pl.* (plans) Vorkehrungen *Pl.;* **make** ∼**s** Vorkehrungen treffen

**arrears** /ə'rɪəz/ *n. pl.* Schulden *Pl.;* **be in** ∼ **with sth.** mit etw. im Rückstand sein; **be paid in** ∼: rückwirkend bezahlt werden

**arrest** /ə'rest/ ① *v.t.* **(a)** verhaften, (temporarily) festnehmen ⟨*Person*⟩
**(b)** (stop) aufhalten
② *n.* Verhaftung, *die;* **under** ∼: festgenommen

**arrival** /ə'raɪvl/ *n.* Ankunft, *die;* **new** ∼**s** Neuankömmlinge

**arrive** /ə'raɪv/ *v.i.* **(a)** ankommen; ∼ **at a conclusion/an agreement** zu einem Schluss/ einer Einigung kommen
**(b)** ⟨*Stunde, Tag, Augenblick:*⟩ kommen

**arrogance** /'ærəgəns/ *n.* Arroganz, *die*

**arrogant** /'ærəgənt/ *adj.* arrogant

**arrow** /'ærəʊ/ *n.* Pfeil, *der*

**arse** /ɑːs/ *n.* (coarse) Arsch, *der* (derb)
■ **arse a'bout, arse a'round** *v. i.* (Brit. coarse) herumalbern (ugs.); herumblödeln (ugs.)

**'arsehole** *n.* (coarse) Arschloch, *das* (derb)

**arsenal** /'ɑːsənl/ *n.* Waffenlager, *das*

**arsenic** /'ɑːsənɪk/ *n.* **(a)** Arsenik, *das*
**(b)** (element) Arsen, *das*

**arson** /'ɑːsn/ *n.* Brandstiftung, *die;* ∼ **attack** Brandanschlag, *der*

**arsonist** /'ɑːsənɪst/ *n.* Brandstifter, *der*/ Brandstifterin, *die*

**art** /ɑːt/ *n.* **(a)** Kunst, *die;* **works of** ∼: Kunstwerke *Pl.;* ∼ **college** *or* **school** Kunsthochschule, *die;* ∼**s and crafts** Kunsthandwerk, *das*
**(b)** *in pl.* (branch of study) Geisteswissenschaften *Pl.*

**artery** /'ɑːtərɪ/ *n.* (Anat.) Schlagader, *die;* Arterie, *die* (bes. fachspr.)

**artful** /'ɑːtfl/ *adj.* schlau

**'art gallery** *n.* Kunstgalerie, *die*

**arthritic** /ɑː'θrɪtɪk/ *adj.* arthritisch

**arthritis** /ɑː'θraɪtɪs/ *n.* Arthritis, *die* (fachspr.); Gelenkentzündung, *die*

**artichoke** /'ɑːtɪtʃəʊk/ *n.* [globe] ∼: Artischocke, *die*

**article** /'ɑːtɪkl/ *n.* **(a)** (in magazine, newspaper; Ling.) Artikel, *der*
**(b)** an ∼ **of furniture/clothing** ein Möbel-/ Kleidungsstück; **an** ∼ **of value** ein Wertgegenstand

**articulate** /ɑːˈtɪkjʊlət/ *adj.* redegewandt; **be ~/not very ~:** sich gut/nicht sehr gut ausdrücken [können]

**articulated** /ɑːˈtɪkjʊleɪtɪd/ *adj.* **~ 'lorry** Sattelzug, *der*

**artificial** /ɑːtɪˈfɪʃl/ *adj.* **(a)** künstlich; Kunst-; (not real) unecht; **~ limb** Prothese, *die* **(b)** (affected) gekünstelt

**artificial: ~ insemi'nation** *n.* künstliche Befruchtung; (of animal) künstliche Besamung; **~ in'telligence** *n.* künstliche Intelligenz; **~ 'language** *n.* Kunstsprache, *die;* **~ respi'ration** *n.* künstliche Beatmung

**artillery** /ɑːˈtɪlərɪ/ *n.* Artillerie, *die*

**artisan** /ˈɑːtɪzn, ɑːtɪˈzæn/ *n.* [Kunst]handwerker, *der*

**artist** /ˈɑːtɪst/ *n.* Künstler, *der*/Künstlerin, *die*

**artiste** /ɑːˈtiːst/ *n.* Artist, *der*/Artistin, *die*

**artistic** /ɑːˈtɪstɪk/ *adj.* **(a)** (of art) Kunst-; künstlerisch **(b)** (naturally skilled in art) künstlerisch veranlagt

**'artless** *adj.* arglos

**art nouveau** /ɑː nuːˈvəʊ/ *n.* Jugendstil, *der*

**'art room** *n.* Zeichensaal, *der*

**'arts centre** *n.* Kunstzentrum, *das*

**'art work** *n.* Bildmaterial, *das*

**as** /əz, *stressed* æz/ ① *adv., conj.* **(a)** he is as tall as I am er ist so groß wie ich; **as quickly as you can/as possible** so schnell du kannst/wie möglich **(b)** (though) **small as he was** obwohl er klein war **(c)** (however much) **try as he might/would, he could not concentrate** sosehr er sich auch bemühte, er konnte sich nicht konzentrieren **(d)** *expr. manner* wie; **as you may already have heard, ...:** wie Sie vielleicht schon gehört haben, ...; **as it were** sozusagen **(e)** *expr. time* als; während; **as we climbed the stairs** als wir die Treppe hinaufgingen; **as we were talking** während wir uns unterhielten **(f)** *expr. reason* da ② *prep.* **(a)** (in the function of) als; **as an artist** als Künstler; **speaking as a mother ...:** als Mutter ... **(b)** (like) wie **(c) the same as ...:** der-/die-/dasselbe wie ...; **such as** wie zum Beispiel ③ **as for ...:** was ... angeht *od.* betrifft; **as [it] is** wie die Dinge liegen; **the place is untidy enough as it is** es ist hier [so] schon unordentlich genug; **as of ...** (Amer.) von ... an; **as to** hinsichtlich (+ *Gen.*); **as yet** bis jetzt; noch

**a.s.a.p.** *abbr.* = **as soon as possible**

**asbestos** /æzˈbestɒs/ *n.* Asbest, *der*

**asbestosis** /æzbesˈtəʊsɪs/ *n.* (Med.) Asbestose, *die*

**ascend** /əˈsend/ ① *v.i.* **(a)** (go up) hinaufsteigen; (climb up) hinaufklettern; (by vehicle) hinauffahren **(b)** (rise) aufsteigen; ⟨Hubschrauber:⟩ höhersteigen **(c)** (slope upwards) ⟨Hügel, Straße:⟩ ansteigen ② *v.t.* **(a)** (go up) hinaufsteigen ⟨Treppe, Leiter, Berg⟩ **(b) ~ the throne** den Thron besteigen

**Ascension Day** /əˈsenʃn/ *n.* Himmelfahrtstag, *der*

**ascent** /əˈsent/ *n.* Aufstieg, *der*

**ascertain** /æsəˈteɪn/ *v.t.* feststellen; ermitteln ⟨Fakten, Daten⟩

**ascribe** /əˈskraɪb/ *v.t.* zuschreiben (**to** *Dat.*)

**asexual** /eɪˈsekʃʊəl/ *adj.* (without sexuality) asexuell

**ash¹** /æʃ/ *n.* (tree) Esche, *die*

**ash²** *n.* (from fire etc.) Asche, *die*

**ashamed** /əˈʃeɪmd/ *adj.* beschämt; **be ~:** sich schämen (**of** wegen)

**ash: ~ bin** *n.* Mülleimer, *der;* **~ blonde** ① *adj.* aschblond; ② *n.* Aschblonde, *der/die;* **~can** (Amer.) ▶ ~ BIN

**ashen** /ˈæʃn/ *adj.* aschfahl ⟨Gesicht⟩

**ashore** /əˈʃɔː(r)/ *adv.* an Land

**'ashtray** *n.* Aschenbecher, *der*

**Ash 'Wednesday** *n.* Aschermittwoch, *der*

**Asia** /ˈeɪʃə/ *pr. n.* Asien (*das*)

**Asian** /ˈeɪʃən/ ① *adj.* asiatisch ② *n.* Asiat, *der*/Asiatin, *die*

**aside** /əˈsaɪd/ *adv.* beiseite; zur Seite

**ask** /ɑːsk/ ① *v.t.* **(a)** fragen; **~ sb. [sth.]** jmdn. [nach etw.] fragen **(b)** (seek to obtain) **~ sth.** um etw. bitten; **how much are you ~ing for that car?** wie viel verlangen Sie für das Auto?; **~ sb. to do sth.** jmdn. [darum] bitten, etw. zu tun **(c)** (invite) einladen ② *v.i.* **~ after sb./sth.** nach jmdm./etw. fragen; **~ for sth./sb.** etw./jmdn. verlangen

**askance** /əˈskæns, əˈskɑːns/ *adv.* **look ~ at sb.** jmdn. befremdet ansehen

**askew** /əˈskjuː/ *adv., pred. adj.* schief

**asleep** /əˈsliːp/ *pred. adj.* schlafend; **be/lie ~:** schlafen; **fall ~:** einschlafen

**asparagus** /əˈspærəgəs/ *n.* Spargel, *der*

**aspect** /ˈæspekt/ *n.* Aspekt, *der*

**aspersion** /əˈspɜːʃn/ *n.* **cast ~s on sb./sth.** jmdn./etw in den Schmutz ziehen

**asphalt** /ˈæsfælt/ *n.* Asphalt, *der*

**asphyxiate** /æsˈfɪksɪeɪt/ *v.t. & i.* ersticken

**aspiration** /æspəˈreɪʃn/ *n.* Streben, *das*

**aspire** /əˈspaɪə(r)/ *v.i.* **~ to** *or* **after sth.** nach etw. streben

**aspirin** /ˈæspərɪn/ *n.* Aspirin Ⓦⓩ, *das;* Kopfschmerztablette, *die*

**ass¹** /æs/ *n.* Esel, *der*

**ass²** (Amer.) ▶ ARSE

**assailant** /əˈseɪlənt/ n. Angreifer, der/ Angreiferin, die

**assassin** /əˈsæsɪn/ n. Mörder, der/ Mörderin, die

**assassinate** /əˈsæsɪneɪt/ v.t. ermorden; **be ~d** einem Attentat zum Opfer fallen

**assassination** /əsæsɪˈneɪʃn/ n. Mord, der (**of** an + Dat.); **~ attempt** Attentat, das (**on** auf + Akk.)

**assault** /əˈsɔːlt/ ⓵ n. Angriff, der; (fig.) Anschlag, der
② v.t. angreifen

**assemble** /əˈsembl/ ⓵ v.t. (a) zusammentragen; zusammenrufen ‹Menschen›
(b) (fit together) zusammenbauen
② v.i. sich versammeln

**assembly** /əˈsemblɪ/ n. (a) (meeting) Versammlung, die; (in school) Morgenandacht, die
(b) (fitting together) Zusammenbau, der

**as'sembly line** n. Fließband, das

**assent** /əˈsent/ ⓵ v.i. zustimmen (**to** Dat.)
② n. Zustimmung, die

**assert** /əˈsɜːt/ v.t. (a) geltend machen; **~ oneself** sich durchsetzen
(b) (declare) behaupten; beteuern ‹Unschuld›

**assertion** /əˈsɜːʃn/ n. (a) Geltendmachen, das
(b) (declaration) Behauptung, die

**assertive** /əˈsɜːtɪv/ adj. energisch ‹Person›; bestimmt ‹Ton, Verhalten›

**assertiveness** /əˈsɜːtɪvnɪs/ n. Bestimmtheit, die

**assess** /əˈses/ v.t. einschätzen; festsetzen ‹Steuer› (**at** auf + Akk.)

**as'sessment** n. (a) Einschätzung, die
(b) (tax to be paid) Steuerbescheid, der

**asset** /ˈæset/ n. (a) Vermögenswert, der
(b) (useful quality) Vorzug, der (**to** für); ( person) Stütze, die; (thing) Hilfe, die

**'asset-stripping** n.: Ankauf unrentabler Unternehmen, von denen einzelne Teile Gewinn bringend weiterverkauft werden

**assiduous** /əˈsɪdjʊəs/ adj. (a) (diligent) eifrig
(b) (conscientious) gewissenhaft

**assign** /əˈsaɪn/ v.t. (a) (allot) zuweisen (**to** Dat.)
(b) (appoint) zuteilen; **~ sb. to do sth.** jmdn. damit betrauen, etw. zu tun

**as'signment** n. (a) (allotment) Zuweisung, die; (appointment) Zuteilung, die
(b) (task) Aufgabe, die

**assimilate** /əˈsɪmɪleɪt/ v.t. angleichen (**to, with** an + Akk.)

**assimilation** /əsɪmɪˈleɪʃn/ n. Angleichung, die (**to, with** an + Akk.)

**assist** /əˈsɪst/ ⓵ v.t. helfen (+ Dat.)
② v.i. helfen; **~ with sth./in doing sth.** bei etw. helfen/helfen, etw. zu tun

**assistance** /əˈsɪstəns/ n. Hilfe, die

**assistant** /əˈsɪstənt/ n. (helper) Helfer, der/ Helferin, die; (subordinate) Mitarbeiter, der/ Mitarbeiterin, die; (of professor, artist) Assistent, der/Assistentin, die; (in shop) Verkäufer, der/Verkäuferin, die; **~ manager** stellvertretender Geschäftsführer

**associate** ⓵ /əˈsəʊʃɪət, əˈsəʊsɪət/ n. ( partner) Partner, der/Partnerin, die; (colleague) Kollege, der/Kollegin, die
② /əˈsəʊʃɪeɪt, əˈsəʊsɪeɪt/ v.t. in Verbindung bringen; **be ~d** in Verbindung stehen
③ /əˈsəʊʃɪeɪt, əˈsəʊsɪeɪt/ v.i. **~ with sb.** mit jmdm. Umgang haben

**association** /əsəʊsɪˈeɪʃn/ n. (a) (organization) Vereinigung, die
(b) (mental connection) Assoziation, die
(c) (connection) Verbindung, die

**assorted** /əˈsɔːtɪd/ adj. gemischt

**assortment** /əˈsɔːtmənt/ n. Sortiment, das; **a good ~ of hats [to choose from]** eine gute Auswahl an Hüten

**Asst.** abbr. = **Assistant** Ass.

**assume** /əˈsjuːm/ v.t. (a) voraussetzen; **assuming that …:** vorausgesetzt, dass …
(b) (undertake) übernehmen ‹Amt, Pflichten›
(c) (take on) annehmen ‹Namen, Rolle›

**assumption** /əˈsʌmpʃn/ n. Annahme, die; **going on the ~ that …:** vorausgesetzt, dass …; **the A~** (Relig.) Mariä Himmelfahrt

**assurance** /əˈʃʊərəns/ n. (a) Zusicherung, die
(b) (self-confidence) Selbstsicherheit, die

**assure** /əˈʃʊə(r)/ v.t. (a) versichern (+ Dat.)
(b) (convince) **~ sb./oneself** jmdn./sich überzeugen
(c) (make certain or safe) gewährleisten

**assured** /əˈʃʊəd/ adj. gewährleistet ‹Erfolg›; **be ~ of sth.** sich (Dat.) einer Sache (Gen.) sicher sein

**asterisk** /ˈæstərɪsk/ n. Sternchen, das

**astern** /əˈstɜːn/ adv. (Naut., Aeronaut.) achtern; (towards the rear) achteraus

**asteroid** /ˈæstərɔɪd/ n. Asteroid, der

**asthma** /ˈæsmə/ n. Asthma, das

**asthmatic** /æsˈmætɪk/ ⓵ adj. asthmatisch
② n. Asthmatiker, der/Asthmatikerin, die

**astonish** /əˈstɒnɪʃ/ v.t. erstaunen

**a'stonishing** adj. erstaunlich

**a'stonishment** n. Erstaunen, das

**astound** /əˈstaʊnd/ v.t. verblüffen

**a'stounding** adj. erstaunlich

**astray** /əˈstreɪ/ adv. **sth. goes ~** (is mislaid) etw. wird verlegt; (is lost) etw. geht verloren; **go/lead ~** (fig.) in die Irre gehen/führen

**astride** /əˈstraɪd/ ⓵ adv. rittlings ‹sitzen›
② prep. rittlings auf (+ Dat.)

**astringent** /əˈstrɪndʒənt/ ⓵ adj. scharf
② n. Adstringens, das

**astrologer** /əˈstrɒlədʒə(r)/ n. Astrologe, der/Astrologin, die

**astrological** /æstrəˈlɒdʒɪkl/ adj. astrologisch

**astrology** /əˈstrɒlədʒɪ/ n. Astrologie, die

**astronaut** /'æstrənɔ:t/ *n.* Astronaut, *der/* Astronautin, *die*

**astronautics** /æstrə'nɔ:tɪks/ *n.* Astronautik, *die;* Raumfahrt, *die*

**astronomer** /ə'strɒnəmə(r)/ *n.* Astronom, *der/*Astronomin, *die*

**astronomical** /æstrə'nɒmɪkl/ *adj.* astronomisch

**astronomy** /ə'strɒnəmɪ/ *n.* Astronomie, *die*

**astrophysics** /æstrəʊ'fɪzɪks/ *n.* Astrophysik, *die*

**astute** /ə'stju:t/ *adj.* scharfsinnig

**asylum** /ə'saɪləm/ *n.* **(a)** (Polit.) Asyl, *das;* **grant sb. ~:** jmdm. Asyl gewähren; **~ seeker** Asylsuchende, *der/die* **(b)** ▶ LUNATIC ASYLUM

**asymmetric** /æsɪ'metrɪk, eɪsɪ'metrɪk/ *adj.* asymmetrisch; unsymmetrisch

**at** /ət, *stressed* æt/ *prep.* **(a)** *expr. place* an (+ *Dat.*); **at the station** am Bahnhof; **at the baker's/butcher's/grocer's** beim Bäcker/ Fleischer/Kaufmann; **at the chemist's** in der Apotheke/Drogerie; **at the supermarket** im Supermarkt; **at the party** auf der Party; **at the office/hotel** im Büro/Hotel; **at Dover** in Dover **(b)** *expr. time* **at Christmas** [zu *od.* an] Weihnachten; **at six o'clock** um sechs Uhr; **at midnight** um Mitternacht; **at midday** am Mittag; **at [the age of] 40** mit 40; im Alter von 40; **at this/the moment** in diesem/im Augenblick *od.* Moment **(c)** *expr. price* **at £2.50 [each]** zu *od.* für [je] 2,50 Pfund **(d)** *expr. speed* **at 30 m.p.h.** *etc.* mit dreißig Meilen pro Stunde *usw.* **(e) at that** (at that point) dabei; (at that provocation) daraufhin; (moreover) noch dazu

**ate** ▶ EAT

**atheism** /'eɪθɪɪzm/ *n.* Atheismus, *der*

**atheist** /'eɪθɪɪst/ *n.* Atheist, *der/*Atheistin, *die*

**Athens** /'æθɪnz/ *pr. n.* Athen (*das*)

**athlete** /'æθli:t/ *n.* Athlet, *der/*Athletin, *die;* (runner, jumper) Leichtathlet, *der/*-athletin, *die*

**athletic** /æθ'letɪk/ *adj.* sportlich

**ath'letics** *n.* Leichtathletik, *die*

**Atlantic** /ət'læntɪk/ **1** *adj.* atlantisch; **~ Ocean** Atlantischer Ozean **2** *pr. n.* Atlantik, *der*

**atlas** /'ætləs/ *n.* Atlas, *der*

**ATM** *abbr.* = **automated teller machine**

**atmosphere** /'ætməsfɪə(r)/ *n.* Atmosphäre, *die*

**atmospheric** /ætməs'ferɪk/ *adj.* **(a)** atmosphärisch **(b)** (fig.: evocative) stimmungsvoll

**atom** /'ætəm/ *n.* Atom, *das*

**'atom bomb** *n.* Atombombe, *die*

**atomic** /ə'tɒmɪk/ *adj.* Atom-

**atomizer** /'ætəmaɪzə(r)/ *n.* Zerstäuber, *der*

**atone** /ə'təʊn/ *v.i.* es wieder gutmachen; **~ for sth.** etw. wieder gutmachen

**a'tonement** *n.* Buße, *die*

**atrocious** /ə'trəʊʃəs/ *adj.* grauenhaft; scheußlich ⟨*Wetter, Benehmen*⟩

**a'trociously** *adv.* grauenhaft; scheußlich ⟨*sich benehmen*⟩

**atrocity** /ə'trɒsɪtɪ/ *n.* **(a)** (wickedness) Grauenhaftigkeit, *die* **(b)** (deed) Gräueltat, *die*

**attach** /ə'tætʃ/ *v.t.* **(a)** (fasten) befestigen (**to** an + *Dat.*); **please find ~ed a copy of the letter** beigeheftet ist eine Kopie des Briefes **(b)** (fig.) **~ importance to sth.** einer Sache (*Dat.*) Gewicht beimessen

**attaché** /ə'tæʃeɪ/ *n.* Attaché, *der*

**at'taché case** *n.* Diplomatenkoffer, *der*

**attached** /ə'tætʃt/ *adj.* (emotionally) **be ~ to sb./sth.** an jmdm./etw. hängen

**at'tachment** *n.* **(a)** (act or means of fastening) Befestigung, *die* **(b)** (affection) Anhänglichkeit, *die* (**to** an + *Akk.*) **(c)** (accessory) Zusatzgerät, *das* **(d)** (Comp.) Attachment, *das;* Anlage, *die*

**attack** /ə'tæk/ **1** *v.t.* **(a)** angreifen; (ambush, raid) überfallen; (fig.: criticize) attackieren **(b)** (affect) ⟨*Krankheit:*⟩ befallen **2** *v.i.* angreifen **3** *n.* Angriff, *der;* (ambush) Überfall, *der;* (fig.: criticism) Attacke, *die;* (of illness) Anfall, *der*

**at'tacker** *n.* Angreifer, *der/*Angreiferin, *die*

**attacking** /ə'tækɪŋ/ *adj.* offensiv ⟨*Spielweise, Spieler*⟩; angreifend ⟨*Truppen*⟩

**attain** /ə'teɪn/ *v.t.* erreichen

**attainable** /ə'teɪnəbl/ *adj.* erreichbar ⟨*Ziel*⟩; realisierbar ⟨*Hoffnung, Ziel*⟩

**at'tainment** *n.* Verwirklichung, *die*

**attempt** /ə'tempt/ **1** *v.t.* versuchen **2** *n.* Versuch, *der*

**attend** /ə'tend/ **1** *v.i.* **(a)** (give care and thought) aufpassen; (apply oneself) **~ to sth.** (deal with sth.) sich um etw. kümmern **(b)** (be present) anwesend sein (**at** bei) **2** *v.t.* **(a)** (be present at) teilnehmen an (+ *Dat.*); (go regularly to) besuchen **(b)** (wait on) bedienen (+ *Dat.*) **(c)** ⟨*Arzt:*⟩ behandeln

**attendance** /ə'tendəns/ *n.* Anwesenheit, *die;* (number of people) Teilnehmerzahl, *die*

**attendant** /ə'tendənt/ *n.* **(a)** [lavatory] **~:** Toilettenmann, *der/*-frau, *die;* [cloakroom] **~:** Garderobenmann, *der/*-frau, *die;* **museum ~:** Museumswärter, *der/*-wärterin, *die* **(b)** (member of entourage) Begleiter, *der/* Begleiterin, *die*

**attention** /ə'tenʃn/ **1** *n.* **(a)** Aufmerksamkeit, *die;* **attract [sb.'s] ~:** [jmdn.] auf sich (*Akk.*) aufmerksam machen; **pay ~ to sb./sth.** jmdn./etw. beachten; **pay** ⋯⋗

**a**

∼! gib Acht!; pass auf!; **hold sb.'s** ∼: jmds.
Interesse wach halten; ∼ **Miss Jones** (on
letter) zu Händen [von] Miss Jones
**(b)** (Mil.) **stand to** ∼: stillstehen
2 *int.* **(a)** Achtung
**(b)** (Mil.) stillgestanden

**attentive** /ə'tentɪv/ *adj.* aufmerksam

**attic** /'ætɪk/ *n.* (room) Dachboden, *der;*
(habitable) Dachkammer, *die*

**attire** /ə'taɪə(r)/ *n.* Kleidung, *die*

**attitude** /'ætɪtjuːd/ *n.* **(a)** Haltung, *die*
**(b)** (mental ∼) Einstellung, *die*

**attn.** *abbr.* = **for the attention of**
z. H[d].

**attorney** /ə'tɜːnɪ/ *n.* **(a)** Bevollmächtigte,
*der/die;* **power of** ∼: Vollmacht, *die*
**(b)** (Amer.: lawyer) [Rechts]anwalt, *der/*
-anwältin, *die*

**attract** /ə'trækt/ *v.t.* **(a)** (draw) anziehen; auf
sich (*Akk.*) ziehen ⟨*Interesse, Blick, Kritik*⟩
**(b)** (arouse pleasure in) anziehend wirken auf
(+ *Akk.*)
**(c)** (arouse interest in) reizen (**about** an + *Dat.*)

**attraction** /ə'trækʃn/ *n.* **(a)** Anziehung,
*die;* (force, lit. or fig.) Anziehung[skraft], *die*
**(b)** (fig.: thing that attracts) Attraktion, *die;*
(charm) Verlockung, *die;* Reiz, *der*

**attractive** /ə'træktɪv/ *adj.* **(a)** anziehend
**(b)** (fig.) attraktiv; reizvoll ⟨*Vorschlag,
Möglichkeit, Idee*⟩

**attribute** 1 /'ætrɪbjuːt/ *n.* Eigenschaft, *die*
2 /ə'trɪbjuːt/ *v.t.* zuschreiben (**to** *Dat.*)

**attributive** /ə'trɪbjʊtɪv/ *adj.* (Ling.)
attributiv

**atypical** /eɪ'tɪpɪkl/ *adj.* atypisch; untypisch

**aubergine** /'əʊbəʒiːn/ *n.* Aubergine, *die*

**auburn** /'ɔːbən/ *adj.* rötlich braun

**auction** /'ɔːkʃn/ 1 *n.* Versteigerung, *die*
2 *v.t.* versteigern

**auctioneer** /ɔːkʃə'nɪə(r)/ *n.* Auktionator,
*der/*Auktionatorin, *die*

**audacious** /ɔː'deɪʃəs/ *adj.* **(a)** (daring) kühn;
verwegen
**(b)** (impudent) dreist

**audacity** /ɔː'dæsɪtɪ/ *n.* **(a)** (daringness)
Kühnheit, *die;* Verwegenheit, *die*
**(b)** (impudence) Dreistigkeit, *die*

**audible** /'ɔːdɪbl/ *adj.* hörbar

**audience** /'ɔːdɪəns/ *n.* **(a)** Publikum, *das*
**(b)** (formal interview) Audienz, *die* (**with** bei)

**audio** /'ɔːdɪəʊ/ *adj.* Ton-; ∼ **frequency**
Tonfrequenz, *die;* ∼ **equipment** Audioanlage,
*die*

**audio:** ∼**book** *n.* Hörbuch, *das;*
∼ **cassette** *n.* Audiokassette, *die;*
Tonkassette, *die;* ∼ **typist** *n.* Phonotypist,
*der/*-typistin, *die;* ∼**visual** *adj.* audiovisuell

**audit** /'ɔːdɪt/ 1 *n.* ∼ [**of the accounts**]
Rechnungsprüfung, *die*
2 *v.t.* prüfen

**audition** /ɔː'dɪʃn/ 1 *n.* (singing) Vorsingen,
*das;* (dancing) Vortanzen, *das;* (acting)
Vorsprechen, *das*

2 *v.i.* (sing) vorsingen; (dance) vortanzen;
(act) vorsprechen
3 *v.t.* vorsingen/vortanzen/vorsprechen
lassen

**auditor** /'ɔːdɪtə(r)/ *n.* Buchprüfer, *der/*
-prüferin, *die*

**auditorium** /ɔːdɪ'tɔːrɪəm/ *n.*
Zuschauerraum, *der*

**Aug.** *abbr.* = **August** Aug.

**augment** /ɔːg'ment/ *v.t.* verbessern
⟨*Einkommen*⟩; aufstocken ⟨*Fonds*⟩

**augur** /'ɔːgə(r)/ 1 *v.t.* bedeuten;
versprechen ⟨*Erfolg*⟩
2 *v.i.* ∼ **well/ill for sth./sb.** ein gutes/
schlechtes Zeichen für etw./jmdn. sein

**August** /'ɔːgəst/ *n.* August, *der;* **in** ∼: im
August; **last/next** ∼: letzten/nächsten
August; **the first of/on the first of** ∼: der
erste/am ersten August

**aunt** /ɑːnt/ *n.* Tante, *die*

**auntie, aunty** /'ɑːntɪ/ *n.* (coll.) Täntchen,
*das;* (with name) Tante, *die*

**au pair** /əʊ 'peə(r)/ *n.* Aupairmädchen, *das*

**aura** /'ɔːrə/ *n.* Aura, *die*

**auspices** /'ɔːspɪsɪs/ *n. pl.* **under the** ∼ **of**
**sb./sth.** unter jmds./einer Sache
Schirmherrschaft

**auspicious** /ɔː'spɪʃəs/ *adj.* günstig;
viel versprechend ⟨*Anfang*⟩

**Aussie** /'ɒzɪ/ (coll.) 1 *adj.* australisch
2 *n.* Australier, *der/*Australierin, *die*

**austere** /ɒ'stɪə(r)/ *adj.* **(a)** (strict, stern)
streng
**(b)** (severely simple) karg

**austerity** /ɒ'sterɪtɪ/ *n.* **(a)** (strictness)
Strenge, *die*
**(b)** (severe simplicity) Kargheit, *die*
**(c)** (lack of luxuries) wirtschaftliche
Einschränkung

**Australia** /ɒ'streɪlɪə/ *pr. n.* Australien (*das*)

**Australian** /ɒ'streɪlɪən/ 1 *adj.* australisch;
**sb. is** ∼: jmd. ist Australier/Australierin
2 *n.* Australier, *der/*Australierin, *die*

**Austria** /'ɒstrɪə/ *pr. n.* Österreich (*das*)

**Austrian** /'ɒstrɪən/ 1 *adj.* österreichisch;
**sb. is** ∼ jmd. ist Österreicher/Österreicherin
2 *n.* Österreicher, *der/*Österreicherin, *die*

**authentic** /ɔː'θentɪk/ *adj.* authentisch

**authenticate** /ɔː'θentɪkeɪt/ *v.t.*
authentifizieren; ∼ **sth.** die Echtheit einer
Sache (*Gen.*) bestätigen

**authentication** /ɔːθentɪ'keɪʃn/ *n.*
Bestätigung der Echtheit; (of information, report)
Bestätigung, *die*

**authenticity** /ɔːθen'tɪsɪtɪ/ *n.* Authentizität,
*die*

**author** /'ɔːθə(r)/ *n.* Autor, *der/*Autorin, *die;*
(profession) Schriftsteller, *der/*Schriftstellerin,
*die*

**authoritarian** /ɔːθɒrɪ'teərɪən/ 1 *adj.*
autoritär
2 *n.* autoritäre Person

**authoritative** /ɔːˈθɒrɪtətɪv/ adj.
maßgebend; zuverlässig ⟨Bericht,
Information⟩

**authority** /ɔːˈθɒrɪtɪ/ n. (a) Autorität, die; in
~: verantwortlich
(b) the authorities die Behörde[n]

**authorization** /ɔːθəraɪˈzeɪʃn/ n.
Genehmigung, die

**authorize** /ˈɔːθəraɪz/ v.t. (a) ermächtigen;
bevollmächtigen
(b) (sanction) genehmigen

**auto** /ˈɔːtəʊ/ n., pl. ~s (Amer. coll.) Auto, das

**auto-** /ɔːtəʊ/ in comb. auto-/Auto-

**autobio'graphical** adj. autobiographisch

**autobi'ography** n. Autobiographie, die

**autocrat** /ˈɔːtəkræt/ n. Autokrat, der/
Autokratin, die

**autocratic** /ɔːtəˈkrætɪk/ adj. autokratisch

**'autocross** n. Autocross, das

**Autocue** ® /ˈɔːtəʊkjuː/ n. Teleprompter
Ⓦ, der

**'autofocus** n. (Photog.) Autofokus, der

**autograph** /ˈɔːtəɡrɑːf/ ① n. Autogramm,
das
② v.t. signieren

**auto-im'mune** adj. (Med.) autoimmun;
~ response Autoimmunantwort, die

**automat** /ˈɔːtəmæt/ n. (Amer.) (a) (slot
machine) [Münz]automat, der
(b) (cafeteria) Automatenrestaurant, das

**automate** /ˈɔːtəmeɪt/ v.t. automatisieren

**automated 'teller machine** n.
Geldautomat, der

**automatic** /ɔːtəˈmætɪk/ ① adj.
automatisch; ~ gear system, ~ transmission
Automatikgetriebe, das
② n. (weapon) automatische Waffe; (vehicle)
Fahrzeug mit Automatikgetriebe

**automatically** /ɔːtəˈmætɪkəlɪ/ adv.
automatisch

**automation** /ɔːtəˈmeɪʃn/ n. Automation,
die

**automaton** /ɔːˈtɒmətən/ n., pl. ~s or
automata /ɔːˈtɒmətə/ Automat, der

**automobile** /ˈɔːtəməbiːl/ n. (Amer.) Auto,
das

**autonomous** /ɔːˈtɒnəməs/ adj. autonom

**autonomy** /ɔːˈtɒnəmɪ/ n. Autonomie, die

**'autopilot** n. Autopilot, der; [fly] on ~: mit
Autopilot [fliegen]

**autopsy** /ˈɔːtɒpsɪ/ n. Autopsie, die

**auto:** ~save (Comp.) ① n. automatisches
Speichern; ② v.t. automatisch speichern;
~-suggestion n. Autosuggestion, die;
~timer n. [automatische] Schaltuhr

**autumn** /ˈɔːtəm/ n. Herbst, der; in [the] ~:
im Herbst

**autumnal** /ɔːˈtʌmnl/ adj. herbstlich

**auxiliary** /ɔːɡˈzɪljərɪ/ ① adj. Hilfs-
② n. (a) Hilfskraft, die
(b) (Ling.) Hilfsverb, das

**avail** /əˈveɪl/ ① n. be of no ~: nichts
nützen; to no ~: vergebens
② v. refl. ~ oneself of sth. von etw.
Gebrauch machen

**available** /əˈveɪləbl/ adj. (a) (at one's
disposal) verfügbar
(b) (obtainable) erhältlich; lieferbar ⟨Waren⟩

**avalanche** /ˈævəlɑːnʃ/ n. Lawine, die

**avarice** /ˈævərɪs/ n. Geldgier, die;
Habsucht, die

**avaricious** /ævəˈrɪʃəs/ adj. geldgierig;
habsüchtig

**avenge** /əˈvendʒ/ v.t. rächen

**avenue** /ˈævənjuː/ n. Allee, die; (fig.) Weg,
der (to zu)

**average** /ˈævərɪdʒ/ ① n. Durchschnitt,
der; on ~: im Durchschnitt;
durchschnittlich
② adj. durchschnittlich
③ v.t. (a) (find the ~ of) den Durchschnitt
ermitteln von
(b) (amount on ~ to) durchschnittlich
betragen
④ v.i. ~ out at im Durchschnitt betragen

**averse** /əˈvɜːs/ adj. be ~ to sth. einer
Sache (Dat.) abgeneigt sein

**aversion** /əˈvɜːʃn/ n. Abneigung, die (to
gegen)

**avert** /əˈvɜːt/ v.t. abwenden; verhüten
⟨Unfall⟩

**aviary** /ˈeɪvɪərɪ/ n. Vogelhaus, das

**aviation** /eɪvɪˈeɪʃn/ n. Luftfahrt, die

**avid** /ˈævɪd/ adj. (enthusiastic) begeistert; be
~ for sth. (eager, greedy) begierig auf etw.
(Akk.) sein

**avocado** /ævəˈkɑːdəʊ/ n., pl. ~s: ~ [pear]
Avocado[birne], die

**avoid** /əˈvɔɪd/ v.t. (a) meiden ⟨Ort⟩; ~ a
cyclist einem Radfahrer ausweichen; ~ the
boss when he's in a temper geh dem Chef
aus dem Weg, wenn er schlechte Laune hat
(b) (refrain from, escape) vermeiden

**avoidable** /əˈvɔɪdəbl/ adj. vermeidbar

**avoidance** /əˈvɔɪdəns/ n. Vermeidung, die

**await** /əˈweɪt/ v.t. erwarten

**awake** /əˈweɪk/ ① v.i., awoke /əˈwəʊk/,
awoken /əˈwəʊkn/ erwachen
② v.t., awoke, awoken wecken
③ pred. adj. wach; wide ~: hellwach

**awaken** /əˈweɪkn/ v.t. & i. (esp. fig.)
▶ AWAKE 1, 2

**award** /əˈwɔːd/ ① v.t. verleihen ⟨Preis,
Auszeichnung⟩; zusprechen ⟨Sorgerecht,
Entschädigung⟩; gewähren ⟨Zahlung,
Gehaltserhöhung⟩
② n. (prize) Auszeichnung, die

**a'ward-winning** adj. preisgekrönt

**aware** /əˈweə(r)/ adj. be ~ of sth. sich
(Dat.) einer Sache (Gen.) bewusst sein; be
~ that …: sich (Dat.) [dessen] bewusst sein,
dass …

**a'wareness** n. Bewusstsein, das

**awash** /ə'wɒʃ/ *adj.* be ~ (flooded) unter Wasser stehen

**away** /ə'weɪ/ ① *adv.* (a) (at a distance) entfernt; **play** ~ (Sport) auswärts spielen (b) (to a distance) weg; fort (c) (absent) nicht da ② *adj.* (Sport) auswärts *präd.*; Auswärts-; ~ **match** Auswärtsspiel, *das;* ~ **team** Gastmannschaft, *die*

**awe** /ɔː/ *n.* Ehrfurcht, *die* (of vor + *Dat.*)

**'awe-inspiring** *adj.* Ehrfurcht gebietend; beeindruckend

**awesome** /'ɔːsəm/ *adj.* überwältigend; eindrucksvoll ⟨*Schweigen*⟩; übergroß ⟨*Verantwortung*⟩

**awe:** ~**stricken,** ~**struck** *adj.* [von Ehrfurcht] ergriffen; ehrfurchtsvoll ⟨*Ausdruck, Staunen*⟩

**awful** /'ɔːfl/ *adj.,* **'awfully** *adv.* furchtbar

**awkward** /'ɔːkwəd/ *adj.* (a) (difficult to use) ungünstig; **be** ~ **to use** unhandlich sein (b) (clumsy) unbeholfen (c) (embarrassing) peinlich (d) (difficult) schwierig; ungünstig ⟨*Zeitpunkt*⟩

**awning** /'ɔːnɪŋ/ *n.* (on house) Markise, *die;* (of tent) Vordach, *das*

**awoke, awoken** ▶ AWAKE

**awry** /ə'raɪ/ *adv.* schief; **go** ~ (fig.) schief gehen (ugs.); ⟨*Plan:*⟩ fehlschlagen

**axe** (*Amer.:* **ax**) /æks/ *n.* Axt, *die;* Beil, *das*

**axis** /'æksɪs/ *n., pl.* **axes** /'æksiːz/ Achse, *die*

**axle** /'æksl/ *n.* Achse, *die*

# Bb

**B, b** /biː/ *n.* B, b, *das;* **B road** Straße 2. Ordnung; ≈ Landstraße, *die*

**BA** *abbr.* = **Bachelor of Arts**

**babble** /'bæbl/ *v.i.* (a) (talk incoherently) stammeln (b) (talk foolishly) [dumm] schwatzen (c) ⟨*Bach:*⟩ plätschern

**baboon** /bə'buːn/ *n.* Pavian, *der*

**baby** /'beɪbɪ/ *n.* (a) Baby, *das;* **have a** ~/**be going to have a** ~: ein Kind bekommen; **throw out** *or* **away the** ~ **with the bathwater** (fig.) das Kind mit dem Bade ausschütten (b) (childish person) **be a** ~: sich wie ein kleines Kind benehmen

**baby:** ~ **boom** *n.* Babyboom, *der;* ~**bouncer** *n.: federnd aufgehängter Sitz für Kleinkinder, in dem sie durch Wippen ihre Beine kräftigen sollen;* ~ **buggy,** ~ **carriage** *ns.* (Amer.) Kinderwagen, *der;* ~ **clothes** *n. pl.* Babykleidung, *die;* ~ **food** *n.* Babynahrung, *die*

**'babyish** *adj.* kindlich ⟨*Aussehen*⟩; kindisch ⟨*Benehmen, Person*⟩

**baby:** ~**-minder** *n.* Tagesmutter, *die;* ~**sit** *v.i., forms as* SIT 1: babysitten (ugs.); auf das Kind/die Kinder aufpassen; ~**sitter** *n.* Babysitter, *der*/Babysitterin, *die;* ~**sitting** *n.* Babysitting, *das;* ~**-snatcher** *n.* Kindesentführer, *der* /-entführerin, *die;* ~**-talk** *n.* Babysprache, *die;* ~ **walker** *n.* Laufstuhl, *der;* ~ **wipe** *n.* feuchtes Baby[pflege]tuch

**bachelor** /'bætʃələ(r)/ *n.* (a) Junggeselle, *der*

(b) (Univ.) **B**~ **of Arts**/**Science** Bakkalaureus der philosophischen Fakultät/der Naturwissenschaften

**back** /bæk/ ① *n.* (a) (of person, animal) Rücken, *der;* (of house, cheque) Rückseite, *die;* (of vehicle) Heck, *das;* (inside car) Rücksitz, *der;* **stand** ~ **to** ~: Rücken an Rücken stehen; ~ **to front** verkehrt rum; **turn one's** ~ **on sb.** jmdm. den Rücken zuwenden; (fig.) jmdn. im Stich lassen; **turn one's** ~ **on sth.** (fig.) sich um etw. nicht kümmern; **get** *or* **put sb.'s** ~ **up** (fig.) jmdn. wütend machen; **be glad to see the** ~ **of sb.**/**sth.** (fig.) froh sein, jmdn./ etw. nicht mehr sehen zu müssen; **have one's** ~ **to the wall** (fig.) mit dem Rücken zur Wand stehen; **put one's** ~ **into sth.** (fig.) sich für etw. mit allen Kräften einsetzen; **with the** ~ **of one's hand** mit dem Handrücken; **at the** ~ **[of the book]** hinten [im Buch] (b) (Sport: player) Verteidiger, *der* ② *adj.* hinter... ③ *adv.* zurück; **two miles** ~: vor zwei Meilen; ~ **and forth** hin und her; **there and** ~: hin und zurück; **a week/month** ~: vor einer Woche/vor einem Monat ④ *v.t.* (a) (assist) unterstützen (b) (bet on) wetten *od.* setzen auf (+ *Akk.*) (c) zurücksetzen [mit] ⟨*Fahrzeug*⟩ ⑤ *v.i.* zurücksetzen; ~ **into/out of sth.** rückwärts in etw. (*Akk.*)/aus etw. fahren; ~ **on to sth.** hinten an etw. (*Akk.*) grenzen
∎ **back 'down** *v.i.* nachgeben
∎ **back 'out** *v.i.* rückwärts herausfahren; ~ **out of sth.** (fig.) von etw. zurücktreten
∎ **back 'up** *v.t.* (a) unterstützen; untermauern ⟨*Anspruch, These*⟩

**(b)** (Comp.) sichern ⟨*Daten, Dokumente*⟩; ∼ **up a file on to a floppy disk** von einer Datei eine Sicherungskopie auf Diskette machen

**back:** ∼**ache** *n.* Rückenschmerzen *Pl.;* ∼**-bencher** /bæk'bentʃə(r)/ *n.* (Brit. Parl.) [einfacher] Abgeordneter/[einfache] Abgeordnete; ∼**bone** *n.* Rückgrat, *das;* ∼**chat** *n.* (coll.) [freche] Widerrede; ∼**date** *v.t.* zurückdatieren (**to** auf + *Akk.*); ∼ '**door** *n.* Hintertür, *die*

'**backer** *n.* Geldgeber, *der*

**back:** ∼'**fire** *v.i.* knallen; (fig.) fehlschlagen; **it** ∼**fired on me/him** *etc.* der Schuss ging nach hinten los (ugs.); ∼**gammon** /'bækgæmən/ *n.* (game) Backgammon, *das;* ≈ Tricktrack, *das;* ≈ Puff, *das;* ∼**ground** *n.* Hintergrund, *der;* (social status) Herkunft, *die;* ∼**hand** (Tennis etc.) **1** *adj.* Rückhand-; **2** *n.* Rückhand, *die;* ∼'**handed** *adj.* **(a)** (Tennis etc.) Rückhand-; **(b)** (fig.) indirekt; zweifelhaft ⟨*Kompliment*⟩; ∼'**hander** *n.* (coll.: bribe) Schmiergeld, *das*

'**backing** *n.* (support) Unterstützung, *die*

**back:** ∼ **issue** ▸ ∼ NUMBER; ∼**lash** *n.* (fig.) Gegenreaktion, *die;* ∼**log** *n.* Rückstand, *der;* ∼ **number** *n.* (of periodical, magazine) alte Nummer; ∼**pack** **1** *n.* Rucksack, *der;* **2** *v.i.* mit dem Rucksack [ver]reisen; ∼**packer** *n.* Rucksackreisende, *der/die;* Rucksacktourist, *der/*-touristin, *die;* (hiker) Wanderer, *der/* Wanderin, *die* mit Rucksack; ∼**packing** *n.* das [Ver]reisen mit dem Rucksack; (hiking) das Wandern mit dem Rucksack; *attrib.* ⟨*Reise usw.*⟩ mit dem Rucksack; ∼ **pay** *n.* ausstehender Lohn/ausstehendes Gehalt; **he was reinstated with** ∼ **pay** er wurde wieder eingestellt und erhielt eine Lohn-/ Gehaltsnachzahlung; **she was awarded £7,850 in** ∼ **pay** sie erhielt eine Nachzahlung von 7 850 Pfund; ∼'**pedal** *v.i.* **(a)** die Pedale rückwärts treten; **(b)** (fig.) einen Rückzieher machen (ugs.); ∼**scratching** *n.* (fig. coll.) [mutual] ∼**scratching** Klüngelei, *die* (abwertend); ∼ '**seat** *n.* Rücksitz, *der;* ∼**side** *n.* Hinterteil, *das* (ugs.); ∼**space** *n.* Rücktaste betätigen; ∼'**stage** *adv.* **go** ∼**stage** hinter die Bühne gehen; ∼ **street** *n.* kleine Seitenstraße; ∼**stroke** *n.* Rückenschwimmen, *das;* ∼**track** *v.i.* wieder zurückgehen; (fig.) eine Kehrtwendung machen; ∼**-up** *n.* (support) Unterstützung, *die;* ∼**-up** [copy] (Comp.) Sicherungskopie, *die*

**backward** /'bækwəd/ **1** *adj.* **(a)** rückwärts gerichtet; Rückwärts- **(b)** (reluctant, shy) zurückhaltend **(c)** (underdeveloped) rückständig ⟨*Land, Region*⟩ **2** *adv.* ▸ BACKWARDS

**backwards** /'bækwədz/ *adv.* **(a)** nach hinten; **the child fell [over]** ∼ **into the water** das Kind fiel rückwärts ins Wasser; **bend** *or* **lean over** ∼ **to do sth.** (fig. coll.) sich zerreißen, um etw. zu tun (ugs.) **(b)** (oppositely to normal direction) rückwärts; ∼ **and forwards** hin und her

**back:** ∼**water** *n.* (fig.) Kaff, *das* (ugs.); ∼ '**yard** *n.* Hinterhof, *der*

**bacon** /'beɪkn/ *n.* [Frühstücks]speck, *der*

**bacterial** /bæk'tɪərɪəl/ *adj.* bakteriell

**bacterium** /bæk'tɪərɪəm/ *n., pl.* **bacteria** /bæk'tɪərɪə/ Bakterie, *die*

**bad** /bæd/ *adj.,* **worse** /wɜːs/, **worst** /wɜːst/ **(a)** schlecht; (rotten) schlecht, verdorben ⟨*Fleisch, Fisch, Essen*⟩; faul ⟨*Ei, Apfel*⟩; **not** ∼ (coll.) nicht schlecht; nicht übel **(b)** (naughty) ungezogen, böse ⟨*Kind, Hund*⟩ **(c)** (offensive) [use] ∼ **language** Kraftausdrücke [benutzen] **(d)** (regretful) **feel** ∼ **about sth.** etw. bedauern; **I feel** ∼ **about him** ich habe seinetwegen ein schlechtes Gewissen **(e)** (serious) schlimm ⟨*Sturz, Krise*⟩; schwer ⟨*Fehler, Krankheit, Unfall*⟩ **(f)** (Commerc.) **a** ∼ **debt** eine uneinbringliche Schuld

**bade** ▸ BID 1B

**badge** /bædʒ/ *n.* Abzeichen, *das*

**badger** /'bædʒə(r)/ *n.* Dachs, *der*

'**badly** *adv.,* **worse** /wɜːs/, **worst** /wɜːst/ **(a)** schlecht **(b)** schwer ⟨*verletzt, beschädigt*⟩ **(c)** (urgently) dringend

**bad-mannered** /bæd'mænəd/ *adj.* **be** ∼: schlechte Manieren haben

**badminton** /'bædmɪntən/ *n.* Federball, *der;* (als Sport) Badminton, *das*

**bad-tempered** /bæd'tempəd/ *adj.* griesgrämig

**baffle** /'bæfl/ *v.t.* ∼ **sb.** jmdm. unverständlich sein

**baffling** /'bæflɪŋ/ *adj.* rätselhaft

**bag** /bæg/ **1** *n.* Tasche, *die;* (sack) Sack, *der;* (hand∼) Handtasche, *die;* (plastic ∼) Beutel, *der;* (small paper ∼) Tüte, *die;* ∼**s of** (coll.: large amount) jede Menge **2** *v.t.,* -**gg**-: **(a)** in Säcke/Beutel/Tüten füllen **(b)** (claim possession of) sich (*Dat.*) schnappen (ugs.)

**baggage** /'bægɪdʒ/ *n.* Gepäck, *das*

**baggage:** ∼ **allowance** *n.* Freigepäck, *das;* **be over/within one's** ∼ **allowance** Übergepäck/kein Übergepäck haben; ∼ **handler** *n.* Gepäckverlader, *der/* -verladerin, *die;* ∼ **handling** *n.* Gepäckverladung, *die;* ∼ **reclaim** *n.* Gepäckausgabe, *die*

**baggy** /'bægɪ/ *adj.* weit [geschnitten] ⟨*Kleid, Hose*⟩; (through long use) ausgebeult ⟨*Hose*⟩

'**bagpipe[s]** *n.* [*pl.*] Dudelsack, *der*

**baguette** /bæ'get/ *n.* Baguette, *die;* [französisches] Stangenweißbrot

**Bahamas** /bə'hɑːməz/ pr. n. pl. **the ~:** die Bahamas Pl.

**bail¹** /beɪl/ ① n. Kaution, die; **be [out] on ~:** gegen Kaution auf freiem Fuß sein ② v.t. **~ sb. out** jmdn. gegen Kaution freibekommen; (fig.) jmdm. aus der Klemme helfen (ugs.)

**bail²** v.t. (scoop) **~ [out]** ausschöpfen ■ **'bail out** v.i. ⟨Pilot:⟩ abspringen

**bailiff** /'beɪlɪf/ n. ≈ Gerichtsvollzieher, der

**bait** /beɪt/ ① v.t. mit einem Köder versehen ② n. Köder, der

**bake** /beɪk/ v.t. & i. backen; **~d beans** gebackene Bohnen [in Tomatensoße]; **~d potato** [in der Schale] gebackene Kartoffel

**'baker** n. Bäcker, der

**bakery** /'beɪkərɪ/ n. Bäckerei, die

**baking: ~ powder** n. Backpulver, das; **~ sheet** n. Backblech, das; **~ soda** n. Natron, das; **~ tin** n. Backform, die; **~ tray** n. Kuchenblech, das

**balance** /'bæləns/ ① n. (a) (instrument) Waage, die (b) (fig.) **be** or **hang in the ~:** in der Schwebe sein (c) (steady position) Gleichgewicht, das; **keep/ lose one's ~:** das Gleichgewicht halten/ verlieren; (fig.) sein Gleichgewicht bewahren/ verlieren; **strike a ~ between** (fig.) den Mittelweg finden zwischen (+ Dat.) (d) (Bookk.: difference) Bilanz, die; (state of bank account) Kontostand, der; **on ~** (fig.) alles in allem; **~ sheet** Bilanz, die (e) (Econ.) **~ of payments** Zahlungsbilanz, die; **~ of trade** Handelsbilanz, die (f) (remainder) Rest, der ② v.t. (a) (weigh up) abwägen (b) (bring into or keep in ~) balancieren; auswuchten ⟨Rad⟩ (c) (equal, neutralize) ausgleichen; **~ each other, be ~d** sich (Dat.) die Waage halten

**'balanced** adj. ausgewogen; ausgeglichen ⟨Person, Team, Gemüt⟩

**balcony** /'bælkənɪ/ n. Balkon, der

**bald** /bɔːld/ adj. kahl ⟨Kopf⟩; kahlköpfig, glatzköpfig ⟨Person⟩; **be/go ~:** eine Glatze haben/bekommen

**bald: ~head** n. kahlköpfiger od. glatzköpfiger Mensch; Kahlkopf, der (ugs.); Glatzkopf, der (ugs.); **~-'headed** adj. glatzköpfig; kahlköpfig

**'balding** adj. mit beginnender Glatze nachgestellt; **be ~:** kahl werden

**'baldness** n. Kahlheit, die

**bale** /beɪl/ n. Ballen, der

**balk** /bɔːlk/ ① v.t. **they were ~ed in their plan** ihr Plan wurde blockiert ② v.i. sich sträuben **(at** gegen)

**Balkan** /'bɔːlkn/ ① adj. Balkan- ② n. pl. **the ~s** der Balkan

**ball¹** /bɔːl/ n. (a) Ball, der; (Billiards etc., Croquet) Kugel, die; **be on the ~** (coll.: be alert) auf Zack sein (ugs.)

(b) (of wool, string, fluff, etc.) Knäuel, das

**ball²** n. (dance) Ball, der

**ballad** /'bæləd/ n. Ballade, die

**ballast** /'bæləst/ n. Ballast, der

**ball: ~ 'bearing** n. Kugellager, das; **~boy** n. Balljunge, der; **~cock** n. Schwimmer[regel]ventil, das

**ballerina** /bælə'riːnə/ n. Ballerina, die

**ballet** /'bæleɪ/ n. Ballett, das; **~ dancer** Balletttänzer, der/-tänzerin, die

**'ball game** n. (a) Ballspiel, das (b) (Amer.) Baseballspiel, das; **a whole new ~** (fig. coll.) eine ganz neue Geschichte (ugs.); **a different ~** (fig. coll.) eine andere Sache

**ballistic** /bə'lɪstɪk/ adj. ballistisch; **go ~** (fig. coll.) ausrasten (salopp)

**balloon** /bə'luːn/ n. (a) Ballon, der; **hot-air ~:** Heißluftballon, der (b) (toy) Luftballon, der

**ballot** /'bælət/ n. Abstimmung, die; **[secret] ~:** geheime Wahl

**ballot: ~ box** n. Wahlurne, die; **~ paper** n. Stimmzettel, der

**ball: ~park** n. (Amer.) Baseballfeld, das; **your estimate is not in the right ~park** (fig.) mit deiner Schätzung liegst du völlig falsch (ugs.); **~ pen, ~point 'pen** ns. Kugelschreiber, der; **~room** n. Tanzsaal, der

**balls-up** /'bɔːlzʌp/ n. (coarse) Scheiß, der (salopp abwertend); **make a ~ of sth.** bei etw. Scheiße bauen (derb)

**balm** /bɑːm/ n. Balsam, der

**balmy** /'bɑːmɪ/ adj. (mild) mild

**balsa** /'bɔːlsə, 'bɒlsə/ n. **~ [wood]** Balsaholz, das

**Baltic** /'bɔːltɪk/ ① pr. n. Ostsee, die ② adj. **~ Sea** Ostsee, die

**balustrade** /bælə'streɪd/ n. Balustrade, die

**bamboo** /bæm'buː/ n. Bambus, der

**ban** /bæn/ ① v.t., **-nn-** verbieten; **~ sb. from doing sth.** jmdm. verbieten, etw. zu tun ② n. Verbot, das

**banal** /bə'nɑːl/ adj. banal

**banality** /bə'nælɪtɪ/ n. Banalität, die

**banana** /bə'nɑːnə/ n. Banane, die

**ba'nana skin** n. Bananenschale, die

**band** /bænd/ ① n. (a) Band, das; **a ~ of light/colour** ein Streifen Licht/Farbe (b) (range of values) Bandbreite, die (c) (organized group) Gruppe, die; (of robbers, outlaws, etc.) Bande, die (d) (Mus.) [Musik]kapelle, die; (pop group, jazz ~) Band, die ② v.i. **~ together [with sb.]** sich [mit jmdm.] zusammenschließen

**bandage** /'bændɪdʒ/ ① n. Verband, der; (as support) Bandage, die ② v.t. verbinden; bandagieren ⟨verstauchtes Gelenk usw.⟩

**b. & b.** /biː ən 'biː/ abbr. = **bed & breakfast**

**bandit** /'bændɪt/ *n.* Bandit, *der*

**band: ~stand** *n.* Musiktribüne, *die;*
**~wagon** *n.* climb *or* jump on [to] the
**~wagon** (fig.) auf den fahrenden Zug
aufspringen (fig.)

**bandy¹** /'bændɪ/ *v.t.* they were ~ing words/
insults sie stritten sich/beschimpften sich
gegenseitig

**bandy²** *adj.* krumm; **he is ~-legged** er hat
O-Beine (ugs.)

**bang** /bæŋ/ 1 *v.t.* knallen (ugs.); schlagen;
zuknallen (ugs.) ‹Tür, Fenster, Deckel›;
**~ one's head on sth.** mit dem Kopf an etw.
(Akk.) knallen (ugs.)
2 *v.i.* (strike) **~ [against sth.]** [gegen etw.]
knallen (ugs.); **~ shut** ‹Tür:› zuknallen (ugs.)
3 *n.* (a) (blow) Schlag, *der*
(b) (noise) Knall, *der*
4 *adv.* **go ~** ‹Gewehr, Feuerwerkskörper:›
krachen

**'banger** *n.* (coll.) (a) (sausage) Würstchen,
*das*
(b) (firework) Kracher, *der* (ugs.)
(c) (car) Klapperkiste, *die* (ugs.)

**bangle** /'bæŋgl/ *n.* Armreif, *der*

**banish** /'bænɪʃ/ *v.t.* verbannen (**from** aus)

**banister** /'bænɪstə(r)/ *n.*
[Treppen]geländer, *das*

**banjo** /'bændʒəʊ/ *n., pl.* **~s** *or* **~es** Banjo,
*das*

**bank¹** /bæŋk/ *n.* (a) (slope) Böschung, *die*
(b) (of river) Ufer, *das*

**bank²** 1 *n.* (Finance) Bank, *die*
2 *v.i.* **~ at/with** ...: ein Konto haben bei ...;
**~ on sth.** (fig.) auf etw. (Akk.) zählen
3 *v.t.* zur Bank bringen

**bank: ~ account** *n.* Bankkonto, *das;*
**~ balance** *n.* Kontostand, *der;* **~ book**
*n.* Sparbuch, *das;* **~ card** *n.* Scheckkarte,
*die;* **~ charges** *n. pl.*
Kontoführungskosten *Pl.;* **~ clerk** *n.*
Bankangestellte, *der/die;* **~ draft** *n.*
Bankakzept, *das*

**'banker** *n.* Bankier, *der*

**banker's: ~ card ▶** BANK CARD; **~ draft**
▶ BANK DRAFT; **~ 'order** *n.*
Bankanweisung, *die*

**bank 'holiday** *n.* (Brit.) Feiertag, *der*

**'banking** *n.* Bankwesen, *das*

**bank: ~ loan** *n.* Bankdarlehen, *das;* take
out a **~ loan** bei einer Bank einen Kredit
*od.* ein Darlehen aufnehmen; **~ manager**
*n.* Zweigstellenleiter/-leiterin [einer/der
Bank]; **~note** *n.* Banknote, *die*

**bankrupt** /'bæŋkrʌpt/ 1 *n.* Bankrotteur,
*der*
2 *adj.* **go ~:** Bankrott machen
3 *v.t.* Bankrott machen

**bankruptcy** /'bæŋkrʌptsɪ/ *n.* Konkurs,
*der;* Bankrott, *der*

**'bank statement** *n.* Kontoauszug, *der*

**banner** /'bænə(r)/ *n.* Banner, *das;* (on two
poles) Spruchband, *das*

**banns** /bænz/ *n. pl.* Aufgebot, *das*

**banquet** /'bæŋkwɪt/ *n.* Bankett, *das*

**bap** /bæp/ *n.* ≈ Brötchen, *das*

**baptism** /'bæptɪzm/ *n.* Taufe, *die*

**Baptist** /'bæptɪst/ *n.* Baptist, *der*/Baptistin,
*die*

**baptize** /bæp'taɪz/ *v.t.* taufen

**bar** /bɑː(r)/ 1 *n.* (a) Stange, *die;* (shorter,
thinner also) Stab, *der;* (of cage, prison)
Gitterstab, *der;* **a ~ of soap** ein Stück Seife;
**a ~ of chocolate** eine Tafel Schokolade
(b) (for refreshment) Bar, *die;* (counter) Theke,
*die*
2 *v.t.,* **-rr-:** (a) (fasten) verriegeln
(b) **~ sb.'s way** jmdm. den Weg versperren
(c) (prohibit, hinder) verbieten; **~ sb. from**
doing sth. jmdn. daran hindern, etw. zu tun
3 *prep.* abgesehen von; **~ none** ohne
Einschränkung

**barb** /bɑːb/ *n.* Widerhaken, *der*

**barbarian** /bɑː'beərɪən/ *n.* Barbar, *der*

**barbaric** /bɑː'bærɪk/ *adj.* barbarisch

**barbarity** /bɑː'bærɪtɪ/ *n.* Grausamkeit, *die*

**barbecue** /'bɑːbɪkjuː/ 1 *n.* (a) (party)
Grillparty, *die*
(b) (food) Grillgericht, *das;* **~ sauce**
Grillsoße, *die;* Barbecuesoße, *die*
2 *v.t.* grillen

**barbed wire** /bɑːbd 'waɪə(r)/ *n.*
Stacheldraht, *der*

**barber** /'bɑːbə(r)/ *n.* [Herren]friseur, *der;*
**~'s shop** (Brit.) Friseursalon, *der*

**barbiturate** /bɑː'bɪtjʊrət/ *n.* (Chem.)
Barbiturat, *das*

**bar: ~ chart** *n.* Stabdiagramm, *das;*
**~ code** *n.* Strichcode, *der*

**bare** /beə(r)/ 1 *adj.* nackt; (leafless,
unfurnished) kahl; (empty) leer; äußerst
‹Notwendige›; **do sth. with one's ~ hands**
etw. mit den bloßen Händen tun
2 *v.t.* entblößen ‹Kopf, Arm, Bein›; blecken
‹Zähne›

**bare: ~faced** /'beəfeɪst/ *adj.* (fig.)
unverhüllt; **~foot** 1 *adj.* barfüßig; 2 *adv.*
barfuß

**barely** /'beəlɪ/ *adv.* kaum; knapp
‹vermeiden, entkommen›

**bargain** /'bɑːgɪn/ 1 *n.* (a) (agreement)
Abmachung, *die;* **into the ~:** darüber hinaus
(b) (thing offered cheap) günstiges Angebot;
(thing acquired cheaply) guter Kauf
2 *v.i.* (a) (discuss) handeln
(b) **~ for** *or* on sth. (expect sth.) mit etw.
rechnen

**bargain: ~ 'basement** *n.* Untergeschoss
mit Sonderangeboten; **~ hunter** *n.*
Schnäppchenjäger, *der*/-jägerin, *die;*
**~ price** *n.* Sonderpreis, *der*

**barge** /bɑːdʒ/ 1 *n.* Kahn, *der*
2 *v.i.* **~ into sb.** jmdn. anrempeln; **~ in**
(intrude) hineinplatzen/hereinplatzen (ugs.)

**baritone** /'bærɪtəʊn/ 1 *n.* Bariton, *der*
2 *adj.* Bariton-

**b**

**bark¹** /bɑːk/ n. (of tree) Rinde, die

**bark²** ⟨1⟩ n. (of dog) Bellen, das
⟨2⟩ v.i. bellen; **be ~ing up the wrong tree** auf dem Holzweg sein

**barley** /'bɑːlɪ/ n. Gerste, die

**bar: ~maid** n. (Brit.) Bardame, die; **~man** /'bɑːmən/ n., pl. **~men** /'bɑːmən/ Barmann, der

**barmy** /'bɑːmɪ/ adj. (coll.: crazy) bescheuert (salopp)

**barn** /bɑːn/ n. (Brit.: for grain etc.) Scheune, die; (Amer.: for animals) Stall, der

**barnacle** /'bɑːnəkl/ n. Rankenfüßer, der

**barn: ~ dance** n. ≈ Schottische, der; **~storming** /'bɑːnstɔːmɪŋ/ adj. mitreißend

**barometer** /bə'rɒmɪtə(r)/ n. Barometer, das

**baron** /'bærn/ n. Baron, der; Freiherr, der

**baroness** /'bærənɪs/ n. Baronin, die; Freifrau, die

**baroque** /bə'rɒk/ ⟨1⟩ n. Barock, das
⟨2⟩ adj. barock

**barracks** /'bærəks/ n. pl. Kaserne, die

**barrage** /'bærɑːʒ/ n. (Mil.) Sperrfeuer, das; **a ~ of questions** ein Bombardement von Fragen

**barrel** /'bærl/ n. (a) Fass, das
(b) (of gun) Lauf, der

**barren** /'bærn/ adj. unfruchtbar

**barricade** /bærɪ'keɪd/ ⟨1⟩ n. Barrikade, die
⟨2⟩ v.t. verbarrikadieren

**barrier** /'bærɪə(r)/ n. Barriere, die; (at level crossing etc.) Schranke, die

**barring** /'bɑːrɪŋ/ prep. außer im Falle (+ Gen.)

**barrister** /'bærɪstə(r)/ n. (Brit.) **~[-at-law]** Barrister, der; ≈ [Rechts]anwalt/-anwältin vor höheren Gerichten

**barrow** /'bærəʊ/ n. (a) Karre, die; Karren, der
(b) ▶ WHEELBARROW

**barter** /'bɑːtə(r)/ ⟨1⟩ v.t. [ein]tauschen; **~ sth. for sth.** [else] etw. für od. gegen etw. [anderes] [ein]tauschen
⟨2⟩ v.i. Tauschhandel treiben
⟨3⟩ n. Tauschhandel, der

**base** /beɪs/ ⟨1⟩ n. (a) (of lamp, mountain) Fuß, der; (of cupboard, statue) Sockel, der; (fig.: support) Basis, die
(b) (Mil.) Basis, die; Stützpunkt, der
⟨2⟩ v.t. (a) **be ~d on sth.** sich auf etw. (Akk.) gründen; **~ sth. on sth.** etw. auf etw. (Dat.) aufbauen
(b) in pass. **be ~d in Paris** (permanently) in Paris sitzen; (temporarily) in Paris sein

**base: ~ball** n. Baseball, der; **~line** n. Grundlinie, die

**basement** /'beɪsmənt/ n. Untergeschoss, das; **a ~ flat** eine Kellerwohnung

**'base rate** n. (Finance) Eckzins, der

**bash** /bæʃ/ v.t. [heftig] schlagen

**bashful** /'bæʃfl/ adj. schüchtern

**basic** /'beɪsɪk/ adj. grundlegend; Grund⟨prinzip, -bestandteil, -lohn, -gehalt usw.⟩; Haupt⟨problem, -grund, -sache⟩; **be ~ to sth.** wesentlich für etw. sein

**basically** /'beɪsɪkəlɪ/ adv. im Grunde; grundsätzlich ⟨übereinstimmen⟩; (mainly) hauptsächlich

**basil** /'bæzɪl/ n. Basilikum, das

**basin** /'beɪsn/ n. (a) Becken, das; (wash~) Waschbecken, das; (bowl) Schüssel, die
(b) (of river) Becken, das

**basis** /'beɪsɪs/ n., pl. **bases** /'beɪsiːz/ Basis, die; Grundlage, die

**bask** /bɑːsk/ v.i. sich [wohlig] wärmen

**basket** /'bɑːskɪt/ n. Korb, der

**'basketball** n. Basketball, der

**Basle** /bɑːl/ pr. n. Basel (das)

**bass** /beɪs/ ⟨1⟩ n. (a) Bass, der
(b) (coll.) (double **~**) [Kontra]bass, der; (**~** guitar) Bass, der
⟨2⟩ adj. Bass-

**bass gui'tar** n. Bassgitarre, die

**bassoon** /bə'suːn/ n. Fagott, das

**'bass player** n. Bassist, der/Bassistin, die

**bastard** /'bɑːstəd/ ⟨1⟩ adj. unehelich
⟨2⟩ n. (a) uneheliches Kind
(b) (sl.: disliked person) Schweinehund, der (derb)

**baste** /beɪst/ v.t. [mit Fett] begießen

**bastion** /'bæstɪən/ n. Bastei, die

**bat¹** /bæt/ n. (Zool.) Fledermaus, die

**bat²** ⟨1⟩ n. (Sport) Schlagholz, das; (for table tennis) Schläger, der; **do sth. off one's own ~** (fig.) etw. auf eigene Faust tun
⟨2⟩ v.t., -tt- schlagen

**bat³** v.t. **not ~ an eyelid** nicht mit der Wimper zucken

**batch** /bætʃ/ n. (a) (of loaves) Schub, der
(b) (of people) Gruppe, die; (of books, papers) Stapel, der

**batch: ~ file** n. (Comp.) Stapeldatei, die; **~ 'processing** n. (Comp.) Schub-, Stapelverarbeitung, die

**bated** /'beɪtɪd/ v.t. **with ~ breath** mit angehaltenem Atem

**bath** /bɑːθ/ ⟨1⟩ n., pl. **~s** /bɑːðz/ (a) Bad, das; **have or take a ~:** ein Bad nehmen
(b) (tub) Badewanne, die; **room with ~:** Zimmer mit Bad
(c) usu. in pl. (building) Bad, das
⟨2⟩ v.t. & i. baden

**'bath cubes** n. pl. Badesalz, das

**bathe** /beɪð/ v.t. & i. baden

**bather** /'beɪðə(r)/ n. Badende, der/die

**bathing** /'beɪðɪŋ/ n. Baden, das

**bathing: ~ beach** n. Badestrand, der; **~ costume, ~ suit** ns. Badeanzug, der; **~ trunks** n. pl. Badehose, die

**bath: ~ mat** n. Bademenatte, die; **~robe** n. Bademantel, der; **~room** n. Badezimmer,

*das;* ~ **salts** *n. pl.* Badesalz, *das;*
~ **towel** *n.* Badetuch, *das;* ~**tub** ▶ BATH
1B; ~**water** *n.* Badewasser, *das*

**baton** /'bætn/ *n.* **(a)** (truncheon) Schlagstock,
*der*
**(b)** (Mus.) Taktstock, *der*

**batsman** /'bætsmən/ *n., pl.* **batsmen**
/'bætsmən/ Schlagmann, *der*

**battalion** /bə'tæljən/ *n.* Bataillon, *das*

**batter¹** /'bætə(r)/ *v.t.* (strike) einschlagen
auf (+ *Akk.*)

**batter²** *n.* (Cookery) [Back]teig, *der*

**battery** /'bætərɪ/ *n.* Batterie, *die*

**battery:** ~ **charger** *n.* Batterieladegerät,
*das;* ~ **'chicken** *n.* Batteriehuhn, *das;*
~ **'farming** *n.* Batteriehaltung, *die;*
~ **'hen** *n.* Batteriehuhn, *das;*
~**-operated** *adj.* batteriebetrieben

**battle** /'bætl/ [1] *n.* Schlacht, *die;* (fig.)
Kampf, *der*
[2] *v.i.* kämpfen

**battle:** ~**axe** *n.* (coll.: woman)
Schreckschraube, *die* (ugs.); ~**field,**
~**ground** *ns.* Schlachtfeld, *das*

**battlements** /'bætlmənts/ *n. pl.* Zinnen
*Pl.*

**'battleship** *n.* Schlachtschiff, *das*

**batty** /'bætɪ/ *adj.* (coll.) bekloppt (salopp)

**bauble** /'bɔːbl/ *n.* Flitter, *der*

**baulk** ▶ BALK

**Bavaria** /bə'veərɪə/ *pr. n.* Bayern (*das*)

**Bavarian** /bə'veərɪən/ [1] *adj.* bay[e]risch;
**sb. is** ~: jmd. ist Bayer/Bayerin
[2] *n.* Bayer, *der*/Bayerin, *die*

**bawdy** /'bɔːdɪ/ *adj.* zweideutig; (stronger)
obszön

**bay¹** /beɪ/ *n.* (of sea) Bucht, *die*

**bay²** *n.* **(a)** (space in room) Erker, *der*
**(b)** [parking] ~: Stellplatz, *der*

**bay³** *n.* hold *or* keep sb./sth. at ~: sich
(*Dat.*) jmdn./etw. vom Leib halten

**'bayleaf** *n.* Lorbeerblatt, *das*

**bayonet** /'beɪənɪt/ *n.* Bajonett, *das*

**bayonet:** ~ **fitting** *n.* Bajonettfassung,
*die;* ~ **plug** *n.* Stecker mit
Bajonettverschluss *od.* -fassung; ~ **socket**
*n.* Steckdose mit Bajonettfassung

**bay 'window** *n.* Erkerfenster, *das*

**bazaar** /bə'zɑː(r)/ *n.* Basar, *der*

**BBC** *abbr.* = **British Broadcasting
Corporation** BBC, *die*

**BC** *abbr.* = **before Christ** v.Chr.

**be** /biː/ *v., pres. t.* **I am** /əm, *stressed* æm/, **he
is** /ɪz/, **we are** /ə(r)/, *stressed* ɑː(r)/; *p.t.* **I was**
/wəz, *stressed* wɒz/, **we were** /wə(r)/, *stressed*
wɜː(r)/; *pres.p.* **being** /'biːɪŋ/; *p.p.* **been** /bɪn,
*stressed* biːn/ [1] *copula* **(a)** sein; **she is a
mother/an Italian/a teacher** sie ist Mutter/
Italienerin/Lehrerin; **be sensible!** sei
vernünftig!; **be ill/unwell** krank sein/sich
nicht wohl fühlen; **I am well** es geht mir gut;
**I am hot** mir ist heiß; **I am freezing** mich

friert es; **how are you/is she?** wie gehts
(ugs.)/geht es ihr?; **it is the 5th today** heute
haben wir den Fünften; **who's that?** wer ist
das?; **if I were you** an deiner Stelle; **it's hers**
es ist ihrs
**(b)** (cost) kosten; **how much are the eggs?**
was kosten die Eier?; **two times three is six,
two threes are six** zweimal drei ist *od.* sind
sechs
**(c)** (constitute) bilden
[2] *v.i.* **(a)** (exist) [vorhanden] sein; **there is/
are ...:** es gibt ...; **for the time being**
vorläufig; **be that as it may** wie dem auch
sei
**(b)** (remain) bleiben; **I shan't be a moment** ich
komme sofort; **let it be** lass es sein; **let him/
her be** lass ihn/sie in Ruhe
**(c)** (happen) stattfinden; sein
**(d)** (go, come) **be off with you!** geh/geht!; **I'm
off home** ich gehe jetzt nach Hause; **she's
from Australia** sie stammt *od.* ist aus
Australien
**(e)** (go or come on visit) sein; **have you [ever]
been to London?** bist du schon einmal in
London gewesen?; **has anyone been?** ist
jemand da gewesen?
[3] *v. aux.* **(a)** *forming passive* werden; **the
child was found** das Kind wurde gefunden;
**German is spoken here** hier wird Deutsch
gesprochen
**(b)** *forming continuous tenses, active* **he is
reading** er liest [gerade]; **I am leaving
tomorrow** ich reise morgen [ab]; **the train
was departing when I got there** der Zug fuhr
gerade ab, als ich ankam
**(c)** *forming continuous tenses, passive* **the
house is/was being built** das Haus wird/
wurde [gerade] gebaut
**(d)** *expr. arrangement, obligation* **be to**
sollen; **I am to go/to inform you** ich soll
gehen/Sie unterrichten
**(e)** *expr. destiny* **they were never to meet
again** sie sollten sich nie wieder treffen
**(f)** *expr. condition* **if I were to tell you that
...:** wenn ich dir sagen würde, dass ...
[4] **bride-/husband-to-be** zukünftige Braut/
zukünftiger Ehemann

**beach** /biːtʃ/ *n.* Strand, *der;* **on the** ~: am
Strand; ~ **hat/holiday/shoe** Strandhut/
-urlaub/-schuh, *der*

**beach:** ~**ball** *n.* Wasserball, *der;* ~**wear**
*n.* Strandkleidung, *die*

**beacon** /'biːkn/ *n.* Leuchtfeuer, *das;* (Naut.)
Leuchtbake, *die*

**bead** /biːd/ *n.* Perle, *die;* ~**s** Perlen *Pl.;*
Perlenkette, *die;* ~**s of dew/sweat** Tau-/
Schweißtropfen

**beady** /'biːdɪ/ *adj.* ~ **eyes** Knopfaugen *Pl.*

**beak** /biːk/ *n.* Schnabel, *der*

**beaker** /'biːkə(r)/ *n.* Becher, *der*

**beam** /biːm/ [1] *n.* **(a)** (timber etc.) Balken,
*der*
**(b)** (ray etc.) [Licht]strahl, *der*
[2] *v.i.* **(a)** (shine) strahlen; glänzen  ⋯⊱

**(b)** (smile) strahlen; ∼ **at sb.** jmdn.
anstrahlen

**bean** /biːn/ n. Bohne, die; **full of** ∼s (fig. coll.)
putzmunter (ugs.)

**bean:** ∼**bag** n. **(a)** mit Bohnen gefülltes
Säckchen zum Spielen; **(b)** (cushion)
Knautschsessel, der; ∼ **curd** n.
Soja[bohnen]quark, der; ∼**pole** n. (lit. or fig.)
Bohnenstange, die; ∼**sprout** n.
Sojabohnenkeim, der

**bear**[1] /beə(r)/ n. Bär, der

**bear**[2] [1] v.t., bore /bɔː(r)/, borne /bɔːn/ **(a)**
tragen; aufweisen ⟨Spuren, Ähnlichkeit⟩;
tragen, führen ⟨Namen, Titel⟩; ∼ **some/little
relation to sth.** einen gewissen/wenig Bezug
zu etw. haben
**(b)** (endure, tolerate) ertragen ⟨Schmerz,
Kummer⟩; with neg. ertragen, aushalten
⟨Schmerz⟩; ausstehen ⟨Geruch, Lärm⟩
**(c)** (be fit for) vertragen; **it will not** ∼ **scrutiny**
es hält einer Überprüfung nicht stand; **it
does not** ∼ **thinking about** daran darf man
gar nicht denken
**(d)** (give birth to) gebären ⟨Kind, Junges⟩
[2] v.i., bore, borne: ∼ **left** ⟨Person:⟩ sich
links halten; **the path** ∼s **to the left** der Weg
führt nach links
■ **bear 'out** v.t. (fig.) bestätigen ⟨Bericht,
Erklärung⟩; ∼ **sb. out** jmdm. Recht geben
■ **'bear with** v.t. Nachsicht haben mit

**bearable** /'beərəbl/ adj. erträglich

**beard** /bɪəd/ n. Bart, der

**'bearded** adj. bärtig. **be** ∼: einen Bart
haben

**'bearer** n. (carrier) Träger, der/Trägerin, die;
(of message, cheque) Überbringer, der/
Überbringerin, die

**'bear hug** n. kräftige Umarmung

**'bearing** n. **(a)** (behaviour) Verhalten, das
**(b)** (relation) Bezug, der; **have some/no** ∼ **on
sth.** relevant/irrelevant für etw. sein
**(c)** (Mech. Engin.) Lager, das
**(d)** (compass ∼) Position, die; **take a compass**
∼: den Kompasskurs feststellen; **get one's**
∼s sich orientieren; (fig.) sich zurechtfinden

**beast** /biːst/ n. Tier, das; (fig.: brutal person)
Bestie, die

**'beastly** adj., adv. (coll.) scheußlich

**beat** /biːt/ [1] v.t., beat, beaten /'biːtn/
schlagen; klopfen ⟨Teppich⟩; (surpass) brechen
⟨Rekord⟩; **hard to** ∼: schwer zu schlagen; **it**
∼s **me how/why ...:** es ist mir ein Rätsel
wie/warum ...; ∼ **time** den Takt schlagen;
∼ **it!** (coll.) hau ab! (ugs.); see also BEATEN 2
[2] v.i., beat, beaten schlagen (on auf + Akk.)
⟨Regen, Hagel:⟩ prasseln (against gegen)
[3] n. **(a)** (stroke, throbbing) Schlagen, das;
(Mus.) (rhythm) Takt, der; (single ∼) Schlag,
der
**(b)** (of policeman) Runde, die
■ **beat 'off** v.t. abwehren ⟨Angriff⟩
■ **beat 'up** v.t. zusammenschlagen ⟨Person⟩

**beaten** /'biːtn/ [1] ▶ BEAT 1, 2
[2] adj. **(a) off the** ∼ **track** weit abgelegen

**(b)** gehämmert ⟨Silber, Gold⟩

**'beating** n. **(a)** ( punishment) **a** ∼: Schläge Pl.;
Prügel Pl.
**(b)** (defeat) Niederlage, die
**(c) take some/a lot of** ∼: nicht leicht zu
übertreffen sein

**'beat-up** adj. (coll.) ramponiert (ugs.)

**beautician** /bjuː'tɪʃn/ n. Kosmetiker, der/
Kosmetikerin, die

**beautiful** /'bjuːtɪfl/ adj. schön;
wunderschön ⟨Augen, Aussicht, Morgen⟩

**beautify** /'bjuːtɪfaɪ/ v.t. verschönern

**beauty** /'bjuːtɪ/ n. Schönheit, die; (beautiful
feature) Schöne, das; **the** ∼ **of it** das Schöne
daran

**beauty:** ∼ **competition,** ∼ **contest**
ns. Schönheitswettbewerb, der; ∼ **parlour**
▶ ∼ SALON; ∼ **queen** n. Schönheitskönigin,
die; ∼ **salon** n. Kosmetiksalon, der;
∼ **spot** n. Schönheitsfleck, der; ( place)
schönes Fleckchen [Erde]; ∼ **treatment**
n. Schönheitsbehandlung, die

**beaver** /'biːvə(r)/ n. Biber, der

**became** ▶ BECOME

**because** /bɪ'kɒz/ [1] conj. weil
[2] adv. ∼ **of** wegen (+ Gen.)

**beckon** /'bekn/ v.t. & i. winken (**to sb.**
jmdm.); (fig.) locken

**become** /bɪ'kʌm/ [1] copula, became
/bɪ'keɪm/, become werden; ∼ **a politician**
Politiker werden; ∼ **a nuisance/rule** zu einer
Plage/zur Regel werden
[2] v.i., became, become werden; **what has**
∼ **of him?** was ist aus ihm geworden?
[3] v.t., became, become (suit) ∼ **sb.** jmdm.
stehen

**becoming** /bɪ'kʌmɪŋ/ adj. **(a)** (fitting)
schicklich (geh.)
**(b)** (flattering) vorteilhaft ⟨Hut, Kleid, Frisur⟩

**bed** /bed/ n. **(a)** (without bedstead) Bett, das;
Lager, das; **in** ∼: im Bett; ∼ **and breakfast**
Zimmer mit Frühstück; **get out of/into** ∼:
aufstehen/ins Bett gehen; **go to** ∼: ins Bett
gehen; **put sb. to** ∼: jmdn. ins Bett bringen;
**make the** ∼: das Bett machen
**(b)** (flat base) Unterlage, die; (of machine) Bett,
das
**(c)** (in garden) Beet, das
**(d)** (of sea, lake) Grund, der; (of river) Bett, das

**'bedclothes** n. pl. Bettzeug, das

**bedding** /'bedɪŋ/ n. Matratze und Bettzeug

**'bedding plant** n. Freilandpflanze, die

**bedlam** /'bedləm/ n., no indef. art. Tumult,
der

**bed:** ∼**linen** n. Bettwäsche, die; ∼**pan** n.
Bettpfanne, die

**bedraggled** /bɪ'drægld/ adj. (soaked)
durchnässt; (with mud) verdreckt

**bed:** ∼**ridden** adj. bettlägerig; ∼**room** n.
Schlafzimmer, das; ∼ **set'tee** n. Bettcouch,
die; ∼**side** n. Seite des Bettes, die; ∼**side
table/lamp** Nachttisch, der/Nachttischlampe,
die; ∼**sit,** ∼'**sitter** ns. (coll.)

Wohnschlafzimmer, *das;* ~**spread** *n.*
Tagesdecke, *die;* ~**stead** *n.* Bettgestell,
*das;* ~**time** *n.* Schlafenszeit, *die;* **at** ~**time**
vor dem Zubettgehen; **a** ~**time story** eine
Gutenachtgeschichte; ~**-wetting** *n.*
Bettnässen, *das*

**bee** /biː/ *n.* Biene, *die*

**beech** /biːtʃ/ *n.* Buche, *die*

**beef** /biːf/ ⓵ *n.* **(a)** Rindfleisch, *das*
**(b)** (coll.: muscles) Muskeln *Pl.*
⓶ *v.t.* ~ **up** stärken

**beef:** ~**burger** *n.* Beefburger, *der;*
~**cake** *n.* (Amer. coll.) Muskeln *Pl.;* Bizeps,
*der* (ugs.)

**bee:** ~**hive** *n.* Bienenstock, *der;*
~**-keeper** *n.* Imker, *der*/Imkerin, *die;*
~**-keeping** *n.* Imkerei, *die;* ~**line** *n.*
**make a** ~**line for sth.**/**sb.** schnurstracks auf
etw./jmdn. zustürzen

**been** ▶ BE

**beep** /biːp/ ⓵ *n.* Piepton, *der;* (of car horn)
Tuten, *das*
⓶ *v.i.* piepen; ⟨Signalhorn:⟩ hupen
⓷ *v.t.* (esp. Amer.) ▶ BLEEP 3

**beeper** /ˈbiːpə(r)/ *n.* Piepser, *der*

**beer** /bɪə(r)/ *n.* Bier, *das*

**beer:** ~ **barrel** *n.* Bierfass, *das;* ~ **belly**
*n.* (coll.) Bierbauch, *der* (ugs.); ~ **bottle** *n.*
Bierflasche, *die;* ~ **can** *n.* Bierdose, *die;*
~ **cellar** *n.* Bierkeller, *der;* ~ **drinker** *n.*
Biertrinker, *der;* ~ **garden** *n.* Biergarten,
*der;* ~ **glass** *n.* Bierglas, *das;* ~ **mat** *n.*
Bierdeckel, *der;* Bieruntersetzer, *der;*
~ **mug** *n.* Bierkrug, *der*

**beet** /biːt/ *n.* Rübe, *die*

**beetle** /ˈbiːtl/ *n.* Käfer, *der*

**'beetroot** *n.* rote Beete *od.* Rübe

**before** /bɪˈfɔː(r)/ ⓵ *adv.* **(a)** (of time) vorher;
(already) schon; **the day** ~: am Tag zuvor;
**never** ~: noch nie
**(b)** (ahead in position) vor[aus]
⓶ *prep.* (of time; position) vor (+ *Dat.*);
(direction) vor (+ *Akk.*); **the day** ~ **yesterday**
vorgestern; ~ **now**/**then** früher/vorher;
~ **Christ** vor Christus; ~ **leaving, he phoned**
bevor er wegging, rief er an
⓷ *conj.* bevor

**be'forehand** *adv.* vorher; (in anticipation) im
Voraus

**befriend** /bɪˈfrend/ *v.t.* **(a)** (act as a friend to)
sich anfreunden mit
**(b)** (help) sich annehmen (+ *Gen.*)

**beg** /beg/ ⓵ *v.t.,* **-gg-: (a)** betteln um
**(b)** (ask earnestly for) ~ **sth.** um etw. bitten
⓶ *v.i.,* **-gg-** betteln (**for** um)

**began** ▶ BEGIN

**beggar** /ˈbegə(r)/ *n.* **(a)** Bettler, *der*/
Bettlerin, *die*
**(b)** (coll.) **poor** ~: armer Teufel

**begin** /bɪˈgɪn/ ⓵ *v.t.,* **-nn-,** began /bɪˈgæn/,
begun /bɪˈgʌn/ ~ **sth.** [mit] etw. beginnen;
~ **doing** *or* **to do sth.** anfangen *od.*
beginnen, etw. zu tun

⓶ *v.i.,* **-nn-,** began, begun anfangen;
~ [up]on **sth.** etw. anfangen

**be'ginner** *n.* Anfänger, *der*/Anfängerin, *die*

**be'ginning** *n.* Anfang, *der;* **at** *or* **in the** ~:
am Anfang; **at the** ~ **of February**/**the month**
Anfang Februar/des Monats; **from the** ~:
von Anfang an

**begrudge** /bɪˈgrʌdʒ/ *v.t.* ~ **sb.** **sth.** jmdm.
etw. missgönnen; ~ **doing sth.** etw. ungern
tun

**begun** ▶ BEGIN

**behalf** /bɪˈhɑːf/ *n.* **on** *or* (Amer.) **in** ~ **of sb.**/
**sth.** für jmdn./etw.; (more formally) im Namen
von jmdm./etw.

**behave** /bɪˈheɪv/ ⓵ *v.i.* sich verhalten;
sich benehmen; **well-**/**ill-** *or* **badly** ~**d** brav/
ungezogen
⓶ *v. refl.* ~ **oneself** sich benehmen

**behaviour** /bɪˈheɪvjə(r)/ *n.* Verhalten, *das*

**behead** /bɪˈhed/ *v.t.* enthaupten

**behind** /bɪˈhaɪnd/ ⓵ *adv.* hinten; (further
back) **be miles** ~: kilometerweit
zurückliegen; **stay** ~: dableiben; **leave sb.**/
**sth.** ~: jmdn./etw. zurücklassen; **fall** ~:
zurückbleiben; (fig.) in Rückstand geraten;
**be**/**get** ~ **with one's payments**/**rent** mit
seinen Zahlungen/der Miete im Rückstand
sein/in Rückstand geraten
⓶ *prep.* **(a)** hinter (+ *Dat.*); **one** ~ **the other**
hintereinander
**(b)** (towards rear of) hinter (+ *Akk.*)

**beige** /beɪʒ/ ⓵ *n.* Beige, *das*
⓶ *adj.* beige

**being** /ˈbiːɪŋ/ *n.* **(a)** (existence) Dasein, *das;*
**in** ~: bestehend; **come into** ~: entstehen
**(b)** (person etc.) Wesen, *das*

**belated** /bɪˈleɪtɪd/ *adj.,* **be'latedly** *adv.*
verspätet

**belch** /beltʃ/ ⓵ *v.i.* heftig aufstoßen;
rülpsen (ugs.)
⓶ *n.* Rülpser, *der* (ugs.)

**beleaguer** /bɪˈliːgə(r)/ *v.t.* (lit. or fig.)
belagern

**belfry** /ˈbelfrɪ/ *n.* Glockenturm, *der*

**Belgian** /ˈbeldʒən/ ⓵ *adj.* belgisch; **sb. is**
~: jmd. ist Belgier/Belgierin
⓶ *n.* Belgier, *der*/Belgierin, *die*

**Belgium** /ˈbeldʒəm/ *pr. n.* Belgien (*das*)

**belie** /bɪˈlaɪ/ *v.t.,* **belying** /bɪˈlaɪɪŋ/
hinwegtäuschen über ⟨Tatsachen, wahren
Zustand⟩; nicht erfüllen ⟨Versprechen⟩; nicht
entsprechen ⟨Vorstellung (Dat.)⟩

**belief** /bɪˈliːf/ *n.* **(a)** Glaube, *der* (**in** an
+ *Akk.*); **in the** ~ **that ...**: in der
Überzeugung, dass ...
**(b)** (Relig.) Glaube[n], *der*

**believable** /bɪˈliːvəbl/ *adj.* glaubhaft

**believe** /bɪˈliːv/ ⓵ *v.i.* glauben (**in** an
+ *Dat.*); (have faith) glauben (**in** an + *Akk.*)
⟨Gott, Himmel usw.⟩; **I** ~ **so**/**not** ich glaube
schon/nicht   ···⫶·

2 *v.t.* glauben; ~ sb. jmdm. glauben; I don't ~ you das glaube ich dir nicht; make ~ that ...: so tun, als ob ...

**believer** /brˈliːvə(r)/ *n.* (a) Gläubige, *der/die*
(b) be a great *or* firm ~ in sth. viel von etw. halten

**Belisha beacon** /bəliːʃə ˈbiːkn/ *n.* (Brit.) *gelbes Blinklicht an Zebrastreifen*

**belittle** /brˈlɪtl/ *v.t.* herabsetzen

**bell** /bel/ *n.* Glocke, *die;* (door~) Klingel, *die*

**belligerent** /brˈlɪdʒərənt/ *adj.* Krieg führend ⟨Nation⟩; streitlustig ⟨Person⟩

**bellow** /ˈbeləʊ/ 1 *v.i.* brüllen
2 *v.t.* ~ [out] brüllen ⟨Befehl⟩

**bellows** /ˈbeləʊz/ *n. pl.* Blasebalg, *der*

**bell:** ~**-ringer** *n.* Glöckner, *der;* ~**-ringing** *n.* Glockenläuten, *das*

**belly** /ˈbelɪ/ *n.* Bauch, *der*

**belly:** ~**ache** *n.* Bauchschmerzen *Pl.;* ~ **button** *n.* (coll.) Bauchnabel, *der;* ~ **dance** *n.* Bauchtanz, *der*

**belong** /brˈlɒŋ/ *v.i.* ~ to sb./sth. jmdm./zu etw. gehören; ~ to a club einem Verein angehören; where does this ~? wo gehört das hin?

**be'longings** *n. pl.* Habe, *die;* Sachen *Pl.;* personal ~: persönlicher Besitz; persönliches Eigentum

**beloved** /brˈlʌvɪd/ 1 *adj.* geliebt
2 *n.* Geliebte, *der/die*

**below** /brˈləʊ/ 1 *adv.* (a) (position) unten; (lower down) darunter; from ~: von unten [herauf]
(b) (direction) nach unten; hinunter
2 *prep.* unter (*position:* + *Dat.; direction:* + *Akk.*)

**belt** /belt/ *n.* Gürtel, *der;* (for tools, weapons, ammunition) Gurt, *der;* (of trees) Streifen, *der*
■ **belt along** *v.i.* (coll.) rasen (ugs.)
■ **belt 'up** *v.i.* (Brit. coll.) die Klappe halten (salopp)

**bemused** /brˈmjuːzd/ *adj.* verwirrt

**bench** /bentʃ/ *n.* Bank, *die;* (work table) Werkbank, *die*

**bench:** ~**mark** *n.* Höhenmarke, *die;* (fig.) Maßstab, *der;* Fixpunkt, *der;* ~**marking** *n.* Benchmarking, *das* (fachspr.); Leistungsvergleich, *der;*

**bend** /bend/ 1 *n.* Beuge, *die;* (in road) Kurve, *die*
2 *v.t.,* bent /bent/ biegen; beugen ⟨Arm, Knie⟩; anwinkeln ⟨Bein⟩
3 *v.i.,* bent sich biegen; (bow) sich bücken
■ **bend 'down** *v.i.* sich bücken
■ **bend 'over** *v.i.* sich nach vorn beugen

**beneath** /brˈniːθ/ *prep.* (a) (unworthy of) ~ sb., ~ sb.'s dignity unter jmds. Würde (*Dat.*)
(b) (arch./literary: under) unter (+ *Dat.*)

**benefactor** /ˈbenɪfæktə(r)/ *n.* Wohltäter, *der;* (patron) Gönner, *der*

**beneficial** /benɪˈfɪʃl/ *adj.* nützlich; vorteilhaft ⟨Einfluss⟩

**benefit** /ˈbenɪfɪt/ 1 *n.* (a) Vorteil, *der;* be of ~ to sb./sth. jmdm./einer Sache von Nutzen sein; have the ~ of den Vorteil (+ *Gen.*) haben; with the ~ of mit Hilfe (+ *Gen.*); for sb.'s ~: in jmds. Interesse (*Dat.*)
(b) (allowance) Beihilfe, *die;* unemployment ~: Arbeitslosenunterstützung, *die*
2 *v.t.* nützen (+ *Dat.*)
3 *v.i.* ~ by/from sth. von etw. profitieren

**benevolent** /brˈnevələnt/ *adj.* (a) gütig
(b) wohltätig ⟨Institution, Verein⟩

**benign** /brˈnaɪn/ *adj.* gütig; (Med.) gutartig

**bent** /bent/ 1 ▶ BEND 2, 3
2 *n.* (liking) Neigung, *die* (for zu)
3 (a) *adj.* krumm
(b) (Brit. sl.: corrupt) link (salopp)

**bequeath** /brˈkwiːð/ *v.t.* ~ sth. to sb. jmdm. etw. hinterlassen

**bequest** /brˈkwest/ *n.* Legat, *das* (to an + *Akk.*)

**bereaved** /brˈriːvd/ *n.* the ~: der/die Hinterbliebene/die Hinterbliebenen

**bereavement** /brˈriːvmənt/ *n.* Trauerfall, *der*

**beret** /ˈbereɪ/ *n.* Baskenmütze, *die*

**Berlin** /bɜːˈlɪn/ *pr. n.* Berlin (*das*)

**Berne** /bɜːn/ *pr. n.* Bern (*das*)

**berry** /ˈberɪ/ *n.* Beere, *die*

**berserk** /bəˈsɜːk/ *adj.* rasend; go ~: durchdrehen (ugs.)

**berth** /bɜːθ/ *n.* (for ship) Liegeplatz, *der;* (sleeping place) (in ship) Koje, *die;* (in train) Schlafwagenbett, *das*

**beside** /brˈsaɪd/ *prep.* (a) neben (+ *Dat.*); ~ the sea/lake am Meer/See
(b) be ~ the point nichts damit zu tun haben
(c) ~ oneself außer sich

**besides** /brˈsaɪdz/ 1 *adv.* außerdem
2 *prep.* außer

**besiege** /brˈsiːdʒ/ *v.t.* belagern

**besotted** /brˈsɒtɪd/ *adj.* be ~ by *or* with sb. in jmdn. vernarrt sein

**bespectacled** /brˈspektəkld/ *adj.* bebrillt

**best** /best/ 1 *adj.* best...; the ~ part of an hour fast eine ganze Stunde
2 *adv.* am besten
3 *n.* the ~: der/die/das Beste; do one's ~: sein Bestes tun; make the ~ of it das Beste daraus machen; at ~: bestenfalls

**best:** ~**-before date** *n.* Mindesthaltbarkeitsdatum, *das;* ~ 'friend *n.* bester Freund/beste Freundin; be ~ friends with sb. sehr gut mit jmdm. befreundet sein; ~ 'man *n.* Trauzeuge, *der* (des Bräutigams); ~ 'seller *n.* Bestseller, *der;* (author) Bestsellerautor, *der;* ~**-selling** *attrib. adj.* meistverkauft ⟨Schallplatte⟩; ~**-selling book/novel** Bestseller, *der;* a ~**-selling author/novelist** ein Bestsellerautor

**bet** /bet/ 1 *v.t. & i.,* -tt-, ~ *or* ~ted wetten; I ~ him £10 ich habe mit ihm um 10 Pfund gewettet; ~ on sth. auf etw. (*Akk.*) setzen

2 *n.* Wette, *die;* (fig. coll.) Tipp, *der*
**beta-blocker** /'bi:təblɒkə(r)/ *n.* (Med.)
Beta[rezeptoren]blocker, *der*
**betray** /bɪ'treɪ/ *v.t.* verraten (**to** an + *Akk.*)
**betrayal** /bɪ'treɪəl/ *n.* Verrat, *der*
**better** /'betə(r)/ 1 *adj.* besser; ∼ **and** ∼:
immer besser; **be much** ∼ (recovered) sich
viel besser fühlen; **get** ∼ (recover) besser
werden; **the** ∼ **part of sth.** der größte Teil
einer Sache (*Gen.*)
2 *adv.* besser; ∼ **'off** (financially) [finanziell]
besser gestellt; **be** ∼ **off than sb.** besser als
jmd. dran sein (ugs.); **be** ∼ **off without sb./
sth.** ohne jmdn./etw. besser dran sein; **I'd**
∼ **be off now** ich gehe jetzt besser
3 *n.* **get the** ∼ **of sb./sth.** jmdn./etw.
unterkriegen (ugs.); **a change for the** ∼: eine
vorteilhafte Veränderung
4 *v.t.* übertreffen
**better-'quality** *attrib. adj.* qualitativ
besser
**'betting shop** *n.* Wettbüro, *das*
**between** /bɪ'twi:n/ 1 *prep.* **(a)** [in] ∼:
zwischen (*position:* + *Dat.; direction:* + *Akk.*)
**(b)** (amongst) unter (+ *Dat.*); ∼ **ourselves,**
∼ **you and me** unter uns (*Dat.*) gesagt
**(c)** ∼ **them/us** (by joint action of) gemeinsam;
∼ **us** we had 40p wir hatten zusammen 40
Pence
2 *adv.* **[in]** ∼: dazwischen; (in time)
zwischendurch
**beverage** /'bevərɪdʒ/ *n.* Getränk, *das*
**beware** /bɪ'weə(r)/ *v.t. & i.; only in imper.
and inf.* ∼ **[of] sb./sth.** sich vor jmdm./etw.
in Acht nehmen; ∼ **of doing sth.** sich davor
hüten, etw. zu tun; **'**∼ **of the dog'** „Vorsicht,
bissiger Hund!"
**bewilder** /bɪ'wɪldə(r)/ *v.t.* verwirren
**be'wildering** *adj.* verwirrend
**be'wilderment** *n.* Verwirrung, *die*
**bewitch** /bɪ'wɪtʃ/ *v.t.* verzaubern; (fig.)
bezaubern
**beyond** /bɪ'jɒnd/ 1 *adv.* **(a)** (in space)
jenseits; (on other side of wall, mountain range,
etc.) dahinter
**(b)** (in time) darüber hinaus
**(c)** (in addition) außerdem
2 *prep.* **(a)** (at far side of) jenseits (+ *Gen.*)
**(b)** (later than) nach
**(c)** (out of reach or comprehension or range) über
... (+ *Akk.*) hinaus
**bias** /'baɪəs/ 1 *n.* Voreingenommenheit, *die*
2 *v.t.,* **-s-** *or* **-ss-** beeinflussen; **be** ∼**ed in
favour of/against sth./sb.** für etw./jmdn.
eingestellt sein/gegen etw./jmdn.
voreingenommen sein
**bib** /bɪb/ *n.* Lätzchen, *das*
**Bible** /'baɪbl/ *n.* Bibel, *die*
**biblical** /'bɪblɪkl/ *adj.* biblisch
**bibliography** /bɪblɪ'ɒgrəfɪ/ *n.*
Bibliographie, *die*
**biceps** /'baɪseps/ *n.* Bizeps, *der*
**bicker** /'bɪkə(r)/ *v.i.* sich zanken

**bicycle** /'baɪsɪkl/ 1 *n.* Fahrrad, *das;*
*attrib.* Fahrrad-
2 *v.i.* Rad fahren
**bicycle:** ∼ **clip** *n.* Hosenklammer, *die;*
∼ **courier** *n.* Fahrradkurier, *der/*
-kurierin, *die;* ∼ **lane** *n.* (reserved for cyclists)
Radfahrstreifen, *der;* (with priority for cyclists)
Schutzstreifen, *der* [für Radfahrer]; ∼ **path**
*n.* [Fahr]radweg, *der*
**bid** /bɪd/ 1 *v.t.* **(a)** -dd-, bid (at auction)
bieten
**(b)** -dd-, bade /bæd, beɪd/ *or* bid, bidden
/'bɪdn/ *or* bid: ∼ **sb. welcome/goodbye**
jmdn. willkommen heißen/sich von jmdm.
verabschieden
2 *v.i.,* -dd-, bid **(a)** werben (**for** um)
**(b)** (at auction) bieten
3 *n.* **(a)** (at auction) Gebot, *das*
**(b)** (attempt) Versuch, *der*
**bidden** ▶ BID 1B
**'bidder** *n.* Bieter, *der*/Bieterin, *die*
**bide** /'baɪd/ *v.t.* ∼ **one's time** den richtigen
Augenblick abwarten
**biennial** /baɪ'enɪəl/ *n.* (Bot.) zweijährige
Pflanze; Bienne, *die* (fachspr.)
**bifocal** /baɪ'fəʊkl/ 1 *adj.* Bifokal-
2 *n. in pl.* Bifokalgläser *Pl.*
**big** /bɪg/ *adj.* groß
**bigamist** /'bɪgəmɪst/ *n.* Bigamist, *der*/
Bigamistin, *die*
**bigamy** /'bɪgəmɪ/ *n.* Bigamie, *die*
**big:** ∼**head** *n.* (coll.) Fatzke, *der* (ugs.
abwertend); ∼**-'headed** *adj.* (coll.)
eingebildet
**bigot** /'bɪgət/ *n.* bornierter Mensch; (Relig.)
bigotter Mensch
**bigoted** /'bɪgətɪd/ *adj.* borniert
**big:** ∼ **'toe** *n.* große Zehe; ∼ **'top** *n.*
Zirkuszelt, *das;* ∼ **'wheel** *n.* (at fair)
Riesenrad, *das*
**bike** /baɪk/ (coll.) 1 *n.* (bicycle) Rad, *das;*
(motor cycle) Maschine, *die*
2 *v.i.* Rad fahren/[mit dem] Motorrad
fahren
**bike:** ∼ **courier,** ∼ **messenger** *ns.* (on
motorbike) Motorradkurier, *der*/-kurierin, *die;*
(on bicycle) Fahrradkurier, *der*/-kurierin, *die;*
∼ **path** (esp. Amer.) ▶ BICYCLE PATH
**bikini** /bɪ'ki:nɪ/ *n.* Bikini, *der*
**bilingual** /baɪ'lɪŋgwəl/ *adj.* zweisprachig
**bilious** /'bɪljəs/ *adj.* (Med.) Gallen-; ∼ **attack**
Gallenanfall, *der*
**bill**[1] /bɪl/ *n.* (of bird) Schnabel, *der*
**bill**[2] *n.* **(a)** (Parl.) Gesetzentwurf, *der*
**(b)** (note of charges) Rechnung, *die;* **could we
have the** ∼ **please?** wir möchten zahlen
**(c)** (poster) '[stick] no ∼s' „[Plakate]
ankleben verboten"
**'billboard** *n.* Reklametafel, *die*
**billet** /'bɪlɪt/ 1 *n.* Quartier, *das*
2 *v.t.* einquartieren (**with, on** bei)
**'billfold** *n.* (Amer.) Brieftasche, *die*

**'billiard ball** n. Billardkugel, *die*

**billiards** /'bɪljədz/ n. Billard[spiel], *das*

**billion** /'bɪljən/ n. **(a)** (thousand million) Milliarde, *die* **(b)** (esp. Brit. dated: million million) Billion, *die*

**billionaire** /bɪljə'neə(r)/ n. (Amer.) Milliardär, *der*

**billy goat** /'bɪlɪgəʊt/ n. Ziegenbock, *der*

**bimbo** /'bɪmbəʊ/ n. (coll. derog.) Puppe, *die* (salopp)

**bin** /bɪn/ n. Behälter, *der;* (for bread) Brotkasten, *der;* (for rubbish) Mülleimer, *der*

**binary** /'baɪnərɪ/ adj. binär

**'bin bag** n. Müllbeutel, *der*

**bind** /baɪnd/ v.t., **bound** /baʊnd/ **(a)** fesseln ⟨Person, Tier⟩; (bandage) wickeln ⟨Glied, Baum⟩; verbinden ⟨Wunde⟩ **(with** mit) **(b)** (fasten together) zusammenbinden **(c)** binden ⟨Buch⟩ **(d) be bound up with sth.** (fig.) eng mit etw. verbunden sein **(e) be bound to do sth.** (required) verpflichtet sein, etw. zu tun; (certain) etw. ganz bestimmt tun; **it is bound to rain** es wird bestimmt regnen

**'binder** n. (for papers) Hefter, *der;* (for magazines) Mappe, *die*

**'binding** [1] adj. bindend ⟨Vertrag, Abkommen⟩ (**on** für) [2] n. (of book) Einband, *der*

**bingo** /'bɪŋgəʊ/ n. Bingo, *das*

**'bin liner** n. Müllbeutel, *der*

**binoculars** /bɪ'nɒkjʊləz/ n. pl. **[pair of]** ∼: Fernglas, *das*

**bio'chemistry** n. Biochemie, *die*

**biodegradable** /baɪəʊdɪ'greɪdəbl/ adj. biologisch abbaubar

**biode'grade** v.i. sich biologisch abbauen

**biographer** /baɪ'ɒgrəfə(r)/ n. Biograph, *der*/Biographin, *die*

**biographical** /baɪə'græfɪkl/ adj. biographisch

**biography** /baɪ'ɒgrəfɪ/ n. Biographie, *die*

**biological** /baɪə'lɒdʒɪkl/ adj. biologisch

**biological:** ∼ **'clock** n. biologische Uhr; ∼ '**warfare** n. biologische Kriegführung; Bakterienkrieg, *der;* ∼ '**waste** n. Bio-Abfall, *der;* Biomüll, *der*

**biologist** /baɪ'ɒlədʒɪst/ n. Biologe, *der*/Biologin, *die*

**biology** /baɪ'ɒlədʒɪ/ n. Biologie, *die*

**biopsy** /'baɪɒpsɪ/ n. Biopsie, *die*

**'biorhythm** n. Biorhythmus, *der*

**'biosphere** n. Biosphäre, *die*

**biotech'nology** n. Biotechnologie, *die*

**birch** /bɜːtʃ/ n. Birke, *die*

**bird** /bɜːd/ n. Vogel, *der*

**bird:** ∼ **bath** n. Vogelbad, *das;* ∼ **cage** n. Vogelkäfig, *der;* ∼**'s-eye 'view** n. Vogelperspektive, *die;* ∼**'s nest** n. Vogelnest, *das;* ∼ **table** n. Futterstelle für

Vögel, ∼**watcher** n. Vogelbeobachter, *der*/-beobachterin, *die;* ∼**-watching** n. das Beobachten von Vögeln

**Biro** ® /'baɪrəʊ/ n., pl. ∼**s** Kugelschreiber, *der;* Kuli, *der* (ugs.)

**birth** /bɜːθ/ n. **(a)** Geburt, *die;* **give** ∼ ⟨Frau:⟩ entbinden; ⟨Tier:⟩ jungen; werfen; **give** ∼ **to a child** ein Kind zur Welt bringen **(b)** (of movement, fashion, etc.) Aufkommen, *das*

**birth:** ∼ **certificate** n. Geburtsurkunde, *die;* ∼ **control** n. Geburtenkontrolle, *die;* ∼**day** n. Geburtstag, *der; attrib.* Geburtstags-

**'birthing pool** n. Gebärwanne, *die*

**birth:** ∼**mark** n. Muttermal, *das;* ∼**place** n. Geburtsort, *der;* ∼ **rate** n. Geburtenrate, *die*

**biscuit** /'bɪskɪt/ n. (Brit.) Keks, *der*

**bisect** /baɪ'sekt/ v.t. halbieren

**bisexual** /baɪ'seksjʊəl/ [1] adj. bisexuell [2] n. Bisexuelle, *der*/*die*

**bishop** /'bɪʃəp/ n. **(a)** (Eccl.) Bischof, *der* **(b)** (Chess) Läufer, *der*

**bit¹** /bɪt/ n. **(a)** (for horse) Gebiss, *das* **(b)** (of drill) [Bohr]einsatz, *der*

**bit²** n. (piece) Stück, *das;* **not a** or **one** ∼ (not at all) überhaupt nicht; **a** ∼ **tired/too early** ein bisschen müde/zu früh; **be a** ∼ **of a coward/ bully** ein ziemlicher Feigling sein/den starken Mann markieren (ugs.)

**bit³** n. (Comp.) Bit, *das*

**bit⁴** ▶ BITE 1, 2

**bitch** /bɪtʃ/ n. **(a)** (dog) Hündin, *die* **(b)** (sl. derog.: woman) Miststück, *das* (derb)

**bitchy** /'bɪtʃɪ/ adj. (coll.) gemein; gehässig

**bite** /baɪt/ [1] v.t., **bit** /bɪt/, **bitten** /'bɪtn/ beißen; ⟨Moskito usw.:⟩ stechen [2] v.i., **bit**, **bitten** beißen/stechen; (take bait) anbeißen [3] n. Biss, *der;* (piece) Bissen, *der;* (wound) Bisswunde, *die;* (by mosquito etc.) Stich, *der* ▪ **bite 'off** v.t. abbeißen

**'bite-size** adj. mundgerecht

**biting** /'baɪtɪŋ/ adj. beißend

**bitten** ▶ BITE 1, 2

**bitter** /'bɪtə(r)/ adj. bitter

**'bitterly** adv. bitterlich ⟨weinen, sich beschweren⟩; ∼ **cold** bitterkalt

**'bitterness** n. Bitterkeit, *die*

**bizarre** /bɪ'zɑː(r)/ adj. bizarr

**black** /blæk/ [1] adj. **(a)** schwarz; ∼ **and blue** (fig.) grün und blau; **in** ∼ **and white** (fig.) schwarz auf weiß; ∼ **and white film** Schwarzweißfilm, *der;* **in the** ∼ (in credit) in den schwarzen Zahlen **(b)** B∼ (dark-skinned) schwarz [2] n. **(a)** Schwarz, *das* **(b)** B∼ (person) Schwarze, *der*/*die* [3] v.t. bestreiken ⟨Betrieb⟩; boykottieren ⟨Arbeit⟩ ▪ **black 'out** [1] v.t. verdunkeln [2] v.i. das Bewusstsein verlieren

**black:** ~**berry** /'blækbərɪ/ *n.* Brombeere,
*die;* ~**bird** *n.* Amsel, *die;* ~**board** *n.*
[Wand]tafel, *die;* ~ '**box** *n.* (flight recorder)
Flugschreiber, *der;* ~'**currant** *n.* schwarze
Johannisbeere

**blacken** /'blækn/ *v.t.* schwärzen;
verfinstern ⟨*Himmel*⟩

**black:** ~ '**eye** *n.* blaues Auge;
**B**~ '**Forest** *pr. n.* Schwarzwald, *der;*
~ '**hole** *n.* (Astron.) schwarzes Loch; ~ '**ice**
*n.* Glatteis, *das;* ~**leg** *n.* (Brit.)
Streikbrecher, *der/*-brecherin, *die;* ~ **list** *n.*
schwarze Liste; ~**list** *v.t.* auf die schwarze
Liste setzen; ~**mail** [1] *v.t.* erpressen; [2] *n.*
Erpressung, *die;* ~ **market** *n.* schwarzer
Markt

'**blackness** *n.* Schwärze, *die;* (darkness)
Finsternis, *die*

**black:** ~**out** *n.* (a) Verdunkelung, *die;*
(Theatre, Radio) Blackout, *der;* (b) (Med.) **have
a** ~**out** das Bewusstsein verlieren;
~ '**pudding** *n.* Blutwurst, *die;* **B**~ '**Sea**
*pr. n.* Schwarze Meer, *das;* ~**smith** *n.*
Schmied, *der;* ~ **spot** *n.* Gefahrenstelle, *die*

**bladder** /'blædə(r)/ *n.* Blase, *die*

**blade** /bleɪd/ *n.* (a) (of sword, knife, razor, etc.)
Klinge, *die;* (of saw, oar, propeller) Blatt, *das*
(b) (of grass) Spreite, *die*

**Blairite** /'bleəraɪt/ [1] *adj.* blairsch;
Blairsch
[2] *n.* Blair-Anhänger, *der/*-Anhängerin, *die*

**blame** /bleɪm/ [1] *v.t.* ~ **sb.** [**for sth.**] jmdm.
die Schuld [an etw. (*Dat.*)] geben; **be to**
~ [**for sth.**] an etw. (*Dat.*) schuld sein;
~ **sth.** [**for sth.**] etw. [für etw.]
verantwortlich machen
[2] *n.* Schuld, *die*

'**blameless** *adj.* untadelig

**blancmange** /blə'mɒnʒ/ *n.* Flammeri, *der*

**bland** /blænd/ *adj.* mild; (suave) verbindlich

**blank** /blæŋk/ [1] *adj.* (a) leer; kahl ⟨*Wand,
Fläche*⟩
(b) (empty) frei
[2] *n.* (a) (space) Lücke, *die*
(b) (cartridge) Platzpatrone, *die*
(c) **draw a** ~: kein Glück haben

**blank 'cheque** *n.* Blankoscheck, *der;* (fig.)
Blankovollmacht, *die*

**blanket** /'blæŋkɪt/ *n.* Decke, *die;* **wet** '~
(fig.) Trauerkloß, *der* (ugs.)

**blare** /'bleə(r)/ [1] *v.i.* ⟨*Lautsprecher:*⟩
plärren; ⟨*Trompete:*⟩ schmettern
[2] *v.t.* ~ [**out**] [hinaus]plärren ⟨*Worte*⟩;
[hinaus]schmettern ⟨*Melodie*⟩

**blasé** /'blɑːzeɪ/ *adj.* blasiert

**blasphemous** /'blæsfəməs/ *adj.* lästerlich

**blasphemy** /'blæsfəmɪ/ *n.* Blasphemie, *die*

**blast** /blɑːst/ [1] *n.* (a) **a** ~ [**of wind**] ein
Windstoß
(b) (of horn) Tuten, *das*
[2] *v.t.* (blow up) sprengen
[3] *int.* verdammt
■ **blast 'off** *v.i.* abheben

**blasted** /'blɑːstɪd/ *adj.* (damned) verdammt
(salopp)

'**blast-off** *n.* Abheben, *das*

**blatant** /'bleɪtənt/ *adj.* (a) (flagrant) eklatant
(b) (unashamed) unverhohlen; unverfroren
⟨*Lüge*⟩

'**blatantly** *adv.* ▶ BLATANT: eklatant;
unverhohlen

**blaze** /bleɪz/ [1] *n.* Feuer, *das*
[2] *v.i.* brennen; lodern (geh.)

**blazer** /'bleɪzə(r)/ *n.* Blazer, *der*

**bleach** /bliːtʃ/ [1] *v.t.* bleichen
[2] *n.* Bleichmittel, *das*

**bleak** /'bliːk/ *adj.* (a) öde ⟨*Landschaft usw.*⟩
(b) (unpromising) düster

**bleat** /bliːt/ *v.i.* ⟨*Schaf:*⟩ blöken; ⟨*Ziege:*⟩
meckern

**bled** ▶ BLEED

**bleed** /bliːd/ *v.i.,* **bled** /bled/ bluten

**bleep** /bliːp/ [1] *n.* Piepen, *das*
[2] *v.i.* ⟨*Geigerzähler, Funksignal:*⟩ piepen
[3] *v.t.* ~ **sb.** jmdn. über seinen
Kleinempfänger *od.* (ugs.) Piepser rufen

**bleeper** /'bliːpə(r)/ *n.* Kleinempfänger, *der;*
Piepser, *der* (ugs.)

**blemish** /'blemɪʃ/ *n.* Fleck, *der*

**blend** /blend/ [1] *v.t.* mischen
[2] *v.i.* sich mischen lassen
[3] *n.* Mischung, *die*

'**blender** *n.* Mixer, *der*

**bless** /bles/ *v.t.* segnen; ~ **you!** (after sb.
sneezes) Gesundheit!

**blessed** /'blesɪd/ *adj.* (a) (revered) heilig
(b) (cursed) verdammt (salopp)

'**blessing** *n.* Segen, *der*

**blew** ▶ BLOW[1]

**blight** /blaɪt/ *n.* (fig.) Fluch, *der*

**blind** /blaɪnd/ [1] *adj.* blind; ~ **in one eye**
auf einem Auge blind
[2] *adv.* blindlings
[3] *n.* (a) Jalousie, *die;* (made of cloth) Rouleau,
*das;* (of shop) Markise, *die*
(b) *pl.* **the n**~: die Blinden *Pl.*
[4] *v.t.* blenden

**blind:** ~ '**alley** *n.* (lit. or fig.) Sackgasse, *die;*
~ '**corner** *n.* unübersichtliche Ecke;
~ '**date** *n.* Verabredung mit einem/einer
Unbekannten; ~**fold** [1] *v.t.* die Augen
verbinden (+ *Dat.*); [2] *adj.* mit verbundenen
Augen *nachgestellt*

'**blinding** *adj.* blendend; **a** ~ **headache**
rasende Kopfschmerzen *Pl.*

'**blindly** *adv.* [wie] blind; (fig.) blindlings

'**blindness** *n.* Blindheit, *die*

'**blind spot** *n.* (Motor Veh.) toter Winkel; (fig.:
weak spot) schwacher Punkt;

**blink** /blɪŋk/ *v.i.* (a) blinzeln
(b) (shine intermittently) blinken

'**blinkers** *n. pl.* Scheuklappen *Pl.*

**bliss** /blɪs/ *n.* [Glück]seligkeit, *die*

'**blissful** /'blɪsfl/ *adj.* [glück]selig

**blister** /'blɪstə(r)/ [1] *n.* Blase, *die*   ⋯⋗

2 *v.i.* ⟨*Haut:*⟩ Blasen bekommen; ⟨*Anstrich:*⟩ Blasen werfen

**'blister pack** *n.* Klarsichtpackung, *die*

**blizzard** /'blɪzəd/ *n.* Schneesturm, *der*

**bloated** /'bləʊtɪd/ *adj.* (having overeaten) aufgedunsen; **I feel ∼**: ich bin voll (ugs.)

**blob** /blɒb/ *n.* (drop) Tropfen, *der;* (small mass) Klacks, *der* (ugs.)

**block** /blɒk/ 1 *n.* (a) Klotz, *der;* (for chopping on) Hackklotz, *der;* (of concrete or stone, building stone) Block, *der*
(b) (building) [Häuser]block, *der;* **∼ of flats/ offices** Wohnblock, *der*/Bürohaus, *das*
2 *v.t.* versperren ⟨*Tür, Straße, Durchgang, Sicht*⟩; verstopfen ⟨*Pfeife, Abfluss*⟩; verhindern ⟨*Fortschritt*⟩
■ **block 'out** *v.t.* ausschließen ⟨*Licht, Lärm*⟩
■ **block 'up** *v.t.* verstopfen; versperren ⟨*Eingang*⟩

**blockade** /blɒ'keɪd/ 1 *n.* Blockade, *die*
2 *v.t.* blockieren

**blockage** /'blɒkɪdʒ/ *n.* Block, *der;* (of pipe, gutter) Verstopfung, *die*

**block:** ∼ **'booking** *n.* Gruppenbuchung, *die;* ∼**buster** *n.* (a) (bomb) [große] Fliegerbombe; (b) (fig.) Knüller, *der* (ugs.); ∼ **'capital** *n.* Blockbuchstabe, *der;* ∼**head** *n.* Dummkopf, *der;* ∼ **'letters** *pl.* Blockschrift, *die*

**bloke** /bləʊk/ *n.* (Brit. coll.) Typ, *der* (ugs.)

**blonde** /blɒnd/ 1 *adj.* blond
2 *n.* Blondine, *die*

**blood** /blʌd/ *n.* Blut, *das*

**blood:** ∼ **bank** *n.* Blutbank, *die;* ∼**bath** *n.* Blutbad, *das;* ∼ **cell** *n.* Blutkörperchen, *das;* ∼ **clot** *n.* Blutgerinnsel, *das;* ∼ **donor** *n.* Blutspender, *der*/-spenderin, *die;* ∼ **group** *n.* Blutgruppe, *die;* ∼**hound** *n.* Bluthund, *der;* ∼ **plasma** *n.* Blutplasma, *das;* ∼ **poisoning** *n.* Blutvergiftung, *die;* ∼ **pressure** *n.* Blutdruck, *der;* ∼ **sample** *n.* Blutprobe, *die;* ∼**shed** *n.* Blutvergießen, *das;* ∼**shot** *adj.* blutunterlaufen; ∼ **sports** *n. pl.* Hetzjagd, *die;* ∼**stain** *n.* Blutfleck, *der;* ∼**stained** *adj.* blutbefleckt; ∼**stream** *n.* Blutstrom, *der;* ∼ **sugar** *n.* Blutzucker, *der;* ∼ **test** *n.* Blutprobe, *die;* ∼**thirsty** *adj.* blutrünstig; ∼ **transfusion** *n.* Bluttransfusion, *die;* ∼ **vessel** *n.* Blutgefäß, *das*

**'bloody** 1 *adj.* (a) blutig; (running with blood) blutend
(b) (sl.: damned) verdammt (salopp)
2 *adv.* (sl.: damned) verdammt (salopp)

**bloom** /bluːm/ 1 *n.* Blüte, *die;* **be in ∼**: in Blüte stehen
2 *v.i.* blühen

**blossom** /'blɒsəm/ 1 *n.* (flower) Blüte, *die;* (mass) Blütenmeer, *das* (geh.)
2 *v.i.* blühen; ⟨*Mensch:*⟩ aufblühen

**blot** /blɒt/ 1 *n.* (of ink) Tintenklecks, *der;* (stain) Fleck, *der*
2 *v.t.,* **-tt-** ablöschen ⟨*Tinte, Papier*⟩

■ **blot 'out** *v.t.* (fig.) auslöschen

**blotchy** /'blɒtʃɪ/ *adj.* fleckig

**'blotting paper** *n.* Löschpapier, *das*

**blouse** /blaʊz/ *n.* Bluse, *die*

**blow¹** /bləʊ/ 1 *v.i.,* blew /bluː/, blown /bləʊn/ ⟨*Wind:*⟩ wehen; ⟨*Sturm:*⟩ blasen
2 *v.t.,* blew, blown: (a) blasen; ⟨*Wind:*⟩ wehen; machen ⟨*Seifenblase*⟩; ∼ **sb. a kiss** jmdm. eine Kusshand zuwerfen
(b) ∼ **one's nose** sich ⟨*Dat.*⟩ die Nase putzen
(c) ∼ **sth. to pieces** etw. in die Luft sprengen
■ **blow 'out** 1 *v.t.* ausblasen
2 *v.i.* ausgeblasen werden
■ **blow 'over** 1 *v.i.* umgeblasen werden; ⟨*Streit, Sturm:*⟩ sich legen
2 *v.t.* umblasen
■ **blow 'up** 1 *v.t.* (a) (shatter) [in die Luft] sprengen
(b) aufblasen ⟨*Ballon*⟩; aufpumpen ⟨*Reifen*⟩
(c) (coll.: exaggerate) hochspielen
2 *v.i.* (explode) explodieren

**blow²** *n.* (a) Schlag, *der;* (with axe) Hieb, *der;* **come to ∼s** handgreiflich werden
(b) (disaster) [schwerer] Schlag

**blow:** ∼**dry** *v.t.* fönen; ∼**lamp** *n.* Lötlampe, *die*

**blown** ▶ BLOW¹

**blow:** ∼**torch** (Amer.) ▶ ∼LAMP; ∼**up** *n.* (coll.: enlargement) Vergrößerung, *die*

**blubber** /'blʌbə(r)/ *n.* Walspeck, *der*

**blue** /bluː/ 1 *adj.* blau
2 *n.* (a) Blau, *das*
(b) **have the ∼s** deprimiert sein
(c) (Mus.) **the ∼s** der Blues
(d) **out of the ∼**: aus heiterem Himmel

**blue:** ∼**bell** *n.* Glockenblume, *die;* ∼ **'blood** *n.* blaues Blut; ∼**bottle** *n.* Schmeißfliege, *die;* ∼ **'cheese** *n.* Blauschimmelkäse, *der;* Edelpilzkäse, *der;* ∼**collar** *adj.* ∼-collar worker Arbeiter, *der*/Arbeiterin, *die;* ∼**eyed** *adj.* blauäugig; **be ∼-eyed** blaue Augen haben; ∼ **'jeans** *pl.* Blue jeans *Pl.;* ∼ **'moon** *n.* **once in a ∼ moon** alle Jubeljahre (ugs.); ∼**print** *n.* (fig.) Entwurf, *der;* ∼ **tit** *n.* (Ornith.) Blaumeise, *die;* ∼ **'whale** *n.* Blauwal, *der*

**bluff** /blʌf/ 1 *n.* Bluff, *der* (ugs.); **call sb.'s ∼**: es darauf ankommen lassen (ugs.)
2 *v.i. & t.* bluffen (ugs.)

**blunder** /'blʌndə(r)/ 1 *n.* [schwerer] Fehler
2 *v.i.* (a) (make mistake) einen [schweren] Fehler machen
(b) (move blindly) tappen

**blunt** /blʌnt/ 1 *adj.* (a) stumpf
(b) (outspoken) direkt; glatt (ugs.) ⟨*Ablehnung*⟩
2 *v.t.* ∼ [**the edge of**] stumpf machen

**'bluntly** *adv.* direkt; glatt ⟨*ablehnen*⟩

**blur** /blɜː(r)/ 1 *v.t.,* **-rr-**: (a) verwischen
(b) (become indistinct) verschwimmen; **his vision was ∼red** er sah alles verschwommen
2 *n.* (smear) Fleck, *der;* (dim image) verschwommener Fleck

**blurt** /blɜːt/ v.t. ~ **out** herausplatzen mit (ugs.)

**blush** /blʌʃ/ ① v.i. rot werden
② n. Rotwerden, das

**bluster** /'blʌstə(r)/ v.i. sich aufplustern (ugs.)

**blustery** /'blʌstərɪ/ adj. stürmisch

**BO** abbr. (coll.) = **body odour**
Körpergeruch, der

**boar** /bɔː(r)/ n. [wild] ~: Keiler, der

**board** /bɔːd/ ① n. **(a)** Brett, das; (black~)
Tafel, die; (notice~) schwarzes Brett; **above**
~ (fig.) einwandfrei; korrekt
**(b)** (Commerc.) ~ [of directors] Vorstand, der;
(supervisory ~) Aufsichtsrat, der
**(c)** (Naut., Aeronaut.) **on** ~: an Bord
**(d)** ~ **and lodging** Unterkunft und
Verpflegung; **full** ~: Vollpension, die
② v.t. ~ **the ship/plane** an Bord des
Schiffes/Flugzeuges gehen; ~ **the train/bus**
in den Zug/Bus einsteigen
■ **board 'up** v.t. mit Brettern vernageln

**'boarder** n. (Sch.) Internatsschüler, der/
-schülerin, die

**'board game** n. Brettspiel, das

**boarding:** ~ **house** n. Pension, die;
~ **pass** n. Bordkarte, die; ~ **school** n.
Internat, das

**board:** ~ **meeting** n. Vorstandssitzung,
die; ~**room** n. Sitzungssaal, der

**boast** /bəʊst/ v.i. prahlen

**boastful** /'bəʊstfl/ adj. prahlerisch

**boat** /bəʊt/ n. Boot, das

**boat:** ~**house** n. Bootshaus, das; ~ **trip**
n. Bootsfahrt, die

**bob**[1] /bɒb/ v.i., **-bb-:** ~ [up and down] sich
auf und nieder bewegen

**bob**[2] n. (~sled) Bob, der

**bobbin** /'bɒbɪn/ n. Spule, die

**bob:** ~**sled,** ~**sleigh** ns. Bobschlitten,
der

**bodice** /'bɒdɪs/ n. Mieder, das; (part of dress)
Oberteil, das

**bodily** /'bɒdɪlɪ/ adj. körperlich; ~ **needs**
leibliche Bedürfnisse

**body** /'bɒdɪ/ n. **(a)** Körper, der
**(b)** (corpse) Leiche, die
**(c)** (group) Gruppe, die; (with particular function)
Organ, das

**body:** ~ **bag** n. Leichensack, der;
~**building** ① n. Bodybuilding, das;
② adj. ~building food Aufbaukost, die;
~ **clock** ▶ BIOLOGICAL CLOCK; ~**guard** n.
(single) Leibwächter, der; (group) Leibwache,
die; ~ **language** n. Körpersprache, die;
~ **odour** n. Körpergeruch, der;
~ **piercing** n. Piercing, das; ~ **weight**
n. Körpergewicht, das; ~**work** n.
Karosserie, die

**bog** /bɒg/ ① n. Moor, das; (marsh, swamp)
Sumpf, der
② v.t., **-gg-:** be/get ~ged down (fig.) sich
verzettelt haben/sich verzetteln

**boggle** /'bɒgl/ v.i. (coll.) **the mind** ~**s** da
kann man nur [noch] staunen

**bogus** /'bəʊgəs/ adj. falsch

**boil**[1] /bɔɪl/ ① v.i. & t. kochen
② n. **come to/go off the** ~: zu kochen
anfangen/aufhören; **bring to the** ~: zum
Kochen bringen
■ **boil 'down** v.i. ~ **down to sth.** (fig.) auf
etw. hinauslaufen
■ **boil 'over** v.i. überkochen

**boil**[2] n. (Med.) Furunkel, der

**'boiler** n. Kessel, der

**boiler:** ~**room** n. Kesselraum, der;
~ **suit** n. Overall, der

**'boiling point** n. Siedepunkt, der

**boisterous** /'bɔɪstərəs/ adj. ausgelassen

**bold** /bəʊld/ adj. **(a)** (courageous) mutig;
(daring) kühn
**(b)** auffallend ⟨Farbe, Muster⟩

**'boldly** adv. (courageously) mutig; (daringly)
kühn

**Bolivia** /bə'lɪvɪə/ pr. n. Bolivien (das)

**bollard** /'bɒlɑːd/ n. (Brit.) Poller, der

**bollocks** /'bɒləks/ (coarse) ① n. pl. Eier
(derb)
② int. Scheiße

**bolster** /'bəʊlstə(r)/ ① n. (pillow)
Nackenrolle, die
② v.t. (fig.) stärken

**bolt** /bəʊlt/ ① n. **(a)** (on door or window)
Riegel, der; (on gun) Kammerverschluss, der
**(b)** (metal pin) Schraube, die; (without thread)
Bolzen, der
② v.i. davonlaufen; ⟨Pferd:⟩ durchgehen;
⟨Fuchs, Kaninchen:⟩ flüchten
③ v.t. **(a)** verriegeln ⟨Tür, Fenster⟩
**(b)** (fasten with ~s) verschrauben/mit Bolzen
verbinden
**(c)** ~ [down] hinunterschlingen ⟨Essen⟩
④ adv. ~ **upright** kerzengerade

**bomb** /bɒm/ ① n. Bombe, die; ~ **attack**
Bombenanschlag, der
② v.t. bombardieren

**bombard** /bɒm'bɑːd/ v.t. beschießen

**bom'bardment** n. Beschuss, der

**bombastic** /bɒm'bæstɪk/ adj. bombastisch

**bomb:** ~ **blast** n. (blast wave) Druckwelle,
die; (explosion) Bombenexplosion, die;
~ **disposal** n. Räumung von Bomben;
~ **disposal squad** Bombenräumkommando,
das

**bomber** /'bɒmə(r)/ n. (Air Force) Bomber,
der (ugs.)

**bombing** /'bɒmɪŋ/ n. Bombardierung, die

**bomb:** ~ **scare** n. Bombendrohung, die;
~**shell** n. Bombe, die; (fig.) Sensation, die

**bond** /bɒnd/ n. **(a)** Band, das; in pl.
(shackles) Fesseln Pl.
**(b)** (adhesion) Verbindung, die
**(c)** (Commerc.) Anleihe, die

**bone** /bəʊn/ ① n. Knochen, der; (of fish)
Gräte, die      ···⊹

2 *v.t.* den/die Knochen herauslösen aus; entgräten ⟨*Fisch*⟩

**bone:** ~ **'china** *n.* Knochenporzellan, *das;* ~ **'dry** *adj.* knochentrocken (ugs.); ~ **'idle** *adj.* stinkfaul (salopp); ~ **marrow** *n.* (Anat.) Knochenmark, *das;* ~**meal** *n.* Knochenmehl, *das*

**bonfire** /'bɒnfaɪə(r)/ *n.* Freudenfeuer, *das;* (for rubbish) Feuer, *das;* B~ **Night** (Brit.) [Abend des] Guy Fawkes Day ⟨*mit Feuerwerk*⟩

**bonnet** /'bɒnɪt/ *n.* (a) (woman's) Haube, *die;* (child's) Häubchen, *das* (b) (Brit. Motor Veh.) Motorhaube, *die*

**bonus** /'bəʊnəs/ *n.* zusätzliche Leistung; (to shareholders) Bonus, *der;* **Christmas** ~: Weihnachtsgratifikation, *die*

**bony** /'bəʊnɪ/ *adj.* (a) Knochen-; (like bone) knochenartig (b) (skinny) knochendürr (ugs.); spindeldürr

**boo** /buː/ 1 *int.* (to surprise sb.) huh; (expr. disapproval, contempt) buh 2 *n.* Buh, *das* (ugs.) 3 *v.t.* ausbuhen (ugs.) 4 *v.i.* buhen (ugs.)

**boob** /buːb/ (Brit. coll.) *n.* (a) (mistake) Fehler, *der;* Schnitzer, *der* (ugs.) (b) (breast) Titte, *die* (derb)

**booby** /'buːbɪ/ *n.* Trottel, *der* (ugs.)

**booby:** ~ **prize** *n.: Preis für den schlechtesten Teilnehmer an einem Wettbewerb;* ~ **trap** *n.* (a) *Falle, mit der man jmdm. einen Streich spielen will;* (b) (Mil.) versteckte Sprengladung

**book** /bʊk/ 1 *n.* Buch, *das;* (for accounts) Rechnungsbuch, *das;* (for exercises) [Schreib]heft, *das* 2 *v.t.* buchen ⟨*Reise, Flug, Platz* [*im Flugzeug*]⟩; [vor]bestellen ⟨*Eintrittskarte, Tisch, Zimmer, Platz* [*im Theater*]⟩ 3 *v.i.* buchen
▪ **book 'in** 1 *v.i.* sich eintragen 2 *v.t.* eintragen
▪ **book 'up** *v.i. & t.* buchen; **be** ~**ed up** ⟨*Hotel usw.:*⟩ ausgebucht sein

**book:** ~**case** *n.* Bücherschrank, *der;* ~ **club** *n.* Buchklub, *der;* Buchgemeinschaft, *die;* ~**ends** *n. pl.* Buchstützen *Pl.*

**bookie** /'bʊkɪ/ *n.* (coll.) Buchmacher, *der*

**'booking office** *n.* [Fahrkarten]schalter, *der*

**book:** ~**keeper** *n.* Buchhalter, *der*/ -halterin, *die;* ~**keeping** *n.* Buchführung, *die;* Buchhaltung, *die*

**booklet** /'bʊklɪt/ *n.* Broschüre, *die*

**book:** ~**maker** *n.* (in betting) Buchmacher, *der;* ~**mark** 1 *n.* (also Comp.) Lesezeichen, *das;* 2 *v.t.* (Comp.) mit einem Lesezeichen versehen; ~**seller** *n.* Buchhändler, *der*/ -händlerin, *die;* ~**shelf** *n.* Bücherbord, *das;* ~**shop** *n.* Buchhandlung, *die;* ~**stall** *n.* Bücherstand, *der;* ~**store** *n.* (Amer.)

Buchhandlung, *die;* ~ **token** *n.* Büchergutschein, *der;* ~**worm** *n.* Bücherwurm, *der*

**boom¹** /buːm/ *n.* (a) (for camera or microphone) Ausleger, *der* (b) (Naut.) Baum, *der*

**boom²** 1 *v.i.* (a) dröhnen (b) ⟨*Geschäft, Verkauf, Gebiet:*⟩ sich sprunghaft entwickeln 2 *n.* (a) Dröhnen, *das* (b) (in business or economy) Boom, *der*

**boomerang** /'buːməræŋ/ *n.* Bumerang, *der*

**boon** /buːn/ *n.* Segen, *der* (**to** für)

**boor** /bʊər/ *n.* Rüpel, *der*

**boorish** /'bʊərɪʃ/ *adj.* rüpelhaft

**boost** /buːst/ 1 *v.t.* ankurbeln ⟨*Wirtschaft*⟩; in die Höhe treiben ⟨*Preis, Wert*⟩; stärken ⟨*Selbstvertrauen, Moral*⟩ 2 *n.* Auftrieb, *der*

**boot** /buːt/ 1 *n.* (a) Stiefel, *der;* **give sb. the** ~ (fig. coll.) jmdn. rausschmeißen (ugs.) (b) (Brit.: of car) Kofferraum, *der* 2 *v.t.* (a) (coll.: kick) kicken (ugs.) (b) (Comp.) ~ [**up**] booten

**bootable** /'buːtəbl/ *adj.* (Comp.) bootbar ⟨*System*⟩; ~ **disk** Bootdiskette, *die*

**'boot disk** *n.* (Comp.) Bootdiskette, *die*

**booth** /buːð/ *n.* (a) Bude, *die* (b) (telephone ~) Zelle, *die*

**'bootleg** *adj.* (illegally sold/distilled) schwarz verkauft/gebrannt

**booze** /buːz/ (coll.) 1 *v.i.* saufen (derb) 2 *n.* Alkohol, *der*

**'booze-up** *n.* (coll.) Besäufnis, *das* (salopp); **have a** ~: saufen gehen (salopp) (ugs.)

**border** /'bɔːdə(r)/ 1 *n.* (a) Rand, *der;* (of tablecloth, handkerchief) Bordüre, *die* (b) (of country) Grenze, *die* (c) (flower bed) Rabatte, *die* 2 *attrib. adj.* Grenz⟨*stadt, -streit*⟩ 3 *v.t.* (a) (adjoin) [an]grenzen an (+ *Akk.*) (b) (put a ~ to, act as ~ to) umranden; einfassen 4 *v.i.* ~ **on** (a) ▶ 3A (b) (resemble) grenzen an (+ *Akk.*)

**border:** ~ **crossing** *n.* Grenzübergang, *der;* ~**line** 1 *n.* Grenzlinie, *die;* 2 *adj.* be ~line auf der Grenze liegen; **a** ~line case/ candidate ein Grenzfall

**bore¹** /bɔː(r)/ 1 *v.t.* bohren 2 *n.* (of firearm) Kaliber, *das*

**bore²** 1 *n.* (a) it's a real ~: es ist wirklich ärgerlich; **what a** ~! wie ärgerlich! (b) (person) Langweiler, *der* (ugs.) 2 *v.t.* langweilen; **be** ~**d** sich langweilen

**bore³** ▶ BEAR²

**boredom** /'bɔːdəm/ *n.* Langeweile, *die*

**'borehole** *n.* Bohrloch, *das*

**boring** /'bɔːrɪŋ/ *adj.* langweilig

**born¹** /bɔːn/ 1 **be** ~: geboren werden 2 *adj.* geboren; **be a** ~ **orator** der geborene Redner sein

**borne** ▶ BEAR²

**borough** /'bʌrə/ *n.* (town) Stadt, *die;* (village) Gemeinde, *die*

**borrow** /'bɒrəʊ/ *v.t.* leihen (**from** von, bei); (from library) entleihen

'**borrower** *n.* (from bank) Kreditnehmer, *der;* (from library) Entleiher, *der*

**Bosnia** /'bɒznɪə/ *n.* Bosnien (*das*)

**Bosnian** /'bɒznɪən/ ⟨1⟩ *adj.* bosnisch; **sb. is ∼:** jmd. ist Bosnier/Bosnierin
⟨2⟩ *n.* Bosnier, *der*/Bosnierin, *die*

**bosom** /'bʊzəm/ *n.* Brust, *die*

**boss** /bɒs/ (coll.) ⟨1⟩ *n.* Boss, *der* (ugs.); Chef, *der*
⟨2⟩ *v.t.* ∼ [**about** *or* **around**] herumkommandieren (ugs.)

'**bossy** *adj.* (coll.) herrisch

**botanical** /bə'tænɪkl/ *adj.* botanisch

**botanist** /'bɒtənɪst/ *n.* Botaniker, *der*/Botanikerin, *die*

**botany** /'bɒtənɪ/ *n.* Botanik, *die*

**botch** /bɒtʃ/ ⟨1⟩ *v.t.* pfuschen bei (ugs.)
⟨2⟩ *v.i.* pfuschen (ugs.)
■ **botch 'up** *v.t.* (bungle) verpfuschen (ugs.)

**both** /bəʊθ/ ⟨1⟩ *adj.* beide; ∼ [**the**] **brothers** beide Brüder
⟨2⟩ *pron.* beide; ∼ [**of them**] **are dead** beide sind tot; ∼ **of you/them are ...:** ihr seid/sie sind beide ...
⟨3⟩ *adv.* ∼ **A and B** sowohl A als [auch] B; **he and I were** ∼ **there** er und ich waren beide da

**bother** /'bɒðə(r)/ ⟨1⟩ *v.t.* (a) **I can't be** ∼**ed** ich habe keine Lust
(b) (annoy) lästig sein (+ *Dat.*); ⟨*Lärm, Licht:*⟩ stören; ⟨*Schmerz, Zahn:*⟩ zu schaffen machen (+ *Dat.*); **I'm sorry to** ∼ **you, but ...:** es tut mir Leid, wenn ich Sie störe, aber ...
(c) (worry) Sorgen machen (+ *Dat.*); ⟨*Problem, Frage:*⟩ beschäftigen
⟨2⟩ *v.i.* **don't** ∼ **to do it** Sie brauchen es nicht zu tun; **you needn't/shouldn't have** ∼**ed** das wäre nicht nötig gewesen; **don't** ∼! nicht nötig!
⟨3⟩ *n.* (a) (trouble) Ärger, *der*
(b) (effort) Mühe, *die*
⟨4⟩ *int.* (coll.) wie ärgerlich!

**bottle** /'bɒtl/ ⟨1⟩ *n.* Flasche, *die;* **a** ∼ **of beer** eine Flasche Bier
⟨2⟩ *v.t.* (a) ( put into ∼s) in Flaschen [ab]füllen
(b) ∼**d beer** Flaschenbier, *das*
(c) ( preserve in jars) einmachen
■ **bottle 'up** *v.t.* (a) (conceal) in sich (*Dat.*) aufstauen
(b) (trap) einschließen

**bottle:** ∼ **bank** *n.* Altglasbehälter, *der;* ∼**neck** *n.* (fig.) Flaschenhals, *der* (ugs.); ∼**-opener** *n.* Flaschenöffner, *der;* ∼ **top** *n.* Flaschenverschluss, *der*

**bottom** /'bɒtəm/ ⟨1⟩ *n.* (a) unteres Ende; (of cup, glass, box) Boden, *der;* (of valley, well, shaft) Sohle, *die;* (of hill, cliff, stairs) Fuß, *der*
(b) (buttocks) Hinterteil, *das* (ugs.)
(c) (of sea, lake) Grund, *der*

(e) (farthest point) **at the** ∼ **of the garden/street** hinten im Garten/am Ende der Straße
(e) (underside) Unterseite, *die*
(f) (fig.) **start at the** ∼: ganz unten anfangen; **be** ∼ **of the class** der/die Letzte in der Klasse sein
⟨2⟩ *adj.* (a) (lowest) unterst...; (lower) unter...
(b) (fig.: last) letzt...

'**bottomless** *adj.* bodenlos; unendlich tief ⟨*Meer, Ozean*⟩

'**botulism** /'bɒtjuːlɪzm/ *n.* (Med.) Botulismus, *der*

**bough** /baʊ/ *n.* Ast, *der*

**bought** ▶ BUY 1

**boulder** /'bəʊldə(r)/ *n.* Felsbrocken, *der*

**boulevard** /'buːləvɑːd/ *n.* Boulevard, *der*

**bounce** /baʊns/ ⟨1⟩ *v.i.* (a) springen
(b) (coll.) ⟨*Scheck:*⟩ platzen (ugs.)
⟨2⟩ *v.t.* aufspringen lassen ⟨*Ball*⟩
⟨3⟩ *n.* Aufprall, *der*

'**bouncer** *n.* (coll.) Rausschmeißer, *der* (ugs.)

**bouncing** /'baʊnsɪŋ/ *adj.* stramm ⟨*Baby*⟩

**bouncy** /'baʊnsɪ/ *adj.* gut springend ⟨*Ball*⟩; (fig.: lively) munter

**bound¹** /baʊnd/ ⟨1⟩ *n., usu. in pl.* (limit) Grenze, *die;* **within the** ∼**s of possibility** im Bereich des Möglichen; **sth. is out of** ∼**s [to sb.]** der Zutritt zu etw. ist [für jmdn.] verboten
⟨2⟩ *v.t.* **be** ∼**ed by sth.** durch etw. begrenzt werden

**bound²** ⟨1⟩ *v.i.* hüpfen
⟨2⟩ *n.* Satz, *der*

**bound³** *pred. adj.* **be** ∼ **for home/Frankfurt** auf dem Heimweg/nach Frankfurt unterwegs sein; **homeward** ∼: auf dem Weg nach Hause

**bound⁴** ▶ BIND

**boundary** /'baʊndərɪ/ *n.* Grenze, *die*

'**boundless** *adj.* grenzenlos

**bounty** /'baʊntɪ/ *n.* Kopfgeld, *das*

**bouquet** /bʊ'keɪ/ *n.* [Blumen]strauß, *der*

**bourgeois** /'bʊəʒwɑː/ ⟨1⟩ *n., pl. same* Bürger, *der*/Bürgerin, *die*
⟨2⟩ *adj.* bürgerlich

**bout** /baʊt/ *n.* (a) (contest) Wettkampf, *der*
(b) (fit) Anfall, *der*

**boutique** /buː'tiːk/ *n.* Boutique, *die*

**bow¹** /bəʊ/ *n.* (a) (curve, weapon, Mus.) Bogen, *der*
(b) (knot, ribbon) Schleife, *die*

**bow²** /baʊ/ ⟨1⟩ *v.i.* (a) ∼ [**to sb.**] sich [vor jmdm.] verbeugen
(b) (submit) sich beugen (**to** *Dat.*)
⟨2⟩ *n.* Verbeugung, *die*

**bow³** /baʊ/ *n.* (Naut.) Bug, *der*

**bowel** /'baʊəl/ *n.* (Anat.) ∼**s** *pl.,* (Med.) ∼: Darm, *der*

**bowl¹** /bəʊl/ *n.* (basin) Schüssel, *die;* (shallower) Schale, *die;* (of spoon) Schöpfteil, *der;* (of pipe) Kopf, *der*

**bowl²** ⟨1⟩ *n.* (a) (ball) Kugel, *die*

⋯⟶

**(b)** *in pl.* (game) Bowls, *das*
2 *v.i.* **(a)** ( play ~s) Bowls spielen
**(b)** (Cricket) werfen

**bow-legged** /'bəʊlegɪd/ o-beinig (ugs.)

**bowler¹** /'bəʊlə(r)/ *n.* (Cricket) Werfer, *der*

**bowler²** *n.* ~ [hat] Bowler, *der*

**'bowling** *n.* [tenpin] ~: Bowling, *das;* go ~: bowlen gehen

**bowling:** ~ **alley** *n.* Bowlingbahn, *die;* ~ **green** *n.:* Rasenfläche für Bowls

**bow** /bəʊ/: ~**string** *n.* Bogensehne, *die;* ~ **'tie** *n.* Fliege, *die;* ~ **window** *n.* Erkerfenster, *das*

**box¹** /bɒks/ *n.* **(a)** Kasten, *der;* (bigger) Kiste, *die;* (of cardboard) Schachtel, *die*
**(b)** the ~ (coll.: television) der Kasten (ugs. abwertend); die Flimmerkiste (scherzh.)

**box²** 1 *n.* he gave him a ~ on the ear[s] er gab ihm eine Ohrfeige
2 *v.t.* **(a)** he ~ed his ears *or* ~ed him round the ears er ohrfeigte ihn
**(b)** (Sport) ~ sb. gegen jmdn. boxen
3 *v.i.* (Sport) boxen
■ **box 'in** *v.t.* (enclose tightly) einklemmen

**'boxer** *n.* Boxer, *der*

**'boxer shorts** *n. pl.* Boxershorts *Pl.*

**'boxing** *n.* Boxen, *das*

**boxing: B~ Day** *n.* zweiter Weihnachtsfeiertag; ~ **glove** *n.* Boxhandschuh, *der;* ~ **match** *n.* Boxkampf, *der;* ~ **ring** *n.* Boxring, *der*

**box:** ~ **junction** *n.* (Brit.) *gelb markierter Kreuzungsbereich, in den man bei Stau nicht einfahren darf;* ~ **number** *n.* (at newspaper office) Chiffre, *die;* (at post office) Postfach, *das;* ~ **office** *n.* Kasse, *die;* be a ~ office success ein Kassenerfolg sein; ~**room** *n.* (Brit.) Abstellraum, *der*

**boy** /bɔɪ/ *n.* Junge, *der*

**'boy band** *n.* Boyband, *die*

**boycott** /'bɔɪkɒt/ 1 *v.t.* boykottieren
2 *n.* Boykott, *der*

**'boyfriend** *n.* Freund, *der*

**'boyish** *adj.* jungenhaft

**boy 'scout** ▶ SCOUT 1A

**bra** /brɑː/ *n.* BH, *der* (ugs.)

**brace** /breɪs/ 1 *n.* **(a)** (connecting piece) Klammer, *die;* (strut) Strebe, *die;* (Dent.) [Zahn]spange, *die*
**(b)** *in pl.* (trouser straps) Hosenträger *Pl.*
2 *v. refl.* ~ oneself for sth. sich auf etw. (*Akk.*) vorbereiten

**bracelet** /'breɪslɪt/ *n.* Armband, *das*

**bracing** /'breɪsɪŋ/ *adj.* belebend

**bracken** /'brækn/ *n.* [Adler]farn, *der*

**bracket** /'brækɪt/ 1 *n.* **(a)** (support) Konsole, *die*
**(b)** (mark) Klammer, *die*
2 *v.t.* einklammern

**brag** /bræg/ *v.i. & t.,* -gg- prahlen (about mit)

**braid** /breɪd/ 1 *n.* **(a)** ( plait) Flechte, *die* (geh.); Zopf, *der*
**(b)** (woven band) Borte, *die;* (on uniform) Litze, *die*
2 *v.t.* flechten

**Braille** /breɪl/ *n.* Blindenschrift, *die*

**brain** /breɪn/ *n.* Gehirn, *das*

**brain:** ~**child** *n.* (coll.) Geistesprodukt, *das;* ~**-dead** *adj.* **(a)** (Med.) hirntot; **(b)** (coll. derog.) hirnlos ⟨Person⟩; ~**less** *adj.* hirnlos; ~**storm** *n.* **(a)** Anfall geistiger Umnachtung; **(b)** (Amer. coll.) ▶ ~WAVE; ~**storming** *n.* Brainstorming, *das;* ~ **tumour** *n.* Gehirntumor, *der;* ~**wash** *v.t.* einer Gehirnwäsche unterziehen; ~**wave** *n.* (coll.: inspiration) genialer Einfall

**'brainy** *adj.* intelligent

**brake** /breɪk/ 1 *n.* Bremse, *die*
2 *v.t. & i.* bremsen

**brake:** ~ **block** *n.* Bremsklotz, *der;* ~ **cable** *n.* Bremszug, *der;* Bremsseil, *das;* ~ **fluid** *n.* Bremsflüssigkeit, *die;* ~ **light** *n.* Bremslicht, *das;* ~ **pad** *n.* Bremsbelag, *der;* ~ **shoe** *n.* Bremsbacke, *die*

**'braking distance** *n.* Bremsweg, *der*

**bramble** /'bræmbl/ *n.* Dornenstrauch, *der*

**bran** /bræn/ *n.* Kleie, *die*

**branch** /brɑːntʃ/ 1 *n.* **(a)** (bough) Ast, *der;* (twig) Zweig, *der*
**(b)** (of artery, antlers) Ast, *der*
**(c)** (office) Zweigstelle, *die;* (shop) Filiale, *die*
2 *v.i.* sich verzweigen
■ **branch 'off** *v.i.* abzweigen
■ **branch 'out** *v.i.* (fig.) ~ out into sth. sich auch mit etw. befassen

**branch:** ~ **line** *n.* (Railw.) Nebenstrecke, *die;* ~ **manager** *n.* Filialleiter, *der/* -leiterin, *die;* ~ **office** *n.* Zweigstelle, *die*

**brand** /brænd/ *n.* **(a)** (trade mark) Markenzeichen, *das;* (goods of particular make) Marke, *die*
**(b)** (mark) Brandmal, *das*

**'brand image** *n.* Markenimage, *das*

**brandish** /'brændɪʃ/ *v.t.* schwenken; schwingen ⟨Waffe⟩

**brand:** ~ **leader** *n.* ( product) marktführendes Produkt; (brand) führende Marke; ~ **name** *n.* Markenname, *der;* ~-**'new** *adj.* nagelneu (ugs.)

**brandy** /'brændɪ/ *n.* Weinbrand, *der;* Kognak, *der*

**brash** /bræʃ/ *adj.* dreist

**brass** /brɑːs/ *n.* Messing, *das; attrib.* Messing-; the ~ (Mus.) das Blech; ~ **player** (Mus.) Blechbläser, *der;* get down to ~ tacks zur Sache kommen

**brass 'band** *n.* Blaskapelle, *die*

**brassière** /'bræzɪə(r)/ *n.* Büstenhalter, *der*

**brat** /bræt/ *n.* Balg, *das od. der* (ugs.)

**bravado** /brə'vɑːdəʊ/ *n.* do sth. out of ~: so waghalsig sein, etw. zu tun

**brave** /breɪv/ 1 *adj.* tapfer
2 *n.* [indianischer] Krieger

3 *v.t.* trotzen (+ *Dat.*)

**'bravely** *adv.* tapfer

**bravery** /'breɪvərɪ/ *n.* Tapferkeit, *die*

**bravo** /brɑ:'vəʊ/ *int.* bravo

**brawl** /brɔ:l/ 1 *v.i.* sich schlagen
2 *n.* Schlägerei, *die*

**brawny** /'brɔ:nɪ/ *adj.* muskulös

**bray** /breɪ/ 1 Iah, *das*
2 *v.i.* ⟨*Esel:*⟩ iahen

**brazen** /'breɪzn/ 1 *adj.* dreist; (shameless) schamlos
2 *v.t.* ~ [out] trotzen (+ *Dat.*); ~ it out (deny guilt) es abstreiten; (not admit guilt) es nicht zugeben

**brazier** /'breɪzɪə(r)/ *n.* Kohlenbecken, *das*

**Brazil** /brə'zɪl/ *pr. n.* Brasilien (*das*)

**Bra'zil nut** *n.* Paranuss, *die*

**breach** /bri:tʃ/ 1 *n.* (a) (violation) Verstoß, *der* (of gegen); ~ of faith/duty Vertrauensbruch, *der*/Pflichtverletzung, *die*
(b) (of relations) Bruch, *der*
(c) (gap) Bresche, *die;* (fig.) Riss, *der*
2 *v.t.* durchbrechen

**bread** /bred/ *n.* Brot, *das;* a piece of ~ and butter ein Butterbrot

**bread:** ~ **bin** *n.* Brotkasten, *der;* ~**board** *n.* [Brot]brett, *das;* ~**crumb** *n.* Brotkrume, *die;* ~**crumbs** (coating) Paniermehl, *das;* ~ **knife** *n.* Brotmesser, *das;* ~**line** *n.* be or live on/below the ~**line** gerade noch/nicht einmal mehr das Notwendigste zum Leben haben; ~ **'roll** *n.* Brötchen, *das*

**breadth** /bredθ/ *n.* Breite, *die*

**'breadwinner** *n.* Ernährer, *der*/ Ernährerin, *die*

**break** /breɪk/ 1 *v.t.*, broke /brəʊk/, broken /'brəʊkn/ (a) brechen; (so as to damage) zerbrechen; kaputtmachen (ugs.); zerreißen ⟨*Seil*⟩; (fig.: interrupt) unterbrechen; brechen ⟨*Bann, Zauber, Schweigen*⟩; the TV/my watch is broken der Fernseher/meine Uhr ist kaputt (ugs.); ~ the habit es sich (*Dat.*) abgewöhnen
(b) (fracture) sich (*Dat.*) brechen ⟨*Arm, Bein usw.*⟩
(c) brechen ⟨*Vertrag, Versprechen*⟩; verstoßen gegen ⟨*Regel, Gesetz*⟩
(d) (surpass) brechen ⟨*Rekord*⟩
(e) (cushion) auffangen ⟨*Schlag, jmds. Fall*⟩
2 *v.i.*, broke, broken (a) kaputtgehen (ugs.); ⟨*Faden, Seil:*⟩ [zer]reißen; ⟨*Glas, Tasse, Teller:*⟩ zerbrechen; ⟨*Eis:*⟩ brechen; ~ in two/ in pieces durchbrechen/zerbrechen
(b) ~ into einbrechen in (+ *Akk.*) ⟨*Haus*⟩; aufbrechen ⟨*Auto, Safe*⟩; ~ into laughter/ tears in Gelächter/Tränen ausbrechen; ~ into a trot/run zu traben/laufen anfangen
(c) (escape) ~ out of prison aus dem Gefängnis ausbrechen; ~ free or loose sich losreißen
(d) ⟨*Welle:*⟩ sich brechen (on/against an + *Dat.*)
(e) ⟨*Tag:*⟩ anbrechen; ⟨*Sturm:*⟩ losbrechen

(f) sb's voice is ~ing jmd. kommt in den Stimmbruch
3 *n.* (a) Bruch, *der;* (of rope) Reißen, *das;* a ~ with sb./sth. ein Bruch mit jmdm./etw.
(b) (gap) Lücke, *die;* (broken place) Sprung, *der*
(c) (dash) they made a sudden ~: sie stürmten plötzlich davon
(d) (interruption) Unterbrechung, *die;* (pause, holiday) Pause, *die;* take or have a ~: Pause machen
(e) (coll.: chance) Chance, *die*

■ **break 'down** 1 *v.i.* zusammenbrechen; ⟨*Verhandlungen:*⟩ scheitern; ⟨*Auto:*⟩ eine Panne haben
2 *v.t.* (a) aufbrechen ⟨*Tür*⟩; brechen ⟨*Widerstand*⟩; niederreißen ⟨*Barriere, Schranke*⟩
(b) (analyse) aufgliedern

■ **break 'in** 1 *v.i.* (into building etc.) einbrechen
2 *v.t.* (a) zureiten ⟨*Pferd*⟩
(b) einlaufen ⟨*Schuhe*⟩
(c) ~ the door in die Tür aufbrechen

■ **'break into** ► ~ 2B

■ **break 'off** 1 *v.t.* abbrechen; abreißen ⟨*Faden*⟩; auflösen ⟨*Verlobung*⟩
2 *v.i.* (a) abbrechen
(b) (cease) aufhören

■ **break 'out** *v.i.* ausbrechen; ~ out in spots/a rash Pickel/einen Ausschlag bekommen

■ **break 'up** 1 *v.t.* (a) (~ into pieces) zerkleinern; ausschlachten ⟨*Auto*⟩; aufbrechen ⟨*Erde*⟩
(b) (disband) auflösen
2 *v.i.* (a) (~ into pieces, lit. or fig.) zerbrechen
(b) (disband) sich auflösen; ⟨*Schule:*⟩ schließen; ⟨*Schüler, Lehrer:*⟩ in die Ferien gehen
(c) ~ up [with sb.] sich [von jmdm.] trennen

**breakable** /'breɪkəbl/ 1 *adj.* zerbrechlich
2 *n.* ~s zerbrechliche Dinge

**breakage** /'breɪkɪdʒ/ *n.* Zerbrechen, *das;* ~s must be paid for zerbrochene Ware muss bezahlt werden

**'breakdown** *n.* (a) (of vehicle) Panne, *die;* (in machine) Störung, *die;* ~ truck/van Abschleppwagen, *der*
(b) (Med.) Zusammenbruch, *der*
(c) (analysis) Aufschlüsselung, *die*

**'breaker** *n.* (a) (wave) Brecher, *der*
(b) ~'s [yard] Autoverwertung, *die*

**breakfast** /'brekfəst/ 1 *n.* Frühstück, *das;* for ~: zum Frühstück
2 *v.i.* frühstücken

**breakfast:** ~ **cereal** *n.* ≈ Frühstücksflocken *Pl.;* ~ **'television** *n.* Frühstücksfernsehen, *das*

**'break-in** *n.* Einbruch, *der*

**'breaking** *n.* ~ and entering (Law) Einbruch, *der;* be at a ~ point (mentally) die Grenze der Belastbarkeit erreicht haben

**break:** ~**neck** *adj.* halsbrecherisch;  ⋯

**∼through** n. Durchbruch, der; **∼-up** n. Auflösung, die; (of relationship) Bruch, der; **∼water** n. Wellenbrecher, der

**breast** /brest/ n. Brust, die

**breast: ∼bone** n. Brustbein, das; **∼ cancer** n. Brustkrebs, der; **∼feed** v.t. & i. stillen; **∼stroke** n. Brustschwimmen, das

**breath** /breθ/ n. (a) Atem, der; get one's **∼ back** wieder zu Atem kommen; hold one's **∼**: den Atem anhalten; be out of **∼**: außer Atem sein; say sth. under one's **∼**: etw. vor sich (Akk.) hin murmeln (b) (one respiration) Atemzug, der

**Breathalyser** (Brit.), **Breathalyzer** ® /ˈbreθəlaɪzə(r)/ n. Alcotest-Röhrchen Ⓦ, das; **∼ test** Alcotest Ⓦ, der

**breathe** /briːð/ [1] v.i. atmen; **∼ in** einatmen; **∼ out** ausatmen [2] v.t. (a) **∼ [in/out]** ein-/ausatmen (b) (utter) hauchen

**breather** /ˈbriːðə(r)/ n. Verschnaufpause, die

**breathing space** n. Zeit zum Luftholen; (fig.) Atempause, die

**breathless** adj. atemlos (with vor + Dat.)

**breath: ∼taking** adj. atemberaubend; **∼ test** n. Alcotest Ⓦ, der

**bred** ▶ BREED 1, 2

**breeches** /ˈbrɪtʃɪz/ n. pl. [pair of] **∼**: [Knie]bundhose, die; [riding]**∼**: Reithose, die

**breed** /briːd/ [1] v.t., bred /bred/ (a) (cause) erzeugen (b) züchten ⟨Tiere, Pflanzen⟩ [2] v.i., bred sich vermehren [3] n. (of animals) Rasse, die

**breeding** n. [good] **∼**: gute Erziehung

**breeding ground** n. (lit. or fig.) Brutstätte, die

**breeze** /briːz/ n. Brise, die

**breeze block** n. (Building) ≈ Leichtstein, der

**breezy** /ˈbriːzɪ/ adj. windig

**brevity** /ˈbrevɪtɪ/ n. Kürze, die

**brew** /bruː/ [1] v.t. brauen ⟨Bier⟩; **∼ [up]** kochen ⟨Kaffee, Tee usw.⟩ [2] v.i. (a) ⟨Bier:⟩ gären; ⟨Kaffee, Tee:⟩ ziehen (b) ⟨Unwetter:⟩ sich zusammenbrauen [3] n. (brewed beer/tea) Bier, das/Tee, der

**brewer** n. Brauer, der; (firm) Brauerei, die

**brewery** /ˈbruːərɪ/ n. Brauerei, die

**bribe** /braɪb/ [1] n. Bestechung, die [2] v.t. bestechen; **∼ sb. to do/into doing sth.** jmdn. bestechen, damit er etw. tut

**bribery** /ˈbraɪbərɪ/ n. Bestechung, die

**brick** /brɪk/ [1] n. Ziegelstein, der; (toy) Bauklötzchen, das [2] adj. Ziegelstein-

**brick: ∼layer** n. Maurer, der; **∼laying** n. Mauern, das; **∼ 'wall** n. Backsteinmauer, die; bang one's head against a **∼ wall** (fig.) mit dem Kopf gegen die Wand rennen (fig.)

**bridal** /ˈbraɪdl/ adj. Braut-

**bride** /braɪd/ n. Braut, die

**bridegroom** n. Bräutigam, der

**bridesmaid** /ˈbraɪdzmeɪd/ n. Brautjungfer, die

**bridge**[1] /brɪdʒ/ [1] n. (a) Brücke, die (b) (Naut.) [Kommando]brücke, die (c) (of nose) Nasenbein, das (d) (of spectacles) Steg, der [2] v.t. eine Brücke bauen über (+ Akk.)

**bridge**[2] n. (Cards) Bridge, das

**bridging loan** n. (Commerc.) Überbrückungskredit, der

**bridle** /ˈbraɪdl/ n. Zaum, der

**bridle path** n. Reitweg, der

**brief**[1] /briːf/ adj. (a) kurz; gering ⟨Verspätung⟩ (b) (concise) knapp; in **∼**, to be **∼**: kurz gesagt

**brief**[2] [1] n. (instructions) Instruktionen Pl.; (Law: case) Mandat, das [2] v.t. Instruktionen geben (+ Dat.); (inform) unterrichten

**briefcase** n. Aktentasche, die

**briefing** n. Briefing, das; (of reporters) Unterrichtung, die

**briefly** adv. (a) kurz (b) (concisely) knapp; kurz

**briefs** /briːfs/ n. pl. [pair of] **∼**: Slip, der

**brigade** /brɪˈgeɪd/ n. (Mil.) Brigade, die

**brigadier** /brɪgəˈdɪə(r)/ n. Brigadegeneral, der

**bright** /braɪt/ adj. (a) hell; grell ⟨Scheinwerfer[licht], Sonnenlicht⟩; strahlend ⟨Sonnenschein, Augen, Tag⟩; leuchtend ⟨Farbe, Blume⟩; **∼ intervals/periods** Aufheiterungen Pl. (b) (cheerful) fröhlich (c) (clever) intelligent

**brighten** /ˈbraɪtn/ [1] v.t. **∼ [up]** aufhellen [2] v.i. the weather or it is **∼ing [up]** es klärt sich auf

**brightly** adv. (a) hell (b) (cheerfully) fröhlich

**brightness** n. ▶ BRIGHT: (a) Helligkeit, die; Grelle, die; Strahlen, das; Leuchtkraft, die (b) Fröhlichkeit, die (c) Intelligenz, die

**brilliance** /ˈbrɪlɪəns/ n. ▶ BRILLIANT: (a) Helligkeit, die; Leuchten, das (b) Genialität, die; Glanz, der

**brilliant** /ˈbrɪljənt/ adj. (a) hell ⟨Licht⟩; leuchtend ⟨Farbe⟩ (b) genial ⟨Mensch, Gedanke, Leistung⟩; glänzend ⟨Verstand, Aufführung, Idee⟩

**brim** /brɪm/ [1] n. Rand, der; (of hat) [Hut]krempe, die [2] v.i., -mm-: be **∼ming with sth.** randvoll mit etw. sein

**brim-'full** pred. adj. randvoll (with mit)

**brine** /braɪn/ n. Salzwasser, das

**bring** /brɪŋ/ *v.t.*, **brought** /brɔːt/ **(a)** bringen; (as a present or favour) mitbringen; ~ sth. with one etw. mitbringen
**(b)** ~ sb. to do sth. jmdn. dazu bringen, etw. zu tun; I could not ~ myself to do it ich konnte es nicht über mich bringen, es zu tun
■ **bring a'bout** *v.t.* verursachen
■ **bring 'back** *v.t.* **(a)** (return) zurückbringen; (from a journey) mitbringen
**(b)** (recall) in Erinnerung bringen
**(c)** (restore, reintroduce) wieder einführen
■ **bring 'down** *v.t.* **(a)** herunterbringen
**(b)** (kill, wound) zur Strecke bringen
**(c)** senken ⟨Preise, Inflationsrate, Fieber⟩
■ **bring 'forward** *v.t.* **(a)** nach vorne bringen
**(b)** vorbringen ⟨Argument⟩; zur Sprache bringen ⟨Fall, Angelegenheit⟩
**(c)** vorverlegen ⟨Termin⟩ (to auf + Akk.)
■ **bring 'in** *v.t.* hereinbringen; einbringen ⟨Gesetzesvorlage, Verdienst, Summe⟩
■ **bring 'off** *v.t.* (conduct successfully) zustande bringen
■ **bring 'on** *v.t.* **(a)** (cause) verursachen
**(b)** (Sport) einsetzen
■ **bring 'out** *v.t.* **(a)** herausbringen
**(b)** hervorheben ⟨Unterschied⟩
**(c)** einführen ⟨Produkt⟩; herausbringen ⟨Buch, Zeitschrift⟩
■ **bring 'up** *v.t.* **(a)** heraufbringen
**(b)** (educate) erziehen; (rear) aufziehen
**(c)** zur Sprache bringen ⟨Angelegenheit, Thema, Problem⟩

**brink** /brɪŋk/ *n.* Rand, *der;* be on the ~ of doing sth. nahe daran sein, etw. zu tun
**brisk** /brɪsk/ *adj.* flott ⟨Gang⟩; forsch ⟨Person, Art⟩; frisch ⟨Wind⟩; (fig.) rege ⟨Handel, Nachfrage⟩; lebhaft ⟨Geschäft⟩
**'briskly** *adv.* flott
**bristle** /'brɪsl/ ① *n.* Borste, *die*
② *v.i.* **(a)** ~ [up] ⟨Haare:⟩ sich sträuben
**(b)** ~ with (fig.) starren vor (+ Dat.)
**bristly** /'brɪslɪ/ *adj.* borstig
**Brit** /brɪt/ *n.* (coll.) Brite, *der*/Britin, *die;* Engländer, *der*/Engländerin, *die* (ugs.)
**Britain** /'brɪtn/ *pr. n.* Großbritannien (das)
**British** /'brɪtɪʃ/ ① *adj.* britisch; he/she is ~: er ist Brite/sie ist Britin
② *n. pl.* the ~: die Briten
**British 'Isles** *pr. n. pl.* Britische Inseln
**Briton** /'brɪtn/ *n.* Brite, *der*/Britin, *die*
**Brittany** /'brɪtənɪ/ *pr. n.* Bretagne, *die*
**brittle** /'brɪtl/ *adj.* spröde ⟨Material⟩
**broach** /brəʊtʃ/ *v.t.* anschneiden ⟨Thema⟩
**broad** /brɔːd/ *adj.* **(a)** breit; (extensive) weit ⟨Ebene, Land⟩; ausgedehnt ⟨Fläche⟩
**(b)** (explicit) klar ⟨Hinweis⟩; breit ⟨Lächeln⟩
**(c)** (main) grob; (generalized) allgemein
**(d)** stark ⟨Akzent⟩
**broad 'bean** *n.* Saubohne, *die*
**broadcast** /'brɔːdkɑːst/ ① *n.* Sendung, *die;* (live) Übertragung, *die*

② *v.t.*, **broadcast** senden; übertragen ⟨Livesendung⟩
③ *v.i.*, **broadcast** senden
**'broadcaster** *n.* (Radio, Telev.) *jmd., der durch häufige Auftritte im Rundfunk und Fernsehen, besonders als Interviewpartner, Diskussionsteilnehmer od. Kommentator, bekannt ist*
**'broadcasting** *n.* Senden, *das;* (live) Übertragen, *das;* work in ~: beim Funk arbeiten
**broaden** /'brɔːdn/ ① *v.t.* **(a)** verbreitern
**(b)** ausweiten ⟨Diskussion⟩
② *v.i.* sich verbreitern; (fig.) sich erweitern
**'broadly** *adv.* **(a)** deutlich ⟨hinweisen⟩; breit ⟨grinsen, lächeln⟩
**(b)** (in general) allgemein ⟨beschreiben⟩; ~ speaking allgemein gesagt
**broad: ~'minded** *adj.* tolerant;
~sheet *n.* **(a)** (Printing) Einblattdruck, *der;*
**(b)** (pamphlet) Flugblatt, *das;*
~'shouldered *adj.* breitschultrig;
~side *n.* Breitseite, *die*
**brocade** /brə'keɪd/ *n.* Brokat, *der*
**broccoli** /'brɒkəlɪ/ *n.* Brokkoli, *der*
**brochure** /'brəʊʃə(r)/ *n.* Broschüre, *die;* Prospekt, *der*
**broil** /'brɔɪl/ *v.t.* (esp. Amer.) grillen
**broke** /brəʊk/ ① ▶ BREAK 1, 2
② *pred. adj.* (coll.) pleite (ugs.)
**broken** /'brəʊkn/ ① ▶ BREAK 1, 2
② *adj.* **(a)** zerbrochen; gebrochen ⟨Bein, Hals⟩; verletzt ⟨Haut⟩; abgebrochen ⟨Zahn⟩; gerissen ⟨Seil⟩; kaputt (ugs.) ⟨Uhr, Fernsehen, Fenster⟩; ~ glass Glasscherben *Pl.*
**(b)** (imperfect) gebrochen; in ~ English in gebrochenem Englisch
**(c)** (fig.) ruiniert ⟨Ehe⟩; gebrochen ⟨Mensch, Herz⟩
**broken: ~-down** *adj.* baufällig ⟨Gebäude⟩; kaputt (ugs.) ⟨Wagen⟩;
~'hearted *adj.* untröstlich
**broker** /'brəʊkə(r)/ *n.* Makler, *der*
**brolly** /'brɒlɪ/ *n.* (Brit. coll.) [Regen]schirm, *der*
**bronchitis** /brɒŋ'kaɪtɪs/ *n.* Bronchitis, *die*
**bronze** /brɒnz/ ① *n.* Bronze, *die*
② *attrib. adj.* Bronze-; (coloured like ~) bronzefarben
**brooch** /brəʊtʃ/ *n.* Brosche, *die*
**brood** /bruːd/ ① *n.* Brut, *die*
② *v.i.* [vor sich (Akk.) hin] brüten
**brook** /brʊk/ *n.* Bach, *der*
**broom** /bruːm/ *n.* **(a)** Besen, *der*
**(b)** (Bot.) Ginster, *der*
**broom: ~ cupboard** *n.* Besenschrank, *der;* ~stick *n.* Besenstiel, *der*
**broth** /brɒθ/ *n.* Brühe, *die*
**brothel** /'brɒθl/ *n.* Bordell, *das*
**brother** /'brʌðə(r)/ *n.* Bruder, *der;* my ~s and sisters meine Geschwister ⋯⟩

**'brotherhood** *n.* (organization) Bruderschaft, *die*

**'brother-in-law** *n., pl.* brothers-in-law Schwager, *der*

**brought** ▸ BRING

**brow** /braʊ/ *n.* (a) (eye⁓) Braue, *die* (b) (forehead) Stirn, *die* (c) (of hill) Kuppe, *die*

**'browbeat** *v.t., forms as* BEAT 1 einschüchtern

**brown** /braʊn/ **1** *adj.* braun **2** *n.* Braun, *das*

**brown:** ⁓ **'bread** *n.* ≈ Mischbrot, *das;* ⁓**-eyed** *adj.* braunäugig; **be** ⁓**-eyed** braune Augen haben

**Brownie** /'braʊnɪ/ *n.* Wichtel, *die*

**brown:** ⁓ **'paper** *n.* Packpapier, *das;* ⁓ **'rice** *n.* Naturreis, *der*

**browse** /braʊz/ *v.i.* **1** (a) weiden (b) (in shop) sich umsehen; (read) blättern (**through** in + *Dat.*) (c) (Comp.) suchen; ⁓ **through sth.** etw. durchsuchen **2** (a) abgrasen ⟨*Weide*⟩; abfressen ⟨*Blätter*⟩ (b) (Comp.) ⁓ **sth** in etw. (*Dat.*) suchen

**browser** /'braʊzə(r)/ *n.* (Comp.) Browser, *der*

**bruise** /bruːz/ **1** *n.* (a) (Med.) blauer Fleck (b) (on fruit) Druckstelle, *die* **2** *v.t.* quetschen ⟨*Obst, Pflanzen*⟩; ⁓ **oneself/one's leg** sich stoßen/sich am Bein stoßen

**brunch** /brʌntʃ/ *n.* (coll.) Brunch, *der;* ausgedehntes, spätes Frühstück

**brunette** /bruːˈnet/ **1** *n.* Brünette, *die* **2** *adj.* brünett

**brunt** /brʌnt/ *n.* **bear the** ⁓ **of the attack/ financial cuts** vom Angriff/von den Einsparungen am meisten betroffen sein

**brush** /brʌʃ/ **1** *n.* (a) Bürste, *die;* (for sweeping) Besen, *der;* (with short handle) Handfeger, *der;* (for painting or writing) Pinsel, *der* (b) (skirmish) Zusammenstoß, *der* (c) (light touch) flüchtige Berührung **2** *v.t.* (a) kehren; fegen; abbürsten ⟨*Kleidung*⟩; ⁓ **one's teeth/hair** sich (*Dat.*) die Zähne putzen/die Haare bürsten (b) (touch in passing) streifen **3** *v.i.* ⁓ **past sb./sth.** jmdn./etw. streifen ▪ **brush 'up** *v.t. & i.* ⁓ **up [on]** auffrischen ⟨*Kenntnisse usw.*⟩

**brusque** /bruːsk/ *adj.,* **'brusquely** *adv.* schroff

**Brussels** /'brʌslz/ *pr. n.* Brüssel (*das*)

**Brussels 'sprouts** *n. pl.* Rosenkohl, *der*

**brutal** /'bruːtl/ *adj.* brutal

**brutality** /bruːˈtælɪtɪ/ *n.* Brutalität, *die*

**brutally** /'bruːtəlɪ/ *adv.* brutal

**brute** /bruːt/ **1** *n.* (a) (animal) Bestie, *die* (b) (person) Rohling, *der* **2** *attrib. adj.* **by** ⁓ **force** mit roher Gewalt

**B.Sc.** *abbr.* = **Bachelor of Science**

**BSE** *abbr.* = **bovine spongiform encephalopathy** BSE

**BST** *abbr.* = **British Summer Time** Britische Sommerzeit

**bubble** /'bʌbl/ **1** *n.* Blase, *die;* (small) Perle, *die* **2** *v.i.* ⟨*Wasser, Schlamm, Lava:*⟩ Blasen bilden

**bubble:** ⁓ **bath** *n.* Schaumbad, *das;* ⁓ **pack** *n.* Klarsichtpackung, *die;* ⁓**-wrapped** *adj.* in Luftpolsterfolie verpackt

**buck¹** /bʌk/ *n.* (deer, chamois) Bock, *der;* (rabbit, hare) Rammler, *der*

**buck²** *n.* **pass the** ⁓ **to sb.** jmdm. die Verantwortung aufhalsen

**buck³** (coll.) **1** *v.i.* ⁓ **'up (a)** (make haste) sich ranhalten (ugs.) (b) (cheer up) ⁓ **up!** Kopf hoch! **2** *v.t.* ⁓ **one's ideas up** (coll.) sich zusammenreißen

**buck⁴** *n.* (Amer. coll.) Dollar, *der*

**bucket** /'bʌkɪt/ *n.* Eimer, *der*

**bucketful** /'bʌkɪtfʊl/ *n.* Eimer [voll]

**bucket:** ⁓ **seat** *n.* Schalensitz, *der;* ⁓ **shop** *n.* [nicht ganz seriöses] Maklerbüro; (for air tickets) Reisebüro (*das vor allem Billigflüge vermittelt*)

**buckle** /'bʌkl/ **1** *n.* Schnalle, *die* **2** *v.t.* (a) zuschnallen; ⁓ **sth. on/up** etw. anschnallen/festschnallen (b) verbiegen ⟨*Stoßstange, Rad*⟩ **3** *v.i.* ⟨*Rad, Metallplatte:*⟩ [sich] verbiegen

**bud** /bʌd/ **1** *n.* Knospe, *die;* **come into** ⁓/**be in** ⁓: Knospen treiben **2** *v.i.,* -dd- Knospen treiben

**Buddha** /'bʊdə/ *n.* Buddha, *der*

**Buddhism** /'bʊdɪzm/ *n.* Buddhismus, *der*

**Buddhist** /'bʊdɪst/ **1** *n.* Buddhist, *der/* Buddhistin, *die* **2** *adj.* buddhistisch

**budge** /bʌdʒ/ **1** *v.i.* sich rühren; ⟨*Gegenstand:*⟩ sich bewegen **2** *v.t.* bewegen

**budgerigar** /'bʌdʒərɪɡɑː(r)/ *n.* Wellensittich, *der*

**budget** /'bʌdʒɪt/ **1** *n.* Etat, *der;* Haushalt[splan], *der* **2** *v.i.* ⁓ **for sth.** etw. [im Etat] einplanen

**'budget account** *n.* Konto für laufende Zahlungen

**budgie** /'bʌdʒɪ/ *n.* (coll.) Wellensittich, *der*

**buff** /bʌf/ **1** *adj.* gelbbraun **2** *n.* (coll.: enthusiast) Fan, *der* (ugs.)

**buffalo** /'bʌfələʊ/ *n., pl.* ⁓**es** or same Büffel, *der*

**buffer** /'bʌfə(r)/ *n.* Prellbock, *der;* (on vehicle; also fig.) Puffer, *der*

**buffet** /'bʊfeɪ/ *n.* Büfett, *das*

**'buffet car** *n.* Büfettwagen, *der*

**bug** /bʌɡ/ *n.* (also coll.: microphone) Wanze, *die*

**bugger** /'bʌgə(r)/ (coarse) ① *n.* (as insult) Scheißkerl, *der* (derb)
② *v.t.* (damn) ~ you/him du kannst/der kann mich mal (derb); ~ it! ach du Scheiße! (derb)
■ ~ 'off *v.i.* abhauen (ugs.)

**buggy** /'bʌgɪ/ *n.* (pushchair) Sportwagen, *der*

**bugle** /'bju:gl/ *n.* Bügelhorn, *das*

**build** /bɪld/ ① *v.t., built* /bɪlt/ bauen; (fig.) aufbauen ⟨System, Gesellschaft, Zukunft⟩
② *v.i., built* bauen
③ *n.* Körperbau, *der*
■ **build 'in** *v.t.* einbauen
■ **build 'on** *v.t.* aufbauen auf (+ *Dat.*); bebauen ⟨Gebiet⟩
■ **build 'up** ① *v.t.* aufhäufen ⟨Reserven, Mittel⟩; kräftigen ⟨Personen, Körper⟩; steigern ⟨Produktion, Kapazität⟩; stärken ⟨[Selbst]vertrauen⟩; aufbauen ⟨Firma, Geschäft⟩
② *v.i.* ⟨Spannung, Druck:⟩ zunehmen; ⟨Schlange, Rückstau:⟩ sich bilden; ⟨Verkehr:⟩ sich verdichten

**'builder** *n.* Bauunternehmer, *der*

**'building** *n.* (a) Bau, *der*
(b) (structure) Gebäude, *das*

**building:** ~ **site** *n.* Baustelle, *die;*
~ **society** *n.* (Brit.) Bausparkasse, *die*

**built** ▶ BUILD 1, 2

**built:** ~-**in** *adj.* (a) eingebaut; Einbau⟨schrank, küche usw.⟩; (b) (fig.: instinctive) angeboren; ~-**up** *adj.* bebaut; ~-**up area** Wohngebiet, *das;* (Motor Veh.) geschlossene Ortschaft

**bulb** /bʌlb/ *n.* (a) (Bot., Hort.) Zwiebel, *die*
(b) (of lamp) [Glüh]birne, *die*

**Bulgaria** /bʌl'geərɪə/ *pr. n.* Bulgarien (*das*)

**Bulgarian** /bʌl'geərɪən/ ① *adj.* bulgarisch; **sb. is** ~: jmd. ist Bulgare/Bulgarin
② *n.* (a) (person) Bulgare, *der*/Bulgarin, *die*
(b) (language) Bulgarisch, *das; see also* ENGLISH 2A

**bulge** /bʌldʒ/ ① *n.* Ausbeulung, *die;* ausgebeulte Stelle
② *v.i.* sich wölben

**bulimia (nervosa)** /bʊ'li:mɪə (nɜːˈvəʊsə)/ *n.* Bulimie, *die;* Bulimia nervosa (fachspr.)

**bulimic** /bʊ'lɪmɪk/ ① *n.* Bulimiker, *der*/Bulimikerin, *die*
② *adj.* bulimisch

**bulk** /bʌlk/ *n.* (a) (large quantity) **in** ~: in großen Mengen
(b) (large shape) massige Gestalt
(c) (size) Größe, *die*
(d) (greater part) der größte Teil; (of population, votes) Mehrheit, *die*

**bulk 'buying** *n.* Großeinkauf, *der*

**'bulky** *adj.* sperrig ⟨Gegenstand⟩; massig ⟨Gestalt, Körper⟩

**bull** /bʊl/ *n.* Bulle, *der;* (esp. for bullfight) Stier, *der*

**bull:** ~ **bar** *n.* Rammschutz, *der;* Rammbügel, *der;* ~**dog** *n.* Bulldogge, *die*

**bulldozer** /'bʊldəʊzə(r)/ *n.* Planierraupe, *die*

**bullet** /'bʊlɪt/ *n.* Kugel, *die*

**'bullet hole** *n.* Einschuss, *der;* Einschussloch, *das*

**bulletin** /'bʊlɪtɪn/ *n.* Bulletin, *das*

**'bulletin board** *n.* (Comp.) schwarzes Brett

**'bulletproof** *adj.* kugelsicher

**bull:** ~**fight** *n.* Stierkampf, *der;* ~**fighter** *n.* Stierkämpfer, *der;* ~**fighting** *n.* Stierkämpfe *Pl.*

**bullion** /'bʊljən/ *n.* **gold** ~: Goldbarren *Pl.*

**'bull neck** *n.* Stiernacken, *der*

**'bullock** /'bʊlək/ *n.* Ochse, *der*

**bull:** ~**ring** *n.* Stierkampfarena, *die;*
~**seye** *n.* (of target) Schwarze, *das;* ~**shit** (coarse) *n.* Scheiße, *die* (salopp abwertend)

**bully** /'bʊlɪ/ ① *n.* (schoolboy etc.) ≈ Rabauke, *der;* (boss) Tyrann, *der*
② *v.t.* schikanieren; (frighten) einschüchtern

**bullying** /'bʊlɪŋ/ *n.* Schikanieren, *das*

**bum**[1] /bʌm/ *n.* (Brit. coll.) Hintern, *der* (ugs.)

**bum**[2] *n.* (Amer. coll.: tramp) Penner, *der* (salopp)

**bumble-bee** /'bʌmblbi:/ *n.* Hummel, *die*

**bumf** /bʌmf/ *n.* (Brit. coll. derog.: papers) Papierkram, *der* (ugs.)

**bump** /bʌmp/ ① *n.* (a) (sound) Bums, *der;* (impact) Stoß, *der*
(b) (swelling) Beule, *die*
(c) (hump) Buckel, *der* (ugs.)
② *adv.* bums
③ *v.t.* anstoßen
■ **'bump into** *v.t.* (a) stoßen an (+ *Akk.*)
(b) (meet by chance) zufällig [wieder]treffen

**'bumper** ① *n.* Stoßstange, *die;* ~-**to**-~ Stoßstange an Stoßstange
② *attrib. adj.* Rekord⟨ernte, -jahr⟩

**'bumpy** *adj.* holp[e]rig ⟨Straße, Fahrt, Fahrzeug⟩; uneben ⟨Fläche⟩; unruhig ⟨Flug⟩

**bun** /bʌn/ *n.* süßes Brötchen; (currant ~) Korinthenbrötchen, *das*

**bunch** /bʌntʃ/ *n.* (a) (of flowers) Strauß, *der;* (of grapes, bananas) Traube, *die;* (of parsley, radishes) Bund, *das;* ~ **of flowers/grapes** Blumenstrauß, *der*/Traube, *die;* **a** ~ **of keys** ein Schlüsselbund
(b) (lot) Anzahl, *die;* **the best** *or* **pick of the** ~: der/die/das Beste [von allen]
(c) (of people) Haufen, *der* (ugs.)

**bundle** /'bʌndl/ *n.* Bündel, *das;* (of papers) Packen, *der*

**bung** /bʌŋ/ ① *n.* Spund, *der*
② *v.t.* (coll.) schmeißen (ugs.)
■ **bung 'up** *v.i.* be/get ~ed up verstopft sein/verstopfen

**bungalow** /'bʌŋgələʊ/ *n.* Bungalow, *der*

**'bungee jumping** /'bʌndʒɪ/ *n.* Bungeespringen, *das*

**bungle** /'bʌŋgl/ *v.t.* stümpern bei

**bunk** /bʌŋk/ *n.* (in ship, lorry) Koje, *die;* (in sleeping car) Bett, *das;* (~ **bed**) Etagenbett, *das*

**bunker** /'bʌŋkə(r)/ *n.* Bunker, *der*

**bunny** /'bʌnɪ/ *n.* Häschen, *das*

**buoy** /bɔɪ/ *n.* Boje, *die*

**buoyancy** /'bɔɪənsɪ/ *n.* Auftrieb, *der*

**buoyant** /'bɔɪənt/ *adj.* (a) schwimmend; **be ~:** schwimmen

(b) (fig.) rege, lebhaft ‹*Markt*›; heiter, munter ‹*Person*›; **in ~ spirits** in Hochstimmung

**burden** /'bɜːdn/ 1 *n.* Last, *die;* **become a ~** (fig.) zur Last werden

2 *v.t.* belasten (**with** mit)

**bureau** /'bjʊərəʊ, bjʊə'rəʊ/ *n.* (a) (Brit.: writing desk) Sekretär, *der*

(b) (office) Büro, *das*

**bureaucracy** /bjʊə'rɒkrəsɪ/ *n.* Bürokratie, *die*

**bureaucrat** /'bjʊərəkræt/ *n.* Bürokrat, *der*/Bürokratin, *die*

**bureaucratic** /bjʊərə'krætɪk/ *adj.* bürokratisch

**burger** /'bɜːgə(r)/ *n.* (coll.) Hamburger, *der*

**'burger bar** *n.* (coll.) Hamburgerlokal, *das*

**burglar** /'bɜːglə(r)/ *n.* Einbrecher, *der*

**burglar: ~ alarm** *n.* Alarmanlage, *die;* **~-proof** *adj.* einbruch[s]sicher

**burglary** /'bɜːglərɪ/ *n.* Einbruch, *der*

**burgle** /'bɜːgl/ *v.t.* einbrechen in (+ *Akk.*); **the shop/he was ~d** in dem Laden/bei ihm wurde eingebrochen

**burial** /'berɪəl/ *n.* Begräbnis, *das*

**burly** /'bɜːlɪ/ *adj.* stämmig

**Burma** /'bɜːmə/ *pr. n.* Birma (*das*)

**Burmese** /bɜː'miːz/ 1 *adj.* birmanisch; **sb. is ~:** jmd. ist Birmane/Birmanin

2 *n., pl. same* (a) (person) Birmane, *der*/Birmanin, *die*

(b) (language) Birmanisch, *das; see also* ENGLISH 2A

**burn** /bɜːn/ 1 *n.* (on the skin) Verbrennung, *die;* (on material) Brandfleck, *der*

2 *v.t.,* ~t /bɜːnt/ *or* ~ed (a) verbrennen; **~ oneself/one's hand** sich verbrennen/sich (*Dat.*) die Hand verbrennen; **~ a hole in sth.** ein Loch in etw. (*Akk.*) brennen

(b) als Brennstoff verwenden ‹*Gas, Öl usw.*›; heizen mit ‹*Kohle, Holz, Torf*›

(c) (spoil) anbrennen lassen ‹*Fleisch, Kuchen*›; **be ~t** angebrannt sein

3 *v.i.,* ~t *or* ~ed brennen; **~ to death** verbrennen; **she ~s easily** sie bekommt leicht einen Sonnenbrand

■ **burn 'down** *v.t. & i.* niederbrennen

**'burned-out** *adj.* (lit. or fig.) ausgebrannt

**'burner** *n.* Brenner, *der*

**'burning** *adj.* glühend ‹*Leidenschaft, Hass, Wunsch*›; brennend ‹*Wunsch, Frage, Problem*›

**'burn-out** *n.* Burn-out, *das* (Med.); totale Erschöpfung *od.* Entkräftung; **risk ~:** Gefahr laufen, sich zu übernehmen

**burnt** ▸ BURN 2, 3

**'burnt-out** ▸ BURNED-OUT

**burp** /bɜːp/ (coll.) 1 *n.* Rülpser, *der* (ugs.)

2 *v.i.* rülpsen (ugs.)

**burrow** /'bʌrəʊ/ 1 *n.* Bau, *der*

2 *v.i.* [sich (*Dat.*)] einen Gang graben

**burst** /bɜːst/ 1 *n.* (a) (split) Bruch, *der*

(b) (of firing) Salve, *die*

(c) (fig.) **a ~ of applause/cheering** ein Beifallsausbruch/Beifallsrufe *Pl.*

2 *v.t.,* burst zum Platzen bringen; platzen lassen ‹*Luftballon*›; **~ pipe** Rohrbruch, *der*

3 *v.i.,* burst (a) platzen; ‹*Bombe:*› explodieren; ‹*Damm:*› brechen; ‹*Flussufer:*› überschwemmt werden; ‹*Furunkel, Geschwür:*› aufgehen

(b) **be ~ing with sth.** zum Bersten voll sein mit etw.; **be ~ing with pride/impatience/excitement** vor Stolz/Ungeduld platzen/vor Aufregung außer sich sein

■ **'burst into** *v.t.* (a) eindringen in

(b) **~ into tears/laughter** in Tränen/Gelächter ausbrechen; **~ into flames** in Brand geraten

■ **burst 'out** *v.i.* (a) herausstürzen

(b) (exclaim) losplatzen

(c) **~ out laughing/crying** in Lachen/Tränen ausbrechen

**bury** /'berɪ/ *v.t.* (a) begraben

(b) (hide) vergraben; **~ one's face in one's hands** das Gesicht in den Händen vergraben

(c) **~ one's teeth in sth.** seine Zähne in etw. (*Akk.*) graben

**bus** /bʌs/ *n.* Bus, *der*

**bus: ~ company** *n.* ≈ Verkehrsbetrieb, *der;* **~ conductor** *n.* Busschaffner, *der*/-schaffnerin, *die;* **~ depot** ▸ ~ GARAGE; **~ driver** *n.* Busfahrer, *der*/-fahrerin, *die;* **~ fare** *n.* [Bus]fahrpreis, *der;* **~ garage** *n.* Busdepot, *das*

**bush** /bʊʃ/ *n.* (a) Busch, *der*

(b) (shrubs) Gebüsch, *das*

**'bushy** *adj.* buschig

**busily** /'bɪzɪlɪ/ *adj.* eifrig

**business** /'bɪznɪs/ *n.* (a) (trading operation) Geschäft, *das;* (company, firm) Betrieb, *der;* (large) Unternehmen, *das;* **how's ~ with you?** (lit. or fig.) was machen die Geschäfte [bei Ihnen]?; **~ is ~** (fig.) Geschäft ist Geschäft; **go out of ~:** Pleite gehen (ugs.); **go into ~:** Geschäftsmann/-frau werden

(b) (buying and selling) Geschäfte *Pl.*

(c) (task, province) Aufgabe, *die;* **mind your own ~!** kümmere dich um deine [eigenen] Angelegenheiten!

(d) (difficult matter) Problem, *das*

**business: ~ address** *n.* Geschäftsadresse, *die;* **~ card** *n.* Geschäftskarte, *die;* **~ class** 1 *n., no pl.* Businessklasse, *die; attrib.* Businessklasse-; 2 *adv.* **fly/travel ~ class** in der Businessklasse fliegen/reisen; **~ correspondence** *n.* Geschäftskorrespondenz, *die;* **~ hours** *n.pl.* Geschäftszeit, *die;* (in office) Dienstzeit, *die;* **~ letter** *n.* Geschäftsbrief, *der;* **~-like**

adj. geschäftsmäßig ⟨Art⟩; geschäftstüchtig ⟨Person⟩; ~ **lunch** n. Arbeitsessen, das; ~**man** n. Geschäftsmann, der; ~ **park** n. Gewerbepark, der; ~ **plan** n. Geschäftsplan, der; ~ **premises** n. pl. Geschäftsräume Pl.; ~ **school** n. kaufmännische Fachschule; ~ **studies** n. pl. Wirtschaftslehre, die; ~ **trip** n. Geschäftsreise, die; on a ~ trip auf Geschäftsreise; ~**woman** n. Geschäftsfrau, die

**busker** /'bʌskə(r)/ n. Straßenmusikant, der

**bus:** ~ **lane** n. (Brit.) Busspur, die; ~ **ride** n. Busfahrt, die; B. is only an hour's ~ ride away B. ist nur eine Busstunde entfernt; ~ **route** n. Buslinie, die; ~ **service** n. Omnibusverkehr, der; (specific service) Busverbindung, die; ~ **shelter** n. Wartehäuschen, das; ~ **station** n. Omnibusbahnhof, der; ~ **stop** n. Bushaltestelle, die

**bust**¹ /bʌst/ n. (a) (sculpture) Büste, die (b) ~ [measurement] Oberweite, die

**bust**² (coll.) ① adj. kaputt (ugs.)
② v.t., ~ed or bust (break) kaputtmachen (ugs.); ~ sth. open etw. aufbrechen
③ v.i., ~ed or bust kaputtgehen (ugs.)

**bus:** ~ **terminal** n. Busbahnhof, der; ~ **ticket** n. Busfahrkarte, die; Busfahrschein, der

**bustle** /'bʌsl/ ① v.i. ~ about geschäftig hin und her eilen
② n. Betrieb, der

**bustling** /'bʌslɪŋ/ adj. belebt ⟨Straße, Stadt, Markt usw.⟩; rege ⟨Tätigkeit⟩

**busy** /'bɪzɪ/ ① adj. (a) beschäftigt (at, with mit); arbeitsreich ⟨Leben⟩; ziemlich hektisch ⟨Zeit⟩; I'm ~ now ich habe jetzt zu tun; he was ~ packing er war mit Packen beschäftigt
(b) (Amer. Teleph.) besetzt
② v. refl. ~ oneself sich beschäftigen (with mit)

**'busybody** n. G[e]schaftlhuber, der

**but** ① /bət, stressed bʌt/ conj. aber; correcting after a negative sondern; not that book ~ this one nicht das Buch, sondern dieses
② /bət/ prep. außer (+ Dat.); the next/last ~ one der/die/das übernächste/vorletzte

**butcher** /'bʊtʃə(r)/ ① n. Fleischer, der/ Fleischerin, die
② v.t. (murder) niedermetzeln

**butler** /'bʌtlə(r)/ n. Butler, der

**butt**¹ /bʌt/ n. (a) (of rifle) Kolben, der
(b) (of cigarette, cigar) Stummel, der

**butt**² n. (object of teasing or ridicule) Zielscheibe, die

**butt**³ ① n. (push) (by person) [Kopf]stoß, der; (by animal) Stoß [mit den Hörnern]
② v.t. & i. mit dem Kopf/den Hörnern stoßen

▪ **butt 'in** v.i. dazwischenreden

**butter** /'bʌtə(r)/ ① n. Butter, die

② v.t. buttern

**butter:** ~ **bean** n. Mondbohne, die; ~**cup** n. Butterblume, die; ~ **dish** n. Butterdose, die; ~**fingers** n. sing. Tollpatsch, der (beim Fangen usw.); ~**fly** n. (a) Schmetterling, der; (b) ~fly [stroke] Delphinstil, der; ~ **mountain** n. Butterberg, der

**buttock** /'bʌtək/ n. Hinterbacke, die; Gesäßhälfte, die; ~s Gesäß, das

**button** /'bʌtn/ ① n. Knopf, der
② v.t. ~ [up] zuknöpfen

**'buttonhole** ① n. (a) Knopfloch, das
(b) (flower) Knopflochblume, die
② v.t. zu fassen kriegen (ugs.)

**buttress** /'bʌtrɪs/ n. (Archit.) Mauerstütze, die

**buxom** /'bʌksəm/ adj. drall

**buy** /baɪ/ ① v.t., bought /bɔːt/ kaufen; ~ sb./oneself sth. jmdm./sich etw. kaufen
② n. [Ein]kauf, der; be a good ~: preiswert sein

▪ **buy 'up** v.t. aufkaufen

**'buyer** n. (a) Käufer, der/Käuferin, die
(b) (Commerc.) Einkäufer, der/Einkäuferin, die

**'buying power** /'baɪɪŋ/ n. Kaufkraft, die

**'buyout** n. Aufkauf, der; Management-Buy-Out, das (Wirtsch.)

**buzz** /bʌz/ ① n. Summen, das
② v.i. summen

▪ **buzz 'off** v.i. (coll.) abhauen (salopp)

**'buzzer** n. Summer, der

**by** /baɪ/ ① prep. (a) (near, beside) an (+ Dat.); bei; (next to) neben; ~ the window/river am Fenster/Fluss
(b) (to position beside) zu
(c) (about, in the possession of) bei
(d) [all] by herself/himself etc. [ganz] allein[e]
(e) (along) entlang; (via) über (+ Akk.)
(f) (passing) vorbei an (+ Dat.)
(g) (during) bei; by day/night bei Tag/Nacht
(h) (through the agency of) von; written by …: geschrieben von …
(i) (through the means of) durch; by bus/ship etc. mit dem Bus/Schiff usw.; by air/sea mit dem Flugzeug/Schiff
(j) (not later than) bis; by now/this time inzwischen
(k) (indicating unit) pro; by the minute/hour pro Minute/Stunde; day by day/month by month Tag für Tag/Monat für Monat; 10 ft. by 20 ft. 10 [Fuß] mal 20 Fuß
(l) (indicating amount) one by one einzeln; two by two/three by three zu zweit/dritt
(m) (indicating factor) durch; 8 divided by 2 is 4 8 geteilt durch 2 ist 4
(n) (indicating extent) um; wider by a foot um einen Fuß breiter
(o) (according to) nach
② adv. (a) (past) vorbei
(b) (near) close/near by in der Nähe
(c) by and large im Großen und Ganzen

**bye[-bye]** /'baɪ(baɪ)/ *int.* (coll.) tschüs (ugs.)

**bye-law** ▶ BY-LAW

**'by-election** *n.* Nachwahl, *die*

**bygone** /'baɪgɒn/ *adj.* vergangen

**'by-law** *n.* (esp. Brit.) Verordnung, *die*

**'bypass** [1] *n.* (a) Umgehungsstraße, *die*
(b) (Med.) Bypass, *der;* ~ **surgery** (Med.) eine
Bypassoperation/Bypassoperationen *Pl.*
[2] *v.t.* (a) **the road** ~**es the town** die Straße
führt um die Stadt herum

(b) (fig.) übergehen

**'by-product** *n.* Nebenprodukt, *das*

**'byroad** *n.* Nebenstraße, *die*

**bystander** /'baɪstændə(r)/ *n.* Zuschauer,
*der*/Zuschauerin, *die*

**byte** /'baɪt/ *n.* (Comp.) Byte, *das*

**'byway** *n.* Seitenweg, *der*

**'byword** *n.* Inbegriff, *der* (**for** *Gen.*)

---

# Cc

---

**C, c** /siː/ *n.* C, c, *das*

**C.** *abbr.* (a) = **Celsius** C
(b) = **Centigrade** C

**cab** /kæb/ *n.* (a) (taxi) Taxi, *das*
(b) (of lorry, truck) Fahrerhaus, *das;* (of train)
Führerstand, *der*

**cabaret** /'kæbəreɪ/ *n.* Varietee, *das;*
(satirical) Kabarett, *das*

**cabbage** /'kæbɪdʒ/ *n.* Kohl, *der;* **red/white**
~: Rot-/Weißkohl, *der*

**'cab driver** *n.* Taxifahrer, *der*/-fahrerin, *die*

**cabin** /'kæbɪn/ *n.* (in ship) (for passengers)
Kabine, *die;* (for crew) Kajüte, *die;* (in aircraft)
Kabine, *die*

**cabinet** /'kæbɪnɪt/ *n.* (a) Schrank, *der;* (in
bathroom, for medicines) Schränkchen, *das;*
[display] ~: Vitrine, *die*
(b) **the C**~ (Polit.) das Kabinett; **C**~ **Minister**
Minister, *der*

**cable** /'keɪbl/ [1] *n.* (a) (rope) Kabel, *das;* (of
~ car etc.) Seil, *das*
(b) (Electr., Teleph.) Kabel, *das*
(c) (message) Kabel, *das*
[2] *v.t.* kabeln ⟨Mitteilung, Nachricht⟩

**cable:** ~ **car** *n.* Drahtseilbahn, *die;*
~ **'television,** ~ **'TV** *ns.* Kabelfernsehen,
*das*

**'cab rank** *n.* (Brit.) Taxistand, *der;*
Droschken[halte]platz, *der* (Amtsspr.)

**cache** /kæʃ/ *n.* geheimes [Waffen-/Proviant-]
lager

**cackle** /'kækl/ [1] *n.* (a) (of hen) Gackern,
*das*
(b) (laughter) [meckerndes] Gelächter
[2] *v.i.* (a) ⟨Henne:⟩ gackern
(b) (laugh) meckernd lachen

**cactus** /'kæktəs/ *n., pl.* **cacti** /'kæktaɪ/ or
~**es** Kaktus, *der*

**CAD** *abbr.* = **computer-aided design**
CAD

**caddie** /'kædɪ/ *n.* (Golf) Caddie, *der*

**caddy** /'kædɪ/ *n.* Dose, *die*

**cadet** /kə'det/ *n.* Offiziersschüler, *der;*
**naval/police** ~: Marinekadett/Anwärter für
den Polizeidienst

**cadge** /kædʒ/ *v.t.* [sich (*Dat.*)] erbetteln

**café, cafe** /'kæfeɪ/ *n.* Lokal, *das;* (tea room)
Café, *das*

**cafeteria** /kæfɪ'tɪərɪə/ *n.* Cafeteria, *die*

**cafetière** /kæfə'tjeə/ *n.* Kaffeebereiter, *der*

**caffeinated** /'kæfɪneɪtɪd/ *adj.* koffeinhaltig

**caffeine** /'kæfiːn/ *n.* Koffein, *das*

**cage** /keɪdʒ/ [1] *n.* (a) Käfig, *der*
(b) (of lift) Fahrkabine, *die*
[2] *v.t.* einsperren

**cagey** /'keɪdʒɪ/ *adj.* (coll.) zugeknöpft (ugs.);
**be** ~ **about sth.** mit etw. hinterm Berg
halten (ugs.)

**Cairo** /'kaɪərəʊ/ *pr. n.* Kairo (*das*)

**cajole** /kə'dʒəʊl/ *v.t.* ~ **sb. into sth./doing**
**sth.** jmdm. etw. einreden/jmdm. einreden,
etw. zu tun

**cake** /keɪk/ [1] *n.* Kuchen, *der;* **a** ~ **of soap**
ein Riegel *od.* Stück Seife
[2] *v.t.* verkrusten; ~**d with dirt/blood**
schmutz-/blutverkrustet

**cal.** *abbr.* = **calorie[s]** cal.

**calamity** /kə'læmɪtɪ/ *n.* Unheil, *das*

**calcium** /'kælsɪəm/ *n.* Kalzium, *das*

**calculate** /'kælkjʊleɪt/ [1] *v.t.* (a)
berechnen; (by estimating) ausrechnen
(b) **be** ~**d to do sth.** darauf abzielen, etw. zu
tun
[2] *v.i.* ~ **on doing sth.** damit rechnen, etw.
zu tun

**'calculated** *adj.* kalkuliert ⟨Risiko⟩;
vorsätzlich ⟨Handlung⟩

**calculation** /kælkjʊ'leɪʃn/ *n.* (a) (result)
Rechnung, *die;* **he is out in his** ~**s** er hat
sich verrechnet
(b) (calculating) Berechnung, *die*

**calculator** /'kælkjʊleɪtə(r)/ *n.* Rechner, *der*

**calculus** /'kælkjuːləs/ *n.* differential/ integral ~: Differenzial-/Integralrechnung, *die*

**calendar** /'kælɪndə(r)/ *n.* Kalender, *der; attrib.* Kalender-

**calf**[1] /kɑːf/ *n., pl.* **calves** Kalb, *das*

**calf**[2] *n., pl.* **calves** (Anat.) Wade, *die*

**calibre** (*Brit.; Amer.:* **caliber**) /'kælɪbə(r)/ *n.* Kaliber, *das*

**calico** /'kælɪkəʊ/ *n.* Kattun, *der*

**California** /kælɪ'fɔːnɪə/ *pr. n.* Kalifornien (*das*)

**caliper** ▶ CALLIPER

**call** /kɔːl/ [1] *v.i.* (a) rufen; ~ to sb. jmdm. etwas zurufen; ~ [out] for help um Hilfe rufen
  (b) (pay brief visit) [kurz] besuchen (at *Akk.*); ~ on sb. jmdn. besuchen; ~ round vorbeikommen (ugs.); ~ at a port/station einen Hafen anlaufen/an einem Bahnhof halten
  (c) (Teleph.) who is ~ing, please? wer spricht da, bitte?; thank you for ~ing vielen Dank für Ihren Anruf!
  [2] *v.t.* (a) rufen; aufrufen 〈Namen, Nummer〉
  (b) (cry to, summon) rufen; (to a duty, to do sth.) aufrufen
  (c) (by radio/telephone) rufen/anrufen; (initially) Kontakt aufnehmen mit
  (d) (rouse) wecken
  (e) einberufen 〈Konferenz〉; ausrufen 〈Streik〉
  (f) (name) nennen; he is ~ed Bob er heißt Bob; what is it ~ed in English? wie heißt das auf Englisch?
  [3] *n.* (a) Ruf, *der;* a ~ for help ein Hilferuf; be on ~: Bereitschaftsdienst haben
  (b) (visit) Besuch, *der;* make *or* pay a ~ on sb., make *or* pay sb. a ~: jmdn. besuchen
  (c) (telephone ~) Anruf, *der;* give sb. a ~: jmdn. anrufen; make a ~: telefonieren
  (d) (invitation, summons) Aufruf, *der*
  (e) (need, occasion) Anlass, *der*
■ **call 'back** [1] *v.t.* zurückrufen
  [2] *v.i.* zurückrufen; (come back) zurückkommen
■ **'call for** *v.t.* (a) (send for, order) bestellen
  (b) (collect) abholen
  (c) (require, demand) erfordern; this ~s for a celebration das muss gefeiert werden
■ **call 'in** [1] *v.i.* vorbeikommen (ugs.) (on bei)
  [2] *v.t.* zu Rate ziehen 〈Fachmann usw.〉
■ **call 'off** *v.t.* absagen 〈Treffen, Verabredung〉; rückgängig machen 〈Geschäft〉; lösen 〈Verlobung〉; (end) abbrechen 〈Streik〉
■ **'call on** *v.t.* (a) ▶ ~ 1B
  (b) ▶ ~ [UP]ON
■ **call 'out** [1] *v.t.* alarmieren 〈Truppen〉; zum Streik aufrufen 〈Arbeitnehmer〉
  [2] *v.i.* ▶ ~ 1A
■ **call 'up** *v.t.* (a) (by telephone) anrufen
  (b) (Mil.) einberufen
■ **'call [up]on** *v.t.* ~ upon sb.'s generosity

an jmds. Großzügigkeit (*Akk.*) appellieren; ~ [up]on sb. to do sth. jmdn. auffordern, etw. zu tun

**'call box** *n.* Telefonzelle, *die*

**'caller** *n.* (visitor) Besucher, *der*/Besucherin, *die;* (on telephone) Anrufer, *der*/Anruferin, *die*

**'call girl** *n.* Callgirl, *das*

**'calling** *n.* Beruf, *der*

**calliper** /'kælɪpə(r)/ *n.* (a) [a pair of] ~s Tasterzirkel, *der*
  (b) (Med.) Beinschiene, *die*

**callous** /'kæləs/ *adj.* gefühllos; herzlos 〈Handlung, Verhalten〉

**'call-up** *n.* (Mil.) Einberufung, *die*

**calm** /kɑːm/ [1] *n.* (stillness) Stille, *die;* (serenity) Ruhe, *die*
  [2] *adj.* ruhig
  [3] *v.t.* ~ sb. [down] jmdn. beruhigen
  [4] *v.i.* ~ [down] sich beruhigen

**'calmly** *adv.* ruhig; gelassen

**'calmness** *n.* Ruhe, *die;* (of water) Stille, *die*

**Calor gas** ® /'kælə gæs/ *n.* Butangas, *das*

**calorie** /'kælərɪ/ *n.* Kalorie, *die*

**calorific** /kælə'rɪfɪk/ *adj.* ~ value Heizwert, *der*

**calves** *pl. of* CALF[1], [2]

**CAM** *abbr.* = **computer-aided manufacturing** CAM

**camber** /'kæmbə(r)/ *n.* Wölbung, *die*

**camcorder** /'kæmkɔːdə(r)/ *n.* Camcorder, *der;* Kamerarecorder, *der*

**came** ▶ COME

**camel** /'kæml/ *n.* Kamel, *das*

**camera** /'kæmərə/ *n.* Kamera, *die*

**camera:** ~ case *n.* Kameratasche, *die;* ~ crew *n.* Kamerateam, *das;* ~man *n.* Kameramann, *der;* ~work *n., no indef. art.* Kameraführung, *die*

**camomile** /'kæməmaɪl/ *n.* Kamille, *die;* ~ tea Kamillentee, *der*

**camouflage** /'kæməflɑːʒ/ [1] *n.* Tarnung, *die*
  [2] *v.t.* tarnen

**camp** /kæmp/ [1] *n.* Lager, *das*
  [2] *v.i.* ~ [out] campen; (in tent) zelten; go ~ing Campen/Zelten fahren/gehen

**campaign** /kæm'peɪn/ [1] *n.* (a) (Mil.) Feldzug, *der*
  (b) (organized action) Kampagne, *die;* publicity ~: Werbekampagne, *die*
  [2] *v.i.* ~ for/against sth. sich für etw. einsetzen/gegen etw. etwas unternehmen; be ~ing 〈Politiker〉: im Wahlkampf stehen

**'camp bed** *n.* Campingliege, *die*

**'camper** *n.* (person) Camper, *der*/Camperin, *die*

**'campfire** *n.* Lagerfeuer, *das*

**'camping** *n.* Camping, *das;* (in tent) Zelten, *das*

**camping:** ~ ground ▶ ~ SITE;

~ **holiday** n. Campingurlaub, der; ~ **site** n. Campingplatz, der; ~ **stove** n. Campingkocher, der

'**campsite** n. Campingplatz, der

**campus** /'kæmpəs/ n. Campus, der

**can¹** /kæn/ ① n. (milk ~, watering ~) Kanne, die; (for oil, petrol) Kanister, der; (Amer.: for refuse) Eimer, der
(b) (for preserving) [Konserven]dose, die; a ~ of tomatoes/beer eine Dose Tomaten/Bier
② v.t., -nn- konservieren

**can²** /kən, stressed kæn/ v. aux., only in pres. **can**, neg. **cannot** /'kænət/, (coll.) **can't** /kɑːnt/, past **could** /kʊd/, neg. (coll.) **couldn't** /'kʊdnt/ können; (have right, be permitted) dürfen; können; **I can't do that** das kann ich nicht; (it would be wrong) das kann ich nicht tun; **you can't smoke here** hier dürfen Sie nicht rauchen; **could you ring me tomorrow?** könnten Sie mich morgen anrufen?; **I could have killed him** ich hätte ihn umbringen können; [**that**] **could be** [**so**] das könnte od. kann sein

**Canada** /'kænədə/ pr. n. Kanada (das)

**Canadian** /kə'neɪdɪən/ ① adj. kanadisch; **sb. is** ~: jmd. ist Kanadier/Kanadierin
② n. Kanadier, der/Kanadierin, die

**canal** /kə'næl/ n. Kanal, der

**canary** /kə'neərɪ/ n. Kanarienvogel, der

**Ca'nary Islands** pr. n. pl. Kanarische Inseln Pl.

**cancel** /'kænsl/ ① v.t., (Brit.) -ll- (a) absagen ⟨Besuch, Urlaub, Reise, Sportveranstaltung⟩; ausfallen lassen ⟨Veranstaltung, Vorlesung, Zug, Bus⟩; fallen lassen ⟨Pläne⟩; rückgängig machen ⟨Einladung, Vertrag⟩; zurücknehmen ⟨Befehl⟩; stornieren ⟨Bestellung, Auftrag⟩; kündigen ⟨Abonnement⟩; abbestellen ⟨Zeitung⟩
(b) (Comp.) abbrechen
② v.i., (Brit.) -ll-: (a) ~ [out] sich [gegenseitig] aufheben
(b) (Comp.) abbrechen

**cancellation** /kænsə'leɪʃn/ n. ▶ CANCEL 1A: Absage, die; Ausfall, der; Fallenlassen, das; Rückgängigmachen, das; Zurücknahme, die; Stornierung, die; Kündigung, die; Abbestellung, die

**cancer** /'kænsə(r)/ n. (a) (Med.) Krebs, der; ~ **of the liver** Leberkrebs, der
(b) C~ (Astrol., Astron.) der Krebs

**candelabra** /kændɪ'lɑːbrə/ n. Leuchter, der

**candid** /'kændɪd/ adj. offen; ehrlich ⟨Ansicht, Bericht⟩

**candidate** /'kændɪdət, 'kændɪdeɪt/ n. Kandidat, der/Kandidatin, die

**candle** /'kændl/ n. Kerze, die

**candle:** ~**light** n. Kerzenlicht, das; ~**stick** n. Kerzenhalter, der; (elaborate) Leuchter, der; ~**wick** n. (material) Frottierplüsch, der

**candour** (Brit., Amer.: **candor**) /'kændə(r)/ n. ▶ CANDID: Offenheit, die; Ehrlichkeit, die

**candy** /'kændɪ/ n. (Amer.) (sweets) Süßigkeiten Pl.; (sweet) Bonbon, das od. der

'**candyfloss** /'kændɪflɒs/ n. Zuckerwatte, die

**cane** /keɪn/ ① n. (a) (stem) Rohr, das; (of raspberry, blackberry) Spross, der
(b) (material) Rohr, das
(c) (stick) [Rohr]stock, der
② v.t. [mit dem Stock] schlagen

'**cane sugar** n. Rohrzucker, der

**canine** /'keɪnaɪn/ adj. (a) (of dog[s]) Hunde-
(b) ~ **tooth** Eckzahn, der

**canister** /'kænɪstə(r)/ n. Büchse, die; (for petrol, oil, etc.) Kanister, der

**cannabis** /'kænəbɪs/ n. (hashish) Haschisch, das; (marijuana) Marihuana, das

**canned** /kænd/ adj. Dosen-; in Dosen nachgestellt; ~ **meat/fruit** Fleisch-/Obstkonserven Pl.; ~ **beer** Dosenbier; ~ **food** [Lebensmittel]konserven Pl.; ~ **music** Musikkonserve, die

**cannibal** /'kænɪbl/ n. Kannibale, der/Kannibalin, die

**cannibalism** /'kænɪbəlɪzm/ n. Kannibalismus, der

**cannon** /'kænən/ ① n. Kanone, die
② v.i. (Brit.) ~ **into sb./sth.** mit etw./jmdm. zusammenprallen

'**cannon ball** n. Kanonenkugel, die

**cannot** ▶ CAN²

**canny** /'kænɪ/ adj. (shrewd) schlau

**canoe** /kə'nuː/ n. Paddelboot, das; (Indian ~, Sport) Kanu, das

**canoeing** /kə'nuːɪŋ/ n. Paddeln, das; (Sport) Kanufahren, das; Kanusport, der

**canoeist** /kə'nuːɪst/ n. Paddelbootfahrer, der/-fahrerin, die

**canon** /'kænən/ n. (a) (general law, criterion) Grundregel, die
(b) (Eccl.: person) Kanoniker, der

**canonize** /'kænənaɪz/ v.t. kanonisieren ⟨Heiligen⟩; heilig sprechen ⟨Märtyrer⟩

'**can-opener** n. Dosenöffner, der

**canopy** /'kænəpɪ/ n. Baldachin, der; (over entrance) Vordach, das

**can't** /kɑːnt/ (coll.) = CANNOT; ▶ CAN²

**cantankerous** /kæn'tæŋkərəs/ adj. streitsüchtig

**canteen** /kæn'tiːn/ n. Kantine, die

**canter** /'kæntə(r)/ ① n. Handgalopp, der
② v.i. leicht galoppieren

**canvas** /'kænvəs/ n. Leinwand, die

**canvass** /'kænvəs/ ① v.t. Wahlwerbung treiben in ⟨einem Wahlkreis, Gebiet⟩; Wahlwerbung treiben bei ⟨Wählern, Bürgern⟩
② v.i. werben (**on behalf of** für); ~ **for votes** um Stimmen werben

'**canvasser** n. (for votes) Wahlhelfer, der/

-helferin, *die*

**canyon** /'kænjən/ *n.* Cañon, *der*

**cap** /kæp/ ① *n.* **(a)** Mütze, *die;* (nurse's, servant's) Haube, *die;* (with peak) Schirmmütze, *die;* (skull~) Kappe, *die* **(b)** (of bottle, jar) [Verschluss]kappe, *die;* (petrol ~, radiator ~) Deckel, *der* ② *v.t.,* -pp-: **(a)** verschließen ‹*Flasche*›; zudecken ‹*Bohrloch*›; mit einer Schutzkappe versehen ‹*Zahn*› **(b)** (fig.) überbieten; **to ~ it all** obendrein

**CAP** *abbr.* = **Common Agricultural Policy** gemeinsame Agrarpolitik

**capability** /keɪpə'bɪlɪtɪ/ *n.* Fähigkeit, *die*

**capable** /'keɪpəbl/ *adj.* **(a) be ~ of sth.** ‹*Person.:*› zu etw. imstande sein **(b)** (gifted, able) fähig

**capacity** /kə'pæsɪtɪ/ *n.* **(a)** Fassungsvermögen, *das;* **the machine is working to ~:** die Maschine ist voll ausgelastet; **a seating ~ of 300** 300 Sitzplätze **(b)** (measure) Rauminhalt, *der;* Volumen, *das;* **measure of ~:** Hohlmaß, *das* **(c)** (position) Eigenschaft, *die;* **in his ~ as …:** in seiner Eigenschaft als …

**cape¹** /keɪp/ *n.* (garment) Umhang, *der;* Cape, *das*

**cape²** *n.* (Geog.) Kap, *das;* **the C~** [**of Good Hope**] das Kap der Guten Hoffnung; **C~ Town** Kapstadt (*das*)

**caper** /'keɪpə(r)/ *v.i.* **~ [about]** [herum]tollen

**capful** /'kæpfʊl/ *n.* **one ~:** der Inhalt einer Verschlusskappe

**capillary** /kə'pɪlərɪ/ *n.* Kapillare, *die* (fachspr.)

**capital** /'kæpɪtl/ ① *attrib. adj.* **(a)** Todes‹*strafe, -urteil*›; Kapital‹*verbrechen*› **(b)** groß, Groß‹*buchstabe*› **(c)** (principal) Haupt‹*stadt*› ② *n.* **(a)** (letter) Großbuchstabe, *der* **(b)** (city, town) Hauptstadt, *die* **(c)** (stock, wealth) Kapital, *das*

**capitalism** /'kæpɪtəlɪzm/ *n.* Kapitalismus, *der*

**capitalist** /'kæpɪtəlɪst/ ① *n.* Kapitalist, *der*/Kapitalistin, *die* ② *adj.* kapitalistisch

**capitalize** /'kæpɪtəlaɪz/ ① *v.t.* großschreiben ‹*Buchstaben, Wort*› ② *v.i.* **~ on sth.** aus etw. Kapital schlagen (ugs.)

**capital 'punishment** *n.* Todesstrafe, *die*

**capitulate** /kə'pɪtjʊleɪt/ *v.i.* kapitulieren

**capitulation** /kəpɪtjʊ'leɪʃn/ *n.* Kapitulation, *die*

**cappuccino** /kɑːpʊ'tʃiːnəʊ/ *n., pl.* ~s Cappuccino, *der*

**capricious** /kə'prɪʃəs/ *adj.* launisch

**Capricorn** /'kæprɪkɔːn/ *n.* (Astrol., Astron.) der Steinbock

**capsize** /kæp'saɪz/ ① *v.t.* zum Kentern bringen

② *v.i.* kentern

**capsule** /'kæpsjuːl/ *n.* Kapsel, *die*

**Capt.** *abbr.* = **Captain** Kapt.; Hptm.

**captain** /'kæptɪn/ ① *n.* Kapitän, *der;* (Army) Hauptmann, *der* ② *v.t.* **~ a team** Kapitän einer Mannschaft sein

**caption** /'kæpʃn/ *n.* (heading) Überschrift, *die;* (under photograph, drawing) Bildunterschrift, *die;* (Cinemat., Telev.) Untertitel, *der*

**captivate** /'kæptɪveɪt/ *v.t.* fesseln

**captivating** /'kæptɪveɪtɪŋ/ *adj.* bezaubernd; einnehmend ‹*Lächeln*›

**captive** /'kæptɪv/ ① *adj.* gefangen; **be taken ~:** gefangen genommen werden; **~ audience** unfreiwilliges Publikum ② *n.* Gefangener, *der*/Gefangene, *die*

**captivity** /kæp'tɪvɪtɪ/ *n.* Gefangenschaft, *die;* **be held in ~:** gefangen gehalten werden

**captor** /'kæptə(r)/ *n.* **his ~:** der, der/die, die ihn gefangen nahm

**capture** /'kæptʃə(r)/ ① *n.* **(a)** (of thief etc.) Festnahme, *die;* (of town) Einnahme, *die* **(b)** (thing, person) Fang, *der* ② *v.t.* festnehmen ‹*Person*›; [ein]fangen ‹*Tier*›; einnehmen ‹*Stadt*›; gefangen nehmen ‹*Fantasie*›

**car** /kɑː(r)/ *n.* Auto, *das;* Wagen, *der;* **by ~:** mit dem Auto

**carafe** /kə'ræf/ *n.* Karaffe, *die*

**caramel** /'kærəməl/ *n.* Karamell, *der;* (toffee) Karamellbonbon, *das*

**carat** /'kærət/ *n.* Karat, *das;* **a 22-~ gold ring** ein 22-karätiger Goldring

**caravan** /'kærəvæn/ *n.* (Brit.) Wohnwagen, *der*

**'caravan site** *n.* Campingplatz für Wohnwagen

**carbohydrate** /kɑːbəʊ'haɪdreɪt/ *n.* Kohlenhydrat, *das*

**'car bomb** *n.* Autobombe, *die*

**carbon** /'kɑːbən/ *n.* Kohlenstoff, *der*

**carbon:** **~ 'copy** *n.* Durchschlag, *der;* **~ dioxide** /- daɪ'ɒksaɪd/ *n.* Kohlendyoxid, *das;* **~ mo'noxide** /-mə'nɒksaɪd/ *n.* (Chem.) Kohlenmonoxyd, *das;* **~ paper** *n.* Kohlepapier, *das*

**car 'boot sale** *n.:* Trödelmarkt, bei dem die Händler ihre Waren aus dem Kofferraum ihrer Autos heraus verkaufen

**carburettor** (*Amer.:* **carburetor**) /kɑːbə'retə(r)/ *n.* Vergaser, *der*

**carcass** (Brit. also: **carcase**) /'kɑːkəs/ *n.* Kadaver, *der*

**'car crash** *n.* Autounfall, *der*

**card** /kɑːd/ *n.* Karte, *die;* **play ~s** Karten spielen

**card:** **~board** *n.* Pappe, *die;* **~board 'box** *n.* [Papp]karton, *der;* (smaller) [Papp]schachtel, *die;* **~ game** *n.* Kartenspiel, *das;* **~holder** *n.* Karteninhaber, *der*/-inhaberin, *die*

**cardiac** /'kɑ:dɪæk/ *adj.* (of heart) Herz-
**cardiac ar'rest** *n.* Herzstillstand, *der*
**cardigan** /'kɑ:dɪgən/ *n.* Strickjacke, *die*
**cardinal** /'kɑ:dɪnl/ ①*adj.* grundlegend
⟨*Frage, Doktrin, Pflicht*⟩; Kardinal⟨*fehler,
-problem*⟩; Haupt⟨*punkt, -merkmal*⟩
② *n.* (Eccl.) Kardinal, *der*
**cardinal:** ~ **'number** *n.* Kardinalzahl,
*die;* ~ **'sin** *n.* Todsünde, *die*
**'cardphone** *n.* Kartentelefon, *das*
**care** /keə(r)/ ① *n.* **(a)** (anxiety) Sorge, *die*
**(b)** (pains) Sorgfalt, *die*
**(c)** (caution) Vorsicht, *die;* **take** ~: aufpassen
**(d)** medical ~: ärztliche Betreuung
**(e)** (charge) Obhut, *die* (geh.); **put sb. in** ~/
**take sb. into** ~: jmdn. in Pflege geben/
nehmen; ~ **of** (on letter) bei; **take** ~ **of sb./sth.**
(ensure safety of) auf jmdn./etw. aufpassen;
(attend to) sich um jmdn./etw. kümmern
② *v.i.* ~ **for sb./sth.** (look after) sich um
jmdn./etw. kümmern; (like) jmdn./etw. mögen;
~ **to do sth.** etw. tun mögen; **I don't**
~ [**whether/how/what** *etc.*] es ist mir
gleich[, ob/wie/was *usw.*]
**career** /kə'rɪə(r)/ ① *n.* Beruf, *der*
② *v.i.* rasen; ⟨*Pferd, Reiter:*⟩ galoppieren
**career:** ~ **break** *n.* Karriereknick, *der;*
~**s adviser** *n.* Berufsberater, *der*/
-beraterin, *die;* ~**s** [**advisory**] **service**
*n.* Berufsberatung, *die;* ~ **woman** *n.*
Karrierefrau, *die*
**'carefree** *adj.* sorgenfrei
**careful** /'keəfl/ *adj.* (thorough) sorgfältig;
(cautious) vorsichtig; [**be**] ~! Vorsicht!; **be**
~ **of sb./sth.** (be cautious of) sich vor jmdm./
etw. in Acht nehmen; **be** ~ **with sb./sth.**
vorsichtig mit jmdm./etw. umgehen
**'carefully** *adv.* (thoroughly) sorgfältig;
(attentively) aufmerksam; (cautiously) vorsichtig
**careless** /'keəlɪs/ *adj.* **(a)** (inattentive)
unaufmerksam; (thoughtless) gedankenlos;
leichtsinnig ⟨*Fahrer*⟩; nachlässig ⟨*Arbeiter,
Arbeit*⟩; gedankenlos ⟨*Bemerkung,
Handlung*⟩; unachtsam ⟨*Fahren*⟩
**(b)** (nonchalant) ungezwungen
**'carelessly** *adv.* (without care) nachlässig;
(thoughtlessly) gedankenlos
**'carelessness** *n.* (lack of care)
Nachlässigkeit, *die;* (thoughtlessness)
Gedankenlosigkeit, *die*
**carer** /'keərə(r)/ *n.* (for sick person) Pfleger,
*der*/Pflegerin, *die*
**caress** /kə'res/ ① *n.* Liebkosung, *die*
② *v.t.* liebkosen
**'caretaker** *n.* Hausmeister, *der*/-meisterin,
*die*
**'car ferry** *n.* Autofähre, *die*
**cargo** /'kɑ:gəʊ/ *n.* Fracht, *die*
**'cargo boat, 'cargo ship** *ns.* Frachter,
*der*
**'car hire** *n.* Autovermietung, *die*
**Caribbean** /kærɪ'bi:ən/ ① *n.* **the** ~: die
Karibik

② *adj.* karibisch
**caricature** /'kærɪkətjʊə(r)/ ① *n.*
Karikatur, *die*
② *v.t.* karikieren
**caring** /'keərɪŋ/ *adj.* sozial ⟨*Gesellschaft*⟩;
fürsorglich ⟨*Person*⟩
**carnage** /'kɑ:nɪdʒ/ *n.* Gemetzel, *das*
**carnal** /'kɑ:nl/ *adj.* sinnlich
**carnation** /kɑ:'neɪʃn/ *n.* [Garten]nelke, *die*
**carnet** /'kɑ:neɪ/ *n.* (of motorist) Triptyk, *das;*
[camping] ~: Ausweis für Camper
**carnival** /'kɑ:nɪvl/ *n.* Volksfest, *das*
**carnivorous** /kɑ:'nɪvərəs/ *adj.* Fleisch
fressend
**carol** /'kærl/ *n.* [Christmas] ~:
Weihnachtslied, *das*
**'car owner** *n.* Autobesitzer, *der*/-besitzerin,
*die*
**carp** /kɑ:p/ *n., pl. same* Karpfen, *der*
**car:** ~ **park** *n.* Parkplatz, *der;* (building)
Parkhaus, *das;* ~ **parking** *n.* Parken, *das;*
~ **parking facilities are available** Parkplätze
[sind] vorhanden
**carpenter** /'kɑ:pɪntə(r)/ *n.* Zimmermann,
*der;* (for furniture) Tischler, *der*/Tischlerin, *die*
**carpentry** /'kɑ:pɪntrɪ/ *n.*
Zimmerhandwerk, *das;* (in furniture)
Tischlerhandwerk, *das*
**carpet** /'kɑ:pɪt/ *n.* Teppich, *der*
**carpet:** ~ **slipper** *n.* Hausschuh, *der;*
~ **sweeper** *n.* Teppichkehrer, *der*
**car:** ~ **phone** *n.* Autotelefon, *das;* ~**port**
*n.* Einstellplatz, *der;* ~ **radio** *n.* Autoradio,
*das;* ~ **rental** ▶ CAR HIRE
**carriage** /'kærɪdʒ/ *n.* **(a)** (horse-drawn)
Kutsche, *die*
**(b)** (Railw.) Wagen, *der*
**'carriageway** *n.* Fahrbahn, *die*
**'car ride** *n.* Autofahrt, *die*
**carrier** /'kærɪə(r)/ *n.* **(a)** (bearer) Träger, *der*
**(b)** (firm) Transportunternehmen, *das*
**carrier:** ~ **bag** *n.* Tragetasche, *die;*
~ **pigeon** *n.* Brieftaube, *die*
**carrot** /'kærət/ *n.* Möhre, *die*
**carry** /'kærɪ/ *v.t.* **(a)** tragen; (emphasizing
destination) bringen
**(b)** (possess) besitzen ⟨*Autorität, Gewicht*⟩
■ **carry a'way** *v.t.* forttragen; **be** *or* **get
carried away** sich hinreißen lassen
■ **carry 'on** ① *v.t.* fortführen; ~ **on** [**doing
sth.**] weiterhin etw. tun
② *v.i.* weitermachen
■ **carry 'out** *v.t.* durchführen; ausführen
⟨*Anweisung, Auftrag*⟩; vornehmen
⟨*Verbesserungen*⟩
**carry:** ~**cot** *n.* Babytragetasche, *die;*
~**-out** *n.* ~-out [meal] Essen *od.* Mahlzeit
zum Mitnehmen; **get a** ~**-out** sich (*Dat.*) in
einem Restaurant was zu essen holen
**carsick** *adj.* **children are often** ~: Kindern
wird beim Autofahren oft schlecht
**cart** /kɑ:t/ ① *n.* Wagen, *der*

2 *v.t.* (coll.) schleppen

'**car thief** *n.* Autodieb, *der*/-diebin, *die*

**cartilage** /'kɑːtɪlɪdʒ/ *n.* Knorpel, *der*

**carton** /'kɑːtn/ *n.* [Papp]karton, *der;* (of drink) Tüte, *die;* (of cream, yoghurt) Becher, *der*

**cartoon** /kɑː'tuːn/ *n.* humoristische Zeichnung; (satirical) Karikatur, *die;* (film) Zeichentrickfilm, *der*

**cartridge** /'kɑːtrɪdʒ/ *n.* (a) (for gun) Patrone, *die*
(b) (of film; cassette) Kassette, *die*

'**cartwheel** *n.* (Gymnastics) Rad, *das;* **turn** or **do** ∼s Rad schlagen

**carve** /kɑːv/ 1 *v.t.* (a) tranchieren ⟨*Fleisch, Braten, Hähnchen*⟩
(b) (from wood) schnitzen; (from stone) meißeln
2 *v.i.* ∼ **in wood/stone** in Holz schnitzen/in Stein meißeln

**carving** /'kɑːvɪŋ/ *n.* (in or from wood) Schnitzerei, *die;* (in or from stone) Skulptur, *die*

'**carving knife** *n.* Tranchiermesser, *das*

'**car wash** *n.* Waschanlage, *die*

**cascade** /kæs'keɪd/ *n.* Kaskade, *die*

**case¹** /keɪs/ *n.* (a) (instance, matter, set of arguments) Fall, *der;* **it is** [**not**] **the** ∼ **that** ...: es trifft [nicht] zu, dass ...; **in** ∼ ...: falls ...; [**just**] **in** ∼: für alle Fälle; **in** ∼ **of emergency** im Notfall; **in that** ∼: in diesem Fall; **in any** ∼ (regardless of anything else) jedenfalls; **I don't need it in any** ∼: ich brauche es sowieso nicht
(b) (Med., Police, Soc. Serv., etc.) Fall, *der*
(c) (Law) Fall, *der;* (action) Verfahren, *das*
(d) (Ling.) Fall, *der;* Kasus, *der* (fachspr.)

**case²** *n.* (a) Koffer, *der;* (brief∼) [Akten]tasche, *die*
(b) (for spectacles, cigarettes) Etui, *das*
(c) (crate) Kiste, *die*
(d) [**display**] ∼: Schaukasten, *der*

**cash** /kæʃ/ 1 *n.* Bargeld, *das;* **pay** [**in**] ∼, **pay** ∼ **down** bar zahlen
2 *v.t.* einlösen ⟨*Scheck*⟩

**cash:** ∼ **account** *n.* Kassekonto, *das;* ∼ **and 'carry** *n.* cash and carry; (store) Cash-and-carry-Laden, *der;* ∼**back** *n., no art.:* Barauszahlung eines Differenzbetrages bei Kauf mit Geldkarte; ∼**card** *n.* Geldautomatenkarte, *die;* ∼ **desk** *n.* (Brit.) Kasse, *die;* ∼ **discount** *n.* Skonto, *der* od. *das;* Barzahlungsrabatt, *der;* ∼ **dispenser** *n.* Geldautomat, *der*

**cashew nut** /'kæʃuː/ *n.* Cashewnuss, *die*

'**cash flow** *n.* Cashflow, *der*

**cashier** /kæ'ʃɪə(r)/ *n.* Kassierer, *der*/ Kassiererin, *die*

'**cashless** *adj.* bargeldlos; **the** ∼ **society** die bargeldlose Gesellschaft

**cashmere** /'kæʃmɪə(r)/ *n.* Kaschmir, *der;* ∼ **wool/sweater** Kaschmirwolle, *die*/ Kaschmirpullover, *der*

**cash:** ∼ **payment** *n.* Barzahlung, *die;*

**make** ∼ **payment** bar bezahlen; ∼**point** *n.* Geldautomat, *der;* ∼ **register** *n.* [Registrier]kasse, *die*

**casino** /kə'siːnəʊ/ *n.* Kasino, *das*

**cask** /kɑːsk/ *n.* Fass, *das*

**casket** /'kɑːskɪt/ *n.* (a) Kästchen, *das*
(b) (Amer.: coffin) Sarg, *der*

**casserole** /'kæsərəʊl/ *n.* Schmortopf, *der*

**cassette** /kə'set/ *n.* Kassette, *die*

**cassette:** ∼ **deck** *n.* Kassettendeck, *das;* ∼ **player** *n.* Kassettengerät, *das;* ∼ **recorder** *n.* Kassettenrekorder, *der*

**cast** /kɑːst/ 1 *v.t.,* **cast** (a) werfen
(b) (shape, form) gießen
(c) abgeben ⟨*Stimme*⟩
2 *n.* (a) (Med.) Gipsverband, *der*
(b) (actors) Besetzung, *die*
■ **cast a'side** *v.t.* beiseite schieben ⟨*Vorschlag*⟩; vergessen ⟨*Sorgen*⟩; fallen lassen ⟨*Hemmungen*⟩
■ **cast 'off** *v.i. & t.* (Naut.) losmachen

**castanets** /kæstə'nets/ *n. pl.* Kastagnetten *Pl.*

'**castaway** *n.* Schiffbrüchige, *der*/*die*

**caste** /kɑːst/ *n.* Kaste, *die*

**cast 'iron** *n.* Gusseisen, *das*

**castle** /'kɑːsl/ *n.* Burg, *die;* (mansion) Schloss, *das*

'**cast-offs** *n. pl.* abgelegte Sachen *Pl.*

**castor** /'kɑːstə(r)/ *n.* (wheel) Rolle, *die*

**castor:** ∼ **'oil** *n.* Rizinusöl, *das;* ∼ **sugar** *n.* Raffinade, *die*

**castrate** /kæ'streɪt/ *v.t.* kastrieren

**castration** /kæ'streɪʃn/ *n.* Kastration, *die*

**casual** /'kæʒjʊəl/ *adj.* ungezwungen; leger ⟨*Kleidung*⟩; beiläufig ⟨*Bemerkung*⟩; flüchtig ⟨*Bekannter, Bekanntschaft, Blick*⟩; unbekümmert ⟨*Haltung, Einstellung*⟩

**casual 'labour** *n.* Gelegenheitsarbeit, *die*

'**casually** *adv.* ungezwungen; beiläufig ⟨*bemerken*⟩; flüchtig ⟨*anschauen*⟩; leger ⟨*sich kleiden*⟩

**casualty** /'kæʒjʊəltɪ/ *n.* (a) (injured person) Verletzte, *der*/*die;* (in battle) Verwundete, *der*/*die;* (dead person) Tote, *der*/*die*
(b) (hospital department) Unfallstation, *die*

'**casualty ward** *n.* Unfallstation, *die*

**cat** /kæt/ *n.* Katze, *die*

**catalogue** (*Amer.:* **catalog**) /'kætəlɒg/
1 *n.* Katalog, *der*
2 *v.t.* katalogisieren

**catalyst** /'kætəlɪst/ *n.* Katalysator, *der*

**catalytic** /kætə'lɪtɪk/ *adj.* ∼ **converter** Katalysator, *der*

**catamaran** /kætəmə'ræn/ *n.* Katamaran, *der*

**catapult** /'kætəpʌlt/ 1 *n.* Katapult, *das*
2 *v.t.* katapultieren

**cataract** /'kætərækt/ *n.* (a) Katarakt, *der*
(b) (Med.) grauer Star

**catarrh** /kə'tɑː(r)/ *n.* Katarrh, *der*

**catastrophe** /kə'tæstrəfɪ/ n. Katastrophe, die

**catastrophic** /kætə'strɒfɪk/ adj. katastrophal

**catch** /kætʃ/ ① v.t., caught /kɔːt/ (a) fangen; ~ hold of sb./sth. jmdn./etw. festhalten; (to stop oneself falling) sich an jmdm./etw. festhalten; get sth. caught or ~ sth. on/in sth. mit etw. an/in etw. (Dat.) hängen bleiben; ~ one's finger in the door sich (Dat.) den Finger in der Tür einklemmen
(b) (travel by) nehmen; (be in time for) [noch] erreichen
(c) (surprise) ~ sb. doing sth. jmdn. [dabei] erwischen, wie er etw. tut (ugs.)
(d) (become infected with) sich (Dat.) zuziehen; ~ sth. from sb. sich bei jmdm. mit etw. anstecken; ~ a cold sich erkälten; ~ it (fig. coll.) etwas kriegen (ugs.)
(e) ~ sb.'s attention/interest jmds. Aufmerksamkeit erregen/jmds. Interesse wecken
② v.i., caught (a) (begin to burn) [anfangen zu] brennen
(b) (become hooked up) hängenbleiben; ⟨Haar, Faden:⟩ sich verfangen
③ n. (a) (of ball) make a ~: fangen
(b) (amount caught, lit. or fig.) Fang, der
(c) (difficulty) Haken, der (in an + Dat.)
(d) (of door) Schnapper, der
■ **catch 'on** v.i. (coll.) (a) (become popular) [gut] ankommen (ugs.)
(b) (understand) kapieren (ugs.)
■ **catch 'up** ① v.t. ~ sb. up, ~ up with s.b. jmdn. einholen
② v.i. ~ up gleichziehen; ~ up on sth. etw. nachholen

**'catching** adj. ansteckend

**'catchphrase** n. Slogan, der

**'catchy** adj. eingängig

**'cat door** n. Katzentür, die

**categorical** /kætɪ'gɒrɪkl/ adj. kategorisch

**categorize** (**categorise**) /'kætɪgəraɪz/ v.t. kategorisieren

**category** /'kætɪgərɪ/ n. Kategorie, die

**cater** /'keɪtə(r)/ v.i. ~ for sb./sth. für jmdn./etw. [die] Speisen und Getränke liefern; (fig.) auf jmdn./etw. eingestellt sein

**'caterer** n. Lieferant von Speisen und Getränken

**'catering** n. (a) (trade) Gastronomie, die
(b) (service) Lieferung von Speisen und Getränken

**caterpillar** /'kætəpɪlə(r)/ n. Raupe, die

**'cat flap** ▶ CAT DOOR

**cathedral** /kə'θiːdrl/ n. Dom, der

**Catherine wheel** /'kæθrɪn wiːl/ n. Feuerrad, das

**Catholic** /'kæθəlɪk/ ① adj. katholisch
② n. Katholik, der/Katholikin, die

**Catholicism** /kə'θɒlɪsɪzm/ n. Katholizismus, der

**catkin** /'kætkɪn/ n. (Bot.) Kätzchen, das

**'Cat's-eye** ® n. (Brit.: on road) Bodenrückstrahler, der

**cattle** /'kætl/ n. pl. Rinder Pl.

**'cattle market** n. Viehmarkt, der; (fig.) Fleischbeschau, die (ugs. scherzh.)

**'catwalk** n. Laufsteg, der

**caught** ▶ CATCH 1, 2

**cauldron** /'kɔːldrən/ n. Kessel, der

**cauliflower** /'kɒlɪflaʊə(r)/ n. Blumenkohl, der

**cause** /kɔːz/ ① n. (a) Ursache, die (of für od. Gen.); (person) Verursacher, der/ Verursacherin, die; be the ~ of sth. etw. verursachen
(b) (reason) Grund, der; ~ for sth. Grund zu etw.
(c) (object of support) Sache, die; [in] a good ~: [für] eine gute Sache
② v.t. verursachen; erregen ⟨Aufsehen, Ärgernis⟩; hervorrufen ⟨Unruhe, Verwirrung⟩; ~ sb. worry/pain jmdm. Sorge/ Schmerzen bereiten; ~ sb. to do sth. jmdn. veranlassen, etw. zu tun

**causeway** /'kɔːzweɪ/ n. Damm, der

**caustic** /'kɔːstɪk/ adj. ätzend; (fig.) bissig; beißend ⟨Spott⟩

**caution** /'kɔːʃn/ ① n. (a) Vorsicht, die
(b) (warning) Warnung, die
② v.t. (warn) warnen; (warn and reprove) verwarnen (for wegen)

**cautious** /'kɔːʃəs/ adj., **'cautiously** adv. vorsichtig

**cavalry** /'kævəlrɪ/ n. Kavallerie, die

**cave** /keɪv/ n. Höhle, die
■ **cave 'in** v.i. einbrechen

**'caveman** n. Höhlenbewohner, der

**cavern** /'kævən/ n. Höhle, die

**cavernous** /'kævənəs/ adj. höhlenartig

**caviar[e]** /'kævɪɑː(r)/ n. Kaviar, der

**cavity** /'kævɪtɪ/ n. Hohlraum, der; (in tooth) Loch, das

**'cavity wall** n. Hohlmauer, die

**CB** abbr. = **citizen's band** CB

**cc** /siː'siː/ abbr. = **cubic centimetre(s)** $cm^3$

**CCTV** abbr. = **closed-circuit television** CCTV

**CD** abbr. = **compact disc** CD, die; CD player CD-Spieler, der

**CD-ROM** /siːdiː'rɒm/ n. CD-ROM, die; ~ drive CD-ROM-Laufwerk, das

**cease** /siːs/ ① v.i. aufhören
② v.t. (a) (stop) aufhören
(b) (end) aufhören mit; einstellen ⟨Bemühungen⟩

**'ceasefire** n. Waffenruhe, die

**cedar** /'siːdə(r)/ n. Zeder, die

**Ceefax** ® /'siːfæks/ n. (Brit.) Bildschirmtextdienst der BBC

**ceiling** /'siːlɪŋ/ n. (a) Decke, die
(b) (upper limit) Maximum, das

**celebrate** /'selɪbreɪt/ v.t. & i. feiern
**'celebrated** adj. berühmt
**celebration** /selɪ'breɪʃn/ n. Feier, die
**celebrity** /sɪ'lebrɪtɪ/ n. Berühmtheit, die
**celery** /'selərɪ/ n. Sellerie, der od. die
**celibate** /'selɪbət/ adj. zölibatär (Rel.);
ehelos
**cell** /sel/ n. Zelle, die
**cellar** /'selə(r)/ n. Keller, der
**cellist** /'tʃelɪst/ n. Cellist, der/Cellistin, die
**cello** /'tʃeləʊ/ n., pl. ~s Cello, das
**Cellophane** ® /'seləfeɪn/ n. Cellophan
ⓌⓏ, das
**cellular 'phone** /'seljʊlə(r)/ n.
Mobiltelefon, das
**cellulite** /'seljʊlaɪt/ n., no indef. art.:
überschüssige Fettdepots an Oberschenkeln
und Hüften
**Celsius** /'selsɪəs/ adj. Celsius
**cement** /sɪ'ment/ ① n. Zement, der
② v.t. zementieren; (stick together)
zusammenkleben
**ce'ment mixer** n. Betonmischmaschine,
die
**cemetery** /'semɪtərɪ/ n. Friedhof, der
**censor** /'sensə(r)/ ① n. Zensor, der
② v.t. zensieren
**'censorship** n. Zensur, die
**censure** /'senʃə(r)/ v.t. tadeln
**census** /'sensəs/ n. Volkszählung, die
**cent** /sent/ n. Cent, der
**centenary** /sen'tiːnərɪ/ adj. & n.
~ [celebrations] Hundertjahrfeier, die
**center** (Amer.) ▶ CENTRE
**centigrade** /'sentɪɡreɪd/ ▶ CELSIUS
**centimetre** (Brit.; Amer.: **centimeter**)
/'sentɪmiːtə(r)/ n. Zentimeter, der
**centipede** /'sentɪpiːd/ n. Tausendfüßler,
der
**central** /'sentrl/ adj. zentral
**Central:** ~ **A'merica** pr. n.
Mittelamerika (das); ~ **'Europe** pr. n.
Mitteleuropa (das); ~ **Euro'pean** adj.
mitteleuropäisch; **c**~ **'heating** n.
Zentralheizung, die
**centralize** /'sentrəlaɪz/ v.t. zentralisieren
**central:** ~ **'locking** n. (Motor Veh.)
Zentralverriegelung, die; ~ **'nervous
system** n. Zentralnervensystem, das;
~ **'processing unit** n. (Comp.)
Zentraleinheit, die; ~ **reservation** n.
(Brit.) Mittelstreifen, der
**centre** /'sentə(r)/ (Brit.) ① n. (a) Mitte, die;
(of circle) Mittelpunkt, der
(b) (of area, city) Zentrum, das
② adj. mittler...
③ v.i. ~ **on sth.** sich auf etw. (Akk.)
konzentrieren; ~ **[a]round sth.** sich um etw.
drehen
④ v.t. (a) in der Mitte anbringen

(b) (concentrate) be ~d [a]round sth. etw. zum
Mittelpunkt haben; ~ **sth. on sth.** etw. auf
etw. (Akk.) konzentrieren
**centre 'forward** n. Mittelstürmer, der
**centrifugal** /sentrɪ'fjuːɡl/ adj. ~ **force**
Zentrifugalkraft, die; Fliehkraft, die
**century** /'sentʃərɪ/ n. (hundred-year period from
a year ..00) Jahrhundert, das; (hundred years)
hundert Jahre
**ceramic** /sɪ'ræmɪk/ adj. keramisch
**cereal** /'sɪərɪəl/ n. Getreide, das; (breakfast
dish) Getreideflocken Pl.
**cerebral** /'serɪbrl/ adj. (intellectual)
intellektuell
**ceremonial** /serɪ'məʊnɪəl/ ① adj.
feierlich; (prescribed for ceremony) zeremoniell
② n. Zeremoniell, das
**ceremony** /'serɪmənɪ/ n. Feier, die; (formal
act) Zeremonie, die
**certain** /'sɜːtn, 'sɜːtɪn/ adj. (a) (settled,
definite) bestimmt
(b) be ~ **to do sth.** etw. bestimmt tun
(c) (confident, sure to happen) sicher
(d) (indisputable) unbestreitbar
(e) a ~ Mr Smith ein gewisser Herr Smith;
to a ~ extent in gewisser Weise
**'certainly** adv. (a) (admittedly) sicher[lich];
(definitely) bestimmt
(b) (in answer) [aber] sicher; [most] ~ 'not!
auf [gar] keinen Fall!
**certainty** /'sɜːtntɪ, 'sɜːtɪntɪ/ n. (a) be a ~:
sicher sein
(b) (absolute conviction) Gewissheit, die
**certificate** /sə'tɪfɪkət/ n. Urkunde, die; (of
action performed) Schein, der
**certify** /'sɜːtɪfaɪ/ v.t. bescheinigen;
bestätigen; **this is to** ~ **that** ...: hiermit wird
bescheinigt od. bestätigt, dass ...
**cf.** abbr. = **compare** vgl.
**CFC** abbr. = **chlorofluorocarbon**
FCKW, das; ~-**free** FCKW-frei
**chafe** /tʃeɪf/ v.t. wund scheuern
**chaff** /tʃɑːf/ n. Spreu, die
**chaffinch** /'tʃæfɪntʃ/ n. Buchfink, der
**chagrin** /'ʃæɡrɪn/ n. Kummer, der
**chain** /tʃeɪn/ ① n. Kette, die; ~ **of shops/
hotels** Laden-/Hotelkette, die
② v.t. [an]ketten (to an + Akk.)
**chain:** ~ **re'action** n. Kettenreaktion,
die; ~**saw** n. Kettensäge, die; ~-**smoke**
v.t. & i. Kette rauchen (ugs.); ~-**smoker** n.
Kettenraucher, der/-raucherin, die;
~ **store** n. Kettenladen, der
**chair** /tʃeə(r)/ ① n. (a) Stuhl, der; (arm~,
easy ~) Sessel, der
(b) (professorship) Lehrstuhl, der
(c) (at meeting) Vorsitz, der; (~person)
Vorsitzende, der/die
② v.t. den Vorsitz haben bei
**chair:** ~ **back** n. Rückenlehne, die; ~**lift**
n. Sessellift, der; ~**man** /'tʃeəmən/ n., pl. ⋯⟫

**~men** /'tʃeəmən/ Vorsitzende, *der/die;*
**~person** *n.* Vorsitzende, *der/die;*
**~woman** *n.* Vorsitzende, *die*

**chalet** /'ʃæleɪ/ *n.* Chalet, *das*

**chalk** /tʃɔːk/ ① *n.* Kreide, *die*
② *v.t.* mit Kreide schreiben/malen *usw*

**challenge** /'tʃælɪndʒ/ ① *n.*
Herausforderung, *die*
② *v.t.* **(a)** (to contest etc.) herausfordern
**(b)** (fig.) auffordern; (question) infrage stellen

**challenged** /'tʃælɪndʒd/ *adj.* (euphem. or
joc.) behindert; **mentally ~**: geistig behindert

'**challenger** *n.* Herausforderer, *der/*
Herausforderin, *die*

**challenging** /'tʃælɪndʒɪŋ/ *adj.*
herausfordernd; fesselnd ⟨*Problem*⟩;
anspruchsvoll ⟨*Arbeit*⟩

**chamber** /'tʃeɪmbə(r)/ *n.* Kammer, *die*

**chamber: ~maid** *n.* Zimmermädchen,
*das;* **~ music** *n.* Kammermusik, *die;*
**C~ of 'Commerce** *n.* Industrie- und
Handelskammer, *die;* **~ pot** *n.* Nachttopf,
*der*

**chameleon** /kə'miːljən/ *n.* Chamäleon, *das*

**chamois** /'ʃæmwɑː/ *n.* **(a)** Gämse, *die*
**(b)** /'ʃæmɪ/ **~ [leather]** Chamois[leder], *das*

**champagne** /ʃæm'peɪn/ *n.* Sekt, *der;* (from
Champagne) Champagner, *der*

**cham'pagne glass** *n.* Sektglas, *das*

**champion** /'tʃæmpɪən/ ① *n.* **(a)** (defender)
Verfechter, *der/*Verfechterin, *die*
**(b)** (Sport) Meister, *der/*Meisterin, *die*
② *v.t.* verfechten ⟨*Sache*⟩; sich einsetzen für
⟨*Person*⟩

'**championship** *n.* Meisterschaft, *die*

**chance** /tʃɑːns/ ① *n.* **(a)** (fortune, trick of fate)
Zufall, *der; attrib.* zufällig; **~ encounter**
Zufallsbegegnung, *die;* **game of ~**:
Glücksspiel, *das;* **by ~**: zufällig; **take a ~**: es
riskieren; **the ~s are that …**: es ist
wahrscheinlich, dass …; **by [any] ~, by some
~ or other** zufällig
**(b)** (opportunity, possibility) Chance, *die;* **get a/the
~ to do sth.** eine/die Gelegenheit haben,
etw. zu tun
② *v.t.* riskieren

**chancellor** /'tʃɑːnsələ(r)/ *n.* Kanzler, *der;*
**C~ of the Exchequer** (Brit.) Schatzkanzler, *der*

**chandelier** /ʃændə'lɪə(r)/ *n.* Kronleuchter,
*der*

**change** /tʃeɪndʒ/ ① *n.* **(a)** Veränderung,
*die;* Änderung, *die;* (of job, surroundings,
government, etc.) Wechsel, *der*
**(b)** (for the sake of variety) Abwechslung, *die;*
**for a ~**: zur Abwechslung
**(c)** (money) Wechselgeld, *das;* **[loose** *or* **small]
~**: Kleingeld, *das;* **[here is] £5 ~**:
5 Pfund zurück; **keep the ~**: [es] stimmt so
② *v.t.* **(a)** (switch) wechseln; auswechseln
⟨*Glühbirne, Batterie*⟩; **~ one's clothes** sich
umziehen; **~ one's address/name** seine
Anschrift/seinen Namen ändern; **~ trains/
buses** umsteigen

**(b)** (transform) verwandeln (**into** in + *Akk.*);
(alter) ändern
**(c)** (exchange) eintauschen (**for** für); wechseln
⟨*Geld*⟩
③ *v.i.* **(a)** (alter) sich ändern; ⟨*Person, Land:*⟩
sich verändern
**(b)** (into something else) sich verwandeln
**(c)** (put on other clothes) sich umziehen
**(d)** (**~trains**, buses, etc.) umsteigen
■ **change 'over** *v.i.* **~ over from sth. to
sth.** von etw. zu etw. übergehen

**changeable** /'tʃeɪndʒəbl/ *adj.*
veränderlich

'**change[-giving] machine** *n.*
Geldwechsler, *der*

'**changeover** *n.*Wechsel, *der;* **~ from sth.
to sth.** Umstellung von etw. auf etw. (*Akk.*)

'**changing room** *n.* (Brit.) Umkleideraum,
*der*

**channel** /'tʃænl/ ① *n.* (also Telev., Radio)
Kanal, *der;* **the C~** (Brit.) der [Ärmel]kanal
② *v.t.* (fig.) lenken

**Channel: c~-hop** *v.i.* (coll.) **(a)** (Telev.)
zappen (ugs.); **(b)** (cross the English Channel)
kurz mal über den Kanal fahren;
**~ Islands** *pr. n. pl.* Kanalinseln *Pl.;*
**~ 'Tunnel** *n.* [Ärmel]kanaltunnel, *der*

**chant** /tʃɑːnt/ ① *v.t.* skandieren; (Eccl.)
singen
② *v.i.* Sprechchöre anstimmen; (Eccl.) singen
③ *n.* Sprechchor, *der;* (Eccl.) Gesang, *der*

**chaos** /'keɪɒs/ *n.* Chaos, *das*

**chaotic** /keɪ'ɒtɪk/ *adj.* chaotisch

**chap**[1] /tʃæp/ *n.* (Brit. coll.) Bursche, *der;* Kerl,
*der*

**chap**[2] *v.t.,* **-pp-** aufplatzen lassen

**chapel** /'tʃæpl/ *n.* Kapelle, *die*

**chaperon** /'ʃæpərəʊn/ ① *n.*
Anstandsdame, *die*
② *v.t.* beaufsichtigen

**chaplain** /'tʃæplɪn/ *n.* Kaplan, *der*

**chapter** /'tʃæptə(r)/ *n.* Kapitel, *das*

**char** /tʃɑː(r)/ *v.t. & i.,* **-rr-** verkohlen

**character** /'kærɪktə(r)/ *n.* **(a)** Charakter,
*der*
**(b)** (in novel etc.) Figur, *die*
**(c)** (coll.: extraordinary person) Original, *das*
**(d)** (symbol) Zeichen, *das*

**characteristic** /kærɪktə'rɪstɪk/ ① *adj.*
charakteristisch (**of** für)
② *n.* charakteristisches Merkmal

**characterize** /'kærɪktəraɪz/ *v.t.*
charakterisieren

'**characterless** *adj.* nichts sagend

**charade** /ʃə'rɑːd/ *n.* Scharade, *die;* (fig.)
Farce, *die*

**charcoal** /'tʃɑːkəʊl/ *n.* Holzkohle, *die*

**charge** /tʃɑːdʒ/ ① *n.* **(a)** (price) Preis, *der;*
(for services) Gebühr, *die*
**(b) be in ~ of sth.** für etw. die
Verantwortung haben; **take ~**: die
Verantwortung übernehmen
**(c)** (Law: accusation) Anklage, *die*

**(d)** (attack) Angriff, *der*
**(e)** (of explosives, electricity) Ladung, *die*
**②** *v.t.* **(a)** ~ sb. sth., ~ sth. to sb. jmdm. etw. berechnen
**(b)** (Law: accuse) anklagen (**with** wegen)
**(c)** (Electr.) [auf]laden ‹*Batterie*›
**(d)** (rush at) angreifen
**③** *v.i.* **(a)** (attack) angreifen
**(b)** (coll.: hurry) sausen

**charge:** ~ **account** *n.* (Amer.) Kreditkonto, *das;* ~ **card** *n.* Kreditkarte, *die*

**charisma** /kəˈrɪzmə/ *n.* Charisma, *das*

**charitable** /ˈtʃærɪtəbl/ *adj.* **(a)** wohltätig
**(b)** (lenient) großzügig

**charity** /ˈtʃærɪtɪ/ *n.* **(a)** Wohltätigkeit, *die*
**(b)** (organization) wohltätige Organisation

**charity:** ~ **concert** *n.* Benefizkonzert, *das;* ~ **match** *n.* Benefizspiel, *das;* ~ **performance** *n.* Benefizvorstellung, *die;* Wohltätigkeitsvorstellung, *die;* ~ **shop** *n.:* Secondhandladen, dessen Erlöse einem wohltätigen Zweck dienen

**charlady** /ˈtʃɑːleɪdɪ/ *n.* (Brit.) Putzfrau, *die*

**charlatan** /ˈʃɑːlətən/ *n.* Scharlatan, *der*

**charm** /tʃɑːm/ **①** *n.* **(a)** (act) Zauber, *der*
**(b)** (talisman) Talisman, *der*
**(c)** (attractiveness) Reiz, *der;* (of person) Charme, *der*
**②** *v.t.* bezaubern

'**charming** *adj.* bezaubernd

**chart** /tʃɑːt/ **①** *n.* **(a)** (map) Karte, *die*
**(b)** (graph etc.) Schaubild, *das*
**(c)** the ~s die Hitliste
**②** *v.t.* (fig.: describe) schildern

**charter** /ˈtʃɑːtə(r)/ **①** *n.* **(a)** Charta, *die*
**(b)** on ~ gechartert
**②** *v.t.* chartern ‹*Schiff, Flugzeug*›

**chartered:** ~ **ac'countant** *n.* (Brit.) Wirtschaftsprüfer, *der/*-prüferin, *die;* ~ '**aircraft** *n.* Charterflugzeug, *das;* Chartermaschine, *die*

**charter:** ~ **flight** *n.* Charterflug, *der;* ~ **plane** ▶ CHARTERED AIRCRAFT

**charwoman** /ˈtʃɑːwʊmən/ *n.* Putzfrau, *die*

**chase** /tʃeɪs/ **①** *n.* Verfolgungsjagd, *die*
**②** *v.t.* ( pursue) jagen; ~ sth. (fig.) einer Sache (*Dat.*) nachjagen
**③** *v.i.* ~ **after** sb./sth. hinter jmdm./etw. herjagen
■ **chase 'up** *v.t.* (coll.) ausfindig machen

**chasm** /ˈkæzm/ *n.* Kluft, *die*

**chassis** /ˈʃæsɪ/ *n., pl. same* /ˈʃæsɪz/ Chassis, *das;* Fahrgestell, *das*

**chaste** /tʃeɪst/ *adj.* keusch

**chastening** /ˈtʃeɪsənɪŋ/ *adj.* ernüchternd

**chastise** /tʃæˈstaɪz/ *v.t.* züchtigen

**chastity** /ˈtʃæstɪtɪ/ *n.* Keuschheit, *die*

**chat** /tʃæt/ **①** *n.* Schwätzchen, *das*
**②** *v.i.,* -tt-: **(a)** plaudern; ~ **with** *or* **to** sb. **about** sth. mit jmdm. von etw. plaudern
**(b)** (Comp.) chatten
■ **chat 'up** *v.t.* (Brit. coll.) anmachen (ugs.)

**chat:** ~ **line** *n.* Chatline, *die;* ~ **room** *n.* (Comp.) Chat-Room, *der;* ~ **show** *n.* Talkshow, *die*

**chattels** /ˈtʃætəlz/ *n. pl.* bewegliche Habe (geh.)

**chatter** /ˈtʃætə(r)/ **①** *v.i.* **(a)** schwatzen
**(b)** ‹*Zähne:*› klappern
**②** *n.* Schwatzen, *das*

'**chatterbox** *n.* Quasselstrippe, *die* (ugs.)

**chatty** /ˈtʃætɪ/ *adj.* gesprächig

**chauffeur** /ˈʃəʊfə(r)/ **①** *n.* Fahrer, *der;* Chauffeur, *der*
**②** *v.t.* fahren

**chauvinist** /ˈʃəʊvɪnɪst/ *n.* Chauvinist, *der/* Chauvinistin, *die*

**chauvinistic** /ʃəʊvɪˈnɪstɪk/ *adj.* chauvinistisch

**cheap** /tʃiːp/ *adj., adv.* billig

**cheapen** /ˈtʃiːpn/ *v.t.* (fig.) herabsetzen

'**cheaply** *adv.* billig

**cheat** /tʃiːt/ **①** *n.* Schwindler, *der/* Schwindlerin, *die*
**②** *v.t. & i.* betrügen

**check¹** /tʃek/ **①** *n.* **(a)** Kontrolle, *die;* make/keep a ~ **on** kontrollieren
**(b)** (Amer.: bill) Rechnung, *die*
**②** *v.t.* **(a)** (restrain) unter Kontrolle halten
**(b)** (examine) nachprüfen; kontrollieren ‹*Fahrkarte*›
**(c)** (stop) aufhalten
**③** *v.i.* ~ **on** sth. etw. überprüfen; ~ **with** sb. bei jmdm. nachfragen
■ **check 'in** *v.t. & i.* (at airport) einchecken
■ **check 'out** **①** *v.t.* überprüfen
**②** *v.i.* abreisen
■ **check 'up** *v.i.* ~ **up** [**on**] überprüfen

**check²** *n.* (pattern) Karo, *das*

**checkers** /ˈtʃekəz/ (Amer.) ▶ DRAUGHTS

**check:** ~-**in** *n.* Abfertigung, *die;* ~**list** *n.* Checkliste, *die;* ~**mate** **①** *n.* [Schach]matt, *das;* **②** *int.* [schach]matt; ~**out** [**desk**] *n.* Kasse, *die;* ~**point** *n.* Kontrollpunkt, *der;* ~-**up** *n.* (Med.) Untersuchung, *die*

**cheek** /tʃiːk/ *n.* **(a)** Backe, *die;* Wange, *die* (geh.)
**(b)** (impertinence) Frechheit, *die*

'**cheekbone** *n.* Backenknochen, *der*

'**cheekily** *adv.,* '**cheeky** *adj.* frech

**cheep** /tʃiːp/ **①** *v.i.* piep[s]en
**②** *n.* Piep[s]en, *das*

**cheer** /tʃɪə(r)/ **①** *n.* **(a)** (applause) Beifallsruf, *der*
**(b)** *in pl.* (Brit. coll.: as a toast) prost!
**(c)** (Brit. coll.: thank you) danke
**②** *v.t.* **(a)** (applaud) ~ sth./sb. etw. bejubeln/ jmdm. zujubeln
**(b)** (gladden) aufmuntern
**③** *v.i.* jubeln
■ **cheer 'on** *v.t.* anfeuern ‹*Sportler*›
■ **cheer 'up** **①** *v.t.* aufheitern
**②** *v.i.* bessere Laune bekommen; ~ **up**! Kopf hoch!

**cheerful** /'tʃɪəfl/ adj. (in good spirits)
fröhlich; (bright, pleasant) heiter

**'cheerfully** adv. vergnügt

**'cheering** ⬚1 adj. fröhlich stimmend
⬚2 n. Jubeln, das

**cheerio** /tʃɪərɪ'əʊ/ int. (Brit. coll.) tschüs
(ugs.)

**'cheery** adj. fröhlich

**cheese** /tʃiːz/ n. Käse, der

**cheese:** ∼**board** n. Käseplatte, die;
∼**cake** n. Käsetorte, die

**cheetah** /'tʃiːtə/ n. Gepard, der

**chef** /ʃef/ n. Küchenchef, der; (as profession)
Koch, der

**chemical** /'kemɪkl/ ⬚1 adj. chemisch
⬚2 n. Chemikalie, die

**chemical 'warfare** n. chemische
Krieg[s]führung

**chemist** /'kemɪst/ n. (a) (scientist) Chemiker,
der/Chemikerin, die
(b) (Brit.: pharmacist) Drogist, der/Drogistin,
die; ∼**'s [shop]** Drogerie, die

**chemistry** /'kemɪstrɪ/ n. Chemie, die

**chemotherapy** /kiːmə'θerəpɪ/ n.
Chemotherapie, die

**cheque** /tʃek/ n. Scheck, der; **pay by** ∼:
mit [einem] Scheck bezahlen

**cheque:** ∼**book** n. Scheckbuch, das;
∼**book 'journalism** n.
Scheckbuchjournalismus, der; ∼ **card** n.
Scheckkarte, die

**cherish** /'tʃerɪʃ/ v.t. hegen ⟨Hoffnung,
Gefühl⟩; in Ehren halten
⟨[Erinnerungs]gegenstand⟩

**cherry** /'tʃerɪ/ n. Kirsche, die

**chess** /tʃes/ n., no art. das Schach[spiel]

**chess:** ∼**board** n. Schachbrett, das;
∼**man** n. Schachfigur, die; ∼ **player** n.
Schachspieler, der/-spielerin, die

**chest** /tʃest/ n. (a) Kiste, die
(b) (Anat.) Brust, die; **get sth. off one's** ∼ (fig.
coll.) sich (Dat.) etw. von der Seele reden
(c) ∼ [measurement] Brustumfang, der

**chestnut** /'tʃesnʌt/ ⬚1 n. (a) Kastanie, die
(b) (colour) Kastanienbraun, das
⬚2 adj. (colour) ∼[-brown] kastanienbraun

**'chestnut tree** n. Kastanie, die

**chest of 'drawers** n. Kommode, die

**chew** /tʃuː/ v.t. & i. kauen

**'chewing gum** n. Kaugummi, der od. das

**chic** /ʃiːk/ adj. schick; elegant

**chick** /tʃɪk/ n. (a) Küken, das
(b) (sl.: young woman) Biene, die (ugs.)

**chicken** /'tʃɪkɪn/ ⬚1 n. (a) Huhn, das;
(grilled, roasted) Hähnchen, das
(b) (coll.: coward) Angsthase, der
⬚2 adj. (coll.) feig[e]
⬚3 v.i. ∼ **out** (coll.) kneifen

**chicken:** ∼**pox** /-pɒks/ n. Windpocken Pl.;
∼ **'soup** n. Hühnersuppe, die; ∼ **wire** n.
Maschendraht, der

**'chickpea** n. Kichererbse, die

**chicory** /'tʃɪkərɪ/ n. (plant) Chicorée, der od.
die; (for coffee) Zichorie, die

**chief** /tʃiːf/ ⬚1 n. (a) Oberhaupt, das; (of
tribe) Häuptling, der
(b) (of department) Leiter, der; ∼ **of police**
Polizeipräsident, der
⬚2 adj., usu. attrib. (a) Haupt-
(b) (leading) führend

**'chiefly** adv. hauptsächlich

**chieftain** /'tʃiːftən/ n. Stammesführer, der

**chilblain** /'tʃɪlbleɪn/ n. Frostbeule, die

**child** /tʃaɪld/ n., pl. ∼**ren** /'tʃɪldrən/ Kind,
das

**child:** ∼ **abuse** n. Kindesmisshandlung,
die; ∼**bearing** ⬚1 n. Schwangerschaften
Pl.; ⬚2 adj. ∼**bearing age** Gebäralter, das; of
∼**bearing age** im gebärfähigen Alter;
∼**birth** n. Geburt, die; ∼**care** n.
Kinderbetreuung die

**'childhood** n. Kindheit, die

**childish** /'tʃaɪldɪʃ/ adj., **'childishly** adv.
kindisch

**'childishness** n. (behaviour) kindisches
Benehmen

**child:** ∼**less** adj. kinderlos; ∼**like** adj.
kindlich; ∼**minder** /-maɪndə(r)/ n. (Brit.)
Tagesmutter, die; ∼**proof** adj. kindersicher;
∼**proof door lock** (in car) Kindersicherung,
die

**children** pl. of CHILD

**'child's play** n. (fig.) ein Kinderspiel

**Chile** /'tʃɪlɪ/ pr. n. Chile (das)

**chill** /tʃɪl/ ⬚1 n. Kühle, die; (illness)
Erkältung, die
⬚2 v.t. kühlen
■ **chill out** v.i. (coll.) (relax) sich entspannen;
(calm down) sich abregen (ugs.)

**chilli** /'tʃɪlɪ/ n., pl. ∼**es** Chili, der

**chilling** /'tʃɪlɪŋ/ adj. (fig.) ernüchternd

**'chilly** adj. kühl; **I am rather** ∼: mir ist
ziemlich kühl

**chime** /tʃaɪm/ ⬚1 n. Geläute, das
⬚2 v.i. läuten; ⟨Turmuhr:⟩ schlagen

**chimney** /'tʃɪmnɪ/ n. Schornstein, der

**chimney:** ∼ **breast** n. Kaminmantel, der;
∼ **pot** n. ≈ Schornsteinkopf, der;
∼ **sweep** n. Schornsteinfeger, der

**chimpanzee** /tʃɪmpən'ziː/ n. Schimpanse,
der

**chin** /tʃɪn/ n. Kinn, das

**china** n. Porzellan, das; (crockery) Geschirr,
das

**China** /'tʃaɪnə/ pr. n. China (das)

**Chinese** /tʃaɪ'niːz/ ⬚1 adj. chinesisch; **sb.
is** ∼: jmd. ist Chinese/Chinesin
⬚2 n. (a) pl. same (person) Chinese, der/
Chinesin, die
(b) (language) Chinesisch, das; see also
ENGLISH 2A

**chink** n. (gap) Spalt, der

**chip** /tʃɪp/ ⬚1 n. (a) Splitter, der
(b) in pl. (Brit.: potato ∼s) Pommes frites Pl.

(c) (Gambling, Comp.) Chip, *der*
2 *v.t.*, **-pp-** anschlagen

■ **chip 'in** (coll.) 1 *v.i.* (a) (interrupt) sich
einmischen
(b) (contribute money) etwas beisteuern
2 *v.t.* (contribute) beisteuern

'**chipboard** *n.* Spanplatte, *die*

**chipmunk** /'tʃɪpmʌŋk/ *n.* Chipmunk, *das*

**chippy** /'tʃɪpɪ/ *n.* (Brit. coll.) Pommes-frites-
Bude, *die;* Frittenbude, *die* (ugs.)

'**chip shop** (Brit.) ▶ CHIPPY

**chiropodist** /kɪ'rɒpədɪst/ *n.* Fußpfleger,
*der*/-pflegerin, *die*

**chiropody** /kɪ'rɒpədɪ/ *n.* Fußpflege, *die*

**chirp** /tʃɜːp/ 1 *v.i.* zwitschern; ⟨Grille:⟩
zirpen
2 *n.* Zwitschern, *das;* Zirpen, *das*

**chisel** /'tʃɪzl/ 1 *n.* Meißel, *der;* (for wood)
Stemmeisen, *das*
2 *v.t.*, (Brit.) **-ll-** meißeln; (in wood) hauen

**chit** /tʃɪt/ *n.* Notiz, *die*

**chit-chat** /'tʃɪttʃæt/ *n.* Plauderei, *die*

**chivalrous** /'ʃɪvlrəs/ *adj.* ritterlich

**chivalry** /'ʃɪvlrɪ/ *n.* Ritterlichkeit, *die*

**chives** /tʃaɪvz/ *n.* Schnittlauch, *der*

**chloride** /'klɔːraɪd/ *n.* Chlorid, *das*

**chlorine** /'klɔːriːn/ *n.* Chlor, *das*

**chlorofluorocarbon**
/klɔːrəʊflʊərəʊ'kɑːbən/ *n.*
Chlorfluorkohlenstoff, *der*

**chock** /tʃɒk/ *n.* Bremsklotz, *der*

'**chock-a-block** *pred adj.* voll gepfropft

**chocolate** /'tʃɒklət/ *n.* Schokolade, *die*

**chocolate 'biscuit** *n.* Schokoladenkeks,
*der*

**choice** /tʃɔɪs/ 1 *n.* (a) Wahl, *die;* from ~:
freiwillig
(b) (variety) Auswahl, *die*
2 *adj.* ausgewählt

**choir** /kwaɪə(r)/ *n.* Chor, *der*

'**choirboy** *n.* Chorknabe, *der*

**choke** /tʃəʊk/ 1 *v.t.* (a) ersticken
(b) (block up) verstopfen
2 *v.i.* (temporarily) keine Luft [mehr]
bekommen; (permanently) ersticken (on an
+ *Dat.*)
3 *n.* (Motor Veh.) Choke, *der*

**cholera** /'kɒlərə/ *n.* Cholera, *die*

**cholesterol** /kə'lestərɒl/ *n.* Cholesterin,
*das*

**choose** /tʃuːz/ 1 *v.t.*, chose /tʃəʊz/,
chosen /'tʃəʊzn/ (a) wählen
(b) (decide) ~/~ not to do sth. sich dafür/
dagegen entscheiden, etw. zu tun
2 *v.i.*, chose, chosen wählen (between
zwischen); ~ from sth. aus etw./(from several)
unter etw. (*Dat.*) [aus]wählen

**choos[e]y** /'tʃuːzɪ/ *adj.* wählerisch

**chop** /tʃɒp/ 1 *n.* (a) Hieb, *der*
(b) (of meat) Kotelett, *das*
(c) get the ~ (coll.: be dismissed) rausgeworfen
werden (ugs.)

2 *v.t.*, **-pp-** hacken ⟨Holz⟩; klein schneiden
⟨Fleisch, Gemüse⟩

'**chopper** *n.* (axe) Beil, *das;* (cleaver)
Hackbeil, *das*

'**chopping board** *n.* Hackbrett, *das*

'**choppy** *adj.* bewegt

'**chopstick** *n.* [Ess]stäbchen, *das*

**choral** /'kɔːrl/ *adj.* Chor-

**chord** /kɔːd/ *n.* (Mus.) Akkord, *der*

**chore** /tʃɔː(r)/ *n.* [lästige] Routinearbeit

**choreographer** /kɒrɪ'ɒɡrəfə(r)/ *n.*
Choreograph, *der*/Choreographin, *die*

**choreography** /kɒrɪ'ɒɡrəfɪ/ *n.*
Choreographie, *die*

**chortle** /'tʃɔːtl/ 1 *v.i.* vor Lachen glucksen
2 *n.* Glucksen, *das*

**chorus** /'kɔːrəs/ *n.* (a) Chor, *der*
(b) (of song) Refrain, *der;* (in jazz) Chorus, *der*

**chose, chosen** ▶ CHOOSE

**chow** /tʃaʊ/ *n.* (Amer. sl.: food) Futter, *das*
(salopp)

**Christ** /kraɪst/ *n.* Christus (*der*)

**christen** /'krɪsn/ *v.t.* taufen

'**christening** *n.* Taufe, *die*

**Christian** /'krɪstjən/ 1 *adj.* christlich
2 *n.* Christ, *der*/Christin, *die*

**Christianity** /krɪstɪ'ænɪtɪ/ *n.* das
Christentum

'**Christian name** *n.* Vorname, *der*

**Christmas** /'krɪsməs/ *n.* Weihnachten, *das*
*od. Pl.;* merry *or* happy ~: frohe *od.*
fröhliche Weihnachten; at ~: [zu]
Weihnachten

**Christmas:** ~ **cake** *n.*
Weihnachtskuchen, *der;* ~ **card** *n.*
Weihnachtskarte, *die;* ~ '**carol** *n.*
Weihnachtslied, *das;* ~ '**Day** *n.* erster
Weihnachtsfeiertag; ~ '**Eve** *n.* Heiligabend,
*der;* ~ **present** *n.* Weihnachtsgeschenk,
*das;* ~ **tree** *n.* Weihnachtsbaum, *der*

**chrome** /krəʊm/**, chromium**
/'krəʊmɪəm/ *ns.* Chrom, *das*

'**chromium-plated** *adj.* verchromt

**chromosome** /'krəʊməsəʊm/ *n.*
Chromosom, *das*

**chronic** /'krɒnɪk/ *adj.* chronisch; ~ **fatigue
syndrome** chronisches Müdigkeitssyndrom

**chronically** /'krɒnɪkəlɪ/ *adv.* chronisch

**chronicle** /'krɒnɪkl/ *n.* Chronik, *die*

**chronological** /krɒnə'lɒdʒɪkl/ *adj.*
chronologisch

**chrysalis** /'krɪsəlɪs/ *n., pl.* ~**es** Puppe, *die*

**chrysanthemum** /krɪ'sænθɪməm/ *n.*
Chrysantheme, *die*

**chubby** /'tʃʌbɪ/ *adj.* pummelig

**chuck** /tʃʌk/ *v.t.* (coll.) schmeißen (ugs.)

■ **chuck 'away, chuck 'out** *v.t.* (coll.)
wegschmeißen (ugs.)

**chuckle** /'tʃʌkl/ 1 *v.i.* leise [vor sich hin]
lachen (at über + *Akk.*)
2 *n.* leises, glucksendes Lachen

**chug** /tʃʌg/ v.i., -gg- tuckern

**chum** /tʃʌm/ n. (coll.) Kumpel, der (salopp)

**chunk** /tʃʌŋk/ n. dickes Stück

**'chunky** adj. (a) (small and sturdy) stämmig (b) dick ‹Pullover›

**Chunnel** /'tʃʌnl/ n. (Brit. coll.) [Ärmel]kanaltunnel, der

**church** /tʃɜːtʃ/ n. Kirche, die; **go to** ∼: in die Kirche gehen; **the C**∼ **of England** die Kirche von England

**'churchyard** n. Friedhof, der (bei einer Kirche); Kirchhof, der (veralt.)

**churlish** /'tʃɜːlɪʃ/ adj. (ill-bred) ungehobelt; (surly) griesgrämig

**churn** /tʃɜːn/ n. (Brit.) Butterfass, das

**churn 'out** v.t. massenweise produzieren (ugs.)

**chute** /ʃuːt/ n. Schütte, die; (for persons) Rutsche, die

**chutney** /'tʃʌtnɪ/ n. Chutney, das

**CIA** abbr. (Amer.) = **Central Intelligence Agency** CIA, der od. die

**cicada** /sɪ'kɑːdə/ n. Zikade, die

**CID** abbr. (Brit.) = **Criminal Investigation Department** C.I.D.; **the** ∼: die Kripo

**cider** /'saɪdə(r)/ n. ≈ Apfelwein, der

**cigar** /sɪ'gɑː(r)/ n. Zigarre, die

**cigarette** /sɪgə'ret/ n. Zigarette, die

**cigarette:** ∼ **end** n. Zigarettenstummel, der; ∼ **lighter** n. Feuerzeug, das; ∼ **packet** n. Zigarettenschachtel, die; ∼ **paper** n. Zigarettenpapier, das

**cinders** /'sɪndəz/ n. pl. Asche, die

**cine** /'sɪnɪ/**:** ∼ **camera** n. Filmkamera, die; ∼ **film** n. Schmalfilm, der

**cinema** /'sɪnɪmə/ n. Kino, das; **go to the** ∼: ins Kino gehen

**cinema:** ∼ **complex** n. Kinocenter, das; ∼**-goer** n. (Brit.) Kinogänger, der/-gängerin, die

**cinematography** /sɪnɪmə'tɒgrəfɪ/ n. Kinematographie, die

**cinnamon** /'sɪnəmən/ n. Zimt, der

**cipher** /'saɪfə(r)/ n. Geheimschrift, die; **in** ∼: chiffriert

**circle** /'sɜːkl/ ① n. Kreis, der ② v.i. kreisen ③ v.t. umkreisen

**circuit** /'sɜːkɪt/ n. (a) (Electr.) Schaltung, die (b) (Motor racing) Rundkurs, der

**circular** /'sɜːkjʊlə(r)/ ① adj. (round) kreisförmig ② n. (letter, notice) Rundbrief, der; Rundschreiben, das; (advertisement) Werbeprospekt, der

**circular:** ∼ **'letter** ▶ CIRCULAR 2; ∼ **'saw** n. Kreissäge, die

**circulate** /'sɜːkjʊleɪt/ ① v.i. zirkulieren; ‹Personen, Wein usw.:› herumgehen (ugs.) ② v.t. in Umlauf setzen; herumgehen lassen ‹Buch, Bericht› (**around** in + Dat.)

**circulation** /sɜːkjʊ'leɪʃn/ n. (a) (Physiol.) Kreislauf, der; **poor** ∼: Kreislaufstörungen Pl. (b) (copies sold) verkaufte Auflage

**circulatory** /sɜːkjʊ'leɪtərɪ, 'sɜːkjʊleɪtərɪ/ adj. (Physiol., Bot.) Kreislauf-; ∼ **system** Kreislauf, der

**circumcise** /'sɜːkəmsaɪz/ v.t. beschneiden

**circumcision** /sɜːkəm'sɪʒn/ n. Beschneidung, die

**circumference** /sə'kʌmfərəns/ n. Umfang, der

**circumstances** /'sɜːkəmstənsɪz/ n. pl. Umstände Pl.; **in** or **under the** ∼: unter diesen Umständen; **under no** ∼: unter keinen Umständen

**circus** /'sɜːkəs/ n. Zirkus, der

**CIS** abbr. = **Commonwealth of Independent States** GUS

**cissy** /'sɪsɪ/ ▶ SISSY

**cistern** /'sɪstən/ n. Wasserkasten, der; (in roof) Wasserbehälter, der

**citation** /saɪ'teɪʃn/ n. Zitat, das

**cite** /saɪt/ v.t. (quote) zitieren; anführen ‹Beispiel›

**citizen** /'sɪtɪzən/ n. (a) (of town, city) Bürger, der/Bürgerin, die (b) (of state) [Staats]bürger, der/-bürgerin, die

**'citizenship** n. Staatsbürgerschaft, die

**citrus** /'sɪtrəs/ n. ∼ [**fruit**] Zitrusfrucht, die

**city** /'sɪtɪ/ n. [Groß]stadt, die

**city 'centre** n. Stadtzentrum, das

**civic** /'sɪvɪk/ adj. [staats]bürgerlich; ∼ **centre** Verwaltungszentrum der Stadt

**civil** /'sɪvl/ adj. (a) (not military) zivil (b) (polite, obliging) höflich (c) (Law) Zivil-

**civil:** ∼ **engi'neer** n. Bauingenieur, der/ -ingenieurin, die; ∼ **engi'neering** n. Hoch- und Tiefbau, der

**civilian** /sɪ'vɪljən/ ① n. Zivilist, der ② adj. Zivil-

**civility** /sɪ'vɪlɪtɪ/ n. Höflichkeit, die

**civilization** /sɪvɪlaɪ'zeɪʃn/ n. Zivilisation, die

**civilized** /'sɪvɪlaɪzd/ adj. zivilisiert

**civil:** ∼ **'law** n. Zivilrecht, das; ∼ **'rights** n. pl. Bürgerrechte Pl.; ∼ **'servant** n. ≈ Staatsbeamte, der/-beamtin, die; **C**∼ **'Service** n. öffentlicher Dienst; ∼ **'war** n. Bürgerkrieg, der

**CJD** abbr. = **Creutzfeldt-Jakob disease**

**clad** /klæd/ adj. (arch./literary) gekleidet (**in** in + Akk.)

**claim** /kleɪm/ ① v.t. (a) beanspruchen ‹Thron, Gebiete›; fordern ‹Lohnerhöhung, Schadensersatz›; beantragen ‹Sozialhilfe usw.› (b) (assert) behaupten ② v.i. (Insurance) Ansprüche geltend machen

**3** *n.* Anspruch, *der* (**to** auf + *Akk.*); **lay ~ to sth.** auf etw. (*Akk.*) Anspruch erheben

**claimant** /'kleɪmənt/ *n.* Antragsteller, *der*/-stellerin, *die*

'**claim form** *n.* (a) (Insurance) Antragsformular, *das* (b) (for expenses) Spesenabrechnungsformular, *das*

**clairvoyant** /kleə'vɔɪənt/ **1** *n.* Hellseher, *der*/Hellseherin, *die* **2** *adj.* hellseherisch

**clam** /klæm/ **1** *n.* Klaffmuschel, *die* **2** *v.i.,* -**mm**-: ~ **up** (coll.) den Mund nicht [mehr] aufmachen

**clamber** /'klæmbə(r)/ *v.i.* klettern

**clammy** /'klæmɪ/ *adj.* feucht; kalt und schweißig ⟨*Haut*⟩; klamm ⟨*Kleidung*⟩

**clamour** (*Brit.; Amer.:* **clamor**) /'klæmə(r)/ **1** *n.* (noise, shouting) Lärm, *der;* lautes Geschrei **2** *v.i.* ~ **for sth.** nach etw. schreien

**clamp** /klæmp/ **1** *n.* Klammer, *die;* (for holding) Schraubzwinge, *die* **2** *v.t.* klemmen; einspannen ⟨*Werkstück*⟩ **3** *v.i.* (fig.) ~ **down on sb./sth.** gegen jmdn./etw. rigoros vorgehen

**clan** /klæn/ *n.* Sippe, *die;* (of Scottish Highlanders) Clan, *der*

**clandestine** /klæn'destɪn/ *adj.* heimlich

**clang** /klæŋ/ **1** *n.* (of bell) Läuten, *das;* (of hammer) Klingen, *das* **2** *v.i.* ⟨*Glocke:*⟩ läuten; ⟨*Hammer:*⟩ klingen

**clap** /klæp/ **1** *n.* (a) Klatschen, *das* (b) ~ **of thunder** Donnerschlag, *der* **2** *v.i.,* -**pp**- klatschen **3** *v.t.,* -**pp**-: ~ **one's hands** in die Hände klatschen; ~ **sth.** etw. beklatschen; ~ **sb.** jmdm. Beifall klatschen

'**clapping** *n.* Applaus, *der*

**claret** /'klærət/ **1** *n.* roter Bordeauxwein **2** *adj.* weinrot

**clarification** /klærɪfɪ'keɪʃn/ *n.* Klarstellung, *die*

**clarify** /'klærɪfaɪ/ *v.t.* klären ⟨*Situation usw.*⟩; (by explanation) klarstellen; erläutern ⟨*Bedeutung, Aussage*⟩

**clarinet** /klærɪ'net/ *n.* Klarinette, *die*

**clarity** /'klærɪtɪ/ *n.* Klarheit, *die*

**clash** /klæʃ/ **1** *v.i.* (a) scheppern (ugs.) (b) (meet in conflict) zusammenstoßen (c) (disagree) sich streiten (d) ⟨*Interesse, Ereignis:*⟩ kollidieren; ⟨*Farbe:*⟩ sich beißen (ugs.) (**with** mit) **2** *v.t.* gegeneinander schlagen **3** *n.* (a) (of cymbals) Dröhnen, *das* (b) (meeting in conflict) Zusammenstoß, *der* (c) (disagreement) Auseinandersetzung, *die;* (of personalities, colours) Unverträglichkeit, *die;* (of events) Überschneidung, *das*

**clasp** /klɑːsp/ **1** *n.* Verschluss, *der* **2** *v.t.* umklammern

**class** /klɑːs/ **1** *n.* Klasse, *die;* (in society) Gesellschaftsschicht, *die;* (Sch.: lesson) Stunde, *die* **2** *v.t.* einstufen (**as** als)

'**class-conscious** *adj.* klassenbewusst

**classic** /'klæsɪk/ **1** *adj.* klassisch **2** *n.* Klassiker, *der;* ~**s** Altphilologie, *die*

**classical** /'klæsɪkl/ *adj.* klassisch

**classifiable** /'klæsɪfaɪəbl/ *adj.* klassifizierbar

**classification** /klæsɪfɪ'keɪʃn/ *n.* Klassifikation, *die*

**classified** /'klæsɪfaɪd/ *adj.* (a) (secret) geheim (b) ~ **advertisement** Kleinanzeige, *die*

**classify** /'klæsɪfaɪ/ *v.t.* klassifizieren

'**classless** *adj.* klassenlos ⟨*Gesellschaft*⟩

**class**: ~**mate** *n.* Klassenkamerad, *der*/-kameradin, *die;* ~**room** *n.* Klassenzimmer, *das;* ~ **trip** *n.* Klassenfahrt, *die;* Klassenausflug, *der*

'**classy** *adj.* (coll.) klasse

**clatter** /'klætə(r)/ **1** *n.* Klappern, *das* **2** *v.i.* (a) klappern (b) (move or fall with a ~) poltern

**clause** /klɔːz/ *n.* (a) Klausel, *die* (b) (Ling.) Teilsatz, *der;* [**subordinate**] ~: Nebensatz, *der*

**claustrophobia** /klɒstrə'fəʊbɪə/ *n.* Klaustrophobie, *die*

**claustrophobic** /klɒstrə'fəʊbɪk/ *adj.* beengend ⟨*Ort*⟩

**claw** /klɔː/ **1** *n.* Kralle, *die;* (of crab etc.) Schere, *die* **2** *v.t.* kratzen

**clay** /kleɪ/ *n.* Lehm, *der;* (for pottery) Ton, *der*

**clean** /kliːn/ **1** *adj.* sauber; frisch ⟨*Wäsche, Hemd*⟩ **2** *adv.* glatt **3** *v.t.* sauber machen; putzen ⟨*Zimmer, Schuh*⟩; reinigen ⟨*Teppich, Kleidung, Wunde*⟩; ~ **one's teeth** sich (*Dat.*) die Zähne putzen **4** *n.* **give sth. a** ~: etw. putzen

■ **clean 'out** *v.t.* (a) sauber machen (b) (coll.) ~ **sb. out** (take all sb.'s money) jmdn. [total] schröpfen (ugs.)

■ **clean 'up** **1** *v.t.* (a) aufräumen (b) (fig.) säubern **2** *v.i.* aufräumen

'**clean-cut** *adj.* klar [umrissen]; **his** ~ **features** seine klar geschnittenen Gesichtszüge

'**cleaner** *n.* (a) Raumpfleger, *der*/-pflegerin, *die;* (woman also) Putzfrau, *die* (b) *usu. in pl.* (dry-~) Reinigung, *die;* **take sth. to the** ~'**s** etw. in die Reinigung bringen

**cleanliness** /'klenlɪnɪs/ *n.* Reinlichkeit, *die*

'**clean-living** *adj.* von untadeligem Lebenswandel *nachgestellt*

**cleanly** /'kliːnlɪ/ *adv.* sauber

**cleanse** /klenz/ v.t. [gründlich] reinigen

'**cleanser** n. Reinigungsmittel, das

'**clean-shaven** adj. glatt rasiert

'**cleansing cream** n. Reinigungscreme, die

**clear** /klɪə(r)/ 1 adj. (a) klar; scharf ⟨Bild⟩; make oneself ∼: sich deutlich [genug] ausdrücken; **make it** ∼ **[to sb.] that ...:** [jmdm.] klar und deutlich sagen, dass ... (b) (complete) **three** ∼ **days** volle drei Tage (c) (unobstructed) frei; **keep sth.** ∼ (not block) etw. freihalten
2 adv. **keep** ∼ **of sth./sb.** etw./jmdn. meiden; **please stand** or **keep** ∼ **of the door** bitte von der Tür zurücktreten
3 v.t. (a) räumen ⟨Straße⟩; abräumen ⟨Schreibtisch⟩; freimachen ⟨Abfluss, Kanal⟩; ∼ **a space for sb./sth.** für jmdn./etw. Platz machen (b) (empty) räumen; leeren ⟨Briefkasten⟩ (c) (remove) wegräumen; beheben ⟨Verstopfung⟩ (d) (show to be innocent) freisprechen (e) (get permission for) ∼ **sth. with sb.** etw. von jmdm. genehmigen lassen
4 v.i. (a) ⟨Wetter, Himmel:⟩ sich aufheitern (b) (disperse) sich verziehen
5 n. **we're in the** ∼ (free of suspicion) auf uns fällt kein Verdacht; (free of trouble) wir haben es geschafft
■ **clear 'off** v.i. abhauen (salopp)
■ **clear 'out** 1 v.t. ausräumen
2 v.i. (coll.) verschwinden
■ **clear 'up** 1 v.t. (a) wegräumen ⟨Abfall⟩; aufräumen ⟨Platz, Sachen⟩ (b) (explain) klären
2 v.i. (a) aufräumen (b) ⟨Wetter:⟩ sich aufhellen

**clearance** /'klɪərəns/ n. (a) (of obstruction) Beseitigung, die (b) (clear space) Spielraum, der

'**clearance sale** n. Räumungsverkauf, der

'**clear cut** adj. klar umrissen; klar ⟨Abgrenzung, Ergebnis⟩

'**clearing** n. Lichtung, die

'**clearing bank** n. Clearingbank, die

'**clearly** adv. (a) (distinctly) klar; deutlich ⟨sprechen⟩ (b) (manifestly, unambiguously) eindeutig; klar ⟨denken⟩

'**clearway** n. (Brit.) Straße mit Halteverbot

**cleavage** /'kliːvɪdʒ/ n. (between breasts) Dekolleté, das

**cleaver** /'kliːvə(r)/ n. Hackbeil, das

**clef** /klef/ n. Notenschlüssel, der

**cleft** /kleft/ n. Spalte, die

**clematis** /'klemətɪs, klə'meɪtɪs/ n. Klematis, die

**clementine** /'klemənti:n, 'kleməntaɪn/ n. Klementine, die

**clench** /klentʃ/ v.t. zusammenpressen; ∼ **one's fist** or **fingers** die Faust ballen; ∼ **one's teeth** die Zähne zusammenbeißen

**clergy** /'klɜːdʒɪ/ n. pl. Geistlichkeit, die; Klerus, der

**clergyman** /'klɜːdʒɪmən/ n., pl. ∼**men** /'klɜːdʒɪmən/ Geistliche, der

**clerical** /'klerɪkl/ adj. Büro⟨arbeit, -personal⟩; ∼ **error** Schreibfehler, der

**clerk** /klɑːk/ n. (in bank) Bankangestellte, der/die; (in office) Büroangestellte, der/die

**clever** /'klevə(r)/ adj. (a) klug (b) (skilful) geschickt (c) (ingenious) geistreich ⟨Idee, Argument⟩ (d) (smart, cunning) clever

'**cleverly** adv. (a) klug (b) (skilfully) geschickt

**cliché** /'kliːʃeɪ/ n. Klischee, das

**click** /klɪk/ 1 n. Klicken, das
2 v.i. klicken
3 v.t. (Comp.) drücken ⟨Maustaste⟩
■ **click on** v.t. (Comp.) anklicken

**client** /'klaɪənt/ n. (a) Klient, der/Klientin, die (b) (customer) Kunde, der/Kundin, die

**clientele** /kliːɒn'tel/ n. (of shop) Kundschaft, die

**cliff** /klɪf/ n. Kliff, das

'**cliffhanger** n. Thriller, der

**climate** /'klaɪmət/ n. Klima, das

**climatic** /klaɪ'mætɪk/ adj. klimatisch

**climax** /'klaɪmæks/ n. Höhepunkt, der

**climb** /klaɪm/ 1 v.t. hinaufsteigen; klettern auf ⟨Baum⟩; ⟨Auto:⟩ hinaufkommen ⟨Hügel⟩
2 v.i. (a) klettern (**up** auf + Akk.) (b) ⟨Flugzeug, Sonne:⟩ aufsteigen
3 n. Aufstieg, der
■ **climb 'down** v.i. (a) hinunterklettern (b) (fig.) nachgeben

'**climbdown** n. Rückzieher, der (ugs.)

**climber** /'klaɪmə(r)/ n. Bergsteiger, der

'**climbing frame** n. Klettergerüst, das

**clinch** /klɪntʃ/ 1 v.t. zum Abschluss bringen; perfekt machen (ugs.) ⟨Geschäft⟩
2 n. (Boxing) Clinch, der

**cling** /klɪŋ/ v.i., **clung** /klʌŋ/ sich klammern (**to** an + Akk.)

'**cling film** n. Klarsichtfolie, die

**clinic** /'klɪnɪk/ n. Klinik, die

**clinical** /'klɪnɪkl/ adj. (a) (Med.) klinisch (b) (dispassionate) nüchtern

**clink** /klɪŋk/ 1 n. (of glasses) Klirren, das; (of coins) Klimpern, das
2 v.i. ⟨Flaschen:⟩ klirren; ⟨Münzen:⟩ klimpern
3 v.t. klirren mit ⟨Glas⟩; klimpern mit ⟨Kleingeld⟩

**clip¹** /klɪp/ 1 n. Klammer, die; (for paper) Büroklammer, die
2 v.t., **-pp-** klammern (**[on] to** an + Akk.)

**clip²** v.t., **-pp-** (cut) schneiden ⟨Fingernägel, Haar, Hecke⟩; stutzen ⟨Flügel⟩

**clip:** ∼**board** n. (a) Klemmbrett, das; (b) (Comp.) Zwischenablage, die; ∼ **frame** n. [rahmenloser] Bilderhalter

**clipping** /'klɪpɪŋ/ n. (a) (piece clipped off)
Schnipsel, der od. das
(b) (newspaper cutting) Ausschnitt, der

**clique** /kli:k/ n. Clique, die

**clitoris** /'klɪtərɪs/ n. Kitzler, der; Klitoris,
die (fachspr.)

**cloak** /kləʊk/ ⬛1⬛ n. Umhang, der
⬛2⬛ v.t. [ein]hüllen

**'cloakroom** n. Garderobe, die; (Brit.
euphem.: lavatory) Toilette, die

**clock** /klɒk/ ⬛1⬛ n. (a) Uhr, die; [work]
against the ∼: gegen die Zeit [arbeiten];
round the ∼: rund um die Uhr
(b) (coll.) (speedometer) Tacho, der (ugs.);
(milometer) ≈ Kilometerzähler, der
⬛2⬛ v.t. ∼ [up] zu verzeichnen haben
⟨Erfolg⟩; erreichen ⟨Geschwindigkeit⟩
■ **clock 'in, clock 'on** v.i. [bei
Arbeitsantritt] stechen
■ **clock 'off, clock 'out** v.i. [bei
Arbeitsschluss] stechen

**clock 'radio** n. Radiowecker, das

**'clockwise** adv., adj. im Uhrzeigersinn

**'clockwork** n. Uhrwerk, das; a ∼ car ein
Aufziehauto; as regular as ∼ (fig.) absolut
regelmäßig

**clod** /klɒd/ n. (of earth) Scholle, die

**clog** /klɒg/ ⬛1⬛ n. Clog, der; (traditional)
Holzschuh, der
⬛2⬛ v.t., -gg-: ∼ [up] verstopfen

**cloister** /'klɔɪstə(r)/ n. Kreuzgang, der

**clone** /kləʊn/ ⬛1⬛ n. Klon, der
⬛2⬛ v.t. klonen

**close** ⬛1⬛ /kləʊs/ adj. (a) (in space) dicht;
nahe; be ∼ to sth. nahe bei od. an etw.
(Dat.) sein; at ∼ quarters aus der Nähe
betrachtet
(b) (in time) nahe (to an + Dat.)
(c) eng ⟨Freund, Zusammenarbeit⟩; nahe
⟨Verwandte, Bekanntschaft⟩
(d) eingehend ⟨Untersuchung, Prüfung usw.⟩
(e) hart ⟨Wett[kampf], Spiel⟩; knapp
⟨Ergebnis⟩; that was a ∼ call or shave! (coll.)
das war knapp!
⬛2⬛ /kləʊs/ adv. nah[e]; ∼ by in der Nähe;
∼ to sb./sth. nahe bei jmdm./etw.
⬛3⬛ /kləʊz/ v.t. (a) (shut) schließen; zuziehen
⟨Vorhang⟩; schließen ⟨Laden, Fabrik⟩;
sperren ⟨Straße⟩
(b) (conclude) schließen ⟨Diskussion,
Versammlung⟩
⬛4⬛ /kləʊz/ v.i. (a) (shut) sich schließen
(b) ⟨Laden, Fabrik:⟩ schließen, (ugs.)
zumachen
⬛5⬛ /kləʊz/ n. Ende, das; Schluss, der; come
or draw to a ∼: zu Ende gehen; bring or
draw sth. to a ∼: etw. zu Ende bringen
■ **close 'down** /kləʊz/ ⬛1⬛ v.t. schließen;
stilllegen ⟨Werk⟩
⬛2⬛ v.i. geschlossen werden; ⟨Werk:⟩
stillgelegt werden
■ **close 'in** v.i. ⟨Nacht, Dunkelheit:⟩
hereinbrechen; ⟨Tage:⟩ kürzer werden; ∼ in
on umzingeln

■ **close 'off** v.t. [ab]sperren

**close-cropped** /'kləʊskrɒpt/ adj. kurz
geschoren

**closed** /kləʊzd/ adj. geschlossen; we're ∼:
wir haben geschlossen

**'closed-circuit** adj. ∼ television interne
Fernsehanlage; (for supervision)
Videoüberwachungsanlage, die

**close-down** /'kləʊzdaʊn/ n. (Radio, Telev.)
Sendeschluss, der

**closed 'shop** n. Closed Shop, der

**'close-knit** /kləʊs'nɪt/ adj. fest
zusammengewachsen

**closely** /'kləʊslɪ/ adv. (a) dicht
(b) (intimately) eng
(c) genau ⟨befragen, prüfen⟩; streng
⟨bewachen⟩

**'close-range** /'kləʊsreɪndʒ/ adj. ⟨Sicht,
Betrachtung⟩ aus nächster Nähe

**closet** /'klɒzɪt/ n. (Amer.: cupboard) Schrank,
der

**close-up** /'kləʊsʌp/ n. ∼ [picture/shot]
Nahaufnahme, die

**closing** /'kləʊzɪŋ/: ∼ **date** n. (for
competition) Einsendeschluss, der; (to take part)
Meldefrist, die; ∼ **time** n. (of pub)
Polizeistunde, die

**closure** /'kləʊʒə(r)/ n. Schließung, die; (of
road) Sperrung, die

**clot** /klɒt/ ⬛1⬛ n. (a) (blood) Gerinnsel, das
(b) (Brit. coll.: stupid person) Trottel, der
⬛2⬛ v.i., -tt- ⟨Blut:⟩ gerinnen

**cloth** /klɒθ/ n., pl. ∼s /klɒθs/ (a) Stoff, der;
Tuch, das
(b) (dish∼) Spültuch, das; (table∼)
[Tisch]decke, die

**clothe** /kləʊð/ v.t. kleiden

**clothes** /kləʊðz/ n. pl. Kleider Pl.; put
one's ∼ on sich anziehen; take one's ∼ off
sich ausziehen

**clothes:** ∼ **brush** n. Kleiderbürste, die;
∼ **hanger** n. Kleiderbügel, der; ∼ **horse**
n. Wäscheständer, der; ∼ **line** n.
Wäscheleine, die; ∼ **peg** (Brit.), ∼**pin**
(Amer.) ns. Wäscheklammer, die

**clothing** /'kləʊðɪŋ/ n. Kleidung, die

**clotted cream** /klɒtɪd 'kri:m/ n. sehr
fetter Rahm

**cloud** /klaʊd/ n. (a) Wolke, die; every ∼ has
a silver lining (prov.) es hat alles sein Gutes
(b) ∼ of dust/smoke Staub-/Rauchwolke, die
■ **cloud 'over** v.i. sich bewölken

**'cloudburst** n. Wolkenbruch, der

**'cloudless** adj. wolkenlos

**'cloudy** adj. bewölkt ⟨Himmel⟩; trübe
⟨Wetter, Flüssigkeit, Glas⟩

**clout** /klaʊt/ (coll.) ⬛1⬛ n. Schlag, der
⬛2⬛ v.t. hauen (ugs.)

**clove**[1] /kləʊv/ n. ∼ [of garlic]
[Knoblauch]zehe, die

**clove**[2] n. (spice) [Gewürz]nelke, die

**clover** /'kləʊvə(r)/ n. Klee, der

**'cloverleaf** n. Kleeblatt, *das*
**clown** /klaʊn/ ① n. Clown, *der*
　② v.i. ~ [about or around] den Clown
　spielen
**cloying** /'klɔɪɪŋ/ adj. süßlich
**club** /klʌb/ ① n. (a) (weapon) Keule, *die;* (golf
　~) Schläger, *der*
　(b) (association) Klub, *der;* Verein, *der*
　(c) (Cards) Kreuz, *das;* ~s are trumps Kreuz
　ist Trumpf; **the ace/seven of** ~s das
　Kreuzas/die Kreuzsieben
　② v.t., -bb- (beat) prügeln; (with ~) knüppeln
　③ v.i., -bb-: ~ **together** (to buy something)
　zusammenlegen
**club 'sandwich** n. (Amer.) Club-Sandwich,
　*das;* Doppeldecker, *der* (ugs.)
**cluck** /klʌk/ ① n. Gackern, *das*
　② v.i. gackern
**clue** /klu:/ n. Anhaltspunkt, *der;* (in criminal
　investigation) Spur, *die;* **not have a** ~: keine
　Ahnung haben
**'clueless** adj. (coll.) unbedarft (ugs.)
**clump** /klʌmp/ n. Gruppe, *die;* (of grass)
　Büschel, *das*
**clumsily** /'klʌmzɪlɪ/ adv. ▶ CLUMSY:
　schwerfällig; unbeholfen; plump
**clumsiness** /'klʌmzɪnɪs/ n. ▶ CLUMSY:
　Schwerfälligkeit, *die;* Plumpheit, *die*
**clumsy** /'klʌmzɪ/ adj. schwerfällig,
　unbeholfen ‹Person, Bewegung›; plump
　‹Form, Figur, Nachahmung›
**clung** ▶ CLING
**cluster** /'klʌstə(r)/ ① n. (of grapes, berries)
　Traube, *die;* (of fruit, flowers) Büschel, *das;* (of
　stars, huts) Haufen, *der*
　② v.i. ~ [a]round sb./sth. sich um jmdn./
　etw. scharen *od.* drängen
**clutch** /klʌtʃ/ ① v.t. umklammern
　② v.i. ~ at sth. nach etw. greifen; (fig.) sich
　an etw. (Akk.) klammern
　③ n. (a) in pl. (fig.: control) Klauen Pl.
　(b) (Motor Veh.) Kupplung, *die*
**clutter** /'klʌtə(r)/ ① n. Durcheinander, *das*
　② v.t. ~ [up] the table/room überall auf dem
　Tisch/im Zimmer herumliegen
**cm.** abbr. = **centimetre[s]** cm
**c/o** abbr. = **care of** bei; c/o
**Co.** abbr. (a) = **company** Co.
　(b) = **county**
**coach** /kəʊtʃ/ ① n. (a) (horse-drawn)
　Kutsche, *die*
　(b) (Railw.) Wagen, *der*
　(c) (bus) [Reise]bus, *der;* **by** ~: mit dem Bus
　(d) (Sport) Trainer, *der/*Trainerin, *die*
　② v.t. trainieren
**coaching** /'kəʊtʃɪŋ/ n. (a) (teaching)
　Privatunterricht, *der*
　(b) (Sport) Training, *das*
**coach:** ~ **party** n. Reisegesellschaft, *die;*
　~ **station** n. Busbahnhof, *der;* ~ **tour** n.
　Rundreise [im Omnibus]
**coagulate** /kəʊ'ægjʊleɪt/ ① v.t. gerinnen
　lassen

　② v.i. gerinnen
**coal** /kəʊl/ n. Kohle, *die*
**coal:** ~**field** n. Kohlenrevier, *das;*
　~ **fire** n. Kohlenfeuer, *das;* ~**-fired** adj. mit
　Kohle beheizt; kohlebeheizt
**coalition** /kəʊə'lɪʃn/ n. (Polit.) Koalition, *die*
**coal:** ~ **mine** n. [Kohlen]bergwerk, *das;*
　~ **miner** n. [im Kohlenbergbau tätiger]
　Grubenarbeiter; ~ **mining** n.
　Kohlenbergbau, *der*
**coarse** /kɔ:s/ adj. (a) (in texture) grob
　(b) (unrefined, obscene) derb
**coast** /kəʊst/ ① n. Küste, *die*
　② v.i. im Freilauf fahren
**coastal** /'kəʊstl/ adj. Küsten-
**'coaster** n. (a) (mat) Untersetzer, *der*
　(b) (ship) Küstenmotorschiff, *das*
**coast:** ~**guard** n. Küstenwache, -wacht,
　*die;* ~**line** n. Küste, *die*
**coat** /kəʊt/ ① n. (a) Mantel, *der*
　(b) (layer) Schicht, *die;* (of paint) Anstrich, *der*
　(c) (animal's hair, fur, etc.) Fell, *das*
　② v.t. überziehen; (with paint) streichen
**'coat hanger** n. Kleiderbügel, *der*
**'coating** n. Schicht, *die*
**coat of 'arms** n. Wappen, *das*
**coax** /kəʊks/ v.t. überreden
**cobble** /'kɒbl/ n. Kopfstein, *der*
**cobbler** /'kɒblə(r)/ n. Schuster, *der*
**'cobblestone** ▶ COBBLE
**cobra** /'kəʊbrə/ n. Kobra, *die*
**cobweb** /'kɒbweb/ n. Spinnengewebe, *das;*
　Spinnennetz, *das*
**cocaine** /kə'keɪn/ n. Kokain, *das*
**cock** /kɒk/ ① n. Hahn, *der*
　② v.t. spitzen ‹Ohren›; ~ a/the gun den
　Hahn spannen
**cock-a-hoop** /kɒkə'hu:p/ adj.
　überschwänglich
**cockatoo** /kɒkə'tu:/ n. Kakadu, *der*
**'cockcrow** n. at ~: beim ersten
　Hahnenschrei
**cockerel** /'kɒkərəl/ n. junger Hahn
**cock-eyed** /'kɒkaɪd/ adj. (a) (crooked)
　schief
　(b) (absurd) verrückt
**cockle** /'kɒkl/ n. Herzmuschel, *die*
**cockney** /'kɒknɪ/ ① adj. Cockney-
　② n. Cockney, *der*
**'cockpit** n. Cockpit, *das*
**cockroach** /'kɒkrəʊtʃ/ n. [Küchen-, Haus-]
　schabe, *die*
**cocktail** /'kɒkteɪl/ n. Cocktail, *der*
**cocktail:** ~ **cabinet** n. Hausbar, *die;*
　~ **party** n. Cocktailparty, *die*
**cocoa** /'kəʊkəʊ/ n. Kakao, *der*
**coconut** /'kəʊkənʌt/ n. Kokosnuss, *die*
**cocoon** /kə'ku:n/ n. (Zool.) Kokon, *der*
**cod** /kɒd/ n., pl. same Kabeljau, *der*
**COD** abbr. = **cash on delivery,** (Amer.)
　= **collect on delivery** p. Nachn.

**code** /kəʊd/ ⟨1⟩ *n.* (a) (statutes etc.)
Gesetzbuch, *das;* ~s of behaviour
Verhaltensnormen
(b) (system of signals) Code, *der;* be in ~:
verschlüsselt sein
⟨2⟩ *v.t.* chiffrieren; verschlüsseln
**code:** ~ **name** *n.* Deckname, *der;*
~ **word** *n.* Kennwort, *das*
**cod-liver 'oil** *n.* Lebertran, *der*
**co-driver** /'kəʊdraɪvə(r)/ *n.* Beifahrer, *der/*
-fahrerin, *die*
**coed** /'kəʊed/ (esp. Amer. coll.) ⟨1⟩ *n.*
Studentin, *die*
⟨2⟩ *adj.* ~ **school** gemischte Schule
**coeducational** /kəʊedjʊ'keɪʃənl/ *adj.*
koedukativ; Koedukations-
**coerce** /kəʊ'ɜːs/ *v.t.* zwingen; ~ **sb. into**
**sth.** jmdn. zu etw. zwingen
**coercion** /kəʊ'ɜːʃn/ *n.* Zwang, *der*
**coexist** /kəʊɪg'zɪst/ *v.i.* koexistieren
**coexistence** /kəʊɪg'zɪstəns/ *n.*
Koexistenz, *die*
**C. of E.** /siːəv'iː/ *abbr.* = **Church of**
**England**
**coffee** /'kɒfɪ/ *n.* Kaffee, *der;* **three black/**
**white** ~s drei [Tassen] Kaffee ohne/mit
Milch
**coffee:** ~ **bar** *n.* Café, *das;* ~ **bean** *n.*
Kaffeebohne, *die;* ~ **break** *n.* Kaffeepause,
*die;* ~ **cup** *n.* Kaffeetasse, *die;*
~ **machine,** ~ **maker** *ns.*
Kaffeeautomat, *der;* ~ **pot** *n.* Kaffeekanne,
*die;* ~ **shop** *n.* Kaffeestube, *die;* ~ **table**
*n.* Couchtisch, *der*
**coffin** /'kɒfɪn/ *n.* Sarg, *der*
**cog** /kɒg/ *n.* (Mech.) Zahn, *der*
**cogent** /'kəʊdʒənt/ *adj.* überzeugend
⟨*Argument*⟩; zwingend ⟨*Grund*⟩
**cognac** /'kɒnjæk/ *n.* Cognac, *der* ⟨Wz⟩
**cog:** ~ **railway** *n.* Zahnradbahn, *die;*
~**wheel** *n.* Zahnrad, *das*
**cohabit** /kəʊ'hæbɪt/ *v.i.* zusammenleben;
in eheähnlicher Gemeinschaft leben
(Rechtsspr.)
**cohere** /kəʊ'hɪə(r)/ *v.i.* zusammenhalten
**coherent** /kəʊ'hɪərənt/ *adj.*
zusammenhängend
**coherently** /kəʊ'hɪərəntlɪ/ *adv.*
zusammenhängend; im Zusammenhang
**coil** /kɔɪl/ ⟨1⟩ *v.t.* aufwickeln; (twist)
aufdrehen
⟨2⟩ *v.i.* ~ **round sth.** etw. umschlingen
⟨3⟩ *n.* (a) ~s **of rope/wire** aufgerollte Seile
*Pl.*/aufgerollter Draht
(b) (single turn) Windung, *die*
(c) (Electr.) Spule, *die*
**'coil spring** *n.* Spiralfeder, *die*
**coin** /kɔɪn/ ⟨1⟩ *n.* Münze, *die*
⟨2⟩ *v.t.* prägen ⟨*Wort, Redewendung*⟩
**coincide** /kəʊɪn'saɪd/ *v.i.* (a) (in time)
zusammenfallen
(b) (agree) übereinstimmen (**with** mit)

**coincidence** /kəʊ'ɪnsɪdəns/ *n.* Zufall, *der*
**coincidental** /kəʊɪnsɪ'dentl/ *adj.* zufällig
**coincidentally** /kəʊɪnsɪ'dentlɪ/ *adv.*
gleichzeitig; (by coincidence) zufälligerweise
**'coin-operated** *adj.* Münz-
**coke** /kəʊk/ *n.* Koks, *der*
**Col.** *abbr.* = **Colonel** Obst.
**colander** /'kʌləndə(r)/ *n.* Sieb, *das*
**cold** /kəʊld/ ⟨1⟩ *adj.* (a) kalt; I am/feel ~:
mir ist kalt
(b) (fig.) [betont] kühl ⟨*Person, Aufnahme,*
*Begrüßung*⟩
⟨2⟩ *adv.* kalt
⟨3⟩ *n.* (a) Kälte, *die*
(b) (illness) Erkältung, *die;* ~ [in the head]
Schnupfen, *der;* have a ~: eine Erkältung/
[einen] Schnupfen haben
**cold-blooded** /'kəʊldblʌdɪd/ *adj.* (a)
wechselwarm ⟨*Tier*⟩
(b) kaltblütig ⟨*Person, Mord*⟩
**'coldly** *adv.* [betont] kühl
**cold:** ~'**shoulder** *v.t.* schneiden (fig.);
~ '**storage** *n.* Kühllagerung, *die;* ~ '**war**
*n.* kalter Krieg
**coleslaw** /'kəʊlslɔː/ *n.* Krautsalat, *der*
**collaborate** /kə'læbəreɪt/ *v.i.* (a)
zusammenarbeiten; ~ [**with sb.**] **on sth.**
zusammen [mit jmdm.] an etw. (*Dat.*)
arbeiten
(b) (with enemy) kollaborieren
**collaboration** /kəlæbə'reɪʃn/ *n.*
Zusammenarbeit, *die;* (with enemy)
Kollaboration, *die*
**collaborator** /kə'læbəreɪtə(r)/ *n.*
Mitarbeiter, *der/*-arbeiterin, *die;* (with enemy)
Kollaborateur, *der/*Kollaborateurin, *die*
**collage** /'kɒlɑːʒ/ *n.* Collage, *die*
**collapse** /kə'læps/ ⟨1⟩ *n.* (a) (of person)
Zusammenbruch, *der*
(b) (of structure) Einsturz, *der*
(c) (of negotiations) Scheitern, *das;* (of company)
Zusammenbruch, *der*
⟨2⟩ *v.i.* (a) ⟨*Person:*⟩ zusammenbrechen
(b) ⟨*Stuhl:*⟩ zusammenbrechen; ⟨*Gebäude:*⟩
einstürzen
(c) ⟨*Verhandlungen:*⟩ scheitern;
⟨*Unternehmen:*⟩ zusammenbrechen
(d) (fold down) ⟨*Regenschirm, Fahrrad, Tisch:*⟩
sich zusammenklappen lassen
**collapsible** /kə'læpsɪbl/ *adj.* Klapp⟨*stuhl,*
*-tisch, -fahrrad*⟩
**collar** /'kɒlə(r)/ ⟨1⟩ *n.* (a) Kragen, *der*
(b) (for dog) [Hunde]halsband, *das*
⟨2⟩ *v.t.* schnappen (ugs.)
**'collarbone** *n.* Schlüsselbein, *das*
**colleague** /'kɒliːg/ *n.* Kollege, *der/*
Kollegin, *die*
**collect** /kə'lekt/ ⟨1⟩ *v.i.* sich versammeln;
⟨*Staub, Müll usw.:*⟩ sich ansammeln
⟨2⟩ *v.t.* sammeln; aufsammeln ⟨*Müll, leere*
*Flaschen usw.*⟩; (fetch) abholen ⟨*Menschen,*
*Dinge*⟩; ~ **one's wits/thoughts** seine
Gedanken sammeln

**col'lected** adj. (a) (gathered) gesammelt
(b) (calm) gesammelt; gelassen

**collection** /kə'lekʃn/ n. (a) (collecting)
Sammeln, das; (of goods, persons) Abholen, das
(b) (amount of money collected) Sammlung, die;
(in church) Kollekte, die
(c) (from postbox) Leerung, die
(d) (of stamps etc.) Sammlung, die

**collective** /kə'lektɪv/ adj. kollektiv *nicht
präd*

**collective 'bargaining** n.
Tarifverhandlungen Pl.

**collector** /kə'lektə(r)/ n. (a) (of stamps etc.)
Sammler, der/Sammlerin, die
(b) (of taxes) Einnehmer, der/Einnehmerin,
die

**col'lector's item, col'lector's piece**
ns. Sammlerstück, das

**college** /'kɒlɪdʒ/ n. (a) (esp. Brit. Univ.)
College, das
(b) (place of further education) Fach[hoch]schule,
die; **go to ~** (esp. Amer.) studieren

**collide** /kə'laɪd/ v.i. zusammenstoßen (**with**
mit)

**collie** /'kɒlɪ/ n. Collie, der

**colliery** /'kɒljərɪ/ n. Kohlengrube, die

**collision** /kə'lɪʒn/ n. Zusammenstoß, der;
**on a ~ course** (lit. or fig.) auf Kollisionskurs

**colloquial** /kə'ləʊkwɪəl/ adj.
umgangssprachlich

**collusion** /kə'lu:ʒn/ n. geheime Absprache

**cologne** ▶ EAU-DE-COLOGNE

**Cologne** /kə'ləʊn/ ① pr. n. Köln (das)
② attrib. adj. Kölner

**Colombia** /kə'lɒmbɪə/ pr. n. Kolumbien
(das)

**colon¹** /'kəʊlən/ n. Doppelpunkt, der

**colon²** /'kəʊlən, 'kəʊlɒn/ n. (Anat.)
Grimmdarm, der

**colonel** /kɜ:nl/ n. Oberst, der

**colonial** /kə'ləʊnɪəl/ adj. Kolonial-; kolonial

**colonize** /'kɒlənaɪz/ v.t. kolonisieren

**colony** /'kɒlənɪ/ n. Kolonie, die

**color** etc. (Amer.) ▶ COLOUR etc.

**colossal** /kə'lɒsl/ adj. ungeheuer; gewaltig
⟨Bauwerk⟩

**colour** /'kʌlə(r)/ (Brit.) ① n. Farbe, die; **what
~ is it?** welche Farbe hat es?; **change ~:** die
Farbe ändern; **he is off ~:** ihm ist nicht gut
② v.t. (a) (give ~ to) Farbe geben (+ Dat.)
(b) (paint) malen
(c) (stain, dye) färben
③ v.i. **~ [up]** erröten

**'colour-blind** adj. farbenblind

**coloured** /'kʌləd/ (Brit.) ① adj. (a) farbig
(b) (of non-white descent) farbig; **~ people**
Farbige Pl.
② n. Farbige, der/die

**colour: ~-fast** adj. farbecht; **~ film** n.
Farbfilm, der

**colourful** /'kʌləfl/ adj. (Brit.) bunt;
anschaulich ⟨Sprache, Stil, Bericht⟩

**'colouring** n. (Brit.) (a) (colours) Farben Pl.
(b) **~ [matter]** (in food etc.) Farbstoff, der

**'colourless** adj. (Brit.) farblos

**colour: ~ photograph** n.
Farbaufnahme, die; **~ printer** n.
Farbdrucker, der; **~ scheme** n.
Farb[en]zusammenstellung, die;
**~ supplement** n. Farbbeilage, die;
**~ television** n. Farbfernsehen, das; (set)
Farbfernsehgerät, das; **~ transparency**
n. Farbdia, das

**colt** /kəʊlt/ n. [Hengst]fohlen, das

**column** /'kɒləm/ n. (a) Säule, die
(b) (of page) Spalte, die; **sports ~:** Sportteil,
der

**columnist** /'kɒləmɪst/ n. Kolumnist, der/
Kolumnistin, die

**coma** /'kəʊmə/ n. Koma, das; **in a ~:** im
Koma

**comb** /kəʊm/ ① n. Kamm, der
② v.t. (a) kämmen; **~ sb.'s/one's hair**
jmdm./sich die Haare kämmen
(b) (search) durchkämmen

**combat** /'kɒmbæt/ ① n. Kampf, der
② v.t. bekämpfen

**combatant** /'kɒmbətənt/ n. Kombattant,
der

**combination** /kɒmbɪ'neɪʃn/ n.
Kombination, die; **in ~:** zusammen

**combi'nation lock** n.
Kombinationsschloss, das

**combine** ① /kəm'baɪn/ v.t.
zusammenfügen (**into** zu); verbinden
⟨Substanzen⟩
② v.i. (join together) ⟨Stoffe:⟩ sich verbinden
③ /'kɒmbaɪn/ n. **~ [harvester]** Mähdrescher,
der

**combustible** /kəm'bʌstɪbl/ adj. brennbar

**combustion** /kəm'bʌstʃn/ n.
Verbrennung, die

**come** /kʌm/ v.i., **came** /keɪm/, **come** /kʌm/
kommen; **~ here!** komm [mal] her!; **[I'm]
coming!** [ich] komme schon!; **the train came
into the station** der Zug fuhr in den Bahnhof
ein; **Christmas is coming** bald ist
Weihnachten; **the handle has ~ loose** der
Griff ist lose; **nothing came of it** es ist nichts
daraus geworden

■ **come a'bout** v.i. passieren

■ **come across** ① /--'-/ v.i. (be understood)
verstanden werden
② /'--/ v.t. begegnen (+ Dat.)

■ **come a'long** v.i. (coll.) (a) (hurry up)
**~ along!** komm/kommt!
(b) (make progress) **~ along nicely** gute
Fortschritte machen
(c) (to place) mitkommen (**with** mit)

■ **come 'back** v.i. zurückkommen

■ **come by** ① /--'/ v.t. (obtain) bekommen
② /-'-/ v.i. vorbeikommen

■ **come 'down** v.i. (a) (fall) ⟨Schnee, Regen,
Preis:⟩ fallen
(b) (~ lower) herunterkommen
(c) (land) [not]landen; (crash) abstürzen

■ **come 'in** v.i. (enter) hereinkommen; ～ **in!** herein!

■ **'come into** v.t. (a) (enter) hereinkommen in (+ Akk.)
(b) (inherit) erben

■ **come off** 1 /-'-/ v.i. (a) ⟨Griff, Knopf:⟩ abgehen; (be removable) sich abnehmen lassen
(b) (succeed) ⟨Pläne, Versuche:⟩ Erfolg haben
(c) (take place) stattfinden
2 /'--/ v.t. ～ **off a horse/bike** vom Pferd/ Fahrrad fallen; ～ **'off it!** (coll.) nun mach mal halblang! (ugs.)

■ **come on** 1 /-'-/ v.i. (a) (continue coming, follow) kommen; ～ **on!** komm, komm/kommt, kommt!; (encouraging) na, komm!
(b) (make progress) ～ **on very well** gute Fortschritte machen
2 /'--/ v.t. ▶ ～ UPON

■ **come 'out** v.i. (a) herauskommen
(b) (fig.) ⟨Sonne, Wahrheit, Buch:⟩ herauskommen
(c) ～ **out with** herausrücken mit (ugs.)

■ **come 'over** 1 v.i. herüberkommen
2 v.t. kommen über (+ Akk.)

■ **come 'round** v.i. (a) (visit) vorbeischauen
(b) (recover) wieder zu sich kommen

■ **come 'through** 1 v.i. durchkommen
2 v.t. (survive) überleben

■ **come to** 1 /'--/ v.t. (amount to) ⟨Rechnung, Kosten:⟩ sich belaufen auf (+ Akk.), machen
2 /-'-/ v.i. wieder zu sich kommen

■ **'come under** v.t. (a) (be classed as or among) kommen unter (+ Akk.)
(b) (be subject to) kommen unter (+ Akk.)

■ **come 'up** v.i. (a) (～ higher) hochkommen
(b) ～ **up to sb.** (approach for talk) auf jmdn. zukommen
(c) (present itself) sich ergeben
(d) ～ **up to** (reach) reichen bis an (+ Akk.); entsprechen (+ Dat.) ⟨Erwartungen⟩
(e) ～ **up against sth.** (fig.) auf etw. (Akk.) stoßen
(f) ～ **up with** vorbringen ⟨Vorschlag⟩; wissen ⟨Lösung, Antwort⟩

■ **'come upon** v.t. (meet by chance) begegnen (+ Dat.)

**'comeback** n. (to profession etc.) Come-back, das

**comedian** /kə'mi:dɪən/ n. Komiker, der

**comedienne** /kəmi:dɪ'en/ n. Komikerin, die

**'comedown** n. Abstieg, der

**comedy** /'kɒmɪdɪ/ (a) n. Lustspiel, das; Komödie, die
(b) (humour) Witz, der; Witzigkeit, die

**comer** /'kʌmə(r)/ n. **the competition is open to all** ～s an dem Wettbewerb kann sich jeder beteiligen; **the first** ～: derjenige, der zuerst kommt

**comet** /'kɒmɪt/ n. Komet, der

**comeuppance** /kʌm'ʌpəns/ n. **get one's** ～: die Quittung kriegen (fig.)

**comfort** /'kʌmfət/ 1 n. (a) (consolation) Trost, der

(b) (physical well-being) Behaglichkeit, die
(c) in pl. Komfort, der
2 v.t. trösten

**comfortable** /'kʌmfətəbl/ adj. (a) bequem ⟨Bett, Schuhe⟩; komfortabel ⟨Haus, Zimmer⟩; **a** ～ **victory** ein leichter Sieg
(b) (at ease) **be/feel** ～: sich wohl fühlen

**comfortably** /'kʌmfətəblɪ/ adv. bequem; leicht ⟨gewinnen⟩

**comforting** /'kʌmfətɪŋ/ adj. beruhigend ⟨Gedanke⟩; tröstend ⟨Worte⟩; wohlig ⟨Wärme⟩

**'comfort station** n. (Amer.) öffentliche Toilette

**comfy** /'kʌmfɪ/ adj. (coll.) bequem; gemütlich ⟨Haus, Zimmer⟩

**comic** /'kɒmɪk/ 1 adj. komisch
2 n. (a) (comedian) Komiker, der/Komikerin, die
(b) (periodical) Comicheft, das

**comical** /'kɒmɪkl/ adj. komisch

**coming** /'kʌmɪŋ/ 1 adj. **in the** ～ **week** kommende Woche
2 n. ～**s and goings** das Kommen und Gehen

**comma** /'kɒmə/ n. Komma, das

**command** /kə'mɑ:nd/ 1 v.t. (a) (order) befehlen (**sb.** jmdm.)
(b) (be in ～ of) befehligen ⟨Schiff, Armee⟩
(c) verfügen über (+ Akk.) ⟨Gelder, Wortschatz⟩
2 n. (a) Kommando, das; (in writing) Befehl, der; **have/take** ～ **of** das Kommando über (+ Akk.) ... haben/übernehmen
(b) (mastery, possession) Beherrschung, die

**commandeer** /kɒmən'dɪə(r)/ v.t. requirieren

**com'mander** n. Führer, der

**com'manding** adj. (a) gebieterisch ⟨Erscheinung, Stimme⟩; imposant ⟨Gestalt⟩
(b) beherrschend ⟨Ausblick, Lage⟩

**commanding 'officer** n. Befehlshaber, der/Befehlshaberin, die

**com'mandment** n. Gebot, das

**commemorate** /kə'meməreɪt/ v.t. gedenken (+ Gen.)

**commemoration** /kəmemə'reɪʃn/ n. Gedenken, das; **in** ～ **of** zum Gedenken an (+ Akk.)

**commemorative** /kə'memərətɪv/ adj. Gedenk-; ～ **of** zum Gedenken an (+ Akk.)

**commence** /kə'mens/ v.t. & i. beginnen

**com'mencement** n. Beginn, der

**commend** /kə'mend/ v.t. (praise) loben

**commendable** /kə'mendəbl/ adj. lobenswert; löblich

**commendation** /kɒmen'deɪʃn/ n. (praise) Lob, das; (official) Belobigung, die; (award) Auszeichnung, die

**comment** /'kɒment/ 1 n. Bemerkung, die (**on** über + Akk.); (note) Anmerkung, die (**on** über + Akk.); **no** ～**!** (coll.) kein Kommentar! ···꙳

**2** *v.i.* ~ **on sth.** über etw. (*Akk.*)
Bemerkungen machen; **he ~ed that ...:** er
bemerkte, dass ...

**commentary** /'kɒməntərɪ/ *n.* (a)
Kommentar, *der* (on zu)
(b) (Radio, Telev.) [**live** *or* **running**] ~:
Livereportage, *die*

**commentate** /'kɒmənteɪt/ *v.i.* ~ **on sth.**
etw. kommentieren

**commentator** /'kɒmənteɪtə(r)/ *n.*
Kommentator, *der*/Kommentatorin, *die;*
(Sport) Reporter, *der*/Reporterin, *die*

**commerce** /'kɒmɜːs/ *n.* Handel, *der*

**commercial** /kə'mɜːʃl/ **1** *adj.* Handels-;
kaufmännisch ⟨*Ausbildung*⟩
**2** *n.* Werbespot, *der*

**commercial:** ~ **'bank** *n.* private
Geschäftsbank; ~ **'break** *n.* Werbepause,
*die*

**commercialism** /kə'mɜːʃəlɪzm/ *n.*
Kommerzialismus, *der*

**commercialize** /kə'mɜːʃəlaɪz/ *v.t.*
kommerzialisieren

**commercial:** ~ **'radio** *n.* Werbefunk,
*der;* ~ **'television** *n.* Werbefernsehen,
*das;* ~ **'traveller** *n.* Handelsvertreter, *der*/
-vertreterin, *die;* ~ **'vehicle** *n.*
Nutzfahrzeug, *das*

**commiserate** /kə'mɪzəreɪt/ *v.i.* ~ **with sb.**
jmdm. sein Mitgefühl aussprechen (on zu)

**commission** /kə'mɪʃn/ **1** *n.* (a) (official
body) Kommission, *die*
(b) (instruction, piece of work) Auftrag, *der*
(c) (Mil.) Ernennungsurkunde, *die*
(d) (pay of agent) Provision, *die*
(e) **in/out of** ~ ⟨*Auto, Maschine*⟩ in/außer
Betrieb
**2** *v.t.* beauftragen ⟨*Künstler*⟩; in Auftrag
geben ⟨*Gemälde usw.*⟩

**commissionaire** /kəmɪʃə'neə(r)/ *n.* (esp.
Brit.) Portier, *der*

**commissioner** /kə'mɪʃənə(r)/ *n.* (of police)
Präsident, *der*

**commit** /kə'mɪt/ *v.t.*, **-tt-:** (a) begehen
⟨*Verbrechen, Fehler, Ehebruch*⟩
(b) (pledge, bind) ~ **oneself/sb. to doing sth.**
sich/jmdn. verpflichten, etw. zu tun
(c) (entrust) anvertrauen (**to** *Dat.*)
(d) ~ **sb. for trial** jmdn. dem Gericht
überstellen

**com'mitment** *n.* Verpflichtung (**to**
gegenüber)

**com'mitted** *adj.* engagiert

**committee** /kə'mɪtɪ/ *n.* Ausschuss, *der*

**commodity** /kə'mɒdɪtɪ/ *n.* (a) **household**
~: Haushaltsartikel, *der*
(b) (St. Exch.) [vertretbare] Ware; (raw material)
Rohstoff, *der*

**common** /'kɒmən/ **1** *adj.* (a) (belonging to
all) gemeinsam
(b) (public) öffentlich
(c) (usual) gewöhnlich; (frequent) häufig;
allgemein verbreitet ⟨*Sitte, Redensart*⟩

(d) (vulgar) ordinär
**2** *n.* (a) (land) Gemeindeland, *das*
(b) **have sth./nothing/a lot in** ~ [**with sb.**]
etw./nichts/viel [mit jmdm.] gemein[sam]
haben

**common 'cold** *n.* Erkältung, *die*

**'commoner** *n.* Bürgerliche *der*/*die*

**common:** ~ **'ground** *n.* gemeinsame
Basis; ~ **'knowledge** *n.* **it's** [**a matter of**]
~ **knowledge that ...** es ist allgemein
bekannt, dass ...; ~**-law** *adj.* **she's his**
~**-law wife** sie lebt mit ihm in eheähnlicher
Gemeinschaft

**'commonly** *adv.* im Allgemeinen

**common:** **C~ 'Market** *n.* gemeinsamer
Markt; ~**place** **1** *n.* Gemeinplatz, *der;*
**2** *adj.* alltäglich; ~ **room** *n.* (Brit.)
Gemeinschaftsraum, *der;* (for lecturers)
Dozentenzimmer, *das*

**Commons** /'kɒmənz/ *n. pl.* **the** [**House of**]
~: das Unterhaus

**common:** ~ **'sense** *n.* gesunder
Menschenverstand; ~**-sense** *adj.*
vernünftig; gesund ⟨*Ansicht, Standpunkt*⟩;
~**wealth** *n.* **the** [**British**] **C~wealth** das
Commonwealth

**commotion** /kə'məʊʃn/ *n.* Tumult, *der*

**communal** /'kɒmjʊnl/ *adj.* (a) (of or for the
community) gemeindlich
(b) (for common use) gemeinsam

**commune** /'kɒmjuːn/ *n.* Kommune, *die*

**communicate** /kə'mjuːnɪkeɪt/ **1** *v.t.*
übertragen ⟨*Krankheit*⟩; übermitteln
⟨*Informationen*⟩; vermitteln ⟨*Gefühle, Ideen*⟩
**2** *v.i.* ~ **with sb.** mit jmdm. kommunizieren

**communication** /kəmjuːnɪ'keɪʃn/ *n.* (a)
(of information) Übermittlung, *die*
(b) (message) Mitteilung, *die* (**to** an + *Akk.*)

**communication:** ~ **cord** *n.* Notbremse,
*die;* ~**s satellite** *n.* Nachrichtensatellit,
*der*

**communicative** /kə'mjuːnɪkətɪv/ *adj.*
gesprächig

**Communion** /kə'mjuːnɪən/ *n.* [**Holy**] ~
(Protestant Ch.) das [heilige] Abendmahl; (RC
Ch.) die [heilige] Kommunion

**communiqué** /kə'mjuːnɪkeɪ/ *n.*
Kommuniqué, *das*

**communism** /'kɒmjʊnɪzm/ *n.*
Kommunismus, *der;* **C~:** der Kommunismus

**Communist, communist** /'kɒmjʊnɪst/
**1** *n.* Kommunist, *der*/Kommunistin, *die*
**2** *adj.* kommunistisch

**community** /kə'mjuːnɪtɪ/ *n.* (a) (organized
body) Gemeinwesen, *das;* **the Jewish** ~: die
jüdische Gemeinde
(b) *no pl.* (public) Öffentlichkeit, *die*

**community:** ~ **'care** *n.* ≈ ambulante
Betreuung; ~ **centre** *n.*
Gemeindezentrum, *das;* ~ **'charge** *n.* (Brit.)
Gemeindesteuer, *die;* ~ **'service** *n.*:

[*freiwilliger od. als Strafe auferlegter*]
*sozialer Dienst;* ~ **spirit** *n.*
Gemeinschaftsgeist, *der*
**commute** /kə'mjuːt/ [1] *v.t.* umwandeln
⟨*Strafe*⟩ (**to** in + *Akk.*)
[2] *v.i.* pendeln
**commuter** /kə'mjuːtə(r)/ *n.* Pendler, *der*/
Pendlerin, *die*
**com'muter:** ~ **belt** *n.* großstädtischer
Einzugsbereich; ~ **train** *n.* Pendlerzug, *der*
**compact**¹ /kəm'pækt/ *adj.* kompakt
**compact**² /'kɒmpækt/ *n.* Puderdose [mit
Puder(stein)]
**compact 'disc** *n.* Compactdisc, *die;*
~ **player** CD-Spieler, *der*
**companion** /kəm'pænjən/ *n.* Begleiter,
*der*/Begleiterin, *die*
**com'panionship** *n.* Gesellschaft, *die*
**company** /'kʌmpənɪ/ *n.* (a) (persons
assembled, companionship) Gesellschaft, *die;*
**expect** ~: Besuch *od.* Gäste erwarten; **keep
sb.** ~: jmdm. Gesellschaft leisten
(b) (firm) Gesellschaft, *die;* ~ **car**
Firmenwagen, *der;* ~ **policy**
Unternehmenspolitik, *die;* Firmenpolitik, *die*
(c) (of actors) Truppe, *die;* Ensemble, *das*
(d) (Mil.) Kompanie, *die*
**comparable** /'kɒmpərəbl/ *adj.*
vergleichbar (**to, with** mit)
**comparably** /'kɒmpərəblɪ/ *adv.* in
vergleichbarer Weise; vergleichbar
**comparative** /kəm'pærətɪv/ [1] *adj.* (a)
(relative) relativ; **in** ~ **comfort** relativ
komfortabel
(b) (Ling.) komparativ (fachspr.); **a**
~ **adjective/adverb** ein Adjektiv/Adverb im
Komparativ
[2] *n.* (Ling.) Komparativ, *der*
**com'paratively** *adv.* verhältnismäßig
**compare** /kəm'peə(r)/ [1] *v.t.* vergleichen
(**to, with** mit); ~**d with** or **to sb./sth.**
verglichen mit *od.* im Vergleich zu jmdm./
etw.
[2] *v.i.* sich vergleichen lassen
**comparison** /kəm'pærɪsn/ *n.* Vergleich,
*der;* **in** or **by** ~ [**with sb./sth.**] im Vergleich
[zu jmdm./etw.]
**compartment** /kəm'pɑːtmənt/ *n.* (in
drawer, desk, etc.) Fach, *das;* (of railway carriage)
Abteil, *das*
**compass** /'kʌmpəs/ *n.* (a) in *pl.* [**a pair of**]
~**es** ein Zirkel
(b) (for navigating) Kompass, *der*
**compassion** /kəm'pæʃn/ *n.* Mitgefühl,
*das* (**for** mit)
**compassionate** /kəm'pæʃənət/ *adj.*
mitfühlend; **on** ~ **grounds** aus persönlichen
Gründen; (for family reasons) aus familiären
Gründen
**compatibility** /kəmpætɪ'bɪlɪtɪ/ *n.*
Vereinbarkeit, *die;* (of people)
Zueinanderpassen, *das;* (Comp.)
Kompatibilität, *die*

**compatible** /kəm'pætɪbl/ *adj.* vereinbar;
zueinander passend ⟨*Personen*⟩; (Comp.)
kompatibel
**compel** /kəm'pel/ *v.t.,* **-ll-** zwingen
**compelling** /kəm'pelɪŋ/ *adj.* bezwingend
**compendium** /kəm'pendɪəm/ *n.*
Kompendium, *das*
**compensate** /'kɒmpenseɪt/ [1] *v.i.* ~ **for**
sth. etw. ersetzen
[2] *v.t.* ~ **sb. for sth.** jmdn. für etw.
entschädigen
**compensation** /kɒmpen'seɪʃn/ *n.* Ersatz,
*der;* (for damages, injuries, etc.)
Schaden[s]ersatz, *der*
**compère** /'kɒmpeə(r)/ *n.* (Brit.)
Conférencier, *der*
**compete** /kəm'piːt/ *v.i.* konkurrieren (**for**
um); (Sport) kämpfen
**competence** /'kɒmpɪtəns/ *n.* Fähigkeiten
*Pl.*
**competent** /'kɒmpɪtənt/ *adj.* fähig; **not**
~ **to do sth.** nicht kompetent, etw. zu tun
**'competently** *adv.* kompetent
**competition** /kɒmpɪ'tɪʃn/ *n.* (a) (contest)
Wettbewerb, *der;* (in magazine etc.)
Preisausschreiben, *das*
(b) (those competing) Konkurrenz, *die*
**competitive** /kəm'petɪtɪv/ *adj.*
wettbewerbsfähig ⟨*Preis, Unternehmen*⟩;
~ **sports** Leistungssport, *der*
**competitor** /kəm'petɪtə(r)/ *n.* Konkurrent,
*der*/Konkurrentin, *die;* (in contest, race)
Teilnehmer, *der*/-nehmerin, *die*
**compile** /kəm'paɪl/ *v.t.* zusammenstellen
**complacency** /kəm'pleɪsənsɪ/ *n.*
Selbstzufriedenheit, *die*
**complacent** /kəm'pleɪsənt/ *adj.*
selbstzufrieden
**complain** /kəm'pleɪn/ *v.i.* sich beklagen
(**about, at** über + *Akk.;* **to** bei); ~ **of sth.**
über etw. (*Akk.*) klagen
**complaint** /kəm'pleɪnt/ *n.* (a) Beschwerde,
*die*
(b) (ailment) Leiden, *das*
**complement** [1] /'kɒmplɪmənt/ *n.* (a)
(what completes) Vervollständigung, *die*
(b) (full number) **a [full]** ~: die volle Zahl; (of
people) die volle Stärke
[2] /'kɒmplɪment/ *v.t.* ergänzen
**complementary** /kɒmplɪ'mentərɪ/ *adj.*
(a) (completing) ergänzend
(b) (completing each other) einander ergänzend
**complementary 'medicine** *n.*
Komplementärmedizin, *die*
**complete** /kəm'pliːt/ [1] *adj.* (a)
vollständig; (in number) vollzählig
(b) (finished) fertig
(c) (absolute) völlig ⟨*Idiot*⟩; absolut
⟨*Katastrophe*⟩; total, (ugs.) blutig ⟨*Anfänger*⟩
[2] *v.t.* (a) (finish) beenden; fertig stellen
⟨*Gebäude, Arbeit*⟩
(b) ausfüllen ⟨*Formular*⟩

C

**com'pletely** *adv.* völlig; absolut ⟨*erfolgreich*⟩

**completion** /kəm'pli:ʃn/ *n.* Beendigung, *die;* (of building, work) Fertigstellung, *die*

**complex** /'kɒmpleks/ **1** *adj.* kompliziert **2** *n.* Komplex, *der*

**complexion** /kəm'plekʃn/ *n.* Gesichtsfarbe, *die;* (fig.) Gesicht, *das*

**-complexioned** /kəm'plekʃnd/ *adj.* in *comb.* sallow-/fair-~: mit gelblichem Teint/ mit hellem Teint

**complexity** /kəm'pleksıtı/ *n.* Kompliziertheit, *die*

**complicate** /'kɒmplıkeıt/ *v.t.* komplizieren.

**'complicated** *adj.* kompliziert

**complication** /kɒmplı'keıʃn/ *n.* Komplikation, *die*

**complicity** /kəm'plısıtı/ *n.* Mittäterschaft, *die* (in bei)

**compliment** **1** /'kɒmplımənt/ *n.* Kompliment, *das; in pl.* (formal greetings) Grüße *Pl.;* **pay sb. a ~:** jmdn. ein Kompliment machen **2** /'kɒmplıment/ *v.t.* **~ sb. on sth.** jmdm. Komplimente wegen etw. machen

**complimentary** /kɒmplı'mentərı/ *adj.* **(a)** schmeichelhaft **(b)** (free) Frei-

**comply** /kəm'plaı/ *v.i.* **~ with sth.** sich nach richten; **he refused to ~:** er wollte sich nicht danach richten

**component** /kəm'pəʊnənt/ **1** *n.* Bestandteil, *der* **2** *adj.* **a ~ part** ein Bestandteil

**compose** /kəm'pəʊz/ *v.t.* **(a)** bilden; **be ~d of** sich zusammensetzen aus **(b)** verfassen ⟨*Rede, Gedicht*⟩; abfassen ⟨*Brief*⟩ **(c)** (Mus.) komponieren

**com'posed** *adj.* (calm) gefasst

**com'poser** *n.* Komponist, *der/* Komponistin, *die*

**composition** /kɒmpə'zıʃn/ *n.* **(a)** (constitution) (of soil etc.) Zusammensetzung, *die;* (of picture) Aufbau, *der* **(b)** (essay) Aufsatz, *der;* (Mus.) Komposition, *die*

**compost** /'kɒmpɒst/ *n.* Kompost, *der*

**compostable** /'kɒmpɒstəbl/ *adj.* kompostierbar

**'compost heap** *n.* Komposthaufen, *der*

**composure** /kəm'pəʊʒə(r)/ *n.* Gleichmut, *der*

**compound¹** **1** /'kɒmpaʊnd/ *adj.* **(a)** zusammengesetzt **(b)** (Med.) **~ fracture** komplizierter Bruch **2** /'kɒmpaʊnd/ *n.* **(a)** (mixture) Mischung, *die* **(b)** (Ling.) Kompositum, *das* **(c)** (Chem.) Verbindung, *die* **3** /'kɒm'paʊnd/ *v.t.* verschlimmern ⟨*Schwierigkeiten, Verletzung usw.*⟩

**compound²** /'kɒmpaʊnd/ *n.* umzäuntes Gelände

**compound 'interest** *n.* Zinseszinsen *Pl.*

**comprehend** /kɒmprı'hend/ *v.t.* verstehen

**comprehensible** /kɒmprı'hensıbl/ *adj.* verständlich

**comprehension** /kɒmprı'henʃn/ *n.* Verständnis, *das*

**comprehensive** /kɒmprı'hensıv/ **1** *adj.* **(a)** umfassend **(b) ~ school** Gesamtschule, *die* **(c)** (insurance) Vollkasko- **2** *n.* Gesamtschule, *die*

**compress** **1** /kəm'pres/ *v.t.* **(a)** (squeeze) zusammenpressen (into zu) **(b)** komprimieren ⟨*Luft, Gas, Bericht*⟩ **(c)** (Comp.) komprimieren **2** /'kɒmpres/ *n.* Kompresse, *die*

**compression** /kəm'preʃn/ *n.* Kompression, *die*

**compressor** /kəm'presə(r)/ *n.* Kompressor, *der*

**comprise** /kəm'praız/ *v.t.* (include) umfassen; (consist of) bestehen aus

**compromise** /'kɒmprəmaız/ **1** *n.* Kompromiss, *der* **2** *v.i.* Kompromisse/einen Kompromiss schließen **3** *v.t.* kompromittieren

**compromising** /'kɒmprəmaızıŋ/ *adj.* kompromittierend

**compulsion** /kəm'pʌlʃn/ *n.* Zwang, *der;* **be under no ~ to do sth.** keineswegs etw. tun müssen

**compulsive** /kəm'pʌlsıv/ *adj.* **(a)** zwanghaft; **he is a ~ gambler** er ist dem Spiel verfallen **(b) this book is ~ reading** von diesem Buch kann man sich nicht losreißen

**compulsory** /kəm'pʌlsərı/ *adj.* obligatorisch

**compunction** /kəm'pʌŋkʃn/ *n.* Schuldgefühle

**computer** /kəm'pju:tə(r)/ *n.* Computer, *der*

**computer: ~-aided** *adj.* computergestützt; **~ ani'mation** *n.* Computeranimation, *die;* **~-assisted** *adj.* computergestützt; **~ 'dating** *n.* Partnervermittlung per Computer; **~ dating agency/service** Computer-Partnervermittlung[sagentur], *die;* **~ game** *n.* Computerspiel, *das;* **~ 'graphics** *n. pl.* Computergraphik, *die*

**computerisation, computerise** ▶ COMPUTERIZ-

**computerization** /kəmpju:təraı'zeıʃn/ *n.* Computerisierung, *die*

**computerize** /kəm'pju:təraız/ *v.t.* computerisieren

**computer: ~-'literate** *adj.* mit Computern vertraut; **~-'operated** *adj.* computergesteuert; rechnergesteuert; **~ program** *n.* Programm, *das;*

~ **programmer** *n.* Programmierer, *der*/ Programmiererin, *die;* ~ **programming** *n.* Programmieren, *das;* ~ **room** *n.* Computerraum, *der;* ~ **'science** *n.* Computerwissenschaft, *die;* ~ **terminal** *n.* Terminal, *das;* ~ **'typesetting** *n.* Computersatz, *der;* ~ **virus** *n.* [Computer]virus, *das od. der*

**computing** /kəm'pju:tɪŋ/ *n.* EDV, *die;* elektronische Datenverarbeitung; ~ **skills** Computerkenntnisse *Pl.*

**comrade** /'kɒmreɪd, 'kɒmrɪd/ *n.* Kamerad, *der*/Kameradin, *die*

**'comradeship** *n.* Kameradschaft, *die*

**con** /kɒn/ (coll.) ⟨1⟩ *n.* Schwindel, *der* ⟨2⟩ *v.t.,* **-nn-** reinlegen (ugs.); ~ **sb. into sth.** jmdm. etw. aufschwatzen (ugs.)

**concave** /'kɒnkeɪv/ *adj.* konkav

**conceal** /kən'si:l/ *v.t.* verbergen **(from** vor + *Dat.*)

**con'cealment** *n.* Verbergen, *das*

**concede** /kən'si:d/ *v.t.* zugeben

**conceit** /kən'si:t/ *n.* Einbildung, *die*

**con'ceited** *adj.* eingebildet

**conceivable** /kən'si:vəbl/ *adj.* vorstellbar; **it is scarcely** ~ **that** ...: man kann sich (*Dat.*) kaum vorstellen, dass ...

**conceivably** /kən'sɪ:vəblɪ/ *adj.* möglicherweise; **he cannot** ~ **have done it** er kann es unmöglich getan haben

**conceive** /kən'si:v/ ⟨1⟩ *v.t.* **(a)** empfangen ⟨*Kind*⟩ **(b)** (form in mind) sich (*Dat.*) vorstellen; haben ⟨*Idee, Plan*⟩ ⟨2⟩ *v.i.* **(a)** (become pregnant) empfangen **(b)** ~ **of sth.** sich (*Dat.*) etw. vorstellen

**concentrate** /'kɒnsəntreɪt/ ⟨1⟩ *v.t.* konzentrieren ⟨2⟩ *v.i.* sich konzentrieren **(on** auf + *Akk.*)

**'concentrated** *adj.* konzentriert

**concentration** /kɒnsən'treɪʃn/ *n.* Konzentration, *die*

**concen'tration camp** *n.* Konzentrationslager, *das;* KZ, *das*

**concentric** /kən'sentrɪk/ *adj.* konzentrisch

**concept** /'kɒnsept/ *n.* Begriff, *der;* (idea) Vorstellung, *die*

**conception** /kən'sepʃn/ **(a)** Vorstellung, *die* (of von) **(b)** (of child) Empfängnis, *die*

**conceptual** /kən'septjʊəl/ *adj.* begrifflich

**conceptualize** /kən'septjʊəlaɪz/ *v.t.* begrifflich fassen

**concern** /kən'sɜ:n/ ⟨1⟩ *v.t.* **(a)** (affect) betreffen; **so far as ... is** ~**ed** was ... betrifft; **'to whom it may** ~**'** ≈ „Bestätigung"; (on certificate, testimonial) ≈ „Zeugnis" **(b)** (interest) ~ **oneself with** *or* **about sth.** sich mit etw. befassen **(c)** (trouble) beunruhigen ⟨2⟩ *n.* **(a)** (anxiety) Besorgnis, *die;* (interest) Interesse, *das*

**(b)** (matter) Angelegenheit, *die* **(c)** (firm) Unternehmen, *das*

**con'cerned** /kən'sɜ:nd/ *adj.* **(a)** (involved) betroffen; (interested) interessiert; **as** *or* **so far as I'm** ~: was mich betrifft **(b)** (troubled) besorgt

**con'cerning** *prep.* bezüglich

**concert** /'kɒnsət/ *n.* Konzert, *das*

**concerted** /kən'sɜ:tɪd/ *adj.* vereint

**concert:** ~**goer** *n.* Konzertbesucher, *der*/-besucherin, *die;* ~ **hall** *n.* Konzertsaal, *der*

**concertina** /kɒnsə'ti:nə/ *n.* Konzertina, *die*

**concerto** /kən'tʃeətəʊ/ *n.* Konzert, *das*

**concession** /kən'seʃn/ *n.* Konzession, *die*

**concessionary** /kən'seʃənərɪ/ *adj.* Konzessions-; ~ **rate/fare** ermäßigter Tarif

**conciliatory** /kən'sɪljətərɪ/ *adj.* versöhnlich

**concise** /kən'saɪs/ *adj.* kurz und prägnant; knapp, konzis ⟨*Stil*⟩

**conclude** /kən'klu:d/ ⟨1⟩ *v.t.* **(a)** (end) beschließen **(b)** (infer) schließen **(from** aus) **(c)** (reach decision) beschließen ⟨2⟩ *v.i.* (end) schließen

**concluding** /kən'klu:dɪŋ/ *adj.* abschließend

**conclusion** /kən'klu:ʒn/ *n.* **(a)** (end) Abschluss, *der;* **in** ~: zum Abschluss **(b)** (result) Ausgang, *der* **(c)** (inference) Schluss, *der;* **draw** *or* **reach a** ~: zu einem Schluss kommen

**conclusive** /kən'klu:sɪv/ *adj.,* **con'clusively** *adv.* schlüssig

**concoct** /kən'kɒkt/ *v.t.* zubereiten; zusammenbrauen ⟨*Trank*⟩

**concoction** /kən'kɒkʃn/ *n.* Gebräu, *das*

**concourse** /'kɒnkɔ:s/ *n.* Halle, *die;* **station** ~: Bahnhofshalle, *die*

**concrete** /'kɒnkri:t/ ⟨1⟩ *adj.* konkret ⟨2⟩ *n.* Beton, *der; attrib.* Beton-; aus Beton präd

**concrete**/'kɒnkri:t/**:** ~ **mixer** *n.* Betonmischer, *der;* Betonmischmaschine, *die;* ~ **'poetry** *n.* konkrete Poesie

**concur** /kən'kɜ:(r)/ *v.i.,* **-rr-** ~ **[with sb.] [in sth.]** [jmdm.] [in etw. (*Dat.*)] zustimmen

**concurrent** /kən'kʌrənt/ *adj.,* **con'currently** *adv.* gleichzeitig

**concussion** /kən'kʌʃn/ *n.* Gehirnerschütterung, *die*

**condemn** /kən'dem/ *v.t.* **(a)** (censure) verdammen **(b)** (Law: sentence) verurteilen **(to** zu) **(c)** für unbewohnbar erklären ⟨*Gebäude*⟩

**condemnation** /kɒndem'neɪʃn/ *n.* Verdammung, *die*

**condensation** /kɒnden'seɪʃn/ *n.* **(a)** (condensing) Kondensation, *die* **(b)** (water) Kondenswasser, *das*

**condense** /kən'dens/ [1] *v.t.* **(a)** komprimieren; ~d milk Kondensmilch, *die* **(b)** (Phys., Chem.) kondensieren [2] *v.i.* kondensieren

**condescend** /kɒndɪ'send/ *v.i.* ~ to do sth. sich dazu herablassen, etw. zu tun

**conde'scending** *adj.* herablassend

**condescension** /kɒndɪ'senʃn/ *n.* (derog.: patronizing manner) Herablassung, *die*

**condiment** /'kɒndɪmənt/ *n.* Gewürz, *das*

**condition** /kən'dɪʃn/ *n.* **(a)** (stipulation) [Vor]bedingung, *die;* on [the] ~ that ...: unter der Voraussetzung, dass ... **(b)** *in pl.* (circumstances) Umstände *Pl.;* weather/living ~s Witterungs-/ Wohnverhältnisse; working ~s Arbeitsbedingungen **(c)** (of athlete etc.) Form, *die;* (of thing) Zustand, *der;* (of patient) Verfassung, *die* **(d)** (Med.) Leiden, *das*

**conditional** /kən'dɪʃənl/ *adj.* **(a)** bedingt; be ~ [up]on sth. von etw. abhängen **(b)** (Ling.) Konditional-

**con'ditioner** *n.* Frisiermittel, *das*

**condolence** /kən'dəʊləns/ *n.* Anteilnahme, die; letter of ~: Beileidsbrief, *der*

**condom** /'kɒndɒm/ *n.* Kondom, *das od. der*

**condominium** /kɒndə'mɪnɪəm/ *n.* (Amer.) Appartementhaus [mit Eigentumswohnungen]

**condone** /kən'dəʊn/ *v.t.* hinwegsehen über (+ *Akk.*); (approve) billigen

**conducive** /kən'djuːsɪv/ *adj.* be ~ to sth. einer Sache (*Dat.*) förderlich sein

**conduct** [1] /'kɒndʌkt/ *n.* **(a)** (behaviour) Verhalten, *das* **(b)** (way of ~ing) Führung, *die* [2] /kən'dʌkt/ *v.t.* **(a)** führen **(b)** (Mus.) dirigieren **(c)** (Phys.) leiten **(d)** ~ed tour Führung, *die*

**conduction** /kən'dʌkʃn/ *n.* (Phys.) Leitung, *die*

**conductor** /kən'dʌktə(r)/ *n.* **(a)** (Mus.) Dirigent, *der*/Dirigentin, *die* **(b)** (of bus, tram) Schaffner, *der*

**conductress** /kən'dʌktrɪs/ *n.* Schaffnerin, *die*

**conduit** /'kɒndjʊɪt/ *n.* **(a)** Leitung, *die;* Kanal, *der* (auch fig.) **(b)** (Electr.) Isolierrohr, *das*

**cone** /kəʊn/ *n.* **(a)** Kegel, *der;* (traffic ~) Leitkegel, *der* **(b)** (Bot.) Zapfen, *der* **(c)** ice-cream ~: Eistüte, *die*

**confectioner** /kən'fekʃənə(r)/ *n.* ~'s [shop] Süßwarengeschäft, *das*

**con'fectionery** *n.* Süßwaren *Pl.*

**confederate** /kən'fedərət/ *adj.* verbündet

**confederation** /kənfedə'reɪʃn/ *n.* [Staaten]bund, *der*

**confer** /kən'fɜː(r)/ [1] *v.t.*, -rr-: ~ sth. [up]on sb. jmdm. etw. verleihen [2] *v.i.*, -rr-: ~ with sb. sich mit jmdm. beraten

**conference** /'kɒnfərəns/ *n.* **(a)** Konferenz, *die* **(b)** be in ~: in einer Besprechung sein

**conference:** ~ **room** *n.* Konferenzraum, *der;* ~ **table** *n.* Konferenztisch, *der*

**confess** /kən'fes/ [1] *v.t.* **(a)** gestehen **(b)** (Eccl.) beichten [2] *v.i.* **(a)** ~ to sth. etw. gestehen **(b)** (Eccl.) beichten (to sb. jmdm.)

**confession** /kən'feʃn/ *n.* **(a)** Geständnis, *das* **(b)** (Eccl.: of sins etc.) Beichte, *die*

**confetti** /kən'fetɪ/ *n.* Konfetti, *das*

**confidant** /'kɒnfɪdænt, kɒnfɪ'dænt/ *n.* Vertraute, *der*

**confidante** /'kɒnfɪdænt, kɒnfɪ'dænt/ *n.* Vertraute, *die*

**confide** /kən'faɪd/ [1] *v.i.* ~ in sb. sich jmdm. anvertrauen [2] *v.t.* ~ sth. to sb. jmdm. etw. anvertrauen

**confidence** /'kɒnfɪdəns/ *n.* **(a)** (firm trust) Vertrauen, *das;* have ~ in sb./sth. Vertrauen zu jmdm./etw. haben; have [absolute] ~ that ...: [absolut] sicher sein, dass ... **(b)** (assured expectation) Gewissheit, *die* **(c)** (self-reliance) Selbstvertrauen, *das* **(d)** in ~: im Vertrauen; this is in [strict] ~: das ist [streng] vertraulich

'**confidence trick** *n.* (Brit.) Trickbetrug, *der*

**confident** /'kɒnfɪdənt/ *adj.* zuversichtlich (about in Bezug auf + *Akk.*)

**confidential** /kɒnfɪ'denʃl/ *adj.* vertraulich

**confidentiality** /kɒnfɪdenʃɪ'ælɪtɪ/ *n.* Vertraulichkeit, *die*

**confi'dentially** *adv.* vertraulich

'**confidently** *adv.* zuversichtlich

**confiding** /kən'faɪdɪŋ/ *adj.*, **con'fidingly** *adv.* vertrauensvoll

**confine** /kən'faɪn/ *v.t.* **(a)** einsperren; be ~d to bed/the house ans Bett/Haus gefesselt sein **(b)** (fig.) ~ oneself to doing sth. sich darauf beschränken, etw. zu tun

**con'fined** *adj.* begrenzt

**con'finement** *n.* (imprisonment) Einsperrung, *die*

**confines** /'kɒnfaɪnz/ *n. pl.* Grenzen

**confirm** /kən'fɜːm/ *v.t.* bestätigen

**confirmation** /kɒnfə'meɪʃn/ *n.* **(a)** Bestätigung, *die* **(b)** (Protestant Ch.) Konfirmation, *die;* (RC Ch.) Firmung, *die*

**con'firmed** *adj.* eingefleischt ‹*Junggeselle*›; überzeugt ‹*Vegetarier*›

**confiscate** /'kɒnfɪskeɪt/ *v.t.* beschlagnahmen

**confiscation** /kɒnfɪsˈkeɪʃn/ n.
Beschlagnahme, *die*

**conflict** ⓵ /ˈkɒnflɪkt/ n. (a) (fight) Kampf,
*der*
(b) (clashing) Konflikt, *der*
⓶ /kənˈflɪkt/ v.i. (be incompatible) sich (*Dat.*)
widersprechen; ~ **with sth.** einer Sache
(*Dat.*) widersprechen
**con'flicting** adj. widersprüchlich

**conform** /kənˈfɔːm/ v.i. (a) entsprechen (**to**
*Dat.*)
(b) (comply) sich einfügen; ~ **to** or **with sth.**/
**with sb.** sich nach etw./jmdm. richten

**conformist** /kənˈfɔːmɪst/ n. Konformist,
*der*/Konformistin, *die*

**conformity** /kənˈfɔːmɪtɪ/ n.
Übereinstimmung, *die* (**with, to** mit)

**confound** /kənˈfaʊnd/ v.t. (a) (defeat)
vereiteln
(b) (confuse) verwirren

**con'founded** adj. (coll. derog.) verdammt

**confront** /kənˈfrʌnt/ v.t. (a)
gegenüberstellen; ~ **sb. with sth.**/**sb.** jmdn.
mit etw./[mit] jmdm. konfrontieren
(b) (stand facing) gegenüberstehen (+ *Dat.*)

**confrontation** /kɒnfrənˈteɪʃn/ n.
Konfrontation, *die*

**confuse** /kənˈfjuːz/ v.t. (a) (disorder)
durcheinander bringen
(b) (mix up mentally) verwechseln
(c) (perplex) verwirren

**con'fused** adj. konfus; wirr ‹*Gedanken,*
*Gerüchte*›; verworren ‹*Lage, Situation*›

**confusing** /kənˈfjuːzɪŋ/ adj. verwirrend

**confusion** /kənˈfjuːʒn/ n. (a) Verwirrung,
*die*; (mixing up) Verwechslung, *die*
(b) (embarrassment) Verlegenheit, *die*

**congeal** /kənˈdʒiːl/ v.i. gerinnen

**congenial** /kənˈdʒiːnɪəl/ adj. (agreeable)
angenehm

**congenital** /kənˈdʒenɪtl/ adj. angeboren;
kongenital (fachspr.)

**conger** /ˈkɒŋɡə(r)/ n. ~ [**eel**] Seeaal, *der*

**congested** /kənˈdʒestɪd/ adj. verstopft
‹*Straße, Nase*›

**congestion** /kənˈdʒestʃn/ n. (of traffic)
Stauung, *die*; **nasal ~**: verstopfte Nase

**conglomerate** /kənˈɡlɒmərət/ n.
(Commerc.) Großkonzern, *der*

**conglomeration** /kənɡlɒməˈreɪʃn/ n.
Anhäufung, *die*

**congratulate** /kənˈɡrætjʊleɪt/ v.t.
gratulieren (+ *Dat.*); ~ **sb.**/**oneself on sth.**
jmdm./sich zu etw. gratulieren

**congratulations** /kənɡrætjʊˈleɪʃnz/
⓵ int. ~**!** herzlichen Glückwunsch! (**on** zu);
(on passing exam etc.) ich gratuliere!
⓶ n. pl. Glückwünsche Pl.

**congregate** /ˈkɒŋɡrɪɡeɪt/ v.i. sich
versammeln

**congregation** /kɒŋɡrɪˈɡeɪʃn/ n. (Eccl.)
Gemeinde, *die*

**congress** /ˈkɒŋɡres/ n. Kongress, *der;* **C~**
(Amer.) der Kongress

**congressional** /kənˈɡreʃənl/ adj.
Kongress-

**conical** /ˈkɒnɪkl/ adj. kegelförmig

**conifer** /ˈkɒnɪfə(r)/ n. Nadelbaum, *der*

**coniferous** /kəˈnɪfərəs/ adj. Nadel-; ~ **tree**
Nadelbaum, *der;* Konifere, *die*

**conjecture** /kənˈdʒektʃə(r)/ ⓵ n.
Vermutung, *die*
⓶ v.t. vermuten
⓷ v.i. Vermutungen anstellen

**conjugate** /ˈkɒndʒʊɡeɪt/ v.t. (Ling.)
konjugieren

**conjugation** /kɒndʒʊˈɡeɪʃn/ n. (Ling.)
Konjugation, *die*

**conjunction** /kənˈdʒʌŋkʃn/ n. (a)
Verbindung, *die;* **in ~ with** in Verbindung
mit
(b) (Ling.) Konjunktion, *die*

**conjure** /ˈkʌndʒə(r)/ v.i. zaubern; **conjuring**
**trick** Zaubertrick, *der*
■ **conjure 'up** v.t. heraufbeschwören

**conjurer, conjuror** /ˈkʌndʒərə(r)/ n.
Zauberkünstler, *der*/-künstlerin, *die*

**connect** /kəˈnekt/ ⓵ v.t. verbinden (**to,**
**with** mit)
⓶ v.i. ~ **with sth.** mit etw.
zusammenhängen

**con'nected** adj. zusammenhängend

**connection,** (Brit. also) **connexion**
/kəˈnekʃn/ n. (a) (act, state) Verbindung, *die*
(b) (fig.: of ideas) Zusammenhang, *der;* **in**
~ **with** im Zusammenhang mit
(c) (train, bus, etc.) Anschluss, *der*

**connoisseur** /kɒnəˈsɜː(r)/ n. Kenner, *der*

**connotation** /kɒnəˈteɪʃn/ n. Assoziation,
*die*

**conquer** /ˈkɒŋkə(r)/ v.t. besiegen; erobern
‹*Land*›

**conqueror** /ˈkɒŋkərə(r)/ n. (of a country)
Eroberer, *der*

**conquest** /ˈkɒŋkwest/ n. Eroberung, *die*

**conscience** /ˈkɒnʃəns/ n. Gewissen, *das;*
**have a clear/guilty ~:** ein gutes/schlechtes
Gewissen haben

**'conscience-stricken,**
**'conscience-struck** adjs.
schuldbewusst

**conscientious** /kɒnʃɪˈenʃəs/ adj.
pflichtbewusst; (meticulous) gewissenhaft;
~ **objector** Wehrdienstverweigerer [aus
Gewissensgründen]

**consci'entiously** adv. pflichtbewusst;
(meticulously) gewissenhaft

**conscious** /ˈkɒnʃəs/ adj. (a) **he is not**
~ **of it** es ist ihm nicht bewusst
(b) pred. (awake) bei Bewusstsein präd.
(c) (realized by doer) bewusst ‹*Versuch,*
*Bemühung*›

**'consciously** adv. bewusst

**'consciousness** n. Bewusstsein, *das*

**conscript** [1] /kən'skrɪpt/ v.t. einberufen
[2] /'kɒnskrɪpt/ n. Einberufene, der/die
**conscription** /kən'skrɪpʃn/ n.
Wehrpflicht, die
**consecrate** /'kɒnsɪkreɪt/ v.t. weihen
**consecutive** /kən'sekjʊtɪv/ adj.
aufeinander folgend ⟨Monate, Jahre⟩;
fortlaufend ⟨Zahlen⟩
**con'secutively** adj. hintereinander
**consensus** /kən'sensəs/ n. Einigkeit, die
**consent** /kən'sent/ [1] v.i. zustimmen
[2] n. (agreement) Zustimmung, die (to zu); by
common or general ∼: nach allgemeiner
Auffassung; **age of** ∼: Ehemündigkeitsalter,
das
**consequence** /'kɒnsɪkwəns/ n. (a) (result)
Folge, die; in ∼: folglich; **as a** ∼:
infolgedessen
(b) (importance) Bedeutung, die
**consequent** /'kɒnsɪkwənt/ adj. daraus
folgend
**'consequently** adv. infolgedessen
**conservation** /kɒnsə'veɪʃn/ n. Erhaltung,
die; **wildlife** ∼: Schutz wild lebender
Tierarten
**conser'vation area** n. (Brit.) (rural)
Landschaftsschutzgebiet, das; (urban) unter
Denkmalschutz stehendes Gebiet
**conservationist** /kɒnsə'veɪʃənɪst/ n.
Naturschützer, der/-schützerin, die
**conservative** /kən'sɜːvətɪv/ [1] adj. (a)
konservativ
(b) vorsichtig ⟨Schätzung⟩
(c) C∼ (Brit. Polit.) konservativ; **the C∼ Party**
die Konservative Partei
[2] n. C∼ (Brit. Polit.) Konservative, der/die
**con'servatively** adv. vorsichtig
⟨geschätzt⟩
**conservatory** /kən'sɜːvətərɪ/ n.
Wintergarten, der
**conserve** /kən'sɜːv/ v.t. erhalten; schonen
⟨Kräfte⟩
**consider** /kən'sɪdə(r)/ v.t. (a) (think about)
∼ sth. an etw. (Akk.) denken; **he's** ∼**ing
emigrating** er denkt daran, auszuwandern
(b) (reflect on) sich (Dat.) überlegen
(c) (regard as) halten für; **all things** ∼**ed** alles
in allem
**considerable** /kən'sɪdərəbl/ adj.,
**con'siderably** adv. erheblich
**considerate** /kən'sɪdərət/ adj.
rücksichtsvoll; (thoughtfully kind)
entgegenkommend
**considerately** /kən'sɪdərətlɪ/ adv.
rücksichtsvoll; (obligingly) entgegenkommend
**consideration** /kənsɪdə'reɪʃn/ n. (a)
Überlegung, die; **take sth. into** ∼: etw.
berücksichtigen; **the matter is under** ∼: die
Angelegenheit wird geprüft
(b) (thoughtfulness) Rücksichtnahme, die
**considered** /kən'sɪdəd/ adj. (a) ∼ **opinion**
feste od. ernsthafte Überzeugung

(b) **be highly** ∼ **[by others]** [bei anderen] in
hohem Ansehen stehen
**con'sidering** prep. ∼ sth. wenn man etw.
bedenkt; ∼ [that] …: wenn man bedenkt,
dass …
**consign** /kən'saɪn/ v.t. anvertrauen (**to**
Dat.)
**con'signment** n. (Commerc.) Sendung, die;
(large) Ladung, die
**consist** /kən'sɪst/ v.i. ∼ **of** bestehen aus
**consistency** /kən'sɪstənsɪ/ n. (a) (density)
Konsistenz, die
(b) (being consistent) Konsequenz, die
**consistent** /kən'sɪstənt/ adj. (a) (compatible)
[miteinander] vereinbar
(b) (uniform) gleich bleibend ⟨Qualität⟩
(c) (unchanging) konsequent
**consolation** /kɒnsə'leɪʃn/ n. Trost, der
**conso'lation prize** n. Trostpreis, der
**console** /kən'səʊl/ v.t. trösten
**consolidate** /kən'sɒlɪdeɪt/ v.t. festigen
**consolidation** /kənsɒlɪ'deɪʃn/ n.
Festigung, die
**consoling** /kən'səʊlɪŋ/ adj. tröstlich
**consonant** /'kɒnsənənt/ n. Konsonant, der
**consort** /kən'sɔːt/ v.i. verkehren (**with** mit)
**consortium** /kən'sɔːtɪəm/ n., pl. **consortia**
/kən'sɔːtɪə/ Konsortium, das
**conspicuous** /kən'spɪkjʊəs/ adj. (a)
(visible) unübersehbar
(b) (obvious) auffallend
**con'spicuously** adv. (a) (visibly)
unübersehbar
(b) (obviously) auffallend
**conspiracy** /kən'spɪrəsɪ/ n. (conspiring)
Verschwörung, die; (plot) Komplott, das
**conspire** /kən'spaɪə(r)/ v.i. sich
verschwören
**constable** /'kʌnstəbl, 'kɒnstəbl/ n. (Brit.)
Polizist, der/Polizistin, die
**constabulary** /kən'stæbjʊlərɪ/ n. Polizei,
die
**constant** /'kɒnstənt/ adj. (a) (unceasing)
ständig
(b) (unchanging) gleich bleibend
**'constantly** adv. (a) (unceasingly) ständig
(b) (unchangingly) konstant
**constellation** /kɒnstə'leɪʃn/ n. Sternbild,
das
**consternation** /kɒnstə'neɪʃn/ n.
Bestürzung, die
**constipated** /'kɒnstɪpeɪtɪd/ adj. **be** ∼: an
Verstopfung leiden
**constipation** /kɒnstɪ'peɪʃn/ n.
Verstopfung, die
**constituency** /kən'stɪtjʊənsɪ/ n.
Wahlkreis, der
**constituent** /kən'stɪtjʊənt/ n. (a) (part)
Bestandteil, der
(b) (Polit.) Wähler, der/Wählerin, die
**constitute** /'kɒnstɪtjuːt/ v.t. (a) (form, be)
sein; ∼ **a threat to** eine Gefahr sein für

**(b)** (make up) bilden

**constitution** /kɒnstɪˈtjuːʃn/ n. **(a)** (of person) Konstitution, *die*
**(b)** (of state) Verfassung, *die*

**constitutional** /kɒnstɪˈtjuːʃnl/ adj. (of constitution) der Verfassung *nachgestellt;* (in harmony with constitution) verfassungsmäßig

**constrain** /kənˈstreɪn/ v.t. zwingen

**constraint** /kənˈstreɪnt/ n. (limitation) Einschränkung, *die*

**constrict** /kənˈstrɪkt/ v.t. verengen

**constriction** /kənˈstrɪkʃn/ n. Verengung, *die*

**construct** /kənˈstrʌkt/ v.t. bauen; (fig.) erstellen ⟨*Plan*⟩

**construction** /kənˈstrʌkʃn/ n. **(a)** (constructing) Bau, *der;* **be under ∼:** im Bau sein
**(b)** (thing constructed) Bauwerk, *das*

**constructive** /kənˈstrʌktɪv/ adj. konstruktiv

**consul** /ˈkɒnsl/ n. Konsul, *der*

**consulate** /ˈkɒnsjʊlət/ n. Konsulat, *das*

**consult** /kənˈsʌlt/ v.t. konsultieren ⟨*Arzt, Fachmann*⟩; **∼ a book** in einem Buch nachsehen

**consultant** /kənˈsʌltənt/ n. Berater, *der*/ Beraterin, *die;* (Med.) Chefarzt, *der*/-ärztin, *die*

**consultation** /kɒnsəlˈteɪʃn/ n. Beratung, *die*

**con'sulting room** n. Sprechzimmer, *das*

**consume** /kənˈsjuːm/ v.t. verbrauchen; (eat, drink) konsumieren

**con'sumer** n. Verbraucher, *der*/ Verbraucherin, *die*

**con'sumer goods** n. pl. Konsumgüter Pl.

**consumerism** /kənˈsjuːmərɪzm/ n., no art. Konsumerismus, *der*

**consumer: ∼ pro'tection** n. Verbraucherschutz, *der;* **∼ research** n. Verbrauchsforschung, *die;* Konsumforschung, *die*

**consumption** /kənˈsʌmpʃn/ n. Verbrauch, *der* **(of an** + *Dat.*); (eating or drinking) Verzehr, *der* **(of** von)

**cont.** abbr. = **continued** Forts.

**contact** ⟨**1**⟩ /ˈkɒntækt/ n. Berührung, *die;* (fig.) Kontakt, *der;* **be in ∼ with sth.** etw. berühren; **be in ∼ with sb.** (fig.) mit jmdm. Kontakt haben
⟨**2**⟩ /ˈkɒntækt, kənˈtækt/ v.t. sich in Verbindung setzen mit

**'contact lens** n. Kontaktlinse, *die*

**contagious** /kənˈteɪdʒəs/ adj. ansteckend

**contain** /kənˈteɪn/ v.t. **(a)** (hold, include) enthalten
**(b)** (prevent from spreading) aufhalten

**con'tainer** n. Behälter, *der;* (cargo ∼) Container, *der;* **cardboard/wooden ∼:** Pappkarton, *der*/Holzkiste, *die*

**contaminate** /kənˈtæmɪneɪt/ v.t. verunreinigen; (with radioactivity) verseuchen

**contamination** /kənˌtæmɪˈneɪʃn/ n. Verunreinigung, *die;* (with radioactivity) Verseuchung, *die*

**contemplate** /ˈkɒntəmpleɪt/ v.t. **(a)** betrachten; (mentally) nachdenken über (+ *Akk.*)
**(b)** (expect) rechnen mit; (consider) ∼ **sth./ doing sth.** an etw. *(Akk.)* denken/daran denken, etw. zu tun

**contemplation** /kɒntəmˈpleɪʃn/ n. Betrachtung, *die;* (mental) Nachdenken, *das* **(of** über + *Akk.*)

**contemporary** /kənˈtempərəri/ ⟨**1**⟩ adj. zeitgenössisch
⟨**2**⟩ n. Zeitgenosse, *der*/-genossin, *die*

**contempt** /kənˈtempt/ n. Verachtung, *die* **(of, for** für)

**contemptible** /kənˈtemptɪbl/ adj. verachtenswert

**contemptuous** /kənˈtemptjʊəs/ adj. verächtlich

**contend** /kənˈtend/ v.i. **be able/have to ∼ with** fertig werden können/müssen mit

**con'tender** n. Bewerber, *der*/Bewerberin, *die*

**content¹** /ˈkɒntent/ n. **(a)** in pl. Inhalt, *der;* **[table of] ∼s** Inhaltsverzeichnis, *das*
**(b)** (amount contained) Gehalt, *der* **(of an** + *Dat.*)

**content²** /kənˈtent/ ⟨**1**⟩ pred. adj. zufrieden
⟨**2**⟩ v.t. zufrieden stellen; **∼ oneself with sth./ sb.** sich mit etw./jmdm. zufrieden geben

**con'tented** adj., **con'tentedly** adv. zufrieden

**contention** /kənˈtenʃn/ n. **(a)** Streit, *der*
**(b)** (point asserted) Behauptung, *die*

**contentious** /kənˈtenʃəs/ adj. strittig ⟨*Punkt, Thema*⟩

**con'tentment** n. Zufriedenheit, *die*

**contest** ⟨**1**⟩ /ˈkɒntest/ n. Wettbewerb, *der*
⟨**2**⟩ /kənˈtest/ v.t. **(a)** bestreiten; infrage stellen ⟨*Behauptung*⟩
**(b)** (Brit.: compete for) kandidieren für

**contestant** /kənˈtestənt/ n. (competitor) Teilnehmer, *der*/Teilnehmerin, *die*

**context** /ˈkɒntekst/ n. Kontext, *der;* **in/out of ∼:** im/ohne Kontext; **in this ∼:** in diesem Zusammenhang

**contextual** /kənˈtekstjʊəl/ adj. kontextuell

**contextualize** /kənˈtekstjʊəlaɪz/ v.t. ( place in context) in einen Kontext einordnen

**continent** /ˈkɒntɪnənt/ n. Kontinent, *der;* **the C∼:** das europäische Festland

**continental** /kɒntɪˈnentl/ adj. **(a)** . kontinental
**(b)** C∼ (mainland European) kontinental[europäisch]

**continental: ∼ 'breakfast** n. kontinentales Frühstück; **∼ 'quilt** n. (Brit.) [Stepp]federbett, *das*

**con'tingency plan** /kən'tɪndʒənsɪ/ *n.*
Alternativplan, *der*

**contingent** /kən'tɪndʒənt/ *n.* Kontingent,
*das*

**continual** /kən'tɪnjʊəl/ *adj.*,
**con'tinually** *adv.* (frequent[ly]) ständig;
(without stopping) unaufhörlich

**continuation** /kəntɪnjʊ'eɪʃn/ *n.*
Fortsetzung, *die*

**continue** /kən'tɪnjuː/ 1 *v.t.* fortsetzen; '∼d
on page 2' „Fortsetzung auf Seite 2";
∼ doing *or* to do sth. etw. weiter tun; it ∼d
to rain es regnete weiter
2 *v.i.* (persist) ⟨Wetter, Zustand, Krise usw.:⟩
andauern; (persist in doing sth.) nicht aufhören;
∼ with sth. mit etw. fortfahren

**continuity** /kɒntɪ'njuːɪtɪ/ *n.* Kontinuität,
*die*

**continuous** /kən'tɪnjʊəs/ *adj.* (a)
ununterbrochen; anhaltend ⟨Regen,
Sonnenschein⟩; ständig ⟨Kritik, Streit⟩;
durchgezogen ⟨Linie⟩
(b) (Ling.) ∼ [form] Verlaufsform, *die*
**con'tinuously** *adv.* ununterbrochen;
ständig ⟨sich ändern⟩

**contort** /kən'tɔːt/ *v.t.* verdrehen

**contortion** /kən'tɔːʃn/ *n.* Verdrehung, *die*

**contour** /'kɒntʊə(r)/ *n.* Kontur, *die;* ∼ map
Höhenlinienkarte, *die*

**contraband** /'kɒntrəbænd/ *n.*
Schmuggelware, *die*

**contraception** /kɒntrə'sepʃn/ *n.*
Empfängnisverhütung, *die*

**contraceptive** /kɒntrə'septɪv/ 1 *adj.*
empfängnisverhütend
2 *n.* Verhütungsmittel, *das*

**contract** 1 /'kɒntrækt/ *n.* Vertrag, *der;*
∼ of employment Arbeitsvertrag, *der;* be
under ∼ to do sth. vertraglich verpflichtet
sein, etw. zu tun
2 /kən'trækt/ *v.t.* (Med.) sich (*Dat.*) zuziehen
3 /kən'trækt/ *v.i.* (a) ∼ to do sth. sich
vertraglich verpflichten, etw. zu tun
(b) (become smaller, be drawn together) sich
zusammenziehen

**contraction** /kən'trækʃn/ *n.* Kontraktion,
*die*

**'contract killer** *n.* Auftragskiller, *der/*
-killerin, *die*

**contractor** /kən'træktə(r)/ *n.*
Auftragnehmer, *der/*-nehmerin, *die*

**contradict** /kɒntrə'dɪkt/ *v.t.*
widersprechen (+ *Dat.*)

**contradiction** /kɒntrə'dɪkʃn/ *n.*
Widerspruch, *der;* in ∼ to sb./sth. im
Widerspruch zu jmdm./etw.

**contradictory** /kɒntrə'dɪktərɪ/ *adj.*
widersprüchlich

**contraflow** /'kɒntrəfləʊ/ *n.* ∼ system
Gegenverkehr auf einem Fahrstreifen

**contralto** /kən'træltəʊ/ *n., pl.* ∼s Alt, *der*

**contraption** /kən'træpʃn/ *n.* (coll.)
[komisches] Gerät

**contrary** /'kɒntrərɪ/ 1 *adj.* (a)
entgegengesetzt; be ∼ to sth. im Gegensatz
zu etw. stehen
(b) /kən'treərɪ/ (perverse) widerspenstig
2 *n.* the ∼: das Gegenteil; on the ∼: im
Gegenteil
3 *adv.* ∼ to sth. entgegen einer Sache

**contrast** 1 /kən'trɑːst/ *v.t.*
gegenüberstellen
2 /'kɒntrɑːst/ *n.* Kontrast, *der* (with zu); in
∼, ...: im Gegensatz dazu, ...; [be] in ∼ with
sth. im Gegensatz zu etw. [stehen]

**con'trasting** *adj.* gegensätzlich

**contravene** /kɒntrə'viːn/ *v.t.* verstoßen
gegen

**contravention** /kɒntrə'venʃn/ *n.* Verstoß,
*der* (of gegen)

**contribute** /kən'trɪbjuːt/ 1 *v.t.* ∼ sth. [to
*or* towards sth.] etw. [zu etw.] beitragen
2 *v.i.* ∼ to charity für karitative Zwecke
spenden; ∼ to the success of sth. zum Erfolg
einer Sache (*Gen.*) beitragen

**contribution** /kɒntrɪ'bjuːʃn/ *n.* Beitrag,
*der;* (for charity) Spende, *die* (to für); make a
∼: einen Beitrag leisten; (to charity) etwas
spenden

**contributor** /kən'trɪbjʊtə(r)/ *n.* (to
encyclopaedia etc.) Mitarbeiter, *der/*
Mitarbeiterin, *die*

**'con trick** (Brit. coll.) ▶ CONFIDENCE TRICK

**contrite** /'kɒntraɪt/ *adj.* zerknirscht

**contrive** /kən'traɪv/ *v.t.* ∼ to do sth. es
fertig bringen, etw. zu tun

**contrived** /kən'traɪvd/ *adj.* künstlich

**control** /kən'trəʊl/ 1 *n.* (a) Kontrolle, *die*
(of über + *Akk.*); keep ∼ of sth. etw. unter
Kontrolle halten; be in ∼ [of sth.] die
Kontrolle [über etw. (*Akk.*)] haben; [go *or*
get] out of ∼: außer Kontrolle [geraten]; [get
sth.] under ∼: [etw.] unter Kontrolle
[bringen]
(b) (device) Regler, *der;* ∼s Schalttafel, *die*
2 *v.t.*, -ll- kontrollieren; lenken ⟨Auto⟩;
zügeln ⟨Zorn⟩; regeln ⟨Verkehr⟩

**control:** ∼ **centre** *n.* Kontrollzentrum,
*das;* ∼ **con'trol desk** *n.* Schaltpult, *das*

**con'troller** *n.* (director) Leiter, *der/*Leiterin,
*die*

**control:** ∼ **panel** *n.* Schalttafel, *die;*
∼ **room** *n.* Kontrollraum, *der;* ∼ **tower**
*n.* Kontrollturm, *der*

**controversial** /kɒntrə'vɜːʃl/ *adj.*
umstritten

**controversy** /'kɒntrəvɜːsɪ, kən'trɒvəsɪ/ *n.*
Auseinandersetzung, *die*

**conurbation** /kɒnɜː'beɪʃn/ *n.* Konurbation,
*die* (Soziol.); ≈ Stadtregion, *die*

**convalesce** /kɒnvə'les/ *v.i.* genesen

**convalescence** /kɒnvə'lesəns/ *n.*
Genesung, *die*

**convection** /kən'vekʃn/ *n.* (Phys., Meteorol.)
Konvektion, *die*

**convector** /kən'vektə(r)/ *n.* Konvektor, *der*

**convene** /kən'vi:n/ **1** *v.t.* einberufen **2** *v.i.* zusammenkommen

**convenience** /kən'vi:nɪəns/ *n.* **(a)** for sb.'s ~ zu jmds. Bequemlichkeit; **at your ~:** wann es Ihnen passt **(b)** (toilet) **[public]** ~: [öffentliche] Toilette

**con'venience food** *n.* Fertignahrung, *die*

**convenient** /kən'vi:nɪənt/ *adj.* günstig; (useful) praktisch; **would it be ~ to** *or* **for you?** würde es Ihnen passen?

**con'veniently** *adv.* **(a)** günstig ‹gelegen, angebracht› **(b)** (opportunely) angenehmerweise

**convent** /'kɒnvənt/ *n.* Kloster, *das*

**convention** /kən'venʃn/ *n.* **(a)** Brauch, *der* **(b)** (assembly) Konferenz, *die* **(c)** (agreement) Konvention, *die*

**conventional** /kən'venʃənl/ *adj.* konventionell

**converge** /kən'vɜ:dʒ/ *v.i.* ~ [on each other] aufeinander zulaufen

**conversant** /kən'vɜ:sənt/ *pred. adj.* vertraut **(with** mit)

**conversation** /kɒnvə'seɪʃn/ *n.* Unterhaltung, *die;* **have a ~:** ein Gespräch führen

**conversational** /kɒnvə'seɪʃənl/ *adj.* ~ **English** gesprochenes Englisch

**converse¹** /kən'vɜ:s/ *v.i.* (formal) ~ **[with sb.]** [about *or* on sth.] sich [mit jmdm.] [über etw. (*Akk.*)] unterhalten

**converse²** /'kɒnvɜ:s/ **1** *adj.* entgegengesetzt; umgekehrt ‹Fall, Situation› **2** *n.* Gegenteil, *das*

**conversely** /kən'vɜ:slɪ/ *adj.* umgekehrt

**conversion** /kən'vɜ:ʃn/ *n.* **(a)** Umwandlung, *die* **(into** in + *Akk.*) **(b)** (adaptation) Umbau, *der* **(c)** (of person) Bekehrung, *die* **(to** zu)

**con'version table** *n.* Umrechnungstabelle, *die*

**convert** **1** /kən'vɜ:t/ *v.t.* umwandeln **(into** in + *Akk.*); (Comp.) konvertieren ‹Daten›; ~ **sb.** [to sth.] jmdn. [zu etw.] bekehren **2** /kən'vɜ:t/ *v.i.* ~ **into sth.** sich in etw. (*Akk.*) umwandeln lassen **3** /'kɒnvɜ:t/ *n.* Konvertit, *der*/Konvertitin, *die*

**convertible** /kən'vɜ:tɪbl/ **1** *adj.* be ~ **into** sth. sich in etw. (*Akk.*) umwandeln lassen **2** *n.* Kabrio[lett], *das*

**convex** /'kɒnveks/ *adj.* konvex

**convey** /kən'veɪ/ *v.t.* **(a)** befördern **(b)** (impart) vermitteln

**conveyance** /kən'veɪəns/ *n.* **(a)** (transportation) Beförderung, *die* **(b)** (formal: vehicle) Beförderungsmittel, *das*

**con'veyancing** *n.* (Law) ~ **[of property]** [Eigentums]übertragung, *die*

**conveyor** /kən'veɪə(r)/ *n.* ~ **[belt]** Förderband, *das*

**convict** **1** /'kɒnvɪkt/ *n.* Strafgefangene, *der/die* **2** /kən'vɪkt/ *v.t.* verurteilen

**conviction** /kən'vɪkʃn/ *n.* **(a)** (Law) Verurteilung, *die* **(for** wegen) **(b)** (belief) Überzeugung, *die*

**convince** /kən'vɪns/ *v.t.* überzeugen; ~ **sb. that ...:** jmdn. davon überzeugen, dass ...; **be ~d that ...:** davon überzeugt sein, dass ...

**convincing** /kən'vɪnsɪŋ/ *adj.*, **con'vincingly** *adv.* überzeugend

**convivial** /kən'vɪvɪəl/ *adj.* fröhlich

**convoluted** /'kɒnvəlu:tɪd/ *adj.* (complex) kompliziert

**convoy** /'kɒnvɔɪ/ *n.* Konvoi, *der;* **in ~:** im Konvoi

**convulse** /kən'vʌls/ *v.t.* **be ~d with** sich krümmen vor (+ *Dat.*)

**convulsions** /kən'vʌlʃnz/ *n. pl.* Krämpfe *Pl.*

**convulsive** /kən'vʌlsɪv/ *adj.*, **con'vulsively** *adv.* konvulsivisch

**coo** /ku:/ *v.i.* gurren

**cook** /kʊk/ **1** *n.* Koch, *der*/Köchin, *die* **2** *v.t.* kochen ‹Mahlzeit›; (fry, roast) braten; (boil) kochen **3** *v.i.* kochen

■ **cook 'up** *v.t.* erfinden ‹Geschichte›

**'cookbook** *n.* (Amer.) Kochbuch, *das*

**'cooker** *n.* (Brit.) Herd, *der*

**cookery** /'kʊkərɪ/ *n.* Kochen, *das*

**'cookery book** *n.* (Brit.) Kochbuch, *das*

**cookie** /'kʊkɪ/ *n.* **(a)** (Amer.) Keks, *der* **(b)** (Comp.) Cookie, *der*

**'cooking** *n.* Kochen, *das*

**cooking:** ~ **apple** *n.* Kochapfel, *der;* ~ **utensil** *n.* Küchengerät, *das*

**cool** /ku:l/ **1** *adj.* **(a)** kühl; **store in a ~ place** kühl aufbewahren **(b)** (unemotional, unfriendly) kühl; (calm) ruhig **2** *n.* Kühle, *die* **3** *v.i.* abkühlen **4** *v.t.* kühlen; (from high temperature) abkühlen

■ **cool 'down, cool 'off** *v.i. & t.* abkühlen

**cool:** ~ **box** *n.* Kühlbox, *die;* ~**-headed** *adj.* kühl; nüchtern

**coolly** /'ku:llɪ/ *adv.* (calmly) ruhig; (unemotionally) kühl

**coop** /ku:p/ **1** *n.* (for poultry) Hühnerstall, *der* **2** *v.t.* ~ **up** einpferchen

**cooperate** /kəʊ'ɒpəreɪt/ *v.i.* mitarbeiten (**in** bei); (with each other) zusammenarbeiten (**in** bei)

**cooperation** /kəʊɒpə'reɪʃn/ *n.* Zusammenarbeit, *die*

**cooperative** /kəʊ'ɒpərətɪv/ **1** *adj.* kooperativ; (helpful) hilfsbereit **2** *n.* Genossenschaft, *die*

**coordinate** /kəʊ'ɔ:dɪneɪt/ *v.t.* koordinieren

**coordination** /kəʊɔːdɪˈneɪʃn/ *n.*
Koordination, *die*

**co-owner** /kəʊˈəʊnə(r)/ *n.* Miteigentümer,
*der*/-eigentümerin, *die*; (of business)
Mitinhaber, *der*/-inhaberin, *die*

**cop** /kɒp/ *n.* (coll.: police officer) Bulle, *der*
(salopp)

**cope** /kəʊp/ *v.i.* ~ **with sb./sth.** mit jmdm./
etw. fertig werden

**Copenhagen** /kəʊpnˈheɪgn/ *pr. n.*
Kopenhagen (*das*)

**copier** /ˈkɒpɪə(r)/ *n.* (machine) Kopiergerät,
*das*

**co-pilot** /ˈkəʊpaɪlət/ *n.* Kopilot, *der*/
Kopilotin, *die*

**copious** /ˈkəʊpɪəs/ *adj.* reichhaltig

**'cop-out** *n.* (coll.) Drückebergerei, *die* (ugs.
abwertend); **that's a** ~: das ist Drückebergerei
(ugs. abwertend)

**copper¹** /ˈkɒpə(r)/ *n.* Kupfer, *das*

**copper²** (Brit. coll.) ▶ COP

**coppice** /ˈkɒpɪs/, **copse** /kɒps/ *ns.*
Wäldchen, *das*

**'cop shop** *n.* (Brit. coll.) Wache, *die*; Revier,
*das*

**copula** /ˈkɒpjʊlə/ *n.* (Ling.) Kopula, *die*

**copulate** /ˈkɒpjʊleɪt/ *v.i.* kopulieren

**copy** /ˈkɒpɪ/ ① *n.* (a) (reproduction) Kopie, *die*
(b) (specimen) Exemplar, *das*
② *v.t. & i.* kopieren; (transcribe) abschreiben

**copy:** ~**cat** *n.* (coll.) you're such a ~cat! du
musst immer alles nachmachen!; ~ **editor**
*n.* Redakteur, *der*/Redakteurin, *die* (der/die nur
nach schriftlichen Vorlagen arbeitet);
~ **protection** *n.* (Comp.) Kopierschutz,
*der*; ~**right** *n.* Urheberrecht, *das* ~**writer**
*n.* [Werbe]texter, *der*/-texterin, *die*

**coral** /ˈkɒrl/ *n.* Koralle, *die*

**cord** /kɔːd/ *n.* (a) Kordel, *die*; (strong string)
Schnur, *die*
(b) (cloth) Cord, *der*
(c) *in pl.* (trousers) [pair of] ~s Cordhose, *die*

**cordial** /ˈkɔːdɪəl/ ① *adj.* herzlich
② *n.* (drink) Sirup, *der*

**cordiality** /kɔːdɪˈælɪtɪ/ *n.* Herzlichkeit, *die*

**'cordially** *adv.* herzlich

**'cordless phone** /ˈkɔːdlɪs/ *n.*
Schnurlostelefon, *das*

**cordon** /ˈkɔːdn/ ① *n.* Kordon, *der*
② *v.t.* ~ [off] absperren

**corduroy** /ˈkɔːdərɔɪ, ˈkɔːdjʊrɔɪ/ *n.*
Cordsamt, *der*

**core** /kɔː(r)/ ① *n.* (of fruit) Kerngehäuse, *das*
② *v.t.* entkernen

**co-respondent** /kəʊrɪˈspɒndənt/ *n.*
Mitbeklagte, *der/die* (im *Scheidungsprozess*)

**cork** /kɔːk/ ① *n.* (a) (bark) Kork, *der*
(b) (bottle stopper) Korken, *der*
② *v.t.* zukorken

**cork:** ~**screw** *n.* Korkenzieher, *der*;
~ **'tile** *n.* Korkplatte, *die*

**cormorant** /ˈkɔːmərənt/ *n.* Kormoran, *der*

**corn¹** /kɔːn/ *n.* Getreide, *das*

**corn²** *n.* (on foot) Hühnerauge, *das*

**cornea** /ˈkɔːnɪə/ *n.* (Anat.) Hornhaut, *die*;
Cornea, *die* (fachspr.)

**corned beef** /kɔːnd ˈbiːf/ *n.* Cornedbeef,
*das*

**corner** /ˈkɔːnə(r)/ ① *n.* (a) Ecke, *die*; (curve)
Kurve, *die*; **on the** ~: an der Ecke/in der
Kurve
(b) (of mouth, eye) Winkel, *der*
② *v.t.* (fig.) in die Enge treiben
③ *v.i.* die Kurve nehmen

**corner:** ~ **kick** *n.* (Footb.) Eckball, *der*;
~ **shop** *n.* Tante-Emma-Laden, *der* (ugs.);
~**stone** *n.* (fig.) Eckpfeiler, *der*

**cornet** /ˈkɔːnɪt/ *n.* (a) (Brit.: for ice cream)
[Eis]tüte, *die*
(b) (Mus.) Kornett, *das*

**corn:** ~**flakes** *n. pl.* Cornflakes *Pl.*;
~**flour** (Brit.) *n.* Maismehl, *das*; ~**flower** *n.*
Kornblume, *die*; ~ **starch** (Amer.) *n.*
Maismehl, *das*

**'corny** *adj.* (coll.: trite) abgedroschen

**coronary** /ˈkɒrənərɪ/ ① *adj.* (Anat.) koronar
② *n.* (Med.) ▶ CORONARY THROMBOSIS

**coronary:** ~ **'artery** *n.* Herzkranzarterie,
*die*; Koronararterie, *die* (fachspr.);
~ **throm'bosis** *n.* Koronarthrombose, *die*

**coronation** /kɒrəˈneɪʃn/ *n.* Krönung, *die*

**coroner** /ˈkɒrənə(r)/ *n.* Coroner, *der*;
*Beamter, der gewaltsame od. unnatürliche*
*Todesfälle untersucht*

**coronet** /ˈkɒrənet/ *n.* Krone, *die*

**corporal¹** /ˈkɔːpərl/ *adj.* körperlich

**corporal²** *n.* ≈ Hauptgefreite, *der*

**corporate** /ˈkɔːpərət/ *adj.* körperschaftlich

**corporation** /kɔːpəˈreɪʃn/ *n.*
Stadtverwaltung, *die*

**corpo'ration tax** *n.* Körperschaftssteuer,
*die*

**corps** /kɔː(r)/ *n.*, *pl. same* /kɔːz/ Korps, *das*

**corpse** /kɔːps/ *n.* Leiche, *die*

**corpulent** /ˈkɔːpjʊlənt/ *adj.* korpulent

**Corpus Christi** /kɔːpəs ˈkrɪstɪ/ *n.* (Eccl.)
Fronleichnam (*der*)

**corpuscle** /ˈkɔːpəsl/ *n.* [blood] ~
Blutkörperchen, *das*

**corral** /kəˈrɑːl/ (Amer.) ① *n.* Pferch, *der*
② *v.t.*, **-ll-** einpferchen

**correct** /kəˈrekt/ ① *v.t.* korrigieren
② *adj.* korrekt; **that is** ~: das stimmt

**correction** /kəˈrekʃn/ *n.* Korrektur, *die*

**cor'rectly** *adv.* korrekt

**correspond** /kɒrɪˈspɒnd/ *v.i.* (a) ~ [**to**
**each other**] einander entsprechen; ~ **to sth.**
einer Sache (*Dat.*) entsprechen
(b) (communicate) ~ **with sb.** mit jmdm.
korrespondieren

**correspondence** /kɒrɪˈspɒndəns/ *n.* (a)
Übereinstimmung, *die* (with, to mit)
(b) (communication) Briefwechsel, *der*

**corre'spondence course** *n.* Fernkurs, *der*

**correspondent** /kɒrɪ'spɒndənt/ *n.* (reporter) Korrespondent, *der*/ Korrespondentin, *die*

**corre'sponding** *adj.* entsprechend (**to** *Dat.*)

**corre'spondingly** *adv.* entsprechend

**corridor** /'kɒrɪdɔː(r)/ *n.* (a) Flur, *der* (b) (Railw.) [Seiten]gang, *der*

**corroborate** /kə'rɒbəreɪt/ *v.t.* bestätigen

**corroboration** /kərɒbə'reɪʃn/ *n.* Bestätigung, *die*

**corrode** /kə'rəʊd/ ① *v.t.* zerfressen ② *v.i.* zerfressen werden

**corrosion** /kə'rəʊʒn/ *n.* Korrosion, *die*

**corrugated** /'kɒrəgeɪtɪd/ *adj.* ~ **cardboard** Wellpappe, *die;* ~ **iron** Wellblech, *das*

**corrupt** /kə'rʌpt/ ① *adj.* (depraved) verdorben (geh.); (influenced by bribery) korrupt ② *v.t.* (deprave) korrumpieren; (bribe) bestechen

**corruption** /kə'rʌpʃn/ *n.* (moral deterioration) Verdorbenheit, *die* (geh.); (corrupt practices) Korruption, *die*

**corset** /'kɔːsɪt/ *n.* Korsett, *das*

**Corsica** /'kɔːsɪkə/ *pr. n.* Korsika (*das*)

**cortège** /kɔː'teɪʒ/ *n.* Trauerzug, *der*

**cortisone** /'kɔːtɪzəʊn/ *n.* Kortison, *das;* Cortison, *das* (fachspr.)

**cosh** /kɒʃ/ (Brit. coll.) ① *n.* Totschläger, *der* ② *v.t.* niederknüppeln

**cosmetic** /kɒz'metɪk/ ① *adj.* kosmetisch ② *n.* Kosmetikum, *das*

**cosmic** /'kɒzmɪk/ *adj.* kosmisch

**cosmonaut** /'kɒzmənɔːt/ *n.* Kosmonaut, *der*/Kosmonautin, *die*

**cosmopolitan** /kɒzmə'pɒlɪtən/ *adj.* kosmopolitisch

**cosmos** /'kɒzmɒs/ *n.* Kosmos, *der*

**cosset** /'kɒsɪt/ *v.t.* [ver]hätscheln

**cost** /kɒst/ ① *n.* (a) Kosten *Pl.* (b) (fig.) Preis, *der;* **at all** ~**s, at any** ~: um jeden Preis ② *v.t.* (a) *p.t., p.p.* **cost** (lit. or fig.) kosten; **how much does it** ~? was kostet es? (b) *p.t., p.p.* **costed** (Commerc.: fix price of) ~ **sth.** den Preis für etw. kalkulieren

**co-star** /'kəʊstɑː(r)/ (Cinemat., Theatre) ① *n.* **be a/the** ~: eine der Hauptrollen/die zweite Hauptrolle spielen ② *v.i.,* **-rr-:** eine der Hauptrollen spielen ③ *v.t.,* **-rr-: the film** ~**red Robert Redford** der Film zeigte Robert Redford in einer der Hauptrollen

**cost:** ~ **cutting** *n.* Kostensenkung, *die;* ~-**cutting** *adj.* Spar-; ~-**effective** *adj.* rentabel

**'costly** *adj.* teuer

**cost:** ~ **of 'living** *n.*

Lebenshaltungskosten *Pl.;* ~-**of-living index** Lebenshaltungsindex, *der;* ~ **price** *n.* Selbstkostenpreis, *der*

**costume** /'kɒstjuːm/ *n.* Kleidermode, *die;* (theatrical ~) Kostüm, *das*

**costume 'jewellery** *n.* Modeschmuck, *der*

**cosy** /'kəʊzɪ/ *adj.* gemütlich

**cot** /kɒt/ *n.* Kinderbett, *das*

**'cot death** *n.* (Brit.) plötzlicher Kindstod; Cot-death, *der* (Med.)

**cottage** /'kɒtɪdʒ/ *n.* Cottage, *das*

**cottage:** ~ **'cheese** *n.* Hüttenkäse, *der;* ~ **'hospital** *n.: kleines* [*Land*]*krankenhaus ohne ständige ärztliche Betreuung;* ~ **industry** *n.* Heimarbeit, *die;* ~ **'pie** *n.: mit Kartoffelbrei überbackenes Hackfleisch*

**cotton** /'kɒtən/ ① *n.* Baumwolle, *die;* (thread) Baumwollgarn, *das* ② *attrib. adj.* Baumwoll- ③ *v.i.* ~ **'on** (coll.) kapieren (ugs.)

**cotton:** ~ **reel** *n.* [Näh]garnrolle, *die;* ~ **'wool** *n.* Watte, *die*

**couch** /kaʊtʃ/ *n.* Couch, *die*

**couchette** /kuː'ʃet/ *n.* (Railw.) Liegewagenplatz, *der*

**couch po'tato** *n.* (coll.) Couchpotato[e], *der*

**cough** /kɒf/ ① *n.* Husten, *der* ② *v.i.* husten

**cough:** ~ **medicine** *n.* Hustenmittel, *das;* ~ **mixture** *n.* Hustensaft, *der*

**could** ▶ CAN²

**couldn't** /'kʊdnt/ (coll.) = **could not;** ▶ CAN²

**council** /'kaʊnsl/ *n.* Rat, *der;* **local** ~: Gemeinderat, *der;* **city/town** ~: Stadtrat, *der;* **C**~ **of Ministers** Ministerrat, *der*

**council:** ~ **estate** *n.* Wohnviertel mit Sozialwohnungen; ~ **flat** *n.* Sozialwohnung, *die;* ~ **house** *n.* Haus des sozialen Wohnungsbaus; ~ **housing** *n.* sozialer Wohnungsbau

**councillor** /'kaʊnsələ(r)/ *n.* Ratsmitglied, *das*

**'council tax** *n.* (Brit.) Gemeindesteuer, *die*

**counsel** /'kaʊnsl/ ① *n.* (a) Rat[schlag], *der* (b) *pl. same* (Law) Rechtsanwalt, *der*/ -anwältin, *die* ② *v.t.,* (Brit.) **-ll-** beraten

**counselling** (*Amer.:* **counseling**) /'kaʊnsəlɪŋ/ *n.* Beratung, *die;* **marriage** ~: Eheberatung, *die*

**counsellor,** (*Amer.* **counselor**) /'kaʊnsələ(r)/ *n.* Berater, *der*/Beraterin, *die*

**count¹** /kaʊnt/ ① *n.* Zählen, *das;* **keep** ~ [**of sth.**] [etw.] zählen; **lose** ~: sich verzählen ② *v.t.* (a) zählen (b) (include) mitzählen; **not** ~**ing** abgesehen von (c) (consider) halten für; ~ **oneself lucky** sich glücklich schätzen können ⋯⟩

**3** *v.i.* **(a)** zählen; ∼ **[up] to ten** bis zehn zählen

**(b)** (be included) zählen

■ **'count on** *v.t.* ∼ **on sb./sth.** sich auf jmdn./etw. verlassen

■ **count 'up** *v.t.* zusammenzählen

**count²** *n.* (nobleman) Graf, *der*

**'countdown** *n.* Count-down, *der od. das*

**countenance** /'kaʊntɪnəns/ **1** *n.* (literary: face) Antlitz, *das*

**2** *v.t.* (formal: approve) gutheißen

**counter¹** /'kaʊntə(r)/ *n.* **(a)** (in shop) Ladentisch, *der;* (in cafeteria) Büfett, *das;* (in bank) Schalter, *der*

**(b)** (for games) Spielmarke, *die*

**counter²** **1** *adj.* Gegen-

**2** *v.t.* **(a)** (oppose) begegnen (+ *Dat.*)

**(b)** (act against) kontern

**3** *adv.* **go** ∼ **to** zuwiderlaufen (+ *Dat.*)

**counter:** ∼**'act** *v.t.* entgegenwirken (+ *Dat.*); ∼**attack** *n.* Gegenangriff, *der;* ∼**balance** *v.t.* (fig.) ausgleichen; ∼**'espionage** *n.* Spionageabwehr, *die*

**counterfeit** /'kaʊntəfɪt/ **1** *adj.* gefälscht; ∼ **money** Falschgeld, *das*

**2** *v.t.* fälschen

**'counterfeiter** *n.* Fälscher, *der*/Fälscherin, *die*

**counterfoil** /'kaʊntəfɔɪl/ *n.* Kontrollabschnitt, *der*

**counter:** ∼**part** *n.* Gegenstück, *das* (of zu); ∼**pro'ductive** *adj.* sth. is ∼productive bewirkt das Gegenteil des Gewünschten; ∼**sign** *v.t.* gegenzeichnen; ∼**weight** *n.* Gegengewicht, *das*

**countess** /'kaʊntɪs/ *n.* Gräfin, *die*

**'countless** *adj.* zahllos

**countrified** /'kʌntrɪfaɪd/ *adj.* ländlich

**country** /'kʌntrɪ/ *n.* **(a)** Land, *das;* sb's **[home]** ∼: jmds. Heimat

**(b)** (∼side) Landschaft, *die;* **in the** ∼: auf dem Land; ∼ **road/air** Landstraße, *die*/Landluft, *die*

**country 'dancing** *n.* Kontertanz, *der*

**countryfied** ▶ COUNTRIFIED

**country:** ∼**man** /'kʌntrɪmən/, *n. pl.* ∼**men** /'kʌntrɪmən/ Landsmann, *der;* ∼**side** *n.* **(a)** (rural areas) Land, *das;* **(b)** (rural scenery) Landschaft, *die*

**county** /'kaʊntɪ/ *n.* (Brit.) Grafschaft, *die*

**coup** /kuː/ *n.* **(a)** Coup, *der*

**(b)** ▶ COUP D'ÉTAT

**coup d'état** /kuː deɪ'taː/ *n.* Staatsstreich, *der*

**coupé** /'kuːpeɪ/ *n.* Coupé, *das*

**couple** /'kʌpl/ **1** *n.* **(a)** (pair) Paar, *das;* (married) [Ehe]paar, *das*

**(b) a** ∼ **[of]** (a few) ein paar; (two) zwei

**2** *v.t.* koppeln

**coupon** /'kuːpɒn/ *n.* **(a)** (for rations) Marke, *die*

**(b)** (in advertisement) Coupon, *der*

**courage** /'kʌrɪdʒ/ *n.* Mut, *der*

**courageous** /kə'reɪdʒəs/ *adj.,* **cou'rageously** *adv.* mutig

**courgette** /kʊə'ʒet/ *n.* (Brit.) Zucchino, *der*

**courier** /'kʊrɪə(r)/ *n.* **(a)** (Tourism) Reiseleiter, *der*/-leiterin, *die*

**(b)** (messenger) Kurier, *der*

**'courier company** *n.* Kurierdienst, *der*

**course** /kɔːs/ *n.* **(a)** (of ship, plane) Kurs, *der;* ∼ **[of action]** Vorgehensweise, *die*

**(b) of** ∼: natürlich

**(c) in due** ∼: zu gegebener Zeit; **in the** ∼ **of the day/his life** im Lauf[e] des Tages/seines Lebens

**(d)** (of meal) Gang, *der*

**(e)** (Sport) Kurs, *der;* **[golf]**∼: [Golf]platz, *der*

**(f)** (Educ.) Kurs[us], *der;* **go to** *or* **attend/do a** ∼ **in sth.** einen Kurs in etw. (*Dat.*) besuchen/machen

**(g)** (Med.) **a** ∼ **of treatment** eine Kur

**court** /kɔːt/ **1** *n.* **(a)** Hof, *der*

**(b)** (Tennis, Squash) Platz, *der*

**(c)** (Law) Gericht, *das*

**2** *v.t.* ∼ **sb.** jmdn. umwerben

**courteous** /'kɜːtɪəs/ *adj.* höflich

**courtesy** /'kɜːtəsɪ/ *n.* Höflichkeit, *die*

**'courtesy light** *n.* (Motor Veh.) Innenbeleuchtung, *die*

**court:** ∼ **house** *n.* (Law) Gerichtsgebäude, *das;* ∼ **'martial** *n., pl.* ∼**s martial** (Mil.) Kriegsgericht, *das;* ∼**room** *n.* (Law) Gerichtssaal, *der*

**courtship** /'kɔːtʃɪp/ *n.* Werben, *das*

**court:** ∼ **shoe** *n.* Pumps, *der;* ∼**yard** *n.* Hof, *der*

**cousin** /'kʌzn/ *n.* **[first]** ∼: Cousin, *der*/Cousine, *die*

**couturier** /kuː'tjʊərjeɪ/ *n.* Couturier, *der;* Modeschöpfer, *der*

**cove** /kəʊv/ *n.* (Geog.) [kleine] Bucht

**covenant** /'kʌvənənt/ *n.* formelle Übereinkunft

**cover** /'kʌvə(r)/ **1** *n.* **(a)** (piece of cloth) Decke, *die;* (of cushion, bed) Bezug, *der;* (lid) Deckel, *der;* (of hole, engine, typewriter, etc.) Abdeckung, *die*

**(b)** (of book) Einband, *der;* (of magazine) Umschlag, *der*

**(c) [send sth.] under separate** ∼: [etw.] mit getrennter Post [schicken]

**(d) take** ∼ **[from sth.]** Schutz [vor etw. (*Dat.*)] suchen; **under** ∼ (from rain) überdacht

**2** *v.t.* **(a)** bedecken; beziehen ⟨Sessel, Kissen⟩; zudecken ⟨Pfanne⟩; **the roses are** ∼**ed with greenfly** die Rosen sind voller Blattläuse

**(b)** (include) abdecken

**(c)** (Journ.) berichten über (+ *Akk.*)

**(d)** decken ⟨Kosten⟩

■ **cover 'up** **1** *v.t.* zudecken; (fig.) vertuschen

**2** *v.i.* ∼ **up for sb.** jmdn. decken

**coverage** /'kʌvərɪdʒ/ *n.* (Journ.) Berichterstattung, *die*

'**cover charge** n. [Preis für das] Gedeck

'**covering** n. Decke, die; (of chair, bed) Bezug, der

'**covering letter** n. Begleitbrief, der

'**cover story** n. (Journ.) Titelgeschichte, die

**covert** /'kʌvət/ adj. versteckt

**cover: ⁀-up** n. Verschleierung, die; ⁀ **version** n. Coverversion, die

**covet** /'kʌvɪt/ v.t. begehren (geh.)

**covetous** /'kʌvɪtəs/ adj. begehrlich (geh.)

**cow** /kaʊ/ n. Kuh, die

**coward** /'kaʊəd/ n. Feigling, der

**cowardice** /'kaʊədɪs/ n. Feigheit, die

'**cowardly** adj. feig[e]

'**cowboy** n. Cowboy, der

**cower** /'kaʊə(r)/ v.i. sich ducken

**cowherd** n. Kuhhirte, der

'**co-worker** n. Kollege, der/Kollegin, die

**cow: ⁀ parsley** n. (Bot.) Wiesenkerbel, der; ⁀**pat** n. Kuhfladen, der; ⁀**shed** n. Kuhstall, der; ⁀**slip** n. Schlüsselblume, die

**coy** /kɔɪ/ adj. gespielt schüchtern

**cozy** (Amer.) ▶ cosy

**CPU** abbr. (Comp.) = **central processing unit** ZE

**crab** /kræb/ n. Krabbe, die

'**crab apple** n. Holzapfel, der

**crack** /kræk/ ① n. (a) (noise) Krachen, das (b) (in china etc.) Sprung, der; (in rock) Spalte, die; (chink) Spalt, der

(c) (coll.: try) have a ⁀ at sth./doing sth. versuchen, etw. zu tun

(d) (sl.: drug) ⁀ [**cocaine**] Crack, das

② attrib. adj. (coll.) erstklassig

③ v.t. (a) knacken ⟨Nuss, Problem, Kode⟩

(b) (make a ⁀ in) anschlagen ⟨Porzellan usw.⟩

(c) ⁀ a joke einen Witz machen

(d) ⁀ a whip mit einer Peitsche knallen

④ v.i. ⟨Porzellan usw.:⟩ einen Sprung/ Sprünge bekommen

■ **crack 'down** v.i. (coll.) ⁀ down [on sb./ sth.] [gegen jmdn./etw.] [hart] vorgehen

■ **crack 'up** v.i. (coll.) ⟨Person:⟩ zusammenbrechen

'**crack-down** n. (coll.) there will be a ⁀: man wird hart durchgreifen; have/order a ⁀ on sb./sth. drastische Maßnahmen gegen jmdn./etw. ergreifen/anordnen

**cracked** /krækt/ adj. gesprungen ⟨Porzellan usw.⟩; rissig ⟨Verputz⟩

**cracker** /'krækə(r)/ n. (a) [Christmas] ⁀ ≈ Knallbonbon, der od. das

(b) (biscuit) Cracker, der

'**crackers** pred. adj. (Brit. coll.) übergeschnappt (ugs.)

**crackle** /'krækl/ ① v.i. knistern; ⟨Feuer:⟩ prasseln

② n. Knistern, das

**cradle** /'kreɪdl/ ① n. Wiege, die

② v.t. wiegen

**cradle:⁀ -snatch** v.i. (coll.) Your boyfriend/girlfriend is much younger than

you. You're ⁀-snatching Dein Freund/deine Freundin ist viel jünger als du. Du vergreifst dich ja an kleinen Kindern (ugs. scherzh.); ⁀ **-snatcher** n. (fig. coll.) jmd., der mit einer sehr viel jüngeren Person eine Liebesbeziehung eingeht

**craft** /krɑːft/ n. (a) (trade) Handwerk, das; (art) Kunsthandwerk, das

(b) pl. same (boat) Boot, das

**craftily** /'krɑːftɪlɪ/ adv. listig

**craftsman** /'krɑːftsmən/ n., pl. **craftsmen** /'krɑːftsmən/ Handwerker, der

**craftsmanship** /'krɑːftsmənʃɪp/ n. (skilled workmanship) handwerkliches Können

**crafty** /'krɑːftɪ/ adj. listig

**crag** /kræg/ n. Felsspitze, die

'**craggy** adj. (a) felsig

(b) zerfurcht ⟨Gesicht⟩

**cram** /kræm/ ① v.t., -mm- (overfill) voll stopfen (ugs.); (force) stopfen

② v.i., -mm- (for exam) büffeln (ugs.)

**cramp** /kræmp/ ① n. (Med.) Krampf, der

② v.t. einengen

**cramped** /kræmpt/ adj. eng ⟨Raum⟩; gedrängt ⟨Handschrift⟩

**cranberry** /'krænbərɪ/ n. Preiselbeere, die

**crane** /kreɪn/ ① n. Kran, der

② v.t. ⁀ one's neck den Hals recken

**crane: ⁀ driver** n. Kranführer, der/ -führerin, die; ⁀ **fly** n. Schnake, die

**crank¹** /kræŋk/ n. (Mech. Engin.) [Hand]kurbel, die

**crank²** n. Irre, der/die (salopp)

**crank: ⁀ arm** n. (of bicycle) Tretkurbel, die; ⁀**shaft** n. (Mech. Engin.) Kurbelwelle, die

'**cranky** adj. (eccentric) schrullig

**cranny** /'krænɪ/ n. Ritze, die

**crap** /kræp/ n. (coarse) (a) (faeces) Scheiße, die (derb); have a ⁀: scheißen (derb)

(b) (nonsense) Scheiß, der (salopp)

**crash** /kræʃ/ ① n. (a) (noise) Krachen, das (b) (collision) Zusammenstoß, der; have a ⁀: einen Unfall haben

② v.i. (a) (make a noise, go noisily) krachen

(b) (have a collision) einen Unfall haben; ⟨Flugzeug, Flieger:⟩ abstürzen; ⁀ into sth. gegen etw. krachen

(c) (Finance etc., Computing) zusammenbrechen

③ v.t. (a) (smash) schmettern

(b) (cause to have collision) einen Unfall haben mit

**crash: ⁀ barrier** n. Leitplanke, die; ⁀ **course** n. Intensivkurs, der; ⁀ **diet** n. radikale Diät; ≈ Nulldiät, die; ⁀ **helmet** n. Sturzhelm, der; ⁀**land** ① v.t. ⁀-land a plane mit einem Flugzeug bruchlanden; ② v.i. bruchlanden; ⁀**-landing** n. Bruchlandung, die

**crass** /kræs/ adj. haarsträubend ⟨Dummheit, Unwissenheit⟩; (grossly stupid) strohdumm

**crate** /kreɪt/ n. Kiste, die

**crater** /'kreɪtə(r)/ n. Krater, der

**cravat** /krə'væt/ *n.* Krawatte, *die*

**crave** /kreɪv/ *v.t.* **(a)** (beg) erbitten
**(b)** (long for) sich sehnen nach

'**craving** *n.* Verlangen, *das* **(for** nach)

**crawl** /krɔːl/ **1** *v.i.* **(a)** kriechen; ⟨*Baby, Insekt:*⟩ krabbeln
**(b)** (coll.) ~ **to sb.** vor jmdm. kriechen
**2** *n.* **(a) go at a** ~: im Schneckentempo fahren
**(b)** (swimming stroke) Kraulen, *das*

'**crawler lane** *n.* Kriechspur, *die*

**crayfish** /'kreɪfɪʃ/ *n.*, *pl. same* Flusskrebs, *der*

**crayon** /'kreɪən/ *n.* [coloured] ~: Buntstift, *der;* (wax) Wachsmalstift, *der*

**craze** /kreɪz/ *n.* Begeisterung, *die*

**crazy** /'kreɪzɪ/ *adj.* verrückt; **be** ~ **about sb./sth.** (coll.) nach jmdm./etw. verrückt sein (ugs.)

**creak** /kriːk/ **1** *n.* Knarren, *das*
**2** *v.i.* knarren

**cream** /kriːm/ **1** *n.* **(a)** Sahne, *die*
**(b)** (dessert, cosmetic) Creme, *die*
**2** *adj.* ~[-coloured] creme[farben]

**cream:** ~ **cake** *n.* Cremetorte, *die;* (small) Cremetörtchen, *das;* (with whipped ~) Sahnetorte, *die*/Sahnetörtchen, *das;*
~ '**cheese** *n.* ≈ Frischkäse, *der;*
~ '**cracker** *n.* ≈ Cracker, *der;* ~ '**tea** *n.* Tee mit Marmeladetörtchen und Sahne

'**creamy** *adj.* (with cream) sahnig; (like cream) cremig

**crease** /kriːs/ **1** *n.* (pressed) Bügelfalte, *die;* (accidental) Falte, *die*
**2** *v.t.* (press) eine Falte bügeln in (+ *Akk.*); (accidentally) zerknittern
**3** *v.i.* Falten bekommen; knittern

'**crease-resistant** *adj.* knitterfrei

**create** /kriː'eɪt/ *v.t.* schaffen; verursachen ⟨*Verwirrung*⟩; machen ⟨*Eindruck*⟩

**creation** /kriː'eɪʃn/ *n.* Schaffung, *die;* (of the world) Schöpfung, *die* (geh.)

**creative** /kriː'eɪtɪv/ *adj.* kreativ

**creator** /kriː'eɪtə(r)/ *n.* Schöpfer, *der*/Schöpferin, *die*

**creature** /'kriːtʃə(r)/ *n.* Geschöpf, *das*

**crèche** /kreʃ/ *n.* [Kinder]krippe, *die*

**credentials** /krɪ'denʃlz/ *n. pl.* Zeugnis, *das*

**credibility** /kredɪ'bɪlɪtɪ/ *n.* Glaubwürdigkeit, *die*

**credible** /'kredɪbl/ *adj.* glaubwürdig

**credit** /'kredɪt/ **1** *n.* **(a)** (honour) Ehre, *die;* **take the** ~ **for sth.** die Anerkennung für etw. einstecken
**(b)** (Commerc.) Kredit, *der*
**(c)** ~**s,** ~ **titles** (at beginning of film) Vorspann, *der;* (at end) Nachspann, *der*
**2** *v.t.* **(a)** glauben
**(b)** (Finance) gutschreiben

**creditable** /'kredɪtəbl/ *adj.* anerkennenswert

**creditably** /'kredɪtəblɪ/ *adv.* achtbar

**credit:** ~ **account** *n.* Kreditkonto, *das;*
~ **card** *n.* Kreditkarte, *die;* ~ **facilities** *n. pl.* [Kredit]fazilität, *die* (fachspr.); ~ **limit** *n.* Kreditlinie, *die*

**creditor** /'kredɪtə(r)/ *n.* Gläubiger, *der*/Gläubigerin, *die*

**credit:** ~ **rating** *n.* [Einschätzung der] Kreditwürdigkeit; **have a good/bad** ~ **rating** als kreditwürdig/kreditunwürdig eingeschätzt werden; ~**worthy** *adj.* kreditwürdig

**creed** /kriːd/ *n.* Glaubensbekenntnis, *das*

**creek** /kriːk/ *n.* **(a)** (Brit.: of coast) [kleine] Bucht
**(b)** (of river) [kurzer] Flussarm

**creep** /kriːp/ **1** *v.i.,* **crept** [krept] kriechen; (move timidly, slowly, stealthily) schleichen
**2** *n.* **(a)** (coll.: person) Fiesling, *der* (salopp)
**(b)** (coll.) **give sb. the** ~**s** jmdn. nicht [ganz] geheuer sein

'**creeper** *n.* Kletterpflanze, *die*

'**creepy** *adj.* unheimlich

**cremate** /krɪ'meɪt/ *v.t.* einäschern

**cremation** /krɪ'meɪʃn/ *n.* Einäscherung, *die*

**crematorium** /kremə'tɔːrɪəm/ *n.* Krematorium, *das*

**creosote** /'kriːəsəʊt/ *n.* Kreosot, *das*

**crept** ▸ CREEP 1

**crescendo** /krɪ'ʃendəʊ/ *n.*, *pl.* ~**s** (Mus.) Crescendo, *das;* (fig.) Zunahme, *die*

**crescent** /'kresənt/ *n.* Mondsichel, *die*

**cress** /kres/ *n.* Kresse, *die*

**crest** /krest/ *n.* Kamm, *der*

'**crestfallen** *adj.* niedergeschlagen

**Crete** /kriːt/ *pr. n.* Kreta (*das*)

**cretin** /'kretɪn/ *n.* (coll.) Trottel, *der*

**Creutzfeldt-Jakob disease** /'krɔɪtsfelt'jækɒb/ *n.* Creutzfeldt-Jakob-Krankheit, *die*

**crevasse** /krɪ'væs/ *n.* Gletscherspalte, *die*

**crevice** /'krevɪs/ *n.* Spalt, *der*

**crew** /kruː/ *n.* Besatzung, *die*

**crew:** ~**cut** *n.* Bürstenschnitt, *der;*
~ **neck** *n.* enger, runder Halsausschnitt; **a** ~**-neck pullover** ein Pullover mit engem, rundem Halsausschnitt

**crib** /krɪb/ **1** *n.* Krippe, *die*
**2** *v.t.,* **-bb-** (coll.) abkupfern (salopp)

**crick** /krɪk/ *n.* **a** ~ [**in one's neck/back**] ein steifer Hals/Rücken

**cricket¹** /'krɪkɪt/ *n.* Kricket, *das*

**cricket²** *n.* (Zool.) Grille, *die*

**cricket:** ~ **ball** *n.* Kricketball, *der;* ~ **bat** *n.* Schlagholz, *das*

'**cricketer** *n.* Kricketspieler, *der*/-spielerin, *die*

'**cricket match** *n.* Kricketspiel, *das*

**cried** ▸ CRY

**crime** /kraɪm/ *n.* **(a)** Verbrechen, *das*

**(b)** *collect.* **a wave of** ~: eine Welle von
Straftaten; ~ **doesn't pay** Verbrechen
lohnen sich nicht
**crime:** ~ **prevention** *n.*
Verbrechensverhütung, *die;* **C**~ **Prevention**
**Officer** *Polizeibeamter, dessen/-beamtin,*
*deren Aufgabe aktive, vorbeugende*
*Verbrechensbekämpfung ist;* ~ **rate** *n.*
Kriminalitätsrate, *die;* ~ **wave** *n.* Welle
von Straftaten; ~ **writer** *n.*
Kriminalschriftsteller, *der/-*schriftstellerin,
*die*
**criminal** /'krɪmɪnl/ ① *adj.* kriminell;
strafbar; ~ **act** *or* **deed/offence** Straftat, *die*
② *n.* Kriminelle, *der/die*
**criminal:** ~ **charge** *n.* Anklage, *die;* **face**
~ **charges [for sth.]** sich [wegen etw.] vor
Gericht zu verantworten haben; **there are**
~ **charges against him** er steht unter
Anklage; ~ **'court** *n.* Strafgericht, *das;*
~ **'law** *n.* Strafrecht, *das;* ~ **'lawyer** *n.*
Anwalt/Anwältin für Strafsachen;
~ **'record** *n.* Strafregister, *das;* **have a**
~ **record** vorbestraft sein
**crimson** /'krɪmzn/ ① *adj.* purpurrot
② *n.* Purpurrot, *das*
**cringe** /krɪndʒ/ *v.i.* zusammenzucken
**crinkle** /'krɪŋkl/ ① *n.* Knitterfalte, *die*
② *v.t.* zerknittern
③ *v.i.* knittern
**cripple** /'krɪpl/ ① *n.* Krüppel, *der*
② *v.t.* zum Krüppel machen; (fig.) lähmen
**crippled** /'krɪpld/ *adj.* verkrüppelt
**crippling** /'krɪplɪŋ/ *adj.* zur Verkrüppelung
führend ⟨*Krankheit, Verletzung*⟩; (fig.)
erdrückend ⟨*Preise, Inflationsrate, Steuern,*
*Mieten*⟩; lähmend ⟨*Streik, Schmerzen*⟩
**crisis** /'kraɪsɪs/ *n., pl.* **crises** /'kraɪsiːz/
Krise, *die*
**crisis:** ~ **area** *n.* Krisengebiet, *das;*
~ **'management** *n.* Krisenmanagement,
*das*
**crisp** /krɪsp/ ① *adj.* knusprig
② *n.* **(a)** *usu. in pl.* (Brit.: potato ~)
[Kartoffel]chip, *der*
**(b) be burned to a** ~: verbrannt sein
**'crispbread** *n.* Knäckebrot, *das*
**'crispy** *adj.* knusprig
**criss-cross** /'krɪskrɒs/ ① *adj.* ~ **pattern**
Muster aus gekreuzten Linien
② *adv.* kreuz und quer
③ *v.t.* wiederholt schneiden
**criterion** /kraɪ'tɪərɪən/ *n., pl.* **criteria**
/kraɪ'tɪərɪə/ Kriterium, *das*
**critic** /'krɪtɪk/ *n.* Kritiker, *der/*Kritikerin,
*die*
**critical** /'krɪtɪkl/ *adj.* kritisch; **be** ~ **of sb./**
**sth.** jmdn./etw. kritisieren
**critically** /'krɪtɪkəlɪ/ *adv.* kritisch; ~ **ill**
ernstlich krank
**critical 'mass** *n.* (Phys.) kritische Masse
**criticism** /'krɪtɪsɪzm/ *n.* Kritik, *die* (of an
+ *Dat.*)

**criticize** /'krɪtɪsaɪz/ *v.t.* kritisieren (**for**
wegen)
**critique** /krɪ'tiːk/ *n.* Kritik, *die*
**croak** /krəʊk/ ① *n.* (of frog) Quaken, *das;* (of
person) Krächzen, *das*
② *v.i.* ⟨*Frosch:*⟩ quaken; ⟨*Person:*⟩ krächzen
③ *v.t.* krächzen
**Croat** /'krəʊæt/ *n.* **(a)** (person) Kroate, *der/*
Kroatin, *die*
**(b)** (language) Kroatisch, *das*
**Croatia** /krəʊ'eɪʃə/ *pr. n.* Kroatien (*das*)
**Croatian** /krəʊ'eɪʃn/ ① *adj.* kroatisch;
**sb. is** ~: jmd. ist Kroate/Kroatin
② *n.* ▶ CROAT
**crochet** /'krəʊʃeɪ/ ① *n.* Häkelarbeit, *die;*
~ **hook** Häkelhaken, *der*
② *v.t.* häkeln
**crock** /krɒk/ *n.* (coll.) **[old]** ~ (person) altes
Wrack, *das* (fig.); (vehicle) [alte] Klapperkiste
(ugs.)
**crockery** /'krɒkərɪ/ *n.* Geschirr, *das*
**crocodile** /'krɒkədaɪl/ *n.* Krokodil, *das*
**crocus** /'krəʊkəs/ *n.* Krokus, *der*
**croft** /krɒft/ *n.* **(a)** [kleines] Stück Acker-/
Weideland
**(b)** (smallholding) [kleines] Pachtgut
**'crofter** *n.* (Brit.) Pächter, *der/*Pächterin, *die*
**croissant** /'krwɑːsɑ̃/ *n.* Hörnchen, *das*
**crony** /'krəʊnɪ/ *n.* Kumpel, *der* (ugs.)
**crook** /krʊk/ *n.* **(a)** (coll.: rogue) Gauner, *der*
**(b)** (shepherd's) Hirtenstab, *der*
**crooked** /'krʊkɪd/ *adj.* krumm; (fig.:
dishonest) betrügerisch
**crop** /krɒp/ ① *n.* **[Feld]frucht, *die;* (season's
yield) Ernte, *die*
② *v.t.* stutzen ⟨*Haare usw.*⟩
▪ **crop 'up** *v.i.* auftauchen
**'crop dusting** *n.* Schädlingsbekämpfung
aus der Luft
**'cropper** *n.* (coll.) **come a** ~: einen Sturz
bauen (ugs.)
**crop:** ~**-spraying** *n.*
Schädlingsbekämpfung (*mit Sprühmitteln*);
~ **top** *n.* bauch- *od.* nabelfreies Top
**croquet** /'krəʊkeɪ/ *n.* Krocket[spiel], *das*
**croquette** /krə'ket/ *n.* Krokette, *die*
**cross** /krɒs/ ① *n.* **(a)** Kreuz, *das*
**(b)** (mixture) Mischung, *die* (**between** aus)
② *v.t.* **(a)** [über]kreuzen; ~ **one's arms/legs**
die Arme verschränken/die Beine
übereinander schlagen; **keep one's fingers**
~**ed [for sb.]** (fig.) [jmdm.] die *od.* den
Daumen drücken
**(b)** (go across) kreuzen; überqueren ⟨*Straße,*
*Gebirge*⟩; durchqueren ⟨*Land, Zimmer*⟩;
~ **sb.'s mind** (fig.) jmdm. einfallen; '~ **now'**
„Gehen"
**(c)** (Brit.) **a** ~**ed cheque** ein
Verrechnungsscheck
**(d)** ~ **oneself** sich bekreuzigen
③ *v.i.* aneinander vorbeigehen; ~ **[in the**
**post]** ⟨*Briefe:*⟩ sich kreuzen ⸱⸱⸱⊹

**4** *adj.* verärgert; **sb. will be** ∼: jmd. wird ärgerlich *od.* böse werden; **be** ∼ **with sb.** böse auf jmdn. sein

■ **cross 'out** *v.t.* ausstreichen

■ **cross 'over** *v.t.* überqueren; *abs.* hinübergehen

**cross:** ∼**bar** *n.* (a) [Fahrrad]stange, *die;* (b) (Sport) Querlatte, *die;* ∼**bones** *n. pl.* gekreuzte Knochen *Pl. (unter Totenkopf);* ∼**bow** /ˈkrɒsbəʊ/ *n.* Armbrust, *die;* ∼**-breed** **1** *n.* Hybride, *die;* (animal) Bastard, *der;* **2** *v.t.* kreuzen; ∼**-Channel** *adj.* ∼**-Channel traffic/ferry** Verkehr/Fähre über den Kanal; ∼**-check** **1** *n.* Gegenprobe, *die;* **2** *v.t.* [nochmals] nachprüfen; nachkontrollieren; ∼**-country** **1** *adj.* Querfeldein-; **2** *adv.* querfeldein; ∼**-cultural** *adj.* interkulturell; ∼**-dressing** *n.* Crossdressing, *das;* ∼**-examination** *n.* Kreuzverhör, *das;* ∼**-examine** *v.t.* ins Kreuzverhör nehmen; ∼**-eyed** /ˈkrɒsaɪd/ *adj.* [nach innen] schielend; **be** ∼**-eyed** schielen; ∼**-'fertilize** *v.t.* fremdbestäuben; kreuzbefruchten; (fig.) sich gegenseitig befruchten; ∼**fire** *n.* Kreuzfeuer, *das;* **get caught in the** ∼**fire** (fig.) ins Kreuzfeuer geraten

'**crossing** *n.* (a) (act) Überquerung, *die* (b) (pedestrian ∼) Überweg, *der*

**cross-legged** /ˈkrɒslegd/ *adv.* mit gekreuzten Beinen; (with feet across thighs) im Schneidersitz

'**crossly** *adv.* verärgert

**cross:** ∼ '**purposes** *n. pl.* **talk at** ∼ **purposes** aneinander vorbeireden; ∼**-'question** *v.t.* ins Kreuzverhör nehmen; ∼**-refer** *v.i.* einen Querverweis machen (**to** auf + *Akk.*); ∼ **reference** *n.* Querverweis, *der;* ∼**roads** *n. sing.* Kreuzung, *die;* (fig.) Wendepunkt, *der;* ∼ **section** *n.* Querschnitt, *der;* ∼**word** *n.* ∼**word [puzzle]** Kreuzworträtsel, *das*

**crotch** /krɒtʃ/ *n.* (of trousers, body) Schritt, *der*

**crotchet** /ˈkrɒtʃɪt/ *n.* (Brit. Mus.) Viertelnote, *die*

**crouch** /kraʊtʃ/ *v.i.* [sich zusammen]kauern

**croupier** /ˈkruːpɪə(r), ˈkruːpɪeɪ/ *n.* Croupier, *der*

**crow** /krəʊ/ *n.* Krähe, *die;* **as the** ∼ **flies** Luftlinie

'**crowbar** *n.* Brechstange, *die*

**crowd** /kraʊd/ **1** *n.* [Menschen]menge, *die* **2** *v.t.* füllen **3** *v.i.* sich sammeln

'**crowded** *adj.* überfüllt

'**crowd-puller** *n.* (coll.) Publikumsmagnet, *der*

**crown** /kraʊn/ **1** *n.* Krone, *die* **2** *v.t.* (a) krönen (b) überkronen ⟨*Zahn*⟩

**crown 'jewels** *n. pl.* Kronjuwelen *Pl.*

'**crow's-foot** *n., usu. in pl.* Krähenfuß, *der*

**crucial** /ˈkruːʃl/ *adj.* entscheidend (**to** für)

**crucially** /ˈkruːʃəlɪ/ *adv.* entscheidend; **be** ∼ **important** von entscheidender Wichtigkeit sein

**crucifix** /ˈkruːsɪfɪks/ *n.* Kruzifix, *das*

**crucifixion** /kruːsɪˈfɪkʃn/ *n.* Kreuzigung, *die*

**crucify** /ˈkruːsɪfaɪ/ *v.t.* kreuzigen

**crude** /kruːd/ *adj.* (a) roh; ∼ **oil** Rohöl, *das* (b) (fig.) grob ⟨*Entwurf, Worte*⟩

**cruel** /ˈkruːəl/ *adj.* grausam

**cruelty** /ˈkruːəltɪ/ *n.* Grausamkeit, *die*

**cruet** /ˈkruːɪt/ *n.* (a) Essig-/Ölfläschchen, *das* (b) ▶ CRUET STAND

'**cruet stand** *n.* Menage, *die*

**cruise** /kruːz/ **1** *v.i.* (at random) ⟨*Fahrzeug, Fahrer:*⟩ herumfahren **2** *n.* Kreuzfahrt, *die*

'**cruise missile** *n.* Marschflugkörper, *der*

'**cruiser** *n.* Kreuzer, *der*

**crumb** /krʌm/ *n.* Krümel, *der*

**crumble** /ˈkrʌmbl/ **1** *v.t.* zerkrümeln ⟨*Keks, Kuchen*⟩ **2** *v.i.* ⟨*Mauer:*⟩ zusammenfallen

**crumbly** /ˈkrʌmblɪ/ *adj.* krümelig ⟨*Keks, Kuchen*⟩; bröckelig ⟨*Gestein*⟩

**crumpet** /ˈkrʌmpɪt/ *n. weiches Hefeküchlein zum Toasten*

**crumple** /ˈkrʌmpl/ **1** *v.t.* (a) (crush) zerdrücken (b) (wrinkle) zerknittern **2** *v.i.* knittern

'**crumple zone** *n.* (Motor Veh.) Knautschzone, *die*

**crunch** /krʌntʃ/ **1** *v.t.* [geräuschvoll] knabbern ⟨*Keks*⟩ **2** *v.i.* ⟨*Schnee, Kies:*⟩ knirschen **3** *n.* Knirschen, *das;* **when it comes to the** ∼: wenn es hart auf hart geht

'**crunchy** *adj.* knusprig

**crusade** /kruːˈseɪd/ **1** *n.* (Hist.; also fig.) Kreuzzug, *der* **2** *v.i.* (fig.) zu Felde gehen

**cru'sader** *n.* (Hist.) Kreuzfahrer, *der*

**crush** /krʌʃ/ **1** *v.t.* (a) quetschen (b) (powder) zerstampfen (c) (fig.) niederschlagen **2** *n.* (a) (crowd) Gedränge, *das* (b) (coll.) **have/get a** ∼ **on sb.** in jmdn. verknallt sein/sich in jmdn. verknallen (ugs.)

**crush:** ∼ **bar** *n.* Bar, *die (im Foyer eines Theaters);* ∼**-barrier** *n.* Absperrgitter, *das*

**crushing** /ˈkrʌʃɪŋ/ *adj.* niederschmetternd ⟨*Antwort*⟩; vernichtend ⟨*Niederlage, Schlag*⟩

**crust** /krʌst/ *n.* Kruste, *die*

'**crusty** *adj.* knusprig

**crutch** /krʌtʃ/ *n.* Krücke, *die;* **go about on** ∼**es** an Krücken gehen

**crux** /krʌks/ *n.* **the** ∼ **of the matter** der springende Punkt bei der Sache

**cry** /kraɪ/ **1** *n.* (of grief) Schrei, *der;* (of words) Schreien, *das;* **a far ~ from ...** (fig.) etwas ganz anderes als ...
**2** *v.i.* **(a)** rufen; (loudly) schreien
**(b)** (weep) weinen (**over** wegen)
■ **cry 'off** *v.i.* absagen
■ **cry 'out** *v.i.* aufschreien

**'crying** *adj.* **it's a ~ shame** es ist eine wahre Schande

**crypt** /krɪpt/ *n.* Krypta, *die*

**cryptic** /'krɪptɪk/ *adj.* geheimnisvoll

**crystal** /'krɪstl/ **1** *n.* **(a)** Kristall, *der*
**(b)** (glass) Bleikristall, *das*
**2** *adj.* (made of ~ glass) kristallen; Kristalle⟨schale, -vase⟩

**crystal: ~ clear** *adj.* kristallklar; ; (fig.) glasklar; **~ 'glass** *n.* Bleikristall, *das;* Kristallglas, *das*

**crystallize** /'krɪstəlaɪz/ *v.i.* kristallisieren; (fig.) feste Form annehmen

**cub** /kʌb/ *n.* **(a)** Junge, *das;* (of wolf, fox, dog) Welpe, *der*
**(b) Cub** ▶ CUB SCOUT

**Cuba** /'kjuːbə/ *pr. n.* Kuba (*das*)

**cubby[hole]** /'kʌbɪ(həʊl)/ *n.* Kämmerchen, *das*

**cube** /kjuːb/ *n.* Würfel, *der*

**'cube sugar** *n.* Würfelzucker, *der*

**cubic** /'kjuːbɪk/ *adj.* **(a)** würfelförmig
**(b)** Kubik⟨*meter usw.*⟩

**cubicle** /'kjuːbɪkl/ *n.* Kabine, *die*

**cubism** /'kjuːbɪzm/ *n.* (Art) Kubismus, *der*

**cubist** /'kjuːbɪst/ *n.* (Art) Kubist, *der*/ Kubistin, *die*

**'Cub Scout** *n.* Wölfling, *der*

**cuckoo** /'kʊkuː/ *n.* Kuckuck, *der*

**'cuckoo clock** *n.* Kuckucksuhr, *die*

**cucumber** /'kjuːkʌmbə(r)/ *n.* [Salat]gurke, *die*

**cuddle** /'kʌdl/ **1** *n.* enge Umarmung
**2** *v.t.* schmusen mit; hätscheln ⟨*kleines Kind*⟩
**3** *v.i.* schmusen

**cuddly** /'kʌdlɪ/ *adj.* zum Schmusen nachgestellt

**cuddly 'toy** *n.* Plüschtier, *das*

**cudgel** /'kʌdʒl/ *n.* Knüppel, *der*

**cue¹** /kjuː/ *n.* (Billiards etc.) Queue, *das*

**cue²** *n.* (Theatre) Stichwort, *das*

**cuff¹** /kʌf/ *n.* **(a)** Manschette, *die;* **off the ~** (fig.) aus dem Stegreif
**(b)** (Amer.: trouser turn-up) [Hosen]aufschlag, *der*

**cuff²** **1** *v.t.* **~ sb.** jmdm. einen Klaps geben
**2** *n.* Klaps, *der*

**'cuff link** *n.* Manschettenknopf, *der*

**cuisine** /kwɪ'ziːn/ *n.* Küche, *die*

**cul-de-sac** /'kʌldəsæk/ *n.* Sackgasse, *die*

**culinary** /'kʌlɪnərɪ/ *adj.* kulinarisch

**culminate** /'kʌlmɪneɪt/ *v.i.* gipfeln; **~ in sth. in etw.** (*Dat.*) seinen Höchststand erreichen

**culmination** /kʌlmɪ'neɪʃn/ *n.* Höhepunkt, *der*

**culottes** /kjuː'lɒts/ *n. pl.* Hosenrock, *der*

**culpable** /'kʌlpəbl/ *adj.* schuldig ⟨*Person*⟩; strafbar ⟨*Handlung*⟩

**culprit** /'kʌlprɪt/ *n.* Täter, *der*/Täterin, *die*

**cult** /kʌlt/ *n.* Kult, *der*

**cultivate** /'kʌltɪveɪt/ *v.t.* kultivieren (auch fig.); bestellen ⟨*Acker, Land*⟩; anbauen ⟨*Pflanzen*⟩

**cultivated** /'kʌltɪveɪtɪd/ *adj.* kultiviert ⟨*Manieren, Sprache, Geschmack*⟩; kultiviert, gebildet ⟨*Person*⟩

**cultivation** /kʌltɪ'veɪʃn/ *n.* ▶ CULTIVATE: Kultivierung, *die;* Bestellen *das;* Anbau, *der*

**culture** /'kʌltʃə(r)/ *n.* Kultur, *die*

**'cultured** *adj.* kultiviert

**'culture shock** *n.* Kulturschock, *der*

**cumbersome** /'kʌmbəsəm/ *adj.* hinderlich ⟨*Kleider*⟩; sperrig ⟨*Pakete*⟩; schwerfällig ⟨*Arbeitsweise*⟩

**cunning** /'kʌnɪŋ/ **1** *n.* Schläue, *die*
**2** *adj.* schlau

**cup** /kʌp/ *n.* **(a)** Tasse, *die*
**(b)** (prize, competition) Pokal, *der*
**(c)** (~ful) Tasse, *die;* **a ~ of coffee/tea** eine Tasse Kaffee/Tee

**cupboard** /'kʌbəd/ *n.* Schrank, *der*

**'Cup Final** *n.* Pokalendspiel, *das*

**cupful** /'kʌpfl/ *n.* Tasse, *die;* **a ~ of water** eine Tasse Wasser

**'cup tie** *n.* Pokalspiel, *das*

**curable** /'kjʊərəbl/ *adj.* heilbar

**curate** /'kjʊərət/ *n.* Kurat, *der*

**curator** /kjʊə'reɪtə(r)/ *n.* (of museum) Direktor, *der*/Direktorin, *die*

**curb** /kɜːb/ *v.t.* zügeln

**'curd cheese** *n.* ≈ Quark, *der*

**curdle** /'kɜːdl/ *v.i.* gerinnen

**cure** /kjʊə(r)/ **1** *n.* [Heil]mittel, *das* (**for** gegen); (fig.) Mittel, *das*
**2** *v.t.* **(a)** heilen
**(b)** [ein]pökeln ⟨*Fleisch*⟩

**'cure-all** *n.* Allheilmittel, *das*

**curfew** /'kɜːfjuː/ *n.* Ausgangssperre, *die*

**curiosity** /kjʊərɪ'ɒsɪtɪ/ *n.* **(a)** Neugier[de], *die*
**(b)** (object) Wunderding, *das*

**curious** /'kjʊərɪəs/ *adj.* **(a)** (inquisitive) neugierig
**(b)** (strange, odd) seltsam

**curl** /kɜːl/ **1** *n.* Locke, *die*
**2** *v.t.* locken
**3** *v.i.* **(a)** sich locken
**(b)** ⟨*Straße, Fluss:*⟩ sich winden

**'curler** *n.* Lockenwickler, *der*

**'curly** *adj.* lockig

**'curly-haired** adj. lockenköpfig; mit
lockigem Haar

**currant** /'kʌrənt/ n. Korinthe, die

**currency** /'kʌrənsɪ/ n. (money) Währung,
die; **foreign currencies** Devisen Pl.

**current** /'kʌrənt/ ① adj. (a) verbreitet
⟨Meinung⟩; gebräuchlich ⟨Wort⟩
**(b)** laufend ⟨Jahr, Monat⟩
**(c)** (the present) aktuell ⟨Ereignis, Mode⟩;
Tages⟨politik, -preis⟩; ~ **affairs** Tagespolitik,
die
② n. **(a)** (of water, air) Strömung, die
**(b)** (Electr.) Strom, der

**'current account** n. Girokonto, das

**'currently** adv. zur Zeit

**curriculum** /kə'rɪkjʊləm/ n. Lehrplan, der

**curriculum vitae** /- 'vi:taɪ/ n. Lebenslauf,
der

**curry¹** /'kʌrɪ/ n. Curry[gericht], das

**curry²** v.t. ~ **favour [with sb.]** sich [bei
jmdm.] einschmeicheln

**curse** /kɜːs/ ① n. Fluch, der
② v.t. verfluchen
③ v.i. fluchen

**cursor** /'kɜːsə(r)/ n. Läufer, der; (on screen)
Cursor, der; Schreibmarke, die

**cursory** /'kɜːsərɪ/ adj. flüchtig

**curt** /kɜːt/ adj. kurz angebunden; kurz und
schroff ⟨Brief⟩

**curtail** /kɜː'teɪl/ v.t. kürzen; abkürzen
⟨Urlaub⟩; beschneiden ⟨Macht⟩

**curtain** /'kɜːtən/ n. Vorhang, der; **draw** or
**pull the** ~**s** (open) die Vorhänge aufziehen;
(close) die Vorhänge zuziehen

**curtain:** ~ **call** n. Vorhang, der; ~ **hook**
n. Gardinenhaken, der; ~ **rod** n.
Gardinenstange, die

**curtsy** /'kɜːtsɪ/ ① n. Knicks, der
② v.i. einen Knicks machen (**to** vor + Dat.)

**curvaceous** /kɜː'veɪʃəs/ adj. kurvenreich
(ugs.); **a** ~ **figure** eine üppige Figur

**curve** /kɜːv/ ① v.t. krümmen
② v.i. ⟨Straße, Fluss:⟩ eine Biegung machen
③ n. Kurve, die

**cushion** /'kʊʃn/ ① n. Kissen, das
② v.t. dämpfen ⟨Aufprall, Stoß⟩

**cushy** /'kʊʃɪ/ adj. (coll.) bequem

**custard** /'kʌstəd/ n. ≈ Vanillesoße, die

**'custard powder** n. Vanillesoßenpulver,
das

**custodian** /kʌs'təʊdɪən/ n. (of museum)
Wächter, der/Wächterin, die; (of valuables)
Hüter, der/Hüterin, die

**custody** /'kʌstədɪ/ n. **(a)** (care) Obhut, die
**(b)** (imprisonment) **[be] in** ~: in Haft [sein];
**take sb. into** ~: jmdn. verhaften od.
festnehmen

**custom** /'kʌstəm/ n. **(a)** Brauch, der
**(b)** in pl. (duty on imports) Zoll, der

**customary** /'kʌstəmərɪ/ adj. üblich

**'custom-built** adj. spezial[an]gefertigt

**customer** /'kʌstəmə(r)/ n. Kunde, der/
Kundin, die

**customize (customise)** /'kʌstəmaɪz/
v.t. speziell anfertigen; (alter) umbauen

**'custom-made** adj. spezial[an]gefertigt;
maßgeschneidert ⟨Kleidung⟩

**customs:** ~ **duty** n. Zoll, der; ~
**inspection** n. Zollkontrolle, die; ~
**officer** n. Zollbeamter, der/-beamtin, die

**cut** /kʌt/ ① v.t., -tt-, cut **(a)** schneiden;
durchschneiden ⟨Seil⟩; ~ **one's leg** sich (Dat.
od. Akk.) ins Bein schneiden
**(b)** abschneiden ⟨Scheibe⟩; schneiden
⟨Hecke⟩; mähen ⟨Getreide, Gras⟩; ~ **one's
nails** sich (Dat.) die Nägel schneiden
**(c)** (reduce) senken ⟨Preise⟩; kürzen ⟨Lohn⟩;
abbauen ⟨Arbeitsplätze⟩
**(d)** ~ **sth. short** (interrupt) etw. abbrechen
**(e)** (Comp.) ~ **and paste** ausschneiden und
einfügen
② v.i., -tt-, cut **(a)** ⟨Messer:⟩ schneiden
**(b)** ~ **through** or **across the field/park** [quer]
über das Feld/durch den Park gehen
③ n. **(a)** (act of cutting) Schnitt, der
**(b)** (stroke, blow) (with knife) Schnitt, der; (with
sword, whip) Hieb, der
**(c)** (reduction) Kürzung, die; (in prices)
Senkung, die; (in services) Verringerung, die
**(d)** (of meat) Stück, das
■ **cut a'way** v.t. abschneiden
■ **cut 'back** v.t. **(a)** (reduce) einschränken
**(b)** (prune) stutzen
■ **cut 'down** ① v.t. **(a)** fällen ⟨Baum⟩
**(b)** (reduce) einschränken
② v.i. ~ **down on sth.** etw. einschränken
■ **cut 'off** v.t. abschneiden; unterbrechen
⟨Telefongespräch, Sprecher⟩
■ **cut 'out** ① v.t. **(a)** ausschneiden (**of** aus)
**(b)** be ~ **out for** geeignet sein zu
② v.i. ⟨Motor:⟩ aussetzen
■ **cut 'up** v.t. zerschneiden

**cut:** ~**back** n. (reduction) Kürzung, die;
~ **'glass** n. Kristall[glas], das; ~**-glass**
adj. Kristall-

**cutlery** /'kʌtlərɪ/ n. Besteck, das

**cutlet** /'kʌtlɪt/ n. Kotelett, das

**cut:** ~**-off** n. ~**-off point** Trennungslinie,
die; ~**-out** n. (figure) Ausschneidefigur, die;
~**-price** adj. herabgesetzt; ~**-price offer**
Billigangebot, das

**'cutting** ① adj. beißend ⟨Bemerkung,
Antwort⟩
② n. (from newspaper) Ausschnitt, der

**'cutting edge** n. **be at the** ~ **of technology**
auf dem Gebiet der Technologie führend
sein; die Speerspitze der Technologie sein;
**be at the** ~ **of fashion** auf dem Gebiet der
Mode führend sein

**c. v.** abbr. = **curriculum vitae**

**cyber:** ~**cafe** /'saɪbəkæfeɪ/ n. Internet-
Café das; ~**sex** /'saɪbəseks/ n., no art.
Cybersex, der; ~**space** /'saɪbəspeɪs/ n., no
art. Cyberspace, der

**cycle** /'saɪkl/ ① n. **(a)** (recurrent period) Zyklus, der
**(b)** (bicycle) Rad, das
② v.i. Rad fahren

**cycle:** ~ **lane** n. Fahrradspur, die; ~ **race** n. Radrennen, das; ~ **track** n. Rad[fahr]weg, der; (for racing) Radrennbahn, die

**cycling** /'saɪklɪŋ/ n. (activity) Radfahren, das; (sport) Radsport, der; ~ **shorts** Radlerhose, die

**cyclist** /'saɪklɪst/ n. Radfahrer, der/ -fahrerin, die

**cyclone** /'saɪkləʊn/ n. (violent hurricane) Zyklon, der

**cylinder** /'sɪlɪndə(r)/ n. Zylinder, der

**cylindrical** /sɪ'lɪndrɪkl/ adj. zylindrisch

**cymbal** /'sɪmbl/ n. Beckenteller, der; ~s Becken Pl.

**cynic** /'sɪnɪk/ n. Zyniker, der

**cynical** /'sɪnɪkl/ adj. zynisch; bissig ⟨Bemerkung, Worte⟩

**cynicism** /'sɪnɪsɪzm/ n. Zynismus, der

**Cyprus** /'saɪprəs/ pr. n. Zypern (das)

**czar** ▶ TSAR

**Czech** /tʃek/ ① adj. tschechisch; **sb. is** ~: jmd. ist Tscheche/Tschechin
② n. **(a)** (language) Tschechisch, das
**(b)** (person) Tscheche, der/Tschechin, die

**Czechoslovakia** /tʃekəʊslə'vækɪə/ pr. n. (Hist.) die Tschechoslowakei

**Czechoslovakian** /tʃekəʊslə'vækɪən/ (Hist.) ① adj. tschechoslowakisch
② n. Tschechoslowake, der/ Tschechoslowakin, die

**Czech Re'public** pr. n. Tschechische Republik; Tschechien (das)

# Dd

**D, d** /diː/ n. D, d, das

**dab** /dæb/ ① n. Tupfer, der
② v.t., **-bb-** abtupfen; ~ sth. on or against sth. etw. auf etw. (Akk.) tupfen

**dabble** /'dæbl/ v.i. ~ **in sth.** sich in etw. (Dat.) versuchen

**dachshund** /'dækshʊnd/ n. Dackel, der

**dad** /dæd/ n. (coll.) Vater, der

**daddy** /'dædɪ/ n. (coll.) Vati, der (fam.)

**daddy-'long-legs** n. Schnake, die

**daffodil** /'dæfədɪl/ n. Osterglocke, die

**daft** /dɑːft/ adj. doof (ugs.)

**dagger** /'dægə(r)/ n. Dolch, der

**daily** /'deɪlɪ/ ① adj. täglich; ~ **[news]paper** Tageszeitung, die
② adv. täglich
③ n. Tageszeitung, die

**dainty** /'deɪntɪ/ adj. zierlich; anmutig ⟨Bewegung, Person⟩; zart ⟨Gesichtszüge⟩

**dairy** /'deərɪ/ n. **(a)** Molkerei, die
**(b)** (shop) Milchladen, der

**dairy:** ~ **cattle** n. Milchvieh, das; ~ **farm** n. Milchbetrieb, der; ~ **farmer** n. Milchbauer, der; ~ **produce** n., ~ **products** n. pl. Molkereiprodukte

**dais** /'deɪɪs/ n. Podium, das

**daisy** /'deɪzɪ/ n. Gänseblümchen, das

**'daisy chain** n. Kranz aus Gänseblümchen

**dam** /dæm/ ① n. [Stau]damm, der
② v.t., **-mm-:** **(a)** ~ **[up]** sth. etw. abblocken
**(b)** aufstauen ⟨Fluss⟩

**damage** /'dæmɪdʒ/ ① n. Schaden, der

② v.t. beschädigen

**damaging** /'dæmɪdʒɪŋ/ adj. schädlich **(to** für)

**damn** /dæm/ ① v.t. verdammen
② adj., adv., int. (coll.) verdammt (ugs.)
③ n. **he doesn't give** or **care a** ~: ihm ist es völlig wurscht (ugs.)

**damp** /dæmp/ ① adj. feucht
② v.t. ▶ DAMPEN
③ n. Feuchtigkeit, die

**dampen** /'dæmpn/ v.t. befeuchten; (fig.) dämpfen ⟨Begeisterung, Eifer⟩

**'dampness** n. Feuchtigkeit, die

**'damp-proof** adj. feuchtigkeitsbeständig; ~ **course** Sperrschicht, die ⟨gegen aufsteigende Bodenfeuchtigkeit⟩

**dance** /dɑːns/ ① v.i. & t. tanzen
② n. **(a)** Tanz, der
**(b)** (party) Tanzveranstaltung, die; (private) Tanzparty, die

**dance:** ~ **floor** n. Tanzfläche, die; ~ **hall** n. Tanzsaal, der

**'dancer** n. Tänzer, der/Tänzerin, die

**'dance step** n. Tanzschritt, der

**dandelion** /'dændɪlaɪən/ n. Löwenzahn, der

**dandruff** /'dændrʌf/ n. [Kopf]schuppen Pl.

**Dane** /deɪn/ n. Däne, der/Dänin, die

**danger** /'deɪndʒə(r)/ n. Gefahr, die; **in/out of** ~: in/außer Gefahr; **be in** ~ **of doing sth.** ⟨Person:⟩ Gefahr laufen, etw. zu tun

**danger:** ~ **area** n. Gefahrenzone, die; ~ **list** n. be on/off the ~ **list** in/außer Lebensgefahr sein

**dangerous** /'deɪndʒərəs/ adj., **'dangerously** adv. gefährlich

**danger:** ~ **signal** n. Warnzeichen, das; ~ **zone** n. Gefahrenzone, die

**dangle** /'dæŋgl/ 1 v.i. baumeln (**from** an + Dat.) 2 v.t. baumeln lassen

**Danish** /'deɪnɪʃ/ 1 adj. dänisch; **sb. is ~:** jmd. ist Däne/Dänin 2 n. Dänisch, das; see also ENGLISH 2A

**dank** /dæŋk/ adj. feucht

**Danube** /'dænjuːb/ pr. n. Donau, die

**dare** /deə(r)/ 1 v.t. (a) [es] wagen; ~ **to do sth.** [es] wagen, etw. zu tun (b) (challenge) ~ **sb. to do sth.** jmdn. aufstacheln, etw. zu tun; **I** ~ **you!** trau dich! 2 n. Mutprobe, die

**daring** /'deərɪŋ/ adj. (bold) kühn; waghalsig ⟨Kunststück, Tat⟩; (fearless) wagemutig

**dark** /dɑːk/ 1 adj. dunkel; (dark-haired) dunkelhaarig; ~-**blue/-brown** dunkelblau/ -braun; ~ **glasses** dunkle Brille 2 n. (a) Dunkel, das; **in the ~:** im Dunkeln; **keep sb. in the ~** (fig.) jmdn. im Dunkeln lassen (b) no art. (nightfall) Einbruch der Dunkelheit

**darken** /'dɑːkn/ v.t. verdunkeln

**dark:** ~-**haired** adj. dunkelhaarig; ~ **'horse** n. be a ~ **horse** ein stilles Wasser sein

**'darkness** n. Dunkelheit, die

**'darkroom** n. Dunkelkammer, die

**darling** /'dɑːlɪŋ/ n. Liebling, der

**darn** /dɑːn/ v.t. stopfen

**dart** /dɑːt/ 1 n. (a) (missile) Pfeil, der (b) (Sport) Wurfpfeil, der; ~**s** sing. (game) Darts, das 2 v.i. sausen

**'dartboard** n. Dartsscheibe, die

**dash** /dæʃ/ 1 v.i. sausen 2 v.t. (fling) schleudern 3 n. (a) **make a ~:** rasen (ugs.) (**for** zu) (b) (horizontal stroke) Gedankenstrich, der (c) (small amount) Schuss, der

**'dashboard** n. Armaturenbrett, das

**data** /'deɪtə, 'dɑːtə/ n. Daten Pl.

**data:** ~**base** n. Datenbank, die; ~ **capture** n. (Comp.) Datenerfassung, die; ~ **file** n. (Comp.) Datei, die; ~ **highway** n. (Comp.) Datenautobahn, die; ~ **pro'tection** n. (Comp.) Datenschutz, der; ~ **retrieval** n. (Comp.) Retrieval, das; Datenabruf, der; ~ **security** n. (Comp.) Datensicherung, die; ~ **storage** n. (Comp.) Datenspeicherung, die; (capacity) Speicherkapazität, die

**date¹** /deɪt/ n. (Bot.) Dattel, die

**date²** 1 n. (a) Datum, das; (on coin etc.) Jahreszahl, die; ~ **of birth** Geburtsdatum, das; **be out of ~:** altmodisch sein; **to ~:** bis heute (b) (coll.: appointment) Verabredung, die; **have/ make a ~ with sb.** mit jmdm. verabredet sein/sich mit jmdm. verabreden 2 v.t. (a) datieren (b) (coll.: make seem old) alt machen 3 v.i. ~ **back to/~ from** stammen aus

**dated** /'deɪtɪd/ adj. altmodisch

**date:** ~ **line** n. Datumsgrenze, die; ~ **rape** n.: Vergewaltigung der eigenen Freundin oder Vergewaltigung einer Frau während einer Verabredung mit ihr; ~ **stamp** n. Datumsstempel, der; ~-**stamp** v.t. abstempeln; mit einem Datumsstempel versehen

**'dating agency** /'deɪtɪŋ/ n. Partnervermittlung, die

**dative** /'deɪtɪv/ adj. & n. ~ [**case**] Dativ, der

**daub** /dɔːb/ v.t. (smear) beschmieren; (put crudely) schmieren

**daughter** /'dɔːtə(r)/ n. Tochter, die

**'daughter-in-law** n., pl. **daughters-in-law** Schwiegertochter, die

**daunt** /dɔːnt/ v.t. entmutigen

**dawdle** /'dɔːdl/ v.i. bummeln (ugs.)

**dawn** /dɔːn/ 1 v.i. ~ dämmern; **sth. ~s** [**up**]**on sb.** etw. dämmert jmdm 2 n. [Morgen]dämmerung, die; **at ~:** im Morgengrauen

**dawn 'chorus** n. morgendlicher Gesang der Vögel

**day** /deɪ/ n. Tag, der; **all ~** [**long**] den ganzen Tag [lang]; **for two ~s** zwei Tage [lang]; **the ~ before yesterday/after tomorrow** vorgestern/übermorgen; ~ **after ~:** Tag für Tag; ~ **in** ~ **out** tagaus, tagein; **in the ~s when ...:** zu der Zeit, als ...; **these ~s** heutzutage; **in those ~s** damals

**day:** ~**bed** n. Liegesofa, das; ~**break** n. Tagesanbruch, der; ~ **care** n. Ganztagsbetreuung, die; ~**dream** 1 n. Tagtraum, der; 2 v.i. träumen; ~**dreamer** n. Tagträumer, der/-träumerin, die; ~**light** n. Tageslicht, das; **in broad** ~**light** am helllichten Tag[e]; ~ **release** n. (Brit.) [tageweise] Freistellung zur Fortbildung; ~ **re'turn** n. Tagesrückfahrkarte, die; ~**time** n. Tag, der; ~-**to-** ~ adj. [tag]täglich; ~ **trip** n. Tagesausflug, der; ~ **tripper** n. Tagesausflügler, der/ -ausflüglerin, die

**daze** /deɪz/ v.t. benommen machen

**dazed** /'deɪzd/ adj. benommen

**dazzle** /'dæzl/ v.t. blenden

**DC** abbr. = **direct current** GS

**dead** /ded/ 1 adj. (a) tot (b) plötzlich ⟨Halt⟩; genau ⟨Mitte⟩ (c) (numb) taub 2 adv. völlig; ~ **straight** schnurgerade; ~ **easy/slow** kinderleicht/ganz langsam; ~ **on time** auf die Minute; ~ **tired** todmüde 3 n. pl. **the ~:** die Toten Pl.

**deaden** /'dedn/ v.t. dämpfen; betäuben ⟨Schmerz⟩

**dead:** ∼ **'end** n. Sackgasse, die; ∼ **'heat** n. totes Rennen; ∼**line** n. [letzter] Termin; ∼**lock** n. völliger Stillstand; ∼ **'loss** n. (coll.) (worthless thing) totaler Reinfall (ugs.); (person) hoffnungsloser Fall (ugs.)

**deadly** /'dedlɪ/ adj. tödlich; (fig. coll.: boring) todlangweilig

**dead:** ∼**pan** adj. unbewegt; **he looked** ∼**pan** or **had a** ∼**pan expression** er verzog keine Miene; **D**∼ **'Sea** pr. n. Totes Meer; ∼ **'wood** n. **(**fig.**) be just** ∼ **wood** völlig überflüssig sein

**deaf** /def/ adj. 1 taub; ∼ **and dumb** taubstumm
2 n. pl. **the** ∼: die Gehörlosen Pl.

**'deaf aid** n. Hörgerät, das

**deafen** /'defn/ v.t. ∼ sb. bei jmdm. zur Taubheit führen; **I was** ∼**ed by the noise** (fig.) ich war von dem Lärm wie betäubt

**'deafening** adj. ohrenbetäubend

**'deafness** n. Taubheit, die

**deal¹** /di:l/ 1 v.t., **dealt** /delt/ **(a)** (Cards) austeilen
**(b)** ∼ **sb. a blow** jmdm. einen Schlag versetzen
2 v.i., **dealt (a)** (do business) ∼ **in sth.** mit etw. handeln
**(b)** ∼ **with sth.** (occupy oneself) sich mit etw. befassen; (manage) mit etw. fertig werden; (be about) von etw. handeln; ∼ **with sb.** mit jmdm. fertig werden
3 n. (coll.: arrangement) Geschäft, das; **it's a** ∼**!** abgemacht!; **big** ∼**!** (iron.) na, und?
■ **deal 'out** v.t. verteilen

**deal²** n. **a great** or **good** ∼: viel; (often) ziemlich viel; **a great** or **good** ∼ **of** viel

**'dealer** n. **(a)** Händler, der
**(b)** (Cards) Geber, der; **he's the** ∼: er gibt

**'dealings** n. pl. **have** ∼ **with sb.** mit jmdm. zu tun haben

**dealt** ▶ DEAL¹ 1, 2

**dean** /di:n/ n. (Eccl.) Dechant, der

**dear** /dɪə(r)/ 1 adj. **(a)** lieb; **sb./sth. is** ∼ **to sb.['s heart]** jmd. liebt jmdn./etw.; (beginning letter) **D**∼ **Sir/Madam** Sehr geehrter Herr/ Sehr geehrte Dame; **D**∼ **Mr Jones/Mrs Jones** Sehr geehrter Herr Jones/Sehr geehrte Frau Jones; **D**∼ **Malcolm/Emily** Lieber Malcolm/ Liebe Emily
**(b)** (expensive) teuer
2 int. ∼, ∼**!,** ∼ **me!, oh** ∼**!** [ach] du liebe od. meine Güte!

**'dearly** adv. **(a)** von ganzem Herzen
**(b)** (at high price) teuer

**dearth** /dɜ:θ/ n. Mangel, der (**of** an + Dat.)

**death** /deθ/ n. **(a)** Tod, der; ... **to** ∼: zu Tode ...; **bleed to** ∼: verbluten
**(b)** (instance) Todesfall, der

**death:** ∼**bed** n. Totenbett, das; **on one's** ∼**bed** auf dem Sterbebett; ∼ **certificate** n. (from doctor) Totenschein, der

**deathly** /'deθlɪ/ 1 adj. tödlich
2 adv. tödlich; ∼ **still/quiet** totenstill

**death:** ∼ **penalty** n. Todesstrafe, die; ∼ **sentence** n. Todesurteil, das; ∼ **trap** n. lebensgefährliche Sache; ∼ **threat** n. Morddrohung, die

**debatable** /dɪ'beɪtəbl/ adj. (questionable) fraglich

**debate** /dɪ'beɪt/ n. Debatte, die

**debilitating** /dɪ'bɪlɪteɪtɪŋ/ adj. anstrengend ⟨Klima⟩; schwächend ⟨Krankheit⟩

**debit** /'debɪt/ 1 n. Soll, das
2 v.t. belasten ⟨Konto⟩

**debris** /'debri:/ n. Trümmer Pl.

**debt** /det/ n. Schuld, die; **be in** ∼: Schulden haben; **get into** ∼: in Schulden geraten

**debtor** /'detə(r)/ n. Schuldner, der/ Schuldnerin, die

**debug** /di:'bʌg/ v.t., **-gg-** (coll.: remove defects from) von Fehlern befreien

**début** (Amer.: **debut**) /'deɪbu:, 'deɪbju:/ n. Debüt, das

**Dec.** abbr. = **December** Dez.

**decade** /'dekeɪd/ n. Jahrzehnt, das

**decadent** /'dekədənt/ adj. dekadent

**decaf, decaff** /'di:kæf/ n. (coll.) or ® koffeinfreier Kaffee

**decaffeinated** /di:'kæfɪneɪtɪd/ adj. entkoffeiniert

**decanter** /dɪ'kæntə(r)/ n. Karaffe, die

**decay** /dɪ'keɪ/ 1 v.i. verrotten; ⟨Gebäude:⟩ zerfallen; ⟨Zahn:⟩ faul werden
2 n. Verrotten, das; (of building) Zerfall, der; (of tooth) Fäule, die

**deceased** /dɪ'si:st/ 1 adj. verstorben
2 n. Verstorbene, der/die

**deceit** /dɪ'si:t/ n. Täuschung, die

**deceitful** /dɪ'si:tfl/ adj. falsch ⟨Person, Art⟩; hinterlistig ⟨Trick⟩

**deceive** /dɪ'si:v/ v.t. täuschen; (be unfaithful to) betrügen

**December** /dɪ'sembə(r)/ n. Dezember, der; see also AUGUST

**decency** /'di:sənsɪ/ n. Anstand, der

**decent** /'di:sənt/ adj. anständig

**decentralization** /di:sentrəlaɪ'zeɪʃn/ n. Dezentralisierung, die

**decentralize** /di:'sentrəlaɪz/ v.t. dezentralisieren

**deception** /dɪ'sepʃn/ n. Betrug, der; (being deceived) Täuschung, die

**deceptive** /dɪ'septɪv/ adj. trügerisch

**decibel** /'desɪbel/ n. Dezibel, das

**decide** /dɪ'saɪd/ 1 v.t. **(a)** (settle, judge) entscheiden über (+ Akk.)
**(b)** (resolve) ∼ **that** ...: beschließen, dass ...; ∼ **to do sth.** sich entschließen, etw. zu tun
2 v.i. sich entscheiden (**in favour of** zugunsten von, **against** gegen)

**de'cided** adj., **de'cidedly** adv. entschieden

**deciduous** /dɪ'sɪdjʊəs/ adj. ∼ **tree** ≈ Laubbaum, der

**d**

**decimal** /'desɪml/ [1] n. Dezimalbruch, der
[2] adj. Dezimal-

**decimal:** ~ **'currency** n.
Dezimalwährung, die; ~ **'fraction** n.
Dezimalbruch, der; ~ **'point** n. Komma,
das

**decimate** /'desɪmeɪt/ v.t. dezimieren

**decipher** /dɪ'saɪfə(r)/ v.t. entziffern

**decision** /dɪ'sɪʒn/ n. Entscheidung, die

**decisive** /dɪ'saɪsɪv/ adj. entscheidend

**deck** /dek/ n. (a) Deck, das; on ~: an Deck;
below ~[s] unter Deck
(b) (Amer.: pack) a ~ of cards ein Spiel
Karten

**'deckchair** n. Liegestuhl, der

**declaration** /deklə'reɪʃn/ n. Erklärung,
die

**declare** /dɪ'kleə(r)/ v.t. erklären; kundtun
(geh.) ⟨Wunsch, Absicht⟩; ~ sth./sb. [to be]
sth. etw./jmdn. für etw. erklären

**declension** /dɪ'klenʃn/ n. Deklination, die

**decline** /dɪ'klaɪn/ [1] v.i. nachlassen;
⟨Anzahl:⟩ sinken
[2] v.t. (a) ablehnen
(b) (Ling.) deklinieren
[3] n. ▶1: Nachlassen, das/Sinken, das (in
Gen.); be on the ~: nachlassen/sinken

**decode** /di:'kəʊd/ v.t. entziffern

**decommission** /di:kə'mɪʃən/ v.t.
stilllegen; außer Dienst stellen ⟨Schiff⟩

**decompose** /di:kəm'pəʊz/ v.i. sich
zersetzen

**décor** /'deɪkɔ:(r)/ n. Ausstattung, die

**decorate** /'dekəreɪt/ v.t. (a) schmücken
⟨Raum, Straße, Baum⟩; verzieren ⟨Kuchen,
Kleid⟩; (paint) streichen; (wallpaper) tapezieren
(b) (award medal etc. to) auszeichnen

**decoration** /dekə'reɪʃn/ n. (a) Schmücken,
das; (with paint) Streichen, das; (with wallpaper)
Tapezieren, das; (of cake, dress) Verzieren, das
(b) (adornment) Schmuck, der
(c) (medal etc.) Auszeichnung, die

**decorative** /'dekərətɪv/ adj. dekorativ

**decorator** /'dekəreɪtə(r)/ n. Maler, der;
(paperhanger) Tapezierer, der

**decorous** /'dekərəs/ adj., **'decorously**
adv. schicklich (geh.)

**decorum** /dɪ'kɔ:rəm/ n. Schicklichkeit, die
(geh.)

**decoy** /'di:kɔɪ/ n. Lockvogel, der

**decrease** [1] /dɪ'kri:s/ v.i. abnehmen;
⟨Stärke:⟩ nachlassen
[2] /dɪ'kri:s/ v.t. [ver]mindern ⟨Wert, Lärm⟩;
schmälern ⟨Popularität, Macht⟩
[3] /'di:kri:s/ n. Rückgang, der; (in weight)
Abnahme, die; (in strength) Nachlassen, das; (in
value, noise) Minderung, die

**decree** /dɪ'kri:/ [1] n. Dekret, das; Erlass,
der
[2] v.t. verfügen

**decrepit** /dɪ'krepɪt/ adj. altersschwach;
(dilapidated) heruntergekommen

**decriminalize** /di:'krɪmɪnəlaɪz/ v.t.
entkriminalisieren

**dedicate** /'dedɪkeɪt/ v.t. ~ sth. to sb.
jmdm. etw. widmen

**'dedicated** adj. (a) (devoted) be ~ to sth./
sb. nur für etw./jmdn. leben
(b) (to vocation) hingebungsvoll; a ~ teacher
ein Lehrer mit Leib und Seele

**dedication** /dedɪ'keɪʃn/ n. (a) Widmung,
die (to Dat.)
(b) (devotion) Hingabe, die

**deduce** /dɪ'dju:s/ v.t. ~ sth. [from sth.] etw.
[aus etw.] schließen

**deduct** /dɪ'dʌkt/ v.t. ~ sth. [from sth.] etw.
[von etw.] abziehen

**deduction** /dɪ'dʌkʃn/ n. (a) (deducting)
Abzug, der
(b) (deducing, thing deduced) Ableitung, die
(c) (amount) Abzüge Pl.

**deed** /di:d/ n. (a) Tat, die
(b) (Law) Urkunde, die

**deejay** /di:'dʒeɪ/ n. (coll.) Diskjockey, der

**deem** /di:m/ v.t. erachten für

**deep** /di:p/ [1] adj. (lit. or fig.) tief; tiefgründig
⟨Bemerkung⟩; water ten feet ~: drei Meter
tiefes Wasser; take a ~ breath tief Atem
holen; be ~ in thought in Gedanken
versunken sein
[2] adv. tief

**'deepen** [1] v.t. vertiefen
[2] v.i. sich vertiefen

**deep:** ~-'freeze v.t. tiefgefrieren;
~-'fried adj. frittiert

**'deeply** adv. (lit. or fig.) tief; äußerst
⟨interessiert, dankbar⟩

**deep-'rooted** adj. tief ⟨Abneigung⟩; tief
verwurzelt ⟨Tradition⟩

**deer** /dɪə(r)/ n., pl. same Hirsch, der; (roe ~)
Reh, das

**de-escalate** /di:'eskəleɪt/ v.t. deeskalieren

**deface** /dɪ'feɪs/ v.t. verunstalten

**defamation** /defə'meɪʃn/ n. Diffamierung,
die

**defamatory** /dɪ'fæmətərɪ/ adj.
diffamierend

**default** /dɪ'fɔ:lt, dɪ'fɒlt/ [1] n. (a) lose/go by
~: durch Abwesenheit verlieren/nicht zur
Geltung kommen; win by ~: durch
Nichterscheinen des Gegners gewinnen
(b) (Comp.) Voreinstellung, die
[2] v.i. ~ on one's payments/debts seinen
Zahlungsverpflichtungen nicht nachkommen

**defeat** /dɪ'fi:t/ [1] v.t. besiegen
[2] n. (being ~ed) Niederlage, die; (~ing) Sieg,
der (of über + Akk.)

**de'featist** adj. defätistisch

**defect** [1] /'di:fekt/ n. (a) (lack) Mangel, der
(b) (shortcoming) Fehler, der
[2] /dɪ'fekt/ v.i. überlaufen (to zu)

**defection** /dɪ'fekʃn/ n. Flucht, die

**defective** /dɪˈfektɪv/ *adj.* defekt ⟨*Maschine*⟩; fehlerhaft ⟨*Material, Arbeiten, Methode*⟩

**defector** /dɪˈfektə(r)/ *n.* Überläufer, *der*/ -läuferin, *die*

**defence** /dɪˈfens/ *n.* (Brit.) Verteidigung, *die;* (means of ∼) Schutz, *der*

**de'fenceless** *adj.* wehrlos

**de'fence mechanism** *n.* (Physiol., Psych.) Abwehrmechanismus, *der*

**defend** /dɪˈfend/ *v.t.* verteidigen

**defendant** /dɪˈfendənt/ *n.* (Law) (accused) Angeklagte, *der*/*die;* (sued) Beklagte, *der*/*die*

**de'fender** *n.* Verteidiger, *der*

**defense** etc. (*Amer.*) ▶ DEFENCE etc.

**defensive** /dɪˈfensɪv/ ①*adj.* defensiv ② *n.* be on the ∼: in der Defensive sein

**defer**[1] /dɪˈfɜː(r)/ *v.t.,* -rr- aufschieben

**defer**[2] *v.i.,* -rr-: ∼ [to sb.] sich [jmdm.] beugen

**deference** /ˈdefərəns/ *n.* Respekt, *der;* in ∼ to sb./sth. aus Achtung vor jmdm./etw.

**deferential** /defəˈrenʃl/ *adj.* respektvoll

**defiance** /dɪˈfaɪəns/ *n.* Trotz, *der;* in ∼ of sb./sth. jmdm./einer Sache zum Trotz

**defiant** /dɪˈfaɪənt/ *adj.,* **de'fiantly** *adv.* trotzig

**deficiency** /dɪˈfɪʃənsɪ/ *n.* Mangel, *der*

**deficient** /dɪˈfɪʃnt/ *adj.* unzulänglich; **sb.**/ **sth. is** ∼ **in sth.** jmdm./einer Sache mangelt es an etw. (*Dat.*)

**deficit** /ˈdefɪsɪt/ *n.* Defizit, *das* (**of** an + *Dat.*)

**defile** /dɪˈfaɪl/ *v.t.* verpesten ⟨*Luft*⟩; beflecken ⟨*Reinheit, Unschuld*⟩

**define** /dɪˈfaɪn/ *v.t.* definieren

**definite** /ˈdefɪnɪt/ *adj.* bestimmt; eindeutig ⟨*Antwort, Entscheidung, Beschluss, Verbesserung*⟩; klar umrissen ⟨*Ziel, Plan*⟩; klar ⟨*Vorstellung*⟩; genau ⟨*Zeitpunkt*⟩

**'definitely** ①*adv.* bestimmt; eindeutig ⟨*festlegen, größer sein, verbessert*⟩; endgültig ⟨*entscheiden*⟩ ② *int.* (coll.) na, klar (ugs.)

**definition** /defɪˈnɪʃn/ *n.* Definition, *die;* (Telev., Phot.) Schärfe, *die*

**definitive** /dɪˈfɪnɪtɪv/ *adj.* endgültig ⟨*Beschluss, Antwort, Urteil*⟩; (authoritative) maßgeblich

**deflate** /dɪˈfleɪt/ *v.t.* die Luft ablassen aus; (fig.) ernüchtern

**deflation** /dɪˈfleɪʃn/ *n.* (Econ.) Deflation, *die*

**deflect** /dɪˈflekt/ *v.t.* brechen ⟨*Licht*⟩; ∼ **sb./sth. [from sb./sth.]** jmdn./etw. [von jmdm./einer Sache] ablenken

**deforestation** /diːfɒrɪˈsteɪʃn/ *n.* Entwaldung, *die;* Abholzung, *die*

**deform** /dɪˈfɔːm/ *v.t.* deformieren

**deformed** /dɪˈfɔːmd/ *adj.* entstellt ⟨*Gesicht*⟩; verunstaltet ⟨*Person, Körperteil*⟩

**deformity** /dɪˈfɔːmɪtɪ/ *n.* (malformation) Verunstaltung, *die*

**defraud** /dɪˈfrɔːd/ *v.t.* ∼ **sb.** [**of sth.**] jmdn. [um etw.] betrügen

**defray** /dɪˈfreɪ/ *v.t.* bestreiten

**defrost** /diːˈfrɒst/ *v.t.* auftauen ⟨*Speisen*⟩; abtauen ⟨*Kühlschrank*⟩

**deft** /deft/ *adj.,* **'deftly** *adv.* sicher und geschickt

**defunct** /dɪˈfʌŋkt/ *adj.* defekt ⟨*Maschine*⟩; veraltet ⟨*Gesetz*⟩

**defuse** /diːˈfjuːz/ *v.t.* entschärfen

**defy** /dɪˈfaɪ/ *v.t.* (a) (resist openly) ∼ **sb.** jmdm. trotzen (b) (refuse to obey) ∼ **sb./sth.** sich jmdm./ einer Sache widersetzen

**degenerate** /dɪˈdʒenəreɪt/ *v.i.* ∼ [**into sth.**] [zu etw.] verkommen

**degradation** /degrəˈdeɪʃn/ *n.* Erniedrigung, *die*

**degrade** /dɪˈgreɪd/ *v.t.* erniedrigen

**degrading** /dɪˈgreɪdɪŋ/ *adj.* entwürdigend; erniedrigend

**degree** /dɪˈgriː/ *n.* (a) Grad, *der;* 20 ∼s 20 Grad (b) (academic rank) [akademischer] Grad

**de'gree course** *n.* Studium, *das*

**dehydrate** /diːˈhaɪdreɪt/ *v.t.* austrocknen ⟨*Körper*⟩; ∼d dehydratisiert (fachspr.)

**dehydration** /diːhaɪˈdreɪʃn/ *n.* Dehydration, *die* (fachspr.); Austrocknung, *die*

**de-ice** /diːˈaɪs/ *v.t.* enteisen

**deign** /deɪn/ *v.t.* ∼ **to do sth.** sich [dazu] herablassen, etw. zu tun

**deity** /ˈdiːɪtɪ/ *n.* Gottheit, *die*

**dejected** /dɪˈdʒektɪd/ *adj.* niedergeschlagen

**dejection** /dɪˈdʒekʃn/ *n.* Niedergeschlagenheit, *die*

**delay** /dɪˈleɪ/ ①*v.t.* (make late) aufhalten; verzögern ⟨*Ankunft, Abfahrt*⟩; **the train has been** ∼**ed** der Zug hat Verspätung ② *v.i.* warten ③ *n.* (a) Verzögerung, *die* (**to** bei) (b) (Transport) Verspätung, *die*

**delectable** /dɪˈlektəbl/ *adj.* köstlich

**delegate** ①/ˈdelɪgət/ *n.* Delegierte, *der*/ *die* ②/ˈdelɪgeɪt/ *v.t.* delegieren (**to** an + *Akk.*)

**delegation** /delɪˈgeɪʃn/ *n.* Delegation, *die*

**delete** /dɪˈliːt/ *v.t.* streichen (**from** in + *Dat.*); (Comp.) löschen

**de'lete key** *n.* (Comp.) Löschtaste, *die*

**deletion** /dɪˈliːʃn/ *n.* Streichung, *die;* (Comp.) Löschung, *die*

**deli** /ˈdelɪ/ (coll.) ▶ DELICATESSEN

**deliberate** /dɪˈlɪbərət/ *adj.* (a) (intentional) absichtlich; bewusst ⟨*Lüge, Irreführung*⟩ (b) (fully considered) wohl überlegt

**de'liberately** *adv.* absichtlich

**deliberation** /dɪlɪbəˈreɪʃn/ *n.* Überlegung, *die;* (discussion) Beratung, *die*

**delicacy** /ˈdelɪkəsɪ/ *n.* (a) (tactfulness and care) Feingefühl, *das* ⋯❖

**(b)** (food) Delikatesse, *die*

**delicate** /'delɪkət/ *adj.* zart; (requiring careful handling) empfindlich; delikat ⟨*Frage, Angelegenheit*⟩

**delicatessen** /delɪkə'tesən/ *n.* Feinkostgeschäft, *das*

**delicious** /dɪ'lɪʃəs/ *adj.* köstlich

**delight** /dɪ'laɪt/ ①︎ *v.t.* erfreuen
②︎ *v.i.* **sb. ~s in doing sth.** es macht jmdm. Freude, etw. zu tun
③︎ *n.* Freude, *die* (**at** über + *Akk.;* **in** an + *Dat.*)

**de'lighted** *adj.* **be ~** ⟨*Person:*⟩ hocherfreut sein; **be ~ by** *or* **with sth.** sich über etw. (*Akk.*) freuen

**delightful** /dɪ'laɪtfl/ *adj.* wunderbar; köstlich ⟨*Geschmack*⟩; reizend ⟨*Person, Landschaft*⟩

**de'lightfully** *adv.* wunderbar

**delinquent** /dɪ'lɪŋkwənt/ ①︎ *n.* Randalierer, *der*
②︎ *adj.* kriminell

**delirious** /dɪ'lɪrɪəs/ *adj.* **be ~:** im Delirium sein; **be ~ [with sth.]** (fig.) außer sich [vor etw. (*Dat.*)] sein

**delirium** /dɪ'lɪrɪəm/ *n.* Delirium, *das*

**deliver** /dɪ'lɪvə(r)/ *v.t.* **(a)** bringen; liefern ⟨*Ware*⟩; zustellen ⟨*Post, Telegramm*⟩; überbringen ⟨*Botschaft*⟩
**(b)** halten ⟨*Rede*⟩

**delivery** /dɪ'lɪvərɪ/ *n.* Lieferung, *die;* (of letters, parcels) Zustellung, *die*

**delivery: ~ date** *n.* Liefertermin, *der;* **~ note** *n.* Lieferschein, *der;* **~ service** *n.* Zustelldienst, *der;* **~ van** *n.* Lieferwagen, *der*

**delta** /'deltə/ *n.* Delta, *das*

**delude** /dɪ'ljuːd/ *v.t.* täuschen

**deluge** /'deljuːdʒ/ ①︎ *n.* sintflutartiger Regen
②︎ *v.t.* überschwemmen

**delusion** /dɪ'ljuːʒn/ *n.* Illusion, *die*

**de luxe** /də'lʌks/ *adj.* Luxus-

**demand** /dɪ'mɑːnd/ ①︎ *n.* Forderung, *die* (**for** nach); (for commodity) Nachfrage, *die;* **sth./sb. is in ~:** etw. ist gefragt/jmd. ist begehrt
②︎ *v.t.* verlangen (**of, from** von); fordern ⟨*Recht*⟩

**de'manding** *adj.* anspruchsvoll

**demean** /dɪ'miːn/ *v. refl.* (lower one's dignity) **~ oneself [to do sth.]** sich [dazu] erniedrigen[, etw. zu tun]; **~ oneself by sth./ doing sth.** sich durch etw. erniedrigen/sich dadurch erniedrigen, dass man etw. tut

**demeaning** /dɪ'miːnɪŋ/ *adj.* erniedrigend

**demeanour** (*Brit.; Amer.:* **demeanor**) /dɪ'miːnə(r)/ *n.* Benehmen, *das*

**demented** /dɪ'mentɪd/ *adj.* wahnsinnig

**dementia** /dɪ'menʃə/ *n.* (Med.) Demenz, *die*

**demerara** /demə'reərə/ *n.* **~ [sugar]** brauner Zucker; Farin, *der*

**demise** /dɪ'maɪz/ *n.* (death) Ableben, *das* (geh.); (of firm, party, etc.) Untergang, *der*

**demo** /'deməʊ/ *n., pl.* **~s** (coll.) Demo, *die* (ugs.)

**de'mobilize** *v.t.* demobilisieren ⟨*Armee, Kriegsschiff*⟩; aus dem Kriegsdienst entlassen ⟨*Soldat*⟩

**democracy** /dɪ'mɒkrəsɪ/ *n.* Demokratie, *die*

**Democrat** /'deməkræt/ *n.* (Amer. Polit.) Demokrat, *der*/Demokratin, *die*

**democratic** /demə'krætɪk/ *adj.,* **democratically** /demə'krætɪkəlɪ/ *adv.* demokratisch

**demolish** /dɪ'mɒlɪʃ/ *v.t.* abreißen

**demolition** /demə'lɪʃn/ *n.* Abriss, *der;* **~ work** Abbrucharbeit, *die*

**demon** /'diːmən/ *n.* Dämon, *der*

**demonstrably** /'demənstrəblɪ, dɪ'mɒnstrəblɪ/ *adv.* nachweislich

**demonstrate** /'demənstreɪt/ ①︎ *v.t.* zeigen; (be proof of) zeigen; beweisen
②︎ *v.i.* demonstrieren

**demonstration** /demən'streɪʃn/ *n.* (also Pol. etc.) Demonstration, *die;* (proof) Beweis, *der*

**demonstrative** /də'mɒnstrətɪv/ *adj.* **(a)** offen ⟨*Person*⟩
**(b)** (Ling.) Demonstrativ-

**demonstrator** /'demənstreɪtə(r)/ *n.* (Pol. etc.) Demonstrant, *der*/Demonstrantin, *die*

**demoralize** /dɪ'mɒrəlaɪz/ *v.t.* demoralisieren

**demote** /diː'məʊt/ *v.t.* degradieren (**to** zu)

**demotion** /diː'məʊʃn/ *n.* Degradierung, *die* (**to** zu)

**demur** /dɪ'mɜː(r)/ *v.i.,* **-rr-** Einwände erheben

**demure** /dɪ'mjʊə(r)/ *adj.* betont zurückhaltend

**den** /den/ *n.* Höhle, *die*

**denial** /dɪ'naɪəl/ *n.* (refusal) Verweigerung, *die;* (of request) Ablehnung, *die*

**denier** /'denjə(r)/ *n.* Denier, *das;* **20 ~ stockings** 20-den-Strümpfe

**denim** /'denɪm/ *n.* Denim ⓌⓏ, *der;* Jeansstoff, *der;* **~ jacket** Jeansjacke, *die;* **~s** Bluejeans *Pl.*

**Denmark** /'denmɑːk/ *pr. n.* Dänemark (*das*)

**denomination** /dɪnɒmɪ'neɪʃn/ *n.* (Relig.) Konfession, *die*

**denote** /dɪ'nəʊt/ *v.t.* bezeichnen

**dénouement, denouement** /deɪ'nuːmɑ̃/ *n.* Ausgang, *der*

**denounce** /dɪ'naʊns/ *v.t.* denunzieren; (accuse publicly) beschuldigen

**dense** /dens/ *adj.* **(a)** dicht; massiv ⟨*Körper*⟩
**(b)** (stupid) dumm

**'densely** *adv.* dicht; **~ packed** dicht gedrängt

**density** /'densɪtɪ/ *n.* Dichte, *die*

**dent** /dent/ ①︎ *n.* Beule, *die*

② *v.t.* einbeulen
**dental** /'dentl/ *adj.* Zahn-; ~ **care**
Zahnpflege, *die;* ~ **treatment** zahnärztliche
Behandlung
**dental:** ~ **floss** /'dentl flɒs/ *n.* Zahnseide,
*die;* ~ **surgeon** *n.* Zahnarzt, *der/*-ärztin,
*die*
**dentist** /'dentɪst/ *n.* Zahnarzt, *der/*-ärztin,
*die*
**dentistry** /'dentɪstrɪ/ *n.* Zahnheilkunde,
*die*
**denture** /'dentʃə(r)/ *n.* ~[s] Zahnprothese,
*die*
**denunciation** /dɪnʌnsɪ'eɪʃn/ *n.*
Denunziation, *die;* ( public accusation)
Beschuldigung, *die*
**deny** /dɪ'naɪ/ *v.t.* (declare untrue) bestreiten;
(refuse) ~ **sb. sth.** jmdm. etw. verweigern;
~ **sb.'s request** jmdm. seine Bitte
abschlagen
**deodorant** /di:'əʊdərənt/ ① *adj.*
deodorierend
② *n.* Deodorant, *das*
**depart** /dɪ'pɑːt/ *v.i.* (a) (go away) weggehen
(b) (set out, leave) abfahren; (on one's journey)
abreisen
(c) (fig.: deviate) abweichen (**from** von)
**department** /dɪ'pɑːtmənt/ *n.* Abteilung,
*die;* (government ~) Ministerium, *das;* (of
university) Seminar, *das*
**de'partment store** *n.* Kaufhaus, *das*
**departure** /dɪ'pɑːtʃə(r)/ *n.* (a) Abreise, *die;*
(of train, bus, ship) Abfahrt, *die;* (of aircraft)
Abflug, *der*
(b) (deviation) ~ **from sth.** Abweichen von
etw.
**departure:** ~ **gate** *n.* Flugsteig, *der;*
~ **lounge** *n.* Abflughalle, *die;* ~ **time** *n.*
(of train, bus) Abfahrtzeit, *die;* (of aircraft)
Abflugzeit, *die*
**depend** /dɪ'pend/ *v.i.* (a) ~ [up]on
abhängen von; **it/that** ~**s** es kommt drauf an
(b) (rely, trust) ~ [up]on sich verlassen auf
(+ *Akk.*); (have to rely on) angewiesen sein auf
(+ *Akk.*)
**dependable** /dɪ'pendəbl/ *adj.* zuverlässig
**dependant** /dɪ'pendənt/ *n.* Abhängige,
*der/die*
**dependence** /dɪ'pendəns/ *n.*
Abhängigkeit, *die*
**dependent** /dɪ'pendənt/ ① *n.*
▶ DEPENDANT
② *adj.* abhängig
**depict** /dɪ'pɪkt/ *v.t.* darstellen
**deplete** /dɪ'pliːt/ *v.t.* erheblich verringern
**deplorable** /dɪ'plɔːrəbl/ *adj.*
beklagenswert
**deplore** /dɪ'plɔː(r)/ *v.t.* (a) (disapprove of)
verurteilen
(b) (regret) beklagen
**deploy** /dɪ'plɔɪ/ *v.t.* einsetzen
**deport** /dɪ'pɔːt/ *v.t.* ausweisen

**deportation** /diːpɔː'teɪʃn/ *n.* Ausweisung,
*die*
**depose** /dɪ'pəʊz/ *v.t.* absetzen
**deposit** /dɪ'pɒzɪt/ ① *n.* (a) (in bank) Depot,
*das;* (credit) Guthaben, *das;* (Brit.: at interest)
Sparguthaben, *das*
(b) (first instalment) Anzahlung, *die;* **put down**
a ~ **on sth.** eine Anzahlung für etw. leisten
(c) (on bottle) Pfand, *das*
② *v.t.* (a) (lay down) ablegen; abstellen ⟨*etw.*
*Senkrechtes*⟩
(b) (in bank) deponieren
**de'posit account** *n.* (Brit.) Sparkonto,
*das*
**depot** /'depəʊ/ *n.* Depot, *das*
**depraved** /dɪ'preɪvd/ *adj.* verdorben
**depravity** /dɪ'prævɪtɪ/ *n.* Verdorbenheit,
*die*
**depreciate** /dɪ'priːʃɪeɪt/ *v.i.* an Wert
verlieren
**depreciation** /dɪpriːʃɪ'eɪʃn/ *n.*
Wertverlust, *der*
**depress** /dɪ'pres/ *v.t.* (a) (deject)
deprimieren
(b) ( push down) herunterdrücken
**depressed** /dɪ'prest/ *adj.* deprimiert
**de'pressing** *adj.*, **de'pressingly** *adv.*
deprimierend
**depression** /dɪ'preʃn/ *n.* (a) Depression,
*die*
(b) (sunk place) Vertiefung, *die*
(c) (Meteorol.) Tief[druckgebiet], *das*
(d) (Econ.) Wirtschaftskrise, *die*
**deprivation** /deprɪ'veɪʃn/ *n.* Entbehrung,
*die*
**deprive** /dɪ'praɪv/ *v.t.* ~ **sb. of sth.** jmdm.
etw. nehmen; ( prevent from having) jmdm. etw.
vorenthalten
**deprived** /dɪ'praɪvd/ *adj.* benachteiligt
⟨*Kind, Familie usw.*⟩
**depth** /depθ/ *n.* Tiefe, *die;* **in** ~: gründlich;
**in the** ~**s of winter** im tiefsten Winter
**'depth charge** *n.* Wasserbombe, *die*
**deputation** /depjʊ'teɪʃn/ *n.* Abordnung,
*die*
**deputize** /'depjʊtaɪz/ *v.i.* ~ **for sb.** jmdn.
vertreten
**deputy** /'depjʊtɪ/ *n.* [Stell]vertreter, *der/*
-vertreterin, *die; attrib.* stellvertretend
**derail** /dɪ'reɪl/ *v.t.* **be** ~**ed** entgleisen
**de'railment** *n.* Entgleisung, *die*
**deranged** /dɪ'reɪndʒd/ *adj.* [**mentally**] ~:
geistesgestört
**deregulate** /diː'regjʊleɪt/ *v.t.* deregulieren
(fachspr.); dem freien Wettbewerb überlassen
**deregulation** /diːregjʊ'leɪʃn/ *n.*
Deregulation, *die* (fachspr.); Deregulierung,
*die* (fachspr.)
**derelict** /'derɪlɪkt/ ① *adj.* verlassen und
verfallen
② *n.* Ausgestoßene, *der/die*

**d**

**deride** /dɪˈraɪd/ v.t. sich lustig machen über (+ Akk.)

**derision** /dɪˈrɪʒn/ n. Spott, der

**derisive** /dɪˈraɪsɪv/ adj. (ironical) spöttisch; (scoffing) verächtlich

**derisory** /dɪˈraɪzərɪ/ adj. (ridiculously inadequate) lächerlich

**derivation** /derɪˈveɪʃn/ n. Ableitung, die

**derivative** /dɪˈrɪvətɪv/ [1] adj. abgeleitet; (lacking originality) nachahmend [2] n. Ableitung, die

**derive** /dɪˈraɪv/ [1] v.t. ∼ sth. from sth. etw. aus etw. gewinnen; ∼ **pleasure from sth.** Freude an etw. (Dat.) haben [2] v.i. ∼ **from** beruhen auf (+ Dat.)

**derogatory** /dɪˈrɒɡətərɪ/ adj. abfällig

**derrick** /ˈderɪk/ n. [Derrick]kran, der

**derv** /dɜːv/ n. Diesel[kraftstoff], der

**descale** /diːˈskeɪl/ v.t. entkalken

**descend** /dɪˈsend/ [1] v.i. **(a)** (go down) hinuntergehen/-steigen/-klettern/-fahren; (come down) herunterkommen; ⟨Fallschirm, Flugzeug:⟩ niedergehen; **(b)** (slope downwards) abfallen; **(c)** ∼ **on sb.** jmdn. überfallen; [2] v.t. (go/come down) hinunter-/ heruntergehen/-steigen/-klettern/-fahren

**descendant** /dɪˈsendənt/ n. Nachkomme, der

**de'scended** adj. **be** ∼ **from sb.** von jmdm. abstammen

**descent** /dɪˈsent/ n. **(a)** Abstieg, der; (of parachute, plane) Niedergehen, das; **(b)** (lineage) Herkunft, die; **be of Russian** ∼: russischer Abstammung sein

**describe** /dɪˈskraɪb/ v.t. beschreiben

**description** /dɪˈskrɪpʃn/ n. **(a)** Beschreibung, die; **(b)** (sort, class) Art, die

**descriptive** /dɪˈskrɪptɪv/ adj. beschreibend; (vivid) anschaulich; **a purely** ∼ **report** ein reiner Tatsachenbericht

**desecrate** /ˈdesɪkreɪt/ v.t. entweihen

**desert**[1] /ˈdezət/ n. Wüste, die

**desert**[2] /dɪˈzɜːt/ [1] v.t. verlassen [2] v.i. ⟨Soldat:⟩ desertieren

**de'serted** adj. verlassen

**de'serter** n. Deserteur, der

**desertion** /dɪˈzɜːʃn/ n. Desertion, die

**desert 'island** /dezət ˈaɪlənd/ n. einsame Insel

**deserts** /dɪˈzɜːts/ n. pl. **get one's [just]** ∼: das bekommen, was man verdient hat

**deserve** /dɪˈzɜːv/ v.t. verdienen

**deserving** /dɪˈzɜːvɪŋ/ adj. verdienstvoll; **a** ∼ **cause** ein guter Zweck

**design** /dɪˈzaɪn/ [1] n. Entwurf, der; (pattern) Muster, das; (established form of machine, engine, etc.) Bauweise, die; (general idea, construction) Konstruktion, die [2] v.t. entwerfen; **be** ∼**ed to do sth.** etw. tun sollen

**designate** /ˈdezɪɡneɪt/ v.t. **(a)** bezeichnen **(b)** (appoint) designieren (geh.)

**designation** /dezɪɡˈneɪʃn/ n. Bezeichnung, die

**'designer** n. Designer, der/Designerin, die; (of machines) Konstrukteur, der/ Konstrukteurin, die; attrib. Modell⟨-kleidung, -jeans⟩

**desirability** /dɪzaɪərəˈbɪlɪtɪ/ n. Wunschbarkeit, die

**desirable** /dɪˈzaɪərəbl/ adj. wünschenswert

**desire** /dɪˈzaɪə(r)/ [1] n. Wunsch, der (for nach); (longing) Sehnsucht, die (for nach) [2] v.t. sich (Dat.) wünschen; (long for) sich sehnen nach

**desist** /dɪˈzɪst/ v.i. (literary) einhalten (geh.); ∼ **from sth.** von etw. ablassen (geh.)

**desk** /desk/ n. **(a)** Schreibtisch, der; (in school) Tisch, der **(b)** (cash ∼) Kasse, die; (reception ∼) Rezeption, die

**desk:** ∼**-bound** adj. an den Schreibtisch gefesselt (fig.); ∼ **calendar,** ∼ **diary** ns. Tischkalender, der; ∼ **editor** n. Manuskriptbearbeiter, der/-bearbeiterin, die; Lektor, der/Lektorin, die; ∼ **lamp** n. Schreibtischlampe, die; ∼**top** adj. ∼**top publishing** Desktoppublishing, das; ∼**top computer** Tischcomputer, der

**desolate** /ˈdesələt/ adj. trostlos

**desolation** /desəˈleɪʃn/ n. Trostlosigkeit, die

**despair** /dɪˈspeə(r)/ [1] n. Verzweiflung, die; **be the** ∼ **of sb.** jmdn. zur Verzweiflung bringen [2] v.i. verzweifeln

**desperate** /ˈdespərət/ adj. verzweifelt; extrem ⟨Maßnahmen⟩; **be** ∼ **for sth.** etw. dringend brauchen

**desperation** /despəˈreɪʃn/ n. Verzweiflung, die

**despicable** /dɪˈspɪkəbl/ adj. verabscheuungswürdig

**despise** /dɪˈspaɪz/ v.t. verachten

**despite** /dɪˈspaɪt/ prep. trotz

**despondent** /dɪˈspɒndənt/ adj. bedrückt

**despot** /ˈdespɒt/ n. Despot, der

**dessert** /dɪˈzɜːt/ n. Nachtisch, der

**dessert:** ∼**spoon** n. Esslöffel, der; ∼**spoonful** n. Esslöffel, der; ∼ **wine** n. Dessertwein, der

**destabilize** /diːˈsteɪbɪlaɪz/ v.t. (Polit.) destabilisieren

**destination** /destɪˈneɪʃn/ n. Reiseziel, das; (of goods) Bestimmungsort, der; (of train, bus) Zielort, der

**destine** /ˈdestɪn/ v.t. bestimmen; **be** ∼**d to do sth.** dazu bestimmt sein, etw. zu tun

**destiny** /ˈdestɪnɪ/ n. Schicksal, das

**destitute** /ˈdestɪtjuːt/ adj. mittellos

**destroy** /dɪˈstrɔɪ/ v.t. zerstören

**de'stroyer** n. (also Naut.) Zerstörer, der

**destruction** /dɪˈstrʌkʃn/ n. Zerstörung, die

**destructive** /dɪˈstrʌktɪv/ adj. zerstörerisch; verheerend ⟨Sturm, Feuer⟩

**desultory** /ˈdesəltərɪ/ adj. sprunghaft; zwanglos, ungezwungen ⟨Gespräch⟩

**detach** /dɪˈtætʃ/ v.t. entfernen; abnehmen ⟨wieder zu Befestigendes⟩; herausnehmen ⟨innen Befindliches⟩

**detachable** /dɪˈtætʃəbl/ adj. abnehmbar

**detached** /dɪˈtætʃt/ adj. **(a)** (impartial) unvoreingenommen; (unemotional) unbeteiligt **(b)** a ∼ **house** ein Einzelhaus

**de'tachment** n. **(a)** ▶ DETACH: Entfernen, das; Abnehmen, das; Herausnehmen, das **(b)** (Mil.) Abteilung, die

**detail** /ˈdiːteɪl/ n. **1** n. Einzelheit, die; Detail, das; **in** ∼: Punkt für Punkt; **go into** ∼[s] ins Detail gehen **2** v.t. **(a)** einzeln ausführen **(b)** (Mil.) abkommandieren

**detailed** /ˈdiːteɪld/ adj. detailliert; eingehend ⟨Studie⟩

**detain** /dɪˈteɪn/ v.t. **(a)** festhalten; (take into confinement) verhaften **(b)** (delay) aufhalten

**detainee** /diːteɪˈniː/ n. Verhaftete, der/die

**detect** /dɪˈtekt/ v.t. entdecken; wahrnehmen ⟨Bewegung⟩; aufdecken ⟨Irrtum, Verbrechen⟩

**detection** /dɪˈtekʃn/ n. Entdeckung, die; (of error, crime) Aufdeckung, die

**detective** /dɪˈtektɪv/ n. Detektiv, der; **private** ∼: Privatdetektiv, der; ∼ **work** Ermittlungsarbeit, die; ∼ **story** Detektivgeschichte, die

**detector** /dɪˈtektə(r)/ n. Detektor, der

**detention** /dɪˈtenʃn/ n. **(a)** Festnahme, die; (confinement) Haft, die **(b)** (Sch.) Nachsitzen, das

**de'tention centre** n. (Brit.) Jugendstrafanstalt, die

**deter** /dɪˈtɜː(r)/ v.t., **-rr-** abschrecken

**detergent** /dɪˈtɜːdʒənt/ n. Waschmittel, das

**deteriorate** /dɪˈtɪərɪəreɪt/ v.i. sich verschlechtern; ⟨Haus:⟩ verfallen

**deterioration** /dɪtɪərɪəˈreɪʃn/ n. ▶ DETERIORATE: Verschlechterung, die; Verfall, der

**determination** /dɪtɜːmɪˈneɪʃn/ n. Entschlossenheit, die

**determine** /dɪˈtɜːmɪn/ v.t. **(a)** (decide) beschließen **(b)** (be a decisive factor for) bestimmen **(c)** (ascertain) feststellen

**determined** /dɪˈtɜːmɪnd/ adj. **(a)** be ∼ to do sth. etw. unbedingt tun wollen **(b)** (resolute) entschlossen

**deterrent** /dɪˈterənt/ n. Abschreckungsmittel, das (to für)

**detest** /dɪˈtest/ v.t. verabscheuen

**detestable** /dɪˈtestəbl/ adj. verabscheuenswert

**detonate** /ˈdetəneɪt/ **1** v.t. zünden **2** v.i. detonieren

**detonation** /detəˈneɪʃn/ n. Detonation, die

**detonator** /ˈdetəneɪtə(r)/ n. Sprengkapsel, die

**detour** /ˈdiːtʊə(r)/ n. Umweg, der; (diversion) Umleitung, die

**detoxify** /diːˈtɒksɪfaɪ/ v.t. entgiften; unschädlich machen ⟨Gift usw.⟩

**detract** /dɪˈtrækt/ v.i. ∼ from sth. etw. beeinträchtigen

**detriment** /ˈdetrɪmənt/ n. to the ∼ of sth. zum Nachteil einer Sache (Gen.)

**detrimental** /detrɪˈmentl/ adj. schädlich; be ∼ to sth. ⟨Dat.⟩ schaden

**deuce** /djuːs/ n. (Tennis) Einstand, der

**devaluation** /diːvæljuˈeɪʃn/ n. Abwertung, die

**devalue** /diːˈvæljuː/ v.t. abwerten

**devastate** /ˈdevəsteɪt/ v.t. verwüsten; (fig.) niederschmettern

**devastating** /ˈdevəsteɪtɪŋ/ adj. verheerend; (fig.) niederschmetternd

**devastation** /devəˈsteɪʃn/ n. Verwüstung, die

**develop** /dɪˈveləp/ **1** v.t. entwickeln; erschließen ⟨natürliche Ressourcen⟩; bekommen ⟨Krankheit, Fieber, Lust⟩; ∼ a taste for sth. Geschmack an etw. (Akk.) finden **2** v.i. sich entwickeln (from aus; into zu)

**de'veloper** n. **(a)** (Photog.) Entwickler, der **(b)** (of land) Bauunternehmer, der

**developing:** ∼ **country** n. Entwicklungsland, das; ∼ **world** n. Entwicklungsländer Pl.

**de'velopment** n. Entwicklung, die (from aus; into zu); (of natural resources etc.) Erschließung, die

**de'velopment area** n. (Brit.) Entwicklungsgebiet, das

**deviant** /ˈdiːvɪənt/ adj. abweichend

**deviate** /ˈdiːvɪeɪt/ v.i. abweichen

**deviation** /diːvɪˈeɪʃn/ n. Abweichung, die

**device** /dɪˈvaɪs/ n. Gerät, das; (as part of sth.) Vorrichtung, die; leave sb. to his own ∼s jmdn. sich (Dat.) selbst überlassen

**devil** /ˈdevl/ n. Teufel, der; the D∼: der Teufel

**'devilish** adj. teuflisch

**devious** /ˈdiːvɪəs/ adj. **(a)** (winding) verschlungen; ∼ route Umweg, der **(b)** (unscrupulous, insincere) hinterhältig

**devise** /dɪˈvaɪz/ v.t. entwerfen; schmieden ⟨Pläne⟩

**devoid** /dɪˈvɔɪd/ adj. ∼ of sth. (lacking) ohne etw.; (free from) frei von etw.

**devolution** /diːvəˈluːʃn/ n. (Polit.) Dezentralisierung, die

**devote** /dɪˈvəʊt/ v.t. widmen (to Dat.)

**de'voted** *adj.* treu; aufrichtig
⟨*Freundschaft, Liebe, Verehrung*⟩; be ∼ **to sb.**
jmdn. innig lieben

**devotion** /dɪ'vəʊʃn/ *n.* ∼ **to sb./sth.**
Hingabe an jmdn./etw.

**devour** /dɪ'vaʊə(r)/ *v.t.* verschlingen

**devout** /dɪ'vaʊt/ *adj.* fromm

**dew** /djuː/ *n.* Tau, *der*

**'dewdrop** *n.* Tautropfen, *der*

**dexterity** /dek'sterɪtɪ/ *n.* Geschicklichkeit,
*die*

**dextrous** /'dekstrəs/ *adj.* geschickt

**diabetes** /daɪə'biːtiːz/ *n.* Zuckerkrankheit,
*die*

**diabetic** /daɪə'betɪk/ ☐1 *adj.* zuckerkrank
⟨*Person*⟩
　☐2 *n.* Diabetiker, *der*/Diabetikerin, *die*

**diabolical** /daɪə'bɒlɪkl/ *adj.* teuflisch

**diagnose** /daɪəg'nəʊz/ *v.t.* diagnostizieren;
feststellen ⟨*Fehler*⟩

**diagnosis** /daɪəg'nəʊsɪs/ *n., pl.* **diagnoses**
/daɪəg'nəʊsiːz/ Diagnose, *die;* **make a** ∼: eine
Diagnose stellen

**diagonal** /daɪ'ægənl/ ☐1 *adj.* diagonal
　☐2 *n.* Diagonale, *die*

**di'agonally** *adv.* diagonal

**diagram** /'daɪəgræm/ *n.* Diagramm, *das*

**dial** /'daɪəl/ ☐1 *n.* (of clock or watch) Zifferblatt,
*das;* (of gauge, meter, etc.) Skala, *die;* (Teleph.)
Wählscheibe, *die*
　☐2 *v.t. & i.,* (Brit.) **-ll-** (Teleph.) wählen; ∼ **direct**
selbst wählen; (dial extension) durchwählen

**dialect** /'daɪəlekt/ *n.* Dialekt, *der*

**dialling,** (Amer.) **dialing:** ∼ **code** *n.*
Vorwahl, *die;* ∼ **tone** Wählton, *der*

**dialogue** /'daɪəlɒg/ *n.* Dialog, *der*

**'dialogue box** *n.* (Comp.) Dialogbox, *die;*
Dialogfenster, *das*

**'dial tone** *n.* (Amer.) Wählton, *der*

**dialysis** /daɪ'ælɪsɪs/ *n.* [Hämo]dialyse, *die*
(fachspr.); Blutwäsche, *die,* ∼ **machine**
Dialyseapparat, *der*

**diameter** /daɪ'æmɪtə(r)/ *n.* Durchmesser,
*der*

**diametrical** /daɪə'metrɪkl/ *adj.,*
**dia'metrically** *adv.* diametral

**diamond** /'daɪəmənd/ *n.* (a) Diamant, *der*
(b) (figure) Raute, *die*
(c) (Cards) Karo, *das; see also* CLUB 1C

**diaper** /'daɪəpə(r)/ *n.* (Amer.) Windel, *die*

**diaphragm** /'daɪəfræm/ *n.* Diaphragma,
*das* (Fachspr.); ⟨*Anat. also*⟩ Zwerchfell, *das;*
⟨*Photog. also*⟩ Blende, *die*

**diarrhoea** ⟨*Amer.:* **diarrhea**⟩ /daɪə'riːə/
*n.* Durchfall, *der*

**diary** /'daɪərɪ/ *n.* (a) Tagebuch, *das*
(b) (for appointments) Terminkalender, *der*

**dice** /daɪs/ ☐1 *n.* Würfel, *der*
　☐2 *v.t.* (Cooking) würfeln

**dicey** /'daɪsɪ/ *adj.* (coll.) riskant

**Dictaphone** ® /'dɪktəfəʊn/ *n.* Diktaphon,
*das* (fachspr.); Diktiergerät, *das*

**dictate** /dɪk'teɪt/ *v.t. & i.* diktieren;
(prescribe) vorschreiben; ∼ **to** Vorschriften
machen (+ *Dat.*)

**dic'tating machine** *n.* Diktiergerät, *das*

**dictation** /dɪk'teɪʃn/ *n.* Diktat, *das*

**dictator** /dɪk'teɪtə(r)/ *n.* Diktator, *der*

**dictatorial** /dɪktə'tɔːrɪəl/ *adj.* diktatorisch

**dic'tatorship** *n.* Diktatur, *die*

**dictionary** /'dɪkʃənərɪ/ *n.* Wörterbuch, *das*

**did** ▶ DO

**diddle** /'dɪdl/ *v.t.* (coll.) übers Ohr hauen
(ugs.)

**didn't** /'dɪdnt/ (coll.) = **did not;** ▶ DO

**die** /daɪ/ *v.i.,* **dying** /'daɪɪŋ/ sterben (of, from
an + *Dat.*); ⟨*Tier, Pflanze:*⟩ eingehen; **be**
**dying to do sth.** darauf brennen, etw. zu tun;
**be dying for sth.** etw. unbedingt brauchen

■ **die 'down** *v.i.* ⟨*Sturm, Wind, Protest:*⟩
sich legen; ⟨*Flammen:*⟩ kleiner werden;
⟨*Feuer:*⟩ herunterbrennen; ⟨*Lärm:*⟩ leiser
werden

■ **die 'out** *v.i.* aussterben

**'diehard** *n.* Ewiggestrige, *der*/*die*

**diesel** /'diːzl/ *n.* ∼ **[engine]** Diesel[motor],
*der;* ∼ **[fuel]** Diesel[kraftstoff], *der*

**diet** /'daɪət/ ☐1 *n.* Diät, *die;* **be**/**go on a** ∼:
eine Schlankheitskur machen
　☐2 *v.i.* eine Schlankheitskur machen

**'diet sheet** *n.* Diätplan, *der*

**differ** /'dɪfə(r)/ *v.i.* (be different) sich
unterscheiden

**difference** /'dɪfərəns/ *n.* (a) Unterschied,
*der;* **make no** ∼ **[to sb.]** [jmdm.] nichts
ausmachen; **it makes a** ∼: es ist ein *od.* (ugs.)
macht einen Unterschied
(b) (disagreement) Meinungsverschiedenheit,
*die*

**different** /'dɪfərənt/ *adj.* verschieden;
(*pred. also*) anders; (*attrib. also*) ander...; **be**
∼ **from** or (esp. Brit.) **to** or (Amer.) **than** ...:
anders sein als ...

**differentiate** /dɪfə'renʃɪeɪt/ *v.t. & i.*
unterscheiden (**between** zwischen + *Dat.*)

**'differently** *adv.* anders (**from,** *esp. Brit.* **to**
als)

**difficult** /'dɪfɪkəlt/ *adj.* schwierig

**'difficulty** *n.* Schwierigkeit, *die;* **with [great]**
∼: [sehr] mühsam; **get into difficulties** in
Schwierigkeiten kommen

**diffident** /'dɪfɪdənt/ *adj.* zaghaft; (modest)
zurückhaltend

**diffuse** ☐1 /dɪ'fjuːz/ *v.t.* verbreiten
　☐2 *v.i.* sich ausbreiten (**through** in + *Dat.*)
　☐3 /dɪ'fjuːs/ *adj.* diffus

**dig** /dɪg/ ☐1 *v.i.,* **-gg-,** dug /dʌg/ graben (**for**
nach)
　☐2 *v.t.,* **-gg-,** dug graben; umgraben ⟨*Erde,*
*Garten*⟩

■ **dig 'out** *v.t.* ausgraben

■ **dig 'up** *v.t.* ausgraben; umgraben ⟨*Garten*⟩; aufreißen ⟨*Straße*⟩

**digest** /dɪˈdʒest, daɪˈdʒest/ *v.t.* verdauen

**digestion** /dɪˈdʒestʃn, daɪˈdʒestʃn/ *n.* Verdauung, *die*

**'digger** *n.* Bagger, *der*

**digit** /ˈdɪdʒɪt/ *n.* Ziffer, *die*

**digital** /ˈdɪdʒɪtl/ *adj.* Digital-; ∼ **audio tape** Digitaltonband, *das;* ∼ **camera** Digitalkamera, *die;* ∼ **television** Digitalfernsehen, *das;* Digital Video Disc, *die*; ∼ **video disc** DVD, *die;* Digital Video Disc, *die*

**dignified** /ˈdɪɡnɪfaɪd/ *adj.* würdig; (stately) würdevoll

**dignify** /ˈdɪɡnɪfaɪ/ *v.t.* Würde verleihen (+ *Dat.*)

**dignitary** /ˈdɪɡnɪtərɪ/ *n.* Würdenträger, *der;* dignitaries (prominent people) Honoratioren *Pl.*

**dignity** /ˈdɪɡnɪtɪ/ *n.* Würde, *die*

**digress** /daɪˈɡres/ *v.i.* abschweifen

**digression** /daɪˈɡreʃn/ *n.* Abschweifung, *die*

**dike** /daɪk/ *n.* Deich, *der*

**dilapidated** /dɪˈlæpɪdeɪtɪd/ *adj.* verfallen ⟨*Gebäude*⟩; verwahrlost ⟨*Erscheinung*⟩

**dilate** /daɪˈleɪt/ ① *v.i.* sich weiten ② *v.t.* ausdehnen

**dilemma** /dɪˈlemə, daɪˈlemə/ *n.* Dilemma, *das*

**diligence** /ˈdɪlɪdʒəns/ *n.* Fleiß, *der*

**diligent** /ˈdɪlɪdʒənt/ *adj.,* **'diligently** *adv.* fleißig

**dilute** ① /daɪˈljuːt, ˈdaɪljuːt/ *adj.* verdünnt ② /daɪˈljuːt/ *v.t.* verdünnen

**dim** /dɪm/ ① *adj.* (a) schwach ⟨*Licht, Flackern*⟩; dunkel ⟨*Zimmer*⟩; verschwommen ⟨*Gestalt*⟩
(b) (vague) verschwommen
(c) (coll.: stupid) beschränkt
② *v.i.* schwächer werden

**dime** /daɪm/ *n.* (Amer. coll.) Zehncentstück, *das*

**dimension** /dɪˈmenʃn, daɪˈmenʃn/ *n.* Dimension, *die;* ∼**s** (measurements) Abmessungen; Maße

**diminish** /dɪˈmɪnɪʃ/ ① *v.i.* nachlassen; ⟨*Vorräte, Einfluss:*⟩ abnehmen; ⟨*Wert, Ansehen:*⟩ geringer werden
② *v.t.* verringern; schmälern ⟨*Ansehen, Ruf*⟩

**dimple** /ˈdɪmpl/ *n.* Grübchen, *das*

**dim:** ∼**wit** *n.* (coll.) Dummkopf, *der* (ugs.); ∼**-witted** /ˈdɪmwɪtɪd/ *adj.* (coll.) dusselig (salopp)

**din** /dɪn/ *n.* Lärm, *der*

**dine** /daɪn/ *v.i.* [zu Mittag/zu Abend] essen

**'diner** *n.* Gast, *der*

**dinghy** /ˈdɪŋɡɪ, ˈdɪŋɪ/ *n.* Ding[h]i, *das;* (inflatable) Schlauchboot, *das*

**dingy** /ˈdɪndʒɪ/ *adj.* schmuddelig

**dining** /ˈdaɪnɪŋ/**:** ∼ **area** *n.* ≈ Essecke,

*die;* ∼ **car** *n.* Speisewagen, *der;* ∼ **room** *n.* Esszimmer, *das;* (in hotel etc.) Speisesaal, *der;* ∼ **table** *n.* Esstisch, *der*

**dinner** /ˈdɪnə(r)/ *n.* (at midday) Mittagessen, *das;* (in the evening) Abendessen, *das;* (formal) Diner, *das*

**dinner:** ∼ **jacket** *n.* (Brit.) Dinnerjacket, *das;* ∼ **party** *n.* Abendeinladung, *das* (mit *Essen*); (more formal) Abendgesellschaft, *die;* ∼ **plate** *n.* flacher Teller; Essteller, *der;* ∼ **table** *n.* Esstisch, *der;* ∼ **time** *n.* Essenszeit, *die;* **at** ∼ **time** zur Essenszeit; (12-2 p.m.) mittags

**dinosaur** /ˈdaɪnəsɔː(r)/ *n.* Dinosaurier, *der*

**dint** /dɪnt/ *n.* **by** ∼ **of** durch; **by** ∼ **of doing** sth. indem jmd. etw. tut

**dip** /dɪp/ ① *v.t.,* **-pp-:** (a) [ein]tauchen (**in** in + *Akk.*)
(b) ∼ **one's headlights** abblenden
② *v.i.* sinken; (incline) abfallen
③ *n.* (a) (in road) Senke, *die*
(b) (bathe) [kurzes] Bad

**diphtheria** /dɪfˈθɪərɪə/ *n.* Diphtherie, *die*

**diphthong** /ˈdɪfθɒŋ/ *n.* Diphthong, *der*

**diploma** /dɪˈpləʊmə/ *n.* Diplom, *das*

**diplomacy** /dɪˈpləʊməsɪ/ *n.* Diplomatie, *die*

**diplomat** /ˈdɪpləmæt/ *n.* Diplomat, *der/* Diplomatin, *die*

**diplomatic** /dɪpləˈmætɪk/ *adj.,* **diplo'matically** *adv.* diplomatisch

**diplo'matic service** *n.* diplomatischer Dienst

**'dipstick** *n.* [Öl-/Benzin]messstab, *der*

**dire** /ˈdaɪə(r)/ *adj.* furchtbar

**direct** /dɪˈrekt, daɪˈrekt/ ① *v.t.* (a) (turn) richten (**to[wards]** auf + *Akk.*); ∼ **sb. to a place** jmdn. den Weg zu einem Ort weisen
(b) (control) leiten; regeln ⟨*Verkehr*⟩
(c) (order) anweisen
(d) (Theatre, Cinemat., etc.) Regie führen bei
② *adj.* direkt; durchgehend ⟨*Zug*⟩; unmittelbar ⟨*Ursache, Auswirkung, Erfahrung, Verantwortung*⟩; genau ⟨*Gegenteil*⟩; direkt ⟨*Widerspruch*⟩; diametral ⟨*Gegensatz*⟩; ∼ **speech** direkte Rede
③ *adv.* direkt

**direct:** ∼ **'current** *n.* (Electr.) Gleichstrom, *der;* ∼ **'debit** *n.* (Brit.) Lastschriftverfahren, *das;* ∼ **'dialling** *n.* Durchwahl, *die;* **we will soon have** ∼ **dialling** wir werden bald ein Durchwahlsystem haben; ∼ **'flight** *n.* Direktflug, *der;* ∼ **'hit** *n.* Volltreffer, *der*

**direction** /dɪˈrekʃn, daɪˈrekʃn/ *n.* (a) Richtung, *die;* **in the** ∼ **of London** in Richtung London
(b) (guidance) Führung, *die;* (Theatre, Cinemat., etc.) Regie, *die;* Spielleitung, *die*
(c) *usu. in pl.* (order) Anordnung, *die;* ∼**s [for use]** Gebrauchsanweisung, *die*

**di'rectly** *adv.* (a) direkt; unmittelbar ⟨*folgen, verantwortlich sein*⟩ ⋯⋗

**(b)** (exactly) genau
**(c)** (at once) umgehend
**(d)** (shortly) gleich

**di'rect object** *n.* direktes Objekt

**director** /daɪ'rektə(r), dɪ'rektə(r)/ *n.* **(a)** (Commerc.) Direktor, *der*/Direktorin, *die;* **board of** ~**s** Aufsichtsrat, *der* **(b)** (Theatre, Cinemat., etc.) Regisseur, *der*/Regisseurin, *die*

**directory** /daɪ'rektərɪ, dɪ'rektərɪ/ *n.* (telephone ~) Telefonbuch, *das;* (of tradesmen etc.) Branchenverzeichnis, *das;* (Comp.) Verzeichnis, *das;* ~ **enquiries** (Brit.), ~ **information** (Amer.) [Fernsprech]auskunft, *die*

**dirt** /dɜːt/ *n.* Schmutz, *der;* ~ **cheap** (coll.) spottbillig

**'dirty** ① *adj.* schmutzig; **get sth.** ~: etw. schmutzig machen ② *v.t.* schmutzig machen

**disa'bility** *n.* Behinderung, *die*

**disa'bility allowance** *n.* Erwerbsunfähigkeitsentschädigung, *die*

**disabled** /dɪs'eɪbld/ *adj.* behindert

**disad'vantage** *n.* Nachteil, *der;* **at a** ~: im Nachteil

**disad'vantaged** *adj.* benachteiligt

**disa'gree** *v.i.* anderer Meinung sein; ~ **with sb./sth.** mit jmdm./etw. nicht übereinstimmen; ~ **[with sb.] about** *or* **over sth.** sich [mit jmdm.] über etw. (*Akk.*) nicht einig sein

**disa'greeable** *adj.* unangenehm

**disa'greement** *n.* **(a)** (difference of opinion) Uneinigkeit, *die;* **be in** ~ **with sb./sth.** mit jmdm./etw. nicht übereinstimmen **(b)** (quarrel) Meinungsverschiedenheit, *die* **(c)** (discrepancy) Diskrepanz, *die*

**disal'low** *v.t.* verbieten; (Sport) nicht geben ⟨*Tor*⟩

**disap'pear** *v.i.* verschwinden; ⟨*Brauch, Tierart:*⟩ aussterben

**disap'pearance** *n.* Verschwinden, *das*

**disap'point** *v.t.* enttäuschen

**disap'pointed** *adj.* enttäuscht

**disap'pointing** *adj.* enttäuschend

**disap'pointment** *n.* Enttäuschung, *die*

**disap'proval** *n.* Missbilligung, *die*

**disap'prove** *v.i.* dagegen sein; ~ **of sb./sth.** jmdn. ablehnen/etw. missbilligen

**dis'arm** *v.t.* entwaffnen

**disarmament** /dɪs'ɑːməmənt/ *n.* Abrüstung, *die*

**disarray** /dɪsə'reɪ/ *n.* Unordnung, *die;* **in** ~: in Unordnung

**disaster** /dɪ'zɑːstə(r)/ *n.* Katastrophe, *die;* ~ **area** Katastrophengebiet, *das;* ~ **fund** Nothilfefonds, *der*

**disastrous** /dɪ'zɑːstrəs/ *adj.* katastrophal; verhängnisvoll ⟨*Irrtum, Entscheidung, Politik*⟩

**dis'band** ① *v.t.* auflösen

② *v.i.* sich auflösen

**disbe'lief** *n.* Unglaube, *der;* **in** ~: ungläubig

**disbe'lieve** *v.t.* ~ **sb./sth.** jmdm./etw. nicht glauben

**disc** /dɪsk/ *n.* **(a)** Scheibe, *die;* (record) Platte, *die* **(b)** (Comp.) ▶ DISK A

**discard** /dɪs'kɑːd/ *v.t.* wegwerfen; fallenlassen ⟨*Vorschlag, Idee*⟩

**'disc brake** *n.* Scheibenbremse, *die*

**discern** /dɪ'sɜːn/ *v.t.* wahrnehmen

**discernible** /dɪ'sɜːnɪbl/ *adj.* erkennbar

**di'scerning** *adj.* kritisch

**discharge** ① /dɪs'tʃɑːdʒ/ *v.t.* **(a)** entlassen (from aus); freisprechen ⟨*Angeklagte*⟩ **(b)** ablassen ⟨*Flüssigkeit, Gas*⟩ ② /'dɪstʃɑːdʒ/ *n.* **(a)** Entlassung, *die* (from aus); (of defendant) Freispruch, *der* **(b)** (emission) Ausfluss, *der*

**disciple** /dɪ'saɪpl/ *n.* **(a)** (Relig.) Jünger, *der* **(b)** (follower) Anhänger, *der*/Anhängerin, *die*

**disciplinary** /dɪsɪ'plɪnərɪ/ *adj.* disziplinarisch; ~ **action** Disziplinarmaßnahmen *Pl.*

**discipline** /'dɪsɪplɪn/ ① *n.* Disziplin, *die* ② *v.t.* disziplinieren; (punish) bestrafen

**disciplined** /'dɪsɪplɪnd/ *adj.* diszipliniert

**'disc jockey** *n.* Diskjockey, *der*

**dis'claim** *v.t.* abstreiten

**dis'claimer** *n.* Gegenerklärung, *die;* (Law) Verzichterklärung, *die*

**disclose** /dɪs'kləʊz/ *v.t.* enthüllen; bekannt geben ⟨*Information, Nachricht*⟩

**dis'closure** *n.* Enthüllung, *die;* (of information, news) Bekanntgabe, *die*

**disco** /'dɪskəʊ/ *n., pl.* ~**s** (coll.) Disko, *die*

**'disco dancing** *n.* Diskotanz, *der*

**dis'colour** (Brit.; Amer.: **discolor**) *v.t.* verfärben

**dis'comfort** *n.* **(a)** *no pl.* (slight pain) Beschwerden *Pl.* **(b)** (hardship) Unannehmlichkeit, *die*

**'disco music** *n.* Diskomusik, *die*

**disconcert** /dɪskən'sɜːt/ *v.t.* irritieren

**discon'nect** *v.t.* abtrennen; abstellen ⟨*Telefon*⟩

**disconsolate** /dɪs'kɒnsələt/ *adj.* **(a)** (unhappy) unglücklich **(b)** (inconsolable) untröstlich

**discon'tent** *n.* Unzufriedenheit, *die*

**discon'tented** *adj.* unzufrieden

**discon'tinue** *v.t.* einstellen

**discord** /'dɪskɔːd/ *n.* **(a)** Zwietracht, *die* **(b)** (Mus.) Dissonanz, *die*

**discordant** /dɪs'kɔːdənt/ *adj.* **(a)** (conflicting) gegensätzlich **(b)** a ~ **note** ein Misston

**discothèque** /'dɪskətek/ *n.* Diskothek, *die*

**discount** ① /'dɪskaʊnt/ *n.* (Commerc.) Rabatt, *der* (**on** auf + *Akk.*)

**2** /dɪˈskaʊnt/ *v.t.* (disbelieve) unberücksichtigt lassen

**discourage** /dɪˈskʌrɪdʒ/ *v.t.* **(a)** entmutigen
**(b)** (advise against) abraten

**diˈscouragement** *n.* **(a)** Entmutigung, *die*
**(b)** (depression) Mutlosigkeit, *die*

**discouraging** /dɪˈskʌrɪdʒɪŋ/ *adj.* entmutigend

**disˈcourteous** *adj.* unhöflich

**disˈcourtesy** *n.* Unhöflichkeit, *die*

**discover** /dɪˈskʌvə(r)/ *v.t.* entdecken; (by search) herausfinden

**disˈcovery** *n.* Entdeckung, *die*

**disˈcredit** **1** *n.* Misskredit, *der;* bring ～ on sb./sth., bring sb./sth. into ～: jmdn./etw. in Misskredit bringen
**2** *v.t.* in Misskredit bringen

**discreet** /dɪˈskriːt/ *adj.,* **disˈcreetly** *adv.* diskret

**discrepancy** /dɪˈskrepənsɪ/ *n.* Diskrepanz, *die*

**discrepant** /dɪˈskrepənt/ *adj.* [voneinander] abweichend

**discretion** /dɪˈskreʃn/ *n.* (prudence) Umsicht, *die*

**discriminate** /dɪˈskrɪmɪneɪt/ *v.i.* **(a)** unterscheiden
**(b)** ～ against/in favour of sb. jmdn. diskriminieren/bevorzugen

**discrimination** /dɪskrɪmɪˈneɪʃn/ *n.* **(a)** Unterscheidung, *die*
**(b)** Diskriminierung, *die* (against *Gen.*); ～ in favour of Bevorzugung (+ *Gen.*)

**discus** /ˈdɪskəs/ *n.* Diskus, *der*

**discuss** /dɪˈskʌs/ *v.t.* besprechen; (debate) diskutieren über (+ *Akk.*)

**discussion** /dɪˈskʌʃn/ *n.* Gespräch, *das;* (debate) Diskussion, *die*

**disdain** /dɪsˈdeɪn/ **1** *n.* Verachtung, *die*
**2** *v.t.* verachten; ～ to do sth. zu stolz sein, etw. zu tun

**disdainful** /dɪsˈdeɪnfl/ *adj.* verächtlich

**disease** /dɪˈziːz/ *n.* Krankheit, *die*

**diseased** /dɪˈziːzd/ *adj.* krank

**disemˈbark** *v.i.* von Bord gehen

**disenˈchant** *v.t.* ernüchtern; he became ～ed with her/it sie/es hat ihn desillusioniert

**disenˈgage** *v.t.* lösen (from aus, von); ～ the clutch auskuppeln

**disenˈtangle** *v.t.* entwirren; (extricate) befreien (from aus)

**disˈfigure** *v.t.* entstellen

**disgrace** /dɪsˈɡreɪs/ **1** *n.* Schande, *die* (to für)
**2** *v.t.* Schande machen (+ *Dat.*); ～ oneself sich blamieren

**disˈgraceful** /dɪsˈɡreɪsfl/ *adj.* skandalös; it's ～: es ist ein Skandal

**disgruntled** /dɪsˈɡrʌntld/ *adj.* verstimmt

**disguise** /dɪsˈɡaɪz/ **1** *v.t.* verkleiden ⟨Person⟩; verstellen ⟨Stimme⟩; tarnen ⟨Gegenstand⟩
**2** *n.* Verkleidung, *die*

**disgust** /dɪsˈɡʌst/ **1** *n.* (nausea) Ekel, *der* (at vor + *Dat.*); (revulsion) Abscheu, *der* (at vor + *Dat.*); (indignation) Empörung, *die* (at über + *Akk.*)
**2** *v.t.* anwidern; (fill with nausea) ekeln; (fill with indignation) empören

**disˈgusted** *adj.* angewidert; (nauseated) angeekelt; (indignant) empört

**disˈgusting** *adj.* widerlich

**dish** /dɪʃ/ *n.* **(a)** Schale, *die;* (deeper) Schüssel, *die;* ～es (crockery) Geschirr, *das;* wash *or* (coll.) do the ～es Geschirr spülen
**(b)** (type of food) Gericht, *das*

■ **dish ˈout** *v.t.* **(a)** austeilen ⟨Essen⟩
**(b)** (coll.: distribute) verteilen

■ **dish ˈup** *v.t.* auftragen

**ˈdishcloth** *n.* Spültuch, *das*

**disˈhearten** *v.t.* entmutigen

**dishevelled** (*Amer.:* **disheveled**) /dɪˈʃevld/ *adj.* zerzaust ⟨Haar⟩; ungepflegt ⟨Erscheinung⟩

**disˈhonest** *adj.,* **disˈhonestly** *adv.* unehrlich

**disˈhonesty** *n.* Unehrlichkeit, *die*

**disˈhonour** **1** *n.* Unehre, *die*
**2** *v.t.* beleidigen

**dishonourable** /dɪsˈɒnərəbl/ *adj.* unehrenhaft

**dish:** ～ **rack** *n.* Abtropfgestell, *das;* (in dishwasher) Geschirrwagen, *der;* ～**washer** *n.* Geschirrspülmaschine, *die*

**disilˈlusion** **1** *v.t.* ernüchtern
**2** *n.* Desillusion, *die* (with über + *Akk.*)

**disilˈlusionment** *n.* Desillusionierung, *die*

**disincentive** /dɪsɪnˈsentɪv/ *n.* Hemmnis, *das;* act as *or* be a ～ to sb. to do sth. jmdn. davon abhalten, etw. zu tun

**disinˈfect** *v.t.* desinfizieren

**disinfectant** /dɪsɪnˈfektənt/ **1** *adj.* desinfizierend
**2** *n.* Desinfektionsmittel, *das*

**disinformation** /dɪsɪnfəˈmeɪʃn/ *n.* Desinformation, *die*

**disingenuous** /dɪsɪnˈdʒenjʊəs/ *adj.* unaufrichtig

**disˈintegrate** *v.i.* zerfallen

**disinteˈgration** *n.* Zerfall, *der*

**disˈinterested** *adj.* **(a)** (impartial) unvoreingenommen
**(b)** (coll.: uninterested) desinteressiert

**disjointed** /dɪsˈdʒɔɪntɪd/ *adj.* unzusammenhängend

**disk** *n.* **(a)** (Comp.) **[floppy]** ～: Floppydisk, *die;* Diskette, *die;* **[hard]** ～ (exchangeable) [harte] Magnetplatte; (fixed) Festplatte, *die*
**(b)** ▶ DISC A

**'disk drive** n. (Comp.) Diskettenlaufwerk, *das*

**diskette** /dɪ'sket/ n. Diskette, *die*

**dis'like** ① v.t. nicht mögen; ~ **doing sth.** etw. ungern tun
② n. Abneigung, *die* (**of, for** gegen); **take a** ~ **to sb./sth.** eine Abneigung gegen jmdn./ etw. empfinden

**dislocate** /'dɪsləkeɪt/ v.t. ausrenken; auskugeln ⟨Schulter, Hüfte⟩

**dis'lodge** v.t. entfernen (**from** aus)

**dis'loyal** adj. illoyal (**to** gegenüber)

**dis'loyalty** n. Illoyalität, *die* (**to** gegenüber)

**dismal** /'dɪzməl/ adj. trist

**dismantle** /dɪs'mæntl/ v.t. demontieren; abbauen ⟨Schuppen, Gerüst⟩

**dismay** /dɪs'meɪ/ ① v.t. bestürzen
② n. Bestürzung, *die* (**at** über + Akk.)

**dismiss** /dɪs'mɪs/ v.t. entlassen; (reject) ablehnen

**dismissal** /dɪs'mɪsl/ n. Entlassung, *die*

**dismissive** /dɪs'mɪsɪv/ adj. abweisend; (disdainful) abschätzig

**dis'mount** v.i. absteigen

**diso'bedience** n. Ungehorsam, *der*

**diso'bedient** adj. ungehorsam

**diso'bey** v.t. nicht gehorchen (+ Dat.); nicht befolgen ⟨Befehl⟩

**dis'order** n. (a) Durcheinander, *das*
(b) (Med.) Störung, *die*

**dis'orderly** adj. (untidy) unordentlich; ~ **conduct** ungebührliches Benehmen

**dis'organized** adj. chaotisch

**dis'orientated, dis'oriented** adjs. desorientiert

**dis'own** v.t. verleugnen

**disparage** /dɪ'spærɪdʒ/ v.t. herabsetzen

**disparaging** /dɪ'spærɪdʒɪŋ/ adj. abschätzig

**disparity** /dɪ'spærɪtɪ/ n. Ungleichheit, *die*

**dispatch** /dɪ'spætʃ/ ① v.t. (a) schicken
(b) (kill) töten
② n. Bericht, *der*

**di'spatch note** n. Versandanzeige, *die*

**dispel** /dɪ'spel/ v.t., -ll- vertreiben; zerstreuen ⟨Besorgnis, Befürchtung⟩

**dispensable** /dɪ'spensəbl/ adj. entbehrlich

**dispensary** /dɪ'spensərɪ/ n. Apotheke, *die*

**dispense** /dɪ'spens/ v.i. ~ **with** verzichten auf (+ Akk.)

**dispensing 'chemist** n. Apotheker, *der*/ Apothekerin, *die*

**dispersal** /dɪ'spɜ:sl/ n. Zerstreuung, *die*

**disperse** /dɪ'spɜ:s/ ① v.t. zerstreuen
② v.i. sich zerstreuen

**dispirited** /dɪ'spɪrɪtɪd/ adj. entmutigt

**dis'place** v.t. verschieben; (supplant) ersetzen

**displaced 'person** n. Vertriebene, *der*/ *die*

**display** /dɪ'spleɪ/ ① v.t. (a) zeigen; ausstellen ⟨Waren⟩

(b) (Comp.) anzeigen
② n. (a) Ausstellung, *die;* (of goods) Auslage, *die;* (ostentatious show) Zurschaustellung, *die*
(b) (Comp. etc.) Display, *das;* Anzeige, *die*

**dis'please** v.t. ~ **sb.** jmds. Missfallen erregen

**dis'pleasure** n. Missfallen, *das*

**disposable** /dɪ'spəʊzəbl/ adj. Wegwerf-

**disposal** /dɪ'spəʊzl/ n. Beseitigung, *die;* **have sth./sb. at one's** ~: etw./jmdn. zur Verfügung haben; **be at sb.'s** ~: jmdn. zur Verfügung stehen

**dispose** /dɪ'spəʊz/ v.t. ~ **sb. to sth.** jmdn. zu etw. veranlassen; ~ **sb. to do sth.** jmdn. dazu veranlassen, etw. zu tun

■ **di'spose of** v.t. beseitigen; (settle) erledigen

**disposed** /dɪ'spəʊzd/ adj. **be** ~ **to do sth.** dazu neigen, etw. zu tun; **be well** ~ **towards sb./sth.** jmdm. wohl gesinnt sein/einer Sache (Dat.) positiv gegenüberstehen

**disposition** /dɪspə'zɪʃn/ n. Veranlagung, *die;* (nature) Art, *die*

**dis'prove** v.t. widerlegen

**disputable** /dɪ'spju:təbl, 'dɪspjʊtəbl/ adj. strittig

**dispute** /dɪ'spju:t/ ① n. Streit, *der* (**over** um)
② v.t. (a) (discuss) sich streiten über (+ Akk.)
(b) (oppose) bestreiten

**disqualifi'cation** n. Ausschluss, *der;* (Sport) Disqualifikation, *die*

**dis'qualify** v.t. ausschließen (**from** von); (Sport) disqualifizieren

**disre'gard** ① v.t. ignorieren
② n. Missachtung, *die* (**of, for** Gen.); (of wishes, feelings) Gleichgültigkeit, *die* (**for, of** gegenüber)

**dis'reputable** adj. verrufen

**disrepute** /dɪsrɪ'pju:t/ n. Verruf, *der;* **bring sb./sth. into** ~: jmdn./etw. in Verruf bringen

**disre'spect** n. Missachtung, *die;* **show** ~ **for sb./sth.** keine Achtung vor jmdm./etw. haben

**disre'spectful** adj. respektlos

**disrupt** /dɪs'rʌpt/ v.t. stören

**disruption** /dɪs'rʌpʃn/ n. Störung, *die*

**disruptive** /dɪs'rʌptɪv/ adj. störend

**dissatis'faction** n. Unzufriedenheit, *die*

**dis'satisfied** adj. unzufrieden

**dissect** /dɪ'sekt/ v.t. sezieren

**disseminate** /dɪ'semɪneɪt/ v.t. verbreiten

**dissent** /dɪ'sent/ ① v.i. (a) (refuse to assent) nicht zustimmen; ~ **from sth.** mit etw. nicht übereinstimmen
(b) (disagree) ~ **from sth.** von etw. abweichen
② n. Ablehnung, *die;* (from majority) Abweichung, *die*

**dissertation** /dɪsə'teɪʃn/ n. Dissertation, *die*

**dis'service** n. **do sb. a** ~: jmdm. einen schlechten Dienst erweisen

**dissident** /'dɪsɪdənt/ n. Dissident, der/ Dissidentin, die

**dis'similar** adj. unähnlich (**to** Dat.)

**dissociate** /dɪ'səʊʃɪeɪt/ v.t. trennen; ~ **oneself** sich distanzieren (**from** von)

**dissolve** /dɪ'zɒlv/ **1** v.t. auflösen **2** v.i. sich auflösen

**dissuade** /dɪ'sweɪd/ v.t. abbringen (**from** von)

**distance** /'dɪstəns/ n. **(a)** Entfernung, die (**from** zu) **(b)** (way to cover) Strecke, die; **from a ~:** von weitem; **in/into the ~:** in der/die Ferne

**'distance learning** n. Fernstudium, das

**distant** /'dɪstənt/ adj. **(a)** fern; entfernt ⟨Ähnlichkeit, Verwandtschaft, Verwandte⟩ **(b)** (reserved) distanziert

**dis'taste** n. Abneigung, die (**for** gegen)

**dis'tasteful** adj. unangenehm

**distend** /dɪ'stend/ v.t. erweitern

**distil,** (Amer.) **distill** /dɪ'stɪl/ v.t. destillieren; brennen ⟨Branntwein⟩

**distillation** /dɪstɪ'leɪʃn/ n. Destillation, die

**distillery** /dɪ'stɪlərɪ/ n. Brennerei, die

**distinct** /dɪ'stɪŋkt/ adj. deutlich; (different) verschieden

**distinction** /dɪ'stɪŋkʃn/ n. Unterschied, der

**distinctive** /dɪ'stɪŋktɪv/ adj. unverwechselbar

**dis'tinctly** adv. deutlich

**distinguish** /dɪ'stɪŋgwɪʃ/ **1** v.t. **(a)** (make out) erkennen **(b)** (differentiate) unterscheiden **(c)** (characterize) kennzeichnen **(d)** ~ **oneself** [**by sth.**] sich [durch etw.] hervortun **2** v.i. unterscheiden; ~ **between** auseinander halten

**distinguished** /dɪ'stɪŋgwɪʃt/ adj. angesehen; glänzend ⟨Laufbahn⟩; vornehm ⟨Aussehen⟩

**distort** /dɪ'stɔːt/ v.t. verzerren; (fig.) verdrehen

**distortion** /dɪ'stɔːʃn/ n. Verzerrung, die; (fig.) Verdrehung, die

**distract** /dɪ'strækt/ v.t. ablenken; ~ **sb.**['**s attention from sth.**] jmdn. [von etw.] ablenken

**di'stracted** adj. von Sinnen nachgestellt; (mentally far away) abwesend

**distraction** /dɪ'strækʃn/ n. **(a)** (diversion) Ablenkung, die; (interruption) Störung, die **(b)** drive sb. to ~: jmdn. zum Wahnsinn treiben

**distraught** /dɪ'strɔːt/ adj. aufgelöst (**with** vor + Dat.); verstört ⟨Blick⟩

**distress** /dɪ'stres/ **1** n. **(a)** Kummer, der (**at** über + Akk.) **(b)** (pain) Qualen Pl. **(c)** an aircraft/ship in ~: ein Flugzeug in Not/ein Schiff in Seenot

**2** v.t. nahe gehen (+ Dat.)

**di'stressing** adj. erschütternd

**di'stress signal** n. Notsignal, das

**distribute** /dɪ'strɪbjuːt/ v.t. verteilen (**to** an + Akk.; **among** unter + Akk.); (Commerc.) vertreiben

**distribution** /dɪstrɪ'bjuːʃn/ n. Verteilung, die; (Commerc.) Vertrieb, der

**distributor** /dɪ'strɪbjʊtə(r)/ n. Verteiler, der/Verteilerin, die; (Commerc.) Vertreiber, der

**district** /'dɪstrɪkt/ n. Gegend, die; (Admin.) Bezirk, der

**district:** ~ **at'torney** n. (Amer. Law) [Bezirks]staatsanwalt, der/-anwältin, die; ~ **'nurse** n. (Brit.) Gemeindeschwester, die

**dis'trust** /dɪs'trʌst/ **1** n. Misstrauen, das (**of** gegen) **2** v.t. misstrauen (+ Dat.)

**dis'trustful** adj. misstrauisch

**disturb** /dɪ'stɜːb/ v.t. **(a)** stören; '**do not ~!**' „bitte nicht stören!" **(b)** (worry) beunruhigen

**disturbance** /dɪ'stɜːbəns/ n. Störung, die; **political ~s** politische Unruhen

**disturbed** /dɪ'stɜːbd/ adj. besorgt; [**mentally**] ~: geistig gestört

**disturbing** /dɪs'tɜːbɪŋ/ adj. bestürzend

**disuse** /dɪs'juːs/ n. **fall into ~:** außer Gebrauch kommen

**disused** /dɪs'juːzd/ adj. stillgelegt; leer stehend ⟨Gebäude⟩

**ditch** /dɪtʃ/ **1** n. Graben, der **2** v.t. (coll.) sausen lassen ⟨Plan⟩; sitzen lassen ⟨Familie, Freund⟩

**dither** /'dɪðə(r)/ v.i. schwanken

**ditto** /'dɪtəʊ/ n., pl. ~**s** ebenso; ditto; ~ **marks** Unterführungszeichen, das

**divan** /dɪ'væn/ n. [Polster]liege, die

**dive** /daɪv/ **1** v.i., **dived** or (Amer.) **dove** /dəʊv/ **(a)** einen Kopfsprung machen; (when already in water) tauchen **(b)** ⟨Vogel, Flugzeug usw.:⟩ einen Sturzflug machen **2** n. **(a)** Kopfsprung, der; (of bird, aircraft, etc.) Sturzflug, der **(b)** (coll.: place) Spelunke, die

**'diver** n. **(a)** (Sport) Kunstspringer, der/-springerin, die **(b)** (as profession) Taucher, der/Taucherin, die

**diverge** /daɪ'vɜːdʒ/ v.i. auseinander gehen

**divergent** /daɪ'vɜːdʒənt/ adj. auseinander gehend

**diverse** /daɪ'vɜːs/ adj. verschieden

**diversify** /daɪ'vɜːsɪfaɪ, dɪ'vɜːsɪfaɪ/ v.i. ⟨Firma:⟩ sich auf neue Produktions-/Produktbereiche umstellen

**diversion** /daɪ'vɜːʃn/ n. **(a)** Ablenkung, die; **create a ~:** ein Ablenkungsmanöver durchführen **(b)** (Brit.: alternative route) Umleitung, die

**diversity** /daɪ'vɜːsɪtɪ/ n. Vielfalt, die

**d**

**divert** /daɪˈvɜːt/ *v.t.* umleiten ⟨Verkehr, Fluss⟩; ablenken ⟨Aufmerksamkeit⟩

**divide** /dɪˈvaɪd/ **1** *v.t.* (a) teilen; ~ sth. in two etw. [in zwei Teile] zerteilen
(b) (distribute) aufteilen (**among/between** unter + Akk. od. Dat.)
(c) (Math.) dividieren (fachspr.), teilen (**by** durch)
**2** *v.i.* sich teilen; ~ [**from sth.**] von etw. abzweigen

▪ **divide 'out** *v.t.* aufteilen (**among/between** unter + Akk. od. Dat.); (distribute) verteilen an (+ Akk.)

▪ **divide 'up** *v.t.* aufteilen

**dividend** /ˈdɪvɪdend/ *n.* Dividende, *die*

**dividers** /dɪˈvaɪdəz/ *n. pl.* Stechzirkel, *der*

**divine** /dɪˈvaɪn/ *adj.* göttlich

**diving** /ˈdaɪvɪŋ/ *n.* Kunstspringen, *das*

**diving:** ~ **board** *n.* Sprungbrett, *das;* ~ **suit** *n.* Taucheranzug, *der*

**divinity** /dɪˈvɪnɪtɪ/ *n.* (a) Göttlichkeit, *die*
(b) (god) Gottheit, *die*

**divisible** /dɪˈvɪzɪbl/ *adj.* teilbar (**by** durch)

**division** /dɪˈvɪʒn/ *n.* (a) Teilung, *die*
(b) (Math.) Dividieren, *das;* **do** ~: dividieren; **long** ~: ausführliche Division (*mit Aufschreiben der Zwischenprodukte*); **short** ~: verkürzte Division (*ohne Aufschreiben der Zwischenprodukte*)
(c) (section, part) Abteilung, *die*
(d) (group) Gruppe, *die*
(e) (Mil. etc.) Division, *die*
(f) (Footb. etc.) Liga, *die;* Spielklasse, *die;* (in British football) Division, *die*

**divorce** /dɪˈvɔːs/ **1** *n.* [Ehe]scheidung, *die*
**2** *v.t.* ~ **one's husband/wife** sich von seinem Mann/seiner Frau scheiden lassen

**divorcee** /dɪvɔːˈsiː/ *n.* Geschiedene, *der/die;* **be a** ~: geschieden sein

**divorced** /dɪˈvɔːst/ *adj.* geschieden; **get** ~: sich scheiden lassen

**divulge** /daɪˈvʌldʒ/ *v.t.* preisgeben

**DIY** *abbr.* = **do-it-yourself**

**dizzy** /ˈdɪzɪ/ *adj.* schwind[e]lig; **I feel** ~: mir ist schwindlig

**DJ** /diːˈdʒeɪ/ *abbr.* = **disc jockey** Diskjockey, *der*

**DNA** *abbr.* = **deoxyribonucleic acid** DNS

**do** /də, *stressed* duː/ **1** *v.t.,* *neg.* (coll.) **don't** /dəʊnt/, *pres.t.* **he does** /dʌz/, *neg.* (coll.) **doesn't** /ˈdʌznt/, *p.t.* **did** /dɪd/, *neg.* (coll.) **didn't** /ˈdɪdnt/, *pres.p.* **doing** /ˈduːɪŋ/, *p.p.* **done** /dʌn/ (a) machen ⟨Hausaufgaben, Hausarbeit, Examen, Übersetzung, Kopie, Bett, Handstand⟩; erfüllen ⟨Pflicht⟩; verrichten ⟨Arbeit⟩; vorführen ⟨Trick, Nummer, Tanz⟩; durchführen ⟨Test⟩; schaffen ⟨Pensum⟩; (clean) putzen; (arrange) [zurecht]machen ⟨Haare⟩; schminken ⟨Lippen, Augen, Gesicht⟩; machen (ugs.) ⟨Nägel⟩; (cut) schneiden ⟨Nägel⟩; (paint) machen (ugs.) ⟨Zimmer⟩; streichen ⟨Haus,

Möbel⟩; (repair) in Ordnung bringen; **do the shopping/washing-up/cleaning** einkaufen [gehen]/abwaschen/sauber machen; **what can I do for you?** (in shop) was darfs sein?; **do sth. about sth./sb.** etw. gegen etw./jmdn. unternehmen
(b) (cook) braten; **well done** durch[gebraten]
(c) (solve) lösen ⟨Problem, Rätsel⟩; machen ⟨Puzzle, Kreuzworträtsel⟩
(d) (coll.: swindle) reinlegen (ugs.); **do sb. out of sth.** jmdn. um etw. bringen
(e) (satisfy) zusagen (+ Dat.)
**2** *v.i.,* *forms as* 1: (a) (act) tun; **do as they do** mach es wie sie
(b) (fare) **how are you doing?** wie gehts dir?
(c) (get on) vorankommen; (in exams) abschneiden; **do well/badly at school** gut/ schlecht in der Schule sein
(d) **how do you do?** (formal) guten Tag/ Morgen/Abend!
(e) (serve purpose) es tun; (suffice) [aus]reichen; (be suitable) gehen; **that won't do** das geht nicht; **that will do!** jetzt aber genug!
**3** *v. substitute, forms as* 1: **you mustn't act as he does** du darfst nicht so wie er handeln; **You went to Paris, didn't you? – Yes, I did** Du warst doch in Paris, nicht wahr? – Ja[, stimmt]; **come in, do!** komm doch herein!
**4** *v. aux. forms as* 1: **I do love Greece** Griechenland gefällt mir wirklich gut; **little did he know that ...:** er hatte keine Ahnung, dass ...; **do you know him?** kennst du ihn?; **what does he want?** was will er?; **I don't or do not wish to take part** ich möchte nicht teilnehmen; **don't be so noisy!** seid [doch] nicht so laut!
**5** *n.* /duː/, *pl.* **do's** *or* **dos** /duːz/ (Brit. coll.) Feier, *die;* Fete, *die* (ugs.)

▪ **do a'way with** *v.t.* abschaffen

▪ **'do for** *v.t.* (coll.) **do for sb.** jmdn. fertig machen (ugs.); **be done for** erledigt sein

▪ **do 'in** *v.t.* (sl.) kaltmachen (salopp)

▪ **do 'up** *v.t.* (a) (fasten) zumachen; binden ⟨Schnürsenkel, Fliege⟩
(b) (wrap) einpacken

▪ **'do with** *v.t.* **I could do with ...:** ich brauche ...

▪ **'do without** *v.t.* **do without sth.** auf etw. (Akk.) verzichten

**docile** /ˈdəʊsaɪl/ *adj.* sanft; (submissive) unterwürfig

**dock**[1] /dɒk/ **1** *n.* (a) Dock, *das*
(b) usu. in pl. (area) Hafen, *der*
**2** *v.t.* [ein]docken
**3** *v.i.* anlegen

**dock**[2] *n.* (in lawcourt) Anklagebank, *die;* **stand/be in the** ~: ≈ auf der Anklagebank sitzen

**'docker** *n.* Hafenarbeiter, *der*

**dock:** ~**land** *n.* das Hafenviertel; ~**yard** *n.* Schiffswerft, *die*

**doctor** /ˈdɒktə(r)/ **1** *n.* (a) Arzt, *der*/Ärztin, *die; as address* Herr/Frau Doktor
(b) (holder of degree) Doktor, *der*

②  *v.t.* (coll.) verfälschen
**doctorate** /ˈdɒktərət/ *n.* Doktorwürde, *die*
**doctrine** /ˈdɒktrɪn/ *n.* Lehre, *die*
**document** /ˈdɒkjʊmənt/ *n.* (a) Dokument, *das;* Urkunde, *die*
(b) (Comp.) Dokument, *das*
**documentary** /dɒkjʊˈmentərɪ/ ① *adj.* dokumentarisch
② *n.* (film) Dokumentarfilm, *der*
**documentation** /dɒkjʊmenˈteɪʃn/ *n.* (material) beweiskräftige Dokumente *Pl.*
**dodge** /dɒdʒ/ ① *v.i.* ausweichen
② *v.t.* ausweichen (+ *Dat.*) ⟨*Schlag, Hindernis usw.*⟩; entkommen (+ *Dat.*) ⟨*Polizei, Verfolger*⟩
③ *n.* (trick) Trick, *der*
**dodgems** /ˈdɒdʒəmz/ *n. pl.*
[Auto]skooterbahn, *die;* **have a ride/go on the** ∼: Autoskooter fahren
**dodgy** /ˈdɒdʒɪ/ *adj.* (Brit. coll.) (unreliable) unsicher; (risky) gewagt
**doe** /dəʊ/ *n.* (deer) Damtier, *das;* (rabbit) [Kaninchen]weibchen, *das*
**does** /dʌz/ ▶ DO
**doesn't** /ˈdʌznt/ (coll.) = does not; ▶ DO
**dog** /dɒg/ ① *n.* Hund, *der*
② *v.t.,* **-gg-** verfolgen; (fig.) heimsuchen
**dog:** ∼ **biscuit** *n.* Hundekuchen, *der;*
∼ **collar** *n.* [Hunde]halsband, *das;* (joc.: clerical collar) Kollar, *das;* ∼**-eared** *adj.* a ∼**-eared book** ein Buch mit Eselsohren; ∼**-end** *n.* (coll.) Kippe, *die* (ugs.)
**dogged** /ˈdɒgɪd/ *adj.* hartnäckig ⟨*Weigerung, Verurteilung*⟩; zäh ⟨*Durchhaltevermögen, Ausdauer*⟩
**'dog licence** *n.*
Hundesteuerbescheinigung, *die*
**dogma** /ˈdɒgmə/ *n.* Dogma, *das*
**dogmatic** /dɒgˈmætɪk/ *adj.* dogmatisch
**do-gooder** /duːˈgʊdə(r)/ *n.* Wohltäter, *der* (iron.)
**dog:** ∼**sbody** *n.* (Brit. coll.) Mädchen für alles; ∼'**s life** *n.* a ∼'**s life** ein Hundeleben; **give** *or* **lead sb. a** ∼'**s life** jmdn. schäbig behandeln; ∼'**tired** *adj.* hundemüde
**doing** /ˈduːɪŋ/ *n.* Tun, *das*
**do-it-yourself** /duːɪtjəˈself/ ① *adj.* Do-it-yourself-
② *n.* Heimwerken, *das*
**doldrums** /ˈdɒldrəmz/ *n. pl.* **in the** ∼ (in low spirits) niedergeschlagen; (Econ.) in einer Flaute
**dole** /dəʊl/ ① *n.* (coll.) **the** ∼: Stempelgeld, *das* (ugs.); **be/go on the** ∼: stempeln gehen (ugs.)
② *v.t.* ∼ **out** [in kleinen Mengen] verteilen
**doll** /dɒl/ *n.* Puppe, *die*
**dollar** /ˈdɒlə(r)/ *n.* Dollar, *der*
**dollar:** ∼ '**bill** *n.* Dollarnote, *die;* ∼ **sign** *n.* Dollarzeichen, *das*
**dollop** /ˈdɒləp/ *n.* (coll.) Klacks, *der* (ugs.)

'**doll's house** *n.* Puppenhaus, *das*
**dolphin** /ˈdɒlfɪn/ *n.* Delphin, *der*
**domain** /dəˈmeɪn/ *n.* (a) Gebiet, *das*
(b) (Comp.) Domäne, *die;* Domain, *die;*
∼ **name** Domänenname, *der*
**dome** /dəʊm/ *n.* Kuppel, *die*
**domestic** /dəˈmestɪk/ *adj.* (a) (household) häuslich; (family) familiär ⟨*Angelegenheit, Reibereien*⟩
(b) (Econ.) inländisch; Binnen-
(c) ∼ **animal/cat** Haustier, *das*/-katze, *die*
**domesticated** /dəˈmestɪkeɪtɪd/ *adj.* gezähmt ⟨*Tier*⟩; (fig.) häuslich
**domesticity** /dəʊmesˈtɪsɪtɪ, dɒmesˈtɪsɪtɪ/ *n.* (being domestic) Häuslichkeit, *die*
**domestic 'science** *n.*
Hauswirtschaftslehre, *die*
**dominant** /ˈdɒmɪnənt/ *adj.* vorherrschend
**dominate** /ˈdɒmɪneɪt/ *v.t.* beherrschen
**domination** /dɒmɪˈneɪʃn/ *n.*
[Vor]herrschaft, *die* (**over** über + *Akk.*)
**domineering** /dɒmɪˈnɪərɪŋ/ *adj.* herrisch
**domino** /ˈdɒmɪnəʊ/ *n.* Domino[stein], *der;*
∼**es** *sing.* (game) Domino[spiel], *das;* **play** ∼**es** Domino spielen
'**domino effect** *n.* Dominoeffekt, *der*
**don**¹ /dɒn/ *v.t.* (Liter.) anlegen (geh.)
**don**² *n.* (Univ.) Dozent, *der*
**donate** /dəʊˈneɪt/ *v.t.* spenden; (on large scale) stiften
**donation** /dəˈneɪʃn/ *n.* Spende, *die* (**to** für); (large-scale) Stiftung, *die*
**done** /dʌn/ ▶ DO
**donkey** /ˈdɒŋkɪ/ *n.* Esel, *der*
**donor** /ˈdəʊnə(r)/ *n.* Spender, *der*/ Spenderin, *die*
**don't** /dəʊnt/ (coll.) = do not; ▶ DO
**doodle** /ˈduːdl/ *v.i.* [herum]kritzeln
**doom** /duːm/ ① *n.* Verhängnis, *das*
② *v.t.* verurteilen; **be** ∼**ed** verloren sein; **be** ∼**ed to fail** *or* **failure** zum Scheitern verurteilt sein
**door** /dɔː(r)/ *n.* Tür, *die;* (of castle, barn) Tor, *das;* **out of** ∼**s** im Freien; **go out of** ∼**s** nach draußen gehen
**door:** ∼**bell** *n.* Türklingel, *die;* ∼**frame** *n.* Türrahmen, *der;* ∼ **handle** *n.* Türklinke, *die;* ∼**keeper** *n.* Pförtner, *der;* Portier, *der;* ∼**knob** *n.* Türknopf, -knauf, *der;* ∼**man** *n.* Portier, *der;* ∼**mat** *n.* Fußmatte, *die;* ∼**step** *n.* Türstufe, *die;* **on one's/the** ∼**step** (fig.) vor jmds. Tür; ∼**way** *n.* Eingang, *der*
**dope** /dəʊp/ ① *n.* (a) (sl.: narcotic) Stoff, *der* (salopp)
(b) (coll.: fool) Dussel, *der*
② *v.t.* dopen ⟨*Pferd, Athleten*⟩
**dormant** /ˈdɔːmənt/ *adj.* ruhend ⟨*Tier, Pflanze*⟩; untätig ⟨*Vulkan*⟩
**dormitory** /ˈdɔːmɪtərɪ/ *n.* Schlafsaal, *der*
**dormouse** /ˈdɔːmaʊs/ *n., pl.* **dormice** /ˈdɔːmaɪs/ Haselmaus, *die*

**DOS** /dɒs/ *abbr.* (Comp.) = **disk operating system** DOS
**dosage** /'dəʊsɪdʒ/ *n.* (size of dose) Dosis, *die*
**dose** /dəʊs/ ① *n.* Dosis, *die*
② *v.t.* ~ sb. with sth. jmdm. etw. geben
**dot** /dɒt/ *n.* Punkt, *der*; on the ~: auf den Punkt genau
**dot.com** /'dɒtkɒm/ ① *adj.* Dot-com-
② *n.* Dot-com-Firma, *die*
**dote** /dəʊt/ *v.i.* ~ on sb./sth. jmdn./etw. abgöttisch lieben
**'dot matrix** *n.* (Comp.) Punktmatrix, *die*; ~ printer Nadeldrucker, *der*
**dotted** /'dɒtɪd/ *adj.* gepunktet
**dotty** /'dɒtɪ/ *adj.* (coll.) (silly) dümmlich; (feeble-minded) vertrottelt (ugs.); (absurd) blödsinnig (ugs.)
**double** /'dʌbl/ ① *adj.* doppelt; ~ bed/room Doppelbett, *das*/-zimmer, *das*; be ~ the height/width/length doppelt so hoch/breit/lang sein
② *adv.* doppelt
③ *n.* (a) Doppelte, *das*
(b) (twice as much) doppelt so viel; (twice as many) doppelt so viele
(c) (person) Doppelgänger, *der*/-gängerin, *die*
(d) in pl. (Tennis etc.) Doppel, *das*
(e) at the ~ (Mil.) im Laufschritt; (fig.) ganz schnell
④ *v.t.* verdoppeln
⑤ *v.i.* sich verdoppeln
■ **double 'back** *v.i.* kehrtmachen (ugs.).
■ **double 'up** *v.i.* sich krümmen (with vor + *Dat.*)
**double:** ~ 'agent *n.* Doppelagent, *der*/-agentin, *die*; ~-**barrelled** (*Amer.*: ~-barreled) /'dʌblbærəld/ *adj.* doppelläufig; ~-barrelled surname (Brit.) Doppelname, *der*; ~ 'bass *n.* Kontrabass, *der*; ~ 'bill *n.* Doppelprogramm, *das*; ~-breasted /dʌbl'brestɪd/ *adj.* zwei- od. doppelreihig; ~-breasted jacket Zweireiher, *der*; ~-'check *v.t.* (verify twice) zweimal kontrollieren; (verify in two ways) zweifach überprüfen; ~ 'chin *n.* Doppelkinn, *das*; ~-'click (Comp.) ① *v.i.* doppelklicken; ② *v.t.* ~click sth. auf etw. (*Dat.*) doppelklicken; ~ 'cream *n.* Sahne mit hohem Fettgehalt; ~-'cross *v.t.* ein Doppelspiel treiben mit; ~-**decker** /dʌbl'dekə(r)/ *n.* Doppeldeckerbus, *der*
**double entendre** /du:bl ã'tãdr/ *n.* Zweideutigkeit, *die*
**double:** ~-'glazed *adj.* Doppel‹fenster›; ~ 'glazing *n.* Doppelverglasung, *die*; ~-'jointed *adj.* sehr gelenkig; ~-'lesson *n.* Doppelstunde, *die*; ~-'lock *v.t.* zweimal abschließen; ~ 'meaning ▶ DOUBLE ENTENDRE; ~-'page 'spread *n.* the advertisement was a ~-page spread die Anzeige war doppelseitig; ~-'parking *n.* Parken in der zweiten Reihe; ~ 'room *n.* Doppelzimmer, *das*; ~ 'standard *n.* (rule) Doppelmoral, *die*; apply or operate a

~ standard or ~ standards mit zweierlei Maß messen; ~ 'vision *n.* Doppeltsehen, *das*; ~ yellow 'lines *n. pl.*: am Fahrbahnrand verlaufende gelbe Doppellinie, die ein Halteverbot signalisiert
**doubly** /'dʌblɪ/ *adv.* doppelt
**doubt** /daʊt/ ① *n.* Zweifel, *der* (about, as to, of an + *Dat.*); ~[s] [about or as to sth./as to whether ...] (as to future) Ungewissheit, (as to fact) Unsicherheit [über etw. (*Akk.*)/darüber, ob ...]; there's no ~ that ...: es besteht kein Zweifel daran, dass ...; ~[s] (hesitations) Bedenken *Pl.* (about gegen); no ~ (certainly) gewiss; (probably) sicherlich
② *v.i.* zweifeln
③ *v.t.* zweifeln an (+ *Dat.*); I don't ~ that or it ich bezweifle das nicht; I ~ whether or if or that ...: ich bezweifle, dass ...
**doubtful** /'daʊtfl/ *adj.* skeptisch ‹Wesen›; ungläubig ‹Blick›
**doubtless** /'daʊtlɪs/ *adv.* (a) (certainly) gewiss
(b) (probably) sicherlich
**dough** /dəʊ/ *n.* (a) Teig, *der*
(b) (coll.: money) Knete, *die* (salopp)
**'doughnut** *n.* [Berliner] Pfannkuchen, *der*
**douse** /daʊs/ *v.t.* übergießen; (extinguish) ausmachen
**dove¹** /dʌv/ *n.* Taube, *die*
**dove²** /dəʊv/ ▶ DIVE 1
**dovecot, dovecote** /'dʌvkɒt/ *n.* Taubenschlag, *der*; flutter the ~cots (fig.) für einige Aufregung sorgen
**dowdy** /'daʊdɪ/ *adj.* unansehnlich; (shabby) schäbig
**down¹** /daʊn/ *n.* (feathers) Daunen *Pl.*
**down²** /daʊn/ ① *adv.* (a) (to lower place) herunter/hinunter; (in lift) abwärts
(b) (in lower place, downstairs) unten; ~ there/here da/hier unten; the next floor ~: ein Stockwerk tiefer; be ~ with an illness eine Krankheit haben; be three points/games ~: mit drei Punkten/Spielen zurückliegen
② *prep.* herunter/hinunter; lower ~ the river weiter unten am Fluss; walk ~ the hill/road den Berg/die Straße heruntergehen; fall ~ the stairs/steps die Treppe/Stufen herunterstürzen; fall ~ a hole/ditch in ein Loch/einen Graben fallen; go ~ the pub in die Kneipe gehen; live just ~ the road ein Stück weiter unten in der Straße wohnen; be ~ the pub/town in der Kneipe/Stadt sein; I've got coffee [all] ~ my skirt mein ganzer Rock ist voll Kaffee
③ *v.t.* (coll.) schlucken (ugs.) ‹Getränk›; ~ tools die Arbeit niederlegen
**down:** ~-and-'out *n.* Stadtstreicher, *der*/-streicherin, *die*; ~cast *adj.* niedergeschlagen; ~fall *n.* Untergang, *der*; ~-'hearted *adj.* niedergeschlagen; ~'hill *adv.* bergab; ~'load *v.t.* (Comp.) herunterladen; ~market *adj.* weniger anspruchsvoll; ~ payment *n.* Anzahlung, *die*; ~pour *n.* Regenguss, *der*; ~right *adj.*

ausgemacht; glatt ⟨*Lüge*⟩; ∼**size** [1] *v.t.*
verschlanken; [2] *v.i.* abspecken; ∼**stairs**
[1] /-'-/ *adv.* die Treppe hinunter⟨*gehen,
-fallen, -kommen*⟩; unten ⟨*wohnen, sein*⟩;
[2] /'--/ *adj.* im Erdgeschoss *nachgestellt;*
∼'**stream** *adv.* flussabwärts; ∼**-to-
'earth** *adj.* sachlich; ∼**town** *adv.* im/
(direction) ins Stadtzentrum; ∼**trodden** *adj.*
unterdrückt; ∼**turn** *n.* (Econ., Commerc.)
Abschwung, *der;* ∼ '**under** *adv.* (coll.) in/
(to) nach Australien/Neuseeland
**downward** /'daʊnwəd/ [1] *adj.* nach unten
gerichtet
  [2] *adv.* abwärts ⟨*sich bewegen*⟩; nach unten
⟨*sehen, gehen*⟩
**downwards** /'daʊnwədz/ ▶ DOWNWARD 2
**dowry** /'daʊrɪ/ *n.* Aussteuer, *die*
**doz.** *abbr.* = **dozen** Dtzd.
**doze** /dəʊz/ [1] *v.i.* dösen (ugs.)
  [2] *n.* Nickerchen, *das* (ugs.)
■ **doze 'off** *v.i.* eindösen (ugs.)
**dozen** /'dʌzn/ *n.* (a) Dutzend, *das;* half a ∼:
sechs
  (b) *in pl.* (coll.: many) Dutzende *Pl.*
**Dr** *abbr.* = **doctor** Dr.
**drab** /dræb/ *adj.* langweilig; trostlos
⟨*Landschaft*⟩; eintönig ⟨*Leben*⟩
**draft** /drɑːft/ [1] *n.* (a) (of speech) Konzept,
*das;* (of treaty, bill) Entwurf, *der*
  (b) (Amer.) ▶ DRAUGHT
  [2] *v.t.* entwerfen
**drafty** (Amer.) ▶ DRAUGHTY
**drag** /dræg/ [1] *v.t.,* **-gg-** schleppen; (Comp.)
ziehen; ∼ **and drop** ziehen und ablegen
  [2] *v.i.,* **-gg-** schleifen; (fig.: pass slowly) sich
[hin]schleppen
  [3] *n.* (a) (coll.) **in** ∼: in Frauenkleidung
  (b) (coll.: at cigarette) Zug, *der*
■ **drag 'down** *v.t.* nach unten ziehen;
∼ **sb. down** to one's own level (fig.) jmdn.
auf sein Niveau herabziehen
■ **drag 'on** *v.i.* sich [da]hinschleppen
**dragon** /'drægn/ *n.* Drache, *der*
'**dragonfly** *n.* Libelle, *die*
**drain** /dreɪn/ [1] *n.* Abflussrohr, *das;*
(underground) Kanalisationsrohr, *das;* (grating at
roadside) Gully, *der;* go down the ∼ (fig. coll.)
für die Katz sein (ugs.)
  [2] *v.t.* (a) trockenlegen ⟨*Teich*⟩; entwässern
⟨*Land*⟩; ableiten ⟨*Wasser*⟩
  (b) (Cookery) abgießen ⟨*Wasser, Gemüse*⟩
  (c) austrinken ⟨*Glas*⟩
  [3] *v.i.* ⟨*Flüssigkeit:*⟩ ablaufen; ⟨*Geschirr,
Gemüse:*⟩ abtropfen
**drainage** /'dreɪnɪdʒ/ *n.* Kanalisation, *die*
'**draining board** (*Brit.; Amer.:*
'**drainboard**) *n.* Abtropfbrett, *das*
'**drainpipe** *n.* Regen[abfall]rohr, *das*
**drake** /dreɪk/ *n.* Enterich, *der*
**drama** /'drɑːmə/ *n.* Drama, *das*
**dramatic** /drə'mætɪk/ *adj.* dramatisch
**dramatist** /'dræmətɪst/ *n.* Dramatiker,
*der*/Dramatikerin, *die*

**dramatize** /'dræmətaɪz/ *v.t.* dramatisieren
**drank** ▶ DRINK 2
**drape** /dreɪp/ [1] *v.t.* drapieren
  [2] *n.* (Amer.: curtain) Vorhang, *der*
'**draper** *n.* (Brit.) Textilkaufmann, *der;* ∼'s
[shop] Textilgeschäft, *das*
**drastic** /'dræstɪk/ *adj.* drastisch
**draught** /drɑːft/ *n.* [Luft]zug, *der;* there's a
∼: es zieht
**draught:** ∼ '**beer** *n.* Fassbier, *das;*
∼ **board** *n.* (Brit.) Damebrett, *das;*
∼ **excluder** *n.* Abdichtvorrichtung, *die;*
Zugluft-Verhinderer, *der;* ∼**proof** *adj.*
winddicht
**draughts** /drɑːfts/ *n.* (Brit.) Damespiel, *das*
'**draughtsman** /-mən/ *n., pl.*
**draughtsmen** /-mən/ Zeichner, *der*/
Zeichnerin, *die*
'**draughty** *adj.* zugig
**draw** /drɔː/ [1] *v.t.,* **drew** /druː/, **drawn**
/drɔːn/ (a) (pull) ziehen; ∼ **the curtains**/
**blinds** (close) die Vorhänge zuziehen/die
Jalousien herunterlassen; ∼ **sth. towards
one** etw. zu sich heranziehen
  (b) (attract) anlocken; **be** ∼**n to sb.** von
jmdm. angezogen werden
  (c) (take out) herausziehen; schöpfen
⟨*Wasser*⟩; ∼ **money from the bank** Geld bei
der Bank holen/abheben
  (d) beziehen ⟨*Gehalt, Rente,
Arbeitslosenunterstützung*⟩
  (e) ziehen ⟨*Strich*⟩; zeichnen ⟨*geometrische
Figur, Bild*⟩
  (f) ziehen ⟨*Parallele, Vergleich*⟩;
herausstellen ⟨*Unterschied*⟩
  [2] *v.i.* (a) **drew, drawn:** ∼ **to an end** zu Ende
gehen
  (b) (Sport) **they drew [three-all]** sie spielten
[3 : 3] unentschieden
  [3] *n.* (a) (raffle) Tombola, *die*
  (b) (of lottery) Ziehung, *die*
  (c) ([result of] drawn game) Unentschieden, *das;*
**end in a** ∼: mit einem Unentschieden enden
■ **draw 'back** [1] *v.t.* zurückziehen
  [2] *v.i.* zurückweichen
■ **draw 'in** *v.i.* einfahren; ⟨*Tage:*⟩ kürzer
werden
■ **draw 'out** *v.i.* abfahren; ⟨*Tage:*⟩ länger
werden
■ **draw 'up** [1] *v.t.* (a) aufsetzen ⟨*Vertrag*⟩;
aufstellen ⟨*Liste*⟩
  (b) (pull closer) heranziehen
  [2] *v.i.* [an]halten
**draw:** ∼**back** *n.* Nachteil, *der;* ∼**bridge**
*n.* Zugbrücke, *die*
**drawer** /drɔː(r), 'drɔːə(r)/ *n.* Schublade, *die*
'**drawing** *n.* (sketch) Zeichnung, *die*
**drawing:** ∼ **board** *n.* Zeichenbrett, *das;*
∼ **pin** *n.* (Brit.) Reißzwecke, *die;* ∼ **room** *n.*
Salon, *der*
**drawl** /drɔːl/ [1] *v.i.* gedehnt sprechen
  [2] *n.* gedehntes Sprechen
**drawn** ▶ DRAW 1, 2

**d**

**dread** /dred/ 1 v.t. sich sehr fürchten vor
(+ *Dat.*); **the ~ed day/moment** der
gefürchtete Tag/Augenblick
2 n. Angst, die

**dreadful** /'dredfl/ adj. schrecklich; (coll.:
very bad) fürchterlich; **I feel ~** (unwell) ich
fühle mich scheußlich (ugs.)

**'dreadfully** adv. schrecklich; (coll.: very
badly) fürchterlich

**dream** /driːm/ 1 n. Traum, der; attrib.
traumhaft; Traum⟨haus, -auto, -urlaub⟩; **have
a ~ about sb./sth.** von jmdm./etw. träumen
2 v.i. & t. **dreamt** /dremt/ or **dreamed**
träumen

**'dreamer** n. (in sleep) Träumende, der/die;
(day~) Träumer, der/Träumerin, die

**dreary** /'drɪərɪ/ adj. trostlos

**dredge** /dredʒ/ v.t. ausbaggern

**'dredger** n. Bagger, der

**dregs** /dregz/ n. pl. [Boden]satz, der

**drench** /drentʃ/ v.t. durchnässen

**dress** /dres/ 1 n. Kleid, das; (clothing)
Kleidung, die
2 v.t. (a) anziehen; **be well ~ed** gut
gekleidet sein; **get ~ed** sich anziehen
(b) verbinden ⟨*Wunde*⟩
3 v.i. sich anziehen
▪ **dress 'up** v.i. sich fein machen

**dress: ~ circle** n. (Theatre) erster Rang;
**~ designer** n. Modeschöpfer, der/
-schöpferin, die

**'dresser** n. (a) Anrichte, die
(b) (Amer.) ▶ DRESSING TABLE

**'dressing** n. (a) no pl. Anziehen, das
(b) (Cookery) Dressing, das
(c) (Med.) Verband, der

**dressing: ~ gown** n. Bademantel, der;
**~ room** n. (Sport) Umkleideraum, der; (for
actor) Garderobe, die; **~ table** n.
Frisierkommode, die

**dress: ~maker** n. Damenschneider, der/
-schneiderin, die; **~making** n.
Damenschneiderei, die; **~ rehearsal** n.
Generalprobe, die

**drew** ▶ DRAW 1, 2

**dribble** /'drɪbl/ v.i. (a) (slobber) sabbern
(b) (Sport) dribbeln

**dried** /draɪd/ adj. getrocknet; **~ fruit[s]**
Dörrobst, das; **~ milk** Trockenmilch, die

**drier** /'draɪə(r)/ n. (for hair) Trockenhaube,
die; (hand-held) Föhn, der; (for laundry)
[Wäsche]trockner, der

**drift** /drɪft/ 1 n. (a) (of snow or sand)
Verwehung, die
(b) (gist) **get** or **catch the ~ of sth.** etw im
Wesentlichen verstehen
2 v.i. (a) treiben; ⟨*Wolke*⟩ ziehen
(b) ⟨*Sand, Schnee*⟩ zusammengeweht
werden

**'driftwood** n. Treibholz, das

**drill** /drɪl/ 1 n. (a) (tool) Bohrer, der
(b) (Mil.: training) Drill, der
2 v.t. & i. bohren (**for** nach)

**'drill bit** n. Bohrer, der

**drink** /drɪŋk/ 1 n. Getränk, das; (alcoholic)
Glas, das; (not with food) Drink, der; **have a ~:**
[etwas] trinken; (alcoholic) ein Glas trinken
2 v.t. & i. **drank** /dræŋk/, **drunk** /drʌŋk/
trinken

**drinkable** /'drɪŋkəbl/ adj. trinkbar

**'drink-driving** n. Fahren unter
Alkoholeinfluss; Alkohol am Steuer;
**~ offence** Alkoholdelikt, das

**drinker** /'drɪŋkə(r)/ n. Trinker, der/
Trinkerin, die

**drinking** /'drɪŋkɪŋ/: **~ fountain** n.
Trinkbrunnen, der; **~ water** n.
Trinkwasser, das

**drip** /drɪp/ 1 n. (a) Tropfen, das
(b) (coll.: feeble person) Schlappschwanz, der
(salopp)
2 v.i., **-pp-** tropfen; **be ~ping with water/
moisture** triefend nass sein

**'drip-dry** adj. bügelfrei

**'dripping** n. (Cookery) Schmalz, das

**drive** /draɪv/ 1 n. (a) Fahrt, die
(b) (private road) Zufahrt, die; (entrance) (to small
building) Einfahrt, die; (to large building)
Auffahrt, die
(c) (energy) Tatkraft, die
(d) (Psych.) Trieb, der
(e) (Motor Veh.) **left-hand/right-hand ~:** Links-/
Rechtssteuerung, die
2 v.t., **drove** /drəʊv/, **driven** /'drɪvn/ (a)
fahren
(b) treiben ⟨*Tier*⟩
(c) (compel to move) vertreiben (**out of, from**
aus)
(d) (fig.) **~ sb. to sth.** jmdn. zu etw. treiben;
**~ sb. to do sth.** or **into doing sth.** jmdn.
dazu treiben, etw. zu tun
(e) (power) antreiben
3 v.i., **drove**, **driven** (a) fahren; **can you ~?**
kannst du Auto fahren?
(b) (go by car) mit dem [eigenen] Auto fahren
▪ **drive at** v.t. (fig.) hinauswollen auf
(+ *Akk.*); **what are you driving at?** worauf
wollen Sie hinaus?
▪ **drive a'way** 1 v.i. wegfahren
2 v.t. (a) wegfahren
(b) (chase away) vertreiben
▪ **drive 'off** ▶ DRIVE AWAY
▪ **drive 'on** v.i. weiterfahren
▪ **drive 'up** v.i. vorfahren (**to** vor + *Dat.*)

**'drive-in** adj. Drive-in-; **~ cinema** or (Amer.)
movie [theater] Autokino, das

**drivel** /'drɪvl/ n. Gefasel, das (ugs.); **talk ~:**
faseln (ugs.)

**driven** ▶ DRIVE 2, 3

**driver** /'draɪvə(r)/ n. (a) Fahrer, der/
Fahrerin, die; (of locomotive) Führer, der/
Führerin, die; **~'s license** (Amer.)
Führerschein, der
(b) (Comp.) Treiber, der

**driving** /'draɪvɪŋ/ 1 n. Fahren, das
2 adj. peitschend ⟨*Regen*⟩

**driving: ~ force** n. treibende Kraft;

Triebfeder, *die; the* ~ **force behind sth.** die
treibende Kraft hinter etw.; ~ **gloves** *n.*
*pl.* Autohandschuhe *Pl.*; ~ **instructor** *n.*
Fahrlehrer, *der*/-lehrerin, *die;* ~ **lesson** *n.*
Fahrstunde, *die;* ~ **licence** *n.*
Führerschein, *der;* ~ **mirror** *n.*
Rückspiegel, *der;* ~ **school** *n.* Fahrschule,
*die;* ~ **test** *n.* Fahrprüfung, *die*

**drizzle** /'drɪzl/ ⓵ *n.* Nieseln, *das*
 ⓶ *v.i.* **it's drizzling** es nieselt

**drone** /drəʊn/ ⓵ *v.i.* (a) ⟨*Biene:*⟩ summen;
 ⟨*Maschine:*⟩ brummen
 **(b)** ⟨*Rezitator:*⟩ leiern
 ⓶ *n.* ▶ 1: Summen, *das;* Brummen, *das;*
 Geleier, *das*

**drool** /dru:l/ *v.i.* ~ **over** eine kindische
 Freude haben an (+ *Dat.*)

**droop** /dru:p/ *v.i.* herunterhängen; ⟨*Blume:*⟩
 den Kopf hängen lassen

**drop** /drɒp/ ⓵ *n.* (a) Tropfen, *der;* **in** ~**s**
 tropfenweise
 **(b)** (decrease) Rückgang, *der*
 ⓶ *v.i., -pp-:* (a) (fall) (accidentally)
 [herunter]fallen; (deliberately) sich
 [hinunter]fallen lassen
 **(b)** (in amount etc.) sinken; ⟨*Preis, Wert:*⟩
 sinken, fallen; ⟨*Wind:*⟩ sich legen; ⟨*Stimme:*⟩
 sich senken
 ⓷ *v.t., -pp-:* (a) fallen lassen; abwerfen
 ⟨*Bomben, Nachschub*⟩
 **(b)** (discontinue, abandon) fallen lassen; ~ **out**
 **of university/the course** das Studium
 abbrechen *od.* aufgeben
 **(c)** (omit) auslassen
 ▪ **drop 'by, drop 'in** *v.i.* vorbeikommen
 ▪ **drop 'off** ⓵ *v.i.* (a) (fall off) abfallen
 **(b)** (fall asleep) einnicken
 ⓶ *v.t.* absetzen ⟨*Fahrgast*⟩
 ▪ **drop 'out** *v.i.* (a) herausfallen (of aus)
 **(b)** (withdraw) aussteigen (ugs.) (of aus);
 (beforehand) seine Teilnahme absagen

**drop:** ~**-down menu** *n.* (Comp.)
 Dropdownmenü, *das;* ~ **handlebars** *n. pl.*
 Rennlenker, *der;* ~ **kick** *n.* (Football)
 Dropkick, *der*

**droplet** /'drɒplɪt/ *n.* Tröpfchen, *das*

**dropout** /'drɒpaʊt/ *n.* Aussteiger, *der*/
 Aussteigerin, *die*

**dropper** /'drɒpə(r)/ *n.* (esp. Med.) Tropfer,
 *der*

**drop shot** *n.* (Tennis etc.) Stoppball, *der*

**drought** /draʊt/ *n.* Dürre, *die*

**drove** ▶ DRIVE 2, 3

**drown** /draʊn/ ⓵ *v.i.* ertrinken
 ⓶ *v.t.* ertränken; **be** ~**ed** ertrinken

**drowse** /draʊz/ *v.i.* [vor sich hin]dösen

**drowsy** /'draʊzɪ/ *adj.* schläfrig; (on just
 waking) verschlafen

**drudgery** /'drʌdʒərɪ/ *n.* Schufterei, *die*

**drug** /drʌg/ ⓵ *n.* (a) (Med.) [Arznei]mittel,
 *das*
 **(b)** (narcotic) Droge, *die;* **be on** ~**s** Rauschgift
 nehmen

⓶ *v.t., -gg-* betäuben ⟨*Person*⟩; ~ **sb.'s food/
 drink** jmds. Essen/Getränk (*Dat.*) ein
 Betäubungsmittel beimischen

**drug:** ~ **abuse** *n.* Drogenmissbrauch, *der;*
 ~ **abuser** *n.* Drogenmissbrauch
 Treibender/Treibende; ~ **addict** *n.*
 Drogensüchtige, *der*/*die;* ~ **addiction** *n.*
 Drogensucht, *die;* ~ **dealer** *n.*
 Drogenhändler, *der*/-händlerin, *die;* Dealer,
 *der*/Dealerin, *die* (Drogenjargon); ~ **peddler**
 ▶ DRUG DEALER; ~**-related** *adj.*
 Drogen⟨-tote, -kriminalität, -delikt,
 -probleme⟩; ~ **scene** *n.* Drogenszene, *die;*
 ~**store** *n.* (Amer.) Drugstore, *der;*
 ~**-taking** *n.* Drogeneinnahme, *die;*
 ~ **trafficking** *n.* Drogenhandel, *der;*
 ~ **test** *n.* Dopingkontrolle, *die;* Dopingtest,
 *der;* ~**user** *n.* Drogenkonsument, *der*/
 -konsumentin, *die*

**drum** /drʌm/ ⓵ *n.* (a) Trommel, *die*
 **(b)** *in pl.* (in jazz or pop) Schlagzeug, *das*
 **(c)** (container) Fass, *das*
 ⓶ *v.i.* trommeln
 ▪ **drum 'up** *v.i.* auftreiben

**drum beat** *n.* Trommelschlag, *der*

**'drummer** *n.* Schlagzeuger, *der*

**'drumstick** *n.* (a) Trommelschlägel, *der*
 **(b)** (Cookery) Keule, *die*

**drunk** /drʌŋk/ ⓵ *adj.* **be** ~: betrunken
 sein; **get** ~: betrunken werden (**on** von);
 (intentionally) sich betrinken (**on** mit)
 ⓶ *n.* Betrunkene, *der*/*die*

**drunkard** /'drʌŋkəd/ *n.* Trinker, *der*/
 Trinkerin, *die*

**drunken** /'drʌŋkn/ *attrib. adj.* betrunken;
 (habitually) ständig betrunken; ~ **driving**
 Trunkenheit am Steuer

**'drunkenness** *n.* Betrunkenheit, *die;*
 (habitual) Trunksucht, *die*

**dry** /draɪ/ ⓵ *adj.* trocken; trocken, (very ~)
 herb ⟨*Wein*⟩; ausgetrocknet ⟨*Flussbett*⟩; **get**
 *or* **become** ~: trocknen
 ⓶ *v.t.* (a) trocknen ⟨*Haare, Wäsche*⟩;
 abtrocknen ⟨*Geschirr, Baby*⟩; ~ **oneself** sich
 abtrocknen; ~ **one's eyes** *or* **tears/hands**
 sich (*Dat.*) die Tränen abwischen/die Hände
 abtrocknen
 **(b)** (preserve) trocknen; dörren ⟨*Obst,
 Fleisch*⟩
 ⓷ *v.i.* trocknen
 ▪ **dry 'out** *v.t. & i.* trocknen
 ▪ **dry 'up** ⓵ *v.t.* abtrocknen
 ⓶ *v.i.* (a) (~ the dishes) abtrocknen
 **(b)** ⟨*Brunnen, Quelle:*⟩ versiegen; ⟨*Fluss,
 Teich:*⟩ austrocknen

**dry:** ~**-'clean** *v.t.* chemisch reinigen;
 ~**-'cleaner's** *n.* chemische Reinigung;
 ~**-'cleaning** *n.* chemische Reinigung

**'dryer** ▶ DRIER

**dry:** ~**-eyed** *adj.* ohne Rührung; ~ **'ice** *n.*
 Trockeneis, *das*

**drying-'up** *n.* Abtrocknen, *das;* **do the** ~
 abtrocknen; *attrib.* ~ **cloth** Geschirrtuch,
 *das*

**'dryness** *n.* Trockenheit, *die*

**dry 'rot** *n.* Trockenfäule, *die*

**dual** /'dju:əl/ *adj.* doppelt

**dual:** ~ **'carriageway** *n.* (Brit.) Straße mit Mittelstreifen; ~ **con'trol** *n.* (Aeronaut.) Doppelsteuerung, *die;* (Motor Veh.) doppelte Bedienungselemente *Pl.;* ~**-'purpose** *adj.* zweifach verwendbar

**dub** /dʌb/ *v.t.,* **-bb-** (Cinemat.) synchronisieren

**dubious** /'dju:bɪəs/ *adj.* (doubting) unschlüssig; (suspicious) zweifelhaft

**duchess** /'dʌtʃɪs/ *n.* Herzogin, *die*

**duck** /dʌk/ 1 *n.* Ente, *die* 2 *v.i.* sich [schnell] ducken 3 *v.t.* ~ one's head den Kopf einziehen

**duckling** /'dʌklɪŋ/ *n.* Entenküken, *das*

**'duck pond** *n.* Ententeich, *der*

**duct** /dʌkt/ *n.* Rohr, *das;* (for air) Ventil, *das*

**dud** /dʌd/ 1 *n.* (useless thing) Niete, die (ugs.); (counterfeit) Fälschung, *die* 2 *adj.* mies (ugs.); schlecht; (fake) gefälscht; geplatzt ⟨Scheck⟩

**dude** /dju:d, du:d/ *n.* (esp. Amer. coll.) Typ, *der* (ugs.)

**due** /dju:/ 1 *adj.* (a) (owed) geschuldet; zustehend ⟨Eigentum, Recht usw.⟩; there's sth. ~ to me, I've got sth. ~: mir steht etw. zu (b) (immediately payable) fällig (c) (that it is proper to give or use) gebührend; angemessen ⟨Belohnung⟩; be ~ to sb. jmdm. gebühren; with all ~ respect bei allem gebotenen Respekt (d) (attributable) the mistake was ~ to negligence der Fehler war durch Nachlässigkeit verursacht; it's ~ to her that we missed the train ihretwegen verpassten wir den Zug (e) (scheduled, expected); be ~ to do sth. etw. tun sollen; be ~ [to arrive] ankommen sollen (f) (likely to get, deserving) be ~ for sth. etw. verdienen 2 *adv.* (a) ~ north genau nach Norden (b) ~ to aufgrund (+ *Gen.*); auf Grund (+ *Gen.*) 3 *n.* (a) give sb. his ~: jmdm. Gerechtigkeit widerfahren lassen (b) ~s (fees) Gebühren *Pl.*

**duel** /'dju:əl/ *n.* Duell, *das*

**duet** /dju:'et/ *n.* (for voices) Duett, *das;* (instrumental) Duo, *das*

**duffle** /'dʌfl/**:** ~ **bag** *n.* Matchbeutel, *der;* ~ **coat** *n.* Dufflecoat, *der*

**dug** ▶ DIG

**duke** /dju:k/ *n.* Herzog, *der*

**dull** /dʌl/ 1 *adj.* (a) (stupid) beschränkt; (slow to understand) begriffsstutzig (b) (boring) langweilig (c) (gloomy) trübe ⟨Wetter, Tag⟩ 2 *v.t.* abstumpfen ⟨Geist, Sinne, Verstand⟩

**duly** /'dju:lɪ/ *adv.* ordnungsgemäß

**dumb** /dʌm/ *adj.* (a) stumm (b) (coll.: stupid) doof (ugs.)

■ **dumb down** *v.t. & i.* (coll.) verflachen

**dumbfounded** /dʌm'faʊndɪd/ *adj.* sprachlos

**dummy** /'dʌmɪ/ *n.* (a) (of tailor) Schneiderpuppe, *die;* (in shop) Schaufensterpuppe, *die;* (of ventriloquist) Puppe, *die;* (stupid person) Dummkopf, *der* (ugs.); like a stuffed ~: wie ein Ölgötze (ugs.) (b) (imitation) Attrappe, *die* (c) (esp. Brit.: for baby) Schnuller, *der*

**dump** /dʌmp/ 1 *n.* (a) (place) Müllkippe, *die;* (heap) Müllhaufen, *der;* (permanent) Müllhalde, *die* (b) (Mil.) Depot, *das* (c) (coll.: town) Kaff, *das* (ugs.) 2 *v.t.* (dispose of) werfen; (deposit) abladen ⟨Sand, Müll usw.⟩; (leave) lassen; (place) abstellen

**'dumping ground** *n.* Müllkippe, *die;* (fig.) Abstellplatz, *der*

**dumpling** /'dʌmplɪŋ/ *n.* Kloß, *der*

**dumps** /dʌmps/ *n. pl.* be *or* feel down in the ~: ganz down sein (ugs.)

**'dump truck** *n.* Kipper, *der*

**dunce** /dʌns/ *n.* Null, *die* (ugs.)

**dune** /dju:n/ *n.* Düne, *die*

**dung** /dʌŋ/ *n.* Dung, *der*

**dungarees** /dʌŋɡə'ri:z/ *n. pl.* Latzhose, *die*

**dungeon** /'dʌndʒən/ *n.* Kerker, *der*

**dunk** /dʌŋk/ *v.t.* tunken

**dupe** /dju:p/ 1 *v.t.* übertölpeln 2 *n.* Dumme, *der/die*

**duplex** /'dju:pleks/ *adj.* (esp. Amer.) (two-storey) zweistöckig ⟨Wohnung⟩; (two-family) Zweifamilien⟨haus⟩

**duplicate** 1 /'dju:plɪkət/ *adj.* (a) (identical) Zweit- (b) (twofold) doppelt 2 *n.* Kopie, *die;* (second copy of letter/document/key) Duplikat, *das;* in ~: in doppelter Ausfertigung 3 /'dju:plɪkeɪt/ *v.t.* (a) (make a copy of, make in ~) ~ sth. eine zweite Anfertigung von etw. machen (b) (on machine) vervielfältigen (c) (do twice) noch einmal tun

**duplicity** /dju:'plɪsɪtɪ/ *n.* Falschheit, *die*

**durability** /djʊərə'bɪlɪtɪ/ *n.* (of friendship, peace, etc.) Dauerhaftigkeit, *die;* (of garment, material) Haltbarkeit, die

**durable** /'djʊərəbl/ *adj.* haltbar; dauerhaft ⟨Friede, Freundschaft usw.⟩

**duration** /djʊə'reɪʃn/ *n.* Dauer, *die*

**duress** /djʊə'res/ *n.* Zwang, *der*

**during** /'djʊərɪŋ/ *prep.* während; (at a point in) in (+ *Dat.*)

**dusk** /dʌsk/ *n.* Einbruch der Dunkelheit

**dust** /dʌst/ 1 *n.* Staub, *der* 2 *v.t.* abstauben ⟨Möbel⟩; ~ a room/ house in einem Zimmer/Haus Staub wischen 3 *v.i.* Staub wischen

**dust:** ~**bin** *n.* (Brit.) Mülltonne, *die;* ~**cart** *n.* (Brit.) Müllwagen, *der;* ~ **cloth** *n.* Schonbezug, *der;* (duster) Staubtuch, *das*
'**duster** *n.* Staubtuch, *das*
**dust:** ~ **jacket** *n.* Schutzumschlag, *der;* ~**man** /-mən/ *n., pl.* ~**men** /-mən/ (Brit.) Müllmann, *der;* ~**pan** *n.* Kehrschaufel, *die*
'**dusty** *adj.* staubig; verstaubt ‹Bücher, Möbel›
**Dutch** /dʌtʃ/ [1] *adj.* holländisch; **sb. is** ~: jmd. ist Holländer/Holländerin
[2] *n.* (a) (language) Holländisch, *das; see also* ENGLISH 2A
(b) the ~ *pl.* die Holländer *Pl.*
**Dutch:** ~ '**courage** *n.* angetrunkener Mut; ~ '**elm disease** *n.* Ulmensterben, *das;* ~**man** /-mən/ *n., pl.* ~**men** /-mən/ Holländer, *der;* ~**woman** *n.* Holländerin, *die*
**dutiful** /'djuːtɪfl/ *adj.,* '**dutifully** *adv.* pflichtbewusst
**duty** /'djuːtɪ/ *n.* (a) Pflicht, *die;* (task) Aufgabe, *die;* **be on** ~: Dienst haben; **off** ~: nicht im Dienst; **be off** ~: keinen Dienst haben; ‹ab … Uhr› dienstfrei sein
(b) (tax) Zoll, *der;* **pay** ~ **on sth.** Zoll für etw. bezahlen
'**duty-free** *adj., adv.* zollfrei

**duvet** /'duːveɪ/ *n.* Federbett, *das;* ~ **cover** Bettbezug, *der*
**DVD** *abbr.* = **digital video disc** DVD
**dwarf** /dwɔːf/ *n., pl.* ~**s** *or* **dwarves** /'dwɔːvz/ Zwerg, *der*/Zwergin, *die*
**dwell** /dwel/ *v.i.,* **dwelt** /dwelt/ (literary) wohnen
■ '**dwell [up]on** *v.t.* (in discussion) sich ausführlich befassen mit; (in thought) in Gedanken verweilen bei
'**dwelling** *n.* Wohnung, *die*
**dwelt** ▸ DWELL
**dwindle** /'dwɪndl/ *v.i.* ~ **[away]** abnehmen; ‹Unterstützung, Interesse:› nachlassen; ‹Vorräte:› schrumpfen
**dye** /daɪ/ [1] *n.* Färbemittel, *das*
[2] *v.t.,* ~**ing** /'daɪɪŋ/ färben
**dying** /'daɪɪŋ/ *adj.* sterbend; absterbend ‹Baum›
**dyke** ▸ DIKE
**dynamic** /daɪ'næmɪk/ *adj.* dynamisch
**dynamism** /'daɪnəmɪzm/ *n.* Dynamik, *die*
**dynamite** /'daɪnəmaɪt/ *n.* Dynamit, *das*
**dynamo** /'daɪnəməʊ/ *n.* Dynamo, *der;* (in car) Lichtmaschine, *die*
**dynasty** /'dɪnəstɪ/ *n.* Dynastie, *die*
**dysentry** /'dɪsəntrɪ/ *n.* Ruhr, *die*

# Ee

**E, e** /iː/ *n.* E, e, *das*
**E.** *abbr.* (a) = **east** O
(b) = **eastern** ö
**each** /iːtʃ/ [1] *adj.* jeder/jede/jedes; **they cost** *or* **are a pound** ~: sie kosten ein Pfund pro Stück
[2] *pron.* (a) jeder/jede/jedes
(b) ~ **other** sich
**eager** /'iːɡə(r)/ *adj.* eifrig; **be** ~ **to do sth.** etw. unbedingt tun wollen
'**eagerly** *adv.* eifrig; gespannt ‹warten›
**eagle** /'iːɡl/ *n.* Adler, *der*
**eagle-'eyed** *adj.* adleräugig
**ear**[1] /ɪə(r)/ *n.* Ohr, *das;* **up to one's** ~**s in work/debt** bis zum Hals in Arbeit/Schulden; **be[come] all** ~**s** [plötzlich] ganz Ohr sein; **play by** ~ (Mus.) nach dem Gehör spielen
**ear**[2] *n.* (Bot.) Ähre, *die*
**ear:** ~**ache** *n.* Ohrenschmerzen *Pl.;* ~ **clip** *n.* Ohr[en]klipp, *der;* ~ **drops** *n. pl.* (a) (Med.) Ohrentropfen *Pl.;* (b) (earrings) Ohrgehänge, *das;* ~**drum** *n.* Trommelfell, *das*
**earl** /ɜːl/ *n.* Graf, *der*
'**ear lobe** *n.* Ohrläppchen, *das*

**early** /'ɜːlɪ/ [1] *adj.* früh
[2] *adv.* früh; **I am a bit** ~: ich bin etwas zu früh gekommen; ~ **next week** Anfang der nächsten Woche; ~ **in June** Anfang Juni; **from** ~ **in the morning till late at night** von früh [morgens] bis spät [nachts]; ~ **on** schon früh
**early:** ~ '**closing** *n.* **it is** ~ **closing** die Geschäfte haben nachmittags geschlossen; ~**'closing day** *n.:* Tag, an dem die Geschäfte nachmittags geschlossen haben
**ear:** ~**mark** *v.t.* vorsehen; ~**muffs** *n. pl.* Ohrenschützer *Pl.*
**earn** /ɜːn/ *v.t.* verdienen; (bring in as income or interest) einbringen
**earnest** /'ɜːnɪst/ [1] *adj.* ernsthaft
[2] *n.* **in** ~: mit vollem Ernst
**earnings** /'ɜːnɪŋz/ *n. pl.* Verdienst, *der;* (of business etc.) Ertrag, *der*
**ear:** ~**phones** *n. pl.* Kopfhörer, *der;* ~**piece** *n.* Hörmuschel, *die;* ~**piercing** [1] *adj.* durch Mark und Bein gehend ‹Lärm›; [2] *n.* Durchstechen der Ohrläppchen; ~**plug** *n.* Ohropax, *das* (Wz);

**e**

**∼ring** *n.* Ohrring, *der;* **∼shot** *n.* out of/ within ∼shot außer/in Hörweite; **∼splitting** *adj.* ohrenbetäubend

**earth** /ɜ:θ/ ⊡ *n.* (also Brit. Electr.) Erde, *die;* how/what *etc.* on ∼ ...? wie/was *usw.* in aller Welt ...?

⊡ *v.t.* (Brit. Electr.) erden

**earthenware** /'ɜːθnweə(r)/ ⊡ *n.* Tonwaren *Pl.*

⊡ *adj.* Ton-

**earthly** /'ɜːθlɪ/ *adj.* irdisch; no ∼ use *etc.* (coll.) nicht der geringste Nutzen *usw.*

**earth: ∼quake** *n.* Erdbeben, *das;* **∼ sciences** *n. pl.* Geowissenschaften *Pl.;* **∼worm** *n.* Regenwurm, *der*

**'earthy** *adj.* (a) erdig

(b) (coarse) derb

**'earwax** *n.* Ohrenschmalz, *das*

**earwig** /'ɪəwɪg/ *n.* Ohrwurm, *der*

**ease** /iːz/ ⊡ *n.* (a) set sb. at ∼: jmdn. beruhigen; at [one's] ∼: entspannt; be *or* feel at [one's] ∼: sich wohl fühlen; [stand] at ∼! (Mil.) rührt euch!

(b) with ∼ (without difficulty) mit Leichtigkeit ⊡ *v.t.* lindern ⟨*Schmerz, Kummer*⟩; entspannen ⟨*Lage*⟩; verringern ⟨*Belastung, Druck, Spannung*⟩

⊡ *v.i.* nachlassen

**easel** /'iːzl/ *n.* Staffelei, *die*

**easily** /'iːzɪlɪ/ *adv.* leicht

**easiness** /'iːzɪnɪs/ *n.* Leichtigkeit, *die*

**east** /iːst/ ⊡ *n.* (a) Osten, *der;* in/to[wards]/ from the ∼: im/nach/von Osten; to the ∼ of östlich von

(b) *usu.* E∼ (Geog., Polit.) Osten, *der* ⊡ *adj.* östlich; Ost⟨*küste, -wind, -grenze*⟩ ⊡ *adv.* nach Osten; ∼ of östlich von

**'East Ber'lin** *pr. n.* (Hist.) Ostberlin, *das*

**'eastbound** *adj.* ⟨*Zug, Verkehr usw.*⟩ in Richtung Osten

**Easter** /'iːstə(r)/ *n.* Ostern, *das od. Pl.*

**'Easter egg** *n.* Osterei, *das*

**easterly** /'iːstəlɪ/ *adj.* östlich; ⟨*Wind*⟩ aus östlichen Richtungen

**Easter 'Monday** *n.* Ostermontag, *der*

**eastern** /'iːstən/ *adj.* östlich; Ost⟨*grenze, -hälfte, -seite*⟩; ∼ Germany Ostdeutschland (*das*)

**Eastern: ∼ 'Europe** *pr. n.* Osteuropa, (*das*); ∼ **Euro'pean** ⊡ *adj.* osteuropäisch; ⊡ *n.* Osteuropäer, *der/* Osteuropäerin, *die*

**Easter 'Sunday** *n.* Ostersonntag, *der*

**East: ∼ 'German** (Hist.) ⊡ *adj.* ostdeutsch; he/she is ∼ German er ist Ostdeutscher/sie ist Ostdeutsche; ⊡ *n.* Ostdeutsche, *der/die;* ∼ **'Germany** *pr. n.* (Hist.) Ostdeutschland (*das*); ∼ **'Timor** /'tiːmɔː(r)/ *pr. n.* Osttimor (*das*)

**eastward(s)** /'iːstwəd(z)/ *adv.* ostwärts

**easy** /'iːzɪ/ ⊡ *adj.* (a) leicht; on ∼ terms auf Raten ⟨*kaufen*⟩

(b) sorglos ⟨*Leben, Zeit*⟩

(c) (free from constraint) ungezwungen ⊡ *adv.* leicht; easier said than done leichter gesagt als getan; take it ∼! (calm down!) beruhige dich!

**easy: ∼-care** *attrib. adj.* pflegeleicht; ∼ **chair** *n.* Sessel, *der;* ∼**'going** *adj.* gelassen; (lax) nachlässig; ∼ **'money** *n.* leicht verdientes Geld

**eat** /iːt/ *v.t. & i.,* ate /et, eɪt/, eaten /'iːtn/ essen; ⟨*Tier:*⟩ fressen

■ **eat a'way** *v.t.* ⟨*Rost, Säure:*⟩ zerfressen

■ **eat 'out** *v.i.* essen gehen

■ **eat 'up** *v.t.* aufessen; ⟨*Tier:*⟩ auffressen

**'eat-by date** *n.* Verfallsdatum, *das*

**eaten** ▸ EAT

**eating: ∼ apple** *n.* Essapfel, *der;* ∼ **disorder** *n.* Essstörung, *die* (*meist Pl.*)*;* ∼ **place** *n.* Essgelegenheit, *die*

**eau-de-Cologne** /əʊdəkə'ləʊn/ *n.* Kölnischwasser, *das*

**eaves** /iːvz/ *n. pl.* Dachgesims, *das*

**'eavesdrop** *v.i.* lauschen; ∼ on belauschen

**'eavesdropper** *n.* Lauscher, *der/* Lauscherin, *die*

**ebb** /eb/ ⊡ *n.* Ebbe, *die;* be at a low ∼ (fig.) ⟨*Person, Stimmung, Moral:*⟩ auf dem Nullpunkt sein ⊡ *v.i.* zurückgehen; ∼ away (fig.) dahinschwinden

**'ebb tide** *n.* Ebbe, *die*

**ebony** /'ebənɪ/ *n.* Ebenholz, *das*

**EC** *abbr.* = **European Community** EG

**eccentric** /ɪk'sentrɪk/ ⊡ *adj.* exzentrisch ⊡ *n.* Exzentriker, *der/*Exzentrikerin, *die*

**eccentricity** /eksen'trɪsɪtɪ/ *n.* Exzentrizität, *die*

**ecclesiastical** /ɪkliːzɪ'æstɪkl/ *adj.* kirchlich; geistlich ⟨*Musik*⟩

**ECG** *abbr.* = **electrocardiogram** EKG

**echo** /'ekəʊ/ ⊡ *n.* Echo, *das* ⊡ *v.t.* zurückwerfen; (fig.: repeat) wiederholen

**éclair** /eɪ'kleə(r)/ *n.* Eclair, *das*

**eclipse** /ɪ'klɪps/ *n.* (Astron.) Finsternis, *die;* ∼ of the sun Sonnenfinsternis, *die*

**'eco-friendly** *adj.* umweltfreundlich

**ecological** /iːkə'lɒdʒɪkl/ *adj.* ökologisch

**eco'logically** *adv.* ökologisch; ∼ aware/ sound/harmful umweltbewusst/-gerecht/ -schädlich

**ecologist** /iː'kɒlədʒɪst/ *n.* Ökologe, *der/* Ökologin, *die*

**ecology** /iː'kɒlədʒɪ/ *n.* Ökologie, *die*

**e-commerce** /iː'kɒmɜːs/ *n.* (Comp.) elektronischer Handel; E-Commerce, *der*

**economic** /iːkə'nɒmɪk/ *adj.* (a) Wirtschafts⟨*politik, -abkommen, -system, -krise, -wunder*⟩; wirtschaftlich ⟨*Entwicklung, Zusammenbruch*⟩

(b) (giving adequate return) wirtschaftlich

**economical** /iːkə'nɒmɪkl/ *adj.* wirtschaftlich; sparsam ⟨*Person*⟩; be ∼ with sth. mit etw. haushalten

**eco'nomically** *adv.* wirtschaftlich; (not wastefully) sparsam

**economics** /i:kə'nɒmɪks/ *n.* Wirtschaftswissenschaft, *die (meist Pl.)*

**economist** /ɪ'kɒnəmɪst/ *n.* Wirtschaftswissenschaftler, *der*/ -wissenschaftlerin, *die*

**economize** /ɪ'kɒnəmaɪz/ *v.i.* sparen; ~ on sth. etw. sparen

**economy** /ɪ'kɒnəmɪ/ *n.* (a) (frugality) Sparsamkeit, *die* (b) (instance) Einsparung, *die;* **make economies** zu Sparmaßnahmen greifen (c) (of country etc.) Wirtschaft, *die*

**economy:** ~ **class** *n.* Touristenklasse, *die;* Economyklasse, *die;* ~ **size** *n.* Haushaltspackung, *die*

**'ecosystem** *n.* Ökosystem, *das*

**ecstasy** /'ekstəsɪ/ *n.* (a) Ekstase, *die* (b) E~ (drug) Ecstasy, *das*

**ecstatic** /ɪk'stætɪk/ *adj.* ekstatisch

**ecu, ECU** /'eɪkju:/ *abbr.* = **European currency unit** Ecu, *der od. die*

**eddy** /'edɪ/ *n.* Strudel, *der*

**edge** /edʒ/ **1** *n.* (a) (of knife, razor, weapon) Schneide, *die;* **on** ~ (fig.) nervös *od.* gereizt (**about** wegen) (b) (of solid, bed, table) Kante, *die;* (of sheet of paper, road, forest, cliff) Rand, *der* **2** *v.i.* sich schieben

**edgy** /'edʒɪ/ *adj.* nervös

**edible** /'edɪbl/ *adj.* essbar

**edict** /'i:dɪkt/ *n.* Erlass, *der*

**edit** /'edɪt/ *v.t.* herausgeben ⟨*Zeitung*⟩; redigieren ⟨*Buch, Artikel, Manuskript*⟩

**edition** /ɪ'dɪʃn/ *n.* Ausgabe, *die*

**editor** /'edɪtə(r)/ *n.* Redakteur, *der*/ Redakteurin, *die;* (of particular work) Bearbeiter, *der*/Bearbeiterin, *die;* (of newspaper) Herausgeber, *der*/Herausgeberin, *die*

**editorial** /edɪ'tɔ:rɪəl/ **1** *n.* Leitartikel, *der* **2** *adj.* redaktionell

**EDP** *abbr.* = **electronic data processing** EDV

**educate** /'edjʊkeɪt/ *v.t.* (a) (bring up) erziehen; (train mind and character of) bilden (b) (provide schooling for) **he was** ~**d at** ...**:** er hat seine Ausbildung in ... erhalten

**educated** /'edjʊkeɪtɪd/ *adj.* gebildet

**education** /edjʊ'keɪʃn/ *n.* Erziehung, *die;* (system) Erziehungswesen, *das*

**educational** /edjʊ'keɪʃənl/ *adj.* pädagogisch; Lehr⟨*film, -spiele, -anstalt*⟩; Erziehungs⟨*methoden, -arbeit*⟩

**edu'cation system** *n.* Bildungssystem, *das*

**EEC** *abbr.* = **European Economic Community** EWG

**eel** /i:l/ *n.* Aal, *der*

**eerie** /'ɪːrɪ/ *adj.* unheimlich

**eff** /ef/ *v.i.* (sl.) ~ **and blind** fluchen

**effect** /ɪ'fekt/ *n.* (a) Wirkung, *die* (**on** auf + *Akk.*); **the** ~**s of sth. on sth.** die Auswirkungen einer Sache (*Gen.*) auf etw. (*Akk.*); **take** ~: die erwünschte Wirkung erzielen; **in** ~: in Wirklichkeit (b) **come into** ~: gültig werden; ⟨*Gesetz:*⟩ in Kraft treten; **put into** ~: in Kraft setzen ⟨*Gesetz*⟩; verwirklichen ⟨*Plan*⟩; **with** ~ **from 2 November/Monday** mit Wirkung vom 2. November/von Montag (c) **personal** ~**s** persönliches Eigentum; Privateigentum, *das;* **household** ~**s** Hausrat, *der*

**effective** /ɪ'fektɪv/ *adj.* (a) wirksam ⟨*Mittel, Maßnahmen*⟩; **be** ~ ⟨*Arzneimittel:*⟩ wirken (b) (in operation) gültig; ~ **from/as of** mit Wirkung vom

**effectively** *adv.* (in fact) effektiv; (with effect) wirkungsvoll

**effectual** /ɪ'fektjʊəl/ *adj.* wirksam

**effeminate** /ɪ'femɪnət/ *adj.* unmännlich

**effervescent** /efə'vesənt/ *adj.* sprudelnd; (fig.) übersprudelnd

**effete** /e'fi:t/ *adj.* verweichlicht

**efficiency** /ɪ'fɪʃənsɪ/ *n.* (of person) Fähigkeit, *die;* Tüchtigkeit, *die;* (of machine, factory, engine) Leistungsfähigkeit, *die;* (of organization, method) gutes Funktionieren

**efficient** /ɪ'fɪʃənt/ *adj.* fähig ⟨*Person*⟩; tüchtig ⟨*Arbeiter, Sekretärin*⟩; leistungsfähig ⟨*Maschine, Motor, Fabrik*⟩; gut funktionierend ⟨*Methode, Organisation*⟩

**efficiently** *adj.* gut

**effigy** /'efɪdʒɪ/ *n.* Bildnis, *das*

**effing** /'efɪŋ/ *adj.* (sl.) Scheiß- (salopp)

**effluent** /'eflʊənt/ Abwässer *Pl.*

**effort** /'efət/ *n.* (a) Anstrengung, *die;* Mühe, *die;* **make an/every** ~ ( physically) sich anstrengen; (mentally) sich bemühen (b) (attempt) Versuch, *der*

**'effortless** *adj.* mühelos

**effrontery** /ɪ'frʌntərɪ/ *n.* Dreistigkeit, *die;* **have the** ~ **to do sth.** die Stirn besitzen, etw. zu tun

**effusive** /ɪ'fju:sɪv/ *adj.* überschwänglich; exaltiert (geh.) ⟨*Person*⟩

**EFL** *abbr.* = **English as a foreign language**

**e.g.** /i:'dʒi:/ *abbr.* = **for example** z.B.

**egg** /eg/ *n.* Ei, *das* ■ **egg 'on** *v.t.* anstacheln

**egg:** ~**cup** *n.* Eierbecher, *der;* ~**plant** *n.* Aubergine, *die;* (fruit also) Eierfrucht, *die;* ( plant also) Eierpflanze, *die;* ~**shell** *n.* Eierschale, *die;* ~ **timer** *n.* Eieruhr, *die;* ~ **white** *n.* Eiweiß, *das;* ~ **yolk** *n.* Eigelb, *das*

**ego** /'egəʊ, 'i:gəʊ/ *n., pl.* ~**s** (a) (Psych.) Ego, *das* (b) (self-esteem) Selbstbewusstsein, *das*

**egotism** /'egətɪzm/ *n.* (a) Egotismus, *der* (fachspr.); Ichbezogenheit, *die* ⋯⋯

**(b)** (self-conceit) Egoismus, *der;* Selbstgefälligkeit, *die*

**egotist** /'egətɪst/ *n.* Egotist, *der*/Egotistin, *die* (fachspr.); (self-centred person) Egozentriker, *der*/Egozentrikerin, *die*

**egotistic** /egə'tɪstɪk/**, egotistical** /egə'tɪstɪkl/ *adj.* **(a)** ichbezogen ⟨Rede, Gespräch⟩ **(b)** selbstsüchtig, selbstgefällig ⟨Person⟩

**Egypt** /'iːdʒɪpt/ *pr. n.* Ägypten (*das*)

**Egyptian** /ɪ'dʒɪpʃn/ ① *adj.* ägyptisch; **sb. is** ∼: jmd. ist Ägypter/Ägypterin ② *n.* (person) Ägypter, *der*/Ägypterin, *die*

**eiderdown** /'aɪdədaʊn/ *n.* Federbett, *das*

**eight** /eɪt/ ① *adj.* acht; **at** ∼: um acht; **half past** ∼: halb neun; ∼ **thirty** acht Uhr dreißig; ∼ **ten/fifty** zehn nach acht/vor neun; (esp. in timetable) acht Uhr zehn/fünfzig; ∼**-year-old boy** achtjähriger Junge; **an** ∼**-year-old** ein Achtjähriger/eine Achtjährige; **at [the age of]** ∼, **aged** ∼: mit acht Jahren; ∼ **times** achtmal ② *n.* Acht, *die;* **the first/last** ∼: die ersten/ letzten acht; **there were** ∼ **of us present** wir waren [zu] acht

**eighteen** /eɪ'tiːn/ ① *adj.* achtzehn ② *n.* Achtzehn, *die.* See also EIGHT

**eighteenth** /eɪ'tiːnθ/ ① *adj.* achtzehnt... ② *n.* (fraction) Achtzehntel, *das.* See also EIGHTH

**eighth** /eɪtθ/ ① *adj.* acht...; **be/come** ∼: Achter sein/als Achter ankommen; ∼**largest** achtgrößt... ② *n.* (in sequence, rank) Achte, *der/die/das;* (fraction) Achtel, *das;* **the** ∼ **of May** der achte Mai

**eightieth** /'eɪtɪɪθ/ *adj.* achtzigst...

**eighty** /'eɪtɪ/ ① *adj.* achtzig ② *n.* Achtzig, *die;* **the eighties** (years) die Achtzigerjahre; **be in one's eighties** in den Achtzigern sein. See also EIGHT

**Eire** /'eərə/ *pr. n.* Irland, *das;* Eire, *das*

**either** /'aɪðə(r), 'iːðə(r)/ ① *adj.* **(a)** (each) **at** ∼ **end of the table** an beiden Enden des Tisches **(b)** (one or other) [irgend]ein ... [von beiden]; **take** ∼ **one** nimm einen/eine/eins von [den] beiden ② *pron.* **(a)** (each) beide *Pl.;* **I can't cope with** ∼: ich kann mit keinem von beiden fertig werden **(b)** (one or other) einer/eine/ein[e]s [von beiden] ③ *adv.* auch [nicht]; **'I don't like that** ∼: ich mag es auch nicht ④ *conj.* ∼ ... **or** ...: entweder ... oder ...; (after negation) weder ... noch ...

**ejaculate** /ɪ'dʒækjʊleɪt/① *v.t.* (utter suddenly) ausstoßen ② *v.i.* (eject semen) ejakulieren

**eject** /'ɪdʒekt/ ① *v.t.* **(a)** (from hall, meeting) hinauswerfen (from aus) **(b)** ⟨Gerät:⟩ auswerfen, ⟨Person:⟩ herausholen ⟨Kassette⟩

② *v.i.* sich hinauskatapultieren

**ejector seat** /ɪ'dʒektə siːt/ *n.* Schleudersitz, *der*

**eke out** /iːk 'aʊt/ *v.t.* strecken; ∼ **out a living** *sb.* (Dat.) seinen Lebensunterhalt notdürftig verdienen

**elaborate** ① /ɪ'læbərət/ *adj.* kompliziert; kunstvoll [gearbeitet] ⟨Arrangement, Verzierung⟩ ② /ɪ'læbəreɪt/ *v.i.* mehr ins Detail gehen; ∼ **on** näher ausführen

**elapse** /ɪ'læps/ *v.i.* ⟨Zeit:⟩ vergehen

**elastic** /ɪ'læstɪk/ ① *adj.* elastisch ② *n.* (∼ band) Gummiband, *das*

**elastic 'band** *n.* Gummiband, *das*

**elated** /ɪ'leɪtɪd/ *adj.* freudig erregt; **be** *or* **feel** ∼: in Hochstimmung sein

**elation** /ɪ'leɪʃn/ *n.* freudige Erregung

**elbow** /'elbəʊ/ ① *n.* Ell[en]bogen, *der* ② *v.t.* ∼ *sb.* **aside** jmdn. mit dem Ellenbogen zur Seite stoßen

**elbow:** ∼ **grease** *n.* (joc.) Muskelkraft, *die;* ∼ **room** *n.* Ell[en]bogenfreiheit, *die*

**elder¹** /'eldə(r)/ ① *attrib. adj.* älter... ② *n.* **(a)** (senior) Ältere, *der/die* **(b)** (village ∼, church ∼) Älteste, *der/die*

**elder²** *n.* (Bot.) Holunder, *der*

**'elderberry** *n.* Holunderbeere, *die*

**elderly** /'eldəlɪ/ ① *adj.* älter ② *n. pl.* **the** ∼: ältere Menschen

**eldest** /'eldɪst/ *adj.* ältest...

**elect** /ɪ'lekt/ ① *adj. postpos.* gewählt; **the President** ∼: der designierte Präsident ② *v.t.* wählen; ∼ *sb.* **chairman** jmdn. zum Vorsitzenden wählen

**election** /ɪ'lekʃn/ *n.* Wahl, *die;* **general** ∼: allgemeine Wahlen *Pl.;* ∼ **results** Wahlergebnisse *Pl.*

**e'lection campaign** *n.* Wahlkampagne, *die*

**electioneer** /ɪlekʃə'nɪə(r)/ *v.i.* **be/go** ∼**ing** Wahlkampf machen

**elector** /ɪ'lektə(r)/ *n.* Wähler, *der*/Wählerin, *die*

**electoral** /ɪ'lektərl/ *adj.* Wahl-

**electoral 'college** *n.* Wahlmännergremium, *das;* Wahlausschuss, *der*

**electorate** /ɪ'lektərət/ *n.* Wähler *Pl.*

**electric** /ɪ'lektrɪk/ *adj.* elektrisch; Elektro⟨kabel, -motor, -herd, -kessel⟩; Strom⟨versorgung⟩; (fig.) spannungsgeladen ⟨Atmosphäre⟩

**electrical** /ɪ'lektrɪkl/ *adj.* elektrisch; Elektro⟨abteilung, -handel, -geräte⟩

**electric:** ∼ **'blanket** *n.* Heizdecke, *die;* ∼ **'chair** *n.* elektrischer Stuhl; ∼ **cooker** *n.* Elektroherd, *der;* ∼ **'fire** *n.* [elektrischer] Heizofen; ∼ **gui'tar** *n.* elektrische Gitarre; E-Gitarre, *die*

**electrician** /ɪlek'trɪʃn/ *n.* Elektriker, *der*/ Elektrikerin, *die*

**electricity** /ɪlek'trɪsɪtɪ/ n. Elektrizität, *die*
**electricity:** ~ **bill** n. Stromrechnung, *die;*
~ **man** n. (fitter) Elektroinstallateur, *der;*
(meter reader, collector) Stromableser, *der;*
~ **meter** n. Stromzähler, *der*

**electric 'shock** n. Stromschlag, *der*

**electrify** /ɪ'lektrɪfaɪ/ v.t. elektrifizieren;
(fig.) elektrisieren

**electro'cardiogram** n.
Elektrokardiogramm, *das*

**electrocute** /ɪ'lektrəkjuːt/ v.t. durch
Stromschlag töten

**electrode** /ɪ'lektrəʊd/ n. Elektrode, *die*

**electro'magnet** n. Elektromagnet, *der*

**electromag'netic** adj.
elektromagnetisch

**electron** /ɪ'lektrɒn/ n. Elektron, *das*

**electronic** /ɪlek'trɒnɪk/ adj. elektronisch

**electronic:** ~ **'cash** n. elektronisches
Geld; ~ **'mail** n. elektronische Post;
~ **'publishing** n. elektronisches
Publizieren

**electronics** /ɪlek'trɒnɪks/ n. Elektronik,
*die*

**electron 'microscope** n.
Elektronenmikroskop, *das*

**elegance** /'elɪgəns/ n. Eleganz, *die*

**elegant** /'elɪgənt/ adj. elegant

**elegy** /'elɪdʒɪ/ n. Elegie, *die*

**element** /'elɪmənt/ n. (a) Element, *das*
(b) (Electr.) Heizelement, *das*
(c) ~s (rudiments) Grundlagen *Pl.*

**elementary** /elɪ'mentərɪ/ adj. elementar;
grundlegend ⟨*Fakten, Wissen*⟩;
Grundschul⟨*bildung*⟩; Grund⟨*kurs,
-ausbildung, -kenntnisse*⟩

**elementary:** ~ **'particle** n. (Phys.)
Elementarteilchen, *das;* ~ **school** n.
Grundschule, *die*

**elephant** /'elɪfənt/ n. Elefant, *der;* **white** ~
(fig.) nutzloser Besitz; **be a white** ~
⟨*Gebäude, Einkaufszentrum usw.*⟩ reine
Geldverschwendung sein

**elevate** /'elɪveɪt/ v.t. [empor]heben

**elevation** /elɪ'veɪʃn/ n. (a) (height) Höhe,
*die*
(b) (Archit.) Aufriss, *der*

**elevator** /'elɪveɪtə(r)/ n. (Amer.) Aufzug,
*der;* Fahrstuhl, *der*

**eleven** /ɪ'levn/ [1] adj. elf
[2] n. (also Sport) Elf, *die. See also* EIGHT

**elevenses** /ɪ'levnzɪz/ n. sing. or pl. (Brit.
coll.) ≈ zweites Frühstück [gegen elf Uhr]

**eleventh** /ɪ'levnθ/ [1] adj. elft...; **at the**
~ **hour** in letzter Minute
[2] n. (fraction) Elftel, *das. See also* EIGHTH

**elf** /elf/ n., pl. **elves** /elvz/ Elf, *der/* Elfe, *die*

**elicit** /ɪ'lɪsɪt/ v.t. entlocken (**from** *Dat.*);
gewinnen ⟨*Unterstützung*⟩

**eligible** /'elɪdʒɪbl/ adj. **be** ~ **for sth.** (fit) für
etw. geeignet sein; (entitled) zu etw. berechtigt
sein

**eliminate** /ɪ'lɪmɪneɪt/ v.t. (a) (remove)
beseitigen; ausschließen ⟨*Möglichkeit*⟩
(b) (exclude) ausschließen; **be** ~**d** (Sport)
ausscheiden

**elimination** /ɪlɪmɪ'neɪʃn/ n. (a) (removal)
Beseitigung, *die;* **process of** ~:
Ausleseverfahren, *das*
(b) (exclusion) Ausschluss, *der;* (Sport)
Ausscheiden, *das*

**élite** /eɪ'liːt/ n. Elite, *die*

**élitist** /eɪ'liːtɪst/adj. elitär; Elite⟨*denken*⟩

**elk** /elk/ n., pl. ~**s** or same (a) (deer) Elch,
*der*
(b) (moose) Riesenelch, *der*

**ellipse** /ɪ'lɪps/ n. Ellipse, *die*

**elliptical** /ɪ'lɪptɪkl/ adj. elliptisch

**elm** /elm/ n. Ulme, *die*

**elocution** /elə'kjuːʃn/ n. (art) Sprechkunst,
*die*

**elongated** /'iːlɒŋgeɪtɪd/ adj. lang gestreckt

**elope** /ɪ'ləʊp/ v.i. durchbrennen (ugs.)

**eloquence** /'eləkwəns/ n. Beredtheit, *die*

**eloquent** /'eləkwənt/ adj. beredt ⟨*Person*⟩;
gewandt ⟨*Stil, Redner*⟩

**else** /els/ adv. (a) (besides) sonst [noch];
**somebody/something** ~: [noch] jemand
anders/noch etwas; **everybody/everything** ~:
alle anderen/alles andere; **who/what/when/
how** ~? wer/was/wann/wie sonst noch?;
**why** ~? warum sonst?
(b) (instead) ander...; **sb.'s hat** der Hut von
jmd. anders; **anybody/anything** ~?
[irgend]jemand anders/[irgend]etwas
anderes?; **somebody/something** ~: jemand
anders/etwas anderes; **everybody/everything**
~: alle anderen/alles andere
(c) (otherwise) sonst; **or** ~: oder aber; **do it or**
~ ...! tun Sie es, sonst ...!

**'elsewhere** adv. woanders

**elude** /ɪ'ljuːd/ v.t. (avoid) ausweichen
(+ *Dat.*); (escape from) entkommen (+ *Dat.*)

**elusive** /ɪ'ljuːsɪv/ adj. schwer zu erreichen
⟨*Person*⟩; schwer zu fassen ⟨*Straftäter*⟩;
schwer definierbar ⟨*Begriff, Sinn*⟩

**elves** pl. of ELF

**emaciated** /ɪ'meɪsɪeɪtɪd/ adj. abgezehrt

**e-mail** /'iːmeɪl/ [1] n. E-Mail, *die;* ~ **address**
E-Mail-Adresse, *die;* ~ **message** E-Mail, *die*
[2] v.t. per E-Mail übermitteln ⟨*Ergebnisse,
Datei usw.*⟩; ~ **sb.** jmdm. eine E-Mail
schicken

**emancipated** /ɪ'mænsɪpeɪtɪd/ adj.
emanzipiert: **become** ~: sich emanzipieren

**emancipation** /ɪmænsɪ'peɪʃn/ n.
Emanzipation, *die*

**embalm** /ɪm'bɑːm/ v.t. einbalsamieren

**embankment** /ɪm'bæŋkmənt/ n. Damm,
*der*

**embargo** /em'bɑːgəʊ/ n., pl. ~**es** Embargo,
*das;* **put** or **lay an** ~ **on sth.** etw. mit einem
Embargo belegen

e

**embark** /ɪmˈbɑːk/ *v.i.* **(a)** sich einschiffen (for nach)
**(b)** ~ [up]on sth. etw. in Angriff nehmen
**embarkation** /embɑːˈkeɪʃn/ *n.* Einschiffung, *die*
**embarrass** /ɪmˈbærəs/ *v.t.* in Verlegenheit bringen
**embarrassed** /ɪmˈbærəst/ *adj.* verlegen; feel ~: verlegen sein
**em'barrassing** *adj.* peinlich
**em'barrassment** *n.* Verlegenheit, *die*
**embassy** /ˈembəsɪ/ *n.* Botschaft, *die*
**embed** /ɪmˈbed/ *v.t.*, -dd-: **(a)** (fix) einlassen; ~ sth. in cement/concrete etw. einzementieren/einbetonieren; ~ded in the mud im Schlamm versunken; ~ded sentence (Ling.) eingeschobener Satz
**embellish** /emˈbelɪʃ/ *v.t.* beschönigen ⟨Wahrheit⟩; ausschmücken ⟨Geschichte, Bericht⟩
**embers** /ˈembəz/ *n. pl.* Glut, *die*
**embezzle** /ɪmˈbezl/ *v.t.* unterschlagen
**embitter** /ɪmˈbɪtə(r)/ *v.t.* verbittern
**emblem** /ˈembləm/ *n.* Emblem, *das*
**embody** /ɪmˈbɒdɪ/ *v.t.* verkörpern
**embrace** /ɪmˈbreɪs/ ⎡1⎤ *v.t.* umarmen; (fig.: accept, adopt) annehmen ⎡2⎤ *v.i.* sich umarmen ⎡3⎤ *n.* Umarmung, *die*
**embroider** /ɪmˈbrɔɪdə(r)/ *v.t.* sticken ⟨Muster⟩; besticken ⟨Tuch, Kleid⟩; (fig.) ausschmücken
**embroidery** /ɪmˈbrɔɪdərɪ/ *n.* Stickerei, *die*
**embroil** /ɪmˈbrɔɪl/ *v.t.* become/be ~ed in sth. in etw. (Akk.) verwickelt werden/sein
**embryo** /ˈembrɪəʊ/ *n.* Embryo, *der*
**embryonic** /embrɪˈɒnɪk/ *adj.* (Biol., fig.) Embryonal⟨entwicklung, -struktur, -zustand, -stadium⟩; unausgereift ⟨Vorstellung⟩
**emerald** /ˈemərəld/ ⎡1⎤ *n.* Smaragd, *der* ⎡2⎤ *adj.* smaragdgrün; the E~ Isle die Grüne Insel
**emerald 'green** *n.* Smaragdgrün, *das*
**emerge** /ɪˈmɜːdʒ/ *v.i.* auftauchen (from aus, from behind hinter + Dat.); ⟨Wahrheit:⟩ an den Tag kommen; it ~s that ...: es stellt sich heraus, dass ...
**emergency** /ɪˈmɜːdʒənsɪ/ ⎡1⎤ *n.* Notfall, *der;* in an *or* in case of ~: im Notfall; declare a state of ~: den Ausnahmezustand ausrufen ⎡2⎤ *adj.* Not-
**emergency:** ~ exit *n.* Notausgang, *der;* ~ services *n. pl.* Hilfsdienste *Pl.*
**'emery paper** *n.* Schmirgelpapier, *das*
**emetic** /ɪˈmetɪk/ (Med.) *n.* Emetikum, *das* (fachspr.); Brechmittel, *das*
**emigrant** /ˈemɪɡrənt/ *n.* Auswanderer, *der/* Auswanderin, *die*
**emigrate** /ˈemɪɡreɪt/ *v.i.* auswandern (to nach, from aus)

**emigration** /emɪˈɡreɪʃn/ *n.* Auswanderung, *die* (to nach, from aus)
**eminence** /ˈemɪnəns/ *n.* hohes Ansehen
**eminent** /ˈemɪnənt/ *adj.* bedeutend; herausragend
**emission** /ɪˈmɪʃn/ *n.* Emission, *die* (fachspr.); (process also) Abgabe, *die*
**emit** /ɪˈmɪt/ *v.t.*, -tt- abgeben, emittieren (fachspr.) ⟨Wärme, Strahlung usw.⟩; ausstoßen ⟨Rauch⟩
**emoticon** /ɪˈmɒtɪkɒn/ *n.* (Comp.) Emoticon, *das*
**emotion** /ɪˈməʊʃn/ *n.* Gefühl, *das*
**emotional** /ɪˈməʊʃənl/ *adj.* emotional; Gemüts⟨zustand, -störung⟩; gefühlvoll ⟨Stimme⟩
**e'motionally** *adv.* emotional; gefühlvoll ⟨sprechen⟩; ~ disturbed seelisch gestört
**emotive** /ɪˈməʊtɪv/ *adj.* emotional
**empathize** /ˈempəθaɪz/ *v.i.* ~ with sb. sich in jmdn. hineinversetzen; ~ with sth. etw. nachempfinden
**empathy** /ˈempəθɪ/ *n.* Empathie, *die* (Psych.); Einfühlung, *die*
**emperor** /ˈempərə(r)/ *n.* Kaiser, *der*
**emphasis** /ˈemfəsɪs/ *n., pl.* emphases /ˈemfəsiːz/ Betonung, *die;* lay *or* place *or* put ~ on sth. etw. betonen
**emphasize** /ˈemfəsaɪz/ *v.t.* betonen
**emphatic** /ɪmˈfætɪk/ *adj.* nachdrücklich; demonstrativ ⟨Ablehnung⟩; be ~ that ...: darauf bestehen, dass ...
**em'phatically** *adv.* nachdrücklich
**empire** /ˈempaɪə(r)/ *n.* Reich, *das*
**empirical** /ɪmˈpɪrɪkl/ *adj.* empirisch
**employ** /ɪmˈplɔɪ/ *v.t.* **(a)** (take on) einstellen; (have working for one) beschäftigen; be ~ed by a company bei einer Firma arbeiten **(b)** (use) einsetzen (for, in, on für); anwenden ⟨Methode, List⟩ (for, in, on bei)
**employee** (Amer.: **employe**) /emplɔɪˈiː, emˈplɔɪiː/ *n.* Angestellte, *der/die*
**employer** /ɪmˈplɔɪə(r)/ *n.* Arbeitgeber, *der/* -geberin, *die*
**employment** /ɪmˈplɔɪmənt/ *n.* **(a)** (work) Arbeit, *die* **(b)** (regular trade or profession) Beschäftigung, *die*
**employment:** ~ agency *n.* Stellenvermittlung, *die;* ~ office *n.* (Brit.) Arbeitsamt, *das*
**empower** /ɪmˈpaʊə(r)/ *v.t.* (authorize) ermächtigen; (enable) befähigen
**empress** /ˈemprɪs/ *n.* Kaiserin, *die*
**emptiness** /ˈemptɪnɪs/ *n.* Leere, *die*
**empty** /ˈemptɪ/ ⎡1⎤ *adj.* leer; frei ⟨Sitz, Parkplatz⟩ ⎡2⎤ *v.t.* leeren; (pour) schütten (over über + Akk.) ⎡3⎤ *v.i.* sich leeren
**'empty-handed** *adj.* mit leeren Händen

**EMS** *abbr.* = **European Monetary System** EWS

**emu** /ˈiːmjuː/ *n.* (Ornith.) Emu, *der*

**EMU** *abbr.* = **Economic and Monetary Union** WWU

**emulate** /ˈemjʊleɪt/ *v.t.* nacheifern (+ *Dat.*)

**emulsion** /ɪˈmʌlʃn/ *n.* **(a)** Emulsion, *die*
**(b)** ▶ EMULSION PAINT

**e'mulsion paint** *n.* Dispersionsfarbe, *die*

**enable** /ɪˈneɪbl/ *v.t.* ~ sb. to do sth. es jmdm. ermöglichen, etw. zu tun

**enamel** /ɪˈnæml/ ① *n.* Email, *das* ② *v.t.*, (Brit.) **-ll-** emaillieren

**enchant** /ɪnˈtʃɑːnt/ *v.t.* verzaubern; (delight) entzücken

**en'chanted** *adj.* verzaubert

**en'chanting** *adj.* entzückend

**en'chantment** *n.* Verzauberung, *die;* (fig.) Zauber, *der*

**encircle** /ɪnˈsɜːkl/ *v.t.* umgeben

**encl.** *abbr.* = **enclosed, enclosure[s]** Anl.

**enclave** /ˈenkleɪv/ *n.* Enklave, *die*

**enclose** /ɪnˈkləʊz/ *v.t.* **(a)** (surround) umgeben; (shut up or in) einschließen
**(b)** (with letter) beilegen (**with, in** *Dat.*); **please find** ~**d** anbei erhalten Sie

**enclosure** /ɪnˈkləʊʒə(r)/ *n.* **(a)** (in zoo) Gehege, *das*
**(b)** (with letter) Anlage, *die*

**encode** /ɪnˈkəʊd/ *v.t.* verschlüsseln; chiffrieren

**encore** /ˈɒŋkɔː(r)/ ① *int.* Zugabe! ② *n.* Zugabe, *die*

**encounter** /ɪnˈkaʊntə(r)/ ① *v.t.* (as adversary) treffen auf (+ *Akk.*); (by chance) begegnen (+ *Dat.*); stoßen auf (+ *Akk.*) ⟨*Problem, Widerstand usw.*⟩ ② *n.* (chance meeting) Begegnung, *die*

**encourage** /ɪnˈkʌrɪdʒ/ *v.t.* ermutigen; (promote) fördern

**encouragement** *n.* Ermutigung, *die* (**from** durch)

**encroach** /ɪnˈkrəʊtʃ/ *v.i.* ~ **on** eindringen in (+ *Akk.*); in Anspruch nehmen ⟨*Zeit*⟩

**encrypt** /enˈkrɪpt/ *v.t.* (Comp.) verschlüsseln ⟨*Daten etc.*⟩

**encumber** /ɪnˈkʌmbə(r)/ *v.t.* belasten

**encumbrance** /ɪnˈkʌmbrəns/ *n.* Belastung, *die*

**encyclopaedia** /ɪnsaɪkləˈpiːdɪə/ *n.* Lexikon, *das;* Enzyklopädie, *die*

**encyclopaedic** /ɪnsaɪkləˈpiːdɪk/ *adj.* enzyklopädisch

**end** /end/ ① *n.* **(a)** Ende, *das;* (of nose, hair, finger) Spitze, *die;* **from** ~ **to** ~: von einem Ende zum anderen; **at the** ~ **of** 1987/**March** Ende 1987/März; **in the** ~: schließlich; **come to an** ~: ein Ende nehmen; **be at an** ~: zu Ende sein
**(b)** (of box, packet, etc.) Schmalseite, *die;* (top/ bottom surface) Ober-/Unterseite, *die;* **on** ~:

hochkant; **make** ~**s meet** (fig.)
zurechtkommen; **no** ~ **of** (coll.) unendlich viel/viele
**(c)** (remnant) Rest, *der;* (of cigarette) Stummel, *der*
**(d)** (purpose, object) Ziel, *das;* ~ **in itself** Selbstzweck, *der*
② *v.t.* beenden
③ *v.i.* enden

■ **end 'up** *v.i.* enden; ~ **up in** (coll.) landen in (+ *Dat.*); ~ **up [as] a teacher** (coll.) schließlich Lehrer werden

**endanger** /ɪnˈdeɪndʒə(r)/ *v.t.* gefährden

**endear** /ɪnˈdɪə(r)/ *v.t.* ~ **sb./sth./oneself to sb.** jmdn./etw./sich bei jmdm. beliebt machen

**en'dearing** *adj.* reizend; gewinnend ⟨*Lächeln, Art*⟩

**endeavour** (Brit.; Amer.: **endeavor**) /ɪnˈdevə(r)/ ① *v.i.* ~ **to do sth.** sich bemühen, etw. zu tun ② *n.* Bemühung, *die;* (attempt) Versuch, *der*

**'ending** *n.* Schluss, *der;* (of word) Endung, *die*

**endive** /ˈendaɪv/ *n.* Endivie, *die*

**'endless** *adj.* endlos

**'endlessly** *adv.* unaufhörlich ⟨*streiten, schwatzen*⟩

**endorse** /ɪnˈdɔːs/ *v.t.* **(a)** indossieren ⟨*Scheck*⟩
**(b)** beipflichten (+ *Dat.*) ⟨*Meinung*⟩; billigen ⟨*Entscheidung, Handlung*⟩; unterstützen ⟨*Vorschlag*⟩
**(c)** (Brit. Law) einen Strafvermerk machen auf (+ *Akk. od. Dat.*)

**en'dorsement** *n.* **(a)** (of cheque) Indossament, *das*
**(b)** (support) Billigung, *die;* (of proposal) Unterstützung, *die*
**(c)** (Brit. Law) Strafvermerk, *der*

**endow** /ɪnˈdaʊ/ *v.t.* [über Stiftungen/ eine Stiftung] finanzieren; stiften ⟨*Preis, Lehrstuhl*⟩; **be** ~**ed with charm/a talent for music** Charme/musikalisches Talent besitzen

**en'dowment mortgage** *n.* ≈ Tilgungslebensversicherung, *die;*

**end:** ~ **'product** *n.* Endprodukt, *das;* ~ **re'sult** *n.* Ergebnis, *das;* (consequence) Folge, *die*

**endurable** /ɪnˈdjʊərəbl/ *adj.* erträglich

**endurance** /ɪnˈdjʊərəns/ *n.* Ausdauer, *die*

**en'durance test** *n.* Belastungsprobe, *die*

**endure** /ɪnˈdjʊə(r)/ *v.t.* ertragen

**enema** /ˈenəmə/ *n.* Einlauf, *der*

**enemy** /ˈenəmɪ/ ① *n.* Feind, *der* (**of, to** Gen.)
② *adj.* feindlich

**energetic** /enəˈdʒetɪk/ *adj.* energiegeladen; (active) tatkräftig

**energy** /ˈenədʒɪ/ *n.* Energie, *die*

**energy:** ~ **consumption** *n.* Energieverbrauch, *der;* ~ **crisis** *n.*    ···✦

Energiekrise, *die;* ~ **resources** *n. pl.*
Energieressourcen *Pl.;* ~**-saving** *adj.*
Energie sparend; ~**-saving lamp**
Energiesparlampe, *die*

**enforce** /ɪnˈfɔːs/ *v.t.* durchsetzen; sorgen
für ⟨Disziplin⟩; ~**d** erzwungen ⟨Schweigen⟩;
unfreiwillig ⟨Untätigkeit⟩

**ENG** *abbr.* = **electronic news-**
**gathering** elektronische
Berichterstattung; EB

**engage** /ɪnˈɡeɪdʒ/ **1** *v.t.* **(a)** (hire) einstellen
⟨Arbeiter⟩; engagieren ⟨Sänger⟩
**(b)** wecken ⟨Interesse⟩; auf sich (Akk.) ziehen
⟨Aufmerksamkeit⟩
**(c)** ~ **the clutch/first gear** einkuppeln/den
ersten Gang einlegen
**2** *v.i.* ~ **in sth.** sich an etw. (Dat.)
beteiligen; ~ **in politics** sich politisch
engagieren

**engaged** /ɪnˈɡeɪdʒd/ *adj.* **(a)** be ~ [to be
married] [to sb.] [mit jmdm.] verlobt sein; get
~ [to be married] [to sb.] sich [mit jmdm.]
verloben
**(b)** be ~ in sth./in doing sth. mit etw.
beschäftigt sein/damit beschäftigt sein, etw.
zu tun; be otherwise ~: etwas anderes
vorhaben
**(c)** besetzt ⟨Toilette, [Telefon]anschluss,
Nummer⟩; ~ signal *or* tone (Brit.)
Besetzzeichen, *das*

**en'gagement** *n.* **(a)** (to be married)
Verlobung, *die* (**to** mit)
**(b)** (appointment) Verabredung, *die*

**en'gagement ring** *n.* Verlobungsring,
*der*

**engaging** /ɪnˈɡeɪdʒɪŋ/ *adj.* bezaubernd;
einnehmend ⟨Persönlichkeit, Art⟩

**engine** /ˈendʒɪn/ *n.* **(a)** Motor, *der;* (rocket/jet
~) Triebwerk, *das*
**(b)** (locomotive) Lok[omotive], *die*

**'engine driver** *n.* Lok[omotiv]führer, *der*

**engineer** /endʒɪˈnɪə(r)/ **1** *n.* **(a)** Ingenieur,
*der*/Ingenieurin, *die;* (service ~, installation ~)
Techniker, *der*/Technikerin, *die*
**(b)** (Amer.: engine driver) Lok[omotiv]führer,
*der*
**2** *v.t.* arrangieren

**engi'neering** *n.* Technik, *die*

**England** /ˈɪŋɡlənd/ *pr. n.* England (das)

**English** /ˈɪŋɡlɪʃ/ **1** *adj.* englisch; he/she is
~: er ist Engländer/sie ist Engländerin
**2** *n.* **(a)** Englisch, *das;* say sth. in ~: etw.
auf Englisch sagen; I cannot *or* do not speak
~: ich spreche kein Englisch; translate into/
from [the] ~: ins Englische/aus dem
Englischen übersetzen
**(b)** *pl.* the ~: die Engländer *Pl.*

**English:** ~ **breakfast** *n.* englisches
Frühstück; ~ **'Channel** *pr. n.* the
~ Channel der [Ärmel]kanal; ~**man** /-mən/
*n., pl.* ~**men** /-mən/ Engländer, *der;*
~**woman** *n.* Engländerin, *die*

**engrave** /ɪnˈɡreɪv/ *v.t.* gravieren;
eingravieren ⟨Namen, Figur usw.⟩

**engraving** /ɪnˈɡreɪvɪŋ/ *n.* Stich, *der;* (from
wood) Holzschnitt, *der*

**engross** /ɪnˈɡrəʊs/ *v.t.* fesseln; be ~ed in
sth. in etw. (Akk.) vertieft sein; become *or*
get ~ed in sth. sich in etw. (Akk.) vertiefen

**engrossing** /ɪnˈɡrəʊsɪŋ/ *adj.* fesselnd

**engulf** /ɪnˈɡʌlf/ *v.t.* verschlingen

**enhance** /ɪnˈhɑːns/ *v.t.* erhöhen ⟨Wert,
Aussichten, Schönheit⟩; verstärken
⟨Wirkung⟩; heben ⟨Aussehen⟩

**enigma** /ɪˈnɪɡmə/ *n.* Rätsel, *das*

**enigmatic** /enɪɡˈmætɪk/ *adj.* rätselhaft

**enjoy** /ɪnˈdʒɔɪ/ **1** *v.t.* **(a)** I ~ed the book/
work das Buch/die Arbeit hat mir gefallen;
he ~s reading/travelling er liest/reist gern
**(b)** genießen ⟨Rechte, Privilegien, Vorteile⟩
**2** *v. refl.* sich amüsieren

**enjoyable** /ɪnˈdʒɔɪəbl/ *adj.* schön;
angenehm ⟨Empfindung, Arbeit⟩;
unterhaltsam ⟨Buch, Film, Stück⟩

**en'joyment** *n.* Vergnügen, *das* (**of** an
+ *Dat.*)

**enlarge** /ɪnˈlɑːdʒ/ **1** *v.t.* vergrößern;
verbreitern ⟨Straße, Durchgang⟩
**2** *v.i.* ~ [up]on sth. etw. weiter ausführen

**en'largement** *n.* Vergrößerung, *die;*
(making wider) Verbreiterung, *die*

**enlighten** /ɪnˈlaɪtn/ *v.t.* aufklären (on, as to
über + Akk.).

**en'lightenment** *n.* Aufklärung, *die*

**enlist** /ɪnˈlɪst/ **1** *v.t.* (obtain) gewinnen
**2** *v.i.* ~ [for the army/navy] in die Armee/
Marine eintreten; ~ [as a soldier] Soldat
werden

**enliven** /ɪnˈlaɪvn/ *v.t.* beleben

**enmity** /ˈenmɪtɪ/ *n.* Feindschaft, *die*

**enormous** /ɪˈnɔːməs/ *adj.* enorm; riesig,
gewaltig ⟨Figur, Tier, Menge⟩

**e'normously** *adv.* enorm

**enough** /ɪˈnʌf/ **1** *adj.* genug; there's
~ room es ist Platz genug
**2** *n.* genug; be ~ to do sth. genügen, etw.
zu tun; have had ~ [of sb./sth.] genug [von
jmdm./etw.] haben; I've had ~! jetzt reicht's
mir aber!
**3** *adv.* genug; oddly/funnily ~:
merkwürdigerweise/(ugs.) komischerweise

**enquire** /ɪnˈkwaɪə(r)/ **1** *v.i.* sich
erkundigen (about, after nach, of bei); ~ into
untersuchen
**2** *v.t.* sich erkundigen nach ⟨Weg, Namen⟩

**enquiring** /ɪnˈkwaɪərɪŋ/ *adj.* fragend;
forschend ⟨Geist⟩

**enquiry** /ɪnˈkwaɪərɪ/ *n.* **(a)** (question)
Erkundigung, *die* (into über + Akk.); make
enquiries Erkundigungen einziehen; ~ desk,
~ office Auskunft, *die*
**(b)** (investigation) Untersuchung, *die*

**enrage** /ɪnˈreɪdʒ/ *v.t.* wütend machen; be
~d by sth. über etw. (Akk.) wütend werden

**enrich** /ɪnˈrɪtʃ/ *v.t.* reich machen; (fig.)
bereichern

**enrol** (*Amer.*: **enroll**) /ɪnˈrəʊl/ ① *v.i.*, -ll-
sich einschreiben; ~ **for a course** sich zu
einem Kurs anmelden
② *v.t.* einschreiben

**en'rolment** (*Amer.*: **en'rollment**) *n.*
Einschreibung, *die*

**en route** /ɑ̃ ˈruːt/ *adv.* unterwegs; ~ **to
Scotland/for Edinburgh** auf dem Weg nach
Schottland/Edinburgh

**ensign** /ˈensaɪn, ˈensn/ *n.* Hoheitszeichen,
*das*

**enslave** /ɪnˈsleɪv/ *v.t.* versklaven

**ensue** /ɪnˈsjuː/ *v.i.* folgen (**from** aus); **the
discussion which** ~**d** die anschließende
Diskussion

**ensure** /ɪnˈʃʊə(r)/ *v.t.* ~ **that** ... (see to it
that) gewährleisten, dass ...; ~ **sth.** etw.
gewährleisten

**entail** /ɪnˈteɪl/ *v.t.* mit sich bringen; **sth.** ~**s
doing sth.** etw. bedeutet, dass man etw. tun
muss

**entangle** /ɪnˈtæŋgl/ *v.t.* sich verfangen
lassen; **get** *or* **become** ~**d in** *or* **with sth.**
sich in etw. (*Dat.*) verfangen

**enter** /ˈentə(r)/ ① *v.i.* (a) hineingehen;
⟨*Fahrzeug*:⟩ hineinfahren; (come in)
hereinkommen; (into room) eintreten
(b) (register as competitor) sich zur Teilnahme
anmelden (**for** an + *Dat.*)
② *v.t.* (a) [hinein]gehen in (+ *Akk.*);
⟨*Fahrzeug*:⟩ [hinein]fahren in (+ *Akk.*);
betreten ⟨*Gebäude, Zimmer*⟩; einlaufen in
(+ *Akk.*) ⟨*Hafen*⟩; einreisen in (+ *Akk.*)
⟨*Land*⟩; (come into) [herein]kommen in
(+ *Akk.*)
(b) teilnehmen an (+ *Dat.*) ⟨*Rennen,
Wettbewerb*⟩
(c) (in book etc.) eintragen (**in** in + *Akk.*)
(d) (Comp.) eingeben ⟨*Daten usw.*⟩; **press** ~:
'Enter' drücken
■ **'enter into** *v.t.* aufnehmen
⟨*Verhandlungen*⟩; eingehen ⟨*Verpflichtung*⟩;
schließen ⟨*Vertrag*⟩
■ **'enter [up]on** *v.t.* beginnen

**'enter key** *n.* (Comp.) Entertaste, *die;*
Eingabetaste, *die*

**enterprise** /ˈentəpraɪz/ *n.* (a) (undertaking)
Unternehmen, *das;* **free/private** ~: freies/
privates Unternehmertum
(b) (enterprising spirit) Unternehmungsgeist,
*der*

**enterprising** /ˈentəpraɪzɪŋ/ *adj.*
unternehmungslustig

**entertain** /entəˈteɪn/ *v.t.* (a) (amuse)
unterhalten
(b) (receive as guest) bewirten
(c) haben ⟨*Vorstellung*⟩; hegen (geh.) ⟨*Gefühl,
Verdacht, Zweifel*⟩; (consider) in Erwägung
ziehen

**enter'tainer** *n.* Unterhalter, *der/*
Unterhalterin, *die*

**enter'taining** *adj.* unterhaltsam

**enter'tainment** *n.* (a) (amusement)
Unterhaltung, *die*

(b) (performance, show) Veranstaltung, *die*

**enthral** (*Amer.*: **enthrall**) /ɪnˈθrɔːl/ *v.t.*,
-ll- gefangen nehmen (fig.)

**enthuse** /ɪnˈθjuːz/ ① *v.i.* in Begeisterung
ausbrechen (**about** über + *Akk.*)
② *v.t.* begeistern

**enthusiasm** /ɪnˈθjuːzɪæzm/ *n.*
Begeisterung, *die*

**enthusiast** /ɪnˈθjuːzɪæst/ *n.* Enthusiast,
*der;* (for sports) Fan, *der;* **a great DIY** ~: ein
begeisterter Heimwerker

**enthusiastic** /ɪnθjuːzɪˈæstɪk/ *adj.*
begeistert; **not be very** ~ **about doing sth.**
keine große Lust haben, etw. zu tun

**entice** /ɪnˈtaɪs/ *v.t.* locken (**into** in + *Akk.*);
~ **sb. into doing** *or* **to do sth.** jmdn. dazu
verleiten, etw. zu tun

**entire** /ɪnˈtaɪə(r)/ *adj.* (a) (whole) ganz
(b) (intact) vollständig

**en'tirely** *adv.* (a) (wholly) völlig
(b) (solely) ganz ⟨*für sich behalten*⟩; voll
⟨*verantwortlich sein*⟩; **it's up to you** ~: es
liegt ganz bei dir

**entirety** /ɪnˈtaɪərətɪ/ *n.* **in its** ~: in seiner/
ihrer Gesamtheit

**entitle** /ɪnˈtaɪtl/ *v.t.* berechtigen (**to** zu);
~ **sb. to do sth.** jmdn. das Recht geben, etw.
zu tun; **be** ~**d to** [**claim**] **sth.** Anspruch auf
etw. (*Akk.*) haben; **be** ~**d to do sth.** das
Recht haben, etw. zu tun

**entomologist** /entəˈmɒlədʒɪst/ *n.*
Entomologe, *der/*Entomologin, *die*

**entomology** /entəˈmɒlədʒɪ/ *n.*
Entomologie, *die;* Insektenkunde, *die*

**entourage** /ɒntʊˈrɑːʒ/ *n.* Gefolge, *das*

**entrails** /ˈentreɪlz/ *n. pl.* Eingeweide *Pl.*

**entrance¹** /ɪnˈtrɑːns/ *v.t.* hinreißen

**entrance²** /ˈentrəns/ *n.* (way in) Eingang,
*der* (**to** Gen. od. zu); (for vehicles) Einfahrt, *die*

**entrance** /ˈentrəns/**: ~ examination**
*n.* Aufnahmeprüfung, *die;* ~ **fee** *n.*
Eintrittsgeld, *das;* ~ **hall** *n.* Eingangshalle,
*die;* ~ **ticket** *n.* Eintrittskarte, *die*

**entrant** /ˈentrənt/ *n.* (for competition, race, etc.)
Teilnehmer, *der/*Teilnehmerin, *die* (**for** Gen.,
an + *Dat.*)

**entreat** /ɪnˈtriːt/ *v.t.* anflehen

**en'treaty** *n.* flehentliche Bitte

**entrepreneur** /ɒntrəprəˈnɜː(r)/ *n.*
Unternehmer, *der/*Unternehmerin, *die*

**entrepreneurial** /ɒntrəprəˈnɜːrɪəl/ *adj.*
unternehmerisch

**entrust** /ɪnˈtrʌst/ *v.t.* ~ **sb. with sth.** jmdm.
etw. anvertrauen; ~ **sth./sth. to sb./sth.**
jmdn./etw. jmdm./einer Sache anvertrauen;
~ **a task to sb.** jmdn. mit einer Aufgabe
betrauen

**entry** /ˈentrɪ/ *n.* (a) Eintritt, *der* (**into** in
+ *Akk.*); (into country) Einreise, *die;* '**no** ~' (for
people) „Zutritt verboten"; (for vehicles)
„Einfahrt verboten"
(b) (way in) Eingang, *der;* (for vehicle) Einfahrt,
*die*                                        ···⟫

**(c)** (registration, item) Eintragung, *die* (**in, into** in + *Akk. od. Dat.*); (in dictionary, encyclopaedia) Eintrag, *der*

**entry:** ~ **fee** *n.* Eintrittsgeld, *das;* ~ **form** *n.* Anmeldeformular, *das;* ~ **visa** *n.* Einreisevisum, *das*

**envelop** /ɪnˈveləp/ *v.t.* [ein]hüllen (**in** in + *Akk.*); **be** ~**ed in flames** ganz von Flammen umgeben sein

**envelope** /ˈenvələʊp, ˈɒnvələʊp/ *n.* [Brief]umschlag, *der*

**enviable** /ˈenvɪəbl/ *adj.* beneidenswert

**envious** /ˈenvɪəs/ *adj.* neidisch (**of** auf + *Akk.*)

**environment** /ɪnˈvaɪərənmənt/ *n.* Umwelt, *die;* (surrounding objects, region) Umgebung, *die*

**environmental** /ɪnvaɪərənˈmentl/ *adj.* Umwelt⟨*verschmutzung, -schutz, -katastrophe*⟩; **for** ~ **reasons** aus Gründen des Umweltschutzes; ~ **group** Umweltschutzorganisation, *die;* ~ **protection** Umweltschutz, *der*

**environmental 'health** *n.* Umwelthygiene, *die;* ~ **health officer** Umwelthygienebeauftragte, *der/die;* ~ **health department** Umwelthygieneamt, *das*

**environ'mentalist** *n.* Umweltschützer, *der/*-schützerin, *die*

**environ'mentally** *adv.* ~ **friendly** umweltfreundlich; ~ **sensitive** ökologisch sensibel; ~ **sound** umweltverträglich; umweltgerecht

**envisage** /ɪnˈvɪzɪdʒ/, **envision** /ɪnˈvɪʒn/ *v.t.* sich (*Dat.*) vorstellen

**envoy** /ˈenvɔɪ/ *n.* Gesandte, *der/*Gesandtin, *die*

**envy** /ˈenvɪ/ **1** *n.* Neid, *der;* **you'll be the** ~ **of all your friends** alle deine Freunde werden dich beneiden

**2** *v.t.* beneiden; ~ **sb. sth.** jmdn. um etw. beneiden

**enzyme** /ˈenzaɪm/ *n.* Enzym, *das*

**ephemeral** /ɪˈfemərl/ *adj.* kurzlebig

**epic** /ˈepɪk/ **1** *adj.* episch
**2** *n.* Epos, *das*

**epidemic** /epɪˈdemɪk/ **1** *adj.* epidemisch
**2** *n.* Epidemie, *die*

**epilepsy** /ˈepɪlepsɪ/ *n.* Epilepsie, *die*

**epileptic** /epɪˈleptɪk/ **1** *adj.* epileptisch; ~ **fit** epileptischer Anfall
**2** *n.* Epileptiker, *der/*Epileptikerin, *die*

**Epiphany** /ɪˈpɪfənɪ/ *n.* [**Feast of the**] ~: Epiphanias, *das;* Dreikönigsfest, *das;* **at** ~: am Dreikönigstag

**episode** /ˈepɪsəʊd/ *n.* **(a)** Episode, *die*
**(b)** (of serial) Folge, *die*

**epistle** /ɪˈpɪsl/ *n.* Epistel, *die*

**epitaph** /ˈepɪtɑːf/ *n.* Grab[in]schrift, *die*

**epithet** /ˈepɪθet/ *n.* Beiname, *der;* (as term of abuse) Schimpfname, *der*

**epitome** /ɪˈpɪtəmɪ/ *n.* Inbegriff, *der*

**epitomize** /ɪˈpɪtəmaɪz/ *v.t.* ~ **sth.** der Inbegriff einer Sache (*Gen.*) sein

**epoch** /ˈiːpɒk/ *n.* Epoche, *die*

**'epoch-making** *adj.* Epoche machend

**equal** /ˈiːkwl/ **1** *adj.* **(a)** gleich; ~ **in** *or* **of** ~ **height/size/importance** *etc.* gleich hoch/ groß/wichtig *usw.*
**(b) be** ~ **to sth./sb.** (strong, clever, etc. enough) einer Sache/jmdm. gewachsen sein
**2** *n.* Gleichgestellte, *der/die;* **have no** ~: nicht seines-/ihresgleichen haben
**3** *v.t.,* (Brit.) **-ll-:** ~ **sb.** es jmdm. gleichtun; **three times four** ~**s twelve** drei mal vier ist [gleich] zwölf

**equality** /ɪˈkwɒlɪtɪ/ *n.* Gleichheit, *die;* (equal rights) Gleichberechtigung, *die;* ~ **between the sexes** Gleichheit von Mann und Frau

**equalize** /ˈiːkwəlaɪz/ *v.i.* (Sport) den Ausgleich[streffer] erzielen

**'equalizer** *n.* (Sport) Ausgleich[streffer], *der*

**'equally** *adv.* gleich; (just as) ebenso; **in gleiche Teile** ⟨*aufteilen*⟩; gleichmäßig ⟨*verteilen*⟩

**Equal Oppor'tunities Commission** *n.* (Brit.) Ausschuss für Chancengleichheit; ≈ Gleichstellungsausschuss, *der*

**equal oppor'tunity** *n.* Chancengleichheit, *die*

**'equals sign** *n.* (Math.) Gleichheitszeichen, *das*

**equanimity** /ekwəˈnɪmɪtɪ/ *n.* Gelassenheit, *die*

**equate** /ɪˈkweɪt/ *v.t.* gleichsetzen (**with** mit)

**equation** /ɪˈkweɪʒn/ *n.* (Math.) Gleichung, *die*

**equator** /ɪˈkweɪtə(r)/ *n.* Äquator, *der*

**equilibrium** /iːkwɪˈlɪbrɪəm/ *n., pl.* **equilibria** /iːkwɪˈlɪbrɪə/ *or* ~**s** Gleichgewicht, *das*

**equinox** /ˈekwɪnɒks/ *n.* Tagundnachtgleiche, *die*

**equip** /ɪˈkwɪp/ *v.t.,* **-pp-** ausrüsten ⟨*Fahrzeug, Armee*⟩; ausstatten ⟨*Küche*⟩; **fully** ~**ped** komplett ausgerüstet/ausgestattet; ~ **sb./oneself** [**with sth.**] jmdn./sich [mit etw.] ausrüsten

**e'quipment** *n.* Ausrüstung, *die;* (of kitchen, laboratory) Ausstattung, *die;* (needed for activity) Geräte *Pl.*

**equity** /ˈekwɪtɪ/ *n.* **(a)** (fairness) Gerechtigkeit, *die;* **with** ~: gerecht
**(b)** *in pl.* (stocks and shares without fixed interest) [Stamm]aktien *Pl.*
**(c)** (value of shares) Eigenkapital, *das*
**(d)** (net value of mortgaged property) Wert eines Besitzes nach Abzug der Belastungen

**'equity market** *n.* (Commerc.) Aktienmarkt, *der*

**equivalent** /ɪˈkwɪvələnt/ **1** *adj.* gleichwertig; **be** ~ **to sth.** einer Sache (*Dat.*) entsprechen
**2** *n.* **(a)** (thing, person) Pendant, *das;* Gegenstück, *das* (**of** zu)

**(b) be the** ~ **of sth.** (have same result) einer Sache (*Dat.*) entsprechen

**equivocal** /ɪ'kwɪvəkl/ *adj.* zweideutig

**er** /ɜː(r)/ *int.* äh

**era** /'ɪərə/ *n.* Ära, *die*

**eradicate** /ɪ'rædɪkeɪt/ *v.t.* ausrotten

**erase** /ɪ'reɪz/ *v.t.* auslöschen; (with rubber, knife) ausradieren; (from tape, also Comp.) löschen

**e'raser** *n.* [pencil] ~: Radiergummi, *der*

**erect** /ɪ'rekt/ [1] *adj.* aufrecht
[2] *v.t.* errichten; aufstellen ⟨*Standbild, Mast, Verkehrsschild, Gerüst, Zelt*⟩

**erection** /ɪ'rekʃn/ *n.* (a) ▶ ERECT 2: Errichtung, *die;* Aufstellen, *das*
**(b)** (Physiol.) Erektion, *die*

**ergonomic** /ɜːgə'nɒmɪk/ *adj.*,
**ergo'nomically** *adv.* ergonomisch

**ermine** /'ɜːmɪn/ *n.* Hermelin, *der*

**erode** /ɪ'rəʊd/ *v.t.* (a) ⟨*Säure, Rost:*⟩ angreifen; ⟨*Wasser:*⟩ auswaschen; ⟨*Wind:*⟩ verwittern lassen
**(b)** (fig.) unterminieren

**erosion** /ɪ'rəʊʒn/ *n.* (a) ▶ ERODE A: Angreifen, *das;* Auswaschung, *die;* Verwitterung, *die*
**(b)** (fig.) Unterminierung, *die*

**erotic** /ɪ'rɒtɪk/ *adj.* erotisch

**err** /ɜː(r)/ *v.i.* sich irren

**errand** /'erənd/ *n.* Botengang, *der;* (shopping) Besorgung, *die;* **go on** *or* **run an** ~: einen Botengang/eine Besorgung machen

**'errand boy** *n.* Laufbursche, *der*

**erratic** /ɪ'rætɪk/ *adj.* unregelmäßig; sprunghaft ⟨*Wesen, Person, Art*⟩; launenhaft ⟨*Verhalten*⟩

**erroneous** /ɪ'rəʊnɪəs/ *adj.* falsch; irrig ⟨*Schlussfolgerung, Annahme*⟩

**error** /'erə(r)/ *n.* (mistake) Fehler, *der;* (wrong opinion) Irrtum, *der;* **in** ~: irrtümlich[erweise]

**'error message** *n.* (Comp.) Fehlermeldung, *die*

**erudite** /'eruːdaɪt/ *adj.* gelehrt

**erupt** /ɪ'rʌpt/ *v.i.* ausbrechen

**eruption** /ɪ'rʌpʃn/ *n.* Ausbruch, *der*

**escalate** /'eskəleɪt/ *v.i.* [1] sich ausweiten (**into** zu); ⟨*Preise, Kosten:*⟩ [ständig] steigen
[2] *v.t.* ausweiten (**into** zu)

**escalator** /'eskəleɪtə(r)/ *n.* Rolltreppe, *die*

**escapade** /eskə'peɪd/ *n.* Eskapade, *die* (geh.)

**escape** /ɪ'skeɪp/ [1] *n.* Flucht, *die* (**from** aus); **have a narrow** ~: gerade noch einmal davonkommen
[2] *v.i.* (a) fliehen (**from** aus); (successfully) entkommen (**from** *Dat.*)
**(b)** ⟨*Gas:*⟩ ausströmen; ⟨*Flüssigkeit:*⟩ auslaufen
[3] *v.t.* (a) entkommen (+ *Dat.*) ⟨*Verfolger,*

*Feind*⟩; entgehen (+ *Dat.*) ⟨*Bestrafung, Gefangennahme, Tod*⟩; verschont bleiben von ⟨*Zerstörung, Auswirkungen*⟩
**(b)** (not be remembered by) entfallen sein (+ *Dat.*)

**escape:** ~ **artist** ▶ ESCAPOLOGIST;
~ **attempt,** ~ **bid** *ns.* Fluchtversuch, *der;* (from prison) Ausbruchsversuch, *der;*
~ **hatch** *n.* Notausstieg, *der;* (fig.) Rettungsanker, *der;* ~ **key** *n.* (Comp.) Escapetaste, *die;* ~ **road** *n.* Auslaufstrecke, *die;* ~ **route** *n.* Fluchtweg, *der*

**escapism** /ɪ'skeɪpɪzm/ *n.* Realitätsflucht, *die*

**escapologist** /eskə'pɒlədʒɪst/ *n.* (Brit.) Entfesselungskünstler, *der*/-künstlerin, *die*

**escarpment** /ɪ'skɑːpmənt/ *n.* (Geog.) Steilhang, *der*

**escort** [1] /'eskɔːt/ *n.* (a) Begleitung, *die;* (Mil.) Eskorte, *die*
**(b)** (hired companion) Begleiter, *der*/ Begleiterin, *die*
[2] /ɪ'skɔːt/ *v.t.* begleiten; (lead) führen; (Mil.) eskortieren

**Eskimo** /'eskɪməʊ/ [1] *adj.* Eskimo-
[2] *n., pl.* ~**s** *or* **same** Eskimo, *der*/ Eskimofrau, *die;* **the** ~[**s**] die Eskimos

**esoteric** /esəʊ'terɪk/ *adj.* esoterisch

**especial** /ɪ'speʃl/ *attrib. adj.* [ganz] besonder...

**especially** /ɪ'speʃəlɪ/ *adv.* besonders

**espionage** /'espɪənɑːʒ/ *n.* Spionage, *die*

**esplanade** /esplə'neɪd, esplə'nɑːd/ *n.* Esplanade, *die* (geh.)

**espouse** /ɪ'spaʊz/ *v.t.* eintreten für

**espresso** /e'spresəʊ/ *n., pl.* ~**s** (coffee) Espresso, *der*

**e'spresso bar** *n.* Espressobar, *die*

**Esq.** /ɪ'skwaɪə(r)/ *abbr.* = **Esquire** ≈ Hr.; (on letter) ≈ Hrn.; **Jim Smith,** ~: Hr./Hrn. Jim Smith

**essay** /'eseɪ/ *n.* Essay, *der;* Aufsatz, *der* (bes. Schulw.)

**essence** /'esəns/ *n.* (a) Wesen, *das;* (gist) Wesentliche, *das;* **in** ~: im Wesentlichen
**(b)** (Cookery) Essenz, *die*

**essential** /ɪ'senʃl/ [1] *adj.* (a) (fundamental) wesentlich
**(b)** (indispensable) unentbehrlich; lebensnotwendig ⟨*Versorgungseinrichtungen, Güter*⟩; unabdingbar ⟨*Qualifikation, Voraussetzung*⟩; **it is** ~ **that ...:** es ist unbedingt notwendig, dass ...
[2] *n. pl.* **the** ~**s** (fundamentals) das Wesentliche; (items) das Notwendigste

**es'sentially** *adv.* im Grunde

**establish** /ɪ'stæblɪʃ/ *v.t.* (a) schaffen ⟨*Einrichtung, Präzedenzfall*⟩; gründen ⟨*Organisation, Institut*⟩; errichten ⟨*Geschäft, System*⟩
**(b)** (secure acceptance for) etablieren; **become** ~**ed** sich einbürgern
**(c)** (prove) beweisen     ···⟩

**(d)** (discover) feststellen

**established** /ɪ'stæblɪʃt/ *adj.* bestehend ⟨*Ordnung*⟩; etabliert ⟨*Schriftsteller*⟩; (accepted) üblich; fest ⟨*Brauch*⟩; feststehend ⟨*Tatsache*⟩; **become ∼**: sich durchsetzen

**e'stablishment** *n.* **(a)** (setting up, foundation) Gründung, *die*
**(b)** [business] **∼**: Unternehmen, *das*

**estate** /ɪ'steɪt/ *n.* **(a)** (landed property) Gut, *das*
**(b)** (Brit.: housing **∼**) [Wohn]siedlung, *die*
**(c)** (of deceased person) Erbmasse, *die*

**estate: ∼ agent** *n.* (Brit.) Grundstücksmakler, *der/*-maklerin, *die;* **∼ car** *n.* (Brit.) Kombiwagen, *der;* **∼ duty** (Brit.)**, e'state tax** (Amer.) *ns.* Erbschaftssteuer, *die*

**esteem** /ɪ'stiːm/ ⟦1⟧ *n.* Wertschätzung, *die* (geh.) (for *Gen.,* für)
⟦2⟧ *v.t.* schätzen; **highly ∼ed** hoch geschätzt

**estimate** ⟦1⟧ /'estɪmət/ *n.* **(a)** Schätzung, *die;* **at a rough ∼**: grob geschätzt
**(b)** (Commerc.) Kostenvoranschlag, *der*
⟦2⟧ /'estɪmeɪt/ *v.t.* schätzen (**at** auf + *Akk.*)

**estimation** /estɪ'meɪʃn/ *n.* Schätzung, *die;* **in sb.'s ∼**: nach jmds. Schätzung

**Estonia** /e'stəʊnɪə/ *pr. n.* Estland (*das*)

**Estonian** /e'stəʊnɪən/ ⟦1⟧ *adj.* estländisch; estnisch; **sb. is ∼**: jmd. ist Este/Estin
⟦2⟧ *n.* **(a)** (language) Estnisch, *das;* Estländisch, *das; see also* ENGLISH 2A
**(b)** (person) Este, *der/*Estin, *die;* Estländer, *der/*Estländerin, *die*

**estuary** /'estjʊərɪ/ *n.* [Trichter]mündung, *die*

**ETA** *abbr.* = **estimated time of arrival** voraussichtliche Ankunftszeit

**etc.** *abbr.* = **et cetera** usw.

**etch** /etʃ/ *v.t.* ätzen (**on** auf + *Akk.*); (on metal also) ⟨*bes. Künstler:*⟩ radieren; (fig.) einprägen (**in, on** *Dat.*)

**'etching** *n.* (Art) Radierung, *die*

**eternal** /ɪ'tɜːnl/ *adj.,* **e'ternally** *adv.* ewig

**eternity** /ɪ'tɜːnɪtɪ/ *n.* Ewigkeit, *die*

**ether** /'iːθə(r)/ *n.* Äther, *der*

**ethereal** /ɪ'θɪərɪəl/ *adj.* ätherisch

**ethical** /'eθɪkl/ *adj.* ethisch

**ethics** /'eθɪks/ *n.* **(a)** Moral, *die;* (moral philosophy) Ethik, *die*
**(b)** *usu. constr. as pl.* (moral code) Ethik, *die* (geh.)

**Ethiopia** /iːθɪ'əʊpɪə/ *pr. n.* Äthiopien (*das*)

**Ethiopian** /iːθɪ'əʊpɪən/ ⟦1⟧ *adj.* äthiopisch; **sb. is ∼**: jmd. ist Äthiopier/Äthiopierin
⟦2⟧ *n.* Äthiopier, *der/*Äthiopierin, *die*

**ethnic** /'eθnɪk/ *adj.* ethnisch; **∼ minority** ethnische Minderheit

**ethnic 'cleansing** *n.* ethnische Säuberung

**ethnology** /eθ'nɒlədʒɪ/ *n.* Ethnologie, *die*

**ethos** /'iːθɒs/ *n.* (guiding beliefs) Gesinnung, *die;* (fundamental values) Ethos, *das* (geh.); (characteristic spirit) Geist, *der*

**etiquette** /'etɪket/ *n.* Etikette, *die*

**etymology** /etɪ'mɒlədʒɪ/ *n.* Etymologie, *die*

**EU** *abbr.* = **European Union** EU

**eulogy** /'juːlədʒɪ/ *n.* Lobrede, *die*

**euphemism** /'juːfəmɪzm/ *n.* Euphemismus, *der*

**euphemistic** /juːfə'mɪstɪk/ *adj.* verhüllend

**euphoria** /juː'fɔːrɪə/ *n.* Euphorie, *die* (geh.)

**euro** /'jʊərəʊ/ *n.* Euro, *der*

**Euro: ∼cheque** *n.* Euroscheck, *der;* **∼land** *n.* Euroland, *das;* **∼-MP** *n.* Europaabgeordnete, *der/die*

**Europe** /'jʊərəp/ *pr. n.* Europa (*das*)

**European** /jʊərə'piːən/ ⟦1⟧ *adj.* europäisch; **sb. is ∼**: jmd. ist Europäer/Europäerin; **∼ [Economic] Community** Europäische [Wirtschafts]gemeinschaft
⟦2⟧ *n.* Europäer, *der/*Europäerin, *die*

**European: ∼ Central 'Bank** *n.* Europäische Zentralbank; **∼ Com'mission** *n.* Europäische Kommission; **∼ 'Council** *n.* Europäischer Rat; **∼ Court of 'Justice** *n.* Europäischer Gerichtshof; **∼ 'Cup** *n.* (Footb.) Europacup, *der;* Europapokal, *der;* **∼ 'currency unit** *n.* Europäische Währungseinheit; **∼ 'Monetary System** *n.* Europäisches Währungssystem; **∼ Monetary 'Union** *n.* Europäische Währungsunion; **∼ 'Parliament** *n.* Europäisches Parlament; **∼ 'Union** *n.* Europäische Union

**Euro-: ∼rebel** *n.* (esp. Brit.) [innerparteilicher] Europagegner/ [innerparteiliche] Europagegnerin; **∼sceptic** *n.* Euroskeptiker, *der/*-skeptikerin, *die;* **∼star** ® *n.* Eurostar, *der;* **go by ∼star** mit dem Eurostar fahren

**euthanasia** /juːθə'neɪzɪə/ *n.* Euthanasie, *die*

**evacuate** /ɪ'vækjʊeɪt/ *v.t.* evakuieren (**from** aus)

**evacuation** /ɪvækjʊ'eɪʃn/ *n.* Evakuierung, *die* (**from** aus)

**evade** /ɪ'veɪd/ *v.t.* ausweichen (+ *Dat.*) ⟨*Angriff, Angreifer, Schlag, Problem, Frage*⟩; sich entziehen (+ *Dat.*) ⟨*Verhaftung, Verantwortung*⟩; entkommen (+ *Dat.*) ⟨*Verfolger, Verfolgung*⟩; hinterziehen ⟨*Steuern*⟩; **∼ doing sth.** vermeiden, etw. zu tun

**evaluate** /ɪ'væljʊeɪt/ *v.t.* einschätzen; bewerten ⟨*Daten*⟩

**evangelical** /iːvæn'dʒelɪkl/ *adj.* missionarisch (fig.); (Protestant) evangelikal

**evangelist** /ɪ'vændʒəlɪst/ *n.* Evangelist, *der*

**evaporate** /ɪ'væpəreɪt/ ⟦1⟧ *v.i.* verdunsten
⟦2⟧ *v.t.* verdunsten lassen

**evaporated 'milk** *n.* Kondensmilch, *die*

**evaporation** /ɪˌvæpə'reɪʃn/ n.
Verdunstung, *die*

**evasion** /ɪ'veɪʒn/ n. Umgehung, *die;* (of responsibility, question) Ausweichen, *das* (of vor + *Dat.*); **tax** ~: Steuerhinterziehung, *die*

**evasive** /ɪ'veɪsɪv/ *adj.* **(a)** be/become ~: ausweichen
**(b)** ausweichend ⟨*Antwort*⟩

**eve** /iːv/ n. Vorabend, *der* (of *Gen.*); (day) Vortag, *der* (of *Gen.*)

**even** /'iːvn/ ① *adj.* **(a)** eben ⟨*Boden, Fläche*⟩; gleich hoch ⟨*Stapel, Stuhl-, Tischbein*⟩; **be of** ~ **height/length** gleich hoch/lang sein
**(b)** gerade ⟨*Zahl, Seite, Hausnummer*⟩
**(c)** be *or* get ~ **with sb.** (quits) es jmdm. heimzahlen; **break** ~: die Kosten decken
② *adv.* sogar; selbst; sogar noch ⟨*weniger, schlimmer usw.*⟩; ~ **if** selbst wenn; ~ **so** [aber] trotzdem; **not** *or* **never** ~ …: [noch] nicht einmal …
∎ **even 'up** *v.t.* ausgleichen

**evening** /'iːvnɪŋ/ n. Abend, *der;* **this/ tomorrow** ~: heute/morgen Abend; **in the** ~: am Abend; (regularly) abends

**evening:** ~ **class** n. Abendkurs, *der;* ~ **dress** n. Abendkleidung, *die;* ~ **'meal** n. Abendessen, *das;* ~ **'paper** n. Abendzeitung, *die*

**'evenly** *adv.* gleichmäßig

**'even-numbered** *adj.* gerade

**event** /ɪ'vent/ n. **(a)** **in the** ~ **of his dying** *or* **death im** Falle seines Todes; **in the** ~: letzten Endes; **in the** ~ **of rain** bei Regenwetter
**(b)** (occurrence) Ereignis, *das*
**(c)** ( planned public or social occasion) Veranstaltung, *die*

**e'ventful** *adj.* ereignisreich

**eventual** /ɪ'ventjuəl/ *adj.* predict sb.'s ~ **downfall** vorhersagen, dass jmd. schließlich zu Fall kommen wird; **the career of Napoleon and his** ~ **defeat** der Aufstieg Napoleons und schließlich seine Niederlage

**eventuality** /ɪventjʊ'ælɪtɪ/ n. Eventualität, *die*

**e'ventually** *adv.* schließlich

**ever** /'evə(r)/ *adv.* **(a)** (always) immer; **for** ~: für immer; ewig ⟨*lieben, da sein, leben*⟩; ~ **since** [then] seit [dieser Zeit]
**(b)** (at any time) je[mals]; **hardly** ~: so gut wie nie; **as** ~: wie gewöhnlich
**(c)** *in comb. with compar. adj. or adv.* noch; ~**-increasing** ständig zunehmend
**(d)** **what** ~ **does he want?** was will er nur?; **why** ~ **not?** warum denn nicht?

**'ever:** ~**green** ① *adj.* immergrün; ② n. immergrüne Pflanze; ~**lasting** *adj.* **(a)** (eternal) immer während; ewig ⟨*Leben*⟩; unvergänglich ⟨*Ruhm, Ehre*⟩; **(b)** (incessant) endlos

**every** /'evrɪ/ *adj.* **(a)** jeder/jede/jedes; ~ **one** jeder/jede/jedes [einzelne]; **your** ~ **wish** all[e] deine Wünsche; **she comes**

~ **day** sie kommt jeden Tag; ~ **three/few days** alle drei/paar Tage; ~ **other** (~ second, almost ~) jeder/jede/jedes zweite
**(b)** (the greatest possible) all ⟨*Respekt, Aussicht*⟩

**every:** ~**body** n. & pron. jeder; ~**body else** alle anderen; ~**day** *attrib. adj.* alltäglich; Alltags⟨*kleidung, -sprache*⟩; **in** ~**day life** im Alltag; ~**one** ▶ ~BODY; ~**place** (Amer.) ▶ ~WHERE; ~**thing** n. & pron. alles; ~**where** *adv.* überall; ~**where you go/look** wohin man auch geht/sieht

**evict** /ɪ'vɪkt/ *v.t.* ~ **sb.** [from his home] jmdn. zur Räumung [seiner Wohnung] zwingen

**eviction** /ɪ'vɪkʃn/ n. Zwangsräumung, *die;* **the** ~ **of the tenant** die zwangsweise Vertreibung des Mieters

**evidence** /'evɪdəns/ n. **(a)** Beweis, *der;* (indication) Anzeichen, *das;* **be** ~ **of sth.** etw. beweisen
**(b)** (Law) Beweismaterial, *das;* **give** ~: aussagen

**evident** /'evɪdənt/ *adj.* offensichtlich; **be** ~ **to sb.** jmdm. klar sein; **it soon became** ~ **that** …: es stellte sich bald heraus, dass …

**'evidently** *adv.* offensichtlich

**evil** /'iːvl, 'iːvɪl/ ① *adj.* böse; schlecht ⟨*Charakter, Einfluss, System*⟩
② n. **(a)** Böse, *das*
**(b)** (bad thing) Übel, *das*

**evocative** /ɪ'vɒkətɪv/ *adj.* be ~ **of sth.** etw. heraufbeschwören

**evoke** /ɪ'vəʊk/ *v.t.* heraufbeschwören; hervorrufen ⟨*Bewunderung, Überraschung*⟩; erregen ⟨*Interesse*⟩

**evolution** /iːvə'luːʃn/ n. Entwicklung, *die;* (Biol.) Evolution, *die*

**evolve** /ɪ'vɒlv/ ① *v.i.* sich entwickeln (from aus, into zu)
② *v.t.* entwickeln

**ewe** /juː/ n. Mutterschaf, *das*

**ex¹** /eks/ n. (coll.) Verflossene, *der/die* (ugs.)

**ex²** *prep.* (Commerc.) ex works/store ⟨*Güter*⟩ ab Werk/Lager

**ex-** *pref.* Ex-⟨*Freundin, Präsident, Champion*⟩; Alt⟨[bundes]kanzler⟩

**exacerbate** /ek'sæsəbeɪt/ *v.t.* verschärfen ⟨*Lage*⟩; verschlechtern ⟨*Zustand*⟩

**exact** /ɪg'zækt/ ① *adj.* genau
② *v.t.* fordern; erheben ⟨*Gebühr*⟩

**exacting** /ɪg'zæktɪŋ/ n. anspruchsvoll; hoch ⟨*Anforderung*⟩

**exactitude** /ɪg'zæktɪtjuːd/ Genauigkeit, *die*

**exactly** /ɪg'zæktlɪ/ *adv.* genau; **not** ~ (coll. iron.) nicht gerade

**exactness** /ɪg'zæktnɪs/ n. Genauigkeit, *die*

**exaggerate** /ɪg'zædʒəreɪt/ *v.t.* übertreiben

**exaggeration** /ɪgzædʒə'reɪʃn/ n. Übertreibung, *die*

**exam** /ɪg'zæm/ (coll.) ▶ EXAMINATION B

**examination** /ɪgzæmɪˈneɪʃn/ n. **(a)** (inspection; Med.) Untersuchung, die **(b)** (Sch. etc.) Prüfung, die; (final ∼ at university) Examen, das

**exami'nation paper** n. **(a)** ∼[s] schriftliche Prüfungsaufgaben Pl. **(b)** (with candidate's answers) ≈ Klausurarbeit, die

**examine** /ɪgˈzæmɪn/ v.t. **(a)** (inspect; Med.) untersuchen (for auf + Akk.); prüfen ⟨Dokument, Gewissen⟩; kontrollieren ⟨Ausweis, Gepäck⟩ **(b)** (Sch. etc.) prüfen (in in + Dat.) **(c)** (Law) verhören

**examiner** /ɪgˈzæmɪnə(r)/ n. Prüfer, der/ Prüferin, die

**example** /ɪgˈzɑːmpl/ n. Beispiel, das; for ∼: zum Beispiel; **make an ∼ of sb.** ein Exempel an jmdm. statuieren

**exasperate** /ɪgˈzæspəreɪt/ v.t. (irritate) verärgern; (infuriate) zur Verzweiflung bringen

**exasperation** /ɪgˈzæspəreɪʃn/ n. ▶ EXASPERATE: Ärger, der/Verzweiflung, die (with über + Akk.); **in ∼:** verärgert/ verzweifelt

**excavate** /ˈekskəveɪt/ v.t. **(a)** ausschachten; (with machine) ausbaggern **(b)** (Archaeol.) ausgraben

**excavation** /ekskəˈveɪʃn/ n. **(a)** Ausschachtung, die; (with machine) Ausbaggerung, die **(b)** (Archaeol.) Ausgrabung, die

**excavator** /ˈekskəveɪtə(r)/ n. Bagger, der

**exceed** /ɪkˈsiːd/ v.t. **(a)** (be greater than) übertreffen (in an + Dat.); ⟨Kosten, Summe, Anzahl⟩ übersteigen (by um) **(b)** (go beyond) überschreiten; hinausgehen über (+ Akk.) ⟨Auftrag, Befehl⟩

**ex'ceedingly** adv. äußerst; ausgesprochen ⟨hässlich, dumm⟩

**excel** /ɪkˈsel/ ① v.t., **-ll-** übertreffen; ∼ **oneself** (lit. or iron.) sich selbst übertreffen ② v.i., **-ll-** sich hervortun (at, in in + Dat.)

**excellence** /ˈeksələns/ n. hervorragende Qualität

**excellent** /ˈeksələnt/ adj. hervorragend

**except** /ɪkˈsept/ ① prep. ∼ **[for]** außer (+ Dat.); ∼ **for** (in all respects other than) abgesehen von ② v.t. ausnehmen (from bei); ∼**ed** ausgenommen

**ex'cepting** prep. außer (+ Dat.)

**exception** /ɪkˈsepʃn/ n. Ausnahme, die; **take ∼ to** Anstoß nehmen an (+ Dat.)

**exceptional** /ɪkˈsepʃənl/ adj. außergewöhnlich

**ex'ceptionally** adv. **(a)** (as an exception) ausnahmsweise **(b)** (remarkably) ungewöhnlich

**excerpt** /ˈeksɜːpt/ n. Auszug, der (from aus)

**excess** /ɪkˈses/ n. **(a)** Übermaß, das (of an + Dat.); **eat/drink to ∼:** übermäßig essen/ trinken

**(b)** esp. in pl. (over-indulgence) Exzess, der **(c)** **be in ∼ of sth.** etw. übersteigen **(d)** (surplus) Überschuss, der

**excess** /ˈekses/**:** ∼ **'baggage** n. Mehrgepäck, das; ∼ **'fare** n. Mehrpreis, der; **pay the ∼ fare** nachlösen

**excessive** /ɪkˈsesɪv/ adj. übermäßig; übertrieben ⟨Forderung, Lob, Ansprüche⟩; unmäßig ⟨Esser, Trinker⟩

**ex'cessively** adv. übertrieben; unmäßig ⟨essen, trinken⟩

**excess:** ∼ **'luggage** ▶∼ BAGGAGE; ∼ **'postage** n. Nachgebühr, die

**exchange** /ɪksˈtʃeɪndʒ/ ① v.t. **(a)** tauschen ⟨Plätze, Ringe, Küsse⟩; umtauschen ⟨Geld⟩; wechseln ⟨Blicke, Worte⟩; ∼ **insults** sich beleidigen **(b)** (give in place of another) eintauschen (for für, gegen); umtauschen ⟨[gekaufte] Ware⟩ (for gegen) ② n. **(a)** Tausch, der; **in ∼:** dafür; **in ∼ for** sth. für etw. **(b)** (Educ.) Austausch, der; **an ∼ student** ein Austauschstudent/eine Austauschstudentin **(c)** (of money) Umtausch, der; ∼ **rate, rate of** ∼: Wechselkurs, der **(d)** (Teleph.) Fernmeldeamt, das

**exchequer** /ɪksˈtʃekə(r)/ n. (Brit.) Schatzamt, das

**excise** /ˈeksaɪz/ n. Verbrauchsteuer, die; **Customs and E∼** (Brit.) Amt für Zölle und Verbrauchsteuer

**excitable** /ekˈsaɪtəbl/ adj. leicht erregbar

**excite** /ɪkˈsaɪt/ v.t. **(a)** (thrill) begeistern **(b)** (agitate) aufregen

**ex'cited** adj. aufgeregt (at über + Akk.); **get ∼:** sich aufregen

**ex'citement** n. Aufregung, die; (enthusiasm) Begeisterung, die

**exciting** /ɪkˈsaɪtɪŋ/ adj. aufregend; (full of suspense) spannend

**exclaim** /ɪkˈskleɪm/ ① v.t. ausrufen ② v.i. aufschreien

**exclamation** /ekskləˈmeɪʃn/ n. Ausruf, der

**excla'mation mark,** (Amer.) **excla'mation point** ns. Ausrufezeichen, das

**exclude** /ɪkˈskluːd/ v.t. ausschließen

**excluding** /ɪkˈskluːdɪŋ/ prep. ∼ **drinks/VAT** Getränke ausgenommen/ohne Mehrwertsteuer

**exclusion** /ɪkˈskluːʒn/ n. Ausschluss, der

**exclusive** /ɪkˈskluːsɪv/ adj. **(a)** alleinig ⟨Besitzer, Kontrolle⟩; Allein⟨eigentum⟩; (Journ.) Exklusiv⟨bericht, -interview⟩ **(b)** (select) exklusiv **(c)** ∼ **of** ohne

**ex'clusively** adv. ausschließlich

**excommunicate** /ekskəˈmjuːnɪkeɪt/ v.t. exkommunizieren

**excrement** /ˈekskrɪmənt/ n. Kot, der (geh.)

**excrete** /ɪkˈskriːt/ v.t. ausscheiden

**excruciating** /ɪk'skruː'ʃɪeɪtɪŋ/ adj.
unerträglich

**excursion** /ɪk'skɜːʃn/ n. Ausflug, der

**excusable** /ɪk'skjuːzəbl/ adj.
entschuldbar; verzeihlich

**excuse** [1] /ɪk'skjuːz/ v.t. (a)
entschuldigen; ~ oneself sich
entschuldigen; ~ me Entschuldigung
(b) (release, exempt) befreien (from von)
[2] /ɪk'skjuːs/ n. Entschuldigung, die

**ex-di'rectory** adj. (Brit. Teleph.)
Geheim⟨nummer, -anschluss⟩; be ~: nicht
im Telefonbuch stehen

**execute** /'eksɪkjuːt/ v.t. (a) hinrichten
(b) (put into effect) ausführen

**execution** /eksɪ'kjuːʃn/ n. (a)
Hinrichtung, die
(b) (putting into effect) Ausführung, die

**exe'cutioner** n. Scharfrichter, der

**executive** /ɪg'zekjʊtɪv/ [1] n. leitender
Angestellter/leitende Angestellte
[2] adj. leitend ⟨Stellung, Funktion⟩

**executive:** ~ 'stress n. Managerstress,
der; ~ 'toy n. Managerspielzeug, das

**executor** /ɪg'zekjʊtə(r)/ n. (Law)
Testamentsvollstrecker, der

**exemplary** /ɪg'zemplərɪ/ adj. (a) (model)
vorbildlich
(b) (deterrent) exemplarisch

**exemplify** /ɪg'zemplɪfaɪ/ v.t.
veranschaulichen

**exempt** /ɪg'zempt/ [1] adj. [be] ~ [from
sth.] [von etw.] befreit [sein]
[2] v.t. befreien

**exemption** /ɪg'zempʃn/ n. Befreiung, die

**exercise** /'eksəsaɪz/ [1] n. (a) Übung, die
(b) no pl. (physical exertion) Bewegung, die;
take ~: sich (Dat.) Bewegung schaffen
[2] v.t. ausüben ⟨Recht, Macht, Einfluss⟩;
walten lassen ⟨Vorsicht⟩
[3] v.i. sich (Dat.) Bewegung schaffen

**exercise:** ~ **bicycle,** (coll.) ~ **bike** ns.
Heimtrainer, der; ~ **book** n. [Schul]heft,
das

**exert** /ɪg'zɜːt/ [1] v.t. aufbieten ⟨Kraft⟩;
ausüben ⟨Einfluss, Druck⟩
[2] v. refl. sich anstrengen

**exertion** /ɪg'zɜːʃn/ n. (a) (of strength, force)
Aufwendung, die; (of influence, pressure)
Ausübung, die
(b) (effort) Anstrengung, die

**exhale** /eks'heɪl/ v.t. & i. ausatmen

**exhaust** /ɪg'zɔːst/ [1] v.t. erschöpfen;
erschöpfend behandeln ⟨Thema⟩
[2] n. (Motor Veh.) Auspuff, der; (gases)
Auspuffgase Pl.; ~ **emissions** Auspuffabgase
Pl.; ~ **emissions test** Abgasuntersuchung,
die

**ex'hausted** adj. erschöpft

**ex'hausting** adj. anstrengend

**exhaustion** /ɪg'zɔːstʃn/ n. Erschöpfung,
die

**exhaustive** /ɪg'zɔːstɪv/ adj. umfassend

**ex'haust pipe** n. Auspuffrohr, das

**exhibit** /ɪg'zɪbɪt/ [1] v.t. ausstellen; zeigen
⟨Mut, Symptome, Angst usw.⟩
[2] n. Ausstellungsstück, das

**exhibition** /eksɪ'bɪʃn/ n. Ausstellung, die;
make an ~ of oneself sich unmöglich
aufführen

**exhibitionism** /eksɪ'bɪʃənɪzm/ n.
Exhibitionismus, der

**exhibitionist** /eksɪ'bɪʃənɪst/ n.
Exhibitionist, der/Exhibitionistin, die

**exhibitor** /ɪg'zɪbɪtə(r)/ n. Aussteller, der/
Ausstellerin, die

**exhilarated** /ɪg'zɪləreɪtɪd/ adj. belebt

**exhilarating** /ɪg'zɪləreɪtɪŋ/ adj. belebend

**exhilaration** /ɪgzɪlə'reɪʃn/ n. [feeling of]
~: Hochgefühl, das

**exhort** /ɪg'zɔːt/ v.t. ermahnen

**exile** /'eksaɪl/ [1] n. (a) Exil, das; in/into ~:
im/ins Exil
(b) (person) Verbannte, der/die
[2] v.t. verbannen

**exist** /ɪg'zɪst/ v.i. existieren; ⟨Zweifel,
Gefahr, Problem, Einrichtung:⟩ bestehen;
~ on sth. von etw. leben

**existence** /ɪg'zɪstəns/ n. Existenz, die;
(mode of living) Dasein, das; be in/come into
~: existieren/entstehen

**exit** /'eksɪt/ n. (way out) Ausgang, der (from
aus); (for vehicle) Ausfahrt, die

**exit:** ~ **permit** n. Ausreiseerlaubnis, die;
~ **poll** n.: Befragung der ein Wahllokal
verlassenden Wähler; ~ **visa** n.
Ausreisevisum, das

**exonerate** /ɪg'zɒnəreɪt/ v.t. entlasten

**exorbitant** /ɪg'zɔːbɪtənt/ adj. [maßlos]
überhöht

**exorcize** /'eksɔːsaɪz/ v.t. austreiben

**exotic** /ɪg'zɒtɪk/ adj. exotisch

**expand** /ɪk'spænd/ [1] v.i. (a) sich
ausdehnen; (Commerc.) expandieren
(b) ~ on weiter ausführen
[2] v.t. ausdehnen; (Commerc.) erweitern

**expanse** /ɪk'spæns/ n. [weite] Fläche

**expansion** /ɪk'spænʃn/ n. Ausdehnung,
die; (Commerc.) Expansion, die

**expect** /ɪk'spekt/ v.t. (a) erwarten; ~ to do
sth. damit rechnen, etw. zu tun; ~ sb. to do
sth. damit rechnen, dass jmd. etw. tut;
(require) von jmdm. erwarten, dass er etw. tut
(b) (coll.: think, suppose) glauben; I ~ so ich
glaube schon

**expectancy** /ɪk'spektənsɪ/ n. Erwartung,
die

**expectant** /ɪk'spektənt/ adj.
erwartungsvoll; ~ **mother** werdende Mutter

**ex'pectantly** adv. erwartungsvoll;
gespannt ⟨warten⟩

**expectation** /ekspek'teɪʃn/ n. Erwartung,
die

**expedient** /ɪk'spiːdɪənt/ [1] adj.
angebracht ⋯later

2 *n.* Mittel, *das*

**expedition** /ekspɪ'dɪʃn/ *n.* Expedition, *die*

**expel** /ɪk'spel/ *v.t.*, **-ll-** ausweisen (**from** aus); ∼ **sb. from school** jmdn. von der Schule verweisen

**expend** /ɪk'spend/ *v.t.* (a) aufwenden ([up]on für)
(b) (use up) aufbrauchen ([up]on für)

**expendable** /ɪk'spendəbl/ *adj.* entbehrlich; **be** ∼: geopfert werden können

**expenditure** /ɪk'spendɪtʃə(r)/ *n.* (a) (amount spent) Ausgaben *Pl.* (**on** für)
(b) (spending) Ausgabe, *die*

**expense** /ɪk'spens/ *n.* (a) Kosten *Pl.;* **at sb.'s** ∼: auf jmds. Kosten (*Akk.*); **at one's own** ∼: auf eigene Kosten
(b) *usu. in pl.* (Commerc. etc.: amount spent [and repaid]) Spesen *Pl.*
(c) (fig.) [**be**] **at the** ∼ **of sth.** auf Kosten von etw. [gehen]

**ex'pense account** *n.* Spesenabrechnung, *die;* **put sth. on one's** ∼: etw. als Spesen abrechnen

**expensive** /ɪk'spensɪv/ *adj.*, **ex'pensively** *adv.* teuer

**experience** /ɪk'spɪərɪəns/ 1 *n.* Erfahrung, *die;* (incident) Erlebnis, *das*
2 *v.t.* erleben; haben ⟨*Schwierigkeiten*⟩; verspüren ⟨*Kälte, Schmerz, Gefühl*⟩

**ex'perienced** *adj.* erfahren

**experiment** 1 /ɪk'sperɪmənt/ *n.* (a) Experiment, *das,* Versuch, *der* (**on** an + *Dat.*)
(b) (fig.) Experiment, *das*
2 /ɪk'sperɪment/ *v.i.* Versuche anstellen (**on** an + *Dat.*)

**experimental** /ɪksperɪ'mentl/ *adj.* experimentell; Experimentier⟨*theater, -kino*⟩

**expert** /'ekspɜːt/ 1 *adj.* ausgezeichnet; **be** ∼ **in** *or* **at sth.** Fachmann *od.* Experte für etw. sein; **be** ∼ **in** *or* **at doing sth.** etw. ausgezeichnet können
2 *n.* Fachmann, *der;* Experte, *der*/Expertin, *die;* **be an** ∼ **in** *or* **at/on sth.** Fachmann *od.* Experte in etw. (*Dat.*)/für etw. sein

**expertise** /ekspɜː'tiːz/ *n.* Fachkenntnisse *Pl.;* (skill) Können, *das*

**expert:** ∼ **system** *n.* (Comp.) Expertensystem, *das;* ∼ **'witness** *n.* sachverständiger Zeuge

**expire** /ɪk'spaɪə(r)/ *v.i.* ablaufen

**expiry** /ɪk'spaɪərɪ/ *n.* Ablauf, *der*

**explain** /ɪk'spleɪn/ 1 *v.t., also abs.* erklären
2 *v. refl., often abs.* **please** ∼ [**yourself**] bitte erklären Sie mir das
∎ **explain a'way** *v.t.* eine [plausible] Erklärung finden für

**explanation** /eksplə'neɪʃn/ *n.* Erklärung, *die;* **need** ∼: einer Erklärung bedürfen

**explanatory** /ɪk'splænətərɪ/ *adj.* erklärend; erläuternd ⟨*Bemerkung*⟩

**explicable** /ɪk'splɪkəbl/ *adj.* erklärbar

**explicit** /ɪk'splɪsɪt/ *adj.* klar; ausdrücklich ⟨*Zustimmung, Erwähnung*⟩

**ex'plicitly** *adv.* ausdrücklich; deutlich ⟨*beschreiben, ausdrücken*⟩

**explode** /ɪk'spləʊd/ 1 *v.i.* explodieren
2 *v.t.* zur Explosion bringen

**exploit** 1 /'eksplɔɪt/ *n.* Heldentat, *die*
2 /ɪk'splɔɪt/ *v.t.* ausbeuten ⟨*Arbeiter usw.*⟩; ausnutzen ⟨*Gutmütigkeit, Freund, Unwissenheit*⟩

**exploitation** /eksplɔɪ'teɪʃn/ *n.* ▶ EXPLOIT 2: Ausbeutung, *die;* Ausnutzung, *die*

**exploration** /eksplə'reɪʃn/ *n.* Erforschung, *die;* (fig.) Untersuchung, *die*

**exploratory** /ɪk'splɒrətərɪ/ *adj.* Forschungs-

**explore** /ɪk'splɔː(r)/ *v.t.* erforschen; (fig.) untersuchen

**ex'plorer** *n.* Entdeckungsreisende, *der*/*die*

**explosion** /ɪk'spləʊʒn/ *n.* Explosion, *die*

**explosive** /ɪk'spləʊzɪv/ 1 *adj.* explosiv
2 *n.* Sprengstoff, *der*

**export** 1 /ɪk'spɔːt, 'ekspɔːt/ *v.t.* exportieren; ausführen
2 /'ekspɔːt/ *n.* Export, *der*

**export** /'ekspɔːt/: ∼ **drive** *n.* Exportkampagne, *die;* ∼ **duty** *n.* Exportzoll, *der*

**ex'porter** *n.* Exporteur, *der*

**export** /'ekspɔːt/: ∼ **licence** *n.* Ausfuhrlizenz, *die;* ∼ **market** *n.* Exportmarkt, *der;* ∼ **permit** *n.* Exporterlaubnis, *die;* Ausfuhrerlaubnis, *die*

**expose** /ɪk'spəʊz/ *v.t.* (a) (uncover) freilegen; entblößen ⟨*Haut, Körper*⟩
(b) offenbaren ⟨*Schwäche*⟩; aufdecken ⟨*Missstände, Verbrechen*⟩; entlarven ⟨*Täter, Spion*⟩
(c) (subject) ∼ **to sth.** einer Sache (*Dat.*) aussetzen
(d) (Photog.) belichten

**exposed** /ɪk'spəʊzd/ *adj.* (unprotected) ungeschützt; ∼ **position** exponierte Stellung

**exposure** /ɪk'spəʊʒə(r)/ *n.* (a) (to cold etc.) die of/suffer from ∼: an Unterkühlung (*Dat.*) sterben/leiden
(b) (Photog.) (exposing time) Belichtung, *die;* (picture) Aufnahme, *die*

**ex'posure meter** *n.* Belichtungsmesser, *der*

**expound** /ɪk'spaʊnd/ *v.t.* darlegen

**express** /ɪk'spres/ 1 *v.t.* ausdrücken; äußern ⟨*Meinung, Wunsch, Dank, Bedauern*⟩; ∼ **oneself** sich ausdrücken
2 *attrib. adj.* (a) Eil⟨*brief, -bote usw.*⟩; Schnell⟨*paket, -sendung*⟩
(b) ausdrücklich ⟨*Wunsch, Absicht*⟩
3 *adv.* als Eilsache ⟨*senden*⟩
4 *n.* (train) Schnellzug, *der*

**express de'livery** *n.* Eilzustellung, *die*

**expression** /ɪk'spreʃn/ *n.* Ausdruck, *der*

**expressive** /ɪk'spresɪv/ *adj.* ausdrucksvoll

**express:** ∼ **'letter** n. Eilbrief, der; ∼ **'lift** n. Schnellaufzug, der

**ex'pressly** adv. ausdrücklich

**express:** ∼ **'train** n. D-Zug, der; ∼**way** n. (Amer.) Schnellstraße, die

**expulsion** /ɪkˈspʌlʃn/ n. Ausweisung, die (from aus); (from school) Verweisung, die (from von)

**exquisite** /ˈekskwɪzɪt, ɪkˈskwɪzɪt/ adj. erlesen

**ex'quisitely** adv. vorzüglich; kunstvoll ⟨verziert, geschnitzt⟩

**extend** /ɪkˈstend/ ① v.t. verlängern; ausstrecken ⟨Arm, Bein, Hand⟩; ausziehen ⟨Leiter, Teleskop⟩; verlängern lassen ⟨Leihbuch, Visum⟩; ausdehnen ⟨Einfluss, Macht⟩; vergrößern ⟨Haus, Geschäft, Fabrik⟩; gewähren ⟨[Gast]freundschaft, Hilfe, Kredit⟩ (to Dat.); ∼ the time limit den Termin hinausschieben
② v.i. sich erstrecken; the season ∼s from November to March die Saison geht von November bis März

**extended 'family** n. Großfamilie, die

**extension** /ɪkˈstenʃn/ n. (a) Verlängerung, die
(b) (part of house) Anbau, der
(c) (telephone) Nebenanschluss, der; (number) Apparat, der

**extension:** ∼ **cord** (Amer.) ▶ ∼ LEAD; ∼ **ladder** n. Ausziehleiter, die; ∼ **lead** n. (Brit.) Verlängerungsschnur, die

**extensive** /ɪkˈstensɪv/ adj. ausgedehnt; umfangreich ⟨Reparatur, Wissen, Nachforschungen⟩; beträchtlich ⟨Schäden⟩; weit reichend ⟨Änderungen⟩

**ex'tensively** adv. beträchtlich ⟨ändern, beschädigen⟩; ausführlich ⟨berichten, schreiben⟩

**extent** /ɪkˈstent/ n. Ausdehnung, die; (scope) Umfang, der; (of damage) Ausmaß, das; to what ∼? inwieweit?

**exterior** /ɪkˈstɪərɪə(r)/ ① adj. äußer...; Außen⟨fläche, -wand⟩
② n. Äußere, das; (of house) Außenwände Pl.

**exterminate** /ɪkˈstɜːmɪneɪt/ v.t. ausrotten ⟨Nation, Volk⟩; vertilgen ⟨Ungeziefer⟩; liquidieren ⟨Person⟩

**extermination** /ɪkstɜːmɪˈneɪʃn/ n. Ausrottung, die; (of pests) Vertilgung, die

**extermi'nation camp** n. Vernichtungslager, das

**external** /ɪkˈstɜːnl/ adj. äußer...; Außen⟨fläche, -abmessungen⟩; purely ∼: rein äußerlich; for ∼ use only nur äußerlich anzuwenden

**extinct** /ɪkˈstɪŋkt/ adj. erloschen ⟨Vulkan⟩; ausgestorben ⟨Art, Rasse, Gattung⟩

**extinction** /ɪkˈstɪŋkʃn/ n. Aussterben, das

**extinguish** /ɪkˈstɪŋgwɪʃ/ v.t. löschen

**ex'tinguisher** n. Feuerlöscher, der

**extol** /ɪkˈstɒl/ v.t., -ll- rühmen; preisen

**extort** /ɪkˈstɔːt/ v.t. erpressen (out of von)

**extortion** /ɪkˈstɔːʃn/ n. Erpressung, die

**extortionate** /ɪkˈstɔːʃənət/ adj. Wucher⟨preis, -zinsen usw.⟩; maßlos überzogen ⟨Forderung⟩

**extra** /ˈekstrə/ ① adj. zusätzlich; Mehr⟨arbeit, -kosten, -ausgaben⟩; Sonder⟨bus, -zug⟩
② adv. (a) (more than usually) besonders; extra ⟨lang, stark, fein⟩
(b) (additionally) extra; packing and postage ∼: zuzüglich Verpackung und Porto
③ n. (a) (added to services, salary, etc.) zusätzliche Leistung; (on car etc.) Extra, das
(b) (in play, film, etc.) Statist, der/Statistin, die

**extract** ① /ˈekstrækt/ n. (a) Extrakt, der (fachspr. auch: das)
(b) (from book, music, etc.) Auszug, der
② /ɪkˈstrækt/ v.t. ziehen ⟨Zahn⟩; herausziehen ⟨Dorn, Splitter usw.⟩

**extraction** /ɪkˈstrækʃn/ n. (of tooth) Extraktion, die; (of thorn, splinter, etc.) Herausziehen, das

**ex'tractor fan** n. Entlüfter, der

**extra-curricular** /ekstrəkəˈrɪkjʊlə(r)/ adj. extracurricular (fachspr.); ⟨Aktivität⟩ außerhalb des Lehrplans

**extradite** /ˈekstrədaɪt/ v.t. ausliefern

**extradition** /ekstrəˈdɪʃn/ n. Auslieferung, die

**extra'marital** adj. außerehelich

**extraordinary** /ɪkˈstrɔːdɪnərɪ/ adj. außergewöhnlich; merkwürdig ⟨Benehmen⟩; how ∼! wie seltsam!

**extravagance** /ɪkˈstrævəgəns/ n. (a) Extravaganz, die
(b) (extravagant thing) Luxus, der

**extravagant** /ɪkˈstrævəgənt/ adj. verschwenderisch; aufwendig ⟨Lebensstil⟩; teuer ⟨Geschmack⟩

**extreme** /ɪkˈstriːm/ ① adj. (a) äußerst... ⟨Spitze, Rand, Ende⟩; extrem ⟨Gegensätze, Hitze, Kälte⟩; höchst... ⟨Gefahr⟩; äußerst... ⟨Notfall, Höflichkeit, Bescheidenheit⟩; stärkst... ⟨Schmerzen⟩; größt... ⟨Wichtigkeit⟩; at the ∼ edge/left ganz am Rand/ganz links
(b) (not moderate) extrem; drastisch ⟨Maßnahme⟩
② n. Extrem, das; go to ∼s vor nichts zurückschrecken; go from one ∼ to the other von einem Extrem ins andere fallen

**ex'tremely** adv. äußerst

**extremist** /ɪkˈstriːmɪst/ n. Extremist, der/Extremistin, die; attrib. extremistisch

**extremity** /ɪkˈstremɪtɪ/ n. äußerstes Ende

**extricate** /ˈekstrɪkeɪt/ v.t. ∼ sth. from sth. etw. aus etw. herausziehen; ∼ oneself/sb. from sth. sich/jmdn. aus etw. befreien

**extrovert** /ˈekstrəvɜːt/ ① n. extravertierter Mensch; be an ∼: extravertiert sein
② adj. extravertiert

**exuberant** /ɪgˈzjuːbərənt/ adj. be ∼: sich überschwänglich freuen

**exude** /ɪgˈzjuːd/ *v.t.* absondern; (fig.) ausstrahlen

**exult** /ɪgˈzʌlt/ *v.i.* jubeln (**in, at, over** über + *Akk.*)

**eye** /aɪ/ ① *n.* (a) Auge, *das;* **keep an ∼ on sb./sth.** auf jmdn./etw. aufpassen; **see ∼ to ∼:** einer Meinung sein; **with one's ∼s shut** (fig.) blind; (easily) im Schlaf; **be up to one's ∼s in work/debt** bis über beide Ohren in Arbeit/Schulden stecken (ugs.)
(b) (of needle) Öhr, *das;* (metal loop) Öse, *die* ② *v.t.,* beäugen; **∼ sb. up and down** jmdn. von oben bis unten mustern

**eye: ∼ball** *n.* Augapfel, *der;* **∼brow** *n.* Augenbraue, *die;* **∼-catching** *adj.* ins Auge springend *od.* fallend ‹*Inserat, Plakat,* *Buchhülle usw.*›; **be** [**very**] **∼-catching** ein [wirkungsvoller] Blickfang sein; **∼ drops** *n. pl.* (Med.) Augentropfen *Pl.;* **∼ hospital** *n.* Augenklinik, *die;* **∼lash** *n.* Augenwimper, *die;* **∼ level** *n.* Augenhöhe, *die;* **∼-level** *attrib.* in Augenhöhe *nachgestellt;* **at ∼ level** in Augenhöhe; **∼lid** *n.* Augenlid, *das;* **∼ make-up** *n.* Augen-Make-up, *das;* **∼shadow** *n.* Lidschatten, *der;* **∼sight** *n.* Sehkraft, *die;* **have good ∼sight** gute Augen haben; **his ∼sight is poor** er hat schlechte Augen; **∼sore** *n.* Schandfleck, *der;* **∼wash** *n.* (a) (Med.: lotion) Augenwasser, *das;* (b) (coll.) (nonsense) Gewäsch, *das* (ugs.); (concealment) Augen[aus]wischerei, *die* (ugs.); **∼witness** *n.* Augenzeuge, *der*/-zeugin, *die*

# Ff

**F, f** /ef/ *n.* F, f, *das*

**fable** /ˈfeɪbl/ *n.* Fabel, *die;* (myth, lie) Märchen, *das*

**fabric** /ˈfæbrɪk/ *n.* Gewebe, *das*

**fabricate** /ˈfæbrɪkeɪt/ *v.t.* (invent) erfinden

**fabrication** /fæbrɪkeɪʃn/ *n.* Erfindung, *die*

**'fabric softener** /ˈsɒfənə(r)/ *n.* Weichspülmittel, *das;* Weichspüler, *der*

**fabulous** /ˈfæbjʊləs/ *adj.* (a) sagenhaft
(b) (coll.: marvellous) fabelhaft (ugs.)

**façade** /fəˈsɑːd/ *n.* (lit. or fig.) Fassade, *die;* **that's just a ∼** (fig.) das ist alles nur Fassade

**face** /feɪs/ ① *n.* (a) Gesicht, *das;* **lie ∼ down**[**ward**] ‹*Person/Buch:*› auf dem Bauch/Gesicht liegen; **make** *or* **pull a ∼/∼s** Grimassen schneiden; **on the ∼ of it** dem Anschein nach; **in the ∼ of sth.** trotz etw. (*Gen.*)
(b) (of mountain, cliff) Wand, *die;* (of clock, watch) Zifferblatt, *das;* (of dice) Seite, *die;* (of coin, playing card) Vorderseite, *die*
② *v.t.* (a) sich wenden zu; [**stand**] **facing one another** sich (*Dat.*) gegenüber[stehen]
(b) (fig.) ins Auge sehen (+ *Dat.*) ‹*Tod, Vorstellung*›; stehen vor (+ *Dat.*) ‹*Ruin, Entscheidung*›; **the facts** den Tatsachen ins Gesicht sehen; **be ∼d with sth.** sich einer Sache (*Dat.*) gegenübersehen
(c) (coll.: bear) verkraften
③ *v.i.* (in train etc.) **∼ backwards/forwards** ‹*Person:*› entgegen der/in Fahrtrichtung sitzen
▪ **face 'up to** *v.t.* ins Auge sehen (+ *Dat.*); sich abfinden mit ‹*Möglichkeit*›

**face: ∼ cream** *n.* Gesichtscreme, *die;* **∼ flannel** *n.* (Brit.) Waschlappen, *der;* **∼less** /ˈfeɪslɪs/ *adj.* (anonymous) anonym (fig.); **∼lift** *n.* (a) Facelifting, *das;* **have** *or* **get a ∼lift** sich liften lassen; (b) (fig.) Verschönerung, *die;* **∼ pack** *n.* [Gesichts]maske, *die;* **∼-saving** *adj.* zur Wahrung des Gesichts *nachgestellt*

**facet** /ˈfæsɪt/ *n.* Facette, *die;* (fig.) Aspekt, *der*

**facetious** /fəˈsiːʃəs/ *adj.* [gewollt] witzig

**face: ∼-to-∼** *adj.* persönlich ‹*Gespräch, Treffen*›; **∼ value** *n.* Nennwert, *der;* **accept sth. at** [**its**] **∼ value** (fig.) etw. für bare Münze nehmen

**facial** /ˈfeɪʃl/ *adj.* Gesichts-

**facile** /ˈfæsaɪl/ *adj.* nichts sagend

**facilities** /fəˈsɪlɪtɪz/ *n. pl.* Einrichtungen *Pl.;* **cooking/washing ∼:** Koch-/ Waschgelegenheit, *die;* **sports ∼:** Sportanlagen *Pl.;* **shopping ∼:** Einkaufsmöglichkeiten *Pl.*

**facsimile** /fækˈsɪmɪlɪ/ *n.* (a) Faksimile, *das* (b) ▶ FAX 1

**fact** /fækt/ *n.* Tatsache, *die;* **∼s and figures** Fakten und Zahlen; **the ∼ remains that …:** Tatsache bleibt: …; **the true ∼s of the case** *or* **matter** der wahre Sachverhalt; **know for a ∼ that …:** genau wissen, dass …; **in ∼:** tatsächlich

**faction** /ˈfækʃn/ *n.* Splittergruppe, *die*

**factor** /ˈfæktə(r)/ *n.* Faktor, *der*

**factory** /ˈfæktərɪ/ *n.* Fabrik, *die*

**factory: ∼ 'farm** *n.* [voll]automatisierter landwirtschaftlicher Betrieb; **∼ 'farming** *n.* [fabrikmäßige] Massentierhaltung; **the ∼ farming of salmon** die massenweise Lachsproduktion; **∼ worker** *n.* Fabrikarbeiter, *der*/-arbeiterin, *die*

**'fact sheet** *n.* Infoblatt, *das*

**factual** /ˈfæktjʊəl/ *adj.* sachlich

**faculty** /'fækəltɪ/ n. (a) Fähigkeit, die; mental ∼: geistige Kraft
(b) (Univ.) Fakultät, die

**fad** /fæd/ n. Marotte, die

**fade** /feɪd/ v.i. (a) ⟨Blätter, Blumen:⟩ [ver]welken
(b) ∼ [in colour] [ver]bleichen; the light ∼d es dunkelte
(c) ⟨Laut:⟩ verklingen
(d) (fig.) verblassen; ⟨Schönheit:⟩ verblühen; ⟨Hoffnung:⟩ schwinden
(e) (blend) übergehen (into in + Akk.).
■ **fade a'way** v.i. schwinden; ⟨Laut:⟩ verklingen (into in + Dat.)

**faded** /'feɪdɪd/ adj. welk ⟨Blume, Blatt, Laub⟩; verblichen ⟨Stoff, Farbe⟩

**faeces** /'fiːsiːz/ n. pl. Fäkalien Pl.

**fag** /fæg/ n. (a) (Brit. coll.) Schinderei, die (ugs.)
(b) (coll.: cigarette) Stäbchen, das (ugs.)

**fail** /feɪl/ [1] v.i. (a) scheitern; (in examination) nicht bestehen, (ugs.) durchfallen (in in + Dat.)
(b) (become weaker) ⟨Augenlicht, Gehör, Stärke:⟩ nachlassen
(c) (break down, stop) ⟨Versorgung:⟩ zusammenbrechen; ⟨Motor:⟩ aussetzen; ⟨Batterie, Pumpe:⟩ ausfallen; ⟨Bremse:⟩ versagen
[2] v.t. (a) ∼ to do sth. (not succeed in doing) etw. nicht tun [können]; ∼ to achieve one's purpose/aim seine Absicht/sein Ziel verfehlen
(b) (be unsuccessful in) nicht bestehen, (ugs.) durchfallen in (+ Dat.) ⟨Prüfung⟩
(c) (reject) durchfallen lassen (ugs.) ⟨Prüfling⟩
(d) ∼ to do sth. (not do) etw. nicht tun; (neglect to do) [es] versäumen, etw. zu tun; not ∼ to do sth. etw. tun
(e) words ∼ me mir fehlen die Worte; his courage ∼ed him ihn verließ der Mut
[3] n. without ∼: auf jeden Fall

**'failing** [1] n. Schwäche, die
[2] prep. ∼ that andernfalls

**failure** /'feɪljə(r)/ n. (a) (omission, neglect) Versäumnis, das
(b) (lack of success) Scheitern, das; end in ∼: scheitern
(c) (person or thing) Versager, der; our plan/attempt was a ∼: unser Plan/Versuch war fehlgeschlagen

**faint** /feɪnt/ [1] adj. (a) matt ⟨Licht, Farbe, Stimme, Lächeln⟩; schwach ⟨Geruch, Duft⟩; leise ⟨Flüstern, Geräusch, Stimme⟩; entfernt ⟨Ähnlichkeit⟩; undeutlich ⟨Umriss, Linie, Spur, Fotokopie⟩
(b) (giddy, weak) matt; she felt ∼: ihr war schwindelig
[2] v.i. ohnmächtig werden (from vor + Dat.)
[3] n. Ohnmacht, die

**faint-'hearted** adj. hasenherzig; zaghaft ⟨Versuch⟩

**'faintly** adv. schwach; entfernt ⟨sich ähneln⟩

**fair¹** /feə(r)/ n. (fun∼) Jahrmarkt, der; (exhibition) Messe, die; book/trade ∼: Buch-/Handelsmesse, die

**fair²** adj. (a) (just) gerecht; begründet ⟨Beschwerde, Annahme⟩; fair ⟨Spiel, Kampf, Prozess, Preis, Beurteilung, Handel⟩; ∼ play Fairness, die
(b) (not bad, pretty good) ganz gut ⟨Bilanz, Anzahl, Chance⟩; ziemlich ⟨Maß, Geschwindigkeit⟩
(c) (blond) blond ⟨Haar, Person⟩; (light) hell ⟨Haut⟩; (∼-skinned) hellhäutig ⟨Person⟩
(d) schön ⟨Wetter, Tag⟩

**fair:** ∼**ground** n. Festplatz, der; ∼**-haired** adj. blond; ∼**-haired boy** (Amer. fig.) Liebling, der; Favorit, der

**'fairly** adv. (a) fair ⟨kämpfen, spielen⟩; gerecht ⟨bestrafen, beurteilen, behandeln⟩
(b) (rather) ziemlich

**'fair-minded** adj. unvoreingenommen

**'fairness** n. Gerechtigkeit, die; in all ∼ [to sb.] um fair [gegen jmdn.] zu sein

**fairy** /'feərɪ/ n. Fee, die

**fairy:** ∼ **'godmother** n. gute Fee; ∼ **story,** ∼ **tale** ns. Märchen, das

**faith** /feɪθ/ n. (a) (reliance, trust) Vertrauen, das (in zu); have ∼ in oneself Selbstvertrauen haben; in good ∼: in gutem Glauben
(b) (religious belief) Glaube, der

**faithful** /'feɪθfl/ adj. (a) treu (to Dat.)
(b) (conscientious) pflichtbewusst; [ge]treu ⟨Diener⟩
(c) (accurate) [wahrheits]getreu; originalgetreu ⟨Wiedergabe, Kopie⟩

**'faithfully** adv. (a) treu ⟨dienen⟩; pflichtbewusst ⟨überbringen, zustellen⟩; hoch und heilig ⟨versprechen⟩
(b) (accurately) wahrheitsgetreu ⟨erzählen⟩; originalgetreu ⟨wiedergeben⟩; genau ⟨befolgen⟩
(c) yours ∼: hochachtungsvoll

**faith:** ∼ **healer** n. Gesundbeter, der/-beterin, die; ∼ **healing** n. Gesundbeten, das

**fake** /feɪk/ [1] adj. unecht; gefälscht ⟨Dokument, Banknote, Münze⟩
[2] n. (a) Imitation, die; (painting) Fälschung, die
(b) (person) Schwindler, der/Schwindlerin, die
[3] v.t. fälschen ⟨Unterschrift⟩; vortäuschen ⟨Krankheit, Unfall⟩

**falcon** /'fɔːlkn/ n. Falke, der

**fall** /fɔːl/ [1] n. (a) Fallen, das; (of person) Sturz, der; ∼ of snow/rain Schnee-/Regenfall, der; have a ∼: stürzen
(b) (collapse, defeat) Fall, der; (of dynasty, empire) Untergang, der
(c) (decrease) Rückgang, der
(d) (Amer.: autumn) Herbst, der
[2] v.i., fell /fel/, fallen /'fɔːln/ (a) fallen; ⟨Baum:⟩ umstürzen; ⟨Pferd:⟩ stürzen; ∼ off sth., ∼ down from sth. von etw. ··➔

[herunter]fallen; ～ **down** [**into**] **sth.** in etw.
(*Akk.*) [hinein]fallen; ～ **to the ground auf**
**den Boden fallen;** ～ **down the stairs** *or*
**downstairs** die Treppe herunter-/
hinunterfallen
(b) ⟨*Nacht, Dunkelheit:*⟩ hereinbrechen;
⟨*Abend:*⟩ anbrechen
(c) ⟨*Blätter:*⟩ [ab]fallen
(d) (sink) sinken; ⟨*Barometer:*⟩ fallen; ⟨*Absatz,*
*Verkauf:*⟩ zurückgehen; ～ **by 10 per cent/**
**from 10[°C] to 0[°C]** um 10%/von 10[°C] auf
0[°C] sinken
(e) (be killed) ⟨*Soldat:*⟩ fallen
(f) (collapse) einstürzen; ～ **to pieces,** ～ **apart**
auseinander fallen
(g) (occur) fallen (**on** auf + *Akk.*)
■ **fall 'back** *v.i.* zurückweichen
■ **fall 'back on** *v.t.* zurückgreifen auf
(+ *Akk.*)
■ **fall 'down** *v.i.* (a) ▶ FALL 2A
(b) ⟨*Brücke, Gebäude:*⟩ einstürzen
■ **'fall for** *v.t.* (coll.) ～ **for sb.** sich in jmdn.
verknallen (ugs.); ～ **for sth.** auf etw. (*Akk.*)
hereinfallen (ugs.)
■ **fall 'in** *v.i.* (a) hineinfallen
(b) (Mil.) antreten; ～ **in!** angetreten!
(c) ⟨*Gebäude, Wand usw.:*⟩ einstürzen
■ **fall 'off** *v.i.* (a) herunterfallen
(b) (diminish) nachlassen
■ **fall 'out** *v.i.* (a) herausfallen; ⟨*Haare,*
*Federn*⟩ ausfallen
(b) (quarrel) ～ **out** [**with sb.**] sich [mit jmdm.]
streiten
■ **fall 'over** *v.i.* umfallen; ⟨*Person:*⟩
[hin]fallen
■ **fall 'through** *v.i.* (fig.) ins Wasser fallen
(ugs.)
**fallacy** /'fæləsɪ/ *n.* Irrtum, *der*
**fallen** ▶ FALL 2
**fallible** /'fælɪbl/ *adj.* nicht unfehlbar;
fehlbar ⟨*Person*⟩
**'fallout** *n.* radioaktiver Niederschlag
**fallow** /'fæləʊ/ *adj.* brachliegend; ～ **ground/**
**land** Brache, *die*/Brachland, *das;* **lie** ～**:**
brachliegen
**false** /fɔːls, fɒls/ *adj.* falsch; gefälscht
⟨*Urkunde, Dokument*⟩; künstlich ⟨*Wimpern*⟩;
**under a** ～ **name** unter falschem Namen
**false 'alarm** *n.* blinder Alarm
**'falsely** *adv.* falsch; fälschlich[erweise]
⟨*annehmen, glauben, behaupten,*
*beschuldigen*⟩
**false:** ～ **'move** ▶ FALSE STEP;
～ **pre'tences** *n. pl.* Vorspiegelung
falscher Tatsachen; ～ **'start** *n.* Fehlstart,
*der;* ～ **'step** *n.* (lit. or fig.) falscher Schritt;
**make a** ～ **step** einen falschen Schritt tun;
～ **'teeth** *n. pl.* [künstliches] Gebiss
**falsify** /'fɔːlsɪfaɪ/ *v.t.* (alter) fälschen;
(misrepresent) verfälschen ⟨*Tatsachen,*
*Wahrheit*⟩
**falter** /'fɔːltə(r)/ *v.i.* stocken
**fame** /feɪm/ *n.* Ruhm, *der*

**familiar** /fə'mɪljə(r)/ *adj.* (a) vertraut;
bekannt ⟨*Gesicht, Name, Lied*⟩; **he looks** ～**:**
er kommt mir bekannt vor
(b) (informal) ungezwungen ⟨*Sprache, Art*⟩
**familiarity** /fəmɪlɪ'ærɪtɪ/ *n.* Vertrautheit,
*die*
**familiarize** /fə'mɪljəraɪz/ *v.t.* vertraut
machen (**with** mit)
**family** /'fæmǝlɪ/ *n.* Familie, *die*
**family:** ～ **'doctor** *n.* Hausarzt, *der;*
～ **name** *n.* Familienname, *der;*
～ **'planning** *n.* Familienplanung, *die;*
～ **'tree** *n.* Stammbaum, *der*
**famine** /'fæmɪn/ *n.* Hungersnot, *die*
**famished** /'fæmɪʃt/ *adj.* ausgehungert; **I'm**
**absolutely** ～ (coll.) ich sterbe vor Hunger
(ugs.)
**famous** /'feɪməs/ *adj.* berühmt
**fan¹** /fæn/ ①  *n.* Fächer, *der;* (apparatus)
Ventilator, *der*
② *v.t.*, **-nn-** fächeln ⟨*Gesicht*⟩; anfachen
⟨*Feuer*⟩; ～ **oneself/sb.** sich/jmdm. Luft
zufächeln
■ **fan 'out** *v.i.* fächern; ⟨*Soldaten:*⟩
ausfächern
**fan²** *n.* (devotee) Fan, *der*
**fanatic** /fə'nætɪk/ *n.* Fanatiker, *der*/
Fanatikerin, *die*
**fanatical** /fə'nætɪkl/ *adj.* fanatisch
**fanaticism** /fə'nætɪsɪzm/ *n.* Fanatismus,
*der*
**'fan belt** *n.* Keilriemen, *der*
**fanciful** /'fænsɪfl/ *adj.* überspannt
⟨*Vorstellung, Gedanke*⟩; fantastisch ⟨*Gemälde,*
*Design*⟩
**'fan club** *n.* Fanklub, *der*
**fancy** /'fænsɪ/ ①  *n.* (a) (taste, inclination) **he**
**has taken a** ～ **to a new car/her** ein neues
Auto/sie hat es ihm angetan; **take** *or* **catch**
**sb.'s** ～**:** jmdm. gefallen
(b) (whim) Laune, *die;* **tickle sb.'s** ～**:** jmdn.
reizen
② *attrib. adj.* kunstvoll ⟨*Arbeit, Muster*⟩;
fein[st...] ⟨*Kuchen, Spitzen*⟩
③ *v.t.* (a) (imagine) sich (*Dat.*) einbilden;
～ **that!** (coll.) sieh mal einer an!
(b) (suppose) glauben
(c) (wish to have) mögen; **what do you** ～ **for**
**dinner?** was hättest du gern zum
Abendessen?; **do you think she fancies him?**
glaubst du, sie mag ihn?
**fancy 'dress** *n.* [Masken]kostüm, *das;* **in**
～**:** kostümiert; **fancy-dress party** Kostümfest,
*das;* **fancy-dress ball** Maskenball, *der*
**fanfare** /'fænfeə(r)/ *n.* Fanfare, *die*
**fang** /fæŋ/ *n.* Reißzahn, *der;* (of snake)
Giftzahn, *der*
**fan:** ～ **heater** *n.* Heizlüfter, *der;* ～**light**
*n.* Oberlicht, *das;* ～ **mail** *n.* Fanpost, *die;*
～ **oven** *n.* Heißluftofen, *der*
**fantastic** /fæn'tæstɪk/ *adj.* (a) (grotesque,
quaint) bizarr
(b) (coll.: excellent) fantastisch (ugs.)

**fantasy** /'fæntəzɪ/ *n.* Fantasie, *die;* (mental image) Fantasiegebilde, *das*

**FAQ** /fæk/ *abbr.* (Comp.) FAQ

**far** /fɑː(r)/ **1** *adv.* weit; ~ **above/below** hoch über/tief unter (+ *Dat.*); hoch oben/tief unten; **as** ~ **as Munich/the church** bis [nach] München/bis zur Kirche; ~ **and wide** weit und breit; **from** ~ **and wide** von fern und nah; ~ **too** viel zu; ~ **longer/better** weit[aus] länger/besser; **as** ~ **as I remember/know** soweit ich mich erinnere/weiß; **go so** ~ **as to do sth.** so weit gehen und etw. tun; **so** ~ (until now) bisher; **so** ~ **so good** so weit, so gut; **by** ~: bei weitem; ~ **from easy/good** alles andere als leicht/gut

**2** *adj.* (a) (remote) weit entfernt; (in time) fern; **in the** ~ **distance** in weiter Ferne (b) (more remote) weiter entfernt; **the** ~ **bank of the river/side of the road** das andere Flussufer/die andere Straßenseite; **the** ~ **door/wall** *etc.* die hintere Tür/Wand *usw.*

**farce** /fɑːs/ *n.* Farce, *die*

**farcical** /'fɑːsɪkl/ *adj.* (absurd) farcenhaft

**fare** /feə(r)/ *n.* (a) (price) Fahrpreis, *der;* (money) Fahrgeld, *das;* **what** *or* **how much is the** ~? was kostet die Fahrt? (b) (food) Kost, *die*

**Far:** ~ **'East** *n.* **the** ~ **East** der Ferne Osten; ~ **'Eastern** *adj.* fernöstlich; des Fernen Ostens *nachgestellt*

**farewell** /feə'wel/ **1** *int.* leb[e] wohl (veralt.)

**2** *n. attrib.* ~ **speech/gift** Abschiedsrede, *die/*-geschenk, *das*

**far-'fetched** *adj.* weit hergeholt

**farm** /fɑːm/ **1** *n.* [Bauern]hof, *der;* (larger) Gut, *das;* ~ **animals** Nutzvieh, *das*

**2** *v.t.* bebauen ‹*Land*›

**3** *v.i.* Landwirtschaft treiben

**'farmer** *n.* Landwirt, *der/*-wirtin, *die*

**farm:** ~**hand** *n.* Landarbeiter, *der/*-arbeiterin, *die;* ~**house** *n.* Bauernhaus, *das;* (larger) Gutshaus, *das*

**'farming** *n.* Landwirtschaft, *die*

**farm:** ~**land** *n.* Acker- und Weideland, *das;* ~**worker** *n.* Landarbeiter, *der/*-arbeiterin, *die;* ~**yard** *n.* Hof, *der*

**far:** ~-'**reaching** *adj.* weit reichend; ~**sighted** *adj.* (a) (fig.) weit blickend; (b) (Amer.: long-sighted) weitsichtig

**fart** /fɑːt/ (coarse) **1** *v.i.* furzen (derb)

**2** *n.* Furz, *der* (derb)

**farther** /'fɑːðə(r)/ ▸ FURTHER 1A, 2

**farthest** /'fɑːðɪst/ ▸ FURTHEST

**fascinate** /'fæsɪneɪt/ *v.t.* fesseln; bezaubern

**fascinated** /'fæsɪneɪtɪd/ *adj.* fasziniert

**fascinating** /'fæsɪneɪtɪŋ/ *adj.* faszinierend (geh.); bezaubernd; hochinteressant ‹*Thema, Faktum, Meinung*›; spannend, fesselnd ‹*Buch*›

**fascination** /fæsɪ'neɪʃn/ *n.* Zauber, *der;* **have a** ~ **for sb.** einen besonderen Reiz auf jmdn. ausüben

**fascism** /'fæʃɪzm/ *n.* Faschismus, *der*

**fascist** /'fæʃɪst/ **1** *n.* Faschist, *der/* Faschistin, *die*

**2** *adj.* faschistisch

**fashion** /'fæʃn/ **1** *n.* (a) Mode, *die* (b) (manner) Art [und Weise]; **talk/behave in a peculiar** ~: merkwürdig sprechen/sich merkwürdig verhalten

**2** *v.t.* formen (out of, from aus; [in]to zu)

**fashionable** /'fæʃənəbl/ *adj.* modisch; vornehm ‹*Hotel, Restaurant*›; Mode‹*farbe, -autor*›

**fashionably** /'fæʃənəblɪ/ *adv.* modisch

**fashion:** ~**-conscious** *adj.* modebewusst; ~ **designer** *n.* Modeschöpfer, *der/*-schöpferin, *die;* ~ **parade,** ~ **show** *ns.* Mode[n]schau, *die*

**fast¹** /fɑːst/ **1** *v.i.* fasten

**2** *n.* Fasten, *das*

**fast²** **1** *adj.* (a) (fixed, attached) fest; **make [the boat]** ~: das Boot festmachen; **hard and** ~: fest; bindend ‹*Regel*›; klar ‹*Entscheidung*› (b) (rapid) schnell; ~ **train** Schnellzug, *der;* D-Zug, *der* (c) **be [ten minutes]** ~ ‹*Uhr:*› [zehn Minuten] vorgehen

**2** *adv.* (a) **be** ~ **asleep** fest schlafen; (when one should be awake) fest eingeschlafen sein (b) (quickly) schnell

**'fastback** *n.* (back of car) Fließheck, *das;* Fastback, *das;* (car) Wagen mit Fließheck; Fastback, *das*

**fasten** /'fɑːsn/ *v.t.* befestigen (on, to an + *Dat.*); zumachen ‹*Kleid, Spange, Jacke*›; [ab]schließen ‹*Tür*›; anstecken ‹*Brosche*› (to an + *Akk.*); ~ **one's seat belt** sich anschnallen

**'fastener, 'fastening** *ns.* Verschluss, *der*

**fast:** ~ **'food** *n.: im Schnellrestaurant angebotenes Essen;* Fastfood, *das; attrib.* ~**-food restaurant** Schnellrestaurant, *das;* ~ **'forward** *n.* schneller Vorlauf; (playback) Zeitrafferwiedergabe, *die;* ~**-forward** **1** *attrib. adj.* Vorspul‹*taste, -funktion*›; **2** *v.t. & i.* vorspulen

**fastidious** /fæ'stɪdɪəs/ *adj.* wählerisch; (hard to please) heikel

**fast:** ~ **lane** *n.* Überholspur, *die;* **life in the** ~ **lane** (fig.) Leben auf vollen Touren (ugs.); ~ **track** *n.* Überholspur, *die;* **a career on the** ~ **track** eine Blitzkarriere; **be on the** ~ **track** eine Blitzkarriere machen; ~**-track** **1** *v.t.* beschleunigen ‹*Projekt*›; **2** *attrib. adj.* Schnell-

**fat** /fæt/ **1** *adj.* dick; rund ‹*Wangen, Gesicht*›

**2** *n.* Fett, *das;* **animal/vegetable** ~: tierisches/pflanzliches Fett

**fatal** /'feɪtl/ adj. (a) (disastrous) verheerend (to für); it would be ~: das wäre das Ende (b) (deadly) tödlich ⟨Unfall, Verletzung⟩

**fatality** /fə'tælɪtɪ/ n. Todesopfer, das

'**fatally** adv. tödlich; be ~ ill todkrank sein

**fate** /feɪt/ n. Schicksal, das

**fat-free** adj. fettfrei

'**fathead** n. Dummkopf, der (ugs.)

**father** /'fɑːðə(r)/ n. Vater, der

**father: F~ 'Christmas** n. der Weihnachtsmann; ~ **figure** n. Vaterfigur, die

**fatherhood** /'fɑːðəhʊd/ n. Vaterschaft, die

'**father-in-law** n., pl. ~s-in-law Schwiegervater, der

'**fatherly** adj. väterlich

'**Father's Day** n. Vatertag, der

**fathom** /'fæðəm/ 1 n. (Naut.) Faden, der 2 v.t. (comprehend) verstehen; ~ sb./sth. out jmdn./etw. ergründen

**fatigue** /fə'tiːg/ 1 n. Ermüdung, die 2 v.t. ermüden

'**fatness** n. Dicke, die

**fatten** /'fætn/ v.t. herausfüttern ⟨Person⟩; mästen ⟨Tier⟩

'**fattening** adj. be ~: dick machen

**fatty** /'fætɪ/ adj. fett ⟨Fleisch, Soße⟩; fetthaltig ⟨Speise, Nahrungsmittel⟩

**faucet** /'fɔːsɪt/ n. (Amer.) Wasserhahn, der

**fault** /fɔːlt, fɒlt/ n. (a) Fehler, der (b) (responsibility) Schuld, die; it's your ~: du bist schuld; it isn't my ~: ich habe keine Schuld; be at ~: im Unrecht sein (c) (in machinery; also Electr.) Defekt, der

'**faultless** adj. einwandfrei

'**faulty** adj. fehlerhaft; defekt ⟨Gerät, usw.⟩

**fauna** /'fɔːnə/ n., pl. ~e /'fɔːniː/ or ~s Fauna, die

**favor** etc. (Amer.) ▶ FAVOUR etc.

**favour** /'feɪvə(r)/ 1 n. (a) Gunst, die (b) (kindness) Gefallen, der; ask sb. a ~, ask a ~ of sb. jmdn. um einen Gefallen bitten; do sb. a ~, do a ~ for sb. jmdm. einen Gefallen tun; as a ~: aus Gefälligkeit (c) be in ~ of sth. für etw. sein 2 v.t. bevorzugen

**favourable** /'feɪvərəbl/ adj. (Brit.) (a) günstig ⟨Eindruck, Licht⟩; gewogen ⟨Haltung, Einstellung⟩; freundlich ⟨Erwähnung⟩; positiv ⟨Bericht[erstattung], Bemerkung⟩ (b) (helpful) günstig (to für) ⟨Wetter, Wind, Umstand⟩

**favourably** /'feɪvərəblɪ/ adv. (Brit.) wohlwollend; be ~ disposed towards sb./sth. jmdm./einer Sache positiv gegenüberstehen

**favourite** /'feɪvərɪt/ (Brit.) 1 adj. Lieblings- 2 n. (a) Liebling, der; ⟨food/country etc.⟩ Lieblingsessen, das usw.; this/he is my ~: das/ihn mag ich am liebsten (b) (Sport) Favorit, der/Favoritin, die

**favouritism** /'feɪvərɪtɪzm/ n. (Brit.) Begünstigung, die; (when selecting sb. for a post etc.) Günstlingswirtschaft, die

**fawn** /fɔːn/ 1 n. (a) (colour) Rehbraun, das (b) (young deer) [Dam]kitz, das 2 adj. rehfarben

**fax** /fæks/ 1 n. [Tele]fax, das 2 v.t. faxen

**fax: ~ machine** n. Faxgerät, das; ~ **modem** n. (Comp.) Faxmodem, das; ~ **number** n. Faxnummer, die

**FBI** abbr. (Amer.) = **Federal Bureau of Investigation** FBI, das

**fear** /fɪə(r)/ 1 n. Angst, die (of vor + Dat.); (instance) Befürchtung, die; ~ of death or dying/heights Todes-/Höhenangst, die; ~ of doing sth. Angst davor, etw. zu tun; in ~: angstvoll; no ~! (coll.) keine Bange! (ugs.) 2 v.t. (a) ~ sb./sth. vor jmdm./etw. Angst haben; ~ to do or doing sth. Angst haben, etw. zu tun (b) (be worried about) befürchten; ~ [that ...] fürchten[, dass ...]

**fearful** /'fɪəfl/ adj. (a) (terrible) furchtbar (b) (frightened) ängstlich; be ~ of sth./sb. vor etw./jmdm. Angst haben

'**fearless** adj., '**fearlessly** adv. furchtlos

**feasibility** /fiːzɪ'bɪlɪtɪ/ n. Durchführbarkeit, die

**feasible** /'fiːzɪbl/ adj. durchführbar

**feast** /fiːst/ 1 n. (a) (Relig.) Fest, das (b) (banquet) Festessen, das 2 v.i. schlemmen; ~ on sth. sich an etw. (Dat.) gütlich tun

**feat** /fiːt/ n. Meisterleistung, die

**feather** /'feðə(r)/ n. Feder, die

**feather: ~ 'bed** n. mit Federn gefüllte Matratze; ~ '**duster** n. Flederwisch, der; ~**weight** n. (Boxing) Federgewicht, das

**feature** /'fiːtʃə(r)/ 1 n. (a) usu. in pl. (of face) Gesichtszug, der (b) (characteristic) [charakteristisches] Merkmal; be a ~ of sth. charakteristisch für etw. sein (c) (Journ.) Feature, das (d) (Cinemat.) ~ [film] Hauptfilm, der 2 v.t. vorrangig vorstellen; (in film) in der Hauptrolle zeigen 3 v.i. vorkommen; ~ in (be important) eine bedeutende Rolle haben bei

**Feb.** abbr. = **February** Febr.

**February** /'februərɪ/ n. Februar, der

**feces** (Amer.) ▶ FAECES

**fed** /fed/ 1 ▶ FEED 1, 2 2 pred. adj. (coll.) be/get ~ up with sb./sth. jmdn./etw. satt haben/kriegen (ugs.); I'm ~ up ich hab die Nase voll (ugs.)

**federal** /'fedərl/ adj. Bundes-; föderativ ⟨System⟩

**federation** /fedə'reɪʃn/ n. Föderation, die

**fee** /fiː/ n. Gebühr, die; (of doctor, lawyer, etc.) Honorar, das

**feeble** /'fiːbl/ *adj.* schwach; wenig
überzeugend ⟨*Entschuldigung*⟩; zaghaft
⟨*Versuch*⟩; lahm (ugs.) ⟨*Witz*⟩

**feed** /fiːd/ **1** *v.t.,* **fed** /fed/ **(a)** füttern;
∼ **sb./an animal with sth.** jmdm. etw. zu
essen/einem Tier [etw.] zu fressen geben
**(b)** (provide food for) ernähren **(on, with** mit)
**2** *v.i.,* **fed** ⟨*Tier:*⟩ fressen **(from** aus);
⟨*Person:*⟩ essen **(off** von); ∼ **on sth.** ⟨*Tier:*⟩
etw. fressen
**3** *n.* **(a)** (for baby) Mahlzeit, *die*
**(b)** (fodder) Futter, *das*

**'feedback** *n.* Reaktion, *die*

**feel** /fiːl/ **1** *v.t.,* **felt** /felt/ **(a)** (explore by
touch) befühlen
**(b)** (perceive by touch) fühlen; (become aware of)
bemerken; (have sensation of) spüren
⟨*Drang*⟩; ∼ **the cold/heat** unter der Kälte/
Hitze leiden; ∼ **[that]** ...: das Gefühl haben,
dass ...; (think) glauben, dass ...
**2** *v.i.,* **felt: (a)** ∼ **[about] in sth. [for sth.]** in
etw. (*Dat.*) [nach etw.] [herum]suchen
**(b)** (be conscious that one is) sich ... fühlen;
∼ **angry/sure/disappointed** böse/sicher/
enttäuscht sein; ∼ **like sth./doing sth.** auf
etw. (*Akk.*) Lust haben/Lust haben, etw. zu
tun
**(c)** (be consciously perceived as) sich ...
anfühlen

▪ **'feel for** *v.t.* ∼ **for sb.** mit jmdm. Mitleid
haben

**'feeler** *n.* Fühler, *der*

**'feeling** *n.* **(a)** Gefühl, *das;* (sense of touch)
[**sense of**] ∼: Tastsinn, *der;* **hurt sb.'s** ∼**s**
jmdn. verletzen
**(b)** (opinion) Ansicht, *die*

**feet** *pl. of* FOOT

**feign** /feɪn/ *v.t.* vortäuschen; ∼ **to do sth.**
vorgeben, etw. zu tun

**feline** /'fiːlaɪn/ *adj.* (of cat[s]) Katzen-;
(catlike) katzenartig; katzenhaft

**fell**[1] ▶ FALL 2

**fell**[2] /fel/ *v.t.* fällen ⟨*Baum*⟩

**fell**[3] *adj.* **in one** ∼ **swoop** auf einen Schlag

**fellow** /'feləʊ/ **1** *n.* **(a)** (comrade) Kamerad,
*der*
**(b)** (Brit. Univ.) Fellow, *der*
**(c)** (of academy or society) Mitglied, *das*
**(d)** (coll.: man, boy) Kerl, *der* (ugs.)
**2** *attrib. adj.* Mit-; ∼ **man** *or* **human being**
Mitmensch, *der*

**fellowship** /'feləʊʃɪp/ *n.* (companionship)
Gesellschaft, *die*

**felt**[1] /felt/ *n.* Filz, *der*

**felt**[2] ▶ FEEL

**felt[-tipped] 'pen** *n.* Filzstift, *der*

**female** /'fiːmeɪl/ **1** *adj.* weiblich;
Frauen⟨*stimme, -chor, -verein*⟩
**2** *n.* Frau, *die;* (foetus, child) Mädchen, *das;*
(animal) Weibchen, *das*

**feminine** /'femmɪn/ *adj.* weiblich;
Frauen⟨*angelegenheit, -leiden*⟩; (womanly)
feminin

**femininity** /femɪ'nɪnɪtɪ/ *n.* Weiblichkeit,
*die*

**feminism** /'femmɪzm/ *n.* Feminismus, *der*

**feminist** /'femmɪst/ **1** *adj.* feministisch;
Feministen⟨*bewegung, -gruppe*⟩
**2** *n.* Feministin, *die*/Feminist, *der*

**fence** /fens/ **1** *n.* Zaun, *der*
**2** *v.i.* (Sport) fechten
**3** *v.t.* ∼ **[in]** einzäunen

**'fencer** *n.* Fechter, *der*/Fechterin, *die*

**fencing** /'fensɪŋ/ *n.* (Sport) Fechten, *das*

**fend** /fend/ *v.i.* ∼ **for oneself** für sich selbst
sorgen; (in hostile surroundings) sich allein
durchschlagen

▪ **fend 'off** *v.t.* abwehren

**fender** /'fendə(r)/ *n.* **(a)** (for fire)
Kaminschutz, *der*
**(b)** (Amer.) (car bumper) Stoßstange, *die;* (car
mudguard) Kotflügel, *der*

**ferment** /fə'ment/ **1** *v.i.* gären
**2** *v.t.* zur Gärung bringen

**fermentation** /fɜːmen'teɪʃn/ *n.* Gärung,
*die*

**fern** /fɜːn/ *n.* Farnkraut, *das*

**ferocious** /fə'rəʊʃəs/ *adj.* wild

**ferocity** /fə'rɒsɪtɪ/ *n.* Wildheit, *die*

**ferret** /'ferɪt/ *n.* Frettchen, *das*

**ferrous** /'ferəs/ *adj.* (containing iron)
eisenhaltig; Eisen-

**ferry** /'ferɪ/ **1** *n.* Fähre, *die;* (service)
Fährverbindung, *die*
**2** *v.t.* (in boat) ∼ [**across** *or* **over**] übersetzen

**'ferry service** *n.* **(a)** Fährverbindung, *die*
**(b)** (business) Fährbetrieb, *der*

**fertile** /'fɜːtaɪl/ *adj.* (fruitful) fruchtbar;
(capable of developing) befruchtet

**fertility** /fə'tɪlɪtɪ/ *n.* Fruchtbarkeit, *die*

**fer'tility drug** *n.* Hormonpräparat, *das*
(*zur Steigerung der Fruchtbarkeit*)

**fertilization** /fɜːtɪlaɪ'zeɪʃn/ *n.* **(a)** (Biol.)
Befruchtung, *die*
**(b)** (Agric.) Düngung, *die*

**fertilize** /'fɜːtɪlaɪz/ *v.t.* befruchten

**'fertilizer** *n.* Dünger, *der*

**fervent** /'fɜːvənt/ *adj.* leidenschaftlich;
inbrünstig ⟨*Gebet, Wunsch, Hoffnung*⟩

**fervour** (*Brit.; Amer.:* **fervor**) /'fɜːvə(r)/ *n.*
Leidenschaftlichkeit, *die*

**fester** /'festə(r)/ *v.i.* eitern

**festival** /'festɪvl/ *n.* **(a)** (feast day) Fest, *das*
**(b)** (of music etc.) Festival, *das*

**festive** /'festɪv/ *adj.* festlich; fröhlich; **the**
∼ **season** die Weihnachtszeit

**festivity** /fe'stɪvɪtɪ/ *n.* **(a)** (gaiety)
Feststimmung, *die*
**(b)** (celebration) Feier, *die;* **festivities**
Feierlichkeiten *Pl.*

**festoon** /fe'stuːn/ **1** *n.* Girlande, *die*
**2** *v.t.* schmücken (**with** mit)

**fetch** /fetʃ/ v.t. **(a)** holen; (collect) abholen (from von); ∼ **sb. sth.,** ∼ **sth. for sb.** jmdm. etw. holen
**(b)** (be sold for) erzielen ‹Preis›
**'fetching** adj. einnehmend
**fête** /feɪt/ n. [Wohltätigkeits]basar, der
**fetish** /'fetɪʃ/ n. Fetisch, der
**fetishism** /'fetɪʃɪzm/ n. Fetischismus, der
**fetishist** /'fetɪʃɪst/ n. Fetischist, der/ Fetischistin, die
**fetter** /'fetə(r)/ v.t. fesseln
**fetus** (Amer.) ▶ FOETUS
**feud** /fju:d/ n. Fehde, die
**feudal** /'fju:dl/ adj. Feudal-; feudalistisch; ∼ **system** Feudalsystem, das
**fever** /'fi:və(r)/ n. **(a)** (high temperature) Fieber, das; have a [high] ∼: [hohes] Fieber haben
**(b)** (disease) Fieberkrankheit, die
**'feverish** adj. **(a)** (Med.) fiebrig; be ∼: Fieber haben
**(b)** (excited) fiebrig
**'fever pitch** n. Siedepunkt, der (fig.); reach ∼: auf dem Siedepunkt angelangt sein; at ∼: auf dem Siedepunkt
**few** /fju:/ ① adj. **(a)** (not many) wenige; abs. nur wenige; with very ∼ exceptions mit ganz wenigen Ausnahmen; his ∼ belongings seine paar Habseligkeiten; a ∼ ...: wenige ...
**(b)** (some) wenige; a ∼ ...: ein paar ...; a ∼ more ...: noch ein paar ...
② n. **(a)** (not many) wenige; a ∼: wenige; just a ∼ of you/her friends nur ein paar von euch/ihrer Freunde
**(b)** (some) with a ∼ of our friends mit einigen unserer Freunde; quite a ∼: ziemlich viele
**fiancé** /fɪ'ãseɪ/ n. Verlobte, der
**fiancée** /fɪ'ãseɪ/ n. Verlobte, die
**fiasco** /fɪ'æskəʊ/ n., pl. ∼s Fiasko, das
**fib** /fɪb/ ① n. Flunkerei, die (ugs.); tell ∼s flunkern (ugs.)
② v.i., -bb- flunkern (ugs.)
**fibre** (Brit.; Amer.: **fiber**) /'faɪbə(r)/ n. **(a)** Faser, die
**(b)** (material) [Faser]gewebe, das
**fibre:** ∼**glass** n. ( plastic) glasfaserverstärkter Kunststoff; ∼ **optic 'cable** n. Glasfaserkabel, das; ∼ **'optics** n. Faseroptik, die
**fibrous** /'faɪbrəs/ adj. faserig ‹Aufbau, Beschaffenheit, Eigenschaft›; Faser‹gewebe, -holz, -stoff›
**fiche** /fi:ʃ/ n., pl. same or ∼s Mikrofiche, das od. der
**fickle** /'fɪkl/ adj. unberechenbar
**fiction** /'fɪkʃn/ n. erzählende Literatur; a ∼/ ∼s eine Erfindung
**fictional** /'fɪkʃənl/ adj. erfunden ‹Geschichte›; fiktiv ‹Figur›
**'fiction writer** n. Belletrist, der/ Belletristin, die
**fictitious** /fɪk'tɪʃəs/ adj. fingiert; falsch ‹Name, Identität›

**fiddle** /'fɪdl/ ① n. **(a)** (Mus.) (coll./derog.) Fiedel, die; (violin for traditional music) Geige, die; [as] fit as a ∼: kerngesund
**(b)** (coll.: swindle) Gaunerei, die
② v.t. (coll.) frisieren (ugs.) ‹Bücher, Rechnungen›
③ v.i. herumspielen (with mit)
**fiddler** /'fɪdlə(r)/ n. Geiger, der/Geigerin, die
**fiddly** /'fɪdlɪ/ adj. (coll.) knifflig
**fidelity** /fɪ'delɪtɪ/ n. Treue, die (to zu)
**fidget** /'fɪdʒɪt/ ① v.i. ∼ [about] herumrutschen
② n. (person) Zappelphilipp, der (ugs.)
**'fidgety** adj. unruhig; zappelig ‹Kind›
**field** /fi:ld/ n. **(a)** Feld, das
**(b)** (for game) Platz, der; [Spiel]feld, das
**(c)** (subject area) [Fach]gebiet, das; in the ∼ of medicine auf dem Gebiet der Medizin; that is outside my ∼: das fällt nicht in mein Fach
**field:** ∼ **day** n. have a ∼ day seinen großen Tag haben; ∼ **events** n. pl. technische Disziplinen Pl. ∼ **glasses** n. pl. Feldstecher, der; **F**∼ **'Marshal** n. (Brit. Mil.) Feldmarschall, der; ∼ **mouse** n. Brandmaus, die; ∼ **trip** n. Exkursion, die
**fiend** /fi:nd/ n. **(a)** (wicked person) Scheusal, das
**(b)** (evil spirit) böser Geist
**'fiendish** adj. **(a)** teuflisch
**(b)** (very awkward) höllisch
**fierce** /fɪəs/ adj. wild; erbittert ‹Widerstand, Kampf›; scharf ‹Kritik›
**'fiercely** adv. heftig ‹angreifen, Widerstand leisten›; wütend ‹brüllen›; aufs heftigste ‹kritisieren, bekämpfen›
**fiery** /'faɪərɪ/ adj. glühend; (looking like fire) feurig; (blazing red) feuerrot
**fifteen** /fɪf'ti:n/ ① adj. fünfzehn
② n. Fünfzehn, die. See also EIGHT
**fifteenth** /fɪf'ti:nθ/ ① adj. fünfzehnt...
② n. (fraction) Fünfzehntel, das. See also EIGHTH
**fifth** /fɪfθ/ ① adj. fünft...
② n. (in sequence, rank) Fünfte, der/die/das; (fraction) Fünftel, das. See also EIGHTH
**fiftieth** /'fɪftɪθ/ adj. fünfzigst...
**fifty** /'fɪftɪ/ ① adj. fünfzig
② n. Fünfzig, die. See also EIGHT; EIGHTY 2
**fig** /fɪg/ n. Feige, die
**fig.** abbr. = **figure** Abb.
**fight** /faɪt/ ① v.i., fought /fɔːt/ **(a)** kämpfen; (with fists) sich schlagen
**(b)** (squabble) [sich] streiten (about wegen)
② v.t., fought: **(a)** ∼ sb./sth. gegen jmdn./ etw. kämpfen; (using fists) ∼ sb. sich mit jmdm. schlagen
**(b)** (seek to overcome) bekämpfen; (resist) ∼ sb./sth. gegen jmdn./etw. ankämpfen
**(c)** ∼ a battle einen Kampf austragen
**(d)** kandidieren bei ‹Wahl›
③ n. Kampf, der (for um)
■ **'fight against** v.t. kämpfen gegen; ankämpfen gegen ‹Wellen, Wind›

■ **fight 'back** ① *v.i.* zurückschlagen
② *v.t.* (suppress) zurückhalten
■ **fight 'off** *v.t.* abwehren
■ **'fight with** *v.t.* (a) kämpfen mit
(b) (squabble with) [sich] streiten mit
**'fighter** *n.* Kämpfer, *der*/Kämpferin, *die;*
(aircraft) Kampfflugzeug, *das*
**'fighting** *n.* Kämpfe *Pl.*
**fighting 'chance** *n.* have a ∼ of
succeeding/of doing sth. Aussicht auf Erfolg
haben/gute Chancen haben, etw. zu tun
**'fig leaf** *n.* (lit. or fig.) Feigenblatt, *das*
**figment** /'fɪgmənt/ *n.* a ∼ of one's *or* the
imagination pure Einbildung
**'fig tree** *n.* Feigenbaum, *der*
**figurative** /'fɪɡərətɪv/ *adj.* übertragen
**figure** /'fɪɡə(r)/ ① *n.* (a) (shape) Form, *die*
(b) (carving, sculpture, one's bodily shape) Figur,
*die*
(c) (illustration) Abbildung, *die*
(d) (person as seen) Gestalt, *die;* (literary ∼)
Figur, *die*
(e) (numerical symbol) Ziffer, *die;* (number) Zahl,
*die;* (amount of money) Betrag, *der*
(f) ∼ of speech Redewendung, *die*
② *v.i.* (a) vorkommen
(b) that ∼s (coll.) das kann gut sein
■ **figure 'out** *v.t.* (a) (by arithmetic)
ausrechnen
(b) (understand) verstehen
**figure:** ∼**head** *n.* (lit. or fig.) Galionsfigur,
*die;* ∼ **skating** *n.* Eiskunstlauf, *der*
**filament** /'fɪləmənt/ *n.* (a) Faden, *der*
(b) (Electr.) Glühfaden, *der*
**filch** /'fɪltʃ/ *v.t.* stibitzen (ugs.)
**file¹** /faɪl/ ① *n.* Feile, *die*
② *v.t.* feilen ⟨Fingernägel⟩; mit der Feile
bearbeiten ⟨Holz, Eisen⟩
**file²** ① *n.* (a) (holder) Ordner, *der;* (box)
Kassette, *die*
(b) (papers) Ablage, *die;* (cards) Kartei, *die*
② *v.t.* (a) [in die Kartei] einordnen/[in die
Akten] aufnehmen
(b) einreichen ⟨Antrag⟩
**file³** ① *n.* (Mil. etc.) Reihe, *die;* [in] single *or*
Indian ∼: [im] Gänsemarsch
② *v.i.* ∼ [in/out] in einer Reihe [hinein-/
hinaus]gehen
**file copy** *n.* Belegexemplar, *das;* (of letter)
Kopie für die Akten
**filigree** /'fɪlɪɡriː/ *n.* Filigran, *das*
**'filing cabinet** *n.* Aktenschrank, *der*
**filings** /'faɪlɪŋz/ *n. pl.* Späne *Pl.*
**fill** /fɪl/ ① *v.t.* (a) füllen; besetzen
⟨Sitzplätze⟩; (fig.) ausfüllen ⟨Gedanken, Zeit⟩;
(pervade) erfüllen; ∼ed with voller ⟨Reue,
Bewunderung, Neid usw.⟩
(b) (appoint sb. to) besetzen ⟨Posten⟩
② *v.i.* ∼ [with sth.] sich [mit etw.] füllen
③ *n.* eat/drink one's ∼: sich satt essen/
trinken
■ **fill 'in** ① *v.t.* (a) füllen; zuschütten
⟨Erdloch⟩

(b) (complete) ausfüllen
(c) ∼ sb. in [on sth.] (coll.) jmdn. [über etw.
⟨Akk.⟩] ins Bild setzen
② *v.i.* ∼ in for sb. für jmdn. einspringen
■ **fill 'out** *v.t.* ausfüllen
■ **fill 'up** *v.t.* (a) füllen (with mit)
(b) (put petrol into) ∼ up the tank tanken; ∼
her up! (coll.) voll [tanken]!
**fillet** /'fɪlɪt/ ① *n.* Filet, *das*
② *v.t.* entgräten ⟨Fisch⟩
**'filling** *n.* (a) (for teeth) Füllung, *die*
(b) (for pancakes etc.) Füllung, *die;* (for
sandwiches etc.) Belag, *der;* (for spreading)
Aufstrich, *der*
**'filling station** *n.* Tankstelle, *die*
**filly** /'fɪlɪ/ *n.* junge Stute
**film** /fɪlm/ ① *n.* (a) Film, *der*
(b) (thin layer) Schicht, *die*
② *v.t.* filmen; drehen ⟨Kinofilm, Szene⟩
**film:** ∼ **crew** *n.* Kamerateam, *das;*
∼ **director** *n.* Filmregisseur, *der*/
-regisseurin, *die;* ∼ **industry** *n.*
Filmindustrie, *die;* ∼ **music** *n.*
Filmmusik, *die;* ∼ **poster** *n.* Filmplakat,
*das;* ∼ **projector** *n.* Projektor, *der;*
∼ **script** *n.* Drehbuch, *das;* ∼ **set** *n.*
Dekoration, *die;* ∼ **star** *n.* Filmstar, *der;*
∼**strip** *n.* Filmstreifen, *der;* ∼ **studio** *n.*
Filmstudio, *das*
**Filofax** ® /'faɪləʊfæks/ *n.* ≈ Terminplaner,
*der*
**filter** /'fɪltə(r)/ ① *n.* Filter, *der*
② *v.t.* filtern
■ **filter 'through** *v.t.* durchsickern
**filter:** ∼ **ciga'rette** *n.* Filterzigarette, *die;*
∼ **coffee** *n.* Filterkaffee, *der;* ∼ **lane** *n.*
Abbiegespur, *die;* ∼**tip** *n.* (a) Filter, *der;*
(b) ∼-tip [cigarette] Filterzigarette, *die*
**filth** /fɪlθ/ *n.* Dreck, *der*
**'filthy** *adj.* dreckig (ugs.); schmutzig
**fin** /fɪn/ *n.* Flosse, *die*
**final** /'faɪnl/ ① *adj.* letzt...; End⟨spiel,
-stadium, -stufe, -ergebnis⟩; endgültig
⟨Entscheidung⟩
② *n.* (a) (Sport etc.) Finale, *das*
(b) ∼s *pl.* (university examination) Examen, *das*
**finale** /fɪ'nɑːlɪ/ *n.* Finale, *das*
**finalist** /'faɪnəlɪst/ *n.* Teilnehmer/
Teilnehmerin in der Endausscheidung;
(Sport) Finalist, *der*/Finalistin, *die*
**finality** /faɪ'nælɪtɪ/ *n.* Endgültigkeit, *die;* (of
tone of voice) Entschiedenheit, *die*
**finalize** /'faɪnəlaɪz/ *v.t.* [endgültig]
beschließen; (complete) zum Abschluss
bringen
**finally** /'faɪnəlɪ/ *adv.* (a) (in the end)
schließlich; (expressing impatience etc.) endlich
(b) (in conclusion) abschließend
(c) (conclusively) entschieden ⟨sagen⟩
**finance** /faɪ'næns, 'faɪmæns/ ① *n.* (a) *in pl.*
(resources) Finanzen *Pl.*
(b) (management of money) Geldwesen, *das*
(c) (support) Geldmittel *Pl.*                    ⋯⟶

2 *v.t.* finanzieren
'**finance company** *n.*
Finanzierungsgesellschaft, *die*
**financial** /faɪˈnænʃl/ *adj.* finanziell;
Finanz⟨*mittel, -experte, -lage*⟩; ~ year
Geschäftsjahr, *die*
fi'**nancially** *adv.* finanziell
**financier** /faɪˈnænsɪə(r)/ *n.* Finanzexperte,
*der*/-expertin, *die*
**finch** /fɪntʃ/ *n.* Fink[envogel], *der*
**find** /faɪnd/ 1 *v.t.,* **found** /faʊnd/ finden;
(come across unexpectedly) entdecken;
auftreiben ⟨*Geld, Gegenstand*⟩; aufbringen
⟨*Kraft, Energie*⟩; **want to** ~: suchen; ~ **that**
...: herausfinden, dass ...; ~ **sth. necessary**
etw. für nötig erachten; ~ **sth./sb. to be** ...:
herausfinden, dass etw./jmd. ... ist/war; **you
will** ~ [**that**] ...: Sie werden sehen, dass ...
2 *n.* Fund, *der*
■ **find 'out** *v.t.* herausfinden
'**finder** *n.* Finder, *der*/Finderin, *die*
'**findings** *n. pl.* Ergebnisse *Pl.*
**fine**[1] /faɪn/ 1 *n.* Geldstrafe, *die*
2 *v.t.* mit einer Geldstrafe belegen
**fine**[2] *adj.* (a) hochwertig ⟨*Qualität,
Lebensmittel*⟩; fein ⟨*Gewebe, Spitze*⟩; edel
⟨*Holz, Wein*⟩
(b) (delicate) fein; zart ⟨*Porzellan*⟩; (thin)
hauchdünn; **cut** *or* **run it** ~: knapp
kalkulieren
(c) (in small particles) [hauch]fein ⟨*Sand,
Staub*⟩; ~ **rain** Nieselregen, *der*
(d) (sharp) scharf ⟨*Spitze, Klinge*⟩; spitz
⟨*Nadel, Schreibfeder*⟩
(e) (excellent) ausgezeichnet ⟨*Sänger,
Schauspieler*⟩
(f) (satisfactory) schön; **that's** ~ **by** *or* **with me**
ja, ist mir recht
(g) (in good health or state) gut; **feel** ~: sich
wohl fühlen
(h) schön ⟨*Wetter*⟩
**fine 'arts** *n. pl.* schöne Künste *Pl.*
**finery** /ˈfaɪnərɪ/ *n.* Pracht, *die;* (garments etc.)
Staat, *der*
**finger** /ˈfɪŋɡə(r)/ 1 *n.* Finger, *der*
2 *v.t.* berühren; (meddle with) befingern
**finger:** ~**mark** *n.* Fingerabdruck, *der;*
~**nail** *n.* Fingernagel, *der;* ~**print** *n.*
Fingerabdruck, *der;* ~**tip** *n.* Fingerspitze,
*die;* **have sth. at one's** ~**tips** (fig.) etw. im
kleinen Finger haben (ugs.)
**finish** /ˈfɪnɪʃ/ 1 *v.t.* (a) beenden
⟨*Unterhaltung*⟩; erledigen ⟨*Arbeit*⟩;
abschließen ⟨*Kurs, Ausbildung*⟩; **have** ~**ed**
**sth.** etw. fertig haben; ~ **writing/reading sth.**
etw. zu Ende schreiben/lesen
(b) aufessen ⟨*Mahlzeit*⟩; auslesen ⟨*Buch,
Zeitung*⟩; austrinken ⟨*Flasche, Glas*⟩
2 *v.i.* (a) aufhören; **have you** ~**ed?** sind Sie
fertig?; **when does the concert** ~? wann ist
das Konzert aus?; **have you** ~**ed with the
sugar?** brauchen Sie den Zucher noch?; ~
**with one's boyfriend/girlfriend** mit seinem
Freund/seiner Freundin Schluss machen

(b) (in race) das Ziel erreichen
3 *n.* (a) Ende, *das*
(b) (~ing line) Ziel, *das*
■ **finish 'off** *v.t.* abschließen
'**finishing:** ~ **post** *n.* Zielpfosten, *der;*
~ '**touch** *n.* **as a** ~ **touch to sth.** zur
Vollendung *od.* Vervollkommnung einer
Sache; **put the** ~ **touches to sth.** einer Sache
(*Dat.*) den letzten Schliff geben
**finite** /ˈfaɪnaɪt/ *adj.* begrenzt
**Finland** /ˈfɪnlənd/ *pr. n.* Finnland (*das*)
**Finn** /fɪn/ *n.* Finne, *der*/Finnin, *die*
**Finnish** /ˈfɪnɪʃ/ 1 *adj.* finnisch; **sb. is** ~:
jmd. ist Finne/Finnin
2 *n.* Finnisch, *das; see also* ENGLISH 2A
**fiord** /fɪˈɔːd/ *n.* Fjord, *der*
**fir** /fɜː(r)/ *n.* Tanne, *die*
**fire** /ˈfaɪə(r)/ 1 *n.* (a) Feuer, *das;* **be on** ~:
brennen; **catch** ~: Feuer fangen; ⟨*Wald,
Gebäude*⟩ in Brand geraten; **set** ~ **to sth.**
etw. anzünden
(b) (in grate) [offenes] Feuer; (electric or gas ~)
Heizofen, *der;* **light the** ~: den Ofen
anstecken; (in grate) das [Kamin]feuer
anmachen
(c) (destructive burning) Brand, *der*
(d) (of guns) **come/be under** ~: unter
Beschuss geraten/beschossen werden
2 *v.t.* (a) abschießen ⟨*Gewehr*⟩; abfeuern
⟨*Kanone*⟩; abgeben ⟨*Schuss*⟩; ~ **one's gun/
pistol/rifle at sb.** auf jmdn. schießen; **two
shots were** ~**d** es fielen zwei Schüsse; ~
**questions at sb.** jmdn. mit Fragen
bombardieren
(b) (coll.: dismiss) feuern (ugs.)
3 *v.i.* feuern; ~ **at/on** schießen auf (+ *Akk.*);
~! Feuer!
**fire:** ~ **alarm** *n.* Feuermelder, *der;* ~**arm**
*n.* Schusswaffe, *die;* ~**bomb** *n.* Brandsatz,
*der;* (aerial bomb) Brandbombe, *die;*
~ **brigade** (Brit.)**,** ~ **department** (Amer.)
*ns.* Feuerwehr, *die;* ~ **drill** *n.*
Probe[feuer]alarm, *der;* ~ **engine** *n.*
Löschfahrzeug, *das;* ~ **escape** *n.* (staircase)
Feuertreppe, *die;* ~ **exit** *n.* Notausgang,
*der;* ~ **extinguisher** *n.* Feuerlöscher, *der;*
~**fighter** *n.* Feuerwehrmann, *der*/-frau, *die;*
~**fighting** *n.* Feuerbekämpfung, *die;*
Brandbekämpfung, *die;* ~ **hazard** *n.*
Brandrisiko, *das;* ~**lighter** *n.* (Brit.)
Feueranzünder, *der;* ~**man** /ˈfaɪəmən/ *n.,*
*pl.* ~**men** /-mən/ Feuerwehrmann, *der;*
~**place** *n.* Kamin, *der;* ~ **precautions**
*n. pl.* Feuerschutz, *der;* ~**proof** 1 *adj.*
feuerfest; 2 *v.t.* feuerfest machen;
~**resistant** *adj.* feuerbeständig; ~ **risk**
▶ ~ HAZARD; ~**side** *n.* **at** *or* **by the** ~**side**
am Kamin; ~ **station** *n.* Feuerwache, *die;*
~ **tongs** *n. pl.* Feuerzange, *die;* **a pair of**
~ **tongs** eine Feuerzange; ~**wood** *n.*
Brennholz, *das;* ~**work** *n.*
Feuerwerkskörper, *der;* ~**works** (display)
Feuerwerk, *das*
**firm**[1] /fɜːm/ *n.* Firma, *die*

**firm²** *adj.* **(a)** fest; stabil ⟨*Konstruktion, Stuhl*⟩
**(b)** (resolute, strict) bestimmt
**'firmly** *adv.* **(a)** fest
**(b)** (resolutely, strictly) bestimmt
**first** /fɜːst/ ① *adj.* erst...; **he was ∼ to arrive** er kam als Erster an
② *adv.* **(a)** (before anyone else) zuerst; als Erster/Erste ⟨*sprechen, ankommen*⟩; (before anything else) an erster Stelle ⟨*stehen, kommen*⟩; **∼ come ∼ served** wer zuerst kommt, mahlt zuerst (Spr.)
**(b)** (beforehand) vorher
**(c)** (for the ∼ time) zum ersten Mal
**(d)** **∼ of all** zuerst; (in importance) vor allem
③ *n.* **(a) the ∼** (in sequence, rank) der/die/das Erste; *pl.* die Ersten
**(b) at ∼:** zuerst; **from the ∼:** von Anfang an
**first:** **∼ 'aid** *n.* erste Hilfe; **∼-aid box/kit** Verbandkasten, *der*/Erste-Hilfe-Ausrüstung, *die;* **∼-class** ① /'--/ *adj.* **(a)** erster Klasse *nachgestellt;* Erste[r]-Klasse-⟨*Fahrkarte, Abteil, Post, Brief usw.*⟩; **(b)** (excellent) erstklassig; ② /-'-/ *adv.* erster Klasse ⟨*reisen*⟩
**'firstly** *adv.* zunächst [einmal]; (followed by 'secondly') erstens
**first:** **∼ name** *n.* Vorname, *der;* **∼ 'night** *n.* (Theatre) Premiere, *die;* **∼ of'fender** *n.* Ersttäter, *der*/-täterin, *die;* **∼-rate** *adj.* erstklassig; **∼ school** *n.* (Brit.) ≈ Grundschule, *die*
**'fir tree** *n.* Tanne, *die*
**fish** /fɪʃ/ ① *n.* Fisch, *der*
② *v.i.* fischen; (with rod) angeln; **go ∼ing** fischen/angeln gehen
■ **fish 'out** *v.t.* (coll.) herausfischen (ugs.)
**fish:** **∼ bone** *n.* [Fisch]gräte, *die;* **∼ cake** *n.* Fischfrikadelle, *die*
**fisherman** /'fɪʃəmən/ *n., pl.* **fishermen** /'fɪʃəmən/ Fischer, *der;* (angler) Angler, *der*
**fish:** **∼eye lens** *n.* Fischaugenobjektiv, *das;* **∼ farm** *n.* Fischzucht[anlage], *die;* **∼ farming** *n.* Fischzucht, *die;* **∼ 'finger** *n.* Fischstäbchen, *das;* **∼ hook** *n.* Angelhaken, *der*
**'fishing** *n.* Fischen, *das;* (with rod) Angeln, *das*
**fishing:** **∼ boat** *n.* Fischerboot, *das;* **∼ industry** *n.* Fischerei[industrie], *die;* **∼ net** *n.* Fischernetz, *das;* **∼ rod** *n.* Angelrute, *die* **∼ tackle** *n.* Angelgeräte *Pl.;* **∼ vessel** *n.* Fischereifahrzeug, *das;* **∼ village** *n.* Fischerdorf, *das*
**fish:** **∼ kettle** *n.* Fischkessel, *der;* **∼monger** /'fɪʃmʌŋgə(r)/ *n.* (Brit.) Fischhändler, *der*/-händlerin, *die;* **∼ pond** *n.* Fischteich, *der;* **∼ shop** *n.* Fischgeschäft, *das;* **∼ slice** *n.* Wender, *der;* **∼ tank** *n.* Fischkasten, *der;* Fischbehälter, *der*
**'fishy** *adj.* **(a)** fischartig; Fisch⟨*geschmack, -geruch*⟩
**(b)** (coll.: suspicious) verdächtig

**fist** /fɪst/ *n.* Faust, *die*
**fit¹** /fɪt/ *n.* Anfall, *der;* (fig.) [plötzliche] Anwandlung; **be in ∼s of laughter** sich vor Lachen biegen; **in a ∼ of ...:** in einem Anfall von ...
**fit²** ① *adj.* **(a)** (suitable) geeignet; **∼ to eat** essbar
**(b)** (worthy) würdig; wert
**(c)** (proper) richtig; **see** *or* **think ∼ [to do sth.]** es für richtig halten[, etw. zu tun]
**(d)** (healthy) fit (ugs.); **keep ∼:** sich fit halten
② *n.* Passform, *die;* **it is a good/bad ∼:** es sitzt *od.* passt gut/nicht gut
③ *v.t.,* **-tt-:** **(a)** ⟨*Kleider:*⟩ passen (+ *Dat.*); ⟨*Deckel, Bezug:*⟩ passen auf (+ *Akk.*)
**(b)** (put into place) anbringen (to an + *Dat. od. Akk.*); einbauen ⟨*Motor, Ersatzteil*⟩
④ *v.i.,* **-tt-** passen
■ **fit 'in** ① *v.t.* unterbringen
② *v.i.* **(a)** ⟨*Person:*⟩ sich anpassen (**with** an + *Akk.*)
**(b)** (be in accordance with) **∼ in with sth.** mit etw. übereinstimmen
**'fitful** *adj.* unbeständig; unruhig ⟨*Schlaf*⟩; launisch ⟨*Brise*⟩
**'fitment** *n.* Einrichtung, *die*
**'fitness** *n.* **(a)** ( physical) Fitness, *die*
**(b)** (suitability) Eignung, *die*
**'fitness studio** *n.* Fitnessstudio, *das*
**'fitted** *adj.* **(a)** (suited) geeignet (**for** für, zu)
**(b)** (shaped) tailliert ⟨*Kleider*⟩; Einbau⟨*küche, schrank*⟩; **∼ carpet** Teppichboden, *der*
**'fitter** *n.* Monteur, *der;* (of pipes) Installateur, *der;* (of machines) Maschinenschlosser, *der*
**'fitting** ① *adj.* (appropriate) passend; (becoming) schicklich (geh.) ⟨*Benehmen*⟩
② *n.* **(a)** *usu. in pl.* (fixture) Anschluss, *der;* **∼s** (furniture) Ausstattung, *die*
**(b)** (Brit.: size) Größe, *die*
**'fitting-room** *n.* Anprobe, *die*
**five** /faɪv/ ① *adj.* fünf
② *n.* Fünf, *die.* See also EIGHT
**fiver** /'faɪvə(r)/ *n.* (Brit. coll.) Fünfpfundschein, *der*
**five:** **∼-star** *adj.* Fünf-Sterne-⟨*Hotel, General*⟩; (fig.) ausgezeichnet; **∼-'year plan** *n.* Fünfjahresplan, *der*
**fix** /fɪks/ ① *v.t.* **(a)** befestigen
**(b)** festsetzen ⟨*Termin, Preis, Grenze*⟩; (agree on) ausmachen
**(c)** (repair) reparieren
**(d)** (arrange) arrangieren
② *n.* (coll.: predicament) Klemme, *die* (ugs.); **be in a ∼:** in der Klemme sitzen
■ **fix 'up** *v.t.* **(a)** (arrange) arrangieren; festsetzen ⟨*Termin, Treffpunkt*⟩
**(b)** (provide) versorgen; **∼ sb. up with sth.** jmdm. etw. verschaffen
**fixed:** **∼ price** Festpreis, *der;* **∼-rate** *attrib. adj.* Festzins-; mit festem Zins *nachgestellt*
**fixture** /'fɪkstʃə(r)/ *n.* **(a)** (furnishing) eingebautes Teil
**(b)** (Sport) Veranstaltung, *die*

**fizz** /fɪz/ *v.i.* [zischend] sprudeln

**fizzle** /'fɪzl/ *v.i.* zischen

■ **fizzle 'out** *v.i.* ⟨*Kampagne:*⟩ im Sande verlaufen

**fizzy** /'fɪzɪ/ *adj.* sprudelnd; ~ lemonade Brause[limonade], *die*

**flabbergast** /'flæbəgɑːst/ *v.t.* umhauen (ugs.)

**flabby** /'flæbɪ/ *adj.* schlaff

**flag**[1] /flæg/ *n.* Fahne, *die;* (national ~, on ship) Flagge, *die*

**flag**[2] *v.i.,* -gg- ⟨*Person:*⟩ abbauen; ⟨*Kraft, Begeisterung usw.:*⟩ nachlassen

**flagon** /'flægn/ *n.* Kanne, *die*

**'flagpole** *n.* Flaggenmast, *der*

**flagrant** /'fleɪgrənt/ *adj.* eklatant; flagrant ⟨*Verstoß*⟩

**'flagstone** *n.* Steinplatte, *die*

**flair** /fleə(r)/ *n.* Gespür, *das;* (special ability) Talent, *das*

**flak** /flæk/ *n.* Flakfeuer, *das* (Milit.); (gun) Flak, *die* (Milit.); **get a lot of** ~ **for sth.** (fig.) wegen etw. [schwer] unter Beschuss geraten

**flake** /fleɪk/ [1] *n.* Flocke, *die;* (of dry skin) Schuppe, *die*
[2] *v.i.* abblättern

**'flak jacket** *n.* kugelsichere Weste

**flaky** /'fleɪkɪ/ *adj.* blättrig ⟨*Kruste*⟩; ~ **pastry** Blätterteig, *der*

**flamboyant** /flæm'bɔɪənt/ *adj.* extravagant

**flame** /fleɪm/ *n.* Flamme, *die;* **be in** ~**s** in Flammen stehen

**'flameproof** nicht entflammbar; flammfest

**flan** /flæn/ *n.* [fruit] ~: [Obst]torte, *die*

**flank** /flæŋk/ *n.* Seite, *die;* (of animal; also Mil.) Flanke, *die*

**flannel** /'flænl/ *n.* (a) (fabric) Flanell, *der* (b) (Brit.: for washing) Waschlappen, *der*

**flap** /flæp/ [1] *v.t.,* -pp-: ~ **its wings** mit den Flügeln schlagen
[2] *v.i.,* -pp- ⟨*Flügel:*⟩ schlagen; ⟨*Segel, Fahne, Vorhang:*⟩ flattern
[3] *n.* (a) Klappe, *die;* (envelope seal, of shoe) Lasche, *die*
(b) (fig. coll.) **in a** ~: furchtbar aufgeregt

**flare** /fleə(r)/ [1] *v.i.* flackern; (fig.) ausbrechen; **tempers** ~**d** die Gemüter erhitzten sich
[2] *n.* Leuchtsignal, *das*
■ **flare 'up** *v.i.* (a) aufflackern (b) (break out) [wieder] ausbrechen

**flash** /flæʃ/ [1] *n.* Aufleuchten, *das;* (as signal) Lichtsignal, *das;* ~ **of lightning** Blitz, *der;* **in a** ~: (quickly) im Nu
[2] *v.t.* (a) aufleuchten lassen; ~ **one's headlights** die Lichthupe betätigen; ~ **sb. a smile/glance** jmdm. ein Lächeln/einen Blick zuwerfen
(b) (display briefly) kurz zeigen
[3] *v.i.* aufleuchten; ~ **by** or **past** ⟨*Zeit, Ferien:*⟩ wie im Fluge vergehen

**flash:** ~**back** *n.* Rückblende, *die* (to auf

+ *Akk.*); ~ **bulb** *n.* Blitzbirnchen, *das;* ~ **cube** *n.* Blitzwürfel, *der;* ~ **flood** *n.* Überschwemmung, *die* (durch heftige Regenfälle); ~**gun** *n.* Blitzgerät, *das;* ~**light** *n.* (a) (for signals) Blinklicht, *das;* (b) (Amer.: torch) Taschenlampe, *die;* ~**point** *n.* Flammpunkt, *der;* (fig.) Siedepunkt, *der*

**'flashy** *adj.* auffällig

**flask** /flɑːsk/ *n.* (a) ▶ THERMOS
(b) (for wine, oil) [bauchige] Flasche
(c) (Chem.) Kolben, *der*

**flat**[1] /flæt/ *n.* (Brit.) Wohnung, *die*

**flat**[2] [1] *adj.* (a) flach; eben ⟨*Fläche*⟩; platt ⟨*Nase, Reifen*⟩
(b) (downright) glatt (ugs.) ⟨*Absage, Weigerung, Widerspruch*⟩
(c) (Mus.) [um einen Halbton] erniedrigt ⟨*Note*⟩
(d) schal, abgestanden ⟨*Bier, Sekt*⟩
(e) leer ⟨*Batterie*⟩
[2] *adv.* (Mus.) zu tief

**flat:** ~**chested** /flæt'tʃestɪd/ *adj.* flachbrüstig; flachbusig; ~ **'feet** *n. pl.* Plattfüße *Pl.;* ~**'fish** *n.* Plattfisch, *der;* ~**'footed** *adj.* plattfüßig; ~**heeled** *adj.* ⟨*Schuh*⟩ mit flachem Absatz; flach ⟨*Schuh*⟩

**flatlet** /'flætlɪt/ *n.* (Brit.) Appartement, *das*

**'flatly** *adv.* rundweg

**flat:** ~ **mate** *n.* (Brit.) Mitbewohner, *der*/Mitbewohnerin, *die;* **they were** ~ **mates** sie haben zusammen gewohnt; ~ **'out** *adv.* (at top speed) **he ran/worked** ~ **out** er rannte/arbeitete, so schnell er konnte; ~**pack** *adj.* ⟨*Möbel*⟩ zum Selbstbauen; ~ **rate** *n.* Einheitstarif, *der;* ~ **'spin** *n.* (Aeronaut.) Flachtrudeln, *das;* **go into a** ~ **spin** (fig. coll.) durchdrehen (ugs.)

**flatten** /'flætn/ [1] *v.t.* flach drücken ⟨*Schachtel*⟩; **dem Erdboden gleichmachen** ⟨*Stadt, Gebäude*⟩
[2] *v. refl.* ~ **oneself against sth.** sich flach gegen etw. drücken

**flatter** /'flætə(r)/ *v.t.* schmeicheln (+ *Dat.*)

**'flattering** *adj.* schmeichelhaft

**'flattery** *n.* Schmeichelei, *die*

**flat 'tyre** *n.* Reifenpanne, *die*

**flatulence** /'flætjʊləns/ *n.* Blähungen *Pl.;* Flatulenz, *die* (Med.)

**flaunt** /flɔːnt/ *v.t.* zur Schau stellen

**flavor** *etc.* (Amer.) ▶ FLAVOUR *etc.*

**flavour** /'fleɪvə(r)/ (Brit.) [1] *n.* (a) Geschmack, *der*
(b) (fig.) Anflug, *der*
[2] *v.t.* abschmecken

**'flavouring** *n.* (Brit.) Aroma, *das*

**'flavourless** *adj.* (Brit.) fade

**flavoursome** /'fleɪvəsəm/ *adj.* (Brit.) schmackhaft

**flaw** /flɔː/ *n.* Fehler, *der;* (imperfection) Makel, *der;* (in workmanship or goods) Mangel, *der*

**flax** /flæks/ *n.* Flachs, *der*

**flea** /fliː/ *n.* Floh, *der*

**flea:** ∼ **bite** n. Flohbiss, der; ∼ **market** n. (coll.) Flohmarkt, der

**fled** ▶ FLEE

**flee** /fliː/ ① v.i., fled /fled/ fliehen; ∼ **from sth./sb.** aus etw./vor jmdm. flüchten ② v.t., **fled** fliehen aus

**fleece** /fliːs/ ① n. [Schaf]fell, das ② v.t. (fig.) ausplündern

**fleecy** /'fliːsɪ/ adj. flauschig

**fleet** /fliːt/ n. Flotte, die

**fleeting** /'fliːtɪŋ/ adj. flüchtig

**flesh** /fleʃ/ n. Fleisch, das; (of fruit, plant) [Frucht]fleisch, das

**flesh:** ∼-**coloured** adj. fleischfarben; ∼ **wound** n. Fleischwunde, die

**'fleshy** adj. fett; fleischig ⟨Hände⟩

**flew** ▶ FLY² 1, 2

**flex¹** /fleks/ n. (Brit. Electr.) Kabel, das

**flex²** v.t. beugen ⟨Arm, Knie⟩; ∼ **one's muscles** seine Muskeln spielen lassen

**flexible** /'fleksɪbl/ adj. (a) biegsam; elastisch
(b) (fig.) flexibel; ∼ **working hours** or **time** gleitende Arbeitszeit

**flexitime** /'fleksɪtaɪm/ (Brit.), **flextime** /'flekstaɪm/ (Amer.) ns. Gleitzeit, die; **be on** or **work** ∼: gleitende Arbeitszeit haben

**flick** /flɪk/ v.t. schnippen; anknipsen ⟨Schalter⟩; verspritzen ⟨Tinte⟩
■ **'flick through** v.t. durchblättern

**flicker** /'flɪkə(r)/ ① v.i. flackern; ⟨Fernsehapparat:⟩ flimmern ② n. Flackern, das; (of TV) Flimmern, das

**flick knife** n. (Brit.) Schnappmesser, das

**flight¹** /flaɪt/ n. (a) Flug, der
(b) ∼ [of stairs or steps] Treppe, die

**flight²** n. (fleeing) Flucht, die; **take** ∼: die Flucht ergreifen; **put to** ∼: in die Flucht schlagen

**flight:** ∼ **attendant** n. Flugbegleiter, der/-begleiterin, die; ∼ **control** n. ≈ Flugsicherung, die; ∼ **controller** n. (Aeronaut.) Fluglotse, der; ∼ **deck** n. (a) (of aircraft carrier) Flugdeck, das; (b) (of aircraft) Cockpit, das; ∼ **number** n. Flugnummer, die; ∼ **path** n. (Aeronaut.) Flugweg, der; (Astronaut.) Flugbahn, die; ∼ **recorder** n. Flugschreiber, der

**flimsy** /'flɪmzɪ/ adj. (a) dünn; nicht sehr haltbar ⟨Verpackung⟩
(b) (fig.) fadenscheinig ⟨Entschuldigung, Argument⟩

**flinch** /flɪntʃ/ v.i. zurückschrecken (**from** vor + Dat.); (wince) zusammenzucken

**fling** /flɪŋ/ ① n. **have a** or **one's** ∼: sich ausleben ② v.t., **flung** /flʌŋ/ werfen; ∼ **oneself into sth.** (fig.) sich in etw. (Akk.) stürzen

**flint** /flɪnt/ n. Feuerstein, der

**flip** /flɪp/ v.t., -**pp**- schnipsen; ∼ [**over**] (turn over) umdrehen
■ **'flip through** v.t. durchblättern

**flippant** /'flɪpənt/ adj. leichtfertig

**flipper** /'flɪpə(r)/ n. Flosse, die

**'flip side** n. B-Seite, die

**flirt** /flɜːt/ v.i. flirten

**flirtation** /flɜː'teɪʃn/ n. Flirt, der

**flirtatious** /flɜː'teɪʃəs/ adj. kokett ⟨Blick, Art⟩

**flit** /flɪt/ v.i. huschen

**float** /fləʊt/ ① v.i. treiben; (in air) schweben ② n. (for carnival) Festwagen, der ③ v.t. (set afloat) flottmachen; (fig.) lancieren ⟨Plan, Idee⟩

**floating:** ∼ **'dock** n. Schwimmdock, das; ∼ **'voter** n. Wechselwähler, der/-wählerin, die

**flock** /flɒk/ ① n. (a) Herde, die; (of birds) Schwarm, der
(b) (of people) Schar, die ② v.i. strömen; ∼ **round sb.** sich um jmdn. scharen

**flog** /flɒg/ v.t., -**gg**-: (a) auspeitschen
(b) (Brit. coll.: sell) verscheuern (salopp)

**flood** /flʌd/ ① n. (a) Überschwemmung, die; **the F**∼ (Bibl.) die Sintflut ② v.i. ⟨Fluss:⟩ über die Ufer treten; (fig.) strömen ③ v.t. überschwemmen

**flood:** ∼ **damage** n. Hochwasserschaden, der; **the area suffered extensive** ∼ **damage** in dem Gebiet gab es beträchtliche Hochwasserschäden; ∼**gate** n. (Hydraulic Engin.) Schütze, die; **open the** ∼**gates to sth.** (fig.) einer Sache (Dat.) Tür und Tor öffnen; ∼**light** ① n. Scheinwerfer, der. ② v.t., **floodlit** /'flʌdlɪt/ anstrahlen; ∼ **tide** n. Flut, die; ∼ **warning** n. Hochwasserwarnung, die; ∼ **water** n. Hochwasser, das

**floor** /flɔː(r)/ ① n. (a) Boden, der
(b) (storey) Stockwerk, das; **first** ∼ (Amer.) Erdgeschoss, das; **first** ∼ (Brit.), **second** ∼ (Amer.) erster Stock; **ground** ∼: Erdgeschoss, das; Parterre, das ② v.t. (a) (confound) überfordern
(b) (knock down) zu Boden schlagen

**floor:** ∼**board** n. Dielenbrett, das; ∼**cloth** n. (Brit.) Scheuertuch, das; ∼ **polish** n. Bohnerwachs, das; ∼ **show** n. ≈ Unterhaltungsprogramm, das

**flop** /flɒp/ ① v.i., -**pp**-: (a) plumpsen
(b) (coll.: fail) fehlschlagen; ⟨Theaterstück, Show:⟩ durchfallen ② n. (coll.: failure) Reinfall, der (ugs.)

**floppy** /'flɒpɪ/ adj. weich und biegsam

**floppy disk** n. (Comp.) Floppy Disk, die; Diskette, die

**flora** /'flɔːrə/ n. Flora, die

**floral** /'flɔːrl, 'flɒrl/ adj. geblümt ⟨Kleid, Stoff⟩; Blumen⟨muster⟩

**Florence** /'flɒrəns/ pr. n. Florenz (das)

**florid** /'flɒrɪd/ adj. blumig ⟨Stil, Redeweise⟩; gerötet ⟨Teint⟩

**florist** /'flɒrɪst/ n. Florist, der/Floristin, die

**flotsam** /'flɒtsəm/ n. ~ [and jetsam] Treibgut, das

**flounder** /'flaʊndə(r)/ v.i. taumeln

**flour** /'flaʊə(r)/ n. Mehl, das

**flourish** /'flʌrɪʃ/ 1 v.i. gedeihen; ⟨Geschäft:⟩ florieren, gut gehen
2 v.t. schwingen
3 n. do sth. with a ~: etw. schwungvoll tun

**flout** /flaʊt/ v.t. missachten

**flow** /fləʊ/ 1 v.i. fließen; ⟨Körner, Sand:⟩ rinnen, rieseln; ⟨Gas:⟩ strömen
2 n. (a) Fließen, das; ~ of water/people Wasser-/Menschenstrom, der; ~ of information Informationsfluss, der
(b) (of tide, river) Flut, die

**'flow chart** n. Flussdiagramm, das

**flower** /'flaʊə(r)/ 1 n. (blossom) Blüte, die; (plant) Blume, die; come into ~: zu blühen beginnen
2 v.i. blühen

**'flower bed** n. Blumenbeet, das

**flowering** /'flaʊərɪŋ/ adj. ~ cherry/shrub Zierkirsche, die/Blütenstrauch, der

**'flowerpot** n. Blumentopf, der

**flowery** /'flaʊərɪ/ adj. geblümt ⟨Stoff, Muster⟩; (fig.) blumig ⟨Sprache⟩

**flowing** adj. fließend; wallend ⟨Haar⟩

**flown** ▶ FLY² 1, 2

**flu** /fluː/ n. (coll.) Grippe, die

**fluctuate** /'flʌktjʊeɪt/ v.i. schwanken

**fluctuation** /flʌktjʊ'eɪʃn/ n. Schwankung, die

**fluency** /'fluːənsɪ/ n. Gewandtheit, die; (spoken) Redegewandtheit, die

**fluent** /'fluːənt/ adj. gewandt ⟨Stil, Redeweise, Redner, Schreiber⟩; be ~ in Russian, speak ~ Russian fließend Russisch sprechen

**fluff** /flʌf/ n. Flusen Pl.; Fusseln Pl.

**fluffy** /'flʌfɪ/ adj. [flaum]weich ⟨Kissen, Küken⟩; flauschig ⟨Spielzeug, Decke⟩

**fluid** /'fluːɪd/ 1 n. Flüssigkeit, die
2 adj. flüssig

**fluke** /fluːk/ n. (piece of luck) Glücksfall, der

**flung** ▶ FLING 2

**fluorescent** /flʊə'resənt/ adj. fluoreszierend

**fluorescent 'light** n. Leuchtstofflampe, die

**fluoride** /'fluːəraɪd/ n. Fluorid, das; ~ toothpaste fluorhaltige Zahnpasta

**flurry** /'flʌrɪ/ n. (a) Aufregung, die (b) (of rain/snow) [Regen-/Schnee]schauer, der

**flush¹** /flʌʃ/ 1 v.i. rot werden
2 v.t. ausspülen ⟨Becken⟩; ~ the toilet or lavatory spülen
3 n. Rotwerden, das

**flush²** adj. (level) bündig; be ~ with sth. mit etw. bündig abschließen

**flush 'toilet** n. Toilette mit Wasserspülung

**fluster** /'flʌstə(r)/ v.t. aus der Fassung bringen

**flustered** /'flʌstəd/ adj. nervös

**flute** /fluːt/ n. Flöte, die

**flutter** /'flʌtə(r)/ 1 v.i. flattern
2 v.t. flattern mit ⟨Flügel⟩

**flux** /flʌks/ n. in a state of ~: im Fluss

**fly¹** /flaɪ/ n. Fliege, die

**fly²** 1 v.i., flew /fluː/, flown /fləʊn/ (a) fliegen; ~ away or off wegfliegen
(b) (fig.) ~ [by or past] wie im Fluge vergehen
(c) ⟨Fahne:⟩ gehisst sein
2 v.t., flew, flown fliegen ⟨Flugzeug, Fracht, Einsatz usw.⟩; fliegen über (+ Akk.) ⟨Strecke⟩
3 n. in sing. or pl. (on trousers) Hosenschlitz, der

■ **fly 'in** v.i. [mit dem Flugzeug] eintreffen (from aus)

■ **fly 'out** v.i. abfliegen (of von)

**'fly-fishing** n. Fliegenfischerei, die

**flying** /'flaɪɪŋ/: ~ 'doctor n.: Arzt, der seine Krankenbesuche mit dem Flugzeug macht; ~ 'saucer n. fliegende Untertasse; ~ 'start n. (Sport) fliegender Start; ~ 'visit n. Stippvisite, die (ugs.)

**fly:** ~leaf n. Vorsatzblatt, das; ~over n. (Brit.) [Straßen]überführung, die; ~ spray n. Insektenspray, der od. das; ~ swatter n. Fliegenklappe, die; Fliegenklatsche, die

**foal** /fəʊl/ n. Fohlen, das

**foam** /fəʊm/ 1 n. Schaum, der
2 v.i. schäumen

**foam:** ~backed adj. schaumstoffverstärkt; ~ 'mattress n. Schaumgummimatratze, die; ~ 'rubber n. Schaumgummi, der

**fob** /fɒb/ v.t., -bb-: ~ sb. off with sth. jmdn. mit etw. abspeisen (ugs.)

**'focal point** n. Brennpunkt, der (auch fig.)

**focus** /'fəʊkəs/ 1 n., pl. ~es or foci /'fəʊsaɪ/ Brennpunkt, der; out of/in ~: unscharf/scharf eingestellt; unscharf/scharf ⟨Foto, Film usw.⟩; (fig.) be the ~ of attention im Brennpunkt des Interesses stehen
2 v.t., -s- or -ss- einstellen (on auf + Akk.); bündeln ⟨Licht, Strahlen⟩
3 v.i., -s- or -ss- (fig.) sich konzentrieren (on auf + Akk.)

**'focus group** n. Fokusgruppe, die

**fodder** /'fɒdə(r)/ n. [Vieh]futter, das

**foe** /fəʊ/ n. (poet./rhet.) Feind, der

**foetus** /'fiːtəs/ n. Fötus, der

**fog** /fɒg/ n. Nebel, der

**'foglight** n. Nebelscheinwerfer, der

**foggy** /'fɒgɪ/ adj. neblig

**fogy** /'fəʊgɪ/ n. [old] ~: [alter] Opa (salopp)/ [alte] Oma (salopp)

**foible** /'fɔɪbl/ n. Eigenheit, die

**foil¹** /fɔɪl/ n. Folie, die

**foil²** v.t. vereiteln

**foist** /fɔɪst/ v.t. ~ [off] on to sb. jmdm. andrehen (ugs.); auf jmdn. abwälzen ⟨Probleme, Verantwortung⟩

**fold** /fəʊld/ ① *v.t.* [zusammen]falten;
~ one's arms die Arme verschränken
② *v.i.* (a) (become ~ed) sich zusammenfalten
(b) (be able to be ~ed) sich falten lassen
(c) (go bankrupt) Konkurs machen
③ *n.* Falte, *die;* (line made by ~ing) Kniff, *der*
▪ **fold 'up** *v.t.* zusammenfalten ⟨*Laken*⟩;
zusammenklappen ⟨*Stuhl*⟩
**'folder** *n.* (a) Mappe, *die*
(b) (Comp.) Ordner, *der*
**foliage** /'fəʊlɪdʒ/ *n.* Blätter *Pl.;* (of tree also)
Laub, *das*
**folk** /fəʊk/ *n.* (a) Volk, *das*
(b) *in pl.* ~[s] (people) Leute *Pl.*
**folk:** ~ **dance** *n.* Volkstanz, *der;* ~ **hero**
*n.* Volksheld, *der;* ~**lore** /-lɔː(r)/ *n.*
Folklore, *die;* ~ **music** *n.* Volksmusik, *die;*
~ **singer** *n.* Sänger/Sängerin von
Volksliedern; (modern) Folksänger, *der/*
-sängerin, *die;* ~ **song** Volkslied, *das;*
(modern) Folksong, *der*
**follow** /'fɒləʊ/ ① *v.t.* (a) folgen (+ *Dat.*)
(b) entlanggehen/-fahren ⟨*Straße usw.*⟩
(c) (come after) folgen auf (+ *Akk.*)
(d) (result from) die Folge sein von
(e) (treat or take as guide) sich orientieren an
(+ *Dat.*)
(f) folgen (+ *Dat.*) ⟨*Prinzip, Instinkt, Trend*⟩;
verfolgen ⟨*Politik*⟩; befolgen ⟨*Regel,*
*Vorschrift, Rat, Warnung*⟩; sich halten an
(+ *Akk.*) ⟨*Konventionen, Diät*⟩
(g) (grasp meaning of) folgen (+ *Dat.*); **do you**
~ **me?** verstehst du, was ich meine?
② *v.i.* (a) (go, come) ~ **after sb./sth.** jmdm./
einer Sache folgen
(b) (come next in order or time) folgen; **as** ~**s**
wie folgt
(c) ~ **from sth.** (result) die Folge von etw.
sein; (be deducible) aus etw. folgen
▪ **follow 'on** *v.i.* (continue) ~ **on from sth.**
die Fortsetzung von etw. sein
▪ **follow 'up** *v.t.* (a) ausbauen ⟨*Erfolg,*
*Sieg*⟩
(b) nachgehen (+ *Dat.*) ⟨*Hinweis*⟩
**'follower** *n.* Anhänger, *der/*Anhängerin,
*die*
**'following** ① *adj.* folgend; **the** ~:
Folgendes
② *prep.* nach
③ *n.* Anhängerschaft, *die*
**folly** /'fɒlɪ/ *n.* Torheit, *die* (geh.)
**fond** /fɒnd/ *adj.* liebevoll; lieb ⟨*Erinnerung*⟩;
**be** ~ **of sb.** jmdn. mögen; **be** ~ **of doing sth.**
etw. gern tun
**fondle** /'fɒndl/ *v.t.* streicheln
**'fondness** *n.* Liebe, *die;* ~ **for sth.** Vorliebe
für etw.
**font¹** /fɒnt/ *n.* Taufstein, *der*
**font²** *n.* (Comp., Printing) Schrift, *die;* Font, *der*
(fachspr.); ~ **size** Schriftgröße, *die;* Fontgröße,
*die*
**food** /fuːd/ *n.* (a) Nahrung, *die;* (for animals)
Futter, *das*
(b) (as commodity) Lebensmittel *Pl.*

(c) (in solid form) Essen, *das*
(d) (particular kind) Nahrungsmittel, *das;* Kost,
*die*
**food:** ~ **chain** *n.* Nahrungskette, *die;*
~ **poisoning** *n.* Lebensmittelvergiftung,
*die;* ~ **processor** *n.* Küchenmaschine,
*die;* ~ **shop,** ~ **store** *ns.*
Lebensmittelgeschäft, *das;* ~**stuff** *n.*
Nahrungsmittel, *das;* perishable ~stuffs
leicht verderbliche Lebensmittel
**fool** /fuːl/ ① *n.* Dummkopf, *der* (ugs.)
② *v.t.* ~ **sb. into doing sth.** jmdn. [durch
Tricks] dazu bringen, etw. zu tun
▪ **fool a'bout, fool a'round** *v.i.* Unsinn
machen
**foolhardy** /'fuːlhɑːdɪ/ *adj.* tollkühn
**'foolish** *adj.* töricht; verrückt (ugs.) ⟨*Idee,*
*Vorschlag*⟩
**'foolproof** *adj.* (infallible) absolut sicher
**foot** /fʊt/ ① *n., pl.* **feet** /fiːt/ *n.* Fuß, *der;* **on**
~: zu Fuß; **put one's** ~ **in it** (fig. coll.) ins
Fettnäpfchen treten (ugs.)
(b) (far end) unteres Ende; (of bed) Fußende,
*das*
(c) (measure) Fuß, *der* (30,48 cm)
② *v.t.* ~ **the bill** die Rechnung bezahlen
**football** /'fʊtbɔːl/ *n.* (game, ball) Fußball, *der*
**'football boot** *n.* Fußballschuh, *der*
**'footballer** *n.* Fußballspieler, *der/*
-spielerin, *die*
**football:** ~ **pitch** *n.* Fußballplatz, *der;*
~ **pools** *n. pl.* **the** ~ **pools** das Fußballtoto
**foot:** ~ **brake** *n.* Fußbremse, *die;*
~ **bridge** *n.* Fußgängerbrücke, *die;*
~**hold** *n.* Halt, *der*
**'footing** *n.* (a) (fig.) **be on an equal** ~ [**with**
**sb.**] [jmdm.] gleichgestellt sein
(b) (foothold) Halt, *der*
**foot:** ~**note** *n.* Fußnote, *die;*
~ **passenger** *n.* Fußpassagier, *der;*
~**path** *n.* Fußweg, *der;* ~**print** *n.*
Fußabdruck, *der;* ~**rest** *n.* Fußstütze, *die;*
(on bicycle or motorcycle) Fußraste, *die;* ~**step**
*n.* Schritt, *der;* follow in sb.'s ~steps (fig.) in
jmds. Fußstapfen (*Akk.*) treten; ~**stool** *n.*
Fußbank, *die;* Fußschemel, *der;* ~**wear** *n.*
Schuhe *Pl.;* ~**work** *n.* (Sport, Dancing)
Beinarbeit, *die*
**for** /fə(r), *stressed* fɔː(r)/ ① *prep.* (a) für;
**what is it** ~? wofür ist das?; **reason** ~ **living**
Grund zu leben; **a request** ~ **help** eine Bitte
um Hilfe; **study** ~ **a university degree** auf
einen Hochschulabschluss hin studieren;
**take sb.** ~ **a walk** mit jmdm. einen
Spaziergang machen; **be '**~ **doing sth.** (in
favour) dafür sein, etw. zu tun; **cheque/bill**
~ **£5** Scheck/Rechnung über 5 Pfund; **what**
**have you got** ~ **a cold?** was haben Sie
gegen Erkältungen?
(b) (on account of, as penalty of) wegen; **were it**
**not** ~ **you/ your help** ohne dich/deine Hilfe;
~ **fear of** aus Angst vor (+ *Dat.*)
(c) (in spite of) ~ **all** ...: trotz ...; ~ **all that,**
...: trotzdem ...                                    ⋯⁘

**(d)** ~ all I know/care ...: möglicherweise/was mich betrifft, ...; ~ one thing, ...: zunächst einmal ...
**(e)** (during) stay ~ a week eine Woche bleiben; we've/we haven't been here ~ three years wir sind seit drei Jahren hier/nicht mehr hier gewesen
**(f)** walk ~ 20 miles 20 Meilen gehen ② *conj.* denn

**forage** /'fɒrɪdʒ/ ① *n.* Futter, *das* ② *v.i.* ~ for sth. auf der Suche nach etw. sein

**forbad, forbade** ▸ FORBID

**forbid** /fə'bɪd/ *v.t.*, -dd-, forbad /fə'bæd/ *or* forbade /fə'bæd, fə'beɪd/, forbidden /fə'bɪdn/ ~ sb. to do sth. jmdm. verbieten, etw. zu tun; ~ [sb.] sth. [jmdm.] etw. verbieten; it is ~den [to do sth.] es ist verboten[, etw. zu tun]

**forbidden** ▸ FORBID

**for'bidding** *adj.* Furcht einflößend

**force** /fɔːs/ ① *n.* **(a)** (strength, power) Stärke, *die;* (of explosion, storm) Wucht, *die;* (Phys.; physical strength) Kraft, *die;* in ~: mit einem großen Aufgebot
**(b)** (validity) Kraft, *die;* in ~: in Kraft; come into ~ ⟨*Gesetz usw.:*⟩ in Kraft treten
**(c)** (violence) Gewalt, *die;* by ~: gewaltsam
**(d)** (group) (of workers) Kolonne, *die;* Trupp, *der;* (Mil.) Armee, *die;* the ~ (Police) die Polizei; the ~s die Armee; be in the ~s beim Militär sein
② *v.t.* **(a)** zwingen; ~ sth. [up]on sb. jmdm. etw. aufzwingen
**(b)** ~ [open] aufbrechen; ~ one's way in sich (*Dat.*) mit Gewalt Zutritt verschaffen

**forced** /fɔːst/ *adj.* **(a)** (contrived, unnatural) gezwungen
**(b)** (compelled by force) erzwungen; Zwangs⟨*arbeit*⟩

**forced 'landing** *n.* Notlandung, *die*

**'force-feed** *v.t.* zwangsernähren

**forceful** /'fɔːsfl/ *adj.* stark ⟨*Persönlichkeit, Charakter*⟩; energisch ⟨*Person, Art*⟩; eindrucksvoll ⟨*Sprache*⟩

**forceps** /'fɔːseps/ *n., pl. same* [pair of] ~: Zange, *die*

**forcible** /'fɔːsɪbl/ *adj.,* **forcibly** /'fɔːsɪblɪ/ *adv.* gewaltsam

**ford** /fɔːd/ ① *n.* Furt, *die* ② *v.t.* durchqueren; (wade through) durchwaten

**fore** /fɔː(r)/ ① *adj., esp. in comb.* vorder...; Vorder⟨*teil, -front usw.*⟩ ② *n.* to the ~: im Vordergrund

**'forearm** *n.* Unterarm, *der*

**foreboding** /fɔː'bəʊdɪŋ/ *n.* Vorahnung, *die*

**'forecast** ① *v.t.,* forecast *or* forecasted vorhersagen ② *n.* Voraussage, *die*

**'forecaster** *n.* Meteorologe, *der*/Meteorologin, *die*

**'forecourt** *n.* Vorhof, *der*

**'forefather** *n., usu. in pl.* Vorfahr, *der*

**'forefinger** *n.* Zeigefinger, *der*

**'forefront** *n.* [be] in the ~ of in vorderster Linie (+ *Gen.*) [stehen]

**'foregone** *adj.* be a ~ conclusion von vornherein feststehen; (be certain) so gut wie sicher sein

**'foreground** *n.* Vordergrund, *der*

**forehead** /'fɒrɪd, 'fɔːhed/ *n.* Stirn, *die*

**foreign** /'fɒrɪn/ *adj.* **(a)** (from abroad) ausländisch; Fremd⟨*kapital, -sprache*⟩; he is ~: er ist Ausländer
**(b)** (abroad) fremd; Außen⟨*politik, -handel*⟩; from a ~ country aus einem anderen Land; aus dem Ausland; ~ countries Ausland, *das*
**(c)** (from outside) fremd; ~ body/substance Fremdkörper, *der*

**foreign corre'spondent** *n.* (Journ.) Auslandskorrespondent, *der*/-korrespondentin, *die*

**'foreigner** *n.* Ausländer, *der*/Ausländerin, *die*

**foreign:** ~ ex'change *n.* Devisen *Pl.;* ~ 'language *n.* Fremdsprache, *die;* ~-language assistant Fremdsprachenassistent, *der*/-assistentin, *die;* ~-language newspaper/broadcast fremdsprachige Zeitung/Rundfunksendung; ~-language teaching Fremdsprachenunterricht, *der;* F~ 'Minister *n.* Außenminister, *der*/-ministerin, *die;* F~ 'Ministry *n.* Außenministerium, *das;* F~ Office *n.* (Brit. Hist./coll.) Außenministerium, *das;* ~ policy *n.* Außenpolitik, *die;* F~ 'Secretary *n.* (Brit.) Außenminister, *der*/-ministerin, *die;* ~ trade *n.* Außenhandel, *der*

**foreman** /'fɔːmən/ *n., pl.* foremen /'fɔːmən/ Vorarbeiter, *der*

**foremost** /'fɔːməʊst, 'fɔːməst/ ① *adj.* **(a)** vorderst...
**(b)** (fig.) führend ② *adv.* first and ~: zunächst einmal

**'forename** *n.* Vorname, *der*

**forensic** /fə'rensɪk/ *adj.* ~ medicine Gerichtsmedizin, *die;* ~ science Kriminaltechnik, *die*

**'foreplay** *n.* Vorspiel, *das*

**'forerunner** *n.* Vorläufer, *der*/Vorläuferin, *die*

**foresaw** ▸ FORESEE

**foresee** /fɔː'siː/ *v.t., forms as* SEE voraussehen

**foreseeable** /fɔː'siːəbl/ *adj.* vorhersehbar; in the ~ future in nächster Zukunft

**foreseen** ▸ FORESEE

**'foresight** *n.* Weitblick, *der*

**foreskin** *n.* (Anat.) Vorhaut, *die*

**forest** /'fɒrɪst/ *n.* Wald, *der;* (commercially exploited) Forst, *der*

**fore'stall** *v.t.* zuvorkommen (+ *Dat.*)

**forested** /'fɒrɪstɪd/ *adj.* bewaldet

**forestry** /ˈfɒrɪstrɪ/ n. Forstwirtschaft, die

**'foretaste** n. Vorgeschmack, der

**fore'tell** v.t., fore'told voraussagen

**'forethought** n. (prior deliberation) [vorherige] Überlegung; (care for the future) Vorausdenken, das

**forever** /fəˈrevə(r)/ adv. (constantly) ständig

**fore'warn** v.t. vorwarnen

**fore'warning** n. Vorwarnung, die

**'foreword** n. Vorwort, das

**forfeit** /ˈfɔːfɪt/ ① v.t. verlieren; verwirken (geh.) ⟨Recht, jmds. Gunst⟩
② n. Strafe, die; (games) Pfand, das

**forgave** ▶ FORGIVE

**forge¹** /fɔːdʒ/ ① n. (a) (workshop) Schmiede, die
(b) (blacksmith's hearth) Esse, die
② v.t. (a) schmieden (into zu)
(b) (fig.) schmieden ⟨Plan⟩; schließen ⟨Vereinbarung, Freundschaft⟩
(c) (counterfeit) fälschen

**forge²** v.i. ~ ahead [das Tempo] beschleunigen; (fig.) Fortschritte machen

**'forger** n. Fälscher, der/Fälscherin, die

**forgery** /ˈfɔːdʒərɪ/ n. Fälschung, die

**forget** /fəˈget/ ① v.t., -tt-, forgot /fəˈgɒt/, forgotten /fəˈgɒtn/ vergessen; (~ learned ability) verlernen
② v.i., -tt-, forgot, forgotten es vergessen; ~ about sth. etw. vergessen; ~ about it! (coll.) schon gut!

**forgettable** /fəˈgetəbl/ adj. easily ~: leicht zu vergessen

**forgetful** /fəˈgetfl/ adj. vergesslich

**for'getfulness** n. Vergesslichkeit, die

**for'get-me-not** n. (Bot.) Vergissmeinnicht, das

**forgive** /fəˈgɪv/ v.t., forgave /fəˈgeɪv/, forgiven /fəˈgɪvn/ verzeihen; vergeben ⟨Sünden⟩; ~ sb. [sth. or for sth.] jmdm. [etw.] verzeihen

**for'giveness** n. Verzeihung, die; (of sins) Vergebung, die

**for'giving** /fəˈgɪvɪŋ/ adj. versöhnlich

**forgo** /fɔːˈgəʊ/ v.t., forms as GO: verzichten auf (+ Akk.)

**forgone** ▶ FORGO

**forgot, forgotten** ▶ FORGET

**fork** /fɔːk/ ① n. (a) Gabel, die; knives and ~s Besteck, das
(b) (in road) Gabelung, die; (one branch) Abzweigung, die
② v.i. (divide) sich gabeln; (turn) abbiegen; ~ left links abbiegen

■ **fork 'out** v.i. (coll.) blechen (ugs.)

**forked 'lightning** n., no indef. art. Linienblitz, der

**'forklift truck** n. Gabelstapler, der

**forlorn** /fəˈlɔːn/ adj. (a) (desperate) verzweifelt
(b) (forsaken) verlassen

**form** /fɔːm/ ① n. (a) (shape, type, style) Form, die; take ~: Gestalt annehmen
(b) (printed sheet) Formular, das
(c) (Brit. Sch.) Klasse, die
(d) (bench) Bank, die
(e) (Sport: physical condition) Form, die; (fig.) true to ~: wie üblich
② v.t. (a) bilden
(b) (shape) formen, gestalten (into zu)
(c) sich (Dat.) bilden ⟨Meinung, Urteil⟩; gewinnen ⟨Eindruck⟩; fassen ⟨Plan⟩; entwickeln ⟨Vorliebe, Gewohnheit⟩; schließen ⟨Freundschaft⟩
(d) (set up) bilden ⟨Regierung⟩; gründen ⟨Bund, Firma, Partei⟩
③ v.i. sich bilden; ⟨Idee:⟩ Gestalt annehmen

**formal** /ˈfɔːml/ adj. formell; förmlich ⟨Person, Art, Einladung, Begrüßung⟩; (official) offiziell; a ~ 'yes'/'no' eine bindende Zusage/endgültige Absage

**formality** /fɔːˈmælɪtɪ/ n. (a) (requirement) Formalität, die
(b) (being formal) Förmlichkeit, die

**formalize** /ˈfɔːməlaɪz/ v.t. (a) (specify and systematize) formalisieren
(b) (make official) formell bekräftigen

**format** /ˈfɔːmæt/ n. ① (also Comp.) Format, das
② v.t., -tt- (Comp.) formatieren

**formation** /fɔːˈmeɪʃn/ n. (a) ▶ FORM 2A, D: Bildung, die; Gründung, die
(b) (Mil., Aeronaut.) Formation, die

**formative** /ˈfɔːmətɪv/ adj. formend, prägend ⟨Einfluss⟩; the ~ years of life die entscheidenden Lebensjahre

**former** /ˈfɔːmə(r)/ attrib. adj. ehemalig; in ~ times früher; the ~: der/die/das Erstere; pl. die Ersteren

**'formerly** adv. früher

**formidable** /ˈfɔːmɪdəbl/ adj. gewaltig; gefährlich ⟨Herausforderung, Gegner⟩

**formula** /ˈfɔːmjʊlə/ n. Formel, die

**formulate** /ˈfɔːmjʊleɪt/ v.t. formulieren; (devise) entwickeln

**formulation** /fɔːmjʊˈleɪʃn/ n. Formulierung, die

**forsake** /fəˈseɪk/ v.t., forsook /fəˈsʊk/, ~n /fəˈseɪkn/ (a) (give up) verzichten auf (+ Akk.)
(b) (desert) verlassen

**for'saken** adj. verlassen

**forsook** ▶ FORSAKE

**fort** /fɔːt/ n. (Mil.) Fort, das

**forte** /ˈfɔːteɪ/ n. Stärke, die

**forth** /fɔːθ/ adv. and so ~: und so weiter; see also BACK 3

**forthcoming** /ˈ---, -ˈ--/ adj. (a) (approaching) bevorstehend; in Kürze erscheinend ⟨Buch usw.⟩
(b) pred. be ~ ⟨Geld, Antwort:⟩ kommen; ⟨Hilfe:⟩ geleistet werden; not be ~: ausbleiben
(c) (responsive) mitteilsam ⟨Person⟩

**'forthright** adj. direkt

**forth'with** adv. unverzüglich

**fortieth** /'fɔːtɪɪθ/ adj. vierzigst...

**fortify** /'fɔːtɪfaɪ/ v.t. (a) (Mil.) befestigen
(b) (strengthen) stärken

**fortitude** /'fɔːtɪtjuːd/ n. innere Stärke

**fortnight** /'fɔːtnaɪt/ n. vierzehn Tage Pl.

**fortnightly** /'fɔːtnaɪtlɪ/ ①adj.
vierzehntäglich; zweiwöchentlich
②adv. alle vierzehn Tage; alle zwei Wochen

**fortress** /'fɔːtrɪs/ n. Festung, die

**fortuitous** /fɔː'tjuːɪtəs/ adj.,
**for'tuitously** adv. zufällig

**fortunate** /'fɔːtʃənət/ adj. glücklich

**'fortunately** adv. glücklicherweise

**fortune** /'fɔːtʃən, 'fɔːtʃuːn/ n. (a) (wealth)
Vermögen, das
(b) (luck) Schicksal, das; **bad/good** ∼: Pech/
Glück, das

**'fortune teller** n. Wahrsager, der/
Wahrsagerin, die

**forty** /'fɔːtɪ/ ①adj. vierzig; **have** ∼ 'winks
ein Nickerchen machen (ugs.)
②n. Vierzig, die. See also EIGHT; EIGHTY 2

**forum** /'fɔːrəm/ n. Forum, das

**forward** /'fɔːwəd/ ①adv. (a) (in direction
faced) vorwärts
(b) (to the front) nach vorn; vor‹laufen,
-rücken, -schieben›
(c) (closer) heran; **he came** ∼ **to greet me** er
kam auf mich zu, um mich zu begrüßen
(d) **come** ∼ ‹Zeuge, Helfer:› sich melden
②adj. (a) (directed ahead) vorwärts gerichtet
(b) (at or to the front) Vorder-; vorder...
③n. (Sport) Stürmer, der/Stürmerin, die
④v.t. (send on) nachschicken ‹Post› (**to** an
+ Akk.)

**forwarding ad'dress** /'fɔːwədɪŋ/ n.
Nachsendeanschrift, die

**forward:** ∼-**looking** adj.
vorausschauend; ∼ 'planning n.
Vorausplanung, die

**forwards** /'fɔːwədz/ ▶ FORWARD 1A, B

**forwent** ▶ FORGO

**fossil** /'fɒsɪl/ n. Fossil, das; ∼ **fuel** fossiler
Brennstoff

**foster** /'fɒstə(r)/ ①v.t. (a) (fördern; pflegen
‹Freundschaft›
(b) in Pflege haben ‹Kind›
②adj. ∼: Pflege‹kind, -eltern, -sohn usw.›

**fought** ▶ FIGHT 1, 2

**foul** /faʊl/ ①adj. (a) abscheulich ‹Geruch,
Geschmack›
(b) (polluted) verschmutzt ‹Wasser, Luft›;
(putrid) faulig ‹Wasser›; stickig ‹Luft›
(c) (coll.: awful) scheußlich (ugs.); anstößig
‹Sprache›
②n. (Sport) Foul, das
③v.t. (a) beschmutzen; verpesten ‹Luft›
(b) (Sport) foulen

**foul:** ∼-**mouthed** /'faʊlmaʊðd/ adj.
unanständig; unflätig; ∼-**smelling** adj.
übel riechend

**found¹** /faʊnd/ v.t. (a) (establish) gründen;
stiften ‹Krankenhaus, Kloster›; begründen
‹Wissenschaft, Religion›
(b) (fig.: base) begründen; **be** ∼**ed [up]on sth.**
[sich] auf etw. (Akk.) gründen

**found²** ▶ FIND 1

**foundation** /faʊn'deɪʃn/ n. (a) Gründung,
die; (of hospital, monastery) Stiftung, die
(b) usu. in pl. ∼[s] (lit. or fig.) Fundament,
das; **be without** ∼ (fig.) unbegründet sein

**foundation:** ∼ **course** n. (Univ. etc.)
Grundkurs, der; ∼ **cream** n.
Grundierungscreme, die; ∼ **stone** n. (lit. or
fig.) Grundstein, der

**'founder¹** n. Gründer, der/Gründerin, die;
(of hospital) Stifter, der/Stifterin, die

**founder²** v.i. (a) ‹Schiff:› sinken
(b) (fig.: fail) sich zerschlagen

**foundry** /'faʊndrɪ/ n. Gießerei, die

**fountain** /'faʊntɪn/ n. Fontäne, die; (structure)
Springbrunnen, der; (fig.) Quelle, die

**'fountain pen** n. Füllfederhalter, der

**four** /fɔː(r)/ ①adj. vier
②n. Vier, die; **on all** ∼**s** auf allen vieren
(ugs.). See also EIGHT

**four:** ∼-**by**-∼ ①adj. Allrad-; ②n.
Allradler, der; Allradfahrzeug, das; ∼-**door**
attrib. adj. viertürig ‹Auto›; ∼**fold**
/'fɔːfəʊld/ adj., adv. vierfach; **a** ∼**fold**
**increase** ein Anstieg auf das Vierfache;
∼-**legged** /'fɔːlegɪd, 'fɔːlegd/ adj.
vierbeinig; ∼-**letter 'word** n. vulgärer
Ausdruck; (expressing anger) ≈ Kraftausdruck,
der; ∼-**poster** n. Himmelbett, das;
∼**some** /'fɔːsəm/ n. Quartett, das; **go in** or
**as a** ∼**some** zu viert gehen; ∼-**star** n.
∼-**star [petrol]** Super[benzin], das

**fourteen** /fɔː'tiːn/ ①adj. vierzehn
②n. Vierzehn, die. See also EIGHT

**fourteenth** /fɔː'tiːnθ/ ①adj. vierzehnt...
②n. (fraction) Vierzehntel, das. See also
EIGHTH

**fourth** /fɔːθ/ ①adj. viert...
②n. (in sequence, rank) Vierte, der/die/das;
(fraction) Viertel, das. See also EIGHTH

**'fourthly** adv. viertens

**four-wheel 'drive** n. (Motor Veh.) Vier- od.
Allradantrieb, der

**fowl** /faʊl/ n. Haushuhn, das; (collectively)
Geflügel, das

**fox** /fɒks/ ①n. Fuchs, der
②v.t. verwirren

**'fox-hunting** n. Fuchsjagd, die

**foyer** /'fɔɪeɪ/ n. Foyer, das

**fraction** /'frækʃn/ n. (a) (Math.) Bruch, der
(b) (small part) Bruchteil, der

**fracture** /'fræktʃə(r)/ ①n. Bruch, der
②v.t. brechen

**fragile** /'frædʒaɪl/ adj. zerbrechlich

**fragility** /frə'dʒɪlɪtɪ/ n. Zerbrechlichkeit, die

**fragment** /'frægmənt/ n. Bruchstück, das

**fragmentary** /'frægməntərɪ/ adj.
bruchstückhaft

**fragrance** /'freɪgrəns/ n. Duft, der

**fragrant** /'freɪgrənt/ adj. duftend

**frail** /freɪl/ adj. zerbrechlich; gebrechlich
⟨Greis, Greisin⟩

**frame** /freɪm/ ① n. (a) (of vehicle) Rahmen,
der; (of bed) Gestell, das
(b) (border) Rahmen, der; [spectacle] ∼s
[Brillen]gestell, das
② v.t. (a) rahmen
(b) formulieren ⟨Frage, Antwort⟩
(c) (coll.: incriminate) ∼ sb. jmdm. etwas
anhängen (ugs.)

**frame:** ∼**up** n. (coll.) abgekartetes Spiel
(ugs.); ∼**work** n. Gerüst, das

**franc** /fræŋk/ n. Franc, der; (Swiss)
Franken, der

**France** /frɑːns/ pr. n. Frankreich (das)

**franchise** /'fræntʃaɪz/ n. (a) Stimmrecht,
das
(b) (Commerc.) Lizenz, die

**frank¹** adj. offen; freimütig ⟨Geständnis,
Äußerung⟩; **be** ∼ **with sb.** zu jmdm. offen
sein

**frank²** v.t. (Post) frankieren

**frankfurter** /'fræŋkfɜːtə(r)/ (Amer.:
**frankfurt** /'fræŋkfɜːt/) n. Frankfurter
[Würstchen]

**'frankly** adv. offen; (honestly) offen gesagt

**frantic** /'fræntɪk/ adj. (a) verzweifelt
⟨Hilferufe, Gestikulieren⟩; **be** ∼ **with fear/
rage** etc. außer sich (Dat.) sein vor Angst/
Wut usw.
(b) hektisch ⟨Aktivität, Suche⟩

**frantically** /'fræntɪkəlɪ/, **'franticly** adv.
verzweifelt

**fraternal** /frə'tɜːnl/ adj. brüderlich

**fraternize** /'frætənaɪz/ v.i. ∼ [with sb.]
sich verbrüdern [mit jmdm.]

**fraud** /frɔːd/ n. (a) no pl. Betrug, der
(b) (trick) Schwindel, der
(c) (person) Betrüger, der/Betrügerin, die

**fraudulent** /'frɔːdjʊlənt/ adj. betrügerisch

**fraught** /frɔːt/ adj. **be** ∼ **with danger** voller
Gefahren sein

**fray¹** /freɪ/ n. [Kampf]getümmel, das; **enter
or join the** ∼: sich in den Kampf stürzen

**fray²** v.i. [sich] durchscheuern; ⟨Hosenbein,
Teppich, Seilende:⟩ ausfransen; **our nerves/
tempers began to** ∼ (fig.) wir verloren
langsam die Nerven/unsere Gemüter
erhitzten sich

**freak** /friːk/ n. (a) Missgeburt, die; attrib.
ungewöhnlich ⟨Wetter, Ereignis⟩
(b) (coll.: fanatic) Freak, der

**freakish** /'friːkɪʃ/ adj. (capricious) launisch;
verrückt (ugs.); (abnormal) absonderlich

**freaky** /'friːkɪ/ adj.(a) ▶ FREAKISH
(b) (coll.: bizarre) irre (salopp); verrückt (ugs.)

**freckle** /'frekl/ n. Sommersprosse, die

**'freckled** adj. sommersprossig

**free** /friː/ ① adj., **freer** /'friːə(r)/, **freest**
/'friːɪst/ (a) frei; **get** ∼: freikommen; **set** ∼:
freilassen; ∼ **of charge/cost** gebührenfrei/
kostenlos; **sb. is** ∼ **to do sth.** es steht jmdm.
frei, etw. zu tun; ∼ **time** Freizeit, die; **he's**
∼ **in the mornings** er hat morgens Zeit
(b) (without payment) kostenlos; frei
⟨Unterkunft, Verpflegung⟩; Frei⟨karte,
-exemplar⟩; Gratis⟨probe⟩; **'admission** ∼'
„Eintritt frei"; **for** ∼ (coll.) umsonst
② adv. gratis; umsonst
③ v.t. (set at liberty) freilassen; (disentangle)
befreien (of, from von); ∼ **sb./oneself from**
jmdn./sich befreien aus ⟨Gefängnis,
Sklaverei⟩

**free 'agent** n. **be a** ∼: sein eigener Herr
sein

**freedom** /'friːdəm/ n. Freiheit, die; ∼ **of
the press** Pressefreiheit, die; ∼ **of action/
speech/movement** Handlungs-/Rede-/
Bewegungsfreiheit, die; ∼ **of information**
Auskunftsrecht, das

**'freedom fighter** n. Freiheitskämpfer,
der/-kämpferin, die

**free:** ∼ **'enterprise** n. freies
Unternehmertum; ∼ **'fall** n. freier Fall;
∼**-fall** parachuting Fallschirmspringen mit
freiem Fall; **F**∼**fone** ® /'friːfəʊn/ n. ≈
Service 130; **phone us on F**∼**fone 0800 343
027** rufen Sie uns unter 0800 343 027 zum
Nulltarif an; ∼ **'gift** n. Gratisgabe, die;
∼**hold** ① n. Besitzrecht, das; ② adj.
Eigentums-; ∼**holder** n. Grundeigentümer,
der; ∼ **house** n. (Brit.)
brauereiunabhängiges Wirtshaus; ∼ **'kick**
n. (Footb.) Freistoß, der; ∼**lance** ① n.
freier Mitarbeiter/freie Mitarbeiterin;
② adj. freiberuflich; ∼**lancer**
/'friːlɑːnsə(r)/ ▶ ∼LANCE 1

**'freely** adv. (willingly) großzügig; freimütig
⟨eingestehen⟩; (without restriction) frei; (frankly)
offen

**free:** ∼ **'market** n. (Econ.) freier Markt;
**F**∼**mason** n. Freimaurer, der;
**F**∼**phone** ▶ FREEFONE; ∼**-range** adj. frei
laufend ⟨Huhn⟩; ∼**-range eggs** Eier von frei
laufenden Hühnern; ∼ **speech** n.
Redefreiheit; ∼**-standing** adj. frei
stehend; ∼**ware** /'friːweə(r)/ n., no indef.
art. (Comp.) Freeware, die; kostenlose
Software; ∼**way** n. (Amer.) Autobahn, die;
∼**-wheel** v.i. im Freilauf fahren;
∼ **'world** n. freie Welt

**freeze** /friːz/ ① v.i., **froze** /frəʊz/, **frozen**
/'frəʊzn/ (a) frieren; (become covered with ice)
zufrieren; ⟨Straße:⟩ vereisen; ⟨Flüssigkeit:⟩
gefrieren; ⟨Rohr, Schloss:⟩ einfrieren
(b) (become rigid) steif frieren
② v.t., **froze, frozen** (a) (preserve) tiefkühlen
(b) einfrieren ⟨Kredit, Löhne, Preise usw.⟩

**'freeze-dry** v.t. gefriertrocknen

**'freezer** n. Tiefkühltruhe, die; [upright] ∼:
Tiefkühlschrank, der; ∼ **compartment**
Tiefkühlfach, das

**freezing** /'fri:zɪŋ/ ① *adj.* (lit. or fig.) frostig;
it's ∼: es ist eiskalt
② *n.* above/below ∼: über/unter dem/den
Gefrierpunkt

**freezing:** ∼ **'fog** *n.* gefrierender Nebel;
∼ **point** *n.* Gefrierpunkt, *der*

**freight** /freɪt/ *n.* Fracht, *die*

**'freighter** *n.* Frachter, *der*

**'freight train** *n.* Güterzug, *der*

**French** /frentʃ/ ① *adj.* französisch; **he/she
is** ∼: er ist Franzose/sie ist Französin
② *n.* (a) (language) Französisch, *das; see also*
ENGLISH 2A
(b) **the** ∼ *pl.* die Franzosen *Pl.*

**French:** ∼ **'bean** *n.* (Brit.) Gartenbohne,
*die;* ∼ **'bread** *n.* französisches
[Stangen]weißbrot; ∼ **'dressing** *n.*
Vinaigrette, *die;* ∼ **'fries** *n. pl.* Pommes
frites *Pl.;* ∼ **'kiss** *n.* französischer Kuss
(ugs.); Zungenkuss, *der;* ∼**man** /'frentʃmən/
*n., pl.* ∼**men** /'frentʃmən/ Franzose, *der;*
∼ **'polish** *n.* Schellackpolitur, *die;*
∼ **'window** *n.* französisches Fenster;
∼**woman** *n.* Französin, *die*

**frenzied** /'frenzɪd/ *adj.* rasend

**frenzy** /'frenzɪ/ *n.* Wahnsinn, *der;* (fury)
Raserei, *die*

**frequency** /'fri:kwənsɪ/ *n.* (a) Häufigkeit,
*die*
(b) (Phys.) Frequenz, *die*

**frequent** ① /'fri:kwənt/ *adj.* (a) häufig;
**become** ∼: seltener werden
(b) (habitual) eifrig
② /frɪ'kwent/ *v.t.* häufig besuchen ⟨Café,
Klub, usw.⟩

**frequently** /'fri:kwəntlɪ/ *adv.* häufig

**fresco** /'freskəʊ/ *n. pl.* ∼**es** *or* ∼**s** Fresko,
*das*

**fresh** /freʃ/ *adj.* frisch; neu ⟨Beweise,
Anstrich, Mut, Energie⟩; ∼ **supplies**
Nachschub, *der* (**of** an + *Dat.*); **make a**
∼ **start** noch einmal von vorne anfangen;
(fig.) neu beginnen

**freshen** /'freʃn/ *v.i.* auffrischen

■ **freshen 'up** *v.i.* sich auffrischen

**'freshly** *adv.* frisch

**'freshness** *n.* Frische, *die*

**fresh 'water** *n.* Süßwasser, *das*

**fret** /fret/ *v.i.*, **-tt-** sich (*Dat.*) Sorgen machen

**fretful** /'fretfl/ *adj.* verdrießlich; quengelig
(ugs.)

**'fretsaw** *n.* Laubsäge, *die*

**Fri.** *abbr.* = **Friday** Fr.

**friar** /'fraɪə(r)/ *n.* Ordensbruder, *der*

**friction** /'frɪkʃn/ *n.* Reibung, *die*

**Friday** /'fraɪdeɪ, 'fraɪdɪ/ *n.* Freitag, *der;* **on**
∼: [am] Freitag; **on a** ∼, **on a** ∼**s** freitags;
∼ **13 August** Freitag, der 13. August; (at top of
letter etc.) Freitag, den 13. August; **next/last**
∼: [am] nächsten/letzten Freitag; **Good** ∼:
Karfreitag, *der*

**fridge** /frɪdʒ/ *n.* (Brit. coll.) Kühlschrank, *der*

**fried** ▶ FRY¹

**friend** /frend/ *n.* Freund, *der*/Freundin, *die;*
**be** ∼**s with sb.** mit jmdm. befreundet sein;
**make** ∼**s [with sb.]** [mit jmdm.] Freundschaft
schließen

**friendliness** /'frendlɪnɪs/ *n.*
Freundlichkeit, *die*

**'friendly** ① *adj.* freundlich (**to** zu);
freundschaftlich ⟨Rat, Beziehungen,
Wettkampf⟩
② *n.* (Sport) Freundschaftsspiel, *das*

**'friendship** *n.* Freundschaft, *die*

**fries** /fraɪz/ *n. pl.* (Amer.) Pommes frites *Pl.*

**frigate** /'frɪgət/ *n.* (Naut.) Fregatte, *die*

**fright** /fraɪt/ *n.* Schreck, *der;* **take** ∼:
erschrecken

**frighten** /'fraɪtn/ *v.t.* ⟨Explosion, Schuss:⟩
erschrecken; ⟨Gedanke, Drohung:⟩ Angst
machen (+ *Dat.*); **be** ∼**ed at** *or* **by sth.** vor
etw. (*Dat.*) erschrecken

**'frightful** *adj.*, **'frightfully** *adv.* furchtbar

**frigid** /'frɪdʒɪd/ *adj.* frostig; (sexually) frigid[e]

**frill** /frɪl/ *n.* (a) Rüsche, *die*
(b) *in pl.* (embellishments) Beiwerk, *das*

**'frilly** *adj.* mit Rüschen besetzt;
Rüschen⟨kleid, -bluse⟩

**fringe** /frɪndʒ/ *n.* (a) Fransenkante, *die* (**on**
an + *Dat.*)
(b) (hair) [Pony]fransen *Pl.* (ugs.)
(c) (edge) Rand, *der*

**frisk** /frɪsk/ ① *v.i.* ∼ **[about]**
[herum]springen
② *v.t.* (coll.) filzen (ugs.)

**'frisky** *adj.* munter

**fritter¹** /'frɪtə(r)/ *n.* apple *etc.* ∼**s**
Apfelstücke *usw.* in Pfannkuchenteig

**fritter²** *v.t.* ∼ **away** vergeuden

**frivolity** /frɪ'vɒlɪtɪ/ *n.* Oberflächlichkeit, *die*

**frivolous** /'frɪvələs/ *adj.* (a) frivol
(b) (trifling) belanglos

**frizzy** /'frɪzɪ/ *adj.* kraus

**fro** /frəʊ/ *adv.* ▶ TO 2

**frock** /frɒk/ *n.* Kleid, *das*

**frog** /frɒg/ *n.* Frosch, *der*

**frog:** ∼**man** /'frɒgmən/ *n., pl.* ∼**men**
/'frɒgmən/ Froschmann, *der;* ∼**spawn** *n.*
Froschlaich, *der*

**frolic** /'frɒlɪk/ *v.i.*, **-ck-:** ∼ **[about** *or* **around]**
[herum]springen

**from** /frəm, *stressed* frɒm/ *prep.* von;
(∼ within; expr. origin) aus; ∼ **Paris** aus Paris;
∼ **Paris to Munich** von Paris nach München;
**be a mile** ∼ **sth.** eine Meile von etw. entfernt
sein; **where do you come** ∼?, **where are you**
∼? woher kommen Sie?; **painted** ∼ **life** nach
dem Leben gemalt; **weak** ∼ **hunger** schwach
vor Hunger; ∼ **the year 1972** seit 1972; ∼ **[the
age of] 18** ab 18 Jahre; ∼ **4 to 6 eggs** 4 bis 6
Eier

**front** /frʌnt/ ① *n.* (a) Vorderseite, *die;* (of
house) Vorderfront, *die;* **in** *or* **at the** ∼ **[of**

sth.] vorn [in etw. *position: Dat., movement:
Akk.*]; **to the** ~: nach vorn; **in** ~: vorn[e]; **be
in** ~ **of sth./sb.** vor etw./jmdm. sein
**(b)** (Mil.) Front, *die*
**(c)** (at seaside) Strandpromenade, *die*
**(d)** (Meteorol.) Front, *die*
**(e)** (bluff) Fassade, *die*
2 *adj.* vorder...; Vorder⟨*rad, -zimmer,
-zahn*⟩; ~ **garden** Vorgarten, *der;* ~ **row**
erste Reihe

**frontal** /'frʌntl/ *adj.* Frontal-

**front 'door** *n.* (of flat) Wohnungstür, *die;* (of
house) Haustür, *die*

**frontier** /'frʌntɪə(r)/ *n.* Grenze, *die*

**front:** ~ **'page** *n.* Titelseite, *die;*
~**-wheel drive** 1 *n.* Vorderradantrieb,
*der;* Frontantrieb, *der;* 2 *adj.* **a** ~**-wheel
drive vehicle** ein Fahrzeug mit Vorderrad-
od. Frontantrieb

**frost** /frɒst/ 1 *n.* Frost, *der;* **ten degrees of**
~ (Brit.) zehn Grad minus
2 *v.t.* ~**ed glass** Mattglas, *das*

**'frostbite** *n.* Erfrierung, *die*

**'frosting** *n.* (esp. Amer.) Glasur, *die*

**'frosty** *adj.* frostig

**froth** /frɒθ/ 1 *n.* Schaum, *der*
2 *v.i.* schäumen

**'frothy** *adj.* schaumig

**frown** /fraʊn/ 1 *v.i.* die Stirn runzeln
([up]on über + *Akk.*)
2 *n.* Stirnrunzeln, *das*

**froze** ▶ FREEZE

**frozen** /'frəʊzn/ 1 ▶ FREEZE
2 *adj.* **(a)** zugefroren ⟨*Fluss, See*⟩;
eingefroren ⟨*Wasserleitung*⟩; **I'm** ~ (fig.) mir
ist eiskalt
**(b)** (to preserve) tiefgekühlt; ~ **food**
Tiefkühlkost, *die*

**frugal** /'fru:gl/ *adj.* genügsam ⟨*Lebensweise,
Mensch*⟩; frugal ⟨*Mahl*⟩

**fruit** /fru:t/ *n.* Frucht, *die; collect.* Obst, *das*

**'fruit cake** *n.* englischer Teekuchen

**fruitful** /'fru:tfl/ *adj.* fruchtbar

**'fruit juice** *n.* Obstsaft, *der*

**'fruitless** *adj.* nutzlos ⟨*Versuch, Gespräch*⟩;
fruchtlos ⟨*Verhandlung, Suche*⟩

**fruit:** ~ **machine** *n.* (Brit.) Spielautomat,
*der;* ~ **'salad** *n.* Obstsalat, *der*

**'fruity** *adj.* fruchtig ⟨*Geschmack, Wein*⟩

**frustrate** /frʌ'streɪt/ *v.t.* vereiteln ⟨*Plan,
Versuch*⟩; zunichte machen ⟨*Hoffnung,
Bemühungen*⟩

**'frustrated** *adj.* frustriert

**frustration** /frʌ'streɪʃn/ *n.* Frustration,
*die*

**fry**¹ /fraɪ/ *v.t. & i.*, **fried** /fraɪd/ braten; **fried
egg** Spiegelei, *das*

**fry**² *n.* (fishes) Brut, *die;* **small** ~ (fig.)
unbedeutende Leute

**'frying pan** *n.* Bratpfanne, *die*

**ft.** *abbr.* = **feet, foot** ft.

**fuchsia** /'fju:ʃə/ *n.* (Bot.) Fuchsie, *die*

---

**fuck** /fʌk/ (coarse) 1 *v.t. & i.* ficken (vulg.);
[oh,] ~!, [oh,] ~ **it!** [au,] Scheiße! (derb.)
2 *n.* Fick, *der* (vulg.)

**fuddy-duddy** /'fʌdɪdʌdɪ/ (coll.) 1 *adj.*
verkalkt (ugs.)
2 *n.* Fossil, *das* (fig.)

**fudge** /fʌdʒ/ *n.* Karamellbonbon, *der od.
das*

**fuel** /'fju:əl/ *n.* Brennstoff, *der;* (for vehicle)
Kraftstoff, *der;* (for ship, aircraft) Treibstoff, *der*

**fuel:** ~ **consumption** *n.* (of vehicle)
Kraftstoffverbrauch, *der;* ~ **gauge** *n.*
Kraftstoffanzeiger *der;* ~ **injection** *n.*
Benzineinspritzung, *die*

**fugitive** /'fju:dʒɪtɪv/ *n.* Flüchtige, *der/die*

**fugue** /fju:g/ *n.* (Mus.) Fuge, *die*

**fulfil** (*Amer.:* **fulfill**) /fʊl'fɪl/ *v.t.,* **-ll-**
erfüllen; halten ⟨*Versprechen;*⟩ ~ **oneself**
sich selbst verwirklichen

**ful'filment** (*Amer.:* **ful'fillment**) *n.*
Erfüllung, *die*

**full** /fʊl/ 1 *adj.* **(a)** voll; satt ⟨*Person*⟩; ~ **of**
voller; **be** ~ **up** voll [besetzt] sein;
⟨*Behälter:*⟩ randvoll sein; ⟨*Flug:*⟩ völlig
ausgebucht sein; **I'm** ~ [up] (coll.) ich bin
voll [bis obenhin] (ugs.); **be** ~ **of oneself**
sehr von sich eingenommen sein
**(b)** ausführlich ⟨*Bericht, Beschreibung*⟩;
erfüllt ⟨*Leben*⟩; ganz ⟨*Stunde, Jahr, Monat,
Seite*⟩; voll ⟨*Name, Bezahlung, Verständnis*⟩;
~ **details** alle Einzelheiten; **at** ~ **speed** mit
Höchstgeschwindigkeit
**(c)** voll ⟨*Gesicht*⟩; füllig ⟨*Figur*⟩; weit ⟨*Rock*⟩
2 *n.* **in** ~: vollständig
3 *adv.* (exactly) genau

**full:** ~**-blown** *adj.* ausgewachsen
⟨*Skandal*⟩; ausgereift ⟨*Theorie, Plan,
Gedanke*⟩; ~**-blown AIDS** Vollbild-Aids, *das;*
~**-bodied** *adj.* vollmundig, (fachspr.)
körperreich ⟨*Wein*⟩; ~**-cream** *adj.*
~**-cream milk/cheese** Vollmilch, *die/*
Vollfettkäse, *der;* ~ **-length** *adj.* lang
⟨*Kleid*⟩; ~ **'moon** *n.* Vollmond, *der;*
~**-scale** *adj.* **(a)** in Originalgröße; **(b)**
groß angelegt ⟨*Untersuchung, Suchaktion*⟩;
~ **'stop** *n.* Punkt, *der;* ~**-time** *adj.*
ganztägig; Ganztags⟨*arbeit*⟩; ~**-'timer** *n.*
Ganztagsbeschäftigte, *der/die*

**fully** /'fʊlɪ/ *adv.* voll [und ganz]; reich
⟨*belohnt*⟩; ausführlich ⟨*erklären*⟩

**fulsome** /'fʊlsəm/ *adj.* übertrieben

**fumble** /'fʌmbl/ *v.i.* ~ **at** *or* **with**
[herum]fingern an (+ *Dat.*); ~ **in one's
pockets for sth.** in seinen Taschen nach etw.
kramen (ugs.)

**fume** /fju:m/ 1 *n. in pl.* ~**s** Dämpfe *Pl.;*
(from car exhaust) Abgase *Pl.*
2 *v.i.* vor Wut schäumen

**fumigate** /'fju:mɪgeɪt/ *v.t.* ausräuchern

**fun** /fʌn/ *n.* Spaß, *der;* **have** ~! viel Spaß!;
**make** ~ **of sb.** sich über jmdn. lustig
machen; **for** ~, **for the** ~ **of it** zum Spaß

**function** /'fʌŋkʃn/ **1** n. Aufgabe, die;
Funktion, die; (formal event) Veranstaltung, die
**2** v.i. ⟨Maschine, System:⟩ funktionieren;
~ as fungieren als; (serve as) dienen als
**functional** /'fʌŋkʃənl/ adj. (a) (useful)
funktionell
(b) (working) funktionsfähig
**'function key** n. (Comp.) Funktionstaste,
die
**fund** /fʌnd/ **1** n. (a) (money) Fonds, der
(b) (fig.: stock) Fundus, der (of von, an + Dat.)
**2** v.t. finanzieren
**fundamental** /fʌndə'mentl/ adj.
grundlegend (to für); elementar ⟨Bedürfnisse⟩
**fundamentalism** /fʌndə'mentəlɪzm/ n.
Fundamentalismus, der
**fundamentalist** /fʌndə'mentəlɪst/ n.
Fundamentalist, der/Fundamentalistin, die
**funda'mentally** adv. grundlegend; von
Grund auf ⟨verschieden, ehrlich⟩
**fund:** ~**-raiser** /'fʌndreɪzə(r)/ n. (a)
( person) Geldbeschaffer, der/-beschafferin,
die; (b) (event) Benefizveranstaltung, die;
~**-raising** /'fʌndreɪzɪŋ/ n.
Geldbeschaffung, die; attrib. zur
Geldbeschaffung nachgestellt
**funeral** /'fjuːnərl/ n. Beerdigung, die.
~ director Bestattungsunternehmer, der;
~ service Trauerfeier, die
**'funfair** n. (Brit.) Jahrmarkt, der
**fungus** /'fʌŋgəs/ n., pl. fungi /'fʌŋgaɪ,
'fʌndʒaɪ/ or ~es Pilz, der
**funicular** /fjuː'nɪkjʊlə(r)/ adj. & n.
~ [railway] [Stand]seilbahn, die
**'fun-loving** adj. lebenslustig
**funnel** /'fʌnl/ n. Trichter, der; (of ship etc.)
Schornstein, der
**funnily** /'fʌnɪlɪ/ adv. komisch; ~ enough
komischerweise
**funny** /'fʌnɪ/ adj. (a) komisch; lustig; witzig
⟨Mensch, Einfall⟩
(b) (strange) komisch
**'funny bone** n. Musikantenknochen, der
**fur** /fɜː(r)/ n. (a) Fell, das; (garment) Pelz, der;
~ coat Pelzmantel, der
(b) (in kettle) Kesselstein, der
**furious** /'fjʊərɪəs/ adj. wütend; heftig
⟨Streit⟩; wild ⟨Tanz, Tempo, Kampf⟩; be
~ with sb. wütend auf jmdn. sein
**'furiously** adv. wütend; wild ⟨kämpfen⟩: wie
wild (ugs.) ⟨arbeiten⟩
**furl** /fɜːl/ v.t. einrollen ⟨Segel, Flagge⟩
**furnace** /'fɜːnɪs/ n. Ofen, der
**furnish** /'fɜːnɪʃ/ v.t. (a) möblieren
(b) (supply) liefern; ~ sb. with sth. jmdm. etw.
liefern
**'furnishings** n. pl.
Einrichtungsgegenstände Pl.
**furniture** /'fɜːnɪtʃə(r)/ n. Möbel Pl.; piece of
~: Möbel[stück], das

**furniture:** ~ **polish** n. Möbelpolitur, die;
~ **van** n. Möbelwagen, der
**furrow** /'fʌrəʊ/ n. Furche, die
**furry** /'fɜːrɪ/ adj. haarig; ~ animal (toy)
Plüschtier, das
**further** /'fɜːðə(r)/ **1** adj. (a) (in space) weiter
entfernt
(b) (additional) weiter...
**2** adv. weiter
**3** v.t. fördern
**further edu'cation** n. Weiterbildung, die;
(for adults also) Erwachsenenbildung, die
**further'more** adv. außerdem
**'furthermost** adj. äußerst...
**furthest** /'fɜːðɪst/ **1** adj. am weitesten
entfernt
**2** adv. am weitesten ⟨springen, laufen⟩; am
weitesten entfernt ⟨sein, wohnen⟩
**furtive** /'fɜːtɪv/ adj., **furtively** adv.
verstohlen
**fury** /'fjʊərɪ/ n. Wut, die; (of sea, battle) Wüten,
das
**fuse¹** /fjuːz/ **1** v.t. (blend) verschmelzen
(into zu)
**2** v.i. ~ together miteinander verschmelzen
**fuse²** n. [time] ~: [Zeit]zünder, der; (cord)
Zündschnur, die
**fuse³** (Electr.) **1** n. Sicherung, die
**2** v.i. the lights have ~d die Sicherung ist
durchgebrannt
**'fuse box** n. Sicherungskasten, der
**fuselage** /'fjuːzəlɑːʒ/ n. [Flugzeug]rumpf,
der
**fusion** /'fjuːʒn/ n. (a) Verschmelzung, die
(b) (Phys.) Fusion, die
**fuss** /fʌs/ **1** n. Theater, das (ugs.); make a
~ [about sth.] einen Wirbel [um etw.]
machen
**2** v.i. Wirbel machen; (get agitated) sich
[unnötig] aufregen
**'fussy** adj. (fastidious) eigen; penibel; I'm not
~ (I don't mind) ich bin nicht wählerisch
**futile** /'fjuːtaɪl/ adj. vergeblich ⟨Versuch,
Bemühung⟩; zum Scheitern verurteilt ⟨Plan⟩
**futility** /fjuː'tɪlɪtɪ/ n. (of attempt, effort)
Vergeblichkeit, die; (of plan) Zwecklosigkeit,
die
**futon** /'fuːtɒn/ n. Futon, der
**future** /'fjuːtʃə(r)/ **1** adj. [zu]künftig; at
some ~ date zu einem späteren Zeitpunkt;
künftig
**2** n. (a) Zukunft, die; in ~: in Zukunft;
künftig
(b) (Ling.) Futur, das; Zukunft, die
(c) in pl. (Commerc.) Terminware, die;
(contracts) Lieferungsverträge Pl.
**futuristic** /fjuːtʃə'rɪstɪk/ adj. futuristisch
**fuze** /fjuːz/ ▶ FUSE²
**fuzzy** /'fʌzɪ/ adj. (a) (frizzy) kraus
(b) (blurred) verschwommen

# Gg

**G, g** /dʒiː/ *n.* G, g, *das*

**gab** /gæb/ *n.* (coll.) **have the gift of the ~:** reden können

**gabble** /ˈgæbl/ *v.i.* brabbeln (ugs.)

**gable** /ˈgeɪbl/ *n.* Giebel, *der*

**gad** /gæd/ *v.i.*, **-dd-** (coll.) **~ about** herumziehen (ugs.)

**gadget** /ˈgædʒɪt/ *n.* Gerät, *das*

**gadgetry** /ˈgædʒɪtrɪ/ *n.* [hoch technisierte] Ausstattung

**Gaelic** /ˈgeɪlɪk, ˈgælɪk/ 1 *adj.* gälisch
2 *n.* Gälisch, *das*

**gaffe** /gæf/ *n.* Fauxpas, *der*

**gag** /gæg/ 1 *n.* **(a)** Knebel, *der*
**(b)** (joke) Gag, *der*
2 *v.t.*, **-gg-** knebeln

**gaiety** /ˈgeɪətɪ/ *n.* Fröhlichkeit, *die*

**gaily** /ˈgeɪlɪ/ *adv.* fröhlich; in leuchtenden Farben ‹*bemalt, geschmückt*›

**gain** /geɪn/ 1 *n.* **(a)** Gewinn, *der*
**(b)** (increase) Zunahme, *die* (**in** an + *Dat.*)
2 *v.t.* **(a)** gewinnen; finden ‹*Zugang, Zutritt*›; erwerben ‹*Wissen, Ruf*›; erlangen ‹*Freiheit*›; erzielen ‹*Vorteil, Punkte*›; verdienen ‹*Lebensunterhalt, Geldsumme*›; **~ weight/five pounds [in weight]** zunehmen/fünf Pfund zunehmen; **~ speed** schneller werden
**(b)** ‹*Uhr:*› vorgehen um
3 *v.i.* **(a) ~ by sth.** von etw. profitieren
**(b)** ‹*Uhr:*› vorgehen

**gainful** /ˈgeɪnfl/ *adj.* **~ employment** Erwerbstätigkeit, *die*

**gainfully** /ˈgeɪnfəlɪ/ *adv.* **~ employed** erwerbstätig

**gait** /geɪt/ *n.* Gang, *der*

**gala** /ˈgɑːlə, ˈgeɪlə/ *n.* Festveranstaltung, *die; attrib.* Gala‹*abend, -vorstellung*›; **swimming ~:** Schwimmfest, *das*

**galaxy** /ˈgæləksɪ/ *n.* Galaxie, *die*

**gale** /geɪl/ *n.* Sturm, *der*

**gall** /gɔːl/ *n.* Unverschämtheit, *die*

**gallant** /ˈgælənt/ *adj.* (brave) tapfer; (chivalrous) ritterlich

**gallantry** /ˈgæləntrɪ/ *n.* (bravery) Tapferkeit, *die*

**ˈgall bladder** *n.* Gallenblase, *die*

**gallery** /ˈgælərɪ/ *n.* **(a)** Galerie, *die*
**(b)** (Theatre) dritter Rang

**galley** /ˈgælɪ/ *n.* **(a)** (ship's kitchen) Kombüse, *die*
**(b)** (Hist.) Galeere, *die*

**gallivant** /ˈgælɪvænt/ *v.i.* (coll.) herumziehen (ugs.)

**gallon** /ˈgælən/ *n.* Gallone, *die*

**gallop** /ˈgæləp/ 1 *n.* Galopp, *der*
2 *v.i.* ‹*Pferd, Reiter:*› galoppieren

**gallows** /ˈgæləʊz/ *n. sing.* Galgen, *der*

**Gallup poll** ® /ˈgæləp pəʊl/ *n.* Meinungsumfrage, *die*

**galore** /gəˈlɔː(r)/ *adv.* im Überfluss; in Hülle und Fülle

**galvanize** /ˈgælvənaɪz/ *v.t.* wachrütteln; **~ sb. into action** jmdn. veranlassen, sofort aktiv zu werden

**gambit** /ˈgæmbɪt/ *n.* Gambit, *das*

**gamble** /ˈgæmbl/ *v.i.* **(a)** [um Geld] spielen; **~ at cards/on horses** um Geld Karten spielen/auf Pferde wetten
**(b)** (fig.) spekulieren; **~ on sth.** sich auf etw. (*Akk.*) verlassen

**gambler** /ˈgæmblə(r)/ *n.* Glücksspieler, *der*

**gambling** /ˈgæmblɪŋ/ *n.* Spiel[en], *das;* Glücksspiel, *das;* (on horses, dogs) Wetten, *das*

**game¹** /geɪm/ *n.* **(a)** Spiel, *das;* (of [table] tennis, chess, cards, cricket) Partie, *die*
**(b)** (fig.: scheme) Vorhaben, *das*
**(c)** *in pl.* (athletic contests) Spiele *Pl.*; (in school) (sports) Sport, *der;* (athletics) Leichtathletik, *die*
**(d)** (Hunting, Cookery) Wild, *das*

**game²** *adj.* mutig; **be ~ to do sth.** bereit sein, etw. zu tun

**ˈgamekeeper** *n.* Wildheger, *der*

**gamma rays** /ˈgæmə/ *n. pl.* (Phys.) Gammastrahlen *Pl.*

**gammon** /ˈgæmən/ *n.* Räucherschinken, *der*

**gamut** /ˈgæmət/ *n.* Skala, *die*

**gander** /ˈgændə(r)/ *n.* Gänserich, *der*

**gang** /gæŋ/ 1 *n.* Bande, *die;* (of workmen, prisoners) Trupp, *der*
2 *v.i.* **~ up against** *or* **on** (coll.) sich verbünden gegen

**gangling** /ˈgæŋglɪŋ/ schlaksig (ugs.)

**gangster** /ˈgæŋstə(r)/ *n.* Gangster, *der*

**ˈgang warfare** *n.* Bandenkrieg, *der*

**ˈgangway** *n.* Gangway, *die;* (Brit.: between seats) Gang, *der*

**gaol** /dʒeɪl/ ▶ JAIL

**gap** /gæp/ *n.* **(a)** Lücke, *die*
**(b)** (in time) Pause, *die*
**(c)** (divergence) Kluft, *die*

**gape** /geɪp/ *v.i.* **(a)** den Mund aufsperren; ‹*Loch, Abgrund, Wunde:*› klaffen
**(b)** (stare) Mund und Nase aufsperren (ugs.); **~ at sb./sth.** jmdn./etw. mit offenem Mund anstarren

**garage** /'gærɪdʒ/ n. Garage, die; (selling petrol) Tankstelle, die; (for repairing cars) [Kfz-]Werkstatt, die

**garb** /gɑːb/ n. Tracht, die

**garbage** /'gɑːbɪdʒ/ n. (a) Abfall, der; Müll, der (b) (coll.: nonsense) Quatsch, der (salopp)

**garbage:** ∼ **can** n. (Amer.) Mülltonne, die; ∼ **dis'posal unit,** ∼ **disposer** ns. Abfallvernichter, der; Müllwolf, der

**garble** /'gɑːbl/ v.t. verstümmeln

**garden** /'gɑːdn/ n. Garten, der

**garden:** ∼ **centre** n. Gartencenter, das; ∼ **'city** n. Gartenstadt, die

**gardener** /'gɑːdnə(r)/ n. Gärtner, der/ Gärtnerin, die

**gardening** /'gɑːdnɪŋ/ n. Gartenarbeit, die

**garden:** ∼ **'shed** n. Geräteschuppen, der ∼ **'waste** n. Gartenabfälle Pl.; Gartenabfall, der

**gargle** /'gɑːgl/ v.i. gurgeln

**gargoyle** /'gɑːgɔɪl/ n. (Archit.) Wasserspeier, der

**garish** /'geərɪʃ/ adj. grell ⟨Farbe, Licht⟩; knallbunt ⟨Kleidung⟩

**garland** /'gɑːlənd/ n. Girlande, die

**garlic** /'gɑːlɪk/ n. Knoblauch, der

**garment** /'gɑːmənt/ n. Kleidungsstück, das; ∼s pl. (clothes) Kleidung, die; Kleider Pl.

**garnish** /'gɑːnɪʃ/ ① v.t. garnieren ② n. Garnierung, die

**garret** /'gærət/ n. Dachkammer, die

**garrison** /'gærɪsn/ n. Garnison, die

**garter** /'gɑːtə(r)/ n. Strumpfband, das

**gas** /gæs/ ① n. (a) pl. ∼es /'gæsɪz/ Gas, das (b) (Amer. coll.: petrol) Benzin, das ② v.t., -ss- mit Gas vergiften

**gas:** ∼ **chamber** n. Gaskammer, die; ∼ **'cooker** n. (Brit.) Gasherd, der; ∼ **cylinder** n. Gasflasche, die; ∼ **'fire** n. Gasofen, der

**gash** /gæʃ/ ① n. Schnittwunde, die ② v.t. aufritzen ⟨Haut⟩; ∼ one's finger sich (Dat. od. Akk.) in den Finger schneiden

**gas:** ∼ **heater** n. Gasofen, der; ∼ **mask** n. Gasmaske, die; ∼ **meter** n. Gaszähler, der

**gasoline (gasolene)** /'gæsəliːn/ n. (Amer.) Benzin, das

**gasometer** /gæ'sɒmɪtə(r)/ n. Gasometer, der

**gasp** /gɑːsp/ ① v.i. nach Luft schnappen (with vor); he was ∼ing for air er rang nach Luft ② v.t. ∼ out hervorstoßen ③ n. Keuchen, das

**'gas station** n. (Amer.) Tankstelle, die

**gastric:** ∼ **'flu** (coll.), ∼ **influ'enza** ns. Darmgrippe, die; ∼ **'ulcer** n. Magengeschwür, das

**gastro-enteritis** /gæstrəʊentə'raɪtɪs/ n. Gastroenteritis, die (fachspr.); Magen-Darm-Katarrh, der

**gastronomy** /gæ'strɒnəmɪ/ n. Gastronomie, die

**gasworks** n. sing. Gaswerk, das

**gate** /geɪt/ n. Tor, das; (barrier) Sperre, die; (to field etc.) Gatter, das; (of level crossing) [Bahn]schranke, die; (in airport) Flugsteig, der

**gateau** /'gætəʊ/ n., pl. ∼s or ∼x /'gætəʊz/ Torte, die

**gate:** ∼**crasher** /'geɪtkræʃə(r)/ n. ungeladener Gast; ∼**way** n. Tor, das

**gather** /'gæðə(r)/ ① v.t. (a) sammeln; zusammentragen ⟨Informationen⟩; pflücken ⟨Obst, Blumen⟩ (b) (infer, deduce) schließen (from aus) (c) ∼ speed/force schneller/stärker werden ② v.i. sich versammeln; ⟨Wolken:⟩ sich zusammenziehen

**'gathering** n. Versammlung, die

**GATT** /gæt/ abbr. = **General Agreement on Tariffs and Trade** GATT, das

**gauche** /gəʊʃ/ adj. linkisch

**gaudy** /'gɔːdɪ/ adj. protzig; grell ⟨Farben⟩

**gauge** /geɪdʒ/ ① n. ① (a) (measure) Maß, das (b) (instrument) Messgerät, das ② v.t. messen; (fig.) beurteilen

**gaunt** /gɔːnt/ adj. hager

**gauntlet** /'gɔːntlɪt/ n. Stulpenhandschuh, der

**gauze** /gɔːz/ n. Gaze, die

**gave** ▶ GIVE 1, 2

**gay** /geɪ/ ① adj. (a) fröhlich; (brightly coloured) farbenfroh (b) (coll.: homosexual) schwul (ugs.); Schwulen⟨lokal⟩ ② n. (coll.) Schwule, der (ugs.)

**gay 'rights** n. pl. Schwulenrechte Pl.

**gaze** /geɪz/ v.i. blicken; (fixedly) starren; ∼ at sb./sth. jmdn./etw. anstarren

**GB** abbr. = **Great Britain** GB

**GCSE** abbr. (Brit.) = **General Certificate of Secondary Education**

**gear** /gɪə(r)/ ① n. (a) (Motor Veh.) Gang, der; top/bottom ∼ (Brit.) der höchste/erste Gang; change or shift ∼: schalten; put the car into ∼: einen Gang einlegen; out of ∼: im Leerlauf (b) (coll.: clothes) Aufmachung, die (c) (equipment) Gerät, das; Ausrüstung, die ② v.t. ausrichten (to auf + Akk.)

**gear:** ∼**box** n. Getriebekasten, der; ∼ **lever,** (Amer.) ∼ **shift** ns. Schalthebel, der

**geese** pl. of GOOSE

**geezer** /'giːzə(r)/ n. (coll.: old man) Opa, der (ugs.)

**gel** /dʒel/ n. Gel, das

**gelatin** /'dʒelətɪn/, (Brit.) **gelatine**
/'dʒeləti:n/ n. Gelatine, die

**gelignite** /'dʒelɪgnaɪt/ n. Gelatinedynamit,
das

**gem** /dʒem/ n. Edelstein, der

**Gemini** /'dʒemɪnaɪ, 'dʒemɪni/ n. (Astrol.,
Astron.) Zwillinge Pl.

**'gemstone** n. Edelstein, der

**gender** /'dʒendə(r)/ n. (Ling.)
[grammatisches] Geschlecht

**gene** /dʒi:n/ n. (Biol.) Gen, das

**general** /'dʒenrl/ ①  adj. allgemein; weit
verbreitet ⟨Ansicht⟩; (true of [nearly] all cases)
allgemein gültig; ungefähr ⟨Vorstellung,
Beschreibung usw.⟩; **the ~ public** weite
Kreise der Bevölkerung; **in ~ use** allgemein
verbreitet; **as a ~ rule, in ~:** im
Allgemeinen
② n. (Mil.) General, der

**general: ~ e'lection** ▶ ELECTION;
**~ 'hospital** n. Allgemeinkrankenhaus,
das

**generalization** /dʒenrəlaɪ'zeɪʃn/ n.
Verallgemeinerung, die

**generalize** /'dʒenrəlaɪz/ ① v.t.
verallgemeinern
② v.i. **~ about sth.** etw. verallgemeinern

**general 'knowledge** n.
Allgemeinwissen, das

**generally** /'dʒenrəlɪ/ adv. (a) allgemein;
**~ available** überall erhältlich; **~ speaking**
im Allgemeinen
(b) (usually) im Allgemeinen

**general: ~ 'manager** n. [leitender]
Direktor/[leitende] Direktorin;
**~ 'meeting** n. Generalversammlung, die;
Hauptversammlung, die; **~ National
Vo'cational Qualification** n. (Brit.)
staatliches Berufsausbildungsprogramm;
**~ prac'titioner** n. (Med.) Arzt/Ärztin für
Allgemeinmedizin

**generate** /'dʒenəreɪt/ v.t. erzeugen (**from**
aus); (result in) führen zu

**generation** /dʒenə'reɪʃn/ n. (a)
Generation, die
(b) ( production) Erzeugung, die

**generator** /'dʒenəreɪtə(r)/ n. Generator,
der

**generosity** /dʒenə'rɒsɪtɪ/ n.
Großzügigkeit, die

**generous** /'dʒenərəs/ adj. großzügig;
reichlich ⟨Vorrat, Portion⟩

**'generously** adv. großzügig

**genetic** /dʒɪ'netɪk/ adj. genetisch

**genetically** /dʒɪ'netɪkəlɪ/ adv. genetisch;
**~ modified** gentechnisch verändert;
**~ engineered** gentechnisch verändert
⟨Organismus, Pflanzen, Tiere,
Nahrungsmittel⟩; genetisch hergestellt
⟨Medikament, Enzym⟩

**genetic engi'neering** n.
Gentechnologie, die

**genetics** /dʒɪ'netɪks/ n. Genetik, die

**Geneva** /dʒɪ'ni:və/ ①  pr. n. Genf (das)
② attrib. adj. Genfer

**genial** /'dʒi:nɪəl/ adj. freundlich

**genitals** /'dʒenɪtlz/ n. pl.
Geschlechtsorgane Pl.

**genitive** /'dʒenɪtɪv/ adj. & n. **~ [case]**
Genitiv, der

**genius** /'dʒi:nɪəs/ n. (a) ( person) Genie, das
(b) (ability) Talent, das

**genome** /'dʒi:nəʊm/ n. (Biol.) Genom, das

**genre** /'ʒɑ̃rə/ n. Genre, das

**gent** /dʒent/ n. (a) (coll./joc.) Gent, der (iron.)
(b) **the G~s** (Brit. coll.) die Herrentoilette

**genteel** /dʒen'ti:l/ adj. vornehm

**gentle** /'dʒentl/ adj., **~r** /'dʒentlə(r)/, **~st**
/'dʒentlɪst/ sanft; liebenswürdig ⟨Person,
Verhalten⟩; leicht, schwach ⟨Brise⟩; leise
⟨Geräusch⟩; gemächlich ⟨Spaziergang,
Tempo⟩; mäßig ⟨Hitze⟩

**gentleman** /'dʒentlmən/ n., pl. **gentlemen**
/'dʒentlmən/ Herr, der; (well-mannered)
Gentleman, der; **Ladies and Gentlemen!**
meine Damen und Herren!; **'Gentlemen'**
(sign) „Herren"

**'gentleness** n. Sanftheit, die; (of nature)
Sanftmütigkeit, die

**gently** /'dʒentlɪ/ adv. (tenderly) zart; zärtlich;
(mildly) sanft; (carefully) behutsam; (quietly, softly)
leise

**genuine** /'dʒenjʊɪn/ adj. (a) (real) echt
(b) (true) aufrichtig; wahr ⟨Grund, Not⟩

**'genuinely** adv. wirklich

**genus** /'dʒi:nəs, 'dʒenəs/ n., pl. **genera**
/'dʒenərə/ (Biol.) Gattung, die

**geographical** /dʒi:ə'græfɪkl/ adj.
geographisch

**geography** /dʒɪ'ɒgrəfɪ/ n. Geographie, die;
Erdkunde, die (Schulw.)

**geological** /dʒi:ə'lɒdʒɪkl/ adj. geologisch

**geologist** /dʒɪ'ɒlədʒɪst/ n. Geologe, der/
Geologin, die

**geology** /dʒɪ'ɒlədʒɪ/ n. Geologie, die

**geometric** /dʒi:ə'metrɪk/, **geometrical**
/dʒi:ə'metrɪkl/ adj. geometrisch

**geometry** /dʒɪ'ɒmɪtrɪ/ n. Geometrie, die

**geranium** /dʒə'reɪnɪəm/ n. Geranie, die;
Pelargonie, die

**geriatric** /dʒerɪ'ætrɪk/ adj. geriatrisch

**germ** /dʒɜ:m/ n. Keim, der

**German** /'dʒɜ:mən/ ①  adj. deutsch; **he/she
is ~:** er ist Deutscher/sie ist Deutsche
② n. (a) ( person) Deutsche, der/die
(b) (language) Deutsch, das; see also
ENGLISH 2A

**German Democratic Re'public** pr. n.
(Hist.) Deutsche Demokratische Republik

**Germanic** /dʒɜ:'mænɪk/ adj. germanisch

**German 'measles** n. Röteln Pl.

**Germany** /'dʒɜ:mənɪ/ pr. n. Deutschland
(das); **Federal Republic of ~:**
Bundesrepublik Deutschland, die

**germinate** /'dʒɜ:mɪneɪt/ v.i. keimen

**germ 'warfare** n. Bakterienkrieg, der

**gesticulate** /dʒeˈstɪkjʊleɪt/ v.i. gestikulieren

**gesticulation** /dʒestɪkjʊˈleɪʃn/ n. Gesten Pl.

**gesture** /ˈdʒestʃə(r)/ n. Geste, die

**get** /get/ 1 v.t., -tt-, got /gɒt/, got or (Amer.) gotten /ˈgɒtn/ (a) (obtain, receive) bekommen; kriegen (ugs.); sich (Dat.) besorgen ⟨Visum, Genehmigung⟩; sich (Dat.) beschaffen ⟨Geld⟩; (find) finden ⟨Zeit⟩; (fetch) holen; (buy) kaufen; where did you ~ that? wo hast du das her?; ~ sb. a job/taxi, ~ a job/taxi for sb. jmdm. einen Job verschaffen/ein Taxi besorgen; ~ oneself sth. sich (Dat.) etw. zulegen (b) ~ the bus etc. (be in time for, catch) den Bus usw. erreichen od. (ugs.) kriegen; (travel by) den Bus usw. nehmen (c) (prepare) machen (ugs.), zubereiten ⟨Essen⟩ (d) (win) bekommen; finden ⟨Anerkennung⟩; erzielen ⟨Tor, Punkt, Treffer⟩; gewinnen ⟨Spiel, Preis, Belohnung⟩; ~ permission die Erlaubnis erhalten (e) finden ⟨Schlaf, Ruhe⟩; bekommen ⟨Einfall, Vorstellung, Gefühl, Kopfschmerzen, Grippe⟩; gewinnen ⟨Eindruck⟩ (f) have got (coll.: have) haben; have got a cold eine Erkältung haben; have got to do sth. etw. tun müssen (g) (succeed in placing, bringing, etc.) bringen; kriegen (ugs.); ~ a message to sb. jmdm. eine Nachricht zukommen lassen; ~ things going or started die Dinge in Gang bringen (h) ~ everything packed/prepared alles [ein]packen/vorbereiten; ~ sth. ready/done etw. fertig machen; ~ one's feet wet nasse Füße kriegen; ~ one's hands dirty sich (Dat.) die Hände schmutzig machen; ~ one's hair cut sich (Dat.) die Haare schneiden lassen; ~ sb. to do sth. (induce) jmdn. dazu bringen, etw. zu tun (i) ~ sb. [on the telephone] jmdn. [telefonisch] erreichen (j) (coll.) (understand) kapieren (ugs.); (hear) mitkriegen (ugs.) 2 v.i., -tt-, got, got or (Amer.) gotten (a) (succeed in coming or going) kommen; ~ to London before dark London vor Einbruch der Dunkelheit erreichen (b) (come to be) ~ working sich an die Arbeit machen; ~ going or started (leave) losgehen; (become lively or operative) in Schwung kommen; ~ going on or with sth. mit etw. anfangen (c) ~ to know sb. jmdn. kennen lernen (d) (become) werden; ~ ready/washed sich fertig machen/waschen; ~ frightened/hungry Angst/Hunger kriegen

■ **get a'bout** v.i. (a) (travel) herumkommen (b) ⟨Gerücht:⟩ sich verbreiten

■ **get at** v.t. (a) herankommen an (+ Akk.) (b) (find out) [he]rausfinden ⟨Wahrheit usw.⟩; what are you ~ting at? worauf wollen Sie hinaus? (c) (coll.: attack, taunt) anmachen (salopp)

■ **get a'way** v.i. (a) (leave) wegkommen (b) (escape) entkommen

■ **get 'back** 1 v.i. zurückkommen; ~ back home nach Hause kommen 2 v.t. (recover) zurückbekommen; ~ one's own back (coll.) sich rächen

■ **get 'by** v.i. (a) vorbeikommen (b) (coll.: manage) über die Runden kommen (ugs.)

■ **get 'down** 1 v.i. hinunter-/heruntersteigen; ~ down to sth. (start) sich an etw. (Akk.) machen 2 v.t. (a) ~ sb./sth. down jmdn./etw. hinunter-/herunterbringen (b) (coll.: depress) fertig machen (ugs.)

■ **get 'in** 1 v.i. (into bus etc.) einsteigen; (arrive) ankommen 2 v.t. (fetch) reinholen

■ **get 'off** 1 v.i. (a) (alight) aussteigen; (dismount) absteigen (b) (leave) [weg]gehen (c) (escape punishment) davonkommen 2 v.t. (a) (remove) ausziehen ⟨Kleidung usw.⟩; entfernen ⟨Fleck usw.⟩; abbekommen ⟨Deckel usw.⟩ (b) (alight from) aussteigen aus; absteigen von ⟨Fahrrad⟩ (c) ~ off the subject vom Thema abkommen

■ **get 'on** v.i. (a) (mount) aufsteigen; (enter vehicle) einsteigen (b) (make progress) vorankommen; he's ~ting on well es geht ihm gut (c) (manage) zurechtkommen

■ **get 'on with** v.t. (a) weitermachen mit (b) ~ on [well] with sb. mit jmdm. [gut] auskommen

■ **get 'out** 1 v.i. (a) rausgehen/rausfahren (of aus) (b) (alight) aussteigen (c) (escape) ausbrechen (of aus); (fig.) herauskommen; ~ out of (avoid) herumkommen um (ugs.) 2 v.t. (a) (cause to leave) rausbringen (b) (withdraw) abheben ⟨Geld⟩ (of von)

■ **get 'over** v.t. (a) (cross) gehen über (+ Akk.); (climb) klettern über (+ Akk.) (b) (recover from) überwinden; hinwegkommen über (+ Akk.)

■ **get 'round** v.i. ~ round to doing sth. dazu kommen, etw. zu tun

■ **get 'through** v.i. durchkommen

■ **get 'up** v.i. aufstehen

■ **get 'up to** v.t. ~ up to mischief etwas anstellen

**get:** ~**away** n. Flucht, die; attrib. Flucht⟨plan, -wagen⟩; make one's ~away entkommen; ~**together** n. (coll.) gemütliches Beisammensein; ~**up** n. (coll.) Aufmachung, die

**geyser** /ˈgiːzə(r)/ n. (a) (spring) Geysir, der (b) (Brit.) Durchlauferhitzer, der

**ghastly** /ˈgɑːstlɪ/ adj. grauenvoll; entsetzlich ⟨Verletzungen⟩; schrecklich ⟨Fehler⟩

**gherkin** /ˈgɜːkɪn/ n. Essiggurke, die

**ghetto** /'getəʊ/ n., pl. ~s Getto, das
**ghetto blaster** /'getəʊblɑːstə(r)/ n. (coll.) [großer, tragbarer] Radiorekorder
**ghost** /gəʊst/ n. Geist, der; Gespenst, das
**'ghostly** adj. gespenstisch
**ghost:** ~ **story** n. Gespenstergeschichte, die; ~ **writer** n. Ghostwriter, der
**giant** /'dʒaɪənt/ [1] n. Riese, der [2] attrib. adj. riesig
**gibberish** /'dʒɪbərɪʃ/ n. Kauderwelsch, das
**gibe** /dʒaɪb/ n. Stichelei, die
**giblets** /'dʒɪblɪts/ n. pl. [Geflügel]klein, das
**giddiness** /'gɪdɪnɪs/ n. Schwindel, der
**giddy** /'gɪdɪ/ adj. schwind[e]lig
**gift** /gɪft/ n. (a) Geschenk, das; make sb. a ~ of sth., make a ~ of sth. to sb. jmdm. etw. schenken; a ~ box/pack eine Geschenkpackung
(b) (talent) Begabung, die; have a ~ for languages/mathematics sprachbegabt/mathematisch begabt sein
**'gifted** adj. begabt (in, at für)
**gift:** ~ **shop** n. Geschenkboutique, die; Geschenkladen, der; ~ **token,** ~ **voucher** ns. Geschenkgutschein, der; ~-**wrap** v.t. als Geschenk einpacken; in Geschenkpapier einpacken
**gigantic** /dʒaɪ'gæntɪk/ adj. gigantisch; riesig; enorm ⟨Verbesserung, Appetit⟩
**giggle** /'gɪgl/ [1] n. Kichern, das [2] v.i. kichern
**gild** /gɪld/ v.t. vergolden
**gill** /gɪl/ n. Kieme, die
**gilt** /gɪlt/ [1] n. Goldauflage, die; (paint) Goldfarbe, die [2] adj. vergoldet
**gimmick** /'gɪmɪk/ n. (coll.) Gag, der
**gin** /dʒɪn/ n. Gin, der
**ginger** /'dʒɪndʒə(r)/ n. (a) Ingwer, der (b) (colour) Rötlichgelb, das
**ginger:** ~ **'beer** n. Ingwerbier, das; ~**bread** n. Pfefferkuchen, der
**gingerly** /'dʒɪndʒəlɪ/ adv. vorsichtig
**gipsy** ▶ GYPSY
**giraffe** /dʒɪ'rɑːf/ n. Giraffe, die
**girder** /'gɜːdə(r)/ n. Träger, der
**girdle** /'gɜːdl/ n. Hüfthalter, der
**girl** /gɜːl/ n. Mädchen, das; (teenager) junges Mädchen
**'girlfriend** n. Freundin, die
**'girlish** adj. mädchenhaft
**'girl power** n. (coll.) Girlpower, die
**giro** /'dʒaɪərəʊ/ n. (a) Giro, das; attrib. Giro-; bank ~: Giroverkehr, der (b) (cheque) Scheck, der
**girth** /gɜːθ/ n. (a) Umfang, der (b) (for horse) Bauchgurt, der
**gismo** /'gɪzməʊ/ n. (coll.) Ding, das (ugs.)
**gist** /dʒɪst/ n. Wesentliche, das; (of tale, question, etc.) Kern, der

**give** /gɪv/ [1] v.t., gave /geɪv/, given /'gɪvn/ (a) geben (to Dat.)
(b) (as gift) schenken; ~ sb. sth., ~ sth. to sb. jmdm. etw. schenken; ~ and take (fig.) Kompromisse eingehen
(c) (assign) aufgeben ⟨Hausaufgaben usw.⟩; (grant, award, offer, allow to have) geben; verleihen ⟨Preis, Titel usw.⟩; lassen ⟨Wahl, Zeit⟩; verleihen ⟨Gewicht, Nachdruck⟩; bereiten, machen ⟨Freude, Mühe, Kummer⟩; bieten ⟨Schutz⟩; leisten ⟨Hilfe⟩; gewähren ⟨Unterstützung⟩; be ~n sth. etw. bekommen; ~n that (because) da; (if) wenn; ~ sb. hope jmdm. Hoffnung machen
(d) (tell) angeben ⟨Namen, Anschrift, Alter, Grund⟩; nennen ⟨Einzelheiten⟩; geben ⟨Rat, Befehl, Anweisung, Antwort⟩; fällen ⟨Urteil, Entscheidung⟩; sagen ⟨Meinung⟩; bekannt geben ⟨Nachricht⟩; ~ him my best wishes richte ihm meine besten Wünsche aus
(e) (perform, sing, etc.) geben ⟨Vorstellung, Konzert⟩; halten ⟨Vortrag, Seminar⟩
(f) (produce) geben ⟨Licht, Milch⟩; ergeben ⟨Zahlen, Resultat⟩
(g) (make, show) geben ⟨Zeichen, Stoß, Tritt⟩; machen ⟨Satz, Ruck⟩; ausstoßen ⟨Schrei, Seufzer, Pfiff⟩; ~ sb. a [friendly] look jmdm. einen [freundlichen] Blick zuwerfen
(h) (inflict) versetzen ⟨Schlag, Stoß⟩; sth. ~s me a headache von etw. bekomme ich Kopfschmerzen
(i) geben ⟨Party, Essen usw.⟩
[2] v.i., gave, given (yield) nachgeben; ⟨Knie:⟩ weich werden; ⟨Bett:⟩ federn
[3] n. Nachgiebigkeit, die; (elasticity) Elastizität, die

■ **give a'way** v.t. (a) verschenken (b) (in marriage) dem Bräutigam zuführen (c) (betray) verraten
■ **give 'back** v.t. zurückgeben
■ **give in** [1] /'--/ v.t. abgeben [2] /-'-/ v.i. nachgeben (to Dat.)
■ **give 'off** v.t. ausströmen ⟨Geruch⟩; aussenden ⟨Strahlen⟩
■ **give 'up** [1] v.i. aufgeben [2] v.t. aufgeben; widmen ⟨Zeit⟩; ~ sth. up (abandon habit) sich ⟨Dat.⟩ etw. abgewöhnen; ~ oneself up sich stellen
■ **give 'way** v.i. (a) (yield) nachgeben (b) (in traffic) ~ way [to traffic from the right] [dem Rechtsverkehr] die Vorfahrt lassen; 'G~ Way' „Vorfahrt beachten" (c) (collapse) einstürzen

**given** ▶ GIVE 1, 2
**'given name** n. (Amer.) Vorname, der
**give-'way sign** n. (Brit.) Vorfahrtsschild, das
**gizmo** ▶ GISMO
**glacier** /'glæsɪə(r)/ n. Gletscher, der
**glad** /glæd/ adj. froh; be ~ of sth. über etw. (Akk.) froh sein; für etw. dankbar sein
**gladden** /'glædn/ v.t. erfreuen
**glade** /gleɪd/ n. Lichtung, die
**'gladly** adv. gern

**glamor** (Amer.) ▶ GLAMOUR

**glamorous** /ˈglæmərəs/ adj. glanzvoll; glamourös ⟨Filmstar⟩

**glamour** /ˈglæmə(r)/ n. Glanz, der; (of person) Ausstrahlung, die

**glance** /glɑːns/ ①n. Blick, der
②v.i. blicken; ~ at sb./sth. jmdn./etw. anblicken; ~ at one's watch auf seine Uhr blicken; ~ at the newspaper etc. einen Blick in die Zeitung usw. werfen; ~ round [the room] sich [im Zimmer] umsehen

**gland** /glænd/ n. Drüse, die

**glandular** /ˈglændjʊlə(r)/ adj. Drüsen-

**glare** /gleə(r)/ ①n. (a) grelles Licht
**(b)** (hostile look) feindseliger Blick; with a ~: feindselig
②v.i. (glower) [finster] starren; ~ at sb./sth. jmdn./etw. anstarren

**glaring** /ˈgleərɪŋ/ adj. grell; (fig.: conspicuous) schreiend; grob ⟨Fehler⟩; krass ⟨Gegensatz⟩

**glass** /glɑːs/ n. (a) (substance) Glas, das; pieces of/broken ~: Glasscherben Pl.; (smaller) Glassplitter Pl.
**(b)** (drinking ~) Glas, das; a ~ of milk ein Glas Milch
**(c)** (pane) [Glas]scheibe, die
**(d)** in pl. (spectacles) [a pair of] ~es eine Brille

**glass 'ceiling** n. (fig.) unsichtbare Barriere

**'glassy** adj. gläsern

**glaze** /gleɪz/ ①n. Glasur, die
②v.t. (a) glasieren
**(b)** (fit with glass) verglasen

**glazed** /gleɪzd/ adj. glasig ⟨Blick⟩

**glazier** /ˈgleɪzɪə(r)/ n. Glaser, der

**gleam** /gliːm/ ①n. Schein, der; (fainter) Schimmer, der; ~ of hope Hoffnungsschimmer, der
②v.i. ⟨Licht:⟩ scheinen; ⟨Fußboden, Stiefel:⟩ glänzen; ⟨Zähne:⟩ blitzen; ⟨Augen:⟩ leuchten

**'gleaming** adj. glänzend

**glean** /gliːn/ v.t. zusammentragen ⟨Informationen usw.⟩; ~ sth. from sth. einer Sache (Dat.) etw. entnehmen

**glee** /gliː/ n. Freude, die; (gloating joy) Schadenfreude, die

**gleeful** /ˈgliːfl/ adj. freudig; (gloating) schadenfroh

**glen** /glen/ n. [schmales] Tal

**glib** /glɪb/ adj. aalglatt ⟨Person⟩; leicht dahingesagt ⟨Antwort⟩

**glide** /glaɪd/ v.i. gleiten; (through the air) schweben

**'glider** n. Segelflugzeug, das

**glimmer** /ˈglɪmə(r)/ ①n. Schimmer, der (of von); (of fire) Glimmen, das
②v.i. glimmen

**glimpse** /glɪmps/ ①n. [kurzer] Blick; catch or have or get a ~ of sb./sth. jmdn./etw. [kurz] zu sehen bekommen
②v.t. flüchtig sehen

**glint** /glɪnt/ ①n. Schimmer, der
②v.i. blinken; glitzern

**glisten** /ˈglɪsn/ v.i. glitzern

**glitter** /ˈglɪtə(r)/ ①v.i. glitzern; ⟨Juwelen, Sterne:⟩ funkeln
②n. Glitzern, das; (of diamonds) Funkeln, das

**glitz** /glɪts/ n. Glanz, der

**glitzy** /ˈglɪtsɪ/ adj. glanzvoll

**gloat** /gləʊt/ v.i. ~ over sth. sich hämisch über etw. (Akk.) freuen

**global** /ˈgləʊbl/ adj. weltweit; ~ warming globaler Temperaturanstieg; the ~ village das Weltdorf

**globalization** /gləʊbəlaɪˈzeɪʃn/ n. Globalisierung, die

**globalize** /ˈgləʊbəlaɪz/ v.t. globalisieren

**globe** /gləʊb/ n. (a) (sphere) Kugel, die
**(b)** (with map) Globus, der
**(c)** (world) the ~: der Globus; der Erdball

**'globetrotter** n. Globetrotter, der; Weltenbummler, der

**gloom** /gluːm/ n. (a) (darkness) Dunkel, das (geh.)
**(b)** (despondency) düstere Stimmung

**'gloomy** adj. (a) (dark) düster; finster
**(b)** (depressing) düster; (depressed) trübsinnig ⟨Person⟩

**glorify** /ˈglɔːrɪfaɪ/ v.t. verherrlichen; a glorified messenger boy ein besserer Botenjunge

**glorious** /ˈglɔːrɪəs/ adj. (a) (illustrious) ruhmreich ⟨Held, Sieg⟩
**(b)** (delightful) wunderschön; herrlich

**glory** /ˈglɔːrɪ/ ①n. (a) (splendour) Schönheit, die; (majesty) Herrlichkeit, die
**(b)** (fame) Ruhm, der
②v.i. ~ in sth. (be proud of) sich einer Sache (Gen.) rühmen

**gloss** /glɒs/ n. Glanz, der; ~ paint Lackfarbe, die
■ **'gloss over** v.t. bemänteln; beschönigen ⟨Fehler⟩

**glossary** /ˈglɒsərɪ/ n. Glossar, das

**'glossy** ①adj. glänzend; (fig.) glanzvoll
②n. (coll.) (magazine) auf [Hoch]glanzpapier gedruckte Zeitschrift

**glove** /glʌv/ n. Handschuh, der

**glove:** ~ **box** n. (a) ▶ ~ COMPARTMENT; (b) (for toxic material etc.) Handschuhkasten, der; ~ **compartment** n. Handschuhfach, das; ~ **puppet** n. Handpuppe, die

**glow** /gləʊ/ v.i. (a) glühen; ⟨Lampe, Leuchtfarbe:⟩ schimmern, leuchten
**(b)** (fig.) (with warmth or pride) ⟨Gesicht, Wangen:⟩ glühen (with vor + Dat.); (with health or vigour) strotzen (with vor + Dat.)

**glower** /ˈglaʊə(r)/ v.i. finster dreinblicken; ~ at sb. jmdn. finster anstarren

**'glowing** adj. glühend; begeistert ⟨Bericht⟩

**'glow-worm** n. Glühwürmchen, das

**glucose** /ˈgluːkəʊz/ n. Glucose, die

**glue** /gluː/ ①n. Klebstoff, der

**2** *v.t.* kleben; ~ **sth. to sth.** etw. an etw. (*Dat.*) an- *od.* festkleben

**'glue-sniffing** *n.* Schnüffeln, *das* (ugs.); Sniefen, *das* (ugs.)

**glum** /glʌm/ *adj.* verdrießlich

**glut** /glʌt/ *n.* Überangebot, *das* (of an, von + *Dat.*)

**glutton** /'glʌtən/ *n.* Vielfraß, *der* (ugs.); **a ~ for punishment** (iron.) ein Masochist (fig.)

**gluttony** /'glʌtənɪ/ *n.* Gefräßigkeit, *die*

**glycerine** /'glɪsəriːn/ (*Amer.*: **glycerin** /'glɪsərɪn/) *n.* Glyzerin, *das*

**GM** *abbr.* = **genetically modified**; GM crops/food gentechnisch veränderte Feldfrüchte *Pl.*/Nahrungsmittel *Pl.*

**gm.** *abbr.* = **gram[s]** g

**GMO** *abbr.* = **genetically modified organism** GVO

**GMT** *abbr.* = **Greenwich Mean Time** GMT; WEZ

**gnarled** /nɑːld/ *adj.* knorrig; knotig ⟨Hand⟩

**gnash** /næʃ/ *v.t.* ~ **one's teeth** mit den Zähnen knirschen

**gnat** /næt/ *n.* [Stech]mücke, *die*

**gnaw** /nɔː/ **1** *v.i.* ~ **[away] at sth.** an etw. (*Dat.*) nagen
**2** *v.t.* nagen an (+ *Dat.*); abnagen ⟨Knochen⟩

**gnome** /nəʊm/ *n.* Gnom, *der*

**GNVQ** *abbr.* = **General National Vocational Qualification**

**go** /gəʊ/ **1** *v.i., pres.* **he goes** /gəʊz/, *p.t.* **went** /went/, *pres. p.* **going** /'gəʊɪŋ/, *p.p.* **gone** /gɒn/ **(a)** gehen; ⟨Fahrzeug:⟩ fahren; ⟨Flugzeug:⟩ fliegen; ⟨Vierfüßer:⟩ laufen; (on horseback etc.) reiten; (in lift) fahren; (on outward journey) weg-, abfahren; (travel regularly) ⟨Verkehrsmittel:⟩ verkehren (**from ... to** zwischen + *Dat.* ... und); **go by bicycle/car/bus/train** *or* **rail/boat** *or* **sea** *or* **ship** mit dem [Fahr]rad/Auto/Bus/Zug/Schiff fahren; **go by plane** *or* **air** fliegen; **go on foot** zu Fuß gehen; laufen (ugs.); **go on a journey** verreisen; **have far to go** es weit haben; **go to the toilet/cinema/a museum** auf die Toilette/ins Kino/ins Museum gehen; **go to the doctor['s]** *etc.* zum Arzt *usw.* gehen; **go bathing** baden gehen; **go cycling** Rad fahren; **go to see sb.** jmdn. aufsuchen; **go and see whether ...**: nachsehen [gehen], ob ...; **I'll go!** ich geh schon!; (answer phone) ich geh ran *od.* nehme ab; (answer door) ich mache auf
**(b)** (start) losgehen; (in vehicle) losfahren
**(c)** (pass, circulate) gehen; **a shiver went up** *or* **down my spine** ein Schauer lief mir über den Rücken; **go to** (be given to) ⟨Preis, Gelder, Job:⟩ gehen an (+ *Akk.*); ⟨Titel, Besitz:⟩ übergehen auf (+ *Akk.*); **go towards** (be of benefit to) zugute kommen (+ *Dat.*)
**(d)** (act, function effectively) gehen; ⟨Mechanismus, Maschine:⟩ laufen; **keep going** (in movement) weitergehen/-fahren; (in activity) weitermachen; (not fail) sich aufrecht halten; **keep sth. going** etw. in Gang halten; **make sth. go, get/set sth. going** etw. in Gang bringen
**(e) go to work** zur Arbeit gehen; **go to school** in die Schule gehen; **go to a comprehensive school** auf eine Gesamtschule gehen
**(f)** (depart) gehen; ⟨Bus, Zug:⟩ [ab]fahren; ⟨Post:⟩ rausgehen (ugs.)
**(g)** (cease to function) kaputtgehen; ⟨Sicherung:⟩ durchbrennen; (break) brechen; ⟨Seil usw.:⟩ reißen
**(h)** (disappear) weggehen; ⟨Mantel, Hut, Fleck:⟩ verschwinden; ⟨Geruch, Rauch:⟩ sich verziehen; ⟨Geld, Zeit:⟩ draufgehen (ugs.) (**in, on** für)
**(i) to go** (still remaining) **have sth. [still] to go** [noch] etw. übrig haben; **one week** *etc.* **to go to ...**: noch eine Woche *usw.* bis ...; **there's hours to go** es dauert noch Stunden
**(j)** (be sold) weggehen (ugs.); verkauft werden; **going! going! gone!** zum Ersten! zum Zweiten! zum Dritten!; **go to sb.** an jmdn. gehen
**(k)** (run) ⟨Grenze, Straße usw.:⟩ verlaufen, gehen; (lead) gehen; führen; (extend) reichen; **as** *or* **so far as he/it goes** so weit
**(l)** (turn out, progress) ⟨Projekt, Interview, Abend:⟩ verlaufen; **how did your holiday go?** wie war Ihr Urlaub?; **things have been going well/badly** in der letzten Zeit läuft alles gut/schief
**(m)** (be, have form or nature) sein; ⟨Sprichwort, Gedicht, Titel:⟩ lauten; **that's the way it goes** so ist es nun mal; **go hungry** hungern; **go without food/water** es ohne Essen/Wasser aushalten
**(n)** (become) werden; **the tyre has gone flat** der Reifen ist platt
**(o)** (have usual place) kommen; (belong) gehören; **where does the box go?** wo kommt *od.* gehört die Kiste hin?
**(p)** (fit) passen; **go in[to] sth.** in etw. (*Akk.*) gehen *od.* [hinein]passen; **go through sth.** durch etw. [hindurch]gehen
**(q)** (match) passen (**with** zu)
**(r)** ⟨Turmuhr, Gong:⟩ schlagen; ⟨Glocke:⟩ läuten
**(s)** (coll.: be acceptable or permitted) erlaubt sein; **it/that goes without saying** es/das ist doch selbstverständlich. See also GOING 2
**2** *n., pl.* **goes** /gəʊz/ (coll.) **(a)** (attempt, try) Versuch, *der;* (chance) Gelegenheit, *die;* **have a go** es versuchen; **let me have a go/can I have a go?** lass mich [auch ein]mal/kann ich [auch ein]mal? (ugs.); **it's 'my go** ich bin an der Reihe *od.* dran; **at one go** auf einmal; **at the first go** auf Anhieb
**(b)** (vigorous activity) **it's all go** es ist alles eine einzige Hetzerei (ugs.); **be on the go** auf Trab sein (ugs.)
**(c)** (success) **make a go of sth.** mit etw. Erfolg haben

■ **go a'head** *v.i.* **(a)** (in advance) vorausgehen (**of** *Dat.*) ⋯

**(b)** (proceed) weitermachen; (make progress) ⟨*Arbeit:*⟩ fortschreiten, vorangehen
■ **go a'long with** *v.t.* go along with sth. (agree to) sich einer Sache (*Dat.*) anschließen
■ **go a'way** *v.i.* weggehen; (on holiday or business) verreisen
■ **go 'back** *v.i.* zurückgehen/-fahren; (restart) ⟨*Schule, Fabrik:*⟩ wieder anfangen; (fig.) zurückgehen; go back to the beginning noch mal von vorne anfangen
■ **go by** ⟨1⟩ /'--/ *v.t.* go by sth. sich nach etw. richten; (adhere to) sich an etw. (*Akk.*) halten ⟨2⟩ /-'-/ *v.i.* ⟨*Zeit:*⟩ vergehen
■ **go 'down** *v.i.* hinuntergehen/-fahren; ⟨*Sonne:*⟩ untergehen; ⟨*Schiff:*⟩ untergehen; (fall to ground) ⟨*Flugzeug usw.:*⟩ abstürzen.
■ **'go for** *v.t.* go for sb./sth. (go to fetch) jmdn./etw. holen; (apply to) für jmdn./etw. gelten; (like) jmdn./etw. gut finden
■ **go 'in** *v.i.* hineingehen; reingehen (ugs.)
■ **go 'off** ⟨1⟩ *v.i.* **(a)** go off with sb./sth. mit jmdm./etw. auf- und davonmachen (ugs.) **(b)** ⟨*Alarm, Schusswaffe:*⟩ losgehen; ⟨*Wecker:*⟩ klingeln; ⟨*Bombe:*⟩ hochgehen **(c)** (turn bad) schlecht werden **(d)** ⟨*Strom:*⟩ ausfallen ⟨2⟩ *v.t.* (begin to dislike) go off sth. von etw. abkommen
■ **go 'on** *v.i.* **(a)** weitergehen/-fahren **(b)** (continue) weitermachen **(c)** (happen) passieren
■ **go 'out** *v.i.* ausgehen; go out to work/for a meal arbeiten/essen gehen; go out with sb. (date sb.) mit jmdm. gehen (ugs.)
■ **go over** ⟨1⟩ /-'--/ *v.i.* hinübergehen ⟨2⟩ /'---, -'--/ *v.t.* (re-examine) durchgehen
■ **go 'round** *v.i.* **(a)** (call) go round and *or* to see sb. bei jmdm. vorbeigehen (ugs.) **(b)** (look round) sich umschauen **(c)** (suffice) reichen; langen (ugs.) **(d)** (spin) sich drehen
■ **go through** ⟨1⟩ /-'-/ *v.i.* ⟨*Ernennung:*⟩ durchkommen; ⟨*Antrag:*⟩ durchgehen ⟨2⟩ /'--/ **(a)** (rehearse) durchgehen **(b)** (examine) durchsehen **(c)** (endure) durchmachen
■ **go 'through with** *v.t.* zu Ende führen
■ **go 'under** *v.i.* untergehen; (fig.: fail) eingehen
■ **go 'up** *v.i.* **(a)** hinaufgehen/-fahren; ⟨*Ballon:*⟩ aufsteigen; (Theatre) ⟨*Vorhang:*⟩ aufgehen; ⟨*Lichter:*⟩ angehen **(b)** (increase) ⟨*Zahl:*⟩ wachsen; ⟨*Preis, Wert, Niveau:*⟩ steigen; (in price) ⟨*Ware:*⟩ teurer werden
■ **go without** ⟨1⟩ /'--/ *v.t.* verzichten auf (+ *Akk.*) ⟨2⟩ /-'-/ *v.i.* verzichten

**goad** /gəʊd/ *v.t.* ~ sb. into sth./doing sth. jmdn. zu etw. anstacheln/dazu anstacheln, etw. zu tun

**'go-ahead** ⟨1⟩ *adj.* unternehmungslustig; ( progressive) fortschrittlich ⟨2⟩ *n.* give sb./sth. the ~: jmdm./einer Sache grünes Licht geben

**goal** /gəʊl/ *n.* **(a)** (aim) Ziel, *das* **(b)** (Footb., Hockey) Tor, *das;* **score/kick a** ~: einen Treffer erzielen
**goalie** /'gəʊlɪ/ *n.* (coll.) Tormann, *der*
**goal:** ~**keeper** *n.* Torwart, *der;* ~**post** *n.* Torpfosten, *der;* **move the** ~**posts** (fig. coll.) sich nicht an die Spielregeln halten
**goat** /gəʊt/ *n.* Ziege, *die*
**gobble** /'gɒbl/ ⟨1⟩ *v.t.* ~ [down *or* up] hinunterschlingen ⟨2⟩ *v.i.* schlingen
**'go-between** *n.* Vermittler, *der/* Vermittlerin, *die*
**goblet** /'gɒblɪt/ *n.* Kelchglas, *das*
**goblin** /'gɒblɪn/ *n.* Kobold, *der*
**god** /gɒd/ *n.* **(a)** Gott, *der* **(b)** God (Theol.) Gott
**god:** ~**child** *n.* Patenkind, *das;* ~**-daughter** *n.* Patentochter, *die*
**goddess** /'gɒdɪs/ *n.* Göttin, *die*
**god:** ~**father** *n.* Pate, *der;* **G~-forsaken** *adj.* gottverlassen; ~**mother** *n.* Patentante, *die;* ~**send** *n.* Gottesgabe, *die;* be a ~send to sb. für jmdn. ein Geschenk des Himmels sein; ~**son** *n.* Patensohn, *der*
**'go-getter** *n.* Draufgänger, *der*
**'goggle-box** *n.* (Brit. coll.) Glotze, *die* (salopp); Glotzkiste, *die* (salopp)
**goggles** /'gɒglz/ *n. pl.* Schutzbrille, *die*
**going** /'gəʊɪŋ/ ⟨1⟩ *n.* (progress) Vorankommen, *das;* **while the** ~ **is good** solange es noch geht ⟨2⟩ *adj.* **(a)** (available) erhältlich; **there is sth.** ~: es gibt etw. **(b)** be ~ to do sth. etw. tun [werden/wollen]; I was ~ to say ich wollte sagen; it's ~ to snow es wird schneien; a ~ concern eine gesunde Firma **(c)** (current) [derzeit/damals/dann] geltend); **the** ~ **rate of exchange** der augenblickliche Wechselkurs **(d)** a ~ concern eine gesunde Firma
**goings-'on** *n. pl.* Ereignisse *Pl.*
**gold** /gəʊld/ ⟨1⟩ *n.* Gold, *das* ⟨2⟩ *attrib. adj.* golden; Gold⟨*münze, -kette usw.*⟩
**'gold-digger** *n.* Goldgräber, *der;* **she's a** ~**-digger** (fig. coll.) sie ist nur auf das Geld der Männer aus
**golden** /'gəʊldn/ *adj.* golden
**golden 'wedding** *n.* goldene Hochzeit
**gold:** ~**fish** *n.* Goldfisch, *der;* ~**fish bowl** *n.* Goldfischglas, *das;* **like being in a** ~**fish bowl** (fig.) wie auf dem Präsentierteller; ~ **'medal** *n.* Goldmedaille, *die;* ~ **'medallist** *n.* Goldmedaillengewinner, *der/*-gewinnerin, *die;* ~ **mine** *n.* Goldmine, *die;* (fig.) Goldgrube, *die;* ~**'plated** *adj.* vergoldet; ~**smith** *n.* Goldschmied, *der/*-schmiedin, *die*
**golf** /gɒlf/ *n.* Golf, *das*

**golf: ∼ ball** *n.* Golfball, *der;* ∼ **club** *n.* **(a)** (implement) Golfschläger, *der;* **(b)** (association) Golfklub, *der;* ∼**course** *n.* Golfplatz, *der*

**'golfer** *n.* Golfer, *der*/Golferin, *die*

**golf links** *n.* Golfplatz, *der*

**gondola** /'gɒndələ/ *n.* Gondel, *die*

**gondolier** /gɒndə'lɪə(r)/ *n.* Gondoliere, *der*

**gone** /gɒn/ 1 ▸ GO 1
2 *pred. adj.* **(a)** (away) weg; **it's time you were ∼:** es ist *od.* wird Zeit, dass du gehst **(b)** (of time: after) nach; **it's ∼ ten o'clock** es ist zehn Uhr vorbei

**gong** /gɒŋ/ *n.* Gong, *der*

**good** /gʊd/ 1 *adj.,* **better** /'betə(r)/, **best** /best/ **(a)** gut; günstig ⟨Gelegenheit, Angebot⟩; ausreichend ⟨Vorrat⟩; ausgiebig ⟨Mahl⟩; **as ∼ as** so gut wie; **his ∼ eye/leg** sein gesundes Auge/Bein; **in ∼ time** frühzeitig; **all in ∼ time** alles zu seiner Zeit; **be ∼ at sth.** in etw. *(Dat.)* gut sein; **too ∼ to be true** zu schön, um wahr zu sein; **apples are ∼ for you** Äpfel sind gesund; **be too much of a ∼ thing** zu viel des Guten sein; **∼ times** eine schöne Zeit; **feel ∼:** sich wohl fühlen; **take a ∼ look round** sich gründlich umsehen; **give sb. a ∼ beating/scolding** jmdn. tüchtig verprügeln/ausschimpfen; **∼ afternoon/day** guten Tag!; **∼ evening/morning** guten Abend/Morgen!; **∼ night** gute Nacht!
**(b)** (enjoyable) schön ⟨Leben, Urlaub, Wochenende⟩; **the ∼ life** das angenehme[, sorglose] Leben; **have a ∼ time!** viel Spaß!; **have a ∼ journey!** gute Reise!
**(c)** (well-behaved) gut; brav; **be ∼!, be a ∼ girl/boy!** sei brav *od.* lieb!; **[as] ∼ as gold** ganz artig *od.* brav
**(d)** (virtuous) rechtschaffen; (kind) nett; gut ⟨Absicht, Wünsche, Benehmen, Tat⟩; **be ∼ to sb.** gut zu jmdm. sein; **would you be so ∼ as to** *or* **∼ enough to do that?** wären Sie so freundlich *od.* nett, das zu tun?; **that/it is ∼ of you** das ist nett *od.* lieb von dir
**(e)** (commendable) gut; **∼ for 'you** *etc.* (coll.) bravo!
**(f)** (attractive) schön; gut ⟨Figur⟩; **look ∼:** gut aussehen
**(g)** (considerable) [recht] ansehnlich ⟨Menschenmenge⟩; ganz schön, ziemlich (ugs.) ⟨Entfernung, Strecke⟩; gut ⟨Preis, Erlös⟩
**(h) make ∼** (succeed) erfolgreich sein; (compensate for) wieder gutmachen; (indemnify) ersetzen
2 *n.* **(a)** (use) Nutzen, *der;* **be some ∼ to sb./sth.** jmdm./einer Sache nützen; **be no ∼ to sb./sth.** für jmdn./etw. nicht zu gebrauchen sein; **it is no/not much ∼ doing sth.** hat keinen/kaum einen Sinn, etw. zu tun; **what's the ∼ of …?, what ∼ is …?** was nützt …?
**(b)** (benefit) **for your/his** *etc.* **own ∼:** zu deinem/seinem *usw.* Besten; **do no/little ∼:** nichts/wenig helfen *od.* nützen; **do sb./sth.**

∼: jmdm./einer Sache nützen; ⟨Ruhe, Erholung:⟩ jmdm./einer Sache gut tun; ⟨Arznei:⟩ jmdm./einer Sache helfen
**(c)** (goodness) Gute, *das;* **be up to no ∼:** nichts Gutes im Sinn haben
**(d) for ∼** (finally) ein für alle Mal; (permanently) für immer
**(e)** *in pl.* (wares etc.) Waren *Pl.;* (belongings) Habe, *die;* (Brit. Railw.) Fracht, *die; attrib.* Güter⟨wagen, -zug⟩

**good: ∼'bye** (Amer.: ∼'by) *int.* auf Wiedersehen!; (on telephone) auf Wiederhören!; **∼-for-nothing** 1 *adj.* nichtsnutzig; 2 *n.* Taugenichts, *der;* **∼-'looking** *adj.* gut aussehend

**'goodness** 1 *n.* Güte, *die*
2 *int.* **[my] ∼!** meine Güte! (ugs.)

**good: ∼s train** *n.* (Brit.) Güterzug, *der;* **∼-'tempered** *adj.* ausgeglichen; verträglich ⟨Person⟩; **∼'will** *n.* guter Wille; *attrib.* Goodwill⟨botschaft, -reise usw.⟩

**'goody** *n.* (coll.: hero) Gute, *der/die*

**gooey** /'guːɪ/ *adj.,* **gooier** /'guːɪə(r)/, **gooiest** /'guːɪɪst/ (coll.) klebrig

**goose** /guːs/ *n., pl.* **geese** /giːs/ Gans, *die*

**gooseberry** /'gʊzbərɪ/ *n.* Stachelbeere, *die*

**goose bumps** (Amer.), **goose pimples** *ns. pl.* **have ∼:** eine Gänsehaut haben

**gore¹** /gɔː(r)/ *v.t.* [mit den Hörnern] aufspießen *od.* durchbohren

**gore²** *n.* Blut, *das*

**gorge** /gɔːdʒ/ 1 *n.* Schlucht, *die*
2 *v.i. & refl.* ∼ **[oneself]** sich voll stopfen (ugs.) (**on** mit)

**gorgeous** /'gɔːdʒəs/ *adj.* prächtig; hinreißend ⟨Frau, Mann, Lächeln⟩

**gorilla** /gə'rɪlə/ *n.* Gorilla, *der*

**gormless** /'gɔːmlɪs/ *adj.* (Brit. coll.) dämlich (ugs.)

**gorse** /gɔːs/ *n.* Stechginster, *der*

**gory** /'gɔːrɪ/ *adj.* (fig.) blutrünstig

**gosh** /gɒʃ/ *int.* (coll.) Gott!

**'go-slow** *n.* (Brit.) Bummelstreik, *der*

**gospel** /'gɒspl/ *n.* Evangelium, *das*

**'gospel singer** *n.* Gospelsänger, *der*/-sängerin, *die*

**gossamer** /'gɒsəmə(r)/ *n.* Altweibersommer, *der; attrib.* hauchdünn

**gossip** /'gɒsɪp/ 1 *n.* **(a)** (talk) Klatsch, *der* (ugs.)
**(b)** (person) Klatschbase, *die* (ugs.)
2 *v.i.* klatschen (ugs.)

**gossip: ∼ column** *n.* Klatschspalte, *die* (ugs.); **∼ columnist** *n.* Klatschspaltenkolumnist, *der*/-kolumnistin, *die*

**got** ▸ GET

**Gothic** /'gɒθɪk/ *adj.* gotisch

**gotten** ▸ GET

**gouge** /gaʊdʒ/ *v.t.* aushöhlen

**goulash** /'guːlæʃ/ *n.* Gulasch, *das od. der*

**gourmet** /'gʊəmeɪ/ *n.* Gourmet, *der*

**gout** /gaʊt/ *n.* Gicht, *die*

**govern** /'gʌvn/ ① *v.t.* (a) regieren ‹Land, Volk›; verwalten ‹Provinz›
(b) (dictate) bestimmen
② *v.i.* regieren

**governess** /'gʌvənɪs/ *n.* Gouvernante, *die* (veraltet); Hauslehrerin, *die*

**government** /'gʌvnmənt/ *n.* Regierung, *die; attrib.* Regierungs-

**government:** ~ **department** *n.* Regierungsstelle, *die;* ~**-funded** *adj.* staatlich finanziert; ~ **official** *n.* Regierungsbeamte, *der/-*beamtin, *die*

**governor** /'gʌvənə(r)/ *n.* (a) (of province etc.) Gouverneur, *der*
(b) (of institution) Direktor, *der/*Direktorin, *die;* [board of] ~s Vorstand, *der*
(c) (coll.: employer) Boss, *der* (ugs.)

**gown** /gaʊn/ *n.* (a) [elegantes] Kleid
(b) (official or uniform robe) Talar, *der*

**GP** *abbr.* = **general practitioner**

**grab** /græb/ ① *v.t.,* -bb- greifen nach; (seize) packen; ~ **the chance** die Gelegenheit ergreifen; ~ **hold of sb./sth.** sich *(Dat.)* jmdn./etw. schnappen (ugs.)
② *v.i.,* -bb-: ~ **at sth.** nach etw. greifen
③ *n.* **make a** ~ **at** *or* **for sb./sth.** nach jmdm./etw. greifen

**grace** /greɪs/ *n.* (a) (charm) Anmut, *die* (geh.)
(b) (decency) **have the** ~ **to do sth.** so anständig sein und etw. tun
(c) (delay) Frist, *die;* **give sb. a day's** ~: jmdm. einen Tag Aufschub gewähren
(d) (prayers) **say** ~: das Tischgebet sprechen

**graceful** /'greɪsfl/ *adj.* elegant; graziös ‹Bewegung, Eleganz›

**gracious** /'greɪʃəs/ ① *adj.* (a) liebenswürdig
(b) (merciful) gnädig
② *int.* **good** ~! [ach] du meine Güte!

**grade** /greɪd/ ① *n.* (a) Rang, *der;* (Mil.) Dienstgrad, *der*
(b) (position) Stufe, *die*
(c) (Amer. Sch.: class) Klasse, *die*
(d) (Sch., Univ.: mark) Note, *die;* Zensur, *die*
② *v.t.* (a) einstufen ‹Schüler›; [nach Größe/ Qualität] sortieren ‹Eier, Kartoffeln›
(b) (mark) benoten

**gradient** /'greɪdɪənt/ *n.* (ascent) Steigung, *die;* (descent) Gefälle, *das*

**gradual** /'grædʒʊəl/ *adj.,* **'gradually** *adv.* allmählich

**graduate** ① /'grædʒʊət/ *n.* Graduierte, *der/die;* (who has left university) Akademiker, *der/*Akademikerin, *die;* **university** ~: Hochschulabsolvent, *der/-*absolventin, *die*
② /'grædʒʊeɪt/ *v.i.* einen akademischen Grad/Titel erwerben; (Amer. Sch.) die [Schul]abschlussprüfung bestehen (**from an** + *Dat.*)

**graduation** /grædʒʊ'eɪʃn/ *n.* (a) (Univ.) Graduierung, *die*

(b) (Amer. Sch.) Entlassung, *die*

**graffiti** /grə'fiːtiː/ *n. sing. or pl.* Graffiti *Pl.;* ~ **artist** Graffitikünstler, *der/-*künstlerin, *die*

**graft** /grɑːft/ ① *n.* (a) (Bot.) Edelreis, *das*
(b) (Med.) (operation) Transplantation, *die;* (thing ~ed) Transplantat, *das*
(c) (Brit. coll.: work) Plackerei, *die* (ugs.)
② *v.t.* (a) (Bot.) pfropfen
(b) (Med.) transplantieren
③ *v.i.* (Brit. coll.) schuften (ugs.)

**grain** /greɪn/ *n.* (a) Korn, *das; collect.* Getreide, *das*
(b) (particle) Korn, *das*
(c) (in wood) Maserung, *die;* (in paper) Faser, *die;* (in leather) Narbung, *die;* **go against the** ~ [**for sb.**] (fig.) jmdm. gegen den Strich gehen (ugs.)

**'grainy** *adj.* körnig; gemasert ‹Holz›; genarbt ‹Leder›

**gram** /græm/ *n.* Gramm, *das*

**grammar** /'græmə(r)/ *n.* Grammatik, *die*

**grammar:** ~ **book** *n.* Grammatik, *die;* ~ **school** *n.* (Brit.) ≈ Gymnasium, *das*

**grammatical** /grə'mætɪkl/ *adj.* (a) grammat[ikal]isch richtig *od.* korrekt
(b) (of grammar) grammatisch

**grammatically** /grə'mætɪkəlɪ/ *adv.* grammati[kal]isch ‹richtig, falsch›

**gramme** ▶ GRAM

**gramophone** /'græməfəʊn/ *n.* Plattenspieler, *der*

**gran** /græn/ *n.* (coll./child lang.) Oma, *die* (Kinderspr./ugs.)

**granary** /'grænərɪ/ *n.* Getreidesilo, *der od. das;* Kornspeicher, *der*

**'granary bread** *n.* Ganzkornbrot, *das*

**grand** /grænd/ *adj.* (a) (most or very important) groß; ~ **finale** großes Finale
(b) (splendid) grandios
(c) (coll.: excellent) großartig

**grandad** /'grændæd/ *n.* (coll./child lang.); Opa, *der* (Kinderspr./ugs.)

**grand:** ~**child** *n.* Enkel, *der/*Enkelin, *die;* Enkelkind, *das;* ~**dad**[**dy**] /'grændæd(i)/ ▶ GRANDAD; ~**daughter** *n.* Enkelin, *die*

**grandeur** /'grændʒə(r), 'grændjə(r)/ *n.* Erhabenheit, *die*

**'grandfather** *n.* Großvater, *der;* ~ **clock** Standuhr, *die*

**grandiose** /'grændɪəʊs/ *adj.* grandios; (pompous) bombastisch

**grand:** ~**ma** *n.* (coll./child lang.) Oma, *die* (Kinderspr./ugs.); ~**mother** *n.* Großmutter, *die;* ~**pa** *n.* (coll./child lang.) Opa, *der* (Kinderspr./ugs.); ~**parent** *n.* (male) Großvater, *der;* (female) Großmutter, *die;* ~**parents** Großeltern *Pl.;* ~ **pi'ano** *n.* [Konzert]flügel, *der;* ~**son** *n.* Enkel, *der;* ~**stand** *n.* [Haupt]tribüne, *die*

**granite** /'grænɪt/ *n.* Granit, *der*

**granny** /'grænɪ/ *n.* (coll./child lang.) Oma, *die* (Kinderspr./ugs.)

**'granny flat** *n.* Einliegerwohnung, *die*

**grant** /grɑːnt/ ⟦1⟧ *v.t.* **(a)** erfüllen ⟨*Wunsch*⟩; stattgeben (+ *Dat.*) ⟨*Gesuch*⟩
**(b)** (concede, give) gewähren; geben ⟨*Zeit*⟩; bewilligen ⟨*Geldmittel*⟩; zugestehen ⟨*Recht*⟩; erteilen ⟨*Erlaubnis*⟩
**(c)** (in argument) zugeben; **take sb./sth. for** ∼**ed** sich (*Dat.*) jmds. sicher sein/etw. für selbstverständlich halten
⟦2⟧ *n.* Zuschuss, *der;* (financial aid [to student]) [Studien]beihilfe, *die;* (scholarship) Stipendium, *das*

**granulated sugar** /grænjʊleɪtɪd ˈʃʊɡə(r)/ *n.* Kristallzucker, *der*

**granule** /ˈgrænjuːl/ *n.* Körnchen, *das*

**grape** /greɪp/ *n.* Weintraube, *die;* **a bunch of** ∼**s** eine Traube

**grape:** ∼**fruit** *n., pl. same* Grapefruit, *die;* ∼ **juice** *n.* Traubensaft, *der;* ∼**vine** *n.* (fig.) **the** ∼**vine** die Flüsterpropaganda; **I heard on the** ∼**vine that ...:** es wird geflüstert, dass ...

**graph** /grɑːf/ *n.* grafische Darstellung; ∼ **paper** Diagrammpapier, *das*

**graphic** /ˈgræfɪk/ *adj.* **(a)** grafisch
**(b)** (vivid) plastisch; anschaulich

**graphically** /ˈgræfɪkəlɪ/ *adv.* **(a)** (vividly) plastisch
**(b)** (using graphics) grafisch

**graphic 'arts** *n. pl.* Grafik, *die*

**graphics** /ˈgræfɪks/ *n.* (use of diagrams) grafische Darstellung; **computer** ∼: Computergraphik, *die*

**grapple** /ˈgræpl/ *v.i.* handgemein werden; ∼ **with** (fig.) sich auseinander setzen mit

**grasp** /grɑːsp/ ⟦1⟧ *v.i.* ∼ **at** ergreifen; sich stürzen auf (+ *Akk.*) ⟨*Angebot*⟩
⟦2⟧ *v.t.* **(a)** (seize) ergreifen
**(b)** (hold firmly) festhalten
**(c)** (understand) verstehen; erfassen ⟨*Bedeutung*⟩
⟦3⟧ *n.* **(a)** (firm hold) Griff, *der*
**(b)** (mental ∼) **have a good** ∼ **of sth.** etw. gut beherrschen

**'grasping** *adj.* habgierig

**grass** /grɑːs/ *n.* **(a)** Gras, *das*
**(b)** (lawn) Rasen, *der*
**(c)** (Brit. sl.: police informer) Spitzel, *der*

**grass:** ∼**hopper** *n.* Grashüpfer, *der;* ∼**-root[s]** *attrib. adj.* (Polit.) Basis-; ∼ **seed** *n.* Grassamen, *der;* (collect.) Grassamen *Pl.*

**grassy** /ˈgrɑːsɪ/ *adj.* mit Gras bewachsen

**grate¹** /greɪt/ *n.* Rost, *der;* (recess) Kamin, *der*

**grate²** *v.t.* **(a)** reiben; (less finely) raspeln
**(b)** (grind) ∼ **one's teeth** mit den Zähnen knirschen

**grateful** /ˈgreɪtfl/ *adj.* dankbar (**to** *Dat.*)

**'gratefully** *adv.* dankbar

**'grater** *n.* Reibe, *die;* Raspel, *die*

**gratify** /ˈgrætɪfaɪ/ *v.t.* freuen; **be gratified by** *or* **with** *or* **at sth.** über etw. (*Akk.*) erfreut sein

**'gratifying** *adj.* erfreulich

**grating** /ˈgreɪtɪŋ/ *n.* Gitter, *das*

**gratitude** /ˈgrætɪtjuːd/ *n.* Dankbarkeit, *die* (**to** gegenüber)

**gratuitous** /grəˈtjuːɪtəs/ *adj.* (motiveless) grundlos

**gratuity** /grəˈtjuːɪtɪ/ *n.* Trinkgeld, *das*

**grave¹** /greɪv/ *n.* Grab, *das*

**grave²** *adj.* **(a)** (important, solemn) ernst
**(b)** (serious) schwer ⟨*Fehler, Irrtum*⟩; ernst ⟨*Situation, Lage*⟩; groß ⟨*Gefahr*⟩; schlimm ⟨*Nachricht*⟩

**'gravedigger** *n.* Totengräber, *der*

**gravel** /ˈgrævl/ *n.* Kies, *der*

**grave:** ∼**stone** *n.* Grabstein, *der;* ∼**yard** *n.* Friedhof, *der*

**gravity** /ˈgrævɪtɪ/ *n.* **(a)** (of mistake, offence) Schwere, *die;* (of situation) Ernst, *der*
**(b)** (Phys., Astron.) Gravitation, *die;* Schwerkraft, *die*

**gravy** /ˈgreɪvɪ/ *n.* **(a)** (juices) Bratensaft, *der*
**(b)** (dressing) [Braten]soße, *die*

**gravy:** ∼ **boat** *n.* Sauciere, *die;* Soßenschüssel, *die;* ∼ **train** *n.* **ride/board the** ∼ **train** (coll.) leichtes Geld machen (ugs.)

**gray** *etc.* (Amer.) ▶ GREY *etc.*

**graze¹** /greɪz/ *v.i.* grasen; weiden

**graze²** ⟦1⟧ *n.* Schürfwunde, *die*
⟦2⟧ *v.t.* **(a)** (touch lightly) streifen
**(b)** (scrape) abschürfen ⟨*Haut*⟩; zerkratzen ⟨*Oberfläche*⟩

**grease** /griːs/ ⟦1⟧ *n.* Fett, *das;* (lubricant) Schmierfett, *das*
⟦2⟧ *v.t.* einfetten; (lubricate) schmieren

**'greaseproof** *adj.* fettdicht; ∼ **paper** Pergament- *od.* Butterbrotpapier, *das*

**greasy** /ˈgriːsɪ/ *adj.* fettig; fett ⟨*Essen*⟩; (lubricated) geschmiert; (dirty with lubricant) schmierig

**great** /greɪt/ *adj.* **(a)** groß; **a** ∼ **many** sehr viele; sehr gut ⟨*Freund*⟩; (impressive; coll.: splendid) großartig; **be a** ∼ **one for sth.** etw. sehr gern tun
**(b)** (Groß)⟨*onkel, -tante, -neffe, -nichte*⟩; Ur⟨*großmutter, -großvater, -enkel, -enkelin*⟩

**great:** **G**∼ **'Bear** *n.* (Astron.) Großer Bär; **G**∼ **'Britain** *pr. n.* Großbritannien (*das*)

**'greatly** *adv.* sehr; höchst ⟨*verärgert*⟩; stark ⟨*beeinflusst*⟩; bedeutend ⟨*verbessert*⟩

**'greatness** *n.* Größe, *die*

**Great 'War** *n.* Erster Weltkrieg

**Greece** /griːs/ *pr. n.* Griechenland (*das*)

**greed** /griːd/ *n.* Gier, *die* (**for** nach); (gluttony) Gefräßigkeit, *die*

**'greedy** *adj.* gierig; (gluttonous) gefräßig

**Greek** /griːk/ ⟦1⟧ *adj.* griechisch; **sb. is** ∼: jmd. ist Grieche/Griechin
⟦2⟧ *n.* **(a)** (person) Grieche, *der*/Griechin, *die*
**(b)** (language) Griechisch, *das; see also* ENGLISH 2A

**green** /griːn/ ⟦1⟧ *adj.* **(a)** grün
**(b)** (environmentally safe) ökologisch ⋯⋯

**(c)** (gullible) naiv; (inexperienced) grün
**(d)** (Polit.) G~: grün; **the G~s** die Grünen
**2** *n.* **(a)** (colour) Grün, *das*
**(b)** (piece of land) Grünfläche, *die;* **village ~:**
Dorfanger, *der*
**(c)** *in pl.* (~ vegetables) Grüngemüse, *das*
**green: ~ belt** *n.* Grüngürtel, *der;*
~ **'card** *n.* (Motor Veh.) grüne Karte

**greenery** /'gri:nərɪ/ *n.* Grün, *das*

**green: ~fly** *n.* (Brit.) grüne Blattlaus;
~**gage** /'gri:ngeɪdʒ/ *n.* Reineclaude, *die;*
~**grocer** *n.* (Brit.) Obst- und
Gemüsehändler, *der/*-händlerin, *die*

**'greenhouse** *n.* Gewächshaus, *das*

**greenhouse: ~ effect** *n.*
Treibhauseffekt, *der;* ~ **gas** *n.*
Treibhausgas, *das*

**green: ~ light** *n.* **(a)** grünes Licht; (as
signal) Grün, *das;* **(b)** (fig.) **give sb./get the ~:**
jmdm. grünes Licht geben/grünes Licht
erhalten; **G~ Party** *n.* (Polit.) die Grünen
*Pl.*

**greet** /gri:t/ *v.t.* begrüßen; (in passing)
grüßen; (receive) empfangen

**'greeting** *n.* Begrüßung, *die;* (in passing)
Gruß, *der;* (words) Grußformel, *die*

**'greetings card** *n.* Grußkarte, *die;* (for
birthday) Glückwunschkarte, *die*

**gregarious** /grɪ'geərɪəs/ *adj.* gesellig

**grenade** /grɪ'neɪd/ *n.* Granate, *die*

**grew** ▶ GROW

**grey** /greɪ/ **1** *adj.* grau
**2** *n.* Grau, *das*

**grey: ~-haired** *adj.* grauhaarig;
~**hound** *n.* Windhund, *der;* ~**hound
racing** *n.* Windhundrennen, *das*

**greyish** /'greɪɪʃ/ *adj.* gräulich

**grid** /grɪd/ *n.* **(a)** (grating) Rost, *der*
**(b)** (of lines) Gitter[netz], *das*
**(c)** (for supply) Versorgungsnetz, *das*

**grid: ~lock** *n.* Verkehrsinfarkt, *der;* (fig.)
völliger Stillstand; ~**locked** /'grɪdlɒkt/
*adj.* total verstopft ⟨*Straße, Stadt*⟩; (fig.)
festgefahren

**grief** /gri:f/ *n.* Kummer, *der* (over, at über
+ *Akk.,* um); (at loss of sb.) Trauer, *die* (for
um); **come to ~** (fail) scheitern

**'grief-stricken** *adj.* untröstlich (at über
+ *Akk.*)

**grievance** /'gri:vəns/ *n.* (complaint)
Beschwerde, *die;* (grudge) Groll, *der*

**grieve** /gri:v/ **1** *v.t.* betrüben; bekümmern
**2** *v.i.* trauern (for um)

**grievous** /'gri:vəs/ *adj.* schwer
⟨*Verwundung, Krankheit;*⟩ ~ **bodily harm**
(Law) schwere Körperverletzung

**grill**[1] /grɪl/ **1** *v.t.* **(a)** (cook) grillen; (fig.: question)
in die Mangel nehmen (ugs.)
**2** *n.* **(a)** **mixed ~:** gemischte Grillplatte
**(b)** (on cooker) Grill, *der*

**grille (grill**[2]**)** *n.* **(a)** Gitter, *das*
**(b)** (Motor Veh.) [Kühler]grill, *der*

**grim** /grɪm/ *adj.* (stern) streng; grimmig
⟨*Lächeln, Schweigen*⟩; (unrelenting) erbittert
⟨*Widerstand, Kampf*⟩; (ghastly) grauenvoll
⟨*Aufgabe, Nachricht*⟩; trostlos ⟨*Aussichten*⟩

**grimace** /grɪ'meɪs/ **1** *n.* Grimasse, *die.*
**2** *v.i.* Grimassen schneiden; ~ **with pain** vor
Schmerz das Gesicht verziehen

**grime** /graɪm/ *n.* Schmutz, *der*

**grimy** /'graɪmɪ/ *adj.* schmutzig

**grin** /grɪn/ **1** *n.* Grinsen, *das*
**2** *v.i.,* **-nn-** grinsen; ~ **at sb.** jmdn.
angrinsen

**grind** /graɪnd/ **1** *v.t.,* **ground** /graʊnd/ **(a)**
~ **[up]** zermahlen; mahlen ⟨*Kaffee, Pfeffer,
Getreide*⟩
**(b)** (sharpen) schleifen ⟨*Schere, Messer*⟩;
schärfen ⟨*Klinge*⟩
**(c)** (rub harshly) zerquetschen; ~ **one's teeth**
mit den Zähnen knirschen
**2** *v.i.,* **ground:** ~ **to a halt** ⟨*Fahrzeug:*⟩
quietschend zum Stehen kommen; (fig.)
⟨*Verkehr:*⟩ zum Erliegen kommen
**3** *n.* (coll.) Plackerei, *die* (ugs.)

**'grinder** *n.* Schleifmaschine, *die;* (coffee
~ etc.) Mühle, *die*

**'grindstone** *n.* Schleifstein, *der*

**grip** /grɪp/ **1** *n.* **(a)** (firm hold) Halt, *der;* (fig.:
power) Umklammerung, *die;* **have a ~ on sth.**
etw. festhalten; (fig.) etwas im Griff haben;
**loosen one's ~:** loslassen; **lose one's ~** (fig.)
nachlassen
**(b)** (strength or way of ~ping) Griff, *der*
**2** *v.t.,* **-pp-** [fest] halten; ⟨*Reifen:*⟩ greifen;
(fig.) fesseln ⟨*Publikum, Aufmerksamkeit*⟩
**3** *v.i.,* **-pp-** ⟨*Räder, Bremsen usw.:*⟩ greifen

**gripe** /graɪp/ *v.i.* (coll.) meckern (ugs.) (**about**
über + *Akk.*)

**gripping** /'grɪpɪŋ/ *adj.* (fig.) packend

**grisly** /'grɪzlɪ/ *adj.* grausig

**gristle** /'grɪsl/ *n.* Knorpel, *der*

**grit** /grɪt/ **1** *n.* **(a)** Sand, *der*
**(b)** (coll.: courage) Schneid, *der* (ugs.)
**2** *v.t.,* **-tt-: (a)** streuen ⟨*Straßen*⟩
**(b)** ~ **one's teeth** die Zähne
zusammenbeißen (ugs.)

**grizzly** /'grɪzlɪ/ *n.* ~ [**bear**] Grislybär, *der*

**groan** /grəʊn/ **1** *n.* Stöhnen, *das;* (of thing)
Ächzen, *das*
**2** *v.i.* [auf]stöhnen (at bei); ⟨*Tisch, Planken:*⟩
ächzen
**3** *v.t.* stöhnen

**grocer** /'grəʊsə(r)/ *n.* Lebensmittelhändler,
*der/*-händlerin, *die*

**grocery** /'grəʊsərɪ/ *n.* **(a)** *in pl.* (goods)
Lebensmittel *Pl.*
**(b)** ~ [**store**] Lebensmittelgeschäft, *das*

**groggy** /'grɒgɪ/ *adj.* groggy präd. (ugs.)

**groin** /grɔɪn/ *n.* Leistengegend, *die*

**groom** /gru:m, grʊm/ **1** *n.* **(a)** (stable boy)
Stallbursche, *der*
**(b)** (bride~) Bräutigam, *der*
**2** *v.t.* striegeln ⟨*Pferd*⟩; (fig.) vorbereiten (**for**
auf + *Akk.*)

**groove** /gruːv/ n. Rille, die

**grope** /grəʊp/ v.i. tasten **(for** nach)

**gross¹** /grəʊs/ adj. **(a)** (flagrant) grob ⟨Fahrlässigkeit, Fehler⟩
**(b)** (obese) fett
**(c)** (total) Brutto-

**gross²** n., pl. same Gros, das

**'grossly** adj. (flagrantly) äußerst; grob ⟨übertreiben⟩

**grotesque** /grəʊ'tesk/ adj. grotesk

**grotto** /'grɒtəʊ/ n., pl. ~es or ~s Grotte, die

**grotty** /'grɒtɪ/ adj. (Brit. coll.) mies (ugs.)

**ground¹** /graʊnd/ [1] n. **(a)** Boden, der; **get off the** ~ (coll.) konkrete Gestalt annehmen
**(b)** [**sports**] ~: Sportplatz, der
**(c)** in pl. (attached to house) Anlage, die
**(d)** (reason) Grund, der; **on the** ~[**s**] **of** auf Grund (+ Gen.); **on the** ~[**s**] **that** ...: unter Berufung auf die Tatsache, dass ...
**(e)** in pl. (sediment) Satz, der
[2] v.t. (Aeronaut.) am Boden festhalten

**ground²** [1] ▸ GRIND 1, 2
[2] adj. gemahlen ⟨Kaffee, Getreide⟩

**ground:** ~ **control** n. (Aeronaut.: personnel, equipment, etc.;) Flugsicherungskontrolldienst, der; ~ **'floor** ▸ FLOOR 1B; ~ **forces** n. pl. Bodentruppen Pl.; ~ **frost** n. Bodenfrost, der

**'grounding** n. Grundkenntnisse Pl.

**'groundless** adj. unbegründet

**ground:** ~**sheet** n. Bodenplane, die; ~**sman** /'graʊndzmən/ n., pl. -smen /'graʊndzmən/ (Sport) Platzwart, der; ~**work** n. Vorarbeiten Pl.

**group** /gruːp/ [1] n. Gruppe, die
[2] v.t. gruppieren

**group:** ~ **practice** n. Gemeinschaftspraxis, die; ~ **therapy** n. Gruppentherapie, die

**grouse¹** /graʊs/ n., pl. same Raufußhuhn, das; [**red**] ~ (Brit.) Schottisches Moorschneehuhn

**grouse²** v.i. (coll.) meckern (ugs.)

**grove** /grəʊv/ n. Wäldchen, das

**grovel** /'grɒvl/ v.i., (Brit.) **-ll-** (fig.) katzbuckeln

**grow** /grəʊ/ [1] v.i., grew /gruː/, grown /grəʊn/ **(a)** wachsen; ~ **out of** or **from sth.** sich aus etw. entwickeln; (from sth. abstract) von etw. herrühren; ~ **in** gewinnen an (+ Dat.) ⟨Größe, Bedeutung⟩
**(b)** (become) werden; ~ **apart** (fig.) sich auseinander leben; ~ **to love/hate sb./sth.** jmdn./etw. lieben lernen/hassen lernen; ~ **to like sb./sth.** nach und nach Gefallen an jmdn./etw. finden
[2] v.t., grew, grown ziehen; (on a large scale) anpflanzen; züchten ⟨Blumen⟩

■ **grow 'up** v.i. **(a)** aufwachsen; (become adult) erwachsen werden
**(b)** ⟨Legende:⟩ entstehen

**growl** /graʊl/ [1] n. Knurren, das; (of bear) Brummen, das
[2] v.i. knurren; ⟨Bär:⟩ [böse] brummen

**grown** /grəʊn/ [1] ▸ GROW
[2] adj. erwachsen

**'grown-up** [1] n. Erwachsene, der/die
[2] adj. erwachsen

**growth** /grəʊθ/ n. **(a)** Wachstum, das (of, in Gen.); (increase) Zunahme, die (of, in Gen.)
**(b)** (Med.) Gewächs, das

**growth:** ~ **area** n. Wachstumsbereich, der; ~ **industry** n. Wachstumsindustrie, die; ~ **rate** n. Wachstumsrate, die

**grub** /grʌb/ n. **(a)** Larve, die; (maggot) Made, die
**(b)** (coll.: food) Fressen, das (salopp)

**grubby** /'grʌbɪ/ adj. schmudd[e]lig (ugs.)

**grudge** /grʌdʒ/ [1] v.t. ~ **sb. sth.** jmdm. etw. missgönnen; ~ **doing sth.** etw. ungern tun
[2] n. Groll, der; **bear sb. a.** ~ or **a** ~ **against sb.** jmdm. gegenüber nachtragend sein

**grudging** /'grʌdʒɪŋ/ adj. widerwillig; widerwillig gewährt ⟨Zuschuss⟩

**'grudgingly** adv. widerwillig

**gruelling** (Amer.: **grueling**) /'gruːəlɪŋ/ adj. aufreibend; strapaziös ⟨Reise⟩

**gruesome** /'gruːsəm/ adj. grausig

**gruff** /grʌf/ adj. barsch; rau ⟨Stimme⟩

**grumble** /'grʌmbl/ v.i. murren; ~ **about** or **over sth.** sich über etw. (Akk.) beklagen

**grumpily** /'grʌmpɪlɪ/ adv. unleidlich

**grumpy** /'grʌmpɪ/ adj. unleidlich

**grunge** /grʌndʒ/ n. Grunge, der

**grunt** /grʌnt/ [1] n. Grunzen, das
[2] v.i. grunzen

**guarantee** /gærən'tiː/ [1] v.t. **(a)** garantieren für; [eine] Garantie geben auf (+ Akk.); **the clock is** ~**d for a year** die Uhr hat ein Jahr Garantie
**(b)** (promise) garantieren (ugs.); (ensure) bürgen für ⟨Qualität⟩
[2] n. **(a)** (Commerc. etc.) Garantie, die; (document) Garantieschein, der
**(b)** (promise) Garantie, die (ugs.); **give sb. a** ~ **that** ...: jmdm. garantieren, dass ...

**guarantor** /'gærəntə(r), gærən'tɔː(r)/ n. Bürge, der/Bürgin, die

**guaranty** /'gærəntɪ/ n. (basis of security) Garantie, die; Gewähr, die

**guard** /gɑːd/ [1] n. **(a)** (guardsman) Wachtposten, der; (group of soldiers) Wache, die; **be on** ~: Wache haben; **be on [one's]** ~ (lit. or fig.) sich hüten
**(b)** (Brit. Railw.) [Zug]schaffner, der/-schaffnerin, die
**(c)** (Amer.: prison warder) [Gefängnis]wärter, der/-wärterin, die
**(d)** (safety device) Schutz, der
[2] v.t. bewachen; hüten ⟨Geheimnis⟩; schützen ⟨Leben⟩; beschützen ⟨Prominenten⟩ ⋯❖

■ **'guard against** v.t. sich hüten vor (+ Dat.); vorbeugen (+ Dat.) ⟨Krankheit, Irrtum⟩

**guard:** ~ **dog** n. Wachhund, der; ~ **duty** n. Wachdienst, der

**'guarded** adj. zurückhaltend

**guardian** /'gɑːdɪən/ n. (a) Hüter, der; Wächter, der

(b) (Law) Vormund, der

**guardian 'angel** n. Schutzengel, der

**guerrilla** /gə'rɪlə/ n. Guerillakämpfer, der/ -kämpferin, die; attrib. Guerilla-

**guess** /ges/ [1] v.t. (a) (estimate) schätzen; (surmise) raten; (surmise correctly) erraten; raten ⟨Rätsel⟩; ~ **what!** (coll.) stell dir vor!

(b) (esp. Amer.: suppose) **I** ~: ich glaube

[2] v.i. (estimate) schätzen; (make assumption) vermuten; (surmise correctly) es erraten; ~ **at** sth. etw. schätzen; **keep sb.** ~**ing** (coll.) jmdn. im Unklaren lassen

[3] n. Schätzung, die; **make** or **have a** ~: schätzen

**'guesswork** n. be ~: eine Vermutung sein

**guesstimate** /'gestɪmət/ n. (coll.) grobe Schätzung

**guest** /gest/ n. Gast, der

**guest:** ~ **house** n. Pension, die; ~ **list** n. Gästeliste, die; ~ **room** n. Gästezimmer, das; ~ **worker** n. Gastarbeiter, der/ -arbeiterin, die

**guffaw** /gʌ'fɔː/ [1] n. brüllendes Gelächter [2] v.i. brüllend lachen

**guidance** /'gaɪdəns/ n. (a) (leadership) Führung, die; (by teacher etc.) [An]leitung, die

(b) (advice) Rat, der

**guide** /gaɪd/ [1] n. (a) Führer, der/Führerin, die; (Tourism) [Fremden]führer, der/-führerin, die

(b) (indicator) be a [good] ~ **to** sth. ein [guter] Anhaltspunkt für etw. sein; **be no** ~ **to** sth. keine Rückschlüsse auf etw. (Akk.) zulassen

(c) (Brit.) [Girl] **G**~: Pfadfinderin, die

(d) (handbook) Handbuch, das

(e) (for tourists) [Reise]führer, der

[2] v.t. führen; (fig.) bestimmen ⟨Handeln, Urteil⟩; **be** ~**d by** sth./sb. sich von etw./ jmdm. leiten lassen

**'guidebook** n. [Reise]führer, der

**guided 'missile** n. Lenkflugkörper, der

**'guide dog** n. Blinden[führ]hund, der

**guided 'tour** n. Führung, die (**of** durch)

**'guideline** n. Richtlinie, die

**guild** /gɪld/ n. (a) Verein, der

(b) (Hist.) Gilde, die; Zunft, die

**guile** /gaɪl/ n. Hinterlist, die

**guillotine** /'gɪləti:n/ n. Guillotine, die

**guilt** /gɪlt/ n. (a) Schuld, die (**of, for** an + Dat.)

(b) (guilty feeling) Schuldgefühle Pl.

**'guiltless** adj. unschuldig (**of** an + Dat.)

**'guilty** adj. (a) schuldig; **be** ~ **of murder** des Mordes schuldig sein; **find sb.** ~/**not** ~ [**of**

sth.] jmdn. [an etw. (Dat.)] schuldig sprechen/[von etw.] freisprechen; **feel** ~ ein schlechtes Gewissen haben

(b) schuldbewusst ⟨Miene, Blick, Verhalten⟩; schlecht ⟨Gewissen⟩

**guinea:** ~**fowl,** ~ **hen** ns. Perlhuhn, das; ~ **pig** n. (a) (animal) Meerschweinchen, das; (b) (fig.: subject of experiment) (person) Versuchsperson, die; Versuchskaninchen, das (ugs. abwertend); (thing) Versuchsobjekt, das; **act as** ~ **pig** Versuchskaninchen spielen

**guise** /gaɪz/ n. Gestalt, die; **in the** ~ **of** in Gestalt (+ Gen.)

**guitar** /gɪ'tɑː(r)/ n. Gitarre, die

**guitarist** /gɪ'tɑːrɪst/ n. Gitarrist, der/ Gitarristin, die

**gulf** /gʌlf/ n. (a) (Geog.) Golf, der

(b) (wide gap) Kluft, die

**gull** /gʌl/ n. Möwe, die

**gullet** /'gʌlɪt/ n. (a) Speiseröhre, die

(b) (throat) Kehle, die

**gullible** /'gʌlɪbl/ adj. leichtgläubig

**gully** /'gʌlɪ/ n. (artificial channel) Abzugsrinne, die; (drain) Gully, der

**gulp** /gʌlp/ [1] v.t. hinunterschlingen; hinuntergießen ⟨Getränk⟩

[2] n. (a) Schlucken, das

(b) (large mouthful of drink) kräftiger Schluck

■ **gulp 'down** v.t. hinunterschlingen; hinuntergießen ⟨Getränk⟩

**gum**[1] /gʌm/ n. (Anat.) ~[**s**] Zahnfleisch, das

**gum**[2] [1] n. (a) Gummi, das; (glue) Klebstoff, der

(b) (Amer.) ▶ CHEWING GUM

[2] v.t., -mm-: (a) (smear with ~) mit Klebstoff bestreichen; gummieren ⟨Briefmarken, Etiketten usw.⟩

(b) (fasten with ~) kleben

**'gumboot** n. Gummistiefel, der

**gumption** /'gʌmpʃn/ n. (coll.) Grips, der

**gun** /gʌn/ n. Schusswaffe, die; (rifle) Gewehr, das; (pistol) Pistole, die; (revolver) Revolver, der

■ **gun 'down** v.t. niederschießen

**gun:** ~**fight** n. (Amer. coll.) Schießerei, die; ~**fire** n. Geschützfeuer, das; ~ **laws** pl. Waffengesetze Pl.; ~**man** /'gʌnmən/ n., pl. ~**men** /'gʌnmən/ bewaffneter Mann; ~**powder** n. Schießpulver, das; ~**shot** n. Schuss, der; ~**shot wound** Schusswunde, die; ~**smith** n. Büchsenmacher, der

**gurgle** /'gɜːgl/ [1] n. Gluckern, das; (of brook) Plätschern, das

[2] v.i. gluckern; ⟨Bach:⟩ plätschern; ⟨Baby:⟩ lallen; (with delight) glucksen

**guru** /'goru:/ n. Guru, der

**gush** /gʌʃ/ [1] n. Schwall, der

[2] v.i. (a) strömen; ~ **out** herausströmen

(b) (fig.: enthuse) schwärmen

**'gushing** adj. (a) reißend ⟨Strom⟩

(b) (effusive) exaltiert

**gust** /gʌst/ n. ~ [**of wind**] Bö[e], die

**gusto** /'gʌstəʊ/ n. Genuss, der; (vitality) Schwung, der

**'gusty** *adj.* böig

**gut** /gʌt/ ① *n.* **(a)** (material) Darm, *der* **(b)** *in pl.* (bowels) Eingeweide *Pl.;* Gedärme *Pl.* **(c)** *in pl.* (coll.: courage) Schneid, *der* (ugs.) ② *v.t.,* -tt-: **(a)** (remove ∼s of) ausnehmen **(b)** (remove fittings from) ausräumen; **the house was ∼ted [by fire]** das Haus brannte aus ③ *attrib. adj.* ∼ **feeling** instinktives Gefühl; **have a ∼ feeling that ...** es im Gefühl *od.* (salopp) Urin haben, dass ...

**gutter** /'gʌtə(r)/ *n.* (below edge of roof) Dachrinne, *die;* (at side of street) Rinnstein, *der;* Gosse, *die*

**'guttering** *n.* (on roof) Dachrinnen *Pl.*

**gutter 'press** *n.* Sensationspresse, *die*

**guttural** /'gʌtərl/ *adj.* guttural; kehlig

**guy** /gaɪ/ *n.* **(a)** (coll.: man) Typ, *der* (ugs.) **(b)** *in pl.* (Amer.: everyone) **[listen,] you ∼s!** [hört mal,] Kinder! (ugs.)

**'guy rope** *n.* Zelt[spann]leine, *die*

**guzzle** /'gʌzl/ ① *v.t.* (eat) hinunterschlingen; (drink) hinuntergießen

② *v.i.* schlingen

**gym** /dʒɪm/ *n.* (coll.) **(a)** (gymnasium) Turnhalle, *die* **(b)** (gymnastics) Turnen, *das*

**gymnasium** *n.* /dʒɪm'neɪzɪəm/ *n., pl.* ∼s *or* **gymnasia** /dʒɪm'neɪzɪə/ Turnhalle, *die*

**gymnast** /'dʒɪmnæst/ *n.* Turner, *der/* Turnerin, *die*

**gymnastic** /dʒɪm'næstɪk/ *adj.* turnerisch ⟨Können⟩; ∼ **equipment** Turngeräte *Pl.*

**gymnastics** /dʒɪm'næstɪks/ *n.* Gymnastik, *die;* (esp. with apparatus) Turnen, *das*

**'gymslip** *n.* Trägerrock, *der*

**gynaecologist** /gaɪnɪ'kɒlədʒɪst/ *n.* Frauenarzt, *der/-*ärztin, *die*

**gynaecology** /gaɪnɪ'kɒlədʒɪ/ *n.* Gynäkologie, *die*

**gypsy, Gypsy** /'dʒɪpsɪ/ *n.* Zigeuner, *der/* Zigeunerin, *die*

**gyrate** /dʒaɪə'reɪt/ *v.i.* sich drehen

# Hh

**H¹, h** /eɪtʃ/ *n.* H, h, *das*

**haberdashery** /'hæbədæʃərɪ/ *n.* (goods) Kurzwaren *Pl.;* (Amer.: menswear) Herrenmoden *Pl.*

**habit** /'hæbɪt/ *n.* **(a)** Gewohnheit, *die;* **good/ bad ∼:** gute/schlechte [An]gewohnheit; **get** *or* **fall into a** *or* **the ∼ of doing sth.** [es] sich (*Dat.*) angewöhnen, etw. zu tun **(b)** (coll.: addiction) Süchtigkeit, *die*

**habitable** /'hæbɪtəbl/ *adj.* bewohnbar

**habitat** /'hæbɪtæt/ *n.* Habitat, *das*

**habitation** /hæbɪ'teɪʃn/ *n.* **fit/unfit for human ∼:** bewohnbar/unbewohnbar

**habitual** /hə'bɪtjʊəl/ *adj.* **(a)** gewohnt **(b)** (given to habit) gewohnheitsmäßig; Gewohnheits⟨trinker⟩

**ha'bitually** *adv.* (regularly) regelmäßig

**hack¹** /hæk/ *v.t.* **(a)** hacken ⟨Holz⟩; ∼ **sth. to bits** *or* **pieces** etw. in Stücke hacken **(b)** (Comp.) eindringen in (+ *Akk.*) ⟨Computersystem⟩; ∼ **into sth.** in etw. (*Akk.*) eindringen ■ **hack 'off** *v.t.* abhacken ■ **hack 'out** *v.t.* heraushauen **(from** aus) **hack²** *n.* (derog.: writer) Schreiberling, *der*

**hacker** /'hækə(r)/ *n.* (Comp.) Hacker, *der*

**hackneyed** /'hæknɪd/ *adj.* abgegriffen; abgedroschen (ugs.)

**'hacksaw** *n.* [Metall]bügelsäge, *die*

**had** ▶ HAVE

**haddock** /'hædək/ *n., pl. same* Schellfisch, *der*

**hadn't** /'hædnt/ (coll.) = **had not;** ▶ HAVE

**haemoglobin** /hiːmə'gləʊbɪn/ *n.* Hämoglobin, *das*

**haemophilia** /hiːmə'fɪlɪə/ *n.* Hämophilie, *die* (fachspr.); Bluterkrankheit, *die*

**haemophiliac** /hiːmə'fɪlɪæk/ *n.* Bluter, *der/*Bluterin, *die*

**haemorrhage** /'hemərɪdʒ/ *n.* Blutung, *die*

**haemorrhoid** /'hemərɔɪd/ *n.* Hämorrhoide, *die*

**hag** /hæg/ *n.* [alte] Hexe

**haggard** /'hægəd/ *adj.* ausgezehrt; (with worry) abgehärmt

**haggle** /'hægl/ *v.i.* sich zanken (**over, about** wegen); (over price) feilschen (**over, about** um)

**Hague** /heɪg/ *pr. n.* **The ∼:** Den Haag (*das*)

**hail¹** /heɪl/ ① *n.* Hagel, *der* ② *v.i.* **it ∼s** *or* **is ∼ing** es hagelt; ∼ **down** (fig.) niederprasseln (**on** auf + *Akk.*)

**hail²** *v.t.* **(a)** (call out to) anrufen; (signal to) anhalten ⟨Taxi⟩ **(b)** (acclaim) zujubeln (+ *Dat.*); bejubeln (**as** als)

**'hailstone** *n.* Hagelkorn, *das*

**hair** /heə(r)/ *n.* **(a)** (one strand) Haar, *das* ····⟡

**(b)** *collect.* Haar, *das;* Haare *Pl.; attrib.* Haar-; have *or* get one's ∼ done sich *(Dat.)* Haar *od.* die Haare machen lassen (ugs.)

**hair:** ∼**brush** n. Haarbürste, *die;*
∼ **conditioner** n. Pflegespülung, *die;*
∼ **cream** n. Haarcreme, *die;* Pomade, *die;*
∼ **curler** n. Lockenwickler, *der;* ∼**cut** n.
**(a)** (act) Haareschneiden, *das;* go for/need a ∼cut zum Friseur gehen/müssen; get/have a ∼cut sich *(Dat.)* die Haare schneiden lassen;
**(b)** (style) Haarschnitt, *der;* ∼**do** n. (style) Frisur, *die;* ∼**dresser** n. Friseur, *der/* Friseurin, *die;* go to the ∼dresser's zum Friseur gehen; ∼ **dye** n. Haarfärbemittel, *das;* ∼**grip** n. (Brit.) Haarklammer, *die;*
∼**line** n. **(a)** (edge of hair) Haaransatz, *der;* his ∼line is receding, he has a receding ∼line er bekommt eine Stirnglatze; **(b)** (crack) Haarriss; ∼**line fracture** (Med.) Fissur, *die;* ∼**pin** n. Haarnadel, *die;* ∼**pin 'bend** n. Haarnadelkurve, *die;* ∼**raising** /'heəreɪzɪŋ/ *adj.* haarsträubend; ∼**spray** n. Haarspray, *das;* ∼**style** n. Frisur, *die*

**'hairy** *adj.* **(a)** behaart; flauschig ⟨*Pullover, Teppich*⟩
**(b)** (coll.: difficult) haarig

**hale** /heɪl/ *adj.* ∼ and hearty gesund und munter

**half** /hɑːf/ **1** *n., pl.* **halves** /hɑːvz/ **(a)** Hälfte, *die;* ∼ [of sth.] die Hälfte [von etw.]; ∼ of Europe halb Europa; one and a ∼ hours, one hour and a ∼: anderthalb *od.* eineinhalb Stunden; divide sth. in ∼ *or* into halves etw. halbieren; she is three and a ∼: sie ist dreieinhalb
**(b)** (Footb. etc.: period) Halbzeit, *die*
**2** *adj.* halb; ∼ the house/books/time die Hälfte des Hauses/der Bücher/der Zeit; ∼ an hour eine halbe Stunde
**3** *adv.* **(a)** zur Hälfte; halb ⟨*schließen, aufessen, fertig, voll, geöffnet*⟩; (almost) fast ⟨*ersticken, tot sein*⟩; ∼ as much/many halb so viel/viele; only ∼ hear what ...: nur zum Teil hören, was ...
**(b)** ∼ past *or* (coll.) ∼ one/two/three *etc.* halb zwei/drei/vier *usw.;* ∼ past twelve halb eins

**half:** ∼'**board** n. Halbpension, *die;*
∼**caste** n. Mischling, *der;* ∼'**hearted** *adj.* halbherzig; ∼'**hour** n. halbe Stunde;
∼ '**mast** n. be [flown] at ∼ mast auf Halbmast stehen; ∼ '**moon** n. Halbmond, *der;* ∼ **note** n. (Amer. Mus.) halbe Note;
∼'**price** **1** n. halber Preis; **2** *adj.* zum halben Preis *nachgestellt;* **3** *adv.* zum halben Preis; ∼'**term** n. (Brit.) (holiday) ∼term [holiday/break] Ferien in der Mitte des Trimesters; ∼'**time** n. (Sport) Halbzeit, *die;* ∼'**way** **1** *adj.* ∼way point Mitte, *die;* **2** *adv.* die Hälfte des Weges ⟨*begleiten, fahren*⟩; ∼**wit** n. Schwachkopf, *der;* (scatterbrain) Schussel, *der*

**halibut** /'hælɪbət/ *n., pl. same* Heilbutt, *der*

**hall** /hɔːl/ n. **(a)** Saal, *der;* (building) Halle, *die;* school/church ∼: Aula, *die*/Gemeindehaus, *das*

**(b)** (entrance ∼) Flur, *der*
**(c)** (Univ.) ∼ [of residence] Studentenwohnheim, *das*

**'hallmark** n. [Feingehalts]stempel, *der;* (fig.) Kennzeichen, *das*

**hallo** /hə'ləʊ/ *int.* **(a)** (to call attention) hallo
**(b)** (Brit.) ▶ HELLO

**Hallowe'en** /hæləʊ'iːn/ n. Halloween, *das; Abend vor Allerheiligen*

**hallucination** /həluːsɪ'neɪʃn/ n. Halluzination, *die*

**hallucinogen** /hə'luːsɪnədʒen/ n. (Med.) Halluzinogen, *das*

**hallucinogenic** /həluːsɪnə'dʒenɪk/ *adj.* (Med.) halluzinogen

**'hallway** n. Flur, *der*

**halo** /'heɪləʊ/ *n., pl.* ∼es Heiligenschein, *der*

**halt** /hɒlt, hɔːlt/ **1** n. **(a)** Pause, *die;* (interruption) Unterbrechung, *die;* call a ∼ to sth. mit etw. Schluss machen
**(b)** (Brit. Railw.) Haltepunkt, *der*
**2** *v.i.* **(a)** stehen bleiben; ⟨Fahrer:⟩ anhalten; (for a rest) eine Pause machen; (esp. Mil.) Halt machen; ∼, who goes there? (Mil.) halt, wer da?
**(b)** (end) eingestellt werden
**3** *v.t.* anhalten; einstellen ⟨Projekt⟩

**'halting** *adj.* schleppend; zögernd ⟨Antwort⟩

**halve** /hɑːv/ *v.t.* halbieren

**halves** *pl. of* HALF

**ham** /hæm/ n. Schinken, *der*

**hamburger** /'hæmbɜːgə(r)/ n. Hacksteak, *das;* (in roll) Hamburger, *der*

**hamlet** /'hæmlɪt/ n. Weiler, *der*

**hammer** /'hæmə(r)/ **1** n. Hammer, *der*
**2** *v.t.* hämmern
**3** *v.i.* hämmern (at an + *Dat.*)
■ **hammer 'out** *v.t.* ausklopfen ⟨Delle, Beule⟩; (fig.: devise) ausarbeiten

**hammock** /'hæmək/ n. Hängematte, *die*

**hamper¹** /'hæmpə(r)/ n. [Deckel]korb, *der*

**hamper²** *v.t.* behindern

**hamster** /'hæmstə(r)/ n. Hamster, *der*

**'hamstring** **1** n. (Anat.) Kniesehne, *die*
**2** *vt.* (fig.) lähmen

**hand** /hænd/ **1** n. **(a)** Hand, *die;* by ∼ (manually) mit der *od.* von Hand; give *or* lend [sb.] a ∼ [with *or* in sth.] [jmdm.] [bei etw.] helfen
**(b)** (share) have a ∼ in sth. bei etw. seine Hände im Spiel haben
**(c)** (worker) Arbeiter, *der;* (Naut.: seaman) Matrose, *der*
**(d)** (of clock or watch) Zeiger, *der*
**(e)** at ∼: in der Nähe; on the one ∼ ..., [but] on the other [∼] ...: einerseits ..., andererseits ...
**(f)** (Cards) Karte, *die*
**2** *v.t.* geben; ⟨Überbringer:⟩ übergeben ⟨Sendung, Lieferung⟩
■ **hand 'in** *v.t.* abgeben (to, at bei); einreichen ⟨Petition⟩
■ **hand 'out** *v.t.* austeilen

■ **hand 'over** v.t. übergeben (**to** Dat.)

**hand:** ~**bag** n. Handtasche, die; ~ **baggage** n. Handgepäck, das; ~**book** n. Handbuch, das; ~**brake** n. Handbremse, die; ~**cuff** ⟨1⟩ n., usu. in pl. Handschelle, die; ⟨2⟩ v.t. ~cuff sb. jmdm. Handschellen anlegen

**handful** /'hændfʊl/ n. Handvoll, die; **be a** ~: (fig. coll.) einen ständig auf Trab halten (ugs.)

**hand:** ~ **grenade** n. Handgranate, die; ~**gun** n. Faustfeuerwaffe, die; ~**-held** adj. ~-held camera Handkamera, die

**handicap** /'hændɪkæp/ ⟨1⟩ n. (a) (Sport, also fig.) Handikap, das (b) (physical) Behinderung, die ⟨2⟩ v.t., -pp- benachteiligen

**handicapped** /'hændɪkæpt/ adj. [**mentally/physically**] ~: [geistig/körperlich] behindert

**handicraft** /'hændɪkrɑːft/ n. [Kunst]handwerk, das; (needlework, knitting, etc.) Handarbeit, die

**handiwork** /'hændɪwɜːk/ n. handwerkliche Arbeit; **it's all his own** ~: das hat er selbst gemacht

**handkerchief** /'hæŋkətʃɪf/ n., pl. ~s or **handkerchieves** /'hæŋkətʃiːvz/ Taschentuch, das

**handle** /'hændl/ ⟨1⟩ n. Griff, der; (of door) Klinke, die; (of axe, brush, comb, broom, saucepan) Stiel, der; (of cup, jug) Henkel, der ⟨2⟩ v.t. (a) (touch, feel) anfassen (b) (control) handhaben ⟨Fahrzeug, Flugzeug⟩ (c) (deal/cope with) umgehen/fertig werden mit

**'handlebars** n. pl. Lenkstange, die

**'handling charge** /'hændlɪŋ/ n. (Commerc.) Bearbeitungsgebühr, die

**hand:** ~ **lotion** n. Handlotion, die; ~ **luggage** n. Handgepäck, das; ~**made** adj. handgearbeitet; ~**over** n. Übergabe, die; ~**painted** adj. handbemalt; ~**picked** adj. sorgfältig ausgewählt; ~**shake** n. Händedruck, der

**handsome** /'hænsəm/ adj. gut aussehend

**hand:** ~**s-'on** adj. praktisch; ~**stand** n. Handstand, der; ~ **towel** n. [Hände]handtuch, das; ~**writing** n. [Hand]schrift, die; ~**written** adj. handgeschrieben; handschriftlich

**handy** /'hændɪ/ adj. greifbar; **keep/have** sth. ~: etw. greifbar haben

**'handyman** n. Handwerker, der; [**home**] ~: Heimwerker, der

**hang** /hæŋ/ ⟨1⟩ v.t. (a) p.t., p.p. hung /hʌŋ/ hängen; aufhängen ⟨Bild, Gardinen⟩; ankleben ⟨Tapete⟩ (b) p.t., p.p. **hanged** (execute) hängen (**for** wegen); ~ **oneself** sich erhängen ⟨2⟩ v.i., hung (a) hängen; ⟨Kleid usw.:⟩ fallen (b) (be executed) hängen ⟨3⟩ n. **get the** ~ **of** sth. (coll.) mit etw. klarkommen (ugs.)

■ **hang a'bout, hang a'round** v.i. (a) (loiter) herumlungern (salopp) (b) (coll.: wait) warten

■ **hang 'on** v.i. (a) sich festhalten (**to** an + Dat.) (b) (coll.: wait) warten (c) ~ **on to** (coll.: keep) behalten

■ **hang 'out** ⟨1⟩ v.t. aufhängen ⟨Wäsche⟩ ⟨2⟩ v.i. (a) heraushängen (b) (coll.) (live) wohnen; (be often present) sich herumtreiben (ugs.)

■ **hang 'up** v.t. ⟨1⟩ aufhängen ⟨2⟩ v.i. (Teleph.) auflegen

**hangar** /'hæŋə(r)/ n. Hangar, der

**'hanger** n. Bügel, der

**hang:** ~**glider** n. Hängegleiter, der; Drachen, der; ~**glider pilot** Drachenflieger, der/-fliegerin, die; ~**gliding** n. Drachenfliegen, das

**'hanging** ⟨1⟩ n. (execution) Hinrichtung, die [durch den Strang] ⟨2⟩ adj. ~ **basket** Hängekorb, der

**hang:** ~**man** /'hæŋmən/ n., pl. ~**men** /'hæŋmən/ Henker, der; ~**over** n. Kater, der (ugs.); ~**up** n. (coll.) Macke, die (ugs.)

**hanker** /'hæŋkə(r)/ v.i. ~ **after** ein heftiges Verlangen haben nach

**hanky** /'hæŋkɪ/ n. (coll.) Taschentuch, das

**Hanover** /'hænəʊvə(r)/ pr. n. Hannover (das)

**haphazard** /hæp'hæzəd/ adj., **hap'hazardly** adv. willkürlich

**happen** /'hæpn/ v.i. geschehen; ⟨Vorhergesagtes:⟩ eintreffen; ~ **to** sb. jmdm. passieren; ~ **to do** sth./**be** sb. zufällig etw. tun/jmd. sein; **as it** ~s or **it so** ~s **I have** ...: zufällig habe ich ...

**'happening** n. Ereignis, das

**happily** /'hæpɪlɪ/ adv. (a) glücklich ⟨lächeln⟩; vergnügt ⟨spielen, lachen⟩ (b) (gladly) mit Vergnügen

**happiness** /'hæpɪnɪs/ n. ▶ HAPPY A: Glück, das; Heiterkeit, die; Zufriedenheit, die

**happy** /'hæpɪ/ adj. (a) (joyful) glücklich; heiter ⟨Bild, Veranlagung⟩; erfreulich ⟨Erinnerung, Szene⟩; froh ⟨Ereignis⟩; (contented) zufrieden (b) **be** ~ **to do** sth. (glad) etw. gern tun

**happy:** ~ **'ending** n. Happyend, das; ~**-go-'lucky** adj. sorglos

**harass** /'hærəs/ v.t. schikanieren

**harassed** /'hærəst/ adj. geplagt (**with** von); gequält ⟨Blick, Ausdruck⟩

**'harassment** n. Schikanierung, die; **sexual** ~: [sexuelle] Belästigung

**harbour** (Brit.; Amer.: **harbor**) /'hɑːbə(r)/ ⟨1⟩ n. Hafen, der; **in** ~: im Hafen ⟨2⟩ v.t. Unterschlupf gewähren (+ Dat.) ⟨Verbrecher, Flüchtling⟩; hegen (geh.) ⟨Groll, Verdacht⟩

**hard** /hɑːd/ ⟨1⟩ adj. (a) hart; fest ⟨Gelee⟩; stark ⟨Regen⟩; streng ⟨Frost, Winter⟩; gesichert ⟨Beweis, Daten⟩

····⟩

**(b)** (difficult) schwer; **this is ~ to believe** das ist kaum zu glauben; **do sth. the ~ way** es sich (*Dat.*) bei etw. unnötig schwer machen **(c)** (strenuous) hart **(d)** (vigorous) kräftig ‹*Schlag, Stoß, Tritt*› **(e)** (harsh) hart

**2** *adv.* **(a)** (strenuously) hart ‹*arbeiten, trainieren*›; fleißig ‹*studieren, üben*›; genau ‹*überlegen*›; gut ‹*aufpassen, zuhören*›; **try ~:** sich sehr bemühen

**(b)** (vigorously) heftig; fest ‹*schlagen, drücken, klopfen*›

**(c)** (severely) hart; **be ~ up** knapp bei Kasse sein (ugs.); **feel ~ done by** sich schlecht behandelt fühlen

**hard: ~back** *n.* gebundene Ausgabe; **~board** *n.* Hartfaserplatte, *die;* **~-boiled** *adj.* **(a)** hart gekocht ‹*Ei*›; **(b)** (tough) hartgesotten; **~ 'cash** *n.* **in ~ cash** in bar ‹*bezahlen*›; **~ copy** *n.* (Comp.) Hardcopy, *die;* **~-core** *attrib. adj.* hart ‹*Pornographie*›; **~ court** *n.* (Tennis) Hartplatz, *der;* **~ 'currency** *n.* harte Währung; **'disk ▶** DISK A; **~ drug** *n.* harte Droge; **~-earned** *adj.* schwer verdient

**harden** /'hɑːdn/ **1** *v.t.* härten; (fig.) abhärten (**to** gegen)

**2** *v.i.* hart werden; (become confirmed) sich verhärten

**hardened** /'hɑːdnd/ *adj.* abgehärtet (**to** gegen); hartgesotten ‹*Verbrecher*›

**hard: ~ 'hat** *n.* Schutzhelm, *der;* **~-headed** *adj.* nüchtern; **~-hearted** *adj.* hartherzig (**towards** gegenüber); **~-'hitting** *adj.* (fig.) aggressiv ‹*Rede, Politik, Kritik*›; **~ 'labour** *n.* Zwangsarbeit, *die*

**hardly** /'hɑːdlɪ/ *adv.* kaum; **~ anyone** *or* **anybody/anything** fast niemand/nichts; **~ ever** so gut wie nie; **~ at all** fast überhaupt nicht

**'hardness** *n.* Härte, *die*

**hard: ~ porn** (coll.)**, ~ pornography** *ns.* harte Pornographie; harte Pornos *Pl.* (ugs.); **~ 'pressed** *adj.* hart bedrängt; **be ~ pressed** große Schwierigkeiten haben; **~ sell** *n.* aggressive Verkaufsmethoden *Pl.*

**'hardship** *n.* **(a)** Not, *die;* Elend, *das* **(b)** (instance) Notlage, *die*

**hard: ~ 'shoulder** *n.* (Brit.) Standspur, *die;* **~ware** *n.* **(a)** (goods) Eisenwaren *Pl.; attrib.* Eisenwaren‹*geschäft*›; **(b)** (Comp.) Hardware, *die;* **~-wearing** *adj.* strapazierfähig; **~-working** *adj.* fleißig; **~wood** *n.* Hartholz, *das*

**hardy** /'hɑːdɪ/ *adj.* abgehärtet; zäh ‹*Rasse*›; winterhart ‹*Pflanze*›

**hare** /heə(r)/ *n.* Hase, *der*

**harem** /'hɑːriːm, hɑˈriːm/ *n.* Harem, *der*

**hark** /hɑːk/ *v.i.* [just] **~ at him** hör ihn dir/ hört ihn euch nur an!; **~ back to** zurückkommen auf (+ *Akk.*)

**harm** /hɑːm/ **1** *n.* Schaden, *der;* **do sb. ~, do ~ to sb.** jmdm. schaden

**2** *v.t.* etwas [zuleide] tun (+ *Dat.*); schaden (+ *Dat.*) ‹*Beziehungen, Land, Ruf*›

**harmful** /'hɑːmfl/ *adj.* schädlich (**to** für)

**'harmless** *adj.* harmlos

**harmonica** /hɑːˈmɒnɪkə/ *n.* Mundharmonika, *die*

**harmonious** /hɑːˈməʊnɪəs/ *adj.* harmonisch

**harmonize** /'hɑːmənaɪz/ **1** *v.t.* aufeinander abstimmen

**2** *v.i.* harmonieren (**with** mit)

**harmony** /'hɑːmənɪ/ *n.* Harmonie, *die;* **be in ~:** harmonieren

**harness** /'hɑːnɪs/ **1** *n.* Geschirr, *das* **2** *v.t.* anschirren; (fig.) nutzen

**harp** /hɑːp/ **1** *n.* Harfe, *die* **2** *v.i.* **~ on [about] sth.** immer wieder von etw. reden; (critically) auf etw. (*Dat.*) herumreiten (salopp)

**harpoon** /hɑːˈpuːn/ *n.* Harpune, *die*

**harpsichord** /'hɑːpsɪkɔːd/ *n.* Cembalo, *das*

**harrowing** /'hærəʊɪŋ/ *adj.* entsetzlich; grauenhaft ‹*Anblick, Geschichte*›

**harsh** /hɑːʃ/ *adj.* **(a)** rau ‹*Gewebe, Klima*›; schrill ‹*Ton, Stimme*›; grell ‹*Licht*›; hart ‹*Bedingungen, Leben*›

**(b)** (excessively severe) [sehr] hart; [äußerst] streng ‹*Disziplin*›; rücksichtslos ‹*Tyrann, Herrscher, Politik*›

**'harshly** *adv.* [sehr] hart

**harvest** /'hɑːvɪst/ **1** *n.* Ernte, *die* **2** *v.t.* ernten

**harvest 'festival** *n.* Erntedankfest, *das*

**has ▶** HAVE

**has-been** /'hæzbiːn/ *n.* (coll.) **be a ~:** seine besten Jahre hinter sich haben

**hash** /hæʃ/ *n.* **(a)** (Cookery) Haschee, *das* **(b)** **make a ~ of sth.** (coll.) etw. verpfuschen (ugs.)

**'hash browns** *n. pl.:* Bratkartoffeln mit Zwiebeln; ≈ Rösti mit Zwiebeln

**hashish** /'hæʃɪʃ/ *n.* Haschisch, *das*

**hasn't** /'hæznt/ = **has not; ▶** HAVE

**hassle** /'hæsl/ (coll.) **1** *n.* Ärger, *der* **2** *v.t.* schikanieren

**haste** /heɪst/ *n.* Eile, *die;* (rush) Hast, *die;* **make ~:** sich beeilen

**hasten** /'heɪsn/ **1** *v.t.* beschleunigen **2** *v.i.* eilen

**hastily** /'heɪstɪlɪ/ *adv.* (hurriedly) eilig; (rashly) übereilt

**hasty** /'heɪstɪ/ *adj.* eilig; flüchtig ‹*Skizze, Blick*›; (rash) übereilt

**hat** /hæt/ *n.* Hut, *der*

**hatch¹** /hætʃ/ *n.* Luke, *die;* (serving ~) Durchreiche, *die*

**hatch²** **1** *v.t.* ausbrüten **2** *v.i.* [aus]schlüpfen

**■ hatch 'out** **1** *v.i.* ausschlüpfen **2** *v.t.* ausbrüten '**hatchback** *n.* (car) Schräghecklimousine, *die*

**hatchet** /'hætʃɪt/ *n.* Beil, *das;* **bury the ~** (fig.) das Kriegsbeil begraben

**hate** /heɪt/ ① *n.* Hass, *der* ② *v.t.* hassen; **I ~ to say this** (coll.) ich sage das nicht gern

**hateful** /'heɪtfl/ *adj.* abscheulich

'**hate mail** *n.* hasserfüllte Briefe *Pl.*

'**hatpin** *n.* Hutnadel, *die*

**hatred** /'heɪtrɪd/ *n.* Hass, *der*

**hat: ~stand** *n.* Hutständer, *der;* **~ trick** *n.* Hattrick, *der*

**haughty** /'hɔːtɪ/ *adj.* hochmütig

**haul** /hɔːl/ ① *v.i. & t.* ziehen ② *n.* (a) Ziehen, *das* (b) (catch) Fang, *der;* (fig.) Beute, *die*

**haulage** /'hɔːlɪdʒ/ *n.* Transport, *der*

**haunch** /hɔːntʃ/ *n.* **sit on one's/its ~es** auf seinem Hinterteil sitzen

**haunt** /hɔːnt/ *v.t.* **~ a house/castle** in einem Haus/Schloss spuken; **a ~ed house** ein Haus, in dem es spukt

'**haunting** *adj.* sehnsüchtig

**have** ① /hæv/ *v.t., pres.* **he has** /hæz/, *p.t. & p.p.* **had** /hæd/ haben; (obtain) bekommen; (take) nehmen; bekommen ⟨*Kind*⟩; **~ breakfast/dinner/lunch** frühstücken/zu Abend/zu Mittag essen; **~ a cup of tea** eine Tasse Tee trinken; **~ sb. to stay** jmdn. zu Besuch haben; **you've had it now** (coll.) jetzt ist es aus (ugs.); **~ a game of football** Fußball spielen ② /həv/, əv, *stressed* hæv/ *v. aux.,* **he has** /həz/, əz, *stressed* hæz/, **had** /həd/, əd, *stressed* hæd/ **I ~/I had read** ich habe/hatte gelesen; **I ~/I had gone** ich bin/war gegangen; **if I had known ...**: wenn ich gewusst hätte ...; **~ sth. made** etw. machen lassen; **~ to** müssen

■ **have 'on** *v.t.* (a) (wear) tragen (b) (Brit. coll.: deceive) **~ sb. on** jmdn. auf den Arm nehmen (ugs.)

■ **have 'out** *v.t.* (a) **~ a tooth/one's tonsils out** sich (*Dat.*) einen Zahn ziehen lassen/ sich (*Dat.*) die Mandeln herausnehmen lassen (b) **~ it out with sb.** mit jmdm. offen sprechen

**haven** /'heɪvn/ *n.* geschützte Anlegestelle, *die;* (fig.) Zufluchtsort, *der*

**haven't** /'hævnt/ = have not; ▶ HAVE

**haversack** /'hævəsæk/ *n.* Brotbeutel, *der*

**havoc** /'hævək/ *n.* (a) (devastation) Verwüstungen *Pl.;* **cause** *or* **wreak ~**: Verwüstungen anrichten (b) (confusion) Chaos; **play ~ with sth.** etw. völlig durcheinander bringen

**hawk**[1] /hɔːk/ *n.* Falke, *der*

**hawk**[2] *v.t.* hausieren mit

'**hawker** *n.* Hausierer, *der*/Hausiererin, *die*

**hawthorn** /'hɔːθɔːn/ *n.* (Bot.) (white) Weißdorn, *der;* (red) Rotdorn, *der*

**hay** /heɪ/ *n.* Heu, *das*

**hay: ~ fever** *n.* Heuschnupfen, *der;* **~making** *n.* Heuernte, *die;* **~stack** *n.* Heuschober, *der* (südd.); Heudieme, *die* (nordd.); **~wire** *adj.* (coll.) **go ~wire** ⟨*Instrument:*⟩ verrückt spielen (ugs.)

**hazard** /'hæzəd/ ① *n.* Gefahr, *die* ② *v.t.* **~ a guess** es mit Raten probieren

'**hazard lights** *n. pl.* Warnblinkanlage, *die*

**hazardous** /'hæzədəs/ *adj.* gefährlich; **~ waste** Sondermüll, *der*

**hazard 'warning lights** ▶ HAZARD LIGHTS

**haze** /heɪz/ *n.* Dunst[schleier], *der*

**hazel** /'heɪzl/ *adj.* haselnussbraun

**hazelnut** /'heɪzlnʌt/ *n.* Haselnuss, *die*

**hazy** /'heɪzɪ/ *adj.* dunstig; (fig.) vage

**HDTV** *abbr.* = **high-definition television** HDTV

**he** /hɪ, *stressed* hiː/ *pron.* er

**head** /hed/ ① *n.* (a) Kopf, *der;* **~ first** mit dem Kopf voran; **~ over heels** kopfüber; **keep/lose one's ~**: einen klaren Kopf behalten/den Kopf verlieren; **in one's ~**: im Kopf; **enter sb.'s ~**: jmdm. in den Sinn kommen; **use your ~**: gebrauch deinen Verstand; **a** *or* **per ~**: pro Kopf (b) *in pl.* (on coin) **~s** Kopf, *die;* **~s or tails?** Kopf oder Zahl? (c) (leader) Leiter, *der*/Leiterin, *die* (d) (on beer) Blume, *die* ② *attrib. adj.* **~ waiter** Oberkellner, *der;* **~ office** Hauptverwaltung, *die;* **~ boy/girl** ≈ Schulsprecher, *der*/-sprecherin, *die* (*vom Lehrkörper eingesetzt*) ③ *v.t.* (a) (stand at top of) anführen ⟨*Liste*⟩; (lead) leiten; führen ⟨*Bewegung*⟩ (b) (Football) köpfen ④ *v.i.* steuern; **~ for London** ⟨*Flugzeug, Schiff:*⟩ Kurs auf London nehmen; ⟨*Auto:*⟩ in Richtung London fahren; **you're ~ing for trouble** du wirst Ärger bekommen

**head: ~ache** *n.* Kopfschmerzen *Pl.;* **~band** *n.* Stirnband, *das;* **~board** *n.* Kopfende, *das;* **~ count** *n.* Kopfzahl, *die*

'**header** *n.* (Footb.) Kopfball, *der*

'**headgear** *n.* Kopfbedeckung, *die*

'**heading** *n.* Überschrift, *die*

**head: ~lamp** *n.* Scheinwerfer, *der;* **~land** *n.* Landspitze, *die;* **~light** *n.* Scheinwerfer, *der;* **~line** *n.* Schlagzeile, *die;* **be ~line news, make [the] ~lines, hit the ~lines** Schlagzeilen machen; **~long** *adv.* kopfüber; **~master** *n.* Schulleiter, *der;* **~mistress** *n.* Schulleiterin, *die;* **~ 'office** *n.* Hauptsitz, *der;* **~-on** ① /'--/ *adj.* frontal; Frontal⟨*zusammenstoß*⟩; ② /'-'-/ *adv.* frontal; **~phones** *n. pl.* Kopfhörer, *der;* **~'quarters** *n. sing. or pl.* Hauptquartier, *das;* **~rest** *n.* Kopfstütze, *die;* **~room** *n.* [lichte] Höhe, *die;* **~scarf** *n.* Kopftuch, *das;* **~set** *n.* Kopfhörer, *der;* **~stone** *n.* (a) (gravestone) Grabstein, *der;* (b) (of building) Grundstein, *der;* (fig.) Grundpfeiler, *der;* **~strong** *adj.* ⸱⸱⸱❖

**h**

eigensinnig; ~ **'teacher** ▶ ~MASTER;
~MISTRESS; ~**way** n. make ~way
Fortschritte machen; ~ **wind** n.
Gegenwind, der

**heady** /'hedɪ/ adj. berauschend

**heal** /hiːl/ **1** v.t. heilen
**2** v.i. ~ [up] [ver]heilen

**healer** /'hiːlə(r)/ n. (person) Heilkundige,
der/die

**health** /helθ/ n. Gesundheit, die; **in good/
very good** ~: bei guter/bester Gesundheit;
**good** or **your** ~! auf deine Gesundheit!

**health:** ~ **care** n. Gesundheitsfürsorge,
die; ~ **care worker** im Gesundheitswesen
Beschäftigte, der/die; **inadequate** ~ **care**
unzureichende medizinische Versorgung;
~ **centre** n. Poliklinik, die;
~ **certificate** n. Gesundheitszeugnis, das;
~ **check** n. Gesundheitsuntersuchung, die;
~ **farm** n. Gesundheitsfarm, die (ugs.);
~ **food** n. Reformhauskost, die; ~ **food
shop** Reformhaus, das; ~ **hazard** n.
Gesundheitsrisiko, das

**healthily** /'helθɪlɪ/ adv. gesund

**health:** ~ **insurance** n.
Krankenversicherung, die; ~ **resort** n.
Kurort, der; ~ **service** n.
Gesundheitsdienst, der; ~ **visitor** n.
Krankenschwester/-pfleger im Sozialdienst;
~ **warning** n. Warnhinweis, der; Hinweis
auf die Gesundheitsgefährdung

**healthy** /'helθɪ/ adj. gesund

**heap** /hiːp/ **1** n. Haufen, der; ~**s of** (coll.)
jede Menge (ugs.)
**2** v.t. aufhäufen

**hear** /hɪə(r)/ **1** v.t., **heard** /hɜːd/ **(a)** hören
**(b)** (understand) verstehen
**2** v.i., **heard:** ~ **about sb./sth.** von jmdm./
etw. [etwas] hören; **he wouldn't** ~ **of it** er
wollte nichts davon hören
**3** int. **H**~! bravo!; richtig!
∎ **hear 'out** v.t. ausreden lassen

**heard** ▶ HEAR 1, 2

**'hearing** n. Gehör, das; **be hard of** ~:
schwerhörig sein

**'hearing aid** n. Hörgerät, das

**hearsay** /'hɪəseɪ/ n. Gerücht, das; **it's only**
~: es ist nur ein Gerücht

**hearse** /hɜːs/ n. Leichenwagen, der

**heart** /hɑːt/ n. (also Cards) Herz, das; **by** ~:
auswendig; **at** ~: im Grunde seines/ihres
Herzens; **take/lose** ~: Mut schöpfen/
verlieren; **my** ~ **sank** mein Mut sank; **the**
~ **of the matter** der wahre Kern der Sache;
see also CLUB 1C

**heart:** ~**ache** n. [seelische] Qual;
~ **attack** n. Herzanfall, der; (fatal)
Herzschlag, der; ~**beat** n. Herzschlag, der;
~**breaking** adj. herzzerreißend;
~**broken** adj. **she was** ~**broken** ihr Herz
war gebrochen; ~**burn** n. Sodbrennen, das;
~ **disease** n. Herzkrankheiten Pl.

**hearten** /'hɑːtn/ v.t. ermutigen

**'heartening** adj. ermutigend

**heart:** ~ **failure** n. Herzversagen, das;
~**felt** adj. tief empfunden ⟨Beileid⟩;
aufrichtig ⟨Dankbarkeit⟩

**hearth** /hɑːθ/ n.: Platz vor dem Kamin

**'hearthrug** n. Kaminvorleger, der

**heartily** /'hɑːtɪlɪ/ adv. von Herzen; **eat** ~:
tüchtig essen

**'heartless** adj. herzlos

**heart:** ~ **rate** n. Herzfrequenz, die;
~**-shaped** adj. herzförmig; ~**-throb** n.
Idol, das; ~ **transplant** n.
Herztransplantation, die (fachspr.);
~**-warming** adj. herzerfreuend

**hearty** /'hɑːtɪ/ adj. herzlich; ungeteilt
⟨Zustimmung⟩; herzhaft ⟨Mahlzeit⟩

**heat** /hiːt/ **1** n. **(a)** (hotness) Hitze, die
**(b)** (Phys.) Wärme, die
**(c)** (Sport) Vorlauf, der
**2** v.t. heizen
∎ **heat 'up** v.t. heiß machen

**'heated** adj. (angry) hitzig

**'heater** n. Ofen, der; (for water) Boiler, der

**heath** /hiːθ/ n. Heide, die

**heathen** /'hiːðn/ **1** adj. heidnisch
**2** n. Heide, der/Heidin, die

**heather** /'heðə(r)/ n. Heidekraut, das

**'heating** n. Heizung, die

**heat:** ~**proof** adj. feuerfest; ~ **rash** n.
Hitzebläschen Pl.; ~**-resistant** adj.
hitzebeständig; ~**-stroke** n. Hitzschlag, der;
~ **treatment** n. (Med.) Wärmebehandlung,
die; ~**wave** n. Hitzewelle, die

**heave** /hiːv/ **1** v.t. **(a)** heben
**(b)** (coll.: throw) schmeißen (ugs.)
**(c)** ~ **a sigh** aufseufzen
**2** v.i. (pull) ziehen
**3** n. Zug, die

**heaven** /'hevn/ n. Himmel, der; **in** ~: im
Himmel; **for H**~**'s sake!** um Gottes willen!

**'heavenly** adj. himmlisch

**heavily** /'hevɪlɪ/ adj. schwer; (to a great
extent) stark; schwer ⟨bewaffnet⟩; tief
⟨schlafen⟩; dicht ⟨bevölkert⟩; **smoke/drink** ~:
ein starker Raucher/Trinker sein; **it rained/
snowed** ~: es regnete/schneite stark

**heavy** /'hevɪ/ adj. schwer; unmäßig
⟨Trinken, Rauchen⟩; **a** ~ **smoker/drinker** ein
starker Raucher/Trinker; **be a** ~ **sleeper**
sehr fest schlafen

**heavy:** ~**-duty** adj. strapazierfähig
⟨Kleidung, Material⟩; schwer ⟨Werkzeug,
Maschine⟩; ~ **'goods vehicle** n. (Brit.)
Schwerlastwagen, der; ~**-'handed** adj.
(clumsy) ungeschickt ⟨Person⟩; ~ **'industry**
n. Schwerindustrie, die; ~ **'metal** n. **(a)**
Schwermetall, das; **(b)** (Mus.) Heavy metal,
das; ~**weight** n. Schwergewicht, das

**Hebrew** /'hiːbruː/ **1** adj. hebräisch
**2** n. (language) Hebräisch, das

**heckle** /'hekl/ v.t. durch Zwischenrufe
unterbrechen

**heckler** /'heklə(r)/ n. Zwischenrufer, der/ Zwischenruferin, die

**hectic** /'hektɪk/ adj. hektisch

**he'd** /hɪd, stressed hiːd/ (a) = he had; (b) = he would

**hedge** /hedʒ/ [1] n. Hecke, die
[2] v.t. ~ one's bets (fig.) nicht alles auf eine Karte setzen
[3] v.i. sich nicht festlegen

**'hedge clippers** n. pl. Heckenschere, die

**hedgehog** /'hedʒhɒg/ n. Igel, der

**'hedgerow** n. Hecke, die [als Feldbegrenzung]

**hedonism** /'hiːdənɪzm/ n. Hedonismus, der

**hedonist** /'hiːdənɪst/ n. Hedonist, der/ Hedonistin, die

**heed** /hiːd/ [1] v.t. beachten; beherzigen ‹Rat, Lektion›; ~ the danger/risk sich (Dat.) der Gefahr/des Risikos bewusst sein
[2] n. give or pay ~ to, take ~ of Beachtung schenken (+ Dat.)

**'heedless** adj. unachtsam; be ~ of sth. auf etw. (Akk.) nicht achten

**heel** /hiːl/ n. Ferse, die; (of shoe) Absatz, der; Achilles' ~ (fig.) Achillesferse, die; down at ~ (fig.) heruntergekommen; take to one's ~s Fersengeld geben (ugs.)

**hefty** /'heftɪ/ adj. kräftig; (heavy) schwer

**height** /haɪt/ n. (a) Höhe, die; (of person, animal, building) Größe, die
(b) (fig.: highest point) Höhepunkt, der

**heighten** /'haɪtn/ v.t. aufstocken; (fig.) verstärken

**heir** /eə(r)/ n. Erbe, der/Erbin, die

**heiress** /'eərɪs/ n. Erbin, die

**heirloom** /'eəluːm/ n. Erbstück, das

**held** ▶ HOLD² 1, 2

**helicopter** /'helɪkɒptə(r)/ n. Hubschrauber, der

**heliport** /'helɪpɔːt/ n. Heliport, der

**helium** /'hiːlɪəm/ n. Helium, das

**hell** /hel/ n. (a) Hölle, die
(b) (coll.) [oh] ~! verdammter Mist! (ugs.); what the ~! ach, zum Teufel! (ugs.); run like ~: wie der Teufel rennen (ugs.)

**he'll** /hɪl, stressed hiːl/ = he will

**hello** /hə'ləʊ, he'ləʊ/ int. (greeting) hallo; (surprise) holla

**hell's 'angel** n. Rocker, der

**helm** /helm/ n. (Naut.) Ruder, das

**helmet** /'helmɪt/ n. Helm, der

**help** /help/ [1] v.t. (a) ~ sb. [to do sth.] jmdm. helfen[, etw. zu tun]; can I ~ you? (in shop) was möchten Sie bitte?
(b) (serve) ~ oneself sich bedienen; ~ oneself to sth. sich (Dat.) etw. nehmen; (coll.: steal) etw. mitgehen lassen (ugs.)
(c) (avoid) if I/you can ~ it wenn es irgend zu vermeiden ist; (remedy) I can't ~ it ich kann nichts dafür (ugs.); it can't be ~ed es lässt sich nicht ändern
(d) (refrain from) I can't ~ thinking or can't

~ but think that ...: ich kann mir nicht helfen, ich glaube, ...; I can't ~ laughing ich muss einfach lachen
[2] n. Hilfe, die; with the ~ of ...: mit Hilfe ... (+ Gen.); be of [some]/no/much ~ to sb. jmdm. eine gewisse/keine/eine große Hilfe sein
■ **help 'out** [1] v.i. aushelfen
[2] v.t. ~ sb. out jmdm. helfen

**'help desk** n. Help Desk, das (fachspr.); Auskunftsstelle für Computerbenutzer

**'helper** n. Helfer, der/Helferin, die

**helpful** /'helpfl/ adj. (willing) hilfsbereit; (useful) hilfreich; nützlich

**'helping** [1] adj. lend [sb.] a ~ hand [with sth.] (fig.) [jmdm.] [bei etw.] helfen
[2] n. Portion, die

**'helpless** adj., **'helplessly** adv. hilflos

**'helpline** n. Hotline, die

**helter-skelter** /heltə'skeltə(r)/ n. [spiralförmige] Rutschbahn

**hem** /hem/ [1] n. Saum, der
[2] v.t., -mm- säumen
■ **hem 'in** v.t. einschließen; feel ~med in sich eingeengt fühlen

**hemisphere** /'hemɪsfɪə(r)/ n. Halbkugel, die

**'hemline** n. Saum, der

**hemo-** (Amer.) ▶ HAEMO-

**hemp** /hemp/ n. Hanf, der

**hen** /hen/ n. Huhn, das; Henne, die

**hence** /hens/ adv. (therefore) daher

**hence'forth** adv. von nun an

**henchman** /'hentʃmən/ n., pl. henchmen /'hentʃmən/ Handlanger, der

**hen:** ~ **party** n. (coll.) [Damen]kränzchen, das; ~**pecked** /'henpekt/ adj. a ~ husband ein Pantoffelheld, der (ugs.)

**hepatitis** /hepə'taɪtɪs/ n. (Med.) Leberentzündung, die

**her¹** /hə(r), stressed hɜː(r)/ pron. sie; as indirect object ihr; it was ~: sie wars

**her²** poss. pron. attr. ihr

**herald** /'herəld/ [1] n. Herold, der
[2] v.t. ankündigen

**heraldic** /he'rældɪk/ adj. heraldisch

**heraldry** /'herəldrɪ/ n. Heraldik, die

**herb** /hɜːb/ n. Kraut, das

**herbaceous** /hɜː'beɪʃəs/ adj. krautartig; ~ border Staudenrabatte, die

**herbal** /'hɜːbl/ attrib. adj. Kräuter-

**herbivore** /'hɜːbɪvɔː(r)/ n. Pflanzenfresser, der

**'herb tea** n. Kräuteraufguss, der

**herd** /hɜːd/ [1] n. Herde, die; (of wild animals) Rudel, das
[2] v.t. (a) treiben; ~ people together Menschen zusammenpferchen
(b) (tend) hüten

**here** /hɪə(r)/ [1] adv. (a) (in or at this place) hier; down/in/up ~: hier unten/drin/oben; ~ you are (coll.: giving sth.) hier ⋯⋮

**(b)** (to this place) hierher; **in[to]** ∼: hierherein; **come/bring** ∼: hierher kommen/bringen ⟨2⟩ *int.* (attracting attention) he

**here'by** *adv.* (formal) hiermit

**hereditary** /hɪ'redɪtərɪ/ *adj.* **(a)** erblich ⟨*Titel, Amt*⟩
**(b)** (Biol.) angeboren

**heresy** /'herɪsɪ/ *n.* Ketzerei, *die*

**heretic** /'herɪtɪk/ *n.* Ketzer, *der*/Ketzerin, *die*

**heretical** /hɪ'retɪkl/ *adj.* ketzerisch

**here'with** *adv.* in der Anlage

**heritage** /'herɪtɪdʒ/ *n.* Erbe, *das*

**hermetic** /hɜː'metɪk/ *adj.* luftdicht

**hermetically** /hɜː'metɪkəlɪ/ *adv.* hermetisch

**hermit** /'hɜːmɪt/ *n.* Einsiedler, *der*/Einsiedlerin, *die*

**hernia** /'hɜːnɪə/ *n.* Bruch, *der*

**hero** /'hɪərəʊ/ *n., pl.* ∼**es** Held, *der*

**heroic** /hɪ'rəʊɪk/ *adj.* heldenhaft

**heroin** /'herəʊɪn/ *n.* Heroin, *das*

**heroine** /'herəʊɪn/ *n.* Heldin, *die*

**heroism** /'herəʊɪzm/ *n.* Heldentum, *das*

**heron** /'hern/ *n.* Reiher, *der*

**herpes** /'hɜːpiːz/ *n.* (Med.) Herpes, *der*

**herring** /'herɪŋ/ *n.* Hering, *der*

**hers** /hɜːz/ *poss. pron.* ihrer/ihre/ihres; **the book is** ∼: das Buch gehört ihr

**her'self** *pron.* **(a)** *emphat.* selbst; **[all] by** ∼: [ganz] allein[e]
**(b)** *refl.* sich; allein[e] ⟨*tun, wählen*⟩; **younger than/as heavy as** ∼: jünger als/so schwer wie sie selbst

**he's** /hɪz, *stressed* hiːz/ **(a)** = he is;
**(b)** = he has

**hesitant** /'hezɪtənt/ *adj.* zögernd ⟨*Reaktion*⟩; stockend ⟨*Rede*⟩

**hesitate** /'hezɪteɪt/ *v.i.* zögern; (falter) ins Stocken geraten; ∼ **to do sth.** Bedenken haben, etw. zu tun

**hesitation** /hezɪ'teɪʃn/ *n.* **(a)** (indecision) Unentschlossenheit, *die;* **without** ∼: ohne zu zögern
**(b)** (instance of faltering) Unsicherheit, *die*
**(c)** (reluctance) Bedenken *Pl.*

**hetero** /'hetərəʊ/ *n.* (coll.) *n.* Hetero *der*/*die*

**heterosexual** /hetərəʊ'seksjʊəl/ ⟨1⟩ *adj.* heterosexuell
⟨2⟩ *n.* Heterosexuelle, *der*/*die*

**het up** /het 'ʌp/ *adj.* aufgeregt

**hew** /hjuː/ *v.t., p.p.* **hewn** /hjuːn/ *or* **hewed** /hjuːd/ hacken ⟨*Holz*⟩; losschlagen ⟨*Kohle, Gestein*⟩

**hewn** ▸ HEW

**hexagon** /'heksəgən/ *n.* Sechseck, *das*

**hey** /heɪ/ *int.* he; ∼ **presto!** simsalabim!

**heyday** /'heɪdeɪ/ *n.* Blütezeit, *die*

**HGV** *abbr.* (Brit.) = **heavy goods vehicle**

**hi** /haɪ/ *int.* hallo (ugs.)

**hiatus** /haɪ'eɪtəs/ *n.* Unterbrechung, *die*

**hibernate** /'haɪbəneɪt/ *v.i.* Winterschlaf halten

**hibernation** /haɪbə'neɪʃn/ *n.* Winterschlaf, *der*

**hiccup** /'hɪkʌp/ ⟨1⟩ *n.* **(a)** Schluckauf, *der;* **have/get [the]** ∼**s** den Schluckauf haben/bekommen
**(b)** (fig.: stoppage) Störung, *die*
⟨2⟩ *v.i.* schlucksen (ugs.)

**hid** ▸ HIDE[1]

**hidden** ▸ HIDE[1]

**hide**[1] /haɪd/ ⟨1⟩ *v.t.,* **hid** /hɪd/, **hidden** /'hɪdn/ **(a)** verstecken ⟨*Gegenstand, Person usw.*⟩ (from vor + *Dat.*); verbergen ⟨*Gefühle, Sinn usw.*⟩ (from vor + *Dat.*); verheimlichen ⟨*Tatsache, Absicht usw.*⟩ (from *Dat.*)
**(b)** (obscure) verdecken
⟨2⟩ *v.i.,* **hid, hidden** sich verstecken (from vor + *Dat.*)

**hide**[2] *n.* Haut, *die;* (of furry animal) Fell, *das;* (dressed) Leder, *das*

**hide-and-'seek** *n.* Versteckspiel, *das;* **play** ∼: Verstecken spielen

**hideous** /'hɪdɪəs/ *adj.* scheußlich

**'hideout** *n.* Versteck, *das*

**hiding**[1] /'haɪdɪŋ/ *n.* **go into** ∼: sich verstecken; (to avoid police, public attention) untertauchen; **be in** ∼: sich versteckt halten; (to avoid police, public attention) untergetaucht sein

**hiding**[2] *n.* (coll.: beating) Tracht Prügel; **give sb. a [good]** ∼: jmdm. eine [ordentliche] Tracht Prügel verpassen (ugs.)

**'hiding place** *n.* Versteck, *das*

**hierarchic** /haɪə'rɑːkɪk/, **hierarchical** /haɪə'rɑːkɪkl/ *adj.* hierarchisch

**hierarchy** /'haɪərɑːkɪ/ *n.* Hierarchie, *die*

**hi-fi** /'haɪfaɪ/ (coll.) ⟨1⟩ *adj.* Hi-Fi-
⟨2⟩ *n.* Hi-Fi-Anlage, *die*

**high** /haɪ/ ⟨1⟩ *adj.* **(a)** hoch; groß ⟨*Höhe*⟩; stark ⟨*Wind*⟩
**(b)** (coll.: on a drug) high (ugs.)
**(c)** **it's** ∼ **time you left** es ist höchste Zeit, dass du gehst
⟨2⟩ *adv.* hoch; **search** *or* **look** ∼ **and low** überall suchen
⟨3⟩ *n.* **(a)** (∼est level/figure) Höchststand, *der*
**(b)** (Meteorol.) Hoch, *das*
**(c)** (coll.: drug-induced euphoria) Rausch[zustand], *der;* **give sb. a** ∼ ⟨*Droge:*⟩ jmdn. high machen (ugs.)

**high:** ∼**brow** ⟨1⟩ *n.* Intellektuelle, *der*/*die;*
⟨2⟩ *adj.* intellektuell ⟨*Person, Gerede usw.*⟩; hochgestochen (abwertend) ⟨*Person, Musik, Literatur usw.*⟩; ∼ **chair** *n.* Hochstuhl, *der;* ∼**-definition 'television** *n.* hoch auflösendes Fernsehen

**higher edu'cation** *n.* Hochschulbildung, *die*

**high:** ∼ **fi'nance** *n.* Hochfinanz, *die;* ∼**-'flier,** ∼**-'flyer** *n.* (successful person) Senkrechtstarter, *der;* ( person with great

potential) Hochbegabte, *der*/*die;*
~ **'frequency** n. Hochfrequenz, *die;*
~-**'handed** adj. selbstherrlich;
~-**heeled** /haɪ'hiːld/ *adj.* ⟨*Schuhe*⟩ mit
hohen Absätzen; ~-**income** *adj.*
einkommensstark; ~ **jump** n. Hochsprung,
*der;* ~**land** /'haɪlənd/ n. Hochland, *das;*
~**light** ①n. (a) Höhepunkt, *der;* (b) (bright
area) Licht, *das;* ②*v.t.,* ~**lighted** ein
Schlaglicht werfen auf (+ *Akk.*) ⟨*Probleme
usw.*⟩

**'highly** *adv.* sehr; hoch ⟨*angesehen, bezahlt*⟩;
hoch⟨*interessant, -gebildet*⟩; leicht
⟨*entzündlich*⟩; stark ⟨*gewürzt*⟩; **think** ~ **of
sb.**/**sth.** eine hohe Meinung von jmdm./etw.
haben; **speak** ~ **of sb.**/**sth.** jmdn./etw. sehr
loben

**highly-strung** /'haɪlɪstrʌŋ/ *adj.*
übererregbar

**Highness** /'haɪnɪs/ n. **His**/**her** *etc.* ~:
Seine/Ihre *usw.* Hoheit

**high:** ~-**pitched** /'haɪpɪtʃt/ *adj.* hoch
⟨*Ton, Stimme*⟩; ~-**powered** /'haɪpaʊəd/
*adj.* (forceful) dynamisch ⟨*Geschäftsmann*⟩;
~ **'pressure** n. (a) (Meteorol.) Hochdruck,
*der;* (b) (Mech. Engin.) Überdruck, *der;*
~-**rise** *adj.* ~-**rise building** Hochhaus, *das;*
~-**rise block of flats**/**office block** Wohn-/
Bürohochhaus, *das;* ~-**risk** *attrib. adj.*
risikoreich ⟨*gruppe, -sportart*⟩; **a**
~-**risk investment** eine Geldanlage mit
hohem Risiko; ~ **school** n. ≈ Oberschule,
*die;* ~ **'seas** n. pl. **the** ~ **seas** die hohe
See; ~ **season** n. Hochsaison, *die;*
~-**speed** *adj.* ~-**speed train**
Hochgeschwindigkeitszug, *der;* ~ **street**
n. Hauptstraße, *die;* ~ **'tech** (coll.)
▶ ~ TECHNOLOGY; ~-**tech** *adj.* (coll.)
Hightech-; ~ **tech'nology** n.
Spitzentechnologie, *die;* Hochtechnologie,
*die;* ~-**'voltage** *adj.* Hochspannungs-;
~**way** n. öffentliche Straße

**hijack** /'haɪdʒæk/ *v.t.* entführen

**'hijacker** n. Entführer, *der;* (of aircraft)
Hijacker, *der*

**hike** /haɪk/ n. Wanderung, *die*

**'hiker** n. Wanderer, *der*/Wanderin, *die*

**hilarious** /hɪ'leərɪəs/ *adj.* urkomisch

**hill** /hɪl/ n. Hügel, *der;* (higher) Berg, *der;*
(slope) Hang, *der*

**hill:** ~**billy** /'hɪlbɪlɪ/ n. (Amer.)
Hinterwäldler, *der*/Hinterwäldlerin, *die;*
~**side** n. Hang, *der;* ~**top** n. [Berg]gipfel,
*der*

**'hilly** *adj.* hüg[e]lig

**hilt** /hɪlt/ n. Griff, *der;* [up] **to the** ~ (fig.)
voll und ganz

**him** /ɪm, *stressed* hɪm/ *pron.* ihn; *as indirect
object* ihm; **it was** ~: er war's

**Himalayas** /hɪmə'leɪəz/ *pr. n. pl.*
Himalaya, *der*

**him'self** *pron.* (a) *emphat.* selbst
(b) *refl.* sich. *See also* HERSELF

**hind** /haɪnd/ *adj.* hinter...; ~ **legs**
Hinterbeine *Pl.*

**hinder** /'hɪndə(r)/ *v.t.* (impede) behindern;
(delay) verzögern ⟨*Vollendung einer Arbeit,
Vorgang*⟩; aufhalten ⟨*Person*⟩; ~ **sb. from
doing sth.** jmdn. daran hindern, etw. zu tun

**'hindquarters** n. pl. Hinterteil, *das*

**hindrance** /'hɪndrəns/ n. Hindernis, *das*
(to für)

**'hindsight** n. **with** [**the benefit of**] ~: im
Nachhinein

**Hindu** /'hɪnduː, hɪn'duː/ ①n. Hindu, *der*
②*adj.* hinduistisch; Hindu⟨*gott, -tempel*⟩

**Hinduism** /'hɪnduːɪzm/ n. Hinduismus, *der*

**hinge** /hɪndʒ/ ①n. Scharnier, *das*
②*v.t.* mit Scharnieren versehen
③*v.i.* (depend) abhängen ([up]on von)

**hint** /hɪnt/ ①n. (a) (suggestion) Wink, *der*
(b) (slight trace) Spur, *die* (of von); **the** ~/**no**
~ **of a smile** der Anflug/nicht die Spur eines
Lächelns
(c) (information) Tipp, *der* (on für)
②*v.i.* ~ **at** andeuten

**hip** /hɪp/ n. Hüfte, *die*

**hip:** ~ **bone** n. Hüftbein, *das;* ~ **flask** n.
Taschenflasche, *die;* ~ **joint** n. Hüftgelenk,
*das*

**hippie** /'hɪpɪ/ n. (coll.) Hippie, *der*

**hippopotamus** /hɪpə'pɒtəməs/ n.
Nilpferd, *das*

**hippy** ▶ HIPPIE

**hire** /haɪə(r)/ ①n. Mieten, *das;* **be on** ~ [**to
sb.**] [an jmdn.] vermietet sein; **for** ~: zu
vermieten
②*v.t.* (a) (employ) anwerben; engagieren
⟨*Anwalt, Berater usw.*⟩
(b) (obtain use of) mieten; ~ **sth. from sb.**
etw. bei jmdm. mieten
(c) (grant use of) ~ [**out**] vermieten; ~ **sth.**
[**out**] **to sb.** etw. jmdm. od. an jmdn.
vermieten

**hire:** ~ **car** n. Mietwagen, *der;* ~
**'purchase** n. (Brit.) Ratenkauf, *der;* attrib.
Raten-; **pay for**/**buy sth. on** ~ **purchase** etw.
in Raten bezahlen/auf Raten kaufen

**his** /ɪz, *stressed* hɪz/ *poss. pron.* (a) *attrib.*
sein
(b) *pred.* seiner/seine/sein[e]s; *see also* HERS

**hiss** /hɪs/ ①n. Zischen, *das*
②*v.i.* zischen

**historian** /hɪ'stɔːrɪən/ n. Historiker, *der*/
Historikerin, *die*

**historic** /hɪ'stɒrɪk/ *adj.* historisch

**historical** /hɪ'stɒrɪkl/ *adj.* historisch;
geschichtlich ⟨*Belege, Hintergrund*⟩

**history** /'hɪstərɪ/ n. Geschichte, *die*

**hit** /hɪt/ ①*v.t.,* -tt-, hit schlagen; (with missile)
treffen; ⟨*Geschoss, Ball usw.*⟩ treffen;
⟨*Fahrzeug:*⟩ prallen gegen; ⟨*Schiff:*⟩ laufen
gegen; ~ **one's head on sth.** mit dem Kopf
gegen etw. stoßen; ~ **it off with sb.** gut mit
jmdm. auskommen
②*v.i.,* -tt-, hit schlagen ⋯✧

**3** *n.* (a) (blow) Schlag, *der;* (shot or bomb striking target) Treffer, *der*
(b) (success) Erfolg, *der;* (in entertainment) Schlager, *der;* Hit, *der* (ugs.)
■ **hit 'back** *v.t. & i.* zurückschlagen
■ **'hit [up]on** *v.t.* kommen auf (+ *Akk.*) ⟨Idee⟩; finden ⟨richtige Antwort, Methode⟩
**hit-and-'run** *adj.* unfallflüchtig ⟨Fahrer⟩; ~ **accident** Unfall mit Fahrerflucht

**hitch** /hɪtʃ/ **1** *v.t.* (a) binden ⟨Seil⟩ (round um + *Akk.*); [an]koppeln ⟨Anhänger usw.⟩ (to an + *Akk.*); spannen ⟨Zugtier usw.⟩ (to vor + *Akk.*)
(b) ~ **a lift** *or* **ride** (coll.) per Anhalter fahren **2** *n.* (problem) Problem, *das*
■ **hitch 'up** *v.t.* hochheben ⟨Rock⟩

**'hitch-hike** *v.i.* per Anhalter fahren

**'hitch-hiker** *n.* Anhalter, *der*/Anhalterin, *die*

**hit:** ~ **man** *n.* (Amer.) Killer, *der* (salopp); **~-or-'miss** *adj.* (coll.: random) unsicher, unzuverlässig ⟨Methode⟩; ~ **parade** *n.* Hitparade, *die;* ~ **'record** *n.* Hit, *der* (ugs.)

**HIV** *abbr.* = **human immunodeficiency virus** HIV; **~-positive/-negative** HIV-positiv/-negativ

**hive** /haɪv/ *n.* [Bienen]stock, *der*

**HMS** *abbr.* (Brit.) = **Her/His Majesty's Ship** H.M.S.

**hoard** /hɔːd/ **1** *n.* Vorrat, *der*
**2** *v.t.* ~ **[up]** horten; hamstern ⟨Lebensmittel⟩

**hoarding** /'hɔːdɪŋ/ *n.* (fence) Bauzaun, *der;* (Brit.: for advertisements) Reklamewand, *die*

**hoar frost** /'hɔːfrɒst/ *n.* [Rau]reif, *der*

**hoarse** /hɔːs/ *adj.* heiser

**hoax** /həʊks/ **1** *v.t.* anführen (ugs.); foppen
**2** *n.* (deception) Schwindel, *der;* (practical joke) Streich, *der;* (false alarm) blinder Alarm

**hob** /hɒb/ *n.* [Koch]platte, *die*

**hobble** /'hɒbl/ *v.i.* ~ **[about]** [herum]humpeln

**hobby** /'hɒbɪ/ *n.* Hobby, *das*

**'hobby horse** *n.* Steckenpferd, *das*

**hobnailed** /'hɒbneɪld/ *adj.* Nagel⟨schuh, -stiefel⟩

**hobo** /'həʊbəʊ/ *n., pl.* **-es** (Amer.) Landstreicher, *der*/-streicherin, *die*

**hockey** /'hɒkɪ/ *n.* Hockey, *das*

**'hockey stick** *n.* Hockeyschläger, *der*

**hoe** /həʊ/ **1** *n.* Hacke, *die*
**2** *v.t. & i.* hacken

**hog** /hɒg/ **1** *n.* [Mast]schwein
**2** *v.t.,* **-gg-** (coll.) mit Beschlag belegen

**hoist** /hɔɪst/ **1** *v.t.* hochziehen, hissen ⟨Flagge usw.⟩; hieven ⟨Last⟩; setzen ⟨Segel⟩
**2** *n.* [Lasten]aufzug, *der*

**hold¹** /həʊld/ *n.* (of ship) Laderaum, *der;* (of aircraft) Frachtraum, *der*

**hold²** **1** *v.t.,* **held** /held/ (a) halten; (carry)

tragen; (keep fast) festhalten; ~ **the door open for sb.** jmdm. die Tür aufhalten; ~ **sth. in place** etw. halten
(b) (contain) enthalten; (be able to contain) fassen ⟨Liter, Personen usw.⟩
(c) (possess) besitzen; haben
(d) (keep possession of) halten ⟨Stützpunkt, Stadt, Stellung⟩; ~ **the line** (Teleph.) am Apparat bleiben; ~ **one's own** sich behaupten
(e) (cause to take place) stattfinden lassen; abhalten ⟨Veranstaltung, Konferenz, Gottesdienst, Sitzung⟩; veranstalten ⟨Festival, Auktion⟩; austragen ⟨Meisterschaften⟩; führen ⟨Unterhaltung, Gespräch⟩; durchführen ⟨Untersuchung⟩; halten ⟨Vortrag, Rede⟩
(f) (think, believe) ~ **a view** *or* **an opinion** eine Ansicht haben (on über + *Akk.*); ~ **that ...:** der Ansicht sein, dass ...; ~ **oneself responsible for sth.** sich für etw. verantwortlich fühlen; ~ **sth. against sb.** jmdm. etw. vorwerfen
**2** *v.i.,* **held** halten; ⟨Wetter:⟩ sich halten
**3** *n.* (a) (grasp) Griff, *der;* **grab** *or* **seize** ~ **of sth.** etw. ergreifen; **get** *or* **lay** *or* **take** ~ **of sth.** etw. fassen *od.* packen; **keep** ~ **of sth.** etw. festhalten; **get** ~ **of sth.** (fig.) etw. auftreiben; **get** ~ **of sb.** (fig.) jmdn. erreichen
(b) (influence) Einfluss, *der* (on, over auf + *Akk.*)
(c) (Sport) Griff, *der*
■ **hold 'back** **1** *v.t.* zurückhalten
**2** *v.i.* zögern
■ **hold 'on** **1** *v.t.* [fest]halten
**2** *v.i.* (a) sich festhalten; ~ **on to** sich festhalten an (+ *Dat.*); (keep) behalten
(b) (coll.: wait) warten
■ **hold 'out** **1** *v.t.* ausstrecken ⟨Hand, Arm usw.⟩; hinhalten ⟨Tasse, Teller⟩
**2** *v.i.* (resist) sich halten
■ **hold 'up** *v.t.* (a) (raise) hochhalten; heben ⟨Hand, Kopf⟩
(b) (delay) aufhalten
(c) (rob) überfallen
■ **'hold with** *v.t.* not ~ with sth. etw. ablehnen

**'holdall** *n.* Reisetasche, *die*

**'holder** *n.* (a) (of post, title) Inhaber, *der*/ Inhaberin, *die*
(b) ⟨Zigaretten⟩spitze, *die;* ⟨Papier-, Zahnputzglas⟩halter, *der*

**'hold-up** *n.* (a) (robbery) [Raub]überfall, *der*
(b) (delay) Verzögerung, *die*

**hole** /həʊl/ *n.* Loch, *das;* (of fox, badger, rabbit) Bau, *der;* **pick** ~**s in** (fig.) zerpflücken (ugs.)

**holiday** /'hɒlɪdeɪ/ *n.* (a) [arbeits]freier Tag; (public ~) Feiertag, *der*
(b) *in sing. or pl.* (Brit.: vacation) Urlaub, *der;* (Sch.) [Schul]ferien *Pl.*

**holiday:** ~ **home** *n.* Feriendomizil, *das;* ~ **job** *n.* Ferienjob, *der;* ~**maker** *n.* Urlauber, *der*/Urlauberin, *die;* ~ **resort** *n.* Ferienort, *der;* ~ **season** *n.* Urlaubszeit, *die*

**Holland** /'hɒlənd/ *pr. n.* Holland (*das*)

**hollow** /ˈhɒləʊ/ **1** *adj.* hohl; eingefallen ⟨*Wangen, Schläfen*⟩; (fig.) leer ⟨*Versprechen*⟩ **2** *n.* [Boden]senke, *die* **3** *v.t.* ∼ **out** aushöhlen

**holly** /ˈhɒlɪ/ *n.* Stechpalme, *die*

**holocaust** /ˈhɒləkɔːst/ *n.* (destruction) Massenvernichtung, *die;* **the H∼:** der Holocaust

**hologram** /ˈhɒləgræm/ *n.* Hologramm, *der*

**holster** /ˈhəʊlstə(r)/ *n.* [Pistolen]halfter, *die od. das*

**holy** /ˈhəʊlɪ/ *adj.* heilig

**Holy: H∼ ˈBible** *n.* Heilige Schrift; ∼ **ˈGhost** ▶ ∼ SPIRIT; ∼ **Land** *n.* the ∼ Land das Heilige Land; ∼ **ˈSpirit** *n.* Heiliger Geist

**homage** /ˈhɒmɪdʒ/ *n.* Huldigung, *die* (**to** an + *Akk.*); **pay** *or* **do** ∼ **to sb./sth.** jmdm./einer Sache huldigen

**home** /həʊm/ **1** *n.* **(a)** Heim, *das;* (flat) Wohnung, *die;* (house) Haus, *das;* (household) [Eltern]haus, *das;* (native country) Heimat, *die;* **at** ∼: zu Hause; **be/feel at** ∼ (fig.) sich wohl fühlen; **make yourself at** ∼: fühl dich wie zu Hause **(b)** (institution) Heim, *das* **2** *adj.* **(a)** Haus- **(b)** (Sport) Heim-; ∼ **match** Heimspiel, *das* **3** *adv.* nach Hause

**home:** ∼ **address** *n.* Privatanschrift, *die;* ∼ **ˈbanking** *n.* Homebanking, *das;* ∼**-based** /ˈhəʊmbeɪst/ *adj.* zu Hause arbeiten; **be** ∼**-based** zu Hause arbeiten; seinen Arbeitsplatz zu Hause haben; ∼**coming** *n.* Heimkehr, *die;* ∼ **comˈputer** *n.* Heimcomputer, *der;* ∼ **ˈground** *n.* on ∼ ground auf heimischem Boden; (fig.) zu Hause (ugs.); ∼**-grown** *adj.* selbst gezogen; ∼**land** *n.* Heimat, *die*

**ˈhomeless 1** *adj.* obdachlos **2** *n. pl.* **the** ∼: die Obdachlosen *Pl.*

**ˈhomelessness** *n.* Obdachlosigkeit, *die*

**ˈhomely** /ˈhəʊmlɪ/ *adj.* wohnlich ⟨*Zimmer usw.*⟩; behaglich ⟨*Atmosphäre*⟩

**home:** ∼**-made** *adj.* selbst gemacht; selbst gebacken ⟨*Brot*⟩; hausgemacht ⟨*Lebensmittel*⟩; **H∼ Office** *n.* (Brit.) Innenministerium, *das*

**homeopathic** etc. (Amer.) ▶ HOMOEO-

**home:** ∼**owner** *n.* Eigenheimbesitzer, *der/*-besitzerin, *die;* ∼ **page** *n.* (Comp.) Homepage, *die;* **H∼ ˈSecretary** *n.* (Brit.) Innenminister, *der;* ∼ **ˈshopping** *n.* Teleshopping, *das;* ∼**sick** *adj.* heimwehkrank; **become/be** ∼**sick** Heimweh bekommen/haben; ∼**sickness** *n.* Heimweh, *das;* ∼ **ˈtown** *n.* Heimatstadt, *die;* ∼**work** *n.* Hausaufgaben *Pl.;* **piece of** ∼**work** Hausaufgabe, *die*

**homicide** /ˈhɒmɪsaɪd/ *n.* Tötung, *die;* (manslaughter) Totschlag, *der*

**homoeopathic** /həʊmɪəˈpæθɪk, hɒmɪəˈpæθɪk/ *adj.* homöopathisch

**homoeopathy** /həʊmɪˈɒpəθɪ, hɒmɪˈɒpəθɪ/ *n.* Homöopathie, *die*

**homosexual** /həʊməʊˈseksjʊəl/ **1** *adj.* homosexuell **2** *n.* Homosexuelle, *der/die*

**homosexuˈality** *n.* Homosexualität, *die*

**hone** /həʊn/ *v.t.* wetzen

**honest** /ˈɒnɪst/ *adj.* ehrlich

**ˈhonestly** *adv.* ehrlich; redlich ⟨*handeln*⟩; ∼! ehrlich!; (annoyed) also wirklich!

**honesty** /ˈɒnɪstɪ/ *n.* Ehrlichkeit, *die*

**honey** /ˈhʌnɪ/ *n.* Honig, *der*

**honey:** ∼ **bee** *n.* Honigbiene, *die;* ∼**comb** *n.* Honigwabe, *die;* ∼**moon** *n.* Flitterwochen *Pl.;* (journey) Hochzeitsreise, *die;* ∼**suckle** *n.* Geißblatt, *das*

**honk** /hɒŋk/ **1** *v.i.* ⟨*Fahrzeug, Fahrer:*⟩ hupen **2** *n.* Hupen, *das*

**honor, honorable** (Amer.) ▶ HONOUR, HONOURABLE

**honorary** /ˈɒnərərɪ/ *adj.* Ehren⟨*mitglied, -präsident, -doktor, -bürger*⟩

**honour** /ˈɒnə(r)/ (Brit.) **1** *n.* **(a)** Ehre, *die* **(b)** (distinction) Auszeichnung, *die* **2** *v.t.* ehren; (Commerc.) honorieren

**honourable** /ˈɒnərəbl/ *adj.* (Brit.) ehrenwert (geh.)

**ˈhonours degree** *n.* Examen mit Auszeichnung

**hood** /hʊd/ *n.* **(a)** Kapuze, *die* **(b)** (Amer. Motor Veh.) Motorhaube, *die* **(c)** (of pram) Verdeck, *das*

**hoodlum** /ˈhuːdləm/ *n.* Rowdy, *der*

**hoodwink** /ˈhʊdwɪŋk/ *v.t.* hinters Licht führen

**hoof** /huːf/ *n., pl.* ∼**s** or **hooves** /huːvz/ Huf, *der*

**hook** /hʊk/ **1** *n.* Haken, *der;* **by** ∼ **or by crook** mit allen Mitteln **2** *v.t.* **(a)** (grasp) mit Haken/mit einem Haken greifen **(b)** (fasten) mit Haken/mit einem Haken befestigen (**to** an + *Dat.*) **(c)** **be** ∼**ed** [**on sth.**] (addicted) [von etw.] abhängig sein; (harmlessly) auf etw. (*Akk.*) stehen (ugs.)

■ **hook ˈup** *v.t.* festhaken (**to** an + *Akk.*)

**hooligan** /ˈhuːlɪgən/ *n.* Rowdy, *der*

**hooliganism** /ˈhuːlɪgənɪzm/ *n.* Rowdytum, *das*

**hoop** /huːp/ *n.* Reifen, *der*

**hooray** /hʊˈreɪ/ *int.* hurra

**hoot** /huːt/ **1** *v.i.* **(a)** (call out) johlen **(b)** ⟨*Eule:*⟩ schreien **(c)** ⟨*Fahrzeug, Fahrer:*⟩ hupen **2** *n.* **(a)** (shout) ∼**s of derision** verächtliches Gejohle **(b)** (of owl) Schrei, *der* **(c)** (of vehicle) Hupen, *das* '**hooter** *n.* (Brit.: siren) Sirene, *die*

**hoover** /'hu:və(r)/ (Brit.) ① *n.* (a) H~ ®
[Hoover]staubsauger, *der*
(b) (made by any company) Staubsauger, *der*
② *v.t.* staubsaugen

**hooves** *pl. of* HOOF

**hop**¹ /hɒp/ *n.* (a) (plant) Hopfen, *der*
(b) *in pl.* (Brewing) Hopfen, *der*

**hop**² ① *v.i.,* -pp-: (a) hüpfen; ⟨Hase:⟩
hoppeln
(b) (fig. coll.) ~ out of bed aus dem Bett
springen; ~ into the car/on [to] the bus/train
sich ins Auto/in den Bus/Zug schwingen
(ugs.)
② *v.t.,* -pp- (Brit. coll.) ~ it sich verziehen
(ugs.)
③ *n.* (a) Hüpfer, *der*
(b) (Brit. coll.) catch sb. on the ~: jmdn.
überraschen

**hope** /həʊp/ ① *n.* Hoffnung, *die;* sb.'s ~[s]
of sth. jmds. Hoffnung auf etw. (*Akk.*); raise
sb.'s ~s jmdm. Hoffnung machen
② *v.i. & t.* hoffen (for auf + *Akk.*); I ~ so/not
hoffentlich/hoffentlich nicht; ~ for the best
das Beste hoffen

**hopeful** /'həʊpfl/ *adj.* (a) zuversichtlich; be
~ of sth./of doing sth. auf etw. (*Akk.*) hoffen/
voller Hoffnung sein, etw. zu tun
(b) (promising) viel versprechend

'**hopefully** *adv.* (a) (expectantly) voller
Hoffnung
(b) (coll.: it is hoped that) hoffentlich

'**hopeless** *adj.,* '**hopelessly** *adv.* (a)
hoffnungslos
(b) (inadequate) miserabel

'**hopelessness** *n.* Hoffnungslosigkeit, *die*

**hopscotch** /'hɒpskɒtʃ/ *n.* Himmel-und-
Hölle-Spiel, *das*

**horde** /hɔ:d/ *n.* Horde, *die*

**horizon** /hə'raɪzn/ *n.* Horizont, *der;* on the
~: am Horizont; (fig.) broaden one's/sb.'s ~s
seinen/jmds. Horizont erweitern

**horizontal** /hɒrɪ'zɒntl/ *adj.* horizontal;
waagerecht

**hori'zontally** *adv.* horizontal; (flat)
waagerecht

**hormone** /'hɔ:məʊn/ *n.* Hormon, *das*

**hormone re'placement therapy** *n.*
Hormonsubstitutionstherapie, *die*

**horn** /hɔ:n/ *n.* Horn, *das;* (of vehicle) Hupe, *die*

**hornet** /'hɔ:nɪt/ *n.* Hornisse, *die*

'**horny** *adj.* (hard) hornig

**horoscope** /'hɒrəskəʊp/ *n.* Horoskop, *das*

**horrendous** /hə'rendəs/ *adj.* (coll.)
schrecklich (ugs.)

**horrible** /'hɒrɪbl/ *adj.* grauenhaft; grausig
⟨Monster⟩; grauenvoll ⟨Verbrechen,
Albtraum⟩

**horrid** /'hɒrɪd/ *adj.* scheußlich

**horrific** /hə'rɪfɪk/ *adj.* schrecklich

**horrify** /'hɒrɪfaɪ/ *v.t.* mit Schrecken
erfüllen; be horrified (shocked, scandalized)
entsetzt sein (at, by über + *Akk.*)

'**horrifying** *adj.* grauenhaft

**horror** /'hɒrə(r)/ ① *n.* Entsetzen, *das* (at
über + *Akk.*); (repugnance) Grausen, *das;*
(horrifying thing) Gräuel, *der*
② *attrib. adj.* Horror-; ~ film/story
Horrorfilm, *der*/-geschichte, *die*

'**horror-stricken,** '**horror-struck** *adjs.*
von Entsetzen gepackt

**hors d'œuvre** /ɔ:'dɜ:vr/ *n.* Horsd'œuvre,
*das;* ≈ Vorspeise, *die*

**horse** /hɔ:s/ *n.* Pferd, *das*

**horse:** ~**back** *n.* on ~back zu Pferd;
~ '**chestnut** *n.* Rosskastanie, *die;* ~**fly** *n.*
Pferdebremse, *die;* ~**man** /'hɔ:smən/ *n.,* pl.
~**men** /'hɔ:smən/ ([skilled] rider) [guter] Reiter;
~**play** *n.* Balgerei, *die;* ~**power** *n.,* pl.
same (Mech.) Pferdestärke, *die;* ~**racing** *n.*
Pferderennsport, *der;* ~**radish** *n.*
Meerrettich, *der;* ~**shoe** *n.* Hufeisen, *das*

**horticulture** /'hɔ:tɪkʌltʃə(r)/ *n.* Gartenbau,
*der*

**hose** /həʊz/, '**hosepipe** *ns.* Schlauch, *der*

**hospice** /'hɒspɪs/ *n.* (Brit.: for the terminally ill)
Sterbehospiz, *das*

**hospitable** /hɒ'spɪtəbl/ *adj.* gastfreundlich
⟨Person, Wesensart⟩; be ~ to sb. jmdn.
gastfreundlich aufnehmen

**hospital** /'hɒspɪtl/ *n.* Krankenhaus, *das;* in
~ (Brit.), in the ~ (Amer.) im Krankenhaus

'**hospital bed** *n.* Krankenhausbett, *das*

**hospitality** /hɒspɪ'tælɪtɪ/ *n.*
Gastfreundschaft, *die*

'**hospital nurse** *n.* ≈ Krankenschwester,
*die*

**host**¹ /həʊst/ *n.* (large number) Menge, *die;* a
~ of people/children eine Menge Leute/eine
Schar von Kindern

**host**² *n.* Gastgeber, *der*/-geberin, *die*

**hostage** /'hɒstɪdʒ/ *n.* Geisel, *die*

'**host country** *n.* Gastland, *das*

**hostel** /'hɒstl/ *n.* (Brit.) Wohnheim, *das*

**hostess** /'həʊstɪs/ *n.* Gastgeberin, *die;* (in
nightclub) Animierdame, *die*

**hostile** /'hɒstaɪl/ *adj.* (a) feindlich
(b) (unfriendly) feindselig (to[wards]
gegenüber); be ~ to sth. etw. ablehnen

**hostility** /hɒ'stɪlɪtɪ/ *n.* Feindseligkeit, *die*

**hot** /hɒt/ *adj.* (a) heiß; warm ⟨Mahlzeit,
Essen⟩; I am/feel ~: mir ist heiß
(b) (pungent) scharf ⟨Gewürz, Senf usw.⟩;
scharf gewürzt ⟨Essen⟩
(c) (recent) noch warm ⟨Nachrichten⟩
(d) (coll.: illegally obtained) heiß ⟨Ware, Geld⟩

**hot:** ~ '**air** *n.* (coll.) leeres Gerede (ugs.);
~**bed** *n.* (Hort.) Mistbeet, *das;* (fig.: of vice,
corruption) Brutstätte, *die* (of für)

**hotchpotch** /'hɒtʃpɒtʃ/ *n.* Mischmasch,
*der* (ugs.) (of aus)

**hot:** ~-**desking** *n.:* Mehrfachnutzung von
Arbeitsplätzen; ~ **dog** *n.* (coll.) Hotdog, *der*
od. *das*

**hotel** /həʊ'tel/ *n.* Hotel, *das*

**hotelier** /hə'telɪə(r)/ *n.* Hotelier, *der*

**ho'tel room** *n.* Hotelzimmer, *das*

**hot:** ∼**head** *n.* Hitzkopf, *der;* ∼**house** *n.*
Treibhaus, *das;* ∼ **line** *n.* Hotline, *die;*
(Polit.) heißer Draht

**'hotly** *adv.* heftig

**hot:** ∼**plate** *n.* Kochplatte, *die;* (to keep food
∼) Warmhalteplatte, *die;* ∼ **seat** *n.* (coll.)
be in the ∼ **seat** den Kopf hinhalten müssen
(ugs.); ∼**-tempered** *adj.* heißblütig;
∼**-'water bottle** *n.* Wärmflasche, *die*

**hound** /haʊnd/ ⟦1⟧ *n.* Jagdhund, *der*
⟦2⟧ *v.t.* verfolgen

**hour** /'aʊə(r)/ *n.* (a) Stunde, *die;* half an ∼:
eine halbe Stunde; **an** ∼ **and a half**
anderthalb Stunden; **be paid by the** ∼:
stundenweise bezahlt werden; **the**
**24-**∼ **clock** die Vierundzwanzigstundenuhr
(b) (time o'clock) Zeit, *die;* **the small** ∼**s** [**of the**
**morning**] die frühen Morgenstunden; **0100/**
**0200/1700/1800** ∼**s** (on 24-∼ clock) 1.00/2.00/
17.00/18.00 Uhr

**'hourly** *adj., adv.* stündlich; **be paid** ∼:
stundenweise bezahlt werden

**house** ⟦1⟧ /haʊs/ *n., pl.* ∼**s** /'haʊzɪz/ Haus,
*das;* **to/at my** ∼: zu mir [nach Hause]/bei
mir [zu Hause]
⟦2⟧ /haʊz/ *v.t.* (a) ein Heim geben (+ *Dat.*)
(b) (keep, store) unterbringen

**house**/haʊs/**:** ∼ **arrest** *n.* Hausarrest,
*der;* ∼**boat** *n.* Hausboot, *das;* ∼**-bound**
*adj.* ans Haus gefesselt

**household** /'haʊshəʊld/ *n.* Haushalt, *der;*
*attrib.* Haushalts-

**'householder** *n.* Wohnungsinhaber, *der/*
-inhaberin, *die*

**household 'name** *n.* geläufiger Name; **be**
**a** ∼: ein Begriff sein

**house** /haʊs/**:** ∼ **husband** *n.* Hausmann,
*der;* ∼**keeper** *n.* Haushälterin, *die;*
∼**keeping** *n.* Hauswirtschaft, *die;*
∼ **plant** *n.* Zimmerpflanze, *die;* ∼**-proud**
*adj.* he/she is ∼**-proud** Ordnung und
Sauberkeit [im Haushalt] gehen ihm/ihr
über alles; ∼**-sit** *v.i.* das Haus hüten;
∼**-sitter** *n.* Housesitter, *der* (ugs.); *Person,*
*die für jemanden das Haus hütet;*
∼**-trained** *adj.* (Brit.) stubenrein ⟨*Hund,*
*Katze*⟩; ∼**-warming** *n.* ∼**-warming** [**party**]
Einzugsfeier, *die;* ∼**wife** *n.* Hausfrau, *die;*
∼**work** *n.* Hausarbeit, *die*

**housing** /'haʊzɪŋ/ *n.* (dwellings) Wohnungen
*Pl.;* ( provision of dwellings)
Wohnungsbeschaffung, *die*

**housing:** ∼ **association** *n.* (Brit.)
Gesellschaft für sozialen Wohnungsbau;
∼ **benefit** *n.* (Brit.) Wohngeld, *das;*
∼ **estate** *n.* (Brit.) Wohnsiedlung, *die;*
∼ **shortage** *n.* Wohnraummangel, *der*

**hovel** /'hɒvl/ *n.* [armselige] Hütte

**hover** /'hɒvə(r)/ *v.i.* (a) schweben
(b) (linger) sich herumdrücken (ugs.)

**'hovercraft** *n., pl. same* Hovercraft, *das;*
Luftkissenfahrzeug, *das*

**'hover mower** *n.* Luftkissenmäher, *der*

**how** /haʊ/ *adv.* wie; **learn** ∼ **to ride a bike/**
**swim** Rad fahren/schwimmen lernen; ∼ **'are**
**you?** wie geht es dir?; (greeting) guten
Morgen/Tag/Abend!; ∼ **do you 'do?** (formal)
guten Morgen/Tag/Abend!; ∼ **much?**
wieviel?; ∼ **many?** wie viel?; wie viele?

**however** /haʊ'evə(r)/ *adv.* **(a)** wie ... auch
**(b)** (nevertheless) jedoch; aber

**howl** /haʊl/ ⟦1⟧ *n.* (of animal) Heulen, *das;* (of
distress) Schrei, *der;* ∼**s of laughter**
brüllendes Gelächter
⟦2⟧ *v.i.* ⟨*Tier, Wind:*⟩ heulen; (with distress)
schreien
⟦3⟧ *v.t.* [hinaus]schreien

**howler** /'haʊlə(r)/ *n.* (coll.: blunder) Schnitzer,
*der* (ugs.)

**HP** *abbr.* (Brit.) = **hire purchase**

**HQ** *abbr.* = **headquarters** HQ

**HTML** *abbr.* (Comp.) = **hypertext**
**markup language** HTML

**hub** /hʌb/ *n.* [Rad]nabe, *die;* (fig.)
Mittelpunkt, *der*

**hubbub** /'hʌbʌb/ *n.* Lärm, *der;* **a** ∼ **of**
**voices** ein Stimmengewirr

**hub:** ∼**cap** *n.* Radkappe, *die;* ∼ **dynamo**
*n.* Nabendynamo, *der;* ∼ **gear** *n.*
Nabenschaltung, *die*

**huddle** /'hʌdl/ *v.i.* sich drängen; ∼ **together**
sich zusammendrängen
■ **huddle 'up** *v.i.* (nestle up) sich
zusammenkauern; (crowd together) sich
[zusammen]drängen

**hue**[1] /hju:/ *n.* Farbton, *der*

**hue**[2] *n.* ∼ **and cry** lautes Geschrei; ( protest)
Gezeter, *das*

**huff** /hʌf/ ⟦1⟧ *v.i.* ∼ **and puff** schnaufen und
keuchen
⟦2⟧ *n.* **in a** ∼: beleidigt

**hug** /hʌg/ ⟦1⟧ *n.* Umarmung, *die;* **give sb. a**
∼: jmdn. umarmen
⟦2⟧ *v.t.,* -gg- umarmen

**huge** /hju:dʒ/ *adj.* riesig; gewaltig
⟨*Unterschied, Verbesserung, Interesse*⟩

**hulking** /'hʌlkɪŋ/ *adj.* (coll.) ∼ **great** klobig

**hull** /hʌl/ *n.* (Naut.) Schiffskörper, *der*

**hum** /hʌm/ ⟦1⟧ *v.i.,* -mm-: (a) summen;
⟨*Maschine:*⟩ brummen
(b) ∼ **and haw** (coll.) herumdrucksen (ugs.)
⟦2⟧ *v.t.,* -mm- summen
⟦3⟧ *n.* (a) Summen, *das;* (of machinery)
Brummen, *das*
(b) (of voices, conversation) Gemurmel, *das;* (of
traffic) Brausen, *das*

**human** /'hju:mən/ ⟦1⟧ *adj.* menschlich; **the**
∼ **race** die menschliche Rasse
⟦2⟧ *n.* Mensch, *der*

**human 'being** *n.* Mensch, *der*

**humane** /hju:'meɪn/ *adj.* human

**humanitarian** /hju:mænɪ'teərɪən/ *adj.*
humanitär

**humanity** /hjuːˈmænɪtɪ/ n. (a) (mankind)
Menschheit, die; (people collectively) Menschen
Pl.
(b) (being humane) Humanität, die
**human 'rights** n. pl. Menschenrechte Pl.;
~ rights group Menschenrechtsorganisation,
die
**humble** /ˈhʌmbl/ [1] adj. (a) demütig
(b) (modest) bescheiden
(c) (low-ranking) einfach; niedrig ⟨Status, Rang
usw.⟩
[2] v.t. (a) demütigen; ~ oneself sich
demütigen od. erniedrigen
(b) (defeat decisively) [vernichtend] schlagen
**humbly** /ˈhʌmblɪ/ adv. demütig
**humdrum** /ˈhʌmdrʌm/ adj. alltäglich;
eintönig ⟨Leben⟩
**humid** /ˈhjuːmɪd/ adj. feucht
**humidifier** /hjuːˈmɪdɪfaɪə(r)/ n.
Luftbefeuchter, der
**humidify** /hjuːˈmɪdɪfaɪ/ v.t. befeuchten
**humidity** /hjuːˈmɪdɪtɪ/ n. Feuchtigkeit, die
**humiliate** /hjuːˈmɪlɪeɪt/ v.t. demütigen
**humiliation** /hjuːmɪlɪˈeɪʃn/ n. Demütigung,
die
**humility** /hjuːˈmɪlɪtɪ/ n. Demut, die
**humor** (Amer.) ▶ HUMOUR
**humorous** /ˈhjuːmərəs/ adj. lustig,
komisch ⟨Geschichte, Name, Situation⟩;
witzig ⟨Bemerkung⟩
**humour** /ˈhjuːmə(r)/ (Brit.) [1] n. (a) Humor,
der; sense of ~: Sinn für Humor; have no
sense of ~: keinen Humor haben
(b) (mood) Laune, die
[2] v.t. ~ sb. jmdm. seinen Willen lassen
**hump** /hʌmp/ [1] n. (a) (of person) Buckel,
der; (of animal) Höcker, der
(b) (mound) Hügel, der
[2] v.t. (Brit. coll.: carry) schleppen
**humpback 'bridge** n. gewölbte Brücke
**hunch¹** /hʌntʃ/ v.t. ~ [up] hochziehen
**hunch²** n. (feeling) Gefühl, das
**'hunchback** n. (back) Buckel, der; (person)
Bucklige, der/die; be a ~: einen Buckel
haben
**hundred** /ˈhʌndrəd/ [1] adj. hundert; a or
one ~: [ein]hundert; two/several ~:
zweihundert/mehrere hundert; a or one
~ and one hundert[und]eins
[2] n. (a) (number) hundert; a or one/two ~:
[ein]hundert/zweihundert
(b) (written figure; group) Hundert, das
(c) (indefinite amount) ~s Hunderte. See also
EIGHT
**hundredth** /ˈhʌndrədθ/ [1] adj.
hundertst...; a ~ part ein Hundertstel
[2] n. (fraction) Hundertstel, das; (in sequence,
rank) Hundertste, der/die/das
**'hundredweight** n., pl. same (Brit.) 50,8 kg;
≈ Zentner, der
**hung** ▶ HANG 1, 2
**Hungarian** /hʌŋˈgeərɪən/ [1] adj.
ungarisch; sb. is ~: jmd. ist Ungar/Ungarin

[2] n. (a) (person) Ungar, der/Ungarin, die
(b) (language) Ungarisch, das; see also
ENGLISH 2A
**Hungary** /ˈhʌŋgərɪ/ pr. n. Ungarn (das)
**hunger** /ˈhʌŋgə(r)/ [1] n. Hunger, der
[2] v.i. ~ after or for sb./sth. [heftiges]
Verlangen nach jmdm./etw. haben
**'hunger strike** n. Hungerstreik, der; go
on ~: in den Hungerstreik treten
**hung 'over** adj. (coll.) verkatert (ugs.)
**hungry** /ˈhʌŋgrɪ/ adj. hungrig; be ~:
Hunger haben; go ~: hungern
**hunk** /hʌŋk/ n. [großes] Stück
**hunt** /hʌnt/ [1] n. Jagd, die; (search) Suche,
die
[2] v.t. jagen; (search for) Jagd machen auf
(+ Akk.) ⟨Mörder usw.⟩
[3] v.i. jagen; go ~ing auf die Jagd gehen;
~ after or for Jagd machen auf (+ Akk.);
(seek) suchen
**'hunter** n. Jäger, der
**'hunting** n. die Jagd (of auf + Akk.);
(searching) Suche, die (for nach)
**hurdle** /ˈhɜːdl/ n. Hürde, die
**hurl** /hɜːl/ v.t. werfen; (violently) schleudern;
~ insults at sb. jmdm. Beleidigungen ins
Gesicht schleudern
**hurly-burly** /ˈhɜːlɪbɜːlɪ/ n. Tumult, der; the
~ of city life der Großstadttrummel (ugs.)
**hurrah** /hʊˈrɑː/, **hurray** /hʊˈreɪ/ int. hurra
**hurricane** /ˈhʌrɪkən/ n. (tropical cyclone)
Hurrikan, der; (storm, lit. or fig.) Orkan, der
**hurried** /ˈhʌrɪd/ adj. eilig; überstürzt
⟨Abreise⟩; in Eile ausgeführt ⟨Arbeit⟩
**hurry** /ˈhʌrɪ/ [1] n. Eile, die; in a ~: eilig; be
in a ~: es eilig haben; there's no ~: es eilt
nicht
[2] v.t. antreiben ⟨Person⟩; hinunterschlingen
⟨Essen⟩; ~ one's work seine Arbeit in zu
großer Eile erledigen
[3] v.i. sich beeilen; (to or from place) eilen
■ **hurry 'up** [1] v.i. sich beeilen
[2] v.t. antreiben
**hurt** /hɜːt/ [1] v.t., **hurt** (a) wehtun (+ Dat.);
(injure) verletzen; ~ oneself sich (Dat.) weh
tun; (injure oneself) sich verletzen; ~ one's
arm/back sich (Dat.) am Arm/Rücken
wehtun; (injure) sich (Dat.) den Arm/am
Rücken verletzen
(b) (damage, be detrimental to) schaden (+ Dat.)
(c) (upset) verletzen ⟨Person, Stolz⟩
[2] v.i., **hurt** (a) wehtun
(b) (cause damage, be detrimental) schaden
[3] adj. gekränkt ⟨Tonfall, Miene⟩
[4] n. (emotional pain) Schmerz, der
**hurtful** /ˈhɜːtfl/ adj. verletzend
**hurtle** /ˈhɜːtl/ v.i. rasen (ugs.)
**husband** /ˈhʌzbənd/ n. Ehemann, der; my/
your/her ~: mein/dein/ihr Mann; ~ and wife
Mann und Frau
**hush** /hʌʃ/ [1] n. (silence) Schweigen, das;
(stillness) Stille, die

2 *v.t.* (silence) zum Schweigen bringen; (still) beruhigen
3 *v.i.* still sein; ∼! still!
■ **hush 'up** *v.t.* vertuschen
**husk** /hʌsk/ *n.* Spelze, *die*
**husky¹** /'hʌskɪ/ *adj.* heiser
**husky²** *n.* Eskimohund, *der*
**hustle** /'hʌsl/ 1 *v.t.* drängen (**into** zu)
2 *n.* ∼ **and bustle** geschäftiges Treiben
**hut** /hʌt/ *n.* Hütte, *die*
**hutch** /hʌtʃ/ *n.* Stall, *der*
**hyacinth** /'haɪəsɪnθ/ *n.* Hyazinthe, *die*
**hybrid** /'haɪbrɪd/ 1 *n.* Hybride, *die od. der* (**between** aus); (fig.: mixture) Mischung, *die*
2 *adj.* hybrid ⟨*Züchtung*⟩
**hydrangea** /haɪ'dreɪndʒə/ *n.* Hortensie, *die*
**hydrant** /'haɪdrənt/ *n.* Hydrant, *der*
**hydraulic** /haɪ'drɔːlɪk/ *adj.* hydraulisch
**hydrochloric acid** /haɪdrəklɔːrɪk 'æsɪd/ *n.* Salzsäure, *die*
**hydroelectric** /haɪdrəʊɪ'lektrɪk/ *adj.* hydroelektrisch; ∼ **power station** Wasserkraftwerk, *das*
**hydrofoil** /'haɪdrəfɔɪl/ *n.* Tragflächenboot, *das*
**hydrogen** /'haɪdrədʒən/ *n.* Wasserstoff, *der*
**'hydrogen bomb** *n.* Wasserstoffbombe, *die*
**hyena** /haɪ'iːnə/ *n.* Hyäne, *die*
**hygiene** /'haɪdʒiːn/ *n.* Hygiene, *die*
**hygienic** /haɪ'dʒiːnɪk/ *adj.* hygienisch
**hymn** /hɪm/ *n.* Hymne, *die;* (sung in service) Kirchenlied, *das*
**'hymn book** *n.* Gesangbuch, *das*
**hyper** /'haɪpə(r)/ *adj.* (coll.) aufgedreht (ugs.)
**hyperactive** /haɪpə'ræktɪv/ *adj.* überaktiv
**hyperbole** /haɪ'pɜːbəlɪ/ *n.* Hyperbel, *die*
**hyper:** ∼**link** *n.* (Comp.) Hyperlink, *der;* ∼**market** *n.* (Brit.) Verbrauchermarkt, *der;* ∼**text** *n.* (Comp.) Hypertext, *der;* ∼**'ventilate** *v.i.* hyperventilieren

**hyphen** /'haɪfn/ 1 *n.* Bindestrich, *der*
2 *v.t.* mit Bindestrich schreiben
**hyphenate** /'haɪfəneɪt/ ▶ HYPHEN 2
**hyphenation** /haɪfə'neɪʃn/ *n.* Kopplung, *die*
**hypnosis** /hɪp'nəʊsɪs/ *n., pl.* **hypnoses** /hɪp'nəʊsiːz/ Hypnose, *die;* (act, process) Hypnotisierung, *die;* **under** ∼: in Hypnose (*Dat.*)
**hypnotic** /hɪp'nɒtɪk/ *adj.* hypnotisch
**hypnotism** /'hɪpnətɪzm/ *n.* Hypnotik, *die;* (act) Hypnotisieren, *das*
**hypnotist** /'hɪpnətɪst/ *n.* Hypnotiseur, *der/* Hypnotiseurin, *die*
**hypnotize** /'hɪpnətaɪz/ *v.t.* hypnotisieren
**hypochondria** /haɪpə'kɒndrɪə/ *n.* Hypochondrie, *die*
**hypochondriac** /haɪpə'kɒndrɪæk/ *n.* Hypochonder, *der*
**hypocrisy** /hɪ'pɒkrɪsɪ/ *n.* Heuchelei, *die*
**hypocrite** /'hɪpəkrɪt/ *n.* Heuchler, *der/* Heuchlerin, *die*
**hypocritical** /hɪpə'krɪtɪkl/ *adj.* heuchlerisch
**hypodermic** /haɪpə'dɜːmɪk/ *adj. & n.* ∼ [**syringe**] Injektionsspritze, *die*
**hypotenuse** /haɪ'pɒtənjuːz/ *n.* Hypotenuse, *die*
**hypothermia** /haɪpə'θɜːmɪə/ *n.* (Med.) Hypothermie, *die* (fachspr.); Unterkühlung, *die*
**hypothesis** /haɪ'pɒθɪsɪs/ *n., pl.* **hypotheses** /haɪ'pɒθɪsiːz/ Hypothese, *die*
**hypothetical** /haɪpə'θetɪkl/ *adj.* hypothetisch
**hysterectomy** /hɪstə'rektəmɪ/ *n.* (Med.) Hysterektomie, *die* (fachspr.)
**hysteria** /hɪ'stɪərɪə/ *n.* Hysterie, *die*
**hysterical** /hɪ'sterɪkl/ *adj.* hysterisch
**hysterics** /hɪ'sterɪks/ *n. pl.* (laughter) hysterischer Lachanfall; (crying) hysterischer Weinkrampf; **have** ∼: hysterisch lachen/ weinen

# I i

**I¹, i** /aɪ/ *n.* I, i, *das*
**I²** *pron.* ich
**ice** /aɪs/ 1 *n.* (a) Eis, *das;* **feel/be like** ∼ (be very cold) eiskalt sein
(b) (∼ cream) [Speise]eis, *das;* **an** ∼/**two** ∼**s** ein/zwei Eis
2 *v.t.* glasieren ⟨*Kuchen*⟩
■ **ice 'over, ice 'up** *v.i.* ⟨*Gewässer:*⟩ zufrieren

**'ice age** *n.* Eiszeit, *die*
**iceberg** /'aɪsbɜːg/ *n.* Eisberg, *der*
**ice:** ∼**box** *n.* (Amer.) Kühlschrank, *der;* ∼ **bucket** *n.* Eisbehälter, *der;* ∼**cold** *adj.* eiskalt; ∼ **'cream** *n.* Eis, *das;* Eiscreme, *die;* **one** ∼ **cream/two/too many** ∼ **creams** ein/zwei/zu viel Eis; ∼ **'cream parlour** *n.* Eisdiele, *die;* ∼ **cube** *n.* ···❖

Eiswürfel, *die;* ~ **hockey** *n.* Eishockey, *das*

**Iceland** /'aɪslənd/ *pr. n.* Island (*das*)

**Icelandic** /aɪs'lændɪk/ 1 *adj.* isländisch
2 *n.* Isländisch, *das; see also* ENGLISH 2A

**ice:** ~ '**lolly** *n.* Eis am Stiel; ~ **rink** *n.* Eisbahn, *die;* ~ **skate** *n.* Schlittschuh, *der;* ~-**skate** *v.i.* Schlittschuh laufen; ~ **skating** *n.* Schlittschuhlaufen, *das*

**icicle** /'aɪsɪkl/ *n.* Eiszapfen, *der*

**icing** /'aɪsɪŋ/ *n.* Zuckerguss, *der*

'**icing sugar** *n.* (Brit.) Puderzucker, *der*

**icon** /'aɪkɒn/ *n.* (a) Ikone, *die*
(b) (Comp.) Icon, *das*

**icy** /'aɪsɪ/ *adj.* (a) vereist ⟨*Berge, Landschaft, Straße*⟩; eisreich ⟨*Region, Land*⟩; in ~ **conditions** bei Eis
(b) (very cold) eiskalt; eisig; (fig.) frostig

**I'd** /aɪd/ (a) = I had;
(b) = I would

**idea** /aɪ'dɪə/ *n.* Idee, *die;* Gedanke, *der;* (mental picture) Vorstellung, *die;* (vague notion) Ahnung, *die;* **have you any** ~ [**of**] **how ...?** weißt du ungefähr, wie ...?; **have no** ~ [**of**] **where ...:** keine Ahnung haben, wo ...; **not have the slightest** *or* **faintest** ~: nicht die leiseste Ahnung haben

**ideal** /aɪ'dɪəl/ 1 *adj.* ideal; vollendet ⟨*Ehemann, Gastgeber*⟩; vollkommen ⟨*Welt*⟩
2 *n.* Ideal, *das*

**idealism** /aɪ'dɪəlɪzm/ *n.* Idealismus, *der*

**idealist** /aɪ'dɪəlɪst/ *n.* Idealist, *der/* Idealistin, *die*

**idealistic** /aɪdɪə'lɪstɪk/ *adj.* idealistisch

**idealize** /aɪ'dɪəlaɪz/ *v.t.* idealisieren

**ideally** /aɪ'dɪəlɪ/ *adv.* ideal; ~, ...: idealerweise *od.* im Idealfall ...

**identical** /aɪ'dentɪkl/ *adj.* identisch; **be** ~: sich (*Dat.*) völlig gleichen; ~ **twins** eineiige Zwillinge

**identification** /aɪdentɪfɪ'keɪʃn/ *n.* Identifizierung, *die;* (of plants, animals) Bestimmung, *die*

**identifi'cation parade** *n.* (Brit.) Gegenüberstellung [zur Identifizierung], *die*

**identify** /aɪ'dentɪfaɪ/ 1 *v.t.* identifizieren; bestimmen ⟨*Pflanze, Tier*⟩
2 *v.i.* ~ **with sb.** sich mit jmdm. identifizieren

**Identikit** ® /aɪ'dentɪkɪt/ *n.* Phantombild, *das*

**identity** /aɪ'dentɪtɪ/ *n.* Identität, *die;* **proof of** ~: Identitätsnachweis, *der;* [**case of**] **mistaken** ~: [Personen]verwechslung, *die*

**identity:** ~ **card** *n.* [Personal]ausweis, *der;* ~ **crisis** *n.* Identitätskrise, *die;* ~ **parade** ▶ IDENTIFICATION PARADE

**ideological** /aɪdɪə'lɒdʒɪkl/ *adj.* ideologisch

**ideology** /aɪdɪ'ɒlədʒɪ/ *n.* Ideologie, *die*

**idiocy** /'ɪdɪəsɪ/ *n.* Idiotie, *die*

**idiom** /'ɪdɪəm/ *n.* [Rede]wendung, *die*

**idiomatic** /ɪdɪə'mætɪk/ *adj.* idiomatisch

**idiosyncrasy** /ɪdɪə'sɪŋkrəsɪ/ *n.* Eigentümlichkeit, *die*

**idiosyncratic** /ɪdɪəsɪŋ'krætɪk/ *adj.* eigenwillig

**idiot** /'ɪdɪət/ *n.* Idiot, *der* (ugs.)

**idiotic** /ɪdɪ'ɒtɪk/ *adj.* idiotisch (ugs.)

**idle** /'aɪdl/ 1 *adj.* (a) (lazy) faul
(b) (not in use) außer Betrieb *nachgestellt;* **be** ~ ⟨*Maschinen, Fabrik:*⟩ stillstehen
(c) bloß ⟨*Neugier, Spekulation*⟩; leer ⟨*Geschwätz*⟩
2 *v.i.* ⟨*Motor:*⟩ leer laufen

■ **idle a'way** *v.t.* vertun

'**idleness** *n.* Faulheit, *die*

**idol** /'aɪdl/ *n.* Idol, *das*

**idolize** /'aɪdəlaɪz/ *v.t.* vergöttern

**idyllic** /ɪ'dɪlɪk/ *adj.* idyllisch

**i.e.** /aɪ'i:/ *abbr.* = **that is** d.h.; i.e.

**if** /ɪf/ *conj.* (a) wenn; **if anyone should ask ...:** falls jemand fragt, ...; **if I knew what to do ...:** wenn ich wüsste, was ich tun soll ...; **if I were you** an deiner Stelle; **if so/not** wenn ja/ nein *od.* nicht; **if then/that/at all** wenn überhaupt; **as if** als ob; **if I only knew, if only I knew!** wenn ich das nur wüsste!; **if it isn't Ronnie!** das ist doch Ronnie!
(b) (whenever) [immer] wenn
(c) (whether) ob
(d) (though) auch *od.* selbst wenn
(e) (despite being) wenn auch

**iffish** /'ɪfɪʃ/, **iffy** /'ɪfɪ/ *adjs.* (coll.) ungewiss; zweifelhaft

**igloo** /'ɪglu:/ *n.* Iglu, *der od. das*

**ignite** /ɪg'naɪt/ 1 *v.t.* anzünden
2 *v.i.* sich entzünden

**ignition** /ɪg'nɪʃn/ *n.* (a) (igniting) Zünden, *das*
(b) (Motor Veh.) Zündung, *die;* ~ **key** Zündschlüssel, *der*

**ignorance** /'ɪgnərəns/ *n.* Unwissenheit, *die;* **keep sb. in** ~ **of sth.** jmdn. in Unkenntnis über etw. (*Akk.*) lassen

**ignorant** /'ɪgnərənt/ *adj.* unwissend; **be** ~ **of sth.** (uninformed) über etw. (*Akk.*) nicht informiert sein

**ignore** /ɪg'nɔ:(r)/ *v.t.* ignorieren; nicht befolgen ⟨*Befehl, Rat*⟩; übergehen ⟨*Frage, Bemerkung*⟩

**ill** /ɪl/ 1 *adj.,* **worse** /wɜ:s/, **worst** /wɜ:st/ krank; **fall** ~: krank werden
2 *adv.* **be** ~ **at ease** sich nicht wohl fühlen
3 *n.* Übel, *das*

**I'll** /aɪl/ (a) = I shall;
(b) = I will

'**ill-advised** *adj.* unklug

**illegal** /ɪ'li:gl/ *adj.,* **il'legally** *adv.* illegal

**il'legal immigrant** *n.* illegaler Einwanderer/illegale Einwanderin

**illegality** /ɪlɪ'gælɪtɪ/ *n.* Ungesetzlichkeit, *die*

**illegible** /ɪ'ledʒɪbl/ *adj.* unleserlich

**illegitimate** /ɪlɪ'dʒɪtɪmət/ *adj.* unehelich ⟨*Kind*⟩

**ill 'health** n. schwache Gesundheit

**illicit** /ɪˈlɪsɪt/ adj. unerlaubt ⟨Beziehung, [Geschlechts]verkehr⟩; Schwarz⟨handel, -verkauf, -arbeit⟩

**'ill-informed** adj. schlecht informiert

**illiteracy** /ɪˈlɪtərəsɪ/ n. Analphabetentum, das

**illiterate** /ɪˈlɪtərət/ adj. des Lesens und Schreibens unkundig; analphabetisch ⟨Bevölkerung⟩

**illness** /ˈɪlnɪs/ n. Krankheit, die

**illogical** /ɪˈlɒdʒɪkl/ adj. unlogisch

**ill-'treat** v.t. misshandeln

**ill-'treatment** n. Misshandlung, die

**illuminate** /ɪˈluːmɪneɪt/ v.t. beleuchten

**illuminating** /ɪˈluːmɪneɪtɪŋ/ adj. aufschlussreich

**illumination** /ɪluːmɪˈneɪʃn/ n. Beleuchtung, die

**illusion** /ɪˈluːʒn/ n. Illusion, die; be under the ~ that ...: sich (Dat.) einbilden, dass ...

**illusory** /ɪˈluːsərɪ/ adj. illusorisch

**illustrate** /ˈɪləstreɪt/ v.t. (a) (serve as example of) veranschaulichen
**(b)** illustrieren ⟨Buch, Erklärung⟩

**illustration** /ɪləˈstreɪʃn/ n. (a) (example) Beispiel, das (of für)
**(b)** (picture) Abbildung, die

**illustrious** /ɪˈlʌstrɪəs/ adj. berühmt ⟨Person⟩

**ill 'will** n. Böswilligkeit, die

**I'm** /aɪm/ = I am

**image** /ˈɪmɪdʒ/ n. (a) Bildnis, das (geh.)
**(b)** (Optics) Bild, das
**(c)** [public] ~: Image, das

**'image-conscious** adj. imagebewusst

**imaginable** /ɪˈmædʒɪnəbl/ adj. the best solution ~: die denkbar beste Lösung

**imaginary** /ɪˈmædʒɪnərɪ/ adj. imaginär (geh.); eingebildet ⟨Krankheit⟩

**imagination** /ɪmædʒɪˈneɪʃn/ n. (a) Fantasie, die
**(b)** (fancy) Einbildung, die

**imaginative** /ɪˈmædʒɪnətɪv/ adj. fantasievoll; (showing imagination) einfallsreich

**imagine** /ɪˈmædʒɪn/ v.t. (a) sich (Dat.) vorstellen
**(b)** (suppose) glauben
**(c)** (get the impression) ~ that ...: sich (Dat.) einbilden[, dass ...]

**imbalance** /ɪmˈbæləns/ n. Unausgeglichenheit, die

**imbecile** /ˈɪmbɪsiːl/ n. Idiot, der (ugs.)

**IMF** abbr. = **International Monetary Fund** IWF, der

**imitate** /ˈɪmɪteɪt/ v.t. nachahmen

**imitation** /ɪmɪˈteɪʃn/ n. (a) Nachahmung, die
**(b)** (counterfeit) Imitation, die

**immaculate** /ɪˈmækjʊlət/ adj. (spotless) makellos; (faultless) tadellos

**immaterial** /ɪməˈtɪərɪəl/ adj. unerheblich

**immature** /ɪməˈtjʊə(r)/ adj. unreif; noch nicht voll entwickelt ⟨Lebewesen⟩

**immaturity** /ɪməˈtjʊərɪtɪ/ n. Unreife, die

**immediate** /ɪˈmiːdjət/ adj. **(a)** unmittelbar; (nearest) nächst... ⟨Nachbar[schaft], Umgebung, Zukunft⟩; engst... ⟨Familie⟩
**(b)** (occurring at once) prompt; unverzüglich ⟨Handeln, Maßnahmen⟩; umgehend ⟨Antwort⟩

**im'mediately** [1] adv. **(a)** unmittelbar
**(b)** (without delay) sofort
[2] conj. sobald

**immemorial** /ɪmɪˈmɔːrɪəl/ adj. **from time ~:** seit undenklichen Zeiten

**immense** /ɪˈmens/ adj. **(a)** ungeheuer
**(b)** (coll.: great) enorm

**im'mensely** adv. **(a)** ungeheuer
**(b)** (coll.: very much) unheimlich (ugs.)

**immerse** /ɪˈmɜːs/ v.t. [ein]tauchen; **be ~d in thought/one's work** in Gedanken versunken/in seine Arbeit vertieft sein

**immersion** /ɪˈmɜːʃn/ n. Eintauchen, das

**im'mersion heater** n. Heißwasserbereiter, der

**immigrant** /ˈɪmɪgrənt/ [1] n. Einwanderer, der/Einwanderin, die
[2] adj. Einwanderer-; ~ **workers** ausländische Arbeitnehmer Pl.

**immigration** /ɪmɪˈgreɪʃn/ n. Einwanderung die (into nach, from aus); attrib. Einwanderungs⟨kontrolle, -gesetz⟩; ~ **officer** Beamter/Beamtin der Einwanderungsbehörde; ~ **authorities** Einwanderungsbehörden Pl.; **go through ~:** durch die Passkontrolle gehen

**imminent** /ˈɪmɪnənt/ adj. unmittelbar bevorstehend; drohend ⟨Gefahr⟩; **be ~:** unmittelbar bevorstehen/drohen

**immobile** /ɪˈməʊbaɪl/ adj. (immovable) unbeweglich

**immobilize** /ɪˈməʊbɪlaɪz/ v.t. verankern; (fig.) lähmen

**immobilizer** /ɪˈməʊbɪlaɪzə(r)/ n. (Motor Veh.) Wegfahrsperre, die

**immodest** /ɪˈmɒdɪst/ adj. unbescheiden; (improper) unanständig

**immoral** /ɪˈmɒrəl/ adj. unmoralisch; (in sexual matters) sittenlos

**immorality** /ɪməˈrælɪtɪ/ n. Unmoral, die; (in sexual matters) Sittenlosigkeit, die

**immortal** /ɪˈmɔːtl/ adj. unsterblich

**immortality** /ɪmɔːˈtælɪtɪ/ n. Unsterblichkeit, die

**immortalize** /ɪˈmɔːtəlaɪz/ v.t. unsterblich machen

**immovable** /ɪˈmuːvəbl/ adj. unbeweglich; **be ~:** sich nicht bewegen lassen

**immune** /ɪˈmjuːn/ adj. **(a)** (exempt) sicher (from vor + Dat.)
**(b)** (not susceptible) unempfindlich (to gegen) ···⟩

**(c)** (Med.) immun (**to** gegen); ~ **system** Immunsystem, *das*

**immunity** /ɪˈmjuːnɪtɪ/ *n.* **(a)** diplomatic ~: diplomatische Immunität

**(b)** (Med.) Immunität, *die*

**immunization** /ɪmjʊnaɪˈzeɪʃn/ *n.* Immunisierung, *die*

**immunize** /ˈɪmjʊnaɪz/ *v.t.* immunisieren

**immunodeficiency** /ɪˈmjuːnəʊdɪfɪʃənsɪ/ *n.* Immunschwäche, *die*

**immunology** /ɪmjʊˈnɒlədʒɪ/ *n.* Immunologie, *die*

**immutable** /ɪˈmjuːtəbl/ *adj.* unveränderlich

**imp** /ɪmp/ *n.* **(a)** Kobold, *der* **(b)** (fig.: child) Racker, *der* (fam.)

**impact** /ˈɪmpækt/ *n.* **(a)** Aufprall, *der* (**on**, **against** auf + *Akk.*); (collision) Zusammenprall, *der* **(b)** (fig.) Wirkung, *die*

**impair** /ɪmˈpeə(r)/ *v.t.* beeinträchtigen; schaden (+ *Dat.*) ⟨*Gesundheit*⟩

**impale** /ɪmˈpeɪl/ *v.t.* aufspießen

**impart** /ɪmˈpɑːt/ *v.t.* **(a)** (give) [ab]geben (**to** an + *Akk.*) **(b)** (communicate) kundtun (geh.) (**to** *Dat.*); vermitteln ⟨*Kenntnisse*⟩ (**to** *Dat.*)

**impartial** /ɪmˈpɑːʃl/ *adj.* unparteiisch; gerecht ⟨*Entscheidung, Urteil*⟩

**impassable** /ɪmˈpɑːsəbl/ *adj.* unpassierbar (**to** für); (to vehicles) unbefahrbar (**to** für)

**impasse** /ˈæmpɑːs/ *n.* Sackgasse, *die*

**impassive** /ɪmˈpæsɪv/ *adj.* ausdruckslos

**impatience** /ɪmˈpeɪʃəns/ *n.* Ungeduld, *die* (**at** über + *Akk.*)

**impatient** /ɪmˈpeɪʃənt/ *adj.* ungeduldig; ~ **at sth./with sb.** ungeduldig über etw. (*Akk.*)/mit jmdm.

**im'patiently** *adv.* ungeduldig

**impeccable** /ɪmˈpekəbl/ *adj.* makellos; tadellos ⟨*Manieren*⟩

**impeccably** /ɪmˈpekəblɪ/ *adv.* tadellos; makellos ⟨*rein*⟩

**impede** /ɪmˈpiːd/ *v.t.* behindern

**impediment** /ɪmˈpedɪmənt/ *n.* **(a)** Hindernis, *das* (**to** für) **(b)** (speech defect) Sprachfehler, *der*

**impel** /ɪmˈpel/ *v.t.*, **-ll-** treiben; **feel** ~**led to do sth.** sich genötigt *od.* gezwungen fühlen, etw. zu tun

**impending** /ɪmˈpendɪŋ/ *adj.* bevorstehend

**impenetrable** /ɪmˈpenɪtrəbl/ *adj.* undurchdringlich (**by, to** für)

**imperative** /ɪmˈperətɪv/ **1** *adj.* dringend erforderlich **2** *n.* (Ling.) Imperativ, *der*

**imperceptible** /ɪmpəˈseptɪbl/ *adj.* nicht wahrnehmbar; (very slight or gradual) unmerklich

**imperfect** /ɪmˈpɜːfɪkt/ **1** *adj.* **(a)** (incomplete) unvollständig **(b)** (faulty) mangelhaft

**2** *n.* (Ling.) Imperfekt, *das*

**imperfection** /ɪmpəˈfekʃn/ *n.* **(a)** (incompleteness) Unvollständigkeit, *die* **(b)** (fault) Mangel, *der*

**im'perfectly** *adv.* **(a)** (incompletely) unvollständig **(b)** (faultily) fehlerhaft

**imperial** /ɪmˈpɪərɪəl/ *adj.* kaiserlich

**imperialism** /ɪmˈpɪərɪəlɪzm/ *n.* Imperialismus, *der*

**imperil** /ɪmˈperɪl/ *v.t.*, (Brit.) **-ll-** gefährden

**imperious** /ɪmˈpɪərɪəs/ *adj.* herrisch

**impermeable** /ɪmˈpɜːmɪəbl/ *adj.* undurchlässig

**impersonal** /ɪmˈpɜːsənl/ *adj.* unpersönlich

**impersonate** /ɪmˈpɜːsəneɪt/ *v.t.* sich ausgeben als; (to entertain) imitieren; nachahmen

**impersonator** /ɪmˈpɜːsəneɪtə(r)/ *n.* (entertainer) Imitator, *der*/Imitatorin, *die*

**impertinence** /ɪmˈpɜːtɪnəns/ *n.* Unverschämtheit, *die*

**impertinent** /ɪmˈpɜːtɪnənt/ *adj.* unverschämt

**imperturbable** /ɪmpəˈtɜːbəbl/ *adj.* gelassen; **be completely** ~: durch nichts zu erschüttern sein

**impervious** /ɪmˈpɜːvɪəs/ *adj.* undurchlässig; **be** ~ **to sth.** (fig.) unempfänglich für etw. sein

**impetuous** /ɪmˈpetjʊəs/ *adj.* unüberlegt; impulsiv ⟨*Person*⟩

**impetus** /ˈɪmpɪtəs/ *n.* **(a)** Kraft, *die* **(b)** (fig.) Motivation, *die*

**impinge** /ɪmˈpɪndʒ/ *v.i.* ~ **on sth.** auf etw. (*Akk.*) Einfluss nehmen

**'impish** *adj.* lausbübisch

**implacable** /ɪmˈplækəbl/ *adj.* unversöhnlich; erbittert ⟨*Gegner*⟩

**implausible** /ɪmˈplɔːzɪbl/ *adj.* unglaubwürdig

**implement 1** /ˈɪmplɪmənt/ *n.* Gerät, *das* **2** /ˈɪmplɪment/ *v.t.* [in die Tat] umsetzen ⟨*Politik, Plan usw.*⟩

**implicate** /ˈɪmplɪkeɪt/ *v.t.* belasten; **be** ~**d in a scandal** in einen Skandal verwickelt sein

**implication** /ɪmplɪˈkeɪʃn/ *n.* Implikation, *die*; **by** ~: implizit

**implicit** /ɪmˈplɪsɪt/ *adj.* **(a)** (implied) implizit (geh.); unausgesprochen ⟨*Drohung, Zweifel*⟩ **(b)** (resting on authority) unbedingt; blind ⟨*Vertrauen*⟩

**implicitly** /ɪmˈplɪsɪtlɪ/ *adv.* **(a)** (by implication) implizit (geh.) **(b)** (unquestioningly) blind ⟨*vertrauen, gehorchen usw.*⟩

**implode** /ɪmˈpləʊd/ *v.i.* implodieren

**implore** /ɪmˈplɔː(r)/ *v.t.* anflehen (**for** um)

**imply** /ɪmˈplaɪ/ *v.t.* **(a)** implizieren (geh.); (say indirectly) hindeuten auf (+ *Akk.*) **(b)** (insinuate) unterstellen

**impolite** /ɪmpə'laɪt/ *adj.* unhöflich

**import** ① /ɪm'pɔːt/ *v.t.* importieren, einführen ⟨*Waren*⟩ (**from** aus, **into** nach) ② /'ɪmpɔːt/ *n.* (a) (process) Import, *der* (b) (article) Importgut, *das*

**importance** /ɪm'pɔːtəns/ *n.* Wichtigkeit, *die* (**to** für); (significance) Bedeutung, *die;* **be of** ~: wichtig sein; **full of one's own** ~: von seiner eigenen Wichtigkeit überzeugt

**important** /ɪm'pɔːtənt/ *adj.* wichtig (**to** für); (significant) bedeutend

**'import duty** *n.* Einfuhrzoll, *der*

**im'porter** *n.* Importeur, *der*

**impose** /ɪm'pəʊz/ *v.t.* auferlegen (geh.) ⟨*Bürde, Verpflichtung*⟩ ([**up**]**on** *Dat.*); erheben ⟨*Steuer*⟩ (**on** auf + *Akk.*); verhängen ⟨*Kriegsrecht*⟩; anordnen ⟨*Rationierung*⟩ ∎ **im'pose on** *v.t.* ausnutzen ⟨*Gutmütigkeit, Toleranz usw.*⟩; ~ **on sb.** sich jmdm. aufdrängen

**imposing** /ɪm'pəʊzɪŋ/ *adj.* imposant

**imposition** /ɪmpə'zɪʃn/ *n.* (a) Auferlegung, *die;* (of tax) Erhebung, *die* (b) (unreasonable demand) Zumutung, *die*

**impossibility** /ɪmpɒsɪ'bɪlɪtɪ/ *n.* Unmöglichkeit, *die*

**impossible** /ɪm'pɒsɪbl/ *adj.,* **impossibly** /ɪm'pɒsɪblɪ/ *adv.* unmöglich

**impostor** /ɪm'pɒstə(r)/ *n.* Hochstapler, *der*/-staplerin, *die;* (swindler) Betrüger, *der*/ Betrügerin, *die*

**impotence** /'ɪmpətəns/ *n.* (a) (powerlessness) Machtlosigkeit, *die* (b) (lack of sexual power) Impotenz, *die*

**impotent** /'ɪmpətənt/ *adj.* (a) (powerless) machtlos (b) (lacking in sexual power; in popular use: sterile) impotent

**impound** /ɪm'paʊnd/ *v.t.* beschlagnahmen

**impoverished** /ɪm'pɒvərɪʃt/ *adj.* **be**/ **become** ~: verarmt sein/verarmen

**impracticable** /ɪm'præktɪkəbl/ *adj.* undurchführbar

**impractical** /ɪm'præktɪkl/ *adj.* (a) (unpractical) unpraktisch (b) ▶ IMPRACTICABLE

**imprecise** /ɪmprɪ'saɪs/ *adj.* ungenau

**impregnable** /ɪm'pregnəbl/ *adj.* uneinnehmbar ⟨*Festung, Bollwerk*⟩; (fig.) unanfechtbar ⟨*Ruf, Stellung*⟩

**impregnate** /'ɪmpregneɪt/ *v.t.* imprägnieren

**impress** /ɪm'pres/ *v.t.* beeindrucken; *abs.* Eindruck machen; **be** ~**ed by** *or* **with sth.** von etw. beeindruckt sein ∎ **im'press** [**up**]**on** *v.t.* einschärfen (+ *Dat.*); ~ **sth.** [**up**]**on sb.'s memory** jmdm. etw. einschärfen

**impression** /ɪm'preʃn/ *n.* (a) Eindruck, *der;* **form an** ~ **of sb.** sich (*Dat.*) ein Bild von jmdm. machen (b) (impersonation) **do an** ~ **of sb.** jmdn. imitieren; **do** ~**s** andere Leute imitieren

**impressionable** *adj.* beeinflussbar

**impressionist** /ɪm'preʃənɪst/ *n.* Impressionist, *der*/Impressionistin, *die*

**impressive** /ɪm'presɪv/ *adj.* beeindruckend; imponierend

**imprint** ① /'ɪmprɪnt/ *n.* Abdruck, *der;* (fig.) Stempel, *der* ② /ɪm'prɪnt/ *v.t.* aufdrucken; (fig.) einprägen (**on** *Dat.*)

**imprison** /ɪm'prɪzn/ *v.t.* in Haft nehmen; **be** ~**ed** sich in Haft befinden

**im'prisonment** *n.* Haft, *die;* **a long term of** ~: eine lange Haftstrafe

**improbable** /ɪm'prɒbəbl/ *adj.* unwahrscheinlich

**impromptu** /ɪm'prɒmptjuː/ ① *adj.* improvisiert; **an** ~ **speech** eine Stegreifrede ② *adv.* aus dem Stegreif

**improper** /ɪm'prɒpə(r)/ *adj.* (a) (wrong) unrichtig (b) (unseemly) unpassend; (indecent) unanständig

**im'properly** *adv.* ▶ IMPROPER: unrichtig; unpassend; unanständig

**improvable** /ɪm'pruːvəbl/ *adj.* verbesserungsfähig

**improve** /ɪm'pruːv/ ① *v.i.* besser werden; ⟨*Person, Wetter:*⟩ sich bessern ② *v.t.* verbessern ③ *v. refl.* ~ **oneself** sich weiterbilden ∎ **im'prove** [**up**]**on** *v.t.* überbieten ⟨*Rekord, Angebot*⟩; verbessern ⟨*Leistung*⟩

**improvement** /ɪm'pruːvmənt/ *n.* Verbesserung, *die* (**on, over** gegenüber); **make** ~**s to sth.** Verbesserungen an etw. (*Dat.*) vornehmen

**improvisation** /ɪmprəvaɪ'zeɪʃn/ *n.* Improvisieren, *das*

**improvise** /'ɪmprəvaɪz/ *v.t.* improvisieren

**imprudent** /ɪm'pruːdənt/ *adj.* unklug; (showing rashness) unbesonnen

**impudence** /'ɪmpjʊdəns/ *n.* Unverschämtheit, *die;* (brazenness) Dreistigkeit, *die*

**impudent** /'ɪmpjʊdənt/ *adj.,* **impudently** *adv.* unverschämt; (brazen[ly]) dreist

**impulse** /'ɪmpʌls/ *n.* Impuls, *der;* **on [an]** ~: impulsiv

**'impulse buying** *n.* Spontankäufe *Pl.*

**impulsive** /ɪm'pʌlsɪv/ *adj.* impulsiv

**impunity** /ɪm'pjuːnɪtɪ/ *v.t.* **with** ~: ungestraft

**impure** /ɪm'pjʊə(r)/ *adj.* unrein

**impurity** /ɪm'pjʊərɪtɪ/ *n.* Unreinheit, *die;* (foreign body) Fremdstoff, *der*

**impute** /ɪm'pjuːt/ *v.t.* zuschreiben (**to** *Dat.*)

**in** /ɪn/ ① *prep.* (position; also fig.) in (+ *Dat.*); (into) in (+ *Akk.*); **in this heat** bei dieser Hitze; **two feet in diameter** mit einem Durchmesser von zwei Fuß; **there are three feet in a yard** ein Yard hat drei Fuß; **draw in** ⋯⋗

crayon/ink mit Kreide/Tinte zeichnen; pay in pounds/dollars in Pfund/Dollars bezahlen; in fog/rain etc. bei Nebel/Regen usw.; in the 20th century im 20. Jahrhundert; 4 o'clock in the morning/afternoon 4 Uhr morgens/abends; in 1990 [im Jahre] 1990; in three minutes/years in drei Minuten/Jahren; in doing this, he ...: indem er das tut/tat, ... er ...; in that ...: insofern als...

**2** adv. (a) (inside) hinein⟨gehen usw.⟩; herein⟨kommen usw.⟩
(b) (at home, work, etc.) be in da sein
(c) have it in for sb. es auf jmdn. abgesehen haben (ugs.); sb. is in for sth. (about to undergo) jmdm. steht etw. bevor
**3** adj. (coll.: in fashion) in (ugs.)
**4** n. know the ins and outs of sth. sich in einer Sache genau auskennen

**in.** abbr. = **inch[es]**

**ina'bility** n. Unfähigkeit, die

**inaccessible** /ɪnək'sesɪbl/ adj. unzugänglich

**in'accuracy** n. (a) (incorrectness) Unrichtigkeit, die
(b) (imprecision) Ungenauigkeit, die

**in'accurate** adj. (a) (incorrect) unrichtig
(b) (imprecise) ungenau

**in'active** adj. untätig

**inac'tivity** n. Untätigkeit, die

**inadequacy** /ɪn'ædɪkwəsɪ/ n. (a) Unzulänglichkeit, die
(b) (incompetence) mangelnde Eignung

**in'adequate** adj. unzulänglich; (incompetent) ungeeignet; feel ∼: sich überfordert fühlen

**inadvertent** /ɪnəd'vɜːtənt/ adj., **inad'vertently** adv. versehentlich

**inad'visable** adj. nicht ratsam

**inane** /ɪn'eɪn/ adj. dümmlich

**in'animate** adj. unbelebt

**inap'plicable** adj. nicht zutreffend

**inap'propriate** adj. unpassend

**in'apt** adj. unpassend

**inar'ticulate** adj. (a) she's rather/very ∼: sie kann sich ziemlich schlecht/sehr schlecht ausdrücken
(b) (indistinct) unverständlich

**inat'tentive** adj. unaufmerksam (to gegenüber)

**in'audible** adj. unhörbar

**inau'spicious** adj. (ominous) unheilvoll; (unlucky) unglücklich

**'inborn** adj. angeboren (in Dat.)

**'in-box** n. (Comp.) Inbox, die; Posteingang, der

**in'bred** adj. they are/have become ∼: bei ihnen herrscht Inzucht

**in'breeding** n. Inzucht, die

**'inbuilt** adj. jmdm./einer Sache eigen

**Inc.** abbr. (Amer.) = **Incorporated** e. G.

**incalculable** /ɪn'kælkjʊləbl/ adj. (very great) unermesslich

**in'capable** adj. (a) be ∼ of doing sth. außerstande sein, etw. zu tun; be ∼ of sth. zu etw. unfähig sein
(b) be ∼ of nicht zulassen ⟨Beweis, Messung usw.⟩

**incapacitate** /ɪnkə'pæsɪteɪt/ v.t. unfähig machen

**incarcerate** /ɪn'kɑːsəreɪt/ v.t. einkerkern (geh.)

**incarceration** /ɪnkɑːsə'reɪʃn/ n. Einkerkerung, die (geh.)

**incendiary** /ɪn'sendɪərɪ/ adj. & n. ∼ device Brandsatz, der; ∼ [bomb] Brandbombe, die

**incense¹** /'ɪnsens/ n. Weihrauch, der

**incense²** /ɪn'sens/ v.t. erzürnen

**incentive** /ɪn'sentɪv/ n. Anreiz, der

**incessant** /ɪn'sesənt/ adj., **in'cessantly** adv. unablässig

**incest** /'ɪnsest/ n. Inzest, der

**incestuous** /ɪn'sestjʊəs/ adj. inzestuös

**inch** /ɪntʃ/ **1** n. Inch, der; Zoll, der (veralt.)
**2** v.t. & i. ∼ [one's way] forward sich Zoll für Zoll vorwärts bewegen

**incident** /'ɪnsɪdənt/ n. (a) (notable event) Vorfall, der
(b) (clash) Zwischenfall, der

**incidental** /ɪnsɪ'dentl/ adj. beiläufig ⟨Bemerkung⟩; Neben⟨ausgaben, -einnahmen⟩

**incidentally** /ɪnsɪ'dentəlɪ/ adv. nebenbei [bemerkt]

**inci'dental music** n. Begleitmusik, die

**incinerate** /ɪn'sɪnəreɪt/ v.t. verbrennen

**incinerator** /ɪn'sɪnəreɪtə(r)/ n. Verbrennungsofen, der

**incision** /ɪn'sɪʒn/ n. Einschnitt, der

**incisive** /ɪn'saɪsɪv/ adj. schneidend ⟨Ton⟩; scharf ⟨Verstand⟩; scharfsinnig ⟨Kritik, Frage, Bemerkung, Argument⟩

**incite** /ɪn'saɪt/ v.t. anstiften; aufstacheln ⟨Massen, Volk⟩

**in'citement** n. Anstiftung, die/ Aufstachelung, die

**incl.** abbr. = **including** inkl.

**inclination** /ɪnklɪ'neɪʃn/ n. Neigung, die

**incline** **1** /ɪn'klaɪn/ v.t. (a) (bend) neigen
(b) (dispose) veranlassen
**2** v.i. (be disposed) neigen (to[wards] zu)
**3** /'ɪnklaɪn/ n. Steigung, die

**inclined** /ɪn'klaɪnd/ adj. geneigt; they are ∼ to be slow sie neigen zur Langsamkeit; if you feel [so] ∼: wenn Sie Lust [dazu] haben

**include** /ɪn'kluːd/ v.t. einschließen; (contain) enthalten; ∼d in the price im Preis inbegriffen

**including** /ɪn'kluːdɪŋ/ prep. einschließlich (+ Gen.); ∼ VAT inklusive Mehrwertsteuer

**inclusion** /ɪn'kluːʒn/ n. Aufnahme, die

**inclusive** /ɪn'kluːsɪv/ adj. einschließlich; be ∼ of sth. etw. einschließen; from 2 to 6 January ∼: vom 2. bis einschließlich 6. Januar; cost £50 ∼: 50 Pfund kosten, alles inbegriffen

**incognito** /ɪnkɒgˈniːtəʊ/ *adj., adv.*
inkognito

**inco'herent** *adj.* zusammenhanglos

**income** /ˈɪnkəm/ *n.* Einkommen, *das*

**income: ~ bracket, ~ group** *ns.*
Einkommensklasse, *die;* ~ **sup'port** *n.*
(Brit.) zusätzliche Hilfe zum Lebensunterhalt;
~ **tax** *n.* Einkommensteuer, *die;* (on wages,
salary) Lohnsteuer, *die*

**'incoming** *adj.* ankommend; landend
⟨Flugzeug⟩; einfahrend ⟨Zug⟩; eingehend
⟨Telefongespräch, Auftrag⟩

**incomings** /ˈɪnkʌmɪŋz/ *n. pl.* (revenue,
income) Einnahmen *Pl.*

**in'comparable** *adj.* unvergleichlich

**incom'patible** *adj.* unvereinbar; be ~
⟨Menschen:⟩ nicht zueinander passen

**in'competence** /ɪnˈkɒmpɪtəns/ *n.*
Unfähigkeit, *die;* Unvermögen, *das*

**in'competent** *adj.* unfähig

**incom'plete** *adj.* unvollständig

**incompre'hensible** *adj.* unbegreiflich;
unverständlich ⟨Rede, Argument⟩

**incon'ceivable** *adj.* unvorstellbar

**incon'clusive** *adj.* ergebnislos; nicht
schlüssig ⟨Beweis, Argument⟩

**incongruous** /ɪnˈkɒŋgrʊəs/ *adj.*
unpassend

**inconsequential** /ɪnkɒnsɪˈkwenʃl/ *adj.*
belanglos

**incon'siderate** *adj.* rücksichtslos

**incon'sistency** *n.* ▸ INCONSISTENT:
Widersprüchlichkeit, *die;* Inkonsequenz, *die;*
Unbeständigkeit, *die*

**incon'sistent** *adj.* widersprüchlich;
(illogical) inkonsequent; (irregular) unbeständig

**inconsolable** /ɪnkənˈsəʊləbl/ *adj.*
untröstlich

**incon'spicuous** *adj.* unauffällig

**incontinence** /ɪnˈkɒntɪnəns/ *n.* (Med.)
Inkontinenz, *die*

**incontinent** /ɪnˈkɒntɪnənt/ *adj.* (Med.)
inkontinent; be ~: an Inkontinenz leiden

**incontrovertible** /ɪnkɒntrəˈvɜːtəbl/ *adj.*
unbestreitbar; unwiderlegbar ⟨Beweis⟩

**incon'venience** ① *n.*
Unannehmlichkeiten *Pl.* (to für); put sb. to a
lot of ~: jmdm. große Unannehmlichkeiten
bereiten
② *v.t.* Unannehmlichkeiten bereiten
(+ Dat.); (disturb) stören

**incon'venient** *adj.* unbequem; ungünstig
⟨Lage, Standort⟩; come at an ~ time zu
ungelegener Zeit kommen; be ~ for sb.
jmdm. nicht passen

**incorporate** /ɪnˈkɔːpəreɪt/ *v.t.* aufnehmen
(in[to], with in + Akk.)

**incorporated** /ɪnˈkɔːpəreɪtɪd/ *adj.*
eingetragen ⟨[Handels]gesellschaft⟩

**incor'rect** *adj.* (a) unrichtig; be ~: nicht
stimmen; it is ~ to say that ...: es stimmt
nicht, dass ...

(b) (improper) inkorrekt

**incor'rectly** *adv.* (a) unrichtigerweise;
falsch ⟨beantworten, aussprechen⟩
(b) (improperly) inkorrekt

**incorrigible** /ɪnˈkɒrɪdʒɪbl/ *adj.*
unverbesserlich

**increase** ① /ɪnˈkriːs/ *v.i.* zunehmen;
⟨Lärm:⟩ größer werden; ⟨Preise, Nachfrage:⟩
steigen; ~ **in weight/size/price** schwerer/
größer/teurer werden
② *v.t.* (a) (make greater) erhöhen
(b) (intensify) verstärken
③ /ˈɪnkriːs/ *n.* Zunahme, *die* (in Gen.); be on
the ~: ständig zunehmen

**increasing** /ɪnˈkriːsɪŋ/ *adj.* steigend; an
~ **number of people** mehr und mehr
Menschen

**in'creasingly** *adv.* in zunehmendem
Maße; become ~ **apparent** immer deutlicher
werden

**in'credible** *adj.* (also coll.: remarkable)
unglaublich

**in'credibly** *adv.* (also coll.: remarkably)
unglaublich

**incredulity** /ɪnkrɪˈdjuːlɪtɪ/ *n.*
Ungläubigkeit, *die*

**incredulous** /ɪnˈkredjʊləs/ *adj.* ungläubig

**increment** /ˈɪnkrɪmənt/ *n.* Erhöhung, *die;*
(amount of growth) Zuwachs, *der*

**incriminate** /ɪnˈkrɪmɪneɪt/ *v.t.* belasten

**incubate** /ˈɪŋkjʊbeɪt/ *v.t.* bebrüten; (to
hatching) ausbrüten

**incubation** /ɪŋkjʊˈbeɪʃn/ *n.* Bebrütung, *die*

**incubator** /ˈɪŋkjʊbeɪtə(r)/ *n.* Inkubator,
*der;* (for babies also) Brutkasten, *der*

**incur** /ɪnˈkɜː(r)/ *v.t.*, **-rr-** sich (Dat.) zuziehen
⟨Unwillen, Ärger⟩; ~ **debts/expenses/risks**
Schulden machen/Ausgaben haben/Risiken
eingehen

**in'curable** *adj.* unheilbar

**incurably** /ɪnˈkjʊərəblɪ/ *adv.* unheilbar
⟨krank⟩

**incursion** /ɪnˈkɜːʃn/ *n.* Eindringen, *das;* (by
sudden attack) Einfall, *der*

**indebted** /ɪnˈdetɪd/ *pred. adj.* be [much]
~ **to sb. for sth.** jmdm. für etw. [sehr] zu
Dank verpflichtet sein

**in'decency** *n.* Unanständigkeit, *die*

**in'decent** *adj.*, **in'decently** *adv.*
unanständig

**indecipherable** /ɪndɪˈsaɪfərəbl/ *adj.*
unentzifferbar

**inde'cision** *n.* Unentschlossenheit, *die*

**inde'cisive** *adj.* (a) ergebnislos ⟨Streit,
Diskussion⟩; nichtssagend ⟨Ergebnis⟩
(b) (hesitating) unentschlossen

**indeed** /ɪnˈdiːd/ *adv.* (a) in der Tat; thank
you very much ~: haben Sie vielen
herzlichen Dank; ~ **it is** in der Tat
(b) (in fact) ja sogar; ~, **he can ...**: ja, er
kann sogar ...
(c) (admittedly) zugegebenermaßen

**indefatigable** /ɪndɪˈfætɪɡəbl/ adj.
unermüdlich

**indefensible** /ɪndɪˈfensɪbl/ adj. (intolerable)
unverzeihlich

**in'definite** adj. (a) (vague) unbestimmt
(b) (unlimited) unbegrenzt

**in'definitely** adv. (a) (vaguely) unbestimmt
(b) (unlimitedly) unbegrenzt; auf unbestimmte
Zeit ⟨verschieben⟩

**indelible** /ɪnˈdelɪbl/ adj. unauslöschlich;
~ ink Wäschetinte, die

**indelibly** /ɪnˈdelɪblɪ/ adv. unauslöschlich

**indemnify** /ɪnˈdemnɪfaɪ/ v.t. absichern
(against gegen); (compensate) entschädigen

**indemnity** /ɪnˈdemnɪtɪ/ n. Absicherung,
die; (compensation) Entschädigung, die

**indentation** /ɪndenˈteɪʃn/ n. (a) (indenting,
notch) Einkerbung, die
(b) (recess) Einschnitt, der

**inde'pendence** n. Unabhängigkeit, die

**inde'pendent** adj., **inde'pendently**
adv. unabhängig (of von)

**indescribable** /ɪndɪˈskraɪbəbl/ adj.
unbeschreiblich

**indestructible** /ɪndɪˈstrʌktɪbl/ adj.
unzerstörbar

**indeterminable** /ɪndɪˈtɜ:mɪnəbl/ adj.
unbestimmbar

**indeterminate** /ɪndɪˈtɜ:mɪnət/ adj.
unbestimmt; unklar ⟨Konzept⟩

**index** /ˈɪndeks/ ① n. Register, das
② v.t. mit einem Register versehen

**index:** ~**card** n. Karteikarte, die;
~ **finger** n. Zeigefinger, der; ~ **gears** pl.
Indexschaltung, die; ~**linked** adj. (Econ.)
indexiert; dynamisch ⟨Rente⟩; ~ **number**
n. Indexzahl, die

**India** /ˈɪndɪə/ n. Indien (das)

**Indian** /ˈɪndɪən/ ① adj. (a) indisch; sb. is
~: jmd. ist Inder/Inderin
(b) [American] ~: indianisch
② n. (a) Inder, der/Inderin, die
(b) [American] ~: Indianer, der/Indianerin,
die

**Indian:** ~ **'Ocean** pr. n. Indischer Ozean;
~ **'summer** n. Altweibersommer, der

**indicate** /ˈɪndɪkeɪt/ ① v.t. (a) (be a sign of)
erkennen lassen
(b) (state briefly) andeuten
(c) (mark, point out) anzeigen
(d) (suggest, make evident) zum Ausdruck
bringen (to gegenüber)
② v.i. (Motor Veh.) blinken

**indication** /ɪndɪˈkeɪʃn/ n. [An]zeichen, das
(of Gen., für)

**indicative** /ɪnˈdɪkətɪv/ ① adj. (a) be ~ of
sth. auf etw. (Akk.) schließen lassen
(b) (Ling.) indikativisch
② n. (Ling.) Indikativ, der

**indicator** /ˈɪndɪkeɪtə(r)/ n. (on vehicle)
Blinker, der

**indict** /ɪnˈdaɪt/ v.t. anklagen (for, on a
charge of Gen.)

**indie** /ˈɪndɪ/ (coll.) ① adj. Indie-⟨Gruppe,
Szene, Charts etc.⟩
② n. (record company) Indie-Label, das; (band)
Indie-Band, die

**in'difference** n. Gleichgültigkeit, die
(to[wards] gegenüber)

**in'different** adj. (a) gleichgültig
(b) (not good) mittelmäßig

**indigenous** /ɪnˈdɪdʒɪnəs/ adj. einheimisch;
eingeboren ⟨Bevölkerung⟩

**indigestible** /ɪndɪˈdʒestɪbl/ adj. (lit. or fig.)
unverdaulich

**indi'gestion** n. Magenverstimmung, die;
(chronic) Verdauungsstörungen Pl.

**indignant** /ɪnˈdɪɡnənt/ adj. entrüstet (at,
over, about über + Akk.); indigniert ⟨Blick,
Geste⟩

**in'dignantly** adv. entrüstet; indigniert

**indignation** /ɪndɪɡˈneɪʃn/ n. Entrüstung,
die (about, at, against, over über + Akk.)

**in'dignity** n. Demütigung, die

**indigo** /ˈɪndɪɡəʊ/ ① adj. ~ [blue] indigoblau
② n. ~ [blue] Indigoblau, das

**indi'rect** adj. indirekt; ~ **speech** indirekte
Rede

**indi'rectly** adv. indirekt

**indirect 'object** n. indirektes Objekt; (in
German) Dativobjekt, das

**indiscipline** /ɪnˈdɪsɪplɪn/ n., no indef. art.
Disziplinlosigkeit, die

**indi'screet** adj. indiskret

**indi'scretion** n. Indiskretion, die

**indiscriminate** /ɪndɪˈskrɪmɪnət/ adj.
(lacking judgement) unkritisch; (random,
unrestrained) wahllos

**indi'spensable** adj. unentbehrlich (to
für); unabdingbar ⟨Voraussetzung⟩

**indisposed** /ɪndɪˈspəʊzd/ adj. (unwell)
unpässlich; indisponiert ⟨Sänger,
Schauspieler⟩

**indisputable** /ɪndɪˈspju:təbl/ adj.,
**indisputably** /ɪndɪˈspju:təblɪ/ adv.
unbestreitbar

**indi'stinct** adj., **indi'stinctly** adv.
undeutlich

**indi'stinguishable** adj. nicht
unterscheidbar

**individual** /ɪndɪˈvɪdjʊəl/ ① adj. (a) einzeln
(b) (distinctive, characteristic) individuell
② n. Einzelne, der/die

**individualist** /ɪndɪˈvɪdjʊəlɪst/ n.
Individualist, der/Individualistin, die

**individualistic** /ɪndɪvɪdjʊəˈlɪstɪk/ adj.
individualistisch

**individuality** /ɪndɪvɪdjʊˈælɪtɪ/ n. (character)
eigene Persönlichkeit

**indi'vidually** adv. einzeln

**indi'visible** adj. unteilbar

**indoctrinate** /ɪnˈdɒktrɪneɪt/ v.t.
indoktrinieren

**indoctrination** /ɪndɒktrɪˈneɪʃn/ n.
Indoktrination, die

**indolence** /'ɪndələns/ n. Trägheit, *die*

**indolent** /'ɪndələnt/ adj. träge

**indomitable** /ɪn'dɒmɪtəbl/ adj. unbeugsam

**Indonesia** /ɪndə'niːzɪə/ pr. n. Indonesien (*das*)

**'indoor** adj. ~ swimming pool/sports Hallenbad, *das*/-sport, *der;* ~ plants Zimmerpflanzen; ~ games Spiele im Haus; (Sport) Hallenspiele

**indoors** /ɪn'dɔːz/ adv. drinnen; im Haus; go/come ~: nach drinnen gehen/kommen

**indubitable** /ɪn'djuːbɪtəbl/ adj. unzweifelhaft

**indubitably** /ɪn'djuːbɪtəblɪ/ adv. zweifellos; zweifelsohne

**induce** /ɪn'djuːs/ v.t. ~ sb. to do sth. jmdn. dazu bringen, etw. zu tun

**in'ducement** n. (incentive) Anreiz, *der*

**induction** /ɪn'dʌkʃn/ n. Amtseinführung, *die;* ~ course Einführungskurs[us], *der*

**indulge** /ɪn'dʌldʒ/ 1 v.t. (a) nachgeben (+ Dat.) ⟨Wunsch, Verlangen, Verlockung⟩; frönen (geh.) (+ Dat.) ⟨Leidenschaft⟩ (b) (please) verwöhnen
2 v.i. ~ in frönen (geh.) (+ Dat.) ⟨Leidenschaft⟩

**indulgence** /ɪn'dʌldʒəns/ n. (a) Nachsicht, *die;* (humouring) Nachgiebigkeit, *die* (with gegenüber) (b) (thing indulged in) Luxus, *der*

**indulgent** /ɪn'dʌldʒənt/ adj. nachsichtig (with, to[wards] gegenüber)

**industrial** /ɪn'dʌstrɪəl/ adj. industriell; Arbeits⟨unfall, -medizin, -psychologie⟩

**industrial:** ~ 'action n. Arbeitskampfmaßnahmen Pl.; take ~ action in den Ausstand treten; ~ area n. Industriegebiet, *das;* ~ di'sease n. Berufskrankheit, *die;* ~ dispute n. Arbeitskonflikt, *der;* ~ 'espionage n. Industriespionage, *die;* ~ estate n. Industriegebiet, *das* ~ 'injury n. Arbeitsverletzung, *die*

**industrialist** /ɪn'dʌstrɪəlɪst/ n. Industrielle, *der/die*

**industrialization** /ɪndʌstrɪəlaɪ'zeɪʃn/ n. Industrialisierung, *die*

**industrialize** /ɪn'dʌstrɪəlaɪz/ v.t. industrialisieren

**industrial:** ~ park n. Industriegebiet, *das;* ~ plant n. Industrieanlage, *die;* ~ re'lations n. pl. Industrialrelations Pl.; ~ town n. Industriestadt, *die;* ~ tribunal n. Arbeitsgericht, *das;* ~ 'waste n. Industriemüll, *der*

**industrious** /ɪn'dʌstrɪəs/ adj. fleißig; (busy) emsig

**industry** /'ɪndəstrɪ/ n. (a) Industrie, *die* (b) ▶ INDUSTRIOUS: Fleiß, *der;* Emsigkeit, *die*

**inebriated** /ɪ'niːbrɪeɪtɪd/ adj. betrunken

**inebriation** /ɪniːbrɪ'eɪʃn/ n. Betrunkenheit, *die;* betrunkener Zustand

**in'edible** adj. ungenießbar

**ineffective** adj. unwirksam; fruchtlos ⟨Anstrengung, Versuch⟩

**ineffectual** /ɪnɪ'fektjʊəl/ adj. unwirksam; fruchtlos ⟨Versuch, Bemühung⟩; ineffizient ⟨Methode, Person⟩

**inefficiency** n. Leistungsschwäche, *die;* (of organization, method) schlechtes Funktionieren

**inefficient** adj. leistungsschwach; schlecht funktionierend ⟨Organisation, Methode⟩

**in'elegant** adj. unelegant

**in'eligible** adj. ungeeignet; be ~ for nicht infrage kommen für ⟨Beförderung, Position⟩; nicht berechtigt sein zu ⟨Leistungen des Staats usw.⟩

**inept** /ɪ'nept/ adj. unbeholfen

**ineptitude** /ɪ'neptɪtjuːd/ n. Unbeholfenheit, *die*

**ine'quality** n. Ungleichheit, *die*

**inert** /ɪ'nɜːt/ adj. (a) reglos; (sluggish) träge (b) (Chem.) inert; ~ gas Edelgas, *das*

**inertia** /ɪ'nɜːʃə/ n. Trägheit, *die*

**inertia reel 'seat belt** n. Automatikgurt, *der*

**inescapable** /ɪnɪ'skeɪpəbl/ adj. unausweichlich

**ines'sential** adj. unwesentlich; (dispensable) entbehrlich

**inestimable** /ɪn'estɪməbl/ adj. unschätzbar

**inevitable** /ɪn'evɪtəbl/ adj. unvermeidlich; unabwendbar ⟨Ereignis, Krieg, Schicksal⟩; zwangsläufig ⟨Ergebnis, Folge⟩

**inevitably** /ɪn'evɪtəblɪ/ adv. zwangsläufig

**ine'xact** adj. ungenau

**inex'cusable** adj. unverzeihlich

**inexhaustible** /ɪnɪg'zɔːstɪbl/ adj. unerschöpflich; unverwüstlich ⟨Person⟩

**inexorable** /ɪn'eksərəbl/ adj. unerbittlich

**inex'pensive** adj. preisgünstig

**inex'perience** n. Unerfahrenheit, *die*

**inex'perienced** adj. unerfahren; ~ in sth. wenig vertraut mit etw.

**inexpert** /ɪn'ekspɜːt/ adj. unerfahren

**inex'plicable** adj. unerklärlich

**inexpressive** /ɪnɪk'spresɪv/ adj. ausdruckslos ⟨Gesicht, Augen⟩; trocken ⟨Ausdrucksweise, Sprache⟩

**inextricably** /ɪn'ekstrɪkəblɪ/ adv. become ~ entangled sich vollkommen verheddern (ugs.); [be] ~ linked untrennbar verbunden [sein]

**infallibility** /ɪnfælɪ'bɪlɪtɪ/ n. Unfehlbarkeit, *die*

**in'fallible** adj. unfehlbar

**infamous** /'ɪnfəməs/ adj. berüchtigt

**infancy** /'ɪnfənsɪ/ n. frühe Kindheit; be in its ~ (fig.) noch in den Anfängen stecken

**infant** /'ɪnfənt/ n. kleines Kind

**infantile** /'ɪnfəntaɪl/ *adj.* kindlich; (childish) kindisch

**infant mor'tality** *n.* Säuglingssterblichkeit, *die*

**infantry** /'ɪnfəntrɪ/ *n.* Infanterie, *die*

**'infant school** *n.* (Brit.) ≈ Vorschule, *die*

**infatuated** /ɪn'fætjʊeɪtɪd/ *adj.* be ~ with sb. in jmdn. vernarrt sein

**infect** /ɪn'fekt/ *v.t.* anstecken; infizieren; **the wound became** ~ed die Wunde entzündete sich

**infection** /ɪn'fekʃn/ *n.* Infektion, *die;* **throat/ear/eye** ~: Hals-/Ohren-/Augenentzündung, *die*

**infectious** /ɪn'fekʃəs/ *adj.* ansteckend; **be** ~ ⟨*Person:*⟩ eine ansteckende Krankheit haben

**infer** /ɪn'fɜː(r)/ *v.t.,* -rr- schließen (from aus); ziehen ⟨*Schlussfolgerung*⟩

**inference** /'ɪnfərəns/ *n.* [Schluss]folgerung, *die*

**inferior** /ɪn'fɪərɪə(r)/ [1] *adj.* (of lower quality) minderwertig ⟨*Ware*⟩; minder... ⟨*Qualität*⟩; unterlegen ⟨*Gegner*⟩; ~ to sth. schlechter als etw.; **feel** ~: Minderwertigkeitsgefühle haben [2] *n.* Untergebene, *der/die*

**inferiority** /ɪnfɪərɪ'ɒrɪtɪ/ *n.* Minderwertigkeit, *die;* (of opponent) Unterlegenheit, *die*

**inferi'ority complex** *n.* Minderwertigkeitskomplex, *der*

**infernal** /ɪn'fɜːnl/ *adj.* (a) (of hell) höllisch (b) (coll.) verdammt (salopp)

**inferno** /ɪn'fɜːnəʊ/ *n.* Inferno, *das*

**in'fertile** *adj.* unfruchtbar

**infer'tility** *n.* Unfruchtbarkeit, *die*

**infest** /ɪn'fest/ *v.t.* ⟨*Ungeziefer:*⟩ befallen; ⟨*Unkraut:*⟩ überwuchern; ~ed with befallen/überwuchert von

**infestation** /ɪnfes'teɪʃn/ *n.* ~ of rats/insects Ratten-/Insektenplage, *die*

**infidelity** /ɪnfɪ'delɪtɪ/ *n.* Untreue, *die* (to gegenüber)

**'infighting** *n.* (in organization) interne Machtkämpfe *Pl.*

**infiltrate** /'ɪnfɪltreɪt/ *v.t.* (a) infiltrieren; unterwandern ⟨*Partei, Organisation*⟩ (b) einschleusen ⟨*Agenten*⟩

**infinite** /'ɪnfɪnɪt/ *adj.* (a) (endless) unendlich (b) (very great) ungeheuer

**infinitesimal** /ɪnfɪnɪ'tesɪml/ *adj.* (a) (Math.) infinitesimal (b) (very small) äußerst gering; winzig ⟨*Menge*⟩

**infinitive** /ɪn'fɪnɪtɪv/ *n.* Infinitiv, *der*

**infinity** /ɪn'fɪnɪtɪ/ *n.* Unendlichkeit, *die*

**infirm** /ɪn'fɜːm/ *adj.* gebrechlich

**infirmary** /ɪn'fɜːmərɪ/ *n.* (hospital) Krankenhaus, *das*

**infirmity** /ɪn'fɜːmɪtɪ/ *n.* Gebrechlichkeit, *die;* (malady) Gebrechen, *das*

**inflamed** /ɪn'fleɪmd/ *adj.* (Med.) **be/become** ~: entzündet sein/sich entzünden

**inflammable** /ɪn'flæməbl/ *adj.* feuergefährlich

**inflammation** /ɪnflə'meɪʃn/ *n.* (Med.) Entzündung, *die*

**inflammatory** /ɪn'flæmətərɪ/ *adj.* aufrührerisch; **an** ~ **speech** eine Hetzrede

**inflatable** /ɪn'fleɪtəbl/ *adj.* aufblasbar; ~ **dinghy** Schlauchboot, *das*

**inflate** /ɪn'fleɪt/ *v.t.* aufblasen; (with pump) aufpumpen

**inflated** /ɪn'fleɪtɪd/ *adj.* (lit or fig.) aufgeblasen

**inflation** /ɪn'fleɪʃn/ *n.* (Econ.) Inflation, *die*

**in'flexible** *adj.* (a) (stiff) unbiegsam (b) (obstinate) [geistig] unbeweglich

**inflict** /ɪn'flɪkt/ *v.t.* zufügen ⟨*Leid, Schmerzen*⟩, beibringen ⟨*Wunde*⟩, versetzen ⟨*Schlag*⟩ (on *Dat.*)

**infliction** /ɪn'flɪkʃn/ *n.* ▶ INFLICT: Zufügen, *das;* Beibringen, *das;* Versetzen, *das*

**'in-flight** *adj.* Bord⟨*verpflegung, -programm*⟩

**influence** /'ɪnflʊəns/ [1] *n.* Einfluss, *der;* **be a good/bad** ~ **[on sb.]** einen guten/schlechten Einfluss [auf jmdn.] ausüben [2] *v.t.* beeinflussen

**influential** /ɪnflʊ'enʃl/ *adj.* einflussreich

**influenza** /ɪnflʊ'enzə/ *n.* Grippe, *die*

**influx** /'ɪnflʌks/ *n.* Zustrom, *der*

**info** /'ɪnfəʊ/ *n.* (coll.) Infos *Pl.* (ugs.)

**inform** /ɪn'fɔːm/ [1] *n.* informieren (of, about über + *Akk.*); **keep sb.** ~ed jmdn. auf dem Laufenden halten [2] *v.i.* ~ against *or* on sb. jmdn. denunzieren (to bei)

**in'formal** *adj.* (a) zwanglos (b) (unofficial) informell

**infor'mality** *n.* Zwanglosigkeit, *die*

**informant** /ɪn'fɔːmənt/ *n.* Informant, *der/*Informantin, *die*

**information** /ɪnfə'meɪʃn/ *n.* Informationen *Pl.;* **give** ~ **on sth.** Auskunft über etw. (*Akk.*) erteilen; **piece** *or* **bit of** ~: Information, *die*

**information:** ~ **bureau,** ~ **centre** *ns.* Auskunftsbüro, *das;* ~ **desk** *n.* Informationsschalter, *der;* ~ **explosion** *n.* Informationsflut, *die;* ~ **highway** *n.* (Comp.) Datenautobahn, *die;* ~ **office** ▶ ~ BUREAU; ~ **pack** *n.* Informationspaket, *das;* (folder etc.) Informationsmappe, *die;* ~ **retrieval** *n.* (Comp.) Retrieval, *das;* ~ **science** *n.* Informatik, *die;* ~ **superhighway** *n.* (Comp.) Datenautobahn, *die;* Datensuperhighway, *der;* ~ **system** *n.* Informationssystem, *das;* ~ **technology** *n.* Informationstechnologie, *die*

**informative** /ɪn'fɔːmətɪv/ *adj.* informativ; **not very** ~: nicht sehr aufschlussreich ⟨*Dokument, Schriftstück*⟩

**informed** /ɪn'fɔːmd/ *adj.* informiert

**in'former** n. Denunziant, der/
Denunziantin, die

**infra-red** /ˈɪnfrəˈred/ adj. infrarot

**infrastructure** /ˈɪnfrəstrʌktʃə(r)/ n.
Infrastruktur, die

**infrequency** /ɪnˈfriːkwənsɪ/ n. Seltenheit,
die

**in'frequent** adj., **in'frequently** adv.
selten

**infringe** /ɪnˈfrɪndʒ/ v.t. & i. ~ [on]
verstoßen gegen

**in'fringement** n. Verstoß, der (of gegen)

**infuriate** /ɪnˈfjʊərɪeɪt/ v.t. wütend machen;
be ~d wütend sein (by über + Akk.)

**infuriating** /ɪnˈfjʊərɪeɪtɪŋ/ adj. ärgerlich

**ingenious** /ɪnˈdʒiːnɪəs/ adj. einfallsreich;
genial ⟨Methode, Idee⟩; raffiniert ⟨Spielzeug,
Maschine⟩

**ingenuity** /ɪndʒɪˈnjuːɪtɪ/ n. Genialität, die

**ingot** /ˈɪŋɡət/ n. Ingot, der

**ingratiate** /ɪnˈɡreɪʃɪeɪt/ v. refl. ~ oneself
with sb. sich bei jmdm. einschmeicheln

**in'gratitude** n. Undankbarkeit, die
(to[wards] gegenüber)

**ingredient** /ɪnˈɡriːdɪənt/ n. Zutat, die

**ingrowing** /ˈɪnɡrəʊɪŋ/ adj. eingewachsen
⟨Zehennagel usw.⟩

**inhabit** /ɪnˈhæbɪt/ v.t. bewohnen

**inhabitable** /ɪnˈhæbɪtəbl/ adj. bewohnbar

**inhabitant** /ɪnˈhæbɪtənt/ n. Bewohner,
der/Bewohnerin, die

**inhale** /ɪnˈheɪl/ v.t. & i. einatmen;
inhalieren (ugs.) ⟨Zigarettenrauch usw.⟩

**inherent** /ɪnˈhɪərənt, ɪnˈherənt/ adj. adj.
(belonging by nature) innewohnend (geh.);
natürlich ⟨Anmut, Eleganz⟩

**inherit** /ɪnˈherɪt/ v.t. erben

**inheritance** /ɪnˈherɪtəns/ n. Erbe, das;
(inheriting) Erbschaft, die

**in'heritance tax** n. Erbschaftssteuer, die

**inhibit** /ɪnˈhɪbɪt/ v.t. hemmen

**in'hibited** adj. gehemmt

**inhibition** /ɪnhɪˈbɪʃn/ n. Hemmung, die

**inho'spitable** adj. ungastlich ⟨Person,
Verhalten⟩; unwirtlich ⟨Gegend, Klima⟩

**'in-house** adj. hausintern

**in'human** adj. unmenschlich

**inhumane** /ɪnhjuːˈmeɪn/ adj.
unmenschlich

**initial** /ɪˈnɪʃl/ ①adj. anfänglich;
Anfangs⟨stadium, -schwierigkeiten⟩
②n. esp. in pl. Initiale, die
③v.t., (Brit.) -ll- abzeichnen ⟨Scheck,
Quittung⟩; paraphieren ⟨Vertrag, Abkommen
usw.⟩

**initial 'letter** n. Anfangsbuchstabe, der

**i'nitially** adv. anfangs; am Anfang

**initiate** /ɪˈnɪʃɪeɪt/ v.t. (a) (introduce)
einführen (into in + Akk.); (into knowledge,
mystery) einweihen (into in + Akk.)
(b) (begin) einleiten

**initiation** /ɪnɪʃɪˈeɪʃn/ n. (a) (introduction)
Einführung, die
(b) (into knowledge, mystery) Einweihung, die

**initiative** /ɪˈnɪʃətɪv/ n. Initiative, die; lack
~: keine Initiative haben

**inject** /ɪnˈdʒekt/ v.t. [ein]spritzen; injizieren
(Med.)

**injection** /ɪnˈdʒekʃn/ n. Spritze, die;
Injektion, die

**injure** /ˈɪndʒə(r)/ v.t. (a) verletzen; his leg
was ~d er wurde/(state) war am Bein
verletzt
(b) (impair) schaden (+ Dat.)

**injured** /ˈɪndʒəd/ adj. verletzt; verwundet
⟨Soldat⟩

**injury** /ˈɪndʒərɪ/ n. Verletzung, die (to Gen.)

**'injury time** n. (Brit. Footb.) Nachspielzeit,
die; be into/play ~: nachspielen

**in'justice** n. Ungerechtigkeit, die

**ink** /ɪŋk/ n. Tinte, die

**'ink-jet printer** n. Tintenstrahldrucker,
der

**inkling** /ˈɪŋklɪŋ/ n. Ahnung, die; have an
~ of sth. etw. ahnen

**'ink pad** n. Stempelkissen, das

**inland** /ˈɪnlənd, ˈɪnlænd/ adj. Binnen-;
binnenländisch

**Inland 'Revenue** n. (Brit.) ≈ Finanzamt,
das

**'in-laws** n. pl. (coll.) Schwiegereltern Pl.

**inlet** /ˈɪnlet/ n. [schmale] Bucht

**'inmate** n. Insasse, der/Insassin, die

**inn** /ɪn/ n. (hotel) Gasthof, der; (pub)
Wirtshaus, das

**innate** /ɪˈneɪt/ adj. angeboren

**inner** /ˈɪnə(r)/ adj. inner...; Innen⟨hof, -tür,
-fläche, -seite usw.⟩; ~ tube Schlauch, der

**inner 'city** n. Innenstadt, die; ~ areas
Innenbezirke

**innermost** /ˈɪnəməʊst/ adj. innerst...

**'innkeeper** n. [Gast]wirt, der/-wirtin, die

**innocence** /ˈɪnəsəns/ n. (a) Unschuld, die
(b) (naïvity) Naivität, die

**innocent** /ˈɪnəsənt/ adj. (a) unschuldig (of
an + Dat.)
(b) (naïve) naiv

**innocuous** /ɪˈnɒkjʊəs/ adj. harmlos

**innovation** /ɪnəˈveɪʃn/ n. Innovation, die;
(thing, change) Neuerung, die

**innovative** /ˈɪnəvətɪv/ adj. innovativ

**innuendo** /ɪnjuːˈendəʊ/ n., pl. ~es or ~s
versteckte Andeutung

**innumerable** /ɪˈnjuːmərəbl/ adj. unzählig

**innumeracy** /ɪˈnjuːmərəsɪ/ n. Nicht-
Rechnen-Können, das

**innumerate** /ɪˈnjuːmərət/ adj. be ~: nicht
rechnen können

**inoculate** /ɪˈnɒkjʊleɪt/ v.t. impfen

**inoculation** /ɪnɒkjʊˈleɪʃn/ n. Impfung, die

**inof'fensive** adj. harmlos

**inoperable** /ɪnˈɒpərəbl/ *adj.* (Surg.) inoperabel (fachspr.)

**inoperative** /ɪnˈɒpərətɪv/ *adj.* ungültig

**in'opportune** *adj.* unpassend; unangebracht ⟨*Bemerkung*⟩

**inordinate** /ɪˈnɔːdɪnət/ *adj.* unmäßig; ungeheuer ⟨*Menge*⟩

**inor'ganic** *adj.* anorganisch

**'inpatient** *n.* stationär behandelter Patient/ behandelte Patientin

**'input** *n.* Input, *der od. das*

**inquest** /ˈɪŋkwest/ *n.* gerichtliche Untersuchung der Todesursache

**inquire, inquiry** ▶ ENQUIR-

**inquisitive** /ɪnˈkwɪzɪtɪv/ *adj.* neugierig

**'inroad** *n.* Eingriff, *der* (on, into in + *Akk.*); make ~s into sb.'s savings jmds. Ersparnisse angreifen

**in'sane** *adj.* geisteskrank

**in'sanitary** *adj.* unhygienisch

**in'sanity** *n.* Geisteskrankheit, *die*

**insatiable** /ɪnˈseɪʃəbl/ *adj.* unersättlich; unstillbar ⟨*Verlangen*⟩

**inscribe** /ɪnˈskraɪb/ *v.t.* schreiben; (on stone, rock) einmeißeln; mit einer Inschrift versehen ⟨*Denkmal, Grabstein*⟩

**inscription** /ɪnˈskrɪpʃn/ *n.* Inschrift, *die;* (on coin) Aufschrift, *die*

**inscrutable** /ɪnˈskruːtəbl/ *adj.* unergründlich; undurchdringlich ⟨*Miene*⟩

**insect** /ˈɪnsekt/ *n.* Insekt, *das*

**insect:** ~ **bite** *n.* Insektenstich, *der;* ~**-borne** *adj.* durch Insekten übertragen ⟨*Krankheit*⟩

**insecticide** /ɪnˈsektɪsaɪd/ *n.* Insektizid, *das*

**'insect repellent** *n.* Insektenschutzmittel, *das*

**inse'cure** *adj.* unsicher

**inse'curity** *n.* Unsicherheit, *die*

**insemination** /ɪnsemɪˈneɪʃn/ *n.* (of woman) Befruchtung, *die;* (of animal) Besamung, *die*

**in'sensitive** *adj.* (a) gefühllos ⟨*Person, Art*⟩; (unappreciative) unempfänglich (to für) (b) (physically) unempfindlich (to gegen)

**in'separable** *adj.* untrennbar; (fig.) unzertrennlich

**insert** /ɪnˈsɜːt/ *v.t.* (a) einlegen ⟨*Film*⟩; einwerfen ⟨*Münze*⟩; hineinstecken ⟨*Schlüssel*⟩; einstechen ⟨*Nadel*⟩ (b) (Comp.) einfügen; ~ **key** Einfügetaste, *die*

**insertion** /ɪnˈsɜːʃn/ *n.* ▶ INSERT: Einlegen, *das;* Einwerfen, *das;* Hineinstecken, *das;* Einstechen, *das;* Einfügen, *das*

**'inset** *n.* (small map) Nebenkarte, *die;* (small photograph, diagram) Nebenbild, *das*

**inside** ⓵ /-ˈ-/, '-ˈ-/ *n.* (a) (internal side) Innenseite, *die;* on the ~: innen; to/from the ~: nach/von innen (b) (inner part) Innere, *das* ⓶ /'-ˈ-/ *adj.* inner...; Innen⟨*wand, -einrichtung, -ansicht*⟩; (fig.) intern

⓷ /-ˈ-/ *adv.* (on or in the ~) innen; (to the ~) nach innen hinein/herein; (indoors) drinnen; come ~: hereinkommen; take a look ~: hineinsehen; go ~: [ins Haus] hineingehen; turn a jacket ~ out eine Jacke nach links wenden; know sth. ~ out etw. in- und auswendig kennen ⓸ /-ˈ-/ *prep.* (position) in (+ *Dat.*); (direction) in (+ *Akk.*) hinein

**inside-'leg** *adj.* ~ **measurement** Schrittlänge, *die*

**insidious** /ɪnˈsɪdɪəs/ *adj.* heimtückisch

**'insight** *n.* (discernment) Verständnis, *das;* gain an ~ into sth. Einblick in etw. (*Akk.*) gewinnen

**insig'nificant** *adj.* unbedeutend; geringfügig ⟨*Summe*⟩

**insin'cere** *adj.* unaufrichtig

**insin'cerity** *n.* Unaufrichtigkeit, *die*

**insinuate** /ɪnˈsɪnjʊeɪt/ *v.t.* andeuten (to sb. jmdm. gegenüber)

**insinuation** /ɪnsɪnjʊˈeɪʃn/ *n.* Anspielung, *die* (about auf + *Akk.*)

**insipid** /ɪnˈsɪpɪd/ *adj.* fade

**insist** /ɪnˈsɪst/ *v.i.* bestehen ([up]on auf + *Dat.*); ~ on doing sth./on sb.'s doing sth. darauf bestehen, etw. zu tun/dass jmd. etw. tut; if you ~: wenn du darauf bestehst

**insistence** /ɪnˈsɪstəns/ *n.* Bestehen, *das* (on auf + *Dat.*)

**insistent** /ɪnˈsɪstənt/ *adj.* be ~ that ...: darauf bestehen, dass ...

**insolence** /ˈɪnsələns/ *n.* Unverschämtheit, *die;* Frechheit, *die*

**insolent** /ˈɪnsələnt/ *adj.,* **'insolently** *adv.* unverschämt; frech

**in'soluble** *adj.* (a) (esp. Chem.) unlöslich (b) (not solvable) unlösbar

**insolvency** /ɪnˈsɒlvənsɪ/ *n.* Zahlungsunfähigkeit, *die*

**in'solvent** *adj.* zahlungsunfähig

**insomnia** /ɪnˈsɒmnɪə/ *n.* Schlaflosigkeit, *die*

**insomniac** /ɪnˈsɒmnɪæk/ *n.* be an ~: an Schlaflosigkeit leiden

**inspect** /ɪnˈspekt/ *v.t.* prüfend betrachten; (examine officially) überprüfen; kontrollieren ⟨*Räumlichkeiten*⟩

**inspection** /ɪnˈspekʃn/ *n.* Überprüfung, *die;* (of premises) Kontrolle, *die;* Inspektion, *die;* on [closer] ~: bei näherer Betrachtung

**inspector** /ɪnˈspektə(r)/ *n.* (a) (on bus, train, etc.) Kontrolleur, *der*/Kontrolleurin, *die* (b) (Brit.) ≈ Polizeiinspektor, *der*

**inspiration** /ɪnspəˈreɪʃn/ *n.* Inspiration, *die* (geh.)

**inspire** /ɪnˈspaɪə(r)/ *v.t.* (a) inspirieren (geh.) ⟨*Person*⟩ (b) (instil) einflößen (in *Dat.*)

**inspiring** /ɪnˈspaɪərɪŋ/ *adj.* inspirierend (geh.)

**insta'bility** *n.* Instabilität, *die;* (of person) Labilität, *die*

**install** /ɪn'stɔːl/ *v.t.* installieren; einbauen ⟨*Badezimmer*⟩; anschließen ⟨*Telefon, Herd*⟩; ∼ **oneself** sich installieren

**installation** /ɪnstə'leɪʃn/ *n.* **(a)** Installation, *die;* (of bathroom) Einbau, *der;* (of telephone, cooker) Anschluss, *der* **(b)** (apparatus etc. installed) Anlage, *die*

**instalment** (*Amer.:* **installment**) /ɪn'stɔːlmənt/ *n.* **(a)** (part payment) Rate, *die;* **pay by** *or* **in** ∼**s** in Raten zahlen **(b)** (of serial, novel) Fortsetzung, *die;* (Radio, Telev.) Folge, *die*

**instance** /'ɪnstəns/ *n.* (example) Beispiel, *das* (of für); **for** ∼: zum Beispiel; **in many** ∼**s** (cases) in vielen Fällen; **in the first** ∼: zunächst einmal

**instant** /'ɪnstənt/ ⟨1⟩ *adj.* unmittelbar; sofortig ⟨*Wirkung, Linderung, Ergebnis*⟩; ∼ **coffee/tea** Pulverkaffee/Instanttee, *der;* ∼ **potatoes** fertiger Kartoffelbrei ⟨2⟩ *n.* Augenblick, *der;* **at that very** ∼: genau in dem Augenblick; **come here this** ∼: komm sofort her; **in an** ∼: augenblicklich

**instantaneous** /ɪnstən'teɪnɪəs/ *adj.* unmittelbar; **his reaction was** ∼: er reagierte sofort

**'instantly** *adv.* sofort

**instead** /ɪn'sted/ *adv.* stattdessen; ∼ **of doing sth.** [an]statt etw. zu tun; ∼ **of sth.** anstelle einer Sache (*Gen.*); **I will go** ∼ **of you** ich gehe an deiner Stelle

**'instep** *n.* (of foot) Spann, *der;* Fußrücken, *der;* (of shoe) Blatt, *das*

**instigate** /'ɪnstɪgeɪt/ *v.t.* anstiften (to zu); initiieren (geh.) ⟨*Reformen, Projekt usw.*⟩

**instigation** /ɪnstɪ'geɪʃn/ *n.* Anstiftung, *die;* (of reforms, project, etc.) Initiierung, *die;* **at sb.'s** ∼: auf jmds. Betreiben (*Akk.*)

**instil** (*Amer.:* **instill**) /ɪn'stɪl/ *v.t.*, **-ll-** einflößen (**in** *Dat.*); beibringen ⟨*gutes Benehmen, Wissen*⟩ (**in** *Dat.*)

**instinct** /'ɪnstɪŋkt/ *n.* Instinkt, *der*

**instinctive** /ɪn'stɪŋktɪv/ *adj.,* **in'stinctively** *adv.* instinktiv

**institute** /'ɪnstɪtjuːt/ ⟨1⟩ *n.* Institut, *das* ⟨2⟩ *v.t.* einführen; einleiten ⟨*Suche, Verfahren*⟩; anstrengen ⟨*Prozess*⟩

**institution** /ɪnstɪ'tjuːʃn/ *n.* Institution, *die;* (home) Heim, *das;* Anstalt, *die*

**instruct** /ɪn'strʌkt/ *v.t.* **(a)** (teach) unterrichten ⟨*Klasse, Fach*⟩ **(b)** (direct, command) anweisen

**instruction** /ɪn'strʌkʃn/ *n.* **(a)** (teaching) Unterricht, *der* **(b)** *esp. in pl.* (direction, order) Anweisung, *die;* ∼ **manual/**∼**s for use** Gebrauchsanleitung, *die*

**instructive** /ɪn'strʌktɪv/ *adj.* aufschlussreich; lehrreich ⟨*Erfahrung, Buch*⟩

**instructor** /ɪn'strʌktə(r)/ *n.* Lehrer, *der/* Lehrerin, *die;* (Mil.) Ausbilder, *der*

**instrument** /'ɪnstrʊmənt/ *n.* Instrument, *das*

**instrumental** /ɪnstrə'mentl/ *adj.* **(a)** (Mus.) Instrumental- **(b)** (helpful) dienlich (**to** *Dat.*); **he was** ∼ **in finding me a job** er hat mir zu einer Stelle verholfen

**instrumentalist** /ɪnstrʊ'mentəlɪst/ *n.* Instrumentalist, *der/*Instrumentalistin, *die*

**insubordinate** /ɪnsə'bɔːdɪnət/ *adj.* aufsässig

**insubordination** /ɪnsəbɔːdɪ'neɪʃn/ *n.* Aufsässigkeit, *die*

**insubstantial** /ɪnsəb'stænʃl/ *adj.* wenig substanziell (geh.)

**insufferable** /ɪn'sʌfərəbl/ *adj.* (unbearably arrogant) unausstehlich

**insuf'ficient** *adj.* nicht genügend; unzulänglich ⟨*Beweise*⟩; unzureichend ⟨*Versorgung, Beleuchtung*⟩

**insuf'ficiently** *adv.* ungenügend

**insular** /'ɪnsjʊlə(r)/ *adj.* **(a)** Insel-; insular (fachspr.) **(b)** (fig.: narrow-minded) provinziell (abwertend)

**insulate** /'ɪnsjʊleɪt/ *v.t.* isolieren (**against, from** gegen); **insulating tape** Isolierband, *das*

**insulation** /ɪnsjʊ'leɪʃn/ *n.* Isolierung, *die*

**insulin** /'ɪnsjʊlɪn/ *n.* Insulin, *das*

**insult** ⟨1⟩ /'ɪnsʌlt/ *n.* Beleidigung, *die* (**to** *Gen.*) ⟨2⟩ /ɪn'sʌlt/ *v.t.* beleidigen

**insulting** /ɪn'sʌltɪŋ/ *adj.* beleidigend

**insuperable** /ɪn'suːpərəbl/ *adj.* unüberwindlich

**insupportable** /ɪnsə'pɔːtəbl/ *adj.* (unendurable) unerträglich

**insurance** /ɪn'ʃʊərəns/ *n.* Versicherung, *die;* (fig.) Sicherheit, *die;* **take out** ∼ **against/ on sth.** eine Versicherung gegen etw. abschließen/etw. versichern lassen; **travel** ∼: Reisegepäck- und -unfallversicherung, *die*

**insurance:** ∼ **agent** *n.* Versicherungsvertreter, *der/*-vertreterin, *die;* ∼ **broker** *n.* Versicherungsmakler, *der/* -maklerin, *die;* ∼ **claim** *n.* Versicherungsanspruch, *der;* ∼ **company** *n.* Versicherungsgesellschaft, *die;* ∼ **stamp** *n.* (Brit.) Versicherungsmarke, *die*

**insure** /ɪn'ʃʊə(r)/ *v.t.* versichern ⟨*Person*⟩; versichern lassen ⟨*Gepäck, Gemälde usw.*⟩; ∼ **[oneself] against sth.** [sich] gegen etw. versichern

**insurer** /ɪn'ʃʊərə(r)/ *n.* Versicherer, *der*

**insurmountable** /ɪnsə'maʊntəbl/ *adj.* unüberwindlich

**intact** /ɪn'tækt/ *adj.* **(a)** (entire) unbeschädigt; intakt ⟨*Uhr, Maschine usw.*⟩ **(b)** (unimpaired) unversehrt

**'intake** *n.* **(a)** (action) Aufnahme, *die* **(b)** (persons, things) Neuzugänge *Pl.;* (amount) aufgenommene Menge

**in'tangible** *adj.* nicht greifbar; (mentally) unbestimmbar

**integral** /'ıntıgrl/ *adj.* (a) wesentlich ⟨*Bestandteil*⟩
(b) (whole) vollständig

**integrate** /'ıntıgreıt/ *v.t.* integrieren (**into** in + *Akk.*)

**integration** /ıntı'greıʃn/ *n.* Integration, *die* (**into** in + *Akk.*)

**integrity** /ın'tegrıtı/ *n.* Redlichkeit, *die*

**intellect** /'ıntəlekt/ *n.* Verstand, *der;* Intellekt, *der*

**intellectual** /ıntə'lektjʊəl/ ⟦1⟧ *adj.* intellektuell; geistig anspruchsvoll ⟨*Person, Publikum*⟩
⟦2⟧ *n.* Intellektuelle, *der/die*

**intelligence** /ın'telıdʒəns/ *n.* (a) Intelligenz, *die*
(b) (information) Informationen *Pl.*
(c) military ~ (organization) militärischer Geheimdienst

**intelligence: ~ quotient** *n.* Intelligenzquotient, *der;* ~ **test** *n.* Intelligenztest, *der*

**intelligent** /ın'telıdʒənt/ *adj.* intelligent

**intelligible** /ın'telıdʒıbl/ *adj.* verständlich (**to** für)

**intend** /ın'tend/ *v.t.* beabsichtigen; **it was ~ed as a joke** das sollte ein Witz sein

**in'tended** *adj.* beabsichtigt ⟨*Wirkung*⟩; **be ~ for sb./sth.** für jmdn./etw. gedacht sein

**intense** /ın'tens/ *adj.* (a) intensiv; groß ⟨*Hitze, Belastung, Interesse*⟩; stark ⟨*Schmerzen*⟩
(b) (earnest) ernst

**in'tensely** *adv.* äußerst; intensiv ⟨*studieren, fühlen*⟩

**intensify** /ın'tensıfaı/ ⟦1⟧ *v.t.* intensivieren
⟦2⟧ *v.i.* zunehmen

**intensity** /ın'tensıtı/ *n.* ▶ INTENSE A: Intensität, *die;* Größe, *die;* Stärke, *die*

**intensive** /ın'tensıv/ *adj.* intensiv; Intensiv⟨*kurs*⟩; **be in ~ care** auf der Intensivstation sein

**in'tensively** *adv.* intensiv

**intent** /ın'tent/ ⟦1⟧ *n.* Absicht, *die;* **to all ~s and purposes** im Grunde
⟦2⟧ *adj.* **be ~ on achieving sth.** etw. unbedingt erreichen wollen

**intention** /ın'tenʃn/ *n.* Absicht, *die*

**intentional** /ın'tenʃənl/ *adj.*, **in'tentionally** *adv.* absichtlich

**in'tently** *adv.* aufmerksam

**interact** /ıntər'ækt/ *v.i.* interagieren

**interaction** /ıntər'ækʃn/ *n.* Interaktion, *die*

**interactive** /ıntər'æktıv/ *adj.* (Sociol., Psych., Comp.) interaktiv; ~ **television** interaktives Fernsehen

**intercede** /ıntə'si:d/ *v.i.* sich einsetzen (**with** bei; **for, on behalf of** für)

**intercept** /ıntə'sept/ *v.t.* abfangen

**interchange** ⟦1⟧ /'ıntətʃeındʒ/ *n.* (a) Austausch, *der*
(b) (road junction) [Autobahn]kreuz, *das*
⟦2⟧ /ıntə'tʃeındʒ/ *v.t.* austauschen

**interchangeable** /ıntə'tʃeındʒəbl/ *adj.* austauschbar

**inter-city** /ıntə'sıtı/ *adj.* Intercity-; ~ **train** Intercity[-Zug], *der*

**intercom** /'ıntəkɒm/ *n.* (coll.) Gegensprechanlage, *die*

**interconnect** /ıntəkə'nekt/ ⟦1⟧ *v.t.* miteinander verbinden
⟦2⟧ *v.i.* miteinander in Zusammenhang stehen

**intercontinental** /ıntəkɒntı'nentl/ *adj.* interkontinental

**intercourse** /'ıntəkɔ:s/ *n.* (sexual) [Geschlechts]verkehr, *der*

**interest** /'ıntrəst/ ⟦1⟧ *n.* (a) Interesse, *das;* **take** *or* **have an ~ in sb./sth.** sich für jmdn./ etw. interessieren; **[just] for** *or* **out of ~:** [nur] interessehalber; **with ~:** interessiert; **act in one's own/sb.'s ~[s]** im eigenen/in jmds. Interesse handeln; **be of ~:** interessant sein (**to** für)
(b) (Finance) Zinsen *Pl.*
⟦2⟧ *v.t.* interessieren; **be ~ed** sich interessieren (**in** für)

**interest-'free** *adj., adv.* unverzinslich ⟨*Schuldverschreibung*⟩; zinsfrei ⟨*Darlehen*⟩

**'interesting** *adj.* interessant

**'interest rate** *n.* Zinssatz, *der;* Zinsfuß, *der*

**interface** /'ıntəfeıs/ *n.* (Comp.) Schnittstelle, *die*

**interfere** /ıntə'fıə(r)/ *v.i.* sich einmischen (**in** in + *Akk.*); ~ **with sth.** sich (*Dat.*) an etw. (*Dat.*) zu schaffen machen

**interference** /ıntə'fıərəns/ *n.* (a) (interfering) Einmischung, *die*
(b) (Radio, Telev.) Störung, *die*

**interim** /'ıntərım/ ⟦1⟧ *n.* **in the ~:** in der Zwischenzeit
⟦2⟧ *adj.* vorläufig

**interior** /ın'tıərıə(r)/ ⟦1⟧ *adj.* inner...; Innen⟨*fläche, -wand*⟩
⟦2⟧ *n.* Innere, *das*

**interior: ~ deco'ration** *n.* Raumgestaltung, *die;* ~ **'decorator** *n.* Raumgestalter, *der*/-gestalterin, *die;* ~ **de'sign** *n.* Innenarchitektur, *die;* ~ **de'signer** *n.* Innenarchitekt, *der*/ -architektin, *die*

**interject** /ıntə'dʒekt/ *v.t.* einwerfen

**interjection** /ıntə'dʒekʃn/ *n.* Ausruf, *der*

**interloper** /'ıntələʊpə(r)/ *n.* Eindringling, *der*

**interlude** /'ıntəlu:d/ *n.* Pause, *die;* (music) Zwischenspiel, *das*

**intermediary** /ıntə'mi:dıərı/ *n.* Vermittler, *der*/Vermittlerin, *die*

**intermediate** /ıntə'mi:djət/ *adj.* Zwischen-

**interminable** /ın'tɜ:mınəbl/ *adj.* endlos

# intermingle ⋯⋙ intrigue ⋯⋯

**intermingle** /ɪntə'mɪŋgl/ *v.i.* sich vermischen

**intermission** /ɪntə'mɪʃn/ *n.* Pause, *die*

**intermittent** /ɪntə'mɪtənt/ *adj.* in Abständen auftretend

**inter'mittently** *adv.* in Abständen

**intern** /ɪn'tɜːn/ *v.t.* gefangen halten

**internal** /ɪn'tɜːnl/ *adj.* inner...; Innen⟨fläche, -abmessungen⟩

**internalize (internalise)** /ɪn'tɜːnəlaɪz/ *v.t.* (Psych.) verinnerlichen

**internally** /ɪn'tɜːnəlɪ/ *adv.* innerlich

**international** /ɪntə'næʃənl/ [1] *adj.* international
[2] *n.* (a) (Sport) (contest) Länderspiel, *das*
(b) (participant) Nationalspieler, *der/* -spielerin, *die*

**international:** ～ **call** *n.* Auslandsgespräch, *das;* ～ **'law** *n.* Völkerrecht, *das*

**inter'nationally** *adv.* international

**International 'Monetary Fund** *n.* Internationaler Währungsfonds

**internee** /ɪntɜː'niː/ *n.* Internierte, *der/die*

**Internet** /'ɪntənet/ *n.* **the** ～ das Internet; **on the** ～: im Internet

**Internet 'Service Provider** *n.* (Comp.) Internetprovider, *der*

**in'ternment** *n.* Internierung, *die*

**interplay** /'ɪntəpleɪ/ *n.* Zusammenspiel, *das*

**interpret** /ɪn'tɜːprɪt/ [1] *v.t.* (a) interpretieren; deuten ⟨Traum, Zeichen⟩
(b) (between languages) dolmetschen
[2] *v.i.* dolmetschen

**interpretation** /ɪntɜːprɪ'teɪʃn/ *n.* Interpretation, *die;* (of dream, symptoms) Deutung, *die*

**in'terpreter** *n.* Dolmetscher, *der/* Dolmetscherin, *die*

**interrogate** /ɪn'terəgeɪt/ *v.t.* verhören; ausfragen ⟨Freund, Kind usw.⟩

**interrogation** /ɪnterə'geɪʃn/ *n.* Verhör, *das*

**interrogative** /ɪntə'rɒgətɪv/ *adj.* (Ling.) Interrogativ-

**interrogator** /ɪn'terəgeɪtə(r)/ *n.* Vernehmer, *der*

**interrupt** /ɪntə'rʌpt/ [1] *v.t.* unterbrechen; **don't** ～ **me when I'm busy** stör mich nicht, wenn ich zu tun habe
[2] *v.i.* unterbrechen; stören

**interruption** /ɪntə'rʌpʃn/ *n.* Unterbrechung, *die;* Störung, *die*

**intersect** /ɪntə'sekt/ *v.i.* (a) ⟨Straßen:⟩ sich kreuzen
(b) (Geom.) sich schneiden

**intersection** /ɪntə'sekʃn/ *n.* (a) (road junction) Kreuzung, *die*
(b) (Geom.) Schnittpunkt, *der*

**intersperse** /ɪntə'spɜːs/ *v.t.* **be** ～**d with** durchsetzt sein mit

**interval** /'ɪntəvl/ *n.* (a) [Zeit]abstand, *der;* **at** ～**s** in Abständen
(b) (break; also Brit. Theatre etc.) Pause, *die;* **sunny** ～**s** Aufheiterungen *Pl.*

**intervene** /ɪntə'viːn/ *v.i.* (a) [vermittelnd] eingreifen (**in** in + *Akk.*)
(b) **the intervening years** die dazwischenliegenden Jahre

**intervention** /ɪntə'venʃn/ *n.* Eingreifen, *das;* Intervention, *die* (bes. Politik)

**interview** /'ɪntəvjuː/ [1] *n.* (a) (for job) Vorstellungsgespräch, *das*
(b) (Journ., Radio, Telev.) Interview, *das*
[2] *v.t.* ein Vorstellungsgespräch führen mit; interviewen ⟨Politiker, Filmstar usw.⟩

**'interviewer** *n.* Interviewer, *der/* Interviewerin, *die*

**intestine** /ɪn'testɪn/ *n.* Darm, *der*

**intimacy** /'ɪntɪməsɪ/ *n.* (a) Vertrautheit, *die*
(b) (sexual) Intimität, *die*

**intimate** [1] /'ɪntɪmət/ *adj.* (a) eng ⟨Freund, Verhältnis⟩; genau, (geh.) intim ⟨Kenntnis⟩
(b) (sexually) intim
[2] /'ɪntɪmeɪt/ *v.t.* (imply) andeuten

**intimately** /'ɪntɪmətlɪ/ *adv.* genau[estens] ⟨kennen⟩; eng ⟨verbinden⟩

**intimidate** /ɪn'tɪmɪdeɪt/ *v.t.* einschüchtern

**intimidation** /ɪntɪmɪ'deɪʃn/ *n.* Einschüchterung, *die*

**into** /before vowel 'ɪntʊ, before consonant 'ɪntə/ *prep.* in (+ *Akk.*); (against) gegen; **I went out** ～ **the street** ich ging auf die Straße hinaus; **translate sth.** ～ **English** etw. ins Englische übersetzen

**in'tolerable** *adj.* unerträglich

**in'tolerance** *n.* Intoleranz, *die*

**in'tolerant** *adj.* intolerant (**of** gegenüber)

**intonation** /ɪntə'neɪʃn/ *n.* Intonation, *die*

**intoxicant** /ɪn'tɒksɪkənt/ *n.* Rauschmittel, *das*

**intoxicate** /ɪn'tɒksɪkeɪt/ *v.t.* betrunken machen

**intoxication** /ɪntɒksɪ'keɪʃn/ *n.* Rausch, *der*

**intractable** /ɪn'træktəbl/ *adj.* hartnäckig ⟨Problem⟩

**intransigent** /ɪn'trænsɪdʒənt/ *adj.* unnachgiebig

**in'transitive** *adj.* (Ling.) intransitiv

**intra-uterine** /ɪntrə'juːtəraɪn/ *adj.* (Med.) intrauterin; ～ [contraceptive] device Intrauterinpessar, *das*

**intravenous** /ɪntrə'viːnəs/ *adj.* (Med.) intravenös

**'in-tray** *n.* Eingangskorb, *der*

**intrepid** /ɪn'trepɪd/ *adj.* unerschrocken

**intricacy** /'ɪntrɪkəsɪ/ *n.* Kompliziertheit, *die*

**intricate** /'ɪntrɪkət/ *adj.* kompliziert

**intrigue** /ɪn'triːg/ *v.t.* faszinieren

**intriguing** /ɪnˈtriːɡɪŋ/ adj. faszinierend
**intrinsic** /ɪnˈtrɪnsɪk/ adj. innewohnend;
inner...; ~ **value** innerer Wert
**intrinsically** /ɪnˈtrɪnsɪkəlɪ/ adv. im
Wesentlichen
**intro** /ˈɪntrəʊ/ n., pl. ~s (coll.) (presentation)
Vorstellung, die; (Mus.) Einleitung, die
**introduce** /ɪntrəˈdjuːs/ v.t. einführen;
~ **oneself/sb.** [**to sb.**] sich/jmdn. [jmdm.]
vorstellen
**introduction** /ɪntrəˈdʌkʃn/ n. Einführen,
das; Einführung, die; (to person) Vorstellung,
die; (to book) Einleitung, die
**intro'duction agency** n.
Partnervermittlung[sagentur], die
**introductory** /ɪntrəˈdʌktərɪ/ adj.
einleitend; Einführungs⟨kurs, -vortrag⟩
**introspective** /ɪntrəˈspektɪv/ adj. in sich
(Akk.) gerichtet
**introvert** /ˈɪntrəvɜːt/ **1** n. Introvertierte,
der/die; **be an** ~: introvertiert sein
**2** adj. introvertiert
**introverted** /ˈɪntrəvɜːtɪd/ adj. introvertiert
**intrude** /ɪnˈtruːd/ v.i. stören
**in'truder** n. Eindringling, der
**in'truder alarm** n. Einbruchmeldeanlage,
die
**intrusion** /ɪnˈtruːʒn/ n. Störung, die
**intrusive** /ɪnˈtruːsɪv/ adj. aufdringlich
**intuition** /ɪntjuːˈɪʃn/ n. Intuition, die
**intuitive** /ɪnˈtjuːɪtɪv/ adj., **in'tuitively**
adv. intuitiv
**inundate** /ˈɪnəndeɪt/ v.t. überschwemmen
**inure** /ɪˈnjʊə(r)/ v.t. gewöhnen (**to an** + Akk.)
**invade** /ɪnˈveɪd/ v.t. einfallen in (+ Akk.)
**in'vader** n. Angreifer, der
**invalid¹** /ˈɪnvəlɪd/ (Brit.) **1** n. Kranke, der/
die; (disabled) Körperbehinderte, der/die
**2** adj. körperbehindert
**invalid²** /ɪnˈvælɪd/ adj. nicht schlüssig
⟨Argument, Theorie⟩; ungültig ⟨Fahrkarte,
Garantie, Vertrag⟩
**invalidate** /ɪnˈvælɪdeɪt/ v.t. aufheben;
widerlegen ⟨Theorie, These⟩
**in'valuable** adj. unersetzlich ⟨Person⟩;
unschätzbar ⟨Dienst, Hilfe⟩; außerordentlich
wichtig ⟨Rolle⟩
**in'variable** adj. unveränderlich
**invariably** /ɪnˈveərɪəblɪ/ adv. immer;
ausnahmslos ⟨falsch, richtig⟩
**invasion** /ɪnˈveɪʒn/ n. Invasion, die
**invective** /ɪnˈvektɪv/ n. Beschimpfungen
Pl.
**invent** /ɪnˈvent/ v.t. erfinden
**invention** /ɪnˈvenʃn/ n. Erfindung, die
**inventive** /ɪnˈventɪv/ adj. (a) schöpferisch
⟨Person, Begabung⟩
(b) (original) originell
**inventor** /ɪnˈventə(r)/ n. Erfinder, der/
Erfinderin, die

**inventory** /ˈɪnvəntərɪ/ n. Bestandsliste, die;
**make** or **take an** ~ **of sth.** von etw. ein
Inventar aufstellen
**inverse** /ˈɪnvɜːs/ adj. umgekehrt
**invert** /ɪnˈvɜːt/ v.t. umstülpen
**in'vertebrate** n. wirbelloses Tier
**inverted 'commas** n. pl. (Brit.)
Anführungszeichen Pl.
**invest** /ɪnˈvest/ v.t. (a) (Finance) anlegen (**in**
in + Dat.); investieren (**in** in + Dat. od. Akk.)
(b) (fig.) investieren; ~ **sb. with sth.** jmdm.
etw. übertragen; ~ **sth. with sth.** einer Sache
(Dat.) etw. verleihen
**investigate** /ɪnˈvestɪɡeɪt/ v.t. untersuchen
**investigation** /ɪnˌvestɪˈɡeɪʃn/ n.
Untersuchung, die
**investigative** /ɪnˈvestɪɡətɪv/ adj.
detektivisch; ~ **journalism**
Enthüllungsjournalismus, der
**investigator** /ɪnˈvestɪɡeɪtə(r)/ n. **[private]**
~: [Privat]detektiv, der/-detektivin, die
**in'vestment** n. Investition, die; (money
invested) angelegtes Geld; **be a good** ~ (fig.)
sich bezahlt machen
**investor** /ɪnˈvestə(r)/ n. [Kapital]anleger,
der/-anlegerin, die
**inveterate** /ɪnˈvetərət/ adj. eingefleischt
⟨Trinker, Raucher⟩; unverbesserlich
⟨Lügner⟩
**invigilate** /ɪnˈvɪdʒɪleɪt/ v.i. (Brit.: in
examination) Aufsicht führen
**invigilator** /ɪnˈvɪdʒɪleɪtə(r)/ n. (Brit.)
Aufsichtsperson, die
**invigorate** /ɪnˈvɪɡəreɪt/ v.t. stärken;
(physically) kräftigen
**invigorating** /ɪnˈvɪɡəreɪtɪŋ/ adj. kräftigend
⟨Getränk, Klima⟩
**invincible** /ɪnˈvɪnsɪbl/ adj. unbesiegbar
**in'visible** adj. unsichtbar
**invitation** /ɪnvɪˈteɪʃn/ n. Einladung, die; **at
sb.'s** ~: auf jmds. Einladung (Akk.)
**invite** /ɪnˈvaɪt/ v.t. (a) (request to come)
einladen
(b) (request to do sth.) auffordern
(c) (bring on) herausfordern ⟨Kritik,
Verhängnis⟩
**inviting** /ɪnˈvaɪtɪŋ/ adj. einladend;
verlockend ⟨Gedanke, Vorstellung⟩
**in-vitro fertili'zation** /ɪnˈviːtrəʊ
fɜːtɪlaɪˈzeɪʃn/ n. künstliche Befruchtung [im
Reagenzglas]; In-vitro-Fertilisation, die
(fachspr.)
**invoice** /ˈɪnvɔɪs/ **1** n. (bill) Rechnung, die
**2** v.t. ~ **sb.** jmdm. eine Rechnung schicken;
~ **sb. for sth.** jmdm. etw. in Rechnung
stellen
**invoke** /ɪnˈvəʊk/ v.t. anrufen
**in'voluntarily** adv., **in'voluntary** adj.
unwillkürlich
**involve** /ɪnˈvɒlv/ v.t. (a) (implicate)
verwickeln

**(b) become** or **get** ∼**d in a fight** in eine Schlägerei verwickelt werden; **get** ∼**d with sb.** sich mit jmdm. einlassen
**(c)** (entail) mit sich bringen

**involved** /ɪnˈvɒlvd/ adj. verwickelt; (complicated) kompliziert

**invulnerable** /ɪnˈvʌlnərəbl/ adj. unverwundbar; (fig.) unantastbar

**inward** /ˈɪnwəd/ ① adj. inner…
② adv. einwärts ⟨gerichtet, gebogen⟩; **open** ∼: nach innen öffnen

ˈ**inwardly** adv. im Inneren; innerlich

**inwards** /ˈɪnwədz/ ▶ INWARD 2

**iodine** /ˈaɪədiːn/ n. Jod, das

**ion** /ˈaɪən/ n. Ion, das

**iota** /aɪˈəʊtə/ n. **not one** or **an** ∼: nicht ein Jota (geh.)

**IOU** /aɪəʊˈjuː/ n. Schuldschein, der

**IQ** abbr. = **intelligence quotient** IQ, der; IQ-test IQ-Test, der

**IRA** abbr. = **Irish Republican Army** IRA, die

**Iran** /ɪˈrɑːn/ pr. n. Iran, der od. (das)

**Iraq** /ɪˈrɑːk/ pr. n. Irak, der od. (das)

**irate** /aɪˈreɪt/ adj. wütend

**Ireland** /ˈaɪələnd/ pr. n. Irland (das)

**iris** /ˈaɪərɪs/ n. (Bot., Anat.) Iris, die

**Irish** /ˈaɪərɪʃ/ ① adj. irisch; **sb. is** ∼: jmd. ist Ire/Irin
② n. **(a)** (language) Irisch, das; see also ENGLISH 2A
**(b)** constr. as pl. **the** ∼: die Iren Pl.

ˈ**Irish:** ∼**man** /ˈaɪərɪʃmən/ n., pl. ∼**men** /ˈaɪərɪʃmən/ Ire, der; ∼ **Reˈpublic** pr. n. Irische Republik; ∼ ˈ**Sea** pr. n. Irische See; ∼**woman** n. Irin, die

**irk** /ɜːk/ v.t. ärgern

**irksome** /ˈɜːksəm/ adj. lästig

**iron** /ˈaɪən/ ① n. **(a)** (metal) Eisen, das
**(b)** (for smoothing) Bügeleisen, das
② attrib. adj. eisern; Eisen⟨platte usw.⟩
③ v.t. & i. bügeln
▪ **iron ˈout** v.t. herausbügeln; (fig.) aus dem Weg räumen

**Iron ˈCurtain** n. (Hist.) Eiserner Vorhang

**ironic** /aɪˈrɒnɪk/, **ironical** /aɪˈrɒnɪkl/ adj. ironisch

**ironing** /ˈaɪənɪŋ/ n. Bügeln, das; (items) Bügelwäsche, die; **do the** ∼: bügeln

ˈ**ironing board** n. Bügelbrett, das

**ironmonger** /ˈaɪənmʌŋgə(r)/ n. (Brit.) Eisenwarenhändler, der/-händlerin, die

**irony** /ˈaɪrəni/ n. Ironie, die; **the** ∼ **was that** …: die Ironie lag darin, dass …

**irradiate** /ɪˈreɪdɪeɪt/ v.t. bestrahlen

**irrational** /ɪˈræʃənl/ adj. irrational

**irreconcilable** /ɪˈrekənsaɪləbl/ adj. (incompatible) unvereinbar

**irrefutable** /ɪrɪˈfjuːtəbl/ adj. unwiderlegbar

**irregular** /ɪˈregjʊlə(r)/ adj. unregelmäßig; unkorrekt ⟨Verhalten, Handlung usw.⟩

**irregularity** /ɪregjʊˈlærɪti/ n. ▶ IRREGULAR: Unregelmäßigkeit, die; Unkorrektheit, die

**irrelevance** /ɪˈrelɪvəns/, **irrelevancy** /ɪˈrelɪvənsi/ ns. Belanglosigkeit, die; Irrelevanz, die (geh.)

**irrelevant** /ɪˈrelɪvənt/ adj. belanglos; irrelevant (geh.)

**irreparable** /ɪˈrepərəbl/ adj. nicht wieder gutzumachend nicht präd.; irreparabel (geh., Med.)

**irreplaceable** /ɪrɪˈpleɪsəbl/ adj. unersetzlich

**irrepressible** /ɪrɪˈpresɪbl/ adj. nicht zu unterdrückend nicht präd.; **she is** ∼: sie ist nicht unterzukriegen (ugs.)

**irreproachable** /ɪrɪˈprəʊtʃəbl/ adj. untadelig

**irresistible** /ɪrɪˈzɪstɪbl/ adj. unwiderstehlich; bestechend ⟨Argument⟩

**irresolute** /ɪˈrezəluːt/ adj. unentschlossen

**irrespective** /ɪrɪˈspektɪv/ adj. ∼ **of** ungeachtet (+ Gen.)

**irresponsible** /ɪrɪˈspɒnsɪbl/ adj. verantwortungslos ⟨Person⟩; unverantwortlich ⟨Benehmen⟩

**irretrievable** /ɪrɪˈtriːvəbl/ adj. nicht mehr wiederzubekommen nicht attr.

**irreverence** /ɪˈrevərəns/ n. Respektlosigkeit, die

**irreverent** /ɪˈrevərənt/ adj. respektlos

**irreversible** /ɪrɪˈvɜːsɪbl/, **irrevocable** /ɪˈrevəkəbl/ adjs. unwiderruflich

**irrigate** /ˈɪrɪgeɪt/ v.t. bewässern

**irrigation** /ɪrɪˈgeɪʃn/ n. Bewässerung, die

**irritable** /ˈɪrɪtəbl/ adj. (quick to anger) reizbar; (temporarily) gereizt

**irritant** /ˈɪrɪtənt/ n. Reizstoff, der

**irritate** /ˈɪrɪteɪt/ v.t. **(a)** ärgern; **get** ∼**d** ärgerlich werden; **be** ∼**d by sth.** sich über etw. (Akk.) ärgern
**(b)** (Med.) reizen

**irritating** /ˈɪrɪteɪtɪŋ/ adj. lästig

**irritation** /ɪrɪˈteɪʃn/ n. **(a)** Ärger, der
**(b)** (Med.) Reizung, die

**is** ▶ BE

**Islam** /ˈɪzlɑːm/ n. Islam, der

**island** /ˈaɪlənd/ n. Insel, die

ˈ**islander** n. Inselbewohner, der/-bewohnerin, die

**island:** ∼**hop** v.i. **go** ∼**hopping** eine Inselhoppingtour machen; ∼**hopping** n. Inselhopping, das

**isle** /aɪl/ n. Insel, die

**isn't** /ˈɪznt/ (coll.) = **is not;** ▶ BE

**isolate** /ˈaɪsəleɪt/ v.t. isolieren

**isolated** /ˈaɪsəleɪtɪd/ adj. **(a)** (single) einzeln; ∼ **cases/instances** Einzelfälle
**(b)** (remote) abgelegen

**isolation** /aɪsə'leɪʃn/ n. **(a)** (act) Isolierung, *die*
**(b)** (state) Isolation, *die*

**ISP** abbr. = **Internet service provider** ISP

**Israel** /'ɪzreɪl/ pr. n. Israel (*das*)

**Israeli** /ɪz'reɪlɪ/ ⓵ adj. israelisch; **sb. is ~**: jmd. ist Israeli
⓶ n. Israeli, *der/die*

**issue** /'ɪʃuː, 'ɪsjuː/ ⓵ n. **(a)** (point in question) Frage, *die;* **make an ~ of sth.** etw. aufbauschen; **evade** or **dodge the ~**: ausweichen
**(b)** (of magazine etc.) Ausgabe, *die*
**(c)** (result, outcome) Ergebnis, *das*
⓶ v.t. **(a)** (give out) ausgeben; ausstellen ⟨*Pass*⟩; erteilen ⟨*Lizenz, Befehl*⟩; **~ sb. with sth.** etw. an jmdn. austeilen
**(b)** (publish) herausgeben ⟨*Publikation*⟩

**it** /ɪt/ pron. **(a)** es; **I can't cope with it any more** ich halte das nicht mehr länger aus; **what is it?** was ist los?
**(b)** (the thing, animal, young child previously mentioned) er/sie/es; *as direct obj.* ihn/sie/es; *as indirect obj.* ihm/ihr/ihm
**(c)** (the person in question) **who is it?** wer ist da?; **it was the children** es waren die Kinder; **is it you, Dad?** bist du es, Vater?

**IT** abbr. = **information technology** IT

**Italian** /ɪ'tæljən/ ⓵ adj. italienisch; **sb. is ~**: jmd. ist Italiener/Italienerin
⓶ n. **(a)** (person) Italiener, *der/*Italienerin, *die*
**(b)** (language) Italienisch, *das; see also* ENGLISH 2A

**italic** /ɪ'tælɪk/ ⓵ adj. kursiv
⓶ n. *in pl.* Kursivschrift, *die;* **in ~s** kursiv

**Italy** /'ɪtəlɪ/ pr. n. Italien (*das*)

**itch** /ɪtʃ/ ⓵ n. Juckreiz, *der;* **I have an ~**: es juckt mich
⓶ v.i. **(a)** (have a Juckreiz haben; **it ~es** es juckt
**(b)** **~** or **be ~ing to do sth.** darauf brennen, etw. zu tun

**'itchy** adj. kratzig; **be ~** ⟨*Körperteil:*⟩ jucken

**it'd** /'ɪtəd/ (coll.) **(a)** = **it had**
**(b)** = **it would**

**item** /'aɪtəm/ n. **(a)** Ding, *das;* Sache, *die;* (in shop, catalogue) Artikel, *der;* (on radio, TV) Nummer, *die;* **~ of clothing** Kleidungsstück, *das*
**(b)** **~** [of news] Nachricht, *die*

**itemize** /'aɪtəmaɪz/ v.t. einzeln aufführen

**itinerary** /aɪ'tɪnərərɪ/ n. Reiseroute, *die*

**it'll** /ɪtl/ (coll.) = **it will**

**its** /ɪts/ poss. pron. attrib. sein/ihr/sein

**it's** /ɪts/ **(a)** = **it is**
**(b)** = **it has**

**itself** /ɪt'self/ pron. **(a)** emphat. selbst
**(b)** refl. sich

**IUD** abbr. = **intrauterine device** IUP

**I've** /aɪv/ = **I have**

**IVF** abbr. = **in-vitro fertilization** IVF

**ivory** /'aɪvərɪ/ n. Elfenbein, *das; attrib.* elfenbeinern; Elfenbein-

**ivy** /'aɪvɪ/ n. Efeu, *der*

# J j

**J, j** /dʒeɪ/ n. J, j, *das*

**jab** /dʒæb/ ⓵ v.t., **-bb-** stoßen
⓶ n. **(a)** Stoß, *der;* (with needle) Stich, *der*
**(b)** (Brit. coll.: injection) Spritze, *die*

**jabber** /'dʒæbə(r)/ v.i. plappern (ugs.)

**jack** /dʒæk/ n. **(a)** (for car) Wagenheber, *der*
**(b)** (Cards) Bube, *der*

**jackal** /'dʒækl/ n. Schakal, *der*

**jackdaw** /'dʒækdɔː/ n. Dohle, *die*

**jacket** /'dʒækɪt/ n. **(a)** Jacke, *die;* (of suit) Jackett, *das;* sports **~**: Sakko, *der*
**(b)** (of book) Schutzumschlag, *der*
**(c)** **~ potatoes** in der Schale gebackene Kartoffeln

**jack: ~-knife** v.i. **the lorry ~-knifed** der Anhänger des Lastwagens stellte sich quer; **~pot** n. Jackpot, *der;* **hit the ~pot** (fig.) das große Los ziehen

**jacuzzi** (Amer.: ®) /dʒə'kuːzɪ/ n. ≈ Whirlpool, *der*

**jaded** /'dʒeɪdɪd/ adj. abgespannt

**jagged** /'dʒægɪd/ adj. gezackt

**jaguar** /'dʒægjʊə(r)/ n. Jaguar, *der*

**jail** /dʒeɪl/ ⓵ n. Gefängnis, *das*
⓶ v.t. ins Gefängnis bringen

**jail: ~bird** Knastbruder, *der* (ugs.); **~break** n. Gefängnisausbruch, *der*

**jailer, jailor** /'dʒeɪlə(r)/ n. Gefängniswärter, *der/*-wärterin, *die*

**jam¹** /dʒæm/ ⓵ v.t., **-mm-**: **(a)** (between two surfaces) einklemmen
**(b)** (make immovable) blockieren; (fig.) lähmen
⓶ v.i., **-mm-**: **(a)** (become wedged) sich verklemmen
**(b)** ⟨*Maschine:*⟩ klemmen
⓷ n. **(a)** (crush, stoppage) Blockierung, *die*

**(b)** (coll.: dilemma) **be in a** ∼: in der Klemme stecken (ugs.)

■ **jam 'on** *v.t.* ∼ **the brakes [full] on** [voll] auf die Bremse steigen (ugs.)

**jam²** *n.* Marmelade, *die*

**Jamaica** /dʒə'meɪkə/ *pr. n.* Jamaika (*das*)

**jamb** /dʒæm/ *n.* (of doorway, window) Pfosten, *der*

**'jam-packed** *adj.* (coll.) knallvoll (ugs.), proppenvoll (ugs.) **(with** von)

**Jan.** *abbr.* = **January** Jan.

**jangle** /'dʒæŋgl/ ①*v.i.* klimpern; ⟨Klingel:⟩ bimmeln
②*v.t.* rasseln mit

**janitor** /'dʒænɪtə(r)/ *n.* Hausmeister, *der*

**January** /'dʒænjʊərɪ/ *n.* Januar, *der; see also* AUGUST

**Japan** /dʒə'pæn/ *n.* Japan (*das*)

**Japanese** /dʒæpə'niːz/ ①*adj.* japanisch; **sb. is** ∼ jmd. ist Japaner/Japanerin
②*n., pl. same* **(a)** (person) Japaner, *der*/ Japanerin, *die*
**(b)** (language) Japanisch, *das; see also* ENGLISH 2A

**jar¹** /dʒɑː(r)/ ①*v.i., -rr-* quietschen; (fig.) ∼ **on sb./sb.'s nerves** jmdm. auf die Nerven gehen
②*v.t., -rr-* erschüttern

**jar²** *n.* Topf, *der;* (glass ∼) Glas, *das*

**jargon** /'dʒɑːgən/ *n.* Jargon, *der*

**jasmin[e]** /'dʒæsmɪn/ *n.* Jasmin, *der*

**jaundice** /'dʒɔːndɪs/ *n.* (Med.) Gelbsucht, *die*

**jaundiced** /'dʒɔːndɪst/ *adj.* (fig.) verbittert

**jaunt** /dʒɔːnt/ *n.* Ausflug, *der*

**jaunty** /'dʒɔːntɪ/ *adj.* unbeschwert; keck ⟨Hut⟩; **he wore his hat at a** ∼ **angle** er hatte sich (*Dat.*) den Hut keck aufs Ohr gesetzt

**javelin** /'dʒævlɪn/ *n.* **(a)** Speer, *der;*
**(b)** (Sport: event) Speerwerfen, *das*

**jaw** /dʒɔː/ Kiefer, *der*

**'jawbone** *n.* Kieferknochen, *der*

**jay** /dʒeɪ/ *n.* Eichelhäher, *der*

**'jay-walk** *v.i.* als Fußgänger im Straßenverkehr unachtsam sein

**jazz** /dʒæz/ ①*n.* Jazz, *der; attrib.* Jazz-
②*v.t.* ∼ **up** aufpeppen (ugs.)

**jazz:** ∼ **band** *n.* Jazzband, *die;* ∼ **dance** *n.* Jazztanz, *der;* ∼ **'rock** *n.* Jazzrock, *der*

**jazzy** /'dʒæzɪ/ *adj.* poppig; **a** ∼ **sports car** ein aufgemotzter Sportwagen (ugs.)

**jealous** /'dʒeləs/ *adj.* eifersüchtig (**of** auf + *Akk.*)

**'jealousy** *n.* Eifersucht, *die*

**jeans** /dʒiːnz/ *n. pl.* Jeans Pl.

**Jeep** ® /dʒiːp/ *n.* Jeep ⓌⓏ, *der*

**jeer** /dʒɪə(r)/ *v.i.* höhnen (geh.); ∼ **at sb.** jmdn. verhöhnen

**jelly** /'dʒelɪ/ *n.* Gelee, *das;* (dessert) Götterspeise, *die*

**'jellyfish** *n.* Qualle, *die*

**jeopardize** /'dʒepədaɪz/ *v.t.* gefährden

**jeopardy** /'dʒepədɪ/ *n.* **in** ∼: in Gefahr; gefährdet

**jerk** /dʒɜːk/ ①*n.* Ruck, *der*
②*v.t.* reißen an (+ *Dat.*)
③*v.i.* zucken

**jersey** /'dʒɜːzɪ/ *n.* Pullover, *der;* (Sport) Trikot, *das*

**jest** /dʒest/ ①*n.* Scherz, *der;* **in** ∼: im Scherz
②*v.i.* scherzen

**Jesus** /'dʒiːzəs/ *pr. n.* Jesus (*der*)

**jet** /dʒet/ *n.* **(a)** (stream) Strahl, *der*
**(b)** (nozzle) Düse, *die*
**(c)** (aircraft) Düsenflugzeug, *das;* Jet, *der*

**jet:** ∼**-black** *adj.* pechschwarz;
∼ **engine** *n.* Düsentriebwerk, *das;* ∼**foil** *n.* [Jetfoil-]Tragflügelboot, *das;* ∼ **lag** *n.* Jetlag, *der;* ∼**-lagged** *adj.* **sb. is** ∼**-lagged** jmdm. macht der Jetlag zu schaffen;
∼ **plane** *n.* Düsenflugzeug, *das;*
∼**-propelled** *adj.* düsengetrieben;
∼ **pro'pulsion** *n.* Düsen- *od.* Strahlantrieb, *der*

**jetsam** /'dʒetsəm/ *n.* ▶ FLOTSAM

**jet:** ∼ **set** *n.* Jet-set, *der;* ∼ **ski** *n.* Jetski, *der*

**jettison** /'dʒetɪsən/ *v.t.* über Bord werfen; (discard) wegwerfen

**jetty** /'dʒetɪ/ *n.* Landungsbrücke, *die*

**Jew** /dʒuː/ *n.* Jude, *der*/Jüdin, *die*

**jewel** /'dʒuːəl/ *n.* Juwel, *das od. der*

**'jewel box, 'jewel case** *ns.* Schmuckkasten, *der*

**jeweller** (*Amer.:* **jeweler**) /'dʒuːələ(r)/ *n.* Juwelier, *der*

**jewellery** (Brit.), **jewelry** /'dʒuːəlrɪ/ *n.* Schmuck, *der*

**Jewish** /'dʒuːɪʃ/ *adj.* jüdisch; **he/she is** ∼: er ist Jude/sie ist Jüdin

**jib** /dʒɪb/ *v.i., -bb-* sich sträuben (**at** gegen)

**jibe** ▶ GIBE

**jiffy** /'dʒɪfɪ/ *n.* (coll.) **in a** ∼: sofort

**'Jiffy bag** ® *n.* gefütterte Versandtasche

**jig** /dʒɪg/ *n.* Jig, *die*

**'jigsaw** *n.* **(a)** Dekupiersäge, *die;* (electric) Stichsäge, *die*
**(b)** ∼ **[puzzle]** Puzzle, *das*

**jilt** /dʒɪlt/ *v.t.* sitzenlassen (ugs.)

**jingle** /'dʒɪŋgl/ ①*n.* (Commerc.) Werbespruch, *der;* Jingle, *der* (Werbespr.)
②*v.i.* klimpern; ⟨Glöckchen:⟩ bimmeln
③*v.t.* klimpern mit ⟨Münzen, Schlüsseln⟩

**jinx** /dʒɪŋks/ (coll.) ①*n.* Fluch, *der*
②*v.t.* verhexen

**jitters** /'dʒɪtəz/ *n. pl.* (coll.) großes Zittern

**jittery** /'dʒɪtərɪ/ *adj.* (coll.) (nervous) nervös; (frightened) verängstigt

**job** /dʒɒb/ *n.* **(a)** (piece of work) Arbeit, *die;* **I have a** ∼ **for you** ich habe eine Aufgabe für dich
**(b)** (employment) Stelle, *die;* Job, *der* (ugs.)

**job:** ~ **advert** n. Stellenanzeige, die; ~**centre** n. (Brit.) Arbeitsvermittlungsstelle, die; ~ **creation scheme** n. Beschäftigungsprogramm, das; Arbeitsbeschaffungsprogramm, das; ~ **description** n. Arbeitsplatzbeschreibung, die; ~ **evaluation** n. Arbeitsbewertung, die; ~**hunt** v.i. go/be ~hunting auf Arbeits- od. Stellensuche gehen/sein; ~**hunter** n. Stellen- od. Arbeitssuchende, der/die; ~**hunting** n. Arbeitssuche, die; Stellensuche, die

**'jobless** adj. arbeitslos

**job:** ~ **market** n. Arbeitsmarkt, der; Stellenmarkt, der; ~ **offer** n. Stellenangebot, das; ~ **satisfaction** n. Arbeitszufriedenheit, die; ~ **security** n. Arbeitsplatzsicherheit, die; ~**share** ☐ n. geteilter Arbeitsplatz; ☑ v.i. sich (Dat.) einen Arbeitsplatz teilen (with mit); ~**sharing** n. Jobsharing, das

**jockey** /'dʒɒkɪ/ n. Jockei, der

**jockey shorts** n. pl. (Amer.) Unterhose, die; Unterhosen Pl.

**jocular** /'dʒɒkjʊlə(r)/ adj. lustig

**jodhpurs** /'dʒɒdpəz/ n. pl. Reithose, die

**jog** /dʒɒg/ ☐ v.t., **-gg-:** (a) (shake) rütteln (b) (nudge) [an]stoßen (c) ~ **sb.'s memory** jmds. Gedächtnis (Dat.) auf die Sprünge helfen ☑ v.i., **-gg-:** (a) (up and down) auf und ab hüpfen (b) (trot) ⟨Pferd:⟩ [dahin]trotten (c) (Sport) joggen ☐ n. **go for a** ~: joggen gehen

**jogger** /'dʒɒgə(r)/ n. Jogger, der/Joggerin, die

**'jogging** n. Jogging, das

**'jogtrot** n. (lit. or fig.) Trott, der

**john** /dʒɒn/ n. (Amer. sl.: lavatory) Lokus, der (salopp)

**join** /dʒɔɪn/ ☐ v.t. (a) (connect) verbinden (**to** mit) (b) (come into company of) sich gesellen zu (c) eintreten in (+ Akk.) ⟨Armee, Firma, Verein, Partei⟩ ☑ v.i. ⟨Straßen:⟩ zusammenlaufen ■ **join in** ☐ /-'-/ v.i. mitmachen (**with** bei) ☑ /'--/ v.t. mitmachen bei ■ **join up** ☐ v.i. (Mil.) einrücken ☑ v.t. miteinander verbinden

**'joiner** n. Tischler, der/Tischlerin, die

**joinery** /'dʒɔɪnərɪ/ n., no art. (craft) Tischlerei, die; Tischlerhandwerk, das

**joint** /dʒɔɪnt/ ☐ n. (a) (Building) Fuge, die (b) (Anat.) Gelenk, das (c) **a** ~ **[of meat]** ein Stück Fleisch; (for roasting) ein Braten (d) (coll.: place) Laden, der (e) (sl.: marijuana cigarette) Joint, der ☑ adj. (a) (of two or more) gemeinsam (b) Mit⟨autor, -erbe, -besitzer⟩

**'jointly** adv. gemeinsam

**joint 'venture** n. (Commerc.) Jointventure, das

**joist** /dʒɔɪst/ n. (Building) Deckenbalken, der; (steel) [Decken]träger, der

**joke** /dʒəʊk/ ☐ n. Witz, der; Scherz, der ☑ v.i. scherzen, Witze machen (**about** über + Akk.); **joking apart** Scherz beiseite!

**'joker** n. (a) Spaßvogel, der (b) (Cards) Joker, der

**jollity** /'dʒɒlɪtɪ/ n. Fröhlichkeit, die; (merrymaking) Festlichkeit, die

**jolly** /'dʒɒlɪ/ ☐ adj. fröhlich ☑ adv. (Brit. coll.) ganz schön (ugs.); ~ **good!** ausgezeichnet!

**jolt** /dʒəʊlt/ ☐ v.t. ⟨Fahrzeug:⟩ durchrütteln ☑ v.i. ⟨Fahrzeug:⟩ holpern ☐ n. (a) (jerk) Stoß, der; Ruck, der (b) (fig.: shock) Schock, der

**Jordan** /'dʒɔːdn/ pr. n. Jordanien (das)

**jostle** /'dʒɒsl/ ☐ v.i. ~ **[against each other]** aneinander stoßen ☑ v.t. stoßen

**jot** /dʒɒt/ n. **[not] a** ~: [k]ein bisschen ■ **jot 'down** v.t. [rasch] aufschreiben

**jotter** /'dʒɒtə(r)/ n. Notizblock, der

**journal** /'dʒɜːnl/ n. Zeitschrift, die

**journalism** /'dʒɜːnəlɪzm/ n. Journalismus, der

**journalist** /'dʒɜːnəlɪst/ n. Journalist, der/Journalistin, die

**journey** /'dʒɜːnɪ/ n. (a) Reise, die (b) (of vehicle) Fahrt, die

**jovial** /'dʒəʊvɪəl/ adj. herzlich ⟨Gruß⟩; fröhlich ⟨Person⟩

**jowl** /dʒaʊl/ n. (jaw) Unterkiefer, der; (lower part of face) Kinnbacken Pl.; (double chin) Doppelkinn, das

**joy** /dʒɔɪ/ n. Freude, die

**joyful** /'dʒɔɪfl/ adj. froh [gestimmt] ⟨Person⟩; freudig ⟨Blick, Ereignis, Gesang⟩

**joy:** ~**ride** n. (coll.) Spritztour, die [im gestohlenen Auto]; ~**stick** n. (a) (Aeronaut.) Knüppel, der; (b) (on computer etc.) Hebel, der; Joystick, der

**JP** abbr. = **Justice of the Peace**

**jubilant** /'dʒuːbɪlənt/ adj. jubelnd; **be** ~ ⟨Person⟩ frohlocken

**jubilation** /dʒuːbɪ'leɪʃn/ n. Jubel, der

**jubilee** /'dʒuːbɪliː/ n. Jubiläum, das

**Judaism** /'dʒuːdeɪɪzm/ n., no art. Judentum, das; Judaismus, der

**judge** /dʒʌdʒ/ ☐ n. (a) Richter, der/Richterin, die (b) (in contest) Preisrichter, der/-richterin, die (c) (fig.: critic) Kenner, der/Kennerin, die ☑ v.t. (a) (sentence) richten (geh.) (b) (form opinion about) [be]urteilen

**'judg[e]ment** n. (a) Urteil, das (b) (critical faculty) Urteilsvermögen, das

**judicial** /dʒuː'dɪʃl/ adj. gerichtlich

**judiciary** /dʒuː'dɪʃərɪ/ n. Richterschaft, die

**judicious** /dʒuː'dɪʃəs/ adj. klar blickend

**judo** /'dʒuːdəʊ/ n. Judo, das

**jug** /dʒʌg/ n. Krug, der; (with lid, water ~) Kanne, die

**juggernaut** /'dʒʌgənɔːt/ n. (Brit.: lorry) schwerer Brummer (ugs.)

**juggle** /'dʒʌgl/ v.i. jonglieren

**juggler** /'dʒʌglə(r)/ n. Jongleur, der/ Jongleurin, die

**juice** /dʒuːs/ n. Saft, der

**juicy** /'dʒuːsɪ/ adj. saftig

**jukebox** /'dʒuːkbɒks/ n. Jukebox, die; Musikbox, die

**Jul.** abbr. = **July** Jul.

**July** /dʒuˈlaɪ/ n. Juli, der; see also AUGUST

**jumble** /'dʒʌmbl/ **1** v.t. ~ up durcheinander bringen **2** n. Durcheinander, das

**'jumble sale** n. (Brit.) Trödelmarkt, der

**jumbo jet** /dʒʌmbəʊ 'dʒet/ n. Jumbojet, der

**jump** /dʒʌmp/ **1** n. (a) Sprung, der **(b)** (in prices) sprunghafter Anstieg **2** v.i. (a) springen; ~ for joy einen Freudensprung machen **(b)** ~ to conclusions voreilige Schlüsse ziehen **3** v.t. (a) überspringen **(b)** ~ the queue (Brit.) sich vordrängeln ■ **jump a'bout, jump a'round** v.i. herumspringen (ugs.) ■ **'jump at** v.t. (fig.) sofort zugreifen bei ⟨Angebot, Gelegenheit⟩

**jumped-up** /'dʒʌmptʌp/ adj. (coll.) emporgekommen

**'jumper** n. Pullover, der

**jump:** ~ **jet** n. Senkrechtstarter, der; ~ **leads** n. pl. (Brit. Motor Veh.) Starthilfekabel Pl. ; ~**start** **1** v.t. Starthilfe geben (+ Dat.) ⟨Auto⟩; (fig.) [wieder] in Gang bringen; [wieder] ankurbeln ⟨Wirtschaft, Industrie⟩; **2** n. Start durch Starthilfe; (fig.) neuer Impuls od. Auftrieb; ~**suit** n. Overall, der

**jumpy** /'dʒʌmpɪ/ adj. nervös

**Jun.** abbr. = **June** Jun.

**junction** /'dʒʌŋkʃn/ n. (a) (of railway lines, roads) ≈ Einmündung, die **(b)** (crossroads) Kreuzung, die

**'junction box** n. (Electr.) Verteilerkasten, der

**juncture** /'dʒʌŋktʃə(r)/ n. at this ~: zu diesem Zeitpunkt

**June** /dʒuːn/ n. Juni, der; see also AUGUST

**jungle** /'dʒʌŋgl/ n. Dschungel, der

**junior** /'dʒuːnɪə(r)/ adj. (a) (in age) jünger; ~ **team** (Sport) Juniorenmannschaft, die **(b)** (in rank) rangniedriger ⟨Person⟩; niedriger ⟨Rang⟩

**junior:** ~ **'partner** n. Juniorpartner, der/ -partnerin, die; ~ **school** n. (Brit.) Grundschule, die

**junk** /dʒʌŋk/ n. Trödel, der (ugs.); (trash) Ramsch, der (ugs.)

**'junk food** n. minderwertige Kost

**junkie** /'dʒʌŋkɪ/ n. (sl.) Junkie, der (Drogenjargon)

**junk:** ~ **mail** n. Postwurfsendungen Pl.; Reklame, die; ~ **shop** n. Trödelladen, der (ugs.)

**Jupiter** /'dʒuːpɪtə(r)/ pr. n. (Astron.) Jupiter, der

**jurisdiction** /dʒʊərɪsˈdɪkʃn/ n. Gerichtsbarkeit, die

**juror** /'dʒʊərə(r)/ n. Geschworene, der/die

**jury** /'dʒʊərɪ/ n. (a) (in court) the ~: die Geschworenen Pl. **(b)** (in competition) Jury, die

**just** /dʒʌst/ **1** adj. (morally right) gerecht **2** adv. (a) (exactly) genau; ~ then/enough gerade da/genug; ~ as (exactly as) genauso wie; (when) gerade, als; ~ as you like or please ganz wie Sie wünschen/du magst; ~ as good etc. genauso gut usw. **(b)** (barely) gerade [eben]; (with little time to spare) gerade noch; (no more than) nur; ~ under £10 nicht ganz zehn Pfund **(c)** (at this moment) gerade; not ~ now im Moment nicht **(d)** (coll.) (simply) einfach; (only) nur; esp. with imper. mal [eben]; ~ look at that! guck dir das mal an!; ~ a moment einen Moment mal; ~ in case für alle Fälle

**justice** /'dʒʌstɪs/ n. (a) Gerechtigkeit, die **(b)** (magistrate) Schiedsrichter, der/-richterin, die; J~ of the Peace Friedensrichter, der/ -richterin, die

**justifiable** /dʒʌstɪˈfaɪəbl/ adj. berechtigt

**justifiably** /dʒʌstɪˈfaɪəblɪ/ adv. zu Recht

**justification** /dʒʌstɪfɪˈkeɪʃn/ n. Rechtfertigung, die

**justify** /'dʒʌstɪfaɪ/ v.t. rechtfertigen; be justified in doing sth. etw. zu Recht tun

**jut** /dʒʌt/ v.i., -tt-: ~ [out] [her]vorragen; herausragen

**juvenile** /'dʒuːvənaɪl/ **1** adj. (a) jugendlich **(b)** (immature) kindisch **2** n. Jugendliche, der/die

**juvenile delinquency** /dɪˈlɪŋkwənsɪ/ n. Jugendkriminalität, die

**juvenile delinquent** /dɪˈlɪŋkwənt/ n. jugendlicher Straftäter/jugendliche Straftäterin

**juxtapose** /dʒʌkstəˈpəʊz/ v.t. nebeneinander stellen (with, to und)

**juxtaposition** /dʒʌkstəpəˈzɪʃn/ n. Nebeneinanderstellung, die

# K k

**K, k** /keɪ/ n. K, k, das

**kale** /keɪl/ n. Grünkohl, der; Krauskohl, der

**kaleidoscope** /kəˈlaɪdəskəʊp/ n. Kaleidoskop, das

**kangaroo** /kæŋgəˈruː/ n. Känguru, das

**karaoke** /kærɪˈəʊkɪ/ n., no indef. art. Karaoke, das; attrib. Karaoke-

**karate** /kəˈrɑːtɪ/ n. Karate, das

**kebab** /kɪˈbæb/ n. Kebab, der

**keel** /kiːl/ n. [1] (Naut.) Kiel, der
[2] v.i. ~ over umstürzen; ⟨Schiff:⟩ kentern; ⟨Person:⟩ umkippen

**keen** /kiːn/ adj. (a) (sharp) scharf
(b) (cold) schneidend ⟨Wind, Kälte⟩
(c) (eager) begeistert ⟨Fußballfan, Sportler⟩; lebhaft ⟨Interesse⟩; be ~ to do sth. darauf erpicht sein, etw. zu tun; be ~ on doing sth. etw. gern[e] tun
(d) (sensitive) scharf ⟨Augen⟩; fein ⟨Sinne⟩

**'keenly** adv. (a) (sharply) scharf
(b) (eagerly) eifrig; brennend ⟨interessiert sein⟩
(c) (acutely) be ~ aware of sth. sich (Dat.) einer Sache (Gen.) voll bewusst sein

**keep** /kiːp/ [1] v.t., kept /kept/ (a) halten ⟨Versprechen, Schwur, Sabbat, Fasten⟩; einhalten ⟨Verabredung, Vereinbarung⟩; begehen, feiern ⟨Fest⟩
(b) (have charge of) aufbewahren
(c) (retain) behalten; (not lose or destroy) aufheben ⟨Quittung, Rechnung⟩
(d) halten ⟨Bienen, Hund usw⟩
(e) führen ⟨Tagebuch, Geschäft, Ware⟩
(f) (support) versorgen ⟨Familie⟩
(g) (detain) festhalten; ~ sb. waiting jmdn. warten lassen; what kept you? wo bleibst du denn?
(h) (reserve) aufheben
[2] v.i., kept (a) (remain) bleiben; are you ~ing well? gehts dir gut?
(b) ~ [to the] left/right sich links/rechts halten; ~ doing sth. (repeatedly) etw. immer wieder tun; ~ talking/working etc. until ...: weiterreden/-arbeiten usw., bis ...
(c) (remain good) ⟨Lebensmittel:⟩ sich halten
[3] n. (a) (maintenance) Unterhalt, der
(b) for ~s (coll.) auf Dauer
(c) (Hist.: tower) Bergfried, der

■ **keep 'back** [1] v.i. zurückbleiben
[2] v.t. (restrain) zurückhalten ⟨Menschenmenge, Tränen⟩
(b) (withhold) verschweigen ⟨Informationen, Tatsachen⟩ (from Dat.)

■ **keep 'down** [1] v.i. unten bleiben
[2] v.t. (a) niedrig halten ⟨Steuern, Preise usw.⟩; ~ one's weight down nicht zunehmen
(b) keep your voice down! rede nicht so laut!

■ **keep 'off** [1] v.i. ⟨Person:⟩ wegbleiben
[2] v.t. fern halten; '~ off the grass' „Betreten des Rasens verboten"

■ **keep 'on** v.i. weitermachen (with Akk.); ~ on doing sth. etw. [immer] weiter tun; (repeatedly) etw. immer wieder tun

■ **keep 'out** [1] v.i. '~out „Zutritt verboten"
[2] v.t. nicht hereinlassen

■ **keep 'up** [1] v.i. ~ up with sb./sth. mit jmdm./etw. Schritt halten
[2] v.t. aufrechterhalten ⟨Freundschaft, jmds. Moral⟩; ~ one's strength up sich bei Kräften halten; ~ it up! weiter so!

**keep-'fit** n. Fitnesstraining, das

**keep-'fit class** n. Fitnessgruppe, die; go to ~es zu Fitnessübungen gehen

**'keeping** n. be in ~ with sth. einer Sache (Dat.) entsprechen

**'keepsake** n. Andenken, das

**keg** /keg/ n. [kleines] Fass

**kelp** /kelp/ n. [See]tang, der

**kennel** /ˈkenl/ n. Hundehütte, die

**Kenya** /ˈkenjə/ pr. n. Kenia (das)

**kept** ▶ KEEP 1, 2

**kerb** /kɜːb/ n. (Brit.) Bordstein, der

**kerb: ~-crawling** n. (Brit.) (langsames) Fahren auf dem Autostrich zur Kontaktaufnahme mit einer Prostituierten; **~stone** n. (Brit.) Bordstein, der

**kernel** /ˈkɜːnl/ n. Kern, der

**kerosene, kerosine** /ˈkerəsiːn/ n. (Amer., Austral., NZ/as tech. term) Paraffin[öl], das; (for jet engines) Kerosin, das

**kestrel** /ˈkestrəl/ n. Turmfalke, der

**ketch** /ketʃ/ n. Ketsch, die

**ketchup** /ˈketʃʌp/ n. Ketschup, der od. das

**kettle** /ˈketl/ n. [Wasser]kessel, der

**key** /kiː/ [1] n. (a) Schlüssel, der
(b) (on piano, typewriter, computer, etc.) Taste, die
(c) (Mus.) Tonart, die
[2] v.t. (Comp.) eintasten

**key: ~board** n. (of piano etc.) Klaviatur, die; (of typewriter, computer, etc.) Tastatur, die; **~board operator** Taster, der/Tasterin, die; **~boarder** n. Taster, der/Tasterin, die; **~boarding** n. Tasten, das; **~boarding error** Tastfehler, der; **~hole** n. Schlüsselloch, das; **~hole surgery** n. Schlüssellochchirurgie, die; Knopflochchirurgie, die

**'keying** ▶ KEYBOARDING

**key: ~ring** n. Schlüsselring, der; **~stone** n. (Archit.) Schlussstein, der; (fig.) Grundpfeiler, der; **~stroke** n. Anschlag, der

**kg.** *abbr.* = **kilogram[s]** kg

**khaki** /'kɑːkɪ/ ⟨1⟩ *adj.* khakifarben
⟨2⟩ *n.* (cloth) Khaki, *der*

**kick** /kɪk/ ⟨1⟩ *n.* **(a)** [Fuß]tritt, *der;* (Footb.)
Schuss, *der;* **give sb. a** ~: jmdm. einen Tritt
geben

**(b)** (coll.: thrill) **do sth. for** ~s etw. zum Spaß
tun; **he gets a** ~ **out of it** er hat Spaß daran
⟨2⟩ *v.i.* treten; ⟨*Pferd:*⟩ ausschlagen
⟨3⟩ *v.t.* einen Tritt geben (+ *Dat.*) ⟨*Person,
Hund*⟩; treten gegen ⟨*Gegenstand*⟩; kicken
(ugs.), schießen ⟨*Ball*⟩

■ **kick a'bout, kick a'round** *v.t.* [in der
Gegend] herumkicken (ugs.)

■ **kick 'off** *v.i.* (Footb.) anstoßen

■ **kick 'up** *v.t.* (coll.) ~ **up a fuss/row** Krach
schlagen/anfangen (ugs.)

**kick:** ~**off** *n.* (Footb.) Anstoß, *der;*
~**start** ⟨1⟩ *n.* **(a)** Kickstarter, *der;* **(b)** (fig.)
[neuer] Auftrieb; ⟨2⟩ *v.t.* **(a)** [mit dem
Kickstarter] starten; **(b)** (fig.) ankurbeln
⟨*Industrie, Wirtschaft*⟩; vorantreiben,
forcieren ⟨*Friedensprozess, Entwicklung*⟩

**kid** /kɪd/ ⟨1⟩ *n.* **(a)** (young goat) Kitz, *das*
**(b)** (coll.: child) Kind, *das*
⟨2⟩ *v.t.,* **-dd-** (coll.) auf den Arm nehmen (ugs.);
~ **oneself** sich (*Dat.*) was vormachen

**kiddie** /'kɪdɪ/ *n.* (coll.) Kindchen, *das*

**kid-'glove** *adj.* sanft

**kidnap** /'kɪdnæp/ *v.t.,* (Brit.) **-pp-** entführen

**'kidnapper** *n.* Entführer, *der*/Entführerin,
*die*

**kidney** /'kɪdnɪ/ *n.* Niere, *die*

**kidney:** ~ **bean** *n.* Gartenbohne, *die;*
(scarlet runner bean) Feuerbohne, *die;* **red**
~ **bean** Kidneybohne, *die;* ~ **machine** *n.*
künstliche Niere; ~**-shaped** *adj.*
nierenförmig

**kill** /kɪl/ *v.t.* **(a)** töten; (deliberately)
umbringen; **be** ~**ed in action** im Kampf
fallen; **be** ~**ed in a car crash** bei einem
Autounfall ums Leben kommen
**(b)** ~ **time** die Zeit totschlagen

**'killer** *n.* Mörder, *der*/Mörderin, *die*

**'killer whale** *n.* Mörderwal, *der*

**'killing** *n.* **(a)** Töten, *das*
**(b)** **make a** ~ (coll.: great profit) einen
[Mords]reibach machen (ugs.)

**'killjoy** *n.* Spielverderber, *der*/-verderberin,
*die*

**kiln** /kɪln/ *n.* Brennofen, *der*

**kilo** /'kiːləʊ/ *n., pl.* ~**s** Kilo, *das*

**kilogram, kilogramme** /'kɪləgræm/ *n.*
Kilogramm, *das*

**kilometre** (*Brit.; Amer.:* **kilometer**)
/'kɪləmiːtə(r) (Brit.), kɪ'lɒmɪtə(r)/ *n.*
Kilometer, *der*

**kilowatt** *n.* /'kɪləwɒt/ Kilowatt, *das*

**kilt** /kɪlt/ *n.* Kilt, *der*

**kimono** /kɪ'məʊnəʊ/ *n., pl.* ~**s** Kimono, *der*

**kin** /kɪn/ *n.* (relatives) Verwandte *Pl.;* (relative)
Verwandte, *der/die*

**kind¹** /kaɪnd/ *n.* **(a)** (class, sort) Art, *die;*

several ~s **of apples** mehrere Sorten Äpfel;
**all** ~s **of things/excuses** alles Mögliche/alle
möglichen Ausreden; **no ... of any** ~:
keinerlei ...; **what** ~ **is it?** was für einer/
eine/eins ist es?; **what** ~ **of [a] tree is this?**
was für ein Baum ist das?
**(b)** (implying vagueness) **a** ~ **of ...**: [so] eine
Art ...; ~ **of cute** (coll.) irgendwie niedlich
(ugs.)

**kind²** *adj.* liebenswürdig; (showing friendliness)
freundlich; **be** ~ **to animals** gut zu Tieren
sein; **how** ~! wie nett [von ihm/Ihnen *usw.*]!

**kindergarten** /'kɪndəɡɑːtn/ *n.*
Kindergarten, *der*

**kind-hearted** /kaɪnd'hɑːtɪd/ *adj.*
gutherzig

**kindle** /'kɪndl/ (fig.) wecken

**kindly** /'kaɪndlɪ/ ⟨1⟩ *adv.* **(a)** freundlich;
nett
**(b)** *in polite request etc.* freundlicherweise;
**thank you** ~: herzlichen Dank
⟨2⟩ *adj.* freundlich; nett; (kind-hearted) gütig

**'kindness** *n.* **(a)** *no pl.* (kind nature)
Freundlichkeit, *die*
**(b)** **do sb. a** ~ (kind act) jmdm. eine
Gefälligkeit erweisen

**kindred** /'kɪndrɪd/ *adj.* verwandt; ~ **'spirit**
Gleichgesinnte, *der/die*

**king** /kɪŋ/ *n.* König, *der*

**kingdom** /'kɪŋdəm/ *n.* Königreich, *das*

**'kingfisher** *n.* Eisvogel, *der*

**'king-size[d]** *adj.* extragroß; King-size-
⟨*Zigaretten*⟩

**kink** /kɪŋk/ *n.* (in pipe, wire, etc.) Knick, *der;*
(in hair, wool) Welle, *die*

**'kinky** *adj.* (coll.) spleenig; (sexually) abartig

**kinsman** /'kɪnzmən/ *n., pl.* **kinsmen**
/'kɪnzmən/ Verwandte, *der*

**kinswoman** /'kɪnzwʊmn/ *n.* Verwandte,
*die*

**kiosk** /'kiːɒsk/ *n.* **(a)** Kiosk, *der*
**(b)** (telephone booth) [Telefon]zelle, *die*

**kip** /kɪp/ *n.* (Brit. coll.: sleep) **have a/get some**
~: eine Runde pennen (salopp)

**kipper** /'kɪpə(r)/ *n.* Kipper, *der*

**kiss** /kɪs/ ⟨1⟩ *n.* Kuss, *der*
⟨2⟩ *v.t.* küssen; ~ **sb. good night/goodbye**
jmdm. einen Gutenacht-/Abschiedskuss
geben
⟨3⟩ *v.i.* **they** ~**ed** sie küssten sich

**kit** /kɪt/ *n.* **(a)** (Brit.: set of items) Set, *das*
**(b)** (Brit.: clothing etc.) **sports** ~: Sportzeug,
*das;* **riding/skiing** ~: Reit-/Skiausrüstung,
*die*

**'kitbag** *n.* Tornister, *der*

**kitchen** /'kɪtʃɪn/ *n.* Küche, *die; attrib.*
Küchen-

**kitchen:** ~ **paper** *n.* Küchenkrepp, *der;*
~ **roll** *n.* Küchenrolle, *die;* (kitchen paper)
Küchenkrepp, *der;* ~ **'sink** *n.*
[Küchen]ausguss, *der;* ~ **unit** *n.* ⋯❖

Küchenelement, *das;* ∼ **units** Küchenmöbel *Pl.;* ∼ **utensil** *n.* Küchengerät, *das;* ∼**ware** *n.* Küchengeräte *Pl.*

**kite** /kaɪt/ *n.* Drachen, *der*

**kith** /kɪθ/ *n.* ∼ **and kin** Freunde und Verwandte

**kitten** /'kɪtn/ *n.* Kätzchen, *das*

**kitty** /'kɪtɪ/ *n.* (money) Kasse, *die*

**kleptomania** /kleptə'meɪnɪə/ *n.* Kleptomanie, *die*

**kleptomaniac** /kleptə'meɪnɪæk/ *n.* Kleptomane, *der*/Kleptomanin, *die*

**km.** *abbr.* = **kilometre[s]** km

**knack** /næk/ *n.* Talent, *das;* **get the** ∼ [**of doing sth.**] den Bogen rauskriegen [, wie man etw. macht] (ugs.); **have lost the** ∼: es nicht mehr zustande bringen

**knapsack** /'næpsæk/ *n.* Rucksack, *der;* (Mil.) Tornister, *der*

**knead** /niːd/ *v.t.* kneten

**knee** /niː/ *n.* Knie, *das*

**knee:** ∼**cap** *n.* Kniescheibe, *die;* ∼**-deep** *adj.* knietief; ∼**-high** *adj.* kniehoch; ∼**-jerk reaction** *n.* (fig.) automatische Reaktion; ∼ **joint** *n.* Kniegelenk, *das*

**kneel** /niːl/ *v.i.,* **knelt** /nelt/ *or* (esp. Amer.) **kneeled** knien; ∼ **down** niederknien

**'knee-length** *adj.* knielang

**knelt** ▶ KNEEL

**knew** ▶ KNOW

**knickers** /'nɪkəz/ *n. pl.* (Brit.) [Damen]schlüpfer, *der*

**knife** /naɪf/ ① *n., pl.* **knives** /naɪvz/ Messer, *das* ② *v.t.* (stab) einstechen auf (+ *Akk.*); (kill) erstechen

**'knife-edge** *n.* Schneide, *die;* **be [balanced] on a** ∼ (fig.) auf des Messers Schneide stehen

**knight** /naɪt/ *n.* (a) (Hist.) Ritter, *der* (b) (Chess) Springer, *der*

**'knighthood** *n.* Ritterwürde, *die*

**knit** /nɪt/ *v.t.,* **-tt-** stricken; ∼ **one's brow** die Stirn runzeln

**'knitting** *n.* Stricken, *das;* (work being knitted) Strickarbeit, *die*

**'knitting needle** *n.* Stricknadel, *die*

**'knitwear** *n.* Strickwaren *Pl.*

**knives** *pl. of* KNIFE 1

**knob** /nɒb/ *n.* (a) (on door, walking stick, etc.) Knauf, *der* (b) (control on radio etc.) Knopf, *der* (c) (of butter) Klümpchen, *das*

**knock** /nɒk/ ① *v.t.* (a) (strike) (lightly) klopfen an (+ *Akk.*); (forcefully) schlagen gegen *od.* an (+ *Akk.*); ∼ **a hole in sth.** ein Loch in etw. (*Akk.*) schlagen (b) (coll.: criticize) herziehen über (+ *Akk.*) (ugs.) ② *v.i.* klopfen (**at an** + *Akk.*) ③ *n.* Klopfen, *das*

■ **knock 'down** *v.t.* (a) (in car) umfahren (b) (demolish) abreißen

■ **knock 'off** ① *v.t.* (a) ∼ **off work** (coll.: leave) Feierabend machen (b) (deduct) ∼ **five pounds off the price** es fünf Pfund billiger machen (c) (coll.: do quickly) aus dem Ärmel schütteln (ugs.) (d) (coll.: steal) klauen (salopp) ② *v.i.* (coll.) Feierabend machen

■ **knock 'out** *v.t.* (a) (make unconscious) bewusstlos umfallen lassen (b) (Boxing) k.o. schlagen (c) (coll.: exhaust) kaputtmachen (ugs.)

■ **knock 'over** *v.t.* umstoßen; ⟨*Fahrer, Fahrzeug:*⟩ umfahren ⟨*Person*⟩

**'knock-down** *adj.* ∼ **prices** Schleuderpreise

**'knocker** *n.* [Tür]klopfer, *der*

**knock:** ∼**-kneed** /'nɒkniːd/ *adj.* x-beinig ⟨*Person*⟩; ∼**out** *n.* (Boxing) K.-o.-Schlag, *der*

**knot** /nɒt/ ① *n.* Knoten, *der* ② *v.t.,* **-tt-** knoten ⟨*Seil, Faden usw.*⟩

**'knotty** *adj.* (fig.: puzzling) verwickelt

**know** /nəʊ/ *v.t.,* **knew** /njuː/, **known** /nəʊn/ (a) (recognize) erkennen (**by** an + *Dat.,* **for** als + *Akk.*) (b) (be able to distinguish) ∼ **sth. from sth.** etw. von etw. unterscheiden können (c) (be aware of) wissen (d) (have understanding of) können ⟨*ABC, Einmaleins, Deutsch usw.*⟩; ∼ **how to mend fuses** wissen, wie man Sicherungen repariert; ∼ **how to drive a car** Auto fahren können (e) kennen ⟨*Person*⟩

**'know-all** *n.* Neunmalkluge, *der*/*die*

**'know-how** *n.* praktisches Wissen; (technical expertise) Know-how, *das*

**'knowing** *adj.* (a) wissend ⟨*Blick, Lächeln*⟩ (b) (cunning) verschlagen

**'knowingly** *adv.* (a) (intentionally) wissentlich (b) viel sagend ⟨*lächeln, anblicken*⟩

**knowledge** /'nɒlɪdʒ/ *n.* (a) (familiarity) Kenntnisse *Pl.* (**of** in + *Dat.*) (b) (awareness) Wissen, *das;* **have no** ∼ **of sth.** nichts von etw. wissen; keine Kenntnis von etw. haben (geh.) (c) [a] ∼ **of languages/French** Sprach-/Französischkenntnisse *Pl.*

**knowledgeable** /'nɒlɪdʒəbl/ *adj.* **be** ∼ **about** *or* **on sth.** viel über etw. (*Akk.*) wissen

**known** /nəʊn/ ① ▶ KNOW ② *adj.* bekannt

**knuckle** /'nʌkl/ *n.* [Finger]knöchel, *der*

**Koran** /kɔː'rɑːn, kə'rɑːn/ *n.* Koran, *der*

**Korea** /kə'rɪə/ *pr. n.* Korea (*das*)

**Korean** /kə'riːən/ ① *adj.* koreanisch; **sb. is** ∼: jmd. ist Koreaner/Koreanerin ② *n.* (a) (person) Koreaner, *der*/Koreanerin, *die* (b) (language) Koreanisch, *das; see also* ENGLISH 2A

**kosher** /'kəʊʃə(r)/ *adj.* koscher

**Kosovan** /ˈkɒsəvən/ [1] *adj.* ~ town/ immigrant Stadt im Kosovo/Einwanderer aus dem Kosovo; ~ **Albanian** Kosovoalbaner, *der*/-albanerin, *die;* **he/she is** ~: er ist Kosovarer/sie ist Kosovarin
[2] *n.* (person) Kosovare, *der*/Kosovarin, *die*

**Kosovo** /ˈkɒsəvə/ *pr. n.* Kosovo, *der od. das od.* (*das*)

**kudos** /ˈkjuːdɒs/ *n.* Prestige, *das*

**Kurd** /kɜːd/ *n.* Kurde, *der*/Kurdin, *die*

**Kurdish** /ˈkɜːdɪʃ/ [1] *adj.* kurdisch; **sb. is** ~: jmd. ist Kurde/Kurdin
[2] *n.* (language) Kurdisch, *das*

**Kurdistan** /kɜːdɪˈstɑːn/ *pr. n.* Kurdistan (*das*)

**Kuwait** /kʊˈweɪt/ *pr. n.* Kuwait (*das*)

**Kuwaiti** /kʊˈweɪtɪ/ [1] *adj.* kuwaitisch; **sb. is** ~: jmd. ist Kuwaiti
[2] *n.* Kuwaiti, *der*/*die*

**kW** *abbr.* = **kilowatt[s]** kW

# L l

**L, l** /el/ *n.* L, l, *das*

**l.** *abbr.* = **litre[s]** l

**£** *abbr.* = **pound[s]** £; **cost £5** 5 £ *od.* Pfund kosten

**lab** /læb/ *n.* (coll.) Labor, *das*

**label** /ˈleɪbl/ [1] *n.* Schildchen, *das;* (on bottles, in clothes) Etikett, *das;* (tied/stuck to an object) Anhänger/Aufkleber, *der*
[2] *v.t.,* (Brit.) **-ll-:** (a) etikettieren; auszeichnen ‹*Waren*›; (write on) beschriften
(b) (fig.) ~ **sb./sth. [as]** sth. jmdn./etw. als etw. etikettieren

**labor** (Amer.) ▶ LABOUR

**laboratory** /ləˈbɒrətərɪ/ *n.* Labor[atorium], *das*

**labored, laborer** (Amer.) ▶ LABOUR-

**laborious** /ləˈbɔːrɪəs/ *adj.* mühsam

**la'boriously** *adv.* mühevoll

**labour** /ˈleɪbə(r)/ (Brit.) [1] *n.* (a) Arbeit, *die*
(b) (workers) Arbeiterschaft, *die;* **immigrant** ~: ausländische Arbeitskräfte *Pl.*
(c) **L**~, **the L**~ **Party** (Polit.) die Labour Party
(d) (childbirth) Wehen *Pl.;* **be in** ~: in den Wehen liegen
[2] *v.i.* hart arbeiten (**at, on** an + *Dat.*)
[3] *v.t.* ~ **the point** sich lange darüber verbreiten

**laboured** /ˈleɪbəd/ *adj.* (Brit.) mühsam; schwerfällig ‹*Stil*›; **his breathing was** ~: er atmete schwer

**'labourer** *n.* (Brit.) Arbeiter, *der*/Arbeiterin, *die*

**labour:** ~ **pains** *n. pl.* Wehenschmerzen *Pl.;* ~**-saving** *adj.* arbeit[s]sparend

**laburnum** /ləˈbɜːnəm/ *n.* (Bot.) Goldregen, *der*

**labyrinth** /ˈlæbərɪnθ/ *n.* Labyrinth, *das*

**lace** /leɪs/ [1] *n.* (a) (for shoe) Schnürsenkel, *der*
(b) (fabric) Spitze, *die; attrib.* Spitzen-
[2] *v.t.* ~ **[up]** [zu]schnüren

**lacerate** /ˈlæsəreɪt/ *v.t.* aufreißen

**'lace-up** [1] *attrib. adj.* Schnür-
[2] *n.* Schnürschuh/-stiefel, *der*

**lack** /læk/ [1] *n.* Mangel, *der* (**of** an + *Dat.*)
[2] *v.t.* **sb./sth.** ~**s** sth. jmdm./einer Sache fehlt es an etw. (*Dat.*)

**lackey** /ˈlækɪ/ *n.* Lakai, *der*

**'lacking** *adj.* **be** ~: fehlen

**laconic** /ləˈkɒnɪk/ *adj.* lakonisch

**lacquer** /ˈlækə(r)/ *n.* Lack, *der*

**lacrosse** /ləˈkrɒs/ *n.* Lacrosse, *das*

**lacy** /ˈleɪsɪ/ *adj.* Spitzen-

**lad** /læd/ *n.* Junge, *der*

**ladder** /ˈlædə(r)/ [1] *n.* (a) Leiter, *die*
(b) (Brit.: in tights etc.) Laufmasche, *die*
[2] *v.i.* (Brit.) Laufmaschen/eine Laufmasche bekommen
[3] *v.t.* (Brit.) Laufmaschen/eine Laufmasche machen in (+ *Akk.*)

**laden** /ˈleɪdn/ *adj.* beladen (**with** mit)

**ladle** /ˈleɪdl/ *n.* Schöpfkelle, *die*

**lady** /ˈleɪdɪ/ *n.* (a) Dame, *die;* ~**-in-waiting** (Brit.) Hofdame, *die*
(b) '**Ladies**' (WC) „Damen"
(c) (as form of address) **Ladies** meine Damen
(d) (Brit.) (as title) **L**~: Lady

**lady:** ~**bird,** (Amer.) ~**bug** *ns.* Marienkäfer, *der;* ~**like** *adj.* damenhaft

**lag**[1] /læg/ *v.i.,* **-gg-:** ~ [**behind**] zurückbleiben; (fig.) im Rückstand sein

**lag**[2] *v.t.,* **-gg-** (insulate) isolieren

**lager** /ˈlɑːgə(r)/ *n.* Lagerbier, *das*

**'lager lout** *n.* Bier trinkender Rüpel

**'lagging** *n.* Isolierung, *die*

**lagoon** /ləˈguːn/ *n.* Lagune, *die*

**laid** ▶ LAY[2]

**'laid-back** *adj.* (coll.) gelassen

**lain** ▶ LIE[2]

**lair** /leər/ *n.* (of wild animal) Unterschlupf, *der;* (of pirates, bandits) Schlupfwinkel, *der*

**lake** /leɪk/ *n.* See, *der*

**Lake Constance** /leɪk ˈkɒnstəns/ *pr. n.* der Bodensee

**lama** /'lɑːmə/ n. Lama, der
**lamb** /læm/ n. (a) Lamm, das
  (b) (meat) Lamm[fleisch], das
**lamb 'chop** n. Lammkotelett, das
**lambswool** /'læmzwʊl/ n. Lambswool, die
**lame** /leɪm/ adj., **'lamely** adv. lahm
**lament** /lə'ment/ [1] n. Klage, die (for um)
  [2] v.t. ~ that ...: beklagen, dass ...
  [3] v.i. klagen (geh.); ~ over sth. etw.
  beklagen (geh.)
**lamentable** /'læməntəbl/ adj.
  beklagenswert
**laminated** /'læmɪneɪtɪd/ adj. lamelliert;
  ~ glass Verbundglas, das
**lamp** /læmp/ n. Lampe, die; (in street)
  [Straßen]laterne, die
**lamp:** ~ **post** n. Laternenpfahl, der;
  ~shade n. Lampenschirm, der
**lance** /lɑːns/ [1] n. Lanze, die
  [2] v.t. (Med.) mit der Lanzette öffnen
**lance 'corporal** n. Obergefreite, der
**land** /lænd/ [1] n. Land, das; **have** or **own** ~:
  Grundbesitz haben
  [2] v.t. (a) (set ashore) [an]landen
  (b) (Aeronaut.) landen
  (c) ~ **oneself in trouble** sich in
  Schwierigkeiten bringen; ~ sb. with sth.,
  ~ sth. on sb. jmdm. etw. aufhalsen (ugs.)
  [3] v.i. (a) ⟨Boot usw.:⟩ anlegen, landen;
  ⟨Passagier:⟩ aussteigen (from aus); we ~ed at
  Dieppe wir gingen in Dieppe an Land
  (b) (Aeronaut.) landen
  (c) ~ **on one's feet** (fig.) [wieder] auf die
  Füße fallen
**'landed** adj. ~ **gentry/aristrocracy** Landadel,
  der
**'landing** n. (a) (of ship, aircraft) Landung, die
  (b) (on stairs) Treppenabsatz, der; (passage)
  Treppenflur, der
**landing:** ~ **card** n. Landekarte, die;
  ~ **stage** n. Landesteg, der
**land:** ~**lady** n. (a) (of rented property)
  Vermieterin, die; (b) (of public house)
  [Gast]wirtin, die; ~**locked** adj. vom Land
  eingeschlossen ⟨Bucht, Hafen⟩; ⟨Staat⟩ ohne
  Zugang zum Meer; ~**lord** n. (a) (of rented
  property) Vermieter, der; (b) (of public house)
  [Gast]wirt, der; ~**mark** n. (a)
  Orientierungspunkt, der; (b) (fig.) Markstein,
  der; ~ **mass** n. Landmasse, die; ~**mine** n.
  Landmine, die; ~**owner** n. Grundbesitzer,
  der/-besitzerin, die; ~**scape** /'lændskeɪp/
  n. Landschaft, die; ~**scape architect** n.
  Landschaftsarchitekt, der/-architektin, die;
  ~**scape gardener** n.
  Landschaftsgärtner, der/-gärtnerin, die;
  ~**scape gardening** n.
  Landschaftsgärtnerei, die; ~**slide** n.
  Erdrutsch, der; a ~**slide [victory]** (Polit.) ein
  Erdrutsch[wahl]sieg
**lane** /leɪn/ n. (a) (in the country)
  Landsträßchen, das; Weg, der
  (b) (in town) Gasse, die

(c) (part of road) [Fahr]spur, die; **'get in** ~'
  „bitte einordnen"
  (d) (Sport) Bahn, die
**language** /'læŋgwɪdʒ/ n. Sprache, die;
  (style) Ausdrucksweise, die
**language:** ~ **course** n. Sprachkurs[us],
  der; ~ **school** n. Sprachenschule; die;
  ~ **teacher** n. Sprachlehrer, der/-lehrerin,
  die
**languid** /'læŋgwɪd/ adj. träge
**languish** /'læŋgwɪʃ/ v.i. (a) (lose vitality)
  ermatten (geh.)
  (b) ~ **under sth.** unter etw. (Dat.)
  schmachten (geh.)
**lank** /læŋk/ adj. (a) hager
  (b) glatt herabhängend ⟨Haar⟩
**lanky** /'læŋkɪ/ adj. schlaksig (ugs.)
**lantern** /'læntən/ n. Laterne, die
**lap¹** /læp/ n. (part of body) Schoß, der
**lap²** n. (Sport) Runde, die
**lap³** [1] v.i., **-pp-** schlecken
  [2] v.t., **-pp-:** ~ [up] [auf]schlecken
  ■ **lap 'up** v.t. (fig.) schlucken
**'lap belt** n. Beckengurt, der
**lapel** /lə'pel/ n. Revers, das
**Lapland** /'læplænd/ pr. n. Lappland (das)
**lapse** /læps/ [1] n. (a) (interval) a/the ~ **of** ...:
  eine/die Zeitspanne von ...
  (b) (mistake) Fehler, der; ~ **of memory**
  Gedächtnislücke, die
  [2] v.i. (a) ⟨Vertrag, usw.:⟩ ungültig werden
  (b) ~ **into** verfallen in (+ Akk.)
**'laptop** [1] adj. tragbar, Laptop⟨gerät, -PC⟩
  [2] n. Laptop, der; tragbarer PC
**larceny** /'lɑːsənɪ/ n. Diebstahl, der
**lard** /lɑːd/ n. Schweineschmalz, das
**larder** /'lɑːdə(r)/ n. Speisekammer, die
**large** /lɑːdʒ/ [1] adj. groß
  [2] n. **at** ~ (not in prison etc.) auf freiem Fuß
  [3] adv. ▶ BY 2D
**'largely** adv. weitgehend
**larger-than-'life** attrib. adj.
  überlebensgroß
**large:** ~**-scale** attrib. adj. groß angelegt;
  groß ⟨Erfolg, Misserfolg⟩; ⟨Katastrophe⟩
  großen Ausmaßes; ⟨Modell⟩ in großem
  Maßstab; ~**-scale manufacture**
  Massenproduktion, die; ~**-size[d]** adj. groß
**lark¹** /lɑːk/ n. (Ornith.) Lerche, die
**lark²** (coll.) [1] n. Jux, der (ugs.)
  [2] v.i. ~ [about or around] herumalbern
  (ugs.)
**larva** /'lɑːvə/ n., pl. ~**e** /'lɑːviː/ Larve, die
**laryngitis** /lærɪn'dʒaɪtɪs/ n.
  Kehlkopfentzündung, die
**larynx** /'lærɪŋks/ n. Kehlkopf, der
**lascivious** /lə'sɪvɪəs/ adj. lüstern (geh.)
**laser** /'leɪzə(r)/ n. Laser, der
**laser:** ~ **beam** n. Laserstrahl, der;
  ~**disc** n. Laserplatte, die; ~ **printer** n.
  Laserdrucker, der

**lash** /læʃ/ ⓵ *n.* **(a)** (stroke) [Peitschen]hieb, *der*
**(b)** (on eyelid) Wimper, *die*
⓶ *v.i.* ⟨*Welle, Regen:*⟩ peitschen (**against** gegen, **on** auf + *Akk.*)
⓷ *v.t.* **(a)** (fasten) festbinden (**to** an + *Dat.*)
**(b)** (as punishment) auspeitschen
■ **lash 'down** ⓵ *v.t.* festbinden
⓶ *v.i.* ⟨*Regen:*⟩ niederprasseln
■ **lash 'out** *v.i.* **(a)** (hit out) um sich schlagen; ~ **out at sb.** nach jmdm. schlagen
**(b)** ~ **out on sth.** (coll.: spend freely) sich (*Dat.*) etw. leisten
**lashings** /'læʃɪŋz/ *n. pl.* ~ **of sth.** Unmengen von etw.
**lass** /læs/ *n.* Mädchen, *das*
**lasso** /læ'suː/ Lasso, *das*
**last¹** /lɑːst/ ⓵ *adj.* letzt...; **be** ~ **to arrive** als Letzter/Letzte ankommen; ~ **night** gestern Nacht/Abend
⓶ *adv.* **(a)** [ganz] zuletzt; als Letzter/Letzte ⟨*sprechen, ankommen*⟩
**(b)** (on ~ previous occasion) das letzte Mal; zuletzt
⓷ *n.* **(a)** (person or thing) **the** ~: der/die/das Letztere; *pl.* die Letzteren
**(b) at [long]** ~: endlich
**last²** *v.i.* **(a)** (continue) dauern; ⟨*Wetter, Ärger:*⟩ anhalten
**(b)** (suffice) reichen
**'last-ditch** *adj.* ~ **attempt** letzter verzweifelter Versuch
**'lasting** *adj.* bleibend; dauerhaft ⟨*Beziehung*⟩; nachhaltig ⟨*Eindruck, Wirkung*⟩
**'lastly** *adv.* schließlich
**last:** ~**-minute** *attrib. adj.* in letzter Minute vorgebracht ⟨*Plan, Aufruf, Ergänzung, Gesuch, Bewerbung*⟩; ~ **name** *n.* Zuname, *der;* Nachname, *der*
**latch** /lætʃ/ *n.* Riegel, *der;* **on the** ~: nur eingeklinkt
■ **latch 'on to** *v.t.* (coll.:) kapieren (ugs.)
**late** /leɪt/ ⓵ *adj.* **(a)** spät; **am I** ~? komme ich zu spät?; **be** ~ **for the train** den Zug verpassen; **the train is [an hour]** ~: der Zug hat [eine Stunde] Verspätung; ~ **shift** Spätschicht, *die;* ~ **summer** Spätsommer, *der*
**(b)** (dead) verstorben
**(c)** (former) ehemalig. *See also* LATER 1; LATEST
⓶ *adv.* **(a)** (after proper time) verspätet
**(b)** (at/till a ~ hour) spät; **be up** ~: bis spät in die Nacht aufbleiben; **work** ~ **at the office** [abends] lange im Büro arbeiten; **[a bit]** ~ **in the day** (fig. coll.) reichlich spät
⓷ *n.* **of** ~: in letzter Zeit
**latecomer** /'leɪtkʌmə(r)/ *n.* Zuspätkommende, *der/die*
**'lately** *adv.* in letzter Zeit
**'lateness** *n.* **(a)** (delay) Verspätung, *die*
**(b) the** ~ **of the performance** der späte Beginn der Vorstellung

**'late-night** *attrib. adj.* Spät⟨*programm, -vorstellung*⟩
**latent** /'leɪtənt/ *adj.* latent
**later** /'leɪtə(r)/ ⓵ *adv.* ~ **[on]** später
⓶ *adj.* später; (more recent) neuer
**lateral** /'lætərl/ *adj.* seitlich (**to** von); ~ **thinking** Querdenken, *das*
**latest** /'leɪtɪst/ *adj.* **(a)** (modern) neu[e]st...
**(b)** (most recent) letzt...
**(c) at [the]** ~**/the very** ~: spätestens/ allerspätestens
**lathe** /leɪð/ *n.* Drehbank, *die*
**lather** /'lɑːðə(r)/ ⓵ *n.* [Seifen]schaum, *der*
⓶ *v.t.* einschäumen
**Latin** /'lætɪn/ ⓵ *adj.* lateinisch
⓶ *n.* Latein, *das; see also* ENGLISH 2A
**Latin A'merica** *pr. n.* Lateinamerika (*das*)
**Latin-A'merican** *adj.* lateinamerikanisch
**latitude** /'lætɪtjuːd/ *n.* **(a)** (freedom) Freiheit, *die*
**(b)** (Geog.) Breite, *die*
**latrine** /lə'triːn/ *n.* Latrine, *die*
**latter** /'lætə(r)/ *attrib. adj.* letzter...; **the** ~: der/die/das Letztere; *pl.* die Letzteren
**'latterly** *adv.* in letzter Zeit
**lattice** /'lætɪs/ *n.* Gitter, *das*
**laudable** /'lɔːdəbl/ *adj.* lobenswert
**laugh** /lɑːf/ ⓵ *n.* Lachen, *das;* (continuous) Gelächter, *das*
⓶ *v.i.* lachen; ~ **out loud** laut auflachen; ~ **at sb./sth.** über jmdn./etw. lachen; (jeer) jmdn. auslachen/etw. verlachen
■ **laugh 'off** *v.t.* mit einem Lachen abtun
**laughable** /'lɑːfəbl/ *adj.* lachhaft; lächerlich
**'laughing** *n.* **be no** ~ **matter** nicht zum Lachen sein
**laughing:** ~ **gas** *n.* Lachgas, *das;* ~ **stock** *n.* **make sb. a** ~ **stock, make a** ~ **stock of sb.** jmdn. zum Gespött machen
**laughter** /'lɑːftə(r)/ *n.* Lachen, *das;* (continuous) Gelächter, *das*
**'laughter lines** *n. pl.* Lachfältchen *Pl.*
**launch** /lɔːntʃ/ *v.t.* **(a)** zu Wasser lassen ⟨*Boot*⟩; vom Stapel lassen ⟨*neues Schiff*⟩; abschießen ⟨*Harpune, Torpedo*⟩; schleudern ⟨*Speer*⟩
**(b)** (fig.) auf den Markt bringen ⟨*Produkt*⟩; vorstellen ⟨*Buch, Schallplatte, Sänger*⟩; ~ **an attack** einen Angriff durchführen
■ **launch 'out** *v.i.* (fig.) ~ **out into films/a new career/on one's own** sich beim Film versuchen/beruflich etwas ganz Neues anfangen/sich selbstständig machen
**'launching pad, launch pad** *ns.* [Raketen]abschussrampe, *die*
**launder** /'lɔːndə(r)/ *v.t.* waschen und bügeln
**launderette** /lɔːndə'ret/, **laundrette** /lɔːn'dret/, (Amer.) **laundromat** /'lɔːndrəmæt/ *ns.* Waschsalon, *der*

**laundry** /'lɔːndrɪ/ n. (a) (place) Wäscherei, die
(b) (clothes etc.) Wäsche, die

'**laundry basket** n. Wäschekorb, der

**lava** /'lɑːvə/ n. Lava, die

**lavatory** /'lævətərɪ/ n. Toilette, die

**lavender** /'lævɪndə(r)/ n. Lavendel, der

**lavish** /'lævɪʃ/ [1] adj. großzügig
[2] v.t. ~ sth. on sb. jmdn. mit etw. überhäufen

**law** /lɔː/ n. (a) Gesetz, das; **break the** ~: gegen das Gesetz verstoßen; **take the** ~ **into one's own hands** sich (Dat.) selbst Recht verschaffen; ~ **and order** Ruhe und Ordnung
(b) (of game) Regel, die
(c) (as subject) Jura o. Art.

**law:** ~**-abiding** /'lɔːəbaɪdɪŋ/ adj. gesetzestreu; ~**court** n. Gerichtsgebäude, das; (room) Gerichtssaal, der; ~ **firm** n. (Amer.) Anwaltskanzlei, die

**lawful** /'lɔːfl/ adj. rechtmäßig ⟨Besitzer, Erbe⟩; legal, gesetzmäßig ⟨Vorgehen, Maßnahme⟩

'**lawless** adj. gesetzlos

**lawn** /lɔːn/ n. Rasen, der

**lawn:** ~**mower** n. Rasenmäher, der; ~ **sprinkler** n. Rasensprenger, der; ~ **tennis** n. Rasentennis, das

'**law suit** n. Prozess, der

**lawyer** /'lɔːjə(r)/ n. Rechtsanwalt, der/ Rechtsanwältin, die

**lax** /læks/ adj. lax; **be** ~ **about hygiene/ paying the rent** etc. es mit der Hygiene/der Zahlung der Miete usw. nicht so genau nehmen

**laxative** /'læksətɪv/ n. Abführmittel, das

**laxity** /'læksɪtɪ/, '**laxness** ns. Laxheit, die

**lay¹** /leɪ/ adj. Laien-

**lay²** v.t., **laid** /leɪd/ (a) legen ⟨Teppichboden, Rohr, Kabel⟩
(b) (impose) auferlegen ⟨Verantwortung, Verpflichtung⟩ (**on** Dat.); verhängen ⟨Strafe⟩ (**on** über + Akk.)
(c) ~ **the table** den Tisch decken
(d) (Biol.) legen ⟨Ei⟩
■ **lay a'side** v.t. beiseite legen
■ **lay 'by** v.t. beiseite legen
■ **lay 'down** v.t. (a) hinlegen
(b) festlegen ⟨Regeln, Bedingungen⟩
■ **lay 'off** [1] v.t. (from work) vorübergehend entlassen
[2] v.i. (coll.: stop) aufhören
■ **lay 'out** v.t. (a) (spread out) ausbreiten
(b) anlegen ⟨Garten⟩
■ **lay 'up** v.t. (a) (store) lagern
(b) **I was laid up in bed for a week** ich musste eine Woche das Bett hüten

**lay³** ▶ LIE²

**lay:** ~**about** n. (Brit.) Gammler, der (ugs.); ~**-by** n., pl. ~**bys** (Brit.) Parkbucht, die; Haltebucht, die

**layer** /'leɪə(r)/ n. Schicht, die

**layette** /leɪ'et/ n. [baby's] ~: Babyausstattung, die

**lay:** ~**man** /'leɪmən/ n., pl. ~**men** /'leɪmən/ n. Laie, der; ~**out** n. (of garden, park) Anlage, die; (of book, advertisement, etc.) Layout, das

**laze** /leɪz/ v.i. faulenzen; ~ **around** or **about** herumfaulenzen (ugs.)

**lazily** /'leɪzɪlɪ/ adv. faul

**laziness** /'leɪzɪnɪs/ n. Faulheit, die

**lazy** /'leɪzɪ/ adj. faul

'**lazybones** n. sing. Faulpelz, der

**lb.** abbr. = **pound**[s] ≈ Pfd.

**LCD** abbr. = **liquid crystal display** LCD

**lead¹** /led/ [1] n. (a) (metal) Blei, das
(b) (in pencil) [Bleistift]mine, die
[2] attrib. adj. Blei-
[3] v.t. (a) in Blei fassen ⟨Fenster⟩; ~**ed** bleigefasst
(b) ~**ed petrol** bleihaltiges Benzin

**lead²** /liːd/ [1] v.t., **led** /led/ (a) führen; ~ **sb. to do sth.** (fig.) jmdn. dazu bringen, etw. zu tun
(b) (fig.: influence) ~ **sb. to do sth.** jmdn. veranlassen, etw. zu tun; **be easily led** sich leicht beeinflussen lassen; **he led me to believe that ...**: er machte mich glauben, dass ...
(c) (be first in) anführen
(d) (direct) anführen ⟨Bewegung, Abordnung⟩; leiten ⟨Diskussion, Orchester⟩
[2] v.i., **led** (a) ⟨Straße usw., Tür:⟩ führen
(b) (be first) führen; (go in front) vorangehen
[3] n. (a) (precedent) Beispiel, das; (clue) Anhaltspunkt, der; **follow sb.'s** ~: jmds. Beispiel (Dat.) folgen
(b) (first place) Führung, die; **be in the** ~: in Führung liegen
(c) (distance ahead) Vorsprung, der
(d) (leash) Leine, die; **on a** ~: an der Leine
(e) (Electr.) Kabel, das
(f) (Theatre) Hauptrolle, die
■ **lead a'way** v.t. abführen ⟨Gefangenen, Verbrecher⟩
■ **lead 'off** [1] v.t. abführen
[2] v.i. beginnen
■ **lead 'on** [1] v.t. ~ **sb. on** (entice) jmdn. reizen; (deceive) jmdn. auf den Leim führen
[2] v.i. ~ **on to the next topic** etc. zum nächsten Thema usw. führen
■ **lead 'up to** v.t. schließlich führen zu

'**leader** n. (a) Führer, der/Führerin, die; (of political party) Vorsitzende, der/die; (of expedition) Leiter, der/Leiterin, die
(b) (Brit. Journ.) Leitartikel, der

'**leadership** n. Führung, die

'**leader writer** n. Leitartikelschreiber, der/-schreiberin, die; Leitartikler, der/-artiklerin, die (Pressejargon)

**lead-free** /'ledfriː/ adj. bleifrei

**leading** /'liːdɪŋ/ adj. führend

**leading:** ~ '**lady** n. Hauptdarstellerin, die; ~ '**man** n. Hauptdarsteller, der;

~ **'question** n. Suggestivfrage, die;
~ **role** n. Hauptrolle, die; (fig.) führende Rolle

**lead:** ~ **'pencil** /led 'pensl/ n. Bleistift, der; ~ **poisoning** /'led pɔɪzənɪŋ/ n. Bleivergiftung, die; ~ **singer** /liːd 'sɪŋə(r)/ n. Leadsänger der/-sängerin, die; ~ **story** /'liːd stɔːrɪ/ n. (Journ.) Titelgeschichte, die; ~ **time** /'liːd taɪm/ n. (Econ.) Entwicklungszeit, die

**leaf** /liːf/ n., pl. **leaves** /liːvz/ Blatt, das; (of table) Platte die

■ **leaf 'through** v.t. durchblättern

**leaflet** /'liːflɪt/ n. [Hand]zettel, der; (advertising) Reklamezettel, der; (political) Flugblatt, das

**'leafy** adj. belaubt

**league** /liːg/ n. (a) (agreement) Bündnis, das; **be in** ~ **with sb.** mit jmdm. im Bunde sein
(b) (Sport) Liga, die

**league:** ~ **'football** n. Ligafußball, der; ~ **match** n. Ligaspiel, das; ~ **table** n. Tabelle, die (Sport); **be at the top/bottom of the** ~ **table** an der Tabellenspitze/am Tabellenende sein (fig.); an der Spitze rangieren/das Schlusslicht bilden (ugs.) (**of** unter + Dat.)

**leak** /liːk/ 1 n. (a) (hole) Leck, das; (in roof, tent; also fig.) undichte Stelle
(b) (escaping gas) durch ein Leck austretendes Gas
2 v.i. (a) (escape) austreten (**from** aus)
(b) ⟨Fass, Tank, Schiff⟩ lecken; ⟨Rohr, Leitung, Dach⟩ undicht sein; ⟨Gefäß, Füller⟩ auslaufen
(c) (fig.) ~ **[out]** durchsickern
3 v.t. ~ **sth. to sb.** jmdm. etw. zuspielen

**leakage** /'liːkɪdʒ/ n. Auslaufen, das; (of fluid, gas) Ausströmen, das; (fig.: of information) Durchsickern, das

**'leaky** adj. undicht; leck ⟨Boot⟩

**lean**[1] /liːn/ 1 adj. mager
2 n. (meat) Magere, das

**lean**[2] 1 v.i., **leaned** /liːnd, lent/ or (Brit.) **leant** /lent/ (a) sich beugen; ~ **against the door** sich gegen die Tür lehnen; ~ **down/ forward** sich herab-/vorbeugen; ~ **back** sich zurücklehnen
(b) (support oneself) ~ **against/on sth.** sich gegen/an etw (Akk.) lehnen
(c) (be supported) lehnen (**against** an + Dat.)
(d) (fig.) ~ **[up]on sb.** (rely) auf jmdn. bauen; ~ **to[wards] sth.** (tend) zu etw. neigen
2 v.t., **leaned** or (Brit.) **leant** lehnen (**against** gegen od. an + Akk.)

■ **lean 'over** v.i. sich hinüberbeugen

**'leaning** n. Neigung, die

**leant** ▶ LEAN[2]

**leap** /liːp/ 1 v.i., **leaped** /liːpt, lept/ or **leapt** /lept/ (a) springen; ⟨Herz⟩ hüpfen
(b) (fig.) ~ **at the chance** die Gelegenheit beim Schopf packen
2 v.t., **leaped** or **leapt** überspringen

3 n. Sprung, der; **with** or **in one** ~: mit einem Satz; **by** ~**s and bounds** (fig.) mit Riesenschritten

**'leapfrog** 1 n. Bockspringen, das
2 v.i., **-gg-** Bockspringen machen
3 v.t. ~**frog sb.** einen Bocksprung über jmdn. machen
(b) (fig.) übertreffen ⟨Konkurrenz, Kollegen usw.⟩

**leapt** ▶ LEAP 1, 2

**'leap year** n. Schaltjahr, das

**learn** /lɜːn/ 1 v.t., **learned** /lɜːnd, lɜːnt/ or **learnt** /lɜːnt/ (a) lernen; ~ **to swim** schwimmen lernen
(b) (find out) erfahren
2 v.i., **learned** or **learnt** (a) lernen; ~ **about sth.** etwas über etw. (Akk.) lernen
(b) (get to know) erfahren (**of** von)

**learned** /'lɜːnɪd/ adj. gelehrt

**'learner** n. (beginner) Anfänger, der/ Anfängerin, die; ~ **[driver]** Fahrschüler, der/-schülerin, die

**'learning** n. (of person) Gelehrsamkeit, die

**learning:** ~ **difficulties** n. pl. Lernschwierigkeiten Pl.; ~ **disability** n. Lernbehinderung, die

**learnt** ▶ LEARN

**lease** /liːs/ 1 n. (of land, business premises) Pachtvertrag, der; (of house, flat, office) Mietvertrag, der
2 v.t. (a) (grant ~ on) verpachten ⟨Grundstück, Geschäft, Rechte⟩; vermieten ⟨Haus, Wohnung, Büro⟩
(b) (take ~ on) pachten ⟨Grundstück, Geschäft⟩; mieten ⟨Haus, Wohnung, Büro⟩

**'leasehold** n. ▶ LEASE 2: **have the** ~ **of** or **on sth.** etw. gepachtet/gemietet haben

**leash** /liːʃ/ n. Leine, die

**least** /liːst/ 1 adj. (smallest) kleinst...; (in quantity) wenigst...; (in status) geringst...
2 n. Geringste, das; **the** ~ **I can do** das Mindeste, was ich tun kann; **at** ~: mindestens; (anyway) wenigstens; **at the [very]** ~: [aller]mindestens; **not [in] the** ~: nicht im Geringsten
3 adv. am wenigsten

**leather** /'leðə(r)/ 1 n. Leder, das
2 adj. ledern; Leder⟨jacke, -mantel⟩

**'leather goods** n. pl. Lederwaren Pl.

**'leathery** adj. ledern

**leave**[1] /liːv/ n. (a) (permission) Erlaubnis, die
(b) (from duty or work) Urlaub, der; ~ **[of absence]** Urlaub, der
(c) **take one's** ~ sich verabschieden

**leave**[2] v.t., **left** /left/ (a) (make or let remain) hinterlassen; ~ **sb. to do sth.** es jmdm. überlassen, etw. zu tun; (in will) ~ **sb. sth.,** ~ **sth. to sb.** jmdm. etw. hinterlassen
(b) (refrain from doing, using, etc.) stehen lassen ⟨Abwasch, Essen⟩

⋯⋗

**(c)** (in given state) lassen; ∼ **sb. alone** (allow to be alone) jmdn. allein lassen; (stop bothering) jmdn. in Ruhe lassen
**(d)** (refer, entrust) ∼ **sth. to sb./sth.** etw. jmdm./einer Sache überlassen
**(e)** (go away from, quit, desert) verlassen; ∼ **home at 6 a.m.** um 6 Uhr früh von zu Hause weggehen/-fahren; ∼ **Bonn at 6 p.m.** (by car, in train) um 18 Uhr von Bonn abfahren; (by plane) um 18 Uhr in Bonn abfliegen; *abs.* **the train** ∼**s at 8.30 a.m.** der Zug fährt *od.* geht um 8.30 Uhr; ∼ **on the 8 a.m. train/flight** mit dem Achtuhrzug fahren/der Achtuhrmaschine fliegen
▪ **leave a'side** *v.t.* beiseite lassen
▪ **leave be'hind** *v.t.* zurücklassen; (by mistake) vergessen; liegen lassen
▪ **leave 'off** *v.t.* (stop) aufhören mit; *abs.* aufhören
▪ **leave 'out** *v.t.* auslassen
▪ **leave 'over** *v.t.* **be left over** übrig [geblieben] sein

**leaves** *pl. of* LEAF

**Lebanon** /ˈlebənən/ *pr. n.* [the] ∼: [der] Libanon

**lecherous** /ˈletʃərəs/ *adj.* lüstern (geh.)

**lecture** /ˈlektʃə(r)/ ① **(a)** *n.* Vortrag, *der;* (Univ.) Vorlesung, *die*
**(b)** (reprimand) Strafpredigt, *die* (ugs.)
② *v.i.* ∼ **[to sb.] [on sth.]** [vor jmdm.] einen Vortrag/(Univ.) eine Vorlesung [über etw. (*Akk.*)] halten
③ *v.t.* (scold) ∼ **sb.** jmdm. eine Strafpredigt halten

**'lecture hall** *n.* Hörsaal, *der*

**'lecturer** *n.* Vortragende, *der/die;* **senior** ∼: Dozent, *der/*Dozentin, *die*

**'lecture room** *n.* Vortragsraum, *der;* (Univ.) Vorlesungsraum, *der*

**lectureship** /ˈlektʃəʃɪp/ *n.* Dozentur, *die*

**lecture:** ∼ **theatre** *n.* Hörsaal, *der;* ∼ **tour** *n.* Vortragsreise, *die*

**led** ▷ LEAD² 1, 2

**LED** *abbr.* = **light-emitting diode** LED

**ledge** /ledʒ/ *n.* Sims, *der od. das;* (of rock) Vorsprung, *der*

**ledger** /ˈledʒə(r)/ *n.* (Commerc.) Hauptbuch, *das*

**lee** /liː/ *n.* **(a)** (shelter) Schutz, *der*
**(b)** ∼ **[side]** (Naut.) Leeseite, *die*

**leech** /liːtʃ/ *n.* [Blut]egel, *der*

**leek** /liːk/ *n.* Stange Porree *od.* Lauch; ∼**s** Porree, *der;* Lauch, *der*

**leek 'soup** *n.* Lauch[creme]suppe, *die*

**leer** /lɪə(r)/ ① *n.* anzüglicher/spöttischer Blick
② *v.i.* ∼ **at sb.** jmdm. einen anzüglichen/ spöttischen [Seiten]blick zuwerfen

**leeward** /ˈliːwəd/ ① *adj.* **to/on the** ∼ **side of the ship** nach/in Lee
② *n.* Leeseite, *die;* **to** ∼: leewärts

**'leeway** *n.* **(a)** (Naut.) Leeweg, *der;* Abdrift, *die*

---

**(b)** (fig.) Spielraum, *der*

**left¹** ▷ LEAVE²

**left²** /left/ ① *adj.* **(a)** link...; **on the** ∼ **side** auf der linken Seite; links
**(b)** **L**∼ (Polit.) link...
② *adv.* nach links
③ *n.* **(a)** (∼-hand side) linke Seite; **on** *or* **to the** ∼ **[of sb./sth.]** links [von jmdm./etw.]
**(b)** (Polit.) **the L**∼: die Linke

**left:** ∼**-hand** *adj.* link...; ∼**-'handed** ① *adj.* linkshändig; ⟨*Werkzeug*⟩ für Linkshänder; **be** ∼**-handed** Linkshänder/ Linkshänderin sein; ② *adv.* linkshändig; ∼ **'luggage [office]** *n.* (Brit. Railw.) Gepäckaufbewahrung, *die;* ∼**overs** *n. pl.* Reste *Pl.* ∼ **'wing** *n.* linker Flügel; ∼**-wing** *adj.* (Polit.) linksgerichtet; Links⟨*extremist, -intellektueller*⟩; ∼**-'winger** *n.* **(a)** (Sport) Linksaußen, *der;* **(b)** (Polit.) Angehöriger/Angehörige des linken Flügels

**leg** /leg/ *n.* **(a)** Bein, *das;* **pull sb.'s** ∼ (fig.) jmdn. auf den Arm nehmen (ugs.); **stretch one's** ∼**s** sich (*Dat.*) die Beine vertreten
**(b)** ∼ **of lamb** Lammkeule, *die*
**(c)** (of journey) Etappe, *die*

**legacy** /ˈlegəsɪ/ *n.* Vermächtnis, *das* (Rechtsspr.); Erbschaft, *die*

**legal** /ˈliːgl/ *adj.* **(a)** (concerning the law) juristisch; Rechts⟨*beratung, -streit, -experte, -schutz*⟩; gesetzlich ⟨*Vertreter*⟩; rechtlich ⟨*Gründe, Stellung*⟩; Gerichts⟨*kosten*⟩
**(b)** (required by law) gesetzlich ⟨*Verpflichtung*⟩; gesetzlich verankert ⟨*Recht*⟩
**(c)** (lawful) legal; rechtsgültig ⟨*Vertrag, Testament*⟩

**legal:** ∼ **'action** *n.* Gerichtsverfahren, *das;* Prozess, *der;* **take** ∼ **action against sb.** gerichtlich gegen jmdn. vorgehen; ∼ **'aid** *n.* ≈ Prozesskostenhilfe, *die*

**legality** /lɪˈgælɪtɪ/ *n.* Legalität, *die*

**legalization** /liːgəlaɪˈzeɪʃn/ *n.* Legalisierung, *die*

**legalize** /ˈliːgəlaɪz/ *v.t.* legalisieren

**legend** /ˈledʒənd/ *n.* Sage, *die;* (unfounded belief) Legende, *die*

**legendary** /ˈledʒəndərɪ/ *adj.* legendär

**leggings** /ˈlegɪŋz/ *n. pl.* Ledergamaschen *Pl.* (veralt.); (of baby) Strampelhose, *die*

**legibility** /ledʒɪˈbɪlɪtɪ/ *n.* Leserlichkeit, *die*

**legible** /ˈledʒɪbl/ *adj.* leserlich; **easily/ scarcely** ∼: leicht/kaum lesbar

**legion** /ˈliːdʒn/ *n.* Legion, *die*

**legislate** /ˈledʒɪsleɪt/ *v.i.* Gesetze verabschieden

**legislation** /ledʒɪsˈleɪʃn/ *n.* **(a)** (laws) Gesetze *Pl.*
**(b)** (legislating) Gesetzgebung, *die*

**legislative** /ˈledʒɪslətɪv/ *adj.* gesetzgebend

**legislator** /ˈledʒɪsleɪtə(r)/ *n.* Gesetzgeber, *der*

**legislature** /ˈledʒɪsleɪtʃə(r)/ *n.* Legislative, *die*

**legitimacy** /lɪ'dʒɪtɪməsɪ/ *n.* **(a)**
Rechtmäßigkeit, *die;* Legitimität, *die*
**(b)** (of child) Ehelichkeit, *die*

**legitimate** /lɪ'dʒɪtɪmət/ *adj.* **(a)** (lawful)
legitim; rechtmäßig ‹*Besitzer, Regierung*›
**(b)** (valid) berechtigt
**(c)** ehelich ‹*Kind*›

**legitimatize (legitimatise)**
/lɪ'dʒɪtɪmətaɪz/, **legitimize (legitimise)**
/lɪ'dʒɪtɪmaɪz/ *v.t.* legitimieren

**leisure** /'leʒə(r)/ *n.* Freizeit, *die; attrib.*
Freizeit-

'**leisurely** *adj.* gemächlich

'**leisurewear** *n., no indef. art.*
Freizeitkleidung, *die*

**lemon** /'lemən/ *n.* Zitrone, *die*

**lemonade** /lemə'neɪd/ *n.*
[Zitronen]limonade, *die*

**lend** /lend/ *v.t.,* lent /lent/ leihen; ~ sth. to
sb. jmdm. etw. leihen

'**lender** *n.* Verleiher, *der*/Verleiherin, *die*

**length** /leŋθ, leŋkθ/ *n.* **(a)** (also of time)
Länge, *die;* **be six feet in ~:** sechs Fuß lang
sein; **a short ~ of time** kurze Zeit
**(b) at ~** (for a long time) lange; (eventually)
schließlich; **at [great] ~** (in great detail) lang
und breit; **at some ~:** ziemlich ausführlich
**(c) go to any/great ~s** alles nur/alles
Erdenkliche tun
**(d)** ( piece of material) Länge, *die;* Stück, *das*

**lengthen** /'leŋθən/ |1| *v.i.* länger werden
|2| *v.t.* verlängern; länger machen ‹*Kleid*›

**lengthways** /'leŋθweɪz/ *adv.* der Länge
nach; längs

'**lengthy** *adj.* überlang

**lenient** /'li:nɪənt/ *adj.* nachsichtig

**lens** /lenz/ *n.* Linse, *die;* (of spectacles) Glas,
*das*

**lens cap** *n.* Objektivdeckel, *der*

**lent ▶** LEND

**Lent** /lent/ *n.* Fastenzeit, *die*

**lentil** /'lentl/ *n.* Linse, *die*

**Leo** /'li:əʊ/ *n., pl.* ~s (Astrol., Astron.) der
Löwe

**leopard** /'lepəd/ *n.* Leopard, *der*

**leotard** /'li:əta:d/ *n.* Turnanzug, *der*

**leper** /'lepə(r)/ *n.* Leprakranke, *der/die*

**leprosy** /'leprəsɪ/ *n.* Lepra, *die*

**lesbian** /'lezbɪən/ |1| *n.* Lesbierin, *die*
|2| *adj.* lesbisch

**less** /les/ |1| *adj.* weniger; **of ~ value/
importance** weniger wertvoll/wichtig
|2| *adv.* weniger; **~ and ~:** immer weniger;
**~ and ~ [often]** immer seltener
|3| *n.* weniger
|4| *prep.* (deducting) **ten ~ three** zehn weniger
drei

**lessen** /'lesn/ |1| *v.t.* verringern
|2| *v.i.* sich verringern

**lesser** /'lesə(r)/ *attrib. adj.* geringer...

**lessee** /le'si:/ *n.* Pächter, *der*/Pächterin,
*die;* Mieter, *der*/Mieterin, *die*

**lesson** /'lesn/ *n.* **(a)** (class)
[Unterrichts]stunde, *die*
**(b)** (example, warning) Lehre, *die*
**(c)** (Eccl.) Lesung, *die*

**let** /let/ |1| *v.t.,* **-tt-,** let **(a)** (allow to) lassen;
~ sb. do sth. jmdn. etw. tun lassen; ~ alone
(far less) geschweige denn
**(b)** (cause to) ~ sb. know jmdn. wissen
lassen
**(c)** (Brit.: rent out) vermieten
|2| *v. aux.,* **-tt-,** let lassen; **Let's go to the
cinema. – Yes,** ~'s/No, ~'s not Komm/
Kommt, wir gehen ins Kino. – Ja, gut/Nein,
lieber nicht; ~ them come in sie sollen
hereinkommen

■ **let 'down** *v.t.* **(a)** (lower) herunter-/
hinunterlassen
**(b)** (Dressm.) auslassen
**(c)** (disappoint, fail) im Stich lassen

■ **let 'in** *v.t.* **(a)** (admit) herein-/hineinlassen
**(b)** ~ oneself in for sth. sich auf etw. (*Akk.*)
einlassen
**(c)** ~ sb. in on a secret/plan *etc.* jmdn. in
ein Geheimnis/einen Plan *usw.* einweihen

■ '**let into** *v.t.* **(a)** (admit into) lassen in
(+ *Akk.*)
**(b)** (fig.: acquaint with) ~ sb. into a secret
jmdn. in ein Geheimnis einweihen

■ **let 'off** *v.t.* **(a)** (excuse) laufen lassen (ugs.);
~ sb. off sth. jmdm. etw. erlassen
**(b)** (allow to alight) aussteigen lassen
**(c)** abbrennen ‹*Feuerwerk*›

■ **let 'on** (coll.) |1| *v.i.* don't ~ on! nichts
verraten!
|2| *v.t.* sb. ~ on to me that ...: man hat mir
gesteckt, dass ... (ugs.)

■ **let 'out** *v.t.* **(a)** ~ sb./an animal out
jmdn./ein Tier heraus-/hinaus lassen
**(b)** ausstoßen ‹*Schrei*›; ~ out a groan
aufstöhnen
**(c)** verraten ‹*Geheimnis*›
**(d)** (Dressm.) auslassen
**(e)** (Brit.: rent out) vermieten

■ **let 'through** *v.t.* durchlassen

■ **let 'up** *v.i.* (coll.) nachlassen

'**let-down** *n.* Enttäuschung, *die*

**lethal** /'li:θl/ *adj.* tödlich

**lethargic** /lɪ'θɑ:dʒɪk/ *adj.* träge; (apathetic)
lethargisch

**lethargy** /'leθədʒɪ/ *n.* Trägheit, *die;* (apathy)
Lethargie, *die*

**letter** /'letə(r)/ *n.* **(a)** Brief, *der* (to an
+ *Akk.*)
**(b)** (of alphabet) Buchstabe, *der*

**letter:** ~ **bomb** *n.* Briefbombe, *die;*
~ **box** *n.* Briefkasten, *der;* ~head,
~-heading *ns.* Briefkopf, *der*

'**lettering** *n.* Typographie, *die*

**letter:** ~ **pad** *n.* Briefblock, *der;* ~s
**page** *n.* Leserbriefseite, *die*

**lettuce** /'letɪs/ *n.* [Kopf]salat, *der*

**leukaemia,** (Amer.) **leukemia**
/lu:'ki:mɪə/ *n.* Leukämie, *die*

**level** /'levl/ ① n. **(a)** Höhe, die; (storey)
Etage, die
**(b)** (fig.: steady state) Niveau, das; **be on a**
~ **[with sb./sth.]** auf dem gleichen Niveau
sein [wie jmd./etw.]
**(c)** (of computer game) Level, der
② adj. **(a)** waagerecht; eben ⟨Boden, Land⟩
**(b)** (on a ~) **be** ~ **[with sth./sb.]** auf gleicher
Höhe [mit etw./jmdm.] sein
**(c)** (fig.) **keep a** ~ **head** einen kühlen Kopf
bewahren; **do one's** ~ **best** (coll.) sein
Möglichstes tun
③ v.t., (Brit.) **-ll-: (a)** (make ~) ebnen
**(b)** (aim) richten ⟨Blick, Gewehr⟩ (at auf
+ Akk.); (fig.) richten ⟨Kritik usw.⟩ (at gegen)

**level:** ~ **'crossing** n. (Brit. Railw.)
[schienengleicher] Bahnübergang;
~**-'headed** adj. besonnen

**lever** /'li:və(r)/ ① n. Hebel, der
② v.t. ~ **sth. open** etw. aufhebeln

**leverage** /'li:vərɪdʒ/ n. Hebelwirkung, die

**levity** /'levɪtɪ/ n. (frivolity) Unernst, der

**levy** /'levɪ/ ① n. (tax) Steuer, die
② v.t. erheben

**lewd** /lju:d/ adj. geil; anzüglich ⟨Geste⟩;
schlüpfrig ⟨Witz⟩

**lexicon** /'leksɪkən/ n. **(a)** (dictionary)
Wörterbuch, das; Lexikon, das (veralt.)
**(b)** (vocabulary) Wortschatz, der

**liability** /laɪə'bɪlɪtɪ/ n. **(a)** Haftung, die
**(b)** (handicap) Belastung, die (to für)

**liable** /'laɪəbl/ pred. adj. **(a)** (legally bound) be
~ **for sth.** für etw. haftbar sein od. haften
**(b)** (prone) **be** ~ **to sth.** ⟨Person:⟩ zu etw.
neigen; **be** ~ **to do sth.** ⟨Sache:⟩ leicht etw.
tun; ⟨Person:⟩ dazu neigen, etw. zu tun

**liaise** /lɪ'eɪz/ v.i. eine Verbindung
herstellen; ~ **on a project** bei einem Projekt
zusammenarbeiten

**liaison** /lɪ'eɪzɒn/ n. (cooperation)
Zusammenarbeit, die

**liar** /'laɪə(r)/ n. Lügner, der/Lügnerin, die

**libel** /'laɪbl/ ① n. Verleumdung, die
② v.t., (Brit.) **-ll-** verleumden

**libellous** (Amer.: **libelous**) /'laɪbələs/ adj.
verleumderisch

**liberal** /'lɪbərl/ ① adj. **(a)** großzügig
**(b)** (Polit.) liberal; **the L**~ **Democrats** (Brit.) die
Liberaldemokraten
② n. **L**~ (Polit.) Liberale, der/die

**liberate** /'lɪbəreɪt/ v.t. befreien (**from** aus); **a**
~**d woman** eine emanzipierte Frau

**liberation** /lɪbə'reɪʃn/ n. Befreiung, die; see
also WOMEN'S LIBERATION

**liberator** /'lɪbəreɪtə(r)/ n. Befreier, der/
Befreierin, die

**liberty** /'lɪbətɪ/ n. Freiheit, die; **take the**
~ **of doing sth.** sich (Dat.) die Freiheit
nehmen, etw. zu tun; **take liberties with sb.**
sich (Dat.) Freiheiten gegen jmdn.
herausnehmen (ugs.)

**Libra** /'li:brə/ n. (Astrol., Astron.) die Waage

**librarian** /laɪ'breərɪən/ n. Bibliothekar, der/
Bibliothekarin, die

**library** /'laɪbrərɪ/ n. Bibliothek, die; **public**
~: öffentliche Bücherei

**library:** ~ **book** n. Buch aus der
Bibliothek; ~ **ticket** n. Lesekarte, die

**Libya** /'lɪbɪə/ pr. n. Libyen (das)

**lice** pl. of LOUSE

**licence** /'laɪsəns/ ① n. [behördliche]
Genehmigung; Lizenz, die; [driving] ~:
Führerschein, der
② v.t. ▶ LICENSE 1

**'licence fee** n. Lizenzgebühr, die

**license** /'laɪsəns/ ① v.t. ermächtigen; **the**
**restaurant is** ~**d to sell drinks** das
Restaurant hat eine Schankerlaubnis od.
-konzession; ~**d** ⟨Händler, Makler,
Buchmacher⟩ mit [einer] Lizenz; **licensing**
**laws** Schankgesetze; ~**d premises** Gaststätte
mit Schankerlaubnis; **get a car** ~**d** ≈ die
Kfz-Steuer für ein Auto bezahlen
② n. (Amer.) ▶ LICENCE 1

**'license plate** n. (Amer.) Nummernschild,
das

**licentious** /laɪ'senʃəs/ adj. zügellos
⟨Person⟩; unzüchtig ⟨Benehmen⟩

**lichen** /'laɪkn, 'lɪtʃn/ n. Flechte, die

**lick** /lɪk/ ① v.t. **(a)** lecken
**(b)** (coll.: beat) verdreschen (ugs.)
② n. Lecken, das
▪ **lick 'off** v.t. ablecken

**lid** /lɪd/ n. **(a)** Deckel, der
**(b)** (eyelid) Lid, das

**lido** /'li:dəʊ/ n., pl. ~**s** Freibad, das

**lie¹** /laɪ/ ① n. Lüge, die; **tell** ~**s/a** ~: lügen
② v.i., **lying** /'laɪɪŋ/ lügen; ~ **to sb.** jmdn. be-
od. anlügen

**lie²** v.i., **lying** /'laɪɪŋ/ **lay** /leɪ/, **lain** /leɪn/ **(a)**
liegen; (assume horizontal position) sich legen
**(b)** ~ **idle** ⟨Maschine, Fabrik:⟩ stillstehen
▪ **lie a'bout, lie a'round** v.i.
herumliegen (ugs.).
▪ **lie 'back** v.i. sich zurücklegen; (sitting)
sich zurücklehnen
▪ **lie 'down** v.i. sich hinlegen

**lie detector** /'laɪdɪtektə(r)/ n.
Lügendetektor, der

**'lie-in** n. (coll.) **have a** ~: [sich] ausschlafen

**lieu** /lju:/ n. **in** ~ **of sth.** anstelle einer Sache
(Gen.); **get holiday in** ~: stattdessen Urlaub
bekommen

**lieutenant** /lef'tenənt/ n. (Army)
Oberleutnant, der

**life** /laɪf/ n., pl. **lives** /laɪvz/ Leben, das; **for**
~: lebenslänglich ⟨inhaftiert⟩; **true to** ~:
wahrheitsgetreu; **get a** ~ (coll.) was aus
seinem Leben machen

**life:** ~**-and-death** adj. ⟨Kampf⟩ auf Leben
und Tod; (fig.) überaus wichtig ⟨Frage, Brief⟩;
~ **assurance** n. (Brit.)
Lebensversicherung, die; ~**belt** n.
Rettungsring, der; ~**boat** n. Rettungsboot,
das; ~**buoy** n. Rettungsring, der; ~ **cycle**

*n.* Lebenszyklus, *der;* ∼ **expectancy** *n.* Lebenserwartung, *die;* ∼**guard** *n.* Rettungsschwimmer, *der/*-schwimmerin, *die;* ∼ **insurance** *n.* Lebensversicherung, *die;* ∼ **jacket** *n.* Schwimmweste, *die;* ∼**less** *adj.* leblos; (fig.) farblos; ∼**like** *adj.* lebensecht; ∼**line** *n.* Rettungsleine, *die;* (fig.) Rettungsanker, *der;* ∼**long** *adj.* lebenslang

**lifer** /ˈlaɪfə(r)/ *n.* (coll.) Lebenslängliche, *der/die* (ugs.)

**life:** ∼**-saving** *n.* Rettungsschwimmen, *das; attrib.* Rettungs-; ∼ **sciences** *n. pl.* Biowissenschaften *Pl.;* ∼ **sentence** *n.* lebenslängliche Freiheitsstrafe; ∼**-size,** ∼**-sized** *adj.* lebensgroß; in Lebensgröße *nachgestellt;* ∼**span** *n.* Lebenserwartung, *die;* (Biol.) Lebensdauer, *die;* ∼**style** *n.* Lebensstil, *der;* ∼**time** *n.* Lebenszeit, *die;* **during my** ∼**time** während meines Lebens; **once in a** ∼**time** einmal im Leben; ∼ **vest** *n.* Schwimmweste, *die*

**lift** /lɪft/ ⓵ *v.t.* heben; (fig.) erheben ⟨*Gemüt, Geist*⟩

⓶ *n.* (a) (in vehicle) **get a** ∼: mitgenommen werden; **give sb. a** ∼: jmdn. mitnehmen
(b) (Brit.: elevator) Aufzug, *der*
⓷ *v.i.* ⟨*Nebel:*⟩ sich auflösen
■ **'lift off** *v.t. & i.* abheben
■ **lift 'up** *v.t.* hochheben; heben ⟨*Kopf*⟩

**'lift-off** *n.* Abheben, *das*

**ligament** /ˈlɪɡəmənt/ *n.* Band, *das*

**light¹** /laɪt/ ⓵ *n.* (a) Licht, *das;* ∼ **of day** Tageslicht, *das*
(b) (lamp) Licht, *das;* (fitting) Lampe, *die*
(c) (signal to traffic) Ampel, *die;* **as far as the** ∼**s** bis zur Ampel
(d) (to ignite) **have you got a** ∼? haben Sie Feuer? **set** ∼ **to sth.** etw. anzünden
(e) **bring sth. to** ∼: etw. ans [Tages]licht bringen; **throw** *or* **shed** ∼ **[up]on sth.** Licht in etw. (*Akk.*) bringen
(f) (aspect) **in this** ∼: aus dieser Sicht; **seen in this** ∼: so gesehen; **in the** ∼ **of** angesichts (+ *Gen.*); **show sb. in a bad** ∼: ein schlechtes Licht auf jmdn. werfen
⓶ *adj.* hell; ∼**-blue/-brown** *etc.* hellblau/-braun *usw.*
⓷ *v.t.,* **lit** /lɪt/ *or* **lighted** (a) (ignite) anzünden
(b) (illuminate) erhellen
■ **light 'up** ⓵ *v.i.* (a) (become lit) erleuchtet werden
(b) (become bright) aufleuchten (**with** vor)
⓶ *v.t.* (a) (illuminate) erleuchten
(b) anzünden ⟨*Zigarette*⟩

**light²** ⓵ *adj.* leicht; (mild) mild ⟨*Strafe*⟩
⓶ *adv.* **travel** ∼: mit wenig *od.* leichtem Gepäck reisen

**light:** ∼ **'aircraft** *n.* Leichtflugzeug, *das;* ∼**bulb** *n.* Glühbirne, *die*

**'lighted** *adj.* brennend ⟨*Kerze, Zigarette*⟩; angezündet ⟨*Streichholz*⟩

**light-emitting 'diode** /ˈdaɪəʊd/ *n.* Leuchtdiode, *die*

**lighten¹** /ˈlaɪtn/ *v.t.* (make less heavy, difficult) leichter machen

**lighten²** ⓵ *v.t.* (make brighter) aufhellen; heller machen ⟨*Raum*⟩
⓶ *v.i.* sich aufhellen

**'lighter** *n.* Feuerzeug, *das*

**light:** ∼**-'headed** *adj.* leicht benommen; ∼**-'hearted** *adj.* (a) (humorous) unbeschwert; (b) (optimistic) unbekümmert; ∼**house** *n.* Leuchtturm, *der;* ∼ **'industry** *n.* Leichtindustrie, *die*

**'lighting** *n.* Beleuchtung, *die*

**'lightly** *adv.* (a) leicht
(b) (without serious consideration) leichtfertig
(c) (cheerfully) leichthin; **not treat sth.** ∼: etw. nicht auf die leichte Schulter nehmen
(d) **get off** ∼: glimpflich davonkommen

**'light meter** *n.* Lichtmesser, *der;* (exposure meter) Belichtungsmesser, *der*

**'lightness¹** *n.* (of weight; also fig.) Leichtigkeit, *die*

**lightness²** *n.* (of colour) Helligkeit, *die*

**lightning** /ˈlaɪtnɪŋ/ *n.* Blitz, *der;* **flash of** ∼: Blitz, *der*

**lightning:** ∼ **conductor** *n.* Blitzableiter, *der;* ∼ **strike** *n.* Blitzschlag, *der*

**light:** ∼**weight** ⓵ *adj.* leicht. ⓶ *n.* Leichtgewicht, *das;* ∼ **year** *n.* Lichtjahr, *das*

**like¹** /laɪk/ ⓵ *adj.* (a) (resembling) wie; **your dress is** ∼ **mine** dein Kleid ist so ähnlich wie meins; **in a case** ∼ **that** in so einem Fall; **what is sb./sth.** ∼? wie ist jmd./etw.?
(b) (characteristic of) typisch für ⟨*dich, ihn usw.*⟩
(c) (similar) ähnlich
⓶ *prep.* (in the manner of) wie; **[just]** ∼ **that** [einfach] so
⓷ *n.* (a) (equal) **his/her** ∼: seines-/ihresgleichen
(b) (similar things) **the** ∼: so etwas; **and the** ∼: und dergleichen

**like²** ⓵ *v.t.* (be fond of, wish for) mögen; ∼ **vegetables** Gemüse mögen; gern Gemüse essen; ∼ **doing sth.** etw. gern tun; **would you** ∼ **a drink?** möchtest du etwas trinken?; **would you** ∼ **me to do it?** möchtest du, dass ich es tue?; **how do you** ∼ **it?** wie gefällt es dir?; **if you** ∼ *expr. assent* wenn du willst
⓶ *n., in pl.* ∼**s and dislikes** Vorlieben und Abneigungen

**likeable** /ˈlaɪkəbl/ *adj.* nett; sympathisch

**likelihood** /ˈlaɪklɪhʊd/ *n.* Wahrscheinlichkeit, *die*

**likely** /ˈlaɪklɪ/ ⓵ *adj.* wahrscheinlich; **there are** ∼ **to be [traffic] hold-ups** man muss mit [Verkehrs]staus rechnen; **they are [not]** ∼ **to come** sie werden wahrscheinlich [nicht] kommen; **is it** ∼ **to rain tomorrow?** wird es morgen wohl regnen?; **this is not** ∼ **to happen** es ist unwahrscheinlich, dass das geschieht

2 *adv.* wahrscheinlich; **as** ~ **as not** höchstwahrscheinlich; **not** ~! (coll.) auf keinen Fall!

'**like-minded** *adj.* gleich gesinnt

**liken** /'laɪkn/ *v.t.* ~ **sth./sb. to sth./sb. etw./** jmdn. mit etw./jmdm. vergleichen

'**likeness** *n.* Ähnlichkeit, *die* (**to** mit)

'**likewise** /'laɪkwaɪz/ *adv.* ebenso

**liking** /'laɪkɪŋ/ *n.* Vorliebe, *die;* **take a** ~ **to sb./sth.** an jmdm./einer Sache Gefallen finden; **sth. is [not] to sb.'s** ~: etw. ist [nicht] nach jmds. Geschmack

**lilac** /'laɪlək/ 1 *n.* (a) (Bot.) Flieder, *der* (b) (colour) Zartlila, *das* 2 *adj.* zartlila; fliederfarben

**Lilo** ® /'laɪləʊ/ *n.* Luftmatratze, *die*

**lily** /'lɪlɪ/ *n.* Lilie, *die*

**limb** /lɪm/ *n.* (a) (Anat.) Glied, *das* (b) **be out on a** ~ (fig.) exponiert sein

**limber up** /lɪmbər 'ʌp/ *v.i.* (loosen up) die Muskeln lockern

**lime¹** /laɪm/ *n.* [**quick**]~: [ungelöschter] Kalk

**lime²** *n.* (fruit) Limone, *die*

**lime³** ▶ LIME TREE

'**limelight** *n.* **be in the** ~: im Rampenlicht [der Öffentlichkeit] stehen

**limerick** /'lɪmərɪk/ *n.* Limerick, *der*

**lime:** ~**stone** *n.* Kalkstein, *der;* ~ **tree** *n.* Linde, *die*

**limit** /'lɪmɪt/ 1 *n.* (a) Grenze, *die;* **set** *or* **put a** ~ **on sth.** etw. begrenzen; **be over the** ~ ⟨*Autofahrer:*⟩ zu viele Promille haben; **lower/ upper** ~: Untergrenze/Höchstgrenze, *die;* **without** ~: unbegrenzt; **within** ~**s** innerhalb gewisser Grenzen (b) (coll.) **this is the** ~! das ist [doch] die Höhe!; **he/she is the [very]** ~: er/sie ist [einfach] unmöglich 2 *v.t.* begrenzen (**to** auf + *Akk.*); einschränken ⟨*Freiheit*⟩

**limitation** /lɪmɪ'teɪʃn/ *n.* Beschränkung, *die*

'**limited** *adj.* (a) (restricted) begrenzt (b) (intellectually narrow) beschränkt

'**limitless** *adj.* grenzenlos

**limousine** /'lɪmʊziːn/ *n.* Limousine, *die*

**limp¹** /lɪmp/ 1 *v.i.* hinken 2 *n.* Hinken, *das*

**limp²** *adj.* schlaff

'**limply** *adv.* schlaff; (weakly) schwach

**limpet** /'lɪmpɪt/ *n.* (Zool.) Napfschnecke, *die*

**limpid** /'lɪmpɪd/ *adj.* klar

**linctus** /'lɪŋktəs/ *n.* Hustensaft, *der*

**line¹** /laɪn/ 1 *n.* (a) (string, cord, rope, etc.) Leine, *die* (b) (telephone cable) Leitung, *die* (c) (long mark; also Math., Phys.) Linie, *die* (d) (row, series) Reihe, *die;* (Amer.: queue) Schlange, *die;* **bring sb. into** ~: dafür sorgen, dass jmd. nicht aus der Reihe tanzt (ugs.) (e) (row of words on a page) Zeile, *die*

(f) (wrinkle) Falte, *die*
(g) (direction, course) Richtung, *die;* **on the** ~**s of** nach Art (+ *Gen.*); **be on the right/wrong** ~**s** in die richtige/falsche Richtung gehen; **along** *or* **on the same** ~**s** in der gleichen Richtung
(h) (Railw.) Bahnlinie, *die;* (track) Gleis, *das*
(i) (field of activity) Branche, *die*
(j) (Commerc.: product) Artikel, *der;* Linie, *die* (fachspr.)
2 *v.t.* (a) linieren ⟨*Papier*⟩; **a** ~**d face** ein faltiges Gesicht
(b) säumen (geh.) ⟨*Straße, Strecke*⟩

■ **line 'up** 1 *v.t.* antreten lassen ⟨*Gefangene, Soldaten usw.*⟩; [in einer Reihe] aufstellen ⟨*Gegenstände*⟩
2 *v.i.* ⟨*Gefangene, Soldaten:*⟩ antreten; (queue up) sich anstellen

**line²** *v.t.* füttern ⟨*Kleidungsstück*⟩; ausschlagen ⟨*Schublade usw.*⟩

**lineage** /'lɪnɪdʒ/ *n.* Abstammung, *die*

**linear** /'lɪnɪə(r)/ *adj.* linear

**line:** ~ **dance** 1 *n.* Linedance, *der;* 2 *v.i.* Linedance tanzen; ~ **dancing** *n.* Linedance-Tanzen, *das;* ~ **manager** *n.* [unmittelbarer] Vorgesetzter; Linienmanager, *der*

**linen** /'lɪnɪn/ 1 *n.* (a) Leinen, *das* (b) (shirts, sheets, etc.) Wäsche, *die* 2 *adj.* Leinen⟨faden, -bluse⟩; Lein⟨tuch⟩

**linen:** ~ **basket** *n.* (Brit.) Wäschekorb, *der;* ~ **cupboard** *n.* Wäscheschrank, *der*

'**line printer** *n.* (Comp.) Zeilendrucker, *der*

**liner** /'laɪnə(r)/ *n.* Linienschiff, *das*

'**line-up** *n.* Aufstellung, *die*

**linger** /'lɪŋɡə(r)/ *v.i.* verweilen (geh.); bleiben

**lingerie** /'læʒərɪ/ *n.* [**women's**] ~: Damenunterwäsche, *die*

**lingo** /'lɪŋɡəʊ/ *n.* (coll.) Sprache, *die*

**linguist** /'lɪŋɡwɪst/ *n.* Sprachkundige, *der/ die*

**linguistic** /lɪŋ'ɡwɪstɪk/ *adj.* (of ~s) linguistisch; (of language) sprachlich

**linguistics** /lɪŋ'ɡwɪstɪks/ *n.* Linguistik, *die*

**lining** /'laɪnɪŋ/ *n.* (of clothes) Futter, *das;* (of objects, machines, etc.) Auskleidung, *die*

'**lining paper** *n.* Schrankpapier, *das*

**link** /lɪŋk/ 1 *n.* (a) (of chain) Glied, *das* (b) (connection) Verbindung, *die* 2 *v.t.* verbinden; ~ **arms** sich unterhaken

■ **link 'up** *v.t.* miteinander verbinden

**links** /lɪŋks/ *n.* [**golf**] ~: Golfplatz, *der*

**lino** /'laɪnəʊ/ *n., pl.* ~**s** Linoleum, *das*

**linoleum** /lɪ'nəʊlɪəm/ *n.* Linoleum, *das*

**linseed** /'lɪnsiːd/ *n.* Leinsamen, *der*

**linseed 'oil** *n.* Leinöl, *das*

**lint** /lɪnt/ *n.* Mull, *der*

**lintel** /'lɪntl/ *n.* (Archit.) Sturz, *der*

**lion** /'laɪən/ *n.* Löwe, *der*

**lioness** /'laɪənɪs/ *n.* Löwin, *die*

**lip** /lɪp/ *n.* (a) (Anat.) Lippe, *die;* **lower/upper** ~: Unter-/Oberlippe, *die*

**(b)** (of cup) [Gieß]rand, *der;* (of jug) Schnabel, *der*

**liposuction** /'laɪpəʊsʌkʃn, 'lɪpəʊsʌkʃn/ *n.* Fettabsaugung, *die;* Liposuktion, *die*

**lip:** ∼**-read** *v.i.* von den Lippen lesen; ∼**-reading** *n.* Lippenlesen, *das;* ∼ **service** *n.* pay ∼ service to sth. ein Lippenbekenntnis zu etw. ablegen; ∼**stick** *n.* Lippenstift, *der*

**liquefy** /'lɪkwɪfaɪ/ [1] *v.t.* verflüssigen [2] *v.i.* sich verflüssigen

**liqueur** /lɪ'kjʊə(r)/ *n.* Likör, *der*

**liquid** /'lɪkwɪd/ [1] *adj.* flüssig [2] *n.* Flüssigkeit, *die*

**liquidate** /'lɪkwɪdeɪt/ *v.t.* (Commerc.) liquidieren

**liquidation** /lɪkwɪ'deɪʃn/ *n.* (Commerc.) Liquidation, *die*

**liquid crystal dis'play** *n.* Flüssigkristallanzeige, *die*

**liquidize** /'lɪkwɪdaɪz/ *v.t.* auflösen; (Cookery) [im Mixer] pürieren

**'liquidizer** *n.* Mixer, *der*

**liquid 'measure** *n.* Flüssigkeitsmaß, *das*

**liquor** /'lɪkə(r)/ *n.* (drink) Alkohol, *der*

**liquorice** /'lɪkərɪs/ *n.* Lakritze, *die*

**Lisbon** /'lɪzbən/ *pr. n.* Lissabon (*das*)

**lisp** /lɪsp/ [1] *v.i. & t.* lispeln [2] *n.* Lispeln, *das*

**list¹** /lɪst/ [1] *n.* Liste, *die* [2] *v.t.* aufführen; auflisten; (verbally) aufzählen

**list²** *v.i.* (Naut.) Schlagseite haben

**listed 'building** *n.* (Brit.) Gebäude unter Denkmalsschutz

**listen** /'lɪsn/ *v.i.* zuhören; ∼ to music/the radio Musik/Radio hören; they ∼ed to his words sie hörten ihm zu

**listener** /'lɪsnə(r)/ *n.* Zuhörer, *der*/ Zuhörerin, *die;* (to radio) Hörer, *der*/Hörerin, *die*

**listless** /'lɪstlɪs/ *adj.* lustlos

**'list price** *n.* Katalogpreis, *der*

**lit** ▶ LIGHT¹ 3

**litany** /'lɪtənɪ/ *n.* Litanei, *die*

**lite, Lite** ® /laɪt/ [1] *adj.* kalorienreduziert ⟨*Bier, Käse etc.*⟩ [2] *n.* Leichtbier, *das*

**liter** (Amer.) ▶ LITRE

**literacy** /'lɪtərəsɪ/ *n.* Lese- und Schreibfertigkeit, *die*

**literal** /'lɪtərl/ *adj.* **(a)** wörtlich **(b)** (not exaggerated) buchstäblich

**literally** /'lɪtərəlɪ/ *adv.* **(a)** wörtlich **(b)** (actually) buchstäblich **(c)** (coll.: with some exaggeration) geradezu

**literary** /'lɪtərərɪ/ *adj.* literarisch

**literary 'agent** *n.* Literaturagent, *der*/ -agentin, *die*

**literate** /'lɪtərət/ *adj.* des Lesens und Schreibens kundig; (educated) gebildet

**literature** /'lɪtrətʃə(r)/ *n.* Literatur, *die*

**lithe** /laɪð/ *adj.* geschmeidig

**litigation** /lɪtɪ'geɪʃn/ *n.* Rechtsstreit, *der*

**litre** /'liːtə(r)/ *n.* (Brit.) Liter, *der od. das*

**litter** /'lɪtə(r)/ [1] *n.* **(a)** (rubbish) Abfall, *der* **(b)** (of animals) Wurf, *der* [2] *v.t.* verstreuen

**litter:** ∼ **basket** *n.* Abfallkorb, *der;* ∼ **bin** *n.* Abfalleimer, *der;* ∼**bug,** ∼ **lout** *ns.* Schmutzfink, *der* (ugs.)

**little** /'lɪtl/ [1] *adj.,* ∼**r** /'lɪtlə(r)/, ∼**st** /'lɪtlɪst/ (*Note: it is more common to use the compar. and superl. forms* smaller, smallest) **(a)** klein; a ∼ way ein kurzes Stück; after a ∼ while nach kurzer Zeit **(b)** (not much) wenig; there is very ∼ tea left es ist kaum noch Tee da; a ∼ ... (a small quantity of) etwas ...; ein bisschen ... [2] *n.* wenig; a ∼ (a small quantity) etwas; (somewhat) ein wenig; ∼ by ∼: nach und nach

**little:** ∼ 'finger *n.* kleiner Finger; ∼**-known** *adj.* wenig bekannt

**liturgy** /'lɪtədʒɪ/ *n.* Liturgie, *die*

**live¹** /laɪv/ [1] *adj.* **(a)** *attrib.* (alive) lebend **(b)** (Radio, Telev.) ∼ performance Liveaufführung, *die;* ∼ broadcast Livesendung, *die* **(c)** (Electr.) Strom führend [2] *adv.* (Radio, Telev.) live ⟨*übertragen usw.*⟩

**live²** /lɪv/ [1] *v.i.* **(a)** leben **(b)** (make permanent home) wohnen; leben [2] *v.t.* leben

■ **live 'down** *v.t.* Gras wachsen lassen über (+ *Akk.*); he will never be able to ∼ it down das wird ihm ewig anhängen

■ **live on** [1] /'--/ *v.t.* leben von [2] /-'-/ *v.i.* weiterleben

■ **live 'up to** *v.t.* gerecht werden (+ *Dat.*)

**live-in** /'lɪvɪn/ *attrib. adj.* im Haus wohnend ⟨*Personal*⟩

**livelihood** /'laɪvlɪhʊd/ *n.* Lebensunterhalt, *der*

**liveliness** /'laɪvlɪnɪs/ *n.* Lebhaftigkeit, *die*

**lively** /'laɪvlɪ/ *adj.* lebhaft; lebendig ⟨*Schilderung*⟩; rege ⟨*Handel*⟩

**liven up** /laɪvn 'ʌp/ [1] *v.t.* Leben bringen in (+ *Akk.*) [2] *v.i.* ⟨*Person:*⟩ aufleben

**liver** /'lɪvə(r)/ *n.* Leber, *die*

**livery** /'lɪvərɪ/ *n.* Livree, *die*

**lives** *pl. of* LIFE

**live** /laɪv/: ∼**stock** *n. pl.* Vieh, *das;* ∼ 'wire *n.* (fig.) Energiebündel, *das* (ugs.)

**livid** /'lɪvɪd/ *adj.* (Brit. coll.) fuchtig (ugs.)

**living** /'lɪvɪŋ/ [1] *n.* **(a)** Leben, *das* **(b)** make a ∼: seinen Lebensunterhalt verdienen **(c)** *pl.* the ∼: die Lebenden *Pl.* [2] *adj.* lebend; within ∼ memory seit Menschengedenken

**living:** ∼ **room** *n.* Wohnzimmer, *das;* ∼ 'will *n.* Patientenverfügung, *die*

**lizard** /'lɪzəd/ n. Eidechse, die

**llama** /'lɑːmə/ n. Lama, das

**load** /ləʊd/ **1** n. (burden, weight; also fig.) Last, die; (amount carried) Ladung, die

**2** v.t. (a) (put ~ on) beladen; (put as load) ~ **sb. with work** jmdm. Arbeit auftragen
(b) laden ⟨Gewehr⟩; ~ **a camera** einen Film [in einen Fotoapparat] einlegen

■ **load 'up** v.i. laden (with Akk.)

**'loaded** adj. **a** ~ **question** eine suggestive Frage; **be** ~ (coll.: rich) [schwer] Kohle haben (salopp)

**'loading bay** n. Ladeplatz, der

**loaf¹** /ləʊf/ n., pl. **loaves** /ləʊvz/ Brot, das; [Brot]laib, der; **a** ~ **of bread** ein Laib Brot

**loaf²** v.i. ~ **round town/the house** in der Stadt/zu Hause herumlungern (ugs.)

**loan** /ləʊn/ **1** n. (a) (thing lent) Leihgabe, die; **be out on** ~: ausgeliehen sein; **have sth. on** ~ **[from sb.]** etw. [von jmdm.] geliehen haben
(b) (money lent) Darlehen, das

**2** v.t. ~ **sth. to sb.** jmdm. etw. leihen

**loan shark** n. (coll.) Kredithai, der (ugs.)

**loath** /ləʊθ/ pred. adj. **be** ~ **to do sth.** etw. ungern tun

**loathe** /ləʊð/ v.t. verabscheuen

**loathing** /'ləʊðɪŋ/ n. Abscheu, der (of, for vor + Dat.)

**loathsome** /'ləʊðsəm/ adj. abscheulich; widerlich

**loaves** pl. of LOAF¹

**lobby** /'lɒbɪ/ n. (a) (pressure group) Lobby, die
(b) (of hotel) Eingangshalle, die; (of theatre) Foyer, das

**lobe** /ləʊb/ n. (ear~) Ohrläppchen, das

**lobster** /'lɒbstə(r)/ n. Hummer, der

**'lobster pot** n. Hummerkorb, der

**local** /'ləʊkl/ **1** adj. lokal (bes. Zeitungsw.); Kommunal⟨wahl, -abgaben⟩; (of this area) hiesig; (of that area) dortig; ortsansässig ⟨Firma, Familie⟩; ⟨Wein, Produkt, Spezialität⟩ [aus] der Gegend; **she's a** ~ **girl** sie ist von hier/dort

**2** n. (a) (person) Einheimische, der/die
(b) (Brit. coll.: pub) [Stamm]kneipe, die

**local:** ~ **anaes'thetic** n. Lokalanästhetikum, das; ~ **au'thority** n. (Brit.) Kommunalverwaltung, die; ~ **call** n. (Teleph.) Ortsgespräch, das; ~ **'government** n. Kommunalverwaltung, die

**locality** /ləʊ'kælɪtɪ/ n. Ort, der

**'locally** adv. im/am Ort

**locate** /ləʊ'keɪt/ v.t. (a) **be** ~d liegen
(b) (determine position of) ausfindig machen

**location** /ləʊ'keɪʃn/ n. (a) Lage, die
(b) (Cinemat.) Drehort, der; **be on** ~: bei Außenaufnahmen sein

**loch** /lɒx, lɒk/ n. (Scot.) See, der

**lock¹** /lɒk/ n. (of hair) [Haar]strähne, die

**lock²** /lɒk/ **1** n. (a) (of door etc.) Schloss, das

(b) (on canal etc.) Schleuse, die

**2** v.t. zuschließen

**3** v.i. ⟨Tür, Kasten usw.⟩ sich zuschließen lassen

■ **lock a'way** v.t. einschließen; einsperren ⟨Person⟩

■ **lock 'in** v.t. einschließen; (deliberately) einsperren

■ **lock 'out** v.t. aussperren (of aus); ~ **oneself out** sich aussperren

■ **lock 'up** **1** v.i. abschließen
**2** v.t. (a) abschließen ⟨Haus, Tür⟩
(b) (imprison) einsperren

**locker** /'lɒkə(r)/ n. Schließfach, das

**locket** /'lɒkɪt/ n. Medaillon, das

**lock:** ~**jaw** n. (Med.) Kieferklemme, die; ~**out** n. Aussperrung, die; ~**smith** n. Schlosser, der

**locomotive** /ləʊkə'məʊtɪv/ n. Lokomotive, die

**locust** /'ləʊkəst/ n. Heuschrecke, die

**lodge** /lɒdʒ/ **1** n. (a) (cottage) Pförtner-/Gärtnerhaus, das
(b) (porter's room) [Pförtner]loge, die

**2** v.t. (a) einlegen ⟨Beschwerde, Protest usw.⟩
(b) einreichen ⟨Klage⟩

**3** v.i. [zur Miete] wohnen

**'lodger** n. Untermieter, der/Untermieterin, die

**lodging** /'lɒdʒɪŋ/ n. [möbliertes] Zimmer

**loft** /lɒft/ n. (attic) [Dach]boden, der

**lofty** /'lɒftɪ/ adj. (a) (exalted) hoch
(b) (haughty) hochmütig

**log** /lɒg/ n. (a) (timber) [geschlagener] Baumstamm; (as firewood) [Holz]scheit, das
(b) ~**[book]** (Naut.) Logbuch, das

■ **log 'in** ▸ LOG ON

■ **log 'off** v.i. (Comp.) sich abmelden

■ **log 'on** v.i. (Comp.) sich anmelden

■ **log 'out** ▸ LOG OFF

**log:** ~ **'cabin** n. Blockhütte, die; ~ **'fire** n. Holzfeuer, das

**loggerheads** /'lɒgəhedz/ n. pl. **be at** ~ **with sb.** mit jmdm. im Clinch liegen

**logic** /'lɒdʒɪk/ n. Logik, die

**logical** /'lɒdʒɪkl/ adj. logisch; **she has a** ~ **mind** sie denkt logisch

**logically** /'lɒdʒɪkəlɪ/ adv. logisch

**logistics** /lə'dʒɪstɪks/ n. pl. Logistik, die

**logo** /'ləʊgəʊ/ n., pl. ~**s** Signet, das

**loin** /lɔɪn/ n. Lende, die

**'loincloth** n. Lendenschurz, der

**loiter** /'lɔɪtə(r)/ v.i. trödeln; (linger suspiciously) herumlungern

**loll** /lɒl/ v.i. sich lümmeln (ugs.)

**lollipop** /'lɒlɪpɒp/ n. Lutscher, der

**London** /'lʌndən/ **1** pr. n. London (das)
**2** attrib. adj. Londoner

**'Londoner** n. Londoner, der/Londonerin, die

**lone** /ləʊn/ attrib. adj. einsam

**loneliness** /ˈləʊnlɪnɪs/ *n.* Einsamkeit, *die*
**lonely** /ˈləʊnlɪ/ *adj.* einsam
**lone 'parent** *n.* allein erziehender
Elternteil; **she/he is a ~:** sie/er ist allein
erziehend
**loner** /ˈləʊnə(r)/ *n.* Einzelgänger, *der/*
-gängerin, *die*
**lonesome** /ˈləʊnsəm/ *adj.* einsam
**long¹** /lɒŋ/ ① *adj.,* **~er** /ˈlɒŋgə(r)/, **~est**
/ˈlɒŋgɪst/ **(a)** lang; weit ⟨*Reise, Weg*⟩
**(b)** (elongated) länglich; schmal
**(c) in the '~ run** auf die Dauer
② *n.* (~ interval) **take ~:** lange dauern; **for ~:**
lange; (since ~ ago) seit langem; **before ~:**
bald
③ *adv.,* **~er, ~est (a)** lang[e]; **as** *or* **so ~ as**
solange; **you should have finished ~ before
now** du hättest schon längst fertig sein
sollen; **much ~er** viel länger
**(b) as** *or* **so ~ as** ( provided that) solange;
wenn
**long²** *v.i.* **~ for sb./sth.** sich nach jmdm./
etw. sehnen; **~ to do sth.** sich danach
sehnen, etw. zu tun
**long-distance** ① /ˈ---/ *adj.* Fern⟨*gespräch,
-verkehr usw.*⟩; Langstrecken⟨*läufer, -flug
usw.*⟩
② /-ˈ--/ *adv.* **phone ~:** ein Ferngespräch
führen
**longevity** /lɒnˈdʒevɪtɪ/ *n.* Langlebigkeit,
*die*
**long: ~-haired** *adj.* langhaarig;
Langhaar⟨*dackel, -katze*⟩; **~hand** *n.*
Langschrift, *die;* **~-haul** *adj.* Fern⟨*verkehr,
-lastwagen*⟩; Langstrecken⟨*[flug]verkehr*⟩
**'longing** ① *n.* Sehnsucht, *die*
② *adj.* sehnsüchtig
**'longingly** *adv.* sehnsüchtig
**longitude** /ˈlɒŋgɪtjuːd/ *n.* (Geog.) Länge, *die*
**long: ~ jump** *n.* (Brit. Sport) Weitsprung,
*der;* **~-lasting** *adj.* langandauernd;
dauerhaft ⟨*Beziehung, Freundschaft*⟩;
**~-legged** *adj.* langbeinig; **~ 'lens** *n.*
Fernobjektiv, *das;* **~-life** *adj.* haltbar
[gemacht]; **~-life battery** Batterie mit langer
Lebensdauer; **~-life milk** H-Milch, *die;*
**~-lived** /ˈlɒŋlɪvd/ *adj.* langlebig;
**~-playing 'record** *n.* Langspielplatte,
*die;* **~-range** *adj.* **(a)**
Langstrecken⟨*flugzeug, -rakete usw.*⟩; **(b)**
(relating to time) langfristig; **~-sighted**
/lɒŋˈsaɪtɪd/ *adj.* weitsichtig; (fig.)
weitblickend; **~-sleeved** /ˈlɒŋsliːvd/ *adj.*
langärmelig; **~-standing** *attrib. adj.* seit
langem bestehend; alt ⟨*Schulden, Streit*⟩;
**~-suffering** *adj.* schwer geprüft;
**~-term** *adj.* langfristig; **~ wave** *n.*
(Radio) Langwelle, *die;* **~-winded**
/lɒŋˈwɪndɪd/ *adj.* langatmig
**loo** /luː/ *n.* (Brit. coll.) Klo, *das* (ugs.)
**look** /lʊk/ ① *v.i.* **(a)** sehen; gucken (ugs.)
**(b)** (search) nachsehen
**(c)** (face) zugewandt sein **(to[wards]** *Dat.*)

**(d)** (appear) aussehen; **~ well/ill** gut/schlecht
aussehen
② *n.* **(a)** Blick, *der;* **have** *or* **take a ~ at sb./
sth.** sich (*Dat.*) jmdn./etw. ansehen
**(b)** (appearance) Aussehen, *das;* **good ~s**
gutes Aussehen
■ **look 'after** *v.t.* (care for) sorgen für
■ **look a'head** *v.i.* (fig.) an die Zukunft
denken
■ **'look at** *v.t.* **(a)** (regard) ansehen
**(b)** (consider) betrachten
■ **look 'back** *v.i.* **(a)** sich umsehen
**(b) ~ back on** *or* **to sth.** an etw. (*Akk.*)
zurückdenken
■ **look 'down [up]on** *v.t.* **(a)** herunter-/
hinuntersehen auf (+ *Akk.*)
**(b)** (fig.: despise) herabsehen auf (+ *Akk.*)
■ **'look for** *v.t.* **(a)** (seek) suchen nach
**(b)** (expect) erwarten
■ **look 'out** *v.i.* **(a)** hinaus-/heraussehen (of
aus)
**(b)** (take care) aufpassen
**(c) ~ out on sth.** ⟨*Zimmer, Wohnung usw.:*⟩
zu etw. hin liegen
■ **look 'out for** *v.t.* (be prepared for) achten
auf (+ *Akk.*); (keep watching for) Ausschau
halten nach ⟨*Arbeit, Gelegenheit,
Sammelobjekt usw.*⟩
■ **look 'over** *v.t.* **(a)** sehen über (+ *Akk.*)
**(b)** (survey) sich (*Dat.*) ansehen ⟨*Haus*⟩
■ **look 'round** *v.i.* sich umsehen
■ **'look through** *v.t.* **(a) ~ through sth.**
durch etw. [hindurch] sehen
**(b)** (inspect) durchsehen ⟨*Papiere*⟩
■ **'look to** *v.t.* (rely on) **~ to sb./sth. for sth.**
etw. von jmdm./etw. erwarten
■ **look 'up** ① *v.i.* **(a)** aufblicken
**(b)** (improve) besser werden
② *v.t.* nachschlagen ⟨*Wort*⟩; heraussuchen
⟨*Telefonnummer, Zugverbindung usw.*⟩
■ **look 'up to** *v.t.* **~ up to sb.** zu jmdm.
aufsehen
**'look-alike** *n.* Doppelgänger, *der/*-gängerin,
*die*
**looker-'on** *n.* Zuschauer, *der/*Zuschauerin,
*die*
**'looking glass** *n.* Spiegel, *der*
**'lookout** *n., pl.* **~s (a)** (observation post)
Ausguck, *der*
**(b)** ( person) Wache, *die*
**(c)** (Brit. fig.) **that's a bad ~:** das sind
schlechte Aussichten; **that's his ~:** das ist
sein Problem
**(d) keep a ~ [for sb./sth.]** [nach jmdm./etw]
Ausschau halten
**loom¹** /luːm/ *n.* (Weaving) Webstuhl, *der*
**loom²** *v.i.* auftauchen
**loop** /luːp/ ① *n.* **(a)** Schleife, *die*
**(b)** (cord) Schlaufe, *die*
② *v.t.* zu einer Schlaufe formen
**'loophole** *n.* (fig.) Lücke, *die*
**loopy** /ˈluːpɪ/ *adj.* (coll.) verrückt (ugs.)
**loose** /luːs/ *adj.* **(a)** (not firm) locker ⟨*Zahn,
Schraube, Knopf*⟩                                    ⸱⸱⸱>

(b) (not fixed) lose ⟨Knopf, Buchseite, Brett, Stein⟩; offen ⟨Haar⟩
(c) be at a ∼ end (fig.) nichts zu tun haben
(d) (inexact) ungenau

**loose:** ∼**-fitting** adj. bequem geschnitten; ∼**-leaf** adj. Loseblatt-; ∼**-leaf file** Ringbuch, das; ∼**-limbed** adj. gelenkig

'**loosely** adv. locker; lose ⟨zusammenhängen⟩; frei ⟨übersetzen⟩

**loosen** /'luːsn/ v.t. lockern
■ **loosen 'up** v.i. sich auflockern; (relax) auftauen

'**looseness** n. Lockerheit, die

**loot** /luːt/ ① v.t. plündern
② n. Beute, die

'**looter** n. Plünderer, der

**lop** /lɒp/ v.t. ∼ sth. [off or away] etw. abbauen od. abhacken

**lopsided** /lɒp'saɪdɪd/ adj. schief

**loquacious** /lə'kweɪʃəs/ adj. redselig

**lord** /lɔːd/ ① n. (a) (master) Herr, der
(b) L∼ (Relig.) Herr, der
(c) (Brit.: as title) Lord, der; **the House of L**∼**s** (Brit.) das Oberhaus
② int. (coll.) Gott; **oh/good L**∼**!** du lieber Himmel!

'**lordship** n. Lordschaft, die

**lore** /lɔː(r)/ n. Überlieferung, die

**lorry** /'lɒrɪ/ n. (Brit.) Lastwagen, der; Lkw, der

'**lorry driver** n. (Brit.) Lastwagenfahrer, der; Lkw-Fahrer, der

**lose** /luːz/ ① v.t., lost /lɒst/ (a) verlieren; ∼ **one's way** sich verlaufen/verfahren
(b) ⟨Uhr:⟩ nachgehen
(c) (waste) vertun ⟨Zeit⟩; (miss) versäumen ⟨Gelegenheit⟩
(d) ∼ **weight** abnehmen
② v.i., lost (a) (in match, contest) verlieren
(b) ⟨Uhr:⟩ nachgehen

'**loser** n. Verlierer, der/Verliererin, die

**loss** /lɒs/ n. (a) Verlust, der (of Gen.); **sell at a** ∼: mit Verlust verkaufen
(b) **be at a** ∼: nicht [mehr] weiterwissen; **be at a** ∼ **for words** um Worte verlegen sein; **be at a** ∼ **what to do** nicht wissen, was zu tun ist

**loss:** ∼ **adjuster** n. (Finance) Schaden[s]regulierer, der/-reguliererin, die; ∼**-making** adj. mit Verlust arbeitend

**lost** /lɒst/ ① ▶ LOSE
② adj. (a) verloren; **get** ∼ ⟨Person:⟩ sich verlaufen/verfahren; **get** ∼**!** (coll.) verdufte! (salopp); ∼ **cause** aussichtslose Sache
(b) (wasted) vertan ⟨Zeit⟩; (missed) versäumt ⟨Gelegenheit⟩

**lot** /lɒt/ n. (a) (destiny) Los, das
(b) (set of persons) Haufen, der; **the** ∼: [sie] alle
(c) (set of things) Menge, die; **the** ∼: alle/alles
(d) (coll.: large quantity) ∼**s or a** ∼ **of money** etc. viel od. eine Menge Geld usw.; **sing** etc. **a** ∼: viel singen usw.; **like sth. a** ∼: etw. sehr mögen; **have** ∼**s to do** viel zu tun haben

(e) (for choosing) Los, das; **draw/cast/throw** ∼**s [for sth.]** um etw. losen

**lotion** /'ləʊʃn/ n. Lotion, die

**lottery** /'lɒtərɪ/ n. Lotterie, die

'**lottery number** n. Lottozahl, die

**loud** /laʊd/ ① adj. (a) laut; lautstark ⟨Protest, Kritik⟩
(b) (flashy, conspicuous) aufdringlich; grell ⟨Farbe⟩
② adv. laut; **laugh out** ∼: laut auflachen; **say sth. out** ∼: etw. aussprechen

**loud'hailer** n. Megaphon, das

'**loudly** adv. laut

**loud:** ∼**-mouth** n. Großmaul, das; ∼**-mouthed** /'laʊdmaʊðd/ adj. großmäulig (ugs.)

'**loudness** n. Lautstärke, die

**loud'speaker** n. Lautsprecher, der

**lounge** /laʊndʒ/ ① v.i. ∼ **[about or around]** [faul] herumliegen/-sitzen/-stehen
② n. (a) (in hotel) [Hotel]halle, die; (at airport) Wartehalle, die
(b) (sitting room) Wohnzimmer, das

**lounger** /'laʊndʒə(r)/ n. (sunbed) Liege, die

'**lounge suit** n. (Brit.) Straßenanzug, der

**louse** /laʊs/ n., pl. **lice** /laɪs/ Laus, die

**lousy** /'laʊzɪ/ adj. (coll.) (a) (disgusting) ekelhaft
(b) (very poor) lausig (ugs.); **feel** ∼: sich mies (ugs.) fühlen

**lout** /laʊt/ n. Rüpel, der; Flegel, der

**loutish** /'laʊtɪʃ/ adj. rüpelhaft; flegelhaft

**louver, louvre** /'luːvə(r)/ n. ∼ **window** Jalousiefenster, das; ∼ **door** Jalousietür, die

**lovable** /'lʌvəbl/ adj. liebenswert

**love** /lʌv/ ① n. (a) Liebe, die (of, for zu); **in** ∼ **[with]** verliebt [in (+ Akk.)]; **fall in** ∼ **[with]** sich verlieben [in (+ Akk.)]; **for** ∼: aus Liebe; ∼ **from Beth** (in letter) herzliche Grüße von Beth; **send one's** ∼ **to sb.** jmdn. grüßen lassen
(b) (sweetheart) Geliebte, der/die; **[my]** ∼ (coll.: form of address) [mein] Liebling od. Schatz
(c) (Tennis) **fifteen/thirty** ∼: fünfzehn/dreißig null
② v.t. (a) lieben; **our/their** ∼**d ones** unsere/ihre Lieben
(b) (like) **I'd** ∼ **a cigarette** ich hätte sehr gerne eine Zigarette; ∼ **to do or** ∼ **doing sth.** etw. gern tun

**love:** ∼ **affair** n. Liebesverhältnis, das; ∼ **letter** n. Liebesbrief, der; ∼ **life** n. Liebesleben, das

**loveliness** /'lʌvlɪnɪs/ n. Schönheit, die

**lovely** /'lʌvlɪ/ adj. [wunder]schön; herrlich ⟨Tag, Essen⟩

**lover** /'lʌvə(r)/ n. (a) Liebhaber, der; Geliebte, der; (woman) Geliebte, die; **be** ∼**s** ein Liebespaar sein
(b) (person who likes sth.) Freund, der/Freundin, die

**love:** ∼**sick** adj. an Liebeskummer

leidend; liebeskrank (geh.); ~ **song** n.
Liebeslied, das; ~ **story** n.
Liebesgeschichte, die

**loving** /'lʌvɪŋ/ adj. (a) (affectionate) liebend
(b) (expressing love) liebevoll

'**lovingly** adv. liebevoll

**low** /ləʊ/ 1 adj. (a) niedrig; tief
ausgeschnitten ⟨Kleid⟩; tief ⟨Ausschnitt⟩; tief
liegend ⟨Grund⟩
(b) (of humble rank) nieder…; niedrig
(c) (inferior) niedrig; gering ⟨Intelligenz,
Bildung⟩
(d) (in pitch) tief; (in loudness) leise
2 adv. (a) (to a ~ position) tief
(b) (not loudly) leise
(c) lie ~ (hide) untertauchen

**low:** ~-**alcohol** adj. alkoholarm
⟨Getränk⟩; ~**brow** adj. schlicht ⟨Person⟩;
[geistig] anspruchslos ⟨Buch, Programm⟩;
~-**budget** adj. Lowbudget-, Billig⟨film,
-produktion usw.⟩; ~-**calorie** adj.
kalorienarm ⟨Kost, Getränk⟩; ~-**cost** adj.
preiswert; ~-**cut** adj. [tief] ausgeschnitten
⟨Kleid⟩; ~-**cut neck** tiefer Ausschnitt; ~-**cut
shoes** Halbschuhe

**lower**[1] /'ləʊə(r)/ v.t. (a) herab-/hinablassen
(b) senken ⟨Blick⟩; auslassen ⟨Saum⟩;
senken ⟨Preis, Miete, Zins usw.⟩; ~ **one's
voice** leiser sprechen

**lower**[2] 1 compar. adj. unter…;
Unter⟨grenze, -arm, -lippe usw.⟩
2 compar. adv. tiefer

**lower 'case** 1 n. Kleinbuchstaben Pl.;
2 adj. klein ⟨Buchstabe⟩

**low:** ~-**fat** adj. fettarm; ~-**flying** adj. tief
fliegend; ~-**flying aircraft** Tiefflieger, der;
~ '**frequency** n. Niederfrequenz, die;
~-**grade** adj. minderwertig; ~-**income**
adj. einkommensschwach; ~-**income families**
Familien mit niedrigem Einkommen;
~-**key** adj. zurückhaltend; unaufdringlich
⟨Beleuchtung, Unterhaltung⟩; unauffällig
⟨Einsatz⟩; ~**land** /'ləʊlənd/ n. Tiefland, das

**lowly** /'ləʊlɪ/ adj. (modest) bescheiden

**low:** ~-**lying** adj. tief liegend;
~-**nicotine** adj. nikotinarm; ~-**paid** adj.
niedrig bezahlt; ~-**paid families** Familien
mit geringem Einkommen; ~ **point** n.
Tiefpunkt, der; ~ **pressure** n. (Meteorol.)
Tiefdruck, der; ~-**priced** adj. preisgünstig;
~ **season** n. Nebensaison, die; ~-**tech**
adj. Lowtech⟨-system, -ausrüstung etc.⟩;
~-**voltage** adj. Niederspannungs-;
~-**wage** attrib. adj. schlecht bezahlt;
Niedriglohn⟨land⟩

**loyal** /'lɔɪəl/ adj. treu

**loyalty** /'lɔɪəltɪ/ n. Treue, die

'**loyalty card** n. Treuekarte, die (für
Kunden)

**lozenge** /'lɒzɪndʒ/ n. Pastille, die

**LP** abbr. = **long-playing record** LP, die

'**L-plate** n. (Brit.) 'L'-Schild, das; ≈
„Fahrschule"-Schild, das

**Ltd.** abbr. = **Limited** GmbH

**lubricant** /'lu:brɪkənt/ n. Schmiermittel,
das

**lubricate** /'lu:brɪkeɪt/ v.t. schmieren

**lubrication** /lu:brɪ'keɪʃn/ n. Schmierung,
die; attrib. Schmier⟨system, -vorrichtung⟩

**lucid** /'lu:sɪd/ adj. klar

**lucidity** /lu:'sɪdɪtɪ/ n. Klarheit, die

**luck** /lʌk/ n. Glück, das; **good** ~: Glück,
das; **bad** or **hard** ~: Pech, das; **good** ~! viel
Glück!; **be in/out of** ~: Glück/kein Glück
haben; **no such** ~: schön wärs

**luckily** /'lʌkɪlɪ/ adv. glücklicherweise

**lucky** /'lʌkɪ/ adj. (a) glücklich; **be** ~: Glück
haben
(b) (bringing good luck) Glücks⟨zahl, -tag usw.⟩;
~ **charm** Glücksbringer, der

**lucrative** /'lu:krətɪv/ adj. einträglich;
lukrativ

**ludicrous** /'lu:dɪkrəs/ adj. lächerlich;
lachhaft ⟨Angebot, Ausrede⟩

**lug** /lʌg/ v.t., -gg- (drag) schleppen

**luggage** /'lʌgɪdʒ/ n. Gepäck, das

**luggage:** ~ **locker** n.
[Gepäck]schließfach, das; ~ **rack** n.
Gepäckablage, die

**lugubrious** /lu:'gu:brɪəs/ adj. (mournful)
kummervoll; (dismal) düster

**lukewarm** /'lu:kwɔ:m/ adj. lauwarm

**lull** /lʌl/ 1 v.t. (a) (soothe) lullen
(b) (fig.) einlullen; ~ **sb. into a false sense of
security** jmdn. in einer trügerischen
Sicherheit wiegen
2 n. Pause, die

**lullaby** /'lʌləbaɪ/ n. Schlaflied, das

**lumbago** /lʌm'beɪgəʊ/ n., pl. ~s (Med.)
Hexenschuss, der

**lumber** /'lʌmbə(r)/ 1 n. (a) (furniture)
Gerümpel, das
(b) (useless material) Kram, der (ugs.)
(c) (Amer.: timber) [Bau]holz, das
2 v.t. ~ **sb. with sth./sb.** jmdm. etw./jmdn.
aufhalsen (ugs.)

'**lumbering** adj. schwerfällig

**lumberjack** /'lʌmbədʒæk/ n. (Amer.)
Holzfäller, der

**luminous** /'lu:mɪnəs/ adj. [hell] leuchtend;
Leucht⟨anzeige, -zeiger usw.⟩

**lump** /lʌmp/ 1 n. (a) Klumpen, der; (of
sugar, butter, etc.) Stück, das; (of wood) Klotz,
der; (of dough) Kloß, der; (of bread) Brocken,
der
(b) (swelling) Beule, die
2 v.t. ~ **sth. with sth.** etw. und etw.
zusammentun

**lump:** ~ '**payment** n. einmalige Zahlung
[einer größeren Summe]; ~ '**sum** n.
Pauschalsumme, die

'**lumpy** adj. klumpig ⟨Brei⟩; ⟨Kissen,
Matratze⟩ mit klumpiger Füllung

**lunacy** /'lu:nəsɪ/ n. Wahnsinn, der

**lunar** /'lu:nə(r)/ adj. Mond-

**lunatic** /'lu:nətɪk/ ① *adj.* wahnsinnig
② *n.* Wahnsinnige, *der/die;* Irre, *der/die*

**'lunatic asylum** *n.* (Hist.) Irrenanstalt, *die* (veralt., ugs.)

**lunch** /lʌntʃ/ ① *n.* Mittagessen, *das;* **have** *or* **eat [one's]** ~: zu Mittag essen
② *v.i.* zu Mittag essen

**lunch:** ~ **box** *n.* Lunchbox, *die;* ~ **break** ▶ ~ HOUR

**luncheon:** ~ **meat** *n.* Frühstücksfleisch, *das;* ~ **voucher** *n.* (Brit.) Essenmarke, *die*

**lunch:** ~ **hour** *n.* Mittagspause, *die;* ~**time** *n.* Mittagszeit, *die;* **at** ~**time** mittags

**lung** /lʌŋ/ *n.* (right or left) Lungenflügel, *der;* ~**s** Lunge, *die*

**'lung cancer** *n.* Lungenkrebs, *der*

**lunge** /lʌndʒ/ ① *n.* Sprung nach vorn
② *v.i.* ~ **at sb. with a knife** jmdn. mit einem Messer angreifen

**lurch**[1] /lɜ:tʃ/ *n.* **leave sb. in the** ~: jmdn. im Stich lassen

**lurch**[2] ① *n.* Rucken, *das*
② *v.i.* rucken; ⟨*Betrunkener:*⟩ torkeln

**lure** /ljʊə(r), lʊə(r)/ ① *v.t.* locken
② *n.* Lockmittel, *das*

**lurid** /'ljʊərɪd, 'lʊərɪd/ *adj.* (a) (in colour) grell
(b) (sensational) reißerisch

**lurk** /lɜ:k/ *v.i.* lauern

**luscious** /'lʌʃəs/ *adj.* köstlich [süß]; saftig [süß] ⟨*Obst*⟩

**lush** /lʌʃ/ *adj.* saftig ⟨*Wiese*⟩; grün ⟨*Tal*⟩; üppig ⟨*Vegetation*⟩

**lust** /lʌst/ ① *n.* (a) (sexual) Sinnenlust, *die*
(b) (strong desire) Gier, *die* (**for** nach)
② *v.i.* ~ **after** [lustvoll] begehren (geh.)

**lustful** /'lʌstfl/ *adj.* lüstern (geh.)

**lustily** /'lʌstɪlɪ/ *adv.* kräftig; aus voller Kehle ⟨*rufen, singen*⟩

**lustre** /'lʌstə(r)/ *n.* (Brit.) (a) Schimmer, *der*
(b) (fig.: splendour) Glanz, *der*

**lusty** /'lʌstɪ/ *adj.* kräftig

**Luxembourg, Luxemburg** /'lʌksəmbɜ:g/ *pr. n.* Luxemburg (*das*)

**luxuriant** /lʌg'zjʊərɪənt/ *adj.* üppig

**luxuriate** /lʌg'zjʊərɪeɪt/ *v.i.* ~ **in** sich aalen in (+ *Dat.*)

**luxurious** /lʌg'zjʊərɪəs/ *adj.* luxuriös

**luxury** /'lʌkʃərɪ/ *n.* (a) Luxus, *der; attrib.* Luxus-
(b) (article) Luxusgegenstand, *der;* **luxuries** Luxus, *der*

**LW** *abbr.* (Radio) = **long wave** LW

**lying** /'laɪɪŋ/ *adj.* verlogen ⟨*Person*⟩. See also LIE[1] 2

**lymph gland** *n.* Lymphknoten, *der*

**lynch** /lɪntʃ/ *v.t.* lynchen

**lynx** /lɪŋks/ *n.* Luchs, *der*

**lyre** /'laɪə(r)/ *n.* Lyra, *die*

**lyric** /'lɪrɪk/ ① *adj.* lyrisch; ~ **poetry** Lyrik, *die*
② *n.* in *pl.* (of song) Text, *der*

**lyrical** /'lɪrɪkl/ *adj.* (a) lyrisch
(b) (coll.: enthusiastic) gefühlvoll

# M m

**M, m** /em/ *n.* M, m, *das*

**m.** *abbr.* (a) = **masculine** m.
(b) = **metre[s]** m
(c) = **million[s]** Mill.
(d) = **minute[s]** Min.

**MA** *abbr.* = **Master of Arts** M.A.

**mac** /mæk/ *n.* (Brit. coll.) Regenmantel, *der*

**macaroni** /mækə'rəʊnɪ/ *n.* Makkaroni *Pl.*

**Macedonia** /mæsɪ'dəʊnɪə/ *pr. n.* Makedonien (*das*)

**machine** /mə'ʃi:n/ *n.* Maschine, *die*

**machine:** ~ **gun** *n.* Maschinengewehr, *das;* ~**-made** *adj.* maschinell hergestellt; ~ **operator** *n.* [Maschinen]bediener, *der/*-bedienerin, *die;* ~**-readable** *adj.* (Comp.) maschinenlesbar

**machinery** /mə'ʃi:nərɪ/ *n.* (a) (machines) Maschinen *Pl.*
(b) (mechanism) Mechanismus, *der*

**machine:** ~ **tool** *n.* Werkzeugmaschine,

*die;* ~**-wash** *v.t.* in der Waschmaschine waschen; ~**-washable** *adj.* waschmaschinenfest

**machinist** /mə'ʃi:nɪst/ *n.* Maschinist, *der/* Maschinistin, *die;* [sewing] ~: [Maschinen]näherin, *die/*-näher, *der*

**machismo** /mə'tʃɪzməʊ, mə'kɪzməʊ/ *n.* Machismo, *der;* Männlichkeitswahn, *der*

**macho** /'mætʃəʊ/ *adj.* Macho-; **he is** ~: er ist ein Macho

**mackerel** /'mækərl/ *n., pl. same or* ~**s** Makrele, *die*

**mackintosh** /'mækɪntɒʃ/ *n.* Regenmantel, *der*

**macro** /'mækrəʊ/ *n.* (Comp.) Makro, *das*

**macrobiotic** /mækrəʊbaɪ'ɒtɪk/ *adj.* makrobiotisch

**mad** /mæd/ *adj.* (a) (insane) geisteskrank
(b) (frenzied) wahnsinnig; **drive sb. mad** jmdn. um den Verstand bringen

**(c)** (foolish) verrückt (ugs.)
**(d)** (very enthusiastic) **be ∼ about** or **on sb./ sth.** auf jmdn./etw. wild sein (ugs.)
**(e)** (coll.: annoyed) **∼ [with** or **at sb.]** sauer [auf jmdn.] (ugs.)
**(f)** (with rabies) toll[wütig]; **[run** etc.**] like ∼** (coll.) wie wild [laufen usw.]

**madam** /'mædəm/ n. gnädige Frau; **Dear M∼** (in letter) Sehr geehrte Dame

**mad 'cow disease** n. (coll.) Rinderwahnsinn, der

**madden** /'mædn/ v.t. (irritate) [ver]ärgern

**maddening** /'mædənɪŋ/ adj. (irritating) [äußerst] ärgerlich

**made** ▶ MAKE 1

**made-to-'measure** attrib. adj. Maß-

**'madly** adv. (coll.) wahnsinnig (ugs.)

**madman** /'mædmən/ n., pl. **madmen** /'mædmən/ n. Wahnsinnige, der

**'madness** n. Wahnsinn, der

**magazine** /mægə'ziːn/ n. **(a)** Zeitschrift, die
**(b)** (of firearm) Magazin, das

**maggot** /'mægət/ n. Made, die

**magic** /'mædʒɪk/ [1] n. **(a)** Magie, die; **work like ∼:** wie ein Wunder wirken
**(b)** (conjuring) Zauberei, die
[2] adj. **(a)** magisch; Zauber⟨trank, -baum⟩
**(b)** (fig.) wunderbar

**magical** /'mædʒɪkl/ adj. zauberhaft

**magician** /mə'dʒɪʃn/ n. Magier, der/ Magierin, die; (conjurer) Zauberer, der/ Zauberin, die

**magic 'wand** n. Zauberstab, der

**magistrate** /'mædʒɪstreɪt/ n. Friedensrichter, der/-richterin, die

**magnanimity** /mægnə'nɪmɪtɪ/ n. Großmut, die

**magnanimous** /mæg'nænɪməs/ adj. großmütig **(towards** gegen)

**magnate** /'mægneɪt/ n. Magnat, der/ Magnatin, die

**magnesium** /mæg'niːzɪəm/ n. Magnesium, das

**magnet** /'mægnɪt/ n. Magnet, der

**magnetic** /mæg'netɪk/ adj. magnetisch

**magnetic: ∼ 'north** magnetisch Nord, das; **∼ 'tape** n. Magnetband, das

**magnetism** /'mægnɪtɪzm/ n. **(a)** (force, lit. or fig.) Magnetismus, der
**(b)** (fig.: charm) Anziehungskraft, die

**magnetize** /'mægnɪtaɪz/ v.t. magnetisieren

**magnification** /mægnɪfɪ'keɪʃn/ n. Vergrößerung, die

**magnificence** /mæg'nɪfɪsəns/ n. Pracht, die; (beauty) Herrlichkeit, die; (lavishness) Üppigkeit, die

**magnificent** /mæg'nɪfɪsənt/ adj. **(a)** prächtig; herrlich ⟨Garten, Kunstwerk, Wetter⟩; (lavish) üppig ⟨Mahl⟩
**(b)** (coll.: excellent) fabelhaft (ugs.)

**magnifier** /'mægnɪfaɪə(r)/ n. (Optics) Lupe, die

**magnify** /'mægnɪfaɪ/ v.t. **(a)** vergrößern
**(b)** (exaggerate) aufbauschen

**'magnifying glass** n. Lupe, die

**magnitude** /'mægnɪtjuːd/ n. **(a)** (size) Größe, die
**(b)** (importance) Wichtigkeit, die

**magnolia** /mæg'nəʊlɪə/ n. Magnolie, die

**magnum** /'mægnəm/ n. (bottle) Magnum, die

**magpie** /'mægpaɪ/ n. Elster, die

**mahogany** /mə'hɒgənɪ/ n. Mahagoni[holz], das; attrib. Mahagoni-

**maid** /meɪd/ n. Dienstmädchen, das

**maiden** /'meɪdn/ [1] n. Jungfrau, die
[2] adj. **(a)** (unmarried) unverheiratet
**(b)** (first) **∼ voyage/speech** Jungfernfahrt/ -rede, die

**'maiden name** n. Mädchenname, der

**mail** /meɪl/ [1] n. ▶ POST² 1
[2] v.t. abschicken

**mail: ∼bag** n. Postsack, der; **∼box** n. (Amer.) Briefkasten, der; **∼ing address** n. Postanschrift, die; **∼ing list** n. Adressenliste, die; **∼man** n. (Amer.) Briefträger, der; **∼ order** n. Bestellung per Post; **∼ order catalogue** n. Versandhauskatalog, der; **∼ order firm** n. Versandhaus, das; **∼ room** n. Poststelle, die

**maim** /meɪm/ v.t. verstümmeln

**main** /meɪn/ [1] n. **(a)** (channel, pipe) Hauptleitung, die; **∼s** (Electr.) Stromnetz, das
**(b)** **in the ∼:** im Großen und Ganzen
[2] attrib. adj. Haupt-; **the ∼ thing is that ...:** die Hauptsache ist, dass ...

**main: ∼ beam** n. (Motor Veh.) **on ∼ beam** aufgeblendet; **∼ course** n. Hauptgang, der; Hauptgericht, das; **∼frame** n. (Comp.) Großrechner, der; **∼land** /'meɪnlənd/ n. Festland, das; **∼ 'line** n. (Railw.) Hauptstrecke, die; **∼-line station/train** Fernbahnhof/-zug, der

**'mainly** adv. hauptsächlich

**main: ∼ 'road** n. Hauptstraße, die; **∼stay** n. [wichtigste] Stütze; **∼ street** /Brit. -'-, Amer. '--/ n. Hauptstraße, die

**maintain** /meɪn'teɪn/ v.t. **(a)** (keep up) aufrechterhalten
**(b)** (provide for) **∼ sb.** für jmds. Unterhalt aufkommen
**(c)** (preserve) instand halten; warten ⟨Maschine⟩
**(d)** **∼ that ...:** behaupten, dass ...

**maintenance** /'meɪntənəns/ n. **(a)** (keeping up) Aufrechterhaltung, die
**(b)** (preservation) Instandhaltung, die; (of machinery) Wartung, die
**(c)** (Law: money paid to support sb.) Unterhalt, der

**maintenance-'free** adj. wartungsfrei

m

**maison[n]ette** /meɪzə'net/ n.
[zweistöckige] Wohnung

**maize** /meɪz/ n. Mais, der

**majestic** /mə'dʒestɪk/ adj.,
**majestically** /mə'dʒestɪkəlɪ/ adv.
majestätisch

**majesty** /'mædʒɪstɪ/ n. Majestät, die (geh.);
Your/Her etc. M∼: Eure/Seine usw. Majestät

**major** /'meɪdʒə(r)/ **1** adj. (a) attrib. (greater)
größer...
(b) attrib. (important) bedeutend...; (serious)
schwer; ∼ **road** Hauptverkehrsstraße, die
(c) (Mus.) Dur-; **C** ∼: C-Dur
**2** n. (Mil.) Major, der
**3** v.i. (Amer. Univ.) ∼ **in sth.** etw. als
Hauptfach haben

**Majorca** /mə'jɔːkə/ pr. n. Mallorca (das)

**majority** /mə'dʒɒrɪtɪ/ n. Mehrheit, die; **be
in the** ∼: in der Mehrzahl sein

**majority 'rule** n. Mehrheitsregierung, die

**make** /meɪk/ **1** v.t., **made** /meɪd/ (a)
machen (of aus); bauen ‹Straße, Flugzeug›;
anlegen ‹Teich, Weg usw.›; zimmern ‹Tisch,
Regal›; basteln ‹Spielzeug, Vogelhäuschen
usw.›; nähen ‹Kleider›; (manufacture)
herstellen; (prepare) zubereiten ‹Mahlzeit›;
machen, kochen ‹Kaffee, Tee›; backen ‹Brot,
Kuchen›
(b) (establish, enact) treffen ‹Unterscheidung,
Übereinkommen›; ziehen ‹Vergleich›; erlassen
‹Gesetz›; aufstellen ‹Regeln, Behauptung›;
stellen ‹Forderung›; geben ‹Bericht›;
vornehmen ‹Zahlung›; erheben ‹Protest,
Beschwerde›
(c) (cause to be or become) ∼ **happy/known** etc.
glücklich/bekannt usw. machen; ∼ **sb.**
**captain** jmdn. zum Kapitän machen
(d) ∼ **sb. do sth.** (cause) jmdn. dazu bringen,
etw. zu tun; (compel) jmdn. zwingen, etw. zu
tun; **be made to do sth.** etw. tun müssen
(e) (earn) machen ‹Profit, Verlust›; verdienen
‹Lebensunterhalt›
(f) **what do you** ∼ **of him?** was hältst du von
ihm?
(g) (arrive at) erreichen; **make it** (succeed in
arriving) es schaffen
(h) ∼ **'do** vorlieb nehmen; ∼ **'do with/
without sth.** mit/ohne etw. auskommen
**2** n. (brand) Marke, die
▪ **'make for** v.t. zusteuern auf (+ Akk.)
▪ **make 'off** v.i. sich davonmachen
▪ **make 'off with** v.t. ∼ **off with sb./sth.**
sich mit jmdm./etw. auf und davon machen
▪ **make 'out** **1** v.t. (a) (write) ausstellen;
∼ **out a cheque to sb.** einen Scheck auf
jmdn. ausstellen
(b) (claim) behaupten
(c) (manage to see or hear) ausmachen; (manage
to read) entziffern
(d) (pretend) vorgeben
**2** v.i. (coll.) zurechtkommen (**at** bei)
▪ **make 'over** v.t. überschreiben (**to** auf
+ Akk.)
▪ **make 'up** **1** v.t. (a) (assemble)
zusammenstellen

(b) (invent) erfinden
(c) (constitute) bilden; **be made up of ...:**
bestehen aus ...
(d) (apply cosmetics to) schminken; ∼ **up one's
face** sich schminken
**2** v.i. (be reconciled) sich wieder vertragen
▪ **make 'up for** v.t. wieder gutmachen;
∼ **up for lost time** Versäumtes nachholen

**make:** ∼**-believe** **1** n. it's only ∼**-believe**
das ist bloß Fantasie; **2** adj. nicht echt;
∼**-or-'break** attrib. adj. alles
entscheidend; ∼**over** n. (of a person's
appearance) [grundlegende] Verwandlung; (of a
building) Umbau, der

**'maker** n. (manufacturer) Hersteller, der

**make:** ∼**shift** adj. behelfsmäßig; ∼**-up** n.
Make-up, das; ∼**-up bag** Kosmetiktasche, die

**making** /'meɪkɪŋ/ n. **in the** ∼: im
Entstehen; **have the** ∼**s of a leader** das Zeug
zum Führer haben (ugs.)

**maladjusted** /mælə'dʒʌstɪd/ adj.
verhaltensgestört

**malady** /'mælədɪ/ n. Leiden, das

**malaise** /mæ'leɪz/ n. Unbehagen, das

**malaria** /mə'leərɪə/ n. Malaria, die

**Malaysia** /mə'leɪzɪə/ pr. n. Malaysia (das)

**male** /meɪl/ **1** adj. männlich;
Männer‹stimme, -chor, -verein›; ∼ **doctor/
nurse** Arzt, der/Krankenpfleger, der
**2** n. (person) Mann, der; (animal) Männchen,
das

**'male-dominated** adj. von Männern
dominiert

**malevolence** /mə'levələns/ n.
Boshaftigkeit, die

**malevolent** /mə'levələnt/ adj. boshaft

**malfunction** /mæl'fʌŋkʃn/ **1** n. Störung,
die; (Med.) Funktionsstörung, die
**2** v.i. nicht richtig funktionieren

**malice** /'mælɪs/ n. Bosheit, die

**malicious** /mə'lɪʃəs/ adj. böse

**malign** /mə'laɪn/ v.t. verleumden

**malignant** /mə'lɪgnənt/ adj. bösartig

**malinger** /mə'lɪŋgə(r)/ v.i. simulieren

**ma'lingerer** n. Simulant, der/Simulantin,
die

**malleable** /'mælɪəbl/ adj. formbar

**mallet** /'mælɪt/ n. Holzhammer, der

**malnourished** /mæl'nʌrɪʃt/ adj.
unterernährt

**malnutrition** /mælnjuː'trɪʃn/ n.
Unterernährung, die

**malpractice** /mæl'præktɪs/ n. (Law, Med.)
Kunstfehler, der

**malt** /mɔːlt/ n. Malz, das

**Malta** /'mɔːltə/ pr. n. Malta (das)

**maltreat** /mæl'triːt/ v.t. misshandeln

**mal'treatment** n. Misshandlung, die

**malt 'whisky** n. Malzwhisky, der

**mammal** /'mæml/ n. Säugetier, das

**mammoth** /'mæməθ/ **1** n. Mammut, das

2 *adj.* Mammut-; gigantisch ‹*Vorhaben*›

**man** /mæn/ 1 *n.* **(a)** *pl.* **men** [men] Mann, *der*

**(b)** (human race) der Mensch

2 *v.t.*, **-nn-** bemannen ‹*Schiff*›; besetzen ‹*Büro, Stelle usw.*›; bedienen ‹*Telefon, Geschütz*›

**manacle** /ˈmænəkl/ 1 *n.*, *usu. in pl.* [Hand]fessel, *die*

2 *v.t.* Handfesseln anlegen (+ *Dat.*)

**manage** /ˈmænɪdʒ/ 1 *v.t.* **(a)** leiten ‹*Geschäft*›

**(b)** (Sport) betreuen ‹*Mannschaft*›

**(c)** (cope with) schaffen

**(d)** ~ to do sth. es fertig bringen, etw. zu tun; **he** ~**d to do it** es gelang ihm, es zu tun

2 *v.i.* zurechtkommen; ~ **without sth.** ohne etw. auskommen; **I can** ~: es geht

**manageable** /ˈmænɪdʒəbl/ *adj.* leicht frisierbar ‹*Haar*›; fügsam ‹*Person, Tier*›; überschaubar ‹*Größe, Menge*›

**'management** *n.* **(a)** (of a business) Leitung, *die*

**(b)** (managers) **the** ~: die Geschäftsleitung

**management:** ~ **consultancy** *n.* Unternehmensberatung, *die;*

~ **consultant** *n.* Unternehmensberater, *der/*-beraterin, *die*

**'manager** *n.* (of shop or bank) Filialleiter, *der/*-leiterin, *die;* (of football team) [Chef]trainer, *der/*-trainerin, *die;* (of restaurant, shop, hotel) Geschäftsführer, *der/*-führerin, *die*

**manageress** /mænɪdʒəˈres/ *n.* Geschäftsführerin, *die*

**managerial** /mænəˈdʒɪərɪəl/ *adj.* führend, leitend ‹*Stellung*›; ~ **skills** Führungsqualitäten

**managing** /ˈmænɪdʒɪŋ/ *adj.* ~ **director** Geschäftsführer, *der/*-führerin, *die*

**mandarin**¹ /ˈmændərɪn/ *n.* ~ [**orange**] Mandarine, *die*

**mandarin**² *n.* (bureaucrat) Bürokrat, *der/* Bürokratin, *die*

**mandarine** /ˈmændəriːn/ ▶ MANDARIN¹

**mandate** /ˈmændeɪt/ *n.* Mandat, *das*

**mandatory** /ˈmændətərɪ/ *adj.* obligatorisch

**mandolin[e]** /mændəˈlɪn/ *n.* Mandoline, *die*

**mane** /meɪn/ *n.* Mähne, *die*

**maneuver[able]** (Amer.) ▶ MANŒUVR-

**manful** /ˈmænfl/ *adj.*, **manfully** /ˈmænfəlɪ/ *adv.* mannhaft

**manger** /ˈmeɪndʒə(r)/ *n.* Krippe, *die*

**mangetout** /mãˈtuː/ *n.* Zuckererbse, *die*

**mangle** /ˈmæŋgl/ *v.t.* verstümmeln ‹*Person*›; demolieren ‹*Sache*›

**mango** /ˈmæŋgəʊ/ *n.*, *pl.* ~**es** *or* ~**s** (fruit) Mango[frucht], *die*

**mangy** /ˈmeɪndʒɪ/ *adj.* **(a)** (Vet. Med.) räudig

**(b)** (shabby) schäbig

**man:** ~**handle** *v.t.* **(a)** von Hand bewegen ‹*Gegenstand*›; **(b)** grob behandeln ‹*Person*›; ~**hole** *n.* Mannloch, *das*

**'manhood** *n.* Mannesalter, *das*

**man:** ~**-hour** *n.* Arbeitsstunde, *die;* ~**hunt** *n.* Verbrecherjagd, *die*

**mania** /ˈmeɪnɪə/ *n.* Manie, *die*

**maniacal** /məˈnaɪəkl/ *adj.* wahnsinnig

**manicure** /ˈmænɪkjʊə(r)/ 1 *n.* Maniküre, *die*

2 *v.t.* maniküren

**manifest** /ˈmænɪfest/ 1 *adj.* offenkundig

2 *v.t.* (reveal) offenbaren

**'manifestly** *adv.* offenkundig

**manifesto** /mænɪˈfestəʊ/ *n.*, *pl.* ~**s** Manifest, *das*

**manifold** /ˈmænɪfəʊld/ *adj.* (literary) mannigfaltig (geh.)

**manipulate** /məˈnɪpjʊleɪt/ *v.t.* **(a)** manipulieren

**(b)** (handle) handhaben

**manipulation** /mənɪpjʊˈleɪʃn/ *n.* **(a)** Manipulation, *die*

**(b)** (handling) Handhabung, *die*

**manipulative** /məˈnɪpjʊlətɪv/ *adj.* manipulativ

**mankind** /mænˈkaɪnd/ *n.* Menschheit, *die*

**manly** /ˈmænlɪ/ *adj.* männlich

**'man-made** *adj.* künstlich; (synthetic) Kunst‹*faser, -stoff*›

**manned** /mænd/ *adj.* bemannt

**manner** /ˈmænə(r)/ *n.* **(a)** Art, *die;* Weise, *die;* **in this** ~: auf diese Art und Weise

**(b)** (general behaviour) Art, *die*

**(c)** *in pl.* Manieren Pl.

**mannerism** /ˈmænərɪzm/ *n.* Eigenart, *die*

**manœuvrable** /məˈnuːvrəbl/ *adj.* (Brit.) manövrierfähig

**manœuvre** /məˈnuːvə(r)/ (Brit.) 1 *n.* Manöver, *das*

2 *v.t. & i.* manövrieren

**manor** /ˈmænə(r)/ *n.* **(a)** (land) [Land]gut, *das*

**(b)** ▶ MANOR HOUSE

**'manor house** *n.* Herrenhaus, *das*

**'manpower** *n.* Arbeitskräfte Pl.

**mansion** /ˈmænʃn/ *n.* Herrenhaus, *das*

**manslaughter** /ˈmænslɔːtə(r)/ *n.* Totschlag, *der*

**mantel:** ~**piece** /ˈmæntlpiːs/ *n.* **(a)** (above fireplace) Kaminsims, *der od. das;* **(b)** (around fireplace) Kamineinfassung, *die;* ~**shelf** ▶ ~PIECE A

**mantle** /ˈmæntl/ *n.* Umhang, *der*

**manual** /ˈmænjʊəl/ 1 *adj.* **(a)** manuell; ~ **work** Handarbeit; ~ **worker** Handarbeiter, *der/*-arbeiterin, *die*

**(b)** (not automatic) handbetrieben; ‹*Bedienung, Schaltung*› von Hand

2 *n.* Handbuch, *das*

m

**manually** /'mænjʊəlɪ/ *adv.* manuell; a ~ operated machine eine handbetriebene Maschine

**manufacture** /mænjʊ'fæktʃə(r)/ ① *n.* Herstellung, *die* ② *v.t.* herstellen

**manu'facturer** *n.* Hersteller, *der*

**manure** /mə'njʊə(r)/ ① *n.* Dung, *der* ② *v.t.* düngen

**manuscript** /'mænjʊskrɪpt/ *n.* Manuskript, *das*

**many** /'menɪ/ ① *adj.* viele; **how ~ people/ books?** wie viele *od.* wie viel Leute/Bücher? ② *n.* viele [Leute]; **~ of us** viele von uns; **a good/great ~:** eine Menge

**map** /mæp/ ① *n.* [Land]karte, *die;* (street plan) Stadtplan, *der* ② *v.t.,* **-pp-** kartographieren

■ **map 'out** *v.t.* im Einzelnen festlegen

**maple** /'meɪpl/ *n.* Ahorn, *der*

**'map-reading** *n.* Kartenlesen, *das*

**mar** /mɑ:(r)/ *v.t.* verderben

**marathon** /'mærəθən/ *n.* (a) Marathon[lauf], *der* (b) (fig.) Marathon, *das*

**marauder** /mə'rɔ:də(r)/ *n.* Plünderer, *der*

**marble** /'mɑ:bl/ *n.* (a) (stone) Marmor, *der* (b) (toy) Murmel, *die;* [game of] ~s Murmelspiel, *das*

**march** ① *n.* Marsch, *der;* [protest] ~: Protestmarsch, *der* ② *v.i.* marschieren

■ **march 'off** ① *v.i.* losmarschieren ② *v.t.* abführen

■ **march 'past** *v.i.* vorbeimarschieren

**March** /mɑ:tʃ/ *n.* März, *der; see also* AUGUST

**'marcher** *n.* [protest] ~: Demonstrant, *der/* Demonstrantin, *die*

**mare** /meə(r)/ *n.* Stute, *die*

**margarine** /mɑːdʒə'riːn/, (coll.) **marge** /mɑːdʒ/ *ns.* Margarine, *die*

**margin** /'mɑːdʒɪn/ *n.* (a) (of page) Rand, *der* (b) (extra amount) Spielraum, *der;* [profit] ~: [Gewinn]spanne, *die;* **by a narrow ~:** knapp

**marginal** /'mɑːdʒɪnl/ *adj.,* **'marginally** *adv.* unwesentlich

**marigold** /'mærɪɡəʊld/ *n.* Ringelblume, *die*

**marijuana** /mærɪjʊ'ɑːnə/ *n.* Marihuana, *das*

**marina** /mə'riːnə/ *n.* Jachthafen, *der*

**marinade** /mærɪ'neɪd/ ① *n.* Marinade, *die* ② ▶ MARINATE

**marinate** /'mærɪneɪt/ *v.t.* marinieren

**marine** /mə'riːn/ ① *adj.* Meeres-; See⟨*versicherung, -recht usw.*⟩; Schiffs⟨*ausrüstung, -turbine usw.*⟩ ② *n.* (person) Marineinfanterist, *der*

**mariner** /'mærɪnə(r)/ *n.* Seemann, *der*

**marionette** /mærɪə'net/ *n.* Marionette, *die*

**marital** /'mærɪtl/ *adj.* ehelich; **~ status** Familienstand, *der*

**maritime** /'mærɪtaɪm/ *adj.* See-

**mark¹** /mɑːk/ ① *n.* (a) (trace) Spur, *die;* (stain etc.) Fleck, *der;* (scratch) Kratzer, *der* (b) (sign) Zeichen, *das* (c) (Sch.) Note, *die* (d) (target) Ziel, *das* ② *v.t.* (a) (dirty) schmutzig machen; (scratch) zerkratzen (b) ( put distinguishing ~ on) kennzeichnen, markieren (**with** mit) (c) (Sch.) (correct) korrigieren; (grade) benoten (d) ~ **time** auf der Stelle treten

■ **mark 'off** *v.t.* abgrenzen (**from** von, gegen)

■ **mark 'out** *v.t.* markieren

**mark²** *n.* (monetary unit) Mark, *die*

**marked** /mɑːkt/ *adj.,* **markedly** /'mɑːkɪdlɪ/ *adv.* deutlich

**'marker** *n.* Markierung, *die*

**'marker pen** *n.* Markierstift, *der*

**market** /'mɑːkɪt/ ① *n.* Markt, *der* ② *v.t.* vermarkten

**market: ~ day** *n.* Markttag, *der;* **~ e'conomy** *n.* Marktwirtschaft, *die;* **~ 'forces** *n. pl.* Kräfte des freien Marktes; **~ 'gardening** *n.* (Brit.) Gemüseanbau, *der*

**'marketing** *n.* Marketing, *das*

**market: ~ 'leader** *n.* (company, brand) Marktführer, *der;* (product) meistverkauftes Produkt; **the company is the ~ leader in its field** die Firma ist marktführend auf ihrem Gebiet; **~ place** *n.* Marktplatz, *der;* (fig.) Markt, *der;* **~ 'price** *n.* Marktpreis, *der;* **~ 'research** *n.* Marktforschung, *die;* **~ share** *n.* Marktanteil, *der;* **~ town** *n.* Marktort, *der;* **~ 'value** *n.* Marktwert, *der*

**'marking** *n.* (a) Markierung, *die* (b) (on animal) Zeichnung, *die*

**marksman** /'mɑːksmən/ *n., pl.* **marksmen** /'mɑːksmən/ Scharfschütze, *der*

**marmalade** /'mɑːməleɪd/ *n.* [orange] ~: Orangenmarmelade, *die*

**maroon¹** /mə'ruːn/ ① *adj.* kastanienbraun ② *n.* Kastanienbraun, *das*

**maroon²** *v.t.* (a) (Naut.: put ashore) aussetzen (b) ⟨*Flut, Hochwasser:*⟩ von der Außenwelt abschneiden

**marquee** /mɑː'kiː/ *n.* Festzelt, *das*

**marquess, marquis** /'mɑːkwɪs/ *n.* Marquis, *der*

**marquetry** /'mɑːkɪtrɪ/ *n.* Marketerie, *die*

**marriage** /'mærɪdʒ/ *n.* (a) Ehe, *die* (**to** mit) (b) (wedding) Hochzeit, *die*

**marriage: ~ broker** *n.* Heiratsvermittler, *der/*-vermittlerin, *die;* **~ bureau** *n.* Eheanbahnungs- *od.* Ehevermittlungsinstitut, *das;* **~ certificate** *n.* Trauschein, *der;* (record of civil marriage also) Heiratsurkunde, *die;* **~ 'guidance** *n.* Eheberatung, *die;* **~ licence** *n.* Heirats- *od.* Eheerlaubnis, *die*

**married** /'mærɪd/ *adj.* (a) verheiratet; **~ couple** Ehepaar, *das* (b) (marital) Ehe⟨*leben, -name*⟩

**marrow** /'mærəʊ/ *n.* (a) [vegetable] ∼:
Speisekürbis, *der*
(b) (Anat.) [Knochen]mark, *das*

**marry** /'mærɪ/ [1] *v.t.* (a) heiraten
(b) (join) trauen; **they were** *or* **got/have got
married** sie haben geheiratet
[2] *v.i.* heiraten

**Mars** /mɑːz/ *pr. n.* (Astron.) Mars, *der*

**marsh** /mɑːʃ/ *n.* Sumpf, *der*

**marshal** /'mɑːʃl/ [1] *n.* (a) (officer in army)
Marschall, *der*
(b) (Sport) Ordner, *der*
[2] *v.t.*, (Brit.) **-ll-** aufstellen ⟨*Truppen*⟩; ordnen
⟨*Fakten*⟩

**'marshalling yard** *n.* Rangierbahnhof,
*der*

**marshmallow** /mɑːʃ'mæləʊ/ *n.* (sweet) ≈
Mohrenkopf, *der*

**'marshy** *adj.* sumpfig

**marsupial** /mɑː'sjuːpɪəl/ *n.* Beuteltier, *das*

**martial** /'mɑːʃl/ *adj.* kriegerisch

**martial 'law** *n.* Kriegsrecht, *das*

**martyr** /'mɑːtə(r)/ [1] *n.* Märtyrer, *der*/
Märtyrerin, *die*
[2] *v.t.* **be** ∼**ed** den Märtyrertod sterben

**marvel** /'mɑːvl/ [1] *n.* Wunder, *das*
[2] *v.i.*, (Brit.) **-ll-** (literary) ∼ **at sth.** über etw
(*Akk.*) staunen

**marvellous** /'mɑːvələs/ *adj.*,
**'marvellously** *adv.* wunderbar

**marvelous[ly]** (Amer.) ▶ MARVELLOUS[LY]

**Marxism** /'mɑːksɪzm/ *n.* Marxismus, *der*

**Marxist** /'mɑːksɪst/ [1] *n.* Marxist, *der*/
Marxistin, *die*
[2] *adj.* marxistisch

**marzipan** /'mɑːzɪpæn/ *n.* Marzipan, *das*

**mascara** /mæ'skɑːrə/ *n.* Mascara, *das*

**mascot** /'mæskɒt/ *n.* Maskottchen, *das*

**masculine** /'mæskjʊlɪn/ *adj.* männlich

**masculinity** /mæskju'lɪnɪtɪ/ *n.*
Männlichkeit, *die*

**mash** /mæʃ/ [1] *n.* (a) Brei, *der*
(b) (Brit. coll.: ∼ed potatoes) Kartoffelbrei, *der*
[2] *v.t.* zerdrücken; ∼**ed potatoes**
Kartoffelbrei, *der*

**mask** /mɑːsk/ [1] *n.* Maske, *die*
[2] *v.t.* maskieren

**'masking tape** *n.* Abklebeband, *das*

**masochism** /'mæsəkɪzm/ *n.*
Masochismus, *der*

**masochist** /'mæsəkɪst/ *n.* Masochist, *der*/
Masochistin, *die*

**masochistic** /mæsə'kɪstɪk/ *adj.*
masochistisch

**mason** /'meɪsn/ *n.* (a) Steinmetz, *der*
(b) **M**∼ (Free∼) [Frei]maurer, *der*

**Masonic** /mə'sɒnɪk/ *adj.* [frei]maurerisch;
∼ **lodge** [Frei]maurerloge, *die*

**masonry** /'meɪsnrɪ/ *n.* Mauerwerk, *das*

**masquerade** /mæskə'reɪd, mɑːskə'reɪd/
[1] *n.* Maskerade, *die*

[2] *v.i.* ∼ **as sb./sth.** sich als jmd./etw.
ausgeben

**mass¹** /mæs/ *n.* (Eccl.) Messe, *die*

**mass²** [1] *n.* (a) Masse, *die*
(b) **a** ∼ **of ...:** eine Unmenge von ...
(c) *attrib.* (for many people) Massen-
[2] *v.t.* anhäufen
[3] *v.i.* sich ansammeln; ⟨*Truppen:*⟩ sich
massieren

**massacre** /'mæsəkə(r)/ [1] *n.* Massaker,
*das*
[2] *v.t.* massakrieren

**massage** /'mæsɑːʒ/ [1] *n.* Massage, *die*
[2] *v.t.* massieren

**mass communi'cations** *n. pl.*
Massenkommunikation, *die*

**masseur** /mæ'sɜː(r)/ *n.* Masseur, *der*

**masseuse** /mæ'sɜːz/ *n. fem.* Masseurin,
*die*

**mass hy'steria** *n.* Massenhysterie, *die*

**massive** /'mæsɪv/ *adj.* massiv; gewaltig
⟨*Aufgabe*⟩; enorm ⟨*Schulden*⟩

**mass:** ∼ **market** *attrib. adj.* für den
Massenmarkt *nachgestellt;* ∼ **'media** *n. pl.*
Massenmedien *Pl.;* ∼ **'murderer** *n.*
Massenmörder, *der*/-mörderin, *die;*
∼**-pro'duced** *adj.* serienmäßig
produziert; ∼ **pro'duction** *n.*
Massenproduktion, *die*

**mast** /mɑːst/ *n.* Mast, *der*

**mastectomy** /mæ'stektəmɪ/ *n.* (Med.)
Mastektomie, *die*

**master** /'mɑːstə(r)/ [1] *n.* (a) Herr, *der*
(b) (of dog) Herrchen, *das;* (of ship) Kapitän,
*der*
(c) (Sch.: teacher) Lehrer, *der*
(d) (expert, great artist) Meister, *der* (**at** in
+ *Dat.*)
(e) **M**∼ **of Arts/Science** Magister Artium/
rerum naturalium
[2] *adj.* Haupt-
[3] *v.t.* (learn) erlernen; **have** ∼**ed a language**
eine Sprache beherrschen

**masterful** /'mɑːstəfl/ *adj.* (masterly)
meisterhaft

**'master key** *n.* Hauptschlüssel, *der*

**masterly** /'mɑːstəlɪ/ *adj.* meisterhaft

**master:** ∼**mind** [1] *n.* führender Kopf;
[2] *v.t.* ∼**mind the plot** den Kopf des
Komplotts sein; ∼**piece** *n.* (work of art)
Meisterwerk, *das;* ∼ **stroke** *n.*
Geniestreich, *der;* **be a** ∼ **stroke** genial sein;
∼ **switch** *n.* Hauptschalter, *der*

**mastery** /'mɑːstərɪ/ *n.* (a) (skill)
Meisterschaft, *die*
(b) (knowledge) Beherrschung, *die* (**of** *Gen.*)

**masturbate** /'mæstəbeɪt/ *v.i. & t.*
masturbieren

**masturbation** /mæstə'beɪʃn/ *n.*
Masturbation, *die*

**mat** /mæt/ *n.* (a) Matte, *die*
(b) (to protect table etc.) Untersetzer, *der*

**matador** /'mætədɔː(r)/ *n.* Matador, *der*

**m**

**match¹** /mætʃ/ ⓵ n. (a) be no ∼ for sb.
sich mit jmdm. nicht messen können; **meet
one's ∼:** seinen Meister finden
(b) be a [good *etc.*] ∼ for sth. [gut *usw.*] zu
etw. passen
(c) (Sport) Spiel, *das;* (Boxing) Kampf, *der*
⓶ v.t. (a) (equal) ∼ sb. at chess es mit jmdm.
im Schach aufnehmen [können]
(b) (harmonize with) passen zu; **a handbag and
∼ing shoes** eine Handtasche und [dazu]
passende Schuhe; ∼ **each other** zueinander
passen
⓷ v.i. zusammenpassen

**match²** n. (∼stick) Streichholz, *das*

'**matchbox** n. Streichholzschachtel, *die*

'**matchless** adj. unvergleichlich

**match:** ∼**maker** n. Ehestifter, *der*/
Ehestifterin, *die;* ∼**stick** n. Streichholz, *das*

**mate¹** /meɪt/ ⓵ n. (a) Kumpel, *der* (ugs.);
**look** *or* **listen,** ∼, ...: jetzt hör [mir] mal gut
zu, Freundchen, ...
(b) (Naut.) ≈ Kapitänleutnant, *der*
(c) (workman's assistant) Gehilfe, *der*
(d) (Zool.) (male) Männchen, *das;* (female)
Weibchen, *das*
⓶ v.i. sich paaren
⓷ v.t. paaren ‹*Tiere*›

**mate²** (Chess) ▶ CHECKMATE

**material** /mə'tɪərɪəl/ ⓵ adj. (a) materiell
(b) (relevant) wesentlich
⓶ n. (a) ∼[s] Material, *das;* **building/writing
∼s** Bau-/Schreibmaterial, *das*
(b) (cloth) Stoff, *der*

**materialism** /mə'tɪərɪəlɪzm/ n.
Materialismus, *der*

**materialistic** /mətɪərɪə'lɪstɪk/ adj.
materialistisch

**materialize** /mə'tɪərɪəlaɪz/ v.i. ‹*Plan, Idee:*›
sich verwirklichen; ‹*Treffen:*› zustande
kommen

**maternal** /mə'tɜ:nl/ adj. mütterlich;
Mutter‹*instinkt*›

**maternity** /mə'tɜ:nɪtɪ/ n. Mutterschaft, *die*

**maternity:** ∼ **benefit** n.
Mutterschaftsgeld, *das;* ∼ **dress** n.
Umstandskleid, *das;* ∼ **hospital** n.
Entbindungsheim, *das;* ∼ **leave** n.
Mutterschaftsurlaub, *der;* ∼ **nurse** n.
Hebamme, *die;* ∼ **pay** n. Mutterschaftsgeld,
*das;* ∼ **unit,** ∼ **ward** ns.
Entbindungsstation, *die;* ∼ **wear** n.
Umstandskleidung, *die*

**matey** /'meɪtɪ/ adj., **matier** /'meɪtɪə(r)/,
**matiest** /'meɪtɪɪst/ (Brit. coll.)
kameradschaftlich

**math** /mæθ/ (Amer. coll.) ▶ MATHS

**mathematical** /mæθɪ'mætɪkl/ adj.,
**mathematically** /mæθɪ'mætɪkəlɪ/ adv.
mathematisch

**mathematician** /mæθɪmə'tɪʃn/ n.
Mathematiker, *der*/Mathematikerin, *die*

**mathematics** /mæθɪ'mætɪks/ n.
Mathematik, *die*

**maths** /mæθs/ n. (Brit. coll.) Mathe, *die*
(Schülerspr.)

**matinée** /'mætɪneɪ/ n.
Nachmittagsvorstellung, *die*

**matriarchal** /meɪtrɪ'ɑ:kl/ adj.
matriarchalisch

**matriarchy** /'meɪtrɪɑ:kɪ/ n. Matriarchat,
*das*

**matrices** pl. of MATRIX

**matriculate** /mə'trɪkjʊleɪt/ ⓵ v.t.
immatrikulieren (**in** an + *Dat.*)
⓶ v.i. sich immatrikulieren

**matriculation** /mətrɪkjʊ'leɪʃn/ n.
Immatrikulation, *die*

**matrimonial** /mætrɪ'məʊnɪəl/ adj. Ehe-

**matrimony** /'mætrɪmənɪ/ n. Ehestand, *der*

**matrix** /'meɪtrɪks/ n., pl. **matrices**
/'meɪtrɪsi:z/ or ∼**es** Matrix, *die*

**matron** /'meɪtrən/ n. (in school) ≈
Hausmutter, *die;* (in hospital) Oberschwester,
*die*

**matt** /mæt/ adj. matt

'**matted** adj. verfilzt

**matter** /'mætə(r)/ ⓵ n. (a) (affair)
Angelegenheit, *die;* ∼**s** die Dinge; **money** ∼**s**
Geldangelegenheiten
(b) it's a ∼ **of taste** das ist
Geschmackssache; **[only] a** ∼ **of time** [nur
noch] eine Frage der Zeit
(c) **what's the** ∼? was ist [los]?
(d) (physical material) Materie, *die*
⓶ v.i. etwas ausmachen; **what does it** ∼?
was macht das schon?; **[it] doesn't** ∼: [das]
macht nichts (ugs.)

'**matter-of-fact** adj. sachlich

**mattress** /'mætrɪs/ n. Matratze, *die*

**mature** /mə'tjʊə(r)/ ⓵ adj. reif; ausgereift
‹*Stil, Käse, Portwein, Sherry*›
⓶ v.t. reifen lassen
⓷ v.i. reifen

**maturity** /mə'tjʊərɪtɪ/ n. Reife, *die*

**Maundy Thursday** /mɔ:ndɪ 'θɜ:zdɪ/ n.
Gründonnerstag, *der*

**mausoleum** /mɔ:sə'li:əm/ n. Mausoleum,
*das*

**mauve** /məʊv/ adj. mauve

**mawkish** /'mɔ:kɪʃ/ adj. rührselig

**max.** abbr. = **maximum** (adj.) max., (n.)
Max.

**maxim** /'mæksɪm/ n. Maxime, *die*

**maximum** /'mæksɪməm/ ⓵ n., pl. **maxima**
/'mæksɪmə/ Maximum, *das*
⓶ adj. maximal; Maximal-; ∼ **speed/
temperature** Höchstgeschwindigkeit, *die*/
-temperatur, *die*

'**maximum-security** attrib. adj.
Hochsicherheits‹*gefängnis*›trakt›

**may** v. aux., only in pres. **may,** neg. (coll.)
**mayn't** /meɪnt/, past **might** /maɪt/, neg. (coll.)
**mightn't** /'maɪtnt/ (a) (expr. possibility) können;
**it** ∼ **be true** das kann stimmen; **I** ∼ **be wrong**
vielleicht irre ich mich; **it** ∼ **not be possible**

das wird vielleicht nicht möglich sein; **he ~ have missed his train** vielleicht hat er seinen Zug verpasst; **it ~** *or* **might rain** es könnte regnen; **we ~** *or* **might as well go** wir könnten eigentlich ebenso gut [auch] gehen
**(b)** (expr. permission) dürfen
**(c)** (expr. wish) mögen; **~ the best man win!** auf dass der Beste gewinnt!

**May** /meɪ/ *n.* Mai, *der; see also* AUGUST

**maybe** /ˈmeɪbiː, ˈmeɪbɪ/ *adv.* vielleicht

**'May Day** *n.* der Erste Mai; **the ~ holiday** der Maifeiertag

**'mayfly** *n.* Eintagsfliege, *die*

**mayhem** /ˈmeɪhem/ *n.* Chaos, *das*

**mayn't** /meɪnt/ (coll.) = may not; ▶ MAY

**mayonnaise** /meɪəˈneɪz/ *n.* Mayonnaise, *die*

**mayor** /meə(r)/ *n.* Bürgermeister, *der*

**mayoress** /ˈmeərɪs/ *n.* (woman mayor) Bürgermeisterin, *die;* (mayor's wife) [Ehe]frau des Bürgermeisters

**maze** /meɪz/ *n.* Labyrinth, *das*

**MBA** *abbr.* = **Master of Business Administration** *Diplom in Betriebswirtschaft*

**me** /mɪ, *stressed* miː/ *pron.* mich; *as indirect object* mir; **who, me?** wer, ich?; **not me** ich nicht; **it's me** ich bins

**ME** *abbr.* (Med.) = **myalgic encephalomyelitis**

**meadow** /ˈmedəʊ/ *n.* Wiese, *die*

**meagre** /ˈmiːgə(r)/ *adj.* dürftig

**meal** /miːl/ *n.* Mahlzeit, *die;* **go out for a ~:** essen gehen; **enjoy your ~:** guten Appetit!; **~s on wheels** (Brit.) Essen auf Rädern

**meal: ~ ticket** *n.* Essenmarke, *die;* (fig. coll.) melkende Kuh (ugs.); **~time** *n.* Essenszeit, *die;* **~ voucher** *n.* Essenmarke, *die*

**mean¹** /miːn/ *n.* **(a)** Mittelweg, *der*
**(b)** (Math.) Mittelwert, *der*

**mean²** *adj.* **(a)** (miserly) geizig
**(b)** (unkind) gemein
**(c)** (shabby) schäbig

**mean³** *v.t.,* meant /ment/ **(a)** (intend) beabsichtigen; **~ to do sth.** etw. tun wollen
**(b)** (design, destine) **be ~t to do sth.** etw. tun sollen
**(c)** (intend to convey) meinen; **I [really] ~ it** ich meine das ernst; **what do you ~ by that?** was hast du damit gemeint?
**(d)** (signify) bedeuten

**meander** /mɪˈændə(r)/ *v.i.* **(a)** ⟨*Fluss:*⟩ sich winden
**(b)** ⟨*Person:*⟩ schlendern

**'meaning** *n.* Bedeutung, *die;* (of text etc., life) Sinn, *der*

**meaningful** /ˈmiːnɪŋfl/ *adj.* bedeutungsvoll ⟨*Blick, Ergebnis*⟩; sinnvoll ⟨*Aufgabe, Gespräch*⟩

**'meaningless** *adj.* ⟨*Wort, Gespräch:*⟩ ohne Sinn; sinnlos ⟨*Aktivität*⟩

**means** /miːnz/ *n.* **(a)** Möglichkeit, *die;* [Art und] Weise; **by this ~:** hierdurch; **~ of transport** Transportmittel, *das*
**(b)** *pl.* (resources) Mittel *Pl.;* **live within/ beyond one's ~:** seinen Verhältnissen entsprechend/über seine Verhältnisse leben
**(c)** **by all ~!** selbstverständlich!; **by no [manner of] ~:** ganz und gar nicht; **by ~ of** durch; mit [Hilfe von]

**'means test** *n.* Überprüfung der Bedürftigkeit

**meant** ▶ MEAN³

**mean: ~time** ① *n.* **in the ~time** inzwischen; ② *adv* inzwischen; **~while** *adv.* inzwischen

**measles** /ˈmiːzlz/ *n.* Masern *Pl.*

**measly** /ˈmiːzlɪ/ *adj.* (coll.) pop[e]lig (ugs.)

**measurable** /ˈmeʒərəbl/ *adj.* messbar

**measure** /ˈmeʒə(r)/ ① *n.* **(a)** Maß, *das;* **for good ~:** sicherheitshalber; (as an extra) zusätzlich; **made to ~:** maßgeschneidert
**(b)** (degree) **in some/large ~:** in gewisser Hinsicht/ in hohem Maße
**(c)** (for measuring) Maß, *das*
**(d)** (step) Maßnahme, *die;* **take ~s** Maßnahmen treffen
② *v.t.* messen ⟨*Größe, Menge usw.*⟩; ausmessen ⟨*Raum*⟩
③ *v.i.* messen
∎ **measure 'up to** *v.t.* entsprechen (+ *Dat.*)

**'measured** /ˈmeʒəd/ *adj.* gemessen ⟨*Schritt, Worte*⟩

**'measurement** *n.* **(a)** Messung, *die*
**(b)** (dimension) Maß, *das*

**'measuring tape** *n.* Bandmaß, *das*

**meat** /miːt/ *n.* Fleisch, *das*

**'meaty** *adj.* **(a)** fleischig
**(b)** (fig.) gehaltvoll

**mechanic** /mɪˈkænɪk/ *n.* Mechaniker, *der/* Mechanikerin, *die*

**mechanical** /mɪˈkænɪkl/ *adj.* mechanisch

**mechanical engi'neering** *n.* Maschinenbau, *der*

**me'chanically** *adv.* mechanisch

**mechanical 'pencil** *n.* (Amer.) Drehbleistift, *der*

**me'chanics** *n.* **(a)** Mechanik, *die*
**(b)** *pl.* (mechanism) Mechanismus, *der*

**mechanism** /ˈmekənɪzm/ *n.* Mechanismus, *der*

**mechanize** /ˈmekənaɪz/ *v.t.* mechanisieren

**medal** /ˈmedl/ *n.* Medaille, *die;* (decoration) Orden, *der*

**medallion** /mɪˈdæljən/ *n.* [große] Medaille

**medallist** /ˈmedəlɪst/ *n.* Medaillengewinner, *der/*-gewinnerin, *die*

**meddle** /ˈmedl/ *v.i.* **~ with sth.** sich (*Dat.*) an etw. (*Dat.*) zu schaffen machen; **~ in sth.** sich in etw. (*Akk.*) einmischen

**media** /ˈmiːdɪə/ *n.* ▶ MASS MEDIA; MEDIUM 1

**mediaeval** ▶ MEDIEVAL

**'media studies** n. sing.
Medienwissenschaft, die; (school subject)
Medienkunde, die

**mediate** /'mi:dɪeɪt/ v.i. vermitteln

**mediator** /'mi:dɪeɪtə(r)/ n. Vermittler, der/
Vermittlerin, die

**medical** /'medɪkl/ adj. medizinisch;
ärztlich ⟨Behandlung, Untersuchung⟩

**medical:** ~ **certificate** n. Attest, das;
~ **exami'nation** n. ärztliche
Untersuchung; ~ **'history** n. (of person)
Krankengeschichte, die; ~ **insurance** n.
Krankenversicherung, die; **have** ~ **insurance**
krankenversichert sein; ~ **prac'titioner**
n. praktischer Arzt/praktische Ärztin;
~ **report** n. medizinisches Gutachten;
~ **school** n. medizinische Hochschule;
~ **student** n. Medizinstudent, der/
-studentin die

**medicament** /mɪ'dɪkəmənt, 'medɪkəmənt/
n. Medikament, das

**Medicare** /'medɪkeə(r)/ n. (Amer.)
[bundes]staatliches
Krankenversicherungssystem für Personen
über 65 Jahre

**medicated** /'medɪkeɪtɪd/ adj. medizinisch

**medication** /medɪ'keɪʃn/ n. (medicine)
Medikament, das

**medicinal** /mɪ'dɪsɪnl/ adj. medizinisch

**medicine** /'medsən, 'medɪsɪn/ n. **(a)**
(science) Medizin, die
**(b)** (preparation) Medikament, das

**'medicine chest** n.
Medikamentenschränkchen, das; (in home)
Hausapotheke, die

**medieval** /medɪ'i:vl/ adj. mittelalterlich

**mediocre** /mi:dɪ'əʊkə(r)/ adj. mittelmäßig

**mediocrity** /mi:dɪ'ɒkrɪtɪ/ n.
Mittelmäßigkeit, die

**meditate** /'medɪteɪt/ v.i. nachdenken, (esp.
Relig.) meditieren (⟨up⟩on über + Akk.)

**meditation** /medɪ'teɪʃn/ n. **(a)** (act)
Nachdenken, das
**(b)** (Relig.) Meditation, die

**Mediterranean** /medɪtə'reɪnɪən/ pr. n. the
~: das Mittelmeer

**medium** /'mi:dɪəm/ 1 n., pl. media
/'mi:dɪə/ or ~s **(a)** (substance) Medium, das
**(b)** (means) Mittel, das; **by** or **through the**
~ **of** durch
**(c)** pl. ~s (Spiritualism) Medium, das
**(d)** in pl. media (mass media) Medien Pl.
2 adj. mittler ..; medium nur präd. ⟨Steak⟩

**medium-:** ~**-range** adj.
Mittelstrecken⟨flugzeug, -rakete⟩; ~**-size[d]**
adj. mittelgroß

**medley** /'medlɪ/ n. **(a)** buntes Gemisch
**(b)** (Mus.) Potpourri, das

**meek** /mi:k/ adj. **(a)** (humble) sanftmütig
**(b)** (submissive) zu nachgiebig

**meet** /mi:t/ 1 v.t., met /met/ **(a)** treffen;
(collect) abholen

**(b)** (make the acquaintance of) kennen lernen;
**pleased to** ~ **you** [sehr] angenehm
**(c)** (experience) stoßen auf (+ Akk.)
⟨Widerstand, Problem⟩
**(d)** (satisfy) entsprechen (+ Dat.) ⟨Wunsch,
Bedürfnis, Kritik⟩; einhalten ⟨Termin,
Zeitplan⟩
**(e)** (pay) decken ⟨Kosten⟩; bezahlen
⟨Rechnung⟩
2 v.i., met **(a)** (by chance) sich (Dat.)
begegnen; (by arrangement) sich treffen; **we've
met before** wir kennen uns bereits
**(b)** ⟨Komitee, Ausschuss usw.:⟩ tagen

■ **meet 'up** v.i. sich treffen; ~ **up with sb.**
(coll.) sich treffen

■ **'meet with** v.t. **(a)** begegnen (+ Dat.)
**(b)** (experience) haben ⟨Erfolg, Unfall⟩; stoßen
auf (+ Akk.) ⟨Widerstand⟩

**'meeting** n. **(a)** Begegnung, die; (by
arrangement) Treffen, das
**(b)** (assembly) Versammlung, die; (of committee
etc.) Sitzung, die

**'meeting place** n. Treffpunkt, der

**mega** /'megə/ (coll.) 1 adj. **(a)** (enormous)
Mega- (Jugendspr.)
**(b)** (excellent) geil (Jugendspr.)
2 adv. äußerst; **be** ~ **rich** super- od.
(Jugendspr.) megareich sein

**'megabyte** n. (Comp.) Megabyte, das

**megalomania** /megələ'meɪnɪə/ n.
Größenwahn, der

**megaphone** /'megəfəʊn/ n. Megaphon, das

**melancholic** /melən'kɒlɪk/ adj.
melancholisch

**melancholy** /'melənkəlɪ/ 1 n.
Melancholie, die
2 adj. melancholisch

**mellow** /'meləʊ/ 1 adj. **(a)** (softened by age
or experience) abgeklärt
**(b)** (ripe, well-matured) reif
2 v.i. reifen

**melodic** /mɪ'lɒdɪk/**, melodious**
/mɪ'ləʊdɪəs/ adjs.**, me'lodiously** adv.
melodisch

**melodrama** /'melədrɑ:mə/ n. Melodrama,
das

**melodramatic** /melədrə'mætɪk/ adj.
melodramatisch

**melody** /'melədɪ/ n. Melodie, die

**melon** /'melən/ n. Melone, die

**melt** /melt/ 1 v.i. schmelzen
2 v.t. schmelzen; zerlassen ⟨Butter⟩

■ **melt a'way** v.i. [weg]schmelzen

■ **melt 'down** 1 v.i. schmelzen
2 v.t. einschmelzen

**melting:** ~ **point** n. Schmelzpunkt, der;
~ **pot** n. (fig.) Schmelztiegel, der

**member** /'membə(r)/ n. **(a)** Mitglied, das;
**be a** ~: Mitglied sein; ~ **of a/the family**
Familienangehörige, der/die
**(b)** M~ [of Parliament] (Brit.) Abgeordnete
[des Unterhauses], der/die

**'membership** n. (a) Mitgliedschaft, die (of in + Dat.)
(b) (number of members) Mitgliederzahl, die
(c) (members) Mitglieder Pl.

**'member state** n. Mitglied[s]staat, der

**membrane** /'membreɪn/ n. (Biol.) Membran, die

**memento** /mɪ'mentəʊ/ n., pl. ∼es or ∼s Andenken, das (of an + Akk.)

**memo** /'meməʊ/ n., pl. ∼s (coll.)
▶ MEMORANDUM

**memoirs** /'memwɑːz/ n. pl. Memoiren Pl.

**memorable** /'memərəbl/ adj. denkwürdig ⟨Ereignis, Tag⟩; unvergesslich ⟨Film, Buch, Aufführung⟩

**memorandum** /memə'rændəm/ n., pl. **memoranda** /memə'rændə/ or ∼s Mitteilung, die

**memorial** /mɪ'mɔːrɪəl/ **1** adj. Gedenk-
**2** n. Denkmal, das (to für)

**memorize** /'meməraɪz/ v.t. sich (Dat.) merken od. einprägen; (learn by heart) auswendig lernen

**memory** /'meməri/ n. (a) Gedächtnis, das
(b) (thing remembered, act of remembering) Erinnerung, die (of an + Akk.); from ∼: aus dem Gedächtnis; in ∼ of zur Erinnerung an (+ Akk.)
(c) (Comp.) Speicher, der

**'memory bank** n. Speicherbank, die

**men** pl. of MAN

**menace** /'menəs/ **1** v.t. bedrohen
**2** n. Plage, die

**menacing** /'menəsɪŋ/ adj. drohend

**mend** /mend/ **1** v.t. reparieren; ausbessern ⟨Kleidung⟩; kleben ⟨Glas, Porzellan⟩
**2** v.i. ⟨Knochen, Bein usw.:⟩ heilen
**3** n. be on the ∼: auf dem Wege der Besserung sein

**'menfolk** n. pl. Männer Pl.

**menial** /'miːnɪəl/ adj. niedrig; untergeordnet ⟨Aufgabe⟩

**meningitis** /menɪn'dʒaɪtɪs/ n. Hirnhautentzündung, die

**menopause** /'menəpɔːz/ n. Wechseljahre Pl.

**menstrual** /'menstrʊəl/ adj. menstrual (fachspr.)

**menstruate** /'menstrʊeɪt/ v.i. menstruieren

**menstruation** /menstrʊ'eɪʃn/ n. Menstruation, die

**menswear** /'menzweə(r)/ n. Herrenbekleidung, die

**mental** /'mentl/ adj. (a) (of the mind) geistig; Geistes⟨zustand, -störung⟩
(b) (Brit. coll.: mad) verrückt (salopp)

**mental:** ∼ a'rithmetic n. Kopfrechnen, das; ∼ 'health n. seelische Gesundheit; ∼ 'hospital n. Nervenklinik, die (ugs.); ∼ 'illness n. Geisteskrankheit, die

**mentality** /men'tælɪti/ n. Mentalität, die

**'mentally** adv. geistig

**mention** /'menʃn/ **1** n. Erwähnung, die
**2** v.t. erwähnen (to gegenüber); don't ∼ it keine Ursache

**menu** /'menjuː/ n. (a) [Speise]karte, die
(b) (Comp., Telev.) Menü, das

**'menu bar** n. (Comp.) Menüleiste, die

**mercenary** /'mɜːsɪnəri/ **1** adj. gewinnsüchtig
**2** n. Söldner, der

**merchandise** /'mɜːtʃəndaɪz/ n. [Handels]ware, die

**merchant** /'mɜːtʃənt/ n. Kaufmann, der

**merchant:** ∼ 'bank n. Handelsbank, die; ∼ 'navy n. (Brit.) Handelsmarine, die

**merciful** /'mɜːsɪfl/ adj. gnädig

**mercifully** /'mɜːsɪfəli/ adv. (fortunately) glücklicherweise

**merciless** /'mɜːsɪlɪs/ adj., **mercilessly** adv. gnadenlos

**mercury** /'mɜːkjʊri/ **1** n. Quecksilber, das
**2** pr. n. M∼ (Astron.) Merkur, der

**mercy** /'mɜːsi/ n. Erbarmen, das (on mit); show sb. [no] ∼: mit jmdm. [kein] Erbarmen haben; be at the ∼ of sb./sth. jmdm./einer Sache [auf Gedeih und Verderb] ausgeliefert sein

**mere** /mɪə(r)/ adj., **'merely** adv. bloß

**merge** /mɜːdʒ/ **1** v.t. (a) (combine) zusammenschließen
(b) (blend gradually) verschmelzen (with mit)
**2** v.i. (a) (combine) fusionieren (with mit)
(b) ⟨Straße:⟩ zusammenlaufen (with mit)

**merger** /'mɜːdʒə(r)/ n. Fusion, die

**meringue** /mə'ræŋ/ n. Meringe, die; Baiser, das

**merit** /'merɪt/ **1** n. (a) (worth) Verdienst, das
(b) (good feature) Vorzug, der
**2** v.t. verdienen

**mermaid** /'mɜːmeɪd/ n. Nixe, die

**merrily** /'merɪli/ adv. munter

**merriment** /'merɪmənt/ n. Fröhlichkeit, die

**merry** /'meri/ adj. fröhlich; ∼ Christmas! frohe od. fröhliche Weihnachten!

**'merry-go-round** n. Karussell, das

**'merrymaking** n. Feiern, das

**mesh** /meʃ/ n. (a) Masche, die
(b) (netting; also fig.: network) Geflecht, das; wire ∼: Maschendraht, der

**mesmerize** /'mezməraɪz/ v.t. faszinieren

**mess** /mes/ n. (a) (dirty/untidy state) [be] a ∼ or in a ∼: schmutzig/unaufgeräumt [sein]; what a ∼! was für ein Dreck (ugs.)/ Durcheinander!
(b) (bad state) be [in] a ∼: sich in einem schlimmen Zustand befinden; ⟨Person:⟩ schlimm dran sein; get into a ∼: in Schwierigkeiten geraten; make a ∼ of verpfuschen (ugs.) ⟨Arbeit, Leben⟩
(c) (Mil.) Kasino, das ⋯⋗

■ **mess a'bout, mess a'round** ⒈ *v.i.* (potter) herumwerken; (fool about) herumalbern
⒉ *v.t.* ~ **sb. about** *or* **around** mit jmdm. nach Belieben umspringen

■ **mess 'up** *v.t.* (a) (make dirty) schmutzig machen; (make untidy) in Unordnung bringen
(b) (bungle) ~ **it/things up** Mist bauen (ugs.)

**message** /'mesɪdʒ/ *n.* Nachricht, *die;* **give sb. a** ~: jmdm. etwas ausrichten

**messenger** /'mesɪndʒə(r)/ *n.* Bote, *der/* Botin, *die*

**Messiah** /mɪ'saɪə/ *n.* Messias, *der*

**Messrs** /'mesəz/ *n. pl.* (a) (in name of firm) ≈ Fa.
(b) *pl. of* MR; (in list of names) ~ **A and B** die Herren A und B

'**messy** *adj.* (dirty) schmutzig; (untidy) unordentlich

**met** ▶ MEET

**metabolism** /mɪ'tæbəlɪzm/ *n.* Stoffwechsel, *der*

**metal** /'metl/ ⒈ *n.* Metall, *das*
⒉ *adj.* Metall-

'**metal detector** *n.* Metallsuchgerät, *das*

**metallic** /mɪ'tælɪk/ *adj.* metallisch; **have a** ~ **taste** nach Metall schmecken

**metallurgy** /mɪ'tælədʒɪ/ *n.* Metallurgie, *die*

'**metalwork** *n.* (products) Metallarbeiten *Pl.*

**metamorphosis** /metə'mɔːfəsɪs/ *n., pl.* **metamorphoses** /metə'mɔːfəsiːz/ Metamorphose, *die*

**metaphor** /'metəfə(r)/ *n.* Metapher, *die*

**metaphorical** /metə'fɒrɪkl/ *adj.,* **metaphorically** /metə'fɒrɪkəlɪ/ *adv.* metaphorisch

**meteor** /'miːtɪə(r)/ *n.* Meteor, *der*

**meteoric** /miːtɪ'ɒrɪk/ *adj.* (fig.) kometenhaft

**meteorological** /miːtɪərə'lɒdʒɪkl/ *adj.* meteorologisch ‹*Instrument*›; Wetter‹*ballon, -bericht*›

**meteorologist** /miːtɪə'rɒlədʒɪst/ *n.* Meteorologe, *der/*Meteorologin, *die*

**meteorology** /miːtɪə'rɒlədʒɪ/ *n.* Meteorologie, *die*

**meter**[1] /'miːtə(r)/ *n.* (a) Zähler, *der;* (for coins) Münzzähler, *der*
(b) (parking ~) Parkuhr, *die*

**meter**[2] (Amer.) ▶ METRE[1, 2]

**methane** /'miːθeɪn/ *n.* Methan, *das*

**method** /'meθəd/ *n.* Methode, *die*

**methodical** /mɪ'θɒdɪkl/ *adj.,* **me'thodically** *adv.* systematisch

**Methodist** /'meθədɪst/ *n.* Methodist, *der/* Methodistin, *die*

**meths** /meθs/ *n.* (Brit. coll.) [Brenn]spiritus, *der*

**methylated spirit[s]** /meθɪleɪtɪd 'spɪrɪt(s)/ *n.* [*pl.*] Brennspiritus, *der*

**meticulous** /mɪ'tɪkjʊləs/ *adj.,* **me'ticulously** *adv.* (scrupulous[ly]) sorgfältig; (overscrupulous[ly]) übergenau

**metre**[1] /'miːtə/ *n.* (Brit.: poetic rhythm) Metrum, *das*

**metre**[2] *n.* (Brit.: unit) Meter, *der od. das*

**metric** /'metrɪk/ *adj.* metrisch; ~ **system** metrisches System

**metrication** /metrɪ'keɪʃn/ *n.* Umstellung auf das metrische System

**metro** /'metrəʊ/ *n., pl.* ~**s** U-Bahn, *die;* **the Paris M**~ die [Pariser] Metro

**metronome** /'metrənəʊm/ *n.* Metronom, *das*

**metropolis** /mɪ'trɒpəlɪs/ *n.* Metropole, *die*

**metropolitan** /metrə'pɒlɪtən/ *adj.* ~ **New York** der Großraum New York; ~ **London** Großlondon (*das*)

**Mexican** /'meksɪkən/ ⒈ *adj.* mexikanisch; **sb. is** ~: jmd. ist Mexikaner/Mexikanerin
⒉ *n.* Mexikaner, *der/*Mexikanerin, *die*

**Mexico** /'meksɪkəʊ/ *pr. n.* Mexiko (*das*)

**miaow** /mɪ'aʊ/ ⒈ *v.i.* miauen
⒉ *n.* Miauen, *das*

**mice** *pl. of* MOUSE

**microbe** /'maɪkrəʊb/ *n.* Mikrobe, *die*

**micro** /'maɪkrəʊ/: ~**chip** *n.* Mikrochip, *der;* ~**computer** *n.* Mikrocomputer, *der;* ~**dot** *n.* Mikrat, *das;* ~**fibre** *n.* Mikrofaser, *die;* ~**fiche** *n.* Mikrofiche, *das od. der;* ~**film** ⒈ *n.* Mikrofilm, *der;* ⒉ *v.t.* auf Mikrofilm aufnehmen; ~**light** ['aircraft] *n.* Ultraleichtflugzeug, *das*

**microphone** /'maɪkrəfəʊn/ *n.* Mikrofon, *das*

**microprocessor** /maɪkrəʊ'prəʊsesə(r)/ *n.* Mikroprozessor, *der*

**microscope** /'maɪkrəskəʊp/ *n.* Mikroskop, *das*

**microscopic** /maɪkrə'skɒpɪk/ *adj.* mikroskopisch; (fig.: very small) winzig

'**microwave** *n.* Mikrowelle, *die;* ~ [oven] Mikrowellenherd, *der*

**mid-** /mɪd/ *in comb.* in ~**-air** in der Luft; in ~**-sentence** mitten im Satz; ~**-July** Juli; **the** ~**-60s** die Mitte der Sechzigerjahre; **a man in his** ~**-fifties** ein Mittfünfziger; **be in one's** ~**-thirties** Mitte dreißig sein

**midday** /'mɪddeɪ, mɪd'deɪ/ *n.* (a) (noon) zwölf Uhr
(b) (middle of day) Mittag, *der; attrib.* Mittags-

**middle** /'mɪdl/ ⒈ *attrib. adj.* mittler...
⒉ *n.* (a) Mitte, *die;* **in the** ~ **of the forest/night** mitten im Wald/in der Nacht
(b) (waist) Taille, *die*

**middle:** ~ '**age** *n.* mittleres [Lebens]alter; ~-**aged** /'mɪdleɪdʒd/ *adj.* mittleren Alters *nachgestellt;* **M**~ '**Ages** *n. pl.* **the M**~ **Ages** das Mittelalter; ~ '**class** *n.* Mittelstand, *der;* ~**class** *adj.* bürgerlich; **M**~ '**East** *pr. n.* **the M**~ **East** der Nahe [und Mittlere] Osten; **M**~ '**Eastern** *adj.* nahöstlich; ~**man** *n.* (Commerc.) Zwischenhändler, *der/* -händlerin, *die;* (fig.) Vermittler, *der/*

Vermittlerin, *die;* ~ **'management** *n.*
mittleres Management; ~ **name** *n.* zweiter
Vorname

**middling** /'mɪdlɪŋ/ *adj.* mittelmäßig

**'midfield** *n.* (Footb.) Mittelfeld, *das*

**midge** /mɪdʒ/ *n.* Stechmücke, *die*

**midget** /'mɪdʒɪt/ ⬚1 *n.* Liliputaner, *der/*
Liliputanerin, *die*
⬚2 *adj.* winzig

**Midlands** /'mɪdləndz/ *n. pl.* **the** ~ (Brit.)
Mittelengland (*das*)

**midlife crisis** /mɪdlaɪf 'kraɪsɪs/ *n.*
Midlifecrisis, *die*

**'midnight** *n.* Mitternacht, *die*

**'midpoint** *n.* Mitte, *die*

**midriff** /'mɪdrɪf/ *n.* Bauch, *der*

**midst** /mɪdst/ *n.* **in the** ~ **of sth.** mitten in
einer Sache; **in our/their/your** ~: in unserer/
ihrer/eurer Mitte

**midsummer** /'---, -'--/ *n.* die [Zeit der]
Sommersonnenwende

**midway** /'--, -'-/ *adv.* auf halbem Weg[e]
⟨*sich treffen, sich befinden*⟩

**midweek** /'mɪdwiːk, mɪd'wiːk/ *n.* **in** ~: in
der Wochenmitte

**'midwife** *n., pl.* **'midwives** Hebamme, *die*

**midwifery** /'mɪdwɪfrɪ, mɪd'wɪfərɪ/ *n., no
art.* Geburtshilfe, *die*

**mid'winter** *n.* die [Zeit der]
Wintersonnenwende

**might¹** ▶ MAY

**might²** /maɪt/ *n.* (a) (force) Gewalt, *die*
(b) (power) Macht, *die*

**mightn't** /'maɪtnt/ (coll.) = might not; ▶ MAY

**mighty** /'maɪtɪ/ ⬚1 *adj.* mächtig
⬚2 *adv.* (coll.) verdammt (ugs.)

**migraine** /'miːgreɪn/ *n.* Migräne, *die*

**migrant** /'maɪgrənt/ *n.* (a) Auswanderer,
*der/*Auswanderin, *die*
(b) (bird) Zugvogel, *der*

**migrate** /maɪ'greɪt/ *v.i.* (a) (to a town)
abwandern; (to another country) auswandern
(b) ⟨*Vogel:*⟩ fortziehen

**migration** /maɪ'greɪʃn/ *n.* (a) (to a town)
Abwandern, *das;* (to another country)
Auswandern, *das*
(b) (of birds) Zug, *der*

**migratory** /maɪ'greɪtərɪ/ *adj.* ~ **bird/fish**
Zugvogel, *der/*Wanderfisch, *der*

**mike** /maɪk/ *n.* (coll.) Mikro, *das*

**Milan** /mɪ'læn/ *pr. n.* Mailand (*das*)

**mild** /maɪld/ *adj.* mild; sanft ⟨*Person*⟩

**mildew** /'mɪldjuː/ *n.* (a) Schimmel, *der*
(b) (on plant) Mehltau, *der*

**'mildly** *adv.* (a) (gently) mild[e]
(b) (slightly) ein bisschen
(c) **to put it** ~: gelinde gesagt

**mile** /maɪl/ *n.* (a) Meile, *die*
(b) (fig. coll.) ~**s better/too big** tausendmal
besser/viel zu groß; **be** ~**s ahead of sb.**
jmdm. weit voraus sein

**mileage** /'maɪlɪdʒ/ *n.* [Anzahl der] Meilen
*Pl.;* **a low** ~: ein niedriger Meilenstand

**'milestone** *n.* Meilenstein, *der*

**militant** /'mɪlɪtənt/ ⬚1 *adj.* militant
⬚2 *n.* Militante, *die/der/die*

**military** /'mɪlɪtərɪ/ ⬚1 *adj.* militärisch;
Militär⟨*regierung, -akademie, -uniform,
-parade*⟩; ~ **service** Militärdienst, *der*
⬚2 *n.* **the** ~: das Militär

**militate** /'mɪlɪteɪt/ *v.i.* ~ **against/in favour
of sth.** [deutlich] gegen/für etw. sprechen

**militia** /mɪ'lɪʃə/ *n.* Miliz, *die*

**milk** /mɪlk/ ⬚1 *n.* Milch, *die*
⬚2 *v.t.* melken

**milk:** ~ **bottle** *n.* Milchflasche, *die;*
~ **'chocolate** *n.* Milchschokolade, *die;*
~ **float** *n.* (Brit.) Milchwagen, *der*

**milking** /'mɪlkɪŋ/ *n.* Melken, *das*

**milk:** ~ **jug** *n.* Milchkännchen, *das;*
~**man** /'mɪlkmən/ *n., pl.* ~**men** /'mɪlkmən/
Milchmann, *der;* ~ **shake** *n.* Milchshake,
*der;* ~ **tooth** *n.* Milchzahn, der

**'milky** *adj.* milchig

**Milky 'Way** *n.* Milchstraße, *die*

**mill** /mɪl/ ⬚1 *n.* (a) Mühle, *die*
(b) (factory) Fabrik, *die*
⬚2 *v.t.* (a) mahlen ⟨*Getreide*⟩
(b) fräsen ⟨*Metallgegenstand*⟩

**mill a'bout** (Brit.), **mill a'round** *v.i.*
durcheinander laufen

**millennium** /mɪ'lenɪəm/ *n., pl.* ~**s** *or*
**millennia** /mɪ'lenɪə/ Jahrtausend, *das;*
Millennium, *das*

**mil'lennium bug** *n.* (Comp.)
Jahrtausendvirus, *der od. das*

**'miller** *n.* Müller, *der*

**millet** /'mɪlɪt/ *n.* Hirse, *die*

**milligram** /'mɪlɪgræm/ *n.* Milligramm, *das*

**millilitre** (Brit.; Amer.: **milliliter**)
/'mɪlɪliːtə(r)/ *n.* Milliliter, *der od. das*

**millimetre** (Brit.; Amer.: **millimeter**)
/'mɪlɪmiːtə(r)/ *n.* Millimeter, *der od. das*

**milliner** /'mɪlɪnə(r)/ *n.* Modist, *der/*
Modistin, *die*

**'millinery** *n.* Hutmacherei, *die*

**million** /'mɪljən/ ⬚1 *adj.* **a** *or* **one/two** ~:
eine Million/zwei Millionen; **half a** ~: eine
halbe Million
⬚2 *n.* (a) Million, *die*
(b) (indefinite amount) ~**s of people** eine
Unmenge Leute

**millionaire** /mɪljə'neə(r)/ *n.* Millionär,
*der/*Millionärin, *die*

**millionth** /'mɪljənθ/ ⬚1 *adj.* millionst...
⬚2 *n.* (fraction) Millionstel, *das*

**'millstone** *n.* Mühlstein, *der*

**mime** /maɪm/ ⬚1 *n.* (a) (performance)
Pantomime, *die*
(b) (art) Pantomimik, *die*
⬚2 *v.i.* pantomimisch agieren
⬚3 *v.t.* pantomimisch darstellen

**mimic** /'mɪmɪk/ ⬚1 *n.* Imitator, *der* ····ᐳ

**m**

2 *v.t.,* -ck- nachahmen

**min.** *abbr.* (a) = **minute[s]** Min.
(b) = **minimum** (*adj.*) mind., (*n.*) Min.

**mince** /mɪns/ 1 *n.* Hackfleisch, *das*
2 *v.t.* durch den [Fleisch]wolf drehen
⟨*Fleisch*⟩

'**mincemeat** *n.* (a) Hackfleisch, *das*
(b) (sweet) *süße Pastetenfüllung aus Obst, Rosinen, Gewürzen, Nierenfett usw.*

**mince 'pie** *n.* mit „mincemeat" B *gefüllte Pastete*

'**mincer** *n.* Fleischwolf, *der*

**mind** /maɪnd/ 1 *n.* (a) Geist, *der*
(b) (remembrance) bear *or* keep sth. in ∼: an etw. (*Akk.*) denken; have [got] sb./sth. in ∼: an jmdn./etw. denken
(c) (opinion) give sb. a piece of one's ∼: jmdm. gründlich die Meinung sagen; to my ∼: meiner Meinung *od.* Ansicht nach; change one's ∼: seine Meinung ändern; I have a good ∼ to do that ich hätte große Lust, das zu tun; make up one's ∼, make one's ∼ up sich entscheiden
(d) ([normal] mental powers) Verstand, *der;* be out of one's ∼: den Verstand verloren haben
(e) frame of ∼: [seelische] Verfassung
2 *v.t.* (a) I can't afford a bicycle, never ∼ a car ich kann mir kein Fahrrad leisten, geschweige denn ein Auto; we've got some decorations up, - not many, ∼ you wir haben etwas dekoriert, allerdings nicht viel
(b) *usu. neg. or interrog.* (object to) would you ∼ opening the door? würdest du bitte die Tür öffnen?; I wouldn't ∼ a walk ich hätte nichts gegen einen Spaziergang
(c) (take care) ∼ you don't go too near the cliff edge! pass auf, dass du nicht zu nah an den Felsenrand gehst!; ∼ how you go! pass auf!
(d) (have charge of) aufpassen auf (+ *Akk.*)
3 *v.i.* (a) ∼! Vorsicht!; Achtung!
(b) (care, object) do you ∼ if I smoke? stört es Sie, wenn ich rauche?
(c) never ∼ (it's not important) macht nichts
∎ **mind 'out** *v.i.* aufpassen (for auf + *Akk.*); ∼ out! Vorsicht!

**mind:** ∼**bending,** (coll.) ∼**blowing** *adjs.* bewusstseinsverändernd;
∼**boggling** /'maɪndbɒɡlɪŋ/ *adj.* (coll.) wahnsinnig (ugs.)

'**minded** *adj.* mechanically ∼: technisch veranlagt; not politically ∼: unpolitisch

**minder** /'maɪndə(r)/ *n.* (a) (for child) we need a ∼ for the child wir brauchen jemanden, der auf das Kind aufpasst *od.* das Kind betreut
(b) (sl.: protector of criminal) Gorilla, *der* (salopp)

**mindful** /'maɪndfl/ *adj.* be ∼ of sth. etw. berücksichtigen

'**mindless** *adj.* geistlos ⟨*Person*⟩; sinnlos ⟨*Gewalt*⟩

**mine**[1] /maɪn/ *n.* (a) Bergwerk, *das*
(b) (explosive) Mine, *die*

**mine**[2] *poss. pron. pred.* meiner/meine/mein[e]s; *see also* HERS

**mine:** ∼**detector** *n.* Minensuchgerät, *das;* ∼**field** *n.* Minenfeld, *das*

'**miner** *n.* Bergmann, *der*

**mineral** /'mɪnərl/ 1 *adj.* mineralisch; Mineral⟨*salz, -quelle*⟩
2 *n.* (a) Mineral, *das*
(b) (Brit.: soft drink) Erfrischungsgetränk, *das*

'**mineral water** *n.* Mineralwasser, *das*

**minesweeper** /'maɪnswiːpə(r)/ *n.* Minensuchboot, *das*

**mingle** /'mɪŋɡl/ 1 *v.t.* [ver]mischen
2 *v.i.* sich [ver]mischen (with mit)

**mini** /'mɪni/ *n.* (coll.) (a) (car) M∼ ® Mini, *der*
(b) (skirt) Mini, *der* (ugs.)

**mini-** /'mɪni/ *in comb.* Mini-; Klein⟨*bus, -wagen, -taxi*⟩

**miniature** /'mɪnɪtʃə(r)/ 1 *n.* (picture) Miniatur, *die*
2 *adj.* Miniatur-

**mini:** ∼**bus** *n.* Kleinbus, *der;* ∼**cab** *n.* Minicar, *das*

**minim** /'mɪnɪm/ *n.* (Brit. Mus.) halbe Note

**minimal** /'mɪnɪml/ *adj.* minimal

**minimize** /'mɪnɪmaɪz/ *v.t.* (a) (reduce) auf ein Mindestmaß reduzieren
(b) (understate) bagatellisieren

**minimum** /'mɪnɪməm/ 1 *n., pl.* minima /'mɪnɪmə/ Minimum, *das* (of an + *Dat.*)
2 *attrib. adj.* Mindest-

**minimum:** ∼ '**lending rate** *n.* Mindestausleihsatz [*der Bank von England*]; ≈ Mindestdiskontsatz, *der;* ∼ '**wage** *n.* Mindestlohn, *der*

**mining** /'maɪnɪŋ/ *n.* Bergbau, *der; attrib.* Bergbau-

**mining:** ∼ **industry** *n.* Bergbau, *der;* ∼ **town** *n.* Bergbaustadt, *die*

**minion** /'mɪnjən/ *n.* Lakai, *der*

**mini:** ∼ **roundabout** *n.* (Brit.) *sehr kleiner, oft nur aufs Pflaster aufgezeichneter Kreisverkehr;* ∼**skirt** *n.* Minirock, *der*

**minister** /'mɪnɪstə(r)/ 1 *n.* (Polit.) Minister, *der*/Ministerin, *die*
(b) (Eccl.) Geistliche, *der*/*die*; Pfarrer, *der*/Pfarrerin, *die*
2 *v.i.* ∼ to sb. sich um jmdn. kümmern

**ministerial** /mɪnɪˈstɪərɪəl/ *adj.* (Polit.) Minister-; ministeriell

**ministry** /'mɪnɪstri/ *n.* (a) (Polit.) Ministerium, *das*
(b) (Eccl.) geistliches Amt

**mink** /mɪŋk/ *n.* Nerz, *der*

**minnow** /'mɪnəʊ/ *n.* Elritze, *die*

**minor** /'maɪnə(r)/ 1 *adj.* (a) (lesser) kleiner...
(b) (unimportant) weniger bedeutend; (not serious) leicht; ∼ road kleine Straße
(c) (Mus.) Moll-; A ∼: a-Moll
2 *n.* Minderjährige, *der*/*die*

**minority** /maɪˈnɒrɪtɪ, mɪˈnɒrɪtɪ/ *n.*
Minderheit, *die;* **in the** ∼: in der Minderheit

**minstrel** /ˈmɪnstrl/ *n.* fahrender Sänger

**mint¹** /mɪnt/ [1] *n.* (place) Münzanstalt, *die*
[2] *adj.* funkelnagelneu (ugs.); **in** ∼ **condition**
in tadellosem Zustand
[3] *v.t.* prägen

**mint²** *n.* (a) (plant) Minze, *die*
(b) (peppermint) Pfefferminz, *das; attrib.*
Pfefferminz-

**mint 'sauce** *n.* Minzsoße, *die*

**minuet** /mɪnjʊˈet/ *n.* Menuett, *das*

**minus** /ˈmaɪnəs/ *prep.* minus; weniger;
(without) abzüglich (+ *Gen.*)

**minuscule** /ˈmɪnəskjuːl/ *adj.* winzig

**minute¹** /ˈmɪnɪt/ *n.* (a) Minute, *die;*
(moment) Moment, *der*
(b) ∼s (of meeting) Protokoll, *das;* **take the**
∼**s of a meeting** bei einer Sitzung [das]
Protokoll führen

**minute²** /maɪˈnjuːt/ *adj.* (tiny) winzig

**minute hand** /ˈmɪnɪthænd/ *n.*
Minutenzeiger, *der;* großer Zeiger

**minutiae** /maɪˈnjuːʃɪiː, mɪˈnjuːʃɪiː/ *n. pl.*
Details *Pl.*

**miracle** /ˈmɪrəkl/ *n.* Wunder, *das*

**miraculous** /mɪˈrækjʊləs/ *adj.* wunderbar

**mirage** /ˈmɪrɑːʒ/ *n.* Fata Morgana, *die*

**mire** /maɪə(r)/ *n.* Morast, *der*

**mirror** /ˈmɪrə(r)/ [1] *n.* Spiegel, *der*
[2] *v.t.* [wider]spiegeln

**mirror 'image** *n.* Spiegelbild, *das*

**misadventure** /mɪsədˈventʃə(r)/ *n.*
Missgeschick, *das*

**misanthropist** /mɪˈzænθrəpɪst/ *ns.*
Misanthrop, *der* (geh.); Menschenfeind, *der*

**misanthropy** /mɪˈzænθrəpɪ/ *n.*
Menschenfeindlichkeit, *die*

**misapprehension** /mɪsæprɪˈhenʃn/ *n.*
Missverständnis, *das;* **be under a** ∼: einem
Irrtum unterliegen

**misbehave** /mɪsbɪˈheɪv/ *v.i. & refl.* sich
schlecht benehmen

**misbehaviour** (*Amer.:* **misbehavior**)
/mɪsbɪˈheɪvjə(r)/ *n.* schlechtes Benehmen

**miscalculate** /mɪsˈkælkjʊleɪt/ [1] *v.t.*
falsch berechnen; (misjudge) falsch
einschätzen
[2] *v.i.* sich verrechnen

**miscalculation** /mɪskælkjʊˈleɪʃn/ *n.*
Rechenfehler, *der;* (misjudgement)
Fehleinschätzung, *die*

**miscarriage** /mɪsˈkærɪdʒ/ *n.* (a)
Fehlgeburt, *die*
(b) ∼ **of justice** Justizirrtum, *der*

**miscarry** /mɪsˈkærɪ/ *v.i.* (a) (Med.) eine
Fehlgeburt haben
(b) ⟨Plan, Vorhaben usw.⟩ fehlschlagen

**miscellaneous** /mɪsəˈleɪnɪəs/ *adj.* (a)
[kunter]bunt
(b) *with pl. n.* verschieden

**miscellany** /mɪˈselənɪ/ *n.* [bunte]
Sammlung; [buntes] Gemisch

**mischief** /ˈmɪstʃɪf/ *n.* (a) Unfug, *der;* **get
up to** ∼: etwas anstellen
(b) (harm) Schaden, *der*

**mischievous** /ˈmɪstʃɪvəs/ *adj.*
spitzbübisch; schelmisch

**misconception** /mɪskənˈsepʃn/ *n.*
falsche Vorstellung (**about** von); **be
[labouring] under a** ∼ **about sth.** sich (*Dat.*)
eine falsche Vorstellung von etw. machen

**misconduct** /mɪsˈkɒndʌkt/ *n.*
unkorrektes Verhalten

**misconstrue** /mɪskənˈstruː/ *v.t.*
missverstehen

**miscount** /mɪsˈkaʊnt/ [1] *v.i.* sich
verzählen
[2] *v.t.* falsch zählen

**misdeed** /mɪsˈdiːd/ *n.* Missetat, *die* (veralt.,
scherzh.)

**misdemeanour** (*Amer.:*
**misdemeanor**) /mɪsdɪˈmiːnə(r)/ *n.*
Missetat, *die* (veralt., scherzh.)

**misdirect** /mɪsdɪˈrekt, mɪsdaɪˈrekt/ *v.t.*
falsch adressieren ⟨Brief⟩; in die falsche
Richtung schicken ⟨Person⟩

**miser** /ˈmaɪzə(r)/ *n.* Geizhals, *der*

**miserable** /ˈmɪzərəbl/ *adj.* (a)
unglücklich; **feel** ∼: sich elend fühlen
(b) trist ⟨Wetter, Urlaub⟩

**miserably** /ˈmɪzərəblɪ/ *adv.* unglücklich;
jämmerlich ⟨versagen⟩; ∼ **poor** bettelarm

**miserly** /ˈmaɪzəlɪ/ *adj.* geizig

**misery** /ˈmɪzərɪ/ *n.* (a) Elend, *das*
(b) (coll.: discontented person) ∼ **[guts]**
Miesepeter, *der* (ugs.)

**misfire** /mɪsˈfaɪə(r)/ *v.i.* (a) ⟨Motor:⟩
Fehlzündungen haben
(b) ⟨Plan, Versuch:⟩ fehlschlagen; ⟨Streich,
Witz:⟩ danebengehen

**misfit** /ˈmɪsfɪt/ *n.* Außenseiter, *der/*
Außenseiterin, *die*

**misfortune** /mɪsˈfɔːtʃuːn/ *n.* Missgeschick,
*das*

**misgiving** /mɪsˈgɪvɪŋ/ *n.* ∼[s] Bedenken
*Pl.*

**misguided** /mɪsˈgaɪdɪd/ *adj.* töricht

**mishandle** /mɪsˈhændl/ *v.t.* falsch
behandeln

**mishap** /ˈmɪshæp/ *n.* Missgeschick, *das*

**mishear** /mɪsˈhɪə(r)/ [1] *v.i.,* misheard
/mɪsˈhɜːd/ sich verhören
[2] *v.t.,* misheard falsch verstehen

**mishit** [1] /ˈmɪshɪt/ *n.* Fehlschlag, *der*
[2] /mɪsˈhɪt/ *v.t.,* -tt-, mishit verschlagen

**mishmash** /ˈmɪʃmæʃ/ *n.* Mischmasch, *der*
(ugs.) (of aus)

**misinform** /mɪsɪnˈfɔːm/ *v.t.* falsch
informieren

**misinterpret** /mɪsɪnˈtɜːprɪt/ *v.t.* (make
wrong inference from) falsch deuten; missdeuten ····▷

**misinterpretation** /mɪsɪntɜːprɪ'teɪʃn/ *n.* be open to ∼: leicht missdeutet werden können

**misjudge** /mɪs'dʒʌdʒ/ *v.t.* falsch einschätzen; falsch beurteilen ⟨*Person*⟩

**misjudgement, misjudgment** /mɪs'dʒʌdʒmənt/ *n.* Fehleinschätzung, *die;* (of person) falsche Beurteilung

**mislay** /mɪs'leɪ/ *v.t.,* mislaid /mɪs'leɪd/ verlegen

**mislead** /mɪs'liːd/ *v.t.,* misled /mɪs'led/ irreführen

**mis'leading** *adj.* irreführend

**mismanage** /mɪs'mænɪdʒ/ *v.t.* schlecht abwickeln ⟨*Geschäft, Projekt*⟩

**mismanagement** /mɪs'mænɪdʒmənt/ *n.* schlechte Abwicklung

**misnomer** /mɪs'nəʊmə(r)/ *n.* unzutreffende Bezeichnung

**misogynist** /mɪ'sɒdʒɪnɪst/ *n.* Frauenhasser, *der*

**misplace** /mɪs'pleɪs/ *v.t.* an den falschen Platz stellen/legen/setzen *usw.*

**misprint** ⒈ /'mɪsprɪnt/ *n.* Druckfehler, *der* ⒉ /mɪs'prɪnt/ *v.t.* verdrucken

**mispronounce** /mɪsprə'naʊns/ *v.t.* falsch aussprechen

**misquote** /mɪs'kwəʊt/ *v.t.* falsch zitieren; he was ∼d as saying that ...: man unterstellte ihm, gesagt zu haben, dass ...

**misread** /mɪs'riːd/ *v.t.,* misread /mɪs'red/ falsch lesen

**misrepresent** /mɪsreprɪ'zent/ *v.t.* falsch darstellen

**misrepresentation** /mɪsreprɪzen'teɪʃn/ *n.* falsche Darstellung

**miss** ⒈ *n.* Fehlschlag, *der;* (shot) Fehlschuss, *der;* (throw) Fehlwurf, *der* ⒉ *v.t.* **(a)** (fail to hit) verfehlen **(b)** (let slip) verpassen; ∼ an opportunity sich ⟨*Dat.*⟩ eine Gelegenheit entgehen lassen **(c)** (fail to catch) verpassen ⟨*Zug*⟩ **(d)** (fail to take part in) versäumen; ∼ school in der Schule fehlen **(e)** (fail to see) übersehen; (fail to hear) nicht mitbekommen **(f)** (feel the absence of) vermissen; she ∼es him er fehlt ihr ⒊ *v.i.* (not hit sth.) danebentreffen

▪ **miss 'out** ⒈ *v.t.* weglassen ⒉ *v.i.* ∼ out on sth. (coll.) sich ⟨*Dat.*⟩ etw. entgehen lassen

**Miss** /mɪs/ *n.* ∼ Brown (unmarried woman) Frau Brown; Fräulein Brown (veralt.); (girl) Fräulein Brown

**misshapen** /mɪs'ʃeɪpn/ *adj.* missgebildet

**missile** /'mɪsaɪl/ *n.* **(a)** (thrown) [Wurf]geschoss, *das* **(b)** (Mil.) Rakete, *die*

**'missile base, 'missile site** *ns.* Raketenbasis, *die*

**'missing** *adj.* fehlend; be ∼: fehlen; ⟨*Person:*⟩ (Mil. etc.) vermisst werden; (not present) fehlen; ∼ person Vermisste, *der/die*

**mission** /'mɪʃn/ *n.* **(a)** Mission, *die* **(b)** (planned operation) Einsatz, *der*

**missionary** /'mɪʃənərɪ/ *n.* Missionar, *der/* Missionarin, *die*

**'mission statement** *n.* Unternehmensleitbild, *das*

**misspell** /mɪs'spel/ *v.t.,* forms as SPELL[1] falsch schreiben

**mist** /mɪst/ *n.* (fog) Nebel, *der;* (haze) Dunst, *der;* (on windscreen etc.) Beschlag, *der*

▪ **mist 'up** *v.i.* [sich] beschlagen

**mistake** /mɪ'steɪk/ ⒈ *n.* Fehler, *der;* by ∼: versehentlich ⒉ *v.t.,* forms as TAKE 1: **(a)** falsch verstehen **(b)** ∼ x for y x mit y verwechseln

**mistaken** /mɪ'steɪkn/ *adj.* be ∼: sich täuschen; a case of ∼ identity eine Verwechslung

**mi'stakenly** *adv.* irrtümlicherweise

**mistletoe** /'mɪsltəʊ/ *n.* Mistel, *die*

**mistook** ▸ MISTAKE 2

**mistranslate** /mɪstræns'leɪt/ *v.t.* falsch übersetzen

**mistreat** /mɪs'triːt/ *v.t.* schlecht behandeln; (violently) misshandeln

**mistreatment** /mɪs'triːtmənt/ *n.* schlechte Behandlung; (violent) Misshandlung, *die*

**mistress** /'mɪstrɪs/ *n.* **(a)** (Brit. Sch.: teacher) Lehrerin, *die* **(b)** (lover) Geliebte, *die*

**mistrust** /mɪs'trʌst/ ⒈ *v.t.* misstrauen (+ *Dat.*) ⒉ *n.* Misstrauen, *das* (of gegenüber + *Dat.*)

**mistrustful** /mɪs'trʌstfl/ *adj.* misstrauisch (of gegenüber)

**'misty** *adj.* dunstig

**misunderstand** /mɪsʌndə'stænd/ *v.t.,* forms as UNDERSTAND: missverstehen

**misunder'standing** *n.* Missverständnis, *das*

**misuse** ⒈ /mɪs'juːz/ *v.t.* missbrauchen ⒉ /mɪs'juːs/ *n.* Missbrauch, *der*

**mite** /maɪt/ *n.* **(a)** (Zool.) Milbe, *die* **(b)** (small child) Würmchen, *das* (fam.); poor little ∼: armes Kleines

**miter** (Amer.) ▸ MITRE

**mitigate** /'mɪtɪgeɪt/ *v.t.* **(a)** (reduce) lindern **(b)** (make less severe) mildern; mitigating circumstances mildernde Umstände

**mitre** /'maɪtə(r)/ *n.* (Brit. Eccl.) Mitra, *die*

**mitten** /'mɪtn/ *n.* Fausthandschuh, *der*

**mix** /mɪks/ ⒈ *v.t.* [ver]mischen; verrühren ⟨*Zutaten*⟩ ⒉ *v.i.* **(a)** (become ∼ed) sich vermischen **(b)** (be sociable, participate) Umgang mit anderen [Menschen] haben; ∼ with Umgang haben mit; ∼ well kontaktfreudig sein ⒊ *n.* (coll.) Mischung, *die;* [cake] ∼: Backmischung, *die*

■ **mix 'up** *v.t.* **(a)** vermischen
**(b)** (muddle) durcheinander bringen; (confuse)
verwechseln
**(c)** be/get ∼ed up in sth. in etw. (*Akk.*)
verwickelt sein/werden

**mixed** /mɪkst/ *adj.* **(a)** gemischt
**(b)** (diverse) unterschiedlich

**mixed:** ∼ 'bag *n.* bunte Mischung;
∼ 'blessing *n.* be a ∼ blessing nicht nur
Vorteile haben; ∼ 'grill *n.* Mixedgrill, *der*
(Gastr.); gemischte Grillplatte;
∼ 'marriage *n.* Mischehe, *die;* ∼ 'up *adj.*
(fig. coll.) verwirrt, konfus ⟨*Person*⟩; be/feel
very ∼ up völlig durcheinander sein

**'mixer** *n.* (for food) Küchenmaschine, *die;*
hand ∼: Handrührgerät, *das*

**mixture** /'mɪkstʃə(r)/ *n.* **(a)** Mischung, *die*
(of aus)
**(b)** (Med.) Mixtur, *die*

**'mix-up** *n.* Durcheinander, *das;*
(misunderstanding) Missverständnis, *das*

**mm.** *abbr.* = **millimetre[s]** mm

**moan** /məʊn/ ① *n.* **(a)** Stöhnen, *das*
**(b)** have a ∼ (complain) jammern
② *v.i.* **(a)** stöhnen (with vor + *Dat.*)
**(b)** (complain) jammern (about über + *Akk.*)
③ *v.t.* stöhnen

**moat** /məʊt/ *n.* [castle] ∼: Burggraben, *der*

**mob** /mɒb/ ① *n.* **(a)** (rabble) Mob, *der*
**(b)** (coll.: group) Peter and his ∼: Peter und
seine ganze Blase (salopp)
② *v.t.,* -bb- belagern (ugs.) ⟨*Star*⟩

**mobile** /'məʊbaɪl/ ① *adj.* beweglich; (on
wheels) fahrbar; upwardly ∼: sozial
aufsteigend
② *n.* Mobile, *das;* (∼ phone) Handy, *das*

**mobile:** ∼ 'home *n.* transportable
Wohneinheit; ∼ 'phone *n.* Mobiltelefon,
*das*

**mobility** /mə'bɪlɪtɪ/ *n.* Beweglichkeit, *die*

**mobilization** /məʊbɪlaɪ'zeɪʃn/ *n.*
Mobilisierung, *die*

**mobilize** /'məʊbɪlaɪz/ *v.t.* mobilisieren

**moccasin** /'mɒkəsɪn/ *n.* Mokassin, *der*

**mocha** /'mɒkə/ *n.* Mokka, *der*

**mock** /mɒk/ ① *v.t.* sich lustig machen über
(+ *Akk.*)
② *v.i.* sich lustig machen (at über + *Akk.*)
③ *adj.* Schein⟨*kampf, -angriff, -ehe*⟩

**mockery** /'mɒkərɪ/ *n.* Spott, *der;* make a
∼ of sth. etw. zur Farce machen

**'mock-up** *n.* Modell [in Originalgröße]

**mode** /məʊd/ *n.* **(a)** Art [und Weise], *die*
**(b)** (fashion) Mode, *die*

**model** /'mɒdl/ ① *n.* **(a)** Modell, *das*
**(b)** (example to be imitated) Vorbild, *das*
**(c)** (Art) Modell, *das;* (Fashion) Mannequin,
*das;* (male) Dressman, *der*
② *adj.* **(a)** (exemplary) Muster-
**(b)** (miniature) Modell-
③ *v.t.,* (Brit.) -ll-: **(a)** modellieren; ∼ sth. after
or [up]on sth. etw. einer Sache (*Dat.*)
nachbilden

**(b)** (Fashion) vorführen
④ *v.i.* (Fashion) als Mannequin/Dressman
arbeiten; (Art) Modell stehen/sitzen

**modem** /'məʊdem/ *n.* Modem, *der*

**moderate** ① /'mɒdərət/ *adj.* **(a)** gemäßigt
⟨*Ansichten*⟩; maßvoll ⟨*Trinker, Forderungen*⟩
**(b)** mittler... ⟨*Größe, Menge, Wert*⟩;
(reasonable) angemessen ⟨*Preis, Summe*⟩
② /'mɒdərət/ *n.* Gemäßigte, *der/die*
③ /'mɒdəreɪt/ *v.t.* mäßigen
④ *v.i.* nachlassen

**moderately** /'mɒdərətlɪ/ *adv.*
einigermaßen; mäßig ⟨*begeistert, groß,
begabt*⟩

**moderation** /mɒdə'reɪʃn/ *n.* Mäßigkeit,
*die;* in ∼: mit Maßen

**modern** /'mɒdn/ *adj.* modern; heutig
⟨*Zeit[alter], Welt, Mensch*⟩; ∼ art/music
moderne Kunst/Musik; ∼ history neuere
Geschichte; ∼ languages neuere Sprachen

**modernize** /'mɒdənaɪz/ *v.t.* modernisieren

**modest** /'mɒdɪst/ *adj.* bescheiden; einfach
⟨*Haus, Kleidung*⟩

**'modestly** *adv.* bescheiden

**'modesty** *n.* Bescheidenheit, *die*

**modification** /mɒdɪfɪ'keɪʃn/ *n.*
[Ab]änderung, *die*

**modify** /'mɒdɪfaɪ/ *v.t.* [ab]ändern

**modulate** /'mɒdjʊleɪt/ *v.t. & i.* modulieren

**modulation** /mɒdjʊ'leɪʃn/ *n.* Modulation,
*die*

**module** /'mɒdjuːl/ *n.* **(a)** Bauelement, *das*
**(b)** (Astronaut.) command ∼:
Kommandoeinheit, *die*
**(c)** (Educ.) Unterrichtseinheit, *die*

**mohair** /'məʊheə(r)/ *n.* Mohair, *der*

**moist** /mɔɪst/ *adj.* feucht (with von)

**moisten** /'mɔɪsn/ *v.t.* anfeuchten

**moisture** /'mɔɪstʃə(r)/ *n.* Feuchtigkeit, *die*

**moisturize** /'mɔɪstjʊraɪz, 'mɔɪstʃəraɪz/ *v.t.*
befeuchten; ∼ the skin der Haut (*Dat.*)
Feuchtigkeit zuführen; ⟨*Creme:*⟩ der Haut
(*Dat.*) Feuchtigkeit verleihen

**moisturizer** /'mɔɪstʃəraɪzə(r)/,
**moisturizing cream** /'mɔɪstʃəraɪzɪŋ
kriːm/ *ns.* Feuchtigkeitscreme, *die*

**molar** /'məʊlə(r)/ *n.* Backenzahn, *der*

**molasses** /mə'læsɪz/ *n.* Melasse, *die*

**mold** (Amer.) ▶ MOULD¹, ²

**molder, molding, moldy** (Amer.)
▶ MOULD-

**mole¹** /məʊl/ *n.* (on skin) Leberfleck, *der*

**mole²** *n.* (animal) Maulwurf, *der*

**molecular** /mə'lekjʊlə(r)/ *adj.* molekular

**molecule** /'mɒlɪkjuːl/ *n.* Molekül, *das*

**'molehill** *n.* Maulwurfshügel, *der*

**molest** /mə'lest/ *v.t.* belästigen

**mollify** /'mɒlɪfaɪ/ *v.t.* besänftigen

**mollusc,** (Amer.) **mollusk** /'mɒləsk/ *n.*
Weichtier, *das*

m

**mollycoddle** /'mɒlɪkɒdl/ *v.t.*
[ver]hätscheln

**molt** (Amer.) ▶ MOULT

**molten** /'məʊltn/ *adj.* geschmolzen

**mom** /mɒm/ (Amer. coll.) ▶ MUM²

**moment** /'məʊmənt/ *n.* Augenblick, *der;* at
any ~, (coll.) any ~: jeden Augenblick; one
*or* just a *or* wait a ~! einen Augenblick!; in a
~ (very soon) sofort; at the ~: im Augenblick;
the ~ of truth die Stunde der Wahrheit

**momentarily** /'məʊməntərɪlɪ/ *adv.* einen
Augenblick lang

**momentary** /'məʊməntərɪ/ *adj.* kurz

**momentous** /mə'mentəs/ *adj.* (important)
bedeutsam; (of consequence) folgenschwer

**momentum** /mə'mentəm/ *n.* Schwung, *der*

**Mon.** *abbr.* = **Monday** Mo.

**monarch** /'mɒnək/ *n.* Monarch, *der/*
Monarchin, *die*

'**monarchy** *n.* Monarchie, *die*

**monastery** /'mɒnəstrɪ/ *n.* Kloster, *das*

**monastic** /mə'næstɪk/ *adj.* mönchisch

**Monday** /'mʌndeɪ, 'mʌndɪ/ *n.* Montag, *der;*
*see also* FRIDAY

**monetary** /'mʌnɪtərɪ/ *adj.* (a) (of currency)
monetär; Währungs⟨*politik, -system*⟩;
~ union Währungsunion, *die*
(b) (of money) finanziell

**money** /'mʌnɪ/ *n.* Geld, *das;* make ~
⟨*Person:*⟩ [viel] Geld verdienen; ⟨*Geschäft:*⟩
etwas einbringen; for '**my** ~: wenn man
mich fragt

**money:** ~ **bag** *n.* Geldsack, *der;* ~ **belt**
*n.* Geldgürtel, *der;* ~ **box** *n.* Sparbüchse,
*die;* ~**making** *adj.* Gewinn bringend;
~ **order** *n.* Postanweisung, *die*

**Mongolia** /mɒŋ'gəʊlɪə/ *pr. n.* Mongolei, *die*

**Mongolian** /mɒŋ'gəʊlɪən/ ① *adj.*
mongolisch; *sb.* is ~: jmd. ist Mongole/
Mongolin
② *n.* (person) Mongole, *der/*Mongolin, *die*

**mongrel** /'mʌŋgrəl/ *n.* ~ [dog]
Promenadenmischung, *die*

**monitor** /'mɒnɪtə(r)/ ① *n.* (a) (Sch.)
Aufsichtsschüler, *der/*-schülerin, *die*
(b) (Med., Telev., Comp.) Monitor, *der*
② *v.t.* beobachten ⟨*Wetter, Flugzeug*⟩;
abhören ⟨*Sendung, Telefongespräch*⟩

**monk** /mʌŋk/ *n.* Mönch, *der*

**monkey** /'mʌŋkɪ/ *n.* Affe, *der*

**monkey:** ~ **business** *n.* (coll.: mischief)
Schabernack, *der;* ~ **nut** *n.* Erdnuss, *die;*
~ **wrench** *n.*
Universalschraubenschlüssel, *der*

**mono** /'mɒnəʊ/ *adj.* Mono⟨*platte[nspieler],
-wiedergabe*⟩

**monochrome** /'mɒnəkrəʊm/ *adj.*
monochrom (fachspr.); einfarbig;
Schwarzweiß- (Ferns.)

**monocle** /'mɒnəkl/ *n.* Monokel, *das*

**monogamous** /mə'nɒgəməs/ *adj.*
monogam

**monogamy** /mə'nɒgəmɪ/ *n.* Monogamie,
*die;* Einehe, *die*

**monogram** /'mɒnəgræm/ *n.* Monogramm,
*das*

**monogrammed** /'mɒnəgræmd/ *adj.*
monogrammiert; ⟨*Taschentuch usw.:*⟩ mit
Monogramm

**monologue** (*Amer.:* **monolog**)
/'mɒnəlɒg/ *n.* Monolog, *der*

**monopolize** /mə'nɒpəlaɪz/ *v.t.* (Econ.)
monopolisieren; (fig.) mit Beschlag belegen;
~ **the conversation** den/die anderen nicht zu
Wort kommen lassen

**monopoly** /mə'nɒpəlɪ/ *n.* (a) (Econ.)
Monopol, *das* (of auf + *Akk.*)
(b) (exclusive possession) alleiniger Besitz

**monotone** /'mɒnətəʊn/ *n.* gleich
bleibender Ton

**monotonous** /mə'nɒtənəs/ *adj.*,
**mo'notonously** *adv.* eintönig

**monotony** /mə'nɒtənɪ/ *n.* Eintönigkeit, *die*

**monsoon** /mɒn'su:n/ *n.* Monsun, *der*

**monster** /'mɒnstə(r)/ *n.* (a) (creature)
Ungeheuer, *das;* (huge thing) Ungetüm, *das*
(b) (inhuman person) Unmensch, *der*

**monstrosity** /mɒn'strɒsɪtɪ/ *n.* (a)
(outrageous thing) Ungeheuerlichkeit, *die*
(b) (hideous building etc.) Ungetüm, *das*

**monstrous** /'mɒnstrəs/ *adj.* (a) (huge)
riesig
(b) (outrageous) ungeheuerlich
(c) (atrocious) scheußlich

**month** /mʌnθ/ *n.* Monat, *der;* for a ~/~s
einen Monat [lang]/monatelang

'**monthly** ① *adj.* monatlich;
Monats⟨*einkommen, -gehalt*⟩
② *adv.* einmal im Monat
③ *n.* Monatsschrift, *die*

**monument** /'mɒnjʊmənt/ *n.* Denkmal, *das*

**monumental** /mɒnjʊ'mentl/ *adj.* (a)
(massive) monumental
(b) gewaltig ⟨*Misserfolg, Irrtum*⟩

**moo** /mu:/ ① *n.* Muhen, *das*
② *v.i.* muhen

**mooch** /mu:tʃ/ *v.i.* (coll.) ~ about *or* around/
along herumschleichen (ugs.)/zockeln (ugs.)

**mood** /mu:d/ *n.* (a) Stimmung, *die;* be in a
good/bad ~: [bei] guter/schlechter Laune
sein; I'm not in the ~: ich hab keine Lust
dazu
(b) (bad ~) Verstimmung, *die*

'**moody** *adj.* (a) (sullen) missmutig
(b) (subject to moods) launenhaft

**moon** /mu:n/ *n.* Mond, *der*

**moon:** ~**beam** *n.* Mondstrahl, *der;*
~**light** ① *n.* Mondlicht, *das;* Mondschein,
*der;* ② *v.i.* (coll.) nebenberuflich abends
arbeiten; ~**lit** *adj.* mondbeschienen (geh.)

**moor¹** /mʊə(r), mɔ:(r)/ *n.* (Geog.)
[Hoch]moor, *das*

**moor²** *v.t. & i.* festmachen; vertäuen

'**moorhen** *n.* [Grünfüßiges] Teichhuhn

**'mooring** *n.* ~[s] Anlegestelle, *die*
**'mooring post** *n.* Pfahl, *der;*
≈ Duckdalben, *der*

**moorland** /'mʊələnd, 'mɔːlənd/ *n.*
Moorland, *das*

**moose** /muːs/ *n., pl. same* Amerikanischer
Elch

**moot** /muːt/ ① *adj.* umstritten; offen
⟨*Frage*⟩; strittig ⟨*Punkt*⟩
② *v.t.* erörtern ⟨*Frage, Punkt*⟩

**mop** /mɒp/ ① *n.* **(a)** Mopp, *der*
**(b)** ~ [of hair] Wuschelkopf, *der*
② *v.t.,* **-pp-** moppen ⟨*Fußboden*⟩; (wipe)
abwischen ⟨*Träne, Schweiß, Stirn*⟩
▪ **mop 'up** *v.t.* aufwischen

**mope** /məʊp/ *v.i.* Trübsal blasen

**moped** /'məʊped/ *n.* Moped, *das*

**moral** /'mɒrl/ ① *adj.* **(a)** moralisch; sittlich
⟨*Wert*⟩; Moral⟨*begriff, -prinzip*⟩
**(b)** (virtuous) moralisch ⟨*Leben, Person*⟩
② *n.* **(a)** Moral, *die*
**(b)** *in pl.* (habits) Moral, *die*

**morale** /mə'rɑːl/ *n.* Moral, *die;* **low/high** ~:
schlechte/gute Moral

**mo'rale-booster** *n.* be a *or* act as a ~ for
sb. jds. Moral heben *od.* stärken

**morality** /mə'rælɪtɪ/ *n.* Moral, *die*

**moral sup'port** *n.* moralische
Unterstützung

**morbid** /'mɔːbɪd/ *adj.* krankhaft; morbid
(geh.) ⟨*Faszination, Neigung*⟩

**more** /mɔː(r)/ ① *adj.* mehr; **any** *or* **some** ~
(apples, books, etc.) noch welche; **any** *or* **some**
~ (tea, paper, etc.) noch etwas; **any** *or* **some**
~ **apples/tea** noch Äpfel/Tee; **I haven't any**
~ **[apples/tea]** ich habe keine [Äpfel]/keinen
[Tee] mehr; ~ **and** ~: immer mehr
② *n.* mehr; ~ **and** ~: immer mehr; **six or**
~: mindestens sechs
③ *adv.* **(a)** mehr; ~ **interesting**
interessanter
**(b)** (nearer, rather) eher
**(c)** (again) wieder; **no** ~, **not any** ~: nicht
mehr; **once** ~: noch einmal
**(d)** ~ **and** ~: immer mehr; ~ **and** ~ **absurd**
immer absurder
**(e)** ~ **or less** (fairly) mehr oder weniger;
(approximately) annähernd

**moreish** /'mɔːrɪʃ/ *adj.* (coll.) lecker

**more'over** *adv.* und außerdem

**morgue** /mɔːg/ ▶ MORTUARY

**morning** /'mɔːnɪŋ/ *n.* Morgen, *der;* (not
afternoon) Vormittag, *der; attrib.* morgendlich;
Morgen-; **this** ~: heute Morgen; **tomorrow**
~, (coll.) **in the** ~: morgen früh; **[early] in the**
~: am [frühen] Morgen; (regularly)
[früh]morgens

**morning:** ~ **'after** *n.* ~**-'after** [feeling]
(coll.: hangover) Katzenjammer, *der;* ~**-'after**
**pill** *n.* Pille [für den Morgen] danach;
~ **'star** *n.* Morgenstern, *der*

**Moroccan** /mə'rɒkən/ ① *adj.*
marokkanisch; **sb. is** ~: jmd. ist
Marokkaner/Marokkanerin
② *n.* Marokkaner, *der*/Marokkanerin, *die*

**Morocco** /mə'rɒkəʊ/ *pr. n.* Marokko (*das*)

**moron** /'mɔːrɒn/ *n.* (coll.) Schwachkopf, *der*
(ugs.)

**morose** /mə'rəʊs/ *adj.* verdrießlich

**morphine** /'mɔːfiːn/ *n.* Morphin, *das*

**Morse [code]** /mɔːs ('kəʊd)/ *n.*
Morsealphabet, *das*

**morsel** /'mɔːsl/ *n.* (of food) Bissen, *der*

**mortal** /'mɔːtl/ ① *adj.* **(a)** sterblich
**(b)** (fatal) tödlich (**to** für)
② *n.* Sterbliche, *der/die*

**mortality** /mɔː'tælɪtɪ/ *n.* **(a)** Sterblichkeit,
*die*
**(b)** ~ [rate] Sterblichkeitsrate, *die*

**'mortally** *adv.* tödlich

**mortar** /'mɔːtə(r)/ *n.* **(a)** Mörtel, *der*
**(b)** (vessel) Mörser, *der*
**(c)** (weapon) Minenwerfer, *der;* Mörser, *der*

**mortgage** /'mɔːgɪdʒ/ ① *n.* Hypothek, *die*
② *v.t.* mit einer Hypothek belasten

**mortuary** /'mɔːtjʊərɪ/ *n.* (building)
Leichenschauhaus, *das;* (room)
Leichenkammer, *die*

**mosaic** /məʊ'zeɪɪk/ *n.* Mosaik, *das*

**Moscow** /'mɒskəʊ/ *pr. n.* Moskau (*das*)

**Moselle** /məʊ'zel/ *pr. n.* Mosel, *die*

**Moslem** /'mɒzləm/ ▶ MUSLIM

**mosque** /mɒsk/ *n.* Moschee, *die*

**mosquito** /mɒs'kiːtəʊ/ *n., pl.* ~es
Stechmücke, *die;* (in tropics) Moskito, *der*

**mos'quito net** *n.* Moskitonetz, *das*

**moss** /mɒs/ *n.* Moos, *das*

**'mossy** *adj.* moosig

**most** /məʊst/ ① *adj.* (in number, majority of)
die meisten; (in amount) meist…; **make the**
~ **mistakes/the** ~ **noise** die meisten Fehler/
den größten Lärm machen; **for the** ~ **part**
größtenteils
② *n.* **(a)** (greatest amount) **the** ~ **it will cost is**
**£10** es wird höchstens zehn Pfund kosten;
**pay the** ~: am meisten bezahlen
**(b)** (greater part) ~ **of the girls** die meisten
Mädchen; ~ **of his friends** die meisten
seiner Freunde; ~ **of the poem** der größte
Teil des Gedichts; ~ **of the time** die meiste
Zeit
**(c)** (on ~ occasions) meistens
③ *adv.* **(a)** am meisten; **the** ~ **interesting**
**book** das interessanteste Buch; ~ **often** am
häufigsten
**(b)** (exceedingly) äußerst

**'mostly** *adv.* (most of the time) meistens;
(mainly) größtenteils

**MOT** ▶ MOT TEST

**motel** /məʊ'tel/ *n.* Motel, *das*

**moth** /mɒθ/ *n.* Nachtfalter, *der;* (in clothes)
Motte, *die*

**moth:** ~**ball** *n.* Mottenkugel, *die;*
~**-eaten** *adj.* von Motten zerfressen

**mother** /'mʌðə(r)/ ① *n.* Mutter, *die*
② *v.t.* (over-protect) bemuttern

**'motherboard** *n.* (Comp.) Mutterplatine, *die*

**'motherhood** *n.* Mutterschaft, *die*

**Mothering Sunday** /'mʌðərɪŋ sʌndɪ/
(Brit. Eccl.) ▶ MOTHER'S DAY

**mother:** ~**-in-law** *n., pl.* ~**s-in-law**
Schwiegermutter, *die;* ~**land** *n.* Vaterland,
*das*

**motherly** /'mʌðəlɪ/ *adj.* mütterlich; ~ love
Mutterliebe, *die*

**mother:** ~**-of-'pearl** *n.* Perlmutt, *das;*
M~**'s Day** *n.* Muttertag, *der;* ~ **'tongue**
*n.* Muttersprache, *die*

**moth:** ~ **hole** *n.* Mottenloch, *das;* ~**proof**
*adj.* mottenfest

**motif** /məʊ'tiːf/ *n.* Motiv, *das*

**motion** /'məʊʃn/ ① *n.* (a) Bewegung, *die*
(b) (proposal) Antrag, *der*
② *v.t. & i.* ~ [to] sb. to do sth. jmdm.
bedeuten (geh.), etw. zu tun

**'motionless** *adj.* bewegungslos

**motivate** /'məʊtɪveɪt/ *v.t.* motivieren

**motivation** /məʊtɪ'veɪʃn/ *n.* Motivation,
*die*

**motive** /'məʊtɪv/ *n.* Beweggrund, *der;* the
~ for the crime das Tatmotiv

**motley** /'mɒtlɪ/ *adj.* bunt gemischt

**motor** /'məʊtə(r)/ ① *n.* (a) Motor, *der*
(b) (Brit.: ~ car) Auto, *das*
② *adj.* Motor⟨mäher, -jacht usw.⟩
③ *v.i.* (Brit.) [mit dem Auto] fahren

**motor:** ~**bike** *n.* (coll.) Motorrad, *das;*
~ **boat** *n.* Motorboot, *das*

**motorcade** /'məʊtəkeɪd/ *n.* Fahrzeug- od.
Wagenkolonne, *die*

**motor:** ~ **car** *n.* (Brit.) Kraftfahrzeug, *das;*
~ **cycle** *n.* Motorrad, *das;* ~**cyclist** *n.*
Motorradfahrer, *der*/-fahrerin, *die*

**'motoring** *n.* (Brit.) Autofahren, *das*

**'motorist** *n.* Autofahrer, *der*/-fahrerin, *die*

**motorize** /'məʊtəraɪz/ *v.t.* motorisieren

**motor:** ~ **racing** *n.* Autorennsport, *der;*
~ **show** *n.* Auto[mobil]ausstellung, *die;*
~ **vehicle** *n.* Kraftfahrzeug, *das;* ~**way**
*n.* (Brit.) Autobahn, *die*

**MOT test** *n.* (Brit.) ≈ TÜV, *der*

**mottled** /'mɒtld/ *adj.* gesprenkelt

**motto** /'mɒtəʊ/ *n., pl.* ~**es** Motto, *das*

**mould¹** /məʊld/ ① *n.* (hollow container) Form,
*die*
② *v.t.* formen (out of, from aus)

**mould²** *n.* (Bot.) Schimmel, *der*

**moulder** /'məʊldə(r)/ *v.i.* ~ [away]
[ver]modern

**'moulding** *n.* (a) Formteil, *das* (of, in aus);
(Archit.) Zierleiste, *die*
(b) (wooden) Leiste, *die*

**'mouldy** *adj.* schimmlig; go ~: schimmeln

**moult** /məʊlt/ *v.i.* ⟨Vogel:⟩ sich mausern;
⟨Hund, Katze:⟩ sich haaren

**mound** /maʊnd/ *n.* (a) (of earth) Hügel, *der*
(b) (heap) Haufen, *der*

**mount** /maʊnt/ ① *n.* (a) M~ Vesuvius/
Everest der Vesuv/der Mount Everest
(b) (animal) Reittier, *das;* (horse) Pferd, *das*
(c) (of picture, photograph) Passepartout, *das*
(d) (for gem) Fassung, *die*
② *v.t.* (a) hinaufsteigen ⟨Treppe⟩; steigen auf
(+ Akk.) ⟨Plattform, Reittier, Fahrzeug⟩
(b) aufziehen ⟨Bild⟩; einfassen ⟨Edelstein
usw.⟩
(c) inszenieren ⟨Stück, Oper⟩; organisieren
⟨Ausstellung⟩; durchführen ⟨Angriff,
Operation⟩
③ *v.i.* ~ [up] (increase) steigen (to auf + Akk.)

**mountain** /'maʊntɪn/ *n.* Berg, *der;* in the
~s im Gebirge

**mountain:** ~ **bike** *n.* Mountainbike, *das;*
~ **chain** *n.* Gebirgszug, *der*

**mountaineer** /maʊntɪ'nɪə(r)/ *n.*
Bergsteiger, *der*/Bergsteigerin, *die*

**mountai'neering** *n.* Bergsteigen, *das*

**mountainous** /'maʊntɪnəs/ *adj.* (a)
gebirgig
(b) (huge) riesig

**mountain:** ~ **'range** *n.* Gebirgszug, *der;*
~**side** *n.* [Berg][ab]hang, *der;* ~ **top** *n.*
Berggipfel, *der*

**mourn** /mɔːn/ ① *v.i.* trauern; ~ for *or* over
trauern um ⟨Toten⟩
② *v.t.* betrauern

**'mourner** *n.* Trauernde, *der*/*die*

**mournful** /'mɔːnfl/ *adj.* klagend ⟨Stimme,
Ton, Schrei⟩; trauervoll (geh.) ⟨Person⟩

**'mourning** *n.* Trauer, *die;* be in/go into ~:
Trauer tragen/anlegen

**mouse** /maʊs/ *n., pl.* mice /maɪs/ Maus, *die*

**mouse:** ~ **button** *n.* (Comp.) Maustaste,
*die;* ~ **click** *n.* (Comp.) Mausklick, *der;*
~ **mat** *n.* (Comp.) Mauspad, *das;*
~ **pointer** *n.* (Comp.) Mauszeiger, *der;*
~**trap** *n.* Mausefalle, *die*

**mousse** /muːs/ *n.* Mousse, *die*

**moustache** /mə'stɑːʃ/ *n.* Schnurrbart, *der*

**mousy** /'maʊsɪ/ *adj.* (a) mattbraun ⟨Haar⟩
(b) (timid) scheu

**mouth** ① /maʊθ/ *n.* (a) (of person) Mund,
*der;* (of animal) Maul, *das;* with one's ~ open/
full mit offenem/vollem Mund
(b) (harbour entrance) [Hafen]einfahrt, *die;* (of
tunnel, cave) Eingang, *der;* (of river) Mündung,
*die*
② /maʊð/ *v.t.* mit Lippenbewegungen sagen

**mouthful** /'maʊθfʊl/ *n.* Mundvoll, *der*

**mouth:** ~ **organ** *n.* Mundharmonika, *die;*
~**piece** *n.* (a) Mundstück, *das;* (b) (fig.)
Sprachrohr, *das*

**movable** /'muːvəbl/ *adj.* beweglich

**move** /muːv/ ① *n.* (a) (change of home)
Umzug, *der*

**(b)** (action taken) Schritt, *der;* (Footb. etc.)
Spielzug, *der*
**(c)** (turn in game) Zug, *der;* **make a** ~: ziehen;
it's your ~: du bist am Zug
**(d) be on the** ~ ⟨*Person:*⟩ unterwegs sein
**(e) make a** ~ (do sth.) etwas tun; (coll.: leave)
losziehen (ugs.)
**(f) get a** ~ **on** (coll.) einen Zahn zulegen
(ugs.); **get a** ~ **on!** (coll.) [mach] Tempo! (ugs.)
2 *v.t.* **(a)** (change position of) bewegen;
wegräumen ⟨*Hindernis, Schutt*⟩; (transport)
befördern; ~ **sth. to a new position** etw. an
einen neuen Platz bringen; ~ **house**
umziehen
**(b)** (in game) ziehen
**(c)** (affect) bewegen; ~ **sb. to tears** jmdn. zu
Tränen rühren; **be** ~**d by sth.** über etw.
(*Akk.*) gerührt sein
**(d)** (prompt) ~ **sb. to do sth.** jmdn. dazu
bewegen, etw. zu tun
**(e)** (propose) beantragen
3 *v.i.* **(a)** sich bewegen; (in vehicle) fahren
**(b)** (in games) ziehen
**(c)** (do sth.) handeln
**(d)** (change home) umziehen (**to** nach); ~ **into
a flat** in eine Wohnung einziehen; ~ **out of a
flat** aus einer Wohnung ausziehen; ~ **to
London** nach London ziehen
**(e)** (change posture or state) sich bewegen;
**don't** ~**!** keine Bewegung!
▪ **move a'bout** 1 *v.i.* zugange sein; (travel)
unterwegs sein
2 *v.t.* herumräumen
▪ **move a'long** 1 *v.i.* **(a)** gehen/fahren
**(b)** ~ **along, please!** gehen/fahren Sie bitte
weiter!
2 *v.t.* zum Weitergehen/-fahren auffordern
▪ **move 'in** 1 *v.i.* **(a)** (to home etc.)
einziehen
**(b)** ~ **in on** ⟨*Truppen, Polizeikräfte:*⟩
vorrücken gegen
2 *v.t.* hineinbringen
▪ **move 'off** *v.i.* sich in Bewegung setzen
▪ **move 'on** 1 *v.i.* weitergehen/-fahren;
~ **on to another question** (fig.) zu einer
anderen Frage übergehen
2 *v.t.* zum Weitergehen/-fahren auffordern
▪ **move 'out** *v.t.* ausziehen (**of** aus)
▪ **move 'over** *v.i.* rücken
▪ **move 'up** *v.i.* **(a)** rücken
**(b)** (in queue, hierarchy) aufrücken
'**movement** *n.* **(a)** Bewegung, *die;* (trend,
tendency) Tendenz, *die* (**towards** zu)
**(b)** *in pl.* Aktivitäten *Pl.*
**(c)** (Mus.) Satz, *der*
**movie** /'mu:vɪ/ *n.* (Amer. coll.) Film, *der;* **the**
~**s** der Film; **go to the** ~**s** ins Kino gehen
**moving** /'mu:vɪŋ/ *adj.* **(a)** beweglich
**(b)** (affecting) ergreifend
**mow** /məʊ/ *v.t., p.p.* **mown** /məʊn/ *or*
**mowed** /məʊd/ mähen
▪ **mow 'down** *v.t.* (shoot) niedermähen
⟨*Menschen*⟩
'**mower** *n.* Rasenmäher, *der*
**mown** ▶ MOW

**MP** *abbr.* = **Member of Parliament**
**m.p.g.** *abbr.* = **miles per gallon**
**m.p.h.** *abbr.* = **miles per hour**
**MPV** *abbr.* = **multi-purpose vehicle**
**Mr** /'mɪstə(r)/ *n.* Herr; (in an address) Herrn
**Mrs** /'mɪsɪz/ *n.* Frau
**Ms** /mɪz/ *n.* Frau
**MS** *abbr.* (Med.) = **multiple sclerosis**
MS
**Mt.** *abbr.* = **Mount**
**much** /mʌtʃ/ 1 *adj.,* **more** /mɔː(r)/, **most**
/məʊst/ viel; **too** ~: zu viel *indekl*
2 *n.* vieles; ~ **of the day** der Großteil des
Tages; **not be** ~ **to look at** nicht sehr
ansehnlich sein
3 *adv.,* **more, most (a)** viel ⟨*besser, schöner
usw.*⟩; ~ **more lively/attractive** viel lebhafter/
attraktiver
**(b)** mit Abstand ⟨*der/die/das Beste, Klügste
usw.*⟩
**(c)** (greatly) sehr ⟨*lieben, genießen usw.*⟩; (for
~ of the time) viel ⟨*lesen, spielen usw.*⟩; (often)
oft ⟨*sehen, besuchen usw.*⟩
**(d)** [pretty *or* very] ~ **the same** fast [genau]
der-/die-/dasselbe
**muck** /mʌk/ *n.* **(a)** (coll.: something disgusting)
Dreck, *der* (ugs.)
**(b)** (coll.: nonsense) Mist, *der* (ugs.)
▪ **muck a'bout, muck a'round** (Brit.
coll.) *v.i.* **(a)** herumalbern (ugs.)
**(b)** (tinker) herumfummeln (**with** an + *Dat.*)
▪ **muck 'in** *v.i.* (coll.) mit anpacken (**with**
bei)
▪ **muck 'up** *v.t.* **(a)** (Brit. coll.: bungle)
vermurksen (ugs.)
**(b)** (make dirty) dreckig machen (ugs.)
**(c)** (coll.: spoil) vermasseln (salopp)
'**mucky** *adj.* dreckig (ugs.)
**mucus** /'mju:kəs/ *n.* Schleim, *der*
**mud** /mʌd/ *n.* Schlamm, *der*
**muddle** /'mʌdl/ 1 *n.* Durcheinander, *das*
2 *v.t.* ~ [**up**] durcheinander bringen; ~ **up**
(mix up) verwechseln (**with** mit)
▪ **muddle a'long, muddle 'on** *v.i.* vor
sich (*Akk.*) hin wursteln (ugs.)
▪ **muddle 'through** *v.i.* sich
durchwursteln (ugs.)
**muddy** /'mʌdɪ/ *adj.* schlammig; **get** *or*
**become** ~: verschlammen
'**mudguard** *n.* Schutzblech, *das;* (of car)
Kotflügel, *der*
**muesli** /'mju:zlɪ/ *n.* Müsli, *das*
**muff¹** /mʌf/ *n.* Muff, *der*
**muff²** *v.t.* verpatzen (ugs.)
**muffin** /'mʌfɪn/ *n.* Muffin, *der*
**muffle** /'mʌfl/ *v.t.* **(a)** (envelop) ~ [**up**]
einhüllen
**(b)** dämpfen ⟨*Geräusch*⟩
'**muffler** *n.* **(a)** (wrap, scarf) Schal, *der*
**(b)** (Amer. Motor Veh.) Schalldämpfer, *der*
**mug** /mʌg/ 1 *n.* **(a)** Becher, *der* (meist mit
Henkel); (for beer etc.) Krug, *der*
**(b)** (coll.: face, mouth) Visage, *die* (salopp)

···⊹

**(c)** (Brit. coll.: gullible person) Trottel, *der* (ugs.)
② *v.t.*, **-gg-** (rob) überfallen und berauben

'**mugger** *n.* Straßenräuber, *der*/-räuberin, *die*

'**mugging** *n.* Straßenraub, *der*

**muggy** /'mʌgɪ/ *adj.* schwül

**mule** /mjuːl/ *n.* Maultier, *das*

**multi:** ∼**coloured** (Brit.; Amer.: ∼**colored**) *adj.* mehrfarbig; bunt ⟨*Stoff, Kleid*⟩; ∼'**cultural** *adj.* multikulturell; ∼**function button** *n.* Multifunktionstaste, *die;* ∼**media** *n. sing.* Multimedia, *das;* ∼**millio'naire** *n.* Multimillionär, *der*/-millionärin, *die;* ∼**national** /mʌltɪ'næʃənl/ ① *adj.* multinational; ② *n.* multinationaler Konzern, *der;* Multi, *der* (ugs.)

**multiple** /'mʌltɪpl/ *adj.* mehrfach

**multiple:** ∼-'**choice** *adj.* Multiplechoice⟨*test, -frage*⟩; ∼ '**store** *n.* (Brit.) Kettenladen, *der*

**multiplication** /mʌltɪplɪ'keɪʃn/ *n.* Multiplikation, *die*

**multiply** /'mʌltɪplaɪ/ ① *v.t.* multiplizieren, malnehmen (by mit) ② *v.i.* sich vermehren

**multi:** ∼-**purpose** *adj.* Mehrzweck-; ∼-**purpose 'vehicle** *n.* Großraumlimousine, *die;* '∼-**storey** *adj.* mehrstöckig; mehrgeschossig; ∼-**storey car park/block of flats** Parkhaus/Wohnhochhaus, *das;* ∼**track** *adj.* mehrspurig; Mehrspur⟨*aufnahme, -ton, -tonbandgerät*⟩

**multitude** /'mʌltɪtjuːd/ *n.* (crowd) Menge, *die;* (great number) Vielzahl, *die*

**mum**[1] /mʌm/ (coll.) ① *int.* ∼'s the word nicht weitersagen! ② *adj.* keep ∼: den Mund halten (ugs.)

**mum**[2] *n.* (Brit. coll.: mother) Mama, *die* (fam.)

**mumble** /'mʌmbl/ *v.i. & t.* nuscheln (ugs.)

**mummy**[1] *n.* (Brit. coll.: mother) Mutti, *die* (fam.)

**mummy**[2] /'mʌmɪ/ *n.* Mumie, *die*

**mumps** /mʌmps/ *n.* Mumps, *der*

**munch** /mʌntʃ/ *v.t. & i.* ∼ [one's food] mampfen (salopp)

**mundane** /mʌn'deɪn/ *adj.* **(a)** (dull) banal **(b)** (worldly) weltlich

**Munich** /'mjuːnɪk/ *pr. n.* München ⟨*das*⟩

**municipal** /mjʊ'nɪsɪpl/ *adj.* kommunal; Kommunal⟨*politik, -verwaltung*⟩

**munition** /mjuː'nɪʃn/ *n., usu. in pl.* Kriegsmaterial, *das;* ∼[s] **factory** Rüstungsbetrieb, *der*

**mural** /'mjʊərl/ *n.* Wandbild, *das*

**murder** /'mɜːdə(r)/ ① *n.* Mord, *der* (of an + *Dat.*) ② *v.t.* ermorden

'**murderer** *n.* Mörder, *der*/Mörderin, *die*

**murderess** /'mɜːdərɪs/ *n.* Mörderin, *die*

**murderous** /'mɜːdərəs/ *adj.* tödlich; Mord⟨*absicht, -drohung*⟩; mörderisch (ugs.) ⟨*Kampf*⟩

**murk** /mɜːk/ *n.* Dunkelheit, *die*

'**murky** *adj.* **(a)** (dark) düster **(b)** (dirty) schmutzig-trüb ⟨*Wasser*⟩

**murmur** /'mɜːmə(r)/ ① *n.* **(a)** (subdued sound) Rauschen, *das* **(b)** (expression of discontent) Murren, *das* **(c)** (soft speech) Murmeln, *das* ② *v.t.* murmeln ③ *v.i.* ⟨*Person:*⟩ murmeln; (complain) murren

**muscle** /'mʌsl/ *n.* Muskel, *der*

**muscular** /'mʌskjʊlə(r)/ *adj.* **(a)** (Anat.) Muskel- **(b)** (strong) muskulös

**muse** /mjuːz/ (literary) *v.i.* [nach]sinnen (geh.) (on, over über + *Akk.*)

**museum** /mjuː'ziːəm/ *n.* Museum, *das*

**mush** /mʌʃ/ *n.* Brei, *der*

**mushroom** /'mʌʃrʊm, 'mʌʃruːm/ ① *n.* Pilz, *der;* (cultivated) Champignon, *der* ② *v.i.* wie Pilze aus dem Boden schießen

'**mushroom cloud** *n.* Rauchpilz, *der;* (after nuclear explosion) Atompilz, *der*

'**mushy** *adj.* breiig

**music** /'mjuːzɪk/ *n.* **(a)** Musik, *die;* piece of ∼: Musikstück, *das;* set sth. to ∼: etw. vertonen **(b)** (score) Noten *Pl.*

**musical** /'mjuːzɪkl/ ① *adj.* musikalisch; Musik⟨*instrument, -verständnis, -notation, -abend*⟩ ② *n.* Musical, *das*

'**musical box** *n.* (Brit.) Spieldose, *die*

**musician** /mjuː'zɪʃn/ *n.* Musiker, *der*/ Musikerin, *die*

**music:** ∼ **lesson** *n.* Musikstunde, *die;* ∼ **room** *n.* Musiksaal, *der;* ∼ **stand** *n.* Notenständer, *der;* ∼ **teacher** *n.* Musiklehrer, *der*/-lehrerin, *die;* ∼ **video** *n.* Musikvideo, *das*

**Muslim** /'mʊslɪm, 'mʌzlɪm/ ① *adj.* moslemisch ② *n.* Moslem, *der*/Moslime, *die*

**muslin** /'mʌzlɪn/ *n.* Musselin, *der*

**mussel** /'mʌsl/ *n.* Muschel, *die*

**must** /məst, stressed mʌst/ ① *v. aux., only in pres., neg.* (coll.) **mustn't** /'mʌsnt/ müssen; with neg. dürfen ② *n.* (coll.) Muss, *das*

**mustache** ▶ MOUSTACHE

**mustard** /'mʌstəd/ *n.* Senf, *der*

**muster** /'mʌstə(r)/ ① *n.* pass ∼: akzeptabel sein ② *v.t.* versammeln; (Mil., Naut.) [zum Appell] antreten lassen; (fig.) zusammennehmen ⟨*Kraft, Mut, Verstand*⟩ ③ *v.i.* sich [ver]sammeln
■ **muster 'up** *v.t.* aufbringen

**mustn't** /'mʌsnt/ (coll.) = must not; ▶ MUST 1

**musty** /'mʌstɪ/ *adj.* muffig

**mutant** /'mju:tənt/ ① adj. mutiert
② n. Mutante, die
**mutation** /mju:'teɪʃn/ n. Mutation, die
**mute** /mju:t/ ① adj. stumm
② n. Stumme, der/die
**'muted** adj. gedämpft
**mutilate** /'mju:tɪleɪt/ v.t. verstümmeln
**mutilation** /mju:tɪ'leɪʃn/ n.
Verstümmelung, die
**mutinous** /'mju:tɪnəs/ adj. meuternd
**mutiny** /'mju:tɪnɪ/ ① n. Meuterei, die
② v.i. meutern
**mutter** /'mʌtə(r)/ v.i. & t. murmeln
**'muttering** n. Gemurmel, das
**mutton** /'mʌtn/ n. Hammelfleisch, das
**mutual** /'mju:tjʊəl/ adj. (a) gegenseitig
(b) (coll.: shared) gemeinsam
**'mutually** adv. (a) gegenseitig; **be
~ exclusive** sich [gegenseitig] ausschließen
(b) (in common) gemeinsam
**muzak** /'mju:zæk/ n. (often derog.)
Hintergrundmusik, die
**muzzle** /'mʌzl/ ① n. (a) (of dog) Schnauze,
die; (of horse, cattle) Maul, das
(b) (of gun) Mündung, die
(c) (put over animal's mouth) Maulkorb, der
② v.t. (a) einen Maulkorb anlegen (+ Dat.)
⟨Hund⟩
(b) (fig.) mundtot machen (ugs.) (+ Dat.)
**muzzy** /'mʌzɪ/ adj. verschwommen; **feel ~:**
ein dumpfes Gefühl haben
**MW** abbr. (Radio) = **medium wave** MW

**my** /maɪ/ poss. pron. attrib. mein; **my[, my]!,
[my] oh my!** [ach du] meine Güte! (ugs.)
**myalgic encephalomyelitis**
/maɪældʒɪk ensefələʊmaɪə'laɪtɪs/ n. (Med.)
myalgische Enzephalomyelitis
**myopia** /maɪ'ɒpɪə/ n. Kurzsichtigkeit, die
(auch fig.)
**myopic** /maɪ'ɒpɪk/ adj. kurzsichtig (auch
fig.)
**myself** /maɪ'self/ pron. (a) emphat. selbst; **I
thought so ~:** das habe ich auch gedacht
(b) refl. mich/mir. See also HERSELF
**mysterious** /mɪ'stɪərɪəs/ adj. rätselhaft;
geheimnisvoll ⟨Fremder, Orient⟩
**my'steriously** adv. auf rätselhafte Weise;
geheimnisvoll ⟨lächeln usw.⟩
**mystery** /'mɪstərɪ/ n. (a) Rätsel, das
(b) (secrecy) Geheimnis, das
**mystery: ~ tour** n. Fahrt ins Blaue (ugs.);
**~ writer** Kriminalschriftsteller, der/
-schriftstellerin, die
**mystic** /'mɪstɪk/ ① adj. mystisch
② n. Mystiker, der/Mystikerin, die
**mystical** /'mɪstɪkl/ adj. mystisch
**mysticism** /'mɪstɪsɪzm/ n. Mystik, die
**mystify** /'mɪstɪfaɪ/ v.t. verwirren
**myth** /mɪθ/ n. Mythos, der
**mythical** /'mɪθɪkl/ adj. (a) (based on myth)
mythisch
(b) (invented) fiktiv
**mythological** /mɪθə'lɒdʒɪkl/ adj.
mythologisch
**mythology** /mɪ'θɒlədʒɪ/ n. Mythologie, die

**n**

# Nn

**N, n** /en/ n. N, n, das
**N.** abbr. (a) = **north** N
(b) = **northern** n.
**NAAFI** /'næfɪ/ abbr. (Brit.) **Navy, Army and
Air Force Institutes** Kaufhaus für Angehörige
der britischen Truppen
**nab** /næb/ v.t., -bb- (coll.) (a) (arrest)
schnappen (ugs.)
(b) (seize) sich (Dat.) schnappen
**nag** /næg/ v.i. & t. -gg-: **~ [at] sb.** an jmdm.
herumnörgeln; **~ [at] sb. to do sth.** jmdm.
zusetzen (ugs.), dass er etw. tut
**'nagging** ① adj. (persistent) quälend;
bohrend ⟨Schmerz⟩
② n. Genörgel, das
**nail** /neɪl/ ① n. Nagel, der; **hit the ~ on the
head** (fig.) den Nagel auf den Kopf treffen
(ugs.)
② v.t. nageln (**to** an + Akk.)

■ **nail 'down** v.t. festnageln; zunageln
⟨Kiste⟩

**nail: ~ brush** n. Nagelbürste, die;
**~ clippers** n. pl. [pair of] **~ clippers**
Nagelknipser, der; **~ file** n. Nagelfeile, die;
**~ polish** n. Nagellack, der; **~ polish
remover** Nagellackentferner, der;
**~ scissors** n. pl. [pair of] **~ scissors**
Nagelschere, die; **~ varnish** (Brit.)
▶ **~ POLISH**

**naive, naïve** /naɪ'i:v/ adj., **na'ively,
na'ïvely** adv. naiv
**naked** /'neɪkɪd/ adj. nackt; **visible to** or
**with the ~ eye** mit bloßem Auge zu
erkennen
**'nakedness** n. Nacktheit, die
**name** /neɪm/ ① n. (a) Name, der; **what's
your ~/the ~ of this place?** wie heißt du/
dieser Ort?; **my ~ is Jack** ich heiße Jack; ⋯⫶

last ~: Nachname, *der;* by ~: namentlich
⟨*erwähnen, aufrufen usw.*⟩; know sb. by ~:
jmdn. mit Namen kennen
**(b)** (reputation) Ruf, *der;* make a ~ for oneself
sich (*Dat.*) einen Namen machen
**(c)** call sb. ~s jmdn. beschimpfen
[2] *v.t.* **(a)** (give ~ to) einen Namen geben
(+ *Dat.*); ~ sb. John jmdn. John nennen;
~ sb./sth. after *or* (Amer.) for sb. jmdn./etw.
nach jmdm. benennen; be ~d John John
heißen; a man ~d Smith ein Mann namens
Smith
**(b)** (call by right ~) benennen
**(c)** (nominate) ~ sb. [as] sth. jmdn. zu etw.
ernennen
'**name-drop** *v.i.* [scheinbar beiläufig]
bekannte Namen fallen lassen
'**nameless** *adj.* namenlos
'**namely** *adv.* nämlich
'**namesake** /'neɪmseɪk/ *n.* Namensvetter, *der*/
-schwester, *die*
**nanny** /'nænɪ/ *n.* (Brit.) Kindermädchen, *das*
**nanny:** ~ **goat** *n.* Ziege, *die;* ~ '**state** *n.*
(derog.) Versorgungsstaat, *der*
**nap** /næp/ [1] *n.* Nickerchen, *das* (fam.); have
a ~: ein Nickerchen halten
[2] *v.i.,* **-pp-** dösen (ugs.); catch sb. ~ping (fig.)
jmdn. überrumpeln
**nape** /neɪp/ *n.* ~ [of the neck] Nacken, *der;*
Genick, *das*
**napkin** /'næpkɪn/ *n.* Serviette, *die*
**Naples** /'neɪplz/ *pr. n.* Neapel (*das*)
**nappy** /'næpɪ/ *n.* (Brit.) Windel, *die*
**narcissistic** /nɑːsɪ'sɪstɪk/ *adj.* narzisstisch
**narcissus** /nɑː'sɪsəs/ *n., pl.* **narcissi**
/nɑː'sɪsaɪ/ *or* ~**es** Narzisse, *die*
**narcotic** /nɑː'kɒtɪk/ [1] *n.* **(a)** (drug)
Rauschgift, *das*
**(b)** (active ingredient) Betäubungsmittel, *das*
[2] *adj.* **(a)** narkotisch; ~ drug Rauschgift,
*das*
**(b)** (causing drowsiness) einschläfernd
**narrate** /nə'reɪt/ *v.t.* erzählen;
kommentieren ⟨*Film*⟩
**narration** /nə'reɪʃn/ *n.* Erzählung, *die*
**narrative** /'nærətɪv/ [1] *n.* Erzählung, *die*
[2] *adj.* erzählend
**narrator** /nə'reɪtə(r)/ *n.* Erzähler, *der*/
Erzählerin, *die*
**narrow** /'nærəʊ/ [1] *adj.* **(a)** schmal; schmal
geschnitten ⟨*Rock, Hose, Ärmel usw.*⟩; eng
⟨*Tal, Gasse*⟩
**(b)** (limited) eng; begrenzt ⟨*Auswahl*⟩
**(c)** knapp ⟨*Sieg, Mehrheit*⟩; have a ~ escape
mit knapper Not entkommen (from *Dat.*)
**(d)** (not tolerant) engstirnig
[2] *v.i.* sich verschmälern; ⟨*Tal:*⟩ sich
verengen
[3] *v.t.* verschmälern; (fig.) einengen
■ **narrow 'down** *v.t.* einengen (to auf
+ *Akk.*)
**narrow-'minded** *adj.* engstirnig
**nasal** /'neɪzl/ *adj.* **(a)** (Anat.) Nasen-

**(b)** näselnd; speak in a ~ voice näseln
**nastily** /'nɑːstɪlɪ/ *adv.* **(a)** (unpleasantly)
scheußlich
**(b)** (ill-naturedly) gemein; behave ~: hässlich
sein
**nasty** /'nɑːstɪ/ *adj.* **(a)** (unpleasant) scheußlich
⟨*Geruch, Geschmack*⟩; gemein ⟨*Trick,
Person*⟩; hässlich ⟨*Angewohnheit*⟩; that was a
~ thing to say/do das war gemein
**(b)** (ill-natured) böse; be ~ to sb. hässlich zu
jmdm. sein
**(c)** (serious) übel; schlimm ⟨*Krankheit,
Husten, Verletzung*⟩; she had a ~ fall sie ist
übel gefallen
**nation** /'neɪʃn/ *n.* Nation, *die;* (people) Volk,
*das*
**national** /'næʃənl/ [1] *adj.* national;
National⟨*flagge, -held, -theater, -gericht,
-charakter*⟩; Staats⟨*sicherheit, -religion*⟩;
überregional ⟨*Rundfunkstation, Zeitung*⟩;
landesweit ⟨*Streik*⟩
[2] *n.* (citizen) Staatsbürger, *der*/-bürgerin, *die;*
foreign ~: Ausländer, *der*/Ausländerin, *die*
**national:** ~ '**anthem** *n.* Nationalhymne,
*die;* ~ **call** *n.* (Brit. Teleph.) Inlandsgespräch,
*das;* ~ '**costume** *n.* Nationaltracht, *die;*
N~ '**Health [Service]** *n.* (Brit.)
staatlicher Gesundheitsdienst; N~ Health
doctor/patient/spectacles ≈ Kassenarzt, *der*/
-patient, *der*/-brille, *die;* N~ **In'surance**
*n.* (Brit.) Sozialversicherung, *die*
**nationalism** /'næʃənəlɪzm/ *n.*
Nationalismus, *der*
**nationalist** /'næʃənəlɪst/ [1] *n.* Nationalist,
*der*/Nationalistin, *die*
[2] *adj.* nationalistisch
**nationality** /næʃə'nælɪtɪ/ *n.*
Staatsangehörigkeit, *die;* what's his ~?
welche Staatsangehörigkeit hat er?
**nationalization** /næʃənəlaɪ'zeɪʃn/ *n.*
Verstaatlichung, *die*
**nationalize** /'næʃənəlaɪz/ *v.t.*
verstaatlichen
'**nationally** *adv.* landesweit
**National:** n~ '**park** *n.* Nationalpark, *der;*
~ '**Savings** *n. pl.* (Brit.)
Staatsschuldverschreibungen *Pl.;* ~ Savings
certificate Sparkassengutschein, *der;*
öffentlicher Sparbrief; n~ '**service** *n.*
(Brit.) Wehrdienst, *der;* do n~ service seinen
Wehrdienst ableisten; ~ '**Socialist** *n.*
Nationalsozialist, *der*/-sozialistin, *die; attrib.*
nationalsozialistisch; ~ **Vo'cational
Qualification** *n.* (Brit.) staatliches
*Berufsausbildungsprogramm*
**native** /'neɪtɪv/ [1] *n.* **(a)** (of specified place) a
~ of Britain ein gebürtiger Brite/eine
gebürtige Britin
**(b)** (person born in a place) Eingeborene, *der*/
*die*
**(c)** (local inhabitant) Einheimische, *der*/*die*
[2] *adj.* eingeboren; einheimisch ⟨*Pflanze,
Tier*⟩; ~ inhabitant Eingeborene/

Einheimische, *der*/*die;* ~ land Geburts- *od.*
Heimatland, *das;* ~ language
Muttersprache, *die*

**nativity** /nə'tɪvɪtɪ/ *n.* the N~ [of Christ] die
Geburt Christi

**na'tivity play** *n.* Krippenspiel, *das*

**NATO, Nato** /'neɪtəʊ/ *abbr.* = **North
Atlantic Treaty Organization**
NATO, *die*

**natter** /'nætə(r)/ (Brit. coll.) **1** *v.i.* quatschen
(ugs.)
**2** *n.* have a ~: quatschen (ugs.)

**natural** /'nætʃrəl/ *adj.* natürlich;
Natur⟨zustand, -seide, -gewalt⟩

**natural:** ~ **'childbirth** *n.* natürliche
Geburt; ~ **'gas** *n.* Erdgas, *das;*
~ **'history** *n.* Naturkunde, *die*

**naturalism** /'nætʃrəlɪzm/ *n.*
Naturalismus, *der*

**naturalist** /'nætʃrəlɪst/ *n.* Naturforscher,
*der*/-forscherin, *die*

**naturalization** /nætʃrəlaɪ'zeɪʃn/ *n.*
Einbürgerung, *die*

**naturalize** /'nætʃrəlaɪz/ *v.t.* einbürgern

**'naturally** *adv.* (a) (by nature) von Natur aus
⟨blass, fleißig usw.⟩; (in a true-to-life way)
naturgetreu
(b) (of course) natürlich

**'naturalness** Natürlichkeit, *die*

**nature** /'neɪtʃə(r)/ *n.* (a) Natur, *die*
(b) (essential qualities) Beschaffenheit, *die;* in
the ~ of things naturgemäß
(c) (kind) Art, *die;* things of this ~:
derartiges
(d) (character) Wesen, *das;* be proud/friendly
*etc.* by ~: ein stolzes/freundliches *usw.*
Wesen haben

**nature:** ~ **conservation** *n.*
Naturschutz, *der;* ~ **lover** *n.* Naturfreund,
*der*/-freundin, *die;* ~ **reserve** *n.*
Naturschutzgebiet, *das;* ~ **study** *n.*
Naturkunde, *die;* ~ **trail** *n.* Naturlehrpfad,
*der*

**naturist** /'neɪtʃərɪst/ *n.* (nudist) Naturist,
*der*/Naturistin, *die;* FKK-Anhänger, *der*/
FKK-Anhängerin, *die*

**naught** /nɔːt/ *n.* (arch./dial.) come to ~:
zunichte werden

**naughtily** /'nɔːtɪlɪ/ *adv.* ungezogen

**naughtiness** /'nɔːtɪnɪs/ *n.* Ungezogenheit,
*die*

**naughty** /'nɔːtɪ/ *adj.* ungezogen; you
~ boy/dog du böser Junge/Hund

**nausea** /'nɔːzɪə/ *n.* Übelkeit, *die*

**nauseate** /'nɔːzɪeɪt/ *v.t.* (disgust) anwidern

**'nauseating** *adj.* (disgusting) widerlich

**nauseous** /'nɔːzɪəs/ *adj.* sb. is *or* feels ~:
jmdm. ist übel

**nautical** /'nɔːtɪkl/ *adj.* nautisch

**nautical 'mile** *n.* Seemeile, *die*

**naval** /'neɪvl/ *adj.* Marine-; See⟨schlacht,
-macht, -streitkräfte⟩; ~ ship Kriegsschiff,
*das*

**naval:** ~ **base** *n.* Flottenstützpunkt, *der;*
~ **officer** *n.* Marineoffizier, *der*

**nave** /neɪv/ *n.* [Mittel]schiff, *das*

**navel** /'neɪvl/ *n.* Nabel, *der*

**navigate** /'nævɪgeɪt/ *v.t.* (a) navigieren
⟨Schiff, Flugzeug⟩
(b) befahren ⟨Fluss usw.⟩

**navigation** /nævɪ'geɪʃn/ *n.* Navigation, *die*

**navigator** /'nævɪgeɪtə(r)/ *n.* Navigator,
*der*/Navigatorin, *die*

**navy** /'neɪvɪ/ **1** *n.* (a) [Kriegs]marine, *die*
(b) ▶ NAVY BLUE
**2** *adj* ▶ NAVY-BLUE

**navy:** ~ **'blue** *n.* Marineblau, *das;*
~-**blue** *adj.* marineblau

**Nazi** /'nɑːtsɪ/ **1** *n.* Nazi, *der*
**2** *adj.* nazistisch; Nazi-

**NB** *abbr.* = **nota bene** NB

**NCO** *abbr.* = **non-commissioned
officer** Uffz.

**NE** *abbr.* = **north-east** NO

**near** /nɪə(r)/ **1** *adv.* nah[e]; **stand/live
[quite] ~:** [ganz] in der Nähe stehen/
wohnen; **come** *or* **draw ~/~er** ⟨Tag,
Zeitpunkt:⟩ nahen/näher rücken; **get ~er
together** näher zusammenrücken; ~ **at hand**
in Reichweite (*Dat.*); ⟨Ort⟩ ganz in der Nähe;
~ **to** = 2
**2** *prep.* (a) ⟨position⟩ nahe an/bei (+ *Dat.*);
(fig.) in der Nähe (+ *Gen.*); **keep ~ me** halte
dich in meiner Nähe; **it's ~ here** es ist hier
in der Nähe
(b) (motion) nahe an (+ *Akk.*); (fig.) in der
Nähe (+ *Gen.*); **don't come ~ me** komm mir
nicht zu nahe
**3** *adj.* (a) (in space or time) nahe; **in the
~ future** in nächster Zukunft; **the ~est man**
der am nächsten stehende Mann
(b) (in nature) **£30 or ~/~est offer** 30 Pfund
oder nächstbestes Angebot; ~ **escape**
Entkommen mit knapper Not; **that was a
~ miss/thing!** das war knapp!
**4** *v.t.* sich nähern (+ *Dat.*); **the building is
~ing completion** das Gebäude steht kurz
vor seiner Vollendung
**5** *v.i.* ⟨Zeitpunkt:⟩ näher rücken

**'nearby** *adj.* nahe gelegen

**'nearly** *adv.* fast; **be ~ in tears** den Tränen
nahe sein; **it is ~ six o'clock** es ist kurz vor
sechs Uhr; **are you ~ ready?** bist du bald
fertig?

**'nearness** *n.* Nähe, *die*

**'near-sighted** *adj.* (Amer.) kurzsichtig

**neat** /niːt/ *adj.* (a) (tidy) ordentlich
(b) (undiluted) pur
(c) (smart) gepflegt ⟨Erscheinung, Kleidung⟩
(d) (deft) geschickt

**'neatly** *adv.* ▶ NEAT A, C, D: ordentlich;
gepflegt; geschickt

**'neatness** *n.* ▶ NEAT A, C, D: Ordentlichkeit, *die;* Gepflegtheit, *die;* Geschicktheit, *die*

**necessarily** /ˈnesɪˈserɪlɪ/ *adv.* zwangsläufig; **it is not ~ true** es muss nicht [unbedingt] stimmen

**necessary** /ˈnesɪsərɪ/ ⓵ *adj.* nötig; notwendig; **do everything ~**: das Nötige *od.* Notwendige tun ⓶ *n.* **the necessaries of life** das Lebensnotwendige

**necessitate** /nɪˈsesɪteɪt/ *v.t.* erforderlich machen

**necessity** /nɪˈsesɪtɪ/ *n.* **(a)** (need, necessary thing) Notwendigkeit, *die;* **do sth. out of** *or* **from ~**: etw. notgedrungen tun; **of ~**: notwendigerweise **(b)** (want) Not, *der*

**neck** /nek/ *n.* **(a)** Hals, *der;* **be a pain in the ~** (coll.) jmdm. auf die Nerven gehen (ugs.); **break one's ~** (fig. coll.) sich den Hals brechen; **~ and ~**: Kopf an Kopf **(b)** (of garment) Kragen, *der*

**neck: ~lace** /ˈneklɪs/ *n.* [Hals]kette, *die;* (with jewels) Kollier, *das;* **~line** *n.* [Hals]ausschnitt, *der;* **~tie** *n.* Krawatte, *die*

**nectar** /ˈnektə(r)/ *n.* Nektar, *der*

**née** (*Amer.:* **nee**) /neɪ/ *adj.* geborene

**need** /niːd/ ⓵ *n.* **(a)** Notwendigkeit, *die* (for, of *Gen.*); (demand) Bedarf, *der* (for, of an + *Dat.*); **as the ~ arises** nach Bedarf; **if ~ be** nötigenfalls; **there's no ~ for that** [das ist] nicht nötig; **there's no ~ to do sth.** es ist nicht nötig, etw. zu tun; **be in ~ of sth.** etw. brauchen; **there's no ~ for you to come** du brauchst nicht zu kommen **(b)** *no pl.* (emergency) Not, *die;* **in case of ~**: im Notfall **(c)** (thing) Bedürfnis, *das* ⓶ *v.t.* **(a)** (require) brauchen; **sth. that urgently ~s doing** etw., was dringend gemacht werden muss; **it ~s a coat of paint** es muss gestrichen werden **(b)** (expr. necessity) müssen; **I ~ to do it** ich muss es tun; **it ~s/doesn't ~ to be done** es muss getan werden/es braucht nicht getan zu werden **(c)** *pres.* **he ~**, *neg.* **~ not** *or* (coll.) **~n't** /ˈniːdnt/ (expr. desirability) müssen; *with neg.* brauchen zu

**needle** /ˈniːdl/ ⓵ *n.* Nadel, *die* ⓶ *v.t.* (coll.) nerven (ugs.)

**needle: ~cord** *n.* (Textiles) Feinkord, *der;* **~craft** *n.* Nadelarbeit, *die*

**needless** /ˈniːdlɪs/ *adj.* unnötig; **~ to add** *or* **say, ...**: überflüssig zu sagen, dass ...

**'needlessly** *adv.* unnötig

**'needlework** *n.* Handarbeit, *die;* **do ~**: handarbeiten

**needn't** /ˈniːdnt/ (coll.) = **need not**; ▶ NEED 2C

**'needy** *adj.* notleidend; bedürftig

**negation** /nɪˈɡeɪʃn/ *n.* Verneinung, *die*

**negative** /ˈneɡətɪv/ ⓵ *adj.* negativ ⓶ *n.* **(a)** (Photog.) Negativ, *das* **(b)** (~ statement) negative Aussage; (answer) Nein, *das*

**negative 'equity** *n.* Negativwert, *der*

**'negatively** *adv.* negativ

**neglect** /nɪˈɡlekt/ ⓵ *v.t.* vernachlässigen; **she ~ed to write** sie hat es versäumt zu schreiben ⓶ *n.* Vernachlässigung, *die;* **be in a state of ~** ⟨*Gebäude:*⟩ verwahrlost sein

**neglectful** /nɪˈɡlektfl/ *adj.* gleichgültig (of gegenüber); **be ~ of** sich nicht kümmern um

**negligence** /ˈneɡlɪdʒəns/ *n.* Nachlässigkeit, *die;* (Law, Insurance, etc.) Fahrlässigkeit, *die*

**negligent** /ˈneɡlɪdʒənt/ *adj.* nachlässig; **be ~ about sth.** sich um etw. nicht kümmern

**negligible** /ˈneɡlɪdʒɪbl/ *adj.* unerheblich

**negotiable** /nɪˈɡəʊʃəbl/ *adj.* **(a)** verhandlungsfähig ⟨*Forderung, Bedingung*⟩ **(b)** passierbar ⟨*Straße, Fluss*⟩

**negotiate** /nɪˈɡəʊʃɪeɪt/ ⓵ *v.i.* verhandeln (for, on, about über + *Akk.*) ⓶ *v.t.* **(a)** (arrange) aushandeln **(b)** überwinden ⟨*Hindernis*⟩; passieren ⟨*Straße, Fluss*⟩; nehmen ⟨*Kurve*⟩

**negotiation** /nɪɡəʊʃɪˈeɪʃn/ *n.* Verhandlung, *die*

**negotiator** /nɪˈɡəʊʃɪeɪtə(r)/ *n.* Unterhändler, *der/*-händlerin, *die*

**Negress** /ˈniːɡrɪs/ *n.* Negerin, *die*

**Negro** /ˈniːɡrəʊ/ ⓵ *n., pl.* **~es** Neger, *der* ⓶ *adj.* Neger-

**neigh** /neɪ/ ⓵ *v.i.* wiehern ⓶ *n.* Wiehern, *das*

**neighbor** etc. (*Amer.*) ▶ NEIGHBOUR etc.

**neighbour** /ˈneɪbə(r)/ ⓵ *n.* Nachbar, *der/* Nachbarin, *die;* **my next-door ~s** meine Nachbarn von nebenan ⓶ *v.t. & i.* **~ [upon]** grenzen an (+ *Akk.*)

**'neighbourhood** *n.* (district) Gegend, *die;* (neighbours) Nachbarschaft, *die;* **[somewhere] in the ~ of £100** [so] um [die] 100 Pfund

**'neighbourhood watch** *n.*: Programm für Verhütung von Straftaten, bes. von Wohnungseinbrüchen, durch erhöhte Wachsamkeit aller in einem Wohngebiet lebenden Menschen

**'neighbouring** *adj.* Nachbar-; angrenzend ⟨*Felder*⟩

**neighbourly** /ˈneɪbəlɪ/ *adj.* **(a)** (characteristic of neighbours) [gut]nachbarlich **(b)** (friendly) freundlich

**neither** /ˈnaɪðə(r), ˈniːðə(r)/ ⓵ *adj.* keiner/ keine/keins der beiden ⓶ *pron.* keiner/keine/keins von *od.* der beiden ⓷ *adv.* (also not) auch nicht; **~ am I,** (coll.) **me ~**: ich auch nicht ⓸ *conj.* (not either) weder; **~ ... nor ...**: weder ... noch ...

**neo'classical** *adj.* klassizistisch

**neo'fascist** *adj.* neofaszistisch

**neon** /'niːɒn/ *n.* Neon, *das*

**neo-'nazi** [1] *n.* Neonazi, *der*
[2] *adj.* neonazistisch; **a ~ group** eine
Neonazigruppe

**neon:** **~ 'lamp, ~ 'light** *ns.* Neonlampe,
*die;* **~ 'sign** *n.* Neonreklame, *die*

**nephew** /'nevjuː, 'nefjuː/ *n.* Neffe, *der*

**nepotism** /'nepətɪzm/ *n.*
Vetternwirtschaft, *die*

**Neptune** /'neptjuːn/ *pr. n.* (Astron.) Neptun,
*der*

**nerve** /nɜːv/ *n.* Nerv, *der;* **get on sb.'s ~s**
jmdm. auf die Nerven gehen (ugs.); **lose
one's ~:** die Nerven verlieren; **what [a] ~!**
[so eine] Frechheit!

**nerve:** **~ cell** *n.* Nervenzelle, *die;*
**~ centre** *n.* (fig.) Schaltzentrale, *die;*
**~ gas** *n.* Nervengas, *das;* **~-racking** *adj.*
nervenaufreibend

**nervous** /'nɜːvəs/ *adj.* **(a)** (Anat., Med.)
Nerven-; **~ breakdown**
Nervenzusammenbruch, *der*
**(b)** (having delicate nerves) nervös; **be a
~ wreck** mit den Nerven völlig am Ende
sein
**(c)** (Brit.: timid) **be ~ of** *or* **about** Angst haben
vor (+ *Dat.*); **be a ~ person** ängstlich sein

**'nervously** *adv.* nervös

**'nervousness** *n.* Ängstlichkeit, *die*

**nervy** /'nɜːvɪ/ *adj.* **(a)** nervös
**(b)** (Amer. coll.: impudent) unverschämt

**nest** [1] *n.* Nest, *das*
[2] *v.i.* nisten

**'nest egg** *n.* (fig.) Notgroschen, *der*

**nestle** /'nesl/ *v.i.* **(a)** sich schmiegen (**to, up
against** an + *Akk.*)
**(b)** (lie half hidden) eingebettet sein

**net¹** /net/ [1] *n.* **(a)** Netz, *das*
**(b)** **the Net** (Comp.) das Netz
[2] *v.t.,* **-tt-** [mit einem Netz] fangen

**net²** *adj.* **(a)** netto; Netto⟨*einkommen,
-[verkaufs]preis usw.*⟩; **~ weight**
Nettogewicht, *das*
**(b)** (ultimate) End⟨*ergebnis, -effekt*⟩

**net:** **~ball** *n.* Netzball, *der;* **~ 'curtain** *n.*
Store, *der*

**Netherlands** /'neðələndz/ *pr. n. sing. or
pl.* Niederlande *Pl.*

**net 'profit** *n.* Reingewinn, *der*

**'netspeak** *n.* Internetjargon, *der*

**nett** ▸ NET² A

**'netting** *n.* ([piece of] net) Netz, *das;* **wire ~:**
Maschendraht, *der*

**nettle** /'netl/ *n.* Nessel, *die*

**'network** *n.* Netz, *das;* (Comp.) Netzwerk,
*das*

**'network provider** *n.* (Comp)
Netzanbieter, *der*

**neuralgia** /njʊə'rældʒə/ *n.* Neuralgie, *die*

**neurological** /njʊərə'lɒdʒɪkl/ *adj.*
neurologisch

**neurologist** /njʊə'rɒlədʒɪst/ *n.* Neurologe,
*der*/Neurologin, *die*

**neurology** /njʊə'rɒlədʒɪ/ *n.* Neurologie, *die*

**neurosis** /njʊə'rəʊsɪs/ *n., pl.* **neuroses**
/njʊə'rəʊsiːz/ Neurose, *die*

**neurotic** /njʊə'rɒtɪk/ *adj.* **(a)** nervenkrank
**(b)** (coll.) neurotisch

**neuter** /'njuːtə(r)/ *adj.* sächlich

**neutral** /'njuːtrl/ [1] *adj.* neutral
[2] *n.* (~ gear) Leerlauf, *der*

**neutrality** /njuː'trælɪtɪ/ *n.* Neutralität, *die*

**neutralize** /'njuːtrəlaɪz/ *v.t.* neutralisieren

**neutron** /'njuːtrɒn/ *n.* Neutron, *das*

**never** /'nevə(r)/ *adv.* **(a)** nie; **~-ending**
endlos
**(b)** (coll.) **you ~ believed that, did you?** du
hast das doch wohl nicht geglaubt?; **well, I
~ [did]! [na]** so was!

**neverthe'less** *adv.* trotzdem

**new** /njuː/ *adj.* neu

**new:** **New Age** *n.* Newage, *das; attrib.*
Newage-; **~-born** *adj.* neugeboren;
**~comer** /'njuːkʌmə(r)/ *n.*
Neuankömmling, *der;* **~fangled**
/'njuːfæŋgld/ *adj.* neumodisch; **~-found**
*adj.* neu; **~-laid** *adj.* frisch [gelegt]; **New
'Left** *n.* neue Linke; **~ 'look** *n.* (coll.)
neuer Stil

**'newly** *adv.* (recently) neu; **~ married** seit
kurzem verheiratet

**'newly-wed** *n.* Jungverheiratete, *der*/*die*

**new:** **New 'Man** *n.* der neue Mann;
**~ 'moon** *n.* Neumond, *der*

**'newness** *n.* Neuheit, *die*

**news** /njuːz/ *n.* **(a)** Nachricht, *die;* **be in the
~:** Schlagzeilen machen; **good/bad ~:**
schlechte/gute Nachrichten *Pl.*
**(b)** (Radio, Telev.) Nachrichten *Pl.*

**news:** **~ agency** *n.* Nachrichtenagentur,
*die;* **~agent** *n.* Zeitungshändler, *der/*
-händlerin, *die;* **~ bulletin** *n.* Nachrichten
*Pl.;* **~cast** *n.* Nachrichtensendung, *die;*
**~caster** *n.* Nachrichtensprecher, *der/*
-sprecherin, *die;* **~ desk** *n.*
Nachrichtenredaktion, *die;* **this is Joe Smith
at the ~ desk** (Radio) hier ist Joe Smith mit
den Nachrichten; **~flash** *n.* Kurzmeldung,
*die;* **~group** *n.* (Comp.) Newsgroup, *die;*
**~ 'headline** *n.* Schlagzeile, *die;* **~letter**
*n.* Rundschreiben, *das;* **~paper** *n.* **(a)**
Zeitung, *die;* **~paper boy/girl**
Zeitungsausträger, *der/*-austrägerin, *die;* **(b)**
(material) Zeitungspapier, *das;* **~reader** *n.*
Nachrichtensprecher, *der/*-sprecherin, *die;*
**~reel** *n.* Wochenschau, *die;* **~room** *n.*
Nachrichtenredaktion, *die;* **~-sheet** *n.*
Informationsblatt, *das;* **~stand** *n.*
Zeitungskiosk, *der;* Zeitungsstand, *der;*
**~ summary** *n.* Kurznachrichten *Pl.;*
**~ vendor** *n.* Zeitungsverkäufer, *der/*
-verkäuferin, *die;* **~worthy** *adj.* [für die
Medien] interessant

**newt** /njuːt/ *n.* [Wasser]molch, *der*

**n**

**New: new town** *n.*: mit Unterstützung der Regierung völlig neu entstandene Ansiedlung; **new 'year** *n.* Neujahr, *das;* **over the new year** über Neujahr; **a Happy New Year** ein glückliches *od.* gutes neues Jahr; ~ **'Year's** (Amer.), ~ **Year's 'Day** *ns.* Neujahrstag, *der;* ~ **Year's 'Eve** *n.* Silvester, *der od. das;* ~ **Zealand** /- 'ziːlənd/ *pr. n.* Neuseeland (*das*); ~ **'Zealander** *n.* Neuseeländer, *der* /-länderin, *die*

**next** /nekst/ [1] *adj.* nächst...; **the ~ but one** der/die/das Übernächste; ~ **to** (fig.: almost) fast; nahezu; **[the]** ~ **time** das nächste Mal; **the ~ best** der/die/das Nächstbeste; **am I** ~? komme ich jetzt dran?
[2] *adv.* (in the ~ place) als Nächstes; (on the ~ occasion) das nächste Mal; **it's my turn** ~: ich komme als Nächster dran; **sit/stand** ~ **to** sb. neben jmdm. stehen/sitzen; **place sth.** ~ **to sb./sth.** etw. neben jmdn./etw. stellen
[3] *n.* **(a) the week after** ~: [die] übernächste Woche
**(b)** (person) ~ **of kin** nächster/nächste Angehörige; ~, **please!** der Nächste, bitte!

**'next-door** *adj.* gleich nebenan *nachgestellt*

**NHS** *abbr.* (Brit.) = **National Health Service**

**nib** /nɪb/ *n.* Feder, *die*

**nibble** /'nɪbl/ *v.t. & i.* knabbern (**at, on** an + *Dat.*)

**nice** /naɪs/ *adj.* nett; angenehm ‹*Stimme*›; schön ‹*Wetter*›; (iron.: disgraceful, difficult) schön; ~ **[and]** warm/fast schön warm/schnell; ~-**looking** gut aussehen

**'nicely** *adv.* (coll.) **(a)** (well) nett; gut ‹*arbeiten, sich benehmen, platziert sein*› **(b)** (all right) gut; **that will do** ~: das reicht völlig

**niceties** /'naɪsɪtɪz/ *n. pl.* Feinheiten *Pl.*

**niche** /nɪtʃ, niːʃ/ *n.* **(a)** (in wall) Nische, *die* **(b)** (fig.: suitable place) Platz, *der*

**nick** /nɪk/ *n.* **(a)** (notch) Kerbe, *die* **(b)** (sl. prison) Knast, *der* (salopp) **(c)** (Brit.: police station) Wache, *die* **(d) in good/poor** ~ (coll.) gut/nicht gut im Schuss (ugs.) **(e) in the** ~ **of time** gerade noch rechtzeitig
[2] *v.t.* **(a)** einkerben **(b)** (Brit. coll.: arrest) einlochen (salopp) **(c)** (Brit. coll.: steal) klauen (salopp)

**nickel** /'nɪkl/ *n.* **(a)** Nickel, *das* **(b)** (Amer. coll.: coin) Fünfcentstück, *das*

**nickname** /'nɪkneɪm/ *n.* Spitzname, *der;* (affectionate) Koseform, *die*

**nicotine** /'nɪkətiːn/ *n.* Nikotin, *das*

**'nicotine patch** *n.* Nikotinpflaster, *das*

**niece** /niːs/ *n.* Nichte, *die*

**Nigeria** /naɪ'dʒɪərɪə/ *pr. n.* Nigeria (*das*)

**niggardly** /'nɪgədlɪ/ *adj.* knaus[e]rig (ugs.)

**niggling** /'nɪglɪŋ/ *adj.* **(a)** (petty) belanglos **(b)** (trivial) nichts sagend **(c)** (nagging) nagend

**night** /naɪt/ *n.* Nacht, *die;* (evening) Abend, *der;* **the following** ~: die Nacht/der Abend darauf; **the previous** ~: die vorausgegangene Nacht/der vorausgegangene Abend; **on Sunday** ~: Sonntagnacht/[am] Sonntagabend; **for the** ~: über Nacht; **at** ~: nachts/abends; **late at** ~: spätabends

**night:** ~**bird** *n.* (person) Nachteule, *die* (ugs. scherzh.); ~ **blindness** *n.* Nachtblindheit, *die;* ~**cap** *n.* (drink) Schlaftrunk, *der;* ~**clothes** *n. pl.* Nachtwäsche, *die;* ~**club** *n.* Nachtklub, *der;* ~**dress** *n.* Nachthemd, *das;* ~ **duty** *n.* Nachtdienst, *der;* **be on** ~ **duty** Nachtdienst haben; ~**fall** *n.* Einbruch der Dunkelheit

**nightie** /'naɪtɪ/ *n.* (coll.) Nachthemd, *das*

**nightingale** /'naɪtɪŋgeɪl/ *n.* Nachtigall, *die*

**'nightlife** *n.* Nachtleben, *das*

**nightly** /'naɪtlɪ/ [1] *adj.* (happening every night/evening) allnächtlich/allabendlich
[2] *adv.* (every night) jede Nacht; (every evening) jeden Abend

**night:** ~**mare** *n.* Albtraum, *der;* ~**marish** /'naɪtmeərɪʃ/ *adj.* albtraumhaft; ~ **owl** *n.* **(a)** (Ornith.) Eule, *die;* **(b)** (coll.: person) Nachteule, *die* (ugs. scherzh.); ~ **porter** *n.* Nachtportier, *der;* ~ **safe** *n.* Nachttresor, *der;* ~ **school** *n.* Abendschule, *die;* ~ **shelter** *n.* Nachtasyl, *das;* ~ **shift** *n.* Nachtschicht, *die;* ~ **'sky** *n.* Nachthimmel, *der;* ~ **'storage heater** *n.* Nachtspeicherofen, *der;* ~**time** *n.* Nacht, *die;* **in the** *or* **at** ~**time** nachts; ~**'watchman** *n.* Nachtwächter, *der;* ~**wear** *n. sing.* ▶ NIGHTCLOTHES

**nihilistic** /naɪ'lɪstɪk, nɪhɪ'lɪstɪk/ *adj.* nihilistisch

**nil** /nɪl/ *n.* null

**Nile** /naɪl/ *pr. n.* Nil, *der*

**nimble** /'nɪmbl/ *adj.*, **nimbly** /'nɪmblɪ/ *adv.* flink

**nine** /naɪn/ [1] *adj.* neun
[2] *n.* Neun, *die.* See also EIGHT

**nineteen** /naɪn'tiːn/ [1] *adj.* neunzehn
[2] *n.* Neunzehn, *die.* See also EIGHT

**nineteenth** /naɪn'tiːnθ/ [1] *adj.* neunzehnt...
[2] *n.* (fraction) Neunzehntel, *das.* See also EIGHTH

**ninetieth** /'naɪntɪɪθ/ *adj.* neunzigst...

**ninety** /'naɪntɪ/ [1] *adj.* neunzig
[2] *n.* Neunzig, *die.* See also EIGHT; EIGHTY 2

**ninth** /naɪnθ/ [1] *adj.* neunt...
[2] *n.* (in sequence, rank) Neunte, *der/die/das;* (fraction) Neuntel, *das.* See also EIGHTH

**nip** /nɪp/ [1] *v.t.,* **-pp-** zwicken
[2] *v.i.,* **-pp-** (Brit. coll.) ~ **in** hinein-/hereinflitzen (ugs.); ~ **out** hinaus-/herausflitzen (ugs.)
[3] *n.* (pinch, squeeze) Kniff, *der;* (bite) Biss, *der*

**'nipper** *n.* (Brit. coll.: child) Balg, *das* (ugs.)

**nipple** /'nɪpl/ *n.* **(a)** Brustwarze, *die* **(b)** (of feeding bottle) Sauger, *der*

**nitrate** /'naɪtreɪt/ n. (a) (salt) Nitrat, *das*
(b) (fertilizer) Nitratdünger, *der*
**nitric acid** /'naɪtrɪk æsɪd/ n.
Salpetersäure, *die*
**nitrogen** /'naɪtrədʒən/ n. Stickstoff, *der*
'**nitrogen cycle** n. Stickstoffkreislauf, *der*
**nitwit** /'nɪtwɪt/ n. (coll.) Trottel, *der* (ugs.)
**no** /nəʊ/ 1 adj. kein
2 adv. (a) (by no amount) nicht; **no less**
[than] nicht weniger [als]; **no more wine?**
keinen Wein mehr?
(b) (as answer) nein
3 n., pl. **noes** /nəʊz/ Nein, *das*
**No.** abbr. = **number** Nr.
**Noah's ark** /nəʊəz 'ɑːk/ n. die Arche Noah
**Nobel prize** /nəʊbel 'praɪz/ n. Nobelpreis,
*der*
**nobility** /nə'bɪlɪtɪ/ n. Adel, *der;* many of the
~: viele Adlige
**noble** /'nəʊbl/ 1 adj. ad[e]lig; edel
‹Gedanken, Gefühle›
2 n. Adlige, *der/die*
**nobleman** /'nəʊblmən/ n., pl. **noblemen**
/'nəʊblmən/ Adlige, *der*
**nobly** /'nəʊblɪ/ adv. (a) edel [gesinnt]
(b) (generously) edelmütig (geh.)
**nobody** /'nəʊbədɪ/ n. & pron. niemand;
keiner; (person of no importance) Niemand, *der*
**no-'claim[s] bonus** n. (Insurance)
Schadenfreiheitsrabatt, *der*
**nocturnal** /nɒk'tɜːnl/ adj. nächtlich;
~ **animal/bird** Nachttier, *das*/-vogel, *der*
**nod** /nɒd/ 1 v.i., -dd- nicken
2 v.t., -dd-: ~ **one's head [in greeting]** [zum
Gruß] mit dem Kopf nicken
3 n. [Kopf]nicken, *das*
■ **nod 'off** v.i. einnicken (ugs.)
**nodule** /'nɒdjuːl/ n. (a) Klümpchen, *das*
(b) (Bot.) Knötchen, *das*
**no-'fly zone** n. Flugverbotszone, *die*
**no-'go** adj. Sperr‹gebiet, -zone›
'**no-good** adj. (coll.) nichtsnutzig (abwertend)
**no-hoper** /nəʊ'həʊpə(r)/ n. absoluter
Außenseiter; **be a** ~: keine Chance haben
**nohow** /'nəʊhaʊ/ adv. (Amer. coll.) in keiner
Weise
**noise** /nɔɪz/ n. Geräusch, *das;* (loud, harsh,
unwanted) Lärm, *der*
'**noise abatement** n. Lärmbekämpfung,
*die*
'**noiseless** adj., '**noiselessly** adv.
lautlos
**noise:** ~ **level** n. Geräuschpegel, *der;* (of
unpleasant noise) Lärmpegel, *der;*
~ **pollution** n. Lärmbelästigung, *die*
**noisily** /'nɔɪzɪlɪ/ adv., **noisy** /'nɔɪzɪ/ adj.
laut
**nomad** /'nəʊmæd/ n. Nomade, *der*
**nomadic** /nəʊ'mædɪk/ adj. nomadisch;
~ **tribe** Nomadenstamm, *der*
'**no man's land** n. Niemandsland, *das*

**nominal** /'nɒmɪnl/ adj. (a) (in name only)
nominell
(b) (virtually nothing) äußerst gering
**nominally** /'nɒmɪnəlɪ/ adv. namentlich
**nominate** /'nɒmɪneɪt/ v.t. (a) (propose)
nominieren
(b) (appoint) ernennen
**nomination** /nɒmɪ'neɪʃn/ n. ▶ NOMINATE:
Nominierung, *die;* Ernennung, *die*
**nominative** /'nɒmɪnətɪv/ adj. & n.
~ [case] Nominativ, *der*
**nominee** /nɒmɪ'niː/ n. (candidate) Kandidat,
*der*/Kandidatin, *die*
**non-** /nɒn/ pref. nicht-
**non-alco'holic** adj. alkoholfrei
**nonchalant** /'nɒnʃələnt/ adj.
unbekümmert
**non-commissioned 'officer** n.
Unteroffizier, *der*
**non-committal** /nɒnkə'mɪtl/ adj.
unverbindlich; **he was** ~: er hat sich nicht
klar geäußert
**noncon'formist** n. Nonkonformist, *der*/
Nonkonformistin, *die*
**non-con'tributory** adj. beitragsfrei
**nondescript** /'nɒndɪskrɪpt/ adj.
unscheinbar; undefinierbar ‹Farbe›
'**non-drip** adj. nicht tropfend ‹Farbe›
**non-'driver** n. Nicht[auto]fahrer, *die*
**none** /nʌn/ 1 pron. kein...; ~ **of them**
keiner/keine/keines von ihnen; ~ **of this**
nichts davon
2 adv. keineswegs; **I'm** ~ **the wiser now**
jetzt bin ich um nichts klüger; ~ **the less**
nichtsdestoweniger
**nonentity** /nɒ'nentɪtɪ/ n. Nichts, *das*
**non-existent** /nɒnɪg'zɪstənt/ adj. nicht
vorhanden
**non-'fiction** n. Sachliteratur, *die*
**non-'iron** adj. bügelfrei
**non-'member** n. Nichtmitglied, *das*
'**no-no** n., pl. ~**es** (coll.) **be a** ~: nicht
infrage kommen (ugs.)
**non-'payment** n. Nichtzahlung, *die*
**nonplus** /nɒn'plʌs/ v.t., -ss- verblüffen
**non-'profit[-making]** adj. nicht auf
Gewinn ausgerichtet
**non-prolife'ration** n. Nichtverbreitung
von Atomwaffen; ~ **treaty**
Atom[waffen]sperrvertrag, *der*
**non-re'cyclable** adj. nicht recyclebar
**non-'resident** n. (outside a country)
Nichtansässige, *der/die;* **the bar is open to**
~**s** die Bar ist auch für Gäste geöffnet, die
nicht im Hotel wohnen
**nonsense** /'nɒnsəns/ 1 n. Unsinn, *der*
2 int. Unsinn
**nonsensical** /nɒn'sensɪkl/ adj. unsinnig
**non sequitur** /nɒn 'sekwɪtə(r)/ n.
unlogische Folgerung

**non-'smoker** n. (a) (person) Nichtraucher, der/-raucherin, die
(b) (train compartment) Nichtraucherabteil, das
**non-'starter** n. (fig. coll.) Reinfall, der (ugs.)
**non-'stick** adj. ~ frying pan etc. Bratpfanne usw. mit Antihaftbeschichtung
**non-stop** ① /'--/ adj. durchgehend ⟨Zug, Busverbindung⟩; Nonstop⟨flug, -revue⟩
② /-'-/ adv. ohne Unterbrechung ⟨tanzen, reden, reisen, senden⟩; nonstop ⟨fliegen, tanzen, fahren⟩
**'non-toxic** adj. ungiftig
**noodle** /'nu:dl/ n., usu. pl. Nudel, die
**nook** /nʊk/ n. Winkel, der; Ecke, die
**noon** /nu:n/ n. Mittag, der; zwölf Uhr [mittags]; at/before ~: um/vor zwölf [Uhr mittags]
**'no one** pron. ▶ NOBODY
**noose** /nu:s/ n. Schlinge, die
**nor** /nə(r), stressed nɔ:(r)/ conj. noch; **neither/ not ... ~ ...**: weder ... noch ...
**norm** /nɔ:m/ n. Norm, die
**normal** /'nɔ:ml/ ① adj. normal
② n. (a) (~ value) Normalwert, der
(b) (usual state) normaler Stand; **everything is back to** or **has returned to ~**: es hat sich wieder alles normalisiert
**normality** /nɔ:'mælɪtɪ/ Normalität, die
**'normally** adv. (a) (in normal way) normal
(b) (ordinarily) normalerweise
**north** /nɔ:θ/ ① n. (a) Norden, der; **in/ to[wards]/from the ~**: im/nach/von Norden; **to the ~ of** nördlich von
(b) usu. **N~** (Geog., Polit.) Norden, der
② adj. nördlich; Nord⟨wind, -küste, -grenze⟩
③ adv. nach Norden; ~ **of** nördlich von
**north: N~ 'Africa** pr. n. Nordafrika (das);
**N~ A'merica** pr. n. Nordamerika (das);
**N~ A'merican** ① adj. nordamerikanisch;
② n. Nordamerikaner, der/-amerikanerin, die; **~bound** adj. ⟨Zug, Verkehr usw.⟩ in Richtung Norden; **~-'east** ① n. Nordosten, der; ② adj. nordöstlich; nordost⟨wind, -küste⟩; ③ adv. nordostwärts; nach Nordosten; **~-'eastern** adj. nordöstlich
**northerly** /'nɔ:ðəlɪ/ adj. nördlich; ⟨Wind⟩ aus nördlichen Richtungen
**northern** /'nɔ:ðən/ adj. nördlich; Nord⟨grenze, -hälfte, -seite⟩
**northern: N~ 'Ireland** pr. n. Nordirland (das); ~ **'lights** n. pl. Nordlicht, das
**North: ~ 'Germany** pr. n. Norddeutschland (das); ~ **'Pole** pr. n. Nordpol, der; ~ **'Sea** pr. n. Nordsee, die
**northward[s]** /'nɔ:θwəd(z)/ adv. nordwärts
**north: ~-'west** ① n. Nordwesten, der;
② adj. nordwestlich; Nordwest⟨wind, -küste⟩;
③ adv. nordwestwärts; nach Nordwesten;
**~-'western** adj. nordwestlich
**Norway** /'nɔ:weɪ/ pr. n. Norwegen (das)
**Norwegian** /nɔ:'wi:dʒn/ ① adj. norwegisch; **sb. is ~**: jmd. ist Norweger/ Norwegerin

② n. (a) (person) Norweger, der/Norwegerin, die
(b) (language) Norwegisch, das; see also ENGLISH 2A
**Nos.** abbr. = **numbers** Nrn.
**nose** /nəʊz/ ① n. Nase, die
② v.t. ~ **one's way** sich (Dat.) vorsichtig seinen Weg bahnen
③ v.i. sich vorsichtig bewegen
■ **nose a'bout, nose a'round** v.i. (coll.) herumschnüffeln (ugs.)
**nose: ~bleed** n. Nasenbluten, das;
**~dive** ① n. Sturzflug, der; ② v.i. im Sturzflug hinuntergehen
**nosey** ▶ NOSY
**nostalgia** /nɒ'stældʒə/ n. Nostalgie, die; ~ **for sth.** Sehnsucht nach etw.
**nostalgic** /nɒ'stældʒɪk/ adj. nostalgisch
**nostril** /'nɒstrɪl/ n. Nasenloch, das; (of horse) Nüster, die
**nosy** /'nəʊzɪ/ adj. (coll.) neugierig
**not** /nɒt/ adv. nicht; **he is ~ a doctor** er ist kein Arzt; ~ **at all** überhaupt nicht; ~ **... but ...**: nicht ..., sondern ...; ~ **a thing** gar nichts
**notable** /'nəʊtəbl/ adj. bemerkenswert; **be ~ for sth.** für etw. bekannt sein
**notably** /'nəʊtəblɪ/ adv. besonders
**notation** /nəʊ'teɪʃn/ n. Notierung, die
**notch** /nɒtʃ/ ① n. Kerbe, die
② v.t. kerben
■ **notch 'up** v.t. erreichen
**note** /nəʊt/ ① n. (a) (Mus.) (sign) Note, die; (key of piano) Taste, die; (sound) Ton, der
(b) (jotting) Notiz, die; **take** or **make ~s** sich (Dat.) Notizen machen; **take** or **make a ~ of sth.** sich (Dat.) etw. notieren
(c) (comment, footnote) Anmerkung, die
(d) (short letter) [kurzer] Brief
(e) (importance) **a person/something of ~**: eine bedeutende Persönlichkeit/etwas Bedeutendes; **be of ~**: bedeutend sein
② v.t. (a) (pay attention to) beachten
(b) (notice) bemerken
(c) (write) ~ **[down]** [sich (Dat.)] notieren
**'notebook** n. (a) Notizbuch, das; (for lecture notes) Kollegheft, das
(b) **~book [computer]** Notebook, das
**'noted** adj. bekannt (**for** für, wegen)
**note: ~pad** n. Notizblock, der; **~paper** n. Briefpapier, das; **~worthy** adj. bemerkenswert
**nothing** /'nʌθɪŋ/ n. nichts; ~ **interesting** nichts Interessantes; ~ **much** nichts Besonderes; ~ **more than** nur; ~ **more,** ~ **less** nicht mehr, nicht weniger; **next to ~**: so gut wie nichts; **have [got]** or **be ~ to do with sb./sth.** (not concern) nichts zu tun haben mit jmdm./etw.; **have ~ to do with sb.** (avoid) jmdm. aus dem Weg gehen
**notice** /'nəʊtɪs/ ① n. (a) Anschlag, der; (in newspaper) Anzeige, die

**(b)** (warning) **at short/a moment's ~:** kurzfristig/von einem Augenblick zum andern
**(c)** (formal notification) Ankündigung, *die;* **until further ~:** bis auf weiteres
**(d)** (ending an agreement) Kündigung, *die;* **give sb. a month's ~:** jmdm. mit einer Frist von einem Monat kündigen; **hand in one's ~, give ~** (Brit.), **give one's ~** (Amer.) kündigen
**(e)** (attention) **bring sb./sth. to sb.'s ~:** jmdm. auf jmdn./etw. aufmerksam machen; **take no ~ of sb./sth.** (disregard) keine Notiz von jmdm./etw. nehmen; **take no ~:** sich nicht darum kümmern
2 *v.t.* bemerken

**noticeable** /'nəʊtɪsəbl/ *adj.* wahrnehmbar ⟨*Fleck, Schaden, Geruch*⟩; merklich ⟨*Verbesserung*⟩; spürbar ⟨*Mangel*⟩

**noticeably** /'nəʊtɪsəblɪ/ *adv.* sichtlich ⟨*größer, kleiner*⟩; merklich ⟨*verändern*⟩; spürbar ⟨*kälter*⟩

**'noticeboard** *n.* (Brit.) Anschlagbrett, *das;* schwarzes Brett

**notifiable** /'nəʊtɪfaɪəbl/ *adj.* meldepflichtig ⟨*Krankheit*⟩

**notification** /nəʊtɪfɪ'keɪʃn/ *n.* Mitteilung, *die* (**of** sth. über etw. [*Akk.*])

**notify** /'nəʊtɪfaɪ/ *v.t.* **(a)** (make known) ankündigen
**(b)** (inform) benachrichtigen (**of** über + *Akk.*)

**notion** /'nəʊʃn/ *n.* Vorstellung, *die;* **not have the faintest/least ~ of how/what** *etc.* nicht die blasseste/geringste Ahnung haben, wie/was *usw.*

**notoriety** /nəʊtə'raɪətɪ/ *n.* traurige Berühmtheit

**notorious** /nə'tɔːrɪəs/ *adj.* berüchtigt (**for** wegen); notorisch ⟨*Lügner*⟩

**nougat** /'nuːɡɑː/ *n.* Nougat, *das od. der*

**nought** /nɔːt/ *n.* Null, *die*

**noun** /naʊn/ *n.* (Ling.) Substantiv, *das*

**nourish** /'nʌrɪʃ/ *v.t.* ernähren (**on** mit)

**'nourishing** *adj.* nahrhaft

**'nourishment** *n.* Nahrung, *die*

**Nov.** *abbr.* = **November** Nov.

**novel** /'nɒvl/ 1 *n.* Roman, *der*
2 *adj.* neuartig

**novelist** /'nɒvəlɪst/ *n.* Romanautor, *der/* -autorin, *die*

**novella** /nə'velə/ *n.* Novelle, *die*

**novelty** /'nɒvltɪ/ *n.* **(a) be a/no ~:** etwas/ nichts Neues sein
**(b)** (newness) Neuheit, *die*
**(c)** (gadget) Überraschung, *die*

**November** /nə'vembə(r)/ *n.* November, *der; see also* AUGUST

**novice** /'nɒvɪs/ *n.* Anfänger, *der/* Anfängerin, *die*

**now** /naʊ/ 1 *adv.* jetzt; (nowadays) heutzutage; (immediately) [jetzt] sofort; **just ~** (very recently) gerade eben; **[every] ~ and then** *or* **again** hin und wieder; **well ~:** also; **~, ~:** na, na; **~ then** na (ugs.)

2 *conj.* **~ [that]** ...: jetzt, wo ...
3 *n.* **before ~:** früher; **by ~:** inzwischen; **a week from ~:** [heute] in einer Woche

**nowadays** /'naʊədeɪz/ *adv.* heutzutage

**nowhere** /'nəʊweə(r)/ *adv.* nirgends; nirgendwo; (to no place) nirgendwohin

**no-'win** *attrib. adj.* Verlierer-

**noxious** /'nɒkʃəs/ *adj.* giftig

**nozzle** /'nɒzl/ *n.* Düse, *die*

**nuance** /'njuːɑ̃s/ *n.* Nuance, *die*

**nuclear** /'njuːklɪə(r)/ *adj.* Atom-; Kern⟨*explosion*⟩; atomar ⟨*Antrieb, Gefechtskopf, Wettrüsten, Abrüstung*⟩; nuklear ⟨*Sprengkörper*⟩; atomgetrieben ⟨*Unterseeboot*⟩

**nuclear: ~ 'bomb** *n.* Atombombe, *die;* **~ capa'bility** *n.* nukleares Potenzial; **a missile with ~ capability** eine nuklearfähige Rakete; **have ~ capability** nuklearfähig sein; **~ de'terrent** *n.* atomare *od.* nukleare Abschreckung; **~ 'energy** *n.* Atom- *od.* Kernenergie, *die;* **~ 'family** *n.* Kernfamilie, *die;* **~-free** *adj.* atomwaffenfrei ⟨*Zone*⟩; **~ 'fuel** *n.* Kernbrennstoff, *der;* **~ 'physics** *n.* Kernphysik, *die;* **~ 'power** *n.* **(a)** Atom- *od.* Kernkraft, *die;* **(b)** (country) Atom- *od.* Nuklearmacht, *die;* **~-'powered** *adj.* atomgetrieben; **~ 'power station** *n.* Atom- *od.* Kernkraftwerk, *das;* **~ 'test** *n.* Atom[waffen]test, *der;* **~ 'testing** *n.* Atomversuche *Pl.;* **~ 'warfare** *n.* Atomkrieg, *der;* **~ 'waste** *n.* Atommüll, *der*

**nucleus** /'njuːklɪəs/ *n., pl.* **nuclei** /'njuːklɪaɪ/ Kern, *der*

**nude** /njuːd/ 1 *adj.* nackt
2 *n.* **(a)** (figure) Akt, *der*
**(b) in the ~:** nackt

**nudge** /nʌdʒ/ 1 *v.t.* anstoßen
2 *n.* Stoß, *der*

**nudism** /'njuːdɪzm/ *n.* Nudismus, *der;* Freikörperkultur, *die*

**nudist** /'njuːdɪst/ *n.* Nudist, *der/*Nudistin, *die; attrib.* Nudisten-

**nudity** /'njuːdɪtɪ/ *n.* Nacktheit, *die*

**nugget** /'nʌɡɪt/ *n.* Klumpen, *der;* (of gold) Goldklumpen, *der;* (fig.) **~s of wisdom** goldene Weisheiten

**nuisance** /'njuːsəns/ *n.* Ärgernis, *das;* **what a ~!** so etwas Dummes!

**null** /nʌl/ *adj.* **~ and void** null und nichtig

**numb** /nʌm/ 1 *adj.* gefühllos, taub (**with** vor + *Dat.*); (without emotion) benommen
2 *v.t.* betäuben

**number** /'nʌmbə(r)/ 1 *n.* **(a)** (in series) Nummer, *die;* **you've got the wrong ~** (Teleph.) Sie sind falsch verbunden; **dial a wrong ~:** sich verwählen (ugs.)
**(b)** (esp. Math.: numeral) Zahl, *die*
**(c)** (sum, total, quantity) [An]zahl, *die;* **a ~ of people/things** einige Leute/Dinge; **a ~ of times** mehrmals

···⁖

2 *v.t.* **(a)** (assign ∼ to) nummerieren
**(b)** (amount to, comprise) zählen
**(c)** (include) zählen **(among, with** zu)
**(d) sb.'s days are** ∼**ed** jmds. Tage sind gezählt
**'numbering** *n.* Nummerierung, *die*
**'numberless** *adj.* unzählig; zahllos
**'number plate** *n.* Nummernschild, *das*
**numeracy** /'nju:mərəsɪ/ *n.* rechnerische Fähigkeiten *Pl.*
**numeral** /'nju:mərl/ *n.* Ziffer, *die*
**numerate** /nju:mərət/ *adj.* **be** ∼: rechnen können
**numerical** /nju:'merɪkl/ *adj.* numerisch; Zahlen⟨*wert, -folge*⟩; zahlenmäßig ⟨*Stärke, Überlegenheit*⟩
**numerically** /nju:'merɪkəlɪ/ *adv.* numerisch
**numerous** /'nju:mərəs/ *adj.* zahlreich
**nun** /nʌn/ *n.* Nonne, *die*
**nurse** /nɜ:s/ 1 *n.* Krankenschwester, *die;* [male] ∼: Krankenpfleger, *der*
2 *v.t.* **(a)** pflegen ⟨*Kranke*⟩
**(b)** (fig.) hegen (geh.) ⟨*Gefühl, Groll*⟩
**'nursemaid** *n.* (lit. or fig.) Kindermädchen, *das*
**nursery** /'nɜ:sərɪ/ *n.* **(a)** (room) Kinderzimmer, *das*
**(b)** (crèche) Kindertagesstätte, *die*
**(c)** ▶ NURSERY SCHOOL
**(d)** (for plants) Gärtnerei, *die*
**nursery:** ∼ **rhyme** *n.* Kinderreim, *der;* ∼ **school** *n.* Kindergarten, *der;* ∼**-school teacher** *n.* (female) Kindergärtnerin, *die;* Erzieherin, *die;* (male) Erzieher, *der;* ∼ **slopes** *n. pl.* (Skiing) Idiotenhügel, *der* (ugs. scherzh.)

**nursing** /'nɜ:sɪŋ/ *n.* Krankenpflege, *die; attrib.* Pflege⟨*personal, -beruf*⟩
**'nursing home** *n.* Pflegeheim, *das*
**nurture** /'nɜ:tʃə(r)/ *v.t.* (rear) aufziehen; (fig.) nähren
**nut** /nʌt/ *n.* **(a)** Nuss, *die*
**(b)** (Mech. Engin.) [Schrauben]mutter, *die*
**(c)** (crazy person) Verrückte, *der/die* (ugs.)
**nut:** ∼ **case** *n.* (coll.) Verrückte, *der/die* (ugs.); ∼ **crackers** *n. pl.* Nussknacker, *der*
**nutmeg** /'nʌtmeg/ *n.* Muskat, *der*
**nutrient** /'nju:trɪənt/ *n.* Nährstoff, *der*
**nutrition** /nju:'trɪʃn/ *n.* Ernährung, *die;* (food) Nahrung, *die*
**nutritional** /nju:'trɪʃənl/ *adj.* nahrhaft; ∼ **value** Nährwert, *der*
**nutritionist** /nju:'trɪʃənɪst/ *n.* Ernährungswissenschaftler, *der/* -wissenschaftlerin, *die*
**nutritious** /nju:'trɪʃəs/ *adj.* nahrhaft
**'nutshell** *n.* Nussschale, *die;* **in a** ∼ (fig.) hurz [gesagt]
**nutty** /'nʌtɪ/ *adj.* **(a)** (in taste) nussig
**(b)** (coll.: crazy) verrückt (ugs.)
**nuzzle** /'nʌzl/ *v.i.* sich kuscheln **(up to, against** an + *Akk.*)
**NVQ** *abbr.* (Brit.) = **National Vocational Qualification**
**NW** *abbr.* = **north-west** NW
**nylon** /'naɪlɒn/ *n.* **(a)** Nylon, *das; attrib.* Nylon-
**(b)** *in pl.* (stockings) Nylonstrümpfe *Pl.*
**nymph** /nɪmf/ *n.* Nymphe, *die*
**nymphomaniac** /nɪmfə'meɪnɪæk/ *n.* Nymphomanin, *die*
**NZ** *abbr.* = **New Zealand**

# Oo

**O, o** /əʊ/ *n.* O, o, *das*
**oaf** /əʊf/ *n.* Stoffel, *der* (ugs.)
**oak** /əʊk/ *n.* Eiche, *die*
**'oak tree** *n.* Eiche, *die*
**OAP** *abbr.* (Brit.) = **old-age pensioner** Rentner, *der/*Rentnerin, *die*
**oar** /ɔ:(r)/ *n.* Ruder, *das*
**oarsman** /'ɔ:zmən/ *n., pl.* **oarsmen** /'ɔ:zmən/ Ruderer, *der*
**oasis** /əʊ'eɪsɪs/ *n., pl.* **oases** /əʊ'eɪsi:z/ Oase, *die*
**oat** /əʊt/ *n.* ∼**s** Hafer, *der*
**'oatcake** *n.* [flacher] Haferkuchen
**oath** /əʊθ/ *n.* **(a)** Eid, *der;* Schwur, *der;* **take** *or* **swear an** ∼: einen Eid schwören

**(b)** (swear word) Fluch, *der*
**'oatmeal** *n.* Hafermehl, *das*
**obedience** /ə'bi:dɪəns/ *n.* Gehorsam, *der*
**obedient** /ə'bi:dɪənt/ *adj.* gehorsam; **be** ∼ **to sb./sth.** jmdm./einer Sache gehorchen
**o'bediently** *adv.* gehorsam
**obelisk** /'ɒbəlɪsk/ *n.* Obelisk, *der*
**obese** /əʊ'bi:s/ *adj.* fettleibig
**obesity** /əʊ'bi:sɪtɪ/ *n.* Fettleibigkeit, *die*
**obey** /əʊ'beɪ/ 1 *v.t.* gehorchen (+ *Dat.*); sich halten an (+ *Akk.*) ⟨*Vorschrift, Regel*⟩; befolgen ⟨*Befehl*⟩
2 *v.i.* gehorchen
**obituary** /ə'bɪtjʊərɪ/ *n.* Nachruf, *der* **(to, of** auf + *Akk.*)

**object** [1] /'ɒbdʒɪkt/ n. (a) (thing)
Gegenstand, der
(b) (purpose) Ziel, das
(c) (obstacle) money/time etc. is no ∼: Geld/
Zeit usw. spielt keine Rolle
(d) (Ling.) Objekt, das
[2] /əb'dʒekt/ v.i. (a) Einwände/einen
Einwand erheben (to gegen)
(b) (have objection or dislike) etwas dagegen
haben; ∼ to sb./sth. etwas gegen jmdn./etw.
haben
[3] /əb'dʒekt/ v.t. einwenden
**objection** /əb'dʒekʃn/ n. (a) Einwand, der;
raise or make an ∼ [to sth.] einen Einwand
[gegen etw.] erheben
(b) (dislike) Abneigung, die; have an/no ∼ to
sb./sth. etw./nichts gegen jmdn./etw. haben;
have no ∼s nichts dagegen haben
**objectionable** /əb'dʒekʃənəbl/ adj.
unangenehm ⟨Anblick, Geruch⟩; anstößig
⟨Bemerkung, Wort, Benehmen⟩
**objective** /əb'dʒektɪv/ [1] adj. objektiv
[2] n. (goal) Ziel, das
**ob'jectively** adv. objektiv
**objectivity** /ɒbdʒek'tɪvɪtɪ/ n. Objektivität,
die
**obligation** /ɒblɪ'geɪʃn/ n. Verpflichtung,
die; be under an ∼ to sb. jmdm. verpflichtet
sein; without ∼: unverbindlich
**obligatory** /ə'blɪɡətərɪ/ adj. obligatorisch;
it has become ∼ to …: es ist jetzt Pflicht,
zu …
**oblige** /ə'blaɪdʒ/ v.t. (a) (be binding on) ∼ sb.
to do sth. jmdm. vorschreiben, etw. zu tun
(b) (compel) zwingen; be ∼d to do sth.
gezwungen sein, etw. zu tun; feel ∼d to do
sth. sich verpflichtet fühlen, etw. zu tun
(c) (be kind to) ∼ sb. by doing sth. jmdm. den
Gefallen tun und etw. tun
(d) (grateful) be much/greatly ∼d to sb. [for
sth.] jmdm. [für etw.] sehr verbunden sein;
much ∼d! besten Dank!
**obliging** /ə'blaɪdʒɪŋ/ adj.
entgegenkommend
**oblique** /ə'bliːk/ adj. schief ⟨Gerade,
Winkel⟩; (fig.) indirekt
**obliterate** /ə'blɪtəreɪt/ v.t. auslöschen
**oblivion** /ə'blɪvɪən/ n. Vergessenheit, die;
sink or fall into ∼: in Vergessenheit geraten
**oblivious** /ə'blɪvɪəs/ adj. be ∼ to or of sth.
sich (Dat.) einer Sache (Gen.) nicht bewusst
sein
**oblong** /'ɒblɒŋ/ [1] adj. rechteckig
[2] n. Rechteck, das
**obnoxious** /əb'nɒkʃəs/ adj. widerlich
**oboe** /'əʊbəʊ/ n. Oboe, die
**obscene** /əb'siːn/ adj. obszön
**obscenity** /əb'senɪtɪ/ n. Obszönität, die
**obscure** /əb'skjʊə(r)/ [1] adj. (a)
(unexplained) dunkel
(b) (hard to understand) schwer verständlich
⟨Argument, Dichtung, Autor, Stil⟩
(c) (unknown) unbekannt

[2] v.t. (a) (make indistinct) verdunkeln;
versperren ⟨Aussicht⟩
(b) (make unintelligible) unverständlich machen
**obsequious** /əb'siːkwɪəs/ adj. unterwürfig
**observance** /əb'zɜːvəns/ n. Einhaltung,
die
**observant** /əb'zɜːvənt/ adj. aufmerksam
**observation** /ɒbzə'veɪʃn/ n. (a)
Beobachtung, die; be [kept] under ∼:
beobachtet werden; (by police) überwacht
werden
(b) (remark) Bemerkung, die (on über + Akk.)
**obser'vation post** n.
Beobachtungsposten, der
**observatory** /əb'zɜːvətərɪ/ n. (Astron.)
Sternwarte, die
**observe** /əb'zɜːv/ v.t. (a) (watch)
beobachten; (perceive) bemerken
(b) (abide by, keep) einhalten
(c) (say) bemerken
**ob'server** n. Beobachter, der/Beobachterin,
die
**obsess** /əb'ses/ v.t. ∼ sb. von jmdm. Besitz
ergreifen (fig.); be/become ∼ed with or by
sb./sth. von jmdm./etw. besessen sein/
werden
**obsession** /əb'seʃn/ n. Zwangsvorstellung,
die
**obsessive** /əb'sesɪv/ adj. zwanghaft; be
∼ about sth. von etw. besessen sein
**obsolescent** /ɒbsə'lesənt/ adj. veraltend
**obsolete** /'ɒbsəliːt/ adj. veraltet
**obstacle** /'ɒbstəkl/ n. Hindernis, das (to
für)
**obstacle: ∼ course** n.
Hindernisparcours, der; ∼ **race** n.
Hindernisrennen, das
**obstetrics** /ɒb'stetrɪks/ n. (Med.)
Obstetrik, die (fachspr.)
**obstinacy** /'ɒbstɪnəsɪ/ n. ▶ OBSTINATE:
Starrsinn, der; Hartnäckigkeit, die
**obstinate** /'ɒbstɪnət/ adj. starrsinnig;
(adhering to particular course of action) hartnäckig
**obstruct** /əb'strʌkt/ v.t. (a) (block)
blockieren; behindern ⟨Verkehr⟩; ∼ sb.'s
view jmdm. die Sicht versperren
(b) (fig.: impede; also Sport) behindern
**obstruction** /əb'strʌkʃn/ n. Blockierung,
die; (of progress; also Sport) Behinderung, die
**obstructive** /əb'strʌktɪv/ adj. hinderlich;
obstruktiv ⟨Politik, Taktik⟩; be ∼ ⟨Person:⟩
sich quer legen (ugs.)
**obtain** /əb'teɪn/ v.t. bekommen; erzielen
⟨Resultat, Wirkung⟩
**obtainable** /əb'teɪnəbl/ adj. erhältlich
**obtrusive** /əb'truːsɪv/ adj. aufdringlich;
(conspicuous) auffällig
**obtuse** /əb'tjuːs/ adj. (a) stumpf ⟨Winkel⟩
(b) (stupid) begriffsstutzig
**obvious** /'ɒbvɪəs/ adj. offenkundig; (easily
seen) augenfällig; be ∼ [to sb.] that …:
[jmdm.] klar sein, dass …

**O**

'**obviously** *adv.* offenkundig; sichtlich ⟨*enttäuschen, überraschen usw.*⟩

**occasion** /əˈkeɪʒn/ 1 *n.* (a) Gelegenheit, *die;* **rise to the** ~: sich der Situation gewachsen zeigen; **on several** ~**s** bei mehreren Gelegenheiten; **on** ~[**s**] gelegentlich
(b) (special occurrence) Anlass, *der;* **it was quite an** ~: es war ein Ereignis
(c) (reason) Grund, *der* (**for** zu)
2 *v.t.* verursachen

**occasional** /əˈkeɪʒənl/ *adj.* gelegentlich; vereinzelt ⟨*Regenschauer*⟩

**oc'casionally** *adv.* gelegentlich; [**only**] **very** ~: gelegentlich einmal

**occult** /ɒˈkʌlt, ˈɒkʌlt/ *adj.* okkult; **the** ~: das Okkulte

**occupant** /ˈɒkjʊpənt/ *n.* Bewohner, *der*/ Bewohnerin, *die;* (of car, bus, etc.) Insasse, *der*/ Insassin, *die*

**occupation** /ɒkjʊˈpeɪʃn/ *n.* (a) (Mil.) Besetzung, *die;* (period) Besatzungszeit, *die*
(b) (activity) Beschäftigung, *die*
(c) (profession) Beruf, *der*

**occupational** /ɒkjʊˈpeɪʃənl/ *adj.* Berufs⟨*beratung, -risiko*⟩; ~ **therapy** Beschäftigungstherapie, *die;* ~ **therapist** Beschäftigungstherapeut, *der*/-therapeutin, *die*

**occupier** /ˈɒkjʊpaɪə(r)/ *n.* (Brit.) Besitzer, *der*/Besitzerin, *die;* (tenant) Bewohner, *der*/ Bewohnerin, *die*

**occupy** /ˈɒkjʊpaɪ/ *v.t.* (a) (Mil.; as demonstration) besetzen
(b) (live in) bewohnen
(c) (take up, fill) einnehmen; belegen ⟨*Zimmer*⟩; in Anspruch nehmen ⟨*Zeit, Aufmerksamkeit*⟩
(d) (busy, employ) beschäftigen

**occur** /əˈkɜː(r)/ *v.i.,* **-rr-:** (a) (be met with) vorkommen; ⟨*Gelegenheit:*⟩ sich bieten; ⟨*Problem:*⟩ auftreten
(b) (happen) ⟨*Veränderung:*⟩ eintreten; ⟨*Unfall, Vorfall:*⟩ sich ereignen
(c) ~ **to sb.** (be thought of) jmdm. in den Sinn kommen; ⟨*Idee:*⟩ jmdm. kommen

**occurrence** /əˈkʌrəns/ *n.* (a) (incident) Ereignis, *das;* Begebenheit, *die*
(b) (occurring) Vorkommen, *das*

**ocean** /ˈəʊʃn/ *n.* Ozean, *der;* Meer, *das*

**o'clock** /əˈklɒk/ *adv.* **it is two/six** ~: es ist zwei/sechs Uhr; **at two/six** ~: um zwei/sechs Uhr; **six** ~ *attrib.* Sechsuhr⟨*zug, -maschine, -nachrichten*⟩

**Oct.** *abbr.* = **October** Okt.

**octagon** /ˈɒktəgən/ *n.* Achteck, *das*

**octane** /ˈɒkteɪn/ *n.* Oktan, *das*

**octave** /ˈɒktɪv/ *n.* Oktave, *die*

**October** /ɒkˈtəʊbə(r)/ *n.* Oktober, *der; see also* Aᴜɢᴜsᴛ

**octopus** /ˈɒktəpəs/ *n.* Tintenfisch, *der*

**odd** /ɒd/ *adj.* (a) (surplus, spare) übrig ⟨*Stück, Silbergeld*⟩; **£25 and a few** ~ **pence** 25 Pfund und ein paar Pence
(b) (occasional) gelegentlich; ~ **job/**~**-job man** Gelegenheitsarbeit, *die*/-arbeiter, *der*
(c) (one of pair or group) einzeln; ~ **socks** nicht zusammengehörende Socken; **be the** ~ **man out** ⟨*Gegenstand:*⟩ nicht dazu passen
(d) (uneven) ungerade ⟨*Zahl, Seite, Hausnummer*⟩
(e) (plus something) **forty** ~: über vierzig; **twelve pounds** ~: etwas mehr als zwölf Pfund
(f) (strange, eccentric) seltsam

**oddity** /ˈɒdɪtɪ/ *n.* (object, event) Kuriosität, *die*

'**oddly** *adv.* seltsam; ~ **enough** seltsamerweise

**odd 'man** *n.* ~ **out** Außenseiter, *der*/ Außenseiterin, *die;* **be the** ~ **out** (extra person) überzählig sein

'**odd-numbered** *adj.* ungerade

**odds** /ɒdz/ *n. pl.* (a) (Betting) Odds *Pl.*
(b) [**the**] ~ **are that she did it** wahrscheinlich hat sie es getan; **the** ~ **are against/in favour of sb./sth.** jmds. Aussichten/die Aussichten für etw. sind gering/gut
(c) ~ **and ends** Kleinigkeiten; (of food) Reste
(d) **be at** ~ **with sb. over sth.** mit jmdm. in etw. (*Dat.*) uneinig sein
(e) **it makes no/little** ~ [**whether ...**] es ist völlig/ziemlich gleichgültig[, ob ...]

'**odds-on** 1 *adj.* gut ⟨*Chance, Aussicht*⟩; hoch, klar ⟨*Favorit*⟩
2 *adv.* wahrscheinlich

**odious** /ˈəʊdɪəs/ *adj.* widerwärtig

**odor** *etc.* (*Amer.*) ▶ ᴏᴅᴏᴜʀ *etc.*

**odour** /ˈəʊdə(r)/ *n.* Geruch, *der*

'**odourless** *adj.* geruchlos

**oedema** /ɪˈdiːmə/ *n.* Ödem, *das*

**oestrogen** /ˈiːstrədʒən/ *n.* Östrogen, *das*

**œuvre** /ˈɜːvr/ *n.* Œuvre, *das* (geh.); Werk, *das*

**of** /əv, *stressed* ɒv/ *prep.* von; (indicating material, substance) aus; **articles of clothing** Kleidungsstücke; **a friend of mine** ein Freund von mir; **where's that pencil of mine?** wo ist mein Bleistift?; **it was clever of you to do that** es war klug von dir, das zu tun; **the approval of sb.** jmds. Zustimmung; **the works of Shakespeare** Shakespeares Werke; **be made of ...:** aus ... [hergestellt] sein; **the fifth of January** der fünfte Januar; **his love of his father** seine Liebe zu seinem Vater; **person of extreme views** Mensch mit extremen Ansichten; **a boy of 14 years** ein vierzehnjähriger Junge; **the five of us** wir fünf

**off** /ɒf/ 1 *adv.* (a) (away) **be a few miles** ~: wenige Meilen entfernt sein; **the lake is not far** ~: der See ist nicht weit [weg]; **I'm** ~ **now** ich gehe jetzt; ~ **we go!** los gehts!
(b) (not on or attached or supported) ab; **get the lid** ~: den Deckel abbekommen

**(c) be** ~ (switched or turned ~) ‹*Wasser, Gas, Strom:*› abgestellt sein; **the light/radio** *etc.* **is** ~: das Licht/Radio *usw.* ist aus
**(d) the meat** *etc.* **is** ~: das Fleisch *usw.* ist schlecht [geworden]
**(e) be** ~ (cancelled) abgesagt sein; ‹*Verlobung:*› [auf]gelöst sein; ~ **and on** immer mal wieder (ugs.)
**(f)** (not at work) frei; **on my day** ~: an meinem freien Tag; **have a week** ~: eine Woche Urlaub bekommen
**(g)** (no longer available) [the] **soup** *etc.* **is** ~: es gibt keine Suppe *usw.* mehr
**(h)** (situated as regards money etc.) **he is badly** *etc.* ~: er ist schlecht *usw.* gestellt
**2** *prep.* von; **be** ~ **school/work** in der Schule/am Arbeitsplatz fehlen; **be** ~ **one's food** keinen Appetit haben; **just** ~ **the square** ganz in der Nähe des Platzes

**offal** /'ɒfl/ *n.* Innereien *Pl.*

**off:** ~**beat** *adj.* (fig.: eccentric) unkonventionell; ~-**'centre** *adv.* nicht [genau] in der Mitte; ~ **'colour** *adj.* unwohl; ~**cut** *n.* Rest, *der;* ~**duty** *attrib. adj.* Freizeit-; ‹*Polizist usw.*›, der dienstfrei hat

**offence** /ə'fens/ *n.* (Brit.) **(a)** (hurting of sb.'s feelings) Kränkung, *die;* **I meant no** ~: ich wollte Sie/ihn *usw.* nicht kränken
**(b)** (annoyance) **give** ~: Missfallen erregen; **take** ~: verärgert sein
**(c)** (crime) Straftat, *die;* **criminal** ~: strafbare Handlung

**offend** /ə'fend/ **1** *v.i.* verstoßen (**against** gegen)
**2** *v.t.* ~ **sb.** bei jmdm. Anstoß erregen; (hurt feelings of) jmdn. kränken

**offender** *n.* Straffällige, *der/die*

**offense** (Amer.) ▶ OFFENCE

**offensive** /ə'fensɪv/ **1** *adj.* **(a)** (aggressive) offensiv; Angriffs‹*waffe*›
**(b)** (giving offence) ungehörig; (indecent) anstößig
**2** *n.* Offensive, *die;* **take the** *or* **go on the** ~: in die *od.* zur Offensive übergehen

**offer** /'ɒfə(r)/ **1** *v.t.* anbieten; vorbringen ‹*Entschuldigung*›; bieten ‹*Chance*›; aussprechen ‹*Beileid*›; ~ **to help** seine Hilfe anbieten; ~ **resistance** Widerstand leisten
**2** *n.* Angebot, *das;* [have/be] **on** ~: im Angebot [haben/sein]

**'offering** *n.* (thing) Angebot, *das;* (to a deity) Opfer, *das*

**off'hand** **1** *adv.* **(a)** (without preparation) auf Anhieb ‹*sagen, wissen*›; spontan ‹*beschließen, entscheiden*›
**(b)** (casually) leichthin
**2** *adj.* **(a)** (without preparation) spontan
**(b)** (casual) beiläufig; **be** ~ **with sb.** zu jmdm. kurz angebunden sein

**office** /'ɒfɪs/ *n.* **(a)** Büro, *das*
**(b)** (branch) Zweigstelle, *die*
**(c)** (position) Amt, *das;* **hold** ~: amtieren

**office:** ~ **block** *n.* Bürogebäude, *das;* ~ **hours** *n. pl.* Dienststunden *Pl.;* ~ **job** *n.* Bürotätigkeit, *die*

**officer** /'ɒfɪsə(r)/ *n.* **(a)** (Army etc.) Offizier, *der*
**(b)** (official) Beamte, *der*/Beamtin, *die*
**(c)** (constable) Polizeibeamte, *der*/-beamtin, *die*

**office:** ~ **technology** *n.* Bürotechnik, *die;* ~ **worker** *n.* Büroangestellte, *der/die*

**official** /ə'fɪʃl/ **1** *adj.* offiziell; amtlich ‹*Verlautbarung*›; regulär ‹*Streik*›
**2** *n.* Beamte, *der*/Beamtin, *die;* (party, union, or sports ~) Funktionär, *der*/Funktionärin, *die*

**officialdom** /ə'fɪʃldəm/ *n., no art.* Beamtentum, *das;* Bürokratie, *die*

**officially** *adv.* offiziell

**officious** /ə'fɪʃəs/ *adj.* übereifrig

**offing** /'ɒfɪŋ/ *n.* **be in the** ~: bevorstehen; ‹*Gewitter:*› aufziehen

**off:** ~**licence** *n.* (Brit.) ≈ Wein- und Spirituosenladen, *der;* ~**line** (Comp.) **1** /'--/ *adj.* Offline-; **2** /-'-/ *adv.* offline; ~**load** *v.t.* abladen; ~**peak** *attrib. adj.* during ~**peak hours** außerhalb der Spitzenlastzeiten; ~**peak power** *or* **electricity** Nachtstrom, *der;* ~**putting** /'ɒfpʊtɪŋ/ *adj.* (Brit.) abstoßend; ~**print** *n.* Sonderdruck, *der;* ~**road** *attrib. adj.* Gelände-, Offroad‹*fahrzeug, -fahrrad, -wagen, -fahrt, -einsatz*›; ~**road driving** Fahren im Gelände; ~**set** /'--, -'-/ *v.t., forms as* SET: ausgleichen; ~ **season** *n.* Nebensaison, *die;* ~**shore** *adj.* küstennah; ~**side** *adj.* Abseits-; **be** ~**side** abseits sein; ~**spring** *n., pl. same* Nachkommenschaft, *die;* (of animal) Junge *Pl.;* ~**the-peg** *attrib. adj.* Konfektions-; ~**the-shoulder** *attrib. adj.* schulterfrei ‹*Kleid*›; ~**the-wall** *attrib. adj.* (esp. Amer. coll.) ausgeflippt (ugs.); ~-**'white** *adj.* gebrochen weiß

**Oftel** /'ɒftel/ *abbr.* (Brit.) = **Office of Telecommunications** *Regulierungsbehörde für Telekommunikation*

**often** /'ɒfn, 'ɒftn/ *adv.* oft; **every so** ~: gelegentlich

**Ofwat** /'ɒfwɒt/ *abbr.* (Brit.) = **Office of Water Services** *Regulierungsbehörde für Wasserwirtschaft*

**oh** /əʊ/ *int.* oh; *expr. pain* au

**OHP** *abbr.* (Brit.) = **overhead projector** OHP

**oil** /ɔɪl/ **1** *n.* Öl, *das*
**2** *v.t.* ölen

**oil:** ~**burner** *n.* Ölbrenner, *der;* ~**can** *n.* Ölkanne, *die;* ~ **change** *n.* (Motor Veh.) Ölwechsel, *der;* ~ **drum** *n.* Ölfass, *das;* ~**field** *n.* Ölfeld, *das;* ~ **lamp** *n.* Öllampe, *die;* ~ **painting** *n.* Ölgemälde, *das;* ~**producing** *adj.* [Erd]öl fördernd ‹*Land*›; ~ **refinery** *n.* [Erd]ölraffinerie, ····⟫

**O**

*die;* ~ **rig** ▶ RIG¹ 1; ~**skins** *n. pl.* Ölzeug,
*das;* ~ **slick** *n.* Ölteppich, *der;* ~ **tanker**
*n.* Öltanker, *der;* ~ **well** *n.* Ölquelle, *die*

**oily** /'ɔɪlɪ/ *adj.* ölig; ölverschmiert ⟨*Gesicht,
Hände*⟩

**ointment** /'ɔɪntmənt/ *n.* Salbe, *die*

**OK** /əʊ'keɪ/ (coll.) ①*adj.* in Ordnung; okay
(ugs.)
②*adv.* gut
③*int.* okay (ugs.)
④*v.t.* (approve) zustimmen (+ *Dat.*); **be OK'd
by sb.** von jmdm. das Okay bekommen (ugs.)

**okay** /əʊ'keɪ/ ▶ OK

**old** /əʊld/ *adj.* alt; **be [more than] 30 years
~:** [über] 30 Jahre alt sein

**old:** ~ **'age** *n.* [fortgeschrittenes] Alter;
~**-age** *attrib. adj.* Alters⟨*rente, -ruhegeld*⟩;
~**-age pensioner** Rentner, *der*/Rentnerin, *die;*
~**-fashioned** /əʊld'fæʃnd/ *adj.*
altmodisch; ~ **'people's home** *n.*
Altenheim, *das;* Altersheim, *das;* ~ **'wives'
tale** *n.* Ammenmärchen, *das*

**olive** /'ɒlɪv/ *n.* Olive, *die*

**olive 'oil** *n.* Olivenöl, *das*

**Olympic** /ə'lɪmpɪk/ *adj.* olympisch;
~ **Games** Olympische Spiele

**Olympics** /ə'lɪmpɪks/ *n. pl.* Olympiade, *die;*
**Winter ~:** Winterolympiade, *die*

**omelette** ⟨**omelet**⟩ /'ɒmlɪt/ *n.* Omelett,
*das*

**omen** /'əʊmən/ *n.* Vorzeichen, *das*

**ominous** /'ɒmɪnəs/ *adj.* (of evil omen)
ominös; (worrying) beunruhigend

**omission** /ə'mɪʃn/ *n.* Auslassung, *die;*
(failure to act) Unterlassung, *die*

**omit** /ə'mɪt/ *v.t.,* **-tt-** weglassen; ~ **to do sth.**
es versäumen, etw. zu tun

**omnipotence** /ɒm'nɪpətəns/ *n.* Allmacht,
*die* (geh.)

**omnipotent** /ɒm'nɪpətənt/ *adj.* allmächtig

**on** /ɒn/ ①*prep.* auf ⟨*position:* + *Dat.;
direction:* + *Akk.*⟩; (attached to) an (+ *Dat./
Akk.*); (concerning, about) über (+ *Akk.*); (in
expressions of time) an ⟨*einem Abend, Tag
usw.*⟩; **write sth. on the wall** etw. an die Wand
schreiben; **be hanging on the wall** an der
Wand hängen; **have sth. on one** etw. bei sich
haben; **on the bus/train** im Bus/Zug; (by bus/
train) mit dem Bus/Zug; **on Oxford 556767**
unter der Nummer Oxford 556767; **on
Sundays** sonntags; **on [his] arrival** bei seiner
Ankunft; **on entering the room ...:** beim
Betreten des Zimmers ...; **it's just on 9** es ist
fast 9 Uhr; **the drinks are on me** (coll.) die
Getränke gehen auf mich
②*adv.* **with/without a hat/coat on** mit/ohne
Hut/Mantel; **have a hat on** einen Hut
aufhaben; **on and on** immer weiter; **speak/
wait/work** *etc.* **on** weiterreden/-warten/
-arbeiten *usw.;* **from now on** von jetzt an; **the
light/radio** *etc.* **is on** das Licht/Radio *usw.* ist
an; **is Sunday's picnic on?** findet das
Picknick am Sonntag statt?; **what's on at the**

**cinema?** was läuft im Kino?; **on and off**
immer mal wieder (ugs.); **on to, onto** auf
(+ *Akk.*)

**once** /wʌns/ ①*adv.* **(a)** einmal; ~ **a week/
month/year** einmal die Woche/im Monat/im
Jahr; ~ **again** *or* **more** noch einmal; ~ **[and]
for all** ein für alle Mal; **never/not ~:** nicht
ein einziges Mal
**(b)** (multiplied by one) ein mal
**(c)** (formerly) früher einmal; ~ **upon a time
there lived a king** es war einmal ein König
**(d) at ~** (immediately) sofort; (at the same time)
gleichzeitig; **all at ~** (suddenly) plötzlich;
(simultaneously) alle[s] zugleich
②*conj.* wenn; (with past tense) als
③*n.* [just *or* only] **this ~:** [nur] dieses eine
Mal

**'oncoming** *adj.* entgegenkommend
⟨*Fahrzeug, Verkehr*⟩

**one** /wʌn/ ①*adj.* ein; *see also* EIGHT 1;
(single, only) einzig; **no/not ~:** kein; **the
~ thing** das Einzige; **at ~ time** einmal; ~
**morning/night** eines Morgens/Nachts
②*n.* **(a)** eins
**(b)** (number, symbol) Eins, *die*
**(c)** (unit) **in ~s** einzeln
③*pron.* **(a)** ein... (of + *Gen.*); **big ~s and
little ~s** Große und Kleine; **the older/younger
~:** der/die/das Ältere/Jüngere; **this ~:**
dieser/diese/dieses [da]; **that ~:** der/die/das
[da]; **which ~?** welcher/welche/welches?;
**which ~s?** welche?; ~ **by ~:** einzeln; **love/
hate ~ another** sich lieben/hassen; **be kind
to ~ another** nett zueinander sein
**(b)** (people in general; coll.: I, we) man; *as
indirect object* einem; *as direct object* einen;
~**'s** sein

**one:** ~**-night 'stand** *n.* (coll.) [sexuelles]
Abenteuer für eine Nacht; ~**-off** (Brit.) ①*n.*
(article) Einzelstück, *das;* ②*adj.* einmalig;
~**-parent family** *n.* Einelternfamilie, *die*

**onerous** /'əʊnərəs/ *adj.* schwer

**one:** ~**'self** *pron.* **(a)** *emphat.* selbst; **be
~self** man selbst sein; **(b)** *refl.* sich; *see also*
HERSELF; ~**-sided** *adj.* einseitig; ~**-stop
shopping** *n.* Einkaufen in einem
Einkaufszentrum [mit Komplettangebot];
~**-storey** *adj.* eingeschossig; ~**-touch**
*adj.* ~**-touch dialling** Zielwahl, *die;* ~**-track**
*adj.* eingleisig; **have a ~-track mind** (be
obsessed) nur eins im Kopf haben;
~**-upmanship** /wʌn'ʌpmənʃɪp/ *n., no
indef. art.* die Kunst, den anderen immer um
eine Nasenlänge voraus zu sein; ~**-way**
*adj.* **(a)** in einer Richtung *nachgestellt;*
Einbahn⟨*straße, -verkehr*⟩; **(b)** einfach
⟨*Fahrpreis, Flug*⟩

**'ongoing** *adj.* aktuell ⟨*Problem, Debatte*⟩;
andauernd ⟨*Situation*⟩

**onion** /'ʌnjən/ *n.* Zwiebel, *die*

**onion:** ~ **skin** *n.* Zwiebelschale, *die;*
~ **'soup** *n.* Zwiebelsuppe, *die*

**online** (Comp.) ①/'--/ *adj.* Online-
②/-'-/ *adv.* online

**'onlooker** n. Zuschauer, der/Zuschauerin, die

**only** /'əʊnlɪ/ ① attrib. adj. einzig...; the ～ person der/die Einzige; an ～ child ein Einzelkind

② adv. nur; **we had been waiting ～ 5 minutes when** ...: wir hatten erst 5 Minuten gewartet, als ...; **it's ～/～ just 6 o'clock** es ist erst 6 Uhr/gerade erst 6 Uhr vorbei; **he ～ just made it** er hat es gerade noch geschafft; ～ **if** nur [dann] ..., wenn; ～ **the other day/week** erst neulich

**on-screen** adj. (Comp., TV) Bildschirm-

**'onset** n. (of winter) Einbruch, der; (of disease) Ausbruch, der

**onslaught** /'ɒnslɔːt/ n. [heftige] Attacke (fig.)

**'on-target** attrib. adj. ～ **earnings £50,000** Verdienst bei erfolgreicher Tätigkeit 50 000 Pfund

**onto** ▶ ON 2

**onus** /'əʊnəs/ n. **the ～ is on him to do it** es ist seine Sache, es zu tun

**onward[s]** /'ɒnwədz/ adv. (in space) vorwärts; **from X ～**: von X an; **from that day ～**: von diesem Tag an

**onyx** /'ɒnɪks/ n. Onyx, der

**ooze** /uːz/ ① v.i. sickern (**from** aus) ② v.t. triefen von od. vor (+ Dat.); (fig.) ausstrahlen

**op** /ɒp/ n. (coll.) Operation, die

**opaque** /əʊ'peɪk/ adj. lichtundurchlässig; opak (fachspr.)

**open** /'əʊpn/ ① adj. (a) offen; (not blocked or obstructed) frei; (available) frei ⟨Stelle⟩; **in the ～ air** im Freien; **be ～** ⟨Laden, Museum, Bank usw.⟩ geöffnet sein; **have an ～ mind about** or **on sth.** einer Sache gegenüber aufgeschlossen sein
(b) unverhohlen ⟨Bewunderung, Hass, Verachtung⟩
(c) (frank, communicative) offen ⟨Wesen, Streit, Abstimmung, Regierungsstil⟩; (not secret) öffentlich ⟨Wahl⟩
(d) geöffnet ⟨Regenschirm⟩; aufgeblüht ⟨Blume, Knospe⟩; aufgeschlagen ⟨Zeitung, Landkarte⟩
② n. **in the ～** (outdoors) unter freiem Himmel; **[out] in the ～** (fig.) öffentlich bekannt
③ v.t. (a) öffnen
(b) eröffnen ⟨Konferenz, Diskussion, Laden⟩; beginnen ⟨Verhandlungen, Spiel⟩
(c) (unfold, spread out) aufschlagen ⟨Zeitung, Buch, Landkarte⟩; öffnen ⟨Schirm⟩
④ v.i. (a) sich öffnen; ～ **into/on to sth.** zu etw. führen
(b) (become ～ to customers) öffnen; (start trading etc.) eröffnet werden
(c) (start) beginnen; ⟨Ausstellung:⟩ eröffnet werden; ⟨Theaterstück:⟩ Premiere haben
■ **open 'up** ① v.t. öffnen; (establish) eröffnen ② v.i. sich öffnen; ⟨Filiale:⟩ eröffnet werden; ⟨Firma:⟩ sich niederlassen

**open: ～-air** attrib. adj. Openair⟨konzert⟩; ～-air [swimming] pool Freibad, das; ～-and-'shut case n. (coll.) klarer Fall; ～ day n. Tag der offenen Tür

**'opener** n. Öffner, der

**'opening** ① n. (a) Öffnen, das; (becoming open) Sichöffnen, das; (of exhibition, new centre) Eröffnen, das
(b) (establishment, ceremony) Eröffnung, die
(c) (initial part) Anfang, der
(d) (gap, aperture) Öffnung, die
(e) (opportunity) Möglichkeit, die; (vacancy) freie Stelle
② adj. einleitend

**opening: ～ hours** n. pl. Öffnungszeiten Pl.; ～ **time** n. Öffnungszeit, die

**'openly** adv. (a) (publicly) in der Öffentlichkeit; öffentlich ⟨zugeben, verurteilen⟩
(b) (frankly) offen

**open: ～ 'market** n. offener od. freier Markt; ～-'minded adj. aufgeschlossen

**openness** /'əʊpnnɪs/ n. (frankness) Offenheit, die

**open: ～-'plan** adj. ～-plan office Großraumbüro, das; ～ 'prison n. offene Anstalt; ～ 'sandwich n. belegtes Brot

**opera** /'ɒpərə/ n. Oper, die

**opera: ～ glasses** n. pl. Opernglas, das; ～ **house** n. Opernhaus, das; ～ **singer** n. Opernsänger, der/-sängerin, die

**operate** /'ɒpəreɪt/ ① v.i. (a) (be in action) in Betrieb sein; ⟨Bus, Zug usw.:⟩ verkehren
(b) (function) arbeiten; **the torch ～s on batteries** die Taschenlampe arbeitet mit Batterien
(c) ～ [**on sb.**] (Med.) [jmdn.] operieren ② v.t. bedienen ⟨Maschine⟩; unterhalten ⟨Busverbindung, Telefondienst⟩; betätigen ⟨Hebel, Bremse⟩

**operating: ～ system** n. (Comp.) Betriebssystem, das; ～ **theatre** n. (Brit. Med.) Operationssaal, der

**operation** /ɒpə'reɪʃn/ n. (a) (causing to work) (of machine) Bedienung, die; (of bus service, telephone service, etc.) Unterhaltung, die; (of lever, brake) Betätigung, die
(b) **come into ～** ⟨Gesetz, Gebühr usw.:⟩ in Kraft treten; **be in/out of ～** ⟨Maschine, Gerät usw.:⟩ in/außer Betrieb sein
(c) (Med.) Operation, die; **have an ～**: operiert werden

**operational** /ɒpə'reɪʃənl/ adj. (esp. Mil.: ready to function) einsatzbereit

**operative** /'ɒpərətɪv/ adj. **become ～** ⟨Gesetz:⟩ in Kraft treten; **the scheme is ～**: das Programm läuft

**operator** /'ɒpəreɪtə(r)/ n. [Maschinen]bediener, der/-bedienerin, die; (Teleph.) (at exchange) Vermittlung, die; (at switchboard) Telefonist, der/Telefonistin, die

**ophthalmic op'tician** /ɒf'θælmɪk/ n. (Brit.) Augenoptiker, der/-optikerin, die

**opinion** /ə'pɪnjən/ n. Meinung, die (**on** über ····⟶

+ *Akk.*, zu); **have a high/low** ∼ **of sb.** eine/
keine hohe Meinung von jmdm. haben; **in
my** ∼: meiner Meinung nach

**opinionated** /ə'pɪnjəneɪtɪd/ *adj.*
rechthaberisch

**o'pinion poll** *n.* Meinungsumfrage, *die*

**opium** /'əʊpɪəm/ *n.* Opium, *das*

**opponent** /ə'pəʊnənt/ *n.* Gegner, *der*/
Gegnerin, *die*

**opportune** /'ɒpətjuːn/ *adj.* **(a)** (favourable)
günstig
**(b)** (well-timed) zur rechten Zeit *nachgestellt*

**opportunism** /ɒpə'tjuːnɪzm/ *n.*
Opportunismus, *der*

**opportunist** /ɒpə'tjuːnɪst/ *n.* Opportunist,
*der*/Opportunistin, *die*

**opportunity** /ɒpə'tjuːnɪti/ *n.* Gelegenheit,
*die*

**oppose** /ə'pəʊz/ **1** *v.t.* sich wenden gegen
**2** *v.i.* **the opposing team** die gegnerische
Mannschaft

**opposed** /ə'pəʊzd/ *adj.* **as** ∼ **to** im
Gegensatz zu; **be** ∼ **to sth.** ⟨*Person:*⟩ gegen
etw. sein

**opposite** /'ɒpəzɪt/ **1** *adj.* gegenüberliegend
⟨*Straßenseite, Ufer*⟩; entgegengesetzt ⟨*Ende,
Weg, Richtung*⟩; **the** ∼ **sex** das andere
Geschlecht
**2** *n.* Gegenteil, *das* (**of** von)
**3** *adv.* gegenüber
**4** *prep.* gegenüber

**opposite 'number** *n.* (fig.) Pendant, *das*

**opposition** /ɒpə'zɪʃn/ *n.* **(a)** Opposition,
*die;* (resistance) Widerstand, *der* (**to** gegen); **in**
∼ **to** entgegen
**(b)** (Brit. Polit.) **the O**∼: die Opposition

**oppress** /ə'pres/ *v.t.* unterdrücken; (fig.)
⟨*Gefühl:*⟩ bedrücken

**oppression** /ə'preʃn/ *n.* Unterdrückung,
*die*

**oppressive** /ə'presɪv/ *adj.* repressiv; (fig.)
bedrückend ⟨*Ängste, Atmosphäre*⟩; (hot and
close) drückend ⟨*Wetter, Klima, Tag*⟩

**opt** /ɒpt/ *v.i.* sich entscheiden (**for** für); ∼ **to
do sth.** sich dafür entscheiden, etw. zu tun;
∼ **out** nicht mitmachen/(stop taking part) nicht
länger mitmachen (**of** bei)

**optic** /'ɒptɪk/ **1** *adj.* (Anat.) Seh⟨*nerv, -bahn*⟩
**2** *n.* **or O**∼ ® (Brit.: for spirits) Portionierer,
*der*

**optical** /'ɒptɪkl/ *adj.* optisch

**optical 'character reader** *n.* (Comp.)
Klarschriftleser, *der*

**optician** /ɒp'tɪʃn/ *n.* Optiker, *der*/
Optikerin, *die*

**optics** /'ɒptɪks/ *n.* Optik, *die*

**optima** *pl. of* OPTIMUM

**optimise** ▶ OPTIMIZE

**optimism** /'ɒptɪmɪzm/ *n.* Optimismus, *der*

**optimist** /'ɒptɪmɪst/ *n.* Optimist, *der*/
Optimistin, *die*

**optimistic** /ɒptɪ'mɪstɪk/ *adj.* optimistisch

**optimize** /'ɒptɪmaɪz/ *v.t.* (make the most of)
das Beste machen aus

**optimum** /'ɒptɪməm/ **1** *n., pl.* **optima**
/'ɒptɪmə/ Optimum, *das*
**2** *adj.* optimal

**option** /'ɒpʃn/ *n.* (choice) Wahl, *die;* (thing)
Wahlmöglichkeit, *die*

**optional** /'ɒpʃənl/ *adj.* nicht zwingend;
∼ **subject** Wahlfach, *das*

**opulence** /'ɒpjʊləns/ *n.* Wohlstand, *der*

**opulent** /'ɒpjʊlənt/ *adj.* wohlhabend; feudal
⟨*Auto, Haus usw.*⟩

**or** /ə(r), *stressed* ɔː(r)/ *conj.* **(a)** oder; **he
cannot read or write** er kann weder lesen
noch schreiben; **without food or water** ohne
Essen und Wasser; **15 or 20 minutes** 15 bis 20
Minuten; **in a day or two** in ein, zwei Tagen
**(b)** (introducing explanation) das heißt; **or rather**
beziehungsweise

**oracle** /'ɒrəkl/ *n.* Orakel, *das*

**oral** /'ɔːrəl/ *adj.* mündlich; (Med.) oral

**orally** /'ɔːrəli/ *adv.* **take** ∼: einnehmen

**orange** /'ɒrɪndʒ/ **1** *n.* **(a)** (fruit) Orange, *die;*
Apfelsine, *die*
**(b)** (colour) Orange, *das*
**2** *adj.* orange[farben]

**orange:** ∼ **juice** *n.* Orangensaft, *der;*
∼ **peel** *n.* Orangenschale, *die;* ∼ **'squash**
*n.* Orangensaftgetränk, *das*

**orator** /'ɒrətə(r)/ *n.* Redner, *der*/Rednerin,
*die*

**oratory** /'ɒrətəri/ *n.* Redekunst, *die*

**orb** /ɔːb/ *n.* Kugel, *die*

**orbit** /'ɔːbɪt/ **1** *n.* (Astron.) [Umlauf]bahn, *die*
**2** *v.i.* kreisen
**3** *v.t.* umkreisen

**orbital** /'ɔːbɪtl/ *adj.* ∼ **road** Ringstraße, *die*

**orchard** /'ɔːtʃəd/ *n.* Obstgarten, *der;*
(commercial) Obstplantage, *die*

**orchestra** /'ɔːkɪstrə/ *n.* Orchester, *das*

**orchestral** /ɔː'kestrl/ *adj.* Orchester-

**orchestrate** /'ɔːkɪstreɪt/ *v.t.* orchestrieren

**orchid** /'ɔːkɪd/ *n.* Orchidee, *die*

**ordain** /ɔː'deɪn/ *v.t.* **(a)** (Eccl.) ordinieren
**(b)** (decree) verfügen

**ordeal** /ɔː'diːl/ *n.* Qual, *die*

**order** /'ɔːdə(r)/ **1** *n.* **(a)** (sequence)
Reihenfolge, *die;* **out of** ∼: durcheinander
**(b)** (regular arrangement, normal state) Ordnung,
*die;* **be/not be in** ∼: in Ordnung/nicht in
Ordnung sein (ugs.); **be out of/in** ∼ (not in/in
working condition) nicht funktionieren/
funktionieren; **'out of** ∼' „außer Betrieb"; **in
good/bad** ∼: in gutem/schlechtem Zustand
**(c)** (command) Anweisung, *die;* (Mil.) Befehl,
*der*
**(d) in** ∼ **to do sth.** um etw. zu tun
**(e)** (Commerc.) Auftrag, *der* (**for** über + *Akk.*);
(to waiter, ∼ed goods) Bestellung, *die*
**(f) keep** ∼: Ordnung [be]wahren; *see also*
LAW B
**(g)** (religious ∼) Orden, *der*

2 *v.t.* (a) (command) befehlen; ⟨*Richter:*⟩ verfügen; ∼ **sb. to do sth.** jmdn. anweisen/ (Milit.) jmdm. befehlen, etw. zu tun
(b) (Commerc.) bestellen (**from** bei)
(c) (arrange) ordnen
■ **order a'bout, order a'round** *v.t.* herumkommandieren

'**order form** *n.* Bestellformular, *das*

**orderly** /'ɔːdəlɪ/ 1 *adj.* friedlich; diszipliniert ⟨*Menge*⟩; (methodical) methodisch; (tidy) ordentlich
2 *n.* (a) (Mil.) [Offiziers]bursche, *der*
(b) **medical** ∼: ≈ Krankenpflegehelfer, *der*

**ordinal** /'ɔːdɪnl/ *adj. & n.* ∼ [**number**] Ordinalzahl, *die*

**ordinarily** /'ɔːdɪnərɪlɪ/ *adv.* normalerweise; gewöhnlich

**ordinary** /'ɔːdɪnərɪ/ *adj.* (normal) normal ⟨*Gebrauch*⟩; üblich ⟨*Verfahren*⟩; (not exceptional) gewöhnlich

**ordination** /ɔːdɪ'neɪʃn/ *n.* (Eccl.) Ordination, *die;* Ordinierung, *die*

**ordnance 'survey** /'ɔːdnəns/ *n.* (Brit.) amtliche Landesvermessung; ∼ **survey map** amtliche topographische Karte

**ore** /ɔː(r)/ *n.* Erz, *das*

**organ** /'ɔːgən/ *n.* (a) (Mus.) Orgel, *die*
(b) (Biol.) Organ, *das*

'**organ donor** *n.* Organspender, *der*/ -spenderin, *die;* ∼ **card** Organspende[r]ausweis, *der*

**organic** /ɔː'gænɪk/ *adj.* organisch; biologisch-dynamisch ⟨*Ackerbau*⟩; biodynamisch ⟨*Nahrungsmittel*⟩

**organically** /ɔː'gænɪkəlɪ/ *adv.* (a) (also Med.) organisch
(b) (without chemicals) biologisch

**organism** /'ɔːgənɪzm/ *n.* Organismus, *der*

**organist** /'ɔːgənɪst/ *n.* Organist, *der*/ Organistin, *die*

**organization** /ɔːgənaɪ'zeɪʃn/ *n.* Organisation, *die;* ∼ **of time/work** Zeit-/ Arbeitseinteilung, *die*

**organize** /'ɔːgənaɪz/ *v.t.* organisieren; einteilen ⟨*Arbeit, Zeit*⟩; veranstalten ⟨*Konferenz, Festival*⟩; ∼ **into groups** in Gruppen einteilen

**organized** /'ɔːgənaɪzd/ *adj.* organisiert

'**organizer** *n.* Organisator, *der*/ Organisatorin, *die;* (of event, festival) Veranstalter, *der*/Veranstalterin, *die*

'**organ transplant** *n.* Organverpflanzung, *die*

**orgasm** /'ɔːgæzm/ *n.* Orgasmus, *der*

**orgy** /'ɔːdʒɪ/ *n.* Orgie, *die*

**orient** 1 /'ɔːrɪənt/ *n.* **the O**∼: der Orient
2 /'ɒrɪent/ *v.t.* ausrichten (**towards** nach); ∼ **oneself** sich orientieren

**oriental** /ɒrɪ'entl/ 1 *adj.* orientalisch
2 *n.* Asiat, *der*/Asiatin, *die*

**orientate** /'ɒrɪənteɪt/ ▶ ORIENT 2

**orientation** /ɒrɪən'teɪʃn/ *n.* Orientierung, *die*

**orienteering** /ɒrɪən'tɪərɪŋ/ *n.* (Brit.) Orientierungslauf, *der*

**orifice** /'ɒrɪfɪs/ *n.* Öffnung, *die*

**origin** /'ɒrɪdʒɪn/ *n.* (derivation) Herkunft, *die;* (beginnings) Anfänge *Pl.;* (source) Ursprung, *der;* **country of** ∼: Herkunftsland, *das;* **have its** ∼ **in sth.** seinen Ursprung in etw. (*Dat.*) haben

**original** /ə'rɪdʒɪnl/ 1 *adj.* ursprünglich; Ur⟨*text, -fassung*⟩; eigenständig ⟨*Forschung*⟩; (inventive) originell; **an** ∼ **painting** ein Original
2 *n.* Original, *das*

**original 'gravity** *n.* Stammwürze, *die*

**originality** /ərɪdʒɪ'nælɪtɪ/ *n.* Originalität, *die*

**originally** /ə'rɪdʒɪnəlɪ/ *adv.* (a) ursprünglich
(b) originell ⟨*schreiben usw.*⟩

**originate** /ə'rɪdʒɪneɪt/ *v.i.* ∼ **from** entstehen aus; ∼ **in** seinen Ursprung haben in (+ *Dat.*)

**ornament** /'ɔːnəmənt/ *n.* Ziergegenstand, *der*

**ornamental** /ɔːnə'mentl/ *adj.* dekorativ; Zier⟨*pflanze, -naht usw.*⟩

**ornate** /ɔː'neɪt/ *adj.* reich verziert; prunkvoll ⟨*Dekoration*⟩

**ornithologist** /ɔːnɪ'θɒlədʒɪst/ *n..* Ornithologe, *der*/Ornithologin, *die*

**ornithology** /ɔːnɪ'θɒlədʒɪ/ *n.* Ornithologie, *die*

**orphan** /'ɔːfn/ 1 *n.* Waise, *die*
2 *v.t.* **be** ∼**ed** [zur] Waise werden

**orphanage** /'ɔːfənɪdʒ/ *n.* Waisenhaus, *das*

**orthodox** /'ɔːθədɒks/ *adj.* orthodox

**orthopaedic** /ɔːθə'piːdɪk/ *adj.* orthopädisch

**orthopaedics** /ɔːθə'piːdɪks/ *n.* Orthopädie, *die*

**oscillate** /'ɒsɪleɪt/ *v.i.* schwingen

**oscillation** /ɒsɪ'leɪʃn/ *n.* Schwingen, *das;* (single ∼) Schwingung, *die*

**osmosis** /ɒz'məʊsɪs/ *n., pl.* **osmoses** /ɒz'məʊsiːz/ Osmose, *die*

**ostensible** /ɒ'stensɪbl/ *adj.* vorgeschoben

**ostensibly** /ɒ'stensɪblɪ/ *adv.* vorgeblich

**ostentatious** /ɒsten'teɪʃəs/ *adj.* prunkhaft ⟨*Kleidung, Schmuck*⟩; prahlerisch ⟨*Art*⟩

**osteopath** /'ɒstɪəpæθ/ *n.* Osteopath, *der*/ Osteopathin, *die*

**osteoporosis** /ɒstɪəʊpə'rəʊsɪs/ *n.* Osteoporose, *die*

**ostrich** /'ɒstrɪtʃ/ *n.* Strauß, *der*

**other** /'ʌðə(r)/ 1 *adj.* (a) (not the same) ander…; **the** ∼ **two/three** *etc.* (the remaining) die beiden/drei *usw.* anderen; **the** ∼ **one** der/die/das andere; **some** ∼ **time** ein andermal

⋯⟶

**(b)** (further) one ∼ thing noch eins; **some/six ∼ people** noch ein paar/noch sechs [andere *od.* weitere] Leute; **no ∼ questions** keine weiteren Fragen
**(c) ∼ than** (different from) anders als; (except) außer
**(d) the ∼ day/evening** neulich/neulich abends
2 *n.* anderer/andere/anderes; **there are six ∼s** es sind noch sechs andere da; **any ∼:** irgendein anderer/-eine andere/-ein anderes; **not any ∼:** kein anderer/keine andere/kein anderes; **one after the ∼:** einer/eine/eins nach dem/der/dem anderen
3 *adv.* anders; **∼ than that, ...:** abgesehen davon, ...

**otherwise** /'ʌðəwaɪz/ 1 *adv.* **(a)** (in a different way) anders
**(b)** (or else) anderenfalls
**(c)** (in other respects) im Übrigen
2 *pred. adj.* anders

**otter** /'ɒtə(r)/ *n.* [Fisch]otter, *der*

**ouch** /aʊtʃ/ *int.* autsch

**ought** /ɔ:t/ *v. aux. only in pres. and past* ought, *neg.* (coll.) **oughtn't** /'ɔ:tnt/ **I ∼ to do/ have done it** (expr. moral duty) ich müsste es tun/hätte es tun müssen; (expr. desirability) ich sollte es tun/hätte es tun sollen; **∼ not** *or* **∼n't you to have left by now?** müsstest du nicht schon weg sein?; **one ∼ not to do it** man sollte es nicht tun; **he ∼ to be hanged/ in hospital** er gehört an den Galgen/ins Krankenhaus; **that ∼ to be enough** das dürfte reichen; **he ∼ to win** er müsste [eigentlich] gewinnen

**oughtn't** /'ɔ:tnt/ (coll.) = **ought not**

**ounce** /aʊns/ *n.* (measure) Unze, *die*

**our** /'aʊə(r)/ *poss. pron. attrib.* unser

**ours** /'aʊəz/ *poss. pron. pred.* unserer/ unsere/unseres; *see also* HERS

**ourselves** /aʊə'selvz/ *pron.* **(a)** *emphat.* selbst
**(b)** *refl.* uns. *See also* HERSELF

**oust** /aʊst/ *v.t.* verdrängen; **∼ sb. from his job/from power** jmdn. von seinem Arbeitsplatz vertreiben/jmdn. entmachten

**out** /aʊt/ *adv.* **(a)** (away from place) **∼ here/ there** hier/da draußen; **be ∼ in the garden** draußen im Garten sein; **what's it like ∼?** wie ist es draußen?; **go ∼ shopping** *etc.* einkaufen *usw.* gehen; **be ∼** (not at home, not in one's office, etc.) nicht da sein; **she was ∼ all night** sie war eine/die ganze Nacht weg; **have a day ∼ in London** einen Tag in London verbringen; **row ∼ to ...:** hinaus-/ herausrudern zu ...; **be ∼ at sea** auf See sein
**(b)** (Sport, Games) **be ∼** ⟨*Ball:*⟩ aus *od.* im Aus sein; ⟨*Mitspieler:*⟩ ausscheiden; ⟨*Schlagmann:*⟩ aus[geschlagen] sein; **not ∼:** nicht aus
**(c) be ∼** (asleep) weg sein (ugs.); (unconscious) bewusstlos sein
**(d)** (no longer burning) aus[gegangen]

**(e)** (in error) **be 3% ∼ in one's calculations** sich um 3% verrechnet haben; **this is £5 ∼:** das stimmt um 5 Pfund nicht
**(f)** (not in fashion) passee (ugs.); out (ugs.)
**(g) say it ∼ loud** es laut sagen; **∼ with it!** heraus mit der Sprache; **their secret is ∼:** ihr Geheimnis ist bekannt geworden; **[the] truth will ∼:** die Wahrheit wird an den Tag kommen; **the sun/moon is ∼:** die Sonne/der Mond scheint; **the third volume is just ∼:** der dritte Band ist soeben erschienen; **the roses are ∼:** die Rosen blühen
**(h) be ∼ for sth./to do sth.** auf etw. (*Akk.*) aus sein/darauf aus sein, etw. zu tun; **be ∼ for trouble** Streit suchen
**(i)** (to or at an end) **before the day/month was ∼:** am selben Tag/vor Ende des Monats. *See also* OUT OF

**out: ∼back** *n.* (esp. Austral.) Hinterland, *das;* **∼'bid** *v.t.,* ∼bid überbieten; **∼board** *adj.* **∼board motor** Außenbordmotor, *der;* **∼break** *n.* Ausbruch, *der;* **at the ∼break of war** bei Kriegsausbruch; **an ∼break of flu** eine Grippeepidemie; **∼building** *n.* Nebengebäude, *das;* **∼burst** *n.* Ausbruch, *der;* **an ∼burst of weeping/laughter** ein Weinkrampf/Lachanfall; **an ∼burst of temper** ein Wutanfall; **∼cast** *n.* Ausgestoßene, *der/ die;* **a social ∼cast** ein Geächteter/eine Geächtete; **∼come** *n.* Ergebnis, *das;* Resultat, *das;* **∼cry** *n.* [Aufschrei der] Empörung; **∼'dated** *adj.* überholt; **∼'do** *v.t., forms as* DO: überbieten (in an + *Dat.*); **∼door** *adj.* ∼door shoes/things Straßenschuhe/-kleidung, *die;* **∼door games/ pursuits** Spiele/Beschäftigungen im Freien; **∼door swimming pool** Freibad, *das;* **∼'doors** 1 *adv.* draußen; **go ∼doors** nach draußen gehen; 2 *n.* **the [great] ∼doors** die freie Natur

**outer** /'aʊtə(r)/ *adj.* äußer...; Außen⟨*fläche, -seite, -wand, -tür*⟩

**outer 'space** *n.* Weltraum, *der*

**out: ∼fit** *n.* **(a)** (clothes) Kleider *Pl.;* **(b)** (equipment) Ausrüstung, *die;* **(c)** (coll.: organization) Laden, *der* (ugs.); **∼going** 1 *adj.* **(a)** [aus dem Amt] scheidend ⟨*Regierung, Präsident*⟩; **(b)** (friendly) kontaktfreudig ⟨*Person*⟩; 2 *n., in pl.* ∼s (expenditure) Ausgaben *Pl.;* **∼'grow** *v.t., forms as* GROW: herauswachsen aus ⟨*Kleider*⟩; (leave behind) entwachsen (+ *Dat.*); **∼growth** *n.* Auswuchs, *der;* **∼house** *n.* Nebengebäude, *das*

**'outing** *n.* Ausflug, *der*

**out: ∼landish** /aʊt'lændɪʃ/ *adj.* ausgefallen; **∼last** *v.t.* überdauern; überleben ⟨*Person, Jahrhundert*⟩; **∼law** 1 *n.* Bandit, *der/*Banditin, *die;* 2 *v.t.* verbieten; **∼lay** *n.* Ausgaben *Pl.* (on für); **∼let** /'aʊtlet, 'aʊtlɪt/ *n.* **(a)** Ablauf, Abfluss, *der;* Auslauf, Auslass, *der;* **(b)** (fig.) Ventil, *das;* **(c)** (market) Absatzmarkt, *der;* (shop) Verkaufsstelle, *die;* **∼line** 1 *n.* **(a)** *in sing. or pl.* Umriss, *der;* **(b)** (short account)

Grundriss, *der;* (of topic) Übersicht, die (**of** über + *Akk.*); **2** *v.t.* (describe) umreißen; ~**live** /aʊt'lɪv/ *v.t.* überleben; ~**look** *n.* (a) (view) Aussicht, die (**over** über + *Akk.,* **on to** auf + *Akk.*); (fig.; Meteorol.) Aussichten *Pl.;* (**b**) (mental attitude) Einstellung, *die* (**on** zu); ~**lying** *adj.* entlegen; ~**ma'nœuvre** *v.t.* überlisten ⟨*Truppen*⟩; ~**moded** /aʊt'məʊdɪd/ *adj.* antiquiert; ~**number** *v.t.* zahlenmäßig überlegen sein (+ *Dat.*)

'**out of** *prep.* (**a**) (from within) aus; **go** ~ **the door** zur Tür hinausgehen

(**b**) (not within) **be** ~ **the country** im Ausland sein; **be** ~ **town/the room** nicht in der Stadt/ im Zimmer sein; **feel** ~ **it** *or* **things** sich ausgeschlossen fühlen

(**c**) (from among) **one** ~ **every three smokers** jeder dritte Raucher; **58** ~ **every 100** 58 von hundert

(**d**) (beyond range of ) außer ⟨*Reich-/Hörweite, Sicht, Kontrolle*⟩

(**e**) (from) aus; **get money** ~ **sb.** Geld aus jmdm. herausholen; **do well** ~ **sb./sth.** von jmdm./etw. profitieren

(**f**) aus ⟨*Mitleid, Furcht, Neugier usw.*⟩

(**g**) (without) ~ **money** ohne Geld; **we're** ~ **tea** wir haben keinen Tee mehr

(**h**) (away from) von … entfernt; **ten miles** ~ **London** 10 Meilen außerhalb von London

**out:** ~**-of-court settlement** *n.* (Law) (agreement) außergerichtlicher Vergleich; (payment) Vergleichssumme, *die;* ~**-of-'date** *attrib. adj.* veraltet; (expired) ungültig ⟨*Karte*⟩; ~**-of-'pocket** *attrib. adj.* Bar⟨*auslagen*⟩; ~**-of-print** *attrib. adj.* vergriffen; ~**-of-work** *attrib. adj.* arbeitslos; ~**patient** *n.* ambulanter Patient/ambulante Patientin; ~**patients[' department]** Poliklinik, *die;* ~'**play** *v.t.* (Sport) besser spielen als; ~**post** *n.* Außenposten, *der;* (of civilization etc.; also Mil.) Vorposten, *der;* ~**pouring** *n.,* *usu. in pl.* Gefühlsäußerung, *die;* ~**put** *n.* (**a**) (Produktion, *die;* (of liquid, electricity, etc.) Leistung, *die;* (**b**) (Comp.) Ausgabe, *die*

**outrage** **1** /'aʊtreɪdʒ/ *n.* (**a**) (deed) Verbrechen, *das;* (during war) Gräueltat, *die;* (against decency) grober Verstoß

(**b**) (strong resentment) Empörung, *die* (**at** gegen)

**2** /aʊt'reɪdʒ/ *v.t.* empören

**outrageous** /aʊt'reɪdʒəs/ *adj.* unverschämt; unverschämt hoch ⟨*Preis*⟩; unerhört ⟨*Frechheit, Skandal*⟩

**out:** ~**right** **1** /-'-/ *adv.* (**a**) ganz, komplett ⟨*kaufen, verkaufen*⟩; (**b**) (openly) freiheraus ⟨*erzählen, sagen, lachen*⟩; **2** /'--/ *adj.* ausgemacht ⟨*Unehrlichkeit*⟩; glatt (ugs.) ⟨*Ablehnung, Absage, Lüge*⟩; klar ⟨*Sieg, Niederlage, Sieger*⟩; ~**set** *n.* Anfang, *der;* **at the** ~**set** zu Anfang; **from the** ~**set** von Anfang an; ~'**shine** *v.t.,* ~**shone** /aʊt'ʃɒn/ (fig.) in den Schatten stellen

**outside** **1** /-'-, '--/ *n.* (**a**) Außenseite, *die;* **on the** ~: außen; **to/from the** ~: nach/von außen; ~ **lane** Überholspur, *die*

(**b**) (external appearance) Äußere, *das*

(**c**) **at the [very]** ~ äußerstenfalls; höchstens

**2** /'--/ *adj.* (**a**) äußer…; Außen⟨*wand, -antenne, -kajüte, -toilette, -durchmesser*⟩; ~ **lane** Überholspur, *die*

(**b**) **have only an** ~ **chance** nur eine sehr geringe Chance haben

**3** /-'-/ *adv.* (on the ~) draußen; (to the ~) nach draußen

**4** /-'-/ *prep.* (**a**) (position) außerhalb (+ *Gen.*); ~ **the door** vor der Tür

(**b**) (to the ~ of ) aus … hinaus; **go** ~ **the house** nach draußen gehen

**out'sider** *n.* (Sport; also fig.) Außenseiter, *der*

**out:** ~**size** *adj.* überdimensional; ~**size clothes** Kleidung in Übergröße; ~**skirts** *n. pl.* Stadtrand, *der;* **the** ~**skirts of the town** die Außenbezirke der Stadt; ~'**smart** *v.t.* (coll.) ausschmieren (ugs.); ~'**spoken** *adj.* freimütig; **be** ~**spoken about sth.** sich freimütig über etw. äußern; ~'**standing** *adj.* (**a**) (exceptional) hervorragend; überragend ⟨*Bedeutung*⟩; außergewöhnlich ⟨*Person, Mut, Fähigkeit*⟩; (**b**) (not yet settled) ausstehend ⟨*Schuld, Geldsumme*⟩; unbezahlt ⟨*Rechnung*⟩; ungelöst ⟨*Problem*⟩

~'**standingly** *adv.* außergewöhnlich; ~**stretched** *adj.* ausgestreckt; (spread out) ausgebreitet; ~'**strip** *v.t.* (pass in running) überholen; (in competition) überflügeln; ~**tray** *n.* Ablage für Ausgänge; ~'**vote** *v.t.* überstimmen

**outward** /'aʊtwəd/ **1** *adj.* (**a**) (external, apparent) [rein] äußerlich; äußer… ⟨*Erscheinung, Bedingung*⟩

(**b**) Hin⟨*reise, -fracht*⟩

**2** *adv.* nach außen ⟨*aufgehen, richten*⟩

'**outwardly** *adv.* nach außen hin ⟨*Gefühle zeigen*⟩; öffentlich ⟨*Loyalität erklären*⟩

'**outwards** ▶ OUTWARD 2

**out:** ~'**weigh** *v.t.* schwerer wiegen als; überwiegen ⟨*Nachteile*⟩; ~'**wit** *v.t.,* -**tt**- überlisten; ~'**worn** *adj.* veraltet

**oval** /'əʊvl/ **1** *adj.* oval

**2** *n.* Oval, *das*

**ovary** /'əʊvərɪ/ *n.* (Anat.) Eierstock, *der*

**ovation** /əʊ'veɪʃn/ *n.* Ovation, *die;* **a standing** ~: stehende Ovationen *Pl.*

**oven** /'ʌvn/ *n.* [Back]ofen, *der*

**oven:** ~ **cloth** *n.* Topflappen, *der;* ~ **glove** *n.* Topfhandschuh, *der;* ~**proof** *adj.* feuerfest; ~**-ready** *adj.* backfertig ⟨*Pommes frites, Pastete*⟩; bratfertig ⟨*Geflügel*⟩; ~**ware** *n.* feuerfestes Geschirr

**over** /'əʊvə(r)/ **1** *adv.* (**a**) (outward and downward) hinüber; **climb/look/jump** ~: hinüber- od. (ugs.) rüberklettern/-sehen/ -springen

(**b**) (so as to cover surface) **board/cover** ~: zunageln/-decken

(**c**) (across a space) hinüber; (towards speaker) herüber; **he swam** ~ **to us/the other side** er schwamm zu uns herüber/hinüber zur anderen Seite; ~ **here/there** (direction) hier ⋯⋗

herüber/dort hinüber; (location) hier/dort;
[come in, please,] ~ (Radio) übernehmen Sie
bitte; ~ and out (Radio) Ende
(d) (in excess etc.) children of 12 and ~:
Kinder im Alter von zwölf Jahren und
darüber; be [left] ~: übrig [geblieben] sein
(e) (from beginning to end) von Anfang bis
Ende; say sth. twice ~: etw. zweimal sagen;
[all] ~ again, (Amer.) ~: noch einmal [ganz
von vorn]; ~ and ~ [again] immer wieder
(f) (at an end) vorbei; vorüber; be ~: vorbei
sein; ⟨Aufführung:⟩ zu Ende sein; get sth.
~ with etw. hinter sich ⟨Akk.⟩ bringen; be
~ and done with erledigt sein
(g) all ~ (completely finished) aus [und vorbei]; I
ache all ~: mir tut alles weh; be shaking all
~: am ganzen Körper zittern
② prep. (a) (above, on, round about) über
(position: + Dat.; direction: + Akk.); (across)
über (+ Akk.); look ~ a wall über eine Mauer
sehen; fall ~ a cliff von einem Felsen
stürzen; the pub ~ the road die Wirtschaft
gegenüber; hit sb. ~ the head jmdm. auf den
Kopf schlagen; ~ the page auf der nächsten
Seite
(b) (in or across every part of) [überall] in
(+ Dat.); (to and fro upon) über (+ Akk.); (all
through) durch; all ~ (in or on all parts of)
überall in (+ Dat.); travel all ~ the country
das ganze Land bereisen; all ~ Spain in ganz
Spanien; all ~ the world in der ganzen Welt
(c) (on account of) wegen
(d) (engaged with) bei; take trouble ~ sth. sich
(Dat.) mit etw. Mühe geben; be a long time
~ sth. lange für etw. brauchen; ~ work/
dinner bei der Arbeit/beim Essen
(e) (superior to, in charge of) über (+ Akk.); have
command/authority ~ sb. Befehlsgewalt über
jmdn./Weisungsbefugnis gegenüber jmdm.
haben; be ~ sb. (in rank) über jmdm. stehen
(f) (beyond, more than) über (+ Akk.); ~ and
above zusätzlich zu
(g) (throughout, during) über (+ Akk.); ~ the
weekend/summer übers Wochenende/den
Sommer über; ~ the past years in den
letzten Jahren

**over:** ~**'active** adj. hyperaktiv; ~**all**
① n. (Brit.: garment) Arbeitskittel, der; ② adj.
(a) Gesamt⟨breite, -einsparung, -abmessung⟩;
have an ~all majority die absolute Mehrheit
haben; (b) (general) allgemein; ③ /'---, --'-/
adv. (a) (in all parts) insgesamt; (b) (taken as a
whole) im Großen und Ganzen; ~**'anxious**
adj. be ~anxious to do sth. etw. unbedingt
tun wollen; ~**'awe** v.t. Ehrfurcht einflößen
(+ Dat.); ~**'balance** v.i. das Gleichgewicht
verlieren; ~**'bearing** adj. herrisch;
~**'blown** adj. (past its prime, lit. or fig.)
verblühend; ~**board** adv. über Bord; fall
~board über Bord gehen; ~**'cast** adj. trübe;
bewölkt ⟨Himmel⟩; ~**'charge** v.t. (a)
(beyond reasonable price) zu viel abverlangen
(+ Dat.); (b) (beyond right price) zu viel
berechnen (+ Dat.); ~**coat** n. Mantel, der;
~**'come** v.t., forms as COME: (a)
überwinden; bezwingen ⟨Feind⟩; ⟨Dämpfe:⟩

betäuben; (b) he was ~come by grief/with
emotion Kummer/Rührung überwältigte ihn;
~**'confidence** n. übersteigertes
Selbstvertrauen; ~**'confident** adj.
übertrieben zuversichtlich; ~**'cooked** adj.
verkocht; ~**'critical** adj. zu kritisch;
~**'crowded** adj. überfüllt; ~**'crowding**
n. (of room, bus, train) Überfüllung, die; (of city)
Übervölkerung, die; ~**'do** v.t., forms as DO:
(carry to excess) übertreiben; ~do it or things
(work too hard) sich übernehmen; ~**'done**
adj. (a) (exaggerated) übertrieben; (b)
(~cooked) verkocht; verbraten ⟨Fleisch⟩;
~**dose** n. ① Überdosis, die; ② v.i. ~dose
on heroin eine Überdosis Heroin nehmen;
~**draft** n. Kontoüberziehung, die; have an
~draft of £50 sein Konto um 50 Pfund
überzogen haben; ~**'draw** v.t., forms as
DRAW 1: überziehen ⟨Konto⟩; ~**'drawn** adj.
überzogen ⟨Konto⟩; I am ~drawn [at the
bank] mein Konto ist überzogen; ~**drive** n.
Schongang, der; ~**'due** adj. überfällig; the
train is 15 minutes ~due der Zug hat schon
15 Minuten Verspätung; ~**'eager** adj.
übereifrig; ~**'eat** v.i., forms as EAT: zu viel
essen; ~**estimate** ① /-'estɪmeɪt/ v.t.
überschätzen; ② /-'estɪmət/ n. zu hohe
Schätzung; ~**ex'ert** v. refl. sich
überanstrengen; ~**ex'pose** v.t. (Photog.)
überbelichten; ~**'fill** v.t. zu voll machen;
~**flow** ① /--'-/ v.t. laufen über (+ Akk.)
⟨Rand⟩; (flow over brim of) überlaufen aus;
~flow its banks ⟨Fluss:⟩ über die Ufer treten;
② /--'-/ v.i. überlaufen; ③ /'---/ n. ~flow
[pipe] Überlauf, der; ~**'full** adj. zu voll;
übervoll; ~**'grown** adj. überwachsen (with
von); ~**hang** ① /--'-/ v.t., ~hung /əʊvə'hʌŋ/
⟨Felsen, Stockwerk:⟩ hinausragen über
(+ Akk.); ② /'---/ n. Überhang, der;
~**'hanging** adj. überhängend; ~**haul**
① /--'-/ v.t. überholen; überprüfen ⟨System⟩;
② /'---/ n. Überholung, die; ~**head** ① /--'-/
adv. über mir/ihm/uns usw.; ② /'---/ adj.
~head wires Oberleitung, die; ~head
lighting Deckenbeleuchtung, die; ③ /'---/ n.
~heads, (Amer.) ~head (Commerc.)
Gemeinkosten Pl.; ~**'hear** v.t., forms as
HEAR 1 (accidentally) zufällig [mit]hören;
(intentionally) belauschen; ~**'heat** v.i. zu heiß
werden; ⟨Maschine, Lager:⟩ heißlaufen;
~**in'dulge** v.i. es übertreiben; ~**-indulge**
in food and drink sich an Essen und Trinken
mehr als gütlich tun; ~**in'dulgence** n.
übermäßiger Genuss (in von); (towards a
person) zu große Nachgiebigkeit;
~**in'dulgent** adj. unmäßig; (towards a
person) zu nachgiebig

**overjoyed** /əʊvə'dʒɔɪd/ adj. überglücklich
(at über + Akk.)

**over:** ~**land** /--'-/ adv. auf dem Landweg;
~**lap** ① /--'-/ v.t. überlappen; ② /--'-/ v.i.
⟨Flächen, Dachziegel:⟩ sich überlappen;
⟨Aufgaben:⟩ sich überschneiden; ③ n.
Überlappung, die; ~**'leaf** adv. auf der
Rückseite; ~**load** v.t. überladen; ~**look**
v.t. (a) ⟨Hotel, Zimmer, Haus:⟩ Aussicht

bieten auf (+ *Akk.*); **(b)** (ignore, not see)
übersehen; (allow to go unpunished)
hinwegsehen über (+ *Akk.*)
**'overly** *adv.* allzu
**over: ~'man** *v.t.* überbesetzen;
**~'manning** *n.* [personelle] Überbesetzung;
**~'modest** *adj.* zu bescheiden; **~'much**
[1] *adj.* allzu viel; [2] *adv.* allzu sehr;
**~night** [1] /--'-/ *adv.* (also fig.: suddenly) über
Nacht; **stay ~ night** übernachten; [2] /'---/
*adj.* **~night stay** Übernachtung, *die;* **be an
~night success** (fig.) über Nacht Erfolg
haben; **~'pay** *v.t., forms as* PAY 2:
überbezahlen; **~'populated** *adj.*
überbevölkert; **~popu'lation** *n.*
Übervölkerung, *die;* **~'power** *v.t.*
überwältigen; **~'powering** *adj.*
überwältigend; durchdringend ⟨*Geruch*⟩;
**~'priced** *adj.* zu teuer; **~'qualified** *adj.*
überqualifiziert; **~'rate** *v.t.* überschätzen;
**~re'act** *v.i.* unangemessen heftig
reagieren (**to** auf + *Akk.*); **~re'action** *n.*
Überreaktion, *die* (**to** auf + *Akk.*); **~'ride**
*v.t. forms as* RIDE 3: sich hinwegsetzen über
(+ *Akk.*); **~'riding** *adj.* vorrangig; **be of
~riding importance** wichtiger als alles
andere sein; **~'ripe** *adj.* überreif; **~'rule**
*v.t.* aufheben ⟨*Entscheidung*⟩; zurückweisen
⟨*Einwand, Argument*⟩; **~rule sb.** jmds.
Vorschlag ablehnen; **~'run** *v.t., forms as*
RUN 3: **be ~run with** überlaufen sein von
⟨*Touristen*⟩; überwuchert sein von
⟨*Unkraut*⟩; **~seas** [1] /--'-/ *adv.* in Übersee
⟨*leben, sein*⟩; nach Übersee ⟨*gehen*⟩; [2] /'---/
*adj.* Übersee-; **~'see** *v.t., forms as* SEE 1:
überwachen; (manage) leiten ⟨*Abteilung*⟩;
**~'sensitive** *adj.* überempfindlich;
**~-sexed** /əʊvə'sekst/ *adj.* sexbesessen;
**~'shadow** *v.t.* überschatten; **~'shoot**
*v.t., forms as* SHOOT 2: hinausschießen über
(+ *Akk.*); **~shoot [the runway]** ⟨*Pilot,
Flugzeug:*⟩ zu weit kommen; **~'sight** *n.*
Versehen, *das;* **~simplifi'cation** *n.* zu
starke Vereinfachung; **~'simplify** *v.t.* zu
stark vereinfachen; **~'sleep** *v.i., forms as*
SLEEP 2: verschlafen; **~'spend** *v.i., forms
as* SPEND: zu viel [Geld] ausgeben;
**~statement** *n.* Übertreibung, *die;*
**~'stay** *v.t.* überziehen ⟨*Urlaub*⟩; **~'step**
*v.t.* überschreiten; **~'stretch** *v.t.*
überdehnen; (fig.) überfordern
**overt** /əʊ'vɜːt/ *adj.* unverhohlen
**over: ~'take** *v.t., forms as* TAKE:
überholen; **'no ~taking'** (Brit.) „Überholen
verboten"; **~-the-top** *adj.* überzogen;
**~throw** [1] /--'-/ *v.t., forms as* THROW 1:
stürzen; [2] /'---/ *n.* Sturz, *der;* **~time** [1] *n.*
Überstunden *Pl.;* [2] *adv.* **work ~time**
Überstunden machen; **~'tire** *v.t.*
übermüden; **~tire oneself** sich übernehmen
*od.* überanstrengen

**overtly** /'əʊvətlɪ, əʊ'vɜːtlɪ/ *adv.*
unverhohlen
**'overtone** *n.* (fig.) Unterton, *der*
**overture** /'əʊvətjʊə(r)/ *n.* (Mus.) Ouvertüre,
*die*
**over: ~'turn** [1] *v.t.* umstoßen; [2] *v.i.*
⟨*Auto, Boot:*⟩ umkippen; ⟨*Boot:*⟩ kentern;
**~use** /əʊvə'juːz/ *v.t.* zu oft verwenden
**overweening** /əʊvə'wiːnɪŋ/ *adj.* maßlos
⟨*Ehrgeiz, Gier, Stolz*⟩
**'overweight** *adj.* übergewichtig ⟨*Person*⟩;
**be ~weight** Übergewicht haben
**overwhelm** /əʊvə'welm/ *v.t.* überwältigen
**over'whelming** *adj.* überwältigend
**over: ~'work** [1] *v.t.* mit Arbeit
überlasten; [2] *v.i.* sich überarbeiten;
**~'wrought** *adj.* überreizt
**ovulate** /'ɒvjʊleɪt/ *v.i.* (Physiol.) ovulieren
**ovulation** /ɒvjʊ'leɪʃn/ *n.* Ovulation, *die*
**owe** /əʊ/ *v.t., owing* /'əʊɪŋ/ schulden; **~ sb.
sth., ~ sth. to sb.** jmdm. etw. schulden; (fig.)
jmdm. etw. verdanken
**owing** /'əʊɪŋ/ *pred. adj.* ausstehend; **be ~:**
ausstehen
**'owing to** *prep.* wegen
**owl** /aʊl/ *n.* Eule, *die*
**own** /əʊn/ [1] *adj.* eigen; **be sb.'s
~ [property]** jmdm. selbst gehören; **a house/
ideas of one's ~:** ein eigenes Haus/eigene
Ideen; **on one's/its ~:** allein
[2] *v.t.* besitzen; **be ~ed by sb.** jmdm.
gehören
■ **own 'up** *v.i.* gestehen; **~ up to sth.** etw.
zugeben
**'own-brand, 'own-label** [1] *attrib. adjs.*
Eigenmarken-
[2] *n.* Hausmarke, *die*
**'owner** *n.* Besitzer, *der*/Besitzerin, *die;* (of
shop, hotel, firm, etc.) Inhaber, *der*/Inhaberin,
*die*
**owner-'occupier** *n.* (Brit.)
Eigenheimbesitzer, *der*/-besitzerin, *die*
**'ownership** *n.* Besitz, *der*
**own 'goal** *n.* (lit. or fig.) Eigentor, *das*
**ox** /ɒks/ *n., pl.* **oxen** /'ɒksn/ Ochse, *der*
**oxidize (oxidise)** /'ɒksɪdaɪz/ *v.t. & i.*
(Chem.) oxidieren; oxydieren (fachspr.)
**oxtail 'soup** *n.* Ochsenschwanzsuppe, *die*
**oxygen** /'ɒksɪdʒən/ *n.* Sauerstoff, *der*
**'oxygen mask** *n.* Sauerstoffmaske, *die*
**oyster** /'ɔɪstə(r)/ *n.* Auster, *die*
**oz.** *abbr.* = **ounce[s]**
**ozone** /'əʊzəʊn/ *n.* Ozon, *das*
**ozone: ~ depletion** *n.* Ozonabbau, *der;*
**~-friendly** *adj.* ozonsicher; (not using CFCs)
FCKW-frei; **~ hole** *n.* Ozonloch, *das* (ugs.);
**~ layer** *n.* Ozonschicht, *die*

# Pp

**P, p** /piː/ *n.* P, p, *das*

**p.** *abbr.* **(a)** = **page** S.
**(b)** (Brit.) = **penny/pence** p

**pace** /peɪs/ ⊡ *n.* **(a)** (step) Schritt, *der*
**(b)** (speed) Tempo, *das;* **keep ~ with** Schritt
halten mit
⊡ *v.i.* **~ up and down** auf und ab gehen
⊡ *v.t.* auf und ab gehen in (+ *Dat.*)

**'pacemaker** *n.* (Sport, Med.) Schrittmacher,
*der*

**Pacific** /pə'sɪfɪk/ ⊡ *adj.* (Geog.) **~ Ocean**
Pazifischer *od.* Stiller Ozean
⊡ *n.* **the ~:** der Pazifik

**pacifier** /'pæsɪfaɪə(r)/ *n.* (Amer.: dummy)
Schnuller, *der*

**pacifism** /'pæsɪfɪzm/ *n.* Pazifismus, *der*

**pacifist** /'pæsɪfɪst/ ⊡ *n.* Pazifist, *der*/
Pazifistin, *die*
⊡ *adj.* pazifistisch

**pacify** /'pæsɪfaɪ/ *v.t.* besänftigen

**pack** /pæk/ ⊡ *n.* **(a)** (bundle) Bündel, *das;*
(Mil.) Tornister, *der;* (rucksack) Rucksack, *der*
**(b)** (derog.: lot) (people) Bande, *die;* **a ~ of lies/
nonsense** ein Sack voll Lügen/eine Menge
Unsinn
**(c)** (Brit.) **~ [of cards]** [Karten]spiel, *das*
**(d)** (of wolves, wild dogs) Rudel, *das;* (of hounds)
Meute, *die*
**(e)** (packet) Packung, *die*
⊡ *v.t.* **(a)** einpacken; (fill) packen; **~ one's
bags** seine Koffer packen
**(b)** (cram) voll stopfen (ugs.)
**(c)** (wrap) verpacken (**in** in + *Dat. od. Akk.*)
⊡ *v.i.* packen; **send sb. ~ing** (fig.) jmdn.
rausschmeißen (ugs.)
■ **pack 'up** ⊡ *v.t.* zusammenpacken
‹*Sachen, Werkzeug*›; packen ‹*Paket*›
⊡ *v.i.* (coll.: stop) aufhören

**package** /'pækɪdʒ/ ⊡ *n.* Paket, *das*
⊡ *v.t.* verpacken

**package: ~ deal** *n.* Paket, *das;*
**~ holiday, ~ tour** *ns.* Pauschalreise, *die*

**packaging** /'pækɪdʒɪŋ/ *n.* (material)
Verpackung, *die*

**packed** /pækt/ *adj.* **(a)** gepackt; **~ lunch**
Lunchpaket, *das*
**(b)** (crowded) [über]voll; **~ out** gerammelt voll
(ugs.)

**packet** /'pækɪt/ *n.* Päckchen, *das;* (box)
Schachtel, *die;* **a ~ of cigarettes** ein
Päckchen/eine Schachtel Zigaretten; **cost/
earn a ~:** ein Heidengeld kosten (ugs.)/ein
Schweinegeld verdienen (ugs.)

**packet 'soup** *n.* Instantsuppe, *die*

**'packing** *n.* (material) Verpackungsmaterial,
*das;* **postage and ~:** Porto und Verpackung

**'packing case** *n.* [Pack]kiste, *die*

**pact** /pækt/ *n.* Pakt, *der*

**pad¹** /pæd/ ⊡ *n.* Polster, *das;* (block of paper)
Block, *der*
⊡ *v.t.,* **-dd-** polstern ‹*Jacke, Schulter*›
■ **pad 'out** *v.t.* (fig.) auswalzen

**pad²** *v.i.,* **-dd-** tappen

**padded** /'pædɪd/ *adj.* gepolstert

**padded 'envelope** *n.* wattierter
Umschlag

**padding** /'pædɪŋ/ *n., no indef. art.*
Polsterung, *die;* (fig.) Füllsel, *das*

**paddle¹** /'pædl/ ⊡ *n.* [Stech]paddel, *das*
⊡ *v.t. & i.* paddeln

**paddle²** ⊡ *v.i.* (with feet) planschen
⊡ *n.* **have a/go for a ~:** ein bisschen
planschen/planschen gehen

**paddling pool** /'pædlɪŋpuːl/ *n.*
Planschbecken, *das*

**paddock** /'pædək/ *n.* Koppel, *die*

**'padlock** ⊡ *n.* Vorhängeschloss, *das*
⊡ *v.t.* [mit einem Vorhängeschloss]
verschließen

**paediatrician** /piːdɪə'trɪʃn/ *n.* Kinderarzt,
*der*/-ärztin, *die*

**paediatrics** /piːdɪ'ætrɪks/ *n.* Pädiatrie, *die*
(fachspr.); Kinderheilkunde, *die*

**paedophile** /'piːdəfaɪl/ ⊡ *n.* Pädophile,
*der*
⊡ *adj.* pädophil

**pagan** /'peɪgən/ ⊡ *n.* Heide, *der*/Heidin, *die*
⊡ *adj.* heidnisch

**page¹** /peɪdʒ/ *n.* (boy) Page, *der*

**page²** *n.* (of book etc.) Seite, *die*

**pageant** /'pædʒənt/ *n.* (spectacle)
Schauspiel, *das*

**pageantry** /'pædʒəntrɪ/ *n.* Prunk, *der*

**page: ~ break** *n.* (Comp.) Seitenbruch, *der;*
**~ number** *n.* Seitenzahl, *die*

**pager** /'peɪdʒə(r)/ *n.* Piepser, *der* (ugs.)

**paginate** /'pædʒɪneɪt/ *v.t.* paginieren

**pagination** /pædʒɪ'neɪʃn/ *n.* Paginierung,
*die*

**'paging device** ▶ PAGER

**paid** /peɪd/ ⊡ ▶ PAY 2, 3
⊡ *adj.* **(a)** bezahlt ‹*Urlaub, Arbeit*›
**(b) put ~ to** (Brit. coll.) zunichte machen;
kurzen Prozess machen mit (ugs.) ‹*Person*›

**pail** /peɪl/ *n.* Eimer, *der*

**pain** /peɪn/ *n.* **(a)** (suffering) Schmerzen *Pl.;*
(mental **~**) Qualen *Pl.;* **be in ~:** Schmerzen
haben
**(b)** (instance) Schmerz, *der;* **I have a ~ in my
knee/stomach** mein Knie/Magen tut weh

**(c)** *in pl.* (trouble taken) Mühe, *die;* **take** ∼**s** sich (*Dat.*) Mühe geben (**over** mit, bei)

**painful** /'peɪnfl/ *adj.* **(a)** schmerzhaft; **be** ∼ ⟨*Körperteil:*⟩ wehtun **(b)** (distressing) schmerzlich ⟨*Gedanke, Erinnerung*⟩; traurig ⟨*Pflicht*⟩

'**painkiller** *n.* schmerzstillendes Mittel

'**painless** *adj.* schmerzlos; (fig.) unproblematisch

**painstaking** /'peɪnzteɪkɪŋ/ *adj.* gewissenhaft

**paint** /peɪnt/ ① *n.* Farbe, *die;* (on car) Lack, *der*

② *v.t.* (cover, colour) [an]streichen; (make picture of, make by ∼ing) malen; bemalen ⟨*Wand, Vase, Decke*⟩

**paint:** ∼**box** *n.* Malkasten, *der;* ∼**brush** *n.* Pinsel, *der*

'**painter** *n.* Maler, *der*/Malerin, *die*

'**painting** *n.* (art) Malerei, *die;* (picture) Gemälde, *das;* Bild, *das*

'**painting book** *n.* Malbuch, *das*

**paint:** ∼ **stripper** *n.* Abbeizer, *der;* ∼**work** *n.* (on walls etc.) Anstrich, *der;* (of car) Lack, *der*

**pair** /peə(r)/ ① *n.* Paar, *das;* **a** ∼ **of** gloves/ socks/shoes *etc.* ein Paar Handschuhe/ Socken/Schuhe *usw.;* **in** ∼**s** paarweise; **a** ∼ **of** trousers/jeans eine Hose/Jeans ② *v.t.* paaren

■ **pair 'off** *v.i.* Zweiergruppen bilden

**pajamas** /pə'dʒɑːməz/ (Amer.) ▶ PYJAMAS

**Pakistan** /pɑːkɪ'stɑːn/ *pr. n.* Pakistan (*das*)

**Pakistani** /pɑːkɪ'stɑːnɪ/ ① *adj.* pakistanisch; **sb. is** ∼: jmd. ist Pakistani ② *n.* Pakistani, *der*/*die*

**pal** /pæl/ *n.* (coll.) Kumpel, *der* (ugs.)

**palace** /'pælɪs/ *n.* Palast, *der*

**palate** /'pælət/ *n.* Gaumen, *der*

**palatial** /pə'leɪʃl/ *adj.* palastartig

**pale**[1] /peɪl/ *adj.* blass, (nearly white) bleich ⟨*Gesichtsfarbe, Haut, Gesicht*⟩; blass ⟨*Farbe*⟩; fahl ⟨*Licht*⟩; **go** ∼: blass/bleich werden; (fig.) ∼ **imitation** schlechte Nachahmung

**pale**[2] *n.* **beyond the** ∼: unmöglich

**Palestine** /'pælɪstaɪn/ *pr. n.* Palästina (*das*)

**Palestinian** /pælɪ'stɪnɪən/ ① *adj.* palästinensisch; **sb. is** ∼: jmd. ist Palästinenser/Palästinenserin ② *n.* Palästinenser, *der*/Palästinenserin, *die*

**palette** /'pælɪt/ *n.* Palette, *die*

**pall**[1] /pɔːl/ *n.* **(a)** (over coffin) Sargtuch, *das* **(b)** (fig.) Schleier, *der*

**pall**[2] *v.i.* ∼ **[on sb.]** [jmdm.] langweilig werden

**pallor** /'pælə(r)/ *n.* Blässe, *die*

**palm**[1] /pɑːm/ *n.* (tree) Palme, *die*

**palm**[2] *n.* Handteller, *der*

■ **palm 'off** *v.t.* ∼ sth. off on sb., ∼ sb. off with sth. jmdm. etw. andrehen (ugs.)

**palmistry** /'pɑːmɪstrɪ/ *n.* Handlesekunst, *die*

**palm: P**∼ '**Sunday** *n.* Palmsonntag, *der;* ∼**top** *n.* ∼top [computer] Palmtop, *der;* ∼ **tree** *n.* Palme, *die*

**palpitation** /pælpɪ'teɪʃn/ *n. in pl.* (Med.: of heart) Palpitation, *die* (fachspr.); **suffer from** ∼**s** Herzklopfen haben

**paltry** /'pɔːltrɪ, 'pɒltrɪ/ *adj.* schäbig

**pamper** /'pæmpə(r)/ *v.t.* verhätscheln; ∼ **oneself** sich verwöhnen

**pamphlet** /'pæmflɪt/ *n.* (leaflet) Prospekt, *der;* (booklet) Broschüre, *die*

**pan** /pæn/ *n.* [Koch]topf, *der;* (for frying) Pfanne, *die*

**panacea** /pænə'sɪə/ *n.* Allheilmittel, *das*

**Panama** /pænə'mɑː/ *pr. n.* Panama (*das*); ∼ **Ca'nal** Panamakanal, *der*

'**pancake** *n.* Pfannkuchen, *der*

**pancreas** /'pæŋkrɪəs/ *n.* Bauchspeicheldrüse, *die*

**panda** /'pændə/ *n.* Panda, *der*

**pandemonium** /pændɪ'məʊnɪəm/ *n.* Chaos, *das;* (uproar) Tumult, *der*

**pander** /'pændə(r)/ *v.i.* ∼ **to** allzu sehr entgegenkommen (+ *Dat.*)

**pane** /peɪn/ *n.* Scheibe, *die*

**panel** /'pænl/ *n.* **(a)** Paneel, *das* **(b)** (esp. Telev., Radio, etc.) (quiz team) Rateteam, *das;* (in public discussion) Podium, *das*

**panelling** /'pænəlɪŋ/ *n.* Täfelung, *die*

**panellist** /'pænəlɪst/ *n.* (Telev., Radio) (on quiz programme) Mitglied des Rateteams; (on discussion panel) Diskussionsteilnehmer, *der*/ -teilnehmerin, *die*

'**pan-fry** *v.t.* [in der Pfanne] braten

**pang** /pæŋ/ *n.* (of pain) Stich, *der;* **feel** ∼**s of** conscience/guilt Gewissensbisse haben; ∼**[s] of hunger** quälender Hunger

**panic** /'pænɪk/ ① *n.* Panik, *die;* **hit the** ∼ **button** (fig. coll.) Alarm schlagen; (∼) durchdrehen (ugs.) ② *v.i.,* **-ck-** in Panik (*Akk.*) geraten; **don't** ∼! nur keine Panik!

**panic:** ∼ **attack** *n.* Angstanfall, *der;* ∼-**stricken,** ∼-**struck** *adjs.* von Panik erfasst

**panorama** /pænə'rɑːmə/ *n.* Panorama, *das*

**pansy** /'pænzɪ/ *n.* Stiefmütterchen, *das*

**pant** /pænt/ *v.i.* keuchen; ⟨*Hund:*⟩ hecheln

**panther** /'pænθə(r)/ *n.* Panther, *der*

**panties** /'pæntɪz/ *n. pl.* (coll.) **[pair of]** ∼: Schlüpfer, *der*

**pantomime** /'pæntəmaɪm/ *n.* (Brit.) *Märchenspiel im Varieteestil, das um Weihnachten aufgeführt wird*

**pantry** /'pæntrɪ/ *n.* Speisekammer, *die*

**pants** /pænts/ *n. pl.* **(a)** (esp. Amer. coll.: trousers) **[pair of]** ∼: Hose, *die* **(b)** (Brit. coll.: underpants) Unterhose, *die*

**P**

**paparazzo** /pæpæ'rɑːtsəʊ/ *n., pl.* **paparazzi** /pæpæ'rɑːtsi:/ Paparazzo, *der*

**paper** /'peɪpə(r)/ ① *n.* **(a)** (material) Papier, *das*
**(b)** *in pl.* (documents) Unterlagen *Pl.;* (to prove identity etc.) Papiere *Pl.*
**(c)** (in examination) (Univ.) Klausur, *die;* (Sch.) Arbeit, *die*
**(d)** (newspaper) Zeitung, *die*
**(e)** (learned article) Referat, *das*
② *adj.* aus Papier *nachgestellt;* Papier⟨mütze, -taschentuch⟩
③ *v.t.* tapezieren

**paper:** ~**back** ① *n.* Paperback, *das;*
② *adj.* ~**back book** Paperback, *das;* ~ **'bag** *n.* Papiertüte, *die;* ~ **boy** *n.* Zeitungsjunge, *der;* ~ **clip** *n.* Büroklammer, *die;* (larger) Aktenklammer, *die;* ~ **'handkerchief** *n.* Papiertaschentuch, *das;* ~ **mill** *n.* Papierfabrik *od.* -mühle, *die;* ~ **money** *n.* Papiergeld, *das;* ~ **'napkin** *n.* Papierserviette, *die;* ~ **round** *n.* Zeitungenaustragen, *das;* ~ **servi'ette** ▶~ NAPKIN; ~ **'towel** *n.* Papierhandtuch, *das;* ~**weight** *n.* Briefbeschwerer, *der;* ~**work** *n.* Schreibarbeit, *die*

**par** /pɑː(r)/ *n.* **feel below** ~: nicht ganz auf dem Posten sein (ugs.); **be on a** ~ **with sb./ sth.** jmdm./einer Sache gleichkommen

**parable** /'pærəbl/ *n.* Gleichnis, *das*

**parachute** /'pærəʃuːt/ ① *n.* Fallschirm, *der*
② *v.i.* ⟨Truppen:⟩ abspringen (**into** über + *Dat.*)

**parade** /pə'reɪd/ ① *n.* **(a)** (display) Zurschaustellung, *die*
**(b)** (Mil.) Appell, *der*
**(c)** (procession) Umzug, *der;* (of troops) Parade, *die*
② *v.t.* zur Schau stellen
③ *v.i.* paradieren

**pa'rade ground** *n.* Exerzierplatz, *der*

**paradise** /'pærədaɪs/ *n.* Paradies, *das*

**paradox** /'pærədɒks/ *n.* Paradox[on], *das*

**paradoxical** /pærə'dɒksɪkl/ *adj.* paradox

**paraffin** /'pærəfɪn/ *n.* Paraffin, *das;* (Brit.: fuel) Petroleum, *das*

**paragliding** /'pærəglaɪdɪŋ/ *n.* Paragliding, *das*

**paragon** /'pærəgən/ Muster, *das* (**of an** + *Dat.*); ~ **of virtue** Tugendheld, *der/*-heldin, *die*

**paragraph** /'pærəgrɑːf/ *n.* Absatz, *der*

**parallel** /'pærəlel/ ① *adj.* parallel; (fig.: similar) vergleichbar; ~ **bars** Barren, *der*
② *n.* Parallele, *die;* ~ **[of latitude]** Breitenkreis, *die*

**paralyse** /'pærəlaɪz/ *v.t.* lähmen; (fig.) lahm legen ⟨Verkehr, Industrie⟩

**paralysis** /pə'rælɪsɪs/ *n.* Lähmung, *die*

**paralyze** (Amer.) ▶ PARALYSE

**paramedic** /pærə'medɪk/ *n.* medizinische Hilfskraft; (ambulance worker) Sanitäter, *der/* Sanitäterin, *die*

**parameter** /pə'ræmɪtə(r)/ *n.* Faktor, *der*

**paramilitary** /pærə'mɪlɪtərɪ/ *adj.* paramilitärisch

**paramount** /'pærəmaʊnt/ *adj.* größt... ⟨Wichtigkeit⟩; Haupt⟨überlegung⟩; **be** ~: Vorrang haben

**paranoia** /pærə'nɔɪə/ *n.* Paranoia, *die* (Med.); (tendency) Verfolgungswahn, *der*

**paranoid** /'pærənɔɪd/ *adj.* **be** ~ ⟨Person:⟩ an Verfolgungswahn leiden

**parapet** /'pærəpɪt/ *n.* Brüstung, *die*

**paraphernalia** /pærəfə'neɪlɪə/ *n. sing.* Apparat, *der*

**paraphrase** /'pærəfreɪz/ ① *n.* Umschreibung, *die*
② *v.t.* umschreiben

**paraplegic** /pærə'pliːdʒɪk/ ① *adj.* doppelseitig gelähmt
② *n.* doppelseitig Gelähmter/Gelähmte

**parasite** /'pærəsaɪt/ *n.* Schmarotzer, *der*

**parasitic** /pærə'sɪtɪk/ *adj.* **(a)** (Biol.) parasitisch
**(b)** (fig.) schmarotzerhaft

**parasol** /'pærəsɒl/ *n.* Sonnenschirm, *der*

**paratroops** /'pærətruːps/ *n. pl.* Fallschirmjäger *Pl.*

**parcel** /'pɑːsl/ *n.* Paket, *das*

**parched** /pɑːtʃt/ *adj.* ausgedörrt; trocken ⟨Lippen⟩

**parchment** /'pɑːtʃmənt/ *n.* Pergament, *das*

**pardon** /'pɑːdn/ ① *n.* Verzeihung, *die;* **beg sb.'s** ~: jmdn. um Entschuldigung bitten; **I beg your** ~: entschuldigen Sie bitte
② *v.t.* **(a)** ~ **sb. [for] sth.** jmdm. etw. verzeihen
**(b)** (excuse) entschuldigen

**pardonable** /'pɑːdənəbl/ *adj.* verzeihlich

**pare** /peə(r)/ *v.t.* (trim) schneiden; (peel) schälen

**parent** /'peərənt/ *n.* Elternteil, *der;* ~**s** Eltern *Pl.*

**parental** /pə'rentl/ *adj.* Eltern⟨pflicht, -haus, -liebe⟩

**parenthesis** /pə'renθɪsɪs/ *n., pl.* **parentheses** /pə'renθɪsiːz/ (bracket) runde Klammer

**'parents' evening** *n.* Elternabend, *der*

**'parents-in-law** *pl.* Schwiegeeltern *Pl.*

**Paris** /'pærɪs/ *pr. n.* Paris (*das*)

**parish** /'pærɪʃ/ *n.* Gemeinde, *die*

**parish:** ~ **'church** *n.* Pfarrkirche, *die;* ~ **'council** *n.* (Brit.) Gemeinderat, *der*

**parishioner** /pə'rɪʃənə(r)/ *n.* Gemeinde[mit]glied, *das*

**parish 'priest** *n.* Gemeindepfarrer, *der*

**park** /pɑːk/ ① *n.* Park, *der*
② *v.i.* parken
③ *v.t.* abstellen; parken ⟨Kfz⟩; **a** ~**ed car** ein parkendes Auto

**park-and-'ride** n. Park-and-ride-System, das; (place) Park-and-ride-Parkplatz, der

**'parking** n. Parken, das; 'no ~' „Parken verboten"

**parking:** ~ **fine** n. Geldbuße für falsches Parken; ~ **light** n. Parkleuchte, die; ~ **lot** n. (Amer.) Parkplatz, der; ~ **meter** n. Parkuhr, die; ~ **offence** n. Verstoß gegen das Parkverbot; ~ **space** n. (a) no pl. Parkraum, der; (b) (single space) Parkplatz, der; ~ **ticket** n. Strafzettel [für falsches Parken]

**'park-keeper** n. Parkwächter, der/ -wächterin, die

**parliament** /'pɑːləmənt/ n. Parlament, das; [Houses of] P~ (Brit.) Parlament, das

**parliamentary** /pɑːlə'mentərɪ/ adj. parlamentarisch; Parlaments⟨geschäfte, -wahlen, -reform⟩

**parlour** (Brit.; Amer.: **parlor**) /'pɑːlə(r)/ n. (dated) Wohnzimmer, das

**parochial** /pə'rəʊkɪəl/ adj. krähwinklig

**parody** /'pærədɪ/ ①1 n. Parodie, die (of auf + Akk.) ②2 v.t. parodieren

**parole** /pə'rəʊl/ n. bedingter Straferlass (Rechtsw.); on ~: auf Bewährung

**paroxysm** /'pærəksɪzm/ n. Krampf, der; (fit, convulsion) Anfall, der (of von)

**parquet** /'pɑːkɪ, 'pɑːkeɪ/ n. ~ [floor/ flooring] Parkett, das

**parrot** /'pærət/ n. Papagei, der

**parry** /'pærɪ/ v.t. abwehren ⟨Faustschlag⟩; (Fencing; also fig.) parieren

**parsley** /'pɑːslɪ/ n. Petersilie, die

**parsnip** /'pɑːsnɪp/ n. Gemeiner Pastinak, der

**parson** /'pɑːsn/ n. Pfarrer, der

**part** /pɑːt/ ①1 n. (a) Teil, der; the greater ~: der größte Teil; der Großteil; for the most ~: größtenteils; in ~: teilweise; in large ~: groß[en]teils; in ~s zum Teil (b) (of machine) [Einzel]teil, das (c) (share) Anteil, der (d) (Theatre) Rolle, die (e) (Mus.) Part, der; Stimme, die (f) usu. in pl. (region) Gegend, die; (of continent, world) Teil, der (g) (side) Partei, die; take sb.'s ~: jmds. od. für jmdn. Partei ergreifen (h) take [no] ~ [in sth.] sich [an etw. (Dat.)] [nicht] beteiligen (i) take sth. in good ~: etw. nicht übel nehmen ②2 adv. teils ③3 v.t. (a) (divide into ~s) teilen; scheiteln ⟨Haar⟩ (b) (separate) trennen ④4 v.i. ⟨Seil, Tau, Kette:⟩ reißen; ⟨Wege, Personen:⟩ sich trennen; ~ with sich trennen von ⟨Besitz, Geld⟩

**part ex'change** n. accept sth. in ~ for sth. etw. für etw. in Zahlung nehmen; sell sth. in ~: etw. in Zahlung geben

**partial** /'pɑːʃl/ adj. (a) (biased) voreingenommen (b) be/not be ~ to sth. eine Schwäche/keine Vorliebe für etw. haben (c) partiell ⟨Lähmung, Sonnenfinsternis⟩; a ~ success ein Teilerfolg

**'partially** adv. teilweise

**participant** /pɑː'tɪsɪpənt/ n. Beteiligte, der/die (in an + Dat.)

**participate** /pɑː'tɪsɪpeɪt/ v.i. sich beteiligen (in an + Dat.); (in arranged event) teilnehmen (in an + Dat.)

**participation** /pɑːtɪsɪ'peɪʃn/ n. Beteiligung, die (in an + Dat.); (in arranged event) Teilnahme, die (in bei, an + Dat.)

**participle** /'pɑːtɪsɪpl/ n. Partizip, das

**particle** /'pɑːtɪkl/ n. Teilchen, das

**particular** /pə'tɪkjʊlə(r)/ ①1 adj. (a) besonder...; here in ~: besonders hier; nothing/anything [in] ~: nichts/irgendetwas Besonderes (b) (fastidious) genau; I am not ~: es ist mir gleich; be ~ about sth. es mit etw. genau nehmen ②2 n., in pl. Einzelheiten Pl.; Details Pl.; (of person) Personalien Pl.

**par'ticularly** adv. besonders

**'parting** ①1 n. (a) [final] ~: Abschied, der (b) (Brit.: in hair) Scheitel, der ②2 attrib. adj. Abschieds-

**partisan** /'pɑːtɪzæn/ n. Partisan, der/ Partisanin, die

**partition** /pɑː'tɪʃn/ ①1 n. (a) (Polit.) Teilung, die (b) (room divider) Trennwand, die ②2 v.t. (a) (divide) aufteilen ⟨Land, Zimmer⟩ (b) (Polit.) teilen ⟨Land⟩

■ **partition 'off** v.t. abteilen

**'partly** adv. zum Teil; teilweise

**partner** /'pɑːtnə(r)/ n. Partner, der/ Partnerin, die

**'partnership** n. Partnerschaft, die; business ~: [Personen]gesellschaft, die

**'part-owner** n. Mitbesitzer, der/ -besitzerin, die

**partridge** /'pɑːtrɪdʒ/ n., pl. same or ~s Rebhuhn, das

**part:** ~**time** ①1 /'--/ adj. Teilzeit⟨arbeit, -arbeiter⟩; ②2 /-'-/ adv. stundenweise, halbtags ⟨arbeiten, studieren⟩; ~**'timer** n. Teilzeitkraft, die; study as a ~-timer halbtags od. stundenweise studieren

**party** /'pɑːtɪ/ n. (a) (Polit., Law) Partei, die; attrib. Partei- (b) (group) Gruppe, die (c) (social gathering) Party, die

**party:** ~ **po'litical** adj. parteipolitisch; ~ **'politics** n. Parteipolitik, die; ~ **wall** n. Mauer zum Nachbargrundstück/-gebäude

**pass** /pɑːs/ ①1 n. (a) (passing of an ⸱⸱⸱⸱

examination) bestandene Prüfung; '∿' (mark)
Ausreichend, *das;* **get a** ∿ **in maths** die
Mathematikprüfung bestehen
**(b)** (written permission) Ausweis, *der*
**(c)** (Footb.) Pass, *der* (fachspr.); Ballabgabe, *die*
**(d)** (in mountains) Pass, *der*
⟨2⟩ *v.i.* **(a)** (go by) ⟨*Fußgänger:*⟩ vorbeigehen;
⟨*Fahrer, Fahrzeug:*⟩ vorbeifahren; ⟨*Zeit,
Sekunde:*⟩ vergehen; (by chance) ⟨*Person,
Fahrzeug:*⟩ vorbeikommen
**(b)** (come to an end) vorbeigehen; ⟨*Gewitter,
Unwetter:*⟩ vorüberziehen
**(c)** (be accepted) durchgehen (**as** als, **for** für)
**(d)** (in exam) bestehen
⟨3⟩ *v.t.* **(a)** ⟨*Fußgänger:*⟩ vorbeigehen an
(+ *Dat.*); ⟨*Fahrer, Fahrzeug:*⟩ vorbeifahren an
(+ *Dat.*); (by chance) ⟨*Person, Fahrzeug:*⟩
vorbeikommen an (+ *Dat.*)
**(b)** (overtake) vorbeifahren an (+ *Dat.*)
**(c)** bestehen ⟨*Prüfung*⟩
**(d)** (approve) verabschieden ⟨*Gesetzentwurf*⟩;
annehmen ⟨*Vorschlag*⟩; bestehen lassen
⟨*Prüfungskandidaten*⟩
**(e)** (Footb. etc.) abgeben (**to** an + *Akk.*)
**(f)** (spend) verbringen ⟨*Leben, Zeit, Tag*⟩
**(g)** (hand) ∿ **sb. sth.** jmdm. etw. reichen *od.*
geben
**(h)** fällen ⟨*Urteil*⟩; machen ⟨*Bemerkung*⟩
**(i)** ∿ **water** Wasser lassen
▪ **pass a'way** *v.i.* (euphem.) verscheiden
(*geh.*)
▪ **pass 'off** *v.t.* ∿ **sth. off as sth.** etw. als
etw. ausgeben
▪ **pass 'on** *v.t.* weitergeben (**to** an + *Akk.*)
▪ **pass 'out** *v.i.* ohnmächtig werden
▪ **pass 'up** *v.t.* entgehen lassen
⟨*Gelegenheit*⟩; ablehnen ⟨*Angebot*⟩
**passable** /'pɑːsəbl/ *adj.* **(a)** (acceptable)
passabel
**(b)** befahrbar ⟨*Straße*⟩
**passage** /'pæsɪdʒ/ *n.* **(a)** (voyage) Überfahrt,
*die*
**(b)** (way) Durchgang, *der;* (corridor) Korridor,
*der*
**(c)** ( part of book etc.) Textstelle, *die;* (Mus.)
Stelle, *die*
**'passageway** *n.* Gang, *der;* (between houses)
Durchgang, *der*
**passenger** /'pæsɪndʒə(r)/ *n.* Passagier, *der;*
(on train) Reisende, *der/die;* (on bus, in taxi)
Fahrgast, *der;* (in car, on motor cycle) Mitfahrer,
*der/*Mitfahrerin, *die;* (in front seat of car)
Beifahrer, *der/*Beifahrerin, *die*
**passenger:** ∿ **aircraft** *n.*
Passagierflugzeug, *das;* ∿ **door** *n.*
Beifahrertür, *die;* ∿ **lounge** *n.* Warteraum,
*der;* ∿ **plane** *n.* Passagierflugzeug, *das;*
∿ **seat** *n.* Beifahrersitz, *der;* ∿ **service**
*n.* (train) Personenzugverbindung, *die;* (ferry)
Personenfährverbindung, *die*
**passer-by** /pɑːsə'baɪ/ *n.* Passant, *der/*
Passantin, *die*
**'passing** ⟨1⟩ *n.* (of time, years) Lauf, *der;* **in** ∿:
beiläufig ⟨*bemerken usw.*⟩

⟨2⟩ *adj.* **(a)** vorbeifahrend ⟨*Zug, Auto*⟩;
vorbeikommend ⟨*Person*⟩
**(b)** flüchtig ⟨*Blick*⟩; vorübergehend ⟨*Mode,
Interesse*⟩; flüchtig ⟨*Bekanntschaft*⟩
**'passing place** *n.* Ausweichstelle, *die*
**passion** /'pæʃn/ *n.* Leidenschaft, *die;*
(enthusiasm) leidenschaftliche Begeisterung;
**he has a** ∿ **for steam engines** Dampfloks
sind seine Leidenschaft
**passionate** /'pæʃənət/ *adj.*
leidenschaftlich; heftig ⟨*Verlangen*⟩
**passive** /'pæsɪv/ ⟨1⟩ *adj.* **(a)** passiv
**(b)** (Ling.) Passiv-
⟨2⟩ *n.* (Ling.) Passiv, *das*
**pass:** ∿ **key** *n.* (master key) Hauptschlüssel,
*der;* ∿ **mark** *n.* Mindestpunktzahl, *die;*
∿**port** *n.* [Reise]pass, *der; attrib.* Pass-;
∿**port control** Passkontrolle, *die;* **(b)** (fig.)
Schlüssel, *der* (**to** zu); ∿**word** *n.* **(a)** Parole,
*die;* Losung, *die;* **(b)** (Comp.) Passwort, *das*
**past** /pɑːst/ ⟨1⟩ *adj.* **(a)** pred. (over) vorbei
**(b)** attrib. ( previous) früher; vergangen;
ehemalig ⟨*Präsident, Vorsitzende usw.*⟩
**(c)** attrib. ( just gone by) letzt...; vergangen; **in
the** ∿ **few days** während der letzten Tage
**(d)** (Ling.) ∿ **tense** Vergangenheit, *die*
⟨2⟩ *n.* Vergangenheit, *die;* **in the** ∿: früher; **in**
der Vergangenheit ⟨*leben*⟩; **be a thing of the**
∿: der Vergangenheit angehören
⟨3⟩ *prep.* (in time) nach; (in place) hinter
(+ *Dat.*); **half** ∿ **three** halb vier; **five [minutes]**
∿ **two** fünf [Minuten] nach zwei; **gaze/walk**
∿ **sb./sth.** an jmdm./etw. vorbeiblicken/
vorbeigehen; ∿ **repair** nicht mehr zu
reparieren
⟨4⟩ *adv.* vorbei; **hurry** ∿: vorübereilen
**pasta** /'pæstə/ *n.* Teigwaren *Pl.*
**paste** /peɪst/ ⟨1⟩ *n.* **(a)** Brei, *der*
**(b)** (glue) Kleister, *der*
**(c)** (of meat, fish, etc.) Paste, *die*
⟨2⟩ *v.t.* **(a)** kleben; ∿ **sth. into sth.** etw. in
etw. (*Akk.*) einkleben
**(b)** (Comp.) einfügen (**into** in + *Akk.*); *see also*
CUT 1E
**pastel** /'pæstl/ ⟨1⟩ *n.* (crayon) Pastellstift, *der*
⟨2⟩ *adj.* pastellfarben; Pastell⟨*farben, -töne,
-zeichnung*⟩
**pasteurize** /'pɑːstʃəraɪz/ *v.t.*
pasteurisieren
**pastille** /'pæstɪl/ *n.* Pastille, *die*
**pastime** /'pɑːstaɪm/ *n.* Zeitvertreib, *der;*
( person's specific ∿) Hobby, *das*
**past 'master** *n.* (fig.) Meister, *der*
**pastor** /'pɑːstə(r)/ *n.* Pfarrer, *der/*Pfarrerin,
*die;* Pastor, *der/*Pastorin, *die*
**pastoral** /'pɑːstərl/ *adj.* Weide-; ländlich
⟨*Reiz, Idylle, Umgebung*⟩
**pastry** /'peɪstrɪ/ *n.* Teig, *der;* (article of food)
Gebäckstück, *das;* **pastries** collect.
[Fein]gebäck, *das*
**pasture** /'pɑːstʃə(r)/ *n.* Weide, *die*
**'pastureland** *n.* Weideland, *das*
**pasty** /'pæstɪ/ *n.* Pastete, *die*

**pat¹** /pæt/ 1 n. (a) (tap) Klaps, der
(b) (of butter) Stückchen, das
2 v.t., -tt- leicht klopfen auf (+ Akk.);
tätscheln, (once) einen Klaps geben (+ Dat.)
⟨Person, Hund, Pferd⟩; ~ sb. on the arm/
head jmdm. den Arm/Kopf tätscheln

**pat²** adv. have sth. off ~: etw. parat haben

**patch** /pætʃ/ 1 n. (a) Stelle, die; fog ~es
Nebelfelder
(b) (on worn garment) Flicken, der; be not a
~ on sth. (fig. coll.) nichts gegen etw. sein
2 v.t. flicken
▪ **patch 'up** v.t. reparieren; (fig.) beilegen
⟨Streit⟩

**patchwork** n. Patchwork, das

**patchy** /'pætʃɪ/ adj. uneinheitlich
⟨Qualität⟩; ungleichmäßig ⟨Arbeit⟩; sehr
lückenhaft ⟨Wissen⟩

**pâté** /'pæteɪ/ n. Pastete, die

**patent** /'peɪtənt, 'pætənt/ 1 adj. (obvious)
offenkundig
2 n. Patent, das
3 v.t. patentieren lassen

**patent 'leather** n. Lackleder, das;
~ shoes Lackschuhe Pl.

**'patently** adv. offenkundig; ~ obvious
ganz offenkundig

**paternal** /pə'tɜ:nl/ adj. väterlich

**paternity** /pə'tɜ:nɪtɪ/ n. (fatherhood)
Vaterschaft, die

**pa'ternity leave** n. Vaterschaftsurlaub,
der

**path** /pɑ:θ/ n. Weg, der; (line of motion) Bahn,
die

**pathetic** /pə'θetɪk/ adj. (a) (pitiful) Mitleid
erregend
(b) (contemptible) armselig ⟨Entschuldigung⟩;
erbärmlich ⟨Person, Leistung⟩

**pathogen** /'pæθədʒən/ n.
[Krankheits]erreger, der

**pathological** /pæθə'lɒdʒɪkl/ adj. (a)
pathologisch
(b) (fig.: obsessive) krankhaft

**pathologist** /pə'θɒlədʒɪst/ n. Pathologe,
der/Pathologin, die

**pathology** /pə'θɒlədʒɪ/ n. Pathologie, die;
the ~ of a disease das Krankheitsbild

**'pathway** n. Weg, der

**patience** /'peɪʃəns/ n. Geduld, die

**patient** /'peɪʃənt/ 1 adj. geduldig
2 n. Patient, der/Patientin, die

**'patiently** adv. geduldig

**patio** /'pætɪəʊ/ n., pl. ~s Veranda, die;
Terrasse, die

**patio 'door** n. große Glasschiebetür (zum
Garten)

**patriarch** /'peɪtrɪɑ:k/ n. (of family)
Familienoberhaupt, das

**patriarchal** /peɪtrɪ'ɑ:kl/ adj.
patriarchalisch

**patriot** /'peɪtrɪət/ n. Patriot, der/Patriotin,
die

**patriotic** /peɪtrɪ'ɒtɪk/ adj. patriotisch

**patriotism** /'peɪtrɪətɪzm/ n. Patriotismus,
der

**patrol** /pə'trəʊl/ 1 n. (Police) Streife, die;
(Mil.) Patrouille, die; be on ~: patrouillieren
2 v.i. -ll- patrouillieren; ⟨Polizei:⟩ Streife
laufen/fahren
3 v.t. -ll- patrouillieren durch (+ Akk.);
abpatrouillieren ⟨Straßen, Gegend, Lager⟩;
patrouillieren vor (+ Dat.) ⟨Küste, Grenze⟩;
⟨Polizei:⟩ Streife laufen/fahren in (+ Dat.)
⟨Straßen, Stadtteil⟩

**patrol: ~ boat** n. Patrouillenboot, das;
~ **car** n. Streifenwagen, der

**patron** /'peɪtrən/ n. (a) Gönner, der/
Gönnerin, die; (of institution, campaign)
Schirmherr, der/Schirmherrin, die
(b) (customer) (of shop) Kunde, der/Kundin,
die; (of restaurant, hotel) Gast, der; (of theatre,
cinema) Besucher, der/Besucherin, die
(c) ~ [saint] Schutzheilige, der/die

**patronage** /'pætrənɪdʒ/ n. Gönnerschaft,
die; (for campaign, institution) Schirmherrschaft,
die

**patronize** /'pætrənaɪz/ v.t. (a) (frequent)
besuchen
(b) (condescend to) ~ sb. jmdn. herablassend
behandeln

**patronizing** /'pætrənaɪzɪŋ/ adj.
gönnerhaft; herablassend

**patter** /'pætə(r)/ 1 n. (of rain) Prasseln, das;
(of feet) Trappeln, das
2 v.i. ⟨Regen:⟩ prasseln

**pattern** /'pætən/ n. Muster, das; (model)
Vorlage, die; (for sewing) Schnittmuster, das;
(for knitting) Strickmuster, das

**paunch** /pɔːntʃ/ n. Bauch, der

**pauper** /'pɔːpə(r)/ n. Arme, der/die

**pause** /pɔːz/ 1 n. Pause, die
2 v.i. eine Pause machen; ⟨Redner:⟩
innehalten; (hesitate) zögern

**pave** /peɪv/ v.t. befestigen; (with stones)
pflastern; ~ the way for sth. (fig.) einer
Sache (Dat.) den Weg ebnen

**'pavement** n. (a) (Brit.: footway) Bürgersteig,
der
(b) (Amer.: roadway) Fahrbahn, die

**'pavement café** n. Straßencafé, das

**pavilion** /pə'vɪljən/ n. Pavillon, der; (Brit.
Sport) Klubhaus, das

**'paving stone** n. Platte, die; Pflasterstein,
der

**paw** /pɔː/ n. Pfote, die; (of bear, lion, tiger)
Pranke, die

**pawn¹** /pɔːn/ n. (Chess) Bauer, der; (fig.)
Schachfigur, die

**pawn²** 1 n. Pfand, das; in ~: verpfändet
2 v.t. verpfänden

**pawn: ~broker** n. Pfandleiher, der/
-leiherin, die; ~**shop** n. Leihhaus, das

**pay** /peɪ/ 1 n. (wages) Lohn, der; (salary)
Gehalt, das; be in the ~ of sb./sth. für
jmdn./etw. arbeiten

⋯•

2 *v.t.*, **paid** /peɪd/ bezahlen; zahlen ⟨*Geld*⟩; ~ **sb. to do sth.** jmdn. dafür bezahlen, dass er etw. tut; ~ **sb. £10** jmdm. 10 Pfund zahlen 3 *v.i.*, **paid** (a) zahlen; ~ **for sth./sb.** etw./ für jmdn. bezahlen; **sth.** ~**s for itself** etw. macht sich bezahlt
(b) (be profitable) sich lohnen; ⟨*Geschäft:*⟩ rentabel sein; **it** ~**s to be careful** es lohnt sich, vorsichtig zu sein. *See also* PAID
■ **pay 'back** *v.t.* zurückzahlen; **I'll** ~ **you back later** ich gebe dir das Geld später zurück
■ **pay 'in** *v.t.* einzahlen
■ **pay 'off** *v.t.* auszahlen ⟨*Arbeiter*⟩; abbezahlen ⟨*Schulden*⟩; ablösen ⟨*Hypothek*⟩; befriedigen ⟨*Gläubiger*⟩
■ **pay 'out** *v.t.* auszahlen; (spend) ausgeben
■ **pay 'up** *v.i.* zahlen

**payable** /'peɪəbl/ *adj.* zahlbar; **be** ~ **to sb.** an jmdn. zu zahlen sein; **make a cheque** ~ **to the Post Office/to sb.** einen Scheck auf die Post/auf jmds. Namen ausstellen

**pay:** ~ **and display** 1 *n.* Parken mit Parkschein; *attrib.* Parkschein-; 2 *n.* ~ **and display car park** Parkplatz mit Parkscheinautomat; ~ **cheque** *n.* Lohn-/Gehaltsscheck, *der*; ~ **claim** *n.* Lohn-/Gehaltsforderung, *die*; ~ **day** *n.* Zahltag, *der*; ~ **increase** ▶ PAY RISE

**payee** /peɪ'iː/ *n.* Zahlungsempfänger, *der*/-empfängerin, *die*

**paying** /'peɪɪŋ/: ~ **'guest** *n.* zahlender Gast; ~**-'in slip** *n.* (Brit. Banking) Einzahlungsschein, *der*

'**payment** *n.* (a) (of sum, bill, debt, fine) Bezahlung, *die*; (of interest, instalment, tax, fee) Zahlung, *die*; **in** ~ [**for sth.**] als Bezahlung [für etw.]
(b) (amount) Zahlung, *die*

**pay:** ~ **packet** *n.* (Brit.) Lohntüte, *die*; ~**phone** *n.* Münzfernsprecher, *der*; ~ **rise** *n.* Lohn-/Gehaltserhöhung, *die*; ~**roll** *n.* Lohnliste, *die*; **be on sb.'s** ~**roll** für jmdn. arbeiten; ~**slip** *n.* Lohnstreifen, *der*/Gehaltszettel, *der*; ~ **station** *n.* (Amer.) ▶ ~PHONE

**p.c.** *abbr.* = **per cent** v. H.

**PC** *abbr.* (a) (Brit.) = **police constable** Wachtm.
(b) = **personal computer** PC
(c) = **politically correct** politisch korrekt

**PE** *abbr.* = **physical education**

**pea** /piː/ *n.* Erbse, *die*

**peace** /piːs/ *n.* Frieden, *der*; (tranquillity) Ruhe, *die*; ~ **of mind** Seelenfrieden, *der*

**peaceable** /'piːsəbl/ *adj.* friedfertig; (calm) friedlich

**peaceful** /'piːsfl/ *adj.* friedlich; friedfertig ⟨*Person, Volk*⟩

'**peacefully** *adv.* friedlich; **die** ~: sanft entschlafen

**peace:** ~**keeper** *n.* Friedenswächter, *der*; ~**keeping force** Friedenstruppe, *die*;

~**maker** *n.* Friedensstifter, *der*/-stifterin, *die*; ~ **movement** *n.* Friedensbewegung, *die*; ~ **process** *n.* Friedensprozess, *der* ~ **treaty** *n.* Friedensvertrag, *der*

**peach** /piːtʃ/ *n.* Pfirsich, *der*

'**peacock** *n.* Pfau, *der*

'**pea-green** *adj.* erbsengrün; maigrün

**peak** /piːk/ 1 *n.* (a) (of cap) Schirm, *der*
(b) (of mountain) Gipfel, *der*; (fig.) Höhepunkt, *der*
2 *attrib. adj.* Höchst-, Spitzen⟨*preise, -werte*⟩; ~**hour traffic** Stoßverkehr, *der*

**peaked** /piːkt/ *adj.* ~ **cap** Schirmmütze, *die*

'**peak season** *n.* Hochsaison, *die*

**peal** /piːl/ *n.* Läuten, *das*; ~ **of bells** Glockenläuten, *das*; **a** ~/~**s of laughter** schallendes Gelächter

**peanut** /'piːnʌt/ *n.* Erdnuss, *die*; ~ **butter** Erdnussbutter, *die*; ~**s** (coll.: little money) ein paar Kröten (salopp)

**pear** /peə(r)/ *n.* Birne, *die*

**pearl** /pɜːl/ *n.* Perle, *die*

**pear:** ~**-shaped** *adj.* birnenförmig: ~**tree** *n.* Birnbaum, *der*

**peasant** /'pezənt/ *n.* [armer] Bauer, *der*; Landarbeiter, *der*

**pea 'soup** Erbsensuppe, *die*

**peat** /piːt/ *n.* Torf, *der*

**pebble** /'pebl/ *n.* Kiesel[stein], *der*

**peck** /pek/ 1 *v.t.* hacken; picken ⟨*Körner*⟩
2 *v.i.* picken (**at** nach); ~ **at one's food** im Essen herumstochern
3 *n.* (kiss) flüchtiger Kuss

'**pecking order** *n.* Hackordnung, *die*

**peckish** /'pekɪʃ/ *adj.* (coll.) **feel/get** ~: Hunger haben/bekommen

**peculiar** /pɪ'kjuːlɪə(r)/ *adj.* (a) (strange) seltsam; **I feel [slightly]** ~: mir ist [etwas] komisch
(b) (especial) besonder...
(c) (belonging exclusively) eigentümlich (**to** *Dat.*)

**peculiarity** /pɪkjuːlɪ'ærɪtɪ/ *n.* (a) (odd trait) Eigentümlichkeit, *die*
(b) (distinguishing characteristic) [charakteristisches] Merkmal

**pe'culiarly** *adv.* (a) (strangely) seltsam
(b) (especially) besonders

**pedal** /'pedl/ 1 *n.* Pedal, *das*
2 *v.i.*, (Brit.) **-ll-** in die Pedale treten

'**pedal bin** *n.* Treteimer, *der*

**pedalo** /'pedələʊ/ *n., pl.* ~**s** Tretboot, *das*

**pedant** /'pedənt/ *n.* Pedant, *der*/Pedantin, *die*

**pedantic** /pɪ'dæntɪk/ *adj.* pedantisch

**peddle** /'pedl/ *v.t.* auf der Straße verkaufen; (door to door) hausieren mit

**pedestal** /'pedɪstl/ *n.* Sockel, *der*

**pedestrian** /pɪ'destrɪən/ 1 *adj.* (uninspired) trocken; langweilig
2 *n.* Fußgänger, *der*/-gängerin, *die*

**pedestrian 'crossing** *n.* Fußgängerüberweg, *der*

**pedestrianize** (**pedestrianise**) /pɪ'destrɪənaɪz/ v.t. zur Fußgängerzone machen; ~d **zone** Fußgängerzone, die

**pedestrian 'precinct** ▶ PRECINCT A

**pediatrician** etc. ▶ PAEDIATRICIAN etc.

**pedicure** /'pedɪkjʊə(r)/ n., no art. Pediküre, die

**pedigree** /'pedɪɡriː/ ① n. Stammbaum, der ② adj. mit Stammbaum nachgestellt

**pedlar** /'pedlə(r)/ n. Straßenhändler, der/ -händlerin, die; (door to door) Hausierer, der/ Hausiererin, die

**pee** /piː/ (coll.) ① v.i. pinkeln (salopp); Pipi machen (Kinderspr.)
② n. (a) have a ~: pinkeln (salopp)
(b) (urine) Pipi, das (Kinderspr.)

**peek** /piːk/ ▶ PEEP²

**peel** /piːl/ ① v.t. schälen
② v.i. ⟨Person, Haut:⟩ sich schälen; ⟨Farbe:⟩ abblättern
③ n. Schale, die

**'peelings** n. pl. Schalen Pl.

**peep¹** /piːp/ ① v.i. ⟨Maus, Vogel:⟩ piep[s]en
② n. Piepsen, das; (coll.: remark etc.) Piep[s], der

**peep²** ① v.i. gucken (ugs.); (furtively) verstohlen gucken (ugs.)
② n. kurzer/verstohlener Blick

**peep:** ~**hole** n. Guckloch, das; ~**ing 'Tom** n. Spanner, der (ugs.)

**peer¹** /pɪə(r)/ n. Peer, der; (equal) Gleichgestellte, der/die

**peer²** v.i. forschend schauen; (with difficulty) angestrengt schauen; ~ **at sth./sb.** [sich (Dat.)] etw. genau ansehen/jmdn. forschend ansehen; (with difficulty) [sich (Dat.)] etw./ jmdn. angestrengt ansehen

**peerage** /'pɪərɪdʒ/ n. Peerswürde, die

**'peer pressure** n. Gruppenzwang, der

**peevish** /'piːvɪʃ/ adj. nörgelig

**peg** /peɡ/ n. (for holding together) Stift, der; (for tying things to) Pflock, der; (for hanging things on) Haken, der; (clothes ~) Wäscheklammer, die; (tent ~) Hering, der; **off the** ~ (Brit.: ready-made) von der Stange (ugs.)

**pejorative** /pɪ'dʒɒrətɪv/ adj., **pe'joratively** adv. abwertend

**pelican** /'pelɪkən/ n. Pelikan, der

**'pelican crossing** n. (Brit.) Ampelübergang, der

**pellet** /'pelɪt/ n. Kügelchen, das

**pelmet** /'pelmɪt/ n. Blende, die

**pelt¹** /pelt/ n. Fell, das

**pelt²** ① v.t. ~ **sb. with sth.** jmdn. mit etw. bewerfen
② v.i. (a) it was ~ing down [with rain] es goss wie aus Kübeln (ugs.)
(b) (run fast) rasen (ugs.)

**pelvic** /'pelvɪk/ adj. Becken-

**pelvis** /'pelvɪs/ n., pl. **pelves** /'pelviːz/ or ~**es** (Anat.) Becken, das

**pen¹** /pen/ ① n. (enclosure) Pferch, der

② v.t., -nn-: ~ **sb. in a corner** jmdn. in eine Ecke drängen
■ **pen 'in** v.t. einpferchen

**pen²** ① n. Federhalter, der; (fountain ~) Füller, der; (ball ~) Kugelschreiber, der; (felt-tip ~) Filzstift, der
② v.t., -nn- schreiben

**penal** /'piːnl/ adj. Straf-

**penalize** /'piːnəlaɪz/ v.t. bestrafen; (Sport) eine Strafe verhängen gegen

**penalty** /'penltɪ/ n. (a) Strafe, die; **pay the** ~/**the** ~ **for** or **of sth.** dafür/für etw. büßen [müssen]
(b) (Footb.) Elfmeter, der

**penalty:** ~ **box** n. (Footb.) Strafraum, der; (Ice Hockey) Strafbank, die; ~ **kick** n. (Footb.) Strafstoß, der

**penance** /'penəns/ n. Buße, die; **act of** ~: Bußwerk, das; **do** ~: Buße tun

**pence** ▶ PENNY

**pencil** /'pensl/ ① n. Bleistift, der; **red/ coloured** ~: Rot-/Buntstift, der
② v.t., (Brit.) -ll- mit einem Bleistift/Farbstift schreiben

**pencil:** ~ **case** n. Griffelkasten, der; (of soft material) Federmäppchen, das; ~ **sharpener** n. Bleistiftspitzer, der

**pendant** /'pendənt/ n. Anhänger, der

**pending** /'pendɪŋ/ ① adj. unentschieden ⟨Angelegenheit, Sache⟩; schwebend ⟨Verfahren⟩
② prep. ~ **his return** bis zu seiner Rückkehr

**pendulum** /'pendjʊləm/ n. Pendel, das

**penetrate** /'penɪtreɪt/ v.t. eindringen in (+ Akk.); (pass through) durchdringen

**penetrating** /'penɪtreɪtɪŋ/ adj. durchdringend

**penetration** /penɪ'treɪʃn/ n. Eindringen, das (of in + Akk.); (passing through) Durchdringen, das

**'penfriend** n. Brieffreund, der/-freundin, die

**penguin** /'peŋgwɪn/ n. Pinguin, der

**penicillin** /penɪ'sɪlɪn/ n. Penizillin, das

**peninsula** /pɪ'nɪnsjʊlə/ n. Halbinsel, die

**penis** /'piːnɪs/ n. Penis, der

**penitence** /'penɪtəns/ n. Reue, die

**penitent** /'penɪtənt/ adj. reuevoll (geh.); reuig (geh.) ⟨Sünder⟩

**penitentiary** /penɪ'tenʃərɪ/ n. (Amer.) Straf[vollzugs]anstalt, die

**pen:** ~**knife** n. Taschenmesser, das; ~ **light** n. [Mini]stablampe, die

**pennant** /'penənt/ n. Wimpel, der; (on official car etc.) Stander, der

**penniless** /'penɪlɪs/ adj. mittellos

**penny** /'penɪ/ n., pl. usu. **pennies** /'penɪz/ (for separate coins), **pence** /pens/ (for sum of money) Penny, der; **fifty pence** fünfzig Pence; **two/fifty pence** [**piece**] Zwei-/ Fünfzigpencestück, das

P

**pension** /'penʃn/ n. Rente, die; (payment to retired civil servant) Pension, die; widow's ~: Witwenrente, die /-pension, die; be on a ~: eine Rente beziehen

■ **pension 'off** v.t. berenten (Amtsspr.); auf Rente setzen (ugs.); pensionieren ⟨Lehrer, Beamten⟩

**'pensioner** n. Rentner, der/Rentnerin, die; (retired civil servant) Pensionär, der/Pensionärin, die

**pensive** /'pensɪv/ adj. nachdenklich

**pentagon** /'pentəgən/ n. Fünfeck, das; the P~ (Amer. Polit.) das Pentagon

**Pentecost** /'pentɪkɒst/ n. Pfingsten, das

**pent:** ~**house** n. Penthaus, das; ~**-up** adj. angestaut ⟨Ärger, Wut⟩; unterdrückt ⟨Sehnsucht, Gefühle⟩

**penultimate** /pe'nʌltɪmət/ adj. vorletzt...

**people** /'piːpl/ n. (a) constr. as pl. Leute Pl.; Menschen Pl.; (as opposed to animals) Menschen Pl.; city/country ~ (inhabitants) Stadt-/Landbewohner Pl.; local ~: Einheimische Pl.; working ~: arbeitende Menschen; coloured/white ~: Farbige/Weiße Pl.; ~ say ...: man sagt ...; a crowd of ~: eine Menschenmenge
(b) (nation) Volk, das

**pepper** /'pepə(r)/ ① n. (a) Pfeffer, der
(b) (vegetable) Paprikaschote, die; red/green ~: roter/grüner Paprika
② v.t. (a) pfeffern
(b) (pelt) bombardieren (ugs.)

**pepper:** ~**corn** n. Pfefferkorn, das; ~ **mill** n. Pfeffermühle, die; ~**mint** n. (sweet) Pfefferminz, das; ~ **pot** n. Pfefferstreuer, der

**peppery** /'pepərɪ/ adj. pfeff[e]rig; (spicy) scharf

**per** /pə(r), stressed pɜ:(r)/ prep. pro

**perceive** /pə'siːv/ v.t. wahrnehmen; (with the mind) spüren; ~d vermeintlich ⟨Bedrohung, Gefahr, Wert⟩

**per cent** (Brit.; Amer.: **percent**) /pə'sent/ ① adv. ninety ~ effective zu 90 Prozent wirksam
② adj. a 5 ~ increase ein Zuwachs von 5 Prozent
③ n. (a) Prozent, das
(b) ▶ PERCENTAGE

**percentage** /pə'sentɪdʒ/ n. Prozentsatz, der

**per'centage sign** n. Prozentzeichen, das

**perceptible** /pə'septɪbl/ adj. wahrnehmbar

**perception** /pə'sepʃn/ n. (act) Wahrnehmung, die; (result) Erkenntnis, die; (faculty) Wahrnehmungsvermögen, das

**perceptive** /pə'septɪv/ adj. einfühlsam ⟨Person, Bemerkung⟩

**perch** /pɜːtʃ/ ① n. Sitzstange, die
② v.i. (a) sich niederlassen
(b) (be supported) sitzen
③ v.t. setzen/stellen/legen

**percolate** /'pɜːkəleɪt/ v.i. [durch]sickern

**percolator** /'pɜːkəleɪtə(r)/ n. Kaffeemaschine, die

**percussion** /pə'kʌʃn/ n. (Mus.) Schlagzeug, das; ~ **instrument** Schlaginstrument, das

**perennial** /pə'renjəl/ ① adj. (a) (Bot.) ausdauernd
(b) immer wieder auftretend ⟨Problem⟩
② n. (Bot.) ausdauernde Pflanze

**perfect** ① /'pɜːfɪkt/ adj. vollkommen; perfekt ⟨Englisch, Timing⟩; tadellos ⟨Zustand⟩; (coll.: unmitigated) absolut; a ~ stranger ein völlig Fremder
② /pə'fekt/ v.t. vervollkommnen

**perfection** /pə'fekʃn/ n. Perfektion, die; to ~: perfekt

**perfectionism** /pə'fekʃənɪzm/ n. Perfektionismus, der

**perfectionist** /pə'fekʃənɪst/ n. Perfektionist, der/Perfektionistin, die

**'perfectly** adv. (a) (completely) vollkommen; be ~ entitled to do sth. durchaus berechtigt sein, etw. zu tun
(b) (faultlessly) perfekt; tadellos ⟨sich verhalten⟩

**perfect 'pitch** n. (Mus.) absolutes Gehör

**perforate** /'pɜːfəreɪt/ v.t. perforieren; (make opening into) durchlöchern

**perforation** /pɜːfə'reɪʃn/ n. (a) (hole) Loch, das
(b) in pl. ~s Perforation, die; (in sheets of stamps) Zähnung, die

**perform** /pə'fɔːm/ ① v.t. ausführen ⟨Arbeit, Operation⟩; erfüllen ⟨Pflicht, Aufgabe⟩; vollbringen ⟨[Helden]tat, Leistung⟩; ausfüllen ⟨Funktion⟩; vollbringen ⟨Wunder⟩; anstellen ⟨Berechnungen⟩; durchführen ⟨Experiment, Sektion⟩; vorführen ⟨Trick⟩; aufführen ⟨Theaterstück, Scharade⟩; vortragen ⟨Lied, Sonate usw.⟩
② v.i. eine Vorführung geben; (sing) singen; (play) spielen

**performance** /pə'fɔːməns/ n. (a) (of duty, task) Erfüllung, die
(b) ([notable] achievement; Motor Veh.) Leistung, die
(c) (at theatre, cinema, etc.) Vorstellung, die; her ~ as Desdemona ihre Darstellung der Desdemona; the ~ of a play/opera die Aufführung eines Theaterstücks/einer Oper

**performance:** ~ **art** n. Performance-Art, die; ~ **artist** n. Performancekünstler, der/ -künstlerin, die ~**-enhancing** adj. ~-enhancing drug/substance leistungsfördernde od. -steigernde Droge/ Substanz

**per'former** n. Künstler, der/Künstlerin, die

**per'forming** attrib. adj. dressiert ⟨Tier⟩

**performing 'arts** n. pl. darstellende Künste

**perfume** /'pɜːfjuːm/ n. Duft, der; (fluid) Parfüm, das

# perfunctory ⸱⸱⸱⸦ personal ⸱⸱⸱⸱

**perfunctory** /pə'fʌŋktəri/ *adj.*
oberflächlich ⟨Arbeit, Überprüfung⟩; flüchtig
⟨Erkundigung, Bemerkung⟩

**perhaps** /pə'hæps/ *adv.* vielleicht

**peril** /'peril/ *n.* Gefahr, *die*

**perilous** /'perələs/ *adj.* gefahrvoll; **be** ~:
gefährlich sein

**perimeter** /pə'rɪmɪtə(r)/ *n.* [äußere]
Begrenzung; Grenze, *die*

**period** /'pɪərɪəd/ ①*n.* **(a)** (of history or life)
Periode, *die;* Zeit, *die;* (any portion of time)
Zeitraum, *der;* **the Classical/Romantic** ~: die
Klassik/Romantik
**(b)** (Sch.) Stunde, *die;* **chemistry/English** ~:
Chemie-/Englischstunde, *die*
**(c)** (menstruation) Periode, *die*
**(d)** ( punctuation mark) Punkt, *der*
②*adj.* zeitgenössisch ⟨Tracht, Kostüm⟩;
antik ⟨Möbel⟩

**periodic** /pɪərɪ'ɒdɪk/ *adj.* regelmäßig;
(intermittent) gelegentlich

**periodical** /pɪərɪ'ɒdɪkl/ ①*adj.* ▶ PERIODIC
②*n.* Zeitschrift, *die;* **weekly/monthly** ~:
Wochenzeitschrift/Monatsschrift, *die*

**peri'odically** *adv.* regelmäßig; (intermittently)
gelegentlich

**peripheral** /pə'rɪfərl/ ①*adj.* peripher
(geh.); Rand⟨problem, -erscheinung⟩
②*n.* (Comp.) Peripheriegerät, *das*

**periphery** /pə'rɪfəri/ *n.* Peripherie, *die*

**periscope** /'periskəʊp/ *n.* Periskop, *das*

**perish** /'perɪʃ/ *v.i.* **(a)** (die) umkommen
**(b)** (rot) verderben; ⟨Gummi:⟩ altern

**perishable** /'perɪʃəbl/ *adj.* [leicht]
verderblich

**'perishing** (coll.) ①*adj.* mörderisch
⟨Kälte⟩; **it's/I'm** ~: es ist bitterkalt/ich
komme um vor Kälte (ugs.)
②*adv.* mörderisch ⟨kalt⟩

**perjury** /'pɜːdʒəri/ *n.* Meineid, *der;* **commit**
~: einen Meineid leisten

**perk¹** /pɜːk/ (coll.) ①*v.i.* ~ **up** munter
werden
②*v.t.* ~ **up** aufmuntern

**perk²** *n.* (Brit. coll.) [Sonder]vergünstigung,
*die*

**perky** /'pɜːki/ *adj.* lebhaft; munter

**perm** /pɜːm/ ①*n.* Dauerwelle, *die*
②*v.t.* **have one's hair** ~**ed** sich (Dat.) eine
Dauerwelle machen lassen

**permanence** /'pɜːmənəns/ *n.*
Dauerhaftigkeit, *die*

**permanent** /'pɜːmənənt/ *adj.* fest ⟨Sitz,
Bestandteil, Mitglied⟩; ständig ⟨Wohnsitz,
Adresse, Kampf⟩; Dauer⟨stellung, -visum⟩;
bleibend ⟨Schaden⟩

**'permanently** *adv.* dauernd; auf Dauer
⟨verhindern, bleiben⟩

**permanent 'wave** *n.* Dauerwelle, *die*

**permeable** /'pɜːmɪəbl/ *adj.* durchlässig; **be**
~ **to sth.** etw. durchlassen

**permeate** /'pɜːmɪeɪt/ ①*v.t.* dringen
durch; **be** ~**d with** or **by sth.** (fig.) von etw.
durchdrungen sein
②*v.i.* ~ **through sth.** etw. durchdringen

**permissible** /pə'mɪsɪbl/ *adj.* zulässig; **be**
~ **to** or **for sb.** jmdm. erlaubt sein

**permission** /pə'mɪʃn/ *n.* Erlaubnis, *die;*
(given by official body) Genehmigung, *die;* **give
sb.** ~ **to do sth.** jmdm. erlauben, etw. zu tun

**permissive** /pə'mɪsɪv/ *adj.* **the** ~ **society**
die permissive Gesellschaft

**permit** ①/pə'mɪt/ *v.t.,* **-tt-** zulassen
⟨Berufung, Einspruch usw.⟩; ~ **sb. sth.**
jmdm. etw. erlauben; **sb. is** ~**ted to do sth.**
es ist jmdm. erlaubt, etw. zu tun
②*v.i.,* **-tt-** es zulassen
③/'pɜːmɪt/ *n.* Genehmigung, *die*

**pernicious** /pə'nɪʃəs/ *adj.* verderblich;
bösartig ⟨Krankheit⟩

**peroxide** /pə'rɒksaɪd/ *n.* Peroxid, *das;*
~ **blonde** Wasserstoffblondine, *die*

**perpendicular** /pɜːpən'dɪkjʊlə(r)/ *adj.*
senkrecht

**perpetrate** /'pɜːpɪtreɪt/ *v.t.* begehen;
verüben ⟨Gräuel⟩

**perpetual** /pə'petjʊəl/ *adj.* **(a)** (eternal) ewig
**(b)** (continuous; coll.: repeated) ständig

**per'petually** *adv.* **(a)** (eternally) ewig
**(b)** (continuously; coll.: repeatedly) ständig

**perpetuate** /pə'petjʊeɪt/ *v.t.*
aufrechterhalten

**perplex** /pə'pleks/ *v.t.* verwirren

**perplexed** /pə'plekst/ *adj.* verwirrt;
( puzzled) ratlos

**perplexity** /pə'pleksɪti/ *n.* Verwirrung,
*die;* ( puzzlement) Ratlosigkeit, *die*

**persecute** /'pɜːsɪkjuːt/ *v.t.* verfolgen

**persecution** /pɜːsɪ'kjuːʃn/ *n.* Verfolgung,
*die*

**persecutor** /'pɜːsɪkjuːtə(r)/ *n.* Verfolger,
*der*/Verfolgerin, *die*

**perseverance** /pɜːsɪ'vɪərəns/ *n.*
Beharrlichkeit, *die;* Ausdauer, *die*

**persevere** /pɜːsɪ'vɪə(r)/ *v.i.* ausharren;
~ **with** or **at** or **in sth.** bei etw. dabeibleiben

**Persian** /'pɜːʃn/ *adj.* persisch; Perser⟨katze,
-teppich⟩

**persist** /pə'sɪst/ *v.i.* **(a)** nicht nachgeben;
~ **in doing sth.** etw. weiterhin [beharrlich]
tun
**(b)** (continue to exist) anhalten

**persistence** /pə'sɪstəns/ Hartnäckigkeit,
*die*

**persistent** /pə'sɪstənt/ *adj.* **(a)** hartnäckig
**(b)** (constantly repeated) dauernd; hartnäckig
⟨Gerüchte⟩

**per'sistently** *adv.* hartnäckig

**person** /'pɜːsn/ *n.* Mensch, *der;* **in** ~:
persönlich; selbst

**personal** /'pɜːsənl/ *adj.* persönlich; ⸱⸱⸱⸦

Privat⟨*angelegenheit, -leben*⟩; ~ **computer**
Personalcomputer, *der;* ~ **stereo** Walkman,
*der;* ~ **hygiene** Körperpflege, *die*
**personal:** ~ **ad** *n.* Privatanzeige, *die;*
(seeking friendship, romance) Kontaktanzeige, *die;*
~ **as'sistant** *n.* persönlicher Referent/
persönliche Referentin; ~ **'best** *n.* (Sport)
persönliche Bestleistung; ~ **call** *n.* (Brit.
Teleph.) Anruf mit Voranmeldung;
~ **column** *n.* Rubrik für private
[Klein]anzeigen; ~ **identifi'cation
number** *n.* persönliche
Identifikationsnummer; Geheimnummer, *die*
**personality** /pɜːsə'nælɪtɪ/ *n.*
Persönlichkeit, *die*
**'personal loan** *n.* Personal- od.
Privatdarlehen, *das;* Personal- od.
Privatkredit, *der*
**'personally** *adv.* persönlich
**personal:** ~ **'organizer** *n.*
Terminplaner, *der;* ~ **'pension plan** *n.*
persönlicher Renten[vorsorge]plan;
~ **'property** *n.* persönliches Eigentum
**personification** /pəsɒnɪfɪ'keɪʃn/ *n.*
Verkörperung, *die*
**personify** /pə'sɒnɪfaɪ/ *v.t.* verkörpern; **be
kindness personified** die Freundlichkeit in
Person sein
**personnel** /pɜːsə'nel/ *n.* Belegschaft, *die;* (of
shop, restaurant, etc.) Personal, *das; attrib.*
Personal-; ~ **department** Personalabteilung,
*die*
**person-to-'person** *adj.* (Amer. Teleph.)
~ **call** Anruf mit Voranmeldung
**perspective** /pə'spektɪv/ *n.* Perspektive,
*die;* (fig.) Blickwinkel, *der*
**perspiration** /pɜːspɪ'reɪʃn/ *n.* Schweiß, *der*
**perspire** /pə'spaɪə(r)/ *v.i.* schwitzen
**persuade** /pə'sweɪd/ *v.t.* (a) (convince)
überzeugen (of von); ~ **oneself [that]** ...: sich
(*Dat.*) einreden, dass ...
(b) (induce) überreden
**persuasion** /pə'sweɪʒn/ *n.* Überzeugung,
*die;* **it didn't take much** ~: es brauchte nicht
viel Überredungskunst
**persuasive** /pə'sweɪsɪv/ *adj.,*
**per'suasively** *adv.* überzeugend
**pert** /pɜːt/ *adj.* keck
**pertinent** /'pɜːtɪmənt/ *adj.* relevant (**to** für)
**perturb** /pə'tɜːb/ *v.t.* beunruhigen
**Peru** /pə'ruː/ *pr. n.* Peru (*das*)
**Peruvian** /pə'ruːvɪən/ 1 *adj.* peruanisch;
**sb. is** ~: jmd. ist Peruaner/Peruanerin
2 *n.* Peruaner, *der*/Peruanerin, *die*
**peruse** /pə'ruːz/ *v.t.* genau durchlesen; (fig.:
examine) untersuchen
**pervade** /pə'veɪd/ *v.t.* durchdringen
**pervasive** /pə'veɪsɪv/ *adj.* durchdringend
⟨*Geruch, Kälte*⟩; weit verbreitet ⟨*Ansicht*⟩;
sich ausbreitend ⟨*Gefühl*⟩
**perverse** /pə'vɜːs/ *adj.* starrköpfig

**perversion** /pə'vɜːʃn/ *n.* (a) (sexual)
Perversion, *die*
(b) ~ **of justice** Rechtsbeugung, *die*
**pervert** 1 /pə'vɜːt/ *v.t.* (morally) verderben
2 /'pɜːvɜːt/ *n.* perverser Mensch
**perverted** /pə'vɜːtɪd/ *adj.* (sexually) pervers
**pessimism** /'pesɪmɪzm/ *n.* Pessimismus,
*der*
**pessimist** /'pesɪmɪst/ *n.* Pessimist, *der*/
Pessimistin, *die*
**pessimistic** /pesɪ'mɪstɪk/ *adj.*
pessimistisch
**pest** /pest/ *n.* (thing) Ärgernis, *das;* (person)
Nervensäge, *die* (ugs.); (animal) Schädling, *der*
**pester** /'pestə(r)/ *v.t.* belästigen; nerven
(ugs.); ~ **sb. for sth.** jmdm. wegen etw. in den
Ohren liegen
**pesticide** /'pestɪsaɪd/ *n.* Pestizid, *das*
**pestle** /'pesl/ *n.* Stößel, *der*
**pet** /pet/ 1 *n.* (a) (animal) Haustier, *das*
(b) (as term of endearment) Schatz, *der*
2 *adj.* (favourite) Lieblings-
3 *v.i.,* **-tt-** knutschen (ugs.)
**petal** /'petl/ *n.* Blütenblatt, *das*
**peter** /'piːtə(r)/ *v.i.* ~ **out** [allmählich] zu
Ende gehen; ⟨*Weg:*⟩ sich verlieren
**'pet food** *n.* Tierfutter, *das*
**petite** /pə'tiːt/ *adj.* zierlich
**petition** /pə'tɪʃn/ 1 *n.* Petition, *die;*
Eingabe, *die*
2 *v.t.* eine Eingabe richten an (+ *Akk.*)
**petitioner** /pə'tɪʃənə(r)/ *n.* Antragsteller,
*der*/Antragstellerin, *die*
**petrify** /'petrɪfaɪ/ *v.t.* **be petrified with fear/
shock** starr vor Angst/Schrecken sein
**petrol** /'petrl/ *n.* (Brit.) Benzin, *das*
**petrol:** ~ **bomb** *n.* Benzinbombe, *die;*
~ **can** *n.* (Brit.) Benzinkanister, *der;* ~ **cap**
*n.* (Brit.) Tankverschluss, *der*
**petroleum** /pɪ'trəʊlɪəm/ *n.* Erdöl, *das*
**petroleum 'jelly** *n.* Vaseline, *die*
**petrol:** ~ **pump** *n.* (Brit.) Zapfsäule, *die;*
~ **station** *n.* (Brit.) Tankstelle, *die;*
~ **tank** *n.* (Brit.) Benzintank, *der;*
~ **tanker** *n.* (Brit.) Benzintankwagen, *der*
**'pet shop** *n.* Tierhandlung, *die*
**petticoat** /'petɪkəʊt/ *n.* Unterrock, *der*
**petty** /'petɪ/ *adj.* kleinlich ⟨*Vorschrift,
Einwand*⟩; belanglos ⟨*Detail, Sorgen*⟩;
~ **criminal** Kleinkriminelle, *der*/*die;* ~ **theft**
Bagatelldiebstahl, *der;* ~ **thief** kleiner Dieb/
kleine Diebin
**petty 'cash** *n.* kleine Kasse; Portokasse,
*die*
**petulance** /'petjʊləns/ *n.* Bockigkeit, *die*
**petulant** /'petjʊlənt/ *adj.* bockig
**pew** /pjuː/ *n.* Kirchenbank, *die*
**pewter** /'pjuːtə(r)/ *n.* Zinn, *das*
**phallic** /'fælɪk/ *adj.* phallisch; ~ **symbol**
Phallussymbol, *das*
**phantom** /'fæntəm/ *n.* Phantom, *das*

**pharmacist** /'fɑːməsɪst/ n. Apotheker, der/Apothekerin, die

**pharmacy** /'fɑːməsɪ/ n. (dispensary) Apotheke, die

**phase** /feɪz/ n. Phase, die
■ **phase 'in** v.t. stufenweise einführen
■ **phase 'out** v.t. allmählich abschaffen ‹Verfahrensweise, Methode›; (stop producing) [langsam] auslaufen lassen

**Ph.D.** /piːeɪtʃ'diː/ abbr. = **Doctor of Philosophy** Dr. phil.

**pheasant** /'fezənt/ n. Fasan, der

**phenomenal** /fɪ'nɒmɪnl/ adj., **phenomenally** /fɪ'nɒmɪnəlɪ/ adv. phänomenal

**phenomenon** /fɪ'nɒmɪnən/ n., pl. **phenomena** /fɪ'nɒmɪnə/ Phänomen, das

**phew** /fjuː/ int. puh

**philanderer** /fɪ'lændərə(r)/ n. Schürzenjäger, der (spött.)

**philanthropist** /fɪ'lænθrəpɪst/ n. Philanthrop, der/Philanthropin, die (geh.)

**philanthropy** /fɪ'lænθrəpɪ/ n. Philanthropie, die (geh.)

**Philippines** /'filɪpiːnz/ pr. n. pl. Philippinen Pl.

**philistine** /'filɪstaɪn/ n. Banause, der/ Banausin, die

**Phillips** /'filɪps/ n. ~ **screw** ® Kreuz[schlitz]schraube, die; ~ **screwdriver** ® Kreuz[schlitz]schraubenzieher, der

**philosopher** /fɪ'lɒsəfə(r)/ n. Philosoph, der/Philosophin, die

**philosophical** /filə'sɒfɪkl/ adj. (a) philosophisch
(b) (resigned) abgeklärt

**philosophize** (**philosophise**) /fɪ'lɒsəfaɪz/ v.i. philosophieren (about, on über + Akk.)

**philosophy** /fɪ'lɒsəfɪ/ n. Philosophie, die

**phlegm** /flem/ n. Schleim, der

**phobia** /'fəʊbɪə/ n. Phobie, die

**phobic** /'fəʊbɪk/ adj. phobisch

**phone** /fəʊn/ n. (coll.) ① n. Telefon, das; **by** ~: telefonisch; **be on the** ~: Telefon haben; (be phoning) telefonieren
② v.t. & i. anrufen
■ **phone 'back** v.t. & i. zurückrufen; (make further call) wieder anrufen
■ **phone 'up** v.t. & i. anrufen

**phone:** ~ **book** n. Telefonbuch, das; ~ **booth,** ~ **box** ns. Telefonzelle, die; ~ **call** n. Anruf, der; ~ **card** n. Telefonkarte, die; ~**-in** n. ~**-in** [programme] (Radio) Hörersendung, die; (Telev.) Phone-in-Sendung, die (Jargon); ~ **number** n. Telefonnummer, die

**phonetic** /fə'netɪk/ adj. phonetisch

**phonetics** /fə'netɪks/ n. Phonetik, die

**phoney** /'fəʊnɪ/ adj. (coll.) (sham) falsch; gefälscht ‹Brief, Dokument›

**phonograph** /'fəʊnəɡrɑːf/ n. (Amer.) Plattenspieler, der

**phony** ▶ PHONEY

**phosphate** /'fɒsfeɪt/ n. Phosphat, das

**phosphorus** /'fɒsfərəs/ n. Phosphor, der

**photo** /'fəʊtəʊ/ n., pl. ~**s** Foto, das

**photo:** ~ **album** n. Fotoalbum, das; ~**call** n. Fototermin, der; ~**copier** n. Fotokopiergerät, das; ~**copy** ① n. Fotokopie, die; ② v.t. fotokopieren

**photogenic** /fəʊtə'dʒiːnɪk/ adj. fotogen

**photograph** /'fəʊtəɡrɑːf/ ① n. Fotografie, die; Foto, das; **take a** ~ [of sb./sth.] [jmdn./ etw.] fotografieren
② v.t. & i. fotografieren

'**photograph album** n. Fotoalbum, das

**photographer** /fə'tɒɡrəfə(r)/ n. Fotograf, der/Fotografin, die

**photographic** /fəʊtə'ɡræfɪk/ adj. fotografisch; Foto‹ausrüstung, -apparat, -ausstellung›

**photography** /fə'tɒɡrəfɪ/ n. Fotografie, die

**photo:** ~ **session,** ~ **shoot** ns. Shooting, das; ~'**synthesis** n. Photosynthese, die

**phrase** /freɪz/ ① n. [Rede]wendung, die
② v.t. formulieren

'**phrase book** n. Sprachführer, der

**physical** /'fizɪkl/ adj. (a) physisch ‹Gewalt›; dinglich ‹Welt, Universum›
(b) (of physics) physikalisch
(c) (bodily) körperlich

**physical edu'cation** n. (Sch.) Sport, der

'**physically** adv. (relating to the body) körperlich

**physical 'training** n. Sport, der; (Sch.) Sport[unterricht], der

**physician** /fɪ'zɪʃn/ n. Arzt, der/Ärztin, die

**physicist** /'fizɪsɪst/ n. Physiker, der/ Physikerin, die

**physics** /'fizɪks/ n. Physik, die

**physiology** /fizɪ'ɒlədʒɪ/ n. Physiologie, die

**physiotherapist** /fizɪəʊ'θerəpɪst/ n. Physiotherapeut, der/-therapeutin, die

**physiotherapy** /fizɪəʊ'θerəpɪ/ n. Physiotherapie, die

**physique** /fɪ'ziːk/ n. Körperbau, der

**pianist** /'piːənɪst/ n. Pianist, der/Pianistin, die

**piano** /pɪ'ænəʊ/ n., pl. ~**s** (upright) Klavier, das; (grand) Flügel, der

**piano:** ~ **ac'cordion** n. Akkordeon, das; ~ **music** n. Klaviermusik, die; ~ **player** n. Klavierspieler, der/-spielerin, die; ~ **stool** n. Klavierschemel, der; ~ **tuner** n. Klavierstimmer, der/-stimmerin, die

**pick¹** /pɪk/ n. (tool) Spitzhacke, die

**pick²** ① n. (a) (choice) Wahl, die; **take your** ~: du hast die Wahl
(b) (best part) Elite, die; **the** ~ **of the fruit** die besten Früchte ···》

**2** *v.t.* **(a)** pflücken ⟨*Blumen, Äpfel usw.*⟩; lesen ⟨*Trauben*⟩

**(b)** (select) auswählen; ~ **one's way** sich (*Dat.*) vorsichtig [s]einen Weg suchen

**(c)** ~ **one's nose** in der Nase bohren

**(d)** ~ **sb.'s pocket** jmdn. bestehlen; **he had his pocket** ~**ed** er wurde von einem Taschendieb bestohlen

**(e)** ~ **a lock** ein Schloss knacken (salopp)

**3** *v.i.* ~ **and choose** wählerisch sein

■ **'pick at** *v.t.* herumstochern in (+ *Dat.*) ⟨*Essen*⟩

■ **'pick on** *v.t.* (victimize) es abgesehen haben auf (+ *Akk.*)

■ **pick 'out** *v.t.* **(a)** (choose) auswählen; (for oneself) sich (*Dat.*) aussuchen

**(b)** (distinguish) entdecken ⟨*Detail, jmds. Gesicht in der Menge*⟩

■ **pick up** **1** /'--/ *v.t.* **(a)** [in die Hand] nehmen; hochnehmen ⟨*Baby*⟩; (after dropping) aufheben; aufnehmen ⟨*Masche*⟩; ~ **up the telephone** den [Telefon]hörer abnehmen

**(b)** (collect) mitnehmen; (by arrangement) abholen (**at, from** von); (obtain) holen

**(c)** (become infected by) sich (*Dat.*) holen (ugs.) ⟨*Virus, Grippe*⟩

**(d)** ⟨*Bus, Autofahrer:*⟩ mitnehmen

**(e)** (rescue from the sea) [aus Seenot] bergen

**(f)** empfangen ⟨*Signal, Funkspruch usw.*⟩

**(g)** (coll.: make acquaintance of) aufreißen (ugs.)

**2** /-'-/ *v.i.* **(a)** sich bessern

**(b)** ⟨*Wind:*⟩ auffrischen

**'pickaxe** (*Amer.:* **'pickax**) ▶ PICK¹

**picket** /'pɪkɪt/ **1** *n.* Streikposten, *der*

**2** *v.i.* Streikposten stehen

**3** *v.t.* Streikposten stellen vor (+ *Dat.*)

**'picket fence** *n.* Palisadenzaun, *der*

**'picketing** /'pɪkɪtɪŋ/ *n.* Aufstellen von Streikposten

**'picket line** *n.* Streikpostenkette, *die*

**pickle** /'pɪkl/ **1** *n., usu. in pl.* (food) Mixedpickles *Pl.*

**2** *v.t.* einlegen ⟨*Gurken, Zwiebeln, Eier*⟩; marinieren ⟨*Hering*⟩

**pick:** ~**me-up** *n.* Stärkungsmittel, *das;*
~**pocket** *n.* Taschendieb, *der*/-diebin, *die;*
~**up** *n.* **(a)** ~**up** [**truck**] Kleinlastwagen, *der;*
**(b)** (of record player, guitar) Tonabnehmer, *der*

**picnic** /'pɪknɪk/ **1** *n.* Picknick, *das;* **go for** *or* **on**/**have a** ~: ein Picknick machen

**2** *v.i.,* **-ck-** picknicken; Picknick machen

**picnic:** ~ **basket** *n.* Picknickkorb, *der;*
~ **site** *n.* Picknickplatz, *der*

**pictorial** /pɪk'tɔːrɪəl/ *adj.* illustriert ⟨*Bericht, Zeitschrift*⟩; bildlich ⟨*Darstellung*⟩

**.picture** /'pɪktʃə(r)/ **1** *n.* **(a)** Bild, *das;* **get the** ~ (coll.) verstehen[, worum es geht]; **put sb. in the** ~: jmdn. ins Bild setzen

**(b)** (film) Film, *der*

**(c)** *in pl.* (Brit.: cinema) Kino, *das;* **go to the** ~**s** ins Kino gehen; **what's on at the** ~**s?** was läuft im Kino?

**2** *v.t.* ~ [**to oneself**] sich (*Dat.*) vorstellen

**picture:** ~ **book** *n.* Bilderbuch, *das;*
~ **frame** *n.* Bilderrahmen, *der;*
~ **'postcard** *n.* Ansichtskarte, *die*

**picturesque** /pɪktʃə'resk/ *adj.* malerisch

**pidgin** /'pɪdʒɪn/ *n.* Pidgin, *das*

**pidgin 'English** *n.* Pidginenglisch, *das*

**pie** /paɪ/ *n.* (of meat, fish, etc.) Pastete, *die;* (of fruit etc.) ≈ Obstkuchen, *der*

**piece** /piːs/ **1** *n.* **(a)** Stück, *das;* (of broken glass or pottery) Scherbe, *die;* (of jigsaw puzzle, crashed aircraft, etc.) Teil, *der;* (Amer.: distance) [kleines] Stück; **a** ~ **of meat/cake** ein Stück Fleisch/Kuchen; ~ **of furniture/luggage** Möbel-/Gepäckstück, *das;* **a three-**~ **suite** eine dreiteilige Sitzgarnitur; ~ **of luck** Glücksfall, *der;* ~ **of news/gossip/ information** Nachricht, *die*/Klatsch, *der*/ Information, *die*

**(b)** (Chess) Figur, *die*

**(c)** (coin) **gold** ~: Goldstück, *das;* **a 10p** ~: ein 10-Pence-Stück

**(d)** (literary or musical composition) Stück, *das;* ~ **of music** Musikstück, *das*

**2** *v.t.* ~ **to'gether** zusammenfügen (**from** aus)

**piece:** ~**meal** *adv., adj.* stückweise;
~**work** *n.* Akkordarbeit, *die*

**pie:** ~ **chart** *n.* Kreisdiagramm, *das;*
~**crust** *n.* Teigmantel, *der*

**pier** /pɪə(r)/ *n.* (at seaside) Pier, *der*

**pierce** /pɪəs/ *v.t.* (prick) durchstechen; (penetrate) [ein]dringen in (+ *Akk.*) ⟨*Körper, Fleisch, Herz*⟩; ~ **a hole in sth.** ein Loch in etw. (*Akk.*) stechen

**piercing** /'pɪəsɪŋ/ *adj.* durchdringend ⟨*Stimme, Schrei, Blick*⟩

**piety** /'paɪətɪ/ *n.* Frömmigkeit, *die*

**pig** /pɪg/ *n.* **(a)** Schwein, *das;* ~**s might fly** (iron.) da müsste schon ein Wunder geschehen

**(b)** (coll.: greedy person) Vielfraß, *der* (ugs.)

**pigeon** /'pɪdʒɪn/ *n.* Taube, *die*

**'pigeonhole** *n.* [Ablage]fach, *das;* (for letters) Postfach, *das*

**piggy** /'pɪgɪ/: ~**back** *n.* **give sb. a** ~**back** jmdn. huckepack nehmen; ~ **bank** *n.* Sparschwein[chen], *das*

**pig'headed** *adj.* dickschädelig (ugs.)

**piglet** /'pɪglɪt/ *n.* Ferkel, *das*

**pigment** /'pɪgmənt/ *n.* Pigment, *das*

**pigmentation** /pɪgmən'teɪʃn/ *n.* Pigmentierung, *die*

**pig's 'ear** *n.* (Brit. coll.) **make a** ~**'s ear of sth.** etw. verpfuschen *od.* (ugs.) vermurksen

**pig:** ~**sty** *n.* (lit. *or* fig.) Schweinestall, *der;*
~**tail** *n.* (plaited) Zopf, *der;* ~**tails** (at either side of head) Rattenschwänzchen *Pl.* (ugs.)

**pike** /paɪk/ *n., pl. same* Hecht, *der*

**pilchard** /'pɪltʃəd/ *n.* Sardine, *die*

**pile¹** /paɪl/ **1** *n.* **(a)** (of dishes, plates) Stapel, *der;* (of paper, books, letters) Stoß, *der;* (of clothes) Haufen, *der*

**(b)** (coll.: large quantity) Haufen, *der* (ugs.)

**2** *v.t.* (a) (load) [voll] beladen
(b) (heap up) aufstapeln ⟨*Holz, Steine*⟩; aufhäufen ⟨*Abfall, Schnee*⟩
■ **pile 'in** *v.i.* (seen from outside) hineindrängen; (seen from inside) hereindrängen
■ **'pile into** *v.t.* sich zwängen in (+ *Akk.*) ⟨*Auto, Zimmer, Zugabteil*⟩
■ **pile 'on** **1** *v.i.* ▶ PILE IN
**2** *v.t.* (fig.) ~ on the pressure Druck machen
■ **'pile on to** *v.t.* drängen in (+ *Akk.*) ⟨*Bus usw.*⟩
■ **pile 'out** *v.i.* nach draußen drängen
■ **pile 'up** **1** *v.i.* (a) ⟨*Waren, Post, Arbeit, Schnee:*⟩ sich auftürmen; ⟨*Verkehr:*⟩ sich stauen
(b) (crash) aufeinander auffahren
**2** *v.t.* aufstapeln ⟨*Steine, Bücher usw.*⟩; aufhäufen ⟨*Abfall, Schnee*⟩
**pile²** *n.* (of fabric etc.) Flor, *der*
**pile³** *n.* (stake) Pfahl, *der*
**'piledriver** *n.* [Pfahl]ramme, *die*
**piles** /paɪlz/ *n. pl.* (Med.) Hämorrhoiden *Pl.*
**'pile-up** *n.* Massenkarambolage, *die*
**pilfer** /'pɪlfə(r)/ *v.t.* stehlen
**pilgrim** /'pɪlɡrɪm/ *n.* Pilger, *der*/Pilgerin, *die*
**pilgrimage** /'pɪlɡrɪmɪdʒ/ *n.* Pilgerfahrt, *die*
**pill** /pɪl/ *n.* (a) Tablette, *die*; Pille, *die* (ugs.)
(b) (coll.: contraceptive) the ~ or P~: die Pille (ugs.); be on the ~: die Pille nehmen (ugs.)
**pillage** /'pɪlɪdʒ/ *v.t.* [aus]plündern
**pillar** /'pɪlə(r)/ *n.* Säule, *die*
**'pillar box** *n.* (Brit.) Briefkasten, *der*
**'pillbox** *n.* Pillenschachtel, *die*
**pillion** /'pɪljən/ *n.* Beifahrersitz, *der;* ride ~: als Beifahrer/Beifahrerin mitfahren
**pillow** /'pɪləʊ/ *n.* [Kopf]kissen, *das*
**'pillowcase, 'pillowslip** *ns.* [Kopf]kissenbezug, *der*
**'pill-popping** *n.* (coll.) Pillenschluckerei, *die* (ugs.)
**pilot** /'paɪlət/ **1** *n.* (a) (Aeronaut.) Pilot, *der*/Pilotin, *die*
(b) (Naut.) Lotse, *der*
**2** *adj.* Pilot⟨*programm, -studie, -projekt usw.*⟩
**3** *v.t.* (a) (Aeronaut.) fliegen
(b) (Naut.; fig.) lotsen
**'pilot light** *n.* Zündflamme, *die*
**pimp** /pɪmp/ *n.* Zuhälter, *der*
**pimple** /'pɪmpl/ *n.* Pickel, *der*
**pimply** /'pɪmplɪ/ *adj.* pick[e]lig
**pin** **1** *n.* (a) Stecknadel, *die;* ~s and needles (fig.) Kribbeln, *das*
(b) (peg) Stift, *der*
(c) (Electr.) a two-/three-~ plug ein zwei-/dreipoliger Stecker
**2** *v.t.*, **-nn-**: (a) nageln ⟨*Knochen, Bein*⟩; ~ a badge to one's lapel sich (*Dat.*) ein Abzeichen ans Revers stecken
(b) (fig.) ~ one's hopes on sb./sth. seine

[ganze] Hoffnung auf jmdn./etw. setzen; ~ the blame for sth. on sb. jmdm. die Schuld an etw. (*Dat.*) zuschieben
(c) ~ sb. against the wall jmdn. an die Wand drängen
■ **pin 'down** *v.t.* (a) (fig.) festnageln (to *or* on auf + *Akk.*)
(b) (trap) festhalten
■ **pin 'up** *v.t.* aufhängen ⟨*Bild, Foto*⟩; anschlagen ⟨*Bekanntmachung, Liste*⟩; aufstecken ⟨*Haar*⟩; abstecken ⟨*Saum*⟩
**PIN** /pɪn/ *abbr.* = PIN [number]
▶ PERSONAL IDENTIFICATION NUMBER
**pinafore** /'pɪnəfɔː(r)/ *n.* Schürze, *die* (mit Oberteil)
**pincers** /'pɪnsəz/ *n. pl.* (a) [pair of] ~: Beißzange, *die*
(b) (of crab etc.) Schere, *die*
**pinch** /pɪntʃ/ **1** *n.* (a) (squeezing) Kniff, *der;* give sb. a ~ on the arm/cheek jmdn. in den Arm/die Backe kneifen
(b) (fig.) feel the ~: knapp bei Kasse sein (ugs.); at a ~: zur Not
(c) (small amount) Prise, *die*
**2** *v.t.* (a) kneifen; ~ sb.'s cheek/bottom jmdn. in die Wange/den Hintern (ugs.) kneifen
(b) (coll.: steal) klauen (salopp)
**'pincushion** *n.* Nadelkissen, *das*
**pine¹** /paɪn/ *n.* (tree) Kiefer, *die*
**pine²** *v.i.* sich [vor Kummer] verzehren (geh.)
■ **pine a'way** *v.i.* dahinkümmern
**pineapple** /'paɪnæpl/ *n.* Ananas, *die*
**'pine tree** *n.* Kiefer, *die*
**ping-pong** (Amer.: **Ping-Pong**®) /'pɪŋpɒŋ/ *n.* Tischtennis, *das*
**pinhole 'camera** *n.* Lochkamera, *die;* Camera obscura, *die*
**pink** /pɪŋk/ **1** *n.* Rosa, *das*
**2** *adj.* rosa
**pinkie** /'pɪŋkɪ/ *n.* (Amer., Scot.) kleiner Finger
**'pin money** *n.* Taschengeld, *das*
**pinnacle** /'pɪnəkl/ *n.* Gipfel, *der;* (fig.) Höhepunkt, *der*
**pin: ~point** *v.t.* genau festlegen; **~prick** *n.* Nadelstich, *der;* **~stripe** *n.* Nadelstreifen, *der;* **~stripe suit** Nadelstreifenanzug, *der*
**pint** /paɪnt/ *n.* Pint, *das;* ≈ halber Liter
**pint 'mug** *n.* ≈ Halbliterglas, *das od.* -humpen, *der*
**'pin-up** (coll.) *n.* Pin-up-Girl, *das;* (picture) (of beautiful girl) Pin-up[-Foto], *das;* (of sports, film or pop star) Starfoto, *das*
**pioneer** /paɪə'nɪə(r)/ **1** *n.* Pionier, *der*
**2** *v.t.* Pionierarbeit leisten für
**pious** /'paɪəs/ *adj.* fromm
**pip** /pɪp/ *n.* (seed) Kern, *der*
**pipe** /paɪp/ **1** *n.* (a) (tube) Rohr, *das*
(b) (Mus.) Pfeife, *die*
(c) [tobacco] ~: [Tabaks]pfeife, *die* ⋯⊹

2 *v.t.* [durch ein Rohr/durch Rohre] leiten
■ **pipe 'down** *v.i.* (coll.) ruhig sein
■ **pipe 'up** *v.i.* (coll.) etwas sagen
**pipe:** ~ **dream** *n.* Wunschtraum, *der;*
Hirngespinst, *das* (abwertend); ~**line** *n.*
Pipeline, *die;* **in the** ~**line** (fig.) in
Vorbereitung

**piper** /ˈpaɪpə(r)/ *n.* Pfeifer, *der*/Pfeiferin, *die;*
(bagpiper) Dudelsackspieler, *der*/-spielerin, *die*
**piping hot** /ˈpaɪpɪŋ hɒt/ *adj.* kochend heiß
**piquant** /ˈpiːkənt/ *adj.* pikant
**pique** /piːk/ *n.* **in a [fit of]** ~: verstimmt
**piracy** /ˈpaɪrəsɪ/ *n.* Seeräuberei, *die*
**piranha** /pɪˈrɑːnə, pɪˈrɑːnjə/ *n.* Piranha, *der*
**pirate** /ˈpaɪrət/ *n.* **(a)** Pirat, *der;* Seeräuber,
*der*
**(b)** (Radio) ~ **radio station** Piratensender, *der*
**Pisces** /ˈpaɪsiːz/ *n.* (Astrol, Astron.) Fische *Pl.*
**piss** /pɪs/ (coarse) 1 *n.* **(a)** (urine) Pisse, *die*
(derb)
**(b) have a/go for a** ~: pissen/pissen gehen
(derb)
2 *v.i.* pissen (derb)
■ **'piss down** *v.i.* (sl.) ~ **down [with rain]**
schiffen (salopp)
■ **piss 'off** (Brit. sl.) 1 *v.i.* sich verpissen
(salopp)
2 *v.t.* ankotzen (derb)
**pissed** /pɪst/ *adj.* (sl.) **(a)** (drunk) voll (salopp)
**(b)** (Amer.: angry) [stock]sauer (**with** auf
+ *Akk.*) (salopp)
**pissed 'off** *adj.* (sl.) stocksauer (**with** auf
+ *Akk.*) (salopp)
**'piss-up** *n.* (sl.) Sauferei, *die* (salopp)
**pistol** /ˈpɪstl/ *n.* Pistole, *die*
**piston** /ˈpɪstən/ *n.* Kolben, *der*
**pit** /pɪt/ 1 *n.* (hole, mine) Grube, *die;* (natural)
Vertiefung, *die*
2 *v.t.,* -tt-: ~ **one's wits/skill** *etc.* **against sth.**
seinen Verstand/sein Können *usw.* an etw.
(*Dat.*) messen
**'pit bull terrier** *n.* Pitbullterrier, *der*
**pitch**[1] /pɪtʃ/ 1 *n.* **(a)** (Brit.: usual place)
[Stand]platz, *der;* (Sport: playing area) Feld, *das;*
Platz, *der*
**(b)** (Mus.) Tonhöhe, *die*
**(c)** (slope) Neigung, *die*
2 *v.t.* **(a)** (erect) aufschlagen; ~ **camp** ein/
das Lager aufschlagen
**(b)** (throw) werfen
3 *v.i.* stürzen; ⟨Schiff:⟩ stampfen; ~ **forward**
vornüberstürzen
**pitch**[2] *n.* (substance) Pech, *das*
**pitch:** ~**'black** *adj.* pechschwarz;
stockdunkel (ugs.) ⟨Nacht⟩; ~**'dark** *adj.*
stockdunkel (ugs.)
**pitcher** /ˈpɪtʃə(r)/ *n.* [Henkel]krug, *der*
**'pitchfork** *n.* Heugabel, *die*
**'pitfall** *n.* Fallstrick, *der*
**pith** /pɪθ/ *n.* **(a)** (of orange etc.) weiße Haut
**(b)** (fig.) Kern, *der*
**'pith helmet** *n.* Tropenhelm, *der*

**'pithy** *adj.* (fig.) prägnant
**pitiable** /ˈpɪtɪəbl/, **pitiful** /ˈpɪtɪfl/ *adjs.* **(a)**
Mitleid erregend
**(b)** (contemptible) jämmerlich
**pitifully** /ˈpɪtɪfəlɪ/ *adv.* erbärmlich;
jämmerlich
**'pitiless** *adj.* unbarmherzig
**'pit stop** *n.* (Motor racing) Boxenstopp, *der*
**pittance** /ˈpɪtəns/ *n.* Hungerlohn, *der*
**pity** /ˈpɪtɪ/ 1 *n.* Mitleid, *das;* **feel** ~ **for sb.**
Mitgefühl für jmdn. empfinden; **have/take**
~ **on sb.** Erbarmen mit jmdm. haben; [**what
a**] ~**!** [wie] schade!
2 *v.t.* bemitleiden; **I** ~ **you** du tust mir leid
**pivot** /ˈpɪvət/ 1 *n.* [Dreh]zapfen, *der*
2 *v.i.* sich drehen
**pivotal** /ˈpɪvətl/ *adj.* (fig.: crucial) zentral
**pixel** /ˈpɪksel/ *n.* (Comp. etc.) Bildpunkt, *der;*
Pixel, *das*
**pixie** /ˈpɪksɪ/ *n.* Kobold, *der*
**pizza** /ˈpiːtsə/ *n.* Pizza, *die*
**pizzeria** /piːtsəˈriːə/ *n.* Pizzeria, *die*
**placard** /ˈplækɑːd/ *n.* Plakat, *das*
**placate** /pləˈkeɪt/ *v.t.* beschwichtigen
**place** /pleɪs/ 1 *n.* **(a)** (spot) Stelle,
*die;* **a [good]** ~ **to park/to stop** ein [guter]
Platz zum Parken/eine [gute] Stelle zum
Halten; **do you know a good/cheap** ~ **to eat?**
weißt du, wo man gut/billig essen kann?;
~ **of worship** Andachtsort, *der;* **all over the**
~: überall; (coll.: in a mess) ganz
durcheinander (ugs.)
**(b)** (rank, position) Stellung, *die;* **put sb. in his**
~: jmdn. in seine Schranken weisen
**(c)** (country, town) Ort, *der;* ~ **of birth**
Geburtsort, *der;* ~ **of residence** Wohnort,
*der;* **'go** ~**s** (coll.: fig.) es [im Leben] zu was
bringen (ugs.)
**(d)** (coll.: premises) Bude, *die* (ugs.); **she is at
his** ~: sie ist bei ihm
**(e)** (seat etc.) [Sitz]platz, *der;* **change** ~**s [with
sb.]** [mit jmdm.] die Plätze tauschen; (fig.)
[mit jmdm.] tauschen
**(f)** (step, stage) **in the first** ~: zuerst; **why
didn't you say so in the first** ~**?** warum hast
du das nicht gleich gesagt?
**(g)** (proper ~) Platz, *der;* **everything fell into**
~ (fig.) alles wurde klar; **out of** ~: nicht am
richtigen Platz; (several things) in Unordnung
**(h)** (position in competition) Platz, *der*
2 *v.t.* **(a)** (vertically) stellen; (horizontally) legen
**(b)** **in** *p.p.* (situated) gelegen
**(c)** (find situation or home for) unterbringen (**with**
bei)
**(d)** (class) einordnen; einstufen; **be** ~**d
second in the race** im Rennen den zweiten
Platz belegen
**placebo** /pləˈsiːbəʊ/ *n., pl.* ~**s** Placebo, *das*
**'place mat** *n.* Set, *der od.* das
**placement** /ˈpleɪsmənt/ *n.* Platzierung, *die*
**'place name** *n.* Ortsname, *der*
**placenta** /pləˈsentə/ *n., pl.* ~**e** /pləˈsentiː/
*or* ~**s** Plazenta, *die*

**'place setting** n. Gedeck, *das*
**placid** /'plæsɪd/ *adj.* ruhig
**plagiarism** /'pleɪdʒərɪzm/ n. Plagiat, *das*
**plagiarize** /'pleɪdʒəraɪz/ *v.t.* plagiieren
**plague** /pleɪg/ ① n. **(a)** (esp. Hist.: epidemic) Seuche, *die;* **the** ∼ (bubonic) die Pest
**(b)** (infestation) ∼ **of rats** Rattenplage, *die*
② *v.t.* plagen; ∼**d with** *or* **by sth.** von etw. geplagt
**plaice** /pleɪs/ n., pl. same Scholle, *die*
**plain** /pleɪn/ ① *adj.* **(a)** (clear) klar; (obvious) offensichtlich
**(b)** (frank) offen; schlicht ⟨*Wahrheit*⟩; **be** ∼ **sailing** (fig.) [ganz] einfach sein
**(c)** (unsophisticated) einfach; schlicht ⟨*Kleidung*⟩; unliniert ⟨*Papier*⟩; ⟨*Stoff*⟩ ohne Muster
**(d)** wenig attraktiv ⟨*Mädchen*⟩
② *adv.* **(a)** (clearly) deutlich
**(b)** (simply) einfach
③ n. Ebene, *die*
**plain:** ∼ **'chocolate** n. halbbittere Schokolade; ∼ **'clothes** n. pl. **in** ∼ **clothes** in Zivil
**'plainly** *adv.* **(a)** (clearly) deutlich
**(b)** (obviously) offensichtlich; (undoubtedly) eindeutig
**(c)** (frankly) offen
**(d)** (simply) schlicht
**plaintiff** /'pleɪntɪf/ n. Kläger, *der*/Klägerin, *die*
**plaintive** /'pleɪntɪv/ *adj.* klagend
**plait** /plæt/ ① n. Zopf, *der*
② *v.t.* flechten
**plan** /plæn/ ① n. Plan, *der;* **[go] according to** ∼: nach Plan [gehen]; planmäßig [verlaufen]
② *v.t.,* **-nn-** planen; (design) entwerfen
③ *v.i.,* **-nn-** planen
**plane¹** /pleɪn/ n. ∼ **[tree]** Platane, *die*
**plane²** ① n. (tool) Hobel, *der*
② *v.t.* hobeln
**plane³** n. **(a)** (Geom.: fig.) Ebene, *die*
**(b)** (aircraft) Flugzeug, *das;* Maschine, *die* (ugs.)
**'planeload** n. Flugzeugladung, *die*
**planet** /'plænɪt/ n. Planet, *der*
**planetarium** /plænɪ'teərɪəm/ n., pl. ∼**s** *or* **planetaria** /plænɪ'teərɪə/ Planetarium, *das*
**planetary** /'plænɪtərɪ/ *adj.* planetarisch
**plank** /plæŋk/ n. Brett, *das;* (thicker) Bohle, *die;* (on ship) Planke, *die*
**plankton** /'plæŋktən/ n. Plankton, *das*
**planned e'conomy** n. Planwirtschaft, *die*
**'planner** n. Planer, *der*/Planerin, *die*
**'planning** n. Planen, *das;* Planung, *die*
**plant** /plɑːnt/ ① n. **(a)** (Bot.) Pflanze, *die*
**(b)** *no indef. art.* (machinery) Maschinen *Pl.*
**(c)** (factory) Fabrik, *die;* Werk, *das*
② *v.t.* **(a)** pflanzen

**(b)** (coll.: conceal) anbringen ⟨*Wanze*⟩; legen ⟨*Bombe*⟩; ∼ **sth. on sb.** jmdm. etw. unterschieben
**plantation** /plɑːn'teɪʃn/ n. Plantage, *die*
**planter** /'plɑːntə(r)/ n. (container) Pflanzgefäß, *das*
**'plant food** n. Pflanzennahrung, *die*
**plaque** /plɑːk, plæk/ n. **(a)** Platte, *die;* (commemorating sb.) [Gedenk]tafel, *die*
**(b)** (Dent.) Zahnbelag, *der*
**plasma** /'plæzmə/ n. Plasma, *das*
**plaster** /'plɑːstə(r)/ ① n. **(a)** (for walls etc.) [Ver]putz, *der*
**(b)** ∼ **[of Paris]** Gips, *der;* **have one's leg in** ∼: ein Gipsbein haben
**(c)** ▶ STICKING PLASTER
② *v.t.* **(a)** verputzen ⟨*Wand*⟩
**(b)** (daub) ∼ **sth. on sth.** etw. dick auf etw. (*Akk.*) auftragen
**plaster:** ∼**board** n. Gipsplatte, *die;* ∼ **cast** n. (Med.) Gipsverband, *der*
**plastered** /'plɑːstəd/ *adj.* (sl.: drunk) voll (salopp); **get** ∼: sich voll laufen lassen (salopp)
**'plasterer** n. Gipser, *der*
**plastic** /'plæstɪk/ ① n. **(a)** Plastik, *das;* Kunststoff, *der*
**(b)** (coll.: credit cards etc.) Plastikgeld, *das*
② *adj.* aus Plastik *od.* Kunststoff *nachgestellt;* ∼ **bag** Plastiktüte, *die;* ∼ **money** (joc.) Kreditkarten *Pl.*
**plastic 'bullet** n. Plastikgeschoss, *das*
**Plasticine** ® /'plæstɪsiːn/ n. Plastilin, *das*
**plastic:** ∼ **'surgeon** n. Facharzt für plastische Chirurgie; ∼ **'surgery** n. plastische Chirurgie
**plate** /pleɪt/ ① n. **(a)** Teller, *der;* (serving ∼) Platte, *die*
**(b)** (metal ∼ with name etc.) Schild, *das*
**(c)** (for printing) Platte, *die;* (illustration) [Bild]tafel, *die*
② *v.t.* ∼ **sth. [with gold/silver]** etw. vergolden/versilbern
**plateau** /'plætəʊ/ n., pl. ∼**x** /'plætəʊz/ *or* ∼**s** Hochebene, *die;* Plateau, *das*
**plate:** ∼ **'glass** n. Flachglas, *das;* ∼ **rack** n. (Brit.) Abtropfständer, *der;* Geschirrablage, *die*
**platform** /'plætfɔːm/ n. **(a)** (Brit. Railw.) Bahnsteig, *der;* ∼ **4** Gleis 4
**(b)** (stage) Podium, *das*
**platinum** /'plætɪnəm/ n. Platin, *das*
**platitude** /'plætɪtjuːd/ n. Plattitüde, *die* (geh.); Gemeinplatz, *der*
**platonic** /plə'tɒnɪk/ *adj.* platonisch ⟨*Liebe, Freundschaft*⟩
**platoon** /plə'tuːn/ n. (Mil.) Zug, *der*
**plausible** /'plɔːzɪbl/ *adj.* plausibel; einleuchtend
**play** /pleɪ/ ① n. **(a)** (Theatre) [Theater]stück, *das;* **television** ∼: Fernsehspiel, *das*
**(b)** (recreation) Spielen, *das;* Spiel, *das;* ∼ **on words** Wortspiel, *das*
**(c)** (Sport) Spiel, *das*                    ···⫸

**(d) come into** ~, **be brought** or **called into**
~: ins Spiel kommen
2 v.i. **(a)** spielen; ~ **safe** sichergehen; ~ **for**
**time** Zeit gewinnen wollen
**(b)** (Mus.) spielen (on auf + Dat.)
3 v.t. (also Sport, Theatre, Cards, Mus.) spielen;
abspielen ⟨Schallplatte, Tonband⟩; schlagen
⟨Ball⟩; spielen gegen ⟨Mannschaft, Gegner⟩;
~ **the violin** etc. Geige usw. spielen; ~ **a**
**trick/joke on sb.** jmdn. hereinlegen (ugs.)/
jmdm. einen Streich spielen; ~ **one's cards**
**right** (fig.) es richtig anfassen (fig.)
■ **play a'bout, play a'round** v.i.
spielen; **stop** ~**ing about** or **around** hör doch
auf mit dem Unsinn!
■ **play a'long** v.i. mitspielen
■ **play 'back** v.t. abspielen ⟨Tonband⟩
■ **play 'down** v.t. herunterspielen
■ **play 'up** 1 v.i. (coll.) ⟨Kinder:⟩ nichts als
Ärger machen
2 v.t. (coll.: annoy) ärgern
**play:** ~**-acting** n. Theater, das (ugs.);
~ **area** n. Spielplatz, der; ~**back** n.
Wiedergabe, die; **listen to the** ~**back** die
Aufnahme anhören; ~**boy** n. Playboy, der
'**player** n. Spieler, der/Spielerin, die
**playful** /'pleɪfl/ adj. spielerisch; (frolicsome)
verspielt
**play:** ~**ground** n. Spielplatz, der; (Sch.)
Schulhof, der; ~ **group** n. Spielgruppe, die
**playing:** ~ **area** n. (Sport) Spielfeld, das;
~ **card** n. Spielkarte, die; ~ **field** n.
Sportplatz, der
**play:** ~**mate** n. Spielkamerad, der/
-kameradin, die; ~**off** n.
Entscheidungsspiel, das; ~**pen** Laufgitter,
das; ~ **school** n. Kindergarten, der;
~**thing** n. Spielzeug, das; ~**wright**
/'pleɪraɪt/ n. Dramatiker, der/Dramatikerin,
die
**PLC, plc** abbr. (Brit.) = **public limited**
**company** ≈ GmbH
**plea** /pli:/ n. Bitte, die; (public appeal) Appell,
der (for zu)
**plead** /pli:d/ 1 v.i. **(a)** inständig bitten (for
um); (imploringly) flehen (for um); ~ **with sb.**
**for sth.** jmdn. inständig um etw. bitten
**(b)** (Law; also fig.) plädieren
2 v.t. **(a)** inständig bitten; (imploringly) flehen
**(b)** (Law) ~ **guilty/not guilty** sich schuldig/
nicht schuldig bekennen
'**pleading** adj. flehend
**pleasant** /'plezənt/ adj. angenehm
**pleasantry** /'plezəntrɪ/ n. Nettigkeit, die
**please** /pli:z/ 1 v.t. gefallen (+ Dat.);
~ **oneself** tun, was man will; ~ **yourself**
ganz wie du willst
2 v.i. **I come and go as I** ~: ich komme und
gehe, wie es mir gefällt; **if you** ~: bitte schön
3 int. bitte; ~ **do!** aber bitte od. gern!
**pleased** /pli:zd/ adj. (satisfied) zufrieden (**by**
mit); (happy) erfreut (**by** über + Akk.); **be** ~ **at**
or **about sth.** sich über etw. (Akk.) freuen
**pleasing** /'pli:zɪŋ/ adj. gefällig

**pleasure** /'pleʒə(r)/ n. (joy) Freude, die;
(enjoyment) Vergnügen, das; **have the** ~ **of**
**doing sth.** das Vergnügen haben, etw. zu tun;
**with** ~: mit Vergnügen
'**pleasure cruise** n. Vergnügungsfahrt,
die
**pleat** /pli:t/ n. Falte, die
'**pleated** adj. gefältelt; Falten⟨rock⟩
**plebiscite** /'plebɪsɪt, 'plebɪsaɪt/ n. Plebiszit,
das
**pledge** /pledʒ/ 1 n. Versprechen, das
2 v.t. versprechen; geloben ⟨Treue⟩
**plentiful** /'plentɪfl/ adj. reichlich; **be** ~:
reichlich vorhanden sein
**plenty** /'plentɪ/ n. ~ **of** viel; eine Menge;
(coll.: enough) genug
**pleurisy** /'plʊərɪsɪ/ n. Pleuritis, die;
Brustfellentzündung, die
**pliable** /'plaɪəbl/ adj. biegsam
**plied** ▶ PLY
**pliers** /'plaɪəz/ n. pl. [**pair of**] ~: Zange, die
**plight** /plaɪt/ n. Notlage, die
**plimsoll** /'plɪmsl/ n. (Brit.) Turnschuh, der
**plinth** /plɪnθ/ n. Sockel, der
**plod** /plɒd/ v.i., **-dd-** trotten
■ **plod 'on** v.i. (fig.) sich weiterkämpfen
**plonk** /plɒŋk/ n. (coll.) [billiger] Wein
**plot** /plɒt/ 1 n. **(a)** (conspiracy)
Verschwörung, die
**(b)** (of play, novel) Handlung, die
**(c)** (of ground) Stück Land
2 v.t., **-tt-: (a)** [heimlich] planen
**(b)** (mark on map) einzeichnen
3 v.i., **-tt-:** ~ **against sb.** sich gegen jmdn.
verschwören
'**plotter** n. Verschwörer, der/Verschwörerin,
die
**plough** /plaʊ/ 1 n. Pflug, der
2 v.t. pflügen
■ **plough 'back** v.t. (Finance) reinvestieren
**plow** (Amer./arch.) ▶ PLOUGH
**ploy** /plɔɪ/ n. Trick, der
**pluck** /plʌk/ 1 v.t. **(a)** pflücken ⟨Obst⟩;
~ [**out**] auszupfen ⟨Federn, Haare⟩
**(b)** (pull at) zupfen an (+ Dat.)
**(c)** (strip of feathers) rupfen
2 v.i. ~ **at sth.** an etw. (Dat.) zupfen
3 n. Mut, der
■ **pluck 'up** v.t. ~ **up** [**one's**] **courage** all
seinen Mut zusammennehmen
**pluckily** /'plʌkɪlɪ/ adv., '**plucky** adj.
tapfer
**plug** /plʌg/ 1 n. **(a)** (filling hole) Pfropfen, der;
(in cask) Spund, der; (for basin etc.) Stöpsel, der
**(b)** (Electr.) Stecker, der
2 v.t., **-gg-: (a)** ~ [**up**] zustopfen ⟨Loch usw.⟩
**(b)** (coll.: advertise) Schleichwerbung machen
für
■ **plug 'in** v.t. anschließen
'**plughole** n. Abfluss, der
**plum** /plʌm/ n. **(a)** Pflaume, die

**(b)** (fig.) Leckerbissen, *der;* **a ~ job** ein Traumjob (ugs.)

**plumage** /'pluːmɪdʒ/ *n.* Gefieder, *das*

**plumb¹** /plʌm/ 1 *v.t.* [aus]loten 2 *adv.* **(a)** lotrecht **(b)** (fig.) genau

**plumb²** *v.t.* **~ in** fest anschließen

**plumber** /'plʌmə(r)/ *n.* Klempner, *der*

**plumbing** /'plʌmɪŋ/ *n.* **(a)** Klempnerarbeiten *Pl.* **(b)** (waterpipes) Wasserleitungen *Pl.*

**'plumb line** *n.* Lot, *das*

**plume** /pluːm/ *n.* Feder, *die;* (ornamental bunch) Federbusch, *der*

**plummet** /'plʌmɪt/ *v.i.* stürzen

**plump** /plʌmp/ *adj.* mollig; rundlich

■ **'plump for** *v.t.* sich entscheiden für

**plunder** /'plʌndə(r)/ 1 *v.t.* [aus]plündern ⟨Gebäude, Gebiet⟩ 2 *n.* Plünderung, *die;* (booty) Beute, *die*

**plunge** /plʌndʒ/ 1 *v.t.* stecken; (into liquid) tauchen 2 *v.i.* **(a)** **~ into sth.** in etw. (*Akk.*) stürzen **(b)** ⟨Straße usw.:⟩ steil abfallen 3 *n.* Sprung, *der;* **take the ~** (fig. coll.) den Sprung wagen

**plunger** /'plʌndʒə(r)/ *n.* (suction cup) Stampfer, *der*

**plural** /'plʊərl/ 1 *adj.* pluralisch; Plural-; **~ noun** Substantiv im Plural 2 *n.* Mehrzahl, *die;* Plural, *der*

**pluralism** /'plʊərəlɪzm/ *n.* Pluralismus, *der*

**plus** /plʌs/ 1 *prep.* plus (+ *Dat.*) 2 *n.* (advantage) Pluspunkt, *der*

**plush** /plʌʃ/ 1 *n.* Plüsch, *der* 2 *adj.* (coll.) feudal (ugs.)

**Pluto** /'pluːtəʊ/ *pr. n.* (Astron.) Pluto, *der*

**plutonium** /pluː'təʊnɪəm/ *n.* Plutonium, *das*

**ply** /plaɪ/ 1 *v.t.* **(a)** (use) gebrauchen **(b)** nachgehen (+ *Dat.*) ⟨Handwerk, Arbeit⟩ **(c)** (supply) **~ sb. with sth.** jmdn. mit etw. versorgen **(d)** (assail) überhäufen 2 *v.i.* **~ between** zwischen ⟨Orten⟩ [hin- und her]pendeln

**'plywood** *n.* Sperrholz, *das*

**PM** *abbr.* = **Prime Minister**

**p.m.** /piː'em/ *adv.* nachmittags; **one ~:** ein Uhr mittags

**PMT** *abbr.* = **premenstrual tension** PMS

**pneumatic** /njuː'mætɪk/ *adj.* pneumatisch

**pneumatic 'drill** *n.* Pressluftbohrer, *der*

**pneumonia** /njuː'məʊnɪə/ *n.* Lungenentzündung, *die*

**PO** *abbr.* **(a)** = **postal order** PA **(b)** = **Post Office** PA

**poach¹** /pəʊtʃ/ *v.t.* **(a)** (catch illegally) wildern; illegal fangen ⟨Fische⟩ **(b)** stehlen, (ugs.) klauen ⟨Idee⟩

**poach²** *v.t.* (Cookery) pochieren ⟨Ei⟩; dünsten ⟨Fisch, Fleisch, Gemüse⟩; **~ed eggs** verlorene Eier

**'poacher** *n.* Wilderer, *der*

**PO box** ▶ POST OFFICE BOX

**pocket** /'pɒkɪt/ 1 *n.* **(a)** Tasche, *die* **(b)** (fig.) **be in ~:** Geld verdient haben; **be out of ~:** draufgelegt haben 2 *adj.* Taschen⟨rechner, -uhr, -ausgabe⟩ 3 *v.t.* **(a)** einstecken **(b)** (steal) in die eigene Tasche stecken (ugs.)

**pocket: ~book** *n.* (wallet) Brieftasche, *die;* (notebook) Notizbuch, *das;* **~ 'handkerchief** *n.* Taschentuch, *das;* **~ knife** *n.* Taschenmesser, *das;* **~ money** *n.* Taschengeld, *das;* **~-size[d]** *adj.* im Taschenformat *nachgestellt*

**'pockmarked** *adj.* **(a)** pockennarbig ⟨Gesicht, Haut⟩ **(b)** **a wall ~ with bullets** eine mit Einschüssen übersäte Wand

**pod** /pɒd/ *n.* Hülse, *die;* (of pea) Schote, *die*

**podgy** /'pɒdʒɪ/ *adj.* dicklich

**poem** /'pəʊɪm/ *n.* Gedicht, *das*

**poet** /'pəʊɪt/ *n.* Dichter, *der*/Dichterin, *die*

**poetic** /pəʊ'etɪk/ *adj.* dichterisch

**poetry** /'pəʊɪtrɪ/ *n.* [Vers]dichtung, *die;* Lyrik, *die*

**pogrom** /'pɒɡrəm/ *n.* Pogrom, *das od. der*

**poignant** /'pɔɪnjənt/ *adj.* tief ⟨Bedauern, Trauer⟩; ergreifend ⟨Anblick⟩

**point** /pɔɪnt/ 1 *n.* **(a)** (tiny mark, dot) Punkt, *der* **(b)** (of tool, pencil, etc.) Spitze, *die* **(c)** (single item; unit of scoring) Punkt, *der* **(d)** (stage, degree) **up to a ~:** bis zu einem gewissen Grad; **he gave up at this ~:** an diesem Punkt gab es auf **(e)** (moment) Zeitpunkt, *der;* **be on the ~ of doing sth.** etw. gerade tun wollen **(f)** (distinctive trait) Seite, *die;* **best/strong ~:** starke Seite; Stärke, *die* **(g)** (thing to be discussed) **come to** *or* **get to the ~:** zum Thema kommen; **be beside the ~:** keine Rolle spielen; **make a ~ of doing sth.** [großen] Wert darauf legen, etw. zu tun **(h)** (of story, joke, remark) Pointe, *die* **(i)** (purpose) Zweck, *der;* Sinn, *der;* **there's no ~ in protesting** es hat keinen Sinn *od.* Zweck zu protestieren **(j)** (precise place, spot) Punkt, *der;* Stelle, *die;* **~ of view** (fig.) Standpunkt, *der* **(k)** (Brit.) [power *or* electric] **~:** Steckdose, *die* **(l)** *usu in pl.* (Brit. Railw.) Weiche, *die* 2 *v.i.* **(a)** zeigen, weisen (**to, at** auf + *Akk.*) **(b)** **~ towards** *or* **to** (fig.) [hin]deuten auf (+ *Akk.*) 3 *v.t.* richten ⟨Waffe, Kamera⟩ (**at** auf + *Akk.*); **~ one's finger at sth./sb.** mit dem Finger auf etw./jmdn. zeigen

■ **point 'out** *v.t.* hinweisen auf (+ *Akk.*); **~ sth./sb. out to sb.** jmdn. auf etw./jmdn. hinweisen

**point-'blank** ① adj. (lit. or fig.) direkt; glatt ⟨Weigerung⟩; ~ **range** kürzeste Entfernung ② adv. (at very close range) aus kürzester Entfernung

**'pointed** adj. (a) spitz
(b) (fig.) unmissverständlich

**'pointer** n. (a) Zeiger, der; (rod) Zeigestock, der
(b) (coll.: indication) Hinweis, der (to auf + Akk.)

**'pointless** adj. sinnlos; belanglos ⟨Bemerkung, Geschichte⟩

**poise** /pɔɪz/ n. (composure) Haltung, die; (self-confidence) Selbstvertrauen, das

**poised** /pɔɪzd/ adj. selbstsicher

**poison** /'pɔɪzn/ ① n. Gift, das
② v.t. vergiften

**'poisoning** n. Vergiftung, die

**poisonous** /'pɔɪzənəs/ adj. giftig

**poke** ① v.t. (a) ~ **sth.** [with **sth.**] [mit etw.] gegen etw. stoßen; ~ **sth. into sth.** etw. in etw. (Akk.) stoßen; ~ **the fire** das Feuer schüren
(b) stecken ⟨Kopf⟩
② v.i. (a) [herum]stochern (at, in, among in + Dat.)
(b) (pry) schnüffeln (ugs.)
③ n. (thrust) Stoß, der; give sb. a ~ [in the ribs] jmdm. einen [Rippen]stoß versetzen; give the fire a ~: das Feuer [an]schüren
■ **poke a'bout, poke a'round** v.i. herumschnüffeln (ugs.)

**'poker**[1] n. Schüreisen, das

**'poker**[2] n. (Cards) Poker, das od. der

**'poker-faced** adj. mit unbewegter Miene nachgestellt

**poky** /'pəʊkɪ/ adj. winzig

**Poland** /'pəʊlənd/ pr. n. Polen (das)

**polar** /'pəʊlə(r)/ adj. polar ⟨Kaltluft, Gewässer⟩; Polar⟨eis, -gebiet, -fuchs⟩

**polar:** ~ **'bear** n. Eisbär, der; ~ **'cap** n. Polkappe, die

**pole**[1] n. (support) Stange, die; drive sb. up the ~ (Brit. coll.) jmdn. zum Wahnsinn treiben (ugs.)

**pole**[2] n. (Astron., Geog., Magn., Electr., fig.) Pol, der

**Pole** /pəʊl/ n. Pole, der/Polin, die

**pole:** ~ **star** n. Polarstern, der; ~**-vault** n. Stabhochsprung, der; ~ **vaulter** n. Stabhochspringer, der/-springerin, die

**police** /pə'liːs/ ① n. pl. Polizei, die; (members) Polizisten Pl.; attrib. Polizei-
② v.t. [polizeilich] überwachen ⟨Fußballspiel⟩; kontrollieren ⟨Gebiet⟩

**police:** ~ **force** n. the ~ force die Polizei; ~**man** /pə'liːsmən/ n., pl. -**men** /pə'liːsmən/ Polizist, der; ~ **officer** n. Polizeibeamte, der/-beamtin, die; ~ **state** n. Polizeistaat, der; ~ **station** n. Polizeirevier, das; ~**woman** n. Polizistin, die

**policy**[1] /'pɒlɪsɪ/ n. Politik, die

**policy**[2] n. (Insurance) Police, die

**'policy holder** n. Versicherte, der/die

**polio** /'pəʊlɪəʊ/ n., no art. Polio, die; [spinale] Kinderlähmung

**polish** /'pɒlɪʃ/ ① v.t. (a) polieren; bohnern ⟨Fußboden⟩; putzen ⟨Schuhe⟩
(b) (fig.) ausfeilen ⟨Text, Theorie, Stil⟩
② n. (a) (smoothness) Glanz, der
(b) (substance) Politur, die
(c) (fig.) Schliff, der
■ **polish 'off** v.t. (coll.) (a) (consume) verdrücken (ugs.)
(b) (complete quickly) durchziehen (ugs.)
■ **polish 'up** v.t. (a) polieren
(b) ausfeilen ⟨Stil⟩; aufpolieren ⟨Kenntnisse⟩

**Polish** /'pəʊlɪʃ/ ① adj. polnisch; sb. is ~: jmd. ist Pole/Polin
② n. Polnisch, das; see also ENGLISH 2A

**polite** /pə'laɪt/ adj., ~r /pə'laɪtə(r)/, ~st /pə'laɪtɪst/ höflich

**po'liteness** n. Höflichkeit, die

**political** /pə'lɪtɪkl/ adj. politisch

**politically** /pə'lɪtɪkəlɪ/ adv. politisch; ~ **correct** politisch korrekt

**political 'prisoner** n. politischer Gefangener/politische Gefangene

**politician** /pɒlɪ'tɪʃn/ n. Politiker, der/ Politikerin, die

**politicize** (**politicise**) /pə'lɪtɪsaɪz/ v.t. politisieren

**politics** /'pɒlɪtɪks/ n. Politik, die; (of individual) politische Einstellung

**polka** /'pɒlkə, 'pəʊlkə/ n. Polka, die

**'polka dot** n. [großer] Tupfen

**poll** /pəʊl/ ① n. (a) (voting) Abstimmung, die; (to elect sb.) Wahl, die; go to the ~s zur Wahl gehen
(b) (opinion ~) Umfrage, die
② v.t. (a) (take vote[s] of) abstimmen/wählen lassen
(b) (take opinion of) befragen

**pollen** /'pɒlən/ n. Pollen, der; Blütenstaub, der

**'pollen count** n. Pollenmenge, die

**pollinate** /'pɒlɪneɪt/ v.t. bestäuben

**pollination** /pɒlɪ'neɪʃn/ n. Bestäubung, die

**polling** /'pəʊlɪŋ/: ~ **booth** n. Wahlkabine, die; ~ **station** n. (Brit.) Wahllokal, das

**'poll tax** n. Kopfsteuer, die

**pollutant** /pə'luːtənt/ n. [Umwelt]schadstoff, der

**pollute** /pə'luːt/ v.t. verschmutzen ⟨Luft, Boden, Wasser⟩

**pollution** /pə'luːʃn/ n. [environmental] ~: [Umwelt]verschmutzung, die; **noise** ~: Lärmbelästigung, die

**polo** /'pəʊləʊ/ n. Polo, das

**polo:** ~ **neck** n. Rollkragen, der; ~ **shirt** n. Polohemd, das

**poly** /'pɒlɪ/ n., pl. ~**s** (coll.) Polytechnikum, das; ≈ TH, die

**polyester** /pɒlɪ'estə(r)/ n. Polyester, der

**polygamy** /pə'lɪgəmɪ/ n. Polygamie, die

**polystyrene** /pɒlɪ'staɪriːn/ n. Polystyrol, das; ~ **foam** Styropor ⓦ, das

**polytechnic** /pɒlɪ'teknɪk/ n. (Brit.) ≈ technische Hochschule

**polythene** /'pɒlɪθiːn/ n. Polyäthylen, das; ~ **bag** Plastikbeutel, der

**polyunsaturated** /pɒlɪʌn'sætʃəreɪtɪd/ adj. mehrfach ungesättigt

**polyunsaturates** /pɒlɪʌn'sætjʊrəts/ n. pl. mehrfach ungestättigte Fettsäuren Pl.

**pomegranate** /'pɒmɪgrænɪt/ n. Granatapfel, der

**'pommel horse** n. Seitpferd, das

**pomp** /pɒmp/ n. Pomp, der

**pompom** /'pɒmpɒm/ n. Pompon, der; ~ **hat** Pudelmütze, die

**pompous** /'pɒmpəs/ adj. großspurig; gespreizt ⟨Sprache⟩

**pond** /pɒnd/ n. Teich, der

**ponder** /'pɒndə(r)/ [1] v.t. nachdenken über (+ Akk.) ⟨Frage, Ereignis⟩; abwägen ⟨Vorteile, Worte⟩
[2] v.i. nachdenken (**over, on** über + Akk.)

**ponderous** /'pɒndərəs/ adj. schwer

**pong** /pɒŋ/ (Brit. coll.) [1] n. Mief, der (ugs.)
[2] v.i. miefen (ugs.)

**pony** /'pəʊnɪ/ n. Pony, das

**pony:** ~**tail** n. Pferdeschwanz, der; ~**-trekking** /'pəʊnɪtrekɪŋ/ n. (Brit.) Ponyreiten, das

**poodle** /'puːdl/ n. Pudel, der

**pool¹** /puːl/ n. (a) Tümpel, der
(b) (temporary) Lache, die; ~ **of blood** Blutlache, die
(c) (swimming ~) Schwimmbecken, das; (public) Schwimmbad, das; (in house or garden) Pool, der

**pool²** [1] n. (a) (Gambling) [gemeinsame Spiel]kasse; **the** ~**s** (Brit.) das Toto
(b) (common supply) Topf, der; **a** ~ **of experience** ein Erfahrungsschatz
(c) (game) Pool[billard], das
[2] v.t. zusammenlegen ⟨Geld, Ersparnisse⟩; bündeln ⟨Anstrengungen⟩

**'pool table** n. Pool[billard]tisch, der

**poor** /pʊə(r)/ [1] adj. (a) arm
(b) (inadequate) schlecht; schwach ⟨Spiel, Gesundheit, Leistung, Rede⟩; dürftig ⟨Kleidung, Essen, Unterkunft⟩; **of** ~ **quality** minderer Qualität
(c) (paltry) schwach ⟨Trost⟩; schlecht ⟨Aussichten⟩
(d) (unfortunate) arm (auch iron.)
(e) karg ⟨Boden⟩
(f) (deficient) arm (**in** an + Dat.); ~ **in vitamins** vitaminarm
[2] n. pl. **the** ~: die Armen Pl.

**poorly** /'pʊəlɪ/ adv., pred. adj. schlecht

**pop¹** /pɒp/ [1] v.i., **-pp-:** (a) (make sound) knallen
(b) (coll.: go quickly) **let's** ~ **round to Fred's** komm, wir gehen kurz bei Fred vorbei (ugs.)

[2] v.t., **-pp-:** (a) (coll.: put) ~ **the meat in the fridge** das Fleisch in den Kühlschrank tun
(b) platzen ⟨Luftballon⟩
[3] n. (a) Knall, der; Knallen, das
(b) (coll.: drink) Brause, die (ugs.)
[4] adv. **go** ~: knallen
■ **pop 'out** v.i. hervorschießen; ~ **out to the shops** schnell einkaufen gehen

**pop²** (coll.) [1] n. Popmusik, die; Pop, der
[2] adj. Pop⟨star, -musik usw.⟩

**'popcorn** n. Popcorn, das

**pope** /pəʊp/ n. Papst, der/Päpstin, die

**poplar** /'pɒplə(r)/ n. Pappel, die

**'pop music** n. Popmusik, die

**popper** /'pɒpə(r)/ n. (Brit. coll.) Druckknopf, der

**poppy** /'pɒpɪ/ n. Mohn, der

**popular** /'pɒpjʊlə(r)/ adj. (a) (well liked) beliebt; populär ⟨Entscheidung, Maßnahme⟩
(b) (widespread) ⟨Aberglaube, Irrtum, Meinung⟩; allgemein ⟨Wahl, Unterstützung⟩

**popularity** /pɒpjʊ'lærɪtɪ/ n. Beliebtheit, die; (of decision, measure) Popularität, die

**popularize** /'pɒpjʊləraɪz/ v.t. (a) (make popular) populär machen
(b) (make understandable) breiteren Kreisen zugänglich machen

**'popularly** adv. allgemein

**popular 'music** n. Unterhaltungsmusik, die

**populate** /'pɒpjʊleɪt/ v.t. bevölkern; bewohnen ⟨Insel⟩

**population** /pɒpjʊ'leɪʃn/ n. Bevölkerung, die; **Britain has a** ~ **of 56 million** Großbritannien hat 56 Millionen Einwohner; ~ **density** Bevölkerungsdichte, die

**popu'lation explosion** n. Bevölkerungsexplosion, die

**'pop-up** adj. Stehauf⟨buch, -illustration⟩; ~ **toaster** Toaster mit Auswerfmechanismus; ~ **menu** (Comp.) Pop-up-Menü, das

**porcelain** /'pɔːslɪn/ n. Porzellan, das

**porch** /pɔːtʃ/ n. Vordach, das; (with side walls) Vorbau, der; (enclosed) Windfang, der

**porcupine** /'pɔːkjʊpaɪn/ n. Stachelschwein, das

**pore¹** /pɔː(r)/ n. Pore, die

**pore²** v.i. ~ **over** sth. etw. [genau] studieren

**pork** /pɔːk/ n. Schweinefleisch, das; attrib. Schweine-

**pork:** ~ **'chop** n. Schweinekotelett, das; ~ **'pie** n. Schweinepastete, die

**porn** /pɔːn/ n. (coll.) Pornographie, die; Pornos Pl. (ugs.)

**pornographic** /pɔːnə'græfɪk/ adj. pornographisch; Porno- (ugs.)

**pornography** /pɔː'nɒgrəfɪ/ n. Pornographie, die

**porous** /'pɔːrəs/ adj. porös

**porridge** /'pɒrɪdʒ/ n. [Hafer]brei, der

**port¹** /pɔːt/ ① n. (a) Hafen, der
(b) (Naut., Aeronaut.: left side) Backbord, das
② adj. (Naut., Aeronaut.: left) Backbord-;
backbordseitig

**port²** n. (wine) Portwein, der

**portable** /'pɔːtəbl/ adj. tragbar

**port au'thority** n. Hafenbehörde, die

**porter¹** /'pɔːtə(r)/ n. (Brit.: doorman) Pförtner,
der; (of hotel) Portier, der

**porter²** n. [Gepäck]träger, der/-trägerin, die;
(in hotel) Hausdiener, der

**portfolio** /pɔːt'fəʊliəʊ/ n. pl. ~s (a) (Polit.)
Geschäftsbereich, der
(b) (case, contents) Mappe, die

**porthole** /'pɔːthəʊl/ n. (Naut.) Seitenfenster,
das; (round) Bullauge, das

**portion** /'pɔːʃn/ n. (a) (part) Teil, der; (of
ticket) Abschnitt, der
(b) (of food) Portion, die

**portly** /'pɔːtlɪ/ adj. beleibt

**portrait** /'pɔːtrɪt/ n. Porträt, das

**portray** /pɔː'treɪ/ v.t. darstellen; (make
likeness of) porträtieren

**Portugal** /'pɔːtjʊgl/ pr. n. Portugal (das)

**Portuguese** /pɔːtjʊ'giːz/ ① adj.
portugiesisch; sb. is ~: jmd. ist Portugiese/
Portugiesin
② n., pl. same (a) (person) Portugiese, der/
Portugiesin, die
(b) (language) Portugiesisch, das; see also
ENGLISH 2A

**pose** /pəʊz/ ① v.t. aufwerfen ⟨Frage,
Problem⟩; darstellen ⟨Bedrohung⟩; mit sich
bringen ⟨Schwierigkeiten⟩
② v.i. (a) (assume attitude) posieren; (fig.) sich
geziert benehmen
(b) ~ as sich geben als
③ n. Pose, die; strike a ~: eine Pose
einnehmen

**poser** /'pəʊzə(r)/ n. (question) knifflige Frage

**posh** /pɒʃ/ adj. (coll.) vornehm; nobel (spött.);
stinkvornehm (salopp)

**position** /pə'zɪʃn/ ① n. (a) (place occupied)
Platz, der; (of player in team, of plane, ship, etc.)
Position, die; (of hands of clock, words, stars)
Stellung, die; (of building) Lage, die; be in/out
of ~: an seinem Platz/nicht an seinem Platz
sein
(b) (Mil.) Stellung, die
(c) (fig.: mental attitude) Standpunkt, der
(d) (fig.: situation) be in a good ~ [financially]
[finanziell] gut gestellt sein; be in a ~ of
strength eine starke Position haben
(e) (rank) Stellung, die
(f) (job) Stelle, die
(g) (posture) Haltung, die
② v.t. platzieren; postieren ⟨Polizisten,
Wachen⟩; ~ oneself sich stellen/(sit) setzen

**positive** /'pɒzɪtɪv/ adj. (a) (also Math.)
positiv; konstruktiv ⟨Vorschlag⟩; (definite)
eindeutig; (convinced) sicher; I'm ~ of it ich
bin [mir] [dessen] ganz sicher

(b) (Electr.) positiv ⟨Elektrode, Ladung⟩;
Plus⟨platte, -leiter⟩
(c) as intensifier (coll.) echt

**positive: ~ discrimi'nation** n. positive
Diskriminierung; ~ **vetting** n., no indef.
art. (Brit.) Sicherheitsüberprüfung, die

**possess** /pə'zes/ v.t. besitzen; (as faculty or
quality) haben ⟨Furcht usw.⟩ ergreifen; what
~ed you? was ist in dich gefahren?

**possessed** /pə'zest/ adj. besessen

**possession** /pə'zeʃn/ n. (a) (thing possessed)
Besitz, der; some of my ~s einige meiner
Sachen
(b) in pl. (property) Besitz, der
(c) (possessing) Besitz, der; be in ~ of sth. im
Besitz einer Sache (Gen.) sein; take ~ of in
Besitz nehmen; beziehen ⟨Haus, Wohnung⟩

**possessive** /pə'zesɪv/ adj. (a)
besitzergreifend; be ~ about sth./sb. etw.
eifersüchtig hüten/an jmdn. Besitzansprüche
stellen
(b) (Ling.) possessiv; Possessiv⟨pronomen⟩

**possessor** /pə'zesə(r)/ n. Besitzer, der/
Besitzerin, die

**possibility** /pɒsɪ'bɪlɪtɪ/ n. Möglichkeit, die

**possible** /'pɒsɪbl/ adj. möglich; (likely) [gut]
möglich; if ~: wenn möglich; as ... as ~: so
... wie möglich; möglichst ...

**possibly** /'pɒsɪblɪ/ adv. (a) as often as I
~ can sooft ich irgend kann; I cannot
~ commit myself ich kann mich unmöglich
festlegen
(b) (perhaps) möglicherweise

**post¹** /pəʊst/ n. (a) (as support) Pfosten, der
(b) (stake) Pfahl, der
(c) (starting/finishing ~) Start-/Zielpfosten, der

**post²** ① n. (a) (Brit.: one dispatch/delivery of
letters) Postausgang, der/Post[zustellung], die;
by return of ~: postwendend
(b) no indef. art. (Brit.: official conveying) Post,
die; by ~: mit der Post; per Post
(c) (~ office) Post, die
② v.t. (a) abschicken
(b) (fig. coll.) keep sb. ~ed jmdn. auf dem
Laufenden halten

**post³** ① n. (a) (job) Stelle, die; Posten, der
(b) (Mil.; also fig.) Posten, der
② v.t. postieren; aufstellen

**postage** /'pəʊstɪdʒ/ n. Porto, das

**'postage stamp** n. Briefmarke, die

**postal** /'pəʊstl/ adj. Post-; postalisch
⟨Aufgabe, Einrichtung⟩; (by post) per Post
nachgestellt

**'postal order** n. ≈ Postanweisung, die

**post: ~box** n. (Brit.) Briefkasten, der;
**~card** n. Postkarte, die; **~code** n. (Brit.)
Postleitzahl, die; **~'date** v.t. (give later date to)
vordatieren

**poster** /'pəʊstə(r)/ n. Plakat, das

**poste restante** /pəʊst re'stɑ̃t/ n.
Abteilung/Schalter für postlagernde
Sendungen; write to sb. [at the ~] in Rome
jmdm. postlagernd nach Rom schreiben

# posterior ···✦ power····

**posterior** /pɒˈstɪərɪə(r)/ *n.* (joc.) Hinterteil, *das* (ugs.)

**posterity** /pɒˈsterɪtɪ/ *n., no art.* Nachwelt, *die*

**postgrad** /ˈpəʊstˈɡræd/ (coll.)**,**
**postˈgraduate** [1] *adj.* Graduierten-
[2] *n.* Graduierte, *der/die*

**posthumous** /ˈpɒstjʊməs/ *adj.* postum

**post:** ~**man** /ˈpəʊstmən/, *pl.* ~**men**
/ˈpəʊstmən/ *n.* Briefträger, *der;* ~**mark**
[1] *n.* Poststempel, *der;* [2] *v.t.* abstempeln;
~ˈ**modern** ▶ ~MODERNIST 1;
~ˈ**modernist** [1] *adj.* postmodernistisch;
[2] *n.* Postmodernist, *der*/Postmodernistin,
*die*

**postmortem** /pəʊstˈmɔːtəm/ *n.*
Obduktion, *die*

**post:** ~ **office** *n.* **(a)** (organization) the
P~ Office die Post; **(b)** (place) Postamt, *das;*
Post, *die;* ~ **office box** *n.* Postfach, *das*

**postpone** /pəˈspəʊn/ *v.t.* verschieben; (for
an indefinite period) aufschieben

**postˈponement** *n.* Verschiebung, *die/*
Aufschub, *der*

ˈ**post room** *n.* Poststelle, *die*

**postscript** /ˈpəʊskrɪpt/ *n.* Nachschrift, *die;*
(fig.) Nachtrag, *der*

**posture** /ˈpɒstʃə(r)/ *n.* [Körper]haltung, *die*

ˈ**post-war** *adj.* Nachkriegs-; der
Nachkriegszeit *nachgestellt*

**posy** /ˈpəʊzɪ/ *n.* Sträußchen, *das*

**pot**[1] /pɒt/ [1] *n.* **(a)** [Koch]topf, *der;* **go to** ~
(coll.) den Bach runtergehen (ugs.)
**(b)** (container, contents) Topf, *der;* (teapot, coffee
pot) Kanne, *die*
**(c)** (coll.: large sum) **a** ~ **of/**~**s of**
massenweise
[2] *v.t.* ~ **[up]** eintopfen ⟨*Pflanze*⟩

**pot**[2] *n.* (sl.: marijuana) Pot, *das* (Jargon)

**potassium** /pəˈtæsɪəm/ *n.* Kalium, *das*

**potato** /pəˈteɪtəʊ/ *n., pl.* ~**es** Kartoffel, *die*

**potato ˈsalad** *n.* Kartoffelsalat, *der*

**pot:** ~**belly** *n.* Schmerbauch, *der* (ugs.);
~**boiler** *n.* (derog.) Fließbandprodukt, *das*

**potent** /ˈpəʊtənt/ *adj.* [hoch]wirksam
⟨*Droge*⟩; stark ⟨*Schnaps usw.*⟩; schlagkräftig
⟨*Waffe*⟩

**potential** /pəˈtenʃl/ [1] *adj.* potenziell
(geh.); möglich
[2] *n.* Potenzial, *das* (geh.); Möglichkeiten *Pl.*

**potentially** /pəˈtenʃəlɪ/ *adv.* potenziell
(geh.); **he's** ~ **dangerous** er kann gefährlich
werden; **a** ~ **rich country** ein Land, das
reich sein könnte

**pot:** ~**hole** *n.* **(a)** Schlagloch, *das;* **(b)**
(cave) [tiefe] Höhle; ~**holer** *n.*
Höhlenforscher, *der/*-forscherin, *die;*
~ **plant** *n.* Topfpflanze, *die*

**potpourri** /pəʊpʊəˈriː/ *n.* Duftmischung,
*die*

**pot:** ~ **roast** *n.* Schmorbraten, *der;*
~**shot** *n.* **take a** ~**shot** [at sb./sth.] aufs
Geratewohl [auf jmdn./etw.] schießen

ˈ**potted** *adj.* **(a)** (planted) Topf-
**(b)** (abridged) kurz [gefasst]

ˈ**potter**[1] *n.* Töpfer, *der*/Töpferin, *die*

ˈ**potter**[2] *v.i.* ~ **[about]** [he]rumwerkeln
(ugs.)

**pottery** /ˈpɒtərɪ/ *n.* **(a)** Töpferware, *die*
**(b)** (workshop, craft) Töpferei, *die*

**potty**[1] /ˈpɒtɪ/ *adj.* (Brit. coll.) verrückt (ugs.)
(about, on nach)

**potty**[2] *n.* (Brit. coll.) Töpfchen, *das*

**pouch** /paʊtʃ/ *n.* Beutel, *der*

**pouffe** /puːf/ *n.* Sitzpolster, *das*

**poultry** /ˈpəʊltrɪ/ *n.* Geflügel, *das*

**pounce** /paʊns/ *v.i.* **(a)** sich auf sein Opfer
stürzen; ⟨*Raubvogel:*⟩ herabstoßen auf
(+ *Akk.*)
**(b)** (fig.) ~ **[up]on/at** sich stürzen auf
(+ *Akk.*)

**pound**[1] /paʊnd/ *n.* **(a)** (unit of weight)
[britisches] Pfund (*453,6 Gramm*); **two** ~**[s]
of apples** 2 Pfund Äpfel
**(b)** (unit of currency) Pfund, *das*

**pound**[2] *n.* (enclosure) Pferch, *der;* (for stray
dogs) Zwinger, *der;* (for cars) Abstellplatz, *der*

**pound**[3] [1] *v.t.* (crush) zerstoßen
[2] *v.i.* **(a)** (make one's way heavily) stampfen
**(b)** ⟨*Herz:*⟩ heftig schlagen

ˈ**pound[s] sign** *n.* Pfundzeichen, *das*

**pour** /pɔː(r)/ [1] *v.t.* gießen; (into cup, glass)
einschenken
[2] *v.i.* **(a)** (flow) strömen; ⟨*Rauch:*⟩
hervorquellen (from aus); ~ **[with rain]** in
Strömen regnen
**(b)** (fig.) strömen; ~ **in** herein-/
hineinströmen; ~ **out** heraus-/
hinausströmen
■ **pour ˈdown** *v.i.* it's ~ing down es gießt
[in Strömen] (ugs.)

**pout** /paʊt/ [1] *v.i.* einen Schmollmund
machen
[2] *v.t.* aufwerfen ⟨*Lippen*⟩

**poverty** /ˈpɒvətɪ/ *n.* Armut, *die*

**poverty:** ~ **line** *n.* Armutsgrenze, *die;* **be
on the** ~ **line** an der Armutsgrenze liegen;
**live below the** ~ **line** unterhalb der
Armutsgrenze leben; ~**stricken** *adj.* Not
leidend

**powder** /ˈpaʊdə(r)/ [1] *n.* **(a)** Pulver, *das*
**(b)** (cosmetic) Puder, *der*
[2] *v.t.* pudern
**(b)** (reduce to ~) pulverisieren; ~**ed milk**
Milchpulver, *das*

ˈ**powdery** *adj.* pulv[e]rig

**power** /ˈpaʊə(r)/ [1] *n.* **(a)** (ability) Kraft, *die;*
**do all in one's** ~ **to help sb.** alles in seiner
Macht Stehende tun, um jmdn. zu helfen
**(b)** (faculty) Fähigkeit, *die*
**(c)** (strength, intensity) Kraft, *die;* (of blow)
Wucht, *die*                                    ···✦

**p**

**(d)** (authority, political ~) Macht, *die* (over über + *Akk.*); **come into ~:** an die Macht kommen
**(e)** (authorization) Vollmacht, *die*
**(f)** (State) Macht, *die*
**(g)** (Math.) Potenz, *die*
**(h)** (Mech., Electr.) Kraft, *die;* (electric current) Strom, *der*
2 *v.t.* ⟨*Treibstoff, Strom:*⟩ antreiben; ⟨*Batterie:*⟩ mit Energie versorgen

**power: ~-assisted** *adj.* ~-assisted **steering/brakes** Servolenkung, *die/*-bremsen *Pl.;* ~ **brakes** *n. pl.* Servobremsen *Pl.;* ~ **cable** *n.* Hochspannungsleitung, *die;* ~ **cut** *n.* Stromsperre, *die;* ~ **dressing** *n.: das Tragen betont streng wirkender Kleidung;* ~ **failure** *n.* Stromausfall, *der*

**powerful** /'paʊəfl/ *adj.* **(a)** (strong) stark; kräftig ⟨*Tritt, Schlag, Tier*⟩; heftig ⟨*Gefühl, Empfindung*⟩; hell, strahlend ⟨*Licht*⟩
**(b)** mächtig ⟨*Clique, Person, Herrscher*⟩

**'powerless** *adj.* machtlos

**power: ~ plant** ▶ ~ STATION; ~ **point** *n.* (Brit.) Steckdose, *die;* ~ **station** *n.* Kraftwerk, *das;* ~ **steering** *n.* Servolenkung, *die;* ~ **supply** *n.* Energieversorgung, *die* (to *Gen.*)

**pp.** *abbr.* = **pages**

**p.p.** /'piː'piː/ *abbr.* = **by proxy** pp[a].

**practicable** /'præktɪkəbl/ *adj.* durchführbar ⟨*Projekt, Plan*⟩

**practical** /'præktɪkl/ *adj.* **(a)** praktisch; praktisch veranlagt ⟨*Person*⟩
**(b)** (virtual) tatsächlich
**(c)** (feasible) möglich

**practical 'joke** *n.* Streich, *der*

**'practically** *adv.* praktisch; (almost) so gut wie; praktisch (ugs.)

**practice¹** /'præktɪs/ *n.* **(a)** (repeated exercise) Übung, *die;* **be out of ~:** außer Übung sein
**(b)** (session) Übungen *Pl.;* **piano ~:** Klavierüben, *das*
**(c)** (of doctor, lawyer, etc.) Praxis, *die*
**(d)** (action) **put sth. into ~:** etw. in die Praxis umsetzen
**(e)** (custom) Gewohnheit, *die;* **regular ~:** Brauch, *der*

**practice², practiced, practicing** (Amer.) ▶ PRACTIS-

**practise** /'præktɪs/ 1 *v.t.* **(a)** (apply) anwenden; praktizieren
**(b)** ausüben ⟨*Beruf, Religion*⟩
**(c)** trainieren in (+ *Dat.*) ⟨*Sportart*⟩; ~ **the piano/flute** Klavier/Flöte üben
2 *v.i.* üben

**practised** /'præktɪst/ *adj.* geübt

**practising** /'præktɪsɪŋ/ *adj.* praktizierend ⟨*Arzt, Katholik usw.*⟩

**practitioner** /præk'tɪʃənə(r)/ *n.* Fachmann, *der; see also* GENERAL PRACTITIONER

**pragmatic** /præg'mætɪk/ *adj.* pragmatisch

**Prague** /prɑːg/ *pr. n.* Prag (*das*)

**prairie** /'preərɪ/ *n.* Grassteppe, *die;* (in North America) Prärie, *die*

**praise** /preɪz/ 1 *v.t.* loben; (more strongly) rühmen
2 *n.* Lob, *das*

**'praiseworthy** *adj.* lobenswert

**pram** /præm/ *n.* (Brit.) Kinderwagen, *der*

**prance** /prɑːns/ *v.i.* **(a)** ⟨*Pferd:*⟩ tänzeln
**(b)** (fig.) stolzieren; ~ **about** *or* **around** herumhüpfen

**prank** /præŋk/ *n.* Streich, *der*

**prattle** /'prætl/ 1 *v.i.* plappern (ugs.)
2 *n.* Geplapper, *das* (ugs.)

**prawn** /prɔːn/ *n.* Garnele, *die*

**prawn 'cocktail** *n.* Krabbencocktail, *der*

**pray** /preɪ/ *v.i.* beten (for um)

**prayer** /preə(r)/ *n.* **(a)** Gebet, *das*
**(b)** *no art.* (praying) Beten, *das*

**'prayer book** *n.* Gebetbuch, *das*

**preach** /priːtʃ/ 1 *v.i.* predigen (**to** zu, vor + *Dat.;* **on** über + *Akk.*)
2 *v.t.* halten ⟨*Predigt*⟩; predigen ⟨*Evangelium, Botschaft*⟩

**'preacher** *n.* Prediger, *der/*Predigerin, *die*

**pre-arrange** /priːə'reɪndʒ/ *v.t.* vorher absprechen; vorher ausmachen ⟨*Treffpunkt, Zeichen*⟩

**precarious** /prɪ'keərɪəs/ *adj.* **(a)** (uncertain) labil; prekär; **make a ~ living** eine unsichere Existenz haben
**(b)** (insecure, dangerous) gefährlich

**precaution** /prɪ'kɔːʃn/ *n.* Vorsichts-, Schutzmaßnahme, *die;* **as a ~:** vorsichtshalber

**precede** /prɪ'siːd/ *v.t.* (in order or time) vorangehen (+ *Dat.*)

**precedence** /'presɪdəns/ *n.* Priorität, *die* (geh.), Vorrang, *der* (over vor + *Dat.*)

**precedent** /'presɪdənt/ *n.* Präzedenzfall, *der*

**precinct** /'priːsɪŋkt/ *n.* **(a)** [pedestrian] ~: Fußgängerzone, *die*
**(b)** (Amer.: district) Bezirk, *der*

**precious** /'preʃəs/ 1 *adj.* **(a)** kostbar ⟨*Schmuckstück, Zeit*⟩; Edel⟨*metall, -stein*⟩
**(b)** (beloved) lieb
**(c)** (affected) affektiert
2 *adv.* (coll.) herzlich ⟨*wenig, wenige*⟩

**precipice** /'presɪpɪs/ *n.* Abgrund, *der*

**precipitate** 1 /prɪ'sɪpɪtət/ *adj.* eilig ⟨*Flucht*⟩; übereilt ⟨*Entschluss*⟩
2 /prɪ'sɪpɪteɪt/ *v.t.* (hasten) beschleunigen; (trigger) auslösen

**precipitation** /prɪsɪpɪ'teɪʃn/ *n.* (Meteorol.) Niederschlag, *der*

**precipitous** /prɪ'sɪpɪtəs/ *adj.* **(a)** (steep) sehr steil
**(b)** ▶ PRECIPITATE 1

**précis** /'preɪsiː/ *n., pl. same* /'preɪsiːz/ Zusammenfassung, *die*

**precise** /prɪˈsaɪs/ *adj.* genau; präzise; fein ⟨*Instrument*⟩; förmlich ⟨*Art*⟩; **be [more]** ∼: sich präzise[r] ausdrücken

**pre'cisely** *adv.* genau

**precision** /prɪˈsɪʒn/ *n.* Genauigkeit, *die*

**precision 'instrument** *n.* Präzisions[mess]gerät, *das*

**preclude** /prɪˈkluːd/ *v.t.* ausschließen

**precocious** /prɪˈkəʊʃəs/ *adj.* frühreif ⟨*Kind*⟩; altklug ⟨*Äußerung*⟩

**preconceived** /priːkənˈsiːvd/ *adj.* vorgefasst ⟨*Ansicht, Vorstellung*⟩

**preconception** /priːkənˈsepʃn/ *n.* vorgefasste Meinung (**of** über + *Akk.*)

**precondition** /priːkənˈdɪʃn/ *n.* Vorbedingung, *die* (**of** für)

**pre-cooked** /priːˈkʊkt/ *adj.* vorgekocht

**precursor** /priːˈkɜːsə(r)/ *n.* Wegbereiter, *der*/-bereiterin, *die*

**predator** /ˈpredətə(r)/ *n.* Raubtier, *das;* (fish) Raubfisch, *der*

**'predatory** *adj.* räuberisch; ∼ **animal** Raubtier, *das*

**predecessor** /ˈpriːdɪsesə(r)/ *n.* Vorgänger, *der*/-gängerin, *die*

**predestine** /priːˈdestɪn/ *v.t.* von vornherein bestimmen (**to** zu)

**predicament** /prɪˈdɪkəmənt/ *n.* Dilemma, *das*

**predicate** /ˈpredɪkət/ *n.* (Ling.) Prädikat, *das*

**predicative** /prɪˈdɪkətɪv/ *adj.* (Ling.) prädikativ

**predict** /prɪˈdɪkt/ *v.t.* voraus-, vorhersagen; vorhersehen ⟨*Folgen*⟩

**predictable** /prɪˈdɪktəbl/ *adj.* voraussagbar, vorhersehbar ⟨*Ereignis, Reaktion*⟩; berechenbar ⟨*Person*⟩

**prediction** /prɪˈdɪkʃn/ *n.* Vorhersage, *die*

**predominance** /prɪˈdɒmɪnəns/ *n.* (a) (control) Vorherrschaft, *die* (**over** über + *Akk.*) (b) (majority) Überzahl, *die* (**of** von)

**predominant** /prɪˈdɒmɪnənt/ *adj.* (having more power) dominierend; (prevailing) vorherrschend

**pre'dominantly** *adv.* überwiegend

**predominate** /prɪˈdɒmɪneɪt/ *v.i.* (be more powerful) dominierend sein; (be more important) vorherrschen

**pre-eminent** /priːˈemɪnənt/ *adj.* herausragend

**pre-empt** /priːˈempt/ *v.t.* zuvorkommen (+ *Dat.*)

**preen** /priːn/ *v.t.* putzen ⟨*Federn*⟩

**prefab** /ˈpriːfæb/ *n.* (coll.) Fertighaus, *das*

**prefabricated** /priːˈfæbrɪkeɪtɪd/ *adj.* vorgefertigt

**preface** /ˈprefəs/ ①*n.* Vorwort, *das* (**to** *Gen.*) ②*v.t.* (introduce) einleiten

**prefect** /ˈpriːfekt/ *n.* (Sch.) die Aufsicht führender älterer Schüler/führende ältere Schülerin

**prefer** /prɪˈfɜː(r)/ *v.t.*, **-rr-** vorziehen; ∼ **to do sth.** etw. lieber tun; ∼ **sth. to sth.** etw. einer Sache (*Dat.*) vorziehen

**preferable** /ˈprefərəbl/ *adj.* vorzuziehen *präd.;* vorzuziehend *attr.;* besser (**to** als)

**preferably** /ˈprefərəblɪ/ *adv.* am besten; (as best liked) am liebsten; **Wine or beer?** – **Wine,** ∼**!** Wein oder Bier? – Lieber Wein!

**preference** /ˈprefərəns/ *n.* (a) (greater liking) Vorliebe, *die;* **for** ∼ ▶ PREFERABLY; **have a** ∼ **for sth.** [**over sth.**] etw. [einer Sache (*Dat.*)] vorziehen; **do sth. in** ∼ **to sth. else** etw. lieber als etw. anderes tun (b) (thing preferred) **what are your** ∼**s?** was wäre dir am liebsten? (c) **give** ∼ **to sb.** jmdn. bevorzugen

**preferential** /prefəˈrenʃl/ *adj.* bevorzugt ⟨*Behandlung*⟩

**preferred** /prɪˈfɜːd/ *adj.* bevorzugt; **my** ∼ **solution** *etc.* die Lösung *usw.*, der ich den Vorzug gebe

**prefix** /ˈpriːfɪks/ *n.* Präfix, *das*

**pregnancy** /ˈpregnənsɪ/ *n.* (of woman) Schwangerschaft, *die;* (of animal) Trächtigkeit, *die*

**'pregnancy test** *n.* Schwangerschaftstest, *der*

**pregnant** /ˈpregnənt/ *adj.* schwanger ⟨*Frau*⟩; trächtig ⟨*Tier*⟩

**preheat** /priːˈhiːt/ *v.t.* vorheizen ⟨*Backofen*⟩; vorwärmen ⟨*Geschirr, Essen*⟩

**prehistoric** /priːhɪˈstɒrɪk/ *adj.* prähistorisch

**prehistory** /priːˈhɪstərɪ/ Vorgeschichte, *die*

**prejudge** /priːˈdʒʌdʒ/ *v.t.* vorschnell urteilen über (+ *Akk.*)

**prejudice** /ˈpredʒʊdɪs/ ①*n.* Vorurteil, *das* ②*v.t.* beeinflussen

**prejudiced** /ˈpredʒʊdɪst/ *adj.* voreingenommen (**about** gegenüber, **against** gegen)

**preliminary** /prɪˈlɪmɪnərɪ/ ①*adj.* Vor-; vorbereitend ⟨*Forschung, Maßnahme*⟩ ②*n.; usu. in pl.* **preliminaries** Präliminarien *Pl.;* **as a** ∼ **to sth.** als Vorbereitung auf etw. (*Akk.*)

**prelude** /ˈpreljuːd/ *n.* (a) (introduction) Anfang, *der* (**to** *Gen.*) (b) (Theatre, Mus.) Vorspiel, *das*

**premature** /ˈpremətjʊə(r)/ *adj.* (a) (hasty) übereilt (b) (early) vorzeitig ⟨*Altern, Ankunft*⟩; verfrüht ⟨*Bericht, Eile*⟩; ∼ **baby** Frühgeburt, *die*

**prema'turely** *adv.* (early) vorzeitig; zu früh ⟨*geboren werden*⟩; (hastily) übereilt

**premeditated** /priːˈmedɪteɪtɪd/ *adj.* vorsätzlich

**premeditation** /priːmedɪˈteɪʃn/ *n.* Vorsatz, *der*

**p**

**premenstrual** /priːˈmenstrʊəl/ adj. prämenstruell; ∼ **tension** prämenstruelles Syndrom

**premier** /ˈpremɪə(r)/ n. Premier[minister], der/Premierministerin, die

**première** /ˈpremjeə(r)/ n. Premiere, die; Erstaufführung, die

**premise** /ˈpremɪs/ n. **(a)** ∼s pl. (building) Gebäude, das; (buildings and land) Gelände, das; (rooms) Räumlichkeiten Pl.
**(b)** ▶ PREMISS

**premiss** /ˈpremɪs/ n. Prämisse, die

**premium** /ˈpriːmɪəm/ n. Prämie, die; **be at a** ∼ (fig.) sehr gefragt sein

**'Premium Bond** n. (Brit.) Prämienanleihe, die; Losanleihe, die

**premonition** /premǝˈnɪʃn/ n. Vorahnung, die

**pre-natal** /priːˈneɪtl/ adj. pränatal (fachspr.); ∼ **care** Schwangerschaftsfürsorge, die

**preoccupation** /prɪɒkjʊˈpeɪʃn/ n. Sorge, die (with um)

**preoccupied** /prɪˈɒkjʊpaɪd/ adj. (lost in thought) gedankenverloren; (concerned) besorgt (with um)

**pre-'packed** adj. abgepackt

**prepaid** /priːˈpeɪd/ adj. ∼ **envelope** frankierter Umschlag

**preparation** /prepǝˈreɪʃn/ n. Vorbereitung, die; ∼s pl. Vorbereitungen Pl. (for für)

**preparatory** /prɪˈpærətərɪ/ ① adj. vorbereitend ⟨Maßnahme, Schritt⟩; ∼ **work** Vorarbeiten Pl.
② adv. ∼ **to sth.** vor etw. (Dat.)

**prepare** /prɪˈpeə(r)/ ① v.t. **(a)** vorbereiten; ausarbeiten ⟨Plan, Rede⟩; vorbereiten ⟨Person⟩ (for auf + Akk.); **be** ∼**d to do sth.** (be willing) bereit sein, etw. zu tun
**(b)** herstellen ⟨Chemikalie usw.⟩; zubereiten ⟨Essen⟩
② v.i. sich vorbereiten (for auf + Akk.)

**preponderance** /prɪˈpɒndərəns/ n. Überlegenheit, die (over über + Akk.)

**preposition** /prepǝˈzɪʃn/ n. (Ling.) Präposition, die

**prepossessing** /priːpǝˈzesɪŋ/ adj. einnehmend

**preposterous** /prɪˈpɒstərəs/ adj. absurd; grotesk ⟨Äußeres, Kleidung⟩

**'pre-program** v.t., -mm- [vor]programmieren

**prerequisite** /priːˈrekwɪzɪt/ ① n. [Grund]voraussetzung, die
② adj. unbedingt erforderlich

**prerogative** /prɪˈrɒgətɪv/ n. Privileg, das; Vorrecht, das

**Presbyterian** /prezbɪˈtɪərɪən/ ① adj. presbyterianisch
② n. Presbyterianer, der/Presbyterianerin, die

**prescribe** /prɪˈskraɪb/ v.t. **(a)** (impose) vorschreiben
**(b)** (Med.; also fig.) verschreiben

**prescription** /prɪˈskrɪpʃn/ n. **(a)** Vorschreiben, das
**(b)** (Med.) Rezept, das

**pre'scription charge** n. Rezeptgebühr, die

**presence** /ˈprezəns/ n. **(a)** (of person) Anwesenheit, die; (of things) Vorhandensein, das; **in the** ∼ **of** in Anwesenheit (+ Gen.)
**(b)** ∼ **of mind** Geistesgegenwart, die

**present**[1] /ˈprezənt/ ① adj. **(a)** anwesend (at bei); **all those** ∼: alle Anwesenden
**(b)** (existing now) gegenwärtig; jetzig ⟨Bischof, Chef usw.⟩
**(c)** (Ling.) ∼ **tense** Präsens, das; Gegenwart, die
② n. **(a)** **the** ∼: die Gegenwart; **at** ∼: zurzeit; **for the** ∼: vorläufig
**(b)** (Ling.) Präsens, das; Gegenwart, die

**present**[2] ① /ˈprezənt/ n. (gift) Geschenk, das
② /prɪˈzent/ v.t. **(a)** schenken; überreichen ⟨Preis, Medaille, Geschenk⟩; ∼ **sth. to sb.** or **sb. with sth.** jmdm. etw. schenken/ überreichen; ∼ **sb. with difficulties/a problem** jmdn. vor Schwierigkeiten/ein Problem stellen
**(b)** überreichen ⟨Gesuch⟩ (to bei); vorlegen ⟨Scheck, Bericht, Rechnung⟩ (to Dat.); ∼ **one's case** seinen Fall darlegen
**(c)** (exhibit) zeigen; bereiten ⟨Schwierigkeit⟩
**(d)** (introduce) vorstellen (to Dat.); vorlegen ⟨Abhandlung⟩; moderieren ⟨Sendung⟩
③ v. refl. ⟨Problem:⟩ auftreten; ⟨Möglichkeit:⟩ sich ergeben; ∼ **oneself for an interview** zu einem Gespräch erscheinen

**presentable** /prɪˈzentəbl/ adj. ansehnlich; **I'm not** ∼: ich kann mich nicht so zeigen

**presentation** /prezənˈteɪʃn/ n. **(a)** (giving) Schenkung, die; (of prize, medal) Überreichung, die
**(b)** (ceremony) Verleihung, die
**(c)** (of petition) Überreichung, die; (of cheque, report, account) Vorlage, die; (of case) Darlegung, die

**present-day** /ˈprezəntdeɪ/ adj. heutig

**presenter** /prɪˈzentə(r)/ n. (Radio, Telev.) Moderator, der/Moderatorin, die

**presentiment** /prɪˈzentɪmənt/ n. Vorahnung, die

**presently** /ˈprezəntlɪ/ adv. bald; (Amer., Scot.: now) zurzeit

**preservation** /prezəˈveɪʃn/ n. Erhaltung, die; (of leather, wood, etc.) Konservierung, die

**preservative** /prɪˈzɜːvətɪv/ n. Konservierungsmittel, das

**preserve** /prɪˈzɜːv/ ① n. **(a)** in sing. or pl. (fruit) Eingemachte, das
**(b)** (fig.: special sphere) Domäne, die (geh.)
**(c)** **wildlife/game** ∼: Tierschutzgebiet, das/ Wildpark, der
② v.t. **(a)** (keep safe) schützen (from vor + Dat.)
**(b)** bewahren ⟨Brauch⟩; wahren ⟨Anschein, Reputation⟩

**(c)** (keep from decay) konservieren; einmachen ⟨*Obst, Gemüse*⟩
**(d)** (protect) hegen ⟨*Tierart, Wald*⟩
**preside** /prɪ'zaɪd/ *v.i.* präsidieren, vorsitzen (**over** *Dat.*); (at meeting etc.) den Vorsitz haben (**at** bei)
**presidency** /'prezɪdənsɪ/ *n.* **(a)** Präsidentschaft, *die*
**(b)** (of society) Vorsitz, *der*
**president** /'prezɪdənt/ *n.* **(a)** Präsident, *der*/Präsidentin, *die*
**(b)** (of society) Vorsitzende, *der*/*die*
**presidential** /prezɪ'denʃl/ *adj.* Präsidenten-
**press¹** /pres/ **1** *n.* **(a)** (newspapers etc.) Presse, *die*; *attrib.* Presse-
**(b)** ▶ PRINTING PRESS
**(c)** (for flattening, compressing, etc.) Presse, *die*
**2** *v.t.* **(a)** drücken; drücken auf (+ *Akk.*) ⟨*Klingel, Knopf*⟩; treten auf (+ *Akk.*) ⟨*Gas-, Brems-, Kupplungspedal usw.*⟩
**(b)** (urge) drängen ⟨*Person*⟩; (force) aufdrängen (**[up]on** *Dat.*); nachdrücklich vorbringen ⟨*Forderung, Argument*⟩; **he did not ~ the point** er ließ die Sache auf sich beruhen
**(c)** (compress) pressen; auspressen ⟨*Orangen, Saft*⟩; keltern ⟨*Trauben, Äpfel*⟩
**(d)** (iron) bügeln
**(e)** **be ~ed for time/money** zu wenig Zeit/Geld haben
**3** *v.i.* **(a)** (exert pressure) drücken
**(b)** (be urgent) drängen
**(c)** (make demand) **~ for sth.** auf etw. (*Akk.*) drängen
■ **press a'head, press 'on** *v.i.* (continue) [zügig] weitermachen; (continue travelling) [zügig] weitergehen/-fahren; **~ on with one's work** sich mit der Arbeit ranhalten (ugs.)
**press²** *v.t.* **~ into service/use** in Dienst nehmen; einsetzen
**press: ~ agent** *n.* Presseagent, *der*/-agentin, *die*; **~ conference** *n.* Pressekonferenz, *die*; **~ coverage** *n.* Berichterstattung in der Presse; **~ cutting** *n.* (Brit.) Zeitungsausschnitt, *der*
**'pressing** *adj.* (urgent) dringend
**press: ~man** *n.* (Brit.: journalist) Journalist, *der*; **~ release** *n.* Presseinformation, *die*; **~ stud** *n.* (Brit.) Druckknopf, *der*; **~-up** *n.* Liegestütz, *der*
**pressure** /'preʃə(r)/ **1** *n.* Druck, *der*; **put ~ on sb.** jmdn. unter Druck setzen; **atmospheric ~:** Luftdruck, *der*
**2** *v.t.* unter Druck setzen ⟨*Person*⟩; **~ sb. into doing sth.** jmdn. [dazu] drängen, etw. zu tun
**pressure: ~ cooker** *n.* Schnellkochtopf, *der*; **~ group** *n.* Pressuregroup, *die*
**pressurize** /'preʃəraɪz/ *v.t.* **(a)** ▶ PRESSURE 2
**(b)** **~d cabin** Druckkabine, *die*
**prestige** /pre'stiːʒ/ *n.* Prestige, *das*
**prestigious** /pre'stɪdʒəs/ *adj.* angesehen

**presumably** /prɪ'zjuːməblɪ/ *adv.* vermutlich
**presume** /prɪ'zjuːm/ **1** *v.t.* **(a)** **~ to do sth.** sich (*Dat.*) anmaßen, etw. zu tun; (take the liberty) sich (*Dat.*) erlauben, etw. zu tun
**(b)** (suppose) annehmen
**2** *v.i.* **[up]on sth.** etw. ausnützen
**presumption** /prɪ'zʌmpʃn/ *n.* **(a)** (arrogance) Anmaßung, *die*
**(b)** (assumption) Annahme, *die*
**presumptuous** /prɪ'zʌmptjʊəs/ *adj.* anmaßend
**presuppose** /priːsə'pəʊz/ *v.t.* voraussetzen
**pre-teen** /'priːtiːn/ *adj.* ≈ zehn- bis zwölfjährig
**pretence** /prɪ'tens/ *n.* (Brit.) **(a)** (pretext) Vorwand, *der*
**(b)** *no art.* (make-believe, insincere behaviour) Verstellung, *die*; **it is all** *or* **just a ~:** das ist alles nicht echt
**pretend** /prɪ'tend/ **1** *v.t.* **(a)** vorgeben; **she ~ed to be asleep** sie tat, als ob sie schlief[e]
**(b)** (imagine in play) **~ to be sth.** so tun, als ob man etw. sei
**2** *v.i.* sich verstellen; **she's only ~ing** sie tut nur so
**pretense** (Amer.) ▶ PRETENCE
**pretension** /prɪ'tenʃn/ *n.* **(a)** Anspruch, *der* (**to** auf + *Akk.*)
**(b)** (pretentiousness) Überheblichkeit, *die*
**pretentious** /prɪ'tenʃəs/ *adj.* hochgestochen; wichtigtuerisch ⟨*Person*⟩; (ostentatious) großspurig
**pretext** /'priːtekst/ *n.* Vorwand, *der*; **[up]on** *or* **under the ~ of doing sth.** unter dem Vorwand, etw. tun zu wollen
**prettily** /'prɪtɪlɪ/ *adv.* hübsch; sehr schön ⟨*singen, tanzen*⟩
**pretty** /'prɪtɪ/ **1** *adj.* (also iron.) hübsch
**2** *adv.* ziemlich; **I am ~ well** es geht mir ganz gut
**prevail** /prɪ'veɪl/ *v.i.* **(a)** die Oberhand gewinnen (**against, over** über + *Akk.*); **~ [up]on sb. to do sth.** jmdn. dazu bewegen, etw. zu tun
**(b)** (predominate) ⟨*Zustand, Bedingung:*⟩ vorherrschen
**(c)** (be current) herrschen
**prevalence** /'prevələns/ *n.* Vorherrschen, *das*
**prevalent** /'prevələnt/ *adj.* **(a)** (existing) herrschend; weit verbreitet ⟨*Krankheit*⟩
**(b)** (predominant) vorherrschend
**prevent** /prɪ'vent/ *v.t.* (hinder) verhindern; (forestall) vorbeugen; **~ sb. from doing sth., ~ sb.'s doing sth.,** (coll.) **~ sb. doing sth.** jmdn. daran hindern, etw. zu tun
**preventable** /prɪ'ventəbl/ *adj.* vermeidbar
**prevention** /prɪ'venʃn/ *n.* Verhinderung, *die*; (forestalling) Vorbeugung, *die*

**p**

**preventive** /prɪ'ventɪv/ *adj.* vorbeugend; Präventiv⟨*maßnahme*⟩

**preventive 'medicine** *n.* Präventivmedizin, *die*

**preview** /'priːvjuː/ *n.* (of film, play) Voraufführung, *die;* (of exhibition) Vernissage, *die* (geh.)

**previous** /'priːvɪəs/ 1 *adj.* **(a)** früher ⟨*Anstellung, Gelegenheit*⟩; vorherig ⟨*Abend*⟩; vorig ⟨*Besitzer, Wohnsitz*⟩; **the ~ page** die Seite davor
**(b)** ( prior) **~ to** vor (+ *Dat.*)
2 *adv.* **~ to** vor (+ *Dat.*)

**'previously** *adv.* vorher

**pre-war** /'priːwɔː(r)/ *adj.* Vorkriegs-

**prey** /preɪ/ 1 *n., pl. same* **(a)** (animal[s]) Beute, *die;* **beast/bird of ~:** Raubtier, *das/*-vogel, *der*
**(b)** (victim) Opfer, *das*
2 *v.i.* **~ [up]on** ⟨*Raubtier, Raubvogel:*⟩ schlagen; ( plunder) ausplündern ⟨*Person*⟩; Jagd machen auf (+ *Akk.*); **~ [up]on sb.'s mind** jmdm. keine Ruhe lassen

**price** /praɪs/ *n.* (lit. or fig.) Preis, *der;* **at a ~ of** zum Preis von; **what is the ~ of this?** was kostet das?; **at/not at any ~:** um jeden/ keinen Preis

**price: ~ bracket** ▶ ~ RANGE; **~ cut** *n.* Preissenkung, *die;* **~-cutting** *n.* Preisschleuderei, *die;* **~ increase** *n.* Preiserhöhung, *die*

**'priceless** *adj.* **(a)** (invaluable) unbezahlbar;
**(b)** (coll.: amusing) köstlich

**price: ~ list** *n.* Preisliste, *die;* **~ range** *n.* Preisspanne, *die;* **~ rise** *n.* Preisanstieg, *der;* **~ tag** *n.* Preisschild, *das;* **~ war** *n.* Preiskrieg, *der*

**pricey** /'praɪsɪ/ *adj.* (Brit. coll.) teuer

**prick** /prɪk/ 1 *v.t.* stechen; stechen in ⟨*Ballon*⟩; aufstechen ⟨*Blase*⟩
2 *v.i.* stechen
3 *n.* Stich, *der*

■ **'prick up** *v.t.* aufrichten ⟨*Ohren*⟩; **~ up one's/its ears** die Ohren spitzen

**prickle** /'prɪkl/ 1 *n.* **(a)** Dorn, *der*
**(b)** (Zool., Bot.) Stachel, *der*
2 *v.i.* kratzen

**prickly** /'prɪklɪ/ *adj.* dornig; stachelig; (fig.) empfindlich

**pride** /praɪd/ 1 *n.* **(a)** Stolz, *der;* (arrogance) Hochmut, *der;* **take [a] ~ in sb./sth.** auf jmdn./etw. stolz sein; **sb's ~ and joy** jmds. ganzer Stolz
**(b)** (of lions) Rudel, *das*
2 *v. refl.* **~ oneself [up]on sth.** auf etw. (*Akk.*) stolz sein

**pried** ▶ PRY

**priest** /priːst/ *n.* Priester, *der*

**'priesthood** *n.* geistliches Amt

**prig** /prɪg/ *n.* Tugendbold, *der* (ugs., iron.)

**priggish** /'prɪgɪʃ/ *adj.* übertrieben tugendhaft

**prim** /prɪm/ *adj.* spröde; ( prudish) zimperlich

**primarily** /'praɪmərɪlɪ/ *adv.* in erster Linie

**primary** /'praɪmərɪ/ 1 *adj.* **(a)** (first) primär (geh.); grundlegend
**(b)** (chief) Haupt⟨*rolle, -ziel, -zweck*⟩
2 *n.* (Amer.: election) Vorwahl, *die*

**'primary school** *n.* Grundschule, *die*

**primate** /'praɪmeɪt/ *n.* **(a)** (Eccl.) Primas, *der*
**(b)** (Zool.) Primat, *der*

**prime**[1] /praɪm/ 1 *n.* Höhepunkt, *der;* **be in one's ~:** in den besten Jahren sein
2 *adj.* **(a)** Haupt-; hauptsächlich
**(b)** (excellent) erstklassig; vortrefflich ⟨*Beispiel*⟩

**prime**[2] *v.t.* **(a)** (equip) vorbereiten; **~ sb. with information/advice** jmdn. instruieren/ jmdm. Ratschläge erteilen
**(b)** grundieren ⟨*Wand, Decke*⟩
**(c)** schärfen ⟨*Sprengkörper*⟩

**prime: ~ 'minister** *n.* Premierminister, *der/*-ministerin, *die;* **~ 'number** *n.* (Math.) Primzahl, *die*

**'primer** *n.* **(a)** (explosive) Zündvorrichtung, *die*
**(b)** ( paint) Grundierlack, *der*

**'prime time** *n.* Hauptsendezeit, *die;* **~-time** TV Hauptsendezeit im Fernsehen

**primeval** /praɪ'miːvl/ *adj.* urzeitlich; Ur⟨*zeiten, -wälder*⟩

**primitive** /'prɪmɪtɪv/ *adj.* primitiv; ( prehistoric) urzeitlich ⟨*Mensch*⟩

**primrose** /'prɪmrəʊz/ *n.* gelbe Schlüsselblume

**Primus** ® /'praɪməs/ *n.* **~ [stove]** Primuskocher, *der*

**prince** /prɪns/ *n.* Prinz, *der*

**'princely** *adj.* fürstlich

**princess** /prɪn'ses/ *n.* Prinzessin, *die*

**principal** /'prɪnsɪpl/ 1 *adj.* Haupt-; (most important) wichtigst...
2 *n.* (of college) Rektor, *der/*Rektorin, *die*

**principality** /prɪnsɪ'pælɪtɪ/ *n.* Fürstentum, *das*

**'principally** *adv.* in erster Linie

**principle** /'prɪnsɪpl/ *n.* Prinzip, *das;* **on the ~ that ...:** nach dem Grundsatz, dass ...; **in ~:** im Prinzip; **do sth. on ~** *or* **as a matter of ~:** etw. prinzipiell *od.* aus Prinzip tun

**print** /prɪnt/ 1 *n.* **(a)** (impression) Abdruck, *der;* (finger~) Fingerabdruck, *der*
**(b)** (~ed lettering) Gedruckte, *das;* (typeface) Druck, *der*
**(c)** **be in/out of ~** ⟨*Buch:*⟩ erhältlich/ vergriffen sein
**(d)** (~ed picture or design) Druck, *der*
**(e)** (Photog.) Abzug, *der*
2 *v.t.* **(a)** drucken ⟨*Buch, Zeitschrift usw.*⟩
**(b)** (write) in Druckschrift schreiben

■ **print 'out** *v.t.* (Comp.) ausdrucken

**'printed** *adj.* **(a)** gedruckt
**(b)** ( published) veröffentlicht

**'printed matter** *n.* (Post) Drucksachen *Pl.*

**'printer** *n.* **(a)** (worker) Drucker, *der/* Druckerin, *die;* (firm) Druckerei, *die*

**(b)** (Comp.) Drucker, *der*

**'printing** *n.* **(a)** Drucken, *das*
**(b)** (writing like print) Druckschrift, *die*
**(c)** (edition) Auflage, *die*

**'printing press** *n.* Druckerpresse, *die*

**print: ~out** *n.* (Comp.) Ausdruck, *der;*
~ **run** *n.* (Publishing) Auflage, die; **what is
the ~ run?** wie hoch ist die Auflage?

**prion** /'pri:ɒn/ *n.* (Biol.) Prion, *das*

**prior** /'praɪə(r)/ 1 *adj.* vorherig ‹*Warnung,
Zustimmung usw.*›; früher ‹*Verabredung*›;
Vor‹*geschichte, -kenntnis*›
2 *adv.* ~ **to** vor (+ *Dat.*); ~ **to doing sth.**
bevor man etw. tut/tat; ~ **to that** vorher

**priority** /praɪ'ɒrɪtɪ/ *n.* **(a)** (precedence)
Vorrang, *der; attrib.* vorrangig; **have** *or* **take
~:** Vorrang haben (**over** vor + *Dat.*); **have ~**
(on road) Vorfahrt haben; **give ~ to sb./sth.**
jmdm./einer Sache den Vorrang geben; **give
top ~ to sth.** einer Sache (*Dat.*) höchste
Priorität einräumen
**(b)** (matter) vordringliche Angelegenheit

**prioritize ( prioritise)** /praɪ'ɒrɪtaɪz/ *v.t.*
nach Vordringlichkeit ordnen

**prism** /'prɪzm/ *n.* Prisma, *das*

**prison** /'prɪzn/ *n.* **(a)** Gefängnis, *das; attrib.*
Gefängnis-
**(b)** (custody) Haft, *die;* **in ~:** im Gefängnis; **go
to ~:** ins Gefängnis gehen

**'prison camp** *n.* Gefangenenlager, *das*

**'prisoner** *n.* Gefangene, *der/die;* **take sb. ~:**
jmdn. gefangen nehmen

**prisoner of 'war** *n.* Kriegsgefangene,
*der/die*

**prison: ~ sentence** *n.* Gefängnisstrafe,
*die;* ~ **service** *n.* Strafvollzugsbehörde,
*die*

**pristine** /'prɪstiːn/ *adj.* unberührt; **in
~ condition** in tadellosem Zustand

**privacy** /'prɪvəsɪ/ *n.* Privatsphäre, *die;*
(being undisturbed) Ungestörtheit, *die;* **invasion
of ~:** Eindringen in die Privatsphäre; **in the
strictest ~:** unter strengster Geheimhaltung

**private** /'praɪvət/ 1 *adj.* **(a)** (outside State
system) privat; Privat‹*schule, -industrie,
-klinik usw.*›
**(b)** persönlich ‹*Dinge, Meinung, Interesse*›;
nichtöffentlich ‹*Versammlung, Sitzung*›;
privat ‹*Telefongespräch, Vereinbarung*›;
Privat‹*strand, -parkplatz, -leben*›; geheim
‹*Verhandlung, Geschäft*›; persönlich
‹*Gründe*›; (confidential) vertraulich
2 *n.* **(a)** (Brit. Mil.) einfacher Soldat
**(b) in ~:** privat; in kleinem Kreis ‹*feiern*›;
(confidentially) ganz im Vertrauen

**private: ~ de'tective** *n.*
[Privat]detektiv, *der/*-detektivin, *die;*
~ **'enterprise** *n.* das freie
Unternehmertum; [**spirit of**] ~ **enterprise**
(fig.) Unternehmungsgeist, *der;* ~ **'income**
*n.* private Einkünfte *Pl.;* ~ **investigator**
*n.* Privatdetektiv, *der/*-detektivin, *die*

**'privately** *adv.* privat ‹*erziehen, zugeben*›;
vertraulich ‹*jmdn. sprechen*›; insgeheim
‹*denken, glauben*›; ~ **owned** in Privatbesitz

**private: ~ 'parts** *n. pl.* Geschlechtsteile
*Pl.;* ~ **'practice** *n.* (Med.) Privatpraxis,
*die;* ~ **'property** *n.* Privateigentum, *das;*
~ **'view[ing]** *n.* (Art) Vernissage, *die*

**privation** /praɪ'veɪʃn/ *n.* Not, *die;* **suffer
many ~s** viele Entbehrungen erleiden

**privatize** /'praɪvətaɪz/ *v.t.* privatisieren

**privet** /'prɪvɪt/ *n.* Liguster, *der*

**privilege** /'prɪvɪlɪdʒ/ *n.* (right, immunity)
Privileg, *das;* (special benefit) Sonderrecht,
*das;* (honour) Ehre, *die*

**'privileged** *adj.* privilegiert

**privy** /'prɪvɪ/ *adj.* **be ~ to sth.** in etw. (*Akk.*)
eingeweiht sein

**prize**[1] /praɪz/ 1 *n.* **(a)** (reward, money) Preis,
*der;* **win** *or* **take first ~:** den ersten Preis
gewinnen
**(b)** (in lottery) Gewinn, *der*
2 *v.t.* ~ **sth. [highly]** etw. hoch schätzen

**prize**[2] *v.t.* ~ **[open]** aufstemmen

**prize: ~-giving** *n.* Preisverleihung, *die;*
~ **money** *n.* Geldpreis, *der;* (Sport)
Preisgeld, *das;* ~**winner** *n.* Preisträger,
*der/*-trägerin, *die;* (in lottery) Gewinner, *der/*
Gewinnerin, *die*

**pro** /prəʊ/ *n. in pl.* **the ~s and cons** das Pro
und Kontra

**proactive** /prəʊ'æktɪv/ *adj.* aktiv
‹*Haltung, Rolle*›; **be ~** ‹*Person:*› [selbst] die
Initiative ergreifen

**probability** /prɒbə'bɪlɪtɪ/ *n.*
Wahrscheinlichkeit, *die;* **in all ~:** aller
Wahrscheinlichkeit nach

**probable** /'prɒbəbl/ *adj.* wahrscheinlich;
**highly ~:** höchstwahrscheinlich

**probably** /'prɒbəblɪ/ *adv.* wahrscheinlich

**probation** /prə'beɪʃn/ *n.* **(a)** Probezeit, *die*
**(b)** (Law) Bewährung, *die;* **on ~:** auf
Bewährung

**probationary** /prə'beɪʃənərɪ/ *adj.* Probe-;
~ **period** Probezeit, *die*

**pro'bation officer** *n.* Bewährungshelfer,
*der/*-helferin, *die*

**probe** /prəʊb/ 1 *n.* **(a)** Untersuchung, *die*
(**into** Gen.)
**(b)** (Med., Astron.) Sonde, *die*
2 *v.t.* untersuchen

**problem** /'prɒbləm/ *n.* Problem, *das;*
(puzzle) Rätsel, *das;* **what's the ~?** (coll.) wo
fehlts denn?; **the ~ about** *or* **with sb./sth.**
das Problem mit jmdm./bei etw.

**problematic** /prɒblə'mætɪk/,
**problematical** /prɒblə'mætɪkl/ *adj.*
problematisch

**procedure** /prə'siːdjə(r)/ *n.* Verfahren, *das*

**proceed** /prə'siːd/ *v.i.* (formal) **(a)** (on foot)
gehen; (as or by vehicle) fahren; (after
interruption) weitergehen/-fahren          ⋯⫶

**(b)** (begin and carry on) beginnen; (after interruption) fortfahren; ~ **in** or **with sth.** (begin) [mit] etw. beginnen; (continue) etw. fortsetzen
**(c)** (be under way) ⟨*Verfahren:*⟩ laufen; (be continued after interruption) fortgesetzt werden

**pro'ceedings** *n. pl.* **(a)** (events) Vorgänge *Pl.*
**(b)** (Law) Verfahren, *das;* **legal** ~: Gerichtsverfahren, *das;* **start/take [legal]** ~: gerichtlich vorgehen (**against** gegen)

**proceeds** /'prəʊsiːdz/ *n. pl.* Erlös, *der* (**from** aus)

**process¹** /'prəʊses/ ⟨1⟩ *n.* **(a)** (of time or history) Lauf, *der;* **he learnt a lot in the** ~: er lernte eine Menge dabei; **be in the** ~ **of doing sth.** gerade etw. tun
**(b)** (proceeding, natural operation) Vorgang, *der*
**(c)** (method) Verfahren, *das*
⟨2⟩ *v.t.* verarbeiten ⟨*Rohstoff, Signal, Daten*⟩; bearbeiten ⟨*Antrag, Akte*⟩; (Photog.) entwickeln ⟨*Film*⟩

**process²** /prəʊ'ses/ *v.i.* ziehen

**'process cheese** (Amer.), **'processed cheese** *ns.* Schmelzkäse, *der*

**procession** /prə'seʃn/ *n.* Zug, *der;* (religious) Prozession, *die;* (festive) Umzug, *der;* **go/ march in** ~: ziehen

**proclaim** /prə'kleɪm/ *v.t.* erklären ⟨*Absicht*⟩; geltend machen ⟨*Recht, Anspruch*⟩; verkünden ⟨*Amnestie*⟩; ausrufen ⟨*Republik*⟩

**proclamation** /prɒklə'meɪʃn/ *n.* **(a)** (proclaiming) Verkündung, *die*
**(b)** (notice) Bekanntmachung, *die;* (decree) Erlass, *der*

**procreation** /prəʊkrɪ'eɪʃn/ *n.* Fortpflanzung, *die*

**procure** /prə'kjʊə(r)/ *v.t.* beschaffen

**prod** /prɒd/ ⟨1⟩ *v.t.,* **-dd-** (poke) stupsen (ugs.); stoßen mit ⟨*Stock, Finger usw.*⟩; ~ **sb. gently** jmdn. anstupsen
⟨2⟩ *n.* Stupser, *der;* **give sb. a** ~: jmdm. einen Stupser geben

**prodigal** /'prɒdɪgl/ *adj.* verschwenderisch; ~ **son** verlorener Sohn

**prodigious** /prə'dɪdʒəs/ *adj.* ungeheuer

**prodigy** /'prɒdɪdʒɪ/ *n.* [außergewöhnliches] Talent; **child** ~: Wunderkind, *das*

**produce** ⟨1⟩ /'prɒdjuːs/ *n.* Produkte *Pl.;* Erzeugnisse *Pl.*
⟨2⟩ /prə'djuːs/ *v.t.* **(a)** vorzeigen ⟨*Pass, Fahrkarte*⟩
**(b)** produzieren ⟨*Show, Film*⟩; inszenieren ⟨*Theaterstück, Hörspiel*⟩; herausgeben ⟨*Schallplatte, Buch*⟩
**(c)** (manufacture) herstellen; (in nature; Agric.) produzieren
**(d)** (cause) hervorrufen; bewirken ⟨*Änderung*⟩
**(e)** (bring into being) erzeugen; führen zu ⟨*Situation*⟩
**(f)** (yield) geben ⟨*Milch*⟩; legen ⟨*Eier*⟩
**(g)** ⟨*Baum, Blume:*⟩ tragen ⟨*Früchte, Blüten*⟩; entwickeln ⟨*Triebe*⟩; bilden ⟨*Keime*⟩

**producer** /prə'djuːsə(r)/ *n.* **(a)** (Cinemat., Theatre, Radio, Telev.) Produzent, *der/* Produzentin, *die*
**(b)** (Brit. Theatre/Radio/Telev.) Regisseur, *der/* Regisseurin, *die*

**product** /'prɒdʌkt/ *n.* **(a)** Produkt, *das;* (of industrial process) Erzeugnis, *das;* (of art or intellect) Werk, *das*
**(b)** (result) Folge, *die*
**(c)** (Math.) Produkt, *das* (**of** aus)

**production** /prə'dʌkʃn/ *n.* **(a)** (Cinemat.) Produktion, *die;* (Theatre) Inszenierung, *die;* (of record, book) Herausgabe, *die*
**(b)** (making) Produktion, *die;* (manufacturing) Herstellung, *die;* (thing produced) Produkt, *das;* (thing created) Werk, *das*
**(c)** (yielding) Produktion, *die;* (yield) Ertrag, *der*

**production:** ~ **line** *n.* Fertigungsstraße, *die;* ~ **manager** *n.* Produktionsleiter, *der/*-leiterin, *die*

**productive** /prə'dʌktɪv/ *adj.* leistungsfähig ⟨*Betrieb, Bauernhof*⟩; fruchtbar ⟨*Gespräch, Verhandlungen*⟩

**productivity** /prɒdʌk'tɪvɪtɪ/ *n.* Produktivität, *die*

**'product range** *n.* Produktpalette, *die*

**Prof.** /prɒf/ *abbr.* = **Professor** Prof.

**profane** /prə'feɪn/ *adj.* **(a)** (irreligious) gotteslästerlich
**(b)** (secular) weltlich
**(c)** (irreverent) respektlos ⟨*Bemerkung*⟩; profan ⟨*Sprache*⟩

**profess** /prə'fes/ *v.t.* **(a)** (declare openly) bekunden ⟨*Vorliebe, Abneigung*⟩; ~ **to be/do sth.** erklären, etw. zu sein/tun
**(b)** (claim) vorgeben; ~ **to be/do sth.** behaupten, etw. zu sein/tun

**profession** /prə'feʃn/ *n.* **(a)** Beruf, *der;* **be a pilot by** ~: von Beruf Pilot sein
**(b)** (body of people) Berufsstand, *der*

**professional** /prə'feʃənl/ ⟨1⟩ *adj.* **(a)** Berufs⟨*ausbildung, -leben*⟩; beruflich ⟨*Qualifikation*⟩
**(b)** (worthy of profession) (in technical expertise) fachmännisch; (in attitude) professionell; (in experience) routiniert
**(c)** ~ **people** Angehörige *Pl.* hoch qualifizierter Berufe
**(d)** (by profession) gelernt; (not amateur) Berufs⟨*musiker, -sportler*⟩; Profi⟨*sportler*⟩
**(e)** ( paid) Profi⟨*sport, -boxen*⟩
⟨2⟩ *n.* (trained person) Fachmann, *der/*Fachfrau, *die;* (non-amateur; also Sport) Profi, *der*

**professor** /prə'fesə(r)/ *n.* **(a)** (Univ.) Professor, *der/*Professorin, *die* (**of** für)
**(b)** (Amer.: teacher at university) Dozent, *der/* Dozentin, *die*

**proficiency** /prə'fɪʃənsɪ/ *n.* Können, *das*

**proficient** /prə'fɪʃənt/ *adj.* fähig; gut ⟨*Pianist, Reiter usw.*⟩; geschickt ⟨*Radfahrer, Handwerker*⟩; **be** ~ **at** or **in maths** viel von Mathematik verstehen

**profile** /'prəʊfaɪl/ *n.* **(a)** (side aspect) Profil, *das*

# profit ···❯ promise ····

**(b)** (biographical sketch) Porträt, *das*
**(c)** (fig.) keep a low ∼: sich zurückhalten
**profit** /'prɒfɪt/ *n.* Gewinn, *der;* Profit, *der;*
make a ∼ from *or* out of sth. mit etw. Geld
verdienen; **make [a few pence]** ∼ **on sth.**
[ein paar Pfennige] an etw. (*Dat.*) verdienen;
∼ **and loss** Gewinn und Verlust; ∼**-and-loss**
**account** Gewinn-und-Verlust-Rechnung, *die*
■ '**profit by** *v.t.* profitieren von; Nutzen
ziehen aus ⟨*Fehler, Erfahrung*⟩
■ '**profit from** *v.t.* profitieren von
**profitable** /'prɒfɪtəbl/ *adj.* rentabel;
einträglich; (fruitful) nützlich
**profiteer** /prɒfɪ'tɪə(r)/ ① *n.* Profitmacher,
*der*/-macherin, *die*
② *v.i.* sich bereichern
**profi'teering** *n.* Wucher, *der*
**profit:** ∼ **margin** *n.* Gewinnspanne, *die;*
∼**-sharing** *n.* Gewinnbeteiligung, *die*
**profligate** /'prɒflɪgət/ *adj.*
verschwenderisch; **be** ∼ **of** *or* **with sth.**
verschwenderisch umgehen mit etw.
**profound** /prə'faʊnd/ *adj.* tief; nachhaltig
⟨*Wirkung, Einfluss*⟩; tief greifend ⟨*Wandel,*
*Veränderung*⟩; tief empfunden ⟨*Beileid,*
*Mitgefühl*⟩; tief sitzend ⟨*Misstrauen*⟩
**prognosis** /prɒg'nəʊsɪs/ *n., pl.* prognoses
/prɒg'nəʊsiːz/ Prognose, *die*
**program** /'prəʊgræm/ ① *n.* **(a)** (Amer.)
▶ PROGRAMME 1
**(b)** (Comp.) Programm, *das;* ∼ **file**
Programmdata, *die*
② *v.t.,* **-mm-** (Comp.) programmieren
**programme** /'prəʊgræm/ *n.* **(a)** ([notice of]
events) Programm, *das*
**(b)** (Radio, Telev.) Sendung, *die*
**(c)** (plan, instructions for machine) Programm,
*das*
**programmer** /'prəʊgræmə(r)/ *n.* (Comp.)
Programmierer, *der*/Programmiererin, *die*
**progress** ① /'prəʊgres/ *n.* **(a)** *no pl., no*
*indef. art.* (onward movement)
[Vorwärts]bewegung, *die*
**(b)** (advance) Fortschritt, *der;* **make** ∼:
vorankommen; ⟨*Student, Patient:*⟩
Fortschritte machen; **in** ∼: im Gange
② /prə'gres/ *v.i.* **(a)** (move forward)
vorankommen
**(b)** (be carried on, develop) Fortschritte machen
**progression** /prə'greʃn/ *n.* **(a)**
(development) Fortschritt, *der*
**(b)** (succession) Folge, *die*
**progressive** /prə'gresɪv/ *adj.* **(a)**
fortschreitend ⟨*Verbesserung,*
*Verschlechterung*⟩; schrittweise ⟨*Reform*⟩;
allmählich ⟨*Veränderung*⟩
**(b)** (favouring reform; in culture) fortschrittlich;
progressiv
**pro'gressively** *adv.* immer ⟨*schlechter,*
*weiter*⟩
**prohibit** /prə'hɪbɪt/ *v.t.* (forbid) verbieten;
∼ **sb.'s doing sth.,** ∼ **sb. from doing sth.**
jmdm. verbieten, etw. zu tun

**prohibition** /prəʊhɪ'bɪʃn, prəʊɪ'bɪʃn/ *n.*
Verbot, *das*
**prohibitive** /prə'hɪbɪtɪv/ *adj.*
unerschwinglich ⟨*Preis, Miete*⟩; untragbar
⟨*Kosten*⟩
**project** ① /prə'dʒekt/ *v.t.* werfen ⟨*Schein*⟩;
senden ⟨*Strahl*⟩; (Cinemat.) projizieren
② /prə'dʒekt/ *v.i.* (jut out) ⟨*Felsen:*⟩
vorspringen; ⟨*Zähne, Brauen:*⟩ vorstehen
③ /'prɒdʒekt/ *n.* Projekt, *das*
**projectile** /prə'dʒektaɪl/ *n.* Geschoss, *das*
**projection** /prə'dʒekʃn/ *n.* **(a)** (protruding
thing) Vorsprung, *der*
**(b)** (estimate) Hochrechnung, *die;* (forecast)
Voraussage, *die*
**projectionist** /prə'dʒekʃənɪst/ *n.* (Cinemat.)
Filmvorführer, *der*/-vorführerin, *die*
**pro'jection room** *n.* (Cinemat.)
Vorführraum, *der*
**projector** /prə'dʒektə(r)/ *n.* Projektor, *der*
**proletarian** /prəʊlɪ'teərɪən/ ① *adj.*
proletarisch
② *n.* Proletarier, *der*/Proletarierin, *die*
'**pro-life** *adj.* Lebensschutz-
'**pro-lifer** *n.* Verfechter, *der*/Verfechterin,
*die* des Rechts auf Leben
**proliferate** /prə'lɪfəreɪt/ *v.i.* (increase) sich
ausbreiten
**proliferation** /prəlɪfə'reɪʃn/ *n.* starke
Zunahme
**prolific** /prə'lɪfɪk/ *adj.* **(a)** (fertile) fruchtbar
**(b)** (productive) produktiv
**prologue** (Amer.: **prolog**) /'prəʊlɒg/ *n.*
Prolog, *der* (**to** zu)
**prolong** /prə'lɒŋ/ *v.t.* verlängern
**prolonged** /prə'lɒŋd/ *adj.* lang; lang
anhaltend ⟨*Beifall*⟩
**promenade** /prɒmə'nɑːd/ *n.* Promenade,
*die*
**prominence** /'prɒmɪnəns/ *n.* **(a)**
(conspicuousness) Auffälligkeit, *die*
**(b)** (distinction) Bekanntheit, *die*
**prominent** /'prɒmɪnənt/ *adj.* **(a)**
(conspicuous) auffallend
**(b)** (foremost) herausragend; **he was** ∼ **in**
**politics** er war ein prominenter Politiker
**(c)** (projecting) vorspringend; vorstehend
⟨*Backenknochen, Brauen*⟩
**promiscuity** /prɒmɪ'skjuːɪtɪ/ *n.*
Promiskuität, *die* (geh.)
**promiscuous** /prə'mɪskjʊəs/ *adj.*
promiskuitiv (geh.); **a** ∼ **man** ein Mann, der
häufig die Partnerin wechselt
**promise** /'prɒmɪs/ ① *n.* **(a)** Versprechen,
*das; sb.'s* ∼**s** jmds. Versprechungen; **give** *or*
**make a** ∼ **[to sb.]** [jmdm.] ein Versprechen
geben; **give** *or* **make a** ∼ **[to sb.] to do sth.**
[jmdm.] versprechen, etw. zu tun
**(b)** (fig.: reason for expectation) Hoffnung, *die;* **a**
**painter of** *or* **with** ∼: ein viel versprechender
Maler
② *v.t.* **(a)** versprechen; ∼ **sth. to sb.,** ∼ **sb.**
**sth.** jmdm. etw. versprechen
····❯

**(b)** (fig.: give reason for expectation of) verheißen (geh.); ~ **sb. sth.** jmdm. etw. in Aussicht stellen

③ *v.i.* ~ **well** *or* **favourably** viel versprechend sein; **I can't** ~: ich kann es nicht versprechen

**promising** /'prɒmɪsɪŋ/ *adj.* viel versprechend

**promote** /prə'məʊt/ *v.t.* **(a)** (to more senior job) befördern

**(b)** (encourage) fördern

**(c)** (publicize) Werbung machen für

**(d)** (Footb.) **be ~d** aufsteigen

**pro'moter** *n.* Veranstalter, *der*/ Veranstalterin, *die*

**promotion** /prə'məʊʃn/ *n.* **(a)** Beförderung, *die;* **win** *or* **gain** ~: befördert werden

**(b)** (furtherance) Förderung, *die*

**(c)** (publicization) Werbung, *die;* (instance) Werbekampagne, *die*

**(d)** (Footb.) Aufstieg, *der*

**promotional** /prə'məʊʃənl/ *adj.* Werbe⟨kampagne, -broschüre usw.⟩

**prompt** /prɒmpt/ ① *adj.* **(a)** (ready to act) bereitwillig; **be** ~ **in doing sth.** *or* **to do sth.** etw. unverzüglich tun

**(b)** (done readily) sofortig; **her** ~ **answer** ihre prompte Antwort; **take** ~ **action** sofort handeln

**(c)** (punctual) pünktlich

② *adv.* pünktlich; **at 6 o'clock** ~: Punkt 6 Uhr

③ *v.t.* **(a)** (incite) veranlassen

**(b)** (supply with words) soufflieren (+ *Dat.*); (give suggestion to) weiterhelfen (+ *Dat.*)

**(c)** hervorrufen ⟨Kritik⟩; provozieren ⟨Antwort⟩

**'promptly** *adv.* **(a)** (quickly) prompt

**(b)** (punctually) pünktlich

**prone** /prəʊn/ *adj.* (liable) **be** ~ **to** anfällig sein für ⟨Krankheiten⟩; **be** ~ **to do sth.** dazu neigen, etw. zu tun

**prong** /prɒŋ/ *n.* (of fork) Zinke, *die*

**pronoun** /'prəʊnaʊn/ *n.* (Ling.) Pronomen, *das;* Fürwort, *das*

**pronounce** /prə'naʊns/ ① *v.t.* **(a)** (declare) verkünden; ~ **sb./sth. [to be] sth.** jmdn./etw. für etw. erklären; ~ **sb. fit for work** jmdn. für arbeitsfähig erklären

**(b)** aussprechen ⟨Wort, Buchstaben usw.⟩

② *v.i.* ~ **on sth.** zu etw. Stellung nehmen; ~ **for** *or* **in favour of/against sth.** sich für/ gegen etw. aussprechen

**pronounced** /prə'naʊnst/ *adj.* (marked) ausgeprägt

**pro'nouncement** *n.* Erklärung, *die;* **make a** ~ **[about sth.]** eine Erklärung [zu etw.] abgeben

**pronunciation** /prənʌnsɪ'eɪʃn/ *n.* Aussprache, *die;* **what is the** ~ **of this word?** wie wird dieses Wort ausgesprochen?

**proof** /pruːf/ ① *n.* **(a)** (fact, evidence) Beweis, *der*

**(b)** *no indef. art.* (Law) Beweismaterial, *das*

**(c)** (proving) **in** ~ **of** zum Beweis (+ *Gen.*)

**(d)** *no art.* (standard of strength) Proof *o. Art.;* **100°** ~ (Brit.), **128°** ~ (Amer.) 64 Vol.-% Alkohol

② *adj.* **(a)** **be** ~ **against sth.** unempfindlich gegen etw. sein; (fig.) gegen etw. immun sein

**(b)** *in comb.* ⟨kugel-, einbruch-, idioten⟩sicher; ⟨schall-, wasser⟩dicht; **flame-** ~: nicht brennbar

**proof ~-read** *v.t.* Korrektur lesen; **~-reader** *n.* Korrektor, *der*/Korrektorin, *die*

**prop**[1] /prɒp/ ① *n.* Stütze, *die;* (Mining) Strebe, *die*

② *v.t.,* **-pp-** stützen; **the ladder was** ~**ped against the house** die Leiter war gegen das Haus gelehnt

■ **prop 'up** *v.t.* stützen; (fig.) vor dem Konkurs bewahren ⟨Firma⟩; stützen ⟨Regierung⟩

**prop**[2] *n.* (Theatre, Cinemat.: also fig.) Requisit, *das*

**propaganda** /prɒpə'gændə/ *n.* Propaganda, *die*

**propagate** /'prɒpəgeɪt/ ① *v.t.* **(a)** (Hort., Agric.) vermehren **(from, by** durch)

**(b)** (spread) verbreiten

② *v.i.* **(a)** (Bot.) sich vermehren

**(b)** (spread) sich ausbreiten

**propagation** /prɒpə'geɪʃn/ *n.* **(a)** (Hort., Agric.) Züchtung, *die*

**(b)** (Bot.) Vermehrung, *die*

**(c)** (spreading) Verbreitung, *die*

**propel** /prə'pel/ *v.t.,* **-ll-** antreiben

**propellant** /prə'pelənt/ *n.* **(a)** Treibstoff, *der*

**(b)** (of aerosol spray) Treibgas, *das*

**pro'peller** *n.* Propeller, *der*

**propelling 'pencil** *n.* (Brit.) Drehbleistift, *der*

**propensity** /prə'pensɪtɪ/ *n.* **have a** ~ **to do sth.** *or* **for doing sth.** dazu neigen, etw. zu tun

**proper** /'prɒpə(r)/ *adj.* **(a)** (accurate) richtig; zutreffend ⟨Beschreibung⟩; eigentlich ⟨Wortbedeutung⟩

**(b)** *postpos.* (strictly so called) im engeren Sinn *nachgestellt;* **in London** ~: in London selbst

**(c)** (genuine) echt; richtig ⟨Wirbelsturm, Schauspieler⟩

**(d)** (satisfactory) richtig; zufrieden stellend ⟨Antwort⟩

**(e)** (suitable) angemessen; (morally fitting) gebührend; **do sth. the** ~ **way** etw. richtig machen

**(f)** *attrib.* (coll.: thorough) richtig

**'properly** *adv.* richtig; (rightly) zu Recht; ~ **speaking** genau genommen

**proper 'name, proper 'noun** *ns.* (Ling.) Eigenname, *der*

**property** /'prɒpətɪ/ *n.* **(a)** (possession[s]) Eigentum, *das;* **lost** ~ **[department** *or* **office]** Fundbüro, *das*

**(b)** (estate) Besitz, *der;* Immobilie, *die* (fachspr.)
**(c)** (attribute) Eigenschaft, *die;* (effect, special power) Wirkung, *die*
**'property developer** *n.* ≈ Bauunternehmer, *der*/-unternehmerin, *die*
**prophecy** /ˈprɒfɪsɪ/ *n.* (prediction) Vorhersage, *die;* (prophetic utterance) Prophezeiung, *die*
**prophesy** /ˈprɒfɪsaɪ/ *v.t.* (predict) vorhersagen; (fig.) prophezeien ⟨*Unglück*⟩; (as fortune teller) weissagen
**prophet** /ˈprɒfɪt/ *n.* Prophet, *der*
**prophetic** /prəˈfetɪk/ *adj.* prophetisch
**proportion** /prəˈpɔːʃn/ ① *n.* **(a)** (portion) Teil, *der*
**(b)** (ratio) Verhältnis, *das;* the ∼ of sth. to sth. das Verhältnis von etw. zu etw.
**(c)** (correct relation; Math.) Proportion, *die;* be in ∼ [to *or* with sth.] im richtigen Verhältnis [zu *od.* mit etw.] stehen; keep things in ∼ (fig.) die Dinge im richtigen Licht sehen; be out of ∼/all *or* any ∼ [to *or* with sth.] in keinem/keinerlei Verhältnis zu etw. stehen
**(d)** *in pl.* (size) Dimensionen *Pl.*
② *v.t.* proportionieren
**proportional** /prəˈpɔːʃənl/ *adj.* **(a)** (in proportion) entsprechend; be ∼ to sth. einer Sache (*Dat.*) entsprechen
**(b)** (Math.) be directly/indirectly ∼ to sth. einer Sache (*Dat.*) direkt/umgekehrt proportional sein
**proportionate** /prəˈpɔːʃənət/
▶ PROPORTIONAL A
**proposal** /prəˈpəʊzl/ *n.* Vorschlag, *der;* (offer) Angebot, *das;* ∼ [of marriage] [Heirats]antrag, *der*
**propose** /prəˈpəʊz/ ① *v.t.* **(a)** vorschlagen; ∼ sth. to sb. jmdm. etw. vorschlagen; ∼ marriage [to sb.] [jmdm.] einen Heiratsantrag machen
**(b)** (nominate) ∼ sb. as/for sth. jmdn. als/für etw. vorschlagen
**(c)** (intend) ∼ doing *or* to do sth. beabsichtigen, etw. zu tun
② *v.i.* (offer marriage) ∼ [to sb.] jmdm. einen Heiratsantrag machen
**proposition** /prɒpəˈzɪʃn/ *n.* **(a)** (proposal) Vorschlag, *der;* make *or* put a ∼ to sb. jmdm. einen Vorschlag machen
**(b)** (statement; Logic) Aussage, *die*
**propound** /prəˈpaʊnd/ *v.t.* darlegen
**proprietary** /prəˈpraɪətərɪ/ *adj.* ∼ name *or* term Markenname, *der*
**proprietor** /prəˈpraɪətə(r)/ *n.* Inhaber, *der*/ Inhaberin, *die*
**propriety** /prəˈpraɪətɪ/ *n.* Anstand, *der;* breach of ∼: Verstoß gegen die guten Sitten
**propulsion** /prəˈpʌlʃn/ *n.* Antrieb, *der*
**prosaic** /prəˈzeɪɪk/ *adj.* prosaisch (geh.); nüchtern
**proscribe** /prəˈskraɪb/ *v.t.* verbieten

**prose** /prəʊz/ *n.* Prosa, *die; attrib.* Prosa⟨*werk, -stil*⟩
**prosecute** /ˈprɒsɪkjuːt/ ① *v.t.* strafrechtlich verfolgen; ∼ sb. for sth./doing sth. jmdn. wegen etw. strafrechtlich verfolgen/jmdn. strafrechtlich verfolgen, weil er etw. tut/getan hat
② *v.i.* Anzeige erstatten
**prosecution** /prɒsɪˈkjuːʃn/ *n.* (bringing to trial) [strafrechtliche] Verfolgung; (court procedure) Anklage, *die;* (prosecuting party) Anklage[vertretung], *die;* the ∼: die Anklage
**prosecutor** /ˈprɒsɪkjuːtə(r)/ *n.* Ankläger, *der*/Anklägerin, *die;* public ∼ ≈ Generalstaatsanwalt, *der*/-anwältin, *die*
**prospect** ① /ˈprɒspekt/ *n.* **(a)** (expectation) Erwartung, *die* (of hinsichtlich); [at the] ∼ of sth./doing sth. [bei der] Aussicht auf etw. (*Akk.*)/[darauf], etw. zu tun
**(b)** *in pl.* (hope of success) Zukunftsaussichten *Pl.;* a man with [good] ∼s ein Mann mit Zukunft; sb.'s ∼s of sth./doing sth. jmds. Chancen auf etw. (*Akk.*)/darauf, etw. zu tun; the ∼s for sb./sth. die Aussichten für jmdn./ etw.
② /prəˈspekt/ *v.i.* nach Bodenschätzen suchen
**prospective** /prəˈspektɪv/ *adj.* voraussichtlich; zukünftig ⟨*Erbe, Braut*⟩; potenziell ⟨*Käufer, Kandidat*⟩
**prospector** /prəˈspektə(r)/ *n.* Prospektor, *der;* (for gold) Goldsucher, *der*
**prospectus** /prəˈspektəs/ *n.* Prospekt, *der;* (Brit. Univ.) Studienführer, *der*
**prosper** /ˈprɒspə(r)/ *v.i.* gedeihen; ⟨*Geschäft:*⟩ florieren; ⟨*Berufstätiger:*⟩ Erfolg haben
**prosperity** /prɒˈsperɪtɪ/ *n.* Wohlstand, *der*
**prosperous** /ˈprɒspərəs/ *adj.* wohlhabend; florierend ⟨*Unternehmen*⟩
**prostitute** /ˈprɒstɪtjuːt/ *n.* Prostituierte, *die*
**prostitution** /prɒstɪˈtjuːʃn/ *n.* Prostitution, *die*
**prostrate** ① /ˈprɒstreɪt/ *adj.* [auf dem Bauch] ausgestreckt
② /prəˈstreɪt/ *v. refl.* ∼ oneself [at sth./ before sb.] sich [vor etw./jmdm.] niederwerfen
**protagonist** /prəˈtæɡənɪst/ *n.* (Lit.) Protagonist, *der*/Protagonistin, *die*
**protect** /prəˈtekt/ *v.t.* **(a)** schützen (from vor + *Dat.,* against gegen)
**(b)** (preserve) unter [Natur]schutz stellen ⟨*Pflanze, Tier*⟩
**protection** /prəˈtekʃn/ *n.* Schutz, *der* (from vor + *Dat.,* against gegen)
**protective** /prəˈtektɪv/ *adj.* schützend; Schutz⟨*hülle, -anstrich, -vorrichtung, -maske*⟩; be ∼ towards sb. fürsorglich gegenüber jmdm. sein
**protein** /ˈprəʊtiːn/ *n.* Protein, *das* (fachspr.); Eiweiß, *das*

**protest** ⟦1⟧ /'prəʊtest/ *n.* **(a)** Beschwerde, *die;* **make** *or* **lodge a ~ [against sb./sth.]** eine Beschwerde [gegen jmdn./etw.] einreichen **(b)** (gesture of disapproval) **~[s]** Protest, *der;* **under ~:** unter Protest; **in ~ [against sth.]** aus Protest [gegen etw.] **(c)** *no art.* (dissent) Protest, *der* ⟦2⟧ /prə'test/ *v.t.* (affirm) beteuern ⟦3⟧ /prə'test/ *v.i.* protestieren **(about** gegen); **(make written or formal ~)** Protest einlegen **(to** bei)

**Protestant** /'prɒtɪstənt/ ⟦1⟧ *n.* Protestant, *der*/Protestantin, *die* ⟦2⟧ *adj.* protestantisch; evangelisch

**Protestantism** /'prɒtɪstəntɪzm/ *n., no art.* Protestantismus, *der*

**pro'tester** *n.* Protestierende, *der*/*die;* (at demonstration) Demonstrant, *der*/Demonstrantin, *die*

**protocol** /'prəʊtəkɒl/ *n.* Protokoll, *das*

**proton** /'prəʊtən/ *n.* Proton, *das*

**prototype** /'prəʊtətaɪp/ *n.* Prototyp, *der*

**protract** /prə'trækt/ *v.t.* verlängern

**protractor** /prə'træktə(r)/ *n.* (Geom.) Winkelmesser, *der*

**protrude** /prə'truːd/ *v.i.* herausragen **(from** aus); ⟨Zähne⟩ vorstehen

**protuberance** /prə'tjuːbərəns/ *n.* Auswuchs, *der*

**proud** /praʊd/ ⟦1⟧ *adj.* **(a)** stolz; **~ to do sth.** *or* **to be doing sth.** stolz darauf, etw. zu tun; **~ of sb./sth./doing sth.** stolz auf jmdn./etw./darauf, etw. zu tun **(b)** (arrogant) hochmütig ⟦2⟧ *adv.* (Brit. coll.) **do sb. ~:** jmdn. verwöhnen

**'proudly** *adv.* **(a)** stolz **(b)** (arrogantly) hochmütig

**provable** /'pruːvəbl/ *adj.* beweisbar

**prove** /pruːv/ ⟦1⟧ *v.t., p.p.* **~d** *or* **proven** /'pruːvn/ beweisen; nachweisen ⟨Identität⟩; **~ one's ability** sein Können unter Beweis stellen; **~ sb. right/wrong** ⟨Ereignis:⟩ jmdm. recht/unrecht geben; **be ~d wrong** *or* **to be false** ⟨Theorie:⟩ widerlegt werden; **~ one's/sb.'s case** *or* **point** beweisen, dass man recht hat/jmdm. recht geben ⟦2⟧ *v. refl., p. p.* **proved** *or* **proven: ~ oneself** sich bewähren ⟦3⟧ *v.i., p. p.* **proved** *or* **proven: ~ [to be]** sich erweisen als

**proven** ▸ PROVE

**proverb** /'prɒvɜːb/ *n.* Sprichwort, *das*

**proverbial** /prə'vɜːbɪəl/ *adj.* sprichwörtlich

**provide** /prə'vaɪd/ *v.t.* **(a)** besorgen; liefern ⟨Beweis⟩; bereitstellen ⟨Dienst, Geld⟩; **~ a home/a car for us** jmdm. Unterkunft/ein Auto [zur Verfügung] stellen **(b)** ⟨Vertrag, Gesetz:⟩ vorsehen ▪ **pro'vide for** *v.t.* **(a)** (make provision for) vorsorgen für; ⟨Plan, Gesetz:⟩ vorsehen **(b)** (maintain) sorgen für, versorgen ⟨Familie, Kind⟩

**pro'vided** *conj.* **~ [that]** ...: vorausgesetzt, [dass] ...

**providence** /'prɒvɪdəns/ *n.* **(a)** [divine] **~:** die [göttliche] Vorsehung **(b)** P**~** (God) der Himmel

**province** /'prɒvɪns/ *n.* **(a)** Provinz, *die* **(b) the ~s** (regions outside capital) die Provinz **(c)** (sphere of action) [Tätigkeits]bereich, *der;* (area of responsibility) Zuständigkeitsbereich, *der*

**provincial** /prə'vɪnʃl/ *adj.* Provinz-

**provision** /prə'vɪʒn/ *n.* **(a)** (providing) Bereitstellung, *die;* **make ~ for** vorsorgen od. Vorsorge treffen für ⟨Notfall⟩ **(b) ~s** *pl.* (food) Lebensmittel *Pl.*

**provisional** /prə'vɪʒənl/ *adj.,* **provisionally** /prə'vɪʒənəlɪ/ *adv.* vorläufig; provisorisch

**proviso** /prə'vaɪzəʊ/ *n., pl.* **~s** Vorbehalt, *der*

**provocation** /prɒvə'keɪʃn/ *n.* Provokation, *die*

**provocative** /prə'vɒkətɪv/ *adj.* provozierend; (sexually) aufreizend

**provoke** /prə'vəʊk/ *v.t.* **(a)** provozieren ⟨Person⟩; reizen ⟨Person, Tier⟩; **~ sb. into doing sth.** jmdn. so sehr provozieren, dass er etw. tut **(b)** (give rise to) hervorrufen; erregen

**prow** /praʊ/ *n.* (Naut.) Bug, *der*

**prowl** /praʊl/ ⟦1⟧ *v.i.* streifen ⟦2⟧ *v.t.* durchstreifen ⟦3⟧ *n.* **be on the ~:** auf einem Streifzug sein

**proximity** /prɒk'sɪmɪtɪ/ *n.* Nähe, *die*

**proxy** /'prɒksɪ/ *n.* **by ~:** durch einen Bevollmächtigten/eine Bevollmächtigte

**prude** /pruːd/ *n.* prüder Mensch

**prudence** /'pruːdəns/ *n.* Besonnenheit, *die*

**prudent** /'pruːdənt/ *adj.* **(a)** (careful) besonnen **(b)** (circumspect) vorsichtig

**prudish** /'pruːdɪʃ/ *adj.* prüde

**prune**[1] /pruːn/ *n.* Backpflaume, *die*

**prune**[2] *v.t.* **(a)** (trim) [be]schneiden **(b)** (fig.) reduzieren

**pry** /praɪ/ *v.i.* neugierig sein ▪ **'pry into** *v.t.* seine Nase stecken in (+ *Akk.*) (ugs.) ⟨Angelegenheit⟩

**PS** *abbr.* = **postscript** PS

**psalm** /sɑːm/ *n.* Psalm, *der*

**pseudo** /'sjuːdəʊ/ ⟦1⟧ *adj.* **(a)** (sham) unecht **(b)** (insincere) verlogen ⟦2⟧ *n., pl.* **~s** (pretentious person) Möchtegern, *der* (ugs. spött.)

**pseudonym** /'sjuːdənɪm/ *n.* Pseudonym, *das*

**psychiatric** /saɪkɪ'ætrɪk/ *adj.* psychiatrisch

**psychiatrist** /saɪ'kaɪətrɪst/ *n.* Psychiater, *der*/Psychiaterin, *die*

**psychiatry** /saɪ'kaɪətrɪ/ *n.* Psychiatrie, *die*

**psychic** /'saɪkɪk/ adj. be ∼:
übernatürliche Fähigkeiten haben

**psychoanalyse** /saɪkəʊ'ænəlaɪz/ v.t.
psychoanalysieren

**psychoa'nalysis** n. Psychoanalyse, die

**psycho'analyst** n. Psychoanalytiker,
der/-analytikerin, die

**psychological** /saɪkə'lɒdʒɪkl/ adj.
psychologisch; psychisch ⟨Problem⟩

**psychologist** /saɪ'kɒlədʒɪst/ n.
Psychologe, der/Psychologin, die

**psychology** /saɪ'kɒlədʒɪ/ n. Psychologie,
die

**psychopath** /'saɪkəpæθ/ n. Psychopath,
der/Psychopathin, die

**psychopathic** /saɪkə'pæθɪk/ adj.
psychopathisch

**psychosis** /saɪ'kəʊsɪs/ n., pl. **psychoses**
/saɪ'kəʊsiːz/ Psychose, die

**psychotherapist** /saɪkəʊ'θerəpɪst/ n.
Psychotherapeut, der/-therapeutin, die

**psycho'therapy** n. Psychotherapie, die

**psychotic** /saɪ'kɒtɪk/ adj. psychotisch

**PTO** abbr. = **please turn over** b.w.

**pub** /ʌb/ n. (Brit. coll.) Kneipe, die (ugs.)

**'pub crawl** n. (Brit. coll.) Zechtour, die (ugs.)

**puberty** /'pjuːbətɪ/ n., no art. Pubertät, die

**'pub grub** n. (Brit. coll.) Kneipenessen, das
(ugs.)

**pubic** /'pjuːbɪk/ adj. Scham-

**public** /'pʌblɪk/ ① adj. öffentlich; **make
sth.** ∼: etw. bekannt machen
② n., sing. or pl. (a) (the people)
Öffentlichkeit, die
(b) (section of community) Publikum, das
(c) **in** ∼: öffentlich

**publican** /'pʌblɪkən/ n. (Brit.) [Gast]wirt,
der/-wirtin, die

**publication** /pʌblɪ'keɪʃn/ n.
Veröffentlichung, die

**public:** ∼ **'building** n. öffentliches
Gebäude; ∼ **con'venience** n. öffentliche
Toilette; ∼ **'figure** n. Persönlichkeit des
öffentlichen Lebens; ∼ **'footpath** n.
öffentlicher Fußweg; ∼ **'holiday** n.
gesetzlicher Feiertag; ∼ **'house** n. (Brit.)
Gastwirtschaft, die; Gaststätte, die

**publicity** /pʌb'lɪsɪtɪ/ n. Publicity, die;
(advertising) Werbung, die; ∼ **campaign**
Werbekampagne, die

**pub'licity agent** n. Publicitymanager,
der/-managerin, die

**publicize** /'pʌblɪsaɪz/ v.t. publik machen
⟨Ungerechtigkeit⟩; werben für, Reklame
machen für ⟨Produkt⟩

**public:** ∼ **'library** n. öffentliche Bücherei;
∼ **limited company** n. (Brit.) ≈
Aktiengesellschaft, die

**'publicly** adv. öffentlich; ∼ **owned**
staatseigen

**public:** ∼ **property** n. Staatsbesitz, der;
∼ **re'lations** n., sing. or pl.

Publicrelations Pl.; ∼ **school** n. (a) (Brit.)
Privatschule, die; (b) (Scot., Amer.) staatliche
od. öffentliche Schule; ∼ **'servant** n.
Inhaber/Inhaberin eines öffentlichen Amtes;
∼ **'transport** n. öffentlicher
Personenverkehr

**publish** /'pʌblɪʃ/ v.t. ⟨Verlag:⟩ verlegen
⟨Buch, Zeitschrift, Musik usw.⟩; ⟨Autor:⟩
veröffentlichen ⟨Text⟩

**'publisher** n. Verleger, der/Verlegerin, die;
∼[s] (company) Verlag, der

**'publishing** n., no art. Verlagswesen, das

**puck** /pʌk/ n. (Ice Hockey) Puck, der

**pucker** /'pʌkə(r)/ ① v.t. ∼ [up] runzeln
⟨Brauen, Stirn⟩; kräuseln ⟨Lippen⟩
② v.i. ∼ [up] ⟨Stoff:⟩ sich kräuseln

**pudding** /'pʊdɪŋ/ n. (a) Pudding, der
(b) (dessert) süße Nachspeise

**puddle** /'pʌdl/ n. Pfütze, die

**puerile** /'pjʊəraɪl/ adj. kindisch

**puff** /pʌf/ ① n. (a) Stoß, der; ∼ **of breath/
wind** Atem-/Windstoß, der
(b) ∼ **of smoke** Rauchstoß, der
(c) (pastry) Blätterteigteilchen, das
② v.i. (a) ∼ [and blow] schnaufen [und
keuchen]
(b) (∼ cigarette smoke etc.) paffen (ugs.) (at an
+ Dat.)
(c) ⟨Person:⟩ keuchen; ⟨Zug, Lokomotive⟩
schnaufend fahren
③ v.t. blasen ⟨Rauch⟩; stäuben ⟨Puder⟩

■ **puff 'out** v.t. (a) bauschen ⟨Segel⟩
(b) (put out of breath) außer Atem bringen
⟨Person⟩; **be** ∼**ed [out]** außer Atem sein

**puff 'pastry** n. Blätterteig, der

**puffy** /'pʌfɪ/ adj. verschwollen

**pugnacious** /pʌg'neɪʃəs/ adj. kampflustig

**puke** /pjuːk/ (coarse) ① v.i. kotzen (salopp)
② n. Kotze, die (salopp)

**pull** /pʊl/ ① v.t. (a) (draw, tug) ziehen an
(+ Dat.); ziehen ⟨Hebel⟩; ∼ **sb.'s** or **sb. by
the hair/ears/sleeve** jmdn. an den Haaren/
Ohren/am Ärmel ziehen; ∼ **sth. over one's
ears/head** sich (Dat.) etw. über die Ohren/
den Kopf ziehen; ∼ **to pieces** in Stücke
reißen; (fig.) zerpflücken ⟨Argument usw.⟩
(b) (extract) [her]ausziehen; [heraus]ziehen
⟨Zahn⟩
(c) (strain) sich (Dat.) zerren ⟨Muskel⟩
② v.i. (a) ziehen; 'P∼' „Ziehen"
(b) ∼ [to the left/right] ⟨Auto, Boot:⟩ [nach
links/rechts] ziehen
(c) (pluck) ∼ **at** sth. ziehen an (+ Dat.); ∼ **at sb.'s
sleeve** jmdn. am Ärmel ziehen
③ n. (a) Zug, der
(b) (influence) Einfluss, der (with auf + Akk.,
bei)

■ **pull a'part** v.t. (a) (take to pieces)
auseinander nehmen
(b) (fig.: criticize) zerpflücken; verreißen
⟨Buch, [literarisches] Werk⟩

■ **pull 'down** v.t. (a) herunterziehen
(b) (demolish) abreißen

■ **pull 'in** ① v.t. hereinziehen ···⟩

2 *v.i.* (a) ⟨*Zug:*⟩ einfahren
(b) (move to side of road) an die Seite fahren; (stop) anhalten
■ **pull 'off** *v.t.* (a) (remove) abziehen; (violently) abreißen
(b) (accomplish) an Land ziehen (ugs.)
■ **pull 'out** 1 *v.t.* herausziehen
2 *v.i.* (a) (depart) abfahren
(b) (away from roadside) ausscheren
■ **pull 'through** *v.i.* ⟨*Patient:*⟩ durchkommen
■ **pull to'gether** *v. refl.* sich zusammennehmen
■ **pull 'up** 1 *v.t.* (a) hochziehen
(b) [he]rausziehen ⟨*Unkraut, Pflanze*⟩
(c) (reprimand) zurechtweisen
2 *v.i.* (stop) anhalten
'**pull-down menu** *n.* (Comp.) Pull-down-Menü, *das*
**pulley** /'pʊlɪ/ *n.* Rolle, *die*
**pullover** /'pʊləʊvə(r)/ *n.* Pullover, *der*
**pulp** /pʌlp/ 1 *n.* Brei, *der*
2 *v.t.* zerdrücken ⟨*Rübe*⟩; einstampfen ⟨*Druckerzeugnis*⟩
**pulpit** /'pʊlpɪt/ *n.* Kanzel, *die*
**pulsate** /pʌl'seɪt/ *v.i.* pulsieren
**pulse**[1] /pʌls/ *n.* Puls, *der;* (single beat) Pulsschlag, *der*
**pulse**[2] *n.* (Cookery) Hülsenfrucht, *die*
'**pulse rate** *n.* Pulsfrequenz, *die*
**pulverize** /'pʌlvəraɪz/ *v.t.* pulverisieren
**puma** /'pjuːmə/ *n.* Puma, *der*
**pumice** /'pʌmɪs/ *n.* ~ [stone] Bimsstein, *der*
**pummel** /'pʌml/ *v.t.,* (Brit) -ll- einschlagen auf (+ *Akk.*)
**pump** /pʌmp/ 1 *n.* Pumpe, *die*
2 *v.i.* pumpen
3 *v.t.* pumpen; ~ sth. dry etw. leer pumpen; ~ sb. for information Auskünfte aus jmdm. herausholen; ~ up aufpumpen
'**pump-action** *adj.* ~ spray Pumpspray, *das od. der*
**pumpkin** /'pʌmpkɪn/ *n.* Kürbis, *der*
**pun** /pʌn/ *n.* Wortspiel, *das*
**punch**[1] 1 *v.t.* (a) (with fist) boxen
(b) (pierce) lochen; ~ a hole ein Loch stanzen; ~ a hole/holes in sth. etw. lochen
2 *n.* (a) (blow) Faustschlag, *der*
(b) (for making holes) (in leather, tickets) Lochzange, *die;* (in paper) Locher, *der*
**punch**[2] *n.* (drink) Punsch, *der*
**punch:** ~ **line** *n.* Pointe, *die;* ~-**up** *n.* (Brit. coll.) Prügelei, *die*
**punctual** /'pʌŋktjʊəl/ *adj.* pünktlich
**punctuality** /pʌŋktjʊ'ælɪtɪ/ *n.* Pünktlichkeit, *die*
'**punctually** *adv.* pünktlich
**punctuate** /pʌŋktjʊeɪt/ *v.t.* mit Satzzeichen versehen
**punctuation** /pʌŋktjʊ'eɪʃn/ *n.* Zeichensetzung, *die*

**punctu'ation mark** *n.* Satzzeichen, *das*
**puncture** /'pʌŋktʃə(r)/ 1 *n.* (a) (flat tyre) Reifenpanne, *die*
(b) (hole) Loch, *das*
2 *v.t.* durchstechen; be ~d ⟨*Reifen:*⟩ platt sein
**pundit** /'pʌndɪt/ *n.* Experte, *der*/Expertin, *die*
**pungent** /'pʌndʒənt/ *adj.* beißend, ätzend ⟨*Rauch*⟩; scharf ⟨*Soße*⟩; stechend riechend ⟨*Gas*⟩
**punish** /'pʌnɪʃ/ *v.t.* bestrafen
**punishable** /'pʌnɪʃəbl/ *adj.* strafbar
'**punishment** *n.* (a) (punishing) Bestrafung, *die*
(b) (penalty) Strafe, *die*
**punitive** /'pjuːnɪtɪv/ *adj.* (a) (penal) Straf-
(b) (severe) [allzu] rigoros
**punk** /pʌŋk/ *n.* (a) (Amer. sl.: worthless person) Dreckskerl, *der* (salopp)
(b) (admirer of ~ rock) Punk, *der;* (performer) Punk[rock]er, *der*/-[rock]erin, *die*
(c) (music) Punkrock, *der*
**punnet** /'pʌnɪt/ *n.* (Brit.) Körbchen, *das*
**punt** /pʌnt/ *n.* Stechkahn, *der*
**punter** *n.* (coll.) the ~s (customers) die Leutchen (ugs.)
**puny** /'pjuːnɪ/ *adj.* (a) (undersized) zu klein ⟨*Baby, Junge*⟩
(b) (feeble) gering ⟨*Kraft*⟩; schwach ⟨*Waffe, Person*⟩
**pup** /pʌp/ *n.* Welpe, *der*
**pupa** /'pjuːpə/ *n., pl.* ~e /'pjuːpiː/ Puppe, *die*
**pupate** /pjuː'peɪt/ *v.i.* sich verpuppen
**pupil** /'pjuːpɪl/ *n.* (a) Schüler, *der*/Schülerin, *die*
(b) (Anat.) Pupille, *die*
**puppet** /'pʌpɪt/ *n.* Puppe, *die;* (marionette; also fig.) Marionette, *die*
**puppy** /'pʌpɪ/ *n.* Hundejunge, *das;* Welpe, *der*
**puppy:** ~ **fat** *n.* (Brit.) Babyspeck, *der;* ~ **love** *n.* Jugendschwärmerei, *die*
**purchase** /'pɜːtʃəs/ 1 *n.* (a) Kauf, *der;* make a ~: etwas kaufen
(b) (hold) Halt, *der;* (leverage) Hebelwirkung, *die*
2 *v.t.* kaufen
'**purchase price** *n.* Kaufpreis, *der*
'**purchaser** *n.* Käufer, *der*/Käuferin, *die*
'**purchasing power** *n.* Kaufkraft, *die*
**pure** /pjʊə(r)/ *adj.* rein
**purée** /'pjʊəreɪ/ *n.* Püree, *das*
'**purely** *adv.* (a) (solely) rein
(b) (merely) lediglich
**purgatory** /'pɜːgətərɪ/ *n.* it was ~ (fig.) es war eine Strafe
**purge** /pɜːdʒ/ 1 *v.t.* (a) (cleanse) reinigen (of von)
(b) (remove) entfernen
(c) (rid) säubern ⟨*Partei*⟩ (of von)
2 *n.* Säuberung[saktion], *die*

**purification** /pjʊərɪfɪˈkeɪʃn/ n. Reinigung, die

**purify** /ˈpjʊərɪfaɪ/ v.t. reinigen

**purist** /ˈpjʊərɪst/ n. Purist, der/Puristin, die

**puritan,** (Hist.) **Puritan** /ˈpjʊərɪtn/ n. Puritaner, der/Puritanerin, die

**puritanical** /pjʊərɪˈtænɪkl/ adj. puritanisch

**purity** /ˈpjʊərɪtɪ/ n. Reinheit, die

**purl** /pɜːl/ ① n. linke Masche
② v.t. links stricken; ~ three [stitches] drei linke Maschen stricken

**purple** /ˈpɜːpl/ ① adj. lila; violett
② n. Lila, das; Violett, das

**purport** /pəˈpɔːt/ v.t. ~ to do sth. (profess) [von sich] behaupten, etw. zu tun; (be intended to seem) den Anschein erwecken sollen, etw. zu tun

**purpose** /ˈpɜːpəs/ n. (a) (object) Zweck, der; (intention) Absicht, die; what is the ~ of doing that? was hat es für einen Zweck, das zu tun?; on ~: mit Absicht; absichtlich
(b) (effect) to no ~: ohne Erfolg; to some/good ~: mit einigem/gutem Erfolg
(c) (determination) Entschlossenheit, die

**'purpose-built** adj. [eigens] zu diesem Zweck errichtet ⟨Gebäude⟩

**purposeful** /ˈpɜːpəsfl/ adj. zielstrebig; (with specific aim) entschlossen

**'purposely** adv. absichtlich

**'purpose-made** adj. spezialgefertigt

**purr** /pɜː(r)/ ① v.i. schnurren
② n. Schnurren, das

**purse** /pɜːs/ ① n. Portemonnaie, das
② v.t. kräuseln ⟨Lippen⟩

**purser** /ˈpɜːsə(r)/ n. Zahlmeister, der/-meisterin, die

**pursue** /pəˈsjuː/ v.t. (a) (chase) verfolgen
(b) (look into) nachgehen (+ Dat.)
(c) (engage in) betreiben

**pursuer** /pəˈsjuːə(r)/ n. Verfolger, der/Verfolgerin, die

**pursuit** /pəˈsjuːt/ n. (a) Verfolgung, die; (of knowledge, truth, etc.) Streben, das (of nach); in ~ of auf der Jagd nach ⟨Wild, Dieb usw.⟩; in Ausführung (+ Gen.) ⟨Beschäftigung⟩; with the police in [full] ~: mit der Polizei [dicht] auf den Fersen
(b) (pastime) Beschäftigung, die

**pus** /pʌs/ n. Eiter, der

**push** /pʊʃ/ ① v.t. (a) schieben; (make fall) stoßen; drücken gegen ⟨Tür⟩; ~ one's way through/into/on to etc. sth. sich (Dat.) einen Weg durch/in/auf usw. etw. (Akk.) bahnen
(b) (fig.: impel) drängen
(c) (tax) ~ sb. [hard] jmdn. [stark] fordern; be ~ed for sth. (coll.: find it difficult to provide sth.) mit etw. knapp sein; be ~ed for money or cash knapp bei Kasse sein (ugs.)
(d) (sell illegally, esp. drugs) pushen (Drogenjargon)

② v.i. (a) schieben; (in queue) drängeln; (at door) drücken; ~ and shove schubsen und drängeln
(b) (make demands) ~ for sth. etw. fordern
(c) (make one's way) he ~ed between us er drängte sich zwischen uns; ~ through the crowd sich durch die Menge drängeln
③ n. (a) Stoß, der; give sth. a ~: etw. schieben
(b) (effort) Anstrengungen Pl.; (Mil.: attack) Vorstoß, der
(c) (crisis) when it comes to the ~, (Amer. coll.) when ~ comes to shove wenn es ernst wird
(d) (Brit. coll.: dismissal) get the ~: rausfliegen (ugs.)

■ **push a'head** v.i. ~ ahead with sth. etw. vorantreiben

■ **push 'in** v.i. sich hineindrängen

■ **push 'off** v.i. (a) (Boating) abstoßen
(b) (coll.: leave) abhauen (salopp)

■ **push 'on** ① v.i. (with plans etc.) weitermachen
② v.t. draufdrücken ⟨Deckel usw.⟩

■ **push 'up** v.t. hochschieben; (fig.) hochtreiben

**push: ~bike** n. (Brit. coll.) Fahrrad, das; **~-button** n. [Druck]knopf, der; Drucktaste, die; **~chair** n. (Brit.) Sportwagen, der

**pusher** /ˈpʊʃə(r)/ n. (seller of drugs) Dealer, der/Dealerin, die

**'pushover** n. (coll.) Kinderspiel, das

**pushy** /ˈpʊʃɪ/ adj. (coll.) [übermäßig] ehrgeizig ⟨Person⟩

**pussy** /ˈpʊsɪ/ n. (child lang.: cat) Miezekatze, die (fam.)

**put** /pʊt/ ① v.t., -tt-, put (a) (place) tun; (vertically) stellen; (horizontally) legen; ~ plates on the table Teller auf den Tisch stellen; ~ a stamp on the letter eine Briefmarke auf den Brief kleben; ~ the letter in an envelope/the letter box den Brief in einen Umschlag/in den Briefkasten stecken; ~ sth. in one's pocket etw. in die Tasche stecken; ~ petrol in the tank Benzin in den Tank füllen; ~ the car in[to] the garage das Auto in die Garage stellen; ~ the plug in the socket den Stecker in die Steckdose stecken; ~ one's hands over one's eyes sich (Dat.) die Hände auf die Augen legen; where shall I ~ it? wo soll ich es hintun (ugs.)/-stellen/-legen usw.?; (fig.) be ~ in a difficult position in eine schwierige Lage geraten; ~ sb. on to sth. jmdn. auf etw. (Akk.) hinweisen; ~ sb. to work jmdn. arbeiten lassen; ~ sb. on antibiotics jmdn. auf Antibiotika setzen; ~ oneself in sb.'s place or situation sich in jmds. Lage (Akk.) versetzen
(b) (submit) unterbreiten ⟨Vorschlag, Plan⟩ (to Dat.)
(c) (express) ausdrücken; let's ~ it like this: ...: sagen wir so: ...; ~ sth. into English etc. etw. ins Englische usw. übertragen; ~ sth. into words etw. in Worte fassen
(d) (write) schreiben; ~ one's name on the ···⟶

list seinen Namen auf die Liste setzen;
~ **sth. on the bill** etw. auf die Rechnung
setzen
**(e)** (stake) setzen **(on** auf + *Akk.*)
**(f)** (estimate) ~ **sb./sth. at** jmdn./etw.
schätzen auf (+ *Akk.*)
[2] *v.i.* **-tt-, put** (Naut.) ~ [out] to sea in See
stechen
■ **put a'cross** *v.t.* **(a)** (communicate)
vermitteln **(to** *Dat.*)
**(b)** (make acceptable) ankommen mit
■ **put a'way** *v.t.* **(a)** wegräumen; reinstellen
⟨*Auto*⟩; (in file) abheften
**(b)** (save) beiseite legen
**(c)** (coll.) (eat) verdrücken (ugs.); (drink)
runterkippen (ugs.)
**(d)** (coll.: confine) einsperren (ugs.)
■ **put 'back** *v.t.* **(a)** ~ **the book back** das
Buch zurücktun
**(b)** ~ **the clock back** die Uhr zurückstellen
**(c)** (postpone) verschieben
■ **put 'down** *v.t.* **(a)** (set down) (vertically)
hinstellen; (horizontally) hinlegen; auflegen
⟨*Hörer*⟩
**(b)** (suppress) niederwerfen
**(c)** (humiliate) herabsetzen
**(d)** (kill) töten
**(e)** (write) notieren
**(f)** (attribute) ~ **sth. down to sth.** etw. auf etw.
⟨*Akk.*⟩ zurückführen
■ **put 'forward** *v.t.* **(a)** (propose) aufwarten
mit
**(b)** (nominate) vorschlagen
**(c)** ~ **the clock forward** die Uhr vorstellen
■ **put 'in** [1] *v.t.* **(a)** (install) einbauen
**(b)** (submit) stellen ⟨*Forderung*⟩; einreichen
⟨*Bewerbung*⟩
**(c)** (devote) aufwenden ⟨*Mühe*⟩; (perform)
einlegen ⟨*Sonderschicht, Überstunden*⟩
[2] *v.i.* ~ **in for** sich bewerben um ⟨*Stellung*⟩;
beantragen ⟨*Urlaub*⟩
■ **put 'off** *v.t.* **(a)** (postpone) verschieben
**(until** auf + *Akk.*); (postpone engagement with)
vertrösten **(until** auf + *Akk.*)
**(b)** (switch off) ausmachen
**(c)** (repel) abstoßen; ~ **sb. off sth.** jmdm. etw.
verleiden
**(d)** (distract) stören
**(e)** (dissuade) ~ **sb. off doing sth.** jmdn.
davon abbringen, etw. zu tun
■ **put 'on** *v.t.* **(a)** anziehen ⟨*Kleidung, Hose
usw.*⟩; aufsetzen ⟨*Hut, Brille*⟩; draufsetzen
⟨*Deckel*⟩; ~ **it on** (coll.) [nur] Schau machen
(ugs.)
**(b)** anmachen ⟨*Radio, Licht*⟩; aufsetzen
⟨*Wasser, Kessel*⟩

**(c)** (gain) ~ **on weight** zunehmen
**(d)** (stage) spielen ⟨*Stück*⟩; zeigen ⟨*Film*⟩
■ **put 'out** *v.t.* **(a)** rausbringen
**(b)** ausmachen ⟨*Licht*⟩; löschen ⟨*Feuer*⟩
**(c)** (inconvenience) in Verlegenheit bringen
■ **put 'through** *v.t.* **(a)** (carry out)
durchführen ⟨*Plan, Programm*⟩
**(b)** (Teleph.) verbinden **(to** mit)
■ **put 'up** [1] *v.t.* **(a)** heben ⟨*Hand*⟩; errichten
⟨*Gebäude, Denkmal*⟩; aufstellen ⟨*Gerüst*⟩
**(b)** (display) aushängen
**(c)** hochnehmen ⟨*Fäuste*⟩; leisten
⟨*Widerstand, Gegenwehr*⟩
**(d)** (propose) vorschlagen; (nominate) aufstellen
**(e)** (incite) ~ **sb. up to sth.** jmdn. zu etw.
anstiften
**(f)** (accommodate) unterbringen
**(g)** (increase) [he]raufsetzen ⟨*Preis, Miete*⟩
[2] *v.i.* (lodge) übernachten
■ **put 'up with** *v.t.* sich (*Dat.*) bieten lassen
⟨*Beleidigung, Benehmen*⟩; sich abfinden mit
⟨*Lärm, Elend*⟩; sich abgeben mit ⟨*Person*⟩

**'put-down** *n.* Herabsetzung, *die;* (snub)
Abfuhr, *die*

**putrefaction** /pjuːtrɪ'fækʃn/ *n., no indef.
art.* Zersetzung, *die*

**putrefy** /'pjuːtrɪfaɪ/ *v.i.* sich zersetzen

**putrid** /'pjuːtrɪd/ *adj.* (rotten) faul; ~ **smell**
Fäulnisgeruch, *der*

**putt** /pʌt/ (Golf) [1] *v.i. & t.* putten
[2] *n.* Putt, *der*

**'putter** *n.* Putter, *der*

**putty** /'pʌtɪ/ *n.* Kitt, *der*

**'put-up** *adj.* **a** ~ **job** ein abgekartetes Spiel
(ugs.)

**puzzle** /'pʌzl/ [1] *n.* (problem, enigma) Rätsel,
*das;* (toy) Geduldsspiel, *das*
[2] *v.t.* rätselhaft *od.* ein Rätsel sein (+ *Dat.*)
[3] *v.i.* ~ **over** *or* **about sth.** sich (*Dat.*) über
etw. den Kopf zerbrechen

**puzzled** /'pʌzld/ *adj.* ratlos

**puzzling** /'pʌzlɪŋ/ *adj.* rätselhaft

**PVC** *abbr.* = **polyvinyl chloride** PVC,
*das*

**pygmy** /'pɪgmɪ/ *n.* Pygmäe, *der*

**pyjamas** /pɪ'dʒɑːməz/ *n. pl.* [pair of] ~:
Schlafanzug, *der*

**pylon** /'paɪlən/ *n.* Mast, *der*

**pyramid** /'pɪrəmɪd/ *n.* Pyramide, *die*

**Pyrenees** /pɪrə'niːz/ *pr. n. pl.* the ~: die
Pyrenäen

**python** /'paɪθən/ *n.* Python, *der*

# Qq

**Q, q** /kju:/ *n.* Q, q, *das*

**quack** /kwæk/ [1] *v.i.* ‹*Ente:*› quaken
[2] *n.* Quaken, *das*

**quadrangle** /'kwɒdræŋgl/ *n.* [viereckiger] Innenhof

**quadruped** /'kwɒdrʊped/ *n.* Vierfüßler, *der*

**quadruple** /'kwɒdrʊpl/ [1] *adj.* vierfach
[2] *v.t.* vervierfachen
[3] *v.i.* sich vervierfachen

**quagmire** /'kwægmaɪə(r)/ *n.* Sumpf, *der;* Morast, *der*

**quail¹** /kweɪl/ *n.* (Ornith.) Wachtel, *die*

**quail²** *v.i.* ‹*Person:*› [ver]zagen

**quaint** /kweɪnt/ *adj.* drollig ‹*Häuschen, Einrichtung*›; malerisch ‹*Ort*›; (odd) kurios ‹*Bräuche, Anblick*›

**quake** /kweɪk/ [1] *n.* (coll.) [Erd]beben, *das*
[2] *v.i.* beben; ~ **with fear** vor Angst zittern

**Quaker** /'kweɪkə(r)/ *n.* Quäker, *der/* Quäkerin, *die*

**qualification** /kwɒlɪfɪ'keɪʃn/ *n.* (a) Qualifikation, *die;* (condition) Voraussetzung, *die*
(b) (limitation) Vorbehalt, *der;* **without** ~: vorbehaltlos

**qualified** /'kwɒlɪfaɪd/ *adj.* (a) qualifiziert; (by training) ausgebildet
(b) (restricted) nicht uneingeschränkt; **a** ~ **success** kein voller Erfolg; ~ **acceptance** bedingte Annahme

**qualify** /'kwɒlɪfaɪ/ [1] *v.t.* (a) (make competent) berechtigen (**for** zu)
(b) (modify) einschränken
[2] *v.i.* (a) ~ **in law/medicine** seinen [Studien]abschluss in Jura/Medizin machen; ~ **as a doctor/lawyer** sein Examen als Arzt/ Anwalt machen
(b) (fulfil a condition) in Frage kommen (**for** für)
(c) (Sport) sich qualifizieren

**qualifying** /'kwɒlɪfaɪɪŋ/ *adj.* (Sport) ~ **match** Qualifikationsspiel, *das*

**quality** /'kwɒlɪtɪ/ [1] *n.* (a) Qualität, *die*
(b) (characteristic) Eigenschaft, *die*
[2] *adj.* Qualitäts-

**quality:** ~ **control** *n.* Qualitätskontrolle, *die;* ~ **time** *n.:* ganz dem Miteinander gewidmete Zeit

**qualm** /kwɑːm/ *n.* Bedenken, *das* (**over, about** gegen)

**quandary** /'kwɒndərɪ/ *n.* Dilemma, *das*

**quantify** /'kwɒntɪfaɪ/ *v.t.* quantifizieren

**quantity** /'kwɒntɪtɪ/ *n.* (a) Quantität, *die*
(b) (amount, sum) Menge, *die*

**'quantity surveyor** *n.* Baukostenkalkulator, *der/*-kalkulatorin, *die*

**quantum:** ~ **jump,** ~ **leap** *ns.* (Phys.; also fig.) Quantensprung, *der;* ~ **me'chanics** *n.* Quantenmechanik, *die*

**quarantine** /'kwɒrəntiːn/ *n.* Quarantäne, *die;* **be in** ~: unter Quarantäne stehen

**quarrel** /'kwɒrl/ [1] *n.* (a) Streit, *der;* **have/ pick a** ~ **with sb.** [about/over sth.]** sich mit jmdm. [über etw. (*Akk.*)] streiten/mit jmdm. [wegen etw.] Streit anfangen
(b) (cause of complaint) Einwand, *der* (**with** gegen)
[2] *v.i.,* (Brit.) -**ll**- [sich] streiten (**over** um, **about** über + *Akk.*); ~ **with each other** [sich] [miteinander] streiten; (fall out) sich [zer]streiten (**over** um, **about** über + *Akk.*)

**quarrelsome** /'kwɒrlsəm/ *adj.* streitsüchtig

**quarry¹** /'kwɒrɪ/ *n.* Steinbruch, *der*

**quarry²** *n.* (prey) Beute, *die*

**quart** /kwɔːt/ *n.* Quart, *das*

**quarter** /'kwɔːtə(r)/ [1] *n.* (a) Viertel, *das;* **a or one** ~ **of** ein Viertel (+ *Gen.*); **a** ~ **of a mile/an hour** eine Viertelmeile/-stunde
(b) (of year) Quartal, *das;* Vierteljahr, *das*
(c) [a] ~ **to/past six** Viertel vor/nach sechs
(d) (direction) Richtung, *die*
(e) (area of town) [Stadt]viertel, *das*
(f) ~s *pl.* (lodgings) Quartier, *das* (bes. Milit.); Unterkunft, *die*
(g) (Amer. coin) Vierteldollar, *der*
[2] *v.t.* (a) (divide) vierteln
(b) (lodge) einquartieren ‹*Soldaten*›

**quarter-'final** *n.* Viertelfinale, *das*

**'quarterly** [1] *adj.* vierteljährlich
[2] *n.* Vierteljahr[es]schrift, *die*

**quarter-'pounder** *n.* Viertelpfünder, *der*

**quartet** /kwɔː'tet/ *n.* Quartett, *das*

**quartz** /kwɔːts/ *n.* Quarz, *der*

**quash** /kwɒʃ/ *v.t.* (a) (annul) aufheben
(b) (suppress) niederschlagen

**quaver** /'kweɪvə(r)/ [1] *n.* (Brit. Mus.) Achtelnote, *die*
[2] *v.i.* (vibrate) zittern

**quay** /kiː/, **'quayside** *ns.* Kai, *der*

**queasy** /'kwiːzɪ/ *adj.* unwohl

**queen** /kwiːn/ *n.* (a) Königin, *die*
(b) (Chess, Cards) Dame, *die*

**queen:** ~ **'bee** *n.* Bienenkönigin, *die;* ~ **'mother** *n.* Königinmutter, *die*

**queer** /kwɪə(r)/ [1] *adj.* (a) (strange) sonderbar; (eccentric) verschroben
(b) (shady) merkwürdig
(c) (Brit. coll. dated: out of sorts) unwohl    ···❖

**(d)** (sl. derog.: homosexual) schwul (ugs.)
[2] *n.* (sl. derog.: homosexual) Schwule, *der* (ugs.)

**quell** /kwel/ *v.t.* (literary) niederschlagen
⟨*Aufstand*⟩; zügeln ⟨*Furcht*⟩

**quench** /kwentʃ/ *v.t.* löschen

**query** /'kwɪərɪ/ [1] *n.* Frage, *die*
[2] *v.t.* in Frage stellen ⟨*Anweisung,*
*Glaubwürdigkeit*⟩; beanstanden ⟨*Rechnung*⟩

**quest** /kwest/ *n.* Suche, *die* (**for** nach)

**question** /'kwestʃn/ [1] *n.* **(a)** Frage, *die;*
**ask sb. a** ~: jmdm. eine Frage stellen
**(b)** (doubt, objection) Zweifel, *der* (**about** an
+ *Dat.*); **there is no** ~ **about sth.** es besteht
kein Zweifel an etw. (*Dat.*); **beyond all** *or*
**without** ~: ohne Frage
**(c)** ( problem, concern) Frage, *die;* **sth./it is only**
**a** ~ **of time** etw./es ist [nur] eine Frage der
Zeit; **it is [only] a** ~ **of doing sth.** es geht
[nur] darum, etw. zu tun; **the person/thing in**
~: die fragliche Person/Sache; **sth./it is out**
**of the** ~: etw./es ist ausgeschlossen
[2] *v.t.* **(a)** befragen; ⟨*Polizei, Gericht usw.:*⟩
vernehmen
**(b)** (throw doubt upon, raise objections to)
bezweifeln

**questionable** /'kwestʃənəbl/ *adj.*
fragwürdig

**'question mark** *n.* Fragezeichen, *das*

**questionnaire** /kwestʃə'neə(r)/ *n.*
Fragebogen, *der*

**queue** /kjuː/ [1] *n.* Schlange, *die;* **join the** ~:
sich anstellen
[2] *v.i.* ~ [**up**] Schlange stehen

**'queue-jumping** *n.* (Brit.) Vordrängen, *das*

**quibble** /'kwɪbl/ [1] *n.* Spitzfindigkeit, *die*
[2] *v.i.* streiten

**quibbling** /'kwɪblɪŋ/ *adj.* spitzfindig

**quiche** /kiːʃ/ *n.* Quiche, *die*

**quick** /kwɪk/ [1] *adj.* schnell; kurz ⟨*Rede,*
*Pause*⟩; flüchtig ⟨*Kuss, Blick*⟩; **be** ~! mach
schnell! (ugs.); **be** ~ **to do sth.** etw. schnell
tun; **a** ~ **temper** ein aufbrausendes Wesen
[2] *adv.* schnell
[3] *n.* empfindliches Fleisch; **be cut to the** ~
(fig.) tief getroffen sein

**quicken** /'kwɪkn/ [1] *v.t.* beschleunigen
[2] *v.i.* sich beschleunigen

**'quickly** *adv.* schnell

**'quickness** *n.* **(a)** (speed) Schnelligkeit, *die*
**(b)** (~ of perception) Schärfe, *die*

**quick:** ~**sand** *n.* Treibsand, *der;*
~**-tempered** /-'tempəd/ *adj.* hitzig; **be**
~**-tempered** leicht aufbrausen; ~**-witted**
*adj.* geistesgegenwärtig

**quid** /kwɪd/ *n., pl. same* (Brit. coll.) Pfund, *das*

**quiet** /'kwaɪət/ [1] *adj.,* ~**er** /'kwaɪətə(r)/,
~**est** /'kwaɪətɪst/ *adj.* **(a)** (silent) still; (not loud)
leise; **keep** ~ **about sth.** (fig.) etw. geheim
halten
**(b)** (peaceful, not busy) ruhig
**(c)** (not overt) versteckt; **on the** ~: still und
heimlich
[2] *n.* Ruhe, *die;* (silence, stillness) Stille, *die*

**quieten** /'kwaɪətn/ *v.t.* beruhigen
■ **quieten 'down** *v.i.* sich beruhigen

**'quietly** *adv.* **(a)** (silently) still; (not loudly) leise
**(b)** ( peacefully) ruhig

**'quietness** *n.* (absence of noise) Stille, *die;*
( peacefulness) Ruhe, *die*

**quill** /kwɪl/ *n.* (feather) Kielfeder, *die;* (of
porcupine) Stachel, *der*

**quilt** /kwɪlt/ [1] *n.* Schlafdecke, *die*
[2] *v.t.* wattieren

**quince** /kwɪns/ *n.* Quitte, *die*

**quintessential** /kwɪntɪ'senʃl/ *adj.*
typisch; wesentlich

**quintet** /kwɪn'tet/ *n.* Quintett, *das*

**quip** /kwɪp/ [1] *n.* Witzelei, *die*
[2] *v.i.,* **-pp-** witzeln (**at** über + *Akk.*)

**quirk** /kwɜːk/ *n.* Marotte, *die;* **a** ~ **of fate**
eine Laune des Schicksals

**quirky** /'kwɜːkɪ/ *adj.* schrullig (ugs.)

**quit** /kwɪt/ *v.t.,* **-tt-,** (Amer.) quit **(a)** (give up)
aufgeben; (stop) aufhören mit; ~ **doing sth.**
aufhören, etw. zu tun; **they were given notice**
**to** ~ [**the flat**] ihnen wurde [die Wohnung]
gekündigt
**(b)** (Comp.) beenden

**quite** /kwaɪt/ *adv.* **(a)** (entirely) ganz; völlig;
fest ⟨*entschlossen*⟩; ~ [**so**]! [ja,] genau!
**(b)** (to some extent) ziemlich; ganz ⟨*gern*⟩; ~ **a**
**few** ziemlich viele

**quits** /kwɪts/ *pred. adj.* **be** ~ [**with sb.**] [mit
jmdm.] quitt sein (ugs.)

**quiver**[1] /'kwɪvə(r)/ *v.i.* zittern (**with** vor
+ *Dat.*); ⟨*Stimme, Lippen:*⟩ beben (geh.); ⟨*Lid:*⟩
zucken

**quiver**[2] *n.* (for arrows) Köcher, *der*

**quiz** /kwɪz/ [1] *n., pl.* ~**zes** Quiz, *das*
[2] *v.t.,* **-zz-** ausfragen (**about sth.** nach etw.,
**about sb.** über jmdn.)

**quizzical** /'kwɪzɪkl/ *adj.* fragend

**'quiz programme, 'quiz show** *ns.*
(Radio, Telev.) Quizsendung, *die*

**quoit** /kɔɪt/ *n.* [Gummi]ring, *der*

**quorum** /'kwɔːrəm/ *n.* Quorum, *das*

**quota** /'kwəʊtə/ *n.* **(a)** (share) Anteil, *der*
**(b)** (goods to be produced)
Produktionsmindestquote, *die*
**(c)** (maximum number) Höchstquote, *die*

**quotation** /kwəʊ'teɪʃn/ *n.* **(a)** Zitieren, *das;*
( passage) Zitat, *das*
**(b)** (estimate) Kosten[vor]anschlag, *der*

**quo'tation marks** *n. pl.*
Anführungszeichen *Pl.*

**quote** /kwəʊt/ [1] *v.t. also abs.* zitieren
(from aus); zitieren aus ⟨*Buch, Text*⟩; (mention)
anführen; nennen ⟨*Preis*⟩
[2] *n.* (coll.) **(a)** ( passage) Zitat, *das*
**(b)** (estimate) Kosten[vor]anschlag, *der*
**(c)** *usu. in pl.* (quotation mark)
Anführungszeichen, *das*

**quotient** /'kwəʊʃnt/ *n.* (Math.) Quotient, *der;*
*see also* INTELLIGENCE QUOTIENT

# Rr

**R, r** /ɑː(r)/ *n.* R, r, *das*

**R.** *abbr.* = **River** Fl.

**rabbi** /'ræbaɪ/ *n.* Rabbi[ner], *der;* (as title) Rabbi, *der*

**rabbit** /'ræbɪt/ *n.* Kaninchen, *das*

**rabbit:** ∼ **burrow** *n.* Kaninchenbau, *der;* ∼ **hutch** *n.* (also fig.) Kaninchenstall, *der;* ∼ **warren** *n.* Kaninchengehege, *das;* (fig.) Labyrinth, *das*

**rabble** /'ræbl/ *n.* Mob, *der*

**rabid** /'ræbɪd/ *adj.* **(a)** tollwütig **(b)** (extreme) fanatisch

**rabies** /'reɪbiːz/ *n.* Tollwut, *die*

**race¹** /reɪs/ [1] *n.* Rennen, *das;* (fig.) a ∼ **against time** ein Wettlauf mit der Zeit [2] *v.i.* **(a)** (in swimming, running, etc.) um die Wette schwimmen/laufen *usw.* (**with, against** mit) **(b)** ⟨*Motor:*⟩ durchdrehen; ⟨*Puls:*⟩ jagen **(c)** (rush) sich sehr beeilen; ∼ **after sb.** jmdn. hinterherhetzen [3] *v.t.* um die Wette schwimmen/laufen *usw.* mit

**race²** *n.* (Anthrop., Biol.) Rasse, *die;* **the human** ∼: die Menschheit

**race:** ∼**course** *n.* Rennbahn, *die;* ∼ **hatred** *n.* Rassenhass, *der;* ∼**horse** *n.* Rennpferd, *das;* ∼ **meeting** *n.* Renntag, *der;* (on successive days) Renntage *Pl.* ∼ **relations** *n. pl.* Beziehung zwischen den Rassen; ∼ **riot** *n.* Rassenkrawall, *der;* ∼**track** *n.* Rennbahn, *die*

**racial** /'reɪʃl/ *adj.* Rassen⟨*diskriminierung, -konflikt, -gleichheit, -spannung, -vorurteil*⟩; rassisch ⟨*Gruppe, Minderheit*⟩

**racialism** /'reɪʃəlɪzm/ *n.* Rassismus, *der*

**racialist** /'reɪʃəlɪst/ [1] *n.* Rassist, *der/* Rassistin, *die* [2] *adj.* rassistisch

**racially** /'reɪʃəlɪ/ *adv.* rassisch; **be** ∼ **prejudiced** Rassenvorurteile haben

**racing** /'reɪsɪŋ/ *n.* Rennsport, *der;* (with horses) Pferdesport, *der*

**racing:** ∼ **bicycle** *n.* Rennrad, *das;* Rennmaschine, *die;* ∼ **car** *n.* Rennwagen, *der;* ∼ **driver** *n.* Rennfahrer, *der/*-fahrerin, *die*

**racism** /'reɪsɪzm/ *n.* Rassismus, *der*

**racist** /'reɪsɪst/ [1] *n.* Rassist, *der/*Rassistin, *die* [2] *adj.* rassistisch

**rack** /ræk/ [1] *n.* (for luggage) Ablage, *die;* (for toast, plates) Ständer, *der;* (on bicycle, motor cycle) Gepäckträger, *der*

[2] *v.t.* ∼ **one's brain[s]** (fig.) sich (*Dat.*) den Kopf zerbrechen (ugs.)

**racket¹** /'rækɪt/ *n.* Schläger, *der*

**racket²** *n.* **(a)** (disturbance) Lärm, *der;* Krach, *der* **(b)** (scheme) Schwindelgeschäft, *das* (ugs.)

**racketeer** /rækɪ'tɪə(r)/ *n.* Ganove, *der;* (profiteer) Wucherer, *der*

**racketeering** /rækɪ'tɪərɪŋ/ *n.* kriminelle Geschäfte *Pl.*

**racoon** /rə'kuːn/ *n.* Waschbär, *der*

**racy** /'reɪsɪ/ *adj.* flott (ugs.) ⟨*Stil*⟩

**radar** /'reɪdɑː(r)/ *n.* Radar, *das od. der*

**'radar screen** *n.* Radarschirm, *der*

**radiant** /'reɪdɪənt/ *adj.* strahlend; fröhlich ⟨*Stimmung*⟩; **be** ∼: strahlen (**with** vor + *Dat.*)

**radiate** /'reɪdɪeɪt/ [1] *v.i.* **(a)** ⟨*Hitze, Wärme:*⟩ ausstrahlen; ⟨*Schein, Wellen:*⟩ ausgehen (**from** von) **(b)** (from central point) strahlenförmig ausgehen (**from** von) [2] *v.t.* ausstrahlen ⟨*Licht, Wärme; Glück, Liebe*⟩; aussenden ⟨*Strahlen, Wellen*⟩

**radiation** /reɪdɪ'eɪʃn/ *n.* (of energy) Emission, *die;* (of signals) Ausstrahlung, *die;* (energy transmitted) Strahlung, *die*

**radiator** /'reɪdɪeɪtə(r)/ *n.* **(a)** (for heating) Heizkörper, *der* **(b)** (Motor Veh.) Kühler, *der*

**'radiator cap** *n.* Kühlverschraubung, *die*

**radical** /'rædɪkl/ *adj.* [1] **(a)** (thorough; also Polit.) radikal; drastisch ⟨*Maßnahme*⟩ **(b)** (progressive) radikal **(c)** (fundamental) grundlegend [2] *n.* (Polit.) Radikale, *der/die*

**radio** /'reɪdɪəʊ/ [1] *n., pl.* ∼**s** **(a)** no indef. art. Funk, *der;* (for private communication) Sprechfunk, *der* **(b)** no indef. art. (Broadcasting) Rundfunk, *der;* **on the** ∼: im Radio **(c)** (apparatus) Radio, *das* [2] *attrib. adj.* (Broadcasting) Rundfunk-; Radio⟨*welle, -teleskop*⟩; Funk⟨*mast, -turm, -taxi*⟩ [3] *v.t.* funken

**radio:** ∼'**active** *adj.* radioaktiv; ∼**ac'tivity** *n.* Radioaktivität, *die;* ∼ **cas'sette player** *n.* Kassettenradio, *das;* Radio mit Kassettenteil; ∼**con'trolled** *adj.* funkgesteuert; ∼ **frequency** *n.* Hochfrequenz, *die; attrib.* ∼**-frequency** Hochfrequenz-; ∼ **play** *n.* Hörspiel, *das;* ∼ **station** *n.* Rundfunkstation, *die;* Rundfunk- *od.* ⋯⟩

Radiosender, *der;* ~ **'telescope** *n.*
Radioteleskop, *das;* ~**'therapy** *n.*
Strahlentherapie, *die*
**radish** /'rædɪʃ/ *n.* Rettich, *der;* (small, red)
Radieschen, *das*
**radius** /'reɪdɪəs/ *n., pl.* **radii** /'reɪdɪaɪ/ *or*
~**es** (Math.) Radius, *der;* (fig.) Umkreis, *der*
**RAF** /ɑːreɪ'ef, (coll.) ræf/ *abbr.* = **Royal Air Force**
**raffle** /'ræfl/ **1** *n.* Tombola, *die;* ~ **ticket**
Los, *das*
    **2** *v.t.* ~ **[off]** verlosen
**raft** /rɑːft/ *n.* Floß, *das*
**rafter** /'rɑːftə(r)/ *n.* Sparren, *der*
**rag¹** /ræg/ *n.* **(a)** [Stoff]fetzen, *der*
    **(b)** *in pl.* (old and torn clothes) Lumpen *Pl.*
    **(c)** (derog.: newspaper) Käseblatt, *das* (salopp)
**rag²** *v.t.,* **-gg-** (tease) aufziehen
**rag:** ~**bag** *n.* (fig.) Sammelsurium, *das;*
~ **doll** *n.* Stoffpuppe, *die*
**rage** /reɪdʒ/ **1** *n.* **(a)** (violent anger) Wut, *die;*
(fit of anger) Wutausbruch, *der*
    **(b)** sth. is [all] the ~: etw. ist [ganz] groß in Mode
    **2** *v.i.* **(a)** (rave) toben; ~ **at** *or* **against sth./
    sb.** gegen etw./jmdn. wüten
    **(b)** (be violent, unchecked) toben; ⟨*Krankheit:*⟩ wüten
**ragged** /'rægɪd/ *adj.* zerrissen
**'rag trade** *n.* (coll.) Modebranche, *die* (ugs.)
**raid** /reɪd/ **1** *n.* Einfall, *der;* Überfall, *der;*
(Mil.) Überraschungsangriff, *der;* (by police)
Razzia, *die* (on in + *Dat.*)
    **2** *v.t.* ⟨*Polizei:*⟩ eine Razzia machen auf
    (+ *Akk.*); ⟨*Räuber, Soldaten:*⟩ überfallen
**'raider** *n.* Räuber, *der/*Räuberin, *die*
**rail** /reɪl/ *n.* **(a)** Stange, *die;* (on ship) Reling,
*die;* (as protection against contact) Barriere, *die*
    **(b)** (Railw.: of track) Schiene, *die*
    **(c)** (~way) [Eisen]bahn, *die; attrib.* Bahn-; **by**
    ~: mit der Bahn
**'rail card** *n.* Bahnkarte, *die*
**railing** /'reɪlɪŋ/ *n.* (round park) Zaun, *der;* (on
staircase) Geländer, *das*
**rail:** ~**road** (Amer.) ▶ ~WAY; **R~track** *n.,*
*no art.* (Brit.) *Betreibergesellschaft des
britischen Schienennetzes;* ~**way** *n.* **(a)**
(track) Bahnlinie, *die;* Bahnstrecke, *die;* **(b)**
(system) [Eisen]bahn, *die*
**railway:** ~ **carriage** *n.* Eisenbahnwagen,
*der;* ~ **crossing** *n.* Bahnübergang, *der;*
~ **engine** *n.* Lokomotive, *die;* ~ **line** *n.*
[Eisen]bahnlinie, *die;* ~ **station** *n.*
Bahnhof, *der;* ~ **worker** *n.* Bahnarbeiter,
*der/*-arbeiterin, *die*
**rain** /reɪn/ **1** *n.* **(a)** Regen, *der*
    **(b)** (fig.: of arrows, blows, etc.) Hagel, *der*
    **2** *v.i. impers.* **it is** ~**ing** es regnet
    **3** *v.t.* hageln lassen ⟨*Schläge, Hiebe*⟩
**rain:** ~**bow** /'reɪnbəʊ/ *n.* Regenbogen, *der;*
~ **check** *n.* (Amer. fig.) **take a** ~ **check on
sth.** auf etw. (*Akk.*) später wieder
zurückkommen; ~ **cloud** *n.* Regenwolke,

*die;* ~**coat** *n.* Regenmantel, *der;* ~**fall** *n.*
Niederschlag, *der;* ~**forest** *n.* Regenwald,
*der;* ~**proof** *adj.* regendicht; ~**water** *n.*
Regenwasser, *das;* ~**wear** *n.*
Regenkleidung, *die*
**'rainy** *adj.* regnerisch ⟨*Tag, Wetter*⟩;
regenreich ⟨*Gebiet, Sommer*⟩; ~ **season**
Regenzeit, *die;* **keep sth. for a** ~ **day** (fig.) sich
(*Dat.*) etw. für schlechte Zeiten aufheben
**raise** /reɪz/ *v.t.* **(a)** (lift up) heben; erhöhen
⟨*Temperatur, Miete, Gehalt*⟩; hochziehen
⟨*Fahne*⟩; aufziehen ⟨*Vorhang*⟩; hochheben
⟨*Arm*⟩; ~ **one's glass to sb.** das Glas auf
jmdn. erheben
    **(b)** (set upright) aufrichten; erheben ⟨*Banner*⟩;
    ~ **sb.'s spirits** jmds. Stimmung heben
    **(c)** erheben ⟨*Forderungen, Einwände*⟩;
    aufwerfen ⟨*Frage*⟩; zur Sprache bringen
    ⟨*Thema, Problem*⟩
    **(d)** aufziehen ⟨*Vieh,* [*Haus*]*tiere*⟩; großziehen
    ⟨*Familie, Kinder*⟩
    **(e)** aufbringen ⟨*Geld, Betrag*⟩
    **(f)** aufheben ⟨*Belagerung, Blockade,
    Embargo, Verbot*⟩
**raisin** /'reɪzn/ *n.* Rosine, *die*
**rake** /reɪk/ **1** *n.* Rechen, *der;* Harke, *die*
    **2** *v.t.* **(a)** harken
    **(b)** ~ **the fire** die Asche entfernen
    **(c)** (with eyes, shots) bestreichen
■ **rake 'in** *v.t.* (coll.) scheffeln (ugs.).
■ **rake 'up** *v.t.* zusammenharken; (fig.)
wieder ausgraben
**'rake-off** *n.* (coll.) [Gewinn]anteil, *der*
**rakish** /'reɪkɪʃ/ *adj.* flott; kess
**rally** /'rælɪ/ **1** *v.i.* (regain health) sich wieder
[ein wenig] erholen
    **2** *v.t.* **(a)** (reassemble) wieder zusammenrufen
    **(b)** einigen ⟨*Partei, Kräfte*⟩; sammeln
    ⟨*Anhänger*⟩
    **3** *n.* **(a)** (mass meeting) Versammlung, *die*
    **(b)** [motor] ~: Rallye, *die*
    **(c)** (Tennis) Ballwechsel, *der*
**ram** /ræm/ **1** *n.* (Zool.) Schafbock, *der;*
Widder, *der*
    **2** *v.t.,* **-mm-: (a)** (force) stopfen; ~ **a post into
    the ground** einen Pfosten in die Erde
    rammen; ~ **sth. home to sb.** jmdm. etw.
    deutlich vor Augen führen
    **(b)** (collide with) rammen
**RAM** /ræm/ *abbr.* (Comp.) = **random
access memory** RAM
**ramble** /'ræmbl/ **1** *n.* [nature] ~:
Wanderung, *die*
    **2** *v.i.* **(a)** (walk) umherstreifen (**through, in** in
    + *Dat.*)
    **(b)** (in talk) zusammenhangloses Zeug reden;
    **keep rambling on about sth.** sich endlos über
    etw. (*Akk.*) auslassen
**rambler** /'ræmblə(r)/ *n.* Wanderer, *der/*
Wanderin, *die*
**rambling** /'ræmblɪŋ/ **1** *n.* Wandern, *das*
    **2** *adj.* **(a)** (irregularly arranged) verschachtelt;
    verwinkelt ⟨*Straßen*⟩

**(b)** (incoherent) unzusammenhängend
⟨*Erklärung*⟩
**(c)** ∼ **rose** Kletterrose, *die*
**ramp** /ræmp/ *n.* Rampe, *die*
**rampage** **1** /'ræmpeɪdʒ/ *n.* Randale, *die*
(ugs.); **be/go on the** ∼ (coll.) randalieren
**2** /ræm'peɪdʒ/ *v.i.* randalieren
**rampant** /'ræmpənt/ *adj.* zügellos ⟨*Gewalt,
Rassismus*⟩; steil ansteigend ⟨*Inflation*⟩;
üppig ⟨*Wachstum*⟩
**rampart** /'ræmpɑːt/ *n.* Wehrgang, *der*
**ram:** ∼ **raid** **1** *v.t.* [durch Rammen mit
einem Fahrzeug] einbrechen in (+ *Akk.*);
**2** *n.* [durch Rammen eines Gebäudes
verübter] Einbruch; ∼**-raider** *n.*:
*Einbrecher, der sich durch Einrammen bes.
eines Schaufensters mit einem Fahrzeug
Zutritt verschafft*
'**ramshackle** *adj.* klapprig ⟨*Auto*⟩;
verkommen ⟨*Gebäude*⟩
**ran** ▶ RUN 2, 3
**ranch** /rɑːntʃ/ *n.* Ranch, *die*
'**ranch hand** *n.* Farmarbeiter, *der*/
-arbeiterin, *die*
**rancid** /'rænsɪd/ *adj.* ranzig
**rancour** (*Brit.; Amer.:* **rancor**)
/'ræŋkə(r)/ *n.* [tiefe] Verbitterung
**R&B** *abbr.* = **rhythm and blues** R&B
**R&D** *abbr.* = **research and
development** F&E
**random** /'rændəm/ **1** *n.* **at** ∼: wahllos;
willkürlich; (aimlessly) ziellos; **choose at** ∼:
aufs Geratewohl wählen
**2** *adj.* willkürlich
**random 'access memory** *n.* (Comp.)
Schreib-Lese-Speicher, *der*
**randy** /'rændɪ/ *adj.* geil; scharf (ugs.)
**rang** ▶ RING[2] 2, 3
**range** /reɪndʒ/ **1** *n.* **(a)** ∼ **of mountains**
Bergkette, *die*
**(b)** (of subjects) Palette, *die*; (of knowledge, voice)
Umfang, *der*
**(c)** (of missile etc.) Reichweite, *die*; **at a** ∼ **of
200 metres** auf eine Entfernung von 200
Metern
**(d)** (series, selection) Kollektion, *die*
**(e)** (stove) Herd, *der*
**2** *v.i.* ⟨*Preise, Temperaturen:*⟩ schwanken,
sich bewegen (**from** ... **to** zwischen [+ *Dat.*]
... und)
'**ranger** *n.* Förster, *der*/Försterin, *die*
**rank¹** /ræŋk/ **1** *n.* **(a)** (position in hierarchy)
Rang, *der*; (Mil. also) Dienstgrad, *der*
**(b)** (social position) [soziale] Stellung
**(c)** (row) Reihe, *die*; **the** ∼ **and file** (fig.) die
breite Masse; **the** ∼**s** (enlisted men) die
Mannschaften und Unteroffiziere
**2** *v.t.* ∼ **among** zählen zu
**3** *v.i.* ∼ **among** zählen zu
**rank²** *adj.* **(a)** krass ⟨*Außenseiter*⟩
**(b)** ∼ **weeds** [wild]wucherndes Unkraut
**rankings** /'ræŋkɪŋz/ *n. pl.* (Sport) Rangliste,

*die;* **the team has fallen in the** ∼: die
Mannschaft ist in der Tabelle nach unten
gerutscht
**ransack** /'rænsæk/ *v.t.* **(a)** (search)
durchsuchen (**for** nach)
**(b)** (pillage) plündern
**ransom** /'rænsəm/ *n.* ∼ **[money]** Lösegeld,
*das;* **hold to** ∼: als Geisel festhalten
**rant** /rænt/ *v.i.* ∼ **[and rave]** wettern (ugs.)
(**about** über + *Akk.*)
**rap** /ræp/ **1** *n.* [energisches] Klopfen
**2** *v.t.,* -pp- klopfen
**3** *v.i.,* -pp- klopfen (**on** an + *Akk.*)
**rape¹** /reɪp/ **1** *n.* Vergewaltigung, *die*
**2** *v.t.* vergewaltigen
**rape²** *n.* (Bot., Agric.) Raps, *der*
**rape:** ∼**seed** *n.* Rapssamen, *der;* ∼**seed
oil** *n.* Rapsöl, *das*
**rapid** /'ræpɪd/ **1** *adj.* schnell ⟨*Bewegung,
Wachstum, Puls*⟩; rasch ⟨*Fortschritt,
Ausbreitung*⟩
**2** *n.* in *pl.* Stromschnellen *Pl.*
**rapid-'fire** *adj.* Schnellfeuer⟨*waffe,
-schießen*⟩; (fig.) schnell aufeinander folgend
⟨*Wiederholung*⟩; Schnellfeuer⟨*witze, -fragen*⟩
**rapidity** /rə'pɪdɪtɪ/ *n.* Schnelligkeit, *die*
'**rapidly** *adv.* schnell
**rapist** /'reɪpɪst/ *n.* Vergewaltiger, *der*
**rapport** /rə'pɔː(r)/ *n.* [harmonisches]
Verhältnis
**rapt** /ræpt/ *adj.* gespannt ⟨*Miene*⟩
**rapture** /'ræptʃə(r)/ *n.* **[state of]** ∼:
Verzückung, *die*
**rapturous** /'ræptʃərəs/ *adj.* begeistert
**rare¹** /reə(r)/ *adj.,* '**rarely** *adv.* selten
**rare²** *adj.* (Cookery) englisch gebraten
**rarefied** /'reərɪfaɪd/ *adj.* dünn ⟨*Luft*⟩; (fig.)
exklusiv
**rarity** /'reərɪtɪ/ *n.* Seltenheit, *die*
**rash¹** /ræʃ/ *n.* [Haut]ausschlag, *der*
**rash²** *adj.* voreilig ⟨*Urteil, Entscheidung*⟩;
überstürzt ⟨*Versprechung*⟩
**rasher** /'ræʃə(r)/ *n.* Speckscheibe, *die*
'**rashly** *adv.* voreilig
**rasp** /rɑːsp/ **1** *n.* (tool) Raspel, *die*
**2** *v.t.* (say gratingly) schnarren
**raspberry** /'rɑːzbərɪ/ *n.* Himbeere, *die*
**rat** /ræt/ *n.* **(a)** Ratte, *die;* **smell a** ∼ (fig.)
Lunte riechen (ugs.)
**(b)** (coll. derog.: person) Ratte, *die* (derb)
**ratchet** /'rætʃɪt/ *n.* **(a)** (Mech. Engin.) (set of
teeth) Zahnkranz, *der*
**(b)** ∼ **[wheel]** Klinkenrad, *das*
'**ratchet screwdriver** *n.*
Drillschraubenzieher, *der*
**rate** /reɪt/ **1** *n.* **(a)** (proportion) Rate, *die;*
∼ **of inflation** Inflationsrate, *die*
**(b)** (tariff) Satz, *der;* ∼ **[of pay]** Lohnsatz, *der*
**(c)** (speed) Geschwindigkeit, *die;* Tempo, *das*
**(d)** (Brit.: levy) **[local** *or* **council]** ∼**s**
Gemeindeabgaben *Pl.*
**(e)** (coll.) **at any** ∼ (at least) zumindest;              ···⟩

wenigstens; (whatever happens) auf jeden Fall;
at this ~ we won't get any work done so
kriegen wir gar nichts fertig (ugs.)
**2** *v.t.* **(a)** einschätzen ⟨*Intelligenz, Leistung*⟩
**(b)** (consider) betrachten; rechnen (**among** zu)
**3** *v.i.* ~ **as** gelten als

'**ratepayer** *n.* (Brit.) Realsteuerpflichtige,
*der/die*

**rather** /'rɑːðə(r)/ *adv.* **(a)** (by preference)
lieber
**(b)** (somewhat) ziemlich; **I** ~ **think that ...:** ich
bin ziemlich sicher, dass ...
**(c)** (more truly) vielmehr; **or** ~:
beziehungsweise

**ratification** /rætɪfɪ'keɪʃn/ *n.* Ratifizierung,
*die*

**ratify** /'rætɪfaɪ/ *v.t.* ratifizieren

**rating** /'reɪtɪŋ/ *n.* **(a)** (estimated standing)
Einschätzung, *die*
**(b)** (Radio, Telev.) [popularity] ~:
Einschaltquote, *die*
**(c)** (Brit. Navy) Matrose, *der*

**ratio** /'reɪʃɪəʊ/ *n., pl.* ~s Verhältnis, *das*

**ration** /'ræʃn/ **1** *n.* ~[s] Ration, *die* (**of** an
+ *Dat.*)
**2** *v.t.* rationieren ⟨*Benzin, Zucker usw.*⟩

**rational** /'ræʃnl/ *adj.* (having reason)
rational ⟨*Wesen*⟩; (sensible) vernünftig ⟨*Person,
Art usw.*⟩

**rationalist** /'ræʃnəlɪst/ *n.* Rationalist,
*der/Rationalistin, die*

**rationalize** /'ræʃnəlaɪz/ *v.t.*
rationalisieren

**rationing** /'ræʃnɪŋ/ *n.* Rationierung, *die*

**rat:** ~ **poison** *n.* Rattengift, *das;* ~ **race**
*n.* erbarmungsloser Konkurrenzkampf;
~ **run** *n.* (Brit. coll.) Schleichweg, *der*

**rattle** /'rætl/ **1** *v.i.* **(a)** ⟨*Fenster:*⟩ klappern;
⟨*Flaschen:*⟩ klirren; ⟨*Kette:*⟩ rasseln
**(b)** ⟨*Zug, Bus:*⟩ rattern
**2** *v.t.* **(a)** klappern mit ⟨*Würfel, Geschirr*⟩;
klirren lassen ⟨*Fenster[scheiben]*⟩; rasseln
mit ⟨*Kette*⟩
**(b)** (coll.: disconcert) ~ **sb.,** get **sb.** ~**d** jmdn.
durcheinander bringen
**3** *n.* **(a)** (of baby) Rassel, *die*
**(b)** (sound) Klappern, *das*
■ **rattle 'off** *v.t.* (coll.) herunterrasseln (ugs.)

'**rattlesnake** *n.* Klapperschlange, *die*

**raucous** /'rɔːkəs/ *adj.* rau

**raunchy** /'rɔːntʃɪ/ *adj.* (lewd) vulgär;
(suggestive) scharf (salopp)

**ravage** /'rævɪdʒ/ **1** *v.t.* heimsuchen
⟨*Gebiet, Stadt*⟩
**2** *n. in pl.* verheerende Wirkung

**rave** /reɪv/ **1** *v.i.* **(a)** (talk wildly) irrereden
**(b)** (speak admiringly) schwärmen (**about** von)
**2** *attrib. adj.* (coll.) begeistert ⟨*Kritik*⟩
**3** *n.* (coll.: dancing party) Rave, *der od. das*

**raven** /'reɪvn/ *n.* Rabe, *der*

**ravenous** /'rævənəs/ *adj.* **I'm** ~: ich habe
einen Bärenhunger (ugs.)

'**rave-up** *n.* (Brit. coll.) [wilde] Fete (ugs.)

**ravine** /rə'viːn/ *n.* Schlucht, *die*

**raving** /'reɪvɪŋ/ **1** *adj.* irreredend ⟨*Idiot*⟩
**2** *adv.* **be** ~ **mad** völlig verrückt sein (ugs.)

**ravish** /'rævɪʃ/ *v.t.* (charm) entzücken

'**ravishing** *adj.* bildschön ⟨*Anblick, Person*⟩;
hinreißend ⟨*Schönheit*⟩

**raw** /rɔː/ *adj.* **(a)** (uncooked) roh
**(b)** (inexperienced) unerfahren
**(c)** (stripped of skin) blutig ⟨*Fleisch*⟩; offen
⟨*Wunde*⟩
**(d)** (chilly) nasskalt

**raw ma'terial** *n.* Rohstoff, *der*

**Rawlplug** ® /'rɔːlplʌg/ *n.* Dübel, *der*

**ray** /reɪ/ *n.* Strahl, *der;* ~ **of sunshine/light**
Sonnen-/Lichtstrahl, *der*

**raze** /reɪz/ *v.t.* ~ **to the ground** dem
Erdboden gleichmachen

**razor** /'reɪzə(r)/ *n.* Rasiermesser, *das;*
[electric] ~: [elektrischer] Rasierapparat

**razor:** ~ **blade** *n.* Rasierklinge, *die;*
~**-sharp** *adj.* sehr scharf ⟨*Messer*⟩; (fig.)
messerscharf ⟨*Verstand, Intellekt*⟩;
scharfsinnig ⟨*Person*⟩

**RC** *abbr.* = **Roman Catholic** r.-k.;
röm.-kath.

**Rd.** *abbr.* = **Road** Str.

**re** /riː/ *prep.* (Commerc.) betreffs

**RE** *abbr.* (Brit.) = **Religious Education**
Religionslehre, *die*

**reach** /riːtʃ/ **1** *v.t.* **(a)** (arrive at) erreichen;
ankommen in (+ *Dat.*) ⟨*Stadt, Land*⟩;
erzielen ⟨*Übereinstimmung*⟩; kommen zu
⟨*Entscheidung; Ausgang, Eingang*⟩; **you can**
~ **her at this number** du kannst sie unter
dieser Nummer erreichen
**(b)** (extend to) ⟨*Straße:*⟩ führen bis zu; ⟨*Leiter,
Haar:*⟩ reichen bis zu
**2** *v.i.* **(a)** (stretch out hand) ~ **for sth.** nach
etw. greifen; ~ **across the table** über den
Tisch langen
**(b)** (be long/tall enough) sth. **will/won't** ~: etw.
ist/ist nicht lang genug; **I can't** ~: ich
komme nicht daran
**(c)** (go as far as) ⟨*Wasser, Gebäude, Besitz:*⟩
reichen ([**up**] to bis [hinauf] zu)
**3** *n.* Reichweite, *die;* **be within easy** ~ ⟨*Ort:*⟩
leicht erreichbar sein; **be out of** ~ ⟨*Ort:*⟩
nicht erreichbar sein; ⟨*Gegenstand:*⟩ außer
Reichweite sein
■ **reach 'out** *v.i.* die Hand ausstrecken (**for**
nach)

**react** /rɪ'ækt/ *v.i.* reagieren (**to** auf + *Akk.*)

**reaction** /rɪ'ækʃn/ *n.* Reaktion, *die* (**to** auf
+ *Akk.*)

**reactionary** /rɪ'ækʃənərɪ/ (Polit.) **1** *adj.*
reaktionär
**2** *n.* Reaktionär, *der/Reaktionärin, die*

**reactor** /rɪ'æktə(r)/ *n.* [nuclear] ~:
Kernreaktor, *der*

**read** /riːd/ **1** *v.t.,* **read** /red/ **(a)** lesen; ~ **sb.**
**sth.,** ~ **sth. to sb.** jmdm. etwas vorlesen;
~ **the gas meter** das Gas ablesen

**(b)** (interpret) deuten; ~ **between the lines** zwischen den Zeilen lesen
**(c)** (study) studieren
**2** *v.i.*, **read (a)** lesen; ~ **to sb.** jmdm. vorlesen
**(b)** (convey meaning) lauten; **the contract** ~s **as follows** der Vertrag hat folgenden Wortlaut
■ **read 'out** *v.t.* laut vorlesen
■ **read 'over, read 'through** *v.t.* durchlesen
■ **read 'up** *v.t.* sich informieren (**on** über + *Akk.*)

**readable** /'riːdəbl/ *adj.* **(a)** (pleasant to read) lesenswert
**(b)** (legible) leserlich

**'reader** *n.* **(a)** Leser, *der*/Leserin, *die*
**(b)** (book) Lesebuch, *das*

**'readership** *n.* Leserschaft, *die*

**readily** /'redɪlɪ/ *adv.* **(a)** (willingly) bereitwillig
**(b)** (easily) ohne weiteres

**readiness** /'redmɪs/ *n.* Bereitschaft, *die;* **be in** ~: bereit sein (**for** für)

**'reading** *n.* **(a)** Lesen, *das*
**(b)** (figure shown) Anzeige, *die*
**(c)** (recital) Lesung, *die* (**from** aus)
**(d)** (Parl.) Lesung, *die*

**reading:** ~ **glasses** *n. pl.* Lesebrille, *die;* ~ **lamp,** ~ **light** *ns.* Leselampe, *die;* ~ **matter** *n.* Lesestoff, *der;* Lektüre, *die*

**readjust** /riːə'dʒʌst/ **1** *v.t.* neu einstellen; neu anpassen ⟨*Gehalt, Zinssatz*⟩
**2** *v. refl. & i.* ~ [**oneself**] **to** sich wieder gewöhnen an (+ *Akk.*)

**read** /riːd/: ~-'**only memory** *n.* (Comp.) Fest[wert]speicher, *der;* ~-**out** *n.* (Comp.) Ausgabe, *die;* ~-**write** *n. attrib.* (Comp.) Schreib-Lese-; ~-**write head** Schreib-Lese-Kopf, *der*

**ready** /'redɪ/ **1** *adj.* **(a)** (prepared) fertig; **be** ~ **to do sth.** bereit sein, etw. zu tun; **get** ~: sich fertig machen
**(b)** (willing) bereit
**(c)** (within reach) griffbereit
**2** *adv.* fertig
**3** *n.* **at the** ~ ⟨*Schusswaffe*⟩ im Anschlag

**ready:** ~ '**cash** ▶ ~ MONEY; ~-**cooked** *adj.* vorgekocht; ~-**cooked meal** Fertiggericht, *das;* Fertigmahlzeit, *die;* ~-'**made** *adj.* **(a)** Konfektions⟨*anzug, -kleidung*⟩; **(b)** (fig.) vorgefertigt; ~ '**money** *n.* Bargeld, *das;* ~-**to-eat** *adj.* Fertig⟨*mahlzeit, -dessert*⟩; ~-**to-serve** *adj.* tischfertig; ~-**to-wear** *adj.* Konfektions⟨*anzug, -kleidung*⟩

**real** /rɪəl/ *adj.* **(a)** (actually existing) real ⟨*Ereignis, Lebewesen*⟩; wirklich ⟨*Macht*⟩
**(b)** (genuine) echt ⟨*Interesse, Gold, Seide*⟩
**(c)** (complete) total (ugs.) ⟨*Desaster, Enttäuschung*⟩

**(d)** (true) wahr ⟨*Grund, Name, Glück*⟩; echt ⟨*Mitleid, Sieg*⟩; **the** ~ **thing** der/die/das Echte
**(e) be for** ~ (coll.) echt sein

**'real estate** *n.* (Amer.) Immobilien *Pl.*

**realism** /'rɪəlɪzm/ *n.* Realismus, *der*

**'realist** *n.* Realist, *der*/Realistin, *die*

**realistic** /rɪə'lɪstɪk/ *adj.* realistisch

**reality** /rɪ'ælɪtɪ/ *n.* Realität, *die;* **in** ~: in Wirklichkeit

**realization** /rɪəlaɪ'zeɪʃn/ *n.* Erkenntnis, *die*

**realize** /'rɪəlaɪz/ *v.t.* **(a)** (be aware of) bemerken; erkennen ⟨*Fehler*⟩; **I didn't** ~ *abs.* ich habe es nicht gewusst; ~ [**that**] ...: merken, dass ...
**(b)** (make happen) verwirklichen
**(c)** erbringen ⟨*Summe, Preis*⟩

**real-life** *attrib. adj.* real

**really** /'rɪəlɪ/ *adv.* wirklich; **not** ~: eigentlich nicht; [**well,**] ~! [also] so was!

**realm** /relm/ *n.* Reich, *das*

**realtor** /'rɪəltə(r)/ (Amer.) Grundstücksmakler, *der*

**reap** /riːp/ *v.t.* (cut) schneiden ⟨*Getreide*⟩; (gather in) einfahren ⟨*Getreide, Ernte*⟩

**reappear** /riːə'pɪə(r)/ *v.i.* wieder auftauchen; (come back) [wieder] zurückkommen

**rear¹** /rɪə(r)/ **1** *n.* **(a)** (back part) hinterer Teil
**(b)** (back) Rückseite, *die*
**(c)** (Mil.) Rücken, *der*
**2** *adj.* hinter...; ~ **axle** Hinterachse, *die*

**rear²** **1** *v.t.* großziehen ⟨*Kind, Familie*⟩; halten ⟨*Vieh*⟩
**2** *v.i.* ⟨*Pferd:*⟩ sich aufbäumen

**rear:** ~**guard** *n.* (Mil.) Nachhut, *die;* ~ **light** *n.* Rücklicht, *das;* ~-**wheel drive** **1** *n.* Hinterradantrieb, *der;* **2** *adj.* a ~-**wheel drive vehicle** ein Fahrzeug mit Hinterradantrieb

**rearm** /riː'ɑːm/ *v.i. & t.* wieder aufrüsten

**rearrange** /riːə'reɪndʒ/ *v.t.* umräumen ⟨*Möbel*⟩; verlegen ⟨*Spiel*⟩ (**for** auf + *Akk.*); ändern ⟨*Programm*⟩

**rear-view 'mirror** *n.* Rückspiegel, *der*

**reason** /'riːzn/ **1** *n.* **(a)** (cause) Grund, *der;* **have no** ~ **to complain** sich nicht beklagen können; **for that** [**very**] ~: aus [eben] diesem Grund
**(b)** (power to understand; sense) Vernunft, *die;* (power to think) Verstand, *der;* **in** *or* **within** ~: innerhalb eines vernünftigen Rahmens; **it stands to** ~ **that** ...: es ist unzweifelhaft, dass ...
**2** *v.i.* **(a)** schlussfolgern (**from** aus)
**(b)** ~ **with** diskutieren mit (**about, on** über + *Akk.*); **you can't** ~ **with her** mit ihr kann man nicht vernünftig reden
**3** *v.t.* schlussfolgern

**reasonable** /'riːzənəbl/ *adj.* **(a)** vernünftig
**(b)** (inexpensive) günstig ┈┈▸

**r**

**reasonably** /'riːzənəblɪ/ adv. (a) (within reason) vernünftig
(b) (fairly) ganz ⟨gut⟩; ziemlich ⟨gesund⟩
**reasoned** /'riːznd/ adj. durchdacht
**reasoning** /'riːzənɪŋ/ n. logisches Denken
**reassurance** /riːə'ʃʊərəns/ n. (a) (calming) give sb. ∼: jmdn. beruhigen
(b) (confirmation) Bestätigung, die
**reassure** /riːə'ʃʊə(r)/ v.t. beruhigen; ∼ sb. about his health. jmdm. versichern, dass er gesund ist
**reassuring** /riːə'ʃʊərɪŋ/ adj. beruhigend
**rebate** /'riːbeɪt/ n. (a) (refund) Rückzahlung, die
(b) (discount) Preisnachlass, der (on auf + Akk.)
**rebel** ⟨1⟩ /'rebl/ n. Rebell, der/Rebellin, die
⟨2⟩ attrib. adj. Rebellen-
⟨3⟩ /rɪ'bel/ v.i., -ll- rebellieren
**rebellion** /rɪ'beljən/ n. Rebellion, die
**rebellious** /rɪ'beljəs/ adj. rebellisch
**rebirth** /riː'bɜːθ/ n. (revival) Wiederaufleben, das
**reboot** /riː'buːt/ (Comp.) v.t. & i. neu booten
**rebound** ⟨1⟩ /rɪ'baʊnd/ v.i. (a) (spring back) abprallen (from von)
(b) (fig.) zurückfallen (upon auf + Akk.)
⟨2⟩ /'riːbaʊnd/ n. Abprall, der
**rebuff** /rɪ'bʌf/ ⟨1⟩ n. [schroffe] Abweisung
⟨2⟩ v.t. [schroff] zurückweisen
**rebuild** /riː'bɪld/ v.t., rebuilt /riː'bɪlt/ wieder aufbauen
**rebuke** /rɪ'bjuːk/ ⟨1⟩ v.t. tadeln, rügen (for wegen)
⟨2⟩ n. Rüge, die
**recall** ⟨1⟩ /rɪ'kɔːl/ v.t. (a) (remember) sich erinnern an (+ Akk.)
(b) (serve as reminder of) erinnern an (+ Akk.)
(c) abberufen ⟨Botschafter⟩
⟨2⟩ /rɪ'kɔːl, 'riːkɔːl/ n. (a) [powers of] ∼: Gedächtnis, das
(b) beyond ∼: unwiderruflich
**recant** /rɪ'kænt/ v.i. [öffentlich] widerrufen
**recap** /'riːkæp/ v.t. & i., -pp- (coll.) rekapitulieren
**recapitulate** /riːkə'pɪtjʊleɪt/ v.t. & i. rekapitulieren
**recapture** /riː'kæptʃə(r)/ v.t. wieder ergreifen ⟨Gefangenen⟩; wieder einfangen ⟨Tier⟩
**recede** /rɪ'siːd/ v.i. ⟨Hochwasser, Flut:⟩ zurückgehen; ∼ [into the distance] in der Ferne verschwinden
**receding** /rɪ'siːdɪŋ/ adj. fliehend ⟨Kinn, Stirn⟩
**receipt** /rɪ'siːt/ n. (a) (receiving) Empfang, der
(b) (written acknowledgement) Quittung, die
(c) in pl. (amount received) Einnahmen Pl. (from aus)
**receive** /rɪ'siːv/ v.t. (a) (get) erhalten; beziehen ⟨Gehalt, Rente⟩

(b) (accept) entgegennehmen ⟨Strauß, Lieferung⟩
(c) (entertain) empfangen ⟨Gast⟩
**re'ceiver** n. (a) Empfänger, der/ Empfängerin, die
(b) (Teleph.) [Telefon]hörer, der
(c) (of stolen goods) Hehler, der/Hehlerin, die
**recent** /'riːsənt/ adj. jüngst... ⟨Ereignisse, Vergangenheit usw.⟩; the ∼ closure of the factory die kürzlich erfolgte Schließung der Fabrik
**'recently** adv. (a short time ago) vor kurzem; (in the recent past) in der letzten Zeit
**receptacle** /rɪ'septəkl/ n. Behälter, der; Gefäß, das
**reception** /rɪ'sepʃn/ n. (a) (welcome) Aufnahme, die
(b) (party) Empfang, der
(c) (Brit.: foyer) die Rezeption
**reception:** ∼ com'mittee n. Empfangskomitee, das; ∼ desk n. Rezeption, die
**re'ceptionist** n. (in hotel) Empfangschef, der/-dame, die; (at doctor's) Sprechstundenhilfe, die
**receptive** /rɪ'septɪv/ adj. aufgeschlossen, empfänglich (to für)
**recess** /rɪ'ses, 'riːses/ n. (a) (alcove) Nische, die
(b) (Brit. Parl.; Amer.: short vacation) Ferien Pl.; (Amer. Sch.; between classes) Pause, die
**recession** /rɪ'seʃn/ n. (Econ.) Rezession, die (fachspr.); Konjunkturrückgang, der
**recharge** /riː'tʃɑːdʒ/ v.t. aufladen ⟨Batterie⟩
**rechargeable** /riː'tʃɑːdʒəbl/ adj. wieder aufladbar
**recipe** /'resɪpɪ/ n. Rezept, das
**recipient** /rɪ'sɪpɪənt/ n. Empfänger, der/ Empfängerin, die
**reciprocal** /rɪ'sɪprəkl/ adj. gegenseitig ⟨Abkommen, Zuneigung⟩
**reciprocate** /rɪ'sɪprəkeɪt/ v.t. erwidern
**recital** /rɪ'saɪtl/ n. (performance) [Solisten]konzert, das; (of literature also) Rezitation, die
**recitation** /resɪ'teɪʃn/ n. Rezitation, die
**recite** /rɪ'saɪt/ v.t. (a) rezitieren ⟨Gedicht⟩
(b) (list) aufzählen
**reckless** /'reklɪs/ adj. unbesonnen; rücksichtslos ⟨Fahrweise⟩; ∼ of the dangers/ consequences ungeachtet der Gefahren/ Folgen
**reckon** /'rekn/ v.t. (a) (work out) ausrechnen ⟨Kosten⟩; bestimmen ⟨Position⟩
(b) (consider) halten (as für)
(c) (estimate) schätzen
■ **'reckon on** v.t. (a) (rely on) zählen auf (+ Akk.)
(b) (expect) rechnen mit
■ **'reckon with** v.i. rechnen mit
**'reckoning** n. Berechnung, die; by my ∼: nach meiner Rechnung

**reclaim** /rɪˈkleɪm/ v.t. **(a)** zurückbekommen ⟨*Steuern*⟩ **(b)** urbar machen ⟨*Land*⟩

**recline** /rɪˈklaɪn/ v.i. liegen; **reclining seat** Liegesitz, *der*

**recluse** /rɪˈkluːs/ n. Einsiedler, *der*/ Einsiedlerin, *die*

**recognition** /rekəgˈnɪʃn/ n. **(a)** Wiedererkennen, *das;* **be beyond all** ~: nicht wieder zu erkennen sein **(b)** (acknowledgement) Anerkennung, *die;* **in** ~ **of** als Anerkennung für

**recognize** /ˈrekəgnaɪz/ v.t. **(a)** (know again) wieder erkennen **(by** an + *Dat.,* **from** durch) **(b)** (acknowledge) erkennen; anerkennen ⟨*Gültigkeit, Land*⟩; **be** ~**d as** gelten als

**recoil** ☐ /rɪˈkɔɪl/ v.i. zurückfahren ☐ /ˈriːkɔɪl, rɪˈkɔɪl/ n. Rückstoß, *der*

**recollect** /rekəˈlekt/ ☐ v.t. sich erinnern an (+ *Akk.*) ☐ v.i. sich erinnern

**recollection** /rekəˈlekʃn/ n. Erinnerung, *die*

**recommend** /rekəˈmend/ v.t. empfehlen

**recommendation** /rekəmenˈdeɪʃn/ n. Empfehlung, *die;* **on sb.'s** ~: auf jmds. Empfehlung (*Akk.*)

**recompense** /ˈrekəmpens/ ☐ v.t. entschädigen ☐ n. Entschädigung, *die*

**reconcile** /ˈrekənsaɪl/ v.t. **(a)** (restore to friendship) versöhnen **(b)** ~ **oneself to sth.** sich mit etw. versöhnen

**reconciliation** /rekənsɪlɪˈeɪʃn/ n. Versöhnung, *die*

**recondition** /riːkənˈdɪʃn/ v.t. [general]überholen; ~**ed engine** Austauschmotor, *der*

**reconnaissance** /rɪˈkɒnɪsəns/ n. (Mil.) Aufklärung, *die*

**reconnoitre** (Brit.; Amer.: **reconnoiter**) /rekəˈnɔɪtə(r)/ v.i. auf Erkundung [aus]gehen

**reconsider** /riːkənˈsɪdə(r)/ v.t. [noch einmal] überdenken

**reconstruct** /riːkənˈstrʌkt/ v.t. wieder aufbauen; (fig.) rekonstruieren

**reconstruction** /riːkənˈstrʌkʃn/ n. Wiederaufbau, *der;* (thing reconstructed) Rekonstruktion, *die*

**record** ☐ /rɪˈkɔːd/ v.t. **(a)** aufzeichnen; ~ **a new CD** eine neue CD aufnehmen **(b)** (register officially) dokumentieren; protokollieren ⟨*Verhandlung*⟩ ☐ /ˈrekɔːd/ n. **(a)** **be on** ~ ⟨*Prozess, Verhandlung, Besprechung:*⟩ protokolliert sein; **have sth. on** ~: etw. dokumentiert haben **(b)** (report) Protokoll, *das* **(c)** (document) Dokument, *das;* **[strictly] off the** ~: [ganz] inoffiziell **(d)** (for ~ player) [Schall]platte, *die*

**(e)** **have a [criminal/police]** ~: vorbestraft sein **(f)** (Sport) Rekord, *der*

**record** /ˈrekɔːd/: ~**-breaking** adj. Rekord-; ~ **deck** n. Plattenspieler, *der*

**recorded** /rɪˈkɔːdɪd/ adj. aufgezeichnet ⟨*Konzert, Rede*⟩; ~ **music** Musikaufnahmen *Pl.*

**recorded deˈlivery** n. (Brit. Post.) eingeschriebene Sendung (ohne Versicherung)

**recorder** /rɪˈkɔːdə(r)/ n. (Mus.) Blockflöte, *die*

**ˈrecord holder** n. (Sport) Rekordhalter, *der*/-halterin, *die*

**recording** /rɪˈkɔːdɪŋ/ n. **(a)** (process) Aufzeichnung, *die* **(b)** (what is recorded) Aufnahme, *die*

**recording:** ~ **head** n. Aufnahmekopf, *der;* ~ **studio** n. Tonstudio, *das*

**record** /ˈrekɔːd/: ~ **player** n. Plattenspieler, *der;* ~ **sleeve** n. Plattenhülle, *die;* ~ **token** n. [Schall]plattengutschein, *der*

**re-count** ☐ /riːˈkaʊnt/ v.t. [noch einmal] nachzählen ☐ /ˈriːkaʊnt/ n. Nachzählung, *die*

**recoup** /rɪˈkuːp/ v.t. [wieder] hereinbekommen ⟨*[Geld]einsatz*⟩

**recourse** /rɪˈkɔːs/ n. **have** ~ **to sb./sth.** bei jmdm./zu etw. Zuflucht nehmen

**recover** /rɪˈkʌvə(r)/ ☐ v.t. zurückbekommen ☐ v.i. ~ **from sth.** sich von etw. [wieder] erholen; **be [fully]** ~**ed** [völlig] wiederhergestellt sein

**recovery** /rɪˈkʌvərɪ/ n. Erholung, *die;* **make a quick/good** ~: sich schnell/gut erholen

**recovery:** ~ **position** n. (Med.) stabile Seitenlage; ~ **vehicle** n. Bergungsfahrzeug, *das*

**recreation** /rekrɪˈeɪʃn/ n. Freizeitbeschäftigung, *die;* Hobby, *das*

**recreational** /rekrɪˈeɪʃənl/ adj. Freizeit-

**recreational:** ~ **ˈdrug** n. Freizeitdroge, *die;* ~ **ˈvehicle** n. (Amer.) Wohnmobil, *das*

**recreˈation centre** n. Freizeitzentrum, *das*

**recrimination** /rɪkrɪmɪˈneɪʃn/ n. Gegenbeschuldigung, *die*

**recruit** /rɪˈkruːt/ ☐ n. **(a)** (Mil.) Rekrut, *der* **(b)** (new member) neues Mitglied ☐ v.t. (Mil.: enlist) anwerben; (into party etc.) werben ⟨*Mitglied*⟩; einstellen ⟨*neuen Mitarbeiter*⟩

**reˈcruitment** n. (Mil.) Anwerbung, *die;* (of new staff) Neueinstellung, *die;* ~ **of members** Mitgliederwerbung, *die*

**rectangle** /ˈrektæŋgl/ n. Rechteck, *das*

**rectangular** /rekˈtæŋgjʊlə(r)/ adj. rechteckig

**rector** /ˈrektə(r)/ n. **(a)** Pfarrer, *der* **(b)** (Univ.) Rektor, *der*/Rektorin, *die*   ···⟩

**r**

**rectory** /'rektərɪ/ n. Pfarrhaus, das

**recuperate** /rɪ'kju:pəreɪt/ v.i. sich erholen

**recuperation** /rɪkju:pə'reɪʃn/ n. Erholung, die

**recur** /rɪ'kə:(r)/ v.i., **-rr-** sich wiederholen; ⟨Krankheit:⟩ wiederkehren; ⟨Symptom:⟩ wieder auftreten

**recurrence** /rɪ'kʌrəns/ n. Wiederholung, die; (of illness, thought, feeling) Wiederkehr, die; (of symptom) Wiederauftreten, das

**recurrent** /rɪ'kʌrənt/ adj. immer wiederkehrend

**recycle** /ri:'saɪkl/ v.t. wieder verwerten; ∼d paper Recyclingpapier, das

**recyclable** /ri:'saɪkləbl/ adj. recycelbar

**recycling** /ri:'saɪklɪŋ/ n. Recycling, das

**red** /red/ ① adj. rot
② n. (a) Rot, das
(b) (debt) [be] in the ∼: in den roten Zahlen [sein]

**red:** ∼ **'card** n. (Footb.) rote Karte, die; **Red 'Cross** n. Rotes Kreuz; ∼**'currant** n. [rote] Johannisbeere

**redden** /'redn/ v.i. ⟨Gesicht, Himmel:⟩ sich röten; ⟨Person:⟩ rot werden

**reddish** /'redɪʃ/ adj. rötlich

**redecorate** /ri:'dekəreɪt/ v.t. renovieren; (with wallpaper) neu tapezieren; (with paint) neu streichen

**redeem** /rɪ'di:m/ v.t. (a) [wieder] einlösen ⟨Pfand⟩; einlösen ⟨Gutschein, Coupon⟩
(b) (save) retten

**redemption** /rɪ'dempʃn/ n. (from sin) Erlösung, die

**redeploy** /ri:dɪ'plɔɪ/ v.t. woanders einsetzen ⟨Arbeitskräfte⟩

**red:** ∼**'handed** adj. catch sb. ∼**-handed** jmdn. auf frischer Tat ertappen; ∼ **'herring** n. (fig.) Ablenkungsmanöver, das; ∼**-hot** adj. [rot] glühend

**redial** ① /ri:'daɪəl/ v.t. noch einmal wählen ⟨Telefonnummer⟩
② /'ri:daɪəl/ n. Wahlwiederholung, die; ∼ **button** Wahlwiederholungstaste, die

**Red 'Indian** (Brit.) ① n. Indianer, der/ Indianerin, die
② adj. Indianer-

**redirect** /ri:daɪ'rekt/ v.t. nachsenden ⟨Post, Brief usw.⟩; umleiten ⟨Verkehr⟩

**rediscover** /ri:dɪ'skʌvə(r)/ v.t. wieder entdecken

**redistribute** /ri:dɪ'strɪbju:t/ v.t. umverteilen ⟨Besitz, Einkommen⟩

**redistribution** /ri:dɪstrɪ'bju:ʃn/ n. (of land, wealth) Umverteilung, die

**red:** ∼**'letter day** n. großer Tag; ∼ **'light** n. rotes Warnlicht; (traffic light) rote Ampel; drive through a ∼ light bei Rot über die Ampel fahren; ∼**-'light district** n. Strich, der (salopp); ∼ **meat** n. dunkles Fleisch (z.B. vom Rind)

**redo** /ri:'du:/ v.t. forms as DO: noch einmal machen ⟨Bett, Hausaufgabe⟩; neu frisieren ⟨Haare⟩

**redouble** /ri:'dʌbl/ v.t. verdoppeln

**red 'pepper** n. rote Paprika[schote]

**redress** /rɪ'dres/ ① n. Entschädigung, die
② v.t. wieder gutmachen; ∼ **the balance** das Gleichgewicht wiederherstellen

**red 'tape** n. (fig.) [unnötige] Bürokratie

**reduce** /rɪ'dju:s/ v.t. (a) senken ⟨Preis, Gebühr, Fieber, Aufwendungen, Blutdruck usw.⟩; reduzieren ⟨Geschwindigkeit, Gewicht⟩; at ∼d prices zu herabgesetzten Preisen
(b) ∼ **to silence/tears** verstummen lassen/ zum Weinen bringen

**reduction** /rɪ'dʌkʃn/ n. (in price, costs, speed, etc.) Senkung, die (in Gen.); ∼ **in wages/ weight** Lohnsenkung, die/Gewichtsabnahme, die

**redundancy** /rɪ'dʌndənsɪ/ n. (Brit.) Arbeitslosigkeit, die; **redundancies** Entlassungen Pl.; take or accept voluntary ∼: seiner betriebsbedingten Kündigung zustimmen

**re'dundancy payment** n. Abfindung, die

**redundant** /rɪ'dʌndənt/ adj. (Brit.) arbeitslos; be made ∼: den Arbeitsplatz verlieren; make ∼: entlassen

**red 'wine** n. Rotwein, der

**reed** /ri:d/ n. Schilf[rohr], das

**re-educate** /ri:'edjukeɪt/ v.t. umerziehen

**reef** /ri:f/ n. Riff, das

**'reef knot** n. Kreuzknoten, der

**reek** /ri:k/ v.i. stinken (of nach)

**reel** /ri:l/ ① n. ⟨Garn-, Angel⟩rolle, die; ⟨Film-, Tonband⟩spule, die
② v.i. (a) (be in a whirl) sich drehen
(b) (sway) torkeln

**re-establish** /ri:ɪ'stæblɪʃ/ v.t. wiederherstellen

**re-examine** /ri:ɪg'zæmɪn/ v.t. (scrutinize) erneut überprüfen

**ref** /ref/ n. (Sport coll.) Schiri, der (Sportjargon)

**ref.** abbr. = **reference** Verw.; **your/our ref.** Ihr/unser Zeichen

**refashion** /ri:'fæʃn/ v.t. umgestalten

**refectory** /rɪ'fektərɪ/ n. Mensa, die

**refer** /rɪ'fə:(r)/ ① v.i., **-rr-:** (a) ∼ **to** (allude to) sich beziehen auf (+ Akk.) ⟨Buch, Person usw.⟩; (speak of) sprechen von ⟨Person, Problem usw.⟩
(b) ∼ **to** (apply to, relate to) betreffen
(c) ∼ **to** (consult, cite as proof) nachsehen in (+ Dat.)
② v.t., **-rr-:** ∼ **sb./sth. to sb./sth.** jmdn./etw. an jmdn./auf etw. (Akk.) verweisen

**referee** /refə'ri:/ (Sport) ① n. (umpire) Schiedsrichter, der/-richterin, die; (Boxing) Ringrichter, der
② v.t. als Schiedsrichter/-richterin leiten

**reference** /'refrəns/ n. (a) (allusion) Hinweis, der (to auf + Akk.); **make no ~ to sth.** etw. nicht ansprechen
(b) (testimonial) Zeugnis, das
**reference: ~ book** n. Nachschlagewerk, das; **~ number** n. [Kenn]nummer, die; **~ point** n. Bezugspunkt, der
**referendum** /refə'rendəm/ n. Volksentscheid, der
**refill** [1] /ri:'fɪl/ v.t. nachfüllen; **~ the glasses** nachschenken
[2] /'ri:fɪl/ n. (for ball pen) Ersatzmine, die
**refine** /rɪ'faɪn/ v.t. (a) (purify) raffinieren
(b) (make cultured) kultivieren
(c) (improve) verbessern; verfeinern ⟨Stil, Technik⟩
**refined** /rɪ'faɪnd/ adj. kultiviert
**re'finement** n. Kultiviertheit, die; (improvement) Verbesserung, die
**refinery** /rɪ'faɪnərɪ/ n. Raffinerie, die
**reflate** /ri:'fleɪt/ v.t. (Econ.) ankurbeln
**reflation** /ri:'fleɪʃn/ n. (Econ.) Reflation, die
**reflect** /rɪ'flekt/ v.t. (a) reflektieren
(b) (fig.) widerspiegeln ⟨Ansichten⟩
(c) (contemplate) nachdenken über (+ Akk.); **~ what/how ...:** überlegen, was/wie ...
■ **re'flect [up]on** v.t. (a) (consider) nachdenken über (+ Akk.)
(b) **~ badly [up]on sb./sth.** auf jmdn./etw. ein schlechtes Licht werfen
**reflection** /rɪ'flekʃn/ n. (a) Reflexion, die; (by surface of water) Spiegelung, die
(b) (image) Spiegelbild, das
(c) (consideration) Nachdenken, das (**upon** über + Akk.); **on ~:** bei weiterem Nachdenken
**reflective** /rɪ'flektɪv/ adj. (a) reflektierend
(b) (thoughtful) nachdenklich
**reflector** /rɪ'flektə(r)/ n. Rückstrahler, der
**reflex** /'ri:fleks/ [1] n. Reflex, der
[2] adj. **~ action** Reflexhandlung, die
**reflexive** /rɪ'fleksɪv/ adj. (Ling.) reflexiv
**reforestation** /ri:fɒrɪ'steɪʃn/ n. Wiederaufforstung, die
**reform** /rɪ'fɔ:m/ [1] v.t. (make better) bessern ⟨Person⟩; reformieren ⟨Institution⟩
[2] n. Reform, die (**in** Gen.)
**reformation** /refə'meɪʃn/ n. (of character) Wandlung, die; **the R~** (Hist.) die Reformation
**re'former** n. [political] **~:** Reformpolitiker, der/-politikerin, die
**refract** /rɪ'frækt/ v.t. (Phys.) brechen
**refrain¹** /rɪ'freɪn/ n. Refrain, der
**refrain²** v.i. **~ from doing sth.** es unterlassen, etw. zu tun
**refresh** /rɪ'freʃ/ v.t. erfrischen
**re'fresher course** n. Auffrischungskurs, der
**re'freshing** adj. erfrischend; wohltuend ⟨Abwechslung⟩
**re'freshment** n. Erfrischung, die

**refrigerate** /rɪ'frɪdʒəreɪt/ v.t. (a) kühl lagern ⟨Lebensmittel⟩
(b) (chill) kühlen; (freeze) einfrieren
**refrigeration** /rɪfrɪdʒə'reɪʃn/ n. kühle Lagerung; (chilling) Kühlung, die; (freezing) Einfrieren, das
**refrigerator** /rɪ'frɪdʒəreɪtə(r)/ n. Kühlschrank, der
**refuel** /ri:'fju:əl/, (Brit.) -ll-: [1] v.t. auftanken
[2] v.i. [auf]tanken
**refuge** /'refju:dʒ/ n. Zuflucht, die; **take ~ in** Schutz od. Zuflucht suchen in (+ Dat.) (**from** vor + Dat.); **women's ~:** Frauenhaus, das
**refugee** /refjʊ'dʒi:/ n. Flüchtling, der
**refu'gee camp** n. Flüchtlingslager, das
**refund** [1] /ri:'fʌnd/ v.t. (pay back) zurückzahlen ⟨Geld⟩; erstatten ⟨Kosten⟩
[2] /'ri:fʌnd/ n. Rückzahlung, die; (of expenses) [Rück]erstattung, die
**refundable** /ri:'fʌndəbl/ adj. **be ~:** zurückerstattet werden
**refurbish** /ri:'fɜ:bɪʃ/ v.t. renovieren ⟨Haus⟩
**refurnish** /ri:'fɜ:nɪʃ/ v.t. neu einrichten
**refusal** /rɪ'fju:zl/ n. Ablehnung, die; (after a period of time) Absage, die; **~ to do sth.** Weigerung, etw. zu tun
**refuse¹** /rɪ'fju:z/ [1] v.t. ablehnen; verweigern ⟨Zutritt, Einreise, Erlaubnis⟩; **~ sb. admittance/entry/permission** jmdn. den Zutritt/die Einreise/die Erlaubnis verweigern; **~ to do sth.** sich weigern, etw. zu tun
[2] v.i. ablehnen; (after request) sich weigern
**refuse²** /'refju:s/ n. Abfall, der
**refuse** /'refju:s/ **~ collection** n. Müllabfuhr, die; **~ collector** n. Müllwerker, der; **~ disposal** n. Abfallbeseitigung, die
**refute** /rɪ'fju:t/ v.t. widerlegen
**regain** /rɪ'geɪn/ v.t. zurückgewinnen ⟨Zuversicht, Vertrauen, Augenlicht⟩; **~ one's strength** wieder zu Kräften kommen
**regal** /'ri:gl/ adj. majestätisch
**regalia** /rɪ'geɪlɪə/ n. pl. (of royalty) Krönungsinsignien Pl.
**regard** /rɪ'gɑ:d/ [1] v.t. (a) (look at) betrachten
(b) (give heed to) beachten
(c) (fig.: look upon, contemplate) betrachten; **~ sb. as a friend/fool/genius** jmdn. als Freund betrachten/für einen Dummkopf/ein Genie halten; **be ~ed as** gelten als
(d) (concern, have relation to) betreffen; **as ~s sb./sth., ~ing sb./sth.** was jmdn./etw. angeht od. betrifft
[2] n. (a) (attention) **pay** or **have ~ to sb./sth.** jmdm./etw. Beachtung schenken; **without ~ to** ohne Rücksicht auf (+ Akk.)
(b) (esteem) Achtung, die; **hold sb./sth. in high ~:** jmdn./etw. sehr schätzen
(c) **in** pl. Grüße Pl.; **give her my ~s** grüße sie von mir; **with kind[est] ~s** mit herzlich[st]en Grüßen

r

**re'gardless** *adj.* ohne Rücksicht (of auf + *Akk.*)

**regatta** /rɪ'gætə/ *n.* Regatta, *die*

**regenerate** /rɪ'dʒenəreɪt/ *v.t.* erneuern

**reggae** /'regeɪ/ *n.* Reggae, *der*

**regime, régime** /reɪ'ʒiːm/ *n.* [Regierungs]system, *das*

**regiment** /'redʒɪmənt/ *n.* Regiment, *das*

**regimental** /redʒɪ'mentl/ *adj.* Regiments-

**region** /'riːdʒn/ *n.* (a) (area) Gebiet, *das* (b) (administrative division) Bezirk, *der;* **in the ~ of** (fig.) ungefähr

**regional** /'riːdʒənl/ *adj.* regional

**regionalism** /'riːdʒənəlɪzm/ *n.* (Polit., Ling.) Regionalismus, *der*

**regionalize** /'riːdʒənəlaɪz/ *v.t.* regionalisieren

**register** /'redʒɪstə(r)/ ⓵ *n.* Register, *das;* (at school) Klassenbuch, *das* ⓶ *v.t.* (a) (enter) registrieren; (cause to be entered) registrieren lassen; anmelden ⟨*Auto, Patent*⟩; (at airport) einchecken ⟨*Gepäck*⟩; *abs.* (at hotel) sich ins Fremdenbuch eintragen; **~ with the police** sich polizeilich anmelden (b) (enrol) anmelden; (Univ.) sich einschreiben (c) zum Ausdruck bringen ⟨*Überraschung*⟩; **~ a protest** Protest anmelden

**registered** /'redʒɪstəd/ *adj.* eingetragen ⟨*Firma*⟩; eingeschrieben ⟨*Student, Brief*⟩; **~ trade mark** eingetragenes Warenzeichen; **by ~ post** per Einschreiben

**registrar** /'redʒɪstrɑː(r)/ *n.* Standesbeamte, *der/*-beamtin, *die*

**registration** /redʒɪ'streɪʃn/ *n.* Registrierung, *die;* (enrolment) Anmeldung, *die;* (of students) Einschreibung, *die*

**registration: ~ document** *n.* (Brit.) Kraftfahrzeugbrief, *der;* **~ form** *n.* Anmeldeformular, *das;* **~ number** *n.* amtliches Kennzeichen; **~ plate** *n.* (Motor Veh.) Nummernschild, *das*

**registry** /'redʒɪstrɪ/ *n.* **~ [office]** Standesamt, *das*

**regret** /rɪ'gret/ ⓵ *v.t.,* **-tt-** bedauern; **I ~ to say that …:** ich muss leider sagen, dass … ⓶ *n.* Bedauern, *das;* **have no ~s** nichts bereuen

**regretfully** /rɪ'gretfəlɪ/ *adv.* mit Bedauern

**regrettable** /rɪ'gretəbl/ *adj.* bedauerlich

**regrettably** /rɪ'gretəblɪ/ *adv.* bedauerlicherweise

**regroup** /riː'gruːp/ ⓵ *v.t.* umgruppieren ⓶ *v.i.* (a) (form new group) sich neu gruppieren (b) (Mil.) sich neu formieren

**regular** /'regjʊlə(r)/ ⓵ *adj.* regelmäßig; geregelt ⟨*Arbeit*⟩; fest ⟨*Anstellung*⟩; **~ customer** Stammkunde, *der/*-kundin, *die;* **~ army** reguläre Armee ⓶ *n.* (coll.: ~ customer) Stammkunde, *der/* -kundin, *die;* (in pub) Stammgast, *der*

**regularity** /regjʊ'lærɪtɪ/ *n.* Regelmäßigkeit, *die*

**'regularly** *adv.* regelmäßig

**regulate** /'regjʊleɪt/ *v.t.* (control) regeln; (restrict) begrenzen; (adjust) regulieren

**regulation** /regjʊ'leɪʃn/ *n.* (a) ▶ REGULATE: Regelung, *die;* Begrenzung, *die;* Regulierung, *die* (b) (rule) Vorschrift, *die*

**rehabilitate** /riːhə'bɪlɪteɪt/ *v.t.* rehabilitieren; **~ [back into society]** wieder [in die Gesellschaft] eingliedern

**rehabilitation** /riːhəbɪlɪ'teɪʃn/ *n.* **~ [in society]** Wiedereingliederung, *die* [in die Gesellschaft]

**rehash** ⓵ /riː'hæʃ/ *v.t.* aufwärmen ⓶ /'riːhæʃ/ *n.* Aufguss, *der*

**rehearsal** /rɪ'hɜːsl/ *n.* Probe, *die*

**rehearse** /rɪ'hɜːs/ *v.t.* proben

**reheat** /riː'hiːt/ *v.t.* wieder erwärmen; aufwärmen ⟨*Essen*⟩

**rehouse** /riː'haʊz/ *v.t.* umquartieren

**reign** /reɪn/ ⓵ *n.* Herrschaft, *die* ⓶ *v.i.* herrschen (over über + *Akk.*)

**reimburse** /riːɪm'bɜːs/ *v.t.* [zurück]erstatten ⟨[*Un*]*kosten, Spesen*⟩; entschädigen ⟨*Person*⟩

**rein** /reɪn/ *n.* Zügel, *der*

**reincarnation** /riːɪnkɑː'neɪʃn/ *n.* (Relig.) Reinkarnation, *die*

**reindeer** /'reɪndɪə(r)/ *n., pl. same* Ren[tier], *das*

**reinforce** /riːɪn'fɔːs/ *v.t.* verstärken; **~d concrete** Stahlbeton, *der*

**rein'forcement** *n.* Verstärkung, *die;* **~[s]** (additional men etc.) Verstärkung, *die*

**reinstate** /riːɪn'steɪt/ *v.t.* (in job) wieder einstellen

**reintegrate** /riː'ɪntɪgreɪt/ ⓵ *v.t.* wieder eingliedern (into in + *Akk.*) ⓶ *v. refl.* sich wieder eingliedern (into in + *Akk.*)

**reintegration** /riːɪntɪ'greɪʃn/ *n.* Wiedereingliederung, *die* (into in + *Akk.*)

**reinvigorate** /riːɪn'vɪgəreɪt/ *v.t.* neu beleben; **feel ~d** sich gestärkt fühlen

**reissue** /riː'ɪʃuː/ *v.t.* neu herausbringen

**reiterate** /riː'ɪtəreɪt/ *v.t.* wiederholen

**reject** ⓵ /rɪ'dʒekt/ *v.t.* ablehnen; zurückweisen ⟨*Bitte, Annäherungsversuch*⟩ ⓶ /'riːdʒekt/ (thing) Ausschuss, *der*

**rejection** /rɪ'dʒekʃn/ *n.* Ablehnung, *die/* Zurückweisung, *die*

**re'jection slip** *n.* Absage, *die*

**rejoice** /rɪ'dʒɔɪs/ *v.i.* sich freuen (over, at über + *Akk.*)

**rejoin**[1] /rɪ'dʒɔɪn/ *v.t.* (reply) erwidern (to auf + *Akk.*)

**rejoin**[2] /riː'dʒɔɪn/ *v.t.* wieder eintreten in (+ *Akk.*) ⟨*Partei, Verein*⟩

**rejoinder** /rɪ'dʒɔɪndə(r)/ *n.* Erwiderung, *die* (to auf + *Akk.*)

**rejuvenate** /rɪ'dʒuːvəneɪt/ *v.t.* verjüngen

**rekindle** /riːˈkɪndl/ v.t. wieder anfachen; wieder aufleben lassen ⟨Verlangen, Hoffnungen⟩

**relapse** /rɪˈlæps/ ① v.i. ⟨Kranker:⟩ einen Rückfall bekommen
② n. Rückfall, der

**relate** /rɪˈleɪt/ ① v.t. (a) erzählen ⟨Geschichte⟩; erzählen von ⟨Abenteuer⟩
(b) (bring into relation) in Zusammenhang bringen (to, with mit)
② v.i. (a) ~ to (have reference) in Zusammenhang stehen mit; betreffen ⟨Person⟩
(b) ~ to (feel involved with) eine Beziehung haben zu

**reˈlated** adj. verwandt (to mit)

**relation** /rɪˈleɪʃn/ n. (a) (connection) Beziehung, die, Zusammenhang, der (of … and zwischen … und); in or with ~ to in Bezug auf (+ Akk.)
(b) in pl. (dealings) Verhältnis, das (with zu)
(c) (relative) Verwandte, der/die

**reˈlationship** n. (a) (mutual tie) Beziehung, die (with zu)
(b) (kinship) Verwandtschaftsverhältnis, das
(c) (connection) Beziehung, die; (between cause and effect) Zusammenhang, der
(d) (sexual) Verhältnis, das

**relative** /ˈrelətɪv/ ① n. Verwandte, der/die
② adj. relativ; Relativ⟨satz, -pronomen⟩

**ˈrelatively** adv. relativ; verhältnismäßig

**relative ˈpronoun** n. (Ling.) Relativpronomen, das

**relax** /rɪˈlæks/ ① v.t. (a) entspannen ⟨Muskel, Körper[teil]⟩; lockern ⟨Griff⟩
(b) (make less strict) lockern ⟨Gesetz, Disziplin⟩
② v.i. sich entspannen

**relaxation** /riːlækˈseɪʃn/ n. Entspannung, die; for ~: zur Entspannung

**relaxed** /rɪˈlækst/ adj. entspannt, gelöst ⟨Atmosphäre, Person⟩

**reˈlaxing** adj. entspannend

**relay** ① /ˈriːleɪ/ n. (a) (race) Staffel, die
(b) (gang) Schicht, die; work in ~s schichtweise arbeiten
(c) (Electr.) Relais, das
② /riːˈleɪ/ v.t. (a) weiterleiten
(b) (Radio, Telev.) übertragen

**ˈrelay race** n. Staffellauf, der; (Swimming) Staffelschwimmen, das

**release** /rɪˈliːs/ ① v.t. (a) (free) freilassen ⟨Tier, Häftling, Sklaven⟩; (from jail) entlassen (from aus)
(b) (let go) loslassen; lösen ⟨Handbremse⟩
(c) (make known) veröffentlichen ⟨Erklärung, Nachricht⟩; (issue) herausbringen ⟨Film, Schallplatte⟩
② n. (a) ▶ 1A: Freilassung, die; Entlassung, die
(b) (of published item) Veröffentlichung, die
(c) (handle, lever, button) Auslöser, der

**relegate** /ˈrelɪɡeɪt/ v.t. (a) ~ sb. to the position of …: jmdn. zu … degradieren

(b) (Sport) absteigen lassen; be ~d absteigen (to in + Akk.)

**relegation** /relɪˈɡeɪʃn/ n. (Sport) Abstieg, der

**relent** /rɪˈlent/ v.i. nachgeben

**reˈlentless** adj., **reˈlentlessly** adv. unerbittlich

**relevance** /ˈrelɪvəns/ n. Relevanz, die (to für)

**relevant** /ˈrelɪvənt/ adj. relevant (to für); wichtig ⟨Information⟩

**reliability** /rɪlaɪəˈbɪlɪti/ n. Zuverlässigkeit, die

**reliable** /rɪˈlaɪəbl/ adj., **reliably** /rɪˈlaɪəblɪ/ adv. zuverlässig

**reliance** /rɪˈlaɪəns/ n. Abhängigkeit, die (on von)

**reliant** /rɪˈlaɪənt/ adj. be ~ on sb./sth. auf jmdn./etw. angewiesen sein

**relief¹** /rɪˈliːf/ n. (a) Erleichterung, die; give [sb.] ~ [from pain] [jmdm.] [Schmerz]linderung verschaffen; what a ~!, that's a ~! da bin ich aber erleichtert!
(b) (assistance) Hilfe, die

**relief²** n. (Art) Relief, das

**relief:** ~ **bus** n. Entlastungsbus, der; (as replacement) Ersatzbus, der; ~ **map** n. Reliefkarte, die; ~ **road** n. Entlastungsstraße, die; ~ **worker** n. Helfer, der

**relieve** /rɪˈliːv/ v.t. (a) erleichtern; unterbrechen ⟨Eintönigkeit⟩; abbauen ⟨Anspannung⟩; stillen ⟨Schmerzen⟩; I am or feel ~d to hear that …: es erleichtert mich zu hören, dass …
(b) ablösen ⟨Wache, Truppen⟩

**religion** /rɪˈlɪdʒn/ n. Religion, die

**religious** /rɪˈlɪdʒəs/ adj. religiös; Religions⟨freiheit, -unterricht⟩

**reˈligiously** adv. (conscientiously) gewissenhaft

**relinquish** /rɪˈlɪŋkwɪʃ/ v.t. (a) (give up) aufgeben
(b) ~ one's hold or grip on sb./sth. jmdn./ etw. loslassen

**relish** /ˈrelɪʃ/ ① n. (a) (liking) Vorliebe, die; do sth. with [great] ~: etw. mit [großem] Genuss tun
(b) (condiment) Relish, das
② v.t. genießen

**relive** /riːˈlɪv/ n. noch einmal durchleben

**reload** /riːˈləʊd/ v.t. nachladen ⟨Schusswaffe⟩

**relocate** /riːləˈkeɪt/ ① v.t. verlegen ⟨Fabrik, Büro⟩; versetzen ⟨Angestellten⟩
② v.i. (settle) sich niederlassen

**relocation** /riːləˈkeɪʃn/ n. (of factory, office) Verlegung, die; (of employee) Versetzung, die; ~ **expenses** Umzugskosten Pl.

**reluctance** /rɪˈlʌktəns/ n. Widerwille, der; have a [great] ~ to do sth. etw. nur mit Widerwillen tun

**reluctant** /rɪˈlʌktənt/ *adj.* unwillig; **be ∼ to do sth.** etw. nur ungern tun

**reˈluctantly** *adv.* nur ungern

**rely** /rɪˈlaɪ/ *v.i.* (have trust) sich verlassen/(be dependent) angewiesen sein ([up]on auf + *Akk.*)

**remain** /rɪˈmeɪn/ *v.i.* (a) (be left over) übrigbleiben

(b) (stay) bleiben; **∼ behind** noch dableiben

(c) (continue to be) bleiben; **it ∼s to be seen** es wird sich zeigen

**remainder** /rɪˈmeɪndə(r)/ *n.* Rest, *der*

**reˈmaining** *adj.* restlich

**reˈmains** *n. pl.* (a) Reste *Pl.*

(b) (human) sterbliche [Über]reste *Pl.* (verhüll.)

**remand** /rɪˈmɑːnd/ ⟨1⟩ *v.t.* **∼ sb.** [in custody] jmdn. in Untersuchungshaft behalten

⟨2⟩ *n.* **on ∼:** in Untersuchungshaft

**remark** /rɪˈmɑːk/ ⟨1⟩ *v.t.* bemerken (**to** gegenüber)

⟨2⟩ *v.i.* eine Bemerkung machen ([up]on zu, über + *Akk.*)

⟨3⟩ *n.* Bemerkung, *die* (on über + *Akk.*)

**remarkable** /rɪˈmɑːkəbl/ *adj.* (a) (notable) bemerkenswert

(b) (extraordinary) außergewöhnlich

**remarkably** /rɪˈmɑːkəblɪ/ *adv.* (a) (notably) bemerkenswert

(b) (exceptionally) außergewöhnlich

**remarry** /riːˈmærɪ/ *v.i. & t.* wieder heiraten

**remedy** /ˈremɪdɪ/ ⟨1⟩ *n.* [Heil]mittel, *das* (for gegen)

⟨2⟩ *v.t.* beheben ⟨*Problem*⟩; retten ⟨*Situation*⟩

**remember** /rɪˈmembə(r)/ *v.t.* (a) sich erinnern an (+ *Akk.*); **I ∼ed to bring the book** ich habe daran gedacht, das Buch mitzubringen; **an evening to ∼:** ein unvergesslicher Abend

(b) (convey greetings) **∼ me to them** grüße sie von mir

**remembrance** /rɪˈmembrəns/ *n.* Gedenken, *das;* **in ∼ of sb.** zu jmds. Gedächtnis

**Remembrance Day, Remembrance Sunday** *ns.* (Brit.) ≈ Volkstrauertag, *der*

**remind** /rɪˈmaɪnd/ *v.t.* erinnern (of an + *Akk.*); **∼ sb. to do sth.** jmdn. daran erinnern, etw. zu tun; **that ∼s me, ...:** dabei fällt mir ein, ...

**reˈminder** *n.* Erinnerung, *die* (of an + *Akk.*); (letter) Mahnung, *die;* Mahnbrief, *der*

**reminisce** /remɪˈnɪs/ *v.i.* sich in Erinnerungen (*Dat.*) ergehen (**about** an + *Akk.*)

**reminiscences** /remɪˈnɪsənsɪz/ *n. pl.* Erinnerungen *Pl.*; (memoirs) [Lebens]erinnerungen *Pl.*

**reminiscent** /remɪˈnɪsənt/ *adj.* **be ∼ of sth.** an etw. (*Akk.*) erinnern

**remiss** /rɪˈmɪs/ *adj.* nachlässig (of von)

**remission** /rɪˈmɪʃn/ *n.* (a) (of debt, punishment) Erlass, *der*

(b) (of prison sentence) Straferlass, *der*

**remit** /rɪˈmɪt/ *v.t.,* **-tt-** (send) überweisen ⟨*Geld*⟩

**remittance** /rɪˈmɪtəns/ *n.* Überweisung, *die*

**remnant** /ˈremnənt/ *n.* Rest, *der*

**remonstrate** /ˈremənstreɪt/ *v.i.* protestieren (**against** gegen); **∼ with sb.** jmdm. Vorhaltungen machen (**about, on** wegen)

**remorse** /rɪˈmɔːs/ *n.* Reue, *die* (**for, about** über + *Akk.*)

**reˈmorseful** /rɪˈmɔːsfl/ *adj.* reumütig

**reˈmorseless** *adj.* unerbittlich

**remote** /rɪˈməʊt/ *adj.,* **∼r** /rɪˈməʊtə(r)/, **∼st** /rɪˈməʊtɪst/ (a) fern ⟨*Vergangenheit, Zukunft, Zeit*⟩; abgelegen ⟨*Ort, Gebiet*⟩; **∼ from** weit entfernt von

(b) (slight) gering ⟨*Chance*⟩

**remote: ∼ conˈtrol** *n.* (of vehicle) Fernlenkung, *die;* (for TV set) Fernbedienung, *die;* **∼-conˈtrol[led]** *adj.* ferngelenkt; fernbedient ⟨*Anlage*⟩

**reˈmotely** *adv.* entfernt ⟨*verwandt*⟩; **they are not ∼ alike** sie haben nicht die entfernteste Ähnlichkeit miteinander

**removable** /rɪˈmuːvəbl/ *adj.* abnehmbar; entfernbar ⟨*Trennwand*⟩; herausnehmbar ⟨*Futter*⟩

**removal** /rɪˈmuːvl/ *n.* (a) Entfernung, *die;* (of obstacle, problem) Beseitigung, *die*

(b) (transfer of furniture) Umzug, *der*

**removal: ∼ expenses** *n. pl.* Umzugskosten *Pl.;* **∼ firm** *n.* Spedition, *die;* **∼ man** *n.* Möbelpacker, *der;* **∼ van** *n.* Möbelwagen, *der*

**remove** /rɪˈmuːv/ *v.t.* entfernen; beseitigen ⟨*Spur, Hindernis*⟩; (take off) abnehmen; ausziehen ⟨*Kleidungsstück*⟩; **∼ a book from the shelf** ein Buch vom Regal nehmen

**reˈmover** *n.* (a) (of paint/varnish/hair/rust) Farb-/Lack-/Haar-/Rostentferner, *der*

(b) (man) Möbelpacker, *der;* [firm of] **∼s** Spedition[sfirma], *die*

**remunerate** /rɪˈmjuːnəreit/ *v.t.* bezahlen

**remuneration** /rɪmjuːnəˈreɪʃn/ *n.* Bezahlung, *die*

**Renaissance** /rəˈneɪsəns, rɪˈneɪsəns/ *n.* (Hist.) Renaissance, *die*

**rename** /riːˈneɪm/ *v.t.* umbenennen

**render** /ˈrendə(r)/ *v.t.* (a) (make) machen

(b) erweisen ⟨*Dienst*⟩

(c) (translate) übersetzen (by mit)

**ˈrendering** *n.* (translation) Übersetzung, *die*

**rendezvous** /ˈrɒndeɪvuː/ *n., pl. same* /ˈrɒndeɪvuːz/ (a) (meeting place) Treffpunkt, *der*

(b) (meeting) Verabredung, *die*

**renegade** /ˈrenɪgeɪd/ ⟨1⟩ *n.* Abtrünnige, *der/die*

⟨2⟩ *adj.* abtrünnig

**renegotiate** /riːnɪˈgəʊʃɪeɪt/ *v.t.* neu aushandeln

**renew** /rɪ'njuː/ v.t. erneuern; fortsetzen ⟨Angriff, Bemühungen⟩; (extend) erneuern ⟨Vertrag, Ausweis usw.⟩; ~ **a library book** ⟨Bibliothekar/Benutzer:⟩ ein Buch [aus der Bücherei] verlängern/verlängern lassen

**re'newable** /rɪ'njuːəbl/ adj. regenerationsfähig ⟨Energiequelle⟩; verlängerbar ⟨Vertrag, Genehmigung, Ausweis⟩

**renewal** /rɪ'njuːəl/ n. Erneuerung, die

**renounce** /rɪ'naʊns/ v.t. verzichten auf (+ Akk.); verstoßen ⟨Person⟩; ~ **the devil/one's faith** dem Teufel/seinem Glauben abschwören

**renovate** /'renəveɪt/ v.t. renovieren ⟨Gebäude⟩; restaurieren ⟨Möbel usw.⟩

**renovation** /renə'veɪʃn/ n. ▶ RENOVATE: Renovierung, die; Restaurierung, die

**renown** /rɪ'naʊn/ n. Renommee, das

**renowned** /rɪ'naʊnd/ adj. berühmt (for wegen, für)

**rent** /rent/ ① n. (for house etc.) Miete, die; (for land) Pacht, die

② v.t. **(a)** (use) mieten ⟨Haus, Wohnung usw.⟩; pachten ⟨Land⟩; mieten ⟨Auto⟩

**(b)** (let) vermieten ⟨Haus, Auto usw.⟩ (to Dat., an + Akk.); verpachten ⟨Land⟩ (to Dat., an + Akk.)

■ **rent 'out** v.t. ▶ RENT 2B

**rental** /'rentl/ n. Miete, die

**rent:** ~ **boy** n. (coll.) Strichjunge, der (salopp); ~ **rebate** n. Mietermäßigung, die; ~ **tribunal** n. Mietgericht, das

**renunciation** /rɪnʌnsɪ'eɪʃn/ n. ▶ RENOUNCE: Verzicht, der; Verstoßung, die

**reopen** /riː'əʊpn/ ① v.t. wieder öffnen; wieder aufmachen; wieder eröffnen ⟨Geschäft, Lokal usw.⟩; wieder aufnehmen ⟨Diskussion, Verhandlung⟩

② v.i. ⟨Geschäft, Lokal usw.:⟩ wieder öffnen

**reorder** /riː'ɔːdə(r)/ v.t. **(a)** (Commerc.) nachbestellen ⟨Ware⟩

**(b)** (rearrange) umordnen

**reorganization** /riːɔːgənəɪ'zeɪʃn/ n. Umorganisation, die; (of time, work) Neueinteilung, die

**reorganize** /riː'ɔːgənaɪz/ v.t. umorganisieren; neu einteilen ⟨Zeit, Arbeit⟩

**rep** /rep/ n. (coll.: representative) Vertreter, der/ Vertreterin, die

**repaid** ▶ REPAY

**repair** /rɪ'peə(r)/ ① v.t. (mend) reparieren; ausbessern ⟨Kleidung, Straße⟩

② n. Reparatur, die; **be in good/bad** ~: in gutem/schlechtem Zustand sein

**repair:** ~ **man** n. Mechaniker, der; (in house) Handwerker, der; ~ **shop** n. Reparaturwerkstatt, die

**repaper** /riː'peɪpə(r)/ v.t. neu tapezieren

**repatriate** /riː'pætrieɪt/ v.t. repatriieren

**repatriation** /riːpætrɪ'eɪʃn/ n. Repatriierung, die

**repay** /riː'peɪ/ v.t., **repaid** /riː'peɪd/ zurückzahlen ⟨Schulden usw.⟩; erwidern ⟨Besuch, Gruß, Freundlichkeit⟩; ~ **sb. for sth.** jmdm. etw. vergelten

**re'payment** n. Rückzahlung, die

**re'payment mortgage** n. Tilgungshypothek, die

**repeal** /rɪ'piːl/ ① v.t. aufheben ⟨Gesetz, Erlass usw.⟩

② n. Aufhebung, die

**repeat** /rɪ'piːt/ ① n. Wiederholung, die

② v.t. wiederholen; **please** ~ **after me:** ...: sprich/sprecht/sprechen Sie mir bitte nach: ...

**re'peated** adj. wiederholt; (several) mehrere; **make** ~ **efforts to** ...: wiederholt od. mehrfach versuchen, ...zu...

**re'peatedly** adv. mehrmals

**repel** /rɪ'pel/ v.t., **-ll-: (a)** (drive back) abwehren

**(b)** (be repulsive to) abstoßen

**repellent** /rɪ'pelənt/ ① adj. abstoßend

② n. [insect] ~: Insektenschutzmittel, das

**repent** /rɪ'pent/ v.i. bereuen (of Akk.)

**repentance** /rɪ'pentəns/ n. Reue, die

**repentant** /rɪ'pentənt/ adj. reuig

**repercussion** /riːpə'kʌʃn/ n., usu. in pl. Auswirkung, die ([up]on auf + Akk.)

**repertoire** /'repətwɑː(r)/ n. Repertoire, das

**repertory** /'repətərɪ/ n. (Theatre) Repertoiretheater, das

**'repertory company** n. Repertoiretheater, das

**repetition** /repɪ'tɪʃn/ n. Wiederholung, die

**repetitious** /repɪ'tɪʃəs/ adj. sich immer wiederholend attr.

**repetitive** /rɪ'petɪtɪv/ adj. eintönig

**repetitive 'strain injury** n. chronisches Überlastungssyndrom

**rephrase** /riː'freɪz/ v.t. umformulieren; **I'll** ~ **that** ich will es anders ausdrücken

**replace** /rɪ'pleɪs/ v.t. **(a)** (vertically) zurückstellen; (horizontally) zurücklegen

**(b)** (take place of) ersetzen; ~ **A with** or **by B** A durch B ersetzen

**(c)** (exchange) austauschen, auswechseln ⟨Maschinen[teile] usw.⟩

**re'placement** n. **(a)** ▶ REPLACE A: Zurückstellen, das; Zurücklegen, das

**(b)** (provision of substitute for) Ersatz, der; attrib. Ersatz-

**(c)** (substitute) Ersatz, der; ~ [part] Ersatzteil, das

**replay** ① /riː'pleɪ/ v.t. wiederholen ⟨Spiel⟩; nochmals abspielen ⟨Tonband usw.⟩

② /'riːpleɪ/ n. Wiederholung, die; (match) Wiederholungsspiel, das

**replenish** /rɪ'plenɪʃ/ v.t. auffüllen

**replica** /'replɪkə/ n. Nachbildung, die

**reply** /rɪ'plaɪ/ ① v.i. ~ **[to sb./sth.]** [jmdm./ auf etw. (Akk.)] antworten

② v.t. ~ **that** ...: antworten, dass ...

③ n. Antwort, die (to auf + Akk.)

**re'ply-paid** adj. ～-paid telegram
RP-Telegramm, das; ～-paid envelope
Freiumschlag, der

**repopulate** /riː'pɒpjʊleɪt/ v.t. neu
besiedeln

**report** /rɪ'pɔːt/ ① v.t. (a) (relate) berichten/
(in writing) einen Bericht schreiben über
(+ Akk.); (state formally also) melden
(b) (name to authorities) melden (to Dat.); (for
prosecution) anzeigen (to bei)
② v.i. (a) Bericht erstatten (on über + Akk.);
berichten (on über + Akk.)
(b) (present oneself) sich melden (to bei)
③ n. (a) (account) Bericht, der (on, about
über + Akk.)
(b) (Sch.) Zeugnis, das
(c) (of gun) Knall, der

**reportedly** /rɪ'pɔːtɪdlɪ/ adv. wie verlautet

**reported 'speech** n. indirekte Rede

**re'porter** n. Reporter, der/Reporterin, die

**repossess** /riːpə'zes/ v.t. wieder in Besitz
nehmen

**reprehensible** /reprɪ'hensɪbl/ adj.
tadelnswert

**represent** /reprɪ'zent/ v.t. (a) darstellen
(as als)
(b) (act for) vertreten

**representation** /reprɪzen'teɪʃn/ n. (a)
(depicting, image) Darstellung, die
(b) (acting for sb.) Vertretung, die
(c) make ～s to sb. bei jmdm. Protest
einlegen

**representative** /reprɪ'zentətɪv/ ① n. (a)
(Commerc.) Vertreter, der/Vertreterin, die
(b) R～ (Amer. Polit.) Abgeordnete, der/die
② adj. (typical) repräsentativ (of für)

**repress** /rɪ'pres/ v.t. (a) unterdrücken
⟨Aufruhr, Gefühle, Lachen usw.⟩
(b) (Psych.) verdrängen ⟨Gefühle⟩ (from aus)

**repressed** /rɪ'prest/ adj. unterdrückt;
(Psych.) verdrängt

**repression** /rɪ'preʃn/ n. Unterdrückung,
die

**repressive** /rɪ'presɪv/ adj. repressiv

**reprieve** /rɪ'priːv/ ① v.t. ～ sb. (postpone
execution) jmdm. Strafaufschub gewähren;
(remit execution) jmdm. begnadigen
② n. Strafaufschub, der (of für)/
Begnadigung, die; (fig.) Gnadenfrist, die

**reprimand** /'reprɪmɑːnd/ ① n. Tadel, der
② v.t. tadeln

**reprint** ① /riː'prɪnt/ v.t. wieder abdrucken
② /'riːprɪnt/ n. Nachdruck, der

**reprisal** /rɪ'praɪzl/ n. Vergeltungsakt, der
(for gegen)

**reproach** /rɪ'prəʊtʃ/ ① v.t. ～ sb. jmdm.
Vorwürfe machen
② n. Vorwurf, der

**reproachful** /rɪ'prəʊtʃfl/ adv. vorwurfsvoll

**reproduce** /riːprə'djuːs/ ① v.t.
wiedergeben
② v.i. (multiply) sich fortpflanzen

**reproduction** /riːprə'dʌkʃn/ n. (a)
Wiedergabe, die
(b) (producing offspring) Fortpflanzung, die
(c) (copy) Reproduktion, die

**reproductive** /riːprə'dʌktɪv/ adj.
Fortpflanzungs-

**reprove** /rɪ'pruːv/ v.t. tadeln

**reptile** /'reptaɪl/ n. Reptil, das

**republic** /rɪ'pʌblɪk/ n. Republik, die

**republican** /rɪ'pʌblɪkən/ ① adj.
republikanisch
② n. R～ (Amer. Polit.) Republikaner, der/
Republikanerin, die

**repudiate** /rɪ'pjuːdɪeɪt/ v.t. zurückweisen

**repugnance** /rɪ'pʌgnəns/ n. Abscheu, der
(to[wards] vor + Dat.)

**repugnant** /rɪ'pʌgnənt/ adj. widerlich (to
Dat.)

**repulse** /rɪ'pʌls/ v.t. abwehren

**repulsion** /rɪ'pʌlʃn/ n. (disgust) Widerwille,
der (towards gegen)

**repulsive** /rɪ'pʌlsɪv/ adj. abstoßend

**reputable** /'repjʊtəbl/ adj. angesehen
⟨Person, Beruf, Zeitung usw.⟩; anständig
⟨Verhalten⟩; seriös ⟨Firma⟩

**reputably** /'repjʊtəblɪ/ adv. anständig

**reputation** /repjʊ'teɪʃn/ n. (a) Ruf, der;
have a ～ for or of doing/being sth. in dem
Ruf stehen, etw. zu tun/sein
(b) (good name) Name, der

**repute** /rɪ'pjuːt/ ① v.t. in pass. be ～d [to
be] sth. als etw. gelten; she is ～d to have/
make ...: man sagt, dass sie ... hat/macht
② n. Ruf, der

**reputed** /rɪ'pjuːtɪd/ adj., **re'putedly** adv.
angeblich

**request** /rɪ'kwest/ ① v.t. bitten; ～ sth. of
or from sb. jmdn. um etw. bitten
② n. Bitte, die (for um); at sb.'s ～: auf jmds.
Bitte (Akk.) [hin]

**re'quest stop** n. (Brit.) Bedarfshaltestelle,
die

**require** /rɪ'kwaɪə(r)/ v.t. (a) (need) brauchen
(b) (order, demand) verlangen (of von); be ～d
to do sth. etw. tun müssen

**re'quirement** n. (a) (need) Bedarf, der
(b) (condition) Erfordernis, das

**requisite** /'rekwɪzɪt/ ① adj. notwendig (to,
for für)
② n. in pl. toilet/travel ～s Toiletten-/
Reiseartikel Pl.

**requisition** /rekwɪ'zɪʃn/ ① n. (order for sth.)
Anforderung, die (for Gen.)
② v.t. anfordern

**rescind** /rɪ'sɪnd/ v.t. für ungültig erklären

**rescue** /'reskjuː/ ① v.t. retten (from aus)
② n. Rettung, die; attrib. Rettungs⟨dienst,
-mannschaft⟩; go/come to the/sb.'s ～: jmdm.
zu Hilfe kommen

**rescuer** /'reskjuːə(r)/ n. Retter, der/
Retterin, die

**'rescue worker** n. [Einsatz]helfer, der/ -helferin, die

**research** /rɪ'sɜːtʃ, 'riːsɜːtʃ/ **1** n. Forschung, die (**into, on** über + Akk.) **2** v.i. forschen; ~ **into sth.** etw. erforschen

**research as'sistant** n. wissenschaftlicher Assistent/ wissenschaftliche Assistentin

**researcher** /-'--, '---/ n. Forscher, der/ Forscherin, die

**research:** ~ **student** n. ≈ Doktorand, der/Doktorandin, die; ~ **work** n. Recherchen Pl.; (medical, scientific) Forschungsarbeit, die; ~ **worker** n. ≈ Rechercheur, der/Rechercheurin, die; (medical, scientific) Forscher, der/Forscherin, die

**resell** /riː'sel/ v.t., **resold** /riː'səʊld/ weiterverkaufen (**to** an + Akk.)

**resemblance** /rɪ'zembləns/ n. Ähnlichkeit, die (**to** mit)

**resemble** /rɪ'zembl/ v.t. ähneln, gleichen (+ Dat.)

**resent** /rɪ'zent/ v.t. übel nehmen

**resentful** /rɪ'zentfl/ adj. übelnehmerisch, nachtragend ⟨Person, Art⟩; be ~ **of** or feel ~ **about sth.** etw. übel nehmen

**re'sentment** n. Groll, der (geh.); feel ~ **towards** or **against sb.** einen Groll auf jmdn. haben

**reservation** /rezə'veɪʃn/ n. (a) Reservierung, die; have a ~ **[for a room]** ein Zimmer reserviert haben (b) (doubt) Vorbehalt, der (**about** gegen); Bedenken (**about** bezüglich + Gen.); without ~: ohne Vorbehalt

**reserve** /rɪ'zɜːv/ **1** v.t. reservieren lassen ⟨Zimmer, Tisch, Platz⟩; (set aside) reservieren; ~ **the right to do sth.** sich (Dat.) [das Recht] vorbehalten, etw. zu tun **2** n. (a) (extra amount) Reserve, die (**of** an + Dat.) **have/hold** or **keep sth. in** ~: etw. in Reserve haben/halten (b) (place set apart) Reservat, das (c) (Sport) Reservespieler, der/-spielerin, die; **the R~s** die Reserve (d) (reticence) Zurückhaltung, die

**reserved** /rɪ'zɜːvd/ adj. (reticent) reserviert

**reservoir** /'rezəvwɑː(r)/ n. ([artificial] lake) Reservoir, das

**reshape** /riː'ʃeɪp/ v.t. umgestalten

**reshuffle** /riː'ʃʌfl/ **1** v.t. (a) umbilden ⟨Kabinett⟩ (b) (Cards) neu mischen **2** n. Umbildung, die

**reside** /rɪ'zaɪd/ v.i. (formal) wohnen; wohnhaft sein (Amtsspr.)

**residence** /'rezɪdəns/ n. (a) (abode) Wohnsitz, der; (of ambassador etc.) Residenz, die (b) (stay) Aufenthalt, der

**'residence permit** n. Aufenthaltsgenehmigung, die

**resident** /'rezɪdənt/ **1** adj. wohnhaft; be ~ **in England** seinen Wohnsitz in England haben **2** n. (inhabitant) Bewohner, der/Bewohnerin, die; (at hotel) Hotelgast, der

**residential** /rezɪ'denʃl/ adj. Wohn⟨gebiet, -siedlung, -straße⟩; ~ **hotel** Hotel für Dauergäste

**residential 'care** n. stationäre Pflege

**resident's 'parking** n. Parken nur für Anlieger

**residual** /rɪ'zɪdjʊəl/ adj. zurückgeblieben

**residue** /'rezɪdjuː/ n. (a) Rest, der (b) (Chem.) Rückstand, der

**resign** /rɪ'zaɪn/ **1** v.t. zurücktreten von ⟨Amt⟩ **2** v. refl. ~ **oneself to sth./to doing sth.** sich mit etw. abfinden/sich damit abfinden, etw. zu tun **3** v.i. ⟨Arbeitnehmer:⟩ kündigen; ⟨Regierungsbeamter:⟩ zurücktreten (**from** von)

**resignation** /rezɪg'neɪʃn/ n. (a) ▶ RESIGN 3: Kündigung, die; Rücktritt, der; **tender one's** ~: seine Kündigung/seinen Rücktritt einreichen (b) (being resigned) Resignation, die; **with** ~: resigniert

**resigned** /rɪ'zaɪnd/ adj. resigniert; be ~ **to sth.** sich mit etw. abgefunden haben

**resilience** /rɪ'zɪliəns/ n. (a) Elastizität, die (b) (fig.) Unverwüstlichkeit, die

**resilient** /rɪ'zɪliənt/ adj. elastisch; (fig.) unverwüstlich

**resin** /'rezɪn/ n. Harz, das

**resist** /rɪ'zɪst/ **1** v.t. (a) standhalten (+ Dat.) ⟨Frost, Hitze, Feuchtigkeit usw.⟩ (b) (oppose) sich widersetzen (+ Dat.); widerstehen (+ Dat.) ⟨Versuchung⟩ **2** v.i. ▶ 1B: sich widersetzen; widerstehen

**resistance** /rɪ'zɪstəns/ n. Widerstand, der (**to** gegen)

**re'sistance movement** n. Widerstandsbewegung, die

**resistant** /rɪ'zɪstənt/ adj. (a) (opposed) be ~ **to** sich widersetzen (+ Dat.) (b) (having power to resist) widerstandsfähig (**to** gegen)

**reskill** /riː'skɪl/ v.t. fort- od. weiterbilden; umschulen ⟨Arbeitslose⟩

**resold** ▶ RESELL

**resolute** /'rezəluːt/ adj. resolut, energisch ⟨Person⟩; entschlossen ⟨Tat⟩

**resolution** /rezə'luːʃn/ n. (a) (firmness) Entschlossenheit, die (b) (decision) Entschließung, die; (Polit. also) Resolution, die (c) (resolve) Vorsatz, der; **make a** ~: einen Vorsatz fassen

**resolve** /rɪ'zɒlv/ **1** v.t. (a) lösen ⟨Problem, Rätsel⟩; ausräumen ⟨Schwierigkeit⟩ (b) (decide) beschließen ⋯⟩

**(c)** (settle) beilegen ⟨*Streit*⟩; regeln
⟨*Angelegenheit*⟩
2 *n.* **(a)** Vorsatz, *der*
**(b)** (resoluteness) Entschlossenheit, *die*
**resolved** /rɪ'zɒlvd/ *adj.* ~ [to do sth.]
entschlossen[, etw. zu tun]
**resonant** /'rezənənt/ *adj.* hallend ⟨*Ton,
Klang*⟩
**resort** /rɪ'zɔːt/ 1 *n.* **(a)** (place)
Aufenthalt[sort], *der;* [holiday] ~: Ferienort,
*der;* **ski** ~: Skiurlaubsort, *der;* **seaside** ~:
Seebad, *das*
**(b)** (recourse) **as a last** ~: als letzter Ausweg
2 *v.i.* ~ **to sth./sb.** zu etw. greifen/sich an
jmdn. wenden (**for** um)
**resound** /rɪ'zaʊnd/ *v.i.* widerhallen
**re'sounding** *adj.* hallend ⟨*Lärm*⟩;
überwältigend ⟨*Sieg, Erfolg*⟩
**resource** /rɪ'sɔːs, rɪ'zɔːs/ *n. usu. in pl.*
(stock) Mittel *Pl.;* Ressource, *die*
**resourceful** /rɪ'sɔːsfl, rɪ'zɔːsfl/ *adj.* findig
⟨*Person*⟩
**respect** /rɪ'spekt/ 1 *n.* **(a)** (esteem)
Respekt, *der,* Achtung, *die* (**for** vor + *Dat.*);
**show** ~ **for sb./sth.** Respekt vor jmdm./etw.
zeigen
**(b)** (aspect) Hinsicht, *die;* **in some** ~s in
mancher Hinsicht
**(c)** **with** ~ **to** ...: in Bezug auf ... (*Akk.*); was
... [an]betrifft
2 *v.t.* respektieren; achten
**respectable** /rɪ'spektəbl/ *adj.* angesehen
⟨*Bürger usw.*⟩; ehrenwert ⟨*Motive*⟩; (decent)
ehrbar (geh.) ⟨*Leute, Kaufmann*⟩; anständig,
respektabel ⟨*Beschäftigung usw.*⟩
**respectful** /rɪ'spektfl/ *adj.* respektvoll
(to[wards] gegenüber)
**re'spectfully** *adv.* respektvoll
**respective** /rɪ'spektɪv/ *adj.* jeweilig
**re'spectively** *adv.* beziehungsweise
**respiration** /respɪ'reɪʃn/ *n.* Atmung, *die*
**respiratory** /'respərətərɪ/ *adj.*
Atmungs⟨*system, -organ, -funktion*⟩
**respite** /'respaɪt/ *n.* Ruhepause, *die;* (delay)
Aufschub, *der;* **without** ~: ohne Pause
**resplendent** /rɪ'splendənt/ *adj.* prächtig
**respond** /rɪ'spɒnd/ 1 *v.i.* **(a)** (answer)
antworten (**to** auf + *Akk.*)
**(b)** (react) reagieren (**to** auf + *Akk.*); ⟨*Patient,
Bremsen:*⟩ ansprechen (**to** auf + *Akk.*)
2 *v.t.* antworten; erwidern
**response** /rɪ'spɒns/ *n.* **(a)** (answer) Antwort,
*die* (**to** auf + *Akk.*); **in** ~ [**to**] als Antwort [auf
(+ *Akk.*)]
**(b)** (reaction) Reaktion, *die*
**responsibility** /rɪspɒnsɪ'bɪlɪtɪ/ *n.* **(a)** (being
responsible) Verantwortung, *die*
**(b)** (duty) Verpflichtung, *die*
**responsible** /rɪ'spɒnsɪbl/ *adj.* **(a)**
verantwortlich; **be** ~ **to sb.** jmdm.
gegenüber verantwortlich sein (**for** für)
**(b)** (trustworthy) verantwortungsvoll

**responsibly** /rɪ'spɒnsɪblɪ/ *adv.*
verantwortungsbewusst
**responsive** /rɪ'spɒnsɪv/ *adj.*
aufgeschlossen ⟨*Person*⟩; **be** ~ **to sth.** auf
etw. (*Akk.*) reagieren
**rest**[1] /rest/ 1 *v.i.* ruhen; ~ **on** ruhen auf
(+ *Dat.*); ~ **from sth.** sich von etw. ausruhen;
~ **assured that** ...: seien Sie versichert, dass
...; ~ **with sb.** ⟨*Verantwortung:*⟩ bei jmdm.
liegen
2 *v.t.* **(a)** ~ **sth. against sth.** etw. an etw.
(*Akk.*) lehnen
**(b)** ausruhen ⟨*Augen*⟩
3 *n.* **(a)** (repose) Ruhe, *die*
**(b)** (break, relaxation) Ruhe[pause], *die;*
Erholung, *die* (**from** von); **take a** ~: sich
ausruhen (**from** von); **give it a** ~! (coll.) hör
jetzt mal auf damit!
**(c)** (pause) **have a** ~: [eine] Pause machen;
~ **period** [Ruhe]pause, *die*
**rest**[2] *n.* **the** ~: der Rest; **we'll do the** ~:
alles Übrige erledigen wir
**restaurant** /'restərɒnt/ *n.* Restaurant, *das*
**'restaurant car** *n.* (Brit. Railw.)
Speisewagen, *der*
**rest:** ~ **cure** *n.* Erholungskur, *die;* ~ **day**
*n.* Ruhetag, *der*
**'rested** *adj.* ausgeruht
**restful** /'restfl/ *adj.* ruhig ⟨*Tag, Woche*⟩
**'rest home** *n.* Pflegeheim, *das*
**restive** /'restɪv/ *adj.* unruhig
**'restless** *adj.* unruhig ⟨*Nacht, Schlaf,
Bewegung*⟩; ruhelos ⟨*Person*⟩
**restoration** /restə'reɪʃn/ *n.* **(a)** (of peace,
health) Wiederherstellung, *die;* (of work of art,
building) Restaurierung, *die*
**(b)** **the R**~ (Brit. Hist.) die Restauration
**restore** /rɪ'stɔː(r)/ *v.t.* **(a)** (give back)
zurückgeben
**(b)** restaurieren ⟨*Bauwerk, Kunstwerk usw.*⟩;
~ **sb. to health** jmdn. wiederherstellen
**(c)** wiederherstellen ⟨*Ordnung, Ruhe*⟩
**restrain** /rɪ'streɪn/ *v.t.* zurückhalten
⟨*Gefühl, Lachen, Person*⟩; bändigen
⟨*unartiges Kind, Tier*⟩; ~ **sb./oneself from
doing sth.** jmdn. davon abhalten/sich
zurückhalten, etw. zu tun
**restrained** /rɪ'streɪnd/ *adj.* zurückhaltend
⟨*Wesen, Kritik*⟩; beherrscht ⟨*Reaktion, Worte*⟩
**restraint** /rɪ'streɪnt/ *n.* **(a)** (restriction)
Einschränkung, *die*
**(b)** (reserve) Zurückhaltung, *die*
**(c)** (self-control) Selbstbeherrschung, *die*
**restrict** /rɪ'strɪkt/ *v.t.* beschränken (**to** auf
+ *Akk.*)
**re'stricted** *adj.* beschränkt
**restriction** /rɪ'strɪkʃn/ *n.* Beschränkung,
*die* (**on** *Gen.*)
**restrictive** /rɪ'strɪktɪv/ *adj.* restriktiv
**'rest room** *n.* (esp. Amer.) Toilette, *die*
**restyle** /riː'staɪl/ *v.t.* neu stylen; ~ **sb.'s
hair** jmdm. eine neue Frisur machen

**result** /rɪ'zʌlt/ ① *v.i.* (a) (follow) ~ **from sth.** die Folge einer Sache (*Gen.*) sein (b) (end) ~ **in sth.** in etw. (*Dat.*) resultieren ② *n.* Ergebnis, *das;* **be the** ~ **of sth.** die Folge einer Sache (*Gen.*) sein; **as a** ~ **[of this]** infolgedessen

**re'sultant** /rɪ'zʌltənt/ *attrib. adj.* daraus resultierend

**resume** /rɪ'zjuːm/ *v.t.* wieder aufnehmen; fortsetzen ⟨*Reise*⟩

**résumé** /'rezʊmeɪ/ *n.* (a) (summary) Zusammenfassung, *die* (b) (Amer.: curriculum vitae) Lebenslauf, *der*

**resumption** /rɪ'zʌmpʃn/ *n.* Wiederaufnahme, *die*

**resurface** /riː'sɜːfɪs/ ① *v.t.* ~ **a road** den Belag einer Straße erneuern ② *v.i.* (lit. or fig.) wieder auftauchen

**resurgence** /rɪ'sɜːdʒəns/ *n.* Wiederaufleben, *das*

**resurrection** /rezə'rekʃn/ *n.* Auferstehung, *die*

**resuscitate** /rɪ'sʌsɪteɪt/ *v.t.* wieder beleben

**resuscitation** /rɪsʌsɪ'teɪʃn/ *n.* Wiederbelebung, *die*

**retail** /'riːteɪl/ ① *adj.* Einzel⟨*handel*⟩; Einzelhandels⟨*geschäft, -preis*⟩ ② *adv.* **buy/sell** ~: en détail kaufen/ verkaufen

'**retailer** *n.* Einzelhändler, *der*/-händlerin, *die*

'**retailing** /'riːteɪlɪŋ/ *n., no art.* Einzelhandel, *der*

**retail 'price index** *n.* (Brit.) Preisindex des Einzelhandels

**retain** /rɪ'teɪn/ *v.t.* behalten; ein-, zurückbehalten ⟨*Gelder*⟩

**retaining:** ~ **fee** *n.* Honorarvorschuss, *der;* ~ **wall** *n.* Böschungsmauer, *die*

**retaliate** /rɪ'tælɪeɪt/ *v.i.* Vergeltung üben (**against** an + *Dat.*)

**retaliation** /rɪtælɪ'eɪʃn/ *n.* Vergeltung, *die;* **in** ~ **for** als Vergeltung für

**retarded** /rɪ'tɑːdɪd/ *adj.* [**mentally**] ~: [geistig] zurückgeblieben

**retch** /retʃ/ *v.i.* würgen

**retentive** /rɪ'tentɪv/ *adj.* gut ⟨*Gedächtnis*⟩

**rethink** /riː'θɪŋk/ *v.t.,* **rethought** /riː'θɔːt/ noch einmal überdenken

**reticence** /'retɪsəns/ *n.* Zurückhaltung, *die*

**reticent** /'retɪsənt/ *adj.* zurückhaltend (**on, about** in Bezug auf + *Akk.*)

**retina** /'retɪnə/ *n.* Netzhaut, *die*

**retinue** /'retɪnjuː/ *n.* Gefolge, *das*

**retire** /rɪ'taɪə(r)/ *v.i.* (a) ⟨*Angestellter, Arbeiter:*⟩ in Rente (*Akk.*) gehen; ⟨*Beamter, Militär:*⟩ in Pension *od.* den Ruhestand gehen (b) (withdraw) sich zurückziehen (**to** in + *Akk.*)

**retired** /rɪ'taɪəd/ *adj.* aus dem Berufsleben ausgeschieden; ⟨*Beamter, Soldat*⟩ im Ruhestand, pensioniert

**re'tirement** *n.* Ruhestand, *der;* **take early** ~ ⟨*Selbstständiger:*⟩ sich vorzeitig zur Ruhe setzen; ⟨*Angestellter, Arbeiter:*⟩ vorzeitig in Rente (*Akk.*) gehen; ⟨*Beamter, Militär:*⟩ sich vorzeitig pensionieren lassen

**retirement:** ~ **age** *n.* Altersgrenze, *die;* ~ **home** *n.* (a) (house, flat) Alters- *od.* Ruhesitz, *der;* (b) (institution) Alters- *od.* Altenheim, *das;* ~ **pay,** ~ **pension** *ns.* [Alters]rente, *die*

**retiring** /rɪ'taɪərɪŋ/ *adj.* (shy) zurückhaltend

**retort** /rɪ'tɔːt/ ① *n.* Entgegnung, *die* (**to** auf + *Akk.*) ② *v.t.* entgegnen

**retrace** /rɪ'treɪs/ *v.t.* zurückverfolgen; ~ **one's steps** denselben Weg noch einmal zurückgehen

**retract** /rɪ'trækt/ *v.t.* zurücknehmen

**retrain** /riː'treɪn/ ① *v.i.* [sich] umschulen [lassen] ② *v.t.* umschulen

**re'training** *n.* Umschulung, *die*

**retreat** /rɪ'triːt/ ① *n.* (a) (withdrawal) Rückzug, *der;* **beat a** ~ (fig.) das Feld räumen (b) (place) Zufluchtsort, *der* ② *v.i.* sich zurückziehen

**retribution** /retrɪ'bjuːʃn/ *n.* Vergeltung, *die*

**retrieval** /rɪ'triːvl/ *n.* (a) (of situation) Rettung, *die;* **beyond** *or* **past** ~: hoffnungslos (b) (rescue) Rettung, *die;* (from wreckage) Bergung, *die*

**retrieve** /rɪ'triːv/ *v.t.* (a) (rescue) retten (**from** aus); (from wreckage) bergen (**from** aus) (b) (recover) zurückholen ⟨*Brief*⟩; wiederholen ⟨*Ball*⟩; wiederbekommen ⟨*Geld*⟩ (c) (Comp.) wieder auffinden ⟨*Informationen*⟩ (d) ⟨*Hund:*⟩ apportieren (e) retten ⟨*Situation*⟩

**re'triever** *n.* Apportierhund, *der;* (breed) Retriever, *der*

**retrospect** /'retrəspekt/ *n.* **in** ~: im Nachhinein

**retrospective** /retrə'spektɪv/ ① *adj.* retrospektiv (geh.) ② *n.* (Art) Retrospektive, *die* (geh.)

**retrovirus** /'retrəʊvaɪrəs/ *n.* Retrovirus, *das od. der*

**returf** /riː'tɜːf/ *v.t.* neuen Rasen verlegen auf (+ *Dat.*)

**return** /rɪ'tɜːn/ ① *v.i.* (come back) zurückkommen; (go back) zurückgehen; (by vehicle) zurückfahren ② *v.t.* (a) (bring back) zurückbringen; zurückgeben ⟨*geliehenen/gestohlenen Gegenstand*⟩; ~**ed with thanks** mit Dank zurück ····⟩

**(b)** erwidern ⟨*Besuch, Gruß, Liebe*⟩; sich revanchieren für (ugs.) ⟨*Freundlichkeit, Gefallen*⟩
**(c)** (elect) wählen ⟨*Kandidaten*⟩
**(d)** ∼ a verdict of guilty/not guilty ⟨*Geschworene:*⟩ auf „schuldig"/„nicht schuldig" erkennen
**3** *n.* **(a)** Rückkehr, *die;* many happy ∼s [of the day]! herzlichen Glückwunsch [zum Geburtstag]!
**(b)** by ∼ [of post] postwendend
**(c)** (ticket) Rückfahrkarte, *die;* (for flight) Rückflugschein, *der*
**(d)** ∼[s] (proceeds) Gewinn, *der* (on, from aus)
**(e)** (bringing back) Zurückbringen, *das;* (of property, goods, book) Rückgabe, *die* (to an + *Akk.*); receive/get sth. in ∼ [for sth.] etw. [für etw.] bekommen

**returnable** /rɪˈtɜːnəbl/ *adj.* Mehrweg⟨*behälter, -flasche usw.*⟩; rückzahlbar ⟨*Gebühr, Kaution*⟩; ∼ bottle Pfandflasche, *die;* ∼ deposit Pfand, *der*

**return:** ∼ **'fare** *n.* Preis für eine Rückfahrkarte/(for flight) einen Rückflugschein; ∼ **'flight** *n.* Rückflug, *der;* ∼ **'journey** *n.* Rückreise, *die;* Rückfahrt, *die;* ∼ **'match** *n.* Rückspiel, *das;* ∼ **'ticket** *n.* (Brit.) Rückfahrkarte, *die;* (for flight) Rückflugschein, *der;* ∼ **'trip** *n.* **(a)** (trip back) Rückweg, *der;* Rückfahrt, *die;* **(b)** (trip out and back) Hin- und Rückfahrt, *die;* Hin- und Rückreise, *die*

**retype** /riːˈtaɪp/ *v.t.* neu tippen

**reunification** /riːjuːnɪfɪˈkeɪʃn/ *n.* Wiedervereinigung, *die*

**reunify** /riːˈjuːnɪfaɪ/ *v.t.* wieder vereinigen

**reunion** /riːˈjuːnjən/ *n.* (gathering) Treffen, *das*

**reunite** /riːjʊˈnaɪt/ *v.t.* wieder zusammenführen

**reusable** /riːˈjuːzəbl/ *adj.* wieder verwendbar

**reuse** **1** /riːˈjuːz/ *v.t.* wieder verwenden **2** /riːˈjuːs/ *n.* Wiederverwendung, *die*

**rev** /rev/ (coll.) **1** *n., usu. in pl.* Umdrehung, *die*
**2** *v.i.,* **-vv-** hochtourig laufen
**3** *v.t.,* **-vv-** aufheulen lassen
■ **rev 'up** *v.t.* aufheulen lassen

**Rev.** /ˈrevərənd, (coll.) rev/ *abbr.* = **Reverend** Rev.

**reveal** /rɪˈviːl/ *v.t.* enthüllen (geh.); be ∼ed ⟨*Wahrheit:*⟩ ans Licht kommen

**re'vealing** *adj.* aufschlussreich

**revel** /ˈrevl/ *v.i.,* (Brit.) **-ll-** genießen (in *Akk.*); ∼ in doing sth. es [richtig] genießen, etw. zu tun

**revelation** /revəˈleɪʃn/ *n.* **(a)** Enthüllung, *die* (geh.); be a ∼: einem die Augen öffnen
**(b)** (Relig.) Offenbarung, *die*

**reveller** /ˈrevələ(r)/ *n.* Feiernde, *der/die*

**revelry** /ˈrevəlrɪ/ *n.* Feiern, *das*

**revenge** /rɪˈvendʒ/ **1** *v.t.* rächen ⟨*Person, Tat*⟩
**2** *n.* (action) Rache, *die;* take ∼ or have one's ∼ [on sb.] [for sth.] Rache [an jmdm.] [für etw.] nehmen; in ∼ for sth. als Rache für etw

**revengeful** /rɪˈvendʒfl/ *adj.* rachsüchtig (geh.)

**revenue** /ˈrevənjuː/ *n.* ∼[s] Einnahmen *Pl.*

**revere** /rɪˈvɪə(r)/ *v.t.* verehren

**reverence** /ˈrevərəns/ *n.* Ehrfurcht, *die*

**Reverend** /ˈrevərənd/ *adj.* the ∼ John Wilson Hochwürden John Wilson

**reverent** /ˈrevərənt/ *adj.* ehrfürchtig

**reverie** /ˈrevərɪ/ *n.* Träumerei, *die*

**reversal** /rɪˈvɜːsl/ *n.* Umkehrung, *die*

**reverse** /rɪˈvɜːs/ **1** *adj.* entgegengesetzt ⟨*Richtung*⟩; Rück⟨*seite*⟩; umgekehrt ⟨*Reihenfolge*⟩
**2** *n.* **(a)** (contrary) Gegenteil, *das*
**(b)** (Motor Veh.) Rückwärtsgang, *der;* put the car into ∼, go into ∼: den Rückwärtsgang einlegen
**3** *v.t.* **(a)** umkehren ⟨*Reihenfolge*⟩; ∼ the charge[s] (Brit.) ein R-Gespräch anmelden
**(b)** zurücksetzen ⟨*Fahrzeug*⟩
**4** *v.i.* zurücksetzen; rückwärts fahren

**reverse:** ∼'**charge** *adj.* (Brit.) make a ∼-charge call ein R-Gespräch führen; ∼ '**gear** *n.* (Motor Veh.) Rückwärtsgang, *der; see also* GEAR 1A

**reversible** /rɪˈvɜːsɪbl/ *adj.* beidseitig tragbar ⟨*Kleidungsstück*⟩; Wende⟨*mantel, -jacke*⟩

**re'versing light** *n.* Rückfahrscheinwerfer, *der*

**revert** /rɪˈvɜːt/ *v.i.* ∼ to zurückkommen auf (+ *Akk.*) ⟨*Thema, Frage*⟩; ∼ to savagery in den Zustand der Wildheit zurückfallen

**review** /rɪˈvjuː/ **1** *n.* **(a)** (survey) Überblick, *der* (of über + *Akk.*)
**(b)** (re-examination) [nochmalige] Überprüfung
**(c)** (of book, play, etc.) Kritik, *die;* Rezension, *die*
**2** *v.t.* **(a)** (survey) untersuchen; prüfen
**(b)** (re-examine) überprüfen
**(c)** (Mil.) inspizieren
**(d)** (write a criticism of) rezensieren

**re'viewer** *n.* Rezensent, *der*/Rezensentin, *die*

**revile** /rɪˈvaɪl/ *v.t.* schmähen (geh.)

**revise** /rɪˈvaɪz/ *v.t.* **(a)** (check over) durchsehen ⟨*Manuskript*⟩
**(b)** (for exam) wiederholen; *abs.* lernen

**revision** /rɪˈvɪʒn/ *n.* **(a)** (checking over) Durchsicht, *die*
**(b)** (amended version) revidierte Fassung
**(c)** (for exam) Wiederholung, *die*

**revisit** /riːˈvɪzɪt/ *v.t.* wieder besuchen

**revitalize** /riːˈvaɪtəlaɪz/ *v.t.* neu beleben

**revival** /rɪˈvaɪvl/ *n.* Neubelebung, *die*

**revive** /rɪˈvaɪv/ **1** *v.i.* (come back to consciousness) wieder zu sich kommen; (be reinvigorated) zu neuem Leben erwachen

2 *v.t.* **(a)** (restore to consciousness) wieder beleben; (reinvigorate) wieder zu Kräften kommen lassen
**(b)** wieder wecken ⟨*Lebensgeister, Interesse*⟩
**revoke** /rɪ'vəʊk/ *v.t.* aufheben ⟨*Entscheidung*⟩; widerrufen ⟨*Befehl, Erlaubnis, Genehmigung*⟩
**revolt** /rɪ'vəʊlt/ 1 *v.i.* revoltieren (**against** gegen)
2 *v.t.* mit Abscheu erfüllen
3 *n.* Revolte, *die* (auch fig.); Aufstand, *der*
**re'volting** *adj.* abscheulich; (unpleasant) widerlich
**revolution** /revə'lu:ʃn/ *n.* Revolution, *die*
**revolutionary** /revə'lu:ʃənərɪ/ 1 *adj.* revolutionär
2 *n.* Revolutionär, *der*/Revolutionärin, *die*
**revolve** /rɪ'vɒlv/ 1 *v.t.* drehen
2 *v.i.* sich drehen (**round, about, on** um)
**revolver** /rɪ'vɒlvə(r)/ *n.* [Trommel]revolver, *der*
**revolving** /rɪ'vɒlvɪŋ/ *attrib. adj.* Dreh⟨*bühne, -tür*⟩
**revue** /rɪ'vju:/ *n.* Kabarett, *das;* (musical show) Revue, *die*
**revulsion** /rɪ'vʌlʃn/ *n.* Abscheu, *der* (**at** vor + *Dat.*, **gegen**)
**reward** /rɪ'wɔ:d/ 1 *n.* Belohnung, *die*
2 *v.t.* belohnen
**re'warding** *adj.* lohnend; **be ~/financially ~**: sich lohnen/einträglich sein
**rewind** /ri:'waɪnd/ *v.t.*, **rewound** /ri:'waʊnd/ **(a)** wieder aufziehen ⟨*Uhr*⟩
**(b)** zurückspulen ⟨*Film, Band*⟩
**'rewind button** *n.* (on camera) Rückspulknopf, *der;* (on cassette recorder etc.) Rücklauftaste, *die*
**reword** /ri:'wɜ:d/ *v.t.* umformulieren
**rewrite** /ri:'raɪt/ *v.t.*, **rewrote** /ri:'rəʊt/, **rewritten** /ri:'rɪtn/ noch einmal [neu] schreiben; (write differently) umschreiben
**rhetoric** /'retərɪk/ *n.* [**art of**] **~:** Redekunst, *die;* Rhetorik, *die*
**rhetorical** /rɪ'tɒrɪkl/ *adj.* rhetorisch
**rheumatic** /ru:'mætɪk/ *adj.* rheumatisch
**rheumatism** /'ru:mətɪzm/ *n.* Rheumatismus, *der;* Rheuma, *das* (ugs.)
**Rhine** /raɪn/ *pr. n.* Rhein, *der*
**rhino** /'raɪnəʊ/ *n., pl.* **same or ~s** (coll.)**, rhinoceros** /raɪ'nɒsərəs/ *n., pl.* **same or ~es** Nashorn, *das;* Rhinozeros, *das*
**rhododendron** /rəʊdə'dendrən/ *n.* Rhododendron, *der*
**rhubarb** /'ru:bɑ:b/ *n.* Rhabarber, *der*
**rhyme** /raɪm/ 1 *n.* Reim, *der;* **without ~ or reason** ohne Sinn und Verstand
2 *v.i.* sich reimen (**with** auf + *Akk.*)
**rhythm** /'rɪðm/ *n.* Rhythmus, *der*
**rhythmic** /'rɪðmɪk/**, rhythmical** /'rɪðmɪkl/ *adj.* rhythmisch
**rib** /rɪb/ 1 *n.* Rippe, *die*
2 *v.t.*, **-bb-** (coll.) aufziehen (ugs.)

**ribald** /'rɪbəld/ *adj.* zotig
**ribbon** /'rɪbn/ *n.* Band, *das;* (on typewriter) [Farb]band, *das*
**'ribcage** *n.* Brustkorb, *der*
**rice** /raɪs/ *n.* Reis, *der*
**rice: ~ 'pudding** *n.* Milchreis, *der;* **~ wine** *n.* Reiswein, *der*
**rich** /rɪtʃ/ 1 *adj.* **(a)** reich (**in** an + *Dat.*); (fertile) fruchtbar ⟨*Land, Boden*⟩
**(b)** (splendid) prachtvoll
**(c)** (containing much fat, oil, eggs, etc.) gehaltvoll
**(d)** (deep, full) voll[tönend] ⟨*Stimme*⟩; voll ⟨*Ton*⟩; satt ⟨*Farbe, Farbton*⟩
2 *n. pl.* **the ~:** die Reichen *Pl.*; **~ and poor** Arm und Reich
**riches** /'rɪtʃɪz/ *n. pl.* Reichtum, *der*
**'richly** *adv.* **(a)** (splendidly) reich; üppig ⟨*ausgestattet*⟩; prächtig ⟨*gekleidet*⟩
**(b)** (fully) voll und ganz; **~ deserved** wohlverdient
**'richness** *n.* **(a)** (of food) Reichhaltigkeit, *die*
**(b)** (of voice) voller Klang; (of colour) Sattheit, *die*
**rickets** /'rɪkɪts/ *n.* Rachitis, *die*
**rickety** /'rɪkɪtɪ/ *adj.* wack[e]lig
**ricochet** /'rɪkəʃeɪ/ 1 *n.* **(a)** Abprallen, *das*
**(b)** (hit) Abpraller, *der*
2 *v.i.*, **~ed** /'rɪkəʃeɪd/ abprallen (**off** von)
**rid** /rɪd/ *v.t.*, **-dd-, rid: ~ sth. of sth.** etw. von etw. befreien; **~ oneself of sb./sth.** sich von jmdm./etw. befreien; **be ~ of sb./sth.** jmdn./etw. los sein (ugs.); **get ~ of sb./sth.** jmdn./etw. loswerden
**riddance** /'rɪdəns/ *n.* **good ~!** Gott sei Dank ist er/es *usw.* weg!
**ridden** ▶ RIDE 2, 3
**riddle**[1] /'rɪdl/ *n.* Rätsel, *das*
**riddle**[2] *v.t.* durchlöchern; **~d with bullets** von Kugeln durchsiebt
**ride** /raɪd/ 1 *n.* (on horseback) [Aus]ritt, *der;* (in vehicle, at fair) Fahrt, *die;* **~ in a train/ coach** Zug-/Busfahrt, *die;* **go for a ~:** ausreiten; **go for a [bi]cycle ~:** Rad fahren; **go for a ~ [in the car]** [mit dem Auto] wegfahren; **take sb. for a ~** (fig. coll.: deceive) jmdn. reinlegen (ugs.)
2 *v.i.*, **rode** /rəʊd/, **ridden** /'rɪdn/ (on horse) reiten; (on bicycle, in vehicle) fahren; **~ to town on one's bike/in one's car/on the train** mit dem Rad/Auto/Zug in die Stadt fahren
3 *v.t.*, **rode, ridden** reiten ⟨*Pferd usw.*⟩; fahren mit ⟨*Fahrrad*⟩
■ **ride a'way, ride 'off** *v.i.* wegreiten/ -fahren
**'rider** *n.* **(a)** Reiter, *der*/Reiterin, *die;* (of cycle) Fahrer, *der*/Fahrerin, *die*
**(b)** (addition) Zusatz, *der*
**ridge** /rɪdʒ/ *n.* **(a)** (of roof) First, *der*
**(b)** (long hilltop) Grat, *der;* Kamm, *der*
**(c)** (Meteorol.) **~ [of high pressure]** lang gestrecktes Hoch
**ridicule** /'rɪdɪkju:l/ 1 *n.* Spott, *der*

② *v.t.* verspotten

**ridiculous** /rɪ'dɪkjʊləs/ *adj.* lächerlich

**riding** /'raɪdɪŋ/ *n.* Reiten, *das*

**riding:** ∼ **lesson** *n.* Reitstunde, *die;*
  ∼ **school** *n.* Reitschule, *die*

**rife** /raɪf/ *pred. adj.* weit verbreitet

**riff-raff** /'rɪfræf/ *n.* Gesindel, *das*

**rifle** /'raɪfl/ ① *n.* Gewehr, *das*
  ② *v.t.* durchwühlen
  ③ *v.i.* ∼ **through** sth. etw. durchwühlen

**rift** /rɪft/ *n.* Unstimmigkeit, *die*

**rig¹** /rɪg/ *n.* (for oil well) [Öl]förderturm, *der;*
  (off shore) Förderinsel, *die*
  ▪ **rig 'out** *v.t.* ausstaffieren
  ▪ **rig 'up** *v.t.* aufbauen

**rig²** *v.t.,* -gg- manipulieren ‹[*Wahl*]*ergebnis*›;
  fälschen ‹*Wahl*›

**rigging** /'rɪgɪŋ/ *n.* Takelung, *die*

**right** /raɪt/ ① *adj.* (a) (just, morally good,
  sound) richtig
  (b) (correct, true) richtig; **you're** [quite] ∼: du
  hast [völlig] recht; **be** ∼ **in** sth. Recht mit
  etw. haben; **is that clock** ∼? geht die Uhr da
  richtig?; **put** *or* **set** ∼: richtig stellen
  ‹*Irrtum, Behauptung*›; wieder gutmachen
  ‹*Unrecht*›; berichtigen ‹*Fehler*›; richtig
  stellen ‹*Uhr*›; **put** *or* **set** sb. ∼: jmdn.
  berichtigen; **that's** ∼: ja[wohl]; so ist es; **is
  that** ∼? stimmt das?; (indeed?) aha!; **[am I]** ∼?
  nicht [wahr]?
  (c) (preferable, most suitable) richtig; recht; **do**
  sth. **the** ∼ **way** etw. richtig machen
  (d) (opposite of left) recht...; **on the** ∼ **side**
  rechts
  (e) **R**∼ (Polit.) recht...
  ② *v.t.* aus der Welt schaffen ‹*Unrecht*›
  ③ *n.* (a) (fair claim, authority) Recht, *das;* **have
  a/no** ∼ **to** sth. ein/kein Anrecht *od.* Recht
  auf etw. (*Akk.*) haben; **in one's own** ∼: aus
  eigenem Recht; ∼ **of way** Vorfahrtsrecht,
  *das;* **have** ∼ **of way** Vorfahrt haben
  (b) (what is just) Recht, *das;* **by** ∼[s] von
  Rechts wegen; **in the** ∼: im Recht
  (c) (∼-hand side) rechte Seite; **on** *or* **to the**
  ∼ [**of** sb./sth.] rechts [von jmdm./etw.]
  (d) (Polit.) **the R**∼: die Rechte
  ④ *adv.* (a) (correctly) richtig
  (b) (to the ∼-hand side) nach rechts
  (c) (completely) ganz
  (d) (exactly) genau; ∼ '**now** im Moment; jetzt
  sofort ‹*handeln*›
  (e) (straight) direkt

'**right angle** *n.* rechter Winkel; **at** ∼**s to**
  sth. rechtwinklig zu etw.

**righteous** /'raɪtʃəs/ *adj.* rechtschaffen

**rightful** /'raɪtfl/ *adj.* rechtmäßig ‹*Besitzer,
  Herrscher*›

**right:** ∼-'**hand** *adj.* recht...; ∼-'**handed**
  ① *adj.* rechtshändig; ‹*Werkzeug*› für
  Rechtshänder; **be** ∼-**handed** ‹*Person.*›
  Rechtshänder/Rechtshänderin sein; ② *adv.*
  rechtshändig; ∼-**hand** '**man** *n.* rechte
  Hand

'**rightly** *adv.* zu Recht

**right:** ∼-'**minded** *adj.* gerecht denkend;
  ∼-**to-**'**life** *attrib. adj.* Recht-auf-Leben-;
  ∼ '**wing** *n.* rechter Flügel; ∼-**wing** *adj.*
  (Polit.) rechtsgerichtet; Rechts‹*extremist,
  -intellektueller*›; ∼-**winger** *n.* (a) (Sport)
  Rechtsaußen, *der;* (b) (Polit.) Rechte, *der/die*

**rigid** /'rɪdʒɪd/ *adj.* (a) starr; (stiff) steif
  (b) (strict) streng; unbeugsam ‹*System*›

**rigidity** /rɪ'dʒɪtɪ/ *n.* ▸ RIGID: Starrheit, *die;*
  Steifheit, *die;* Strenge, *die*

**rigmarole** /'rɪgmərəʊl/ *n.* (a) (talk)
  langatmiges Geschwafel (ugs.)
  (b) (procedure) Zirkus, *der*

**rigor** /'rɪgə(r)/ (Amer.) ▸ RIGOUR

**rigor mortis** /rɪgə 'mɔːtɪs/ *n.* Totenstarre,
  *die*

**rigorous** /'rɪgərəs/ *adj.* streng

**rigour** /'rɪgə(r)/ *n.* (Brit.) Strenge, *die*

**rile** /raɪl/ *v.t.* (coll.) ärgern

**rim** /rɪm/ *n.* Rand, *der;* (of wheel) Felge, *die*

**rind** /raɪnd/ *n.* (of fruit) Schale, *die;* (of cheese)
  Rinde, *die;* (of bacon) Schwarte, *die*

**ring¹** /rɪŋ/ ① *n.* (a) Ring, *der*
  (b) (Boxing) Ring, *der;* (in circus) Manege, *die*
  ② *v.t.* (surround) umringen; einkreisen ‹*Wort
  usw.*›

**ring²** ① *n.* (a) (act of sounding bell) Läuten,
  *das;* Klingeln, *das*
  (b) (Brit. coll.: telephone call) Anruf, *der;* **give** sb.
  **a** ∼: jmdn. anrufen
  (c) (fig.: impression) **have the** ∼ **of truth** [about
  it] glaubhaft klingen
  ② *v.i.,* rang /ræŋ/, rung /rʌŋ/ (a) (sound
  clearly) [er]schallen; ‹*Hammer:*› [er]dröhnen
  (b) (be sounded) ‹*Glocke, Klingel, Telefon:*›
  läuten; ‹*Wecker, Telefon, Kasse:*› klingeln; **the
  doorbell rang** es klingelte
  (c) (∼ bell) läuten (**for** nach)
  (d) (Brit.: make telephone call) anrufen
  ③ *v.t.,* rang, rung (a) läuten ‹*Glocke*›; ∼ **the
  [door]bell** läuten; klingeln; **it** ∼**s a bell** (fig.
  coll.) es kommt mir [irgendwie] bekannt vor
  (b) (Brit.: telephone) anrufen
  ▪ **ring 'back** (Brit.) *v.t. & i.* (a) (again) wieder
  anrufen
  (b) (in return) zurückrufen
  ▪ **ring 'off** *v.i.* (Brit.) auflegen
  ▪ **ring 'out** *v.i.* ertönen
  ▪ **ring 'up** *v.t.* (Brit.: telephone) anrufen

**ring:** ∼ **binder** *n.* Ringbuch, *das;*
  ∼ **finger** *n.* Ringfinger, *der*

**ringing** /'rɪŋɪŋ/ *n.* Läuten, *das;* (Brit. Teleph.)
  ∼ **tone** Freiton, *der*

'**ringleader** *n.* Anführer, *der*/Anführerin,
  *die*

**ringlet** /'rɪŋlɪt/ *n.* [Ringel]löckchen, *das*

'**ring road** *n.* Ringstraße, *die*

**rink** /rɪŋk/ *n.* (for ice skating) Eisbahn, *die;* (for
  roller skating) Rollschuhbahn, *die*

**rinse** /rɪns/ ① *v.t.* (a) (wash out) ausspülen
  ‹*Mund, Gefäß usw.*›
  (b) [aus]spülen ‹*Wäsche usw.*›; abspülen
  ‹*Hände, Geschirr*›

2 *n.* Spülen, *das; give sth. a* [good/quick] ∼: etw. [gut/schnell] ausspülen/abspülen/spülen

■ **rinse 'out** *v.t.* ausspülen

**riot** /'raɪət/ 1 *n.* Aufruhr, *der;* ∼s Unruhen *Pl.; run* ∼: randalieren
2 *v.i.* randalieren

'**rioter** *n.* Randalierer, *der*

'**riot gear** *n.* Schutzkleidung *od.* -ausrüstung

**riotous** /'raɪətəs/ *adj.* (a) gewalttätig
(b) (unrestrained) wild

**rip** /rɪp/ 1 *n.* Riss, *der*
2 *v.t.,* **-pp-** zerreißen; ∼ **open** aufreißen
■ **rip 'off** *v.t.* (a) (remove from) reißen von; (remove) abreißen
(b) (coll.: defraud) übers Ohr hauen (ugs.)
■ **rip 'out** *v.t.* herausreißen (of aus)

**RIP** *abbr.* = **rest in peace** R.I.P.

'**ripcord** *n.* Reißleine, *die*

**ripe** /raɪp/ *adj.* reif (for zu)

**ripen** /'raɪpn/ 1 *v.t.* zur Reife bringen
2 *v.i.* reifen

'**ripeness** *n.* Reife, *die*

'**rip-off** *n.* (coll.) Nepp, *der* (ugs.)

**riposte** /rɪ'pɒst/ 1 *n.* (retort) [rasche] Entgegnung
2 *v.i.* [rasch] antworten

**ripple** /'rɪpl/ 1 *n.* kleine Welle
2 *v.i.* ⟨See:⟩ sich kräuseln; ⟨Welle:⟩ plätschern
3 *v.t.* kräuseln

**rise** /raɪz/ 1 *n.* (a) (advancement) Aufstieg, *der*
(b) (in value, price, cost) Steigerung, *die;* (in population, temperature) Zunahme, *die*
(c) (Brit.) [pay] ∼ (in wages) Lohnerhöhung, *die;* (in salary) Gehaltserhöhung, *die*
(d) (hill) Anhöhe, *die*
(e) give ∼ to führen zu; Anlass geben zu ⟨Spekulation⟩
2 *v.i., rose* /rəʊz/, *risen* /'rɪzn/ (a) (go up) aufsteigen
(b) ⟨Sonne, Mond:⟩ aufgehen
(c) (increase, reach higher level) steigen
(d) (advance) ⟨Person:⟩ aufsteigen
(e) ⟨Teig, Kuchen:⟩ aufgehen
(f) (Theatre) ⟨Vorhang:⟩ aufgehen
(g) ⟨Fluss:⟩ entspringen
■ **rise 'up** *v.i.* (a) ∼ up [in revolt] aufbegehren (geh.)
(b) ⟨Berg:⟩ aufragen

**risen** ▶ RISE 2

'**riser** *n.* early ∼: Frühaufsteher, *der*/Frühaufsteherin, *die*

**rising** /'raɪzɪŋ/ 1 *n.* (of sun, moon, etc.) Aufgang, *der*
2 *adj.* (a) aufgehend ⟨Sonne, Mond usw.⟩
(b) steigend ⟨Kosten, Temperatur, Wasser, Flut⟩
(c) (sloping upwards) ansteigend

**risk** /rɪsk/ 1 *n.* Gefahr, *die;* (chance taken) Risiko, *das; at one's own* ∼: auf eigene Gefahr *od.* eigenes Risiko; *take the* ∼ *of doing sth.* es riskieren, etw. zu tun; *be at* ∼ ⟨Zukunft, Plan:⟩ gefährdet sein
2 *v.t.* riskieren; I'll ∼ it ich lasse es darauf ankommen

'**risky** *adj.* gefährlich; gewagt ⟨Experiment, Projekt⟩

**risotto** /rɪ'zɒtəʊ/ *n., pl.* ∼s Risotto, *der od. das*

**risqué** /'rɪskeɪ/ *adj.* gewagt

**rissole** /'rɪsəʊl/ *n.* Frikadelle, *die*

**rite** /raɪt/ *n.* Ritus, *der*

**ritual** /'rɪtʃʊəl/ 1 *adj.* rituell; Ritual⟨mord, -tötung⟩
2 *n.* Ritual, *das*

**rival** /'raɪvl/ 1 *n.* (competitor) Rivale, *der*/Rivalin, *die; business* ∼s Konkurrenten *Pl.*
2 *v.t.,* (Brit.) **-ll-** nicht nachstehen (+ *Dat.*)

**rivalry** /'raɪvlrɪ/ *n.* Rivalität, *die* (geh.)

**river** /'rɪvə(r)/ *n.* Fluss, *das*

**river:** ∼ **bank** Flussufer, *der;* ∼ **basin** *n.* Stromgebiet, *das;* ∼ **bed** *n.* Flussbett, *das* ∼**side** 1 *n.* Flussufer, *das;* 2 *attrib. adj.* am Fluss gelegen; am Fluss *nachgestellt*

**rivet** /'rɪvɪt/ 1 *n.* Niete, *die*
2 *v.t.* (a) [ver]nieten
(b) (fig.) fesseln

'**riveting** *adj.* fesselnd

**rivulet** /'rɪvjʊlɪt/ *n.* Bach, *der*

**RN** *abbr.* (Brit.) = **Royal Navy** Königl. Mar.

**road** /rəʊd/ *n.* Straße, *die; across or over the* ∼ [from us] [bei uns] gegenüber; *by* ∼ (by car/bus/lorry) per Auto/Bus/Lkw; *be on the* ∼: auf Reisen *od.* unterwegs sein; ⟨Theaterensemble usw.:⟩ auf Tournee *od.* Tour sein

**road:** ∼ **accident** *n.* Verkehrsunfall, *der;* ∼ **atlas** *n.* Autoatlas, *der;* ∼**block** *n.* Straßensperre, *die;* ∼ **bridge** *n.* Straßenbrücke, *die;* ∼ **haulage** *n.* Gütertransport auf der Straße; ∼ **hog** *n.* Verkehrsrowdy, *der;* ∼ **hump** ▶ SPEED BUMP

**roadie** /'rəʊdɪ/ *n.* (coll.) Roadie, *der*

**road:** ∼ **manager** *n.* Roadmanager, *der;* ∼ **map** *n.* Straßenkarte, *die;* ∼**mender** *n.* Straßen[bau]arbeiter, *der*/-arbeiterin, *die;* ∼ **rage** *n.:* häufig zu gewalttätigen Ausbrüchen führende Wut eines Autofahrers; ∼ **safety** *n.* Verkehrssicherheit, *die;* ∼ **sense** *n.* Gespür für Verkehrssituationen; ∼**side** *n.* Straßenrand, *der at or by/along the* ∼side am Straßenrand; ∼ **sign** *n.* Verkehrszeichen, *das;* Straßenschild, *das* (ugs.); ∼ **sweeper** *n.* Straßenkehrer, *der*/-kehrerin, *die;* ∼ **tax** *n.* (Brit.) Kraftfahrzeugsteuer, *die;* Kfz-Steuer, *die;* ∼ **transport** *n.* Personen- und Güterbeförderung auf der Straße; **form of** ∼ **transport** Verkehrsmittel der Straße; ∼ **user** *n.* Verkehrsteilnehmer, *der*/  ⋯⃗

r

-teilnehmerin, *die;* ~**way** *n.* Fahrbahn, *die;*
~**works** *n. pl.* Straßenbauarbeiten *Pl.;*
~**worthy** *adj.* fahrtüchtig

**roam** /rəʊm/ ⟨1⟩ *v.i.* umherstreifen
⟨2⟩ *v.t.* streifen durch

**roar** /rɔː(r)/ ⟨1⟩ *n.* (of wild beast) Gebrüll, *das;*
(of applause) Tosen, *das;* (of engine, traffic)
Dröhnen, *das;* ~s/a ~ [of laughter]
dröhnendes Gelächter
⟨2⟩ *v.i.* brüllen (**with** vor + *Dat.*); ⟨*Motor:*⟩
dröhnen

'**roaring** *adj.* (a) bullernd (ugs.) ⟨*Feuer*⟩
(b) a ~ **success** ein Bombenerfolg; **do a**
~ **trade** ein Bombengeschäft machen

**roast** /rəʊst/ ⟨1⟩ *v.t.* braten; rösten
⟨*Kaffeebohnen, Kastanien*⟩
⟨2⟩ *attrib. adj.* gebraten ⟨*Fleisch, Ente usw.*⟩;
Brat⟨*hähnchen, -kartoffeln*⟩; Röst⟨*kastanien*⟩;
~ **beef** (sirloin) Roastbeef, *das*
⟨3⟩ *n.* Braten, *der*

**rob** /rɒb/ *v.t.,* -**bb**- ausrauben ⟨*Bank, Safe,*
*Kasse*⟩; berauben ⟨*Person*⟩

**robber** /'rɒbə(r)/ *n.* Räuber, *der/*Räuberin,
*die*

**robbery** /'rɒbərɪ/ *n.* Raub, *der;* **robberies**
Raubüberfälle *Pl.*

**robe** /rəʊb/ *n.* Gewand, *das* (geh.); (of judge,
vicar) Talar, *der*

**robin** /'rɒbɪn/ *n.* ~ [**redbreast**] Rotkehlchen,
*das*

**robot** /'rəʊbɒt/ *n.* Roboter, *der*

**robotics** /rəʊ'bɒtɪks/ *n.* Robotertechnik,
*die;* Robotik, *die*

**robust** /rəʊ'bʌst/ *adj.* robust

**rock¹** /rɒk/ *n.* (a) (piece of ~) Fels, *der*
(b) (large ~, hill) Felsen, *der*
(c) (substance) Fels, *der;* (esp. Geol.) Gestein,
*das*
(d) (boulder) Felsbrocken, *der;* (Amer.: stone)
Stein, *der*
(e) stick of ~: Zuckerstange, *die*
(f) **be on the** ~**s** (fig. coll.) ⟨*Ehe, Firma:*⟩
kaputt sein (ugs.)

**rock²** ⟨1⟩ *v.t.* wiegen; (in cradle) schaukeln
⟨2⟩ *v.i.* (a) schaukeln
(b) (sway) schwanken
⟨3⟩ *n.* (Mus.) Rock, *der; attrib.* Rock-; ~ **and** *or*
'**n' roll** [music] Rock and Roll, *der*

**rock:** ~-'**bottom** (coll.) ⟨1⟩ *adj.* ~-**bottom**
**prices** Schleuderpreise *Pl.* (ugs.); ⟨2⟩ *n.* **reach**
*or* **touch** ~-**bottom** ⟨*Handel, Preis:*⟩ in den
Keller fallen (ugs.); **her spirits reached**
~-**bottom** ihre Stimmung war auf dem
Tiefpunkt; ~ **climber** *n.* Kletterer, *der/*
Kletterin, *die;* ~ **climbing** *n.*
[Fels]klettern, *das*

**rocker** /'rɒkə(r)/ *n.* **be off one's** ~ (fig. coll.)
übergeschnappt *od.* durchgedreht sein (ugs.)

**rockery** /'rɒkərɪ/ *n.* Steingarten, *der*

**rocket** /'rɒkɪt/ ⟨1⟩ *n.* Rakete, *die*
⟨2⟩ *v.i.* ⟨*Preise:*⟩ in die Höhe schnellen
**rocket:** ~ **base** *n.* (Mil.)

Raketen[abschuss]basis, *die;* ~ **launcher**
*n.* Raketenwerfer, *der;* ~-**propelled** *adj.*
raketengetrieben

**rock:** ~ **face** *n.* Felswand, *die;* ~**fall** *n.*
Steinschlag, *der;* ~ **formation** *n.*
Gesteinsformation, *die;* ~ **garden** *n.*
Steingarten, *der;* ~-**hard** *adj.* steinhart

**rocking:** ~ **chair** *n.* Schaukelstuhl, *der;*
~ **horse** *n.* Schaukelpferd, *das*

**rock:** ~ **plant** *n.* Felsenpflanze, *die;* (Hort.)
Steingartengewächs, *das;* ~ **salt** *n.*
Steinsalz, *das*

'**rocky** *adj.* (a) felsig
(b) (coll.: unsteady) wackelig (ugs.)

**rod** /rɒd/ *n.* Stange, *die;* (for punishing) Rute,
*die;* (for fishing) [Angel]rute, *die*

**rode** ▶ RIDE 2, 3

**rodent** /'rəʊdənt/ *n.* Nagetier, *das*

**rodeo** /'rəʊdɪəʊ, rəʊ'deɪəʊ/ *n., pl.* ~**s** Rodeo,
*der od. das*

**roe¹** /rəʊ/ *n.* (of fish) [**hard**] ~: Rogen, *der;*
[**soft**] ~: Milch, *die*

**roe²** *n.* ~ [**deer**] Reh, *das*

**rogue** /rəʊg/ *n.* Gauner, *der*

**role, rôle** /rəʊl/ *n.* Rolle, *die*

**role:** ~ **model** *n.* Leitbild, *das;*
~ **playing** *n.* Rollenspiel, *das;*
~ **reversal** *n.* Rollentausch, *der*

**roll¹** /rəʊl/ *n.* (a) Rolle, *die;* (of cloth etc.)
Ballen, *der;* ~ **of film** Rolle Film
(b) [**bread**] ~: Brötchen, *das*
(c) **be on a** ~ (coll.) eine Glückssträhne
haben

**roll²** ⟨1⟩ *n.* (of drum) Wirbel, *der*
⟨2⟩ *v.t.* (a) rollen; (between surfaces) drehen
(b) (shape by ~ing) rollen; drehen ⟨*Zigarette*⟩
(c) walzen ⟨*Rasen, Metall usw.*⟩; ausrollen
⟨*Teig*⟩
⟨3⟩ *v.i.* (a) rollen
(b) ⟨*Maschine:*⟩ laufen; **get sth.** ~**ing** (fig.)
etw. ins Rollen bringen
(c) **be** ~**ing in money** *or* **in it** (coll.) im Geld
schwimmen (ugs.)
■ **roll a'bout** *v.i.* herumrollen; ⟨*Schiff:*⟩
schlingern; ⟨*Kind, Hund:*⟩ sich wälzen
■ **roll 'back** *v.t.* zurückrollen
■ **roll 'by** *v.i.* ⟨*Zeit:*⟩ vergehen
■ **roll 'in** *v.i.* (coll.) ⟨*Briefe, Geldbeträge:*⟩
eingehen
■ **roll 'out** *v.t.* ausrollen ⟨*Teig, Teppich*⟩
■ **roll 'over** *v.i.* ⟨*Person:*⟩ sich umdrehen, (to
make room) sich zur Seite rollen
■ **roll 'up** ⟨1⟩ *v.t.* aufrollen ⟨*Teppich*⟩;
zusammenrollen ⟨*Landkarte, Dokument*
*usw.*⟩; hochkrempeln ⟨*Ärmel*⟩
⟨2⟩ *v.i.* (coll.: arrive) aufkreuzen (salopp)

'**roll-call** *n.* Ausrufen aller Namen; (Mil.)
Zählappell, *der*

**rolled 'oats** *n. pl.* Haferflocken *Pl.*

'**roller** *n.* (a) Rolle, *die;* (for lawn, road, etc.)
Walze, *die*
(b) (for hair) Lockenwickler, *der*

**roller:** **R**~**blade** ® *n.* Rollerblade, *der;*

Inliner, der; ~**blade** v.i. Rollerblades fahren; ~ **blind** n. Rouleau, das; ~ **coaster** n. Achterbahn, die; ~ **skate** n. Rollschuh, der; ~**skate** v.i. Rollschuh laufen; ~ **skating** n. Rollschuhlaufen, das

'**roll film** n. Rollfilm, der

'**rolling** adj. wellig ⟨Gelände⟩; ~ **hills** sanfte Hügel Pl.

**rolling:** ~ **pin** n. Teigrolle, die; ~ **stock** n. (Brit. Railw.) Fahrzeugbestand, der

**roll:** ~**-neck** ①n. Rollkragen, der; ② adj. Rollkragen-; ~**-on** ~**-off** adj. ~-on ~-off ship/ferry Roll-on-roll-off-Schiff, das/-Fähre, die; ~**over** n. (von Auslosung zu Auslosung) aufgestockter Jackpot; ~**-up** (Brit. coll.)**,** ~**-your-own** (esp. Amer. coll.) ns. Selbstgedrehte, die

**ROM** /rɒm/ abbr. (Comp.) **= read only memory** ROM

**Roman** /'rəʊmən/ ① n. Römer, der/ Römerin, die ② adj. römisch

**Roman 'Catholic** ① adj. römisch- katholisch ② n. Katholik, der/Katholikin, die; sb. is a ~: jmd. ist römisch-katholisch

**romance** /rə'mæns/ n. (a) (love affair) Romanze, die (b) (love story) [romantische] Liebesgeschichte

**Romania** /rəʊ'meɪnɪə/ pr. n. Rumänien (das)

**Romanian** /rəʊ'meɪnɪən/ ① adj. rumänisch; sb. is ~: jmd. ist Romäne/ Romänin ② n. (a) (person) Rumäne, der/Rumänin, die (b) (language) Rumänisch, das; see also ENGLISH 2A

**Roman 'numeral** n. römische Ziffer

**romantic** /rəʊ'mæntɪk/ adj. romantisch

**romanticism** /rəʊ'mæntɪsɪzm/ n. (Lit., Art., Mus.) Romantik, die

**romanticize** /rəʊ'mæntɪsaɪz/ v.t. romantisieren

'**roman type** n. (Printing) Antiquaschrift, die

**Romany** /'rəʊmənɪ/ ① (a) (person) Rom, der (b) (language) Romani, das ② adj. Roma-; (Ling.) Romani-

**Rome** /rəʊm/ pr. n. Rom (das)

**romp** /rɒmp/ ① v.i. (a) [herum]tollen (b) ~ home or in (coll.: win easily) spielend gewinnen ② n. Tollerei, die

**rompers** /'rɒmpəz/ n. pl. Spielhöschen, das

**roof** /ruːf/ ① n. (a) Dach, das (b) ~ of the mouth Gaumen, der ② v.t. bedachen

'**roof garden** Dachgarten, der

'**roofing** n. (material) Deckung, die

'**roof:** ~ **rack** n. Dachgepäckträger, der; ~**top** n. Dach, das

**rook**[1] /rʊk/ n. (Ornith.) Saatkrähe, die

**rook**[2] n. (Chess) Turm, der

**rookery** /'rʊkərɪ/ n. Saatkrähenkolonie, die

**room** /ruːm, rʊm/ n. (a) (in building) Zimmer, das; (for function) Saal, der (b) (space) Platz, der; make ~ [for sb./sth.] [jmdm./einer Sache] Platz machen; there is still ~ for improvement in his work seine Arbeit ist noch verbesserungsfähig

**room:** ~**-mate** n. Zimmergenosse, der/ -genossin, die; ~ **service** n. Zimmerservice, der; ~ **temperature** n. Zimmertemperatur, die

**roomy** /'ruːmɪ/ adj. geräumig

**roost** /ruːst/ ① n. [Sitz]stange, die ② v.i. ⟨Vogel:⟩ sich [zum Schlafen] niederlassen

**root**[1] /ruːt/ ① n. Wurzel, die; put down ~s/ take ~: Wurzel schlagen ② v.i. ⟨Pflanze:⟩ wurzeln ③ v.t. stand ~ed to the spot wie angewurzelt dastehen ■ **root 'out** v.t. ausrotten

**root**[2] v.i. (a) (turn up ground) wühlen (for nach) (b) (coll.) ~ **for** (cheer) anfeuern

'**root crop[s]** n. [pl.] Hackfrüchte Pl.

'**rooted** adj. eingewurzelt

'**rootless** adj. wurzellos

'**root vegetable** n. Wurzelgemüse, das

**rope** /rəʊp/ ① n. (a) (cord) Seil, das (b) know the ~s sich auskennen ② v.t. festbinden ■ **rope 'in** v.t. (fig.) einspannen (ugs.)

**rope 'ladder** n. Strickleiter, die

**ro-ro** /'rəʊrəʊ/ adj. Ro-Ro-⟨Schiff, Fähre⟩

**rosary** /'rəʊzərɪ/ n. Rosenkranz, der

**rose**[1] /rəʊz/ n. (a) (plant, flower) Rose, die (b) (colour) Rosa, das

**rose**[2] ▶ RISE 2

**rosé** /'rəʊzeɪ, 'rəʊzeɪ/ n. Rosé, der

**rose:** ~ **bed** n. Rosenbeet, das; ~**bud** n. Rosenknospe, die; ~ **bush** n. Rosenstrauch, der; ~ **hip** n. Hagebutte, die

**rosemary** /'rəʊzmərɪ/ n. Rosmarin, der

'**rose petal** n. Rosen[blüten]blatt, das

**rosette** /rəʊ'zet/ n. Rosette, die

**roster** /'rɒstə(r)/ n. Dienstplan, der

**rostrum** /'rɒstrəm/ n., pl. **rostra** /'rɒstrə/ or ~s Podium, das

**rosy** /'rəʊzɪ/ adj. rosig

**rot** /rɒt/ ① n. (a) ▶ 2: Verrottung, die; Fäulnis, die; (fig.: deterioration) Verfall, der; stop the ~ (fig.) dem Verfall Einhalt gebieten (b) (coll.: nonsense) Quark, der (salopp) ② v.i., **-tt-** verrotten; ⟨Fleisch, Gemüse, Obst:⟩ verfaulen ③ v.t., **-tt-** verrotten lassen; verfaulen lassen ⟨Fleisch, Gemüse, Obst⟩; zerstören ⟨Zähne⟩

**rota** /'rəʊtə/ n. (Brit.) (order of rotation) Turnus, der; (list) Arbeitsplan, der

**rotary** /'rəʊtərɪ/ adj. rotierend

**r**

**rotate** /rəʊˈteɪt/ ① *v.i.* (revolve) rotieren; sich drehen
② *v.t.* in Rotation versetzen
**rotation** /rəʊˈteɪʃn/ *n.* (a) Rotation, *die,* Drehung, *die* (about um)
(b) (succession) turnusmäßiger Wechsel; **in** *or* **by** ∼: im Turnus
**rote** /rəʊt/ *n.* **by** ∼: auswendig
**rotten** /ˈrɒtn/ *adj.,* ∼**er** /ˈrɒtənə(r)/, ∼**est** /ˈrɒtənɪst/ (a) (decayed) verrottet; verfault 〈*Obst, Gemüse*〉; faul 〈*Ei, Holz, Zähne*〉; ∼ **to the core** (fig.) verdorben bis ins Mark
(b) (corrupt) verdorben
(c) (coll.: bad) mies (ugs.)
**rotund** /rəʊˈtʌnd/ *adj.* (a) (round) rund
(b) ( plump) rundlich
**rouble** /ˈruːbl/ *n.* Rubel, *der*
**rouge** /ruːʒ/ *n.* Rouge, *das*
**rough** /rʌf/ ① *adj.* (a) (coarse, uneven) rau; holp[e]rig 〈*Straße usw.*〉; uneben 〈*Gelände*〉; unruhig 〈*Überfahrt*〉
(b) (violent) grob 〈*Person, Worte, Behandlung*〉
(c) (trying) hart; **this is** ∼ **on him** das ist hart für ihn; **sth. is** ∼ **going** etw. ist nicht einfach
(d) (approximate) grob 〈*Skizze, Schätzung*〉; vag 〈*Vorstellung*〉; ∼ **paper/notebook** Konzeptpapier, *das*/Kladde, *die*
(e) (coll.: ill) angeschlagen (ugs.)
② *n.* [**be**] **in** ∼: [sich] im Rohzustand [befinden]
③ *adv.* rau 〈*spielen*〉; **sleep** ∼: im Freien schlafen
④ *v.t.* ∼ **it** primitiv leben
▪ **rough** ˈ**out** *v.t.* grob entwerfen
▪ **rough** ˈ**up** *v.t.* (coll.) zusammenschlagen
**roughage** /ˈrʌfɪdʒ/ *n.* Ballaststoffe *Pl.*
**rough:** ∼**-and-ready** *adj.* provisorisch; ∼ **and** ˈ**tumble** *n.* [milde] Rauferei; ∼ **copy,** ∼ **draft** *ns.* grobe Skizze; grober Entwurf; ∼ ˈ**diamond** *n.* (fig.) ungehobelter, aber guter Mensch
**roughen** /ˈrʌfn/ *v.t.* aufrauen
**rough:** ∼ ˈ**justice** *n.* ziemlich willkürliche Urteile *Pl.*; ∼ ˈ**luck** *n.* Pech, *das*
ˈ**roughly** *adv.* (a) (violently) roh; grob
(b) (crudely) leidlich; grob 〈*skizzieren, bearbeiten, bauen*〉
(c) (approximately) ungefähr; grob 〈*geschätzt*〉
ˈ**roughness** *n.* (a) Rauheit, *die;* (unevenness) Unebenheit, *die*
(b) (violence) Rohheit, *die*
ˈ**roughshod** *adj.* **ride** ∼ **over sb./sth.** jmdn./etw. mit Füßen treten
**roulette** /ruːˈlet/ *n.* Roulette, *das*
**round** /raʊnd/ ① *adj.* rund; **in** ∼ **figures** rund gerechnet
② *n.* (a) (recurring series) Serie, *die;* ∼ **of talks/ negotiations** Gesprächs-/Verhandlungsrunde, *die;* **the daily** ∼: der Alltag
(b) (of ammunition) Ladung, *die;* **50** ∼**s** [**of ammunition**] 50 Schuss Munition
(c) (of game or contest) Runde, *die*
(d) (burst) ∼ **of applause** Beifallssturm, *der*
(e) ∼ [**of drinks**] Runde, *die*

(f) (regular calls) Runde, *die;* Tour, *die;* **go** [**on**] *or* **make one's** ∼**s** seine Runden machen
(g) **a** ∼ **of toast/sandwiches** eine Scheibe Toast/eine Portion Sandwiches
③ *adv.* (a) **all the year** ∼: das ganze Jahr hindurch; **the third time** ∼: beim dritten Mal; **have a look** ∼: sich umsehen; **ask sb.** ∼ [**for a drink**] jmdn. [zu einem Gläschen zu sich] einladen
(b) (by indirect way) herum; **walk** ∼: außen herum gehen
(c) (here) hier; (there) dort; **I'll go** ∼ **tomorrow** ich gehe morgen hin
④ *prep.* (a) um [... herum]; **travel** ∼ **England** durch England reisen; **run** ∼ **the streets** durch die Straßen rennen; **walk** ∼ **and** ∼ **sth.** immer wieder um etw. herumgehen
(b) (in various directions from) um [... herum]; rund um 〈*einen Ort*〉
⑤ *v.t.* ∼ **a bend** um eine Kurve fahren/ gehen/kommen *usw*
▪ **round** ˈ**off** *v.t.* abrunden
▪ **round** ˈ**up** *v.t.* verhaften 〈*Verdächtige*〉; zusammentreiben 〈*Vieh*〉
**round:** ∼ **a**ˈ**bout** *adv.* (on all sides) ringsum; ∼**about** ① *n.* (a) (Brit.: merry-go-round) Karussell, *das;* (b) (Brit.: road junction) Kreisverkehr, *der.* ② *adj.* umständlich; ∼ ˈ**brackets** *n. pl.* runde Klammern *Pl.*
**rounded** /ˈraʊndɪd/ *adj.* (a) rund
(b) harmonisch 〈*Person*〉
**rounders** /ˈraʊndəz/ *n. sing.* (Brit.) Rounders, *das;* ≈ Schlagball, *der*
**round:** ∼ ˈ**number** *n.* runde Zahl; ∼ ˈ**robin** *n.* Petition, *die;* ∼**-shouldered** /raʊndˈʃəʊldəd/ *adj.* 〈*Person*〉 mit einem Rundrücken; ∼**-the-**ˈ**clock** *adj.* rund um die Uhr *nachgestellt;* ∼ ˈ**trip** *n.* Rundreise, *die;* ∼**-up** *n.* (a) (of animals) Zusammentreiben, *das;* (b) (summary) Zusammenfassung, *die*
**rouse** /raʊz/ *v.t.* wecken (**from** aus)
**rousing** /ˈraʊzɪŋ/ *adj.* mitreißend 〈*Lied*〉; leidenschaftlich 〈*Rede*〉
**rout** /raʊt/ ① *n.* [wilde] Flucht; (defeat) verheerende Niederlage
② *v.t.* aufreiben 〈*Feind, Truppen*〉; vernichtend schlagen 〈*Gegner*〉
**route** /ruːt/ *n.* Route, *die;* Weg, *der*
ˈ**route march** *n.* (Mil.) Übungsmarsch, *der*
**routine** /ruːˈtiːn/ ① *n.* (a) Routine, *die*
(b) (coll.: set speech) Platte, *die* (ugs.)
(c) (Theatre) Nummer, *die;* (Dancing, Skating) Figur, *die*
② *adj.* routinemäßig; Routine〈*arbeit*〉
**roux** /ruː/ *n.* Mehlschwitze, *die*
**row**¹ /raʊ/ ① (coll.) *n.* (a) (noise) Krach, *der;* **make a** ∼: Krach machen
(b) (quarrel) Krach, *der* (ugs.); **have/start a** ∼: Krach haben/anfangen (ugs.)
② *v.i.* sich streiten
**row**² /rəʊ/ *n.* Reihe, *die;* **in a** ∼: in einer Reihe
**row**³ /rəʊ/ *v.i. & t.* (with oars) rudern

**rowan** /'rəʊən/ n. ~ [tree] Eberesche, *die*
**rowboat** /'rəʊbəʊt/ n. (Amer.) Ruderboot, *das*
**rowdy** /'raʊdɪ/ ⟦1⟧ *adj.* rowdyhaft; **the party was ~:** auf der Party ging es laut zu ⟦2⟧ n. Krawallmacher, *der*
**rower** /'rəʊə(r)/ n. Ruderer, *der*/Ruderin, *die*
**rowing** /'rəʊɪŋ/ n. Rudern, *das*
**rowing: ~ boat** n. (Brit.) Ruderboot, *das;* ~ **machine** n. Rudergerät, *das*
**royal** /'rɔɪəl/ *adj.* königlich
**royal: R~ 'Air Force** n. (Brit.) Königliche Luftwaffe; ~ **'blue** n. (Brit.) Königsblau, *das;* ~ **'family** n. königliche Familie; **R~ 'Navy** n. (Brit.) Königliche Kriegsmarine
**royalty** /'rɔɪəltɪ/ n. (a) (payment) Tantieme, *die* (**on** für) (b) *collect.* (royal persons) Mitglieder *Pl.* des Königshauses
**RSI** *abbr.* = **repetitive strain injury**
**RSPCA** *abbr.* (Brit.) = **Royal Society for the Prevention of Cruelty to Animals** *britischer Tierschutzverein*
**rub** /rʌb/ ⟦1⟧ *v.t.,* **-bb-** reiben (**on, against** an + *Dat.*); (to remove dirt etc.) abreiben; (to dry) trockenreiben; ~ **sth. off sth.** etw. von etw. [ab]reiben ⟦2⟧ *v.i.,* **-bb-** reiben ([up]**on, against** an + *Dat.*) ⟦3⟧ n. **give it a ~:** reib es ab; **there's the ~** (fig.) da liegt der Haken [dabei] (ugs.)
■ **rub 'down** *v.t.* abreiben
■ **rub 'in** *v.t.* einreiben; **there's no need to** *or* **don't ~ it in** (fig.) reib es mir nicht [dauernd] unter die Nase
■ **rub 'off** *v.t.* wegreiben; wegwischen
■ **rub 'out** ⟦1⟧ *v.t.* ausreiben; (using eraser) ausradieren ⟦2⟧ *v.i.* sich ausreiben/sich ausradieren lassen
**rubber** /'rʌbə(r)/ n. (a) Gummi, *das od. der* (b) (eraser) Radiergummi, *der*
**rubber: ~ 'band** n. Gummiband, *das;* ~ **'glove** n. Gummihandschuh, *der;* ~ **'plant** n. Gummibaum, *der;* ~ **'stamp** n. Gummistempel, *der;* ~**-stamp** *v.t.* (fig.) absegnen (ugs.)
**rubbery** /'rʌbərɪ/ *adj.* gummiartig; (tough) zäh
**rubbish** /'rʌbɪʃ/ ⟦1⟧ n. (a) (refuse) Abfall, *der;* (to be collected and dumped) Müll, *der* (b) (worthless material) Plunder, *der* (ugs.); **be ~:** nichts taugen (c) (nonsense) Quatsch, *der* (ugs.) ⟦2⟧ *int.* Quatsch (ugs.)
**rubbish: ~ bin** n. Abfall-/Mülleimer, *der;* (in factory) Abfall-/Mülltonne, *die;* ~ **chute** n. Müllschlucker, *der;* ~ **collection** n. Müllabfuhr, *die;* ~ **dump** n. Müllkippe, *die;* ~ **heap** n. Müllhaufen, *der;* ~ **tip** n. Müllablageplatz, *der*

**rubbishy** /'rʌbɪʃɪ/ *adj.* mies (ugs.)
**rubble** /'rʌbl/ n. Trümmer *Pl.*
**rubella** /rʊ'belə/ n. (Med.) Röteln *Pl.*
**ruby** /'ru:bɪ/ n. Rubin, *der*
**ruby 'wedding** n. Rubinhochzeit, *die*
**rucksack** /'rʌksæk, 'rʊksæk/ n. Rucksack, *der*
**rudder** /'rʌdə(r)/ n. [Steuer]ruder, *das*
**ruddy** /'rʌdɪ/ *adj.* (a) (reddish) rötlich (b) (Brit. coll.: bloody) verdammt (salopp)
**rude** /ru:d/ *adj.* (a) unhöflich; (stronger) rüde; **be ~ to sb.** zu jmdm. grob unhöflich sein/jmdn. rüde behandeln (b) (abrupt) unsanft; ~ **awakening** böses Erwachen
**'rudely** *adv.* (a) (impolitely) unhöflich; rüde (b) (abruptly) jäh (geh.)
**'rudeness** n. (bad manners) ungehöriges Benehmen
**rudimentary** /ru:dɪ'mentərɪ/ elementar; primitiv ⟨*Gebäude*⟩
**rudiments** /'ru:dɪmənts/ n. pl. Grundlagen *Pl.*
**rueful** /'ru:fl/ *adj.* reumütig
**ruffian** /'rʌfɪən/ n. Rohling, *der*
**ruffle** /'rʌfl/ *v.t.* (a) kräuseln; ~ **sb.'s hair** jmdm. durch die Haare fahren (b) (upset) aus der Fassung bringen
**rug** /rʌg/ n. [kleiner, dicker] Teppich; **Persian ~:** Perserbrücke, *die*
**rugby** /'rʌgbɪ/ n. Rugby, *das*
**rugby: ~ ball** n. Rugbyball, *der;* ~ **tackle** n. tiefes Fassen; **the policeman brought him down with a ~ tackle** der Polizist warf sich auf ihn und riss ihn zu Boden
**rugged** /'rʌgɪd/ *adj.* (a) (uneven) zerklüftet; unwegsam ⟨*Land*⟩; zerfurcht ⟨*Gesicht*⟩ (b) (sturdy) robust
**ruin** /'ru:ɪn/ ⟦1⟧ n. (a) *in sing. or pl.* (remains) Ruine, *die;* **in ~s** in Trümmern (b) (downfall) Ruin, *der* ⟦2⟧ *v.t.* ruinieren; verderben ⟨*Urlaub, Abend*⟩; ~**ed** (reduced to ruins) verfallen; **a ~ed castle/church** eine Burg-/Kirchenruine
**ruinous** /'ru:ɪnəs/ *adj.* ruinös
**rule** /ru:l/ ⟦1⟧ n. (a) Regel, *die;* **the ~s of the game** die Spielregeln; **be against the ~s** regelwidrig sein; (fig.) gegen die Spielregeln verstoßen; **as a ~:** in der Regel; ~ **of thumb** Faustregel, *die* (b) *no pl.* (government) Herrschaft, *die* (**over** über + *Akk.*) ⟦2⟧ *v.t.* (a) (control) beherrschen (b) (be the ruler of) regieren ⟨*Monarch, Diktator usw.*⟩ herrschen über (+ *Akk.*) ⟦3⟧ *v.i.* (a) (govern) herrschen (b) (decide) entscheiden (**against** gegen; **in favour of** für)
■ **rule 'out** *v.t.* ausschließen; (prevent) unmöglich machen
**'rule book** n. Regeln
**ruled** /ru:ld/ *adj.* liniert ⟨*Papier*⟩

**ruler** /'ruːlə(r)/ *n.* **(a)** (person) Herrscher, *der*/Herrscherin, *die*
**(b)** (for measuring) Lineal, *das*

**ruling** /'ruːlɪŋ/ ① *adj.* herrschend ‹*Klasse*›; regierend ‹*Partei*›
② *n.* Entscheidung, *die*

**rum** /rʌm/ *n.* Rum, *der*

**Rumania** etc. /ruːˈmeɪnɪə/ ▶ ROMANIA etc.

**rumble** /'rʌmbl/ ① *n.* Grollen, *das*
② *v.i.* **(a)** grollen; ‹*Magen:*› knurren
**(b)** ‹*Fahrzeug:*› rumpeln (ugs.)

**ruminate** /'ruːmɪneɪt/ *v.i.* ~ **on** *or* **over sth.** über etw. (Akk.) grübeln

**rummage** /'rʌmɪdʒ/ *v.i.* wühlen; ~ **through sth.** etw. durchwühlen (ugs.)

**rummy** /'rʌmɪ/ *n.* Rommé, *das*

**rumour** (Brit.; Amer.: **rumor**) /'ruːmə(r)/
① *n.* Gerücht, *das;* **there is a ~ that ...**: es geht das Gerücht, dass ...
② *v.t.* **it is ~ed that ...**: es geht das Gerücht, dass ...

**rump** /rʌmp/ *n.* **(a)** (buttocks) Hinterteil, *das* (ugs.)
**(b)** (remnant) Rest, *der*

**rumple** /'rʌmpl/ *v.t.* **(a)** (crease) zerknittern
**(b)** (tousle) zerzausen

**'rump steak** *n.* Rumpsteak, *das*

**rumpus** /'rʌmpəs/ *n.* (coll.) Krach, *der* (ugs.); **kick up** *or* **make a ~**: einen Spektakel veranstalten (ugs.)

**'rumpus room** *n.* (Amer.) Spielzimmer, *das*

**run** /rʌn/ ① *n.* **(a)** Lauf, *der;* **go for a ~**: laufen gehen; **on the ~** (fleeing) auf der Flucht
**(b)** (trip in vehicle) Fahrt, *die;* (for pleasure) Ausflug, *der*
**(c)** (continuous stretch) Länge, *die*
**(d)** (spell) **she has had a long ~ of success** sie war lange [Zeit] erfolgreich; **have a long ~** ‹*Stück, Show:*› viele Aufführungen erleben
**(e)** (succession) Serie, *die;* (Cards) Sequenz, *die;* **a ~ of victories** eine Siegesserie
**(f)** (use) **have the ~ of sth.** etw. zu seiner freien Verfügung haben
**(g)** (enclosure) Auslauf, *der*
**(h)** (in stocking etc.) Laufmasche, *die*
② *v.i.*, **-nn-**, **ran** /ræn/, **run (a)** laufen; ~ **for the bus** laufen, um den Bus zu kriegen (ugs.); ~ **to help sb.** jmdm. zu Hilfe eilen
**(b)** (roll, slide) laufen; ‹*Ball, Kugel:*› rollen, laufen; ‹*Schlitten, [Schiebe]tür:*› gleiten
**(c)** ‹*Rad, Maschine:*› laufen
**(d)** (operate on a schedule) fahren; ~ **between two places** ‹*Zug, Bus:*› zwischen zwei Orten verkehren
**(e)** (flow) laufen; ‹*Fluss:*› fließen; ‹*Augen:*› tränen; **his nose was ~ning** ihm lief die Nase
**(f)** ‹*Vertrag, Theaterstück:*› laufen
**(g)** (have wording) lauten; ‹*Geschichte:*› gehen (fig.)
**(h)** ‹*Butter, Eis:*› zerlaufen; ‹*Farben:*› auslaufen

**(i)** (in election) kandidieren
③ *v.t.*, **-nn-**, **ran**, **run (a)** laufen lassen; (drive) fahren; ~ **one's hand/fingers through/along** *or* **over sth.** mit der Hand/den Fingern durch etw. fahren/über etw. (Akk.) streichen; ~ **an** *or* **one's eye along** *or* **down** *or* **over sth.** (fig.) etw. überfliegen
**(b)** (cause to flow) [ein]laufen lassen; ~ **a bath** ein Bad einlaufen lassen
**(c)** (organize, manage) führen, leiten ‹*Geschäft usw.*›; veranstalten ‹*Wettbewerb*›
**(d)** (operate) bedienen ‹*Maschine*›; verkehren lassen ‹*Verkehrsmittel*›; einsetzen ‹*Sonderbus, -zug*›; laufen lassen ‹*Motor*›
**(e)** (own and use) sich (Dat.) halten ‹*Auto*›
**(f)** ~ **sb. into town** etc. jmdn. in die Stadt usw. fahren

■ **run a'cross** *v.t.* ~ **across sb./sth.** jmdm. treffen/auf etw. (Akk.) stoßen

■ **run a'way** *v.i.* **(a)** (flee) weglaufen; fortlaufen
**(b)** (abscond) ~ **away [from home]** [von zu Hause] weglaufen

■ **run 'down** ① *v.t.* **(a)** (collide with) überfahren
**(b)** (criticize) heruntermachen (ugs.)
**(c)** (reduce) abbauen
② *v.i.* **(a)** hin-/herunterlaufen
**(b)** (decline) sich verringern
**(c)** ‹*Uhr, Spielzeug:*› ablaufen; ‹*Batterie*› leer werden

■ **run into** *v.t.* **(a)** ~ **into a tree** gegen einen Baum fahren
**(b)** (meet) ~ **into sb.** jmdm. in die Arme laufen (ugs.)
**(c)** stoßen auf (+ Akk.) ‹*Schwierigkeiten, Widerstand usw.*›
**(d)** (amount to) ~ **into thousands** in die tausende gehen

■ **run 'off** ① *v.i.* weglaufen
② *v.t.* abziehen ‹*Kopien*›

■ **run 'out** *v.i.* **(a)** hin-/herauslaufen
**(b)** ‹*Vorräte, Bestände:*› zu Ende gehen

■ **run 'out of** *v.t.* **sb. ~s out of sth.** jmdm. geht etw. aus; **I'm ~ning out of patience** meine Geduld geht zu Ende

■ **run 'over** ① /'---/ *v.t.* (knock down) überfahren
② /'-'--/ *v.i.* überlaufen

■ **'run through** *v.t.* durchspielen ‹*Theaterstück*›; durchgehen ‹*Plan*›

■ **'run to** *v.t.* **(a)** (amount to) sich belaufen auf (Akk.)
**(b)** (be sufficient for) **sth. will ~ to sth.** etw. reicht für etw.

■ **run 'up** ① *v.i.* hinlaufen; **come ~ning up** hingelaufen kommen
② *v.t.* **(a)** rasch nähen ‹*Kleidungsstück*›
**(b)** zusammenkommen lassen ‹*Schulden, Rechnung*›

■ **run 'up against** *v.t.* stoßen auf (+ Akk.) ‹*Probleme, Widerstand usw.*›

**run:** ~**about** *n.* (coll.) [little] ~**about** Kleinwagen, *der;* ~**around** *n.* (coll.) **give sb. the ~around** jmdn. an der Nase herumführen (ugs.); ~**away** ① *n.*

Ausreißer, *der*/Ausreißerin, *die* (ugs.);
[2] *attrib. adj.* durchgegangen ‹*Pferd*›; außer
Kontrolle geraten ‹*Fahrzeug, Preise*›;
galoppierend ‹*Inflation*›; ∼**down** /'--/ *n.*
(coll.: briefing) Übersicht, *die* (**on** über + *Akk.*);
∼**-down** /-'-/ *adj.* (tired) mitgenommen
**rung¹** /rʌŋ/ *n.* Sprosse, *die*
**rung²** ▶ RING² 2, 3
'**runner** *n.* (a) Läufer, *der*/Läuferin, *die*
(b) (Bot.) Ausläufer, *der*
(c) (on sledge) Kufe, *die*
'**runner bean** *n.* (Brit.) Stangenbohne, *die*
**runner-'up** *n.* Zweite, *der*/*die;* **the runners-
up** die Platzierten *Pl.*
'**running** [1] *n.* (a) (management) Leitung, *die*
(b) (action) Laufen, *das;* **in/out of the ∼:** im/
aus dem Rennen
[2] *adj.* (in succession) hintereinander; **win for
the third year ∼:** schon drei Jahre
hintereinander gewinnen
**running:** ∼ '**commentary** *n.*
(Broadcasting; also fig.) Livekommentar, *der;*
∼ **costs** *n. pl.* Betriebskosten *Pl.;*
∼ **shoe** *n.* Rennschuh, *der;* ∼ '**total** *n.*
fortlaufende Summe; ∼ **track** *n.*
Aschenbahn, *die;* ∼ '**water** *n.* **hot and cold
∼ water** fließendes kaltes und warmes
Wasser
**runny** /'rʌnɪ/ *adj.* (a) laufend ‹*Nase*›
(b) zu dünn ‹*Farbe, Marmelade*›
**run:** ∼**-of-the-'mill** *adj.* ganz gewöhnlich;
∼**-up** *n.* (a) during *or* in the ∼**-up to an
event** im Vorfeld eines Ereignisses; (b)
(Sport) Anlauf, *der;* ∼**way** *n.* (for take-off)
Startbahn, *die;* (for landing) Landebahn, *die*
**rupture** /'rʌptʃə(r)/ [1] *n.* Bruch, *der*
[2] *v.t.* ∼ **oneself** sich (*Dat.*) einen Bruch
zuziehen
**rural** /'rʊərl/ *adj.* ländlich
**ruse** /ruːz/ *n.* List, *die*
**rush¹** /rʌʃ/ *n.* (Bot.) Binse, *die*
**rush²** [1] *n.* (a) (hurry) Eile, *die;* **what's all the
∼?** wozu diese Hast?; **be in a [great] ∼:** in
[großer] Eile sein

(c) (period of great activity) Hochbetrieb, *der;*
(∼ hour) Stoßzeit, *die*
(c) **make a ∼ for sth.** sich auf etw. (*Akk.*)
stürzen
[2] *v.t.* (a) ∼ **sb./sth. somewhere** jmdn./etw.
auf schnellstem Wege irgendwohin bringen;
**be ∼ed** (have to hurry) in Eile sein; ∼ **sb. into
doing sth.** jmdn. dazu drängen, etw. zu tun
(b) (perform quickly) auf die Schnelle
erledigen; ∼ **it** zu schnell machen
[3] *v.i.* (a) (move quickly) eilen; ‹*Hund, Pferd:*›
laufen; ∼ **to help sb.** jmdm. zu Hilfe eilen
(b) (hurry unduly) sich zu sehr beeilen; **don't
∼!** nur keine Eile!
◾ **rush a'bout, rush a'round** *v.i.*
herumhetzen
**rush:** ∼ **hour** *n.* Stoßzeit, *die;* ∼ **job** *n.*
eilige Arbeit
**rusk** /rʌsk/ *n.* Zwieback, *der*
**Russia** /'rʌʃə/ *pr. n.* Russland (*das*)
**Russian** /'rʌʃn/ [1] *adj.* russisch; **sb. is ∼:**
jmd. ist Russe/Russin
[2] *n.* (a) (person) Russe, *der*/Russin, *die*
(b) (language) Russisch, *das; see also* ENGLISH
2A
**rust** /rʌst/ [1] *n.* Rost, *der*
[2] *v.i.* rosten
**rustic** /'rʌstɪk/ *adj.* (a) ländlich
(b) rustikal ‹*Mobiliar*›
**rustle** /'rʌsl/ [1] *n.* Rascheln, *das*
[2] *v.i.* rascheln
[3] *v.t.* (a) rascheln lassen
(b) (Amer.: steal) stehlen
◾ **rustle 'up** *v.t.* zusammenzaubern
‹*Mahlzeit*›
'**rustproof** *adj.* rostfrei
'**rusty** *adj.* rostig
**rut** /rʌt/ *n.* Spurrille, *die;* **be in a ∼** (fig.) aus
dem [Alltags]trott nicht mehr
herauskommen
**ruthless** /'ruːθlɪs/ *adj.* rücksichtslos
**RV** *abbr.* (Amer.) = **recreational
vehicle**
**rye** /raɪ/ *n.* Roggen, *der*
'**rye bread** *n.* Roggenbrot, *das*

# Ss

**S, s** /es/ *n.* S, s, *das*
**S.** *abbr.* (a) = **south** S
(b) = **southern** s.
**sabbath** /'sæbəθ/ *n.* Sabbat, *der*
**sabbatical** /sə'bætɪkl/ [1] *adj.* ∼ **term/year**
Forschungssemester/-jahr, *das*
[2] *n.* Forschungsurlaub, *der*
**sabotage** /'sæbətɑːʒ/ [1] *n.* Sabotage, *die*

[2] *v.t.* einen Sabotageakt verüben auf
(+ *Akk.*); (fig.) sabotieren
**saboteur** /sæbə'tɜː(r)/ *n.* Saboteur, *der*
**saccharin** /'sækərɪn/ *n.* Saccharin, *das*
**sachet** /'sæʃeɪ/ *n.* Beutel, *der;* (cushion-
shaped) Kissen, *das*
**sack** /sæk/ [1] *n.* (a) Sack, *der*     ····❖

**(b)** (coll.: dismissal) Rausschmiss, *der* (ugs.); **get the** ∼: rausgeschmissen werden (ugs.); **give sb. the** ∼: jmdn. rausschmeißen (ugs.) 2 *v.t.* (coll.) rausschmeißen (ugs.) **(for** wegen)

**sacking** /'sækıŋ/ *n.***(a)** (coll.: dismissal) Rausschmiss, *der* (ugs.)
**(b)** (coarse fabric) Sackleinen, *das*

**sacrament** /'sækrəmənt/ *n.* Sakrament, *das*

**sacred** /'seıkrıd/ *adj.* heilig

**sacrifice** /'sækrıfaıs/ 1 *n.* Opfer, *das* 2 *v.t.* opfern

**sacrilege** /'sækrılıdʒ/ *n.* [act of] ∼: Sakrileg, *das*

**sad** /sæd/ *adj.* traurig **(at, about** über + *Akk.*); schmerzlich ⟨*Tod, Verlust*⟩; **feel** ∼: traurig sein

**sadden** /'sædn/ *v.t.* traurig stimmen

**SAD** *abbr.* = **seasonal affective disorder**

**saddle** /'sædl/ 1 *n.* Sattel, *der* 2 *v.t.* **(a)** satteln ⟨*Pferd usw.*⟩
**(b)** (fig.) ∼ **sb. with sth.** jmdm. etw. aufbürden (geh.)

**'saddlebag** *n.* Satteltasche, *die*

**sadism** /'seıdızm/ *n.* Sadismus, *der*

**sadist** /'seıdıst/ *n.* Sadist, *der*/Sadistin, *die*

**sadistic** /sə'dıstık/ *adj.,* **sa'distically** *adv.* sadistisch

**'sadly** *adv.* **(a)** (with sorrow) traurig
**(b)** (unfortunately) leider

**'sadness** *n.* Traurigkeit, *die*

**sadomasochism** /seıdəʊ'mæsəkızm/ *n.* Sadomasochismus, *der*

**s.a.e.** /eseı'iː/ *abbr.* = **stamped addressed envelope** adressierter Freiumschlag

**safari** /sə'faːrı/ *n.* Safari, *die;* **on** ∼: auf Safari

**safe** /seıf/ 1 *n.* Safe, *der;* Geldschrank, *der* 2 *adj.* **(a)** (out of danger) sicher **(from** vor + *Dat.*); **he's** ∼: er ist in Sicherheit; ∼ **and sound** sicher und wohlbehalten
**(b)** (free from danger) ungefährlich; sicher ⟨*Ort, Hafen*⟩; **wish sb. a** ∼ **journey** jmdm. eine gute Reise wünschen; **to be on the** ∼ **side** zur Sicherheit
**(c)** (reliable) sicher ⟨*Methode, Investition*⟩

**safe:** ∼**guard** 1 *n.* Schutz, *der;* 2 *v.t.* schützen; ∼ **'haven** *n.* **(a)** (safe place) Zuflucht, *die;* **(b)** (Polit.) Schutzzone, *die*

**safely** /'seıflı/ *adv.* sicher; **did the parcel arrive** ∼? ist das Paket heil angekommen?

**safe 'sex** Safersex, *der*

**safety:** ∼ **belt** *n.* Sicherheitsgurt, *der;* ∼ **catch** *n.* (of gun) Sicherungshebel, *der;* ∼ **helmet** *n.* Schutzhelm, *der;* ∼ **margin** *n.* Spielraum, *der;* ∼ **pin** *n.* Sicherheitsnadel, *die;* ∼ **valve** *n.* Sicherheitsventil, *das;* (fig.) Ventil, *das*

**'safe zone** *n.* (Polit.) Schutzzone, *die*

**saffron** /'sæfrən/ *n.* Safran, *der*

**sag** /sæg/ *v.i.,* **-gg-** durchhängen; (sink) sich senken

**saga** /'saːgə/ *n.* **(a)** (story of adventure) Heldenepos, *das;* (medieval narrative) Saga, *die*
**(b)** (long involved story) [ganzer] Roman (fig.)

**sage¹** /seıdʒ/ *n.* (Bot.) Salbei, *der od. die*

**sage²** 1 *adj.* weise 2 *n.* Weise, *der*

**Sagittarius** /sædʒı'teərıəs/ *n.* (Astrol; Astron.) der Schütze

**Sahara** /sə'haːrə/ *pr. n.* **the** ∼ [Desert] die [Wüste] Sahara

**said** ▶ SAY 1

**sail** /seıl/ 1 *n.* **(a)** Segelfahrt, *die* **(b)** (piece of canvas) Segel, *das* 2 *v.i.* **(a)** (travel on water) fahren; (in sailing boat) segeln
**(b)** (start voyage) auslaufen **(for** nach) 3 *v.t.* **(a)** steuern ⟨*Boot, Schiff*⟩; segeln mit ⟨*Segeljacht, -schiff*⟩
**(b)** durchfahren/⟨*Segelschiff:*⟩ durchsegeln ⟨*Meer*⟩

**sail:** ∼**board** *n.* Surfbrett, *das* (*zum Windsurfen*); ∼**boarding** *n.* Windsurfen, *das;* ∼**boat** *n.* (Amer.) Segelboot, *das*

**'sailing** *n.* Segeln, *das*

**sailing:** ∼ **boat** *n.* Segelboot, *das;* ∼ **ship** *n.* Segelschiff, *das*

**sailor** /'seılə(r)/ *n.* Seemann, *der;* (in navy) Matrose, *der*

**saint** 1 /sənt/ *adj.* S∼ **Michael** der heilige Michael; Sankt Michael 2 /seınt/ *n.* Heilige, *der/die*

**'saintly** /'seıntlı/ *adj.* heilig

**sake** /seık/ *n.* **for the** ∼ **of** um ... (*Gen.*) willen; **for my** *etc.* ∼: um meinetwillen *usw.;* mir *usw.* zuliebe

**salad** /'sæləd/ *n.* Salat, *der*

**salad:** ∼ **cream** *n.* ≈ Mayonnaise, *die;* ∼ **dressing** *n.* Salatsoße, *die;* ∼ **servers** *n. pl.* Salatbesteck, *die*

**salary** /'sælərı/ *n.* Gehalt, *das*

**sale** /seıl/ *n.* **(a)** Verkauf, *der;* (at reduced prices) Ausverkauf, *der;* (at end of season) Schlußverkauf, *der;* [up] **for** ∼: zu verkaufen
**(b)** ∼s (amount sold) Verkaufszahlen *Pl.* **(of** für); Absatz, *der*
**(c)** [jumble *or* rummage] ∼: [Wohltätigkeits]basar, *der*

**'sale price** *n.* **(a)** (retail price) Verkaufspreis, *der*
**(b)** (price in sale) Ausverkaufspreis, *der*

**sales:** ∼ **assistant** (Brit.), ∼ **clerk** (Amer.) *ns.* Verkäufer, *der*/Verkäuferin, *die;* ∼**man** /'seılzmən/ *n., pl.* ∼**men** /'seılzmən/ Verkäufer, *der*

**'salesmanship** *n.* Kunst des Verkaufens

**sales:** ∼ **rep** (coll.)**,** ∼ **representative** *ns.* [Handels]vertreter, *der*/-vertreterin, *die;* ∼**woman** *n.* Verkäuferin, *die*

**salient** /'seılıənt/ *adj.* auffallend

**saliva** /sə'laıvə/ *n.* Speichel, *der*

**sallow** /'sæləʊ/ adj. blassgelb

**salmon** /'sæmən/ n. Lachs, der

**saloon** /sə'luːn/ n. (a) (Brit.) ~ [bar] *separater Teil eines Pubs mit mehr Komfort* (b) (Brit.) ~ [car] Limousine, die

**salt** /sɔːlt, sɒlt/ ① n. [common] ~: [Koch]salz, das
② adj. (containing or tasting of ~) salzig; (preserved with ~) gepökelt ⟨Fleisch⟩; gesalzen ⟨Butter⟩
③ v.t. (a) salzen
(b) (cure) [ein]pökeln
(c) ~ the roads Salz auf die Straßen streuen

**salt:** ~ **cellar** n. Salzfässchen, das; ~ '**water** n. Salzwasser, das

'**salty** adj. salzig

**salute** /sə'luːt/ ① v.t. grüßen
② v.i. (Mil., Navy) [militärisch] grüßen
③ n. Salut, der; militärischer Gruß

**salvage** /'sælvɪdʒ/ ① n. Bergung, die
② v.t. bergen

**salvation** /sæl'veɪʃn/ n. Erlösung, die

**Salvation 'Army** n. Heilsarmee, die

**salvo** /'sælvəʊ/ n. Salve, die

**Samaritan** /sə'mærɪtən/ n. good ~: [barmherziger] Samariter; the ~s (organization) ≈ die Telefonseelsorge

**same** /seɪm/ ① adj. the ~: der/die/das gleiche; the ~ [thing] (identical) der-/die-/dasselbe
② adv. all or just the ~: trotzdem

**sample** /'sɑːmpl/ ① n. (example) [Muster]beispiel, das; (specimen) Probe, die; [commercial] ~: Muster, das
② v.t. probieren

'**sample letter** n. Musterbrief, der

**sampler** /'sɑːmplə(r)/ n. (trial pack) Probe[packung], die

**sanatorium** /sænə'tɔːrɪəm/ n. Sanatorium, das

**sanctify** /'sæŋktɪfaɪ/ v.t. heiligen

**sanctimonious** /sæŋktɪ'məʊnɪəs/ adj. scheinheilig

**sanction** /'sæŋkʃn/ ① n. Sanktion, die
② v.t. sanktionieren

**sanctity** /'sæŋktɪtɪ/ n. Heiligkeit, die

**sanctuary** /'sæŋktʃʊərɪ/ n. (a) (holy place) Heiligtum, das
(b) (refuge) Zufluchtsort, der
(c) (for animals) Naturschutzgebiet, das

**sand** /sænd/ ① n. Sand, der
② v.t. ~ sth. [down] etw. [ab]schmirgeln

**sandal** /'sændl/ n. Sandale, die

**sandalwood** n. Sandelholz, das

**sand:** ~**bag** ① n. Sandsack, der; ② v.t. mit Sandsäcken schützen; ~**bank** n. Sandbank, die; ~**castle** n. Sandburg, die; ~ **dune** n. Düne, die; ~**paper** ① n. Sandpapier, das; ② v.t. [mit Sandpapier] [ab]schmirgeln; ~**pit** n. Sandkasten, der; ~**stone** n. Sandstein, der

**sandwich** /'sænwɪdʒ/ ① n. Sandwich, der od. das; ≈ [zusammengeklapptes] belegtes Brot; **cheese** ~: Käsebrot, das
② v.t. einschieben (**between** zwischen + Akk.; **into** in + Akk.)

'**sandy** adj. (a) sandig; Sand⟨boden, -strand⟩
(b) rotblond ⟨Haar⟩

**sane** /seɪn/ adj. (a) geistig gesund
(b) (sensible) vernünftig

**sang** ▶ SING

**sanitary** /'sænɪtərɪ/ adj. sanitär ⟨Verhältnisse, Anlagen⟩

'**sanitary napkin** (Amer.), '**sanitary towel** (Brit.) ns. Damenbinde, die

**sanitation** /sænɪ'teɪʃn/ n. Kanalisation und Abfallbeseitigung

**sanitize** (**sanitise**) /'sænɪtaɪz/ v.t. (fig.) entschärfen

**sanity** /'sænɪtɪ/ n. geistige Gesundheit; **lose one's** ~: den Verstand verlieren

**sank** ▶ SINK 2, 3

**Santa Claus** /'sæntə klɔːz/ n. der Weihnachtsmann

**sap** /sæp/ ① n. Saft, der
② v.t., **-pp-** zehren an (+ Dat.)

**sapling** /'sæplɪŋ/ n. junger Baum

**sapphire** /'sæfaɪə(r)/ n. Saphir, der

**sarcasm** /'sɑːkæzm/ n. Sarkasmus, der

**sarcastic** /sɑː'kæstɪk/ adj. sarkastisch

**sardine** /sɑː'diːn/ n. Sardine, die

**Sardinia** /sɑː'dɪnɪə/ pr. n. Sardinien (das)

**sardonic** /sɑː'dɒnɪk/ adj. höhnisch; sardonisch ⟨Lächeln⟩

**sash** /sæʃ/ n. Schärpe, die

**sash 'window** n. Schiebefenster, das

**sat** ▶ SIT

**Sat.** abbr. = **Saturday** Sa.

**Satan** /'seɪtən/ pr. n. Satan, der

**satanic** /sə'tænɪk/ adj. satanisch

**satchel** /'sætʃl/ n. [Schul]ranzen, der

**satellite** /'sætəlaɪt/ n. Satellit, der

**satellite:** ~ '**broadcasting** n. Satellitenfunk, der; ~ **dish** n. Satellitenschüssel, die; ~ **receiver** n. Satellitenempfänger, der; ~ **technology** n. Satellitentechnik, die; ~ '**television** n. Satellitenfernsehen, das; ~ **town** n. Satelliten- od. Trabantenstadt, die

**satin** /'sætɪn/ n. Satin, der

**satire** /'sætaɪə(r)/ n. Satire, die (**on** auf + Akk.)

**satirical** /sə'tɪrɪkl/ adj. satirisch

**satisfaction** /sætɪs'fækʃn/ n. Befriedigung, die (**at, with** über + Akk.); **meet with sb.'s [complete]** ~: jmdn. [in jeder Weise] zufrieden stellen

**satisfactory** /sætɪs'fæktərɪ/ adj. zufrieden stellend

**satisfied** /'sætɪsfaɪd/ adj. (a) (contented) zufrieden
(b) (convinced) überzeugt (**of** von)

**S**

**satisfy** /'sætɪsfaɪ/ *v.t.* **(a)** befriedigen; zufrieden stellen ⟨*Kunden*⟩; stillen ⟨*Hunger, Durst*⟩
**(b)** (convince) ~ **sb.** [**of sth.**] jmdn. [von etw.] überzeugen

**'satisfying** *adj.* befriedigend; sättigend ⟨*Gericht, Speise*⟩

**saturate** /'sætʃəreɪt/ *v.t.* durchnässen; [mit Feuchtigkeit durch]tränken ⟨*Boden, Erde*⟩

**saturated** /'sætʃəreɪtɪd/ *adj.* durchnässt

**saturation** /sætʃə'reɪʃn/ *n.* Durchnässung, *die*

**Saturday** /'sætədeɪ, 'sætədɪ/ *n.* Samstag, *der; see also* FRIDAY

**'Saturday job** *n.* Samstagsjob, *der* (ugs.)

**Saturn** /'sætən/ *pr. n.* (Astron.) Saturn, *der*

**sauce** /sɔːs/ *n.* **(a)** Soße, *die*
**(b)** (impudence) Frechheit, *die*

**sauce:** ~ **boat** *n.* Sauciere, *die;* ~**pan** /'sɔːspən/ *n.* Kochtopf, *der;* (with straight handle) [Stiel]kasserolle, *die*

**saucer** /'sɔːsə(r)/ *n.* Untertasse, *die*

**saucy** /'sɔːsɪ/ *adj.* **(a)** (rude) frech
**(b)** ( pert, jaunty) keck

**Saudi Arabia** /saʊdɪ ə'reɪbɪə/ *pr. n.* Saudi-Arabien (*das*)

**sauna** /'sɔːnə, 'saʊnə/ *n.* Sauna, *die*

**saunter** /'sɔːntə(r)/ *v.i.* schlendern

**sausage** /'sɒsɪdʒ/ *n.* Wurst, *die*

**sausage:** ~ **meat** *n.* Wurstmasse, *die;* ~ **'roll** *n.:* Blätterteig mit Wurstfüllung

**savage** /'sævɪdʒ/ [1] *adj.* **(a)** (uncivilized) primitiv; wild ⟨*Volksstamm*⟩; unzivilisiert ⟨*Land*⟩
**(b)** (fierce) brutal; wild ⟨*Tier*⟩
[2] *n.* Wilde, *der/die* (veralt.)

**savagery** /'sævɪdʒrɪ/ *n.* Brutalität, *die*

**save** /seɪv/ [1] *v.t.* **(a)** (rescue) retten (**from** vor + *Dat.*); ~ **oneself from falling** sich [beim Hinfallen] fangen
**(b)** ( put aside) aufheben; sparen ⟨*Geld*⟩; sammeln ⟨*Briefmarken usw.*⟩; (conserve) sparsam umgehen mit
**(c)** (make unnecessary) sparen ⟨*Geld, Zeit, Energie*⟩; ~ **sb./oneself sth.** jmdm./sich etw. ersparen
**(d)** (Sport) abwehren ⟨*Schuss, Ball;*⟩
**(e)** (Comp.) speichern; sichern; ~ **sth. on** [**to**] **a disk** etw. auf Diskette abspeichern
[2] *v.i.* sparen (**on** *Akk.*)
[3] *n.* (Sport) Abwehr, *die*
■ **save 'up** [1] *v.t.* sparen
[2] *v.i.* sparen (**for** für, auf + *Akk.*)

**'saver** *n.* Sparer, *der/*Sparerin, *die*

**saving** /'seɪvɪŋ/ [1] *n. in pl.* Ersparnisse *Pl.*
[2] *adj.* ⟨*kosten-, benzin*⟩sparend

**savings:** ~ **account** *n.* Sparkonto, *das;* ~ **bank** *n.* Sparkasse, *die*

**saviour** /'seɪvjə(r)/ *n.* **(a)** Retter, *der/*Retterin, *die*
**(b)** (Relig.) **the S**~: der Heiland

**savor** etc. (*Amer.*) ▶ SAVOUR etc.

**savour** /'seɪvə(r)/ (Brit.) [1] *n.* (flavour) Geschmack, *der*
[2] *v.t.* genießen

**savoury** /'seɪvərɪ/ (Brit.) [1] *adj.* **(a)** pikant; salzig
**(b)** (appetizing) appetitanregend
[2] *n.* [pikantes] Häppchen

**saw**[1] /sɔː/ [1] *n.* Säge, *die*
[2] *v.t., p.p.* **sawn** /sɔːn/ *or* **sawed** [zer]sägen; ~ **in half** in der Mitte durchsägen
[3] *v.i., p.p.* **sawn** *or* **sawed** sägen; ~ **through** sth. etw. durchsägen

**saw**[2] ▶ SEE

**saw:** ~**dust** *n.* Sägemehl, *das;* ~**mill** *n.* Sägemühle, *die*

**sawn** ▶ SAW[1] 2, 3

**'sawn-off** *adj.* (Brit.) ⟨*Gewehr*⟩ mit abgesägtem Lauf

**saxophone** /'sæksəfəʊn/ *n.* Saxophon, *das*

**saxophonist** /sæk'sɒfənɪst/ *n.* Saxophonist, *der/*Saxophonistin, *die*

**say** /seɪ/ [1] *v.t. pres. t.* **he says** /sez/, *p.t. & p.p.* **said** /sed/ **(a)** sagen; **that is to** ~: das heißt; **do as** *or* **what I** ~: tun Sie, was ich sage; **when all is said and done** letzten Endes; **go without** ~**ing** sich von selbst verstehen; **she is said to be clever/to have done it** man sagt, sie sei klug/habe es getan
**(b)** (recite) sprechen ⟨*Gebet, Text*⟩
**(c)** (have specified wording or reading) sagen; ⟨*Zeitung:*⟩ schreiben; ⟨*Uhr:*⟩ zeigen ⟨*Uhrzeit*⟩; **what does it** ~ **here?** was steht hier?
[2] *n.* **have a** *or* **some** ~: ein Mitspracherecht haben (**in** bei); **have no** ~: nichts zu sagen haben; **have one's** ~: seine Meinung sagen

**'saying** *n.* Redensart, *die*

**scab** /skæb/ *n.* [Wund]schorf, *der*

**scaffold** /'skæfəld/ *n.* Schafott, *das*

**'scaffolding** *n.* Gerüst, *das*

**'scaffolding pole** *n.* Gerüststange, *die*

**scald** /skɔːld, skɒld/ [1] *n.* Verbrühung, *die*
[2] *v.t.* verbrühen

**scale**[1] /skeɪl/ *n.* **(a)** (of fish, reptile, etc.) Schuppe, *die*
**(b)** (in kettle etc.) Kesselstein, *der;* (on teeth) Zahnstein, *der*

**scale**[2] *n.* **(a)** *in sing. or pl.* (weighing instrument) ~[**s**] Waage, *die*
**(b)** (dish of balance) Waagschale, *die*

**scale**[3] [1] *n.* **(a)** (series of degrees) Skala, *die*
**(b)** (Mus.) Tonleiter, *die*
**(c)** (dimensions) Ausmaß, *das;* **be on a small** ~: bescheidenen Umfang haben
**(d)** (ratio of reduction) Maßstab, *der;* **what is the** ~ **of the map?** welchen Maßstab hat diese Karte?
**(e)** (indication) (on map) Maßstab, *der;* (on thermometer) [Anzeige]skala, *die*
[2] *v.t.* ersteigen ⟨*Mauer, Leiter, Gipfel*⟩
■ **scale 'down** *v.t.* [entsprechend] drosseln ⟨*Produktion*⟩; Abstriche machen bei ⟨*Planungen*⟩

**scalp** /skælp/ *n.* Kopfhaut, *die*

**scalpel** /'skælpl/ n. Skalpell, *das*

**scam** /skæm/ n. (coll.) Masche, *die* (ugs.)

**scamper** /'skæmpə(r)/ v.i. ‹Person:› flitzen; ‹Tier:› huschen

**scampi** /'skæmpɪ/ n. pl. Scampi Pl.

**scan** /skæn/ ⒈ v.t., -nn-: (a) (search thoroughly) absuchen (**for** nach)
(b) (look over cursorily) flüchtig ansehen; überfliegen ‹Zeitung, Liste usw.› (**for** auf der Suche nach)
(c) (Med.) szintigraphisch untersuchen
(d) (Comp.) scannen
⒉ v.i., -nn- ‹Vers[zeile]:› das richtige Versmaß haben
⒊ n. (Med.) szintigraphische Untersuchung, *die*; (image) Szintigramm, *das*

**scandal** /'skændl/ n. (a) Skandal, *der* (**about/of** um); (story) Skandalgeschichte, *die*
(b) (outrage) Empörung, *die*
(c) (gossip) Klatsch, *der* (ugs.)

**scandalize** /'skændəlaɪz/ v.t. schockieren

**scandalous** /'skændələs/ adj. skandalös; schockierend ‹Bemerkung›

**Scandinavia** /skændɪ'neɪvɪə/ pr. n. Skandinavien (*das*)

**Scandinavian** /skændɪ'neɪvɪən/ ⒈ adj. skandinavisch; **sb. is ~:** jmd. ist Skandinavier/Skandinavierin
⒉ n.(a) (person) Skandinavier, *der*/ Skandinavierin, *die*
(b) (Ling.) skandinavische Sprachen Pl.

**scant** /skænt/ adj. wenig

**scanty** /'skæntɪ/ adj. spärlich; knapp ‹Bikini›

**scapegoat** /'skeɪpɡəʊt/ n. Sündenbock, *der*; **make sb. a ~:** jmdn. zum Sündenbock machen

**scar** /skɑː(r)/ ⒈ n. Narbe, *die*
⒉ v.t., -rr-: **~ sb./sb.'s face** bei jmdm./in jmds. Gesicht (*Dat.*) Narben hinterlassen

**scarce** /skeəs/ adj. (a) (insufficient) knapp
(b) (rare) selten; **make oneself ~** (coll.) sich aus dem Staub machen (ugs.)

**'scarcely** adv. kaum

**scarcity** /'skeəsɪtɪ/ n. Knappheit, *die* (**of** an + *Dat.*)

**scare** /skeə(r)/ ⒈ n. (a) (sensation of fear) Schreck[en], *der*; **give sb. a ~:** jmdm. einen Schreck[en] einjagen
(b) (general alarm) [allgemeine] Hysterie; **bomb ~:** Bombendrohung, *die*
⒉ v.t. (frighten) Angst machen (+ *Dat.*); (startle) erschrecken
■ **scare a'way, scare 'off** v.t. verscheuchen

**'scarecrow** n. Vogelscheuche, *die*

**scared** /skeəd/ adj. **be ~ of sb./sth.** vor jmdm./etw. Angst haben; **be ~ of doing/to do sth.** sich nicht [ge]trauen, etw. zu tun

**scaremongering** /'skeəmʌŋɡərɪŋ/ n. Panikmache, *die*

**scarf** /skɑːf/ n., pl. ~s or scarves /skɑːvz/ Schal, *der*; (square) Halstuch, *das*; (worn over hair) Kopftuch, *das*

**scarlet** /'skɑːlɪt/ ⒈ n. Scharlach, *der*
⒉ adj. scharlachrot

**scarlet 'fever** n. Scharlach, *der*

**scarves** ▶ SCARF

**scary** /'skeərɪ/ adj. Furcht erregend ‹Anblick›; schaurig ‹Film, Geschichte›

**scathing** /'skeɪðɪŋ/ adj. bissig ‹Person, Humor, Bemerkung›

**scatter** /'skætə(r)/ ⒈ v.t. (a) vertreiben; auseinander treiben ‹Menge›
(b) (distribute irregularly) verstreuen
⒉ v.i. sich auflösen; ‹Menge:› sich zerstreuen; (in fear) auseinander stieben

**scattered** /'skætəd/ adj. verstreut; vereinzelt ‹Regenschauer›

**scatty** /'skætɪ/ adj. (Brit. coll.) dusslig (salopp)

**scavenge** /'skævɪndʒ/ v.i. **~ for sth.** nach etw. suchen

**'scavenger** n. (animal) Aasfresser, *der*; (fig. derog.: person) Aasgeier, *der* (ugs.)

**scenario** /sɪ'nɑːrɪəʊ/ n., pl. ~s Szenario, *das*

**scene** /siːn/ n. (a) (place of event) Schauplatz, *der*; **~ of the crime** Tatort, *der*
(b) (division of act) Auftritt, *der*
(c) (view) Anblick, *der*
(d) **behind the ~s** hinter den Kulissen
(e) **the political/drug/artistic ~:** die politische-/Drogen-/Kunstszene

**scenery** /'siːnərɪ/ n. (a) Landschaft, *die*
(b) (Theatre) Bühnenbild, *das*

**scenic** /'siːnɪk/ adj. landschaftlich schön

**scent** /sent/ ⒈ n. (a) (smell) Duft, *der*
(b) (Hunting; also fig.: trail) Fährte, *die*; **be on the ~ of sb./sth.** (fig.) jmdm./einer Sache auf der Spur sein
(c) (Brit.: perfume) Parfüm, *das*
⒉ v.t. wittern

**scented** /'sentɪd/ adj.(a) (having smell) duftend
(b) (perfumed) parfümiert

**sceptic** /'skeptɪk/ n. Skeptiker, *der*/ Skeptikerin, *die*

**sceptical** /'skeptɪkl/ adj. skeptisch; **be ~ about** or **of sb./sth.** jmdm./einer Sache skeptisch gegenüberstehen

**scepticism** /'skeptɪsɪzm/ n. Skepsis, *die*

**schedule** /'ʃedjuːl/ ⒈ n. (a) (list) Tabelle, *die*; (for event) Programm, *das*
(b) (of work) Zeitplan, *der*
(c) **on ~:** plangemäß
⒉ v.t. zeitlich planen

**'scheduled flight** n. Linienflug, *der*

**scheme** /skiːm/ n. (a) (arrangement) Anordnung, *die*
(b) (plan) Programm, *das*; (project) Projekt, *das*
(c) (dishonest plan) Intrige, *die*

**schizophrenia** /skɪtsə'friːnɪə/ n. Schizophrenie, *die*

**schizophrenic** /skɪtsə'frenɪk, skɪtsə'friːnɪk/ *adj.* schizophren
**scholar** /'skɒlə(r)/ *n.* Gelehrte, *der/die*
**'scholarly** *adj.* wissenschaftlich; gelehrt ⟨*Person*⟩
**'scholarship** *n.* (a) (award) Stipendium, *das* (b) (scholarly work) Gelehrsamkeit, *die*
**school** /skuːl/ *n.* Schule, *die;* (Amer.: college) Hochschule, *die;* **be at** *or* **in** ∼: in der Schule sein; (attend ∼) zur Schule gehen; **go to** ∼: zur Schule gehen; ∼ **holidays/exchange** Schulferien *Pl.*/Schüleraustausch, *der*
**school:** ∼ **age** *n.* Schulalter, *das;* ∼**bag** *n.* Schultasche, *die;* ∼**boy** *n.* Schüler, *der;* ∼**child** *n.* Schulkind, *das;* ∼ **friend** *n.* Schulfreund, *der*/-freundin, *die;* ∼**girl** *n.* Schülerin, *die;* ∼ **'governor** *n.:* Mitglied des Schulbeirats; ∼**kid** *n.* (coll.) Schulkind, *das;* ∼ **leaver** *n.* (Brit.) Schulabgänger, *der*/-abgängerin, *die;* ∼**master** *n.* Lehrer, *der;* ∼**mistress** *n.* Lehrerin, *die;* ∼ **'rule** *n.* Schulvorschrift, *die;* Schulregel, *die;* **it is a** ∼ **rule that** ...: an der Schule ist es Vorschrift, dass ...; ∼**teacher** *n.* Lehrer, *der*/Lehrerin, *die;* ∼ **'uniform** *n.* Schuluniform, *die;* ∼ **work** *n.* Schularbeiten *Pl.;* ∼ **'year** *n.* Schuljahr, *das*
**sciatica** /saɪ'ætɪkə/ *n.* Ischias, *der od. das*
**science** /'saɪəns/ *n.* Wissenschaft, *die*
**science 'fiction** *n.* Sciencefiction, *die*
**scientific** /saɪən'tɪfɪk/ *adj.* wissenschaftlich
**scientist** /'saɪəntɪst/ *n.* Wissenschaftler, *der*/Wissenschaftlerin, *die*
**sci-fi** /'saɪfaɪ/ *n.* (coll.) Sciencefiction, *die*
**scintillating** /'sɪntɪleɪtɪŋ/ *adj.* (fig.) geistsprühend
**scissors** /'sɪzəz/ *n. pl.* **[pair of]** ∼: Schere, *die*
**scoff¹** /skɒf/ *v.i.* (mock) spotten; ∼ **at** sich lustig machen über (+ *Akk.*)
**scoff²** *v.t.* (coll.: eat greedily) verschlingen
**scold** /skəʊld/ *v.t.* ausschimpfen (**for** wegen); **she** ∼**ed him for being late** sie schimpfte ihn aus, weil er zu spät kam
**scone** /skɒn, skəʊn/ *n.: weicher, oft zum Tee gegessener kleiner Kuchen*
**scoop** /skuːp/ ⓵ *n.* (a) Schaufel, *die;* (for ice cream etc.) Portionierer, *der* (b) (Journ.) Knüller, *der* (ugs.) ⓶ *v.t.* schaufeln ⟨*Kohlen, Zucker*⟩; schöpfen ⟨*Flüssigkeit*⟩
■ **scoop 'out** *v.t.* (a) (hollow out) aushöhlen; schaufeln ⟨*Loch, Graben*⟩ (b) [her]ausschöpfen ⟨*Flüssigkeit*⟩; auslöffeln ⟨*Fruchtfleisch*⟩; (with a knife) herausschneiden ⟨*Gehäuse, Fruchtfleisch*⟩
■ **scoop 'up** *v.t.* schöpfen ⟨*Flüssigkeit, Suppe*⟩; schaufeln ⟨*Erde*⟩
**scooter** /'skuːtə(r)/ *n.* (a) (toy) Roller, *der* (b) [motor] ∼: [Motor]roller, *der*

**scope** /skəʊp/ *n.* (a) Bereich, *der;* (of discussion etc.) Rahmen, *der* (b) (opportunity) Entfaltungsmöglichkeiten *Pl.*
**scorch** /skɔːtʃ/ *v.t.* versengen
**scorched 'earth policy** *n.* Politik der verbrannten Erde
**scorching** /'skɔːtʃɪŋ/ *adj.* glühend heiß
**score** /skɔː(r)/ ⓵ *n.* (a) (points) [Spiel]stand, *der;* (made by one player) Punktzahl, *die;* **keep [the]** ∼: zählen (b) (Mus.) Partitur, *die;* (Cinemat.) [Film]musik, *die* (c) *pl. same or* ∼**s** (group of 20) zwanzig (d) *in pl.* (great numbers) ∼**s [and** ∼**s] of** zig (ugs.); Dutzende [von] (e) **on that** ∼: was das betrifft (f) **pay off** *or* **settle an old** ∼ (fig.) eine alte Rechnung begleichen ⓶ *v.t.* erzielen ⟨*Erfolg, Punkt usw.*⟩; ∼ **a goal** ein Tor schießen ⓷ *v.i.* (a) (make ∼) Punkte/einen Punkt erzielen; (∼ goal/goals) ein Tor/Tore schießen/werfen (b) (keep ∼) aufschreiben
**'scoreboard** *n.* Anzeigetafel, *die*
**'scorer** *n.* (a) (recorder) Anschreiber, *der*/Anschreiberin, *die* (b) (Footb.) Torschütze, *der*/-schützin, *die*
**'scoresheet** *n.* Anschreibebogen, *der*
**scorn** /skɔːn/ ⓵ *n.* Verachtung, *die* ⓶ *v.t.* verachten; in den Wind schlagen ⟨*Rat*⟩; ausschlagen ⟨*Angebot*⟩
**scornful** /'skɔːnfl/ *adj.* verächtlich ⟨*Lächeln, Blick*⟩; **be** ∼ **of sth.** für etw. nur Verachtung haben
**Scorpio** /'skɔːpɪəʊ/ *n.* (Astrol; Astron.) der Skorpion
**scorpion** /'skɔːpɪən/ *n.* Skorpion, *der*
**Scot** /skɒt/ *n.* Schotte, *der*/Schottin, *die*
**scotch** *v.t.* den Boden entziehen (+ *Dat.*) ⟨*Gerücht*⟩; zunichte machen ⟨*Plan*⟩
**Scotch** /skɒtʃ/ ⓵ *adj.* ▶ SCOTTISH ⓶ *n.* Scotch, *der;* schottischer Whisky
**Scotch:** ∼ **'egg** *n.:* hart gekochtes Ei in Wurstbrät, *der;* ∼ **'whisky** *n.* schottischer Whisky
**scot-'free** *adj.* **[get off/go]** ∼: ungeschoren [davonkommen *od.* bleiben]
**Scotland** /'skɒtlənd/ *pr. n.* Schottland (*das*)
**Scots** /skɒts/ ⓵ *adj.* (esp. Scot.) schottisch; **sb. is** ∼: jmd. ist Schotte/Schottin ⓶ *n.* (dialect) Schottisch, *das*
**Scotsman** /'skɒtsmən/ *n., pl.* **Scotsmen** /'skɒtsmən/ Schotte, *der*
**'Scotswoman** *n.* Schottin, *die*
**Scottish** /'skɒtɪʃ/ *adj.* schottisch; **sb. is** ∼: jmd. ist Schotte/Schottin
**scoundrel** /'skaʊndrl/ *n.* Schuft, *der*
**scour¹** /skaʊə(r)/ *v.t.* (search) durchkämmen (**for** nach)
**scour²** *v.t.* scheuern ⟨*Topf, Metall*⟩
**'scourer** *n.* Topfreiniger, *der*

**scourge** /skɜːdʒ/ n. Geißel, die
**scout** /skaʊt/ ① n. (a) [Boy] S~:
Pfadfinder, der
(b) (Mil.) Späher, der
② v.i. ~ for Ausschau halten nach
**scowl** /skaʊl/ ① v.i. ein mürrisches
Gesicht machen
② n. mürrischer [Gesichts]ausdruck
**scram** /skræm/ v.i., -mm- (coll.) abhauen
(salopp)
**scramble** /'skræmbl/ ① v.i. (a) (clamber)
klettern; ~ through a hedge sich durch eine
Hecke zwängen
(b) (move hastily) rennen (ugs.); ~ for sth. um
etw. rangeln
② v.t. (Teleph., Radio) verschlüsseln
**scrambled 'egg** n. Rührei, das
**scrap¹** /skræp/ ① n. (a) (of paper) Fetzen,
der; (of food) Bissen, der
(b) in pl. (odds and ends) (of food) Reste Pl.
(c) (smallest amount) not a ~ of kein bisschen;
(of sympathy, truth also) nicht ein Fünkchen;
not a ~ of evidence nicht die Spur eines
Beweises
(d) ~ [metal] Schrott, der; ~ iron Alteisen,
das
② v.t., -pp- wegwerfen; (send for ~)
verschrotten; (fig.) aufgeben
**scrap²** (coll.) ① n. (fight) Rauferei, die
② v.i., -pp- sich raufen
**'scrapbook** n. [Sammel]album, das
**scrape** /skreɪp/ ① v.t. (a) (make smooth)
schaben ⟨Häute, Möhren, Kartoffeln usw.⟩;
abziehen ⟨Holz⟩; (damage) verschrammen
⟨Fußboden, Auto⟩
(b) (remove) [ab]kratzen ⟨Farbe, Schmutz,
Rost⟩ (off, from von)
(c) (draw along) schleifen
(d) ~ together (raise) zusammenkratzen
(ugs.); (save up) zusammensparen
② v.i. (a) (move with sound) schleifen
(b) (emit scraping noise) ein schabendes
Geräusch machen
(c) (rub) streifen (against, over Akk.)
③ n. (a) (act, sound) Kratzen, das (against an
+ Dat.)
(b) (predicament) Schwulitäten Pl. (ugs.)
■ **scrape 'by** v.i. (fig.) sich über Wasser
halten (on mit)
■ **scrape 'out** v.t. (a) (excavate) buddeln
(ugs.); scharren
(b) (clean) auskratzen
■ **scrape through** ① /'--/ v.t. sich
zwängen durch; (fig.) mit Hängen und
Würgen kommen durch ⟨Prüfung⟩
② /'--/ v.i. sich durchzwängen; (fig.: in
examination) mit Hängen und Würgen
durchkommen
**'scraper** n. (for shoes) Kratzeisen, das; (grid)
Abtreter, der; (tool, kitchen utensil) Schaber,
der; (for removing ice from car windows)
[Eis]kratzer, der

**scrap:** ~ **heap** n. Schrotthaufen, der;

~ **merchant** n. Schrotthändler, der/
-händlerin, die; ~ **'paper** n.
Schmierpapier, das

**scrappy** /'skræpɪ/ adj. lückenhaft
**'scrapyard** n. Schrottplatz, der
**scratch** /skrætʃ/ ① v.t. (a) (score surface of)
zerkratzen; (score skin of) kratzen
(b) (get scratch[es] on) ~ oneself/one's hands
etc. sich schrammen/sich (Dat.) die Hände
usw. zerkratzen
(c) (scrape without marking) kratzen; kratzen an
(+ Dat.) ⟨Insektenstich usw.⟩; ~ oneself/
one's arm sich kratzen/sich (Dat.) den Arm
od. am Arm kratzen
② v.i. kratzen; (~ oneself) sich kratzen
③ n. (a) (mark, wound) Kratzer, der (ugs.);
Schramme, die
(b) (sound) Kratzen, das
(c) have a [good] ~: sich [ordentlich]
kratzen
(d) start from ~: bei Null anfangen (ugs.); be
up to ~ ⟨Arbeit, Leistung:⟩ nichts zu
wünschen übrig lassen; ⟨Person:⟩ den
Anforderungen genügen
■ **scratch a'bout, scratch a'round**
v.i. scharren; (fig.: search) suchen (for nach)
**'scratch card** n. Rubbellos, das
**scrawl** /skrɔːl/ ① v.t. hinkritzeln
② v.i. kritzeln
③ n. Gekritzel, das; (handwriting) Klaue, die
(salopp)
**scrawny** /'skrɔːnɪ/ adj. hager; dürr
**scream** /skriːm/ ① v.i. schreien (with vor
+ Dat.)
② v.t. schreien
③ n. Schrei, der; (of jet engine) Heulen, das;
~s of pain Schmerzensschreie Pl.
**screech** /skriːtʃ/ ① v.i. & t. kreischen
② n. Kreischen, das
**screen** /skriːn/ ① n. (a) (partition)
Trennwand, die; (piece of furniture)
Wandschirm, der
(b) (of trees, persons, fog) Wand, die
(c) (Cinemat.) Leinwand, die; [TV] ~:
Bildschirm, der
② v.t. (a) (shelter) schützen (from vor
+ Dat.); (conceal) verdecken
(b) vorführen ⟨Film⟩
(c) (for disease) untersuchen
**screening** /'skriːnɪŋ/ n. (a) (in cinema)
Vorführung, die; (on TV) Sendung, die
(b) (Med.) Untersuchung, die
**screen:** ~**play** n. Drehbuch, das;
~ **saver** n. (Comp.) Bildschirmschoner, der;
~**writer** n. Filmautor, der/-autorin, die
**screw** /skruː/ ① n. Schraube, die; he has a
~ loose (coll. joc.) bei ihm ist eine Schraube
locker od. lose (salopp)
② v.t. (a) schrauben (to an + Akk.);
~ together zusammenschrauben; ~ down
festschrauben
(b) ~ you! (coarse) leck mich am Arsch!
(salopp)

S

■ **screw 'up** v.t. (a) (crumple up) zusammenknüllen ⟨Blatt Papier⟩
(b) verziehen ⟨Gesicht⟩; zusammenkneifen ⟨Augen, Mund⟩
(c) (sl.: bungle) vermurksen (salopp); ~ it/ things up Mist bauen (salopp)

**screw:** ~ **cap** n. Schraubverschluss, der; ~**driver** n. Schraubenzieher, der

**'screwed-up** adj. (fig. coll.) neurotisch

**'screw top** ▶ ~ CAP

**screwy** /'skru:ɪ/ adj. (coll.) spinnig (ugs.)

**scribble** /'skrɪbl/ 1 v.t. hinkritzeln
2 v.i. kritzeln
3 n. Gekritzel, das

**script** /skrɪpt/ n. (a) (handwriting) Handschrift, die
(b) (of play) Regiebuch, das; (of film) [Dreh]buch, das
(c) (for broadcaster) Manuskript, das

**scripture** /'skrɪptʃə(r)/ n. (a) [Holy] S~, the [Holy] S~s die [Heilige] Schrift
(b) (Sch.) Religion, die

**'scriptwriter** n. (of film) Drehbuchautor, der/-autorin, die

**scroll** /skrəʊl/ 1 n. (roll) Rolle, die
2 v.t. (Comp.) scrollen

**scrollable** /'skrəʊləbl/ adj. (Comp.) scrollbar

**'scroll bar** n. (Comp.) Rollballen, der

**scrounge** /skraʊndʒ/ (coll.) 1 v.t. schnorren (ugs.) (**off, from** von)
2 v.i. schnorren (ugs.) (**from** bei)

**'scrounger** n. (coll.) Schnorrer, der/ Schnorrerin, die (ugs.)

**scrub¹** /skrʌb/ 1 v.t. -bb-: (a) schrubben (ugs.); scheuern
(b) (coll.: cancel) zurücknehmen ⟨Befehl⟩; sausen lassen (ugs.) ⟨Plan⟩
2 v.i., -bb- schrubben (ugs.); scheuern
3 n. give sth. a ~: etw. schrubben (ugs.) od. scheuern

**scrub²** n. (brushwood) Buschwerk, das; (area) Buschland, das

**scruff¹** /skrʌf/ n. by the ~ of the neck beim Genick

**scruff²** n. (Brit. coll.) (man) vergammelter Typ (ugs.); (woman, girl) Schlampe, die

**'scruffy** adj. vergammelt (ugs.)

**scrum** /skrʌm/ n. Gedränge, das

**scruple** /'skru:pl/ n. Skrupel, der; **have no** ~**s about doing sth.** keine Skrupel haben, etw. zu tun

**scrupulous** /'skru:pjʊləs/ adj. gewissenhaft ⟨Person⟩; unbedingt ⟨Ehrlichkeit⟩; peinlich ⟨Sorgfalt⟩

**scrutinize** /'skru:tɪnaɪz/ v.t. [genau] untersuchen ⟨[Forschungs]gegenstand⟩; [über]prüfen ⟨Rechnung, Pass, Fahrkarte⟩; mustern ⟨Person⟩

**scrutiny** /'skru:tɪnɪ/ n. (a) (critical gaze) musternder Blick
(b) (examination) (of recruit) Musterung, die; (of bill, passport, ticket) [Über]prüfung, die

**scuff** /skʌf/ 1 v.t. streifen; verschrammen ⟨Schuhe, Fußboden⟩
2 n. Schramme, die

**scuffle** /'skʌfl/ 1 n. Handgreiflichkeiten Pl.
2 v.i. handgreiflich werden (**with** gegen)

**scullery** /'skʌlərɪ/ n. Spülküche, die

**sculptor** /'skʌlptə(r)/ n. Bildhauer, der/-hauerin, die

**sculpture** /'skʌlptʃə(r)/ n. (a) (art) Bildhauerei, die
(b) (piece of work) Skulptur, die; Plastik, die; (pieces collectively) Skulpturen Pl.

**scum** /skʌm/ n. (a) Schmutzschicht, die; (film) Schmutzfilm, der
(b) (fig. derog.) Abschaum, der

**'scumbag** n. (sl. derog.) Schwein, das (salopp)

**scurry** /'skʌrɪ/ v.i. huschen

**scuttle¹** /'skʌtl/ n. Kohlenfüller, der

**scuttle²** (Naut.) v.t. versenken

**scuttle³** v.i. rennen; flitzen (ugs.); ⟨Maus, Krabbe:⟩ huschen

**scythe** /saɪð/ n. Sense, die

**SE** abbr. = **south-east** SO

**sea** /si:/ n. (a) Meer, das; the ~: das Meer; die See; **by** ~: mit dem Schiff; **by the** ~: am Meer; **at** ~: auf See ⟨Dat.⟩; **be all at** ~ (fig.) nicht mehr weiter wissen; **put [out] to** ~: in See ⟨Akk.⟩ gehen
(b) (specific tract of water) Meer, das

**sea:** ~ **'air** n. Seeluft, die; ~**'bed** n. Meeresboden, der; ~**'bird** n. Seevogel, der; ~ **breeze** n. Seewind, der; ~**food** n. Meeresfrüchte Pl.; attrib. Fisch⟨restaurant⟩; ~**gull** n. [See]möwe, die

**seal¹** /si:l/ n. (Zool.) Robbe, die; [common] ~: [Gemeiner] Seehund

**seal²** 1 n. (wax etc., stamp, impression) Siegel, das
2 v.t. (a) (stamp, affix ~ to) siegeln ⟨Dokument⟩; (fasten with ~) verplomben ⟨Tür, Stromzähler⟩
(b) (close securely) abdichten ⟨Behälter, Rohr usw.⟩; zukleben ⟨Umschlag, Paket⟩
(c) (stop up) verschließen; abdichten ⟨Leck⟩; verschmieren ⟨Riss⟩

■ **seal 'off** v.t. abriegeln

**sea:** ~ **lane** n. See[schifffahrts]straße, die; ~ **legs** n. pl. Seebeine Pl. (Seemannsspr.); **get** or **find one's** ~ **legs** sich ⟨Dat.⟩ Seebeine wachsen lassen; ~**level** n. Meeresspiegel, der

**'sealing wax** n. Siegellack, der

**'sea lion** n. Seelöwe, der

**seam** /si:m/ n. (a) Naht, die
(b) (of coal) Flöz, das

**sea:** ~**man** /'si:mən/ n., pl. ~**men** /'si:mən/ Matrose, der; ~ **mist** n. Küstennebel, der

**'seamless** adj. nahtlos

**'seamy** adj. the ~ **side** [of life etc.] (fig.) die Schattenseite[n] [des Lebens usw.]

**seance** /'seɪəns/, **séance** /'seɪɑ̃s/ n. Séance, die

**sea:** ∼**plane** n. Wasserflugzeug, das; ∼**port** n. Seehafen, der; ∼ **power** n. Seemacht, die

**sear** /'sɪə(r)/ v.t. versengen

**search** /sɜːtʃ/ ①①① v.t. durchsuchen (**for** nach); absuchen ⟨Gebiet, Fläche⟩ (**for** nach); (fig.: probe) erforschen ⟨Herz, Gewissen⟩; suchen in (+ Dat.) ⟨Gedächtnis⟩ (**for** nach) ②① v.i. suchen (**for** nach) ③① n. Suche, die (**for** nach); (of building, room, etc.) Durchsuchung, die; **in** ∼ **of sb./sth.** auf der Suche nach jmdm./etw

**'search engine** n. (Comp.) Suchmaschine, die

**'searching** adj. prüfend, forschend ⟨Blick⟩; bohrend ⟨Frage⟩

**search:** ∼**light** n. Suchscheinwerfer, der; ∼ **party** n. Suchtrupp, der; ∼ **warrant** n. Durchsuchungsbefehl, der

**sea:** ∼ **salt** n. Meersalz, das; Seesalz, das; ∼**shore** n. [Meeres]küste, die; (beach) Strand, der; ∼**sick** adj. seekrank; ∼**sickness** n. Seekrankheit, die; ∼**side** n. [Meeres]küste, die; **by/to/at the** ∼**side** am/ ans/am Meer; ∼**side town** Seestadt, die

**season** /'siːzn/ ①① n. (a) Jahreszeit, die; **nesting** ∼: Nistzeit, die
(b) ( period of social activity) [opera/football] ∼: [Opern-/Fußball]saison, die; **holiday** or (Amer.) **vacation** ∼: Urlaubszeit, die; **tourist** ∼: Reisezeit, die
(c) **raspberries are in/out of** or **not in** ∼: jetzt ist die/nicht die Saison od. Zeit für Himbeeren; **be in** ∼ (on heat) brünstig sein
(d) ▶ SEASON TICKET
②① v.t. würzen ⟨Fleisch, Rede⟩

**seasonable** /'siːzənəbl/ adj. der Jahreszeit gemäß

**seasonal** /'siːzənl/ adj. Saison⟨arbeit, -geschäft⟩; saisonabhängig ⟨Preise⟩

**seasonal affective disorder** /siːzənl əˈfektɪv dɪsɔːdə(r)/ n. (Med.) saisonabhängige Depression

**'seasoned** adj. (fig.) erfahren

**'seasoning** n. Gewürze Pl.; Würze, die

**'season ticket** n. Dauerkarte, die

**seat** /siːt/ ①① n. (a) Sitzgelegenheit, die; (in vehicle, cinema, etc.) Sitz, der; (of toilet) [Klosett]brille, die (ugs.)
(b) ( place) Platz, der; (in vehicle) [Sitz]platz, der; **have** or **take a** ∼: sich [hin]setzen
(c) ( part of chair) Sitzfläche, die
(d) (buttocks) Gesäß, das; ( part of clothing) Gesäßpartie, die; (of trousers) Sitz, der
②① v.t. (a) (cause to sit) setzen; ⟨Platzanweiser:⟩ einen Platz anweisen (+ Dat.); ∼ **oneself** sich setzen
(b) (have ∼s for) Sitzplätze bieten (+ Dat.); ∼ **500 people** 500 Sitzplätze haben

**'seat belt** n. Sicherheitsgurt, der

**'seat-belt tensioner** /'tenʃnə(r)/n. Gurtstraffer, der

**'seated** adj. sitzend; **remain** ∼: sitzen bleiben

**'seating** n. Sitzplätze Pl.; attrib. Sitz⟨ordnung, -plan⟩

**sea:** ∼ **urchin** n. Seeigel, der; ∼ **wall** n. Strandmauer, die; ∼ **water** n. Meerwasser, das; ∼**weed** n. [See]tang, der; ∼**worthy** adj. seetüchtig

**secateurs** /sekəˈtɜːz/ n. pl. (Brit.) Gartenschere, die

**secluded** /sɪˈkluːdɪd/ adj. (hidden) versteckt; (isolated) abgelegen; zurückgezogen ⟨Leben⟩

**seclusion** /sɪˈkluːʒn/ n. (remoteness) Abgelegenheit, die; ( privacy) Zurückgezogenheit, die

**second¹** /'sekənd/ ①① adj. zweit...; ∼ **largest/highest** etc. zweitgrößt.../-höchst... usw.; **come/be** ∼: Zweiter/Zweite werden/ sein
②① n. (a) (unit of time or angle) Sekunde, die
(b) (coll.: moment) Sekunde, die (ugs.); **wait a few** ∼**s** einen Moment warten; **in a** ∼ (immediately) sofort (ugs.); (very quickly) im Nu (ugs.); **just a** ∼! (coll.) einen Moment!
(c) **the** ∼ (in sequence, rank) der/die/das Zweite
(d) in pl. (helping of food) zweite Portion
③① v.t. (support) unterstützen

**second²** /sɪˈkɒnd/ v.t. (transfer) vorübergehend versetzen

**secondary** /'sekəndərɪ/ adj. (of less importance) zweitrangig; Neben⟨sache⟩; **be** ∼ **to sth.** einer Sache (Dat.) untergeordnet sein

**'secondary school** n. höhere Schule

**second:** ∼-**best** ①① /'---/ adj. zweitbest...; ②① /--'-/ n. Zweitbeste, der/die/das; ∼-**class** ①① /'---/ adj. (of lower class) zweiter Klasse nachgestellt; Zweite[r]-Klasse-⟨Fahrkarte, Abteil, Post, Brief usw.⟩; ∼-**class stamp** Briefmarke für einen Zweiter-Klasse-Brief; ②① /--'-/ adv. zweiter Klasse ⟨fahren⟩; ∼ '**floor** ▶ FLOOR 1B; ∼ '**hand** n. Sekundenzeiger, der; ∼-**hand** ①① /'---/ adj. (a) gebraucht ⟨Kleidung, Auto usw.⟩; antiquarisch ⟨Buch⟩; (b) (selling used goods) Gebrauchtwaren-; Secondhand⟨laden⟩; (c) ⟨Nachrichten, Bericht⟩ aus zweiter Hand; ②① /--'-/ adv. aus zweiter Hand; ∼ '**home** n. Zweitwohnung, die

**'secondly** adv. zweitens

**second:** ∼ **name** n. Nachname, der; ∼-'**rate** adj. zweitklassig; ∼ '**thoughts** n. pl. **have** ∼ **thoughts** (about) sich (Dat.) anders überlegen (**about** mit); **we've had** ∼ **thoughts about buying it** wir wollen es nun doch nicht kaufen; **but on** ∼ **thoughts** ...: wenn ich's mir [noch mal] überlege, ...

**secrecy** /'siːkrɪsɪ/ n. (a) (keeping of secret) Geheimhaltung, die
(b) (secretiveness) Heimlichtuerei, die
(c) **in** ∼: im Geheimen

**secret** /'siːkrɪt/ ①① adj. geheim; ⋯⋯

Geheim⟨*fach, -tür, -abkommen, -kode*⟩;
heimlich ⟨*Trinker, Liebhaber*⟩; **keep sth.** ∼:
etw. geheim halten (**from** vor + *Dat.*)
**2** *n.* (a) Geheimnis, *das;* **make no** ∼ **of sth.**
kein Geheimnis aus etw. machen; (fig.)
keinen Hehl aus etw. machen; **keep** ∼s/ **a** ∼:
schweigen (fig.)
(b) **in** ∼: im Geheimen

**secret 'agent** *n.* Geheimagent, *der*/
-agentin, *die*

**secretarial** /sekrə'teərɪəl/ *adj.*
Sekretärinnen⟨*kursus, -tätigkeit*⟩; ⟨*Arbeit*⟩ als
Sekretärin

**secretary** /'sekrətərɪ/ *n.* Sekretär, *der*/
Sekretärin, *die*

**secret 'ballot** *n.* geheime Abstimmung

**secretive** /'siːkrɪtɪv/ *adj.* verschlossen
⟨*Person*⟩: **be** ∼: geheimnisvoll tun (**about**
mit)

**'secretly** *adv.* heimlich; insgeheim ⟨*etw.
glauben*⟩

**sect** /sekt/ *n.* Sekte, *die*

**section** /'sekʃn/ *n.* (a) ( part cut off)
Abschnitt, *der;* Stück, *das;* ( part of divided
whole) Teil, *der*
(b) (of firm) Abteilung, *die;* (of organization)
Sektion, *die*
(c) (of chapter, book) Abschnitt, *der;* (of statute
etc.) Paragraph, *der*

**sector** /'sektə(r)/ *n.* Sektor, *der*

**secular** /'sekjʊlə(r)/ *adj.* weltlich

**secure** /sɪ'kjʊə(r)/ **1** *adj.* sicher; (firmly
fastened) fest; ∼ **against burglars** gegen
Einbruch geschützt
**2** *v.t.* (a) sichern (**for** *Dat.*); beschaffen
⟨*Auftrag*⟩ (**for** *Dat.*); (for oneself) sich (*Dat.*)
sichern
(b) (fasten) sichern

**se'curely** *adv.* (firmly) fest ⟨*verriegeln,
zumachen*⟩; sicher ⟨*befestigen, untergebracht
sein*⟩

**security** /sɪ'kjʊərɪtɪ/ *n.* (a) Sicherheit, *die;*
∼ **[measures]** Sicherheitsmaßnahmen *Pl.*
(b) (Finance) **securities** *pl.* Wertpapiere *Pl.*

**security:** ∼ **check** *n.*
Sicherheitskontrolle, *die;* ∼ **forces** *n. pl.*
Sicherheitskräfte *Pl.;* ∼ **guard** *n.* Wächter,
*der*/Wächterin, *die;* ∼ **risk** *n.*
Sicherheitsrisiko, *das;* ∼ **van** *n.*
gepanzerter Transporter; (for money)
Geldtransporter, *der*

**sedan** /sɪ'dæn/ *n.* (Amer. Motor Veh.)
Limousine, *die*

**sedate** /sɪ'deɪt/ **1** *adj.* bedächtig; gesetzt
⟨*alte Dame*⟩; gemächlich ⟨*Tempo, Leben*⟩
**2** *v.t.* sedieren

**sedation** /sɪ'deɪʃn/ *n.* Sedation, *die;* **be
under** ∼: sediert sein

**sedative** /'sedətɪv/ **1** *n.*
Beruhigungsmittel, *das*
**2** *adj.* sedativ

**sedentary** /'sedəntərɪ/ *adj.* sitzend

**sediment** /'sedɪmənt/ *n.* Ablagerung, *die;*
(of tea, coffee, etc.) Bodensatz, *der*

**seduce** /sɪ'djuːs/ *v.t.* verführen

**seduction** /sɪ'dʌkʃn/ *n.* Verführung, *die*

**seductive** /sɪ'dʌktɪv/ *adj.* verführerisch;
verlockend ⟨*Angebot*⟩

**see** /siː/ **1** *v.t.*, **saw** /sɔː/, **seen** /siːn/ (a)
sehen; **I can** ∼ **it's hard for you** ich verstehe,
dass es nicht leicht für dich ist; **I** ∼ **what
you mean** ich verstehe[, was du meinst]
(b) (meet [with]) sehen; treffen; (meet socially)
sich treffen mit; **I'll** ∼ **you there/at five** wir
sehen uns dort/um fünf; ∼ **you!, [I'll] be
**∼**ing you!** (coll.) bis bald! (ugs.)
(c) (speak to) sprechen ⟨*Person*⟩ (**about**
wegen); (visit) gehen zu ⟨*Arzt, Anwalt usw.*⟩;
(receive) empfangen
(d) (find out) feststellen; (by looking) nachsehen
(e) (make sure) ∼ **[that]** …: darauf achten,
dass …
(f) (imagine) sich (*Dat.*) vorstellen
(g) (escort) begleiten
**2** *v.i.*, **saw, seen** (a) sehen
(b) (make sure) nachsehen
(c) **I** ∼: ich verstehe; **you** ∼: weißt du/wisst
ihr/wissen Sie

■ **'see about** *v.t.* sich kümmern um

■ **see 'off** *v.t.* (a) (say goodbye to)
verabschieden
(b) (chase away) vertreiben

■ **see 'out** *v.t.* (escort) hinausbegleiten (**of**
aus); ∼ **oneself out** allein hinausfinden

■ **see through** *v.t.* (a) /'--/ hindurchsehen
durch; (fig.) durchschauen
(b) /-'-/ (not abandon) zu Ende bringen

■ **'see to** *v.t.* sich kümmern um

**seed** /siːd/ **1** *n.* (a) Samen, *der;* (of grape
etc.) Kern, *der*
(b) *no pl., no indef. art.* (∼s collectively)
Samen[körner] *Pl.;* (as collected for sowing)
Saatgut, *das;* (for birds) Körner *Pl.;* **go** or **run
to** ∼: Samen bilden; (fig.) herunterkommen
(ugs.)
(c) (Sport) gesetzter Spieler/gesetzte Spielerin
**2** *v.t.* (a) ( place ∼s in) besäen
(b) (Sport) setzen ⟨*Spieler*⟩; **be** ∼**ed number
one** als Nummer eins gesetzt werden/sein

**'seed bed** *n.* [Saat]beet, *das*

**'seedless** *adj.* kernlos

**seedling** /'siːdlɪŋ/ *n.* Sämling, *der*

**'seedy** *adj.* (a) (coll.: unwell) **feel** ∼: sich
[leicht] angeschlagen fühlen
(b) (shabby) schäbig, (ugs.) vergammelt
⟨*Aussehen*⟩; heruntergekommen ⟨*Stadtteil*⟩
(c) (disreputable) zweifelhaft

**'seeing** *conj.* ∼ **[that]** …: in Anbetracht
dessen, dass …

**seek** /siːk/ *v.t.*, **sought** /sɔːt/ suchen;
anstreben ⟨*Posten, Amt*⟩; sich bemühen um
⟨*Anerkennung, Interview, Einstellung*⟩; (try to
reach) aufsuchen

**seem** /siːm/ *v.i.* scheinen; **you** ∼ **tired** du
wirkst müde; **she** ∼s **nice** sie scheint nett zu
sein

**'seeming** *adj.* scheinbar

**'seemingly** *adv.* **(a)** (evidently) offensichtlich
**(b)** (to outward appearance) scheinbar

**seemly** /'si:mlɪ/ *adj.* schicklich

**seen** ▶ SEE

**seep** /si:p/ *v.i.* ~ [away] [ab]sickern

**'see-saw** *n.* Wippe, *die*

**seethe** /si:ð/ *v.i.* **(a)** ~ [with anger/ inwardly] vor Wut/innerlich schäumen
**(b)** ⟨*Straßen usw.:*⟩ wimmeln (**with** von)

**'see-through** *adj.* durchsichtig

**segment** /'segmənt/ *n.* (of orange, pineapple, etc.) Scheibe, *die*

**segregate** /'segrɪgeɪt/ *v.t.* trennen; (racially) absondern

**segregation** /segrɪ'geɪʃn/ *n.* Trennung, *die;* [racial] ~: Rassentrennung, *die*

**seismic** /'saɪzmɪk/ *adj.* seismisch

**seize** /si:z/ ① *v.t.* **(a)** ergreifen; ~ **power** die Macht ergreifen; ~ **sb. by the arm/collar** jmdn. am Arm/Kragen packen; ~ **the opportunity [to do sth.]** die Gelegenheit ergreifen [und etw. tun]; ~ **any/a** *or* **the chance [to do sth.]** jede/die Gelegenheit nutzen[, um etw. zu tun]; **be ~d with remorse/panic** von Gewissensbissen geplagt/ von Panik ergriffen werden
**(b)** (capture) gefangen nehmen ⟨*Person*⟩; kapern ⟨*Schiff*⟩; mit Gewalt übernehmen ⟨*Flugzeug, Gebäude*⟩; einnehmen ⟨*Festung, Brücke*⟩
**(c)** (confiscate) beschlagnahmen
② *v.i.* ▶ ~ UP

■ **'seize on** *v.t.* sich (*Dat.*) vornehmen ⟨*Einzelheit, Aspekt, Schwachpunkt*⟩; aufgreifen ⟨*Idee, Vorschlag*⟩

■ **seize 'up** *v.i.* sich festfressen

**seizure** /'si:ʒə(r)/ *n.* **(a)** ▶ SEIZE 1B, C: Gefangennahme, *die;* Kapern, *das;* Übernahme, *die;* Einnahme, *die;* Beschlagnahme, *die*
**(b)** (Med.) Anfall, *der*

**seldom** /'seldəm/ *adv.* selten

**select** /sɪ'lekt/ ① *adj.* ausgewählt
② *v.t.* auswählen

**selection** /sɪ'lekʃn/ *n.* **(a)** (what is selected [from]) Auswahl, *die* (**of** an + *Dat.*, **from** aus)
**(b)** (act of choosing) [Aus]wahl, *die*

**selective** /sɪ'lektɪv/ *adj.* (using selection) selektiv; (careful in one's choice) wählerisch

**self** /self/ *n., pl.* **selves** [selvz] Selbst, *das* (geh.); Ich, *das*

**self-** *pref.* selbst-/Selbst-

**self:** ~-**ab'sorbed** *adj.* mit sich selbst beschäftigt; ~-**ad'dressed** *adj.* ~-**addressed envelope** adressierter Rückumschlag; ~-**ad'hesive** *adj.* selbstklebend; ~-**ap'pointed** *adj.* selbst ernannt; ~-**as'surance** *n.* Selbstsicherheit, *die;* ~-**as'sured** *adj.* selbstsicher; ~-**a'wareness** *n.* Selbsterkenntnis, *die;* ~-**'catering** ① *adj.*

mit Selbstversorgung *nachgestellt;* ② *n.* Selbstversorgung, *die;* ~-**'centred** *adj.* egozentrisch; ~-**con'fessed** *adj.* erklärt; ~-**'confidence** *n.* Selbstbewusstsein, *das;* ~-**'confident** *adj.* selbstbewusst; ~-**'conscious** *adj.* unsicher; ~-**'consciousness** *n.* Unsicherheit, *die;* ~-**con'tained** *adj.* abgeschlossen ⟨*Wohnung*⟩; ~-**con'trol** *n.* Selbstbeherrschung, *die;* ~-**con'trolled** *adj.* voller Selbstbeherrschung *nachgestellt;* ~-**'critical** *adj.* selbstkritisch; ~-**de'ception** *n.* Selbsttäuschung, *die;* ~-**de'feating** *adj.* unsinnig; ~-**de'fence** *n.* Notwehr, *die;* **in** ~-**defence** aus Notwehr; ~-**de'lusion** *n.* Selbsttäuschung, *die;* ~-**de'nial** *n.* Selbstverleugnung, *die;* ~-**de'structive** *adj.* selbstzerstörerisch; ~-**'discipline** *n.* Selbstdisziplin, *die;* ~-**'drive** *adj.* ~-**drive hire [company]** Autovermietung, *die;* ~-**drive vehicle** Mietwagen, *der;* ~-**em'ployed** *adj.* selbstständig; ~-**e'steem** *n.* Selbstachtung, *die;* ~-**'evident** *adj.* offenkundig; ~-**ex'planatory** *adj.* ohne weiteres verständlich; **be** ~-**explanatory** für sich selbst sprechen; ~-**ful'filling** *adj.* zur eigenen Bestätigung mit beitragend; ~-**'help** *n.* Selbsthilfe, *die;* ~-**im'portant** *adj.* eingebildet; ~-**in'dulgent** *adj.* maßlos; ~-**in'flicted** *adj.* selbst beigebracht ⟨*Wunde*⟩; selbst auferlegt ⟨*Strafe*⟩; ~-**'interest** *n.* Eigeninteresse, *das*

**'selfish** *adj.,* **'selfishly** *adv.* selbstsüchtig

**'selfishness** *n.* Selbstsucht, *die*

**self-'knowledge** *n.* Selbsterkenntnis, *die*

**selfless** /'selflɪs/ *adj.* selbstlos

**self:** ~-**'motivated** *adj.* von sich aus motiviert; ~-**ob'sessed** *adj.* ichbesessen; ~-**o'pinionated** *adj.* eingebildet; ~-**'pity** *n.* Selbstmitleid, *das;* ~-**'portrait** *n.* Selbstporträt, *das;* ~-**pos'sessed** *adj.* selbstbeherrscht; ~-**preser'vation** *n.* Selbsterhaltung, *die;* ~-**'raising flour** *n.* (Brit.) mit Backpulver versetztes Mehl; ~-**re'liant** *adj.* selbstbewusst; ~-**re'spect** *n.* Selbstachtung, *die;* ~-**re'specting** *adj.* **no** ~-**respecting person ...:** niemand, der etwas auf sich hält, ...; ~-**'righteous** *adj.* selbstgerecht; ~-**'sacrifice** *n.* Selbstaufopferung, *die;* ~-**'satisfied** *adj.* selbstzufrieden; (smug) selbstgefällig; ~-**'service** *n.* Selbstbedienung, *die; attrib.* Selbstbedienungs-; ~-**suf'ficient** *adj.* unabhängig; selbstständig ⟨*Person*⟩; ~-**'taught** *adj.* autodidaktisch; ~-**taught person** Autodidakt, *der*/Autodidaktin, *die;* ~-**'willed** *adj.* eigenwillig

**sell** /sel/ ① *v.t.,* **sold** /səʊld/ ~ **sth. to sb.,** ~ **sb. sth.** jmdm. etw. verkaufen; **be sold out** ausverkauft sein
② *v.i.,* **sold** sich verkaufen; ⟨*Person:*⟩ verkaufen ⋯⟶

S

■ **sell 'off** *v.t.* verkaufen

■ **sell 'out** ⓵ *v.t.* **(a)** ausverkaufen
**(b)** (coll.: betray) verraten
⓶ *v.i.* **we have** *or* **are sold out** wir sind
ausverkauft

**'sell-by date** *n.* ≈
Mindesthaltbarkeitsdatum, *das*

**'seller** *n.* **(a)** Verkäufer, *der*/Verkäuferin,
*die*
**(b)** (product) **be a good/slow** ∼: sich gut/nur
langsam verkaufen

**'selling point** *n.* **a [good]** ∼ **point** (fig.) ein
Pluspunkt

**'sellotape** *v.t.* mit Tesafilm kleben

**Sellotape** ® /'seləteɪp/ *n.* ≈ Tesafilm, *der*
Ⓦⓩ

**'sell-out** *n.* **be a** ∼: ausverkauft sein; (coll.:
betrayal) Verrat sein

**selves** *pl. of* SELF

**semaphore** /'seməfɔː(r)/ ⓵ *n.* (system)
Winken, *das*
⓶ *v.i.* ∼ **to sb.** jmdm. ein Winksignal
übermitteln

**semblance** /'sembləns/ *n.* Anschein, *der*

**semen** /'siːmən/ *n.* Samen, *der*

**semester** /sɪ'mestə(r)/ *n.* Semester, *das*

**semi-** /semɪ/ *pref.* halb-/Halb-

**semi:** ∼**bold** *adj.* (Printing) halbfett;
∼**breve** *n.* (Brit. Mus.) ganze Note; ∼**circle**
*n.* Halbkreis, *der;* ∼**'circular** *adj.*
halbkreisförmig; ∼**'colon** *n.* Semikolon,
*das;* ∼**-de'tached** *adj. & n.* ∼**-detached**
[**house**] Doppelhaushälfte, *die;* ∼**-'final** *n.*
Halbfinale, *das*

**seminar** /'semɪnɑː(r)/ *n.* Seminar, *das*

**semi:** ∼**-'precious** *adj.* ∼**-precious stone**
Halbedelstein, *der;* ∼**-skimmed** ⓵ *adj.*
teilentrahmt; ⓶ *n.* teilentrahmte Milch;
∼**tone** *n.* (Mus.) Halbton, *der*

**semolina** /semə'liːnə/ *n.* Grieß, *der*

**senate** /'senət/ *n.* Senat, *der*

**senator** /'senətə(r)/ *n.* Senator, *der*

**send** /send/ *v.t.,* **sent** [sent] schicken;
senden (geh.)

■ **send a'way** ⓵ *v.t.* wegschicken
⓶ *v.i.* ∼ **away [to sb.] for sth.** etw. [bei
jmdm.] anfordern

■ **send 'back** *v.t.* zurückschicken

■ **'send for** *v.t.* **(a)** (tell to come) holen lassen;
rufen ‹Polizei, Arzt usw.›
**(b)** (order from elsewhere) anfordern

■ **send 'off** *v.t.* ⓵ **(a)** (dispatch) abschicken
‹Sache›
**(b)** (Sport) vom Platz stellen
⓶ *v.i.* ▶ SEND AWAY 2

■ **send 'up** *v.t.* (Brit. coll.: parody) parodieren

**'sender** *n.* Absender, *der*

**'send-off** *n.* Verabschiedung, *die*

**senile** /'siːnaɪl/ *adj.* senil

**senile de'mentia** *n.* senile Demenz

**senility** /sɪ'nɪlɪtɪ/ *n.* Senilität, *die*

**senior** /'siːnɪə(r)/ ⓵ *adj.* **(a)** (older) älter

**(b)** höher ‹Rang, Beamter, Stellung›; leitend
‹Angestellter, Stellung›; ∼ **manager** obere
Führungskraft; ∼ **management** oberer
Führungskreis
⓶ *n.* (older) Ältere, *der*/*die;* (of higher rank)
Vorgesetzte, *der*/*die*

**senior 'citizen** *n.* Senior, *der*/Seniorin,
*die*

**seniority** /siːnɪ'ɒrɪtɪ/ *n.* (greater length of
service) höheres Dienstalter; (higher rank)
höherer Rang

**senior 'partner** *n.* Seniorpartner, *der*/
-partnerin, *die*

**sensation** /sen'seɪʃn/ *n.* **(a)** (feeling) Gefühl,
*das*
**(b)** (person, event, etc.) Sensation, *die*

**sensational** /sen'seɪʃənl/ *adj.* sensationell

**sensationalise** ▶ SENSATIONALIZE

**sensationalism** /sen'seɪʃənəlɪzm/ *n.*
Sensationshascherei, *die*

**sensationalist** /sen'seɪʃənəlɪst/ *adj.*
sensationslüstern

**sensationalize** /sen'seɪʃənəlaɪz/ *v.t.*
∼ **sth.** etw. zur Sensation aufbauschen

**sense** /sens/ ⓵ *n.* **(a)** (faculty) Sinn, *der;*
∼ **of smell/touch/taste** Geruchs-/Tast-/
Geschmackssinn, *der;* **come to one's** ∼**s** das
Bewusstsein wiedererlangen
**(b)** *in pl.* (normal state of mind) Verstand, *der;*
**have taken leave of one's** ∼**s** den Verstand
verloren haben
**(c)** (consciousness) Gefühl, *das;* ∼ **of
responsibility/guilt** Verantwortungs-/
Schuldgefühl, *das*
**(d)** (practical wisdom) Verstand, *der;* **sound** *or*
**good** ∼: [gesunder Menschen]verstand; **not
have the** ∼ **to do sth.** nicht so schlau sein,
etw. zu tun; **there is no** ∼ **in doing that** es
hat keinen Sinn, das zu tun
**(e)** (meaning) Sinn, *der;* (of word) Bedeutung,
*die;* **make** ∼: einen Sinn ergeben; **in a** *or* **one**
∼: in gewisser Hinsicht; **make** ∼ **of sth.** etw.
verstehen
⓶ *v.t.* spüren

**'senseless** *adj.* **(a)** (unconscious) bewusstlos
**(b)** (purposeless) sinnlos

**sensible** /'sensɪbl/ *adj.* **(a)** (reasonable)
vernünftig
**(b)** (practical) zweckmäßig

**sensibly** /'sensɪblɪ/ *adv.* **(a)** (reasonably)
vernünftig
**(b)** (practically) zweckmäßig

**sensitive** /'sensɪtɪv/ *adj.* empfindlich; **be**
∼ **to sth.** empfindlich auf etw. (*Akk.*)
reagieren

**sensitivity** /sensɪ'tɪvɪtɪ/ *n.*
Empfindlichkeit, *die*

**sensory** /'sensərɪ/ *adj.* Sinnes-

**sensual** /'sensjʊəl/ *adj.* sinnlich

**sensuous** /'sensjʊəs/ *adj.* sinnlich

**sent** ▶ SEND

**sentence** /'sentəns/ ⓵ *n.* **(a)** (Law)
[Straf]urteil, *das*

**(b)** (Ling.) Satz, *der*
2 *v.t.* verurteilen (**to** zu)
**sentiment** /'sentɪmənt/ *n.* **(a)** Gefühl, *das*
**(b)** (sentimentality) Sentimentalität, *die*
**(c)** (thought) Gedanke, *der*
**sentimental** /sentɪ'mentl/ *adj.*
sentimental
**sentimentality** /sentɪmen'tælɪtɪ/ *n.*
Sentimentalität, *die*
**sentimentalize** /sentɪ'mentəlaɪz/ *v.t.*
sentimental darstellen
**sentry** /'sentrɪ/ *n.* Wache, *die*
**separable** /'sepərəbl/ *adj.* trennbar
**separate** 1 /'sepərət/ *adj.* verschieden
⟨*Fragen, Probleme, Gelegenheiten*⟩; gesondert
⟨*Teil*⟩; separat ⟨*Eingang, Toilette, Blatt
Papier, Abteil*⟩; (one's own, individual) eigen
⟨*Zimmer, Identität, Organisation*⟩; **keep two
things** ~: zwei Dinge auseinander halten
2 /'sepəreɪt/ *v.t.* trennen; **they are** ~**d** (no
longer live together) sie leben getrennt
3 *v.i.* **(a)** (disperse) sich trennen
**(b)** ⟨*Ehepaar:*⟩ sich trennen
**separately** /'sepərətlɪ/ *adv.* getrennt
**separation** /sepə'reɪʃn/ *n.* Trennung, *die*
**Sept.** *abbr.* = **September** Sept.
**September** /sep'tembə(r)/ *n.* September,
*der; see also* Aᴜɢᴜsᴛ
**septic** /'septɪk/ *adj.* septisch; **go** ~: eitrig
werden
**sequel** /'si:kwl/ *n.* **(a)** (consequence, result)
Folge, *die* (**to** von)
**(b)** (continuation) Fortsetzung, *die*
**sequence** /'si:kwəns/ *n.* **(a)** Reihenfolge,
*die*
**(b)** (part of film) Sequenz, *die*
**sequin** /'si:kwɪn/ *n.* Paillette, *die*
**Serbia** /'sɜ:bɪə/ *pr. n.* Serbien, *das*
**Serbian** /'sɜ:bɪən/ 1 *adj.* serbisch; **sb. is**
~: jmd. ist Serbe/Serbin
2 *n.* **(a)** (Ling.) serbischer Dialekt
**(b)** (person) Serbe, *der*/Serbin, *die. See also*
Eɴɢʟɪsʜ 2ᴀ
**serenade** /serə'neɪd/ 1 *n.* Ständchen, *das*
2 *v.t.* ~ **sb.** jmdm. ein Ständchen bringen
**serene** /sɪ'ri:n/ *adj.* gelassen
**serenity** /sɪ'renɪtɪ/ *n.* Gelassenheit, *die*
**sergeant** /'sɑ:dʒənt/ *n.* (Mil.) Unteroffizier,
*der;* (police officer) ≈ Polizeimeister, *der*
**sergeant 'major** *n.* ≈
[Ober]stabsfeldwebel, *der*
**serial** /'sɪərɪəl/ *n.* Fortsetzungsgeschichte,
*die;* (Radio, Telev.) Serie, *die*
**serialize** /'sɪərɪəlaɪz/ *v.t.* in Fortsetzungen
veröffentlichen; (Radio, Telev.) in
Fortsetzungen senden
**'serial killer** *n.* Serienmörder, *der*
**series** /'sɪəri:z, 'sɪərɪz/ *n., pl. same* **(a)**
(sequence) Reihe, *die;* (of events, misfortunes)
Folge, *die*
**(b)** (set of successive issues) Serie, *die;* **radio/TV**
~: Hörfunkreihe/Fernsehserie, *die*

**(c)** (set of books) Reihe, *die*
**serious** /'sɪərɪəs/ *adj.* **(a)** (earnest) ernst
**(b)** (important, grave) ernst ⟨*Angelegenheit,
Lage, Problem, Zustand*⟩; ernsthaft ⟨*Frage,
Einwand, Kandidat*⟩; schwer ⟨*Krankheit,
Unfall, Fehler, Niederlage*⟩; ernst zu
nehmend ⟨*Rivale*⟩; ernstlich ⟨*Gefahr,
Bedrohung*⟩; bedenklich ⟨*Mangel*⟩
**'seriously** *adv.* **(a)** (earnestly) ernst; **take
sth./sb.** ~: etw./jmdn. ernst nehmen
**(b)** (severely) ernstlich; schwer ⟨*verletzt*⟩
**'seriousness** *n.* Ernst, *der;* **in all** ~: ganz
im Ernst
**sermon** /'sɜ:mən/ *n.* Predigt, *die*
**serpent** /'sɜ:pənt/ *n.* Schlange, *die*
**serrated** /se'reɪtɪd/ *adj.* gezackt; ~ **knife**
Sägemesser, *das*
**serum** /'sɪərəm/ *n.* Serum, *das*
**servant** /'sɜ:vənt/ *n.* Diener, *der*/Dienerin,
*die*
**serve** /sɜ:v/ 1 *v.t.* **(a)** (work for) dienen
(+ *Dat.*)
**(b)** (be useful to) dienlich sein (+ *Dat.*)
**(c)** (meet needs of) nutzen (+ *Dat.*); ~ **a/no
purpose** einen Zweck erfüllen/keinen Zweck
haben
**(d)** durchlaufen ⟨*Lehre*⟩; verbüßen
⟨*Haftstrafe*⟩
**(e)** (dish up) servieren; (pour out) einschenken
(**to** *Dat.*)
**(f)** ~**[s]** *or* **it** ~**s him right!** [das] geschieht
ihm recht!
2 *v.i.* **(a)** dienen; ~ **as chairman** das Amt
des Vorsitzenden innehaben; ~ **as a Member
of Parliament** Mitglied des Parlaments sein;
~ **on a jury** Geschworener/Geschworene
sein
**(b)** (be of use) ~ **to do sth.** dazu dienen, etw.
zu tun; ~ **to show sth.** etw. zeigen; ~ **for** *or*
**as** dienen als
**(c)** (Sport) aufschlagen
3 *n.* ▸ sᴇʀᴠɪᴄᴇ 1ɢ
■ **serve 'up** *v.t.* **(a)** servieren
**(b)** (offer for consideration) auftischen (ugs.)
**server** /'sɜ:və(r)/ *n.* (Comp.) Server, *der*
**service** /'sɜ:vɪs/ 1 *n.* **(a)** Dienst, *der;* **do
sb. a** ~: jmdm. einen guten Dienst erweisen
**(b)** (Eccl.) Gottesdienst, *der*
**(c)** (attending to customer) Service, *der;* (in shop,
garage, etc.) Bedienung, *die*
**(d)** (system of transport) Verbindung, *die;* **there
is no [bus]** ~ **on Sundays** sonntags
verkehren keine Busse
**(e)** (provision of maintenance) **[after-sale]** ~:
Kundendienst, *der;* **take one's car in for a** ~:
sein Auto zur Inspektion bringen
**(f)** (operation) Betrieb, *der;* **out of** ~: außer
Betrieb
**(g)** (Sport) Aufschlag, *der;* **whose** ~ **is it?**
wer hat Aufschlag?
**(h)** (crockery set) Service, *das*
**(i)** (assistance) **can I be of** ~ **[to you]?** kann
ich Ihnen behilflich sein?; **I'm at your** ~: ich
stehe zu Ihren Diensten ····⦂

**(j)** (Mil.) the [armed *or* fighting] ∼s die
Streitkräfte *Pl.*; **in the** ∼s beim Militär
**(k)** [motorway] ∼s [Autobahn]raststätte, *die*
2 *v.t.* warten ⟨*Wagen, Waschmaschine,
Heizung*⟩

**serviceable** /'sɜːvɪsəbl/ *adj.* **(a)** (useful)
nützlich
**(b)** (durable) haltbar

**service:** ∼ **area** *n.* Raststätte, *die;*
∼ **charge** *n.* Bedienungsgeld, *das;*
∼ **hatch** *n.* Durchreiche, *die;*
∼ **industry** *n.* Dienstleistungsbetrieb, *der;*
∼**man** *n.* /'sɜːvɪsmən/ *n., Pl.* ∼**men**
/'sɜːvɪsmən/ Militärangehörige, *der;*
∼ **provider** *n.* (Comp.) Provider, *der;*
**Internet** ∼ **provider** Internetanbieter, *der;*
∼ **station** *n.* Tankstelle, *die*

**serviette** /sɜːvɪ'et/ *n.* (Brit.) Serviette, *die*

**servile** /'sɜːvaɪl/ *adj.* unterwürfig

**servility** /sɜː'vɪlɪtɪ/ *n.* Unterwürfigkeit, *die*

**serving** /'sɜːvɪŋ/ *n.* Portion, *die*

**'serving spoon** *n.* Vorlegelöffel, *der*

**servitude** /'sɜːvɪtjuːd/ *n.* Knechtschaft, *die*

**sesame** /'sesəmɪ/ *n.* ∼ [**seed**] Sesamkorn,
*das*

**session** /'seʃn/ *n.* (meeting) Sitzung, *die;* **be
in** ∼: tagen

**set** /set/ 1 *v.t.,* **-tt-, set (a)** (put) (horizontally)
legen; (vertically) stellen; ∼ **sb. ashore** jmdn.
an Land setzen; ∼ **sth./things right** *or* **in
order** etw./die Dinge in Ordnung bringen
**(b)** (apply) setzen; ∼ **a match to sth.** ein
Streichholz an etw. (*Akk.*) halten; *see also*
FIRE 1A; LIGHT¹ 1D
**(c)** (adjust) einstellen (**at** auf + *Akk.*);
aufstellen ⟨*Falle*⟩; stellen ⟨*Uhr*⟩; ∼ **the alarm
for 5.30 a.m.** den Wecker auf 5.30 Uhr stellen
**(d)** be ∼ ⟨*Buch, Film*⟩ spielen (**in** in + *Dat.*)
**(e)** (specify) festlegen ⟨*Bedingungen*⟩;
festsetzen ⟨*Termin, Ort usw.*⟩ (**for** auf
+ *Akk.*); ∼ **limits** Grenzen setzen
**(f)** ∼ **sb. thinking that** ...: jmdn. auf den
Gedanken bringen, dass ...
**(g)** (put forward) stellen ⟨*Frage, Aufgabe*⟩;
aufgeben ⟨*Hausaufgabe*⟩; aufstellen ⟨*Rekord*⟩;
(compose) zusammenstellen ⟨*Rätsel, Fragen*⟩;
∼ **sb. an example,** ∼ **an example to sb.**
jmdm. ein Beispiel geben; ∼ **sb. a task/
problem** jmdm. eine Aufgabe stellen/jmdn.
vor ein Problem stellen; ∼ [**sb./oneself**] **a
target** [jmdm./sich] ein Ziel setzen
**(h)** (Med.: put into place) [ein]richten;
einrenken ⟨*verrenktes Gelenk*⟩
**(i)** legen ⟨*Haare*⟩
**(j)** decken ⟨*Tisch*⟩; auflegen ⟨*Gedeck*⟩
**(k)** fassen ⟨*Edelstein*⟩
2 *v.i.,* **-tt-, set (a)** (solidify) fest werden
**(b)** (go down) ⟨*Sonne, Mond*⟩ untergehen
3 *n.* **(a)** (group) Satz, *der;* ∼ [**of two**] Paar,
*das;* **a** ∼ **of chairs** eine Sitzgruppe
**(b)** (radio, TV) Gerät, *das*
**(c)** (Tennis) Satz, *der*
**(d)** (of hair) Legen, *das*

**(e)** (Theatre: scenery) Bühnenbild, *das; (area of
performance)* (*of film*) Drehort, *der;* (*of play*)
Bühne, *die*
**(f)** (of people) Kreis, *der*
**(g)** (Math.) Menge, *die*
4 *adj.* **(a)** (fixed) fest ⟨*Absichten,
Zielvorstellungen, Zeitpunkt*⟩; **be** ∼ **in one's
ways** *or* **habits** in seinen Gewohnheiten
festgefahren sein; ∼ **meal** *or* **menu** Menü,
*das*
**(b)** vorgeschrieben ⟨*Buch, Lektüre*⟩
**(c)** (ready) **be** [**all**] ∼ **for sth.** zu etw. bereit
sein; **be** [**all**] ∼ **to do sth.** bereit sein, etw. zu
tun
**(d)** (determined) **be** ∼ **on sth./doing sth.** zu
etw. entschlossen sein/entschlossen sein,
etw. zu tun
■ **'set about** *v.t.* ∼ **about sth.** sich an etw.
(*Akk.*) machen; ∼ **about doing sth.** sich
daranmachen, etw. zu tun
■ **set a'side** *v.t.* **(a)** beiseite legen
**(b)** aufheben ⟨*Urteil, Entscheidung*⟩
■ **set 'back** *v.t.* **(a)** aufhalten
⟨*Entwicklung*⟩; zurückwerfen ⟨*Projekt,
Programm*⟩
**(b)** (coll.: cost) kosten ⟨*Person*⟩
**(c)** (place at a distance) zurücksetzen
■ **set 'down** *v.t.* **(a)** absetzen ⟨*Fahrgast*⟩
**(b)** (record) niederschreiben
■ **set 'off** 1 *v.i.* (begin journey) aufbrechen;
(start to move) loslaufen; ⟨*Fahrzeug:*⟩ losfahren
2 *v.t.* **(a)** (cause to explode) explodieren
lassen; abbrennen ⟨*Feuerwerk*⟩
**(b)** auslösen ⟨*Reaktion, Alarmanlage*⟩
■ **set 'out** 1 *v.i.* **(a)** (begin journey)
aufbrechen (**for** nach/zu)
**(b)** ∼ **out to do sth.** sich (*Dat.*) vornehmen,
etw. zu tun
2 *v.t.* darlegen
■ **set 'up** 1 *v.t.* **(a)** errichten
⟨*Straßensperre, Denkmal*⟩; aufbauen ⟨*Zelt,
Klapptisch*⟩
**(b)** (establish) gründen ⟨*Firma, Organisation*⟩;
einrichten ⟨*Büro*⟩
2 *v.i.* ∼ **up in business** ein Geschäft
aufmachen

**'setback** *n.* Rückschlag, *der*

**settee** /se'tiː/ *n.* Sofa, *das*

**'setting** *n.* **(a)** (Mus.) Vertonung, *die*
**(b)** (surroundings) Rahmen, *der;* (of novel etc.)
Schauplatz, *der*

**'setting lotion** *n.* Haarfestiger, *der*

**settle** /'setl/ 1 *v.t.* **(a)** (horizontally)
[sorgfältig] legen; (vertically) [sorgfältig]
stellen; (at an angle) [sorgfältig] lehnen
**(b)** (determine, resolve) sich einigen auf ⟨*Preis*⟩;
beilegen ⟨*Streit, Konflikt,
Meinungsverschiedenheit*⟩; ausräumen
⟨*Zweifel*⟩; entscheiden ⟨*Frage, Spiel*⟩
**(c)** bezahlen ⟨*Rechnung, Betrag*⟩; erfüllen
⟨*Forderung, Anspruch*⟩; ausgleichen ⟨*Konto*⟩
2 *v.i.* **(a)** (become established) sich
niederlassen; (as colonist) sich ansiedeln
**(b)** (pay) abrechnen
**(c)** (in chair, in front of fire, etc.) sich

niederlassen; (to work etc.) sich konzentrieren (**to** auf + *Akk.*); (into way of life, retirement, etc.) sich gewöhnen (**into** an + *Akk.*)

(**d**) (subside) ⟨*Haus, Fundament, Boden:*⟩ sich senken

(**e**) ⟨*Schnee:*⟩ liegen bleiben

■ **settle 'down** ①*v.i.* (**a**) (make oneself comfortable) sich niederlassen (**in** in + *Dat.*)

(**b**) (in town or house) heimisch werden

②*v.t.* (**a**) ~ oneself down sich [gemütlich] hinsetzen

(**b**) (calm down) beruhigen

■ **'settle for** *v.t.* (agree to) sich zufrieden geben mit

■ **'settle 'in** *v.i.* (in new home) sich einleben

■ **'settle on** *v.t.* (decide on) sich entscheiden für

■ **settle 'up** *v.i.* abrechnen; ~ up with the waiter beim Kellner bezahlen

**'settlement** *n.* (**a**) (of argument, conflict, dispute, differences) Beilegung, *die;* (of question) Klärung, *die;* (of bill, account) Bezahlung, *die;* (of court case) Vergleich, *der*

(**b**) (colony) Siedlung, *die*

**settler** /'setlə(r)/ *n.* Siedler, *der*/Siedlerin, *die*

**set:** ~**to** *n., pl.* ~**tos:** have a ~-to Streit haben; (with fists) sich prügeln; ~**-up** *n.* System, *das*

**seven** /'sevn/ ①*adj.* sieben

②*n.* Sieben, *die. See also* EIGHT

**seventeen** /sevn'ti:n/ ①*adj.* siebzehn

②*n.* Siebzehn, *die. See also* EIGHT

**seventeenth** /sevn'ti:nθ/ ①*adj.* siebzehnt…

②*n.* (fraction) Siebzehntel, *das. See also* EIGHTH

**seventh** /'sevnθ/ ①*adj.* sieb[en]t…

②*n.* (in sequence, rank) Sieb[en]te, *der/die/ das;* (fraction) Sieb[en]tel, *das. See also* EIGHTH

**seventieth** /'sevntɪɪθ/ *adj.* siebzigst…

**seventy** /'sevntɪ/ ①*adj.* siebzig

②*n.* Siebzig, *die. See also* EIGHT; EIGHTY 2

**sever** /'sevə(r)/ *v.t.* (**a**) (cut) durchtrennen; (fig.) abbrechen ⟨*Beziehungen*⟩

(**b**) (separate) abtrennen; (with axe etc.) abhacken

**several** /'sevrl/ ①*adv.* mehrere; einige; ~ **times** mehrmals

②*pron.* einige; ~ **of us** einige von uns; ~ **of the buildings** einige od. mehrere [der] Gebäude

**severe** /sɪ'vɪə(r)/ *adj.,* ~**r** /sɪ'vɪərə(r)/, ~**st** /sɪ'vɪərɪst/ hart ⟨*Urteil, Strafe, Kritik, Test, Prüfung*⟩; streng ⟨*Frost, Stil, Schönheit*⟩; schwer ⟨*Dürre, Verlust, Behinderung, Verletzung, Krankheit*⟩; rau ⟨*Wetter*⟩; heftig ⟨*Anfall, Schmerz*⟩; bedrohlich ⟨*Mangel, Knappheit*⟩; stark ⟨*Blutung*⟩

**se'verely** *adv.* hart; schwer ⟨*verletzt, behindert*⟩

**severity** /sɪ'verɪtɪ/ *n.* Strenge, *die;* (of drought, shortage) großes Ausmaß; (of criticism) Schärfe, *die*

**sew** /səʊ/ *v.t. & i., p.p.* **sewn** /səʊn/ *or* **sewed** /səʊd/ nähen

■ **sew 'on** *v.t.* annähen ⟨*Knopf*⟩; aufnähen ⟨*Abzeichen, Band*⟩

■ **sew 'up** *v.t.* nähen ⟨*Saum, Naht, Wunde*⟩

**sewage** /'sju:ɪdʒ/ *n.* Abwasser, *das*

**'sewage disposal** *n.* Abwasserbeseitigung, *die*

**sewer** /'sju:ə(r), 'su:ə(r)/ *n.* (tunnel) Abwasserkanal, *der;* (pipe) Abwasserleitung, *die*

**'sewing** *n.* Näharbeit, *die*

**'sewing machine** *n.* Nähmaschine, *die*

**sewn** ▶ SEW

**sex** /seks/ *n.* (**a**) Geschlecht, *das*

(**b**) (sexuality; coll.: intercourse) Sex, *der* (ugs.); **have** ~ **with sb.** (coll.) mit jmdm. schlafen; Sex mit jmdm. haben (salopp)

**sex:** ~ **appeal** *n.* Sexappeal, *der;* ~ **change** *n.* Geschlechtsumwandlung, *die;* ~ **discrimination** *n.* sexuelle Diskriminierung; ~ **education** *n.* Sexualerziehung, *die*

**sexism** /'seksɪzm/ *n.* Sexismus, *der*

**sexist** /'seksɪst/ *adj.* sexistisch

**sex:** ~ **life** *n.* Geschlechtsleben, *das;* Sexualleben, *das;* ~ **maniac** *n.* Triebverbrecher, *der;* **you** ~ **maniac!** (coll.) du geiler Bock! (ugs.); ~ **offender** *n.* Sexual[straf]täter, *der*/-täterin, *die*

**sexploitation** /seksplɔɪ'teɪʃn/ *n.* [kommerzielle] Ausbeutung der Sexualität

**sex:** ~ **shop** *n.* Sexshop, *der;* ~ **symbol** *n.* Sexidol, *das*

**sexual** /'seksʊəl/ *adj.* sexuell

**sexual:** ~ **a'buse** *n.* sexueller Missbrauch; ~ **'harassment** *n.* sexuelle Belästigung; ~ **'intercourse** *n.* Geschlechtsverkehr, *der*

**sexuality** /seksʊ'ælɪtɪ/ *n.* Sexualität, *die*

**sexual:** ~ **'organs** *n. pl.* Geschlechtsorgane *Pl.;* ~ **'partner** *n.* Sexualpartner, *der*/-partnerin, *die*

**'sexy** *adj.* sexy (ugs.)

**sh** /ʃ/ *int.* sch; pst

**shabbily** /'ʃæbɪlɪ/ *adv.,* **shabby** /'ʃæbɪ/ *adj.* schäbig

**shack** /ʃæk/ *n.* [armselige] Hütte

**shackle** /'ʃækl/ ①*n., usu. in pl.* Fessel, *die*

②*v.t.* anketten (**to** an + *Akk.*)

**shade** /ʃeɪd/ ①*n.* (**a**) Schatten, *der*

(**b**) (colour) Ton, *der;* (fig.) Schattierung, *die*

(**c**) (lamp~) [Lampen]schirm, *der*

②*v.t.* (**a**) (screen) beschatten

(**b**) (darken with lines) ~ **[in]** [ab]schattieren

③*v.i.* übergehen (**into** in + *Akk.*)

**shadow** /'ʃædəʊ/ ①*n.* Schatten, *der*

②*v.t.* (follow) beschatten

S

'**shadowy** *adj.* (indistinct) schattenhaft

**shady** /'ʃeɪdɪ/ *adj.* (a) schattig
(b) (disreputable) zwielichtig

**shaft** /ʃɑːft/ *n.* (a) (of tool, golf club) Schaft,
*der*
(b) (Mech. Engin.) Welle, *die*
(c) (of mine, lift) Schacht, *der*
(d) (of light, lightning) Strahl, *der*

**shaggy** /'ʃægɪ/ *adj.* zottelig

**shake** /ʃeɪk/ ① *n.* Schütteln, *das; give sb./
sth. a* ~: jmdn./etw. schütteln
② *v.t.*, **shook** /ʃʊk/, **shaken** /'ʃeɪkn/ (a) (move
violently) schütteln; ~ *one's fist/a stick at sb.*
jmdm. mit der Faust/einem Stock drohen;
~ *hands* sich (*Dat.*) die Hand geben
(b) (cause to tremble) erschüttern ⟨*Gebäude
usw.*⟩; ~ *one's head* den Kopf schütteln
(c) (shock) erschüttern
③ *v.i.*, **shook**, **shaken** wackeln; ⟨*Boden,
Stimme:*⟩ beben; ⟨*Hand:*⟩ zittern
▪ **shake 'off** *v.t.* abschütteln
▪ **shake 'up** *v.t.* (a) (upset, shock) einen
Schrecken einjagen (+ *Dat.*)
(b) (reorganize) umkrempeln (ugs.)

**shaken** ▸ SHAKE 2, 3

**shaky** /'ʃeɪkɪ/ *adj.* wack[e]lig ⟨*Möbelstück,
Leiter*⟩; zittrig ⟨*Hand, Stimme, Greis*⟩; **feel** ~:
sich zittrig fühlen

**shall** /ʃl, *stressed* ʃæl/ *v. aux. only in pres.*
shall, *neg.* (coll.) **shan't** /ʃɑːnt/, *past* **should**
/ʃəd, *stressed* ʃʊd/, *neg.* (coll.) **shouldn't**
/'ʃʊdnt/ (a) (expr. simple future) werden
(b) (expr. conditional) würde/würdest/
würden/würdet; **I should have been killed if I
had let go** ich wäre getötet worden, wenn ich
losgelassen hätte; **if we should be defeated**
falls wir unterliegen [sollten]
(c) (expr. will or intention) **what** ~ **we do?** was
sollen wir tun?; **let's go in,** ~ **we?** gehen wir
doch hinein, oder?; **we should be safe by
now** jetzt dürften wir in Sicherheit sein; **he
shouldn't do things like that!** er sollte so
etwas nicht tun!

**shallot** /ʃə'lɒt/ *n.* Schalotte, *die*

**shallow** /'ʃæləʊ/ *adj.* seicht ⟨*Wasser, Fluss*⟩;
flach ⟨*Schüssel, Teller, Wasser*⟩; (fig.) flach
⟨*Person*⟩

**sham** /ʃæm/ ① *adj.* unecht; imitiert ⟨*Leder,
Holz, Pelz*⟩
② *n.* (pretence) Heuchelei, *die;* (person)
Heuchler, *der*/Heuchlerin, *die*
③ *v.t.*, **-mm-** vortäuschen
④ *v.i.*, **-mm-** simulieren

**shambles** /'ʃæmblz/ *n.* (coll.) Chaos, *das;
the room was a* ~: das Zimmer glich einem
Schlachtfeld

**shambolic** /ʃæm'bɒlɪk/ *adj.* (coll.)
chaotisch

**shame** /ʃeɪm/ *n.* (a) Scham, *die*
(b) (state of disgrace) Schande, *die;* **put sb./sth.
to** ~: jmdn. beschämen/etw. in den Schatten
stellen
(c) **what a** ~! wie schade!

'**shamefaced** *adj.* betreten

**shameful** /'ʃeɪmfl/ *adj.* beschämend

'**shameless** *adj.* schamlos

**shampoo** /ʃæm'puː/ ① *v.t.* schamponieren
② *n.* Shampoo[n], *das*

**shamrock** /'ʃæmrɒk/ *n.* Klee, *der*

**shandy** /'ʃændɪ/ *n.* Bier mit Limonade;
Radlermaß, *die* (bes. südd.)

**shan't** /ʃɑːnt/ (coll.) = shall not

**shanty**[1] /'ʃæntɪ/ *n.* (hut) [armselige] Hütte

**shanty**[2] *n.* (song) Shanty, *das*

'**shanty town** *n.* Bidonville, *das*

**shape** /ʃeɪp/ ① *v.t.* formen; bearbeiten
⟨*Holz, Stein*⟩ (into zu)
② *n.* Form, *die;* **take** ~: Gestalt annehmen
▪ **shape 'up** *v.i.* sich entwickeln

'**shapeless** *adj.* formlos; unförmig ⟨*Kleid,
Person*⟩

**shapely** /'ʃeɪplɪ/ *adj.* wohlgeformt ⟨*Beine,
Busen*⟩; gut ⟨*Figur*⟩

**share** /ʃeə(r)/ ① *n.* (a) (portion) Teil, *der od.
das;* [fair] ~: Anteil, *der;* **fair** ~**s** gerechte
Teile; **do more than one's [fair]** ~ **of the work**
mehr als seinen Teil zur Arbeit beitragen
(b) (Commerc.) Aktie, *die*
② *v.t.* teilen; gemeinsam tragen
⟨*Verantwortung*⟩
③ *v.i.* ~ **in** teilnehmen an (+ *Dat.*); beteiligt
sein an (+ *Dat.*) ⟨*Gewinn*⟩; teilen ⟨*Freude,
Erfahrung*⟩
▪ **share 'out** *v.t.* aufteilen (among unter
+ *Akk.*)

**share:** ~ **certificate** *n.* Aktienurkunde,
*die;* ~**holder** *n.* Aktionär, *der*/Aktionärin,
*die;* ~ **index** *n.* Aktienindex, *der;* ~**out**
*n.* Aufteilung, *die;* ~**ware** *n.* (Comp.)
Shareware, *die*

**shark** /ʃɑːk/ *n.* Hai[fisch], *der*

**sharp** /ʃɑːp/ ① *adj.* (a) scharf; spitz ⟨*Nadel,
Bleistift, Gipfel, Winkel*⟩; deutlich
⟨*Unterscheidung*⟩; sauer ⟨*Apfel*⟩; herb ⟨*Wein*⟩;
(shrill, piercing) schrill ⟨*Schrei, Pfiff*⟩; heftig
⟨*Schmerz, Krampf, Kampf*⟩; begabt ⟨*Schüler,
Student*⟩
(b) (derog.: dishonest) gerissen
(c) (Mus.) [um einen Halbton] erhöht ⟨*Note*⟩
② *adv.* (a) (punctually) **at six o'clock** ~: Punkt
sechs Uhr
(b) **turn** ~ **right/left** scharf nach rechts/links
abbiegen
(c) **look** ~! halt dich ran! (ugs.)
(d) (Mus.) zu hoch ⟨*singen, spielen*⟩

**sharpen** /'ʃɑːpn/ *v.t.* schärfen; [an]spitzen
⟨*Bleistift*⟩

'**sharpener** *n.* (for pencils) Spitzer, *der* (ugs.)

'**sharp-eyed** *adj.* scharfäugig; **be** ~:
scharfe Augen haben

'**sharpish** *adv.* (coll.) (quickly) rasch; (promptly)
unverzüglich; sofort

'**sharply** *adv.* scharf; in scharfem Ton
⟨*antworten*⟩

'**sharpness** *n.* Schärfe, *die;* (fineness of point)
Spitzheit, *die*

'**sharp-witted** *adj.* scharfsinnig

**shatter** /'ʃætə(r)/ **1** *v.t.* zertrümmern; zerbrechen ⟨*Glas, Fenster*⟩; zerschlagen ⟨*Hoffnungen*⟩
**2** *v.i.* zerbrechen

**shattered** /'ʃætəd/ *adj.* (a) zerbrochen ⟨*Glas, Fenster*⟩; (fig.) zerstört ⟨*Hoffnungen*⟩; zerrüttet ⟨*Nerven*⟩
(b) (coll.: greatly upset) **she was ~ by the news** die Nachricht hat sie schwer mitgenommen; **I'm ~!** ich bin ganz erschüttert!; (Brit. coll.: exhausted) ich bin kaputt! (ugs.)

**'shattering** *adj.* verheerend ⟨*Wirkung*⟩; vernichtend ⟨*Schlag, Niederlage*⟩

**shave** /ʃeɪv/ **1** *v.t.* rasieren; abrasieren ⟨*Haare*⟩
**2** *v.i.* sich rasieren
**3** *n.* Rasur, *die;* **have a ~:** sich rasieren
■ **shave 'off** *v.t.* abrasieren

**'shaven** /'ʃeɪvn/ *adj.* rasiert; [kahl] geschoren ⟨*Kopf*⟩

**'shaver** *n.* Rasierapparat, *der*

**'shaver point** *n.* Anschluss, *der* für den Rasierapparat

**shaving** /'ʃeɪvɪŋ/ *n.* (a) Rasieren, *das*
(b) *in pl.* (of wood, metal, etc.) Späne *Pl.*

**shaving: ~ brush** *n.* Rasierpinsel, *der;* **~ cream** *n.* Rasiercreme, *die;* **~ foam** *n.* Rasierschaum, *der* **~ soap** *n.* Rasierseife, *die;* **~ stick** *n.* Stangenrasierseife, *die*

**shawl** /ʃɔ:l/ *n.* Schultertuch, *das*

**she** /ʃɪ, stressed ʃi:/ *pron.* sie

**sheaf** /ʃi:f/ *n., pl.* **sheaves** /ʃi:vz/ (of corn etc.) Garbe, *die;* (of paper, arrows, etc.) Bündel, *das*

**shear** /ʃɪə(r)/ *v.t., p.p.* **shorn** /ʃɔ:n/ *or* **sheared** (clip) scheren

**shears** /ʃɪəz/ *n. pl.* [pair of] ~: Schere, *die;* **garden ~:** Gartenschere, *die*

**sheath** /ʃi:θ/ *n., pl.* **~s** /ʃi:ðz, ʃi:θs/ (a) (for knife, sword, etc.) Scheide, *die*
(b) (condom) Gummischutz, *der*

**sheaves** *pl. of* SHEAF

**shebang** /ʃɪ'bæŋ/ *n.* (Amer. coll.) **the whole ~:** der ganze Kram (ugs.)

**shed¹** /ʃed/ *v.t.,* **-dd-, shed** (a) verlieren; abwerfen ⟨*Laub, Geweih*⟩
(b) vergießen ⟨*Blut, Tränen*⟩
(c) verbreiten ⟨*Licht*⟩

**shed²** *n.* Schuppen, *der*

**she'd** /ʃɪd, stressed ʃi:d/ (a) = **she had;**
(b) = **she would**

**sheen** /ʃi:n/ *n.* Glanz, *der*

**sheep** /ʃi:p/ *n., pl. same* Schaf, *das*

**sheep: ~ dip** *n.* Desinfektionsbad für Schafe; **~dog** *n.* Hütehund, *der;* Schäferhund, *der;* **Old English S~dog** Bobtail, *der*

**sheepish** /'ʃi:pɪʃ/ *adj.* verlegen

**sheep: ~ shearer** /'ʃi:p ʃɪərə(r)/ *n.* Schafscherer, *der;* **~-shearing** *n.* Schafschur, *die;* **~skin** *n.* Schaffell, *das*

**sheer** /ʃɪə(r)/ *adj.* (a) rein; blank ⟨*Unsinn, Gewalt*⟩; **by ~ chance** rein zufällig
(b) schroff ⟨*Felsen, Abfall*⟩

**sheet** /ʃi:t/ *n.* (a) Laken, *das*
(b) (of thin metal or plastic) Folie, *die;* (of iron, tin) Blech, *das;* (of glass) Platte, *die;* (of paper) Bogen, *der;* Blatt, *das*
(c) ⟨*Eis-, Nebel*⟩decke, *die*

**sheet: ~ lightning** *n.* Flächenblitz, *der;* **~ music** *n.* Notenblätter *Pl.*

**sheik[h]** /ʃeɪk, ʃi:k/ *n.* Scheich, *der*

**shelf** /ʃelf/ *n., pl.* **shelves** /ʃelvz/ Brett, *das;* Bord, *das;* **shelves** (set) Regal, *das*

**shelf life** *n.* Lagerfähigkeit, *die*

**shell** /ʃel/ **1** *n.* (a) Schale, *die;* (of snail) Haus, *das;* (of turtle, tortoise) Panzer, *der;* (on beach) Muschel, *die*
(b) (Mil.) (bomb) Granate, *die*
**2** *v.t.* (a) (take out of ~) schälen
(b) (Mil.) [mit Artillerie] beschießen
■ **shell 'out** *v.t. & i.* (coll.) blechen (ugs.) (**on** für)

**she'll** /ʃɪl, stressed ʃi:l/ = **she will**

**shell: ~fish** *n., pl. same* (a) Schal[en]tier, *das;* (oyster, clam) Muschel, *die;* (crustacean) Krebstier, *das;* (b) *in pl.* (Gastr.) Meeresfrüchte *Pl.;* **~ shock** *n.* Kriegsneurose, *die;* **~ suit** *n.* Trilobanzug, *der*

**shelter** /'ʃeltə(r)/ **1** *n.* (a) (shield) Schutz, *der* (**against** vor + *Dat.,* gegen); **bomb** *or* **air-raid ~:** Luftschutzraum, *der;* **get under ~:** sich unterstellen
(b) *no pl.* (place of safety) Zuflucht, *die*
**2** *v.t.* schützen (**from** vor + *Dat.*); Unterschlupf gewähren (+ *Dat.*) ⟨*Flüchtling*⟩
**3** *v.i.* Schutz suchen (**from** vor + *Dat.*)

**'sheltered** /'ʃeltəd/ *adj.* geschützt; behütet ⟨*Leben;*⟩ **live in ~ housing** in einer Altenwohnung/in Altenwohnungen leben

**shelve** /ʃelv/ **1** *v.t.* (defer) auf Eis legen (ugs.)
**2** *v.i.* (slope) abfallen

**shelves** *pl. of* SHELF

**'shelving** *n.* Regale *Pl.*

**shepherd** /'ʃepəd/ **1** *n.* Schäfer, *der*
**2** *v.t.* führen

**'shepherdess** *n.* Schäferin, *die*

**shepherd: ~'s 'crook** *n.* Schäferstock, *der;* **~'s 'pie** *n.: Auflauf aus Hackfleisch mit einer Schicht Kartoffelbrei darüber*

**sheriff** /'ʃerɪf/ *n.* Sheriff, *der*

**sherry** /'ʃerɪ/ *n.* Sherry, *der*

**she's** /ʃɪz, stressed ʃi:z/ (a) = **she is;**
(b) = **she has**

**shield** /ʃi:ld/ **1** *n.* Schild, *der*
**2** *v.t.* schützen (**from** vor + *Dat.*)

**shift** /ʃɪft/ **1** *v.t.* (a) (move) umstellen ⟨*Möbel*⟩; wegnehmen ⟨*Arm, Hand, Fuß*⟩; wegräumen ⟨*Schutt*⟩; entfernen ⟨*Schmutz, Fleck*⟩; **~ the responsibility/blame on to sb.** die Verantwortung/Schuld auf jmdn. schieben

(b) (Amer. Motor Veh.) ~ **gears** schalten
[2] *v.i.* (a) ⟨*Wind:*⟩ drehen (**to** nach);
⟨*Ladung:*⟩ verrutschen
(b) (coll.: move quickly) rasen
[3] *n.* (a) a ~ **in emphasis** eine Verlagerung
des Akzents; a ~ **in public opinion** ein
Umschwung der öffentlichen Meinung
(b) (for work) Schicht, *die;* **eight-hour/late** ~:
Achtstunden-/Spätschicht, *die;* **do** *or* **work
the late** ~: Spätschicht haben

'**shift work** *n.* Schichtarbeit, *die*

**shifty** /'ʃɪftɪ/ *adj.* verschlagen

**shilling** /'ʃɪlɪŋ/ *n.* (Hist.) Shilling, *der*

**shilly-shally** /'ʃɪlɪʃælɪ/ *v.i.* zaudern; **stop
~ing!** entschließ dich endlich!

**shimmer** /'ʃɪmə(r)/ [1] *v.i.* schimmern
[2] *n.* Schimmer, *der*

**shin** /ʃɪn/ [1] *n.* Schienbein, *das*
[2] *v.i.,* -nn-: ~ **up/down a tree** *etc.* einen
Baum *usw.* hinauf-/hinunterklettern

'**shin bone** *n.* Schienbein, *das*

**shine** /ʃaɪn/ [1] *v.i.,* shone /ʃɒn/ ⟨*Lampe,
Licht, Stern:*⟩ leuchten; ⟨*Sonne, Mond:*⟩
scheinen; (reflect light) glänzen
[2] *v.t.,* shone: ~ **a light on sth./in sb.'s eyes**
etw. anleuchten/jmdm. in die Augen
leuchten
[3] *n.* Glanz, *der*

**shingle** /'ʃɪŋgl/ *n.* (pebbles) Kies, *der*

'**shingles** *n.* (Med.) Gürtelrose, *die*

**shin:** ~ **guard,** ~ **pad** *ns.*
Schienbeinschutz, *der*

**shiny** /'ʃaɪnɪ/ *adj.* glänzend

**ship** /ʃɪp/ [1] *n.* Schiff, *das*
[2] *v.t.,* -pp- (transport by sea) verschiffen; (send
by road, train, or air) verschicken ⟨*Waren*⟩

'**shipbuilding** *n.* Schiffbau, *der*

'**shipment** *n.* (a) Versand, *der;* (by sea)
Verschiffung, *die*
(b) (amount) Sendung, *die*

'**shipowner** *n.* Schiffseigentümer, *der/*
-eigentümerin, *die;* (of several ships) Reeder,
*der/*Reederin, *die*

'**shipper** *n.* Spediteur, *der/*Spediteurin, *die;*
(company) Spedition, *die*

'**shipping** *n.* (a) (ships) Schiffe *Pl.;* (traffic)
Schifffahrt, *die*
(b) (transporting) Versand, *der*

**shipping:** ~ **agent** *n.* Schiffsagent, *der;*
~ **forecast** *n.* Seewetterbericht, *der;*
~ **lane** *n.* Schifffahrtsweg, *der*

**ship:** ~**shape** *adj.* in bester Ordnung;
~**wreck** [1] *n.* Schiffbruch, *der;* [2] *v.t.* be
~**wrecked** Schiffbruch erleiden; ~**yard** *n.*
[Schiffs]werft, *die*

**shirk** /ʃɜːk/ *v.t.* sich drücken vor (+ *Dat.*)

'**shirker** *n.* Drückeberger, *der/*
Drückebergerin, *die* (ugs.)

**shirt** /ʃɜːt/ *n.* [man's] ~: [Herren- *od.*
Ober]hemd, *das;* [woman's] ~: Hemdbluse,
*die*

'**shirtsleeve** *n.* Hemdsärmel, *der;* **in** ~**s** in
Hemdsärmeln

**shit** /ʃɪt/ (coarse) [1] *v.i.,* -tt-, shitted *or* shit
scheißen (derb)
[2] *n.* (a) Scheiße, *die* (derb); **have** (Brit.) *or*
(Amer.) **take a** ~: scheißen (derb)
(b) (person) Scheißkerl, *der* (derb)
(c) (nonsense) Scheiß, *der* (salopp)

**shiver** /'ʃɪvə(r)/ [1] *v.i.* zittern (**with** vor
+ *Dat.*)
[2] *n.* Schau[d]er, *der* (geh.)

**shoal** /ʃəʊl/ *n.* (of fish) Schwarm, *der*

**shock** /ʃɒk/ [1] *n.* (a) Schock, *der;* **give sb. a**
~: jmdm. einen Schock versetzen
(b) (violent impact) Erschütterung, *die* (of
durch)
(c) (Electr.) Schlag, *der*
(d) (Med.) Schock, *der*
[2] *v.t.* ~ **sb.** [deeply] ein [schwerer] Schock
für jmdn. sein; (scandalize) jmdn. schockieren

'**shock absorber** *n.* Stoßdämpfer, *der*

'**shocking** *adj.* (a) schockierend
(b) (coll.: very bad) fürchterlich (ugs.)

**shock:** ~ **jock** *n.* (coll.) Skandal-DJ, *der;*
~**proof** *adj.* stoßfest; ~ **wave** *n.*
Druckwelle, *die* (from *Gen.*); (of earthquake)
Erschütterungswelle, *die* (from *Gen.*)

**shod** ▶ SHOE 2

**shoddy** /'ʃɒdɪ/ *adj.* schäbig; minderwertig
⟨*Arbeit, Stoff, Artikel*⟩

**shoe** /ʃuː/ [1] *n.* Schuh, *der;* (of horse)
[Huf]eisen, *das;* **put oneself into sb.'s** ~**s** (fig.)
sich in jmds. Lage ⟨*Akk.*⟩ versetzen
[2] *v.t.,* ~**ing,** shod /ʃɒd/ beschlagen ⟨*Pferd*⟩

**shoe:** ~**cream** *n.* Schuhcreme, *die;*
~**horn** *n.* Schuhlöffel, *der;* ~**lace** *n.*
Schnürsenkel, *der;* ~**maker** *n.*
Schuhmacher, *der;* ~ **polish** *n.*
Schuhcreme, *die;* ~ **shop** *n.* Schuhgeschäft,
*das;* ~**string** *n.* **on a** ~**string** (coll.) mit ganz
wenig Geld

**shone** ▶ SHINE 1, 2

**shoo** /ʃuː/ [1] *int.* sch
[2] *v.t.* scheuchen; ~ **away** fortscheuchen

**shook** ▶ SHAKE 2, 3

**shoot** /ʃuːt/ [1] *v.i.,* shot /ʃɒt/ (a) schießen
(**at** auf + *Akk.*)
(b) (move rapidly) schießen (ugs.)
[2] *v.t.,* shot (a) (wound) anschießen; (kill)
erschießen; (hunt) schießen; ~ **sb. dead** jmdn.
erschießen
(b) schießen mit ⟨*Bogen, Munition, Pistole*⟩;
abschießen ⟨*Pfeil, Kugel*⟩ (**at** auf + *Akk.*)
(c) (Cinemat.) drehen ⟨*Film, Szene*⟩
[3] *n.* (Bot.) Trieb, *der*

■ **shoot 'down** *v.t.* niederschießen
⟨*Person*⟩; abschießen ⟨*Flugzeug*⟩

■ **shoot 'out** *v.i.* hervorschießen

■ **shoot 'up** *v.i.* in die Höhe schießen;
⟨*Preise, Kosten, Temperatur:*⟩ in die Höhe
schnellen

**shooting:** ~ **range** *n.* Schießstand, *der;*
~ '**star** *n.* Sternschnuppe, *die;* ~ **stick** *n.*
Jagdstock, *der*

'**shoot-out** *n.* Schießerei, *die*

**shop** /ʃɒp/ ① *n.* Laden, *der;* Geschäft, *das;*
go to the ~s einkaufen gehen; talk ~:
fachsimpeln (ugs.)
② *v.i.,* -pp- einkaufen; go ~ping einkaufen
gehen
■ **shop a'round** *v.i.* sich umsehen (**for**
nach)

**shopaholic** /ˈʃɒpəhɒlɪk/ *n.* Kaufsüchtige,
*der/die*

**shop:** ~ **assistant** *n.* (Brit.) Verkäufer,
*der/*Verkäuferin, *die;* ~**front** *n.*
Schaufensterfront, *die;* ~**keeper** *n.*
Ladenbesitzer, *der/*-besitzerin, *die;* ~**lifter**
*n.* Ladendieb, *der/*-diebin, *die;* ~**lifting** *n.*
Ladendiebstahl, *der;* ~**owner** ▶ ~KEEPER

**'shopper** *n.* Käufer, *der/*Käuferin, *die*

**'shopping** *n.* (a) Einkaufen, *das;* do the/
one's ~: einkaufen/[seine] Einkäufe
machen
(b) (items bought) Einkäufe *Pl.*

**shopping:** ~ **bag** *n.* Einkaufstasche, *die;*
~ **basket** *n.* Einkaufskorb, *der;*
~ **centre** *n.* Einkaufszentrum, *das;*
~ **list** *n.* Einkaufszettel, *der;* ~ **mall**
/-mæl/ *n.* Einkaufszentrum, *das;*
~ **precinct** *n.* Einkaufs- od.
Geschäftsviertel, *das;* ~ **street** *n.*
Geschäftsstraße, *die;* ~ **trolley** *n.* (in
supermarket) Einkaufswagen, *der;* (personal)
Einkaufsroller, *der*

**shop:** ~**soiled** *adj.* (Brit.) (slightly damaged)
leicht beschädigt; (slightly dirty) angeschmutzt;
~ **steward** *n.* [gewerkschaftlicher]
Vertrauensmann; ~ **'window** *n.*
Schaufenster, *das*

**shore** /ʃɔː(r)/ *n.* Ufer, *das;* (beach) Strand,
*der*
■ **shore 'up** *v.t.* abstützen ⟨*Mauer, Haus*⟩;
(fig.) stützen

**shorn** ▶ SHEAR

**short** /ʃɔːt/ ① *adj.* (a) kurz; in a ~ time *or*
while (soon) bald; in Kürze; a ~ time *or* while
ago/later vor kurzem/kurze Zeit später; in
~, ...: kurz, ...
(b) klein ⟨*Person, Wuchs*⟩
(c) (deficient, scanty) knapp; go ~ [of sth.] [an
etw. (*Dat.*)] Mangel leiden; sb. is ~ of sth.
jmdm. fehlt es an etw. (*Dat.*); time is getting/
is ~: die Zeit wird/ist knapp; be in
~ supply knapp sein; be ~ [of cash] knapp
[bei Kasse] sein (ugs.)
② *adv.* (a) (abruptly) plötzlich; stop ~:
plötzlich abbrechen; stop sb. ~: jmdm. ins
Wort fallen
(b) stop ~ of doing sth. nicht so weit gehen,
etw. zu tun

**shortage** /ˈʃɔːtɪdʒ/ *n.* Mangel, *der* (**of** an
+ *Dat.*); ~ of fruit/teachers Obstknappheit,
*die/*Lehrermangel, *der*

**short:** ~**bread** *n.* Shortbread, *das;* Kekse
aus Butterteig; ~ **'circuit** *n.* (Electr.)
Kurzschluss, *der;* ~**coming** *n., usu. in pl.*

Unzulänglichkeit, *die;* ~ **'cut** *n.*
Abkürzung, *die;* take a ~ cut den Weg
abkürzen

**shorten** /ˈʃɔːtn/ ① *v.i.* kürzer werden
② *v.t.* kürzen; verkürzen ⟨*Besuch, Wartezeit*⟩

**short:** ~**fall** *n.* Fehlmenge, *die;* ~**haired**
*adj.* kurzhaarig; Kurzhaar⟨*dackel, -katze*⟩;
~**hand** *n.* Stenografie, *die;* ~**hand** typist
Stenotypist, *der/*-typistin, *die;* ~ **list** *n.*
(Brit.) engere Auswahl; **be on/put sb. on the**
~ **list** in der engeren Auswahl sein/jmdn. in
die engere Auswahl nehmen; ~**list** *v.t.* in
die engere Auswahl nehmen; ~**lived** *adj.*
kurzlebig

**'shortly** *adv.* in Kürze; demnächst;
~ before/after sth. kurz vor/nach etw.

**short:** ~ **'pastry** *n.* Mürbeteig, *der;*
~**range** *adj.* (a) Kurzstrecken⟨*flugzeug,*
*-rakete usw.*⟩; (b) (relating to time) kurzfristig

**shorts** /ʃɔːts/ *n. pl.* (a) (trousers) kurze
Hose[n *Pl.*]; Shorts *Pl.*
(b) (Amer.: underpants) Unterhose, *die*

**short:** ~**'sighted** *adj.* kurzsichtig;
~**sleeved** /ˈsliːvd/ *adj.* kurzärm[e]lig;
~**staffed** /ˈstaːft/ *adj.* be [very] ~**staffed**
[viel] zu wenig Personal haben; ~ **'story** *n.*
Kurzgeschichte, *die;* ~**'tempered** *adj.*
aufbrausend; ~**term** *adj.* kurzfristig;
(provisional) vorläufig ⟨*Lösung*⟩; befristet
⟨*Vertrag*⟩; ~ **'trousers** *n. pl.* kurze Hose[n
*Pl.*]; ~ **wave** *n.* (Radio) Kurzwelle, *die*

**shot** /ʃɒt/ ① *n.* (a) Schuss, *der;* fire a ~:
einen Schuss abgeben (**at** auf + *Akk.*); **like a**
~ (fig.) wie der Blitz (ugs.); I'd do it like a ~:
ich würde es auf der Stelle tun
(b) (Athletics) put the ~: die Kugel stoßen;
[putting] the ~: Kugelstoßen, *das*
(c) (Sport: stroke, kick, throw) Schuss, *der*
(d) (Photog.) Aufnahme, *die;* (Cinemat.)
Einstellung, *die*
② ▶ SHOOT 1, 2
③ *adj.* be/get ~ of (coll.) los sein/loswerden

**'shotgun** *n.* [Schrot]flinte, *die*

**should** ▶ SHALL

**shoulder** /ˈʃəʊldə(r)/ ① *n.* Schulter, *die*
② *v.t.* schultern; (fig.) übernehmen

**shoulder:** ~ **bag** *n.* Umhängetasche, *die;*
~ **blade** *n.* Schulterblatt, *das;* ~ **joint** *n.*
Schultergelenk, *das;* ~**length** *adj.*
schulterlang; ~ **pad** *n.* Schulterpolster,
*das;* ~ **strap** *n.* (on garment) Schulterklappe,
*die;* (on bag) Tragriemen, *der*

**shouldn't** /ˈʃʊdnt/ (coll.) = should not;
▶ SHALL

**shout** /ʃaʊt/ ① *n.* Ruf, *der;* (inarticulate)
Schrei, *der*
② *v.i. & t.* schreien
■ **shout 'down** *v.t.* niederschreien
■ **shout 'out** ① *v.i.* aufschreien
② *v.t.* [laut] rufen

**'shouting** *n.* Geschrei, *das*

**shove** /ʃʌv/ ① *n.* Stoß, *der*
② *v.t.* stoßen; schubsen (ugs.); (coll.: put) tun ⋯⊱

■ **shove a'way** v.t. (coll.) wegschubsen (ugs.)

■ **shove 'off** v.i. (coll.: leave) abschieben (ugs.)

**shovel** /'ʃʌvl/ ① n. Schaufel, die ② v.t., (Brit.) -ll- schaufeln

**show** /ʃəʊ/ ① n. **(a)** (entertainment, performance) Show, die; (Theatre) Vorstellung, die; (Radio, Telev.) [Unterhaltungs]sendung, die **(b)** (exhibition) Ausstellung, die; Schau, die; put sth. on ~: etw. ausstellen; be on ~: ausgestellt sein **(c)** (appearance) Anschein, der; be for ~: reine Angeberei sein (ugs.) ② v.t., p.p. shown /ʃəʊn/ **(a)** zeigen; vorzeigen ⟨Pass, Fahrschein usw.⟩; ~ sb. sth., ~ sth. to sb. jmdm. etw. zeigen **(b)** beweisen ⟨Mut, Urteilsvermögen usw.⟩; ~ sb. that ...: jmdm. beweisen, dass ...; ~ [sb.] kindness/mercy freundlich [zu jmdm.] sein/Erbarmen [mit jmdm.] haben **(c)** ⟨Thermometer, Uhr usw.:⟩ anzeigen **(d)** (exhibit in a show) ausstellen; zeigen ⟨Film⟩ ③ v.i., p.p. shown **(a)** (be visible) sichtbar od. zu sehen sein; (come into sight) sich zeigen **(b)** (be ~n) ⟨Film:⟩ laufen; ⟨Künstler:⟩ ausstellen

■ **show 'in** v.t. hinein-/hereinführen

■ **show 'off** v.i. angeben (ugs.); prahlen

■ **show 'out** v.t. hinausführen

■ **show 'round** v.t. herumführen

■ **show 'through** v.i. durchscheinen

■ **show 'up** ① v.t. **(a)** (make visible) [deutlich] sichtbar machen **(b)** (coll.: embarrass) blamieren ② v.i. **(a)** (be visible) [deutlich] zu sehen sein **(b)** (coll.: arrive) sich blicken lassen (ugs.)

**show:** ~ **biz** (coll.)**,** ~ **business** ns., no art. Schaugeschäft, das; ~**case** n. Vitrine, die; (fig.) Schaufenster, das; '~**down** n. (fig.) Kraftprobe, die; **have a** ~**down** [**with sb.**] sich [mit jmdm.] auseinander setzen

**shower** /'ʃaʊə(r)/ ① n. **(a)** Schauer, der; ~ **of rain/hail** Regen-/Hagelschauer, der **(b)** (for washing) Dusche, die; **have** or **take a** [**cold/quick**] ~: [kalt/schnell] duschen ② v.t. (lavish) ~ **sth.** [**up**]**on sb.,** ~ **sb. with sth.** jmdm. mit etw. überhäufen ③ v.i. (have a ~) duschen

**shower:** ~ **cap** n. Duschhaube, die; ~ **curtain** n. Duschvorhang, der; ~ **gel** n. Duschgel, das; ~**proof** adj. [bedingt] regendicht

'**showery** adj. **it is** ~: es gibt immer wieder kurze Schauer; **a** ~ **day** ein Tag mit Schauerwetter

'**showjumping** n. Springreiten, das

**shown** ▶ SHOW 2, 3

**show:** ~**-off** n. (coll.) Angeber, der/ Angeberin, die; ~**piece** n. (of exhibition, collection) Schaustück, das; (highlight) Paradestück, das; ~**room** n. Ausstellungsraum, der; ~ **trial** n. Schauprozess, der

'**showy** adj. protzig (ugs.)

**shrank** ▶ SHRINK

**shred** /ʃred/ ① n. Fetzen, der; (fig.) Spur, die; **tear sth. to** ~**s** etw. zerfetzen; (fig.) etw. zerpflücken ② v.t., -dd- [im Reißwolf] zerkleinern

**shredder** /'ʃredə(r)/ n. (for paper) Reißwolf, der

**shrew** /ʃruː/ n. (Zool.) Spitzmaus, die

**shrewd** /ʃruːd/ adj. klug; genau ⟨[Ein]schätzung⟩

**shriek** /ʃriːk/ ① n. [Auf]schrei, der ② v.i. [auf]schreien ③ v.t. schreien

**shrift** /ʃrɪft/ n. **give sb. short** ~: jmdn. kurz abfertigen (ugs.); **get short** ~ kurz abgefertigt werden (ugs.)

**shrill** /ʃrɪl/ adj. schrill

**shrimp** /ʃrɪmp/ n. Garnele, die

**shrine** /ʃraɪn/ n. (tomb) Grab, das

**shrink** /ʃrɪŋk/ ① v.i., **shrank** /ʃræŋk/, **shrunk** /ʃrʌŋk/ **(a)** schrumpfen; ⟨Kleidung, Stoff:⟩ einlaufen; ⟨Metall, Holz:⟩ sich zusammenziehen **(b)** (recoil) ~ **from sb./sth.** vor jmdm. zurückweichen/vor etw. (Dat.) zurückschrecken; ~ **from doing sth.** sich scheuen, etw. zu tun ② v.t., **shrank, shrunk** einlaufen lassen ⟨Textilien⟩

**shrinkage** /'ʃrɪŋkɪdʒ/ n. (of clothing) Einlaufen, das

**shrink:** ~**-proof,** ~**-resistant** adjs. schrumpffrei; **be** ~**-proof** nicht einlaufen; ~**-wrap** v.t. in einer Schrumpffolie verpacken

**shrivel** /'ʃrɪvl/ v.i., (Brit.) -ll-: ~ [**up**] verschrumpeln; ⟨Pflanze, Blume:⟩ welk werden

**shroud** /ʃraʊd/ ① n. Leichentuch, das ② v.t. ~ **sth. in sth.** etw. in etw. (Akk.) hüllen

**Shrove 'Tuesday** /ʃrəʊv/ n. Fastnachtsdienstag, der

**shrub** /ʃrʌb/ n. Strauch, der

**shrubbery** /'ʃrʌbərɪ/ n. Gesträuch, das

**shrug** /ʃrʌg/ ① v.t. & i., -gg-: ~ [**one's shoulders**] die Achseln zucken ② n. ~ [**of one's** or **the shoulders**] Achselzucken, das

■ **shrug 'off** v.t. in den Wind schlagen

**shrunk** ▶ SHRINK

**shrunken** /'ʃrʌŋkn/ adj. verhutzelt (ugs.) ⟨Person⟩; schrump[e]lig ⟨Apfel⟩

**shudder** /'ʃʌdə(r)/ ① v.i. zittern (**with** vor + Dat.) ② n. Zittern, das

**shuffle** /'ʃʌfl/ ① n. **(a)** Schlurfen, das; **walk with a** ~: schlurfen **(b)** (Cards) Mischen, das; **give the cards a** [**good**] ~: die Karten [gut] mischen ② v.t. **(a)** (Cards) mischen

S

**(b)** ~ **one's feet** von einem Fuß auf den anderen treten

**shun** /ʃʌn/ *v.t.*, **-nn-** meiden

**shunt** /ʃʌnt/ *v.t.* (Railw.) rangieren

**shush** /ʃʊʃ/ *int.* still

**shut** /ʃʌt/ 1 *v.t.*, **-tt-**, **shut** zumachen; schließen; zusammenklappen ⟨*Klappmesser, Fächer*⟩; ~ **one's finger in the door** sich (*Dat.*) den Finger in der Tür einklemmen 2 *v.i.*, **-tt-**, **shut** schließen; ⟨*Blüte:*⟩ sich schließen

■ **shut 'down** 1 *v.t.* **(a)** schließen, zumachen ⟨*Deckel*⟩ **(b)** stilllegen ⟨*Fabrik*⟩; abschalten ⟨*Kernreaktor*⟩ 2 *v.i.* ⟨*Laden, Fabrik:*⟩ geschlossen werden

■ **shut 'out** *v.t.* aussperren

■ **shut 'up** 1 *v.t.* abschließen; einsperren ⟨*Tier, Person*⟩ 2 *v.i.* (coll.: be quiet) den Mund halten

**shutter** /'ʃʌtə(r)/ *n.* **(a)** [Fenster]laden, *der* **(b)** (Photog.) Verschluss, *der;* ~ **release** Auslöser, *der;* ~ **speed** Verschlusszeit, *die*

**shuttle** /'ʃʌtl/ 1 *n.* (in loom) Schiffchen, *das* 2 *v.i.* pendeln

**shuttle:** ~**cock** *n.* Federball, *der;* '~ **service** *n.* Pendelverkehr, *der*

**shy** /ʃaɪ/ *adj.*, ~**er** *or* **shier** /'ʃaɪə(r)/, ~**est** *or* **shiest** /'ʃaɪɪst/ scheu; (diffident) schüchtern

■ **shy a'way** *v.i.* ~ **away from sth./doing sth.** etw. scheuen/sich scheuen, etw. zu tun

**'shyness** *n.* Scheuheit, *die;* (diffidence) Schüchternheit, *die*

**Siamese** /saɪə'miːz/: ~ **'cat** *n.* Siamkatze, *die;* ~ **'twins** *n. pl.* siamesische Zwillinge *Pl.*

**Siberia** /saɪ'bɪərɪə/ *pr. n.* Sibirien (*das*)

**sibling** /'sɪblɪŋ/ *n.* (male) Bruder, *der;* (female) Schwester, *die; in pl.* Geschwister *Pl.*

**Sicily** /'sɪsɪlɪ/ *pr. n.* Sizilien (*das*)

**sick** /sɪk/ 1 *adj.* **(a)** (ill) krank; **be off** ~: krank [gemeldet] sein **(b)** (Brit.: vomiting or about to vomit) **be** ~: sich erbrechen; **I'm going to be** ~: ich muss mich erbrechen; **sb. gets/feels** ~: jmdm. wird/ist [es] übel *od.* schlecht; **be/get** ~ **of sb./sth.** (fig.) jmdn./etw. satt haben/ allmählich satt haben; **make sb.** ~ (disgust) jmdn. anekeln 2 *n. pl.* **the** ~: die Kranken *Pl.*

**sick 'building syndrome** *n.* Sickbuildingsyndrom, *das*

**'sicken** /'sɪkn/ 1 *v.i.* **be** ~**ing for sth.** (Brit.) krank werden; (fig. ausbrüten (ugs.) 2 *v.t.* (disgust) anwidern

**'sickening** *adj.* Ekel erregend, widerlich ⟨*Anblick, Geruch*⟩

**sickle** /'sɪkl/ *n.* Sichel, *die*

**sick:** ~ **leave** *n.* Urlaub wegen Krankheit; **be on** ~ ≈ krank geschrieben sein; ~ **list** *n.* Liste der Kranken, *die;* **on the** ~ **list:** krank [gemeldet/geschrieben]

**'sickly** *adj.* kränklich

**'sickness** *n.* Krankheit, *die;* (nausea) Übelkeit, *die*

**sick:** ~ **pay** *n.* Entgeltfortzahlung im Krankheitsfalle; (paid by insurance) Krankengeld, *das;* ~**room** *n.* Krankenzimmer, *das*

**side** /saɪd/ 1 *n.* **(a)** Seite, *die;* ~ **of beef** Rinderhälfte, *die;* ~ **of bacon** Speckseite, *die;* **walk/stand** ~ **by** ~: nebeneinander gehen/stehen; **work/fight** ~ **by** ~ [**with sb.**] Seite an Seite [mit jmdm.] arbeiten/ kämpfen; **live** ~ **by** ~ [**with sb.**] in [jmds.] unmittelbarer Nachbarschaft leben; **to one** ~: zur Seite; **on one** ~: an der Seite; **on the** ~ (as ~line) nebenbei; **take** ~**s** [**with/against sb.**] [für/gegen jmdn.] Partei ergreifen **(b)** (Sport: team) Mannschaft, *die* 2 *v.i.* ~ **with sb.** sich auf jmds. Seite (*Akk.*) stellen 3 *adj.* Seiten-

**side:** ~**board** *n.* Anrichte, *die;* ~**boards** (coll.), ~**burns** *ns. pl.* (on cheeks) Backenbart, *der;* (in front of the ears) Koteletten *Pl.;* ~**car** *n.* Beiwagen, *der;* ~ **dish** *n.* Beilage, *die;* ~ **door** *n.* Seitentür, *die;* ~ **effect** *n.* Nebenwirkung, *die;* ~ **entrance** *n.* Seiteneingang, *der;* ~ **exit** *n.* Seitenausgang, *der;* ~ **issue** *n.* Randproblem, *das;* ~**kick** *n.* (coll.) Kumpan, *der;* ~**light** *n.* Begrenzungsleuchte, *die;* **drive on** ~**lights** mit Standlicht fahren; ~**line** *n.* (occupation) Nebenbeschäftigung, *die;* ~**long** *adj.* **a** ~**long look/glance** ein Seitenblick; ~ **plate** *n.* kleiner Teller (neben dem Teller für das Hauptgericht); ~ **road** *n.* Seitenstraße, *die;* ~**saddle** *adv.* **ride** ~**saddle** im Damensitz reiten; ~ **salad** *n.* Salat [als Beilage]; **steak with chips and a** ~ **salad** Steak mit Pommes frites und dazu ein Salat; ~**show** *n.* Nebenattraktion, *die;* ~**step** 1 *n.* Schritt zur Seite; 2 *v.t.* ausweichen (+ *Dat.*); ~ **street** *n.* Seitenstraße, *die;* ~ **table** *n.* Beistelltisch, *der;* ~**track** *v.t.* **get** ~**tracked** abgelenkt werden; ~**walk** *n.* (Amer.) Bürgersteig, *der;* ~**ways** /'saɪdweɪz/ 1 *adv.* **look at sb./sth.** ~**ways** jmdn./etw. von der Seite ansehen; 2 *adj.* seitlich; ~ **wind** *n.* Seitenwind, *der*

**siding** /'saɪdɪŋ/ *n.* Abstellgleis, *das*

**sidle** /'saɪdl/ *v.i.* schleichen [**up to** zu]

**siege** /siːdʒ/ *n.* Belagerung, *die;* (by police) Umstellung, *die;* **lay** ~ **to sth.** etw. belagern

**siesta** /sɪ'estə/ *n.* Siesta, *die*

**sieve** /sɪv/ 1 *n.* Sieb, *das* 2 *v.t.* sieben

**sift** /sɪft/ *v.t.* sieben; ~ **sth. from sth.** etw. von etw. trennen

■ **sift 'out** *v.t.* aussieben

**sigh** /saɪ/ 1 *n.* Seufzer, *der;* **breathe** *or* **give** *or* **heave a** ~: einen Seufzer ausstoßen; ~ **of relief/contentment** Seufzer der Erleichterung/Zufriedenheit 2 *v.i.* seufzen; ~ **with relief/despair** erleichtert/verzweifelt seufzen

**S**

**sight** /saɪt/ ⊡ n. (a) (faculty) Sehvermögen, *das;* **know sb. by** ∼: jmdn. vom Sehen kennen
(b) (act of seeing; spectacle) Anblick, *der;* **catch/ lose** ∼ **of sb./sth.** jmdn./etw. erblicken/aus dem Auge verlieren; **at first** ∼: auf den ersten Blick
(c) *in pl.* ∼s ( places of interest) Sehenswürdigkeiten *Pl.;* **see the** ∼s die Sehenswürdigkeiten besichtigen
(d) (range) Sichtweite, *die;* **in** ∼: in Sicht; **within** *or* **in** ∼ **of sb./sth.** (able to see) in jmds. Sichtweite (*Dat.*)/in Sichtweite einer Sache; **out of** ∼: außer Sicht
(e) (of gun) Visier, *das;* **set/have [set] one's** ∼s **on sth.** (fig.) etw. anpeilen
⊡ v.t. sichten ⟨*Land, Schiff, Flugzeug*⟩; sehen ⟨*Entflohenen, Vermissten*⟩

**sighted** /'saɪtɪd/ adj. sehend; **partially** ∼: [hochgradig] sehbehindert

**'sighting** n. Beobachtung, *die*

**sight-read** (Mus.) v.t. & i. ⟨*Pianist usw.:*⟩ vom Blatt spielen; ⟨*Sänger:*⟩ vom Blatt singen

**'sightseeing** n. **go** ∼: Besichtigungen machen

**sightseer** /'saɪtsiːə(r)/ n. Tourist (*der die Sehenswürdigkeiten besichtigt*)

**sign** /saɪn/ ⊡ n. (a) (symbol, signal, indication) Zeichen, *das;* (of future event) Anzeichen, *das;* **as a** ∼ **of** als Zeichen (+ *Gen.*)
(b) (Astrol.) ∼ **[of the zodiac]** Sternzeichen, *das*
(c) (notice; on shop etc.) Schild, *das*
⊡ v.t. & i. unterschreiben; ∼ **one's name** [mit seinem Namen] unterschreiben

▪ **sign 'on** v.i. (as unemployed) sich arbeitslos melden

▪ **sign 'up** v.i. sich [vertraglich] verpflichten (**with** bei); (for course) sich einschreiben

**signal** /'sɪgnl/ ⊡ n. Signal, *das;* **a** ∼ **for sth./to sb.** ein Zeichen zu etw./für jmdn
⊡ v.i., (Brit.) **-ll-** signalisieren; Signale geben; ⟨*Kraftfahrer:*⟩ blinken; (with hand) anzeigen; ∼ **to sb. [to do sth.]** jmdm. ein Zeichen geben[, etw. zu tun]

**signal:** ∼ **box** n. Stellwerk, *das;* ∼ **man** /-mən/ n. Bahnwärter, *der*

**signature** /'sɪgnətʃə(r)/ n. Unterschrift, *die;* (on painting) Signatur, *die*

**'signature tune** n. Erkennungsmelodie, *die*

**'signboard** n. Schild, *das*

**signet ring** /'sɪgnɪt rɪŋ/ n. Siegelring, *der*

**significance** /sɪg'nɪfɪkəns/ n. Bedeutung, *die;* **be of [no]** ∼: [nicht] von Bedeutung sein

**significant** /sɪg'nɪfɪkənt/ adj. (a) (noteworthy, important) bedeutend
(b) (full of meaning) bedeutsam

**sig'nificantly** adv. (a) (meaningfully) bedeutungsvoll; ∼ **[enough]** bedeutsamerweise
(b) (notably) bedeutend

**signify** /'sɪgnɪfaɪ/ v.t. bedeuten

**sign:** ∼ **language** n. Zeichensprache, *die;* ∼**post** n. Wegweiser, *der;* ∼**writer** n. Schildermaler, *der*

**Sikh** /siːk, sɪk/ n. Sikh, *der*

**silence** /'saɪləns/ ⊡ n. Schweigen, *das;* (keeping a secret) Verschwiegenheit, *die;* (stillness) Stille, *die;* **there was** ∼: es herrschte Schweigen/Stille; **in** ∼: schweigend
⊡ v.t. zum Schweigen bringen; (fig.) ersticken ⟨*Proteste*⟩; mundtot machen ⟨*Gegner*⟩

**'silencer** n. (on gun; Brit. Motor Veh.) Schalldämpfer, *der*

**silent** /'saɪlənt/ adj. stumm; (noiseless) unhörbar; (still) still; **be** ∼ (say nothing) schweigen; ∼ **film** Stummfilm, *der*

**'silently** adv. schweigend; stumm ⟨*weinen, beten*⟩; (noiselessly) lautlos

**silent ma'jority** n. schweigende Mehrheit

**silhouette** /sɪlʊ'et/ ⊡ n. (a) ( picture) Schattenriss, *der*
(b) (appearance against the light) Silhouette, *die*
⊡ v.t. **be** ∼**d against sth.** sich als Silhouette gegen etw. abheben

**silicon** /'sɪlɪkən/ n. Silicium, *das;* ∼ **chip** Siliciumchip, *der*

**silicone** /'sɪlɪkəʊn/ n. Silikon, *das;* ∼ **[breast] implant** Silikon[brust]implantat, *das*

**silk** /sɪlk/ ⊡ n. Seide, *die*
⊡ attrib. adj. seiden; Seiden-

**'silkworm** n. Seidenraupe, *die*

**'silky** adj. seidig

**sill** /sɪl/ n. (of door) [Tür]schwelle, *die;* (of window) Fensterbank, *die*

**silly** /'sɪlɪ/ adj. dumm; (imprudent, unwise) töricht; (childish) albern

**silo** /'saɪləʊ/ n., pl. ∼s Silo, *der*

**silt** /sɪlt/ n. Schlamm, *der;* Schlick, *der*

**silver** /'sɪlvə(r)/ ⊡ n. Silber, *das*
⊡ attrib. adj. silbern; Silber⟨*pokal, -münze*⟩

**silver:** ∼ **'jubilee** n. silbernes Jubiläum; ∼ **'medal** n. Silbermedaille, *die;* ∼ **'paper** n. Silberpapier, *das;* ∼**plated** adj. versilbert; ∼**smith** n. Silberschmied, *der/*-schmiedin, *die;* ∼ **'wedding** n. Silberhochzeit, *die*

**similar** /'sɪmɪlə(r)/ adj. ähnlich (**to** *Dat.*)

**similarity** /sɪmɪ'lærɪtɪ/ n. Ähnlichkeit, *die* (**to** mit)

**'similarly** adv. ähnlich; (in exactly the same way) ebenso

**simile** /'sɪmɪlɪ/ n. Vergleich, *der*

**simmer** /'sɪmə(r)/ ⊡ v.i. ⟨*Flüssigkeit:*⟩ sieden; ziehen
⊡ v.t. köcheln *od.* ziehen lassen

▪ **simmer 'down** v.i. sich abregen (ugs.)

**simper** /'sɪmpə(r)/ v.i. affektiert *od.* gekünstelt lächeln

**simple** /'sɪmpl/ adj. einfach; (unsophisticated, not elaborate) schlicht ⟨*Mobiliar, Schönheit,*

*Kunstwerk, Kleidung*); **it was a ~ misunderstanding** es war [ganz] einfach ein Missverständnis

**'simple-minded** *adj.* **(a)** (unsophisticated) schlicht
**(b)** (unintelligent) beschränkt

**simpleton** /'sɪmpltən/ *n.* Einfaltspinsel, *der* (ugs.)

**simplicity** /sɪm'plɪsɪtɪ/ *n.* Einfachheit, *die;* (unpretentiousness, lack of sophistication) Schlichtheit, *die*

**simplification** /sɪmplɪfɪ'keɪʃn/ *n.* Vereinfachung, *die*

**simplify** /'sɪmplɪfaɪ/ *v.t.* vereinfachen

**simplistic** /sɪm'plɪstɪk/ *adj.* [all]zu simpel

**simply** /'sɪmplɪ/ *adv.* einfach; (in an unsophisticated manner) schlicht; (merely) nur; **it ~ isn't true** es ist einfach nicht wahr; **I was ~ trying to help** ich wollte nur helfen

**simulate** /'sɪmjʊleɪt/ *v.t.* **(a)** (feign) vortäuschen
**(b)** simulieren ⟨*Bedingungen, Wetter usw.*⟩

**simulation** /sɪmjʊ'leɪʃn/ *n.* **(a)** (feigning) Vortäuschung, *die*
**(b)** (imitation of conditions) Simulation, *die*
**(c)** (simulated object) Imitation, *die*

**simulator** /'sɪmjʊleɪtə(r)/ *n.* Simulator, *der*

**simultaneous** /sɪml'teɪnɪəs/ *adj.,* **simul'taneously** *adv.* gleichzeitig

**sin** /sɪn/ **1** *n.* Sünde, *die*
**2** *v.i.,* **-nn-** sündigen

**since** /sɪns/ **1** *adv.* seitdem
**2** *prep.* seit; **I have/had been waiting ~** 8 o'clock ich warte/wartete [schon] seit 8 Uhr; **he has lived here ~** his childhood er wohnt seit seiner Kindheit hier; **~ seeing you** ...: seit ich dich gesehen habe; **~ then/ that time** inzwischen
**3** *conj.* **(a)** seit; **it is a long time/so long/not so long ~** ...: es ist lange/so lange/gar nicht lange her, dass ...
**(b)** (seeing that, as) da

**sincere** /sɪn'sɪə(r)/ *adj.,* **~r** /sɪn'sɪərə(r)/, **~st** /sɪn'sɪərɪst/ aufrichtig; herzlich ⟨*Grüße, Glückwünsche usw.*⟩

**sin'cerely** *adv.* aufrichtig; **yours ~:** mit freundlichen Grüßen

**sincerity** /sɪn'serɪtɪ/ *n.* Aufrichtigkeit, *die*

**sinew** /'sɪnjuː/ *n.* Sehne, *die*

**sinful** /'sɪnfl/ *adj.* sündig; (reprehensible) sündhaft; **it is ~ to** ...: es ist eine Sünde, zu ...

**sing** /sɪŋ/ *v.i. & t.,* **sang** /sæŋ/, **sung** /sʌŋ/ singen
■ **sing 'up** *v.i.* lauter singen

**singe** /sɪndʒ/ *v.t. & i.,* **~ing** versengen

**singer** /'sɪŋə(r)/ *n.* Sänger, *der*/Sängerin, *die*

**single** /'sɪŋgl/ **1** *adj.* **(a)** einfach; (sole) einzig; (separate, individual, isolated) einzeln; **not a ~ one** kein Einziger/keine Einzige/kein

Einziges; **every ~ one** jeder/jede/jedes Einzelne; **every ~ day** jeden Tag; **~ ticket** (Brit.) einfache Fahrkarte
**(b)** (for one person) Einzel⟨*bett, -zimmer*⟩
**(c)** (unmarried) ledig; **a ~ man/woman** ein Lediger/eine Ledige; **~ people** Ledige *Pl.*; **~ parent** allein erziehendes Elternteil; **~ mother** allein erziehende *od.* stehende Mutter
**2** *n.* **(a)** (Brit.: ticket) einfache Fahrkarte; **[a] ~/two ~s to Manchester, please** einmal/ zweimal einfach nach Manchester, bitte
**(b)** (record) Single, *die*
**(c)** *in pl.* (Tennis etc.) Einzel, *das*
■ **single 'out** *v.t.* **~ sb./sth. out as/for sth.** jmdn./etw. als/für etw. auswählen

**single: ~ cream** *n.* [einfache] Sahne; **~ 'currency** *n.* Einheitswährung, *die;* **~-decker** **1** *n.* Bus/Straßenbahn mit nur einem Deck; **be a ~-decker** ⟨*Bus, Straßenbahn:*⟩ nur ein Deck haben; **2** *adj.* **~-decker bus/tram** Bus/Straßenbahn mit [nur] einem Deck; **~ [European] market** *n.* [europäischer] Binnenmarkt; **~-'handed** *adv.* allein; **~-lens 'reflex camera** *n.* (Photog.) einäugige Spiegelreflexkamera; **~-minded** *adj.* zielstrebig; **~-mindedly** /sɪŋgl'maɪndɪdlɪ/ *adv.* zielstrebig; **~-sex** *adj.* **~ school** reine Mädchen-/Jungenschule

**'singles bar** *n.* Singlekneipe, *die*

**'single-storey** *adj.* eingeschossig

**singlet** /'sɪŋglɪt/ *n.* (Brit.) (vest) Unterhemd, *das;* (Sport) Trikot, *das*

**singly** /'sɪŋglɪ/ *adv.* einzeln

**singular** /'sɪŋgjʊlə(r)/ **1** *adj.* **(a)** (Ling.) singularisch; Singular-; **~ noun** Substantiv im Singular
**(b)** (extraordinary) einmalig
**2** *n.* (Ling.) Einzahl, *die;* Singular, *der*

**'singularly** *adv.* (extraordinarily) außerordentlich

**sinister** /'sɪnɪstə(r)/ *adj.* finster; (of evil omen) Unheil verkündend

**sink** /sɪŋk/ **1** *n.* Spülbecken, *das*
**2** *v.i.,* **sank** /sæŋk/ *or* **sunk** /sʌŋk/, **sunk** sinken
**3** *v.t.,* **sank** *or* **sunk**, **sunk (a)** versenken ⟨*Schiff*⟩
**(b)** niederbringen ⟨*Schacht*⟩
■ **sink 'in** *v.i.* (fig.) jmdm. ins Bewusstsein dringen; ⟨*Warnung, Lektion:*⟩ verstanden werden

**'sink unit** *n.* Spüle, *die*

**'sinner** *n.* Sünder, *der*/Sünderin, *die*

**sinus** /'saɪnəs/ *n.* Nebenhöhle, *die*

**sinusitis** /saɪnə'saɪtɪs/ *n.* Nebenhöhlenentzündung, *die*

**sip** /sɪp/ **1** *v.t.,* **-pp-: ~ [up]** schlürfen
**2** *v.i.,* **-pp-: ~ at/from sth.** an etw. (*Dat.*) nippen
**3** *n.* Schlückchen, *das*

**siphon** /'saɪfn/ **1** *n.* Siphon, *der* ⋯⧫

**2** *v.t.* [durch einen Saugheber] laufen lassen

**sir** /sɜː(r)/ *n.* **(a)** (formal address) der Herr; (to teacher) Herr Meier/Schmidt *usw.*
**(b)** (in letter) **Dear Sir** Sehr geehrter Herr; **Dear Sirs** Sehr geehrte [Damen und] Herren; **Dear Sir or Madam** Sehr geehrte Dame/Sehr geehrter Herr
**(c) Sir** /sə(r)/ (title of knight etc.) Sir

**siren** /'saɪrən/ *n.* Sirene, *die*

**sirloin** /'sɜːlɔɪn/ *n.* **(a)** (Brit.) Roastbeef, *das;* ∼ **steak** Rumpsteak, *das*
**(b)** (Amer.) Rumpsteak, *das*

**sissy** /'sɪsɪ/ **1** *n.* Waschlappen, *der*
**2** *adj.* feige

**sister** /'sɪstə(r)/ *n.* **(a)** Schwester, *die*
**(b)** (Brit.: nurse) Oberschwester, *die*

**'sister-in-law** *n., pl.* **sisters-in-law** Schwägerin, *die*

**sisterly** /'sɪstəlɪ/ *adj.* schwesterlich

**sit** /sɪt/ **1** *v.i.,* **-tt-, sat** /sæt/ **(a)** (become seated) sich setzen; ∼ **on** a chair/**in** an armchair sich auf einen Stuhl/in einen Sessel setzen
**(b)** (be seated) sitzen
**2** *v.t.,* **-tt-, sat (a)** setzen
**(b)** (Brit.) machen ⟨*Prüfung*⟩

■ **sit 'back** *v.i.* sich zurücklehnen; (fig.) sich im Sessel zurücklehnen

■ **sit 'down** *v.i.* **(a)** (become seated) sich setzen (**on/in** auf/in + *Akk.*)
**(b)** (be seated) sitzen

■ **sit 'up 1** *v.i.* **(a)** (rise) sich aufsetzen
**(b)** (be sitting erect) [aufrecht] sitzen
**(c)** (stay up) aufbleiben
**2** *v.t.* aufsetzen

**sitcom** /'sɪtkɒm/ (coll.) ▶ SITUATION COMEDY

**site** /saɪt/ **1** *n.* **(a)** (land) Grundstück, *das*
**(b)** (location) Sitz, *der;* (of new factory etc.) Standort, *der*
**2** *v.t.* stationieren ⟨*Raketen*⟩; ∼ a factory in London London als Standort einer Fabrik wählen; be ∼d gelegen sein

**siting** /'saɪtɪŋ/ *n.* Standortwahl, *die* (of für); (position) Lage, *die*

**sitter** /'sɪtə(r)/ ▶ BABYSITTER

**'sitting** *n.* Sitzung, *die;* the first ∼ [for lunch] der erste Schub [zum Mittagessen]

**sitting:** ∼ **'duck** *n.* (fig.) leichtes Ziel; ∼ **room** *n.* Wohnzimmer, *das;* ∼ **'target** ▶ ∼ DUCK

**situate** /'sɪtjʊeɪt/ *v.t.* legen

**'situated** *adj.* gelegen; be ∼: liegen

**situation** /sɪtjʊ'eɪʃn/ *n.* **(a)** (location) Lage, *die*
**(b)** (circumstances) Situation, *die*
**(c)** (job) Stelle, *die*

**situation 'comedy** *n.* Situationskomödie, *die*

**six** /sɪks/ **1** *adj.* sechs
**2** *n.* Sechs, *die.* See also EIGHT

**six:** ∼ **'footer** *n.* (person) Zweimetermann, *der/*-frau, *die;* ∼**-pack** *n.* Sechserpack, *der*

**sixteen** /sɪks'tiːn/ **1** *adj.* sechzehn

**2** *n.* Sechzehn, *die.* See also EIGHT

**sixteenth** /sɪks'tiːnθ/ **1** *adj.* sechzehnt...
**2** *n.* (fraction) Sechzehntel, *das.* See also EIGHTH

**sixth** /sɪksθ/ **1** *adj.* sechst...
**2** *n.* (in sequence, rank) Sechste, *der/die/das;* (fraction) Sechstel, *das.* See also EIGHTH

**sixth:** ∼ **form** *n.* (Brit. Sch.) ≈ zwölfte/dreizehnte Klasse; ∼**-form college** *n.* (Brit. Sch.) ≈ Oberstufenzentrum, *das; College, das nur Schüler der zwölften/dreizehnten Klasse aufnimmt;* ∼**-former** *n.* (Brit. Sch.) Schüler/Schülerin der zwölften/dreizehnten Klasse; ∼ **'sense** *n.* sechster Sinn

**sixtieth** /'sɪkstɪɪθ/ *adj.* sechzigst...

**sixty** /'sɪkstɪ/ **1** *adj.* sechzig
**2** *n.* Sechzig, *die.* See also EIGHT; EIGHTY 2

**size** /saɪz/ *n.* Größe, *die;* (of paper) Format, *das;* **be twice the** ∼ **of sth.** zweimal so groß wie etw. sein; **a** ∼ **8 dress** ein Kleid [in] Größe 8; **be** ∼ **8** ⟨*Person:*⟩ Größe 8 haben

■ **size 'up** *v.t.* taxieren ⟨*Lage*⟩

**sizeable** /'saɪzəbl/ *adj.* ziemlich groß; beträchtlich ⟨*Summe, Einfluss*⟩

**sizzle** /'sɪzl/ *v.i.* zischen

**skate** **1** *n.* (ice ∼) Schlittschuh, *der;* (roller ∼) Rollschuh, *der*
**2** *v.i.* (ice-∼) Schlittschuh laufen; (roller-∼) Rollschuh laufen

**'skateboard 1** *n.* Skateboard, *das;* Rollerbrett, *das*
**2** *v.i.* Skateboard fahren

**'skateboarder** *n.* Skateboardfahrer, *der/*-fahrerin, *die*

**'skateboarding** *n.* Skateboardfahren, *das*

**'skater** *n.* (ice ∼) Eisläufer, *der/*-läuferin, *die;* (roller ∼) Rollschuhläufer, *der/*-läuferin, *die*

**skating** /'skeɪtɪŋ/ *n.* (ice ∼) Schlittschuhlaufen, *das;* (roller ∼) Rollschuhlaufen, *das*

**'skating rink** *n.* (ice) Eisbahn, *die;* (for roller skating) Rollschuhbahn, *die*

**skeleton** /'skelɪtn/ *n.* Skelett, *das*

**skeleton:** ∼ **'key** *n.* Dietrich, *der;* ∼ **'staff** *n.* Minimalbesetzung, *die*

**skeptic** *etc.* (Amer.) ▶ SCEPTIC *etc.*

**sketch** /sketʃ/ **1** *n.* **(a)** (drawing) Skizze, *die*
**(b)** (play) Sketch, *der*
**2** *v.t.* skizzieren

**sketch:** ∼**book** *n.* Skizzenbuch, *das;* ∼ **map** *n.* Faustskizze, *die*

**'sketchy** *adj.* skizzenhaft; lückenhaft ⟨*Informationen, Bericht*⟩

**skew** /skjuː/ **1** *adj.* schräg
**2** *n.* **on the** ∼: schief

**skewer** /'skjuːə(r)/ **1** *n.* Bratspieß, *der*
**2** *v.t.* aufspießen

**ski** /skiː/ **1** *n.* **(a)** Ski, *der*
**(b)** (on vehicle) Kufe, *die*
**2** *v.i.* Ski laufen od. fahren

**'ski boot** *n.* Skistiefel, *der*

**skid** /skɪd/ ① *v.i.*, **-dd-** schlittern; (from one side to the other; spinning round) schleudern ② *n.* Schlittern/Schleudern, *das*

**'skid marks** *n. pl.* Schleuderspur, *die*

**skier** /'skiːə(r)/ *n.* Skiläufer, *der*/-läuferin, *die*

**skiing** /'skiːɪŋ/ *n.* Skilaufen, *das;* (Sport) Skisport, *der*

**'ski jumping** *n.* Skispringen, *das*

**skilful** /'skɪlfl/ *adj.* geschickt; gewandt ‹*Redner*›; gut ‹*Beobachter, Lehrer*›

**'ski lift** *n.* Skilift, *der*

**skill** /skɪl/ *n.* (a) (expertness) Geschick, *das;* (of artist) Können, *das* (b) (technique) Fertigkeit, *die;* (of weaving, bricklaying) Technik, *die*

**skilled** /'skɪld/ *adj.* (a) ▶ SKILFUL (b) qualifiziert ‹*Arbeit, Tätigkeit*›; ∼ **trade** Ausbildungsberuf, *der* (c) (trained) ausgebildet

**'skillful** (Amer.) ▶ SKILFUL

**skim** /skɪm/ *v.t.*, **-mm-**: (a) (remove) abschöpfen (b) abrahmen ‹*Milch*› (c) ▶ ∼ THROUGH ■ **skim 'off** *v.t.* abschöpfen ■ **'skim through** *v.t.* überfliegen ‹*Buch, Zeitung*›

**skimmed 'milk** *n.* entrahmte Milch

**skimp** /skɪmp/ ① *v.t.* sparen an (+ *Dat.*) ② *v.i.* sparen (**with,** on an + *Dat.*)

**'skimpy** *adj.* winzig ‹*Badeanzug*›; spärlich ‹*Wissen*›

**skin** /skɪn/ ① *n.* (a) Haut, *die* (b) (fur) Fell, *das* (c) (peel) Schale, *die* ② *v.t.*, **-nn-** häuten; schälen ‹*Frucht*›

**skin:** ∼ **cancer** *n.* Hautkrebs, *der;* ∼ **colour** *n.* Hautfarbe, *die;* ∼ **cream** *n.* Hautcreme, *die;* ∼**'deep** *adj.* (fig.) oberflächlich; ∼ **disease** *n.* Hautkrankheit, *die;* ∼ **diver** *n.* Taucher, *der*/Taucherin, *die;* ∼ **diving** *n.* Tauchen, *das;* ∼**flint** *n.* Geizhals, *der;* ∼ **graft** *n.* Hauttransplantation, *die;* ∼**head** *n.* Skinhead, *der*

**skinny** /'skɪnɪ/ *adj.* mager

**skint** /skɪnt/ *adj.* (Brit. coll.) **be** ∼: blank *od.* pleite sein (ugs.)

**'skin-tight** *adj.* hauteng

**skip¹** /skɪp/ ① *v.i.*, **-pp-**: (a) hüpfen (b) (with skipping rope) seilspringen ② *v.t.*, **-pp-** (omit) überspringen; ∼ **breakfast**/ **lunch** das Frühstück/Mittagessen auslassen ③ *n.* Hüpfer, *der*

**skip²** *n.* (Building) Container, *der*

**ski:** ∼ **pass** *n.* Skipass, *der;* ∼ **pole** *n.* Skistock, *der*

**skipper** /'skɪpə(r)/ *n.* Kapitän, *der*

**'skipping rope** (Brit.)**, 'skip rope** (Amer.) *ns.* Sprungseil, *das*

**'ski resort** *n.* Skiurlaubsort, *der*

**skirmish** /'skɜːmɪʃ/ *n.* (Mil.) Gefecht, *das*

**skirt** /skɜːt/ ① *n.* Rock, *der* ② *v.t.* herumgehen um ■ **skirt 'round** *v.t.* herumgehen um; (fig.) umgehen

**'skirting** *n.* ∼ **[board]** (Brit.) Fußleiste, *die*

**ski:** ∼ **run** *n.* Skihang, *der;* (prepared) [Ski]piste, *die;* ∼**stick** *n.* Skistock, *der*

**skittle** /'skɪtl/ *n.* (a) Kegel, *der* (b) ∼**s** *sing.* (game) Kegeln, *das*

**skive** /skaɪv/ *v.i.* (Brit. coll.) sich drücken (ugs.) ■ **skive 'off** (Brit. coll.) ① *v.i.* sich verdrücken (ugs.) ② *v.t.* schwänzen (ugs.)

**skulk** /skʌlk/ *v.i.* lauern

**skull** /skʌl/ *n.* Schädel, *der*

**skunk** /skʌŋk/ *n.* Stinktier, *das*

**sky** /skaɪ/ *n.* Himmel, *der;* **in the** ∼: am Himmel

**sky:** ∼**diving** *n.* Fallschirmspringen, *das* (als Sport); Fallschirmsport, *der;* ∼**-high** ① *adj.* himmelhoch; astronomisch (ugs.) ‹*Preise usw.*›; ② *adv.* **go** ∼**-high** ‹*Preise usw.*›: in astronomische Höhen klettern (ugs.); ∼**light** *n.* Dachfenster, *das;* ∼**line** *n.* Silhouette, *die;* (characteristic of certain town) Skyline, *die;* ∼**scraper** *n.* Wolkenkratzer, *der*

**slab** /slæb/ *n.* (a) (flat stone etc.) Platte, *die* (b) (thick slice) [dicke] Scheibe; (of cake) [dickes] Stück; (of chocolate, toffee) Tafel, *die*

**slack** /slæk/ ① *adj.* (a) (lax) nachlässig; schlampig (ugs.) (b) (loose) schlaff; locker ‹*Verband*› ② *n.* **take in** *or* **up the** ∼: das Seil/die Schnur *usw.* straffen ③ *v.i.* (coll.) bummeln (ugs.)

**slacken** /'slækn/ ① *v.i.* (a) (loosen) sich lockern (b) (diminish) nachlassen; ‹*Geschwindigkeit:*› sich verringern ② *v.t.* (a) (loosen) lockern (b) (diminish) verringern

**slacker** /'slækə(r)/ *n.* (derog.) Faulenzer, *der*/Faulenzerin, *die*

**slacks** /slæks/ *n. pl.* **[pair of]** ∼: lange Hose; Slacks *Pl.*

**slag** /slæg/ *n.* Schlacke, *die*

**slain** ▶ SLAY

**slake** /sleɪk/ *v.t.* löschen, stillen ‹*Durst*›

**slam** /slæm/ ① *v.t.*, **-mm-**: (a) (shut) zuschlagen (b) (put violently) knallen (ugs.) ② *v.i.*, **-mm-** zuschlagen

**slander** /'slɑːndə(r)/ ① *n.* Verleumdung, *die* (on *Gen.*) ② *v.t.* verleumden

**slanderous** /'slɑːndərəs/ *adj.* verleumderisch

**slang** /slæŋ/ n. Slang, der; ⟨Theater-, Soldaten-, Juristen⟩jargon, der; attrib. Slang⟨wort, -ausdruck⟩

'**slanging match** n. gegenseitige [lautstarke] Beschimpfung

**slangy** /'slæŋɪ/ adj. Slang⟨ausdruck, -wort⟩; salopp ⟨Wortwahl, Redeweise⟩

**slant** /slɑːnt/ **1** v.i. ⟨Fläche:⟩ sich neigen; ⟨Linie:⟩ schräg verlaufen
**2** v.t. **(a)** abschrägen
**(b)** (fig.: bias) [so] hinbiegen (ugs.) ⟨Meldung, Bemerkung⟩
**3** n. Schräge, die; on the or a ~: schräg

**slanting** /'slɑːntɪŋ/ adj. schräg

**slap** /slæp/ **1** v.t., -pp-: **(a)** schlagen
**(b)** (put) knallen (ugs.)
**2** v.i., -pp- schlagen; klatschen
**3** n. Schlag, der
**4** adv. voll; ~ **in the middle** genau in der Mitte

'**slapdash** adj. schludrig (ugs.)

'**slap-up** attrib. adj. (coll.) ⟨Essen⟩ mit allen Schikanen (ugs.)

**slash** /slæʃ/ **1** v.t. **(a)** aufschlitzen
**(b)** (fig.) [drastisch] reduzieren; [drastisch] kürzen ⟨Gehalt, Umfang⟩
**2** n. **(a)** (slit) Schlitz, der
**(b)** (~ing stroke) Hieb, der

**slat** /slæt/ n. Latte, die

**slate** /sleɪt/ **1** n. **(a)** (Geol.) Schiefer, der
**(b)** (Building) Schieferplatte, die
**2** v.t. (Brit. coll.: criticize) in der Luft zerreißen (ugs.)

**slaughter** /'slɔːtə(r)/ **1** n. Schlachten, das; (massacre) Gemetzel, das
**2** v.t. schlachten; (massacre) abschlachten

**slave** /sleɪv/ **1** n. Sklave, der/Sklavin, die
**2** v.i. ~ [away] schuften (ugs.); sich abplagen (at mit)

'**slave driver** n. (fig.) Sklaventreiber, der/-treiberin, die

**slavery** /'sleɪvərɪ/ n. Sklaverei, die

**slavish** /'sleɪvɪʃ/ adj. sklavisch

**slay** /sleɪ/ v.t., slew /sluː/, slain /sleɪn/ (literary) ermorden

**sleaze** /sliːz/ n. (derog.) Korruption, die

'**sleazebag**, '**sleazeball** ns. (sl. derog.) Drecksack, der (derb abwertend)

**sleazy** /'sliːzɪ/ adj. schäbig; (disreputable) anrüchig

**sled** /sled/, **sledge** /sledʒ/ ns. Schlitten, der

'**sledgehammer** n. Vorschlaghammer, der

**sleek** /sliːk/ adj. (glossy) seidig

**sleep** /sliːp/ **1** n. Schlaf, der; get/go to ~: einschlafen; put to ~: einschläfern ⟨Tier⟩
**2** v.i., slept /slept/ schlafen
**3** v.t. slept: the hotel ~s 80 das Hotel hat 80 Betten
■ **sleep a'round** v.i. (coll.) herumschlafen (ugs.)
■ **sleep 'in** v.i. im Bett bleiben

■ **sleep 'off** v.t. ausschlafen; ~ **it off** seinen Rausch ausschlafen
■ **sleep 'over** v.i. [auswärts] übernachten; our cousin was ~ing over unser Cousin übernachtete bei uns
■ **sleep together** v.i. (also coll. euphem.) miteinander schlafen
■ **sleep with** v.t. ~ **with sb.** (coll. euphem.) mit jmdm. schlafen

'**sleeper** n. **(a)** be a heavy/light ~: einen tiefen/leichten Schlaf haben
**(b)** (Brit. Railw.: support) Schwelle, die
**(c)** (Railw.) (coach) Schlafwagen, der; (train) [night] ~: Nachtzug mit Schlafwagen

**sleeping:** ~ **accommodation** n. Übernachtungsmöglichkeit, die; ~ **bag** n. Schlafsack, der; ~ **car** n. Schlafwagen, der; ~ '**partner** n. (Commerc.) stiller Teilhaber; ~ **pill,** ~ **tablet** ns. Schlaftablette, die

**sleep:** ~**less** adj. schlaflos; ~**walk** v.i. schlafwandeln; ~**walker** n. Schlafwandler, der/-wandlerin, die

'**sleepover** n. Übernachtung außer Haus od. bei anderen Leuten

'**sleepy** adj. schläfrig

**sleet** /sliːt/ **1** n. Schneeregen, der
**2** v.i. impers. **it is** ~**ing** es gibt Schneeregen

**sleeve** /sliːv/ n. **(a)** Ärmel, der; (fig.) have sth. up one's ~: etw. in petto haben (ugs.); roll up one's ~s die Ärmel hochkrempeln (ugs.)
**(b)** (for record) Hülle, die

'**sleeveless** adj. ärmellos

**sleigh** /sleɪ/ n. Schlitten, der

**sleight of 'hand** /slaɪt/ n. Fingerfertigkeit, die

**slender** /'slendə(r)/ adj. **(a)** (slim) schlank; schmal ⟨Buch, Band⟩
**(b)** gering ⟨Chance, Mittel, Hoffnung⟩

**slept** ▶ SLEEP 2, 3

**sleuth** /sluːθ/ n. Detektiv, der

**slew**[1] /sluː/ v.i. & t. schwenken

**slew**[2] ▶ SLAY

**slice** /slaɪs/ **1** n. Scheibe, die; (of apple, melon, peach, cake, pie) Stück, das; a ~ **of cake** ein Stück Kuchen
**2** v.t. in Scheiben schneiden; in Stücke schneiden ⟨Bohnen, Apfel, Kuchen usw.⟩; ~**d bread** Schnittbrot, das

**slick** /slɪk/ **1** adj. **(a)** (dexterous) professionell
**(b)** (pretentiously dexterous) clever (ugs.)
**2** n. [oil] ~: Ölteppich, der

**slid** ▶ SLIDE 1, 2

**slide** /slaɪd/ **1** v.i., slid /slɪd/ rutschen; ⟨Kolben, Schublade, Feder:⟩ gleiten
**2** v.t., slid schieben
**3** n. **(a)** (children's ~) Rutschbahn, die
**(b)** (Photog.) Dia[positiv], das

**slide:** ~ **film** n. Diafilm, der; ~ **projector** n. Diaprojektor, der; ~ **show** n. Diashow, die

**sliding door** /'slaɪdɪŋ/ n. Schiebetür, die

**slight** /slaɪt/ [1] *adj.* leicht; schwach ⟨*Hoffnung, Aussichten, Wirkung*⟩; **not in the ~est** nicht im Geringsten [2] *n.* Verunglimpfung, *die* (on *Gen.*); (lack of courtesy) Affront, *der* (on gegen)

**'slightly** *adv.* ein bisschen; leicht ⟨*verletzen, riechen nach, gewürzt sein, ansteigen*⟩; flüchtig ⟨*jmdn. kennen*⟩; oberflächlich ⟨*etw. kennen*⟩

**slim** /slɪm/ [1] *adj.* schlank; schmal ⟨*Band, Buch*⟩; schwach ⟨*Aussicht, Hoffnung*⟩; gering ⟨*Gewinn, Chancen*⟩ [2] *v.i.*, **-mm-** abnehmen

**slime** /slaɪm/ *n.* Schleim, *der*

**slimmer** /'slɪmə(r)/ *n.* (Brit.) *jmd., der etwas für die schlanke Linie tut;* **advice/a diet for ~s** Ratschläge *Pl.*/eine Diät zum Abnehmen

**slimming** /'slɪmɪŋ/ [1] *n.* Abnehmen, *das; attrib.* Schlankheits- [2] *adj.* schlank machend

**slimy** /'slaɪmɪ/ *adj.* schleimig

**sling** /slɪŋ/ [1] *n.* (Med.) Schlinge, *die* [2] *v.t.*, **slung** /slʌŋ/ (coll.: throw) schmeißen (ugs.)

**sling 'out** *v.t.* (coll.) wegschmeißen (ugs.); **~ sb. out** jmdn. rausschmeißen (ugs.)

**slink** /slɪŋk/ *v.i.*, **slunk** /slʌŋk/ schleichen
■ **slink a'way, slink 'off** *v.i.* davonschleichen

**slip** /slɪp/ [1] *v.i.*, **-pp-**: (a) (slide) rutschen; ⟨*Messer:*⟩ abrutschen; (and fall) ausrutschen (b) (escape) schlüpfen (c) (go) **~ to the butcher's** *etc.* [rasch] zum Fleischer *usw.* rüberspringen (ugs.) [2] *v.t.*, **-pp-**: (a) stecken; **~ the dress over one's head** das Kleid über den Kopf streifen (b) **~ sb.'s mind** *or* **memory** jmdm. entfallen [3] *n.* (a) (fall) **after his ~:** nachdem er ausgerutscht [und gestürzt] war (b) (mistake) Versehen, *das;* **~ of the tongue** Versprecher, *der* (c) (underwear) Unterrock, *der* (d) (piece of paper) Zettel, *der* (e) **give sb. the ~:** jmdm. entwischen (ugs.)
■ **slip a'way** *v.i.* (a) ⟨*Person:*⟩ sich fortschleichen (b) ⟨*Zeit:*⟩ verfliegen
■ **slip 'down** *v.i.* runterrutschen (ugs.)
■ **slip 'in** *v.i.* ⟨*Person:*⟩ sich hineinschleichen
■ **'slip into** *v.t.* schlüpfen in (+ *Akk.*) ⟨*Kleidungsstück*⟩
■ **slip 'off** [1] *v.i.* (a) runterrutschen (ugs.) (b) ▶ SLIP AWAY A [2] *v.t.* abstreifen ⟨*Schmuck, Handschuh*⟩; schlüpfen aus ⟨*Kleid, Schuh*⟩
■ **slip 'on** *v.t.* überstreifen ⟨*Handschuh, Ring*⟩; schlüpfen in (+ *Akk.*) ⟨*Kleid, Schuh*⟩
■ **slip 'out** *v.i.* ⟨*Person:*⟩ sich hinausschleichen
■ **slip 'over** *v.i.* (fall) ausrutschen
■ **slip 'up** *v.i.* (coll.) einen Schnitzer machen (ugs.)

**slipped 'disc** /slɪpt/ *n.* Bandscheibenvorfall, *der*

**'slipper** *n.* Hausschuh, *der*

**slippery** /'slɪpərɪ/ *adj.* schlüpfrig

**slippy** /'slɪpɪ/ (coll.) ▶ SLIPPERY

**slip: ~ road** *n.* (Brit.) (to motorway) Auffahrt, *die;* (from motorway) Ausfahrt, *die;* **~shod** *adj.* schludrig (ugs.); **~-up** *n.* (coll.) Schnitzer, *der*

**slit** /slɪt/ [1] *n.* Schlitz, *der* [2] *v.t.*, **-tt-**, **slit** aufschlitzen; **~ sb.'s throat** jmdm. die Kehle durchschneiden

**slither** /'slɪðə(r)/ *v.i.* rutschen

**sliver** /'slɪvə(r)/ *n.* Splitter, *der*

**slob** /slɒb/ *n.* (coll.) Schwein, *das* (derb)

**slobber** /'slɒbə(r)/ *v.i.* sabbern (ugs.)

**slog** /slɒg/ [1] *v.t.*, **-gg-** (in boxing, fight) voll treffen [2] *v.i.*, **-gg-** (work) schuften (ugs.) [3] *n.* (a) (hit) wuchtiger Schlag (b) (work) Plackerei, *die* (ugs.)

**slogan** /'sləʊgən/ *n.* Slogan, *der;* (advertising ~) Werbeslogan, *der*

**slop** /slɒp/ [1] *v.i.* schwappen (out of, from aus) [2] *v.t.* schwappen; (intentionally) kippen
■ **slop 'over** *v.i.* überschwappen

**slope** /sləʊp/ [1] *n.* (a) (slant) Neigung, *die* (b) (slanting ground) Hang, *der* [2] *v.i.* (slant) sich neigen; ⟨*Boden, Garten:*⟩ abschüssig sein; **~ downwards/upwards** ⟨*Straße:*⟩ abfallen/ansteigen
■ **slope a'way** *v.i.* abfallen
■ **slope 'off** *v.i.* (coll.) sich verdrücken (ugs.)

**sloppy** /'slɒpɪ/ *adj.* schludrig (ugs.)

**slosh** /slɒʃ/ *adj.* [1] *v.i.* platschen (ugs.); ⟨*Flüssigkeit:*⟩ schwappen [2] *v.t.* (coll.: pour clumsily) schwappen

**sloshed** /slɒʃt/ *adj.* (Brit. coll.) blau (ugs.)

**slot** /slɒt/ [1] *n.* (a) (hole) Schlitz, *der* (b) (groove) Nut, *die* [2] *v.t.*, **-tt-**: **~ sth. into place/sth.** etw. einfügen/in etw. (*Akk.*) einfügen
■ **slot 'in** [1] *v.t.* einfügen [2] *v.i.* sich einfügen
■ **slot to'gether** [1] *v.t.* zusammenfügen [2] *v.i.* (lit. or fig.) sich zusammenfügen

**sloth** /sləʊθ/ *n.* (a) (lethargy) Trägheit, *die* (b) (Zool.) Faultier, *das*

**'slot machine** *n.* Automat, *der;* (for gambling) Spielautomat, *der*

**slouch** /slaʊtʃ/ *v.i.* sich schlecht halten

**Slovak** /'sləʊvæk/ [1] *adj.* slowakisch; **sb. is ~:** jmd. ist Slowake/Slowakin [2] *n.* (a) (person) Slowake, *der*/Slowakin, *die* (b) (language) Slowakisch, *das; see also* ENGLISH 2A

**Slovakia** /slə'vɑːkɪə/ *pr. n.* Slowakei, *die*

**Slovene** /'sləʊviːn/ [1] *adj.* slowenisch; **sb. is ~:** jmd. ist Slowene/Slowenin [2] *n.* (a) (person) Slowene, *der*/Slowenin, *die* (b) (language) Slowenisch, *das*

**Slovenia** /slə'viːnɪə/ *pr. n.* Slowenien (*das*)

**S**

**Slovenian** /sləˈviːnɪən/ ▶ SLOVENE

**slovenly** /ˈslʌvnlɪ/ adj. schlampig (ugs.)

**slow** /sləʊ/ ① adj. langsam; langwierig ⟨Arbeit⟩; **be [ten minutes]** ~ ⟨Uhr:⟩ [zehn Minuten] nachgehen
② adv. langsam
③ v.i. langsamer werden; ~ **to a halt** anhalten
∎ **slow 'down, slow 'up** v.i. langsamer werden

**'slowcoach** n. Trödler, der/Trödlerin, die (ugs.)

**'slowly** adv. langsam

**slow 'motion** n. **in** ~: in Zeitlupe

**slowness** n. Langsamkeit, die

**slow:** ~ **'puncture** n. winziges Loch; ~ **train** n. Bummelzug, der (ugs.); ~**-witted** /sləʊˈwɪtɪd/ adj. [geistig] schwerfällig

**sludge** /slʌdʒ/ n. Schlamm, der

**slug** /slʌg/ n. Nacktschnecke, die

**sluggish** /ˈslʌgɪʃ/ adj. träge; schleppend ⟨Nachfrage⟩

**sluice** /sluːs/ ① n. Schütz, das
② v.t. ~ **[down]** abspritzen

**'sluice gate** n. Schütz, das

**slum** /slʌm/ n. Slum, der; (single house or apartment) Elendsquartier, das

**slumber** /ˈslʌmbə(r)/ (poet./rhet.) ① n. ~**[s]** Schlummer, der (geh.)
② v.i. schlummern (geh.)

**slump** /slʌmp/ ① n. Sturz, der (fig.); (in demand, investment, sales) starker Rückgang (in Gen.); (economic depression) Depression, die
② v.i. (a) (Commerc.) stark zurückgehen; ⟨Preise, Kurse:⟩ stürzen
(b) (collapse) ⟨Person:⟩ fallen; ~**ed in a chair** in einem Sessel zusammengesunken

**slung** ▶ SLING 2

**slunk** ▶ SLINK

**slur** /slɜː(r)/ ① v.t., **-rr-:** ~ **one's words/ speech** undeutlich sprechen
② n. Beleidigung, die (on für)

**slurp** /slɜːp/ (coll.) ① v.t. ~ **[up]** schlürfen
② n. Schlürfen, das

**slush** /slʌʃ/ n. Schneematsch, der

**'slush fund** n. Fonds, der für Bestechungsgelder

**'slushy** adj. (a) matschig
(b) (sloppy) sentimental

**slut** /slʌt/ n. Schlampe, die (ugs.)

**sly** /slaɪ/ ① adj. schlau; gerissen (ugs.) ⟨Geschäftsmann, Trick⟩; verschlagen ⟨Blick⟩
② n. **on the** ~: heimlich

**smack¹** /smæk/ ① n. (a) (sound) Klatsch, der
(b) (blow) Schlag, der; (on child's bottom) Klaps, der (ugs.)
② v.t. (a) [mit der flachen Hand] schlagen
(b) ~ **one's lips** [mit den Lippen] schmatzen
③ adv. (coll.) direkt

**smack²** v.i. ~ **of** schmecken nach; (fig.) riechen nach (ugs.)

**small** /smɔːl/ ① adj. klein; gering ⟨Wirkung, Appetit, Fähigkeit⟩; schmal ⟨Taille⟩; dünn ⟨Stimme⟩; **make sb. feel** ~: jmdn. beschämen
② n. ~ **of the back** Kreuz, das
③ adv. klein

**small:** ~ **ad** n. (coll.) Kleinanzeige, die; ~ **'change** n. Kleingeld, das; ~**holding** n. landwirtschaftlicher Kleinbetrieb; ~**'minded** adj. kleinlich; ~**pox** n. Pocken Pl.; ~ **'print** n. (lit. or fig.) Kleingedruckte, das

**smalls** /smɔːlz/ n. pl. (Brit. coll.) Unterwäsche, die

**small:** ~ **'screen** n. (Telev.) Bildschirm, der; ~ **talk** n. leichte Unterhaltung; (at parties) Smalltalk, der; **make** ~ **talk [with sb.]** [mit jmdm.] Konversation machen

**smarmy** /ˈsmɑːmɪ/ adj. (coll.) kriecherisch

**smart** /smɑːt/ ① adj. (a) (clever) clever; (ingenious) raffiniert
(b) (neat) schick; schön ⟨Haus, Garten, Auto⟩
(c) attrib. (fashionable) elegant; smart
② v.i. schmerzen

**smart:** ~ **alec[k]** /smɑːt ˈælɪk/ n. (coll.) Besserwisser, der/Besserwisserin, die; ~ **bomb** n. intelligente Bombe; ~ **card** n. Chipkarte, die; ~ **drug** n. Nootropikum, das

**smarten** /ˈsmɑːtn/ v.t. herrichten; ~ **oneself [up]** auf sein Äußeres achten

**'smartly** adv. (a) (cleverly) clever
(b) (neatly) schmuck ⟨[an]gestrichen⟩; smart, flott ⟨gekleidet, geschnitten⟩

**'smart money** n. **the** ~ **is on ...** Experten setzen auf ...

**smash** /smæʃ/ ① v.t. (a) zerschlagen
(b) ~ **sb. in the face/mouth** jmdm. [hart] ins Gesicht/auf den Mund schlagen
(c) (Tennis etc.) schmettern
② v.i. (a) zerbrechen
(b) (crash) krachen (**into** gegen)
③ n. (a) (sound) Krachen, das
(b) ▶ SMASH-UP
(c) (Tennis) Schmetterball, der
∎ **smash 'in** v.t. zerschmettern; einschlagen ⟨Tür, Schädel⟩
∎ **smash 'up** v.t. zertrümmern

**smash-and-'grab [raid]** n. (coll.) Schaufenstereinbruch, der

**smashed** /smæʃt/ adj. (sl.) (a) (drunk) **get** ~ **on sth.** von etw. besoffen werden (derb); **be** ~ **out of one's head** or **mind** or **brains** sturzbetrunken (ugs.) od. (derb) sturzbesoffen sein
(b) (on drugs) stoned (Drogenjargon)

**'smashing** adj. (coll.) toll (ugs.)

**'smash-up** n. schwerer Zusammenstoß

**smattering** /ˈsmætərɪŋ/ n. **[have] a** ~ **of** German etc. ein paar Brocken Deutsch usw. [können]

S

**smear** /smɪə(r)/ [1] *v.t.* **(a)** (daub)
beschmieren; ( put on or over) schmieren
**(b)** (smudge) verwischen
**(c)** (fig.) in den Schmutz ziehen
[2] *n.* **(a)** (blotch) [Schmutz]fleck, *der*
**(b)** (fig.) Beschmutzung, *die* (on *Gen.*)

**smear: ~ campaign** *n.*
Schmutzkampagne, *die;* ~ **tactics** *n. pl.*
schmutzige Mittel *Pl.*; ~ **test** *n.* (Med.)
Abstrich, *der*

**smell** /smel/ [1] *n.* **(a)** have a good/bad
sense of ~: einen guten/schlechten
Geruchssinn haben
**(b)** (odour) Geruch, *der* (of nach); ( pleasant
also) Duft, *der* (of nach); a ~ of burning/gas
ein Brand-/Gasgeruch
**(c)** (stink) Gestank, *der*
[2] *v.t.,* smelt /smelt/ *or* smelled /smeld/ **(a)**
( perceive) riechen
**(b)** (inhale ~ of ) riechen an (+ *Dat.*)
[3] *v.i.,* smelt *or* smelled **(a)** (emit ~) riechen;
( pleasantly also) duften
**(b)** ~ of sth. (lit. or fig.) nach etw. riechen
**(c)** (stink) riechen

**'smelly** *adj.* stinkend; be ~: stinken

**smelt ▸** SMELL 2, 3

**smile** /smaɪl/ [1] *n.* Lächeln, *das;* give sb. a
~: jmdn. anlächeln
[2] *v.i.* lächeln; ~ at sb./sth. jmdn.
anlächeln/über etw. (*Akk.*) lächeln

**smirk** /smɜːk/ [1] *v.t.* grinsen
[2] *n.* Grinsen, *das*

**smith** /smɪθ/ *n.* Schmied, *der*

**smithereens** /smɪðə'riːnz/ *n. pl.* blow/
smash sth. to ~: etw. in tausend Stücke
sprengen/schlagen

**smock** /smɒk/ *n.* Kittel, *der*

**smog** /smɒg/ *n.* Smog, *der*

**smoke** /sməʊk/ [1] *n.* Rauch, *der*
[2] *v.i. & t.* rauchen

**smoked** /sməʊkt/ *adj.* (Cookery) geräuchert

**'smoke detector** *n.* Rauchmelder, *der*

**'smokeless** *adj.* rauchlos; rauchfrei
⟨Zone⟩

**smoker** /'sməʊkə(r)/ *n.* **(a)** Raucher, *der*/
Raucherin, *die;* ~'s cough Raucherhusten,
*der*
**(b)** (Railw.) Raucherabteil, *das*

**'smokescreen** *n.* [künstliche]
Nebelwand; (fig.) Vernebelung *die* (for *Gen.*)

**smoking** /'sməʊkɪŋ/ *n.* **(a)** Rauchen, *das;*
'no ~' „Rauchen verboten"
**(b)** (seating area) [do you want to sit in] ~ or
non-~? möchten Sie für Raucher oder
Nichtraucher?

**'smoking compartment** *n.* (Railw.)
Raucherabteil, *das*

**smoky** /'sməʊkɪ/ *adj.* (emitting smoke)
rauchend; (smoke-filled) verräuchert

**smooth** /smuːð/ [1] *adj.* **(a)** (even) glatt;
eben ⟨Straße, Weg⟩
**(b)** (mild) weich

**(d)** (not jerky) geschmeidig ⟨*Bewegung*⟩; ruhig
⟨*Fahrt, Flug*⟩; weich ⟨*Landung*⟩
**(d)** (without problems) reibungslos
[2] *v.t.* glätten

**smoothie** /'smuːðɪ/ *n.* (coll. derog.)
aalglatter Typ (ugs.)

**'smoothly** *adv.* **(a)** (evenly) glatt
**(b)** (not jerkily) geschmeidig ⟨*sich bewegen*⟩;
weich ⟨*landen*⟩; reibungslos ⟨*funktionieren*⟩

**smother** /'smʌðə(r)/ *v.t.* ersticken; (fig.)
unterdrücken ⟨*Gähnen*⟩; ersticken
⟨*Gelächter, Schreie*⟩

**smoulder** /'sməʊldə(r)/ *v.i.* schwelen; she
was ~ing with rage Zorn schwelte in ihr

**smudge** /smʌdʒ/ [1] *v.t.* verwischen
[2] *v.i.* schmieren
[3] *n.* Fleck, *der*

**smug** /smʌg/ *adj.* selbstgefällig

**smuggle** /'smʌgl/ *v.t.* schmuggeln
■ **smuggle 'in** *v.t.* einschmuggeln; hinein-/
hereinschmuggeln ⟨*Person*⟩
■ **smuggle 'out** *v.t.* hinaus-/
herausschmuggeln

**smuggler** /'smʌglə(r)/ *n.* Schmuggler, *der*/
Schmugglerin, *die*

**smuggling** /'smʌglɪŋ/ *n.* Schmuggel, *der*

**smutty** /'smʌtɪ/ *adj.* (lewd) schmutzig

**snack** /snæk/ *n.* Imbiss, *der*

**'snackbar** *n.* Schnellimbiss, *der*

**snag** /snæg/ *n.* ( problem) Haken, *der;* what's
the ~? wo klemmt es? (ugs.)

**snail** /sneɪl/ *n.* Schnecke, *die;* at [a] ~'s
pace im Schneckentempo (ugs.)

**'snail mail** *n.* (coll. joc.) Schneckenpost, *die*

**snake** /sneɪk/ *n.* Schlange, *die*

**snap** /snæp/ [1] *v.t.,* -pp-: **(a)** (break)
zerbrechen; ~ sth. in two *or* in half etw. in
zwei Stücke brechen
**(b)** ~ one's fingers mit den Fingern
schnalzen
**(c)** ~ sth. home *or* into place etw.
einschnappen lassen; ~ shut zuschnappen
lassen ⟨*Portemonnaie, Schloss*⟩; zuklappen
⟨*Buch, Etui*⟩; ~ sth. open etw. aufschnappen
lassen
**(d)** (take photograph of ) knipsen
**(e)** (say sharply) fauchen; (speak crisply or curtly)
bellen
[2] *v.i.,* -pp-: **(a)** (break) brechen
**(b)** (fig.: give way under strain) ausrasten (ugs.);
my patience has finally ~ped nun ist mir
der Geduldsfaden aber gerissen
[3] *n.* (Photog.) Schnappschuss, *der*
■ **'snap at** *v.t.* (speak sharply to) anfauchen
(ugs.)
■ **snap 'off** *v.t. & i.* abbrechen
■ **snap 'up** *v.t.* (fig. coll.) [sich (*Dat.*)]
schnappen (ugs.)

**'snapshot** *n.* Schnappschuss, *der*

**snare** /sneə(r)/ [1] *n.* Schlinge, *die*
[2] *v.t.* [in einer Schlinge] fangen

**snarl**[1] /snɑːl/ [1] *v.i.* knurren
[2] *n.* Knurren, *das*

**snarl²** n. (tangle) Knoten, der

■ **snarl 'up** v.t. (bring to a halt) zum Erliegen bringen; **get ~ed up in the traffic** im Verkehr stecken bleiben

**'snarl-up** n. Stau, der

**snatch** /snætʃ/ ①v.t. (a) (grab) schnappen; **~ sth. from sb.** jmdm. etw. wegreißen; **~ some sleep** ein bisschen schlafen (b) (steal) klauen (ugs.)
②v.i. einfach zugreifen
③n. **~es of talk/conversation** Gesprächsfetzen Pl.

**snazzy** /'snæzɪ/ adj. (coll.) [super]schick (ugs.)

**sneak** /sniːk/ ①v.t. schmuggeln; **~ a look at** schielen nach
②v.i. (a) schleichen
(b) (Brit. Sch. coll.: tell tales) petzen (Schülerspr.)
③n. (Brit. Sch. coll.) Petze, die (Schülerspr.)

■ **sneak 'out** v.i. [sich] hinausschleichen

**'sneaker** (Amer.) Turnschuh, der

**'sneaking** attrib. adj. heimlich; leise ⟨Verdacht⟩

**'sneak thief** n. Einschleichdieb, der

**'sneaky** adj. (a) (underhand) hinterhältig
'(b) **have a ~ feeling that ...:** so ein leises Gefühl haben, dass ...

**sneer** /snɪə(r)/ v.i. höhnisch lächeln/grinsen

■ **'sneer at** v.t. höhnisch anlächeln/ angrinsen; (scorn) verhöhnen

**sneeze** /sniːz/ ①v.i. niesen
②n. Niesen, das

**snicker** /'snɪkə(r)/ ▶ SNIGGER

**snide** /snaɪd/ adj. abfällig

**sniff** /snɪf/ ①n. Schnuppern, das; (with running nose, while crying) Schniefen, das
②v.i. schniefen; (to detect a smell) schnuppern
③v.t. riechen od. schnuppern an (+ Dat.); **~ glue/cocaine** Klebstoff schnüffeln/Kokain sniffen (Drogenjargon)

■ **'sniff at** v.t. (a) **~** (b) (show contempt for) die Nase rümpfen über

**sniffer dog** /'snɪfə dɒg/ n. Spürhund, der

**snigger** /'snɪgə(r)/ ①v.i. [boshaft] kichern
②n. [boshaftes] Kichern

**snip** /snɪp/ ①v.t., **-pp-** schnippeln (ugs.), schneiden ⟨Loch⟩; schnippeln (ugs.) od. schneiden an (+ Dat.) ⟨Tuch, Haaren, Hecke⟩; (cut off) abschnippeln (ugs.); abschneiden
②n. (cut) Schnitt, der; Schnipser, der (ugs.)

**snipe** /snaɪp/ v.i. **~ at** aus dem Hinterhalt beschießen

**'sniper** n. Heckenschütze, der

**snippet** /'snɪpɪt/ n. (of information in newspaper) Notiz, die; (of conversation) Gesprächsfetzen, der; **useful ~s of information** nützliche Hinweise

**snivel** /'snɪvl/ v.i., (Brit.) **-ll-** schniefen

**'snivelling** (Amer.: **sniveling**) (fig.) attrib. adj. heulend

**snob** /snɒb/ n. Snob, der

**snobbery** /'snɒbərɪ/ n. Snobismus, der

**snobbish** /'snɒbɪʃ/ adj. snobistisch

**snog** /snɒg/ (Brit. coll.) ①v.i., **-gg-** knutschen (ugs.)
②n. Knutschen, das (ugs.)

**snooker** /'snuːkə(r)/ n. Snooker, das

**snoop** /snuːp/ v.i. schnüffeln (ugs.)

**snooty** /'snuːtɪ/ adj. (coll.) hochnäsig (ugs.)

**snooze** /snuːz/ (coll.) ①v.i. dösen (ugs.)
②n. Nickerchen, das (fam.)

**'snooze button** n. Schlummertaste, die

**snore** /snɔː(r)/ ①v.i. schnarchen
②n. Schnarcher, der (ugs.); **~s** Schnarchen, das

**snorkel** /'snɔːkl/ n. Schnorchel, der

**snort** /snɔːt/ v.i. schnauben (**with, in** vor + Dat.); (sl.: take) **~ [coke]** [Koks] sniffen (Drogenjargon)

**snot** /snɒt/ n. (sl.) Rotz, der (derb)

**snotty** adj. rotznäsig (salopp); **~ child/nose** Rotznase, die (salopp)

**snout** /snaʊt/ n. Schnauze, die; (of pig) Rüssel, der

**snow** /snəʊ/ ①n. Schnee, der
②v.i. impers. **it ~s/is ~ing** es schneit

■ **snow 'in** v.t. **they are ~ed in** sie sind eingeschneit

■ **snow 'under** v.t. **be ~ed under** (with work) erdrückt werden; (with gifts, mail) überschüttet werden

**snow:** **~ball** ①n. Schneeball, der; ②v.i. (fig.) lawinenartig zunehmen; **~ blindness** n. Schneeblindheit, die; **~board** ①n. Snowboard, das; ②v.i. Snowboard fahren; **~boarder** n. Snowboarder, der/ Snowboarderin, die; **~boarding** n. Snowboardfahren, das; Snowboarden, das; **~bound** adj. eingeschneit; **~-capped** adj. schneebedeckt; **~ chains** n. pl. Schneeketten Pl.; **~drift** n. Schneewehe, die; **~drop** n. Schneeglöckchen, das; **~fall** n. Schneefall, der; **~flake** n. Schneeflocke, die; **~man** n. Schneemann, der; **~plough** n. Schneepflug, der; **~storm** n. Schneesturm, der

**'snowy** adj. schneereich ⟨Gegend⟩; schneebedeckt ⟨Berge⟩

**snub** /snʌb/ ①v.t., **-bb-:** (a) (rebuff) brüskieren
(b) (reject) ablehnen
②n. Abfuhr, die

**snub-'nosed** adj. stupsnasig

**snuff¹** /snʌf/ n. Schnupftabak, der; **take a pinch of ~:** eine Prise schnupfen

**snuff²** v.t. **~ [out]** löschen ⟨Kerze⟩

**snuffle** /'snʌfl/ v.i. schnüffeln

**snug** /snʌg/ adj. gemütlich; behaglich; **be a ~ fit** genau passen

**snuggle** /'snʌgl/ v.i. **~ up to sb.** sich an jmdn. kuscheln; **~ together** sich aneinander kuscheln; **~ up** or **down in bed** sich ins Bett kuscheln

**so** /səʊ/ ①adv. (a) so; **as winter draws near, so it gets darker** je näher der Winter rückt, desto dunkler wird es; **so ... as** so ... wie; **so**

**far** bis hierher; (until now) bisher; (to such a distance) so weit; **so much the better** um so besser; **so long!** bis dann! (ugs.); **and so on** [and so forth] und so weiter [und so fort]; **so as to** um ... zu; **so [that]** damit; **I'm so glad/tired!** ich bin ja so froh/müde!; **It's a rainbow! – So it is!** Es ist ein Regenbogen! – Ja, wirklich!; **You suggested it. – So I did** Du hast es vorgeschlagen. – Das stimmt; **is that so?** so? (ugs.); wirklich?; **so am/have/would/could/will/do I** ich auch
**(b)** *pron.* **he suggested that I take the train, and if I had done so, ...:** er riet mir, den Zug zu nehmen, und wenn ich es getan hätte, ...; **I'm afraid so** leider ja; **I told you so** ich habe es dir [ja] gesagt; **a week or so** etwa eine Woche; **very much so** in der Tat
**2** *conj.* (therefore) daher; **so there you 'are!** ich habe also recht!; **so 'there!** [und] fertig!; **so?** na und?; **so you see ...:** du siehst also ...; **so where have you been?** wo warst du denn?

**soak** /səʊk/ **1** *v.t.* **(a)** einweichen ‹Wäsche in Lauge›; eintauchen ‹Brot in Milch›
**(b)** (wet) nass machen
**2** *v.i.* **(a)** (steep) **put sth. in sth. to ~:** etw. in etw. (Dat.) einweichen
**(b)** (drain) ‹Feuchtigkeit, Nässe:› sickern

'**soaking** *adj. & adv.* **~ [wet]** völlig durchnässt

'**so-and-so** *n., pl.* **~'s (a)** (person not named) [Herr/Frau] Soundso
**(b)** (coll.: disliked person) Biest, *das* (ugs.)

**soap** /səʊp/ *n.* **(a)** Seife, *die;* **with ~ and water** mit Wasser und Seife
**(b)** (coll.) ▶ SOAP OPERA

**soap: ~ flakes** *n. pl.* Seifenflocken *Pl.;* **~ opera** *n.* Seifenoper, *die* (ugs.); **~ powder** *n.* Seifenpulver, *das;* **~ suds** *n. pl.* Seifenschaum, *der*

'**soapy** *adj.* seifig; **~ water** Seifenlauge, *die*

**soar** /sɔː(r)/ *v.i.* aufsteigen; (fig.) ‹Preise, Kosten usw.:› in die Höhe schießen (ugs.)

**sob** /sɒb/ **1** *v.i., -bb-* schluchzen (**with** vor + Dat.)
**2** *n.* Schluchzer, *der*

**sober** /'səʊbə(r)/ *adj.* **(a)** (not drunk) nüchtern
**(b)** (serious) ernst

■ **sober 'up 1** *v.i.* nüchtern werden
**2** *v.t.* ausnüchtern

'**sobering** *adj.* ernüchternd

**so-called** /'səʊkɔːld/ *adj.* so genannt; (alleged) angeblich

**soccer** /'sɒkə(r)/ *n.* Fußball, *der*

**sociable** /'səʊʃəbl/ *adj.* gesellig

**social** /'səʊʃl/ *adj.* **(a)** sozial; gesellschaftlich
**(b)** (of ~ life) gesellschaftlich; gesellig ‹Abend, Beisammensein›

'**social club** *n.* Klub für geselliges Beisammensein

**socialism** /'səʊʃəlɪzm/ *n.* Sozialismus, *der*

**socialist** /'səʊʃəlɪst/ **1** *n.* Sozialist, *der/* Sozialistin, *die*
**2** *adj.* sozialistisch

**socialize** /'səʊʃəlaɪz/ *v.i.* gesellige Umgang pflegen; **~ with sb.** (chat) sich mit jmdm. unterhalten

'**social life** *n.* gesellschaftliches Leben; **not have much ~** ‹Person:› nicht viel ausgehen

'**socially** *adv.* **meet ~:** sich privat treffen; **~ deprived** sozial benachteiligt

**social: ~ 'science** *n.* Sozialwissenschaften *Pl.;* Gesellschaftswissenschaften *Pl.;* **~ se'curity** *n.* **(a)** (Brit.: benefit) Sozialhilfe, *die;* **(b)** (system) soziale Sicherheit; **~ 'service** *n.* staatliche Sozialleistung; **~ 'services** *n. pl.* Sozialdienste *Pl.;* **~ work** *n.* Sozialarbeit, *die;* **~ worker** *n.* Sozialarbeiter, *der/-*arbeiterin, *die*

**society** /sə'saɪətɪ/ *n.* **(a)** Gesellschaft, *die;* **high ~:** Highsociety, *die*
**(b)** (club, association) Verein, *der*

**socio-eco'nomic** *adj.* sozioökonomisch

**sociological** /ˌsəʊsɪə'lɒdʒɪkl/ *adj.* soziologisch

**sociologist** /ˌsəʊsɪ'ɒlədʒɪst/ *n.* Soziologe, *der/*Soziologin, *die*

**sociology** /ˌsəʊsɪ'ɒlədʒɪ/ *n.* Soziologie, *die*

**sock**[1] /sɒk/ *n.* Socke, *die*

**sock**[2] *v.t.* (coll.: hit) hauen (ugs.)

**socket** /'sɒkɪt/ *n.* **(a)** (Anat.) (of eye) Höhle, *die;* (of joint) Pfanne, *die*
**(b)** (Electr.) Steckdose, *die*

**soda** /'səʊdə/ *n.* Soda, *das*

'**soda water** *n.* Soda[wasser], *das*

**sodden** /'sɒdn/ *adj.* durchnässt (**with** von)

**sodium** /'səʊdɪəm/ *n.* Natrium, *das*

**sodium: ~ bi'carbonate** *n.* doppeltkohlensaures Natrium; Natriumhydrogenkarbonat, *das;* **~ 'chloride** *n.* Natriumchlorid, *das*

**sofa** /'səʊfə/ *n.* Sofa, *das*

**soft** /sɒft/ *adj.* weich; (quiet) leise; (gentle) sanft; **have a ~ spot for sb.** eine Vorliebe für jmdn. haben

**soft: ~-boiled** *adj.* weich gekocht ‹Ei›; **~-centred** *adj.* ‹Praline usw.› mit weicher Füllung; **~ copy** *n.* (Comp.) Softcopy, *die;* **~ cover** *n.* book with a **~ cover** Buch mit einem Softcover (Verlagsw.) od. mit einem flexiblen Einband; **~ drink** *n.* alkoholfreies Getränk; **~ drug** *n.* weiche Droge

**soften** /'sɒfn/ **1** *v.i.* weicher werden
**2** *v.t.* aufweichen ‹Boden›; enthärten ‹Wasser›; mildern ‹Farbe›

**soft: ~ 'furnishings** *n. pl.* (Brit.) Raumtextilien *Pl.;* **~-'hearted** /sɒft'hɑːtɪd/ *adj.* weichherzig

'**softly** *adv.* (quietly) leise; (gently) sanft

**soft: ~ option** *n.* Weg des geringsten Widerstandes; **~ 'porn** (coll.)**, ~ por'nography** *ns.* Softpornographie, ···⫶·

*die;* ~-**spoken** *adj.* leise sprechend
⟨*Person*⟩; ~ **top** *n.* (a) (roof) Stoffverdeck,
*das;* (b) (car) Cabrio, *das;* ~ '**toy** *n.*
Stoffspielzeug, *das;* (toy animal) Stofftier, *das;*
~ **verge** *n.* (Brit.) Grünstreifen, *der;*
~**ware** *n.* (Comp.) Software, *die*

**soggy** /'sɒgɪ/ *adj.* aufgeweicht

**soil**[1] /sɔɪl/ *n.* Erde, *die;* Boden, *der*

**soil**[2] *v.t.* beschmutzen

**solace** /'sɒləs/ *n.* Trost, *der;* **take** *or* **find**
~ **in sth.** Trost in etw. (*Dat.*) finden

**solar** /'səʊlə(r)/ *adj.* Sonnen-

**solar:** ~ **e'clipse** *n.* Sonnenfinsternis, *die;*
~ '**energy** *n.* Sonnenenergie, *die;*
~ '**panel** *n.* Sonnenkollektor, *der;* (on
satellite) Sonnensegel, *das;* ~-**powered** *adj.*
mit Sonnenenergie betrieben; ~ **system**
*n.* Sonnensystem, *das*

**sold** ▶ SELL

**solder** /'səʊldə(r)/ [1] *n.* Lot, *das*
[2] *v.t.* löten

**soldering iron** /'səʊldərɪŋaɪən/ *n.*
Lötkolben, *der*

**soldier** /'səʊldʒə(r)/ *n.* Soldat, *der*

**sole**[1] /səʊl/ *n.* (of foot/shoe) Sohle, *die*

**sole**[2] *adj.* einzig; alleinig ⟨*Verantwortung,
Recht*⟩; Allein⟨*erbe, -eigentümer*⟩

'**solely** *adv.* einzig und allein

**solemn** /'sɒləm/ *adj.* feierlich; ernst
⟨*Anlass, Gespräch*⟩

**solicitor** /sə'lɪsɪtə(r)/ *n.* (Brit.: lawyer)
Rechtsanwalt, *der*/-anwältin, *die*

**solid** /'sɒlɪd/ [1] *adj.* (a) (rigid) fest
(b) (of the same substance all through) massiv
(c) (well-built) stabil; solide gebaut ⟨*Haus,
Mauer usw.*⟩
(d) (complete) ganz; **a good** ~ **meal** eine
kräftige Mahlzeit
[2] *n.* fester Körper

**solidarity** /sɒlɪ'dærɪtɪ/ *n.* Solidarität, *die*

**solid:** ~ '**fuel** *n.* fester Brennstoff; ~-'**fuel**
*attrib. adj.* Festbrennstoff-; ~-**fuel rocket**
Feststoffrakete

**solidify** /sə'lɪdɪfaɪ/ *v.i.* fest werden

**solitary** /'sɒlɪtərɪ/ *adj.* (a) einsam;
~ **confinement** Einzelhaft, *die*
(b) (sole) einzig

**solitude** /'sɒlɪtjuːd/ *n.* Einsamkeit, *die*

**solo** /'səʊləʊ/ [1] *n., pl.* ~s (Mus.) Solo, *das*
[2] *adj.* (a) (Mus.) Solo-
(b) ~ **flight** Alleinflug, *der*
[3] *adv.* (a) (Mus.) solo
(b) **go/fly** ~ (Aeronaut.) einen Alleinflug
machen

**soloist** /'səʊləʊɪst/ *n.* (Mus.) Solist, *der*/
Solistin, *die*

**solstice** /'sɒlstɪs/ *n.* Sonnenwende, *die*

**soluble** /'sɒljʊbl/ *adj.* (a) (esp. Chem.) löslich
(b) (solvable) lösbar

**solution** /sə'luːʃn/ *n.* (a) (esp. Chem.)
Lösung, *die*

(b) ([result of] solving) Lösung, *die* (**to** *Gen.*);
**find a** ~ **to sth.** eine Lösung für etw. finden;
etw. lösen

**solvable** /'sɒlvəbl/ *adj.* lösbar

**solve** /sɒlv/ *v.t.* lösen

**solvent** /'sɒlvənt/ [1] *adj.* (a) (esp. Chem.)
lösend
(b) (Finance) solvent
[2] *n.* Lösungsmittel, *das*

**sombre** (*Amer.*: **somber**) /'sɒmbə(r)/ *adj.*
dunkel; düster ⟨*Stimmung, Atmosphäre*⟩

**some** /səm, *stressed* sʌm/ [1] *adj.* (a) (one or
other) [irgend]ein; ~ **day** eines Tages
(b) (a considerable quantity of) einig...
(c) (a small quantity of) ein bisschen; **would you
like** ~ **wine/cherries?** möchten Sie [etwas]
Wein/[ein paar] Kirschen?; **do** ~ **shopping/
reading** einkaufen/lesen
(d) (to a certain extent) ~ **guide** eine gewisse
Orientierungshilfe
[2] *pron.* einig...; **would you like** ~**?** möchtest
du etwas/(plural) welche?; ~ ..., **others** ...:
manche ..., andere ...

**somebody** /'sʌmbədɪ/ *n. & pron.* jemand;
~ **or other** irgendjemand

'**somehow** *adv.* ~ **[or other]** irgendwie

**someone** /'sʌmwʌn/ *pron.* ▶ SOMEBODY

**somersault** /'sʌməsɔːlt/ *n.* Purzelbaum,
*der* (ugs.); Salto, *der* (Sport); **turn a** ~: einen
Purzelbaum schlagen (ugs.)/einen Salto
springen

'**something** *n. & pron.* etwas; ~ **new** etwas
Neues; ~ **or other** irgendetwas; **see** ~ **of sb.**
jmdn. sehen

'**sometime** [1] *adj.* ehemalig
[2] *adv.* irgendwann

'**sometimes** *adv.* manchmal

'**somewhat** *adv.* ziemlich

'**somewhere** [1] *adv.* (a) (in a place)
irgendwo
(b) (to a place) irgendwohin
[2] *n.* **look for** ~ **to stay** sich nach einer
Unterkunft umsehen

**son** /sʌn/ *n.* Sohn, *der*

**sonata** /sə'nɑːtə/ *n.* Sonate, *die*

**song** /sɒŋ/ *n.* (a) Lied, *das*
(b) (bird cry) Gesang, *der*

**song:** ~**bird** *n.* Singvogel, *der;* ~**book** *n.*
Liederbuch, *das*

**sonic** /'sɒnɪk/ *attrib. adj.* Schall-; ~ **bang** *or*
**boom** Überschallknall, *der*

'**son-in-law** *n., pl.* **sons-in-law**
Schwiegersohn, *der*

**soon** /suːn/ *adv.* (a) bald; (quickly) schnell
(b) (early) früh; **none too** ~: keinen
Augenblick zu früh; ~**er or later** früher oder
später
(c) **we'll set off as** ~ **as he arrives** sobald er
ankommt, machen wir uns auf den Weg; **as**
~ **as possible** so bald wie möglich
(d) (willingly) **just as** ~ **[as** ...**]** genauso gern
[wie ...]; **she would** ~**er die than** ...: sie
würde lieber sterben, als ...

**soot** /sʊt/ n. Ruß, der

**soothe** /suːð/ v.t. (a) (calm) beruhigen
(b) lindern ‹Schmerz›

**soothing** /'suːðɪŋ/ adj. beruhigend;
wohltuend ‹Bad, Creme, Massage›

'**sooty** adj. verrußt; rußig

**sophisticated** /sə'fɪstɪkeɪtɪd/ adj. (a)
(cultured) kultiviert
(b) (elaborate, complex) hoch entwickelt; subtil
‹Argument, System›

**soporific** /sɒpə'rɪfɪk/ adj. einschläfernd

**sopping** /'sɒpɪŋ/ adj. & adv. ~ [wet] völlig
durchnässt

**soppy** /'sɒpɪ/ adj. (Brit. coll.) rührselig;
sentimental ‹Person›

**soprano** /sə'prɑːnəʊ/ n. Sopran, der; (female
also) Sopranistin, die

**sorbet** /'sɔːbɪt, 'sɔːbeɪ/ n. Sorbet, das

**sorcerer** /'sɔːsərə(r)/ n. Zauberer, der

**sorcery** /'sɔːsərɪ/ n. Zauberei, die

**sordid** /'sɔːdɪd/ adj. dreckig; unerfreulich
‹Detail, Geschichte›

**sore** /sɔː(r)/ [1] adj. weh; (inflamed or injured)
wund; a ~ throat Halsschmerzen Pl.; sb. has
a ~ back/foot etc. jmdm. tut der Rücken/
Fuß usw. weh
[2] n. wunde Stelle

'**sorely** adv. sehr; dringend ‹nötig›;
~ tempted stark versucht

**sorrow** /'sɒrəʊ/ n. Kummer, der

**sorry** /'sɒrɪ/ adj. (a) sb. is ~ that ...: es tut
jmdm. Leid, dass ...; sb. is ~ about sth.
jmdm. tut etwas Leid; I am or feel ~ for him
er tut mir Leid; sb. is or feels ~ for sth.
jmd. bedauert etw.; ~! Entschuldigung!; ~?
wie bitte?; I'm ~ to say leider; you'll be ~!
das wird dir noch Leid tun
(b) (wretched) traurig

**sort** /sɔːt/ [1] n. (a) Art, die; (type) Sorte, die;
a new ~ of bicycle ein neuartiges Fahrrad;
all ~s of ...: alle möglichen ...; there are all
~s of things to do es gibt alles Mögliche od.
allerlei zu tun; ~ of (coll.: more or less) mehr
oder weniger; nothing of the ~: nichts
dergleichen
(b) be out of ~s nicht in Form sein
[2] v.t. sortieren
■ sort '**out** v.t. (a) (settle) klären; schlichten
‹Streit›; beenden ‹Verwirrung›
(b) (select) aussuchen

'**sort code** n. Bankleitzahl, die

**sortie** /'sɔːtɪ/ n. Ausfall, der; (flight) Einsatz,
der

'**sorting office** n. Postverteilstelle, die

**SOS** n. SOS, das

'**so so**, '**so-so** adj., adv. so lala (ugs.)

**soufflé** /'suːfleɪ/ n. Soufflé, das

**sought** ▶ SEEK

**soul** /səʊl/ n. Seele, die; not a ~: keine
Menschenseele

'**soul-destroying** adj. (a) (boring)
nervtötend

(b) (depressing) deprimierend

**soulful** /'səʊlfl/ adj. gefühlvoll; (sad)
schwermütig

**soul:** ~ **mate** n. Seelenverwandte, der/die;
~-**searching** n. Gewissenskampf, der

**sound¹** /saʊnd/ [1] adj. (a) (healthy) gesund;
intakt ‹Gebäude, Mauerwerk›; of ~ mind im
Vollbesitz seiner geistigen Kräfte
(b) (well-founded) vernünftig ‹Argument, Rat›;
klug ‹Wahl›; it makes ~ sense es ist sehr
vernünftig
(c) (Finance: secure) gesund, solide ‹Basis›;
klug ‹Investition›
[2] adv. fest, tief ‹schlafen›

**sound²** [1] n. (a) (Phys.) Schall, der
(b) (noise) Laut, der; (of wind, sea, car, footsteps,
breaking glass or twigs) Geräusch, das; (of voices,
laughter, bell) Klang, der; do sth. without a ~:
etw. lautlos tun
(c) (Radio, Telev., Cinemat.) Ton, der
(d) (fig.: impression) I like the ~ of your plan
ich finde, Ihr Plan hört sich gut an; I don't
like the ~ of this das hört sich nicht gut an
[2] v.i. klingen; it ~s as if .../like ...: es
klingt, als .../wie ...; that ~s a good idea to
me ich finde, die Idee hört sich gut an; that
~s odd to me das hört sich seltsam an,
finde ich; ~s good to me! klingt gut! (ugs.)
[3] v.t. (a) ertönen lassen
(b) (utter) ~ a note of caution zur Vorsicht
mahnen
■ sound '**off** v.i. tönen (ugs.),
schwadronieren (on, about, von)
■ sound '**out** v.i. ausfragen ‹Person›; ~ sb.
out on sth. bei jmdm. wegen etw. vorfühlen

**sound:** ~ **barrier** n. Schallmauer, die;
~ **bite** n. kurzes, prägnantes Zitat;
~ **card** n. (Comp.) Soundkarte, die;
~ **effect** n. Geräuscheffekt, der;
~ **engineer** n. Toningenieur, der/
-ingenieurin, die

'**sounding board** n. (a) (Mus.) Decke, die
(b) (fig.: trial audience) ≈ Testgruppe, die

'**soundless** adj. lautlos

'**soundly** adv. (a) (solidly) stabil, solide
‹bauen›
(b) (deeply) tief, fest ‹schlafen›
(c) (thoroughly) ordentlich (ugs.) ‹verhauen›;
vernichtend ‹schlagen, besiegen›

**sound:** ~**proof** [1] adj. schalldicht; [2] v.t.
schalldicht machen; ~ **system** n.
Tonanlage, die; ~**track** n. Soundtrack, der;
~ **wave** n. Schallwelle, die

**soup** /suːp/ n. Suppe, die; be/land in the ~
(fig. coll.) in der Patsche sitzen/landen (ugs.)

**souped-up** /'suːptʌp/ attrib. adj. (Motor Veh.
coll.) frisiert (ugs.)

**soup:** ~ **plate** n. Suppenteller, der;
~ **spoon** n. Suppenlöffel, der

**sour** /saʊə(r)/ adj. (a) sauer
(b) (morose) griesgrämig; säuerlich ‹Blick›
(c) (unpleasant) bitter

**S**

**source** /sɔːs/ n. Quelle, die; ~ of income/ infection Einkommensquelle, die/ Infektionsherd, der; at ~: an der Quelle

**sour 'cream** n. saure Sahne; Sauerrahm, der

**south** /saʊθ/ ① n. (a) Süden, der; in/ to[wards]/from the ~: im/nach/von Süden; to the ~ of südlich von
(b) usu. S~ (Geog., Polit.) Süden, der ② adj. südlich; Süd⟨küste, -wind, -grenze⟩
③ adv. nach Süden; ~ of südlich von

**South:** ~ 'Africa pr. n. Südafrika (das); ~ 'African adj. südafrikanisch;
~ A'merica pr. n. Südamerika (das); ~ A'merican adj. südamerikanisch;
s~bound adj. ⟨Zug, Verkehr usw.⟩ in Richtung Süden; s~-'east ① n. Südosten, der; ② adj. südöstlich; Südost⟨wind, -küste⟩; ③ adv. südostwärts; nach Südosten;
s~-'eastern adj. südöstlich

**southerly** /'sʌðəlɪ/ adj. südlich; ⟨Wind⟩ aus südlichen Richtungen

**southern** /'sʌðən/ adj. südlich; Süd⟨grenze, -hälfte, -seite⟩

**Southern Europe** pr. n. Südeuropa (das)

**South:** ~ 'Germany pr. n. Süddeutschland (das); ~ 'Pole pr. n. Südpol, der

**southward[s]** /'saʊθwəd(s)/ adv. südwärts

**south:** ~-'west ① n. Südwesten, der; ② adj. südwestlich; Südwest⟨wind, -küste⟩; ③ adv. südwestwärts; nach Südwesten; ~-'western adj. südwestlich

**souvenir** /suːvə'nɪə(r)/ n. Souvenir, das (of aus); Andenken, das

**sovereign** /'sɒvrɪn/ n. (ruler) Souverän, der

**sovereignty** /'sɒvrɪntɪ/ n. Souveränität, die

**Soviet** /'səʊvɪət, 'sɒvɪət/ adj. (Hist.) sowjetisch; Sowjet⟨bürger, -literatur⟩

**Soviet 'Union** pr. n. (Hist.) Sowjetunion, die

**sow¹** /səʊ/ v.t., p.p. sown /səʊn/ or sowed /səʊd/ (a) (plant) [aus]säen
(b) einsäen ⟨Feld, Boden⟩

**sow²** /saʊ/ n. (female pig) Sau, die

**sown** ▶ sow¹

**soya [bean]** /'sɔɪə (biːn)/ n. Sojabohne, die

**soy sauce** /'sɔɪ sɔːs/ n. Sojasoße, die

**sozzled** /'sɒzld/ adj. (coll.) voll (ugs.)

**spa** /spɑː/ n. (a) (place) Bad, das; Badeort, der
(b) (spring) Mineralquelle, die

**space** /speɪs/ n. (a) Raum, der
(b) (interval between points) Platz, der; clear a ~: Platz schaffen
(c) the wide open ~s das weite, flache Land
(d) (Astron.) Weltraum, der
(e) (blank between words) Zwischenraum, der
(f) (interval of time) Zeitraum, der; in the ~ of a minute/an hour innerhalb einer Minute/ Stunde; in a short ~ of time he was back nach kurzer Zeit war er zurück

■ **space 'out** v.t. verteilen

**space:** ~ age n. [Welt]raumzeitalter, das; ~ bar n. Leertaste, die; ~craft n. Raumfahrzeug, das; ~saving adj. Platz sparend; ~ship n. Raumschiff, das; ~suit n. Raumanzug, der; ~ travel n. Raumfahrt, die

**spacious** /'speɪʃəs/ adj. geräumig

**spade** /speɪd/ n. (a) Spaten, der
(b) (Cards) Pik, das; see also CLUB 1C

**spaghetti** /spə'getɪ/ n. Spaghetti Pl.

**Spain** /speɪn/ pr. n. Spanien (das)

**spam** /spæm/ n. (Comput.) Spam, der

**span** /spæn/ ① n. (a) Spanne, die; Zeitspanne, die
(b) (of bridge) Spannweite, die ② v.t., -nn- überspannen ⟨Fluss⟩; umfassen ⟨Zeitraum⟩

**Spaniard** /'spænjəd/ n. Spanier, der/ Spanierin, die

**Spanish** /'spænɪʃ/ ① adj. spanisch; sb. is ~: jmd. ist Spanier/Spanierin
② n. (a) (language) Spanisch, das; see also ENGLISH 2A
(b) the ~ pl. die Spanier Pl.

**spank** /spæŋk/ ① n. ≈ Klaps, der (ugs.) ② v.t. ~ sb. jmdm. einen Klaps geben (ugs.)

**spanner** /'spænə(r)/ n. (Brit.) Schraubenschlüssel, der

**spar** /spɑː(r)/ v.i., -rr-: (a) (Boxing) sparren
(b) (fig.: argue) [sich] zanken

**spare** /speə(r)/ ① adj. (a) (not in use) übrig; ~ time/moment Freizeit, die/freier Augenblick; there is one ~ seat ein Platz ist noch frei
(b) (for use when needed) zusätzlich, Extra⟨bett, -tasse⟩; ~ room Gästezimmer, das ② n. Ersatzteil, das/-reifen, der usw ③ v.t. (a) entbehren; we arrived with ten minutes to ~: wir kamen zehn Minuten früher an
(b) (not inflict on) ~ sb. sth. jmdm. etw. ersparen
(c) (not hurt) [ver]schonen
(d) (fail to use) not ~ any expense/pains or efforts keine Kosten/Mühe scheuen; no expense ~d an nichts gespart

**spare:** ~ 'part n. Ersatzteil, das; ~ 'tyre n. Reserve-, Ersatzreifen, der; ~ 'wheel n. Ersatzrad, das

**sparing** /'speərɪŋ/ adj., **sparingly** adv. sparsam

**spark** /spɑːk/ ① n. (a) Funke, der; (fig.) a ~ of generosity/decency ein Funke[n] Großzügigkeit/Anstand
(b) a bright ~ (coll.: person, also iron.) ein schlauer Kopf
② v.t. ~ [off] zünden; (fig.) auslösen

**sparkle** /'spɑːkl/ ① v.i. (a) ⟨Diamant:⟩ glitzern; ⟨Augen:⟩ funkeln
(b) (be lively) sprühen (with vor + Dat.) ② n. Funkeln, das

**sparkling** /'spɑːklɪŋ/ *adj.* glitzernd ⟨*Diamant*⟩; funkelnd ⟨*Augen*⟩
**sparkling 'wine** *n.* Schaumwein, *der*
**'spark plug** *n.* Zündkerze, *die*
**sparrow** /'spærəʊ/ *n.* Spatz, *der*
**sparse** /spɑːs/ *adj.* spärlich; dünn ⟨*Besiedlung*⟩
**spasm** /'spæzm/ *n.* Krampf, *der*
**spasmodic** /spæz'mɒdɪk/ *adj.* **(a)** (marked by spasms) krampfartig
**(b)** (intermittent) sporadisch
**spastic** /'spæstɪk/ ①︎ *n.* Spastiker, *der*/ Spastikerin, *die*
②︎ *adj.* spastisch
**spat** ▶ SPIT 1, 2
**spate** /speɪt/ *n.* **(a) the river is in [full]** ∼: der Fluss führt Hochwasser
**(b)** (fig.) **a** ∼ **of sth.** eine Flut von etw.; **a** ∼ **of burglaries** eine Einbruchsserie
**spatial** /'speɪʃl/ *adj.* räumlich
**'spatter** /'spætə(r)/ *v.t.* spritzen; ∼ **sb./sth. with sth.** jmdn./etw. mit etw. bespritzen
**spatula** /'spætjʊlə/ *n.* Spachtel, *der od. die*
**spawn** /spɔːn/ ①︎ *v.t.* (fig.) hervorbringen
②︎ *v.i.* (Zool.) laichen
③︎ *n.* (Zool.) Laich, *der*
**speak** /spiːk/ ①︎ *v.i.*, **spoke** /spəʊk/, **spoken** /'spəʊkn/ **(a)** sprechen; ∼ **[with sb.] on** *or* **about sth.** [mit jmdm.] über etw. (*Akk.*) sprechen; ∼ **for/against sth.** sich für/gegen etw. aussprechen
**(b)** (on telephone) **Is Mr Grant there? – S**∼**ing!** Ist Mister Grant da? – Am Apparat!; **who is** ∼**ing, please?** wer ist am Apparat, bitte?
②︎ *v.t.*, **spoke, spoken** sprechen ⟨*Satz, Wort, Sprache*⟩; sagen ⟨*Wahrheit*⟩; ∼ **one's mind** sagen, was man denkt
■ **'speak for** *v.t.* sprechen für; **sth. is spoken for** (reserved) etw. ist schon vergeben
■ **'speak of** *v.t.* sprechen von; ∼**ing of Mary** da wir gerade von Mary sprechen; **nothing to** ∼ **of** nichts Besonderes
■ **'speak to** *v.t.* sprechen *od.* reden mit
■ **speak 'up** *v.i.* lauter sprechen
**'speaker** *n.* **(a)** (in public) Redner, *der*/ Rednerin, *die*
**(b)** (of a language) Sprecher *der*/Sprecherin, *die*; **be a 'French** ∼: Französisch sprechen
**(c)** (loudspeaker) Lautsprecher, *der*
**'speaking** ①︎ *n.* Sprechen, *das*; ∼ **clock** (Brit.) telefonische Zeitansage
②︎ *adv.* **strictly/generally** ∼: genau genommen/im Allgemeinen
**spear** /spɪə(r)/ *n.* Speer, *der*
**'spearhead** ①︎ *n.* (fig.) Speerspitze, *die*
②︎ *v.t.* (fig.) anführen
**'spearmint** *n.* Grüne Minze; ∼ **chewing gum** Pfefferminzkaugummi, *der od. das*
**spec¹** /spek/ (coll.) ▶ SPECIFICATION
**spec²** /spek/ *n.* (coll.: speculation) **on** ∼: auf gut Glück; auf Verdacht (ugs.)
**special** /'speʃl/ *adj.* speziell; besonder...; **nobody** ∼: niemand Besonderes

**special de'livery** *n.* (Post) Eilzustellung, *die*
**special effects** *n. pl.* (Cinemat.) Special effects *Pl.*
**specialist** /'speʃəlɪst/ *n.* **(a)** Spezialist, *der*/Spezialistin, *die* (**in** für)
**(b)** (Med.) Facharzt, *der*/-ärztin, *die*
**speciality** /speʃɪ'ælɪtɪ/ *n.* Spezialität, *die*
**specialization** /speʃəlaɪ'zeɪʃn/ *n.* Spezialisierung, *die*
**specialize** /'speʃəlaɪz/ *v.i.* sich spezialisieren (**in** auf + *Akk.*)
**specialized** /'speʃəlaɪzd/ *adj.* **(a)** (requiring detailed knowledge) speziell; Spezial⟨*kenntnisse, -gebiet*⟩
**(b)** (concentrating on small area) spezialisiert
**'specially** *adv.* **(a)** speziell; **make sth.** ∼: etw. speziell *od.* extra anfertigen
**(b)** (especially) besonders
**special:** ∼ **'needs** *n.* **children with** ∼ **needs** Kinder, die besonders betreut werden müssen; ∼ **needs teacher** Förderlehrer, *der*/-lehrerin, *die*; ∼ **'offer** *n.* Sonderangebot, *das*; **on** ∼ **offer** im Sonderangebot; ∼ **school** *n.* Sonderschule, *die*
**specialty** /'speʃltɪ/ (esp. Amer.) ▶ SPECIALITY
**species** /'spiːʃiːz/ *n., pl. same* Art, *die*
**specific** /sprˈsɪfɪk/ *adj.* bestimmt; **could you be more** ∼? kannst du dich genauer ausdrücken?
**specifically** /sprˈsɪfɪkəlɪ/ *adv.* ausdrücklich; eigens; extra (ugs.)
**specification** /spesɪfɪ'keɪʃn/ *n., often pl.* (details) technische Daten *Pl.*; (for building) Baubeschreibung, *die*
**specify** /'spesɪfaɪ/ *v.t.* ausdrücklich sagen; **unless otherwise specified** wenn nicht anders angegeben
**specimen** /'spesɪmən/ *n.* **(a)** (example) Exemplar, *das*
**(b)** (sample) Probe, *die*
**speck** /spek/ *n.* **(a)** (spot) Fleck, *der*
**(b)** (particle) Teilchen, *das*; ∼ **of soot/dust** Rußflocke, *die*/Staubkörnchen, *das*
**specs** /speks/ *n. pl.* (coll.: spectacles) Brille, *die*
**spectacle** /'spektəkl/ *n.* **(a)** *in pl.* [**pair of**] ∼**s** Brille, *die*
**(b)** (public show) Spektakel, *das*
**(c)** (object of attention) Anblick, *der*
**'spectacle case** *n.* Brillenetui, *das*
**spectacular** /spek'tækjʊlə(r)/ *adj.* spektakulär
**spectator** /spek'teɪtə(r)/ *n.* Zuschauer, *der*/Zuschauerin, *die*
**spec'tator sport** *n.* Publikumssport, *der*
**specter** (Amer.) ▶ SPECTRE
**spectra** *pl. of* SPECTRUM
**spectre** /'spektə(r)/ *n.* (Brit.) **(a)** (ghost) Gespenst, *das*
**(b)** (fig.) Schreckgespenst, *das*

**S**

**spectrum** /'spektrəm/ n., pl. **spectra** /'spektrə/ Spektrum, das

**speculate** /'spekjʊleɪt/ v.i. spekulieren (**about, on** über + Akk.)

**speculation** /spekjʊ'leɪʃn/ n. Spekulation, die (**over** über + Akk.)

**speculative** /'spekjʊlətɪv/ adj. spekulativ

**speculator** /'spekjʊleɪtə(r)/ n. Spekulant, der/Spekulantin, die

**sped** ▶ SPEED 2

**speech** /spiːtʃ/ n. (a) (public address) Rede, die; **make** or **deliver** or **give a ~**: eine Rede halten
(b) (faculty or manner of speaking) Sprache, die

**'speechless** adj. sprachlos (**with** vor + Dat.)

**speed** /spiːd/ ① n. Geschwindigkeit, die; Schnelligkeit, die; **at a ~ of ...**: mit einer Geschwindigkeit von ...
② v.i. (a) p.t. & p.p. **sped** /sped/ or **speeded** schnell fahren; rasen (ugs.)
(b) p.t.&p.p. **speeded** (go too fast) zu schnell fahren; rasen (ugs.)

**speed: ~boat** n. Rennboot, das;
**~ bump** n. Bodenschwelle, die;
**~ camera** n. Geschwindigkeitsüberwachungskamera, die

**'speeding** n. Geschwindigkeitsüberschreitung, die

**'speed limit** n. Geschwindigkeitsbeschränkung, die

**speedo** /'spiːdəʊ/ n., pl. **~s** (Brit. coll.) Tacho, der (ugs.)

**speedometer** /spiː'dɒmɪtə(r)/ n. Tachometer, der od. das

**speed: ~ ramp** n. Bodenschwelle, die;
**~way** n. Speedwayrennen, das

**'speedy** adj. schnell; umgehend, prompt ⟨Antwort⟩

**spell¹** /spel/ ① v.t., **spelt** /spelt/ (Brit.) or **spelled** (a) schreiben; (aloud) buchstabieren
(b) (fig.: mean) bedeuten
② v.i., **spelt** (Brit.) or **spelled** (say) buchstabieren; (write) richtig schreiben

**spell²** n. (period) Weile, die; **a cold ~**: eine Kälteperiode

**spell³** n. (a) (magic charm) Zauberspruch, der; **cast a ~ on sb.** jmdn. verzaubern
(b) (fascination) Zauber, der; **break the ~**: den Bann brechen

**'spellbound** adj. verzaubert

**'spell checker** ▶ SPELLING CHECKER

**'spelling** n. Rechtschreibung, die

**spelling: ~ checker** n. Rechtschreibprogramm, das; **~ mistake** n. Rechtschreibfehler, der

**spelt** ▶ SPELL¹

**spend** /spend/ v.t., **spent** /spent/ (a) (pay out) ausgeben; **~ a penny** (fig. coll.) mal verschwinden (ugs.)
(b) verbringen ⟨Zeit⟩

**'spendthrift** n. Verschwender, der/Verschwenderin, die

**spent** ① ▶ SPEND
② adj. (a) (used up) verbraucht
(b) (drained of energy) erschöpft

**sperm** /spɜːm/ n. pl **~s** or same Sperma, der

**sperm: ~ bank** n. Samenbank, die;
**~ count** n. Spermienzahl, die

**spew** /spjuː/ v.t. spucken

**sphere** /sfɪə(r)/ n. (a) (field of action) Bereich, der; Sphäre, die (geh.)
(b) (Geom.) Kugel, die

**spherical** /'sferɪkl/ adj. kugelförmig

**spice** /spaɪs/ ① n. Gewürz, das; (fig.) Würze, die
② v.t. würzen

**'spice rack** n. Gewürzregal, das

**spicy** /'spaɪsɪ/ adj. pikant; würzig

**spider** /'spaɪdə(r)/ n. Spinne, die

**spider: ~ plant** n. Grünlilie, die; **~'s web** (Amer.: **~ web**) Spinnennetz, das; (fig.) Netz, das

**spike** /spaɪk/ n. Stachel, der

**spiky** /'spaɪkɪ/ adj. stachelig

**spill** /spɪl/ ① v.t., **spilt** /spɪlt/ or **spilled** verschütten ⟨Flüssigkeit⟩; **~ sth. on sth.** etw. auf etw. (Akk.) schütten; **~ the beans** aus der Schule plaudern
② v.i., **spilt** or **spilled** überlaufen

**spilt** ▶ SPILL

**spin** /spɪn/ ① v.t., **-nn-**, **spun** /spʌn/ (a) spinnen; **~ yarn** Garn spinnen
(b) (in washing machine etc.) schleudern
② v.i., **-nn-**, **spun** sich drehen; **my head is ~ning** (fig.) mir schwirrt der Kopf

■ **spin 'out** v.t. (prolong) in die Länge ziehen

**spinach** /'spɪnɪdʒ/ n. Spinat, der

**spinal** /'spaɪnl/ adj. Wirbelsäulen-; Rückgrat[s]-

**spinal: ~ 'column** n. Wirbelsäule, die;
**~ 'cord** n. Rückenmark, das

**spindle** /'spɪndl/ n. Spindel, die

**spindly** /'spɪndlɪ/ adj. spindeldürr

**spin: ~ doctor** n. (coll.) Spin-Doktor, der;
**~ 'drier** n. Wäscheschleuder, die; **~-'dry** v.t. schleudern

**spine** /spaɪn/ n. (a) (backbone) Wirbelsäule, die
(b) (Bot., Zool.) Stachel, der

**'spineless** adj. (fig.) rückgratlos

**'spin-off** n. Nebenprodukt, das

**spinster** /'spɪnstə(r)/ n. ledige Frau

**spiny** /'spaɪnɪ/ adj. stachelig

**spiral** /'spaɪrl/ ① adj. spiralförmig
② n. Spirale, die
③ v.i., (Brit.) **-ll-** ⟨Weg:⟩ sich hochwinden; ⟨Kosten:⟩ in die Höhe klettern; ⟨Rauch:⟩ in einer Spirale aufsteigen

**spiral 'staircase** n. Wendeltreppe, die

**spire** /'spaɪə(r)/ n. Turmspitze, die

**spirit** /'spɪrɪt/ n. (a) in pl. (distilled liquor) Spirituosen Pl.
(b) (mental attitude) Geisteshaltung, die; in the right/wrong ∼: mit der richtigen/falschen Einstellung; take sth. in the wrong ∼: etw. falsch auffassen
(c) (courage) Mut, der
(d) (mental tendency) Geist, der; high ∼s gehobene Stimmung; in poor or low ∼s niedergedrückt

'**spirited** adj. beherzt

'**spirit level** n. Wasserwaage, die

**spiritual** /'spɪrɪtʃʊəl/ adj. spirituell (geh.)

**spit** /spɪt/ 1 v.i., -tt-, spat /spæt/ or spit spucken
2 v.t., -tt-, spat or spit spucken
3 n. Spucke, die
■ **spit 'out** v.t. ausspucken

**spite** /spaɪt/ 1 n. (a) Boshaftigkeit, die
(b) in ∼ of trotz; in ∼ of oneself obwohl man es eigentlich nicht will
2 v.t. ärgern

**spiteful** /'spaɪtfl/ adj. gehässig

**spitting 'image** n. be the ∼ of sb. jmdm. wie aus dem Gesicht geschnitten sein

**spittle** /'spɪtl/ n. Spucke, die

**splash** /splæʃ/ 1 v.t. spritzen; ∼ sth. on [to] or over sb./sth. jmdn./etw. mit etw. bespritzen
2 v.i. (a) spritzen
(b) (in water) platschen (ugs.)
3 n. (a) (liquid) Spritzer, der
(b) (noise) Plätschern, das
■ **splash 'out** vi. (coll.) ∼ out on sth. für etw. unbekümmert Geld ausgeben

**splendid** /'splendɪd/ adj. (excellent) großartig; (magnificent) prächtig

**splendour** (Brit.; Amer.: **splendor**) /'splendə(r)/ n. Pracht, die

**splint** /splɪnt/ n. Schiene, die

**splinter** /'splɪntə(r)/ n. Splitter, der

**split** /splɪt/ 1 n. (a) (tear) Riss, der
(b) (division into parts) [Auf]teilung, die; (fig.) Spaltung, die
2 adj. gespalten; be ∼ on a question [sich (Dat.] in einer Frage uneins sein
3 v.t., -tt-, split (a) (tear) zerreißen
(b) (divide) teilen
4 v.i., -tt-, split (a) ⟨Holz:⟩ splittern; ⟨Stoff, Seil:⟩ reißen; ∼ apart zersplittern
(b) (divide into parts) sich teilen
■ **split 'up** 1 v.t. aufteilen
2 v.i. (coll.) sich trennen; ∼ up with sb. sich von jmdm. trennen

**split:** ∼-**level** adj. mit Zwischengeschoss nachgestellt; auf zwei Ebenen nachgestellt; a ∼-**level lounge** ein Wohnraum auf zwei Ebenen; ∼-**level cooker** Einbauherd, bei dem Kochplatten und Backofen getrennt sind; ∼ '**pea** n. getrocknete [halbe] Erbse; ∼ **perso'nality** n. gespaltene Persönlichkeit; ∼ '**second** n. in a

∼ **second** im Bruchteil einer Sekunde; ∼-**second timing** [zeitliche] Abstimmung auf die Sekunde genau

**splitting** /'splɪtɪŋ/ adj. a ∼ **headache** rasende Kopfschmerzen Pl.

**splutter** /'splʌtə(r)/ v.i. ⟨Person:⟩ prusten; ⟨Motor:⟩ stottern

**spoil** /spɔɪl/ 1 v.t., spoilt /spɔɪlt/ or spoiled
(a) (impair) verderben
(b) (pamper) verwöhnen; be ∼t for choice die Qual der Wahl haben
2 v.i., spoilt or spoiled (a) verderben
(b) be ∼ing for a fight Streit suchen
3 n. ∼[s pl.] Beute, die

'**spoiler** n. (of car, aircraft) Spoiler, der

'**spoilsport** n. Spielverderber, der/ -verderberin, die

**spoilt** ▶ SPOIL 1, 2

**spoke¹** /spəʊk/ n. Speiche, die

**spoke², spoken** ▶ SPEAK

**spokesman** /'spəʊksmən/ n., pl. **spokesmen** /'spəʊksmən/ Sprecher, der

**sponge** /spʌndʒ/ 1 n. Schwamm, der
2 v.t. mit einem Schwamm waschen
■ '**sponge on** v.t. ∼ on sb. bei od. von jmdm. schnorren (ugs.)

**sponge:** ∼ **bag** n. (Brit.) Kulturbeutel, der; ∼ **cake** n. Biskuitkuchen, der

**sponger** /'spʌndʒə(r)/ n. Schmarotzer, der/ Schmarotzerin, die

**spongy** /'spʌndʒɪ/ adj. schwammig

**sponsor** /'spɒnsə(r)/ 1 n. Sponsor, der
2 v.t. (a) sponsern
(b) (Polit.) ∼ sb. jmds. Kandidatur unterstützen

**spontaneity** /spɒntə'niːɪtɪ/ n. Spontaneität, die

**spontaneous** /spɒn'teɪnɪəs/ adj. spontan

**spooky** /'spuːkɪ/ adj. gespenstisch

**spool** /spuːl/ n. Spule, die

**spoon** /spuːn/ n. (a) Löffel, der
(b) (amount) ▶ SPOONFUL

'**spoon-feed** v.t. (fig.) ∼ sb. jmdm. alles vorkauen (ugs.)

**spoonful** /'spuːnfʊl/ n. a ∼ of sugar ein Löffel [voll] Zucker

**sporadic** /spə'rædɪk/ adj. sporadisch

**sporadically** /spə'rædɪkəlɪ/ adv. hin und wieder

**spore** /spɔː(r)/ n. Spore, die

**sport** /spɔːt/ 1 n. (a) Sport, der; ∼s Sportarten Pl.; **water/indoor** ∼: Wasser-/ Hallensport, der
(b) (fun) Spaß, der
(c) be a [real] ∼ (coll.) ein prima Kerl sein (ugs.); **be a** ∼! sei kein Spielverderber!
2 v.t. stolz tragen

'**sporting** adj. (a) sportlich
(b) **give sb. a** ∼ **chance** jmdm. eine [faire] Chance geben

**sports:** ∼ **bra** n. Sport-BH, der; ∼ **car** n. Sportwagen, der; ∼ **centre** n. ⋯⟩

**S**

Sportzentrum, *das;* ~ **channel** *n.*
Sportkanal, *der;* ~ **commentator** *n.*
Sportberichterstatter, *der/*-berichterstatterin,
*die;* ~ **complex** *n.* Sportzentrum, *das;*
~ **field** *n.* Sportplatz, *der;* ~ **hall** *n.*
Sporthalle, *die;* ~ **jacket** *n.* sportlicher
Sakko; ~**man** /'spɔ:tsmən/ *n., pl.* ~**men**
/'spɔ:tsmən/ Sportler, *der;* ~**manship**
/'spɔ:tsmənʃɪp/ *n.* (fairness) [sportliche]
Fairness; ~ **page** *n.* (Journ.) Sportseite, *die;*
~ **section** *n.* (Journ.) Sportteil, *der;*
~**wear** *n.* Sport[be]kleidung, *die;*
~**woman** *n.* Sportlerin, *die*

**'sporty** *adj.* sportlich

**spot** /spɒt/ ① *n.* (a) (precise place) Stelle, *die;*
on this ~: an dieser Stelle; be in a tight ~
(fig. coll.) in der Klemme sitzen (ugs.); put sb.
on the ~ (fig. coll.) jmdn. in Verlegenheit
bringen
(b) (suitable area) Platz, *der*
(c) (dot) Tupfen, *der*
(d) (stain) ~ [of blood/grease/ink] [Blut-/Fett-/
Tinten]fleck, *der*
(e) (Brit. coll.: small amount) do a ~ of work/
sewing ein bisschen arbeiten/nähen
(f) (drop) a ~ or a few ~s of rain ein paar
Regentropfen
(g) (Med.) Pickel, *der*
② *v.t.,* **-tt-** (detect) entdecken; erkennen
‹Gefahr›

**spot:** ~ **'check** *n.* Stichprobe, *die;* ~**less**
*adj.* fleckenlos; her house is absolutely ~**less**
(fig.) ihr Haus ist makellos sauber; ~**light**
*n.* Scheinwerfer, *der;* be in the ~light (fig.) im
Rampenlicht stehen

**spotted** /'spɒtɪd/ *adj.* gepunktet

**'spotty** *adj.* (pimply) picklig

**spouse** /spaʊs/ *n.* [Ehe]gatte, *der/*-gattin,
*die*

**spout** /spaʊt/ ① *n.* Schnabel, *der;* (of tap)
Ausflussrohr, *das*
② *v.i.* (gush) schießen (from aus)

**sprain** /spreɪn/ ① *v.t.* verstauchen
② *n.* Verstauchung, *die*

**sprang** ▶ SPRING 2, 3

**sprawl** /sprɔ:l/ *v.i.* (a) sich ausstrecken;
(fall) der Länge nach hinfallen
(b) (straggle) sich ausbreiten

**'sprawling** *attrib. adj.* wuchernd
‹Großstadt›

**spray**[1] /spreɪ/ (bouquet) Strauß, *der*

**spray**[2] ① *v.t.* spritzen; sprühen ‹Parfüm›;
besprühen ‹Haar, Pflanze›
② *n.* (a) (drops) Sprühnebel, *der*
(b) (liquid) Spray, *der od. das*

**spray:** ~ **can** ▶ AEROSOL A; ~ **gun** *n.*
Spritzpistole, *die*

**spread** /spred/ ① *v.t.,* spread (a)
ausbreiten ‹Tuch, Landkarte› (on auf
+ Dat.); streichen ‹Butter, Farbe, Marmelade›
(b) (extend range of) verbreiten
(c) (distribute) verteilen
② *v.i.,* spread sich ausbreiten

③ *n.* (a) Verbreitung, *die;* (of city, poverty)
Ausbreitung, *die*
(b) (coll.: meal) Festessen, *das*
(c) (paste) Brotaufstrich, *der*
(d) (Printing) the advertisement was a full-
page/double-page ~: die Anzeige war
ganzseitig/doppelseitig
■ **spread 'out** ① *v.t.* ausbreiten
② *v.i.* sich verteilen

**'spreadsheet** *n.* (Comp.) Arbeitsblatt, *das*

**spree** /spri:/ *n.* go on a shopping ~: ganz
groß einkaufen gehen

**'spree killer** *n.* Amokläufer, *der*

**sprig** /sprɪg/ *n.* Zweig, *der*

**sprightly** /'spraɪtlɪ/ *adj.* munter

**spring** /sprɪŋ/ ① *n.* (a) (season) Frühling,
*der;* in [the] ~: im Frühling *od.* Frühjahr
(b) (water) Quelle, *die*
(c) (Mech.) Feder, *die*
(d) (jump) Sprung, *der*
② *v.i.,* sprang /spræŋ/ or (Amer.) sprung
/sprʌŋ/, sprung (a) (jump) springen; ~ to life
(fig.) [plötzlich] zum Leben erwachen
(b) (arise) entspringen (from Dat.)
③ *v.t.,* sprang or (Amer.) sprung, sprung:
~ sth. on sb. jmdn. mit etw. überfallen

**spring:** ~**board** *n.* Sprungbrett, *das;*
~ **'chicken** *n.* be no ~ chicken nicht
mehr der/die Jüngste sein (ugs.); ~**'clean**
① *n.* Frühjahrsputz, *der;* ② *v.t.*
Frühjahrsputz machen in (+ Dat.);
~**loaded** *adj.* mit Sprungfeder
*nachgestellt;* ~ **'onion** *n.* Frühlingszwiebel,
*die;* ~**time** *n.* Frühling, *der*

**springy** /'sprɪŋɪ/ *adj.* elastisch; federnd
‹Schritt, Brett, Boden›

**sprinkle** /'sprɪŋkl/ *v.t.* streuen; sprengen
‹Flüssigkeit›

**sprinkler** /'sprɪŋklə(r)/ *n.* (Hort.) Sprinkler,
*der*

**sprinkling** /'sprɪŋklɪŋ/ *n.* a ~ of snow/
sugar/dust eine dünne Schneedecke/Zucker-/
Staubschicht

**sprint** /sprɪnt/ ① *v.t. & i.* rennen; sprinten
(bes. Sport)
② *n.* Sprint, *der*

**sprout** /spraʊt/ ① *n.* (a) Brussels ~s
Rosenkohl, *der*
(b) (Bot.) Trieb, *der*
② *v.i.* sprießen (geh.)

**spruce** /spru:s/ ① *adj.* gepflegt
② *n.* Fichte, *die*

**sprung** /sprʌŋ/ ① ▶ SPRING 2, 3
② *attrib. adj.* gefedert

**spry** /spraɪ/ *adj.* rege

**spud** /spʌd/ *n.* (coll.) Kartoffel, *die*

**spun** ▶ SPIN

**spunk** /spʌŋk/ *n.* (coll.: courage) Mumm, *der*
(ugs.)

**spur** /spɜ:(r)/ ① *n.* Sporn, *der;* (fig.) Ansporn,
*der;* on the ~ of the moment ganz spontan
② *v.t.,* **-rr-** (fig.) anspornen

**S**

**spurious** /'spjʊərɪəs/ *adj.* gespielt ⟨*Interesse*⟩; unberechtigt ⟨*Anspruch, Anklage*⟩

**spurn** /spɜːn/ *v.t.* zurückweisen

**spurt¹** /spɜːt/ *n.* Spurt, *der;* put on a ~: einen Spurt einlegen

**spurt²** 1 *v.i.* ~ out [from *or* of] herausspritzen [aus]
2 *n.* Strahl, *der*

**spy** /spaɪ/ 1 *n.* Spion, *der*/Spionin, *die*
2 *v.i.* spionieren; ~ on sb. jmdm. nachspionieren

**spy:** ~**master** *n.* Chef, *der* eines Spionagerings; ~ **ring** *n.* Spionagering, *der;* ~ **story** *n.* Spionagegeschichte, *die*

**squabble** /'skwɒbl/ 1 *n.* Streit, *der*
2 *v.i.* sich zanken (**over, about** wegen)

**squad** /skwɒd/ *n.* **(a)** (Mil.) Gruppe, *die* **(b)** (group) Mannschaft, *die*

**squadron** /'skwɒdrən/ *n.* **(a)** (Navy) Geschwader, *das* **(b)** (Air Force) Staffel, *die*

**squalid** /'skwɒlɪd/ *adj.* **(a)** (dirty) schmutzig **(b)** (poor) schäbig

**squall** /skwɔːl/ *n.* (gust) Bö, *die*

**squalor** /'skwɒlə(r)/ *n.* Schmutz, *der*

**squander** /'skwɒndə(r)/ *v.t.* vergeuden

**square** /skweə(r)/ 1 *n.* **(a)** (Geom.) Quadrat, *das* **(b)** (open area) Platz, *der*
2 *adj.* **(a)** quadratisch **(b)** a ~ metre/mile ein Quadratmeter/eine Quadratmeile **(c)** be all ~: [völlig] quitt sein (*ugs.*)
3 *v.t.* **(a)** (Math.) quadrieren **(b)** ~ it with sb. es mit jmdm. klären
4 *v.i.* (agree) übereinstimmen
■ **square 'up** *v.i.* (settle up) abrechnen

**square:** ~ '**brackets** *n. pl.* eckige Klammern *Pl.*; ~ '**meal** *n.* anständige Mahlzeit (ugs.); ~ '**root** *n.* Quadratwurzel, *die*

**squash** /skwɒʃ/ 1 *v.t.* (crush) zerquetschen; ~ sth. flat etw. platt drücken
2 *n.* **(a)** Fruchtsaftgetränk, *das* **(b)** (Sport) Squash, *das*

**squash:** ~ **court** *n.* Squashfeld, *das;* ~ **racket** *n.* Squashschläger, *der*

**squat** /skwɒt/ *v.i.*, -**tt**-: **(a)** (crouch) hocken **(b)** ~ in a house ein Haus besetzen

'**squatter** *n.* Hausbesetzer, *der*/-besetzerin, *die*

**squawk** /skwɔːk/ *v.i.* ⟨*Krähe:*⟩ krähen; ⟨*Huhn:*⟩ kreischen

**squeak** /skwiːk/ 1 *n.* **(a)** (of animal) Quieken, *das* **(b)** (of brakes, hinge, etc.) Quietschen, *das*
2 *v.i.* **(a)** ⟨*Tier:*⟩ quieken **(b)** ⟨*Scharnier, Tür, Bremse, Schuh usw.:*⟩ quietschen

**squeaky** /'skwiːkɪ/ *adj.* quietschend

**squeal** /skwiːl/ 1 *v.i.* **(a)** ~ with pain/in

**fear** ⟨*Person:*⟩ vor Schmerz/Angst aufschreien; ⟨*Tier:*⟩ vor Schmerz/Angst laut quieken **(b)** ⟨*Bremsen, Räder:*⟩ kreischen; ⟨*Reifen:*⟩ quietschen
2 *n.* Kreischen, *das;* (of tyres) Quietschen, *das;* (of animal) Quieken, *das*

**squeamish** /'skwiːmɪʃ/ *adj.* be ~: zart besaitet sein

**squeeze** /skwiːz/ 1 *n.* Druck, *der;* give sth. a small ~: etw. [leicht] drücken
2 *v.t.* **(a)** (press) drücken; drücken auf (+ *Akk.*) ⟨*Tube, Plastikflasche*⟩; (to get juice) auspressen **(b)** (extract) drücken (**out of** aus); ~ out sth. etw. herausdrücken **(c)** (force) zwängen

**squelch** /skweltʃ/ *v.i.* quatschen (ugs.)

**squid** /skwɪd/ *n.* Kalmar, *der*

**squiggle** /'skwɪɡl/ *n.* Schnörkel, *der*

**squint** /skwɪnt/ 1 *n.* Schielen, *das*
2 *v.i.* **(a)** (Med.) schielen **(b)** (with half-closed eyes) blinzeln

**squire** /'skwaɪə(r)/ *n.* ≈ Gutsherr, *der*

**squirm** /skwɜːm/ *v.i.* sich winden (**with** vor + *Dat.*)

**squirrel** /'skwɪrl/ *n.* Eichhörnchen, *das*

**squirt** /skwɜːt/ 1 *v.t.* spritzen; sprühen ⟨*Spray, Puder*⟩; ~ sth. at sb. jmdm. mit etw. bespritzen/besprühen
2 *v.i.* spritzen
3 *n.* Spritzer, *der*

**st.** *abbr.* (Brit.: unit of weight) = **stone**

**St** *abbr.* = **Saint** St.

**St.** *abbr.* = **Street** Str.

**stab** /stæb/ 1 *v.t.*, -**bb**- stechen; ~ sb. in the chest jmdm. in die Brust stechen
2 *v.i.*, -**bb**- stechen
3 *n.* **(a)** Stich, *der* **(b)** (coll.: attempt) make *or* have a ~ [at it] [es] probieren

**stability** /stə'bɪlɪtɪ/ *n.* Stabilität, *die*

**stabilize** /'steɪbɪlaɪz/ 1 *v.t.* stabilisieren
2 *v.i.* sich stabilisieren

**stable¹** /'steɪbl/ *adj.* stabil; gefestigt ⟨*Person*⟩

**stable²** *n.* Stall, *der*

**stack** /stæk/ 1 *n.* **(a)** (pile) Stoß, *der;* Stapel, *der* **(b)** (coll.: large amount) Haufen, *der* (ugs.) **(c)** [chimney] ~: Schornstein, *der*
2 *v.t.* ~ [up] [auf]stapeln

**stadium** /'steɪdɪəm/ *n.* Stadion, *das*

**staff** /stɑːf/ 1 *n.* **(a)** (stick) Stock, *der* **(b)** (personnel) Personal, *das;* (of school) Lehrerkollegium, *das*
2 *v.t.* mit Personal ausstatten

**staff:** ~ **meeting** *n.* [Lehrer]konferenz, *die;* ~**room** *n.* Lehrerzimmer, *das*

**stag** /stæɡ/ *n.* Hirsch, *der*

**stage** /steɪdʒ/ 1 *n.* **(a)** (Theatre) Bühne, *die* **(b)** (part of process) Stadium, *das;* at this ~: ⋯⟶

in diesem Stadium; **do sth. by** ∼**s** etw.
abschnittsweise tun; **in the final** ∼**s** in der
Schlussphase
**(c)** (distance) Etappe, *die*
**2** *v.t.* **(a)** (present) inszenieren
**(b)** (arrange) veranstalten

**stage:** ∼**coach** *n.* Postkutsche, *die;*
∼ **door** *n.* Bühneneingang, *der;* ∼ **effect**
*n.* Bühneneffekt, *der;* ∼ **fright** *n.*
Lampenfieber, *das;* ∼**hand** *n.*
Bühnenarbeiter, *der/*-arbeiterin, *die;*
∼**manage** *v.t.* (fig.) veranstalten;
∼ **name** *n.* Künstlername, *der*

**stagger** /'stægə(r)/ **1** *v.i.* schwanken
**2** *v.t.* (astonish) die Sprache verschlagen
(+ *Dat.*)

**stagnant** /'stægnənt/ *adj.* **(a)** stehend
⟨*Gewässer*⟩
**(b)** (Econ.) stagnierend

**stagnate** /stæg'neɪt/ *v.i.* **(a)** ⟨*Wasser:*⟩
abstehen
**(b)** ⟨*Wirtschaft, Geschäft:*⟩ stagnieren;
⟨*Person:*⟩ abstumpfen

**stagnation** /stæg'neɪʃn/ *n.* **(a)** (of water)
Stehen, *das*
**(b)** (Econ.) Stagnation, *die*

**stag:** ∼ **night** *n.*: Zechabend des
*Bräutigams mit seinen Freunden kurz vor
seiner Hochzeit;* ∼ **party** *n.* Herrenabend,
*der*

**staid** /steɪd/ *adj.* gesetzt

**stain** /steɪn/ **1** *v.t.* **(a)** verfärben; (make ∼s
on) Flecken hinterlassen auf (+ *Dat.*)
**(b)** (colour) beizen ⟨*Holz*⟩
**2** *n.* Fleck, *der*

**stained 'glass** *n.* farbiges Glas;
∼ '**window** Fenster mit Glasmalerei

'**stainless** *adj.* fleckenlos

**stainless 'steel** *n.* Edelstahl, *der*

'**stain remover** *n.* Fleck[en]entferner, *der*

**stair** /steə(r)/ *n.* (step) [Treppen]stufe, *die;*
∼s Treppe, *die*

**stair:** ∼**case** *n.* Treppenhaus, *das;* ∼**way**
*n.* Treppe, *die*

**stake** /steɪk/ *n.* **(a)** (pointed stick) Pfahl, *der*
**(b)** (wager) Einsatz, *der;* **be at** ∼: auf dem
Spiel stehen

**stale** /steɪl/ *adj.* alt; muffig; abgestanden
⟨*Luft*⟩; alt[backen] ⟨*Brot*⟩; schal ⟨*Bier, Wein
usw.*⟩

'**stalemate** *n.* Patt, *das*

**stalk**[1] /stɔːk/ *v.t.* **(a)** sich heranpirschen an
(+ *Akk.*)
**(b)** (follow obsessively) ∼ **sb.** jmdm. nachstellen

**stalk**[2] *n.* (Bot.) (main stem) Stängel, *der;* (of
leaf, flower, fruit) Stiel, *der*

**stalker** /'stɔːkə(r)/ *n.* (obsessive pursuer)
[lästiger] Verfolger

**stall** /stɔːl/ **1** *n.* **(a)** Stand, *der*
**(b)** (Brit. Theatre) ∼s Parkett, *das*
**2** *v.t.* abwürgen (ugs.) ⟨*Motor*⟩
**3** *v.i.* ⟨*Motor:*⟩ stehen bleiben

'**stallholder** *n.* Standinhaber, *der/*
-inhaberin, *die*

**stallion** /'stæljən/ *n.* Hengst, *der*

**stalwart** /'stɔːlwət/ *adj.* (determined)
entschieden; (loyal) treu

**stamen** /'steɪmen/ *n.* Staubblatt, *das*

**stamina** /'stæmɪnə/ *n.* Ausdauer, *die*

**stammer** /'stæmə(r)/ **1** *v.i.* stottern
**2** *v.t.* stammeln
**3** *n.* Stottern, *das*

**stamp** /stæmp/ **1** *v.t.* **(a)** (impress, imprint sth.
on) [ab]stempeln
**(b)** ∼ **one's foot** mit dem Fuß stampfen
**(c)** ( put postage ∼ on) frankieren; ∼**ed
addressed envelope** frankierter
Rückumschlag
**(d)** (become *or* be ∼ed on sb.'s memory *or*
mind) sich jmdm. fest einprägen
**2** *v.i.* aufstampfen
**3** *n.* Marke, *die;* ( postage ∼) Briefmarke, *die;*
(instrument for ∼ing) Stempel, *der*
■ '**stamp on** *v.t.* **(a)** zertreten ⟨*Insekt*⟩;
∼ **on sb's foot** jmdm. auf den Fuß treten
**(b)** (suppress) durchgreifen gegen
■ **stamp 'out** *v.t.* [aus]stanzen; (fig.)
ausmerzen

**stamp:** ∼ **album** *n.* Briefmarkenalbum,
*das;* ∼ **collecting** *n.*
Briefmarkensammeln, *das;* ∼ **collection**
*n.* Briefmarkensammlung, *die;* ∼ **duty** *n.*
Stempelsteuer, *die*

**stampede** /stæm'piːd/ *n.* Stampede, *die*

**stance** /stɑːns/ *n.* (posture; fig.: attitude)
Haltung, *die*

**stanch** /stɑːnʃ/ *v.t.* stillen ⟨*Blut*⟩; abbinden
⟨*Wunde*⟩

**stand** /stænd/ **1** *v.i.,* stood /stʊd/ **(a)**
stehen
**(b)** my offer/promise still ∼s mein Angebot/
Versprechen gilt nach wie vor; **as it** ∼**s,** as
**things** ∼: wie die Dinge [jetzt] liegen; **I'd like
to know where I** ∼ (fig.) ich möchte wissen,
wo ich dran bin
**(c)** (be candidate) kandidieren
**(d)** [not] ∼ **in sb.'s way** (fig.) jmdm. [keine]
Steine in den Weg legen
**(e)** (be likely) ∼ **to win** *or* **gain/lose sth.** etw.
gewinnen/verlieren können
**2** *v.t.,* **stood (a)** (set in position) stellen
**(b)** (endure) ertragen; **I cannot** ∼ [**the sight of**]
**him/her** ich kann ihn/sie nicht ausstehen; **he
can't** ∼ **the pressure/strain** er ist dem Druck/
den Strapazen nicht gewachsen; **I can't** ∼ **it
any longer!** ich halte es nicht mehr aus!
**(c)** (buy) ∼ **sb. sth.** jmdm. etw. spendieren
**3** *n.* **(a)** (support) Ständer, *der*
**(b)** (stall; at exhibition) Stand, *der*
**(c)** (raised structure) Tribüne, *die*
■ **stand a'bout, stand a'round** *v.i.*
herumstehen
■ **stand a'side** *v.i.* zur Seite treten
■ **stand 'back** *v.i.* **(a)** ∼ [**well**] **back** [**from
sth.**] [ein gutes Stück] [von etw.] entfernt
stehen

**(b)** (fig.: distance oneself) zurücktreten

■ '**stand be'tween** *v.t.* **sth.** ~**s between sb. and sth.** (fig.) etw. steht jmdm. bei etw. im Wege

■ **stand by** [1] /-'-/ *v.i.* **(a)** (be near) daneben stehen

**(b)** (be ready) sich zur Verfügung halten

[2] /'--/ *v.t.* **(a)** (support) ~ **by sb./one another** jmdm./sich [gegenseitig] beistehen

**(b)** (adhere to) ~ **by sth.** zu etw. stehen

■ **stand 'down** *v.i.* verzichten

■ '**stand for** *v.t.* **(a)** (signify) bedeuten

**(b)** (coll.: tolerate) sich (*Dat.*) bieten lassen

■ **stand 'in** *v.i.* aushelfen; ~ **in for sb.** für jmdn. einspringen

■ **stand 'out** *v.i.* (be prominent) herausragen; ~ **out a mile** (fig.) nicht zu übersehen sein

■ '**stand over** *v.t.* beaufsichtigen

■ **stand 'up** *v.i.* **(a)** aufstehen; ~ **up straight** sich aufrecht hinstellen

**(b)** ~ **up well [in comparison with sb./sth.]** [im Vergleich zu jmdm./etw.] gut abschneiden; ~ **up for sb./sth.** für jmdn./ etw. Partei ergreifen; ~ **up to sb.** sich jmdm. entgegenstellen

**stand-alone** /'stændə'ləʊn/ *adj.* (Comp.) selbstständig

**standard** /'stændəd/ [1] *n.* **(a)** Maßstab, *der;* **safety** ~**s** Sicherheitsnormen *Pl.;* **above/below/up to** ~: überdurchschnittlich [gut]/unter dem Durchschnitt/der Norm entsprechend

**(b)** (degree) Niveau, *das;* ~ **of living** Lebensstandard, *der*

**(c)** ~**s** (morals) Prinzipien *Pl.*

**(d)** (flag) Standarte, *die*

[2] *adj.* Standard-; **be** ~ **practice** allgemein üblich sein

**standardize** /'stændədaɪz/ *v.t.* standardisieren

'**standard lamp** *n.* Stehlampe, *die*

**stand:** ~**by** [1] *n.* **be on** ~**by** einsatzbereit sein; [2] *adj.* Ersatz-; ~**in** [1] *n.* Ersatz, *der;* [2] *adj.* Ersatz-

'**standing** [1] *n.* **(a)** (repute) Ansehen, *das*

**(b)** (duration) **of long/short** ~: von langer/ kurzer Dauer

[2] *adj.* **(a)** (erect) stehend

**(b)** fest ⟨*Regel, Brauch*⟩

**standing:** ~ '**order** *n.* Dauerauftrag, *der;* ~ **o'vation** *n.* stürmischer Beifall; ~ **room** *n.* Stehplätze *Pl.*

**stand-offish** /stænd'ɒfɪʃ/ *adj.* reserviert

**stand:** ~**pipe** *n.* Standrohr, *das;* ~**point** *n.* (fig.) Standpunkt, *der;* ~**still** *n.* Stillstand, *der;* **be at a** ~**still** stillstehen; **come to a** ~**still** zum Stehen kommen

**stank** ▶ STINK 1

**staple¹** /'steɪpl/ [1] *n.* [Heft]klammer, *die* [2] *v.t.* heften (**on** to an + *Akk.*)

**staple²** [1] *attrib. adj.* **(a)** Grund-; **a** ~ **diet** ein Grundnahrungsmittel

**(b)** (Commerc.) grundlegend; ~ **goods** Haupthandelsartikel *Pl.*

[2] *n.* (Commerc.: major item) Haupterzeugnis, *das*

**stapler** /'steɪplə(r)/ *n.* [Draht]hefter, *der*

**star** /stɑː(r)/ [1] *n.* **(a)** Stern, *der*

**(b)** (prominent person) Star, *der*

[2] *v.i.* ~ **in a film** in einem Film die Hauptrolle spielen

**starboard** /'stɑːbəd/ *n.* Steuerbord, *das*

**starch** /stɑːtʃ/ *n.* Stärke, *die*

**starchy** /'stɑːtʃɪ/ *adj.* stärkehaltig ⟨*Nahrungsmittel*⟩; (fig.: prim) steif

**stardom** /'stɑːdəm/ *n.* Starruhm, *der*

**stare** /steə(r)/ *v.i.* starren; ~ **at sb./sth.** jmdn./etw. anstarren

'**starfish** *n.* Seestern, *der*

**stark** /stɑːk/ [1] *adj.* scharf ⟨*Kontrast, Umriss*⟩

[2] *adv.* völlig; ~ **naked** splitternackt (ugs.)

'**starless** *adj.* stern[en]los

'**starlet** /'stɑːlɪt/ *n.* Starlet[t], *das*

**starling** /'stɑːlɪŋ/ *n.* Star, *der*

'**starlit** *adj.* sternhell

**starry** /'stɑːrɪ/ *adj.* sternklar

**star:** ~ **sign** *n.* Sternzeichen, *das;* ~**-studded** *adj.* ⟨*Show, Film, Besetzung*⟩ mit großem Staraufgebot

**start** /stɑːt/ [1] *v.i.* **(a)** (begin) anfangen; ~ **on sth.** etw. beginnen

**(b)** (set out) aufbrechen

**(c)** (begin to function) anlaufen; ⟨*Auto, Motor usw.:*⟩ anspringen

[2] *v.t.* **(a)** (begin) beginnen [mit]; ~ **doing** or **to do sth.** [damit] anfangen, etw. zu tun

**(b)** (cause) auslösen; anfangen ⟨*Streit, Schlägerei*⟩; legen/(accidentally) verursachen ⟨*Brand*⟩

**(c)** (set up) ins Leben rufen ⟨*Organisation, Projekt*⟩

**(d)** (switch on) einschalten; anlassen ⟨*Motor, Auto*⟩

[3] *n.* **(a)** Anfang, *der;* Beginn, *der;* (of race) Start, *der;* **from the** ~: von Anfang an; **from** ~ **to finish** von Anfang bis Ende; **make a** ~: anfangen (**on** mit); (on journey) aufbrechen

**(b)** (Sport: ~ing place) Start, *der*

'**starter** *n.* **(a)** (food) Vorspeise, *die*

**(b)** (Sport) Starter, *der*

**starting** /'stɑːtɪŋ/**:** ~ **point** *n.* (lit. or fig.) Ausgangspunkt, *der;* ~ **post** *n.* (Sport) Startpfosten, *der;* ~ **salary** *n.* Anfangsgehalt, *das*

**startle** /'stɑːtl/ *v.t.* erschrecken; **be** ~**d by sth.** über etw. (*Akk.*) erschrecken

**startling** /'stɑːtlɪŋ/ *adj.* erstaunlich

**starvation** /stɑː'veɪʃn/ *n.* Verhungern, *das*

**starve** /stɑːv/ *v.i.* ~ **[to death]** verhungern

**stash** /stæʃ/ (coll.) [1] *v.t.* ~ **[away]** verstecken

[2] *n.* [geheimes] Lager

**state** /steɪt/ [1] *n.* **(a)** (condition) Zustand, *der*

**(b)** (nation) Staat, *der*

**(c)** **be in a** ~: aufgeregt sein

**(d)** **lie in** ~: aufgebahrt sein     ···❖

**S**

2 *v.t.* (express) erklären; angeben ⟨*Alter usw.*⟩

**stately** /'steɪtlɪ/ *adj.* majestätisch; stattlich ⟨*Körperbau, Gebäude*⟩

**stately 'home** *n.* Herrensitz, *der*

**'statement** *n.* (a) (stating, account) Aussage, *die;* (declaration) Erklärung, *die* (b) [bank] ∼: Kontoauszug, *der*

**state:** ∼**-of-the-'art** *adj.* auf dem neuesten Stand der Technik *nachgestellt;* ∼ **school** *n.* (Brit.) staatliche Schule; ∼**-owned** *adj.* staatlich

**statesman** /'steɪtsmən/ *n., pl.* **statesmen** /'steɪtsmən/ Staatsmann, *der*

**static** /'stætɪk/ *adj.* statisch

**static elec'tricity** *n.* statische Elektrizität

**station** /'steɪʃn/ 1 *n.* (a) ▶ RAILWAY STATION (b) (status) Rang, *der* 2 *v.t.* aufstellen ⟨*Wache*⟩

**stationary** /'steɪʃənərɪ/ *adj.* stehend; **be** ∼: stehen

**stationer** /'steɪʃənə(r)/ *n.* ∼**'s** [shop] Schreibwarengeschäft, *das*

**stationery** /'steɪʃənərɪ/ *n.* (a) (writing materials) Schreibwaren *Pl.* (b) (writing paper) Briefpapier, *das*

**'station wagon** *n.* (Amer.) Kombiwagen, *der*

**statistic** /stə'tɪstɪk/ *n.* statistische Tatsache

**statistical** /stə'tɪstɪkl/ *attrib. adj.*, **statistically** /stə'tɪstɪkəlɪ/ *adv.* statistisch

**statistics** /stə'tɪstɪks/ *n.* Statistik, *die*

**statue** /'stætʃuː, 'stætjuː/ *n.* Statue, *die*

**statuesque** /stætʃʊ'esk/ *adj.* statuenhaft; (imposing) stattlich

**stature** /'stætʃə(r)/ *n.* Statur, *die;* (fig.) Format, *das*

**status** /'steɪtəs/ *n.* Rang, *der;* **social** ∼: [gesellschaftlicher] Status

**'status symbol** *n.* Statussymbol, *das*

**statute** /'stætjuːt/ *n.* Gesetz, *das*

**statutory** /'stætjʊtərɪ/ *adj.* gesetzlich

**staunch** /stɔːntʃ/ *adj.* treu ⟨*Freund*⟩; überzeugt ⟨*Katholik usw.*⟩

**stave** /steɪv/ *v.t.* ∼ **'off** abwenden; stillen ⟨*Hunger*⟩

**stay** /steɪ/ 1 *n.* Aufenthalt, *der;* (visit) Besuch, *der;* **come/go for a short** ∼ **with sb.** jmdn. kurz besuchen 2 *v.i.* bleiben; ∼ **put** (coll.) ⟨*Person:*⟩ bleiben[, wo man ist]; ∼ **the night in a hotel** die Nacht in einem Hotel verbringen 3 *v.t.* ∼ **the course** (fig.) durchhalten

■ **stay a'head** *v.i.* die Führung halten
■ **stay a'way** *v.i.* wegbleiben
■ **stay be'hind** *v.i.* zurückbleiben
■ **stay 'in** *v.i.* zu Hause bleiben
■ **stay 'out** *v.i.* (a) (not go home) wegbleiben (ugs.) (b) (remain outside) draußen bleiben

■ **stay 'over** *v.i.* (coll.) über Nacht bleiben
■ **stay 'up** *v.i.* aufbleiben

**'staying power** *n.* Durchhaltevermögen, *das*

**stead** /sted/ *n.* (a) **in sb.'s** ∼: an jmds. Stelle (*Dat.*) (b) **stand sb. in good** ∼: jmdm. zustatten kommen

**steadfast** /'stedfɑːst/ *adj.* standhaft; zuverlässig ⟨*Freund*⟩

**steadily** /'stedɪlɪ/ *adv.* (a) (stably) fest (b) (continuously) stetig

**steady** /'stedɪ/ 1 *adj.* (a) (stable) stabil; (not wobbling) standfest (b) (still) ruhig (c) (regular, constant) stetig; gleichmäßig ⟨*Arbeit, Tempo*⟩; stabil ⟨*Preis, Lohn*⟩; gleich bleibend ⟨*Temperatur*⟩; **we had** ∼ **rain/drizzle** wir hatten Dauerregen/es nieselte [bei uns] ständig (d) **a** ∼ **job** eine feste Stelle; **a** ∼ **boyfriend** ein fester Freund 2 *v.t.* festhalten ⟨*Leiter*⟩; beruhigen ⟨*Nerven*⟩

**steak** /steɪk/ *n.* Steak, *das*

**'steak knife** *n.* Messer mit Sägezahnung

**steal** /stiːl/ 1 *v.t.*, **stole** /stəʊl/, **stolen** /'stəʊln/ stehlen (**from** *Dat.*) 2 *v.i.*, **stole, stolen** (a) stehlen; ∼ **from sb.** jmdn. bestehlen (b) ∼ **in/out** sich hinein-/hinausstehlen

**stealth** /stelθ/ *n.* Heimlichkeit, *die;* **by** ∼: heimlich

**stealthy** /'stelθɪ/ *adj.* heimlich

**steam** /stiːm/ 1 *n.* Dampf, *der;* **let off** ∼ (fig.) Dampf ablassen (ugs.); **run out of** ∼ (fig.) den Schwung verlieren; **under one's own** ∼ (fig.) aus eigener Kraft 2 *v.t.* (Cookery) dämpfen; dünsten 3 *v.i.* dämpfen; ∼**ing hot** dampfend heiß

■ **steam a'head** *v.i.* (fig. coll.) rasche Fortschritte machen
■ **steam 'up** *v.i.* beschlagen

**steam:** ∼**boat** *n.* Dampfschiff, *das;* (small) Dampfboot, *das;* ∼ **engine** *n.* Dampflok[omotive], *die;* (stationary) Dampfmaschine, *die*

**'steamer** *n.* Dämpfer, *der*

**steam:** ∼ **iron** *n.* Dampfbügeleisen, *das;* ∼**roller** *n.* Dampfwalze, *die;* ∼ **train** *n.* Dampfzug, *der*

**'steamy** *adj.* dunstig; beschlagen ⟨*Glas*⟩

**steel** /stiːl/ 1 *n.* Stahl, *der* 2 *attrib. adj.* stählern; Stahl⟨*helm, -block, -platte*⟩ 3 *v.t.* ∼ **oneself for/against sth.** sich für/gegen etw. wappnen (geh.); ∼ **oneself to do sth.** allen Mut zusammennehmen, um etw. zu tun

**steel:** ∼ **'band** *n.* (Mus.) Steelband, *die;* ∼ **'drum** *n.* (Mus.) Steeldrum, *die;* ∼ **industry** *n.* Stahlindustrie, *die;* ∼ **'wool** *n.* Stahlwolle, *die;* ∼**works** *n. sing. or pl.* Stahlwerk, *das*

**steep**[1] /sti:p/ adj. (a) steil
(b) (coll.: excessive) happig (ugs.); **the bill is [a bit]** ~: die Rechnung ist [ziemlich] gesalzen (ugs.)

**steep**[2] v.t. (soak) einweichen

**steeped** /sti:pt/ adj. durchdrungen (**in** von)

**steeple** /'sti:pl/ n. Kirchturm, der

**steer** /stɪə(r)/ [1] v.t. steuern; lenken
[2] v.i. steuern; ~ **clear of sb./sth.** (fig. coll.) jmdm./einer Sache aus dem Weg[e] gehen

'**steering** n. (Motor Veh.) Lenkung, die

**steering:** ~ **column** n. Lenksäule, die; ~ **lock** n. Lenkradschloss, das; ~ **wheel** n. Lenkrad, das

**stem**[1] /stem/ [1] n. (a) (Bot.) Stiel, der
(b) (Ling.) Stamm, der
[2] v.i., -mm-: ~ **from sth.** auf etw. (Akk.) zurückzuführen sein

**stem**[2] v.t., -mm- (check, dam up) aufhalten; eindämmen ⟨Flut⟩; stillen ⟨Blutung⟩

**stench** /stentʃ/ n. Gestank, der

**stencil** /'stensl/ n. Schablone, die; (for duplicating) Matrize, die

**step** /step/ [1] n. (a) Schritt, der; **take a ~ back/forwards** einen Schritt zurücktreten/nach vorn treten
(b) (stair) Stufe, die; **a flight of ~s** eine Treppe; [**pair of**] ~s (ladder) Stehleiter, die
(c) **be in** ~: im Schritt sein; (with music) im Takt sein
(d) **take ~s to do sth.** Schritte unternehmen, um etw. zu tun
(e) (stage) ~ **by** ~: Schritt für Schritt; **what is the next** ~? wie geht es weiter?
(f) (grade) Stufe, die
[2] v.i., -pp- treten; ~ **inside** eintreten; ~ **into sb's shoes** (fig.) an jmds. Stelle treten; ~ **over sb./sth.** über jmdn./etw. steigen
■ **step 'back** v.i. zurücktreten
■ **step 'in** v.i. (a) eintreten
(b) (fig.) (take sb.'s place) einspringen; (intervene) eingreifen
■ **step 'up** [1] v.i. (ascend) hinaufsteigen
[2] v.t. erhöhen; verstärken ⟨Anstrengungen⟩

**step:** ~ **aerobics** n. Stepaerobic, das; ~**child** n. Stiefkind, das; ~**daughter** n. Stieftochter, die; ~**father** n. Stiefvater, der; ~**ladder** n. Stehleiter, die; ~**mother** n. Stiefmutter, die

'**stepping stone** n. Trittstein, der; (fig.) Sprungbrett, das (**to** für)

**stereo** /'sterɪəʊ/ [1] n. Stereo, das; (equipment) Stereoanlage, die
[2] adj. stereo; Stereo⟨aufnahme, -platte⟩

**stereophonic** /sterɪə'fɒnɪk/ adj. stereophon

**stereotype** /'sterɪətaɪp/ [1] n. Stereotyp, das
[2] v.t. in ein Klischee zwängen; ~**d** stereotyp

**sterile** /'steraɪl/ adj. steril

**sterility** /stə'rɪlɪtɪ/ n. Sterilität, die

**sterilization** /sterɪlaɪ'zeɪʃn/ n. Sterilisation, die

**sterilize** /'sterɪlaɪz/ v.t. sterilisieren

**sterling** /'stɜ:lɪŋ/ [1] n. Sterling, der; **in** ~: in Pfund [Sterling]
[2] attrib. adj. (a) ~ **silver** Sterlingsilber, das
(b) (fig.) gediegen

**stern**[1] /stɜ:n/ adj. streng; ernst ⟨Warnung⟩

**stern**[2] n. (Naut.) Heck, das

'**sternly** adv. streng

**steroid** /'sterɔɪd/ n. Steroid, das

**stethoscope** /'steθəskəʊp/ n. Stethoskop, das

**stew** /stju:/ [1] n. Eintopf, der
[2] v.t. schmoren [lassen]

**steward** /'stju:əd/ n. (a) (on ship, plane) Steward, der
(b) (at public meeting etc.) Ordner, der

'**stewardess** n. Stewardess, die

**stewed** /stju:d/ adj. (Cookery) geschmort

'**stewing steak** n. [Rinder]schmorfleisch, das

**stick** /stɪk/ [1] v.t., stuck /stʌk/ (a) (thrust point of) stecken; ~ **sth. in[to] sth.** mit etw. in etw. (Akk.) stechen
(b) (coll.: put) stecken; ~ **a picture on the wall/a vase on the shelf** ein Bild an die Wand hängen/eine Vase aufs Regal stellen; ~ **sth. in the kitchen** etw. in die Küche tun (ugs.)
(c) (with glue etc.) kleben
(d) **the car is stuck in the mud** das Auto ist im Schlamm stecken geblieben; **the door is stuck** die Tür klemmt [fest]
[2] v.i., stuck (a) (be fixed by point) stecken
(b) (adhere) kleben; ~ **to sth.** an etw. (Dat.) kleben
(c) (become immobile) ⟨Auto, Räder:⟩ stecken bleiben; ⟨Schublade, Tür, Griff, Bremse:⟩ klemmen; ⟨Schlüssel:⟩ feststecken
[3] n. Stock, der; **a** ~ **of chalk** ein Stück Kreide; **a** ~ **of celery/rhubarb** eine Stange Sellerie/Rhabarber
■ **stick a'bout, stick a'round** v.i. (coll.) dableiben; (wait) warten
■ '**stick by** v.t. (fig.) stehen zu
■ **stick 'on** v.t. (glue on) aufkleben
■ **stick 'out** [1] v.t. (a) herausstrecken ⟨Zunge⟩
(b) ~ **it out** (coll.) durchhalten
[2] v.i. (a) ⟨Bauch:⟩ vorstehen; **his ears** ~ **out** er hat abstehende Ohren
(b) (fig.: be obvious) sich abheben; ~ **out a mile** (coll.) [klar] auf der Hand liegen; ~ **out like a sore thumb** (coll.) ins Auge springen
■ '**stick to** v.t. (a) (be faithful to) halten ⟨Versprechen⟩; bleiben bei ⟨Entscheidung⟩
(b) ~ **to the point** beim Thema bleiben
■ **stick to'gether** v.i. zusammenkleben; (fig.) zusammenhalten
■ **stick 'up** [1] v.t. (a) (coll.) anschlagen ⟨Poster⟩; ~ **up one's hand** die Hand heben ⋯⊹

**(b)** (seal) zukleben
2 *v.i.* ~ **up for sb./sth.** für jmdn./etw. eintreten; ~ **up for yourself!** setz dich zur Wehr!

**stick de'odorant** *n.* Deo[dorant]stift, *der*

'**sticker** *n.* Aufkleber, *der*

'**sticking plaster** *n.* Heftpflaster, *das*

**stickler** /'stɪklə(r)/ *n.* **be a** ~ **for tidiness/authority** es mit der Sauberkeit sehr genau nehmen/in puncto Autorität keinen Spaß verstehen

'**stick-up** *n.* (coll.) bewaffneter Raubüberfall

'**sticky** *adj.* **(a)** klebrig; ~ **label** Aufkleber, *der*
**(b)** (humid) schwül ⟨*Klima, Luft*⟩

**stiff** /stɪf/ *adj.* **(a)** (rigid) steif; hart ⟨*Bürste, Stock*⟩; **be frozen** ~: steif vor Kälte sein
**(b)** (intense, severe) hartnäckig
**(c)** (formal) steif
**(d)** (difficult) hart ⟨*Test*⟩; schwer ⟨*Frage, Prüfung*⟩
**(e)** (coll.) **be bored/scared** ~: sich zu Tode langweilen/eine wahnsinnige Angst haben (ugs.)

**stiffen** /'stɪfn/ 1 *v.t.* steif machen
2 *v.i.* steifer werden; ⟨*Person:*⟩ erstarren

'**stiffness** *n.* Steifheit, *die*

**stifle** /'staɪfl/ 1 *v.t.* ersticken; (fig.) unterdrücken
2 *v.i.* ersticken

**stifling** /'staɪflɪŋ/ *adj.* stickig; drückend ⟨*Hitze*⟩

**stigma** /'stɪgmə/ *n.* Stigma, *das* (geh.)

**stile** /staɪl/ *n.* Zauntritt, *der*

**stiletto** /stɪ'letəʊ/ *n.* ~ **[heel]** Stöckelabsatz, *der*

**still**[1] /stɪl/ 1 *pred. adj.* still; **be** ~: [still] stehen; **hold sth.** ~: etw. ruhig halten; **keep** *or* **stay** ~: stillhalten; **stand** ~: stillstehen
2 *adv.* **(a)** (without change) noch; *expr. surprise or annoyance* immer noch
**(b)** (nevertheless) trotzdem
**(c)** *with comparative* (even) noch

**still**[2] *n.* Destillierapparat, *der*

**still:** ~ **birth** *n.* Totgeburt, *die;* ~**born** *adj.* tot geboren; ~ '**life** *n.* (Art) Stillleben, *das*

**stilt** /stɪlt/ *n.* Stelze, *die*

'**stilted** *adj.* gestelzt

**stimulant** /'stɪmjʊlənt/ *n.* Stimulans, *das*

**stimulate** /'stɪmjʊleɪt/ *v.t.* anregen

**stimulation** /stɪmjʊ'leɪʃn/ *n.* Anregung, *die*

**stimulus** /'stɪmjʊləs/ *n., pl.* **stimuli** /'stɪmjʊlaɪ/ Ansporn, *der*

**sting** /stɪŋ/ 1 *n.* **(a)** (wounding) Stich, *der;* (by jellyfish, nettles) Verbrennung, *die*
**(b)** (from ointment, wind) Brennen, *das*
2 *v.t.,* **stung** /stʌŋ/ stechen
3 *v.i.,* **stung** brennen

'**stinging nettle** *n.* Brennnessel, *die*

**stingy** /'stɪndʒɪ/ *adj.* geizig; knaus[e]rig (ugs.)

**stink** /stɪŋk/ 1 *v.i.,* **stank** /stæŋk/ *or* **stunk** /stʌŋk/, **stunk** stinken (**of** nach)
2 *n.* Gestank, *der*

'**stink bomb** *n.* Stinkbombe, *die*

**stint** /stɪnt/ 1 *v.i.* ~ **on sth.** an etw. (*Dat.*) sparen
2 *n.* [Arbeits]pensum, *das*

**stipulate** /'stɪpjʊleɪt/ *v.t.* (demand) fordern; (lay down) festlegen

**stipulation** /stɪpjʊ'leɪʃn/ *n.* (condition) Bedingung, *die*

**stir** /stɜː(r)/ 1 *v.t.,* **-rr-: (a)** (mix) rühren; umrühren ⟨*Tee, Kaffee*⟩
**(b)** (move) bewegen
2 *v.i.,* **-rr-** (move) sich rühren
3 *n.* Aufregung, *die*
■ **stir 'in** *v.t.* einrühren
■ **stir 'up** *v.t.* **(a)** (disturb) aufrühren
**(b)** (fig.: arouse) wecken ⟨*Interesse, Leidenschaft*⟩

**stirring** /'stɜːrɪŋ/ *adj.* bewegend ⟨*Musik, Poesie*⟩; mitreißend ⟨*Rede*⟩

**stirrup** /'stɪrəp/ *n.* Steigbügel, *der*

**stitch** /stɪtʃ/ 1 *n.* **(a)** (Sewing) Stich, *der;* (Knitting) Masche, *die*
**(b)** (pain) **have a** ~: Seitenstechen haben
2 *v.t.* nähen
■ **stitch 'up** *v.t.* **(a)** nähen; vernähen ⟨*Loch, Riss, Wunde*⟩
**(b)** (Brit. fig. coll.: betray, cheat) reinlegen (ugs.); linken (salopp)

'**stitching** *n.* **(a)** Naht, *die*
**(b)** (ornamental stitches) Stickerei, *die*

**stoat** /stəʊt/ *n.* Hermelin, *das*

**stock** /stɒk/ 1 *n.* **(a)** (origin, family, breed) Abstammung, *die*
**(b)** (supply, store) Vorrat, *der;* (in shop etc.) Warenbestand, *der;* **be in/out of** ~ ⟨*Ware:*⟩ vorrätig/nicht vorrätig sein; **have sth. in** ~: etw. auf Lager haben; **take** ~ **of sth.** (fig.) über etw. (*Akk.*) Bilanz ziehen
**(c)** (Cookery) Brühe, *die*
2 *v.t.* **(a)** (supply with ~) beliefern
**(b)** (Commerc.: keep in ~) auf Lager haben
3 *attrib. adj.* Standard-

**stock:** ~**broker** Effektenmakler, *der/*-maklerin, *die;* ~ **cube** *n.* Brühwürfel, *der;* ~ **exchange** *n.* Börse, *die*

**stocking** /'stɒkɪŋ/ *n.* Strumpf, *der*

'**stockist** *n.* Fachhändler, *der/*-händlerin, *die*

**stock:** ~ **market** *n.* **(a)** Börse, *die;* **(b)** (trading) Börsengeschäft, *das;* ~ **market crash** Börsenkrach, *der;* ~**pile** 1 *n.* Vorrat, *der;* (weapons) Arsenal, *das;* 2 *v.t.* horten; anhäufen ⟨*Waffen*⟩; ~**pot** *n.* Suppentopf, *der;* ~**room** *n.* Lager, *das;* ~-'**still** *pred. adj.* bewegungslos; ~**taking** *n.* Inventur, *die*

**stocky** /'stɒkɪ/ *adj.* stämmig

**stodgy** /'stɒdʒɪ/ *adj.* pappig

**stoical** /'stəʊɪkl/ adj. stoisch

**stoicism** /'stəʊɪsɪzm/ n. Stoizismus, der

**stoke** /stəʊk/ v.t. heizen ⟨Ofen, Kessel⟩; unterhalten ⟨Feuer⟩

**stole** ▸ STEAL

**stolen** /'stəʊln/ [1] ▸ STEAL

⟦2⟧ attrib. adj. heimlich ⟨Vergnügen, Kuss⟩

**stolid** /'stɒlɪd/ adj. stur (ugs.)

**stomach** /'stʌmək/ [1] n. (a) Magen, der

(b) (abdomen) Bauch, der

⟦2⟧ v.t. (fig.: tolerate) ausstehen

**stomach:** ∼ **ache** n. Magenschmerzen Pl.; **have a** ∼ **ache** Magenschmerzen haben; ∼ **upset** n. Magenverstimmung, die

**stone** /stəʊn/ [1] n. (a) Stein, der; **a** ∼**'s throw [away]** (fig.) nur einen Steinwurf weit entfernt; **be written** or **carved** or **set in** ∼ (fig.) unverrückbar sein

(b) (Brit.: weight unit) Gewicht von 6,35 kg

⟦2⟧ adj. steinern; Stein⟨mauer, -brücke⟩

⟦3⟧ v.t. mit Steinen bewerfen

**stone:** **S**∼ **Age** n. Steinzeit, die; ∼**-cold** adj. eiskalt

**stoned** /stəʊnd/ adj. (sl.) stoned (Drogenjargon); (drunk) voll zu (salopp)

**stone:** ∼**-'dead** pred. adj. mausetot (fam.); **kill sth.** ∼**-dead** (fig.) etw. völlig zunichte machen; ∼**-'deaf** adj. stocktaub (ugs.); ∼**mason** n. Steinmetz, der; ∼**'wall** (Brit.) v.i. mauern (fig.); ∼**ware** n., no pl. Steingut, das; attrib. ⟨Krug, Vase⟩ aus Steingut; ∼**washed** adj. mit Steinen ausgewaschen; ∼**work** n. Mauerwerk, das

**stony** /'stəʊnɪ/ adj. steinig

**stood** ▸ STAND 1, 2

**stool** /stuːl/ n. Hocker, der

**stoop** /stuːp/ [1] v.i. ∼ **[down]** sich bücken

⟦2⟧ n. **walk with a** ∼: gebeugt gehen

**stop** /stɒp/ [1] v.t., **-pp-**: (a) anhalten ⟨Person, Fahrzeug⟩; aufhalten ⟨Fortschritt, Verkehr, Feind⟩

(b) (not let continue) unterbrechen ⟨Redner, Spiel, Gespräch⟩; beenden ⟨Krieg, Arbeit⟩; stoppen ⟨Produktion, Uhr⟩; einstellen ⟨Zahlung, Lieferung⟩; ∼ **that!** hör damit auf!; ∼ **smoking/crying** aufhören zu rauchen/ weinen

(c) (not let happen) verhindern ⟨Verbrechen, Unfall⟩; ∼ **sth. [from] happening** verhindern, dass etw. geschieht

(d) (switch off) abstellen ⟨Maschine⟩

(e) (block up) zustopfen ⟨Loch⟩; verschließen ⟨Wasserhahn, Flasche⟩

(f) ∼ **a cheque** einen Scheck sperren lassen

⟦2⟧ v.i., **-pp-**: (a) (not extend further) aufhören; ⟨Zahlungen, Lieferungen:⟩ eingestellt werden

(b) (not move further) ⟨Fahrzeug, Fahrer:⟩ halten ⟨Maschine, Motor:⟩ stillstehen; ⟨Uhr, Fußgänger, Herz:⟩ stehen bleiben

⟦3⟧ n. (a) (halt) Halt, der; **bring to a** ∼: zum Stehen bringen ⟨Fahrzeug⟩; zum Erliegen bringen ⟨Verkehr⟩; unterbrechen ⟨Arbeit⟩; **come to a** ∼: stehen bleiben; ⟨Fahrzeug:⟩

zum Stehen kommen; ⟨Arbeit, Verkehr:⟩ zum Erliegen kommen; **put a** ∼ **to** abstellen ⟨Missstände, Unsinn⟩

(b) (place) Haltestelle, die

■ **stop 'by** v.i. (Amer.) vorbeischauen (ugs.)

■ **stop 'out** v.i. (coll.) draußen bleiben

■ **stop 'over** v.i. (coll.) übernachten (**at** bei)

■ **stop 'up** [1] v.t. zustopfen ⟨Loch, Öffnung⟩

⟦2⟧ v.i. (coll.) ▸ STAY UP

**stop:** ∼**button** n. Stopptaste, die; ∼**cock** n. Abstellhahn, der; ∼**gap** n. Notlösung, die; ∼ **light** n. (traffic light) rotes Licht; ∼**over** n. Stopover, der

**stoppage** /'stɒpɪdʒ/ n. (a) (halt) Stillstand, der; (strike) Streik, der

(b) (deduction) Abzug, der

**stopper** /'stɒpə(r)/ n. Stöpsel, der

**stopping** /'stɒpɪŋ/: ∼ **distance** n. Anhalteweg, der; ∼ **place**, ∼ **point** ns. Station, die

**stop:** ∼**press** n. letzte Meldung/ Meldungen Pl.; ∼ **sign** n. Stoppschild, das; ∼ **signal** n. Haltesignal, das; ∼**watch** n. Stoppuhr, die

**storage** /'stɔːrɪdʒ/ n. Lagerung, die; (of films, books, documents) Aufbewahrung, die; (of data, water, electricity) Speicherung, die

**storage:** ∼ **capacity** n. (Comp.) Speicherkapazität, die; ∼ **device** n. (Comp.) Speichermedium, das; ∼ **heater** n. [Nacht]speicherofen, der; ∼ **space** n. Lagerraum, der; (in house) Platz [zum Aufbewahren], der; ∼ **tank** n. Sammelbehälter, der

**store** /stɔː(r)/ [1] n. (a) (Amer.: shop) Laden, der

(b) (Brit.: large general shop) Kaufhaus, das

(c) (warehouse) Lager, das; **put sth. in** ∼: etw. einlagern

(d) (stock) Vorrat, der (**of** an + Dat.); **be** or **lie in** ∼ **for sb.** jmdn. erwarten

(e) **set [great]** ∼ **by** or **on sth.** [großen] Wert auf etw. (Akk.) legen

⟦2⟧ v.t. einlagern; speichern ⟨Getreide, Energie, Wissen, Daten⟩

■ **store 'up** v.t. speichern; ∼ **up provisions** sich (Dat.) Vorräte anlegen

**store:** ∼ **detective** n. Kaufhausdetektiv, der; ∼**house** n. Lager[haus], das; ∼**keeper** n. (Amer.: shopkeeper) Besitzer eines Einzelhandelsgeschäftes; ∼**room** n. Lagerraum, der

**storey** /'stɔːrɪ/ n. Stockwerk, das

**stork** /stɔːk/ n. Storch, der

**storm** /stɔːm/ [1] n. Unwetter, das; (thunder∼) Gewitter, das

⟦2⟧ v.t. & i. stürmen

**'storm damage** n. Sturmschaden, der (meist Pl.)

**'stormy** adj. stürmisch

**story**[1] /'stɔːrɪ/ n. (a) Geschichte, die

(b) (news item) Bericht, der

(c) (coll.: lie) Märchen, das

**story**[2] (Amer.) ▸ STOREY

**'story book** n. Geschichtenbuch, das; (with fairy tales) Märchenbuch, das

**stout** /staʊt/ adj. (a) (strong) fest (b) (fat) beleibt

**stove** /stəʊv/ n. Ofen, der; (for cooking) Herd, der

**stow** /stəʊ/ v.t. verstauen (**into** in + Dat.)
■ **stow a'way** ①v.t. verwahren
② v.i. als blinder Passagier reisen

**straddle** /'strædl/ v.t. ~ **a fence/chair** rittlings auf einem Zaun/Stuhl sitzen

**straggle** /'strægl/ v.i. ~ [**along**] **behind the others** den anderen hinterherzockeln (ugs.)

**straggler** /'stræglə(r)/ n. Nachzügler, der

**straggly** /'stræglɪ/ zottig ⟨Haar, Bart⟩

**straight** /streɪt/ ① adj. (a) gerade; glatt ⟨Haar⟩; **in a** ~ **line** in gerader Linie (b) (undiluted) **drink whisky** ~: Whisky pur trinken (c) (direct) direkt ⟨Blick, Schuss, Weg⟩; **be** ~ **with sb.** zu jmdm. offen sein; **get sth.** ~ (fig.) etw. genau verstehen; **put** or **set the record** ~: die Sache richtig stellen ② adv. (a) gerade (b) (directly) geradewegs; ~ **after** sofort nach; **come** ~ **to the point** direkt zur Sache kommen; **look sb.** ~ **in the eye** jmdm. direkt in die Augen blicken; ~ **ahead** or **on** immer geradeaus (c) (frankly) aufrichtig (d) (clearly) klar ⟨sehen, denken⟩

**straight a'way** adv. sofort

**straighten** /'streɪtn/ ① v.t. (a) gerade ziehen ⟨Teppich⟩; glätten ⟨Kleidung, Haare⟩ (b) (put in order) aufräumen ② v.i. gerade werden
■ **straighten 'out** ① v.t. (a) gerade biegen; glätten ⟨Decke, Teppich⟩ (b) (clear up) klären ② v.i. gerade werden
■ **straighten 'up** ① v.t. ▶ TIDY UP ② v.i. sich aufrichten

**straight:** ~ **'face** n. **with a** ~ **face** ohne eine Miene zu verziehen; **keep a** ~ **face** keine Miene verziehen; ~**faced** adj. mit unbewegter Miene nachgestellt; ~**forward** adj. (a) (frank) freimütig; schlicht ⟨Stil, Sprache, Bericht⟩; klar ⟨Anweisung, Vorstellungen⟩; (b) (simple) einfach

**strain** /streɪn/ ① n. (a) (pull) Belastung, die; (on rope) Spannung, die (b) (tension) Stress, der; **be under [a great deal of]** ~: unter großem Stress stehen (c) (person, thing) **be a** ~ **on sb./sth.** jmdn./ etw. belasten (d) (muscular injury) Zerrung, die ② v.t. (a) (overexert) überanstrengen; zerren ⟨Muskel⟩ (b) (stretch tightly) [fest] spannen (c) (filter) durchseihen; seihen (**through** durch) ③ v.i. (strive intensely) sich anstrengen

**strained** /streɪnd/ adj. gezwungen ⟨Lächeln⟩; ~ **relations** gespannte Beziehungen Pl.

**'strainer** n. Sieb, das

**strait** /streɪt/ n. (a) in sing. or pl. (Geog.) Meerenge, die (b) usu. in pl. (distress, difficulty) Schwierigkeiten Pl.

**strait:** ~**jacket** n. Zwangsjacke, die; ~**-laced** /streɪt'leɪst/ adj. puritanisch

**strand**[1] /strænd/ n. (thread) Faden, der; (of beads) Kette, die; (of hair) Strähne, die; (of rope) Strang, der

**strand**[2] v.t. (leave behind) trockensetzen; **be [left]** ~**ed** festsitzen; (fig.) seinem Schicksal überlassen sein

**strange** /streɪndʒ/ adj. (peculiar) seltsam; sonderbar; ~ **to say** seltsamerweise; **feel** ~: sich komisch fühlen

**strangely** /'streɪndʒlɪ/ adv. seltsam

**stranger** /'streɪndʒə(r)/ n. Fremde, der/die; **he is a** ~ **here/to the town** er ist hier/in der Stadt fremd; **be a/no** ~ **to sth.** etw. nicht gewöhnt/etw. gewöhnt sein

**strangle** /'stræŋgl/ v.t. erwürgen

**'stranglehold** n. Würgegriff, der

**strangulation** /stræŋgjʊ'leɪʃn/ n. Erwürgen, das

**strap** /stræp/ ① n. (a) (leather) Riemen, der; (textile) Band, das; (shoulder ~) Träger, der; (for watch) Armband, das (b) (to grasp in vehicle) Halteriemen, der ② v.t., -pp-: ~ [**into position**]/**down** festschnallen; ~ **oneself in** sich anschnallen

**'strapless** adj. trägerlos

**strapping** /'stræpɪŋ/ adj. stramm

**strata** pl. of STRATUM

**strategic** /strə'tiːdʒɪk/ adj. strategisch

**strategically** /strə'tiːdʒɪkəlɪ/ adv. strategisch

**strategist** /'strætɪdʒɪst/ n. Stratege, der/ Strategin, die

**strategy** /'strætɪdʒɪ/ n. Strategie, die

**stratosphere** /'strætəsfɪə(r)/ n. Stratosphäre, die

**stratum** /'strɑːtəm/ n., pl. **strata** /'strɑːtə/ Schicht, die

**straw** /strɔː/ n. (a) no pl. Stroh, das (b) (single stalk) Strohhalm, der; **that's the last** or **final** ~: jetzt reichts aber (c) [drinking] ~: Strohhalm, der

**strawberry** /'strɔːbərɪ/ n. Erdbeere, die

**stray** /streɪ/ ① v.i. (a) (wander) streunen (b) (deviate) abweichen (**from** von) ② n. (animal) streunendes Tier ③ adj. (a) streunend (b) (occasional) vereinzelt

**streak** /striːk/ n. Streifen, der; (in hair) Strähne, die; **have a jealous/cruel** ~: zur Eifersucht/Grausamkeit neigen

**'streaky** adj. streifig; ~ **bacon** durchwachsener Speck

**stream** /striːm/ [1] n. (of water) Wasserlauf, der; (brook) Bach, der

[2] v.i. strömen; ⟨Sonnenlicht:⟩ fluten; **have a ~ing cold** einen schlimmen Schnupfen haben

**streamer** /'striːmə(r)/ n. (ribbon) Band, das; (of paper) Luftschlange, die

**'streamline** v.t. [eine] Stromlinienform geben (+ Dat.); **be ~lined** eine Stromlinienform haben

**street** /striːt/ n. Straße, die; **in the ~:** auf der Straße; **in** (Brit.) or **on ... Street** in der ...straße

**street: ~car** n. (Amer.) Straßenbahn, die; **~ cred** /'striːt kred/ (coll.)**, ~ credibility** ns. [glaubwürdiges] Image; **~ crime** n., no indef. art. Straßenkriminalität, die; **~ lamp** n. Straßenlaterne, die; **~ lighting** n. Straßenbeleuchtung, die; **~ map** n. Stadtplan, der; **~ market** n. Straßenmarkt, der; **~ plan** n. Stadtplan, der; **~ sweeper** n. (a) (person) Straßenfeger, der/-fegerin, die (bes. nordd.); Straßenkehrer, der/-kehrerin, die (bes. südd.); (b) (vehicle) Straßenkehrmaschine, die; **~ vendor** n. Straßenhändler, der/ -händlerin, die; **~-wise** adj. (coll.) be **~-wise** wissen, wo es langgeht

**strength** /streŋθ/ n. (power) Kraft, die; (strong point, force, intensity, amount of ingredient) Stärke, die; (of poison, medicine) Wirksamkeit, die; **not know one's own ~:** nicht wissen, wie stark man ist; **give sb. ~:** jmdn. stärken; **go from ~ to ~:** immer erfolgreicher werden; **on the ~ of sth./that** aufgrund einer Sache (Gen.)/dessen; **in full ~:** in voller Stärke; **the police were there in ~:** ein starkes Polizeiaufgebot war da

**strengthen** /'streŋθən/ v.t. stärken; (reinforce, intensify) verstärken

**strenuous** /'strenjʊəs/ adj. (a) (energetic) energisch; gewaltig ⟨Anstrengung⟩ (b) (requiring exertion) anstrengend

**stress** /stres/ [1] n. (a) (strain) Stress, der; **be under ~:** unter Stress (Dat.) stehen (b) (emphasis) Betonung, die [2] v.t. (emphasize) betonen

**'stressed out** adj. (coll.) [völlig] gestresst

**stressful** /'stresfl/ adj. anstrengend

**stress: ~ mark** n. Betonungszeichen, das; **~-related** adj. stressbedingt

**stretch** /stretʃ/ [1] v.t. (a) (lengthen) strecken ⟨Arm, Hand⟩; recken ⟨Hals⟩; dehnen ⟨Gummiband⟩; (tighten) spannen (b) (widen) dehnen [2] (a) v.i. (extend in length) sich dehnen (b) **~ to sth.** (be sufficient for) für etw. reichen [3] v. refl. sich strecken [4] n. (a) **have a ~:** sich strecken (b) **at a ~** (fig.) wenn es sein muss (c) (expanse) Abschnitt, der; **a ~ of road** ein Stück Straße

(d) (period) **a four-hour ~:** eine [Zeit]spanne von vier Stunden; **at a ~:** ohne Unterbrechung [5] adj. Stretch⟨hose, -gewebe⟩

**stretcher** /'stretʃə(r)/ n. [Trag]bahre, die

**stretch: ~ marks** n. pl. Schwangerschaftsstreifen Pl.; **~ pants** n. pl. Stretchhose, die

**stretchy** /'stretʃɪ/ adj. (coll.) dehnbar

**strew** /struː/ v.t., p.p. **strewed** /struːd/ or **strewn** /struːn/ streuen

**stricken** /'strɪkn/ adj. (afflicted) heimgesucht; havariert ⟨Schiff⟩; **be ~ with fear/grief** angsterfüllt/grambeugt

**strict** /strɪkt/ adj. (a) (firm) streng; **in ~ confidence** streng vertraulich (b) (precise) streng

**'strictly** adv. streng; **~ [speaking]** streng genommen

**stride** /straɪd/ [1] n. Schritt, der; **put sb. off his ~** (fig.) jmdn. aus dem Konzept bringen; **take sth. in one's ~** (fig). mit etw. gut fertig werden [2] v.i., **strode** /strəʊd/, **stridden** /'strɪdn/ [mit großen Schritten] gehen

**strident** /'straɪdənt/ adj. schrill

**strife** /straɪf/ n. Streit, der

**strike** /straɪk/ [1] n. (Industry) Streik, der; Ausstand, der; **be on/go [out]** or **come out on ~:** in den Streik getreten sein/in den Streik treten [2] v.t., **struck** /strʌk/ (a) (hit) schlagen; ⟨Schlag, Geschoss:⟩ treffen; ⟨Blitz:⟩ [ein]schlagen in (+ Akk.) (b) (delete) streichen (**from, off** aus) (c) (ignite) anzünden ⟨Streichholz⟩ (d) (chime) schlagen (e) (impress) beeindrucken; **~ sb. as [being] silly** jmdm. dumm erscheinen; **it ~s sb. that ...:** es scheint jmdm., dass ... (f) (occur to) einfallen (+ Dat.) [3] v.i., **struck** (a) (deliver a blow) zuschlagen; ⟨Blitz:⟩ einschlagen; ⟨Unheil, Katastrophe:⟩ hereinbrechen (geh.); (hit) schlagen (**against** gegen, [up]on auf + Akk.) (b) (ignite) zünden (c) (chime) schlagen (d) (Industry) streiken

■ **strike 'back** v.i. zurückschlagen

■ **strike 'off** v.t. (**~ off list**) streichen ⟨Namen⟩; (from professional body) die Zulassung entziehen (+ Dat.)

■ **'strike through** v.t. durchstreichen ⟨Wort⟩; (on list also) ausstreichen

■ **'strike up** v.t. beginnen ⟨Unterhaltung⟩; schließen ⟨Freundschaft⟩

**strike: ~ action** n. Streikaktionen Pl.; **~ pay** n. Streikgeld, das

**'striker** n. (a) (worker on strike) Streikende, der/die (b) (Footb.) Stürmer, der/Stürmerin, die

**striking** /'straɪkɪŋ/ adj. auffallend; erstaunlich ⟨Ähnlichkeit⟩; schlagend ⟨Beispiel⟩

**S**

**'striking distance** n. Reichweite, *die*

**string** /strɪŋ/ ① n. **(a)** (thin cord) Schnur, *die;* (to tie up parcels etc. also) Bindfaden, *der;* **pull [a few or some] ~s** (fig.) seine Beziehungen spielen lassen; **with no ~s attached** ohne Bedingung[en]

**(b)** (of bow) Sehne, *die;* (of racket, musical instrument) Saite, *die*

② v.t., **strung** /strʌŋ/ (thread) auffädeln

■ **string a'long** v.t. (deceive) an der Nase herumführen (ugs.)

■ **string to'gether** v.t. auffädeln; miteinander verknüpfen ⟨*Wörter*⟩

■ **string 'up** v.t. aufhängen

**string: ~ bag** n. [Einkaufs]netz, *das;* **~ 'bean** n. (Amer.) Stangenbohne, *die*

**stringed** /strɪŋd/ attrib. adj. (Mus.) Saiten-

**stringent** /'strɪndʒənt/ adj. streng

**string 'vest** n. Netzhemd, *das*

**strip¹** /strɪp/ ① v.t., **-pp-** ausziehen ⟨*Person*⟩ ② v.i., **-pp-** sich ausziehen

**strip²** n. (narrow piece) Streifen, *der*

**strip: ~ cartoon** n. Comic[strip], *der;* **~ club** n. Stripteaselokal, *das*

**stripe** /straɪp/ n. Streifen, *der*

**striped** /straɪpt/ adj. gestreift

**strip: ~ light** n. Neonröhre, *die;* **~ lighting** n. Neonbeleuchtung, *die*

**stripped pine** /strɪpt 'paɪn/ n. abgebeizte Kiefer

**stripper** /'strɪpə(r)/ n. Stripper, *der/* Stripperin, *die* (ugs.)

**strip'tease** n. Striptease, *der*

**stripy** /'straɪpɪ/ adj. gestreift; Streifen⟨*muster*⟩

**strive** /straɪv/ v.i., **strove** /strəʊv/, **striven** /'strɪvn/ sich bemühen; **~ after or for sth.** nach etw. streben

**strode** ▶ STRIDE 2

**stroke¹** /strəʊk/ n. **(a)** (act of striking) Schlag, *der*

**(b)** (Med.) Schlaganfall, *der*

**(c)** (sudden impact) **~ of lightning** Blitzschlag, *der;* **~ of [good] luck** Glücksfall, *der*

**(d)** **at a or one ~:** auf einen Schlag; **not do a ~ [of work]** keinen [Hand]schlag tun; **~ of genius** genialer Einfall

**(e)** (in swimming) Zug, *der*

**(f)** (of clock) Schlag, *der;* **on the ~ of nine** Punkt neun [Uhr]

**stroke²** ① v.t. streicheln

② n. **give sb./sth. a ~:** jmdn./etw. streicheln

**stroll** /strəʊl/ ① v.i. spazieren gehen

② n. **go for a ~:** einen Spaziergang machen

**strong** /strɒŋ/ adj., **-er** /'strɒŋgə(r)/, **-est** /'strɒŋgɪst/ stark; fest ⟨*Fundament, Schuhe*⟩; robust ⟨*Konstitution, Magen*⟩; kräftig ⟨*Arme, Muskeln, Tritt, Zähne*⟩; leistungsfähig ⟨*Wirtschaft*⟩; gut, handfest ⟨*Grund, Beispiel, Argument*⟩; glühend ⟨*Anhänger*⟩; kräftig ⟨*Geruch, Geschmack, Stimme*⟩; **there is a**

**~ possibility that ...:** es ist sehr wahrscheinlich, dass ...; **take ~ measures/ action** energisch vorgehen

**strong: ~hold** n. Festung, *die;* (fig.) Hochburg, *die;* **~ 'language** n. derbe Ausdrucksweise

**'strongly** adv. stark; solide ⟨*gearbeitet*⟩; energisch ⟨*protestieren, bestreiten*⟩; nachdrücklich ⟨*unterstützen*⟩; dringend ⟨*raten*⟩; fest ⟨*glauben*⟩

**strong: ~man** n. Muskelmann, *der* (ugs.); **~'minded** adj. willensstark; **~room** n. Tresorraum, *der;* **~'willed** adj. willensstark

**stroppy** /'strɒpɪ/ adj. (Brit. coll.) pampig (salopp)

**strove** ▶ STRIVE

**struck** ▶ STRIKE 2, 3

**structural** /'strʌktʃərl/ adj. baulich

**structure** /'strʌktʃə(r)/ n. **(a)** Struktur, *die* **(b)** (something constructed) Konstruktion, *die;* (building) Bauwerk, *das*

**structured** /'strʌktʃəd/ adj. strukturiert; geregelt ⟨*Leben*⟩

**struggle** /'strʌgl/ ① v.i. kämpfen; **~ to do sth.** sich abmühen, etw. zu tun; **~ against or with sb./sth.** mit jmdm./etw. od. gegen jmdn./ etw. kämpfen; **~ with sth.** (try to cope) mit etw. kämpfen

② n. Kampf, *der*

**strum** /strʌm/ ① v.i., **-mm-** klimpern (ugs.) (on auf + *Dat.*)

② v.t., **-mm-** klimpern (ugs.) auf (+ *Dat.*)

**strung** ▶ STRING 2

**strut¹** /strʌt/ ① v.i., **-tt-** stolzieren

② n. stolzierender Gang

**strut²** n. (support) Strebe, *die*

**stub** /stʌb/ ① n. **(a)** (remaining portion) Stummel, *der;* (of cigarette) Kippe, *die* **(b)** (counterfoil) Abschnitt, *der*

② v.t., **-bb-:** **(a)** **~ one's toe** [against or on sth.] sich (*Dat.*) den Zeh [an etw. (*Dat.*)] stoßen

**(b)** ausdrücken ⟨*Zigarette*⟩

■ **stub 'out** v.t. ausdrücken

**stubble** /'stʌbl/ n. Stoppeln *Pl.*

**stubbly** /'stʌblɪ/ adj. stopp[e]lig

**stubborn** /'stʌbən/ adj. **(a)** (obstinate) starrköpfig; störrisch ⟨*Tier, Gesicht, Haltung*⟩

**(b)** (resolute) hartnäckig

**'stubbornness** n. ▶ STUBBORN: Starrköpfigkeit, *die;* Hartnäckigkeit, *die*

**stuck** ▶ STICK 1, 2

**'stuck up** adj. (conceited) eingebildet

**student** /'stjuːdənt/ n. Student, *der/* Studentin, *die;* (in school or training establishment) Schüler, *der/*Schülerin, *die;* **be a ~ of sth.** etw. studieren

**studio** /'stjuːdɪəʊ/ n., pl. **~s** **(a)** (workroom) Atelier, *das*

**(b)** (Cinemat., Radio, Telev.) Studio, *das*

**studio: ~ apartment** (Amer.) ▶ ~ FLAT;

~ **'audience** n. (Radio, Telev.) Publikum im Studio; ~ **flat** n. (Brit.) **(a)** Atelier, das; **(b)** (one-room flat) Einzimmerwohnung, die

**studious** /'stju:dɪəs/ adj. lerneifrig

**study** /'stʌdɪ/ [1] n. **(a)** Studium, das **(b)** (room) Arbeitszimmer, das [2] v.t. studieren; sich (Dat.) [sorgfältig] durchlesen (Prüfungsfragen, Bericht)

**'study group** n. Arbeitsgruppe, die

**stuff** /stʌf/ [1] n. (material[s]) Zeug, das (ugs.) [2] v.t. **(a)** stopfen; zustopfen (Loch, Ohren); (Cookery) füllen; ~ sth. with or full of sth. etw. mit etw. voll stopfen (ugs.) **(b)** (sl.) ~ him! zum Teufel mit ihm!

**stuffed 'shirt** n. (coll. derog.) Spießer, der (ugs. abwertend)

**'stuffing** n. **(a)** (material) Füllmaterial, das **(b)** (Cookery) Füllung, die

**stuffy** /'stʌfɪ/ adj. stickig

**stumble** /'stʌmbl/ v.i. stolpern (over über + Akk.)

**stumbling block** /'stʌmblɪŋblɒk/ n. Stolperstein, der

**stump** /stʌmp/ [1] n. (of tree, branch, tooth) Stumpf, der; (of cigar, pencil) Stummel, der [2] v.t. verwirren; be ~ed ratlos sein

**'stumpy** adj. gedrungen; ~ **tail** Stummelschwanz, der

**stun** /stʌn/ v.t., -nn- (knock senseless) betäuben; be ~ned at or by sth. (fig.) von etw. wie betäubt sein

**stung** ▶ STING 2, 3

**stunk** ▶ STINK 1

**stunner** /'stʌnə(r)/ n. (coll.) be a ~: Spitze sein (ugs.)

**stunning** /'stʌnɪŋ/ adj. (coll.) **(a)** (splendid) hinreißend **(b)** (shocking) bestürzend (Nachricht); (amazing) sensationell

**stunt¹** /stʌnt/ v.t. hemmen

**stunt²** n. halsbrecherisches Kunststück; (Cinemat.) Stunt, der

**'stunt man** n. Stuntman, der

**stupefying** /'stju:pɪfaɪɪŋ/ adj. die Sinne betäubend (Hitze); (fig.: astonishing) unfassbar

**stupendous** /stju:'pendəs/ adj. gewaltig

**stupid** /'stju:pɪd/ adj. dumm; (ridiculous) lächerlich; **it would be** ~ **to do sth.** es wäre töricht, etw. zu tun

**stupidity** /stju:'pɪdɪtɪ/ n. Dummheit, die

**'stupidly** adv. dumm

**stupor** /'stju:pə(r)/ n. Benommenheit, die; **in a drunken** ~: sinnlos betrunken

**sturdy** /'stɜ:dɪ/ adj. kräftig; stämmig (Beine, Arme)

**stutter** /'stʌtə(r)/ [1] v.i. stottern [2] n. Stottern, das

**sty¹** /staɪ/ ▶ PIGSTY

**sty², stye** /staɪ/ n. (Med.) Gerstenkorn, das

**style** /staɪl/ n. Stil, der; [hair]~: Frisur, die; **dress in the latest** ~: sich nach der neuesten Mode kleiden

**styli** pl. of STYLUS

**stylish** /'staɪlɪʃ/ adj. stilvoll; elegant (Kleidung, Auto, Person)

**stylist** /'staɪlɪst/ n. (hair~) Haarstilist, der/ -stilistin, die

**stylus** /'staɪləs/ n., pl. **styli** /'staɪlaɪ/ or ~**es** [Abtast]nadel, die

**suave** /swɑ:v/ adj. gewandt

**sub-** /sʌb/ pref. unter-; sub-

**sub'conscious** [1] adj. unterbewusst [2] n. Unterbewusstsein, das

**sub'continent** n. Subkontinent, der

**'subcontract** v.t. an einen Subunternehmer vergeben

**subcon'tractor** n. Subunternehmer, der/ -unternehmerin, die

**'subculture** n. Subkultur, die

**subdivide** /---, --'-/ v.t. unterteilen

**subdue** /səb'dju:/ v.t. bändigen (Kind, Tier); dämpfen (Zorn, Lärm, Licht)

**subdued** /səb'dju:d/ adj. gedämpft

**'subgroup** n. Untergruppe, die

**'subheading** n. Untertitel, der

**sub'human** adj. unmenschlich

**subject** [1] /'sʌbdʒɪkt/ n. **(a)** Staatsbürger, der/-bürgerin, die; (to monarch) Untertan, der/ Untertanin, die **(b)** (topic) Thema, das; (of study) Fach, das; **change the** ~: das Thema wechseln [2] /'sʌbdʒɪkt/ adj. **be** ~ **to sth.** von etw. abhängen [3] /səb'dʒekt/ v.t. unterwerfen (**to** Dat.); (expose) ~ **sb./sth. to sth.** jmdn./etw. einer Sache (Dat.) aussetzen

**subjective** /səb'dʒektɪv/ adj.,

**sub'jectively** adv. subjektiv

**'subject matter** n., no indef. art. Gegenstand, der

**subjugate** /'sʌbdʒʊgeɪt/ v.t. unterjochen (**to** unter + Akk.)

**subjugation** /sʌbdʒʊ'geɪʃn/ n. Unterjochung, die

**subjunctive** /səb'dʒʌŋktɪv/ n. Konjunktiv, der

**sub'let** v.t., -tt-, **sublet** untervermieten

**sublime** /sə'blaɪm/ adj. erhaben

**submarine** /sʌbmə'ri:n/ n. Unterseeboot, das; U-Boot, das

**submerge** /səb'mɜ:dʒ/ v.t. **(a)** ~ **sth.** [**in the water**] etw. eintauchen **(b)** (flood) überschwemmen (Wasser); **be** ~**d in water** unter Wasser stehen

**submerged** /səb'mɜ:dʒd/ adj. versunken

**submission** /səb'mɪʃn/ n. **(a)** (surrender, meekness) Unterwerfung, die **(b)** (presentation) Einreichung, die (**to** bei)

**submissive** /səb'mɪsɪv/ adj. gehorsam

**submit** /səb'mɪt/ v.t., -tt- (present) einreichen; vorbringen (Vorschlag); ~ **sth. to sb.** jmdm. etw. vorlegen

**S**

**subordinate** ☐1 /səˈbɔːdɪnət/ *adj.*
untergeordnet
☐2 /səˈbɔːdɪnət/ *n.* Untergebene, *der/die*
☐3 /səˈbɔːdɪneɪt/ *v.t.* unterordnen (**to** *Dat.*)

**subscribe** /səbˈskraɪb/ *v.i.* (a) (support) ∼ **to sth.** sich einer Sache anschließen
(b) (make contribution) ∼ **to sth.** eine Spende für etw. zusichern
(c) ∼ **to a newspaper** eine Zeitung abonnieren

**subˈscriber** *n.* (to newspaper etc.) Abonnent, *der*/Abonnentin, *die* (**to** *Gen.*)

**subscription** /səbˈskrɪpʃn/ *n.* (membership fee) Mitgliedsbeitrag, *der* (**to** für); (to newspaper etc.) Abonnement, *das*

**subsequent** /ˈsʌbsɪkwənt/ *adj.* folgend; später ⟨*Gelegenheit*⟩

**ˈsubsequently** *adv.* später; danach

**subservient** /səbˈsɜːvɪənt/ *adj.* untergeordnet (**to** *Dat.*); (servile) unterwürfig

**subside** /səbˈsaɪd/ *v.i.* (a) (sink lower) ⟨*Flut, Fluss:*⟩ sinken; ⟨*Boden, Haus:*⟩ sich senken
(b) (abate) nachlassen

**subsidence** /səbˈsaɪdəns/ *n.* (of ground, structure) Senkung, *die*

**subsidiary** /səbˈsɪdɪərɪ/ ☐1 *adj.* untergeordnet ⟨*Funktion, Stellung*⟩; Neben⟨*fach, -aspekt*⟩
☐2 *n.* (Commerc.) Tochtergesellschaft, *die*

**subsidize** /ˈsʌbsɪdaɪz/ *v.t.* subventionieren

**subsidy** /ˈsʌbsɪdɪ/ *n.* Subvention, *die*

**subsist** /səbˈsɪst/ *v.i.* ∼ **on sth.** von etw. leben

**subsistence** /səbˈsɪstəns/ *n.* [Über]leben, *das*

**ˈsubsoil** *n.* Untergrund, *der*

**substance** /ˈsʌbstəns/ *n.* (a) Stoff, *der*
(b) (solidity) Substanz, *die*
(c) (content) Inhalt, *der*

**ˈsubstance abuse** *n.* Drogen- und Genussmittelmissbrauch, *der*

**subˈstandard** *adj.* unzulänglich

**substantial** /səbˈstænʃl/ *adj.* (a) (considerable) beträchtlich
(b) gehaltvoll ⟨*Essen*⟩
(c) (solid) solide ⟨*Möbel, Haus*⟩; wesentlich ⟨*Unterschied*⟩

**subˈstantially** *adv.* (a) (considerably) wesentlich
(b) (solidly) solide
(c) (essentially) im Wesentlichen

**substitute** /ˈsʌbstɪtjuːt/ ☐1 *n.* (a) ∼[s *pl.*] Ersatz, *der*
(b) (Sport) Ersatzspieler, der/-spielerin, *die*
☐2 *v.t.* ∼ **A for B** B durch A ersetzen

**substitution** /sʌbstɪˈtjuːʃn/ *n.* Ersetzung, *die*; **make a** ∼ (Sport) [einen Spieler] auswechseln

**subterfuge** /ˈsʌbtəfjuːdʒ/ *n.* Täuschungsmanöver *Pl.*

**ˈsubtitle** *n.* Untertitel, *der*

**subtle** /ˈsʌtl/ *adj.* subtil (geh.); zart ⟨*Duft, Parfüm, Hinweis*⟩; fein ⟨*Geschmack, Unterschied, Humor*⟩

**ˈsubtotal** *n.* Zwischensumme, *die*

**subtract** /səbˈtrækt/ *v.t.* abziehen

**subtraction** /səbˈtrækʃn/ *n.* Subtraktion, *die*

**subˈtropical** *adj.* subtropisch

**suburb** /ˈsʌbɜːb/ *n.* Vorort, *der*

**suburban** /səˈbɜːbən/ *adj.* Vorort-; ⟨*Leben, Haus*⟩ am Stadtrand

**suburbia** /səˈbɜːbɪə/ *n.* (derog.) die [eintönigen] Vororte *Pl.*

**subversive** /səbˈvɜːsɪv/ *adj.* subversiv

**ˈsubway** *n.* (a) (passage) Unterführung, *die*
(b) (Amer.: railway) Untergrundbahn, *die;* U-Bahn, *die*

**sub-ˈzero** *adj.* ∼ **temperatures/conditions** Temperaturen unter Null

**succeed** /səkˈsiːd/ ☐1 *v.i.* (a) Erfolg haben; **sb.** ∼**s in sth.** jmdm. gelingt etw.; jmd. schafft etw.; **sb.** ∼**s in doing sth.** es gelingt jmdm., etw. zu tun; jmd. schafft es, etw. zu tun; ∼ **in business/college** geschäftlich/im Studium erfolgreich sein; **I did not** ∼ **in doing it** ich habe es nicht geschafft
(b) (come next) die Nachfolge antreten
☐2 *v.t.* (take place of) ablösen

**success** /səkˈses/ *n.* Erfolg, *der;* **make a** ∼ **of sth.** bei etw. Erfolg haben

**successful** /səkˈsesfl/ *adj.* erfolgreich; **be** ∼ **in sth./doing sth.** Erfolg bei etw. haben/ dabei haben, etw. zu tun

**sucˈcessfully** *adv.* erfolgreich

**succession** /səkˈseʃn/ *n.* (a) Folge, *die;* **in** ∼: hintereinander
(b) (series) Serie, *die*
(c) (to throne) Erbfolge, *die*

**successive** /səkˈsesɪv/ *adj.* aufeinander folgend

**sucˈcessively** *adv.* hintereinander

**successor** /səkˈsesə(r)/ *n.* Nachfolger, *der*/ Nachfolgerin, *die*

**sucˈcess story** *n.* Erfolgsstory, *die* (ugs.)

**succinct** /səkˈsɪŋkt/ *adj.* (a) (terse) knapp
(b) (clear) prägnant

**succulent** /ˈsʌkjʊlənt/ *adj.* saftig

**succumb** /səˈkʌm/ *v.i.* unterliegen; ∼ **to sth.** einer Sache (*Dat.*) erliegen

**such** /sʌtʃ/ ☐1 *adj.* (a) (of that kind) solch...; ∼ **a person** ein solcher Mensch; ∼ **a book** ein solches Buch; ∼ **people** solche Leute; ∼ **things** so etwas; **I said no** ∼ **thing** ich habe nichts dergleichen gesagt; **there is no** ∼ **bird** einen solchen Vogel gibt es nicht; **or some** ∼ **thing** oder so etwas; **you'll do no** ∼ **thing** das wirst du nicht tun; **experiences** ∼ **as these** solche Erfahrungen
(b) (so great) solch...; derartig; **I got** ∼ **a fright that** ...: ich bekam einen derartigen *od.* (ugs.) so einen Schrecken, dass ...; ∼ **was the force of the explosion that** ...: die Explosion war so stark, dass ...; **to** ∼ **an extent** dermaßen

**(c)** *with adj.* so; ~ **a big house** ein so großes
Haus; ~ **a long time** so lange
**2** *pron.* **as ~:** als solcher/solche/solches;
(strictly speaking) im Grunde genommen; an
sich; ~ **as** wie [zum Beispiel]; ~ **is life** so ist
das Leben

**such-and-such** /'sʌtʃənsʌtʃ/ *adj.* **at ~ a
time** um die und die Zeit

'**suchlike** *pron.* derlei

**suck** /sʌk/ **1** *v.t.* saugen (**out of** aus);
lutschen ⟨*Bonbon*⟩
**2** *sth.* ~**s** (esp. Amer. sl.) etw. ist Scheiße
(derb)

■ **suck 'up 1** *v.t.* aufsaugen
**2** *v.i.* ~ **up to sb.** (coll.) jmdm. in den
Hintern kriechen (salopp)

'**sucker** *n.* **(a)** (suction pad) Saugfuß, *der;*
(Zool.) Saugnapf, *der*
**(b)** (coll.: dupe) Dumme, *der/die*

**suckle** /'sʌkl/ *v.t.* säugen

**suction** /'sʌkʃn/ *n.* Saugwirkung, *die*

**Sudan** /suː'dɑːn/ *pr. n.* **[the] ~:** [der] Sudan

**sudden** /'sʌdn/ **1** *adj.* **(a)** (unexpected)
plötzlich
**(b)** (abrupt) jäh ⟨*Abgrund, Übergang, Ruck*⟩;
**there was a ~ bend in the road** plötzlich
machte die Straße eine Biegung
**2** *n.* **all of a ~:** plötzlich

'**suddenly** *adv.* plötzlich

'**suddenness** *n.* Plötzlichkeit, *die*

**suds** /sʌdz/ *n. pl.* **[soap]~:** [Seifen]lauge,
*die;* (froth) Schaum, *der*

**sue** /suː/ **1** *v.t.* verklagen (**for** auf + *Akk.*)
**2** *v.i.* klagen (**for** auf + *Akk.*)

**suede** /sweɪd/ *n.* Wildleder, *das*

**suet** /'suːɪt/ *n.* Talg, *der*

**Suez** /'suːɪz, 'sjuːɪz/ *pr. n.* Suez (*das*);
~ **Canal** Suez-Kanal, *der*

**suffer** /'sʌfə(r)/ **1** *v.t.* erleiden;
durchmachen ⟨*Schweres, Kummer*⟩; dulden
⟨*Unverschämtheit*⟩
**2** *v.i.* leiden

■ '**suffer from** *v.t.* leiden unter (+ *Dat.*);
leiden an (+ *Dat.*) ⟨*Krankheit*⟩

**sufferance** /'sʌfərəns/ *n.* Duldung, *die;* **he
remains here on ~ only** er ist hier bloß
geduldet

'**suffering** *n.* Leiden, *das*

**suffice** /sə'faɪs/ **1** *v.i.* genügen; ~ **it to say
...:** nur so viel sei gesagt: ...
**2** *v.t.* genügen (+ *Dat.*)

**sufficiency** /sə'fɪʃnsɪ/ *n.* Zulänglichkeit,
*die*

**sufficient** /sə'fɪʃənt/ *adj.* genug; ~ **money/
food** genug Geld/genug zu essen; **be ~:**
genügen; ~ **reason** Grund genug; **have you
had ~?** (food, drink) haben Sie schon genug?

**sufficiently** *adv.* genug; (adequately)
ausreichend; ~ **large** groß genug; **a ~ large
number** eine genügend große Zahl

**suffix** /'sʌfɪks/ *n.* Nachsilbe, *die*

**suffocate** /'sʌfəkeɪt/ **1** *v.t.* ersticken; **he
was ~d by the smoke** der Rauch erstickte
ihn
**2** *v.i.* ersticken

**suffocation** /sʌfə'keɪʃn/ *n.* Erstickung,
*die;* **a feeling of ~:** das Gefühl, zu ersticken

**sugar** /'ʃʊgə(r)/ **1** *n.* Zucker, *der;* **two ~s,
please** (lumps) zwei Stück Zucker, bitte;
(spoonfuls) zwei Löffel Zucker, bitte
**2** *v.t.* zuckern

**sugar:** ~ **basin** ▶ ~ BOWL; ~ **beet** *n.*
Zuckerrübe, *die;* ~ **bowl** *n.* Zuckerschale,
*die;* (covered) Zuckerdose, *die;* ~ **cane** *n.*
Zuckerrohr, *das;* ~**coated** *adj.* gezuckert;
mit Zucker überzogen ⟨*Dragee usw.*⟩;
~ **daddy** *n.* (coll.) *spendabler älterer Mann,
der ein junges Mädchen aushält;* ~ **lump** *n.*
Zuckerstück, *das;* (when counted) Stück
Zucker; ~ **tongs** *n. pl.* Zuckerzange, *die*

'**sugary** *adj.* süß; (fig.) süßlich

**suggest** /sə'dʒest/ *v.t.* **(a)** (propose)
vorschlagen; ~ **sth. to sb.** jmdm. etw.
vorschlagen; **he ~ed going to the cinema** er
schlug vor, ins Kino zu gehen
**(b)** (assert) **are you trying to ~ that he is
lying** wollen Sie damit sagen, dass er lügt?
**(c)** (make one think of) suggerieren;
⟨*Symptome, Tatsachen:*⟩ schließen lassen auf
(+ *Akk.*)

**suggestion** /sə'dʒestʃn/ *n.* **(a)** Vorschlag,
*der;* **at or on sb.'s ~:** auf jmds. Vorschlag
(*Akk.*)
**(b)** (insinuation) Andeutungen *Pl.*
**(c)** (fig.: trace) Spur, *die*

**suggestive** /sə'dʒestɪv/ *adj.* **(a) be ~ of
sth.** auf etw. (*Akk.*) schließen lassen
**(b)** (indecent) anzüglich

**suicidal** /suːɪ'saɪdl/ *adj.* selbstmörderisch; **I
felt or was quite ~:** ich hätte mich am
liebsten gleich umgebracht

**suicide** /'suːɪsaɪd/ *n.* Selbstmord, *der*

'**suicide attempt** *n.* Selbstmordversuch,
*der*

**suit** /suːt/ **1** *n.* **(a)** (for men) Anzug, *der;* (for
women) Kostüm, *das*
**(b)** (Law) ~ **[at law]** Prozess, *der*
**(c)** (Cards) Farbe, *die;* **follow ~** (fig.) das
Gleiche tun
**2** *v.t.* **(a)** anpassen (**to** *Dat.*)
**(b) be ~ed** [**to sth./one another**] [zu etw./
zueinander] passen
**(c)** (satisfy needs of) passen (+ *Dat.*); **will
Monday ~ you?** passt Ihnen Montag?; **does
the climate ~ you?** bekommt Ihnen das
Klima?
**(d)** (go well with) passen zu; **does this hat
~ me?** steht mir dieser Hut?; **black ~s her**
Schwarz steht ihr gut
**3** *v. refl.* ~ **oneself** tun, was man will;
~ **yourself!** [ganz] wie du willst!

**suitability** /suːtə'bɪlɪtɪ/ *n.* Eignung, *die* (**for**
für)

**suitable** /'suːtəbl/ *adj.* geeignet;
angemessen ⟨*Kleidung*⟩; (convenient) passend; ⸱⸱⸱▹

~ for children für Kinder geeignet; **Monday is the most ~ day [for me]** Montag passt [mir] am besten

**suitably** /'suːtəblɪ/ adv. angemessen; entsprechend ⟨gekleidet⟩

'**suitcase** n. Koffer, der

**suite** /swiːt/ n. (a) (of furniture) Garnitur, die; **three-piece ~:** Polstergarnitur, die (b) (of rooms) Suite, die

**suitor** /'suːtə(r)/ n. Freier, der

**sulfur, sulfuric** (Amer.) ▶ SULPH-

**sulk** /sʌlk/ v.i. schmollen

'**sulky** adj. schmollend; eingeschnappt (ugs.)

**sullen** /'sʌlən/ adj. mürrisch

**sulphur** /'sʌlfə(r)/ n. Schwefel, der

**sulphuric** /sʌl'fjʊərɪk/ adj. **~ acid** Schwefelsäure, die

**sultan** /'sʌltən/ n. Sultan, der

**sultana** /sʌl'tɑːnə/ n. Sultanine, die

**sultry** /'sʌltrɪ/ adj. schwül

**sum** /sʌm/ n. (a) Summe, die (of aus); ~ **[total]** Ergebnis, das (b) (Arithmetic) Rechenaufgabe, die; **do ~s** rechnen; **she is good at ~s** sie kann gut rechnen

■ **sum 'up** ① v.t. (a) zusammenfassen (b) (Brit.: assess) einschätzen ② v.i. ein Fazit ziehen

**summarily** /'sʌmərɪlɪ/ adv. summarisch; ~ **dismissed** fristlos entlassen

**summarize** /'sʌməraɪz/ v.t. zusammenfassen

**summary** /'sʌmərɪ/ ① adj. summarisch; fristlos ⟨Entlassung⟩ ② n. Zusammenfassung, die

**summer** /'sʌmə(r)/ n. Sommer, der; **in [the] ~:** im Sommer

**summer:** ~ **house** n. [Garten]laube, die; ~ **school** n. Sommerkurs, der; ~ **term** n. Sommerhalbjahr, das; ~**time** n. Sommer, der

'**summery** adj. sommerlich

**summing 'up** n. Zusammenfassung, die

**summit** /'sʌmɪt/ n. Gipfel, der; ~ **conference/meeting** Gipfelkonferenz, die/ -treffen, das

**summon** /'sʌmən/ v.t. (a) rufen (to zu); holen ⟨Hilfe⟩ (b) (Law) vorladen

■ **summon 'up** v.t. aufbringen

**summons** /'sʌmənz/ n. Vorladung, die

**sump** /sʌmp/ n. Ölwanne, die

**sumptuous** /'sʌmptjʊəs/ adj. üppig; luxuriös ⟨Möbel, Kleidung⟩

**sun** /sʌn/ ① n. Sonne, die; **catch the ~** (be in sunny position) viel Sonne abbekommen; (get ~burnt) einen Sonnenbrand bekommen ② v. refl., **-nn-** sich sonnen

**Sun.** abbr. = **Sunday** So.

**sun:** ~**baked** adj. an der Sonne getrocknet ⟨Ziegel⟩; ausgedörrt ⟨Landschaft, Prärie usw.⟩; ~**bathe** v.i. sonnenbaden;

~**bathing** n. Sonnenbaden, das; ~**beam** n. Sonnenstrahl, der; ~**bed** n. (with UV lamp) Sonnenbank, die; (in garden) Gartenliege, die; ~**block** n. Sonnenschutzcreme, die [mit hohem Lichtschutzfaktor]; ~**burn** n. Sonnenbrand, der; ~**burnt** adj. **be/get ~burnt** einen Sonnenbrand haben/ bekommen; ~**cream** n. Sonnencreme, die

**sundae** /'sʌndeɪ/ n. **[ice cream] ~:** Eisbecher, der

**Sunday** /'sʌndeɪ, 'sʌndɪ/ n. Sonntag, der; ~ **opening** die sonntägliche Öffnung; ~ **trading** sonntägliche Ladenöffnung; see also FRIDAY

**sun:** ~**deck** n. Sonnendeck, das; ~**dial** n. Sonnenuhr, die; ~**drenched** adj. sonnenüberflutet (geh.); ~**dress** n. Strand- od. Sonnenkleid, das; ~**dried** adj. an der Sonne getrocknet

**sundry** /'sʌndrɪ/ ① adj. verschieden ② n. in pl. Verschiedenes

'**sunflower** n. Sonnenblume, die

**sung** ▶ SING

**sun:** ~**glasses** n. pl. Sonnenbrille, die; ~**hat** n. Sonnenhut, der

**sunk** ▶ SINK 2, 3

**sun:** ~**lamp** n. Höhensonne, die; ~**lit** adj. sonnenbeschienen; ~**light** n. Sonnenlicht, das

**sunny** /'sʌnɪ/ adj. sonnig; ~ **intervals** Aufheiterungen

**sun:** ~ **protection factor** n. Lichtschutzfaktor, der; ~**ray** n. Sonnenstrahl, der; ~**rise** n. Sonnenaufgang, der; ~**roof** n. (Motor Veh.) Schiebedach, das; ~**set** n. Sonnenuntergang, der; ~**shade** n. Sonnenschirm, der; ~**shine** n. Sonnenschein, der; ~**stroke** n. Sonnenstich, der; ~**tan** n. [Sonnen]bräune, die; **get a ~tan** braun werden; ~**tan lotion** n. Sonnencreme, die; ~**tanned** adj. braun [gebrannt]; ~**tan oil** n. Sonnenöl, das; ~**trap** n. sonniges Plätzchen; ~ **worshipper** n. (lit./joc.) Sonnenanbeter, der/-anbeterin, die

**super** /'suːpə(r)/ adj. (coll.) super (ugs.)

**superb** /suː'pɜːb/ adj. einzigartig; erstklassig ⟨Essen⟩

**superbug** /'suːpəbʌg/ n. multiresistenter Erreger

**supercilious** /suːpə'sɪlɪəs/ adj. hochnäsig

**supercomputer** /'suːpəkəmpjuːtə(r)/ n. Supercomputer, der

**superficial** /suːpə'fɪʃl/ adj. oberflächlich

**superficiality** /suːpəfɪʃɪ'ælɪtɪ/ n. Oberflächlichkeit, die

**superfluous** /suː'pɜːfluəs/ adj. überflüssig

**super:** ~**glue** n. Sekundenkleber, der; ~**human** adj. übermenschlich; ~**highway** n. (a) (Amer.) Autobahn, die; (b) (Comp.) Datenautobahn, die

**superintendent** /suːpərɪn'tendənt/ n. (Brit. Police) Kommissar, der/Kommissarin, die

**superior** /suːˈpɪərɪə(r)/ ⟦1⟧ *adj.* **(a)** (of higher quality) besonders gut ⟨*Restaurant, Qualität, Stoff*⟩; überlegen ⟨*Technik, Intelligenz*⟩; **he thinks he is ~ to us** er hält sich für besser als wir **(b)** (having higher rank) höher...; **be ~ to sb.** einen höheren Rang als jmd. haben ⟦2⟧ *n.* Vorgesetzte, *der/die*

**superiority** /suːpɪərɪˈɒrɪtɪ/ *n.* Überlegenheit, *die* (**to** über + *Akk.*)

**superlative** /suːˈpɜːlətɪv/ ⟦1⟧ *adj.* **(a)** unübertrefflich **(b)** (Ling.) **a ~ adjective/adverb** ein Adjektiv/Adverb im Superlativ ⟦2⟧ *n.* (Ling.) Superlativ, *der*

**super: ~market** *n.* Supermarkt, *der;* **~model** *n.* Supermodel, *das;* **~'natural** *adj.* übernatürlich; **~power** *n.* (Polit.) Supermacht, *die*

**supersede** /suːpəˈsiːd/ *v.t.* ablösen (**by** durch)

**supersonic** /suːpəˈsɒnɪk/ *adj.* Überschall-

**superstar** /ˈsuːpəstɑː(r)/ *n.* Superstar, *der*

**superstition** /suːpəˈstɪʃn/ *n.* Aberglaube, *der*

**superstitious** /suːpəˈstɪʃəs/ *adj.* abergläubisch

**superstore** /ˈsuːpəstɔː(r)/ *n.* Großmarkt, *der*

**supervise** /ˈsuːpəvaɪz/ *v.t.* beaufsichtigen

**supervision** /suːpəˈvɪʒn/ *n.* Aufsicht, *die*

**supervisor** /ˈsuːpəvaɪzə(r)/ *n.* Aufseher, *der/*Aufseherin, *die*

**supper** /ˈsʌpə(r)/ *n.* Abendessen, *das;* **have [one's] ~:** zu Abend essen

**'suppertime** *n.* Abendbrotzeit, *die;* **it's ~:** es ist Zeit zum Abendessen

**supplant** /səˈplɑːnt/ *v.t.* ablösen, ersetzen (**by** durch)

**supple** /ˈsʌpl/ *adj.* geschmeidig

**supplement** /ˈsʌplɪmənt/ ⟦1⟧ *n.* **(a)** Ergänzung, *die* (**to** + *Gen.*); (addition) Zusatz, *der* **(b)** (of book) Nachtrag, *der;* (of newspaper) Beilage, *die* **(c)** (to fare) Zuschlag, *der* ⟦2⟧ *v.t.* ergänzen

**supplementary** /sʌplɪˈmentərɪ/ *adj.* zusätzlich; **~ fare/charge** Zuschlag, *der*

**supplier** /səˈplaɪə(r)/ *n.* (Commerc.) Lieferant, *der/*Lieferantin, *die*

**supply** /səˈplaɪ/ ⟦1⟧ *v.t.* liefern ⟨*Waren usw.*⟩; beliefern ⟨*Kunden, Geschäft*⟩; **~ sth. to sb., ~ sb. with sth.** jmdn. mit etw. versorgen; (Commerc.) beliefern ⟦2⟧ *n.* Vorräte *Pl.;* **military/medical supplies** militärischer/medizinischer Nachschub; **~ and demand** (Econ.) Angebot und Nachfrage

**sup'ply teacher** *n.* Vertretung, *die*

**support** /səˈpɔːt/ ⟦1⟧ *v.t.* **(a)** (hold up) stützen ⟨*Mauer, Verletzten*⟩; (bear weight of) tragen **(b)** unterstützen ⟨*Politik, Verein*⟩; (Footb.) **~ Spurs** Spurs-Fan sein **(c)** (provide for) ernähren ⟨*Familie, sich selbst*⟩ **(d)** (speak in favour of) befürworten ⟦2⟧ *n.* **(a)** Unterstützung, *die;* **in ~:** zur Unterstützung; **speak in ~ of sb./sth.** jmdn. unterstützen/etw. befürworten **(b)** (money) Unterhalt, *der* **(c)** (sb./sth. that ~s) Stütze, *die*

**sup'porter** *n.* Anhänger, *der/*Anhängerin, *die;* **football ~:** Fußballfan, *der*

**sup'porting** *adj.* (Cinemat., Theatre) **~ role** Nebenrolle, *die;* **~ actor/actress** Schauspieler/-spielerin in einer Nebenrolle; **~ film** Vorfilm, *der*

**supportive** /səˈpɔːtɪv/ *adj.* hilfreich; **be very ~ [to sb.]** [jmdm.] eine große Hilfe *od.* Stütze sein

**suppose** /səˈpəʊz/ *v.t.* **(a)** (assume) annehmen; **~ or supposing [that] he ...:** angenommen, [dass] er ... **(b)** (presume) vermuten; **I ~ so** (doubtfully) ja, vermutlich; (more confidently) ich glaube schon **(c)** **be ~d to do/be sth.** (be generally believed to do/be sth.) etw. tun/sein sollen **(d)** (allow) **you are not ~d to do that** das darfst du eigentlich nicht; **I'm not ~d to be here** ich dürfte eigentlich gar nicht hier sein

**supposed** /səˈpəʊzd/ *attrib. adj.* mutmaßlich

**supposedly** /səˈpəʊzɪdlɪ/ *adv.* angeblich

**supposition** /sʌpəˈzɪʃn/ *n.* Annahme, *die;* Vermutung, *die*

**suppress** /səˈpres/ *v.t.* unterdrücken

**suppression** /səˈpreʃn/ *n.* Unterdrückung, *die*

**supremacy** /suːˈpreməsɪ/ *n.* **(a)** (supreme authority) Souveränität, *die* **(b)** (superiority) Überlegenheit, *die*

**supreme** /suːˈpriːm/ *adj.* höchst...

**Supt.** *abbr.* = **Superintendent**

**surcharge** /ˈsɜːtʃɑːdʒ/ *n.* Zuschlag, *der*

**sure** /ʃʊə(r)/ ⟦1⟧ *adj.* sicher; **be ~ of sth.** sich (*Dat.*) einer Sache (*Gen.*) sicher sein; **~ of oneself** selbstsicher; **don't be too ~:** da wäre ich mir nicht so sicher; **there is ~ to be a petrol station** es gibt bestimmt eine Tankstelle; **don't worry, it's ~ to turn out well** keine Sorge, es wird schon alles gut gehen; **for ~** (coll.) auf jeden Fall; **make ~ [of sth.]** sich [einer Sache] vergewissern; **make or be ~ you do it, be ~ to do it** (do not fail to do it) sieh zu, dass du es tust; (do not forget) vergiss nicht, es zu tun; **a ~ winner** ein todsicherer Tipp (ugs.) ⟦2⟧ *adv.* **~ enough** tatsächlich ⟦3⟧ *int.* **~!, ~ thing!** (Amer.) na klar! (ugs.)

**sure: ~fire** *attrib. adj.* (Amer. coll.) todsicher; **~footed** *adj.* trittsicher

**'surely** ⟦1⟧ *adv.* **(a)** *as sentence-modifier* doch; **~ we've met before?** wir kennen uns doch, oder? ⋯⋯

**(b)** (steadily) sicher; **slowly but** ∼: langsam, aber sicher
**(c)** (certainly) sicherlich
[2] *int.* (Amer.) natürlich

**surf** /sɜːf/ *n.* [1] Brandung, *die*
[2] *v.i.* **(a)** surfen
**(b)** (Comp.) surfen; (TV) zappen (ugs.)
[3] *v.t.* (Comp., TV) ∼ **the Internet** im Internet surfen; ∼ **the channels** sich durch die Kanäle zappen (ugs.)

**surface** /'sɜːfɪs/ [1] *n.* Oberfläche, *die; outer* ∼: Außenfläche, *die;* **the earth's** ∼: die Erdoberfläche; **on the** ∼: an der Oberfläche (fig.) oberflächlich betrachtet
[2] *v.i.* auftauchen; (fig.) hochkommen
**surface:** ∼ **area** *n.* Oberfläche, *die;* ∼ **mail** *n.* gewöhnliche Post

**'surfboard** *n.* Surfbrett, *das*
**surfeit** /'sɜːfɪt/ *n.* Übermaß, *das*
**'surfer** *n.* Surfer, *der/*Surferin, *die*
**'surfing** *n.* Surfen, *das*

**surge** /sɜːdʒ/ *v.i.* ⟨Wellen:⟩ branden; **the crowd** ∼**d forward** die Menschenmenge drängte nach vorn

**surgeon** /'sɜːdʒən/ *n.* Chirurg, *der/* Chirurgin, *die*

**surgery** /'sɜːdʒərɪ/ *n.* **(a)** Chirurgie, *die;* **undergo** ∼: sich einer Operation (*Dat.*) unterziehen
**(b)** (Brit.: place) Praxis, *die;* **doctor's/dental** ∼: Arzt-/Zahnarztpraxis, *die*
**(c)** (Brit.: time) Sprechstunde, *die*

**surgical** /'sɜːdʒɪkl/ *adj.* chirurgisch; ∼ **treatment** Operation, *die/*Operationen *Pl.*

**surly** /'sɜːlɪ/ *adj.* mürrisch
**surmise** /sə'maɪz/ [1] *n.* Vermutung, *die*
[2] *v.t.* mutmaßen

**surmount** /sə'maʊnt/ *v.t.* überwinden
**surmountable** /sə'maʊntəbl/ *adj.* überwindbar

**surname** /'sɜːneɪm/ *n.* Nachname, *der;* Zuname, *der*

**surpass** /sə'pɑːs/ *v.t.* übertreffen; ∼ **oneself** sich selbst übertreffen

**surplus** /'sɜːpləs/ [1] *n.* Überschuss, *der* (of an + *Dat.*)
[2] *adj.* überschüssig; **be** ∼ **to sb.'s requirements** von jmdm. nicht benötigt werden

**surprise** /sə'praɪz/ [1] *n.* **(a)** Überraschung, *die;* **take sb. by** ∼: jmdn. überrumpeln; **to my great** ∼, **much to my** ∼: zu meiner großen Überraschung; **it came as a** ∼ **to us** es war für uns eine Überraschung
**(b)** *attrib.* überraschend, unerwartet ⟨Besuch⟩; **a** ∼ **attack** ein Überraschungsangriff
[2] *v.t.* überraschen; überrumpeln ⟨Feind⟩; **I shouldn't be** ∼**d if** ...: es würde mich nicht wundern, wenn ...; **be** ∼**d at sb./sth.** sich über jmdn./etw. wundern

**surprising** /sə'praɪzɪŋ/ *adj.* überraschend

**surprisingly** *adv.* überraschend; ∼ **[enough], he was** ...: überraschenderweise war er ...

**surreal** /sə'riːəl/ *adj.* surrealistisch
**surrealism** /sə'riːəlɪzm/ *n.* Surrealismus, *der*

**surrender** /sə'rendə(r)/ [1] *n.* (to enemy) Kapitulation, *die;* (of possession) Aufgabe, *die*
[2] *v.i.* kapitulieren
[3] *v.t.* aufgeben

**surreptitious** /sʌrəp'tɪʃəs/ *adj.* heimlich; verstohlen ⟨Blick⟩

**surrogate** /'sʌrəgət/ *n.* Ersatz, *der*
**surrogate 'mother** *n.* Leihmutter, *die*

**surround** /sə'raʊnd/ *v.t.* **(a)** (come or be all round) umringen; ⟨Truppen, Heer:⟩ umzingeln ⟨Stadt, Feind⟩
**(b)** (encircle) umgeben; **be** ∼**ed by** or **with sth.** von etw. umgeben sein

**sur'rounding** *adj.* umliegend; **the** ∼ **countryside** die [Landschaft in der] Umgebung

**sur'roundings** *n. pl.* Umgebung, *die*

**surveillance** /sə'veɪləns/ *n.* Überwachung, *die;* **be under** ∼: überwacht werden

**survey** [1] /sə'veɪ/ *v.t.* betrachten; überblicken ⟨Landschaft⟩; inspizieren ⟨Gebäude⟩; bewerten ⟨Situation⟩
[2] /'sɜːveɪ/ *n.* Überblick, *der* (of über + *Akk.*); (poll) Umfrage, *die;* (Surv.) Vermessung, *die*

**surveyor** /sə'veɪə(r)/ *n.* (of building) Gutachter, *der/*Gutachterin, *die;* (of land) Landvermesser, *der/*-vermesserin, *die*

**survival** /sə'vaɪvl/ *n.* Überleben, *das;* **fight for** ∼: Existenzkampf, *der*

**sur'vival kit** *n.* Notausrüstung, *die*

**survive** /sə'vaɪv/ [1] *v.t.* überleben
[2] *v.i.* ⟨Person:⟩ überleben; ⟨Schriften, Traditionen:⟩ erhalten bleiben

**survivor** /sə'vaɪvə(r)/ *n.* Überlebende, *der/* *die*

**sus** /sʌs/ (Brit. coll.) *v.t.,* **-ss-** spitzkriegen (ugs.); **get sb.** ∼**sed** jmdn. durchschauen
■ **sus 'out** *v.t.* (coll.) checken (ugs.); spannen (ugs.)

**susceptible** /sə'septɪbl/ *adj.* empfänglich (to für); (to illness) anfällig (to für)

**suspect** [1] /sə'spekt/ *v.t.* **(a)** (imagine to be likely) vermuten; ∼ **the worst** das Schlimmste befürchten; ∼ **sb. to be sth.,** ∼ **that sb. is sth.** glauben od. vermuten, dass jmd. etw. ist
**(b)** (mentally accuse) verdächtigen; ∼ **sb. of sth./of doing sth.** jmdn. einer Sache verdächtigen/jmdn. verdächtigen, etw. zu tun
[2] /'sʌspekt/ *adj.* fragwürdig; verdächtig ⟨Stoff, Paket⟩
[3] /'sʌspekt/ *n.* Verdächtige, *der/die*

**suspend** /sə'spend/ *v.t.* **(a)** (hang up) [auf]hängen
**(b)** (stop) suspendieren

**(c)** (from work) ausschließen (**from** von); sperren ⟨*Sportler*⟩

**suspended 'sentence** *n.* (Law) Strafe mit Bewährung

**suspender belt** /sə'spendə belt/ *n.* (Brit.) Strumpfbandgürtel, *der*

**suspenders** /sə'spendəz/ *n. pl.* **(a)** (Brit.: for stockings) Strumpfbänder *Pl.*
**(b)** (Amer.: for trousers) Hosenträger *Pl.*

**suspense** /sə'spens/ *n.* Spannung, *die;* **keep sb. in ~:** jmdn. auf die Folter spannen

**suspension** /sə'spenʃn/ *n.* (Motor Veh.) Federung, *die*

**su'spension bridge** *n.* Hängebrücke, *die*

**suspicion** /sə'spɪʃn/ *n.* **(a)** (uneasy feeling) Misstrauen, *das* (of gegenüber); (unconfirmed belief) Verdacht, *der;* **have a ~ that ...:** den Verdacht haben, dass ...
**(b)** (suspecting) Verdacht, *der* (of auf + *Akk.*); **on ~ of murder** wegen Mordverdachts; **be under ~:** verdächtigt werden

**suspicious** /sə'spɪʃəs/ *adj.* **(a)** (tending to suspect) misstrauisch (of gegenüber); **be ~ of sb./sth.** jmdm./einer Sache misstrauen
**(b)** (arousing suspicion) verdächtig

**sustain** /sə'steɪn/ *v.t.* **(a)** (support) tragen ⟨*Gewicht*⟩; (fig.) aufrechterhalten
**(b)** erleiden ⟨*Verlust, Verletzung*⟩

**sustainable** /sʌ'steɪnəbl/ *adj.* (Ecology) nachhaltig

**sustenance** /'sʌstɪnəns/ *n.* Nahrung, *die*

**SW** *abbr.* **(a)** = **south-west** SW
**(b)** (Radio) = **short wave** KW

**swab** /swɒb/ *n.* (Med.: pad) Tupfer, *der*

**swagger** /'swægə(r)/ *v.i.* großspurig stolzieren

**swallow¹** /'swɒləʊ/ ①*v.t.* schlucken; (by mistake) verschlucken
②*v.i.* schlucken
③*n.* Schluck, *der*
■ **swallow 'up** *v.t.* verschlucken

**swallow²** *n.* Schwalbe, *die*

**swam** ▶ SWIM 1

**swamp** /swɒmp/ ①*n.* Sumpf, *der*
②*v.t.* überschwemmen

**'swampy** *adj.* sumpfig

**swan** /swɒn/ *n.* Schwan, *der*

**'swansong** *n.* (fig.) Schwanengesang, *der*

**swap** /swɒp/ ①*v.t.,* **-pp-** tauschen (**for** gegen)
②*v.i.,* **-pp-** tauschen
③*n.* Tausch, *der*

**swarm** /swɔːm/ ①*n.* Schwarm, *der*
②*v.i.* schwärmen; (teem) wimmeln (**with** von)

**swarthy** /'swɔːðɪ/ *adj.* dunkel

**swastika** /'swɒstɪkə/ *n.* Hakenkreuz, *das*

**swat** /swɒt/ *v.t.,* **-tt-** totschlagen

**sway** /sweɪ/ ①*v.i.* [hin und her] schwanken; (gently) sich wiegen
②*v.t.* **(a)** wiegen
**(b)** (influence) beeinflussen

③*n.* (fig.) Herrschaft, *die;* **hold ~ over sb.** über jmdn. herrschen

**swear** /sweə(r)/ ①*v.t.,* **swore** /swɔː(r)/, **sworn** /swɔːn/ schwören ⟨*Eid usw.*⟩
②*v.i.,* **swore, sworn (a)** fluchen
**(b)** **~ to sth.** etw. beschwören
■ **'swear at** *v.t.* beschimpfen
■ **'swear by** *v.t.* (coll.) schwören auf (+ *Akk.*)

**'swear word** *n.* Kraftausdruck, *der*

**sweat** /swet/ ①*n.* Schweiß, *der*
②*v.i.* schwitzen

**'sweatband** *n.* Schweißband, *das*

**sweater** /'swetə(r)/ *n.* Pullover, *der*

**sweat: ~shirt** *n.* Sweatshirt, *das;*
**~shop** *n.* ausbeuterische [kleine] Klitsche (ugs.)

**'sweaty** *adj.* schweißig

**swede** *n.* Kohlrübe, *die*

**Swede** /swiːd/ *n.* Schwede, *der*/Schwedin, *die*

**Sweden** /'swiːdn/ *pr. n.* Schweden (*das*)

**Swedish** /'swiːdɪʃ/ ①*adj.* schwedisch; **sb. is ~:** jmd. ist Schwede/Schwedin
②*n.* Schwedisch, *das; see also* ENGLISH 2A

**sweep** /swiːp/ ①*v.t.,* **swept** /swept/ **(a)** fegen; kehren
**(b)** **~ the country** ⟨*Epidemie, Mode:*⟩ das Land überrollen
②*v.i.,* **swept (a)** fegen; kehren
**(b)** (go fast) ⟨*Person, Auto:*⟩ rauschen; ⟨*Wind usw.:*⟩ fegen
③*n.* **(a)** **give sth. a ~:** etw. fegen *od.* kehren
**(b)** (curve) Bogen, *der*
■ **sweep 'up** *v.t.* zusammenfegen; zusammenkehren

**'sweeping** *adj.* pauschal; weit reichend ⟨*Einsparung*⟩; umwälzend ⟨*Veränderung*⟩

**sweet** /swiːt/ ①*adj.* süß; reizend ⟨*Wesen, Gesicht, Mädchen*⟩; **have a ~ tooth** gern Süßes mögen; **how ~ of you!** wie nett *od.* lieb von dir!
②*n.* (Brit.) **(a)** (candy) Bonbon, *das od. der*
**(b)** (dessert) Nachtisch, *der*

**sweet: ~-and-'sour** *attrib. adj.* süßsauer; **~ corn** *n.* Zuckermais, *der*

**sweeten** /'swiːtn/ *v.t.* süßen

**'sweetener** *n.* Süßstoff, *der*

**'sweetheart** *n.* Schatz, *der*

**'sweetness** *n.* Süße, *die*

**sweet: ~ 'pea** *n.* Wicke, *die;* **~ po'tato** *n.* Batate, *die;* **~shop** *n.* (Brit.) Süßwarengeschäft, *das;* **~ talk** (Amer.) *n.* Süßholzgeraspel, *das* (ugs.); **~-talk** *v.t.* **~-talk sb. [into doing sth.]** jmdn. beschwatzen[, etw. zu tun]

**swell** /swel/ ①*v.t.,* **swelled, swollen** /'swəʊlən/ *or* **swelled** anschwellen lassen
②*v.i.,* **swelled, swollen** *or* **swelled (a)** (expand) ⟨*Körperteil:*⟩ anschwellen; ⟨*Segel:*⟩ sich blähen; ⟨*Material:*⟩ aufquellen
**(b)** ⟨*Anzahl:*⟩ zunehmen

'**swelling** *n.* Schwellung, *die*

**swelter** /'sweltə(r)/ *v.i.* ∼ **in the heat** in der Hitze schmoren (ugs.) ∼**ing** glühend heiß ⟨*Tag, Wetter*⟩; ∼**ing heat** Bruthitze, *die*

**swept** ▶ SWEEP 1, 2

**swerve** /swɜːv/ ① *v.i.* einen Bogen machen; ∼ **to the right/left** nach rechts/links [aus]schwenken
② *n.* Bogen, *der*

**swift** /swɪft/ ① *adj.* schnell
② *n.* Mauersegler, *der*

'**swiftly** *adv.* schnell

**swig** /swɪg/ (coll.) Schluck, *der*

**swill** /swɪl/ *v.t.* ∼ **[out]** [aus]spülen

**swim** /swɪm/ ① *v.i.*, **-mm-, swam** /swæm/, **swum** /swʌm/ schwimmen; **my head was** ∼**ming** mir war schwindelig
② *n.* **have a/go for a** ∼: schwimmen/ schwimmen gehen

'**swimmer** *n.* Schwimmer, *der*/ Schwimmerin, *die*; **be a good/poor** ∼: gut/ schlecht schwimmen können

'**swimming** *n.* Schwimmen, *das*

**swimming:** ∼ **baths** *n. pl.* Schwimmbad, *das;* ∼ **costume** *n.* Badeanzug, *der;* ∼ **lesson** *n.* Schwimmstunde, *die;* ∼ **lessons** Schwimmunterricht, *der;* ∼ **pool** *n.* Schwimmbecken, *das;* (building) Schwimmbad, *das;* ∼ **trunks** *n. pl.* Badehose, *die*

'**swimsuit** *n.* Badeanzug, *der*

**swindle** /'swɪndl/ ① *v.t.* betrügen; ∼ **sb. out of sth.** jmdn. um etw. betrügen
② *n.* Schwindel, *der;* Betrug, *der*

**swindler** /'swɪndlə(r)/ *n.* Schwindler, *der*/ Schwindlerin, *die*

**swine** /swaɪn/ *n.* Schwein, *das*

**swing** /swɪŋ/ ① *n.* (a) Schaukel, *die*
(b) (∼ing) Schaukeln, *das;* **in full** ∼ (fig.) in vollem Gang[e]
② *v.i.*, **swung** /swʌŋ/ (a) schwingen; (in wind) schaukeln
(b) (go in sweeping curve) schwenken
③ *v.t.*, **swung** schwingen

**swing:** ∼**bin** *n.* Schwingdeckel[müll]eimer, *der;* ∼ '**door** *n.* Pendeltür, *die*

**swipe** /swaɪp/ (coll.) ① *v.t.* (a) (hit) knallen (ugs.)
(b) (coll.: steal) klauen (ugs.)
(c) ∼ **the card through the swipe reader** die Karte durch das [Karten]lesegerät ziehen
② *n.* (device) ∼ **[reader]** [Karten]lesegerät, *das*

'**swipe card** *n.* Magnetkarte, *die*

**swirl** /swɜːl/ ① *v.i.* wirbeln
② *v.t.* umherwirbeln
③ *n.* Spirale, *die*

**swish** /swɪʃ/ ① *v.i.* zischen
② *n.* Zischen, *das*
③ *adj.* (coll.) schick (ugs.)

**Swiss** /swɪs/ ① *adj.* Schweizer; schweizerisch; **sb. is** ∼: jmd. ist Schweizer/ Schweizerin

② *n.* Schweizer, *der*/Schweizerin, *die;* **the** ∼ *pl.* die Schweizer *Pl.*

**Swiss 'roll** *n.* Biskuitrolle, *die*

**switch** /swɪtʃ/ ① *n.* (a) (esp. Electr.) Schalter, *der*
(b) (change) Wechsel, *der*
② *v.t.* (a) (change) ∼ **sth. [over] to sth.** etw. auf etw. (*Akk.*) umstellen *od.* (Electr.) umschalten
(b) (exchange) tauschen
③ *v.i.* wechseln; ∼ **[over] to sth.** auf etw. (*Akk.*) umstellen *od.* (Electr.) umschalten

■ **switch 'off** *v.t. & i.* ausschalten; (also fig. coll.) abschalten

■ **switch 'on** ① *v.t.* einschalten; anschalten
② *v.i.* sich anschalten

**switch:** ∼**back** *n.* Achterbahn, *die;* ∼**blade** *n.* Springmesser, *das;* ∼**board** *n.* [Telefon]zentrale, *die*

**Switzerland** /'swɪtsələnd/ *pr. n.* die Schweiz

**swivel** /'swɪvl/ ① *v.i.*, **-ll-** sich drehen
② *v.t.*, **-ll-** drehen

'**swivel chair** *n.* Drehstuhl, *der*

**swollen** /'swəʊlən/ ① ▶ SWELL
② *adj.* geschwollen; angeschwollen ⟨*Fluss*⟩

**swoon** /swuːn/ (literary) *v.i.* ohnmächtig werden

**swoop** /swuːp/ ① *n.* (a) Sturzflug, *der*
(b) (coll.: raid) Razzia, *die*
② *v.i.* herabstoßen; ∼ **on sb.** sich auf jmdn. stürzen

**swop** ▶ SWAP

**sword** /sɔːd/ *n.* Schwert, *das*

'**swordfish** *n.* Schwertfisch, *der*

**swore, sworn** ▶ SWEAR

**swot** /swɒt/ (Brit. coll.) ① *n.* Streber, *der*/ Streberin, *die*
② *v.i.*, **-tt-** büffeln (ugs.)

**swum** ▶ SWIM 1

**swung** ▶ SWING 2, 3

'**swung dash** *n.* Tilde, *die*

**sycamore** /'sɪkəmɔː(r)/ *n.* Bergahorn, *der*

**sycophant** /'sɪkəfænt/ *n.* Kriecher, *der*

**syllable** /'sɪləbl/ *n.* Silbe, *die*

**syllabus** /'sɪləbəs/ *n.* Lehrplan, *der;* (for exam) Studienplan, *der*

**symbol** /'sɪmbl/ *n.* Symbol, *das* (**of** für)

**symbolic** /sɪm'bɒlɪk/**, symbolical** /sɪm'bɒlɪkl/ *adj.* symbolisch

**symbolism** /'sɪmbəlɪzm/ *n.* Symbolik, *die*

**symbolize** /'sɪmbəlaɪz/ *v.t.* symbolisieren

**symmetrical** /sɪ'metrɪkl/ *adj.* symmetrisch

**symmetry** /'sɪmɪtrɪ/ *n.* Symmetrie, *die*

**sympathetic** /sɪmpə'θetɪk/ *adj.* mitfühlend

**sympathize** /'sɪmpəθaɪz/ *v.i.* (a) ∼ **with sb.** mit jmdm. [mit]fühlen
(b) ∼ **with** (understand) Verständnis haben für

**sympathy** /'sɪmpəθɪ/ *n.* Mitgefühl, *das;* **in deepest ~:** mit aufrichtigem Beileid
**symphonic** /sɪm'fɒnɪk/ *adj.* sinfonisch
**symphony** /'sɪmfənɪ/ *n.* Sinfonie, *die*
**'symphony orchestra** *n.* Sinfonieorchester, *das*
**symposium** /sɪm'pəʊzɪəm/ *n., pl.* **symposia** /sɪm'pəʊzɪə/ Symposion, *das*
**symptom** /'sɪmptəm/ *n.* Symptom, *das*
**symptomatic** /sɪmptə'mætɪk/ *adj.* symptomatisch (**of** für)
**synagogue** (*Amer.:* **synagog**) /'sɪnəgɒg/ *n.* Synagoge, *die*
**sync** /sɪŋk/ (coll.) *n.* **be in ~/out of ~:** harmonieren/nicht harmonieren (**with** mit)
**synchromesh** /'sɪŋkrəmeʃ/ *n.* (Motor Veh.) Synchrongetriebe, *das*
**synchronize** /'sɪŋkrənaɪz/ *v.t.* synchronisieren; gleichstellen ⟨*Uhren*⟩
**syndicate** /'sɪndɪkət/ *n.* Syndikat, *das*
**syndrome** /'sɪndrəʊm/ *n.* Syndrom, *das*
**synonym** /'sɪnənɪm/ *n.* Synonym, *das*
**synonymous** /sɪ'nɒnɪməs/ *adj.* (a) (Ling.) synonym (**with** mit)
(b) **~ with** (fig.) gleichbedeutend mit
**synopsis** /sɪ'nɒpsɪs/ *n., pl.* **synopses** /sɪ'nɒpsi:z/ Inhaltsangabe, *die*

**syntactic** /sɪn'tæktɪk/ *adj.* syntaktisch
**syntax** /'sɪntæks/ *n.* Syntax, *die*
**synthesis** /'sɪnθɪsɪs/ *n., pl.* **syntheses** /'sɪnθɪsi:z/ Synthese, *die*
**synthesize** /'sɪnθɪsaɪz/ *v.t.* zur Synthese bringen; (Chem.) synthetisieren
**synthesizer** /'sɪnθɪsaɪzə(r)/ *n.* (Mus.) Synthesizer, *der*
**synthetic** /sɪn'θetɪk/ *adj.* synthetisch
**syphilis** /'sɪfɪlɪs/ *n.* Syphilis, *die*
**syphon** ▶ SIPHON
**Syria** /'sɪrɪə/ *pr. n.* Syrien (*das*)
**syringe** /sɪ'rɪndʒ/ ① *n.* Spritze, *die*
② *v.t.* spritzen; ausspritzen ⟨*Ohr*⟩
**syrup** /'sɪrəp/ *n.* Sirup, *der*
**system** /'sɪstəm/ *n.* System, *das*
**systematic** /sɪstə'mætɪk/ *adj.*, **systematically** /sɪstə'mætɪkəlɪ/ *adv.* systematisch
**systematize** /'sɪstəmətaɪz/ *v.t.* systematisieren
**system: ~ disk** *n.* (Comp.) Systemdiskette, *die;* **~ error** *n.* (Comp.) Systemfehler, *der;* **~s analyst** *n.* Systemanalytiker, *der*/-analytikerin, *die;* **~ software** *n.* (Comp.) Systemsoftware, *die*

# Tt

**T, t** /ti:/ *n.* T, t, *das;* **to a T** ganz genau; **T-junction** Einmündung, *die;* **T-bone steak** T-Bone-Steak, *das;* **T-shirt** T-Shirt, *das*
**ta** /tɑː/ *int.* (Brit. coll.) danke
**tab** /tæb/ ① *n.* (a) (projecting flap) Zunge, *die;* (on clothing) Etikett, *das;* (with name) Namensschild, *das*
(b) **pick up the ~** (Amer. coll.) die Zeche bezahlen
(c) **keep ~s** *or* **a ~ on** (watch) [genau] beobachten
(d) (Comp.) Tabulator, *der*
② *v.t.* (Comp.) tabellarisieren
**tabby** /'tæbɪ/ *n.* **~ [cat]** Tigerkatze, *die*
**'tab key** *n.* (Comp.) Tabulatortaste, *die*
**table** /'teɪbl/ ① *n.* (a) Tisch, *der*
(b) (list) Tabelle, *die;* **~ of contents** Inhaltsverzeichnis, *das*
② *v.t.* einbringen
**tableau** /'tæbləʊ/ *n., pl.* **~x** /'tæbləʊz/ Tableau, *das*
**table: ~cloth** *n.* Tischdecke, *die;* **~ leg** *n.* Tischbein, *das;* **~ linen** *n.* Tischwäsche, *die;* **~ manners** *n. pl.* Tischmanieren *Pl.;* **~ mat** *n.* Set, *das;*

**~ salt** *n.* Tafelsalz, *das;* **~spoon** *n.* Servierlöffel, *der;* **~spoonful** *n.* Servierlöffel [voll]
**tablet** /'tæblɪt/ *n.* (a) Tablette, *die*
(b) (of soap) Stück, *das*
**table: ~ tennis** *n.* Tischtennis, *das;* **~ tennis bat** Tischtennisschläger, *der;* **~ wine** *n.* Tischwein, *der*
**tabloid** /'tæblɔɪd/ *n.* Boulevardzeitung, *die;* **the ~s** (derog.) die Boulevardpresse; **~ journalism** Sensationsjournalismus, *der*
**taboo, tabu** /tə'buː/ ① *n.* Tabu, *das*
② *adj.* Tabu⟨*wort*⟩; **be ~:** tabu sein
**tabulate** /'tæbjʊleɪt/ *v.t.* tabellarisch darstellen
**tabulator** /'tæbjʊleɪtə(r)/ *n.* Tabulator, *der*
**tacit** /'tæsɪt/ *adj.*, **'tacitly** *adv.* stillschweigend
**taciturn** /'tæsɪtɜːn/ *adj.* schweigsam; wortkarg
**tack** /tæk/ ① *n.* (a) (nail) kleiner Nagel
(b) (stitch) Heftstich, *der*
(c) (Naut., also fig.) Kurs, *der*
② *v.t.* (a) (nail) festnageln
(b) (stitch) heften

····ᐳ

③ *v.i.* (Naut.) kreuzen

**tackle** /ˈtækl/ ① *v.t.* (a) angehen ⟨*Problem usw.*⟩; ∼ **sb. about/on/over sth.** jmdn. auf etw. (*Akk.*) ansprechen; (ask for sth.) jmdn. um etw. angehen
(b) (Sport) angreifen ⟨*Spieler*⟩; (Amer. Footb.; Rugby) fassen
② *n.* (a) (equipment) Ausrüstung, *die*
(b) (Sport) Angriff, *der;* (sliding ∼) Tackling, *das;* (Amer. Footb.; Rugby) Fassen und Halten

**tacky** /ˈtækɪ/ *adj.* (a) (sticky) klebrig
(b) (coll. derog.: tasteless) geschmacklos

**tact** /tækt/ *n.* Takt, *der;* **he has no** ∼: er hat kein Taktgefühl

**tactful** /ˈtæktfl/ *adj.*, **'tactfully** *adv.* taktvoll

**tactical** /ˈtæktɪkl/ *adj.* taktisch

**tactics** /ˈtæktɪks/ *n. pl.* Taktik, *die*

**'tactless** *adj.*, **'tactlessly** *adv.* taktlos

**tadpole** /ˈtædpəʊl/ *n.* Kaulquappe, *die*

**tag¹** /tæg/ ① *n.* (a) Schild, *das*
(b) (electronic device) (on person) elektronische Fessel; (on goods) Sicherungsetikett, *das*
(c) (Comp.) Tag, *das;* Markierung, *die*
② *v.t.,* **-gg-:** (Comp.) taggen; markieren
■ **tag a'long** *v.i.* mitkommen

**tag²** *n.* (game) Fangen, *das*

**tail** /teɪl/ ① *n.* (a) Schwanz, *der*
(b) *in pl.* (on coin) ∼s [**it is**] Zahl
② *v.t.* (coll.: follow) beschatten
■ **tail 'back** *v.i.* sich stauen
■ **tail 'off** *v.i.* (a) zurückgehen
(b) (into silence) verstummen

**tail:** ∼**back** *n.* (Brit.) Rückstau, *der;* ∼ **end** *n.* Ende, *das;* ∼**gate** ① *n.* (Motor Veh.) Heckklappe, *die;* ② *v.i.* zu dicht auffahren; ∼ **light** *n.* Rücklicht, *das*

**tailor** /ˈteɪlə(r)/ *n.* Schneider, *der/* Schneiderin, *die*

**tailored** /ˈteɪləd/, **'tailor-made** *adjs.* maßgeschneidert

**'tail wind** *n.* Rückenwind, *der*

**taint** /teɪnt/ *v.t.* verderben; **be** ∼**ed with sth.** mit etw. behaftet sein (geh.)

**Taiwan** /taɪˈwɑːn/ *pr. n.* Taiwan (*das*)

**take** /teɪk/ ① *v.t.,* took /tʊk/, taken /ˈteɪkn/
(a) (get hold of, grasp, seize) nehmen
(b) (capture) einnehmen ⟨*Stadt, Festung*⟩; machen ⟨*Gefangenen*⟩
(c) (gain, earn) ⟨*Laden:*⟩ einbringen; ⟨*Person:*⟩ einnehmen; ⟨*Film, Stück:*⟩ einspielen; (win) gewinnen ⟨*Satz, Spiel, Preis, Titel*⟩
(d) (∼ away with one) mitnehmen; (steal) mitnehmen (verhüll.); ∼ **place** stattfinden; (spontaneously) sich ereignen; ⟨*Wandlung:*⟩ sich vollziehen
(e) (avail oneself of, use) nehmen; machen ⟨*Pause, Ferien, Nickerchen*⟩; ∼ **the opportunity to do/of doing sth.** die Gelegenheit dazu benutzen, etw. zu tun
(f) (carry, guide, convey) bringen; ∼ **sb. to visit sb.** jmdn. zu Besuch bei jmdm. mitnehmen;

∼ **home** mit nach Hause nehmen; (earn) nach Hause bringen ⟨*Geld*⟩; (accompany) nach Hause bringen
(g) (remove) nehmen; (deduct) abziehen; ∼ **sth./sb. from sb.** jmdm. etw./jmdm. wegnehmen
(h) (make) machen ⟨*Foto, Kopie*⟩; (photograph) aufnehmen; aufnehmen ⟨*Brief, Diktat*⟩; machen ⟨*Prüfung, Sprung, Spaziergang, Reise*⟩; ablegen ⟨*Gelübde, Eid*⟩; treffen ⟨*Entscheidung*⟩
(i) (conduct) halten ⟨*Gottesdienst, Unterricht*⟩; **Ms X** ∼**s us for maths** in Mathe haben wir Frau X
(j) (eat, drink) nehmen ⟨*Zucker, Milch, Tabletten, Überdosis*⟩; trinken ⟨*Tee, Kaffee, Kognak usw.*⟩
(k) (need, require) brauchen ⟨*Platz, Zeit*⟩; haben ⟨*Objekt, Plural-s*⟩; gebraucht werden mit ⟨*Kasus*⟩; **sth.** ∼**s an hour/a year/all day** etw. dauert eine Stunde/ein Jahr/einen ganzen Tag
(l) (ascertain and record) notieren ⟨*Namen, Adresse, Autonummer usw.*⟩; fühlen ⟨*Puls*⟩; messen ⟨*Temperatur, Größe usw.*⟩
(m) (assume) ∼ **it** [**that**] ...: annehmen, dass ...; ∼ **sb./sth. for/to be sth.** jmdn./etw. für etw. halten
(n) (react to) aufnehmen; ∼ **sth. well/badly** etw. gut/nur schwer verkraften; ∼ **sth. calmly** *or* **coolly** etw. gelassen [auf]nehmen
(o) (accept) annehmen
(p) (adopt, choose) ergreifen ⟨*Maßnahmen*⟩; unternehmen ⟨*Schritte*⟩; ∼ **the wrong road** die falsche Straße nehmen/gehen
(q) **be** ∼**n ill** krank werden
(r) ∼ **sth. to bits** *or* **pieces** etw. auseinander nehmen
② *v.i.,* took, taken (a) ⟨*Transplantat:*⟩ vom Körper angenommen werden; ⟨*Sämling, Pflanze:*⟩ angehen
(b) (detract) ∼ **from sth.** etw. schmälern
■ **'take after** *v.t.* ∼ **after sb.** (resemble) jmdm. ähnlich sein; (∼ **as one's example**) es jmdm. gleichtun
■ **take a'way** *v.t.* (a) (remove) wegnehmen; (to a distance) mitnehmen; ∼ **sth. away from sb.** jmdm. etw. abnehmen; **to** ∼ **away** ⟨*Pizza, Snack usw.*⟩ zum Mitnehmen
(b) (Math.: deduct) abziehen
■ **take a'way from** *v.t.* schmälern
■ **take 'back** *v.t.* zurücknehmen; (return) zurückbringen
■ **take 'down** *v.t.* (a) (carry or lead down) hinunterbringen
(b) abnehmen ⟨*Bild, Ankündigung, Weihnachtsschmuck*⟩; herunterziehen ⟨*Hose*⟩; ∼ **sth. down from a shelf** etw. von einem Regal herunternehmen
(c) (write down) aufnehmen
■ **take 'in** *v.t.* (a) hineinbringen; (bring indoors) hereinholen
(b) enger machen ⟨*Kleidungsstück*⟩
(c) (understand) begreifen
(d) (cheat) hereinlegen (ugs.); (deceive) täuschen

■ **take 'off** 1 *v.t.* **(a)** abnehmen ⟨*Deckel, Hut, Tischtuch, Verband*⟩; abziehen ⟨*Kissenbezug*⟩; ausziehen ⟨*Schuhe, Handschuhe*⟩; ablegen ⟨*Mantel, Schmuck*⟩ **(b)** (deduct) abziehen; ~ **sth. off sth.** etw. von etw. abziehen **(c)** ~ **a day** *etc.* off sich (*Dat.*) einen Tag *usw.* frei nehmen (ugs.) **(d)** (mimic) nachahmen 2 *v.i.* (Aeronaut.) starten

■ **take 'on** *v.t.* **(a)** (undertake) übernehmen; auf sich (*Akk.*) nehmen ⟨*Bürde*⟩ **(b)** (employ) einstellen **(c)** (as opponent) es aufnehmen mit; (Sport: meet) antreten gegen

■ **take 'out** *v.t.* **(a)** (remove) herausnehmen; ziehen ⟨*Zahn*⟩; ~ **sth. out of sth.** etw. aus etw. [heraus]nehmen **(b)** (withdraw) abheben ⟨*Geld*⟩ **(c)** (go out with) ~ **sb. out** mit jmdm. ausgehen; ~ **sb. out to** *or* **for lunch** jmdn. zum Mittagessen einladen **(d)** (get issued) abschließen ⟨*Versicherung*⟩; ausleihen ⟨*Bücher*⟩; ~ **out a subscription to sth.** etw. abonnieren **(e)** ~ **it out on sb.** seine Wut an jmdm. auslassen

■ **take 'over** 1 *v.t.* übernehmen 2 *v.i.* übernehmen; ⟨*Manager, Firmenleiter:*⟩ die Geschäfte übernehmen; ⟨*Regierung, Präsident:*⟩ die Amtsgeschäfte übernehmen; ~ **over from sb.** jmdn. ersetzen; (temporarily) jmdn. vertreten

■ **'take to** *v.t.* **(a)** (get into habit of) ~ **to doing sth.** es sich (*Dat.*) angewöhnen, etw. zu tun **(b)** (like) sich hingezogen fühlen zu ⟨*Person*⟩; sich erwärmen für ⟨*Sache*⟩

■ **take 'up** 1 *v.t.* **(a)** (lift up) hochheben; (pick up) aufheben; herausreißen ⟨*Dielen*⟩; aufreißen ⟨*Straße*⟩ **(b)** (carry or lead up) hinaufbringen **(c)** in Anspruch nehmen ⟨*Zeit*⟩; brauchen/ (undesirably) wegnehmen ⟨*Platz*⟩ **(d)** (start) ergreifen ⟨*Beruf*⟩; anfangen ⟨*Tennis, Schach, Gitarre usw.*⟩; aufnehmen ⟨*Arbeit, Kampf*⟩; antreten ⟨*Stelle*⟩; ~ **up a hobby** sich (*Dat.*) ein Hobby zulegen **(e)** (pursue further) ~ **sth. up with sb.** sich in einer Sache an jmdn. wenden 2 *v.i.* ~ **up with sb.** (coll.) sich mit jmdm. einlassen

**'takeaway** *n.* (meal) Essen zum Mitnehmen; (restaurant) Restaurant mit Straßenverkauf

**taken** ▶ TAKE

**take:** ~**-off** *n.* **(a)** (Aeronaut.) Start, *der;* **(b)** (coll.: caricature) Parodie, *die;* ~**over** *n.* Übernahme, *die*

**takings** /ˈteɪkɪŋz/ *n. pl.* Einnahmen *Pl.*

**talc** /tælk/ *n.* Talkum, *das*

**talcum** /ˈtælkəm/ *n.* ~ **[powder]** Körperpuder, *der*

**tale** /teɪl/ *n.* Erzählung, *die;* Geschichte, *die* (of von, about über + *Akk.*)

**talent** /ˈtælənt/ *n.* Talent, *das;* have [great/ no *etc.*] ~ [for sth.] [viel/kein *usw.*] Talent [zu *od.* für etw.] haben

**'talented** *adj.* talentiert

**'talent-spotting** *n.* Talentsuche, *die*

**talk** /tɔːk/ 1 *n.* **(a)** (discussion) Gespräch, *das;* have a ~ [with sb.] [about sth.] [mit jmdm.] [über etw. (*Akk.*)] sprechen; have *or* hold ~s [with sb.] [mit jmdm.] Gespräche führen; there is [much/some] ~ of ...: man hört [häufig/öfter] von ... **(b)** (speech, lecture) Vortrag, *der* 2 *v.i.* sprechen (with, to mit); (lecture) sprechen; (converse) sich unterhalten; (have ~s) Gespräche führen; (gossip) reden; ~ **on the phone** telefonieren 3 *v.t.* reden; ~ **sb. into/out of sth.** jmdn. zu etw. überreden/jmdm. etw. ausreden

■ **talk 'over** *v.t.* besprechen

■ **talk 'round** *v.t.* ~ **sb. round** jmdn. überreden

**talkative** /ˈtɔːkətɪv/ *adj.* gesprächig

**talking:** ~ **point** *n.* Gesprächsthema, *das;* ~**-to** *n.* (coll.) Standpauke, *die* (ugs.)

**'talk show** *n.* Talkshow, *die*

**tall** /tɔːl/ *adj.* hoch; groß ⟨*Person, Tier*⟩; that's a ~ **order** das ist ziemlich viel verlangt; ~ **story** unglaubliche Geschichte

**tally** /ˈtælɪ/ 1 *n.* keep a ~ of sth. über etw. (*Akk.*) Buch führen 2 *v.i.* übereinstimmen

**talon** /ˈtælən/ *n.* Klaue, *die*

**tambourine** /tæmbəˈriːn/ *n.* Tamburin, *das*

**tame** /teɪm/ 1 *adj.* zahm; (fig.: spiritless) lahm (ugs.) 2 *v.t.* zähmen

**tamper** /ˈtæmpə(r)/ *v.i.* ~ **with** sich (*Dat.*) zu schaffen machen an (+ *Dat.*)

**tampon** /ˈtæmpɒn/ *n.* Tampon, *der*

**tan** /tæn/ 1 *v.t.,* -**nn**- gerben ⟨*Tierhaut, Fell*⟩ 2 *v.i.,* -**nn**- braun werden 3 *n.* **(a)** (colour) Gelbbraun, *das* **(b)** (sun~) Bräune, *die;* have/get a ~: braun sein/werden 4 *adj.* gelbbraun

**tandem** /ˈtændəm/ *n.* ~ **[bicycle]** Tandem, *das*

**tang** /tæŋ/ *n.* (taste) Geschmack, *der;* (smell) Geruch, *der*

**tangent** /ˈtændʒənt/ *n.* Tangente, *die;* go off at a ~ (fig.) plötzlich vom Thema abschweifen

**tangerine** /tændʒəˈriːn/ *n.* (fruit) ~ **[orange]** Tangerine, *die*

**tangible** /ˈtændʒɪbl/ *adj.* greifbar; spürbar ⟨*Unterschied, Verbesserung*⟩; handfest ⟨*Beweis*⟩

**tangle** /ˈtæŋgl/ 1 *n.* Gewirr, *das;* (in hair) Verfilzung, *die* 2 *v.t.* verheddern (ugs.); verfilzen ⟨*Haar*⟩

■ **tangle 'up** *v.t.* verheddern (ugs.)

**tango** /'tæŋgəʊ/ *n., pl.* ~s Tango, *der*

**tank** /tæŋk/ *n.* **(a)** Tank, *der*
**(b)** (Mil.) Panzer, *der*

**tankard** /'tæŋkəd/ *n.* Krug, *der*

**tanker** /'tæŋkə(r)/ *n.* (ship) Tanker, *der;*
(vehicle) Tank[last]wagen, *der*

**tanned** /tænd/ *adj.* braun gebrannt

**tantalize** /'tæntəlaɪz/ *v.t.* reizen

**tantalizing** /'tæntəlaɪzɪŋ/ *adj.* verlockend

**tantamount** /'tæntəmaʊnt/ *adj.* be ~ to
sth. gleichbedeutend mit etw. sein

**tantrum** /'tæntrəm/ *n.* Wutanfall, *der;* (of
child) Trotzanfall, *der;* **throw a** ~: einen
Wutanfall/Trotzanfall bekommen

**tap¹** /tæp/ [1] *n.* Hahn, *der;* **hot/cold[-water]**
~: Warm-/Kaltwasserhahn, *der;* **be on** ~ (fig.)
zur Verfügung stehen
[2] *v.t.,* **-pp-: (a)** erschließen ⟨Reserven,
Markt⟩
**(b)** (Teleph.) abhören; anzapfen (ugs.)

**tap²** [1] *v.t.,* **-pp-** klopfen an (+ Akk.); (on
upper surface) klopfen auf (+ Akk.)
[2] *v.i.,* **-pp-:** ~ **at/on sth.** an etw. ⟨Akk.⟩
klopfen; (on upper surface) auf etw. ⟨Akk.⟩
klopfen
[3] *n.* Klopfen, *das*

'**tap dance** [1] *n.* Stepp[tanz], *der*
[2] *v.i.* Stepp tanzen; steppen

**tape** /teɪp/ [1] *n.* **(a)** Band, *das;* **adhesive** *or*
(coll.) **sticky** ~: Klebeband, *das*
**(b)** (for recording) [Ton]band, *das* (of mit);
**make a** ~ **of sth.** etw. auf Band aufnehmen
[2] *v.t.* **(a)** (record on ~) [auf Band] aufnehmen
**(b)** (bind with ~) [mit Klebeband] zukleben
**(c) have got sb./sth.** ~**d** (coll.) jmdn.
durchschaut haben/etw. im Griff haben

**tape:** ~ **cassette** *n.* Tonbandkassette,
*die;* ~ **deck** *n.* Tapedeck, *das;*
~ **measure** *n.* Bandmaß, *das*

**taper** /'teɪpə(r)/ [1] *v.i.* sich verjüngen; ~ [to
a point] spitz zulaufen
[2] *n.* [wax] ~: Wachsstock, *der*

**tape:** ~ **recorder** *n.* Tonbandgerät, *das;*
~ **recording** *n.* Tonbandaufnahme, *die*

**tapestry** /'tæpɪstrɪ/ *n.* Gobelingewebe, *das;*
(wall-hanging) Bildteppich, *der*

'**tapeworm** *n.* Bandwurm, *der*

'**tap water** *n.* Leitungswasser, *das*

**tar** /tɑː(r)/ [1] *n.* Teer, *der;* **high-~/low-~**
**cigarette** Zigarette mit hohem/niedrigem
Teergehalt
[2] *v.t.,* **-rr-** teeren

**target** /'tɑːgɪt/ [1] *n.* **(a)** Ziel, *das;* **hit/miss**
**the/its** ~: [das Ziel] treffen/das Ziel
verfehlen; **production/export/savings** ~:
Produktions-/Export-/Sparziel, *das;* **be**
**above/below** ~ (fig.) das Ziel über-/
unterschritten haben
**(b)** (Sport) Zielscheibe, *die*
[2] *v.t.* (fig.) zielen auf ⟨Käufergruppe⟩

**target:** ~ **date** *n.* vorgesehener Termin;
~ **figure** *n.* (esp. Commerc.) Ziel, *das*

**tariff** /'tærɪf/ *n.* **(a)** (tax) Zoll, *der*

**(b)** (list of charges) Tarif, *der*

**tarnish** /'tɑːnɪʃ/ [1] *v.t.* stumpf werden
lassen ⟨Metall⟩; (fig.) beflecken ⟨Ruf⟩
[2] *v.i.* stumpf werden

**tarpaulin** /tɑː'pɔːlɪn/ *n.* Plane, *die*

**tart¹** /tɑːt/ *adj.* herb; sauer ⟨Obst⟩; (fig.)
scharfzüngig

**tart²** *n.* **(a)** (Brit.) (filled pie) ≈ Obstkuchen,
*der;* (small pastry) Obsttörtchen, *das*
**(b)** (sl.: prostitute) Nutte, *die* (salopp)
■ **tart 'up** *v.t.* (Brit. coll.) ~ **oneself up, get**
~**ed up** sich auftakeln (ugs.)

**tartan** /'tɑːtən/ [1] *n.* Schotten[stoff], *der*
[2] *adj.* Schotten⟨rock, -jacke⟩

**tartar** /'tɑːtə(r)/ *n.* Zahnstein, *der*

**tartar sauce** /'tɑːtə 'sɔːs/ *n.*
Remoulade[nsoße], *die*

**task** /tɑːsk/ *n.* Aufgabe, *die;* **take sb. to** ~:
jmdm. eine Lektion erteilen

**task:** ~**bar** *n.* (Comp.) Taskleiste, *die;*
~ **force** *n.* Sonderkommando, *das*

**tassel** /'tæsl/ *n.* Quaste, *die*

**taste** /teɪst/ [1] *v.t.* **(a)** schmecken; (try a little)
probieren
**(b)** (recognize flavour of) [heraus]schmecken
[2] *v.i.* schmecken (of nach); **not** ~ **of**
anything nach nichts schmecken
[3] *n.* **(a)** (flavour) Geschmack, *der;* [sense of]
~: Geschmack[ssinn], *der*
**(b)** (discernment) Geschmack, *der*
**(c)** (sample) Kostprobe, *die*

**tasteful** /'teɪstfl/ *adj.,* '**tastefully** *adv.*
geschmackvoll

'**tasteless** *adj.* geschmacklos

**tasty** /'teɪstɪ/ *adj.* lecker

**tat** /tæt/ *n.* ▶ TIT²

**tattered** /'tætəd/ *adj.* zerlumpt ⟨Kleidung⟩;
zerfleddert ⟨Buch⟩

**tatters** /'tætəz/ *n. pl.* Fetzen *Pl.;* **be in** ~: in
Fetzen sein; (fig.) ruiniert sein

**tattoo** /tə'tuː/ [1] *v.t.* tätowieren
[2] *n.* Tätowierung, *die*

**tattooer** /tə'tuːə(r)/**, tattooist** /tə'tuːɪst/
*ns.* Tätowierer, *der*/Tätowiererin, *die*

**tatty** /'tætɪ/ *adj.* (coll.) schäbig

**taught** ▶ TEACH

**taunt** /tɔːnt/ [1] *v.t.* verspotten (about
wegen)
[2] *n.* spöttische Bemerkung

**Taurus** /'tɔːrəs/ *n.* (Astrol., Astron.) der Stier

**taut** /tɔːt/ *adj.* straff ⟨Seil, Kabel⟩; gespannt
⟨Muskel⟩

**tavern** /'tævən/ *n.* Schenke, *die*

**tawny** /'tɔːnɪ/ *adj.* gelbbraun

**tax** /tæks/ [1] *n.* Steuer, *die;* **before/after** ~:
vor Steuern/nach Abzug der Steuern; **for**
~ **reasons** aus steuerlichen Gründen
[2] *v.t.* **(a)** besteuern; versteuern
⟨Einkommen⟩
**(b)** (fig.) strapazieren ⟨Kräfte, Geduld⟩

**taxable** /'tæksəbl/ *adj.* steuerpflichtig

**tax:** ~ **allowance** *n.* Steuerfreibetrag, *der;* ~ **assessment** *n.* Steuerbescheid, *der*

**taxation** /tæk'seɪʃn/ *n.* Besteuerung, *die;* (taxes payable) Steuern *Pl.*

**tax:** ~ **avoidance** *n.* Steuerumgehung, *die;* ~ **bill** *n.* Steuerbescheid, *der;* (amount) Steuerschuld, *die;* ~ **bracket** *n.* Stufe im Steuertarif; ~**deductible** *adj.* steuerabzugsfähig; [steuerlich] absetzbar; ~ **demand** *n.* Steuerforderung, *die;* ~ **disc** *n.* (Motor Veh.) Steuerplakette, *die;* ~ **evasion** *n.* Steuerhinterziehung, *die;* ~ **exile** *n.* (person) Steuerflüchtling, *der;* ~ **form** *n.* Steuerformular, *das;* ~**free** *adj.* steuerfrei; ~ **haven** *n.* Steueroase, *die* (ugs.)

**taxi** /'tæksɪ/ ① *n.* Taxi, *das* ② *v.i.,* ~**ing** *or* **taxiing** ⟨*Flugzeug:*⟩ rollen

'**taxi driver** *n.* Taxifahrer, *der*/-fahrerin, *die*

**tax:** ~ **incentive** *n.* steuerlicher Anreiz; ~ **inspector** *n.* Steuerinspektor, *der*/ -inspektorin, *die*

**taxi:** ~ **rank** (Brit.), ~ **stand** (Amer.) *ns.* Taxistand, *der*

**tax:** ~**man** *n.* (coll.) Finanzbeamte, *der*/ -beamtin, *die;* ~ **office** *n.* Finanzamt, *das* ~**payer** *n.* Steuerzahler, *der*/-zahlerin, *die;* ~ **return** *n.* Steuererklärung, *die;* ~ **relief** *n.* Steuererleichterung, *die;* ~ **year** *n.* Steuerjahr, *das*

**TB** *abbr.* = **tuberculosis** Tb, *die*

**tbsp.** *abbr., pl. same or* ~**s: tablespoon**

**tea** /tiː/ *n.* (a) Tee, *der* (b) (meal) [**high**] ~: Abendessen, *das*

**tea:** ~ **bag** *n.* Teebeutel, *der;* ~ **break** *n.* (Brit.) Teepause, *die;* ~ **caddy** *n.* Teebüchse, *die*

**teach** /tiːtʃ/ ① *v.t.,* **taught** /tɔːt/ unterrichten; (at university) lehren; ~ **sb.**/ **oneself**/**an animal sth.** jmdm./sich/einem Tier etw. beibringen; ~ **sb. to ride** jmdm. das Reiten beibringen ② *v.i.,* **taught** unterrichten

'**teacher** *n.* Lehrer, *der*/Lehrerin, *die*

**teacher:** ~ **training** *n.* Lehrerausbildung, *die;* ~**training college** *n.* ≈ pädagogische Hochschule

'**teaching profession** *n.* Lehrberuf, *der*

**tea:** ~ **cloth** *n.* Geschirrtuch, *das;* ~ **cosy** *n.* Teewärmer, *der;* ~**cup** *n.* Teetasse, *die*

**teak** /tiːk/ *n.* Teak[holz], *das*

'**tea leaf** *n.* Teeblatt, *das*

**team** /tiːm/ *n.* Team, *das;* (Sport also) Mannschaft, *die*

◼ **team 'up** *v.i.* sich zusammentun (ugs.)

**team:** ~ **effort** *n.* Team- od. Gemeinschaftsarbeit, *die;* ~ **game** *n.* Mannschaftsspiel, *das;* ~ **leader** *n.* Gruppenleiter, *der*/-leiterin, *die;* ~**mate** *n.* Mannschaftskamerad, *der*/-kameradin, *die;*

~ '**spirit** *n.* Teamgeist, *der;* (Sport also) Mannschaftsgeist, *der;* ~**work** *n.* Teamarbeit, *die*

'**teapot** *n.* Teekanne, *die*

**tear¹** /teə(r)/ ① *n.* Riss, *der* ② *v.t.,* **tore** /tɔː(r)/, **torn** /tɔːn/ (a) (rip) zerreißen; (pull apart) auseinander reißen; (damage) aufreißen; ~ **open** aufreißen ⟨*Brief, Paket*⟩ (b) ~ **sth. out of sb.'s hands** jmdm. etw. aus der Hand reißen ③ *v.i.,* **tore, torn (a)** (rip) [zer]reißen (b) (move hurriedly) rasen (ugs.)

◼ **tear a'way** *v.t.* wegreißen; ~ **oneself away** (fig.) sich losreißen

◼ **tear 'up** *v.t.* zerreißen

**tear²** /tɪə(r)/ *n.* Träne, *die*

**tearful** /'tɪəfl/ *adj.* weinend

**tear** /tɪə(r)/**:** ~**drop** *n.* Träne, *die;* ~ **gas** *n.* Tränengas, *das*

**tease** /tiːz/ ① *v.t.* necken (about wegen); aufziehen (ugs.) (about mit) ② *v.i.* seine Späße machen

**tea:** ~ **service,** ~**set** *ns.* Teeservice, *das;* ~ **shop** *n.* (Brit.) ≈ Café, *das;* ~**spoon** *n.* Teelöffel, *der;* ~ **strainer** *n.* Teesieb, *das*

**teat** /tiːt/ *n.* (a) Zitze, *die* (b) (of rubber or plastic) Sauger, *der*

**tea:** ~**time** *n.* Teezeit, *die;* ~ **towel** *n.* Geschirrtuch, *das;* ~ **trolley** *n.* Teewagen, *der;* ~ **urn** *n.* Teebehälter, *der*

**techie** /'tekɪ/ *n.* (coll.) Technikfreak, *der;* (computer expert) Computerfreak, *der*

**technical** /'teknɪkl/ *adj.* technisch ⟨*Problem, Daten, Fortschritt*⟩; Fach⟨*kenntnis, -sprache, -begriff, -wörterbuch*⟩; ~ **college** Fachhochschule, *die;* ~ **term** Fachbegriff, *der;* Fachausdruck, *der*

**technicality** /teknɪ'kælɪtɪ/ *n.* technisches Detail

**technician** /tek'nɪʃn/ *n.* Techniker, *der*/ Technikerin, *die*

**technique** /tek'niːk/ *n.* Technik, *die;* (procedure) Methode, *die*

**techno** ① *adj.* Techno- ② *n.* Techno, *der od. das*

**technological** /teknə'lɒdʒɪkl/ *adj.* technisch; technologisch

**technology** /tek'nɒlədʒɪ/ *n.* Technik, *die;* (application of science) Technologie, *die*

**technophobe** /'teknəʊfəʊb/ *n.* Mensch mit einer Technikphobie

**teddy** /'tedɪ/ *n.* ~ [**bear**] Teddy[bär], *der*

**tedious** /'tiːdɪəs/ *adj.* langwierig ⟨*Reise, Arbeit*⟩; (uninteresting) langweilig

**tee** /tiː/ (Golf) Tee, *das*

**teem** /tiːm/ *v.i.* wimmeln (with von)

**teen¹** /tiːn/ *adj.* Teenager-

**teenage[d]** /'tiːneɪdʒ(d)/ *attrib. adj.* im Teenageralter *nachgestellt*

**teenager** /'tiːneɪdʒə(r)/ *n.* Teenager, *der;* (loosely) Jugendliche, *der/die*

**teens** /tiːnz/ *n. pl.* Teenagerjahre *Pl.*

**'tee shirt** *n.* T-Shirt, *das*

**teeter** /'tiːtə(r)/ *v.i.* wanken; ∼ **on the edge of sth.** schwankend am Rande einer Sache (*Gen.*) stehen

**teeth** *pl. of* TOOTH

**teething troubles** /'tiːðɪŋ trʌblz/ *n. pl.* have ∼ (fig.) Anfangsschwierigkeiten haben

**teetotal** /tiː'təʊtl/ *adj.* abstinent lebend

**teetotaller** /tiː'təʊtələ(r)/ *n.* Abstinenzler, *der*/Abstinenzlerin, *die*

**TEFL** /'tefl/ *abbr.* = **teaching of English as a foreign language**

**Teflon** ® /'teflɒn/ *n.* Teflon Ⓦⓩ, *das*

**Tel., tel.** *abbr.* = **telephone** Tel.

**telebanking** /'telɪbæŋkɪŋ/ *n.* Telebanking, *das*

**telecommunications** /telɪkəmjuːnɪ'keɪʃnz/ *n. pl.* Fernmelde- *od.* Nachrichtentechnik, *die*

**telecommute** /'telɪkəmjuːt/ *v.i.* Telearbeit verrichten

**telecommuting** /'telɪkəmjuːtɪŋ/ *n.* Telearbeit, *die*

**teleconference** /'telɪkɒnfərəns/ *n.* Telekonferenz, *die*

**telecottage** /'telɪkɒtɪdʒ/ *n.: jedermann zugängliche Einrichtung, die bes. Telearbeitern Zugang zu einem ans Internet angeschlossenen Computer bietet*

**telegram** /'telɪgræm/ *n.* Telegramm, *das*

**telegraph** /'telɪgrɑːf/ *n.* Telegraf, *der;* ∼ **pole** Telegrafenmast, *der*

**telemarketing** /'telɪmɑːkɪtɪŋ/ *n.* Telefonmarketing, *das*

**telepathy** /tɪ'lepəθɪ/ *n.* Telepathie, *die*

**telephone** /'telɪfəʊn/ 1 *n.* Telefon, *das; attrib.* Telefon-; **answer the** ∼: Anrufe entgegennehmen; (on one occasion) ans Telefon gehen; (speak) sich melden; **be on the** ∼: Telefon haben; (be speaking) telefonieren (**to** mit)
2 *v.t.* anrufen
3 *v.i.* anrufen; ∼ **for a taxi** nach einem Taxi telefonieren

**telephone:** ∼ **'answering machine** *n.* Anrufbeantworter, *der;* ∼ **'banking** *n.* Telefonbanking, *das;* ∼ **book** *n.* Telefonbuch, *das;* ∼ **booth,** (Brit.) ∼ **box** *ns.* Telefonzelle, *die;* ∼ **call** *n.* Telefongespräch, *das;* ∼ **connection** *n.* Telefonverbindung, *die;* ∼ **directory** *n.* Telefonverzeichnis, *das;* ∼ **exchange** *n.* Fernmeldeamt, *das;* ∼ **number** *n.* Telefonnummer, *die;* ∼ **operator** *n.* Telefonist, *der*/Telefonistin, *die*

**telephonist** /tɪ'lefənɪst/ *n.* Telefonist, *der*/Telefonistin, *die*

**telephoto** /telɪ'fəʊtəʊ/ *adj.* ∼ **lens** Teleobjektiv, *das*

**teleprinter** /'telɪprɪntə(r)/ *n.* Fernschreiber, *der*

**'telesales** *n. pl.* Telefonverkauf, *der;* Verkauf per Telefon

**telescope** /'telɪskəʊp/ *n.* Teleskop, *das;* Fernrohr, *das*

**telescopic** /telɪ'skɒpɪk/ *adj.* (collapsible) ausziehbar; Teleskop⟨antenne⟩

**Teletex** ® /'telɪteks/ *n.* Teletex, *das*

**teletext** /'telɪtekst/ *n.* Teletext, *der*

**televise** /'telɪvaɪz/ *v.t.* im Fernsehen senden *od.* übertragen

**television** /'telɪvɪʒn, telɪ'vɪʒn/ *n.* (a) *no art.* das Fernsehen; **on** ∼: im Fernsehen; **watch** ∼: fernsehen
(b) (∼ set) Fernsehapparat, *der;* Fernseher, *der* (ugs.)

**television:** ∼ **aerial** *n.* Fernsehantenne, *die;* ∼ **channel** *n.* [Fernseh]kanal, *der;* ∼ **coverage** *n.* Fernsehberichterstattung, *die;* ∼ **licence** *n.* (Brit.) Fernsehgenehmigung, *die* (*die jährlich gegen Zahlen der Gebühren erneuert wird*); ∼ **licence fee** Fernsehgebühren *Pl.;* ∼ **lounge** *n.* Fernsehraum, *der;* ∼ **personality** *n.* Fernsehgröße, *die* (ugs.); ∼ **picture** *n.* Fernsehbild, *das;* ∼ **programme** *n.* Fernsehsendung, *die;* ∼ **screen** *n.* Bildschirm, *der;* ∼ **serial** *n.* Fernsehserie, *die;* ∼ **set** *n.* Fernsehgerät, *das;* ∼ **studio** *n.* Fernsehstudio, *das;* ∼ **viewer** *n.* Fernsehzuschauer, *der*/ -zuschauerin, *die*

**teleworking** /'telɪwɜːkɪŋ/ *n.* Telearbeit, *die*

**telex** /'teleks/ 1 *n.* Telex, *das*
2 *v.t.* ein Telex schicken (+ *Dat.*); telexen ⟨*Nachricht*⟩

**tell** /tel/ 1 *v.t.,* told /təʊld/ (a) (relate) erzählen; (make known) sagen ⟨*Name, Adresse*⟩; anvertrauen ⟨*Geheimnis*⟩; ∼ **sb. sth.** *or* **sth. to sb.** jmdm. etw. erzählen/sagen/ anvertrauen; ∼ **sb. the way to the station** jmdm. den Weg zum Bahnhof beschreiben; ∼ **sb. the time** jmdm. die Uhrzeit sagen; ∼ **tales** (lie) Lügengeschichten erzählen; (gossip) tratschen (ugs.)
(b) (instruct) sagen; ∼ **sb.** [**not**] **to do sth.** jmdm. sagen, er soll[e] etw. [nicht] tun
(c) (determine) feststellen; (see, recognize) erkennen (**by** an + *Dat.*); (with reference to the future) [vorher]sagen
(d) (distinguish) unterscheiden
(e) **all told** insgesamt
2 *v.i.,* told (a) (determine) **how can you** ∼? wie kann man das feststellen *od.* wissen?; **you never can** ∼: man kann nie wissen
(b) (give information) erzählen (**of, about** von)
(c) (reveal secret) es verraten; **time will** ∼: das wird sich zeigen
(d) (produce an effect) sich auswirken

■ **tell a'part** *v.t.* auseinander halten

■ **tell 'off** *v.t.* (coll.) ∼ **sb. off** [**for sth.**] jmdn. [für *od.* wegen etw.] ausschimpfen

**teller** /'telə(r)/ *n.* (a) (in bank) ▶ CASHIER

**(b)** (counting votes) Stimmenzähler, *der/* -zählerin, *die*

**telly** /'telɪ/ *n.* (Brit. coll.) Fernseher, *der* (ugs.); **on ～:** im Fernsehen; **watch ～ :** Fernsehen gucken (ugs.)

**temp** /temp/ *n.* (Brit. coll.) Zeitarbeitskraft, *die*

**temper** /'tempə(r)/ ⟦1⟧ *n.* **(a)** Naturell, *das;* **be in a good/bad ～:** gute/schlechte Laune haben; **keep/lose one's ～:** sich beherrschen/die Beherrschung verlieren **(b)** (anger) **fit of ～:** Wutanfall, *der;* **have a ～:** jähzornig sein ⟦2⟧ *v.t.* mäßigen; mildern ⟨*Kritik*⟩

**temperament** /'temprəmənt/ *n.* (nature) Veranlagung, *die;* Natur, *die;* (disposition) Temperament, *das*

**temperamental** /temprə'mentl/ *adj.* launenhaft

**temperate** /'tempərət/ *adj.* gemäßigt

**temperature** /'temprɪtʃə(r)/ *n.* Temperatur, *die;* **have *or* run a ～** (coll.) Temperatur *od.* Fieber haben

**template** /'templɪt/ *n.* **(a)** Schablone, *die* **(b)** (Comp.) Schablone, *die;* Template, *das*

**temple¹** /'templ/ *n.* Tempel, *der*

**temple²** *n.* (Anat.) Schläfe, *die*

**tempo** /'tempəʊ/ *n., pl.* **～s** *or* **tempi** /'tempi:/ Tempo, *das*

**temporarily** /'tempərərɪlɪ/ *adv.* vorübergehend

**temporary** /'tempərərɪ/ ⟦1⟧ *adj.* vorübergehend; provisorisch ⟨*Gebäude, Büro,*⟩ **～ job** Aushilfstätigkeit, *die* ⟦2⟧ *n.* Aushilfe, *die;* Aushilfskraft, *die*

**tempt** /tempt/ *v.t.* **(a)** **～ sb. to do sth.** jmdn. geneigt machen, etw. zu tun; **be ～ed to do sth.** versucht sein, etw. zu tun; **～ sb. out** jmdn. hinauslocken **(b)** (provoke) herausfordern; **～ fate** das Schicksal herausfordern

**temptation** /temp'teɪʃn/ *n.* **(a)** *no pl.* (attracting) Verlockung, *die;* (being attracted) Versuchung, *die* **(b)** (thing) Verlockung, *die*

**'tempting** *adj.* verlockend

**ten** /ten/ ⟦1⟧ *adj.* zehn ⟦2⟧ *n.* Zehn, *die. See also* EIGHT

**tenable** /'tenəbl/ *adj.* haltbar ⟨*Theorie*⟩; vertretbar ⟨*Standpunkt*⟩

**tenacious** /tɪ'neɪʃəs/ *adj.* hartnäckig

**tenacity** /tɪ'næsɪtɪ/ *n.* Hartnäckigkeit, *die*

**tenant** /'tenənt/ *n.* (of flat, residential building) Mieter, *der/*Mieterin, *die;* (of farm, shop) Pächter, *der/*Pächterin, *die*

**tend¹** /tend/ *v.i.* **～ to do sth.** dazu neigen *od.* tendieren, etw. zu tun; **～ to sth.** zu etw. neigen; **he ～s to get upset if ...:** er regt sich leicht auf, wenn ...

**tend²** *v.t.* sich kümmern um; hüten ⟨*Schafe*⟩; bedienen ⟨*Maschine*⟩

**tendency** /'tendənsɪ/ *n.* (inclination) Tendenz, *die;* **have a ～ to do sth.** dazu neigen, etw. zu tun

**tender¹** /'tendə(r)/ *adj.* **(a)** (not tough) zart **(b)** (loving) zärtlich **(c)** (sensitive) empfindlich

**tender²** ⟦1⟧ *v.t.* **(a)** (present) einreichen ⟨*Rücktritt*⟩; vorbringen ⟨*Entschuldigung*⟩ **(b)** (offer as payment) anbieten ⟦2⟧ *n.* Angebot, *das*

**'tenderly** *adv.* (gently) behutsam; (lovingly) zärtlich

**'tenderness** *n.* ▶ TENDER¹: Zartheit, *die;* Zärtlichkeit, *die;* Empfindlichkeit, *die*

**tendon** /'tendən/ *n.* (Anat.) Sehne, *die*

**tenement** /'tenɪmənt/ *n.* Mietshaus, *das*

**tenet** /'tenɪt/ *n.* Grundsatz, *der*

**tenner** /'tenə(r)/ *n.* (Brit. coll.) Zehnpfundschein, *der*

**tennis** /'tenɪs/ *n.* Tennis, *das*

**tennis: ～ ball** *n.* Tennisball, *der;* **～ club** *n.* Tennisverein, *der;* **～ court** *n.* (for lawn ～) Tennisplatz, *der;* (indoor) Tennishalle, *die;* **～ 'elbow** *n., no art.* (Med.) Tennisell[en]bogen, *der;* **～ match** *n.* Tennismatch, *das;* Tennisspiel, *das;* **～ racket** *n.* Tennisschläger, *der;* **～ shoe** *n.* Tennisschuh, *der*

**tenor** /'tenə(r)/ *n.* (Mus.) Tenor, *der*

**tense¹** /tens/ *n.* (Ling.) Zeit, *die;* **in the present/future** *etc.* **～:** im Präsens/Futur *usw.*

**tense²** ⟦1⟧ *adj.* gespannt ⟦2⟧ *v.i.* **sb. ～s** jmds. Muskeln spannen sich an ⟦3⟧ *v.t.* anspannen

**tension** /'tenʃn/ *n.* **(a)** Spannung, *die* **(b)** (mental strain) Anspannung, *die*

**tent** /tent/ *n.* Zelt, *das*

**tentacle** /'tentəkl/ *n.* Tentakel, *der od. das*

**tentative** /'tentətɪv/ *adj.* **(a)** (not definite) vorläufig **(b)** (hesitant) zaghaft

**tenterhooks** /'tentəhʊks/ *n. pl.* **be on ～:** [wie] auf glühenden Kohlen sitzen

**tenth** /tenθ/ ⟦1⟧ *adj.* zehnt... ⟦2⟧ *n.* (in sequence, rank) Zehnte, *der/die/das;* (fraction) Zehntel, *das. See also* EIGHTH

**tent: ～ peg** *n.* Zeltpflock, *der;* **～ pole** *n.* Zeltstange, *die*

**tenuous** /'tenjʊəs/ *adj.* dünn ⟨*Atmosphäre*⟩; dürftig ⟨*Argument*⟩; unbegründet ⟨*Anspruch*⟩

**tepid** /'tepɪd/ *adj.* lauwarm

**term** /tɜːm/ ⟦1⟧ *n.* **(a)** [Fach]begriff, *der* **(b)** *in pl.* (conditions) Bedingungen *Pl.;* **come to ～s with sth.** mit etw. zurechtkommen; (resign oneself to sth.) sich mit etw. abfinden **(c)** *in pl.* (charges) Konditionen *Pl.* **(d)** **in the short/long/medium ～:** kurz-/lang-/ mittelfristig **(e)** (Sch.) Halbjahr, *das;* (Univ.: one of two/three divisions per year) Semester, *das/*Trimester, *das* ⋯⟶

**(f)** (limited period) Zeitraum, *der;* ~ [of office] Amtszeit, *die*
**(g)** *in pl.* (mode of expression) Worte *Pl.*
**(h)** *in pl.* (relations) **be on good/bad ~s with sb.** mit jmdm. auf gutem/schlechtem Fuß stehen
②*v.t.* nennen
**terminal** /'tɜːmɪnl/ ①*n.* **(a)** (for train or bus) Bahnhof, *der;* (for airline passengers) Terminal, *der od. das*
**(b)** (Teleph., Comp.) Terminal, *das*
②*adj.* (Med.) unheilbar
**terminally** /'tɜːmɪnəlɪ/ *adv.* ~ **ill** unheilbar krank
**terminate** /'tɜːmɪneɪt/ *v.t.* **(a)** beenden; lösen ‹*Vertrag*›
**(b)** (Med.) unterbrechen ‹*Schwangerschaft*›
**termination** /tɜːmɪ'neɪʃn/ *n.* **(a)** *no pl.* Beendigung, *die;* (of lease) Ablauf, *der*
**(b)** (Med.) Schwangerschaftsabbruch, *der*
**termini** *pl. of* TERMINUS
**terminology** /tɜːmɪ'nɒlədʒɪ/ *n.* Terminologie, *die*
**terminus** /'tɜːmɪnəs/ *n., pl.* ~**es** *or* **termini** /'tɜːmɪnaɪ/ Endstation, *die*
**terrace** /'terəs, 'terɪs/ *n.* Terrasse, *die;* (row of houses) Häuserreihe, *die*
**terraced house** /'terəst haʊs, 'terɪst haʊs/ *n.* Reihenhaus, *das*
**terracotta** /terə'kɒtə/ *n., no indef. art.* Terrakotta, *die*
**terrain** /te'reɪn/ *n.* Gelände, *das*
**terrestrial** /tə'restrɪəl/ *adj.* terrestrisch ‹*Raumschiff, Fernsehen, Bevölkerung*›; Erd‹*satellit, -bevölkerung*›
**terrible** /'terɪbl/ *adj.* **(a)** (coll.: very great or bad) schrecklich (ugs.)
**(b)** (coll.: incompetent) schlecht
**(c)** (causing terror) furchtbar
**terribly** /'terɪblɪ/ *adv.* **(a)** (coll.: very) unheimlich (ugs.)
**(b)** (appallingly) furchtbar (ugs.)
**(c)** (coll.: incompetently) schlecht
**(d)** (fearfully) auf erschreckende Weise
**terrier** /'terɪə(r)/ *n.* Terrier, *der*
**terrific** /tə'rɪfɪk/ *adj.* (coll.) **(a)** (great, intense) irrsinnig (ugs.)
**(b)** (magnificent) sagenhaft (ugs.)
**(c)** (highly expert) klasse (ugs.)
**terrify** /'terɪfaɪ/ *v.t.* **(a)** Angst machen (+ *Dat.*); **be terrified that ...:** Angst haben, dass ...
**(b)** (scare) Angst einjagen (+ *Dat.*)
**'terrifying** *adj.* entsetzlich ‹*Erlebnis, Buch*›; Furcht erregend ‹*Anblick*›; beängstigend ‹*Geschwindigkeit*›
**terrine** /tə'riːn/ *n.* **(a)** (dish) Steinguttopf, *der*
**(b)** (Gastr.) Terrine, *die*
**territorial** /terɪ'tɔːrɪəl/ *adj.* territorial; Gebiets‹*anspruch usw.*›
**territory** /'terɪtrɪ/ *n.* Gebiet, *das*
**terror** /'terə(r)/ *n.* [panische] Angst; Schrecken, *der*

**terrorism** /'terərɪzm/ *n.* Terrorismus, *der;* (terrorist acts) Terror, *der*
**'terrorist** *n.* Terrorist, *der*/Terroristin, *die*
**terrorize** /'terəraɪz/ *v.t.* **(a)** (frighten) in [Angst und] Schrecken versetzen
**(b)** (coerce) terrorisieren
**terse** /tɜːs/ *adj.* **(a)** (concise) kurz und bündig
**(b)** (curt) knapp
**test** /test/ ①*n.* **(a)** (Sch.) Klassenarbeit, *die;* (Univ.) Klausur, *die;* **put sb./sth. to the ~:** jmdn./etw. erproben
**(b)** (analysis) Test, *der*
②*v.t.* untersuchen ‹*Wasser, Augen*›; testen ‹*Gehör, Augen*›; prüfen ‹*Schüler*›; ~ **sb. for Aids** jmdn. auf Aids untersuchen
■ **'test out** *v.t.* ausprobieren ‹*Produkte*› (on an + *Dat.*); erproben ‹*Theorie, Idee*›
**Testament** /'testəmənt/ *n.* **Old/New ~** (Bibl.) Altes/Neues Testament
**test:** ~ **ban** *n.* Atom[waffen]teststopp, *der;* ~ **ban treaty** *n.* [Atom]teststopp-Abkommen, *das;* ~ **drive** *n.* Probefahrt, *die;* ~**-drive** *v.t.* Probe fahren
**testicle** /'testɪkl/ *n.* Testikel, *der* (fachspr.); Hoden, *der*
**testify** /'testɪfaɪ/ ①*v.i.* **(a)** ~ **to sth.** etw. bezeugen
**(b)** (Law) ~ **against sb.** gegen jmdn. aussagen
②*v.t.* bestätigen
**testimonial** /testɪ'məʊnɪəl/ *n.* Zeugnis, *das;* Referenz, *die*
**testimony** /'testɪmənɪ/ *n.* Aussage, *die*
**test:** ~ **pilot** *n.* Testpilot, *der*/-pilotin, *die;* ~ **tube** *n.* Reagenzglas, *das;* ~**-tube baby** *n.* (coll.) Retortenbaby, *das* (ugs.)
**testy** /'testɪ/ *adj.* leicht reizbar ‹*Person*›; gereizt ‹*Antwort*›
**tetanus** /'tetənəs/ *n.* Tetanus, *der*
**tetchy** /'tetʃɪ/ *adj.* leicht reizbar; gereizt
**tether** /'teðə(r)/ ①*n.* **be at the end of one's ~:** am Ende [seiner Kraft] sein
②*v.t.* anbinden (**to** an + *Dat. od. Akk.*)
**text** /tekst/ *n.* Text, *der*
**text:** ~**book** *n.* Lehrbuch, *das;* ~**book case** Paradefall, *der;* ~ **file** *n.* (Comp.) Textdatei, *die*
**textile** /'tekstaɪl/ *n.* Stoff, *der;* ~**s** Textilien *Pl.*
**'text processing** *n.* (Comp.) Textverarbeitung, *die*
**texture** /'tekstʃə(r)/ *n.* Beschaffenheit, *die;* (of fabric) Struktur, *die*
**Thai** /taɪ/ ①*adj.* thailändisch; **sb. is ~:** jmd. ist Thai
②*n.* **(a)** *pl. same or* ~**s** Thai, *der*/*die*
**(b)** (language) Thai, *das*
**Thailand** /'taɪlænd/ *pr. n.* Thailand (*das*)
**Thames** /temz/ *pr. n.* Themse, *die*
**than** /ðən, *stressed* ðæn/ *conj.* als; **I know you better ~ [I do]** him ich kenne dich besser als ihn

**thank** /θæŋk/ *v.t.* ~ sb. [for sth.] jmdm.
[für etw.] danken; ~ **God** *or* **goodness** *or*
**heaven[s]** Gott sei Dank; [I] ~ **you** danke;
**no,** ~ **you** nein, danke; **yes,** ~ **you** ja, bitte;
~ **you very much** vielen herzlichen Dank

**thankful** /'θæŋkfl/ *adj.* dankbar

**thankfully** /'θæŋkfəlɪ/ *adv.* **(a)** (gratefully)
dankbar
**(b)** (as sentence-modifier: fortunately)
glücklicherweise

'**thankless** *adj.* undankbar

**thanks** /θæŋks/ *n. pl.* **(a)** (gratitude) Dank,
*der;* ~ **to** (with the help of) dank; (on account of
the bad influence of) wegen
**(b)** (formula expr. gratitude) danke; **no,** ~: nein,
danke; **yes,** ~: ja, bitte; **many** ~ (coll.) vielen
Dank

**thanksgiving** /'θæŋksgɪvɪŋ/ *n.* **T**~ [**Day**]
(Amer.) [amerikanisches] Erntedankfest;
Thanksgiving Day, *der*

'**thank-you** *n.* (coll.) Dankeschön, *das*

**that** [1] /ðæt/ *adj., pl.* **those** /ðəʊz/ **(a)**
dieser/diese/dieses
**(b)** (coupled or contrasted with 'this') der/die/das
[2] /ðæt/ *pron., pl.* **those (a)** der/die/das;
**what bird is** ~? was für ein Vogel ist das?;
**like** ~: so; [**just**] **like** ~ (without effort, thought)
einfach so; ~'**s right!** gut *od.* recht so; (iron.)
nur so weiter!; ~ **will do** das reicht
**(b)** (Brit.) **who is** ~? wer ist da?; (on telephone)
wer ist am Apparat?
[3] /ðət/ *rel. pron., pl.* **same** der/die/das;
**everyone** ~ **I know** jeder, den ich kenne; **this
is all** [**the money**] ~ **I have** das ist alles
[Geld], was ich habe
[4] /ðæt/ *adv.* (coll.) so
[5] /ðət/ *rel. adv.* der/die/das; **the day** ~ **I
first met her** der Tag, an dem ich sie zum
ersten Mal sah
[6] /ðət, *stressed* ðæt/ *conj.* dass; [**in order**]
~: damit

**thatch** /θætʃ/ *n.* (of straw) Strohdach, *das;*
(of reeds) Schilfdach, *das;* (roofing)
Dachbedeckung, *die*

**thatched** /θætʃt/ *adj.* stroh-/schilfgedeckt

**thaw** /θɔː/ [1] *n.* Tauwetter, *das*
[2] *v.i.* **(a)** tauen
**(b)** (melt) auftauen
[3] *v.t.* auftauen
■ **thaw 'out** ▶ THAW 2, 3

**the** /*before vowel* ðɪ, *before consonant* ðə,
*when stressed* ðiː/ [1] *def. art.* der/die/das
[2] *adv.* ~ **more I practise** ~ **better I play** je
mehr ich übe, desto *od.* umso besser spiele
ich; **so much** ~ **worse for sb./sth.** umso
schlimmer für jmdn./etw

**theatre** (Amer.: **theater**) /'θɪətə(r)/ *n.* **(a)**
Theater, *das*
**(b)** (lecture ~) Hörsaal, *der*
**(c)** (Brit. Med.) ▶ OPERATING THEATRE

**theatrical** /θɪˈætrɪkl/ *adj.* **(a)**
schauspielerisch
**(b)** (showy) theatralisch

**theft** /θeft/ *n.* Diebstahl, *der*

**their** /ðeə(r)/ *poss. pron. attrib.* ihr

**theirs** /ðeəz/ *poss. pron. pred.* ihrer/ihre/
ihres

**them** /ðəm, *stressed* ðem/ *pron.* sie; (as
indirect object) ihnen; *see also* HER[1]

**theme** /θiːm/ *n.* Thema, *das*

**theme:** ~ **music** *n.* Titelmelodie, *die;*
~ **park** *n.:* Freizeitpark, *dessen
Attraktionen und Einrichtungen auf ein
bestimmtes Thema bezogen sind;* ~ **song** *n.*
Erkennungssong, *der;* ~ **tune**
Erkennungsmelodie, *die*

**themselves** /ðəm'selvz/ *pron.* **(a)** *emphat.*
selbst
**(b)** *refl.* sich ⟨*waschen usw.*⟩; sich selbst ⟨*die
Schuld geben, regieren*⟩. See also HERSELF

**then** /ðen/ [1] *adv.* **(a)** (at that time) damals;
~ **and there** auf der Stelle
**(b)** (after that) dann; ~ [**again**] (and also)
außerdem; **but** ~ (after all) aber schließlich
**(c)** (in that case) dann; **but** ~ **again** aber
andererseits
[2] *n.* **before** ~: vorher; davor; **from** ~ **on**
von da an; **since** ~: seitdem
[3] *adj.* damalig

**theological** /θiːəˈlɒdʒɪkl/ *adj.* theologisch;
Theologie⟨*student*⟩

**theology** /θɪˈɒlədʒɪ/ *n.* Theologie, *die*

**theoretical** /θɪəˈretɪkl/ *adj.* theoretisch

**theory** /'θɪərɪ/ *n.* Theorie, *die;* **in** ~:
theoretisch

**therapeutic** /θerəˈpjuːtɪk/ *adj.*
therapeutisch

**therapist** /'θerəpɪst/ *n.* Therapeut, *der/*
Therapeutin, *die*

**therapy** /'θerəpɪ/ *n.* Therapie, *die*

**there** /ðeə(r)/ [1] *adv.* **(a)** (in/at that place) da;
dort; (fairly close) da; **be down/in/up** ~: da
unten/drin/oben sein
**(b)** (calling attention) **hello** *or* **hi** ~! hallo!; **you**
~! Sie da!
**(c)** (in that respect) da; **so** ~: und damit basta
(ugs.)
**(d)** (to that place) dahin, dorthin ⟨*gehen,
fahren, rücken*⟩; **down/up** ~: dort hinunter/
hinauf
**(e)** /ðə(r), *stressed* ðeə(r)/ **was** ~ **anything in
it?** war da irgendwas drin?; ~ **was once** es
war einmal; ~ **is enough food** es gibt genug
zu essen
[2] *int.* ~, ~: na, na (ugs.); ~ [**you are**]! da,
siehst du!
[3] *n.* da; dort; **near** ~: da *od.* dort in der
Nähe

**thereabouts** /'ðeərəbaʊts/ *adv.* **(a)** da [in
der Nähe]
**(b)** (near that number) ungefähr

**therefore** /'ðeəfɔː(r)/ *adv.* deshalb; also

**thermal** /'θɜːml/ *adj.* thermisch;
~ **underwear** kälteisolierende Unterwäsche

**thermal imaging** /θɜːml 'ɪmɪdʒɪŋ/ *n.*
Thermographie, *die*

**thermometer** /θə'mɒmɪtə(r)/ n.
Thermometer, das

**Thermos, thermos** ® /'θɜːməs/ n.
~ [flask/jug/bottle] Thermosflasche, die ⓌⓏ

**thermostat** /'θɜːməstæt/ n. Thermostat,
der

**these** pl. of THIS

**thesis** /'θiːsɪs/ n., pl. **theses** /'θiːsiːz/ (a)
(proposition) These, die
(b) (dissertation) Dissertation, die (on über
+ Akk.)

**they** /ðeɪ/ pron. (a) sie
(b) (people in general) man

**they'd** /ðeɪd/ (a) = they would
(b) = they had

**they'll** /ðeɪl/ = they will

**they're** /ðeə(r)/ = they are

**they've** /ðeɪv/ = they have

**thick** /θɪk/ 1 adj. (a) dick; a rope two
inches ~, a two-inch ~ rope ein zwei Zoll
starkes od. dickes Seil
(b) (dense) dicht ⟨Haar, Nebel, Wolken usw.⟩
(c) (filled) ~ with voll von
(d) dickflüssig ⟨Sahne⟩; dick ⟨Suppe,
Schlamm, Kleister⟩
(e) (stupid) dumm
2 n. in the ~ of mitten in (+ Dat.)

**thick 'ear** n. give sb. a ~ (Brit. coll.) jmdm.
ein paar hinter die Ohren geben (ugs.)

**thicken** /'θɪkn/ 1 v.t. dicker machen;
eindicken ⟨Sauce⟩
2 v.i. (a) dicker werden
(b) ⟨Nebel:⟩ dichter werden
(c) the plot ~s die Sache wird kompliziert

**'thickly** adv. (a) (in a thick layer) dick
(b) (densely) dicht

**'thickness** n. (a) Dicke, die; be two metres
in ~: zwei Meter dick sein
(b) (denseness) Dichte, die

**thick:** ~**set** adj. gedrungen; ~**-skinned**
adj. (fig.) dickfellig (ugs.)

**thief** /θiːf/ n., pl. **thieves** /θiːvz/ Dieb, der/
Diebin, die

**thieve** /θiːv/ v.i. stehlen

**thieves** pl. of THIEF

**thigh** /θaɪ/ n. Oberschenkel, der

**thimble** /'θɪmbl/ n. Fingerhut, der

**thin** /θɪn/ 1 adj. (a) dünn; a tall, ~ man ein
großer, hagerer Mann
(b) (sparse) dünn, schütter ⟨Haar⟩
2 adv. dünn
3 v.t., -nn-: (a) dünner machen
(b) (dilute) verdünnen

■ **thin 'out** v.i. ⟨Menschenmenge:⟩ sich
verlaufen; ⟨Verkehr:⟩ abnehmen

**thing** /θɪŋ/ n. (a) Sache, die; Ding, das;
what's that ~ in your hand? was hast du da
in der Hand?; be a rare ~: etwas Seltenes
sein
(b) (action) it was the right ~ to do es war das
einzig Richtige; that was a foolish/friendly
~ to do das war eine große Dummheit/das
war sehr freundlich

(c) (fact) [Tat]sache, die; it's a strange ~ that
...: es ist seltsam, dass ...; the best/worst
~ about her das Beste/Schlimmste an ihr
(d) (idea) say the first ~ that comes into
one's head das sagen, was einem gerade so
einfällt; what a ~ to say! wie kann man nur
so etwas sagen!
(e) (task) she has a reputation for getting ~s
done sie ist für ihre Tatkraft bekannt; a big
~ to undertake ein großes Unterfangen
(f) (affair) Sache, die; Angelegenheit, die
(g) (circumstance) take ~s too seriously alles
zu ernst nehmen; how are ~s? wie gehts
[dir]?
(h) (individual, creature) Ding, das
(i) in pl. (personal belongings, clothes) Sachen Pl.
(j) (product of work) Sache, die; the latest ~:
der letzte Schrei
(k) (what is important or proper) das Richtige; the
~ is ... (question) die Frage ist ...

**thingamy** /'θɪŋəmɪ/, **thingumabob**
/'θɪŋəməbɒb/, **thingumajig** /'θɪŋəmədʒɪg/,
**thingummy** /'θɪŋəmɪ/, **thingy** /'θɪŋɪ/ ns.
(coll.) Dings, der/die/das (salopp); Dingsbums,
der/die/das (ugs.)

**think** /θɪŋk/ 1 v.t., thought /θɔːt/ (a)
(consider) meinen; we ~ [that] he will come
wir denken od. glauben, dass er kommt;
what do you ~? was meinst du? do you
really ~ so? findest du wirklich?; what do
you ~ of him/it? was hältst du von ihm/
davon?; ..., don't you ~? ... , findest od.
meinst du nicht auch?; I ~ so/not ich glaube
schon/nicht; I ~ I'll try ich glaube, ich werde
es versuchen
(b) (imagine) sich (Dat.) vorstellen
2 v.i., thought [nach]denken; I need time to
~: ich muss es mir erst überlegen; I've been
~ing ich habe nachgedacht; ~ twice es sich
(Dat.) zweimal überlegen
■ **'think of** v.t. (a) denken an (+ Akk.); he
~s of everything er denkt einfach an alles
(b) (have as idea) we'll ~ of something wir
werden uns etwas einfallen lassen; can you
~ of anyone who ...? fällt dir jemand ein,
der ...?
(c) (remember) sich erinnern an (+ Akk.); I
just can't ~ of her name ich komme einfach
nicht auf ihren Namen
(d) ~ little/nothing of sb./sth. (consider
contemptible) wenig/nichts von jmdm./etw.
halten; not ~ much of sb./sth. nicht viel von
jmdm./etw. halten
■ **think 'over** v.t. sich (Dat.) überlegen
■ **think 'through** v.t. [gründlich]
durchdenken
■ **think 'up** v.t. (coll.) sich (Dat.) ausdenken

**'thinker** n. Denker, der/Denkerin, die

**'think tank** n. Beraterstab, der

**'thin-skinned** adj. (fig.) empfindlich;
dünnhäutig (geh.)

**third** /θɜːd/ 1 adj. dritt...
2 n. (in sequence, rank) Dritte, der/die/das;
(fraction) Drittel, das. See also EIGHTH

**'thirdly** adv. drittens

**third:** ~ **'party** n. attrib. ~**-party insurance** Haftpflichtversicherung, die; ~**-rate** adj. drittklassig; **T**~ **'World** n. Dritte Welt; **countries of the T**~ **World, T**~ **World countries** Länder der Dritten Welt

**thirst** /θɜːst/ ① n. Durst, der; **die of** ~: verdursten

② v.i. ~ **for revenge/knowledge** nach Rache/Wissen dürsten (geh.)

**'thirsty** adj. durstig; **be** ~: Durst haben

**thirteen** /θɜːˈtiːn/ ① adj. dreizehn

② n. Dreizehn, die. See also EIGHT

**thirteenth** /θɜːˈtiːnθ/ adj. dreizehnt... See also EIGHTH

**thirtieth** /ˈθɜːtɪɪθ/ ① adj. dreißigst...

② n. (fraction) Dreißigstel, das. See also EIGHTH

**thirty** /ˈθɜːtɪ/ ① adj. dreißig

② n. Dreißig, die. See also EIGHT; EIGHTY 2

**'thirty-something** ① adj. **be** ~: in den Dreißigern sein

② n. Dreißiger, der/-in, die

**this** /ðɪs/ ① adj., pl. **these** /ðiːz/ dieser/diese/dieses; (with less emphasis) der/die/das; **at** ~ **time** zu dieser Zeit; **by** ~ **time** inzwischen; mittlerweile; **these days** heut[zutag]e; **these** ~ **time** vorher; zuvor; **all** ~ **week** die[se] ganze Woche; ~ **morning/ evening** etc. heute Morgen/Abend usw.; **these last three weeks** die letzten drei Wochen; ~ **Monday** (to come) nächsten Montag

② pron., pl. **these (a) what's** ~? was ist [denn] das?; **fold it like** ~: falte es so!

**(b)** (the present) **before** ~: bis jetzt

**(c)** (Brit. Teleph.: person speaking) ~ **is Andy** hier [spricht od. ist] Andy; (Amer. Teleph.) **who did you say** ~ **was?** wer ist am Apparat?

**(d)** ~ **and that** dies und das

**thistle** /ˈθɪsl/ n. Distel, die

**thorn** /θɔːn/ n. **(a)** (part of plant) Dorn, der

**(b)** (plant) Dornenstrauch, der

**'thorny** adj. **(a)** dornig

**(b)** (fig.) heikel

**thorough** /ˈθʌrə/ adj. gründlich

**thorough:** ~**bred** n. reinrassiges Tier; (horse) Rassepferd, das; ~**fare** n. Durchfahrtsstraße, die; **'no** ~**fare'** „Durchfahrt verboten"; (on foot) „kein Durchgang"

**'thoroughly** adv. gründlich ⟨untersuchen⟩; gehörig ⟨erschöpft⟩; so richtig ⟨genießen⟩; zutiefst ⟨beschämt⟩; total ⟨verdorben, verwöhnt⟩; **be** ~ **fed up with sth.** (coll.) von etw. die Nase gestrichen voll haben (ugs.)

**'thoroughness** n. Gründlichkeit, die

**those** ▶ THAT 1, 2

**though** /ðəʊ/ ① conj. **(a)** (despite the fact that) obwohl; **late** ~ **it was** obwohl es so spät war;

**the car,** ~ **powerful, is also economical** der Wagen ist zwar stark, aber [zugleich] auch wirtschaftlich

**(b)** (but nevertheless) aber; **a slow** ~ **certain method** eine langsame, aber od. wenn auch sichere Methode

**(c)** (even if) [even] ~: auch wenn

**(d)** (and yet) ~ **you never know** obwohl man nie weiß

② adv. (coll.) trotzdem

**thought** /θɔːt/ ① ▶ THINK

② n. **(a)** no pl. Denken, das

**(b)** no pl., no art. (reflection) Überlegung, die; Nachdenken, das

**(c)** (consideration) Rücksicht, die **(for** auf + Akk.)

**(d)** (idea, conception) Gedanke, der; **it's the** ~ **that counts** der gute Wille zählt; **give up all** ~**[s] of sth.** sich (Dat.) etw. aus dem Kopf schlagen

**thoughtful** /ˈθɔːtfl/ adj. **(a)** nachdenklich

**(b)** (considerate) rücksichtsvoll; (helpful) aufmerksam

**'thoughtfully** adv. **(a)** nachdenklich

**(b)** (considerately) rücksichtsvollerweise

**'thoughtless** adj. **(a)** gedankenlos

**(b)** (inconsiderate) rücksichtslos

**'thoughtlessly** adv. **(a)** gedankenlos

**(b)** (inconsiderately) aus Rücksichtslosigkeit

**thought:** ~ **process** n. Denkprozess, der; ~**-provoking** adj. nachdenklich stimmend; **be** ~**-provoking** nachdenklich stimmen

**thousand** /ˈθaʊznd/ ① adj. **(a)** tausend; **a or one** ~: eintausend; **two/several** ~: zweitausend/mehrere tausend; **a or one** ~ **and one** [ein]tausend[und]eins

**(b) a** ~ **[and one]** (fig.: innumerable) tausend (ugs.)

② n. **(a)** (number) tausend; **a or one/two** ~: ein-/zweitausend

**(b)** (written figure; group) Tausend, das

**(c)** (indefinite amount) ~**s** tausende

**thousandth** /ˈθaʊzndθ/ ① adj. tausendst...

② n. (fraction) Tausendstel, das; (in sequence) Tausendste, der/die/das

**thrash** /θræʃ/ v.t. **(a)** verprügeln

**(b)** (defeat) vernichtend schlagen

■ **thrash 'out** v.t. ausdiskutieren

**thrashing** /ˈθræʃɪŋ/ n. (beating) Prügel Pl.; **give sb. a** ~: jmdm. eine Tracht Prügel verpassen (ugs.)

**thread** /θred/ ① n. **(a)** Faden, der

**(b)** (of screw) Gewinde, das

② v.t. **(a)** einfädeln; auffädeln ⟨Perlen⟩

**(b)** ~ **one's way through sth.** sich durch etw. schlängeln

**'threadbare** adj. abgenutzt; abgetragen ⟨Kleidung⟩; (fig.) abgedroschen ⟨Argument⟩

**threat** /θret/ n. Drohung, die

**threaten** /ˈθretn/ v.t. **(a)** bedrohen; ~ **sb. with sth.** jmdm. etw. androhen

**(b)** ~ **to do sth.** damit drohen, etw. zu tun

**(c)** drohen mit ⟨Gewalt, Rache usw.⟩

**t**

**threatening** /'θretnɪŋ/ adj. drohend

**three** /θriː/ ①adj. drei

②n. Drei, die. See also EIGHT

**three:** ~**dimensional** /θriːdɪ'menʃənl/ adj. dreidimensional; ~**fold** adj., adv. dreifach; **a** ~**fold increase** ein Anstieg auf das Dreifache; ~**lane** adj. dreispurig; ~**pin** ▶ PIN 1 C; ~**quarters** ①n. drei Viertel pl. (of + Gen.); ~**quarters of an hour** eine Dreiviertelstunde; ②adv. drei viertel ⟨voll⟩; ~**some** /'θriːsəm/ n. Dreigespann, das; Trio, das

**thresh** /θreʃ/ v.t. dreschen

**threshold** /'θreʃəʊld/ n. Schwelle, die

**threw** ▶ THROW 1

**thrift** /θrɪft/ n. Sparsamkeit, die

**'thrifty** adj. sparsam

**thrill** /θrɪl/ ①v.t. (a) (excite) faszinieren (b) (delight) begeistern ②n. (a) Erregung, die (b) (exciting experience) aufregendes Erlebnis

**'thriller** n. Thriller, der

**'thrilling** adj. aufregend; spannend ⟨Buch, Film⟩

**thrive** /θraɪv/ v.i., thrived or throve /θrəʊv/, thrived or thriven /'θrɪvn/ (a) ⟨Pflanze:⟩ wachsen und gedeihen (b) (prosper) aufblühen (on bei)

**throat** /θrəʊt/ n. Hals, der; (esp. inside) Kehle, die; **a [sore]** ~: Halsschmerzen Pl.

**throb** /θrɒb/ ①v.i., -bb- pochen; ⟨Motor:⟩ dröhnen ②n. Pochen, das; (of engine) Dröhnen, das

**throes** /θrəʊz/ n. pl. Qual, die; **be in the** ~ **of sth.** (fig.) mitten in etw. (Dat.) stecken (ugs.)

**thrombosis** /θrɒm'bəʊsɪs/ n., pl. **thromboses** /θrɒm'bəʊsiːz/ Thrombose, die

**throne** /θrəʊn/ n. Thron, der

**throng** /θrɒŋ/ n. [Menschen]menge, die

**throttle** /'θrɒtl/ v.t. erdrosseln

**through** /θruː/ ①prep. (a) durch (b) (Amer.: up to and including) bis [einschließlich] (c) (by reason of) durch; infolge von ⟨Vernachlässigung, Einflüssen⟩ ②adv. (a) **let sb.** ~: jmdn. durchlassen (b) (Teleph.) **be** ~: durch sein (ugs.); **be** ~ **to sb.** mit jmdm. verbunden sein ③attrib. adj. durchgehend ⟨Zug⟩

**through'out** ①prep. ~ **the war/period** den ganzen Krieg/die ganze Zeit hindurch; ~ **the country** im ganzen Land ②adv. (entirely) ganz; (always) stets; die ganze Zeit [hindurch]

**throve** ▶ THRIVE

**throw** /θrəʊ/ ①v.t., threw /θruː/, thrown /θrəʊn/ (a) werfen; ~ **sth. to sb.** jmdm. etw. zuwerfen; ~ **sth. at sb.** etw. nach jmdm. werfen (b) (bring to the ground) zu Boden werfen; abwerfen ⟨Reiter⟩

(c) (coll.: disconcert) ⟨Frage:⟩ aus der Fassung bringen ②n. Wurf, der

■ **throw a'way** v.t. (a) wegwerfen (b) (lose by neglect) verschenken ⟨Vorteil, Spiel usw.⟩

■ **throw 'up** ①v.t. (a) hochwerfen ⟨Arme, Hände⟩ (b) (produce) hervorbringen ⟨Ideen usw.⟩ ②v.i. (coll.) brechen (ugs.)

**'throwaway** adj. (a) Wegwerf-; Einweg- (b) beiläufig ⟨Bemerkung⟩

**thrown** ▶ THROW 1

**thrush** /θrʌʃ/ n. (Ornith.) Drossel, die

**thrust** /θrʌst/ ①v.t., thrust stoßen; ~ **aside** (fig.) beiseite schieben ②n. Stoß, der

**thud** /θʌd/ n. dumpfer Schlag

**thug** /θʌɡ/ n. Schläger, der; **football** ~**s** Fußballrowdys Pl.

**thuggish** /'θʌɡɪʃ/ adj. aggressiv ⟨Verhalten, Fußballfan⟩

**thumb** /θʌm/ ①n. Daumen, der; **get the** ~**s up** ⟨Person, Projekt:⟩ akzeptiert werden; **be under sb.'s** ~: unter jmds. Fuchtel stehen ②v.t. ~ **a lift** per Anhalter fahren

■ **'thumb through** v.t. durchblättern

**thumb:** ~ **index** n. Daumenregister, das; ~**nail** n. Daumennagel, der; ~**tack** n. (Amer.) Reißzwecke, die

**thump** /θʌmp/ ①v.t. [mit Wucht] schlagen ②v.i. (a) hämmern (at, on gegen) (b) ⟨Herz:⟩ heftig pochen ③n. (blow) Schlag, der; (sound) Bums, der (ugs.); dumpfer Schlag

**thunder** /'θʌndə(r)/ ①n. Donner, der ②v.i. donnern

**thunder:** ~**clap** n. Donnerschlag, der; ~**storm** n. Gewitter, das

**thundery** /'θʌndərɪ/ adj. gewittrig

**Thurs.** abbr. = **Thursday** Do.

**Thursday** /'θɜːzdeɪ, 'θɜːzdɪ/ n. Donnerstag, der; see also FRIDAY

**thus** /ðʌs/ adv. so

**thwart** /θwɔːt/ v.t. durchkreuzen ⟨Pläne⟩; vereiteln ⟨Versuch⟩; ~ **sb.** jmdm. einen Strich durch die Rechnung machen

**thyme** /taɪm/ n. Thymian, der

**thyroid** /'θaɪrɔɪd/ n. Schilddrüse, die

**tiara** /tɪ'ɑːrə/ n. Diadem, das

**tick** /tɪk/ ①v.i. ticken ②v.t. (a) mit einem Häkchen versehen (b) ▶ ~ OFF A ③n. (a) (of clock etc.) Ticken, das (b) (mark) Häkchen, das

■ **tick 'off** v.t. (a) (cross off) abhaken (b) (coll.: reprimand) rüffeln (ugs.)

**ticket** /'tɪkɪt/ n. Karte, die; (for bus, train) Fahrschein, der; (for aeroplane) Flugschein, der; (for lottery, raffle) Los, das; (for library) Ausweis, der; **price** ~: Preisschild, das

**ticket:** ~ **agency** n. Kartenvorverkaufsstelle, die; ~ **agent** n.

Inhaber/Inhaberin einer
Kartenvorverkaufsstelle; ∼ **collector** *n.*
(on train) Schaffner, *der*/Schaffnerin, *die;* (on
station) Fahrkartenkontrolleur, *der*/
-kontrolleurin, *die;* ∼ **dispenser** *n.*
Kartenautomat, *der;* (for train etc.) Fahrschein-
od. Fahrkartenautomat, *der;* ∼ **holder** *n.*
Besitzer/Besitzerin einer Eintrittskarte;
∼ **machine** ▶ ∼ DISPENSER; ∼ **office** *n.*
Fahrkartenschalter, *der;* (for advance booking)
Kartenvorverkaufsstelle, *die*

**tickle** /'tɪkl/ *v.t. & i.* kitzeln

**ticklish** /'tɪklɪʃ/ *adj.* kitzlig

**tidal** /'taɪdl/ *adj.* Gezeiten

'**tidal wave** *n.* Flutwelle, *die*

**tiddlywinks** /'tɪdlɪwɪŋks/ *n. sing.* (game)
Flohhüpfen, *das*

**tide** /taɪd/ **1** *n.* Tide, *die* (nordd.); **high** ∼:
Flut, *die;* **low** ∼: Ebbe, *die;* **the** ∼**s** die
Gezeiten; **the** ∼ **is in/out** es ist Flut/Ebbe
**2** *v.t.* ∼ **sb. over** jmdm. über die Runden
helfen (ugs.)

**tidiness** /'taɪdnɪs/ *n.* Ordentlichkeit, *die*

**tidy** /'taɪdɪ/ **1** *adj.* ordentlich; aufgeräumt
⟨*Zimmer, Schreibtisch*⟩
**2** *v.t.* aufräumen; ∼ **oneself** sich
zurechtmachen
▪ **tidy 'up** *v.i.* aufräumen

**tie** /taɪ/ **1** *v.t.,* **tying** /'taɪɪŋ/ binden (**to an**
+ *Akk.,* **into** zu); ∼ **a knot** einen Knoten
machen; (Sport) ∼ **the match** unentschieden
spielen
**2** *v.i.,* **tying** **(a)** (be fastened) **it** ∼**s at the
back** es wird hinten gebunden
**(b)** (have equal scores) ∼ **for second place** mit
gleicher Punktzahl den zweiten Platz
erreichen
**3** *n.* **(a)** Krawatte, *die*
**(b)** (bond) Band, *das;* (restriction) Bindung, *die*
**(c)** (equality of scores) Punktgleichheit, *die*
**(d)** (Sport: match) Begegnung, *die*
▪ **tie 'in** *v.i.* ∼ **with sth.** zu etw. passen
▪ **tie 'up** *v.t.* **(a)** festbinden; ∼ **up a parcel**
ein Paket verschnüren
**(b)** (keep busy) beschäftigen

**tier** /tɪə(r)/ *n.* **(a)** Rang, *der*
**(b)** (unit) Stufe, *die*

**tiger** /'taɪgə(r)/ *n.* Tiger, *der*

**tiger e'conomy** *n.* Tigerstaat, *der*

**tight** /taɪt/ **1** *adj.* **(a)** (firm) fest; fest
angezogen ⟨*Schraube, Mutter*⟩; fest sitzend
⟨*Deckel*⟩
**(b)** (close-fitting) eng ⟨*Kleid, Schuh usw.*⟩
**(c)** (impermeable) ∼ **seal/joint** dichter
Verschluss/dichte Fuge
**(d)** (taut) straff
**(e)** (difficult to negotiate) **a** ∼ **corner** eine enge
Kurve; **be in a** ∼ **corner** (fig.) in der Klemme
sein (ugs.)
**(f)** (strict) streng ⟨*Kontrolle, Disziplin*⟩
**(g)** (coll.: stingy) knauserig (ugs.)
**(h)** (coll.: drunk) voll (salopp)
**2** *adv.* fest; **hold** ∼! halt dich fest!

**3** *n. in pl.* **(a)** (Brit.) **[pair of]** ∼**s**
Strumpfhose, *die*
**(b)** (of dancer etc.) Trikothose, *die*

**tighten** /'taɪtn/ **1** *v.t.* **(a)** [fest] anziehen
⟨*Knoten, Schraube*⟩; straff ziehen ⟨*Seil*⟩
**(b)** verschärfen ⟨*Kontrolle*⟩
**2** *v.i.* sich spannen

**tight-fisted** /taɪt'fɪstɪd/ *adj.* geizig

'**tightrope** *n.* Drahtseil, *das*

**tile** /taɪl/ **1** *n.* (on roof) Ziegel, *der;* (on floor)
Fliese, *die;* (on wall) Kachel, *die*
**2** *v.t.* [mit Ziegeln] decken ⟨*Dach*⟩; fliesen
⟨*Fußboden*⟩; kacheln ⟨*Wand*⟩

**till¹** /tɪl/ **1** *prep.* bis; (followed by article +
noun) bis zu; **not** […] ∼: erst
**2** *conj.* bis

**till²** *n.* Kasse, *die*

'**till receipt** *n.* Kassenzettel, *der*

**tilt** /tɪlt/ **1** *v.i.* kippen
**2** *v.t.* kippen; neigen ⟨*Kopf*⟩
**3** *n.* **(a)** Schräglage, *die;* **a** 45° ∼: eine
Neigung von 45°
**(b)** **[at] full** ∼: mit voller Wucht

**timber** /'tɪmbə(r)/ *n.* [Bau]holz, *das*

**time** /taɪm/ **1** *n.* **(a)** Zeit, *die;* **in** [**the
course of**] ∼, **as** ∼ **goes on/went on** mit der
Zeit; im Laufe der Zeit; **in** ∼, **with** ∼ (sooner
or later) mit der Zeit; **in** [**good**] ∼ (not late)
rechtzeitig; **all the** *or* **this** ∼: die ganze Zeit;
(without ceasing) ständig; **a short** ∼ **ago** vor
kurzem; ∼ **off** *or* **out** freie Zeit; **in** '**no** ∼: im
Handumdrehen; **in a week's/year's** ∼: in
einer Woche/in einem Jahr; **harvest/
Christmas** ∼: Ernte-/Weihnachtszeit, *die;* **on**
∼ (punctually) pünktlich; **ahead of** ∼: zu früh
⟨*ankommen*⟩; vorzeitig ⟨*fertig werden*⟩; **have
a good** ∼: sich amüsieren; Spaß haben
(ugs.); **have no** ∼ **for sb./sth.** (fig.) für jmdn./
etw. ist einem seine Zeit zu schade
**(b)** (occasion) Mal, *das;* **for the first** ∼: zum
ersten Mal; **at** ∼**s** gelegentlich; ∼ **and again,**
∼ **after** ∼: immer [und immer] wieder; **at
one** ∼, **at** [**one and**] **the same** ∼
(simultaneously) gleichzeitig; **one at a** ∼:
einzeln; **two at a** ∼: jeweils zwei
**(c)** (point in day etc.) [Uhr]zeit, *die;* **tell the** ∼:
die Uhr lesen; **what** ∼ **is it?, what is the** ∼?
wie spät ist es?; **by this/that** ∼: inzwischen;
**by the** ∼ [**that**] **we arrived** bis wir hinkamen;
**T**∼! (Brit.: in pub) Feierabend!; ∼, [**ladies and**]
**gentlemen, please!** wir machen Feierabend,
meine [Damen und] Herren!
**(d)** (multiplication) mal; **three** ∼**s four** drei mal
vier
**(e)** (Mus.) Takt, *der;* **in** ∼: im Takt
**2** *v.t.* **(a)** zeitlich abstimmen; **be well** ∼**d**
zur richtigen Zeit kommen
**(b)** (set to operate at correct ∼) einstellen
**(c)** (measure ∼ taken by) stoppen

**time:** ∼ **bomb** *n.* Zeitbombe, *die;*
∼-**consuming** *adj.* **(a)** (taking ∼)
zeitaufwendig; **(b)** (wasteful of ∼)
zeitraubend; ∼ **lag** *n.* zeitliche
Verzögerung

**timeless** /ˈtaɪmlɪs/ *adj.* zeitlos

**'time limit** *n.* Frist, *die*

**timely** /ˈtaɪmlɪ/ *adj.* rechtzeitig

**time:** ~**scale** *n.* Zeitskala, *die;* ~ **sheet** *n.* Stundenzettel, *der;* ~ **switch** *n.* Zeitschalter, *der;* ~**table** *n.* **(a)** (scheme of work) Zeitplan, *der;* (Educ.) Stundenplan, *der;* **(b)** (Transport) Fahrplan, *der;* ~ **warp** *n.* Verwerfung im Raum-Zeit-Kontinuum; ~ **zone** *n.* Zeitzone, *die*

**timid** /ˈtɪmɪd/ *adj.* **(a)** scheu ⟨*Tier*⟩ **(b)** zaghaft ⟨*Mensch*⟩; (shy) schüchtern

**timing** /ˈtaɪmɪŋ/ *n.* **(a)** that was perfect ~! du kommst gerade im richtigen Augenblick! **(b)** (Theatre, Sport) Timing, *das*

**tin** /tɪn/ ⟨1⟩ *n.* **(a)** (metal) Zinn, *das;* ~[plate] Weißblech, *das* **(b)** (Brit.: for preserving) [Konserven]dose, *die* ⟨2⟩ *v.t.,* **-nn-** (Brit.) zu Konserven verarbeiten

**tin 'foil** *n.* Stanniol, *das;* Alufolie, *die*

**tinge** /tɪndʒ/ ⟨1⟩ *v.t.,* ~**ing** /ˈtɪndʒɪŋ/ tönen ⟨2⟩ *n.* [leichte] Färbung; (fig.) Hauch, *der*

**tingle** /ˈtɪŋgl/ *v.i.* kribbeln

**tinker** /ˈtɪŋkə(r)/ ⟨1⟩ *n.* Kesselflicker, *der* ⟨2⟩ *v.i.* ~ **with sth.** an etw. (*Dat.*) herumbasteln (ugs.)

**tinkle** /ˈtɪŋkl/ ⟨1⟩ *n.* Klingeln, *das* ⟨2⟩ *v.i.* klingeln

**tinned** /tɪnd/ *adj.* (Brit.) Dosen-

**tin:** ~**opener** *n.* (Brit.) Dosenöffner, *der;* ~**pot** *attrib. adj.* (derog.) schäbig

**tinsel** /ˈtɪnsl/ *n.* Lametta, *das*

**tint** /tɪnt/ ⟨1⟩ *n.* Farbton, *der* ⟨2⟩ *v.t.* tönen; kolorieren ⟨*Zeichnung*⟩

**tiny** /ˈtaɪnɪ/ *adj.* winzig

**tip¹** /tɪp/ *n.* (end, point) Spitze, *die*

**tip²** ⟨1⟩ *v.i.,* **-pp-** (lean, fall) kippen; ~ **over** umkippen ⟨2⟩ *v.t.,* **-pp-:** **(a)** (make tilt) kippen **(b)** (make overturn) umkippen; (Brit.: discharge) kippen **(c)** voraussagen ⟨*Sieger*⟩; ~ **sb. to win** auf jmds. Sieg tippen **(d)** (reward) ~ **sb.** jmdm. Trinkgeld geben ⟨3⟩ *n.* **(a)** (money) Trinkgeld, *das* **(b)** (special information) Hinweis, *der;* Tipp, *der* (ugs.) **(c)** (Brit.) Müllkippe, *die* ∎ **tip 'off** *v.t.* ~ **sb. off** jmdm. einen Hinweis *od.* (ugs.) Tipp geben

**'tip-off** *n.* Hinweis, *der*

**tipsy** /ˈtɪpsɪ/ *adj.* (coll.) angeheitert; beschwipst (ugs.)

**tip:** ~**toe** ⟨1⟩ *v.i.* auf Zehenspitzen gehen; ⟨2⟩ *n.* **on** ~**toe[s]** auf Zehenspitzen; ~**top** *adj.* tipptopp (ugs.)

**tire¹** /ˈtaɪə(r)/ (Amer.) ▶ TYRE

**tire²** ⟨1⟩ *v.t.* ermüden ⟨2⟩ *v.i.* müde werden; ermüden; ~ **of sth.**/ **doing sth.** einer Sache (*Gen.*) überdrüssig werden ∎ **tire 'out** *v.t.* erschöpfen; ~ **oneself out doing sth.** etw. bis zur Erschöpfung tun

**tired** /ˈtaɪəd/ *adj.* **(a)** (weary) müde **(b)** (fed up) **be** ~ **of sth.**/**doing sth.** etw. satt haben/es satt haben, etw. zu tun

**tiredness** /ˈtaɪədnɪs/ *n.* Müdigkeit, *die*

**'tireless** *adj.* unermüdlich

**tiresome** /ˈtaɪəsəm/ *adj.* **(a)** (wearisome) mühsam **(b)** (annoying) lästig

**tiring** /ˈtaɪərɪŋ/ *adj.* ermüdend

**tissue** /ˈtɪʃuː, ˈtɪsjuː/ *n.* **(a)** Gewebe, *das* **(b)** [paper] ~: Papiertuch, *das;* (handkerchief) Papiertaschentuch, *das* **(c)** ~ [paper] Seidenpapier, *das*

**tit¹** /tɪt/ *n.* (Ornith.) Meise, *die*

**tit²** *n.* **it's** ~ **for tat** wie du mir, so ich dir

**'titbit** *n.* **(a)** (food) Häppchen, *das* (ugs.) **(b)** (piece of news) Neuigkeit, *die*

**titchy** /ˈtɪtʃɪ/ *adj.* (coll.) klitzeklein (ugs.)

**titillate** /ˈtɪtɪleɪt/ *v.t.* erregen

**titillation** /tɪtɪˈleɪʃn/ *n.* Kitzel, *der*

**title** /ˈtaɪtl/ *n.* Titel, *der*

**title:** ~ **deed** *n.* (Law) Eigentumsurkunde, *die;* ~**holder** *n.* (Sport) Titelhalter, *der/* -halterin, *die;* ~ **page** *n.* Titelseite, *die;* ~ **role** *n.* Titelrolle, *die*

**tittle-tattle** /ˈtɪtltætl/ *n.* Klatsch, *der* (ugs.)

**'T-junction** *n.* Einmündung, *die*

**to** ⟨1⟩ /before vowel tʊ, before consonant tə, stressed tuː/ *prep.* **(a)** (in the direction of and reaching) zu; (with name of place) nach; **go to work/to the theatre** zur Arbeit/ins Theater gehen; **to France** nach Frankreich **(b)** (as far as) bis zu; **from London to Edinburgh** von London [bis] nach Edinburgh; **increase from 10% to 20%** von 10% auf 20% steigen **(c)** (introducing relationship or indirect object) **to sb./ sth.** jmdm./einer Sache (*Dat.*); **lend/explain** *etc.* **sth. to sb.** jmdm. etw. leihen/erklären *usw.;* **speak to sb.** mit jmdm. sprechen; **that's all there is to it** mehr ist dazu nicht zu sagen; **what's that to you?** was geht das dich an?; **to me** (in my opinion) meiner Meinung nach; **14 miles to the gallon** 14 Meilen auf eine Gallone **(d)** (until) bis; **to the end** bis zum Ende; **to this day** bis heute; **five [minutes] to eight** fünf [Minuten] vor acht **(e)** (with infinitive of a verb) zu; (expr. purpose, or after) too um [...] zu; **want to know** wissen wollen; **do sth. to annoy sb.** etw. tun, um jmdn. zu ärgern; **too hot to drink** zu heiß zum Trinken; **he would have phoned but forgot to** er hätte angerufen, aber er vergaß es ⟨2⟩ *adv.* /tuː/ **to and fro** hin und her

**toad** /təʊd/ *n.* (also fig. derog.) Kröte, *die*

**'toadstool** *n.* Giftpilz, *der*

**toast** /təʊst/ ⟨1⟩ *n.* **(a)** no pl. Toast, *der;* **a piece of** ~: eine Scheibe Toast **(b)** (call to drink) Toast, *der;* **drink a** ~ **to sb./ sth.** auf jmdn./etw. trinken ⟨2⟩ *v.t.* **(a)** rösten; toasten ⟨*Brot*⟩

**(b)** (drink to) trinken auf (+ *Akk.*)

'**toaster** *n.* Toaster, *der*

'**toast rack** *n.* Toastständer, *der*

**tobacco** /təˈbækəʊ/ *n., pl.* ~s Tabak, *der*

**tobacconist** /təˈbækənɪst/ *n.* Tabak[waren]händler, *der*/-händlerin, *die*

**toboggan** /təˈbɒgən/ **1** *n.* Schlitten, *der* **2** *v.i.* Schlitten fahren

**tod** /tɒd/ *n.* (Brit. coll.) on one's ~: [ganz] allein

**today** /təˈdeɪ/ **1** *n.* heute; ~'s newspaper die Zeitung von heute **2** *adv.* heute

**toddler** /ˈtɒdlə(r)/ *n.* ≈ Kleinkind, *das*

**to-do** /təˈduː/ *n.* Getue, *das* (ugs.)

**toe** /təʊ/ **1** *n.* Zeh, *der;* Zehe, *die;* (of footwear) Spitze, *die* **2** *v.t.,* ~ing (fig.) ~ the line *or* (Amer.) mark sich einordnen

'**toenail** *n.* Zeh[en]nagel, *der*

**toffee** /ˈtɒfɪ/ *n.* Karamell, *der;* (Brit.: piece) Toffee, *das;* Sahnebonbon, *das*

'**toffee apple** *n.* mit Karamell überzogener Apfel am Stiel

**tofu** /ˈtəʊfuː/ *n., no indef. art.* Tofu, *der*

**together** /təˈgeðə(r)/ *adv.* **(a)** (in or into company) zusammen **(b)** (simultaneously) gleichzeitig **(c)** (one with another) miteinander

**toggle** /ˈtɒgl/ **1** *n.* **(a)** (button) Knebelknopf, *der* **(b)** (Comp.) [Kipp]schalter, *der;* Umschalttaste, *die* **2** *v.i.* (Comp.) [hin und her] schalten

**toil** /tɔɪl/ **1** *v.i.* schwer arbeiten **2** *n.* [harte] Arbeit

**toilet** /ˈtɔɪlɪt/ *n.* Toilette, *die;* go to the ~: auf die Toilette gehen

**toilet:** ~ **bag** *n.* Kulturbeutel, *der;* ~ **brush** *n.* Klosettbürste, *die;* ~ **paper** *n.* Toilettenpapier, *das*

**toiletries** /ˈtɔɪlɪtrɪz/ *n. pl.* Körperpflegemittel *Pl.;* Toilettenartikel *Pl.*

**toilet:** ~ **roll** *n.* Rolle Toilettenpapier; ~ **seat** *n.* Klosettbrille, *die* (ugs.); Toilettensitz, *der;* ~ **tissue** ▶ ~ PAPER; ~ **water** *n.* Toilettenwasser, *das;* Eau de Toilette, *das*

**token** /ˈtəʊkn/ **1** *n.* **(a)** (voucher) Gutschein, *der* **(b)** (counter, disc) Marke, *die* **(c)** (sign) Zeichen, *das* **2** *attrib. adj.* symbolisch ⟨*Preis*⟩

**Tokyo** /ˈtəʊkjəʊ/ *pr. n.* Tokio (*das*)

**told** ▶ TELL

**tolerable** /ˈtɒlərəbl/ *adj.* **(a)** (endurable) erträglich (**to, for** für) **(b)** (fairly good) leidlich; annehmbar

**tolerance** /ˈtɒlərəns/ *n.* Toleranz, *die*

**tolerant** /ˈtɒlərənt/ *adj.* tolerant (**of, towards** gegen[über])

**tolerate** /ˈtɒləreɪt/ *v.t.* dulden; (bear) ertragen ⟨*Schmerzen*⟩

**toleration** /tɒləˈreɪʃn/ *n.* Tolerierung, *die* (geh.)

**toll¹** /təʊl/ *n.* **(a)** (tax, duty) Gebühr, *die* **(b)** (damage etc.) Aufwand, *der;* take its ~ of sth. einen Tribut an etw. (*Dat.*) fordern (fig.)

**toll²** *v.i.* ⟨*Glocke:*⟩ läuten

**toll:** ~ **bridge** *n.* gebührenpflichtige Brücke; ~**road** *n.* gebührenpflichtige Straße; Mautstraße, *die* (bes. österr.)

**tom** /tɒm/ *n.* (cat) Kater, *der*

**tomato** /təˈmɑːtəʊ/ *n., pl.* ~es Tomate, *die*

**tomato:** ~ **juice** *n.* Tomatensaft, *der;* ~ '**ketchup** *n.* Tomatenketchup, *der od. das;* ~ '**purée** *n.* Tomatenmark, *das*

**tomb** /tuːm/ *n.* Grab, *das;* (monument) Grabmal, *das*

'**tomboy** *n.* Wildfang, *der*

'**tombstone** *n.* Grabstein, *der*

'**tomcat** *n.* Kater, *der*

**tome** /təʊm/ *n.* dicker Band; Wälzer, *der* (ugs.)

**tomfoolery** /tɒmˈfuːlərɪ/ *n.* Blödsinn, *der* (ugs.)

**tomorrow** /təˈmɒrəʊ/ **1** *n.* morgen; ~ **morning/afternoon/evening/night** morgen früh *od.* Vormittag/Nachmittag/Abend/ Nacht; ~'s newspaper die morgige Zeitung **2** *adv.* morgen; see you ~! (coll.) bis morgen!; the day after ~: übermorgen

**ton** /tʌn/ *n.* Tonne, *die*

**tone** /təʊn/ **1** *n.* **(a)** (sound) Klang, *der;* (Teleph.) Ton, *der* **(b)** (style of speaking) Ton, *der* **(c)** (tint, shade) [Farb]ton, *der* **(d)** (fig.: character) **lower/raise** the ~ of sth. das Niveau einer Sache (*Gen.*) senken/ erhöhen; set the ~: den Ton angeben **2** *v.t.* tönen; abtönen ⟨*Farbe*⟩ ■ **tone 'down** *v.t.* [ab]dämpfen ⟨*Farbe*⟩; (fig.) mäßigen ⟨*Sprache*⟩

**tone:** ~'**deaf** *adj.* ohne musikalisches Gehör; ~ **dialling** (Teleph.) *n.* Tonwahl, *die*

**tongs** /tɒŋz/ *n. pl.* [pair of] ~: Zange, *die*

**tongue** /tʌŋ/ *n.* Zunge, *die;* bite one's ~ (lit. or fig.) sich auf die Zunge beißen; find one's ~: seine Sprache wieder finden; hold one's ~: stillschweigen; he made the remark ~ in cheek (fig.) er meinte die Bemerkung nicht ernst

**tongue:** ~**tied** *adj.* schüchtern; ~**twister** *n.* Zungenbrecher, *der* (ugs.)

**tonic** /ˈtɒnɪk/ **1** *n.* **(a)** (Med.) Tonikum, *das* **(b)** (fig.: invigorating influence) Wohltat, *die* (geh.) **(c)** (~ water) Tonic, *das* **2** *attrib. adj.* kräftigend; (fig.) wohltuend ⟨*Wirkung*⟩

'**tonic water** *n.* Tonic[wasser], *das*

**tonight** /təˈnaɪt/ **1** *n.* **(a)** (this evening) heute Abend; ~'s performance die heutige [Abend]vorstellung **(b)** (this or the coming night) heute Nacht ···⬧

2 *adv.* **(a)** (this evening) heute Abend
**(b)** (during this or the coming night) heute Nacht;
[I'll] see you ~! bis heute Abend!

**tonne** /tʌn/ *n.* [metrische] Tonne

**tonsil** /'tɒnsl/ *n.* [Gaumen]mandel, *die;* have
one's ~s out sich (*Dat.*) die Mandeln
herausnehmen lassen

**tonsillitis** /tɒnsə'laɪtɪs/ *n.*
Mandelentzündung, *die*

**too** /tuː/ *adv.* **(a)** (excessively) zu; ~ difficult a
task eine zu schwierige Aufgabe
**(b)** (also) auch
**(c)** (coll.: very) besonders; not ~ pleased nicht
gerade erfreut

**took** ▶ TAKE

**tool** /tuːl/ *n.* **(a)** Werkzeug, *das;* (garden ~)
Gerät, *das;* [set of] ~s Werkzeug, *das*
**(b)** (Comp.) Tool, *das;* Werkzeug, *das*
**(c)** (fig.: means) [Hilfs]mittel, *das*

**tool:** ~**bar** *n.* (Comp.) Werkzeugleiste, *die;*
~**box** *n.* Werkzeugkasten, *der;* ~ **kit** *n.*
Werkzeug, *das*

**toot** /tuːt/ 1 *v.i.* (on car etc. horn) hupen
2 *n.* Tuten, *das*

**tooth** /tuːθ/ *n., pl.* teeth /tiːθ/ **(a)** Zahn, *der*
**(b)** (of rake, fork, comb) Zinke, *die;* (of cogwheel,
saw) Zahn, *der*

**tooth:** ~**ache** *n.* Zahnschmerzen *Pl.;*
~**brush** *n.* Zahnbürste, *die;* ~ **decay** *n.*
Zahnverfall, *der;* ~**glass** *n.* Zahnputzglas,
*das;* ~ **mug** *n.* Zahnputzbecher, *der;*
~**paste** *n.* Zahnpasta, *die;* ~**pick** *n.*
Zahnstocher, *der;* ~ **powder** *n.*
Zahnpulver, *das*

**top¹** /tɒp/ 1 *n.* **(a)** (highest part) Spitze, *die;*
(of table) Platte, *die;* (~ end) oberes Ende; (of
tree) Wipfel, *der;* (~ floor) oberstes Stockwerk;
(rim of glass) Rand, *der;* on ~ of one another
aufeinander; on ~ of sth. (fig.: in addition)
zusätzlich zu etw.; from ~ to bottom von
oben bis unten; at the ~: oben; at the ~ of
the building/hill/pile/stairs oben im Gebäude/
[oben] auf dem Hügel/[oben] auf dem Stapel/
oben an der Treppe
**(b)** (highest rank) Spitze, *die;* ~ of the table
(Sport) Tabellenspitze, *die;* be [at the] ~ of the
class der/die Klassenbeste sein
**(c)** (upper surface) Oberfläche, *die;* (of cupboard,
chest) Oberseite, *die;* on ~ of sth. [oben] auf
etw. (*position: Dat.; direction: Akk.*)
**(d)** (folding roof) Verdeck, *das*
**(e)** (upper deck of bus) Oberdeck, *das*
**(f)** (cap of pen) [Verschluss]kappe, *die*
**(g)** (upper garment) Oberteil, *das*
**(h)** (lid) Deckel, *der;* (of bottle) Stöpsel, *der*
2 *adj.* oberst...; höchst... ⟨Ton, Preis⟩;
~ end oberes Ende; the ~ pupil der beste
Schüler; ~ speed Spitzen- od.
Höchstgeschwindigkeit, *die*
3 *v.t.* **(a)** (be taller than) überragen
**(b)** (surpass) übertreffen
■ **top 'up** (Brit. coll.) *v.t.* auffüllen ⟨Tank,
Flasche, Glas⟩

**top²** *n.* (toy) Kreisel, *der*

**top:** ~**-flight** *attrib. adj.* erstrangig;
Spitzen⟨sportler, -politiker⟩; ~ '**hat** *n.*
Zylinder[hut], *der;* ~**-heavy** *adj.* oberlastig

**topic** /'tɒpɪk/ *n.* Thema, *das*

**topical** /'tɒpɪkl/ *adj.* aktuell

'**topless** *adj.* a ~ dress/swimsuit ein
busenfreies Kleid/ein Oben-ohne-Badeanzug;
go/bathe ~: oben ohne gehen/baden

**top-level** *attrib. adj.* Gipfel⟨treffen,
-konferenz⟩; ~-level negotiations/deals
Verhandlungen/Vereinbarungen auf
höchster Ebene

**topmost** /'tɒpməʊst, 'tɒpməst/ *adj.*
oberst...; höchst... ⟨Gipfel, Note⟩

**top-'notch** *adj.* (coll.) fantastisch (ugs.).

**topple** /'tɒpl/ 1 *v.i.* fallen
2 *v.t.* stürzen
■ **topple 'down** *v.i.* hinab-/herabfallen
■ **topple 'over** *v.i.* umfallen

**top:** ~**-quality** *adj.* [qualitativ]
hochwertig; ~**-ranking** *attrib. adj.*
Spitzen⟨funktionär, -beamter, -politiker,
-sportler⟩; hochrangig ⟨Offizier⟩; ~ '**secret**
*adj.* streng geheim; ~**soil** *n.* Mutterboden,
*der*

**topsy-turvy** /tɒpsɪ'tɜːvɪ/ *adv.* verkehrtrum
(ugs.); turn sth. ~: etw. auf den Kopf stellen
(ugs.)

'**top-up** *n.* (coll.) Auffüllung, *die;* I need a ~:
ich muss mir noch mal nachgießen/
nachgießen lassen

**torch** /tɔːtʃ/ *n.* (Brit.) Taschenlampe, *die*

'**torchlight** *n.* Licht der/einer
Taschenlampe; by ~light im Schein einer
Taschenlampe

**tore, torn** ▶ TEAR¹ 2, 3

**torment** 1 /'tɔːment/ *n.* Qual, *die*
2 /tɔː'ment/ *v.t.* quälen

**tornado** /tɔː'neɪdəʊ/ *n., pl.* ~es
Wirbelsturm, *der;* (in North America) Tornado,
*der*

**torpedo** /tɔː'piːdəʊ/ 1 *n., pl.* ~es Torpedo,
*der*
2 *v.t.* torpedieren

**torrent** /'tɒrənt/ *n.* reißender Bach; (fig.)
Flut, *die*

**torrential** /tə'renʃl/ *adj.* wolkenbruchartig
⟨Regen⟩

**torso** /'tɔːsəʊ/ *n., pl.* ~s Rumpf, *der;* bare ~:
nackter Oberkörper

**tortoise** /'tɔːtəs/ *n.* Schildkröte, *die*

**tortoiseshell** /'tɔːtəsʃel/ *n.* Schildpatt, *das*

**tortuous** /'tɔːtjʊəs/ *adj.* verschlungen; (fig.)
umständlich

**torture** /'tɔːtʃə(r)/ 1 *n.* Folter, *die*
2 *v.t.* foltern; (fig.) quälen

**Tory** /'tɔːrɪ/ (Brit. Polit. coll.) *n.* Tory, *der*

**toss** /tɒs/ 1 *v.t.* **(a)** (throw upwards)
hochwerfen; ~ a pancake einen
Pfannkuchen [durch Hochwerfen] wenden
**(b)** (throw casually) werfen; schmeißen (ugs.)
**(c)** ~ a coin eine Münze werfen

(d) (Cookery: mix) wenden; mischen ‹*Salat*›
[2] *v.i.* (a) ~ **and turn** sich [schlaflos] im Bett wälzen
(b) ‹*Schiff:*› hin und her geworfen werden
(c) (~ coin) eine Münze werfen; ~ **for sth.** mit einer Münze um etw. losen
[3] *n.* (a) ~ **of a coin** Hochwerfen einer Münze
(b) (throw) Wurf, *der*
(c) **I couldn't give a** ~ (fig. Brit. sl.) es ist mir scheißegal (salopp)
■ **toss 'up** *v.i.* eine Münze werfen; ~ **up for sth.** mit einer Münze um etw. losen

**tot¹** /tɒt/ *n.* (coll.) (a) kleines Kind
(b) (of liquor) Gläschen, *das*

**tot²** (coll.) *v.t.*, **-tt-:** ~ **'up** zusammenziehen (ugs.)

**total** /'təʊtl/ [1] *adj.* (a) gesamt; Gesamt‹*gewicht, -wert, usw.*›
(b) (absolute) völlig *nicht präd.;* **a** ~ **beginner** ein absoluter Anfänger
[2] *n.* (number) Gesamtzahl, *die;* (amount) Gesamtbetrag, *der;* (result of addition) Summe, *die;* **a** ~ **of 200** insgesamt 200; **in** ~: insgesamt
[3] *v.t.*, (Brit.) **-ll-:** (a) addieren, zusammenzählen ‹*Zahlen*›
(b) (amount to) [insgesamt] betragen

**total e'clipse** *n.* (Astron.) totale Finsternis

**totalitarian** /təʊtælɪ'teərɪən/ *adj.* totalitär

**'totally** *adv.* völlig

**totter** /'tɒtə(r)/ *v.i.* wanken; taumeln

**touch** /tʌtʃ/ [1] *v.t.* (a) berühren
(b) (harm) anrühren
(c) (fig.: rival) ~ **sth.** an etw. (*Akk.*) heranreichen
(d) (affect emotionally) rühren
[2] *v.i.* sich berühren; **don't** ~! nicht anfassen!
[3] *n.* (a) Berührung, *die*
(b) *no art.* (faculty) [**sense of**] ~: Tastsinn, *der*
(c) (small amount) **a** ~ **of salt/pepper** *etc.* eine Spur Salz/Pfeffer *usw.;* **a** ~ **of irony** *etc.* ein Anflug von Ironie *usw.*
(d) (fig.) Detail, *das*
(e) (communication) **be in/out of** ~ [**with sb.**] [mit jmdm.] Kontakt/keinen Kontakt haben; **get in** ~: mit jmdm. Kontakt aufnehmen
■ **touch 'down** *v.i.* ‹*Flugzeug:*› landen
■ **'touch on** *v.t.* (mention) ansprechen
■ **touch 'up** *v.t.* (improve) ausbessern

**'touch:** ~**-and-go** *adj.* **it is** ~**-and-go** [**whether...**] es steht auf des Messers Schneide [, ob...]; ~**down** *n.* (Aeronaut.) Landung, *die*

**'touching** *adj.* rührend

**touch:** ~**line** *n.* (Footb., Rugby) Seitenlinie, *die;* ~**paper** *n.* Zündpapier, *das;* (on firework) Papierlunte, *die;* ~**-tone** *adj.* **a** ~**-tone telephone** ein Telefon mit Mehrfrequenzwahl; ~**-type** *v.i.* blind schreiben; ~**-typing** *n.* Blindschreiben, *das*

**touchy** /'tʌtʃɪ/ *adj.* empfindlich; heikel ‹*Thema*›

**tough** /tʌf/ *adj.* (a) fest ‹*Material, Stoff*›; zäh ‹*Fleisch; fachspr.:* Werkstoff, Metall›; widerstandsfähig ‹*Belag, Glas, Haut*›; strapazierfähig ‹*Kleidung*›
(b) (hardy) zäh ‹*Person*›
(c) (difficult) schwierig
(d) (severe, harsh) hart
(e) (coll.) ~ **luck** Pech, *das*

**toughen** /'tʌfn/ *v.t.* ~ [**up**] abhärten ‹*Person*›; verschärfen ‹*Gesetz*›

**toupee, toupet** /'tu:peɪ/ *n.* Toupet, *das*

**tour** /tʊə(r)/ [1] *n.* (a) [Rund]reise, *die;* Tour, *die* (ugs.)
(b) (Theatre, Sport) Tournee, *die*
(c) (of house etc.) Besichtigung, *die*
(d) ~ [**of duty**] Dienstzeit, *die*
[2] *v.i.* (a) ~/**go** ~**ing in** *or* **through a country** eine Reise *od.* (ugs.) Tour durch ein Land machen
(b) (Theatre, Sport) eine Tournee machen
[3] *v.t.* (a) besichtigen ‹*Stadt, Gebäude*›; ~ **a country/region** eine Reise *od.* (ugs.) Tour durch ein Land/Gebiet machen
(b) (Theatre, Sport) ~ **a country/the provinces** eine Tournee durch das Land/die Provinz machen

**tour de force** /tʊə də 'fɔ:s/ *n., pl.* **tours de force** /tʊə də 'fɔ:s/ Glanzleistung, *die*

**'tour guide** *n.* Reiseführer, *der*/ Reiseführerin, *die;* (book) Reiseführer, *der* (to, of von)

**'touring holiday** *n.* **have a** ~ **in a country** in den Ferien/im Urlaub durch ein Land fahren

**tourism** /'tʊərɪzm/ *n.* (a) Tourismus, *der*
(b) (operation of tours) Touristik, *die*

**tourist** /'tʊərɪst/ [1] *n.* Tourist, *der*/ Touristin, *die*
[2] *attrib. adj.* Touristen-

**tourist:** ~ **agency** *n.* Reisebüro, *das;* ~ **attraction** *n.* Touristenattraktion, *die;* ~ **board** *n.* (Brit.) Amt für Fremdenverkehrswesen; ~ **class** *n.* Touristenklasse, *die;* ~ **hotel** *n.* Touristenhotel, *das;* ~ **industry** *n.* Tourismusindustrie, *die;* ~ **infor'mation centre,** ~ **office** *ns.* Fremdenverkehrsbüro, *das;* Touristeninformation, *die* (ugs.); ~ **season** *n.* Touristensaison, *die;* ~ **trade** ▶ ~ INDUSTRY

**touristy** /'tʊərɪstɪ/ *adj.* (derog.) auf Tourismus getrimmt (ugs.); Touristen‹*stadt, -nest, -gegend*› (ugs. abwertend)

**'tour leader** *n.* Reiseleiter, *der*/-leiterin, *die*

**tournament** /'tʊənəmənt/ *n.* (Hist.; Sport) Turnier, *das*

**tourniquet** /'tʊənɪkeɪ/ *n.* (Med.) Tourniquet, *das*

**'tour operator** *n.* Reiseveranstalter, *der*/ -veranstalterin, *die*

**tousle** /'taʊzl/ *v.t.* zerzausen

**tout** /taʊt/ ① *v.i.* ∼ **for customers** Kunden anreißen (ugs.) *od.* werben
② *n.* Anreißer, *der*/Anreißerin, *die* (ugs.); **ticket** ∼: Kartenschwarzhändler, *der*/ -händlerin, *die*

**tow** /təʊ/ ① *v.t.* schleppen; ziehen ⟨Anhänger, Wasserskiläufer⟩
② *n.* Schleppen, *das;* **give a car a** ∼: einen Wagen schleppen; **on** ∼: im Schlepp[tau]
■ **tow a'way** *v.t.* abschleppen

**toward** /tə'wɔːd/, **towards** /tə'wɔːdz/ *prep.* **(a)** (in direction of) ∼ **sb./sth.** auf jmdn./ etw. zu; **turn** ∼ **sb.** sich zu jmdm. umdrehen **(b)** (in relation to) gegenüber; **feel sth.** ∼ **sb.** jmdm. gegenüber etw. empfinden **(c)** (for) **a contribution** ∼ **sth.** ein Beitrag zu etw.; **proposals** ∼ **solving a problem** Vorschläge zur Lösung eines Problems **(d)** (near) gegen; ∼ **the end of May** [gegen] Ende Mai

'**tow bar** *n.* (Motor Veh.) Anhängerkupplung, *die*

**towel** /'taʊəl/ *n.* Handtuch, *das*

**towelling** (*Amer.:* **toweling**) /'taʊəlɪŋ/ *n., no indef. art.* Frottierware, *die*

'**towel rail** *n.* Handtuchhalter, *der*

**tower** /'taʊə(r)/ ① *n.* Turm, *der*
② *v.i.* in die Höhe ragen
■ '**tower above** *v.t.* ∼ **above sb./sth.** jmdn./etw. überragen

'**tower block** *n.* Hochhaus, *das*

'**towering** *attrib. adj.* hoch aufragend; (fig.) herausragend ⟨Leistung⟩

**town** /taʊn/ *n.* Stadt, *die;* **the** ∼ **of Cambridge** die Stadt Cambridge; **in** [**the**] ∼: in der Stadt; **the** ∼ (people) die Stadt; **be in/ out of** ∼: in der Stadt/nicht in der Stadt sein

**town:** ∼ '**centre** *n.* Stadtmitte, *die;* Stadtzentrum, *das;* ∼ '**council** *n.* (Brit.) Stadtrat, *der;* ∼ '**councillor** *n.* (Brit.) Stadtrat, *der*/-rätin, *die;* ∼ '**hall** *n.* Rathaus, *das;* ∼ **house** *n.* (residence in ∼) Stadthaus, *das;* (terrace house) Reihenhaus, *das*

**townie** /'taʊni;/ *n.* Stadtmensch, *der*

**town:** ∼ '**planner** *n.* Stadtplaner, *der*/ -planerin, *die;* ∼ '**planning** *n.* Stadtplanung, *die*

**tow:** ∼**path** *n.* Leinpfad, *der;* ∼ **rope** *n.* Abschleppseil, *das*

**toxic** /'tɒksɪk/ *adj.* giftig

**toxicity** /tɒk'sɪsɪti/ *n.* Giftigkeit, *die*

**toxic 'waste** *n.* Giftmüll *der;* ∼ **tip** *or* **dump** Giftmülldeponie, *die*

**toxin** /'tɒksɪn/ *n.* Toxin, *das*

**toy** /tɔɪ/ ① *n.* Spielzeug, *das;* ∼**s** Spielzeug, *das*
② *adj.* Spielzeug-
③ *v.i.* ∼ **with the idea of doing sth.** mit dem Gedanken spielen, etw. zu tun

**toy:** ∼ **boy** *n.* (coll.) Gespiele, *der* (scherzh.); ∼**shop** *n.* Spielwarengeschäft, *das*

**trace** /treɪs/ ① *v.t.* **(a)** (copy) durchpausen; abpausen **(b)** zeichnen ⟨Linie⟩ **(c)** (follow track of) folgen (+ *Dat.*); verfolgen **(d)** (find) finden
② *n.* Spur, *die*

'**trace element** *n.* (Chem.) Spurenelement, *das*

'**tracing paper** /'treɪsɪŋ peɪpə(r)/ *n.* Pauspapier, *das*

**track** /træk/ ① *n.* **(a)** Spur, *die;* (of wild animal) Fährte, *die;* ∼**s** (footprints) [Fuß]spuren; (of animal also) Fährte, *die;* **keep** ∼ **of sb./sth.** jmdn./etw. im Auge behalten **(b)** (path) Weg, *der;* (footpath) Pfad, *der* **(c)** (Sport) Bahn, *die;* **cycling/greyhound** ∼: Radrennbahn, *die*/Windhundrennbahn, *die* **(d)** (Railw.) Gleis, *das* **(e)** (course taken) Route, *die;* (of rocket, satellite) Bahn, *die*
② *v.t.* ∼ **an animal** die Spur/Fährte eines Tieres verfolgen; **the police** ∼**ed him** [**to Paris**] die Polizei folgte seiner Spur [bis nach Paris]
■ **track 'down** *v.t.* aufspüren

'**trackball, 'tracker ball** *ns.* (Comp.) Rollball, *der*

'**track events** *n. pl.* Laufwettbewerbe *Pl.*

'**tracking station** *n.* (Astronaut.) Bahnverfolgungsstation, *die*

'**track:** ∼**shoe** *n.* Rennschuh, *der;* ∼**suit** *n.* Trainingsanzug, *der*

**tract¹** /trækt/ *n.* (area) Gebiet, *das*

**tract²** *n.* (pamphlet) [Flug]schrift, *die*

**tractor** /'træktə(r)/ *n.* Traktor, *der*

**trad** /træd/ (Mus. coll.) *adj.* traditional (Jargon); ∼ **jazz** Traditional Jazz, *der*

**trade** /treɪd/ ① *n.* **(a)** (line of business) Gewerbe, *das;* **he's a butcher/lawyer** *etc.* **by** ∼: er ist von Beruf Metzger/Rechtsanwalt *usw.* **(b)** *no indef. art* (commerce) Handel, *der* **(c)** (craft) Handwerk, *das*
② *v.i.* (buy and sell) Handel treiben
③ *v.t.* tauschen; austauschen ⟨Waren, Grüße⟩; sich (*Dat.*) sagen ⟨Beleidigungen⟩; ∼ **sth. for sth.** etw. gegen etw. tauschen
■ **trade 'in** *v.t.* in Zahlung geben
■ **trade 'up** *v.t.* sich verbessern

**trade:** ∼ **balance** *n.* Handelsbilanz, *die;* ∼ **deficit** *n.* passive Handelsbilanz; Handelsbilanzdefizit, *das;* ∼ '**discount** *n.* Branchenrabatt, *der;* ∼ **fair** *n.* [Fach]messe, *die;* ∼ **journal** *n.* Fachzeitschrift, *die;* ∼ **mark** *n.* Warenzeichen, *das;* **leave one's** ∼ **mark on sth.** (fig.) einer Sache (*Dat.*) seinen Stempel aufdrücken; ∼ **name** *n.* Fachbezeichnung, *die;* (proprietary name) Markenname, *der;* ∼ **price** *n.* Einkaufspreis, *der*

'**trader** *n.* Händler, *der*/Händlerin, *die*

**trade:** ∼ '**secret** *n.* Geschäftsgeheimnis, *das;* ∼**sman** /'treɪdzmən/ *n., pl.* ∼**smen** /'treɪdzmən/ (shopkeeper) [Einzel]händler, *der;*

(craftsman) Handwerker, *der;* ~ **'union** *n.*
Gewerkschaft, *die; attrib.* Gewerkschafts-;
~ **'unionist** *n.* Gewerkschaft[l]er, *der/*
Gewerkschaft[l]erin, *die*

**trading** /'treɪdɪŋ/ *n.* Handel, *der*

**trading:** ~ **estate** *n.* (Brit.)
Gewerbegebiet, *das;* ~ **hours** *n. pl.*
Geschäftszeit, *die;* **during/outside** ~ **hours**
während/außerhalb der Geschäftszeit;
'Trading hours: ...' „Geschäftszeiten: ...";
~ **partner** *n.* Handelspartner, *der*

**tradition** /trə'dɪʃn/ *n.* Tradition, *die*

**traditional** /trə'dɪʃənl/ *adj.* traditionell;
herkömmlich ⟨*Erziehung, Methode*⟩

**tra'ditionally** *adv.* traditionell

**traffic** /'træfɪk/ ①*n.* (a) *no indef. art.*
Verkehr, *der*
**(b)** (trade) Handel, *der*
②*v.i.,* **-ck-:** ~ **in sth.** mit etw. handeln

**traffic:** ~ **calming** *n.*
Verkehrsberuhigung, *die;* ~ **circle** *n.*
(Amer.) Kreisverkehr, *der;* ~ **cone** *n.*
Pylon, *der;* Leitkegel, *der;* ~ **island** *n.*
Verkehrsinsel, *die;* ~ **jam** *n.*
[Verkehrs]stau, *der*

**trafficker** /'træfɪkə(r)/ *n.* Händler, *der/*
Händlerin, *die;* ~ **in drugs:** Drogenhändler,
*der/*-händlerin, *die*

**traffic:** ~ **lights** *n. pl.* [Verkehrs]ampel,
*die;* ~ **police** *n.* Verkehrspolizei, *die;*
~ **report** *n.* Verkehrsübersicht, *die;* (on
radio) Verkehrsservice, *der;* ~ **sign** *n.*
Verkehrszeichen, *das;* ~ **signals**
▶ ~ LIGHTS; ~ **warden** *n.* (Brit.)
Hilfspolizist, *der;* (woman) Hilfspolizistin, *die;*
Politesse, *die*

**tragedy** /'trædʒɪdɪ/ *n.* Tragödie, *die*

**tragic** /'trædʒɪk/ *adj.* tragisch

**trail** /treɪl/ ①*n.* (a) Spur, *die;* ~ **of smoke/**
**dust** Rauch-/Staubfahne, *die*
**(b)** (Hunting) Spur, *die;* Fährte, *die*
**(c)** (path) Pfad, *der;* Weg, *der*
②*v.t.* (a) (pursue) verfolgen
**(b)** (drag) ~ **sth.** [after *or* behind one] etw.
hinter sich (*Dat.*) herziehen
③*v.i.* (a) (be dragged) schleifen
**(b)** (lag) hinterhertrotten
**(c)** ⟨*Pflanze:*⟩ kriechen

**trailer** /'treɪlə(r)/ *n.* (a) Anhänger, *der;*
(Amer.: caravan) Wohnanhänger, *der*
**(b)** (Cinemat., Telev.) Trailer, *der*

**train** /treɪn/ ①*v.t.* (a) ausbilden (in in
+ *Dat.*); erziehen ⟨*Kind*⟩; abrichten ⟨*Hund*⟩;
dressieren ⟨*Tier*⟩
**(b)** (Sport) trainieren
**(c)** (Hort.) ziehen
②*v.i.* (a) eine Ausbildung machen; **he is**
~**ing as** *or* **to be a doctor/engineer** er macht
eine Arzt-/Ingenieursausbildung
**(b)** (Sport) trainieren
③*n.* (a) (Railw.) Zug, *der;* **on the** ~: im Zug
**(b)** (of skirt etc.) Schleppe, *die*
**(c)** ~ **of thought** Gedankengang, *der*

**'train driver** *n.* Lokomotivführer, *der/*
-führerin, *die*

**trained** /treɪnd/ *adj.* ausgebildet ⟨*Arbeiter,*
*Lehrer, Arzt, Stimme*⟩; abgerichtet ⟨*Hund*⟩;
dressiert ⟨*Tier*⟩; geschult ⟨*Geist, Auge, Ohr*⟩

**trainee** /treɪ'niː/ *n.* Auszubildende, *der/die*

**'trainer** *n.* [Konditions]trainer, *der/*
-trainerin, *die*

**'train fare** *n.* Fahrpreis, *der*

**'training** *n.* (a) Ausbildung, *die*
**(b)** (Sport) Training, *das*

**training:** ~ **camp** *n.* (Sport)
Trainingslager, *das;* ~ **college** *n.*
berufsbildende Schule; ~ **course** *n.*
Lehrgang, *der;* ~ **scheme** *n.*
Ausbildungsprogramm, *das;* ~ **shoes** *n.*
*pl.* Trainingsschuhe *Pl.*

**train:** ~ **journey** *n.* Bahnfahrt, *die;* (long)
Bahnreise, *die;* ~ **service** *n.*
Zugverbindung, *die;* ~ **set** *n.*
[Modell]eisenbahn, *die;* ~**spotting** *n.:* das
*Aufschreiben von Lokomotivnummern als*
*Hobby;* ~ **station** *n.* (Amer.) Bahnhof, *der*

**traipse** /treɪps/ *v.i.* (coll.) latschen (salopp)
■ **traipse about, traipse around** *v.i.*
rumlatschen (salopp)

**trait** /treɪt/ *n.* Eigenschaft, *die*

**traitor** /'treɪtə(r)/ *n.* Verräter, *der/*
Verräterin, *die*

**traitorous** /'treɪtərəs/ *adj.* verräterisch

**trajectory** /trə'dʒektərɪ/ *n.* [Flug]bahn, *die*

**tram** /træm/ *n.* (Brit.) Straßenbahn, *die;*
~**lines** Straßenbahnschienen *Pl.*

**tramp** /træmp/ ①*n.* Landstreicher, *der/*
-streicherin, *die;* (in city) Stadtstreicher, *der/*
-streicherin, *die*
②*v.i.* (a) (tread heavily) trampeln
**(b)** (walk) marschieren

**trample** /'træmpl/ ①*v.t.* zertrampeln
②*v.i.* trampeln
■ **'trample on** *v.t.* herumtrampeln auf
(+ *Dat.*)

**trampoline** /'træmpəliːn/ *n.* Trampolin,
*das*

**'tram stop** *n.* Straßenbahnhaltestelle, *die*

**trance** /trɑːns/ *n.* Trance, *die;* **be in a** ~: in
Trance sein

**tranquil** /'træŋkwɪl/ *adj.* ruhig

**tranquillity** /træŋ'kwɪlɪtɪ/ Ruhe, *die*

**tranquillizer** /'træŋkwɪlaɪzə(r)/ *n.*
Beruhigungsmittel, *das*

**transact** /træn'zækt/ *v.t.* ~ **business**
Geschäfte tätigen

**transaction** /træn'zækʃn/ *n.* Geschäft,
*das;* (financial) Transaktion, *die*

**transatlantic** /trænsət'læntɪk/ *adj.*
transatlantisch

**transcend** /træn'send/ *v.t.* übersteigen

**transcript** /'trænskrɪpt/ *n.* Abschrift, *die;*
(of trial) Protokoll, *das*

**transfer** ① /træns'fɜː(r)/ *v.t.,* **-rr-:** ⋯⃗

**(a)** (move) verlegen **(to** nach); überweisen ⟨*Geld*⟩ **(to** auf + *Akk.*); übertragen ⟨*Befugnis, Macht*⟩ **(to** *Dat.*)
**(b)** übereignen ⟨*Gegenstand, Grundbesitz*⟩ **(to** *Dat.*)
**(c)** versetzen ⟨*Arbeiter, Angestellte*⟩; (Footb.) transferieren
2 /træns'fɜː(r)/ *v.i.*, **-rr-: (a)** (when travelling) umsteigen
**(b)** (change job etc.) wechseln
3 /'trænsfɜː(r)/ *n.* **(a)** (moving) Verlegung, *die;* (of powers) Übertragung, *die* **(to** an + *Akk.*); (of money) Überweisung, *die*
**(b)** (of employee etc.) Versetzung, *die;* (Footb.) Transfer, *der*
**(c)** (picture) Abziehbild, *das*

**transferable** /træns'fɜːrəbl/ *adj.* übertragbar

'**transfer:** ∼ **fee** *n.* (Footb.) Ablösesumme, *die;* Transfersumme, *die* (fachspr.); ∼ **list** *n.* (Footb.) Transferliste, *die*

**transform** /træns'fɔːm/ *v.t.* verwandeln
**transformation** /trænsfə'meɪʃn/ *n.* Verwandlung, *die*
**trans'former** *n.* (Electr.) Transformator, *der*
**transfusion** /træns'fjuːʒn/ *n.* (Med.) Transfusion, *die*
**transient** /'trænzɪənt/ *adj.* kurzlebig; vergänglich
**transistor** /træn'zɪstə(r)/ *n.* Transistor, *der*
**transit** /'trænsɪt/ *n.* **in** ∼: auf der Durchreise; ⟨*Waren*⟩ auf dem Transport; **passengers in** ∼: Transitreisende *Pl.*
**transition** /træn'sɪʒn, træn'zɪʃn/ *n.* Übergang, *der;* Wechsel, *der*
**transitional** /træn'zɪʃənl/ *adj.* Übergangs-
**transitive** /'trænsɪtɪv/ *adj.* (Ling.) transitiv
'**transit lounge** *n.* Transithalle, *die*
**transitory** /'trænsɪtərɪ/ *adj.* vergänglich; (fleeting) flüchtig
'**transit passenger** *n.* Transitpassagier, *der*
**translate** /træns'leɪt/ *v.t.* übersetzen
**translation** /træns'leɪʃn/ *n.* Übersetzung, *die*
**translator** /træns'leɪtə(r)/ *n.* Übersetzer, *der*/Übersetzerin, *die*
**translucent** /træns'luːsənt/ *adj.* durchscheinend
**transmission** /træns'mɪʃn/ *n.* **(a)** Übertragung, *die*
**(b)** (Motor Veh.) Antrieb, *der;* (gearbox) Getriebe, *das*
**transmit** /træns'mɪt/ *v.t.*, **-tt-: (a)** (pass on) übersenden; übertragen
**(b)** durchlassen ⟨*Licht*⟩; leiten ⟨*Wärme*⟩
**trans'mitter** *n.* Sender, *der*
**transparency** /træns'pærənsɪ/ *n.* **(a)** Durchsichtigkeit, *die*
**(b)** (Photog.) Transparent, *das;* (slide) Dia, *das*
**transparent** /træns'pærənt/ *adj.* durchsichtig

**transparently** /træns'pærəntlɪ/ *adv.* offenkundig; ∼ **obvious** ganz offenkundig
**transpire** /træn'spaɪə(r)/ *v.i.* sich herausstellen; (coll.: happen) passieren
**transplant** 1 /træns'plɑːnt/ *v.t.* **(a)** verpflanzen ⟨*Organ*⟩
**(b)** (plant in another place) umpflanzen
2 /'trænsplɑːnt/ *n.* (Med.) Transplantation, *die;* Verpflanzung, *die*
**transport** 1 /træns'pɔːt/ *v.t.* transportieren; befördern
2 /'trænspɔːt/ *n.* **(a)** Transport, *der;* Beförderung, *die; attrib.* Beförderungs-
**(b)** (means of conveyance) Verkehrsmittel, *das;* **be without** ∼: kein [eigenes] Fahrzeug haben
'**transport café** *n.* (Brit.) Fernfahrerlokal, *das*
**transpose** /træns'pəʊz/ *v.t.* vertauschen; umstellen
**transsexual** /træns'seksjʊəl/ 1 *adj.* transsexuell
2 *n.* Transsexuelle, *der/die*
**transvestite** /træns'vestaɪt/ *n.* Transvestit, *der*
**trap** /træp/ 1 *n.* **(a)** Falle, *die;* **set** *or* **lay a** ∼ **for an animal** eine Falle für ein Tier legen *od.* aufstellen; **set** *or* **lay a** ∼ **for sb.** (fig.) jmdm. eine Falle stellen; **fall into a/sb.'s** ∼ (fig.) in die/jmdm. in die Falle gehen
**(b)** (sl.: mouth) Klappe, *die* (salopp)
2 *v.t.*, **-pp-: (a)** [in *od.* mit einer Falle] fangen ⟨*Tier*⟩; (fig.) in eine Falle locken ⟨*Person*⟩; **be** ∼**ped** (fig.) in eine Falle gehen/in der Falle sitzen; **be** ∼**ped in a cave/by the tide** in einer Höhle festsitzen/von der Flut abgeschnitten sein
**(b)** (confine) einschließen; einklemmen ⟨*Körperteil*⟩
**trap'door** *n.* Falltür, *die*
**trapeze** /trə'piːz/ *n.* Trapez, *das*
**tra'peze artist** *n.* Trapezkünstler, *der/*-künstlerin, *die*
**trash** /træʃ/ *n.* **(a)** (rubbish) Abfall, *der*
**(b)** (badly made thing) Mist, *der* (ugs.); (bad literature) Schund, *der* (ugs.)
**trauma** /'trɔːmə/ *n., pl.* ∼**ta** /'trɔːmətə/ *or* ∼**s** Trauma, *das*
**traumatic** /trɔː'mætɪk/ *adj.* traumatisch
**traumatize** /'trɔːmətaɪz/ *v.t.* traumatisieren
**travel** /'trævl/ 1 *n.* Reisen, *das; attrib.* Reise-
2 *v.i.*, (Brit.) **-ll-** reisen; (go in vehicle) fahren
3 *v.t.*, (Brit.) **-ll-** zurücklegen ⟨*Strecke, Entfernung*⟩; benutzen ⟨*Weg, Straße*⟩; **we had** ∼**led 10 miles** wir waren 10 Meilen gefahren
■ **travel a'bout, travel a'round** *v.i.* umherreisen
**travel:** ∼ **agency** *n.* Reisebüro, *das;* ∼ **agent** *n.* Reisebürokaufmann, *der/*-kauffrau, *die;* ∼ **brochure** *n.* Reiseprospekt, *der;* ∼ **bureau** *n.* Reisebüro, *das*

**traveler, traveling** (Amer.) ▶ TRAVELL-

**'travel insurance** n. Reiseversicherung, *die*

**traveller** /'trævlə(r)/ n. (Brit.) **(a)** Reisende, *der/die*
**(b)** *in pl.* (gypsies etc.) fahrendes Volk

**'traveller's cheque** n. Reisescheck, *der*

**travelling** /'trævlıŋ/ *attrib. adj.* (Brit.) Wander‹*zirkus, -ausstellung*›

**travelling:** ~ **clock** n. Reisewecker, *der;* ~ **'salesman** n. Vertreter, *der*

**travel:** ~**-sick** *adj.* reisekrank; ~**-sickness** n. Reisekrankheit, *die;* ~**-sickness pill** n. Tablette gegen Reisekrankheit

**trawler** /'trɔːlə(r)/ n. [Fisch]trawler, *der*

**tray** /treɪ/ n. Tablett, *das;* (for correspondence) Ablagekorb, *der*

**treacherous** /'tretʃərəs/ *adj.* **(a)** treulos ‹*Person*›
**(b)** (deceptive) tückisch

**treachery** /'tretʃərɪ/ n. Verrat, *der*

**treacle** /'triːkl/ n. (Brit.) Sirup, *der*

**tread** /tred/ ①n. **(a)** (of tyre, boot, etc.) Lauffläche, *die;* **2 millimetres of** ~ **on a tyre** 2 Millimeter Profil auf einem Reifen
**(b)** (sound of walking) Schritt, *der*
② *v.i.,* trod /trɒd/, trodden /'trɒdn/ *or* trod treten (**in/on** in/auf + *Akk.*); (walk) gehen
③ *v.t.* trod, trodden *or* trod treten auf (+ *Akk.*); stampfen ‹*Weintrauben*›

**'treadmill** n. (lit. or fig.) Tretmühle, *die*

**treason** /'triːzn/ n. **[high]** ~: Hochverrat, *der*

**treasure** /'treʒə(r)/ ①n. Schatz, *der;* Kostbarkeit, *die;* **art** ~**s** Kunstschätze *Pl.*
② *v.t.* in Ehren halten

**treasure:** ~ **house** n. [wahre] Fundgrube; ~ **hunt** n. Schatzsuche, *die*

**treasurer** /'treʒərə(r)/ n. Kassenwart, *der/* -wartin, *die*

**treasury** /'treʒərɪ/ n. **the T**~: das Finanzministerium

**treat** /triːt/ ①n. **(a)** [besonderes] Vergnügen
**(b)** (entertainment) *Vergnügen, für dessen Kosten jmd. anderes aufkommt;* **lay on a special** ~ **for sb.** jmdm. etwas Besonderes bieten; **it's my** ~: ich lade ein
② *v.t.* **(a)** behandeln; ~ **sth. as a joke** etw. als Witz nehmen; ~ **sth. with contempt** für etw. nur Verachtung haben
**(b)** (Med.) behandeln; ~ **sb. for sth.** jmdn. wegen etw. behandeln; *(before confirmation of diagnosis)* jmdn. auf etw. (*Akk.*) behandeln
**(c)** klären ‹*Abwässer*›
**(d)** ( provide with at own expense) einladen; ~ **sb. to sth.** jmdm. etw. spendieren; ~ **oneself to a new hat** sich (*Dat.*) einen neuen Hut leisten

**treatise** /'triːtɪs, 'triːtɪz/ n. Abhandlung, *die*

**'treatment** n. Behandlung, *die*

**treaty** /'triːtɪ/ n. [Staats]vertrag, *der*

**treble** /'trebl/ ① *adj.* **(a)** dreifach
**(b)** (Brit. Mus.) ~ **voice** Sopranstimme, *die*
② n. **(a)** (~ quantity) Dreifache, *das*
**(b)** (Mus.) **he is a** ~: er singt Sopran
③ *v.t.* verdreifachen
④ *v.i.* sich verdreifachen

**'treble clef** n. (Mus.) Violinschlüssel, *der*

**tree** /triː/ n. Baum, *der*

**'tree house** n. Baumhaus, *das*

**'treeless** *adj.* baumlos

**tree:** ~**-lined** *adj.* von Bäumen gesäumt; ~ **surgeon** n. Baumchirurg, *der;* ~ **surgery** n. Baumchirurgie, *die;* ~**top** n. [Baum]wipfel, *der;* ~ **trunk** n. Baumstamm, *der*

**trek** /trek/ ① *v.i.,* **-kk-** ziehen (**across** durch)
② n. [schwierige] Reise

**trellis** /'trelɪs/ n. Gitter, *das;* (for plants) Spalier, *das*

**tremble** /'trembl/ *v.i.* zittern (**with** vor + *Dat.*)

**trembling** /'tremblıŋ/ ① *adj.* zitternd
② n. Zittern, *das*

**tremendous** /trɪ'mendəs/ *adj.* gewaltig; (coll.: wonderful) großartig

**tremor** /'tremə(r)/ n. **(a)** Zittern, *das*
**(b)** [earth] ~: leichtes Erdbeben

**trench** /trentʃ/ n. Graben, *der;* (Mil.) Schützengraben, *der*

**trench 'warfare** n. Grabenkrieg, *der*

**trend** /trend/ n. **(a)** Trend, *der;* **upward** ~: steigende Tendenz
**(b)** (fashion) Mode, *die;* [Mode]trend, *der*

**trendiness** n. (Brit. coll.) modische Art

**'trendsetter** n. Trendsetter, *der*

**'trendy** *adj.* (Brit. coll.) modisch; Schickimicki‹*kneipe*› (ugs.)

**trepidation** /trepɪ'deɪʃn/ n. Beklommenheit, *die*

**trespass** /'trespəs/ *v.i.* ~ **on** unerlaubt betreten ‹*Grundstück*›

**'trespasser** n. Unbefugte, *der/die*

**trial** /'traɪəl/ n. **(a)** (Law) [Gerichts]verfahren, *das;* **be on** ~ **[for murder]** [wegen Mordes] vor Gericht stehen
**(b)** (testing) Test, *der;* **employ sb. on** ~: jmdn. probeweise einstellen; **[by]** ~ **and error** [durch] Ausprobieren
**(c)** (trouble) Problem, *das*
**(d)** (Sport) (competition) Prüfung, *die;* (for selection) Testspiel, *das*

**trial 'run** n. (of car) Testfahrt, *die;* (fig.) Probelauf, *der*

**triangle** /'traɪæŋgl/ n. **(a)** Dreieck, *das*
**(b)** (Mus.) Triangel, *der od. das*

**triangular** /traɪ'æŋgjʊlə(r)/ *adj.* dreieckig

**tribal** /'traɪbl/ *adj.* Stammes-

**tribalism** /'traɪbəlɪzm/ n. Tribalismus, *der* (fachspr.)

**tribe** /traɪb/ n. Stamm, der
**tribulation** /trɪbjʊˈleɪʃn/ n. Kummer, der
**tribunal** /traɪˈbjuːnl/ n. Schiedsgericht, das
**tributary** /ˈtrɪbjʊtərɪ/ n. Nebenfluss, der
**tribute** /ˈtrɪbjuːt/ n. Tribut, der (**to** an
+ Akk.); **pay a ~ to sb./sth.** jmdm./einer Sache
den schuldigen Tribut zollen (geh.)
**trice** /traɪs/ n. **in a ~:** im Handumdrehen
**trick** /trɪk/ ①️ n. (a) Trick, der; **it was all a
~:** das war [alles] nur Bluff
(b) (feat of skill etc.) Kunststück, das; **that
should do the ~** (coll.) damit dürfte es
klappen (ugs.)
(c) (knack) **get** or **find the ~ [of doing sth.]**
den Dreh finden[, wie man etw. tut]
(d) (prank) Streich, der; **play a ~ on sb.**
jmdm. einen Streich spielen
(e) (Cards) Stich, der
②️ v.t. täuschen; hereinlegen; **~ sb. out of/
into sth.** jmdm. etw. ablisten
③️ adj. **~ photograph** Trickaufnahme, die;
**~ question** Fangfrage, die
**trickery** /ˈtrɪkərɪ/ n. [Hinter]list, die
**trickle** /ˈtrɪkl/ v.i. rinnen; (in drops) tröpfeln
**trickster** /ˈtrɪkstə(r)/ n. Schwindler, der/
Schwindlerin, die
**'tricky** adj. verzwickt (ugs.)
**tricycle** /ˈtraɪsɪkl/ n. Dreirad, das
**tried** ▶ TRY 2, 3
**trifle** /ˈtraɪfl/ n. (a) (Brit. Gastron.) Trifle, das
(b) (thing of slight value) Kleinigkeit, die
**trifling** /ˈtraɪflɪŋ/ adj. unbedeutend
⟨Angelegenheit⟩; gering ⟨Wert⟩
**trigger** /ˈtrɪgə(r)/ ①️ n. (a) (of gun) Abzug,
der; (of machine) Drücker, der
(b) (fig.) Auslöser, der
②️ v.t. **~ [off]** auslösen
**trigonometry** /trɪgəˈnɒmɪtrɪ/ n.
Trigonometrie, die
**trilingual** /traɪˈlɪŋgwəl/ adj. dreisprachig
**trill** /trɪl/ ①️ n. Trillern, das; (Mus.) Triller,
der
②️ v.i. trillern
**trillion** /ˈtrɪljən/ n. (million million) Billion, die
**trilogy** /ˈtrɪlədʒɪ/ n. Trilogie, die
**trim** /trɪm/ ①️ v.t., **-mm-:** (a) schneiden
⟨Hecke⟩; [nach]schneiden ⟨Haar⟩;
beschneiden ⟨Papier, Hecke, Budget⟩
(b) (ornament) besetzen (with mit)
②️ adj. proper; gepflegt ⟨Garten⟩
③️ n. (a) **be in ~** (healthy) in Form od. fit sein
(b) (cut) Nachschneiden, das
**'trimming** n. (a) (decorations) Verzierung, die
(b) in pl. (coll.: accompaniments) Beilagen Pl.;
**with all the ~s** mit allem Drum und Dran
(ugs.)
**Trinity** /ˈtrɪnɪtɪ/ n. (Theol.) **the [Holy] ~:** die
Heilige Dreieinigkeit
**trinket** /ˈtrɪŋkɪt/ n. kleines, billiges
Schmuckstück
**trio** /ˈtriːəʊ/ n., pl. **~s** Trio, das

**trip** /trɪp/ ①️ n. (a) Reise, die; (shorter)
Ausflug, der
(b) (coll.: drug-induced hallucinations) Trip, der
②️ v.i., **-pp-** stolpern (**on** über + Akk.)
■ **trip 'over** v.t. stolpern über (+ Akk.)
■ **trip 'up** ①️ v.i. (a) stolpern
(b) (fig.) einen Fehler machen
②️ v.t. (a) stolpern lassen
(b) (fig.) aufs Glatteis führen (fig.)
**tripe** /traɪp/ n. (a) Kaldaunen Pl.
(b) (coll.: rubbish) Quatsch, der (ugs.)
**triple** /ˈtrɪpl/ ①️ adj. (a) (threefold) dreifach
(b) (three times greater than) **~ the ...:** der/die/
das dreifache ...
②️ n. Dreifache, das
③️ v.i. sich verdreifachen
④️ v.t. verdreifachen
**'triple jump** n. (Sport) Dreisprung, der
**triplet** /ˈtrɪplɪt/ n. Drilling, der
**triplicate** /ˈtrɪplɪkət/ n. **in ~:** in dreifacher
Ausfertigung
**trip 'mileage recorder** n. (Motor Veh.)
Tageskilometerzähler, der
**tripod** /ˈtraɪpɒd/ n. Dreibein, das
**'tripper** n. (Brit.) Ausflügler, der/
Ausflüglerin, die
**'tripwire** n. Stolperdraht, der
**trite** /traɪt/ adj. banal
**triumph** /ˈtraɪəmf, ˈtraɪʌmf/ ①️ n. Triumph,
der (**over** über + Akk.)
②️ v.i. triumphieren (**over** über + Akk.)
**triumphant** /traɪˈʌmfənt/ adj. (a) siegreich
(b) triumphierend ⟨Blick⟩
**trivia** /ˈtrɪvɪə/ n. pl. Belanglosigkeiten Pl.
**trivial** /ˈtrɪvɪəl/ adj. belanglos
**triviality** /trɪvɪˈælɪtɪ/ n. Belanglosigkeit, die
**trivialize** /ˈtrɪvɪəlaɪz/ v.t. auf eine
belanglose Ebene bringen
**trod, trodden** ▶ TREAD 2, 3
**trolley** /ˈtrɒlɪ/ n. (a) (for serving food)
Servierwagen, der
(b) [supermarket] **~:** Einkaufswagen, der
**trombone** /trɒmˈbəʊn/ n. Posaune, die
**troop** /truːp/ ①️ n. (a) in pl. Truppen Pl.
(b) (fig.) Schar, die
②️ v.i. **~ in/out** hinein-/hinausströmen
**troop: ~ carrier** n. Truppentransporter,
der; **~ship** n. Truppentransporter, der
**trophy** /ˈtrəʊfɪ/ n. Trophäe, die
**tropic** /ˈtrɒpɪk/ n. **the T~s** (Geog.) die
Tropen; **the ~ of Cancer/Capricorn** (Astron.,
Geog.) der Wendekreis des Krebses/
Steinbocks
**tropical** /ˈtrɒpɪkl/ adj. tropisch;
Tropen⟨krankheit, -kleidung⟩
**tropical: ~ 'medicine** n.
Tropenmedizin, die; **~ 'rainforest** n.
tropischer Regenwald
**trot** /trɒt/ ①️ n. (coll.) **on the ~:**
hintereinander; **be on the ~:** auf Trab sein
(ugs.)
②️ v.i., **-tt-** traben

# trouble ···⟩ tuba ····

**trouble** /'trʌbl/ **1** n. (a) Ärger, der; Schwierigkeiten Pl.; **there'll be** ~ [if …] es wird Ärger geben, [wenn …]; **what's the** ~? was ist denn?
(b) **engine/brake** ~: Probleme mit dem Motor/der Bremse; **suffer from heart/liver** ~: herz-/leberkrank sein
(c) (inconvenience) Mühe, die; **take a lot of** ~: sich (Dat.) sehr viel Mühe geben; **it's more** ~ **than it's worth** es lohnt sich nicht
(d) in sing. or pl. (unrest) Unruhen Pl.
**2** v.t. (a) (agitate) beunruhigen; **don't let it** ~ **you** mach dir deswegen keine Sorgen
(b) (inconvenience) stören
**3** v.i. (make an effort) sich bemühen

**troubled** /'trʌbld/ adj. (a) (worried) besorgt
(b) (restless) unruhig

**trouble:** ~**-free** adj. problemlos; ~**maker** n. Unruhestifter, der/-stifterin, die

**troublesome** /'trʌblsəm/ adj. schwierig; lästig ⟨Krankheit⟩

**trough** /trɒf/ n. Trog, der

**troupe** /truːp/ n. Truppe, die

**trouser** /'traʊzə/**:** ~ **leg** n. Hosenbein, das; ~ **press** n. Bügelpresse, die; Hosenbügler, der

**trousers** /'traʊzəz/ n. pl. [**pair of**] ~: Hose, die

**'trouser suit** n. (Brit.) Hosenanzug, der

**trousseau** /'truːsəʊ/ n., pl. ~s or ~x /'truːsəʊz/ Aussteuer, die

**trout** /traʊt/ n., pl. same Forelle, die

**trout:** ~ **farm** n. Forellenzuchtbetrieb, der; ~**-fishing** n. Forellenfang, der

**trowel** /'traʊəl/ n. Kelle, die; (Hort.) Pflanzkelle, die

**truant** /'truːənt/ n. **play** ~: [die Schule] schwänzen (ugs.)

**truce** /truːs/ n. Waffenstillstand, der

**truck** /trʌk/ n. (a) Last[kraft]wagen, der; Lkw, der
(b) (Brit. Railw.) offener Güterwagen

**'truck driver, trucker** /'trʌkə(r)/ ns. Lastwagenfahrer, der/-fahrerin, die; (long-distance) Fernfahrer, der/-fahrerin, die

**truculent** /'trʌkjʊlənt/ adj. aufsässig

**trudge** /trʌdʒ/ v.i. trotten; (through snow etc.) stapfen

**true** /truː/ adj., ~r /'truːə(r)/, ~st /'truːɪst/ (a) wahr; wahrheitsgetreu ⟨Bericht⟩; richtig ⟨Vorteil⟩; (rightly so called) eigentlich; echt, wahr ⟨Freund⟩; **is it** ~ **that …?** stimmt es, dass …?; ~ **to life** lebensecht
(b) (loyal) treu

**truffle** /'trʌfl/ n. Trüffel, die od. (ugs.) der

**truism** /'truːɪzm/ n. Binsenweisheit, die

**truly** /'truːlɪ/ adv. (a) wirklich
(b) (accurately) zutreffend; **yours** ~: mit freundlichen Grüßen

**trump** /trʌmp/ (Cards) **1** n. Trumpf, der
**2** v.t. übertrumpfen

**'trump card** n. (lit. or fig.) Trumpf, der

**trumped up** /'trʌmpt ʌp/ adj. falsch ⟨Beschuldigung usw.⟩

**trumpet** /'trʌmpɪt/ n. Trompete, die

**'trumpeter** n. Trompeter, der/ Trompeterin, die

**truncheon** /'trʌntʃn/ n. Schlagstock, der

**trundle** /'trʌndl/ v.t. & i. rollen

**trunk** /trʌŋk/ n. (a) (of elephant etc.) Rüssel, der
(b) (large box) Schrankkoffer, der
(c) (of tree) Stamm, der
(d) (of body) Rumpf, der
(e) (Amer.: of car) Kofferraum, der
(f) in pl. (Brit.) [**swimming**] ~s Badehose, die

**truss** /trʌs/ n. (Med.) Bruchband, das

**trust** /trʌst/ **1** n. (a) Vertrauen, das; **place** or **put one's** ~ **in sb./sth.** sein Vertrauen auf od. in jmdn./etw. setzen; **take sth. on** ~: etw. einfach glauben
(b) (organization managed by trustees) Treuhandgesellschaft, die; [**charitable**] ~: Stiftung, die; (association of companies) Trust, der
(c) (Law) **hold in** ~: treuhänderisch verwalten
**2** v.t. (rely on) trauen (+ Dat.); vertrauen (+ Dat.) ⟨Person⟩; ~ **sb. with sth.** jmdm. etw. anvertrauen
**3** v.i. (a) ~ **to** sich verlassen auf (+ Akk.)
(b) (believe) ~ **in sb./sth.** auf jmdn./etw. vertrauen

**trustee** /trʌ'stiː/ n. Treuhänder, der/ Treuhänderin, die

**trustful** /'trʌstfl/, **'trusting** adjs. vertrauensvoll

**trust:** ~ **fund** n. Treuhandvermögen, das; ~**worthy** adj. vertrauenswürdig

**truth** /truːθ/ n., pl. ~s /truːðz, truːθs/ Wahrheit, die; **tell the** [**whole**] ~: die [ganze] Wahrheit sagen

**truthful** /'truːθfl/ adj. ehrlich

**try** /traɪ/ **1** n. Versuch, der; **have a** ~ **at sth./doing sth.** etw. versuchen/versuchen, etw. zu tun; **give a** ~, **have a** ~: es versuchen
**2** v.t. (a) (attempt) versuchen
(b) (test usefulness of) probieren
(c) (test) auf die Probe stellen ⟨Fähigkeit, Kraft, Geduld⟩
(d) (Law: take to trial) ~ **a case** einen Fall verhandeln; ~ **sb.** [**for sth.**] jmdn. [wegen einer Sache] vor Gericht stellen
**3** v.i. es versuchen; ~ **hard/harder** sich (Dat.) viel/mehr Mühe geben
■ **try 'on** v.t. anprobieren ⟨Kleidungsstück⟩
■ **try 'out** v.t. ausprobieren

**'trying** adj. (a) (testing) schwierig
(b) (difficult to endure) anstrengend

**tsar** /zɑː(r)/ n. (Hist.) Zar, der

**'T-shirt** n. T-Shirt, das

**tub** /tʌb/ n. Kübel, der; (for ice cream etc.) Becher, der

**tuba** /'tjuːbə/ n. (Mus.) Tuba, die

**tubby** /'tʌbɪ/ *adj.* rundlich

**tube** /tju:b/ *n.* **(a)** (for conveying liquids etc.) Rohr, *das*
**(b)** (small cylinder) Tube, *die;* (for sweets, tablets) Röhrchen, *das*
**(c)** (Anat., Zool.) Röhre, *die*
**(d)** (of TV etc.) Röhre, *die*
**(e)** (Brit. coll.: underground railway) U-Bahn, *die*

**tuber** /'tju:bə(r)/ *n.* (Bot.) Knolle, *die*

**tuberculosis** /tju:bɜ:kjʊ'ləʊsɪs/ *n.* Tuberkulose, *die*

**tube:** ~ **station** *n.* (Brit. coll.) U-Bahnhof, *der;* ~ **train** *n.* (Brit. coll.) U-bahn-Zug, *der*

**tubing** /'tju:bɪŋ/ *n.* Rohre *Pl.*

**tubular** /'tju:bjʊlə(r)/ *adj.* röhrenförmig

**tuck** /tʌk/ ⓵ *v.t.* stecken
⓶ *n.* (in fabric) (for decoration) Biese, *die;* (to tighten) Abnäher, *der*
■ **tuck 'in** ⓵ *v.t.* hineinstecken
⓶ *v.i.* (coll.) zulangen (ugs.)
■ **tuck 'up (a)** hochkrempeln ⟨*Ärmel, Hose*⟩; hochnehmen ⟨*Rock*⟩
**(b)** (cover snugly) zudecken

**Tue., Tues.** *abbrs.* = **Tuesday** Di.

**Tuesday** /'tju:zdeɪ, 'tju:zdɪ/ *n.* Dienstag, *der; see also* FRIDAY

**tuft** /tʌft/ *n.* Büschel, *das*

**tug** /tʌg/ ⓵ *n.* **(a)** Ruck, *der;* ~ of war Tauziehen, *das*
**(b)** ~ [boat] Schlepper, *der*
⓶ *v.t.,* -gg- ziehen
⓷ *v.i.,* -gg- zerren (at an + *Dat.*)

**tuition** /tju:'ɪʃn/ *n.* Unterricht, *der*

**tulip** /'tju:lɪp/ *n.* Tulpe, *die*

**tumble** /'tʌmbl/ ⓵ *v.i.* stürzen; fallen
⓶ *n.* Sturz, *der*

**tumble:** ~**down** *adj.* verfallen; ~**-drier** *n.* Wäschetrockner, *der;* ~**-dry** *v.t.* im Automaten trocknen

**tumbler** /'tʌmblə(r)/ *n.* (short) Whiskyglas, *das;* (long) Wasserglas, *das*

**tummy** /'tʌmɪ/ *n.* (child lang./coll.) Bäuchlein, *das*

**tummy:** ~ **ache** *n.* (child lang./coll.) Bauchweh, *das;* ~ **button** *n.* (child lang./coll.) Bauchnabel, *der;* ~ **upset** *n.* (child lang./coll.) Magenverstimmung, *die*

**tumour** (*Brit.; Amer.:* **tumor**) /'tju:mə(r)/ *n.* Tumor, *der*

**tumult** /'tju:mʌlt/ *n.* Tumult, *der*

**tuna** /'tju:nə/ *n., pl. same or* ~s Thunfisch, *der*

**tune** /tju:n/ ⓵ *n.* **(a)** (melody) Melodie, *die;* **change one's** ~ (fig.) sein Verhalten ändern; **call the** ~: den Ton angeben
**(b)** (correct pitch) **sing in/out of** ~: richtig/ falsch singen; **be in/out of** ~ ⟨*Instrument:*⟩ richtig gestimmt/verstimmt sein
⓶ *v.t.* **(a)** (Mus.: put in ~) stimmen
**(b)** (Radio, Telev.) einstellen (**to** auf + *Akk.*)
**(c)** einstellen ⟨*Motor, Vergaser*⟩

**tune 'in** *v.i.* (Radio, Telev.) ~ **to a station** einen Sender einstellen

**tuneful** /'tju:nfl/ *adj.* melodisch

**tuner** /'tju:nə(r)/ *n.* **(a)** (Mus.) Stimmer, *der/* Stimmerin, *die*
**(b)** (radio) Tuner, *der*

**tunic** /'tju:nɪk/ *n.* (of soldier) Uniformjacke, *die;* (of schoolgirl) Kittel, *der*

**'tuning fork** /'tju:nɪŋfɔ:k/ *n.* Stimmgabel, *die*

**Tunisia** /tju:'nɪzɪə/ *pr. n.* Tunesien (*das*)

**tunnel** /'tʌnl/ ⓵ *n.* Tunnel, *der;* (dug by animal) Gang, *der*
⓶ *v.i.,* (Brit.) -ll- einen Tunnel graben

**turban** /'tɜ:bən/ *n.* Turban, *der*

**turbine** /'tɜ:baɪn/ *n.* Turbine, *die*

**turbocharged** /'tɜ:bəʊtʃɑːdʒd/ *adj.* mit Turbolader *nachgestellt*

**turbot** /'tɜ:bət/ *n.* Steinbutt, *der*

**turbulence** /'tɜ:bjʊləns/ *n.* **(a)** Aufgewühltheit, *die;* (fig.) Aufruhr, *der*
**(b)** (Phys.) Turbulenz, *die*

**turbulent** /'tɜ:bjʊlənt/ *adj.* **(a)** aufgewühlt
**(b)** (Phys.) turbulent

**turd** /tɜ:d/ *n.* (coarse) Scheißhaufen, *der* (derb)

**tureen** /tjʊə'ri:n/ *n.* Terrine, *die*

**turf** /tɜ:f/ *n., pl.* ~s *or* **turves** /tɜ:vz/ **(a)** *no pl.* Rasen, *der*
**(b)** (segment) Rasenstück, *das*
■ **turf 'out** *v.t.* (coll.) rausschmeißen (ugs.)

**Turk** /tɜ:k/ *n.* Türke, *der/*Türkin, *die*

**turkey** *n.* Truthahn, *der/*Truthenne, *die;* (esp. as food) Puter, *der/*Pute, *die*

**Turkey** /'tɜ:kɪ/ *pr. n.* die Türkei

**Turkish** /'tɜ:kɪʃ/ ⓵ *adj.* türkisch; **sb. is** ~: jmd. ist Türke/Türkin
⓶ *n.* Türkisch, *das; see also* ENGLISH 2A

**turmoil** /'tɜ:mɔɪl/ *n.* Aufruhr, *der*

**turn** /tɜ:n/ ⓵ *n.* **(a)** (it is sb.'s ~ to do sth.) jmd. ist an der Reihe, etw. zu tun); **it's your** ~ [next] du bist als Nächster/Nächste dran (ugs.) *od.* an der Reihe; **out of** ~: außer der Reihe; (fig.) an der falschen Stelle ⟨*lachen*⟩; **take [it in]** ~s sich abwechseln
**(b)** (rotary motion) Drehung, *die*
**(c)** (change of direction) Wende, *die;* **take a** ~ **to the right/left, do** *or* **take a right/left** ~: nach rechts/links abbiegen; (fig.) **take a favourable** ~ sich zum Guten wenden; **the** ~ **of the year/century** die Jahres-/Jahrhundertwende
**(d)** (bend) Kurve, *die;* (corner) Ecke, *die*
**(e)** (short performance) Nummer, *die*
**(f)** (service) **do sb. a good** ~: jmdm. einen guten Dienst erweisen
**(g)** (coll.: fright) **give sb. quite a** ~: jmdm. einen gehörigen Schrecken einjagen (ugs.)
⓶ *v.t.* **(a)** (make revolve) drehen
**(b)** (reverse) umdrehen; wenden ⟨*Pfannkuchen, Auto, Heu*⟩; ~ **sth. upside down** *or* **on its head** (lit. *or* fig.) etw. auf den Kopf stellen; ~ **the page** umblättern
**(c)** (give new direction to) drehen, wenden ⟨*Kopf*⟩; ~ **a hose/gun on sb./sth.** einen

Schlauch/ein Gewehr auf jmdn./etw. richten; ~ **one's attention/mind to sth.** sich/ seine Gedanken einer Sache (*Dat.*) zuwenden

**(d)** ~ **sb. loose on sb./sth.** jmdn. auf jmdn./ etw. loslassen

**(e)** (cause to become) verwandeln; ~ **the lights [down] low** das Licht dämpfen; ~ **a play/ book into a film** ein Theaterstück/Buch verfilmen

**(f)** (shape in lathe) drechseln ⟨*Holz*⟩; drehen ⟨*Metall*⟩

**(g)** drehen ⟨*Pirouette*⟩; schlagen ⟨*Purzelbaum*⟩

③ *v.i.* **(a)** (revolve) sich drehen

**(b)** (reverse direction) ⟨*Person:*⟩ sich herumdrehen; ⟨*Auto:*⟩ wenden

**(c)** (take new direction) sich wenden; (~ round) sich umdrehen; ~ **to the left/right** nach links/rechts abbiegen

**(d)** (become) werden; ~ **[in]to sth.** zu etw. werden; (be transformed) sich in etw. (*Akk.*) verwandeln

**(e)** (become sour) ⟨*Milch:*⟩ sauer werden

■ **turn a'way** ① *v.i.* sich abwenden

② *v.t.* **(a)** (avert) abwenden

**(b)** (send away) wegschicken

■ **turn 'down** *v.t.* **(a)** herunterschlagen ⟨*Kragen*⟩

**(b)** niedriger stellen ⟨*Heizung*⟩; herunterdrehen ⟨*Gas*⟩; leiser stellen ⟨*Ton, Radio, Fernseher*⟩

**(c)** (reject) ablehnen; abweisen ⟨*Kandidaten usw.*⟩

■ **turn 'in** ① *v.t.* **(a)** nach innen drehen

**(b)** (hand in) abgeben

② *v.i.* **(a)** (enter) einbiegen

**(b)** (coll.: go to bed) in die Falle gehen (salopp)

■ **turn 'off** ① *v.t.* abschalten; abstellen ⟨*Wasser, Gas*⟩; zudrehen ⟨*Wasserhahn*⟩

② *v.i.* abbiegen

■ **turn on** *v.t.* **(a)** /-'-/ anschalten; aufdrehen ⟨*Wasserhahn, Gas*⟩

**(b)** /'--/ (attack) angreifen

■ **turn 'out** ① *v.t.* **(a)** (expel) hinauswerfen (ugs.)

**(b)** (switch off) ausschalten; abdrehen ⟨*Gas*⟩

**(c)** (produce) produzieren

**(d)** (Brit.) (empty) ausräumen; leeren; (get rid of) wegwerfen

② *v.i.* **(a)** (prove to be) sb./sth. ~**s out to be sth.** jmd./etw. stellt sich als jmd./etw. heraus; **everything** ~**ed out well/all right in the end** alles endete gut

**(b)** (appear) ⟨*Fans usw.:*⟩ erscheinen

■ **turn 'over** ① *v.t.* umdrehen

② *v.i.* **(a)** (tip over) umkippen; ⟨*Boot:*⟩ kentern; ⟨*Auto, Flugzeug:*⟩ sich überschlagen

**(b)** (from one side to the other) sich umdrehen

**(c)** (~ a page) umblättern

■ **turn 'round** *v.i.* sich umdrehen

■ **'turn to** *v.t.* (fig.) ~ **to sb.** sich an jmdn. wenden; ~ **sb. for help/advice** bei jmdm. Hilfe/Rat suchen; ~ **to drink** sich in den Alkohol flüchten

■ **turn 'up** ① *v.i.* **(a)** ⟨*Person:*⟩ erscheinen

**(b)** (present itself) auftauchen; ⟨*Gelegenheit:*⟩ sich bieten

② *v.t.* **(a)** hochschlagen ⟨*Kragen*⟩

**(b)** lauter stellen ⟨*Ton, Radio, Fernseher*⟩; aufdrehen ⟨*Heizung, Gas*⟩; heller machen ⟨*Licht*⟩

**'turnaround** *n.* **(a)** (change) [Kehrt]wende, *die*

**(b)** (of aircraft, ship, vehicle) Abfertigung, *die*

**turned-up** /'tɜːndʌp/ *adj.* ~ **nose** Stupsnase, *die* (ugs.)

**'turning** *n.* Abzweigung, *die*

**'turning point** *n.* Wendepunkt, *der*

**turnip** /'tɜːnɪp/ *n.* [weiße] Rübe

**turn:** ~**out** *n.* (of people) Beteiligung, *die* (for an + *Dat.*); ~**over** *n.* **(a)** (Commerc.) Umsatz, *der;* (of stock) Umschlag, *der;* **(b)** (of staff) Fluktuation, *die;* ~**pike** *n.* (Amer.) gebührenpflichtige Autobahn; ~**stile** *n.* Drehkreuz, *das;* ~**table** *n.* Plattenteller, *der;* ~**-up** *n.* (Brit. Fashion) Aufschlag, *der*

**turpentine** /'tɜːpntaɪn/ *n.* Terpentin, *das*

**turps** /tɜːps/ *n.* (coll.) Terpentin, *das* (ugs.)

**turquoise** /'tɜːkwɔɪz/ ① *n.* **(a)** Türkis, *der*

**(b)** (colour) Türkis, *das*

② *adj.* türkis[farben]

**turret** /'tʌrɪt/ *n.* Türmchen, *das*

**turreted** /'tʌrɪtɪd/ *adj.* ⟨*Schloss*⟩ mit Mauertürmchen

**turtle** /'tɜːtl/ *n.* **(a)** Meeresschildkröte, *die*

**(b)** (Amer.: freshwater reptile) Wasserschildkröte, *die*

**'turtleneck** *n.* ~**neck pullover** Pullover mit Stehbund

**turves** ▶ TURF B

**tusk** /tʌsk/ *n.* Stoßzahn, *der*

**tussle** /'tʌsl/ ① *n.* Gerangel, *das* (ugs.)

② *v.i.* sich balgen

**tutor** /'tjuːtə(r)/ *n.* [private] ~: [Privat]lehrer, *der*/-lehrerin, *die*

**tut[-tut]** /tʌt('tʌt)/ ① *int.* na[, na]

② *v.i.,* -tt-: ~ [with disapproval] [missbilligend] „na, na!" sagen

**tutu** /'tuːtuː/ *n.* Tutu, *das*

**tuxedo** /tʌk'siːdəʊ/ *n., pl.* ~**s** *or* ~**es** (Amer.) Smoking, *der*

**TV** /tiː'viː/ *n.* **(a)** Fernsehen, *das*

**(b)** (television set) Fernseher, *der* (ugs.)

**twaddle** /'twɒdl/ *n.* Gewäsch, *das* (ugs.)

**twang** /twæŋ/ ① *v.t.* zupfen ⟨*Saite*⟩

② *n.* [nasal] ~: Näseln, *das*

**tweed** /twiːd/ *n.* Tweed, *der*

**tweezers** /'twiːzəz/ *n. pl.* [pair of] ~: Pinzette, *die*

**twelfth** /twelfθ/ ① *adj.* zwölft...

② *n.* (fraction) Zwölftel, *das. See also* EIGHTH

**twelve** /twelv/ ① *adj.* zwölf

② *n.* Zwölf, *die. See also* EIGHT

**twentieth** /'twentɪɪθ/ ① *adj.* zwanzigst...

② *n.* (fraction) Zwanzigstel, *das. See also* EIGHTH

t

**twenty** /'twentɪ/ ① *adj.* zwanzig
  ② *n.* Zwanzig, *die. See also* EIGHT; EIGHTY 2
**twice** /twaɪs/ *adv.* (a) zweimal
  (b) (doubly) doppelt
**twiddle** /'twɪdl/ *v.t.* herumdrehen an
  (+ *Dat.*) (ugs.); ∼ **one's thumbs** (lit. or fig.)
  Däumchen drehen
**twig¹** /twɪg/ *n.* Zweig, *der*
**twig²** (coll.) ① *v.t.*, **-gg-** kapieren (ugs.)
  ② *v.i.*, **-gg-** es kapieren (ugs.)
**twilight** /'twaɪlaɪt/ *n.* (a) (evening light)
  Dämmerlicht, *das*
  (b) (period of half-light) Dämmerung, *die*
**twin** /twɪn/ ① *attrib. adj.* (a) Zwillings-
  (b) (forming a pair) Doppel-
  ② *n.* Zwilling, *der*
  ③ *v.t.* Bottrop is ∼ned with Blackpool
  Bottrop und Blackpool sind Partnerstädte
**twin 'beds** *n. pl.* zwei Einzelbetten *Pl.*
**twine** /twaɪn/ ① *n.* Bindfaden, *der*
  ② *v.i.* sich winden (**about, around** um)
**twinge** /twɪndʒ/ *n.* Stechen, *das;* ∼[s] of
  **conscience** (fig.) Gewissensbisse *Pl.*
**twinkle** /'twɪŋkl/ ① *v.i.* funkeln (**with** vor
  + *Dat.*)
  ② *n.* Funkeln, *das*
**twinkling** /'twɪŋklɪŋ/ *n.* in a ∼, in the ∼ of
  an eye im Handumdrehen
**'twin town** *n.* (Brit.) Partnerstadt, *die*
**twirl** /twɜːl/ ① *v.t.* [schnell] drehen
  ② *v.i.* wirbeln (**around** über + *Akk.*)
**twist** /twɪst/ ① *v.t.* (a) verdrehen ⟨*Worte,
  Bedeutung*⟩; ∼ **one's ankle** sich (*Dat.*) den
  Knöchel verrenken; ∼ **sb.'s arm** jmdm. den
  Arm umdrehen; (fig.) jmdm. [die]
  Daumenschrauben anlegen
  (b) (rotate) drehen
  ② *v.i.* sich winden
  ③ *n.* (a) (motion) Drehung, *die*
  (b) (unexpected occurrence) überraschende
  Wendung
**'twisted** *adj.* verbogen; (fig.) verdreht (ugs.
  abwertend) ⟨*Geist*⟩; verquer ⟨*Humor*⟩
**twit** /twɪt/ *n.* (Brit. coll.) Trottel, *der* (ugs.)
**twitch** /twɪtʃ/ ① *v.i.* ⟨*Mund, Lippe:*⟩ zucken
  ② *n.* Zucken, *das*
**twitter** /'twɪtə(r)/ ① *n.* Zwitschern, *das*
  ② *v.i.* zwitschern
**two** /tuː/ ① *adj.* zwei

  ② *n.* Zwei, *die. See also* EIGHT
**two:** ∼**-bit** *adj.* (Amer.) (of poor quality) mies
  (ugs.) ∼**-faced** /'tuːfeɪst/ *adj.* (fig.) falsch;
  ∼**fold** *adj., adv.* zweifach; **a** ∼**fold increase**
  ein Anstieg auf das Doppelte; ∼**-lane** *adj.*
  zweispurig; ∼**-piece** ① *n.* Zweiteiler, *der;*
  ② *adj.* zweiteilig; ∼**-seater** /-'-/ *n.*
  Zweisitzer, *der;* ∼**some** /'tuːsəm/ *n.* Paar,
  *das;* ∼**-storey** *adj.* zweigeschossig;
  ∼**-tone** *adj.* zweifarbig; ∼**-up** ∼**-down** *n.*
  kleines [Reihen]haus; ∼**-way** *adj.* (a)
  zweibahnig (Verkehrsw.); '∼**-way traffic ahead**'
  „Achtung Gegenverkehr"; (b) ∼**-way mirror**
  Einwegspiegel, *der*
**tycoon** /taɪ'kuːn/ *n.* Magnat, *der*
**tying** ▶ TIE 1, 2
**type** /taɪp/ ① *n.* (a) Art, *die;* (person) Typ,
  *der;* **what** ∼ **of car ...?** was für ein Auto ...?
  (b) (Printing) Drucktype, *die*
  ② *v.t.* [mit der Maschine] schreiben; tippen
  (ugs.)
  ③ *v.i.* Maschine schreiben
  ■ **type 'out** *v.t.* [mit der Schreibmaschine]
  abschreiben; abtippen (ugs.)
**type:** ∼**cast** *v.t.* [auf eine bestimmte Rolle]
  festlegen; ∼**face** *n.* Schriftbild, *das;*
  ∼**script** *n.* maschine[n]geschriebene
  Fassung; ∼**setter** *n.* [Schrift]setzer, *der*/
  -setzerin, *die;* ∼**setting** *n.* [Schrift]setzen,
  *das;* ∼**writer** *n.* Schreibmaschine, *die;*
  ∼**written** *adj.* maschine[n]geschrieben
**typhoid** /'taɪfɔɪd/ *n.* ∼ **[fever]** Typhus, *der*
**typhoon** /taɪ'fuːn/ *n.* Taifun, *der*
**typical** /'tɪpɪkl/ *adj.* typisch (**of** für)
**typify** /'tɪpɪfaɪ/ *v.t.* ∼ **sth.** als typisches
  Beispiel für etw. dienen
**typing** /'taɪpɪŋ/ *n.* Maschineschreiben, *das*
**'typing error** *n.* Tippfehler, *der*
**typist** /'taɪpɪst/ *n.* Schreibkraft, *die*
**typography** /taɪ'pɒgrəfɪ/ *n.* Typographie,
  *die*
**tyrannical** /tɪ'rænɪkl/ *adj.* tyrannisch
**tyranny** /'tɪrənɪ/ *n.* Tyrannei, *die*
**tyrant** /'taɪərənt/ *n.* Tyrann, *der*
**tyre** /'taɪə(r)/ *n.* Reifen, *der*
**'tyre pressure** *n.* Reifendruck, *der*
**tzar** *etc.* ▶ TSAR *etc.*

# Uu

**U, u** /juː/ *n.* U, u, *das*

**'U-bend** *n.* U-Rohr, *das*

**ubiquitous** /juːˈbɪkwɪtəs/ *adj.* allgegenwärtig

**udder** /ˈʌdə(r)/ *n.* Euter, *das*

**UFO** /ˈjuːfəʊ/ *n.*, *pl.* ~s Ufo, *das*

**ugh** /ʌh, ʊh, ɜːh/ *int.* bah

**ugliness** /ˈʌɡlɪnɪs/ *n.* Hässlichkeit, *die*

**ugly** /ˈʌɡlɪ/ *adj.* (a) hässlich
(b) (nasty) übel ⟨Wunde, Laune usw.⟩

**UHF** *abbr.* = **ultra-high frequency** UHF

**UHT** *abbr.* = **ultra heat-treated** ultrahoch erhitzt

**UK** *abbr.* = **United Kingdom**

**Ukraine** /juːˈkreɪn/ *pr. n.* Ukraine, *die*

**Ukrainian** /juːˈkreɪnɪən/ **1** *adj.* ukrainisch; **sb. is** ~: jmd. ist Ukrainer/ Ukrainerin
**2** *n.* (a) (person) Ukrainer, *der*/Ukrainerin, *die*
(b) (language) Ukrainisch, *das; see also* ENGLISH 2 A

**ulcer** /ˈʌlsə(r)/ *n.* Geschwür, *das*

**ulterior** /ʌlˈtɪərɪə(r)/ *adj.* hintergründig; ~ **motive** Hintergedanke, *der*

**ultimate** /ˈʌltɪmət/ **1** *attrib. adj.* (a) (final) letzt...; (eventual) endgültig ⟨Sieg⟩
(b) (fundamental) tiefst...
**2** *n.* **the** ~ **in comfort/luxury** der Gipfel an Bequemlichkeit/Luxus

**'ultimately** *adv.* (a) (in the end) schließlich
(b) (in the last analysis) letzten Endes

**ultimatum** /ʌltɪˈmeɪtəm/ *n.*, *pl.* ~s *or* **ultimata** /ʌltɪˈmeɪtə/ Ultimatum, *das*

**ultra'sound** *n.* Ultraschall, *der*

**ultra'violet** *adj.* (Phys.) ultraviolett; UV- ⟨Lampe, Filter⟩

**umbilical cord** /ʌmˈbɪlɪkl kɔːd/ *n.* Nabelschnur, *die*

**umbrage** /ˈʌmbrɪdʒ/ *n.* **take** ~ [**at sth.**] [an etw. (+ *Dat.*)] Anstoß nehmen

**umbrella** /ʌmˈbrelə/ *n.* [Regen]schirm, *der*

**um'brella stand** *n.* Schirmständer, *der*

**umpire** /ˈʌmpaɪə(r)/ *n.* Schiedsrichter, *der*/ -richterin, *die*

**umpteen** /ʌmpˈtiːn/ *adj.* (coll.) zig (ugs.); x (ugs.)

**unabashed** /ʌnəˈbæʃt/ *adj.* ungeniert

**unable** /ʌnˈeɪbl/ *pred. adj.* **be** ~ **to do sth.** etw. nicht tun können

**unabridged** /ʌnəˈbrɪdʒd/ *adj.* ungekürzt

**unac'ceptable** *adj.* unannehmbar

**unaccompanied** /ʌnəˈkʌmpənɪd/ *adj.* ohne Begleitung *nachgestellt*

**unac'countable** *adj.* unerklärlich

**unaccountably** /ʌnəˈkaʊntəblɪ/ *adv.* unerklärlicherweise

**unac'customed** *adj.* ungewohnt; **be** ~ **to sth.** etw. (Akk.) nicht gewöhnt sein

**unadulterated** /ʌnəˈdʌltəreɪtɪd/ *adj.* (a) (pure) unverfälscht
(b) (utter) völlig

**unadventurous** /ʌnədˈventʃərəs/ *adj.* bieder ⟨Person⟩; ereignislos ⟨Leben⟩

**unafraid** /ʌnəˈfreɪd/ *adj.* **be** ~ [**of sb./sth.**] keine Angst [vor jmdm./etw.] haben

**unaided** /ʌnˈeɪdɪd/ *adj.* ohne fremde Hilfe

**unalike** /ʌnəˈlaɪk/ *pred. adj.* unähnlich

**unambiguous** /ʌnæmˈbɪɡjʊəs/ *adj.* unzweideutig

**unambitious** /ʌnæmˈbɪʃəs/ *adj.* ⟨Person⟩ ohne Ergeiz

**unanimity** /juːnəˈnɪmɪtɪ/ *n.* Einmütigkeit, *die*

**unanimous** /juːˈnænɪməs/ *adj.* einstimmig; **be** ~ **in doing sth.** etw. einmütig tun

**u'nanimously** *adv.* einstimmig

**unannounced** /ʌnəˈnaʊnst/ *adj.* unangemeldet

**unappetizing** /ʌnˈæpɪtaɪzɪŋ/ *adj.* unappetitlich

**unarmed** /ʌnˈɑːmd/ *adj.* unbewaffnet; ~ **combat** Kampf ohne Waffen

**unassuming** /ʌnəˈsjuːmɪŋ/ *adj.* bescheiden

**unattached** /ʌnəˈtætʃt/ *adj.* (a) nicht befestigt
(b) (without a partner) ungebunden

**unat'tended** *adj.* (a) ~ **to** (not dealt with) unerledigt; nicht bedient ⟨Kunde⟩; nicht behandelt ⟨Patient⟩
(b) (not supervised) unbewacht ⟨Parkplatz, Gepäck⟩

**unat'tractive** *adj.* unattraktiv

**unauthorized** /ʌnˈɔːθəraɪzd/ *adj.* unbefugt; **no entry for** ~ **persons** Zutritt für Unbefugte verboten

**una'vailable** *adj.* nicht erhältlich ⟨Ware⟩; **be** ~ **for comment** zur Stellungnahme nicht zur Verfügung stehen

**una'voidable** *adj.* unvermeidlich

**unaware** /ʌnəˈweə(r)/ *adj.* **be** ~ **of sth.** sich (Dat.) einer Sache (Gen.) nicht bewusst sein

**unawares** /ʌnəˈweəz/ *adv.* **catch sb.** ~: jmdn. überraschen

**unbalanced** /ʌnˈbælənst/ adj. **(a)** unausgewogen
**(b)** (mentally ∼) unausgeglichen

**un'bearable** adj., **unbearably** /ʌnˈbeərəblɪ/ adv. unerträglich

**unbeatable** /ʌnˈbiːˈtəbl/ adj. unschlagbar (ugs.)

**un'beaten** adj. **(a)** ungeschlagen
**(b)** (not surpassed) unerreicht; ungebrochen ⟨Rekord⟩

**unbe'lievable** adj. **(a)** unglaublich
**(b)** (tremendous) unwahrscheinlich

**unbiased, unbiassed** /ʌnˈbaɪəst/ adj. unvoreingenommen

**unblemished** /ʌnˈblemɪʃt/ adj. makellos ⟨Haut, Ruf⟩

**un'block** v.t. frei machen

**un'bolt** v.t. aufriegeln ⟨Tür⟩

**unborn** /ʌnˈbɔːn, attrib. ˈʌnbɔːn/ adj. ungeboren

**un'breakable** adj. unzerbrechlich

**unburden** /ʌnˈbɜːdn/ v.t. ∼ oneself sein Herz ausschütten

**un'button** v.t. aufknöpfen

**uncalled-for** /ʌnˈkɔːldfɔː(r)/ adj. unangebracht

**uncanny** /ʌnˈkænɪ/ adj. unheimlich

**uncared-for** /ʌnˈkeədfɔː(r)/ adj. vernachlässigt

**uncaring** /ʌnˈkeərɪŋ/ adj. gleichgültig

**unceasing** /ʌnˈsiːsɪŋ/ adj. unaufhörlich

**unceremonious** /ʌnserɪˈməʊnɪəs/ adj. **(a)** (informal) formlos
**(b)** (abrupt) brüsk

**uncere'moniously** adv. ohne Umschweife

**un'certain** adj. **(a)** (not sure) be ∼ [whether ...] sich (Dat.) nicht sicher sein[, ob ...]
**(b)** (not clear) ungewiss ⟨Ergebnis, Zukunft⟩; of ∼ age/origin unbestimmten Alters/ unbestimmter Herkunft
**(c)** (ambiguous) vage; in no ∼ terms ganz eindeutig

**uncertainty** /ʌnˈsɜːtntɪ/ n. **(a)** Ungewissheit, die
**(b)** (hesitation) Unsicherheit, die

**unchanged** /ʌnˈtʃeɪndʒd/ adj. unverändert

**uncharacteristic** /ʌnkærɪktəˈrɪstɪk/ adj. uncharakteristisch (of für)

**un'charitable** adj., **uncharitably** /ʌnˈtʃærɪtəblɪ/ adv. lieblos

**un'civil** adj. unhöflich

**uncle** /ˈʌŋkl/ n. Onkel, der

**un'comfortable** adj. **(a)** unbequem
**(b)** (feeling discomfort) be ∼: sich unbehaglich fühlen
**(c)** (uneasy, disconcerting) unangenehm; peinlich ⟨Stille⟩

**un'comfortably** adv. unbequem; be ∼ aware of sth. sich (Dat.) einer Sache peinlich bewusst sein

**un'common** adj. ungewöhnlich

**uncompli'mentary** adj. wenig schmeichelhaft

**uncompromising** /ʌnˈkɒmprəmaɪzɪŋ/ adj. kompromisslos

**uncon'ditional** adj. bedingungslos ⟨Kapitulation⟩; kategorisch ⟨Ablehnung⟩; ⟨Versprechen⟩ ohne Vorbehalte

**unconfirmed** /ʌnkənˈfɜːmd/ adj. unbestätigt

**un'conscious** ⒈ adj. **(a)** (Med.) bewusstlos
**(b)** (unaware) be ∼ of sth. sich einer Sache (Gen.) nicht bewusst sein
**(c)** (not intended; Psych.) unbewusst
⒉ n. Unbewusste, das

**un'consciously** adv. unbewusst

**uncontrollable** /ʌnkənˈtrəʊləbl/ adj. unkontrollierbar; the child is ∼: das Kind ist nicht zu bändigen

**uncon'ventional** adj., **uncon'ventionally** adv. unkonventionell

**unconvinced** /ʌnkənˈvɪnst/ adj. nicht überzeugt; remain ∼: sich nicht überzeugen lassen

**uncooked** /ʌnˈkʊkt/ adj. roh

**unco'operative** adj. unkooperativ; (unhelpful) wenig hilfsbereit

**uncoordinated** /ʌnkəʊˈɔːdɪneɪtɪd/ adj. unkoordiniert

**un'cork** v.t. entkorken

**uncouth** /ʌnˈkuːθ/ adj. ungehobelt ⟨Person, Benehmen⟩; grob ⟨Bemerkung⟩

**un'cover** v.t. aufdecken

**undaunted** /ʌnˈdɔːntɪd/ adj. unverzagt

**undecided** /ʌndɪˈsaɪdɪd/ adj. **(a)** (not settled) nicht entschieden
**(b)** (hesitant) unentschlossen

**undeclared** /ʌndɪˈkleəd/ adj. ∼ income (for tax) nicht angegebenes Einkommen

**'undelete** v.t. (Comp.) wiederherstellen

**undemanding** /ʌndɪˈmɑːndɪŋ/ adj. anspruchslos

**unde'niable** adj., **undeniably** /ʌndɪˈnaɪəblɪ/ adv. unbestreitbar

**under** /ˈʌndə(r)/ ⒈ prep. **(a)** (underneath, below) unter ⟨position: + Dat.; motion: + Akk.⟩; from ∼ the table/bed unter dem Tisch/Bett hervor
**(b)** (undergoing) ∼ treatment in Behandlung; ∼ repair in Reparatur; ∼ construction im Bau
**(c)** (in conditions of) bei ⟨Stress, hohen Temperaturen usw.⟩
**(d)** (subject to) unter (+ Dat.); ∼ the terms of the contract nach den Bestimmungen des Vertrags
**(e)** (with the use of) unter (+ Dat.); ∼ an assumed name unter falschem Namen
**(f)** (less than) unter (+ Dat.)
⒉ adv. **(a)** (in or to a lower or subordinate position) darunter

**(b)** (in/into a state of unconsciousness) be ∿/put sb. ∿: in Narkose liegen/jmdn. in Narkose versetzen

**under:** ∿a'**chieve** *v.i.* unter dem erreichbaren Leistungsniveau bleiben; ∿**-age** *adj.* minderjährig; ∿**carriage** *n.* Fahrwerk, *das;* ∿**clothes** *n. pl.,* ∿**clothing** *n.* ▶ UNDERWEAR; ∿**coat** *n.* (layer of paint) Grundierung, *die;* (paint) Grundierfarbe, *die;* ∿'**cover** *adj.* (disguised) getarnt; (secret) verdeckt; ∿cover agent Geheimagent, *der;* ∿**current** *n.* Unterströmung, *die;* (fig.) Unterton, *der;* ∿'**cut** *v.t.,* ∿cut unterbieten; ∿**dog** *n.* (a) (in fight) Unterlegene, *der/die;* **(b)** (fig.) Benachteiligte, *der/die;* ∿'**done** *adj.* halb gar; ∿**estimate** /ʌndər'estɪmeɪt/ 1 *v.t.* unterschätzen; 2 /ʌndər'estɪmət/ *n.* Unterschätzung, *die;* ∿'**fed** *adj.* unterernährt; ∿'**foot** *adv.* am Boden; be trampled ∿foot mit Füßen zertrampelt werden; ∿'**go** *v.t., forms as* GO 1: durchmachen; ∿go treatment sich einer Behandlung unterziehen; ∿go a change sich verändern; ∿'**graduate** *n.* ∿graduate [student] Student/Studentin vor der ersten Prüfung; ∿**ground** 1 /-'-'-/ *adv.* **(a)** unter der Erde; (Mining) unter Tage; **(b)** (fig.) (in hiding) im Untergrund; (into hiding) in den Untergrund; 2 /'---/ *adj.* unterirdisch ⟨Höhle, See⟩; ∿ground railway Untergrundbahn, *die;* U-Bahn, *die;* ∿ground car park Tiefgarage, *die;* 3 /'---/ *n.* (railway) U-Bahn, *die;* ∿ground station/train U-Bahnhof, *der/*U-Bahn-Zug, *der;* ∿**growth** *n.* Unterholz, *das;* ∿**hand**, ∿'**handed** *adj.* **(a)** (secret) heimlich; **(b)** (crafty) hinterhältig; ∿**lay** *n.* Unterlage, *die;* ∿'**lie** *v.t., forms as* LIE[2]: ∿lie sth. (fig.) einer Sache ⟨Dat.⟩ zugrunde liegen; ∿**lying cause** eigentliche Ursache; ∿'**line** *v.t.* unterstreichen

**underling** /'ʌndəlɪŋ/ *n.* Untergebene, *der/die*

**under:** ∿'**lying** ▶ UNDERLIE; ∿'**mine** *v.t.* **(a)** unterhöhlen; **(b)** (fig.) untergraben; unterminieren ⟨Autorität⟩

**underneath** /ʌndə'ni:θ/ 1 *prep.* unter (*position:* + *Dat.; motion:* + *Akk.*) 2 *adv.* darunter

**under:** ∿'**nourished** *adj.* unterernährt; ∿'**paid** *adj.* unterbezahlt; ∿**pants** *n. pl.* Unterhose, *die;* ∿**pass** *n.* Unterführung, *die;* ∿'**play** *v.t.* herunterspielen; ∿'**privileged** *adj.* unterprivilegiert; ∿'**rate** *v.t.* unterschätzen; ∿**seal** *n.* Unterbodenschutz, *der;* ∿**signed** /ʌndə'saɪnd/ *adj.* (esp. Law) the ∿signed der/die Unterzeichnete/(*pl.*) die Unterzeichneten (Papierdt.); ∿'**staffed** *adj.* unterbesetzt; be ∿staffed an Personalmangel leiden

**understand** /ʌndə'stænd/ 1 *v.t.,* **understood** /ʌndə'stʊd/ **(a)** verstehen; make oneself understood sich verständlich machen **(b)** (have heard) gehört haben

**(c)** (take as implied) it was understood that ...: es wurde allgemein angenommen, dass ... 2 *v.i.,* **understood (a)** verstehen **(b)** (gather, hear) if I ∿ correctly wenn ich mich nicht irre; he is, I ∿, no longer here er ist, wie ich höre, nicht mehr hier

**understandable** /ʌndə'stændəbl/ *adj.* verständlich

**understandably** /ʌndə'stændəblɪ/ *adv.* verständlicherweise

**under'standing** 1 *adj.* verständnisvoll 2 *n.* **(a)** (agreement) Verständigung, *die;* reach an ∿ with sb. sich mit jmdm. verständigen; on the ∿ that ...: unter der Voraussetzung, dass ... **(b)** (intelligence) Verstand, *der* **(c)** (insight) Verständnis, *das* (of, for für)

**under:** ∿**statement** *n.* Untertreibung, *die;* ∿**study** *n.* Ersatzspieler, *der/* -spielerin, *die;* ∿'**take** *v.t., forms as* TAKE 1: unternehmen; ∿take a task eine Aufgabe übernehmen; ∿take to do sth. sich verpflichten, etw. zu tun; ∿**taker** *n.* Leichenbestatter, *der/*-bestatterin, *die;* ∿'**taking** *n.* **(a)** (task) Aufgabe, *die;* **(b)** (pledge) Versprechen, *das;* ∿**tone** *n.* in ∿tones or an ∿tone mit gedämpfter Stimme; ∿tone of criticism kritischer Unterton, *der;* ∿**tow** *n.* Unterströmung, *die;* ∿'**value** *v.t.* unterbewerten; ∿**water** 1 /'----/ *attrib. adj.* Unterwasser-; 2 /--'--/ *adv.* unter Wasser; ∿**wear** *n.* Unterwäsche, *die;* ∿'**weight** *adj.* untergewichtig; ∿**world** *n.* Unterwelt, *der*

**undeserved** /ʌndɪ'zɜ:vd/ *adj.* unverdient

**unde'sirable** *adj.* unerwünscht; it is ∿ that ...: es ist nicht wünschenswert, dass ...

**undeveloped** /ʌndɪ'veləpt/ *adj.* **(a)** (immature) nicht voll ausgebildet **(b)** (not built on) nicht bebaut

**undies** /'ʌndɪz/ *n. pl.* (coll.) Unterwäsche, *die*

**un'dignified** *adj.* blamabel

**undisciplined** /ʌn'dɪsɪplɪnd/ *adj.* undiszipliniert

**undiscovered** /ʌndɪ'skʌvəd/ *adj.* unentdeckt

**undisguised** /ʌndɪs'gaɪzd/ *adj.* unverhohlen

**undisturbed** /ʌndɪ'stɜ:bd/ *adj.* (not interrupted) ungestört

**undo** /ʌn'du:/ *v.t.,* **undoes** /ʌn'dʌz/, **undoing** /ʌn'du:ɪŋ/, **undid** /ʌn'dɪd/, **undone** /ʌn'dʌn/ (unfasten) aufmachen

**un'done** *adj.* **(a)** (not accomplished) unerledigt **(b)** (not fastened) offen

**undoubted** /ʌn'daʊtɪd/ *adj.* unzweifelhaft

**un'doubtedly** *adv.* zweifellos

**un'dress** 1 *v.t.* ausziehen; get ∿ed sich ausziehen 2 *v.i.* sich ausziehen

**undrinkable** /ʌn'drɪŋkəbl/ *adj.* nicht trinkbar; ungenießbar

**un'due** *attrib. adj.* übertrieben; übermäßig

**undulating** /'ʌndjʊleɪtɪŋ/ *adj.* Wellen⟨linie⟩; ~ **country** sanfte Hügellandschaft

**unduly** /ʌn'dju:lɪ/ *adv.* übermäßig

**undying** /ʌn'daɪɪŋ/ *adj.* ewig; unsterblich ⟨Ruhm⟩

**unearth** /ʌn'ɜ:θ/ *v.t.* (a) ausgraben (b) (fig.: discover) aufdecken

**unearthly** /ʌn'ɜ:θlɪ/ *adj.* unheimlich; **at an** ~ **hour** in aller Herrgottsfrühe

**un'easy** *adj.* (a) (anxious) besorgt; **he felt** ~: ihm war unbehaglich zumute (b) (restless) unruhig

**uneatable** /ʌn'i:təbl/ *adj.* ungenießbar

**uneco'nomic** *adj.* unrentabel

**uneco'nomical** *adj.* ~ [to run] unwirtschaftlich

**uneducated** /ʌn'edjʊkeɪtɪd/ *adj.* ungebildet

**unemotional** /ʌnɪ'məʊʃənl/ *adj.* emotionslos; nüchtern

**unemployed** /ʌnɪm'plɔɪd/ ① *adj.* arbeitslos ② *n. pl.* **the** ~: die Arbeitslosen *Pl.*

**unem'ployment** *n.* Arbeitslosigkeit, *die*

**unem'ployment benefit** *n.* Arbeitslosengeld, *das*

**un'ending** *adj.* endlos

**un'equal** *adj.* unterschiedlich; ungleich ⟨Kampf⟩; **be** ~ **to sth.** einer Sache (*Dat.*) nicht gewachsen sein

**unequalled** (*Amer.*: **unequaled**) /ʌn'i:kwld/ *adj.* unerreicht

**une'quivocal** *adj.* eindeutig

**unerring** /ʌn'ɜ:rɪŋ/ *adj.* unfehlbar

**un'ethical** *adj.* unmoralisch

**un'even** *adj.* (a) (not smooth) uneben (b) (not uniform) ungleichmäßig (c) (odd) ungerade ⟨Zahl⟩

**un'evenly** *adv.* ungleichmäßig

**uneventful** /ʌnɪ'ventfl/ *adj.* ereignislos

**unexciting** /ʌnɪk'saɪtɪŋ/ *adj.* wenig aufregend; (boring) langweilig

**unex'pected** *adj.* unerwartet

**unexplained** /ʌnɪk'spleɪnd/ *adj.* ungeklärt

**un'fair** *adj.* unfair; ungerecht

**un'fairly** *adv.* (a) (unjustly) ungerecht; unfair ⟨spielen⟩ (b) (unreasonably) zu Unrecht

**un'fairness** *n.* Ungerechtigkeit, *die*

**un'faithful** *adj.* untreu

**unfa'miliar** *adj.* (a) (strange) unbekannt; ungewohnt ⟨Arbeit⟩ (b) **be** ~ **with sth.** sich mit etw. nicht auskennen

**un'fasten** *v.t.* (a) öffnen (b) (detach) lösen

**un'favourable** *adj.* ungünstig

**un'favourably** *adv.* ungünstig; **be** ~ **disposed towards sb./sth.** jmdm./etw. gegenüber ablehnend eingestellt sein

**un'feeling** *adj.* gefühllos

**unfinished** /ʌn'fɪnɪʃt/ *adj.* unvollendet ⟨Werk⟩; unerledigt ⟨Arbeit⟩

**un'fit** *adj.* (a) ungeeignet (b) (not physically fit) nicht fit (ugs.); ~ **for military service** [wehrdienst]untauglich

**un'flattering** *adj.* wenig schmeichelhaft

**un'flinching** *adj.* unerschrocken

**un'fold** ① *v.t.* entfalten; ausbreiten ⟨Zeitung, Landkarte⟩ ② *v.i.* sich entfalten; (develop) sich entwickeln

**unfore'seen** *adj.* unvorhergesehen

**unforgettable** /ʌnfə'getəbl/ *adj.* unvergesslich

**unforgivable** /ʌnfə'gɪvəbl/ *adj.* unverzeihlich

**un'fortunate** *adj.* unglücklich

**un'fortunately** *adv.* leider

**un'founded** *adj.* (fig.) unbegründet

**un'freeze** *v.t. & i.,* **unfroze** /ʌn'frəʊz/, **unfrozen** /ʌn'frəʊzn/ auftauen

**un'friendly** *adj.* unfreundlich; feindlich ⟨Staat⟩

**unfulfilled** /ʌnfʊl'fɪld/ *adj.* unerfüllt ⟨Person⟩

**un'furl** ① *v.t.* aufrollen; losmachen ⟨Segel⟩ ② *v.i.* sich aufrollen

**un'furnished** *adj.* unmöbliert

**ungainly** /ʌn'geɪnlɪ/ *adj.* unbeholfen

**ungram'matical** *adj.* ungrammatisch

**un'grateful** *adj.* undankbar

**un'happily** *adv.* (a) unglücklich (b) (unfortunately) leider

**un'happiness** *n.* Bekümmertheit, *die*

**un'happy** *adj.* unglücklich; (not content) unzufrieden (about with); **be** *or* **feel** ~ **about doing sth.** Bedenken haben, etw. zu tun

**un'harmed** *adj.* unbeschädigt; (uninjured) unverletzt

**un'healthy** *adj.* ungesund

**unheard-of** /ʌn'hɜ:dɒv/ *adj.* (unknown) [gänzlich] unbekannt; (unprecedented) beispiellos; (outrageous) unerhört

**un'helpful** *adj.* wenig hilfsbereit ⟨Person⟩; ⟨Bemerkung, Kritik⟩ die einem nicht weiterhilft

**un'hook** *v.t.* vom Haken nehmen; aufhaken ⟨Kleid⟩

**un'hurt** *adj.* unverletzt

**unhy'gienic** *adj.* unhygienisch

**unicorn** /'ju:nɪkɔ:n/ *n.* Einhorn, *das*

**uni'dentified** *adj.* nicht identifiziert; ~ **flying object** unbekanntes Flugobjekt

**unification** /ju:nɪfɪ'keɪʃn/ *n.* Einigung, *die*

**uniform** /'ju:nɪfɔ:m/ ① *adj.* einheitlich; **be** ~ **in shape/size** die gleiche Form/Größe haben

**2** *n.* Uniform, *die;* **in/out of** ∼: in/ohne Uniform

**uniformity** /juːnɪˈfɔːmɪtɪ/ *n.* Einheitlichkeit, *die*

**'uniformly** *adv.* einheitlich

**unify** /ˈjuːnɪfaɪ/ *v.t.* einigen

**unilateral** /juːnɪˈlætərl/ *adj.* einseitig

**uni'maginable** *adj.* unvorstellbar

**uni'maginative** *adj.* fantasielos

**unim'portant** *adj.* unwichtig; bedeutungslos

**unimpressed** /ʌnɪmˈprest/ *adj.* nicht beeindruckt

**unin'habitable** *adj.* unbewohnbar

**unin'habited** *adj.* unbewohnt

**un'injured** *adj.* unverletzt

**uninspired** /ʌnɪnˈspaɪəd/ *adj.* einfallslos; **I am/feel** ∼: mir fehlt die Inspiration

**uninspiring** /ʌnɪnˈspaɪərɪŋ/ *adj.* langweilig

**unin'telligent** *adj.* nicht intelligent

**unin'telligible** *adj.* unverständlich

**unin'tended** *adj.* unbeabsichtigt

**unin'tentional** *adj.,* **unin'tentionally** *adv.* unabsichtlich

**un'interested** *adj.* desinteressiert (**in an** + *Dat.*)

**un'interesting** *adj.* uninteressant

**uninterrupted** /ʌnɪntəˈrʌptɪd/ *adj.* ununterbrochen

**uninvited** /ʌnɪnˈvaɪtɪd/ *adj.* ungeladen

**union** /ˈjuːnɪən/ *n.* (a) (trade ∼) Gewerkschaft, *die* (b) (Polit.) Union, *die*

**Union 'Jack** *n.* (Brit.) Union Jack, *der*

**unique** /juːˈniːk/ *adj.* einzigartig

**unisex** /ˈjuːnɪseks/ *adj.* Unisex⟨*mantel, -kleidung*⟩; ∼ **hairdresser** Damen-und-Herren-Frisör, *der*

**unison** /ˈjuːnɪsən/ *n.* Unisono, *das;* **in** ∼: einstimmig; **act in** ∼ (fig.) vereint handeln

**unit** /ˈjuːnɪt/ *n.* (a) (also Mil., Math.) Einheit, *die;* ∼ **of length/monetary** ∼: Längen-/Währungseinheit, *die* (b) (piece of furniture) Element, *das;* **kitchen** ∼: Küchenelement, *das*

**unite** /juːˈnaɪt/ **1** *v.t.* vereinigen; einen, einigen ⟨*Partei, Mitglieder*⟩ **2** *v.i.* sich vereinigen

**u'nited** *adj.* (a) (harmonious) einig (b) (combined) gemeinsam

**United:** ∼ **'Kingdom** *pr. n.* Vereinigtes Königreich [Großbritannien und Nordirland]; ∼ **'Nations** *pr. n. sing.* Vereinte Nationen *Pl.;* ∼ **States [of A'merica]** *pr. n. sing.* Vereinigte Staaten [von Amerika] *Pl.*

**unit 'price** *n.* Stückpreis, *der*

**unity** /ˈjuːnɪtɪ/ *n.* Einheit, *die*

**universal** /juːnɪˈvɜːsl/ *adj.,* **uni'versally** *adv.* allgemein

**universe** /ˈjuːnɪvɜːs/ *n.* Universum, *das*

**university** /juːnɪˈvɜːsɪtɪ/ *n.* Universität, *die; attrib.* Universitäts-

**uni'versity place** *n.* Studienplatz, *der*

**un'just** *adj.* ungerecht

**unjustified** /ʌnˈdʒʌstɪfaɪd/ *adj.* ungerechtfertigt

**unkempt** /ʌnˈkempt/ *adj.* ungepflegt

**un'kind** *adj.,* **un'kindly** *adv.* unfreundlich

**un'kindness** *n.* Unfreundlichkeit, *die*

**un'known** **1** *adj.* unbekannt **2** *adv.* ∼ **to sb.** ohne dass jmd. davon weiß/wusste

**un'lawful** *adj.* ungesetzlich

**unleaded** /ʌnˈledɪd/ *adj.* bleifrei ⟨*Benzin*⟩

**unless** /ənˈles/ *conj.* es sei denn; wenn ... nicht

**un'like** **1** *adj.* nicht ähnlich **2** *prep.* **be** ∼ **sb./sth.** jmdm./einer Sache nicht ähnlich sein; ∼ **him,** ...: im Gegensatz zu ihm ...

**un'likely** *adj.* unwahrscheinlich; **be** ∼ **to do sth.** etw. wahrscheinlich nicht tun

**un'limited** *adj.* unbegrenzt

**un'load** *v.t.* entladen ⟨*Lastwagen, Waggon*⟩; löschen ⟨*Schiff, Schiffsladung*⟩; ausladen ⟨*Gepäck*⟩

**un'lock** *v.t.* aufschließen

**un'lucky** *adj.* (a) unglücklich; (not successful) glücklos; **be [very]** ∼: [großes] Pech haben (b) (bringing bad luck) **an** ∼ **number** eine Unglückszahl; **be** ∼: Unglück bringen

**unmanageable** /ʌnˈmænɪdʒəbl/ *adj.* widerspenstig ⟨*Kind, Pferd*⟩; unkontrollierbar ⟨*Situation*⟩

**un'manned** *adj.* unbemannt

**un'married** *adj.* unverheiratet; ledig

**un'mask** *v.t.* (fig.) entlarven

**unmi'stakable** /ʌnmɪˈsteɪkəbl/ *adj.* deutlich; unverwechselbar ⟨*Handschrift, Stimme*⟩

**unmistakably** /ʌnmɪˈsteɪkəblɪ/ *adv.* unverkennbar

**un'mitigated** *adj.* vollkommen; **be an** ∼ **disaster** (coll.) eine einzige Katastrophe sein

**unmotivated** /ʌnˈməʊtɪveɪtɪd/ *adj.* unmotiviert

**un'natural** *adj.,* **un'naturally** *adv.* unnatürlich; (abnormal) nicht normal

**un'necessarily** *adv.,* **un'necessary** *adj.* unnötig

**unnerve** /ʌnˈnɜːv/ *v.t.* entnerven

**unnerving** /ʌnˈnɜːvɪŋ/ *adj.* entnervend

**unnoticed** /ʌnˈnəʊtɪst/ *adj.* unbemerkt

**unobservant** /ʌnəbˈzɜːvənt/ *adj.* unaufmerksam

**unobserved** /ʌnəbˈzɜːvd/ *adj.* unbeobachtet

**u**

**unob'tainable** *adj.* nicht erhältlich; **number** ~ (Teleph.) kein Anschluss unter dieser Nummer

**unofficial** *adj.,* **unofficially** *adv.* inoffiziell

**un'pack** *v.t. & i.* auspacken

**un'paid** *adj.* unbezahlt; nicht bezahlt; ~ **for** nicht bezahlt

**unpalatable** /ʌn'pælətəbl/ *adj.* ungenießbar

**un'paralleled** *adj.* beispiellos

**un'pardonable** *adj.* unverzeihlich

**un'pleasant** *adj.,* **un'pleasantly** *adv.* unangenehm

**un'pleasantness** *n.* (bad feeling) Verstimmung, *die*

**un'plug** *v.t.,* -gg-: ~ **a lamp** den Stecker einer Lampe herausziehen

**un'popular** *adj.* unbeliebt ⟨*Lehrer, Regierung usw.*⟩; unpopulär ⟨*Maßnahme, Politik*⟩ (with bei)

**un'precedented** *adj.* beispiellos

**unpre'dictable** *adj.* unberechenbar

**unpre'pared** *adj.* unvorbereitet

**unprepos'sessing** *adj.* wenig attraktiv

**unpre'tentious** *adj.* einfach ⟨*Wein, Stil, Haus*⟩; bescheiden ⟨*Person*⟩

**unprincipled** /ʌn'prɪnsɪpld/ *adj.* skrupellos

**unprintable** /ʌn'prɪntəbl/ *adj.* nicht druckreif

**unpro'ductive** *adj.* fruchtlos ⟨*Diskussion, Nachforschung*⟩; unproduktiv ⟨*Zeit, Arbeit*⟩

**unpro'fessional** *adj.* (contrary to standards) standeswidrig

**un'profitable** *adj.* unrentabel

**un'promising** *adj.* nicht sehr viel versprechend

**unpublished** /ʌn'pʌblɪʃt/ *adj.* unveröffentlicht

**un'qualified** *adj.* (a) unqualifiziert (b) (absolute) uneingeschränkt; voll ⟨*Erfolg*⟩

**un'questionable** *adj.* unbezweifelbar ⟨*Tatsache*⟩; unbestreitbar ⟨*Recht, Ehrlichkeit*⟩

**unquestionably** /ʌn'kwestʃənəblɪ/ *adv.* ohne Frage

**unquote** /ʌn'kwəʊt/ *v.i.* ..., **quote,** ..., **~:** ..., Zitat, ..., Ende des Zitats

**unravel** /ʌn'rævl/ ⟨1⟩ *v.t.,* (Brit.) -ll- entwirren; (undo) aufziehen; (fig.) ~ **a mystery/the truth** ein Geheimnis enträtseln/ die Wahrheit aufdecken ⟨2⟩ *v.i.,* (Brit.) -ll- sich aufziehen

**un'real** *adj.* unwirklich

**unrea'listic** *adj.* unrealistisch

**un'reasonable** *adj.* unvernünftig; übertrieben ⟨*Ansprüche, Forderung, Preis, Kosten*⟩

**unrecognizable** /ʌn'rekəɡnaɪzəbl/ *adj.* be [absolutely *or* quite] ~: [überhaupt] nicht wieder zu erkennen sein

**unre'lated** *adj.* **be** ~: nicht miteinander zusammenhängen; (by family) nicht verwandt sein

**unrelenting** /ʌnrɪ'lentɪŋ/ *adj.* unvermindert, nicht nachlassend ⟨*Hitze, Kälte*⟩

**unre'liable** *adj.* unzuverlässig

**unrequited** /ʌnrɪ'kwaɪtɪd/ *adj.* unerwidert

**unreservedly** /ʌnrɪ'zɜːvɪdlɪ/ *adv.* uneingeschränkt

**unresolved** /ʌnrɪ'zɒlvd/ *adj.* (a) (not solved) ungelöst (b) (undecided) **be** ~: sich [noch] nicht entschieden haben

**un'rest** *n.* Unruhen *Pl.*

**unre'stricted** *adj.* unbeschränkt; uneingeschränkt

**un'ripe** *adj.* unreif

**un'rivalled** (Amer.: **un'rivaled**) *adj.* unübertroffen

**un'roll** ⟨1⟩ *v.t.* aufrollen ⟨2⟩ *v.i.* sich aufrollen

**unromantic** /ʌnrə'mæntɪk/ *adj.* unromantisch

**unruly** /ʌn'ruːlɪ/ *adj.* ungebärdig

**un'safe** *adj.* nicht sicher; **feel** ~: sich unsicher fühlen

**un'said** *adj.* ungesagt

**un'salted** *adj.* ungesalzen

**unsatis'factory** *adj.* unbefriedigend

**unsatisfying** /ʌn'sætɪsfaɪɪŋ/ *adj.* unbefriedigend

**un'savoury** (Amer.: **un'savory**) *adj.* unangenehm; zweifelhaft ⟨*Angelegenheit*⟩; unerfreulich ⟨*Einzelheiten*⟩

**unscathed** /ʌn'skeɪðd/ *adj.* unversehrt

**unscented** /ʌn'sentɪd/ *adj.* nicht parfümiert ⟨*Seife, Shampoo*⟩

**un'screw** ⟨1⟩ *v.t.* abschrauben ⟨2⟩ *v.i.* sich abschrauben lassen

**un'scrupulous** *adj.* skrupellos

**unsecured** /ʌnsɪ'kjʊəd/ *adj.* (Finance) ohne Sicherheit[en] *nachgestellt*

**un'seemly** *adj.* unschicklich

**unself'conscious** *adj.* unbefangen

**un'selfish** *adj.* selbstlos

**un'selfishness** *n.* Selbstlosigkeit, *die*

**un'settled** *adj.* (changeable) wechselhaft; (fig.) ruhelos ⟨*Leben*⟩; unruhig ⟨*Zeit, Land*⟩

**un'settling** *adj.* störend

**unshak[e]able** /ʌn'ʃeɪkəbl/ *adj.* unerschütterlich

**un'shaven** *adj.* unrasiert

**un'sightly** *adj.* unschön

**un'skilled** *adj.* ungelernt ⟨*Arbeiter*⟩

**un'skimmed** *adj.* ~ **milk** Vollmilch, *die*

**un'sociable** *adj.* ungesellig

**unsolved** /ʌn'sɒlvd/ *adj.* unaufgeklärt ⟨*Verbrechen*⟩

**unso'phisticated** *adj.* einfach

**un'sound** *adj.* **(a)** (diseased) nicht gesund; krank
**(b)** baufällig ⟨*Gebäude*⟩
**(c)** (ill-founded) wenig stichhaltig; nicht vertretbar ⟨*Ansicht, Methode*⟩
**(d)** of ∼ **mind** unzurechnungsfähig
**un'speakable** /ʌn'spiːkəbl/ *adj.* unbeschreiblich; (very bad) unsäglich
**unspecified** /ʌn'spesɪfaɪd/ *adj.* nicht näher bezeichnet
**unspoken** /ʌn'spəʊkn/ *adj.* ungesagt
**un'stable** *adj.* nicht stabil; [mentally/ emotionally] ∼: [psychisch] labil
**un'steadily** *adv.* unsicher
**un'steady** *adj.* unsicher; wackelig ⟨*Leiter, Tisch*⟩
**unstoppable** /ʌn'stɒpəbl/ *adj.* unhaltbar ⟨*Schuss aufs Fußballtor*⟩; (fig.) unaufhaltsam
**un'stuck** *adj.* **come** ∼: sich lösen; (fig. coll.: fail) ⟨*Person:*⟩ baden gehen (ugs.) (**over** mit)
**unsuc'cessful** *adj.* erfolglos; **be** ∼: keinen Erfolg haben
**unsuc'cessfully** *adv.* erfolglos
**un'suitable** *adj.* ungeeignet
**unsu'specting** *adj.* nichtsahnend
**un'sweetened** *adj.* ungesüßt
**unsympa'thetic** *adj.* wenig mitfühlend; **be** ∼: kein Mitgefühl zeigen
**untalented** /ʌn'tæləntɪd/ *adj.* untalentiert
**untenable** /ʌn'tenəbl/ *adj.* unhaltbar
**unthinkable** /ʌn'θɪŋkəbl/ *adj.* unvorstellbar
**unthinking** /ʌn'θɪŋkɪŋ/ *adj.*, **un'thinkingly** *adv.* gedankenlos
**un'tidily** *adv.* unordentlich
**un'tidiness** *n.* ▶ UNTIDY: Ungepflegtheit, *die*; Unaufgeräumtheit, *die*
**un'tidy** *adj.* ungepflegt ⟨*Äußeres, Person, Garten*⟩; unaufgeräumt ⟨*Zimmer*⟩
**un'tie** *v.t.*, **untying** aufknüpfen ⟨*Seil, Paket*⟩; aufbinden ⟨*Knoten*⟩; losbinden ⟨*Pferd, Boot*⟩
**until** /ən'tɪl/ ⓵ *prep.* bis; ∼ **[the] evening** bis zum Abend; ∼ **then** bis dahin; **not** ∼ [Christmas/the summer] erst [Weihnachten/im Sommer]
⓶ *conj.* bis
**un'timely** *adj.* **(a)** ungelegen
**(b)** (premature) vorzeitig
**un'tiring** *adj.* unermüdlich
**un'told** *adj.* unbeschreiblich; unermesslich ⟨*Reichtümer, Anzahl*⟩
**untoward** /ʌntə'wɔːd, ʌn'təʊəd/ *adj.* ungünstig; **nothing** ∼ **happened** es gab keine Schwierigkeiten
**untranslatable** /ʌntræns'leɪtəbl/ *adj.* unübersetzbar
**untreated** /ʌn'triːtɪd/ *adj.* unbehandelt
**un'true** *adj.* unwahr; **that's** ∼: das ist nicht wahr
**un'trustworthy** *adj.* unzuverlässig
**un'truth** *n.* Unwahrheit, *die*

**un'truthful** *adj.* verlogen
**un'typical** *adj.* untypisch (**of** für)
**unusable** /ʌn'juːzəbl/ *adj.* unbrauchbar
**unused¹** /ʌn'juːzd/ *adj.* (new, fresh) unbenutzt; (not utilized) ungenutzt
**unused²** /ʌn'juːst/ *adj.* (unaccustomed) **be** ∼ **to sth./doing sth.** etw. (*Akk.*) nicht gewohnt sein/nicht gewohnt sein, etw. zu tun
**un'usual** *adj.*, **un'usually** *adv.* ungewöhnlich
**unvarnished** /ʌn'vɑːnɪʃt/ *adj.* unlackiert; (fig.) ungeschminkt ⟨*Wahrheit*⟩
**un'veil** *v.t.* enthüllen; (fig.) vorstellen ⟨*Produkt*⟩; enthüllen ⟨*Plan*⟩
**un'versed** *adj.* nicht bewandert (**in** in + *Dat.*)
**un'wanted** *adj.* unerwünscht
**un'warranted** *adj.* ungerechtfertigt
**un'welcome** *adj.* unwillkommen
**un'well** *adj.* unwohl; **look** ∼: nicht wohl *od.* gut aussehen; **he feels** ∼ (poorly) er fühlt sich nicht wohl
**un'wholesome** *adj.* (lit. or fig.) ungesund
**unwieldy** /ʌn'wiːldɪ/ *adj.* sperrig
**un'willing** *adj.* widerwillig; **be** ∼ **to do sth.** etw. nicht tun wollen
**un'willingly** *adv.* widerwillig
**unwind** /ʌn'waɪnd/ ⓵ *v.t.*, **unwound** /ʌn'waʊnd/ abwickeln
⓶ *v.i.*, **unwound** **(a)** sich abwickeln
**(b)** (coll.: relax) sich entspannen
**un'wise** *adj.* unklug
**unwitting** /ʌn'wɪtɪŋ/ *adj.*, **un'wittingly** *adv.* unwissentlich
**un'workable** *adj.* undurchführbar ⟨*Plan*⟩
**un'worthy** *adj.* unwürdig; **be** ∼ **of sth.** einer Sache (*Gen.*) nicht würdig sein; **be** ∼ **of sb./sth.** ⟨*Verhalten:*⟩ einer Person/ Sache (*Gen.*) unwürdig sein
**un'wrap** *v.t.*, **-pp-** auswickeln
**un'written** *adj.* ungeschrieben
**un'zip** *v.t.*, **-pp-**: **(a)** ∼ **a dress/bag** *etc.* den Reißverschluss eines Kleides/einer Tasche *usw.* öffnen
**(b)** (Comp.) entpacken ⟨*Datei*⟩

**up** /ʌp/ ⓵ *adv.* **(a)** (to higher place) nach oben; (in lift) aufwärts; **the bird flew up to the roof** der Vogel flog aufs Dach [hinauf]; **up into the air** in die Luft [hinauf]; **up here/there** hier herauf/dort hinauf; **higher/a little way up** höher/ein kurzes Stück hinauf; **come on up!** komm [hier/weiter] herauf!
**(b)** (to upstairs) herauf/hinauf; nach oben
**(c)** (in higher place, upstairs) oben; **up here/there** hier/da oben; **the next floor up** ein Stockwerk höher
**(d)** (out of bed) **be up** auf sein
**(e)** (in price, value, amount) **prices have gone up/are up** die Preise sind gestiegen; **butter is up [by ...]** Butter ist [...] teurer ····⋗

**(f)** (as far as) **up to** sth. bis zu etw.; **up to here/there** bis hier[hin]/bis dorthin

**(g)** [not] be/feel **up to** sth. (capable of sth.) einer Sache (*Dat.*) [nicht] gewachsen sein/sich einer Sache (*Dat.*) [nicht] gewachsen fühlen; [not] be/feel **up to** doing sth. [nicht] in der Lage sein/sich [nicht] in der Lage fühlen, etw. zu tun

**(h)** be **up to** (doing) etw. anstellen (ugs.); **it is** [not] **up to** sb. **to do** sth. (sb.'s duty) es ist [nicht] jmds. Sache, etw. zu tun

**(i)** be three points/games **up** mit drei Punkten/Spielen vorn liegen

**(j)** walk **up** and down auf und ab gehen

**(k)** time is **up** die Zeit ist abgelaufen

**2** *prep.* herauf/hinauf; walk **up** the hill/road den Berg/die Straße hinaufgehen; walk **up** and down the platform auf dem Bahnsteig auf und ab gehen; **further up** the ladder/coast weiter oben auf der Leiter/an der Küste; **live just up** the road ein Stück weiter oben in der Straße wohnen

**3** *adj.* (coll.: amiss) what's **up**? was ist los? (ugs.); something is **up** irgendwas ist los (ugs.)

**4** *v.t.*, **-pp-** (coll.: increase) erhöhen

**'up-and-coming** *adj.* (coll.) aufstrebend

**'up-and-up** *n.* (coll.) be on the ~: auf dem aufsteigenden Ast sein (ugs.)

**'upbeat** **1** *n.* (Mus.) Auftakt, *der*

**2** *adj.* (coll.) (optimistic) optimistisch; (cheerful) fröhlich

**'upbringing** *n.* Erziehung, *die*

**up'date** *v.t.* auf den aktuellen Stand bringen

**up 'front** *adv.* (coll.: as down payment) im Voraus

**upgrade** **1** /-'-/ *v.t.* **(a)** aufwerten ⟨*Stellung*⟩

**(b)** (improve) verbessern

**(c)** (Comp.) aufrüsten, nachrüsten ⟨*Computer*⟩

**2** /'--/ *n.* (Comp.) (act of upgrading) Nachrüsten, *die*; Erweiterung, *die*; (upgraded version) erweiterte Version; Upgrade, *der* (fachspr.)

**upheaval** /ʌp'hi:vl/ *n.* Aufruhr, *der*; (disturbance) Durcheinander, *das*

**up'hill** **1** *adj.* (fig.) an ~ task/struggle eine mühselige Aufgabe/ein harter Kampf

**2** *adv.* bergauf

**uphold** *v.t.*, **upheld** unterstützen; wahren ⟨*Tradition*⟩

**upholster** /ʌp'həʊlstə(r)/ *v.t.* polstern

**up'holsterer** *n.* Polsterer, *der*/Polsterin, *die*

**up'holstery** *n.* **(a)** (craft) Polster[er]handwerk, *das*

**(b)** (padding) Polsterung, *die*

**'upkeep** *n.* Unterhalt, *der*

**up'lifting** *adj.* erhebend

**'uplighter** *n.* Deckenfluter, *der*

**up'load** *v.t.* (Comp.) hinaufladen ⟨*Datei, Daten*⟩

**'upmarket** *adj.* exklusiv

**upon** /ə'pɒn/ *prep.* auf (*direction:* + *Akk.*; *position:* + *Dat.*)

**upper** /'ʌpə(r)/ **1** *compar. adj.* ober...; Ober⟨*grenze, -lippe, -arm usw.*⟩; ~ **circle** oberer Rang; ~ **class[es]** Oberschicht, *die*; **have/get/gain the** ~ **hand** die Oberhand haben/gewinnen/erhalten

**2** *n.* Oberteil, *das*

**upper 'deck** *n.* Oberdeck, *das*

**'uppermost** **1** *adj.* oberst...

**2** *adv.* ganz oben

**'upright** *adj.* aufrecht

**'uprising** *n.* Aufstand, *der*

**'uproar** *n.* Aufruhr, *der*

**up'root** *v.t.* [her]ausreißen; ⟨*Sturm*⟩ entwurzeln

**upset** **1** /ʌp'set/ *v.t.*, **-tt-**, **upset** **(a)** (overturn) umkippen; (accidentally) umstoßen ⟨*Tasse, Milch usw.*⟩

**(b)** (distress) erschüttern; (make angry) aufregen; **don't let it** ~ **you** nimm es nicht so schwer

**(c)** (make ill) sth. ~s sb. etw. bekommt jmdm. nicht

**(d)** durcheinander bringen ⟨*Plan*⟩

**2** *v.i.*, **-tt-**, **upset** umkippen

**3** *adj.* (distressed) bestürzt; (agitated) aufgeregt; **get** ~ [**about/over** sth.] sich [über etw. (*Akk.*)] aufregen

**4** /'ʌpset/ *n.* **(a)** (agitation) Aufregung, *die*; (annoyance) Verärgerung, *die*

**(b)** **stomach** ~: Magenverstimmung, *die*

**(c)** (upheaval) Aufruhr, *der*

**up'setting** *adj.* erschütternd; (sad) traurig; (annoying) ärgerlich

**'upshot** *n.* Ergebnis, *das*

**upside 'down** **1** *adv.* verkehrt herum; **turn** sth. ~: etw. auf den Kopf stellen

**2** *adj.* auf dem Kopf stehend ⟨*Bild*⟩; **be** ~: auf dem Kopf stehen

**upstairs** **1** /-'-/ *adv.* nach oben ⟨*gehen, kommen*⟩; oben ⟨*sein, sein usw.*⟩

**2** /'--/ *adj.* im Obergeschoss *nachgestellt*

**'upstart** *n.* Emporkömmling, *der*

**up'stream** *adv.* flussaufwärts

**'uptake** *n.* be quick/slow on the ~ (coll.) schnell begreifen/schwer von Begriff sein (ugs.)

**uptight** /-'-, '-/ *adj.* (coll.: tense) nervös (**about** wegen)

**up to 'date** *adj.* be/keep ~: auf dem neuesten Stand sein/bleiben; **bring** sth. ~: etw. auf den neuesten Stand bringen

**up-to-'date** *attrib. adj.* (current) aktuell; (modern) modern

**up-to-the-'minute** *adj.* hochaktuell

**'upturn** *n.* Aufschwung, *der* (**in** *Gen.*)

**upturned** /'ʌptɜ:nd/ *adj.* umgedreht; ~ **nose** Stupsnase, *die*

**upward** /'ʌpwəd/ **1** *adj.* nach oben gerichtet

**2** *adv.* aufwärts ⟨*sich bewegen*⟩; nach oben ⟨*sehen, gehen*⟩

**upwards** /ˈʌpwədz/ adv. (a) ▶ UPWARD 2
(b) ~ of über (+ Akk.)

**uranium** /jʊəˈreɪnɪəm/ n. Uran, das

**Uranus** /ˈjʊərənəs, jʊəˈreɪnəs/ pr. n.
(Astron.) Uranus, der

**urban** /ˈɜːbn/ adj. städtisch; Stadt⟨gebiet,
-bevölkerung, -planung⟩

**urbane** /ɜːˈbeɪn/ adj. weltmännisch

**urchin** /ˈɜːtʃɪn/ n. Strolch, der

**urge** /ɜːdʒ/ [1] v.t. ~ sb. to do sth. jmdn.
drängen, etw. zu tun
[2] n. Trieb, der

■ **urge 'on** v.t. antreiben; (encourage)
anfeuern

**urgency** /ˈɜːdʒənsɪ/ n. Dringlichkeit, die

**urgent** /ˈɜːdʒənt/ adj. dringend; (to be dealt
with immediately) eilig; **be in ~ need of sth.**
etw. dringend brauchen

**'urgently** adv. dringend; (immediately) eilig

**urinal** /jʊəˈraɪnl/ n. [public] ~: [öffentliche]
Herrentoilette; Pissoir, das

**urinary** /ˈjʊərɪnərɪ/ adj. Harn-

**urinate** /ˈjʊərɪneɪt/ v.i. urinieren

**urine** /ˈjʊərɪn/ n. Urin, der; Harn, der

**URL** abbr. (Comp.) = **uniform resource
locator** URL, der

**urn** /ɜːn/ n. (a) tea/coffee ~: Tee-/
Kaffeemaschine, die
(b) (vessel) Urne, die

**Uruguay** /ˈjʊərəgwaɪ/ pr. n. Uruguay (das)

**us** /əs, stressed ʌs/ pron. uns; **it's us** wir
sinds (ugs.)

**US** abbr. = **United States** USA

**USA** abbr. = **United States of
America** USA

**usage** /ˈjuːzɪdʒ, ˈjuːsɪdʒ/ n. (a) Brauch, der
(b) (Ling.) Sprachgebrauch, der

**use** [1] /juːs/ n. (a) Gebrauch, der; (of
dictionary, calculator, room) Benutzung, die; (of
word, pesticide, spice) Verwendung, die; [not] **be
in ~:** [nicht] in Gebrauch sein; **be no longer
in ~:** nicht mehr verwendet werden; **make
~ of sb./sth.** jmdn./etw. gebrauchen/(exploit)
ausnutzen; **make good ~ of, turn** or **put to
good ~:** gut nutzen ⟨Zeit, Talent, Geld⟩; **put
sth. to ~:** etw. verwenden
(b) (usefulness) Nutzen, der; **is it of [any] ~?**
ist das [irgendwie] von Nutzen?; **be [of] no
~ [to sb.]** [jmdm.] nicht nützen; **it's no
~ [doing that]** es hat keinen Sinn[, das zu
tun]
(c) (purpose) Verwendung, die; **have/find a
~ for sth./sb.** für etw./jmdn. Verwendung
haben/finden; **have no/not much ~ for sth./
sb.** etw./jmdn. nicht/kaum brauchen
[2] /juːz/ v.t. (a) benutzen; nutzen
⟨Gelegenheit⟩; anwenden ⟨Gewalt⟩; in
Anspruch nehmen ⟨Firma, Dienstleistung⟩;
nutzen ⟨Zeit, Gelegenheit⟩; verwenden
⟨Kraftstoff, Butter, Wort⟩
(b) ~**d to** /ˈjuːst tə/ **I ~d to live in London**
früher habe ich in London gelebt

■ **use 'up** v.t. aufbrauchen; verbrauchen
⟨Geld, Energie⟩

**use-by date** /ˈjuːzbaɪ/ n. (esp. Brit.)
[Mindest]haltbarkeitsdatum, das

**used** [1] adj. (a) /juːzd/ gebraucht;
gestempelt ⟨Briefmarke⟩; ~ **car**
Gebrauchtwagen, der
(b) /juːst/ ~ **to sth.** [an] etw. (Akk.) gewöhnt
[2] /juːst/ ▶ USE 2B

**useful** /ˈjuːsfl/ adj. nützlich; praktisch
⟨Werkzeug⟩; hilfreich ⟨Rat, Idee⟩

**'usefulness** n. Nützlichkeit, die

**useless** /ˈjuːslɪs/ adj. unbrauchbar
⟨Werkzeug, Rat, Idee⟩; nutzlos ⟨Wissen,
Information, Protest, Anstrengung, Kampf⟩;
zwecklos ⟨Widerstand, Protest⟩

**user** /ˈjuːzə(r)/ n. Benutzer, der/Benutzerin,
die

**user:** ~**-friendly** adj. benutzerfreundlich;
~ **group** n. Benutzergruppe, die;
~ **interface** n. (Comp.)
Benutzerschnittstelle, die; ~ **name** n.
(Comp.) Benutzername, der

**usher** /ˈʌʃə(r)/ [1] n. (in court)
Gerichtsdiener, der; (at cinema, church)
Platzanweiser, der
[2] v.t. führen

■ **usher 'in** v.t. hineinführen; (fig.)
einläuten

**usherette** /ʌʃəˈret/ n. Platzanweiserin, die

**USSR** abbr. (Hist.) = **Union of Soviet
Socialist Republics** UdSSR, die

**usual** /ˈjuːʒʊəl/ adj. üblich

**usually** /ˈjuːʒʊəlɪ/ adv. gewöhnlich

**usurp** /juːˈzɜːp/ v.t. sich (Dat.)
widerrechtlich aneignen

**utensil** /juːˈtensɪl/ n. Utensil, das; writing
~s Schreibutensilien Pl.; **kitchen** ~s
Küchengeräte Pl.

**uterus** /ˈjuːtərəs/ n. Gebärmutter, die

**utilitarian** /juːtɪlɪˈteərɪən/ adj. funktionell

**utility** /juːˈtɪlɪtɪ/ n. (a) Nutzen, der
(b) [public] ~: öffentlicher
Versorgungsbetrieb

**u'tility room** n.: Raum, in dem [größere]
Haushaltsgeräte (z.B. Waschmaschine)
installiert sind

**utilize** /ˈjuːtɪlaɪz/ v.t. nutzen

**utmost** /ˈʌtməʊst/ [1] adj. äußerst...;
größt... ⟨Höflichkeit, Eleganz, Einfachheit,
Geschwindigkeit⟩
[2] n. Äußerste, das; **do** or **try one's ~ to do
sth.** mit allen Mitteln versuchen, etw. zu tun

**utter¹** /ˈʌtə(r)/ adj. völlig; vollkommen;
~ **fool** Vollidiot, der (ugs.)

**utter²** v.t. (a) von sich geben ⟨Schrei,
Seufzer⟩
(b) (say) sagen

**utterance** /ˈʌtərəns/ n. Worte Pl.

**'utterly** adv. völlig; vollkommen; äußerst
⟨dumm, lächerlich⟩

u

**'U-turn** *n.* Wende [um 180°]; (fig.)
Kehrtwendung, *die;* **make a** ~: wenden; **'No**
~**s'** „Wenden verboten"

**UV** *abbr.* = **ultraviolet** UV

# Vv

**V¹, v** /viː/ *n.* V, v, *das*
**V²** *abbr.* = **volt[s]** V

**v.** *abbr.* = **versus** gg.

**vacancy** /'veɪkənsɪ/ *n.* (a) (job) freie Stelle
(b) (room) freies Zimmer; **'vacancies'**
„Zimmer frei"; **'no vacancies'** „belegt"

**vacant** /'veɪkənt/ *adj.* (a) frei; **'situations**
~**'** „Stellenangebote"
(b) (mentally) leer

**vacate** /və'keɪt/ *v.t.* räumen

**vacation** /və'keɪʃn/ *n.* (a) (Brit. Univ.) Ferien
*Pl.*
(b) (Amer.) ▶ HOLIDAY B

**vaccinate** /'væksɪneɪt/ *v.t.* impfen

**vaccination** /væksɪ'neɪʃn/ *n.* Impfung, *die;*
**have a** ~: geimpft werden

**vaccine** /'væksiːn/ *n.* Impfstoff, *der*

**vacillate** /'væsɪleɪt/ *v.i.* schwanken

**vacuum** /'vækjʊəm/ ⬜1 *n.* (a) Vakuum, *das;*
**live in a** ~: im luftleeren Raum leben
(b) (coll.: ~ cleaner) Staubsauger, *der* (ugs.)
⬜2 *v.t. & i.* [staub]saugen

**vacuum:** ~ **cleaner** *n.* Staubsauger, *der;*
~ **flask** *n.* (Brit.) Thermosflasche, *die;*
~**-packed** *adj.* vakuumverpackt

**vagaries** /'veɪgərɪz/ *n. pl.* Launen *Pl.*

**vagina** /və'dʒaɪnə/ *n.* Scheide, *die*

**vagrant** /'veɪgrənt/ *n.* Landstreicher, *der/*
-streicherin, *die;* (in cities) Stadtstreicher, *der/*
-streicherin, *die*

**vague** /veɪg/ *adj.* vage; verschwommen
⟨*Form, Umriss*⟩; (absent-minded)
geistesabwesend; **not have the** ~**st idea** *or*
**notion** nicht die blasseste *od.* leiseste
Ahnung haben

**'vaguely** *adv.* vage; entfernt ⟨*bekannt sein,*
*erinnern an*⟩; schwach ⟨*sich erinnern*⟩

**vain** /veɪn/ *adj.* (a) (conceited) eitel
(b) (useless) leer; vergeblich ⟨*Hoffnung,*
*Versuch*⟩; **in** ~: vergeblich

**'vainly** *adv.* vergebens

**vale** /veɪl/ *n.* (arch./poet.) Tal, *das*

**valentine** /'væləntaɪn/ *n.* ~ [**card**]
Grußkarte zum Valentinstag; **St. V**~**'s Day**
Valentinstag, *der*

**valet** /'væleɪ/ *n.* Kammerdiener, *der*

**valiant** /'vælɪənt/ *adj.,* **'valiantly** *adv.*
tapfer

**valid** /'vælɪd/ *adj.* (a) (legally acceptable)
gültig; berechtigt ⟨*Anspruch*⟩
(b) (justifiable) stichhaltig ⟨*Argument*⟩; triftig
⟨*Grund*⟩; begründet ⟨*Einwand,*
*Entschuldigung*⟩

**validate** /'vælɪdeɪt/ *v.t.* rechtskräftig
machen

**validity** /və'lɪdɪtɪ/ *n.* Gültigkeit, *die*

**valley** /'vælɪ/ *n.* Tal, *das*

**valour** (*Amer.:* **valor**) /'vælə(r)/ *n.*
Tapferkeit, *die*

**valuable** /'væljʊəbl/ ⬜1 *adj.* wertvoll; **be**
~ **to sb.** für jmdn. wertvoll sein
⬜2 *n.* ~**s** Wertsachen *Pl.*

**valuation** /væljʊ'eɪʃn/ *n.* Schätzung, *die*

**value** /'væljuː/ ⬜1 *n.* Wert, *der;* **be of great/**
**little/some/no** ~ [**to sb.**] [für jmdn.] von
großem/geringem/einigem/keinerlei Nutzen
sein; **know the** ~ **of sth.** wissen, was etw.
wert ist; **something/nothing of** ~: etwas/
nichts Wertvolles
⬜2 *v.t.* schätzen

**value added 'tax** *n.* Mehrwertsteuer, *die*

**valued** /'væljuːd/ *adj.* geschätzt

**'value judgement** *n.* Werturteil, *das*

**'valueless** *adj.* wertlos

**valuer** /'væljʊə(r)/ *n.* Schätzer, *der;* Taxator,
*der*

**valve** /vælv/ *n.* (a) Ventil, *das*
(b) (Anat.) Klappe, *die*

**vampire** /'væmpaɪə(r)/ *n.* Vampir, *der*

**van** /væn/ *n.* [**delivery**] ~: Lieferwagen, *der*

**vandal** /'vændl/ *n.* Rowdy, *der*

**vandalism** /'vændəlɪzm/ *n.* Wandalismus,
*der*

**vandalize** /'vændəlaɪz/ *v.t.* [mutwillig]
beschädigen

**vanilla** /və'nɪlə/ ⬜1 *n.* Vanille, *die*
⬜2 *adj.* Vanille-

**vanish** /'vænɪʃ/ *v.i.* verschwinden

**vanity** /'vænɪtɪ/ *n.* Eitelkeit, *die*

**'vanity bag** *n.* Kosmetiktäschchen, *das*

**vantage point** /'vɑːntɪdʒ pɔɪnt/ *n.*
Aussichtspunkt, *der*

**vapour** (*Brit.; Amer.:* **vapor**) /'veɪpə(r)/ *n.*
Dampf, *der*

**'vapour trail** *n.* (Aeronaut.) Kondensstreifen,
*der*

**variable** /'veərɪəbl/ adj. (a) (alterable) veränderbar; **be ~:** verändert werden können
**(b)** (inconsistent) unbeständig ‹Wetter, Wind, Leistung›; wechselhaft ‹Wetter, Launen, Qualität›
**variance** /'veərɪəns/ n. **be at ~ [with sth.]** [mit etw.] nicht übereinstimmen
**variant** /'veərɪənt/ n. Variante, die
**variation** /veərɪ'eɪʃn/ n. **(a)** (varying) Veränderung, die; (difference) Unterschied, der
**(b)** (variant) Variante, die **(of, on** Gen.)
**varicose vein** /værɪkəʊs 'veɪn/ n. Krampfader, die
**varied** /'veərɪd/ adj. unterschiedlich; abwechslungsreich ‹Diät, Leben›
**variety** /və'raɪətɪ/ n. **(a)** (diversity) Vielfältigkeit, die; (in diet, routine) Abwechslung, die; **add** or **give ~ to sth.** etw. abwechslungsreicher gestalten
**(b)** (assortment) Auswahl, die **(of** an + Dat., von); **for a ~ of reasons** aus verschiedenen Gründen
**(c)** (Theatre) Varietee, das
**(d)** (form) Art, die; (of fruit, vegetable) Sorte, die; (cultivated) Züchtung, die
**various** /'veərɪəs/ adj. **(a)** pred. (different) verschieden; unterschiedlich
**(b)** attrib. (several) verschiedene; **at ~ times** mehrere Male
**'variously** adv. unterschiedlich
**varnish** /'vɑːnɪʃ/ ① n. Lasur, die
② v.t. lasieren
**vary** /'veərɪ/ ① v.t. verändern; ändern ‹Bestimmungen, Programm, Methode, Route›; (add variety to) abwechslungsreicher gestalten
② v.i. (become different) sich ändern; ‹Preis, Qualität:› schwanken; (be different) unterschiedlich sein
**'varying** adj. wechselnd; (different) unterschiedlich
**vase** /vɑːz/ n. Vase, die
**vast** /vɑːst/ adj. **(a)** (huge) riesig; weit ‹Fläche, Meer›
**(b)** (coll.: great) enorm; Riesen‹menge, -summe›
**'vastly** adv. (coll.) enorm; weitaus ‹besser›; weit ‹überlegen, unterlegen›
**vat** /væt/ n. Bottich, der
**VAT** /viːeɪ'tiː, væt/ abbr. **= value added tax** MwSt.
**Vatican** /'vætɪkən/ pr. n. Vatikan, der
**vault¹** /vɔːlt, vɒlt/ n. **(a)** (Archit.) Gewölbe, das
**(b)** (in bank) Tresorraum, der
**(c)** (tomb) Gruft, die
**vault²** ① v.i. sich schwingen
② v.t. sich schwingen über (+ Akk.)
③ n. Sprung, der
**VD** n. Geschlechtskrankheit, die
**VDU** abbr. **= visual display unit**

**veal** /viːl/ n. Kalb[fleisch], das; attrib. Kalbs-
**veer** /vɪə(r)/ v.i. ‹Auto:› ausscheren
▪ **veer a'way, veer 'off** v.i. ‹Auto:› ausscheren; ‹Fahrer, Straße:› abbiegen
**veg** /vedʒ/ n., pl. same (coll.) Gemüse, das
**vegan** /'viːgən/ ① n. Veganer, der/ Veganerin, die
② adj. vegan
**vegetable** /'vedʒɪtəbl/ n. Gemüse, das; **fresh ~s** frisches Gemüse; attrib. Gemüse‹suppe, -extrakt, -garten›
**'vegetable oil** n. Pflanzenöl, das
**vegetarian** /vedʒɪ'teərɪən/ ① n. Vegetarier, der/Vegetarierin, die
② adj. vegetarisch; **sb. is ~:** jmd. ist Vegetarier/Vegetarierin; **eat ~ [food]** vegetarisch essen
**vegetarianism** /vedʒɪ'teərɪənɪzm/ n. Vegetarismus, der
**vegetate** /'vedʒɪteɪt/ v.i. nur noch [dahin]vegetieren
**vegetation** /vedʒɪ'teɪʃn/ n. Vegetation, die
**veggie** /'vedʒɪ/ (coll.) ① adj. vegetarisch; **~ burger** Bratling, der
② n. Vegetarier, der/Vegetarierin, die
**vehement** /'viːəmənt/ adj., **'vehemently** adv. heftig
**vehicle** /'viːɪkl/ n. **(a)** Fahrzeug, das **(b)** (fig.: medium) Vehikel, das
**vehicular** /vɪ'hɪkjʊlə(r)/ adj. Fahrzeug-
**veil** /veɪl/ ① n. Schleier, der
② v.t. verschleiern
**veiled** /veɪld/ adj. verschleiert; (fig.) versteckt
**vein** /veɪn/ n. **(a)** Vene, die; (any blood vessel) Ader, die
**(b)** (fig.: mood) Stimmung, die; **in a similar ~:** vergleichbarer Art
**Velcro** ® /'velkrəʊ/ n. Klettverschluss, der ⒲
**velocity** /vɪ'lɒsɪtɪ/ n. Geschwindigkeit, die
**velvet** /'velvɪt/ ① n. Samt, der
② adj. aus Samt nachgestellt; Samt-
**'velvety** adj. samtig
**vendetta** /ven'detə/ n. Hetzkampagne, die; (feud) Fehde, die
**vending machine** /'vendɪŋ məʃiːn/ n. [Verkaufs]automat, der
**vendor** /'vendə(r)/ n. Verkäufer, der/ Verkäuferin, die
**veneer** /vɪ'nɪə(r)/ n. Furnier, das
**venerable** /'venərəbl/ adj. ehrwürdig
**venerate** /'venəreɪt/ v.t. verehren
**ve'nereal disease** n. (Med.) Geschlechtskrankheit, die
**venetian blind** /vɪ'niːʃn blaɪnd/ n. Jalousie, die
**Venezuela** /venɪ'zweɪlə/ pr. n. Venezuela (das)

V

**vengeance** /'vendʒəns/ n. **(a)** Rache, die; take ~ [up]on sb. [for sth.] sich an jmdm. [für etw.] rächen **(b)** with a ~ (coll.) gewaltig (ugs.)

**Venice** /'venɪs/ pr. n. Venedig (das)

**venison** /'venɪsn, 'venɪzn/ n. Hirsch, der; Hirschfleisch, das; (roe deer) Reh[fleisch], das

**venom** /'venəm/ n. Gift, das

**venomous** /'venəməs/ adj. giftig

**vent¹** /vent/ [1] n. **(a)** Öffnung, die **(b)** (fig.) Ventil, das (fig.); give ~ to Luft machen (+ Dat.) [2] v.t. (fig.) Luft machen (+ Dat.)

**vent²** n. (in garment) Schlitz, der

**ventilate** /'ventɪleɪt/ v.t. belüften

**ventilation** /ventɪ'leɪʃn/ n. Belüftung, die

**ventilator** /'ventɪleɪtə(r)/ n. **(a)** Ventilator, der **(b)** (Med.) Beatmungsgerät, das

**ventriloquist** /ven'trɪləkwɪst/ n. Bauchredner, der/-rednerin, die

**venture** /'ventʃə(r)/ [1] n. Unternehmung, die [2] v.i. **(a)** (dare) wagen **(b)** (dare to go) sich wagen [3] v.t. wagen

■ **venture 'out** v.i. sich hinauswagen

**venue** /'venju:/ n. (Sport) [Austragungs]ort, der; (Mus., Theatre) [Veranstaltungs]ort, der; (meeting place) Treffpunkt, der

**Venus** /'vi:nəs/ pr. n. (Astron.) Venus, die

**veranda[h]** /və'rændə/ n. Veranda, die

**verb** /vɜ:b/ n. Verb, das

**verbal** /'vɜ:bl/ adj., **verbally** /'vɜ:bəlɪ/ adv. **(a)** (relating to words) sprachlich **(b)** (oral[ly]) mündlich

**verbatim** /və'beɪtɪm/ adj., adv. [wort]wörtlich

**verbose** /və'bəʊs/ adj. weitschweifig ⟨Roman, Autor⟩; langatmig ⟨Rede, Redner⟩

**verdict** /'vɜ:dɪkt/ n. Urteil, das; ~ of guilty/ not guilty Schuld-/Freispruch, der; reach a ~: zu einem Urteil kommen

**verge** /vɜ:dʒ/ n. **(a)** Rasensaum, der; (on road) Bankette, die **(b)** (fig.) be on the ~ of war/tears am Rande des Krieges stehen/den Tränen nahe sein; be on the ~ of doing sth. kurz davor stehen, etw. zu tun

■ **'verge on** v.t. [an]grenzen an (+ Akk.)

**verger** /'vɜ:dʒə(r)/ n. Küster, der

**verifiable** /'verɪfaɪəbl/ adj. nachprüfbar

**verification** /verɪfɪ'keɪʃn/ n. **(a)** (check) Überprüfung, die **(b)** (confirmation) Bestätigung, die

**verify** /'verɪfaɪ/ v.t. **(a)** (check) überprüfen **(b)** (confirm) bestätigen

**veritable** /'verɪtəbl/ adj. richtig

**vermin** /'vɜ:mɪn/ n. Ungeziefer, das

**vermouth** /'vɜ:məθ/ n. Wermut[wein], der

**vernacular** /və'nækjʊlə(r)/ n. Landessprache, die

**versatile** /'vɜ:sətaɪl/ adj. vielseitig; (having many uses) vielseitig verwendbar

**versatility** /vɜ:sə'tɪlɪtɪ/ n. Vielseitigkeit, die

**verse** /vɜ:s/ n. **(a)** (stanza) Strophe, die **(b)** (poetry) Lyrik, die; write some ~: einige Verse schreiben; piece of ~: Gedicht, das; written in ~: in Versform **(c)** (in Bible) Vers, der

**versed** /vɜ:st/ adj. be [well] ~ in sth. sich in etw. (Dat.) [gut] auskennen

**version** /'vɜ:ʃn/ n. Version, die; (in another language) Übersetzung, die; (of vehicle, machine, tool) Modell, das

**versus** /'vɜ:səs/ prep. gegen

**vertebra** /'vɜ:tɪbrə/ n., pl. ~e /'vɜ:tɪbri:/ Wirbel, der

**vertebrate** /'vɜ:tɪbrət/ n. Wirbeltier, das

**vertical** /'vɜ:tɪkl/ adj. senkrecht; be ~: senkrecht stehen

**vertically** /'vɜ:tɪkəlɪ/ adv. senkrecht

**vertigo** /'vɜ:tɪgəʊ/ n. Schwindel, der

**verve** /vɜ:v/ n. Schwung, der

**very** /'verɪ/ [1] attrib. adj. **(a)** (precise, exact) genau; you're the ~ person I wanted to see genau dich wollte ich sehen; at the ~ moment when ...: im selben Augenblick, als ...; at the ~ centre genau in der Mitte; the ~ thing genau das Richtige **(b)** (extreme) at the ~ back/front ganz hinten/ vorn; at the ~ end/beginning ganz am Ende/ Anfang; from the ~ beginning von Anfang an; only a ~ little nur ein ganz kleines bisschen **(c)** (mere) bloß ⟨Gedanke⟩ **(d)** (absolute) absolut ⟨Minimum, Maximum⟩; the ~ most I can offer is ...: ich kann allerhöchstens ... anbieten; for the ~ last time zum allerletzten Mal **(e)** emphat. before their ~ eyes vor ihren Augen [2] adv. **(a)** (extremely) sehr; it's ~ near es ist ganz in der Nähe; ~ probably höchstwahrscheinlich; not ~ much nicht sehr; ~ little [nur] sehr wenig ⟨verstehen, essen⟩; thank you [~,] ~ much [vielen,] vielen Dank **(b)** (absolutely) aller⟨best..., -letzt..., -leichtest...⟩; at the ~ latest allerspätestens **(c)** (precisely) the ~ same one genau der-/ die-/dasselbe

**vessel** /'vesl/ n. **(a)** (receptacle) Gefäß, das; [drinking] ~: Trinkgefäß, das **(b)** (Naut.) Schiff, das

**vest** /vest/ [1] n. **(a)** (Brit.) Unterhemd, das **(b)** (Amer.: waistcoat) Weste, die [2] v.t. ~ sb. with sth., ~ sth. in sb. jmdm. etw. verleihen

**'vested** adj. have a ~ interest in sth. ein persönliches Interesse an etw. (Dat.) haben

**vestige** /'vestɪdʒ/ n. Spur, die; not a ~ of truth kein Fünkchen Wahrheit

**v**

**vestment** /'vestmənt/ *n.* [Priester]gewand, *das*

**vestry** /'vestrɪ/ *n.* Sakristei, *die*

**vet** /vet/ ① *n.* Tierarzt, *der*/-ärztin, *die* ② *v.t.*, **-tt-** überprüfen

**veteran** /'vetərən/ *n.* Veteran, *der*/ Veteranin, *die*

**veteran 'car** *n.* (Brit.) Veteran, *der*

**veterinarian** /veterɪ'neərɪən/ *n.* (Amer.) Tierarzt, *der*/-ärztin, *die*

**veterinary** /'vetərmərɪ/ *adj.* tiermedizinisch

**veterinary 'surgeon** *n.* (Brit.) Tierarzt, *der*/-ärztin, *die*

**veto** /'viːtəʊ/ ① *n.*, *pl.* ~es Veto, *das* ② *v.t.* sein Veto einlegen gegen

**vex** /veks/ *v.t.* [ver]ärgern; (cause to worry) beunruhigen; **be ~ed with sb.** sich über jmdn. ärgern

**vexation** /vek'seɪʃn/ *n.* Verärgerung, *die*

**vexed** /vekst/ *adj.* **(a)** verärgert **(b)** ~ **question** viel diskutierte Frage

**VHF** *abbr.* = **Very High Frequency** UKW

**via** /'vaɪə/ *prep.* über (+ *Akk.*) ⟨*Ort, Sender, Telefon*⟩; durch ⟨*Eingang, Schornstein, Person*⟩; per ⟨*Post*⟩

**viability** /vaɪə'bɪlɪtɪ/ *n.* (feasibility) Realisierbarkeit, *die*

**viable** /'vaɪəbl/ *adj.* (feasible) realisierbar

**viaduct** /'vaɪədʌkt/ *n.* Viadukt, *das od. der*

**Viagra** ® /vaɪ'ægrə/ *n.* Viagra, *das*

**vibrant** /'vaɪbrənt/ *adj.* lebensprühend ⟨*Atmosphäre*⟩; lebhaft ⟨*Farbe*⟩

**vibrate** /vaɪ'breɪt/ ① *v.i.* vibrieren; (under strong impact) beben ② *v.t.* vibrieren lassen

**vibration** /vaɪ'breɪʃn/ *n.* Vibrieren, *das;* (under strong import) Beben, *das*

**vicar** /'vɪkə(r)/ *n.* Pfarrer, *der*

**vicarage** /'vɪkərɪdʒ/ *n.* Pfarrhaus, *das*

**vicarious** /vɪ'keərɪəs/ *adj.* nachempfunden

**vice¹** /vaɪs/ *n.* Laster, *das*

**vice²** *n.* (Brit.: tool) Schraubstock, *der*

**vice:** ~'**chairman** *n.* stellvertretender Vorsitzender; ~'**president** *n.* Vizepräsident, *der*/-präsidentin, *die;* ~ **squad** *n.* Sittenpolizei, *die*

**vice versa** /vaɪsɪ 'vɜːsə/ *adv.* umgekehrt

**vicinity** /vɪ'sɪnɪtɪ/ *n.* Umgebung, *die;* **in the** ~ **[of a place]** in der Nähe [eines Ortes]

**vicious** /'vɪʃəs/ *adj.* **(a)** (malicious) böse; bösartig ⟨*Tier*⟩ **(b)** (violent) brutal

**vicious 'circle** *n.* Teufelskreis, *der*

**'viciously** *adv.* **(a)** (maliciously) boshaft **(b)** (violently) brutal

**victim** /'vɪktɪm/ *n.* Opfer, *das;* (of sarcasm, abuse) Zielscheibe, *die* (fig.).

**victimization** /vɪktɪmaɪ'zeɪʃn/ *n.* Schikanierung, *die*

**victimize** /'vɪktɪmaɪz/ *v.t.* schikanieren

**victor** /'vɪktə(r)/ *n.* Sieger, *der*/Siegerin, *die*

**victorious** /vɪk'tɔːrɪəs/ *adj.* siegreich

**victory** /'vɪktərɪ/ *n.* Sieg, *der* (**over** über + *Akk.*); *attrib.* Sieges-

**video** /'vɪdɪəʊ/ ① *adj.* Video- ② *n.*, *pl.* ~s (~ recorder) Videorekorder, *der;* (~tape, ~ recording) Video, *das* (ugs.) ③ *v.t.* ▶ VIDEOTAPE 2

**video:** ~ **camera** *n.* Videokamera, *die;* ~ **cas'sette** *n.* Videokassette, *die;* ~ **cas'sette recorder** *n.* Videokassettenrekorder, *der;* ~ **clip** *n.* Videoclip, *der;* ~ **film** *n.* Videofilm, *der;* ~ **game** *n.* Videospiel, *das;* ~ **library** *n.* Videothek, *die;* ~ **machine** *n.* Videogerät, *das;* ~ **'nasty** *n.* Horrorvideo, *das;* ~**-on-demand** *n.* Video-on-Demand, *das;* ~ **player** *n.* Video-Player, *der;* ~ **recorder** *n.* Videorekorder, *der;* ~ **recording** *n.* Videoaufnahme, *die;* ~**tape** ① *n.* Videoband, *das;* ② *v.t.* [auf Videoband (*Akk.*)] aufnehmen

**vie** /vaɪ/ *v.i.*, **vying** /'vaɪɪŋ/ ~ **[with sb.] for** sth. [mit jmdm.] um etw. wetteifern

**Vienna** /vɪ'enə/ ① *pr. n.* Wien (*das*) ② *attrib. adj.* Wiener

**Viennese** /vɪə'niːz/ ① *adj.* Wiener ② *n.*, *pl. same* Wiener, *der*/Wienerin, *die*

**Vietnam** /vɪet'næm/ *pr. n.* Vietnam (*das*)

**Vietnamese** /vɪetnə'miːz/ ① *adj.* vietnamesisch; **sb. is** ~: jmd. ist Vietnamese/Vietnamesin ② *n.*, *pl. same* **(a)** (person) Vietnamese, *der*/ Vietnamesin, *die* **(b)** (language) Vietnamesisch, *das*

**view** /vjuː/ ① *n.* **(a)** (range of vision) Sicht, *die;* **be out of/in** ~: nicht zu sehen/zu sehen sein **(b)** (what is seen) Aussicht, *die* **(c)** (picture) Ansicht, *die* **(d)** (opinion) Ansicht, *die;* **what is your** ~ **or are your** ~**s on this?** was meinst du dazu?; **hold** *or* **take the** ~ **that** ...: der Ansicht sein, dass ...; **in my** ~: meiner Ansicht nach **(e)** **be on** ~: besichtigt werden können; **in** ~ **of sth.** (fig.) angesichts einer Sache; **with a** ~ **to doing sth.** in der Absicht, etw. zu tun ② *v.t.* **(a)** (look at) sich (*Dat.*) ansehen **(b)** (consider) betrachten **(c)** (inspect) besichtigen ③ *v.i.* (Telev.) fernsehen

**viewdata** /'vjuː deɪtə/ *n.* Bildschirmtextsystem, *das*

**'viewer** *n.* **(a)** (Telev.) [Fernseh]zuschauer, *der*/-zuschauerin, *die;* **(b)** (for slides) Diabetrachter, *der*

**viewfinder** *n.* Sucher, *der*

**viewing** /'vjuːɪŋ/ *n.* (Telev.) Fernsehen, *das;* ~ **figures** Einschaltquoten *Pl.;* **at peak** ~ **time** zur besten Sendezeit

**'viewpoint** *n.* Standpunkt, *der*

**vigil** /'vɪdʒɪl/ n. Wachen, das; keep ∼: wachen

**vigilance** /'vɪdʒɪləns/ n. Wachsamkeit, die

**vigilant** /'vɪdʒɪlənt/ adj. wachsam

**vigilante** /vɪdʒɪ'læntɪ/ n. Mitglied einer/der Bürgerwehr

**vigor** (Amer.) ▸ VIGOUR

**vigorous** /'vɪgərəs/ adj. kräftig; heftig ⟨Attacke, Protest⟩; energisch ⟨Versuch, Anstrengung, Leugnen, Maßnahme⟩

**'vigorously** adv. heftig; kräftig ⟨schrubben, drücken⟩

**vigour** /'vɪgə(r)/ n. (Brit.) (of person) Vitalität, die; (of body) Kraft, die; (of protest, attack) Heftigkeit, die

**vile** /vaɪl/ adj. gemein ⟨Verleumdung⟩; vulgär ⟨Sprache⟩; (repulsive) widerwärtig; (coll.: very unpleasant) scheußlich (ugs.)

**villa** /'vɪlə/ n. (a) [holiday] ∼: Ferienhaus, das

(b) [country] ∼: Landhaus, das

**village** /'vɪlɪdʒ/ n. Dorf, das; attrib. Dorf-

**village:** ∼ **'green** n. Dorfwiese, die; ∼ **'hall** n. Dorfgemeinschaftshaus, das

**villager** /'vɪlɪdʒə(r)/ n. Dorfbewohner, der/ -bewohnerin, die

**villain** /'vɪlən/ n. (a) Verbrecher, der

(b) (Theatre) Bösewicht, der

**villainous** /'vɪlənəs/ adj. gemein

**vindicate** /'vɪndɪkeɪt/ v.t. (a) (justify) rechtfertigen

(b) (clear) rehabilitieren

**vindication** /vɪndɪ'keɪʃn/ n. (a) (justification) Rechtfertigung, die

(b) (clearing) Rehabilitierung, die

**vindictive** /vɪn'dɪktɪv/ adj. nachtragend

**vine** /vaɪn/ n. Weinrebe, die

**vinegar** /'vɪnɪgə(r)/ n. Essig, der

**vinegary** /'vɪnɪgərɪ/ adj. sauer

**vineyard** /'vɪnjɑːd, 'vɪnjəd/ n. Weinberg, der

**vintage** /'vɪntɪdʒ/ ① n. Jahrgang, der ② adj. erlesen ⟨Wein⟩

**vintage 'car** n. (Brit.) Oldtimer, der

**vintner** /'vɪntnə(r)/ n. Weinhändler, der/ -händlerin, die

**vinyl** /'vaɪnɪl/ n. Vinyl, das

**viola** /vɪ'əʊlə/ n. Bratsche, die

**violate** /'vaɪəleɪt/ v.t. (a) verletzen; brechen ⟨Vertrag, Versprechen, Gesetz⟩

(b) (profane, rape) schänden

**violation** /vaɪə'leɪʃn/ n. ▸ VIOLATE: Verletzung, die; Bruch, der; Schändung, die

**violence** /'vaɪələns/ n. (a) (force) Heftigkeit, die; (of blow) Wucht, die

(b) (brutality) Gewalt, die; (at public event) Gewalttätigkeiten Pl.; resort to or use ∼: Gewalt anwenden

**violent** /'vaɪələnt/ adj. gewalttätig; (fig.) heftig; wuchtig ⟨Schlag, Stoß⟩; Gewalt⟨verbrecher, -tat⟩

**'violently** adv. brutal; (fig.) heftig

**violet** /'vaɪələt/ ① n. (a) Veilchen, das

(b) (colour) Violett, das ② adj. violett

**violin** /vaɪə'lɪn/ n. Violine, die; Geige, die

**vio'linist** n. Geiger, der/Geigerin, die

**VIP** /viːaɪ'piː/ n. Prominente, der/die; the ∼s die Prominenz

**viper** /'vaɪpə(r)/ n. Viper, die

**virgin** /'vɜːdʒɪn/ ① n. (a) Jungfrau, die

(b) the [Blessed] V∼ [Mary] die [Heilige] Jungfrau [Maria] ② adj. (unspoiled) unberührt; ∼ olive oil natives Olivenöl

**virginity** /və'dʒɪnɪtɪ/ n. Unschuld, die

**Virgo** /'vɜːgəʊ/ n., pl. ∼s (Astrol., Astron.) die Jungfrau

**virile** /'vɪraɪl/ adj. männlich

**virility** /vɪ'rɪlɪtɪ/ n. Männlichkeit, die

**virology** /vaɪə'rɒlədʒɪ/ n. Virologie, die

**virtual** /'vɜːtjʊəl/ adj. a ∼ ...: so gut wie ein/eine ...; the traffic came to a ∼ standstill der Verkehr kam praktisch zum Stillstand (ugs.)

**'virtually** adv. so gut wie; praktisch (ugs.)

**virtual re'ality** n. (Comp.) virtuelle Realität

**virtue** /'vɜːtjuː/ n. (a) (moral excellence) Tugend, die

(b) (advantage) Vorteil, der

(c) by ∼ of aufgrund (+ Gen.)

**virtuoso** /vɜːtjʊ'əʊzəʊ/ n., pl. virtuosi /vɜːtjʊ'əʊziː/ or ∼s Virtuose, der/Virtuosin, die

**virtuous** /'vɜːtjʊəs/ adj. rechtschaffen ⟨Person⟩; tugendhaft ⟨Leben⟩

**virulent** /'vɪrʊlənt/ adj. (a) (Med.) virulent; stark wirkend ⟨Gift⟩

(b) (fig.) heftig; scharf ⟨Angriff⟩

**virus** /'vaɪərəs/ n. (a) Virus, das

(b) (Comp.) [Computer]virus, das od. der

**visa** /'viːzə/ n. Visum, das

**vis-à-vis** /viːzɑː'viː/ prep. (in relation to) bezüglich (+ Gen.)

**viscosity** /vɪs'kɒsɪtɪ/ n. Dickflüssigkeit, die

**viscount** /'vaɪkaʊnt/ n. Viscount, der

**viscous** /'vɪskəs/ adj. dickflüssig

**visibility** /vɪzɪ'bɪlɪtɪ/ n. (a) Sichtbarkeit, die

(b) (range of vision) Sicht, die; (Meteorol.) Sichtweite, die

**visible** /'vɪzɪbl/ adj. sichtbar

**'visibly** adv. sichtlich

**vision** /'vɪʒn/ n. (a) (sight) Sehkraft, die

(b) (dream) Vision, die

(c) usu. pl. (imaginings) Fantasien Pl.

(d) (insight, foresight) Weitblick, der

**visit** /'vɪzɪt/ ① v.t. besuchen; aufsuchen ⟨Arzt⟩

② v.i. einen Besuch/Besuche machen ③ n. Besuch, der; pay or make a ∼ to sb., pay sb. a ∼: jmdm. einen Besuch abstatten (geh.)

**'visiting:** ∼ **card** n. Visitenkarte, die; ∼ **hours** n. pl. Besuchszeiten Pl.

**visitor** /'vɪzɪtə(r)/ *n.* Besucher, *der/*
Besucherin, *die;* (to hotel) Gast, *der;* **have ~s/**
**a ~:** Besuch haben
**'visitors' book** *n.* Gästebuch, *das;* **sign**
**the ~:** sich ins Gästebuch eintragen
**visual** /'vɪzjʊəl, 'vɪʒjʊəl/ *adj.* visuell;
optisch ⟨*Eindruck, Darstellung*⟩
**visual: ~ aids** *n. pl.*
Anschauungsmaterial, *das;* **~ dis'play**
**unit** *n.* Bildschirmgerät, *das*
**visualization** /vɪzjʊəlaɪ'zeɪʃn/ *n.*
Veranschaulichung, *die;* (imagining)
Sichvorstellen, *das*
**visualize** /'vɪzjʊəlaɪz, 'vɪʒjʊəlaɪz/ *v.t.* (a)
(imagine) sich (*Dat.*) vorstellen
(b) (envisage) voraussehen
**'visually** *adv.* bildlich
**vital** /'vaɪtl/ *adj.* (a) (essential to life)
lebenswichtig
(b) (essential) unbedingt notwendig
(c) (crucial) entscheidend (**to** für); **it is ~ that**
**you ...:** es ist von entscheidender
Bedeutung, dass Sie ...
**vitality** /vaɪ'tælɪtɪ/ *n.* Vitalität, *die*
**'vitally** *adv.* **~ important** von allergrößter
Wichtigkeit; (crucial) von entscheidender
Bedeutung
**vitamin** /'vɪtəmɪn, 'vaɪtəmɪn/ *n.* Vitamin,
*das*
**vitamin pill** *n.* Vitamintablette, *die*
**vitriolic** /vɪtrɪ'ɒlɪk/ *adj.* ätzend
**vivacious** /vɪ'veɪʃəs/ *adj.* lebhaft
**vivacity** /vɪ'væsɪtɪ/ *n.* Lebhaftigkeit, *die*
**vivid** /'vɪvɪd/ *adj.* lebhaft ⟨*Farbe,*
*Erinnerung*⟩; lebendig ⟨*Schilderung*⟩
**'vividly** *adv.* lebendig ⟨*beschreiben*⟩;
**remember sth. ~:** sich lebhaft an etw. (*Akk.*)
erinnern
**vixen** /'vɪksn/ *n.* Füchsin, *die*
**vocabulary** /və'kæbjʊlərɪ/ *n.* (a) (list)
Vokabelverzeichnis, *das;* **learn ~:** Vokabeln
lernen
(b) (range of language) Wortschatz, *der*
**vocal** /'vəʊkl/ *adj.* (a) (concerned with voice)
stimmlich
(b) lautstark ⟨*Minderheit, Protest*⟩
**'vocal cords** *n. pl.* Stimmbänder *Pl.*
**vocalist** /'vəʊkəlɪst/ *n.* Sänger, *der/*
Sängerin, *die*
**vocation** /və'keɪʃn/ *n.* Berufung, *die*
**vocational** /və'keɪʃənl/ *adj.* berufsbezogen
**vocational: ~ college** *n.* Berufsschule,
*die;* **~ guidance** *n.* Berufsberatung, *die;*
**~ training** *n.* berufliche Bildung
**vociferous** /və'sɪfərəs/ *adj.* laut; lautstark
⟨*Forderung, Protest*⟩
**vodka** /'vɒdkə/ *n.* Wodka, *der*
**vogue** /vəʊg/ *n.* Mode, *die;* **be in/come into**
**~:** in Mode sein/kommen
**voice** /vɔɪs/ ①*n.* Stimme, *die;* **in a firm/**
**loud/soft ~:** mit fester/lauter/sanfter
Stimme

②*v.t.* zum Ausdruck bringen
**voice: ~mail** *n.* Voicemail, *die;* **~-over**
*n.* Begleitkommentar, *der;*
**~ recognition** *n.* (Comp.)
Spracherkennung, *die*
**void** /vɔɪd/ ①*adj.* (a) (empty) leer
(b) (invalid) ungültig
(c) **~ of** ohne [jeden/jedes/jede]
②*n.* Nichts, *das*
**vol.** *abbr.* = **volume** Bd.
**volatile** /'vɒlətaɪl/ *adj.* (a) (Chem.) flüchtig
(b) (fig.) impulsiv; brisant ⟨*Lage*⟩
**volcanic** /vɒl'kænɪk/ *adj.* vulkanisch
**volcano** /vɒl'keɪnəʊ/ *n., pl.* **~es** Vulkan,
*der*
**vole** /vəʊl/ *n.* Wühlmaus, *die*
**volition** /və'lɪʃn/ *n.* Wille, *der;* **of one's own**
**~:** aus eigenem Willen
**volley** /'vɒlɪ/ *n.* (a) (of missiles) Salve, *die;* **a**
**~ of arrows** ein Hagel von Pfeilen
(b) (Tennis) Volley, *der*
**'volleyball** *n.* Volleyball, *der*
**volt** /vəʊlt/ *n.* Volt, *das*
**voltage** /'vəʊltɪdʒ/ *n.* Spannung, *die*
**voluble** /'vɒljʊbl/ *adj.* redselig
**volume** /'vɒljuːm/ *n.* (a) (book) Band, *der*
(b) (loudness) Lautstärke, *die;* (of voice)
Volumen, *das*
(c) (space) Rauminhalt, *der;* (amount of
substance) Teil, *der*
**'volume control** *n.* Lautstärkeregler, *der*
**voluntarily** /'vɒləntərɪlɪ/ *adv.,*
**voluntary** /'vɒləntərɪ/ *adj.* freiwillig
**volunteer** /vɒlən'tɪə(r)/ ①*n.* Freiwillige,
*der/die*
②*v.t.* anbieten ⟨*Hilfe, Dienste*⟩;
herausrücken mit ⟨*Informationen*⟩
③*v.i.* sich [freiwillig] melden; **~ to do** *or*
**~ for the shopping** sich zum Einkaufen
bereit erklären
**voluptuous** /və'lʌptjʊəs/ *adj.* üppig
**vomit** /'vɒmɪt/ ①*v.t.* erbrechen
②*v.i.* sich übergeben
③*n.* Erbrochene, *das*
**voodoo** /'vuːduː/ *n.* Wodu, *der*
**voracious** /və'reɪʃəs/ *adj.* gefräßig
⟨*Person*⟩; unbändig ⟨*Appetit*⟩
**vote** /vəʊt/ ①*n.* (a) (individual ~) Stimme,
*die*
(b) (act of voting) Abstimmung, *die;* **take a**
**~ on sth.** über etw. (*Akk.*) abstimmen
(c) (right to ~) Stimmrecht, *das*
②*v.i.* abstimmen; (in election) wählen; **~ for/**
**against** stimmen für/gegen; **~ to do sth.**
beschließen, etw. zu tun; **~ Labour/**
**Conservative** *etc.* Labour/die Konservativen
*usw.* wählen
③*v.t.* **~ sb. Chairman/President** *etc.* jmdn.
zum Vorsitzenden/Präsidenten *usw.* wählen
■ **vote 'in** *v.t.* wählen
**'voter** *n.* Wähler, *der/*Wählerin, *die*
**'vote-catching** *n.* Stimmenfang, *der*

**V**

**voting** /'vəʊtɪŋ/ n. Abstimmen, das; (in election) Wählen, das

**voting:** ~ **age** n. Wahlalter, das; ~ **slip** n. Wahlzettel, der; Stimmzettel, der; ~ **system** n. Wahlsystem, das

**vouch** /vaʊtʃ/ ① v.t. ~ **that** ...: sich dafür verbürgen, dass ... ② v.i. ~ **for sb./sth.** sich für jmdn./etw. verbürgen

**'voucher** n. Gutschein, der

**vow** /vaʊ/ ① n. Gelöbnis, das; (Relig.) Gelübde, das ② v.t. geloben

**vowel** /'vaʊəl/ n. Vokal, der

**voyage** /'vɔɪdʒ/ ① n. Reise, die; (sea ~) Seereise, die; **outward/homeward** ~, ~ **out/** home Hin-/Rückreise, die; a ~ **to the moon** ein Mondflug ② v.i. (literary) reisen

**voyeur** /vwɑːˈjɜː(r)/ n. Voyeur, der

**voyeurism** /vwɑːˈjɜːrɪzm/ n. Voyeurismus, der

**vulgar** /'vʌlgə(r)/ adj. vulgär; ordinär ⟨Person, Benehmen, Witz⟩

**vulgarity** /vʌlˈgærɪtɪ/ n. Vulgarität, die

**vulnerable** /'vʌlnərəbl/ adj. **(a)** (exposed to danger) angreifbar; **be** ~ **to sth.** für etw. anfällig sein; **be** ~ **to attack/in a** ~ **position** leicht angreifbar sein **(b)** (without protection) schutzlos

**vulture** /'vʌltʃə(r)/ n. Geier, der

**vying** ▶ VIE

---

# Ww

---

**W¹, w** /'dʌblju:/ n. W, w, das

**W²** abbr. = **watt[s]** W

**W.** abbr. **(a)** = **west** W. **(b)** = **western** w.

**wad** /wɒd/ n. **(a)** Knäuel, das; (smaller) Pfropfen, der **(b)** (of papers) Bündel, das

**wadding** /'wɒdɪŋ/ n. Futter, das

**waddle** /'wɒdl/ ① v.i. watscheln ② n. watschelnder Gang

**wade** /weɪd/ v.i. waten
■ **'wade through** v.t. (fig. coll.) durchackern (ugs.) ⟨Buch⟩

**wafer** /'weɪfə(r)/ n. Waffel, die

**'wafer-thin** adj. hauchdünn

**waffle¹** /'wɒfl/ n. (Gastr.) Waffel, die

**waffle²** (Brit. coll.: talk) ① v.i. schwafeln (ugs.) ② n. Geschwafel, das (ugs.)

**waft** /wɒft, wɑːft/ ① v.t. wehen ② v.i. ziehen

**wag** /wæg/ ① v.t., **-gg-** ⟨Hund:⟩ wedeln mit ⟨Schwanz⟩; ~ **one's finger at sb.** jmdm. mit dem Finger drohen ② v.i., **-gg-** ⟨Schwanz:⟩ wedeln

**wage** /weɪdʒ/ ① n. in sing. or pl. Lohn, der ② v.t. führen ⟨Krieg⟩

**wage:** ~ **claim** n. Lohnforderung, die; ~ **earner** n. Lohnempfänger, der/ -empfängerin, die; **be the** ~ **earner of the family** der Ernährer/die Ernährerin der Familie sein; ~ **freeze** n. Lohnstopp, der; ~ **increase** n. Lohnerhöhung, die; ~ **packet** n. Lohntüte, die

**wager** /'weɪdʒə(r)/ (dated/formal) ① n. Wette, die; **lay a** ~ **on sth.** auf etw. (Akk.) wetten ② v.t. & i. wetten

**wage:** ~ **rise** n. Lohnerhöhung, die; ~ **scale** n. Tarif, der; ~ **slave** n. Lohnsklave, der

**waggle** /'wægl/ (coll.) ① v.t. ~ **its tail** ⟨Hund:⟩ mit dem Schwanz wedeln ② v.i. hin und her schlagen

**waggon** (Brit.)**, wagon** /'wægən/ n. Wagen, der

**waif** /weɪf/ n. (child) verlassenes Kind

**wail** /weɪl/ ① v.i. klagen (geh.) **(for um);** ⟨Kind:⟩ heulen ② n. klagender Schrei; ~**s** Geheul, das

**waist** /weɪst/ n. Taille, die; **tight round the** ~: eng in der Taille

**'waistband** n. Gürtelbund, der; (of trousers) [Hosen]bund, der; (of skirt) [Rock]bund, der

**waistcoat** /'weɪskəʊt/ n. (Brit.) Weste, die

**'waistline** n. Taille, die; **be bad for the** ~: schlecht für die schlanke Linie sein

**wait** /weɪt/ ① v.i. **(a)** warten; ~ **[for] an hour** eine Stunde warten; ~ **a moment** Moment mal; **keep sb.** ~**ing, make sb.** ~: jmdn. warten lassen **(b)** ~ **at table** servieren ② v.t. (await) warten auf (+ Akk.); ~ **one's turn** warten, bis man drankommt ③ n. **(a) after a long/short** ~: nach langer/ kurzer Wartezeit **(b) lie in** ~ **for sb./sth.** jmdm./einer Sache auflauern
■ **wait be'hind** v.i. noch dableiben
■ **'wait for** v.t. warten auf (+ Akk.); ~ **for sb. to do sth.** darauf warten, dass jmd. etw. tut; ~ **for the rain to stop** warten, bis der Regen aufhört
■ **'wait on** v.t. (serve) bedienen
■ **wait 'up** v.i. aufbleiben **(for wegen)**

**'waiter** *n.* Kellner, *der;* ~! Herr Ober!

**'waiting:** ~ **list** *n.* Warteliste, *die;*
~ **room** *n.* Wartezimmer, *das;* (Railw.)
Warteraum, *der*

**waitress** /'weɪtrɪs/ *n.* Serviererin, *die;* ~!
Fräulein! (veralt.)

**waive** /weɪv/ *v.t.* verzichten auf (+ *Akk.*)

**wake¹** /weɪk/ 1 *v.i.,* woke /wəʊk/, woken
/'wəʊkn/ aufwachen
2 *v.t.,* woke, woken wecken
3 *n.* (by corpse) Totenwache, *die*
■ **wake 'up** 1 *v.i.* aufwachen; ~ up to sth.
(fig.: realize) etw. erkennen
2 *v.t.* (a) wecken
(b) (fig.: enliven) wachrütteln

**wake²** *n.* Kielwasser, *das;* in the ~ of sth.
(fig.) im Gefolge von etw.

**waken** /'weɪkn/ 1 *v.t.* wecken
2 *v.i.* aufwachen

**'wake-up call** (esp. Amer.) ▶ ALARM CALL

**Wales** /weɪlz/ *pr. n.* Wales (das)

**walk** /wɔːk/ 1 *v.i.* (a) laufen; (not run)
gehen; (not drive) zu Fuß gehen; **learn to** ~:
laufen lernen
(b) (exercise) gehen
2 *v.t.* (a) (lead) führen; ausführen ⟨Hund⟩
(b) (accompany) bringen
3 *n.* (a) Spaziergang, *der;* go [out] for or
take *or* have a ~: einen Spaziergang
machen; ten minutes' ~ from here zehn
Minuten zu Fuß von hier
(b) (gait) Gang, *der*
(c) (path) [Spazier]weg, *der*
■ **walk a'way with** *v.t.* (coll.: win easily)
spielend leicht gewinnen
■ **'walk into** *v.t.* (hit by accident) laufen
gegen ⟨Pfosten, Laternenpfahl⟩; ~ into sb.
mit jmdm. zusammenstoßen; ~ into a trap
in eine Falle gehen
■ **walk 'off with** *v.t.* sich davonmachen
mit
■ **walk 'out** *v.i.* (a) (leave in protest) aus
Protest den Saal verlassen
(b) (go on strike) in den Streik treten
■ **walk 'out of** *v.t.* (leave in protest) aus
Protest verlassen
■ **walk 'out on** *v.t.* verlassen

**'walker** *n.* (a) Spaziergänger, *der/*
-gängerin, *die;* (rambler) Wanderer, *der/*
Wanderin, *die*
(b) (baby-~) Laufstuhl, *der*

**walkie-talkie** /wɔːkɪ'tɔːkɪ/ *n.* Walkie-
Talkie, *das*

**'walking** *n.* [Spazieren]gehen, *das;* at
~ pace im Schritttempo; be within
~ distance zu Fuß zu erreichen sein

**walking:** ~ **frame** *n.* Gehbock, *der;*
Gehgestell, *das;* ~ **holiday** *n.*
Wanderurlaub, *der;* ~ **shoe** *n.*
Wanderschuh, *der;* ~ **stick** *n.*
Spazierstock, *der;* ~ **tour** *n.* Wanderung,
*die*

**Walkman** ® /'wɔːkmən/ *n., pl.* Walkmans
Walkman, *der* (Wz)

**walk:** ~**out** *n.* Arbeitsniederlegung, *die;*
~**over** *n.* (fig.: easy victory) Spaziergang, *der*
(ugs.); ~**way** *n.* Fußweg, *der;* (over machinery
etc.) Laufsteg, *der*

**wall** /wɔːl/ *n.* Wand, *die;* (freestanding) Mauer,
*die;* **drive sb. up the** ~ (fig. coll.) jmdn. auf die
Palme bringen (ugs.); **go to the** ~ (fig.) an die
Wand gedrückt werden
■ **wall 'up** *v.t.* zumauern

**wall:** ~**chart** *n.* Schautafel, *die;*
~ **cupboard** *n.* Hängeschrank, *der*

**wallet** /'wɒlɪt/ *n.* Brieftasche, *die*

**wall:** ~**flower** *n.* Goldlack, *der;*
~ **hanging** *n.* Wandbehang, *der;* ~ **light**
*n.* Wandlampe, *die*

**wallop** /'wɒləp/ (coll.) 1 *v.t.* schlagen
2 *n.* Schlag, *der*

**wallow** /'wɒləʊ/ *v.i.* (a) sich wälzen
(b) (fig.) schwelgen (in in + *Dat.*)

**wall:** ~ **painting** *n.* Wandgemälde, *das;*
~**paper** 1 *n.* (a) Tapete, *die;* (b) (Comp.)
Hintergrund, *der;* (pattern)
Hintergrundmuster, *das;* 2 *v.t.* tapezieren;
~**-to-**~ *adj.* ~**-to-**~ carpeting
Teppichboden, *der;* ~ **unit** *n.*
Hängeelement, *das*

**walnut** /'wɔːlnʌt/ *n.* Walnuss, *die*

**walrus** /'wɔːlrəs/ *n.* Walross, *das*

**waltz** /wɔːlts, wɒls/ 1 *n.* Walzer, *der*
2 *v.i.* Walzer tanzen

**wan** /wɒn/ *adj.* bleich

**wand** /wɒnd/ *n.* Stab, *der*

**wander** /'wɒndə(r)/ 1 *v.i.* (go aimlessly)
umherirren; (walk slowly) bummeln
2 *v.t.* wandern durch
3 *n.* (coll.) Spaziergang, *der*
■ **wander a'bout** *v.i.* sich herumtreiben
■ **wander 'off** *v.i.* (stray) weggehen

**wane** /weɪn/ *v.i.* abnehmen

**wangle** /'wæŋgl/ *v.t.* (coll.) organisieren
(ugs.)

**wannabe** /'wɒnəbɪ/ *n.* (coll. derog.)
Möchtegern, *der; attrib.* Möchtegern-

**want** /wɒnt/ 1 *v.t.* (a) (desire) wollen; ~ to
do sth. etw. tun wollen; I ~ it done by
tonight ich will, dass es bis heute Abend
fertig wird
(b) (require, need) brauchen; 'W~ed – cook'
„Koch/Köchin gesucht"; you're ~ed on the
phone du wirst am Telefon verlangt; the
windows ~ painting die Fenster müssten
gestrichen werden; you ~ to be [more]
careful du solltest vorsichtig[er] sein
(c) ~ed [by the police] [polizeilich] gesucht
2 *n.* (a) (lack) Mangel, *der* (of an + *Dat.*); for
~ of sth. aus Mangel an etw. (*Dat.*)
(b) (need) Not, *der*
(c) (desire) Bedürfnis, *das*
■ **'want for** *v.t.* sb. ~s for nothing *or*
doesn't ~ for anything jmdm. fehlt es an
nichts

**'wanting** *adj.* be ~: fehlen; sb./sth. is ~ in ···⟩

sth. jmdm./einer Sache fehlt es an etw.
(*Dat.*); **be found** ∼: für unzureichend
befunden werden

**wanton** /'wɒntən/ *adj.*, **'wantonly** *adv.*
mutwillig

**war** /wɔː(r)/ *n.* Krieg, *der;* **between the** ∼**s**
zwischen den Weltkriegen; **declare** ∼: den
Krieg erklären (**on** *Dat.*); **be at** ∼: sich im
Krieg befinden; **make** ∼: Krieg führen (**on**
gegen)

**warble** /'wɔːbl/ *v.t. & i.* trällern

**war:** ∼ **correspondent** *n.*
Kriegsberichterstatter, *der/*
-berichterstatterin, *die;* ∼ **crime** *n.*
Kriegsverbrechen, *das;* ∼ **criminal** *n.*
Kriegsverbrecher, *der/*-verbrecherin, *die*

**ward** /wɔːd/ *n.* **(a)** (in hospital) Station, *die;*
she's in W∼ 3 sie liegt auf Station 3
**(b)** (child) Mündel, *das od. die*
**(c)** (electoral division) Wahlbezirk, *der*
■ **ward 'off** *v.t.* abwehren

**'war damage** *n.* Kriegsschäden *Pl.*

**warden** /'wɔːdn/ *n.* **(a)** (of hostel) Heimleiter,
*der/*-leiterin, *die;* (of youth hostel)
Herbergsvater, *der/*-mutter, *die*
**(b)** (supervisor) Aufseher, *der/*Aufseherin, *die*

**'warder** *n.* (Brit.) Wärter, *der*

**wardrobe** /'wɔːdrəʊb/ *n.* **(a)**
Kleiderschrank, *der*
**(b)** (clothes) Garderobe, *die*

**warehouse** /'weəhaʊs/ *n.* Lagerhaus, *das;*
( part of building) Lager, *das*

**wares** /weəz/ *n. pl.* Ware, *die*

**warfare** /'wɔːfeə(r)/ *n.* Krieg, *der*

**war:** ∼ **game** *n.* Kriegsspiel, *das;*
∼ **grave** *n.* Kriegs- od. Soldatengrab, *das;*
∼**head** *n.* Sprengkopf, *der*

**warily** /'weərɪlɪ/ *adv.* vorsichtig; (suspiciously)
misstrauisch

**'warlike** *adj.* kriegerisch

**warm** /wɔːm/ ▮1▮ *adj.* **(a)** warm; **I am** [**very**]
∼: mir ist [sehr] warm
**(b)** (enthusiastic) herzlich ⟨*Grüße, Dank*⟩
▮2▮ *v.t.* wärmen; warm machen ⟨*Flüssigkeit*⟩;
∼ **one's hands** sich (*Dat.*) die Hände
wärmen
▮3▮ *v.i.* ∼ **to sb./sth.** (come to like) sich für
jmdn./etw. erwärmen
■ **warm 'up** ▮1▮ *v.i.* warm werden;
⟨*Sportler:*⟩ sich aufwärmen
▮2▮ *v.t.* aufwärmen ⟨*Speisen*⟩; erwärmen
⟨*Raum, Zimmer*⟩

**warm-blooded** /'wɔːmblʌdɪd/ *adj.*
warmblütig

**'war memorial** *n.* Kriegerdenkmal, *das*

**warm-hearted** /'wɔːmhɑːtɪd/ *adj.*
warmherzig ⟨*Person*⟩

**'warmly** *adv.* **(a)** warm
**(b)** (fig.) herzlich ⟨*willkommen heißen,
gratulieren, begrüßen, grüßen, danken*⟩

**warmonger** /'wɔːmʌŋgə(r)/ *n.*
Kriegshetzer, *der/*-hetzerin, *die*

**warmth** /wɔːmθ/ *n.* **(a)** Wärme, *die*

**(b)** (fig.) Herzlichkeit, *die*

**'warm-up** *n.* **have a** ∼ (Sport) sich
aufwärmen; ∼ [**lap**] (Motor Racing)
Aufwärmrunde, *die*

**warn** /wɔːn/ *v.t.* **(a)** (inform, give notice)
warnen (**against, of, about** vor + *Dat.*); ∼ **sb.**
**that** ...: jmdm. darauf hinweisen, dass ...;
∼ **sb. not to do sth.** jmdn. davor warnen,
etw. zu tun
**(b)** (admonish) ermahnen; (officially) abmahnen

**warning** ▮1▮ *n.* **(a)** (advance notice)
Vorwarnung, *die*
**(b)** (lesson) **let that be a** ∼ **to you** lass dir das
eine Warnung sein
**(c)** (caution) Verwarnung, *die;* (less official)
Warnung, *die*
▮2▮ *adj.* Warn⟨*schild, -signal usw.*⟩

**'warning triangle** *n.* Warndreieck, *das*

**warp** /wɔːp/ ▮1▮ *v.i.* sich verbiegen; ⟨*Holz,
Schallplatte:*⟩ sich verziehen
▮2▮ *v.t.* **(a)** verbiegen
**(b)** (fig.) **a** ∼**ed sense of humour** ein
abartiger Humor

**war:** ∼**path** *n.* **be on the** ∼**path** (fig.) in
Rage sein; ∼**plane** *n.* Kampfflugzeug, *das*

**warrant** /'wɒrənt/ ▮1▮ *n.* (for sb.'s arrest)
Haftbefehl, *der;* [**search**] ∼:
Durchsuchungsbefehl, *der*
▮2▮ *v.t.* **(a)** ( justify) rechtfertigen
**(b)** (guarantee) garantieren

**'warranty** *n.* Garantie, *die*

**warrior** /'wɒrɪə(r)/ *n.* (esp. literary) Krieger,
*der* (geh.)

**Warsaw** /'wɔːsɔː/ ▮1▮ *pr. n.* Warschau (*das*)
▮2▮ *attrib. adj.* Warschauer; ∼ **Pact** (Hist.)
Warschauer Pakt

**'warship** *n.* Kriegsschiff, *das*

**wart** /wɔːt/ *n.* Warze, *die*

**war:** ∼**time** *n.* **(a)** Kriegszeit, *die;* **in** *or*
**during** ∼: im Krieg; **(b)** *attrib.*
Kriegs⟨*rationierung, -evakuierung usw.*⟩;
∼**torn** *adj.* kriegsgeschunden

**wary** /'weərɪ/ *adj.* vorsichtig; (suspicious)
misstrauisch (**of** gegenüber); **be** ∼ **of sb./sth.**
sich vor jmdn./etw. in Acht nehmen

**'war zone** *n.* Kriegsgebiet, *das*

**was** ▶ BE

**wash** /wɒʃ/ ▮1▮ *v.t.* **(a)** waschen; ∼ **oneself**
sich waschen; ∼ **one's hands/face/hair** sich
(*Dat.*) die Hände/das Gesicht/die Haare
waschen; ∼ **the clothes** Wäsche waschen;
∼ **the dishes** [Geschirr] spülen; ∼ **the floor**
den Fußboden aufwischen
**(b)** (remove) waschen ⟨*Fleck*⟩ (**out of** aus);
abwaschen ⟨*Schmutz*⟩ (**off** von)
**(c)** (carry along) spülen
▮2▮ *v.i.* **(a)** sich waschen
**(b)** ⟨*Stoff, Kleidungsstück:*⟩ sich waschen
lassen
▮3▮ *n.* **(a)** **give sb./sth. a** [**good**] ∼: jmdn./etw.
[gründlich] waschen
**(b)** (laundering) Wäsche, *die*
**(c)** (of ship) Sog, *der*

■ **wash 'down** *v.t.* abspritzen ‹Auto, Deck, Hof›

■ **wash 'off** [1] *v.t.* ~ sth. off etw. abwaschen
[2] *v.i.* abgehen; (from fabric etc.) herausgehen

■ **wash 'out** *v.t.* ausscheuern ‹Topf›; ausspülen ‹Mund›; ~ dirt/marks out of clothes Schmutz/Flecken aus Kleidern [her]auswaschen

■ **wash 'up** [1] *v.t.* (Brit.) ~ the dishes up das Geschirr spülen
[2] *v.i.* abwaschen; spülen

**washable** /'wɒʃəbl/ *adj.* waschbar

**'washbasin** *n.* Waschbecken, *das*

**washed-'out** *adj.* verwaschen (fig.: exhausted) abgespannt

**washed-'up** *adj.* (coll.) kaputt (ugs.)

**washer** /'wɒʃə(r)/ *n.* (of tap) Dichtungsring, *der*

**'washing** *n.* Wäsche, *die;* do the ~: waschen

**washing:** ~ **machine** *n.* Waschmaschine, *die;* ~ **powder** *n.* Waschpulver, *das;* ~-'up *n.* (Brit.) Abwasch, *der;* do the ~-up abwaschen; spülen; ~-'up **liquid** *n.* Spülmittel, *das*

**'washtub** *n.* Waschbottich, *der*

**wasn't** /'wɒznt/ (coll.) = was not; ▶ BE

**wasp** *n.* Wespe, *die*

**waste** /weɪst/ [1] *n.* (a) (useless remains) Abfall, *der;* kitchen ~: Küchenabfälle *Pl.*
(b) (extravagant use) Verschwendung, *die;* it's a ~ of time/money/energy das ist Zeit-/Geld-/Energieverschwendung
[2] *v.t.* (squander) verschwenden; all his efforts were ~d all seine Mühe war umsonst; don't ~ my time! stehlen Sie mir nicht die Zeit!
[3] *adj.* (a) ~ material Abfall, *der*
(b) lay sth. ~: etw. verwüsten

■ **waste a'way** *v.i.* immer mehr abmagern

**waste:** ~**basket** ▶ WASTE-PAPER BASKET;
~ **disposal** *n.* Abfallbeseitigung, *die;*
~ **disposal site** *n.* [Müll]deponie *die;*
~ **disposal unit** *n.* Müllzerkleinerer, *der*

**wasteful** /'weɪstfl/ *adj.* (a) (extravagant) verschwenderisch
(b) (causing waste) unwirtschaftlich

**waste:** ~**land** *n.* Ödland, *das;*
~ **management** *n.* Abfallmanagement, *das;* Müllmanagement, *das;* ~'**paper** *n.* Papierabfall, *der;* ~-'**paper basket** *n.* Papierkorb, *der;* ~ **pipe** *n.* Abflussrohr, *das;* ~ **reduction** *n.* Abfallverminderung, *die;* Müllreduzierung, *der*

**watch** /wɒtʃ/ [1] *n.* (a) [wrist/pocket] ~: [Armband-/Taschen]uhr, *die*
(b) keep ~: Wache halten; keep [a] ~ for sb./sth. auf jmdn./etw. achten
(c) (Naut.) Wache, *die*
[2] *v.i.* ~ for sb./sth. auf jmdn./etw. warten
[3] *v.t.* (a) (observe) sich ‹Dat.› ansehen ‹Sportveranstaltung, Fernsehsendung›;

~ [the] television *or* TV fernsehen; ~ sb. do *or* doing sth. zusehen, wie jmd. etw. tut; we are being ~ed wir werden beobachtet
(b) (be careful of, look after) achten auf (+ Akk.)

■ **watch 'out** *v.i.* (a) (be careful) aufpassen; ~ out! Vorsicht!
(b) (look out) ~ out for sb./sth. auf jmdn./etw. achten

**'watchdog** *n.* Wachhund, *der;* (fig.) [public] ~: [Leiter/Leiterin einer] Aufsichtsbehörde

**watchful** /'wɒtʃfl/ *adj.* wachsam

**watch:** ~**maker** *n.* Uhrmacher, *der/* -macherin, *die;* ~**man** /'wɒtʃmən/ *n., pl.* ~**men** /'wɒtʃmən/ Wachmann, *der;*
~ **strap** *n.* [Uhr]armband, *das;* ~**tower** *n.* Wachturm, *der*

**water** /'wɔːtə(r)/ [1] *n.* (a) Wasser, *das*
(b) *in pl.* (part of the sea etc.) Gewässer *Pl.*
[2] *v.t.* (a) bewässern ‹Land›; wässern ‹Pflanzen›; ~ the flowers die Blumen [be]gießen
(b) verwässern ‹Bier usw.›
(c) tränken ‹Tier›
[3] *v.i.* ‹Augen:› tränen; my mouth was ~ing mir lief das Wasser im Munde zusammen

■ **water 'down** *v.t.* verwässern

**water:** ~**bed** *n.* Wasserbett, *das;* ~ **birth** *n.* Unterwassergeburt, *die;* ~ **biscuit** *n.* Cracker, *der;* ~ **bottle** *n.* Wasserflasche, *die;* ~ **butt** *n.* Regentonne, *die;* ~ **closet** *n.* Toilette, *die;* WC, *das;* Wasserklosett, *das* (veralt.); ~**colour** *n.* (a) (paint) Wasserfarbe, *die;* (b) (picture) Aquarell, *das;* ~**cress** *n.* Brunnenkresse, *die;* ~**fall** *n.* Wasserfall, *der;* ~**front** *n.* Ufer, *das;* a ~front location eine Gegend am Wasser; ~ **heater** *n.* Heißwassergerät, *das;* ~**hole** *n.* Wasserloch, *das*

**watering:** ~ **can** *n.* Gießkanne, *die;* ~ **place** *n.* (for animals) Wasserstelle, *die*

**water:** ~ **level** *n.* Wasserstand, *der;* ~**lily** *n.* Seerose, *die;* ~**line** *n.* (Naut.) Wasserlinie, *die;* ~**logged** /'wɔːtəlɒgd/ *adj.* nass ‹Boden›; aufgeweicht ‹Sportplatz›; ~ **main** *n.* Hauptwasserleitung, *die;* ~**mark** *n.* Wasserzeichen, *das;* ~**melon** *n.* Wassermelone, *die;* ~ **meter** *n.* Wasseruhr, *die;* ~ **pipe** *n.* Wasserrohr, *das;* ~ **pistol** *n.* Wasserpistole, *die;* ~ **polo** *n.* Wasserball, *der;* ~**proof** [1] *adj.* wasserdicht; wasserfest ‹Farbe›; [2] *v.t.* wasserdicht machen; imprägnieren ‹Stoff›; ~ **rates** *n. pl.* the ~ rates die Wassergebühren *Pl.;* ~**repellent** *adj.* Wasser abstoßend; ~**resistant** *adj.* wasserundurchlässig; wasserfest ‹Farbe›; ~**shed** *n.* (fig.) Wendepunkt, *der;* ~**ski** [1] *n.* Wasserski, *der;* [2] *v.i.* Wasserski laufen; ~**skiing** *n.* Wasserskilaufen, *das;* ~ **softener** /'sɒfnə(r)/ *n.* Wasserenthärter, *der;* ~**soluble** *adj.* wasserlöslich; ~ **supply** *n.* Wasserversorgung, *die;* ~ **table** *n.* Grundwasserspiegel, *der;* ~ **tap** *n.* Wasserhahn, *der;* ~**tight** *adj.* wasserdicht;

**W**

∼ **tower** n. Wasserturm, der; ∼**way** n. Wasserstraße, die; ∼ **vapour** n. Wasserdampf, der; ∼**works** n. sing., pl. same (establishment) Wasserwerk, das; (system) Wasserversorgungssystem, das

'**watery** adj. wässrig

**watt** /wɒt/ n. Watt, das

**wattage** /'wɒtɪdʒ/ n. Wattzahl, die

**wave** /weɪv/ |1| n. (a) Welle, die
(b) (gesture) give sb. a ∼: jmdm. zuwinken; with a ∼ of one's hand mit einem Winken
|2| v.i. (a) ⟨Fahne, Flagge, Wimpel:⟩ wehen; ⟨Baum, Gras, Korn:⟩ sich wiegen
(b) (with hand) winken; ∼ at or to sb. jmdm. zuwinken
|3| v.t. schwenken; schwingen ⟨Schwert⟩; ∼ one's hand at or to sb. jmdm. zuwinken; ∼ goodbye to sb. jmdm. zum Abschied zuwinken
▪ **wave a'side** v.t. (a) abtun ⟨Zweifel, Einwand⟩
(b) (signal to move) ∼ sb. aside [jmdm.] abwinken

**wave:** ∼**band** n. Wellenbereich, der; ∼**length** n. Wellenlänge, die; be on the same ∼**length** [as sb.] (fig.) die gleiche Wellenlänge [wie jmd.] haben

**waver** /'weɪvə(r)/ v.i. schwanken

**wavy** /'weɪvɪ/ adj. wellig; ∼ line Schlangenlinie, die

**wax**[1] /wæks/ |1| n. (a) Wachs, das
(b) (in ear) Schmalz, das
|2| v.t. wachsen

**wax**[2] v.i. (a) ⟨Mond:⟩ zunehmen
(b) (become) werden

**wax 'crayon** n. Wachsmalstift, der

**waxed** /wækst/ adj. gewachst; ∼ paper Wachspapier, das

**wax:** ∼**work** n. Wachsfigur, die; ∼**works** n. sing., pl. same Wachsfigurenkabinett, das

'**waxy** adj. wachsweich

**way** /weɪ/ |1| n. (a) Weg, der; ask the or one's ∼: nach dem Weg fragen; 'W∼ In/Out' „Ein-/Ausgang"; by ∼ of Switzerland über die Schweiz; lead the ∼: vorausgehen; go out of one's ∼: einen Umweg machen; (fig.) keine Mühe scheuen
(b) (method) Art und Weise, die; do it this ∼: mach es so
(c) (distance) Stück, das; it's a long ∼ off or a long ∼ from here es ist weit weg von hier; all the ∼: den ganzen Weg
(d) (direction) Richtung, die; she went this/that/the other ∼: sie ist in diese/die/die andere Richtung gegangen; stand sth. the right/wrong ∼ up etw. richtig/falsch herum stellen
(e) (respect) in [exactly] the same ∼: [ganz] genauso; in some ∼s in gewisser Hinsicht; in one ∼: auf eine Art; in every ∼: in jeder Hinsicht; in a ∼: auf eine Art
(f) (custom) Art, die
(g) get or have one's [own] ∼, have it one's [own] ∼: seinen Willen kriegen; be in sb.'s

or the ∼: [jmdm.] im Weg sein; make ∼ for sth. für etw. Platz machen; (fig.) einer Sache (Dat.) Platz machen; in a bad ∼: schlecht; either ∼: so oder so; by the ∼: übrigens
|2| adv. weit; ∼ back (coll.) vor langer Zeit

**way:** ∼**bill** n. Frachtbrief, der; ∼'**lay** v.t., forms as LAY[2] 1: (a) (ambush) überfallen; (b) (stop for conversation) abfangen; ∼'**out** adj. (coll.) extrem; verrückt; ∼**side** n. Wegrand, der; fall by the ∼**side** (fig.) auf der Strecke bleiben (ugs.)

**wayward** /'weɪwəd/ adj. eigenwillig

**WC** abbr. = **water closet** WC, das

**we** /wɪ, stressed wiː/ pl. pron. wir

**weak** /wiːk/ adj. (a) schwach; (easily led) labil ⟨Charakter, Person⟩
(b) dünn ⟨Getränk⟩

**weaken** /'wiːkn/ |1| v.t. schwächen; beeinträchtigen ⟨Augen⟩
|2| v.i. ⟨Entschlossenheit, Kraft:⟩ nachlassen

**weak-kneed** /'wiːkniːd/ adj. (fig.) feige

**weakling** /'wiːklɪŋ/ n. Schwächling, der

'**weakly** adv. schwach

'**weakness** n. Schwäche, die

'**weak-willed** adj. willensschwach

**wealth** /welθ/ n. (a) (abundance) Fülle, die
(b) (riches, being rich) Reichtum, der

'**wealthy** |1| adj. reich
|2| n. pl. the ∼: die Reichen Pl.

'**wealth tax** n. Vermögenssteuer, die

**wean** /wiːn/ v.t. abstillen; ∼ sb. [away] from sth. (fig.) jmdm. etw. abgewöhnen

**weapon** /'wepən/ n. Waffe, die

**weaponry** /'wepənrɪ/ n. Waffen Pl.

**wear** /weə(r)/ |1| n. (a) ∼ [and tear] Abnutzung, die
(b) (clothes) Kleidung, die
|2| v.t., wore /wɔː(r)/, worn /wɔːn/ (a) (have on) tragen ⟨Schmuck, Brille, Kleidung, Perücke⟩; I haven't a thing to ∼: ich habe überhaupt nichts anzuziehen
(b) (rub) abtragen ⟨Kleidungsstück⟩; abnutzen ⟨Teppich⟩; a [badly] worn tyre ein [stark] abgefahrener Reifen
|3| v.i., wore, worn (a) ⟨Kleider:⟩ sich durchscheuern; ⟨Absätze:⟩ sich ablaufen; ⟨Teppich:⟩ sich abnutzen
(b) (endure rubbing) halten; ∼ well/badly sich gut/schlecht tragen
▪ **wear a'way** |1| v.t. abschleifen
|2| v.i. sich abnutzen
▪ **wear 'down** v.t. (fig.) zermürben
▪ **wear 'off** v.i. ⟨Schicht:⟩ abgehen; ⟨Wirkung, Schmerz:⟩ nachlassen
▪ **wear 'out** |1| v.t. (a) aufbrauchen; auftragen ⟨Kleidungsstück⟩
(b) (fig.: exhaust) kaputtmachen (ugs.); be worn out kaputt sein (ugs.)
|2| v.i. kaputtgehen (ugs.)
▪ **wear 'through** |1| v.i. sich durchscheuern
|2| v.t. durchscheuern

**wearable** /'weərəbl/ *adj.* sth. is [not] ∼: man kann etw. [nicht] anziehen

**wearer** /'weərə(r)/ *n.* Träger, *der*/Trägerin, *die*

**wearily** /'wɪərɪlɪ/ *adv.* müde

**wearing** /'weərɪŋ/ *adj.* ermüdend

**wearisome** /'wɪərɪsəm/ *adj.* ermüdend

**weary** /'wɪərɪ/ 1 *adj.* (a) (tired) müde (b) be ∼ of sth. einer Sache (*Gen.*) überdrüssig sein
2 *v.t.* be wearied by sth. durch etw. erschöpft sein
3 *v.i.* ∼ of sth./sb. einer Sache/jmds. überdrüssig werden

**weasel** /'wiːzl/ *n.* Wiesel, *das*

**weather** /'weðə(r)/ 1 *n.* Wetter, *das;* what's the ∼ like? wie ist das Wetter?; in all ∼s bei jedem Wetter; he is feeling under the ∼ (fig.) er ist [zur Zeit] nicht ganz auf dem Posten
2 *v.t.* abwettern ‹*Sturm*›; (fig.) durchstehen ‹*schwere Zeit*›

**weather:** ∼**-beaten** *adj.* wettergegerbt ‹*Gesicht*›; verwittert ‹*Felsen, Gebäude*›; ∼ **chart** *n.* Wetterkarte, *die;* ∼**cock** *n.* Wetterhahn, *der;* ∼ **conditions** *n. pl.* Witterungsverhältnisse *Pl.;* ∼ **forecast** *n.* Wettervorhersage, *die*

**weathering** /'weðərɪŋ/ *n., no indef. art.* Verwitterung, *die*

**weather:** ∼**man** *n.* Meteorologe, *der;* ∼ **map** *n.* Wetterkarte, *die;* ∼**proof** *adj.* wetterfest; ∼ **report** *n.* Wetterbericht, *der;* ∼ **vane** *n.* Wetterfahne, *die*

**weave¹** /wiːv/ 1 *n.* Bindung, *die*
2 *v.t.,* **wove** /wəʊv/, **woven** /'wəʊvn/ (a) weben; flechten ‹*Korb, Kranz*› (b) (fig.) einflechten ‹*Thema usw.*› (into in + *Akk.*)

**weave²** *v.i.* (take intricate course) sich schlängeln

**'weaver** *n.* Weber, *der*/Weberin, *die*

**web** /web/ *n.* (a) Netz, *das;* spider's ∼: Spinnennetz, *das* (b) the Web (Comp.) das Web (fachspr.); das Netz

**webbed feet** /webd 'fiːt/ *n. pl.* Schwimmfüße *Pl.*

**Web:** ∼ **browser** *n.* (Comp.) Web-Browser, *der;* ∼ **page** *n.* (Comp.) Webseite, *die;* ∼ **site** *n.* (Comp.) Website, *die*

**we'd** /wɪd, *stressed* wiːd/ (a) = we had; (b) = we would

**Wed.** *abbr.* = **Wednesday** Mi.

**wedding** /'wedɪŋ/ *n.* Hochzeit, *die*

**wedding:** ∼ **anniversary** *n.* Hochzeitstag, *der;* ∼ **cake** *n.* Hochzeitskuchen, *der;* ∼ **day** *n.* Hochzeitstag, *der;* ∼ **dress** *n.* Brautkleid, *das;* ∼ **present** *n.* Hochzeitsgeschenk, *das;* ∼ **ring** *n.* Ehering, *der*

**wedge** /wedʒ/ 1 *n.* Keil, *der*

2 *v.t.* verkeilen; ∼ a door/window open eine Tür/ein Fenster festklemmen, damit sie/es offen bleibt

**'wedge-shaped** *adj.* keilförmig

**wedlock** /'wedlɒk/ *n.* born in/out of ∼: ehelich/unehelich geboren

**Wednesday** /'wenzdeɪ, 'wenzdɪ/ *n.* Mittwoch, *der; see also* FRIDAY

**wee¹** /wiː/ *adj.* (child lang./Scot.) klein

**wee²** ▶ WEE-WEE

**weed** /wiːd/ 1 *n.* ∼[s] Unkraut, *das*
2 *v.t.* jäten

■ **weed 'out** *v.t.* (fig.) aussieben

**'weedkiller** *n.* Unkrautvertilgungsmittel, *das*

**'weedy** *adj.* spillerig (ugs.) ‹*Person*›

**week** /wiːk/ *n.* Woche, *die;* for several ∼s mehrere Wochen lang; once a ∼, every ∼: einmal in der Woche; three times a ∼: dreimal in der Woche; a two-∼ visit ein zweiwöchiger Besuch; a ∼ today/tomorrow heute/morgen in einer Woche; a ∼ on Monday, Monday ∼: Montag in einer Woche

**'weekday** *n.* Wochentag, *der*

**weekend** /-'-, '--/ *n.* Wochenende, *das;* at the ∼: am Wochenende; go away for the ∼: übers Wochenende wegfahren

**weekly** /'wiːklɪ/ 1 *adj.* wöchentlich; Wochen‹*zeitung, -zeitschrift, -lohn*›
2 *adv.* wöchentlich
3 *n.* (newspaper) Wochenzeitung, *die;* (magazine) Wochenzeitschrift, *die*

**weep** /wiːp/ *v.i. & t.,* **wept** /wept/ weinen

**weepie** /'wiːpɪ/ *n.* (coll.) Schmachtfetzen, *der* (salopp)

**weeping 'willow** *n.* Trauerweide, *die*

**weepy** /'wiːpɪ/ 1 *adj.* weinerlich
2 *n.* ▶ WEEPIE

**'wee-wee** (coll.) 1 *n.* Pipi, *das* (ugs.); do a ∼: Pipi machen (ugs.)
2 *v.i.* Pipi machen (ugs.)

**weigh** /weɪ/ *v.t. & i.* wiegen

■ **weigh 'down** *v.t.* (fig.: depress) niederdrücken

■ **weigh 'up** *v.t.* abwägen

**'weighing machine** *n.* Waage, *die*

**weight** /weɪt/ *n.* Gewicht, *das;* what is your ∼? wie viel wiegen Sie?; be under/over ∼: zu wenig/zu viel wiegen

**'weighting** *n.* Zulage, *die*

**'weightlessness** *n.* Schwerelosigkeit, *die*

**weight:** ∼**lifter** *n.* Gewichtheber, *der/* -heberin, *die;* ∼**lifting** *n.* Gewichtheben, *das* ∼**train** *v.i.* mit Hanteln trainieren; ∼ **training** *n.* Hanteltraining, *das;* ∼**watcher** *n.* Schlankheitsbewusste, *der/ die*

**'weighty** *adj.* (a) (heavy) schwer (b) (important) gewichtig

**weir** /wɪə(r)/ *n.* Wehr, *das*

**weird** /wɪəd/ *adj.* (coll.: odd) bizarr

**weirdie** /'wɪədɪ/ *n.* (coll.) Freak, *der* (ugs.)

W

**weirdo** /ˈwɪədəʊ/ *n., pl.* ~s ▶ WEIRDIE

**welcome** /ˈwelkəm/ **1** *int.* willkommen; ~ home/to England! willkommen zu Hause/ in England!
**2** *n.* (a) Willkommen, *das*
(b) (reception) Empfang, *der*
**3** *v.t.* begrüßen
**4** *adj.* (a) willkommen; gefällig ⟨Anblick⟩
(b) *pred.* you are ~ to take it du kannst es gern nehmen; you're ~: gern geschehen!

**welcoming** /ˈwelkəmɪŋ/ *adj.* einladend

**weld** /weld/ *v.t.* (join) verschweißen; (repair, make, attach) schweißen (⟨on⟩ to an + *Akk.*)

**'welder** *n.* Schweißer, *der*/Schweißerin, *die*

**'welding** *n.* Schweißen, *das*

**welfare** /ˈwelfeə(r)/ *n.* (a) (health and prosperity) Wohl, *das*
(b) (social work; payments etc.) Sozialhilfe, *die;* be on ~ (Amer.) Sozialhilfe bekommen

**welfare:** W~ **'State** *n.* Wohlfahrtsstaat, *der;* ~ **work** *n.* Sozialarbeit, *die;* ~ **worker** *n.* Sozialarbeiter, *der*/ -arbeiterin, *die*

**well¹** /wel/ *n.* (a) Brunnen, *der*
(b) ▶ OIL WELL
(c) (stair~) Treppenloch, *das*

**well²** **1** *int.* ~! meine Güte!; ~, let's forget that na ja, lassen wir das; ~, who was it? nun *od.* also, wer war's?; oh ~[, never mind] na ja[, macht nichts]; ~? na?
**2** *adv.*, **better** /ˈbetə(r)/, **best** /best/ gut; gründlich ⟨trocknen, schütteln⟩; the business/ patient is doing ~: das Geschäft geht gut/ dem Patienten geht es gut; ~ done! großartig!; he is ~ over forty er ist weit über vierzig; as ~ (in addition) auch; A as ~ as B B und auch [noch] A
**3** *adj.* (in good health) How are you feeling now? – Quite ~, thank you Wie fühlen Sie sich jetzt? – Ganz gut, danke; look ~: gut aussehen; feel ~: sich wohl fühlen; he isn't [very] ~: es geht ihm nicht [sehr] gut; get ~ soon! gute Besserung!; make sb. ~: jmdn. gesund machen

**we'll** /wɪl, *stressed* wiːl/ = we will

**well:** ~-**aimed** *adj.* gezielt; ~-**balanced** *adj.* ausgeglichen ⟨Person⟩; ~-**behaved** ▶ BEHAVE 1; ~-**being** *n.* Wohl, *das;* ~-**bred** *adj.* anständig; ~-**built** *adj.* ⟨Person⟩ mit guter Figur; be ~-built eine gute Figur haben; ~-**chosen** *adj.* wohlgesetzt ⟨Worte⟩; ~-**connected** *adj.* ⟨Person⟩ mit guten Beziehungen; ~ **done** *adj.* (Cookery) durchgebraten; ~-**dressed** *adj.* gut gekleidet; ~-**educated** *adj.* gebildet; ~-**fed** *adj.* wohlgenährt; ~-**founded** *adj.* [wohl] fundiert; ~-**heeled** *adj.* (coll.) gut betucht (ugs.)

**wellington** /ˈwelɪŋtən/ *n.* ~ [boot] Gummistiefel, *der*

**well:** ~-**intentioned** /ˈwelɪntenʃənd/ *adj.* gut gemeint; ~-**known** *adj.* bekannt; ~ **made** *adj.* gut [gearbeitet]; ~-**mannered** *adj.* ⟨Person⟩ mit guten

Manieren; be ~-**mannered** gute Manieren haben; ~-**meaning** *adj.* wohlmeinend; be ~-**meaning** es gut meinen; ~-**meant** *adj.* gut gemeint; ~ **off** *adj.* wohlhabend; sb. is ~ off jmdm. geht es [finanziell] gut; ~ **paid** *adj.* gut bezahlt; ~-**read** /ˈwelred/ *adj.* belesen; ~-**spoken** *adj.* sprachlich gewandt; ~-**timed** *adj.* zeitlich gut gewählt; ~-**to-do** *adj.* wohlhabend; ~-**tried** *adj.* bewährt; ~-**wisher** *n.* Sympathisant, *der*/Sympathisantin, *die*

**Welsh** /welʃ/ **1** *adj.* walisisch; sb. is ~: jmd. ist Waliser/Waliserin
**2** *n.* (a) (language) Walisisch, *das; see also* ENGLISH 2A
(b) *pl.* the ~: die Waliser *Pl.*

**Welsh:** ~**man** /ˈwelʃmən/ *n., pl.* ~**men** /ˈwelʃmən/ Waliser, *der;* ~ **'rabbit,** ~ **rarebit** /ˈreəbɪt/ *ns.* Käsetoast, *der*

**went** ▶ GO 1

**wept** ▶ WEEP

**were** ▶ BE

**we're** /wɪə(r)/ = we are; ▶ BE

**weren't** (coll.) = were not; ▶ BE

**west** /west/ **1** *n.* (a) Westen, *der;* in/ to[wards]/from the ~: im/nach/von Westen; to the ~ of westlich von
(b) *usu.* W~ (Geog., Polit.) Westen, *der*
**2** *adj.* westlich; West⟨küste, -wind, -grenze, -tor⟩
**3** *adv.* nach Westen; ~ of westlich von

**West:** ~ **Ber'lin** *pr. n.* (Hist.) West-Berlin (*das*); **w~bound** *adj.* ⟨Zug, Verkehr usw.⟩ in Richtung Westen; ~ **Country** *n.* (Brit.) Westengland, *das;* ~ **'End** *n.* (Brit.) Westend, *das*

**westerly** /ˈwestəlɪ/ *adj.* westlich; ⟨Wind⟩ aus westlichen Richtungen

**western** /ˈwestən/ **1** *adj.* westlich; West⟨grenze, -hälfte, -seite⟩; ~ Germany Westdeutschland, *das*
**2** *n.* Western, *der*

**Western 'Europe** *pr. n.* Westeuropa (*das*)

**West:** ~ **'German** (Hist.) **1** *adj.* westdeutsch; he/she is ~ German er ist Westdeutscher/sie ist Westdeutsche; **2** *n.* Westdeutsche, *der*/die; ~ **'Germany** *pr. n.* (Hist.) Westdeutschland (*das*); ~ **'Indian** **1** *adj.* westindisch; sb. is ~ Indian jmd. ist Westinder/-inderin; **2** *n.* Westinder, *der*/ -inderin, *die;* ~ **'Indies** *pr. n. pl.* Westindische Inseln *Pl.*

**westward[s]** /ˈwestwəd(z)/ *adv.* westwärts

**wet** /wet/ **1** *adj.* (a) nass
(b) (rainy) regnerisch; feucht ⟨Klima⟩
(c) frisch ⟨Farbe⟩; '~ paint„ „frisch gestrichen"
(d) (coll.: feeble) schlapp (ugs.)
**2** *v.t.*, wet *or* wetted befeuchten
**3** *n.* (a) (moisture) Feuchtigkeit, *die*
(b) in the ~: im Regen

**'wetness** *n.* Nässe, *die*

**'wet suit** *n.* Tauchanzug, *der*

**we've** /wɪv, *stressed* wiːv/ = we have

**whack** /wæk/ (coll.) **1** *v.t.* hauen (ugs.)
**2** *n.* Schlag, *der*

**whacked** /wækt/ *adj.* (Brit. coll.: tired out)
erledigt (ugs.); kaputt (ugs.)

**whale** /weɪl/ *n.* **(a)** Wal, *der*
**(b)** (coll.) **we had a ∼ of a [good] time** wir
haben uns bombig (ugs.) amüsiert

'**whalebone** *n.* Fischbein, *das*

**whaler** /'weɪlə(r)/ *n.* Walfänger, *der*

**whaling** /'weɪlɪŋ/ *n.* Walfang, *die*

**wharf** /wɔːf/ *n., pl.* **wharves** /wɔːvz/ *or* ∼s
Kai, *der*

**what** /wɒt/ **1** *adj.* welch...; ∼ **book?**
welches Buch?; ∼ **time does it start?** um wie
viel Uhr fängt es an?; ∼ **kind of man is he?**
was für ein Mensch ist er?; ∼ **a fool you
are!** was für ein Dummkopf du doch bist!;
∼ **cheek/luck!** was für eine Frechheit/ein
Glück!; **I will give you ∼ help I can** ich
werde dir helfen, so gut ich kann
**2** *adv.* ∼ **do I care?** was kümmerts mich?;
∼ **does it matter?** was machts?
**3** *pron.* was; ∼? wie?; was? (ugs.); ∼ **is your
name?** wie heißt du/heißen Sie?; ∼ **about
...?** (∼ will become of ...?) was ist mit ...?;
∼ **about a game of chess?** wie wärs mit
einer Partie Schach?; ∼**'s-his/-her/-its-name**
wie heißt er/sie/es noch; ∼ **for?** wozu?; ∼ **is
it like?** wie ist es?; **so ∼?** na und?; **do ∼ I
tell you** tu, was ich dir sage

**whatever** /wɒt'evə(r)/ **1** *adj.* ∼ **problems
you have** was für Probleme Sie auch haben;
**nothing ∼:** absolut nichts
**2** *pron.* **do ∼ you like** mach, was du willst;
∼ **happens, ...:** was auch geschieht, ...; **or
∼:** oder was auch immer; ∼ **does he want?**
(coll.) was will er nur?

**whatsit** /'wɒtsɪt/ *n.* (coll.) (thing) Dingsbums,
*das* (ugs.); ( person) Dingsda, *der* (ugs.)

**wheat** /wiːt/ *n.* Weizen, *der*

**wheedle** /'wiːdl/ *v.t.* ∼ **sb. into doing sth.**
jmdm. so lange gut zureden, bis er etw. tut;
∼ **sth. out of sb.** jmdm. etw. abschwatzen
(ugs.)

**wheel** /wiːl/ **1** *n.* **(a)** Rad, *das;* **[potter's]**
∼**:** Töpferscheibe, *die*
**(b)** (steering ∼) Lenkrad, *das;* (ship's ∼)
Steuerrad, *das;* **at** *or* **behind the** ∼ (of car)
am Steuer
**2** *v.t.* ( push) schieben
**3** *v.i.* **(a)** (turn round) kehrtmachen
**(b)** (circle) kreisen

**wheel:** ∼**barrow** *n.* Schubkarre, *die;*
∼ **brace** *n.* Radschlüssel, *der;* ∼**chair** *n.*
Rollstuhl, *der;* ∼ **clamp** *n.* Parkkralle, *die*

**wheeler-dealer** /wiːlə'diːlə(r)/ *n.*
Mauschler, *der*/Mauschlerin, *die;* (financial)
Geschäftemacher, *der*/-macherin, *die*

'**wheelie bin** *n.* (Brit. coll.) Müllcontainer,
*der* auf Rollen

'**wheel reflector** *n.* (on bicycle)
Speichenreflektor, *der*

**wheeze** /wiːz/ *v.t.* schnaufen

**whelk** /welk/ *n.* Wellhornschnecke, *die*

**when** /wen/ **1** *adv.* wann; **the time ∼ ...:**
die Zeit, zu der/(with past tense) als ...; **the day
∼ ...:** der Tag, an dem/(with past tense) als ...
**2** *conj.* **(a)** (at the time that) als; (with present or
future tense) wenn; ∼ **reading [a newspaper]**
beim Lesen [einer Zeitung]
**(b)** (whereas) **why do you go abroad ∼ it's
cheaper here?** warum fährst du ins
Ausland, wo es doch hier billiger ist?
**3** *pron.* **by/till ∼ ...?;** bis wann ...?; **since
∼ ...?** seit wann ...?

**whence** /wens/ *adv., conj.* (arch./literary)
woher

**whenever** /wen'evə(r)/ **1** *adv.* wann
immer; **or ∼:** oder wann immer; ∼ **did he
do it?** (coll.) wann hat er es nur getan?
**2** *conj.* jedes Mal wenn

**where** /weə(r)/ **1** *adv.* **(a)** ( position) wo;
∼ **shall we sit?** wohin wollen wir uns
setzen?
**(b)** (to ∼) wohin
**2** *conj.* wo
**3** *pron.* **near/not far from ∼ it happened**
nahe der Stelle/nicht weit von der Stelle, wo
es passiert ist

**whereabouts 1** /weərə'baʊts/ *adv.*
(where) wo; (to where) wohin
**2** /'weərəbaʊts/ *n., sing. or pl.* (of thing)
Verbleib, *der;* (of person) Aufenthalt[sort], *der*

**where:** ∼**'as** *conj.* während; **he is very
quiet,** ∼**as she is an extrovert** er ist sehr
ruhig, sie dagegen ist eher extravertiert;
∼**'by** *adv.* mit dem/der/denen; ∼**upon**
/weərə'pɒn/ *adv.* worauf

**wherever** /weər'evə(r)/ **1** *adv.* **(a)**
( position) wo immer; **sit ∼ you like** setz dich,
wohin du magst; **or ∼:** oder wo immer
**(b)** (direction) wohin immer; **or ∼:** oder
wohin immer
**(c)** ∼ **have you been?** (coll.) wo hast du bloß
gesteckt?
**2** *conj.* **(a)** ( position) überall [da], wo;
∼ **possible** wo od. wenn [irgend] möglich
**(b)** (direction) wohin auch; ∼ **he went** wohin
er auch ging

**wherewithal** /'weəwɪðɔːl/ *n.* (coll.) **the ∼:**
das nötige Kleingeld (ugs.)

**whet** /wet/ *v.t.,* **-tt-:** **(a)** (sharpen) wetzen
**(b)** (fig.) anregen ‹Appetit›

**whether** /'weðə(r)/ *conj.* ob; **I don't know
∼ to go [or not]** ich weiß nicht, ob ich
gehen soll [oder nicht]

**which** /wɪtʃ/ **1** *adj.* welch...; ∼ **one**
welcher/welche/welches; ∼ **ones** welche;
∼ **way** (how) wie; (in ∼ direction) wohin
**2** *pron.* **(a)** interrog. welcher/welche/
welches; ∼ **of you?** wer von euch?
**(b)** rel. der/die/das; **of ∼:** dessen/deren;
**after ∼:** worauf[hin]

**whichever** /wɪtʃ'evə(r)/ **1** *adj.* welcher/
welche/welches ... auch    ⋯⋮

W

**2** *pron.* **(a)** welcher/welche/welches ... auch **(b)** (coll.) ~ **could it be?** welcher/welche/welches könnte das nur sein?

**whiff** /wɪf/ *n.* ( puff; fig.: trace) Hauch, *der;* (smell) leichter Geruch

**while** /waɪl/ **1** *n.* Weile, *die;* [for] a ~: eine Weile; **a long** ~: lange; **for a little** *or* **short** ~: eine kleine Weile; **[only] a little** *or* **short** ~ **ago** [erst] kürzlich *od.* vor kurzem; **be worth sb.'s** ~: sich [für jmdn.] lohnen **2** *conj.* **(a)** während; (as long as) solange **(b)** (although) obgleich **(c)** (whereas) während

■ **while a'way** *v.t.* ~ **away the time** sich (*Dat.*) die Zeit vertreiben (**by, with** mit)

**whilst** /waɪlst/ (Brit.) ▶ WHILE 2

**whim** /wɪm/ *n.* Laune, *die*

**whimper** /'wɪmpə(r)/ **1** *n.* ~[s] Wimmern, *das;* (of dog etc.) Winseln, *das* **2** *v.i.* wimmern; ⟨*Hund:*⟩ winseln

**whimsical** /'wɪmzɪkl/ *adj.* launenhaft; (odd, fanciful) spleenig

**whine** /waɪn/ **1** *v.i.* **(a)** heulen; ⟨*Hund:*⟩ jaulen **(b)** (complain) jammern **2** *n.* **(a)** Heulen, *das;* (of dog) Jaulen, *das* **(b)** (complaint) ~[s] Gejammer, *das*

**whip** /wɪp/ **1** *n.* **(a)** Peitsche, *die* **(b)** (Brit. Parl.) Fraktionsgeschäftsführer, *der/* -führerin, *die* **2** *v.t.,* **-pp-: (a)** peitschen **(b)** (Cookery) schlagen **(c)** (move quickly) reißen **(d)** (coll.: steal) klauen (ugs.)

■ **whip 'out** *v.t.* [blitzschnell] herausziehen

■ **whip 'up** *v.t.* **(a)** (arouse) anheizen (ugs.) **(b)** (coll.: make quickly) schnell hinzaubern ⟨*Gericht, Essen*⟩

**whiplash** *n.* ~lash [injury] Peitschenschlagverletzung, *die*

**whipped 'cream** *n.* Schlagsahne, *die*

**'whipping cream** *n.* (flüssige) Schlagsahne

**'whip-round** *n.* (Brit. coll.) Sammlung, *die*

**whirl** /wɜːl/ **1** *v.t.* [im Kreis] herumwirbeln **2** *v.i.* wirbeln **3** *n.* **(a)** Wirbeln, *das;* **she was** *or* **her thoughts were in a** ~ (fig.) ihr schwirrte der Kopf **(b)** (bustle) Trubel, *der*

■ **whirl 'round** **1** *v.t.* [im Kreis] herumwirbeln **2** *v.i.* [im Kreis] herumwirbeln; ⟨*Rad, Rotor:*⟩ wirbeln

**whirl:** ~**pool** *n.* Strudel, *der;* (bathing pool) Whirlpool, *der;* ~**wind** *n.* Wirbelwind, *der*

**whirr** /wɜː(r)/ **1** *v.i.* surren **2** *n.* Surren, *das*

**whisk** /wɪsk/ **1** *n.* (Cookery) Schneebesen, *der;* ( part of mixer) Rührbesen, *der* **2** *v.t.* **(a)** (Cookery) [mit dem Schnee-/Rührbesen] schlagen **(b)** (convey rapidly) in Windeseile bringen

■ **whisk a'way** *v.t.* **(a)** (remove suddenly) ~ **sth. away** [**from sb.**] [jmdm.] etw. [plötzlich] wegreißen **(b)** (convey rapidly) in Windeseile wegbringen

**whisker** /'wɪskə(r)/ *n.* **(a)** ~**s** (on man's cheek) Backenbart, *der* **(b)** (of cat, mouse, rat) Schnurrhaar, *das*

**whiskey** (Amer., Ir.), **whisky** /'wɪskɪ/ *n.* Whisky, *der;* (American *or* Irish) Whiskey, *der*

**whisper** /'wɪspə(r)/ **1** *v.i.* flüstern; ~ **to sb.** jmdm. etwas zuflüstern **2** *v.t.* flüstern; ~ **sth. to sb.** jmdm. etw. zuflüstern **3** *n.* **(a)** Flüstern, *das;* **in a** ~, **in** ~**s** im Flüsterton **(b)** (rumour) Gerücht, *das*

**whistle** /'wɪsl/ **1** *v.i.* pfeifen; ~ **at sb.** (in disapproval) jmdn. auspfeifen **2** *v.t.* pfeifen **3** *n.* **(a)** (sound) Pfiff, *der;* (whistling) Pfeifen, *das* **(b)** (instrument) Pfeife, *die;* **blow a/one's** ~: pfeifen

**whistling 'kettle** *n.* Pfeifkessel, *der*

**white** /waɪt/ **1** *adj.* weiß **2** *n.* **(a)** (colour) Weiß, *das* **(b)** (of egg) Eiweiß, *das* **(c)** W~ (person) Weiße, *der/die*

**white:** ~ **bread** *n.* Weißbrot, *das;* ~ **cell** *n.* weißes Blutkörperchen; ~ **'coffee** *n.* (Brit.) Kaffee mit Milch; ~**'collar worker** *n.* Angestellte, *der/die;* ~ **corpuscle** ▶ ~ CELL; ~ **'elephant** ▶ ELEPHANT; **W~ House** *pr. n.* (Amer. Polit.) **the W~ House** das Weiße Haus; ~**knuckle ride** *n.* Fahrt mit äußerstem Nervenkitzel; ~ **'lie** ▶ LIE¹ 1; ~ **'meat** *n.* weißes Fleisch [und Geflügel]

**whiten** /'waɪtn/ **1** *v.t.* weiß machen; weißen ⟨*Wand, Schuhe*⟩ **2** *v.i.* weiß werden

**'whiteness** *n.* Weiß, *das*

**white: W~ 'Paper** *n.* (Brit.) *öffentliches Diskussionspapier über Vorhaben der Regierung;* ~ **'sauce** *n.* weiße *od.* helle Soße; ~**wash** **1** *n.* [weiße] Tünche; (fig.) Schönfärberei, *die;* **2** *v.t.* [weiß] tünchen; ~ **'wedding** *n.* Hochzeit, *die* in Weiß; ~ **'wine** *n.* Weißwein, *der*

**Whit 'Monday** /wɪt/ *n.* Pfingstmontag, *der*

**Whitsun** /'wɪtsn/ *n.* Pfingsten, *das od. Pl.;* **at** ~: zu *od.* an Pfingsten

**whittle** /'wɪtl/**:** ~ **a'way** *v.t.* ~ **away sb.'s rights/power** jmdm. nach und nach alle Rechte/Macht nehmen; ~ **'down** *v.t.* allmählich reduzieren ⟨*Anzahl, Gewinn*⟩; verkürzen ⟨*Liste*⟩

**whiz, whizz** /wɪz/ **1** *v.i.,* **-zz-** zischen **2** *n.* Zischen, *das*

**'whiz[z]-kid** *n.* (coll.) Senkrechtstarter, *der*

**who** /huː, *stressed* huː/ *pron.* **(a)** *interrog.* wer; (coll.: whom) wen; (coll.: to whom) wem **(b)** *rel.* der/die/das; *pl.* die; (coll.: whom) den/

die/das; (coll.: to whom) dem/der/denen;
**anyone/those** ~ ...: wer ...; **everybody** ~ ...:
jeder, der ...

**whoa** /wəʊ/ int. brr

**who'd** /hʊd, stressed huːd/ (a) = **who had**;
(b) = **who would**

**whoever** /huːˈevə(r)/ pron. (a) wer
[immer]
(b) (no matter who) wer ... auch
(c) (coll.) ~ **could it be?** wer könnte das nur
sein?

**whole** /həʊl/ ⏹ adj. ganz; **the** ~ **lot** [of
**them**] [sie] alle
⏹ n. Ganze, das; **the** ~: das Ganze; **the** ~ **of**
**my money/the village/London** mein ganzes
Geld/das ganze Dorf/ganz London; **as a** ~:
als Ganzes; **on the** ~: im Großen und
Ganzen

**whole:** ~**food** n. Vollwertkost, die;
~**hearted** /həʊlˈhɑːtɪd/ adj. herzlich
⟨Dank[barkeit]⟩; rückhaltlos
⟨Unterstützung⟩; ~**meal** adj. Vollkorn-;
~ ˈ**milk** n. Vollmilch, die; ~ **note** n.
(Amer. Mus.) ganze Note; ~ ˈ**number** n.
ganze Zahl; ~**sale** ⏹ adj. (a)
Großhandels-; (b) (fig.: on a large scale)
massenhaft; Massen-; ⏹ adv. (a) en gros;
(b) (fig.: on a large scale) massenweise;
~**saler** /ˈhəʊlseɪlə(r)/ n. Großhändler, der/
-händlerin, die

**wholesome** /ˈhəʊlsəm/ adj. gesund

**who'll** /hʊl, stressed huːl/ = **who will**

**wholly** /ˈhəʊllɪ/ adv. völlig

**whom** /huːm/ pron. (a) interrog. wen; as
indirect object wem
(b) rel. den/die/das; pl. die; as indirect object
dem/der/dem; pl. denen

**whooping cough** /ˈhuːpɪŋ kɒf/ n.
Keuchhusten, der

**whopper** /ˈwɒpə(r)/ n. (coll.) (a) Riese, der
(b) (lie) faustdicke Lüge

**whopping** /ˈwɒpɪŋ/ adj. (coll.) riesig;
Riesen- (ugs.); faustdick ⟨Lüge⟩

**whore** /hɔː(r)/ n. Hure, die

**who's** /huːz/ (a) = **who is**
(b) = **who has**

**whose** /huːz/ pron. (a) interrog. wessen;
~ [**book**] **is that?** wem gehört das [Buch]?
(b) rel. dessen/deren/dessen; pl. deren

**who've** /hʊv, stressed huːv/ = **who have**

**why** /waɪ/ ⏹ adv. (a) (for what reason)
warum; (for what purpose) wozu; ~ **is that?**
warum das?
(b) (on account of which) **the reason** ~ **he did it**
der Grund, warum er es tat
⏹ int. ~, **certainly/of course!** aber sicher!

**wick** /wɪk/ n. Docht, der

**wicked** /ˈwɪkɪd/ adj. böse

**ˈwickedness** n. Bosheit, die

**wicker** /ˈwɪkə(r)/ n. Korbgeflecht, das;
attrib. Korb⟨waren, -stuhl⟩

**ˈwickerwork** n. (a) (material) Korbgeflecht,
das

(b) (articles) Korbwaren Pl.

**wicket** /ˈwɪkɪt/ n. (Cricket) Tor, das

**ˈwicketkeeper** n. (Cricket) Torwächter,
der/-wächterin, die

**wide** /waɪd/ ⏹ adj. (a) (broad) breit; groß
⟨Abstand, Winkel⟩; **three feet** ~: drei Fuß
breit
(b) (extensive) weit; umfassend ⟨Lektüre,
Wissen, Kenntnisse⟩; reichhaltig ⟨Auswahl,
Sortiment⟩
(c) (off target) **be** ~ **of sth.** etw. verfehlen
⏹ adv. (a) ~ **awake** hellwach
(b) (off target) **shoot** ~: danebenschießen; **go**
~: das Ziel verfehlen

**wide:** ~-**angle** ˈ**lens** n. (Photog.)
Weitwinkelobjektiv, das; ~-**eyed** adj.
(surprised) mit großen Augen nachgestellt

**ˈwidely** adv. (a) (over a wide area) weit
⟨verbreitet, gestreut⟩
(b) (by many people) weithin ⟨bekannt,
akzeptiert⟩; **a** ~ **held view** eine weit
verbreitete Ansicht
(c) (greatly) erheblich ⟨sich unterscheiden⟩

**widen** /ˈwaɪdn/ ⏹ v.t. verbreitern
⏹ v.i. sich verbreitern

**wide:** ~-**open** attrib. adj., ~ ˈ**open** pred.
adj. weit geöffnet ⟨Fenster, Tür⟩; weit
aufgerissen ⟨Mund, Augen⟩; **be** ~ **open**
⟨Fenster, Tür:⟩ weit offen stehen;
~-**ranging** /ˈwaɪdreɪndʒɪŋ/ adj. weit
gehend ⟨Maßnahme, Veränderung⟩;
ausführlich ⟨Diskussion, Gespräch⟩;
~ ˈ**screen** n. Breitwand, die; ~**screen**
**television**, ~**screen TV** ns.
Breitwandfernsehen, das; ~**spread** adj.
weit verbreitet

**widow** /ˈwɪdəʊ/ n. Witwe, die

**widowed** /ˈwɪdəʊd/ adj. verwitwet

**widower** /ˈwɪdəʊə(r)/ n. Witwer, der

**width** /wɪdθ/ n. Breite, die; (of garment)
Weite, die

**wield** /wiːld/ v.t. schwingen; (fig.) ausüben
⟨Macht, Einfluss⟩

**wife** /waɪf/ n., pl. **wives** /waɪvz/ Frau, die

**ˈwife battering** n. Misshandlung, die der
[Ehe]frau

**wig** /wɪg/ n. Perücke, die

**wiggle** /ˈwɪgl/ (coll.) ⏹ v.t. hin und her
bewegen
⏹ v.i. wackeln

**wild** /waɪld/ ⏹ adj. (a) wild lebend ⟨Tier⟩;
wild wachsend ⟨Pflanze⟩
(b) wild ⟨Landschaft⟩
(c) (unrestrained) wild ⟨Erregung⟩; **run** ~
⟨Pferd, Hund:⟩ frei herumlaufen; ⟨Kind:⟩
herumtoben; **send** or **drive sb.** ~: jmdn.
rasend vor Erregung machen
(d) (coll.: very keen) **be** ~ **about sb./sth.** wild
auf jmdn./etw. sein
⏹ n. **the** ~[**s**] die Wildnis; **see an animal in**
**the** ~: ein Tier in freier Wildbahn sehen

**W**

**wild:** ~ **'boar** n. Wildschwein, das;
~ **card** n. wilde Karte; ~**cat** n. Wildkatze,
die

**wilderness** /'wɪldənɪs/ n. Wildnis, die;
(desert) Wüste, die

**wild:** ~ **'goose chase** n. (fig.)
aussichtslose Suche; ~**life** n. die Tier- und
Pflanzenwelt; ~life park/reserve/sanctuary
Naturpark, der/-reservat, das/-schutzgebiet,
das

**'wildly** adv. wild; be ~ excited about sth.
über etw. (Akk.) ganz aus dem Häuschen
sein (ugs.); ~ inaccurate völlig ungenau

**wilful** /'wɪlfl/ adj., **wilfully** /'wɪlfəlɪ/ adv.
(a) (deliberate[ly]) vorsätzlich
(b) (obstinate[ly]) starrsinnig

**will¹** /wɪl/ v. aux., only in: pres. will, neg.
(coll.) won't /wəʊnt/, past would /wʊd/, neg.
(coll.) wouldn't /'wʊdnt/ He won't help me.
W~/Would you? Er will mir nicht helfen.
Bist du bereit?; the car won't start das Auto
springt nicht an; ~/would you pass the salt,
please? gibst du bitte mal das Salz rüber?/
würdest du bitte mal das Salz rübergeben?/
~ you be quiet! willst du wohl ruhig sein!;
he ~ sit there hour after hour er pflegt dort
stundenlang zu sitzen; he '~ insist on doing
it er besteht unbedingt darauf, es zu tun;
~ you have some more cake? möchtest od.
willst du noch etwas Kuchen?; the box
~ hold 5 lb. of tea in die Kiste gehen
5 Pfund Tee; tomorrow he ~ be in Oxford
morgen ist er in Oxford; I promise I won't do
it again ich verspreche, ich mach's nicht
noch mal; if he tried, he would succeed wenn
er es versuchen würde, würde er es
schaffen; ~ you please tidy up würdest du
bitte aufräumen?

**will²** n. (a) (faculty) Wille, der
(b) (Law: testament) Testament, das
(c) (desire) at ~: nach Belieben; ~ to live
Lebenswille, der; against one's/sb.'s ~:
gegen seinen/jmds. Willen

**'willing** adj. willig; ready and ~: bereit; be
~ to do sth. bereit sein, etw. zu tun

**'willingly** adv. (a) (with pleasure) gern[e]
(b) (voluntarily) freiwillig

**'willingness** n. Bereitschaft, die

**willow** /'wɪləʊ/ n. Weide, die

**willowy** /'wɪləʊɪ/ adj. gertenschlank

**'will power** n. Willenskraft, die

**willy-nilly** /'wɪlɪ'nɪlɪ/ adv. wohl oder übel
⟨etw. tun müssen⟩

**wilt** /wɪlt/ v.i. ⟨Pflanze, Blumen:⟩ welk
werden, welken

**wily** /'waɪlɪ/ adj. listig; gewieft ⟨Person⟩

**wimp** /wɪmp/ n. (coll.) Schlappschwanz, der
(ugs.)

**wimpish** /'wɪmpɪʃ/ adj. (coll.) lahm (ugs.)

**win** /wɪn/ ① v.t., -nn-, won /wʌn/ gewinnen;
bekommen ⟨Stipendium, Vertrag, Recht⟩;
~ sb. sth. jmdm. etw. einbringen
② v.i., -nn-, won gewinnen

③ n. Sieg, der; have a ~: gewinnen

■ **win 'over, win 'round** v.t. bekehren;
(to one's side) auf seine Seite bringen;
(convince) überzeugen

■ **win 'through** v.i. Erfolg haben

**wince** /wɪns/ v.i. zusammenzucken (at bei)

**winch** /wɪntʃ/ ① n. Winde, die
② v.t. winden; ~ up hochwinden

**wind¹** /wɪnd/ ① n. Wind, der; (Med.)
Blähungen Pl.; get ~ of sth. (fig.) Wind von
etw. bekommen; be in the ~ (fig.) in der Luft
liegen; get/have the ~ up (coll.) Manschetten
(ugs.) kriegen/haben
② v.t. the blow ~ed him der Schlag nahm
ihm den Atem

**wind²** /waɪnd/ ① v.i., wound /waʊnd/ (a)
(curve) sich winden; (move) sich schlängeln
(b) (coil) sich wickeln
② v.t., wound (a) (coil) wickeln; ~ sth. on
[to] sth. etw. auf etw. (Akk.) [auf]wickeln
(b) aufziehen ⟨Uhr⟩

■ **wind 'down** v.t. (a) herunterdrehen
⟨Autofenster⟩
(b) (fig.: reduce gradually) einschränken

■ **wind 'up** ① v.t. (a) hochdrehen
⟨Autofenster⟩
(b) (coil) aufwickeln
(c) aufziehen ⟨Uhr⟩
(d) (coll.: annoy deliberately) auf die Palme
bringen (ugs.)
(e) beschließen ⟨Debatte⟩
(f) (Finance, Law) auflösen
② v.i. (a) (conclude) schließen
(b) (coll.: end up) ~ up in prison/hospital [zum
Schluss] im Gefängnis/Krankenhaus landen
(ugs.)

**wind** /wɪnd/: ~-**blown** adj. vom Wind
zerzaust ⟨Haar⟩; ~**break** n. Windschutz,
der; ~**breaker** (Amer.), ~**cheater** (Brit.)
ns. Windjacke, die; ~ **chill factor** n.
Wind-chill-Index, der

**winded** /'wɪndɪd/ adj. be ~: außer Atem
sein

**winder** /'waɪndə(r)/ n. (of watch) Krone, die;
(of clock, toy) Aufziehschraube, die

**wind** /wɪnd/: ~**fall** n. (a) (fruit) ~falls
Fallobst, das; (b) (fig.) warmer Regen (ugs.);
~fall tax (einmalige) Sondersteuer auf
Privatisierungsgewinne; ~ **farm** n.
Windpark, der; ~ **force** n. Windstärke, die;
~ **instrument** n. Blasinstrument, das;
~**mill** n. Windmühle, die

**window** /'wɪndəʊ/ n. (also Comp.) Fenster,
das; (shop ~) [Schau]fenster, das; break a ~:
eine Fensterscheibe zerbrechen

**window:** ~ **box** n. Blumenkasten, der;
~ **cleaner** n. Fensterputzer, der/-putzerin,
die; ~ **cleaning** n. Fensterputzen, das;
~ **display** n. Schaufensterauslage, die;
~ **dresser** n. Schaufensterdekorateur,
der/-dekorateurin, die; ~ **dressing** n. (fig.)
Schönfärberei, die; ~ **frame** n.
Fensterrahmen, der; ~ **ledge** n. (inside)
Fensterbank, die; (outside) Fenstersims, der

*od. das;* ~ **pane** *n.* Fensterscheibe, *die;*
~ **shopping** *n.* Schaufensterbummeln,
*das;* go ~ shopping einen
Schaufensterbummel machen; ~ **sill** *n.*
(inside) Fensterbank, *die;* (outside)
Fenstersims, *der od. das*

**wind** /wɪnd/: ~**pipe** *n.* (Anat.) Luftröhre,
*die;* ~ **power** *n.* Windkraft, *die;* ~**proof**
*adj.* windabweisend; ~**proof** jacket
Windjacke, *die;* ~**screen,** (Amer.)
~**shield** *ns.* Windschutzscheibe, *die;*
~screen/~shield wiper Scheibenwischer,
*der;* ~screen/~shield washer
Scheibenwaschanlage, *die;* ~**surfer** *n.*
Windsurfer, *der;* ~**surfing** *n.* Windsurfen,
*das;* ~**swept** *adj.* windgepeitscht; vom
Wind zerzaust ⟨*Person, Haare*⟩; ~ **tunnel**
*n.* Windkanal, *der*

**windward** /'wɪndwəd/ *adj.* ~ **side**
Windseite, *die*

'**windy** *adj.* windig

**wine** /waɪn/ *n.* Wein, *der*

**wine:** ~ **bar** *n.* Weinstube, *die;* ~ **bottle**
*n.* Weinflasche, *die;* ~ **cellar** *n.*
[Wein]keller, *das;* ~ **cooler** *n.*
Weinkühler, *der;* ~**glass** *n.* Weinglas, *das;*
~**grower** *n.* Winzer, *der*/Winzerin, *die;*
~**growing** ① *n.* Weinbau, *der;* ② *adj.*
~-growing area Weingegend, *die;* ~ **list** *n.*
Weinkarte, *die;* ~ **merchant** *n.*
Weinhändler, *der*/-händlerin, *die;*
~ merchants (business) Weinhandlung, *die;*
~ **tasting** /'waɪnteɪstɪŋ/ *n.* Weinprobe,
*die;* ~ **vault** *n.* Weinkeller, *der;*
~ '**vinegar** *n.* Weinessig, *der*

**wing** /wɪŋ/ *n.* (a) (Ornith., Archit., Sport) Flügel,
*der*
(b) (Aeronaut.) Tragfläche, *die*
(c) (Brit. Motor. Veh.) Kotflügel, *der*

**winged** /wɪŋd/ *adj.* geflügelt

**winger** /'wɪŋə(r)/ *n.* (Sport) Außenstürmer,
*der*/-stürmerin, *die*

**wing:** ~ **mirror** *n.* (Brit. Motor Veh.)
Außenspiegel, *der;* ~**span** *n.*
[Flügel]spannweite, *die;* ~ **tip** *n.*
Flügelspitze, *die*

**wink** /wɪŋk/ ① *v.i.* (a) blinzeln; (as signal)
zwinkern; ~ **at sb.** jmdm. zuzwinkern
(b) (flash) blinken
② *n.* (a) Blinzeln, *das;* (signal) Zwinkern,
*das;* **give sb. a ~:** jmdm. zuzwinkern
(b) **not sleep a ~:** kein Auge zutun

'**winner** *n.* Sieger, *der*/Siegerin, *die;* (of
competition or prize) Gewinner, *der*/
Gewinnerin, *die*

'**winning** *adj.* (a) *attrib.* siegreich;
~ number Gewinnzahl, *die*
(b) (charming) einnehmend; gewinnend
⟨*Lächeln*⟩

'**winning post** *n.* Zielpfosten, *der*

'**winnings** *n. pl.* Gewinn, *der*

**winter** /'wɪntə(r)/ *n.* Winter, *der;* **in [the] ~:**
im Winter

**winter 'sports** *n. pl.* Wintersport, *der*

**wintry** /'wɪntrɪ/ *adj.* winterlich; ~ shower
Schneegestöber, *das*

**wipe** /waɪp/ ① *v.t.* (a) abwischen;
[auf]wischen ⟨*Fußboden*⟩; (dry) abtrocknen;
~ one's mouth/eyes/nose sich (*Dat.*) den
Mund/die Tränen/die Nase abwischen;
~ one's feet/shoes [sich (*Dat.*)] die Füße/
Schuhe abtreten
(b) (get rid of) [ab]wischen; ~ one's/sb.'s
tears sich/jmdm. die Tränen abwischen
② *n.* **give sth. a ~:** etw. abwischen
▪ **wipe 'down** *v.t.* abwischen; (dry)
abtrocknen
▪ **wipe 'off** *v.t.* (a) (remove) wegwischen;
löschen ⟨*Bandaufnahme*⟩
(b) (pay off) zurückzahlen ⟨*Schulden*⟩
▪ **wipe 'out** *v.t.* (a) (remove) wegwischen;
(erase) auslöschen
(b) (cancel) tilgen; zunichte machen ⟨*Vorteil,
Gewinn usw.*⟩
(c) (destroy) ausrotten ⟨*Rasse, Tierart,
Feinde*⟩; ausmerzen ⟨*Seuche, Korruption*⟩
▪ **wipe 'up** *v.t.* (a) aufwischen
(b) (dry) abtrocknen

'**wiper** *n.* (Motor Veh.) Wischer, *der*

**wire** /'waɪə(r)/ ① *n.* (a) Draht, *der*
(b) (Electr., Teleph.) Leitung, *die*
(c) (coll.: telegram) Telegramm, *das*
② *v.t.* (a) (fasten) ~ sth. together etw. mit
Draht verbinden
(b) (Electr.) ~ sth. to sth. etw. an etw. (*Akk.*)
anschließen; ~ a house in einem Haus die
Stromleitungen legen

**wire:** ~ '**brush** *n.* Drahtbürste, *die;*
~ **cutters** *n. pl.* Drahtschneider, *der*

'**wireless** *n.* (Brit. dated) Radio, *das*

**wire:** ~ '**netting** *n.* Maschendraht, *der;*
~ **strippers** *n. pl.* Abisolierzange, *die;*
~ '**wool** *n.* Stahlwolle, *die*

**wiring** /'waɪərɪŋ/ *n.* [elektrische] Leitungen
*Pl.*

**wisdom** /'wɪzdəm/ *n.* (a) Weisheit, *die*
(b) (prudence) Klugheit, *die*

'**wisdom tooth** *n.* Weisheitszahn, *der*

**wise** /waɪz/ *adj.* (a) weise; vernünftig
⟨*Meinung*⟩
(b) (prudent) klug
(c) **be none the ~r** kein bisschen klüger als
vorher sein

**wise:** ~**crack** (coll.) *n.* witzige
Bemerkung; ~ **guy** *n.* (coll.) Klugscheißer,
*der* (salopp)

'**wisely** *adv.* weise; (prudently) klug

**wish** /wɪʃ/ ① *v.t.* wünschen; I ~ I was *or*
were rich ich wollte, ich wäre reich; I ~ **to**
go ich möchte gehen; ~ **sb. luck/success**
*etc.* jmdm. Glück/Erfolg *usw.* wünschen;
~ **sb. well** jmdm. alles Gute wünschen
② *v.i.* wünschen; ~ **for sth.** sich (*Dat.*) etw.
wünschen
③ *n.* Wunsch, *der;* **make a ~:** sich (*Dat.*)
etwas wünschen; **get** *or* **have one's ~:**
seinen Wunsch erfüllt bekommen

**wishful thinking** /ˌwɪʃfl ˈθɪŋkɪŋ/ n. Wunschdenken, das

**'wishing well** n. Wunschbrunnen, der

**wishy-washy** /ˈwɪʃɪwɒʃɪ/ adj. labberig (ugs.); (fig.) lasch

**wisp** /wɪsp/ n. (of straw) Büschel, das; ~ of hair Haarsträhne, die; ~ of cloud/smoke Wolkenfetzen, der/Rauchfahne, die

**wistful** /ˈwɪstfl/ adj., **'wistfully** adv. wehmütig

**wit** /wɪt/ n. (a) (humour) Witz, der (b) (intelligence) Geist, der; be at one's ~'s or ~s' end sich (Dat.) keinen Rat mehr wissen; be frightened or scared out of one's ~s Todesangst haben; have/keep one's ~s about one auf Draht (ugs.) sein/nicht den Kopf verlieren (c) (person) geistreicher Mensch

**witch** /wɪtʃ/ n. Hexe, die

**witch:** ~**craft** n. Hexerei, die; ~ **doctor** n. Medizinmann, der; ~**-hunt** n. Hexenjagd, die (for auf + Akk.)

**with** /wɪð/ prep. mit; **put sth.** ~ **sth.** etw. zu etw. stellen/legen; **have nothing to write** ~: nichts zum Schreiben haben; **I'm not '**~ **you** (coll.) ich komme nicht mit; **tremble** ~ **fear** vor Angst zittern; **I have no money** ~ **me** ich habe kein Geld dabei od. bei mir; **sleep** ~ **the window open** bei offenem Fenster schlafen

**with'draw** ① v.t., forms as DRAW 1: zurückziehen; abziehen ⟨Truppen⟩; ~ **sth. from an account** etw. von einem Konto abheben
② v.i., forms as DRAW 1: sich zurückziehen

**withdrawal** /wɪðˈdrɔːəl/ n. (a) Zurücknahme, die; (of troops) Abzug, der; (of money) Abhebung, die (b) (from drugs) Entzug, der; ~ **symptoms** Entzugserscheinungen Pl.

**with'drawn** adj. (unsociable) verschlossen

**wither** /ˈwɪðə(r)/ ① v.t. verdorren lassen
② v.i. [ver]welken
∎ **wither a'way** v.i. dahinwelken (geh.)

**withered** /ˈwɪðəd/ adj. verwelkt ⟨Gras, Pflanze⟩; verkrüppelt ⟨Gliedmaße⟩

**withering** /ˈwɪðərɪŋ/ adj. vernichtend ⟨Blick⟩

**with'hold** v.t., forms as HOLD²: ~ **sth. from sb.** jmdm. etw. vorenthalten

**within** /wɪˈðɪn/ prep. innerhalb; **stay/be** ~ **the law** den Boden des Gesetzes nicht verlassen; ~ **eight miles of sth.** acht Meilen im Umkreis von etw.

**without** /wɪˈðaʊt/ prep. ohne; ~ **doing sth.** ohne etw. zu tun; ~ **his knowing** ohne dass er davon weiß/wusste

**with'stand** v.t., withstood /wɪðˈstʊd/ standhalten (+ Dat.); aushalten ⟨Beanspruchung, hohe Temperaturen⟩

**witness** /ˈwɪtnɪs/ ① n. Zeuge, der/Zeugin, die (of, to Gen.)
② v.t. (a) (see) ~ **sth.** Zeuge/Zeugin einer Sache (Gen.) sein (b) bestätigen ⟨Unterschrift⟩

**'witness box** (Brit.), **'witness stand** (Amer.) ns. Zeugenstand, der

**witticism** /ˈwɪtɪsɪzm/ n. Witzelei, die

**wittingly** /ˈwɪtɪŋlɪ/ adv. wissentlich

**witty** /ˈwɪtɪ/ adj. witzig; geistreich ⟨Person⟩

**wives** pl. of WIFE

**wizard** /ˈwɪzəd/ n. Zauberer, der

**wizardry** /ˈwɪzədrɪ/ n. Zauberei, die

**wizened** /ˈwɪzənd/ adj. runz[e]lig

**wobble** /ˈwɒbl/ v.i. wackeln

**wobbly** /ˈwɒblɪ/ adj. wack[e]lig

**woe** /wəʊ/ n. (arch./literary/joc.) ~[s] Jammer, der; ~ **betide you!** wehe dir!

**woebegone** /ˈwəʊbɪgɒn/ adj. jammervoll

**woeful** /ˈwəʊfl/ adj. (deplorable) beklagenswert; (distressed) jammervoll

**wok** /wɒk/ n. (Cookery) Wok, der

**woke, woken** ▶ WAKE¹ 1, 2

**wolf** /wʊlf/ ① n., pl. wolves /wʊlvz/ Wolf, der
② v.t. ~ **[down]** verschlingen

**woman** /ˈwʊmən/ n., pl. women /ˈwɪmɪn/ Frau, die; ~ **doctor** Ärztin, die; ~ **friend** Freundin, die

**womanize** /ˈwʊmənaɪz/ v.i. den Frauen nachstellen

**womanizer** /ˈwʊmənaɪzə(r)/ n. Schürzenjäger, der

**'womanly** adj. fraulich

**womb** /wuːm/ n. Gebärmutter, die

**women** pl. of WOMAN

**women:** ~**folk** n. pl. Frauen Pl.; **W**~**'s 'Lib** (coll.), **W**~**'s Libe'ration** ns. die Frauenbewegung, die; ~**'s movement** n. Frauenbewegung, die; ~**'s 'prison** n. Frauengefängnis, das; ~**'s 'refuge** n. Frauenhaus, das; ~**'s 'rights** n. pl. die Rechte der Frau

**won** ▶ WIN 1, 2

**wonder** /ˈwʌndə(r)/ ① n. (a) (thing) Wunder, das (b) (feeling) Staunen, das
② adj. Wunder-
③ v.i. sich wundern; staunen (at über + Akk.)
④ v.t. sich fragen; **I** ~ **what the time is** wie viel Uhr mag es wohl sein?; **I** ~ **whether I might open the window** dürfte ich vielleicht das Fenster öffnen?

**wonderful** /ˈwʌndəfl/ adj., **wonderfully** /ˈwʌndəfəlɪ/ adv. wunderbar

**wondering** /ˈwʌndərɪŋ/ adj., **wonderingly** /ˈwʌndərɪŋlɪ/ adv. staunend

**won't** /wəʊnt/ (coll.) = will not; ▶ WILL¹

**woo** /wuː/ v.t. (a) (literary: court) ~ **sb.** um jmdn. werben (geh.) (b) umwerben ⟨Kunden, Wähler⟩

**wood** /wʊd/ n. (a) Holz, das; **touch** ~ (Brit.), **knock on** ~ (Amer.) unberufen!

**(b)** (trees) Wald, *der*

**wood:** ∼ **carving** *n.* (object) Holzschnitzerei, *die;* ∼**craft** *n.* (∼work) Holzschnitzerei, *die;* ∼**cut** *n.* Holzschnitt, *der;* ∼**cutter** *n.* Holzfäller, *der*

**'wooded** *adj.* bewaldet

**wooden** /'wʊdn/ *adj.* **(a)** hölzern; Holz- **(b)** (fig.: stiff) hölzern

**wood:** ∼**land** /'wʊdlənd/ *n.* Waldland, *das;* ∼**pecker** *n.* Specht, *der;* ∼ **pigeon** *n.* Ringeltaube, *die;* ∼**shed** *n.* Holzschuppen, *der;* ∼**wind** *n.* the ∼wind [section] die Holzbläser *Pl.;* ∼wind instrument Holzblasinstrument, *das;* ∼**work** *n.* **(a)** (craft) Arbeiten mit Holz; **(b)** (things) Holzarbeit[en *Pl.*]; ∼**worm** *n.* Holzwurm, *der;* **it's got** ∼worm da ist der Holzwurm drin (ugs.)

**'woody** *adj.* **(a)** (wooded) waldreich **(b)** (consisting of wood) holzig

**wool** /wʊl/ *n.* Wolle, *die; attrib.* Woll-

**woollen** (*Amer.:* **woolen**) /'wʊlən/ **1** *adj.* wollen **2** *n.* ∼s Wollsachen *Pl.*

**'woolly** *adj.* **(a)** (wollig, Woll⟨pullover, -mütze⟩ **(b)** (confused) verschwommen

**woozy** /'wuːzɪ/ *adj.* (coll.) **(a)** (dizzy) duselig (ugs.) **(b)** (drunk) angeduselt (salopp)

**word** /wɜːd/ **1** *n.* Wort, *das;* ∼s (of song or actor) Text, *der;* **in other** ∼s mit anderen Worten; ∼ **for** ∼: Wort für Wort; **too funny** *etc.* **for** ∼s unsagbar komisch *usw.;* **have** ∼s einen Wortwechsel haben; **have a** ∼ [**with sb.**] **about sth.** [mit jmdm.] über etw. (*Akk.*) sprechen; **could I have a** ∼ [**with you**]? kann ich dich mal sprechen?; **say a few** ∼s ein paar Worte sprechen; **keep/break one's** ∼: sein Wort halten/brechen; **by** ∼ **of mouth** durch mündliche Mitteilung; **send** ∼ **that** ...: Nachricht geben, dass ... **2** *v.t.* formulieren

**'wording** *n.* Formulierung, *die*

**word:** ∼ **order** *n.* Wortstellung, *die;* ∼**play** *n.* Wortspiel, *das;* ∼ **processing** *n.* Textverarbeitung, *die;* ∼ **processor** *n.* Textverarbeitungssystem, *das*

**wordy** /'wɜːdɪ/ *adj.* weitschweifig

**wore** ▶ WEAR 2, 3

**work** /wɜːk/ **1** *n.* **(a)** Arbeit, *die;* **at** ∼ (engaged in ∼ing) bei der Arbeit; (fig.: operating) am Werk; (at job) auf der Arbeit; **out of** ∼: arbeitslos; **be in** ∼: eine Stelle haben; **set to** ∼ ⟨*Person:*⟩ sich an die Arbeit machen; **go out to** ∼: arbeiten gehen **(b)** ∼s *sing. or pl.* (factory) Werk, *das* **(c)** ∼s *pl.* (∼ing parts) Werk, *das;* (operations) Arbeiten *Pl.* **(d)** (thing made or achieved) Werk, *das;* **a** ∼ **of art/literature** ein Kunstwerk/literarisches Werk **2** *v.i.* **(a)** arbeiten

**(c)** (function effectively) funktionieren; **make the television** ∼: den Fernsehapparat in Ordnung bringen **(c)** (have an effect) wirken (**on** auf + *Akk.*) **(d)** ∼ **loose** sich lockern **3** *v.t.* **(a)** bedienen ⟨Maschine⟩; betätigen ⟨Bremse⟩ **(b)** (get labour from) arbeiten lassen **(c)** ausbeuten ⟨Steinbruch, Grube⟩ **(d)** (cause to go gradually) führen; ∼ **one's way up/into sth.** sich hocharbeiten/in etw. hineinarbeiten

▪ **work 'off** *v.t.* **(a)** (get rid of) loswerden; abreagieren ⟨Wut⟩ **(b)** abarbeiten ⟨Schuld⟩

▪ **'work on** *v.t.* **(a)** ∼ **on sth.** an etw. (*Dat.*) arbeiten **(b)** (try to persuade) ∼ **on sb.** jmdn. bearbeiten (ugs.)

▪ **work 'out** **1** *v.t.* **(a)** (calculate) ausrechnen **(b)** (solve) lösen **(c)** (devise) ausarbeiten **2** *v.i.* **(a)** sth. ∼s out at £2 etw. ergibt 2 Pfund **(b)** (have result) laufen; **things** ∼**ed out** [**well**] **in the end** es ist schließlich doch alles gut gegangen

▪ **work 'up** **1** *v.t.* (excite) aufpeitschen ⟨Menge⟩; **get** ∼**ed up** sich aufregen **2** *v.i.* ∼ **up to sth.** ⟨Musik:⟩ sich zu etw. steigern; ⟨Geschichte, Film:⟩ auf etw. (*Akk.*) zusteuern

**workable** /'wɜːkəbl/ *adj.* (feasible) durchführbar

**workaholic** /wɜːkə'hɒlɪk/ *n.* (coll.) arbeitswütiger Mensch

**work:** ∼**bench** *n.* Werkbank, *die;* ∼**day** *n.* Werktag, *der*

**'worker** *n.* Arbeiter, *der*/Arbeiterin, *die*

**'worker bee** *n.* Arbeiterbiene, *die*

**work:** ∼ **ethic** *n.* Arbeitsethos, *das;* ∼ **experience** *n.* (for schoolchildren) Praktikum, *das;* ∼**force** *n.* Belegschaft, *die;*

**'working** *adj.* **(a)** (in work) werktätig **(b)** ∼ **model** funktionsfähiges Modell

**working:** ∼ **'capital** *n.* Betriebskapital, *das;* ∼ **'class** *n.* Arbeiterklasse, *die;* ∼**-class** *adj.* der Arbeiterklasse *nachgestellt;* **sb. is** ∼**-class** jmd. gehört zur Arbeiterklasse; ∼ **clothes** *n. pl.* Arbeitskleidung, *die;* ∼ **'day** *n.* **(a)** (portion of day) Arbeitstag, *der;* **(b)** (day when work is done) Werktag, *der;* ∼ **'hours** *n. pl.* Arbeitszeit, *die;* ∼ **'knowledge** *n.* ausreichende Kenntnis (**of** in + *Dat.*); ∼ **'mother** *n.* berufstätige Mutter; ∼ **'order** *n.* **be in** [**good**] ∼ **order** betriebsbereit sein; ⟨Auto:⟩ fahrbereit sein; ∼**-'over** *n.* (sl.) Abreibung, *die* (ugs.); ∼ **'week** *n.* Arbeitswoche, *die;* **a 35-hour** ∼ **week** eine 35-Stunden-Woche; ∼ **'wife** *n.* berufstätige Ehefrau

**work:** ∼**load** *n.* Arbeitslast, *die;* ∼**man** ····⋗

**W**

/'wɜːkmən/ *n., pl.* ~**men** /'wɜːkmən/
Arbeiter, *der;* ~**manship** /'wɜːkmənʃɪp/ *n.*
(quality) Kunstfertigkeit, *die;* ~**out** *n.*
[Fitness]training, *das;* ~ **permit** *n.*
Arbeitserlaubnis, *die;* ~**sheet** *n.* (a)
(recording work done) Arbeitszettel, *der;* (b) (for
student) Formular mit Prüfungsfragen;
~**shop** *n.* (a) (room) Werkstatt, *die;* (b)
(building) Werk, *das;* ~**station** *n.* (Comp.)
Workstation, *die;* ~ **table** *n.* Arbeitstisch,
*der;* ~**-to-'rule** *n.* Dienst nach Vorschrift
**world** /wɜːld/ *n.* (a) Welt, *die;* in the ~: auf
der Welt; the tallest building in the ~: das
höchste Gebäude der Welt; all over the ~: in
*od.* auf der ganzen Welt
(b) (vast amount) it will do him a *or* the ~ of
good es wird ihm unendlich gut tun; a ~ of
difference ein weltweiter Unterschied
**world: W**~ 'Bank *n.* Weltbank, *die;*
~ 'champion *n.* Weltmeister, *der/*
-meisterin, *die;* **W**~ 'Cup *n.* Worldcup, *der;*
~**-famous** *adj.* weltberühmt
'**worldly** *adj.* weltlich; weltlich eingestellt
⟨Person⟩
worldly 'wise *adj.* weltklug
**world:** ~ 'power *n.* Weltmacht, *die;*
~ 'record *n.* Weltrekord, *der;* ~-record
holder Weltrekordhalter, *der/*-halterin, *die;*
~**-shaking** *adj.* welterschütternd;
~ **view** *n.* Weltsicht, *die;* ~ 'war *n.*
Weltkrieg, *der;* the First/Second W~ War,
W~ War I/II der Erste/Zweite Weltkrieg; der
1./2. Weltkrieg; ~**wide** /'--/ *adj.* weltweit
*nicht präd.;* **W**~ Wide 'Web *n.* (Comp.)
World Wide Web, *das*
**worm** /wɜːm/ [1] *n.* Wurm, *der*
[2] *v.t.* (a) ~ oneself into sb.'s favour sich in
jmds. Gunst (*Akk.*) schleichen
(b) ~ sth. out of sb. etw. aus jmdm.
herausbringen (ugs.)
'**worm-eaten** *adj.* wurmstichig
**worn** ▶ WEAR 2, 3
'**worn-out** *adj.* (a) abgetragen
⟨Kleidungsstück⟩; abgenutzt ⟨Teppich⟩
(b) erschöpft ⟨Person⟩
**worried** /'wʌrɪd/ *adj.* besorgt
**worry** /'wʌrɪ/ [1] *v.t.* (a) beunruhigen
(b) (bother) stören
[2] *v.i.* sich (*Dat.*) Sorgen machen
[3] *n.* Sorge, *die;* sth. is the least of sb.'s
worries etw. ist jmds. geringste Sorge
'**worrying** *adj.* (a) (causing worry)
beunruhigend
(b) (full of worry) sorgenvoll ⟨Zeit, Woche⟩
**worse** /wɜːs/ [1] *adj.* schlechter; schlimmer
⟨Schmerz, Krankheit, Benehmen⟩
[2] *adv.* schlechter; schlimmer, schlechter
⟨sich benehmen⟩
[3] *n.* Schlimmeres
**worsen** /'wɜːsn/ [1] *v.t.* verschlechtern
[2] *v.i.* sich verschlechtern
**worship** /'wɜːʃɪp/ [1] *v.t.*, (Brit.) -pp-: (a)
anbeten
(b) (idolize) abgöttisch verehren

[2] *v.i.*, (Brit.) -pp- am Gottesdienst teilnehmen
[3] *n.* (a) Anbetung, *die;* (service) Gottesdienst,
*der*
(b) Your/His W~: ≈ Euer/seine Ehren
'**worshipper** (*Amer.*: **worshiper**) *n.*
Gottesdienstbesucher, *der/*-besucherin, *die*
**worst** /wɜːst/ [1] *adj.* schlechtest...;
schlimmst... ⟨Schmerz, Krankheit,
Benehmen⟩
[2] *adv.* am schlechtesten/schlimmsten
[3] *n.* (a) the ~: der/die/das Schlimmste; get
*or* have the ~ of it (suffer the most) am meisten
zu leiden haben; if the ~ comes to the ~:
wenn es zum Schlimmsten kommt
(b) (poorest in quality) Schlechteste, *der/die/das*
**worsted** /'wʊstɪd/ *n.* Kammgarn, *das*
**worth** /wɜːθ/ [1] *adj.* wert; it's ~ £80 es ist
80 Pfund wert; is it ~ hearing/the effort? ist
es hörenswert/der Mühe wert?; is it
~ doing? lohnt es sich?; it isn't ~ it es lohnt
sich nicht
[2] *n.* Wert, *der;* ten pounds' ~ of petrol
Benzin für zehn Pfund
'**worthless** *adj.* (a) (valueless) wertlos
(b) (having bad qualities) nichtswürdig
**worthwhile** *adj.* lohnend
**worthy** /'wɜːðɪ/ *adj.* würdig
**wouldn't** /'wʊdnt/ (coll.) = would not;
▶ WILL[1]
**wound**[1] /wuːnd/ [1] *n.* Wunde, *die*
[2] *v.t.* verwunden; (fig.) verletzen
**wound**[2] ▶ WIND[2]
**wove, woven** ▶ WEAVE[1] 2
**wrangle** /'ræŋgl/ [1] *v.i.* [sich] streiten
[2] *n.* Streit, *der*
**wrap** /ræp/ [1] *v.t.*, -pp- einwickeln; (fig.)
hüllen; ~**ped** abgepackt ⟨Brot usw.⟩; ~ sth.
[a]round sth. etw. um etw. wickeln
[2] *n.* Umschlag[e]tuch, *das*
■ **wrap 'up** *v.t.* (a) einwickeln
(b) (conclude) abschließen
(c) be ~ped up in one's work in seine Arbeit
völlig versunken sein
'**wrapper** *n.* (a) sweet/toffee ~[s]
Bonbonpapier, *das*
(b) (of book) Schutzumschlag, *der*
'**wrapping** *n.* Verpackung, *die*
'**wrapping paper** *n.* (strong) Packpapier,
*das;* (decorative) Geschenkpapier, *das*
**wrath** /rɒθ/ *n.* Zorn, *der*
**wreak** /riːk/ *v.t.* (a) (cause) anrichten
(b) ~ vengeance on sb. an jmdm. Rache
nehmen
**wreath** /riːθ/ *n., pl.* **wreaths** /riːðz, riːθs/
Kranz, *der*
**wreck** /rek/ [1] *n.* (a) Wrack, *das*
(b) (destruction of ship) Schiffbruch, *der*
[2] *v.t.* (a) (destroy) ruinieren; zu Schrott
fahren ⟨Auto⟩; be ~ed (shipwrecked)
Schiffbruch erleiden
(b) (fig.: ruin) zerstören; ruinieren
⟨Gesundheit, Urlaub⟩

**W**

**wreckage** /'rekɪdʒ/ n. Wrackteile Pl.; (fig.) Trümmer Pl.

**wren** n. Zaunkönig, der

**wrench** /rentʃ/ ①n. (a) (esp. Amer.: spanner) Schraubenschlüssel, der (b) (violent twist) Verrenkung, die (c) (fig.) be a great ∼ [for sb.] sehr schmerzhaft für jmdn. sein ②v.t. (a) reißen; ∼ sth. from sb. jmdm. etw. entreißen (b) ∼ one's ankle sich (Dat.) den Knöchel verrenken

**wrest** /rest/ v.t. ∼ sth. from sb. jmdm. etw. entreißen

**wrestle** /'resl/ v.i. ringen

**wrestler** /'reslə(r)/ n. Ringer, der/ Ringerin, die

**wrestling** /'reslɪŋ/ n. Ringen, das

**wretch** /retʃ/ n. Kreatur, die

**wretched** /'retʃɪd/ adj. (a) (miserable) unglücklich (b) (coll.: damned) elend (c) (very bad) erbärmlich

**wriggle** /'rɪgl/ ①v.i. (a) sich winden; ⟨Fisch:⟩ zappeln (b) (move) sich schlängeln ②v.t. ∼ one's way sich schlängeln ③n. Windung, die

**wring** /rɪŋ/ v.t., wrung /rʌŋ/ (a) wringen; ∼ out auswringen (b) ∼ sb.'s hand jmdm. fest die Hand drücken; ∼ the neck of an animal einem Tier den Hals umdrehen (c) ∼ sth. from or out of sb. (fig.) jmdm. etw. abpressen

**wringing 'wet** adj. tropfnass

**wrinkle** /'rɪŋkl/ ①n. Falte, die; (in paper) Knick, der ②v.t. falten ③v.i. sich in Falten legen

**wrinkled** /'rɪŋkld/ adjs. runz[e]lig

**wrinkly** /'rɪŋklɪ/ ①adj. runz[e]lig ②n. (coll.) Grufti, der (ugs.)

**wrist** /rɪst/ n. Handgelenk, das

**'wristwatch** n. Armbanduhr, die

**writ** /rɪt/ n. (Law) Verfügung, die

**write** /raɪt/ ①v.i., wrote /rəʊt/, written /'rɪtn/ schreiben; ∼ to sb./a firm jmdm./an eine Firma schreiben ②v.t., wrote, written schreiben; ausschreiben ⟨Scheck⟩; the written language die Schriftsprache; written applications schriftliche Anträge Pl.

■ **write 'back** v.i. zurückschreiben

■ **write 'down** v.t. aufschreiben

■ **write 'off** ①v.t. (a) abschreiben ⟨Schulden, Verlust⟩ (b) (destroy) zu Schrott fahren ②v.i. ∼ off for sth. etw. [schriftlich] anfordern

**'write-off** n. Totalschaden, der

**writer** /'raɪtə(r)/ n. Schriftsteller, der/ Schriftstellerin, die; (of letter, article) Verfasser, der/Verfasserin, die

**'write-up** n. (by critic) Kritik, die

**writhe** /raɪð/ v.i. sich winden

**writing** /'raɪtɪŋ/ n. (a) Schreiben, das; put sth. in ∼: etw. schriftlich machen (ugs.) (b) (handwriting, something written) Schrift, die

**'writing paper** n. Schreibpapier, das

**written** ▶ WRITE

**wrong** /rɒŋ/ ①adj. (a) (morally bad) unrecht (geh.); (unfair) ungerecht (b) (mistaken) falsch; be ∼ ⟨Person:⟩ sich irren; the clock is ∼: die Uhr geht falsch (c) (not suitable) falsch; give the ∼ answer eine falsche Antwort geben; [the] ∼ way round verkehrt herum (d) (out of order) nicht in Ordnung; what's ∼? was ist los? ②adv. falsch ③n. Unrecht, das; do ∼: Unrecht tun ④v.t. ∼ sb. jmdn. ungerecht behandeln

**'wrongdoer** n. Übeltäter, der/-täterin, die; Missetäter, der/-täterin, die (geh.)

**'wrongdoing** n. no indef. art. Missetaten Pl. (geh.)

**wrongful** /'rɒŋfl/ adj. (a) (unfair) unrecht (geh.) (b) (unlawful) rechtswidrig

**'wrongfully** adv. (a) (unfairly) unrecht (geh.) ⟨handeln⟩; zu Unrecht ⟨beschuldigen⟩ (b) (unlawfully) rechtswidrig

**'wrongly** adv. (a) (unfairly) falsch (b) (mistakenly) zu Unrecht (c) ▶ WRONGFULLY A

**wrote** ▶ WRITE

**wrought iron** /rɔːt 'aɪən/ n. Schmiedeeisen, das; attrib. schmiedeeisern

**wrung** ▶ WRING

**wry** /raɪ/ adj., ∼er or wrier /'raɪə(r)/, ∼est or wriest /'raɪɪst/ ironisch ⟨Blick⟩; fein ⟨Humor, Witz⟩

**WWW** abbr. = **World Wide Web** WWW

**W**

# Xx

**X, x** /eks/ *n.* X, x, *das*
**xenophobia** /zenəˈfəʊbɪə/ *n.*
Fremdenfeindlichkeit, *die*
**xenophobic** /zenəˈfəʊbɪk/ *adj.*
fremdenfeindlich
**Xerox** ®, **xerox** /ˈzɪərɒks/ [1] *n.* (copy)
Xerokopie, *die*

[2] **xerox** *v.t.* xerokopieren

**Xmas** /ˈkrɪsməs, ˈeksməs/ *n.* (coll.)
Weihnachten, *das*

**'X-ray** [1] *n.* (picture) Röntgenaufnahme, *die*
[2] *v.t.* röntgen; durchleuchten ⟨*Gepäck*⟩

# Yy

**Y, y** /waɪ/ *n.* Y, y, *das*
**yacht** /jɒt/ *n.* (a) (for racing) Segeljacht, *die*
(b) (for pleasure) Jacht, *die*
**'yachting** *n.* Segeln, *das*
**yachtsman** /ˈjɒtsmən/ *n.*, *pl.* **yachtsmen**
/ˈjɒtsmən/ Segler, *der*
**yank** (coll.) [1] *v.t.* reißen an (+ *Dat.*)
[2] *n.* Reißen, *das*
**Yank** /jæŋk/ *n.* (Brit. coll.: American) Ami, *der*
(ugs.)
**yap** /jæp/ *v.i.*, **-pp-** kläffen
**yard¹** /jɑːd/ *n.* (measure) Yard, *das*
**yard²** *n.* (a) (attached to building) Hof, *der*; **in
the** ∼: auf dem Hof
(b) (for storage) Lager, *das*
(c) (Amer: garden) Garten, *der*
**'yardstick** *n.* (fig.) Maßstab, *der*
**yarn** /jɑːn/ *n.* (a) (thread) Garn, *das*
(b) (coll.: story) Geschichte, *die*
**yawn** /jɔːn/ [1] *n.* Gähnen, *das*
[2] *v.i.* gähnen
**'yawning** *adj.* gähnend
**year** /jɪə(r)/ *n.* (a) Jahr, *das*; **for [many]** ∼**s**
jahrelang; **once a** ∼, **every** ∼: einmal im
Jahr; **a ten-**∼**-old** ein Zehnjähriger/eine
Zehnjährige
(b) (group of students, vintage of wine) Jahrgang,
*der*
**'yearbook** *n.* Jahrbuch, *das*
**'yearly** [1] *adj.* jährlich;
Einjahres⟨*abonnement*⟩
[2] *adv.* jährlich
**yearn** /jɜːn/ *v.i.* ∼ **for** *or* **after sth./for sb.**
sich nach etw./jmdm. sehnen; ∼ **to do sth.**
sich danach sehnen, etw. zu tun
**'yearning** *n.* Sehnsucht, *die*
**yeast** /jiːst/ *n.* Hefe, *die*
**yell** /jel/ [1] *n.* gellender Schrei

[2] *v.t. & i.* [gellend] schreien
**yellow** /ˈjeləʊ/ [1] *adj.* gelb
[2] *n.* Gelb, *das*
**yellow:** ∼ **'card** *n.* (Footb.) gelbe Karte;
∼ **'fever** *n.* Gelbfieber, *das*
**yellowish** /ˈjeləʊɪʃ/ *adj.* gelblich
**Yellow 'Pages** *n. pl.* ® gelbe Seiten *Pl.*
**yelp** /jelp/ [1] *v.i.* jaulen
[2] *n.* Jaulen, *das*
**yen** /jen/ *n.* (coll.: longing) **sb. has a** ∼ **to do
sth.** es drängt jmdn. danach, etw. zu tun
**yes** /jes/ [1] *adv.* ja; (in contradiction) doch
[2] *n.*, *pl.* ∼**es** Ja, *das*
**'yes-man** *n.* (coll. derog.) Jasager, *der*
(abwertend)
**yesterday** /ˈjestədeɪ, ˈjestədɪ/ [1] *n.*
gestern; **the day before** ∼: vorgestern; ∼**'s
paper** die gestrige Zeitung
[2] *adv.* gestern; **the day before** ∼:
vorgestern
**yet** /jet/ [1] *adv.* (a) (still) noch; ∼ **again** noch
einmal
(b) (hitherto) bisher; **his best** ∼: sein bisher
bestes
(c) *neg.* **not [just]** ∼: [jetzt] noch nicht
(d) (before all is over) doch noch; **he could win**
∼: er könnte noch gewinnen
(e) *with compar.* (even) noch
(f) (nevertheless) doch
[2] *conj.* doch
**yew** /juː/ *n.* ∼ **[tree]** Eibe, *die*
**Yiddish** /ˈjɪdɪʃ/ [1] *adj.* jiddisch
[2] *n.* Jiddisch, *das*; *see also* ENGLISH 2A
**yield** /jiːld/ [1] *v.t.* (give) bringen;
hervorbringen ⟨*Ernte*⟩; abwerfen ⟨*Gewinn*⟩
[2] *v.i.* (a) sich unterwerfen
(b) (give right of way) Vorfahrt gewähren
[3] *n.* Ertrag, *der*

**yob** /jɒb/ n. (Brit. coll.) Rowdy, *der*

**yobbish** /'jɒbɪʃ/ adj. (Brit. coll.) rowdyhaft

**yobbo** /'jɒbəʊ/ n. pl. ~s ▶ YOB

**yodel** /'jəʊdl/ v.i. & t., (Brit.) -ll- jodeln

**yoga** /'jəʊgə/ n. Joga, *der od. das*

**yoghurt, yogurt** /'jɒgət/ n. Joghurt, *der od. das*

**yoke** /jəʊk/ n. Joch, *das*

**yokel** /'jəʊkl/ n. [Bauern]tölpel, *der*

**yolk** /jəʊk/ n. Dotter, *der od. das;* Eigelb, *das*

**yonder** /'jɒndə(r)/ (literary) **1** adj. ~ **tree** jener Baum dort (geh.)
  **2** adv. dort drüben

**Yorkshire 'pudding** n.
  Yorkshirepudding, *der*

**you** /jʊ, stressed juː/ pron. (a) sing./pl. du/ ihr; (polite) sing. or pl. Sie; as direct object dich/euch/Sie; as indirect object dir/euch/ Ihnen; refl. dich/dir/euch; (polite) sich; **it was ~**: du warst/ihr wart/Sie waren es
  **(b)** (one) man

**you'd** /jʊd, stressed juːd/ **(a)** = you had
  **(b)** = you would

**you'll** /jʊl, stressed juːl/ **(a)** = you will
  **(b)** = you shall

**young** /jʌŋ/ **1** adj., ~er /'jʌŋgə(r)/, ~est /'jʌŋgɪst/ jung
  **2** n. pl. (of animals) Junge Pl.; **the ~** (~ people) die jungen Leute

**youngish** adj. ziemlich jung

**youngster** /'jʌŋstə(r)/ n. **(a)** (child) Kleine, *der/die/das*
  **(b)** (young person) Jugendliche, *der/die*

**your** /jə(r), stressed jʊə(r), jɔː(r)/ poss. pron. attrib.: sing. dein; pl. euer; (polite) sing. or pl. Ihr

**you're** /jə(r), stressed jʊə(r), jɔː(r)/ = you are

**yours** /jʊəz, jɔːz/ poss. pron. pred.: sing. deiner/deine/dein[e]s; pl. eurer/eure/eures; (polite) sing. or pl. Ihrer/Ihre/Ihr[e]s; see also HERS

**yourself** /jə'self, jʊə'self, jɔː'self/ pron. **(a)** emphat. selbst
  **(b)** refl. dich/dir/(polite) sich. See also HERSELF

**yourselves** /jə'selvz, jʊə'selvz, jɔː'selvz/ pron. **(a)** emphat. selbst
  **(b)** refl. euch/(polite) sich. See also HERSELF

**youth** /juːθ/ n. **(a)** Jugend, *die*
  **(b)** pl. ~s /juːðz/ (young man) Jugendliche, *der*

**youth:** ~ **centre** n. Jugendzentrum, *das;* ~ **club** n. Jugendklub, *der*

**youthful** /'juːθfl/ adj. jugendlich

**'youth hostel** n. Jugendherberge, *die*

**you've** /jʊv, stressed juːv/ = you have

**yo-yo** ® /'jəʊjəʊ/ n., pl. ~s Jo-Jo, *das*

**Yugoslav** /'juːgəslɑːv/ ▶ YUGOSLAVIAN

**Yugoslavia** /juːgə'slɑːvɪə/ pr. n. Jugoslawien (das); **ex-~**: Ex-Jugoslawien (das)

**Yugoslavian** /juːgə'slɑːvɪən/ **1** adj. jugoslawisch; **sb. is ~**: jmd. ist Jugoslawe/ Jugoslawin
  **2** n. Jugoslawe, *der*/Jugoslawin, *die*

**yuk** /jʌk/ int. (coll.) bäh

**yummy** /'jʌmɪ/ (coll.) int. lecker

**yuppie** /'jʌpɪ/ n. (coll.) Yuppie, *der*

**yuppie 'flu** n. (coll.) Yuppie-Grippe, *die*

# Zz

**Z, z** /zed, (Amer.) ziː/ n. Z, z, *das*

**Zaire** /zɑː'ɪə(r)/ pr. n. Zaire (das)

**Zambia** /'zæmbɪə/ pr. n. Sambia (das)

**zany** /'zeɪnɪ/ adj. irre komisch (ugs.); Wahnsinns⟨humor, -komiker⟩

**zap** /zæp/ (coll.) v.i. -pp- (Telev. coll.) zappen (ugs.)

**zapper** /'zæpə(r)/ n. (Telev. coll.) Drücker, *der* (ugs.)

**zeal** /ziːl/ n. Eifer, *der*

**zealous** /'zeləs/ adj. eifrig

**zebra** /'zebrə, 'ziːbrə/ n. Zebra, *das*

**zebra 'crossing** n. (Brit.) Zebrastreifen, *der*

**zenith** /'zenɪθ/ n. Zenit, *der*

**zero** /'zɪərəʊ/ n., pl. ~s Null, *die*

**zero:** ~**-'rated** adj. ~-rated goods nicht mehrwertsteuerpflichtige Güter;
  ~ **'tolerance** n. Nulltoleranz, *die* (for, to, of gegenüber)

**zest** /zest/ n. (enthusiasm) Begeisterung, *die;* ~ **for living** Lebenslust, *die*

**zigzag** /'zɪgzæg/ **1** adj. zickzackförmig; Zickzack⟨muster, -anordnung⟩
  **2** n. Zickzacklinie, *die*

**Zimbabwe** /zɪm'bɑːbwɪ/ pr. n. Simbabwe (das)

**zinc** /zɪŋk/ n. Zink, *das*

**zip** /zɪp/ **1** n. Reißverschluss, *der*   ··⟶

⊡ *v.t.*, -pp-: (a) ∼ [up] sth. den
Reißverschluss an etw. (*Dat.*) zuziehen
(b) (Comp.) ∼ [up] packen ⟨*Datei*⟩

'**zip bag** *n.* Tasche, *die* mit Reißverschluss

'**Zip code** *n.* (Amer.) Postleitzahl, *die*

**zip fastener** ▶ ZIP 1

**zipper** /'zɪpə(r)/ ▶ ZIP 1

**zither** /'zɪðə(r)/ *n.* Zither, *die*

**zodiac** /'zəʊdɪæk/ *n.* Tierkreis, *der;* sign of
the ∼: Tierkreiszeichen, *das*

**zombie** (*Amer.*: **zombi**) /'zɒmbɪ/ *n.*
Zombie, *der*

**zone** /zəʊn/ *n.* Zone, *die*

**zoo** /zuː/ *n.* Zoo, *der*

'**zookeeper** *n.* Zoowärter, *der*/-wärterin,
*die*

**zoological** /zuːə'lɒdʒɪkl/ *adj.* zoologisch

**zoologist** /zuːˈɒlədʒɪst/ *n.* Zoologe, *der*/
Zoologin, *die*

**zoology** /zuːˈɒlədʒɪ/ *n.* Zoologie, *die*

**zoom** /zuːm/ *v.i.* rauschen
∎ **zoom 'in on** *v.t.* zoomen auf (+ *Akk.*)

'**zoom lens** *n.* Zoomobjektiv, *das*

**zucchini** /zʊ'kiːnɪ/ *n.*, *pl. same or* ∼**s** (esp.
Amer.) Zucchino, *der*

**Z**

# Contents

### Grammar Reference

# Glossary of grammatical terms

**Abbreviation** A shortened form of a word or phrase: **etc.** = **usw.**

**Absolute use** The use of a transitive verb without an expressed object, as in: **I didn't** *realize*

**Accusative** The case of a direct object; some German prepositions take the accusative

**Active** In the active form the subject of the verb performs the action: **he asked** = **er hat gefragt**

**Adjective** A word describing a noun: **a** *red* **pencil** = **ein** *roter* **Stift**

**Adverb** A word that describes or changes the meaning of a verb, an adjective, or another adverb: **she sings** *beautifully* = **sie singt** *schön*

**Article** The definite article, **the** = **der/die/das**, and indefinite article, **a/an** = **ein/eine/ein**, used in front of a noun

**Attributive** An adjective or noun is attributive when it is used directly before a noun: **the** *black* **dog** = **der** *schwarze* **Hund**; *farewell* **speech** = **Abschiedsrede**

**Auxiliary verb** One of the verbs – as German **haben, sein, werden** - used to form the perfect or future tense: **I** *will* **help** = **ich** *werde* **helfen**

**Cardinal number** A whole number representing a quantity: **one/two/three** = **eins/zwei/drei**

**Case** The form of a noun, pronoun, adjective, or article that shows the part it plays in a sentence; there are four cases in German - nominative, accusative, genitive, and dative

**Clause** A self-contained section of a sentence that contains a subject and a verb

**Collective noun** A noun that is singular in form but refers to a group of individual persons or things, e.g. **royalty, grain**

**Collocate** A word that regularly occurs with another; in German, **Buch** is a typical collocate of the verb **lesen**.

**Comparative** The form of an adjective or adverb that makes it "more": **smaller** = **kleiner, more clearly** = **klarer**

**Compound adjective** An adjective formed from two or more separate words: **selbstbewusst (selbst + bewusst)** = **self-confident**

**Compound noun** A noun formed from two or more separate words: **der Flughafen (Flug+ Hafen)** = **airport**

**Compound verb** A verb formed by adding a prefix to a simple verb; in German, some compound verbs are separable **(an|fangen)**, and some are inseparable **(verlassen)**

**Conditional tense** A tense of a verb that expresses what might happen if something else occurred: **he would go** = **er würde gehen**

**Conjugation** Variation of the form of a verb to show tense, person, mood, etc.

**Conjunction** A word used to join clauses together: **and** = **und, because** = **weil**

**Consonant** In German, all the letters of the alphabet other than **a, e, i, o, u, ä, ö, ü**

**Copula** A verb, such as **be** or **become**, which links a **subject** and **predicate**

**Dative** The case of an indirect object; many German prepositions take the dative

**Declension** The form of a noun, pronoun, or adjective that corresponds to a particular case, number, or gender; some German nouns decline like adjectives, e.g. **Beamte, Taube**

**Definite article:** **the** = **der/die/das**

**Demonstrative adjective:** an adjective indicating the person or thing referred to; *this* **table** = *dieser* **Tisch**

**Demonstrative pronoun** A pronoun indicating the person or thing referred to; *this* **is my bicycle** = *das* **ist mein Fahrrad**

**Direct object** The noun or pronoun directly affected by the verb: **he caught** *the ball* = **er fing** *den Ball*

**Direct speech** A speaker's actual words or the use of these in writing

**Elliptical** Having a word or words omitted, especially where the sense can be guessed from the context

**Ending** Letters added to the stem of verbs, as well as to nouns and adjectives, according to tense, case, etc.

**Feminine** One of the three noun genders in German: **die Frau** = **the woman**

**Future tense** The tense of a verb that refers to something that will happen in the future: **I will go** = **ich werde gehen**

# Glossary of grammatical terms

**Gender** One of the three groups of nouns, pronouns, and adjectives in German: masculine, feminine, or neuter

**Genitive** The case that shows possession; some prepositions in German take the genitive

**Imperative** A form of a verb that expresses a command: **go away! = geh weg!**

**Imperfect tense** The tense of a verb that refers to an uncompleted or a habitual action in the past: **I went there every Friday = ich ging jeden Freitag dorthin**

**Impersonal verb** A verb in English used only with 'it', and in German only with 'es': **it is raining = es regnet**

**Indeclinable adjective** An adjective that has no inflected forms, as German **klasse, Moskauer**

**Indefinite article:** a/an = **ein/eine/ein**

**Indefinite pronoun** A pronoun that does not identify a specific person or object: **one = man, something = etwas**

**Indicative form** The form of a verb used when making a statement of fact or asking questions of fact: **he is just coming = er kommt gleich**

**Indirect object** The noun or pronoun indirectly affected by the verb, at which the direct object is aimed: **I gave *him* the book = ich gab *ihm* das Buch**

**Indirect speech** A report of what someone has said which does not reproduce the exact words

**Infinitive** The basic part of a verb: **to play = spielen**

**Inflect** To change the ending or form of a word to show its tense or its grammatical relation to other words: **gehe** and **gehst** are inflected forms of the verb **gehen**

**Inseparable verb** A verb with a prefix that can never be separated from it: **verstehen, ich verstehe**

**Interjection** A sound, word, or remark expressing a strong feeling such as anger, fear, or joy: **oh! = ach!**

**Interrogative pronoun** A pronoun that asks a question: **who? = wer?**

**Intransitive verb** A verb that does not have a direct object: **he died suddenly = er ist plötzlich gestorben**

**Irregular verb** A verb that does not follow one of the set patterns and has its own individual forms

**Masculine** One of the three noun genders in German: **der Mann = the man, der Stuhl = the chair**

**Modal verb** A verb that is used with another verb (not a modal) to express permission, obligation, possibility, etc., as German **können, sollen**, English **might, should**

**Negative** expressing refusal or denial; **there aren't any = es gibt keine**

**Neuter** One of the three noun genders in German: **das Buch = the book, das Kind = the child**

**Nominative** The case of the subject of a sentence; in sentences with **sein** and **werden** the noun after the verb is in the nominative: **that is my car = das ist mein Auto**

**Noun** A word that names a person or a thing

**Number** The state of being either singular or plural

**Object** The word or words naming the person or thing acted upon by a verb or preposition, as 'Buch' in **er las das Buch** or 'ihm' in **ich traue ihm**

**Ordinal number** A number that shows a person's or thing's position in a series: **the *twenty-first* century = das *einundzwanzigste* Jahrhundert, the *second* door on the left = die *zweite* Tür links**

**Part of speech** A grammatical term for the function of a word; noun, verb, adjective, etc., are parts of speech.

**Passive** In the passive form the subject of the verb experiences the action rather than performs it: **he was asked = er wurde gefragt**

**Past participle** The part of a verb used to form past tenses: **she had gone, er hat gelogen**

**Perfect tense** The tense of a verb that refers to a completed action in the past or an action that started in the past and is still going on: **I have already eaten = ich habe schon gegessen; I have been reading all day = ich habe den ganzen Tag gelesen**

**Person** Any of the three groups of personal pronouns and forms taken by verbs; the **first person** (e.g. I/ich) refers to the person(s) speaking, the **second person** (e.g. you/du) refers to the person(s) spoken to; the **third person** (e.g. he/er) refers to the persons spoken about

**Personal pronoun** A pronoun that refers to a person or thing: **he/she/it = er/sie/es**

**Phrasal verb** A verb in English combined with a preposition or an adverb to have a particular meaning: **run away = weglaufen**

**Phrase** A self-contained section of a sentence that does not contain a full verb

**Pluperfect tense** The tense of a verb that refers to something that happened before a particular point in the past: als ich ankam, *war* er schon *losgefahren* = when I arrived, he *had* already *left*

**Plural** Of nouns etc., referring to more than one: **the trees = die Bäume**

**Possessive adjective** An adjective that shows possession, belonging to someone or something; **my = mein/meine/mein**

**Possessive pronoun** A pronoun that shows possession, belonging to someone or something: **mine = meiner/meine/meins**

**Postpositive** Placed after the word to which it relates, as **in stock** in the phrase **items in stock**

**Predicate** The part of a sentence that says something about the **subject**, e.g. **went home** in **John went home**

**Predicative** An adjective is predicative when it comes after a verb such as **be** or **become** in English, or after **sein** or **werden** in German: **she is beautiful = sie ist schön**

**Prefix** A letter or group of letters added to the beginning of a word to change its meaning; in German, the prefix can move from separable verbs (**an|fangen**), but stays fixed to inseparable verbs (**verlassen**)

**Preposition** A word that stands in front of a noun or pronoun, relating it to the rest of the sentence; in German prepositions are always followed by a particular case, usually either the accusative or dative, but occasionally the genitive: **with = mit (+ dative), for = für (+ accusative), because of = wegen (+ genitive)**

**Present participle** The part of a verb that in English ends in –ing, and in German adds –d to the infinitive: **asking = fragend**

**Present tense** The tense of a verb that refers to something happening now: **I make = ich mache**

**Pronoun** A word that stands instead of a noun: **he = er, she = sie, mine = meiner/meine/meins**

**Proper noun** A name of a person, place, institution, etc., in English written with a capital letter at the start; **Germany**, the **Atlantic**, **Karl**, **Europa** are all proper nouns

**Reflexive pronoun** A pronoun that goes with a reflexive verb: in German **mich, dich, sich, uns, euch, sich**

**Reflexive verb** A verb whose object is the same as its subject; in German, it is used with a reflexive pronoun: **du sollst dich waschen = you should wash yourself**

**Regular verb** A verb that follows a set pattern in its different forms

**Relative pronoun** A pronoun that introduces a subordinate clause, relating to a person or thing mentioned in the main clause: **the man** *who* **visited us = der Mann,** *der* **uns besucht hat**

**Reported Speech** Another name for **Indirect speech**

**Root** The part of a word to which inflections are added; **fahr-** is the root of the verb **fahren**

**Sentence** A sequence of words, with a subject and a verb, that can stand on their own to make a statement, ask a question, or give a command

**Separable verb** A verb with a prefix that can be separated from it in some tenses: **anfangen, anzufangen, angefangen**, but **ich fange an, du fingst an**

**Singular** Of nouns etc., referring to just one: **the tree = der Baum**

**Stem** The part of a verb to which endings are added; **fahr-** is the stem of **fahren**

**Subject** In a clause or sentence, the noun or pronoun that causes the action of the verb: *he* **caught the ball =** *er* **fing den Ball**

**Subjunctive** A verb form that is used to express doubt or unlikelihood: **if I were to tell you that … = wenn ich dir sagen würde, dass …**

**Subordinate clause** A clause which adds information to the main clause of a sentence but cannot be used as a sentence by itself

**Suffix** A letter or group of letters joined to the end of a word to make another word, as **-heit** in **Schönheit**

**Superlative** The form of an adjective or adverb that makes it "most": **the** *smallest* **house = das** *kleinste* **Haus, most clearly = am klarsten**

**Syllable** A division of a word that contains a vowel sound that is pronounced as a single unit: **Helikopter** has four syllables, **he-li-kop-ter**

**Tense** The form of a verb that tells when the action takes place: present, future, imperfect, perfect, pluperfect

**Transitive verb** A verb form that is used with a direct object: **she read the book = sie las das Buch**

**Verb** A word or group of words that describes an action: **the children** *are playing* **= die Kinder** *spielen*

**Vowel** In German, one of the following letters: **a, e, i, o, u, ä, ö, ü**

# Summary of German grammar

## 1 Verbs

### 1.1 Regular verbs

Most German verbs are regular and add the same endings to their stem.
You find the stem by taking away the **-en** (or sometimes just **-n**) from the
end of the infinitive. The infinitive of the verb, for example the regular
verb **machen**, is the form you look up in the dictionary. The stem of
**machen** is **mach-**. There are six endings for each tense, to go with the
different pronouns:

ich = *I*      du = *you*      er/sie/es = *he/she/it*
wir = *we*      ihr = *you*      sie/Sie = *they/you* (*polite form*).

### 1.2 Irregular verbs

Some German verbs are irregular and change their stem or add different
endings. All the irregular verbs that appear in the dictionary are given in
the section *German irregular verbs* on pages 944–947.

### 1.3 Present tense

For example, *I make, I am making*, or *I do make*:

| infinitive | ich | du | er/sie/es | wir | ihr | sie/Sie |
| --- | --- | --- | --- | --- | --- | --- |
| machen | mache | machst | macht | machen | macht | machen |

### 1.4 Imperfect tense

For example, *I made, I was making*, or *I used to make*:

| infinitive | ich | du | er/sie/es | wir | ihr | sie/Sie |
| --- | --- | --- | --- | --- | --- | --- |
| machen | machte | machtest | machte | machten | machtet | machten |

### 1.5 Future tense

For example, *I will make* or *I shall make*. The future is formed by using the
present tense of **werden**, which is the equivalent of *will* or *shall*, with the
infinitive of the main verb: **ich werde machen**.

| infinitive | ich | du | er/sie/es | wir | ihr | sie/Sie |
| --- | --- | --- | --- | --- | --- | --- |
| werden | werde | wirst | wird | werden | werdet | werden |

### 1.6 Perfect tense

For example, *I made* or *I have made*. Most German verbs form the perfect
tense with the present tense of **haben**, which is the equivalent of *have*,
plus the past participle: **ich habe gemacht**. Some verbs form the perfect
tense with **sein** instead of **haben**, and these are all marked (*sein*) in the

dictionary. They are either verbs expressing motion and involving a change of place:

> er ist heute nach Berlin gefahren = *he drove to Berlin today*
> *he went out* = er ist hinausgegangen

or, they express a change of state, and this includes verbs meaning to happen (**geschehen, passieren, vorkommen**):

> er ist aufgewacht = *he woke up*
> sie ist gestern gestorben = *she died yesterday*

| infinitive | ich | du | er/sie/es | wir | ihr | sie/Sie |
|---|---|---|---|---|---|---|
| haben | habe | hast | hat | haben | habt | haben |
| sein | bin | bist | ist | sind | seid | sind |

## 1.7 The subjunctive

This is a form of the verb that is used to express speculation, hope, and doubt, and in reported speech. (It is rarely used in English; one example is: *if I were you*, instead of *if I was you*.) The subjunctive is used in both written and spoken German.

> es könnte wahr sein = *it could be true*
> wenn ich du wäre, … = *if I were you,* …
> er sagt, dass er selten in die Stadt gehe = *he says he seldom goes into town*

### Present subjunctive

| infinitive | ich | du | er/sie/es | wir | ihr | sie/Sie |
|---|---|---|---|---|---|---|
| machen | mache | machest | mache | machen | machet | machen |
| sein | sei | sei(e)st | sei | seien | seid | seien |

### Imperfect subjunctive

For regular verbs this is the same as the normal imperfect forms, but irregular verbs vary.

| infinitive | ich | du | er/sie/es | wir | ihr | sie/Sie |
|---|---|---|---|---|---|---|
| machen | machte | machtest | machte | machten | machtet | machten |
| werden | würde | würdest | würde | würden | würdet | würden |
| sein | wäre | wär(e)st | wäre | wären | wär(e)t | wären |

## 1.8 Conditional tense

The conditional tense expresses what would happen if something else occurred. The imperfect subjunctive of **werden** (**würde, würdest**, etc) is used with the infinitive to form the conditional tense.

> er würde gehen = *he would go*
> das würde ich nicht machen = *I wouldn't do that*

## 1.9 Reflexive verbs

The object of a reflexive verb is the same as its subject. In German, the object is a reflexive pronoun. This is usually in the accusative (**ich wasche mich** = *I wash myself*). The reflexive pronouns of some verbs are in the

· · · · · · · · · · · · · · · · · · · · · · · · · · · · · · · · · · · · · · · · · ·

dative (**ich stelle mir vor** = *I imagine*), and these are marked in both halves of the dictionary with the label (*Dat*).

| *infinitive* | ich | du | er/sie/es | wir | ihr | sie/Sie |
|---|---|---|---|---|---|---|
| sich waschen | wasche mich | wäschst dich | wäscht sich | waschen uns | wascht euch | waschen sich |
| sich vorstellen | stelle mir vor | stellst dir vor | stellt sich vor | stellen uns vor | stellt euch vor | stellen sich vor |

## 1.10 The passive

In the passive, the subject of the verb experiences the action rather than performs it: **er wurde gefragt** = *he was asked*. In German, the passive is formed as follows:

| PRESENT PASSIVE | es wird gemacht (present tense of **werden** + past participle) | *it is done* |
|---|---|---|
| IMPERFECT PASSIVE | es wurde gemacht (imperfect tense of **werden** + past participle) | *it was done* |
| FUTURE PASSIVE | es wird gemacht werden (present tense of **werden** + past participle + **werden**) | *it will be done* |
| PERFECT PASSIVE | es ist gemacht worden (present tense of **sein** + past participle + **worden**) | *it has been done* |

When forming the perfect passive, note that the past participle of **werden** used is **worden** rather than **geworden**.

## 1.11 Separable verbs

Some German verbs have stressed separable prefixes, such as **ab-, an-, aus-, her-, hin-, nach-, vor-, zu-**. These prefixes become detached from the main verb in the simple tenses: **hinausgehen: ich gehe hinaus, sie ging hinaus**. In compound tenses formed with the past participle, for example the perfect tense, the **ge-** of the past participle comes between the prefix and the verb:

er/sie/es hat angefangen = *he/she/it has begun*
er/sie/es ist angekommen = *he/she/it has arrived*

## 1.12 Inseparable verbs

The following unstressed prefixes are never separated from their verb in either simple or compound tenses and do not take **ge-** in the past participle:

be-, emp-, ent-, er-, ge-, ver-, zer-.
er begleitet seinen Bruder = *he is accompanying his brother*
er wurde nicht begleitet = *he was not accompanied*

· · · · · · · · · · · · · · · · · · · · · · · · · · · · · · · · · · · · · · · · · ·

# 2 Articles

The definite article (*the*) can be translated in the nominative case by **der, die** or **das** in German. Similarly the indefinite article (*a*) can be translated by **ein, eine**, or **ein**.

There are three genders of nouns in German: masculine (**der Mann** = *the man*), feminine (**die Frau** = *the woman*), and neuter (**das Buch** = *the book*). There are two forms of number: singular (**der Baum** = *the tree*) and plural (**die Bäume** = *the trees*). And there are four cases, which show the part a noun plays in a sentence: nominative (for the subject), accusative (for the object), genitive (to show possession), and dative (for the indirect object). The plural forms of the definite article are the same for all three genders. More information on gender is given below.

### 2.1 Definite article: der/die/das, (*plural*) die = *the*

|  | SINGULAR | | | PLURAL |
| --- | masculine | feminine | neuter | all genders |
| NOMINATIVE | **der** Mann | **die** Frau | **das** Buch | **die** Bäume |
| ACCUSATIVE | **den** Mann | **die** Frau | **das** Buch | **die** Bäume |
| GENITIVE | **des** Mannes | **der** Frau | **des** Buches | **der** Bäume |
| DATIVE | **dem** Mann | **der** Frau | **dem** Buch | **den** Bäumen |

### 2.2 Indefinite article

ein/eine/ein = *a* or *an*. This article can only be singular.

|  | masculine | feminine | neuter |
| --- | --- | --- | --- |
| NOMINATIVE | **ein** Mann | **eine** Frau | **ein** Buch |
| ACCUSATIVE | **einen** Mann | **eine** Frau | **ein** Buch |
| GENITIVE | **eines** Mannes | **einer** Frau | **eines** Buches |
| DATIVE | **einem** Mann | **einer** Frau | **einem** Buch |

## 3 Nouns

In German, all nouns take an initial capital letter wherever they appear in a sentence: **der Baum**, **die Schule**, **das Buch**.

### 3.1 Gender

All German nouns belong to one of the three genders: masculine (**der Mann** = *the man*), feminine (**die Frau** = *the woman*), and neuter (**das Buch** = *the book*). These three examples are logical, with masculine for a male person, feminine for a female person, and neuter for an object. But genders of German nouns do not always follow logic. For example, **der Fluss** (= *the river*), **die Menge** (= *the quantity/crowd*), **das Haus** (= *the house*). **Das Mädchen** (= *the girl*) is neuter and not feminine, because the ending **-chen** is always neuter.

The gender of German nouns is given in both sides of the dictionary by adding **der**, **die**, or **das** after each noun. There are some general rules regarding the gender of groups of nouns, but these cover only a small proportion of them and in many cases a noun's gender can only be established by looking it up.

# Summary of German grammar

. . . . . . . . . . . . . . . . . . . . . . . . . . . . . . . . . . . . . . . . . . . . . . .

### 3.2 Masculine nouns

- male persons and animals: **der Arbeiter** = *worker*; **der Bär** = *bear*

- 'doers' and 'doing' instruments ending in **-er** in German: **der Gärtner** = *gardener*; **der Computer** = *computer*

- days, months, and seasons: **(der) Montag** = *Monday*; **(der) März** = *March*; **der Frühling** = *spring*

- words ending in **-ich**, **-ig**, and **-ling**: **der Strich** = line; **der Honig** = *honey*; **der Lehrling** = *apprentice*

- words ending in **-ismus**, **-ist**, and **-ant**: **der Kapitalismus** = *capitalism*; **der Kriminalist** = *detective*; **der Diamant** = *diamond*

### 3.3 Feminine nouns

- female persons and animals: **die Schauspielerin** = *actress*; **die Henne** = *hen*. The feminine form of professions and animals is made by adding **-in** to the masculine: **der Schauspieler/die Schauspielerin** = *actor/actress*

- nouns ending in **-ei**, **-ie**, **-ik**, **-in**, **-ion**, **-heit**, **-keit**, **-schaft**, **-tät**, **-ung**, **-ur**: **die Gärtnerei** = *gardening*; **die Energie** = *energy*; **die Million** = *million*; **die Freiheit** = *freedom*; **die Freundlichkeit** = *friendliness*; **die Feindschaft** = *enmity*; **die Universität** = *university*; **die Verwaltung** = *management*; **die Natur** = *nature*

- many nouns ending in **-e**: **die Blume** = *flower*. Note that there are many common exceptions, including **der Name** = *name*; **der Käse** = *cheese*; **das Ende** = *end*

### 3.4 Neuter nouns

- names of continents, most countries, and towns: **(das) Europa** = *Europe*; **(das) Deutschland** = *Germany*; **(das) Köln** = *Cologne*

- nouns ending in **-chen** and **-lein** (diminutive suffixes): **das Mädchen**, **das Fräulein** = *girl*

- most (but not all) nouns beginning with **Ge-** or ending in **-nis**, **-tel**, or **-um**: **das Geheimnis** = *secret*; **das Viertel** = *quarter*; **das Zentrum** = *centre*

- infinitives of verbs used as nouns: **das Lachen** = *laughter*; **das Essen** = *food*

### 3.5 Compound nouns

When two nouns combine to make a compound noun, the gender of the compound is that of the second noun:

der Brief + die Marke = die Briefmarke (= *stamp*).

### 3.6 Plural

There are no hard and fast rules for the the formation of plural nouns in German. An ending is generally added. Masculine nouns frequently add -e (**der Freund, die Freunde**). When the vowels -a- or -u- appear in the stem of a noun, they may add an umlaut to give: -ä-, -ü- as in: (**der Gast, die Gäste; das Haus, die Häuser**). Feminine words ending in -heit, -keit, and -**ung** always add -**en** to make the plural (**die Abbildung, die Abbildungen**).

The plurals of all nouns are shown in the German-English part of the dictionary.

### 3.7 Case

There are four cases, which show the part a noun plays in a sentence: nominative, accusative, genitive, and dative. The noun's article changes according to the case, and the ending of the noun changes in some cases:

| SINGULAR | masculine | feminine | neuter |
|---|---|---|---|
| NOMINATIVE | der Mann | die Frau | das Buch |
| ACCUSATIVE | den Mann | die Frau | das Buch |
| GENITIVE | des **Mann(e)s** | der Frau | des **Buch(e)s** |
| DATIVE | dem Mann | der Frau | dem Buch |

| PLURAL | masculine | feminine | neuter |
|---|---|---|---|
| NOMINATIVE | die Männer | die Frauen | die Bücher |
| ACCUSATIVE | die Männer | die Frauen | die Bücher |
| GENITIVE | der Männer | der Frauen | der Bücher |
| DATIVE | den **Männern** | den Frauen | den **Büchern** |

The nominative is used for the subject of a sentence. It is important to note that in sentences with **sein** (*to be*) and **werden** (*to become*), the noun after the verb is in the nominative.

> der Hund bellte = *the dog barked*
> das ist mein Wagen = *that is my car*

The accusative is used for the direct object and after some prepositions (listed on page 941):

> sie hat einen Sohn = *she has a son*

The genitive shows possession, and is also used after some prepositions (listed on page 941):

> der Hund meines Mannes = *my husband's dog*

The dative is used for the indirect object. Some German verbs, such as **helfen**, take the dative when you might have expected the accusative. This information is given in both halves of the dictionary. The dative is also used after some prepositions (listed on page 941):

> sie gab den Kindern die Bücher = *she gave the books to the children*
> er hilft der Frau = *he is helping the woman*

# Summary of German grammar

The following sentence combines all four cases:

> der Mann gibt der Frau den Bleistift = *the man gives the woman the girl's pencil*
> des Mädchens

der Mann *is the subject* (*in the nominative*)
gibt *is the verb*
der Frau *is the indirect object* (*in the dative*)
den Bleistift *is the direct object* (*in the accusative*)
des Mädchens *is in the genitive* (*showing possession*).

## 4 Adjectives

An adjective is a word qualifying a noun. In German, an adjective in front of a noun adds endings that vary with the noun's gender, number, and case. Adjectives that come after a noun do not add endings.

**4.1** Adjectives following the definite article **der**, **die**, **das** take the following endings:

|  | SINGULAR masculine | feminine | neuter | PLURAL all genders |
|---|---|---|---|---|
| NOMINATIVE | der rote Hut | die rote Lampe | das rote Buch | die roten Autos |
| ACCUSATIVE | den roten Hut | die rote Lampe | das rote Buch | die roten Autos |
| GENITIVE | des roten Hutes | der roten Lampe | des roten Buches | der roten Autos |
| DATIVE | dem roten Hut | der roten Lampe | dem roten Buch | den roten Autos |

**4.2** German demonstrative adjectives follow the pattern of the definite article, and adjectives after them change their endings in the same way as after **der/die/das**. For example, **dieser/diese/dieses** (= *this*):

|  | SINGULAR masculine | feminine | neuter | PLURAL all genders |
|---|---|---|---|---|
| NOMINATIVE | dieser | diese | dieses | diese |
| ACCUSATIVE | diesen | diese | dieses | diese |
| GENITIVE | dieses | dieser | dieses | dieser |
| DATIVE | diesem | dieser | diesem | diesen |

Other adjectives of this type are:

jeder, jede, jedes = *every, each*
jener, jene, jenes = *that*
mancher, manche, manches = *many a, some*

solcher, solche, solches = *such*
welcher, welche, welches = *which*

**4.3** Adjectives following the indefinite article **ein**, **eine**, **ein** take the following endings:

| | SINGULAR | | |
| | masculine | feminine | neuter |
| --- | --- | --- | --- |
| NOMINATIVE | ein roter Hut | eine rote Lampe | ein rotes Buch |
| ACCUSATIVE | einen roten Hut | eine rote Lampe | ein rotes Buch |
| GENITIVE | eines roten Hutes | einer roten Lampe | eines roten Buches |
| DATIVE | einem roten Hut | einer roten Lampe | einem roten Buch |

Other German adjectives that follow the pattern of the indefinite article, and take the same endings as **ein**, **eine**, **ein**, are:

dein = *your*     ihr = *her/their*     mein = *my*     kein = *no*
euer = *your*     sein = *his/its*     unser = *our*
Ihr = *your*

These adjectives can also be used in the plural: **keine Autos** = *no cars*; **deine Eltern** = *your parents*; **unsere Lehrer** = *our teachers*, etc. The endings of adjectives that follow them are the same in the plural regardless of gender:

| | PLURAL |
| | all genders |
| --- | --- |
| NOMINATIVE | keine roten Autos |
| ACCUSATIVE | keine roten Autos |
| GENITIVE | keiner roten Autos |
| DATIVE | keinen roten Autos |

**4.4** Adjectives in front of a noun, without an article, take the following endings:

| | SINGULAR | | | PLURAL |
| | masculine | feminine | neuter | all genders |
| --- | --- | --- | --- | --- |
| NOMINATIVE | guter Wein | frische Milch | kaltes Bier | alte Leute |
| ACCUSATIVE | guten Wein | frische Milch | kaltes Bier | alte Leute |
| GENITIVE | guten Weins | frischer Milch | kalten Biers | alter Leute |
| DATIVE | gutem Wein | frischer Milch | kaltem Bier | alten Leuten |

## 4.5 Adjectives as nouns

In German, adjectives can be used as nouns, spelt with a capital letter: **alt** = *old*, **ein Alter** = *an old man*, **eine Alte** = *an old woman*.

With the definite article (**der**, **die**, **das**), these nouns take the following endings:

| | SINGULAR | | | PLURAL |
| | masculine | feminine | neuter | all genders |
| --- | --- | --- | --- | --- |
| NOMINATIVE | der Alte | die Alte | das Alte | die Alten |
| ACCUSATIVE | den Alten | die Alte | das Alte | die Alten |
| GENITIVE | des Alten | der Alten | des Alten | der Alten |
| DATIVE | dem Alten | der Alten | dem Alten | den Alten |

Adjectives can be used in this way in the neuter, usually to express an abstract concept: **das Gute** = *the good* (nominative and accusative), **des Guten** (genitive), **dem Guten** (dative).

• • • • • • • • • • • • • • • • • • • • • • • • • • • • • • • • • • • • • • • • • • • • •

With the indefinite article (**ein**, **eine**, **ein**), these nouns take the following endings:

|  | SINGULAR | | | PLURAL |
|---|---|---|---|---|
|  | masculine | feminine | neuter | all genders<br>without an article |
| NOMINATIVE | ein Alter | eine Alte | ein Altes | Alte |
| ACCUSATIVE | einen Alten | eine Alte | ein Altes | Alte |
| GENITIVE | eines Alten | einer Alten | eines Alten | Alter |
| DATIVE | einem Alten | einer Alten | einem Alten | Alten |

## 4.6 Comparatives and superlatives of adjectives

In English, the comparative of the adjective *small* is *smaller*, and of *difficult* is *more difficult*. The superlatives are *smallest* and *most difficult*. In German, there is just one way to form the comparative and superlative: by adding the endings **-er** and **-(e)st**:

> klein, kleiner, der/die/das kleinste = *small, smaller, smallest*

Many adjectives whose stem vowel is **-a-**, **-o-**, or **-u-** take an umlaut to become **-ä-**, **-ö-** or **-ü-**, in the comparative and superlative:

> kalt, kälter, der/die/das kälteste = *cold, colder, coldest*
> grob, gröber, der/die/das gröbste = *rude, ruder, rudest*
> jung, jünger, der/die/das jüngste = *young, younger, youngest*

Some important adjectives are irregular:

> groß, größer, der/die/das größte = *big, bigger, biggest*
> gut, besser, der/die/das beste = *good, better, best*
> hoch, höher, der/die/das höchste = *high, higher, highest*
> viel, mehr, der/die/das meiste = *much, more, most*
> nah, näher, der/die/das nächste = *near, nearer, nearest*

Comparative and superlative adjectives take the same endings as basic adjectives:

> ein kleineres Kind = *a smaller child*
> ein billigerer Hut = *a cheaper hat*
> der kälteste Monat = *the coldest month*
> die nächste Bushaltestelle = *the nearest bus stop*

• • • • • • • • • • • • • • • • • • • • • • • • • • • • • • • • • • • • • • • • • • • • •

# 5 Adverbs

**5.1** In German almost all adjectives can also be used as adverbs. Adverbs can modify a verb, an adjective, or another adverb.

> sie singt schön (adverb: schön + verb: singt) = *she sings beautifully*
> sie war schnell fertig (adverb: schnell + adjective: fertig) = *she was ready quickly*
> er fährt sehr langsam (adverb: sehr + adverb: langsam) = *he drives very slowly*

The following important adverbs are invariable: **auch** = *also*, **fast** = *almost*, **immer** = *always*, **sehr** = *very*, **leider** = *unfortunately*

> sie ist sehr klug = *she is very clever*

. . . . . . . . . . . . . . . . . . . . . . . . . . . . . . . . . . . . . . . . . . . . .

## 5.2 Comparatives and superlatives of adverbs

The comparative is formed by adding **-er** to the basic adverb, and the superlative by adding the ending **-(e)sten** to the basic adverb and putting **am** in front:

> klar, klarer, am klarsten = *clearly, more clearly, most clearly*

Some important adverbs are irregular:

> bald, früher, am frühesten = *soon, earlier, at the earliest*
> gut, besser, am besten = *well, better, best*
> gern, lieber, am liebsten = *willingly, more willingly, most willingly*

## 5.3 Adverbs of time

There are many adverbs and adverbial expressions of time. They are invariable. Some common ones are:

> morgens = *in the morning*　　　　wochenlang, jahrelang *etc* = *for weeks, for years* etc
> nachmittags = *in the afternoon*　　montags, dienstags *etc* = *on Mondays, Tuesdays* etc
> nachts = *in the night*
>
> bald = *soon*　　　　　　　　　　　jetzt = *now*
> endlich = *in the end*　　　　　　　kürzlich = *recently*
> immer, stets = *always*　　　　　　wieder = *again*

## 5.4 Adverbs of order

The use of adverbs and adverbial expressions to convey order is frequent in German. Here are some common patterns of usage:

> erstens = *firstly*　　　　　　　　zum ersten Mal = *for the first time*
> zweitens = *secondly*　　　　　　zum zweiten Mal = *for the second time*
> drittens = *thirdly*　　　　　　　zum dritten Mal = *for the third time*

. . . . . . . . . . . . . . . . . . . . . . . . . . . . . . . . . . . . . . . . . . . . .

# 6 Pronouns

Pronouns are words that can replace a noun. Examples in English are: *I, you, he, she, it, which, theirs, mine, yours.*

## 6.1 Personal pronouns

These pronouns, such as **er, sie, es** = *he/she/it*, refer to people or things.

|            | I    | you  | he/it   | she/it | it  | we   | you  | they  | you   |
| ---------- | ---- | ---- | ------- | ------ | --- | ---- | ---- | ----- | ----- |
| NOMINATIVE | ich  | du   | er      | sie    | es  | wir  | ihr  | sie   | Sie   |
|            | me   | you  | him/it  | her/it | it  | us   | you  | them  | you   |
| ACCUSATIVE | mich | dich | ihn     | sie    | es  | uns  | euch | sie   | Sie   |
| DATIVE     | mir  | dir  | ihm     | ihr    | ihm | uns  | euch | ihnen | Ihnen |

The genitive form is not given, because it is so rarely used.

# Summary of German grammar

In German there are two forms for you, **du** and **Sie**. **Du** (plural **ihr**) is informal and is used when speaking to a child, a member of your family, or someone you know well. When speaking to a person or a group of people you do not know very well, use the polite form, **Sie**.

German pronouns agree in gender with the noun they refer to. In the nominative case, 'it' can be be translated by **er** or **sie**, as well as **es**:

er (der Bleistift) ist rot = *it (the pencil) is red*
sie (die Rose) ist schön = *it (the rose) is beautiful*
es (das Auto) ist teuer = *it (the car) is expensive*

## 6.2 Possessive pronouns

The possessive pronouns are:

meiner/meine/mein(e)s = *mine*　unserer/unsere/unser(e)s = *ours*
deiner/deine/dein(e)s = *yours*　eurer/eure/eures = *yours*
(informal singular)　(informal plural)
seiner/seine/sein(e)s = *his*　ihrer/ihre/ihr(e)s = *theirs*
ihrer/ihre/ihr(e)s = *hers*　Ihrer, Ihre, Ihr(e)s = *yours* (polite)
seiner/seine/sein(e)s = *its*

They all take endings like **meiner/meine/mein(e)s**, as follows:

| | SINGULAR | | | PLURAL |
| | masculine | feminine | neuter | all genders |
|---|---|---|---|---|
| NOMINATIVE | meiner | meine | mein(e)s | meine |
| ACCUSATIVE | meinen | meine | mein(e)s | meine |
| GENITIVE | meines | meiner | meines | meine |
| DATIVE | meinem | meiner | meinem | meinen |

As can be seen in the table, in the neuter form an -e- can be added (making **meines**). This applies to all the possessive pronouns, but the extra -e- is rare.

## 6.3 Relative pronouns

Relative pronouns link a main clause to a subordinate clause. In English they are *who*, *which*, *that*, and *what*. In German they are **der**, **die**, or **das**, depending on the noun referred to:

| | SINGULAR | | | PLURAL |
| | masculine | feminine | neuter | all genders |
|---|---|---|---|---|
| NOMINATIVE | der | die | das | die |
| ACCUSATIVE | den | die | das | die |
| GENITIVE | dessen | deren | dessen | deren |
| DATIVE | dem | der | dem | denen |

Relative pronouns can be left out in English, but never in German:

das Buch, das ich lese　　= *the book (that) I'm reading*

They agree in gender and number with the noun they refer back to:

der Mann, der uns besucht hat　　= *the man who visited us*

(**der** is masculine singular)

. . . . . . . . . . . . . . . . . . . . . . . . . . . . . . . . . . . . . . . . . . . . . . . . . . .

der Mann, dessen Frau den Wagen = *the man, whose wife had rented the car,*
vermietet hatte, wusste es nicht *did not know about it*

The case of the pronoun depends on its function in the clause it
introduces:

der Bleistift, den ich gestern gekauft habe = *the pencil I bought yesterday*

(**den** is masculine singular, and accusative, because it is the object of the
clause it introduces)

## 6.4 Interrogative pronouns

These pronouns are used to ask questions:

wer? = *who?*  was? = *what?*  welcher/welche/welches? = *which?*

**Wer** changes as follows:

NOMINATIVE wer?  ACCUSATIVE wen?  GENITIVE wessen?  DATIVE wem?

wer sprach? = *who was speaking?*
wen trafst du? = *who (whom) did you meet?*
wessen Buch ist das? = *whose book is that?*
mit wem spricht er? = *who is he talking to?*

**Was?** is invariable.

was ist das? = *what is that?*

**Welcher**: The forms are the same as those given for dieser on page 934.

welche Zeitung hast du gekauft? = *which newspaper have you bought?*

**Was für ein ... ?** This expression means 'what kind or sort of ...?' **Ein**
takes the endings according to whether the noun qualified is the subject,
object, or indirect object.

was für ein Mann/eine Frau ist das? (subject) = *what sort of a man/woman is that?*
was für ein Geschenk bekam er? (object) = *what sort of a present did he get?*
was für Zeitungen haben Sie? (plural object) = *what sort of newspapers do you have?*

## 6.5 Reflexive pronouns

The object of a reflexive verb is the same as its subject. In German, the
object is a reflexive pronoun. This is usually in the accusative (**ich wasche
mich** = *I wash myself*). The reflexive pronouns of some verbs are in the
dative (**ich stelle mir vor** = *I imagine*).

The following table shows which accusative reflexive pronoun
corresponds to the normal (nominative) personal pronoun.

| ich | mich | wir | uns |
|---|---|---|---|
| du | dich | ihr | euch |
| er, sie, es, man | sich | sie, Sie | sich |

sie erinnern sich daran = *they remember it*
es bewegt sich = *it's moving*

The dative forms are the same as the above, except for the **ich** and **du**
forms: **ich**: **mir**; **du**: **dir**.

## 6.6 Indefinite pronouns

Some of these pronouns take endings according to whether they are the subject, object, or indirect object in the sentence. Among those that do are: **jemand** = *someone* or *somebody*, **niemand** = *no one* or *nobody*, **irgend jemand** = *anyone* or *anybody*.

|  | someone | no one | anyone |
| --- | --- | --- | --- |
| NOMINATIVE | jemand | niemand | irgend jemand |
| ACCUSATIVE | jemanden | niemanden | irgend jemanden |
| DATIVE | jemandem | niemandem | irgend jemandem |

jemand hat mein Fahrrad genommen = *someone has taken my bicycle*
sie sah niemanden = *she saw no one*
er gab es jemandem = *he gave it to someone*

The genitive case is rarely used.

## 6.7 One

The pronoun *one* is translated by **einer**, **eine**, **eines** or **eins**, which take the endings already given on page 938 for singular possessive pronouns, according to their function in the sentence.

trinken wir ein(e)s? (ein Bier) = *shall we have one? (a beer)*
einer von uns muss es tun = *one of us must do it*

Similarly **keiner**, **keine**, **keines** or **keins** = *no one* or *nobody*, *nothing* (neuter) take the endings according to their function in the sentence.

keiner will ihn begleiten = *no one wants to go with him*

Indefinite pronouns which are invariable are:

*something* = etwas; *everything* = alles; *nothing* = nichts
gefällt noch etwas? = *would you like something else?*
sie nahm alles = *she took everything*
er weisst nichts = *he knows nothing*

Note that *something/everything/nothing good* is translated by **etwas/alles/nichts Gutes**

*something good has happened* = etwas Gutes ist geschehen

## 7 Prepositions

Prepositions are words like *above, in, under* that convey the idea of place and come in front of a noun or pronoun. In German, the noun following a preposition always has to be in one of three cases: dative, accusative, or genitive.

Prepositions can also be prefixes and form separable verbs:

die Straße entlanggehen = *to walk along the street*
er geht die Straße entlang = *he is walking along the street*

In the dictionary, the case governed by a preposition is given as follows:

mit 1 *Präp mit Dat.*

This means that **mit** always takes the dative case.

The following prepositions always take the dative:

aus   bei   mit   nach   seit   von   zu

The following prepositions always take the accusative:

bis   durch   entlang   für   gegen   ohne   um

The following prepositions always take the genitive:

anstatt   während   trotz   wegen

There is a group of prepositions that can take the dative or the accusative, depending on the sense of the sentence.

They are:

an   auf   außer   hinter   in   unter   neben   vor   über   zwischen

If the speaker wishes to convey the idea that someone or something is stationary, the dative case is used:

sie saß in der Küche = *she sat in the kitchen*
es liegt auf dem Tisch = *it's lying on the table*

But if the speaker wishes to convey the idea of movement the accusative case is used:

sie ging in die Küche = *she went into the kitchen*
er legte den Beutel auf den Tisch = *he put the bag on the table*

Note the expressions **nach Hause** and **zu Hause**: **nach Hause** = *home (homewards)*, and **zu Hause** = *at home*.

Some forms of the definite article are usually shortened when used with certain prepositions:

**am** (an dem); **ans** (an das); **aufs** (auf das); **beim** (bei dem)
**durchs** (durch das); **fürs** (für das); **im** (in dem); **ins** (in das)
**ums** (um das); **vom** (von dem); **zum** (zu dem); **zur** (zu der)

## 8 Conjunctions

Conjunctions are words, such as **und** = *and*, **aber** = *but*, which link clauses in a sentence.

Some common conjunctions are:

aber = *but*   denn = *for*   oder = *or*   sondern = *but (on the contrary)*   und = *and*

These conjunctions do not change normal word order in the two clauses:

ich gehe und er kommt auch = *I am going and he is coming too*

This is because the clauses are of equal weight or importance.

Conjunctions which introduce a subordinate clause make the verb in the subordinate clause appear at the end:

| als = *when, = as* | bevor = *before* | bis = *until* | da = *since* | dass = *that* |
| ob = *whether* | während = *while* | wenn = *when, = if* | weil = *because* | |

| als er das erfuhr, wollte er nicht mitkommen | = *when he found out, he didn't want to come* |
| er konnte nicht in die Schule gehen, weil er krank war | = *he couldn't go to school, because he was ill* |
| wenn sie in die Stadt geht, nimmt sie immer ihre Handtasche | = *when she goes to town, she always takes her handbag* |

## 9 Word order

The basic rule for German word order is that the verb comes second in a sentence. The subject of the sentence usually comes before the verb:

> meine Mutter fährt am Freitag nach Köln = *my mother is going to Cologne on Friday*

When the verb used is in a compound tense, such as the perfect and the future tenses, the auxiliary verb comes second in the sentence, while the past participle (in the perfect) or infinitive (in the future tense) goes to the end:

> wir haben sehr lang gewartet = *we waited a very long time*
> sie wird sicher bald kommen = *she is sure to come soon*

Infinitives go to the end in other sentences too, as when used with modal verbs or the verb **lassen**:

> ich kann dieses Lied nicht leiden = *I can't stand this song*
> du musst hier bleiben = *you must stay here*
> ich lasse mir die Haare schneiden = *I'm going to have my hair cut*

In questions the normal order of the subject and the verb is inverted, as in English:

> kommst du heute Abend? = *are you coming this evening?*

In commands the verb is placed first:

> komm schnell rein! = *come in quickly!*

### Subordinate clauses

A speaker or writer may start a sentence with a subordinate clause in order to introduce variety or for effect. In this case the verb stays in second place, after the subordinate clause, and the subject of the main clause follows the verb; **blieb** in the example below:

> da ich kein Geld hatte, blieb ich zu Hause = *since I had no money, I stayed at home*

In the subordinate clause itself, the verb goes to the end; *cf.* **hatte** in the previous example and **war** in the following one:

> er konnte nicht in die Schule gehen, weil er krank war

The relative pronouns **der**, **die**, and **das**, as well as conjunctions such as **als** = *when*, **dass** = *that*, **weil** = *because*, introduce subordinate clauses and therefore cause the verb to go to the end of the subordinate clause.

(See the section on Conjunctions for more examples.)

| | |
|---|---|
| der Junge, der hier wohnt, ist in der Schule | = *the boy, who lives here, is at school* |
| die Soldaten, die gestern hier waren, haben nicht bezahlt | = *the soldiers, who were here yesterday, did not pay* |

When separable verbs separate, the prefix goes to the end:

| | |
|---|---|
| der Film fängt um acht Uhr an | = *the film starts at 8 o'clock* |
| wann kommt der Zug an? | = *when does the train arrive?* |

When there are a number of phrases in a sentence, the usual order for the different elements is: 1 time, 2 manner, 3 place:

wir fahren heute mit dem Auto nach München = *we are driving to Munich today*

(*time* = heute; *manner* = mit dem Auto; *place* = nach München)

# German irregular verbs / Deutsche unregelmäßige Verben

Irregular and partly irregular verbs are listed alphabetically by infinitive. 1st, 2nd, and 3rd person present and imperative forms are given after the infinitive, and preterite subjunctive forms after the preterite indicative, where they take an umlaut, change *e* to *i*, etc.

Verbs with a raised number in the German-English section of the Dictionary have the same number in this list.

Compound verbs (including verbs with prefixes) are only given if a) they do not take the same forms as the corresponding simple verb, e.g. *befehlen*, or b) there is no corresponding simple verb, e.g. *bewegen*.

An asterisk (*) indicates a verb which is also conjugated regularly.

| Infinitive<br>*Infinitiv* | Preterite<br>*Präteritum* | Past Participle<br>*2. Partizip* |
|---|---|---|
| **abwägen** | wog (wöge) ab | abgewogen |
| **backen** (du bäckst, er bäckt; *auch:* du backst, er backt) | backte, *älter:* buk (büke) | gebacken |
| **befehlen** (du befiehlst, er befiehlt; befiehl!) | befahl (beföhle, befähle) | befohlen |
| **beginnen** | begann (begänne, *seltener:* begönne) | begonnen |
| **beißen** | biss | gebissen |
| **bergen** (du birgst, er birgt; birg!) | barg (bärge) | geborgen |
| **bersten** (du birst, er birst; birst!) | barst (bärste) | geborsten |
| **besinnen** | besann (besänne) | besonnen |
| **bewegen**[2] | bewog (bewöge) | bewogen |
| **biegen** | bog (böge) | gebogen |
| **bieten** | bot (böte) | geboten |
| **binden** | band (bände) | gebunden |
| **bitten** | bat (bäte) | gebeten |
| **blasen** (du bläst, er bläst) | blies | geblasen |
| **bleiben** | blieb | geblieben |
| **bleichen*** | blich | geblichen |
| **braten** (du brätst, er brät) | briet | gebraten |
| **brechen** (du brichst, er bricht; brich!) | brach (bräche) | gebrochen |
| **brennen** | brannte (brennte) | gebrannt |
| **bringen** | brachte (brächte) | gebracht |
| **denken** | dachte (dächte) | gedacht |
| **dreschen** (du drischst, er drischt; drisch!) | drosch (drösche) | gedroschen |
| **dringen** | drang (dränge) | gedrungen |
| **dürfen** (ich darf, du darfst, er darf) | durfte (dürfte) | gedurft |
| **empfehlen** (du empfiehlst, er empfiehlt, empfiehl!) | empfahl (empföhle, *seltener:* empfähle) | empfohlen |
| **erklimmen** | erklomm (erklömme) | erklommen |
| **erlöschen** (du erlischst, er erlischt; erlisch!) | erlosch (erlösche) | erloschen |

| Infinitive | Preterite | Past Participle |
|---|---|---|
| *Infinitiv* | *Präteritum* | *2. Partizip* |

**erschallen\*** ...........erscholl (erschölle) ...........erschollen
**erschrecken**[1,3] (du erschrickst, er .......erschrak (erschäke) ...........erschrocken
erschrickt; erschrick!)
**erwägen**...........erwog (erwöge)...........erwogen
**essen** (du isst, er isst; iss!) ...........aß (äße) ...........gegessen
**fahren** (du fährst, er fährt) ...........fuhr (führe)...........gefahren
**fallen** (du fällst, er fällt) ...........fiel ...........gefallen
**fangen** (du fängst, er fängt) ...........fing...........gefangen
**fechten** (du fichtst, er ficht; ficht!) .......focht (föchte) ...........gefochten
**finden** ...........fand (fände)...........gefunden
**flechten** (du flichtst, er flicht; ...........flocht (flöchte) ...........geflochten
flicht!)
**fliegen** ...........flog (flöge) ...........geflogen
**fliehen** ...........floh (flöhe)...........geflohen
**fließen** ...........floss (flösse) ...........geflossen
**fressen** (du frisst, er frisst; friss!) .......fraß (fräße) ...........gefressen
**frieren** ...........fror (fröre) ...........gefroren
**gären\*** ...........gor (gäre)...........gegoren
**gebären** (*geh.:* du gebierst, sie ...........gebar (gebäre) ...........geboren
gebiert; gebier!)
**geben** (du gibst, er gibt; gib!) ...........gab (gäbe) ...........gegeben
**gedeihen** ...........gedieh ...........gediehen
**gehen**...........ging ...........gegangen
**gelingen** ...........gelang (gelänge) ...........gelungen
**gelten** (du giltst, er gilt; gilt!) ...........galt (gölte, gälte) ...........gegolten
**genesen** ...........genas (genäse) ...........genesen
**genießen** ...........genoss (genösse) ...........genossen
**geschehen** (es geschieht) ...........geschah (geschähe) ...........geschehen
**gewinnen** ...........gewann (gewönne, gewänne) ......gewonnen
**gießen** ...........goss (gösse) ...........gegossen
**gleichen** ...........glich ...........geglichen
**gleiten** ...........glitt ...........geglitten
**glimmen** ...........glomm (glömme) ...........geglommen
**graben** (du gräbst, er gräbt) ...........grub (grübe) ...........gegraben
**greifen** ...........griff ...........gegriffen
**haben** (du hast, er hat) ...........hatte (hätte) ...........gehabt
**halten** (du hältst, er hält) ...........hielt ...........gehalten
**hängen**[1] ...........hing ...........gehangen
**hauen** ...........haute, *geh.:* hieb ...........gehauen
**heben** ...........hob (höbe) ...........gehoben
**heißen** ...........hieß ...........geheißen
**helfen** (du hilfst, er hilft; hilf!) ...........half (hülfe, *selten:* hälfe) ...........geholfen
**kennen** ...........kannte (kennte) ...........gekannt
**klingen** ...........klang (klänge) ...........geklungen
**kneifen** ...........kniff ...........gekniffen
**kommen** ...........kam (käme) ...........gekommen
**können** (ich kann, du kannst, er ...........konnte (könnte) ...........gekonnt
kann)
**kriechen** ...........kroch (kröche) ...........gekrochen
**laden**[1,2] (du lädst, er lädt) ...........lud (lüde) ...........geladen
**lassen** (du lässt, er lässt) ...........ließ ...........gelassen
**laufen** (du läufst, er läuft) ...........lief ...........gelaufen
**leiden** ...........litt ...........gelitten
**leihen** ...........lieh ...........geliehen
**lesen**[1,2] (du liest, er liest; lies!) ...........las (läse) ...........gelesen
**liegen** ...........lag (läge) ...........gelegen
**lügen** ...........log (löge) ...........gelogen
**mahlen** ...........mahlte ...........gemahlen
**meiden** ...........mied ...........gemieden

| Infinitive | Preterite | Past Participle |
| --- | --- | --- |
| *Infinitiv* | *Präteritum* | *2. Partizip* |

**melken\*** (du milkst, er milkt; ...........molk (mölke) ....................gemolken
milk!; du melkst, er melkt;
melke!)

**messen** (du misst, er misst; miss!) ........maß (mäße) ......................gemessen

**misslingen** ...........................misslang (misslänge) .............misslungen

**mögen** (ich mag, du magst, er ...........mochte (möchte) .................gemocht
mag)

**müssen** (ich muss, du musst, er ..........musste (müsste) .................gemusst
muss)

**nehmen** (du nimmst, er nimmt; ..........nahm (nähme) ...................genommen
nimm!)

**nennen** ................................nannte (nennte) .................genannt

**pfeifen** ................................pfiff ..............................gepfiffen

**preisen** ................................pries .............................gepriesen

**quellen** (du quillst, er quillt; ...........quoll (quölle) ....................gequollen
quill!)

**raten** (du rätst, er rät) ..................riet ..............................geraten

**reiben** .................................rieb ..............................gerieben

**reißen** .................................riss ..............................gerissen

**reiten** .................................ritt ..............................geritten

**rennen** ................................rannte (rennte) .................gerannt

**riechen** ................................roch (röche) .....................gerochen

**ringen** .................................rang (ränge) .....................gerungen

**rinnen** .................................rann (ränne, *seltener:* rönne) .......geronnen

**rufen** ..................................rief ..............................gerufen

**salzen\*** ................................salzte .............................gesalzen

**saufen** (du säufst, er säuft) ..............soff (söffe) .......................gesoffen

**saugen\*** ...............................sog (söge) ........................gesogen

**schaffen\*** ..............................schuf (schüfe) ....................geschaffen

**schallen\*** ..............................scholl (schölle) ...................geschallt

**scheiden** ...............................schied ............................geschieden

**scheinen** ...............................schien ............................geschienen

**scheißen** ...............................schiss ............................geschissen

**schelten** (du schiltst, er schilt; ..........schalt (schölte) ..................gescholten
schilt!)

**scheren**[1] ..............................schor (schöre) ....................geschoren

**schieben** ...............................schob (schöbe) ...................geschoben

**schießen** ...............................schoss (schösse) ..................geschossen

**schinden** ...............................schindete ........................geschunden

**schlafen** (du schläfst, er schläft) .........schlief ............................geschlafen

**schlagen** (du schlägst, er schlägt) ........schlug (schlüge) ..................geschlagen

**schleichen** ..............................schlich ...........................geschlichen

**schleifen**[1] .............................schliff ............................geschliffen

**schließen** ...............................schloss (schlösse) .................geschlossen

**schlingen** ..............................schlang (schlänge) ...............geschlungen

**schmeißen** .............................schmiss ..........................geschmissen

**schmelzen** (du schmilzt, er ..............schmolz ..........................geschmolzen
schmilzt; schmilz!)

**schneiden** ..............................schnitt ...........................geschnitten

**schrecken\*** (du schrickst, er ............schrak (schräke) ..................geschreckt
schrickt; schrick!)

**schreiben** ..............................schrieb ...........................geschrieben

**schreien** ...............................schrie ............................geschrie[e]n

**schreiten** ...............................schritt ...........................geschritten

**schweigen** ..............................schwieg ..........................geschwiegen

**schwellen** (du schwillst, er .............schwoll (schwölle) ...............geschwollen
schwillt; schwill!)

**schwimmen** ...........................schwamm (schwömme, *sel-* ........geschwommen
...................................*tener:* schwämme)

**schwinden** .............................schwand (schwände) .............geschwunden

| Infinitive | Preterite | Past Participle |
|---|---|---|
| *Infinitiv* | *Präteritum* | *2. Partizip* |
| **schwingen** | schwang (schwänge) | geschwungen |
| **schwören** | schwor (schwüre) | geschworen |
| **sehen** (du siehst, er sieht; sieh[e]!) | sah (sähe) | gesehen |
| **sein** (ich bin, du bist, er ist, wir sind, ihr seid, sie sind; sei!) | war (wäre) | gewesen |
| **senden\*** | sandte (sendete) | gesandt |
| **sieden\*** | sott (sötte) | gesotten |
| **singen** | sang (sänge) | gesungen |
| **sinken** | sank (sänke) | gesunken |
| **sitzen** | saß (säße) | gesessen |
| **sollen** (ich soll, du sollst, er soll) | sollte | gesollt |
| **spalten\*** | spaltete | gespalten |
| **speien** | spie | gespie[e]n |
| **spinnen** | spann (spönne, spänne) | gesponnen |
| **sprechen** (du sprichst, er spricht; sprich!) | sprach (spräche) | gesprochen |
| **sprießen** | spross (sprösse) | gesprossen |
| **springen** | sprang | gesprungen |
| **stechen** (du stichst, er sticht; stich!) | stach (stäche) | gestochen |
| **stehen** | stand (stünde, *auch:* stände) | gestanden |
| **stehlen** (du stiehlst, er stiehlt; stiehl!) | stahl (stähle, *seltener:* stöhle) | gestohlen |
| **steigen** | stieg | gestiegen |
| **sterben** (du stirbst, er stirbt; stirb!) | starb (stürbe) | gestorben |
| **stinken** | stank (stänke) | gestunken |
| **stoßen** (du stößt, er stößt) | stieß | gestoßen |
| **streichen** | strich | gestrichen |
| **streiten** | stritt | gestritten |
| **tragen** (du trägst, er trägt) | trug (trüge) | getragen |
| **treffen** (du triffst, er trifft; triff!) | traf (träfe) | getroffen |
| **treiben** | trieb | getrieben |
| **treten** (du trittst, er tritt; tritt!) | trat (träte) | getreten |
| **triefen\*** | troff (tröffe) | getroffen |
| **trinken** | trank (tränke) | getrunken |
| **trügen** | trog (tröge) | getrogen |
| **tun** | tat (täte) | getan |
| **verderben** (du verdirbst, er verdirbt; verdirb!) | verdarb (verdürbe) | verdorben |
| **verdrießen** | verdross (verdrösse) | verdrossen |
| **vergessen** (du vergisst, er vergisst, vergiss!) | vergaß (vergäße) | vergessen |
| **verlieren** | verlor (verlöre) | verloren |
| **verschleißen\*** | verschliss | verschlissen |
| **verzeihen** | verzieh | verziehen |
| **wachsen**[1] (du wächst, er wächst) | wuchs (wüchse) | gewachsen |
| **waschen** (du wäschst, er wäscht) | wusch (wüsche) | gewaschen |
| **weichen** | wich | gewichen |
| **weisen** | wies | gewiesen |
| **wenden**[2]**\*** | wandte (wendete) | gewandt |
| **werben** (du wirbst, er wirbt; wirb!) | warb (würbe) | geworben |
| **werden** (du wirst, er wird; werde!) | wurde, *dichter.:* ward (würde) | geworden; *als Hilfsv.:* worden |
| **werfen** (du wirfst, er wirft; wirf!) | warf (würfe) | geworfen |
| **wiegen**[1] | wog (wöge) | gewogen |
| **winden** | wand (wände) | gewunden |
| **wissen** (ich weiß, du weißt, er weiß) | wusste (wüsste) | gewusst |

| Infinitive | Preterite | Past Participle |
|---|---|---|
| *Infinitiv* | *Präteritum* | *2. Partizip* |
| **wollen** (ich will, du willst, er ............. wollte ........................... gewollt will) | | |
| **wringen** ........................... wrang (wränge) ................. gewrungen | | |
| **ziehen** .............................. zog (zöge) ....................... gezogen | | |
| **zwingen** ........................... zwang (zwänge) ................. gezwungen | | |

# English irregular verbs / Englische unregelmäßige Verben

Ein Sternchen (*) weist darauf hin, dass die korrekte Form von der jeweiligen Bedeutung abhängt.

| Infinitive / *Infinitiv* | Past Tense / *Präteritum* | Past Participle / *2. Partizip* |
|---|---|---|
| arise | arose | arisen |
| awake | awoke | awoken |
| be | was *sing.*, were *pl.* | been |
| bear | bore | borne |
| beat | beat | beaten |
| become | became | become |
| begin | began | begun |
| bend | bent | bent |
| bet | bet, betted | bet, betted |
| bid | *bade, bid | *bidden, bid |
| bind | bound | bound |
| bite | bit | bitten |
| bleed | bled | bled |
| blow | blew | blown |
| break | broke | broken |
| breed | bred | bred |
| bring | brought | brought |
| broadcast | broadcast | broadcast |
| build | built | built |
| burn | burnt, burned | burnt, burned |
| burst | burst | burst |
| bust | bust, busted | bust, busted |
| buy | bought | bought |
| cast | cast | cast |
| catch | caught | caught |
| choose | chose | chosen |
| cling | clung | clung |
| come | came | come |
| cost | *cost, costed | *cost, costed |
| creep | crept | crept |
| cut | cut | cut |
| deal | dealt | dealt |
| dig | dug | dug |
| dive | dived, (*Amer.*) dove | dived |
| do | did | done |
| draw | drew | drawn |
| dream | dreamt, dreamed | dreamt, dreamed |
| drink | drank | drunk |
| drive | drove | driven |
| dwell | dwelt | dwelt |
| eat | ate | eaten |
| fall | fell | fallen |
| feed | fed | fed |
| feel | felt | felt |
| fight | fought | fought |

| Infinitive / *Infinitiv* | Past Tense / *Präteritum* | Past Participle / *2. Partizip* |
|---|---|---|
| find | found | found |
| flee | fled | fled |
| fling | flung | flung |
| floodlight | floodlit | floodlit |
| fly | flew | flown |
| forbid | forbade, forbad | forbidden |
| forecast | forecast, forecasted | forecast, forecasted |
| foretell | foretold | foretold |
| forget | forgot | forgotten |
| forgive | forgave | forgiven |
| forsake | forsook | forsaken |
| freeze | froze | frozen |
| get | got | got, (*Amer.*) gotten |
| give | gave | given |
| go | went | gone |
| grind | ground | ground |
| grow | grew | grown |
| hang | *hung, hanged | *hung, hanged |
| have | had | had |
| hear | heard | heard |
| hew | hewed | hewn, hewed |
| hide | hid | hidden |
| hit | hit | hit |
| hold | held | held |
| hurt | hurt | hurt |
| keep | kept | kept |
| kneel | knelt, (*esp. Amer.*) kneeled | knelt, (*esp. Amer.*) kneeled |
| know | knew | known |
| lay | laid | laid |
| lead | led | led |
| lean | leaned, (*Brit.*) leant | leaned, (*Brit.*) leant |
| leap | leapt, leaped | leapt, leaped |
| learn | learnt, learned | learnt, learned |
| leave | left | left |
| lend | lent | lent |
| let | let | let |
| lie[3] | lay | lain |
| light | lit, lighted | lit, lighted |
| lose | lost | lost |
| make | made | made |

| Infinitive | Past Tense | Past Participle |
|---|---|---|
| Infinitiv | Präteritum | 2. Partizip |
| mean | meant | meant |
| meet | met | met |
| mow | mowed | mown, mowed |
| overhang | overhung | overhung |
| pay | paid | paid |
| prove | proved | proved, proven |
| put | put | put |
| quit | quitted, (Amer.) quit | quitted, (Amer.) quit |
| read /ri:d/ | read /red/ | read /red/ |
| rid | rid | rid |
| ride | rode | ridden |
| ring[3] | rang | rung |
| rise | rose | risen |
| run | ran | run |
| saw | sawed | sawn, sawed |
| say | said | said |
| see | saw | seen |
| seek | sought | sought |
| sell | sold | sold |
| send | sent | sent |
| set | set | set |
| sew | sewed | sewn, sewed |
| shake | shook | shaken |
| shear | sheared | shorn, sheared |
| shed | shed | shed |
| shine | shone | shone |
| shit | shitted, shit | shitted, shit |
| shoe | shod | shod |
| shoot | shot | shot |
| show | showed | shown |
| shrink | shrank | shrunk |
| shut | shut | shut |
| sing | sang | sung |
| sink | sank, sunk | sunk |
| sit | sat | sat |
| slay | slew | slain |
| sleep | slept | slept |
| slide | slid | slid |
| sling | slung | slung |
| slink | slunk | slunk |
| slit | slit | slit |
| smell | smelt, smelled | smelt, smelled |
| sow | sowed | sown, sowed |
| speak | spoke | spoken |
| speed | *sped, speeded | *sped, speeded |
| spell | spelled, (Brit.) spelt | spelled, (Brit.) spelt |

| Infinitive | Past Tense | Past Participle |
|---|---|---|
| Infinitiv | Präteritum | 2. Partizip |
| spend | spent | spent |
| spill | spilt, spilled | spilt, spilled |
| spin | spun | spun |
| spit | spat, spit | spat, spit |
| split | split | split |
| spoil | spoilt, spoiled | spoilt, spoiled |
| spread | spread | spread |
| spring | sprang, (Amer.) sprung | sprung |
| stand | stood | stood |
| steal | stole | stolen |
| stick | stuck | stuck |
| sting | stung | stung |
| stink | stank, stunk | stunk |
| strew | strewed | strewed, strewn |
| stride | strode | stridden |
| strike | struck | struck |
| string | strung | strung |
| strive | strove | striven |
| sublet | sublet | sublet |
| swear | swore | sworn |
| sweep | swept | swept |
| swell | swelled | swollen, swelled |
| swim | swam | swum |
| swing | swung | swung |
| take | took | taken |
| teach | taught | taught |
| tear | tore | torn |
| tell | told | told |
| think | thought | thought |
| thrive | thrived, throve | thrived, thriven |
| throw | threw | thrown |
| thrust | thrust | thrust |
| tread | trod | trodden, trod |
| understand | understood | understood |
| undo | undid | undone |
| wake | woke | woken |
| wear | wore | worn |
| weave[1] | wove | woven |
| weep | wept | wept |
| wet | wet, wetted | wet, wetted |
| win | won | won |
| wind[2] /waɪnd/ | wound /waʊnd/ | wound /waʊnd/ |
| wring | wrung | wrung |
| write | wrote | written |

# Numbers / Zahlen

| Cardinal numbers | *Kardinalzahlen* | Ordinal numbers | *Ordinalzahlen* |
|---|---|---|---|
| 1 one | 1 eins, ein… | 1st first | 1. erst… |
| 2 two | 2 zwei | 2nd second | 2. zweit… |
| 3 three | 3 drei | 3rd third | 3. dritt… |
| 4 four | 4 vier | 4th fourth | 4. viert… |
| 5 five | 5 fünf | 5th fifth | 5. fünft… |
| 6 six | 6 sechs | 6th sixth | 6. sechst… |
| 7 seven | 7 sieben | 7th seventh | 7. siebt…, siebent… |
| 8 eight | 8 acht | 8th eighth | 8. acht… |
| 9 nine | 9 neun | 9th ninth | 9. neunt… |
| 10 ten | 10 zehn | 10th tenth | 10. zehnt… |
| 11 eleven | 11 elf | 11th eleventh | 11. elft… |
| 12 twelve | 12 zwölf | 12th twelfth | 12. zwölft… |
| 13 thirteen | 13 dreizehn | 13th thirteenth | 13. dreizehnt… |
| 14 fourteen | 14 vierzehn | 14th fourteenth | 14. vierzehnt… |
| 15 fifteen | 15 fünfzehn | 15th fifteenth | 15. fünfzehnt… |
| 16 sixteen | 16 sechzehn | 16th sixteenth | 16. sechzehnt… |
| 17 seventeen | 17 siebzehn | 17th seventeenth | 17. siebzehnt… |
| 18 eighteen | 18 achtzehn | 18th eighteenth | 18. achtzehnt… |
| 19 nineteen | 19 neunzehn | 19th nineteenth | 19. neunzehnt… |
| 20 twenty | 20 zwanzig | 20th twentieth | 20. zwanzigst… |
| 21 twenty-one | 21 einundzwanzig | 21st twenty-first | 21. einundzwanzigst… |
| 30 thirty | 30 dreißig | 30th thirtieth | 30. dreißigst… |
| 40 forty | 40 vierzig | 40th fortieth | 40. vierzigst… |
| 50 fifty | 50 fünfzig | 50th fiftieth | 50. fünfzigst… |
| 60 sixty | 60 sechzig | 60th sixtieth | 60. sechzigst… |
| 70 seventy | 70 siebzig | 70th seventieth | 70. siebzigst… |
| 80 eighty | 80 achtzig | 80th eightieth | 80. achtzigst… |
| 90 ninety | 90 neunzig | 90th ninetieth | 90. neunzigst… |
| 100 one hundred | 100 [ein]hundert | 100th [one] hundredth | 100. [ein]hundertst… |
| 101 one hundred and one | 101 [ein]hundert[und]eins | 101st [one] hundred and first | 101. [ein]hundert[und]erst… |
| 1,000 one thousand | 1 000 [ein]tausend | 1,000th [one] thousandth | 1 000. [ein]tausendst… |
| 1,001 one thousand and one | 1 001 [ein]tausend[und]eins | 1,001st one thousand and first | 1 001. [ein]tausend[und]erst… |
| 10,000 ten thousand | 10 000 zehntausend | 10,000th ten thousandth | 10 000. zehntausendst… |
| 13,438 thirteen thousand, four hundred and thirty-eight | 13 438 dreizehntausendvierhundert[und]achtunddreißig | 13,438th thirteen thousand, four hundred and thirty-eighth | 13 438. dreizehntausendvierhundert[und]achtunddreißigst… |
| 100,000 one hundred thousand | 100 000 [ein]hunderttausend | 100,000th [one] hundred thousandth | 100 000. [ein]hunderttausendst… |
| 1,000,000 one million | 1 000 000 eine Million | 1,000,000th [one] millionth | 1 000 000. millionst… |
| 2,000,000 two million | 2 000 000 zwei Millionen | 2,000,000th two millionth | 2 000 000. zweimillionst… |
| 1,000,000,000 one thousand million (Brit.);one billion (Amer.) | 1 000 000 000 eine Milliarde | 1,000,000,000th [one] thousand millionth (Brit.); one billionth (Amer.) | 1 000 000 000. milliardst… |

## Vulgar fractions and mixed numbers /
## Brüche (gemeine Brüche) und gemischte Zahlen

| in figures<br>*in Zahlen* | in words | *in Worten* |
|---|---|---|
| 1/2 | a/one half | *ein halb* |
| 1/3 | a/one third | *ein drittel* |
| 1/4 | a/one quarter | *ein viertel* |
| 1/10 | a/one tenth | *ein zehntel* |
| 2/3 | two-thirds | *zwei drittel* |
| 1/1 | one over one | *ein eintel* |
| 4/1 | four over one | *vier eintel* |
| m/n | m over n | *m n-tel* |
| x/6 | x over six | *x sechstel* |
| 1 1/2 | one and a half | *ein[und]einhalb* |

## Decimal numbers / Dezimalzahlen

| written as | *geschrieben* | spoken as | *gesprochen* |
|---|---|---|---|
| 0.1 | *0,1* | nought point one | *null Komma eins* |
| 0.015 | *0,015* | nought point nought one five | *null Komma null eins fünf* |
| 1.40 | *1,40* | one point four o [əʊ] | *eins Komma vier null* |

# Weights and Measures / Maße und Gewichte

## Weight / Gewichte

| | | |
|---|---|---|
| 1,000 milligrams (mg) . . . . . . . . . . . . . . . . . . . . | = 1 gram (g) . . . . . . . . . . . . . . . . | = 15.43 grains |
| 1 000 Milligramm (mg) . . . . . . . . . . . . . . . . . . . | = 1 Gramm (g) | |
| 1,000 grams. . . . . . . . . . . . . . . . . . . . . . . . . . . . | = 1 kilogram (kg). . . . . . . . . . . . . | = 2.205 pounds |
| 1 000 Gramm. . . . . . . . . . . . . . . . . . . . . . . . . | = 1 Kilogramm (kg). . . . . . . . . . . | |
| 1,000 kilograms. . . . . . . . . . . . . . . . . . . . . . . . | = 1 tonne (t). . . . . . . . . . . . . . . . . | = 19.684 hundredweight |
| 1 000 Kilogramm. . . . . . . . . . . . . . . . . . . . . . | = 1 Tonne (t) | |
| | 1 ounce (oz.) . . . . . . . . . . . . . . | = 28.35 g |
| 16 ounces . . . . . . . . . . . . . . . . . . . . . . . . . . . . | = 1 pound (lb.). . . . . . . . . . . . . . . | = 0.454 kg |
| 14 pounds . . . . . . . . . . . . . . . . . . . . . . . . . . . . | = 1 stone (st.) . . . . . . . . . . . . . . . | = 6.35 kg |
| 112 pounds . . . . . . . . . . . . . . . . . . . . . . . . . . | = 1 hundredweight . . . . . . . . . . . | = 50.8 kg |
| 20 hundredweight . . . . . . . . . . . . . . . . . . . . . . | = 1 ton (t.) . . . . . . . . . . . . . . . . . | = 1,016.05 kg |

## Length / Längenmaße

| | | |
|---|---|---|
| 10 millimetres (mm) . . . . . . . . . . . . . . . . . . . . | = 1 centimetre (cm) . . . . . . . . . . | = 0.394 inch |
| 10 Millimeter (mm) . . . . . . . . . . . . . . . . . . . . . | = 1 Zentimeter (cm) | |
| 100 centimetres. . . . . . . . . . . . . . . . . . . . . . . . | = 1 metre (m) . . . . . . . . . . . . . . | = 39.4 inches/1.094 yards |
| 100 Zentimeter . . . . . . . . . . . . . . . . . . . . . . . . | = 1 Meter (m) | |
| 1,000 metres . . . . . . . . . . . . . . . . . . . . . . . . . | = 1 kilometre (km). . . . . . . . . . . | = 0.6214 mile/ 5/8 mile |
| 1 000 Meter . . . . . . . . . . . . . . . . . . . . . . . . . . | = 1 Kilometer (km) . . . . . . . . . . | |
| | 1 inch (in.) . . . . . . . . . . . . . . . . | = 25.4 mm |
| 12 inches . . . . . . . . . . . . . . . . . . . . . . . . . . . . | = 1 foot (ft.) . . . . . . . . . . . . . . . . | = 30.48 cm |
| 3 feet . . . . . . . . . . . . . . . . . . . . . . . . . . . . . . . | = 1 yard (yd.). . . . . . . . . . . . . . . | = 0.914 m |
| 220 yards . . . . . . . . . . . . . . . . . . . . . . . . . . . . | = 1 furlong . . . . . . . . . . . . . . . . . | = 201.17 m |
| 8 furlongs. . . . . . . . . . . . . . . . . . . . . . . . . . . . | = 1 mile (m.) . . . . . . . . . . . . . . . | = 1.609 km |
| 1,760 yards . . . . . . . . . . . . . . . . . . . . . . . . . . | = 1 mile . . . . . . . . . . . . . . . . . . | = 1.609 km |

## Square measure / Flächenmaße

| | | |
|---|---|---|
| 100 square metres (sq. m) . . . . . . . . . . . . . . . . | = 1 are . . . . . . . . . . . . . . . . . . . | = 0.025 acre |
| 100 Quadratmeter (m²). . . . . . . . . . . . . . . . . . | = 1 Ar (a) | |
| 100 ares. . . . . . . . . . . . . . . . . . . . . . . . . . . . . . | = 1 hectare (ha) . . . . . . . . . . . . | = 2.471 acres |
| 100 Ar. . . . . . . . . . . . . . . . . . . . . . . . . . . . . . . | = 1 Hektar (ha) | |
| 100 hectares . . . . . . . . . . . . . . . . . . . . . . . . . | = 1 square kilometre (sq.km). . . . | = 0.386 square miles |
| 100 hektar . . . . . . . . . . . . . . . . . . . . . . . . . . . | = 1 Quadratkilometer (km²) | |
| | 1 square inch . . . . . . . . . . . . . . | = 6.452cm² |
| 144 square inches. . . . . . . . . . . . . . . . . . . . . . | = 1 square foot . . . . . . . . . . . . . | = 929.03 cm² |
| 9 square feet . . . . . . . . . . . . . . . . . . . . . . . . . | = 1 square yard. . . . . . . . . . . . . . | = 0.836 m² |
| 4,840 square yards . . . . . . . . . . . . . . . . . . . . . | = 1 acre . . . . . . . . . . . . . . . . . . . | = 0.405 ha |
| 640 acres. . . . . . . . . . . . . . . . . . . . . . . . . . . . | = 1 square mile . . . . . . . . . . . . . . | = 2.59k²/259 ha |

## Cubic measure / Raummaße

| | | |
|---|---|---|
| 1 cubic centimetre (cc) *1 Kubikzentimeter (cm³)* | | = 0.06 cubic inches |
| 1,000,000 cubic centimetres *1 000 000 Kubikzentimeter* | = 1 cubic metre (cu. m) = *1 Kubikmeter (m³)* | = 35.714 cubic feet/ 1.307 cubic yards |
| | 1 cubic inch | = 16.4 cm³ |
| 1,728 cubic inches | = 1 cubic foot | = 0.028 m³ |
| 27 cubic feet | = 1 cubic yard | = 0.764 m³ |

## Capacity / Hohlmaße

| | | |
|---|---|---|
| 10 millilitres (ml) *10 Milliliter (ml)* | = 1 centilitre (cl) = *1 Zentiliter (cl)* | |
| 100 centilitres *100 Zentiliter* | = 1 litre (l) = *1 Liter (l)* | = 1.76 pints (2.1 US pints)/ 0.22 gallons (0.264 US gallons) |
| 4 gills | = 1 pint (pt.) (1.201 US pints) | = 0.568 l |
| 2 pints | = 1 quart (qt.) (1.201 US quarts) | = 1.136 l |
| 4 quarts | = 1 gallon (gal) (1.201 US gallons) | = 4.546 l |

# Also available from Oxford University Press

## Oxford-Duden German Dictionary

- Over 800,000 words, phrases, and translations

0-19-860365-7
0-19-860248-0
(US edition)

## Concise Oxford-Duden German Dictionary

- Over 400,000 words, phrases, and translations

0-19-864230-X
0-19-860464-5
(Book and CD-ROM)

## Oxford Colour German Dictionary Plus

- Over 100,000 words, phrases, and translations

0-19-864561-9
0-19-864565-1
(US edition)

## Oxford German Minidictionary

- Over 100,000 words, phrases, and translations

0-19-860468-8

## Oxford Take off in German

- Language learning course with almost 5 hours of audio

0-19-8602944
(Book + 4 CDs)
0-19-860275-8
(Book + 4 cassettes)

## Quick Take off in German

- Language learning course with almost 3 hours of audio

0-19-860655-9
(Book + 2 CDs)
0-19-860654-0
(Book + 2 cassettes)

OXFORD
UNIVERSITY PRESS